guide to THE ANTIQUE SHOPS of BRITAIN 1992

1992 Edition

compiled by Carol Adams

FRONT COVER: *A rare Queen Anne walnut shepherd's crook armchair retaining its original needlework. English, circa 1710. Mallett and Son (Antiques) Ltd., 40 New Bond Street, London, W1Y 0BS.*

BACK COVER: *A Regency ebony, ormolu, mother-of-pearl, pewter and brass inlaid inkwell, probably by George Bullock, circa 1810-20. Rothman, 103 Pimlico Road, London, SW1 W8PH.*

ISBN 1 85149 146 5

British Library CIP Data
Guide to the antique shops of Britain.—1992
(June 1991 - June 1992)
1. Great Britain. Antiques trades :
Directories - Serials
I. Antique Collectors' Club
380.1'457451'02541

Printed in England by Antique Collectors' Club Ltd., Woodbridge, Suffolk.
Telephone: (0394) 385501

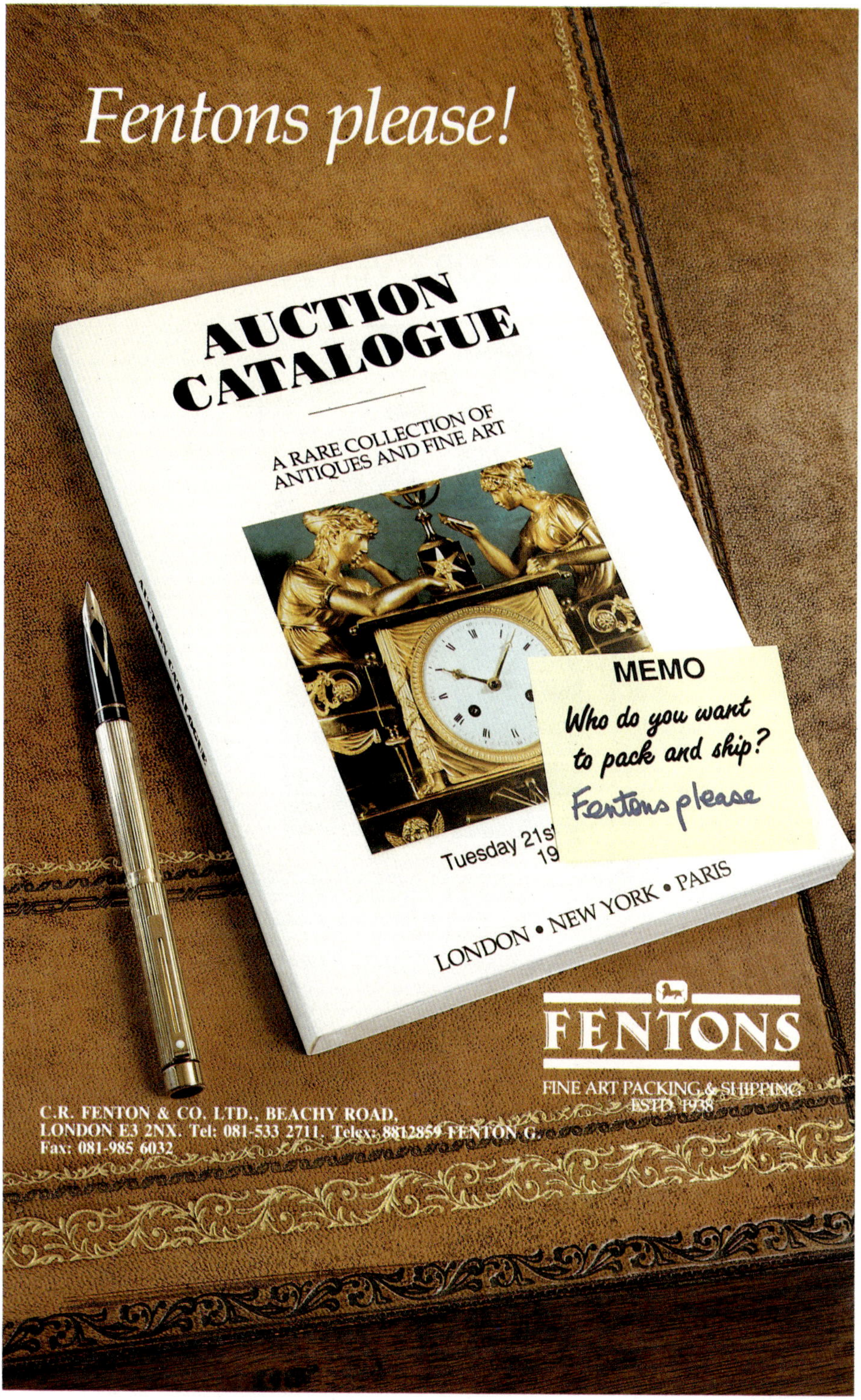

Fentons please!
AUCTION CATALOGUE
A RARE COLLECTION OF ANTIQUES AND FINE ART
AUCTION CATALOGUE
MEMO
Who do you want to pack and ship?
Fentons please
LONDON • NEW YORK • PARIS
FENTONS
FINE ART PACKING & SHIPPING
ESTD. 1938
C.R. FENTON & CO. LTD., BEACHY ROAD,
LONDON E3 2NX. Tel: 081-533 2711. Telex: 8812859 FENTON G.
Fax: 081-985 6032

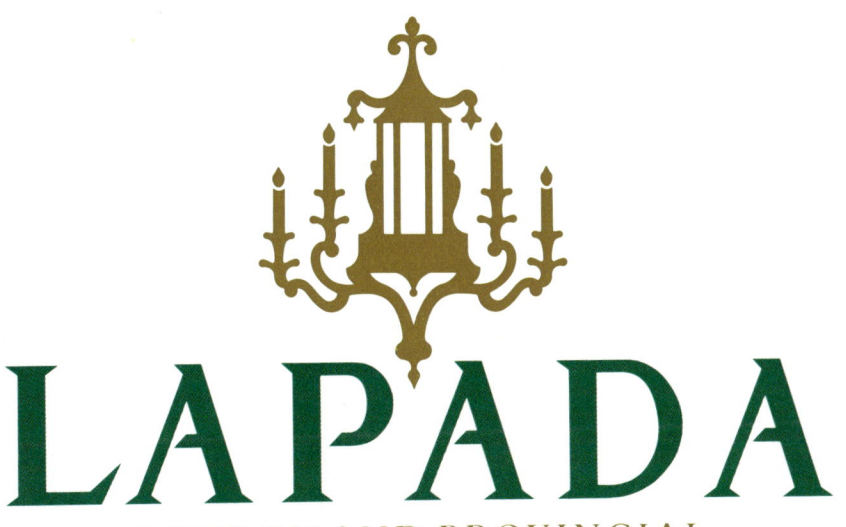

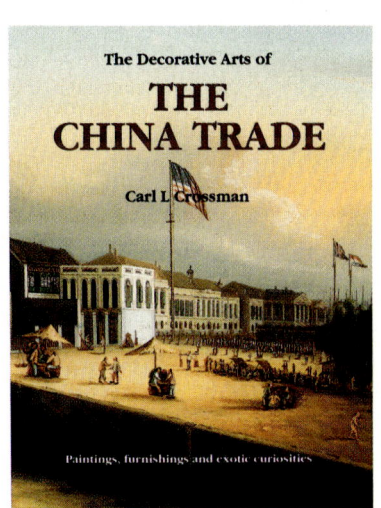

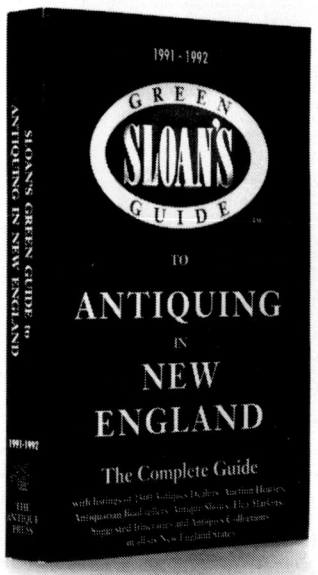

New Publication

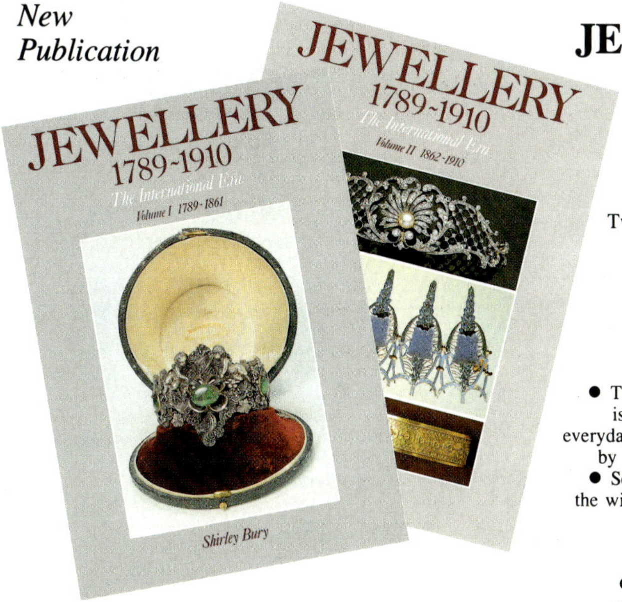
JEWELLERY
1789~1910
The International Era
Volume I 1789-1861
Shirley Bury
JEWELLERY
1789~1910
The International Era
Volume II 1862-1910

JEWELLERY

1789-1910

The International Era
by Shirley Bury

Two volumes £47.50 each (£95 the set).

- This richly illustrated account (215 colour plates) is destined to become the standard work.
- The historical background is examined from popular everyday jewellery to that worn by royalty and the nobility.
- Sets British jewellery into the wider context of European and American jewellery manufacture.

- Shirley Bury, FSA, is arguably Britain's leading jewellery historian.

Books from the Antique Collectors' Club

The Price Guide to Jewellery 3000BC-1950AD

by Michael Poynder

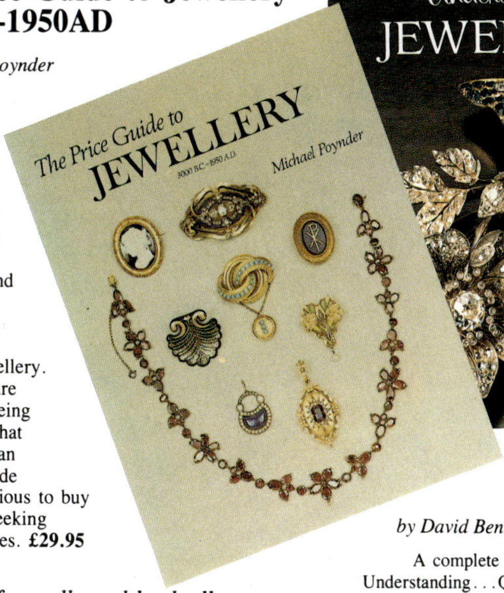
The Price Guide to
JEWELLERY
3000 BC–1950 AD
Michael Poynder

388pp., 340 b. & w.. 44 colour illus. Describes and illustrates hundreds of examples of popular jewellery. The prices are constantly being updated so that the book is an essential guide to those anxious to buy as well as seeking relative values. **£29.95**

Understanding
JEWELLERY
David Bennett &
Daniela Mascetti

Understanding Jewellery

by David Bennett and Daniela Mascetti

A complete guide to identification
Understanding. . .QUALITY
Understanding. . .PASTES FROM GEMSTONES
Understanding. . .FAKES FROM ORIGINALS
Understanding. . .VALUE **£35.00**

Available from all good booksellers or in the case of difficulty direct from Antique Collectors' Club.

5 Church Street, Woodbridge, Suffolk, IP12 1DS. Tel: (0394) 385501.

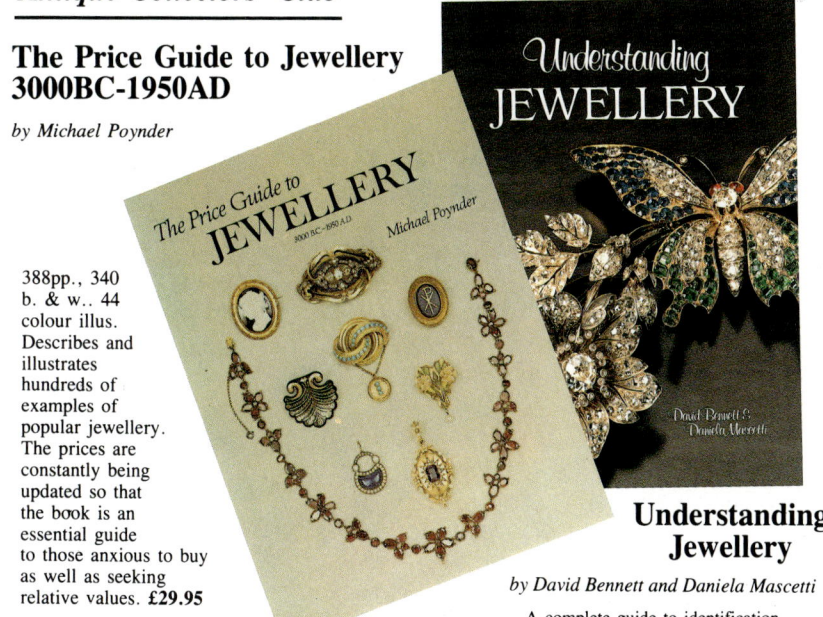

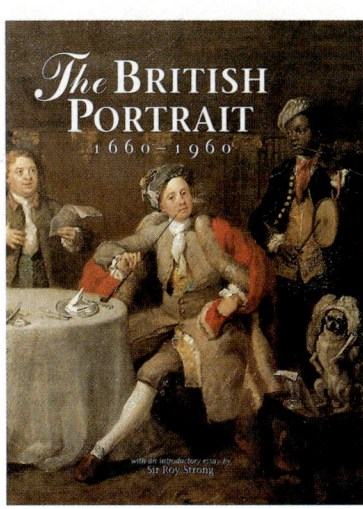

Contents

Acknowledgements

Our main sources of information are still trade magazines, papers, catalogues and so on, but we would like to thank the increasing number of antique dealers, private collectors and members of the Antique Collectors' Club who provide much of our information about new shops and passing on comments which go to make our information complete. Without this assistance our job would be more difficult.

We would also like to thank dealers who supported us with advertising and those who sent in information about their own, as well as other, establishments. Each year we include a form at the end of the Guide which dealers can use to update details about their own business. In anticipation of next year's Guide, we are grateful to those dealers who make use of this form.

Finally, thanks must go to the editorial team of The Guide to the Antique Shops of Britain, which carries out the mammoth task of compiling and indexing the entries.

C.A.

Editor **Carol Adams**

Advertisement Sales **Alistair Layzell Jean Johnson**

Editorial Team **Jill Ringrose Judith Neal Diana Dutson**

Introduction

This is the 20th edition of the **Guide to the Antique Shops of Britain** which is universally accepted as *the* guide for anybody who wishes to buy antiques in Britain.

This year we have listed nearly 7,000 establishments, plus the last minute entries included in the Stop Press section. Each of the entries is checked annually, which as the reader will readily understand is a colossal task. Increasingly, serious dealers recognise the importance of the Guide and send us very detailed information without having to be reminded that it is due. At the other end of the scale we send hundreds of reminders and make telephone calls, together costing thousands of pounds, to make sure that shops are still there. It is indicative of the high regard in which the Guide is held that dealers are kind enough to tell us about the shops that have opened or closed in their locality and we are most grateful for this unsolicited help.

For the price of a few gallons of petrol, the risk of visiting non-existent shops is drastically reduced but perhaps more importantly, time spent in fruitless journeys may be saved. The provision of motorways is very poor by international standards and many foreign visitors tend to underestimate how long it will take to make a visit.

We would stress that quantity of entries is meaningless without detail and here we pride ourselves that the range of information is more detailed and up-to-date than has been available elsewhere. Indeed, much of it is unique giving not only obvious facts — name of proprietor, address, telephone number, opening hours, stock, but also an indication of size of showrooms and price ranges. It is felt that these, although only general, give an indication of the quantity and quality of stock likely to be seen, facts which may well influence a prospective buyer's decision whether to visit a shop or not — in fact a time saver.

Additional information gives details of dealers' trade association memberships, the date the shop was established, and location and parking guidance plus street maps for those towns with over 25 entries. None of these points are necessarily decisive in themselves but, in conjunction with other details, valuable aids which build up a useful picture of the sort of establishment you are likely to find should you decide to visit. However, we strongly recommend that if you know the sort of pieces you want to buy, telephone first and plan the trip accordingly. Dealers questioned this way are normally very honest about their stock.

We start preparing the next Guide in early 1992 and so we should be grateful if dealers would let us know of any changes in their businesses — alterations in type of stock, price range, opening hours are especially important; to assist with this a form appears at the back of the Guide. Notes of changes to other establishments in the area would also be an enormous help.

We are always interested to receive your views about the Guide. How it can be improved or changes that you feel can be made. So please write if you feel that you have something to contribute.

Some Questions and Answers about this Book

You claim that this Guide is far and away the best. Why?
At the time of going to press the Guide lists more antique shops, galleries, warehouses and other antique businesses than are listed in any other publication. The individual entries are detailed, listing items such as stock — often in considerable depth, how to find the shop — which is often not easy. hours of business, and other information not normally available.

But surely any directory must contain some out-of-date entries?
Yes, but to make sure entries are as up to date as possible, each one is checked every year as near publication as possible. And because the Guide to the Antique Shops of Britain is accepted by dealers and collectors alike as *the* directory, over 75 per cent of dealers up date or confirm their annual entry. Where there is an element of doubt, the editorial team check, if need be, by telephone. We have a four figure editorial telephone bill!

Normally a £12.95 book only has 150 to 200 pages. This one has over 900; why is it so cheap?
Dealers like the Guide and, realising that buyers find it essential, give their active support by advertising. Without advertising revenue each copy would cost £18.00.

I bought a copy last year; do I really need to buy this new edition?
Obviously some businesses stay exactly as they are each year. But, perhaps surprisingly, well over half the entries in this edition have been changed in some respect since the last edition. Some dealers go into different types of antiques, often because they cannot get enough of the items in which they previously specialised. Others, approaching retirement, curtail their business hours. Locations and proprietors change. All this is in addition to those who set up new businesses, while others give up or retire. It is a constantly changing scene. Motoring costs around 45p a mile, so you have only to save a 30 mile round trip to pay for a new guide, and that does not include your time.

How to use this Guide

The Guide is set out under six main headings: London, England, Channel Islands, Northern Ireland, Scotland and Wales. Counties are listed alphabetically (with the exception of Scotland); within counties there is a listing of towns and within the towns an index of shops, or galleries. London is divided into postal districts. In Scotland, as the majority of shops are concentrated in the central part and some counties have very few, we felt it would be easier for users of the Guide if towns were listed in alphabetical order rather than separated into their respective counties.

To make route planning easier, there is a map at the beginning of each county, coded to show the number of antique shops in any one town, city or village. The roads indicated on the map are only a broad intimation of the routes available and it is advisable to use an up- to-date road map showing the latest improvements in the road system.

Apart from the six main headings mentioned above, there are further helpful lists; an alphabetical list of towns indicating the counties in which they appear for those not familiar with the location of towns within counties, e.g. Woodbridge is shown in the county of Suffolk. One therefore turns to the Suffolk section to look up Woodbridge. This listing is a valuable aid to the overseas visitor. The second is particularly important to British collectors and dealers, giving an alphabetical list of the name of every shop, proprietor and company director known to be connected with the antique shop or gallery. Thus, if A. Bloggs and B. Brown own an antique shop called Castle Antiques, there will be entries included under Bloggs, A., Brown, B. and Castle Antiques. Listings of specialist dealers, auctioneers, and shippers and packers are also included.

One point that collectors and dealers alike constantly seem to miss is that use of the telephone offers great savings of time and money. Nearly all dealers have to make unscheduled calls during opening hours and the 'back in 5 minutes' notice which has been in the window of a small shop for 20 minutes is a cause of great irritation to the potential buyer. If you have to be a hundred miles along the road in two hours, but there is something in the back of the shop which looks interesting, then the decision to wait or not to wait is even more agonising. A telephone call in advance can forestall such frustrations. When you telephone, it is usually quite acceptable to describe what you are looking for in terms of Antique Collectors' Club books. Increasingly one sees advertisements referring to page numbers. Most dealers have at least some of the books and use them as a basis for communicating information.

All but a handful of dealers are factual and reasonably accurate in describing their stock to us, but there are probably one or two who insist on listing their stock on the basis of what they would like to have, rather than as it is. Information on such dealers from those who use the Guide is greatly appreciated as are any suggestions and ideas; indeed it has been the kindness of so many collectors and dealers who take the trouble to drop us a postcard or telephone (0394) 385501 and tell us about misleading entries or closures that has helped us to ensure that the Guide has become Britain's premier listing of antique shops and galleries.

Abbreviations in entries

In order to cut the bulk of this book as much as possible without curtailing the amount of information, we have made some very simple contractions in the entries.

BADA: Members are indicated by using a bold type face.

EST: Shows the year in which the shop was established or the number of years the dealer or firm has been trading.

CL: Days when the business is normally closed. It is followed by hours of opening. In some small businesses these may prove erratic, as it is often necessary for the dealer to go out at short notice. Unless otherwise stated, it would be wise to assume that shops are closed on Sundays. If making a long journey, it is advisable to telephone and make an appointment.

SIZE: A guide to the size of the showrooms is given to indicate the quantity of stock likely to be seen. Small is under 600 sq.ft. (60 sq. metres), medium between 600 and 1,500 sq.ft. (60 and 150 sq. metres) and large over 1,500 sq.ft. (150 sq. metres).

STOCK: Dealers are asked to list their stock in order of importance, so that the items listed can be expected to comprise a significant part of the stock. The price range is of very general application and is designed to give some idea to prospective buyers of the type of items to be seen. In an age of inflation the price levels quoted will often be too low, but nevertheless it is felt that they act as a useful general indication of the level of quality. Not stocked items are indicated after those which are stocked. The items listed are not normally to be found in this shop. Advertisements often give extra information on the size of showrooms, etc.

LOC: Location of shop. This is a description given by the owner designed to help the would-be caller. Road numbers in the entries are not necessarily shown on the county maps of the Guide, which are merely general aids to direction.

PARK: This indicates how easy it is for a car to park for 15 minutes outside the shop. Where parking is not easy, alternative suggestions for parking are often given.

TEL: Telephone. Where no exchange or STD code is indicated, this will be the same as for the town or village under which the shop is listed. In addition to their business numbers some dealers have listed their home telephone numbers, so customers can ring for an appointment outside business hours. Clearly callers should use discretion and only make out-of-business calls where they are seriously interested and in any event not late at night or early in the morning.

SER: Additional services which the dealer offers. Where 'buys at auction' is shown in this section, it indicates that if an auction is one which a dealer might normally attend, he may be approached to act as bidder on behalf of someone else. Check the cost of this service, and any others offered, beforehand.

VAT: Indicates which of the two VAT schemes, standard or special, are operated. In some cases both schemes are in operation and some very small shops are not registered.

London

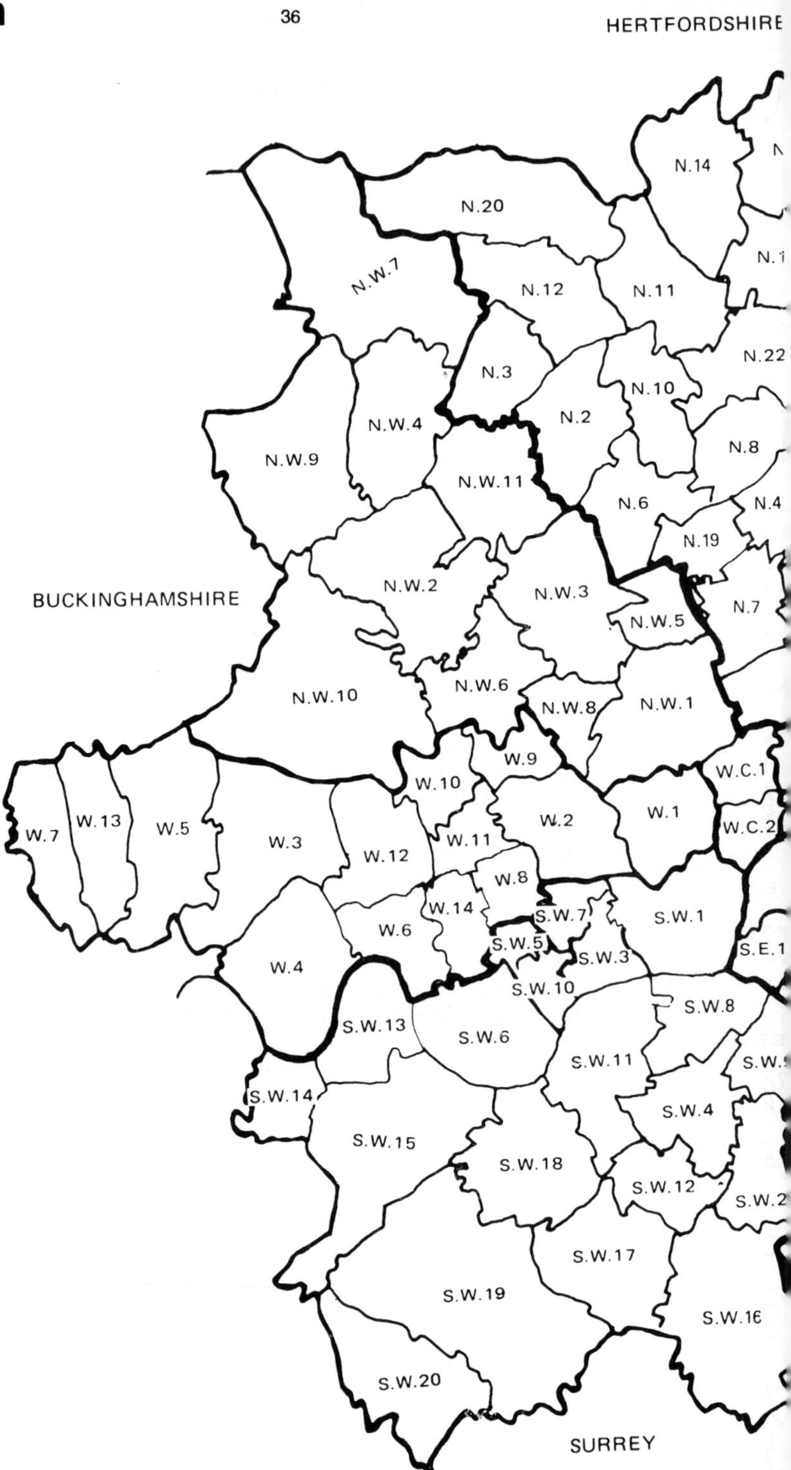
HERTFORDSHIRE
N.14
N.20
N.W.7
N.12
N.11
N.22
N.3
N.10
N.W.4
N.2
N.8
N.W.9
N.W.11
N.6
N.4
N.19
N.W.2
BUCKINGHAMSHIRE
N.W.3
N.7
N.W.5
N.W.10
N.W.6
N.W.8
N.W.1
W.9
W.10
W.C.1
W.7
W.13
W.5
W.3
W.2
W.1
W.C.2
W.11
W.12
W.8
W.14
S.W.7
S.W.1
W.6
S.W.5
S.W.3
S.E.1
W.4
S.W.10
S.W.8
S.W.13
S.W.6
S.W.11
S.W.14
S.W.4
S.W.15
S.W.18
S.W.12
S.W.17
S.W.19
S.W.20
SURREY

London postal districts

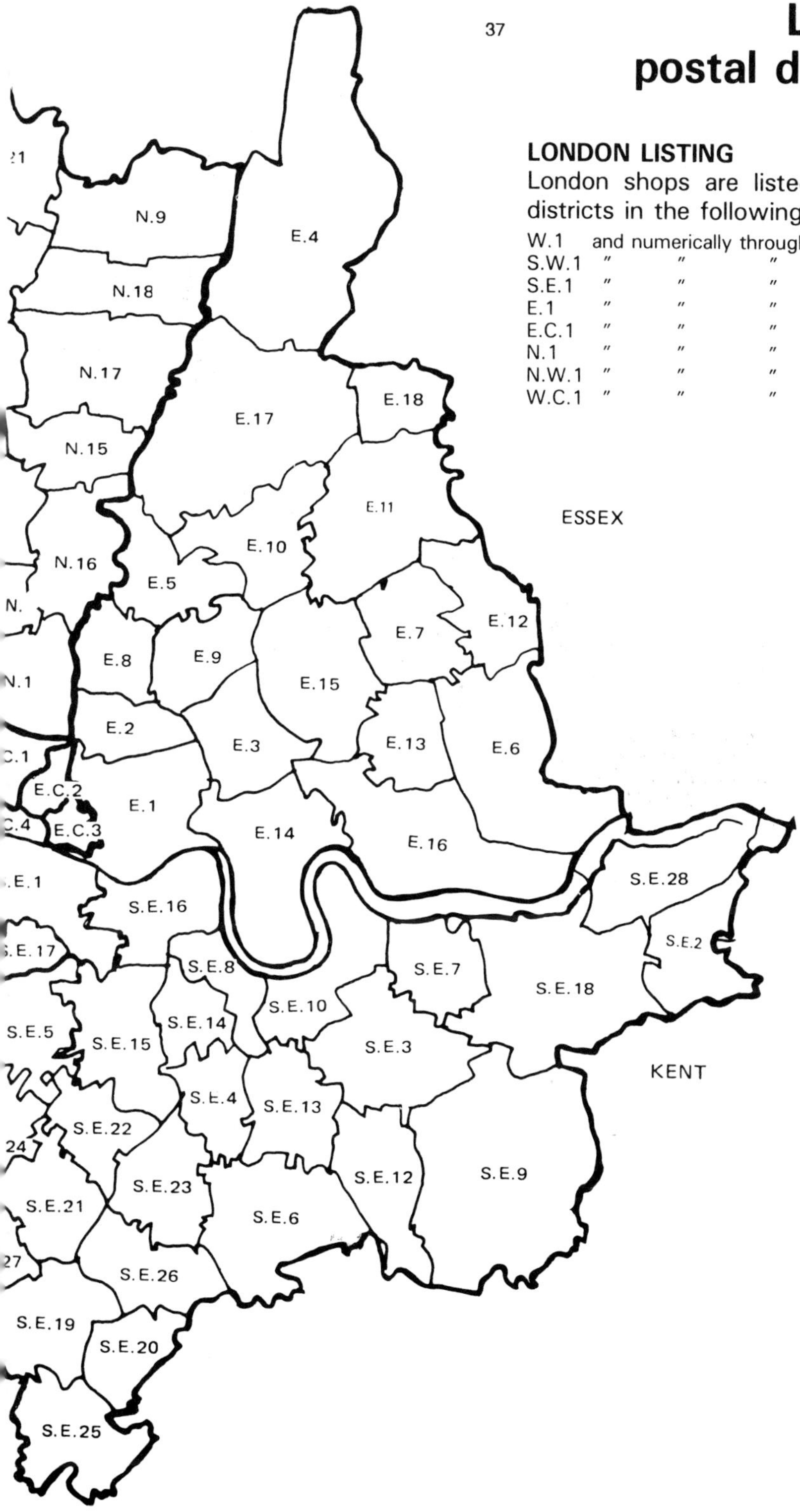
N.9
E.4
N.18
N.17
E.18
E.17
N.15
E.11
ESSEX
E.10
N.16
E.5
E.12
E.7
E.8
E.9
E.15
E.2
E.3
E.13
E.6
E.C.2
E.1
E.C.3
E.14
E.16
S.E.28
S.E.16
S.E.2
S.E.8
S.E.7
S.E.18
S.E.10
S.E.14
S.E.5
S.E.15
S.E.3
KENT
S.E.4
S.E.13
S.E.22
S.E.12
S.E.9
S.E.23
S.E.21
S.E.6
S.E.26
S.E.19
S.E.20
S.E.25

LONDON LISTING

London shops are listed by postal districts in the following order:

W.1	and numerically through to				W.14
S.W.1	"	"	"	"	S.W.20
S.E.1	"	"	"	"	S.E.26
E.1	"	"	"	"	E.18
E.C.1	"	"	"	"	E.C.4
N.1	"	"	"	"	N.21
N.W.1	"	"	"	"	N.W.11
W.C.1	"	"	"	"	W.C.2

London W.1

A.D.C. Heritage Ltd BADA LAPADA
2 Old Bond St. (F. and T. Raeymaekers, E. Bellord and K. Grant-Peterkin) Open 9.30-5.30, Sat. 10-1. *STOCK: Silver, old Sheffield plate.* TEL: 071 493 5088; fax - 071 495 0062. SER: Valuations; restorations; buys at auction.

Aaron Gallery LAPADA
34 Bruton St. (M. and D. Aaron) Est: 1910. Open 10-6, Sat. by appointment. *STOCK: Islamic and ancient art, Oriental carpets.* TEL: 071 499 9434/5; fax - 071 499 0072.

Arthur Ackermann & Son Ltd BADA
33 New Bond St. SLAD. Est: 1783. Open 9.30-6, Sat. 10-1. SIZE: Medium. *STOCK: English sporting paintings and colour prints, 1700-1900.* PARK: Meters. TEL: 071 493 3288/629 0592. SER: Buys at auction. VAT: Stan/Spec.

Addison Fine Art
24 Davies St. (Mrs. D. Geddes) Est: 1978. Open 11-4. SIZE: Small. *STOCK: British and continental post-impressionist paintings.* LOC: Parallel to Bond St.. TEL: 071 493 7185. SER: Valuations; restorations; buys at auction (paintings). FAIRS: 20th C British Art (Sept.); Olympia (June). VAT: Spec.

Thomas Agnew & Sons Ltd BADA
43 Old Bond St, and 3 Albemarle St. Est: 1817. Open 9.30-5.30, Thurs. 9.30-6.30. CL: Sat. SIZE: Large. *STOCK: Paintings, drawings, watercolours, engravings and sculptures of all schools.* TEL: 071 629 6176. VAT: Spec.

Albemarle Gallery
18 Albemarle St. (R. Capstick-Dale and M. Glazebrook) Est: 1986. Open 10-5, Sat. 11-1. SIZE: Medium. *STOCK: British, French, and American paintings and sculptures, 20th C, £200-£100,000.* LOC: Past Ritz Hotel up Albemarle St., opposite Browns Hotel. PARK: Easy. TEL: 071 355 1880. SER: Valuations; restorations; buys at auction. VAT: Stan/Spec.

Alexander and Berendt Ltd
1A Davies St. Open 9.30-5.30. CL: Sat. SIZE: Large. *STOCK: Fine 17th-18th C French and other continental furniture and works of art.* PARK: Meters. TEL: 071 499 4775. VAT: Spec.

Antique Porcelain Co. Ltd
149 New Bond St. (Mrs R Beiny) Est: 1946. Open 9-6, Fri. till 5. CL: Sat. SIZE: Medium. *STOCK: Porcelain, faience, French furniture, 18th C.* PARK: Meters. TEL: 071 629 1254. SER: Restorations; buys at auction. VAT: Stan/Spec.

Philip Antrobus Ltd
11 New Bond St. Est: 1815. *STOCK: Jewellery.* TEL: 071 493 4557/8.

W.1 continued

Aqua Libra
1 Whitehorse St.,, Shepherds Market. (R.D. Rush) Open 10-6. *STOCK: Staffordshire ware, objets vertu, British and continental porcelain, paintings and prints.* TEL: 071 493 3954.

Argyll Etkin Gallery
48 Conduit St, New Bond St., (Argyll Etkin Ltd.). Est: 1954. Open 9-5.30. CL: Sat. SIZE: Medium. *STOCK: Classic postage stamps, postal history and covers, historical documents and antique letters, 1400-1950, £50-£25,000; stamp boxes and associated writing equipment, 1700-1930, £50-£500.* LOC: Near Oxford Circus. PARK: Savile Row. TEL: 071 437 7800 (6 lines). SER: Valuations; buys collections. FAIRS: Major stamp worldwide. VAT: Stan.

Armitage BADA
4 Davies St, Berkeley Sq. (R. Tadj Saadat) Open 9.30-5.30, Sat. by appointment. SIZE: Medium. *STOCK: English silver, 16th-20th C.* PARK: Easy. TEL: 071 408 0675. SER: Valuations; buys at auction.

Armour-Winston Ltd
43 Burlington Arcade. Est: 1952. Open 9-5. CL: Sat.. SIZE: Small. *STOCK: Jewellery, especially Victorian; gentlemen's cufflinks.* LOC: Off Piccadilly. Between Green Park and Piccadilly tube stations. PARK: Savile Row. TEL: 071 493 8937. SER: Valuations; restorations. VAT: Stan/Spec.

Asprey plc BADA
165-169 New Bond St. Est: 1781. Open 9-5.30. CL: Sat. p.m.. SIZE: Large. *STOCK: Furniture, works of art, longcase and bracket clocks, silver, jewellery, Fabergé and objets de vertu, carriage clocks, ships' chronometers, glass.* PARK: Albemarle St., entrance No.22. TEL: 071 493 6767. SER: Valuations; restorations (furniture, jewellery, clocks, silver). VAT: Stan/Spec.

Astarte Gallery
Shop 5, Britannia Hotel, Grosvenor Sq.. (A.G. Davies) Est: 1956. Open daily, Sat. and Sun. by appointment. SIZE: Medium. *STOCK: Roman, Greek and Egyptian art and artifacts, necklaces and other jewellery, £5-£15,000; medallions, some ancient coins, general antiques; books relating to stock.* PARK: Easy. TEL: 071 409 1875; hotel - 071 629 9400, ext. 7002. SER: Buys at auction (antiquities). VAT: Stan/Spec.

Atlantic Bay Carpets
7 Sedley Pl. (W. Grodzinski and Z. Golebiowski) Est: 1945. Open 9-5, Sat. 9-1. SIZE: Medium. *STOCK: Oriental and European carpets and textiles.* LOC: Near Bond/Oxford St. PARK: Easy. TEL: 071 355 3301; fax - 071 355 3760. SER: Valuations; restorations; buys at auction (as stock). VAT: Stan/Spec.

W.1 continued

Gregg Baker Oriental Works of Art

34 Brook St. Est: 1985. Open 10-5, weekends by appointment. SIZE: Small. *STOCK: Japanese and Chinese works of art and porcelain, mainly 18th and 19th C, £100-£10,000.* LOC: Close to Bond St./Brook St. junction. PARK: Meters. TEL: 071 629 7926; home - 071 792 0673. SER: Valuations. VAT: Stan/Spec.

Barling of Mount St Ltd — BADA

112 Mount St. Est: 1946. Open 10-6. CL: Sat. SIZE: Medium. *STOCK: Chinese Ming and Ch'ing furniture; early English and continental oak and walnut furniture, 15th to late 17th C; contemporary sculpture, metalwork and textiles.* LOC: Between Berkeley and Grosvenor Squares. PARK: Easy, meters. TEL: 071 499 2858; fax - 071 493 1186. VAT: Stan/Spec.

Barrett and James

8 South Molton St. Est: 1974. Open by appointment. *STOCK: Silver - Tiffany, Japanese influenced and American, £500-£1,000.* LOC: Off Bond St. PARK: Easy. TEL: 071 629 3389. FAIRS: Olympia, Miami, Chicago, New York Pier. VAT: Stan/Spec.

John and Arthur Beare — BADA

7 Broadwick St. (J & A Beare Ltd) Est: 1892. Open 9-12.15 and 1.30-5. CL: Sat. *STOCK:*

John and Arthur Beare continued

***Violins,violas, cellos, bows and accessories.* TEL: 071 437 1449. SER: Valuations. VAT: Stan/Spec.**

Brian Beet — LAPADA

3b Burlington Gdns. (B.H. Beet) Est: 1979. *STOCK: Unusual silver including Chinese export; brass, wine antiques.* TEL: 071 437 4975.

Paul Bennett — LAPADA

75 George St. (M Dubiner) Open 9.15-6. CL: Sat. SIZE: Large. *STOCK: Silver, 1740-1963, £10-£10,000; Sheffield plate.* PARK: Meters. TEL: 071 935 1555/486 8836. VAT: Stan/Spec.

Bentley & Co Ltd

65 New Bond St, and 19 Burlington Arcade.Open 10-5 CL: Sat.; Burlington Arcade - 9.30-5.30 including Sat. *STOCK: Jewellery, Fabergé, objets d'art.* PARK: Meters. TEL: 071 629 0651/495 3783. SER: Valuations. VAT: Stan/Spec.

W.1 continued

Bernheimer Fine Arts Ltd BADA
32 St. George St. (K.O. Bernheimer) Est: 1985. Open 10-5.30, weekends by appointment. SIZE: Large. *STOCK: European furniture, 17th-19th C, £2,000-£100,000; Oriental porcelain, 16th-18th C, £1,500-£10,000; Oriental carpets, textiles, works of art, 15th-18th C, £1,000-£120,000.* LOC: Parallel to Bond St. PARK: Hanover Sq. TEL: 071 499 0293. SER: Valuations; buys at auction. FAIRS: Grosvenor House. VAT: Spec.

Peter Biddulph
35 St George St. Open 9.30-6.30. CL: Sat. *STOCK: Violins, violas and cellos.* TEL: 071 491 8621.

Bilby and Holloway
13a Grafton St. (D Bilby and B Holloway) Open 9-5.30, Sat. 9-1. *STOCK: Silver, jewellery and objets d'art.* TEL: 071 495 4636.

H. Blairman and Sons Ltd., BADA
119 Mount St. (G.J., M.P. and W.Y Levy and L.G. Hannen) Est: 1884. Open daily. CL: Sat. SIZE: Medium. *STOCK: English and French mid-18th to early 19th C antiques; works of art, mounted porcelain, Chinese mirror pictures; architect designed furniture, 19th C.* TEL: 071 493 0444; fax - 071 495 0766. FAIRS: Grosvenor House. VAT: Spec.

Anne Bloom Fine Jewellery
10a New Bond St. Est: 1960. Open 9.30-6. *STOCK: Fine jewellery, 1890-1955; period silver frames and mirrors.* TEL: 071 491 1213; fax - 071 409 0777. SER: Valuations. VAT: Stan/Spec.

N Bloom & Son (Antiques) Ltd LAPADA
40/41 Conduit St. (I Harris) Est: 1912. Open 10-6. CL: Sat.. SIZE: Medium. *STOCK: Silver, 16th C to second-hand, jewellery, including art deco paste items, 18th-20th C, £100-£50,000.* Not stocked: Furniture, glass, china. LOC: Next to Westbury Hotel. TEL: 071 629 5060; fax - 071 437 5026. SER: Valuations; restorations, repairs; buys at auction. VAT: Stan/Spec.

Bluett and Sons Ltd BADA
60 Brook St. (A.W. Carter and R.B Bluett) Est: 1884. CL: Sat. *STOCK: Oriental works of art.* TEL: 071 629 3397/629 4018; fax - 071 495 0326. VAT: Spec.

Blunderbuss Antiques
29 Thayer St. (T. Greenaway) Open 9.30-4.30. *STOCK: Arms and armour, militaria.* TEL: 071 486 2444.

Bobinet Ltd BADA
102 Mount St. (A. Crisford and S Whitestone) Est: 1973. *STOCK: Watches, clocks, globes, English furniture, 17th-20th*

Bobinet continued

***C, £500-£500,000.* TEL: 071 408 0333/4. SER: Valuations; restorations; buys at auction (clocks, watches, globes). VAT: Stan/Spec.**

Bond Street Antiques Centre
124 New Bond St, (Atlantic Antique Centres Ltd.). Est: 1970. Open 10-5.45, Sat. 10-4. There are 29 dealers selling a wide range of general antiques especially jewellery. TEL: 071 351 5353. Below are listed some of the many specialist dealers at this market.

Emmy Abe
Stand 33. *Jewellery.* TEL: 071 629 1826.

Eli Abramov LAPADA
Stand 2. (Morelle Davidson) *Jewellery, silver and objets d'art.* TEL: 071 629 4764/408 0066.

Accurate Trading Co
Stand 21/22. (E Fahimian) *Jewellery.* TEL: 071 629 0277.

Appleby (A. Lee and Co.)
Stand 41. *Watches and clocks.* TEL: 071 493 5527.

Clayre Armitage
Stand 14. *Jewellery and watches.* TEL: 071 493 5830.

Art-Antica
Stand 16. (P Rovati) *Art nouveau and deco, porcelain, objets d'art, glass.* TEL: 071 491 2327.

Ronald Benjamin
Stand 1a/b. *Jewellery.* TEL: 071 408 0173/493 3937.

C Cavey
Stands 19/20. *Gemology, fossils and jewellery.* TEL: 071 495 1743.

Rachel Child
Stand 1c. *Jewellery.* TEL: 071 408 4447.

Collection
Stands 5/6. (J Shockett) *Jewellery.* TEL: 071 493 2654.

Collings and Ashford
Stand 17. *Jewellery.* TEL: 071 409 7031.

Adele de Havilland
Stand 18. *Oriental porcelain, netsuke, jade, jewellery and hardstone carvings.* TEL: 071 499 7127.

S Deacon
Stand 23. *Silver.* TEL: 071 493 5839.

Robert Deblinger & Co LAPADA
Stand 34. *Jewellery.* TEL: 071 409 1961.

David Duggan
Stands 10/11. *Vintage watches.* TEL: 071 408 0134.

K Edward and Gloria
Stand 12. *Oriental porcelain.*

Elisabeth's Antiques
Stands 42/43. (Mrs E Hage) *Jewellery.* TEL: 071 491 1723.

Anthony Green Antiques
Stand 39. *General antiques.* TEL: 071 409 2854.

Grosvenor Jewellery
Stand 31. (Miss S Lewis) *Jewellery.* TEL: 071 409 1350.

Bond Street Antiques Centre continued

Hoffman BADA LAPADA
Stand 16. *English and continental clocks and barometers; period furniture.* TEL: 071 491 2327.

T Kaczer
Stand 1D. *Glass.* TEL: 071 499 1441/313 0990.

Limner Antiques
Stands 25/26. *Portrait miniatures, 16th to mid-19th C.* TEL: 071 629 5314.

Lydia and Anita's Antiques
Stand 40. (Mrs L Chagnon) *Jewellery.* TEL: 071 409 2107.

Meileng Collection
Stand 13. (Mrs T Leveridge-Koh) *Oriental porcelain and bronzes.* TEL: 071 629 2996.

Myra Antiques and JLA Ltd
Stands 29/30. *Jewellery and objects.* TEL: 071 408 1508.

Nonesuch Antiques
Stand 3. (Mrs E Michelson) *Jewellery and objects.* TEL: 071 629 6783.

Place Vendome
Stand 38. (D Shenny) *Silver, jewellery and objects.* TEL: 071 629 3008.

Sadi and Nasser
Stand 4. *Jewellery and glass.* TEL: 071 491 2081.

Vinci Antiques
Stands 7/8/9. *Silver, jewellery, objets d'art.* TEL: 071 499 1041.

Vipul
Stand 15. (V Lodhia) *Jewellery.*

Xelana Antiques
Stand 32. (Mrs A.M Sanchez-Martin) *Clocks and ivory.* TEL: 071 629 9415.

Bond Street Silver Galleries

111-112 New Bond St. Open 9-5.30. CL: Sat. PARK: Meters. TEL: 071 493 6180. Below are listed the dealers at these galleries. *Mainly trade.*

Arthur Black Ltd
Silver, Sheffield plate. TEL: 071 493 6184. SER: Valuations.

A and B Bloomstein Ltd BADA LAPADA
***Silver, Sheffield plate.* TEL: 071 493 6180. SER:: Valuations; restorations.**

John Bull (Antiques) Ltd LAPADA
Open 9-4.30. *Silver and plate.* TEL: 071 629 1251; fax - 071 495 3001. VAT: Stan/Spec.

Peter Cameron LAPADA
Silver and old Sheffield plate. TEL: 071 499 0330.

Alistair Crawford LAPADA
Silver and old Sheffield plate. TEL: 071 499 8442.

Phillip Cull
Silver and Sheffield plate. TEL: 071 493 2047.

Fortunoff Silver Sales Incorporated
Silver including Victorian, plate. TEL: 071 493 6184.

Bond Street Silver Galleries continued

N and I Franklin (Antiques) LAPADA
Silver and Sheffield plate. TEL: 071 499 1296.

O Frydman
Silver, Sheffield and Victorian plate. TEL: 071 493 4895. VAT: Stan/Spec.

Peter Gaunt
Silver and Sheffield plate. TEL: 071 629 1072.

P Greenhalgh
Silver and old Sheffield plate, books on silver. TEL: 071 491 9178.

R Holt
Silver and old Sheffield plate. TEL: 071 409 7032.

A Pash & Son LAPADA
Silver and old Sheffield plate. TEL: 071 493 5176.

Julian Pawle Ltd LAPADA
(J Pawle and N.R Shaw) *Antique and secondhand silver and Sheffield plate, £100-£10,000.* TEL: 071 499 8442; fax - 071 408 0819.

Ross Antiques
Silver and Sheffield plate. TEL: 071 495 3977.

Michael Smith
Silver and old Sheffield plate. TEL: 071 499 2558.

E Swonnell (Silverware) Ltd LAPADA
Silver, Sheffield plate. TEL: 071 629 9649. VAT: Stan/Spec.

Howard White
Silver and Sheffield plate. TEL: 071 495 1144.

Henry Willis LAPADA
Silver and Sheffield plate. TEL: 071 491 8949.

Browse and Darby Ltd

19 Cork St. Est: 1977. *STOCK: French and British paintings, drawings and sculpture, 19th and 20th C.* TEL: 071 734 7984. VAT: Spec.

Bruford and Heming Ltd BADA

28 Conduit St. NAG. Open 9-5.30. CL: Sat. *STOCK: Domestic silverware, especially flatware, jewellery.* PARK: Meters. TEL: 071 499 7644/629 4289; fax - 071 493 5879. SER: Valuations; restorations. VAT: Stan/Spec.

Burlington Gallery Ltd

10 Burlington Gdns. (A.S. Lloyd, N.C Potter and W.M Lloyd) Est: 1980. Open 9.30-5.30, Sat. 10-5. SIZE: Large. *STOCK: Sporting and decorative prints, 1600-1860, and works by Cecil Aldin.* LOC: Between Bond St. and Regent St. PARK: Old Burlington St. TEL: 071 734 9228; fax - 071 494 3770. SER: Valuations; buys at auction. VAT: Stan/Spec.

W.1 continued

Burlington Paintings Ltd
12 Burlington Gdns. (A Lloyd and M Day) Est: 1981. Open 9.30-5.30, Sat. 10-5. SIZE: Small. *STOCK: English and continental oil paintings and watercolours, 19th to early 20th C, from £500.* LOC: Between Old Bond St. and Regent St., facing Savile Row. PARK: APCOA Old Burlington St. TEL: 071 734 9984. SER: Valuations; restorations (lining, cleaning, reframing oils and watercolours); buys at auction (pictures). VAT: Stan/Spec.

The Button Queen
19 Marylebone Lane. (T. and M Frith) Est: 1953. Open 10-6, Sat. 10-1.30. SIZE: Large. *STOCK: Buttons, antique to modern horn and blazer buttons; buckles, mainly 19th C and Edwardian.* LOC: Off Wigmore St. TEL: 071 935 1505. VAT: Stan.

Helen Buxton Ltd LAPADA
97 Mount St. Est: 1975. Open 10-5.30. CL: Sat. *STOCK: Chinese and Japanese ceramics and works of art.* TEL: 071 409 2685.

Carrington and Co Ltd
170 Regent St. Open 9.30-5.30. *STOCK: Regimental jewellery and silver, trophies, watches, clocks.* TEL: 071 734 3727/8.

Lumley Cazalet Ltd
24 Davies St. Est: 1967. Open 10-6. CL: Sat. *STOCK Late 19th and 20th C original prints including Braque, Chagall, Miro, Matisse, Picasso; also drawings and sculpture by Matisse.* TEL: 071 491 4767.

Antoine Cheneviere Fine Arts BADA
94 Mount St. Open 9.30-6. CL: Sat. *STOCK: 18th-19th C furniture and paintings, objets d'art from Russia, Italy, Austria, Sweden and Germany.* TEL: 071 491 1007.

J Christie BADA LAPADA
26 Burlington Arcade. (P.S Christie) CINOA, ADS. Est: 1947. Open 9.30-5.30, Sat. by appointment. SIZE: Small. *STOCK: Animalier and figurative bronze sculpture, 19th and 20th C.* PARK: Meters, car park. TEL: 071 629 3070/409 0111; fax - 071 409 0631. VAT: Stan/Spec.

Colefax and Fowler
39 Brook St. Est: 1933. Open 9.30-1 and 2-5.30. CL: Sat. SIZE: Medium. *STOCK: Decorative furniture, pictures, lamps and carpets, 18th-19th C.* PARK: Meters. TEL: 071 493 2231. VAT: Stan/Spec.

Collingwood of Bond Street Ltd
171 New Bond St. Est: 1817. Open 9-5. *STOCK: Jewellery, silver, objets d'art and clocks.* PARK: Meters. TEL: 071 734 2656; fax - 071 629 5418. SER: Valuations; design and production. VAT: Stan/Spec.

W.1 continued

P. and D Colnaghi & Co Ltd BADA
14 Old Bond St. Est: 1760. Open 9.30-6. SIZE: Large. *STOCK: Master paintings and drawings, 14th-19th C; English paintings, European sculpture.* TEL: 071 491 7408. SER: Valuations. VAT: Spec.

Connaught Brown plc
2 Albemarle St. (A Brown) Est: 1980. Open 10-6, Sat. 10-12.30. SIZE: Medium. *STOCK: Post Impressionist and modern works, from £5,000+; contemporary, from £500+.* LOC: Off Piccadilly and parallel to Bond St. PARK: Berkeley Sq. TEL: 071 408 0362. SER: Valuations; restorations (paintings, drawings, watercolours and sculpture). FAIRS: Chicago International Art Exposition. VAT: Stan/Spec.

Crawley and Asquith BADA
16 Savile Row. Open 9.30-5. CL: Sat. *STOCK: 18th-19th C paintings, watercolours, prints, books.* TEL: 071 439 2755.

Sandra Cronan Ltd LAPADA
18 Burlington Arcade. Est: 1975. Open 10-5.30. *STOCK: Unusual jewellery, especially horse and polo related, 18th C to 1940's, £800-£15,000.* LOC: Off Bond St. TEL: 071 491 4851; fax - 071 493 2758. SER: Valuations; design commissions. FAIRS: International Silver and Jewellery; Olympia. VAT: Stan/Spec.

Barry Davies
1 Davies St. Open 10-6. CL: Sat. *STOCK: Japanese works of art, netsuke, lacquer and bronzes.* TEL: 071 408 0207.

A. B Davies Ltd
18 Brook St, (Corner of New Bond St). Est: 1920. Open 10-5. CL: Sat. *STOCK: Antique and secondhand jewellery, small silver items and objets d'art.* TEL: 071 629 1053; 071 242 7357 (ansaphone). SER: Valuations; repairs (jewellery and silver). VAT: Stan/Spec.

Richard Day Ltd
173 New Bond St. Open 10-5. CL: Sat. *STOCK: Old Master prints and drawings.* TEL: 071 629 2991; fax - 071 493 7569. VAT: Stan.

Jehanne de Biolley Oriental Art
at A.D. Orsay Ltd, 1st Floor, 28 Conduit St. Est: 1990. Open 10-6, Sat. by appointment. SIZE: Medium. *STOCK: Works of art in bronze, porcelain, jade, wood, lacquer and glass, Japanese, Chinese, Korean and Indian, 12th-19th C, £350-£10,000.* LOC: Opposite Westbury Hotel, off New Bond St. TEL: 071 493 5047; fax - 071 495 0329. SER: Valuations; restorations; buys at auction. FAIRS: San Francisco Fall.

Demas
31 Burlington Arcade. (Mrs E Paul) Est: 1953. Open 10-5. CL: Sat.p.m. *STOCK: Georgian, Victorian and art deco jewellery.* TEL: 071 493 9496. VAT: Stan.

W.1 continued

The Dial Marylebone
13 Westmoreland StMarylebone(B Somerset) Est: 1948. Open 11-6.30. SIZE: Medium. *STOCK: Clocks, 18th C, £500-£5,000.* LOC: Off New Cavendish St. PARK: Meters. TEL: 071 935 2201. SER: Valuations (clocks); restorations (clock movements, cabinets, gilt and French polishing); buys at auction (longcase or bracket). VAT: Stan.

Anthony D'Offay
9, 21 and 23 Dering St, New Bond St. SLAD. Est: 1965. Open 10-5.30; Sat. 10-1. SIZE: Large. *STOCK: Contemporary international paintings, sculpture and drawings.* LOC: Near Oxford Circus and Bond St. tube stations. PARK: Meters in Hanover Sq. TEL: 071 499 4100; fax - 071 493 4443. VAT: Stan/Spec.

A Douch
28 Conduit St. NAG. Est: 1940. Open by appointment only. *STOCK: Jewellery, silver and glass.* TEL: 071 493 9413. SER: Valuations. VAT: Stan/Spec.

Charles Ede Ltd
20 Brook St. Est: 1970. Open 12.30-4.30, or by appointment. CL: Sat., Mon. *STOCK: Greek, Roman and Egyptian antiquities, £50-£25,000.* PARK: Meters. TEL: 071 493 4944. SER: Valuations; buys at auction. VAT: Spec.

Editions Graphiques Gallery
3 Clifford St. (V Arwas) Est: 1966. Open 10-6, Sat. 10-2. SIZE: Large. *STOCK: Art nouveau and art deco, glass, ceramics, bronzes, sculpture, furniture, jewellery, silver, pewter, books and posters 1880-1940, £25-£50,000; paintings, watercolours and drawings, 1880 to date, £100-£20,000; original graphics, lithographs, etchings, woodcuts, 1890 to date, £5-£10,000.* LOC: Between New Bond St and Savile Row. PARK: 50yds. TEL: 071 734 3944. SER: Valuations; buys at auction. VAT: Stan/Spec.

D.H Edmonds Ltd
27 Burlington Arcade, Piccadilly. Open 10-5.30. *STOCK: Jewellery, silver, objets d'art, watches, £50-£20,000.* TEL: 071 495 3127.

Andrew Edmunds
44 Lexington St. Open 10-6. CL: Sat. *STOCK: 18th and early 19th C caricature and decorative prints and drawings.* TEL: 071 437 8594; fax - 071 439 2551. VAT: Stan/Spec.

Emanoeul Antiques Ltd LAPADA
64 South Audley St. (E Naghi) Est: 1974. Open 9.30-6; Sat. 9-1. *STOCK: Important Islamic and fine works of art, 18th and 19th C.* TEL: 071 493 4350; fax - 071 629 3125. VAT: Stan/Spec.

W.1 continued

Entwistle
37 Old Bond St. Open 10-5.30. CL: Sat. *STOCK: Modern, 19th C and Old Master paintings; African and Oceanic art.* TEL: 071 409 3484; fax - 071 499 5795.

Ermitage Ltd
14 Hay Hill. Est: 1985. Open 10-5. CL: Sat. SIZE: Medium. *STOCK: Fabergé objects, £2,000-£60,000+; continental silver, 17th-18th C, £1,000-£50,000+; Russian art, 17th-20th C, £800-£25,000+.* LOC: Mayfair area, between Bond St. and Berkeley Sq. PARK: Berkeley Sq. TEL: 071 499 5459; fax - same. SER: Valuations. FAIRS: London Silver and Jewellery; The Orangerie, Berlin. VAT: Stan/Spec.

Eskenazi Ltd BADA
Foxglove House, 166 Piccadilly. (J.E Eskenazi, L Bandini and P Constantinidi) Est: 1960. Open 9.30-6, Sat. by appointment. SIZE: Large. *STOCK: Early Chinese ceramics; bronzes, sculpture, works of art; Japanese netsuke and lacquer.* LOC: Opposite Old Bond St. TEL: 071 493 5464. VAT: Spec.

Essie Carpets
62 Piccadilly. (E Sakhai) Est: 1766. Open 9.30-6.30, Sun. 10.30-6.30. CL: Sat. SIZE: Large. *STOCK: Persian and Oriental carpets and rugs.* LOC: Opposite St. James St. and Ritz Hotel. PARK: Easy. TEL: 071 493 7766; home - 071 586 3388. SER: Valuations; restorations; commissions undertaken. VAT: Stan/Spec.

Brian Fielden BADA
3 New Cavendish St. Open 9.30-1 and 2-5.30, Sat. 9.30-1. SIZE: Medium. *STOCK: English walnut and mahogany furniture, 18th to early 19th C; mirrors and barometers.* LOC: 5 minutes walk north of Bond St. PARK: Meters. TEL: 071 935 6912. VAT: Spec.

The Fine Art Society plc. BADA
148 New Bond St. SLAD. Est: 1876. Open 9.30-5.30; Sat. 10-1. SIZE: Large. *STOCK: British art, paintings, watercolours, drawings, sculpture, decorative arts, 19th and early 20th C.* PARK: 300yds. TEL: 071 629 5116. SER: Buys at auction. VAT: Stan/Spec.

Fine Jewellery at Liberty's
Liberty plc, Regent St. Est: 1912. Open 9.30-6, Thurs. till 7.30. SIZE: Medium. *STOCK: Jewellery, Georgian to art nouveau, art deco and 'fifties, £100-£10,000.* Not stocked: Furniture, porcelain, pictures. TEL: 071 734 1234. SER: Restorations (jewellery). VAT: Stan/Spec.

W.1 continued

Liliane Flowerdew at Trianon LAPADA

27 Conduit St. Est: 1978. Open 10-5.30. SIZE: Large. *STOCK: Jewellery, 18th to mid 20th C, £500-£100,000; objets d'art, 18th-20th C, £100-£60,000.* LOC: Off Regent St., opposite Liberty's; shop opposite Westbury Hotel. PARK: Hanover Sq. TEL: 071 491 2764; fax - 071 409 1587. FAIRS: Olympia. VAT: Stan/Spec.

Sam Fogg

14 Old Bond St. Est: 1971. Open by appointment. *STOCK: Rare books, manuscripts, all periods.* TEL: 071 495 2333. SER: Valuations; buys at auction.

Forman of Piccadilly Ltd

99 Mount St. Est: 1962. Open 10-6. CL: Sat. *STOCK: General antiques, works of art, militaria, small furniture, curios and unusual items.* TEL: 071 493 2174. SER: Valuations.

Fortnum and Mason plc

Piccadilly. Open 9-5.30. SIZE: Medium. *STOCK: English furniture, 18th C.* PARK: Meters. TEL: 071 734 8040.

Peter Francis BADA

34 Aybrook St. Open by appointment only. *STOCK: Furniture, 1760-1840.* LOC: Baker St., left into Blandford St., left into Aybrook St. TEL: 071 582 7377.

J.A Fredericks and Son BADA

Correspondence only to:99 Hercies Rd, Hillingdon, Middlesex. (J.A. and C.J Fredericks) Est: 1938. Open by appointment. *STOCK: English furniture.* TEL: 0895 55462. VAT: Spec. *Trade Only.*

H Fritz-Denneville Fine Arts Ltd

31 New Bond St. Open 9.30-6, Sat. by appointment. *STOCK: Paintings and drawings especially Old Masters, German, 19th C and modern.* TEL: 071 629 2466. SER: Valuations; restorations; buys at auction.

Frost and Reed Ltd BADA

16 Old Bond St. Est: 1808. Open 9-5.30. CL: Sat. *STOCK: Fine 19th C British and continental paintings, marine and sporting pictures, Impressionist drawings and watercolours; works by Marcel Dyf.* PARK: Meters. TEL: 071 629 2457; fax - 071 499 0299. VAT: Stan/Spec.

Deborah Gage (Works of Art) Ltd

38 Old Bond St. Est: 1982. Open 9.30-5.30. CL: Sat. *STOCK: European decorative arts and paintings, 17th-18th C; French and British pictures, late 19th to early 20th C, from £5,000.* TEL: 071 493 3249; fax - 071 495 1352. SER: Valuations; cataloguing; buys at auction. VAT: Stan/Spec.

W.1 continued

Garrard & Co Ltd (The Crown Jewellers) BADA

112 Regent St. (E.M Green) Est: 1723. Open 9-5.30, Sat. 9.30-1. SIZE: Large. *STOCK: Silver, clocks, jewellery, from £100.* TEL: 071 734 7020. SER: Restorations (antique silver and clocks). FAIRS: Grosvenor House and Burlington House. VAT: Stan.

Marilyn Garrow Antique Textiles

Liberty PLC, Regent St. Open 9.30-6, Thurs. 9.30-7.30. *STOCK: Basement - Oriental textiles.* TEL: 071 734 1234, ext. 2283.

Christopher Gibbs Ltd

8 Vigo St. Est: 1960. Open 9.30-5.30. CL: Sat. SIZE: Large. *STOCK: Pictures of the major painters of all periods; furniture, works of art, garden statuary.* TEL: 071 439 4557. VAT: Spec.

Thomas Gibson Fine Art Ltd

44 Old Bond St. Open 10-5. CL: Sat. *STOCK: 19th-20th C Masters and selected Old Masters.* TEL: 071 499 8572; fax - 071 495 1924.

Attilio Gilberti

70 Wigmore St. Open 10-5.30. CL: Sat. *STOCK: Fine Oriental carpets.* TEL: 071 487 3167/935 4339.

M. and R Glendale

9a New Cavendish St. (entrance Marylebone St.). (R Sands and M.D Sears) ABA. Open 10-6. CL: Sat. *STOCK: Books including children's, illustrated and cookery.* TEL: 071 487 5348.

Thomas Goode and Co (London) Ltd BADA

19 South Audley St. Est: 1827. Open 9.30-5.30. SIZE: Large. *STOCK: China, glass, tableware, ornamental.* TEL: 071 499 2823. SER: Restorations. VAT: Spec.

A. and F Gordon BADA

120a Mount St. Est: 1935. Open 9.30-5.30. CL: Sat. SIZE: Medium. *STOCK: English and continental furniture, paintings, bronzes, porcelain, marbles.* TEL: 071 499 5596. VAT: Stan/Spec.

Gillian Gould

at Captain O.M. Watts,49 Albemarle St, Piccadilly. Open 9-6, Thurs. 9-8, Sat. 9.30-5. SIZE: Small. *STOCK: Nautical antiques and collectables, £30-£1,000.* LOC: Near Bond St. PARK: Meters. TEL: 071 493 8845; home 081 905 5180. SER: Restorations; (scientific instruments); buys at auction (nautical and scientific instruments); hire. VAT: Stan.

W.1 continued

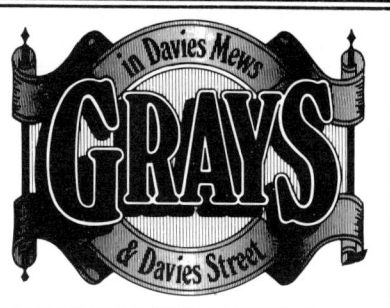

Graus Antiques **LAPADA**
39-41 New Bond St. (E. and H Graus) Est: 1948. Open 9.30-5.30. CL: Sat. SIZE: Medium. *STOCK: Watches, jewellery, enamels, objets d'art.* PARK: Meters. TEL: 071 629 6680. VAT: Stan/Spec.

Grays Antique Market
58 Davies St. Open 10-6. CL: Sat. TEL: 071 629 7034. Below are listed the dealers at this market.

Abacus Antiques
Stand 313. *Jewellery and objects.* TEL: 071 629 9681.
A and G Antiques
Stand 168/9. *Jewellery.* TEL: 071 493 7564.
Arca
Stand 351/2/3. *Ivory, treen, tortoiseshell.* TEL: 071 629 2729.
Armada Antiques **LAPADA**
Stand 122. *Antique weapons.* TEL: 071 499 1087.
Armoury Antiques **LAPADA**
Stand 123. *Antique weapons.* TEL: 071 408 0176.
Sean Arnold
Stand 316. *Golf and polo items.* TEL: 071 409 7358.
Osman Aytac
Stand 331. *Pens and watches.*
R and R Badir
Stand 144. *Jewellery and objets d'art.* TEL: 071 629 6467.
Benjamin/Cook
Stand 127. *Oriental items.* TEL: 071 499 4340.
Colin Bowdell **LAPADA**
Stand 123. *Arms and armour.* TEL: 071 408 0176.
David Bowden
Stand 303. *Oriental items including netsuke.* TEL: 071 495 1773.
Stanhope Bowry
Stand 104. *Leather and antique luggage.* TEL: 071 629 6194.
Patrick Boyd-Carpenter/Philip Bret-Day
Stand 108. *Watercolours and prints.* TEL: 071 491 7623.

Grays Antique Market continued

Britannia
Stand 101. *Commemorative, Doulton and studio pottery.* TEL: 071 629 6772.
Patricia Byrne
Stand 321. *Jewellery.* TEL: 071 629 5011.
Carol and Jeffrey Groombridge
Stand 335. *Jewellery.* TEL: 071 629 0225.
Cekay Antiques
Stand 172. *Objets d'art - glass, pictures, walking sticks.* TEL: 071 629 5130.
Cerberus
Stand 372/3. *Walking canes, silver, watches.* TEL: 071 499 4340.
T A Cherrington
Stand 107. *Atlases, maps, books, prints, watercolours.* TEL: 071 495 1630.
Joy Continuum
Stand 124. *Oriental and tribal arts.* TEL: 071 493 4909.
Cozy World
Stand 385. *Cameras, lighters and watches.* TEL: 071 409 0269.
Croesus/Westleigh Antiques **LAPADA**
Stand 323. *Jewellery and silver.* TEL: 071 493 0624.
J.M Davies (Jewellers) Ltd **LAPADA**
Stand 323. *Jewellery.* TEL: 071 493 0624.
J and P Dowling
Stand 365. *Prints.* TEL: 071 629 4150.
Evonne
Stand 338. *Silver and objets d'art.* TEL: 071 499 4340.
William Ewer
Stand 133. *Antiquarian prints.* TEL: 071 629 5130.
Ronald Falloon
Stand 371. *Glass and drink related objects.* TEL: 071 499 0158.
Jack First
Stand 310. *Silver.* TEL: 071 409 2722.
Adrian Forman
Stand 120. *Aeronautical prints.* TEL: 071 629 6599.
The Gilded Lily **LAPADA**
Stand 131. *Jewellery.* TEL: 071 499 6260.
K N Grant
Stand 176. *Brass and pewter.* TEL: 071 629 5130.

Grays Antique Market continued

Solveig and Anita Gray **LAPADA**
Stand 307/8. *Oriental porcelain, continental silver, objects.* TEL: 071 408 1638.
Susan Haines
Stand 375. *Photographs.* TEL: 071 499 1038.
Hallmark **LAPADA**
Stand 359. *Jewellery, silver, art deco and nouveau.* TEL: 071 409 2937.
Diana Harby
Stand 148/149. *Lace.* TEL: 071 629 5130.
Brian Harkins
Stand 126. *Chinese and Japanese items.* TEL: 071 409 2530.
Hoffman Antiques
Stand 379. *Silver.* TEL: 071 499 4340.
David Hogg
Stand 109. *Tools, instruments and gadgets.* TEL: 071 493 0208.
Holland Antiques
Stand 152/3. *Jewellery.* TEL: 071 629 6502.
Lynn and Brian Holmes **LAPADA**
Stand 304/5/6. *Jewellery, silver.* TEL: 071 629 7327.
Adrienne Hutter
Stand 339. *Clothing and hats.* TEL: 071 629 3534.
Giulia Irving **LAPADA**
Stand 384. Est: 1973. *English porcelain, 18th-19th C, £50-£5,000.* TEL: 071 499 1038. FAIRS: Olympia, Wakefield Ceramic, NEC (Aug.). VAT: Spec.
John Jaffa
Stand 301. *Objets d'art.* TEL: 071 491 7162.
John Joseph **LAPADA**
Stand 345. *Jewellery.* TEL: 071 629 1140.
Felicity Kearney
Stand 327. *Jewellery.*
Roy Kemp
Stand 367. *Lalique and china.* TEL: 071 629 5011.
Kunio Kikuchi
Stand 357/8. *Tobacco jars, pipes, jewellery.* TEL: 071 629 6808.
Barbara Lancaster
Stand 139. *Jewellery.* TEL: 071 499 4340.
Pat Lennard
Stand 149. *English glass.* TEL: 071 629 5130.
Licht and Morrison **LAPADA**
Stand 158. *Jewellery.* TEL: 071 493 7497.
Monty Lo
Stand 369. *Meissen and Berlin porcelain.* TEL: 071 493 9457.
C Lucbernet/Francoise Brown
Stand 329/330. *Objets d'art and jewellery.* TEL: 071 493 1219.
Sue Maddon
Stand 128. *Lace, quilts and textiles.* TEL: 071 493 1307.
Peggy Malone
Stand 322. *Jewellery, china, objets d'art.* TEL: 071 493 7621.
Fiandaca Myers
Stand 386. *Silver.* TEL: 071 493 0768.

Grays Antique Market continued

Howard Neville Antiques
Stand 177/178. *European works of art; marine and scientific instruments.* TEL: 071 493 1148.
Steven O'Donnell **LAPADA**
Stand 156. *Scientific instruments and general furniture.* TEL: 071 491 8852.
David Odling
Stand 137. *Paintings and clocks.* TEL: 071 629 5130.
Nadine Okker
Stand 384. *Porcelain.* TEL: 071 499 4340.
Omniphil
Stand 114. *Antiquarian books, and prints.* TEL: 071 629 3223.
David Paskin **LAPADA**
Stand 347. *Jewellery.* TEL: 071 408 1129.
Puzzle House Antiques **LAPADA**
Stand 108. *Inlaid writing and other boxes; paintings and decorative items.* TEL: Home - 0594 60653. VAT: Stan/Spec.
R B R Group
Stand 175. *Jewellery.* TEL: 071 629 4769.
S D P
Stand 325. *Silver.* TEL: 071 629 5991.
Satoe
Stand 161. *Paste and marcasite jewellery.* TEL: 071 629 4296.
Shapiro and Co
Stand 378/380. *Silver, watches and objets d'art.* TEL: 071 491 2710.
Thimble Society
Stands 134/136. *Thimbles.* TEL: 071 493 0560.
Trianon **LAPADA**
Stand 154. *Jewellery.* TEL: 071 491 2764.
Vintage
Stand 371. *Glass and drink related items, English porcelain and objets d'art.* TEL: 071 483 9457.
Mary Wellard
Stand 164/5. *Small furniture, objects, glass.* TEL: 071 629 5130.
Westminster Group **LAPADA**
Stand 139/50. *Jewellery.* TEL: 071 493 8672.
Wheatley Antiques **LAPADA**
Stand 106. *Oriental porcelain.* TEL: 071 408 1528.
Wimpole Antiques **LAPADA**
Stand 344. *Jewellery and objets d'art.* TEL: 071 499 2889.
Craig Wyncoll
Stand 125. *Prints.* TEL: 071 409 1498.

Grays Mews

1-7 Davies Mews. Open 10-6. CL: Sat. TEL: 071 629 7034. Below are listed some of the dealers at this market.

Allison's
J17/18. *Victorian jet, paste and art deco jewellery.* TEL: 071 629 3788.
Patricia Angeli
L16. *Jewellery.* TEL: 071 629 1184.

Grays Mews continued

The Antique Connoisseur plc LAPADA
M17/19. *Watches and silver.* TEL: 071 629 3272.
Armand Antiques
C22. *Oriental works of art.* TEL: 071 493 6692.
Arms and Armour/Chris Seidler
G12. *Arms and armour.* TEL: 071 629 2851.
Elias Assad
A16/17. B14. *Eastern art.* TEL: 071 499 4778.
Colin Baddiel
C12/B25. *Toys.* TEL: 071 629 2813.
Baddiel/Golfiana
B12/A27/8. *Books on golf.* TEL: 071 408 1239.
David Baker
H23. *Oriental.* TEL: 071 629 3788.
Baudey and Bricher
A29. *Medals.* TEL: 071 629 2823.
Judy Bebber
L14. *Dolls.* TEL: 071 499 6600.
Sylvie Bedwell
J26. *Jewellery.* TEL: 071 629 3501.
Linda Bee
M20. *Art deco.* TEL: 071 629 5921.
Beslali
K33. *Jewellery and silver.* TEL: 071 629 1184.
Ruth Bogojevic
A12/13. *Prints.* TEL: 071 629 2813.
Sue Brown and John Weysom
M14/16. *Jewellery and objects.* TEL: 071 491 4287.
Ruth Clark
K32. *Objects and jewellery.* TEL: 071 629 3788.
Teresa Clayton
L24. *Jewellery and Victoriana.* TEL: 071 629 1184.
Yonna Cohen
C17. *Toys.* TEL: 071 629 3644.
Stuart Cropper
C26. *Mechanical toys.* TEL: 071 499 6600.
Alan Darer
A22. *General.* TEL: 071 629 3644.
Sandy Dickinson
A18/19.
Domus
H24. *Furniture, pictures, bronzes, boxes.* TEL: 071 629 1319.
Donohoe BADA
L25/7, M10/12. *Jewellery, silver and vertu; European needlework, all £50-£15,000.* TEL: 071 629 5633; home - 081 455 5507.
Rosemary Ebrich
C26. *General.* TEL: 071 629 2526.
Ester and Leslie
M13. *Jewellery and silver.* TEL: 071 629 3596.
Sue Flegg Antiques
C20. *Decorative smalls and folding chairs.* TEL: 071 629 3785.

Grays Mews continued

Galerie Harounoff
K20/21. *19th-20th C oil paintings and watercolours.* TEL: 071 408 0803.
Trevor Gilbert
G10/11. *Silver.* TEL: 071 408 0028.
Ora Gordon
J27. *19th C china boxes and decorative items.* TEL: 071 629 3788.
Patrick and Susan Gould
L17. *Art nouveau and art deco glass.* TEL: 071 408 0129.
Anthony Gray
H26/7/8. *Oriental works of art.* TEL: 071 408 1252.
Colin Gross
K10. *Oriental works of art.* TEL: 071 629 3788.
Alice Gulessarian
J15. *Jewellery, collectables.* TEL: 071 629 3788.
Hawkin
K17. *Oriental.* TEL: 071 629 1134.
Heian Gallery
C19. *Oriental ceramics and works of art.* TEL: 071 629 3644.
Keats
J29. *Silver.* TEL: 071 499 2382.
P H McAskie
D10/11. *Toys.* TEL: 071 629 2813.
Robert McPherson
G16. *Oriental porcelain.* TEL: 071 629 3788.
Mankowitz
C31/32. *Tribal antiquities and Oriental works of art.* TEL: 071 629 2526.
Minoo and Andre
G22/23. *Jewellery, silver and clocks.* TEL: 071 629 1200.
Ali Mohammed
C24. *Oriental porcelain.* TEL: 071 629 2526.
Namdar
B21/22/C15/6. *Oriental and Islamic works of art.* TEL: 071 629 1183.
J O'Callaghan
J25. *Antiquarian and fine books.* TEL: 071 629 3788.
Orion Antiques
K24. *Oriental.* TEL: 071 408 0434.
Madeline Popper LAPADA
L12. *Antique, secondhand and art deco jewellery, including goldwork and cameos; cut steel, Berlin iron, objets de vertu and antiquities.* TEL: 071 408 1089.
Lily Randall
J16. *Collectors' items, silver and jewellery.* TEL: 071 629 3788.
Remember When
B13. *Toys, transport ephemera and collectors' tins.*
Pat Richardson
G12/13. *Prints.* TEL: 071 629 1533.
Jonathan Robinson
K24. *Chinese, porcelain and works of art.* TEL: 071 629 3644; 071 493 0592.

Grays Mews continued

Samiramis Ltd **LAPADA**
E18/21. *Islamic works of art and carpets.* TEL: 071 629 1161.
Shadad Antiques
B14. *Antiquities including Islamic.* TEL: 071 499 0572.
Boris Sosna
K32. *Jewellery and silver.* TEL: 071 629 2371.
Stanley, Ian and Mandy
L18. *Jewellery.* TEL: 071 629 4083.
Surena Antiques
K37. *Antiquities and coins.* TEL: 071 493 6762.
Tapsell Antiques
E14/17. *Oriental porcelain, furniture, ivories and netsuke.*
Trotter/Parsons
A10/11. *Antiquities, tribal.* TEL: 071 629 2813.
Vandekar Antiques
G19/20. H13/14/15. *Oriental works of art.* TEL: 071 499 0010.
Betty and Vera Vandekar
D13/14/15/16. *Oriental, English and continental porcelain.* TEL: 071 493 0701.
Ailie Warren
G18. *Paintings.* TEL: 071 629 3788.
Aura Williamson
L10. *Oriental antiques.* TEL: 071 629 3788.

Grays Mews continued

R Wolkowinski
B15. *Oriental, netsuke, ojime.* TEL: 071 629 3644.
Linda Wrigglesworth **LAPADA**
A20/21/23. *Chinese textiles.* TEL: 071 408 0177.

Richard Green **BADA**

44 and 39 Dover St. and 4 New Bond St. Open 9.30-5.30, Sat. 10-12.30. *STOCK: Paintings - Old Master and British; French impressionist and modern British; Victorian sporting and British marine.* PARK: Meters. TEL: 071 493 3939; fax - 071 629 2609. VAT: Stan/Spec.

Simon Griffin Antiques Ltd

3 Royal Arcade, 28 Old Bond St. (S.J Griffin) Est: 1979. Open 10-5, Sat. 10-12. *STOCK: Silver, old Sheffield plate.* TEL: 071 491 7367. VAT: Stan/Spec.

Hadji Baba Ancient Art

34a Davies St. (R.R. Soleimani) Est: 1939. Open 9.30-6, Sat. and Sun. by appointment. SIZE: Medium. *STOCK: Ancient and Islamic art, carpets and rugs.* LOC: Next to Claridges Hotel. PARK: Meters. TEL: 071 499 9363/9384. SER: Valuations.

Bank of England
BANK of ENGLAND

An enamelled £5 brooch in a stamped frame, impounded by the Bank of England between 1878 and 1887 under the Forgery Act. Other banknote brooches imitating £10 and £20 notes were regarded as so good that they represented a threat to the currency. Imported by traders from France and Austria, they caused considerable agitation in the Bank of England. BANK OF ENGLAND MUSEUM
From ***Jewellery 1789-1910 — The International Era,*** Volume II, by Shirley Bury, published by the **Antique Collectors' Club** in 1991. £47.50 each volume.

W.1 continued

Hadleigh Jewellers

30A Marylebone High St. Open 9.30-5.30. *STOCK: Jewellery, some silver.* TEL: 071 935 4074. SER: Valuations; repairs; hand-made jewellery. VAT: Stan/Spec.

Hahn and Son Fine Art Dealers

47 Albemarle St. (P Hahn) Est: 1897. Open 9.30-5.30. CL: Sat. *STOCK: English oil paintings, 18th-19th C.* TEL: 071 493 9196. VAT: Stan.

Halcyon Days BADA

14 Brook St. (S Benjamin) Est: 1950. 9.15-5.30, Sat. 9.30-4.30. *STOCK: 18th to early 19th C enamels, papier mâché, tôle, objects of vertu, treen, Staffordshire pottery figures, prints, small unusual Georgian furniture.* LOC: Hanover Sq. end of Book St. PARK: Meters and in Hanover Sq. TEL: 071 629 8811; fax - 071 409 0280. FAIRS: Grosvenor House. VAT: Stan/Spec.

Hancocks and Co (Jewellers) Ltd BADA

1 Burlington Gardens. Est: 1849. Open 9.30-5. CL: Sat. SIZE: Medium. *STOCK: Jewellery, 1800-1940, £250-£50,000; especially signed pieces; silver, especially Omar Ramsden, 17th-20th C, £50-£50,000.* LOC: Opposite top of Burlington Arcade, off Piccadilly. TEL: 071 493 8904; fax - 071 493 8905. SER: Valuations; restorations (silver and jewellery); buys at auction. FAIRS: International Silver and Jewellery, Park Lane Hotel; International Antique Dealers', New York. VAT: Stan/Spec.

Hancocks and Co (Jewellers) Ltd continued

Harcourt Antiques

5 Harcourt Street. (J Christophe) Est: 1961. Open 10-5 or by appointment. CL: Mon. *STOCK: English, continental and Oriental porcelain, pre-1830.* PARK: Easy. TEL: 071 723 5919. VAT: Stan. *Trade Only.*

David Harrington Gallery

27 Berkeley Sq. Open 10-6, Sat. 10-1 or by appointment. *STOCK: Russian and Soviet paintings, 19th-20th C.* TEL: 071 495 3194; fax - 071 409 3175. SER: Valuations. VAT: Stan.

S.H Harris and Son (London) Ltd BADA

17-18 Old Bond St. (B.C. and R.H Harris) Est: 1885. Open 9-5. CL: Sat. SIZE: Small. *STOCK: Jewellery and silver.* LOC: 50yds from Piccadilly. PARK: Burlington St. TEL: 071 499 0352. SER: Valuations. VAT: Stan/Spec. *Trade Only.*

W.1 continued

Harvey and Gore **BADA**
4 Burlington Gdns. (B.E Norman) Est: 1723. Open 9.30-5. CL: Sat. SIZE: Small. ***STOCK: Jewellery, £150-£150,000; silver, £50-£15,000, old Sheffield plate, £65-£6,000; antique paste.*** **LOC: Near top of Burlington Arcade, off Piccadilly. PARK: 100yds. New Burlington St. TEL: 071 493 2714; fax - 071 493 0324. SER: Valuations; restorations (jewellery and silver); buys at auction. VAT: Stan/Spec.**

W.R Harvey & Co (Antiques) Ltd **BADA**
5 Old Bond St. (W.R., G.M. and A.D Harvey) Est: 1952. Open 10-5.30. SIZE: Large. ***STOCK: Fine English furniture, clocks, barometers, mirrors, paintings, framed engravings and objets d'art, 1675-1830.*** **LOC: 50yds from Piccadilly. TEL: 071 499 8385; fax - 071 495 0209. SER: Valuations; restorations. FAIRS: Park Lane. VAT: Stan/Spec.**

Brian Haughton Antiques
3b Burlington Gdns, Old Bond St. Est: 1965. Open 10-5.30. SIZE: Large. *STOCK: British and European ceramics, porcelain and pottery, 18th and 19th C, £100-£50,000.* PARK: Nearby, Savile Row N.C.P. TEL: 071 734 5491. SER: Buys at auction (porcelain and pottery). FAIRS:

Brian Haughton Antiques continued

International Ceramics and International Silver and Jewellery - Park Lane Hotel (organiser), International Antique Dealers Show (organiser). VAT: Spec.

Hennell Ltd. Founded 1736 (incorporating Frazer and Haws (1868) and E. Lloyd Lawrence (1830)) **BADA**
12 New Bond St. Open 9-5.30, Sat. 10-4. SIZE: Medium. ***STOCK: Fine jewellery, silver.*** **PARK: Meters. TEL: 071 629 6888. SER: Valuations; restorations (silver, jewellery). VAT: Stan/Spec.**

Heskia **BADA**
19 Mount St. Est: 1877. Open 9.30-6. CL: Sat. ***STOCK: Oriental carpets, rugs and tapestries.*** **TEL: 071 629 1483. SER: Valuations; cleaning and repairs.**

G Heywood Hill Ltd
10 Curzon St. (D Bacon) Open 9-5.30, Sat. 9-12.30. *STOCK: Books, Victorian illustrated, children's and natural history.* TEL: 071 629 0647.

W.1 continued

Holland and Holland Ltd
31 and 33 Bruton St. Est: 1835. Open 9.30-5.30, Sat. 10-4. CL: Sat. Jan.-July (No.33 only). SIZE: Medium. *STOCK: Modern and antique guns, rifles, weapons and associated items; sporting prints and pictures; field sports and wildlife books.* PARK: Meters at Berkeley Sq. TEL: 071 499 4411. SER: Valuations. VAT: Stan/Spec.

Holmes Ltd BADA
29 Old Bond St., also at 24 Burlington Arcade. (A.N., B.J. and I.J Neale) Open 9-5.30. CL: Sat. p.m. *STOCK: Jewels and silver.* TEL: 071 493 1396/629 8380. SER: Valuations; restorations. VAT: Stan.

Dennis Hotz Fine Art Ltd
1st Floor, 9 Cork St. Open 10-6, Sat. by appointment. *STOCK: 19th-20th C works of art and sculpture.* TEL: 071 287 8324; fax - 071 287 9713.

How of Edinburgh
1st Floor, 28 Albemarle St. (Mrs G.E.P How) Est: 1930. Open 9.45-5.30. CL: Sat. *STOCK: Silver, to 1800.* PARK: Easy. TEL: 071 408 1867. VAT: Stan/Spec.

Howard Antiques
8 Davies St, Berkeley Sq. Est: 1955. Open 9-6, Sat. by appointment. SIZE: Medium. *STOCK:*

Howard Antiques continued

English and continental furniture, objects. PARK: N.C.P. nearby. TEL: 071 629 2628. SER: Valuations. VAT: Stan/Spec.

C John (Rare Rugs) Ltd BADA
70 South Audley St, Mayfair. Est: 1947. Open 9-5. CL: Sat. *STOCK: Textiles, pre-1800, carpets, tapestries, embroideries.* TEL: 071 493 5288. VAT: Stan/Spec.

Johnson Walker & Tolhurst Ltd BADA
64 Burlington Arcade. Est: 1849. Open 9.30-5.30. *STOCK: Antique and secondhand jewellery, objets d'art, silver.* TEL: 071 629 2615. SER: Restorations (jewellery, pearl-stringing). VAT: Stan/Spec.

E Joseph Antiquarian Bookseller (Est 1876) BADA
1 Vere St. ABA. Open 9.30-5.30 or by appointment. CL: Sat. *STOCK: Rare and fine books specialising in English literature, colour plate, illustrated and press books, fine bindings, Churchilliana, library sets in leather and original cloth; original watercolours by illustrators, from £100.* LOC: Opposite New Bond St., north side of Oxford St. TEL: 071 493 8353/4/5; fax - 071 629 2579. SER: Valuations; buys at auction. VAT: Stan/Spec.

W.1 continued

Alexander Juran and Co BADA

74 New Bond St. Est: 1951. Open 9.15-5.30. CL: Sat. *STOCK: Caucasian rugs, nomadic and tribal; carpets, rugs, tapestries.* TEL: 071 629 2550 /493 4484. SER: Valuations; repairs. VAT: Stan/Spec.

Kennedy Carpets and Kelims LAPADA

9A Vigo St. (M Kennedy) Est: 1974. Open 9.30-6. SIZE: Large. *STOCK: Decorative carpets, collectable rugs and kelims, mid-19th to early 20th C, £200-£50,000.* LOC: Off Regent St., up Sackville St. from Piccadilly, left into Vigo St., shop on left-hand side. PARK: Brewer St. TEL: 071 439 8873; fax - 071 437 1201. SER: Valuations; restorations and cleaning (carpets and kelims). VAT: Stan.

Robin Kennedy

29 New Bond St. Open 10-6 or by appointment. CL: Sat. *STOCK: Japanese prints and paintings.* TEL: 071 408 1238; home - 081 940 3281.

Richard Kruml

P.O. Box 4ER. Est: 1966. Open by appointment. *STOCK: Japanese prints, paintings and books, £25-£10,000.* TEL: 071 499 0790; fax - 071 499 0746. VAT: Stan.

Lady Newborough

1 Whitehorse St, Shepherd's Market. (R.D Rush) Est: 1946. Open 10-6. *STOCK: Jewellery, silverware, objets d'art.* TEL: 071 493 3954. VAT: Stan.

Lane Fine Art Ltd BADA LAPADA

123 New Bond St. (C Foley and A Nelson) Open 10-6, Sat. 10-1. *STOCK: Oil paintings, 1500-1850 especially English portraits and sporting paintings, landscapes and marines 18th C, £5,000-£5000,000.* TEL: 071 499 5020. VAT: Stan/Spec.

D.S Lavender (Antiques) Ltd BADA

16b Grafton St. Est: 1945. Open 9.30-5. CL: Sat. SIZE: Medium. *STOCK: Jewels, miniatures, works of art.* PARK: Meters. TEL: 071 629 1782. SER: Valuations. VAT: Stan/Spec.

Ronald A Lee (Fine Arts) Ltd BADA

1-9 Bruton Pl. (R.A. and C.B Lee) Est: 1930. Open 10-5. CL: Sat. SIZE: Large. *STOCK: Clocks, furniture, pictures, works of art.* PARK: Meters. TEL: 071 629 5600/499 6266. VAT: Spec.

Lefevre Gallery

30 Bruton St. (A Reid and Lefevre Ltd) Est: 1871. Open 10-5. CL: Sat. SIZE: Medium. *STOCK: Impressionist paintings, 19th-20th C.* LOC: Between Berkeley Sq. and Bond St. PARK: Meters, Berkeley Sq. TEL: 071 493 2107. SER: Valuations. VAT: Spec.

W.1 continued

The Leger Galleries Ltd BADA

13 Old Bond St. (D.W Posnett, L.J Libson and R.V Craig) SLAD. Est: 1892. Open 9-5.30, Sat. by appointment. SIZE: Large. *STOCK: Old Masters, English paintings, early English watercolours.* PARK: Meters. TEL: 071 629 3538. SER: Valuations; restorations.

Liberty

Regent St. Est: 1875. Open 9.30-6, Thurs. till 7.30. SIZE: Large. *STOCK: General antiques, 19th C; Victoriana, Edwardiana, arts and crafts, art nouveau and jewellery.* LOC: Regent St. joins Piccadilly and Oxford Circus. PARK: Meters and underground in Cavendish Sq. TEL: 071 734 1234. VAT: Stan.

M. and L. Silver Co Ltd LAPADA

2 Woodstock St. (C Lasher) Est: 1952. Open 9-5, weekends by appointment. *STOCK: Silver, plate, 1750-1900, £100-£25,000.* LOC: 100yds. from Bond St. Station. TEL: 071 499 5392/5170.

Maas Gallery

15a Clifford St, New Bond St. (J.S Maas) Est: 1960. Open 10-5. CL: Sat. SIZE: Medium. *STOCK: Victorian paintings, drawings, watercolours, illustrations.* LOC: Between New Bond St. and Cork St. PARK: Easy. TEL: 071 734 2302; fax - 071 287 4836. SER: Valuations; buys at auction. VAT: Spec.

MacConnal-Mason Gallery BADA

15 Burlington Arcade, Piccadilly. Est: 1893. Open 9-5.30. SIZE: Medium. *STOCK: Pictures 19th-20th C.* PARK: Meters. TEL: 071 499 6991. SER: Valuations; restorations. VAT: Spec.

Maggs Bros Ltd BADA

50 Berkeley Sq. (J.F., B.D. and E.F Maggs, P Harcourt, R Harding, H Bett and J Collins) ABA. Est: 1853. Open 9.30-5. CL: Sat. SIZE: Large. *STOCK: Rare books, manuscripts, autograph letters, and western miniatures.* PARK: Meters. TEL: 071 493 7160 (4 lines); fax - 071 499 2007. VAT: Stan/Spec.

Mahboubian Gallery

65 Grosvenor St. (H Mahboubian) TEL: 071 493 9112.

Mallett and Son (Antiques) Ltd BADA

141 New Bond St. Est: 1870. Open 9.15-5.15. CL: Sat. SIZE: Large. *STOCK: English furniture, 1690-1835; clocks, 17th-18th C; china, needlework, decorative pictures and objects.* PARK: Meters in Berkeley Sq. TEL: 071 499 7411; fax - 071 495 3179.

Mallett at Bourdon House Ltd

2 Davies St. Open 9.30-5.30. CL: Sat. SIZE: Large. *STOCK: Continental furniture, clocks, objets d'art; garden statuary and ornaments.* PARK: Meters, Berkeley Sq. TEL: 071 629 2444. VAT: Stan/Spec.

W.1 continued

Mansour Gallery
46 Davies St. (M Mokhtarzadeh) Open 9.30-5.30, Sat. by appointment. *STOCK: Islamic works of art, miniatures, carpets; ancient glass and glazed wares; also Greek, Roman and Egyptian antiquities.* TEL: 071 491 7444/499 0510. VAT: Stan.

Marks Antiques Ltd LAPADA
49 Curzon St. (A Marks) Est: 1945. Open 9.30-6 including bank holidays. SIZE: Large. *STOCK: Silver, Sheffield plate.* LOC: Green Park tube, opposite Washington Hotel. PARK: Meters. TEL: 071 499 1788. SER: Valuations; buys at auction. VAT: Stan/Spec.

Marlborough Fine Art (London) Ltd
6 Albemarle St. Est: 1946. Open 10-5.30, Sat. 10-12.30. *STOCK: Masters, 19th-20th C.* PARK: Meters or near Cork St. TEL: 071 629 5161.

Marlborough Rare Books Ltd
144 New Bond St. Est: 1946. Open 9.30-5.30. CL: Sat. SIZE: Small. *STOCK: Illustrated books of all periods; rare and out of print books on fine and applied arts.* PARK: Meters. TEL: 071 493 6993. SER: Buys at auction.

Jeremy J Mason Oriental Art
29 New Bond St. Est: 1968. Open 11-4, appointment advisable. *STOCK: Oriental art, especially Japanese lacquer; porcelain, works of art, Chinese ceramics and jades.* TEL: 071 629 3410; home - 081 874 4173.

Massada Antiques LAPADA
45 New Bond St. (B. and C Yacobi) Est: 1970. Open 10-5.30, Thurs. 10-6.30. CL: Sat. SIZE: Large. *STOCK: Jewellery, 18th to early 20th C, £50-£25,000; decorative silver £30-£2,500.* LOC: Near Sotheby's. PARK: Grosvenor Garage. TEL: 071 493 4792/493 5610. SER: Valuations; restorations (jewellery). VAT: Stan/Spec.

Mayfair Carpet Gallery Ltd
41 New Bond St. *STOCK: Persian, Oriental rugs and carpets.* TEL: 071 493 0126.

Mayfair Gallery
36 Davies St. (M Sinai) Open 10-6, Sat. by appointment. *STOCK: 19th-20th C antique and decorative art; Gallé, Daum and Lalique glass; Mucha lithographs.* TEL: 071 491 3435; fax - 071 491 3437.

Melton's
27 Bruton Pl. (C Neal) Open 9.30-5.30. CL: Sat. *STOCK: Decorative items and accessories.* TEL: 071 409 2938.

W.1 continued

David Messum BADA
34 St George St. SLAD. Est: 1960. Open 9-6. SIZE: Large. *STOCK: Pictures including British Impressionists, 1880-1940; 18th-19th C and contemporary.* TEL: 071 408 0243. SER: Valuations; restorations (oil paintings). VAT: Stan/Spec.

Roy Miles Gallery
29 Bruton St. Open 10-6, Sat. 10-1. *STOCK: Major British and Russian paintings.* TEL: 071 495 4747.

Nigel Milne Ltd
16c Grafton St. Est: 1979. Open 9.30-5.30, Sat. by appointment. SIZE: Small. *STOCK: Jewellery, Victorian to 1950's, £200-£100,000; silver frames, Edwardian, £300-£1,500.* LOC: Corner Grafton St. and Albemarle St., off New Bond St. PARK: Easy. TEL: 071 493 9646/491 2504. SER: Valuations; buys at auction. VAT: Stan/Spec.

John Mitchell and Son BADA
160 New Bond St (1st Floor). Est: 1931. Open 9.30-5. CL: Sat. SIZE: Small. *STOCK: Old Master paintings, drawings and watercolours, Dutch, 17th C; English, 18th C; French, 19th C; especially flower paintings.* LOC: Nearest tube Green Park. PARK: Meters. TEL: 071 493 7567. SER: Valuations; restorations (pictures); buys at auction.

Paul Mitchell Ltd BADA
99 New Bond St. Open 9.30-5.30. CL: Sat. *STOCK: Picture frames.* TEL: 071 493 8732/0860.

Bashir Mohamed Ltd
46 Montagu Sq. Open 10-5 by appointment only. CL: Sat. *STOCK: Islamic art, Indian, Moghul and south east Asian manuscripts and objects.* TEL: 071 723 1844. VAT: Spec.

Moira
22-23 New Bond St. Open 10-5.30. *STOCK: Fine antique and art deco jewellery.* TEL: 071 629 0160. VAT: Valuations.

Sydney L Moss Ltd BADA
51 Brook St. (P.G. and E.M Moss) Est: 1910. Open 10-5. CL: Sat. SIZE: Large. *STOCK: Chinese and Japanese paintings and works of art, ceramics, 1500BC-1950; Japanese netsuke, 18th-20th C; reference books (as stock).* LOC: From Grosvenor Sq., up Brook St. to Claridges. PARK: Meters. TEL: 071 629 4670/493 7374; fax - 071 491 9278. SER: Valuations and advice; buys at auction. FAIRS: Grosvenor House. VAT: Spec.

W.1 continued

Anthony Mould Ltd
1st Floor, 173 New Bond St. Open by appointment. *STOCK: Historic portraits, Old Master and English paintings.* TEL: 071 491 4627.

Paul Nels Ltd LAPADA
44 South Molton St. (P.J Nels) Open 8.30-5.30. CL: Sat. p.m. *STOCK: Rugs, carpets, tapestries and textiles.* TEL: 071 629 1909.

L Newland and Son
17 Picton Pl. Est: 1963. Open 9.30-2 and 3.30-6. CL: Sat. SIZE: Medium. *STOCK: Secondhand jewellery, £10-£1,000.* LOC: 1 minute from Selfridges. PARK: Easy, Selfridges. TEL: 071 935 2864. SER: Valuations; restorations and repairs (jewellery, enamel, ivory, tortoiseshell, antique watches, clocks); testing precious metals and gem stones; buys at auction. VAT: Stan.

Noortman
40-41 Old Bond St. Open 9.30-5.30. *STOCK: Old Masters, French 19th-20th C.* TEL: 071 491 7284.

Richard Ogden Ltd BADA
28 and 29 Burlington Arcade, Piccadilly. Est: 1948. Open 9.30-5.15, Sat. 9.30-4. SIZE: Medium. *STOCK: Antique jewellery, rings.* LOC: Near Piccadilly Circus. PARK: Meters. TEL: 071 493 9136/7. SER: Valuations; repairs. VAT: Spec.

Oriental Bronzes Ltd BADA
96 Mount St. Open 10-5.30. CL: Sat. SIZE: Medium. *STOCK: Chinese archaeology, 5000BC to 1300AD.* LOC: Between Park Lane and Berkeley Sq. PARK: Easy. TEL: 071 493 0309; fax - 071 629 2665.

Partridge Fine Arts plc
144-146 New Bond St. Est: 1911. Open 9-5.30. CL: Sat. SIZE: Large. *STOCK: English and French furniture, silver; paintings of English, Italian and French Schools.* LOC: North of Bruton St., opp. Sotheby's. PARK: Meters. TEL: 071 629 0834; fax - 071 495 6266. SER: Buys at auction. VAT: Spec.

W.H Patterson Fine Arts Ltd BADA
19 Albemarle St. (W.H and Mrs. P.M Patterson and J White) SLAD. Open 9.30-6. SIZE: Large. *STOCK: 19th C and contemporary paintings and sculpture.* LOC: Near Green Park tube station. PARK: Meters. TEL: 071 629 4119. SER: Valuations; restorations. VAT: Spec.

Ronald Phillips Ltd BADA
26 Bruton St. Est: 1952. *STOCK: English furniture and objets d'art.* TEL: 071 493 2341. VAT: Mainly spec.

W.1 continued

S.J Phillips Ltd BADA
139 New Bond St. (M.S., N.E.L., J.P. and F.E Norton) Est: 1869. Open 10-5. CL: Sat. SIZE: Large. *STOCK: Silver, jewellery, gold boxes, miniatures.* LOC: Near Bond St. tube station. PARK: Meters. TEL: 071 629 6261; fax - 071 495 6180. SER: Valuations; restorations; buys at auction. FAIRS: Grosvenor House. VAT: Stan/Spec.

Piccadilly Gallery
16 Cork St. Est: 1952. Open 10-5.30, Sat. 10-12.30. CL: Sat. Aug. and Sept. *STOCK: Symbolist and art nouveau works, 20th C; drawings and watercolours.* PARK: Meters. TEL: 071 499 4632; fax - 071 499 0431. VAT: Spec.

Jonathan Potter Ltd BADA LAPADA
21 Grosvenor St, Mayfair. ABA. Est: 1975. Open 9.30-5.30, Sat. by appointment. SIZE: Medium. *STOCK: Maps, 16th-19th C, £15-£10,000; prints of London, 18th-19th C, £5-£1,000; atlases and travel books, 16th-19th C, £50-£10,000.* PARK: Meters. TEL: 071 491 3520; fax - 071 491 9754. SER: Valuations; restorations; colouring, framing; buys at auction (maps and prints); catalogue available. VAT: Stan.

Bernard Quaritch Ltd (Booksellers)
5-8 Lower John St, Golden Sq. Est: 1847. Open 9.30-5.30. CL: Sat. SIZE: Large. *STOCK: Antiquarian books.* PARK: Meters, 50yds. TEL: 071 734 2983; fax - 071 437 0967. SER: Buys at auction. VAT: Stan.

Rabi Gallery Ltd
94 Mount St, Mayfair. (R. and V Soleymani) Est: 1978. Open 10-6. CL: Sat. *STOCK: Ancient and Islamic works of art, carpets and rugs.* TEL: 071 499 8886/7.

William Redford BADA
9 Mount St. Open 9.30-5.30. CL: Sat. SIZE: Large. *STOCK: French furniture, works of art, bronzes , some porcelain.* TEL: 071 629 1165.

David Richards and Sons LAPADA
12 New Cavendish St. (M., H. and E Richards) Open 9.30-5.30. CL: Sat. SIZE: Large. *STOCK: Silver and plate.* LOC: Off Harley St., at corner of Marylebone High St. PARK: Easy. TEL: 071 935 3206/0322; fax - 071 224 4423. SER: Valuations; restorations. VAT: Stan/Spec.

The Richmond Gallery
8 Cork St. (T Pringle and J Molony) Open 10-6. CL: Sat. *STOCK: European paintings, 19th-20th C.* TEL: 071 437 9422 (ansaphone).

Russell Rare Books
18 Queen St, Mayfair. (C Russell) Open 10-5.30, Sat. 10-1. *STOCK: Antiquarian books.* TEL: 071 629 0532; fax - 071 499 2983.

W.1 continued

Rutland Gallery
32a St. George St. Open 10-5. CL: Sat. and Mon. *STOCK: British primitive paintings and watercolours, 18th-19th C.* TEL: 071 499 5636.

Robert G Sawers
PO Box 4QA. Open by appointment. *STOCK: Books on the Orient, Japanese prints, screens, paintings.* TEL: 071 409 0863; fax - 071 409 0817.

Scarisbrick and Bate Ltd
111 Mount St. (A.C Bate) Est: 1958. Open 9.30-5.30. CL: Sat. SIZE: Medium. *STOCK: Furniture, decorative items, mid-18th C to early 19th C.* Not stocked: Glass and china. LOC: By Connaught Hotel (off Park Lane). PARK: Meters. TEL: 071 499 2043/4/5; fax - 071 499 2897. SER: Restorations (furniture); buys at auction. VAT: Stan.

The Schuster Gallery
14 Maddox St. Open 10-5.30, Sat. 10-2. *STOCK: Decorative and rare prints, 1500-1880, £30-£3,000.* LOC: Near Regent St. TEL: 071 491 2208; fax - 071 491 9872. FAIRS: London, New York, Tokyo, San Francisco, Los Angeles.

Thomas E Schuster
14 Maddox St. Est: 1973. Open by appointment only. *STOCK: Fine and rare colour plate books and atlases, 1490-1900, £300-£20,000.* TEL: 071 491 2208; fax - 071 491 9872. FAIRS: ABA, Park Lane.

Schwartz, Sackin & Co. Ltd
17 Old Bond St. (L Sackin) Open 10-6, Sat. 10-5. *STOCK: Rembrandt and Durer etchings and engravings; 17th-19th C oils and watercolours.* TEL: 071 629 4511.

The Scottish Gallery
28 Cork St. Open 10-6, Sat. 10-1. *STOCK: 20th C and contemporary artists.* TEL: 071 287 2121. VAT: Stan/Spec.

The Scripophily Shop
Georgian Arcade, Britannia Hotel, Grosvenor Sq. (K Hollender) Est: 1979. Open 10-5.30, Sat. and Sun. by appointment. SIZE: Small. *STOCK: Old bonds and shares, 1800-1950, £5-£2,000.* TEL: 071 495 0580. SER: Valuations. VAT: Stan/Spec.

B.A Seaby Ltd
7 Davies St. Est: 1926. Open 9.30-5, Sat. by appointment. SIZE: Medium. *STOCK: Ancient Greek and Roman coins; British coins; numismatic books, antiquities.* LOC: Just north of Berkeley Sq., near Green Park and Bond St. underground. TEL: 071 495 2590; fax - 071 491 1595. SER: Valuations; buys at auction; monthly coin and medal bulletin. VAT: Stan/Spec.

W.1 continued

Shaikh and Son (Oriental Rugs) Ltd
16 Brook St. (M Shaikh) Open 10-6. CL: Sat. p.m. *STOCK: Persian carpets, rugs, £100-£10,000.* TEL: 071 629 3430. SER: Repairing and cleaning.

Sheppard and Cooper Ltd BADA
11 St George St. Open 10-5.30. CL: Sat. *STOCK: Glass, works of art, Roman and Greek antiquities.* TEL: 071 629 6489; fax - 071 495 2905.

Sherena Cedar Gallery
14 New Quebec St, Portman Sq. Open 10-6, Sat. by appointment. *STOCK: Victorian watercolours.* TEL: 071 723 1255.

Silver
3-5 Burlington Gdns. (B Silver) Open 10-5. CL: Sat. *STOCK: Antique, art nouveau and art deco jewellery.* LOC: Off Bond St. PARK: Easy. TEL: 071 437 7034. SER: Valuations; restorations; buys at auction. FAIRS: Park Lane. VAT: Stan/Spec.

Michael Simpson Ltd
11 Savile Row. Open 9.30-5.30. CL: Sat. *STOCK: Old Masters, prints, drawings, English watercolours, paintings.* TEL: 071 437 5414. VAT: Spec.

W Sitch and Co Ltd
48 Berwick St. (H Sitch) Est: 1776. Open 8-5, Sat. 8-1. SIZE: Large. *STOCK: Edwardian and Victorian lighting fixtures and floor standards.* LOC: Off Oxford St. TEL: 071 437 3776. SER: Valuations; restorations; repairs. VAT: Stan.

The Sladmore Gallery
32 Bruton Place, Berkeley Sq. (E.F Horswell and J.A Hazandras) Open 10-6. CL: Sat. SIZE: Large. *STOCK: Bronze sculptures, 19th C - Mene, Barye, Fremiet, Bonheur; Impressionist, Bugatti, Troubetskoy, Pompon; contemporary, Geoffrey Dashwood birds, wildlife; Gill Parker, sporting, polo.* TEL: 071 499 0365. SER: Valuations; restorations. VAT: Stan/Spec.

Stephen Somerville Ltd
at Bernheimers, 32 St George St. Est: 1987. Open 10-5, Sat. and Sun. by appointment. SIZE: Small. *STOCK: Old Master prints and drawings; English paintings, watercolours, prints and drawings, 17th-20th C, £50-£50,000.* LOC: Off Hanover Sq., parallel to New Bond St. TEL: 071 493 8363; home - 071 289 0363. SER: Buys at auction (as stock). FAIRS: World of Watercolours. VAT: Spec.

Henry Sotheran Ltd
2/5 Sackville St, Piccadilly. Est: 1761. Open 9.30-6, Sat. 10-4. *STOCK: Antiquarian books and prints, including John Gould prints.* TEL: 071 439 6151. SER: Restorations and binding (books, prints); buys at auction. VAT: Stan.

W.1 continued

South Audley Antiques
36 South Audley St. (F. and V Ghassemi and R.S Idenden) Open 10-6, Sat. 10-2. *STOCK: Fine Victorian and European paintngs, continental and English furniture, porcelain, bronzes, glass, K.P.M. plaques; enamels, Persian carpets.* TEL: 071 499 3178/3195. SER: Interior design. VAT: Spec.

John Sparks Ltd BADA
128 Mount St. Est: 1879. Open 9.30-5. CL: Sat. SIZE: Large. *STOCK: Chinese works of art, B.C. to late 18th C; pottery, porcelain, jade, hardstones.* PARK: Meters. TEL: 071 499 1932/2265. SER: Valuations. VAT: Stan.

Alfred Speelman BADA
129 Mount St. Est: 1931. Open 10-5. SIZE: Large. *STOCK: Chinese and Japanese works of art, Shang era to 19th C.* TEL: 071 499 5126. SER: Valuations; buys at auction. VAT: Spec.

W.1 continued

Edward Speelman Ltd
175 Piccadilly. Est: 1931. Open 10-1 and 2-5. CL: Sat. SIZE: Medium. *STOCK: Old Master painting.* PARK: Meters. TEL: 071 493 0657. SER: Valuations; restorations. VAT: Spec.

H.J Spiller's Ltd
99 New Bond St. Est: 1909. Open 9-5.30. CL: Sat. SIZE: Large. *STOCK: Carved frames.* PARK: Meters. TEL: 071 493 8732. VAT: Stan/Spec.

Spring Antiques
(B Snyder) Est: 1970. Open by appointment. *STOCK: Sporting and decorative prints, mezzotints and acquatints, 18th-19th C, £5-£1,000; Old Master engravings, 15th-19th C, £50-£5,000; oil paintings, 19th C, £20-£500.* TEL: 071 486 4207. SER: Valuations; restorations; buys at auction.

Lady Agnew, by John Singer Sargent. Painted c.1892-93, the new spontaneity of vision apparent in the portrait can be put down partly to the increasing use of and advances in photography. From ***The British Portrait 1660-1969***, published by the **Antique Collectors' Club** in 1991. £45.00

W.1 continued

Stair and Company Ltd **BADA**
120 Mount St. CINOA. Est: 1911. Open 9-5.30. CL: Sat. SIZE: Large. *STOCK: 18th C English furniture, works of art, mirrors, chandeliers, barometers, needlework, lamps, clocks, prints.* LOC: Past Connaught Hotel, towards Berkeley Sq. PARK: Meters, and Adam's Row. TEL: 071 499 1784/5; fax - 071 629 1050. SER: Restorations; buys at auction. VAT: Spec.

Stoppenbach and Delestre Ltd
25 Cork St. Open 10-5.30, Sat. 10-1. *STOCK: French paintings, drawings and sculpture, 19th and 20th C.* TEL: 071 734 3534.

The Taylor Gallery
4 Royal Arcade, Old Bond St. (J Taylor) Est: 1986. Open 10-5. CL: Sat. SIZE: Large. *STOCK: Irish paintings, 20th C; British Impressionists and R.A. artists: Spear, Weight.* TEL: 071 493 4111. SER: Restorations; buys at auction (paintings).

F Teltscher Ltd
17 Crawford St. Est: 1956. Open 11-5. CL: Sat. *STOCK: Pictures, wood carvings, works of art.* PARK: Meters. TEL: 071 935 0525. SER: Valuations; restorations. VAT: Spec.

Tessiers Ltd **BADA**
26 New Bond St. (A.L. and R.F Parsons) Open 9.30-5. CL: Sat. *STOCK: Silver, jewellery, objets d'art.* TEL: 071 629 0458; fax - 071 629 5110. SER: Valuations; restorations. VAT: Spec.

Toynbee-Clarke Interiors Ltd
95 Mount St. (G. and D Toynbee-Clarke) Est: 1953. Open 9-5.30. CL: Sat. SIZE: Medium. *STOCK: Decorative English and continental furniture and objects, 17th-18th C. Chinese hand painted wallpapers, 18th C. French scenic wallpapers, early 19th C. Chinese and Japanese paintings and screens, 17th-19th C.* LOC: Between north-west corner of Berkeley Sq. and Park Lane. PARK: Meters. TEL: 071 499 4472. SER: Buys at auction. VAT: Stan/Spec.

Tradition - Military Antiques
5a Shepherd St, Mayfair. (R Belmont-Maitland) Open 9-6. CL: Sat. *STOCK: Military uniforms, arms, model soldiers.* TEL: 071 493 7452/491 7077. VAT: Stan/Spec.

M Turpin **LAPADA**
27 Bruton St. Open 10-5, or by appointment. CL: Sat. SIZE: Large. *STOCK: English and continental furniture, mirrors, chandeliers and objets d'art, 18th C.* LOC: Between Berkeley Sq. and Bond St. PARK: Limited and meters. TEL: 071 493 3275/736 3417; fax - 071 244 6254/408 1869.

W.1 continued

Under Two Flags
4 St Christopher's Pl. (A.C Coutts) Est: 1973. Open 10-5. CL: Mon. SIZE: Small. *STOCK: Toy soldiers, old military prints; books, porcelain, bronzes of military interest.* TEL: 071 935 6934.

Nicholas Vandekar Antiques Ltd **BADA**
2nd Floor, Dudley House, 169 Piccadilly. Est: 1980. Open 9.30-5.30, Sat. by appointment. SIZE: Small. *STOCK: Ceramics, worldwide, 17th-19th C, £1,000-£50,000; Oriental furniture and works of art, 18th-19th C, to £5,000.* LOC: Opposite end of Old Bond St. PARK: NCP nearby. TEL: 071 409 2272; fax - 071 409 2340. SER: Valuations; restorations; buys at auction (ceramics). FAIRS: Grosvenor House; International Ceramics. VAT: Stan/Spec.

Venners Antiques
7 New Cavendish St. (Mrs S Davis) Open 10.15-4.15, Sat. 10-1. CL: Mon. *STOCK: 18th and 19th C English porcelain and pottery.* PARK: Meters. TEL: 071 935 0184. SER: Valuations; buys at auction. VAT: Spec.

Vigo Carpet Gallery **LAPADA**
6a Vigo St. Open 9-5.30, Fri. 9-5. CL: Sat. *STOCK: Oriental and European rugs and carpets, tapestries and needlework.* TEL: 071 439 6971; fax - 071 439 2353. SER: Design.

Vigo-Sternberg Galleries **BADA LAPADA**
37 South Audley St. (V Roffe and C Sternberg) Est: 1920. Open 9-5.30. CL: Sat. *STOCK: European tapestries, 15th C to contemporary; Oriental and European rugs, 1650-1850.* PARK: Meters. TEL: 071 629 8307. VAT: Stan/Spec.

Angela Grafin von Wallwitz **BADA**
c/o Bernheimer Fine Arts Ltd, 32 St. George St. Open by appointment only. SIZE: Large. *STOCK: Fine and rare continental pottery and porcelain, 15th C to early 19th C.* LOC: Parallel to Bond St., opposite Sotheby's rear entrance. TEL: 071 373 2502; home - same. SER: Valuations; buys at auction (continental ceramics). FAIRS: Grosvenor House; Basle. VAT: Spec.

Walpole Gallery
38 Dover St. Open 9.30-5.30. Cl: Sat. except when exhibitions held. *STOCK: Italian Old Master paintings.* TEL: 071 499 6626.

Wartski Ltd **BADA**
14 Grafton St. Est: 1865. Open 9.30-5. CL: Sat. SIZE: Medium. *STOCK: Jewellery, 18th C gold boxes, Fabergé, Russian works of art, silver.* PARK: Meters. TEL: 071 493 1141. SER: Restorations; buys at auction. FAIRS: Grosvenor House, International Silver and Jewellery. VAT: Stan/Spec.

W.1 continued

Waterhouse and Dodd
1st Floor, 110 New Bond St. (R Waterhouse and J Dodd) Est: 1975. Open 10-6, Sat. and Sun. by appointment. SIZE: Medium. *STOCK: British and European oil paintings, watercolours and drawings, 1850-1950, £2,000-£10,000.* LOC: Corner of Brook St. and Bond St. - entrance on Brook St. TEL: 071 491 9293. SER: Valuations; restorations; buys at auction (paintings). FAIRS: 20th C British Art; City of London Antiques and Fine Art; World of Watercolours; Olympia. VAT: Spec.

The Weiss Gallery
1B Albemarle St. Open 10-6. CL: Sat. *STOCK: Elizabethan, Jacobean and early European portraits.* TEL: 071 409 0035. SER: Valuations; restorations.

The Welbeck Gallery
18 Thayer St. (D. and S Spellman) Est: 1975. Open 10-5, Sat. 10.30-12.30. *STOCK: Prints, topographical, natural history, military, birds, 17th-20th C, etchings, engraving, lithographs.* PARK: Meters. TEL: 071 935 4825; home - 071 340 7130. SER: Framing. VAT: Stan.

William Weston Gallery
7 Royal Arcade, Albemarle St. Est: 1964. Open 9.30-5. CL: Sat. SIZE: Small. *STOCK: Etchings, lithographs, drawings, 1800-1960.* LOC: Off Piccadilly. TEL: 071 493 0722; fax - 071 491 9240. VAT: Spec.

Wildenstein and Co Ltd
147 New Bond St. Est: 1934. Open 10-5.30. CL: Sat. SIZE: Large. *STOCK: Old Master and impressionist paintings and drawings.* PARK: Meters. TEL: 071 629 0602; fax - 071 493 3924.

Wilkins and Wilkins
1 Barrett St, St Christophers Pl. (M Wilkins) Est: 1981. Open 11-5. CL: Sat. SIZE: Small. *STOCK: English 18th C portraits and decorative paintings, £700-£20,000.* LOC: Near Selfridges. TEL: 071 935 9613. SER: Restorations; framing. VAT: Stan/Spec.

Williams and Son
2 Grafton St. (J.R Williams) Est: 1931. Open 9.30-6. CL: Sat. SIZE: Large. *STOCK: 19th C, British and European paintings.* LOC: Between Bond St. and Berkeley Sq. TEL: 071 493 4985/5751. VAT: Stan/Spec.

Young and Stephen Ltd LAPADA
1 Burlington Gdns, New Bond St. (Mr and Mrs S Burton) Est: 1975. Open 9.30-5.45, Sat. 10.30-3.30. *STOCK: Fine Edwardian, art nouveau and art deco jewellery.* TEL: 071 499 7927; fax - 071 495 0570.

Zadah Gallery
29 Conduit St. Est: 1976. Open 9.30-6, appointment advisable. *STOCK: Oriental and European carpets, rugs, tapestries and textiles.* TEL: 071 493 2622/2673.

London W.2

Bayswater Books
27a Craven Terr, Lancaster Gate (Crofter's Lane Ltd.). Est: 1984. Open 11-7. SIZE: Small. *STOCK: Antiquarian books, maps and prints, £5-£500; secondhand books, photographica, ephemera, £1-£500.* LOC: One-way street running south from Craven Rd. to Bayswater Rd. PARK: Meters or NCP 200 metres. TEL: 071 402 7398. SER: Buys at auction (as stock); book search and mail order. FAIRS: PBFA.

Claude Bornoff BADA
20 Chepstow Corner, Pembridge Villas. Est: 1949. Open 9.30-5.30. CL: Sat. SIZE: Medium. *STOCK: English and continental furniture, china, metalware and unusual items.* PARK: Meters. TEL: 071 229 8947. VAT: Stan/Spec.

Garrick D Coleman LAPADA
18 Westbourne Gdns. (G.D. and G.E Coleman) Est: 1944. Open by appointment. SIZE: Medium. *STOCK: Furniture, 1680-1900, £150-£12,000; chess sets, 1750-1880, £100-£4,000; decorative items, arms, pictures, £50-£2,000.* PARK: Easy. TEL: 071 221 6228. VAT: Stan/Spec.

Connaught Galleries
44 Connaught St. (M Hollamby) Est: 1966. Open 10-6.30, Sat. 10-1. SIZE: Medium. *STOCK: Antique and reproduction sporting, historical, geographical and decorative prints.* LOC: Near Marble Arch. PARK: Meters. TEL: 071 723 1660. SER: Picture framing. VAT: Spec.

Craven Gallery
30 Craven Terr. (C. and A Quaradeghini) Est: 1974. Open 11-6, Sat. 3-7, other times by appointment. SIZE: Large and warehouse. *STOCK: Silver and plate, 19th-20th C; furniture, china and glass, Victorian.* LOC: Off Bayswater Rd. PARK: Easy. TEL: 071 402 2802; home - 081 998 0769. VAT: Stan. *Trade Only.*

S Franses Conservation
11 Spring St. Open 9-5.30. *STOCK: Decorative tapestries, carpets and textiles.* TEL: 071 262 1153. SER: Restorations; cleaning. VAT: Spec.

Hosains Books and Antiques
25 Connaught St. Est: 1979. Open 10.30-5.30. CL: Sat. p.m. and Mon. *STOCK: Scarce books, manuscripts, miniatures and prints on Islamic world, Tibet, Central Asia and India.* TEL: 071 262 7900.

W.2 continued

Paul Hughes Textiles
3a Pembridge Sq, Resident. Est: 1977. Open by appointment. CL: Mon. SIZE: Large. *STOCK: Coptic, pre-Columbian, African and European items, 14th-20th C; English textiles and costumes, 17th C.* LOC: Portobello Rd. PARK: Easy. TEL: 071 243 8598. SER: Valuations; restorations; buys at auction (textiles). FAIRS: Royal Academy. VAT: Stan/Spec.

Manya Igel Fine Arts Ltd LAPADA
21/22 Peters Court, Porchester Rd. (M Igel and B.S Prydal) Est: 1977. Open 10-5.30 by appointment only. SIZE: Large. *STOCK: Watercolours, £300-£3,000; oils, £600-£35,000; both 19th C to contemporary.* LOC: Off Queensway. PARK: Nearby. TEL: 071 229 1669/8429. VAT: Spec.

Marcus Kirsch
18 Chepstow Corner, 1 Pembridge Villas (Marcus Kirsch Ltd.). Est: 1959. Open 9.30-5.30, Sat. 9.30-2. SIZE: Medium. *STOCK: Furniture and objects, late 18th to early 19th C, £150-£4,000.* LOC: Westbourne Grove. PARK: Easy. TEL: 071 727 5980; home - 071 372 7617. SER: Valuations; restorations; French polishing; buys at auction (18th-19th C furniture). VAT: Spec.

Ian Lieber
The Shop, 29 Craven Terr., Lancaster Gate. Est: 1965. Open by appointment. SIZE: Medium. *STOCK: Furniture, early 19th C and decorative; porcelain, objets d'art, paintings.* LOC: Near Bayswater Rd. TEL: 071 262 5505. SER: Buys at auction. FAIRS: Olympia. VAT: Stan/Spec. *Trade only.*

M McAleer LAPADA
(M.J McAleer and Mrs M McAleer) Est: 1969. Open by appointment. SIZE: Small. *STOCK: Small collectable and Irish and Scottish provincial silver.* LOC: Near Whiteleys, Bayswater. TEL: 071 727 7979. SER: Buys at auction (silver). VAT: Stan/Spec.

Daniel Mankowitz
16 Pembridge Sq. Est: 1970. Open by appointment only. SIZE: Medium. *STOCK: Furniture, English and continental, 16th-18th C, £100-£10,000; works of art, English and continental, 15th-19th C, £50-£5,000; tapestries, 16th-18th C, £200-£3,000.* LOC: Between Kensington Church St. and Westbourne Grove. PARK: Easy. TEL: 071 229 9270; home - same; fax - 071 792 2141. FAIRS: Olympia. VAT: Spec. *Trade Only.*

William C Mansell
24 Connaught St. *STOCK: Gold, silver, clocks, watches and jewellery.* TEL: 071 723 4154. SER: Restorations; repairs.

W.2 continued

The Mark Gallery BADA
9 Porchester Pl, Marble Arch. (H Mark) CINOA. Est: 1969. Open 10-1 and 2-6, Sat. 11-1. SIZE: Medium. *STOCK: Russian icons, 16th-19th C; modern graphics - French school.* LOC: Near Marble Arch. TEL: 071 262 4906; fax - 071 224 9416. SER: Valuations; restorations; buys at auction. VAT: Stan/Spec.

Orchard Antiques
52 Porchester Rd. (R Orchard) Est: 1974. Open 12-5. *STOCK: Glass, china and early kitchenware.* TEL: 071 221 0154.

Vivien C Youlten
28 Chepstow Rd, Bayswater. Est: 1968. Open by appointment. *STOCK: Unusual decorative items, including peinte, toleware and vizagapatum, 18th to early 19th C, £50-£1,000; small lacquer and bamboo furniture, 19th C; exotic textiles, medical and pharmaceutical items, 18th-19th C, all £500-£1,500.* LOC: Off Westbourne Grove. PARK: Easy. TEL: 071 243 8202; home - same. FAIRS: Decorative Antiques and Textiles. *Trade Only.*

London W.3

Z.J Okolski
14 Princes Ave. Est: 1973. Open any time by appointment. SIZE: Medium. *STOCK: Oil paintings, 1750-1950.* LOC: 1/2 mile from Chiswick flyover, off North Circular Rd; 1/4 mile from Acton Town underground (Piccadilly line). PARK: Easy. TEL: 081 992 7032; home - same. SER: Valuations. VAT: Spec.

London W.4

Antiques 132
132 Chiswick High Rd. (D Evans) Est: 1974. Open 10.30-6, Sun. 12-5. SIZE: Small. *STOCK: Furniture - aesthetic movements, arts and crafts, art nouveau, art deco; related artefacts and ceramics, £10-£10,000.* LOC: 1 mile from end of M4. PARK: Easy. TEL: 081 995 3952. SER: Valuations; buys at auction. VAT: Stan/Spec.

Bishop's Antiques
61 South Parade, Chiswick. (J Bishop) Open 10-6. CL: Mon. *STOCK: Furniture.* TEL: 081 995 4170.

Dick Coats
32 Grantham Rd. Open by appointment. *STOCK: 19th-20th C sculpture and paintings.* TEL: 081 995 9733.

Adrian Hornsey Ltd
The Old Cinema, 160 Chiswick High Rd. Open daily. *STOCK: General antiques and decorative accessories.* TEL: 081 995 4166. SER: Courier

W.4 continued

Mangate Gallery **LAPADA**
3 Chiswick Lane. (Mrs S Beamish) Est: 1968. Open by appointment only. SIZE: Medium. *STOCK: English and continental watercolours and oils, 1800-1950, £150-£10,000.* LOC: Off Chiswick High Rd., or Hogarth roundabout Gt. West Rd.. PARK: Easy. TEL: 081 995 9867; weekends - 098 683 524. SER: Cleaning and framing. VAT: Spec.

The Old Cinema Antique Store
160 Chiswick High Rd. Est: 1977. Open 10-6, Sun. 12-5. SIZE: Large. There are 15 dealers selling. *STOCK: a wide range of antiques including furniture, gardenalia, decorative and architectural items, 1800-1940, £100-£6,000.* PARK: Easy. TEL: 081 995 4166. SER: Restorations. VAT: Stan/Spec.

Strand Antiques
166 Thames Rd,Strand-on-the-Green, Chiswick. Est: 1977. Open 12-5 including Sun. or by appointment. SIZE: Large. *STOCK: Books, kitchen items, glass, furniture, jewellery, paintings, prints, fabrics, china, silver, clothes, and collectors' items, £1-£500.* LOC: Behind Bull's Head Public House, about 400yds. from Kew Bridge. PARK: Easy. TEL: 081 994 1912.

Stratton-Quinn Antiques Etc
164 Thames Rd,Strand-on-the-Green, Chiswick. (N.J Quinn) Est: 1980. Open daily including Sun. 10.30-6. SIZE: Medium. *STOCK: 19th C furniture and decorative items including pine, painted and fruitwood armoires, sleighbeds and dressers, £250-£1,200.* LOC: North side of Thames, east of Kew Bridge, near junction of north and south circulars. PARK: Easy. TEL: 081 994 3140; home - same.

Terry Antiques
The Old Cinema, 160 Chiswick High Rd. (T.H Murphy) Open 10-6, Sun. 12-5. *STOCK: Furniture - mahogany, walnut, rosewood, some oak, mid 18th to mid 19th C, £100-£3,000; objets d'art, grandfather clocks.* TEL: 081 995 4166; home - 081 889 9781. VAT: Stan.

London W.5

Aberdeen House Antiques
75 St Mary's Rd. (N Schwartz) Est: 1971. Open 10-5.30. SIZE: Medium. *STOCK: Furniture and pictures, £50-£2,000; decorative items and textiles, £25-£2,000; china, glass and silver, £25-£1,000; all 18th-20th C.* LOC: On B455 1 mile north of A4. PARK: Easy and at rear. TEL: 081 567 1223/5194. SER: Valuations. FAIRS: Olympia and Barbican. VAT: Stan.

The Badger
12 St Mary's Rd. (M. and E Aalders) Est: 1967. Open 9.30-6. SIZE: Medium. *STOCK: Furniture, £100-£2,000; clocks, £1,000-£3,000; both 18th-19th C; ceramics, 19th C, £50-£1,000.* PARK: Easy. TEL: 081 567 5601. SER: Valuations;

The Badger continued

restorations (furniture and clocks); buys at auction (clocks and watches). VAT: Stan/Spec.

S Bensiglio Ltd **LAPADA**
41 The Ridings. (Mr and Mrs S Bensiglio) Open by appointment. *STOCK: Rugs and carpets.* TEL: 081 997 2140.

Ealing Gallery
78 St. Mary's Rd, Ealing. (Mrs N Lane) Open 10.30-5.30. CL: Mon. *STOCK: Oil paintings, £100-£5,000; watercolours, £50-£3,000; both 19th to early 20th C; contemporary paintings, £30-£250.* PARK: Nearby. TEL: 081 840 7883. SER: Valuations; restorations (oils and watercolours); framing. VAT: Spec.

Harold's Place
148 South Ealing Rd. (H Bowman) Est: 1977. Open 10-6. CL: Wed. SIZE: Medium. *STOCK: Wall plates, commemoratives, porcelain, all 19th to early 20th C, £5-£100.* LOC: 1/2 mile north of A4/M4 at Ealing. TEL: 081 579 4825.

Terrace Antiques
10 South Ealing Rd. (N Schwartz) Est: 1971. Open 10-5.30, Sat. 11-5.30. SIZE: Medium. *STOCK: Victorian furniture and pine, 1850-1920, £50-£500; china, glass and pictures, silver and plate, 1850-1950, £10-£200.* LOC: 1 1/2 miles north of A4 on B455. PARK: Easy and opposite. TEL: 081 567 5194/1223. SER: Valuations. FAIRS: Olympia and Barbican. VAT: Stan.

London W.6

Architectural Antiques
351 King St. (G.P.A Duc) Est: 1985. Open 10-5, Sat. 10-4. SIZE: Medium. *STOCK: Marble chimney pieces, 18th-19th C, £500-£5,000; French furniture, 19th C, £500-£1,000.* PARK: Easy and Black Lion Lane. TEL: 081 741 7883; fax - 081 741 1109. SER: Valuations; cleaning and polishing (marble chimney pieces on site); repair. VAT: Stan. *Trade Only.*

N Davighi
117 Shepherd's Bush Rd. Est: 1950. Open 9.30-5. SIZE: Medium. *STOCK: Chandeliers, light fittings, general antiques, all Georgian and Victorian.* PARK: Easy. TEL: 071 603 5357. SER: Valuations; restorations (ormolu, chandeliers and brass).

Nina Ghiggini
Open by appointment. *STOCK: Primitive and glass paintings, needlework and decorative items.* TEL: 081 748 6393.

C Kent (Fireplaces)
14 Greyhound Rd. (C Kent and J Gregory) Est: 1977. Open 10-5, Sat. 9.30-4. CL: Mon. *STOCK: Restored cast iron fireplaces, mainly Victorian.* LOC: Just south of Charing Cross Hospital. PARK: Easy. TEL: 071 385 1494.

W.6 continued

M.L Waroujian

110-112 Hammersmith Rd. Est: 1959. *STOCK: Antique Oriental carpets and rugs.* TEL: 081 748 7509. SER: Cleaning, repairs (Persian and Oriental carpets). VAT: Spec.

London W.8

Al Mashreq Galleries

110 Kensington Church St. (J.H Mantoura) Est: 1983. Open 10-6. SIZE: Medium. *STOCK: Islamic decorative art and antiques.* PARK: Meters. TEL: 071 229 5453. VAT: Spec.

The Antique Home BADA

104A Kensington Church St. (M Priestley and B.T.W Rolleston) Est: 1950. Open 10-1 and 2.30-6. CL: Sat p.m.. SIZE: Large. *STOCK: English furniture, 18th C, £1,500-£50,000.* PARK: Easy. TEL: 071 229 5892. VAT: Spec.

Valerie Arieta

97b Kensington Church St. Open 10.30-5.30. *STOCK: American, English, continental antiques and American Indian art.* TEL: 071 243 1074/794 7613.

Eddy Bardawil BADA

106 Kensington Church St. (E.S Bardawil) Est: 1979. Open 10-1 and 2-5.30, Sat. 10-1.30. SIZE: Medium. *STOCK: English furniture - mahogany, satinwood, walnut; mirrors, brassware, tea-caddies, all pre-1830, £300-£20,000; prints, 18th C.* LOC: Corner premises, Berkeley Gardens/Church St. PARK: Easy. TEL: 071 221 3967; fax - 071 221 5124. SER: Valuations; restorations (furniture); polishing. VAT: Stan/Spec.

Barker-Mill Design Associates

24 Iverna Gdns, Kensington. Open by appointment only. *STOCK: Oriental carpets, small rugs and cushions, European and Oriental textiles, £200-£10,000.* LOC: Kensington High St., tube. TEL: 071 937 9145. SER: Repairs; cushion making to order; cleaning (as stock).

Barnet Antiques BADA

79 Kensington Church St. (R Gerry) Est: 1959. SIZE: 18th and early 19th C furniture and accessories. TEL: 071 376 2817.

Baumkotter Gallery

63a Kensington Church St. (Mrs L Baumkotter) Est: 1968. Open 9.30-6. CL: Sat. SIZE: Large. *STOCK: 17th-19th C oil paintings.* TEL: 071 937 5171. VAT: Spec.

Anthony Belton LAPADA

14 Holland St. Est: 1969. Open 10-1 and 2-6, Sat. 10-4.30, or by appointment. SIZE: Medium. *STOCK: English and European pottery; decorative and unusual furniture and objects; primitive, topographical and marine watercolours and oil paintings; mainly pre-1830.* Not stocked: Silver, glass, jewellery, coins. LOC: 1st left going up Kensington Church St. from Kensington High St. PARK: Meters or under Kensington Town Hall. TEL: 071 937 1012; home - same. SER: Valuations; restorations (paintings, ceramics); buys at auction. FAIRS: Olympia; West London Kensington Town Hall (Jan. and Aug.). VAT: Mainly Spec.

Bonrose Antiques

207-211 Kensington Church St. *STOCK: French clocks; furniture, porcelain and silver.* TEL: 071 221 3139/727 6597.

David Brower Antiques LAPADA

113 Kensington Church St. Est: 1965. Open 10-6. CL: Sat. SIZE: Medium. *STOCK: Oriental and continental decorative porcelain, £100-£5,000; French and Oriental furniture, bronzes and clocks.* PARK: Meters nearby. TEL: 071 221 4155. SER: Buys at auction. VAT: Stan/Spec.

The Cameo Gallery LAPADA

38 Kensington Church St. (M Levy) Est: 1974. Open 10-5.30, Sun. by appointment. *STOCK: Art nouveau, art deco glass, furniture and bronzes, 1870-1940, £300-£50,000.* LOC: Off Kensington High St. PARK: Nearby. TEL: 071 938 4114; fax - 071 376 0686. SER: Valuations; buys at auction (as stock). VAT: Stan/Spec.

The Lucy B. Campbell Gallery

123 Kensington Church St. Est: 1983. Open 10-4, Sat. 10-5. SIZE: Medium. *STOCK: Fine decorative prints, 17th-19th C; contemporary originals.* Not stocked: Maps and sporting prints. PARK: Meters. TEL: 071 727 2205. SER: Framing. FAIRS: Stan.

Simon Castle LAPADA

38B Kensington Church St. Est: 1975. Open 10-5.30, Sat. 10.30-3.30. *STOCK: Decorative carvings and treen.* TEL: 071 937 2268.

Church Street Galleries Ltd BADA

77 Kensington Church St. (G.A Meyer) Est: 1954. Open 9-6, Sat. 10-4 or by appointment. SIZE: Large. *STOCK: Late 17th to early 19th C English furniture and mirrors.* PARK: Meters. TEL: 071 937 2461. VAT: Stan/Spec.

Coats Oriental Carpets

4 Kensington Church Walk, (off Holland St). (A Coats) Est: 1973. Open 11-5, Sat. 11-3 or by appointment. SIZE: Medium. *STOCK: Oriental carpets and rugs, kelims, all £50-£2,000; Oriental textiles and embroideries, £10-£100; all 19th C.* LOC: Small pedestrian alleyway just off Holland St., off south end of Kensington Church St. PARK: Easy. TEL: 071 937 0983; home - 071 370 2355. SER: Valuations; restorations (re-weaving); buys at auction. VAT: Stan/Spec.

W.8 continued

Mary Cooke Antiques Ltd BADA
121A Kensington Church St. Open 9.30-5.30, Sat. a.m. by appointment. *STOCK: Silver.* TEL: 071 792 8077. SER: Valuations; restorations; buys at auction. FAIRS: Chelsea Spring and Autumn. VAT: Stan/Spec.

Belinda Coote Tapestries
29 Holland St. Resident. Est: 1970. Open 10-5.30, Sat. 10-1. *STOCK: Old textiles, paisleys; reproduction tapestry, wall hangings, fabrics, cushions, painted furniture.* Not stocked: Glass, enamel, metalwork. LOC: 1st left off Kensington Church St. from Kensington High St. TEL: 071 937 3924. VAT: Stan.

Mrs. M.E Crick
166 Kensington Church St. Est: 1897. CL: Sat. *STOCK: Chandeliers, 18th C to modern English and continental, crystal, cut glass and ormolu.* PARK: Meters. TEL: 071 229 1338; fax - 071 792 1073. VAT: Stan.

George Dare
9 Launceston Pl, Kensington. Est: 1980. Open anytime by appointment. SIZE: Medium. *STOCK: English watercolours and oil paintings, mainly 18th and 19th C, £100-£2,500.* LOC: Turn left off London bound section of Cromwell Rd., opposite the Forum Hotel. PARK: Easy. TEL: 071 937 7072; home - same. SER: Restorations; framing; buys at auction (as stock). VAT: Stan.

Davies Antiques LAPADA
40A and 44A Kensington Church St. (H.Q.V Davies) Est: 1976. Open 9.30-5.30, Sat. 10-3. *STOCK: Maps and prints, continental porcelain, 1710-1930.* TEL: 071 937 3379/937 9216.

Richard Dennis
144 Kensington Church St. Est: 1967. Open 10-6, Sat. 10-2. SIZE: Medium. *STOCK: English studio pottery, especially Moorcroft, Martin, Doulton, Pilkington and Parian, 1870-1950.* LOC: Near Notting Hill Gate tube. TEL: 071 727 2061. VAT: Stan/Spec.

Denton Antiques
156 Kensington Church St. (M.T. and M.E Denton) Open 9.30-5.30. CL: Sat. *STOCK: Cut glass, including decorative, and objects, mainly 19th C.* TEL: 071 229 5866; fax - 071 792 1073.

Kay Desmonde
17 Kensington Church Walk. Est: 1964. Open Sat 11-3. *STOCK: Dolls, dolls' houses, dolls' house furniture and accessories.* TEL: 071 937 2602; home - 04606 3280.

W.8 continued

H and W Deutsch Antiques LAPADA
111 Kensington Church St. Est: 1897. Open 10-5. CL: Tues., Wed. and Sat. SIZE: Large. *STOCK: 18th-19th C continental and English porcelain and glassware; silver, plate and enamel ware, miniature portraits; Oriental porcelain, cloisonne, bronzes, £20-£3,000.* TEL: 071 727 5984. VAT: Stan/Spec.

Philip Dombey LAPADA
174 Kensington Church St. Est: 1951. Open 10-4, Tues.-Thurs. SIZE: Medium. *STOCK: French clocks.* LOC: Near Notting Hill Gate tube station. PARK: Meters. TEL: 071 229 7100. SER: Valuations; restorations. VAT: Stan/Spec.

Fine Art Investments
48 Kensington Church St. (W.F Lowe) Open 10-6, Sat. 10-2. *STOCK: 17th-19th C paintings.* TEL: 071 937 8891. SER: Valuations; restorations.

The French Glasshouse
36b Kensington Church St. Open 10.30-5.30, Sat. 11-4. *STOCK: Art nouveau, works of art in glass, 19th C Japanese art.* TEL: 071 937 6474; home - 081 789 3069; fax - 071 937 6476.

Michael C German BADA LAPADA
38B Kensington Church St. Est: 1954. Open 10-5, Sat. 10-3. *STOCK: European and Oriental arms and armour; specialist in walking sticks.* TEL: 071 937 2771.

Geoffrey Godden
at Klaber and Klaber, 2A Bedford Gdns, Kensington Church St. Est: 1900. Open 10-1 and 2-5, Sat. 10.30-4. *STOCK: English ceramics, 19th C.* PARK: Meters. TEL: 071 727 4573.

Graham and Oxley (Antiques) Ltd BADA
101 Kensington Church St. Open 10-5.30. *STOCK: Porcelain, prints and decorative accessories, 18th-19th C.* TEL: 071 229 1850.

Eila Grahame
97c Kensington Church St. Open 9-5.30. *STOCK: Glass, 17th-18th C; early prints, needlework; instruments, scientific and medical; pottery, porcelain, 18th C.* TEL: 071 727 4132. VAT: Spec.

Green's Antique Galleries
117 Kensington Church St. (S Green) Open 9-5. SIZE: Medium. *STOCK: Jewellery, 18th C to date; pre-1930 clothes and lace; dolls, china, silver, furniture, paintings, masonic and crocodile and leather items.* PARK: Easy. TEL: 071 229 9618/9. VAT: Stan/Spec.

W.8 continued

Grosvenor Antiques Ltd **BADA**
27 Holland St, Kensington. (S.C and E Lorie) Est: 1950. *STOCK: English and continental porcelain and works of art.* TEL: 071 937 8649. VAT: Spec.

Robert Hales Antiques Ltd
131 Kensington Church St. Est: 1967. Open 9.30-5.30. CL: Mon. and Sat. SIZE: Small. *STOCK: Islamic, Oriental and ethnographic arms and armour; oceanic art, 16th-19th C.* PARK: Easy. TEL: 071 229 3887. SER: Valuations; buys at auction. VAT: Spec.

Jonathan Harris **BADA**
54 Kensington Church St. Open 9.30-6. CL: Sat. SIZE: Large. *STOCK: English, continental, Oriental furniture; works of art.* LOC: Near Kensington High St. tube station. PARK: Meters. TEL: 071 937 3133. VAT: Spec.

Haslam and Whiteway
105 Kensington Church St. (T.M Whiteway) Est: 1969. Open 10-6, Sat. 10-2. SIZE: Small. *STOCK: British furniture, £80-£10,000; British decorative arts, £20-£5,000; continental and American decorative arts, £5-£500, all 1850-1930.* Not stocked: Pre-Victorian items. LOC: From Notting Hill Gate tube station, down Kensington Church St. Shop is approx. 300yds. down on right. PARK: Meters. TEL: 071 229 1145. SER: Valuations; buys at auction. VAT: Stan.

Jeanette Hayhurst Fine Glass
32A Kensington Church St. Open 10-5, Sat. 11-4. *STOCK: Glass - 18th C English drinking, fine 19th C engraved, table decanters, contemporary art, scent bottles, Roman and continental.* TEL: 071 938 1539.

D Holmes
47c Earls Court Rd(in Abingdon Villas), Kensington. Est: 1965. Open Fri. 2-7 and Sat. 10-5, or by appointment. *STOCK: Decorative items and furniture, 18th-19th C.* TEL: 071 937 3415 or 020 888 0254. SER: Restorations (furniture). VAT: Stan/Spec.

W.8 continued

Hope and Glory
131a Kensington Church St. (E.L Titmuss) Open 10-5. CL: Sat. p.m. and Mon. *STOCK: Royal commemorative china and glass.* TEL: 071 727 8424.

Jonathan Horne **BADA**
66b & 66c Kensington Church St. Est: 1968. Open 9.30-5.30. CL: Sat. and Sun. except by appointment. SIZE: Medium. *STOCK: Early English pottery, needlework and works of art.* TEL: 071 221 5658; fax - 071 792 3090. VAT: Stan/Spec.

Bone china jug freely painted with flowers and insects on a Summerly shape, c.1865. From ***The Dictionary of Minton*** by Paul Atterbury and Maureen Batkin published by the **Antique Collectors' Club** in 1990. £35.00.

W.8 continued

Valerie Howard **LAPADA**
131E Kensington Church St. Open 10-5.30, Sat. 10-4. *STOCK: Mason's and English Ironstone china, 1810-1860, £50-£10,000; French faience from Quimper and Rouen regions, 1850-1920, £20-£3,000; mirrors, 19th C, £150-£2,000.* LOC: Corner of Peel St. TEL: 071 792 9702 (ansaphone at night). SER: Valuations; restorations (ceramics); buys at auction (as stock). FAIRS: Olympia. VAT: Spec.

Iona Antiques **BADA**
PO Box 285. Est: 1974. Open by appointment only. SIZE: Large. *STOCK: 19th C animal paintings, £1,000-£40,000.* LOC: 3 minutes walk from Odeon Cinema, Kensington High St. PARK: Nearby. TEL: 071 602 1193; fax - 071 371 2843. FAIRS: Grosvenor House, Olympia.

Japanese Gallery
66d Kensington Church St. (Mr. and Mrs C.D Wertheim) Est: 1977. Open 10-6. *STOCK: Japanese wood-cut prints; books, screens, netsuke.* TEL: 071 229 2934. SER: Authentification; exhibitions.

Melvyn Jay Antiques and Objets d'Art **LAPADA**
64a Kensington Church St. Est: 1960. Open 9-5.45, Sat. 11-2. SIZE: Medium. *STOCK: Mid-19th C French decorative furniture, clocks;*

Melvyn Jay Antiques continued

continental porcelain, bronzes and silver, £5-£5,000; English and continental furniture. LOC: From Marble Arch to Kensington High St. Bus No.73. PARK: Easy. TEL: 071 937 6832. SER: Valuations; buys at auction. VAT: Stan/Spec.

John Jesse

160 Kensington Church St. Open 10-6, Sat. 11-4. *STOCK: Decorative arts, 1880-1950, especially art nouveau, art deco, silver, glass, bronzes and jewellery.* TEL: 071 229 0312; fax - 071 229 4732.

Howard Jones LAPADA

43 Kensington Church St. (H Howard-Jones) Est: 1971. Open 10-5. SIZE: Small. *STOCK: Silver, porcelain, bronzes, £20-£5,000.* Not stocked: Furniture. PARK: Nearby. TEL: 071 937 4359. VAT: Stan/Spec.

Peter Kemp

174a Kensington Church St. Est: 1975. Open 10-5. CL: Sat. SIZE: Medium. *STOCK: Chinese porcelain, 10th-19th C; Japanese porcelain, 17th-19th C; continental porcelain, 18th C, Oriental works of art and porcelain, 18th-19th C.* LOC: 200yds. from Notting Hill tube station. PARK: Meters nearby. TEL: 071 229 2988. SER: Valuations; restorations (porcelain); buys at auction (Oriental and continental porcelain). VAT: Spec.

Kensington Church Street Antiques Centre

58-60 Kensington Church St. Open 10-6. SIZE: Below are listed some of the dealers at this centre.

A E Gallery
Unit 5. *Fine oil paintings and watercolours.* TEL: 071 376 0425; home - 071 727 3853.

Abstract
Unit 1. (Fenn Ltd. and Noonstar Ltd.). *Cameo glass and decorative items, both 20th C.* TEL: 071 376 2652. VAT: Stan/Spec.

Bloomsbury Antiques
Units 3 and 4. (H Lyons) *Art pottery, £20-£1,500; furniture, £400-£1,500; metalwork, £50-£600; all 1880-1939.* TEL: 071 376 2810; home - 071 820 0601; fax - 071 937 3400. VAT: Stan/Spec.

Henry Boxer
Unit 12. *20th C paintings and drawings.* TEL: 071 948 1633; mobile - 0836 388771.

Didier Antiques
Unit 2. *Jewellery and silver, objets d'art, 1860-1960, £50-£7,000.* TEL: 071 938 2537. VAT: Stan/Spec.

Carol Hammond and David Somerville
Unit 8. *Decorative arts, 20th C.* TEL: 071 376 0425; fax - 071 937 3400.

Kensington Church Street Antiques Centre continued

J A G
Unit 6. *Art glass, including Loetz, Murano, 1880-1960, pewter, WMF, Liberty; ceramics, bronzes and ivories.* TEL: 071 938 4404; fax - 071 937 3400.

Kensington Fine Arts

46 Kensington Church St. (Mrs S Lowe) Open 10-6, Sat. 10-2. *STOCK: 17th-19th C paintings.* TEL: 071 937 5317. SER: Valuations; restorations.

Klaber and Klaber BADA

2a Bedford Gdns, Kensington Church St. (Mrs B Klaber and Miss P Klaber) Est: 1968. Open 10-1 and 2-5, Sat. 10-4, other times by appointment. SIZE: Medium. *STOCK: English and continental porcelain and enamels, 18th-19th C.* LOC: Turning off Kensington Church St. about half way along. PARK: Meters. TEL: 071 727 4573. SER: Restoration (porcelain); buys at auction (porcelain, enamels). FAIRS: Grosvenor House; Bath. VAT: Spec.

The Lacquer Chest

71 and 75 Kensington Church St. (G. and V Andersen) Est: 1959. Open 9.30-5.30. CL: Sat. p.m. SIZE: Large. *STOCK: Furniture and unusual items.* LOC: Half-way up left-hand side from High St. PARK: Meters. TEL: 071 937 1306. VAT: Stan/Spec.

Lev (Antiques) Ltd

97 Kensington Church St. (Mrs Lev) Est: 1882. Open 10-1 and 2-5. SIZE: Medium. *STOCK: Jewellery, silver, plate, curios.* PARK: Meters. TEL: 071 727 9248. SER: Restorations (pictures); repairs (jewellery, silver).

Libra Antiques

131d Kensington Church St. *STOCK: Blue and white pottery, lustre ware.* TEL: 071 727 2990.

Lindsay Antiques BADA

99 Kensington Church St. (T Jellinek and L Shand) Est: 1965. Open 10-1 and 2.15-5.30, Sat. a.m. by appointment. SIZE: Large. *STOCK: Early English pottery; decorative, unusual objects, 18th-19th C; both £100-£10,000.* PARK: Nearby. TEL: 071 727 2333. FAIRS: Olympia Antiques and Olympia Decorative. VAT: Spec.

Eric Lineham and Sons

62 Kensington Church St. Est: 1953. Open 9.30-5.30. CL: Sat. SIZE: Small. *STOCK: English, continental and Oriental porcelain, English and continental glass, objets d'art, clocks and watches, art nouveau, chandeliers, enamels.* LOC: Half way along Kensington Church St. PARK: Meters. TEL: 071 937 9650. VAT: Stan/Spec.

W.8 continued

Little Winchester Gallery
36a Kensington Church St. (I Berge) Est: 1966. Open 11-6. SIZE: Small. *STOCK: French, Dutch and English paintings, 19th-20th C.* PARK: Easy. TEL: 071 937 8444 (24 hr.). VAT: Spec.

Lucerne Gallery
7 Kensington Mall, Kensington Church St. Est: 1976. Open 10-6. *STOCK: Paintings, sculpture, furniture, works of art.* TEL: 071 727 1726. VAT: Spec.

C.H Major (Antiques) Ltd
154 Kensington Church St. (A.H Major) Est: 1905. Open 10-6. SIZE: Large. *STOCK: English mahogany furniture, from 1760, £200-£25,000.* Not stocked: China, glass. PARK: Easy. TEL: 071 229 1162; home - 081 997 9018. VAT: Stan.

E and H Manners
66a Kensington Church St. Est: 1979. Open 10-5.30, Sat. and Sun. by appointment. *STOCK: European and Oriental ceramics, £100-£6,000; Oriental works of art, £100-£4,000; all pre-19th C.* TEL: 071 229 5516; home - 081 741 7084. SER: Valuations; restorations; buys at auction (ceramics). FAIRS: International Ceramic, Park Lane. VAT: Spec.

W.8 continued

S Marchant and Son **BADA**
120 Kensington Church St. (R.P Marchant) Est: 1925. Open 9.30-5.30. CL: Sat. *STOCK: Chinese and Japanese pottery and porcelain, jades, cloisonné, Chinese furniture and paintings.* PARK: Easy. TEL: 071 229 5319/3770. SER: Valuations; restorations (porcelain); buys at auction. VAT: Stan/Spec.

J and J May **BADA**
40 Kensington Church St, Books and articles on commemorative items. Est: 1967. Open 10-1.30 and 2.30-6. SIZE: Small. *STOCK: Commemorative pottery, 1750-1850; commemorative porcelain, enamels, glass pictures, textiles, objets de vertu.* LOC: Underground stations: Notting Hill Gate and Kensington High St. PARK: 25yds. Vicarage Gate. TEL: 071 937 3575. SER: Valuations; buys at auction. VAT: Stan/Spec.

W.8 continued

D Mellor and A.L. Baxter BADA LAPADA

121 Kensington Church St. Open 10-6.30, Sat. 10-4. *STOCK: Leather bound literary sets; antiquarian books on history, science, medicine, travel and exploration; 16th and 17th C books on literature, history and medieval manuscripts.* TEL: 071 229 2033/221 8822; fax - 071 792 0214.

Michael Coins

6 Hillgate St (off Notting Hill Gate). (M Gouby) Est: 1966. Open 10-5. CL: Sat. SIZE: Small. *STOCK: Coins, English and foreign, 1066 A.D. to date; stamps, banknotes and collectors' items.* LOC: From Marble Arch to Notting Hill Gate, turn left at corner of Coronet Cinema. PARK: Easy. TEL: 071 727 1518. SER: Valuations; buys at auction. VAT: Stan/Spec.

D.C Monk and Son

132-134 Kensington Church St. Open 10.30-5. CL: Sat. *STOCK: Oriental porcelain.* TEL: 071 229 3727. VAT: Stan/Spec.

Oliver-Sutton Antiques BADA

34c Kensington Church St. (A Oliver and P Sutton) Est: 1967. Open 10-5, Sat. 10-2. CL: Aug. *STOCK: Staffordshire, Walton, Sherratt pottery; 19th C portrait figures, animals, cottages.* TEL: 071 937 0633. VAT: Spec.

Paravent

(M Aldbrook and M Brittle) Est: 1988. Open by appointment. *STOCK: Screens, 17th-20th C, £500-£10,000.* LOC: Off Kensington High St. TEL: 071 602 2044; home - 089 288 3398. SER: Restorations. FAIRS: Olympia. VAT: Stan/Spec.

Henry Phillips BADA

2 Campden St. Open 9.30-5.30. SIZE: Small. *STOCK: English furniture, 18th to early 19th C.* LOC: Near Kensington Church St. TEL: 071 727 4079; home - 071 937 3448. SER: Buys at auction (English furniture).

The Pruskin Gallery LAPADA

73 Kensington Church St. *STOCK: Fine art nouveau and art deco glass, bronzes, silver, furniture, ceramics, paintings, posters and prints.* TEL: 071 937 1994; evenings - 071 243 1939.

Raffety Ltd BADA LAPADA

34 Kensington Church St. Open 10-5, Sat. by appointment. *STOCK: Fine English longcase and bracket clocks, 17th-18th C; carriage clocks and barometers.* TEL: 071 938 1100; fax - 071 938 3301. SER: Valuations; buys at auction. VAT: Stan/Spec.

Paul Reeves

32B Kensington Church St. Est: 1976. Open 10-6. *STOCK: Architect designed furniture and artifacts 1860-1960.* TEL: 071 937 1594.

W.8 continued

Reindeer Antiques (Reindeer International Ltd.)

81 Kensington Church St. (J.W Butterworth) Open 9.30-1 and 2-6. CL: Sat. *STOCK: Period English and continental furniture, and works of art.* PARK: Meters. TEL: 071 937 3754. VAT: Stan/Spec.

Roderick Antique Clocks LAPADA

23 Vicarage Gate, Kensington. (R Mee) Est: 1975. Open 10-5.15, Sat. 10-4. SIZE: Small. *STOCK: Clocks - French decorative and carriage, 19th C, £250-£2,000; English longcase and bracket, 18th-19th C, £2,000-£7,500.* LOC: At junction of Kensington Church St. PARK: Easy. TEL: 071 937 8517. SER: Valuations; restorations (English and French movements and cases). VAT: Spec.

J Roger (Antiques) Ltd BADA

17 Uxbridge St. (J Roger and C Bayley) Open by appointment. *STOCK: Late 18th to early 19th C small elegant pieces furniture, mirrors, prints, porcelain and boxes.* TEL: 071 603 7627/381 2884.

Roundfield House Antiques Ltd

172 Kensington Church St. (F.R Hudson) Open 10-6. *STOCK: General antiques including furniture and paintings.* TEL: 071 229 5486.

Sabin Galleries Ltd BADA

Campden Lodge, 82 Campden Hill Rd. (S.F, E.P. and P.G Sabin) SLAD. Open by appointment only. *STOCK: English paintings and drawings, pre-1830.* TEL: 071 937 0471.

St . Jude's Antiques LAPADA

107 Kensington Church St. Open 10.30-5.30. CL: Mon. *STOCK: Male figurative paintings 16th-20th C.* TEL: 071 727 8737. VAT: Spec.

Patrick Sandberg Antiques BADA

140-142 Kensington Church St. (P.C.F Sandberg) Est: 1983. Open 10-6, Sat. 10-4. SIZE: Large. *STOCK: 18th and early 19th C English furniture and accessories - candlesticks, tea caddies, clocks and prints, £500-£25,000.* TEL: 071 229 0373; fax - 071 792 3467. FAIRS: Olympia, Cafe Royal, Park Lane. VAT: Spec.

A.V. Santos BADA

1 Campden St. Open 10-1 and 2-6. CL: Sat. *STOCK: Chinese porcelain, 17th-18th C.* TEL: 071 727 4872; fax - 071 229 4801. VAT: Spec.

Arthur Seager Antiques Ltd LAPADA

25a Holland St, Resident. (A.A Seager) Est: 1972. Open 10-5.30, Sun. by appointment. SIZE: Medium. *STOCK: Oak furniture, 17th-18th C; pottery, treen and metalware, £500-£10,000.* LOC: Off Kensington Church St. PARK: Easy. TEL: 071 937 3262. SER: Valuations; restorations (furniture); buys at auction (furniture and pottery). VAT: Stan/Spec.

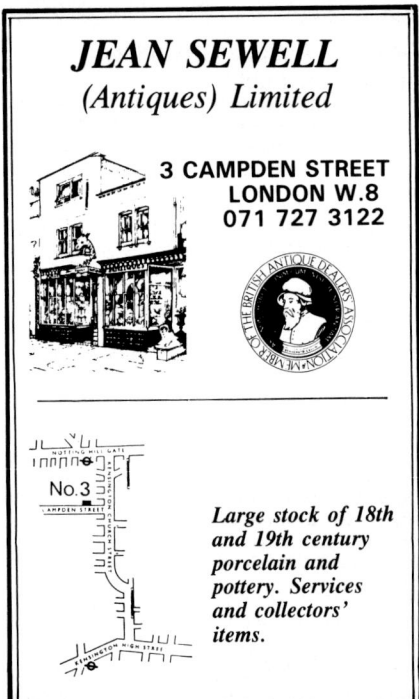

W.8 continued

Select Antiques Gallery Ltd
219 Kensington Church St. (M Vargha and A Youssefian) Open 10-6, Sat. 10-3. *STOCK: French furniture.* TEL: 071 727 4783/229 8732.

M. and D Seligmann **BADA**
37 Kensington Church St. Est: 1948. Open 10-6, Sat. 11-3, or by appointment. SIZE: Medium. *STOCK: 17th-18th C English country furniture, pottery, treen, objets d'art.* LOC: Nearest underground Kensington High St. TEL: 071 937 0400; home - 071 722 4315. SER: Valuations; buys at auction. FAIRS: Fine Arts (Olympia), Chelsea (Spring and Autumn), Café Royal (Spring), Park Lane, Barbican. VAT: Stan/Spec.

Jean Sewell (Antiques) Ltd **BADA**
3 Campden St. (R. and J Sewell) Est: 1956. Open 10-5.30. SIZE: Medium. *STOCK: Pottery and porcelain, 18th-19th C, £1-£10,000.* Not stocked: Silver, furniture and china after 1880. LOC: From Notting Hill Gate down Kensington Church St., fourth street on right at Churchill public house. PARK: Easy. TEL: 071 727 3122. VAT: Stan/Spec.

W.8 continued

Sinai Antiques Ltd **LAPADA**
221 Kensington Church St. (E. and M Sinai) Open 9.30-6. CL: Sat. *STOCK: Carpets, Oriental arts, silver, fine arts.* TEL: 071 229 6190.

Simon Spero
109 Kensington Church St, Author of 'The Price Guide to 18th C English Porcelain'. Est: 1964. Open 10-5, Sat. 10-1. CL: Mon. except by appointment. SIZE: Medium. *STOCK: 18th C English ceramics, enamels and watercolours.* PARK: Meters. TEL: 071 727 7413. SER: Valuations; buys at auction. VAT: Spec.

Constance Stobo
31 Holland St, off Kensington Church St. *STOCK: English lustreware, pottery and Staffordshire animals, Wemyss, 18th-19th C.* TEL: 071 937 6282.

Stockspring Antiques **LAPADA**
114 Kensington Church St. (A Agnew and F Marno) Open 10-5.30, Sat. 10-1. *STOCK: English, European and Oriental pottery and porcelain.* TEL: 071 727 7995. VAT: Spec.

Jacob Stodel **BADA LAPADA**
116 Kensington Church St. Est: 1949. *STOCK: Continental furniture, objets d'art, ceramics, English furniture.* TEL: 071 221 2652. VAT: Spec.

Sukmano Antiques
133 Kensington Church St. Open 10-6. *STOCK: Oriental items.* TEL: 071 229 4323.

Pamela Teignmouth and Son
108 Kensington Church St. (P Teignmouth and T Meyer) Est: 1982. Open 10-6, Sat. 10-4. SIZE: Medium. *STOCK: Papier mâché and tôleware, 19th C, £100-£2,000; English furniture, 18th-19th C; decorative items.* TEL: 071 229 1602. FAIRS: Olympia and Decorators. VAT: Spec.

Murray Thomson Ltd **LAPADA**
152 Kensington Church St. Est: 1966. Open 10-6, Sat. 10-4. SIZE: Large. *STOCK: English furniture, 18th-19th C.* TEL: 071 727 1727; fax - 071 727 1825. VAT: Stan/Spec.

Through the Looking Glass Ltd
137 Kensington Church St. (J.J.A. and D.A Pulton) Est: 1958. Open 10-5.30. SIZE: Medium. *STOCK: Mirrors, 19th C, £500-£1,000.* LOC: 200yds. from Notting Hill Gate. PARK: Side roads. TEL: 071 221 4026. SER: Gilding. VAT: Spec.

Toubian Antiques Ltd
180 Kensington Church St. (N Toubian) Open 10-6. CL: Sat. *STOCK: General antiques.* TEL: 071 221 6476.

W.8 continued

Mary Wise BADA

27 Holland St, Kensington. Est: 1959. *STOCK: English porcelain, Chinese ceramics and jade, works of art, bronzes.* Not stocked: English pottery, jewellery. TEL: 071 937 8649. SER: Buys at auction (Chinese and English porcelain). VAT: Spec.

Yacob's Gallery

176 Kensington Church St. Open 10-6. CL: Sat. *STOCK: Objets d'art and Islamic works of art.* TEL: 071 229 7841. SER: Valuations.

London W.9

Fluss and Charlesworth Ltd

1 Lauderdale Rd. (E Fluss and J Charlesworth) Est: 1970. Open by appointment. *STOCK: 18th to early 19th C furniture and works of art.* TEL: 071 286 8339. SER: Interior decor. FAIRS: Cafe Royal; Olympia.

Robert Hall BADA

140 Sutherland Ave. Est: 1976. Open by appointment. *STOCK: Chinese snuff bottles, Ching dynasty; Oriental works of art, jade carvings, 17th-19th C; all £300-£20,000. Chinese contemporary paintings.* PARK: Easy. TEL: 071 286 0809; fax - 071 289 3287. SER: Valuations; restorations; buys at auction. VAT: Stan/Spec.

Beryl Kendall, The English Watercolour Gallery

2 Warwick Pl, Little Venice. Est: 1953. Open 2-6, Sat. by appointment. CL: Mon. *STOCK: English watercolours, 18th-20th C.* TEL: 071 286 9902.

Charles Spencer

24a Ashworth Rd. Open by appointment. *STOCK: Prints, portraits and original designs relating to the history of the theatre from 17th C to date, £50-£10,000.* LOC: Off Elgin Ave., close Maida Vale station. TEL: 071 286 9396. SER: Valuations; buys at auction (theatrical items). VAT: Stan.

Vale Antiques

245 Elgin Ave, Maida Vale. (P Gooley) *STOCK: General antiques.* TEL: 071 328 4796.

London W.10

Clive Loveless BADA

29 Kelfield GdnsNorth Kensington, Resident. Est: 1968. Open by appointment. SIZE: Small. *STOCK: Near Eastern tribal rugs and kilims, 18th-19th C; textiles - Ottoman, 16th-17th C, Central Asian and African, 18th-19th C.* LOC: Nr. Ladbroke Grove. PARK: Easy. TEL: 081 969 5831. SER: Valuations; restorations (antique rugs); buys at auction. VAT: Stan/Spec.

W.10 continued

Tower Antiques

463 Harrow Rd. (F Jackson) Open 10-5.30. SIZE: Small. *STOCK: Furniture.* LOC: Between Gt. Western Rd. and Ladbroke Grove. PARK: Easy. TEL: 081 969 0535. SER: Valuations; restorations (polishing, wood work); buys at auction.

Andrew White Furnishings

17 The Quadrant, Kilburn Lane. Est: 1969. Open 9-6. SIZE: Small. *STOCK: Chairs, 18th and early 19th C, £500-£1,000+.* LOC: 300 metres north of Ladbroke Grove. PARK: Easy. TEL: 081 960 3452; home - 081 960 1782. SER: Restoration and refinishing (upholstery and chairs). VAT: Stan.

London W.11

Alice's

86 Portobello Rd. (D Carter) Est: 1960. Open 9-5. SIZE: Large. *STOCK: General antiques and decorative items.* TEL: 071 229 8187; fax - 071 792 2456.

The Antique Textile Company LAPADA

100 Portland Rd, Holland Park. (S Franklyn and J Wentworth) Est: 1982. Open 10-6. CL: Sat. *STOCK: Kashmir, paisley, Norwich and French shawls; chintz, quilts, patchworks, period costume, lace, 1600-1850.* LOC: From Notting Hill Gate, 2nd right after Holland Park tube station. PARK: Easy. TEL: 071 221 7730; fax - 071 229 8612. SER: Buys at auction; hire.

Axia Art Consultants Ltd

121 Ledbury Rd. Est: 1974. *STOCK: Works of art, icons, textiles, metalwork, woodwork and ceramics, Islamic and Byzantine.* TEL: 071 727 9724.

B. and T. Antiques

79 Ledbury Rd. (Mrs B Lewis) Open 10-6. *STOCK: Furniture, silver, objets d'art, paintings, 18th C to art deco.* TEL: 071 229 7001.

Serge Baillache

189 Westbourne Grove. Est: 1959. Open 9.30-5.30. CL: Sat. SIZE: Medium. *STOCK: English, continental and decorative furniture, 18th and 19th C.* PARK: Meters. TEL: 071 229 2270. VAT: Stan/Spec.

Barham Antiques

83 Portobello Rd. Est: 1954. Open 9.30-5, Sat. 7-5. SIZE: Large. *STOCK: Victorian walnut and inlaid continental furniture, writing boxes, tea caddies, inkwells and inkstands, glass epergnes, silver plate, clocks, paintings.* TEL: 071 727 3845. SER: Valuations; buys at auction.

W.11 continued

P.R Barham
111 Portobello Rd. Est: 1951. Open 9-5. SIZE: Large. *STOCK: Victorian, Edwardian, continental furniture, Oriental porcelain, objets d'art, silver, plate and clocks.* TEL: 071 727 3397. SER: Valuations; buys at auction.

Beagle Gallery
303 Westbourne Grove. (A. and J Beagle) Open 10.30-5. CL: Mon. *STOCK: Indian, Asian and decorative items.* TEL: 071 229 9524.

David Black Oriental Carpets BADA LAPADA
96 Portland Rd, Holland Park. Est: 1966. Open 11-6. SIZE: Large. *STOCK: Antique and new Oriental room size decorative carpets; tribal rugs, kilims, dhurries, embroideries, £500-£25,000.* LOC: From Notting Hill Gate, second right after Holland Park tube station. PARK: Meters. TEL: 071 727 2566; fax - 071 229 4599. SER: Valuations; restorations; cleaning underfelt. VAT: Spec.

Norman Blackburn
32 Ledbury Road. Est: 1974. Open 10-6. *STOCK: Framed prints - decorative, stipple and mezzotints, floral, sporting, marine and views, pre-1860.* LOC: Two roads east of Portobello. TEL: 071 229 5316. VAT: Spec.

Books and Things
Dolphin Arcade, 157 Portobello Rd. (M Steenson) ABA, PBFA. Est: 1972. Open Sat. 9-4, Mon.-Fri. by appointment. SIZE: Small. *STOCK: Antiquarian books, £25-£500; posters, £50-£500; both 20th C.* PARK: Meters. TEL: 071 370 5593. SER: Valuations; buys at auction; catalogues issued. FAIRS: PBFA London, Oxford, Bath.

F.E.A Briggs Ltd
73 Ledbury Rd. Est: 1962. Open 8.30-5.30, Sat. 10-4. SIZE: Large and warehouse. *STOCK: Furniture and textiles, Victorian, Edwardian and Georgian.* TEL: 071 727 0909/221 4950. SER: Valuations. VAT: Stan/Spec.

John Bull (Antiques) Ltd
163 Portobello Rd. Est: 1940. Open Sat. only, 7.30-11. *STOCK: Silver including frames, plate, jewellery.* TEL: 071 629 1251. VAT: Stan/Spec.

Butchoff Antiques LAPADA
229 and 233 Westbourne Grove. Est: 1962. Open 10-6, Sat. 10-2. SIZE: Large. *STOCK: Furniture and decorative smalls, paintings, 18th-20th C, £500-£30,000.* TEL: 071 221 8174; fax - 071 792 8923.

Caelt Gallery
182 Westbourne Grove. (E.T Crawshaw) Est: 1967. Open 9.30-6. SIZE: Large. *STOCK: Oil paintings, 17th-20th C, £200-£10,000.* PARK: Easy. TEL: 071 229 9309; home - 071 229 0303. VAT: Spec.

W.11 continued

Canonbury Antiques Ltd
174 Westbourne Grove. Est: 1966. Open 9.30-5.30. SIZE: Large. *STOCK: Furniture, porcelain, bronzes, clocks.* TEL: 071 229 2786. VAT: Stan/Spec.

Jack Casimir Ltd BADA LAPADA
The Brass Shop, 23 Pembridge Rd. Est: 1933. Open 10-5.30. SIZE: Medium. *STOCK: Brass, copper, pewter.* Not stocked: Silver, china, jewellery. LOC: 2 mins. walk from Notting Hill Gate station. PARK: 100yds. TEL: 071 727 8643. SER: Exports. VAT: Stan.

Cassio Antiques
68 Ledbury Rd. Est: 1963. Open 10-5.30. SIZE: Large. *STOCK: Furniture.* TEL: 071 727 0678. VAT: Stan/Spec.

Chanticleer Antiques
105 Portobello Rd. (S Wilkinson) Est: 1967. Open Sat. 7-5.30 or by appointment. SIZE: Large. *STOCK: Decorative and collectors items, 18th-19th C, £100-£2,000; European and Oriental works of art.* LOC: Westbourne Grove. PARK: Nearby. TEL: 071 385 0919. SER: Restorations. VAT: Stan/Spec.

Graham Charge Antiques
305 Westbourne Grove. Est: 1975. Open 9.30-5, Sat. 9-5.30. SIZE: Medium. *STOCK: Furniture, 18th-19th C.* LOC: 50yds. off Portobello Rd. PARK: Easy. TEL: 071 229 7907. VAT: Stan/Spec.

Chimney Pieces
227 Westbourne Grove. (E O'Keeffe) Open 10-5.30. CL: Wed. *STOCK: Marble fireplaces, mirrors, grates.* TEL: 071 727 0102.

Cohen and Pearce (Oriental Porcelain) BADA
84 Portobello Rd. (M Cohen and R Pearce) Est: 1974. Open Fri. 10-4, Sat. 8-4 otherwise by appointment. *STOCK: Chinese porcelain, bronzes, works of art; Japanese prints.* TEL: 071 229 9458. SER: Valuations; buys at auction. VAT: Spec.

The Corner Portobello Antiques Supermarket
282,284,288,290 Westbourne Grove. (W Lipka Ltd. LAPADA) Open Fri. 12-4, Sat. 7-6. There are 150 dealers. *STOCK: A wide range of general miniature antiques, silver and jewellery.* TEL: 071 727 2027. SER: Valuations; restorations.

Curá Antiques
34 Ledbury Rd. (G Antichi) Open 11-6, Sat. 10.30-1. *STOCK: Continental furniture, sculptures, majolica and paintings.* TEL: 071 229 6880.

W.11 continued

John Dale
87 Portobello Rd. Est: 1950. Open 9.30-5. CL: Thurs. SIZE: Medium. *STOCK: Georgian furniture, general antiques.* TEL: 071 727 1304. VAT: Stan.

Michael Davidson
52 and 54 Ledbury Rd. Est: 1961. Open 9.45-12.45 and 1.15-5. CL: Sat. p.m. in winter. *STOCK: Regency and period furniture, objets d'art.* TEL: 071 229 6088. SER: Valuations. VAT: Stan/Spec.

Delehar
146 Portobello Rd. Est: 1919. Open Sat. 9-4. SIZE: Medium. *STOCK: General antiques, works of art.* Not stocked: Furniture. TEL: 071 727 9860 or 081 450 9998. VAT: Stan/Spec.

Peter Delehar
146 Portobello Rd. Est: 1919. Open Sat. 10-4. SIZE: Medium. *STOCK: Unusual scientific instruments.* TEL: 071 727 9860 or 081 866 8659. FAIRS: International Scientific and Medical Instrument (Organiser). VAT: Stan/Spec.

Demetzy Books
113 Portobello Rd. (P. and M Hutchinson) ABA, PBFA. Est: 1972. Open Sat. 7.30-3.30. SIZE: Medium. *STOCK: Antiquarian leather bound books, 18th-19th C, £5-£1,000; Dickens' first editions; children's and illustrated books, 18th-20th C, both £5-£200.* LOC: 20yds. from junction with Westbourne Grove, opposite Earl of Lonsdale public house. PARK: Meters. TEL: 0993 702209. SER: Valuations; buys at auction (books). FAIRS: ABA Park Lane; PBFA Russell Hotel, London (monthly); Randolph Hotel, Oxford; ABAA New York, Los Angeles, San Francisco.

E and A Di Michele Antiques LAPADA
36 Ledbury Rd. Est: 1973. Open 9.30-1 and 2-5, resident so usually available. *STOCK: Continental furniture and Dutch marquetry.* TEL: 071 229 1823.

W.11 continued

Dodo Old Advertising
286 Westbourne Grove. (E Farrow) Est: 1960. Open Sat. 7-4 or by appointment. *STOCK: English, American and continental posters, enamels and signs, tins; crate, beer, wine and perfume labels; display figures, pub mirrors, showcards.* Not stocked: Furniture, silver, general antiques. LOC: Near Portobello Rd. TEL: 071 229 3132.

Dolphin Arcade
155-157 Portobello Rd. Open Sat. 7-5.30. SIZE: Large (34 stalls). *STOCK: Jewellery, silver, Oriental porcelain, English pottery, general antiques.* TEL: 071 727 4883. VAT: Stan/Spec.

Elliott and Snowdon Ltd LAPADA
61A Ledbury Rd. Open 10.30-5, Sat. 9.30-12.30. *STOCK: European works of art.* TEL: 071 229 6900.

The Facade
196 Westbourne Grove. Est: 1973. Open 10.30-5.30. *STOCK: Decorative items, 1900-1930 lighting and furniture - mainly French.* PARK: Easy. TEL: 071 727 2159. VAT: Stan.

Jack Fairman (Carpets) Ltd LAPADA
218 Westbourne Grove. (D.R.J. and S.J Page) Open 9.30-6, Sun. by appointment. CL: Sat. p.m. *STOCK: Persian and Oriental carpets and rugs; tapestries.* TEL: 071 229 2262; fax - 071 229 2263. SER: Valuations; repairs; cleaning. VAT: Stan.

Fleur de Lys Gallery
227a Westbourne Grove. (H.S Coronel) Est: 1967. Open 10-5. SIZE: Medium. *STOCK: Oil paintings, 19th C, £500-£3,000.* Not stocked: Prints. PARK: Easy, but limited. TEL: 071 727 8595; fax - same; home - 0372 67934.

Judy Fox LAPADA
81 Portobello Rd, and 176 Westbourne Grove. Est: 1970. Open 10-5. SIZE: Large. *STOCK: Furniture and decorative items, 18th-20th C; inlaid furniture, mainly 19th C; pottery and porcelain.* TEL: 071 229 8130.

W.11 continued

J Freeman **LAPADA**
85a Portobello Rd. Est: 1962. Open 9.30-1 and 2-5.30, Sat. 9-6. SIZE: Medium. *STOCK: Victorian silver plate, 1830-1870, £10-£150; Sheffield plate, 1790-1830, £20-£100; Victorian and later silver, £5-£200.* LOC: Nearest tube station Notting Hill Gate. PARK: Easy. TEL: 071 221 5076; fax - 071 221 5329. VAT: Stan.

Gallery 287 and Gallery 289
287-289 Westbourne Grove. (J Harding) Open Sat. 6-5. There are 25 units here selling. *STOCK: general antiques.* TEL: 071 727 2817.

Philip Garrick Antiques
42 Ledbury Rd. Open 9.30-6. *STOCK: Furniture, bronzes, works of art, 17th-19th C.* Not stocked: Shipping goods. TEL: 071 243 0500.

The Good Fairy Open Air Market
100 Portobello Rd. (S Pardoe) Est: 1978. Open Sat. 5-5. SIZE: Large. There are 80 dealers at this market. *STOCK: A wide variety of general antiques including jewellery and silver, 18th-20th C, £5-£2,000.* LOC: Enter Portobello Rd. at Chepstow Villas, market 150 metres along on right-hand side. PARK: Nearby. TEL: 071 351 5950; Sat. only - 071 221 8977.

Graham and Green
4 Elgin Cres. (A Graham, R Harrison and U Downie) Est: 1974. Open 10-6, Sat. 9.30-6. SIZE: Medium. *STOCK: Turkish kelim rugs, pine and other furniture, re-upholstered Victorian chairs and decorative objects.* LOC: Near Portobello Rd. PARK: Meters nearby. TEL: 071 727 4594. VAT: Stan.

Gavin Graham Gallery
47 Ledbury Rd. SLAD. Est: 1973. *STOCK: Oil paintings.* TEL: 071 229 4848; fax - 071 792 9697. VAT: Spec.

Graham-Stewart
293a Westbourne Grove. (M Graham-Stewart) Est: 1980. Open by appointment. SIZE: Small. *STOCK: African, Polynesian, North and South African ethnographica art and artifacts, £500-£5,000; topographical, ethnographical paintings.* LOC: Between Portobello Rd. and Kensington Park Rd. PARK: Easy. TEL: 071 229 6959. SER: Valuations; buys at auction (ethnographia). VAT: Spec.

Grays Portobello
138 Portobello Rd. Open Sat. 7-4. TEL: 071 221 3069; fax - 071 724 0999.

C Bailey
Stand 3. *English and Chinese pottery and porcelain.*
David Baker
Stand 18. *Oriental ceramics and works of art.*

Grays Portobello continued

Rahmat Bamad
Stand 1. *Oriental and Islamic works of art, carpets, textiles.*
Ann Barlow and Marguerite Harrison
Stand 22. *French faience, Quimper.*
Peter Barlow
Stand 8. *Early Chinese ceramics.*
Pat Bedford and Guy Robbins
Stand 19/20. *Fine art, objets de vertu, antiquities and general antiques.*
Rob Boys
Stand 12. *Oriental antiques.*
Charles Carey
Stand 14/15. *Oriental and European ceramics and antiquities.*
Paul Carnell
Stand 25/26. *European and Oriental works of art, rare antiquities.*
Mrs Davies
Stand 27/28. *Oriental art, netsuke, snuff bottles, jade and bronze.*
Jo de Sousa
Stand 4. *English ceramics.*
Ewa Hall
Stand 13. *Oriental and European works of art.*
J Hill and L Denney
Stand 11. *Oriental art and textiles, European bronzes.*
Steven Hyder
Stand 21. *Oriental works of art and porcelain.*
Diane Leloup
Stand 10. *Oriental and ethnic art and jewellery.*
Ken Leong
Stand 3. *Oriental works of art.*
Jenny Levine
Stand 23. *English, continental and Oriental antiquities.*
Mrs Liv
Stand 9. *Oriental and general antiques.*
A Mohammed
Stand 20. *Oriental porcelain.*
Miranda Rothschild
Stand 17. *Oriental and Chinese.*
Simpsons Textiles
Stand 24. (R Simpson) *Cashmere and European paisley shawls, quilts, tribal carpets, textiles.*
Peter Sloane
Stand 16. *Ancient Islamic and Far Eastern art.*
Angela Strange
Stand 21. *Staffordshire figures and cottages, English pottery.*
G M Thomas
Stand 5/6. *Japanese and Chinese porcelain, woodblocks, prints, ivory and hardstone carving.*
Anita Vandenberg
Stand 7. *Oriental ceramics and antiquities.*
C D Wertheim
Stand 5/6. *Japanese wood cut prints, ceramics, scrolls, paintings.*

W.11 continued

Mark Hales Antiques
69 Portobello Rd Open Sat 7-3. *STOCK: Staffordshire figures and European ceramics.* TEL: Home (0737) 245848.

Hamilton Fine Arts **LAPADA**
61 Ledbury Rd. (V Hamilton) Open 10-6. *STOCK: 18th-20th C paintings, watercolours and bronzes.* TEL: 071 792 8779; evenings - (081) 455 7410. SER: Restorations; framing.

Hancock Gallery
184 Westbourne Grove. Open 10-6.30, Sat. 10-5. *STOCK: 19th C paintings and contemporary art.* TEL: 071 229 7827.

Patricia Harbottle
Stand 16, Geoffrey Van Arcade, 107 Portobello Rd. (Mrs P Harbottle) Est: 1989. Open Sat. 7-5. SIZE: Small. *STOCK: Glass, corkscrews, wine and drink related items, 18th-20th C, £5-£500.* TEL: 071 221 1806; home - 071 731 1972. SER: Valuations; restorations; buys at auction. FAIRS: Putney Hill; Ardingly. VAT: Stan/Spec.

W Hildreth Ltd
141 Portobello Rd. Open Sat. 8-5. SIZE: Large. Over 60 stalls. *STOCK: General antiques.* TEL: 071 727 5242.

Hirst Antiques
59 Pembridge Rd. Est: 1963. Open 10-6. SIZE: Medium. *STOCK: Four poster and half-tester beds; decorative furniture and articles.* LOC: End of Portobello Rd., near Notting Hill Gate tube station. TEL: 071 727 9364. SER: Valuations.

Eric Hudes **LAPADA**
142 Portobello Rd. Est: 1946. Open 9-4.15 Sat. only. *STOCK: Oriental ceramics and works of art, 10th-19th C; early English and European pottery, 17th-19th C, all £100-£1,000.* TEL: 071 727 4643; home - (0376) 83767. SER: Worldwide postal transactions. FAIRS: Buxton and Harrogate. VAT: Spec.

Hyde Park Antiques
191 Westbourne Grove. (G.E. and J.E Baldwin) Open 10-1 and 3-5.30. CL: Sat. *STOCK: Silver and plate.* TEL: 071 727 1585.

George Johnson Antiques Ltd **LAPADA**
First Floor, 120 Kensington Park Rd. Open by appointment. *STOCK: English furniture, walnut and mahogany, 17th to early 19th C; longcase clocks, barometers.* TEL: 071 229 3119; fax - 071 727 4093. VAT: Stan/Spec.

Jones
194 Westbourne Grove. (J Jones) Est: 1978. Open 9.30-6 or by appointment. SIZE: Large. *STOCK: Decorative original interior lighting, 1860-1960.* TEL: 071 229 6866; fax - same. SER: Repairs; valuations; prop hire. VAT: Stan.

W.11 continued

W Jones and Son (Antiques) Ltd
295 Westbourne Grove. (W Jones) Est: 1889. Open 9-1 and 2-5, Sat. 9-5. CL: Mon. SIZE: Large. *STOCK: Victorian and Edwardian furniture, £50-£1,000.* LOC: Near Portobello Rd. PARK: Easy. TEL: 071 727 7051. VAT: Stan.

L'Acquaforte
49A Ledbury Rd. (G. and B Chighine) Est: 1971. Open 9.30-5.30, Sat. by appointment. SIZE: Medium. *STOCK: Continental watercolours and drawings, 18th-19th C, £200-£15,000; natural history, botanical, topographical and other decorative prints, 16th-19th C, £5-£5,000.* LOC: Near Westbourne Grove. PARK: Easy. TEL: 071 221 3388. VAT: Stan/Spec.

Lacy Gallery
38 Ledbury Rd, and 203 Westbourne Grove. Est: 1960. Open 10-5.30, Sat. 10-5. SIZE: Large. *STOCK: Period frames, 1700-1940; sporting and decorative paintings; antique toiles de jouy textiles and decorative art; art reference books.* LOC: Two roads east of Portobello Rd. PARK: Easy. TEL: 071 229 9105/229 6340. VAT: Spec.

L'Aiglon Antique Centre
220 Westbourne Grove, (London Restoration Centre). Open 10-6. There are 12 dealers at this centre. *STOCK: A wide range of general antiques.* TEL: 071 727 6596.

S Lampard and Son Ltd
32 Notting Hill Gate. (J.P Barnett) Est: 1847. Open 9.30-4.30. CL: Sat. SIZE: Medium. *STOCK: Jewellery, silver, clocks.* TEL: 071 229 5457. SER: Valuations; restorations. VAT: Stan/Spec.

Joan Leigh
153 Portobello Rd. Est: 1959. *STOCK: Art nouveau, art deco.* TEL: 071 727 6848.

M and D Lewis
1 Lonsdale Rd,172, 179, 193 and 212 Westbourne Grove, 83 and 85 Ledbury Rd. Est: 1960. Open 9.30-5.30, Sat. 9.30-4. *STOCK: Continental and Victorian furniture, porcelain, bronzes.* TEL: 071 727 3908. VAT: Stan.

J Lipitch Ltd **BADA**
177 Westbourne Grove. Est: 1955. Open 9.30-1 and 2-5.30, Sat. 10-1.30. *STOCK: English and continental furniture, 17th and 18th C; bronze, ormolu and porcelain.* TEL: 071 229 0783. VAT: Spec.

M.C.N. Antiques
183 Westbourne Grove. Open 9.30-6 or by appointment. *STOCK: Oriental and Japanese furniture, porcelain, bronzes, jade, ivory, netsuke, lacquer work.* LOC: Near Portobello Rd. market. PARK: Easy. TEL: 071 727 3796; fax - 071 229 8839. SER: Buys at auction. VAT: Stan.

W.11 continued

Magus Antiques LAPADA
187 Westbourne Grove. (G.R Walpole) Est: 1973. Open 10-6. SIZE: Medium. *STOCK: Metalware including brass, bronze and ormolu; pictures, lighting, furniture, £100-£15,000.* LOC: 300yds. off Portobello Rd. PARK: Easy. TEL: 071 229 0267. SER: Valuations; buys at auction. FAIRS: Olympia. VAT: Stan.

Robin Martin
44 Ledbury Rd. Est: 1972. Open 10-5.30. SIZE: Medium. *STOCK: General antiques, furniture, works of art, early metalware, garden furniture, decorative items.* LOC: Westbourne Grove area. TEL: 071 727 1301. VAT: Stan.

Mayflower Antiques
117 Portobello Rd. (J.W Odgers) Open Sat. 7-3. *STOCK: Clocks, mechanical music, scientific and marine instruments, furniture and general antiques.* TEL: 071 727 0381; mobile - (0860) 315101. VAT: Stan/Spec.

Mercury Antiques BADA
1 Ladbroke Rd. (L Richards) Est: 1963. Open 10-5.30. SIZE: Medium. *STOCK: English porcelain, 1750-1850; English pottery and Delft, 1700-1850; glass, 1780-1850.* Not stocked: Jewellery, silver, plate, art nouveau. LOC: Half minute from Notting Hill Gate underground station, turn into Pembridge Rd. and bear left. TEL: 071 727 5106. VAT: Mainly spec.

Milne and Moller
35 Colville Terrace. (Mr and Mrs C Moller) Est: 1976. Open during exhibitions and Sat. 10-4, other times by appointment. SIZE: Small. *STOCK: Watercolours, oils and sculpture, 19th C to contemporary, £50-£3,000.* LOC: Near junction of Westbourne Grove and Ledbury Rd. PARK: Easy. TEL: 071 727 1679; home - same. SER: Valuations; restorations; framing; buys at auction (watercolours). FAIRS: 20th C British Art, Cumberland Hotel; Olympia. VAT: Spec.

Terence Morse and Son Ltd
197-199 and 237 Westbourne Grove. Est: 1947. Open 9-5. CL: Sat. SIZE: Large. *STOCK: Furniture, 18th-19th C, £1,000+.* LOC: 200yds. from Portobello Rd. PARK: Easy. TEL: 071 229 9380/229 4059. VAT: Stan/Spec.

Myriad Antiques
131 Portland Rd, Holland Park Ave. (S Nickerson) Est: 1970. Open 11-6. SIZE: Medium. *STOCK: Decorative furniture and objects, mostly 19th C, £10-£1,000.* LOC: Between Notting Hill Gate and Shepherds Bush roundabout. TEL: 071 229 1709. VAT: Stan.

Nanking Porcelain Co
84 Portobello Rd. (M Hyams and E Porter) Est: 1967. Open 10-4, Sat. 8-4, Sun. and Mon. by appointment. *STOCK: Fine Chinese export porcelain, 18th-19th C, £250-£20,000; Orientalia,*

Nanking Porcelain Co continued

18th-19th C, £100-£5,000. LOC: Near Notting Hill Gate tube station. TEL: 071 229 9458; home - 071 924 2349. SER: Valuations; buys at auction (Orientalia). VAT: Spec.

Eva Nieradzik Antiques
69 Portobello Rd. Est: 1984. Open Sat. 7-3. *STOCK: Unusual decorative objects, samplers and textiles, 17th-19th C.* PARK: Meters. TEL: Home - 081 840 2014. FAIRS: Little Chelsea; Olympia, Sandown Park.

Noble Antiques
195 Westbourne Grove. (G Lee) Open 9.30-1 and 2-5.30, Sat. 9.30-1. *STOCK: English and continental furniture, 18th-19th C; decorative items.* TEL: 071 229 9575.

Pat Nye
Geoffrey Van Arcade, 105 Portobello Rd. Est: 1963. Open Sat. only 7-3.30 or by appointment. SIZE: Small. *STOCK: Needlework samplers, 18th-19th C, £80-£350; brass, £15-£200; snuff boxes and pipe tampers, £15-£150; pottery - gaudy Welsh, £10-£200; all 18th to early 19th C.* LOC: Near Westbourne Grove. PARK: Powys Sq. TEL: Home - 081 948 4314. FAIRS: West London and Chelsea. VAT: Stan/Spec.

E.R O'Connor and A. and C. Elliott
61A Ledbury Rd. Est: 1951. Open 10-5.30, Sat. 9.30-12.30. SIZE: Medium. *STOCK: Sculpture, metalwork, 16th to early 19th C; decorative and architectural items, 15th-19th C.* LOC: Off Westbourne Grove. PARK: Easy. TEL: 071 229 6900. VAT: Stan/Spec.

Old Father Time Clock Centre
First Floor, 101 Portobello Rd. (J Denvir) Open Fri. 9.30-2, Sat. 6-4. *STOCK: Clocks and barometers.* TEL: 081 546 6299. SER: Spares.

The Old Haberdasher
139 Portobello Rd. (L Lundie and E Harvey) Est: 1974. Open Sat. 8-4.30. SIZE: Small. *STOCK: Antique ribbons, laces and all trimmings; embroideries, tapestries and lace; bridal dresses.* LOC: Opposite Collectors Corner. PARK: Meters until 1.30. TEL: 081 904 6001; home - same. VAT: Stan.

Ormonde Gallery
156 Portobello Rd. (F Ormonde) Open 11-5, Sat. 7-5, or by appointment. *STOCK: Specialist dealers in early Chinese ceramics; Oriental items including textiles, furniture, collectables, porcelain, netsuke, ivory, jade, snuff bottles, ceramics, bronzes, paintings, Middle Eastern items and carpets.* TEL: 071 229 9800 /042482 226. VAT: Stan/Spec.

Pembridge Art Gallery
57 Pembridge Rd, Notting Hill Gate. (D Ewen) Open 9.30-6. *STOCK: Decorative paintings, 19th-20th C.* TEL: 071 792 2717.

W.11 continued

E.S Phillips and Sons

99 Portobello Rd. Est: 1962. Open 10-5.30. *STOCK: Architectural antiques, stained glass windows.* TEL: 071 229 2113. *Export Only.*

Philp BADA

59 Ledbury Rd. (R Philp) SLAD. Est: 1961. Open 10-6. *STOCK: 16th-17th C English portraiture and Old Master paintings, medieval sculpture, early furniture and 20th C drawings, £50-£40,000.* PARK: Easy. TEL: 071 727 7915. VAT: Spec.

Portland Gallery

2 Holland Park Terrace, Portland Rd. (T.A Hewlett) Est: 1980. Open 10-6, Sat. 11-5. SIZE: Medium. *STOCK: Scottish pictures, 20th C, £200-£100,000.* LOC: Corner of Holland Park Ave. and Portland Rd. PARK: Easy. TEL: 071 221 0294. SER: Valuations; buys at auction. VAT: Spec.

Portobello Antique Co

133 Portobello Rd. (L Meltzer and A Goldsmith) Open Fri. 11-4.30, Sat. 8-4.30, other times by appointment. *STOCK: Porcelain, small furniture, reproduction silver plate and cutlery.* LOC: Off Westbourne Grove. PARK: Easy. TEL: 071 221 0344; home - 081 958 7333. VAT: Stan/Spec.

Portobello Antique Store LAPADA

79 Portobello Rd. (J.F Ewing and H Gregory) Est: 1971. Open 10-4, Sat. 8-5. CL: Mon. SIZE: Large. *STOCK: Silver and plate, general antiques, £2-£3,000.* LOC: Notting Hill end of Portobello Rd. PARK: Easy weekdays. TEL: 071 221 1994. SER: Export. VAT: Stan/Spec.

Richard Price

101 Portobello Rd. Est: 1975. Open Sat. 9-2.30. SIZE: Small. *STOCK: Watches and small clocks, 1750-1900, £300-£3,000.* TEL: Home - 0784 452990. SER: Valuations; restorations; buys at auction (watches and clocks). FAIRS: Olympia, Barbican, Kensington (Penman). VAT: Spec.

The Red Lion Market (Portobello Antiques Market)

165/169 Portobello Rd. Est: 1951. Open 5.30-5. There are over 200 dealers selling. *STOCK: a wide range of general antiques including ethnic antiquities, bronzes, ivory statues, jade, precious metals, dolls, silver and plate, drinking vessels, costumes, Oriental and Western porcelain, furniture, collectables, prints, lace, linen, books, manuscripts, stamps, coins, banknotes, paintings, etchings, sporting memorabilia and curios.* TEL: 071 221 4964 (24-hours)/221 7638/229 4010. SER: Valuations; shipping.

Rex Antiques

63 Ledbury Rd. (D Cura) Open 9-6, Sat. 9-1. *STOCK: Victorian and decorative furniture.* TEL: 071 229 6203.

W.11 continued

A Rezai Persian Carpets

123 Portobello Rd. Open 9-5. *STOCK: Oriental carpets, kilims, tribal rugs and silk embroideries, £70-£1,500.* TEL: 071 221 5012.

Rod's Antiques

82B Portobello Rd. (R Buck) Est: 1970. Open 9-5. SIZE: Large. *STOCK: Barometers, English and European copper, brass, boat models, nautical goods, scientific instruments, interior decorating items.* TEL: 071 229 2544. VAT: Stan.

Roger's Antiques Gallery

65 Portobello Rd, (Atlantic Antiques Centres Ltd.). Open 7-4 every Sat. There are 60 dealers selling. *STOCK: a wide range of general antiques.* TEL: Enquiries - 071 351 5353.

St John's Collection Ltd

208 Westbourne Grove. (W.J Richards) Est: 1964. Open 10-6, Sat. by appointment. SIZE: Medium. *STOCK: Decorative prints, 17th to late 19th C, £100-£2,000.* LOC: Near Portobello Rd. market. PARK: Easy. TEL: 071 229 4687. SER: Valuations; hand-made frames. VAT: Stan.

G Sarti Antiques Ltd

186 Westbourne Grove. SLAD. Open 9.30-1 and 2-5.30. *STOCK: Cabinets, European and English furniture, marbles, paintings, 16th-19th C.* TEL: 071 221 7186/727 3493.

Schredds of Portobello LAPADA

107 Portobello Rd. (H.J. and G.R Schrager) Est: 1969. Open Sat. 7.30-3.30 or by appointment. SIZE: Small. *STOCK: Collectors' silver, 17th-19th C, £10-£1,000; Delft, 17th-18th C; English porcelain, 18th C.* TEL: 081 348 3314; home - same. SER: Valuations; buys at auction. FAIRS: West Kensington, Jan. and Aug; City of London, Nov. VAT: Stan/Spec.

Bernard T Shapero Rare Books LAPADA

80 Holland Park Av. Est: 1979. Open 10-7, Sat. 10-5. SIZE: Large. *STOCK: Antiquarian books - travel, natural history and literature (old and modern).* LOC: Between Shepherds Bush roundabout and Notting Hill Gate. TEL: 071 493 0876. SER: Valuations; restorations (antiquarian books); buys at auction. FAIRS: Book - London, Paris, New York, San Francisco.

Justin Skrebowski

82E Portobello Rd. Est: 1985. Open 1-6.30, Sat. 7-6, Sun., Mon. and mornings by appointment. SIZE: Small. *STOCK: Prints, engravings and lithographs, 1700-1850, £50-£500; oil paintings, 1700-1900, £200-£1,500; watercolours, drawings including Old Masters, 1600-1900, £50-£1,000.* PARK: Meters. TEL: 071 792 9742; home - 081 871 4295. SER: Valuations. VAT: Stan/Spec.

W.11 continued

David Slater

170 Westbourne Grove. Est: 1961. Open 9.30-1 and 2-5.30, Sat. 10-1. SIZE: Large. *STOCK: General antiques, decorative items.* PARK: Easy. TEL: 071 727 3336. VAT: Stan.

Colin Smith and Gerald Robinson Antiques

The Geoffrey Van Arcade, 105 Portobello Rd. Est: 1979. Open Sat., Mon. a.m. and Fri. by appointment. SIZE: Small. *STOCK: Tortoiseshell, £100-£2,000; silver, ivory and crocodile items.* TEL: 081 994 3783. FAIRS: Olympia. VAT: Stan.

Louis Stanton BADA

299 and 301 Westbourne Grove. (L.R. and S.A Stanton) CINOA. Est: 1965. Open 9.30-1 and 2-5.30, Sat. 9-6. SIZE: Medium. *STOCK: Early English oak and walnut furniture, tapestries, sculpture, metalware, objets d'art, pre-1750, £20-£25,000; fine English 18th and early 19th C furniture, clocks and unusual decorative items.* PARK: Easy. TEL: 071 727 9336. SER: Valuations; buys at auction. VAT: Stan/Spec.

Stern Art Dealers

46 Ledbury Rd. (M Stern and Son) Est: 1952. Open 10-6. SIZE: Medium. *STOCK: Oil paintings, 19th-20th C, £200-£5,000.* LOC: Off Westbourne Grove near Portobello. PARK: Easy. TEL: 071 229 6187. SER: Valuations; restorations. VAT: Stan.

Stouts Antique Arcade

144 Portobello Rd. Open Sat. only. Below are listed some of the dealers at this arcade.

David Beaumont Antiques
Est. 1972. *Silver, from 1600.*

Court Galleries
(R Cleland) Est. 1969. *Curios of character, fine art.* TEL: 0225 44730.

K and M Antiques
(M G Harris) *Oriental ceramics, European porcelain, jewellery, all from 1870.* TEL: 071 229 2178; home - 081 908 1783; mobile - 0860 878345.

Kleanthous Antiques LAPADA
(C and C Kleanthous) Est. 1969. *Jewellery, watches, clocks, silver and works of art, 1750-1950.* TEL: 071 727 3649. VAT: Stan/Spec.

Rosa Antiques
(J de Perez) *European porcelain, glass, silver, religious objects, watches, from 1800.* TEL: 071 724 7820.

S and G Antiques
(G Sirett) *Objets d'art and collectables.* TEL: 071 229 2178; 081 907 1389; mobile - 0860 863360. VAT: Stan.

Ric Saunders
Est. 1975. *Wrist watches, 1910-1950, £100-£5,000.* TEL: 071 836 8371. VAT: Stan.

Stouts Antique Arcade continued

Sirett Antiques Ltd
(Mrs A M Sirett) Est. 1976. *Fine reproduction Chinese porcelain, ivory and objets d'art, £10-£10,000.* TEL: 071 229 2178; home - 081 907 1389/7140. VAT: Stan/Spec. *Trade Only.*

L. and M Sutton

91 Portobello Rd. Open Sat. 10-5. SIZE: Medium. *STOCK: Jewellery.* TEL: 071 727 0386. SER: Stan.

M. and C Telfer-Smollett

88 Portobello Rd. Est: 1958. Open Thurs, Fri. and Sat. 10-5. SIZE: Medium. *STOCK: Oriental furniture, fabrics, Middle Eastern screens, tables, natural history specimens and tribal art.* TEL: 071 727 0117. VAT: Stan/Spec.

Temple Gallery

6 Clarendon Cross. (R.C.C Temple) Est: 1959. Open 10-6, weekends and evenings by appointment. SIZE: Large. *STOCK: Icons, Russian and Greek, 12th-16th C, £1,000-£50,000.* PARK: Easy. TEL: 071 727 3809; fax - 071 727 1546. SER: Valuations; restorations; buys at auction (icons). VAT: Spec.

Themes and Variations

231 Westbourne Grove. (L Fawcett and G Medda) Open 10-1 and 2-6, Mon. and Sat 10-6. *STOCK: Decorative items, furniture, glass, ceramics, carpets, lamps, jewellery, art nouveau, art deco and 1950s.* TEL: 071 727 5531.

Nicholas Thomas Antiques

57 Ledbury Rd. *STOCK: Paintings, continental furniture, ormolu, pottery and porcelain.* TEL: 071 243 0669.

Igor Tociapski

39 Ledbury Rd. Est: 1959. Open 10-5.30. CL: Sat and Fri p.m.. SIZE: Small. *STOCK: Clocks, watches, scientific instruments and mechanical music, 1500-1900.* Not stocked: Tapestries. PARK: Easy. TEL: 071 229 8317. SER: Restorations (clocks); buys at auction.

Trench Enterprises

The Corner Portobello Antiques Supermarket Basement, 290 Westbourne Grove. Open Sat. only 7-5. *STOCK: Antique and old jigsaw and mechanical puzzles.* TEL: (0284) 760909. SER: Valuations; restorations; searches undertaken.

Christina Truscott

The Hildreth Arcade, 139 Portobello Rd. Est: 1967. Open Sat. 7.30-3.30. *STOCK: Chinese lacquer, tea caddies, work boxes, small decorative items, late 18th to early 19th C, £100-£500.* TEL: Home - (0403) 730554.

Village Gallery

32 Uxbridge St. (T Malvasi) Open by appointment. *STOCK: 19th C English and European paintings.* TEL: 071 229 8928.

W.11 continued

Virginia
98 Portland Rd, Holland Park. (V Bates) Est: 1971. Open 11-6. SIZE: Medium. *STOCK: Decorative items, £50-£2,000; textiles, clothes and lace, £25-£500; bathroom fittings, £15-£600; all 19th-20th C.* LOC: Holland Park Ave. PARK: Easy. TEL: 071 727 9908. VAT: Stan.

Johnny Von Pflugh Antiques
289 Westbourne Grove. Est: 1985. Open Sat., other times by appointment. SIZE: Small. *STOCK: European works of art, Italian oil paintings, gouaches, 17th-19th C, £300-£1,500; fine ironware, 17th-18th C, £300-£800; medical and scientific instruments, 18th-19th C, £200-£1,000.* LOC: Off Portobello Rd. PARK: Easy. TEL: 081 740 5306; home - same. SER: Valuations; buys at auction (keys, caskets, medical instruments, Italian oil paintings, and gouaches). FAIRS: Olympia; Little Chelsea (Scientific and Medical). VAT: Spec.

Trude Weaver LAPADA
71 Portobello Rd. Est: 1968. Open 9.30-5, Sat. 9-5. SIZE: Medium. *STOCK: English and continental furniture, decorative objects, textiles.* PARK: Easy. TEL: 071 229 8738. SER: Valuations.

A.M Web LAPADA
93 Portobello Rd. (J Donovan) Open Thurs., Fri. and Sat. 11-5. *STOCK: Musical boxes, unusual clocks, automata, old toys and other mechanical antiques.* TEL: 071 727 1485. VAT: Stan.

Wellington Antiques
2-5 Wellington Close. (F.E.A Briggs Ltd) Open 8.30-1 and 2-5.30, Sat. 10-4, Sun. by appointment. SIZE: Large. *STOCK: Furniture, mainly mahogany, instruments, 18th-20th C.* LOC: Off Ledbury Rd., near Westbourne Grove. TEL: 071 221 4950. VAT: Stan/Spec.

Westbourne Gallery LAPADA
206 Westbourne Grove. (G Cocozza) Open 10-6, Sat. 10-1. *STOCK: Furniture, objets d'art, decorative items.* TEL: 071 221 1535/229 3908.

Neil Wibroe Antiques Ltd
185 Westbourne Grove. Est: 1984. Open 9.30-6, Sat. 9.30-5. SIZE: Medium. *STOCK: Furniture and works of art, 18th C, £500-£5,000.* PARK: Easy. TEL: 071 229 6334; home - same. SER: Valuations; restorations (furniture); buys at auction (furniture). VAT: Stan/Spec.

World Famous Portobello Market
177 Portobello Rd, and 1-3 Elgin Cres. Est: 1951. Open Sat. 5-6. There are over 200 dealers. *STOCK: A wide range of general antiques including ethnic antiquities, bronzes, ivory statues, jade, precious metals, dolls, silver and plate, drinking vessels and costumes; also specialist golf shop.* TEL: 071 221 4964 (24-hour answering service). SER: Valuations; restorations; shipping.

W.11 continued

The Wyllie Gallery
12 Needham Rd. (J.G Wyllie) Open 9-1 and 2-6, Sat. 10-1 or by appointment. *STOCK: 19th-20th C marine paintings and etchings especially works by the Wyllie family.* TEL: 071 727 0606.

Wynyards Antiques (Lastlodge Ltd.)
5 Ladbroke Rd. Est: 1983. Open 10-5.30, Sat. 10.30-5.30. SIZE: Medium. *STOCK: Treen, £5-£500; small furniture, £35-£2,000; objects of art and interest, £3-£600, all 17th-19th C.* LOC: Near Notting Hill Gate tube station. PARK: Meters. TEL: 071 221 7936. SER: Restorations (furniture); polishing; caning; upholstery. FAIRS: Ravenscott at Chelsea Town Hall. VAT: Mainly spec.

London W.13

Chiswick Antiques
97 Northfield Ave, Ealing. (Mrs D Rout) Est: 1957. Open 9-5.30, CL: Thurs. SIZE: Medium. *STOCK: Furniture; china, glass, £5-£25; silver, £5-£50, all 18th-19th C.* PARK: Easy. TEL: 081 579 3071/567 4162.

Quest Antiques
90 Northfields Ave, Ealing. (W.A Turner) Est: 1979. Open 10.30-5, Sat. 9.30-4. CL: Mon. and Wed. SIZE: Small. *STOCK: Furniture, 19th C, to £1,000; objects and bric-a-brac, 19th-20th C, £5-£300.* PARK: Easy. TEL: 081 840 2349; home - same. VAT: Stan.

Rupert's
151 Northfield Ave. (R Loftus Brigham) Open 10-6 or by appointment. CL: Sat. *STOCK: Pre-broadcast and 1920's items.* TEL: 081 567 1368.

W.13 Antiques
10 The Avenue, Ealing. Open Tues., Thurs. and Sat. 10-5, or by appointment. SIZE: Medium. *STOCK: Furniture, china and general antiques, 18th-20th C.* LOC: Off Uxbridge Rd., West Ealing. PARK: Easy. TEL: 081 998 0390. SER: Valuations. VAT: Stan.

London W.14

Andy's All Pine
Olivia Bridge Quay (OBQ), 70 Russell Rd., Kensington. (A Gibb) Open 9.30-6.30, weekends by appointment. *STOCK: Pine.* TEL: 071 602 0856; fax - 081 740 5504. SER: Stripping.

Alyson Burdon
4 Anley Rd. Est: 1975. Open by appointment. SIZE: Small. *STOCK: Decorative items including textiles, costume, £4-£1,000.* LOC: Off Shepherd's Bush Rd. PARK: Easy. TEL: 071 602 1973; home - same. SER: Valuations; buys at auction (textiles and interesting decorative items). FAIRS: Olympia. VAT: Stan.

W.14 continued

Charleville Gallery
7 Charleville Rd, West Kensington. (F King) Est: 1986. Open Wed. 10-7, Thurs. and Fri. 10-6 or by appointment. *STOCK: Textiles, shawls, cushions, bedspreads, linen, £5-£1,000.* LOC: 2 min. walk from West Kensington station or off M4 onto North End Rd. PARK: Easy. TEL: 071 385 3795; home 071 727 2625.

Sheila Cook
62 Blythe Rd. Est: 1970. CL: Mon. SIZE: Medium. *STOCK: Textiles and jewellery, £50-£500; decorative furniture, £50-£1,000; all 1800-1940.* LOC: Behind Olympia Exhibition Hall, off Hammersmith Rd. PARK: Easy. TEL: 071 603 6602. SER: Valuations; buys at auction (textiles). VAT: Stan.

Stephen Garratt (Fine Paintings) BADA
60 Addison Rd. Open by appointment only. *STOCK: Oils and watercolours, 18th-20th C.* TEL: 071 603 0861.

Richard Joslin
Gordon Mansions, 150 Addison Gardens. Est: 1971. Open by appointment. *STOCK: English and continental oils and watercolours, 19th-20th C, £500-£20,000.* LOC: Off Shepherd's Bush Rd., turn into Blythe Rd., 2nd turning on left. PARK: Easy. TEL: 071 603 6435; fax - same; home - same. SER: Valuations; restorations (oils and watercolours); framing; buys at auction (oils and watercolours, worldwide). VAT: Spec.

Mahine Lak Ltd
44 Palace Mansions, Earsby St. Open by appointment. *STOCK: Archeological objects, works of art.* TEL: 071 602 9284.

D Parikian
3 Caithness Rd. Open by appointment. *STOCK: Antiquarian books, mythology, iconography, emblemata, continental books pre-1800.* TEL: 071 603 8375; fax - 071 602 1178.

Simpsons - Pine Mirrors
Blythe Hall, 100 Blythe Rd. (S Yardy) Open by appointment. *STOCK: Antique and new hand carved mirrors.* TEL: 071 603 8625.

London S.W.1

Didier Aaron (London)Ltd BADA
21 Ryder St, St. James's. Open 10-6. CL: Sat. SIZE: Large. *STOCK: French furniture, 18th C, £5,000-£500,000; Old Master and 19th C pictures, £5,000-£500,000; objets d'art, £1,000-£50,000.* LOC: 200yds. from Christie's. TEL: 071 839 4716/7. FAIRS: Grosvenor House; Winter Antiques Show, New York. VAT: Stan/Spec.

S.W.1 continued

Addison-Ross Gallery
40 Eaton Terrace, Belgravia. (T.C.A. and D.A.A Ross) *STOCK: Paintings and prints especially sporting and natural history.* TEL: 071 730 1536. SER: Interior design (pictures).

Ahuan (UK) Ltd
17 Eccleston St. (O. Hoare) Est: 1975. Open 9.30-5.30. CL: Sat. *STOCK: Early Persian and Islamic works of art.* TEL: 071 730 9382. VAT: Spec.

Armin B Allen BADA
3 Bury St, St. James's. Est: 1980. Open 9.30-5.30. CL: Sat. *STOCK: European pottery and porcelain, works of art, 18th to early 19th C.* TEL: 071 930 4732; 071 930 0729; fax - 071 839 8942. SER: Valuations.

J.A Allen & Co. (The Horseman's Bookshop) Ltd.
, 1 Lower Grosvenor Pl. Est: 1926. Open 9-5.30. CL: Sat p.m.. *STOCK: Horse books, from 1600.* PARK: Meters. TEL: 071 834 5606; fax - 071 834 5836. VAT: Stan.

John Allsopp Antiques
26 Pimlico Rd. Open 9.30-6, Sat. 10-1. *STOCK: Decorative furniture and objects, 18th-19th C.* TEL: 071 730 9347.

Verner Amell Ltd
4 Ryder St, St. James's. Open 10-5.30. CL: Sat. *STOCK: Dutch and Flemish Old Masters, 16th-17th C; French 18th C and Scandinavian, 19th C paintings.* TEL: 071 925 2759.

Albert Amor Ltd
37 Bury St, St. James's. Est: 1837. Open 9.30-4.30. CL: Sat. SIZE: Small. *STOCK: 18th C English ceramics, especially first period Worcester and blue and white porcelain.* PARK: Meters. TEL: 071 930 2444; fax - 071 930 9067. SER: Valuations; buys at auction. VAT: Spec.

Anno Domini Antiques BADA
66 Pimlico Rd. (F Bartman) Est: 1960. Open 10-1 and 2.15-6. CL: Sat. p.m. SIZE: Large. *STOCK: Furniture, 17th to early 19th C, £500-£10,000; mirrors, 17th-19th C, £300-£3,000; glass, screens, decorative items and tapestries, £10-£5,000.* Not stocked: Silver, jewellery, arms, carpets, coins. LOC: From Sloane Sq. go down Lower Sloane St., turn left at traffic lights. PARK: Easy. TEL: 071 730 5496; home - 071 352 3084. SER: Buys at auction. VAT: Stan/Spec.

Antiquités
227 Ebury St. (A De Cacqueray) Open 10-6, Sat. 11-4. *STOCK: French and continental furniture, objets d'art.* TEL: 071 730 5000.

S.W.1 continued

Antiquus

90-92 Pimlico Rd. (E Amati) Open 9.30-5.30. SIZE: Large. *STOCK: Classical, medieval and Renaissance works of art, paintings, textiles and glass.* LOC: Near Sloane Sq. underground station. PARK: Meters in Holbein Place. TEL: 071 730 8681.

Michael Appleby LAPADA

7 St. James's Chambers, 2 -10 Ryder St., St. James's. (M.A Appleby) Open by appointment. *STOCK: Drawings, watercolours, to early 20th C; British, continental and marine oil paintings.* TEL: 071 839 7635.

The Armoury of St. James's Military Antiquarians

17 Piccadilly Arcade, Piccadilly. Open 9.30-6. CL: Sat. SIZE: Small. *STOCK: British and foreign orders, decorations and medals, 18th C to date, £1-£50,000; collectors and toy handpainted soldiers, £2-£400.* LOC: Between Piccadilly and Jermyn St. TEL: 071 493 5082. SER: Valuations; buys at auction (orders, medals and decorations). VAT: Stan/Spec.

Artemis Fine Arts Limited

15 Duke St, St. James's. Open 10-5. CL: Sat. *STOCK: Old Master, 19th C and modern paintings, drawings and prints.* TEL: 071 930 8733.

Maurice Asprey Ltd BADA

41 Duke St, St. James's. Est: 1956. Open 9.30-5.30, Sat. during Dec. only. SIZE: Small. *STOCK: Antique silver, jewellery, portrait miniatures, objets de vertu and Russian works of art.* LOC: South of Jermyn St. TEL: 071 930 3921. SER: Valuations; restorations, repairs, restringing; gold stamping. FAIRS: International Silver and Jewellery (Park Lane Hotel); Grosvenor House; New York International. VAT: Stan/Spec.

Astleys

109 Jermyn St. Est: 1862. CL: Sat. p.m. SIZE: Medium. *STOCK: Meerschaum pipes, 19th C, £30-£1,500; pottery, porcelain, primitive and Oriental pipes, £30-£1,500; smoking accessories, cigar boxes, smoking cabinets, tobacco jars, 19th C, £20-£200.* LOC: Near Piccadilly Circus. PARK: Meters. TEL: 071 930 1687. SER: Valuations; restorations (pipes). VAT: Stan.

Beaton-Brown Fine Paintings

20 Motcomb St. (P Beaton-Brown) Open 10-6, Sat. 10-1. *STOCK: 19th C continental and British paintings.* TEL: 071 823 2240; fax - 071 259 6702.

S.W.1 continued

Chris Beetles Ltd Watercolours and Paintings

10 Ryder St, St. James's. Open 10-5.30, by appointment at weekends. SIZE: Large. *STOCK: English watercolours, 18th-20th C, £500-£50,000.* LOC: 100yds. from Royal Academy. PARK: Meters. TEL: 071 839 7551. SER: Valuations; framing. VAT: Spec.

Belgrave Carpet Gallery Ltd

91 Knightsbridge. (A.H Khawaja) Open 9.30-6.30. *STOCK: Hand knotted Oriental carpets and rugs.* TEL: 071 235 2541/245 9749.

Belgrave Gallery

22 Mason's Yard, Duke St., St. James's. Open 10-6. CL: Sat. *STOCK: 20th C British paintings, watercolours and sculpture.* TEL: 071 930 0294.

Raymond Benardout BADA

4 William St, Knightsbridge. Est: 1961. Open 9.30-6, Sat. by appointment. *STOCK: Antique and decorative rugs and carpets, tapestry.* LOC: Next to Park Tower Hotel. TEL: 071 235 3360; fax - 071 823 1345. SER: Valuations; restorations (hand cleaning). VAT: Stan/Spec.

Bennison

91 Pimlico Rd. Open 9.30-7, Sat. and Sun by appointment. *STOCK: 17th-19th C furniture, pictures, objects and carpets.* PARK: Meters. TEL: 071 730 3370. VAT: Stan/Spec.

Blanchard and Alan Ltd.

86/88 Pimlico Rd. Est: 1990. Open 10-6, Sat. 10-3. SIZE: Medium. *STOCK: English and continental furniture, lighting and objets d'art.* LOC: Near Sloane Sq. underground station. TEL: 071 823 6310; fax - 071 823 6303. SER: Valuations; restorations; buys at auction. VAT: Stan/Spec.

N Bloom and Son (Antiques Ltd.) LAPADA

at Harrods Ltd., Fine Jewellery Room, Brompton Rd., Knightsbridge. (I Harris) Est: 1912. Author. Open 9-6, Wed. 9-7. *STOCK: Silver, 16th C to second-hand; jewellery, including art deco paste items, 18th-20th C, £100-£50,000.* TEL: 071 730 1234, ext. 4062/4072. SER: Valuations; restorations; repairs; buys at auction. VAT: Stan/Spec.

John Bly BADA

27 Bury St, St. James's. (F., N., J. and V Bly) Est: 1891. Open 9-5.30, Sat. 10-3 and by appointment. *STOCK: English furniture, silver, glass, porcelain and pictures, 18th-19th C.* TEL: 071 930 1292.

J H Bourdon-Smith Ltd BADA

24 Mason's Yard, Duke St, St. James's. Est: 1954. Open 9.30-6. CL: Sat. SIZE: Medium. *STOCK: Silver, 1680-1830, £50-£15,000; Victorian and modern silver, 1830 to date,*

J H Bourdon-Smith Ltd continued

£25-£10,000. **PARK: Meters. TEL: 071 839 4714/5. SER: Valuations; restorations (silver); buys at auction. FAIRS: Chelsea, British International (Birmingham), Harrogate, Grosvenor House, International Silver and Jewellery, Park Lane. VAT: Stan/Spec.**

Bourne Fine Art
14 Masons Yard, Duke St., St. James's. Est: 1978. Open 10-6. CL: Sat. SIZE: Small. *STOCK: Scottish paintings, 1800-1950.* PARK: Easy. TEL: 071 930 4215/6. SER: Valuations; restorations; framing; buys at auction. VAT: Stan/Spec.

Bowmore Gallery
8 Halkin Arcade, Motcombe St. Open 10-7.30, Sat. a.m. and Sun. by appointment. SIZE: Small. *STOCK: Oil paintings and watercolours, 1850-1950 and selected contemporary artists, £100-£25,000.* LOC: 2 minutes from Sloane St. or Belgrave Sq. PARK: Kinnerton St. TEL: 071 823 1829; home - 071 736 4111. SER: Valuations; restorations (oils and watercolours); re-gilding of frames; framing; buys at auction (19th-20th C paintings).

Box House Antiques BADA
100 Eaton Terrace. (J Maas) Est: 1963. Open by appointment. ***STOCK: Furniture, 17th-19th C; needlework, samplers, pictures.*** **TEL: 071 730 9257.**

Brisigotti Antiques Ltd
44 Duke St, St. James's. Open 9.30-1 and 2-5.30. *STOCK: European works of art, Old Master paintings.* TEL: 071 839 4441/2.

Brod Gallery
24 St. James's St. SLAD. Open 9.30-5.30, Sat. by appointment. *STOCK: European paintings, 16th-19th C.* PARK: Meters. TEL: 071 839 3871. SER: Valuations. VAT: Spec.

Clive A Burden Ltd
93 Lower Sloane St. Open 10-5.30, appointment preferred. SIZE: Medium. *STOCK: Maps, 1500-1860, antiquarian prints, 1600-1900, both £1-£1,000; antiquarian books, pre-1870, £10-£5,000; Vanity Fair prints.* TEL: 071 823 5053. SER: Valuations; buys at auction (maps, prints, books). VAT: Stan.

Marie-Louise Burness Antiques
69 Pimlico Rd. Est: 1988. Open 10-6, Sat. 11-4. SIZE: Medium. *STOCK: English and continental furniture, decorative objects including porcelain, bronzes and gilt mirrors, 18th-19th C.* LOC: Near Sloane Sq. PARK: Fairly easy. TEL: 071 730 7206. VAT: Spec.

Bury Street Gallery
11 Bury St, St. James's. Est: 1977. *STOCK: 19th C European paintings and drawings especially Scandinavian.* TEL: 071 930 2902.

S.W.1 continued

Camerer Cuss and Co BADA
17 Ryder St, St. James's (The Cuss Clock Co. Ltd.). Est: 1788. Open 9.30-5. CL: Sat. SIZE: Medium. ***STOCK: Clocks, 1600-1910, £250-£30,000; watches, 1600-1930, £100-£35,000.*** **TEL: 071 930 1941. SER: Valuations; restorations (clocks and watches); buys at auction. VAT: Stan/Spec.**

David Carritt Limited
15 Duke St, St. James's. Open 9.30-5.30. CL: Sat. *STOCK: Old Master and modern paintings.* TEL: 071 930 8733.

Odile Cavendish BADA
14 Lowndes St. Est: 1971. Open by appointment. SIZE: Large. ***STOCK: Mainly Oriental, furniture, screens, paintings, works of art.*** **PARK: Meters. TEL: 071 243 1668. VAT: Spec.**

Chaucer Fine Arts
45 Pimlico Rd. Open 10-6, Sat. 10-1. *STOCK: Old Master paintings, sculpture and works of art.* TEL: 071 730 2972/5872.

Ciancimino Ltd
99 Pimlico Rd. Open 10-6, Sat. by appointment. *STOCK: English, European and Oriental fine and decorative works of art, 18th and 19th C.* TEL: 071 730 9950; fax - 071 730 5365.

Cobra and Bellamy
149 Sloane St. (V Manussis and T Hunter) Est: 1976. Open 10.30-6. SIZE: Medium. *STOCK: Decorative art and jewellery, 20th C, £50-£1,000.* TEL: 071 730 2823. VAT: Stan.

Edward Cohen
40 Duke St, St. James's. *STOCK: Paintings.* TEL: 071 839 5180. VAT: Spec.

The Connoisseur Gallery
14/15 Halkin Arcade, Motcomb St., Belgravia. (M.Z Irani) ABA. Est: 1966. Open 10-6. SIZE: Medium. *STOCK: Antiquarian books of the Middle East; Oriental paintings, Islamic works of art, 8th-19th C, £50-£10,000+.* LOC: Between Motcomb St. and Lowndes St. PARK: Easy. TEL: 071 245 6431/2. SER: Valuations; restorations; buys at auction. VAT: Spec.

Cornucopia
12 Upper Tachbrook St. Est: 1967. Open 11-6. SIZE: Large. *STOCK: Jewellery, 20th C clothing; accessories.* PARK: Meters. TEL: 071 828 5752.

Cox and Company
37 Duke St, St. James's. (Mr and Mrs R Cox) Est: 1972. Open 10-5.30, Sat. by appointment. SIZE: Small. *STOCK: European paintings, 19th-20th C, £1,000-£20,000.* LOC: Off Piccadilly. TEL: 071 930 1987. SER: Valuations; restorations; buys at auction. VAT: Spec.

S.W.1 continued

Crane Gallery
171a Sloane Street, 1st Floor. *STOCK: English folk art and 'Americana', furniture, paintings, quilts, weathervanes.* LOC: 2 mins. from Harrods. TEL: 071 235 2464.

Csaky's Antiques
20 Pimlico Rd. Open 10-6. *STOCK: Early English and continental oak furniture; carvings, works of art, unusual items.* TEL: 071 730 2068.

Peter Dale Ltd — LAPADA
11/12 Royal Opera Arcade, Pall Mall. Est: 1955. Open 9.30-5. CL: Sat. SIZE: Medium. *STOCK: Firearms, 16th-19th C; edged weapons, armour, 14th-19th C; militaria.* LOC: Arcade behind Her Majesty's Theatre and New Zealand House. PARK: 350yds. Whitcomb St., Public Garage. TEL: 071 930 3695. SER: Valuations; buys at auction. FAIRS: Arms, spring and autumn. VAT: Spec.

Arthur Davidson Ltd — BADA LAPADA
78/79 Jermyn St. (A. and L Davidson) CINOA. Est: 1962. Open 9.30-5.30. CL: Sat p.m.. SIZE: Medium. *STOCK: Works of art, £1,000-£20,000; curiosities, £1,000-£10,000; early furniture, 16th-18th C, £5,000-£50,000.* Not stocked: China and glass. LOC: Opposite Dunhills. PARK: Easy. TEL: 071 930 6687. SER: Valuations. FAIRS: Grosvenor House. VAT: Spec.

S.W.1 continued

Kenneth Davis
15 King St, St. James's. Open 9-5. CL: Sat. *STOCK: Silver and works of art.* TEL: 071 930 0313.

Shirley Day Ltd — BADA
91b Jermyn St. Est: 1967. *STOCK: Japanese works of art, paintings, screens, sculptures, ceramics, lacquers; early Chinese, Indian and Korean works of art.* TEL: 071 839 2804. VAT: Stan/Spec.

de Havilland (Antiques) Ltd — LAPADA
5 Pont St. Est: 1964. *STOCK: 18th C furniture, silver and clocks.* TEL: 071 235 3534.

The Delightful Muddle
11 Upper Tachbrook St, Victoria. (M. and J Storey) Est: 1935. Open Thurs., Fri. and Sat. 12-6. SIZE: Small. *STOCK: China, glass, objets d'art, Victorian and Edwardian, £1-£100; lace, £1-£50; linen, general antiques and bric-a-brac, £3-£65, all to Victorian.* LOC: Near Victoria Station, Upper Tachbrook St. runs into Vauxhall Bridge Rd. at Queen Mother Sports Centre. PARK: Meters.

Douwes Fine Art Ltd
38 Duke St, St. James's. Est: 1805. Open 9.30-5.30. CL: Sat. SIZE: Medium. *STOCK: Old Master paintings, drawings, watercolours, prints.* PARK: Meters. TEL: 071 839 5795. VAT: Spec.

William R Drown
41 St. James's Pl. Est: 1938. Open 9.30-5.30. CL: Sat. SIZE: Medium. *STOCK: Old Master paintings.* PARK: Meters. TEL: 071 493 4711. SER: Restorations. VAT: Spec.

Eaton Gallery
34 Duke St, St. James's and 9 and 12a Princes Arcade, Jermyn St. (D. George) Open 10-5.30, Sat. by appointment. *STOCK: Fine European paintings, 19th-20th C.* TEL: 071 930 5950.

Annamaria Edelstein at Robin Symes
94 Jermyn St. Open 10-5.30. CL: Sat. *STOCK: Old Master drawings.* PARK: Meters. TEL: 071 930 5300.

Owen Edgar Gallery — BADA
9 West Halkin St. Est: 1977. Open 10-6, Sat. by appointment. *STOCK: Paintings, 18th-19th C and major Victorian.* TEL: 071 235 8989. VAT: Spec.

Christopher Edwards Ltd
62 Pimlico Rd. Open 10-6. *STOCK: 19th C art furniture and applied arts.* TEL: 071 730 4025; fax - 071 823 6873. FAIRS: Olympia. VAT: Stan/Spec.

M Ekstein Ltd — BADA
90 Jermyn St. (L Ekstein and B Forster) Est: 1946. *STOCK: Jewellery, porcelain, enamel, silver, objets d'art, glass.* TEL: 071 930 2024.

S.W.1 continued

Faustus Fine Art Ltd
1st Floor, 90 Jermyn St. Open 9.30-5.30. *STOCK: British and European prints, ancient jewellery, antiquities.* TEL: 071 930 1864. VAT: Spec.

Fernandes and Marche **LAPADA**
23 Motcomb St. Est: 1956. Open 9.30-5.30. CL: Sat. and Sun. except by appointment. SIZE: Medium. *STOCK: English furniture; giltwood (mirrors, consoles, etc.), both 18th C.* PARK: Meters. TEL: 071 235 6773; fax - 071 823 2234. VAT: Spec.

Kate Foster Ltd **BADA**
9 Halkin Arcade, Motcomb St. (Mrs K. and C.M.E Davson) Est: 1974. Open 9.30-5.30. CL: Sat. SIZE: Medium. *STOCK: European porcelain and ceramics, 18th C.* LOC: Belgravia, behind Carlton Tower Hotel. PARK: Off Motcomb St. TEL: 071 245 9848; home - (0797) 222661. SER: Valuations; buys at auction. FAIRS: International Ceramic; I.A.D.S., New York. VAT: Stan/Spec.

J.A.L Franks Ltd
7 Allington St. Est: 1948. *STOCK: Worldwide maps and stamps; framed cigarette cards.* LOC: Opposite stage door - Victoria Palace Theatre. TEL: 071 834 8697.

S Franses Ltd
Jermyn St. at Duke St, St. James's. Est: 1909. Open 9-5. CL: Sat. SIZE: Large. *STOCK: Historic and decorative tapestries, carpets, fabrics and textiles.* TEL: 071 976 1234. SER: Valuations; restorations; cleaning. VAT: Spec.

Victor Franses Gallery **BADA**
57 Jermyn St, St. James's. Est: 1948. Open 10-5.30. CL: Sat. *STOCK: Oriental and European rugs and carpets, tapestries, needlework; 19th C animalier bronzes.* TEL: 071 493 6284/629 1144. SER: Valuations; restorations.

Galerie Moderne Ltd
10 Halkin Arcade, Motcomb St. Open 9.30-6, Sat. by appointment. *STOCK: Rene Lalique glass, and 20th C Sevres porcelain.* TEL: 071 245 6907.

Gallery '25
4 Halkin Arcade, Motcombe St., Belgravia. (D Iglesis and R Lawrence) Est: 1969. Open 9.30-5.30, Sat. 10-2. SIZE: Medium. *STOCK: Art glass, £100-£5,000; signed furniture, £1,000-£10,000; decorative fine art, £500-£5,000; all 1900-1930.* LOC: Arcade between Motcomb St and West Halkin St. PARK: Easy. Cadogan Sq. TEL: 071 235 5178. SER: Valuations; buys at auction (as stock). FAIRS: Park Lane; Olympia. VAT: Stan/Spec.

S.W.1 continued

Gallery Lingard
50 Pall Mall. Open 10-5.30 or by appointment. CL: Sat. *STOCK: Architectural drawings and watercolours.* TEL: 071 930 1645.

General Trading Co Ltd **LAPADA**
144 Sloane St. (E Barlow) Est: 1920. Open 9-5.30, Sat. 9-2. SIZE: Medium. *STOCK: English furniture, £100-£2,000; china, pewter, prints, £20-£500; all 18th-19th C.* PARK: 50yds., underground garage (Cadogan Place). TEL: 071 730 0411. VAT: Stan/Spec.

Joss Graham
10 Eccleston St. Open 10-6, Sat. 10-4. *STOCK: Textiles, jewellery and furniture - Indian, Middle Eastern, African and Central Asian including cushions, wall hangings, bed covers and costume.* TEL: 071 730 4370.

Martyn Gregory Gallery **BADA**
34 Bury Street, St. James's. Open 10-6. CL: Sat. SIZE: Medium. *STOCK: Early English watercolours, 18th-20th C; British paintings, both £500-£100,000; specialists in pictures relating to China.* TEL: 071 839 3731. SER: Valuations. VAT: Spec.

Grove Antiques
at Harvey Nichols, Knightsbridge. (Mrs W.C.M Hines and F.J Van Der Breggen) Est: 1985. Open 10-7, Sat. 10-6. *STOCK: English and continental furniture, £100-£7,000; clocks, decorative metalwork, paintings and architectural items, £25-£3,000.* Not stocked: Silver, gold and jewellery. TEL: 071 235 5000; fax - 071 235 8560. VAT: Spec.

Laurence Hallett
104 Keyes House, Dolphin Sq. Est: 1973. Open by appointment. SIZE: Medium. *STOCK: Watercolours and oil paintings, 19th-20th C, £150-£2,500.* LOC: Nr. St. George's Sq., Pimlico. PARK: Meters. TEL: 071 828 8606; home - same. SER: Free monthly catalogue by post on request. VAT: Spec.

S.W.1 continued

Halsey International Enterprises

CINOA. Est: 1950. Consultancy strictly by appointment. *STOCK: Fine examples of 17th-18th C English and continental furniture and works of art, displayed in period room settings in the Haute Epoque manner may be viewed by those seeking the services listed.* LOC: Thames Embankment, nr. Pimlico underground station. PARK: Easy. TEL: Head office Kingsbridge, Devon (0548) 852440 (24 hr. answering service); fax - (0548) 857246. SER: Commissions undertaken internationally for interiors (individual rooms or entire houses); valuations; antiques purchased for catalogue subscribers of major auction houses; courier service and customised seminars (April-Sept). All correspondence to Halsey Antiques and Interiors, Kingsbridge, Devon, TQ7 2DH.

Rosemary Hamilton

44 Moreton St. Est: 1985. Open 9.30-5.30. SIZE: Small. *STOCK: Small furniture, 1840-1890, £500-£1,000; porcelain and fabrics, £100-£500.* LOC: Off Lupus St., Pimlico. PARK: Easy. TEL: 071 828 5018; home - same. SER: Restorations; gilding; polishing. VAT: Stan.

Ross Hamilton Ltd Antiques LAPADA

73 & 95 Pimlico Rd. Open 9.30-6, Sat. 11-2. *STOCK: Furniture, porcelain, paintings and works of art, 17th-19th C.* TEL: 071 730 3015.

S.W.1 continued

Harari and Johns Ltd

12 Duke St, St. James's. Open 9.30-6. *STOCK: Old Master paintings.* TEL: 071 839 7671; fax - 071 930 0986.

M Harris and Sons BADA

Gayfere House, 22/23 Gayfere St. (R.M Harris) Est: 1868. Open by appointment. SIZE: Small. *STOCK: English period furniture and works of art.* PARK: Meters. TEL: 071 222 8161. SER: Buys at auction. VAT: Spec.

Harrods Ltd

Brompton Rd, Knightsbridge. Open 9-6, Tues. 9.30-6, Wed. 9.30-8. SIZE: Large. *STOCK: Fine Victorian, Edwardian and period furniture, paintings, objets d'art.* PARK: Own - Brompton Rd. TEL: 071 730 1234 ext 2759/2808.

Julian Hartnoll

Second Floor, 14 Mason's Yard, Duke St., St. James's. Est: 1968. Open 2.30-5. *STOCK: 19th C British paintings, drawings and prints especially pre-Raphaelite.* TEL: 071 839 3842. VAT: Spec.

S.W.1 continued

Hazlitt, Gooden and Fox Ltd
38 Bury St, St. James's. Open 9.30-5.30. CL: Sat. SIZE: Large. *STOCK: Paintings, drawings and sculpture.* PARK: Meters. TEL: 071 930 6422. SER: Valuations; restorations. VAT: Spec.

Heim Gallery
59 Jermyn St. Open 10-6. CL: Sat. SIZE: Large. *STOCK: Old Master and English paintings and sculpture.* PARK: Meters. TEL: 071 493 0688. VAT: Spec.

Thomas Heneage and Co Ltd BADA
42 Duke St, St. James's. Est: 1975. Open 10-6, Sat. 10-2, other times by appointment. *STOCK: Art reference books.* TEL: 071 720 1503; fax - 071 720 3158.

Heraz
25 Motcomb St. (M.J Puttick) Est: 1974. Open 11-6. CL: Sat. *STOCK: Textiles cushions, European and Oriental carpets and tapestries.* TEL: 071 245 9497. SER: Valuations; restorations.

Hermitage Antiques
97 Pimlico Rd. (B Vieux-Pernon) Est: 1967. Open 10-6, Sat. 10-4, Sun. by appointment. SIZE: Large. *STOCK: Empire and Biedermeier furniture, oil paintings, decorative arts and French provincial furniture.* Not stocked: Silver and jewellery. LOC: Off Sloane Square. PARK: Easy. TEL: 071 730 1973; fax - 071 730 6586. VAT: Stan/Spec.

Carlton Hobbs BADA
46 Pimlico Rd. Est: 1975. Open 9-6. *STOCK: English and continental furniture, paintings, chandeliers, works of art, £4,000-£850,000.* TEL: 071 730 3640/3517; fax - 071 730 6080.

Hodsoll McKenzie
50 Pimlico Rd. Open 10-7. *STOCK: 18th-19th C decorative furniture, carpets and rugs, paintings, English and Oriental pottery and porcelain.* TEL: 071 730 9835.

Hotspur Ltd BADA
14 Lowndes St. (R.A.B. and B.S Kern) Est: 1924. Open 8.30-6, Sat. 9.30-1. SIZE: Large. *STOCK: English furniture, 1690-1800.* LOC: Between Belgrave Sq and Lowndes Sq. PARK: 2 underground within 100yds. TEL: 071 235 1918. VAT: Spec.

Howe
36 Bourne St. (C Howe) Est: 1982. Open 9.30-7, Sat. 10-4.30, Sun. by appointment. SIZE: Medium. *STOCK: English furniture, late 18th to 19th C, £500-£20,000; objects and lighting, early 19th C, £100-£10,000.* LOC: Near Sloane Sq. and just off Pimlico Rd. PARK: Easy. TEL: 071 730 7987; home - same. SER: Valuations; buys at auction (18th-19th C English furniture and accessories). VAT: Stan/Spec.

S.W.1 continued

Christopher Hull Gallery
17 Motcomb St. Open 10-6, Sat. 10-1. *STOCK: Modern British paintings.* TEL: 071 235 0500.

Sally Hunter Fine Art
11/12 Halkin Arcade, Motcomb St. Open 10-6. CL: Sat. *STOCK: Britist art 1920 to date.* TEL: 071 235 0934.

Iconastas
5 Piccadilly Arcade. Open 10-6 or by appointment. CL: Sat. *STOCK: Russian and Greek icons, Russian works of art, Fabergé, Palekh lacquer, 16th to early 20th C.* TEL: 071 629 1433.

Brand Inglis BADA
9 Halkin Arcade, Motcomb St. Open 9-5, or any time by appointment. CL: Sat. *STOCK: Silver, mainly pre-19th C English.* TEL: 071 235 6604.

David James (Fine Victorian Watercolours) BADA
3 Halkin Arcade, Motcomb St. (D. and E. James) SLAD. Est: 1980. Open 11-6, Mon. and Sat. by appointment. *STOCK: Fine Victorian watercolours.* TEL: 071 235 5552.

Jeremy Ltd BADA
29 Lowndes St. (G.M. and J. Hill) Est: 1946. Open 8.30-6. SIZE: Large. *STOCK: English and French furniture, objets d'art, glass chandeliers, 18th to early 19th C, to £30,000.* PARK: Easy. TEL: 071 823 2923. FAIRS: Grosvenor House, I.A.D., New York. VAT: Spec.

Oscar and Peter Johnson Ltd BADA
Lowndes Lodge Gallery, 27 Lowndes St. Est: 1963. Open 9.30-5. CL: Sat. p.m. SIZE: Medium. *STOCK: English paintings, 18th-20th C.* PARK: Meters. TEL: 071 235 6464. SER: Valuations; restorations. VAT: Spec.

R. and J Jones
6 Bury St, St. James's. Open 9.30-5.30, Sat. by appointment. *STOCK: Dutch, Flemish and Italian paintings, 17th-18th C, £2,000-£80,000.* LOC: Between Jermyn St. and King St. and next to Duke St. TEL: 071 925 2079. SER: Valuations; buys at auction.

David Ker Fine Art
85 Bourne St. Est: 1981. Open 9.30-5.30, Sat. and Sun. by appointment. SIZE: Medium. *STOCK: Watercolours, 1780-1950, £30-£1,500; decorative prints, 1780-1930, £50-£250; decorative oils, 1750-1950, £100-£50,000; antique paste jewellery.* LOC: 2 mins. from Sloane Sq. tube station; Bourne St. is parallel to Eaton Terrace. PARK: Easy. TEL: 071 730 8365; fax - 071 730 3352. SER: Valuations; restorations; framing; cleaning and repair; buys at auction. VAT: Spec.

S.W.1 continued

Khachadourian Gallery

60 Pall Mall. (S. and M Khachadourian) Est: 1965. Open 9.30-6. CL: Sat. SIZE: Large. *STOCK: Automobile art and posters, car mascots and bronzes, £500-£50,000.* PARK: Easy. TEL: 071 930 5727. SER: Valuations.

Dominic King Antique Glass

85 Ebury St, Belgravia. (D. and A King) Est: 1986. Open Mon.-Thurs. 10-6, other times by appointment. SIZE: Small. *STOCK: Georgian rummers and decanters, £50-£200; coloured glass - Bristol, Nailsea, scent bottles, 19th C, £50-£150.* LOC: On foot from Victoria Station via Eccleston St. exit. PARK: Nearby. TEL: 071 824 8319; home - same. FAIRS: N.E.C. and Stourbridge.

King Street Galleries

17 King St, St. James's. (H. O'Nians) Open 9.30-5.30, Sat. 9.30-1. *STOCK: Paintings and watercolours, 19th-20th C.* TEL: 071 930 3993/9392.

Knightsbridge Coins

43 Duke St, St. James's. Open 10-6. CL: Sat. *STOCK: Coins - British, American and South African; medals.* TEL: 071 930 7597/930 8215.

S.W.1 continued

Leggatt Brothers

17 Duke St, St. James's. (Sir Hugh Leggatt) Est: 1820. Open 9.30-5. CL: Sat. SIZE: Large. *STOCK: Oil paintings, 17th to early 19th C.* LOC: Next to Cavendish Hotel. PARK: Easy. TEL: 071 930 3772.

Arthur S Lewis LAPADA

at Harrods Ltd, Antique Clocks and Musical Boxes Dept., Brompton Rd., Knightsbridge. Est: 1969. *STOCK: Clocks and musical boxes, 19th C, from £1,000+.* TEL: 071 730 1234, ext. 2360. VAT: Stan/Spec.

M. and D Lewis

84 Pimlico Rd. Open 10-5, Sat. 10-1. *STOCK: Continental and Victorian furniture, porcelain, bronzes.* TEL: 071 730 1015. VAT: Stan.

Lion, Witch and Lampshade

89 Ebury St. (Mr. and Mrs N Dixon) Est: 1984. Open 10.30-5.30, Wed. 12.30-5.30, prior telephone call advisable. CL: Sat. *STOCK: Unusual decorative objects, 18th to early 20th C, £5-£150; lamps, wall brackets, chandeliers and candlesticks, £50-£1,000.* PARK: Easy. TEL: 071 730 1774. SER: Restorations (porcelain and glass). VAT: Stan/Spec.

S.W.1 continued

Paul Longmire Ltd

12 Bury St, St. James's. Open 9-5. *STOCK: Antique jewellery, cufflinks, signet rings, objects of art and virtue.* LOC: Coming from Piccadilly, down Duke St., right into King St. first right into Bury St. PARK: Easy. TEL: 071 930 8720. SER: Enamelling and engraving cufflinks, heraldic seal engravings.

MacConnal-Mason Gallery BADA

14 Duke St, St. James's. Est: 1893. Open 9-6. SIZE: Large. *STOCK: Pictures, 19th-20th C.* PARK: Meters. TEL: 071 839 7693/499 6991. SER: Valuations; restorations. VAT: Spec.

Rodd McLennan

24 Holbein Place. Est: 1971. Open 11-1 and 2-5.30. CL: Sat. *STOCK: Biedermeier, Empire, bronze, ormolu, marble accessories.* TEL: 071 730 6330. VAT: Spec.

The Mall Galleries

The Mall. Open 10-5 seven days. *STOCK: Paintings.* LOC: Near Admiralty Arch. TEL: 071 930 6844; fax - 071 839 7830. SER: Contemporary art exhibitions held.

Paul Mason Gallery BADA LAPADA

149 Sloane St. Est: 1969. Open 9-6, Wed. 9-7, Sat. 9-1. *STOCK: Marine, sporting and decorative paintings and prints, 18th-19th C; period and old frames, portfolio stands, ship models.* LOC: Sloane Sq. end of Sloane St. PARK: Easy. TEL: 071 730 3683/7359. SER: Valuations; restorations (prints, paintings); buys at auction. FAIRS: England and Europe. VAT: Stan/Spec.

Mathaf Gallery Ltd LAPADA

24 Motcomb St. Est: 1975. Open 9.30-5.30. *STOCK: Paintings, Middle East subjects, 19th C.* TEL: 071 235 0010. SER: Valuations.

Matthiesen Fine Art Ltd. and Matthiesen Works of Art Ltd

7-8 Mason's Yard, Duke St., St. James's. Est: 1978. Open 10-6 or by appointment. CL: Sat. *STOCK: Fine Italian Old Master paintings, 1300-1800; French and Spanish Old Master paintings.* TEL: 071 930 2437; fax - 071 930 1387. SER: Valuations; buys at auction.

Adrian Maynard

91c Jermyn St, St. James's. Est: 1949. Open 9.30-5.30. CL: Sat. SIZE: Medium. *STOCK: Indian and South-East Asian art, to 12th C, from £1,000+.* LOC: Behind St. James's church, Piccadilly. TEL: 071 930 8008; fax - 071 930 2165. SER: Valuations; buys at auction (as stock). VAT: Spec.

Mayorcas Ltd BADA

38 Jermyn St. (J.D. and L.G Mayorcas) Est: 1930. Open 9.30-5.30, Sat. 9.30-1. SIZE: Medium. *STOCK: Tapestries, textiles, embroideries, needlework, church vest-- ments, European carpets and rugs.* TEL: 071 629 4195. SER: Valuations; restorations. VAT: Stan/Spec.

Mayorcas Ltd. continued

I.J Mazure and Co. Ltd BADA

90 Jermyn St. *STOCK: Gold, objets de vertu, Russian works of art including Fabergé.* TEL: 071 839 3101/2.

Christopher Mendez incorporating Craddock and Barnard

58 Jermyn St. Est: 1966. Open 10-5.30. CL: Sat. SIZE: Small. *STOCK: Old Master prints.* TEL: 071 491 0015; fax - 071 495 4949. SER: Valuations; buys at auction. VAT: Stan.

Richard Miles Antiques

8 Holbein Pl. Est: 1974. Open 9.30-1 and 2-5.30. CL: Sat. except by appointment. SIZE: Medium. *STOCK: Unusual furniture and works of art, especially Anglo-Indian and Chinese colonial, 18th to early 19th C, £500-£5,000.* LOC: Between Sloane Sq. and Pimlico Rd. PARK: Easy. TEL: 071 730 1957; fax - 071 824 8865. SER: Buys at auction. VAT: Spec.

Lennox Money (Antiques) Ltd

93 Pimlico Rd. (L.B Money) Est: 1964. Open 9.45-6. CL: Sat. p.m. SIZE: Large. *STOCK: Indian colonial and furniture made of unusual woods; chandeliers.* LOC: 200yds. south of Sloane Sq. TEL: 071 730 3070. VAT: Spec.

Mrs Monro Ltd

16 Motcomb St. Open 9.30-5.30, Fri. 9.30-5. CL: Sat. SIZE: Medium. *STOCK: Small decorative furniture, £500-£1,000+; china, £50-£100; rugs, prints, pictures and general decorative items, from £50; all 18th-19th C.* LOC: Between Lowndes Sq. and Belgrave Sq. PARK: Garage nearby. TEL: 071 235 0326. SER: Restorations (furniture and china). VAT: Stan/Spec.

Moreton Street Gallery

40 Moreton St, (W.M. Pearson-Frasco International Ltd.). Est: 1972. Open 9-1 and 2-6. CL: Sat. SIZE: Medium. *STOCK: Contemporary oils, watercolours, limited editions, posters; early engravings - Bunbury, Rowlandson, Hogarth, Gilray and Heath.* LOC: Off Belgrave Sq. PARK: Easy. TEL: 071 834 7773/5 or 7834. SER: Valuations; restorations; buys at auction (originals and engravings). VAT: Stan.

Guy Morrison

91 Jermyn St. Open 9.30-5.30. CL: Sat. *STOCK: British paintings from 1900.* TEL: 071 839 1454.

Peter Nahum BADA

5 Ryder St. Open 9.30-5.30. CL: Sat. and Sun. except by appointment. SIZE: Large. *STOCK: British and European paintings, drawings and bronzes, 19th-20th C, £500-£50,000+.* LOC: 100yds. from Royal Academy. PARK: Meters. TEL: 071 930 6059. SER: Valuations. VAT: Spec.

Leicester

DATE	MARKS
1570	

Lewes

DATE	MARKS
c.1640	

Lincoln

DATE	MARKS
c.1570	

Liverpool

DATE	MARKS
Early 18th C	
c.1710	

Plymouth

DATE	MARKS
1600-50	
c.1695	
1697-1700	

Salisbury

DATE	MARKS
Late 16th e.17th C	
1620-40	
1640-50	
1670	

Sherborne

DATE	MARKS
Early 17th C	

Southampton

DATE	MARKS
c.1680	

Taunton

DATE	MARKS
c.1660-80	
c.1690	

Truro

DATE	MARKS
c.1610-20	

Waveney Valley

DATE	MARKS
c.1650	

Some of the English provincial marks illustrated in ***Pocket Edition Jackson's Hallmarks*** edited by Ian Pickford and published by the **Antique Collectors' Club** in 1991. £12.50.

S.W.1 continued

Ning Ltd
58 Cambridge St. (Mrs P Grant) Est: 1963. Open 10-6. CL: Sat. *STOCK: Decorative furniture pre-1860; period pine; Spode, Wedgwood, Davenport and blue and white porcelain; small decorative items.* PARK: Meters. TEL: 071 834 3292. VAT: Spec.

Oakstar Ltd
(Mrs P Bromage) Est: 1982. Strictly by appointment only. SIZE: Small. *STOCK: Papier mâché trays, £750-£4,000; mirrors, prints and objets d'art, £100-£2,000; small French and English furniture, £200-£5,000; all 18th-19th C.* LOC: Clarendon Rd. TEL: 071 630 1822. SER: Restorations (lacquer). FAIRS: Decorative Antiques and Textiles; Olympia Decorative. VAT: Stan/Spec.

The Old Ephemera and Newspaper Shop
37 Kinnerton St, Belgravia. Est: 1972. Open 10-5, Fri. 11-4. CL: Sat. SIZE: Large. *STOCK: Ephemera and antiquarian newspapers, from 1642 to 20th C.* LOC: Kinnerton St. runs from Wilton Place (off Knightsbridge) to Motcomb St. PARK: Underground nearby. TEL: 071 235 7788.

Old London Galleries
4 Royal Opera Arcade, Pall Mall. (Mrs V Malmed) Open 10.30-5, Sat. 11.30-1.30. *STOCK: 18th-19th C hand coloured prints, all subjects, from £5.* LOC: Near the Haymarket. TEL: 071 930 7679. SER: Framing; decorative mount cutting.

Old Maps and Prints LAPADA
4th Floor, Harrods, Knightsbridge. Est: 1976. *STOCK: Maps, 16th C to 1880; prints, watercolours and oils, sporting restrikes; Christie's signed, limited edition graphics.* TEL: 071 730 1234 ext 2124.

Omell Galleries LAPADA
22 Bury St, St. James's. Est: 1949. Open 9.30-5.30. CL: Sat. SIZE: Large. *STOCK: English and continental paintings, 19th-20th C, £1,000-£15,000.* LOC: From Jermyn St. last street on left hand side (coming from Piccadilly to St. James's St.). PARK: Easy. TEL: 071 839 4274. SER: Restorations. VAT: Stan/Spec.

Omell Galleries LAPADA
43a Duke St, St. James's. Open 9.30-5, Sat. by appointment. SIZE: Large. *STOCK: Scandinavian, European and Russian oil paintings, 19th C, £5,000-£100,000.* LOC: Corner of Ryder St. TEL: 071 930 7744; fax - 071 839 1235. SER: Restorations; framing.

S.W.1 continued

N.R Omell
43a Duke St, St. James's. Est: 1968. *STOCK: 19th C English landscape and marine oil paintings.* TEL: 071 839 6223/4; fax - 071 839 1235. SER: Catalogues issued. VAT: Spec.

O'Shea Gallery BADA
89 Lower Sloane St. ABA. Open 9.30-6, Sat. 9.30-1. *STOCK: Maps, topographical, decorative, natural history, sporting and marine prints; rare atlases, illustrated books, 15th-19th C, £5-£25,000.* LOC: Near Sloane Sq. TEL: 071 730 0081; fax - 071 730 1386. SER: Decorative framing; restorations. VAT: Stan/Spec.

A. and M Ossowski
83 Pimlico Rd. Est: 1956. Open 9-6. CL: Sat p.m.. SIZE: Medium. *STOCK: Carved gilt, 18th C; mirrors, wood carvings.* TEL: 071 730 3256. SER: Valuations; restorations (gilt furniture). VAT: Stan/Spec.

The Parker Gallery BADA
28 Pimlico Rd, (Thomas H. Parker Ltd.). SLAD. Est: 1750. Open 9.30-5.30. CL: Sat. SIZE: Medium. *STOCK: Historical prints, £30-£1,000; English paintings, £450-£15,000; ship models, £70-£20,000; all 1700-1950.* LOC: 5 minutes from Sloane Sq. TEL: 071 730 6768. SER: Restorations (as stock); mounting; framing. FAIRS: Grosvenor House. VAT: Stan/Spec.

Michael Parkin Fine Art Ltd
11 Motcomb St. Open 10-6, Sat. 10-1. *STOCK: British paintings, watercolours, drawings and prints, 1850-1950, £50-£10,000.* PARK: Easy. TEL: 071 235 8144/1845; fax - 071 245 9846. VAT: Spec.

Pawsey and Payne BADA
90 Jermyn St, St. James's. (Hon N.V.B. and L.N.J Wallop) SLAD. Est: 1910. Open 9.30-5.30. CL: Sat. *STOCK: English oils and watercolours, 18th-19th C.* PARK: Meters. TEL: 071 930 4221; fax - 071 839 1903. SER: Valuations; restorations. VAT: Spec.

Trevor Philip and Sons Ltd LAPADA
75a Jermyn St, St. James's. (T. and R Waterman) Est: 1972. Open 9-6, Sat. 10-4. SIZE: Medium. *STOCK: Early medical, scientific and marine instruments; clocks and decorative items, especially globes.* PARK: At rear. TEL: 071 930 2954/5. SER: Valuations; restorations (clocks and scientific instruments); buys at auction. VAT: Stan/Spec.

S.W.1 continued

Pickering and Chatto Ltd

Incorporating Dawsons of Pall Mall, 17 Pall Mall. Est: 1820. Open 9.30-5.30. CL: Sat. SIZE: Large. *STOCK: English literature, economics, politics, philosophy, science, medicine, manuscripts and autographs.* LOC: 300yds. on right from Trafalgar Sq. PARK: Easy. TEL: 071 930 2515.

Polak Gallery BADA

21 King St, St. James's. Est: 1854. Open 9.30-5.30. CL: Sat. SIZE: Medium. *STOCK: English and continental, 19th-20th C oils and watercolours.* PARK: Meters. TEL: 071 839 2871. SER: Valuations; restorations. VAT: Spec.

Michael Priest Antiques

27a Motcomb St, Belgrave Sq. Est: 1979. Open 9.30-5. CL: Sat. SIZE: Medium. *STOCK: Fine mahogany and walnut, paintings - Old Masters, and primitives, late 17th C to mid-19th C, £500-£20,000.* TEL: 071 235 7241. SER: Valuations; restorations (English furniture, oil paintings). VAT: Spec.

Pyms Gallery BADA

13 Motcomb St, Belgravia. (A. and M Hobart) Est: 1975. Open 10-6. CL: Sat. *STOCK: British, Irish and French paintings, 19th-*

Pyms Gallery continued

***20th C.* TEL: 071 235 3050; fax - 071 235 1002. SER: Valuations; restorations; buys at auction. VAT: Spec.**

Geoffrey Rose Ltd BADA

77 Pimlico Rd. Est: 1961. Open 10-1 and 2.15-6 and most Sat. mornings. CL: Sat. p.m.. SIZE: Medium. *STOCK: English furniture, late 18th to early 19th C.* TEL: 071 730 3004.

Rothman

103 Pimlico Rd. (J.A.F. and S.P.J Rothman) Est: 1981. Open 10-7, Sat. 11-4. SIZE: Large. *STOCK: Regency furniture, 1790-1830; giltwood mirrors and furniture, 1750-1830; French clocks and objects, 1780-1830.* TEL: 071 730 2558; home - 071 730 7200. VAT: Stan/Spec.

Sabin and Vanderkar (Fine Paintings) Ltd. and G.B. Vanderkar

43 Duke St, St. James's. Est: 1939. Open by appointment. CL: Sat. *STOCK: Dutch, Flemish paintings, all periods.* PARK: Meters. TEL: 071 839 1091. VAT: Spec.

Barry Sainsbury

145 Ebury St. *STOCK: Chinese and Japanese furniture and lacquer.* TEL: 071 730 3393. VAT: Spec.

S.W.1 continued

Saint George's Gallery Books Ltd
8 Duke St, St. James's. Est: 1948. Open 10-6. CL: Sat. *STOCK: Books and catalogues on fine and decorative arts.* PARK: Meters. TEL: 071 930 0935. SER: Catalogues available; postal (worldwide).

The St. James's Art Group
91 Jermyn St. (D Bathurst, P Hook and H Wyndham) Open 10-5. CL: Sat. SIZE: Medium. *STOCK: European pictures, 18th-20th C, £1,000-£1,000,000+.* PARK: Meters. TEL: 071 321 0233. SER: Valuations; buys at auction (European pictures, 18th-20th C).

Sanaiy Carpets
57 Pimlico Rd. (H Sanaiy) Open 9-6.30. *STOCK: Antique Persian and Oriental carpets and tapestries.* TEL: 071 730 4742; fax - 071 259 9194.

Gerald Sattin Ltd **BADA**
14 King St, St. James's. (G. and M Sattin) Est: 1966. Open 9-5.30. CL: Sat. p.m. SIZE: Medium. *STOCK: English and continental porcelain, 1720-1900; English glass, 1700-1900, both £55-£2,500; English silver, 1680-1920, £55-£5,000.* Not stocked: Oriental and post 1920 items. LOC: Close to Christie's. PARK: Meters. TEL: 071 493 6557. SER: Buys at auction. VAT: Stan/Spec.

Timothy Schroder Ltd
9 Halkin Arcade, Motcomb St. Open 9-6. CL: Sat. SIZE: Medium. *STOCK: English and continental silver, 16th-20th C, £200-£50,000.* LOC: Between Sloane St. and Belgrave Sq. PARK: Motcomb St. TEL: 071 259 6878. SER: Valuations; restorations; buys at auction (silver and works of art). VAT: Spec.

Seago **BADA**
22 Pimlico Rd. (T.P. and L.G Seago) Open 9-5.30, Sat. 10.30-5. *STOCK: Fine 17th-19th C garden sculpture and ornaments in marble, stone, bronze, lead, terracotta, cast and wrought iron.* TEL: 071 730 7502; fax - 071 730 9179.

Julian Simon Fine Art Ltd
70 Pimlico Rd. (M. and J Brookstone) Open 10-6, Sat. 10-4 or by appointment. *STOCK: 18th-20th C fine English and continental pictures.* TEL: 071 730 8673; fax - 071 823 6116.

Sims, Reed Ltd
58 Jermyn St. Open 10-6, Sat. by appointment. *STOCK: Rare and out-of-print books on the fine and applied arts; illustrated books.* TEL: 071 493 5660/0952; fax - 071 493 8468.

John Carlton Smith **BADA**
17 Ryder St, St. James's. Open 9.30-5.30. CL: Sat. *STOCK: Clocks, barometers, chronometers, 17th-19th C.* TEL: 071 930 6622. SER: Valuations. VAT: Spec.

S.W.1 continued

Peta Smyth - Antique Textiles
42 Moreton St, Pimlico. Est: 1977. Open 10-5.30. CL: Sat. *STOCK: European textiles and needlework, 17th-19th C, £10-£1,000; tapestries and cushions.* PARK: Easy. TEL: 071 630 9898. SER: Restorations (textiles). FAIRS: Olympia. VAT: Spec.

Somlo Antiques
7 Piccadilly Arcade. (G. and S Somlo) Est: 1972. Open 10-5.30 or by appointment. CL: Sat. SIZE: Medium. *STOCK: Pocket and wrist watches, from 17th C, from £100; clocks.* LOC: Between Piccadilly and Jermyn St. PARK: Meters. TEL: 071 499 6526. SER: Valuations; restorations. VAT: Stan/Spec.

Sotheran's
80 Pimlico Rd. Open 10-6, Sat. 10-4. *STOCK: Architectural, ornamental and topographical prints and drawings.* TEL: 071 730 8756.

Michael and Henrietta Spink Ltd
91c Jermyn St, St. James's. Est: 1989. Open 9.30-5.30. CL: Sat. SIZE: Small. *STOCK: Islamic and Indian jewellery, 12th-19th C; Indian miniature paintings, 17th-19th C; Islamic and Indian works of art, 10th-19th C; all £500-£25,000.* PARK: St. James's Sq. TEL: 071 930 8008. SER: Valuations; restorations (Indian and Islamic works of art). VAT: Stan/Spec.

Spink and Son Ltd **BADA**
5-7 King St, St. James's. Est: 1666. Open 9.30-5.30. CL: Sat. SIZE: Large. *STOCK: English paintings, watercolours, silver, jewellery; Chinese, Japanese, Indian, South East Asian, Persian and Islamic works of art; paperweights, textiles, haute couture; Greek and Roman to present day coins, banknotes, bullion, orders, medals and decorations, numismatic books.* PARK: Meters. TEL: 071 930 7888. SER: Valuations; buys at auction; commission sales on behalf of private collectors; coin auctions. VAT: Stan/Spec.

Gerald Spyer and Son(Antiques)Ltd
18 Motcombe St, Belgrave Sq. Est: 1860. Open 10-6. CL: Sat. SIZE: Large. *STOCK: Furniture, mostly English, pre-1830; gilt mirrors, 18th C; bronze and ormolu decorative items, all £750-£125,000.* LOC: In area between Sloane Sq. Hyde Park Corner and Knightsbridge. PARK: Easy. TEL: 071 235 3348; fax - 071 823 2234. SER: Buys at auction. VAT: Spec.

Jeremy and Guy Steel
8 Princes Arcade, Jermyn St. Open 10.30-5. CL: Sat. *STOCK: Jewellery.* TEL: 071 287 2528.

Pamela Streather
The Pink House, 4 Studio Pl, Kinnerton St. CINOA. Est: 1964. Open by appointment. *STOCK: Works of art, paintings; furniture, 17th-19th C.* TEL: 071 235 3450. VAT: Spec.

S.W.1 continued

Robin Symes Ltd
3 Ormond Yard, Duke of York St., St. James's and 94 Jermyn St. Open 10-5.30. CL: Sat. SIZE: Large. *STOCK: Antiquities, ancient art.* PARK: Meters. TEL: 071 930 9856/7 5300.

Bill Thomson - Albany Gallery
1 Bury St, St. James's. (W.B Thomson) Open 9-6, Sat. by appointment. *STOCK: British drawings, watercolours and paintings, 1700-1850 and some 20th C.* TEL: 071 839 6119.

William Thuillier
10a West Halkin St. Open by appointment. *STOCK: Old Master paintings and drawings; Post Impressionists.* TEL: 071 235 3543.

William Tillman Ltd BADA
30 St. James's St. Open 9.30-5.30, Sat. 9.30-1 and by appointment. *STOCK: English furniture, 18th C.* TEL: 071 839 2500.

Peter Tillou Works of Art
39 Duke St, St. James's. (S Rich) Open daily, Sat. by appointment. SIZE: Medium. *STOCK: Master paintings, 16th-19th C; arms and armour, objets d'art, collectors items.* LOC: Just off Piccadilly. PARK: St. James's Sq. TEL: 071 930 9308; fax - 071 930 2088. SER: Valuations; restorations; buys at auction. FAIRS: Maastricht, Holland. VAT: Spec. *Trade Only.*

Trafalgar Galleries BADA
35 Bury St, St. James's. ((B Cohen and Sons)) Open 9.30-6. CL: Sat. *STOCK: Old Master and 19th C paintings.* LOC: Just south of Piccadilly. TEL: 071 839 6466/7.

Trove
71 Pimlico Rd. (P.S Roe and J.P.D Smith) Est: 1969. Open 10-6. CL: Sat. p.m. SIZE: Medium. *STOCK: Furniture, bronzes, sporting paintings and decorative items.* PARK: Easy. TEL: 071 730 6514. SER: Restorations (paintings and furniture); buys at auction. VAT: Spec.

Rafael Valls Ltd BADA
11 Duke St, St. James's. SLAD. Est: 1976. Open 9.30-6. CL: Sat. *STOCK: Old Master, 18th and 19th C paintings.* TEL: 071 930 1144; fax - 071 976 1596. VAT: Spec.

Johnny Van Haeften Ltd BADA
13 Duke St, St. James's. (J. and S Van Haeften) SLAD. Est: 1978. Open 10-6, Sat. and Sun. by appointment. SIZE: Medium. *STOCK: Dutch and Flemish Old Master paintings, 16th-17th C, £5,000-£500,000.* LOC: Middle of Duke St. TEL: 071 930 3062/3; fax - 071 839 6303. SER: Valuations; restorations (Old Masters); buys at auction (Old Masters and other paintings). VAT: Spec.

S.W.1 continued

Edric Van Vredenburgh Ltd BADA
37 Bury St, St. James's. Est: 1961. Open 10-1 and 2-5.30. CL: Sat. SIZE: Small. *STOCK: European decorative arts, 1500-1800; sculpture, early objects; Oriental decorative arts, 18th-19th C.* LOC: Around corner from Christies. PARK: Easy. TEL: 071 839 5818/9; home - same. SER: Valuations; buys at auction. VAT: Stan/Spec.

Rupert Wace Ancient Art Ltd
1st Floor, 107 Jermyn St. Open by appointment. *STOCK: Egyptian and near Eastern antiquities.* TEL: 071 495 1623.

Waterman Fine Art Ltd
74a Jermyn St, St. James's. Open 9-6.30, Sat. 10-4, Sun. 2-5. *STOCK: Fine 20th C paintings, especially British Post Impressionists; British and European contemporary art and ceramics.* TEL: 071 839 5203; fax - 071 321 0212.

Watts and Christensen
54 Cambridge St. (C.E.H Watts and H.O Christensen) Est: 1979. Open 9-6 but resident so usually available at other times. CL: Sat. *STOCK: Continental and English furniture, 18th-19th C, £100-£3,000; unusual continental and English pieces, £50-£1,500.* LOC: One minute from Pimlico Rd. over Ebury Bridge. PARK: Easy. TEL: 071 834 3554. VAT: Spec.

Westenholz Kime Ltd
76 Pimlico Rd. (P Von Westenholz) Open 10-6, Sat. 11-2. *STOCK: Furniture, 18th-19th C.* TEL: 071 824 8090.

David Weston Ltd
44 Duke St, St. James's. (D.A Weston) Est: 1968. Open 9.30-1 and 2-5.30, appointment advisable. CL: Sat. SIZE: Medium. *STOCK: Globes, scientific instruments, marine items, 17th-18th C, £300-£25,000; marine antiques.* LOC: Near Christie's. PARK: Meters. TEL: 071 839 1051/2/3. SER: Valuations. VAT: Stan/Spec.

Philip Whyte
32 Bury St, St. James's. Est: 1972. Open Tues., Wed., Thurs., other times by appointment. SIZE: Medium. *STOCK: Clocks, watches, marine chronometers and other horological items.* LOC: Between Jermyn St. and St. James's St. PARK: Meters. TEL: 071 321 0353; fax - 071 321 0350. VAT: Stan/Spec.

Arnold Wiggins and Sons Ltd BADA
4 Bury St, St. James's. (P Mason and M Gregory) Open 10-5. CL: Sat. *STOCK: Picture frames, 16th-19th C.* TEL: 071 925 0195.

S.W.1 continued

Christopher Wood Gallery BADA
15 Motcomb St, Belgravia. SLAD. Est: 1977. Open 9-5.30. CL: Sat. *STOCK: Victorian, Edwardian and pre-Raphaelite paintings, drawings, watercolours, sculpture, studio pottery, Gothic furniture.* TEL: 071 235 9141/2. VAT: Spec.

London S.W.3

Norman Adams Ltd BADA
8/10 Hans Rd, Knightsbridge. Est: 1923. Open 9-5.30, Sat. and Sun. by appointment. SIZE: Large. *STOCK: English furniture, 18th C, £650-£250,000; objets d'art (English and French) £500-£50,000; mirrors, glass pictures, 18th C.* LOC: 30yds. off the Brompton Rd. opp. west side entrance to Harrods. TEL: 071 589 5266; fax - 071 589 1968. FAIRS: Grosvenor House. VAT: Spec.

Maria Andipa Icon Gallery BADA LAPADA
162 Walton St. CINOA. Est: 1968. Open 11-6, Sat. till 2. *STOCK: Icons, Greek, Russian, Byzantine, Coptic, Syrian; country furniture, crosses, crucifixes, embroidery, ethnic jewellery; lacquer eggs and silver icons.* TEL: 071 589 2371. SER: Valuations, restorations; buys at auction. FAIRS: Park Lane Hotel. VAT: Spec.

S.W.3 continued

Antiquarius
135/141 King's Rd, (Atlantic Antiques Centres Ltd.). Est: 1970. Open 10-6. SIZE: Below are listed some of the many specialist dealers at this market. LOC: On the corner of King's Rd. and Flood St., next to Chelsea Town Hall. TEL: Enquiries 071 351 5353.

Trevor Allen
U2-3. *Jewellery, and objets d'art, rings, 18th-19th C.* TEL: 071 352 7061.

Nigel Appleby - Jarona Antiques
P2. *General antiques, lighting and corkscrews.* TEL: 071 352 8734.

S Arena
E5. *General antiques, silver plate.* TEL: 071 352 7989.

S Aritaka
E3. *Watches, pens and lighters, general.* TEL: 071 376 5394.

Natasha Babic
L10. *General antiques.* TEL: 071 352 4690.

Mr and Mrs Bach
P14/15. *Art deco and art nouveau, glass and china.* TEL: 071 376 5394.

Shaun Balster and Tony Williams
A9-11. *Silver, jewellery and objets d'art.* TEL: 071 351 6442/6004.

Bernice Barker
R7. *Brass and copper.* TEL: 071 352 8882.

Antiquarius continued

B Barkoff
R3/4. *General, inkwells, silver.* TEL: 071 351 5883.
M Bashir
E6. *Jewellery.* TEL: 071 352 7989.
P Beedles
A13. *Art nouveau and art deco, including Clarice Cliff.* TEL: 071 352 4545.
Miss B Bentel
K3/K4. *Jewellery.* TEL: 071 351 1102.
Clark Berger
G2-3. *Decorative arts, 1850-1950.* TEL: 071 352 5452.
D Billing
M7. *Jewellery.* TEL: 071 376 8252.
Alexandra Bolla
J1. *Jewellery.* TEL: 071 352 7989.
William McLeod Brown
L5-7. *Prints, especially botanicals, books.* TEL: 071 352 4690.
Miss T Buchinger
Q3. *Jewellery and silver.* TEL: 071 352 8734.
H P Budhu
A3. *Silver, furniture and general antiques.* TEL: 071 352 7989.
Alisdair Burns
Q1/Q16. *Decorative antiques.*
C Butterworth
C1. *Decorative antiques including lighting.* TEL: 071 352 3583.
Jasmin Cameron **LAPADA**
J6. *Antique fountain pens, £55-£1,000; writing materials, £6-£2,000; artist and drawing materials, £35-£1,000; all 18th-19th C.* TEL: 071 351 4154; home - 0474 873875. SER: SER: Valuations (fountain pens); restorations (fountain pens). VAT: Stan.
Mrs V Carroll
P6. *Jewellery and small objects.* TEL: 071 352 8882.
Bill Chapman
K6. *Silver.* TEL: 071 352 7989.
Chelsea Clocks
H3-4, R1-2. *Clocks and general.* TEL: 071 352 8646.
Eli Cohen
Q2. *General antiques, Oriental art.* TEL: 071 352 8734.
S Collins
Q14-15. *Minerals and gems.* TEL: 071 351 6548.
Jane Course
K5. *General antiques - clocks, boxes, treen.* TEL: 071 352 7989.
J Cowan
D1. *Objets de vertu.* TEL: 071 376 8048.
Crocodile Shop
Q7/8. *Crocodile goods.* TEL: 071 376 5112.
P Defresne t/a Beaux Bijoux
Q9-10. *Costume jewellery.* TEL: 071 352 8882.
Mrs E Earl
Q11. *Clocks.* TEL: 071 352 1295.

Antiquarius continued

S Emerson
M12. *Corkscrews, small instruments.* TEL: 071 352 0872.
Patricia Evans
U4. *Dolls and accessories.* TEL: 071 352 7989.
David Fielden
U1. *Wedding dresses and evening wear.* TEL: 071 351 1745/0002; 071 376 8148.
Frontiers
M1. *Ethnic jewellery.* TEL: 071 352 7989.
Paddy Frost
P1. *Tiles.* TEL: 071 352 2203.
S A Geris
N2/3. *Watches.* TEL: 071 352 8734.
C Gibson
M10. *Silver and plate, general antiques.* TEL: 071 352 4690
Mr Gill
A14-16. *Prints, etchings and lithographs.* TEL: 071 352 8734.
Maurizio and Loretta Giordani
B4/B5. *Watches.* TEL: 071 351 4853.
T Giorgi and S Dwyer
Q12. *Jewellery.*
J Goullet
L1. *Lace.* TEL: 071 352 7989.
Christopher Gower
T5-6. *Mirrors, furniture, decorative accessories.* TEL: 071 351 5353 ext. 26.
B Guittot
A6. *Art deco.* TEL: 071 352 7989.
Mrs B Gunn
N13/N14. *Fans, small silver.* TEL: 071 352 4690.
Mrs B Hamadani
P5. *Gold and silver, general.* TEL: 071 352 8734.
W Harvey and Hilary Conquy
N6/N7. *Decorative arts, china.* TEL: 071 352 8734.
Hayman and Hayman
M14/15, L2. *General antiques, frames, watercolours, treen, scent and ink bottles.* TEL: 071 351 6568.
M Healey
P7/8. *Jewellery and general antiques.* TEL: 071 352 5884.
R Henson
P4. *Coins and medals.* TEL: 071 352 8734.
Maurice Hickey
D2. *Jewellery, especially cuff-links.* TEL: 071 352 8201.
House of Frames
J2/3. *Pictures.* TEL: 071 352 7989.
Mrs B Johnston
K1/K2. *Metalware, burnished steel, copper and brass.* TEL: 071 352 7989.
K and M Antiques
M2. *Oriental porcelain.* TEL: 071 352 3216.
Mrs P A Kaskimo
C2. *General antiques.* TEL: 071 352 7989.
D Kelly
L3. *Books.* TEL: 071 352 4690.

Antiquarius continued

C Kikas
N1. *Prints.* TEL: 071 352 8734.
M Klein
L8/9. *Rare books.* TEL: 071 351 3820.
La Verite Ltd
Q7/8. *Jewellery and objects.* TEL: 071 351 5999.
R Lamari
M3/M4. *Jewellery and watches.* TEL: 071 352 7989.
Mr and Mrs Lehan
B1/6. *Leather items.* TEL: 071 352 7989.
M Lexton
N8/9/10/11. *Silver.* TEL: 071 351 5980.
A Llanos
L1. *Ivory, bronzes, objets d'art.* TEL: 071 352 7989.
Fay Lucas
B4/5. *Silver and objects.* TEL: 071 351 2170.
Mrs N McDonald-Hobley
A4. *Jewellery.* TEL: 071 351 0154.
Mrs M McLean
V23. *General antiques and jewellery.* TEL: 071 352 4739.
Magna Carta Antiques
R3/R4. *General antiques, inkwells, silver, flatware.* TEL: 071 351 5883.
M Mara
A17. *General.* TEL: 071 352 7989.
M Markov
F1/F6. *Decorative arts.* TEL: 071 352 4545.
G S Mathias
R5-6. *Victorian, Edwardian furniture, general, clocks.* TEL: 071 351 0484.
R Mee
A5/6. *Clocks, bronzes, pocket watches.* TEL: 071 351 7031.
A Mehta
E2. *Jewellery.* TEL: 071 351 0697.
P Miller
J4/5/P3. *Jewellery.* TEL: 071 352 4690/8734.
Mrs E Mitchell and S Cordas
D3/D4. *Silver and plate.* TEL: 071 352 7989.
T M Molloy
M6. *Oil paintings.* TEL: 071 352 7989.
Mrs Morrison
J2/J3. *Silver and plate.* TEL: 071 352 7989.
R S and S Necus and Mrs Cremer-Price
A19/H1/H2. *Silver, plate, objets de vertu.* TEL: 071 352 2405.
Sue Norman
L4. *Blue and white transfer ware, photographica.* TEL: 071 352 7217.
Aytac Osman
Q4/Q5. *General antiques, china, from 1900.* TEL: 071 352 2099.
H J and Miss J Palmer
M8/9. *Jewellery and silver.* TEL: 071 352 0431.
Mr Peterson
N4-5/P13. *Art deco and general.* TEL: 071 376 5394.

Antiquarius continued

Miss E Pollock and Mrs N Leon
G1/G4-6. *General antiques, small silver, jewellery and glass.* TEL: 071 352 8734.
The Purple Shop
J9/J10/J11. *Antique and period jewellery and art nouveau, art deco.* TEL: 071 352 1127.
D Raynor
N4/N5. *General antiques, china, decorative items.* TEL: 071 352 2203.
K Reilly
N15/N16. *Art nouveau and art deco.* TEL: 071 352 8734/7989.
Mrs G M Riley
D5. *Porcelain and china.* TEL: 071 352 7989.
Edina Ronay
U7. *Clothing and hand-knitted sweaters.* TEL: 071 352 1085.
Joel Rothman and Elizabeth
Q9/10. *Costume jewellery, art deco beauty and beasts and bronze animals.* TEL: 071 351 5149.
Mrs Michele Rowan
N12. *General and jewellery.* TEL: 071 352 8744.
S and G Antiques
P1. *General.* TEL: 071 352 8734.
Miss J Scott
P9-P11. *General antiques and jewellery.* TEL: 071 352 8882.
H Sedler **LAPADA**
F2-F5. *Silver, glass, general antiques.* TEL: 071 351 5000.
D Shorn (Scalpay Ltd.)
B3. *Jewellery and collector's items.* TEL: 071 352 8687.
M Simpson
E1. *Antique ivory.* TEL: 071 352 7989.
W Stewart
W7. *Art nouveau and art deco jewellery.* TEL: 071 352 4739.
Mrs Barbara Stone
L8. *Antiquarian books.* TEL: 071 351 0983/3820.
Sue Thompson
T1/T2. *General, silver.* TEL: 071 352 3494.
S Thorpe
T3-4. *Silver.* TEL: 071 351 2911.
Brian Tipping
P12. *Antique pipes.* TEL: 071 352 8882.
A Williams
A12. *Silver and objects.* TEL: 071 352 6442.
Catherine Williams Antiques
A1/A2. *General antiques and collectors' items.* TEL: 071 352 7989.

Apter Fredericks Ltd BADA

265-267 Fulham Rd. (B and Mrs. C Apter) Open 9.30-6. CL: Sat. *STOCK: English furniture, 17th to early 19th C.* TEL: 071 352 2188; fax - 071 376 5619. VAT: Stan/Spec.

S.W.3. continued

H.C Baxter and Sons BADA

53 Stewarts Grove. (R.C., T.J., M.J. and G.J Baxter) Est: 1928. Open 8.30-5.15. CL: Sat. and Mon. SIZE: Medium. *STOCK: English furniture, 1730-1830, £1,000-£35,000.* LOC: Next to Royal Marsden hospital, South Kensington nearest station. PARK: Meters. TEL: 071 352 9826/0807. VAT: Spec.

Boodle and Dunthorne Ltd

58 Brompton Rd. Open 9-6. *STOCK: English jewellery, £100-£30,000.* TEL: 071 584 6363.

Joanna Booth BADA

247 King's Rd, Chelsea. Est: 1963. Open 10-6. SIZE: Medium. *STOCK: Wood carvings, oak furniture, 17th C, £50-£5,000; Old Master drawings, textiles, tapestry.* Not stocked: Silver, glass, pottery, clocks. PARK: Meters. TEL: 071 352 8998. SER: Buys at auction. VAT: Spec.

Tony Bunzl LAPADA

344 King's Rd. Open 10-1 and 2-5.30. SIZE: Medium. *STOCK: European vernacular furniture, 17th-18th C.* PARK: Easy. TEL: 071 352 3697. VAT: Stan/Spec.

W.G.T Burne (Antique Glass) Ltd BADA

11 Elystan St. (Mrs G., R.V. and A.T.G Burne) Est: 1936. Open 9-5. CL: Thurs p.m. and Sat p.m.. SIZE: Large. *STOCK: Glass, collectors' pieces, chandeliers, candelabra, cut glass tableware.* PARK: Meters. TEL: 071 589 6074; fax - 081 944 1977. SER: Valuations; renovations and repairs. VAT: Stan/Spec.

Butler and Wilson

189 Fulham Rd. *STOCK: Jewellery, art deco, crocodile and leather accessories.* TEL: 071 352 3045.

John Campbell Picture Frames Ltd

164 Walton St. Open 9.30-5.30. *STOCK: 20th C impressionist and modern British oils and watercolours.* TEL: 071 584 9268. SER: Restorations (oils and watercolours); mount cutting; gilding; framing.

Century Gallery

100 Fulham Rd, Chelsea. (W Westley-Richards) Est: 1979. Open 10-6. *STOCK: Oil paintings especially Russian 20th C, from £1,000+.* LOC: Opposite Brompton Hospital. PARK: Easy. TEL: 071 581 1589; fax - 071 589 9468. SER: Valuations; restorations; buys at auction (paintings). VAT: Stan/Spec.

Chelsea Antique Market

245A and 253 King's Rd. Est: 1965. Open 10-6. SIZE: Large covered market with approximately 50 dealers. *STOCK: General antiques, especially books and prints.* LOC: From South Kensington underground along Sidney Street to King's Rd., turn right. TEL: 071 352 5689; stall-holders - 071 352 9695/1424. VAT: Stan.

Chelsea Rare Books

313 King's Rd. (L.S Bernard) Est: 1968. Open 10-6. *STOCK: Antiquarian books and prints.* TEL: 071 351 0950. VAT: Stan.

Chenil Galleries

181-183 King's Rd, Chelsea (Atlantic Antiques Centres Ltd.). Est: 1978. Open 10-6. Below are listed some of the many specialist dealers at this market. LOC: Next to Chelsea Town Hall. PARK: Sydney St. TEL: 071 351 5353. VAT: Stan/Spec.

G Accossato
D15. *Small silver, walking sticks and collectables.* TEL: 071 352 2123.

Trevor Allen
E9/10. *Jewellery.* TEL: 071 352 7061.

Mrs M Alves
G4. *Prints.* TEL: 071 352 2123.

K Andrea
E5. *Porcelain, glass and collectables.* TEL: 071 352 8653.

Nicolaus Boston and Martine
K5-7. *Furniture and objects.* TEL: 071 352 8790.

B Boycott-Enigma
Z2. *Period clothing.* TEL: 071 352 8581.

M Bristow and Jane
C6-7. *Silver, frames and flatware.* TEL: 071 352 1285.

A Brown
M3-4. *Staffordshire, imari and blue and white.* TEL: 071 352 7384.

Steve Clark
N1-3 and N9-10. *Dolls, toys, teddy bears.* TEL: 071 351 9338.

T Coakley **LAPADA**
D13/D14. *Art deco, art nouveau.* TEL: 071 351 2914.

John Cox (Baptista Arts) **LAPADA**
K1/2/10. *Decorative art.* TEL: 071 352 5793.

Mrs D Crowley and Mrs A Fothergill
D11/12. *Period clothing and textiles.* TEL: 071 351 0011.

Jesse Davis
C5. *China, furniture, silver, majolica.* TEL: 071 351 1607.

G Dewart
C3. *Prints.* TEL: 071 352 7384.

Paul Dowling
A6/7. *Decorative prints.*

G Drey
R16/17. *Modern paintings.* TEL: 071 351 2921.

Tony Durante and Claude Colot
J1-J5. *Decorative objects 1900-1970, Gaunmont and Saint-Lambert.* TEL: 071 351 2479.

Peter Fiell
A1-A4. *Decorative art.* TEL: 071 351 7172.

Chenil Galleries continued

Flight of Fancy
B4/5. *Furniture, objets d'art, silver, porcelain.* TEL: 071 352 4314.
B Gordon **LAPADA**
C4. *Fine silver and Sheffield plate.* TEL: 071 352 5808.
Pamela Haywood
Z3. *Period clothing.* TEL: 071 352 8581.
Il Libro
C8-9. (G Toscani) *Books and prints.* TEL: 071 352 9041/823 3248.
Janus Antiques
P5. (Mrs J Shourbaji) *Decorative items.*
Mrs Gwynneth Jones
Z5. *Period clothing.* TEL: 071 352 8581.
P Jones
A8/A11/A12. *Textiles, 16th-19th C.* TEL: 071 351 2005.
D Kingston
R3-4. *Blue and white porcelain.* TEL: 071 352 7384.
Mrs V Krell
R11. *General antiques.* TEL: 071 352 2123.
La Verite
R5-8. (K and C Bird) *Jewellery, glass and china.* TEL: 071 351 5999.
Claude and Martine Latreville
B1-2. *Fine silver and jewellery.* TEL: 071 352 5964.
Myra Lustigman
E8. *Victorian silver and jewellery.* TEL: 071 352 8653.
Marie and Gerry McClean
R1-2. *Jewellery and Vienna bronzes.* TEL: 071 352 8653.
Agnus McNeill Fine Art
H3. *Oil paintings, 19th C.* TEL: 071 351 5075.
H Man
P1/2. *Chinese items.* TEL: 071 376 8037.
D Martin
D5-6. *Moorcroft porcelain.* TEL: 071 351 5829.
P Mizza
L2-9. *Continental furniture.* TEL: 071 376 5867.
A. Montilla and Acevedoa
M1-2 and M5. *Jewellery, objets d'art.* TEL: 071 351 0314.
Mrs R Muggleton
G5. *Silver and plate.* TEL: 071 352 2123.
G Nelson
H1/2/L1. *Fine oil paintings.* TEL: 071 351 0957.
Miss J Ondaatje
R13-14. *Leatherware.* TEL: 071 351 5903.
John Pearman
R12. *China, glass, bronzes and objects.* TEL: 071 352 2123.
Maria Perez
A5. *Jewellery.* TEL: 071 351 1986.
Ms Pinhas
D1. *Art nouveau, art deco jewellery and objects.* TEL: 071 352 2123.

Chenil Galleries continued

Joanne Piotrowska
G1/2. *Mirrors and lacquered furniture.* TEL: 071 352 7384.
Mr Pyrah
C2. *Art nouveau and art deco.* TEL: 071 351 1836.
G Raffaelli
B7. *Lighters.* TEL: 071 352 6834.
Patricia Rhodes
R9-10. *General antiques.* TEL: 071 352 8653.
S Richards and S Willis
E4. *Prints and objects.* TEL: 071 352 8653.
Matthew Shaw
E7. *General antiques.* TEL: 071 352 8653.
N Sonmez
N6-7. *Persian carpets.* TEL: 071 351 6611.
L Stanton
P3-4. *Art nouveau, art deco.* TEL: 071 352 2183.
Mr and Mrs S Tolkien
E1/2. *American designer jewellery.* TEL: 071 376 3660.
Mrs C Van der Steen
E6. *Porcelain and glass.* TEL: 071 352 8653.
C A Willcocks
G3. *Prints.* TEL: 071 352 2123.
Mrs Y P Willcocks
K3/K4/K8/K9. *Books and fans.* TEL: 071 352 7384.
Basia Zarzycka
E3. *Couture masks and accessories.* TEL: 071 351 7276.

Richard Courtney Ltd BADA
112-114 Fulham Rd. Est: 1959. Open 9.30-1 and 2-6. CL: Sat. SIZE: Large. *STOCK: English furniture, 18th C, £500-£20,000.* PARK: Easy. TEL: 071 370 4020. VAT: Spec.

Zal Davar LAPADA
c/o 344 King's Rd. Est: 1961. Open 9.30-5. CL: Sat. *STOCK: Furniture, 19th C; decorative items.* TEL: 071 351 5730. VAT: Stan/Spec. *Trade and Export Only.*

Colin Denny Ltd
18 Cale St. Est: 1968. Open 10-6. *STOCK: Marine works of art, 19th C.* TEL: 071 584 0240. VAT: Stan/Spec.

Robert Dickson Antiques Ltd BADA
263 Fulham Rd. Est: 1969. Open 9.30-5.30. CL: Sat. SIZE: Medium. *STOCK: Late 18th and early 19th C furniture and works of art, £500-£50,000.* PARK: Easy. TEL: 071 351 0330. VAT: Spec.

Dragons of Walton St. Ltd
23 Walton St. (R Fisher) *STOCK: Mainly painted and decorated furniture; hand decorated children's furniture, decorative items.* LOC: Close to Harrods. PARK: Hasker St. or First St. TEL: 071 589 3795/0548 /5007.

S.W.3 continued

Forty-Eight Walton Street
48 Walton St, (Joan of Art Ltd.). Est: 1976. Open 10-5.30. SIZE: Medium. *STOCK: English and continental furniture and decorative works of art, 18th-19th C, £25-£5,000.* PARK: Easy. TEL: 071 581 0213. SER: Buys at auction.

Michael Foster BADA
118 Fulham Rd, Chelsea. Open 9-6, Sat. 9-1. *STOCK: 18th C English furniture and works of art.* TEL: 071 373 3636/3040. SER: Valuations; restorations.

C Fredericks and Son BADA
92 Fulham Rd. (R.F Fredericks) Open 9.30-5.30, Sat. by appointment. SIZE: Large. *STOCK: Furniture, 18th C, £500-£15,000.* LOC: Near to South Kensington underground station. PARK: Easy. TEL: 071 589 5847. VAT: Stan/Spec.

Gallery Arcticus
56 Fulham Rd. (P Bertelsen) Open 10-6, Sat. 11-3. CL: Mon. *STOCK: 19th-20th C Scandinavian art.* TEL: 071 589 1458; fax - 071 823 9061.

David Gill LAPADA
60 Fulham Rd. Est: 1986. Open 10-6. SIZE: Medium. *STOCK: 1920's to 1950's and contemporary decorative and fine arts items.* PARK: Onslow Sq. TEL: 071 589 5946. VAT: Stan.

Godson and Coles Ltd BADA
310 King's Rd. Est: 1978. Open 9.30-6, Sat. 10-4. *STOCK: English furniture, 18th to early 19th C.* TEL: 071 352 8509.

Daphne Graham and Robert Stephenson
1 Elystan Street, Chelsea Green. Open 10-6, Mon. 2-6, Sat. 10-1. *STOCK: Decorative carpets and kilims, including floral; kilim-upholstered furniture.* TEL: 071 584 8724/225 2343.

Green and Stone
259 Kings Rd. (R.J.S Baldwin) Est: 1927. Open 9-5.30, Sat. 9.30-6. *STOCK: Writing and artists' materials, watercolours, 18th-19th C; drawings, 19th C.* LOC: At junction of King's Rd. and Old Church St. PARK: Meters. TEL: 071 352 0837/6521. SER: Restorations (pictures). VAT: Stan.

Robin Greer
30 Sloane Court West. Est: 1965. Open by appointment. *STOCK: Children's and illustrated books, original illustrations.* TEL: 071 730 7392. SER: Catalogues issued.

Halliday's LAPADA
28 Beacuchamp Pl. Est: 1948. Open 10-6. *STOCK: Mantelpieces, fire grates, fenders, fire-*

Halliday's continued

place accessories, room panelling, all 18th-20th C. TEL: 071 589 5534; fax - 071 589 2477. VAT: Stan/Spec.

William Handford Antiques
172 Brompton Rd. Est: 1974. Open 9.30-5.30. SIZE: Medium. *STOCK: Period English and continental furniture, works of art, lamps by Tiffany.* TEL: 071 823 9039. VAT: Stan/Spec.

James Hardy and Co
235 Brompton Rd. Open 9.30-5.30. *STOCK: Silver tableware; silver and jewellery.* PARK: Meters. TEL: 071 589 5050. SER: Valuations.

Hooper and Purchase
303 Kings Rd. (S Purchase) Est: 1969. Open 10-5.30, evenings and Sat. by appointment only. *STOCK: Chandeliers; English and continental furniture.* PARK: Meter (King's Rd.). TEL: 071 351 3985; home - 071 352 1391. VAT: Stan/Spec.

Stephanie Hoppen Ltd BADA
17 Walton St. Est: 1962. Open 9-6, Sat. 11-4. *STOCK: Prints, paintings and watercolours - botanical, natural history, architecture, interiors, portraits, modern artists.* TEL: 071 589 3678.

Malcolm Innes Gallery
172 Walton St. Est: 1973. Open 9.30-6 and some Sats. 10-1. *STOCK: Scottish and sporting pictures.* TEL: 071 584 0575/5559. SER: Restorations; framing. VAT: Spec.

Anthony James and Son Ltd BADA
88 Fulham Rd. Est: 1949. Open 9.30-6, Sat. by appointment. SIZE: Large. *STOCK: Furniture, 1700-1880, £200-£50,000; mirrors, bronzes, ormolu and decorative items, £200-£20,000.* PARK: Easy. TEL: 071 584 1120; fax - 071 823 7618. SER: Valuations; buys at auction. VAT: Spec.

Annabel Jones
52 Beauchamp Pl, Knightsbridge. Open 10-5.30. CL: Sat. *STOCK: Jewellery, silver and Sheffield plate.* TEL: 071 589 3215.

Paul Jones
Chenil Galleries, 183 King's Rd. Est: 1983. Open 10-6. SIZE: Large. *STOCK: Textiles, tapestries, needleworks and paisley shawls, £100-£20,000; decorative objects, furniture, £30-£4,000; all 16th-19th C; tassels, period upholstery trims, 18th-19th C, £20-£500.* LOC: Near Chelsea Town Hall. PARK: Side streets. TEL: 071 351 2005. SER: Valuations. VAT: Stan.

Lewis M Kaplan Associates Ltd LAPADA
50 Fulham Rd. (L.M Kaplan and G.D Watson) Est: 1977. Open 11-6. *STOCK: Art deco and art nouveau glass and furniture, £500-£10,000; signed art deco and art nouveau jewellery*

Lewis M Kaplan Associates Ltd continued

especially 1940's 'cocktail', £1,000-£10,000; both 1890-1945. LOC: At junction of Sydney St. and Fulham Rd. PARK: Sydney St. TEL: 071 589 3108/584 6328. SER: Valuations; buys at auction (art nouveau and art deco). VAT: Stan/Spec.

John Keil Ltd **BADA**
154 Brompton Rd. Est: 1959. Open 9-6. CL: Sat. except by appointment. SIZE: Large. *STOCK: English furniture, 18th to early 19th C from £500.* LOC: Near Knightsbridge underground station. PARK: 200yds. TEL: 071 589 6454. SER: Restorations (fine pieces). VAT: Spec.

Stanley Leslie
15 Beauchamp Pl. Open 9-5. *STOCK: Silver and Sheffield plate.* PARK: Meters. TEL: 071 589 2333.

Michael Lipitch Ltd.
98 Fulham Rd. *STOCK: 18th C to early 19th C English furniture, decoration and works of art.* TEL: 071 589 7327; fax - 071 823 9106.

Peter Lipitch Ltd **BADA**
120/124 Fulham Rd. Est: 1954. Open 9.30-5.30, Sat. by appointment. SIZE: Large. *STOCK: Fine English furniture and mirrors.* TEL: 071 373 3328. VAT: Spec.

Gwyneth Lloyd Antique Textiles
Open by appointment. *STOCK: Antique and decorative embroideries and hangings; shawls.* TEL: 071 352 4864.

L'Odeon
173 Fulham Rd. (N Tovey) Open 11-6. *STOCK: Art deco.* TEL: 071 736 4216.

McKenna and Co **LAPADA**
28 Beauchamp Pl. (C Macmillan and M McKenna) Est: 1982. Open 10-6. SIZE: Medium. *STOCK: Fine jewellery, Georgian to post war, £50-£10,000; some silver and objects.* Not stocked: Pictures and furniture. LOC: Off Brompton Rd., near Harrods. PARK: Meters. TEL: 071 584 1966; fax - 071 225 2893. SER: Valuations; restorations. FAIRS: Olympia. VAT: Stan/Spec.

The Map House
54 Beauchamp Pl. (Hon. C.A and Mrs. Savile, Lord Mexborough, Countess of Mexborough and Simon Pointer) Est: 1907. Open 9.45-5.45, Sat. 10.30-5 or by appointment. *STOCK: Antique and rare maps, atlases, engravings and globes.* TEL: 071 589 4325/584 8559; fax - 071 589 1041. VAT: Stan.

Mathon Gallery
38 Cheyne Walk, Chelsea (Phipps and Co. Ltd.). Est: 1980. Open 9.30-5.30 or by appointment, including Sun. SIZE: Medium. *STOCK: British oils, watercolours and sculpture, 19th-20th C, £100-£30,000.* TEL: 071 352 5381; (0684)

Mathon Gallery continued

892242. SER: Valuations; buys at auction (British paintings and sculpture). VAT: Spec.

Merola
178 Walton St. (M Merola) Open 10-6. *STOCK: Jewellery, handbags, hats and accessories, 1900-1960.* TEL: 071 589 0365.

Monro Heywood Ltd
336 Kings Rd. (J Monro and E Heywood) Open 10-5. CL: Sat. *STOCK: Pictures and prints, furniture, china, objects, 18th-19th C, £30-£3,500.* LOC: Opposite Paultons Sq. PARK: Easy. TEL: 071 351 1477. VAT: Spec.

Moss Galleries-Rachel Moss **LAPADA**
238 Brompton Rd. Est: 1970. Open 10.30-6, Sat. 11-4. SIZE: Small. *STOCK: English and Scottish watercolours, 18th-20th C.* LOC: Round corner from V. and A. TEL: 071 225 3389. SER: Valuations; restorations; buys at auction. FAIRS: Olympia; World of Watercolours; Twentieth Century. VAT: Spec.

Guy Nevill Fine Paintings Ltd
251A Fulham Rd. Open by appointment 10-5.30. CL: Sat. SIZE: Large. *STOCK: Sporting, country and animal pictures, 18th-20th C, £100-£300,000.* PARK: Easy. TEL: 071 351 4292. VAT: Stan.

H.W Newby (A.J. Waller) and H.C. Mote **BADA**
15 Walton St. Est: 1949. Open 10-1 and 2-5.30. CL: Sat. SIZE: Large. *STOCK: Porcelain, faience, pottery, pre-1830, £50-£5,000; English and continental glass.* Not stocked: Silver, jewellery. LOC: Between Ovington St. and Hasker St. PARK: Meters. TEL: 071 589 2752. SER: Valuations; buys at auction. VAT: Spec.

Old Church Galleries
320 King's Rd. (Mrs M Harrington) Open 10-6. *STOCK: Prints including decorative and sporting, 18th-19th C, £5-£2,000; maps, from 17th C.* TEL: 071 351 4649. SER: Restorations; picture framing.

Jacqueline Oosthuizen **LAPADA**
23 Cale St, (Off Sydney St.), Chelsea Green. Est: 1960. Open 10-6, Sat. by chance or appointment, Sun. by appointment. SIZE: Small. *STOCK: Staffordshire figures, animals, cottages and toby jugs, 18th-19th C, £50-£10,000; jewellery, 19th-20th C, £15-£5,000; decorative ceramics including Poole pottery, 19th-20th C, £20-£1,000.* LOC: Near King's Rd. and Fulham Rd. PARK: Easy. TEL: 071 352 6071; answering service 081 528 9001, pager no.806930. SER: Buys at auction (Staffordshire and jewellery). VAT: Stan/Spec.

S.W.3 continued

Pelham Galleries **BADA**
163-165 Fulham Rd. (A. and L Rubin) Est: 1928. *STOCK: Furniture, English, continental; tapestries; decorative works of art, musical instruments.* TEL: 071 589 2686; fax - 071 823 9398. VAT: Spec.

David Pettifer Ltd **BADA**
269 King's Rd. Est: 1963. Open 9.30-1 and 2-6. SIZE: Large. *STOCK: English furniture, 18th C; paintings and watercolours, 18th-19th C.* LOC: From Sloane Sq., 11, 19 or 22 bus. PARK: Easy. TEL: 071 352 3088. SER: Buys at auction. VAT: Stan/Spec.

Prides of London
15 Paultons House, Paultons Sq. Open by appointment only. *STOCK: Fine furniture, objets d'art.* TEL: 071 586 1227. SER: Interior design.

The Purple Shop
15 Flood St, Chelsea. (A.J Gardner and O.M Becker) Est: 1967. Open 10-6. *STOCK: Antique and period jewellery, especially art nouveau, art deco, studio pottery.* LOC: Near Chelsea Town Hall. PARK: Meters and nearby. TEL: 071 352 1127. SER: Valuations. VAT: Stan.

Rogers de Rin **LAPADA**
76 Royal Hospital Rd, Chelsea. (V de Rin) Est: 1950. Open 10-5.30. SIZE: Small. *STOCK: Wemyss pottery, objets d'art, decorative*

Rogers de Rin continued

furnishings (Regency style), collectors' specialities, all 18th-19th C, £50-£10,000. LOC: Just beyond Royal Hospital, corner of Paradise Walk. PARK: Easy. TEL: 071 352 9007. SER: Buys at auction. VAT: Stan/Spec.

Alistair Sampson Antiques Ltd. inc.
Tobias Jellinek Antiques **BADA**
156 Brompton Rd. (A.H Sampson) Open 9.30-5.30. SIZE: Large. *STOCK: English pottery, oak and country furniture, metalwork, needlework, primitive pictures, decorative and interesting items, all 17th-18th C.* PARK: Meters. TEL: 071 589 5272/581 2267; fax - 071 823 8142. VAT: Spec.

Charles Saunders Antiques
255 Fulham Rd. Open 9.30-5.30, Sat. 10-5.30. *STOCK: Decorative furniture,objects and lamps,18th-19th C.* TEL: 071 351 5242. VAT: Spec.

Christine Schell **LAPADA**
15 Cale St. (B King and C Davies) Est: 1971. Open 10-5.30, Sat. 10-1. SIZE: Small. *STOCK: Unusual tortoiseshell, silver and enamel objects, late 19th to early 20th C, £150-£2,500.* LOC: North of King's Rd., between Sloane Ave. and Sydney St. PARK: Easy. TEL: 071 352 5563. SER: Valuations; restorations (tortoiseshell, ivory, shagreen, crocodile, leather, enamels, silver and hairbrush re-bristling). FAIRS: Olympia. VAT: Stan/Spec.

S.W.3 continued

Mark Senior
240 Brompton Rd. Est: 1980. Open 10.30-6, Sat. 11-3. SIZE: Medium. *STOCK: English watercolours, 19th C, £100-£3,000.* LOC: Near Victoria and Albert Museum. PARK: Meters. TEL: 071 589 5811. SER: Valuations; restorations; framing; buys at auction (watercolours). VAT: Spec.

Oliver Swann Galleries
170 Walton St. Est: 1975. Open 10-6, Sat. by appointment. SIZE: Medium. *STOCK: Marine and yachting paintings, 19th and 20th C; ships models, all £150-£50,000.* PARK: Easy. TEL: 071 581 4229/584 8684. SER: Valuations; restorations; buys at auction. VAT: Spec.

Alan G Thomas
c/o National Westminster Bank, 300 King's Rd. Est: 1956. Open by appointment. *STOCK: Manuscripts, early printing, bindings, literature.* PARK: Meters, opposite. TEL: 071 352 5130.

David Tron Antiques BADA LAPADA
275 King's Rd. Open 9.30-1 and 2-6. *STOCK: Furniture, 17th-19th C; works of art. (Also trade department).* TEL: 071 352 5918.

S.W.3 continued

Valerie Wade
108 Fulham Rd. Open 10-6, Sat. 10-5. *STOCK: Decorative furniture including Regency; Victorian papier mâché furniture and trays; needlepoint carpets.* TEL: 071 225 1414.

Walker-Bagshawe LAPADA
73 Walton St. (C Walker and N Bagshawe) Est: 1975. Open 10-6. SIZE: Medium. *STOCK: English and European oils and watercolours, 1870-1930, £2,000-£150,000; arts and crafts furniture, 1900's, £200-£5,000.* LOC: Behind Harrods. PARK: Meters. TEL: 071 589 4582. SER: Valuations; restorations (oils, watercolours, prints); framing; buys at auction (paintings). FAIRS: Olympia, World of Watercolours, 20th C British Art, Maastricht. VAT: Spec.

R Wearn and Son Ltd
322 King's Rd. Est: 1928. Open 10-5, Sat. 10-2. *STOCK: General antiques, furniture, 18th and 19th C, £200-£4,000.* TEL: 071 352 3918. VAT: Stan/Spec.

O.F Wilson Ltd BADA LAPADA
Queens Elm Parade, Old Church St (corner of Fulham Rd.), Chelsea. (P. and V.E Jackson and M.E Briscoe-Knight) Est: 1935. Open 9.30-5.30, Sat. 10.30-1. *STOCK: English and French furniture, mantelpieces, objets d'art.* TEL: 071 352 9554. SER: Valuations. VAT: Spec.

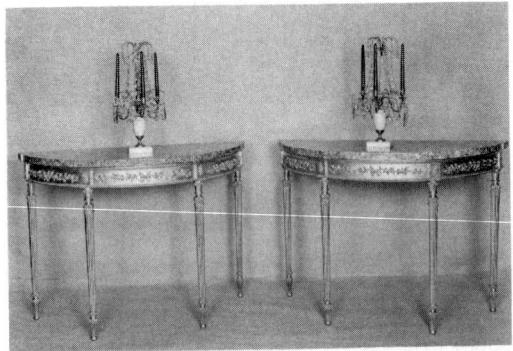

S.W.3 continued

Clifford Wright Antiques Ltd BADA

104-106 Fulham Rd. Est: 1964. Open 9-6. CL: Sat. p.m. *STOCK: Furniture, 18th and early 19th C; period mirrors and giltwood furniture.* TEL: 071 589 0986. VAT: Spec.

London S.W.4

HRW Antiques

4a Kings Avenue, Clapham. Open 10-5, Sat. 10-1, other times by appointment. SIZE: Large. *STOCK: Furniture, porcelain, paintings and objects, 18th-19th C.* TEL: 071 978 1026.

Trowbridge Gallery

17 Turret Grove. (M Trowbridge) Est: 1980. Open by appointment. SIZE: Small. *STOCK: Decorative prints, 17th-19th C, £50-£150.* LOC: Near North St., Clapham. PARK: Easy. TEL: 071 738 8354. SER: Valuations; restorations (paper, colouring); buys at auction (antiquarian books and prints); hand-made frames; decorative mounting. FAIRS: City of London; Decorative Antiques and Textiles. VAT: Stan.

Wingfield Sporting Gallery

35 Sibella Rd, Clapham. (Mrs M Wingfield) Open by appointment. *STOCK: Paintings and prints covering over 50 sports.* TEL: 071 622 6301.

London S.W.5

Stephen Anson

67 Courtfield Gdns, Resident. Est: 1978. Open by appointment. SIZE: Medium. *STOCK: Furniture, 17th-18th C, £500-£20,000; early oak furniture.* LOC: Off Cromwell Rd. PARK: Meters. TEL: 071 373 4612/7080 (ansaphone). SER: Valuations; buys at auction (furniture).

Antique and Modern Furniture Ltd

160 Earls Court Rd. Est: 1941. Open 9.30-1 and 2.30-6. CL: Thurs. *STOCK: Furniture, mainly 18th-19th C.* TEL: 071 373 2935.

Beaver Coin Room

Beaver Hotel, 57 Philbeach Gdns. (J Lis) Est: 1971. Open by appointment. SIZE: Small. *STOCK: European coins, 10th-18th C, commemorative medals, 15th-20th C; all £5-£5,000.* LOC: 2 mins. walk from Earls Court Rd. PARK: Easy. TEL: 071 373 4553; fax - 071 373 4555. SER: Valuations; buys at auction (coins and medals). FAIRS: London Coin and Coinex. VAT: Stan.

David Tremayne Ltd BADA

Flat 5, 20 Bolton Gdns. (D Salmon) Open by appointment only. *STOCK: Chinese hardwood furniture and Oriental works of art.* TEL: 071 370 1962/1682.

HRW ANTIQUES

A LARGE SELECTION OF PERIOD ANTIQUES AND DECORATIVE ITEMS PRICES RANGING FROM £100 TO £10,000

OPEN: MONDAY-FRIDAY 10am – 5pm
SATURDAY 10am – 1pm
OR BY APPOINTMENT

4A KINGS AVENUE, CLAPHAM, SW4 8BD
TEL: 071-978-1026
FAX: 071-498-6376

London S.W.6

20th Century Gallery
821 Fulham Rd. (D Sims, E Brandl and H Chapman) Open 10-6. SIZE: Small. *STOCK: Post impressionist and modern British oils and watercolours; original prints.* LOC: Nr. Munster Rd. junction. PARK: Easy. TEL: 071 731 5888/736 0497. SER: Restorations (paintings); framing. VAT: Spec.

(55) For Decorative Living
55 New King's Rd, Chelsea. (Mrs J Rhodes) Open 10-5.30. *STOCK: Pine, country and fruitwood furniture, decorative items especially carved mirrors.* TEL: 071 736 5623.

634 Kings Rd
Chelsea(J Thornton) Open 10-5.30. *STOCK: Antiquarian books.* TEL: 071 736 6181.

And So To Bed Limited
638/640 King's Rd. Est: 1970. Open 10-6. SIZE: Large. *STOCK: Brass, lacquered and wooded beds.* LOC: End of King's Rd., towards Fulham. PARK: Easy. TEL: 071 731 3593/4/5. SER: Restorations; spares; interior design. VAT: Stan.

Antique Carpets Gallery
150 Wandsworth Bridge Rd, Fulham. (M Taregwian) Est: 1984. Open 10-6.30, Wed. 10-7.30, Sun. 12-3.30. SIZE: Large. *STOCK: Carpets, 19th C, £400-£40,000; rugs, 18th-20th C, £300-£3,000; textiles, 19th C, £70-£1,500.* PARK: Easy. TEL: 071 371 9619/9620; home - 081 648 1703. SER: Valuations; restorations; buys at auction (Oriental and European carpets, rugs and textiles, tapestries). VAT: Stan/Spec.

Karin Armelin Antiques
592 King's Rd. Open 10-5.30. SIZE: Medium. *STOCK: 18th-19th C English and French furniture, decorative prints.* PARK: Easy. TEL: 071 736 0375. SER: Valuations. VAT: Stan/Spec.

Barclay Samson Ltd
39 Inglethorpe St. Open by appointment only. *STOCK: Pre 1940 original lithographic posters; English and continental watercolours, oil paintings and prints, mainly 19th C.* TEL: 071 381 4341; fax - 071 601 0434. VAT: Spec.

Robert Barley Antiques
48 Fulham High St. (R.A Barley) Est: 1965. Open 9.30-5.30. CL: Sat. SIZE: Medium. *STOCK: Decorative furniture, objects, textiles.* LOC: Near Putney Bridge. PARK: Easy. TEL: 071 736 4429. VAT: Stan/Spec.

Beresford-Clark
558 King's Rd, Chelsea. Est: 1976. Open 10-5.30, Sat. by appointment. SIZE: Medium. *STOCK: Furniture, decorative paintings, textiles, unusual objects and china.* PARK: Easy. TEL: 071 731 5079.

S.W.6 continued

Big Ben Antique Clocks
5 Broxholme House, New King's Rd. (R Lascelles) Est: 1978. Open 10-5.30. *STOCK: Clocks, especially longcase, from £600.* LOC: At junction of Wandsworth Bridge Rd. and New King's Rd. TEL: 071 736 1770; fax - 071 384 1957. SER: Repairs (clocks); buys at auction.

Bishops Park Antiques
53-55 Fulham High St. Open 10-6. *STOCK: Pine, especially English and continental, 18th-19th C.* TEL: 071 736 4573.

Bookham Galleries
164 Wandsworth Bridge Rd. (J.H. and J Rowe) Est: 1969. Open 10-5.30. CL: Mon. and Thurs. *STOCK: Furniture, 18th-19th C; Oriental rugs.* TEL: 071 736 5125.

Brandt Oriental Antiques
771 Fulham Rd. (R Brandt) Est: 1981. Open daily, Sat. and Sun. by appointment. SIZE: Medium. *STOCK: Oriental furniture, works of art, £200-£5,000.* LOC: Parsons Green end of Fulham Rd. PARK: Easy. TEL: 071 731 6835; home - 071 731 1192. SER: Restorations including gilding. VAT: Spec.

Alasdair Brown Antiques
569 King's Rd. (A.J.C Brown) Est: 1984. Open 9.30-6. SIZE: Medium. *STOCK: English and continental furniture, £300-£10,000; decorative items, £100-£5,000; all 18th-19th C; pictures, some porcelain, tapestries, 17th-19th C, £150-£3,500.* Not stocked: Silver and jewellery. LOC: Past World's End, over small bridge. PARK: Easy. TEL: 071 736 8077. SER: Valuations. FAIRS: Olympia (June and Oct.). VAT: Stan/Spec.

I. and J.L Brown
632 and 636 King's Rd. Usually open 9.30-5.30. *STOCK: English country and French provincial furniture including tables and country chairs; metalware and decorative items.* TEL: 071 736 4141. SER: Restorations.

Arthur Brown's Number Three Ltd
64 Fulham High St. Open 9.30-1 and 2-5.30. CL: Sat. SIZE: Medium. *STOCK: Furniture, gilt, lacquer and painted, 18th-19th C; decorative and unusual items, especially four poster beds.* PARK: Easy. TEL: 071 385 4218. VAT: Spec.

Buhler Galleries
15c Farm Lane Trading Estate, Farm Lane. (M Buhler) Open by appointment. *STOCK: Oriental carpets and European tapestries.* TEL: 071 386 5023. SER: Restorations.

S.W.6 continued

Rupert Cavendish Antiques LAPADA
610 King's Rd. Est: 1980. Open 10-6. SIZE: Large. *STOCK: Empire and Biedermeier furniture and objets d'art; watercolours and prints.* LOC: Just before New King's Rd. PARK: Easy. TEL: 071 731 7041; fax - 071 731 8302. SER: Valuations. VAT: Spec.

Rupert Cavendish Antiques LAPADA
98 Waterford Rd. Open 10-6. *STOCK: Neo-classical furniture, late 18th and early 19th C, and fabrics, wallpapers and borders.* TEL: 071 384 2642; fax - 071 731 8302.

The Chair Co
180 Wandsworth Bridge Rd, Fulham. (H.A Lowe) Est: 1987. Open 10-5.30, Sat. 12-4. SIZE: Small. *STOCK: Decorative chairs, £30-£1,000.* LOC: Off King's Rd., towards river on right. PARK: Easy. TEL: 071 736 3112. SER: Screens, cushions, upholstery.

Chelsea Clocks and Antiques
479 Fulham Rd, Chelsea. (P Dixon and D Torr) Est: 1976. Open 12-5.30. CL: Sat. and Mon. *STOCK: Longcase clocks, £800-£4,000; mantel and wall clocks, £50-£450; decorative and collectors' items, £5-£500.* LOC: Opp. Chelsea Football Ground. PARK: Easy. TEL: 071 731 5704. FAIRS: Olympia. VAT: Stan.

Chelsea Fine Furniture Ltd LAPADA
40 Fulham High St. (D.N Ward) Open 10-6. *STOCK: Decorative items including mirrors, 18th-19th C furniture, botanical and decorative prints.* TEL: 071 384 2373.

John Clay
263 New King's Rd, Fulham. Est: 1974. Open 8.30-6, Sat. 10-6. SIZE: Medium. *STOCK: Furniture, £50-£5,000; objets d'art and animal objects, silver and clocks, £10-£1,500; all 18th-19th C.* Not stocked: Pine. LOC: Close to Parsons Green, A3. PARK: Easy. TEL: 071 731 5677. SER: Restorations (furniture, objets d'art). VAT: Stan/Spec.

Fergus Cochrane Antiques
570 King's Rd. (F.V Cochrane) Est: 1981. Open 10-6. SIZE: Medium. *STOCK: Decorative lighting, 1700-1930, £100-£2,000.* PARK: Easy. TEL: 071 736 9166. VAT: Stan/Spec.

Peter Collins
92 Waterford Rd. Est: 1971. Open 10-1 and 3-6. CL: Tues. *STOCK: Furniture - country woods or painted, 17th to early 19th C; decorative items.* TEL: 071 736 4149.

The Constant Reader Bookshop
627 Fulham Rd. (G. and A Mullett) Open 10.30-7. *STOCK: Books, some antiquarian, especially Japan and Far East.* TEL: 071 731 0218.

Cooper Fine Arts Ltd LAPADA
768 Fulham Rd. (J Hill-Reid) Est: 1976. Open 10-6.30. SIZE: Medium. *STOCK: Oils and water-*

S.W.6 continued

colours, £200-£5,000; bronzes, £200-£1,000; all 1850-1950. LOC: Putney Bridge end of Fulham Rd. PARK: Easy. TEL: 071 731 3421; home - same. SER: Valuations; restorations; framing; buys at auction. VAT: Stan/Spec.

J Crotty and Son Ltd
74 New King's Rd, Parsons Green. Est: 1945. Open 9.30-5. CL: Sat. p.m. SIZE: Medium. *STOCK: Fire grates, light fittings, fenders, 18th-19th C; marble and pine mantelpieces, fire irons, fire screens.* PARK: In adjacent side street. TEL: 071 731 4209. SER: Restorations (antique metal fireplace equipment); buys at auction. VAT: Stan.

T Crowther and Son Ltd
282 North End Rd, Fulham. Est: 1882. Open 9-5.30. CL: Sat. SIZE: Large. *STOCK: Oak and pine panelling, mainly 17th-18th C; carved wood and marble chimney pieces and Georgian furniture, 1700-1830, £500-£100,000; garden ornaments, 18th-19th C, £500-£50,000.* LOC: Up North End Rd. from Fulham Broadway, on left hand side opposite fruit market, corner of Coomer Place. PARK: Easy. TEL: 071 385 1375/7. SER: Valuations. VAT: Spec.

David Alexander Antiques
102 Waterford Rd. (R.D.A Robertson and K Thurlow) Est: 1970. Appointment advisable. SIZE: Medium. *STOCK: English and continental furniture, 16th to early 18th C.* LOC: Turn left at junction of King's Rd. and New King's Rd. PARK: Easy. TEL: 071 731 4644. SER: Valuations; restorations; buys at auction. VAT: Spec.

Charles Edwards LAPADA
582 King's Rd. Open 9.30-6. *STOCK: Furniture 18th-19th C; architectural and decorative items mirrors, British oil paintings, rugs, carpets, garden furniture and statuary.* TEL: 071 736 8490; fax - 071 371 5436.

English Period Interiors
6 Fulham High St. (J Southwell) Est: 1987. Open 10-6, Mon. by appointment. SIZE: Medium. *STOCK: Furniture, fine 17th-18th C English copies, £500-£3,000; small general antiques and accessories, £50-£100.* LOC: Near Putney Bridge underground. TEL: 071 736 9088. VAT: Stan.

Fairfax Fireplaces and Antiques
568 King's Rd. (H Fairfax) Open 10-5. *STOCK: Fireplaces - cast-iron and pine; railings and balustrades.* TEL: 071 736 5023. SER: Restorations; metal polishing; fabricating.

Five Five Six Antiques LAPADA
556 King's Rd. Est: 1961. Open 10-6. SIZE: Medium. *STOCK: General decorative items - early and unusual furniture, primitive paintings, watercolours, samplers, needlework cushions,*

Five Five Six Antiques continued

wool and silk works, decorators' accessories. TEL: 071 731 2016; home - 071 624 5173. SER: Valuations; interior decoration. VAT: Stan.

George Floyd Ltd
592 Fulham Rd. Open 8.30-5.30. SIZE: Large. *STOCK: 18th and early 19th C furniture and accessories.* TEL: 071 736 1649. VAT: Stan/Spec.

Gerald Freedman
P.O. Box 458, Fulham. Est: 1961. Open by appointment. *STOCK: 17th-18th C Chinese porcelain also European ceramics including Delft, faience and maiolica.* LOC: End of King's Rd., 1 minute from Putney Bridge (District Line station). TEL: 071 736 8666. SER: Valuations.

George Leuchars
793 Fulham Rd. (H Leuchars and A George) Est: 1979. Open 9.30-5.30. *STOCK: English furniture, 1690-1820, £1,000-£30,000.* PARK: Easy. TEL: 071 736 2387. SER: Valuations; restorations. FAIRS: Harrogate. VAT: Spec.

Goodwin and Wadhwa
590 King's Rd. (P Goodwin and M Wadhwa) Open 10-6, Sat. 11-3. SIZE: Medium. *STOCK: English and continental furniture, 1600-1900, £500-£10,000; decorative European and Oriental works of art and paintings, 1500-1900; globes and scientific instruments, 1650-1880; both £200-£10,000.* PARK: Easy. TEL: 071 384 2169. SER: Valuations; restorations; buys at auction. FAIRS: Olympia. VAT: Stan/Spec.

Imogen Graham
585 King's Rd. Est: 1969. Open 10-5.30. SIZE: Large. *STOCK: Furniture, decorative items, oil paintings, watercolours, samplers.* TEL: 071 736 2465. VAT: Stan/Spec.

Robert Gray Antiques
at Carless and Gray, 608 King's Rd. Open 10-5.30. *STOCK: Decorative antiques and textiles.* TEL: 071 731 3837. FAIRS: Olympia; Decorative Antiques and Textiles.

S.W.6 continued

Judy Greenwood
657 Fulham Rd. Est: 1978. Open 10-5. *STOCK: Textiles including paisleys, quilts, curtains; decorative furniture.* TEL: 071 736 6037.

Gregory, Bottley and Lloyd
8-12 Rickett St. Est: 1850. SIZE: Medium. *STOCK: Mineral specimens, £1-£5,000; fossils, £5-£500.* LOC: Behind West Brompton underground. PARK: Easy. TEL: 071 381 5522; home - (081) 878 5202. SER: Valuations. VAT: Stan.

Guinevere Antiques
574/580 King's Rd. Open 9.30-6, Sat. 10-6. SIZE: Large. *STOCK: Period and decorative antiques and accessories.* TEL: 071 736 2917; fax - 071 736 8267.

Han-Shan Tang Ltd
717 Fulham Rd. (C von der Burg) Open 10-6, Sat. by appointment. *STOCK: Second-hand and antiquarian books and periodicals on Chinese, Japanese, Korean and central Asian art and culture.* TEL: 071 731 2447; fax - 071 731 8009.

Nicholas Harris **BADA LAPADA**
564 King's Rd. Est: 1971. Open 10-6, Sat. 10.30-1.30. *STOCK: Silver and objets d'art; jewellery by prior appointment.* TEL: 071 371 9711; fax - 071 371 9537. SER: Valuations; restorations (silver). VAT: Stan/Spec.

Hollingshead and Co
783 Fulham Rd. (D Hollingshead) Est: 1946. Open 10-1 and 2-5. CL: Sat. p.m. SIZE: Medium. *STOCK: Marble and wood mantelpieces, grates, fenders, fire irons, chandeliers, £50-£20,000.* Not stocked: Furniture. PARK: Easy. TEL: 071 385 8519. SER: Valuations; restorations (marblework and wood mantelpieces). VAT: Stan.

House of Mirrors
597 King's Rd. (Z Wigek) Est: 1960. Open 10-6. *STOCK: Mirrors.* TEL: 071 736 5885.

S.W.6 continued

Peter Hurford
618-620 King's Rd. Open 10-5.30. *STOCK: Continental and British decorative objects and furniture, screens and mirrors, 18th and 19th C, £100-£10,000.* TEL: 071 731 4655. VAT: Spec.

P.L James
681 Fulham Rd. Open 7-5. CL: Sat. *STOCK: Gilded mirrors, English and Oriental lacquer, period objects and furniture.* TEL: 071 736 0183. SER: Restorations (painted and lacquer furniture, gilding, carving). VAT: Stan/Spec.

Patrick Jefferson
561 Kings Rd. Est: 1979. Open 9.30-6, Sat. 10-5. SIZE: Medium. *STOCK: Fine 18th-19th C English furniture, works of art, decorative items, garden statuary and curiosities.* PARK: Easy. TEL: 071 371 9088. SER: Valuations; restorations (furniture including upholstery and gilding); buys at auction (furniture and works of art). FAIRS: Olympia; Northern. VAT: Stan/Spec.

Peter Jeffs at Nicholas Harris
564 King's Rd. Est: 1974. Open daily. SIZE: Medium. *STOCK: Silver and decorative art, 19th-20th C, £100-£10,000.* LOC: On corner King's Rd and Holmead Rd. PARK: Easy. TEL: 071 371 9711. SER: Restorations (silver); buys at auction (as stock). FAIRS: Olympia. VAT: Stan/Spec.

The Kilim House
951-953 Fulham Rd. Est: 1989. Open 10-6, Sat. 10-5 and by appointment. SIZE: Medium. *STOCK: Kilims from Asia Minor and beyond, and E. Europe, £50-£8,000.* LOC: Near Putney Bridge Tube, at end of Fulham Rd. PARK: Easy. TEL: 071 731 4912; fax - same.

Eric King Antiques
11 Crondace Road. Est: 1966. Open by appointment. *STOCK: Decorative furniture and accessories, 18th-20th C.* PARK: Easy. TEL: 071 731 2554.

L and E Kreckovic
62 Fulham High St. Open 9.30-5, Sat. 10-5 or by appointment. *STOCK: 19th C furniture especially leather chairs.* TEL: 071 736 0753.

The Lamp Gallery
355 New King's Rd. (G Jones) Est: 1986. Open 10-6. SIZE: Medium. *STOCK: Interior lighting including art nouveau and art deco lamps, 1860-1960, £10-£1,000+.* LOC: 400yds. from junction with Fulham High St. PARK: Side streets. TEL: 071 736 6188. SER: Valuations. VAT: Stan.

M Lassota
596 King's Rd. Open 10-5. *STOCK: Victorian, Regency, Hepplewhite furniture.* TEL: 071 736 3932.

S.W.6 continued

Lunn Antiques
86 New King's Rd. (S Lunn) Est: 1975. Open 10-6.30. *STOCK: Victorian and Edwardian hand worked linens, sheets, bedspreads, pillowcases, tablecloths, Oriental embroidery, pre-war clothing, some early lace and costume.* TEL: 071 736 4638. VAT: Stan.

Magpies
152 Wandsworth Bridge Rd, Fulham. Open 10--6. SIZE: 5 dealers. *STOCK: China, glass, kitchenalia, collectables and furniture.* TEL: 071 736 3738.

Michael Marriott Ltd
588 Fulham Rd. Est: 1979. Open 9-5.30. CL: Sat. p.m. and Sun. except by appointment. SIZE: Large. *STOCK: English furniture, 1700-1850, £400-£15,000; leather upholstery, £250-£1,500; prints, £30-£800.* LOC: Junction of Fulham Rd. and Parsons Green Lane. PARK: Easy. TEL: 071 736 3110/736 0568. SER: Valuations; restorations. FAIRS: Olympia, Kensington, Kenilworth (Spring and Autumn), London Antique Dealers' (Cafe Royal). VAT: Stan/Spec.

David Martin-Taylor Antiques
56 Fulham High St. Open 9.30-5.30. CL: Sat. SIZE: Medium. *STOCK: Decorative furniture and unusual items, 18th-19th C; early English and American wickers.* LOC: Off Putney Bridge between Fulham Rd. and New King's Rd. PARK: Easy. TEL: 071 731 4135. SER: Hire. VAT: Stan/Spec.

Mark Maynard Antiques
651 Fulham Rd. Est: 1977. Open 10-5, Sun. by appointment. SIZE: Medium. *STOCK: Decorative items, £25-£300.* LOC: Near Fulham Broadway underground. PARK: Easy. TEL: 071 731 3533; home - 071 373 4681. VAT: Stan/Spec.

Mill House Antiques
at Carless and Gray, 608 King's Rd. (R. and J Carless) Est: 1978. Open 10-5.30. *STOCK: Decorative antiques and textiles.* TEL: 071 731 3837. FAIRS: Olympia; Decorative Antique and Textiles.

Ian Moggach Antiques
723 Fulham Road. Open 9.30-5.30. CL: Sat. SIZE: Large. *STOCK: 19th C, furniture, including desks, writing tables and bookcases, French marble fireplaces, £400-£2,500.* TEL: 071 731 4883.

Sylvia Napier Ltd
554 King's Rd. Est: 1972. Open 10-6. SIZE: Large. *STOCK: Furniture - decorative European, 18th-19th C, £100-£15,000; decorative Oriental, 17th-19th C, £200-£7,000; garden, 19th C, £150-£7,000; objets d'art.* LOC: Near junction

Sylvia Napier Ltd. continued

with Lots Rd. PARK: Easy. TEL: 071 371 5881; home - 071 221 7247. SER: Restorations. FAIRS: Olympia. VAT: Stan/Spec.

New King's Road and Hurlingham Gallery

297 New King's Rd. (A Levy) Est: 1985. Open 9.30-6.30, Sat. 10-5. SIZE: Medium. *STOCK: British and European oils and watercolours, 19th to early 20th C, £200-£55,000.* PARK: Easy. TEL: 071 731 4363; home - 731 4111; mobile - (0836) 373404. SER: Valuations; restorations (cleaning, framing); buys at auction (oils and watercolours). VAT: Spec.

Old Pine

594 King's Rd. (S. and R Rippingale) Open 10-5.30. *STOCK: Painted and pine furniture.* TEL: 071 736 5999. VAT: Stan.

Old World Trading Co

565 King's Rd. (R.J Campion) Est: 1970. Open 9.30-6. *STOCK: Fireplaces, chimney pieces and accessories, chandeliers, mirrors, furniture including decorative, works of art.* TEL: 071 731 4708; fax - 071 731 1291.

Paul Orssich

117 Munster Rd, Fulham. Open 10-6, Sat. and other times by appointment. *STOCK: Antiquarian maps and books, especially on Hispanic studies, 16th-19th C, from £25; art deco illustrations, 1898-1935, £15-£500.* TEL: 071 736 3869.

Osterley Antiques Ltd

595 King's Rd. Est: 1960. Open 9.30-5.30. SIZE: Large. *STOCK: Furniture, 18th C.* TEL: 071 731 0334. SER: Valuations; restorations. VAT: Stan/Spec.

Pageant Antiques

122 Dawes Rd, Fulham. (A Kopriva) Est: 1974. Open 10-5. SIZE: Medium. *STOCK: Life-size period sculpture, fine chimney pieces.* LOC: Off North End Rd. PARK: Easy. TEL: 071 385 7739.

M Pauw Antiques

606 King's Rd. Est: 1985. SIZE: Medium. *STOCK: English and continental furniture, 18th and 19th C; decorative items, lighting fixtures, £500-£20,000.* PARK: Easy. TEL: 071 731 4022; fax - 071 731 7356. VAT: Stan/Spec.

The Pine Mine (Crewe-Read Antiques)

100 Wandsworth Bridge Rd, Fulham. (D Crewe-Read) Est: 1971. Open 9.45-5.45, Sat. till 4.30. SIZE: Large. *STOCK: Georgian and Victorian pine, Welsh dressers, farmhouse tables, chests of drawers, boxes and some architectural items.* LOC: From Sloane Sq., down King's Rd., into New King's Rd., left into Wandsworth Bridge Rd. PARK: Outside. TEL: 071 736 1092. SER: Furniture made from old wood; stripping; export.

S.W.6 continued

The Pine Village

162 Wandsworth Bridge Rd. Est: 1973. Open 10-6 everyday. SIZE: Large. *STOCK: Stripped pine furniture, £15-£1,000.* LOC: West down King's Rd., into New King's Rd., turn left at Parsons Green, shop corner of Beltran Rd. PARK: Easy. TEL: 071 736 2242. VAT: Stan.

Peter Place Antiques

636 King's Rd. Usually open 9.30-5.30. *STOCK: 18th-19th C metalware, decorative items, paintings, folk art.* TEL: 071 736 9945.

Pryce and Brise Antiques

79 Moore Park Rd, Fulham. (N Pryce and J Brise) Est: 1983. Open 10-6, Sat. 10-4. CL: Mon. SIZE: Medium. *STOCK: English glass, 18th-19th C.* LOC: From King's Rd., going west, turn right before Wandsworth Bridge Rd., into Waterford Rd., shop at junction.. PARK: Easy. TEL: 071 736 1864. SER: Valuations; restorations; buys at auction (glass). VAT: Stan/Spec.

Barrie Quinn Antiques

3 & 4 Broxholme House, New King's Rd. (B.J Quinn) Est: 1968. Open 10-5.30, Sun. by appointment. SIZE: Large. *STOCK: Period and country furniture, mirrors, decorative accessories, statuary and garden items; wirework.* LOC: Nr. Parson's Green, Wandsworth Bridge Rd. PARK: Easy. TEL: 071 736 4747. VAT: Stan/Spec.

Lesley Rendall Antiques BADA

572 Kings Rd. Est: 1970. Open 9.30-6. *STOCK: Furniture, 18th to mid 19th C; decorative objects.* TEL: 071 736 2520. FAIRS: Olympia, Gold Sec. VAT: Stan/Spec.

Peter Reynolds

67 New King's Rd. Est: 1974. Open 10-5.30, Sat. 10-4. SIZE: Medium. *STOCK: Unusual decorative furniture and objects, £20-£2,000.* Not stocked: Jewellery. LOC: Nr. junction with Wandsworth Bridge Rd. PARK: Easy. TEL: 071 736 7797. VAT: Stan/Spec.

Paul Richards

16 Fulham High St. Est: 1980. Open 9.30-5.30. SIZE: Medium. *STOCK: Chandeliers, lighting and decorative furniture, light fixtures, 1800-1930.* LOC: Off Putney Bridge between end of Fulham Rd. and New King's Rd. PARK: Easy. TEL: 071 736 0976. VAT: Stan/Spec.

Richardson and Kailas Icons

65 Rivermead Court, Ranelagh Gardens. (C Richardson and M Kailas) Open by appointment. *STOCK: Icons and frescoes.* TEL: 071 371 0491.

Robin Sanders and Sons LAPADA

590 Fulham Rd. Open 10-6, Sat. 10-1. CL: Mon. *STOCK: English furniture, 1650-1800; 19th C Staffordshire pottery; 18th C glass and pictures.* TEL: 071 736 0586.

S.W.6 continued

Savile Pine
560 King's Rd. (F.S Tucker and D.M Savile) Est: 1962. Open 10-5.30. SIZE: Medium. *STOCK: Country pine furniture.* PARK: In side roads. TEL: 071 736 3625. VAT: Stan.

Sensation Ltd
66 Fulham High St. (M Fenwick) Est: 1958. Open 9-5. C: Sat. and Sun. except by appointment. SIZE: Large. *STOCK: English furniture, pottery, porcelain, silver and objets d'art, 17th-19th C; decorative items and painted furniture.* PARK: At rear. TEL: 071 736 4135; fax - 071 385 4218. SER: Valuations; restorations; buys at auction. VAT: Stan/Spec.

David Seyfried Antiques
759 Fulham Rd. Est: 1984. Open 10-6, Sat. 10.30-3.30. SIZE: Small. *STOCK: Furniture, 19th C; sofas, stools, Turkish kilims, £250-£400.* Not stocked: Silver. LOC: 130yds. west of Parsons Green Lane. PARK: Easy in side streets. TEL: 071 731 4230; home -071 736 6730. VAT: Spec.

William Sheppee
77 Waterford Rd. (W Hiley and A Cox) Est: 1989. Open 10-6, Sun. by appointment. SIZE: Small. *STOCK: Anglo-Indian and Indian furniture, 19th C, £500-£1,000; treen, £50-£250.* LOC: Off King's Rd. PARK: Easy. TEL: 071 371 7432. SER: Valuations. VAT: Stan.

George Sherlock
588 King's Rd. Est: 1968. Open 9.30-5.30. SIZE: Large. *STOCK: General antiques and decorative furniture, 1650-1900, £20-£5,000.* PARK: Easy. TEL: 071 736 3955; fax - 071 371 5179. VAT: Stan/Spec.

Shield and Allen Ltd
584 and 586 King's Rd. Est: 1968. Open 9.30-6. SIZE: Medium. *STOCK: Early furniture, works of art and paintings.* PARK: Easy. TEL: 071 736 7145. VAT: Spec.

R. and H Short
464 Fulham Rd, Fulham Broadway. (P Evanson) Est: 1933. Open 10-4. *STOCK: General antiques and furniture.* TEL: 071 385 4185.

The Singing Tree
69 New King's Rd. Est: 1975. Open 10-5.30. SIZE: Small. *STOCK: Dolls' houses and miniatures.* LOC: Fulham end of King's Rd. PARK: Easy. TEL: 071 736 4527. SER: Catalogues issued. FAIRS: All dolls, dolls' houses and doll's house accessories. VAT: Stan.

Spencer-Bowles Antiques
54 Fulham High St. (A Bowles) Open 10-7. *STOCK: Costume, linen and lace.* TEL: 071 384 1493.

S.W.6 continued

Spice
2 Wandon Rd, King's Rd. (S Dix. Resident) Open 9.30-6.30. *STOCK: Early furniture and decorative items.* TEL: 071 736 4619. SER: Export; interior design.

John Spink
14 Darlan Rd, Fulham. Open by appointment. *STOCK: English watercolours, 1720-1920.* TEL: 071 731 8292.

Thornhill Galleries Ltd
76 New King's Rd. Est: 1880. Open 10-5, Sat. 10-3. CL: Thurs. a.m. SIZE: Large. *STOCK: English and French marble, stone and wood chimney-pieces, and panelled rooms; architectural features and wood carvings, fire grates and fenders; all 17th-19th C. Decorative iron interiors and other fire accessories, 17th-20th C.* LOC: Continuation of King's Rd. Coming from Sloane Sq. shop is on right-hand side. PARK: Easy. TEL: 071 736 5830. SER: Valuations; restorations (architectural items); buys at auction (architectural items). FAIRS: T.B.A. VAT: Stan/Spec.

Through the Looking Glass Ltd
563 King's Rd. (J.J.A. and D.A Pulton) Est: 1966. Open 9.30-5.30. SIZE: Large. *STOCK: Mirrors, 18th and 19th C.* TEL: 071 736 7799. SER: Restorations. VAT: Spec.

Ferenc Toth
598A King's Rd. (F. and E Toth) Est: 1978. Open 9.30-5.30. SIZE: Medium. *STOCK: Mirrors, £50-£3,000; paintings and furniture, 18th and 19th C.* LOC: Fulham end of King's Rd., Chelsea. PARK: Easy. TEL: 071 731 2063; fax - same; home - 071 602 1771. SER: Valuations; buys at auction. VAT: Spec.

Francois Valcke
610 King's Rd. Est: 1982. Open 10-6. SIZE: Medium. *STOCK: 17th-19th C drawings, prints and oil paintings.* LOC: Past World's End. PARK: Easy. TEL: 071 736 6024; fax - 071 731 8302. SER: Restorations; framing. VAT: Spec.

Vaughan
156-160 Wandsworth Bridge Rd. (M.J Vaughan and Vaughan Ltd) Est: 1980. Open 10-5. CL: Sat. SIZE: Large. *STOCK: Decorative furniture and objects, 18th-19th C; lamps and light fittings.* PARK: Easy. TEL: 071 731 3133. VAT: Stan/Spec.

Meldrum Walker Gallery
27 Filmer Rd, Fulham. (M. and D Meldrum Walker) Open 10-6. *STOCK: 19th and 20th C oils and watercolours.* TEL: 071 385 2305. SER: Framing.

Leigh Warren Antiques
566 King's Rd. Open 10-5. *STOCK: General antiques and decorative items.* TEL: 071 736 2485.

S.W.6 continued

Whiteway and Waldron Ltd
305 Munster Rd, Fulham. (M Whiteway and G Kirkland) Est: 1976. Open 10-6, Sat. 11-4. SIZE: Large. *STOCK: Stained glass, from 1850, £20-£3,000; architectural fittings including panelling, doors, fire surrounds and ironwork, from 1750; religious antiques including candlesticks, statuary, gothic and carved church woodwork.* LOC: At junction of Lillie Rd. and Munster Rd. PARK: On forecourt for loading, or Strode Rd. TEL: 071 381 3195. SER: Restorations (stained glass); buys at auction (stained glass and architectural items). VAT: Stan.

Christopher Wray's Lighting Emporium
600-606 King's Rd. Est: 1964. Open 10-6. SIZE: Large. *STOCK: Decorative light fittings of 1880s, brass, antiques, decorative objects.* LOC: From Sloane Sq. over Stanley Bridge. PARK: Own. TEL: 071 736 8434; fax - 071 731 3507. VAT: Stan.

London S.W.7

Anglo Persian Carpet Co
6 South Kensington Station Arcade. Est: 1910. Open 9.30-6. *STOCK: Carpets and rugs.* TEL: 071 589 5457. SER: Valuations; restorations (carpets and rugs); cleaning.

Aubrey Brocklehurst **BADA**
124 Cromwell Rd. Est: 1942. Open 9-1 and 2-6, Sat. 10-1. SIZE: Medium. *STOCK: English clocks and barometers.* TEL: 071 373 0319. SER: Valuations; restorations, furniture and clock repairs; buys at auction. VAT: Spec.

Julie Collino
15 Glendower Pl, South Kensington. Est: 1971. Open 11-6, Sat. 2-6, Sun. by appointment. *STOCK: Watercolours, oils, etchings, £25-£1,000; china, £25-£500; both 19th-20th C; furniture, £50-£2,000.* LOC: Off Harrington Rd. TEL: 071 584 4733; home - 071 373 5353. FAIRS;: Olympia. VAT: Stan/Spec.

Robert Hershkowitz Ltd
94 Queens Gate. Est: 1976. Open by appointment only. *STOCK: 19th C photographs.* TEL: 071 373 8994 or (0447) 2240.

M.P Levene Ltd **BADA**
5 Thurloe Pl. Est: 1926. Open 9.30-6. CL: Sat. p.m. *STOCK: Silver, old Sheffield plate, various, all prices.* LOC: Few minutes past Harrods nr. South Kensington Station. PARK: Easy. TEL: 071 589 3755. SER: Valuations; buys at auction. VAT: Stan/Spec.

A. and H Page
66 Gloucester Rd. Open 9-5.30, Sat. 9-12. *STOCK: Silver, jewellery, objets d'art.* TEL: 071 584 7349. SER: Buys at auction.

S.W.7 continued

Michael and Margaret Parker Antiques
24 Cheval Pl. Est: 1971. Open 10-1 and 2-5; Sat. by appointment. SIZE: Medium. *STOCK: Painted and lacquer furniture and objects, 18th and early 19th C, £100-£3,000; French Provincial furniture, English fruitwood, walnut, 18th C, £1,000-£6,000.* LOC: Off Brompton Rd., opposite Harrods. PARK: Easy. TEL: 071 589 0133. VAT: Spec.

Period Brass Lights
9a Thurloe Pl, Brompton Rd. (M Beattie) Est: 1967. *STOCK: Brass reproduction and antique light fittings; suits of armour.* PARK: Meters. TEL: 071 589 8305.

M Turpin Ltd **LAPADA**
21 Manson Mews, Queen's Gate. Est: 1946. Open by appointment only. *STOCK: English and continental 18th C furniture, mirrors, chandeliers, objets d'art.* PARK: Meters. TEL: 071 373 8490/589 6524 /736 3417; fax - 071 244 6254. VAT: Spec.

Thomas Williams (Fine Art) Ltd
10 Exhibition Rd, South Kensington. Open by appointment. SIZE: Medium. *STOCK: Old and modern Master drawings, £300-£150,000.* PARK: Meters. TEL: 071 584 1113. SER: Valuations; buys at auction (paintings and drawings).

London S.W.8

Nicholas Beech
787 Wandsworth Rd. (N.A Beech) Est: 1981. Open 10-5.30, Sun. by appointment. SIZE: Medium. *STOCK: Pine furniture, Georgian, Victorian and Edwardian, £20-£1,000; decorative items, especially kitchen items.* LOC: Over Chelsea Bridge (south side), straight over roundabout. At 3rd set of traffic lights turn left, shop 100yds. on right. PARK: Easy. TEL: 071 720 8552. SER: Restorations (pine); buys at auction (pine and decorative items); pine stripping. VAT: Stan.

Capital Clocks
190 Wandsworth Rd. Est: 1969. Resident. Open 9.30-5. CL: Thurs. *STOCK: Clocks, including longcase and carriage, £300-£10,000.* LOC: 1/2 mile south of Vauxhill Bridge. PARK: Easy. TEL: 071 720 6372 (24hr.). SER: Valuations; restorations (movements and cases). VAT: Spec.

Secondhand Rose
763-765 Wandsworth Rd. (C George) Open 9.30-5.30. CL: Mon. *STOCK: Furniture, kitchenalia and collectables.* TEL: 071 498 1359.

Wagner Antiques
789 Wandsworth Rd. (D Wagner) Open 9.30-5.30. *STOCK: Pine and general antiques.* TEL: 071 720 6351.

London S.W.9

Scallywag
224 Clapham Rd, Stockwell. (J.A Butterworth) Est: 1970. Open 9.30-5.30 including Sun., Thurs. 9.30-7. SIZE: Large. *STOCK: Pine, 18th-19th C, £1-£10,000.* LOC: 200yds. from Stockwell tube station, on A3 between The Oval and Stockwell. TEL: 071 735 2444; fax - 071 735 0787. SER: Restorations (pine stripping). VAT: Stan/Spec.

London S.W.10

Antique Patchwork Quilts
20 Ifield Rd, Chelsea. (J Kasmin) Open by appointment. *STOCK: Patchwork quilts.* TEL: 071 352 0746.

Christopher Armelin Interiors
The Plaza, 535 King's Rd. Open 9.30-6. *STOCK: General antiques, decorative items and art deco pochoirs, 18th-19th C; modern customised furniture, needlepoint rugs and lamps.* TEL: 071 352 3626; fax 071 376 8300.

John Boyle and Co
40 Drayton Gdns, ABA. Open by appointment only. *STOCK: Antiquarian books - political economy, printing and the mind of Man first editions, science and medicine, English literature.* TEL: 071 373 8247.

T.F Buckle Ltd
427 King's Rd. Open 10-6. CL: Sat. *STOCK: Fireplaces.* TEL: 071 352 0952.

Jonathan Clark
18 Park Walk, Chelsea. Open 10-6.30, Sat. 11-5. *STOCK: Modern British and European paintings and sculpture.* TEL: 071 351 3555.

Furniture Cave
533 King's Rd. (R.I.G Taylor) Est: 1967. Open 10-6. SIZE: Large. *STOCK: Furniture, Victorian, pine, oak, country.* LOC: Corner of Lots Rd. PARK: In yard. TEL: 071 352 4229. SER: Restorations; shipping; forwarding. VAT: Stan/Spec. There are fifteen dealers some of whom are listed below.

Philip and R Allison
Chinese ceramics, kelim and leather seating; reproduction furniture. TEL: 071 351 6543.

B D I
Decorative English and continental furniture, 18th-19th C; architectural items, sculpture, fabrics and carpets. TEL: 071 352 9803.

Jean Brown
French furniture and objets d'art, mainly 19th C; English furniture especially upholstered, small architectural items and shop fittings. TEL: 071 352 1575.

First Floor **LAPADA**
(Brown's, June Metcalf, Woodstock, Robert Grothier, Stuart Duggan). *Furniture, art*

Furniture Cave continued

nouveau, art deco, carpets, paintings and prints. TEL: 071 352 2046/351 7232.

N J A Gifford-Mead and Miles d'Agar Antiques **LAPADA**
Architectural items including ornamental metalwork, sculpture and garden ornaments, to 19th C; rare Regency and Victorian garden seats; stained glass, fireplaces and unusual items. TEL: 071 352 9904/6143.

Kings Road Gallery
Decorative prints and books.

M S M
Country furniture, especially beds. TEL: 071 352 7305.

Anthony Outred
English and continental furniture, 17th-19th C; decorative items, light fittings and Oriental rugs. TEL: 071 352 8840.

Anthony Redmile Ltd
Unusual decorative objects and antler furniture. TEL: 071 351 3813.

William Handford Antiques
515-517 King's Rd. Est: 1974. Open 9.30-6. SIZE: Large. *STOCK: Period and decorative antiques and accessories.* LOC: World's End, Chelsea. PARK: Easy. TEL: 071 351 2768. VAT: Stan/Spec.

Hares Antiques
498 King's Rd. (J Colborne and A. Hare) Est: 1972. Open 10-6. *STOCK: Furniture especially dining tables, 18th to early 19th C, £100-£20,000; upholstery and decorative items.* TEL: 071 351 1442. SER: Valuations; restorations (upholstery); buys at auction. VAT: Spec.

Marina Henderson Gallery
11 Langton St. Open 11-6. CL: Mon. *STOCK: Theatrical and ballet design, from 1800.* TEL: 071 352 1667.

Hollywood Road Gallery
12 Hollywood Rd, Chelsea. (P. and C Kennaugh) Open 11-7. *STOCK: Oils, watercolours, decorative items, 19th-20th C, £100-£2,000.* TEL: 071 351 1973.

Hünersdorff Rare Books and Manuscripts
P.O. Box 582. ABA. Est: 1969. Open by appointment only. *STOCK: Continental books in rare editions, early printing, science and medicine, illustrated books, Latin America, horticulture.* TEL: 071 373 3899; fax - 071 370 1244.

IA Gallery
21 Chelsea Garden Mkt, Chelsea Harbour. Est: 1981. Open 9.30-5.30, Sat. by appointment. *STOCK: European Post-Impressionist and modern British and Russian paintings and watercolours, 1800-1950, £500-£50,000.* LOC: Bottom of Lots Rd. PARK: Easy. TEL: 071 351 3883; fax - 071 351 7245. SER: Valuations; buys at auction. VAT: Stan/Spec.

S.W.10 continued

Stephen Lacey Gallery
Redcliffe Sq. (S.W.H Lacey) Est: 1982. Open by appointment only. *STOCK: British and French oils, watercolours and drawings, 19th-20th C.* TEL: 071 370 7785. VAT: Spec.

Langford **LAPADA**
The Plaza, 535 King's Rd. (L.L Langford) NAG. Est: 1941. *STOCK: Ships models, antique and marine objects.* TEL: 071 351 4881; fax - 071 352 0763. SER: Valuations; restorations. VAT: Stan/Spec.

Stephen Long
348 Fulham Rd. Est: 1966. Open 9-1 and 2.15-5.30. CL: Sat. p.m. and Sun. except by appointment. SIZE: Small. *STOCK: English pottery, 18th-19th C, to £200; English painted furniture, 18th to early 19th C; toys and games, household and kitchen items, chintz, materials and patchwork, to £500.* Not stocked: Stripped pine, large brown furniture, fashionable antiques. LOC: From South Kensington along road on right between Ifield Rd. and Billing Rd. PARK: Easy. TEL: 071 352 8226. VAT: Stan/Spec.

McVeigh and Charpentier
498 King's Rd. Open 10-5.30, other times by appointment. CL: Sat. *STOCK: Furniture and objets d'art, 18th-19th C.* TEL: 071 937 6459.

McWhirter
22 Park Walk. (A.J.K McWhirter) Est: 1988. Open 9.30-6, Sat. 11-2.30. SIZE: Medium. *STOCK: Fine furniture, porcelain, lamps, textiles, decorative objects, 1700-1880.* LOC: Near St. Stephen's Hospital. PARK: Easy. TEL: 071 351 5399. SER: Valuations; buys at auction. VAT: Spec.

Park Walk Gallery
20 Park Walk, Chelsea. (J Cooper) Est: 1988. Open 10-7, Sat. 11-5. SIZE: Medium. *STOCK: Paintings, £250-£100,000; watercolours, £250-£20,000; drawings, £200-£15,000; all 19th-20th C English and Continental.* LOC: Off Fulham Rd. PARK: Easy. TEL: 071 351 0410. SER: Valuations; restorations. FAIRS: 20th C British, Park Lane; The World of Watercolours. VAT: Spec.

H.W Poulter and Son
279 Fulham Rd. Est: 1946. Open 9.30-5. CL: Sat. p.m. SIZE: Large. *STOCK: English and French marble chimney pieces, grates, fenders, fire-irons, brass, chandeliers.* PARK: Meters. TEL: 071 352 7268. SER: Restorations (marble work). VAT: Stan/Spec.

David Randolph Antiques Ltd
498 King's Rd. (Lord Rendlesham and D Randolph) Est: 1973. Open 10-6. SIZE: Large. *STOCK: Furniture, £400-£6,000; mirrors, £500-£3,500; both 18th-19th C; decorative items, 18th-20th C, £25-£2,000.* LOC: World's End.

David Randolph Antiques Ltd. continued

PARK: Easy. TEL: 071 351 1442; home - 071 381 9893. SER: Valuations; restorations (furniture, china); buys at auction (furniture). FAIRS: Olympia. VAT: Stan/Spec.

Rare Carpets Gallery
496 King's Rd, Chelsea. Est: 1963. Open 10-6. SIZE: Large. *STOCK: European and Oriental decorative carpets, tapestries.* TEL: 071 351 3296; fax - 071 376 4876. SER: Valuations; restorations; part exchange (Oriental and hand-made carpets). VAT: Stan.

Rendlesham Antiques Ltd
498 King's Rd. Est: 1970. Open 10-6, Sat. 11-2. SIZE: Medium. *STOCK: English and Continental furniture, objets d'art.* TEL: 071 351 1442.

Harriet Wynter Ltd. Arts and Sciences **BADA**
50 Redcliffe Rd. Est: 1956. Open by appointment. SIZE: Medium. *STOCK: Early scientific instruments and works of art.* TEL: 071 352 6494; fax - 071 352 9312. SER: Valuations; collection counselling; restorations (globes and instruments); film hire; catalogues. VAT: Stan/Spec.

London S.W.11

Antiques and Things
91 Eccles Rd. (Mrs V Crowther) Est: 1986. Open 10-5, Sat. 10-6. SIZE: Medium. *STOCK: Linen, lace, textiles, Victorian to Edwardian, £1-£500; china, glass, kitchenalia, 18th-19th C, £5-£500; English and French furniture, decorative items, 19th C, £20-£2,000.* Not stocked: Coins, stamps, bottles. LOC: Off Lavender Hill, near Clapham junction. TEL: 071 350 0597; home - 071 622 2081.

S.W.11 continued

Christopher Bangs BADA LAPADA

CINOA. Est: 1971. Open by appointment only. *STOCK: Domestic metalwork and metalware, works of art and decorative objects; early lighting and smoothing irons.* PARK: Easy. TEL: 071 223 5676 (24hr.); fax - 071 223 4933; mobile - 0836 333532. SER: Valuations; commission buys at auction; finder. VAT: Stan/Spec.

Christopher Antiques

173 St. John's Hill, Battersea. (C Blom) Est: 1982. Open 10-6. SIZE: Small. *STOCK: British country furniture, 1600-1850, £50-£2,000; decorative items, from £10; early domestic ironwork, from £20.* LOC: Near Clapham Junction station, just off South Circular. PARK: Easy. TEL: 071 978 5132; home - 081 979 2717. FAIRS: Brocante. VAT: Stan/Spec.

Tony Davis plc

23 Battersea Rise. Est: 1955. Open 11-4. CL: Mon. SIZE: Large. *STOCK: Furniture, bric-a-brac, books, pictures, Victorian and Edwardian items.* LOC: Near Clapham junction. TEL: 071 228 1370/1. SER: Buys at auction (worldwide).

Eccles Road Antiques

60 Eccles Rd, Battersea. (H Rix) Open 10-5. *STOCK: General antiques, pine furniture and smalls.* TEL: 071 228 1638.

S.W.11 continued

Just a Second Antiques Ltd

27 Battersea Rise. (J Bastillo) Open by appointment. *STOCK: Furniture, Georgian, Victorian and Edwardian, silver, china, general antiques, £10-£1,500.* TEL: 071 223 5341. VAT: Stan.

Keith. Old Advertising

Unit 14Northcote Rd. Antiques Market, 155a Northcote Rd., Battersea. (K Gretton) Open 10-6, Sun. 12-5. *STOCK: Advertising, signs, bottles, packaging and display.* LOC: Near Clapham Junction. PARK: Easy. TEL: 071 228 6850; home - 071 228 0741. SER: Valuations.

Northcote Road Antiques Market

155A Northcote Rd, Battersea. (H Rix) Open 10-6, Sun. 12-5. There are 30 dealers at this arcade. *STOCK: Art deco, collectables, silver, glass, furniture, lighting, textiles, linen, jewellery, old advertising.* TEL: 071 228 6850.

Howard Walwyn Antiques

Est: 1985. Open by appointment. SIZE: Small. *STOCK: English oak and country furniture, 17th-18th C, £100-£6,000; English longcase clocks and barometers, £300-£10,000.* PARK: Easy. TEL: 071 223 9332; home - same. SER: Restorations (barometers, clocks and furniture); buys at auction. VAT: Spec.

S.W.11 continued

Robert Young Antiques

68 Battersea Bridge Rd. Est: 1974. Open 10-6, Sat. 10-5. CL: Mon. SIZE: Medium. *STOCK: English oak and country furniture, 17th and 18th C, £500-£10,000; English and European treen and objects of folk art, £20-£10,000; English and European provincial pottery and metalwork, £20-£2,500.* LOC: Turn off King's Rd. or Chelsea Embankment into Beaufort St., cross over Battersea Bridge Rd., 9th shop on right. PARK: Opp. in side street. TEL: 071 228 7847. SER: Valuations; buys at auction (treen and country furniture). FAIRS: Olympia, Chelsea. VAT: Stan/Spec.

London S.W.12

The Kilim Warehouse Ltd

28A Pickets St. (J Luczyc-Wyhowska) Est: 1982. Open 10-4, and by appointment. SIZE: Medium. *STOCK: Kilims from Asia Minor and beyond, £50-£10,000.* LOC: Near Clapham South tube station and Nightingale Lane. PARK: Easy. TEL: 081 675 3122; fax - 081 675 8494. SER: Restorations; cleaning. VAT: Stan.

Twentieth Century

14 Blandfield Rd, Nightingale Lane. (M Taylor) Est: 1986. Open Thurs., Fri. and Sat. 11-6, Sun. by appointment. SIZE: Small. *STOCK: Art deco, art nouveau, arts and crafts, decorative items, £50-£100.* PARK: Easy. TEL: 081 675 6511; home - 081 673 1568. SER: Buys at auction (art deco). FAIRS: Greenwich Art Deco and Kensington Decorative Arts. VAT: Stan.

London S.W.13

Alton Gallery

72 Church Rd, Barnes. Open 10-5. CL: Wed. *STOCK: 19th-20th C British art.* TEL: 081 748 0606. SER: Framing.

Christine Bridge Antiques LAPADA

78 Castelnau, Barnes. Est: 1971. Open by appointment. SIZE: Medium. *STOCK: Glass - 18th C collectors and 19th C decorative, £50-£6,000; small decorative items - papier mâché, bronzes, needlework, ceramics.* LOC: Main road from Hammersmith Bridge. PARK: Easy. TEL: 081 741 5501; fax - same. SER: Valuations; restorations; buys at auction. FAIRS: Olympia; British International, Birmingham; Cumberland Ceramics; Decorative; City of London; West London. VAT: Stan/Spec.

Beverley Brook Antiques

29 Grove Rd, Barnes. (N McCormick) Est: 1976. Open by appointment. SIZE: Medium. *STOCK: Glass, china, silver plate.* PARK: Side roads. TEL: Home - 081 878 5656. SER: Silver re-plating and cleaning.

Campion

71 White Hart Lane, Barnes. (J Richards) Est: 1983. Open 10-1 and 2-5.30. SIZE: Small. *STOCK: Jewellery, quilts, cushions, carpets, Turkish kilims, local prints, small furniture, £5-£50.* LOC: Along river from Barnes High St., turn left at White Hart public house. PARK: Easy. TEL: 081 878 6688; home - same. SER: Framing.

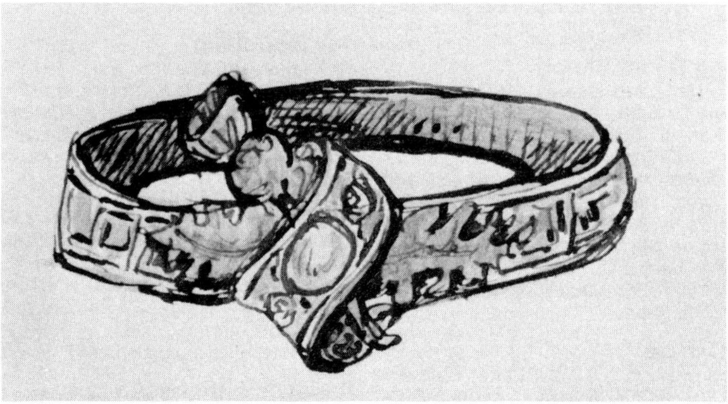

Prince Albert's sketch of a plaid and thistle bracelet, one of his wedding anniversary gifts to the Queen on 10 February 1845. The plaid was executed in turquoise enamel and the ribbon scroll which holds the thistle was set with a large pearl. The writing is the Queen's. ROYAL ARCHIVES, WINDSOR CASTLE
From ***Jewellery 1789-1910 — The International Era,*** Volume II, by Shirley Bury, published by the **Antique Collectors' Club** in 1991. £47.50 each volume.

S.W.13 continued

Simon Coleman Antiques
40 White Hart Lane, Barnes. Est: 1974. SIZE: Large. *STOCK: Country furniture, oak, fruitwood, pine, French and English farm tables, all 18th-19th C.* PARK: Easy. TEL: 081 878 5037. VAT: Stan/Spec.

The Dining Room Shop
62/64 White Hart Lane, Barnes. (K Dyson) Est: 1985. Open 10-5.30, Sun. by appointment. SIZE: Medium. *STOCK: Dining room furniture, 18th-19th C, £500-£10,000; glasses, china especially dinner services; cutlery, damask and lace table linen, 19th C; associated small and decorative items.* LOC: Near Barnes railway bridge, turning opposite White Hart public house. PARK: Easy. TEL: 081 878 1020; home - 081 876 5212. SER: Valuations; restorations; finder. VAT: Stan/Spec.

Marilyn Garrow
6 The Broadway, White Hart Lane, Barnes. Open 10-5.30. *STOCK: European textiles.* TEL: 081 392 1655.

John Haines Antiques Ltd BADA
59 Elm Grove Rd. (J. and S.D Haines) Est: 1960. Open by appointment. SIZE: Small. *STOCK: Furniture and objects, 17th-18th C, £500-£5,000.* PARK: Easy. TEL: 081 876 4215; home - same. SER: Valuations. FAIRS: Olympia. VAT: Spec. *Trade Only.*

S.W.13 continued

David Loman Ltd
12 Suffolk Rd. ABA. Open by appointment only. *STOCK: Antiquarian books and manuscripts on Oriental travel, history, culture, linguistics.* TEL: 081 748 0254.

Joy McDonald
50 Station Rd, Barnes. Est: 1966. Resident. SIZE: Small. *STOCK: Furniture, 18th-19th C; oak, fruitwood, unusual items, large mirrors.* Not stocked: China, glass. PARK: Easy. TEL: 081 876 6184. SER: Restorations (furniture).

New Grafton Gallery
49 Church Rd, Barnes. (D Wolfers) Est: 1968. Open 10-5.30. CL: Mon. SIZE: Medium. *STOCK: British paintings and drawings, £150-£3,000.* LOC: Off Castelnau which runs from Hammersmith Bridge. PARK: Easy. TEL: 081 748 8850; home - 081 876 6294. SER: Valuations; buys at auction. VAT: Stan/Spec.

Randalls Antiques
46/52 Church Rd, Barnes. (E Appleton) Open 10-5. *STOCK: Furniture, 18th-19th C; jewellery, textiles, decorative arts.* TEL: 081 748 1858; evenings - 081 948 1260.

Remember When Ltd
6 and 7 Rocks Lane, Barnes. Est: 1975. Open 9.30-7 including Sun. *STOCK: Pine furniture.* TEL: 081 878 2817.

S.W.13 continued

Jeremy Seale Antiques
56 White Hart Lane, Barnes. Est: 1979. Open 9.30-5.30, Sat. 10-5, Sun. by appointment. SIZE: Medium. *STOCK: Furniture, 18th-19th C, £300-£6,000; decorative items, 19th C; pictures and prints, 18th-19th C; both £50-£500.* LOC: From M3 into London, just off A316 (sign to Mortlake and Barnes), White Hart Lane on right on Barnes approach. PARK: Easy. TEL: 081 876 1041. SER: Finder. VAT: Stan/Spec.

Tobias and The Angel
66-68 White Hart Lane, Barnes. (A Hughes) Est: 1985. Open 10-6. SIZE: Medium. *STOCK: Quilts and textiles, from 1820, from £100+; English pottery, 19th C, from £10+; country furniture, mainly 19th C, from £100+.* LOC: Parallel to Barnes High St. PARK: Easy. TEL: 081 878 8902; home - 0206 391003. SER: Valuations; restorations (furniture, textiles). VAT: Stan/Spec.

Wren Antiques
49b Church Rd, Barnes. (M.A Smith) Est: 1980. Open 10-5.30. CL: Mon. SIZE: Small. *STOCK: Georgian and 19th C furniture, £200-£5,000; 18th-19th C clocks, pictures, £200-£3,000; mirrors and overmantels, barometers, boxes, chandeliers, books.* LOC: Near A3003. PARK: Easy. TEL: 081 741 7841. SER: Valuations; restorations (furniture).

The Wykeham Galleries
51 Church Rd, Barnes. (R Harvie-Watt) Est: 1989. Open 10-5. CL: Mon. *STOCK: Paintings, sculptures, 20th C, £100-£500.* LOC: From Hammersmith Bridge down Castlenau. PARK: Easy. TEL: 081 741 1277.

London S.W.14

Age of Elegance
61 Sheen Lane, East Sheen. (S Elliott) Open 11-7, Mon. 10-5, Fri. 10-7, Sat. 11-6, or by appointment. CL: Wed. *STOCK: Linen, lace, china, glass, cutlery and costume jewellery.* TEL: 081 876 0878.

Dixon's Antique Centre
471 Upper Richmond Rd West, East Sheen. Est: 1981. Open 10-5.30, Sun. 1.30-5.30. CL: Wed. SIZE: Large. There are 25 dealers at this centre. *STOCK: Furniture, porcelain, Doulton, clocks, art glass, silver, art deco, books, pictures, Victorian lace.* LOC: South Circular Rd. between Richmond and Putney. PARK: Easy. TEL: 081 878 6788.

Hallam Gallery
325 Upper Richmond Rd West, East Sheen. (J Adams and P Hallam) Est: 1985. Open 10-5.30. CL: Mon. SIZE: Medium. *STOCK: Victorian watercolours, £800-£5,000; modern British figurative paintings, £200-£5,000.* LOC: South Circular, midway Putney and Richmond. PARK:

Hallam Gallery continued

Easy. TEL: 081 876 2573. SER: Valuations; restorations; buys at auction (paintings). VAT: Spec.

Helius Antiques
487-493 Upper Richmond Rd West. (Mrs M Rowlands) Est: 1965. Open 10-5, Sat. 10.30-12.45. CL: Sun. and Wed., except by appointment. SIZE: Large. *STOCK: Pedestal desks, bureaux, 18th to early 20th C writing tables, secretaires and bookcases; general antiques, decorative furniture.* LOC: On South Circular rd. PARK: Easy. TEL: 081 876 5721. VAT: Stan/Spec.

Sheen Gallery
370 Upper Richmond Rd West, East Sheen. (M.S Wardle) Open 10-6. CL: Wed. *STOCK: Watercolours, oil paintings and prints.* TEL: 081 878 1100. SER: Restorations; gilding and framing.

Yesterday's Antiques
315 Upper Richmond Rd West. (H Rau) Open 9.30-6, Sun. 9.30-5. *STOCK: Old pine and country furniture.* TEL: 081 876 7536.

London S.W.15

R.A Barnes Antiques LAPADA
26 Lower Richmond Rd. Open 10-5. CL: Sat. SIZE: Large. *STOCK: English, Oriental and continental porcelain, antiques and collectables; Wedgwood, ironstone, china, brass, copper, 19th C; art glass, Regency, Victorian and some 18th C small furniture, primitive paintings.* TEL: 081 789 3371. VAT: Stan/Spec.

The Clock Clinic Ltd LAPADA
85 Lower Richmond Rd. (P.M.L Banks and R.S Pedler, FBHI) Est: 1971. Open 9-6, Sat. 9-1. CL: Mon. *STOCK: Clocks and barometers.* TEL: 081 788 1407. SER: Valuations (as stock); restorations (as stock); buys at auction. VAT: Stan/Spec.

A. and R Dockerill Ltd
78 Deodar Rd, Putney. Est: 1880. Open 9-5.15, Sat. 10-12.30. SIZE: Large. *STOCK: French, English marble and wood chimney pieces; panelling, oak and pine.* PARK: Easy. TEL: 081 874 2101. SER: Restorations. VAT: Stan.

Harwood Antiques
24 Lower Richmond Rd, Putney. (G.M Harwood) Est: 1962. SIZE: Medium. *STOCK: Decorative items and furniture, £150-£2,500; textiles, £150-£500; mirrors, oils, watercolours and prints, £100-£550; all 18th-19th C.* LOC: Continuation of King's Rd., over Putney Bridge. PARK: Nearby. TEL: 081 788 7444.

S.W.15 continued

Jorgen Antiques
40 Lower Richmond Rd, Putney. (A.J Dolleris) Est: 1960. Open 11-5. CL: Mon. and Sat. SIZE: Large. *STOCK: English and continental furniture, 18th to early 19th C, £50-£5,000.* LOC: Between Putney Bridge and Putney Common. PARK: Easy. TEL: 081 789 7329. VAT: Spec.

Kate House
139 Lower Richmond Rd, Putney. (M Shamsa) Open 10-5. CL: Mon. *STOCK: Pine, linen, lace, china, bric-a-brac.* TEL: 081 785 9944.

A.V Marsh and Son
Vale House, Kingston Vale. Est: 1960. Open 9-6. *STOCK: Furniture, 18th to early 19th C.* TEL: 081 546 5996. VAT: Stan/Spec.

Richard Maude Tools
22 Parkfields, Putney. (R.M.C Maude) Est: 1977. Open by appointment only. SIZE: Medium. *STOCK: Woodworking tools, 18th-19th C, £5-£1,000; ornamental turning lathes, 19th C, £500-£5,000; books and old trade catalogues relating to previous items, 18th-19th C, £5-£250; medical and dental instruments; some early ironwork and keys.* LOC: 1/2 mile west of Putney High St., off Upper Richmond Rd. PARK: Easy. TEL: 081 788 2991. SER: Valuations; buys at auction. VAT: Spec.

Michael Phelps Antiquarian Books
19 Chelverton Rd, Putney. Open by appointment. *STOCK: Antiquarian books - medicine, science, technology, natural history.* TEL: 081 785 6766.

Dorothy Rose
32 Lacy Rd. Est: 1967. Open 10-6. CL: Thurs. SIZE: Small. *STOCK: Jewellery, bric-a-brac, objets d'art, general antiques.* PARK: Easy. TEL: 081 789 1410.

Serena Stapleton Antiques
75 Lower Richmond Rd, Putney. Est: 1984. Open 10-5. CL: Mon. and Sat. SIZE: Small. *STOCK: Decorative furniture, pictures, objects, 18th-19th C, £50-£5,000.* LOC: 200yds. from Putney Bridge. PARK: Easy. TEL: 081 789 4245. SER: Valuations; restorations; buys at auction. VAT: Spec.

Alan Stone Antiques
3 Wadham Rd, Putney. Open 9-6. *STOCK: General antiques.* TEL: 081 870 1606/642 6877. SER: Restorations.

Thornhill Galleries Ltd
78 Deodar Rd, Putney. Est: 1880. Open 9-5.15, Sat. 10-12.30. SIZE: Large. *STOCK: English and French marble, stone and wood chimney-pieces, English and French panelled rooms, architectural features and wood carvings, fire grates and fenders; all 17th-19th C; decorative iron interiors and other fire accessories, 17th-20th C.* LOC: Off Putney Bridge Rd., at rear of

Thornhill Galleries Ltd. continued

78 Deodor Rd. (large Georgian house). PARK: Easy. TEL: 081 874 2101/5669. SER: Valuations; restorations (architectural items); buys at auction (architectural items). FAIRS: T.B.A. VAT: Stan/Spec.

London S.W.16

S Farrelly
634 Streatham High Rd. Est: 1958. Open 9-5. CL: Wed. p.m. SIZE: Medium. *STOCK: General antiques.* PARK: In side roads. TEL: 081 764 4028. VAT: Stan/Spec.

A. and J Fowle
542 Streatham High Rd. Est: 1962. Open 9.30-7. SIZE: Large. *STOCK: General antiques, Victorian and Edwardian furniture.* LOC: From London take A23 towards Brighton. PARK: Easy. TEL: 081 764 2896. VAT: Stan/Spec.

Rapscallion Antiques Ltd
25 Shrubbery Rd, Streatham. (Mrs P Barry) Open 10-5. CL: Mon. and Wed. *STOCK: General antiques and bric-a-brac.* TEL: 081 769 8078.

William Reeves Bookseller Ltd
1a Norbury Crescent. Est: 1871. Open by appointment. SIZE: Medium. *STOCK: Books about music, 1800-1970, £1-£100.* LOC: From station under railway bridge, first left. PARK: Easy. TEL: 081 764 2108.

Streatham Traders and Shippers Market
United Reform Church Hall, Streatham High St. Est: 1973. Open Tues. 8-3. SIZE: 35 to 60 dealers. *STOCK: General small antiques.* LOC: Between the ice rink and bus garage. TEL: 059 84 596.

London S.W.17

Clifford and Roger Dade
884 Garratt Lane, Tooting. Est: 1937. Open 9.30-6, Sat. and Sun. by appointment. SIZE: Medium. *STOCK: Mahogany furniture, 18th to early 19th C, £200-£3,000.* LOC: 300yds. from Tooting Broadway tube. PARK: Easy. TEL: 081 767 5000; home - 081 330 1831. VAT: Spec. *Trade Only.*

Ted Few
97 Drakefield Rd, Resident. Est: 1975. Open by appointment. SIZE: Medium. *STOCK: Paintings and sculpture, 1700-1940, £500-£5,000.* LOC: 5 mins. walk from Tooting Bec underground station. TEL: 081 767 2314. SER: Valuations; buys at auction. VAT: Spec.

Brian R Verrall and Co
20 Tooting Bec Rd. Est: 1957. Open 10-6. SIZE: Large. *STOCK: Vintage and veteran motor cycles, motor cars.* LOC: 50yds. from Tooting

Brian R. Verrall and Co. continued

Bec underground station. PARK: Easy. TEL: 081 672 1144. SER: Valuations; buys at auction. VAT: Stan/Spec.

London S.W.18

Rodney Brooke Antiques LAPADA
P.O. Box 587. Open by appointment only. *STOCK: Decorative, rare and unusual furniture, 17th-19th C.* TEL: 081 870 7055.

S.A.G. Art Galleries
589 Garratt Lane, Wandsworth. (S.A Gaphar) Open 9-5, Sun. 12-5. *STOCK: 19th and 20th C oils, watercolours, etchings, limited edition prints.* TEL: 081 944 1404; fax - 081 947 8174.

Mr Wandle's Workshop
202 Garratt Lane, Wandsworth. (D Taylor) Open 9-5.30. *STOCK: Victorian and Edwardian fireplaces and surrounds especially cast iron.* TEL: 081 870 5873.

London S.W.19

Acanthus Antiques
171 Arthur Rd, Wimbledon Park. (I.K Von Lobkowitz and J Pol) Est: 1983. Open 9.30-1.30 and 2-5.30, Wed. and Sat. 9.30-1.30. CL: Mon. *STOCK: Pianos and accessories, 19th C to 1940, £500-£3,000; furniture, 18th-19th C, £50-£2,000; pottery, porcelain and glass, 18th-20th C, £20-£500.* LOC: 50yds. from Wimbledon Park tube station. TEL: 081 944 8404. SER: Restorations (pianos). VAT: Stan/Spec.

Adams Room Antiques Ltd LAPADA
18-20 Ridgway, Wimbledon Village. Est: 1971. Open 9.30-5. SIZE: Large. *STOCK: 18th and 19th C English and French furniture especially dining; decorative Regency chairs, silver.* LOC: 4 miles from King's Rd., Chelsea; 1 mile off Kingston by-pass, M3. TEL: 081 946 7047/947 4784. SER: Export orders arranged. VAT: Spec.

Chelsea Bric-a-Brac Shop Ltd
16 Hartfield Rd, Wimbledon. (P. and C Wirth) Est: 1960. Open 10-6. CL: Wed. SIZE: Medium. *STOCK: Furniture - antique, Victorian, pine, and shipping, 1800-1930, £20-£1,500; brass, copper, steel, £1-£500; bric-a-brac, £1-£250; all from Victorian.* Not stocked: Jewellery, weapons. LOC: Left from Wimbledon station, first turning on right, shop 100yds. on left. PARK: 100yds. TEL: 081 946 6894; home - 081 542 5509. SER: Restorations (wood and upholstery); continental export. VAT: Stan.

Clunes Antiques
9 West Pl, Wimbledon Common. Est: 1973. Open 10-5. CL: Mon. *STOCK: General small antiques, Staffordshire figures, theatricalia.* TEL: 081 946 1643.

S.W.19 continued

Hicks Gallery
2 and 4 Leopold Rd, Wimbledon. (J. Hicks) Open 10-6, Sun. and Mon. 10-4, Thurs. 10-8, Fri. 10-5, Sat. 10-7. *STOCK: English and Continental 18th-20th C oil paintings and watercolours £50-£5,000; modern British and living artists.* LOC: 1/2 mile from Wimbledon station. PARK: Easy. TEL: 081 944 7171. SER: Valuations; restorations; buys at auction. FAIRS: N.E.C., Barbican. VAT: Stan/Spec.

The Lighthouse Ltd LAPADA
67 Ridgway, Wimbledon Village. (Mrs E Kingston) Est: 1969. Open 10-5.30, Sat. 10-6. *STOCK: Oriental and continental table lamps, brass and glass chandeliers and wall lights, furniture, 18th-20th C, £600-£6,000.* PARK: Easy. TEL: 081 946 2050.

Richard Maryan and Daughters
177 Merton Rd. Est: 1966. Open 10-5. CL: Wed. p.m. and Mon. SIZE: Large. *STOCK: General antiques.* PARK: Reasonable. TEL: 081 542 5846.

Stefani Antiques
179 Kingston Rd. (K Stefani) Open 10-6. CL: Mon. *STOCK: Furniture, to 1910, £300-£1,000; jewellery, £25-£500; pottery, pictures, silver and plate.* TEL: 081 542 4696.

Mark J West - Cobb Antiques Ltd
39B High St, Wimbledon Village. Open 10-6, other times by appointment. SIZE: Medium. *STOCK: Table glass, 18th-19th C, £100-£800; decorators' items, glass, ceramics, £50-£1,000; collectors' glass, small furniture, £100-£1,000.* PARK: Easy. TEL: 081 946 2811/540 7982. SER: Valuations; buys at auction. FAIRS: Olympia.

London S.W.20

Hamilton's Corner
407A Kingston Rd. (P. and W Hamilton) Est: 1972. Open 10-5. CL: Wed. SIZE: Medium. *STOCK: Edwardian furniture; stripped pine, shipping goods, £25-£500.* LOC: From A3 at New Malden follow A298 Merton for 1 mile. PARK: Easy. TEL: 081 540 1744. VAT: Stan.

London S.E.1

Antique Warehouse
175d Bermondsey St. Open 10-5. CL: Sat. SIZE: The dealers are listed below. *STOCK: Edwardian, Victorian and shipping furniture, lighting, porcelain and glass..*

David Astley
June McDonald
Robin Boys Shipping
Victorian Antiques

S.E.1 continued

Sebastiano Barbagallo
Universal House, 294-304 St. James Rd. Est: 1985. Open by appointment. CL: Sat. SIZE: Large. *STOCK: Chinese, Indian, Tibetan and S.E. Asian antiques and crafts.* LOC: Near Elephant and Castle. PARK: Easy. TEL: 071 231 3680; home - 071 602 8563. FAIRS: Birmingham; Olympia. *Trade Only.*

Nigel A Bartlett **BADA**
67 St. Thomas St. Open 9.30-5.30. CL: Sat. *STOCK: Marble, pine and stone chimney pieces.* TEL: 071 378 7895/6; fax - 071 378 0388.

Bermondsey Antique Market
Corner of Long Lane and Bermonsey St, (Atlantic Antiques Centre Ltd.). Est: 1959. Open Fri. 5a.m.-2p.m. or by appointment. SIZE: 250 stalls. *STOCK: General antiques and collectors' items.* TEL: Enquiries - 071 351 5353.

Bermondsey Antique Warehouse
173 Bermondsey St. Est: 1974. Open 9.30-5.30. CL: Sat. and Sun. except by appointment. SIZE: Large. Below are listed the dealers at this warehouse. TEL: 071 407 2040/403 0022.

A Andrews
General antiques.
Grasvenor Antiques
General antiques.
Mr Pickwick Antiques **LAPADA**
(J Sturton) Est: 1965. *Clocks, shipping goods, general antiques.* TEL: Home - 071 599 6744. VAT: Stan.
G Viventi
General antiques.

Victor Burness Antiques and Scientific Instruments
241 Long Lane, Bermondsey. (V.G Burness) Est: 1975. Open Fri. 6am-1pm or by appointment. SIZE: Small. *STOCK: Scientific instruments, marine items, 19th C, £20-£1,500.* PARK: Easy. TEL: Home - (0732) 454591. SER: Valuations. FAIRS: Portman Hotel.

The Compactum
1 Newhams Row, Bermondsey. CL: Sat. SIZE: Large. The dealers are listed below. *STOCK: Furniture, including Art Deco, and shipping goods.* TEL: 071 357 7304.

Enfield Antiques
TMT Antiques
Ian Wilson Antiques

Oola Boola Antiques London **LAPADA**
166 Tower Bridge Rd. (R. and S Scales) Est: 1968. Open 9-5.30. CL: Sat. SIZE: Large. *STOCK: Furniture, £5-£3,000; mahogany, Victorian and Edwardian shipping goods.* TEL: 071 403 0794; home - 081 693 5050.

S.E.1 continued

Penny Farthing Antiques
177 Bermondsey St. Est: 1976. Open 10-5. CL: Sat. SIZE: Medium. *STOCK: Furniture, including shipping, £25-£1,000; longcase clocks, £200-£1,000; general small antiques and shipping items, £5-£200.* LOC: 5 mins. from Tower Bridge. PARK: Usually easy. TEL: 071 407 5171. VAT: Stan.

Tower Bridge Antique Warehouse Ltd **LAPADA**
159/161 Tower Bridge Rd. Open 9-5, Fri. 9-4. CL: Sat. *STOCK: Victorian and Georgian furniture, shipping goods.* TEL: 071 403 3660. VAT: Stan.

George Wissinger and Antonio Mendoza
166 Bermondsey St. Open 9-6. CL: Sat. SIZE: Large. *STOCK: Furniture and paintings.* TEL: 071 407 5795.

London S.E.3

Michael Silverman
PO Box 350. *STOCK: Manuscripts, autograph letters, historical documents.* TEL: 081 319 4452. SER: Catalogue available. *Postal Only.*

Vale Stamps and Antiques
21 Tranquil Vale, Blackheath. (H.J. and R.P Varnham) Est: 1952. Open 10-5.30. CL: Thurs. SIZE: Small. *STOCK: Pottery, 3000 BC-500 AD, jewellery, Roman, all £20-£200; bronzes, £50-£350; Georgian and Victorian jewellery, £25-£250.* LOC: Village centre, 100yds. from station. PARK: Nearby. TEL: 081 852 9817. SER: Valuations; buys at auction (antiquities). VAT: Stan/Spec.

Wallace Antiques Ltd
56 Tranquil Vale, Blackheath. Open 9.30-5.30. *STOCK: Furniture, including reproduction.* TEL: 081 852 2647.

London S.E.5

Davis and Davis Architectural Antiques
Arch 266Urlwin St, Camberwell. (K. and D Davis) Est: 1988. Open 9.30-6. CL: Mon. SIZE: Medium. *STOCK: Architectural furnishings, early 19th C to 1930s, £50-£500; garden furniture, unusual and interesting items.* LOC: North up Camberwell Rd. towards Elephant and Castle, turn left at junction with Walworth Rd. PARK: Easy. TEL: 071 703 6525. SER: Restorations (fireplaces); pine stripping; buys at auction (as stock).

Franklin's Camberwell Antiques Market
161 Camberwell Rd. (R Franklin) Est: 1968. Open 10-6, Sun. 1-6. SIZE: Large. There are five floors at this market. *STOCK: A range of*

Franklin's Camberwell Antiques Market continued

general antiques, furniture, brass, copper, silver, clocks, pictures, prints, architectural and garden items. LOC: 1 mile from Elephant and Castle via Walworth Rd. PARK: 50yds. behind building, outside premises on Sunday. TEL: 071 703 8089. VAT: Stan/Spec.

London S.E.6

Silver Sixpence
14 Catford Hill. (D Clark) Est: 1968. Open 10-12 and 12.30-6. CL: Mon. SIZE: Large. *STOCK: Clocks, brass fenders, stripped pine.* LOC: 2 mins. Catford Bridge railway station. PARK: Easy. TEL: 081 690 0046. SER: Stripping (pine).

R Wilkinson and Son
5 Catford Hill. Est: 1947. Open 9-5. CL: Sat. SIZE: Medium. *STOCK: Glass, especially chandeliers, 18th C and reproduction, art metal work.* LOC: Opposite Catford Bridge railway station. Entrance through Wickes D.I.Y. car park. PARK: Easy. TEL: 081 314 1080. SER: Restorations and repairs (glass, metalwork).

London S.E.7

Village Time
43 The Village, Charlton. Open 9-5.30, Sat. 9-5. CL: Thurs. SIZE: Small. *STOCK: Clocks, watches and jewellery.* LOC: B210. PARK: Easy and opposite. TEL: 081 858 2514. SER: Valuations; restorations; repairs (clocks, watches and jewellery). VAT: Stan/Spec.

Ward Antiques
267 Woolwich Rd, Charlton. (T. and M Ward) Est: 1981. Open 9.30-5.30, Sun. 10-2. SIZE: Medium. *STOCK: Victorian fireplaces, Victorian and Edwardian furniture, £50-£1,000.* LOC: From A102 M take Woolwich/Woolwich ferry turn, 100yds. from roundabout, immediately under railway bridge across the road. PARK: Easy. TEL: 081 305 0963; home - 081 461 2877/591 3451 and (0836) 231090.

London S.E.8

Antique Warehouse
9-14 Deptford Broadway, Deptford. Est: 1976. Open 10-6, Sun. 11-4. *STOCK: Furniture, 18th-20th C, £5-£5,000.* LOC: A2. PARK: Limited. TEL: 081 469 0295. VAT: Stan.

London S.E.9

R.E Rose FBHI
731 Sidcup Rd, Eltham. Est: 1976. Open 9-5. CL: Thurs. SIZE: Small. *STOCK: Clocks, 1750-1930, £50-£2,500.* LOC: A20 from London, shop on left just past fiveways traffic lights at Green Lane. PARK: Easy. TEL: 081 859 4754; home - 081 464 2653. SER: Restorations (clocks and barometers); spare parts for antique clocks, watches and barometers. VAT: Stan/Spec.

London S.E.10

Antique Mini-Market
15 Greenwich Church St. Open seven days 10-5.30. SIZE: There are 17 dealers at this market. *STOCK: Mainly antique and reproduction furniture and bric-a-brac.*

Badgers Antiques
320-322 Creek Rd, Greenwich. (P.D. and J.M Dempsey) Est: 1979. Open 9-5 including Sun., Wed. and Thurs. by appointment. SIZE: Medium. *STOCK: Victorian and Edwardian furniture, collectables, Pedigree toys, unusual items, £5-£2,000.* LOC: 2 mins. from Cutty Sark, Greenwich Pier. PARK: Nearby. TEL: 081 853 1394; home - same. SER: Valuations; restorations (leather lining, French polishing, cabinet work and upholstery); buys at auction. VAT: Stan.

Christopher Alan
114 Greenwich South St. (J Davison) Open 10-6, Sun. 11-4. *STOCK: Furniture especially Dutch pine.* LOC: A2. PARK: Easy. TEL: 081 692 4047.

The Green Parrot
2 Turnpin Lane, Greenwich. (J Randerson) Est: 1971. *STOCK: Porcelain, bric-a-brac, small furniture, stripped pine chests.* LOC: Off Greenwich Church St. TEL: 081 858 6690. VAT: Stan.

Greenwich Antique and Ironware Co
14/15 King William Walk, Greenwich. Open seven days 10-6. *STOCK: English and continental furniture; antique and reproduction garden furniture in wrought and cast iron and stone; bric-a-brac and decorative items, £20-£15,000.* LOC: 3/4 mile off A2 towards River Thames. TEL: 081 858 7557. SER: Valuations; restorations (furniture and pictures); buys at auction.

Greenwich Antiques Market
Greenwich High Rd. Est: 1972. Open Sun. 7.30-4.30; June-Sept. and every Sat. SIZE: There are 80 stalls at this market. *STOCK: A wide range of antiques and bric-a-brac.* LOC: Almost opposite railway station. PARK: Adjacent.

The Greenwich Gallery
9 Nevada St. (R.F Moy) Est: 1965. Open 10-5.30. *STOCK: Mainly English oil paintings and watercolours, 18th C to 1950.* TEL: 081 365 1666. SER: Restorations; framing; exhibitions. VAT: Spec.

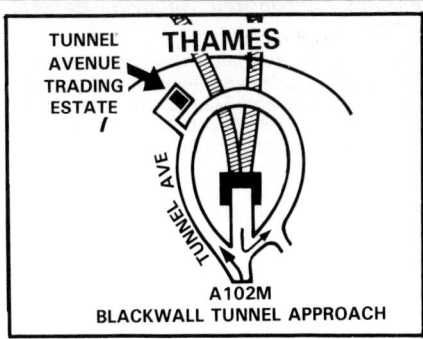

S.E.10 continued

Lamont Antiques Ltd. LAPADA
Tunnel Avenue Antique Warehouse, Tunnel Avenue Trading Estate, Greenwich. (N Lamont and F Llewellyn) Open 9-5.30. CL: Sat. SIZE: Large. *STOCK: Architectural fixtures and fittings, bars, stained glass; pub mirrors and signs; shipping furniture, all £5-£25,000.* PARK: Own. TEL: 081 305 2230; fax - 081 305 1805. SER: Container packing.

Peter Laurie Antiques
28 Greenwich Church St. Open 10.30-5.30 including Sun. *STOCK: Curiosities, nautical items, pine, weapons, scientific instruments.* TEL: 081 853 5777.

The Warwick Leadlay Gallery
5 Nelson Rd, Greenwich. Est: 1973. Open 9.30-5.30, Sun. and Bank Holidays, 11-5.30. SIZE: Large. *STOCK: Antiquarian prints, maps and illustrated books, 17th-19th C.* LOC: 2 mins. walk from Cutty Sark. PARK: Nearby. TEL: 081 858 0317; home - 081 852 7484. SER: Valuations; restorations, cleaning, colouring; mounting, framing. VAT: Stan.

Main Street Antiques
24 Woolwich Rd. (B Sessacar) Open 10-6 including Sun. CL: Thurs. *STOCK: Victorian pine and fireplaces.* TEL: 081 305 1971.

S.E.10 continued

A Polly
26 Greenwich Church St. *STOCK: Furniture, clocks.* TEL: 081 858 4048. VAT: Spec.

Relcy Antiques
9 Nelson Rd, Greenwich. (R Challis) Est: 1958. Open 10-6. CL: Sun. except by appointment. SIZE: Large. *STOCK: English furniture, especially bureaux and bookcases, £50-£15,000; English and continental pictures, especially marine and sporting, £20-£5,000; instruments and marine items, ships' heads, sextants, telescopes, models, £20-£15,000, all 18th and 19th C.* Not stocked: Reproduction and art deco. LOC: 3/4 mile off A2 towards River Thames. TEL: 081 858 2812. SER: Valuations, restorations (furniture and pictures); buys at auction (Georgian and Victorian furniture, pictures). VAT: Stan/Spec.

Rogers Turner Books Ltd
22 Nelson Rd, Greenwich. Est: 1975. Open 10-6. *STOCK: Antiquarian books especially on clocks and scientific instruments.* TEL: 081 853 5271/Paris (010 33) 13912 1191. SER: Buys at auction (British and European); catalogues available.

S.E.10 continued

South London Antique and Book Centre
18-19 Stockwell St, Greenwich. Open Wed. and Thurs. 10-6, Sat. and Sun. 9-5. *STOCK: Books, records, printed ephemera, some furniture, general antiques and collectables.* TEL: 081 853 2151.

Spread Eagle Antiques
8 Nevada St. (R.F Moy) Est: 1954. Open 10-5.30, including Sun. SIZE: Large. *STOCK: Books, period costume, curios, china, bric-a-brac, prints, postcards.* Not stocked: Furniture. LOC: A202. From London follow A2, then turn left at Deptford - or follow riverside road from Tower Bridge. PARK: Easy. TEL: 081 305 1666. SER: Valuations; restorations (furniture, china, pictures). VAT: Stan/Spec.

Spread Eagle Antiques
1 Stockwell St. (R.F Moy) Est: 1954. Open 10-5.30. CL: Thurs. p.m.. SIZE: Large. *STOCK: Furniture, pictures and decorative items, 18th-19th C.* PARK: Easy. TEL: 081 305 1666; home - 081 692 1618. SER: Valuations; restorations (pictures, furniture). VAT: Stan/Spec.

Stuart Antiques
12-14 Greenwich Church St. Open 10-6. CL: Sun. except by appointment. *STOCK: Small English, Oriental and continental furniture; interior decoration pieces, 18th-19th C; bric-a-brac, prints and pictures, soft furnishings, £20-£10,000.* LOC: 3/4 mile off A2 towards River Thames. TEL: 081 858 1975. SER: Valuations; restorations (furniture and pictures); buys at auction.

Robert Whitfield Antiques LAPADA
Tunnel Avenue Antique Warehouse, Tunnel Avenue Trading Estate, Greenwich. Open 10-5. CL: Sat. *STOCK: Edwardian, Victorian and secondhand furniture, especially bentwood chairs.* TEL: 081 305 2230; fax - 081 305 1805. SER: Container packing.

London S.E.11

John Speed (Maps)
33c Chester Way, Kennington. Est: 1972. Open by appointment only. *STOCK: Maps, £10-£2,000; atlases, travel and topographical books, £10-£1,000.* TEL: 071 820 1639 or (0424) 812200.

London S.E.13

Robert Morley and Co Ltd BADA
34 Engate St, Lewisham. Est: 1881. Open 9-5. *STOCK: Pianos, harpsichords, clavichords, spinets, virginals.* TEL: 081 318 5838; fax - 081 297 0720. SER: Restorations (musical instruments). VAT: Stan.

S.E.13 continued

Whitworth and O'Donnell Ltd
282 Lewisham High St. (A O'Donnell) Est: 1950. Open 10-5. CL: Thurs. SIZE: Medium. *STOCK: Jewellery, £10-£500.* TEL: 081 690 1282. SER: Restorations (jewellery). VAT: Stan.

London S.E.15

Peter Allen Antiques Ltd. World Wide Antique Exporters LAPADA
17-17a Nunhead Green, Peckham. Est: 1966. Open 8-5. CL: Sat. SIZE: Large. *STOCK: Fine Victorian furniture.* TEL: 071 732 1968.

G Austin and Sons Ltd
11-23 Peckham Rye. (H., A., D. and V Austin) Est: 1870. Open 8.30-5. CL: Thurs. p.m. SIZE: Large. *STOCK: Furniture, silver, porcelain, pictures, glass, books.* PARK: Easy. TEL: 071 639 3163. SER: Free delivery up to 20 miles. VAT: Stan/Spec.

A Fagiani
30 Wagner St. Est: 1965. Open 8-1 and 2-6, Sat. 8-1. *STOCK: Bookcases, pedestal desks.* LOC: Off Kent Rd. and Ilderton Rd. TEL: 071 732 7188. SER: Valuations; restorations (furniture); French polishing. VAT: Stan.

London S.E.19

Crystal Palace Collectors Market
Jasper Rd, Westow Hill, Crystal Palace. Open 9.30-4, Sun. 11-3. CL: Mon. and Tues. SIZE: Approximately 50 stalls selling. *STOCK: a wide range of general antiques especially collectables.* TEL: 081 761 3735.

London S.E.20

Black Cat
202 High St, Penge. (B Aust) Open 10-6. CL: Wed. *STOCK: Furniture, 19th C; general antiques.* LOC: Opposite Kent House Rd., Beckenham. TEL: 081 778 4230.

London S.E.21

Acorn Antiques
111 Rosendale Rd, West Dulwich. (Mrs G Kingham) Open 10-6.30, Sat. 10-5.30. *STOCK: Jewellery, china, glass, pictures, silver and plate, some furniture including pine, fire irons and fenders.* TEL: 081 761 3349.

London S.E.22

Collectors' Corner - Militaria
1 North Cross Rd, East Dulwich. (J.H Joslyn) Est: 1968. Open by appointment only. *STOCK: Wings and insignia; U.S.A. and German military items; helmets, badges, medals, uniforms, reference books.* Not stocked: Guns, firearms. LOC: From Victoria, No.185 bus. From Elephant and Castle No.12 to Upland Rd. PARK: Easy. TEL: 081 693 6285. SER: Film and T.V. suppliers.

London S.E.23

Bygone Bathrooms
39 Honour Oak Park, Brockley. (P Kelly) Open 9.30-6. *STOCK: Victorian and Edwardian bathrooms and fittings.* TEL: 081 291 4733.

Oddiquities
61 Waldram Park Rd, and 20 Sunderland Rd., Forest Hill. (Mrs S.A Butler) Est: 1966. Open 10-6, Sat. 10-4. CL: Sun. except by appointment and Thurs.. SIZE: Medium. *STOCK: Oil lamps, gas and electric light fitments, 1800-1930; fire furnishings, 1780-1920; all £20-£500; general antiques, 1800-1920, £15-£1,000.* Not stocked: Coins, stamps, medals, jewellery. LOC: On South Circular Rd., between Catford and Forest Hill. PARK: Opposite. TEL: 081 699 9574. VAT: Stan.

Reubens
44 Honour Oak Park, Brockley. (R.E Reubens) Est: 1960. Open 11-6. CL: Sat. SIZE: Medium. *STOCK: Tribal weapons, shields and curios, mainly 19th C, £20-£500; electrical items, mechanical bygones, scientific instruments, occasional musical items, 19th C.* LOC: 200yds. from Honour Oak station. PARK: Easy. TEL: 081 291 1786; home - same. SER: Finder. FAIRS: Ardingly, Newark, Peterborough. VAT: Stan.

London S.E.26

Abbott Antiques and Country Pine (formerly Olwen Carthew)
109 Kirkdale. Est: 1972. Open 10-5.30, Thurs, 10-3, Sat. 10-5, Sun. 1-5. *STOCK: Victorian and Edwardian furniture, country pine and kitchen items.* LOC: 1/2 mile from South Circular Rd. at Forest Hill. TEL: 081 699 1363. VAT: Stan.

David E Green Gallery
188 Dartmouth Rd. Est: 1972. CL: Mon. *STOCK: Fine early English watercolours and drawings.* TEL: 081 699 5461. SER: Restorations; framing and mounting, commissions undertaken. VAT: Stan/Spec.

Hillyers
301 Sydenham Rd. Est: 1952. Open 8.30-4, Sat. 8.30-2. CL: Wed. SIZE: Small. *STOCK: Furniture, silver, plate, porcelain, glass, books, bric-a-brac.* PARK: Easy. TEL: 081 778 6361; home - 081 777 2506. SER: Valuations. VAT: Stan/Spec.

S.E.26 continued

Kirkdale Pianos
251 Dartmouth Rd. Open 9.30-6. *STOCK: Pianos.* TEL: 081 699 1928. SER: Export.

Vintage Cameras Ltd — LAPADA
254 and 256 Kirkdale, Sydenham. (J Jenkins) Est: 1968. Open 9-5. SIZE: Large. *STOCK: Vintage cameras, 1840-1950, £50-£5,000; scientific instruments, 18th C to date, £50-£200; general photographica, 1840-1950, £5-£50, images, £5-£500.* LOC: Near South Circular Rd. PARK: Nearby. TEL: 081 778 5841/5416. SER: Valuations. VAT: Stan.

London E.1

Cutler Street Antique Market
Goulston St, (Atlantic Antiques Centres Ltd.). Open Sun. only 7a.m. to 2p.m. *STOCK: Gold, silver, jewellery, gems, coins and stamps.* LOC: Aldgate end of Goulston St. TEL: Enquiries - 071 351 5353.

London E.2

George Rankin Coin Co. Ltd
325 Bethnal Green Rd. Open 10-5. *STOCK: Coins, medals, medallions and jewellery.* TEL: 071 739 1840/729 1280; fax - 071 729 5023.

St. Peters Organ Works
St. Peters Close, Warner Pl. (J.P Mander and I Bell) Est: 1935. CL: Sat. SIZE: Large. *STOCK: Antique pipe organs.* LOC: Opposite children's hospital, Hackey Rd. PARK: Own. TEL: 071 739 4747. SER: Valuations; restorations. VAT: Stan.

London E.4

Albert and Victoria
Station Approach, Station Rd., Chingford. (S Salter) Est: 1972. Open 10-4, Fri. and Sat. 10-6. CL: Mon. and Thurs. SIZE: Small. *STOCK: General antiques, handworked linen, fashion clothes and accessories, 19th-20th C, £5-£500.* LOC: In forecourt of North Chingford railway station. PARK: Easy. TEL: 081 529 6361.

Gardiner Antiques
1 The Broadway. Open 9.30-5. *STOCK: General antiques.* TEL: 081 527 0182.

London E.5

Hoffman — LAPADA
251 Evering Rd. (J.E Hoffman) Est: 1966. Open by appointment. *STOCK: English and continental clocks and barometers, 17th-19th C, from £200; period furniture.* PARK: Easy. TEL: 081 806 6638. SER: Valuations. VAT: Stan/Spec.

London E.8

Curious Grannies
2 Middleton Rd, Hackney. (A. and J O'Kelly)

Curious Grannies continued

Est: 1974. Open Sat. 10-6, other days by appointment. SIZE: Medium. *STOCK: Boxes - caddies, sewing, writing and snuff, £100-£300; musical instruments mainly plucked string, £250-£750; wooden carvings, torcheres, face screens, £500-£1,000; all 17th-19th C.* LOC: Off Kingsland Rd., continuation of Bishopsgate. PARK: Easy. TEL: 071 254 7074; home - same. SER: Valuations; restorations (exceptional instruments only); buys at auction (as stock).

London E.10

J.C. Antiques

12 Warwick Terrace, corner of Halford Rd. (S.A Logie) Est: 1975. Open 10-6.30, Sun. 10-1. SIZE: Large. *STOCK: General antiques, period and pre-1870.* LOC: On A104 out of London at Whipps Cross. PARK: Easy. TEL: 081 539 4275 or (0376) 43467.

London E.11

K.N. and P Blake - Old Cottage Antiques

8 High St, Wanstead. Est: 1920. Open Thurs. and Fri. 10.30-5.30. SIZE: Medium. *STOCK: Furniture, pre 1840; paintings, 19th and 20th C.* LOC: Near Wanstead station and Snaresbrook. TEL: 081 989 2317/504 9264. SER: Valuations; buys at auction. VAT: Stan/Spec.

London E.12

Liza Doolittles

20 Station Rd, Manor Park. (Mrs E Rose) Open 9-6. *STOCK: General antiques.* TEL: 081 514 8382.

London E.14

San Fairy Ann

110 Salmon Lane. (Mr. and Mrs J McDermott) Est: 1977. SIZE: Small. *STOCK: General antiques, to 1950's, £50-£500; glass.* LOC: Just off Commercial Rd., between Blackwall and Rotherhithe tunnel. PARK: Easy. TEL: 071 987 5771.

London E.15

Cobblers

49 West Ham Lane. (J Levinsky) Open 9-6. *STOCK: General antiques and bric-a-brac; old gold and jewellery.* TEL: 081 519 8237.

Serendipity Emporium

18A-20 Leytonstone Rd, Stratford. (Mr. and Miss Stewart) Est: 1988. Open 10-6. CL: Thurs. SIZE: Small. *STOCK: Art deco and collectors' items, £5-£500.* LOC: Near Stratford underground. TEL: 081 519 3240/534 7883. SER: Buys at auction. VAT: Stan.

London E.17

Antique City

98 Wood St. Est: 1978. Open 9.30-5.00. CL: Thurs. and Sun., except by appointment. SIZE: Large. *STOCK: General antiques, 19th C, £5-£500.* PARK: In side road opposite. TEL: 081 520 4032. *Trade Only.*

Georgian Village Antiques Market

100 Wood St, Walthamstow. Est: 1972. Open 10-5. CL: Thurs.. SIZE: 10 shops. *STOCK: 19th C furniture, clocks, barometers, porcelain, postcards, collectables, jewellery, country items, brass, copper, stamps, violins.* LOC: 50yds. from Dukes Head. PARK: Adjacent. TEL: 081 520 6638.

Georgiana's Antiques

132-134 Palmerston Rd, Walthamstow. (G.P Webb) Open 10-5. CL: Wed. *STOCK: Victorian and Edwardian furniture and china.* TEL: 081 520 7015.

The Junk Shop

101 Wood St, Walthamstow. (K.A.C Yardley) Est: 1968. Open 9-5.30. CL: Sun. except by appointment. *STOCK: Trade furniture, small porcelain, jewellery, silver, linen, period costume, pine (unstripped), small glass cabinets, books, art deco.* PARK: Easy. TEL: 081 521 0014.

London E.18

Simply Capital

33 Victoria Rd, South Woodford. Open 10-6. *STOCK: Pine including reproduction, satinwood; Victorian fireplaces, surrounds, smalls.* TEL: 081 530 6229. SER: Installations (fireplaces).

London E.C.1

City Clocks

31 Amwell St. (J Rosson. FBHI) Est: 1960. Open 8.30-6. SIZE: Medium. *STOCK: Clocks, watches, some furniture, 18th-19th C, £100-£7,000.* PARK: Easy. TEL: 071 278 1154. SER: Valuations; restorations (clocks and watches); buys at auction. VAT: Stan.

Eldridge London

99-101 Farringdon Rd. (B Eldridge) Est: 1953. Open 10-5, Sat. 10-1. SIZE: Large. *STOCK: Furniture, decorative items.* PARK: Easy. TEL: 071 837 0379. VAT: Stan/Spec.

Essie C Harris **LAPADA**

63-66 Hatton Garden (office). (E.C. and D Harris) Est: 1958. Open 10-5. CL: Sat. *STOCK: Jewellery, £50-£20,000.* PARK: Nearby. TEL: 071 242 9115/242 1558. SER: Valuations. FAIRS: Basle, Switzerland and Munich, Germany. VAT: Stan/Spec.

E.C.1 continued

Hirsh Fine Jewels **LAPADA**
Diamond House, Hatton Garden and 10 Hatton Garden. (A Hirsh) Open 10-6. *STOCK: Fine jewellery and objets d'art.* TEL: 071 405 6080/404 4392 (24hrs.).

R Holt and Co. Ltd
98 Hatton Garden. Est: 1948. Open 9.30-5.30. CL: Sat. *STOCK: Chinese artifacts.* TEL: 071 405 0197/405 5286. SER: Valuations; restorations (gem stones); gem stone cutting; gem testing; bead stringing; holistic crystals.

House of Buckingham (Antiques) **LAPADA**
113-117 Farringdon Rd. (B.B White) Est: 1970. Open 9-6. *STOCK: Boxes, clocks, furniture, brass, nautical goods.* TEL: 071 278 2013. VAT: Stan/Spec.

Joseph and Pearce Ltd **LAPADA**
63-66 Hatton Garden. Est: 1896. Open by appointment. *STOCK: Jewellery, 1800-1960, £100-£2,500.* LOC: City. TEL: 071 405 4604/7; fax - 071 242 1902. VAT: Stan/Spec. *Trade Only.*

R.I McKay
88/90 Hatton Garden. Est: 1951. Open by appointment only. SIZE: Small. *STOCK: Jewellery, all periods, from £100.* LOC: Centre

R.I McKay continued

of Hatton Garden. PARK: Easy and multi-storey nearby. TEL: 071 405 7544. VAT: Stan/Spec. *Trade Only.*

Priory Antiques
45 Cloth Fair, West Smithfield. (B Heath and P Timothy) Est: 1975. Open 10-4. CL: Sat. and Mon. SIZE: Small. *STOCK: Jewellery and silver, Victorian to 1950's, £50-£3,000.* LOC: Near St. Bartholomew's Church Hospital and West Smithfield market. PARK: Easy. TEL: 071 606 9060. SER: Valuations; restorations. VAT: Stan/Spec.

A.R Ullmann Ltd
10 Hatton Garden. (J.S Ullmann) Est: 1939. Open 9-6. CL: Sat. SIZE: Small. *STOCK: Jewellery, gold, silver and diamond; silver and objets d'art.* LOC: Very close to Farringdon and Chancery Lane tube stations. PARK: Multi-storey in St. Cross St. TEL: 071 405 1877; home - (081) 346 2546. SER: Restorations. VAT: Stan/Spec.

C.J Vander (Antiques) Ltd
Dunstan House, 14a Cross St. Est: 1946. Open 9.30-1 and 2-5. CL: Sat. SIZE: Large. *STOCK: Silver, Sheffield plate.* TEL: 071 831 6741; fax - 071 831 9695. *Trade Only.*

London E.C.2

The London Architectural Salvage and Supply Co. Ltd. (LASSCo)
St. Michael's Church, Mark St (off Paul St.). Est: 1977. Open 10-5. *STOCK: Architectural relics including doors and door furniture, chimney pieces, flooring, panelled rooms, railings, ironwork, garden and street furniture, glass and ecclesiastical joinery.* TEL: 071 739 0448; fax - 071 729 6853.

Westland Pilkington
The former St. Michael's Church, Leonard St. (G Westland and P Pilkington) Est: 1986. Open 8.30-6. SIZE: Large. *STOCK: English and continental furniture and objects, £100-£20,000; sculpture and statuary, £100-£5,000; garden decoration, architectural items including panelling, £100-£50,000; all English and continental, 18th-20th C.* LOC: Off Gt. Eastern St. PARK: Easy. TEL: 071 739 8094; fax - 071 729 3620. Correspondence: The Clergy House, Mark St., London, EC2A 4ER.

London E.C.3

Ash Rare Books
25 Royal Exchange. (L Worms) Est: 1946. Open 10-5.30. CL: Sat. SIZE: Medium. *STOCK: Books, 1550-1980, £20-£10,000; maps, 1550-1850, £25-£2,000; prints, 1650-1900, £20-£1,000.* LOC: On the Threadneedle St. side of the Royal Exchange, opposite Bank of England. PARK: Nearby. TEL: 071 626 2665. SER: Buys at auction (books and maps); picture framing and mount cutting. VAT: Stan.

E.C.3 continued

Asprey (City Branch) Ltd
153 Fenchurch St. Est: 1780. Open 9-5. CL: Sat. SIZE: Small. *STOCK: Silver, clocks, jewellery.* PARK: Meters. TEL: 071 626 2160. SER: Valuations; restorations. VAT: Stan/Spec.

Halcyon Days **BADA**
4 Royal Exchange. (S Benjamin) Est: 1950. Open 10-5.30. *STOCK: 18th to early 19th C enamels, papier mâché, tôle, objects of vertu, treen, Staffordshire pottery figures, prints, unusual small Georgian furniture.* TEL: 071 629 8811; fax - 071 409 0280. FAIRS: Grosvenor House. VAT: Stan/Spec.

Nanwani and Co
2 Shopping Arcade, Bank Station, Cornhill. Est: 1958. CL: Sat. *STOCK: Precious and semi-precious stones, Oriental items, objets d'art.* TEL: 071 623 8232; fax - 071 283 2548. VAT: Stan.

Royal Exchange Art Gallery
14 Royal Exchange. Est: 1974. Open 10.30-5.15. CL: Sat. *STOCK: Oil paintings and watercolours, 19th and 20th C; especially marine and landscape, etchings.* TEL: 071 283 4400.

Searle and Co Ltd
1 Royal Exchange. Est: 1893. Open 9-5.30. SIZE: Medium. *STOCK: Silver and jewellery.* PARK: Meters. TEL: 071 626 2456. SER: Valuations; restorations; repairs. VAT: Stan/Spec.

London E.C.4

J Clarke-Hall Ltd
7 Bride Court, and 22 Bride Lane. ABA. Est: 1934. Open 10.30-6.30. CL: Sat. Bride Lane - open 12-4. SIZE: Small. *STOCK: 18th C English literature, especially Dr. Samuel Johnson, Lewis Carroll and their contemporaries; books on printing; illustrated books and 19th C prints, modern first editions, £3-£2,500.* LOC: Off Bride Lane, which is off bottom of Fleet St., near Ludgate Circus. PARK: Meters. TEL: 071 353 4116/5483. SER: Restorations (book repairs, rebinding, pictures); framing. VAT: Stan.

London N.1

Angel Arcade
116-118 Islington High St, Camden Passage. Open Wed. and Sat. Other days access available to the shops.. SIZE: Large. *STOCK: General antiques.*

Annie's Antique Clothes
10 Camden Passage, Islington. (A Moss) Open 11-5. CL: Mon. TEL: 071 359 0796.

The Antique Trader **LAPADA**
357 Upper St, Islington. (D Rothera and B Thompson) Est: 1968. Open 10-5. SIZE: Large.

N.1 continued

STOCK: Furniture, Biedermeier, 18th and 19th C, arts and crafts, £150-£10,000. LOC: Camden Passage Antiques Centre. PARK: Easy. TEL: 071 359 2019/359 4188. VAT: Stan/Spec.

At the Sign of the Chest of Drawers
281 Upper St, Islington. (A Harms) Open 10-6 including Sun. *STOCK: Pine, country furniture.* TEL: 071 359 5909.

Ian Auld
1 Gateway Arcade, Camden Passage, Islington. Est: 1968. Open Wed. and Sat. 10-5. SIZE: Small. *STOCK: Ethnographic items, African, Oceanic, £25-£1,000; antiquities, especially pottery, £25-£250; Coptic and pre-Columbian textiles.* Not stocked: Victoriana. LOC: Near Angel tube station. PARK: Easy. TEL: 071 359 1440.

Banbury Fayre
6 Pierrepont Arcade, Camden Passage, Islington. (N Steel) Est: 1984. Open Wed. and Sat. SIZE: Small. *STOCK: Collectors' items, porcelain, glass, brass, pictures, shipping memorabilia.* PARK: 200yds. TEL: Home - (081) 852 5675.

William Bedford plc **LAPADA**
The Merchants Hall, 46 Essex Rd, Islington. (J Bedford and P Hardy) Est: 1959. Open 9.30-5.30. SIZE: Large. *STOCK: English period furniture and accessories.* LOC: 100yds. Camden Passage. PARK: Easy. TEL: 071 226 9648; fax - 071 226 6225. VAT: Stan/Spec.

Boutique Fantasque
13 Pierrepont Row, Camden Passage, Islington. (Mrs M.A.B Gates) Est: 1962. Open Wed. and Sat. SIZE: Small. *STOCK: Watercolours and prints, general antiques, porcelain, jewellery, small collectors' items.* LOC: From Piccadilly, No.19 bus. Tube to Angel station. PARK: 200yds. TEL: Home - (025 126) 2287.

Buck and Payne Antiques **LAPADA**
5 Camden Passage, Islington. (W.M Buck and M.H Payne) Open 10-5, Wed. 8.30-5. *STOCK: French country furniture; unusual and decorative items.* TEL: 071 226 4326/354 3603.

Bushe Antiques **LAPADA**
52/3 Camden Passage, Islington. Open 9-5. CL: Mon. *STOCK: Furniture, longcase and decorative mantel clocks.* TEL: 071 354 1047; (081) 802 0156/7. SER: Restorations; spares.

Bushwood Antiques **LAPADA**
317 Upper St, Islington. (A Bush) Est: 1967. Open 9.30-5.30, Sat. 10-4 or by appointment. SIZE: Large. *STOCK: Furniture including Victorian and Edwardian; bric-a-brac, decorator's items, clocks, works of art.* LOC: 100yds. from Camden Passage. PARK: 50yds. TEL: 071 359 2095; fax - 071 704 9578. VAT: Stan.

N.1 continued

Camden Passage Antiques Centre
357 Upper St, Islington(S Lemkow) Est: 1960. Open weekdays 10.30-5.30. SIZE: 350 shops and boutiques some of which are listed alphabetically in this section. Also 100 stalls open on certain market days, Wed., general antiques, 8-3, Thurs., books, 9-4, Sat., general antiques, 9-5. LOC: Behind the Angel, Islington. TEL: 071 359 0190.

Canonbury Antiques
13 Canonbury Pl. (A.C Holyome) Est: 1965. Open 9-6. CL: Sat. p.m. *STOCK: General antiques, upholstered furniture.* TEL: 071 359 2246. SER: Restorations (upholstery).

Patric Capon BADA LAPADA
350 Upper St, Islington. Est: 1970. Open Wed. and Sat. or by appointment. SIZE: Medium. *STOCK: Unusual carriage clocks, 19th C, £450-£6,000; 8-day and 2-day marine chronometers, 19th C, £850-£4,500; clocks and barometers, 18th-19th C, £400-£6,500.* LOC: Adjacent Camden Passage. PARK: Easy. TEL: 071 354 0487; home - (081) 467 5722. SER: Valuations; restorations. FAIRS: Olympia. VAT: Stan/Spec.

Chancery Antiques Ltd
357a Upper St, Islington. (R. and D Rote) Est: 1950. Open 10.30-5, or by appointment. CL: Mon. and Thurs. SIZE: Medium. *STOCK: Oriental works of art especially Japanese Meiji period.* TEL: 071 359 9035. VAT: Stan/Spec.

Peter Chapman Antiques LAPADA
10 Theberton St, Islington. (P.J Chapman) Est: 1971. Open 9.30-1 and 2-6. CL: Sun. and public holidays except by appointment. SIZE: Medium. *STOCK: Furniture, 1700-1900, £100-£10,000; paintings, drawings and prints, 17th to early 20th C; stained glass; all £50-£5,000, architectural items.* LOC: 5 mins. walk from Camden Passage down Upper St. PARK: Easy. TEL: 071 226 5565; fax - 081 348 4846. SER: Valuations; restorations (furniture and period objects); buys at auction. VAT: Stan/Spec.

Chapter One
2 Pierrepont Row, Camden Passage, Islington. (Lady Ruth Wolfson) Est: 1981. Open Wed. and Sat. 10-4.30, other afternoons by appointment. CL: Fri. SIZE: Small. *STOCK: Fine leather bindings, £20-£800; art books, 19th C.* PARK: Nearby. TEL: 071 359 1185. SER: Valuations; restorations (leather bindings); buys at auction (antiquarian books).

Chevenix-Trench Antiques
13 Camden Passage, Islington. (S Chevenix-Trench) Open 10-5. CL: Mon. *STOCK: French and English furniture, boxes and decorative smalls.* TEL: 071 359 1200.

N.1 continued

Judy Cole at Twenty Eight Camden Passage
28 Camden Passage, Islington. Open Wed., Fri. and Sat. 10-4.30. *STOCK: Metal items - fireplaces, 18th-19th C, £50-£1,000; spiral staircases, £300-£1,000; balconies, railings, garden furniture, £50-£500, all 19th C; small brass decorative items.* TEL: 071 226 4539; home - 071 226 5913. SER: Valuations; restorations (welding, polishing, sandblasting).

"Commemoratives"
3 Pierrepont Arcade, Camden Passage, Islington. (F Annesley) Est: 1971. Open all day Wed. and Sat. and Fri. p.m. *STOCK: Royal and political mugs, English decorative pottery, 1880-1960; decorative perfume bottles, 1900-1990.* LOC: Northern line underground to Angel. PARK: Meters.

Corrigan Antiques
114 Islington High St, Islington. Open 10-4. CL: Thurs. SIZE: Small. *STOCK: Furniture and decorative items, pre-1900.* Not stocked: Weapons. LOC: Near Camden Passage. PARK: Nearby. TEL: 071 704 0678; home - 071 251 8047. VAT: Stan/Spec.

Davidson Brothers
33 Camden Passage, Islington. (S. and C. Davidson) Est: 1981. Open 10-5. SIZE: Medium. *STOCK: Decorative items, £150-£1,000; unusual furniture, £500-£2,500.* LOC: Near Charlton Place. PARK: Meters. TEL: 071 226 7491. FAIRS: Olympia. VAT: Stan/Spec.

Dome Antiques (Exports) Ltd LAPADA
75 Upper St, Islington. (P., A. and P Woolf) Est: 1961. Open 9.30-5.30. SIZE: Large. *STOCK: English furniture, 1700-1900, £100-£5,000; desks, library and dining tables.* Not stocked: Silver. LOC: Opposite Islington Green. PARK: Easy. TEL: 071 226 7227; home - 071 226 1070. SER: Valuations. VAT: Stan/Spec.

Donay Antiques
35 Camden Passage, Islington. (N Donay) Est: 1980. Open 9-5.30. SIZE: Large. *STOCK: Games, £30-£500; artists' colour boxes, £400-£800; decorative items; Staffordshire; fitted boxes; maps and cards.* LOC: Near Angel tube or bus station. PARK: Nearby. TEL: 071 359 1880.

D.J Ferrant Antiques
21a Camden Passage, Islington. (J Ferrant) Est: 1963. Open 9.30-4. SIZE: Large. *STOCK: Georgian furniture; clocks, bronzes; general antiques.* PARK: Easy. TEL: 071 359 2597. SER: Buys at auction. VAT: Stan/Spec.

N.1 continued

Michael Finney Antique Prints and Books

15 Pierrepont Arcade, Camden Passage, Islington. Open 10.30-4.30. CL: Mon. and Tues. *STOCK: Prints, 17th-19th C; plate books, watercolours especially David Roberts, Egypt, Holy Land and Spain, £1-£1,000F.* PARK: Meters. TEL: 071 226 9280.

"The Fleamarket"

7 Pierrepont Row, Camden Passage, Islington. Open 9.30-6. CL: Mon. SIZE: Large. 26 Standholders. *STOCK: Jewellery, furniture, objets d'art, militaria, guns, swords, pistols, porcelain, coins, medals, stamps, 18th-19th C, £1-£500; antiquarian books, prints, fine art, china, silver, glass and general antiques.* PARK: Easy. TEL: 071 226 8211. SER: Valuations; buys at auction; weapon repairs.

Vincent Freeman

1 Camden Passage, Islington. Est: 1966. Open 10-5. CL: Mon. and Thurs. SIZE: Large. *STOCK: Music boxes, also porcelain, glass and decorative items, £50-£1,500.* TEL: 071 226 6178. VAT: Stan/Spec.

Furniture Vault

50 Camden Passage, Islington. Open 9.30-4.30. *STOCK: Furniture, 18th-20th C; decorative bronzes.* TEL: 071 354 1047.

Georgian Village

Islington Green. Open 10-4, Wed. and Sat. 7-5. PARK: Nearby. TEL: 071 226 1571.

"Get Stuffed"

105 Essex Rd, Islington. Est: 1975. Open 10.30-4.30, Thurs. 10.30-1. *STOCK: Stuffed birds, fish, animals, trophy heads; rugs; butterflies, insects.* TEL: 071 226 1364. SER: Restorations; taxidermy; glass domes and cases supplied.

David Graham Antiques LAPADA

104 Islington High St, Camden Passage, Islington. Est: 1973. Open 10-5, Wed. 8-5, Sat. 10-6. CL: Mon. SIZE: Large. *STOCK: Silver, 1750-1930, £100-£15,000; Victorian silver plate, £50-£40,000; Sheffield plate, £100-£5,000; Victorian oil paintings, £2,000-£25,000; Victorian decorative furniture, £1,000-£15,000.* LOC: 2 mins. from Angel Underground. PARK: Easy. TEL: 071 354 2112. VAT: Stan.

Gordon Gridley

41 Camden Passage, Islington. Est: 1968. CL: Mon. SIZE: Medium. *STOCK: English and continental furniture and paintings, decorative objects, metalwork, statuary, scientific instruments, all 17th-19th C, £50-£5,000.* PARK: Nearby, in Charlton Place. TEL: 071 226 0643. SER: Valuations; restorations. VAT: Stan/Spec.

Grove Antiques

33 Essex Rd, Islington. (Mrs W.C.M Hines and F.J Van Der Breggen) Est: 1984. Open 9.15-6,

Grove Antiques continued

Sun. and Mon. by appointment. SIZE: Medium. *STOCK: English and continental furniture, £100-£7,000; clocks, decorative metalwork, paintings and architectural items, £25-£3,000.* Not stocked: Silver, gold, jewellery. LOC: 100yds. from Camden Passage. PARK: Easy. TEL: 071 354 1596; home - 081 207 4413/341 3433. SER: Buys at auction. VAT: Stan/Spec.

Linda Gumb LAPADA

9 Camden Passage, Islington. Est: 1981. Open 9.30-4.30, Wed. 7.30-5, Sat. 9-5. SIZE: Medium. *STOCK: Textiles, 18th-19th C; decorative objects, 19th C; all £10-£5,000.* PARK: Easy. TEL: 071 354 1184. SER: Buys at auction. FAIRS: Olympia. VAT: Stan.

Rosemary Hart

4 Gateway Arcade, Camden Passage, Islington. Est: 1980. Open 11-4, Wed. and Sat. 9-5. CL: Mon. and Thurs. SIZE: Small. *STOCK: Silver and plate, £5-£400.* LOC: Near Angel tube station. TEL: 071 359 6839.

Hart and Rosenberg

2 and 3 Gateway Arcade, Camden Passage, Islington. (E Hart and H Rosenberg) Est: 1968. Open 10-5, Wed. 9-5. CL: Mon. and Thurs. SIZE: Medium. *STOCK: Chinese, Japanese and European porcelain, works of art, decorative items, some furniture, £25-£5,000.* LOC: Near Angel tube station. PARK: Nearby. TEL: 071 359 6839. SER: Valuations; buys at auction. VAT: Stan/Spec.

Sherry Hatcher

5 Gateway Arcade, Camden Passage, Upper St, Islington. Est: 1966. Open 10.30-5. CL: Mon. and Thurs. SIZE: Small. *STOCK: Perfume bottles, sugar shakers, silver, boxes and interesting silver items.* LOC: Near Angel tube station. PARK: Easy. TEL: 071 226 5679; home - 226 8496. VAT: Stan.

Brian Hawkins Antiques LAPADA

73 Upper St, Islington. Open 9.30-5. *STOCK: Furniture, 19th to early 20th C, £50-£1,000+.* TEL: 071 359 3957.

Heather Antiques

11 Camden Passage, Islington. Est: 1965. Open 10-4.30, Wed. 9-5, Thurs. 10-1.30. CL: Mon. SIZE: Medium. *STOCK: Silver and plate.* TEL: 071 226 2412. VAT: Stan.

Linda Helm Antiques LAPADA

Islington. Open by appointment. *STOCK: Country and painted furniture, treen, pottery and floral watercolours.* TEL: 071 609 2716.

Heritage Antiques LAPADA

112 Islington High St, Camden Passage. (A Daniel) Est: 1975. Open Wed. 8-4.30 and Sat. 9-5, or by appointment. SIZE: Large. *STOCK: Metalware, £50-£2,000; oak and country*

Heritage Antiques continued

furniture, 17th-19th C, £100-£5,000; domestic and decorative items. TEL: 071 226 7789. VAT: Stan/Spec.

Robert Hirschhorn
Open by appointment. *STOCK: Early English and European furniture and works of art.* TEL: 071 609 9285.

House of Steel Antiques
400 Caledonian Rd. (J Cole) Est: 1974. Open 10.30-5.30, Sat. by appointment. SIZE: Warehouse. *STOCK: Metal items - fireplaces, 18th-19th C, £50-£1,000; spiral staircases, £300-£1,000; balconies, railings, garden furniture, £50-£500; all 19th C.* LOC: Near King's Cross. PARK: Own. TEL: 071 607 5889; home - 071 226 5913. SER: Valuations; restorations (welding, polishing, sandblasting). VAT: Stan.

Diana Huntley **LAPADA**
8 Camden Passage, Islington. Est: 1970. Open Wed. 7.30-5, Fri. 10-5, Sat. 9-5, Tues. and Thurs. by appointment. CL: Mon. *STOCK: European porcelain, £50-£2,000; glass objets d'art, all 19th C.* TEL: 071 226 4605. SER: Valuations. VAT: Stan/Spec.

Inheritance
8/9/10 Gateway Arcade, Camden Passage, Islington. (A Pantelli) Est: 1969. Open 10.30-5. CL: Mon. SIZE: Small. *STOCK: Jewellery, Oriental and European ceramics, ivories, furniture, cloisonné, clocks, bronzes.* TEL: 071 226 8305. SER: Valuations. VAT: Stan/Spec.

Intercol London
at Donay, 35 Camden Passage. (Y Beresiner) Est: 1977. Open 9-5. CL: Mon. SIZE: Large. *STOCK: Playing cards, maps and banknotes, including related literature, £5-£1,000+..* LOC: Camden Passage. PARK: Easy. TEL: 071 354 2599; fax - (081) 346 9539. SER: Valuations; restorations (maps including colouring); buys at auction (playing cards, maps, banknotes and books). FAIRS: Major specialist European, U.S.A. and Far Eastern. VAT: Stan/Spec.

Islington Artefacts
12 and 14 Essex Rd. (C.C Hill and D.A Magee) Open 9-6. *STOCK: Pine furniture.* TEL: 071 226 6867.

Japanese Gallery
23 Camden Passage, Islington. Open 9.30-4.30. *STOCK: Japanese woodcut prints; books, porcelain, screens, kimonos, scrolls, furniture, general Japanese antiques.* TEL: 071 226 3347. SER: Framing.

Jubilee
10 Pierrepont Row, Camden Passage, Islington. (B Vosburgh) Est: 1970. Open Wed. and Sat. 10.30-5 or by appointment. SIZE: Small. *STOCK: Photographica - apparatus, images, daguerreotypes, ambrotypes, tintypes, vintage paper prints, stereoscopic cards and viewers,*

Jubilee continued

magic lanterns and slides, family-albums, topographical, cabinet cards and cartes de visite, 10p-£1,000. LOC: From Piccadilly Circus, take 19 bus to Angel, Islington. PARK: Meters. TEL: Home - 071 607 5462. SER: Buys at auction.

Julian Antiques **LAPADA**
54 Duncan St. Est: 1964. Open Wed. 8.30-2 and Sat. 9.30-4 and by appointment. *STOCK: French clocks, fireplaces, bronzes, fenders, mirrors.* TEL: 071 833 0835.

Kausmally Antiques
99 St. Pauls Rd. (A Kausmally) Open 10-6. *STOCK: Victorian and Georgian furniture.* TEL: 071 359 0741.

Cassandra Keen Antiques **LAPADA**
Shop 18, Ground Floor, Georgian Village, 30 Islington Green. Est: 1983. Open Wed. 7.30-4, Sat. 8.30-4, Tues. and Fri. by appointment. SIZE: Small. *STOCK: Decorative items and small English and French furniture, 18th-19th C, from £100+.* LOC: Part of Camden Passage. PARK: Meters. TEL: 071 226 1571; home - 071 359 6534. SER: Buys at auction (French items). VAT: Stan/Spec.

Thomas Kerr Antiques Ltd **LAPADA**
11 Theberton St. Est: 1977. Open 10-6, Sat. by appointment. SIZE: Large. *STOCK: English and continental furniture, works of art, paintings and decorative objects 17th-20th C, £100-£20,000.* LOC: 5 mins. walk down Upper St. towards Highbury and Islington tube. PARK: Easy. TEL: 071 226 0626. VAT: Stan/Spec.

Carol Ketley Antiques
9 Georgian Village, 30/31 Islington Green, Camden Passage. Est: 1979. Open Wed. 8.30-4, Sat. 10-4; other days by appointment. SIZE: Small. *STOCK: Decanters, drinking glasses, English pottery, 1780-1900, £10-£1,000.* PARK: Nearby. TEL: 071 359 5529. FAIR: Olympia;City of London; Little Chelsea. VAT: Spec.

N.1 continued

Judith Lassalle
7 Pierrepont Arcade, Camden Passage, Islington. Est: 1955. Open Wed. 7.30-5, Sat. 9-5, other times by appointment. *STOCK: Decorative maps and prints; children's games and rocking horses, 17th to early 20th C, £25-£5,000.* PARK: Nearby. TEL: 071 607 7121. SER: Valuations; restorations; buys at auction; framing. FAIRS: Olympia; Ephemera.

John Laurie **LAPADA**
352 Upper St, Islington. (J Gewirtz) Est: 1962. Open 9.30-5. SIZE: Medium. *STOCK: Silver, Sheffield plate.* TEL: 071 226 0913/226 6969. SER: Restorations; shipping. VAT: Stan.

Sara Lemkow
12 Camden Passage. Open 10-5. *STOCK: Oil lamps, brass, iron, copper, kitchen utensils.* TEL: 071 359 0190.

Nellie Lenson and Roy Smith
16 Camden Passage, Islington. *STOCK: Decorative items, Vienna bronzes, early brass, animalia, French furniture.* TEL: 071 226 2423.

Michael Lewis Antiques
16 Essex Rd, Islington. Est: 1977. Open 8-6, Sat. 8-5, Sun. by appointment. SIZE: Large. *STOCK: Pine furniture, 18th-20th C, £100-*

Michael Lewis Antiques continued

£6,500. LOC: 100yds. north of Camden Passage. PARK: Easy. TEL: 071 359 7733. VAT: Stan.

Wan Li
7 Gateway Arcade, 355 Upper St., Camden Passage, Islington. Est: 1969. *STOCK: Mainly Chinese works of art, porcelain, some European, fans.* VAT: Stan/Spec.

London Militaria Market
Angel Arcade, Camden Passage, Islington. (S Bosley and M Warren) Est: 1987. Open Sat. 8-2. SIZE: Large. There are 35 dealers at this market selling. *STOCK: a wide range of militaria, 1800 to date.* LOC: Near Angel tube station. PARK: Meters and car parks nearby. TEL: (062882) 2503 or (04555) 56971.

Heather Lotinga
York Arcade, Stand 2, 80 Islington High St. Open Wed. and Sat. 8-5. SIZE: Small. *STOCK: Decorative and animal items (especially dog related) including jewellery.* PARK: Nearby. TEL: 071 223 6272. SER: Buys at auction; courier. VAT: Stan.

Finbar MacDonnell
17 Camden Passage, Islington. Open 10-6. *STOCK: Decorative prints, mainly pre-1850.* TEL: 071 226 0537.

N.1. continued

The Mall Antiques Arcade

359 Upper St, Islington, (Atlantic Antiques Centres Ltd.). Est: 1979. Open 10-5, Wed. 7.30-5, Sat. 9-6. CL: Mon. SIZE: Below are listed the dealers at this Arcade. LOC: 5 mins. from Angel tube station. PARK: Meters. TEL: 071 354 2839; enquiries - 071 351 5353.

S and J Afford
G21. *Art nouveau, art deco, glass, ceramics.*

Alma Antiques
G17. (T and A Goldstrom) *Miniatures, objects, watercolours and jewellery.* TEL: 071 359 9045.

Christopher Ashton
G23. *Copper, brass and steel, 18th-19th C, £100-£2,000.* TEL: 071 359 9533.

Audley Art
G20. (A Singer) *19th C English and continental porcelain, clocks, oil paintings.* TEL: 071 704 9507.

Louise Bannister
G4/5. *Decorative items.* TEL: 071 226 6665.

Sonia Bottrill
G1. *Silver, glass and jewellery.* TEL: 071 354 2839.

David Bowden
G8. *Oriental art.* TEL: 071 359 3541.

Collectables
G18. (Mrs C Levy) *Unusual decorative items, papier mâché, tôle, watercolours, glass.* TEL: 071 226 3964.

Decodence
G13. (G Sassower) *Bakelite items, £10-£2,000; radios, early 20th C, £500-£1,000.* TEL: 071 354 4473; home - 081 458 4665.

Josephine Edwards
G6. *Lighting items.* TEL: 071 888 5576.

Norman Gibbs
G27. *Carpets, rugs, Eastern artefacts.*

Griffen Antiques
G10. (J Gardner) *Copper, brass and furniture.* TEL: 071 359 8416.

Jazy Antiques
G14/15. (Mrs J Zaziemski) *Porcelain.* TEL: 071 354 2333.

Patricia Kleinman
G3. *English watercolours, 19th to early 20th C.* TEL: 071 704 0798.

Andrew Lineham
G19. *Glass and porcelain.* TEL: 071 704 0195.

Maureen McEvoy
G9. *Fine jewellery.* TEL: 071 359 6694.

Monika
G16. (M Jartelius) *Fine period costume jewellery and accessories, 1920's-1950's.* TEL: 071 354 3125.

Linda Morgan Antiques
G26. *Early 20th C jewellery; silver.* TEL: 071 359 0654.

Piers Rankin
G24/25. *Silver and Sheffield plate.* TEL: 071 354 3349.

The Mall Antiques Arcade continued

Ritzy
G7. *Vintage jewellery, accessories and objects.* TEL: 071 704 0127.

Mike Weedon
G12. *Art nouveau, art deco.* TEL: 071 226 5319.

Doreen White
G2. *Glass.* TEL: 071 354 3349.

Craig Wyncoll
G11. *Antiquarian prints and maps.* TEL: 071 704 8438.

Michael Young
G22. *Decorative items.* TEL: 071 226 2225.

The Lower Mall

Antique Clocks - Terence Plank LAPADA
B7. *Clocks - longcase, bracket, wall, regulators, small mantel, carriage, skeleton and lantern; barographs and barometers.* TEL: 071 226 2426; home - 0689 831431.

Alexander Baillie Antiques
B6. *English mahogany, oak and walnut furniture, 18th-19th C, £500-£5,000; decorative items - clocks, figures and mirrors, 19th C, £150-£1,000.* TEL: 071 359 9768.

Barry Cotton
B4. *18th-19th C furniture, paintings and decorative accessories.*

Peter Lehmann
B8. *Furniture.* TEL: 071 704 0701.

Riley Antiques
B1. (G Riley) *Edwardian and Victorian furniture.* TEL: 071 354 1719.

Malcolm D Stevens
B9/10. *Furniture.* TEL: 071 359 1020.

G Whittal
B2/3. *Antique and decorative furniture, paintings, silver and accessories.*

Graham Woodage
B5. *Furniture, clocks and accessories.*

Laurence Mitchell Antiques LAPADA

13 Camden Passage, Islington(L.P.J Mitchell) Est: 1972. Open 10-4.30, Wed. 8.30-5. CL: Mon. *STOCK: Oriental, European and English ceramics especially Meissen; glass, Mason ironstone; Oriental and English small furniture.* TEL: 071 359 7579/226 1738. VAT: Stan/Spec.

Number Nineteen

19 Camden Passage, Islington. (D Griffiths and J Wright) Open 10-5. *STOCK: Decorative antiques including bentwood, cane, garden and lacquered bamboo furniture; fairground animals and pub fittings.* TEL: 071 226 1126.

Old Woodworking Tools

41 Cross St, Islington. (T Barwick) Open 9.30-6. *STOCK: Woodworking tools.* TEL: 071 359 9313.

Jacqueline Oosthuizen

1st Floor, Georgian Village, Camden Passage, Islington. Est: 1960. Open Wed. and Sat. 8-4. SIZE: Small. *STOCK: Staffordshire figures,*

Jacqueline Oosthuizen continued

18th-19th C, £50-£10,000; jewellery, 19th-20th C; Oriental, European and English ceramics, 18th-20th C. PARK: Nearby. TEL: 071 226 5393/352 6071; answering service 081 528 9001; pager no.806930. SER: Buys at auction (Staffordshire). VAT: Stan/Spec.

Kevin Page Oriental Art
2, 4 and 6 Camden Passage, Islington. Est: 1968. Open 10-4. CL: Mon. SIZE: Large. *STOCK: Oriental porcelain and furniture, cloisonné, bronzes, ivories.* LOC: 1 min. from Angel tube station. PARK: Easy. TEL: 071 226 8558. SER: Valuations. VAT: Stan.

Persian Market
48 Upper St, Islington. Open 10-6, Wed. 9-6. SIZE: 4 floors. *STOCK: Porcelain, bronze, ivory, furniture, carpets and rugs, clocks, glass, silver.* LOC: 200yds. along Upper St. from Angel Underground. PARK: At rear. TEL: 071 226 7927. SER: Valuations; restorations (porcelain and bronze). VAT: Stan/Spec.

Rookery Farm Antiques
12 Camden Passage. *STOCK: Pine and country furniture.* TEL: 071 359 0190.

Marcus Ross Antiques
14/16 Pierrepont Row, Camden Passage, Islington. Est: 1972. Open 10.30-4.30. CL: Mon. *STOCK: Oriental porcelain, general antiques, Victorian walnut furniture.* TEL: 071 359 8494.

Rumours Decorative Arts
10 The Mall, Upper St., Islington. (J Donovan and A Stones) Open Wed. and Sat. 8-4. *STOCK: Decorative arts, especially Moorcroft pottery.* TEL: (0582) 873561; mobile - (0836) 277274. SER: Valuations.

Robin Sims
7 Camden Passage, Islington. Est: 1970. Open 10-4, Wed. and Sat. 8-5. CL: Mon. SIZE: Small. *STOCK: General antiques, Victoriana, 1840-1920, £5-£5,000.* Not stocked: Large furniture. LOC: Near Angel underground station. PARK: Easy. TEL: 071 226 2393. VAT: Stan.

Keith Skeel Antique Warehouse LAPADA
7-9 Elliotts Pl. SIZE: Large. *STOCK: Interesting and unusual furniture.* TEL: 071 226 7012. *Trade Only.*

Keith Skeel Antiques and Eccentricities LAPADA
94/98 Islington High St. Est: 1969. Open 9-6. SIZE: Large. *STOCK: Interesting and unusual decorative items.* LOC: 1 min. from the Angel underground station. TEL: 071 359 9894/226 7012. VAT: Stan. *Trade Only.*

Strike One (Islington) Ltd BADA
51 Camden Passage, Islington. (J Mighell) Est: 1968. Open Wed. and Sat. 9-5 or by

Strike One (Islington) Ltd. continued

appointment. SIZE: Medium. *STOCK: Clocks, pre-1870, especially early English wall and Act of Parliament, £2,000-£15,000; English longcase, 1675-1820, £3,000-£40,000; English bracket, lantern, skeleton and French carriage clocks; Vienna regulators; barometers, horological books.* PARK: Easy. TEL: 071 226 9709; home - 071 359 6459. SER: Valuations; restorations (clocks, barometers); catalogue available. VAT: Stan/Spec.

The Studio
2 Charlton Pl. Open 10-5.30. *STOCK: Art deco and art nouveau jewellery, fine art; original graphics and sculpture, especially 1920s-1930s.* TEL: 071 226 5625.

Style
1 Ground Floor, Georgian Village, Camden Passage. (M Webb and P Coakley) Open Wed. 8-3, Sat. 9-4, other times by appointment. *STOCK: Art nouveau and art deco pewter, bronzes, jewellery, ceramics and glass.* TEL: 071 359 7867; home - 081 449 2588.

Swan Fine Art
120 Islington High St, Camden Passage. (P Child) Open 10-5, Wed. and Sat. 9-5 or by appointment. SIZE: Medium. *STOCK: Paintings, fine and decorative sporting and animal, portraits, 17th-19th C, £500-£25,000+.* PARK: Easy, except Wed. and Sat.. TEL: 071 226 5335; mobile - (0860) 795336. VAT: Spec.

Tadema Gallery
10 Charlton PlCamden Passage, Islington. (S. and D Newell-Smith) Est: 1978. Open 10-5 and by appointment. CL: Mon. and Thurs. SIZE: Medium. *STOCK: Modern British and continental paintings and sculpture; 20th C decorative art including jewellery.* PARK: Reasonable. TEL: 071 359 1055 (ansaphone). SER: Valuations. VAT: Stan.

Eugene Tiernan
Shop 3, Angel Arcade, Camden Passage. Open Wed. and Sat. 7-4.30, other times by appointment. *STOCK: Furniture, marble, prints, textiles, mirrors, tôle and papier mâché.* TEL: 071 354 5336.

"Turn On" Lighting Ltd
116/118 Islington High St, Camden Passage. Est: 1976. *STOCK: Lighting, 1840-1940.* TEL: 071 359 7616.

Leigh Underhill Gallery
100 Islington High St. Est: 1950. Open 9-6. CL: Mon. and Tues. SIZE: Medium. *STOCK: Paintings, drawings, sculpture, etchings, works of art.* PARK: Meters. TEL: 071 226 5673. VAT: Spec.

N.1. continued

Vane House Antiques

15 Camden Passage, Islington. (M Till and B Snyder) Est: 1950. Open 10-5. *STOCK: 18th to early 19th C furniture.* TEL: 071 359 1343. VAT: Stan/Spec.

Marie West Antiques

4/5 Pierrepont ArcadeCamden Passage, Islington. Est: 1981. Open Wed. 7.30-3.30, Sat. 9.30-4.30, other days by appointment. SIZE: Small. *STOCK: Painted and country furniture, decorative and unusual items, £5-£500.* PARK: Meters. TEL: 071 226 7505. VAT: Stan/Spec.

Mark J West - Cobb Antiques Ltd

15 Georgian VillageCamden Passage, Islington. Open Wed. and Sat., or by appointment. *STOCK: 18th-19th C glass including decanters, sets of glasses; 19th C pottery and decorators' items.* TEL: 071 359 8686; home - 081 540 7982. SER: Valuations. FAIRS: Olympia. VAT: Stan.

Yesterday Child **LAPADA**

Angel Arcade, 118 Islington High St. (D Barrington) Est: 1970. Open Wed. 7.30-3, Sat. 9-2. SIZE: Small. *STOCK: Dolls, 1800-1925, £25-£5,000.* PARK: Easy. TEL: 071 354 1601; home - 0908 583403. SER: Valuations; restorations; buys at auction (dolls). FAIRS: April and September Cumberland Hotel International Doll. VAT: Stan/Spec.

N.1. continued

York Arcade

80 Islington High St, Camden Passage. Open 10-5, Wed. and Sat. 8-5. CL: Mon. SIZE: Large. There are twelve dealers at this arcade. *STOCK: A wide range of silver, art deco, miniature soldiers, porcelain, linen, mirrors, crocodile luggage, jewellery, rugs and carpets, prints, small collectables.* LOC: At top of Camden Passage. PARK: Duncan St. TEL: 071 833 2640.

London N.2

Amazing Grates

Phoenix House, 61-63 High Rd., East Finchley. (E Martin. Resident) Est: 1971. Open 10-6. SIZE: Large. *STOCK: Mantelpieces, grates and fireside items, £200-£5,000; Victorian tiling, £2-£20; early ironwork, all 19th C.* LOC: 100yds. north of East Finchley tube station. PARK: Own. TEL: 081 883 9590/6017. SER: Valuations; restorations (ironwork, welding of cast iron and brazing, polishing); installations. VAT: Stan.

The Antique Shop (Valantique)

9 Fortis Green. (Mrs V Steel) Open 11-6. SIZE: Medium. *STOCK: General antiques especially original lighting and fenders; small furniture, pottery, porcelain, glass, oil paintings, watercolours, prints, mirrors, copper, brass, unusual items, £5-£500.* LOC: 2 mins. from East Finchley tube station. PARK: Side street. TEL: 081 883 7651. SER: Buys at auction.

Martin Henham (Antiques)

218 High Rd, East Finchley. Open 10-6. SIZE: Medium. *STOCK: Furniture, 1710-1920, £5-£1,700; paintings, 1650-1900, £10-£1,000; porcelain, 1750-1910, £5-£450.* PARK: Easy. TEL: 081 444 5274. SER: Valuations; restorations (furniture and paintings); buys at auction. VAT: Stan/Spec.

Lauri Stewart - Fine Art

36 Church Lane. Open 10-5. CL: Thurs. *STOCK: Watercolours, oils and engravings, 19th-20th C; books.* TEL: 081 883 7719. SER: Restorations (oils, watercolours); framing.

London N.3

Park Galleries

20 Hendon Lane, Finchley. Est: 1978. Open 10-6. *STOCK: English watercolours, 18th-20th C; oil paintings and prints.* TEL: 081 346 2176.

London N.4

Marion Gray

33 Crouch Hill. (R.J Orton) Est: 1955. Open 10-6. CL: Sun., except by appointment. SIZE: Large. *STOCK: Furniture, 17th-19th C, objets d'art.* LOC: Next to Crouch Hill station. TEL: 071 272 0372. SER: Restorations; upholstery. VAT: Stan/Spec.

London N.5

North London Clock Shop Ltd
72 Highbury Park. (D.S Tomlin) Est: 1960. Open 9-6. CL: Sat. SIZE: Medium. *STOCK: Clocks, longcase, bracket, carriage, skeleton, 18th-19th C.* LOC: Turn off Seven Sisters Rd. into Blackstock Rd., continue on to Highbury Park. PARK: Easy. TEL: 071 226 1609. SER: Restorations (clocks and barometer); wheel cutting, hand engraving, dial painting, clock reconversions. FAIRS: Olympia. VAT: Stan.

Petherton Antiques
124 Petherton Rd. (V.E Illingworth. Resident) Est: 1987. Open 10.30-7, Thurs. by appointment. CL: Mon. SIZE: Small. *STOCK: Furniture, Georgian to early 20th C, £30-£2,000; boxes, pottery and porcelain, paintings and prints, silver, small decorative items, Victorian and early 20th C, £5-£800.* LOC: Off Balls Pond Rd. PARK: Easy. TEL: 071 226 6597; home - 071 359 4969. SER: Restorations (furniture); buys at auction (furniture).

G.W Walford
15 Calabria Rd, Highbury Fields. Est: 1951. Open 9.30-5.30. CL: Sat. *STOCK: Antiquarian books especially illustrated.* TEL: 071 226 5682.

London N.6

John Beer
c/o Richardsons of Highgate, 191-199 Archway Rd., Highgate. Open 9-1 and 2-5. CL: Thurs. *STOCK: Furniture, 1830-1960s especially English arts and crafts, Gothic and art deco.* LOC: 300yds. south Highgate tube station. PARK: Easy. TEL: (0242) 576080 and (0860) 767194. SER: Valuations; buys at auction. VAT: Stan/Spec.

Centaur Gallery
82 Highgate High St, Highgate Village. (J. and D Wieliczko) Est: 1960. Open 11-6. *STOCK: 18th to early 19th C oil paintings, watercolours, prints, sculpture, ethnic and folk art, unusual items.* TEL: 081 340 0087.

Fisher and Sperr
46 Highgate High St. (J.R Sperr) Est: 1945. Open daily 10.30-6. SIZE: Large. *STOCK: Books, 15th C to date.* LOC: From centre of Highgate Village, nearest underground stations Archway (Highgate), Highgate. PARK: Easy. TEL: 081 340 7244. SER: Valuations; restorations (books); buys at auction. VAT: Stan.

Betty Gould and Julian Gonnevmann Antiques
408-410 Archway Rd, Highgate. Est: 1964. Open 10-5.30, Sat. 9.30-5.30. CL: Thurs. SIZE: Medium. *STOCK: Furniture, 18th-20th C, £50-£5,000.* LOC: On A1, just below Highgate tube station. PARK: Shepherds Hill. TEL: 081 340 4987. SER: Restorations; French polishing; upholstery.

N.6. continued

Home to Home
355c Archway Rd. Open 10-5.30. CL: Wed. *STOCK: Victorian, Edwardian and some Georgian furniture; antiquarian books.* TEL: 081 340 8354. SER: Restorations; upholstery.

D.M. and P. Manheim (Peter Manheim) Ltd BADA
P.O. Box 1259. (P Manheim) Est: 1926. Open by appointment only. *STOCK: English porcelain, pottery and enamels.* TEL: 081 340 9211. VAT: Spec.

London N.7

Princedale Antiques
56 Eden Grove. (G.M Sykes) Est: 1969. Open 10.30-6.30. *STOCK: Pine furniture, decorative items, hand-painted furniture, 19th to early 20th C, £30-£1,000.* TEL: 071 607 6376. VAT: Stan.

Tsar Architectural
487 Liverpool Rd. (A Purcell and C Turner) Open 9.30-7. *STOCK: Fireplaces and associated items.* TEL: 071 609 4238. SER: Restorations.

London N.8

Crouch End Antiques
47 Park Rd, Crouch End. (M.V Kairis) Est: 1979. Open 10-6. SIZE: Medium. *STOCK: Furniture, 19th C, £100-£1,000.* LOC: Corner of Shanklin Rd. TEL: 081 348 7652. SER: Valuations; renovation materials supplied. FAIRS: Alexandra Palace. VAT: Stan/Spec.

Sandra Lummis Fine Art
Flat 7, 17 Haslemere Rd. (Mrs S and Dr T Lummis) Est: 1985. Open by appointment. CL: Aug. *STOCK: British art (Modernist school), 20th C from Sickert to contemporary, especially Bloomsbury painters, £500-£50,000.* LOC: From Highgate Hill, along Hornsey Lane, left at 'T' junction, then 1st right. PARK: Easy. TEL: 081 340 2293; home - same. SER: Valuations; restorations; buys at auction (as stock). VAT: Spec.

London N.10

M.E Korn
47 Tetherdown, Muswell Hill. (E Korn) ABA, PBFA. Est: 1971. Open by appointment. *STOCK: Books - natural history, medical, science, art and literature, 16th-19th C, £10-£100.* TEL: 081 883 5251. SER: Valuations; buys at auction (antiquarian books). FAIRS: PBFA, Russell Hotel monthly; York, Oxford, Cambridge; ABAA in California, Boston, New York and Toronto.

London N.12

Finchley Fine Art Galleries

983 High Rd, North Finchley. (S Greenman) Est: 1972. Open 12.30-7 including Sun; Mon. and Wed. by appointment. SIZE: Large. *STOCK: 18th-20th C watercolours, paintings, etchings, prints, mostly English, £25-£10,000; Georgian, Victorian, Edwardian furniture, to £4,000; china and porcelain - Moorcroft, Doulton, Worcester, Clarice Cliff, £5-£2,000; musical and scientific instruments, bronzes, early photographic apparatus, fire-arms, shotguns.* LOC: Take exit 23, M25, St. Albans road. Gallery 3 miles south of Barnet on rightF. PARK: Easy. TEL: 081 446 4848. SER: Valuations; restorations; framing.

London N.13

Trader Antiques

484 Green Lanes, Palmers Green. (M Webb) Open 10-6. *STOCK: Stripped pine, glass, furniture and general antiques.* TEL: 081 886 9552.

London N.14

C.J Martin (Coins) Ltd

85 The Vale, Southgate. Open by appointment. *STOCK: Ancient and medieval coins and ancient artefacts.* TEL: 081 882 1509/4359.

London N.16

139 Antiques

139 Green Lanes. (F Clifton) Open 9-5. CL: Thurs. *STOCK: General antiques mainly tables and chairs.* TEL: (071) 354 2466.

W Forster

83a Stamford Hill. Est: 1952. Open by appointment. *STOCK: Bibliography and books about books.* LOC: Nearest station Manor House (Piccadilly Line) or 253 bus to Stamford Hill Broadway. PARK: Easy. TEL: 081 800 3919.

London N.20

The Totteridge Gallery

61 Totteridge Lane. Est: 1979. Open daily, Sun. by appointment. SIZE: Small. *STOCK: Oil paintings, £1,000-£25,000; watercolours, £300-£10,000; both 18th to early 20th C. Limited edition Russell Flint prints, 20th C, £500-£3,000.* LOC: Opposite Totteridge and Whetstone tube station. PARK: Easy. TEL: 081 446 7896. SER: Valuations; restorations; frame repairs. VAT: Stan/Spec.

London N.21

The Little Curiosity Shop

24 The Green, Winchmore Hill. (Mrs H Freedman) Est: 1967. Open 10.30-5. CL: Wed. *STOCK: Clocks, porcelain, general antiques, mostly Victorian, bronzes, silver, music boxes, jewellery and diamond items.* LOC: Nearest stations - Winchmore Hill (Eastern Region), and Southgate (Piccadilly Line underground). PARK: Easy. TEL: 081 886 0925. VAT: Stan. *Trade Only.*

Piermont Antiques Ltd

7 Wades Hill, Winchmore Hill. (G. and K Pierssene) Est: 1969. Open 10-5, Fri. until 5.30, Sat. 10-1 and 2.15-6. CL: Wed. SIZE: Small. *STOCK: Furniture, porcelain, jewellery and silver, linen and collectables, all pre-1939, £1-£700.* PARK: Easy. TEL: 081 886 2486. SER: Valuations.

N.21 continued

Rochefort Antiques Gallery
32-34 The Green, Winchmore Hill. (L.W. and Mrs Stevens-Wilson) Est: 1963. Open 10-6. CL: Wed.. SIZE: 12 dealers. *STOCK: Porcelain, English and continental, 18th-19th C, £1-£1,000; furniture, glass, silver, jewellery, copper, brass, pictures, prints, lamps, books, £1-£2,000; lace and linen.* LOC: From London north through Wood Green and Palmers Green - branch off between Palmers Green and Enfield. PARK: Easy. TEL: 081 886 4779; home - 081 363 0910. SER: Valuations; silver plating; repairs (clocks and metalware). VAT: Stan/Spec.

Winchmore Antiques Ltd
14 The Green, Winchmore Hill. (D Hicks and S Christian) Open 10-6. SIZE: Medium. *STOCK: General antiques, £1-£500; architectural brass fittings, vintage lamps and spare parts; all 19th-20th C.* LOC: Junction of 5 roads, at east end of Broadwalk. PARK: Easy. TEL: 081 882 4800; home - 081 361 9499. SER: Valuations; restorations (metal polishing, silver plating, oil lamps). VAT: Stan.

London N.W.1

Acquisitions (Fireplaces) Ltd
269 Camden High St. (K Kennedy) Est: 1970. Open 9.30-5. SIZE: Medium. *STOCK:Fire-*

Acquisitions (Fireplaces) Ltd. continued

places, including Georgian, Victorian, Edwardian and reproduction and fire-side accessories, £195-£595. LOC: 3 mins. walk from Camden Town tube station (Camden High St.). PARK: Easy. TEL: 071 485 4955. VAT: Stan.

Adams Antiques
47 Chalk Farm Rd. Open 10-6, seven days a week. *STOCK: Pine, especially Irish and continental, 18th and 19th C.* TEL: 071 267 9241.

Art Furniture (London) Ltd
158 Camden St. Open 10-6, Sun. 12-6, Thurs. 10-7.30. SIZE: Warehouse. *STOCK: Arts and crafts, art nouveau and art deco furniture, fixtures and fittings, £50-£5,000; bentwood and Lloyd loom.* LOC: Under railway bridge on Camden St. going south. PARK: Easy. TEL: 071 267 4324. SER: Restorations; repolishing. VAT: Stan.

Barkes and Barkes
76 Parkway. (J N and P R Barkes) Est: 1976. Open Thurs., Fri. and Sat. 12-6. SIZE: Small. *STOCK: Paintings and watercolours, 20th C, £200-£5,000.* LOC: Just north of Regents Park. PARK: Next street. TEL: 071 284 1550. VAT: Spec.

Ian Crispin Antiques
95 Lisson Grove. Est: 1971. Open 10-5. *STOCK: General antiques and shipping goods.* TEL: 071 402 6845. VAT: Stan. *Trade Only.*

Dreams
34 Chalk Farm Rd. (L Amato) Open every day, 10.30-6. *STOCK: Brass bedsteads, bedspreads and quilts.* TEL: 071 267 8194.

East-Asia Co
103 Camden High St. Est: 1972. Open 10-6. *STOCK: Oriental antiquarian books on history and culture; Japanese and Chinese paintings and prints; jade, netsuke, objets d'art; books on Oriental art.* TEL: 071 388 5783; fax - 071 387 5766.

Galerie 1900
267 Camden High St. (B Rose and N Polyviou) Est: 1970. Open 10-5.30. SIZE: Medium. *STOCK: Glass, pottery, metalware, silver, jewellery, lighting and furnishings, 1800-1950, £100-£1,000.* LOC: Between Camden Town tube station and Camden Lock. PARK: Easy. TEL: 071 485 1001; home - 081 969 1803.

Haverstock Antiques LAPADA
Flat 24, Harley House, 28/32 Marylebone Rd. (J Newton) Est: 1976. Open 10-5. SIZE: Medium. *STOCK: Mahogany, walnut, elm, oak, rosewood furniture, Regency, Georgian and Victorian, especially dining and upholstered chairs.* PARK: Easy. TEL: 071 935 9813. SER: Restorations; courier; buys at auction. VAT: Stan/Spec.

N.W.1 continued

Hearth and Home

13 Chalk Farm Rd. (C Heath and M.P.W Smith) Open 10-6 including Sun. *STOCK: Pine and garden furniture; statuary, general antiques.* LOC: Opposite Camden Lock market. PARK: Easy. TEL: 071 485 9687. SER: Valuations. VAT: Stan/Spec.

Jazzy Art Deco

67 Camden Rd. (J Eccles) Open 12-6, Sat. 11-6. CL: Mon. *STOCK: Art deco furniture and decorative items.* LOC: Close to Camden Tube Station. TEL: 071 267 3342; home - 081 960 8988.

Richard Kihl Wine Antiques and Accessories

164 Regents Park Rd. Est: 1978. Open 9.30-5, Sat. 11-5. CL: Mon. SIZE: Small. *STOCK: Wine related antiques - decanters, claret jugs, coasters, glass, decanting cradles, corkscrews, glass funnels, old bottles, 1750-1910, £5-£5,000.* LOC: Close to London Zoo and Primrose Hill. PARK: Easy. TEL: 071 586 3838/5911; fax - 071 586 2960. VAT: Stan.

Laurence Corner Militaria

126-130 Drummond St, and 62-64 Hampstead Rd. (Victor Laurence Ltd.). Est: 1967. Open 9-5.30. SIZE: Large. *STOCK: Uniforms - ambassadorial and court dress, swords, helmets, drums; theatrical costumes, prints and paintings.* LOC: From Tottenham Court Rd. - Warren St. end - continue into Hampstead Rd., then Drummond St. is first turning on right by traffic lights. PARK: Easy. TEL: 071 388 6811.

David Miles

Open by appointment. *STOCK: Musical instruments.* TEL: 071 485 1329.

Chas. L Nyman and Co. Ltd

230 and 242 Camden High St. Est: 1920. Open 9.30-5.30. CL: Thurs. p.m. and Sat. *STOCK: English and continental 19th C furniture and porcelain.* TEL: 071 485 1907. VAT: Spec. *Trade Only.*

The Patchwork Dog and The Calico Cat Ltd

21 Chalk Farm Rd. (J Zinni-Lask) Est: 1977. Open Tues.-Sun. 10-6. SIZE: Large. *STOCK: American and English patchwork quilts, 1850-1930, £100-£900.* LOC: Near Camden Lock. PARK: Easy. TEL: 071 485 1239. SER: Restorations (quilt repairs). VAT: Stan/Spec.

Putnams

55 Regents Park Rd. Est: 1977. Open 10-6. SIZE: Small. *STOCK: Staffordshire transfer printed china, decorative items, quilts; fabrics based on antique Staffordshire china designs.* TEL: 071 431 2935.

N.W.1 continued

Regent Antiques

9-10 Chester Court, Albany St. (T Quaradeghini) Est: 1983. Open 10-5.30, Sat. by appointment. SIZE: Large and warehouse. *STOCK: Furniture, 18th C to Edwardian, £50-£5,000+; decorative items and bric-a-brac, 19th-20th C, £10-£1,000.* LOC: 1/4 mile from Gt. Portland St. station towards Camden Town. PARK: Easy. TEL: 071 935 6944; fax - 071 935 7814. SER: Restorations (furniture); gilding. VAT: Stan. *Trade Only.*

Relic Antiques Trade Warehouse

127 Pancras Rd. (M Gliksten and G Gower) Est: 1968. Open 10-5.30. CL: Sat. *STOCK: Showcases, counters, cabinets, shop fittings and interiors, French country furniture and decorative objects, architectural items, naive, advertising and fairground art, toys, games and models, £50-£800.* PARK: Meters. TEL: 071 387 6039; home - 071 586 0594; fax - 071 388 2691. SER: Valuations. VAT: Stan.

Spatz

4 Castlehaven Rd. (P Ebbinkhuyson and S Anchor) Est: 1979. Open Fri. 12-5.30, Sat. and Sun. 11-5.30. SIZE: Small. *STOCK: Victorian lace pillowcases and nightdresses, £25-£40; 1940's dresses, blouses and other daywear, £20-£60.* LOC: At Camden Lock. PARK: NCP nearby. TEL: 071 482 3785. VAT: Stan.

A Spigard

236 Camden High St. Open 9-6. *STOCK: General antiques and furniture.* TEL: 071 485 4095. SER: Restorations. VAT: Spec.

This and That (Furniture)

50 and 51 Chalk Farm Rd. (R.P Schanzer) Est: 1974. Open 10.30-6 every day. SIZE: Medium. *STOCK: Country furniture, stripped pine, oak and walnut, 1880-1900.* LOC: Between Roundhouse and Camden Lock. PARK: Easy. TEL: 071 267 5433. VAT: Stan.

Tomkinson's Stained Glass Windows and Architectural Antiques

129 Pancras Rd. (S Tomkinson) Open 9-5 or by appointment. CL: Sat. *STOCK: Mainly stained-glass windows.* TEL: 071 388 3239 or 071 267 1669. VAT: Stan.

Townsends

3A Prowse Pl, Camden Town. (M Townsend) *STOCK: Stained glass, doors, mirrors, shop fittings, fireplaces, ironwork, flooring and other architectural items.* TEL: 071 485 8611; fax - 071 267 5159. SER: Valuations; restorations (stained glass); stained glass design.

N.W.1 continued

W.E Walker
277/279 Camden High St. Est: 1930. Open 10-6, weekends by appointment. SIZE: Medium. *STOCK: Furniture, 17th-19th C; modern paintings and ceramics.* PARK: Easy. TEL: 071 485 6210/4433. SER: Valuations; restorations (china). VAT: Spec.

London N.W.2

The Corner Cupboard
679 Finchley Rd. (M Fry and R Fischelis) Est: 1950. Open 9.30-5.30. SIZE: Small. *STOCK: Jewellery, 18th-19th C, from £5; silver, china, glass.* LOC: Number 2 or 13 bus from Central London. PARK: Easy. TEL: 071 435 4870. VAT: Stan.

G. and F Gillingham Ltd **LAPADA**
62 Menelik Rd. Est: 1960. Open by appointment. SIZE: Warehouse. *STOCK: 19th C English and continental furniture and decorative items.* PARK: Easy. TEL: 071 435 5644.

Gunter Fine Art
4 Randall Ave. (G.A. and A.M Goodwin) Est: 1977. Open by appointment only. SIZE: Small. *STOCK: Watercolours, 18th-20th C, £100-£1,500; oil paintings, 19th C, £200-£2,000.* LOC: North Circular Rd., near Brent Cross shopping centre. PARK: Easy. TEL: 081 452 3997. SER: Buys at auction. *Trade Only.*

Elizabeth Harvey-Lee
1 Belton Rd, Willesden. Est: 1986. Open by appointment. *STOCK: Original prints 15th-20th C, etchings, engravings, lithographs, £50-£6,000.* TEL: 081 459 7623. SER: Stock catalogues to subscribers (£8 per annum); valuations; buys at auction; collections catalogued. FAIRS: London Original Print; Royal Academy; City of London, Barbican; West London, Kensington; New York, Fine Print. VAT: Spec.

"The Stove Shop"
(P. Crabb) Open by appointment. *STOCK: Original Scandinavian, French and English stoves and cooking ranges.* TEL: 081 208 0925. SER: Restorations; installations; hire and consultancy.

London N.W.3

Nan S Ashcroft
10a Daleham Gdns. Open by appointment. *STOCK: Fine and rare wine related artefacts and glass.* TEL: 071 794 6658.

Patricia Beckman **LAPADA**
Est: 1968. Open by appointment. *STOCK: Furniture, 18th and 19th C.* TEL: 071 435 5050. VAT: Spec.

N.W.3 continued

Tony Bingham
11 Pond St. Est: 1964. *STOCK: Musical instruments, books, music, oil paintings, engravings of musical interest.* TEL: 071 794 1596. VAT: Stan/Spec.

The Catto Gallery
100 Heath St, Hampstead. (Mrs G Catto) Est: 1986. Open 10-6, Sun. 2.30-6. CL: Mon. SIZE: Large. *STOCK: Victorian watercolours, £1,000-£25,000; contemporary watercolours, pastels and oils, £500-£6,000.* LOC: 1 min. from Hampstead tube station. PARK: Adjacent. TEL: 071 435 6660. SER: Valuations; restorations (watercolours); buys at auction (watercolours). VAT: Stan/Spec.

P.G de Lotz
20 Downside Cres, Hampstead. ABA. Est: 1967. *STOCK: Antiquarian books on history warfare - naval, military and aviation.* TEL: 071 794 5709; fax - 071 284 3058. SER: Catalogue available; search. *Postal Only.*

Dolphin Coins
2c England's Lane, Hampstead. (R Ilsley) BNTA. Est: 1966. Open 9.30-5. SIZE: Medium. *STOCK: British and world coins, early and medieval, from 100BC, £20-£50,000.* LOC: Off Haverstock HIll. PARK: Easy. TEL: 071 722 4116. SER: Valuations; buys at auction (coins). VAT: Spec.

Stephen Farrelly
152 Fleet Rd. Est: 1948. Open 10-6. CL: Thurs. *STOCK: Pictures, furniture, porcelain, general antiques.* TEL: 071 485 2089. VAT: Stan/Spec.

Keith Fawkes
1-3 Flask Walk, Hampstead. Est: 1970. Open 10-5.30. *STOCK: Antiquarian and general books.* TEL: 071 435 0614.

Otto Haas (A. and M. Rosenthal)
49 Belsize Park Gdns. Est: 1866. Open 9.30-5 or by appointment. CL: Sat. *STOCK: Manuscripts, printed music, autographs, rare books on music.* TEL: 071 722 1488.

Hampstead Antique Emporium
12 Heath St, Hampstead. Est: 1967. Open 10-6. CL: Mon. SIZE: Approx. 25 dealers. *STOCK: Jewellery, furniture, silver, paintings, prints, metalware, glass, lighting, porcelain, nomadic kelims, tribal weavings, collectors' items and objets d'art, all 18th-19th C.* LOC: 2 mins. walk from Hampstead underground. TEL: 071 794 3297; office - 431 0240. SER: Advice (interior decor). The following are a few of the dealers at the Emporium.

Ala Ryba
Jewellery and glass.
Barbara
Tiles, paperweights and collectables.

Hampstead Antique Emporium continued

Caray Antiques
Furniture, brass including lamps, decorative items.
Deborah
Collectors' items, prints, silver and plate.
Diana
Lighting and furniture.
E Gardner
Furniture, boxes and early prints.
Garvin Antiques
Furniture.
Jackson Antiques
Small furniture, boxes and bronzes.
Lee and Stacey
General antiques, furniture, silver, fine art.
Meadway Books
Children's and illustrated books, modern first editions.
Micawber
Books and postcards; horse racing memorabilia and prints.
Mount Gallery
18th-20th C pictures.
E O'Dwyer
Porcelain, glass, small furniture.
Ross Pye
19th C furniture, decorative items, mirrors and small collectables.
D Quastel
Silver frames and cutlery.
Scorpio Antiques
Jewellery and silver.
Shelagh
Small furniture and objets d'art.
Trio
(Miss S Mendoza) *Furniture, porcelain and glass.* VAT: Stan.

Platon Hobson

34 Belsize Park Gdns. Est: 1980. Open by appointment. *STOCK: Cushions- 17th C tapestry, 18th C Beauvais tapestries, Aubussons and needleworks, some 19th C, £60-£1,000; decorative objects, furniture and pictures, 18th-19th C, from £100.* LOC: 5 mins. from Belsize Park tube station. PARK: Easy.

Platon Hobson continued

TEL: 071 722 3703; home - same. SER: Restorations (textiles, some furniture). FAIRS: Decorative. VAT: Stan/Spec. *Trade Only.*

Just Desks LAPADA

6 Erskine Rd. (G Gordon and N Finch) Est: 1967. Open 9-5.30 or by appointment. *STOCK: Victorian and Edwardian pedestal and partner desks, writing tables, swivel chairs, file cabinets.* PARK: Easy. TEL: 071 722 4902; fax - 071 722 2185. VAT: Stan.

N.W.3 continued

Kendal Antiques
91A Heath St, Hampstead. (T.R.G Brazier) Open Tues.-Sat. 10-6. SIZE: Small. *STOCK: English Georgian, Victorian and Edwardian furniture, china, porcelain, copper, brass, smalls, oils and watercolours.* LOC: Hampstead Village. PARK: Nearby. TEL: 071 435 4351; work-shop - 0480 411 811. SER: Restorations. VAT: Stan/Spec.

John Lyons Gallery
18 South Hill Park, Hampstead. Est: 1968. Resident. Appointment essential. SIZE: Small. *STOCK: Art nouveau, art deco, 20th C paintings, studio ceramics and art glass.* PARK: Easy. TEL: 071 794 3537. SER: Buys at auction.

Duncan R Miller Fine Arts
17 Flask Walk, Hampstead. Open 10-6, Sat. 11-5, Sun. 2-5. SIZE: Small. *STOCK: Modern British and European paintings, drawings and sculpture, especially Scottish Colourist paintings, from £500.* LOC: Off Hampstead High St., near underground station. PARK: Nearby. TEL: 071 435 5462. SER: Valuations; restorations (conservation and restoration of oils and works on paper and Oriental rugs); buys at auction. FAIRS: Contemporary Art; Fine Art, Olympia; 20th C British Art; World of Watercolours. VAT: Spec.

Frederick Mulder
83 Belsize Park Gdns. Open by appointment. *STOCK: Old Master and modern original prints; modern illustrated books.* TEL: 071 722 2105; fax - 071 483 4228.

Newman and Cooling Ltd
c/o Box 1608. Open by appointment only. *STOCK: Oil paintings, 1800-1930, from £1,000.* TEL: 071 722 2537. SER: Valuations; restorations (oil paintings and drawings). VAT: Spec.

London N.W.4

Antiques (Hendon) Ltd
18 Parson St, Hendon. (G Frankl) Est: 1960. Open 9.30-6. CL: Wed. p.m. SIZE: Medium. *STOCK: Furniture and paintings, £100-£1,000; china, £10-£300; all 18th-19th C.* LOC: Coming from Golders Green, cross the North Circular Rd. and proceed to the end of Brent St. PARK: Easy. TEL: 081 203 1194. SER: Valuations; restorations (paintings and furniture); buys at auction. VAT: Stan/Spec.

Talking Machine
30 Watford Way, Hendon. Open 10-5.30, Sat. 11-5. *STOCK: Mechanical music, old gramophones, phonographs, vintage records and 78's, needles and spare parts, early radio, typewriters, sewing machines, juke boxes, early telephones.* TEL: 081 202 3473. SER: Buys at auction. VAT: Stan.

London N.W.5

Antiquum
147 Highgate Rd. (K. and T Kyriacou) Est: 1979. Open 9-6, Mon. and Thurs. 1-6. SIZE: Medium. *STOCK: Georgian and Victorian furniture, £500-£3,000.* LOC: North of Kentish Town, opposite Esso petrol station at junction with Gordon House Rd. PARK: Easy. TEL: 071 485 9501. SER: Restorations (furniture); buys at auction (as stock). VAT: Spec.

Y. and B. Bolour
53-79 Highgate Rd. Open 9.30-5.30. CL: Sat. *STOCK: Decorative carpets, rugs and tapestries.* TEL: 071 485 6262; fax - 071 267 7351.

Game Advice
23 Holmes Rd. (S Elithorn) Est: 1976. Open by appointment only. SIZE: Small. *STOCK: Games, puzzles, jigsaws, cards, educational toys, chess sets; chess, cookery and children's books, £25-£100; ephemera, £5-£50; all 18th-19th C.* LOC: Just off Kentish Town Rd. PARK: Easy. TEL: 071 485 4226. SER: Valuations; restorations; buys at auction. VAT: Stan.

Joseph Lavian
Block 'F', 53-79 Highgate Rd. Est: 1950. Open 9-6. SIZE: Large. *STOCK: Oriental carpets, rugs, kelims, tapestries and needlework, Aubusson, Savonnerie and textiles, 18th-19th C.* LOC: Kentish Town Station. PARK: Own. TEL: 071 485 7955/482 1234; fax - 071 267 9222. SER: Valuations; restorations.

Barrie Marks Ltd
11 Laurier Rd. ABA. Open by appointment only. *STOCK: Antiquarian books - illustrated private press, colourplate, colour printing; modern first editions.* TEL: 071 482 5684; fax - 071 284 3149.

Zoulfaghari
Unit D, 4th Floor, 53-79 Highgate Rd. Est: 1974. Open 9.30-5.30. CL: Sat. SIZE: Large. *STOCK: Oriental carpets and rugs.* LOC: Kentish Town. PARK: Own. TEL: 071 267 5973 (24hr.). SER: Valuations; restorations; buys at auction; cleaning.

London N.W.6

H Baron
76 Fortune Green Rd. Open Fri. and Sat. 1-6. *STOCK: Antiquarian music, books on music and iconography, autograph music and letters.* TEL: 071 794 4041; office and fax - 081 459 2035.

Mr. Temple Brooks
12 Mill Lane, West Hampstead. Est: 1936. Resident. Always available. *STOCK: Clocks.* TEL: 081 452 9696. VAT: Spec.

John Denham Gallery
50 Mill Lane, West Hampstead. Open 10-5. CL: Sat. *STOCK: Paintings, drawings and prints,*

John Denham Gallery continued

17th-20th C, £5-£5,000. TEL: 071 794 2635. SER: Restorations; conservation; re-framing. VAT: Spec.

Gallery Kaleidoscope
66 Willesden Lane. (K Barrie) Est: 1965. Open 10-6. SIZE: Medium. *STOCK: Oils, watercolours and prints, 18th-20th C.* LOC: 10 mins. from Marble Arch. PARK: Easy. TEL: 071 328 5833. SER: Restorations; framing; artists' materials. VAT: Stan/Spec.

Scope Antiques
64-66 Willesden Lane. (K Barrie) Est: 1966. Open 10-6. SIZE: Large. *STOCK: Furniture, general antiques, decorative items, silver, bric-a-brac.* PARK: Easy. TEL: 071 328 5833. SER: Restorations (silver). VAT: Stan/Spec.

G.T Siden
69 Compayne Gdns. Open by appointment only. *STOCK: 16th-19th C drawings.* TEL: 071 624 9045.

London N.W.7

Gerald Clark Antiques LAPADA
1 High St, Mill Hill Village. (G.J Clark) Est: 1976. Open by appointment. SIZE: Medium. *STOCK: Early English and Victorian Staffordshire pottery, porcelain, small furniture, watercolours and plaques, 18th-19th C.* PARK: Easy. TEL: 081 906 0342/958 4295. SER: Valuations; buys at auction. FAIRS: Olympia (June); Kensington (Jan. and Aug.); Barbican (Nov.). VAT: Spec.

London N.W.8

Alfies Antique Market
13-25 Church St. (B Gray) Open 10-6. CL: Mon. SIZE: There are 370 stands on 5 floors selling general antiques and collectables. TEL: 071 723 6066.

Beth Adams
Stand G43/4. *Art deco.* TEL: 071 723 5613.
Sormeh Afshar
Stand G30. *Jewellery.* TEL: 071 723 1513.
Manfred Alan
Stand S14. *Ceramics and glass.* TEL: 071 723 6105.
An Eye for Art
Stand F18. *Paintings.* TEL: 071 723 1370.
Stanley Beal
Stand G130-132, 140-143. *Silver and plate.* TEL: 071 724 6643.
R S Benjamin
Stand S121/134. *Paperweights, glass, pottery.* TEL: 071 723 5731.
David Bennett
Stand G124. *General.* TEL: 071 724 3437.
Ursula and Jurgen Berger
Stand 51/52/62. *Jewellery, ceramics and glass.* TEL: 071 724 3439.

Alfies Antique Market continued

Manley Joseph Black
Stand F61. *Unusual and decorative objects, furniture.* TEL: 071 723 0678.
Oonagh Black
Stand S103. *Furniture and accessories.* TEL: 071 723 5731.
Sophia Blanchard
Stand S41. *Samplers, country furniture.* TEL: 071 723 6105.
Barry Bowman
Stand G101/2/3. *Ceramics, silver and glass.* TEL: 071 724 6643.
Catherine Braithwaite
Stand S7. *Royal Doulton.* TEL: 071 402 0941.
B Bruno
Stand F10. *Clocks, watches.* TEL: 071 723 1370.
S Brunswick
Stand G16/17 and G20-22. *Furniture, accessories, carpets, textiles and decorative objects.* TEL: 071 723 1513.
Ursula Burnstock
Stand G56/7. *General antiques, furniture.* TEL: 071 723 5613.
David Casolani
Stand F107/8. *Paintings.* TEL: 071 723 1370.
Fred Cheeseman
Stand F116. *General.* TEL: 071 723 1370.
Sylvie Chilvers
Stand S59/60. *Carpets, general.* TEL: 071 723 6105.
P Y Chin
Stand B9. *Old Master drawings, watercolours and objects.* TEL: 071 724 3437.
Brenda Klare Gerwat Clark
Stand S1/3. *Dolls and toys, furniture and accessories.* TEL: 071 706 4699.
Joanne Cohen
Stand T105. *Small collectables, ceramics, glass and silver.* TEL: 071 706 2969.
Collectors' Paradise
Stand S5. *Mechanical items.* TEL: 071 724 1488.
Connie and Steven
Stand S115-8 and S126-9. *Furniture and accessories.* TEL: 071 723 5731.
Ruth Davis
Stand F79/80. *Silver, glass and porcelain.* TEL: 071 723 0429.
James Deighton
Stand S112/3/4. *Furniture and accessories.* TEL: 071 723 5731.
Jo del Grosso
Stand F17. *Books.* TEL: 071 724 7231.
Drake
Stand G38/9. *Architectural items, brass.* TEL: 071 723 5613.
M Druks
Stand S46/47. *General antiques.* TEL: 071 723 6105.

Alfies Antique Market continued

East Gates Antiques
Stand G4/6. *Glass, china, cameras.* TEL: 071 724 5650.
Farrow and Werth
Stand F100. *English, American and continental posters.* TEL: 071 706 1545.
Final Whistle
Stand S61/3. *Football items.* TEL: 071 262 3423.
Jean Fleming and Bea Korniczky
Stand G64/5. *Ceramics, objets d'art, Oriental items, general antiques.* TEL: 071 723 0449.
Mrs P M Fogg
Stand S12. *Pens.* TEL: 071 402 0732.
Sally Fox
Stand S111/120/2. *Paintings, furniture, accessories.* TEL: 071 723 5731.
E Freestone
Stand S6. *Marine items.* TEL: 071 723 6105.
Helen Gardiner Antiques
Stand F132-5. *Furniture and accessories.* TEL: 071 723 1370.
Robin Gardiner
Stand B13. *Prints and drawings.* TEL: 071 724 3437.
William Garraway
Stand G11. *Prints, postcards and smalls.* TEL: 071 723 1513.
Genie
Stand S57/8. *General.* TEL: 071 723 6105.
Richard Gibbon
Stand G60. *20th C furniture and accessories.* TEL: 071 723 0449.
Glade Antiques
Stand G144/5. *General antiques.* TEL: 071 723 1513.
Helen Gmur
Ceramics and jewellery.
Goldsmith and Perris **LAPADA**
Stand G53/62/58. *Silver and plate.* TEL: 071 724 7051.
Teresa Gore
Stand S106. *Ceramics and glass; general.* TEL: 071 723 5731.
Marie Gottlieb
Stand B45/46/49. *Art deco furniture and artefacts.* TEL: 071 402 1976.
Gramophone Workshop
Stand B35/6. *Mechanical items.* TEL: 071 724 3437.
Linette Greco
Stand G118. *Jewellery.* TEL: 071 723 0564.
Ena Green Antiques
Stand F74-78. *Furniture and decorative accessories.* TEL: 071 723 0429.
Mary Griffiths
Stand G127. *General.* TEL: 071 723 0564.
Vera Habberley
Stand F70. *Textiles and clothing, linen and lace.* TEL: 071 723 0429.

Alfies Antique Market continued

J Hall
Stand F13. *Furniture and accessories.* TEL: 071 723 0678.
John Hamilton
Stand G115. *General and jewellery.* TEL: 071 723 0564.
Richard Harrison
Stand B19. *Paintings.* TEL: 071 724 3437.
M Heidarieh/A Bagdhi
Stand G1. *Clocks and watches, general.* TEL: 071 724 5650.
Alastair Hendy
Stand B58/59, G79/80. *Art deco furniture, lighting, figures, mirrors, glass, pottery including Clarice Cliff, S. Cooper, Shelley, Poole and Keith Murray, 1920-1940, £10-£1,500.* TEL: 071 706 3907. SER: Valuations.
Tina Henning
Stand F14. *18th-19th C oil paintings.* TEL: 071 723 8964.
Peter Herbert
Stand G56/9/61. *Bathroom fittings, lighting.* TEL: 071 724 2200.
Frances Houlding
Stand G116/7/128/9. *Costume jewellery.* TEL: 071 402 2689.
J Howard
Stand S53. *Carpets.* TEL: 071 723 6105.
Dudley Howe
Stand S55/56/67. *General antiques, commemoratives.* TEL: 071 723 6105.
Virginia Hoyer-Millar
Stand S105. *Furniture and accessories.* TEL: 071 723 5731.
Incisioni
Stand F40-43. *Original prints, drawings and rare books.* TEL: 071 706 2970.
J and G Antiques
Stand B20/21. *General.* TEL: 071 724 3437.
Peter Jacques
Stand S11. *Brass architectural fixtures and fittings.* TEL: 071 723 6105.
Roderick Jones
Stand B2/30-32. *Paintings, frames.* TEL: 071 724 3437.
Mary Keays
Stand G119. *Jewellery.* TEL: 071 723 0564.
Eric Kent
Stand B55/6. *General, postcards, ephemera.* TEL: 071 724 3439.
Mrs Khawaia
Stand G122/3. *Jewellery.* TEL: 071 706 2971.
Simon Kluth
Stand S8. *Furniture and accessories.* TEL: 071 723 6105.
Kotobuki
Stand F113/4/125/6/G95. *Oriental items.* TEL: 071 402 0723.
Lamb Silverware
Stand F118/121. *Silver and plate.* TEL: 071 723 1370.

Alfies Antique Market continued

Marilyn Lancer
Stand G18. *Objets d'art.* TEL: 071 723 1513.
Anthony Lask
Stand F127-9. *Silver and plate.* TEL: 071 723 1370.
Madeline Lawrence
Stand F101/2/138/9/40. *General antiques, kitchenalia, linen and lace.* TEL: 071 723 1370.
Celia Levy/Sheila Hart
Stand S104. *Furniture and accessories.* TEL: 071 723 5731.
Sara Lewis
Stand S16. *Furniture and accessories.* TEL: 071 723 6105.
John Lyons
Stand B5. *Decorative arts, paintings.* TEL: 071 724 3437.
J MacDonald
Stand F13. *Silver.* TEL: 071 723 1370.
Nigel MacDonald
Stand F23. *Decorative items, furniture and accessories.* TEL: 071 723 1370.
M MacLeod
Stand S59/60. *Handbags, costume, general, porcelain and jewellery.* TEL: 071 723 6105.
McLean/Black/Somerville
Stand S4. *Art deco ceramics.* TEL: 071 723 6105.
Daniel Maman
Stand G120. *Jewellery.* TEL: 071 723 0564.
Iris Margolis
Stand G104/5. *General.* TEL: 071 723 0564.
Nigel Martin
Stand S40. *Textiles.* TEL: 071 723 6105.
Francesca Martire
Stand B10/11. *Jewellery, pictures, objects.* TEL: 071 724 3437.
Margaret Miall
Stand G14/15/19. *Light fittings, ceramics and glass.* TEL: 071 723 1513.
J Miles
Stand G31. *Silver.* TEL: 071 723 1513.
Bill Miller
Stand S13. *General and paintings.* TEL: 071 723 6105.
M Miller
Stand G37. *Decorative items, 1890-1920's and some 1950's.* TEL: 071 723 5613.
M O Mohamed
Stand G125/6/134. *Period accessories and costume jewellery.* TEL: 071 723 0564.
Gavin Morgan
Stand F50/1. *20th C furniture and accessories.* TEL: 071 723 0678.
Pat Newcomb
Stand B25. *Clocks.* TEL: 071 724 3437.
Norcliffe Fine Art
Stand F44/5. *Paintings.* TEL: 071 723 0678.
Nordmark and King
Stand F57. *Furniture, French mirrors and fireplaces.* TEL: 071 723 0429.
Michael Nunn/Christine McCabe
Stand B26/7. *General.* TEL: 071 724 3437.

Alfies Antique Market continued

Ms N Oakley
Ceramics.
Obelisk
Stand F106. *Furniture and accessories.* TEL: 071 723 1370.
Susan Oliver
Stand F109-11. *Furniture and accessories.* TEL: 071 723 1370.
The Originals
Stand G49. *Radios; 20th C items.* TEL: 071 723 0449.
A J Partners
Stand F104. *Art deco ceramics.* TEL: 071 723 1370.
M S Payne
Stand G100. *Jewellery, ceramics and glass, clocks and watches.* TEL: 071 402 1136.
Geoffrey Peake
Stand G82/4. *Art deco items; ceramics especially Susie Cooper.* TEL: 071 723 0449.
Bob and Angela Phillips
Stand B60/1. *Silver, plate and jewellery.* TEL: 071 724 3439.
Phoenix
Stand G36. *General, kitchenalia.* TEL: 071 723 5613.
Matteo Picasso
Stand B50. *Silver and plate, clocks and watches.* TEL: 071 724 3439.
Tom Power
Stand S10. *Royal Doulton.* TEL: 071 706 4586.
Shoshi Preiss
Stand F48/49/71/72. *Paintings, furniture and accessories.* TEL: 071 723 0678.
L Preston
Stand F81/4. *Furniture and accessories.* TEL: 071 723 1370.
RMB Art
Stand S109/130. *Pictures, frames.* TEL: 071 723 5731.
Re-Design
Stand F54-56. *Furniture, accessories.* TEL: 071 723 0678.
Angela Regana
Stand S110. *Carpets, general.* TEL: 071 723 5731.
Celia Reynolds
Stand S52. *Furniture and accessories.* TEL: 071 723 6105.
Gareth Roberts
Stand B39. *20th C furniture and accessories.* TEL: 071 724 3439.
C Robinson
Stand G75-78/91/2. *Art deco furniture and accessories.* TEL: 071 723 0449.
Jo Robinson
Stand S108. *Furniture and accessories.* TEL: 071 723 5731.
A C Rockman
Stand G28/9. *Bric-a-brac, Victoriana, commemoratives, ceramics and glass.* TEL: 071 723 1513.

Alfies Antique Market continued

B Rockman
Stand G23/24/25. *Victoriana and general antiques, commemoratives, ceramics and glass.* TEL: 071 723 1513.
Alvin Ross
Stand G9-11. *Dolls and toys.* TEL: 071 723 1513.
Rowe and Lorenzo
Stand S9. *20th C glass.* TEL: 071 723 6105.
SPV Antiques
Stand G35. *General.* TEL: 071 723 5613.
Yakup Saatcioglu
Stand B53. *Carpets.* TEL: 071 724 3439.
Dick Salveson
Stand B43/4. *General antiques.* TEL: 071 724 3439.
Samii
Stand S102/133. *Ceramics and glass, general.* TEL: 071 723 5731.
Patrick Scola
Stand G63. *China.* TEL: 071 723 0449.
Jeremy Sewell
Stand G12/13/144/5. *Watercolours, frames and prints.* TEL: 071 723 1513.
Trudi and Bob Share
Stand F19/22/73. *Art deco and later items.* TEL: 071 723 0429.
A and Z Shine
Stand G2. *Silver and general.* TEL: 071 724 5640.
Roswitha Siptroth
Stand F101/2. *Art deco ceramics.* TEL: 071 723 1370.
Rosemary and Claire Smale
Stand G93/4. *Art deco ceramics.* TEL: 071 723 0449.
Murray Small
Stand S54. *Art deco, ceramics.* TEL: 071 723 6105.
Connie Speight
Stand G107/8/9/124. *Art deco furniture and accessories.* TEL: 071 723 0564.
Kelvin Spooner
Stand B54. *Prints and drawings.* TEL: 071 724 3439.
Colin George Steer
Stand G15/16/7/8. *Paintings.* TEL: 071 724 3437.
Marion Swycher
Stand G111/121. *Ceramics, Staffordshire and glass.* TEL: 071 723 0564.
Elsie Taylor
Stand G135. *20th C furniture and accessories.* TEL: 071 723 0564.
David Tilleke
Stand G7/8. *Paintings, prints.* TEL: 071 723 1370.
Tina Art
Stand B3/4/6/8 and G45-49. *Furniture, textiles and accessories.*
Vintage Sounds
Stand B1. *Mechanical items.* TEL: 071 724 3437.

Alfies Antique Market continued

Sara Viventi
Stand G120. *Silver, jewellery and general.* TEL: 071 723 0564.
Catherine Wallis
19th C French decorative items.
D Wallis
Stand F15. *Scientific instruments, corkscrews.* TEL: 071 402 1038.
Carol Warner
Stand F52/3. *Art nouveau, art deco.* TEL: 071 723 0678.
Marie Warner
Stand G136/7/8. *Jewellery, ceramics and glass.* TEL: 071 706 3727.
Steven Watson
Stand G70/4. *20th C glass.* TEL: 071 723 0678.
J J White
Stand G66-69/87. *Art deco.* TEL: 071 723 0449.
C Wickham
Stand G33/4. *Lighting.* TEL: 071 723 5613.
Norman Wilcocks
Stand G3. *General.* TEL: 071 724 5650.
Rod Woolley
Stand F20/1. *Art deco ceramics.* TEL: 071 723 0678.

Amadeus Gallery
21 St. John's Wood, High St. (E Badraie) Open 10-6. SIZE: Medium. *STOCK: Paintings, 19th-20th C, £2,500-£45,000; works of art, 18th-19th C.* PARK: Meters. TEL: 071 722 5883. SER: Valuations; restorations (paintings and works of art); buys at auction (paintings and sculpture). FAIRS: Olympia. VAT: Stan/Spec.

Beverley
30 Church St, Marylebone. Open 11-7 or by appointment. *STOCK: Art nouveau, art deco, decorative objects.* TEL: 071 262 1576.

D. and A Binder
34 Church St. Open 10-6. SIZE: Medium. *STOCK: Traditional shop-fittings, counters, cabinets, vitrines and display stands.* LOC: Near Lisson Grove. TEL: 071 723 0542; fax - 071 724 0837.

Bizarre
24 Church St. (A Taramasco) Open 10-5. *STOCK: Art deco.* TEL: 071 724 1305.

Camden Art Gallery
22 Church St. (A Silver and A Woda) Est: 1968. Open 10-6. SIZE: Medium. *STOCK: Victorian and continental oils, £300-£10,000; modern British oils and watercolours, £100-£10,000.* LOC: Off Edgware Rd. PARK: Easy. TEL: 071 262 3613. SER: Valuations; restorations (framing and cleaning); buys at auction (oil paintings). FAIRS: Barbican. VAT: Spec.

N.W.8 continued

China Repairers incorporating Mair and Drayson Antiques LAPADA
64 Charles Lane, St. John's Wood. (P Mair, H Howard and V Baron) Est: 1952. Open 9.30-1 and 2.15-5.30. CL: Sat. *STOCK: Early Meissen, English pottery and porcelain, 18th C, £50-£500.* PARK: Meters. TEL: 071 722 8407. SER: Restorations (pottery, porcelain, early Tang); restoration courses. VAT: Stan/Spec.

Church Street Antiques
8 Church St. (S Shuster) Est: 1974. Open 10-5.30. SIZE: Medium. *STOCK: Walnut, mahogany and oak furniture, 19th to early 20th C, £50-£2,500; decorative items - bronze, crystal and ormulu.* LOC: Near Lisson Grove. PARK: Easy. TEL: 071 723 7415. VAT: Stan.

Nicholas Drummond/Wrawby Moor Art Gallery Ltd
6 St. John's Wood Rd. (J.N Drummond) Est: 1972. Open by appointment only. *STOCK: English and European oils, £250-£30,000; works on paper.* LOC: Pass Lords entrance and next lights, house last bow front on left, facing down Hamilton Terrace. TEL: 071 286 6452; home - same. SER: Valuations; restorations (oils); buys at auction. VAT: Spec.

Robert Franses and Sons
5 Nugent Terrace, St. John's Wood. Est: 1969. Open 9-1 or by appointment. CL: Sat. SIZE: Small. *STOCK: European and Oriental carpets, tapestries, needlework, Turkish village rugs, early Chinese rugs.* TEL: 071 286 6913; home - 071 328 0949. SER: Restorations. VAT: Stan/Spec.

The Furniture Store Ltd
35/37 Church St. Open 10-6 or by appointment. *STOCK: Decorative furniture and accessories, Gothic, arts and crafts, art nouveau, art deco, 1950s and 1960s, garden furniture, Lloyd loom, bentwood, lighting, ceramics, glass and pictures.* TEL: 071 723 2776. SER: Hire.

The Gallery of Antique Costume and Textiles
2 Church St, Marylebone. Open 10-5.30. *STOCK: Curtains, needlework, paisley shawls, silk robes and English quilts, 19th-20th C; tassles, decorative borders, silk panels, velvets and brocades, £5-£50,000.* LOC: 500yds. from Marylebone tube and 1/2 mile from Marble Arch. PARK: Easy. TEL: 071 723 9981 (ansaphone).

The Gallery on Church Street
12 Church St. (E Phillips) Open 10-5.30 or by appointment. SIZE: Small. *STOCK: Jewellery, fine art, art nouveau, art deco, watercolours.* PARK: Easy. TEL: 071 723 3389.

N.W.8 continued

Milne Henderson **BADA**
112 Clifton Hill. (S Milne Henderson) Est: 1970. Open by appointment. *STOCK: Japanese, Chinese and Korean paintings and screens.* TEL: 071 328 2171; fax - 071 624 7274. SER: Valuations; buys at auction. VAT: Stan.

Just Desks **LAPADA**
20 Church St. (G Gordon and N Finch) Est: 1967. Open 9.30-6 or by appointment. *STOCK: Victorian and Edwardian desks, writing tables, davenports, bureaux, chairs, filing cabinets, roll tops.* PARK: Meters. TEL: 071 723 7976; fax - 071 402 6416. VAT: Stan.

Magus Antiques **LAPADA**
4 Church St. (D.A Robinson) Est: 1973. Open 10-6. CL: Mon. SIZE: Medium. *STOCK: Porcelain and glass, European and Oriental, £10-£15,000; bronzes, furniture, £100-£15,000.* LOC: Left off Edgware Rd., 200yds. north of Marylebone flyover. PARK: Easy. TEL: 071 724 1278. SER: Valuations; buys at auction. FAIRS: Olympia. VAT: Stan.

Raffles Antiques
40/42 Church St. (D Greengrass and D Tupman) Est: 1971. Open 10-6, Sun. by appointment. SIZE: Large. *STOCK: General antiques and decorative art, 18th-20th C, to £10,000.* LOC: Off Lisson Grove. PARK: Easy. TEL: 071 724 6384/706 2497. FAIRS: Olympia. VAT: Stan.

Risky Business
44 Church St. (P.R John and Mrs C.M Dobson) Est: 1976. Open 10-6. SIZE: Medium. *STOCK: Decorative furnishings, 1900-1930; vintage sporting paraphernalia, luggage; cane, rattan and club style furniture.* LOC: Near Lisson Grove. PARK: Easy. TEL: 071 724 2194. VAT: Stan.

S. and H. Antiques
7 Church St. (W Hyde and G Sinclair) Open 10.30-1 and 2-5.30. *STOCK: Continental porcelain, silver, bronze and decorative items, paintings and works of art, 18th-19th C.* LOC: Near Lisson Grove. PARK: Easy. TEL: 071 724 7118; home - 071 724 5804. SER: Valuations; buys at auction.

Silver Belle
48 Church St. (B and A Bowman) Est: 1986. Open 9.30-5.30, Sun. and Mon. by appointment. SIZE: Medium. *STOCK: Silver and Sheffield plate, china including tea sets.* PARK: Easy. TEL: 071 723 2908; 081 443 0614. SER: Valuations; restorations (re-plating). VAT: Stan/Spec.

Tara Antiques
6 Church St. (P Petrou and G Robinson) Est: 1971. Open 10-6. CL: Mon. SIZE: Medium. *STOCK: Unusual marble and bronze statuary; Vienna bronzes, silver, furniture, paintings, ivory and tortoiseshell.* PARK: Easy. TEL: 071 724 2405. SER: Buys at auction. VAT: Stan.

Townsends
1 Church St. (M Townsend) Open 10-6. CL: Mon. *STOCK: Tiles, door furniture, lighting, garden furniture and ornaments.* TEL: 071 724 3746.

Townsends
81 Abbey Rd, St. John's Wood. (M Townsend) Est: 1972. Open 10-6. CL: Mon. SIZE: Large. *STOCK: Fireplaces, £100-£3,000; stained glass, £30-£200; architectural items, £10-£300; mainly 19th C.* LOC: Corner of Abbey Rd. and Boundary Rd. PARK: Easy. TEL: 071 624 4756. SER: Valuations. VAT: Stan.

Simon Tracy Gallery
18 Church St. Est: 1983. Open 10-7, Thurs. 10-9, Sun. and other times by appointment. *STOCK: British furniture and accessories - arts and crafts, aesthetic movement, architect designed, Gothic revival, art nouveau, 1860-1940, from £100.* TEL: 071 724 5890; fax - 071 262 0274. SER: Valuations; restorations; buys at auction. VAT: Stan/Spec.

Trading Places
22 Church St. Open 9.30-5. SIZE: Medium. *STOCK: General antiques, chaises longues.* PARK: Reasonable. TEL: 071 262 1338. SER: Restorations and upholstery.

N.W.8 continued

Wellington Gallery **LAPADA**
1 St John's Wood High St. (Mr and Mrs K Barclay) Open 10-5.30. *STOCK: Fine furniture, 18th and 19th C; paintings, Georgian glass, porcelain, silver and Sheffield plate, general antiques.* TEL: 071 586 2620.

London N.W.9

B.C Metalcrafts Ltd
69 Tewkesbury Gdns. Est: 1946. Open by appointment only. *STOCK: Lighting, ormolu and marble lamps; Oriental and European vases; clocks, pre-1900, £5-£500.* Not stocked: Silver. TEL: 081 204 2446. SER: Restorations and conversions; buys at auction. VAT: Stan/Spec. *Trade Only.*

The Witch Ball
51A Blackbird Hill, Kingsbury. (L.C.M Drecker) Est: 1941. Open 10-6. SIZE: Medium. *STOCK: Victorian furniture, button chairs.* TEL: 081 200 4937. SER: Restorations; buys at auction.

London N.W.10

David Malik and Son Ltd
5 Metro Centre, Britannia Way, Park Royal. Open 9-5. CL: Sat. *STOCK: Chandeliers, wall lights.* PARK: Easy. TEL: 081 965 4232; fax - 081 965 2401. VAT: Stan.

London N.W.11

Delieb Antiques Ltd
31 Woodville Rd. (E Delieb) Est: 1953. Open by appointment only. CL: Sat. *STOCK: Collectors' silver and rarities.* TEL: 081 458 2083. SER: Valuations (silver). VAT: Spec.

Christopher Eimer
P.O. Box 352. *STOCK: Medals.* TEL: 081 458 9933. *Postal Only.*

London W.C.1

Abbott and Holder
30 Museum St. Est: 1938. Open 9.30-6, Thurs. till 7. *STOCK: Pictures, especially watercolours.* TEL: 071 637 3981. VAT: Spec.

Atlantis Bookshop
49a Museum St. Open 10-5.30, Sat. 11-5. *STOCK: Antiquarian books on the occult and paranormal.* TEL: 071 405 2120.

Austin/Desmond Fine Art
Pied Bull Yard, 15a Bloomsbury Sq. (J Austin and W Desmond) Open 10.30-6.30, Sat. 10.30-2.30. *STOCK: Modern and contemporary British paintings and prints.* TEL: 071 242 4443.

W.C.1 continued

Barometer Fair
Pied Bull Yard, Bury Pl., Bloomsbury. (J.M.W Forster) Open 10-5.30, Sat. 11-3. SIZE: Small. *STOCK: Barometers, 1760-1880, £50-£5,000; old Sheffield plate, scientific instruments, prints.* LOC: Near British Museum. PARK: Nearby. TEL: 071 404 4521. SER: Restorations.

Louis W Bondy
16 Little Russell St. ABA. Est: 1947. Open 10.30-6.30, Sat. 10.30-5.15. SIZE: Small. *STOCK: Rare books.* LOC: Near British Museum. PARK: Fairly easy. TEL: 071 405 2733. SER: Valuations. VAT: Stan.

Cartographia Ltd
Pied Bull Yard, Bury Pl., Bloomsbury. (K Marsden) Est: 1976. Open 10-5.30, Sat. 11-4, other times by appointment. SIZE: Medium. *STOCK: Maps, world-wide, especially British Isles and North America; topographical engravings especially London; decorative engravings including flowers, fashion and theatre.* LOC: Near British Museum. PARK: Nearby. TEL: 071 404 4050/4521.

Cinema Bookshop
13-14 Great Russell St. (F Zentner) Est: 1969. Open 10.30-5.30. SIZE: Small. *STOCK: Books, magazines, posters and stills.* LOC: First right off Tottenham Court Rd. PARK: Easy. TEL: 071 637 0206. SER: Mail order. VAT: Stan.

W.C.1 continued

George and Peter Cohn
Unit 21, 21 Wren St. Est: 1947. Open 9-5, Sat. and Fri. p.m. by appointment. *STOCK: Decorative lights.* PARK: Forecourt. TEL: 071 278 3749. SER: Restorations (chandeliers and wall-lights). *Trade Only.*

Sebastian D'Orsai Ltd
39 Theobalds Rd. (A Brooks) Open 9.30-5. CL: Sat. *STOCK: Framed watercolours.* TEL: 071 405 6663. SER: Restorations (paintings and prints); framing; gilding. VAT: Stan.

J.A.L Franks Ltd
7 New Oxford St. Est: 1947. *STOCK: Stamps, maps, postcards, cigarette cards.* TEL: 071 405 0274.

Jessop Classic Photographica
67 Great Russell St. Open 9-6, Sat. 9-5. *STOCK: Classic photographic equipment, cameras and optical toys.* TEL: 071 831 3640; fax - 071 831 3956.

Marchmont Bookshop
39 Burton St. (D Holder) Open 11-6.30. CL: Sat. *STOCK: Literature, including modern first editions.* TEL: 071 387 7989.

Nihon Token
23 Museum St. (M. and H Dean) Est: 1965. Open 10-5. CL: Sat. SIZE: Medium. *STOCK: Japanese netsuke, swords, fittings, lacquer, armour, furniture, prints, pottery, porcelain, paintings, sculpture, inro, 6th C BC to 19th C, £30-£20,000.* Not stocked: Non-Japanese items. LOC: Opposite British Museum. Nearest tube station - Tottenham Court Rd. and Holborn. PARK: Meters. TEL: 071 580 6511. VAT: Spec.

Nortonbury Antiques
BCM Box 5345. Open by appointment. *STOCK: Silver, 17th-19th C.* TEL: 0984 31668.

The Print Room
37 Museum St. (A Balfour-Lynn and K Surya) Est: 1984. Open 10-6, Sat. 10-4, other times by appointment. *STOCK: Prints, including natural history, views of London, costume plates and caricatures, 1580-1850, £10-£3,000.* LOC: Off Gt. Russell St., opposite British Museum. PARK: N.C.P. Bloomsbury Sq. TEL: 071 430 0159. SER: Valuations; buys at auction (antiquarian books and prints).

Arthur Probsthain
41 Great Russell St. Est: 1902. Open 9.30-6, Sat. 11-4. *STOCK: Books, Oriental and African.* TEL: 071 636 1096. VAT: Stan.

S.J Shrubsole Ltd BADA LAPADA
43 Museum St. (C.J Shrubsole) Est: 1918. Open 9-5.30. CL: Sat. SIZE: Medium. *STOCK: Silver, late 17th to mid-19th C, £50-£25,000; old Sheffield plate, mid-18th to mid-19th C, £10-£5,000.* LOC: 1 min. from British

S.J Shrubsole Ltd continued

Museum. PARK: Easy. TEL: 071 405 2712. SER: Valuations; restorations (silver); buys at auction. VAT: Stan/Spec.

Skoob Books Ltd
15 Sicilian Ave, Southampton Row, Holborn. Est: 1978. Open 10.30-6.30. SIZE: Medium. *STOCK: Books, second-hand literary, technical and scientific.* LOC: In pedestrian arcade, near Holburn Underground. PARK: Easy. TEL: 071 404 3063.

Skoob Two t/a I.K. Ong
19 Bury Pl. Open 10.30-6.30. SIZE: Small. *STOCK: Secondhand and antiquarian books on occult, Oriental studies, esoterica, magic, archaeology, anthropology and classics.* TEL: 071 405 0030.

London W.C.2

Anchor Antiques Ltd
26 Charing Cross Rd. (K.B Embden and H Samne) Est: 1964. Open by appointment. *STOCK: Continental and Oriental ceramics, European works of art and objets de vertu.* TEL: 071 836 5686. VAT: Spec. *Trade Only.*

Apple Market
Covent Garden. Open Mon. only 7-7 in winter, 7-8 in summer.. SIZE: 40 stalls. *STOCK: A wide range of general antiques and collectables.* TEL: 071 836 9137.

A.H Baldwin and Sons Ltd BADA
11 Adelphi Terrace. IAPN, BNTA. Est: 1872. Open 9-5. CL: Sat. SIZE: Medium. *STOCK: Coins, 600 BC to present; commemorative medals, 16th C to present, numismatic literature.* LOC: Off Robert St., near Charing Cross. TEL: 071 930 6879/839 1310; fax - 071 930 9450. SER: Valuations; auction agents for selling and purchasing. VAT: Stan/Spec.

Bell, Book and Radmall
4 Cecil Court. Est: 1974. Open 10-5.30. CL: Sat. *STOCK: First editions of 19th and 20th C English and American literature including detective and fantasy fiction.* TEL: 071 240 2161.

M Bord (Gold Coin Exchange)
16 Charing Cross Rd. Est: 1969. Open 9.30-6. SIZE: Small. *STOCK: Gold, silver and copper coins, Roman to Elizabeth II, all prices.* LOC: Near Leicester Sq. underground station. TEL: 071 836 0631/240 0479. SER: Valuations; buys at auction. FAIRS: All major coin. VAT: Stan/Spec.

Covent Garden Flea Market
Jubilee Market, Covent Garden (Sherman and Waterman Associates Ltd.). Est: 1975. Open Mon. and Bank Holidays only, 6.30-5. SIZE; Over 200 stalls. *STOCK: A wide range of general antiques.* LOC: South side of piazza,

Covent Garden Flea Market continued

just off The Strand, via Southampton St. PARK: Easy and N.C.P. Drury Lane. TEL: 071 836 2139/240 7405.

Ann Creed Books Ltd
22 Cecil Court. Open 10-7 or by appointment. *STOCK: Antiquarian, fine and applied art books.* TEL: 071 836 7757.

Dicken's Old Curiosity Shop
13/14 Portsmouth St. (D. and T Goldband) Est: 1780. Open 9.30-5.30 seven days. Closed Christmas Day and Good Friday. SIZE: Small. *STOCK: General antiques and Dickensiana.* LOC: Off Kingsway, close to Lincoln's Inn Fields. Nearest tube station: Holborn. PARK: Meters. TEL: 071 405 9891. VAT: Stan.

The Dolls House Toys Ltd
29 The Market, Covent Garden. Open 10-8. *STOCK: Dolls' houses, miniature furniture.* TEL: 071 379 7243. VAT: Stan.

H.M Fletcher
27 Cecil Court, Charing Cross Rd. Est: 1905. Open 9.30-5. CL: Sat. SIZE: Medium. *STOCK: Books, rare, antiquarian.* LOC: Between Charing Cross Rd. and St. Martin's Lane. PARK: Meters. TEL: 071 836 2865; fax - 071 497 8023.

W. and G Foyle Ltd
113-119 Charing Cross Rd. Est: 1904. *STOCK: Antiquarian books.*

Frognal Rare Books
18 Cecil Court, Charing Cross Rd. (E Finer) ABA. Est: 1958. Open 11-6. CL: Sat. SIZE: Medium. *STOCK: Antiquarian books -law (pre-1850) and legal history, banking, currency, economics, history, philosophy, French, German, Italian, 1500-1900, £2-£1,000+; also books on literature, travel, art and topography.* LOC: Between Charing Cross Rd. and St. Martin's Lane. PARK: Meters and nearby. TEL: 071 240 2815.

Stanley Gibbons
399 Strand. Est: 1856. Open 9-6. CL: Sat. p.m. SIZE: Large. *STOCK: Popular and specialised stamps, postal history, catalogues, albums, accessories.* LOC: Opposite Savoy Hotel. TEL: 071 836 8444; fax - 071 836 7342. SER: Valuations. VAT: Stan/Spec.

Grosvenor Prints
28/32 Shelton St, Covent Garden. Est: 1975. Open 10-6, Sat. 11-4. SIZE: Large. *STOCK: Engravings, lithographs and etchings, especially topographical and dog portraits.* LOC: Within one-way system near Neal St. PARK: Easy. TEL: 071 836 1979; fax - 071 379 6695. SER: Valuations; restorations; buys at auction. VAT: Stan/Spec.

W.C.2 continued

S. and H Jewell Ltd
26 Parker St. Est: 1830. Open 9-5.30, Sat. by appointment. SIZE: Large. *STOCK: Furniture.* TEL: 071 405 8520. SER: Valuations; restorations. VAT: Stan/Spec.

Thomas Kettle Ltd
53a Neal St. (J King. Resident) Est: 1974. Open 10-7. SIZE: Medium. *STOCK: Wrist watches, 1910-1950, £350-£5,000; contemporary designer jewellery, £40-£2,000.* LOC: Near Covent Garden tube. PARK: Leicester Sq. TEL: 071 379 3579. SER: Valuations; restorations (wrist watches). VAT: Stan.

The London Silver Vaults
Chancery House, 53-65 Chancery Lane. Est: 1892. Open 9-5.30. CL: Sat. p.m. *STOCK: Silver, plate, jewellery, objets d'art, clocks, watches, collectors' items.* TEL: 071 242 3844. The following are some of the dealers at these vaults.

Lawrence Block
Vault 28 and 65. Est: 1959. *Silver especially flatware; jewellery.* TEL: 071 242 0749. SER: Valuations; restorations; buys at auction.

A Bloom
Vault 27. TEL: 071 242 6189.

Luigi Brian Antiques LAPADA
Vault 56. TEL: 071 405 2484.

B L Collins
Vault 20. TEL: 071 404 0628.

P Daniel
Vault 51. TEL: 071 430 1327.

R Feldman Ltd LAPADA
Vault 4/6. TEL: 071 405 6111.

I Franks LAPADA
Vault 9/11. Est: 1926. TEL: 071 242 4035.

Jules Golding and Co
Vault 2. (D Golding) Est: 1926. TEL: 071 242 3217. VAT: Stan/Spec.

Hamilton Antiques
Vault 46. TEL: 071 831 7030.

E and C T Koopman and Son Ltd BADA
(The Provincial Antique Silver Co.). Est: 1967. *Silver and jewellery.* TEL: 071 242 7624/8365. SER: Valuations.

S Kyle Antiques
Vault 68. TEL: 071 242 1708. VAT: Stan/Spec.

B Lampert
Vault 19.

Langfords LAPADA
Vault 8/10. NAG. Est: 1940. *Silver and plate, especially cutlery.* TEL: 071 351 4881; fax - 071 405 6401. SER: Valuations. VAT: Stan/Spec.

Leon Antiques Ltd
Vault 57.

Nat Leslie Ltd
Vault 21. Est: 1940. TEL: 071 242 4787. VAT: Stan/Spec.

London Silver Vaults continued

Linden and Co. (Antiques) Ltd
Vault 7. (H, F, H M and S C Linden) TEL: 071 242 4863. VAT: Stan/Spec.
C and T Mammon
TEL: 071 405 2397.
J Mammon Antiques
Vault 30. TEL: 071 242 4704. *Trade Only.*
H Miller (Antiques) Ltd **LAPADA**
TEL: 071 242 7073. VAT: Stan/Spec.
I Nagioff (Jewellery)
Vault 63 and 69. (I and R Nagioff) Est: 1955. *Jewellery, 18th-20th C, £5-£2,000+; objets d'art, 19th C, to £200.* TEL: 071 405 3766. SER: Valuations; restorations (jewellery). VAT: Stan.
Percy's **LAPADA**
Vault 16/17. *Candelabra, candlesticks, flatware and collectables.* TEL: 071 242 3618.
H Perovetz
Vault 13/15.
Rare Art
Vault 25. TEL: 071 405 9968.
David S Shure and Co
Vault 1. (S Bulka) Est: 1900. Book on silver. TEL: 071 405 0011. SER: Valuations; restorations. VAT: Stan.
Silstar
Vault 29. (H Stern) Est: 1955. TEL: 071 242 6740. VAT: Stan/Spec.
B Silverman **BADA**
Vault 26. (S and R Silverman) Est: 1927. TEL: 071 242 3269. SER: Valuations; buys at auction. VAT: Stan/Spec.
Jack Simons (Antiques) Ltd **LAPADA**
Vault 35 and 37. Est: 1955. TEL: 071 242 3221. VAT: Stan/Spec.
S and J Stodel
Vault 24. TEL: 071 405 7009; fax - 071 242 6366.
A Urbach
Vault 50.
William Walter Antiques Ltd **BADA LAPADA**
Vault 3/5. (R W Walter) Est: 1927. TEL: 071 242 3248. SER: Valuations; restorations (silver, plate).
A and G Weiss
Vault 42/44. TEL: 071 242 7310. VAT Stan.
Peter K Weiss
Vault 18/42/44/106. Est: 1955. *Watches, clocks.* TEL: 071 242 8100/7310. VAT: Stan.
Wolfe (Jewellery)
Vault 41. TEL: 071 405 2101. VAT: Stan/Spec.

Arthur Middleton Ltd LAPADA

12 New Row, Covent Garden. Est: 1968. Open 10-6 or by appointment. SIZE: Small. *STOCK: Scientific instruments - navigation, astronomy, surveying and medical; globes, scales, 18th-19th C, £50-£20,000.* LOC: New Row runs between Leicester Square and Covent Garden.

Arthur Middleton Ltd. continued

Shop 300yds. east from Leicester Square. TEL: 071 836 7042/836 7062; fax - 071 497 9386. SER: Valuations; buys at auction; prop hire. VAT: Stan.

Avril Noble

2 Southampton St, Covent Garden. PBFA. Est: 1964. Open 10-6, Sat. 10-4, Sun. by appointment. SIZE: Large. *STOCK: Maps and engravings of the world, 16th-19th C, £10-£3,000.* LOC: Off the Strand, opposite the Savoy Hotel. PARK: Meters. TEL: 071 240 1970. SER: Buys at auction. FAIRS: International Map, London; Bonnington Hotel. VAT: Stan.

Pearl Cross Ltd

35 St. Martin's Court. (D Strange) Est: 1897. Open 9.30-4.45. CL: Sat. *STOCK: Jewellery, silver, clocks, watches.* PARK: Meters. TEL: 071 836 2814/240 0795. SER: Valuations; restorations (jewellery, silver). VAT: Stan/Spec.

H Perovetz Ltd BADA LAPADA

50/52 Chancery Lane. Est: 1945. Open 9-6. SIZE: Large. *STOCK: Silver, Sheffield plate.* TEL: 071 405 8868; fax - 071 242 1211. SER: Valuations. VAT: Stan/Spec.

Pleasures of Past Times

11 Cecil Court, Charing Cross Rd. (D.B Drummond) Est: 1962. Open 11-2.30 and 3.30-5.45. CL: Sat. (except first one in the month 11-2.15). SIZE: Medium. *STOCK: Scarce and out-of-print books of the performing arts; early juvenile and illustrated books; vintage postcards, valentines, entertainment ephemera.* Not stocked: Coins, stamps, medals, jewellery, cigarette cards. LOC: In pedestrian court between Charing Cross Rd. and St. Martin's Lane. TEL: 071 836 1142. VAT: Stan.

Henry Pordes Books Ltd

58/60 Charing Cross Rd. Open 10-7. *STOCK: Antiquarian and secondhand books, modern first editions, cinema, Judaica and general.* TEL: 071 836 9031.

Reg and Philip Remington

18 Cecil Court, Charing Cross Rd. ABA. Est: 1979. Open 10-5, Sat. by appointment. SIZE: Medium. *STOCK: Voyages and travels, 17th-20th C, £5-£1,000.* LOC: Near Trafalgar Sq. TEL: 071 836 9771. SER: Buys at auction. FAIRS: Edinburgh Book, London Book, Park Lane Hotel. VAT: Stan.

Bertram Rota Ltd

9-11 Langley Court. Est: 1923. Open 9.30-5.30, Sat. by appointment. *STOCK: Antiquarian and secondhand books, especially first editions, private presses, English literature, and literary autographs.* TEL: 071 836 0723.

The Silver Mouse Trap

56 Carey St. (A Woodhouse) Est: 1690. Open 9.30-5.30. CL: Sat. SIZE: Medium. *STOCK: Jewellery, silver.* LOC: South of Lincoln's Inn

The Silver Mouse Trap continued

Fields. TEL: 071 405 2578. SER: Valuations; restorations. VAT: Spec.

Spatz
48 Monmouth St. (P Ebbinkhuyson and S Anchor) Est: 1979. Open 11.30-7. SIZE: Small. *STOCK: Victorian lace pillowcases and nightdresses, £25-£40; 1940's dresses, blouses and other day wear, £20-£60.* LOC: Near Seven Dials, 2 mins. from Long Acre. PARK: NCP nearby. TEL: 071 379 0703. VAT: Stan.

Stage Door Prints
1 Cecil Court, Charing Cross Rd. (A Reynold) Open 11-6. *STOCK: Prints of performing arts, sports and topographical; signed photographs, maps, Victorian cards, valentines.* TEL: 071 240 1683.

Harold T Storey
3 Cecil Court, Charing Cross Rd. (Man. T Kingswood) Est: 1929. Open 10-6. *STOCK: Prints, especially naval and military; antiquarian books.* LOC: Between Charing Cross Rd. and St. Martin's Lane. PARK: Trafalgar Square garage. TEL: 071 836 3777.

Tooley Adams & Co. Ltd
13 Cecil Court, Charing Cross Rd. (D Adams and S Luck) ABA. Est: 1964. Open 9-6. SIZE: Large. *STOCK: Antiquarian maps, atlases, prints; travel and map related reference books.* LOC: Between St. Martin's Lane and Charing Cross Rd. PARK: Gerard St. TEL: 071 240 4406; fax - 071 240 8058. SER: Valuations; restorations; buys at auction. FAIRS: Bonnington Map; Imcos Map. VAT: Stan.

W.C.2 continued

Travis and Emery
17 Cecil Court, Charing Cross Rd. (V Emery) ABA. Est: 1960. Open 10-6. CL: Sat. p.m. SIZE: Medium. *STOCK: Musical literature, music and prints.* LOC: Between Charing Cross Rd. and St. Martin's Lane opposite Odeon. PARK: Meters. TEL: 071 240 2129. VAT: Stan.

Watkins Books Ltd
19 & 21 Cecil Court, Charing Cross Rd. Est: 1880. Open 10-6, Wed. 10.30-6. *STOCK: Mysticism, occultism, Oriental religions, astrology and contemporary spirituality, new and secondhand books.* TEL: 071 836 2182.

The Witch Ball
2 Cecil Court, Charing Cross Rd. (R Glassman. Resident) Est: 1969. Open 10.30-6. SIZE: Small. *STOCK: Prints relating to the performing arts, from 17th C, topographical prints, 20th C posters.* LOC: 2 mins. from Leicester Sq. tube station. PARK: NCP nearby. TEL: 071 836 2922. VAT: Stan.

Zeno Booksellers and Publishers
6 Denmark St. Est: 1944. Open 9.30-6, Sat. till 5. SIZE: Medium. *STOCK: Antiquarian books on Greece, Cyprus, Turkey, Middle East, and the Balkans.* LOC: From Tottenham Court Rd., into Charing Cross Rd., first turning on left. TEL: 071 836 2522.

A Zwemmer Ltd
24 Litchfield St. Est: 1921. Open 9.30-6, Sat. 10-6. SIZE: Large. *STOCK: Books on art and fine art; rare and out-of-print catalogue raisonnés.* LOC: Just south of Cambridge Circus, Leicester Sq. underground. TEL: 071 379 7886.

Please note this is only a rough map designed to show dealers the number of shops in the various towns, and is not necessarily totally accurate.

○ 1–2
⊖ 3–5
◒ 6–12
● 13+

Key to number of shops in this area.

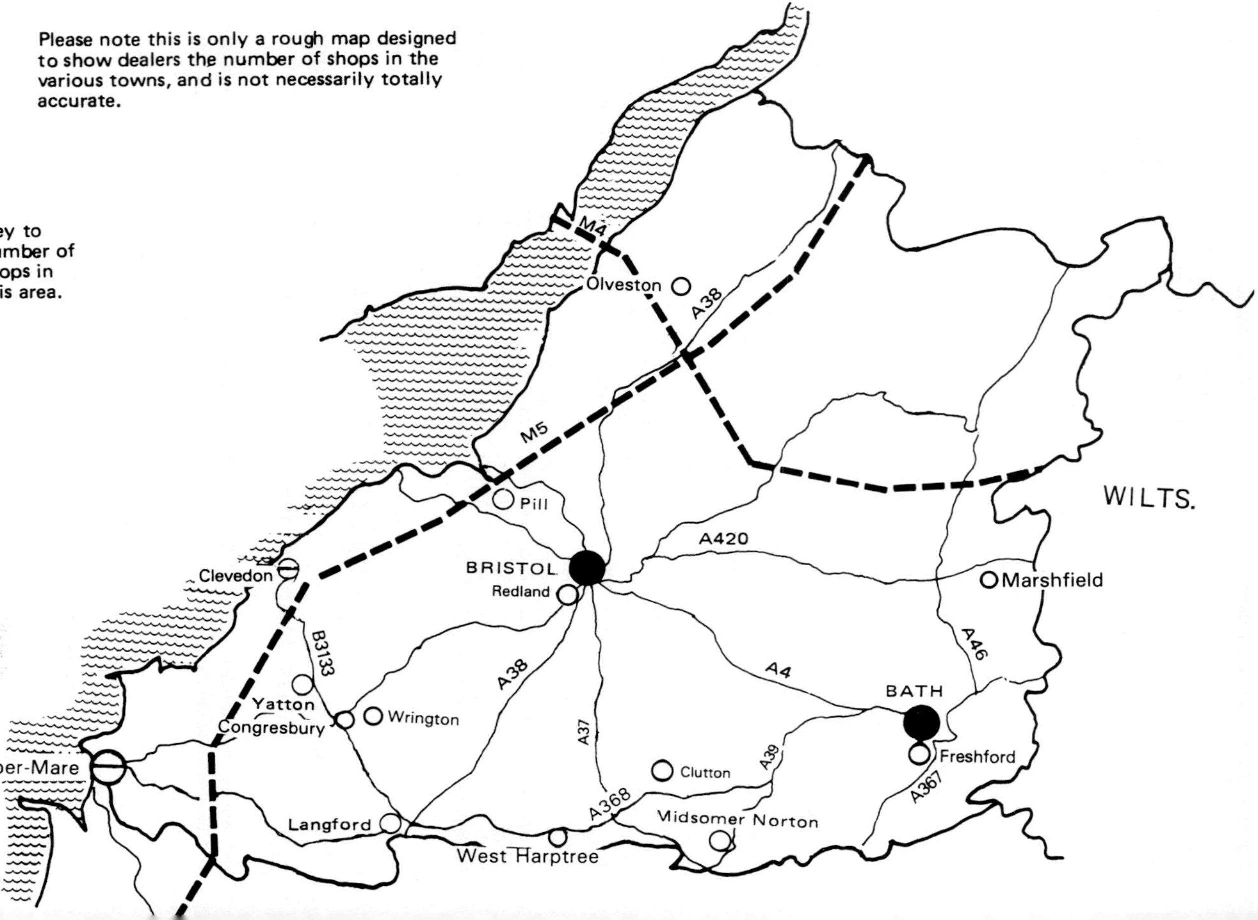

M4
Olveston
A38
M5
Pill
WILTS.
A420
BRISTOL
Redland
Marshfield
Clevedon
B3133
A38
A46
A4
BATH
Yatton
Congresbury
Wrington
A37
A39
Weston-super-Mare
Clutton
Freshford
A368
A367
Langford
Midsomer Norton
West Harptree

ABBOTS LEIGH, Nr. Bristol

David March Ceramics LAPADA
Oak Wood Lodge, Stoke Leigh Woods. (D and S March) Est: 1981. Open by appointment. *STOCK: Interesting and unusual English porcelain including figures, 18th to 19th C; Welsh porcelain, early 19th C.* PARK: Easy. TEL: 0275 372422; home - same. SER: Buys at auction (as stock). FAIRS: Wakefield Ceramic; NEC. VAT: Spec.

BATH

"27a"
27a Belvedere Rd, Lansdown. (P.M Farnham) Est: 1970. Open 9.30-5.30, Sat. 10-4, Sun. by appointment. SIZE: Medium. *STOCK: Interesting items.* PARK: Easy. TEL: 0225 428256. SER: Buys at auction.

Abbey Galleries
9 Abbey Churchyard. (R Dickson) Est: 1930. Open 10.30-5.30. *STOCK: Jewellery, £50; Oriental, £100; both 18th-19th C; silver, 18th C, £100.* Not Stocked: Furniture. TEL: 0225 460565. SER: Valuations; restorations (jewellery and clocks); buys at auction. VAT: Stan.

Adam Gallery
13 John St. (P. and P Dye) Open 9.30-5.30 or by appointment. *STOCK: Late Victorian and Modern British oil paintings and watercolours, especially figurative and landscape, £200-£10,000.* TEL: 0225 480406.

Alderson BADA
23 Brock St. (C.J.R Alderson) Est: 1975. Open 9.30-5.30. *STOCK: Furniture, 17th-18th C; period metalwork, glass, silver.* LOC: Between the Circus and Royal Crescent. PARK: Easy. TEL: 0225 421652. SER: Valuations. VAT: Spec.

Arkea Antiques
10A Monmouth Pl. (G Harmandian) Est: 1972. *STOCK: Furniture, china, silver, clocks.* TEL: 0225 429413; home - 0225 835382.

Aspidistra
46 St. James Parade. (J. and J Waggoner) Est: 1972. Open 10.30-4.30. SIZE: Medium. *STOCK: Books and prints, music and musical instruments, curiosities, bygones.* LOC: 2 mins. walk from Bath Abbey, opposite Technical College. PARK: Easy, 20 mins. Multi-storey 1 min. TEL: 0225 461948. SER: Valuations.

G.A Baines of Bath
14/15 John St. (G. and J Baines) Open 10-5, Sat. 10-6. *STOCK: English furniture, 18th to early 19th C.* TEL: 0225 332566. VAT: Spec.

Bartlett Street Antique Centre
5-10 Bartlett St. Open 9.30-5, Wed. 8-5. SIZE: 52+ dealers. *STOCK: Wide range of general antiques.* TEL: 0225 466689, stallholders - 0225 330267/310457.

Bath continued

Bath Antiques Market
Guinea Lane, Paragon. Est: 1968. Open Wed. only, 6.30-2.30. SIZE: 80 dealers. *STOCK: General antiques.* LOC: From London A4 across two sets of traffic lights after entering Bath. Right at third set (Landsdown Rd.) and first right again. PARK: Nearby. TEL: Enquiries - 071 351 5353; centre - 0225 422510.

Bath Galleries
33 Broad St. (J Griffiths) Open 9.30-5. SIZE: Medium. *STOCK: Furniture, paintings, porcelain, jewellery, clocks, barometers, silver.* LOC: 50yds. from Central Post Office. PARK: Walcot St. multi-park, 30yds. TEL: 0225 462946. SER: Valuations; restorations; buys at auction. VAT: Stan/Spec.

Bath Saturday Antiques Market
Walcot St. (A Whittingham) Est: 1978. Open Sat. 7-5. SIZE: 100 stalls. *STOCK: Wide variety of general antiques, £1-£500.* LOC: Close to Beaufort Hotel. PARK: Multi-storey.

Bath Stamp and Coin Shop
Pulteney Bridge. (H. and A Swindells) Est: 1946. Open 9.30-5.30. *STOCK: Coins (Roman, hammered, early milled, G.B. gold, silver and copper, some foreign); literature and accessories; banknotes; medals, stamps and postal history.* PARK: Laura Place; Walcott multi-storey. SER: Valuations. VAT: Stan.

George Bayntun
Manvers St. (H.H Bayntun-Coward) Est: 1829. Open 9-1 and 2-5.30, Sat. 9.30-1. SIZE: Large. *STOCK: Rare books. First or fine editions of English literature, standard sets, illustrated and sporting books, poetry, biography and travel, mainly in new leather bindings; also large stock of antiquarian books in original bindings.* LOC: By railway and bus stations. PARK: 50yds. by station. TEL: 0225 466000; fax 0225 482122. SER: Restorations (rare books). VAT: Stan.

Beau Nash House Antiques
Beau Nash House, Union Passage. (D. and S Johnson) Resident. Est: 1973. Open 10-6.30, Sun. by appointment. SIZE: Large. *STOCK: Furniture, 1700-1860, £750-£30,000; paintings, 1700-1900, £1,500-£20,000; decorative objects, 1700-1880, £100-£1,500.* LOC: 70yds. north of abbey. PARK: Walcot St. TEL: 0225 447806. SER: Valuations; restorations (furniture and pictures); buys at auction (furniture and pictures). VAT: Spec.

Bladud House Antiques
8 Bladud Buildings. (Mrs E Radosenska) Open 9.30-1 and 2-4.30. CL: Mon. and Thurs. *STOCK: Jewellery and small items.* Not Stocked: Furniture. TEL: 0225 462929.

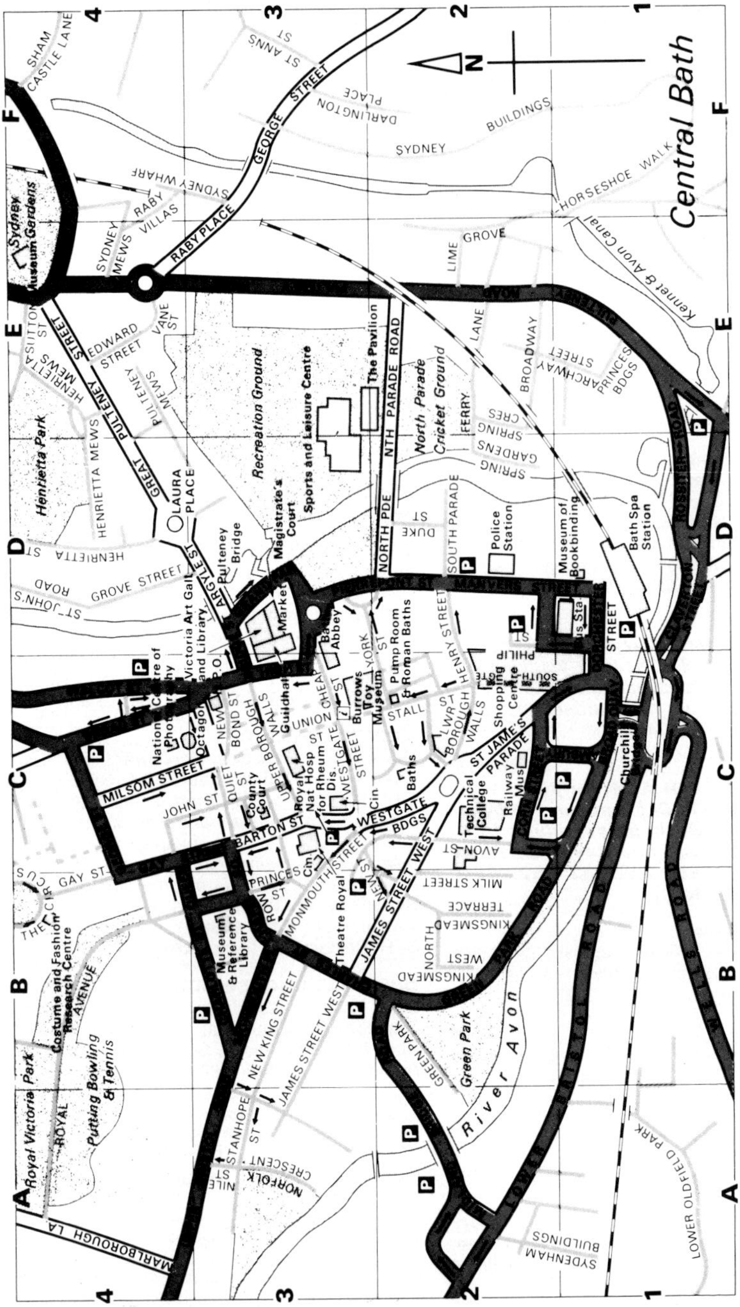
Central Bath
Kennet & Avon Canal
HORSESHOE WALK
SYDNEY BUILDINGS
DARLINGTON PLACE
ST ANNS ST
GEORGE STREET
RABY PLACE
SYDNEY WHARF
RABY VILLAS
SYDNEY MEWS
Sydney Gardens
Museum
LIME GROVE
GREAT PULTENEY STREET
HENRIETTA MEWS
Henrietta Park
HENRIETTA ST
LAURA PLACE
Recreation Ground
Sports and Leisure Centre
The Pavilion
NTH PARADE ROAD
North Parade Cricket Ground
SPRING GARDENS
SOUTH PARADE
Police Station
Museum of Bookbinding
Bath Spa Station
Pulteney Bridge
Magistrate's Court
Market
Abbey
Pump Room & Roman Baths
Guildhall
Victoria Art Gall. and Library
MILSOM STREET
JOHN ST
QUIET ST
County Court
BARTON ST
GAY ST
Technical College
Railway Mus
Green Park
River Avon
LOWER BRISTOL ROAD
WELLS ROAD
JAMES STREET WEST
NEW KING STREET
Museum & Reference Library
Royal Victoria Park
Putting Bowling & Tennis
Costume and Fashion Research Centre
MARLBOROUGH LA
NORFOLK CRESCENT
SYDENHAM BUILDINGS
LOWER OLDFIELD PARK

Key to Town Plan

AA Recommended roads		Car Parks	P
Other roads		Parks and open spaces	
Restricted roads		AA Service Centre	AA
Buildings of interest			

Bath continued

Blyth Antiques
28 Sydney Buildings. (B Blyth) Resident. Est: 1971. Open by appointment. *STOCK: Small furniture, samplers, brass and unusual decorative items.* LOC: Off Bathwick Hill. PARK: Easy. TEL: 0225 469766. VAT: Spec.

Lawrence Brass and Son
93-95 Walcot St. Est: 1973. Open 8-5, Sun. by appointment. SIZE: Small. *STOCK: Furniture, 16th-19th C, £50-£5,000.* Not Stocked: Ceramics, silver, glass. LOC: Main road into town centre. PARK: Easy. TEL: 0225 464057; home - same. SER: Restorations (furniture, clocks and barometers). VAT: Stan/Spec.

Breeze and Behan
6 George St. (R Behan and G. Breeze) Open 10-5.30. *STOCK: Furniture, 18th-20th C.* TEL: 0225 466499. VAT: Stan/Spec.

Bryers Antiques
12a Manvers St, and entrance of Guildhall Market. (S Bryers) Est: 1940. *STOCK: Furniture, decorative items, porcelain, glass, silver and Victorian plate.* LOC: Near the bus station. TEL: 0225 466352/460535. VAT: Stan/Spec.

Casemate
12 Bartlett St. (S Moss) Open 9.30-5, Wed. 8.30-5. SIZE: Small. *STOCK: General antiques, 18th-20th C, £10-£2,000.* Not Stocked: Furniture. LOC: Near Gt. Western Antique Centre. PARK: Alfred St. TEL: 0225 465142. VAT: Stan/Spec.

Robin and Jan Coleman Antiques
at Pennard House, 3/4 Piccadilly, London Rd. Open 9.30-5.30. *STOCK: Interesting and decorative items.* LOC: A4 from east when entering city. TEL: 0225 313791. VAT: Stan/Spec.

Sheila Cooper t/a Sheila Smith Antiques
Bartlett St. Antique Centre, 7-10 Bartlett St. (S.M Cooper) Est: 1967. Open 9.30-5. *STOCK: Fans, needlework tools and accessories, glass, collectors' items, bobbins.* LOC: A4 into city. At 3rd set of traffic lights, turn right into Lansdown then 2nd left into Alfred St. TEL: 0225 330267/310457.

Corridor Stamp Shop
7a The Corridor. (G.H. and S.M Organ) Est: 1970. Open 9.30-5.30. CL: Thurs. p.m.. SIZE: Small. *STOCK: Stamp and postal history, 1700 to date, 5p-£500; albums, reference books; picture postcards, cigarette cards, 1895-1940.* LOC: Within 200yds. of Abbey. PARK: Walcot St. TEL: 0225 463368; home - 0225 316445. SER: Valuations. FAIRS: Stampex, London, Bristol. VAT: Stan.

Bath continued

Brian and Caroline Craik Ltd **LAPADA**
8 Margaret's Buildings. *STOCK: Decorative items, metalwork, furniture, 18th and 19th C.* TEL: 0225 337161.

John Croft Antiques **LAPADA**
3 George St. Open 9.15-5.30. SIZE: Medium. *STOCK: Furniture, 17th to early 19th C; clocks, barometers, decorative objects, paintings.* LOC: A4, turn left at top of Milsom St., opp. 'Hole in the Wall' restaurant. PARK: Broad St. 100yds. TEL: 0225 466211. VAT: Spec.

Andrew Dando **BADA**
4 Wood St, Queen Sq. (G. and V Dando) Est: 1930. Open 9.30-1.15 and 2.30-5.30, Sat. 10-1. SIZE: Large. *STOCK: English, continental, Oriental porcelain and pottery, 17th to mid-19th C; furniture, 18th to mid-19th C.* LOC: 200yds. from bottom of Milsom St. towards Queen Sq. TEL: 0225 422702. SER: Valuations. VAT: Stan/Spec.

Bath continued

D. and B Dickinson **BADA**
22 New Bond St. (S.G., D. and N.W Dickinson and Mrs E.M Dickinson) Est: 1917. Open 9.30-1 and 2.15-5. CL: Mon. and Sat. p.m. SIZE: Small. *STOCK: Jewellery, 1770-1900, £20-£2,000; silver, 1750-1900, £25-£3,000; Sheffield plate, 1770-1845, £50-£1,000.* LOC: Next to Post Office. PARK: 100yds. at bottom of street, turn left then right for multi-storey. TEL: 0225 466502. VAT: Stan/Spec.

Martin Dodge Interiors Ltd
15-16 Broad St. (M.J Dodge) Est: 1969. Open 9.30-5.30. SIZE: Medium. *STOCK: Furniture,*

Martin Dodge Interiors Ltd. continued

18th-19th C; watercolours, oil paintings, decorative items, especially papier mâché, mainly 19th C, £1,000-£10,000. LOC: Main road into city from A4. PARK: Easy, at rear. TEL: 0225 462202.

Dollin and Daines **BADA**
2 Church St, York St. Est: 1968. Open 10.30-1 and 2-4. CL: Thurs. and Sat. *STOCK: Violins, violas, cellos and bows.* TEL: 0225 462752. SER: Restorations (as stock).

Brian and Angela Downes Antiques **LAPADA**
9 Broad St. Est: 1968. Open 9-5.30, Sat. 9-5. SIZE: Medium. *STOCK: Mahogany, walnut and rosewood furniture, 1760-1900, £300-£3,000;English porcelain, 1790-1860, £50-£5,000; clocks, decorative items, boxes and brass.* Not Stocked: Jewellery and silver. LOC: Town centre, 50yds. from main Post Office. PARK: Nearby. TEL: 0225 465352. SER: Valuations; buys at auction (furniture and porcelain). FAIRS: Kensington; N.E.C. Birmingham; Olympia and specialist porcelain. VAT: Stan/Spec.

Peter Dryden Ltd
5/6 Bartlett St. Open 10-5. *STOCK: English and continental furniture; works of art.* TEL: 0225 423038. VAT: Spec.

Frank Dux Antiques
33 Belvedere, Lansdown Rd. (F Dux and M Hopkins) Resident. Open 10-6. SIZE: Medium. *STOCK: Georgian and earlier furniture (mainly oak), £250-£5,000; 18th C and later glass, £10-£1,000; unusual decorative items - pottery, pewter, pictures, rugs.* LOC: From Broad St. up Lansdown Hill, on right 100yds. past Guinea Lane. PARK: Easy. TEL: 0225 312367. SER: Restorations (furniture); replicas made to order; search service. VAT: Spec.

Anthony Emm **BADA**
York St. Open 9.30-5.30, Sat. 11-1 and 2-5. SIZE: Large. *STOCK: English furniture, 18th to early 19th C; works of art, decorative and*

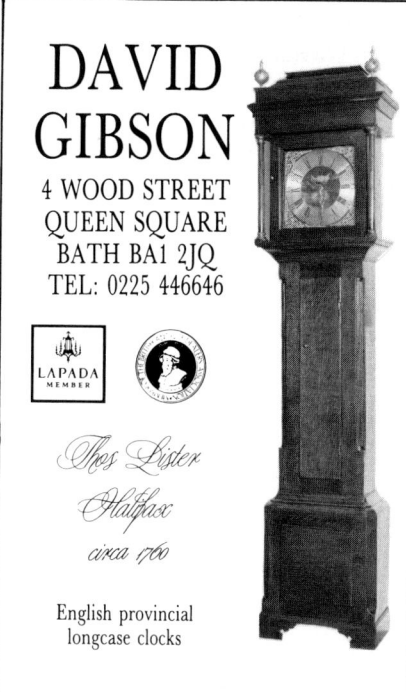

Anthony Emm continued

Chinese export items. **LOC: Adjacent south side Roman Baths, drive up Stall St. PARK: Nearby. TEL: 0225 447992. VAT: Spec.**

Gene and Sally Foster (Antiques)
27B Belvedere, Lansdown. Est: 1969. Open daily. SIZE: Medium. *STOCK: Decorative and unusual items, 17th-19th C; continental and English painted furniture, paintings, needlework, prints and metalware, £25-£2,500.* Not Stocked: Silver, jewellery, arms and armour. TEL: 0225 316216. VAT: Stan/Spec.

Simon Freeman Antiques
11 Walcot Buildings, London Rd. Est: 1981. Open 10-5, Wed. 9-5. CL: Sat. SIZE: Medium. *STOCK: General antiques, smalls and decorative items.* PARK: Easy. TEL: 0225 311547; home - 0225 334803. VAT: Stan/Spec.

The Galleon
33 Monmouth St. (D.L Gwilliam and M.J Wren) Est: 1972. Open 10-5.30, Sat. 10-6, or by appointment. SIZE: Medium. *STOCK: Furniture, jewellery, silver, general collectables and antiques, Georgian to art deco, £5-£1,500.* LOC: Near rear of Theatre Royal. PARK: Easy. TEL: 0225 312330. SER: Buys at auction. VAT: Stan/Spec.

Bath continued

David Gibson BADA LAPADA
4 Wood St, Queen Sq. Est: 1975. Open 10-5.30. CL: Mon. SIZE: Medium. ***STOCK: Longcase clocks, £2,500-£20,000; barometers and musical boxes.*** **LOC: 200yds. from bottom of Milson St. towards Queen Sq. 1st floor above Andrew Dando. PARK: Easy. TEL: 0225 446646. SER: Valuations. FAIRS: West of England, Cafe Royal, Kenilworth, Olympia, N.E.C., and Northern (Harrogate). VAT: Spec.**

Graylow and Co
George St. Open 10-5. *STOCK: Furniture and decorative accessories, mainly George III.* TEL: 0225 469859.

Great Western Antique Centre Ltd
Bartlett St. Open 10-5, Wed. 8.30-5. SIZE: 50 stands on the ground floor. There is an additional mkt. every Wed. and Sat. with 20 stands. LOC: Adjacent to the Assembly Rooms and Museum of Costume. TEL: 0225 424243; stand holders 0225 310388/428731.

Ancestors
Stands 31 and 32. (S Rosser-Rees) *Paintings, small objets d'art and porcelain.*

Antique Linen and Lace
Stands 7 and 8. (R Mellor) *Silver, plate and small decorative items.*

Great Western Antique Centre Ltd. continued

Avril Antiques
Stand 25. (A Brown) *Silver, plate and small decorative items.*
Brunel Antiques
Stands 33 and 34. (J and S Mildred) *Art pottery, arts and crafts, furniture and glass, 1850-1950.*
Churchstoke Booksellers
Stand 39. (B Howard) *Rare books and fine editions.*
Country Interiors
Stand 10. (L Macrae-Stewart) *Pine furniture.*
Crofton Antiques
Stands 13 and 14. (R A Gresham) *Pine furniture.*
Deja Vu
Stand 26. (M P Nunan) *Music boxes, jewellery, Oriental items, silver plate.*
G Frayling
Stand 24. *Clocks, watches and furniture.*
Jessie's Button Box
Stand 9. (J Partt) *Collectors' and designers' buttons.*
Thomas S and Janeien E Kiernan
Stands 29 and 30. *Fine antiques, arms and armour.*
L B Antiques
Stand 6. (L Brine) *Scent bottles and smalls.*
Christopher Lincoln
Stand 22. *Restored pianos.*
P Livani
Stand 11. *European and Middle Eastern works of art and furniture.*
Elizabeth Lyons
Stand 2. *Jewellery.*
Macbeth
Stand 28. *Decorative smalls and silver frames.*
Not Cartier
Stand 48. (G Tinne) *Semi-precious and Venetian glass jewellery.*
Notts Pine
Stand 21. *Pine furniture.*
Jenny and Lindy Notts Pine
Stand 38. *Pine furniture.*
Off the Rails
Stands 46 and 47. (S Relph) *Antique and period clothes and accessories.*
Ray's
Stand 51. (R Harris) *Jewellery.*
R C Southern
Stand 51. *English and continental pine.*
Victoria
Stands 44 and 45. (V Taylor) *Pre 1960's clothes, accessories, textiles and small items.*
Winstone Stamp Co and S D Postcards
Stand 1. (D Winstone) *Postal history, postcards, collectors' items.*
Mike Woodford
Stands 15 and 20. *Silver and general antiques.*

Bath continued

Great Western Antique Centre Ltd. - The Wednesday and Saturday Market

Bartlett St. Open Wed. 7.30-4, Sat. 8.30-4. The market has its own separate entrance. Below are listed some of the dealers at this market. SIZE: 20 dealers on the lower ground floor. *STOCK: General antiques.*

R B Crisp
Stand 4. *Glass, instruments and general antiques.*
Jill Cullimore
Stand 20. *General antiques and auto-h mobilia.*
M Downworth
Stand 6. *Dolls and general antiques.*
M C Fitter
Stand 3. *Silver and general antiques.*
D E Gyles
Stand 12. *Furniture and general antiques.*
E Kilbane
Stand 16. *General antiques.*
D R and P E Martin
Stand 18. *Radios, gramophones and 78 rpm records.*
A Nethercott
Stand 19. *General antiques.*
S Urquhart
Stand 5. *Decorative and general antiques.*
Whittingham
Stand 1. *Furniture and general antiques.*

George Gregory

Manvers St. (H.H Bayntun-Coward) Est: 1845. Open 9-1 and 2-5.30, Sat. 9.30-1. SIZE: Large. *STOCK: Books, 1600 to date; engravings.* LOC: By rail station. PARK: By rail station. TEL: 0225 466055. SER: Restorations (fine books). VAT: Stan.

Haliden Oriental Rug Shop

98 Walcot St. (B.W Dennis) Est: 1963. Open 10-5. CL: Thurs. SIZE: Medium. *STOCK: Caucasian, Turkish, Persian, Chinese, Afghan and tribal rugs and carpets, 19th C, £50-£3,000; some Oriental textiles - coats, embroideries, wall hangings, 19th C, £50-£750; Chinese porcelain and Oriental works of art, Ming or earlier, £50-£1,500.* LOC: Off main London road into town. PARK: Walcot St. multi-storey. TEL: 0225 469240. SER: Valuations; cleaning; restorations (as stock); buys at auction (as stock). VAT: Spec.

Heirloom and Howard Ltd

12 Miles's Buildings, George St. (D.S Howard) Est: 1972. Open 9.30-6, Sat. 11-5. SIZE: Medium. *STOCK: Porcelain including Chinese armorial, 18th C, £200-£10,000; heraldic items, 18th-19th , £10-£1,000; portrait engravings, 17th-19th C, £10-£50.* LOC: Courtyard off George St (A4). PARK: Nearby. TEL: 0225 442544; fax - 0225 442650. SER: Valuations; restorations (Chinese porcelain, heraldic

Bath continued

paintings); buys at auction (Chinese porcelain). FAIRS: International Ceramics. VAT: Spec.
Bath continued

Helena Hood and Co
3 Margarets Buildings, Brock St. (Mrs L.M Hood) Est: 1973. Open 9.30-1 and 2.15-5.30, Sat. 10.30-1. CL: Mon. SIZE: Medium. *STOCK: Decorative items - furniture, carpets, prints, paintings and porcelain, 18th-19th C, £50-£2,500.* LOC: Pedestrian walkway running north from Brock St. PARK: Easy. TEL: 0225 424438. SER: Restorations. VAT: Stan/Spec.

M.A. and D.A Hughes **LAPADA**
11 Pulteney Bridge. Open 10-5. *STOCK: Silver.* TEL: 0225 465782. VAT: Stan/Spec.

Illuminated Objects
57 Walcot St. (Mr. and Mrs T Smily) Est: 1985. Open 9.30-5.30. SIZE: Medium. *STOCK: Light fittings, 19th to early 20th C, £100-£3,000.* LOC: Near London Rd. PARK: Easy. TEL: 0225 462411; home - same. SER: Valuations; restorations (converting old columns and vases). VAT: Stan.

Jadis Ltd
The Old Bank, 17 Walcot Buildings, London Rd. (N.A Mackay and S.H Creese-Parsons) Est: 1970. Open 9.30-6, Sun. by appointment. SIZE: Medium. *STOCK: Furniture, English and European, 18th-19th C; decorative items.* LOC: On left hand side of A4 London Rd., entering Bath. PARK: Easy and at rear. TEL: 0225 338797; home - 317378. VAT: Stan/Spec.

Orlando Jones
10b Monmouth Pl, Upper Bristol Rd. Open 9.30-5.30. *STOCK: Victorian and Edwardian brass bedsteads.* TEL: 0225 422750.

Josephine
142/144 Walcot St. Open 10-5. *STOCK: Decorative objects and furniture.* TEL: 0225 445069.

Ann King
38 Belvedere, Lansdown Rd. Est: 1977. Open 10-4, Wed. 12-3.30. CL: Thurs. SIZE: Small. *STOCK: Period clothes, 19th C to 1960; baby clothes, shawls, bead dresses, linen, cushions, quilts and textiles.* LOC: Around corner from Guinea Lane Antique Market. PARK: Easy. TEL: 0225 336245; home - 0373 864747.

Kingsley Gallery
16 Margarets Buildings, Brock St. (W Pelly) Open 10-5.30 or by appointment. SIZE: Medium. *STOCK: Mainly oils, 16th-20th C, £100-£10,000.* LOC: Off Brock St. between circus and Royal Crescent. PARK: Nearby. TEL: 0225 448432; home - 0225 421714. VAT: Spec.

Bath continued

Lansdown Antiques

23 Belvedere, Lansdown Rd. (C.P. and A.M Kemp) Open 9-6, Sat. 9-5, Sun. by appointment. *STOCK: Painted pine and country furniture, 17th-19th C; metalware, unusual and decorative items.* LOC: From A4/A46 junction across 2 sets of traffic lights, right at 3rd set, shop 350yds. on left. PARK: Easy. TEL: 0225 313417; home - same. VAT: Stan/Spec.

Lantern Gallery BADA

9 George St. (A Campbell Macinnes) ABA. Est: 1966. Open 9.30-5.30; Sat. 10-4.30. *STOCK: Old decorative, natural history, botanical and topographical prints and maps, 1570-1880.* TEL: 0225 463727. SER: Restorations; framing; export. VAT: Spec.

Carr Linford

10-11 Walcot Buildings, London Rd. (N., J. and A Carr Linford) SIZE: Medium. *STOCK: Period and decorative furniture, 18th and early 19th C; caddies, small items.* LOC: Near pelican crossing. PARK: Opposite. TEL: 0225 317516. FAIRS: Olympia; West London. VAT: Spec.

E.P Mallory and Son Ltd BADA

1-4 Bridge St, and 5 Old Bond St. Est: 1898. *STOCK: Period silver and Sheffield plate, jewellery, objets de vertu; clocks, £200-£20,000.* TEL: 0225 465885. VAT: Stan/Spec.

Bath continued

No.12 Queen Street

12 Queen St. (C Roberts and K Stables) Open 9.30-5.30, other times by appointment. *STOCK: Small furniture; textiles, needlework, samplers, decorative items.* TEL: 0225 462363; home - 0225 314846. SER: Interior decorating. VAT: Spec.

Paragon Antiques and Collectors Market

3 Bladud Buildings, The Paragon. (T.J Clifford and Son Ltd) Est: 1978. Open Wed. 6.30-3.30. SIZE: Large. LOC: Milsom St./Broad St. PARK: 50yds. TEL: 0225 463715.

William Pelly

Upper Langridge Farm, Lansdown. (W.R.B Pelly) Est: 1962. Open by appointment only. *STOCK: Oil paintings, 17th-20th C, £50-£5,000; watercolours and drawings, £50-£1,000.* LOC: Opposite Blathwayt Arms Public House, 1/2 mile down track. PARK: Easy. TEL: 0225 421714. SER: Valuations. VAT: Spec.

Bath continued

Pennard House Antiques LAPADA

3/4 Piccadilly, London Rd. (M. and S Dearden) Est: 1966. Open 9.30-5.30. SIZE: Large. *STOCK: Pine, 18th-19th C, £100-£2,000; French provincial furniture, 17th-19th C; £500-£2,500; decorative items, 19th C, £30-£350.* LOC: On A4 from east when entering city. PARK: Easy and at rear. TEL: 0225 313791; home - 074 986 266. SER: Valuations; restorations (furniture). VAT: Stan/Spec.

Robert Pugh LAPADA

Open by appointment. *STOCK: English and Welsh pottery, oak, painted and garden furniture, unusual smalls.* TEL: 0225 314713. FAIRS: Olympia, West London, Harrogate, Chester.

Queens Parade Antiques Ltd

35 Gay St. (S Isbell) Open 9.30-5.30, Sat. 10-5.30, other times by appointment. SIZE: Medium. *STOCK: Furniture, 18th and 19th C English and continental, £500-£12,000; decorative items, including period lamps, £100-£3,000; pictures, £300-£10,000.* LOC: Right-hand side of hill leading from Queens Sq. PARK: Opposite. TEL: 0225 420337. VAT: Spec.

Bath continued

Street Antiques

3 Quiet St. (K Hastings-Spital and R Windebank) Est: 1985. Open 10-6. SIZE: Large. *STOCK: Furniture, 1750-1870, £250-£6,000; objects including bronzes, caddies, boxes, mirrors, £50-£2,000; Royal Worcester porcelain, £30-£2,000; clocks including longcase, wall, bracket and carriage, 1750-1900, £150-£5,000.* LOC: 25yds. from Milsom Sq. PARK: Nearby. TEL: 0225 315727; home - 0225 332399. SER: Buys at auction (furniture and clocks). VAT: Spec.

P.R Rainsford

23a Manvers St. Est: 1967. *STOCK: Architecture, fine and applied art.* TEL: 0225 445107. VAT: Stan.

T.E Robinson BADA

3 and 4 Bartlett St. Est: 1957. *STOCK: Period furniture, glass, unusual and rare items.* TEL: 0225 463982; home - 0225 832307. VAT: Spec.

M Sainsbury

35 Gay St. Est: 1930. Open by appointment. *STOCK: Antiquities, pre 1800.* Not Stocked: Fine pictures, silver. TEL: 0225 424808. SER: Valuations. VAT: Spec.

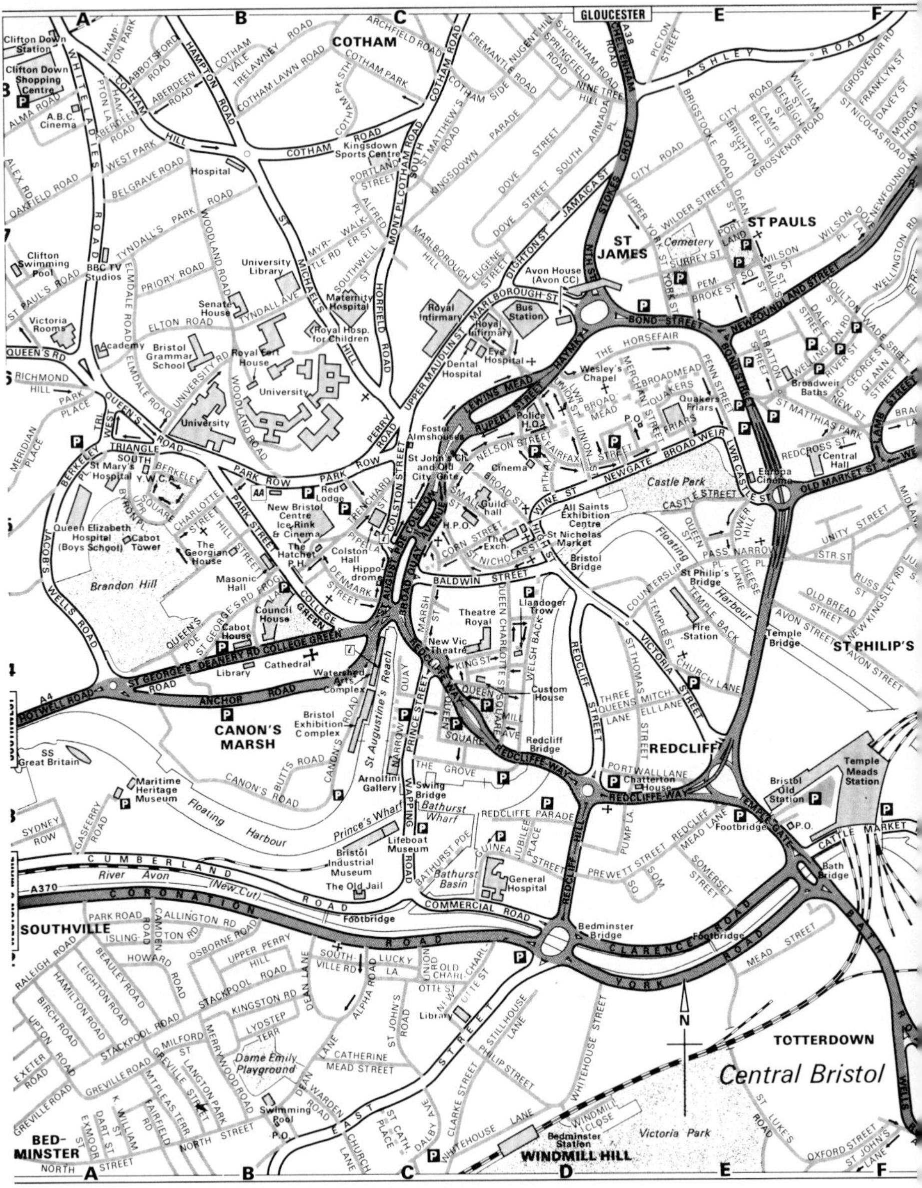
GLOUCESTER
A
B
C
E
F
D
COTHAM
ST PAULS
ST JAMES
CANON'S MARSH
REDCLIFF
ST PHILIP'S
SOUTHVILLE
BED-MINSTER
TOTTERDOWN
WINDMILL HILL
Central Bristol
Clifton Down Station
Clifton Down Shopping Centre
A.B.C. Cinema
Hospital
Clifton Swimming Pool
BBC TV Studios
University Library
Senate House
Victoria Rooms
Academy
Bristol Grammar School
Royal Fort House
University
Maternity Hospital
Royal Hosp. for Children
Royal Infirmary
Bus Station
Dental Hospital
Eye Hospital
Avon House (Avon CC)
Kingsdown Sports Centre
Wesley's Chapel
Quakers Friars
Broadweir Baths
Central Hall
Europa Cinema
Police H.Q.
Foster Almshouses
St John's Ch. and Old City Gate
Cinema
Guildhall
H.P.O.
The Exch.
St Nicholas Market
All Saints Exhibition Centre
Castle Park
Bristol Bridge
St Mary's Hospital
Y.W.C.A.
Queen Elizabeth Hospital (Boys School)
Cabot Tower
The Georgian House
Brandon Hill
Masonic Hall
Council House
Cabot House
Library
Cathedral
Watershed Arts Complex
New Bristol Centre Ice Rink & Cinema
Red Lodge
The Hatchet P.H.
Colston Hall
Hippodrome
Theatre Royal
New Vic Theatre
Llandoger Trow
Custom House
Redcliff Bridge
Fire Station
Temple Bridge
Temple Meads Station
Bristol Old Station
P.O.
Chatterton House
Bristol Exhibition Complex
St Augustine's Reach
Arnolfini Gallery
Swing Bridge
Bathurst Wharf
Lifeboat Museum
Bristol Industrial Museum
The Old Jail
Bathurst Basin
General Hospital
SS Great Britain
Maritime Heritage Museum
Floating Harbour
River Avon
(New Cut)
Footbridge
Bedminster Bridge
Bath Bridge
Dame Emily Playground
Swimming Pool
Library
Bedminster Station
Victoria Park
N
A4
A38
A370
HOTWELL ROAD
ANCHOR ROAD
CUMBERLAND ROAD
CORONATION ROAD
COMMERCIAL ROAD
CLARENCE ROAD
YORK ROAD
BATH ROAD
TEMPLE GATE
REDCLIFFE WAY
REDCLIFF HILL
VICTORIA STREET
BOND STREET
NEWFOUNDLAND STREET
OLD MARKET ST
ASHLEY ROAD
CITY ROAD
STOKES CROFT
CHELTENHAM ROAD
COTHAM ROAD
COTHAM HILL
WHITELADIES ROAD
PARK ROW
PARK STREET
COLLEGE GREEN
DEANERY RD
ST GEORGE'S RD
QUEEN'S ROAD
BALDWIN STREET
BROAD QUAY
COLSTON AVENUE
RUPERT STREET
LEWINS MEAD
MARLBOROUGH ST
HAYMARKET
THE HORSEFAIR
BROADMEAD
NEWGATE
CASTLE STREET
BROAD WEIR
WINE ST
CORN STREET
KING ST
QUEEN SQUARE
PRINCE STREET
WAPPING ROAD
REDCLIFFE PARADE
PORTWALL LANE
TEMPLE ST
ST THOMAS ST
EAST STREET
NORTH STREET
WHITEHOUSE LANE
WHITEHOUSE STREET
CATHERINE MEAD STREET
OXFORD STREET

Key to Town Plan

AA Recommended roads		Car Parks	P
Other roads		Parks and open spaces	
Restricted roads		AA Service Centre	AA
Buildings of interest			

Bath continued

Saville House plc
1 Saville Row. Est: 1985. Open 9.45-5.00, Sat. 9.45-3, Sun. by appointment. SIZE: Medium. *STOCK: Furniture, 18th-19th C, £100-£10,000; works of art, 19th C, £200-£6,000; smalls, 18th-20th C, £100-£5,000.* LOC: Near London Rd. TEL: 0225 334595 (24hrs.). SER: Valuations; restorations (furniture and frames). VAT: Stan/Spec.

Scott Antiques
11 London St. Open 10-5.30. *STOCK: General antiques, Victoriana, bric-a-brac.* TEL: Home - 0225 462423. VAT: Stan/Spec.

Town and Country Antiques
11 Queen St. (R Drewett) Open 10.30-5.30, other times by appointment. *STOCK: Fine period and country furniture, metalware and decorative items.* PARK: Nearby. TEL: 0225 463176. VAT: Spec.

Trimbridge Galleries
2 Trimbridge. (Mr and Mrs A Anderson) Est: 1973. SIZE: Medium. *STOCK: Watercolours and drawings, £50-£3,000; prints and oil paintings; all 18th-early 20th C.* LOC: Just off lower end of Milsom St. PARK: Easy. TEL: 0225 466390.

Walcot Reclamation
108 Walcot St. Est: 1977. Open 8.30-5.30, Sat. 9-5. SIZE: Large. *STOCK: Architectural items - English, Irish and continental chimney pieces in marble and pine; garden statuary, Victorian baths and fittings; traditional building materials.* PARK: Own and multi-storey nearby. TEL: 0225 444404/335532. SER: Valuations; restorations. VAT: Stan.

Derek and Glenda Wallis
6 Chapel Row, Queen Sq. ABA. Est: 1971. Open 10-5.30. SIZE: Large. *STOCK: General antiquarian, early and Victorian children's books, illustrated; folklore, Canadiana and prints.* LOC: Corner Queen Sq. (city centre). PARK: Easy. TEL: 0225 424677.

Widcombe Antiques and Pine
9 Claverton Buildings, Widcombe. (Mrs F.J Winter) Est: 1972. Open 10.30-5.30. SIZE: Medium. *STOCK: Stripped pine, Georgian and Victorian, £15-£1,000; brass, copper, especially fenders and fire items.* LOC: A36. PARK: Own at rear. TEL: 0225 428767. VAT: Stan/Spec.

Nick Woodbridge
15a George St. Open by appointment. *STOCK: 18th-19th C paintings and works of art especially topographical works, marine paintings and artifacts, naive and primitive, all subjects.* TEL: 0225 338477.

BRISTOL

Alexander Gallery
122 Whiteladies Rd. (J.A Fardon) Open 9-5.30, Wed. 9-1. *STOCK: 19th-20th C paintings.* TEL: 0272 734692.

Antique Beds
3 Litfield Pl. (Mrs V Dewdney) Est: 1973. Open at all times but appointment advisable. SIZE: Medium. *STOCK: Four-poster beds, 18th-19th C, £995-£5,000.* LOC: Near suspension bridge. PARK: Easy. TEL: 0272 735134; home - same.

The Barometer Shop
3 Lower Park Row. (R Cookson and R Worthington) Est: 1965. Open 10-5.30 or by appointment. *STOCK: Barometers, clocks and watches, scientific instruments, 18th-19th C; furniture and early metalware.* TEL: 0272 272565. SER: Valuations; restorations; spare parts for barometers and clocks.

Bizarre Antiques
208 Gloucester Rd, Bishopston. (P.J Parkin) Open 8.15-5. *STOCK: General antiques.* TEL: 0272 427888; home - 0272 503498.

Bristol Antique Market
St.Nicholas Markets, The Exchange, Corn St. (M.R Harper) Est: 1975. Open Fri. 9-3. SIZE: 12 dealers. *STOCK: Antiques and collectors' items.* TEL: 0272 224014.

Bristol Guild of Applied Art Ltd
68/70 Park St. Est: 1908. Open 9-5.30, Sat. 9-5. *STOCK: Furniture, late 19th-20th C.* TEL: 0272 265548.

Bristol Trade Antiques
192 Cheltenham Rd and 451 Bath Rd, Brislington. (L Dike) Est: 1970. Open by appointment. SIZE: Large and warehouse. *STOCK: General antiques.* TEL: 0272 717959/422790. *Trade Only.*

Robin Butler BADA
20 Clifton Rd. Est: 1978. Open 9.30-5.30, Sat. 10-3. SIZE: Medium. *STOCK: Fine furniture, silver, wine antiques, glass and works of art, 1600-1850, from £50.* Not Stocked: Victoriana, weapons, carpets, shipping goods. LOC: Map showing location sent on request. PARK: Easy, in drive to left of shop. TEL: 0272 733017. SER: Valuations. FAIRS: West of England and Olympia. VAT: Spec.

Carnival Antiques LAPADA
607 Sixth Avenue, Central Business Park, Hengrove. (A.J Williams) Est: 1967. Open 9.30-5.30. *STOCK: Glass, china, brass, copper, furniture.* TEL: 0272 892166; home - 0272 835223; fax - 0272 891333. SER: Shipping and packing. VAT: Stan/Spec.

Bristol continued

Cleeve Antiques
282 Lodge Causeway, Fishponds. (T. and S.E Scull) Est: 1978. Open 9.30-5.30. CL: Wed. *STOCK: Furniture and bric-a-brac.* TEL: 0272 658366; home - 0272 567008.

Clifton Antiques Market
26/28 The Mall, Clifton. (Tritec Investments Ltd.)Est: 1974. Open 10-6. CL: Mon. SIZE: Large - 60 dealers. *STOCK: A wide selection of general antiques and collectors' items, £5-£1,000.* LOC: Near Clifton suspension bridge. PARK: Easy. TEL: 0272 761919. Below are listed some of the dealers.

Ali Baba
Small silver, toys, Victoriana, postcards. **TEL: 0272 739429.**
G Barnes
Jewellery.
Bees and Graves
Furniture and small items.
P Biggs/S Bristow
Silver, general antiques.
J Brindle
Small items.
Mrs P Coles
China, general antiques. **TEL: 0272 734698.**
S Coles
Porcelain, brass and copper.
Jeanne Crosse
General small decorative items and textiles.
G Dowling
Picture framing and gilding.
Miss S Foster
Unusual diamond and gold jewellery. **TEL: 0272 736996; home - 0272 738390. VAT: Stan.**
Grove Side Antiques
(A Metcalfe) ***Prints.***
P Jones
Furniture.
R Jones
Clocks, watches. **SER: Repairs.**
Mrs M Jubb
General antiques, furniture. **TEL: 0272 734698; home - 0272 738520.**
Mrs M T Kerridge
Silver, jewellery, small items. **TEL: 0272 738504.**
Mrs R Littlejohn
Jewellery.
Mac-Smith
(P Mackenzie-Smith) ***Furniture.*** **TEL: 0272 735678.**
Jan Morrison
Small items.
J Oakes
Architectural antiques.
Rachel
Book-binding.
Mrs M Risdale
Silver, gold, jewellery, china. **TEL: 0272 734698.**

Clifton Antiques Market continued

The Silver Stall
(Mrs I Healey, Mrs M Holmes) ***Silver frames, silver, general antiques and jewellery.*** **TEL: 0272 734531.**
Slade
(Miss N Slade) ***Small general antiques, bric-a-brac, art deco.*** **TEL: 0272 734698.**
S Trickey
Jewellery. **SER: Repairs.**
B Yardley
China, glass and pictures.

Cotham Galleries
22 Cotham Hill, Cotham. (D Jury) Est: 1960. Open 9-5.30. SIZE: Small. *STOCK: Furniture, glass, metal.* LOC: From city centre up Park St. into Whiteladies Rd. Turn right at Clifton Down station. PARK: Easy. TEL: 0272 736026. SER: Valuations.

Cotham Hill Bookshop
39A Cotham Hill, Cotham. (R Plant and M Garbett) Open 9.30-5.30. *STOCK: Antiquarian and secondhand books especially fine art.* TEL: 0272 732344.

David Cross (Fine Art)
3A Boyces Ave, Clifton. Est: 1969. Open 9.30-6. SIZE: Medium. *STOCK: British paintings, especially marine, Bristol school; related drawings, prints and watercolours.* LOC: Between Victoria Sq. and Regent St. PARK: Easy. TEL: 0272 732614. SER: Valuations; restorations (oils, watercolours, frames); buys at auction; framing. VAT: Spec.

Richard Essex Antiques
Est: 1969. *STOCK: General antiques from mid-18th C.* TEL: 0272 733949.

Frocks and Tails
39A Cotham Hill, Cotham. (A.G Haig-Harrison) Est: 1977. Open 10.30-5.30. *STOCK: 1920's period evening wear.* LOC: Off Whiteladies Rd. PARK: Easy. TEL: 0272 737461. SER: Evening dress and costume hire.

George's Antiquarian and Secondhand Bookshop
52 Park St. Est: 1847. Open 9-5.30. *STOCK: Books, antiquarian and secondhand.* TEL: 0272 276602; fax - 0272 251854.

Grey-Harris and Co BADA
12 Princess Victoria St, Clifton. Est: 1963. Open 9.30-5.30. ***STOCK: Jewellery, Victorian; silver, old Sheffield plate.*** **TEL: 0272 737365. SER: Valuations. VAT: Stan/Spec.**

Chris Grimes Militaria
13 Lower Park Row. Open 11-5.30. *STOCK: Militaria, scientific instruments, nautical items.* TEL: 0272 298205.

Bristol continued

A.R Heath
62 Pembroke Rd, Clifton. Open by appointment only. *STOCK: Rare books, pamphlets, broadsides, pre-1850.* TEL: 0272 741183.

Kemps
9 Carlton Court, Westbury-on-Trym. (P.M Kemp) Open 9-5.30. *STOCK: Jewellery.* TEL: 0272 505090.

The Mall Gallery
16 The Mall, Clifton. (C.R.H Warren) Est: 1971. Open 10-5.30. CL: Mon. and Sat. *STOCK: Paintings, £500-£5,000; watercolours, £100-£2,000.* TEL: 0272 736263. SER: Buys at auction. VAT: Spec.

The Mall Jewellers
4 The Mall, Clifton. *STOCK: Jewellery, silver, plate.* TEL: 0272 733178. VAT: Stan/Spec.

Michael's Antiques
150 Wells Rd. (M Beese) Resident. TEL: 0272 713943.

Robert Mills Architectural Antiques Ltd
Unit 3 Satellite Business Park, Blackswarth Rd, Redfield. Est: 1969. Open 9.30-5, Sat. 9-12. SIZE: Large. *STOCK: Architectural items, panelled rooms, shop interiors, Gothic Revival, stained glass, church woodwork, bar and restaurant fittings, 1750-1920, £50-£30,000.* LOC: A420 from Bristol, turn right at Fire Engine public house, then left towards Crews Hole, first yard on right. PARK: Easy. TEL: 0272 556542; home - 0272 555824; fax - 0272 558146. VAT: Stan.

Oldwoods
1 Colston Yard. (S Wilcox and S Duck) Open 10-4, Fri. and Sat. 10-5.30. CL: Mon. *STOCK: Pine and fireplaces.* TEL: 0272 299023. SER: Restorations.

The Oriental Carpet Centre
Maples Store, 3 Queen's Rd, Clifton. (A.R Hill) Open 9-5.30. *STOCK: Oriental carpets and rugs.* TEL: 0272 290165.

Pelter/Sands Art Gallery
43-45 Park St. Open 10-5.30. CL: Mon. SIZE: Large. *STOCK: Oil paintings, watercolours, Victorian, modern British and contemporary.* TEL: 0272 293988. SER: Restorations (oil paintings).

Potter's Antiques and Coins
60 Colston St. (B.C Potter) Est: 1965. Open 10.30-5.30. SIZE: Small. *STOCK: Antiquities, 500 B.C. to 1600 A.D., £5-£500; commemoratives, 1770-1953, £4-£300; coins, 500 B.C. to 1967, £1-£100; drinking glass, 1770-1953, £3-£200; small furniture, from 1837, £10-£200.* LOC: Near top of Christmas Steps, close to city

Potter's Antiques and Coins continued

centre. PARK: N.C.P. Park Row. TEL: 0272 262551. SER: Valuations; buys at auction. VAT: Stan/Spec.

Queens Road Antiques
88a Queens Rd, Clifton. Est: 1979. Open 10-5.30, Wed. 10-1. SIZE: Small. *STOCK: Furniture and bric-a-brac, 19th C, £50-£500.* LOC: Next to Victoria Rooms. TEL: 0272 238215. SER: Valuations. FAIRS: Shepton Mallet; Stoneleigh; Newark; Birmingham. VAT: Stan/Spec.

Quinney's Jewellery
17 The Mall, Clifton. (B Richardson) Est: 1960. Open 10.30-5. CL: Mon. and Sat. *STOCK: Jewellery.* TEL: 0272 735877.

Relics - Pine Furniture
109 St. George's Rd, Hotwells. (R Seville and S Basey) Est: 1972. Open 10-6. SIZE: Large. *STOCK: Victorian pine furniture, £25-£600.* LOC: Near cathedral, 1/2 mile from city centre. PARK: Easy. TEL: 0272 268453. VAT: Stan.

John Roberts Bookshop
43 Triangle West, Clifton. (J.T Roberts) Est: 1955. Open 9-5.30. SIZE: Medium. *STOCK: Secondhand and antiquarian books, topographical and other prints.* LOC: Just off Queens Rd. shopping centre. PARK: Nearby, multi-storey. TEL: 0272 268568. SER: Picture framing. VAT: Spec.

Ruskins
426 Wells Rd. (L.M.A Ruskin) Resident. Always available. *STOCK: General antiques and postcards.* TEL: 0272 776456.

R.A Saunders
164 Raleigh Rd, Bedminster. Open 8-5. *STOCK: Furniture; bric-a-brac.* TEL: 0272 631268; home - 0272 662637. SER: Silver and gold plating.

Sedan Chair Antiques
17/19 Portland St, Clifton. (R Horwood) Est: 1970. Open 10-5.30, Sat. 10-1.30. CL: Mon. *STOCK: Furniture, general antiques, decorative items.* TEL: 0272 734020.

John and Sheila Symes
93 Charleton Mead Dr, Westbury-on-Trym. Open by appointment. *STOCK: Stamps, postcards, ephemera and autographs.* TEL: 0272 501074.

Triangle Antiques LAPADA
9 Byron Pl, Clifton. (R Organ and T Smith) Est: 1970. Open 9.30-5.30. *STOCK: Decorative antiques.* TEL: 0272 292502.

The Tudor Gallery of Bristol LAPADA
(P Lake) *STOCK: Early English porcelain, 19th C.* TEL: 0272 834287.

Bristol continued

The Vintage Wireless Co Ltd
Tudor House, Cossham St, Mangotsfield. (T.G Rees) Est: 1972. SIZE: Medium. *STOCK: Valve radio receivers, vintage valve hi-fi, 1920-1950; radio components, historical and technical data.* LOC: A3174. PARK: Easy. TEL: 0272 565472. VAT: Stan. *Mail Order Only.*

The Wise Owl Bookshop
26 Upper Maudlin St. Open 10.30-5.30. *STOCK: Antiquarian and secondhand books especially on music and the performing arts; sheet music and records.* TEL: 0272 262738; evenings - 0272 246936.

CHIPPING SODBURY, Nr. Bath

Sodbury Antiques
70 Broad St. (Mrs M Brown) Est: 1986. CL: Wed. SIZE: Small. *STOCK: Porcelain and china, mainly 18th-19th C, small furniture, £5-£500.* PARK: Easy. TEL: 0454 273369. SER: Buys at auction.

CLEVEDON

Beach Antiques
Adelaide House, 13 The Beach. (D.A Coles) Open 2-5, Sat. and Sun. 11-5. CL: Mon. and Fri. *STOCK: Jewellery, silver frames, china, brass, glass, mainly small items.* PARK: Easy. TEL: 0272 876881.

Clevedon Fine Arts (with Clevedon Books)
Cinema Building, Old Church Rd. Est: 1972. Open 11-5, prior telephone call welcome. CL: Mon. and Wed. *STOCK: Maps, charts, prints, books.* TEL: 0272 875862/872304.

John and Carol Hawley Antique Clocks
The Orchard, Clevedon Lane, Clapton Wick. CMBHI. Est: 1972. Open by appointment. *STOCK: Clocks, especially longcase, bracket, wall and carriage.* TEL: 0272 852052. SER: Valuations; restorations; repairs.

CLUTTON

Ian and Dianne McCarthy
Arcadian Cottage, 112 Station Rd. Resident. Est: 1958. Open by appointment. SIZE: Medium. *STOCK: Lamps - oil, gas, electric for domestic, industrial, shipping and transport usage; unusual candle lamps; copper and brassware, 17th C to 1920, £5-£500.* PARK: Easy and opposite. TEL: 0761 53188. SER: Valuations; restorations (metalware); cleaning; upholstery; rush seating; spares and lamp-shades. FAIRS: Shepton Mallet. *Trade Only.*

CONGRESBURY

D.M.E. Antiques
Fernbank, High St. (D Moore) Est: 1973. Open by appointment. *STOCK: Furniture, 18th-19th C.* TEL: 0934 832100. *Trade and Export Only.*

FRESHFORD, Nr. Bath

Janet Clarke
3 Woodside Cottages. Open by appointment. *STOCK: Antiquarian books on gastronomy, cookery and wine.* TEL: 0225 723186. SER: Catalogue issued.

LANGFORD, Nr. Bristol

James R Cornish
The Old Garden. Est: 1978. Open 9.30-5.30, Sat. and Sun. by appointment. SIZE: Small. *STOCK: Longcase clocks, 1700-1880, £450-£1,500.* LOC: A38 from Bristol, 4 miles past Bristol Airport turn right to Lower Langford, the Old Garden is first gateway on right. PARK: Easy. TEL: 0934 862704; home - same. SER: Valuations (clocks); restorations (clocks); buys at auction (clocks).

MARSHFIELD, Nr. Bath

David Bridgwater
112 High St. Open by appointment. *STOCK: Sculptural items, garden ornaments, metalwork, architectural and decorative items.* TEL: 0225 891623.

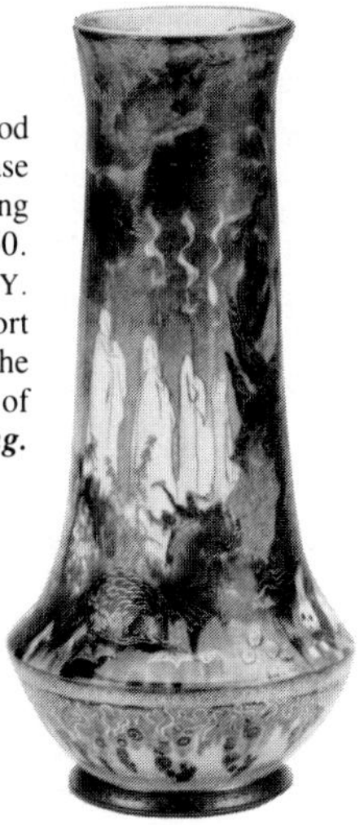

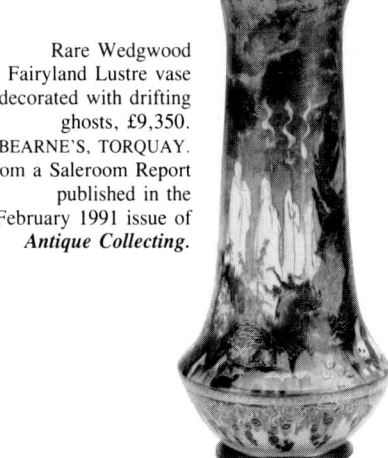

Rare Wedgwood Fairyland Lustre vase decorated with drifting ghosts, £9,350. BEARNE'S, TORQUAY. From a Saleroom Report published in the February 1991 issue of *Antique Collecting.*

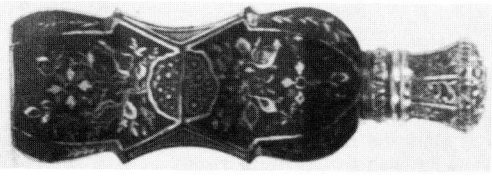

MIDSOMER NORTON

Somervale Antiques BADA LAPADA

6 Radstock Rd. (Wing Cdr R.G Thomas) CINOA. Resident. Open by appointment only. SIZE: Small. *STOCK: Glass - English drinking, decanters, cut and coloured; Bristol and Nailsea bijouterie; glass scent bottles.* LOC: On A362 on Radstock side of town. PARK: Easy. TEL: 0761 412686 (24hrs.). SER: Valuations; buys at auction. FAIRS: Chelsea Spring and Autumn; West of England, Bath. VAT: Stan/Spec.

OLVESTON, Nr. Bristol

Green Farm Antiques

The Green. (V Gillespie) Est: 1985. Usually open by prior telephone call advisable. SIZE: Medium. *STOCK: Oak and country furniture, 17th-18th C, £50-£3,000; decorative items.* LOC: 5 mins. from junction 20, M4 or junction 16, M5 or 3 miles from Severn Bridge. PARK: Easy. TEL: 0454 612362; home - same. FAIRS: Reg Cooper.

PILL

Susan Liddiard Antiques

17 Lodway. Resident. Est: 1970. Open Thurs., Fri. and Sat. 10-5.30, or by appointment. *STOCK: Victorian and Edwardian furniture, some smalls.* LOC: 1 mile from M5 junction 19. TEL: 027 581 2315.

REDLAND, Nr. Bristol

Something Old, Something New

115 Cold Harbour Rd. (Z Bouyamourn) Open 10-5.30. *STOCK: General antiques.* TEL: 0272 247479.

WEST HARPTREE, Nr. Bristol

Tilly Manor Antiques

Tilly Manor. (J.D Scott) Est: 1978. Open 9.30-6, Sun. and other times by appointment. SIZE: Large. *STOCK: Town and country furniture, 18th-19th C, £100-£3,000; brass, copper and metalware, 17th-19th C, decorative collectors items, 18th-19th C; all £5-£500.* LOC: Next to church on A368. PARK: Own. TEL: 0761 221888; home - same. SER: Restorations. VAT: Stan/Spec.

WESTON-SUPER-MARE

Bay Tree House Antiques
Stevens Lane, Lympsham. (N.W. and S.M Adams) Est: 1982. Open 10-5.30 including Sun. SIZE: Warehouse. *STOCK: Stripped pine, satin walnut and mahogany, £25-£2,000.* PARK: Easy. TEL: 0934 750367; home - same.

D.M. Restorations
3 Laburnum Rd. (D Pike) Open 9-5. *STOCK: Small mahogany furniture.* PARK: Easy. TEL: 0934 631681.

Harwood West End AntiquesLAPADA
13 West St. (A. and D.B.M Harwood) Est: 1967. Open 9.15-5. *STOCK: General antiques, jewellery, clocks, Victoriana.* TEL: 0934 629874. VAT: Stan/Spec.

Moorland Antiques
134 Moorland Rd. (T Lim) Open 9-5.30. *STOCK: General antiques.* TEL: 0934 632361.

Sterling Books
43A Locking Rd. Est: 1966. Open 9-1 and 2-6. CL: Thurs. p.m. *STOCK: Antiquarian and secondhand books, ephemera and prints.* TEL: 0934 625056. SER: Catalogues issued.

Toby's Antiques
47 Upper Church Rd. (A. and D White) Open 9-5, Sun. by appointment. *STOCK: Furniture and general antiques.* TEL: 0934 623555.

Winter's Antiques LAPADA
Severn Rd. (R.N., E.P. and L.B Winters) Est: 1967. Open 9-12 and 2-4. CL: Sat. p.m. and Thurs. SIZE: Large. *STOCK: Furniture, clocks, smalls and fine art, all periods.* Not Stocked: Coins, stamps. LOC: Off sea front. PARK: Easy. TEL: 0934 620118/623105/81460.

WRINGTON

Sir William Russell Flint Galleries Ltd
The Georgian House, Broad St. Open 9-5, weekends by appointment. SIZE: Small. *STOCK: Prints, £65-£2,000; engravings, £650-£1,000; books, £75-£1,000; watercolours, £1,000-£25,000; all by Sir William and Francis Murray Russell Flint.* LOC: 3 miles south-west of Bristol Airport. PARK: Easy. TEL: 0934 863149. SER: Valuations; restorations. FAIRS: British International, Birmingham; Gallery 91. VAT: Stan/Spec.

YATTON, Nr. Bristol

Glenville Antiques LAPADA
120 High St. (Mrs S.E.M Burgan) Est: 1969. Open 10.30-5. CL: Sun. except by appointment. SIZE: Small. *STOCK: Glass, £5-£750; small furniture, £25-£2,500; pottery and porcelain, £5-£1,500, all mainly 19th C; collectors' items, sewing items.* Not Stocked: Pewter, guns, antique foreign curios, coins, stamps. LOC: On B3133. PARK: Easy. TEL: 0934 832284. VAT: Stan/Spec.

Lens, Bernard, III 1682-1740)
Handle your Slings. *Etched outline and watercolour, 12in. x 7¼in.*
This is one of a set of 17 watercolours of 'The Granadiers Exercise of the Granade, 1735', which belonged to the Duke of York. The only other known sets are in the Royal Collection and National Army Museum — but beware Lens' son Andrew Benjamin published a set of engravings after them in 1744. ANDREW WYLD
From ***The Dictionary of British Watercolour Artists up to 1920,*** Volume III, by H.L. Mallalieu, published by the **Antique Collectors' Club** in 1990. £35.00.

A postcard of Miss Lily Brayton, the actress, her medieval costume set off by some of her own jewellery. The pendant on a long chain is possibly a German exercise in the Renaissance manner, but the necklace is the Liberty one in Plate 397 (no. 3).

PHOTOGRAPHY BY COURTESY OF JOHN CULME

From ***Jewellery 1789-1910 — The International Era,*** Volume II, by Shirley Bury published by the **Antique Collectors' Club** in 1991. £47.50 each volume.

Bedfordshire

Please note this is only a rough map designed to show dealers the number of shops in the various towns, and is not necessarily totally accurate.

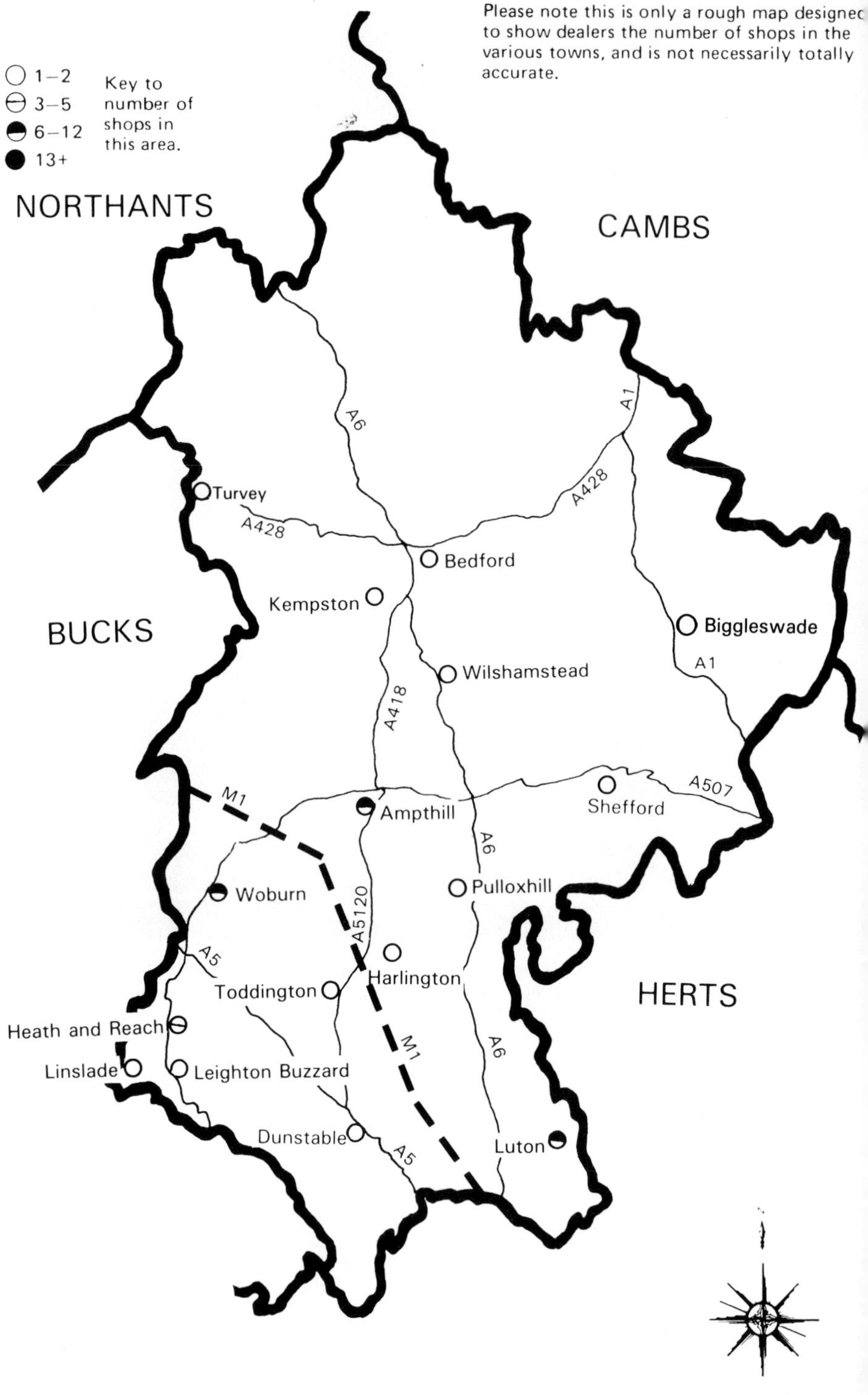

1–2
3–5
6–12
13+
Key to number of shops in this area.
NORTHANTS
CAMBS
BUCKS
HERTS
Turvey
A428
A6
A1
Bedford
Kempston
Biggleswade
Wilshamstead
A418
M1
Ampthill
Shefford
A507
Woburn
A5120
Pulloxhill
Harlington
A5
Toddington
Heath and Reach
Linslade
Leighton Buzzard
Dunstable
Luton

AMPTHILL

Ampthill Antiques
Market Square. (A Olney) Est: 1980. Open 10-5, Sun. 2-5. SIZE: Large. *STOCK: Furniture, collectables, jewellery, watercolours and oil paintings, clocks.* LOC: Town centre. PARK: Easy and at rear. TEL: 0525 403344. SER: Restorations (clocks).

Ampthill Emporium
6 Bedford St. (R.J Bradley) Est: 1978. Open 7 days, 10-5.30. SIZE: Large. *STOCK: Furniture, mainly 19th C, £50-£5,000; decorative items, £5-£500; clocks and pianos, £10-£2,000; pine.* LOC: 5 mins., junction 13, M1. PARK: Easy. TEL: 0525 402131. SER: Valuations; restorations (furniture, stripping, brass polishing). VAT: Stan/Spec.

Pat Bently Antiques
7 Kings Arms Yard. Est: 1976. Open 11-5.30 including Sun. SIZE: Large and barn. *STOCK: Mahogany, oak, pine furniture, smalls.* PARK: Easy. TEL: 0525 404939. VAT: Stan/Spec.

Robert Harman Antiques BADA
11 Church St. (R.H Cannell) Est: 1981. Open 9.30-12.30 and 1.30-5.30, Sun. and evenings by appointment. SIZE: Medium. *STOCK: Furniture and works of art, £500-£30,000; papier mâché, tôle, £200-£5,000; all 18th to early 19th C.* PARK: Easy and opposite. TEL: 0525 402322; home - same. SER: Valuations; restorations (furniture); buys at auction (furniture and works of art). FAIRS: Chelsea Spring & Autumn; Olympia; Café Royal, Park Lane. VAT: Spec.

The Pine Parlour
82a Dunstable St. (L Barker) Est: 1989. Open 10-5. CL: Mon. SIZE: Small. *STOCK: Pine furniture, 19th C, £200-£800; kitchenalia, £5-£60.* PARK: Easy. TEL: 0525 403030; home - same. SER: Valuations.

Ann Roberts Antiques
1 Kings Arms Yard. Est: 1980. Open 11-4.30, Sun. 2-5. CL: Mon. and Tues. SIZE: Medium. *STOCK: Georgian and Victorian fenders, fire irons and wood surrounds; Victorian cast iron fires; brass, copper and iron fire accessories, furniture and clocks.* LOC: Mews off town centre, A507. PARK: 50yds. TEL: 0525 403394.

S. and S Timms Antiques Ltd LAPADA
16, 18 and 20 Dunstable St. Est: 1976. Open 9-6, Sat. 10-4, other times by appointment. SIZE: Large. *STOCK: Furniture, 1700-1900, £500-£15,000; copper, brass.* LOC: A5120. PARK: Easy. TEL: 0525 403067; home - 0525 718829. VAT: Stan/Spec.

Yesterdays Pine
13 Dunstable St. (N.E Chesters) Est: 1975. Open 10-6 and Sun. 2-6. *STOCK: Waxed pine furniture, decorative ceramics, pictures and*

Yesterdays Pine continued

general antiques. TEL: 0525 402260. SER: Furniture made to specification; fitted interiors, bedrooms and kitchens.

BEDFORD

Britcastle Antiques and Interiors
Unit 1, Fenlake Rd. Industrial Estate. (A Rundle) Open Tues.-Sat. 9.30-5.30, or by appointment. *STOCK: General antiques, Victorian and some period items.* PARK: Easy. TEL: 0234 213741.

Stapleton's Antiques
51 Ford End Rd. (D.H Stapleton) Est: 1976. Open 9-5. SIZE: Small and warehouse. *STOCK: General antiques, especially mahogany and oak furniture and clocks, 18th-19th C, £5-£2,000.* LOC: A428. PARK: Easy. TEL: 0234 211087; home - same. SER: Valuations.

BIGGLESWADE

Shortmead Antiques
46 Shortmead St. (S.E Sinfield) Open 10.30-4. CL: Thurs. SIZE: Small. *STOCK: Furniture, 19th C, £50-£1,000+; porcelain, silver, bronzes, paintings and prints, to £1,000; all pre-1930.* LOC: 1/2 mile from A1. TEL: 0767 601780 (ansaphone). FAIRS: Harlequin and some Crown.

DUNSTABLE

Castle Coins and Chiltern International Antiques
47a High St. South. Open 9.30-5. *STOCK: Jewellery, coins and medals, general antiques.* TEL: 0582 606751/602778.

HARLINGTON

Willow Farm Pine Centre
Willow Farm. (M. and A Price) Est: 1974. Open 10-5 every day. SIZE: Large. *STOCK: Country pine.* LOC: Off Barton Rd. PARK: Easy. TEL: 052 55 2052; home - same.

HEATH AND REACH, Nr. Leighton Buzzard

Heath Antique Centre
Woburn Rd. Est: 1985. Open 10-5.30. SIZE: Large. LOC: A418 off A5. PARK: Easy. TEL: 052 523 7831.

Heath and Reach continued

Helton Antiques
Helton House, 28 Birds Hill. (A H Cox) Open 10-6. SIZE: Large. *STOCK: General antiques, shipping goods, collectable items.* TEL: 052 523 474; home - 0525 372887.

Graham Trenchard Ltd. Charterhouse Gallery
14 Birds Hill. Open 9.30-5.30, Sun. by appointment. *STOCK: Watercolours and oils.* PARK: 50yds. TEL: 052 523 379. SER: Valuations; restorations (pictures); framing.

KEMPSTON

Queen Adelaide Gallery
79 High St. (W.T Gibbs) Open 10-6. CL: Mon. *STOCK: Oils, watercolours and some prints, 18th-20th C, £50-£7,000; marquetry and modern ceramics.* LOC: From Bedford, along Kempston Rd., past South Wing Hospital. PARK: Easy. TEL: 0234 854083; home - same. SER: Valuations; restorations (paintings and frames).

Eva Rogers
Spinney Lodge, Ridge Rd. Est: 1962. *STOCK: General antiques and shipping goods.* TEL: 0234 854823; home - same.

LEIGHTON BUZZARD

David Ball Antique and Fine Art LAPADA
59 North St. (D. and J Ball) Est: 1968. Open 10-5. SIZE: Large. *STOCK: Furniture, general antiques and watercolours, 17th-20th C, £3-£2,000.* LOC: A418 to Woburn. PARK: Easy. TEL: 0525 382954; home - 0525 210753. SER: Valuations; restorations. FAIRS: Luton and Dunstable. VAT: Stan/Spec.

LINSLADE, Nr. Leighton Buzzard

Linslade Antiques and Curios
1 New Rd. Est: 1978. Open 9.30-6. *STOCK: General antiques, silver, china, furniture, clocks, toys, prints and paintings.* LOC: 5 mins. walk from Leighton Buzzard station. TEL: 0525 378348. SER: Courier.

LUTON

Bargain Box
4 & 6a Adelaide St. Open 9-6, Wed. 9-1. *STOCK: General antiques.* TEL: 0582 423809.

J Denton (Antiques)
Rear of 440 Dunstable Rd. Est: 1979. Open 10.15-3, or by appointment. CL: Sat. SIZE: Medium. *STOCK: Furniture and small items,*

J Denton (Antiques) continued

Victorian and Edwardian; shipping goods, bric-a-brac. LOC: Corner of Arundel Rd. and Dunstable Rd. PARK: Easy. TEL: 0582 582726; home - 0296 661471. VAT: Stan/Spec.

Foye Gallery
15 Stanley St. Est: 1960. Open 9.30-5, or by appointment. *STOCK: Engravings, etchings, drawings, watercolours, paintings, maps, books.* TEL: 0582 38487. VAT: Stan.

Knight's Gallery
59-61 Guildford St. (J.C Knight) Est: 1973. Open 9-5, Sat. 10-1. SIZE: Small. *STOCK: Watercolours, 19th-20th C, £50-£2,000.* LOC: Rear of Guildford St. PARK: Easy. TEL: 0582 36266; home - 0582 604142. SER: Valuations; restorations; framing; buys at auction (watercolours). VAT: Stan.

Leaside Antiques
(T.G Pepper) Est: 1968. Open by appointment. *STOCK: Furniture, to 1910; jewellery, silver, porcelain, watches, paintings.* TEL: 0582 27957. SER: Repairs (jewellery).

The Old Pine Loft
Kingham Way, Reginald St. Open Sat. only 9.30-4. SIZE: Small. *STOCK: Cast-iron fireplaces, stripped pine doors.* LOC: Off old Bedford Rd., which runs from the station. PARK: Easy. TEL: 0582 459001. SER: Pine stripping.

PULLOXHILL, Nr. Ampthill

Riches
Unit 2, College Farm. (R.J Jennings) Open 10-1 and 2-4.30. CL: Tues. *STOCK: General antiques.* Not Stocked: Jewellery, coins, silver. TEL: 0525 717786. SER: Upholstery; framing.

SHEFFORD

Secondhand Alley
2-4 High St. Open 9-5.30, Wed. and Sat. 9-5. *STOCK: Shipping furniture, bric-a-brac.* PARK: Easy. TEL: 0462 814747. VAT: Stan.

TODDINGTON, Nr. Dunstable

Cobblers Hall Antiques
119/121 Leighton Rd. (A.G. and N.E Huckett) Est: 1974. Open by appointment only. *STOCK: English porcelain, mid-18th to mid-19th C, £25-£400. Georgian and early Victorian writing boxes and slopes, treen and Tunbridgeware.* PARK: Easy. TEL: 052 55 2890. FAIRS: Cheltenham, Worcester, Petersfield, Derby, Felbridge, Harrogate, Oatland Park, Ragley Hall and Worksop.

TURVEY, Nr. Bedford

Fenlan Antiques
Old Working Mens Room, Bamfords Yard, High St. (C Smith and B. and S.L Harrison) Est: 1982. Open 8-5. CL: Sat. SIZE: Medium. *STOCK: Mahogany, rosewood, walnut and oak furniture, 18th to early 20th C, £50-£5,000.* LOC: A428. PARK: Easy. TEL: 023 064 8916; home - 0234 342775. SER: Restorations (cabinet making); restoration products and sundries; French polishing. FAIRS: Newark. VAT: Stan/Spec.

WILSHAMSTEAD, Nr. Bedford

Manor Antiques
The Manor House, Cottonend Rd. (Mrs S Bowen) Est: 1976. Open 10-5, Sun. by appointment. SIZE: Large. *STOCK: Furniture, 19th C to Edwardian, £50-£4,000; copper and brass, Georgian to Victorian; lighting and oil lamps, Victorian to 1920s; general antiques.* LOC: Just off A6, 4 miles south of Bedford. PARK: Own. TEL: 0234 740262; home - same. SER: Restorations (furniture); buys at auction. FAIRS: Luton. VAT: Stan/Spec.

WOBURN

Atrium Antiques and Interiors Ltd
19 Market Pl. (Mrs A Fluitman) Open 9-5.30, Sun. 2-5.30. SIZE: Large. *STOCK: Furniture, paintings, prints and decorative items including lamps.* PARK: Easy. TEL: 0525 290444. VAT: Spec.

Butterworths
14 Bedford St. (M. and J Butterworth) Est: 1964. Open 10-5.30, Sun. 2-5.30. SIZE: Large. *STOCK: Period furniture and accessories, 18th-19th C, £100-£20,000.* LOC: Main st. PARK: Own. TEL: 0525 290545; home -0525 712721. SER: Valuations; restorations (furniture); buys at auction. VAT: Stan/Spec.

George Large Gallery
13/14 Market Pl. Open 10-1 and 2-5.30, Sun. 11-1 and 2-5. *STOCK: British art from 1900.* TEL: 0525 290658.

Questor
13/14 Market Pl. (P Parkinson-Large) Open 10-1 and 2-5.30, Sun. 11-1 and 2-5. *STOCK: Furniture, £50-£1,000; porcelain, jewellery, small antiques.* TEL: 0525 290658.

Christopher Sykes Antiques
The Old Parsonage. (C. and M Sykes) Est: 1949. Open 9-6. SIZE: Large. *STOCK: Furniture, 17th to early 19th C, £30-£2,000; scientific instruments, microscopes, sundials, telescopes, sextants, pewter, candlesticks, £20-£2,000; oil paintings (English Schools),*

Christopher Sykes Antiques continued

porcelain, glass, silver, 19th C, £20-£2,000; pottery, carvings, treen, wine related items and corkscrews, toys, games, metalware. LOC: In main street opposite Post Office on A50. PARK: Easy. TEL: 0525 290259/290467. SER: 130 page illustrated mail order catalogue on corkscrews and wine related antiques available £7 each. VAT: Stan/Spec.

The Woburn Abbey Antiques Centre
Est: 1967. Open every day (including Bank Holidays) 11-5 Nov. to Easter; 10-6 Easter to Oct. CL: 24th-27th Dec. (1991). LOC: On A5. Follow signs to Woburn Abbey and after entering grounds, follow signs. PARK: Easy. TEL: 0525 290350. Below are listed the dealers at this centre.

Applecross Antiques
(A Miller) *Silver, porcelain, pottery (especially blue and white transferware), prints, needlework especially samplers.*

Armigers
Victorian and Edwardian furniture; brass, copper, decorative items.

Mike Armson Antiques
18th and 19th C mahogany and oak furniture, decorative items, copper and brass.

Baroq Antiques
Mahogany furniture, 18th and 19th C; oils, watercolours, porcelain.

Ursula Breese
Victorian jewellery, glass, lace and decorative items.

C K Antiques
Country furniture, 18th and 19th C; decorative items, brass and copper.

Roy Chase
18th-19th C mahogany furniture, nautical objects.

Cottage Antiques
18th-19th C oak and mahogany furniture; decorative items.

Country Life Interiors
Pine furniture, bed and table linen, decorative items and engravings.

Dolphin Antiques
Georgian oak, walnut and mahogany; decorative items.

Duncan House Antiques
18th-19th C mahogany furniture; decorative items.

E and A Antiques
English and continental porcelain, 18th and 19th C; watercolours, decorative items.

G W Ford & Son Ltd **BADA**
18th-19th C furniture; some porcelain, Sheffield plate.

John Ginty
Clocks - wall, longcase, carriage and mantel; country furniture, brass and copper.

Sylvia Grant
Small decorative items, silver and boxes.

Woburn Abbey Antiques Centre

One of the streets on the ground floor.

One of the largest Antiques Centres under one roof in Great Britain and the most original — with 40 independent shops and 12 showrooms comprising 50 established dealers, some of whom are members of L.A.P.A.D.A. and B.A.D.A. — is situated in the magnificent South Court of Woburn Abbey.

We are pleased to offer the dealer and private collector a wide range of Antiques: Clocks, Lamps, Porcelain and Glass, Paintings, Prints, Georgian and Victorian Furniture, Jewellery, Georgian Silver, Painted Furniture, Works of Art, etc., at competitive prices.

Within one hour's drive of Oxford, Cambridge, Birmingham and London (via M1, Exit 12 or 13 signposted Woburn Abbey). Trains from St. Pancras to Flitwick or Euston to Bletchley can be met by prior arrangement. Dealers admitted free and their park entrance refunded at the Antiques Centre. Visiting dealers' car park adjacent to the Antiques Centre.

Interior of one of the shops on the first floor.

OPEN EVERY DAY OF THE YEAR EXCEPT AS SPECIFIED
Including Sundays and Bank Holidays
Easter Sunday to October 10-6 p.m. November to Easter 11-5 p.m.
Closed 24th-27th December

WOBURN ABBEY ANTIQUES CENTRE, WOBURN ABBEY
BEDFORDSHIRE MK43 0TP
Telephone Woburn (0525) 290350

The Woburn Abbey Antiques Centre continued

Irene Hollings Antiques
Furniture and decorative items.
Timothy Jarvis
Georgian furniture and decorative items.
Jean Kershaw
17th-19th C oak and mahogany furniture, brass, copper ware and country items.
Sue Killinger Antiques
Edwardian and Victorian furniture, brass, copper and decorative items.
Marion Langham Ltd
Belleek ware, 19th C porcelain and decorative items.
Gerald Lewis Antiques
18th-19th C oak and mahogany furniture, clocks and barometers.
Mrs Jeanne McPherson
Porcelain, decorative items, silver and glass and small 18th and 19th C furniture.
Mary Malkin
Porcelain and decorative items.
Matsell Antiques Ltd
18th and 19th C furniture, decorative items, mirrors.
Maxim Antiques
Decorative items, lamps and mirrors; Georgian furniture.
Mears and Boyer
Early English country pottery, country furniture, Staffordshire figures.
Sybil Mendoza
19th C mahogany furniture, paintings and decorative items.
Pembroke Antiques
18th and 19th C furniture and porcelain.
Christopher Perry Antiques
18th-19th C oak and mahogany furniture, mirrors, boxes, decorative items.
Ron Perry
Art nouveau, Victoriana and Edwardian furniture, unusual decorative items, light fittings.
Howard Phillips
Early glass.
Valerie Pike
19th C English and continental porcelain, decorative items.

The Woburn Abbey Antiques Centre continued

Rosemary Pratt Antiques
Furniture, treen, lignum vitae, 18th and 19th C; decorative items.
John Rapley Antiques
17th-19th C oak and mahogany furniture; decorative items.
E Robertson
18th-19th C English porcelain, mahogany, walnut and rosewood furniture; boxes.
Guy Roe Antiques
Georgian furniture, porcelain, decorative items and mirrors.
R Rynsard
Silver.
Terry Scudder Antiques
18th-19th C oak and mahogany furniture, Delft tiles, porcelain, watercolours.
Sefton Antiques
(A Miller) *Georgian oak and mahogany furniture; brass and copper, decorative items, papier mâché, treen especially Tunbridgeware.*
Sovereign Art
Decorative items, porcelain and unusual items, period furniture and silver.
S and S Timms Antiques
Georgian and Victorian oak and mahogany furniture.
Christina Tooley and Jacqueline Statham
Clocks, barometers, brass and copper; mahogany, walnut and rosewood furniture, 18th and 19th C.
Town and Country Antiques
18th-19th C furniture, mirrors and decorative items.
Paul Treadaway Antiques
Georgian mahogany furniture, mirrors, engravings, decorative items.
Underwood Antiques
18th-19th C mahogany furniture; decorative items, mirrors.
John Vickers
English and continental porcelain, 18th-19th C.

The Woburn Abbey Antiques Centre continued

Margaret Williams
18th-19th C mahogany and walnut furniture, brass ware, silver and plate; boxes, decorative items, mirrors.
Willow Collectables
Victorian and Edwardian furniture; lamps, decorative items and pine.
Woodstock Antiques
Pictures, decorative items, 18th-19th C furniture; Victorian and Staffordshire figures.

Woburn Fine Arts
12 Market Pl. (Z Bieganski) Est: 1983. Open 2-5.30, Sat. and Sun. 11-1 and 2-5.30 or by appointment. CL: Thurs. SIZE: Medium. *STOCK: Post-impressionist paintings, 1880-1940; European paintings, 17th-18th C; British paintings, 20th C.* PARK: Easy. TEL: 0525 290624. SER: Valuations; restorations (oils and watercolours); framing.

Woburn continued

Yesterday's Pine
Old Chapel, Leighton St. (N.E Chesters) Est: 1975. Open 8-5. CL: Sat. *STOCK: Stripped pine furniture, kitchenalia, decorative ceramics.* TEL: 0525 290526. SER: Handmade furniture from old pine; renovation; stripping; interiors and architectural fitments (kitchens, bedrooms, libraries); containers; shipping and packing.

Captain Benjamin Shreve of Salem, Massachusetts, artist unknown. Miniature on ivory. Circa 1802. In 1819 Shreve undertook a voyage to Canton as captain and supercargo of the ship *Governor Endicott.* His subsequent voyage, shipwreck, dealings with his crew, and trading with the Cantonese hong merchants are followed in detail in Carl Crossman's ***The Decorative Arts of the China Trade,*** published in 1991 by the **Antique Collectors' Club.** £45.00.

Berkshire

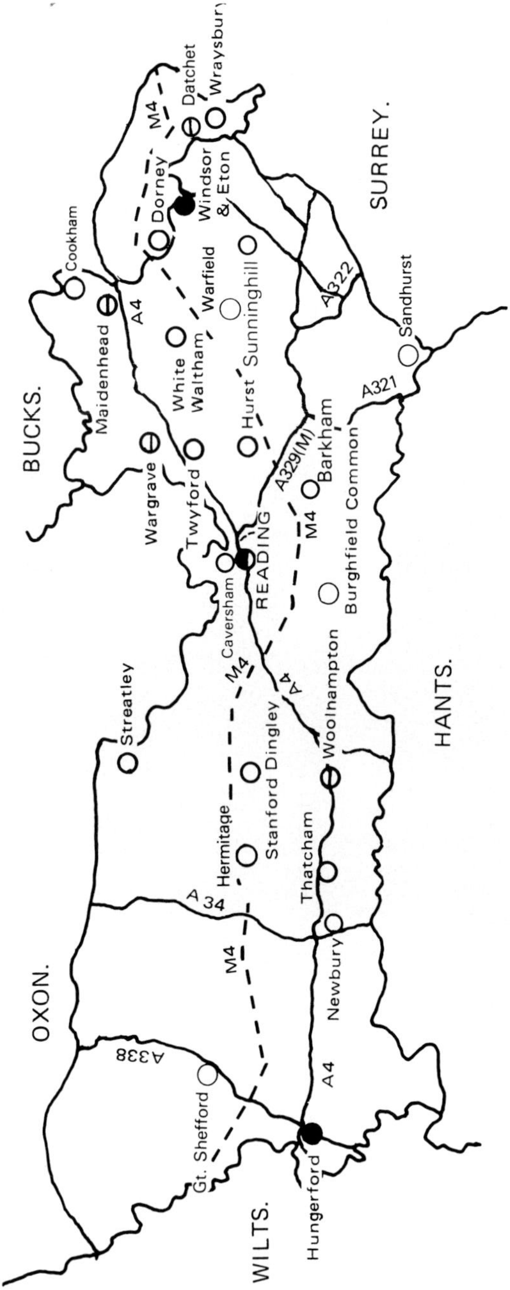
BUCKS.
OXON.
WILTS.
HANTS.
SURREY.
Cookham
Maidenhead
Dorney
Datchet
Wraysbury
Windsor & Eton
Warfield
White Waltham
Sunninghill
Hurst
Wargrave
Twyford
READING
Caversham
Barkham
Burghfield Common
Sandhurst
Streatley
Stanford Dingley
Hermitage
Woolnampton
Thatcham
Newbury
Gt. Shefford
Hungerford
M4
A4
A34
A338
A329(M)
A322
A321

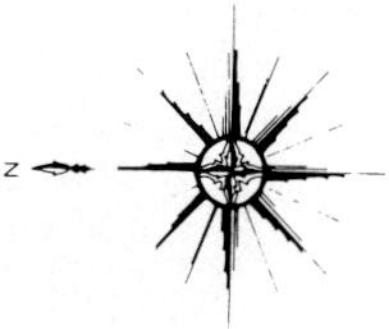
N

○	1–2	Key to number of shops in this area.
⊖	3–5	
◐	6–12	
●	13+	

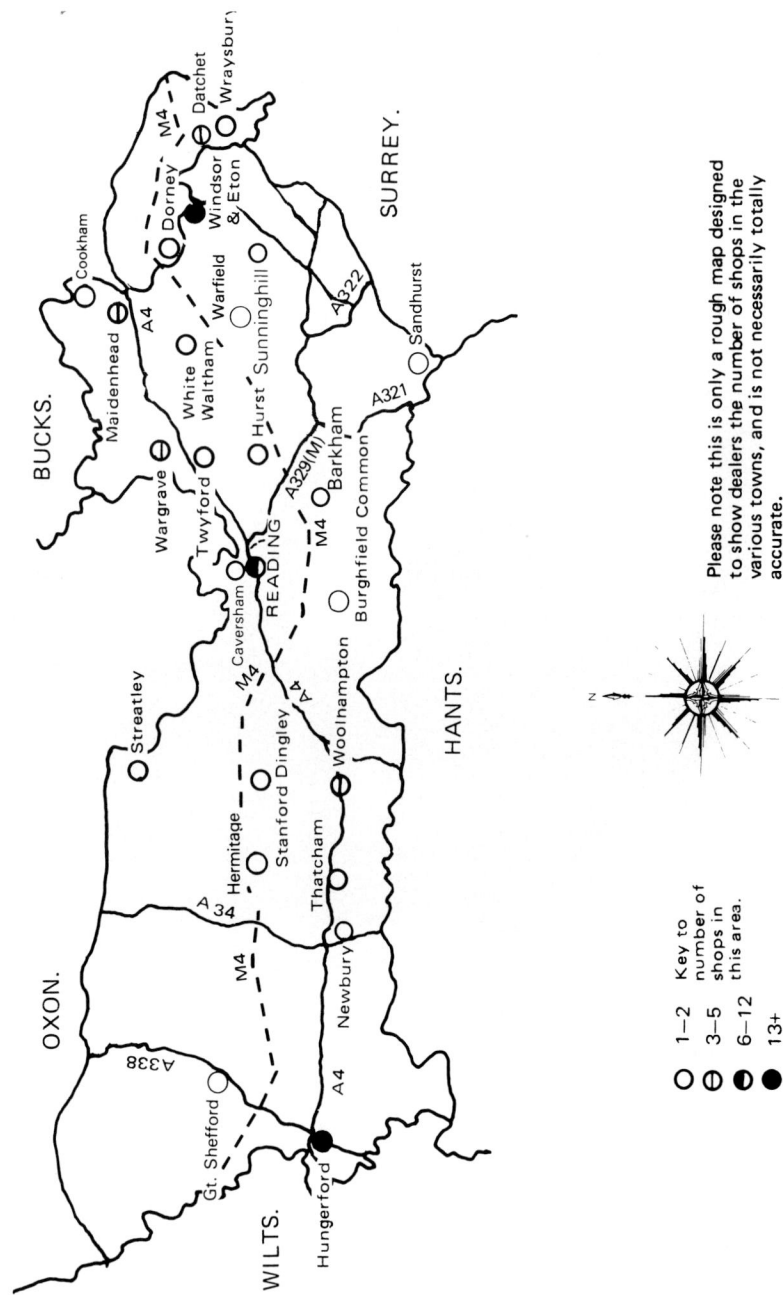

Please note this is only a rough map designed to show dealers the number of shops in the various towns, and is not necessarily totally accurate.

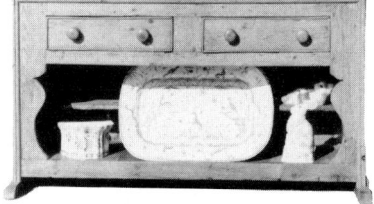

耕織圖

End of a bolt of uncut woven blue silk. Circa 1840. The bolt has been back-lit in photography to show the finely woven medallions, which are in fact very subtle, since the bolt is solid blue. The Chinese merchant's characters can be seen in the uncut fringe. From ***The Decorative Arts of the China Trade,*** by Carl Crossman, published in 1991 by the **Antique Collectors' Club.** £45.00.

BARKHAM, Nr. Wokingham

Barkham Antique and Craft Centre
Barkham St. (E and K Lowes and S and S Bunce) Open 10.30-5 including Sun. SIZE: Large. *STOCK: Tables, chairs, chests, 18th-20th C, £300-£2,500.* LOC: Off M4 junction 10, A329M to Wokingham, over station crossing to Barkham (B3349) left at Bull public house. PARK: Easy. TEL: 0734 761355; home - 0734 783705. SER: Valuations; restorations (china, French polishing, upholstery, cabinet making, caning).

John E Davis Antiques
Edneys Hill Farm, Edneys Hill. Est: 1965. Open every day. SIZE: Large. *STOCK: General antiques.* LOC: M4 junction 10, then A329M to Wokingham, over station crossing to Barkham, left at Barkham sign. PARK: Easy. TEL: 0734 783181; home - same. SER: Valuations; restorations (furniture, clocks and metalwork); buys at auction.

BURGHFIELD COMMON, Nr. Reading

Graham Gallery
(J Steeds) Est: 1976. Open by appointment at any time. SIZE: Medium. *STOCK: English watercolours, £50-£1,500; English oil paintings, £200-£8,000; English prints, £25-£200; all 19th and early 20th C.* LOC: 4 miles from Reading on Burghfield road. PARK: Easy. TEL: 0734 832320. SER: Valuations; restorations (cleaning, framing).

CAVERSHAM, Nr. Reading

The Collectors Gallery
8 Bridge St, Caversham Bridge. (T.B. and H.J Snook) Open 10-5, Sat. 10-4, and by appointment. SIZE: Large. *STOCK: Watercolours, £60-£4,000; oil paintings, £80-£4,000; collectables, prints and engravings; all 18th-19th C.* TEL: 0734 483663/8. SER: Restorations (paintings); monthly exhibitions.

COOKHAM

Phillips and Sons
The Dower House. Open by appointment. *STOCK: British impressionist paintings by the Staithes group, late 19th to early 20th C, £200-£10,000.* TEL: 062 85 29337. SER: Valuations; restorations (pictures); framing. VAT: Spec.

DATCHET

Marian and John Alway Fine Art, BADA LAPADA

Riverside Corner, Windsor Rd. Est: 1978. Open by appointment. *STOCK: Watercolours and oil paintings, 18th to early 20th C, £100-*

W. Anstey-Dollond. Watercolour

Marian and John Alway Fine Art continued

***£10,000.* LOC: Junction 5, M4. On corner of Windsor Rd. and Queens Rd. PARK: Easy. TEL: 0753 41163; home - same. SER: Valuations; restorations (as stock); buys at auction (as stock). VAT: Spec.**

Alasdair Brown Antiques LAPADA
The Manor House, The Green. Open 10-5.30. SIZE: Large. *STOCK: Furniture, 1700-1880, £50-£5,000; general furniture and decorative items.* Not Stocked: Jewellery. LOC: Period house overlooking village green. PARK: Easy. TEL: 0753 42164. SER: Valuations; restorations (upholstery). FAIRS: Olympia (June and Oct.). VAT: Stan/Spec.

DORNEY, Nr.Eton

The Old School Antiques LAPADA
(Lt. Col. V. and Mrs A. Wildish. Resident) Est: 1969. Open 10-5.30 or by appointment. SIZE: Large. *STOCK: Porcelain and English furniture, pre-1850; general antiques.* Not Stocked: Items dated post-1850. LOC: B3026, from M4, junction 7. PARK: Own. TEL: 0628 603247. SER: Valuations; buys at auction. VAT: Spec.

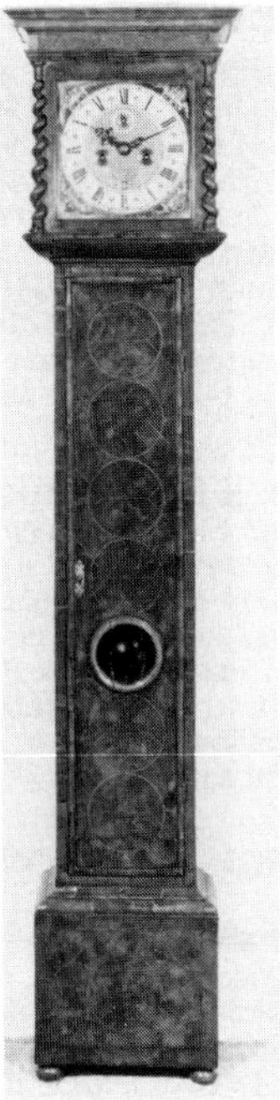

GREAT SHEFFORD, Nr. Hungerford

Ivy House Antiques
Wantage Rd. (J Hodgson) Est: 1972. Open 10-6. *STOCK: Country and pine furniture, kitchenalia, collectors' items, Victoriana.* LOC: A338, 10 minutes from Hungerford towards Wantage. TEL: 048 839 549.

HARE HATCH, Nr. Reading

Ladd's Gallery
Ladd's Garden Centre, Bath Rd. (M. and P Tagg) Est: 1987. Open 10-5 including Sun. SIZE: Medium. LOC: A4. PARK: Easy. TEL: 0734 404334. SER: Restorations (furniture and china); buys at auction (furniture and china). VAT: Stan/Spec. Below are listed the dealers at this centre.

John Collins
19th-20th C furniture.
Katie Collins
19th C china; 19th-20th C furniture and jewellery.
Peter Evans
18th-19th C Oriental items, paintings and furniture.
Patricia Jolliffe
General antiques to 1930.

Ladd's Gallery continued

Knowl Hill Galleries
Georgian and Victorian furniture, china, pottery, glass, prints and paintings, collectables, jewellery and silver.
Susan Ling
General antiques, to 1930.
Pine Time
Pine furniture, British and continental.

HERMITAGE, Nr. Newbury

Richard Barder Antiques
Crossways House. (R.C.R. and P.A Barder) Open 9.30-5.30, but prior telephone call advisable. CL: Mon. SIZE: Large. *STOCK: Clocks - English longcase, bracket, lantern, wall, regulator, carriage, 17th-19th C, £1,000-£50,000.* LOC: Exit 13, M4, on B4009. PARK: Easy. TEL: 0635 200295. SER: Valuations; buys at auction (clocks). VAT: Stan/Spec.

HUNGERFORD

Ashley Antiques
129 High St. Est: 1974. Open 10-5, appointment advisable. SIZE: Medium. *STOCK: Furniture and general antiques.* LOC: Main street. PARK: Easy. TEL: 0488 682771. SER: Restorations (furniture).

Hungerford continued

Mary Bellis Antiques **BADA**
Charnham Close. (E Willson and D Gill) Open 10-5, appointment advisable. ***STOCK: Early English and continental oak furniture and works of art.*** **PARK: Easy. TEL: 0488 682620. VAT: Spec.**

Below Stairs
103 High St. (S Hofgartner) Est: 1974. Open 10-6, including Sun. SIZE: Large. *STOCK: Kitchen and decorative garden items, bedroom furniture, lighting, collectables and interior fittings, mainly 19th C, £20-£2,500.* LOC: Main street. PARK: Easy. TEL: 0488 682317. SER: Valuations. VAT: Stan.

John Bensley - Fine Antique Clocks **LAPADA**
Wilton House, 33 High St. Open by appointment. SIZE: Small. *STOCK: English longcase, bracket and tavern clocks, 1680-1850, £2,500-£75,000; English regulators, 1800-1850, £5,000-£25,000.* LOC: 250yds. south of railway bridge on A338. PARK: Easy. TEL: 0488 682861. SER: Valuations; restorations. VAT: Spec.

Bow House Antiques
3-4 Faulkner Sq, Charnham St. (L.R Herrington) Open 10-5. CL: Thurs. SIZE: Medium. *STOCK: Small period and Victorian furniture.* LOC: A4. PARK: Easy, own. TEL: 0488 683198; home - 0488 684319. VAT: Spec.

Dolls and Toys of Yesteryear at Bow House Antiques
3-4 Faulkner Sq, Charnham St. (D.M Herrington) Open 10-5. CL: Thurs. SIZE: Medium. *STOCK: Dolls, £50-£1,600; toys, £5-£250; dolls' houses, £250-£15,000; dolls' house accessories, £1-£300; rocking horses, all 19th to early 20th C.* PARK: Easy. TEL: 0488 683198; home - 0488 684319. SER: Valuations (dolls); restoration (dolls). FAIRS: Cumberland (London) Doll; Kensington Town Hall.

The Fire Place (Hungerford) Ltd
Hungerford Old Fire Station, Charnham St. (E.B. and E.M Smith) Est: 1976. Open 10-1.30 and 2.15-5. SIZE: Large. *STOCK: Fireplace furnishings and metalware especially fenders.* LOC: On A4. PARK: Opposite. TEL: 0488 683420. VAT: Stan/Spec.

Bibi Harris Antiques
The Old Vicarage, Parsonage Lane. (Mrs B Harris) Est: 1963. Open by appointment only. SIZE: Large. *STOCK: Continental and decorative furniture, some smalls.* TEL: 0488 683382/684616; fax - 0488 684662. VAT: Stan/Spec.

Hungerford continued

Robert and Georgina Hastie **LAPADA**
35a High St. Est: 1987. Open 9.30-5, Sun. by appointment. SIZE: Medium. *STOCK: Decorative items, 1750-1920, £50-£6,000; furniture and clocks, 18th-19th C, £200-£6,000; textiles, 19th C, £50-£1,000.* Not Stocked: Silver, porcelain and dolls. LOC: A338. PARK: Easy. TEL: 0488 682873. VAT: Stan/Spec.

Hungerford Arcade
High St, (Wynsave Investments Ltd.). Est: 1972. Open 9.30-5.30, Sun. 10-6. SIZE: Over 70 stallholders. *STOCK: General antiques and period furniture.* PARK: Easy. TEL: 0488 683701.

Roger King Antiques
111 High St. (Mr and Mrs R.F King) Est: 1974. Open 9.30-5. SIZE: Large. *STOCK: Furniture, 1750-1880, £50-£1,500; china, 19th C; oil paintings.* Not Stocked: Silver, jewellery. LOC: Opposite Hungerford Arcade. PARK: Easy. TEL: 0488 682256. VAT: Spec.

Hungerford continued

Medalcrest Ltd
Charnham House, 29/30 Charnham St. (D.H Farrow) Est: 1981. Open 9.30-5.30, Sat. 10-6, Sun. by appointment. SIZE: Large. *STOCK: 18th-19th C furniture; barometers, longcase, bracket and carriage clocks, metalware, small items.* TEL: 0488 684157. VAT: Spec.

The Old Malthouse **BADA**
(P.F Hunwick) Est: 1963. Open 10-5.30. SIZE: Large. *STOCK: Furniture, 18th and early 19th C walnut and mahogany. English porcelain; clocks, barometers.* Not Stocked: Orientalia. LOC: A338, left at Bear Hotel, shop is approx. 120yds. on left, just before a bridge. PARK: In front of shop. TEL: 0488 682209. SER: Valuations; buys at auction. FAIRS: City of London, Chelsea, Brighton. VAT: Spec.

Paravicini
7 Bridge St. Open 9.30-5.30, Sat. 10-5. SIZE: Medium. *STOCK: Decorative furniture, £300-£15,000; fine art, £100-£25,000; all 17th-19th C; lamps and rugs, £50-£3,000.* LOC: Opposite John O'Gaunt public house. PARK: Easy. TEL: 0488 685173; fax - 0488 685167.

Hungerford continued

Riverside Antiques
Charnham St. (M Stockland) Est: 1976. Open 10-5.30. SIZE: Large. *STOCK: General antiques; furniture, decorative items.* LOC: On A4 just before The Bear Hotel. PARK: Easy. TEL: 0488 682314. VAT: Stan/Spec.

Styles Silver **LAPADA**
12 Bridge St. (P. and D Styles) Est: 1974. Open 10-5.30. CL: Mon. and school holidays. SIZE: Medium. *STOCK: Antique, Victorian and secondhand silver including cutlery.* PARK: Easy. TEL: 0488 683922; home - same. SER: Valuations; repairs; finder. VAT: Stan/Spec.

Victoria's Bedroom
4 Bridge St. (J.A. and M.A Wallbank-Fox) Open 10-6. CL: Mon. *STOCK: Brass and iron beds.* TEL: 0488 682523.

HURST, Nr. Reading

Peter Shepherd Antiques
Penfold, Lodge Rd. Est: 1962. Open by appointment only. *STOCK: Glass, rarities and books.* TEL: 0734 340755. VAT: Stan/Spec.

MAIDENHEAD

Jaspers Fine Arts Ltd
36 Queen St. (T.L Johnson) Open 9-6. *STOCK: Victorian watercolours and paintings; maps and prints.* TEL: 0628 36459. SER: Restorations; framing.

Miscellanea
71 St. Marks Rd. (J Davidson) Open 10-5.30. SIZE: Large. *STOCK: Furniture, books, bric-a-brac, collectors' items.* LOC: 1/2 mile off A4. PARK: Easy. TEL: 0628 23058.

Widmerpool House Antiques
Boulters Lock. Open by appointment only. *STOCK: English furniture, 18th-19th C; oil paintings, watercolours, prints; porcelain, glass, silver, 19th C.* TEL: 0628 23752.

NEWBURY

John Baker Antiques
20 George St, Kingsclere. Est: 1959. Open 9-7, Sat. 10-6. SIZE: Medium. *STOCK: Mahogany, 18th C, £400-£4,000; oak, 17th-18th C, £200-£3,200; desks, Victorian, £480-£1,600.* Not Stocked: Shipping goods. LOC: A339. PARK: Easy (at side). TEL: 0635 298744. SER: Valuations; restorations (furniture); buys at auction. VAT: Stan/Spec.

Newbury continued

Griffons Court
Highclere. (Mr and Mrs T.C Jackson) Est: 1966. Prior telephone call advisable. SIZE: Medium. *STOCK: Fine Georgian furniture, desks, small bookcases, unusual small decorative items, fine paintings.* LOC: 5 miles from Newbury. On A343 at crossroads just inside village boundary. PARK: Easy. TEL: 0635 253247. VAT: Stan/Spec.

READING

Ann Bye Antiques
88 London St. (F.M. and A Easton) Est: 1968. Open 9-5.30. CL: Wed. p.m. *STOCK: Cottage and pine furniture, country and decorative items.* TEL: 0734 582029.

P.D Leatherland Antiques
68 London St. Open 9-5. *STOCK: Furniture and accessories, 18th C to 1920, including shipping.* TEL: 0734 581960.

Reading Emporium
1a Merchants Pl, (off Friar St). Est: 1972. Open 9-5. SIZE: 13 stalls. *STOCK: A wide range of items including Victoriana, advertising items, jewellery and bottles.* TEL: 0734 590290.

Reading continued

Victoria Books
14/16 Eldon Terr. (D.W. and E.J Hutchings) Est: 1961. Open 10-5, Sat. 10-5.30. CL: Wed. *STOCK: Antiquarian books.* TEL: 0734 500303.

SANDHURST, Nr. Camberley

Antiques - Sheila White
Sandhurst Farm Barn, 207 Yorktown Rd, College Town. *STOCK: General antiques.* LOC: Barn at rear of premises. TEL: 0252 873290.

Berkshire Metal Finishers Ltd
Swan Lane Trading Estate. (J.A. and Mrs. J Sturgeon) Est: 1957. Open 8-1 and 2-6, Sat. 8-1 and 2-4, Sun. 9-1. SIZE: Large. *STOCK: Brass, copper and steel metalware; silver plate.* LOC: Off A30 towards Wokingham on A321, 1 1/4 miles turn left into Swan Lane, estate 1st turning right, last factory near car park. PARK: Easy. TEL: 0252 873475; fax - 0252 875434. SER: Restorations (metalware polishing and lacquering).

SONNING-ON-THAMES

Csaky's Antiques
Open by appointment only. *STOCK: Early English and continental oak furniture; carvings, works of art, unusual items.* TEL: 0734 697608.

STANFORD DINGLEY, Nr. Reading

Eliot Antiques
(Lady Cathleen Hudson) Est: 1974. Open 10.30-1, Sun. and afternoons by appointment. CL: Mon. SIZE: Small. *STOCK: English enamels, 18th C, objets de vertu, 18th-19th C, £150-£3,000.* Not Stocked: Furniture, pictures. PARK: Easy. TEL: 0734 744649; home 0734 744346. VAT: Spec.

STREATLEY, Nr. Reading

Vine Cottage Antiques
High St. (B.R. and P.A Wooster) Open 10-5.30. CL: Sun. except by appointment. *STOCK: Furniture and general antiques, 18th-19th C.* TEL: 0491 872425. SER: Restorations; re-upholstery (especially buttoned items). VAT: Spec.

SUNNINGHILL, Nr. Ascot

Antiques of Ascot
3c High St. (K Price) Open 10-4.45. CL: Wed. *STOCK: General antiques.* PARK: Easy. TEL: 0344 872282.

Austin/Desmond Fine Art
3 High St. (J Austin and and W Desmond) Est: 1978. Open 10-5.30. SIZE: Medium. *STOCK: British paintings, 20th C.* PARK: Easy. TEL: 0344 291201. SER: Valuations; buys at auction (modern British paintings). FAIRS: World of Watercolours. VAT: Spec.

THATCHAM

Jackdaw Antiques
Bluecoat School. (C Taylor and C Heron) Open 10-4.30. CL: Mon. and Tues. *STOCK: General antiques.* PARK: Easy. TEL: 0635 65901.

TWYFORD

Cavendish Fine Arts - Janet Middlemiss LAPADA
29 Station Rd. Open 10.30-5.30. *STOCK: Walnut, satinwood, mahogany and oak furniture, £1,000-£15,000; glass and mirrors; all 17th C to c.1820.* LOC: Town centre, in road leading to station. Just off A4 between Reading and Maidenhead, exit 10, M4. TEL: 0734 320795; home - 0734 691904. VAT: Stan/Spec.

WARFIELD

Moss End Antique Centre
Moss End Garden Centre. Open 10.30-5. CL: Mon. SIZE: Large - 25 dealers. *STOCK: General antiques.* LOC: A3095. PARK: Own. TEL: 0344 861942.

WARGRAVE

Millgreen Antiques
86 High St. (K Chate and J Connell and 12 other dealers) Open Wed.-Sun. other times by appointment. SIZE: Large. *STOCK: Furniture, Georgian-Edwardian; small items, china, glass, metal.* PARK: Nearby. TEL: 0734 402955. SER: Restorations (furniture); silver plating; metal polishing.

Wargrave Antiques
66 High St. (K Chate) Open Wed.-Sun. *STOCK: Furniture, Georgian to Edwardian; pine and smalls.* TEL: 0734 402914.

WHITE WALTHAM, Nr. Maidenhead

Braemar Antiques Ltd
Old RAF Mess, Waltham Rd. (J.C White) Open 9-4. CL: Sat. *STOCK: Furniture, 18th-19th C.* TEL: 062 882 3741. VAT: Stan/Spec.

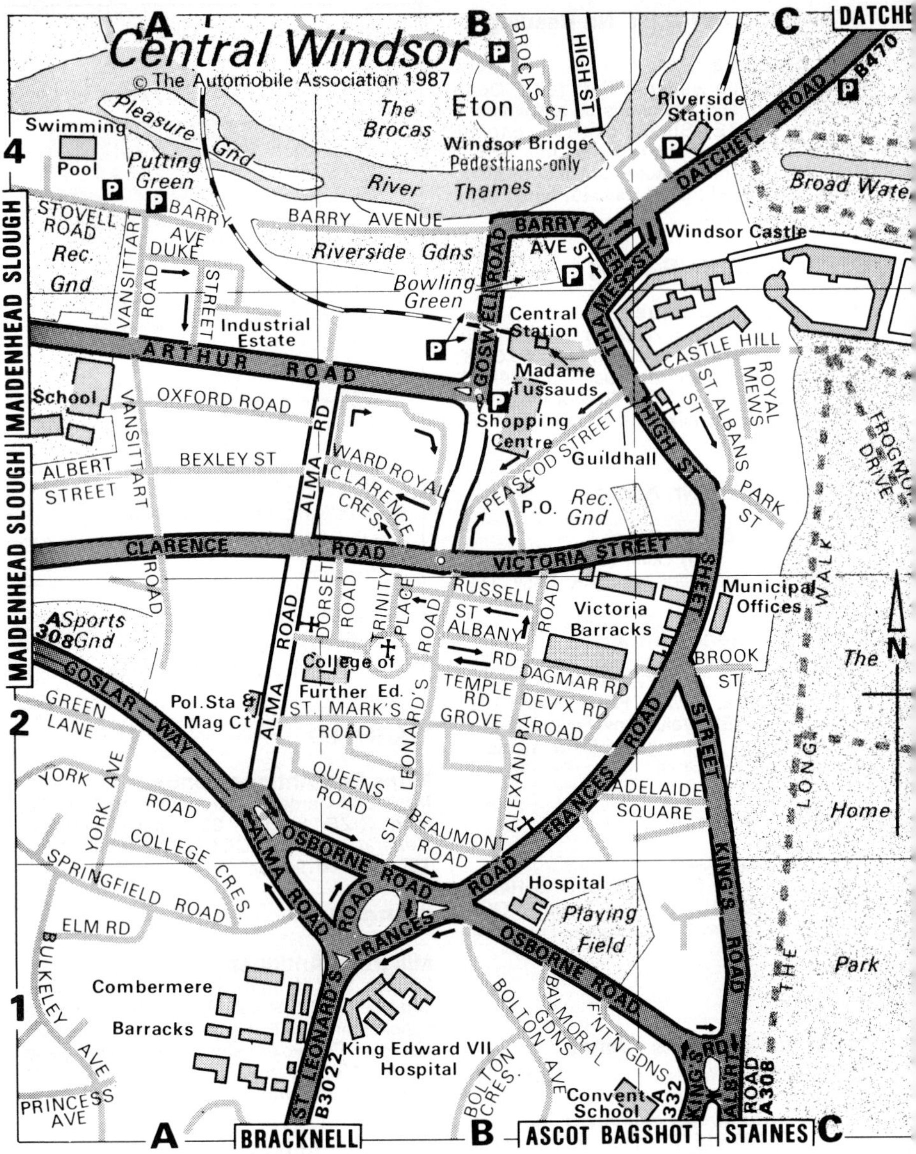
Central Windsor
© The Automobile Association 1987
A
B
C
DATCHET
1
2
4
Eton
The Brocas
Pleasure Gnd
Swimming Pool
Putting Green
River Thames
Windsor Bridge Pedestrians-only
Riverside Station
DATCHET ROAD B470
Broad Water
BROCAS ST
HIGH ST
BARRY AVE
BARRY AVENUE
Riverside Gdns
Bowling Green
Windsor Castle
RIVER ST
THAMES ST
STOVELL ROAD
Rec. Gnd
DUKE STREET
VANSITTART ROAD
Industrial Estate
ARTHUR ROAD
GOSWELL ROAD
Central Station
Madame Tussauds
Shopping Centre
CASTLE HILL
ROYAL MEWS
ST ALBANS ST
PARK ST
FROGMORE DRIVE
School
OXFORD ROAD
BEXLEY ST
ALBERT STREET
WARD ROYAL
CLARENCE CRES
ALMA RD
PEASCOD STREET
Guildhall
HIGH ST
P.O.
Rec. Gnd
MAIDENHEAD SLOUGH
CLARENCE ROAD
VICTORIA STREET
SHEET STREET
LONG WALK
Municipal Offices
RUSSELL ST
DORSET ROAD
TRINITY PLACE
ST LEONARD'S ROAD
ST ALBANY
Victoria Barracks
BROOK ST
A308
Sports Gnd
College of Further Ed.
RD
DAGMAR RD
TEMPLE RD
GROVE
DEV'X RD
ALEXANDRA ROAD
GOSLAR WAY
GREEN LANE
Pol.Sta & Mag Ct
ALMA ROAD
ST. MARK'S ROAD
FRANCES ROAD
ADELAIDE SQUARE
YORK AVE
YORK ROAD
QUEENS ROAD
BEAUMONT ROAD
COLLEGE CRES.
SPRINGFIELD ROAD
OSBORNE ROAD
Hospital
Playing Field
KING'S ROAD
Home Park
The
ELM RD
BULKELEY AVE
Combermere Barracks
ST LEONARD'S B3022
King Edward VII Hospital
BOLTON AVE
BOLTON CRES.
BALMORAL GDNS
F'NT'N GDNS
Convent School
A332
KING'S RD
ALBERT ROAD A308
PRINCESS AVE
BRACKNELL
ASCOT BAGSHOT
STAINES
N

Key to Town Plan

AA Recommended roads
Other roads
Restricted roads
Buildings of interest
Car Parks P
Parks and open spaces
AA Service Centre AA

WINDSOR AND ETON

Addrison Bros
25 King's Rd, Windsor. (Mr and Mrs Addrison) Est: 1980. Open 11-6, Sun. 1-4. SIZE: Small. *STOCK: Furniture including pine, Victorian and Edwardian; Victorian brass and iron beds, £1-£800.* LOC: Close to castle. PARK: Easy. TEL: 0753 863780; home - same.

Antiquus
17 High St, Eton. (Mrs C Thomas) Open 10-5. *STOCK: Furniture, objets d'art, porcelain and textiles.* TEL: 0753 831039; home - 840848.

Roger Barnett
91 High St, Eton. Est: 1975. TEL: 0753 867785.

Guy Bousfield BADA
58 Thames St, Windsor. Est: 1958. Open 8.45-5. CL: Some Wed. SIZE: Medium. *STOCK: Georgian furniture, 1720-1830, £500-£5,000.* LOC: Precinct on castle side of Windsor Bridge. PARK: Easy. TEL: 0753 864575. VAT: Spec.

The Compton Gallery
42 Thames St, Windsor. (B.D. Sutton and K.N Bruendel) Open 10.30-5.30. SIZE: Large. *STOCK: General antiques especially china, glassware, Doulton, Gallé pottery and glass,*

The Compton Gallery continued

jewellery, cards, furniture, silver, toys and dolls, £5-£15,000. TEL: 0753 830100; mobile 0836 206361. SER: Valuations.

Dee's Antiques
89a Grove Rd., Windsor. (D Johnson) Open 10.30-6 or by appointment. SIZE: Small. *STOCK: General antiques.* TEL: 0753 865627; home - 0753 850926.

Eatons of Eton Ltd LAPADA
50 High St, Eton. (P. and P Eaton) Est: 1960. Open 8-5. SIZE: Large. *STOCK: Furniture, 1680-1900, to £4,000; silver, 1730-1900, to £1,500; paintings, £50-£2,000.* PARK: 50yds. almost opposite. TEL: 0753 860337; home - 0628 27413. SER: Valuations. VAT: Spec.

Eton Antique Bookshop
88 High St, Eton. TEL: 0753 855534.

Eton Cottage Antiques
60 High St, Eton. (A Johnson) Open 9.30-5.30, Sun. 2-5. *STOCK: Porcelain, silver, furniture, general antiques.* TEL: 0753 856329.

Eton Gallery Antiques LAPADA
116 High St, Eton. (J Smith) Open 10.30-1 and 2-5, Sun. p.m. by appointment. CL: Mon. and Wed. p.m. *STOCK: Furniture, 18th-19th C; oil paintings; longcase clocks and barometers.* TEL: 0753 865147/860963. VAT: Spec.

Windsor and Eton continued

Grove Gallery
89 Grove Rd, Windsor. *STOCK: Oils, watercolours, prints.* TEL: 0753 865954 or 853658.

Jaspers Fine Arts
67 Victoria St, Windsor. (T.L Johnson) Open 10-5. CL: Wed. *STOCK: Antiquarian maps and prints.* TEL: 0753 854925.

J Manley
27 High St, Eton. Est: 1891. Open 9-5. *STOCK: Watercolours, old prints.* TEL: 0753 865647. SER: Restorations; framing, mounting.

Peter J Martin
40 High St, Eton. Est: 1963. Open 9-1 and 2-5. CL: Sun. SIZE: Large and warehouse. *STOCK: Period, Victorian and decorative furniture and furnishings, £50-£5,000; metalware, £10-£500, all from 1800.* LOC: A332. Middle of Eton High St. PARK: 50yds. opposite. TEL: 0753 864901; home - 0753 863987. SER: Restorations; shipping arranged; buys at auction. VAT: Stan/Spec.

Mostly Boxes
92 High St, Eton. (G.S Munday) Est: 1977. Open 9.30-6. SIZE: Small. *STOCK: Mainly wooden boxes, small furniture.* LOC: Centre of High St. PARK: 100yds. TEL: 0753 858470. SER: Restorations (boxes). VAT: Stan.

O'Connor Brothers
Trinity Yard, 59 St. Leonards Rd, Windsor. *STOCK: Furniture and general antiques.* TEL: 0753 866732. VAT: Stan.

Windsor and Eton continued

Tony L Oliver
Longclose House, Common Rd, Eton Wick. Est: 1959. Open 9-5 by appointment only. *STOCK: Militaria, medals, badges, insignia especially German 1914-1945; civilian and military vehicles, 1914-1955.* TEL: 0753 862637.

John A Pearson Ltd BADA
127-128 High St, Eton. (Mrs J.C Sinclair Hill) Est: 1902. Open 9.30-1 and 2-5.30, but appointment advisable. SIZE: Large. *STOCK: English furniture, 1700-1850, £50-£30,000; oil paintings, 17th-19th C, £50-£50,000; decorative objects.* Not Stocked: Items after mid-19th C. LOC: From London turn off M4, exit 5, past London Airport - approach only via Datchet/Slough (Windsor River Bridge closed). PARK: Easy (2 hours). TEL: 0753 860850/682136. VAT: Spec.

Anthony Seales at Eton Gallery Antiques
116 High St, Eton. Open 10.30-5, Sun. by appointment. CL: Mon. and Wed. p.m. *STOCK: Longcase and bracket clocks, stick and wheel barometers.* TEL: 0753 865147. SER: Valuations; buys at auction. VAT: Stan.

Ulla Stafford BADA
41 High St, Eton. Open daily. SIZE: Large. *STOCK: Georgian and continental furniture, Chinese export porcelain, 18th C; works of art and ceramics, 17th-18th C.* PARK: Easy. TEL: 0753 859625; home - 0734 343208. VAT: Spec.

Windsor and Eton continued

Studio 101
101 High St, Eton. (A Cove) Est: 1959. Open 10.30-5.30, some Sun. p.m.. SIZE: Medium. *STOCK: Mahogany furniture, some 18th C, mainly 19th C, £50-£1,000; brass, silver plate, 19th C, £10-£200.* LOC: Walk over Windsor Bridge from Windsor and Eton Riverside railway station. PARK: Public, at rear of premises. TEL: 0753 863333.

Times Past Antiques Ltd LAPADA
59 High St, Eton. (P Jackson) MBHI. Est: 1970. Open 10-6, Sun. 12-5. SIZE: Medium. *STOCK: Clocks and watches, £100-£3,000; furniture, all 18th-19th C; silver, 19th C, £5-£500.* PARK: Reasonable. TEL: 0753 857018; home - same. SER: Valuations; restorations (clocks and watches); buys at auction (clocks). VAT: Stan/Spec.

Turks Head Antiques
98 High St, Eton. Open 10.30-5. CL: Mon. *STOCK: Silver and plate, jewellery, glass and boxes.* TEL: 0753 863939.

Windsor Antiques LAPADA
80 High St, Eton. (A. and H Procter) CMBHI. Est: 1967. Open 10-5.30, Sun. 11-5.30. SIZE: Large. *STOCK: Longcase and wall clocks, furniture, 18th-19th C.* LOC: Slough East exit from M4 westbound. PARK: Nearby. TEL: 0753 860752; home - same. SER: Exporting; interior design consultants. VAT: Stan/Spec.

WOKINGHAM

Paul Thomas Fine Paintings LAPADA
27 Glebelands Rd. Est: 1986. Open anytime by appointment. *STOCK: Oil paintings and watercolours, 1800-1950, £200-£10,000.* LOC: 1 1/2 miles from A329M on the Henley road. PARK: Easy. TEL: 0734 794671 or 0831 474024. SER: Valuations; restorations; buys at auction (pictures). VAT: Spec.

WOOLHAMPTON, Nr. Reading

The Bath Chair
Woodbine Cottage, Bath Rd. (J.A Lewzey) Est: 1980. Open 10-6. CL: Thurs. SIZE: Small. *STOCK: Furniture and general antiques, £5-£5,000.* LOC: A4. PARK: Easy. TEL: 0734 712225. SER: Valuations; buys at auction.

The Old Bakery
Bath Rd. (D.R Carter) Resident. Est: 1969. *STOCK: Furniture, objets d'art, collectors' items, general antiques.* TEL: 0734 712116.

Woolhampton continued

Old Post House Antiques
Bath Rd. (V.A Liddiard) Est: 1975. Open 10-6. SIZE: Small. *STOCK: Furniture, 18th-19th C, £50-£300; bric-a-brac and brassware, all periods, £2-£100.* LOC: On A4. PARK: Easy. TEL: 0734 712294; home - 0734 713460.

WRAYSBURY

Wyrardisbury Antiques
23 High St. (C Tuffs) Est: 1978. Open Tues., Wed., Fri. and Sat. 10-5; other times by appointment. SIZE: Small. *STOCK: Clocks, £25-£2,000; small furniture, tea caddies, boxes and watercolours, £10-£500; porcelain, £30-£500.* LOC: A376 from Staines by-pass (A30) or from junction 5 M4/A4 via B470, then B376. PARK: Easy. TEL: 0784 483225. SER: Restorations (clocks).

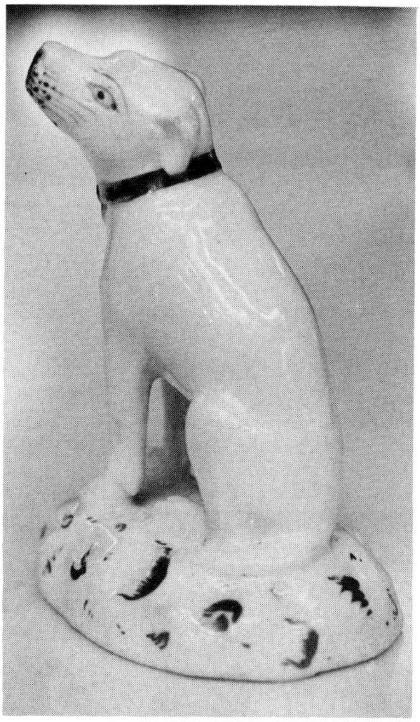

Rockingham white and gilt pointer, looking upwards, seated on an oval base, 3in. (7.6cm) high. Incised 'No 101'. Impressed mark. 1826-30. Cf. the Derby equivalent, figure 121b.

MR AND MRS DUNNINGTON

Buckinghamshire

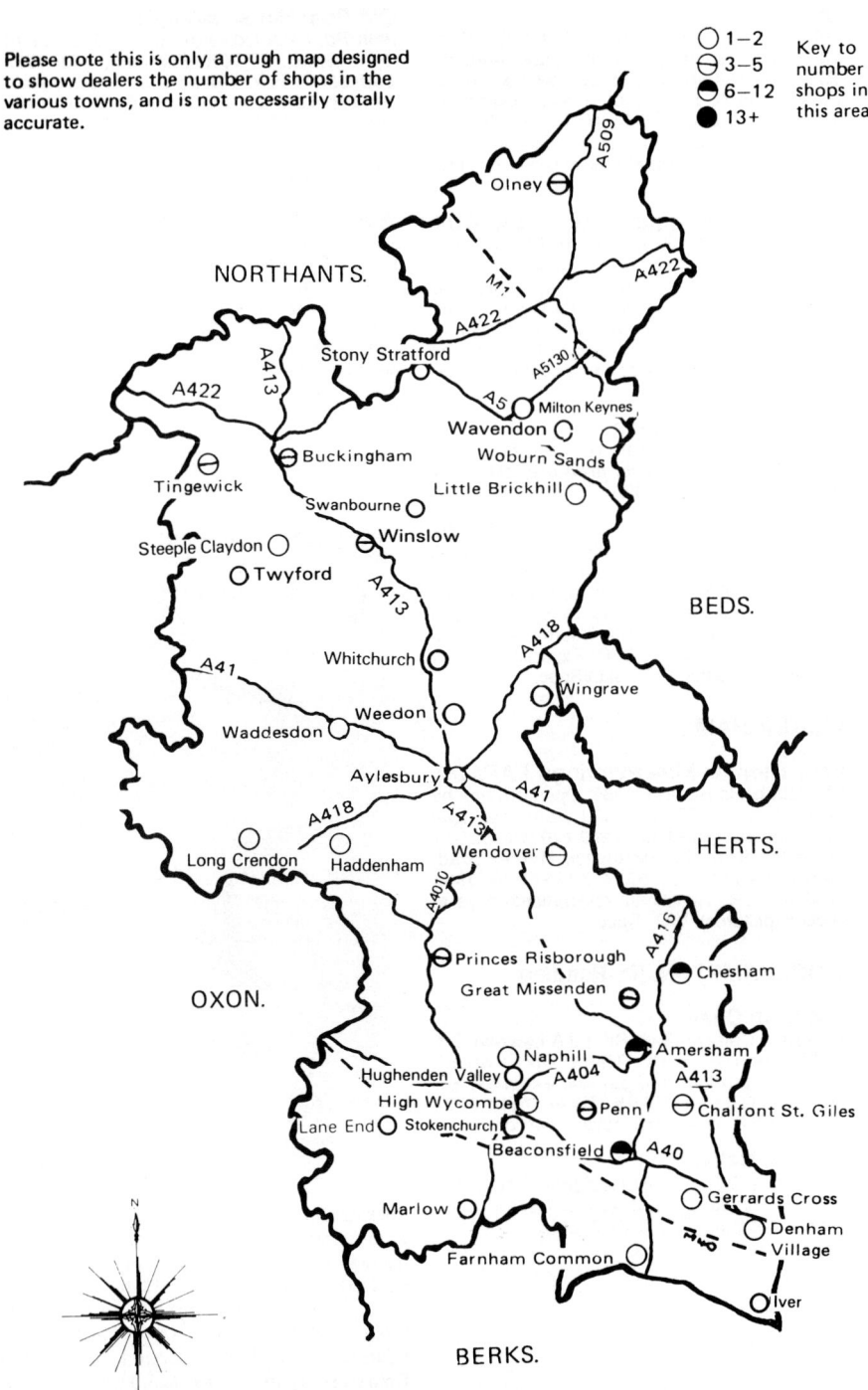

Please note this is only a rough map designed to show dealers the number of shops in the various towns, and is not necessarily totally accurate.

○ 1–2
⊖ 3–5
◓ 6–12
● 13+

Key to number of shops in this area.

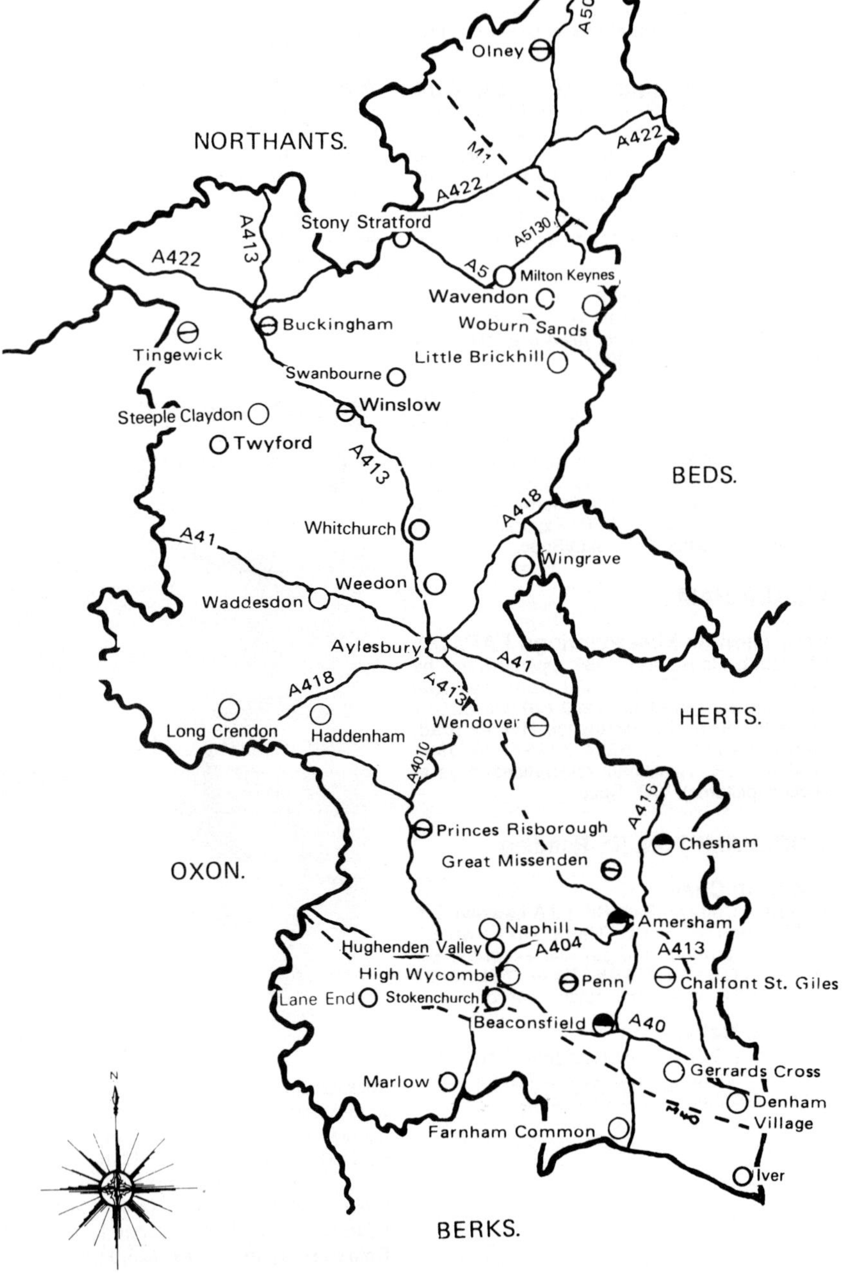

Olney
A509
NORTHANTS.
M1
A422
A422
Stony Stratford
A413
A422
A5130
A5
Milton Keynes
Wavendon
Woburn Sands
Buckingham
Tingewick
Little Brickhill
Swanbourne
Winslow
Steeple Claydon
Twyford
A413
BEDS.
A418
Whitchurch
Wingrave
A41
Weedon
Waddesdon
Aylesbury
A41
A418
A413
Long Crendon
Haddenham
Wendover
HERTS.
A4010
A416
Princes Risborough
Chesham
Great Missenden
OXON.
Amersham
Naphill
A413
Hughenden Valley
A404
High Wycombe
Penn
Chalfont St. Giles
Lane End
Stokenchurch
Beaconsfield
A40
Gerrards Cross
Marlow
Denham Village
M40
Farnham Common
Iver
N
BERKS.

AMERSHAM

Amersham Antiques and Collectors Centre

20-22 Whielden St, Old Amersham. Open 10-6. SIZE: 25-30 dealers. *STOCK: Antiques and collectables.* TEL: 0494 431282.

The Cupboard Antiques LAPADA

80 High St, Old Amersham. (N Lucas) Open 10-5. CL: Fri. *STOCK: Georgian, Regency and early Victorian furniture and decorative items.* PARK: Easy. TEL: 0494 722882.

Fantiques

18-20 Hill Ave. (J Stent and K., M. and P Raven) Est: 1981. Open 9.30-3.30, Sat. all day. SIZE: Medium. *STOCK: Porcelain and glass, 19th C to art deco; fans, prints and maps, 18th-19th C, all £5-£1,000; small furniture, £50-£1,000; English watercolours, £50-£3,000; Victoriana, from £5; mirrors, art deco, £25-£50.* LOC: In road opposite station. PARK: Easy. TEL: 0494 725571. SER: Restorations (fans); framing. FAIRS: Some London hotel.

"Mon Galerie"

The Old Forge, The Broadway, Old Amersham. (A.R. and D.E Guy) Est: 1975. *STOCK: Watercolours, engravings, 19th-20th c, £20-£500; maps.* PARK: Easy. TEL: 0494 721705; workshop 0296 661884. SER: Valuations; restorations, mounting, framing.

Partridges

67 High St, Old Amersham. (Mrs D Krolle) Est: 1976. Open 10.30-5.30. CL: Mon. *STOCK: Antique and decorative items.* PARK: Easy. TEL: 0494 728452.

Michael Quilter

38 High St. Est: 1970. Open 10-5. *STOCK: General antiques, stripped pine, copper, brass.* PARK: Easy. TEL: 0494 433723. VAT: Stan.

Ryecroft Antiques

10 The Broadway. (M Waywell) Open 10-6. CL: Mon. and Tues. SIZE: 15 dealers. *STOCK: China, porcelain, silver and plate, Victorian furniture.* TEL: 0494 433123.

Sundial Antiques LAPADA

19 Whielden St. (A. and Mrs M Macdonald) Est: 1970. Open 9.30-5.30. CL: Thurs. SIZE: Small. *STOCK: English and European brass, copper, metalware, fireplace furniture, 18th-19th C, £5-£500; small period furniture, 1670-1870, £25-£1,500; oil lamps, 1840-1914, £25-£500; decorative items, 1750-1910, £5-£500; weapons, 1600-1860, £25-£1,000; pottery, porcelain; curios, pre-1914, £10-£750.* Not Stocked: Jewellery, clocks, coins, oil paintings, stamps, books, silver. LOC: On A404, in Old Town 200yds. from High St. on right; from High Wycombe, 700yds. from hospital on left. PARK: Easy. TEL: 0494 727955. VAT: Stan/Spec.

AYLESBURY

Morton Harvey Antiques

21 Wendover Rd. (J.M Harvey) Resident. Open 10-5.30. CL: Thurs. *STOCK: 18th C and early Victorian furniture, watercolours; general antiques.* PARK: Rear of premises. TEL: 0296 84307.

Spencer

Verna House, 9 Bicester Rd. (M Spencer) Open by appointment only. *STOCK: Silver.* TEL: 0296 437866.

BEACONSFIELD

Christopher Cole (Fine Paintings) Ltd BADA

1 London End. Est: 1975. Open 9.30-5.30. CL: Mon. *STOCK: Oil paintings and watercolours, 19th and early 20th C.* TEL: 0494 671274.

June Elsworth Beaconsfield Ltd

Clover House, 16 London End. (Mrs J Elsworth) Est: 1983. CL: Mon. SIZE: Small. *STOCK: Fine English furniture, 18th-19th C, £1,000-£2,000; decorative accessories, 19th C, £50-£250; silver, 19th C, £100-£500.* LOC: In old town, on A40. PARK: Easy. TEL: 0494 675611. VAT: Spec.

Grosvenor House Interiors

51 Wycombe End, Beaconsfield Old Town. (T.I Marriott) Est: 1970. Open 9-1 and 2-5.30. SIZE: Large. *STOCK: 18th-19th C furniture, especially upholstered and mid-19th C walnut; fireplaces and accessories.* PARK: Easy. TEL: 0494 677498. SER: Interior architectural design, fireplace specialists. VAT: Stan/Spec.

Norton Antiques

56 London End. (T. and N Hepburn) Est: 1966. Open 10-1 and 2-5.30. CL: Wed. SIZE: Medium. *STOCK: Furniture 1680-1850, £25-£2,500; paintings (oil and watercolour), 19th C, £15-£2,500; clocks, 18th-19th C, £25-£2,000; woodworking and craftsman's hand tools.* LOC: On left shortly after entering Beaconsfield Old Town from the east. PARK: Easy. TEL: 0494 673674. SER: Valuations; buys at auction; pine stripping. FAIRS: Reading, High Wycombe, Oxford. VAT: Stan/Spec.

Old Curiosity Shop

47-49 Wycombe End. (D Barker) Open 9.45-1 and 2.30-5.30. CL: Mon. *STOCK: General antiques, small furniture and interesting items.* TEL: 0494 674473.

Beaconsfield continued

Period Furniture Showrooms
49 London End. (E.W.A. and R.E.W Hearne) Est: 1965. Open 9-5.30. CL: Wed. p.m. SIZE: Large. *STOCK: Furniture, 1700-1900, £50-£3,000.* LOC: A40 Beaconsfield Old Town. PARK: Own. TEL: 0494 674112. SER: Restorations (furniture). VAT: Stan/Spec.

The Spinning Wheel
86 London End. (Mrs M Royle) Est: 1945. Open 10-5. CL: Wed. *STOCK: English furniture, 18th-19th C, mahogany and oak items, porcelain, glass.* TEL: 0494 673055; home - 02407 3294. VAT: Stan/Spec.

BUCKINGHAM

Buckingham Books
20 Market Hill. Appointment advisable. *STOCK: Architectural books.* TEL: 0280 812800.

Flappers
2 High St. (M Goodwin) Open 9.30-1 and 2-5. *STOCK: Stripped pine, oak and mahogany furniture; lace, linen; 1920s and 1930s costume.* TEL: 0280 813115; evenings - 0604 740234.

Yesterdays Pine
4/5 Bridge St. (N.E Chesters) Est: 1975. Open 10-6, Sun. 2-6. *STOCK: Waxed pine furniture, decorative ceramics, pictures and general antiques.* TEL: 0280 822374. SER: Furniture made to specification; fitted interiors, bedrooms and kitchens.

CHALFONT ST. GILES

Bucks House
High St. (Mrs B Buck) Est: 1981. Open 10-5. SIZE: Small. *STOCK: Furniture, paintings and decorative art, 19th-20th C, £10-£300.* LOC: On A413. PARK: Nearby. TEL: 024 07 5711.

Images In Watercolour **LAPADA**
8 The Lagger. (E. and D Parkinson) Est: 1968. Open by appointment. *STOCK: Watercolours, drawings and some oils, 1800-1930.* LOC: Take road to Seer Green from village centre, on left hand side shortly after passing Milton's Cottage. PARK: Easy. TEL: 024 07 5592. VAT: Spec.

T.F.S. Ltd
Smithfield Works, London Rd. (T Smith) Est: 1982. Open 10-5. SIZE: Medium. *STOCK: Furniture, from 1700, £100-£3,000; brass and copper, £20-£500.* LOC: Opposite Pheasant public house. PARK: Easy. TEL: 024 07 3031. SER: Valuations; restorations (including upholstery); buys at auction (furniture). VAT: Stan.

CHESHAM

Albert Bartram
177 Hivings Hill. Est: 1968. Usually open, preferably by appointment. *STOCK: Metalwork, 16th-17th C; pewter, small oak furniture, pottery, £30-£3,000.* LOC: 1 mile from town centre on the road to Bellingdon. PARK: Easy. TEL: 0494 783271. VAT: Spec.

Chess Antiques **LAPADA**
85 Broad St. (M.P Wilder) Est: 1966. Open 9-5, Sat. 10-5. SIZE: Small. *STOCK: Furniture and clocks.* PARK: Easy. TEL: 0494 783043. SER: Valuations; restorations. VAT: Stan/Spec.

For Pine
340 Berkhampstead Rd. (J Morgan and D Hutchin) Open 10-5. CL: Thurs. *STOCK: Restored pine furniture.* TEL: 0494 776119.

Omniphil Ltd
Germains Lodge, Fullers Hill. (A.R.T Muddiman) Est: 1953. Open 9-5.30 or by appointment. CL: Sat. SIZE: Warehouse. *STOCK: Rare prints on all subjects and Illustrated London News from 1842.* TEL: 0494 771851.

Pednor Antiques
109 Church St. (C Simmonds) Est: 1984. CL: Mon. SIZE: Small. *STOCK: Furniture, country and 19th C, £100-£3,000; general decorative items, £5-£100.* LOC: In old town. PARK: Easy. TEL: 0494 778878.

Queen Anne House
57 Church St. (Miss A.E Jackson) Est: 1918. Open Wed., Fri. and Sat. 9.30-5. SIZE: Large. *STOCK: Furniture, decorative and furnishing pieces, porcelain figures, other china, glass, silver plate, copper, brass, Victoriana, clocks, Persian rugs.* Not Stocked: Silver, weapons, jewellery. PARK: Easy. TEL: 0494 783811. SER: Buys at auction. VAT: Stan/Spec.

M.V Tooley, CMBHI
at Chess Antiques, 85 Broad St. Est: 1960. Open 9-6, Sat. 10-5. SIZE: Small. *STOCK: Clocks and barometers.* TEL: 0494 783043. SER: Valuations; restorations; spare parts.

DENHAM VILLAGE

Margaret Elmes Antiques
Denham Gallery. (Mrs M Elmes) Est: 1965. Open 10-12.30 and 2.30-5.30 or by appointment. SIZE: Large. *STOCK: English furniture, pottery and porcelain, glass and metal, late 18th and early 19th C.* LOC: Off A40, 2 miles from Uxbridge. PARK: Easy. TEL: 0895 832244. SER: Restorations (furniture); upholstery. FAIRS: Little Chelsea.

John Wonnacott, b.1940. 'The Grandfather', 1965-9. 93in. x 48in. THOMAS AGNEW & SONS LTD., LONDON.
From ***20th Century Painters and Sculptors*** by Frances Spalding published by the **Antique Collectors' Club** in 1990. £45.00.

FARNHAM COMMON

A Thing of Beauty
5 The Broadway. (K. and B Craven) Est: 1973. Open 9.30-1 and 2.30-5, Wed. and Sat. 9.30-1. SIZE: Medium. *STOCK: English furniture, 1800-1910, £75-£1,000; general antiques, some silver, from 1800, £20-150; European glassware.* Not Stocked: Maps, books, paintings. LOC: Opposite The Foresters public house in High St. PARK: Easy. TEL: 0753 642099 (24hrs.). SER: Valuations; buys at auction (furniture).

Noel Gregory Gallery
4 The Broadway. Open 9-1 and 2-6. *STOCK: Victorian watercolours.* TEL: 028 14 5522.

GERRARDS CROSS

Aristocat LAPADA
19 Packhorse Rd. Est: 1970. CL: Mon. and Wed. *STOCK: Silver and plate, jewellery, metalware.* TEL: 0753 888011. SER: Valuations; metal polishing. VAT: Stan/Spec.

GREAT MISSENDEN

Peter Farrow
Orchard House, Blackthorne Lane, Ballinger Common. Est: 1976. Open by appointment. *STOCK: Victorian furniture, £5-£1,000.* PARK: Easy. TEL: 024 020 403. SER: Valuations; restorations (furniture); polishing; buys at auction (furniture). VAT: Stan.

Gemini Antiques
68a High St. (M Crossley) Open 9-1, Sat. 9-5. *STOCK: General antiques.* PARK: Opposite. TEL: 024 06 6203.

Heritage Antiques and Restorations
36b High St. (J Wilshire) Est: 1974. Open 9-5.30. SIZE: Small. *STOCK: Clocks and small furniture, 18th-19th C, £50-£2,500; curios, £5-£100.* LOC: A413. PARK: Easy. TEL: 024 06 5710. SER: Valuations; restorations; buys at auction. VAT: Stan/Spec.

W.E Hill and Sons BADA
P.O. Box 453. Est: 1742. Open by appointment only. *STOCK: Stringed instruments.* TEL: 0494 678781; fax - 024 06 3655. VAT: Stan/Spec.

The Pine Merchants
52 High St. (D.J Peters) Open 9.30-5.30. CL: Thurs. *STOCK: Stripped pine.* TEL: 024 06 2002.

HADDENHAM

H.S Wellby Ltd
The Malt House, Church End. (C.S Wellby) Est: 1820. Open by appointment 9-6. CL: Sat. *STOCK: 18th and 19th C paintings.* TEL: 0844 290036. SER: Restorations. VAT: Spec.

HAZLEMERE, Nr. High Wycombe

Martin's Gallery
The Beeches, St. John's Rd. (M Jones) Open by appointment. *STOCK: Watercolours, Victorian to contemporary.* TEL: 0494 20768.

HIGH WYCOMBE

Browns' of West Wycombe
Church Lane, West Wycombe. Est: Pre 1900. Open 8-5.30. CL: Sat. *STOCK: Furniture.* LOC: On A40 approximately 3 miles west of High Wycombe on Oxford Rd. PARK: Easy. TEL: 0494 24537. SER: Restorations and hand made copies of period chairs.

Burrell Antiques
Kitchener Works, Kitchener Rd. (G. and P Burrell) Open 8-5.30 (prior telephone call advisable) and Sat. by appointment. SIZE: Medium. *STOCK: Furniture, 1800-1920, £10-£1,000.* LOC: West side of town, near Desborough Rd. shopping area. PARK: Easy. TEL: 0494 23619. SER: Restorations (furniture). VAT: Stan/Spec.

HUGHENDEN VALLEY, Nr. High Wycombe

Pine Reflections
Holly Cottage, Boss Lane. (M Duda) Est: 1978. By appointment only. *STOCK: Period and continental pine.* TEL: 024 024 3598. SER: Export. *Trade Only.*

IVER

"Yester-year"
12 High St. (P.J Frost) Resident. Est: 1969. Open 10.30-6. SIZE: Small. *STOCK: Furniture, porcelain, pottery, glass, metalwork, 18th to early 20th C.* PARK: Easy. TEL: 0753 652072. SER: Valuations; restorations (furniture, pictures); framing; buys at auction.

LANE END, Nr. High Wycombe

Bach Antiques
Essex House, Finings Rd. (C. and Mrs. B Whitby) Est: 1982. Open 11-5. CL: Mon. SIZE; Small. *STOCK: Furniture including pine, general antiques, pre 1920.* LOC: B482 between Marlow and Stokenchurch, Finings Rd. is extension of

Majolica cat and mouse teapot or kettle in the form of an iron, c.1860. From ***The Dictionary of Minton*** by Paul Atterbury and Maureen Batkin, published by the **Antique Collectors' Club** in 1990. £35.00.

Bach Antiques continued

High St. PARK: Easy. TEL: 0494 882683. SER: Valuations; restorations (furniture). FAIRS: Lane End monthly.

LITTLE BRICKHILL

Baroq Antiques

(B Dawson) Est: 1967. Open by appointment only. *STOCK: Pottery and porcelain, £10-£500; paintings and watercolours, 18th-20th C, £100-£1,000; furniture, £100-£1,500.* TEL: 052 526 561; home - 0234 240448; mobile 0860 716818. SER: Buys at auction. VAT: Stan/Spec.

LONG CRENDON

Hollington Antiques

87 Bicester Rd. (J. and V Asta) Est: 1966. Open all week. SIZE: Medium. *STOCK: Books, china, glass, curios, militaria, prints and drawings.* LOC: B4011. Next to "The Chandos Arms". PARK: Easy. TEL: 0844 208294.

MARLOW

Collectors Treasures Ltd

4 Liston Court. (R.J. and D.M Eisler and S.D. and R.J Paessler) Open 9.30-5.30. *STOCK: Maps and prints, 16th-20th C, £3-£2,000; antique wallpaper roller lamps.* TEL: 062 84 73424. SER: Valuations; framing and mounting (maps). VAT: Stan.

Angela Hone Watercolours LAPADA

Open by appointment only. *STOCK: Watercolours, 1850-1920.* TEL: 0628 484170.

MILTON KEYNES

Temple Lighting (Jeanne Temple Antiques)

Stockwell House, Wavendon. Est: 1968. SIZE: Medium. *STOCK: Victorian, Edwardian and 1930's light fittings; 19th C furniture; decorative items.* LOC: Just off main Woburn Sands to Newport Pagnell road. TEL: 0908 583597.

NAPHILL, Nr. High Wycombe

A. and E Foster **BADA**
"Little Heysham", Forge Rd. Est: 1972. Open by appointment only. SIZE: Small. *STOCK: English and continental treen, bygones, metalwork, pre-1830.* Not Stocked: Silver, glass, porcelain. LOC: From High Wycombe take the A4128. Take first left after Hughenden Manor; about 2 miles. PARK: Easy. TEL: 024 024 2024. FAIRS: Chelsea, Fine Arts Fair, Olympia, Grosvenor House, City of London. VAT: Spec.

OLNEY

Market Square Antiques
(J.D. and H Vella) Open 10-5.30, Sun. 2-5.30. *STOCK: Furniture, china, silver, glass, copper, brass, pine.* TEL: 0234 712172. SER: Restorations.

Alan Martin Antiques
Farthing Cottage, Clickers Yard. (A.D Martin) MBHI. Est: 1978. Open 9-5, Sun. by appointment. SIZE: Small. *STOCK: Clocks, £100-£1,500; watches, £50-£500; lacemaking supplies, 18th-19th C.* PARK: Town Square. TEL: 0234 712446. SER: Restorations (clocks).

Olney continued

Olney Antique Centre
Rose Court. (J.D. and H Vella) Open 10-5.30, Sun. 12-5.30. *STOCK: China, furniture, clocks, jewellery, linen, pine, postcards.* TEL: 0234 712172.

John Overland Antiques
Rose Court, Market Pl. Est: 1977. Open 10-5, including Sun. SIZE: Medium. *STOCK: 18th-19th C mahogany and oak furniture, clocks, writing boxes, smalls, brass, copper.* PARK: Market Sq. TEL: 0234 712351. VAT: Stan/Spec.

Robin Unsworth Antiques
1 Weston Rd. (R and Z M Unsworth) Est: 1971. Open 10-5, Sun. 1-5. SIZE: Small. *STOCK: Longcase and wall clocks, £500-£4,000; period and Victorian furniture, £200-£4,000; objects of art, £50-£1,000.* LOC: 6 miles from junction 14, M1. PARK: Easy. TEL: 0234 711210; home - 0908 617193. SER: Valuations; buys at auction (clocks).

PENN, Nr. High Wycombe

Country Furniture Shop **LAPADA**
3 Hazlemere Rd, Potters Cross. (M. and V Thomas) Est: 1955. Open 9.30-1 and 2-5.30. SIZE: Large. *STOCK: Furniture, Georgian, £100-£5,000; Victoriana, £5-£2,500; paintings; large Victorian dining tables.* Not Stocked:

Country Furniture Shop continued

Weapons. LOC: B474. PARK: Easy. TEL: 049 481 2244; home - same. SER: Valuations. VAT: Stan/Spec.

Penn Barn
By the Pond, Elm Rd. (P.J.M Hunnings) ABA. Est: 1968. Open 9.30-1 and 2-5, Sat. 9.30-1; Sat. p.m. and Sun. by appointment. SIZE: Medium. *STOCK: Antiquarian books, maps and prints, 19th C, £5-£250; watercolours and oils, 19th to early 20th C, £50-£500.* LOC: B474. PARK: Easy. TEL: 049 481 5691. SER: Restorations; cleaning and repairs. VAT: Stan/Spec.

Francis Wigram **BADA**
Cottars Barn, Elm Rd. CL: Wed. p.m. *STOCK: General antiques, furniture, English and continental porcelain, works of art, decorative items.* TEL: 049 481 3266.

PRINCES RISBOROUGH

Bell Street Antiques Centre
20/22 Bell St. (J Booth and J Blaik) Est: 1985. Open 9.30-5.30, Sun. 12-5. SIZE: Medium. *STOCK: Furniture, 18th-20th C, from £40; glass, china, collectables, copper, brass, mainly 19th C, from £5.* LOC: A4010. PARK: Easy. TEL: 084 44 3034. VAT: Spec.

White House Antiques
33 High St. (M Amor) Est: 1961. Open by appointment. *STOCK: Marble, chandeliers and furniture, £1,000+.* LOC: Town centre. TEL: 084 44 6976; home - same. SER: Valuations.

STEEPLE CLAYDON

Terence H Porter, Fine Antique European Arms and Armour
"The Beeches". Est: 1963. Open by appointment. *STOCK: Pistols, guns and rifles.* TEL: 029 673 8255. SER: Buys at auction; exchange; bi-monthly lists (send large S.A.E.).

STOKENCHURCH

Amend Antiques
Jardinerie Garden Centre, Oxford Rd, Studley Green. (B Amend) SIZE: Open daily 12-5. *STOCK: General antiques.* PARK: Easy. TEL: 024026 2842.

STONY STRATFORD

Yesterday's Pine
2 High St. (N.E Chesters) Est: 1975. Open 10-6, Sun. 2-6. *STOCK: Waxed pine furniture, decorative ceramics, pictures and general antiques.* TEL: 0908 261337. SER: Furniture made to specification; fitted interiors, bedrooms and kitchens.

SWANBOURNE

Swanbourne Antiques and Cottage Tearooms
26 and 28 Winslow Rd. (F. and Mrs. B Knight) Est: 1987. Open 10-5, Sat. and Sun. 10-6. CL: Thurs. and Fri. SIZE: Medium. *STOCK: Porcelain, glass, brass, collectables, linen, £1-£50; prints, watercolours, £15-£200; furniture, £25-£500; all 19th-20th C.* LOC: Off A413 onto B4032, shop first building in village. PARK: Easy. TEL: 029 672 516; home - same.

TINGEWICK, Nr. Buckingham

Lennard Antiques **LAPADA**
The Laurels, Main St. Est: 1978. Open by appointment. SIZE: Small. *STOCK: Oak and fruitwood country furniture and English delftware, 18th to early 19th C.* LOC: On A421 - next door to post office. TEL: 0280 848371. FAIRS: West London; NEC; Kenilworth; Olympia; Snape.

Tim Marshall Antiques
Main St. Resident. Open 9.30-6, Sun. 12-6. SIZE: Medium. *STOCK: Oak and pine country furniture, 18th and 19th C, £100-£1,000; copper, brass, ceramics and bygones.* TEL: 0280 848546.

Tingewick Antiques Centre
Main St. (B.J. and R Smith) Est: 1973. Open 10.30-5.30 including Sun. SIZE: Large. *STOCK: Furniture including desks, mainly pine and oak, 19th to early 20th C, £5-£1,000; clocks, 18th-19th C, £20-£2,000; collectables, kitchenalia, art deco, pottery, pictures, £1-£1,500.* LOC: On A421. PARK: Easy, layby opposite. TEL: 0280 847922; home - same. SER: Valuations; restorations (copper, brass, spelter); upholstery; French polishing.

Town and Country Antiques Ltd
Heritage House, Main St. Est: 1978. Open 10-5, Sun. 11-6. CL: Mon. SIZE: Medium plus warehouse. *STOCK: Furniture, £25-£3,000; some smalls, £5-£1,000; all Victorian to 1920's.* LOC: A421 towards Bicester, on left just out of village. PARK: Easy. TEL: 0280 848602. SER: Restorations; finder. VAT: Stan/Spec.

TWYFORD, NR. BUCKINGHAM

Adrian Hornsey Ltd
Three Bridge Mill. Open by appointment. SIZE: Large. *STOCK: General antiques, decorative accessories and architectural furniture.* TEL: 0296 738373; fax - 0296 738322. SER: Courier.

WADDESDON

Collectors' Corner
106 High St. (Mrs K Good and Mrs V Grant) Est: 1967. Open 9-5.30. SIZE: Medium. *STOCK: Silver, 18th-20th C, £5-£200; porcelain, jewellery, mainly 19th C, £5-£100; general antiques.* Not Stocked: Coins, militaria. LOC: A41 opp. entrance to Waddesdon Manor. PARK: Easy. TEL: 0296 651563. VAT: Stan.

WAVENDON

Van Riemsdijk Fine Art
Seven Gables, Stockwell Lane. (B Van Riemsdijk) Est: 1974. Open by appointment. SIZE: Medium. *STOCK: Modern British post impressionist, £1,000-£40,000; contemporary, £400-£10,000.* LOC: 2 mins. from junctions 13 and 14, M1. Follow signs for Woburn Sands. PARK: Easy. TEL: 0908 582621; home - same. SER: Valuations; buys at auction (paintings).

Van Riemsdijk Fine Art continued

FAIRS: 20th C British Art, Cumberland Hotel; Barbican, City of London International Art. VAT: Spec.

WEEDON, NR. AYLESBURY

Peter Eaton Booksellers Ltd
Lilies. Open 10-5. *STOCK: Antiquarian and secondhand books.* TEL: 0296 641393. SER: Brochure available.

WENDOVER

Antiques at Wendover
The Old Post Office, 25 High St. (N Gregory) Open 10-5.30, Sun. 11-5.30. SIZE: Large. 30 dealers. *STOCK: General antiques including town and country furniture, 19th C blue and white transfer ware, silver, lamps and lighting, beds and bathroom fittings, tiles, decorative and architectural items, glass, metalware, lace, linen, all pre-1930.* PARK: Own. TEL: 0296 625335; evenings - 0296 624633.

Bowood Antiques
Bowood Lane. (Miss P Peyton-Jones) Est: 1960. Open by appointment. SIZE: Large. *STOCK: Furniture, porcelain, 17th-19th C, £10-£10,000; textiles, prints.* LOC: On A413, signposted at Hunts Green turn-off, between Gt. Missenden and Wendover. PARK: Easy. TEL: 0296 622113; home - same. VAT: Spec.

Sally Turner Antiques LAPADA
Hogarth House, High St. Open 10-5.30. SIZE: Large. *STOCK: Decorative and period furniture, general antiques.* TEL: 0296 624402.

Wendover Antiques
1 South St. (R. and D Davies) Est: 1979. Open 9-5.30, prior telephone call advisable. SIZE: Medium. *STOCK: Furniture, 17th-19th C, £200-£5,000; decorative prints, oils; 18th C silk embroideries, silhouettes, miniatures, Georgian decanters, some silver and Sheffield plate.* LOC: Near village centre on Wendover-Amersham road. PARK: 100yds. TEL: 0296 622078. VAT: Stan/Spec.

WHITCHURCH

Deerstalker Antiques
28 High St. (R.J. and L.L Eichler) Open 10-5.30. CL: Mon. SIZE: Medium. *STOCK: General antiques.* TEL: 0296 641505.

Pair of Staffordshire Dalmatians, each with a support standing on a mound base, their curled-over tails raised in the air, 3½in. (8.9cm) high, c.1830-40.
GROSVENOR ANTIQUES LTD. AND MARY WISE ANTIQUES)
From ***English Porcelain Animals of the 19th Century*** by D.G. Rice published by the **Antique Collectors' Club** in 1989. £25.00.

WINGRAVE, Nr. Aylesbury

Peter Arnold Gallery
Knolls Close. Est: 1978. *STOCK: British watercolours, paintings and etchings, 1750-1950.* TEL: 0296 681568. SER: Exhibition catalogues free.

WINSLOW

Courtyard Clocks
45 Sheep St. (G.A Peacock) Est: 1987. Open by appointment. SIZE: Small. *STOCK: Clocks - mainly longcase, dial and Vienna, some mantel, from 18th C, £75-£4,000.* LOC: 1/2 mile from market square, on A413. TEL: 029 071 4621; home - same. SER: Valuations. VAT: Mainly spec. *Trade Only.*

Medina Antiquarian Maps and Prints
8 High St. (P Williams) Open 9.30-5.30. CL: Thurs. p.m. *STOCK: Maps, prints and watercolours.* TEL: 029 071 2468.

WOBURN SANDS, Nr. Milton Keynes

Haydon House Antiques LAPADA
Haydon House, Station Rd. (G. and M Tyrrell and D Missenden) Est: 1965. Open 10-6, Sat. and Sun. 10-1, other times by appointment. SIZE: Large. *STOCK: Furniture and decorators' items, 18th-19th C, and Edwardian, £25-£2,000; copper, brass, metalware, bygones, prints, £5-£250.* Not Stocked: Coins, silver, jewellery. LOC: 2 miles from exit 13, M1 and 2 miles from Woburn Abbey. PARK: Own. TEL: 0908 582447. VAT: Stan.

Neville's Antiques
1 The Bakery, Russell St. (N.K.T Medcalf) Open 10-5. CL: Mon. and Wed. SIZE: Large. *STOCK: 18th-19th C furniture, oils, metalwork, £20-£3,000.* PARK: Easy. TEL: 0908 584827/ 583024.

Cambridgeshire

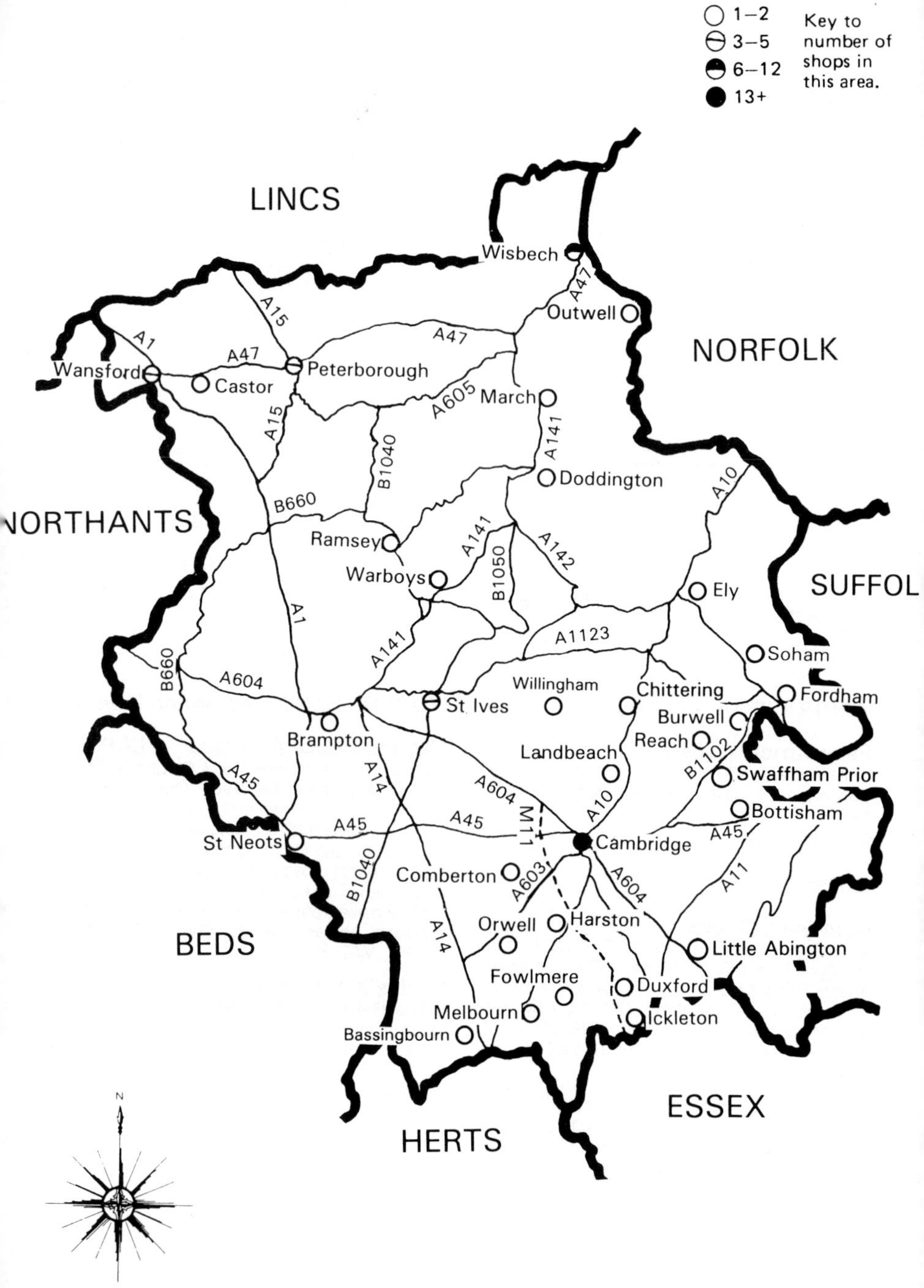
1–2
3–5
6–12
13+
Key to number of shops in this area.
LINCS
NORFOLK
NORTHANTS
SUFFOL
BEDS
HERTS
ESSEX
Wisbech
Outwell
Wansford
Castor
Peterborough
March
Doddington
Ramsey
Warboys
Ely
Soham
Fordham
Willingham
Chittering
Burwell
St Ives
Brampton
Reach
Landbeach
Swaffham Prior
Bottisham
St Neots
Cambridge
Comberton
Orwell
Harston
Little Abington
Fowlmere
Duxford
Melbourn
Ickleton
Bassingbourn
A1
A15
A47
A605
A141
B1040
B660
A142
B1050
A10
A1123
A604
A14
A45
M11
A603
B1102
A11
N

Please note this is only a rough map designed to show dealers the number of shops in the various towns, and is not necessarily totally accurate.

BASSINGBOURN, Nr. Royston (Herts.)

David Bickersteth
4 South End. Est: 1967. Open by appointment. *STOCK: Antiquarian books.* TEL: 0763 245619.

BOTTISHAM, Nr. Cambridge

Cambridge Pine
Hall Farm, Lode Rd. (Mr and Mrs D Weir) Est: 1980. Open seven days. SIZE: Large. *STOCK: Pine, 18th-19th C; pine and oak reproduction; all £25-£1,400.* LOC: Midway between Bottisham and Lode, near Anglesey Abbey. PARK: Easy. TEL: 0223 811208; home - same. SER: Fitted farmhouse kitchens.

BRAMPTON

Brampton Mill Antiques
87 High St. (D.E Clark) Est: 1955. Open by appointment only. SIZE: Large. *STOCK: General antiques.* LOC: 1 mile from A1. TEL: 0480 411204/455593; mobile - 0860 340358. VAT: Stan/Spec.

BURWELL

Peter Norman Antiques and Restorations
Sefton House, 57 North St. (P Norman and A Marpole) Est: 1975. Open 9-12.30 and 2-5.30. SIZE: Medium. *STOCK: Furniture, clocks, arms and Oriental rugs, 17th-19th C, £250-£10,000.* PARK: Easy. TEL: 0638 742197. SER: Valuations; restorations (furniture, oil paintings, clocks, arms). VAT: Stan/Spec.

CAMBRIDGE

20th Century
169 Histon Rd. (S Charles) Open 12-6, Sat. 10-5. CL: Mon. *STOCK: Decorative arts, 1880-1980.* TEL: 0223 359482.

Antiques Etc.
18 King St. (W Heffer) Est: 1970. SIZE: Small. *STOCK: General furniture, silver, china, clocks, watches.* LOC: On the edge of the central shopping district towards Newmarket road. PARK: Multi-storey. TEL: 0223 62825; home - 0223 63634. SER: Valuations; restorations (wood, metalware, silver, china, mother-of-pearl). VAT: Stan/Spec.

Jess Applin Antiques BADA
8 Lensfield Rd. Est: 1968. Open 10-5.30. *STOCK: Furniture, 17th-19th C; works of art.* LOC: Junction Hills Rd. and Lensfield Rd., opposite church. PARK: Meters and nearby. TEL: 0223 315168; evenings - 0223 246851. VAT: Spec.

Cambridge continued

John Beazor and Sons Ltd BADA
78-80 Regent St. Est: 1875. Open 9-5. *STOCK: English furniture, late 17th to early 19th C; clocks, barometers and decorative items.* TEL: 0223 355178. SER: Valuations. VAT: Spec.

Benet Gallery
19 Kings Parade, and 26 Long Rd. (G.H. and J Criddle) Est: 1965. Open 10-5; by appointment (Long Rd.). SIZE: Large. *STOCK: Early maps of Cambridgeshire, engravings of the colleges.* TEL: 0223 353783/248739. VAT: Stan.

The Bookroom (Cambridge)
13A St. Eligius St. (E.A Searle) ABA. Est: 1973. Open 9.30-5, Sat. by appointment. SIZE: Small. *STOCK: Science, medicine, natural history, military, naval and marine, English literature, mainly 19th C; some private press, Folio Society publications including out-of-print.* LOC: Trumpington Rd. end of Bateman St. PARK: Panton St. TEL: 0223 69694; home - 0223 354566. SER: Valuations; buys at auction (books). VAT: Stan.

Buckies LAPADA
31 Trinity St. (G. McC. and P.R Buckie) NAG, GMC. Est: 1972. Open 9.45-5. CL: Mon. SIZE: Medium. *STOCK: Jewellery, silver, objets d'art.* PARK: Multi-storey, nearby. TEL: 0223 357910. SER: Valuations; restorations and repairs. VAT: Stan/Spec.

Cambridge Fine Art Ltd LAPADA
Priesthouse, 33 Church St, Little Shelford. (R. and J Lury) Resident. Est: 1972. Open 10-6, Sun. by appointment. SIZE: Large. *STOCK: British and European paintings, 1780-1900; British paintings, 1880-1930; portraits, 1650-1930.* LOC: Next to church. PARK: Easy. TEL: 0223 842866/843537. SER: Valuations; restorations; buys at auction. VAT: Stan/Spec.

Malcolm G Clark
3 Pembroke St. Est: 1947. Open 9.30-5. CL: Thurs. *STOCK: English furniture, contemporary items.* TEL: 0223 357117. VAT: Spec.

Collectors Centre
The Old Stables, Hope St. Yard, Hope St. (A. and L Carey) Est: 1975. Open 10-5. CL: Wed. and Thurs. SIZE: Small. *STOCK: Pine, general antiques, collectables and bygones, 18th-20th C.* LOC: Off Mill Rd., opposite Co-op. PARK: Easy. TEL: 0223 211632. SER: Valuations; restorations; upholstery. VAT: Stan.

Collectors' Market
Dales Brewery, Gwydir St (off Mill Rd). (Mrs E.M Highmoor) Est: 1976. Open 9.30-5. SIZE: 12 units. *STOCK: Collectors' items from £1.50-£750, including bygones, prints, pine, bric-a-brac, kitchenalia, art deco, furniture.*

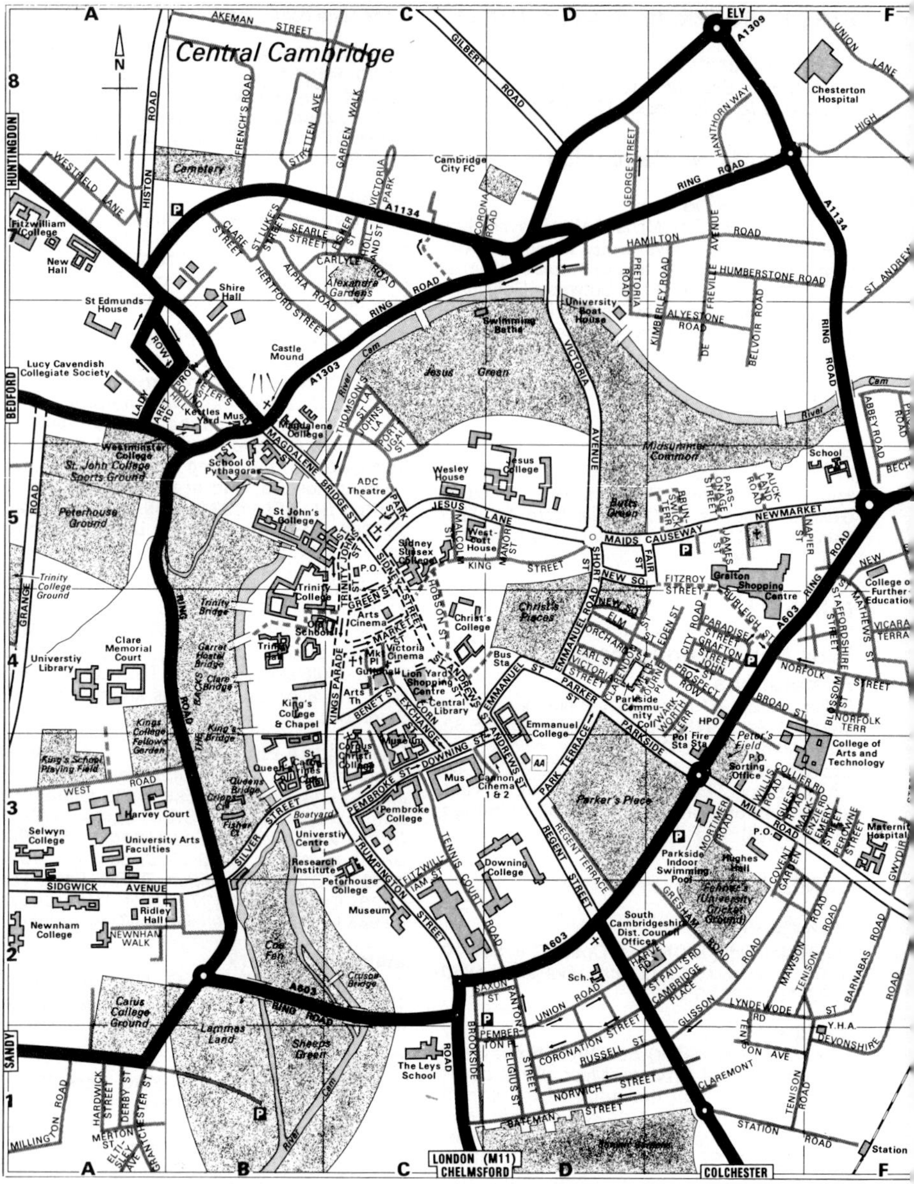
Central Cambridge
N
A
C
D
E
F
ELY
A1309
8
7
5
4
3
2
1
HUNTINGDON
BEDFORD
SANDY
LONDON (M11)
CHELMSFORD
COLCHESTER
AKEMAN STREET
GILBERT ROAD
UNION LANE
Chesterton Hospital
HIGH
FRENCH'S ROAD
STRETTEN AVE
GARDEN WALK
HISTON ROAD
Cemetery
WESTFIELD LANE
VICTORIA PARK
Cambridge City FC
CORONA ROAD
GEORGE STREET
HAWTHORN WAY
RING ROAD
A1134
CLARE STREET
ST LUKE'S STREET
SEARLE STREET
HOLLAND ST
CARLYLE ROAD
Alexandra Gardens
ALPHA ROAD
HERTFORD STREET
HAMILTON ROAD
PRETORIA ROAD
KIMBERLEY ROAD
HUMBERSTONE ROAD
ALYESTONE ROAD
DE FREVILLE AVENUE
BELVOIR ROAD
ST ANDREW'S
Fitzwilliam College
New Hall
St Edmunds House
Shire Hall
Castle Mound
ROW
Lucy Cavendish Collegiate Society
A1303
Swimming Baths
University Boat House
Jesus Green
River Cam
VICTORIA AVENUE
Midsummer Common
ABBEY ROAD
School
LADY MARGARET RD
Kettles Yard
Mus
Magdalene College
THOMSON'S LA
JOHNS LA
PORTUGAL ST
Westminster College
St. John College Sports Ground
School of Pythagoras
MAGDALENE BRIDGE ST
Jesus College
Wesley House
ADC Theatre
Peterhouse Ground
GRANGE ROAD
St John's College
JESUS LANE
PARK ST
Butts Green
BRUNSWICK TERR
PARSONAGE STREET
AUCKLAND ROAD
NEWMARKET
MAIDS CAUSEWAY
NAPIER ST
Trinity College Ground
Sidney Sussex College
MALCOLM ST
West-Cott House
MANOR ST
FAIR ST
JAMES ST
Grafton Shopping Centre
FITZROY STREET
BURLEIGH ST
NEW SQ
ELM ST
Trinity College
P.O.
KING STREET
HOBSON ST
Christ's Pieces
Christ's College
ORCHARD ST
EDEN ST
CITY ROAD
PARADISE STREET
GRAFTON STREET
A603
Trinity Bridge
TRINITY ST
GREEN ST
SIDNEY STREET
Arts Cinema
MARKET
Old Schools
Garret Hostel Bridge
Clare Memorial Court
Universtiy Library
Trinity Hall
Mkt Pl
Victoria Cinema
Guildhall
Lion Yard Shopping Centre
ST ANDREW'S ST
Bus Sta
EMMANUEL ST
EMMANUEL ROAD
EARL ST
VICTORIA STREET
CLARENDON ST
JOHN ST
PROSPECT ROW
NORFOLK STREET
STAFFORDSHIRE STREET
College of Further Education
Clare Bridge
THE BACKS
KINGS PARADE
Arts Th
Central Library
PARKER ST
Parkside Community Coll
WARKWORTH TERR
BROAD ST
BLOSSOM ST
NORFOLK TERR
Kings College Fellows Garden
King's Bridge
King's College & Chapel
BENE'T ST
CORN EXCHANGE ST
Emmanuel College
PARKSIDE
Pol Sta
Fire Sta
HPO
Peter's Field
College of Arts and Technology
King's School Playing Field
WEST ROAD
Queens
Corpus Christi College
Museum
DOWNING ST
ST ANDREWS ST
AA
PARK TERRACE
P.O. Sorting Office
MILL ROAD
WILLIS ROAD
COLLIER RD
GUEST ROAD
MACKENZIE RD
Queens Bridge
Cripps Ct
Fisher Ct
Harvey Court
St Catharines
Mus
Cannon Cinema 1 & 2
Parker's Piece
EMERY ST
PEROWNE STREET
Maternity Hospital
Selwyn College
University Arts Faculties
SILVER STREET
Boatyard
PEMBROKE ST
Pembroke College
University Centre
TRUMPINGTON STREET
REGENT STREET
REGENT TERRACE
MORTIMER ROAD
Parkside Indoor Swimming Pool
Hughes Hall
COVENT GARDEN
GWYDIR
SIDGWICK AVENUE
Ridley Hall
Research Institute
Peterhouse College
FITZWILLIAM ST
TENNIS COURT ROAD
Downing College
Fenner's (University Cricket Ground)
GRESHAM ROAD
Newnham College
NEWNHAM WALK
Museum
South Cambridgeshire Dist. Council Offices
HARVEY RD
ST PAUL'S RD
CAMBRIDGE PLACE
MAWSON ROAD
TENISON ROAD
BARNABAS ROAD
Coe Fen
Crusoe Bridge
Sch.
Caius College Ground
A603
RING ROAD
SAXON ST
UNION ROAD
GLISSON ROAD
LYNDEWODE RD
DEVONSHIRE RD
Y.H.A.
Lammas Land
Sheeps Green
The Leys School
TRUMPINGTON ROAD
BROOKSIDE
PANTON STREET
PEMBERTON PL
CORONATION STREET
RUSSELL ST
TENISON AVE
CLAREMONT
MILLINGTON ROAD
HARDWICK STREET
DERBY ST
MERTON ST
ELTISLEY AVE
GRANCHESTER ST
River Cam
ELIGIUS ST
NORWICH STREET
BATEMAN STREET
STATION ROAD
Station
TENISON ROAD

Key to Town Plan

AA Recommended roads
Other roads
Restricted roads
Buildings of interest
Car Parks
Parks and open spaces
AA Service Centre

Cambridge continued

Collins and Clark
81 Regent St. (J.G Collins) Est: 1895. Open 9.30-5. CL: Thurs. p.m. *STOCK: English furniture, English and Oriental porcelain, silver, glass.* TEL: 0223 353801. VAT: Spec.

Gabor Cossa Antiques
34 Trumpington St. (J Eve) Est: 1948. Open 10-5.15. *STOCK: Early English ceramics, delftware and tiles, 18th C drinking glasses, Oriental porcelain, Japanese woodcuts, prints.* LOC: On main road leading into Cambridge from London opposite Fitzwilliam Museum. PARK: 400yds. - 2 car parks. TEL: 0223 356049. VAT: Spec.

Cottage Antiques
16-18 Lensfield Rd. (Mrs A Owen and Mrs A Yandell) Est: 1981. Open 10-5.30, Sun. by appointment. SIZE: Medium. *STOCK: Pottery, porcelain, country furniture, 18th-19th C; blue and white, pre-1930; Staffordshire figures, antiquities, glass, general antiques, including copper and brass, 19th C.* LOC: Opposite Catholic Church. PARK: Nearby. TEL: 0223 316698.

G David
3-4 and 16 St. Edwards Passage. ABA, PBFA. Est: 1896. Open 9.30-5; No.16 - Open 9-5. CL: Thurs. *STOCK: Antiquarian, secondhand and out of print books, remainders.* TEL: 0223 354619.

Deighton Bell and Co
13 Trinity St. (Heffers Booksellers)ABA, PBFA. Est: 1700. Open 9-5.30. SIZE: Large. *STOCK: Antiquarian, rare and fine old books, most subjects; also bibliography, typography and illustrated books.* PARK: Multi-storey, 300yds. TEL: 0223 353939. SER: Buys at auction. VAT: Stan.

Dolphin Antiques BADA
33 Trumpington St. (R.H Bramwell and L.J Aldred) Open 10-5.30. *STOCK: 18th to early 19th C furniture, metalware and glass.* Not Stocked: Jewellery. LOC: Opposite Fitzwilliam Museum. PARK: Meters or Lion Yard multi-storey. TEL: 0223 354180.

"Flappers"
84 Mill Rd. Open 10-6. *STOCK: Period clothes, Victorian to 1960; jewellery.* TEL: 0223 68442. SER: 20s costume and evening dress hire.

Galloway and Porter Ltd
30 Sidney St, and 3 Green St. ABA. Est: 1900. CL: Sat. *STOCK: Antiquarian and secondhand books.* TEL: 0223 67876.

Derek Gibbons
The Haunted Bookshop, St. Edward's Passage. Est: 1960. Open 9.30-5.30. *STOCK: Antiquarian and illustrated books.* TEL: 0223 312913.

Cambridge continued

Gwydir Street Antiques
Gwydir St. Open 9.30-5, Sat. 9.30-5.30. SIZE: 12 dealers. *STOCK: General antiques including furniture, Georgian to late 1930's; Victorian sofas and chairs, decorative china and objets d'art, Victorian fireplaces.* LOC: Off Mill Rd. PARK: Opposite. TEL: 0223 460548.

Hyde Park Corner Antiques (Antiques Centre)
12 Lensfield Rd. (S.J Cope-Brown) Open 10-5. SIZE: 8 dealers. *STOCK: Pre-1830 English ceramics; glass, silver, furniture, early metalware, pot-lids and Prattware, treen, jewellery and early prints.* TEL: 0223 353654. SER: Valuations; restorations (pottery, porcelain and furniture).

The Oriel Gallery
13 Fair St. (A Wakerley) Est: 1984. Open 10-5, St. 10-4. SIZE: Small. *STOCK: Watercolours, £100-£500; oil paintings, £200-£800; both 1890-1950.* LOC: Between Grafton Shopping Centre and Maids Causeway. PARK: Grafton multi-storey. TEL: 0223 321027. SER: Restorations (oil paintings).

Jean Pain Gallery
7-8 King's Parade. Est: 1967. Open 9.30-5. SIZE: Medium. *STOCK: Local and fine art; reproduction railway posters of '30s, '40s and '50s; prints.* LOC: Opposite King's College. PARK: Lion's Yard. TEL: 0223 313970. VAT: Stan.

Sebastian Pearson Antiques and Paintings
3 Free School Lane, Benet St. Est: 1989. Open 10-5.30. CL: Mon. SIZE: Medium. *STOCK: Oil paintings and watercolours, £500-£4,000; Oriental works of art, £300-£1,500; European, Islamic and Oriental textiles, £50-£500.* LOC: City centre. PARK: Nearby. TEL: 0223 323999; home - 0438 871364. SER: Valuations; buys at auction; picture framing. VAT: Spec.

Quinto of Cambridge
34 Trinity St. Open 9-6. *STOCK: Maps, prints and books.* TEL: 0223 358279.

Cambridge continued

Rose Cottage Antiques
Rose Cottage, Brewery Rd, Pampisford. (A. and A Anness) Open 9-6, Sun. 2-5, other times by appointment. *STOCK: Period furniture, curios; Victorian style solid brass lighting.* PARK: 0223 834631. SER: Restoration (furniture).

Strover Antiques
55 Sturton St. (B.J Strover) Open by chance or by appointment. *STOCK: 18th-19th C primitive and country furniture, mainly pine.* TEL: 0223 66302.

S.J Webster-Speakman BADA
79 Regent St. Open 10-5.30. *STOCK: English furniture, clocks, Staffordshire pottery, general antiques.* TEL: 0223 315048; evenings - 0223 354809. FAIRS: Spring and Autumn Chelsea. VAT: Spec.

CHITTERING, Nr. Cambridge

Simon and Penny Rumble Antiques
The Old School. Usually open but prior telephone call advisable. *STOCK: Early oak and country furniture, pottery, treen, decorative items.* LOC: 6 miles north of Cambridge, off A10. TEL: 0223 861831.

COMBERTON

Comberton Antiques
5a West St. (Mrs M McEvoy) Est: 1980. Open Mon., Fri. and Sat. 10-5, Sun. 2-5. SIZE: Medium. *STOCK: Furniture, 1780-1900, £50-£500; bric-a-brac, 1830-1920, £5-£100; shipping goods.* LOC: 6 miles west of Cambridge, 2 miles west of M11. PARK: Easy. TEL: 0223 262674; home - 0223 263457.

DODDINGTON

Doddington House Antiques
2 Benwick Rd. (B.A Frankland) Est: 1974. *STOCK: Furniture, mirrors, clocks, barometers, pictures and interesting items.* LOC: At Clocktower. PARK: Easy. TEL: 0354 740755. SER: Restoration (chair caning and rushing, barometers).

DUXFORD

Riro D Mooney
4 Moorfield Rd. Est: 1946. Open 9-7. SIZE: Medium. *STOCK: General antiques, 1780-1920, £5-£1,200.* LOC: 1 mile from M11. PARK: Easy. TEL: 0223 832252. VAT: Stan/Spec.

ELY

Mrs. Mills Antiques
1a St. Mary's St. (E.T Mills) FGA. Open 10-1 and 2-5. CL: Tues. *STOCK: General small antiques, porcelain and pottery, 18th-19th C; jewellery, small silver items.* Not Stocked: Furniture. TEL: 0353 664268. SER: Valuations (jewellery); restorations (porcelain).

Waterside Antiques
The Wharf. (G Peters) Est: 1986. Open 9.30-5.30, Sun. 1-5.30. SIZE: Large. *STOCK: General antiques.* LOC: Waterside area. PARK: Easy. TEL: 0353 667066. SER: Valuations.

FORDHAM

Clover Antiques
5-6 Soham Rd. Open Thurs., Fri. and Sat. 9-5.30, or trade by appointment. SIZE: Large and warehouse. *STOCK: Pine, mahogany and oak furniture.* LOC: A142. TEL: 0638 720250. SER: Export.

Fordham continued

Phoenix Antiques
1 Carter St. Est: 1966. Open normal hours, but appointment advisable. CL: Wed. p.m. SIZE: Medium. *STOCK: Early European furniture, domestic metalwork, pottery and delft, carpets, scientific instruments, treen and bygones.* LOC: Centre of village. PARK: Own. TEL: 0638 720363.

FOWLMERE, Nr. Royston (Herts)

Mere Antiques
High St. (R.W Smith) Est: 1979. Open 10-1 and 2-6, including Sun. SIZE: Medium. *STOCK: Furniture, porcelain and clocks, 18th-19th C, to £5,000.* PARK: Easy. TEL: 076 382 477; home - 076 382 495. SER: Valuations. VAT: Spec.

HARSTON

Antique Clocks
1 High St. (C.J Stocker) Open every day. LOC: On A10, 5 miles south of Cambridge. PARK: Easy. TEL: 0223 870264.

IICKLETON, Nr. Saffron Walden (Essex)

Abbey Antiques
18 Abbey St. (K Wilson) Est: 1974. Open 10-5, Sun. 2-5. SIZE: Large. *STOCK: General antiques, 17th-20th C, £1-£1,000.* LOC: Turn off at Stumps Cross at Gt. Chesterford, 1 mile to Ickleton, shop is in main street. PARK: Easy. TEL: 0799 30637. SER: Valuations; restorations (furniture); French polishing.

LANDBEACH

P.R Garner Antiques
104 High St. Est: 1966. Open by appointment only. SIZE: Medium. *STOCK: China, glass, brass, copper, pewter, unrestored furniture,*

P.R Garner Antiques continued

Victorian and earlier, old gramophones, musical boxes, Victorian and Edwardian, shipping goods. LOC: Off A10. PARK: Easy. TEL: 0223 860470. SER: Valuations. VAT: Stan/Spec.

LITTLE ABINGTON, Nr. Cambridge

Abington Books
29 Church Lane. (J Haldane) ABA. Est: 1971. By appointment only. SIZE: Small. *STOCK: Books on Oriental rugs, from 1877, £1-£5,000; books on classical tapestries, from 17th C, £1-£3,000.* PARK: Easy. TEL: 0223 891645; fax - 0223 893724. SER: Valuations; book binding; occasional catalogues; buys at auction (books).

MARCH

Gallery Three
96 and 98 High St. (J Burn) Est: 1970. Open Wed. 10-4, Sat. 10-12, other times by appointment. *STOCK: Porcelain, pottery, glass, silver, small furniture.* PARK: Easy. TEL: 0354 53484/52262. SER: Valuations; restorations.

MELBOURN, Nr. Royston (Herts.)

P.N Hardiman
62 High St. (M. and G.A Hardiman) Est: 1933. Open 8.30-6. CL: Sun. except by appointment. SIZE: Medium. *STOCK: English furniture, 18th and 19th C; general antiques.* LOC: A10 between Royston and Cambridge. PARK: At rear. TEL: 0763 260093. SER: Restorations. VAT: Stan/Spec.

IS YOUR ENTRY CORRECT?
If there is even the slightest inaccuracy in your entry, *please* let us know before 1st January 1992.
GUIDE TO THE
ANTIQUE SHOPS OF BRITAIN
5 Church Street, Woodbridge, Suffolk.
Tel: (0394) 385501

ORWELL

West Farm Antiques LAPADA
High St. (Mrs J Kershaw) Est: 1964. Open Thurs., Sat. and Sun. or by appointment. SIZE: Large. *STOCK: Country furniture and general antiques, 17th-19th C, £5-£3,000.* Not Stocked: Reproductions, silver, clocks, mechanical objects, jewellery. LOC: 5 miles from exit 12, M11, off A603, 1/2 mile past church on right. PARK: Easy. TEL: 0223 207464. FAIRS: Olympia, British International, Birmingham. VAT: Stan/Spec.

OUTWELL, Nr. Wisbech

A.P. and M.A Haylett
Glen-Royd, 393 Wisbech Rd. Open 9-6 including Sun. *STOCK: Country furniture, pottery, treen and metalware, 1750-1900, £5-£500.* Not Stocked: Firearms. LOC: A1101. PARK: Easy. TEL: 0945 772427; home - same. SER: Buys at auction. FAIRS: Snape, Bury St. Edmunds.

PETERBOROUGH

Ivor and Patricia Lewis Antique and Fine Art Dealers
Westfield, 30 Westwood Park Rd. Open by appointment. *STOCK: English and French furniture - some signed, porcelain, bronzes.* TEL: 0733 344567.

Old Soke Books
68 Burghley Rd. (P Clay) Open Fri. and Sat. 10-5, other times by appointment. *STOCK: Antiquarian and secondhand books, small general antiques including furniture, paintings, prints and postcards.* TEL: 0733 64147.

G Smith and Sons (Peterborough)Ltd
1379 Lincoln Rd, Werrington. (M Groucott) Est: 1902. Open 9-1 and 2.15-5. CL: Thurs. p.m. SIZE: Medium. *STOCK: General antiques.* LOC: A15. PARK: Easy. TEL: 0733 71630. SER: Upholstery; restorations. VAT: Stan/Spec.

Peterborough continued

Victorian Pine and Antiques
13 Geneva St. (P Payne) Est: 1985. Open 10-6, Thurs. 10-8. CL: Mon. SIZE: Large. *STOCK: Victorian pine, £100-£600; Georgian and Victorian mahogany and oak, £100-£600.* LOC: 2nd right off city end of Lincoln Rd. PARK: Easy. TEL: 0733 896877; home - same. VAT: Stan.

RAMSEY, Nr. Huntingdon

Abbey Antiques
63 Great Whyte. (R. and J Smith) Est: 1977. Open 10-5 including Sun. CL: Mon. SIZE: Small. *STOCK: Furniture, including pine, 1850-1930, £50-£500; porcelain, Goss and crested china, 1830-1950, £3-£500; brass and copper, 1850-1950, £10-£100.* PARK: Easy. TEL: 0487 814753. FAIRS: Alexandra Palace, Harrow.

Yesteryear Antiques
79/81 High St. (Mr and Mrs S Staley Grace) Est: 1977. Open daily including Sun. CL: Tues. and Wed. SIZE: Medium. *STOCK: Small items, 19th C, £5-£100; furniture, £100-£300; prints, 19th C watercolours and oils.* PARK: Easy. TEL: 0487 815006; home - same. SER: Restorations; picture framing. FAIRS: Clavering.

REACH

Dudley's Antiques and Home Interiors
Vine House, Fair Green. (A.F. and J.A Dudley) Open 9-5, or by appointment. SIZE: Large. *STOCK: General antiques, furniture, copper, brass, porcelain, pictures, prints, country bygones, curios, collectors' items, clocks, bric-a-brac, from 50p.* LOC: Just off B1102. PARK: Easy. TEL: 0638 741989; home - 0638 742171. SER: Valuations; restorations (clocks, barometers, furniture, silver and metal), caning, rushing, framing, wood carving, turning, French polishing, veneering, upholstery and buttoning; design consultant; buys at auction. VAT: Stan/Spec.

ST. IVES

Adams Antiques
Houghton Rd. Open 8.30-5.30, Sat. 10-4. CL: Sat. SIZE: Warehouse. *STOCK: Pine, especially Irish and continental, 18th-19th C.* TEL: 0480 300455.

Broadway Antiques
31 The Broadway. (B.R Norton) Est: 1980. Open 9.30-5. CL: Thurs. SIZE: Small. *STOCK: Furniture, £30-£1,000; metalware, vestas and snuff boxes, treen, corkscrews, £10-£500; all 18th-19th C.* LOC: West end of town, near Norris Museum. PARK: Easy. TEL: 0480 61061; home -0480 68220. SER: Valuations. FAIRS: Bermondsey, Newark, Ardingly, Sandown, Stoneleigh.

B.R Knight and Sons
Quay Court, Bull Lane, Bridge St. (M Knight) Est: 1972. Open 10-4.30. SIZE: Small. *STOCK: Porcelain, pottery, jewellery, paintings, watercolours, prints, decorative arts.* LOC: Off Bridge St. PARK: Nearby. TEL: 0480 68295

ST. NEOTS

Peter John Antiques
38 St. Mary's St, Eynesbury. (K Smith) Open 10-5. CL: Tues. *STOCK: General antiques,*

Peter John Antiques continued

especially jewellery. PARK: Easy. TEL: 0480 216297. SER: Restorations (clocks); repairs (clocks, jewellery).

Tavistock Antiques
Cross Hall Manor, Eaton Ford. Open by appointment. *STOCK: Period English furniture.* TEL: 0480 72082. *Trade Only.*

SOHAM

Audraw Ltd
Staples Lane. (L Audus) Est: 1959. Open by appointment. CL: Wed. SIZE: Warehouse. *STOCK: Furniture, Georgian, Victorian and Edwardian, £10-£1,000; Victorian glass, porcelain, £1-£500; brass, copper.* LOC: On main road between Newmarket and Ely. PARK: Easy. TEL: 0353 720342. VAT: Stan/Spec

SWAFFHAM PRIOR, Nr. Cambridge

Rodney Firmin
Lowfields, Lower End. Est: 1974. Open by appointment only. *STOCK: Clocks - English, French, bracket, longcase and carriage, £500-£20,000.* TEL: 0638 742881. SER: Valuations; restorations; buys at auction. VAT: Spec.

WANSFORD, NR. PETERBOROUGH

Old House Antiques
The Old House, 16 London Rd. (R Rimes and L Ayres) Open 9.30-6 including Sun. CL: Mon. *STOCK: Period lighting.* LOC: On A1 near A47 junction. PARK: Easy. TEL: 0780 783999/783462.

Sydney House Antiques
14 Elton Rd. (G. and R Hancox) Est: 1972. Open 9-5 including Sun., Mon. 2-5.30, other times by appointment. SIZE: Large. *STOCK: Furniture, including marquetry, 19th-20th C, £150-£2,000; Minton, 1850-1920, £100-£2,000; Doulton and Lambeth, £50-£1,000; Royal Worcester, 1860-1940, £100-£1,500.* PARK: Easy. TEL: 0780 782786. SER: Valuations; buys at auction (Minton, Doulton, Royal Worcester, 19th C furniture).

Wansford Antiques and Oriental Pottery
10 London Rd. (P.E Hancox) Open 9-6. *STOCK: Royal Worcester porcelain; French and inlaid furniture.* TEL: 0780 783253.

WARBOYS

'The Golden Drop Antiques'
The Golden Drop, Chatteris Rd. (M Clarke) Open daily. CL: Wed. *STOCK: Golden polished pine; mahogany, oak and walnut, some smalls.* LOC: On A141, 3 miles from Chatteris towards Warboys. TEL: 035 43 2990.

Warboys Antiques
Old Church School. (J Lambden and C Sansean) Est: 1986. Open 10-5. CL: Mon. SIZE: Medium. *STOCK: Decorative smalls, 18th-20th C; sports equipment, advertising items, 19th-20th C; all £1-£500.* LOC: Off A141. PARK: Easy. TEL: 0487 823686. SER: Valuations. FAIRS: Alexandra Palace.

WILLINGHAM

Willingham Antiques and Collectors' Market
25-29 Green St. (K. and Mrs. M Young) Open 10-5. CL: Thurs. SIZE: Medium - 16 dealers. *STOCK: General antiques.* PARK: Easy. TEL: 0945 60283.

WISBECH

Attic Antiques
1 Howletts Hill, Off Norfolk St. (Mrs S Stones) Est: 1978. Open 11-1 and 2-4. CL: Mon. and Wed. SIZE: Small. *STOCK: General antiques, 19th C to art deco, £5-£200.* Not Stocked: Firearms. LOC: Just off Wisbech-Downham Rd. PARK: Easy. TEL: Home - 0945 773014.

Attic Gallery
88 Elm Rd. (B.G Ransome) Est: 1980. Open by appointment. SIZE: Small. *STOCK: Georgian and Victorian silver.* PARK: Easy. TEL: 0945 583734.

Coach House Antiques
55 Elm Rd. (J Ing) Est: 1953. Open 9-5. CL: Sat. and Sun. except by appointment. SIZE: Large. *STOCK: Silver, Georgian and Victorian; furniture, Victorian; prints pre-1820, all to £1,500.* Not Stocked: Firearms, coins, stamps. PARK: Easy. TEL: 0945 583129. SER: Valuations; buys at auction. VAT: Stan/Spec.

Peter A Crofts BADA
Briar Patch, High Rd, Elm. Est: 1949. CL: Sat. *STOCK: General antiques, furniture, porcelain, silver, jewellery.* LOC: A1101. TEL: 0945 584614. VAT: Stan/Spec.

Wisbech continued

Eric Golding
12 North Brink. Open by appointment only. *STOCK: Antiquarian books.* TEL: 0945 582927.

R Wilding
Lanes End, Gadds Lane. *STOCK: Walnut and mahogany furniture, mirrors.* TEL: 0945 588204; home - same. SER: Restorations, re-veneering, polishing, conversions and gilders compo.

Cheshire

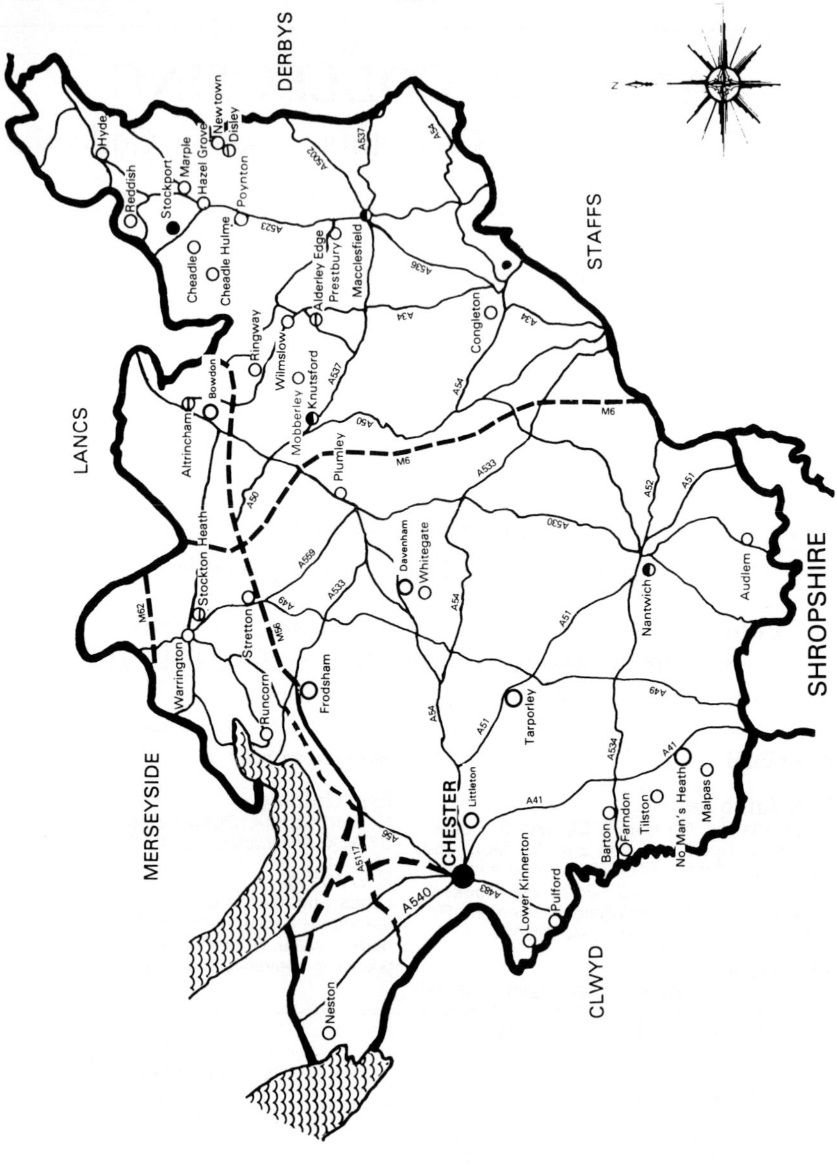

DERBYS
STAFFS
SHROPSHIRE
CLWYD
MERSEYSIDE
LANCS
CHESTER
Hyde
Reddish
Stockport
Marple
Hazel Grove
Newtown
Disley
Poynton
Cheadle
Cheadle Hulme
Alderley Edge
Prestbury
Macclesfield
Ringway
Wilmslow
Congleton
Bowdon
Altrincham
Mobberley
Knutsford
Plumley
Stockton Heath
Warrington
Stretton
Runcorn
Frodsham
Davenham
Whitegate
Nantwich
Audlem
Tarporley
Littleton
Barton
Farndon
Tilston
No Man's Heath
Malpas
Lower Kinnerton
Pulford
Neston
M6
M56
M62
A537
A34
A5002
A523
A536
A54
A50
A533
A52
A51
A530
A559
A49
A534
A41
A56
A5117
A540
A483

○ 1–2 Key to number of shops in this area.
⊖ 3–5
◒ 6–12
● 13+

Please note this is only a rough map designed to show dealers the number of shops in the various towns, and is not necessarily totally accurate.

ALDERLEY EDGE

Alderley Antiques **LAPADA**
17 London Rd. (G Bennett and J Barlow) Est: 1967. Open 10-1 and 2-5. SIZE: Medium. *STOCK: Furniture, £300-£20,000; objets d'art, £100-£4,000; paintings, £100-£5,000, all 17th-19th C.* LOC: Town centre, near station. PARK: Easy. TEL: 0625 583468; home - 0625 584819. FAIRS: British International, Birmingham; Buxton. VAT: Stan/Spec.

Anthony Baker Antiques **LAPADA**
14 London Rd. (G.D.A Price) Est: 1974. Open 10-5.30. CL: Mon. SIZE: Medium. *STOCK: Furniture and clocks, 17th-19th C, £50-£2,000; glass and pottery.* Not Stocked: Jewellery, weapons. LOC: A34, village centre. PARK: Easy. TEL: 0625 582674. VAT: Stan/Spec.

Brook Lane Antiques
93 Brook Lane. (M Goodwin) Est: 1983. Open 11-4 Thurs., Fri. and Sat. SIZE: Small. *STOCK: Stripped Victorian, Edwardian and reproduction pine.* TEL: 0625 584896; evenings - 0625 582717. SER: Stencilling; stripping.

D.J Massey and Son
51a London Rd. Est: 1900. Open 9-5.30, Wed. 9-5. SIZE: Large. *STOCK: Gold and diamond jewellery; silver, all periods.* LOC: On A34. PARK: Easy. TEL: 0625 583565. VAT: Stan/Spec.

ALTRINCHAM

Baron Antiques
64 and 64A Manchester Rd. Open 10-6. *STOCK: General antiques.* TEL: 061 928 2943.

Halo Antiques
97 Hale Rd, and 2a Beech Rd. (P., M. C. and T Oulton) Est: 1976. Open 10-5. CL: Mon. SIZE: Large. *STOCK: Trade items, £5-£5,000; pine.* LOC: Exit 6, M56. A538 for 2 miles. PARK: Easy. TEL: 061 941 1800; fax - 061 929 9565. VAT: Stan.

New Street Antiques
48 New St. (S. and R Redford) Open 10-6. CL: Mon. and Wed. *STOCK: General antiques, furniture, small silver, porcelain.* PARK: Easy. TEL: 061 929 8171; home - 061 928 4827/061 926 8232. SER: Valuations; restorations (furniture, textiles and porcelain); plating and polishing. VAT: Stan/Spec.

Squires Antiques
25 Regent Rd. (V Phillips) Est: 1977. Open10-5. CL: Mon. and Wed. SIZE: Small. *STOCK: Small furniture, 1800-1930, £25-£500; small silver, 1850-1950, £10-£200; brass, copper and bric-a-brac, 1850-1940, £5-£300; jewellery, porcelain, fireplace accessories, lights and interior design items.* Not Stocked: Large furniture, coins and badges. LOC: Adjacent to the hospital, next to large car park. PARK: Easy. TEL: 061 928 0749. SER: Valuations.

AUDLEM

Horn Antiques **BADA**
(Mrs P Hardwick) Est: 1980. Open by appointment. SIZE: Small. *STOCK: Horn items, 17th-19th C; small period country furniture and objects.* Not Stocked: Silver, jewellery. PARK: Easy. TEL: 0270 811545. VAT: Spec.

BARTON, Nr. Malpas

Derek Rayment Antiques **BADA**
Orchard House, Barton Rd. (D.J. and K.M Rayment) Est: 1960. Open by appointment every day. *STOCK: Barometers, 18th-20th C, from £100.* LOC: A534. PARK: Easy. TEL: 0829 270429; home - same. SER: Valuations; restorations (barometers only); buys at auction (barometers). FAIRS: Harrogate; British International Birmingham; Olympia, West London, Chelsea, Penman; Barbican. VAT: Stan/Spec.

BOWDON

Eureka Antiques and Interiors **LAPADA**
7a Church Brow. (N Gibson and A.J O'Donnell) Est: 1965. Open 10-1 and 2-5, other times by appointment. CL: Mon. and Wed. *STOCK: Furniture, 18th-19th C, £100-£8,000; porcelain, 19th C, £60-£500; collectors' items, tartanware, Scottish jewellery.* LOC: Off M6 towards Manchester, straight on after first traffic lights, turn right after large roundabout. Turn left up hill towards church, shop on left. TEL: 061 926 9722.

CHEADLE

Malcolm Frazer Antiques
19 Brooklyn Cres. Open by appointment. *STOCK: Marine, scientific and decorative antiques.* TEL: 061 428 3781.

D.J Massey and Son
79 High St. Est: 1900. Open 9-5.30, Wed. 9-1. *STOCK: Jewellery, gold and diamonds.* PARK: Easy. TEL: 061 428 6953.

CHEADLE HULME

Allan's Antiques and Reproductions
10 Ravenoak Rd. (C Allan) Est: 1979. CL: Wed. *STOCK: Furniture, collectables, general antiques.* TEL: 061 485 3132.

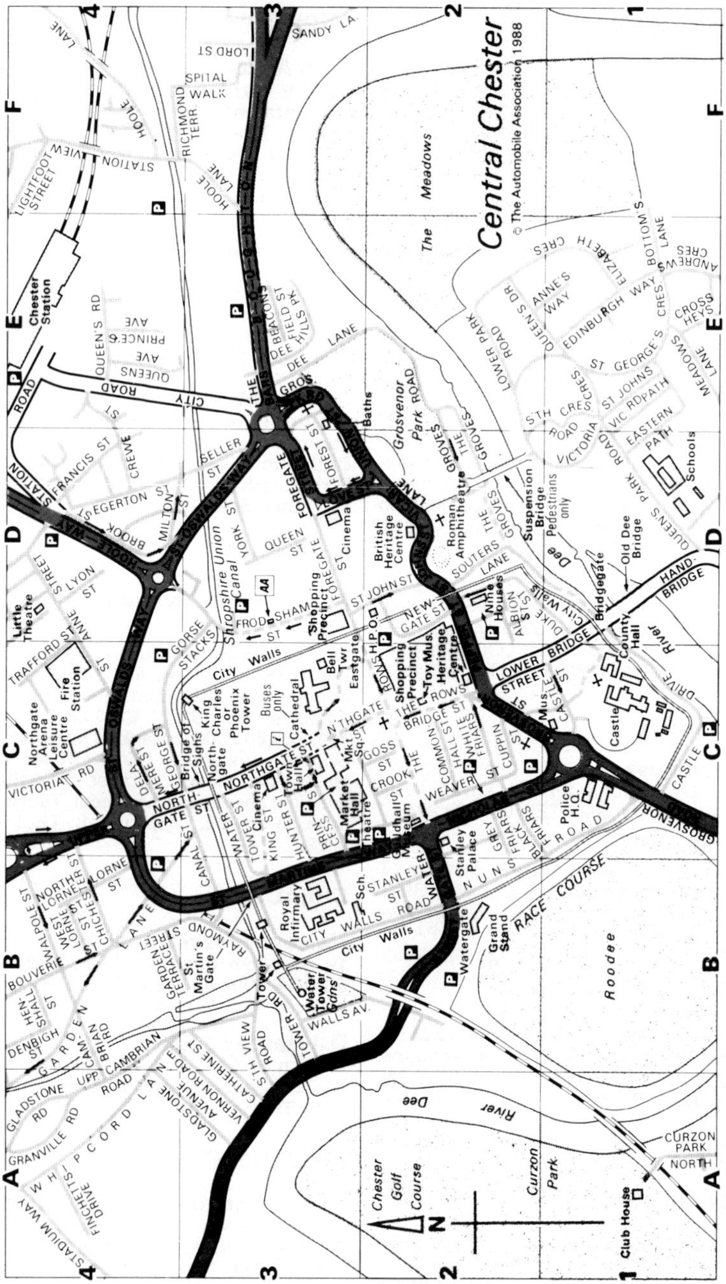
Central Chester
© The Automobile Association 1988
The Meadows
Chester Station
Little Theatre
Fire Station
Northgate Arena Leisure Centre
Shropshire Union Canal
City Walls
King Charles or Phoenix Tower
Cathedral
Bell Twr
Eastgate
Shopping Precinct
Cinema
British Heritage Centre
Roman Amphitheatre
Suspension Bridge
Dee Pedestrians only
Old Dee Bridge
Bridgegate
Nine Houses
County Hall
Castle
Police H.Q.
Town Hall
Market Hall
Theatre
Guildhall Museum
Stanley Palace
Royal Infirmary
Watergate
Grand Stand
RACE COURSE
Roodee
River Dee
Chester Golf Course
Curzon Park
Club House
St Martin's Gate
Water Tower Gdns
Grosvenor Park
Baths
Schools
Toy Mus.
Heritage Centre
Mus.
H.P.O.
Buses only
N

Key to Town Plan

AA Recommended roads		Car Parks	P
Other roads		Parks and open spaces	
Restricted roads		AA Service Centre	AA
Buildings of interest		© Automobile Association 1988.	

CHESTER

Adams Antiques **LAPADA**
65 Watergate Row. (B. and T Adams) Est: 1973. Open 10-5. CL: Sun. except by appointment. SIZE: Medium. *STOCK: English and continental furniture, £200-£4,000; English and French clocks, £150-£4,000; oils, watercolours and objets d'art, £10-£1,000; all 18th-19th C.* PARK: Nearby. TEL: 0244 319421. SER: Valuations; restorations (furniture, clocks, and oil paintings). VAT: Stan/Spec.

Antique Exporters of Chester
Open by appointment only. SIZE: Warehouse. *STOCK: Furniture.* TEL: 0829 41001; home - 0829 570069. SER: Packing. *Export Only.*

Avalon Post Card and Stamp Shop
1 City Walls, Northgate St. (G.E Ellis) *STOCK: Postcards, stamps and collectables.* TEL: 0244 318406.

Baron Fine Art
68 Watergate St. (S. and R Baron) Est: 1984. Open 10-5.15, including Sun. *STOCK: Watercolours and oils, some etchings, late 19th to early 20th C, some contemporary, £200-£25,000.* PARK: Easy. TEL: 0244 342520/349212. SER: Restorations; framing. FAIRS: Tatton Park; Barbican. VAT: Stan/Spec.

Boodle and Dunthorne Ltd
52 Eastgate St. Est: 1798. Open 9-5.30. SIZE: Large. *STOCK: Jewellery, watches, silver, 18th-19th C, £50-£30,000; clocks and clock sets, mid-19th C, £250-£2,000.* Not Stocked: Furniture. PARK: Multi-storey in Pepper St. TEL: 0244 326666. VAT: Stan/Spec.

Olwyn Boustead Antiques **LAPADA**
61 Watergate Row. (Mrs O.L Boustead) Open 10-5.30. *STOCK: Barometers, furniture including beds, 18th-19th C and country; metalware; portraits, 17th-19th C; watercolours, 19th C.* TEL: 0244 342300.

Chester Antiques
49 Watergate Row. (R. and M.D Davison) Est: 1970. *STOCK: Longcase, carriage and mantel clocks; Victorian walnut furniture, oak and mahogany, china and glass, barometers, porcelain, weapons, dolls.* TEL: 0244 311768. VAT: Spec.

Chester Furniture Cave
97a Christleton Rd, Boughton. Open 9.30-5.30. SIZE: Warehouse. *STOCK: Furniture.* PARK: Easy. TEL: 0244 314798.

Farmhouse Antiques
21-23 Christleton Rd, Boughton. (K Appleby) Est: 1973. Open 9-5. SIZE: Large. *STOCK: Farmhouse furniture, longcase clocks, Staffordshire pottery, country bygones, mechanical music.* LOC: 1 mile from City centre on A41. PARK: Easy. TEL: 0244 322478; evenings - 0244 318391. SER: Export. VAT: Stan/Spec.

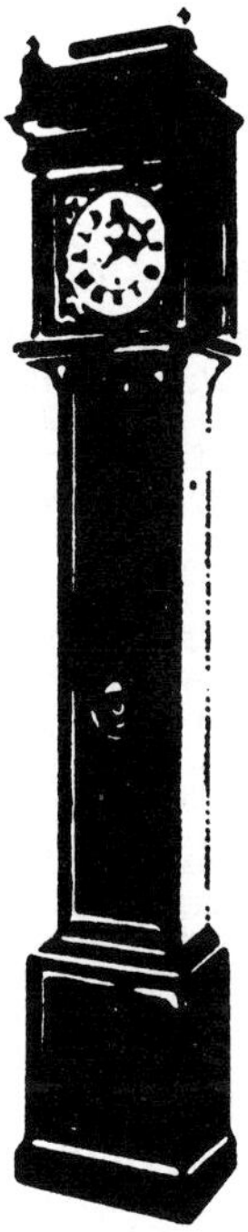

Chester continued

Filkins Antiques

77 Watergate Row. (P. and B Le Rougetel) Est: 1978. Open 10-4.45, Wed. 10-1. SIZE: Medium. *STOCK: English furniture, 1750-1930; lace and linen, clocks, silver and plate, jewellery, copper and brass, china and glass; woodworking hand tools and related literature.* LOC: Town centre. PARK: Nearby. TEL: 0244 318782; home - 0244 343259.

Grosvenor Antiques of Chester

22 Watergate St. (Mrs P.M Jacobi) Est: 1971. Open 9.30-5.30. SIZE: Medium. *STOCK: Jewellery, Georgian and Victorian; furniture, china, porcelain, shipping goods, dolls, silver, Oriental carpets and rugs.* Not Stocked: Stamps, coins. PARK: Easy. TEL: 0244 315201. SER: Valuations; restorations; repairs (jewellery). VAT: Stan/Spec.

Guildhall Fair

Watergate St. Open Thurs. 10-4. SIZE: 20 dealers. *STOCK: General antiques.*

Erica and Hugo Harper

27 Watergate Row. Est: 1964. Open 10-5. CL: Wed. p.m. SIZE: Large. *STOCK: Victoriana, 25p-£300; Victorian and Edwardian copper, glass, china.* Not Stocked: Jewellery, militaria, coins, fine furniture. TEL: 0244 323004; home - 0244 321880.

J. Alan Hulme

The Antique Map and Old Print Gallery, 54 Lower Bridge St. Open 10-5. CL: Wed. *STOCK: Maps, 16th-19th C; prints 18th-19th C.* TEL: 0244 344006/336472.

Jamandic Ltd

22 Bridge St Row. Est: 1975. Open 9.30-5, Sat. 10-1. CL: Sun., except by appointment. SIZE: Medium. *STOCK: Decorative furniture, porcelain, pictures and prints.* TEL: 0244 312822. SER: Interior design; export. VAT: Stan/Spec.

Kayes of Chester

9 St. Michaels Row. (A.M Austin-Kaye and N.J Kaye) NAG. Est: 1948. Open 9-5.30. SIZE: Medium. *STOCK: Diamond rings and jewellery, 1850-1950, £20-£15,000; silver and plate, 1700-1930, £20-£8,000; small objects, oils, watercolours and ceramics, 19th to early 20th C, £50-£1,000.* PARK: Nearby. TEL: 0244 327149. SER: Valuations; restorations (silver, jewellery and plate); buys at auction. VAT: Stan/Spec.

Lowe and Sons

11 Bridge St Row. Est: 1770. *STOCK: Jewellery and silver, Georgian, Victorian and Edwardian; unusual collectors' items, coins and medals.* TEL: 0244 325850. VAT: Stan/Spec.

Chester continued

Made of Honour

11 City Walls. (E Jones) Open 10-5. *STOCK: General antiques, Staffordshire figures, British ceramics, books.* LOC: Next to Eastgate clock, wall level. TEL: 0244 314208.

Melody's Antique Galleries LAPADA

30-32 City Rd. (M Melody) Est: 1977. Open 10-5.30 or by appointment. SIZE: Large. *STOCK: 17th-19th C oak, mahogany, walnut and pine furniture; books, art deco items, lighting, silver and plate.* LOC: 400yds. from station. TEL: 0244 328968. SER: Courier; container packing. VAT: Stan/Spec.

Richard A Nicholson

25 Watergate St. Est: 1961. Open 9.30-1 and 2.15-5. SIZE: Large. *STOCK: Maps, 1540-1840, £1-£1,000; prints, 1650-1890, £1-£300; atlases, £100-£15,000; watercolours and drawings, £4-£200.* LOC: Town centre 100yds. from The Cross. PARK: 200yds. at bottom of street behind church. TEL: 0244 326818; home - 0244 336004. SER: Illustrated monthly catalogue issued. VAT: Stan/Spec.

Christopher Pugh Antiques LAPADA

29 Watergate St. Est: 1964. Open 10-5 or by appointment. SIZE: Large. *STOCK: Furniture, 17th to early 19th C; English pottery, porcelain, glass, watercolours, paintings, metalware, decorative items.* LOC: Town centre. PARK: Nearby. TEL: 0244 314137; home - 0492 348162. SER: Valuations; buys at auction. VAT: Stan/Spec.

Richmond Galleries

1st Floor, Watergate Buildings, New Crane St. (Mrs M Armitage) Est: 1970. Open 10-5.30. SIZE: Large. *STOCK: Stripped pine, decorative items.* LOC: Direction of Sealand Rd. PARK: Own. TEL: 0244 317602; home - 0244 324285.

St .Peters Fine Art Gallery Ltd

St. Peters Churchyard, Northgate St. (D Hellon) Est: 1984. Open 10-5. SIZE: Medium. *STOCK: Watercolours and oil paintings, 19th to early 20th C, £500-£20,000.* LOC: In city centre off Northgate St. PARK: Nearby. TEL: 0244 345500. VAT: Spec.

Bernard Walsh Ltd

11 St. Michaels Row. Est: 1950. Open 9-5. SIZE: Large. *STOCK: Silver, bijouterie, objets d'art, porcelain, glass, jewellery.* PARK: Easy. TEL: 0244 326032.

Watergate Antiques

56 Watergate St. (A Shindler) Est: 1968. Open 9.30-5.30. SIZE: Medium. *STOCK: Silver and plate, porcelain and pottery, furniture, militaria, jewellery.* LOC: From Liverpool first set of traffic lights past Waterfall Roundabout, turn left. PARK: At rear. TEL: 0244 344516; fax - 0244 320350. VAT: Stan.

Chester continued

Joyce and Rod Whitehead
at Made of Honour, 11 City Walls. Open 10-5. *STOCK: Fine art, woolworks, samplers, tapestries, beadwork, textiles and decorative items.* TEL: 0244 314208.

CONGLETON

W Buckley Antiques Exports
35 Chelford Rd. Open 7 days by appointment. *STOCK: Mainly shipping and Victorian furniture.* TEL: 0260 275299. SER: Shipping.

Congleton Antiques
2 Cross St. (D Shaw) Open 9.30-4.30. CL: Wed. *STOCK: Furniture and general antiques.* TEL: 0260 275331.

Pine Too
8/10 Rood Hill. (Mrs J.P Tryon) Open 9-5. *STOCK: Pine.* LOC: Just off A34. PARK: Nearby. TEL: 0260 279228.

DAVENHAM, Nr. Northwich

Davenham Antique Centre
461 London Rd. Est: 1985. Open 10-5. CL: Wed. SIZE: Several dealers. *STOCK: General antiques including small furniture, country items, plated ware, china, brass and copper.* LOC: A533. TEL: 0606 44350.

Magpie Antiques
4 Church St. (Mrs E Bowerman) Est: 1979. Open 11-5, Fri. 2-5. CL: Wed. SIZE: Small. *STOCK: General antiques including country items, pictures, bric-a-brac, curios and small furniture, £2-£150.* LOC: 1/4 mile off Northwich by-pass, left into Church St. PARK: Easy. TEL: Home - 0829 260360.

DISLEY

Crescent Antiques
7 Buxton Rd. (J.P Cooper) Est: 1972. Open 11.30-6.30, Sun. 1.30-6.30. CL: Wed. SIZE: Small. *STOCK: General antiques, including furniture, pottery, silver, 19th C, £20-£500.* PARK: Opposite Co-op. TEL: 0663 65677.

Dystelegh Antiques
1 Buxton Rd. Open 10-5, Sat. 11-5, Sun. 12-5. *STOCK: English and continental furniture, clocks, porcelain, bronzes, objets d'art.* TEL: 0663 66162.

Mill Farm Antiques
50 Market St. (F.E Berry) Est: 1968. Open every day. SIZE: Medium. *STOCK: Pianos, clocks, shipping goods, general antiques, £50-£5,000.* LOC: A6 7 miles south of Stockport. PARK: Easy. TEL: 0663 764045 (24hrs.). SER: Valuations; restorations (clocks, watches, barometers, music boxes). VAT: Stan/Spec.

FARNDON, Nr. Chester

Stephen Meadowcroft Antiques
High St. Open by appointment. *STOCK: Period furniture and decorative objects.* LOC: Take the B5130 from Chester. PARK: Easy. TEL: 0829 270377/0860 267591. SER: Valuations; buys at auction. VAT: Stan/Spec.

FRODSHAM

Lothian Antiques
37 High St. (G Lothian) Open 10-5, Wed. 10-1. CL: Mon. *STOCK: General antiques, mainly furniture.* TEL: 0928 39366.

HAZEL GROVE

Gay's (Hazel Grove) Antiques Ltd LAPADA
34 London Rd. (G.A Yeo) Est: 1956. Open 9-1 and 2-5.30. CL: Sat. SIZE: Large. *STOCK: 18th-19th C furniture.* LOC: On A6. PARK: Easy. TEL: 061 483 5532. VAT: Stan/Spec. *Trade only.*

Highland Antiques
292 London Rd. (E Todd) Est: 1970. SIZE: Medium. *STOCK: Chinese and Japanese pottery, porcelain and furniture, 18th-19th C, to £100,000; silver and plate.* LOC: A6. PARK: Easy. TEL: 061 483 4037. SER: Valuations; restorations; buys at auction. FAIRS: Manchester. VAT: Stan/Spec.

HYDE

Peter Bunting Antiques
238 Higham Lane, Werneth Low, and 274 Stockport Rd., Gee Cross. Est: 1980. Open Wed., Thurs., Fri., Sat. (prior telephone call advisable) and by appointment. SIZE: Medium. *STOCK: Oak, country furniture and decorative items, 17th-18th C.* LOC: Off A560 between Hyde and Romily just outside Gee Cross. PARK: Opposite. TEL: 061 368 5544; home - same. SER: Valuations; restorations. VAT: Stan/Spec.

Armchair. Asian hardwood with caning. Circa 1820. After 1815, furniture styles for the West, as interpreted by Cantonese cabinetmakers, followed the English Regency style, as with this simple but elegant example which is illustrated in Carl Crossman's ***The Decorative Arts of the China Trade,*** published in 1991 by the **Antique Collectors' Club.** £45.00.

KNUTSFORD

David Bedale
5-7 Minshull St. Est: 1977. SIZE: Small. *STOCK: 17th to early 19th C furniture, metalware, objects.* PARK: 25yds. TEL: 0565 653621. VAT: Stan/Spec.

Cranford Clocks
1st Floor, 12 Princess St. (Mr and Mrs M.E Uppink) Est: 1988. Open 10-5 or by appointment. CL: Mon. all day, Wed. p.m. SIZE: Small. *STOCK: Clocks, 1700-1920, £100-£5,000.* LOC: Off M6, junction 19. PARK: Nearby. TEL: 0565 652284; home - 0565 633331. SER: Valuations; restorations (clock movements).

Cranford Galleries
10 King St. (M.R Bentleyf) Est: 1964. Open 9.30-5.30. CL: Wed. SIZE: Small. *STOCK: Pictures, prints and Victoriana.* Not Stocked: Glass. LOC: Main St. PARK: Easy. TEL: 0565 633646. SER: Framing and mounting. VAT: Stan

Glynn Interiors
92 King St. Est: 1963. Open 9-1 and 2-5. CL: Wed. SIZE: Large. *STOCK: Furniture, 1750-1900, £50-£2,000; Victorian chairs, £50-£650.* Not Stocked: Porcelain. LOC: Ten mins. drive

Glynn Interiors continued

after leaving M6 at Exit 19. PARK: Own. TEL: 0565 634418. SER: Restorations (reupholstery) and cabinet repairs. VAT: Stan/Spec.

Knutsford Gallery Antiques
First Floor, 12 Princess St. Open 10-5. CL: Mon., Tues. and Wed. *STOCK: Furniture, paintings, silver, china.* TEL: 0565 652778.

Lion Gallery and Bookshop
15a Minshull St. (R.P Hepner) GMC. Est: 1964. Open Fri. 10.30-4.30, Sat. 10-4.30. *STOCK: Antiquarian maps, prints and books; watercolours, oils; all 16th-20th C; O.S. maps and early directories.* LOC: King St. 3 mins. M6. PARK: Nearby. TEL: 0565 652915. SER: Restorations; binding; cleaning; framing; mounting. VAT: Stan.

Twenty-Two Antiques
22 King St. (T C Batley) Open 10-5, Sun. 2-4.30. CL: Mon. and Wed. *STOCK: Small furniture and small general antiques, £15-£500.* TEL: 0565 633655.

Michael Wisehall BADA
7 Minshull St. Est: 1967. Open by appointment only. SIZE: Medium. *STOCK: Furniture, 18th C, 19th C and decorative; metalware, decorative and architectural items, 18th-19th C.* PARK: 25yds. TEL: 0565 634901. VAT: Stan/Spec.

LITTLETON, Nr. Chester

John Titchner and Sons
Littleton Old Hall, Little Heath Rd. Open 9-5. CL: Sat. *STOCK: Furniture, 18th-19th C.* TEL: 0244 336986.

LOWER KINNERTON, Nr. Chester

Brian Edwards Antique Exports
Gell Farm. (B.H Edwards) Usually open, prior telephone call preferred. SIZE: Warehouse. *STOCK: Georgian, Victorian and Edwardian furniture and some smalls.* LOC: 4 1/2 miles from Chester. TEL: 0244 660240. SER: Container packing; courier. VAT: Stan/Spec. *Trade Only.*

MACCLESFIELD

G Bagshaw Antiques
74 Mill Lane. Est: 1971. Open 10-5.30. CL: Wed. SIZE: Small. *STOCK: General antiques.* Not Stocked: On Leek Rd. PARK: Easy. TEL: 0625 421642; home - 0625 572000. SER: Valuations; restorations (painted clock dials, pottery, porcelain).

Philip Brooks
6 West Bank Rd, Upton. Est: 1983. Open by appointment. SIZE: Small. *STOCK: Watercolours, oil paintings and prints, 1830-1950, £30-£1,000.* LOC: Off Prestbury Rd., by the Conservative Club. PARK: Easy. TEL: 0625 426275; home - same. SER: Valuations; restorations (cleaning and repairs); buys at auction (watercolours, oils and prints). FAIRS: NEC, Birmingham; Buxton; Hopetown House, Edinburgh; Houghton Tower, Preston; Welbeck Abbey, Notts.

Cheshire Antiques
88-90 Chestergate. (D Knight) Open 10-5.30. CL: Sat. SIZE: Medium. *STOCK: Clocks, from 1650, £500-£1,500; furniture, 18th-19th C, £10-£1,000; porcelain, pottery, glass, all periods.* LOC: From A537, shop is on right in one-way system 100yds. from traffic lights. TEL: 0625 423268. SER: Valuations; restorations (porcelain, clocks). VAT: Stan/Spec.

Robert Copperfield
5-7 Chester Rd. Est: 1960. Open 10-6, or by appointment. *STOCK: 17th-19th C furniture, Oriental rugs, carpets, metalware, textiles, paintings, works of art, ethnographia.* TEL: 0625 511233. VAT: Stan/Spec.

Gatehouse Antiques
72 Chestergate. (W.H Livesley) Est: 1973. Open 9-1 and 2-5. CL: Sun. except by appointment and Wed. p.m. *STOCK: Small furniture, silver and plate, glass, brass, copper, pewter, jewellery, 1650-1880.* PARK: At rear. TEL: 0625 426476; home - 0625 612841. VAT: Spec.

Macclesfield continued

Hidden Gem
3 Chester Rd. (Mrs P Tilley) Usually open 9-5, or by appointment. SIZE: Small. *STOCK: Victorian paintings and general antiques.* TEL: 0625 433884; home - 0625 828348.

Hills Antiques
Indoor Market, Grosvenor Centre. (D Hill) Est: 1968. Open 9.30-5.30. CL: Mon. *STOCK: Small furniture, jewellery, collectors' items, stamps, coins, postcards.* LOC: Town Centre. PARK: Easy. TEL: 0625 420777/420467.

Macclesfield Antiques
83/85 Chestergate. (P Bolton) Open 9.30-5.30 or by appointment. SIZE: Medium. *STOCK: 19th C mahogany, walnut and rosewood, including dining room furniture; silver, jewellery, decorative paintings, some collectables.* PARK: At rear. TEL: 0625 433033; home - 0625 572281. VAT: Stan/Spec.

D.J Massey and Son
47 Chestergate. Est: 1900. Open 9-5.30, Wed. 9-1. *STOCK: Jewellery, gold and diamonds, all periods.*

Pictures (Chris Crowe Fine Art)
14 Jordangate. Open Thurs. and Fri. 11-6, Sat. 10-5 or by appointment. *STOCK: British watercolours, 1750-1970, £50-£3,000.* PARK: Multi-storey opposite. TEL: 0625 619203; home - 0625 427240. SER: Valuations; restorations. VAT: Spec.

MALPAS

Stewart Evans
Church St. Est: 1955. Always open. *STOCK: General antiques; furniture to 1835.* TEL: 0948 860214. SER: Hand-made furniture from old timber; repairs. VAT: Stan/Spec. *Trade Only.*

MARPLE

J Milner Antiques
Lower Fold, Marple Bridge. Open 9.30-6, Sun. by appointment. SIZE: Small. *STOCK: Furniture, pottery, pictures and decorative smalls.* LOC: 1 mile from town centre. PARK: Easy. TEL: 061 426 0159 or 0860 611622. SER: Valuations. VAT: Stan/Spec.

Oldfield Cottage Antiques
Town St, Marple Bridge. (Mrs R Potts) Open daily including sun. CL: Mon. and Wed. *STOCK: Pine furniture and kitchens, blue and white.* TEL: 061 427 2751.

MOBBERLEY

English Country Furnishings
95 Town Lane. (Mr and Mrs K Wheatley) Open 11-6 including Sun. CL: Mon. and Wed. *STOCK: Pine and country furniture; general antiques.* PARK: Easy. TEL: 056 587 2225.

NANTWICH

Tim Armitage
99 Welsh Row. (T.J Armitage) Est: 1967. Open Thurs., Fri. and Sat. 10.30-5. SIZE: Small. *STOCK: Tin toys, £25-£750; advertising items, £5-£350; both 19th-20th C; general antiques, 18th-19th C.* LOC: Main road into town from Chester. PARK: Easy. TEL: 0270 626608; home - same. SER: Valuations; buys at auction (toys and models).

Bridge House Antiques
The Old Police Station, Welsh Row. (L. and V Tait) Est: 1950. Open 10-5.30. CL: Wed. p.m. SIZE: Large. *STOCK: Furniture, 19th C, £50-£1,000; china and glass, Victorian, £5-£100; clocks, £100-£500.* Not Stocked: Jewellery. PARK: Easy. TEL: 0270 624035. SER: Valuations.

Chapel Antiques
47 Hospital St. (Miss D.J Atkin) Est: 1983. Open 9.30-5.30, Wed. 9.30-1, or by appointment. CL: Mon. SIZE: Medium. *STOCK: Oak, mahogany and pine furniture, Georgian and Victorian, £100-£3,000; longcase clocks, pre-1830, £1,000-£3,000; copper, brass, silver, glass, porcelain, pottery and small items, 19th C, £10-£500.* LOC: Enter town via Pillory St., turn right into Hospital St. PARK: Easy. TEL: 0270 629508; home - 0270 811437. SER: Valuations; restorations (furniture, clocks).

Stancie Cutler Antique and Collectors Fairs
Nantwich Civic Hall. Est: 1975. Open 1st Thurs. of each month, 12-9, trade from 10 a.m. Bank Holidays and New Year's Day 10-6, trade from 7.30 a.m. SIZE: 75 stands. *STOCK: A wide variety of antiques from large furniture to thimbles, mostly pre-1940. Also 3rd Sat. of each month antique collectors' market, 9-4, trade from 8. There are 70 stands.* PARK: Easy. TEL: Home - 0270 624288 (ansaphone).

Farthings Antiques
50 Hospital St. (P. and A Jones) Est: 1964. Open 9-5.30. CL: Wed. p.m. *STOCK: Furniture, glass, porcelain, silver.* TEL: 0270 625117. VAT: Stan/Spec.

Roderick Gibson LAPADA
2 Chapel Court, Hospital St. Open 9-5. *STOCK: Furniture and smalls.* TEL: 0270 625301. VAT: Stan/Spec.

Nantwich continued

Lions and Unicorns
Kiltearn House, 33 Hospital St. (J Pearson) Open by appointment. SIZE: Small. *STOCK: Commemoratives, pottery, porcelain, £5-£200; Staffordshire, £50-£150; all from early 19th C.* LOC: Town centre, near church. PARK: Easy. TEL: 0270 628892/625678. SER: Restorations (pottery, porcelain, oils and watercolours); re-rushing; buys at auction (commemoratives, Staffordshire, glass and small furniture); repairs (jewellery).

Love Lane Antiques
Love Lane. (M Simon) Open 10-5. CL: Wed. SIZE: Small. *STOCK: General antiques, 19th-20th C, £5-£500.* LOC: Two minutes walk from town square. PARK: Nearby. TEL: 0270 626239; home - 0270 68401

Nantwich Antique Centre
The Old Police Station, Welsh Row. Open 10-5.30. CL: Wed. p.m. SIZE; Six dealers.. *STOCK: General antiques.* PARK: Easy. TEL: 0270 624035.

Nantwich Art Deco and Decorative Arts
87 Welsh Row. (M.J Poole and P.M Savill) Est: 1987. Open 10-5, Tues. and Wed. by appointment. SIZE: Small. *STOCK: Art deco and decorative arts, pottery, china, 1930s lighting, cabinets, £5-£250.* PARK: Easy. TEL: 0270 624876; home - 811541. FAIRS: Loughborough Art Deco; Birmingham 'Wednesday' Rag Market Fair.

Pillory House
18 Pillory St. (D Roberts) Est: 1968. Open 9-5.30. CL: Wed. *STOCK: Hand-carved chimney pieces and oak.* TEL: 0270 623524.

Townwell House Antiques LAPADA
52 Welsh Row. (R Boyer) Open 9-6 and by appointment. SIZE: Large. *STOCK: Period furniture.* TEL: 0270 625953. VAT: Stan/Spec.

Wyche House Antiques LAPADA
50 Welsh Row. (J.A. and E.A Clewlow) Est: 1976. Open 9.30-4.30, Mon. 9.30-1 and 2-4.30. SIZE: Medium. *STOCK: Furniture, silver, china, cranberry glass, brass, copper, 18th-19th C, £25-£5,000.* TEL: 0270 627179. SER: Valuations; buys at auction. FAIRS: Buxton; N.E.C.. VAT: Stan/Spec.

NESTON

The Old Mill Gallery
Leighton Rd. (L Blackburne) Open 10-4.30. CL: Wed. *STOCK: 19th-20th C watercolours and oils; Oriental rugs, kelims and cushions.* TEL: 051 336 1630.

Neston continued

Vine House Antiques
Vine House, Parkgate Rd. (P. and M Prothero) Est: 1969. Open by appointment. SIZE: Medium. *STOCK: Small furniture, mainly 18th-19th C, £20-£400; silver, from late 18th C, £7.50-£500; glass, 18th-19th C, £1-£80; collectors' items.* Not Stocked: Clocks, paintings. LOC: Coming from Chester A540 to West Kirby, 8 miles from Chester turn left to Neston, 50yds. down Parkgate road from village centre. Queen Anne house on right-hand drive in. PARK: Easy. TEL: 051 336 2423. SER: Valuations; buys at auction.

NEWTOWN, Nr. Stockport

Regent House Antiques
8 Buxton Rd. Est: 1961. Open 9-5, Sat. 2-5. *STOCK: English furniture, clocks, Oriental porcelain, oil paintings, watercolours, general antiques.* LOC: A6, near Disley. PARK: Easy. TEL: 0663 742684.

NO MAN'S HEATH, Nr. Malpas

Marcus Moore Antiques
Holly Cottage, Chester Rd. (M.G.J. and M.P Moore) Est: 1980. Usually open but prior telephone call advisable. SIZE: Medium. *STOCK: Oak and country furniture, late 17th to*

Marcus Moore Antiques continued

18th C; Georgian mahogany furniture, 18th to early 19th C; all £50-£2,000; associated items. LOC: A41 Whitchurch/Chester road, opposite Wheatsheaf Inn. PARK: Easy. TEL: 094 885 500. SER: Restorations (furniture); French polishing; buys at auction. VAT: Stan/Spec.

PLUMLEY

Coppelia Antiques
Holford Lodge, Plumley Moor Rd. (V. and R Clements) Resident. Est: 1970. Open every day by appointment. SIZE: Medium. *STOCK: Over 120 clocks, mainly longcase and wall, £1,000-£12,000; Georgian mahogany tables, bureaux, desks, chests of drawers, wine tables, oak gateleg tables, lowboys, coffers, side tables; Victorian suites.* LOC: 4 miles junction 19 M6. PARK: Easy. TEL: 0565 722197. SER: Valuations; restorations (clocks). FAIRS: Kensington, Buxton. VAT: Spec.

POYNTON, Nr. Stockport

Harper Fine Paintings
"Overdale", Woodford Rd. (P.R Harper) Est: 1967. Open by appointment. SIZE: Large. *STOCK: Watercolours, £100-£35,000; oils including European, £250-£60,000; prints,*

FYNS KOMMUNALE
TELEFONSELSKAB

Fyns Kommunale black painted metal telephone with wind up bell. £110.

H.C. CHAPMAN AND SON, SCARBOROUGH
From a Saleroom Report published in the April 1991 issue of ***Antique Collecting.***

Harper Fine Paintings continued

British, £20-£1,000; all mainly 19th-20th C. LOC: From A523 centre of Poynton lights, turn into Chester Rd., over railway. After 1/4 mile turn right, 1st drive on left after railway bridge. PARK: Easy. TEL: 0625 879105; home - same. SER: Valuations; restorations; buys at auction (19th-20th C watercolours and oils). FAIRS: City of London, Barbican. VAT: Stan/Spec.

PRESTBURY, Nr Macclesfield

Prestbury Antiques
4 Swanwick House, The Village. (P Ginsberg) Open 10-5 seven days. *STOCK: Furniture, pictures, silver, glass, ceramics, decorative items and collectables, 18th-20th C.* TEL: 0625 827966. VAT: Stan/Spec.

PULFORD, Nr. Chester

E. and B Rushton
The Old Rectory. Open any time by appointment. *STOCK: Early lighting, porcelain, unusual items, lithophones.* LOC: On A483. TEL: 0244 570150. *Mainly Trade.*

REDDISH, Nr. Stockport

G.E Leigh and Son

Houldsworth Sq. (G.E. and J.E Leigh) CMBHI. Est: 1947. Open 9-5.30. CL: Wed. SIZE: Small. *STOCK: Jewellery, £10-£300; watches, £10-£500; clocks, £20-£1,000; all 19th-20th C.* LOC: From A6 take road to Reddish at Heaton Chapel traffic lights. Turn left in one mile immediately before traffic lights by Clock Tower on Houldsworth Sq. PARK: Easy. TEL: 061 432 2413. SER: Valuations; restorations. VAT: Spec.

RINGWAY, Nr. Altrincham

Cottage Antiques

Hasty Lane. (J. and J.M Gholam) Est: 1967. SIZE: Medium. *STOCK: Furniture, metalware, ceramics, glass, early 18th-mid 19th C.* Not Stocked: Jewellery, jade and ivory. LOC: Off junction 6, M56, off A538, very close to airport. PARK: Easy. TEL: 061 980 7961. SER: Valuations. VAT: Stan/Spec.

RUNCORN

B Braverman

58 High St. CL: Wed. *STOCK: General antiques.* TEL: 0928 572529. FAIRS: Liverpool.

STOCKPORT

Antique Furniture Warehouse

Units 3/4 Royal Oak Buildings, Cooper St. Open 9.30-5.30. SIZE: Large. *STOCK: Furniture, paintings, bronzes, clocks, shipping goods, art deco, arts and crafts furniture, pottery, porcelain and curios, decorative items, architectural, £5-£25,000.* LOC: 2 mins. off M56 towards town centre. PARK: Easy. TEL: 061 429 8590. VAT: Stan.

E.R Antiques Centre

122 Wellington St, off Wellington Rd. South. (E Warburton) Est: 1979. Open 12-5.30. SIZE: Medium. There are 6 dealers at this centre selling. *STOCK: Victorian and cut glass, perfume bottles, blue and white china, pottery, curios, jewellery, pictures, linen, £5-£200.* LOC: Turn into Edwards St. by the Town Hall, at 'T' junction turn left, shop 500yds. on left at bollards. PARK: Easy. TEL: 061 429 6646; home - 061 480 5598.

L Booth Antiques and Reproductions

137 Wellington Road North. Open 10-5. CL: Wed. *STOCK: Victorian and Edwardian furniture.* TEL: 061 431 7494; workshop - 0772 632439. SER: Restorations.

Stockport continued

Carl Bright Antiques

6 Portland Grove, Heaton Moor. Est: 1972. Open 9-1 and 2-5, Wed. 9-1, Sat. 9-5. SIZE: Medium. *STOCK: Furniture, pottery, glass and curios, 18th C, £5-£100.* LOC: Off Heaton Moor road near A6. PARK: Easy. TEL: 061 442 9334; home - 061 431 5685. SER: Restorations.

John and Nick Curbishley

262 Wellington Rd South. Open 9.30-5.30. SIZE: Large. *STOCK: Furniture, stripped pine, prints.* Not Stocked: Art nouveau. LOC: A6. From Manchester, shop on right on south side of Stockport. PARK: Own. TEL: 061 480 3406 or mobile - 0860 423947 or 0836 606899. VAT: Stan/Spec.

Curiosity

83 Moorland Rd, Woodsmoor. (L.E Thompson) Resident. Est: 1981. Open 10-5.30. CL: Wed. SIZE: Medium. *STOCK: Pine furniture including reproduction; pottery and china, Victorian and art deco; jewellery, linen.* LOC: From Stockport, take 1st right past Davenport Cinema, off A6 2nd left is Moorland Rd. PARK: Easy. TEL: 061 456 4022.

Flintlock Antiques

28 and 30 Bramhall Lane. (F Tomlinson and Son) Est: 1968. SIZE: Large. *STOCK: Furniture, clocks, pictures, scientific instruments.* TEL: 061 480 9973. VAT: Stan/Spec.

Grenville Street Bookshop

105 Grenville St, Edgeley. (J.A Heacock) Est: 1978. CL: Mon. *STOCK: Antiquarian, rare and scholarly books.* LOC: Off A6 down Greek St. to roundabout, take second left on to Mercian Way, Grenville St. is at the end on the right. PARK: Easy. TEL: 061 477 1909.

Hole in the Wall Antiques

370 Buxton Rd., Great Moor; warehouses - 1 Lancashire Hill, and Hadfield House, Lancashire Hill. (M. and A Ledger) Est: 1960. Open 9.30-7, Sun. by appointment. SIZE: Large. *STOCK: Furniture, 18th-20th C, smalls, £50-£1,500.* LOC: A6. PARK: Easy. TEL: 061 483 6603; warehouses - 061 477 3804/061 476 4013. SER: Valuations; restorations; buys at auction.

Imperial Antiques LAPADA

295 Buxton Rd, Great Moor. (A Todd) Est: 1972. Open 10-5.30, Sun. by appointment. SIZE: Large. *STOCK: Oriental antiques, English and continental furniture, porcelain, clocks and silver; Persian carpets.* LOC: A6 Buxton Rd., 1 1/2 miles south of town centre. TEL: 061 483 3322; home - 061 428 4152. SER: Buys at auction. VAT: Stan/Spec.

Stockport continued

Nostalgia Architectural Antiques
61 Shaw Heath. (D. and E Durrant) Est: 1975. Open 10-6, Sat. 10-5. CL: Mon. SIZE: Large. *STOCK: Fireplaces, £200-£15,000; bathroom fittings and architectural items, £50-£2,000; all 18th-19th C.* PARK: At rear. TEL: 061 477 7706. SER: Valuations. VAT: Stan/Spec.

Page Antiques
424 Buxton Rd, Great Moor. Open Mon.-Sat. SIZE: Large. *STOCK: Victorian and Georgian furniture, brass, copper, silver, plate, stripped pine.* LOC: A6. TEL: 061 483 9202; home - 061 427 2412. VAT: Stan/Spec.

Zippy Antiques
Units 2 and 3 Royal Oak Building, Cooper St. (M Golding) Est: 1980. Open 9-6, Sun. by appointment. SIZE: Large and warehouse. *STOCK: English ceramics and glass, late 18th C to 1950, £50-£500; furniture, Georgian-1950's, particularly inlaid mahogany; arts and crafts items, £10-£5,000.* PARK: Easy. TEL: 061 477 7953; home - same. SER: Valuations. VAT: Stan.

STOCKTON HEATH, Nr. Warrington

Victoriana Antiques
85a Walton Rd. (Mrs J Taylor) Est: 1976. Open 1-5 or by appointment. CL: Mon. and Thurs. SIZE: Small. *STOCK: Furnishings, to 1930, £50-£1,600; metalware and fireside furniture, to 1910, £30-£800; antique and decorative lighting, to 1930, £15-£500.* LOC: A56 towards Chester, 400yds. from village centre. PARK: Own. TEL: 0925 63263; home - 0925 61035. SER: Valuations; restorations (furniture, metalware). FAIRS: Cumberland Hotel and Deanwater Hotel, Winslow (monthly).

Village Antiques
30 Walton Rd. (Mrs C Kenney) Open 10.30-1 and 2-5. CL: Mon. and Thurs. *STOCK: General antiques especially collectable items.* PARK: Easy. TEL: 0925 68010.

STRETTON, Nr.Warrington

Antiques Etc.
Shepcroft House, London Rd. (Mr and Mrs M.E Clare) Est: 1978. Resident, usually available. SIZE: Medium. *STOCK: Furniture, pine, barometers, clocks, instruments and items of interest, £5-£2,000.* LOC: A49, towards Warrington, through Stretton traffic lights, next turning on left. PARK: Easy. TEL: 092 573 431/0836 570663.

TARPORLEY

Brenda Arden Antiques LAPADA
67 High St. Open by appointment. *STOCK: 18th-19th C oak and mahogany furniture and metalware.* TEL: 0829 733026.

TILSTON, NR. MALPAS

Well House Antiques
The Well House. (S French-Greenslade) Est: 1968. Open by appointment only. SIZE: Small. *STOCK: Collectors' items, china, glass, silver.* LOC: From Whitchurch on A41, take B5395 signposted Malpas. PARK: Easy. TEL: 0892 205332.

WARRINGTON

The Rocking Chair Antiques
Unit 3, St. Peter's Way. (N., M. and J Barratt) Est: 1971. Open 9-5.30. SIZE: Large. *STOCK: Furniture and bric-a-brac, all periods.* LOC: Off Orford Lane. PARK: Easy. TEL: 0925 52409. SER: Valuations; shipping, packing. VAT: Stan.

WHITEGATE, Nr. Northwich

The Antiques Shop
Cinder Hill. (T.H. and B.A Rogerson) Est: 1979. Open 9.30-6 including Sun., Mon. 2-6. CL: Thurs. SIZE: Small. *STOCK: Pottery, porcelain, general antiques, jewellery, silver and plate, £5-£500; furniture, clocks, £100-£2,000; all 18th-19th C; paintings, watercolours, prints, 19th C, £25-£1,000.* LOC: 1 1/2 miles from A556 (Northwich by-pass) near village post office. PARK: Easy. TEL: 0606 882215; home - same.

WILMSLOW

Peter Bosson Antiques
10B Swan St. Est: 1965. Open 10-1 and 2-5.30, or by appointment. CL: Mon. and Wed. SIZE: Small. *STOCK: Clocks, 1675-1900, £5-£2,000; barometers, unusual items.* Not Stocked: Porcelain, silver. LOC: On A34. PARK: 50yds. away. TEL: 0625 525250; home - 0625 527857. SER: Restorations (repair of clocks); buys at auction. VAT: Stan/Spec.

Knutsford Road Antiques
48 Knutsford Rd. (F.G. and A.P Casey) Est: 1969. Open 10.30-1 and 2.30-5. CL: Wed. p.m. and Mon. SIZE: Small. *STOCK: Furniture, £25-£1,000; pottery and porcelain, £5-£200; unsual collectors' items, from £5; small silver, jewellery, glass and metalware.* LOC: B5086. PARK: Easy. TEL: 0625 531829; home - 0625 526043.

Cleveland

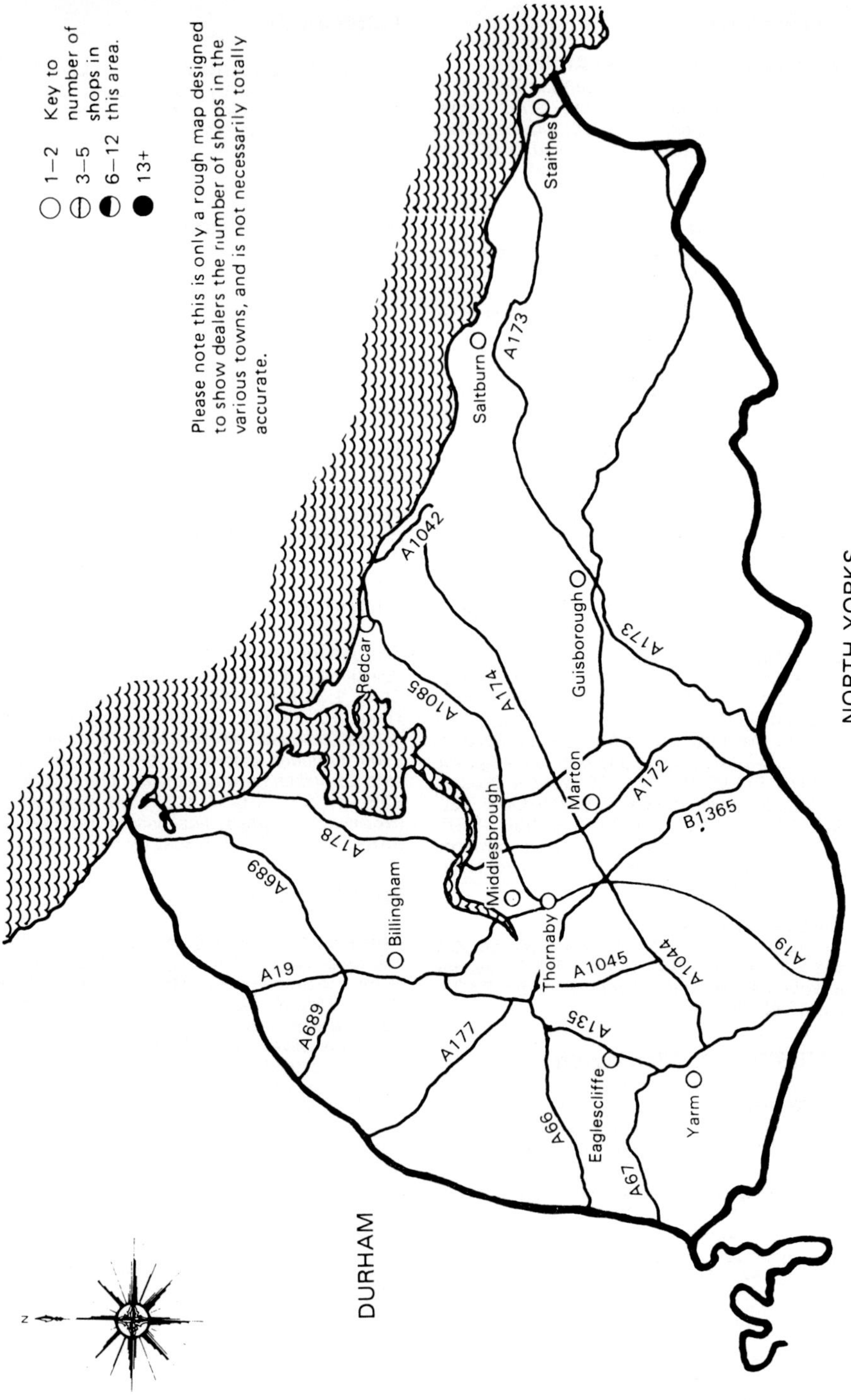
○ 1–2
⊖ 3–5
◐ 6–12
● 13+
Key to number of shops in this area.
Please note this is only a rough map designed to show dealers the number of shops in the various towns, and is not necessarily totally accurate.
Staithes
Saltburn
A173
A1042
Redcar
Guisborough
A173
A1085
A174
NORTH YORKS
Marton
A172
Middlesbrough
B1365
A178
A689
Billingham
Thornaby
A19
A1045
A1044
A19
A689
A177
A135
Eaglescliffe
Yarm
A66
A67
DURHAM
N

BILLINGHAM

Margaret Bedi Antiques LAPADA
5 Station Rd. Est: 1976. Open by appointment. *STOCK: Mainly English period furniture, 1720-1920; oils and watercolours, 19th and 20th C.* LOC: 300yds. off A19, by village green. PARK: Easy. TEL: 0642 607296. VAT: Stan/Spec.

EAGLESCLIFFE, Nr. Stockton-on-Tees

T.B. and R Jordan (Fine Paintings) LAPADA
Aslak, Aislaby. Est: 1974. Open by appointment. *STOCK: Oil paintings and watercolours, 19th-20th C, £200-£3,000.* LOC: Village centre. PARK: Easy. TEL: 0642 782599. SER: Framing. VAT: Spec.

GUISBOROUGH

Atrium Antiques
12 Chaloner St. (W.L. and M.G Richardson) Est: 1967. Open 10-1 and 2-5. CL: Sun., Mon. and Wed., except by appointment. *STOCK: Furniture, silver, pottery, jewellery, clocks, general items.* PARK: Easy. TEL: 0287 632777 anytime.

MARTON, Nr. Middlesbrough

E. and N.R Charlton Fine Art and Porcelain LAPADA
69 Cambridge Ave. Resident. Open by appointment. *STOCK: Fine porcelain, 18th-19th C; Victorian watercolours and paintings; small Regency furniture.* TEL: 0642 319642.

MIDDLESBROUGH

Bradley's Antiques and Jewellery
327 Linthorpe. (P Bradley) Open 10-5. *STOCK: Victorian and shipping items.* TEL: 0642 850518.

Polyera Antiques LAPADA
82 The Avenue, Linthorpe. (M. and A Moor) Est: 1974. Open by appointment. SIZE: Medium. *STOCK: Furniture, clocks, shipping goods, small items.* Not Stocked: Coins, stamps, firearms. LOC: Close to Linthorpe Little Theatre. PARK: Easy. TEL: 0642 824677. VAT: Stan.

REDCAR

Redcar Antiques
4/4a Park Ave. (N.J Bell) Est: 1962. Open 10-4.30, Sat. 10-1, other times by appointment. CL: Wed. SIZE: Small. *STOCK: Ceramics, £10-£300; small and period furniture, clocks, £50-£1,200, all 18th-20th C; paintings and prints, Victorian to date, £20-£300.* LOC: Opposite

Redcar Antiques continued

Zetland Park. PARK: Easy. TEL: 0642 472174; home - 0642 484950. SER: Valuations; buys at auction (as stock). FAIRS: Local. VAT: Stan.

SALTBURN

Endeavour Antiques
The Hollies, Victoria Terrace. (J MacAuliffe) Est: 1969. Open by appointment only. SIZE: Small. *STOCK: General and interesting antiques, especially 18th-19th C pottery and porcelain; Victorian and Edwardian jewellery.* TEL: 0287 623557. VAT: Stan/Spec.

Tessa's Antiques
24 Milton St. (Mrs E Herbert) Open 10-5. CL: Thurs. *STOCK: Jewellery, Georgian to secondhand; furniture, Georgian to Edwardian; porcelain and bric-a-brac.* TEL: 0287 624810; home - 0287 622595.

STAITHES, Nr. Whitby

The Mariners Antiques
High St. Est: 1967. Open July and August daily. Otherwise open Easter-September 30th Sat. and Sun. only 10-6. SIZE: Small. *STOCK: General antiques, 18th-19th C, £1-£100; oil lamps, £10-£100; jewellery, £2-£200; both 19th to early 20th C.* Not Stocked: Coins and firearms. PARK: Easy. TEL: 0947 840565; home - 0642 818377.

THORNABY, Nr. Stockton-on-Tees

Alan Ramsey Antiques LAPADA
4a Thornaby Pl. Est: 1973. Open 10-3, Sat. and Sun. by appointment. CL: Mon. and Wed. SIZE: Warehouse. *STOCK: Victorian and Edwardian shipping goods, including clocks, ornaments, brass, copperware and pine furniture.* LOC: Follow signs for Stockton, turn left immediately before Stockton bridge. PARK: Easy. TEL: 0642 603181; home - 0642 711311. VAT: Stan. *Trade Only.*

YARM

Ruby Snowden Antiques
20 High St. (R.H Snowden) Est: 1977. Open 9-5.30, Wed. 9-5, Sun. by appointment. SIZE: Medium. *STOCK: Furniture, 1700-1930s, £50-£2,000; porcelain and Staffordshire, £5-£200; jewellery, silver, glass, copper and brass.* LOC: Opposite library. PARK: Easy. TEL: 0642 785363; home - 0642 590814. SER: Valuations. VAT: Stan/Spec.

Cornwall

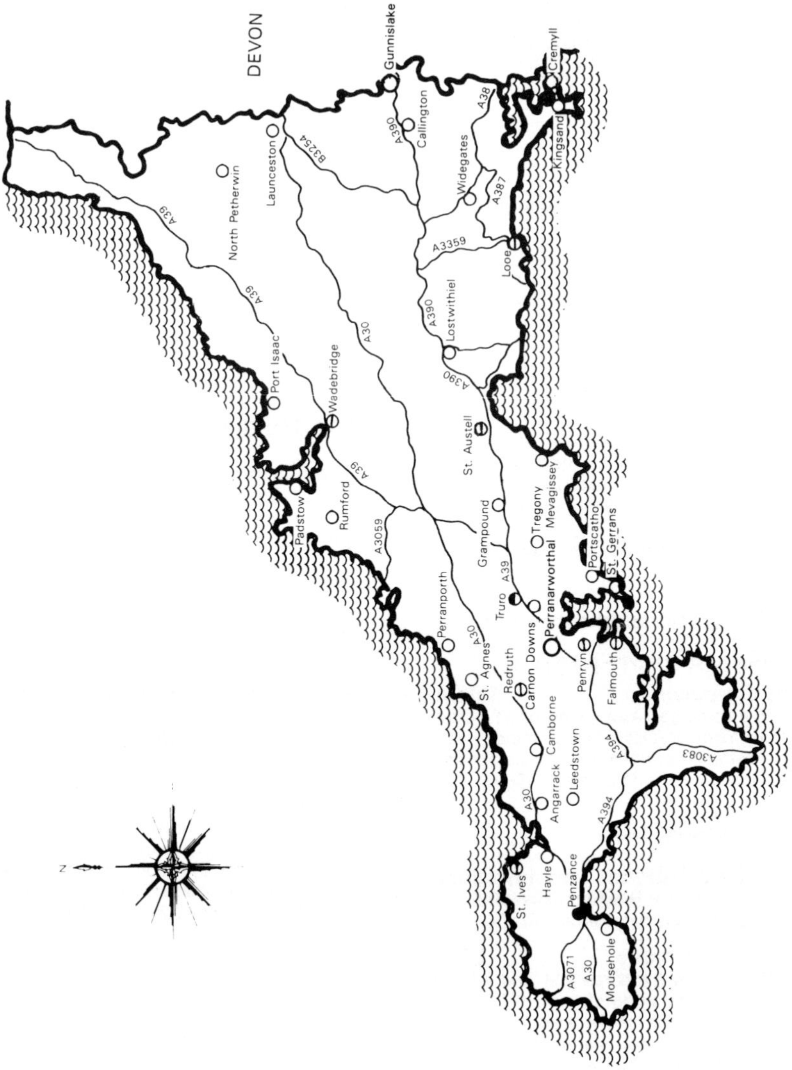

DEVON
Gunnislake
Cremyll
Callington
A390
A38
Launceston
B3254
Widegates
Kingsand
North Petherwin
A387
A39
A3359
Looe
Lostwithiel
A390
A30
Port Isaac
Wadebridge
St. Austell
Padstow
Rumford
A3059
Grampound
Tregony
Mevagissey
Portscatho
St. Gerrans
Perranarworthal
Truro
Perranporth
St. Agnes
Redruth
Carnon Downs
Penryn
Falmouth
Camborne
Leedstown
Angarrack
A394
A3083
St. Ives
Hayle
Penzance
Mousehole
A3071
N

○ 1–2
⊖ 3–5
◒ 6–12
● 13+

Key to number of shops in this area.

Please note this is only a rough map designed to show dealers the number of shops in the various towns, and is not necessarily totally accurate.

ANGARRACK, Nr. Hayle

Paul Jennings Antiques
Millbrook House. Est: 1974. Open by appointment. SIZE: Small. *STOCK: Clocks, furniture, £100-£3,000.* LOC: 1/2 mile from A30. TEL: 0736 754065. VAT: Stan/Spec. *Trade Only.*

CALLINGTON

Chattels
6 Saltash Rd. (P Lightbody) Est: 1968. Open 9.30-5.30, Sat. 9-1. CL: Sun., except by appointment to the Trade. Ring door bell when closed. SIZE: Medium. *STOCK: General antiques and bric-a-brac.* LOC: A388 crossroads A390 (Tavistock-Liskeard; Saltash-Launceston). PARK: 300yds. TEL: 0579 83184.

CAMBORNE

Grate Expectations
West Charles St. (M Swift) Open 9-5 or by appointment. *STOCK: Fireplaces and surrounds.* LOC: 4th turning on left on Helston road out of Camborne. PARK: Own. TEL: 0209 719898; home - 0736 850505.

Victoria Gallery
28 Cross St. (J.P Maker) Open 10-5.30. *STOCK: Books, pictures, general antiques, furniture, silver and jewellery.* TEL: 0209 719268.

CARNON DOWNS, Nr. Truro

Pluvers Folly Antiques
Carnoncrease. (M. and W Bates) Est: 1981. Open 10-5, including Sun. CL: Mon. and Tues. SIZE: Medium. *STOCK: Small furniture, £500-£1,000; china, glass, silver.* LOC: Off A39. PARK: Easy. TEL: 0872 862745; home - same. SER: Valuations.

CREMYLL

Cremyll Antiques
The Cottage, Cremyll Beach, Torpoint. *STOCK: Nautical items, small items, jewellery.* TEL: 0752 822934. SER: Repairs (barometers, barographs, watches, clocks, jewellery).

FALMOUTH

E Cunningham Antiques
5 Webber St. Open 10.30-5.30. *STOCK: General antiques.* TEL: 0326 313207.

Falmouth continued

High Street Antiques and Decor
19 High St. (Cdr R Gealer) Open 10.30-1 and 2-5. SIZE: Large. *STOCK: Maritime antiques, scientific instruments, brass and copper ware, 18th-20th C.* LOC: From centre of Falmouth (The Moor), turn up High St. - 3 mins. walk. PARK: Nearby. TEL: 0326 319105; home - 0326 317739.

John Maggs
54 Church St. (C.C Nunn) Est: 1900. Open 10-1 and 2.15-5. CL: Sat. p.m. and Wed. SIZE: Medium. *STOCK: Antiquarian prints and maps, all periods to 1850.* Not Stocked: Reproductions. LOC: Main street. PARK: At rear of shop. TEL: 0326 313153. SER: Restorations (prints, bindings); framing.

Rosina's
4 High St. (Mrs R Gealer) Open 11-4.30. *STOCK: Dolls and toys, linen and lace, clothes.* TEL: 0326 311406; home - 0326 317739. SER: Restorations.

Waterfront Antiques Market
1st Floor, 4 Quay St. Open 10-5. SIZE: 12 dealers. *STOCK: Furniture, pottery, porcelain, glass, silver, metalware, kitchenalia, pictures, books, clocks, jewellery, decorative and collectors' items.* TEL: 0326 311491.

GRAMPOUND, Nr. Truro

Pine and Period Furniture
Fore St. (S Payne) Open 10-5. CL: Sat. *STOCK: Pine and period furniture.* TEL: 0726 883117.

Radnor House
Fore St. (P Nosworthy) Est: 1972. Open 10-5. SIZE: Medium. *STOCK: Furniture and accessories, pre-1900.* Not Stocked: Jewellery, coins and weapons. LOC: A390. PARK: Easy. TEL: 0726 882921; home - same. SER: Valuations; buys at auction. VAT: Stan/Spec.

GUNNISLAKE

Collectors' Centre
Commercial St. (R Mace) Est: 1984. Open 10.30-5. CL: Wed. SIZE: Medium. *STOCK: Diecast and tin plate toys, from 1930, £5-£500; car accessories, manuals and literature, from 1900, £5-£100; wireless sets, gramophones and spares, 1900-1960, £40-£500.* LOC: Just off A390. PARK: Easy. TEL: 0822 832658.

HAYLE

Copperhouse Gallery - W. Dyer & Sons
14 Fore St. (A.P Dyer) Est: 1900. Open 9-1 and 2-5.30, Wed. 9-1. SIZE: Medium. *STOCK: Watercolours, some oils, including Newlyn and St. Ives Schools, 19th to early 20th C, £25-£1,000.* LOC: Main road. PARK: Easy. TEL: 0736 752787; home - 0736 753362. SER: Restorations (watercolours and oils).

KINGSAND, TORPOINT

Cottage Things
7 Fore St. (Mrs C Drury) Open 10-1 and 2-5. *STOCK: Victoriana and small antiques.* TEL: 0752 822981.

LAUNCESTON

Tamar Gallery (Antiques and Fine Art)
5 Church St. (N. and I Preston) Open 10-1 and 2.30-5, Mon. by appointment. SIZE: Medium. *STOCK: Watercolours, 18th-20th C, £30-£2,000; small furniture, 17th-19th C, £100-£1,200; English pottery and porcelain especially 18th-19th C blue and white, £20-£300; Staffordshire, Victorian glass, copper and brass, objets d'art, decorative items and bygones.* LOC: Near St. Mary Magdalene Church. PARK: Near Church. TEL: 0566 774233; home - 0566 82444. SER: Restorations and cleaning (watercolours). VAT: Stan/Spec.

Westward County Pine
The Old Tannery, Newport Industrial Estate. (R.S Parsonson) Open 10-6, Sat. 10-2. *STOCK: Pine and country furniture.* TEL: 0566 775605.

LEEDSTOWN, Nr. Hayle

A.W Glasby and Son Antiques
(D.E Glasby) Est: 1936. Open 10.15-12.45 and 2.15-5. CL: Sat. and Mon. SIZE: Large. *STOCK: Furniture, porcelain and clocks, £10-£5,000.* Not Stocked: Coins, medals, scientific instruments. LOC: On main road half-way between Hayle and Helston. PARK: Easy. TEL: 0736 850303. VAT: Stan/Spec.

LOOE

Dowling and Bray
Fore St. Est: 1920. *STOCK: General antiques, furniture, pictures.* TEL: 050 36 2797. VAT: Stan.

Looe continued

Tony Martin
Fore St. Est: 1965. Open 9.30-1 and 2-5. Appointment advisable, CL: Thurs. p.m. SIZE: Medium. *STOCK: Porcelain, 18th C; silver, 18th-19th C, both £20-£200; glass, furniture, oils and watercolours.* LOC: Main street. TEL: 050 36 2734; home - 050 36 2228. VAT: Stan/Spec.

West Quay Curios
6 The Quay, West Looe. (C.G Jay and Miss G Jones) Est: 1990. Open 10-7, prior telephone call advisable in winter. SIZE: Small. *STOCK: General small antiques and collectors' items, mainly 19th-20th C, 50p to £500.* PARK: Nearby. TEL: 050 36 4411. SER: Valuations.

LOSTWITHIEL

John Bragg Antiques
35 Fore St. Open 10-5. *STOCK: Furniture, mainly period mahogany and Victorian.* LOC: 100yds. off A390. TEL: 0208 872827.

Old Palace Antiques
Old Palace, Quay St. (D Bryant) Open 10-1 and 2-5. CL: Wed. p.m. *STOCK: Pine, general antiques and collectors' items.* TEL: 0208 872909.

MEVAGISSEY

J Barron and Sons
Fore St. TEL: 0726 842172. VAT: Stan.

MOUSEHOLE

Vanity Fayre
Commercial Rd. (J.L Gillingham, MPS, DBA) Est: 1963. Open 10-1 and 2-5. CL: Thurs. SIZE: Medium. *STOCK: Small furniture and clocks, 1800-1900, £10-£500; copper, brass, metals, silver, porcelain, 1700-1900, £5-£500; items of interest, bric-a-brac, from 1800, £1-£250; stamps and coins.* LOC: Main Penzance road through Newlyn and Mousehole. PARK: Nearby. SER: Buys at auction.

NORTH PETHERWIN, Nr. Launceston

Pine and Country Antiques
Petherwingate. (W Herring) Open 8.30-5.30. SIZE: Medium. *STOCK: Furniture, 19th C including restored and stripped pine, £50-£500; general antiques and bygones.* PARK: Easy. TEL: 056 685 381. SER: Restorations; stripping.

An official photograph of the Queen taken by W. & D. Downey in 1893 and released for her Diamond Jubilee in 1897. Her small coronet of diamond rays was made for her in (probably) 1866. She wears her diamond necklace and earrings of 1858 and, on her right arm, her favourite bracelet set with a miniature of Prince Albert. One of the bracelets on her left wrist is a chain with heart-shaped lockets filled with souvenirs of her family. The Queen's continuing interest in jewellery is attested by the myriad small diamond brooches pinned to her veil and surrounding her tasselled bodice brooch. At least two crescent brooches are among them. From ***Jewellery 1789-1910 — The International Era,*** Volume II, by Shirley Bury published by the **Antique Collectors' Club** in 1991. £47.50 each volume.

PADSTOW

Mayflower Antiques
15 Duke St. (Miss C Hoskin) Est: 1963. Open 10.30-1 and 2.30-5. CL: Afternoons Nov.-Mar. SIZE: Small. *STOCK: Jewellery, £5-£150; copper, brass, £2-£50, all 19th to early 20th C; commemorative ware, £5-£90; Victorian and later pottery and china, £5-£50.* Not Stocked: Weapons, furniture, clocks. LOC: Centre of Padstow. PARK: On Quay. TEL: Home - 0841 532308.

PENRYN

Broad Street Gallery
9 Broad St. (V. and H Harris) Est: 1984. Open 10-5, evenings by appointment. CL: Mon. SIZE: Small. *STOCK: Watercolours, £50-£1,500; oil paintings, £80-£2,500; some prints, £60-£225; all 19th-20th C.* LOC: Main road, Falmouth end of town. PARK: Nearby. TEL: 0326 77216; home - same. SER: Buys at auction (watercolours and oil paintings).

Original Choice
15 Church Rd. (J.M Gavin) Open 8.30-6. *STOCK: General antiques.* TEL: 0326 75092.

Leon Robertson Antiques
7 The Praze. Est: 1972. *STOCK: Furniture, paintings and general antiques.* TEL: 0326 72767.

PENZANCE

Ken Ashbrook Antiques
Leskinnick Place. Est: 1973. Open 10-1 and 2-5, Mon. and Wed. 10-1, Sat. 10.30-1, Tues. and other times by appointment. SIZE: Large. *STOCK: Furniture, 18th-20th C, £100-£5,000.* LOC: 1 min. from railway station. PARK: Nearby. TEL: 0736 65477; home - same. SER: Valuations; restorations (cabinet work); buys at auction (furniture). VAT: Stan/Spec.

Attic Antiques
(In association with The Old Posthouse), 6 The Arcade. (D Richards) Resident. Est: 1969. Open daily 10-1 or by appointment. *STOCK: China, glass, small furniture, curios, decorative items.* TEL: 0736 61232/60320.

Browns Galleries
Bread St. (D. and C Brown) Open 10-4. CL: Wed. SIZE: Medium. *STOCK: Stripped pine, mahogany and oak furniture, general antiques and decorative items, £5-£800.* LOC: 100yds. down from Causeway Head. PARK: Nearby.

Catherine and Mary Antiques
2 Old Brewery Yard, Bread St. (C Farnes and M Palmer) Open 10-5, Wed. 10-1. *STOCK: Textiles, linen, lace, smalls and jewellery.* TEL: 0736 51053.

Penzance continued

Chapel Antiques
10 Chapel St. Open 10-5, Wed. 10-1 in winter. *STOCK: Furniture.* TEL: 0736 63124.

Daphne's Antiques
17 Chapel St. Est: 1976. Open 9-5. SIZE: Medium. *STOCK: Early country furniture, Georgian glass, decorative objects, 18th and 19th C jewellery.* TEL: 0736 61719.

Gallery Tonkin and Gallery Lyonesse
Old Brewery Yard, Bread St. (W.I.J Fisher) Open 10-5, Wed. 10-1. *STOCK: Maps, prints, paintings.* TEL: 0736 69855.

Barbara Howard Antiques
11 Abbey Mall, Abbey St. Open 9-5. *STOCK: General antiques, militaria, smalls.* TEL: 0736 50888.

Brian Humphrys Antiques
1 St. Clare St. Est: 1964. SIZE: Medium. *STOCK: Furniture, clocks, silver, jewellery, 18th-19th C, £25-£4,000.* PARK: Easy opposite. TEL: 0736 65154. SER: Valuations; buys at auction. VAT: Stan/Spec.

Kitts Corner Antiques
51 Chapel St. (B. and D Kirk) Est: 1984. Open 10-1 and 2-4.30. CL: Wed. (Oct.-June). SIZE: Medium. *STOCK: Collectors and decorative ceramics and glass, costume jewellery, kitchenalia and prints, 1880-1960, £5-£150.* PARK: Easy. TEL: 0736 64507; home -0736 63776.

Little Jem's
1 Abbey Mall, Abbey St. (J Lagden) Open 9.30-5. *STOCK: Jewellery, gem stones, costumes, objets d'art, paintings, clocks and watches.* TEL: 0736 51400.

New Generation Antiques Market
61/62 Chapel St. Open 10-5. SIZE: 10 dealers. *STOCK: Furniture, pottery, porcelain, glass, silver, metalware, kitchenalia, pictures, books, clocks, jewellery, decorative and collectors' items.* TEL: 0736 63267.

New Street Antiques
26 New St. Est: 1975. Open 10.30-4.30. SIZE: Medium. *STOCK: Furniture, 18th-19th C, £10-£3,000; brass, china, glass, £1-£300; oils and watercolours, £2-£200.* TEL: 0736 60173. SER: Restorations (furniture); cane seating.

The Old Posthouse
(incorporating Swan Jewellery and The Book Cellar), 9 Chapel St. (D Richards and E Sweet) Open 10-5. *STOCK: China, glass, small furniture, curios, decorative items, pictures, jewellery, small silver, objets d'art, antiquarian and secondhand books, cigarette and postcards.* TEL: 0736 60320.

Penzance continued

Pictures and Things
3 Albert St. (T.J.B Michell) Open 9.30-5.30. CL: Wed. *STOCK: Paintings, small antiques and silverware.* TEL: 0736 63039.

Pinewood Studio
46 Market Jew St. (R Aby) Open 9.30-5.30. *STOCK: Pine.* TEL: 0736 68793.

Tony Sanders Penzance Gallery and Antiques
14 Chapel St. Est: 1972. Open 9-5.30 and evenings in summer 7.30-10. SIZE: Medium. *STOCK: Oils and watercolours including Newlyn and St. Ives schools, 19th-20th C, £50-£8,000; glass, silver, china and small furniture.* TEL: 0736 66620/68461. VAT: Stan.

Leon Suddaby Fine Art
56 Chapel St. Open 10-1 and 2-5.30, Sat. 10-1. *STOCK: Paintings, Newlyn and St. Ives schools, 19th-20th C.* TEL: 0736 50333.

Vive Antiques
Captain Cutters House, 52 Chapel St. (J Buchanan) Open 10-12.30 and 1.30-4.30. SIZE: Small. *STOCK: Furniture, 19th C, £100-£1,000; decorative and interesting items, 18th-20th C, £10-£500.* LOC: Town Centre. PARK: Easy.TEL: 0736 51354; home - same. SER: Valuations; buys at auction. FAIRS: Newark Ardingly, Devon Country. VAT: Stan.

PERRANARWORTHAL

Thomson Antiques
Tryphena, Church Rd. Open by appointment. SIZE: Medium. *STOCK: Mahogany, walnut and oak to 1830.* LOC: Just off A39. PARK: Easy. TEL: 0872 864843. VAT: Stan/Spec.

PERRANPORTH

St. George's Antiques
33 St. George's Hill. (J Holmes) Est: 1983. Open 10-1 and 2-5. CL: Wed. p.m. SIZE: Small. *STOCK: 18th-19th C porcelain and pottery, Victorian and Edwardian furniture, glass and paintings, £10-£1,500.* LOC: B3285, main coast road. PARK: Nearby. TEL: 0872 572947; home - 0872 573469. FAIRS: Exeter; Carlyon Bay, Truro, Sandown Park.

PORT ISAAC

D Holmes
Pilchards Corner, Port Gaverne. Est: 1965. Open by appointment only. *STOCK: Antique and fine furniture.* TEL: 0208 880254. SER: Restorations.

One of a pair of nineteenth century Bath stone finials after a design by the eighteenth century architect James Gibbs, in the Italian Gardens of Belton House, Lincolnshire. Approx. height 72in. An illustration from ***Antique Garden Ornaments*** by John Davis, published by the **Antique Collectors' Club** in 1991. £39.50.

PORTSCATHO, Nr. St. Mawes

Curiosity Antiques
(E. and S Gale) Est: 1965. Open 10-5; Oct.-Mar. by appointment. *STOCK: General antiques, bric-a-brac.* LOC: In main square. PARK: Easy. TEL: 087 258 411.

REDRUTH

Penandrea Gallery
12 Higher Fore St. (W Dyer and Son. FARG) Est: 1900. Open 9-1 and 2-5. CL: Mon. and Thurs. *STOCK: Watercolours, 19th-20th C, £5-£1,000; some oils, prints and Victorian items, £1-£100.* LOC: Upper end of main st. PARK: Easy. TEL: 0209 213134. SER: Valuations; restorations; framing (oils and watercolours).

Victoria Gallery/Victoria Books
Unit 1Jaquemand Estate, New Portreath Rd. (B.J Maker) Open 10-5.30. *STOCK: Books and pictures.* TEL: 0209 843543.

West End Antiques Market
1st Floor, 3 West End. Open 10-5. *STOCK: Furniture, brass and copper, silver, glass, porcelain, pictures, prints, linen, specialist and collectors' items.* TEL: 0209 217001.

Redruth continued

Richard Winkworth Antiques
Unit 6, Station Rd. Open 9-5.30. SIZE: Large. *STOCK: Pine, oak, satin walnut and mahogany furniture; shipping goods, brass, copper, china, glass and smalls.* TEL: 0209 216631.

RUMFORD, Nr. Wadebridge

Henley House Antiques
(P Neale) *STOCK: Juvenilia, small antiques, bric-a-brac.* TEL: 0841 540322.

ST. AGNES

Ages Ago Antiques
1B Churchtown. (D. and M Gregson) Open 10-4.30; Nov.-Mar. 10-1. CL: Wed. p.m. and Sat. p.m. *STOCK: Furniture and ceramics, from 1800.* LOC: Opposite GPO. TEL: 087 255 3820.

ST. AUSTELL

Ancient and Modern LAPADA
32-34 Polkyth Rd. (P.J Watts) Est: 1965. Open 8.30-5. *STOCK: General antiques, paintings, clocks, jewellery, bric-a-brac.* TEL: 0726 73983. VAT: Stan/Spec.

Mrs. Margaret Chesterton
33 Pentewan Rd. Est: 1965. Open 10-5.30, appointment advisable. CL: Sat. p.m. *STOCK: Victoriana, Edwardiana, 1800-1915; some furniture, porcelain, glass, £1-£500; brass, copper, pewter, jewellery, clocks, automata, musical boxes, watercolours.* LOC: Coming from Plymouth, travel direct to St. Austell. Keep on main by-pass until roundabout for Mevagissey and Pentewan Rd. House is 100yds. on left down this road. PARK: Easy. TEL: 0726 72926.

The Furniture Store/St. Austell Antiques Centre
37/39 Truro Rd. (R Nosworthy) Est: 1972. Open 10-4. SIZE: Large. *STOCK: Furniture and decorators' items; some china and glass.* LOC: Town centre, just off A390. PARK: Easy and at rear of warehouse. TEL: 0726 63178; home - 0288 81 548. SER: Valuations; restorations (furniture); buys at auction. VAT: Stan/Spec.

Poldark Antiques
Market House. (P Falconer) Open 9-5. CL: Thurs. p.m. *STOCK: Jewellery, silver, porcelain - Art Deco glass, collectors' items, furniture.* LOC: Opposite parish church. TEL: 0726 72818.

Myles Varcoe
Tregongeeves Farm. Est: 1971. Open by appointment only. *STOCK: Pictures, mainly 19th C marine watercolours and oils, £50-£5,000.* LOC: 1 mile west of town on A390, turn left into lane marked "Golf course". Farm first entrance on right. TEL: 0726 68202. VAT: Spec.

ST. GERRANS, Nr. Portscatho

Turnpike Cottage Antiques and Tearooms
The Square. (T. and S Green) Est: 1988. Open 11-1.30 and 3-6 including Sun. By appointment only in winter. CL: Mon. SIZE: Medium. *STOCK: General antiques, furniture, porcelain, bric-a-brac, £5-£2,000.* Not Stocked: Large items. LOC: Near church. PARK: Easy, at rear. TEL: 087 258 853; home - same. SER: Valuations; restorations (furniture, watercolours).

ST. IVES

Attic Cellar
Street on Garrow. (F Glossop) Open 9-5, seven days a week in summer. SIZE: 10 dealers. *STOCK: General antiques.* TEL: 0736 796633.

Mike Read Antique Sciences
"Ayia Napa"Wheal Whidden, Carbis Bay. Est: 1974. Open by appointment. SIZE: Small. *STOCK: Scientific instruments - navigational, surveying, mining, barometers, telescopes and microscopes, medical, 18th-19th C, £10-£5,000.* LOC: Turn right at St. Ives end of Carbis Bay, 100yds. on right. PARK: Easy. TEL: 0736 798219; home - same. SER: Valuations; restorations. VAT: Spec.

TREGONY, Nr. Truro

Clock Tower Antiques
57 Fore St. (The Warne Family)Est: 1988. Open 10-6, (extended in summer), evenings and Sun. by appointment. SIZE: Medium. *STOCK: Ceramics, including Doulton stoneware, Mason's Ironstone, 19th C blue and white transferware, £10-£500; oils and watercolours, 19th to early 20th C, £50-£1,000; furniture, 18th to early 20th C, £75-£3,000; brass, copper and treen, £10-£300.* Not Stocked: Silver and jewellery. LOC: Village centre, B3287. PARK: Easy. TEL: 087 253 225; home - same.

TRURO

Alan Bennett
24 New Bridge St. Est: 1954. Open 9-5.30. SIZE: Large. *STOCK: Furniture, £50-£5,000; jewellery and porcelain, to 1900, £5-£1,000; paintings and prints, £20-£2,000.* LOC: Eastern side of cathedral. PARK: 100yds. from shop. TEL: 0872 73296. VAT: Stan/Spec.

The Pine Parlour
Blackwater. (S Terrett) Open 9-5.30. *STOCK: Pine.* TEL: 0872 560919. SER: Restorations; stripping.

Pydar Antiques and Gallery
Peoples Palace, Pydar St. (D Severn and J Poole) Est: 1968. Open 10.30-4.30 and by appointment. SIZE: Medium. *STOCK: English furniture, 18th and 19th C, £500-£2,500; Victorian and Edwardian furniture, £50-£1,000; silver, plate, porcelain and glass, prints and watercolours, £5-£500.* PARK: Easy. TEL: Home - 0872 510485 or 0637 872034. FAIRS: West Country.

Peter Stanton Antiques Restoration
The Old Pottery, Chapel Hill. (P. and V Stanton) Open 9-5, Sat. by appointment. SIZE: Small. *STOCK: Furniture, mainly country, £50-£3,500; paintings, 19th-20th C, £50-£1,500.* LOC: Turn right at country hall when coming from by-pass, left down Chapel Hill, premises on left near Bosvigo School. PARK: Easy. TEL: 0872 70262. SER: Valuations; restorations (furniture including French polishing and upholstery).

Strickland and Dorling
Come-to-Good, Feock. (P Strickland and T Dorling) Usually open. *STOCK: Small furniture, pottery, porcelain, silver, pictures, maps of Cornwall, bijouterie and collectors' items.* TEL: 0872 862394.

Richard Winkworth Antiques
Calenick St. Open 10-5. SIZE: Large. *STOCK: Georgian and Victorian furniture, brass, copper, china, glass.* TEL: 0872 40901.

WADEBRIDGE

Bub Doddington Antiques
15 Molesworth St. (M.M. and R.S Young) Resident. Est: 1975. Open 9.30-1 and 2-5. SIZE: Medium. *STOCK: Georgian and earlier oak and mahogany; smalls and decorative lighting.* LOC: On main road. PARK: Nearby. TEL: 0208 813834. SER: Valuations; restorations (furniture, upholstery, plasterwork, caning, etc.); buys at auction.

Wadebridge continued

St. Breock Gallery
St. Breock Churchtown. (R.G.G Haslam-Hopwood) Open 10-5. *STOCK: Watercolours, 19th-20th C; furniture, general antiques and objets d'art.* LOC: Near Royal Cornwall Showground. PARK: Own. TEL: 0208 812543. SER: Restorations; buys at auction.

Victoria Antiques
21 Molesworth St. (M. and S Daly) Open Mon.-Sat. SIZE: Large. *STOCK: Furniture, 17th-19th C, £25-£10,000.* LOC: On A39 between Bude and Newquay. PARK: Nearby. TEL: 0208 814160. SER: Valuations; restorations. VAT: Stan/Spec.

WIDEGATES, Nr. Looe

Pink Cottage Antiques
(I. and B Barrett) Est: 1981. Open 9.30-5, 2-5 Sun., longer hours in summer. SIZE: Medium. *STOCK: Furniture, £50-£2,500; brass and copper, £5-£250; china and glass, £2-£300; oil lamps and clocks; all mainly Victorian and Edwardian, some Georgian.* Not Stocked: Clothing, militaria, jewellery, silver. LOC: A387 from Plymouth, 4 miles before Looe. PARK: At rear. TEL: 050 34 258; home - same. SER: Restorations (furniture).

The Cotswolds

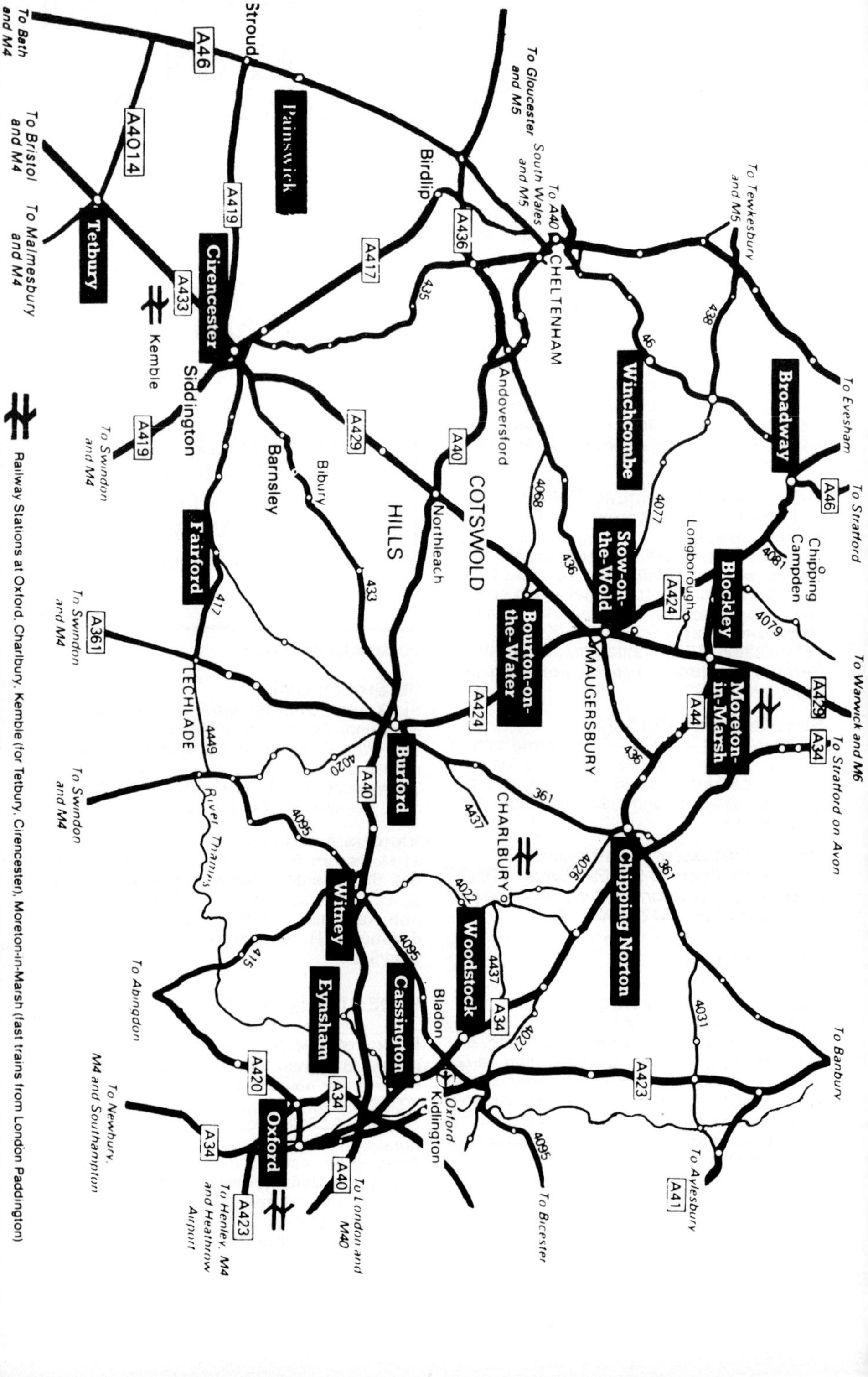

To Bath and M4
A46
Stroud
Painswick
A4014
To Bristol and M4
To Malmesbury and M4
Tetbury
A419
Cirencester
A433
Kemble
Siddington
To Swindon and M4
Birdlip
A417
A436
To Gloucester and M5
South Wales and M5
To A40
CHELTENHAM
435
To Tewkesbury and M5
438
46
Winchcombe
Broadway
To Evesham
A46
To Stratford
Andoversford
A40
A429
Barnsley
Bibury
COTSWOLD
HILLS
Northleach
4068
4077
Stow-on-the-Wold
Longborough
Chipping Campden
4081
Blockley
4079
436
A424
Fairford
433
Bourton-on-the-Water
MAUGERSBURY
A44
Moreton-in-Marsh
A429
To Warwick and M6
A34
To Stratford on Avon
417
To Swindon and M4
A361
LECHLADE
4449
A424
Burford
4020
A40
4437
361
CHARLBURY
River Thames
4095
4026
Chipping Norton
361
4022
Witney
Woodstock
4095
4437
415
To Abingdon
Eynsham
Cassington
Bladon
A34
4027
4031
To Banbury
A423
A420
A34
Oxford
Kidlington
4095
To Newbury, M4 and Southampton
A34
A423
To Henley, M4 and Heathrow Airport
A40
To London and M40
To Bicester
To Aylesbury
A41
Railway Stations at Oxford, Charlbury, Kemble (for Tetbury, Cirencester), Moreton-in-Marsh (fast trains from London Paddington)

THE COTSWOLD ANTIQUE DEALERS' ASSOCIATION

Buy Fine Antiques and Works of Art at provincial prices in England's lovely and historic countryside

The Cotswolds, one of the finest areas of unspoilt countryside in the land, have been called "the essence and the heart of England". The region has a distinctive character created by the use of honey-coloured stone in its buildings and dry stone walls. Within the locality the towns and villages are admirably compact and close to each other and the area is well supplied with good hotels and reasonably priced inns. The Cotswolds are within easy reach of London (1½ hours by road or rail) and several major airports.

Cotswold sheep — which inspired the logo of the Cotswold Antique Dealers' Association — a quatrefoil device with a sheep in its centre — have played an important part in the region's history with much of its wealth created by the woollen industry. As for antiques, shops and warehouses of the CADA offer a selection of period furniture, pictures, porcelain, metalwork, and collectables unrivalled outside London.

With the use of the CADA directory on the following pages, which lists the names of its members, their specialities and opening times, visitors from all over the world can plan their buying visit to the Cotswolds. CADA members will assist all visiting collectors and dealers in locating antiques and works of art. They will give you advice on where to stay in the area, assistance with packing, shipping and insurance and the exchange of foreign currencies. They can advise private customers on what can realistically be bought on their available budgets, and if the first dealer does not have the piece which you are selecting he will know of several other members who will. The CADA welcomes home and overseas buyers in the certain knowledge that there are at least fifty dealers with a good and varied stock, a reputation for fair trading and an annual turnover in excess of £15,000,000.

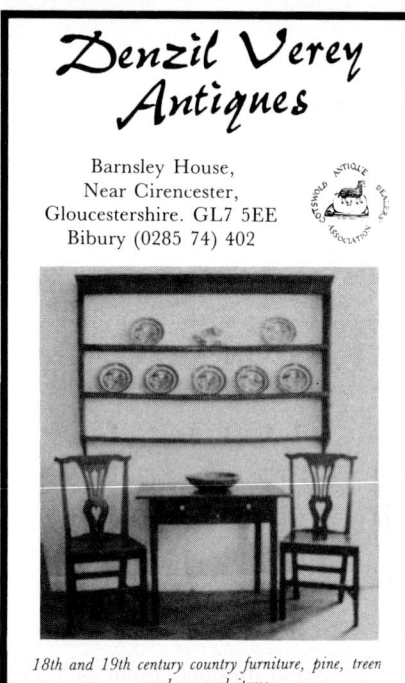

BARNSLEY

Nr. Cirencester

An extremely pretty and totally unspoilt village. Barnsley House Gardens, which have been much written about, are open to the public all year round.

Denzil Verey

Barnsley House. CADA. Resident. Est: 1980. Open 9.30-5.30, Sat. 10.30-1, other times by appointment. SIZE: Large. *STOCK: Country furniture, including pine, 18th-19th C; treen, country and kitchen bygones, unusual and decorative items.* LOC: 4 miles from Cirencester on A433 to Burford, 1st large house in village, set back off road on the right. PARK: Easy. TEL: 0285 74 402. VAT: Stan/Spec.

BROADWAY

Coming via Fish Hill and the Broadway Beacon, which afford magnificent views across the valley, you enter the town along a wide thoroughfare lined with Cotswold houses. The coaching route on

Broadway continued

which Broadway was situated was a major boost to the livelihood of its inhabitants.

Haynes Fine Art BADA

The Bindery Galleries, 69 High St. CADA. Est: 1968. Open 9.30-5.30. SIZE: Large. *STOCK: 16th-20th C British and European paintings, £900-£120,000.* LOC: From Moreton, 50yds. past the Stratford turn off on the left. PARK: Easy. TEL: 0386 852649; home - same. SER: Valuations; restorations; framing. VAT: Spec.

John Noott Fine Paintings LAPADA

14 Cotswold Court, The Green, and 31 High St. CADA. Est: 1972. Open 9-1 and 2-5.30, or by appointment. SIZE: Large. *STOCK: Paintings and watercolours, 19th-20th C, £50-£50,000.* LOC: Centre of village. PARK: Easy. TEL: 0386 852787/858969 (ansaphone 24 hrs.). SER: Valuations; restorations; framing. VAT: Stan/Spec.

BURFORD

William II granted this former market town a charter to hold its markets. Merchants living in the fine imposing houses dealt in dried fish from Aberdeen, dress materials from France, linen from Ireland, metals from Birmingham and local cider.

The Crypt Antiques

109 High St. (P Matthey and M Schotten) CADA. Est: 1957. Open 9.30-1 and 2-5.30 or by appointment. *STOCK: 18th-19th C furniture, antique fishing tackle, golfing collectables.* TEL: 099 382 2302; home - 0993 830254. SER: Restorations.

Jonathan Fyson Antiques

44 and 50 High St. (J.R Fyson) CADA. Est: 1972. Open 9.30-1 and 2-5.30. SIZE: Small. *STOCK: English and continental furniture, decorative brass and steel including lighting and fireplace accessories; papier mâché, tôle, treen, porcelain, glass, jewellery.* LOC: A361. Coming from London on A40 between Oxford and Cheltenham at junction with A361. PARK: Easy. TEL: 099 382 3606/3204; home - 036786 223. SER: Valuations. VAT: Spec.

David Pickup BADA

115 High St. CADA. Est: 1977. Open 9.30-1 and 2-5.30, Sat. 10-1 and 2-4. SIZE: Medium. *STOCK: Fine furniture, from £1,000+; works of art, £500-£10,000; decorative objects, from £100+; all late 17th-19th C.* PARK: Easy. TEL: 099 382 2555. FAIRS: New York International. VAT: Spec.

Burford continued

Swan Gallery
High St. (J. and D Pratt) CADA. Est: 1966. Open 9.30-5.30. SIZE: Large. *STOCK: Furniture - oak, yew, fruitwood and walnut, 17th-19th C, £500-£8,000; oil paintings, sculpture and watercolours, 19th-20th C, £100-£8,000; metalwork, blue and white pottery and porcelain, small decorative items, 18th-20th C, £50-£800.* PARK: Easy. TEL: 099 382 2244. SER: Valuations; restorations (furniture). VAT: Mainly Spec.

CHIPPING NORTON

A charming Cotswold market town situated just off the A34, the main road from Oxford to Stratford-upon-Avon. The name Chipping means trading or dealing, and a weekly market still takes place in the town centre.

Key Antiques **BADA**
11 Horse Fair. (D. and M Robinson) CADA. Resident. Open 9.30-6 or by appointment. SIZE: Medium. *STOCK: Period oak and country furniture, domestic metalware including kitchenware and lighting, early pottery, paintings, needlework, carvings.* LOC: On main road. PARK: Easy. TEL: 0608 643777. VAT: Spec.

Peter Stroud Antiques
35 New St. CADA. Open 9-5.30. SIZE: Medium. *STOCK: 17th-19th C period furniture, oak, walnut, fruitwood and mahogany including tables, chairs, dressers and bureaux.* LOC: 150yds. from Town Hall down hill on the right. PARK: Own. TEL: 0608 642571. SER: Valuations. VAT: Stan/Spec.

CIRENCESTER

This ancient town, founded in AD75, was called Corinium Dobunnorum, was surrounded by a wall two miles in circumference, and an amphitheatre was developed during the second century. If time permits, take a walk through the old streets of the town, Dollar Street, Thomas and Coxwell Street and then Park Street, past the highest yew hedge in England and back to the lovely Market Square.

Cirencester continued

Thomas and Pamela Hudson
At the Sign of the Herald Angel, 19 Park St. CADA. Est: 1959. Open 9-1 and 2-5.30. *STOCK: Old Sheffield, small objets de vertu, netsuke, glass, needlework tools and workboxes, needlework.* LOC: From Market Pl., 100yds. beyond Corinium Museum. TEL: 0285 652972. SER: Valuations; buys at auction. VAT: Spec.

Rankine Taylor Antiques **LAPADA**
34 Dollar St. (Mrs L Taylor) CADA. Est: 1969. Open 9-5.30, Sun. by appointment. SIZE: Large. *STOCK: Furniture, 17th-19th C, £100-£20,000; glass, 18th-20th C, £10-£250; silver and decorative items, 17th-20th C, £20-£8,000.* Not Stocked: Victoriana, militaria. LOC: From Church, turn right up West Market Place, via Gosditch St. into Dollar St. PARK: Abbey grounds via Spittalgate. TEL: 0285 652529. SER: Valuations; buys at auction (furnishing items). VAT: Spec.

William H Stokes **BADA**
The Cloisters, 6/8 Dollar St. (W.H Stokes and P.W Bontoft) CADA. Est: 1968. Open 9.30-5.30, Sat. 10-4. *STOCK: Early oak furniture, £1,000-£30,000; brassware, £150-£5,000; all 16th-17th C.* TEL: 0285 653907. FAIRS: Grosvenor House. VAT: Spec.

P.J Ward Fine Paintings
11 Gosditch St. CADA. Open 9-5. *STOCK: 17th-19th C paintings.* TEL: 0285 658499. SER: Valuations; restorations; framing. VAT: Spec.

Bernard Weaver Antiques
28 Gloucester St. CADA. Open 9.30-6, Sat. 9.30-1. SIZE: Medium. *STOCK: Furniture, 18th-19th C, mahogany and oak; art nouveau and arts and crafts.* LOC: Continuation of Dollar St. PARK: Easy. TEL: 0285 652055; home - same. SER: Valuations.

EYNSHAM

Nr. Oxford

If you approach this pleasant village from South Oxford you will cross the River Thames via the Swinbrook Tollbridge. There has been a crossing here for about 700 years. The toll bridge is privately owned and its income is untaxed to this day. Eynsham is also the site of the oldest documented Cistercian Abbey in the country.

Eynsham continued

David John Ceramics
11 Acre End St. (J Twitchett and D Holborough) CADA. Est: 1959. CL: Mon. SIZE: Medium. *STOCK: English ceramics, 18th-20th C, £15-£5,000; small furniture, decorative items.* TEL: 0865 880786. VAT: Stan/Spec.

FAIRFORD

This is the most easterly of the wool towns, developed in the 17th and 18th centuries. Elegant houses from the period stand round the market square today.

Blenheim Antiques
Market Pl. (N Hurdle) CADA. Resident. Est: 1972. Open 9.30-6.30. *STOCK: 18th-19th C furniture, clocks.* TEL: 0285 712094. VAT: Stan/Spec.

Cirencester Antiques Ltd
High St. (Mr and Mrs R.T.G Chester-Master) CADA. Est: 1959. Open 9-5.30. SIZE: Large. *STOCK: Furniture and works of art, 17th to early 19th C, £50-£50,000.* TEL: 0285 652955.

Gloucester House Antiques Ltd
Market Pl. (Mr and Mrs R Chester-Master) CADA. Est: 1972. Open 9-5.30. SIZE: Large. *STOCK: English and French country furniture in oak, elm, fruitwood, pine; pottery, faiënce and decorative items.* PARK: Easy. TEL: 0285 712790; home - 0285 653066. VAT: Stan/Spec.

LEDBURY

Old George Antiques
Tudor House, 17c High St. (Mrs W Wild and J.G.R Tyndall) CADA. Open 10-5.30, Sat. 10-5, Wed., Sun. and other times by appointment. SIZE: Medium. *STOCK: Furniture, pre-1830, to £2,000; decorative items.* LOC: Tilley's Alley, off High St., opposite Lloyds Bank. PARK: Easy. TEL: 0531 5299 or 0666 503405. SER: Valuations; restorations; buys at auction. FAIRS: Snape; Olympia. VAT: Stan/Spec.

MORETON-IN-MARSH

A thriving market town built on the Fosse Way, the Roman Road running from Bath to Lincoln. The White Hart and the Redesdale Arms were two of Gloucestershire's biggest coaching inns in the era of the stage coach. The 16th century Curfewtrower is the oldest building and its bell is dated 1633.

Moreton-in-Marsh continued

Adams **BADA**
The Old Parsonage, Church St. (Mr and Mrs L Adams) CADA. Open by appointment. *STOCK: 18th C Meissen.* TEL: 0608 51881.

Astley House - Fine Art
Astley House, High St. (D. and N Glaisyer) CADA. Est: 1974. Open 9-5.30. SIZE: Medium. *STOCK: Oil paintings and watercolours, 19th-20th C, £200-£10,000.* LOC: Main street. PARK: Easy. TEL: 0608 50601; fax - 0608 51777. SER: Restorations (oils and watercolours); framing; video valuations. VAT: Spec.

Astley House - Fine Art
Astley House, London Rd. (D. and N Glaisyer) CADA. Est: 1974. Open 10-1 and 2-5.30. SIZE: Large. *STOCK: Oil paintings, 19th-20th C; large decorative paintings and portraits.* LOC: Town centre. PARK: Easy. TEL: 0608 50601; fax - 0608 51777. SER: Restorations (oils and watercolours); porcelain framing. VAT: Spec.

Elizabeth Parker
High St. (P.J King-Smith) CADA. Est: 1975. Open 9-6. SIZE: Large. *STOCK: Furniture, £50-£10,000; English and continental mahogany, satinwood and marquetry, some porcelain, copper and brass, all 18th and 19th C.* LOC: Opposite Manor House Hotel, on Fosseway junction of A44 from Broadway. TEL: 0608 50917. SER: Buys at auction. VAT: Stan/Spec.

STOW-ON-THE-WOLD

The highest town in the Cotswolds at seven hundred feet, Stow lies to one side of the Fosse Way between Cirencester and Moreton-in-Marsh where the road from Cheltenham to Chipping Norton crosses. The beauty of the town is to leave the main roads and enter the unexpectedly large market square to find impressive yet unpretentious buildings all around.

Duncan J Baggott
Woolcomber House, Sheep St. CADA. Est: 1967. Open 9.30-5.30 or by appointment. SIZE: Large. *STOCK: 17th-19th C. English oak, mahogany, walnut and fruitwood furniture, paintings, prints and needlework, metalware and domestic items, garden statuary.* PARK: Own. TEL: 0451 30662.

Duncan J Baggott
Huntsmans Yard, Sheep St. CADA. Est: 1967. Open 9-5 or by appointment. CL: Sat. SIZE: Large. *STOCK: 17th-19th C. English and European furniture, portrait and primitive*

Duncan J Baggott continued

paintings, architectural items and statuary. LOC: 200yds. from Fosseway entrance on right hand side through coaching gates. PARK: Own. TEL: 0451 30662. *Trade Only.*

Baggott Church Street Ltd BADA

Church St. (D.J. and C.M Baggott) CADA. Est: 1978. Open 10-6, Sat. 9.30-5.30 or by appointment. SIZE: Large. *STOCK: English furniture, 17th-19th C; portrait paintings, some metalwork, pottery, treen and decorative items.* LOC: South-west corner of market square. PARK: In market square. TEL: 0451 30370.

Christopher Clarke Antiques Ltd BADA

The Fosse Way. (C.J Clarke) CADA. Est: 1961. Open 9.30-6. SIZE: Medium. *STOCK: Furniture, 17th-19th C, £300-£15,000; walnut, mahogany, metalware, 16th-18th C, £200-£5,000.* Not Stocked: Silver, glass, medals, coins, prints. LOC: Corner of the Fosse Way and Sheep St. PARK: Easy. TEL: 0451 30476.

The Cotswold Galleries

The Square. (R. and C Glaisyer) CADA. Est: 1961. Open 9-5.30, or by appointment. SIZE: Large. *STOCK: Oil paintings, 19th-20th C landscape.* TEL: 0451 30586. SER: Restoration; framing.

The Curiosity Shop

The Square, (Antony Preston Antiques Ltd.). CADA. Est: 1965. Open 9.30-5.30. SIZE: Large. *STOCK: Furniture, clocks, mirrors, 18th to early 19th C, £500-£10,000.* LOC: Off Fosse Way. PARK: Easy. TEL: 0451 31586. VAT: Stan/Spec.

L Greenwold

"Digbeth", Digbeth St. CADA. Est: 1973. Open 10-5. SIZE: Medium. *STOCK: Jewellery, Oriental porcelain, glass.* LOC: Just off the south east corner of market sq. PARK: Easy. TEL: 0451 30398. SER: Valuations. VAT: Spec.

Stow-on-the-Wold continued

Keith Hockin (Antiques) Ltd BADA

The Square. CADA. Est: 1968. Open 9-6. CL: Sun. except by appointment. SIZE: Medium. *STOCK: Oak furniture, 1600-1750; country furniture in oak, fruitwoods, yew, 1700-1850; pewter, copper, brass, ironwork, all periods.* Not Stocked: Mahogany. PARK: Easy. TEL: 0451 31058. SER: Buys at auction (oak, pewter, metalwork). VAT: Stan/Spec.

Huntington Antiques Ltd

The Old Forge, Church St. (M.F., S.P. and N.M.J Golding) CADA. Resident. Est: 1974. Open 9-6 or by appointment. *STOCK: Early period and fine country furniture, metalware, treen and textiles, tapestries and works of art.* TEL: 0451 30842. SER: Valuations; buys at auction. FAIRS: Maastricht; Madrid. VAT: Spec.

Antony Preston Antiques Ltd BADA LAPADA

The Square. CADA. Est: 1968. Open 9.30-6, or by appointment. *STOCK: English and continental furniture and objects, longcase and bracket clocks, barometers, leather upholstery, all 18th and 19th C.* TEL: 0451 31586/31406. VAT: Stan/Spec.

South Bar Antiques

Digbeth St. (R Deeley) CADA. Est: 1974. Open 9-5.30, Sun. by appointment. SIZE: Large. *STOCK: Clocks, jewellery, furniture, Moorcroft, Wemyss, porcelain, silver, paintings, 1640-1920, £50-£40,000.* PARK: Market Sq. TEL: 0451 30236. FAIRS: Café Royal; Barbican; Olympia; British International, Birmingham; Kenilworth. VAT: Spec.

Stow Antiques

The Square. (Mr and Mrs J Hutton-Clarke) CADA. Resident. Est: 1970. Open 9.30-5.30. SIZE: Large. *STOCK: Furniture, mainly period, £200-£20,000; china, silver and plate, glass, copper, 18th C to 1930, £5-£1,500; highly decorative items, 19th-20th C, £5-£5,000.* PARK: Easy. TEL: 0451 30377. SER: Shipping.

STRETTON-ON-FOSSE

Nr. Moreton-in-Marsh

Astley House - Fine Art

The Old School. (D. and N Glaisyer) CADA. Est: 1974. Open by appointment. SIZE: Large. *STOCK: Large decorative oil paintings, 19th-20th C.* LOC: Village centre. PARK: Easy. TEL: 0608 50601; fax - 0608 51777. SER: Valuations; restorations; framing; exhibitions; mailing list. VAT: Spec.

TADDINGTON

Architectural Heritage

Taddington Manor. CADA. Est: 1978. Open 9.30-5.30, Sat. 10.30-4.30. SIZE: Large. *STOCK: Period panelling, oak, mahogany and pine; chimney pieces in marble, stone, oak and mahogany; garden statuary, fountains, seats and urns; complete shop and pub interiors, ornamental gates, stained, leaded and etched glass; doors, decorative and unusual items.* PARK: Easy. TEL: 038 673 414; fax - 038 673 236. VAT: Stan.

TETBURY

An old market town where woolsack races are held each year as a link with the past.

Breakspeare Antiques LAPADA

36 Long St. (M. and S Breakspeare) CADA. Resident. Est: 1962. Open 9.30-5.30, if closed ring bell. CL: Some Thurs. p.m. SIZE: Medium. *STOCK: English period furniture, mainly mahogany, 18th to early 19th C, some early walnut, longcase clocks, barometers.* PARK: Easy. TEL: 0666 503122. VAT: Stan/Spec. *Mainly Trade.*

Old George Antiques and Interiors

3 The Chipping. (Mrs W.M Wild∑ J Tyndall) CADA. Est: 1974. Open 10-5.30, Sun. by appointment. SIZE: Medium. *STOCK: Mahogany, decorated and walnut furniture, 17th C to Regency, to £5,000+; decorative items, porcelain, lighting, £500-£1,000+; paintings and rugs, to 20th C, £500-£2,000.* LOC: 100yds. from town centre, turn off main street at Snooty Fox Hotel into The Chipping car park. PARK: Easy. TEL: 0666 503405. SER: Valuations; restorations; interior decor and design; buys at auction. VAT: Stan/Spec.

Primrose Antiques

45 Long St. (W.T. and B Stickland) CADA. Est: 1972. Open 9.30-5.30. SIZE: Medium. *STOCK: Oak, mahogany and walnut, brass, copper and pewter, 17th-19th C.* PARK: Easy. TEL: 0666 502440; home - same. VAT: Stan/Spec.

WINCHCOMBE

An historic town, displaying fine examples of 17th century architecture, huddled along the narrow meandering High Street. Sudeley Castle lies close by, the splendid home of the Seymours.

Kenulf Fine Art

High St. (E. and J Ford) CADA. Est: 1978. Open 9.30-1 and 2-5.30. *STOCK: 19th to early 20th C oil and watercolour paintings and prints.* TEL: 0242 603204/602776. SER: Valuations; restorations (oils and watercolours); period framing.

WITNEY

To most people the name 'Witney' means blankets which have been made here for upwards of 1,000 years. The traditional sources of Cotswold wealth, fleece and swift water established the trade. Today its blankets, which are known and sold all over the world, can still be bought in the town.

Ian Pout Antiques

99 High St. (I. and J Pout) CADA. Open 10-5.30. *STOCK: 18th and 19th C furniture, decorative objects, vintage teddy bears.* TEL: 0993 702616; home - 0869 40205. VAT: Spec.

Anthony Scaramanga Antiques BADA

108 Newland. CADA. Est: 1969. Open 10-5. CL: Fri. a.m. and Sun. except by appointment. *STOCK: Samplers, 17th-19th C; needlework pictures, lace, small furniture, Staffordshire figures, blue and white pottery.* LOC: From Oxford on A40, turn off bypass onto A4022, shop on left before coming to A147 and Witney. PARK: Easy. TEL: 0993 703472. VAT: Spec.

Witney continued

Windrush Antiques
107 High St. (B Tollett) CADA. Resident. Est: 1978. Open 10-5.30. SIZE: Medium. *STOCK: Furniture, especially 17th-18th C oak and country chairs; Georgian mahogany, some metalware and porcelain.* LOC: A40, corner of Mill St. and High St. PARK: Private at rear. TEL: 0993 772536.

Witney Antiques **BADA**
96/100 Corn St. (L.S.A. and C.J Jarrett) CADA. Est: 1962. Open 9.30-5. SIZE: Large. *STOCK: English furniture, 17th-18th C; bracket and longcase clocks, mahogany, oak and walnut, metalware, needleworks and works of art.* LOC: From Oxford on old A40 through Witney via High St., turn right at T-junction, 400yds. on right. PARK: Easy. TEL: 0993 703902/703887; fax - 0993 779852. SER: Restorations. FAIRS: Chelsea; Park Lane; Grosvenor House. VAT: Spec.

Cumbria

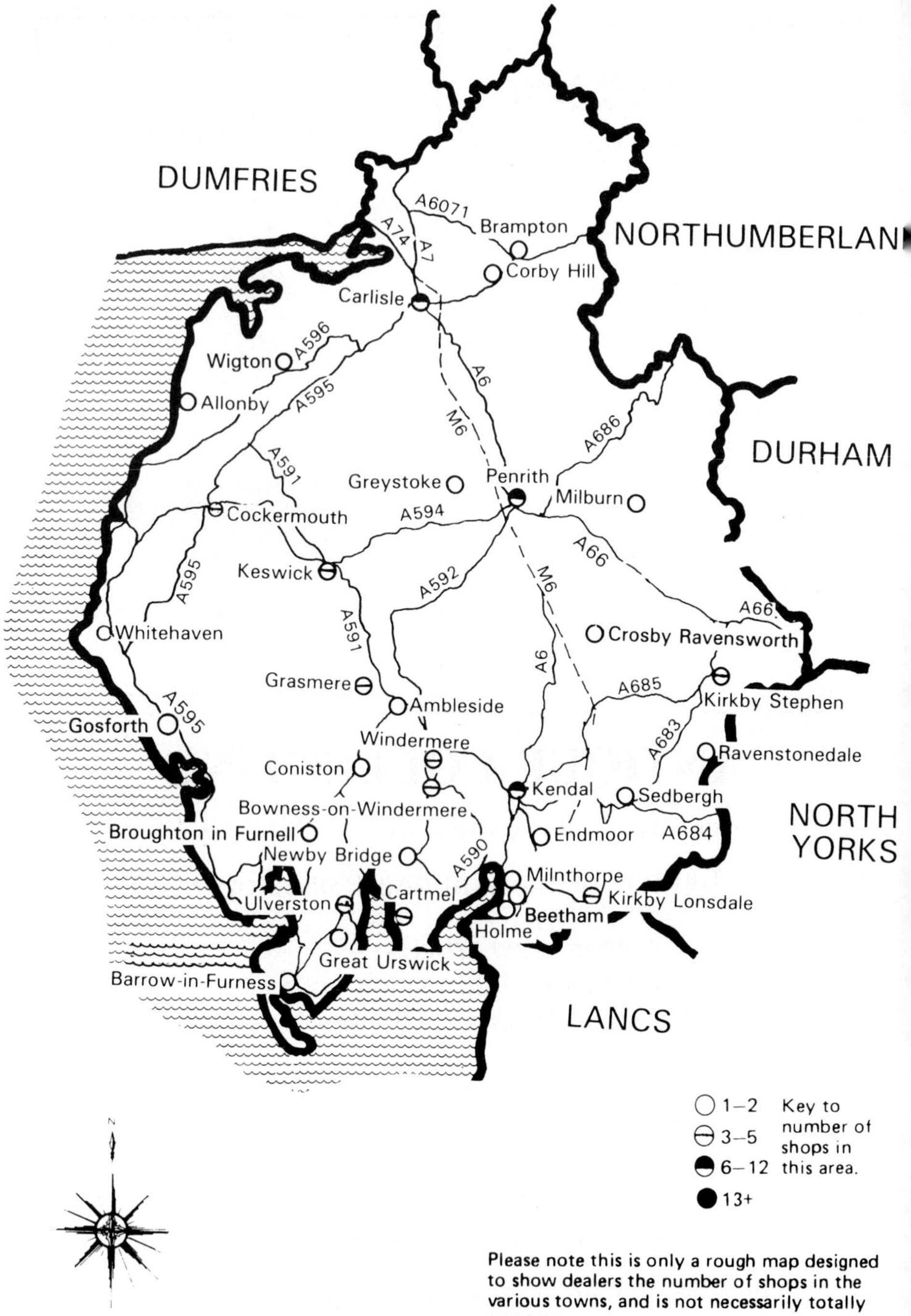
DUMFRIES
NORTHUMBERLAN
DURHAM
NORTH YORKS
LANCS
A6071
A74
A7
Brampton
Corby Hill
Carlisle
Wigton
A596
Allonby
A595
A6
M6
A686
A591
Greystoke
Penrith
Milburn
Cockermouth
A594
Keswick
A66
A595
A592
A66
Whitehaven
A591
Crosby Ravensworth
A6
Grasmere
A685
Kirkby Stephen
Ambleside
Gosforth
A595
Windermere
A683
Ravenstonedale
Coniston
Kendal
Sedbergh
Bowness-on-Windermere
Broughton in Furnell
Endmoor
A684
Newby Bridge
A590
Milnthorpe
Ulverston
Cartmel
Kirkby Lonsdale
Beetham
Holme
Great Urswick
Barrow-in-Furness
1–2
3–5
6–12
13+
Key to number of shops in this area.

Please note this is only a rough map designed to show dealers the number of shops in the various towns, and is not necessarily totally accurate.

ALLONBY

Cottage Curios
Main St. (B Pickering) Est: 1965. Open daily from 2 p.m.

BARROW-IN-FURNESS

Antiques
237 Rawlinson St. (H Vincent) Est: 1965. *STOCK: Jewellery, furniture, paintings, weapons, clocks, brass, copperware, silver, bric-a-brac.* LOC: Off A590 (A6). PARK: Easy. TEL: 0229 823432.

BEETHAM, Nr.Milnthorpe

Mill House Antiques
Temple Bank. (T.E Fitzgerald-moore) Est: 1972. Open by appointment only. *STOCK: 18th and early 19th C furniture, ceramics, collectors and decorative items.* TEL: 0539 562352.

BOWNESS-ON-WINDERMERE

J.W Thornton Antiques Supermarket
North Terrace. SIZE: Large. *STOCK: Fine art, general antiques, furniture, shipping and architectural items, pine, bric-a-brac, paintings, decorators items.* TEL: 096 62 5183/2930 or 0229 869745. SER: Valuations; buys at auction. VAT: Stan/Spec.

Utopia Antiques Ltd
Lake Rd. (P.J. and Mrs J Wilkinson) Open 10-5 including Sun. *STOCK: Pine and country furniture, decorative accessories.* PARK: Easy. TEL: 09662 88464. VAT: Stan.

White Elephant Antiques
66 Quarry Rigg, Lake Rd. (J.C Moore) Est: 1987. Open 9.30-5.30 including Sun. SIZE: Medium. *STOCK: General antiques, 18th-19th C, £5-£200; reproduction Italian inlaid furniture, £25-£200; Persian, Chinese, Indian and Turkish rugs, £25-£400.* LOC: Far end of precinct. PARK: Easy. TEL: 09662 6962; home - 09662 6073. SER: Restorations (rugs); buys at auction. VAT: Spec.

BRAMPTON

Mary Fell Antiques
Collectors' Corner, 32-34 Main St. Est: 1960. Open Tues., Wed., Fri. and Sat. 11-6, other times by appointment. *STOCK: Sheraton and Victorian furniture, porcelain, china, glass, silver and plate, bric-a-brac, early Victorian oil paintings, pictures, prints, jewellery, pot-lids.* Not Stocked: Coins, armour and swords. LOC: Town centre, beside public car park. PARK: Easy. TEL: Home - 0228 22224. SER: Valuations; restorations (furniture); buys at auction.

BROUGHTON-IN-FURNESS

Church Street Antiques
Church St. (Mr and Mrs McAdam-Thomson) Est: 1988. Open 10-5; winter - afternoons only. SIZE: Small. *STOCK: Furniture including small pine pieces, 19th C, £50-£1,000; glass, brass and china, 19th C, £5-£200.* LOC: Off A595. PARK: Nearby. SER: Valuations; restorations (furniture); buys at auction (as stock). FAIRS: Mainly local. VAT: Stan/Spec.

CARLISLE

Carlisle Antique and Craft Centre
Cecil Hall, Cecil St. Open 9.30-5. SIZE: Large plus trade warehouse. LOC: Off Warwick Rd. PARK: Easy. TEL: 0228 21970. Below are listed the dealers at this centre.

Art Deco
Clarice Cliff, Susie Cooper, Charlotte Rhead, light fittings and furnishings, furniture.

Buttons and Beads
Beads, buttons, jewellery components, hand-made jewellery, craft items.

Fine Pine
Stripped pine furniture; mahogany and oak bedroom suites, large furniture, china, quilts.

It's About Time
(B and W Mitton) Est: 1985. *Longcase, bracket and carriage clocks, watches; Royal Worcester fine porcelain, jewellery, textiles.* SER: Valuations; restorations. TEL: 0228 36910.

Revival Antiques and Collectables
China, small furniture, boxes, advertising ephemera, enamel signs, tins, bottles stoneware.

Warwick Antiques
(J Wardrope) CMBHI. *Period furniture, porcelain, wall and bracket clocks, silver.* SER: Valuations (clocks and watches).

Charm Antiques
Lonsdale St. (M Byers) Open 10.30-4. *STOCK: Furniture, Victorian and Edwardian; pine, china, glass and curios.* LOC: Behind bus station. PARK: Easy. TEL: 0228 23035.

James W Clements
19 Fisher St. Est: 1887. Open 9-5. CL: Thurs. *STOCK: Furniture, glass, china, silver, Georgian and Victorian, and Victorian jewellery.* TEL: 0228 25565. VAT: Stan/Spec.

Daisies Antiques
16a Fisher St. (J Cartner) Est: 1985. Open Wed., Fri. and Sat. 11-5. SIZE: Medium. *STOCK: Textiles, costume and clothes, small furniture, decorative furnishings, linen, jewellery and collectables.* LOC: 2 mins. from city centre. PARK: Easy. TEL: 0228 47198.

Carlisle continued

Maurice Dodd
112 Warwick Rd. (G.W. and V.A Keates) Est: 1945. CL: Sun. except by appointment. *STOCK: Books, pictures, prints, general antiques.* TEL: 0228 22087. VAT: Stan/Spec.

Brian Ferguson
38 Lowther Stand The Old School House, Rickerby. (B Ferguson and H.P Senhouse) Est: 1979. Open 10-5.30; by appointment at Rickerby, CL: Thurs. SIZE: Medium. *STOCK: Furniture, £100-£5,000; European and Oriental ceramics, pictures, silver, glass and decorative objects, £50-£2,000; all 18th and early 19th C.* LOC: Leave M6 junction 43, continue into city, turn right at T. junction. PARK: Nearby. TEL: 0228 45181; home - 0228 35094. SER: Valuations; buys at auction (as stock). VAT: Stan/Spec.

Fisher Street Antiques
16 Fisher St. (Mr and Mrs A.M Foreman) Open 11-5. SIZE: Medium. *STOCK: Furniture, pine, paintings, pottery, linen, decorative items, £5-£1,000.* LOC: Near castle. TEL: 0228 49001; home - 0228 60312. SER: Valuations; restorations; buys at auction.

Carlisle continued

A.C Layne
48 Cecil St. Open by appointment. *STOCK: Clocks and watches.* PARK: Easy. TEL: 0228 45019. SER: Repairs (as stock).

Saint Nicholas Galleries (Antiques)Ltd
28 London Rd. (J., C. and F.E Carruthers) Open 9.30-5. CL: Thurs. SIZE: Medium. *STOCK: General antiques, 18th C, £5-£500.* LOC: City centre. PARK: Nearby. TEL: 0228 34425; home - 0228 22249.

Saint Nicholas Galleries Ltd. (Antiques and Jewellery)
39 Bank St. (C.J Carruthers) Open 10-5. CL: Mon. SIZE: Medium. *STOCK: Jewellery, silver, plate, Rolex pocket watches, clocks; collectables; Royal Doulton; Dux, Oriental vases; pottery, porcelain; watercolours, oil paintings; pine furniture; brass and copper.* LOC: City centre. PARK: Nearby. TEL: 0228 44459.

Souvenir Antiques
Treasury Court, Fisher St. (J Higham) Open 10-5. SIZE: Small. *STOCK: Porcelain and pottery, Victorian to art deco, £5-£500; coronation ware, crested china, local prints, maps, postcards, Roman and medieval coins, costume jewellery, small Victorian and later furniture to £500.* Not Stocked: Textiles. LOC: City centre between Fisher St. and Scotch St. PARK: Nearby. TEL: 0228 401281.

CARTMEL

Anthemion - The Antique Shop
(J. and S Wood) Est: 1982. Open 10-5 seven days. SIZE: Large. *STOCK: English period furniture, 17th to early 19th C, £100-£10,000; decorative items, 17th-19th C, from £20; garden furniture, early 19th C, £100-£2,000.* Not Stocked: Militaria, bric-a-brac. LOC: Village centre. PARK: Easy. TEL: 053 95 36295 or 0836 283547; home - 053 95 36234. FAIRS: NEC, Olympia, Barbican, Chester. VAT: Stan/Spec.

Bacchus Antiques -In the Service of Wine
Longlands. (Mrs J.A Johnson) Est: 1979. Open by appointment only. *STOCK: Fine corkscrews.* TEL: 053 95 36475.

Norman Kerr-Gatehouse Bookshop
The Square. Open by appointment only. *STOCK: Antiquarian books.* TEL: 053 95 36247.

Peter Bain Smith (Bookseller)
Bank Court, Market Sq. Open 11.30-4.30. In season open every day 10.30-6. CL: Mon. and Tues. Jan. to Easter. *STOCK: Antiquarian books, especially children's and local topo-*

Peter Bain Smith (Bookseller) continued

graphy. LOC: A590 from Levens Bridge, off roundabout towards new Lindale by-pass through Grange-over-Sands. PARK: Nearby. TEL: 053 95 36369. SER: Valuations.

COCKERMOUTH

Cockermouth Antiques

5 Station St. (E Bell and G Davies) Est: 1983. Open 10-5. SIZE: Large. *STOCK: General antiques especially ceramics, furniture, pictures, glass, books, metalware, quilts.* LOC: Just off A66, in town centre opposite Post Office. PARK: Easy. TEL: 0900 826746.

Cockermouth Antiques Market

Courthouse, Main St. Est: 1979. Open 10-5. SIZE: Large - 7 stallholders. *STOCK: Victorian, Edwardian and art deco items, furniture, printed collectables, postcards, books, linen, china, glass, toys, textiles, jewellery and pictures.* LOC: Town centre, just off A66. PARK: 50yds. TEL: 0900 824346. SER: Restorations (furniture); stripping (pine). VAT: Stan/Spec.

Holmes Antiques

1 Market Pl. (C. and S Holmes) Est: 1972. Open 10-5. CL: Thurs. SIZE: Medium. *STOCK: Furniture, paintings, prints, small antiques, collectors' items.* PARK: Rear of premises. TEL: 0900 826114; home - 07687 82364. VAT: Stan/Spec.

CONISTON

The Old Man Antiques

Yewdale Rd. (R. and Y Williams) Est: 1965. Open daily 9.30-6 Easter-Nov. SIZE: Medium. *STOCK: General antiques especially barometers - 'banjo', from £240 and 'stick' from £450 when available.* LOC: On Ambleside to Ulverston Rd. PARK: Easy. TEL: 053 94 41389. SER: Restorations (barometers, barographs and thermographs).

CORBY HILL, Nr. Carlisle

Langley Antiques

The Forge. (Mrs P Mather) Est: 1976. Open 10.30-5.30. SIZE: Medium. *STOCK: Country oak, period and Edwardian furniture.* LOC: A69. PARK: Easy. TEL: 0228 60899.

CROSBY RAVENSWORTH

David A H Grayling

Lyvennet. Est: 1971. Open by appointment only. *STOCK: Fine and antiquarian books on natural history and all field sports, £5-£2,000.* LOC: Off M6, junction 38 towards Appleby turn left 1/2 mile past Orton. PARK: Easy. TEL: 09315 282; home and fax - same. SER: Valuations; restorations; fine binding.

Crosby Ravensworth continued

Jennywell Hall Antiques

(Mrs M Macadie) Est: 1975. Open weekends 12-6, other times by appointment. SIZE: Medium. *STOCK: Oak, mahogany furniture, paintings, small items, 16th-19th C.* LOC: 5 miles from junction 39, M6. PARK: Easy. TEL: 093 15 288; home - same.

ENDMOOR, Nr. Kendal

Calvert Antiques

Sycamore House. (Mr and Mrs N.A Hutchinson-Shire and Mr and Mrs V.C Bryan) Est: 1986. Open 9.30-5.30, Sun. 10.30-4.30, Tues. and other times by appointment. SIZE: Medium. *STOCK: Furniture, 17th to early 19th C; clocks, 17th-19th C.* Not Stocked: China, silver, treen and jewellery. LOC: On A65. Leave M6 at junction 36 on to Skipton/Kirby Lonsdale rd., first exit left to Endmoor. PARK: Easy. TEL: 044 87 597; home - same. SER: Restorations (furniture). VAT: Stan/Spec.

GOSFORTH

Archie Miles Bookshop

Beck Pl. (Mrs C.M Linsley) Open 10-5, other times by appointment. CL: Mon. *STOCK: Secondhand, antiquarian and out-of-print books, maps and prints.* TEL: 094 67 25792.

GRASMERE, Nr. Ambleside

Aladdin's Cave

Helm House, Langdale Rd. (J Harwood) Est: 1975. Open 10-5 including Sun. SIZE: Medium. *STOCK: General and rural antiques, brass and copper, coloured glass, country furniture; local prints; oils and watercolours, 18th-19th C, £5-£500.* LOC: Behind Red Lion Hotel. Turn past garden centre from church, then 1st right. PARK: Easy. TEL: 096 65 774; home - 096 65 449.

Bev Dennison Antiques

Open by appointment. *STOCK: Oil and electric lighting, 19th-20th C, £50-£1,000; collectables, 18th-20th C, £10-£500; objects du vertu, 19th C, £100-£1,000; decorative items, 19th-20th C, £50-£2,000.* LOC: 1 mile from village. PARK: Easy. TEL: 096 65 733 (Mon.-Fri. only). SER: Buys at auction (as stock). FAIRS: NEC, Olympia, Barbican. VAT: Stan/Spec. *Trade Only.*

The Stables

College St. (J.A. and K.M Saalmans) Est: 1971. Open daily 10-6 Easter-October, other times telephone call advisable. SIZE: Small. *STOCK: Brass and copper items, oil lamps, domestic bygones; pottery, silver, prints, books.* Not Stocked: Weapons, coins. LOC: By the side of Moss Grove Hotel. PARK: Easy. TEL: 096 65 453; home - same. VAT: Stan/Spec.

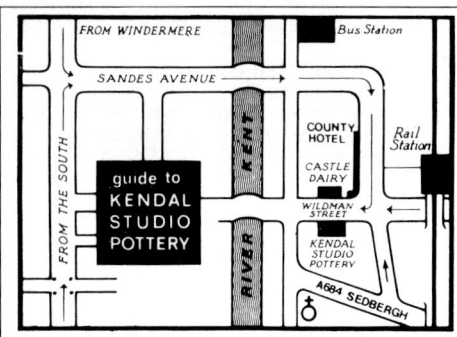

GREAT URSWICK, Nr. Ulverston

Lilian Wood Antiques
Midtown House. Usually open by prior telephone call advisable. *STOCK: Furniture, 17th to early 19th C; paintings and decorative items.* LOC: Off A590, Midtown is second house beyond Derby Arms, turning left. PARK: Easy. TEL: 0229 56297.

GREYSTOKE, Nr. Penrith

Pelican Antiques
Church Rd. (Mrs J Kirkby) Est: 1897. Open daily but phone call advisable. *STOCK: General small antiques, £5-£300.* PARK: Easy. TEL: 085 33 447.

HOLME, Nr. Carnforth

The Holme Fire Co.
Holme Mill. (T. and S Smurthwaite) Est: 1983. Open 10-5, Sun. 12-4. SIZE: Large. *STOCK: Victorian, Georgian fireplaces, tiles, kitchen ranges.* LOC: 4 miles from junctions 35 and 36, M6. PARK: Own. TEL: 0524 781423; home - 0524 422138. SER: Restorations (cast iron); stripping (pine). VAT: Stan.

Utopia Antiques Ltd
Holme Mills. (P.J. and Mrs J Wilkinson) Est: 1970. Open 9-5.30. SIZE: Large. *STOCK: Irish, English and European pine, 18th-19th C, £25-£2,000.* PARK: Easy. TEL: 0524 781739. SER: Restorations (pine); shipping. VAT: Stan.

KENDAL

Below Stairs
78 Highgate. (S Ritchie) Open 10-4. *STOCK: Brass, copper, silver, coloured glass, porcelain, collectables.* LOC: Main street under Shakespeare Inn. TEL: 0539 741278.

Cottage Antiques
80 Highgate. (S Satchell) Est: 1974. Open 11-4.30. CL: Mon. and Thurs. *STOCK: Mainly smalls including pottery, glass, brass, copper, metalware, treen, kitchen items, tool and craft*

Cottage Antiques continued

bygones, small silver, some furniture mainly pine. Not Stocked: Coins. LOC: A6. PARK: Nearby. TEL: 0539 722683; home - 04488 485.

Dower House Antiques
38-40 Kirkland. (B Blakemore) Open 9.15-6, Thurs. 9.15-1. *STOCK: Pottery, porcelain, paintings, furniture and shipping goods.* TEL: 0539 722778.

Keith D Edwards Antiques
Crosscrake Farm, Crosscrake. Open anytime, appointment advisable. *STOCK: General antiques, period oak and mahogany.* LOC: Off A65. TEL: 05395 60313. VAT: Stan/Spec.

Georgian House LAPADA
99 Highgate. (P Gunson and D Jones) Est: 1971. Open 9-5. SIZE: Large. *STOCK: Oak dressers, tables, chairs, tridarns and beds, 17th C, £1,000-£4,000; dining and tea tables, chairs and bureaux, 18th C, £1,000-£3,000.* LOC: On right hand side on A6 (main street). PARK: At rear. TEL: 0539 724527. SER: Valuations; restorations. FAIRS: Cumbrian. VAT: Stan/Spec.

Kendal Studios Antiques
Wildman St. (R. and A.O Aindow) Est: 1950. Open 10.30-1 and 3-6, till 5 on Sat. CL: Thurs. SIZE: Medium. *STOCK: Ceramics, maps and prints, paintings, oak furniture, jewellery, art pottery.* LOC: Leave M6 at junction 37, follow one-way system, shop on left. PARK: Nearby. TEL: 0539 723291 (24 hrs. answering service). SER: Restorations; finder; shipping. VAT: Stan/Spec.

The Silver Thimble
39 All Hallows Lane. (V Ritchie) Est: 1980. Open 10-4. SIZE: Large. *STOCK: Jewellery, silver, glass, linen and lace, porcelain, copper and brass.* LOC: Turn left at second set of traffic lights on main road into Kendal from south, shop 200yds. on right. PARK: Easy. TEL: 0539 731456.

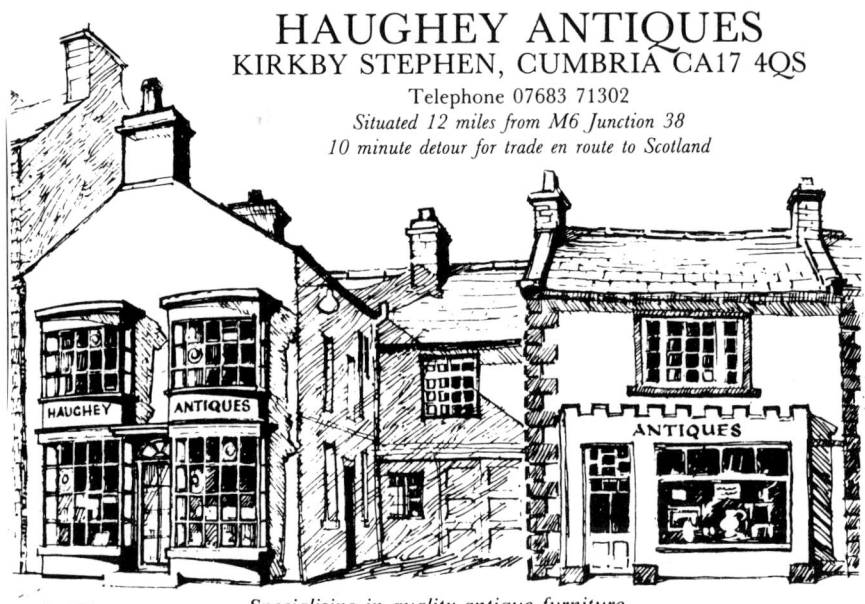

KESWICK

And So To Bed
Lake Rd. (W.I Raw) Est: 1981. Open 9.15-5.15. *STOCK: Brass beds, bedroom furniture, lamps, mirrors, bedding sets and linen, £150-£1,000.* LOC: Top of Main St. TEL: 076 87 74881. VAT: Stan.

Country Living Antiques
1 New St, Packhorse Court. (Miss J.M McCrone) Est: 1990. Open 9.30-5.30, Sun. 2-5 (Whitsun-Nov. inclusive). SIZE: Small. *STOCK: Small Victorian and Edwardian furniture, £50-£3,500; porcelain, pottery, collectables, Georgian-Edwardian, English and European, £5-£1,500; paintings, prints, writing boxes, jewellery, silver and collectors' items, Georgian-Edwardian, £5-£1,500.* Not Stocked: Weapons, stamps, toys and books. LOC: Opposite Motor Museum, halfway up Standish St. PARK: Nearby. TEL: 076 87 71373; home - 076 885 353. SER: Restorations. VAT: Stan/Spec.

John Young and Son (Antiques) LAPADA
12-14 Main St. Est: 1890. Open 9-5.30. SIZE: Large. *STOCK: General antiques, 18th-19th C.* LOC: Town centre. PARK: At rear. TEL: 076 87 73434. VAT: Stan/Spec.

KIRKBY LONSDALE

Alexander Adamson
Tearnside Hall. Est: 1863. *STOCK: Furniture, £200-£40,000; porcelain, £50-£2,000; glass, £50-£800.* PARK: Easy. TEL: 052 42 71989. SER: Valuations; restorations (furniture). VAT: Spec.

Merlin Antiques
8 Market St. (R Udall) Est: 1939. Open 10.30-4.30, other times by appointment. CL: Mon. and Wed. SIZE: Medium. *STOCK: Clocks, furniture, copper, brass, from 1700, £1-£3,000.* LOC: Near Sun Inn. TEL: 052 42 71208; evenings 05396 20719. SER: Restorations.

The Verve Gallery
15 Main St. Est: 1989. Usually open 10-5 but prior telephone call advisable. SIZE: Medium. *STOCK: Prints, watercolours and oil paintings, 17th-20th C.* PARK: Nearby. TEL: 052 42 71805.

KIRKBY STEPHEN

Haughey Antiques LAPADA
Market St. (D.M Haughey) Est: 1969. Open 10-5, Sat. 12-5. SIZE: Large. *STOCK: Furniture, 17th-19th C; garden furniture and statuary.* PARK: Easy. TEL: 076 83 71302. SER: Valuations. VAT: Stan/Spec.

Kirkby Stephen continued

David Hill
36 Market Sq. Est: 1965. Open Mon., Fri. and Sat. 9.30-4. SIZE: Medium. *STOCK: Longcase clocks, £350-£1,500; country furniture, £10-£1,000, all 18th-19th C; curios, £5-£50; shipping goods, kitchenalia, iron and brassware.* LOC: On A685. PARK: Easy. TEL: 076 83 71598. VAT: Stan/Spec.

Mortlake Antiques
32-34 Market St. (C.J. and J.A Bate) Est: 1946. Open 10-5. CL: Tues. (Easter-Oct.), Tues., Wed., Thurs. (Nov.-Easter). SIZE: Medium. *STOCK: Furniture, period, Victorian, Edwardian and country including stripped pine; treen, kitchenalia, bygones, bric-a-brac and metalware.* Not Stocked: Silver, glass, porcelain. LOC: On A685, 12 miles east of junction 38, M6. PARK: Easy. TEL: 076 83 71666 (ansaphone). VAT: Stan/Spec.

MILBURN, Nr. Penrith

Netherley Cottage Antiques
(J Heelis) Est: 1970. Usually open 8.30-8 but appointment advisable. SIZE: Small. *STOCK: Country cottage pottery, porcelain and ornaments, 18th-19th C, £1-£70; kitchen and dairy items, interesting bygones, brass, watercolours, £1-£85; treen, some Oriental items.* Not Stocked: Silver and clocks. TEL: 076 83 61403. SER: Buys at auction.

MILNTHORPE

The Antique Shop
9 Park Rd. Open 10-4.30 Wed. and Fri. SIZE: Medium. *STOCK: General antiques, books, furniture.* LOC: From A6, left at traffic lights in village, opposite Post Office. TEL: 044 82 2253.

NEWBY BRIDGE

Shire Antiques
The Post House, High Newton, Newton-in-Cartmel. (B. and Mrs J Shire) Open by appointment anytime. SIZE: Medium. *STOCK: Early oak furniture, 16th-18th C; Georgian copper, brass, treen.* Not Stocked: Silver and jewellery. LOC: On A590 to Barrow, house is 50yds. from main road in village. PARK: Easy. TEL: 053 95 31431; home - same. SER: Valuations; restorations (furniture). VAT: Stan/Spec.

Townhead Antiques LAPADA
(Mrs C.H. and C.P Townley) Est: 1960. Open 9-5.30. CL: Sun. except by appointment. SIZE: Large. *STOCK: 18th-19th C furniture, silver, porcelain, glass, decorative pieces; clocks, pictures, garden furniture.* LOC: A592. 1 mile from Newby Bridge on the Windermere road. PARK: Easy. TEL: 053 95 31321; fax - 053 95 30019. VAT: Stan/Spec.

PENRITH

Antiques of Penrith
4 Corney Sq. (L Mildwurf and Partners) Est: 1964. Open 10-12 and 1.30-4.45, Sat. 10-12. CL: Wed. SIZE: Large. *STOCK: Early oak; mahogany furniture, clocks, brass, copper, glass, china, silver plate, metal, Staffordshire figures, curios.* Not Stocked: Jewellery, paintings, rugs. LOC: Near Town Hall. PARK: Easy. TEL: 0768 62801. VAT: Stan.

Cornerways
20 Victoria Rd. (P.B. and A.L Clark) Est: 1981. CL: Wed. SIZE: Medium. *STOCK: Furniture including Edwardian, £20-£1,000; collectable items, £2-£500; jewellery, to £900.* LOC: On A6 (south). PARK: Nearby. TEL: 0768 67754; after 6p.m. 63635. VAT: Stan/Spec.

Corney House Antiques
Corney House, 1 Corney Pl. (Mr and Mrs Mawer) Est: 1983. Open 10-1 and 2-5. CL: Wed. SIZE: Medium. *STOCK: Furniture, Georgian and Victorian, and 19th C pine, £100-£3,000; porcelain and pottery, 18th-20th C, £10-£2,000.* LOC: Near town hall. PARK: Easy. TEL: 0768 67665. VAT: Stan/Spec.

The Gallery
54 Castlegate. (K.G Plant) Est: 1969. Open daily, Wed. and Sun. by appointment. SIZE: Small. *STOCK: Paintings and watercolours, 17th-20th C, £50-£20,000.* LOC: From centre of Penrith towards the railway station. TEL: 0768 65538; home - same. SER: Valuations; buys at auction (paintings). VAT: Stan/Spec.

Joseph James Antiques
Corney Sq. (G.R Walker) Est: 1970. Open 9-12.30 and 1.30-5.30. CL: Wed. SIZE: Medium. *STOCK: Furniture and upholstery, 18th C and Victorian, £10-£800; porcelain and pottery, £5-£200; silver and plate, pictures, £2-£500, all 18th-19th C.* LOC: On the one-way system in the town, 100yds. from the main shopping area (Middlegate), 50yds. from the town hall. PARK: Easy (also large car park 100yds.). TEL: 0768 62065. SER: Restorations; re-upholstery. VAT: Stan.

Penrith continued

Penrith Coin and Stamp Centre
37 King St. (Mr and Mrs A Gray) Resident. Est: 1974. Open 9-5.30. CL: Wed. Sept.-May. SIZE: Medium. *STOCK: Coins, B.C. to date, 1p-£500; jewellery, secondhand, £5-£500; Great Britain and Commonwealth stamps.* LOC: Just off town centre. PARK: Behind shop. TEL: 0768 64185. SER: Valuations; jewellery repairs. FAIRS: Many coin. VAT: Stan.

Jane Pollock Antiques
4 Castlegate. Open 9.30-5. CL: Wed. SIZE: Medium. *STOCK: Georgian and Victorian silver, some 20th C small items; Victorian pottery, blue and white lustre; wooden boxes, some small furniture.* LOC: One-way street from town centre towards station. PARK: Easy. TEL: 0768 67211. SER: Valuations (silver); restorations (silver, blue glass liners); buys at auction (silver, pottery). FAIRS: Buxton, Olympia, Edinburgh, Kensington, Harrogate and Grasmere. VAT: Stan/Spec.

RAVENSTONEDALE, Nr. Kirkby Stephen

The Book House
Grey Garth. (C. and M Irwin) PBFA. Est: 1965. Open every day, appointment preferred. *STOCK: Books, mainly 19th-20th C, £1-£1,000; some postcards, 20th C, 25p-£10.* LOC: Off A685. Square house across road triangle from village school. PARK: Easy. TEL: 058 73 634; home - same. SER: Valuations. FAIRS: Northern PBFA. VAT: Stan.

SEDBURGH

R F G Hollett and Son
6 Finkle St. (R F G and C G Hollett) Est: 1951. Open 10-12 and 1.15-5. SIZE: Medium. *STOCK: Antiquarian books, 15th-20th C, £10-£10,000+; maps, prints and paintings, 17th-19th C, £10-£5,000; small general antiques, 17th-19th C, £50-£2,000.* LOC: Town centre. PARK: Nearby. TEL: 05396 20298. SER: Valuations. VAT: Stan.

Sedburgh Antiques and Collectables
59 Main St. (Miss M Brigg and Mrs M J Owens) Est: 1976. Open 9.30-1 and 1.30-5. SIZE: Small. *STOCK: Edwardian and Victorian furniture, £200-£500; Victorian linen, £5-£70; Victorian china, £5-£150.* PARK: Opposite. TEL: 05396 21276; home - 05396 20864. VAT: Stan/Spec.

Stable Antiques
Wheelwright Cottage, 15-16 Back Lane. Est: 1970. Open 10-6. *STOCK: Small furniture, brass, copper, silver, china, prints, small collectors' items.* LOC: 5 miles from exit 37, M6. TEL: 053 96 20251.

ULVERSTON

A1A Antiques
59B Market St. (J.W Thornton) Est: 1960. Open by appointment. SIZE: Large. *STOCK: Bric-a-brac, clocks, furniture, shipping items, pictures, decorators items.* PARK: Easy. TEL: 0229 869745 or 09662 2930/5183. SER: Valuations; restorations; buys at auction. VAT: Stan/Spec.

Elizabeth and Son
Market Hall. (J.R Bevins) Est: 1960. Open 9-5. CL: Wed. SIZE: Medium. *STOCK: Victorian and Georgian glass and silver; brass, copper, books, gold and silver jewellery.* LOC: Town centre. PARK: Easy. TEL: 0229 52763.

WHITEHAVEN

Owen Kelly Antiques
10-11 New St. (V.C Kelly) Appointment advisable. *STOCK: General antiques including china, silver.* TEL: 0946 692879.

Michael Moon
41-43 Roper St. (M. and S Moon) ABA, PBFA. Est: 1969. Open 9.30-5. SIZE: Large. *STOCK: Antiquarian books including Cumbrian topography.* PARK: Nearby. TEL: 0946 62936. FAIRS: PBFA Northern. VAT: Stan.

WIGTON

S.I Jackson Antiques
71 High St. Est: 1987. Open by appointment. CL: Thurs. *STOCK: General antiques and decorative items, £10-£500.* PARK: Easy. TEL: 069 73 45034.

Allen Wright Antiques
Burnfoot Cottage, Burnfoot. Est: 1980. Usually open but prior telephone call advisable. SIZE: Medium. *STOCK: Furniture, 18th-19th C, £1,000-£2,000; general antiques, £5-£2,000; restorations materials.* LOC: Bottom High St. on main Carlisle road, large 17th C house and barn. PARK: Easy. TEL: 069 73 43457; mobile - 0836 237077; home - same. SER: Valuations; restorations (mainly furniture); buys at auction. FAIRS: Newark; Edinburgh; Wales.

WINDERMERE

The Birdcage Antiques
College Rd. (Mrs T.A Griffiths) Est: 1983. Open Wed., Fri. and Sat. 10-5, or by appointment. SIZE: Small. *STOCK: General antiques, glass, brass and copper, oil lamps, country bygones, Staffordshire, 18th C to 1920, small silver, £10-£500; 19th C pottery.* LOC: From A591 through village, past end of one-way system, turn right after 50yds. PARK: Nearby. TEL: 096 62 5063; home - 096 62 3041/3310. VAT: Stan/Spec.

Windermere continued

Century Antiques and Victoria Galleries
Victoria Cottage, 13 Victoria St. (D. and R Hopwood) Est: 1969. Open 9-5.30. CL: Thurs. *STOCK: Furniture, collectors' items, clocks, pictures.* LOC: On main road from station, adjacent to Ellery Hotel. TEL: 096 62 4126.

Joseph Thornton Antiques
4 Victoria St. (J.W Thornton) Est: 1971. Open 10-4.30 or by appointment. SIZE: Large. *STOCK: General antiques, art, architectural and decorators' items, clocks, bric-a-brac.* LOC: 50yds. from railway station. PARK: Easy. TEL: 096 62 2930/5183 or 0229 869745. SER: Valuations; buys at auction. VAT: Stan/Spec.

IS YOUR ENTRY CORRECT?
If there is even the slightest inaccuracy in your entry, *please* let us know before 1st January 1992.
GUIDE TO THE
ANTIQUE SHOPS OF BRITAIN
5 Church Street, Woodbridge, Suffolk.
Tel: (0394) 385501

The Duke of Wellington by Thomas Lawrence, c.1815. Lawrence unhesitatingly flattered his subject as no other painter of Wellington ever did. The black sash that Wellington wears should, by definition, be striped, but Lawrence, who took great care that the picture itself should be an ordered whole, had the presumption to paint out the stripes. 'Never mind', said Wellington, 'they merely constitute me Generalissimo of the Armies of Spain'. It is interesting to compare Lawrence's portrait with Goya's masterpiece of a portrait of Wellington in the National Gallery, for Lawrence's sitter bears not the slightest resemblance to the man painted by Goya, or for that matter to the man caricatured by contemporary political cartoonists. From ***The British Portrait 1660-1960,*** published in 1991 by the **Antique Collectors' Club.** £45.00.

Derbyshire

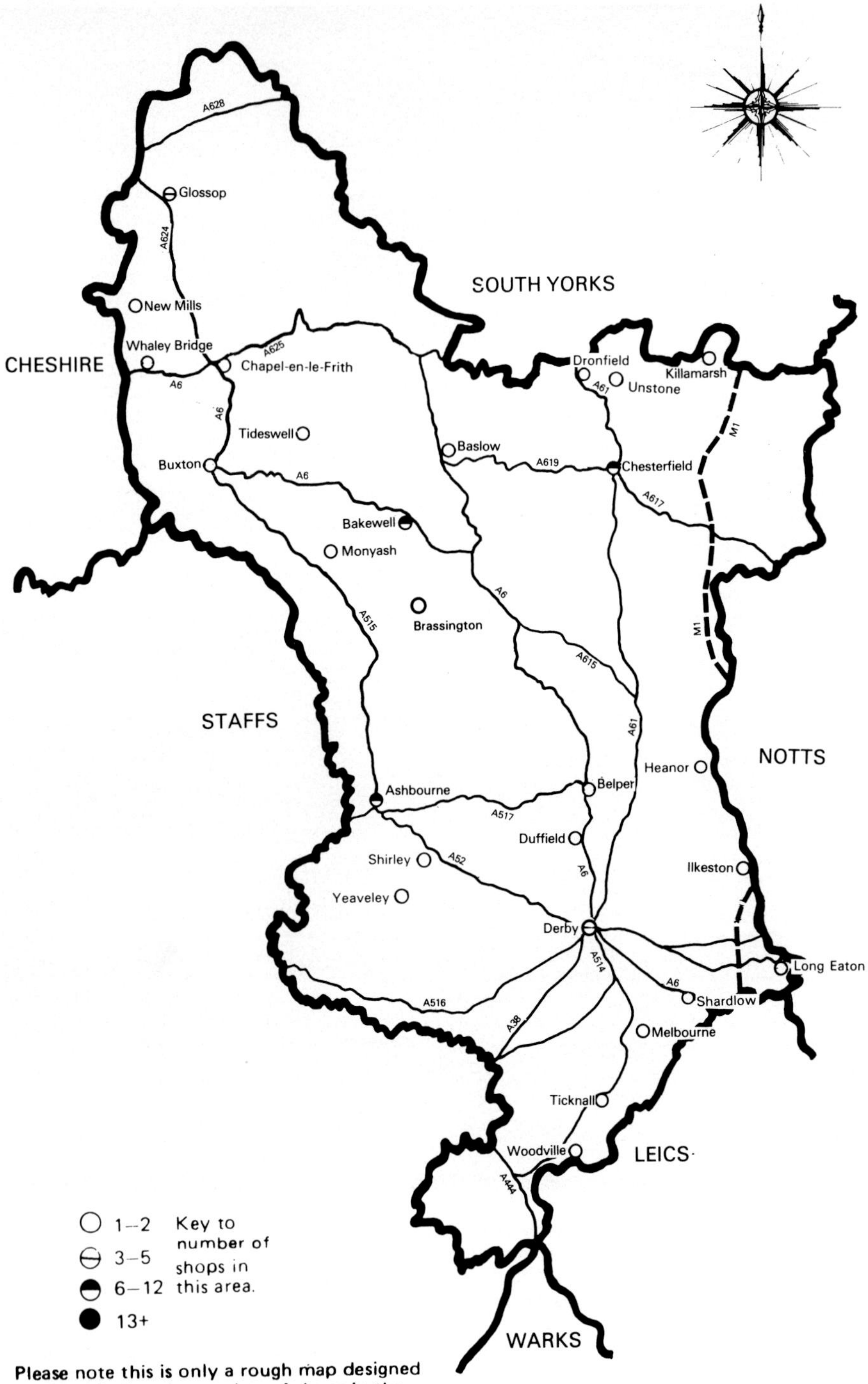

A628
Glossop
A624
New Mills
Whaley Bridge
CHESHIRE
A625
A6
Chapel-en-le-Frith
SOUTH YORKS
Dronfield
A61
Unstone
Killamarsh
M1
Tideswell
Baslow
Buxton
A6
A619
Chesterfield
A617
Bakewell
Monyash
Brassington
A6
A515
A615
M1
STAFFS
A61
NOTTS
Heanor
Belper
Ashbourne
A517
Duffield
Shirley
A52
A6
Ilkeston
Yeaveley
Derby
A514
Long Eaton
A6
Shardlow
A516
A38
Melbourne
Ticknall
Woodville
LEICS
A444
WARKS
1–2
3–5
6–12
13+
Key to number of shops in this area.

Please note this is only a rough map designed to show dealers the number of shops in the various towns, and is not necessarily totally accurate.

The practicality of this expanding dining-table in well figured mahogany with its 'Gillow look' derived from the reeded legs again ensured a strong price of £6,050. From an article entitled 'Only a Few Bargains' by James Storm, published in the March 1991 issue of ***Antique Collecting.***

ASHBOURNE

Yvonne Adams Antiques
47 Church St. (Mrs Y S Adams) Est: 1983. CL: Tues. a.m. and Wed. SIZE: Small. *STOCK: Oak and country furniture, 17th-19th C, £30-£2,000; metalwork, decorative and unusual items.* LOC: A52. PARK: Nearby. TEL: 0335 46466.

Ashbourne Fine Art
Agnes Meadow Farm, Offcote. (S.A. and D.J Smith) Open by appointment only. *STOCK: 19th-20th C oils, watercolours and dolls.* TEL: 0335 44072.

Pamela Elsom - Antiques LAPADA
5 Church St. Est: 1963. Open 10-5. CL: Wed. p.m. SIZE: Medium. *STOCK: Furniture, £20-£5,000, metalware, both 17th-19th C; period smalls, general antiques, treen, pottery, glass, secondhand book dept.* Not Stocked: Coins, militaria. LOC: On A52. PARK: Easy. TEL: 0335 43468. SER: Valuations. VAT: Spec.

Manion Antiques
23 Church St. (Mrs V.J Manion) Est: 1984. Open Thurs., Fri. and Sat. 10-5, other times by appointment. SIZE: Small. *STOCK: Porcelain, silver, jewellery, small furniture, £50-£100+.* PARK: Easy. TEL: 0335 43207; home - same. SER: Valuations.

Ashbourne continued

Out of Time Antiques
21 Church St. (T Wardle and M Locke) Est: 1975. Open 10-5. CL: Wed. SIZE: Medium. *STOCK: Decorative and collectable items, metalware, pottery and textiles; pine, oak and mahogany.* LOC: A52. PARK: Easy. TEL: 0335 42096; home - 0335 42741/42074.

Rose Antiques
37 Church St. Est: 1982. Open 10-5. SIZE: Medium. *STOCK: Furniture, silver, porcelain, jewellery, copper, brass and pine.* LOC: A52. PARK: Easy. TEL: 0335 43822; home - 028 375 301.

Spurrier-Smith Antiques LAPADA
28, 29 and 41 Church St. (I Spurrier-Smith) Est: 1973. Open 9.30-5.30, Sun. by appointment. SIZE: Large. *STOCK: Furniture, oils, watercolours, porcelain, pottery, metalware, instruments, Oriental, bronzes, collectables, pine, decorative items.* TEL: 0335 43669/42198; home - 0629 822502. SER: Valuations. VAT: Stan/Spec.

Ashbourne continued

Tanglewood
9-11 Station St. (R Beech) Est: 1979. Open 8-5, Sat. and Sun. by appointment. SIZE: Large. *STOCK: Irish pine, including dressers and food cupboards, 18th-19th C, £50-£800.* LOC: A52. PARK: Nearby. TEL: 0335 46390; home - 0335 42663. SER: Restorations (pine). VAT: Stan. *Trade Only.*

Kenneth Upchurch
30B Church St. Est: 1972. *STOCK: Oil paintings and watercolours, mainly 19th C; pottery and porcelain.* TEL: 0335 46070/0332 754499.

BAKEWELL

Beedham Antiques Ltd
Holme Hall. (W.H Beedham) Open by appointment. *STOCK: English oak furniture, 16th-17th C.* LOC: Off A619. TEL: 0629 813285. SER: Valuations; buys at auction. VAT: Spec.

K Chappell Antiques and Fine Art BADA
King St. Est: 1940. Open 9-6. *STOCK: 17th-19th C English furniture, oil paintings, porcelain, pottery, metalwork, clocks and decorative items.* TEL: 0629 812496; fax - 0629 814531. VAT: Stan/Spec.

Michael Goldstone BADA
Avenel Court, and The Old Town Hall. (M Goldstone) Est: 1927. Open 9-6 or by appointment. SIZE: Large. *STOCK: Oak furniture, 16th-18th C, from £100; walnut furniture, brass, 18th C, from £500.* PARK: Easy. TEL: 0629 812487; home - same. SER: Valuations; buys at auction. VAT: Spec.

Martin and Dorothy Harper Antiques LAPADA
King St. Open 10-5.30, Sun. by appointment. SIZE: Medium. *STOCK: Furniture, £300-£3,000; metalware, £30-£300; glass, £15-£150; all 17th to late 19th C.* PARK: Easy. TEL: 0629 814757. SER: Valuations; restorations (re-upholstery); buys at auction. VAT: Stan/Spec.

Alan Hill Books
3 Buxton Rd. Est: 1980. Open 10-5.30. *STOCK: Antiquarian books and maps.* TEL: 0629 814841.

Water Lane Antiques
Water Lane. (M. and L Pembery) Est: 1967. Open 9.30-1 and 2-5. SIZE: Medium. *STOCK: Furniture, £500-£4,000; metalware, £100-£1,000; objets d'art, £100-£1,500, all 18th-19th C.* LOC: Off Market Sq. PARK: Nearby. TEL: 0629 814161. SER: Valuations; restorations. VAT: Stan/Spec.

BASLOW

Westfield Antiques
Rigel, Church View Drive. Open by appointment only. *STOCK: 19th C porcelain and Chinese embroidery.* TEL: 0246 582386. FAIRS: Buxton, Thoresby.

BELPER

Sweetings (Antiques 'n' Things)
1 & 1a The Butts. (K.J Sweeting and Miss J.L Bunting) Est: 1971. Open daily. SIZE: Large. *STOCK: Pre 1940's furniture including stripped pine, oak, mahogany, satinwood, £20-£1,000.* LOC: Off A6, near Market Place. PARK: Easy. TEL: 0773 825930/822780. SER: Valuations; restorations (pine and satinwood); shipping. VAT: Stan.

Neil Wayne "The Razor Man"
High Peak ProductsOld Baptist Chapel, rear of 'Riflemans Arms', 72 Bridge St. Resident. Est: 1969. Open every day 9.30-6, prior telephone call essential. SIZE: Medium. *STOCK: Razors and shaving items, 18th to early 19th C, £20-£300; knives including fruit, pocket, hunting and cutlery, 17th-19th C, £20-£500; optical and medical items, 17th-20th C, £10-£1,000.* PARK: Easy. TEL: 0773 827910/820566; fax - 0773 825662.

BRASSINGTON, Nr. Ashbourne

Knights Antiques LAPADA
The Old Barn, Middle Lane. Open by appointment. *STOCK: 18th-19th C English furniture and decorative items.* TEL: 062 985 317. SER: Valuations.

BUXTON

G. and J Antiques
George St. (G. and J Claessens) Est: 1964. Open 10-5, Sat. 10-1, Sun. and Sat. p.m. by appointment. SIZE: Large. *STOCK: Furniture, Georgian, Victorian and continental, clocks and bronzes, from £500+.* LOC: Town centre, on roundabout near Palace Hotel. PARK: Opposite. TEL: 0298 72198; home - 0298 25597. SER: Valuations. VAT: Stan/Spec.

Lewis Antiques
64 Fairfield Rd. (J and S Lewis) Resident. Open 10.30-5, other times by appointment. CL: Mon. and Wed. *STOCK: General antiques, furniture, smalls, linen, collectables.* TEL: 0298 78648.

Buxton continued

The Penny Post Antiques
9 Cavendish Circus. (D and R Hammond) Est: 1978. Open 10-4.30, Sat. 10-5. CL: Mon. and Wed. SIZE: Small. *STOCK: Furniture, 18th to early 20th C, £100-£600; commemoratives and crested china, £5-£75; general antiques.* LOC: Town centre, opposite Palace Hotel. PARK: Easy. TEL: Home - 0298 25965.

West End Galleries
8 Cavendish Circus. (A. and A Needham) Est: 1955. Open 9-5. CL: Sat. SIZE: Large. *STOCK: French, Dutch, English furniture; clocks, paintings, works of art, bronzes.* LOC: A6. PARK: Easy. TEL: 0298 24546. VAT: Stan/Spec.

What Now Antiques
Cavendish Arcade, The Crescent. (L Carruthers) Open 10.30-5.00, Sun. 2-4. *STOCK: Furniture, textiles, garden statues.* TEL: 0298 27178.

CHAPEL-EN-LE-FRITH

The Clock House
48 Manchester Rd. (A.W Thom) MBHI. Resident. Est: 1973. Open 10-6, Sun. 12-6. SIZE: Small. *STOCK: Clocks, 17th-19th C, £25-£5,000; jewellery, 19th-20th C, £10-£500; general antiques, 17th-20th C, £10-£3,000.* LOC: Turn off A6 at town by-pass. PARK: Nearby. TEL: 0298 815174. SER: Valuations; restorations and repairs (clocks).

CHESTERFIELD

Cottage Curios
209 Chatsworth Rd, Brampton. (P Coleman) Est: 1981. Open Thurs. and Fri. 10.30-4.30, Sat. 2-5. SIZE: Small. *STOCK: General antiques, prints and watercolours, late 19th C to 1930, £5-£500.* LOC: A619. PARK: Easy. TEL: 0246 202225. SER: Picture framing.

Anthony D Goodlad
26 Fairfield Rd, Brockwell. Est: 1974. Open by appointment only. *STOCK: General militaria.* LOC: Close to town centre. PARK: Easy. TEL: 0246 204004.

Hackney House Antiques
Hackney Lane, Barlow. (Mrs J.M Gorman) Resident. *STOCK: Furniture, 18th-19th C; silver, prints, jewellery, clocks.* TEL: 0742 890248. VAT: Stan/Spec.

Ian Morris
86 Saltergate, and 479 Chatsworth Rd. Est: 1967. Open 9-5, Sat. 9-1. SIZE: Medium. *STOCK: Furniture, 19th to early 20th C, £100-£1,000; pictures, small items.* LOC: Main thoroughfare, just past town hall. PARK: 100yds.. TEL: 0246 235120. SER: Valuations. VAT: Stan/Spec.

Chesterfield continued

Tilleys Vintage Magazine Shop
29/31 South St, New Whittington. (A.G.J and A.A.J.C Tilley) Est: 1979. Usually open 10-1.30 and 3-5, prior telephone call advisable. SIZE: Large. *STOCK: Magazines, newspapers.* PARK: Easy. TEL: 0246 454270. SER: Mail order.

Brian Yates Antiques
35 Bank St, Brampton. Est: 1977. Open 10-5. SIZE: Small. *STOCK: Furniture, £500-£1,000; boxes, £50-£200; porcelain, copper, brass, £10-£250, all 19th C.* LOC: Off Chatsworth Rd. PARK: Easy. TEL: 0246 220395; home - 0246 230349. SER: Valuations; restorations; cane seating; polishing; buys at auction (period furniture). VAT: Stan/Spec.

DERBY

Abbey House
115 Woods Lane. (S White) Resident. Est: 1959. *STOCK: Dolls and accessories, teddy bears and toys.* TEL: 0332 31426. SER: Repairs (dolls).

Derby Antique Centre
11 Friargate. (D Foddy and J Parkin) Est: 1975. Open 10-5.30, Sun. a.m. by appointment. SIZE: Large. *STOCK: Furniture and clocks, porcelain, 18th-19th C, £25-£3,000; silver and jewellery, 19th-20th C, £5-£500; dolls and toys, cameras, linen, pictures, pine, copper and brass.* LOC: Close to city centre and inner ring road. PARK: Restricted and 200yds. TEL: 0332 385002; home - 0332 841331. SER: Restorations (furniture and clocks). VAT: Stan/Spec.

Derby Antiques Market
52-56 Curzon St. (E.I Corry) Est: 1954. Open 9-5. CL: Wed. p.m. SIZE: Medium. *STOCK: Furniture, paintings, china, silver.* TEL: 0332 41861. VAT: Spec.

Friargate Pine and Antiques Centre
The Pump HouseFriargate Wharf, Stafford St. Entrance. (N J Marianski) Open 9-5. *STOCK: Victorian pine and general antiques.* TEL: 0332 41215.

Laura's Bookshop
58 Osmaston Rd. Est: 1969. CL: Mon. and Wed. *STOCK: Antiquarian and secondhand books, antiquarian maps and prints, especially local history and topography.* PARK: Own. TEL: 0332 47094. VAT: Stan.

Charles H Ward
12 Friar Gate. (M.G Ward) CL: Wed. p.m. *STOCK: Oil paintings, 19th-20th C; watercolours.* TEL: 0332 42893. SER: Restorations.

DRONFIELD

Bardwell Antiques
51 Chesterfield Rd. (S Bardwell) Open 10-5. CL: Mon. *STOCK: General antiques.* TEL: 0246 412183.

DUFFIELD, Nr. Derby

Wayside Antiques
62 Town St. (Mrs J Harding) Est: 1975. *STOCK: Furniture, 18th and 19th C, £50-£2,000; porcelain, pictures, boxes and silver.* TEL: 0332 840346. VAT: Stan/Spec.

GLOSSOP

Antiques for All
Old Chapel, 1 Shrewsbury St. (Mrs F Hickmott) Est: 1980. Open 10-5, Sun. 1-5, other times by appointment. CL: Tues. SIZE: Large. *STOCK: Ceramics, glass, furniture, collectors' items, 18th-20th C.* LOC: Take 3rd turning on right after traffic lights in town centre, travelling towards Manchester. PARK: Easy. TEL: 0457 866960.

Derbyshire Clocks
104 High St. West. (J.A. and T.P Lees) Est: 1975. CL: Mon. and Tues. *STOCK: Clocks.* TEL: 0457 862677. SER: Restorations (clocks).

Glossop continued

Glossop Antique Centre
Brookfield. (E. and M Annal) Open daily including Sun. 10-5. SIZE: 13 dealers. *STOCK: General antiques.* LOC: Opposite Tuson's Garage, on A57. PARK: Easy. TEL: 0457 863904. SER: Valuations; restorations; buys at auction.

Old Cross Gallery
Church St, South, Old Glossop. (Mrs A Lawson) Resident. Est: 1989. Open Thurs.-Sun. 10-5.30, other times by appointment. SIZE: Medium. *STOCK: Country furniture, pictures, frames, mirrors, decorative items, mainly Victorian and Edwardian, £1-£1,000.* Not Stocked: China, silver and jewellery. LOC: Off A57, by Manor Park. PARK: Nearby. TEL: 0457 862555. SER: Valuations; restorations.

HAYFIELD, Nr. New Mills

Michael Allcroft Antiques
1 Church St. Open by appointment. *STOCK: General antiques.* TEL: 0663 742684.

HEANOR

Bygones
23c Derby Rd. (Mrs P Buttifant) Open 10-5. CL: Mon. and Wed. *STOCK: Furniture, porcelain, objets d'art, paintings and prints.* TEL: 0773 768503. SER: Framing.

ILKESTON

Matsell Antiques Ltd
Kingsmill House, 52 King St. (B. and P Matsell) Est: 1945. Open by appointment. *STOCK: English furniture and decorative objects pre-1840.* LOC: Close to M1, junction 25 or 26. TEL: 0602 302446. FAIRS: British International, Birmingham, Kenilworth, City of London, Buxton, Harrogate, Kensington, Cafe Royal. VAT: Stan/Spec.

KILLAMARSH

Havenplan's Architectural Emporium
The Old Station, Station Rd. Est: 1972. Open 10-4. SIZE: Large. *STOCK: Architectural fittings and decorative items, church interiors and furnishings, fireplaces, doors, decorative cast ironwork and masonry, 18th to early 20th C.* LOC: M1, exit 30. Take A616 towards Sheffield, turn right on to B6053, turn right on to B6058 towards Killamarsh, turn right between two railway bridges. PARK: Easy. TEL: 0742 489972; home - 0246 433315. SER: Hire.

LONG EATON

Goodacre Engraving Ltd
Thrumpton Ave(off Chatsworth Ave.), Meadow Lane. Est: 1948. *STOCK: Longcase and bracket clock movements, parts and castings.* TEL: 0602 734387. SER: Hand engraving, movement repairs, silvering and dial repainting. VAT: Stan.

Miss Elany
2 Salisbury St. (D. and Mrs Mottershead) Est: 1977. Open 9-5. SIZE: Medium. *STOCK: Pianos, 1900 to date, £50-£500; general antiques, Victorian and Edwardian, £25-£200.* PARK: Easy. TEL: 0602 734835. VAT: Stan.

MELBOURNE

Melbourne Gallery LAPADA
3 Potter St. (Mr and Mrs J.C Taylor) Est: 1978. Open daily. SIZE: Small. *STOCK: Oils, watercolours and original prints, 18th-20th C, £50-£6,000; porcelain, 19th C, £25-£500.* LOC: 10 mins. from M1, junction 24 towards East Midlands Airport. PARK: Easy. TEL: 0332 864211; home - 0332 864734. SER: Valuations; restorations (frames, ceramics); gilding; buys at auction (pictures). FAIRS: Buxton, British International (Birmingham), Barbican.

Melbourne continued

Melbourne Treasure Chest
60 Potter St. (Mrs W Gee) Open 10.30-4.30. CL: Mon., Thurs. and Sat. *STOCK: General antiques.* TEL: 0332 863399.

MONYASH, Nr. Bakewell

Mrs A Robinson
Chapel St. Est: 1961. Open Sat., Sun. and Mon. 2-6, or by appointment. *STOCK: Oak, mahogany, porcelain, collectors' items, £1-£1,000.* TEL: 062 981 2926.

Shrives Gallery
Chapel St. (Mrs S Allen) Open Sat.-Mon. 2.30-6, or by appointment. *STOCK: Oils and watercolours.* TEL: 062 981 3979.

NEW MILLS

Regent House Antiques
8 Buxton Rd, New Town. Open 10.30-5, Sat. 2-5, or by appointment. CL: Fri. SIZE: Medium. *STOCK: General antiques, period furniture, clocks; copper, brass, decorative items.* PARK: Easy. TEL: 0663 742684. VAT: Stan/Spec.

SHARDLOW, Nr. Derby

Shardlow Antiques Warehouse
24 The Wharf. Open 10.30-5; viewing Sun. p.m. SIZE: Large. *STOCK: Furniture, Georgian to shipping.* LOC: Off M1, junction 24. PARK: Own. TEL: 0332 792899/662899.

SHIRLEY

Antique Exporters U.K
Blake House. (R Allsebrook) Est: 1977. Open by appointment. SIZE: Large. *STOCK: English furniture, 17th-19th C and reproduction.* LOC: 1 mile off A52. PARK: Easy. TEL: 0335 60005; fax - 0335 60121. SER: Restorations; cabinet makers; interior design; packers and shippers. VAT: Stan. *Trade Only.*

TICKNALL

Sam Savage Antiques LAPADA
Hayes Farm, Main St. (S. and M Savage) Resident. Est: 1969. Open 10.30-5.30. CL: Mon. *STOCK: Early period furniture, 17th-19th C; decorative items, Oriental rugs, paintings.* LOC: Centre of Ticknall, on A514, 4 miles from Ashby-de-la-Zouch, 10 miles west from exit 24, M1 and 6 miles east of Ashby turn-off on M42. PARK: Easy. TEL: 0332 862195. SER: Valuations. VAT: Stan/Spec.

TIDESWELL, Nr. Buxton

Yesterday Antiques
6 Commercial Rd. (N.F Thompson) Est: 1983. Open 9.30-5.30, Sun. by appointment. SIZE: Large. *STOCK: Victorian brass, brass and iron beds; 17th-20th C furniture including longcase clocks; silver, paintings, pottery and porcelain.* LOC: Opposite church, off A623. PARK: Easy. TEL: 0298 871932; home - same. SER: Valuations; restorations; buys at auction.

UNSTONE, Nr. Sheffield

G.W. Ford and Son Ltd BADA
15 Cheetham Ave. (I.G.F. Thomson.) Est: 1900. *STOCK: Furniture, 18-19th C, £50-£10,000; some porcelain, old Sheffield plate and general accessoriesicy.* TEL: 0246 410512.

WHALEY BRIDGE

Deane Antiques
105 Buxton Rd. (Mrs J Donelly) Open 9.30-5.30 including Sun. CL: Mon. *STOCK: General antiques.* TEL: 06633 2928.

Nimbus Antiques
5 Lower Macclesfield Rd. (L.M. and H.C Brobbin) Est: 1978. Open 9-6, Sun. 2-6. SIZE: Large. *STOCK: Furniture, mainly mahogany provincial, some country, £500-£1,000; longcase and wall clocks, £200-£1,000; all 18th-19th C; desks and beds, 19th C, £250-£1,000.* LOC: A6. PARK: Easy. TEL: 0663 734248; home - 0663 733332. SER: Valuations; restorations (furniture). VAT: Stan/Spec.

WINSTER

Winster Arts
Kirby House, Main St. (G William) Est: 1981. Open 10.30-6, Sat. 10-6.30. SIZE: Small. *STOCK: General antiques and collectables including ceramics, glass and Oriental, mainly 19th-20th C, £5-£250.* LOC: B5057, 2 miles west of A6 at Darley Dale. PARK: Easy. TEL: 0629 88716; home - same. SER: Restorations (ceramics and furniture). FAIRS: Local.

WOODVILLE

Wooden Box Antiques
32 High St. (Mrs R Bowler) Est: 1982. Open 10-5, some Sun. SIZE: Medium. *STOCK: Furniture, Georgian-Edwardian, £75-£400; writing boxes, tea caddies and mirrors, Georgian-Victorian, £50-£150; country pine furniture, Georgian-Edwardian, £30-£450.* LOC: A50, between Ashby de la Zouch and Burton-on-Trent. PARK: Easy. TEL: 0283 212014; home - same. SER: Restorations (furniture); buys at auction (furniture). FAIRS: Some local.

YEAVELEY, Nr. Ashbourne

Gravelly Bank Pine Antiques
(Mr and Mrs Brassington) Open every day including evenings. *STOCK: Pine, 18th-19th C, £50-£500.* PARK: Easy. TEL: 0335 330237; home - same. SER: Valuations; restorations (pine); buys at auction.

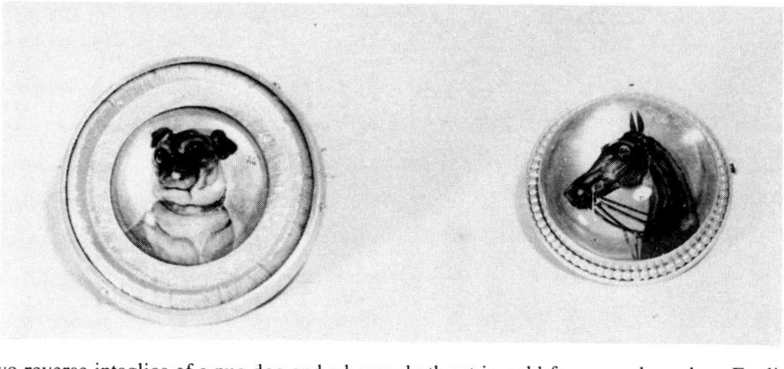

Two reverse intaglios of a pug dog and a horse, both set in gold frames as brooches. English, late nineteenth century. These examples are coloured, like the first examples to attract attention at the International Exhibition held in London in 1862. The exhibitors were Lambert & Rawlings, but a variant, painted with white enamel alone, was shown at the Paris 1878 Exhibition by Marshall's of Edinburgh. This was a short-lived vogue: the polychromatic specimens were much preferred everywhere. MUSEUM OF LONDON

Devonshire

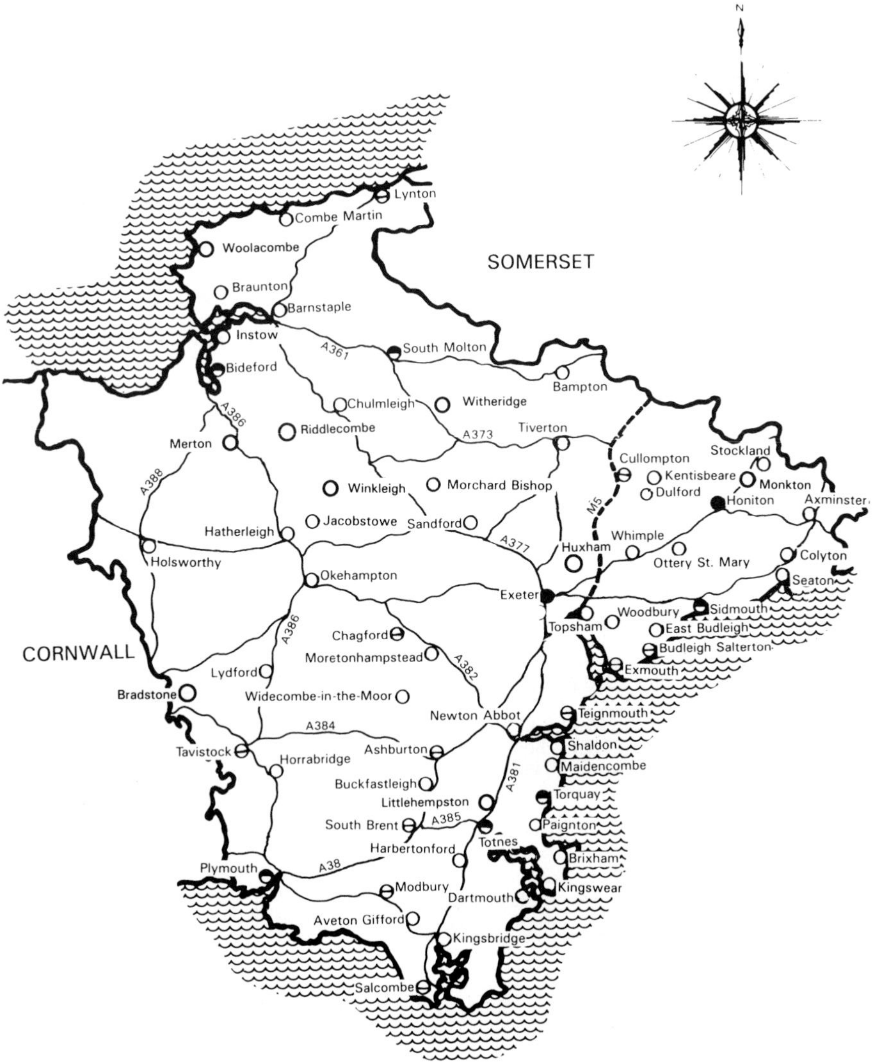
N
SOMERSET
CORNWALL
Lynton
Combe Martin
Woolacombe
Braunton
Barnstaple
Instow
Bideford
South Molton
A361
Bampton
Chulmleigh
Witheridge
A386
Riddlecombe
Merton
A373
Tiverton
Stockland
Cullompton
Kentisbeare
Monkton
Dulford
Honiton
Axminster
A388
Winkleigh
Morchard Bishop
M5
Jacobstowe
Sandford
Hatherleigh
Whimple
A377
Huxham
Ottery St. Mary
Colyton
Holsworthy
Okehampton
Seaton
Exeter
Woodbury
Sidmouth
Topsham
East Budleigh
Chagford
A386
Budleigh Salterton
Moretonhampstead
A382
Exmouth
Lydford
Bradstone
Widecombe-in-the-Moor
Newton Abbot
Teignmouth
A384
Tavistock
Ashburton
Shaldon
Horrabridge
Maidencombe
A381
Buckfastleigh
Torquay
Littlehempston
South Brent
A385
Paignton
Totnes
Harbertonford
Brixham
Plymouth
A38
Modbury
Kingswear
Dartmouth
Aveton Gifford
Kingsbridge
Salcombe

Please note this is only a rough map designed to show dealers the number of shops in the various towns, and is not necessarily totally accurate.

Key to number of shops in this area.

○	1–2
⊖	3–5
◓	6–12
●	13+

ASHBURTON

Ashburton Marbles
6 West St. (A Ager) Est: 1976. Open 9.30-5. CL: Sat. p.m. SIZE: Large. *STOCK: Marble and wooden fire-surrounds, decorative cast iron interiors; scuttles, fenders, overmantels, 1790-1910; architectural and decorative antiques.* PARK: Easy, adjacent. TEL: 0364 53189.

Ashburton Rare Books
20 West St. (R Collicott and N Fereday) Est: 1979. Open 10-5. SIZE: Medium. *STOCK: Books and prints on travel and topography, 18th-19th C, £50-£100.* LOC: Off A38. PARK: Easy. TEL: 0364 53341. SER: Valuations; restorations; book binding. FAIRS: Monthly London PBFA. VAT: Stan.

Dartmoor Antiques Centre
Off West St, (West Country Antiques and Collectors' Fairs, G. Mosdell). ABA. Est: 1984. Open Tues. 9-4. SIZE: 6 dealers. *STOCK: General antiques.* LOC: Opp. town centre car park. PARK: Easy. TEL: 0364 52182. VAT: Stan/Spec.

AVETON GIFFORD, Nr. Kingsbridge

Aune Valley Antiques
Fore St. (J. and E Sharpe) Est: 1976. *STOCK: Furniture, bric-a-brac, dolls.* PARK: Easy. TEL: 0548 550240. VAT: Spec.

AXMINSTER

The Old Curiosity Shop (Antiques)
South St. (N.A. and C Love) Resident. Open 8.30-5.30, Wed. 8.30-1. *STOCK: Furniture, Georgian and Victorian; general antiques and curios, clocks, silver, secondhand books.* LOC: In town centre, next to library. PARK: Easy. TEL: 0297 33016; home - same. SER: Restorations (furniture, china and clocks); re-caning and rushing of chairs; picture framing. VAT: Stan/Spec.

W.G Potter and Son
West St. Est: 1863. Open 9-5. CL: Sat. p.m. SIZE: Medium. *STOCK: Furniture, 17th-19th C, clocks, both £50-£5,000; books, £5-£200; china, £5-£500.* LOC: In main street (A35) opposite church. PARK: Easy. TEL: 0297 32063. SER: Restorations (furniture); buys at auction. VAT: Stan/Spec.

BAMPTON, Nr. Tiverton

Bampton Antiques
9 Castle St. (V.H Strange and J.M Yendell) Est: 1983. Open 10.30-5, Sun. by appointment. CL: Tues. SIZE: Medium. *STOCK: Furniture, porcelain, glass, collectables, fine art, country*

Bampton Antiques continued

furniture. LOC: B3227 from Taunton. PARK: Easy. TEL: 0398 331658. SER: Valuations. FAIRS: Shepton Mallet and Crest Hotel, Taunton.

Robert Byles
7 Castle St. Est: 1966. Open 9-1 and 2-6. CL: Sun. except by appointment. *STOCK: Early oak, local farmhouse tables and settles, metalwork, pottery, unstripped period pine, architectural items.* TEL: 0398 331515. SER: Restoration materials. VAT: Stan/Spec.

BARNSTAPLE

Antique and Collectors Pieces
4 Bear St. (A. and C Pickersgill) Est: 1982. Open 10-4. CL: Wed. SIZE: Small. *STOCK: Ceramics including Royal and political commemoratives, furniture, clothes and linen, glass, 19th-20th C, £5-£500.* LOC: Close to junction with Boutport St. PARK: Nearby. TEL: 0271 74997; home - 0271 73751.

Artavia Gallery
80 Boutport St. (P.J Newcombe) Est: 1972. Open 9.30-5. CL: Wed. p.m. SIZE: Medium. *STOCK: Maps and prints, photographs, oils and watercolours, £1-£500.* TEL: 0271 71025. SER: Picture framing, mounting. VAT: Stan.

Mark Parkhouse Antiques and Jewellery
106 High St. Est: 1976. CL: Wed. *STOCK: Jewellery, furniture, silver, paintings, clocks, glass, porcelain, small collectors' items, 18th-19th C, £100-£10,000.* PARK: Nearby. TEL: 0271 74504. SER: Valuations; buys at auction. VAT: Stan/Spec.

BIDEFORD

Acorn Antiques
11 Rope Walk. (G Crump) Open 9-5. CL: Wed. p.m. *STOCK: Furniture and collectables.* TEL: 0237 470177. SER: Restorations.

Century Galleries
7 Cooper St, (Thomas Williams Antiques Ltd.). *STOCK: General antiques, jewellery, silverware, china.* TEL: 0237 477245. VAT: Stan/Spec.

J. Collins and Son (Est. 1953)

ANTIQUES AND FINE PAINTINGS

The Studio * 63 High Street * Bideford
North Devon * EX39 2AN
Tel: Bideford (0237) 473103

Opening Hours — Monday-Saturday 9.30a.m.-5p.m.
Closed all day Wednesday

With the opening of the North Devon Link Road (A361) we are now 40 minutes from the M5 motorway. Take Exit 27 to Bideford Bridge, at roundabout go left, follow road to the quayside, turn right up High Street with National Westminster Bank on the corner, three quarters to the top, parking outside premises for 30 minutes or in a long term car park, 3 minutes walk.

Five extensive showrooms specialising in Georgian and Regency furniture and two galleries of Victorian oil paintings and watercolours
Our entire stock is now on photographic record.
Colour photographs are now available for clients requiring that 'specific item'.
Why not give us a phone call.

Bideford continued

J Collins and Son
The Studio, 63 and 28 High St. (J., J. and P Biggs) Est: 1953. Open 9.30-5 or by appointment. CL: Wed. SIZE: Large. *STOCK: Period oak and mahogany furniture, general antiques including framed and restored 19th and 20th C oils and watercolours.* LOC: From Bideford Old Bridge turn right, then first left into the High St. PARK: Easy. TEL: 0237 473103; home - 0237 476485. SER: Valuations; restorations (period furniture, paintings and watercolours); cleaning and framing; buys at auction. VAT: Stan/Spec.

Medina Gallery
20 Mill St. (R Jennings) Est: 1973. Open 9.30-5. CL: Wed. p.m. SIZE: Small. *STOCK: Maps and prints, photographs, oils, watercolours, £1-£500.* PARK: Easy. TEL: 0237 476483. SER: Picture framing, mounting. VAT: Stan.

Nick Nack Antiques
3 Cooper St. (L Bayliss) Open 10-5. *STOCK: Brass, copper, china, glass, lace and linen, furniture.* TEL: 0237 478210.

Petticombe Manor Antiques
Petticombe Manor, Monkleigh. (O Wilson) Est: 1971. Open daily until 7 p.m. SIZE: Large. *STOCK: Furniture including dining tables and chairs, desks and bureaux, bookcases and display cabinets, Pembroke and Sutherland tables; china, glass, brass and copper, oils and watercolours, prints and mirrors, hand-stripped pine, mainly 19th to early 20th C.* LOC: Large manor house on A388 Bideford to Holsworthy road. PARK: Own. TEL: 0237 475605; home - same. SER: Restorations (re-upholstery, French polishing, cabinet work). VAT: Stan.

Red House Antiques
25-26 Bridgeland St. (L Turner) Est: 1983. Open 10-1 and 2-5, Sun. by appointment. CL: Wed. SIZE: Small. *STOCK: Furniture, £200-£300; collectables, £5-£25; all 1830-1930.* LOC: Off the quay, shop 1/2 way up on left. PARK: Easy. TEL: 0237 470686; home - same. SER: Valuations.

Riverside Antiques
Rope Walk. (S Duncan) Open 9-1 and 2-5. CL: Wed. p.m. in winter. *STOCK: General antiques especially porcelain.* TEL: 0237 471043; home - 0237 470991.

Scudders Emporium
11 Bridge St. (M.B Chambers) Open 9.30-6. SIZE: Large. *STOCK: General antiques, to 1940's, £5-£1,500.* PARK: Easy. TEL: 0237 479567; home - 02375 665. SER: Valuations; restorations; buys at auction.

BRADSTONE, Nr. Tavistock

Van Kloof Fine Art
The Gallery, Bradstone Coombe Mill. (D Bruce) Open by appointment only. *STOCK: Late 19th to early 20th C British paintings and watercolours.* TEL: 082 287 208.

BRAUNTON

Eileen Cooper Antiques
Challoners Rd. (Mrs M Chugg) Est: 1952. Open 10.30-1 and 2-5 (4.30 in winter), or by appointment, but prior telephone call advisable. CL: Usually Wed. p.m. and Mon. SIZE: Small. *STOCK: General antiques and collectable items including silver, jewellery, paintings, prints, lace, fine linen, christening gowns, embroideries, textiles, pottery, furniture.* Not Stocked: Coins, medals. LOC: From Barnstaple, across traffic lights at Braunton (6 miles), then 200yds. on right. PARK: Easy. TEL: 0271 813320; home - 0271 816005.

Timothy Coward Fine Silver
Marisco, Saunton. Open by appointment. *STOCK: Antique and early 20th C silver.* TEL: 0271 890466.

BRIXHAM

John Prestige Antiques
1 and 2 Greenswood Court. Est: 1971. Open 8.45-6. CL: Sat. and Sun. except by appointment. *STOCK: Period and Victorian furniture.* TEL: 080 45 6141; home - 080 45 3739. SER: Valuations; restorations; desk lining. VAT: Stan/Spec.

BUCKFASTLEIGH

H.V Bendon
33 Market St. Est: 1970. Open 9.30-1 and 2-6; Sun. 10-1. CL: Wed. p.m. *STOCK: Furniture, porcelain and general antiques.* PARK: Adjacent. TEL: 0364 43565.

BUDLEIGH SALTERTON

Lacis
28 Fore St. (Mrs G Parkins) Est: 1988. Open 10-1 and 2-4.30. CL: Mon. and Thurs. SIZE: Small. *STOCK: Lace and linen, jewellery and costume, 19th to early 20th C, £1-£200.* LOC: Continuation of High St., towards the sea. PARK: Nearby. TEL: 039 54 3641; home - 039 54 2544.

Budleigh Salteron continued

New Gallery
Abele Tree House, 9 Fore St. (Mrs P Hull) Est: 1968. Open 10-5 or by appointment. CL: Sun. and Mon. except by appointment. SIZE: Large. *STOCK: Fine art, oil paintings, watercolour drawings, prints from 17th C to modern signed proofs, maps and sculpture.* PARK: Adjacent. TEL: 039 54 3768. SER: Valuations; framing.

The Old Antique Shop
15 Fore St. (C and A Gosling) Est: 1981. Open 10-12.30 and 1.30-5. CL: Thurs. SIZE: Medium. *STOCK: Furniture, 19th C, £25-£500; china, 19th to early 20th C, £15-£250.* LOC: Sea end of town. PARK: Easy. TEL: 0395 271451; home - same. SER: Valuations. FAIRS: Shepton Mallet.

Quinney's
High St. (Miss A Fearfield and Miss S.M Nevill) Est: 1947. Open 9.15-12.45 and 2.15-4.30, Sat. p.m. by appointment. CL: Thurs. *STOCK: Furniture, porcelain, silver, glass.* PARK: Easy. TEL: 039 54 2793. SER: Valuations; minor restorations. VAT: Spec.

David J Thorn
2 High St. Est: 1950. Open Tues. and Fri. 10-1 and 2.15-5.30, Sat. 10-1. SIZE: Small. *STOCK: English, continental and Oriental pottery and porcelain, 1620-1850, £5-£5,000; English furniture, 1680-1870, £20-£5,000; paintings,*

David J Thorn continued

silver, jewellery, £1-£1,000. LOC: From Exeter through Exmouth into Budleigh Salterton or from Honiton. PARK: Easy. TEL: 039 54 2448. SER: Valuations. VAT: Stan/Spec.

CHAGFORD

John Meredith
41 New St, and The Square. (J. and A Meredith) Est: 1979. Open every day 9-1 and 2-5 or by appointment. SIZE: Large. *STOCK: Mahogany, 18th-19th C, £25-£2,000; country oak, 16th-19th C, £5-£1,000; Oriental brass and copper, swords and weapons, large unusual items and large architectural building items.* LOC: 50yds. right of church. PARK: Easy. TEL: 0647 433405 and 433474; home - 0647 433405. SER: Buys at auction. VAT: Stan/Spec.

Mary Payton Antiques
The Old Market House. (Mrs M Payton) Est: 1968. Open 10-1 and 2.30-5. CL: Wed. and Mon. SIZE: Small. *STOCK: English pottery and porcelain, especially Staffordshire, English glass, 18th-19th C; maps and prints (West Country), 17th-19th C.* Not Stocked: Jewellery, firearms, coins, silver, pewter. LOC: Coming from Whiddon Down (A30) by A382, turn right at Easton Court. Shop in the town square. PARK: Easy. TEL: 0647 432428; home -0647 432388.

Whiddons Antiques and Tearooms
6 High St. (D Meldrum) Est: 1979. Open 9.30-5.30. SIZE: Medium. *STOCK: General and country items - furniture including pine, clocks, prints, paintings, copper, brass, books and bric-a-brac.* LOC: Opposite church. PARK: Easy. TEL: 0647 433406; home - 0647 433303.

CHULMLEIGH

W Bagnall
Lingfield. Est: 1965. Open by appointment. *STOCK: Oak, mahogany and walnut furniture, 17th-18th C.* LOC: 3/4 mile west of Chulmleigh. PARK: Easy. TEL: 0769 80576; home - same.

COLYTON

Brookfield Gallery
Market Pl. CL: Wed. *STOCK: General antiques including furniture, pianos and clocks.* TEL: 0297 53541.

Jemms
at Raymond Hicks, Dolphin St. (Mrs J Emmerson) Open 9-5, Bank Holidays 10-4. *STOCK: General antiques and collectables especially lace, linen, quilts, bric-a-brac.* PARK: Easy. TEL: 0297 52339.

COMBE MARTIN, Nr. Ilfracombe

Britannia Restorations
Old Britannia House, Castle St. (S.L Malsom) Open daily and by appointment. *STOCK: Pine, oak and mahogany furniture especially farmhouse and Windsor chairs, metalwork and architectural items.* TEL: 0271 882887. SER: Restoration.

Retrospect Antiques
Sunnymede, King St. Est: 1976. Open 9.15-1. *STOCK: General antiques and bric-a-brac.* TEL: 0271 882346.

CULLOMPTON

Cobweb Antiques
9a Alexandria Industrial Estate, Station Rd, and The Old Tannery, Exeter Rd. (R Holmes) Est: 1980. Open 9-5. SIZE: Large. *STOCK: Pine and country furniture, painted and decorative items, £5-£2,000.* LOC: 100yds. from juction 28, M5. PARK: Easy. TEL: 0884 38207/0395 279253. SER: Stripping; restorations; container packing; courier. VAT: Stan/Spec.

Cullompton Old Tannery Antiques Ltd
Exeter Rd. (Cullompton Antiques Ltd.)Est: 1989. Open 10-5.30, Sat. 10-5. SIZE: Large. *STOCK: Furniture - pine, oak, mahogany, country, 17th C to Edwardian; decorative items, china, earthenware, clocks.* LOC: Leave M5, junction 28, through town centre, premises on right, approximately 1 mile. PARK: Easy. TEL: 0884 38476. VAT: Stan/Spec.

Mills Antiques
The Old Tannery, Exeter Rd. Est: 1979. Open 10-5.30, Sat. 10-5. *STOCK: 17th C to Edwardian decorative items.* PARK: Easy. TEL: 0884 32462. VAT: Stan/Spec.

Sunset Country Antiques
The Old Tannery, Exeter Rd. (R.J. and S.E Reeves) Est: 1981. Open 9.30-5.30. CL: Sat p.m. SIZE: Medium. *STOCK: Furniture - English pine and country especially painted, and decorative items, bric-a-brac and kitchenalia, £10-£2,000.* LOC: M5, junction 28. PARK: Easy. TEL: 0884 32689; home - 0884 32890. SER: Valuations; restorations (stripping and finishing pine).

DARTMOUTH

Anthony Burden Antiques
Duke St. Est: 1963. Open 10-5.30. SIZE: Small. *STOCK: Small furniture, porcelain, silver, clocks.* LOC: Near Boat Pool. TEL: 0803 832723.

Chantry Bookshop and Gallery
11 Higher St. (M.P Merkel) Est: 1969. Open 10.30-5, Sat. 10.30-4. CL: Jan., Feb. and Mar. SIZE: Small. *STOCK: Books, late 19th-20th C;*

Chantry Bookshop and Gallery continued

prints, early to mid-19th C; watercolours, 19th C; maps, 18th-19th C; some sea and battle charts, 18th C; all £5-£1,000. LOC: Next to 'The Cherub' public house. PARK: Nearby. TEL: 0803 832796; home - 0803 834208. SER: Valuations; restorations.

DULFORD, Nr. Cullompton

G Mounter
Bakers Farm. Open by appointment only. *STOCK: Pine, country and painted furniture, early and primitive Windsor chairs.* TEL: 08846 358. *Trade Only.*

EAST BUDLEIGH

Antiques at Budleigh House
Budleigh House. (W Cook) Est: 1982. Open 10-5, Sat. 10-1. CL: Mon. and Wed. SIZE: Small. *STOCK: 18th-19th C small furniture and decorative objects, porcelain, glass, silver and metalware, £5-£1,000.* LOC: Opposite Sir Walter Raleigh public house. PARK: Easy. TEL: 039 54 5368; home - same. SER: Valuations; buys at auction.

EXETER

The Antique Centre on the Quay
The Quay. (Mrs P Crosbie-Smith) Open 10-5. SIZE: Several dealers. *STOCK: General antiques.* TEL: 0392 214180.

Wm Bruford and Son Ltd BADA
1 Bedford St. Est: 1894. Open 9.30-5.30. *STOCK: Jewellery and silver.* Not Stocked: China, glass, furniture, metalware. TEL: 0392 54901. SER: Valuations; restorations (clocks, silver and jewellery). VAT: Stan/Spec.

Lisa Cox
20 Old Tiverton Rd. ABA. Est: 1974. Open by appointment. *STOCK: Music, autographs.* TEL: 0392 55776.

Exeter Antique Wholesalers
Exeter Airport, Clyst Honiton. LOC: A30, 2 miles from exit 30, M5. Below are listed the dealers who are trading as the above. *Trade Only.*

Ash Brothers Antiques
Open 9-6. CL: Sat. *Art deco, unstripped pine, shipping goods.* TEL: 0392 64483. VAT: Stan.

Roy Jones & Son
Shipping goods, pine, general antiques. TEL: 0392 64179. VAT: Stan.

McBains of Exeter
(I G S McBain and Sons) Est: 1963. Open 9-6, weekends by appointment. *Furniture, period and Victorian; decorative and shipping goods.* TEL: 0392 66261; fax - 0392 65572.

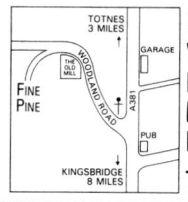

Exeter continued

Exeter Rare Books
Guildhall Shopping Centre. (R Parry) ABA. Est: 1965. Open 10-1 and 2-5. SIZE: Small. *STOCK: Books, antiquarian, secondhand, out-of-print, 17th-20th C, £5-£500.* LOC: City centre. PARK: Easy. TEL: 0392 436021. SER: Valuations; buys at auction. FAIRS: Exeter.

Fagins Antiques
The Old Whiteways Cider Factory, Hele. (C.J Strong) Open 9-5, Sat. 11-5. *STOCK: Furniture, decorative items, architectural and shipping items.* TEL: 0392 882062/0395 27660.

Gold and Silver Exchange
Eastgate House, Princesshay. *STOCK: Jewellery.* TEL: 0392 217478.

Brian Mortimer
87 Queen St. CL: Wed. p.m. *STOCK: General antiques, jewellery, silver, Victoriana.* TEL: 0392 79994. VAT: Stan/Spec.

John Nathan Antiques
153/154 Cowick St, St Thomas. (I Doble) Est: 1950. Open 9-5.30. SIZE: Small. *STOCK: Silver and jewellery, £5-£5,000; clocks, including Georgian and Victorian, £25-£3,000.* LOC: From Exeter inner by-pass over new Exe Bridge, take A30 Okehampton Rd. under railway arch, shop on right. PARK: Easy. TEL: 0392 78216. SER: Valuations; restorations (silver and jewellery); buys at auction. VAT: Stan.

Exeter continued

Pirouette
5 West St. (L Duriez) Open 10-5. *STOCK: Lace, shawls, babywear, linen, 1920's costume, Victorian and Edwardian bridal wear.* TEL: 0392 432643.

Priory Antiques
19/20 Friernhay St. (Miss P.M Small) Resident. Est: 1986. Open Thurs., Fri. and Sat. 10.30-5 or by appointment. SIZE: Medium. *STOCK: Oak, 17th-18th C; hardwood country furniture, 17th-19th C; tribal art.* LOC: Off Fore St. PARK: Adjacent. TEL: 0392 53813.

The Quay Gallery
43 The Quay. Est: 1984. Open 10-5. SIZE: Large - 9 dealers. *STOCK: Furniture, marine items, clocks, decorative textiles.* LOC: Next to H.M. Customs. PARK: Easy. TEL: 0392 213283.

C Samuels and Sons Ltd
17-19 Waterbeer St, Guildhall Shopping Centre. Est: 1872. Large. *STOCK: Watercolours; prints and maps of Devon.* PARK: Nearby. TEL: 0392 73219. SER: Restorations; picture-framing; mounting. VAT: Stan.

Peter Wadham
5 Cathedral Close. Est: 1967. Open 9-5.30. SIZE: Large. *STOCK: English and decorative furniture, 1650-1850; glass, metalware, pottery and general collectors' items, local prints.* LOC: Centre of city, facing Cathedral, north tower. PARK: Own. TEL: 0392 439741. VAT: Spec.

A.T Whitton
151/152 Fore St. Est: 1953. Open 9-5. *STOCK: General antiques, stripped pine.* TEL: 0392 73377. VAT: Stan.

Youll's Antique Centre
Baker's Yard, Alphinbrook Rd. (B Youll) Open 10-5. There are 10 dealers at this centre selling. *STOCK: general antiques.* TEL: 0392 438775.

EXMOUTH

Boase and Vaughan Antiques and Jewellery
5 High St. Est: 1965. Open 10-5. *STOCK: Jewellery, silver and small items for export.* LOC: Town centre. PARK: Easy. TEL: 0395 271528.

Treasures
32-34 Exeter Rd. (L Treasure) Open 9-5. *STOCK: General antiques.* TEL: 0395 273258.

HARBERTONFORD

Fine Pine Antiques
Woodland Rd. Est: 1973. Open 9.30-5. *STOCK: Stripped pine and country furniture.* TEL: 080 423 465. SER: Restorations, stripping.

HATHERLEIGH

Hatherleigh Antiques BADA

22 Bridge St. (S. and M Dann) Open 9-1 and 2-5, anytime by appointment. CL: Wed. and Thurs. SIZE: Medium. *STOCK: Collectors' furniture and works of art, pre-1700.* PARK: Easy. TEL: 0837 810159; home - 0837 810500. SER: Buys at auction. VAT: Spec.

HOLSWORTHY

Victoria Antiques

Victoria Hill. (P. and R Nosworthy) SIZE: Shop and warehouse. *STOCK: Furniture and related items.* PARK: Easy. TEL: 0409 253815; home - 0288 81 548. SER: Valuations; restorations; buys at auction. VAT: Stan/Spec.

HONITON

The Antique Centre Abingdon House

136 High St. (M.V Melliar-Smith and J.J Butler) Est: 1985. Open 10-5. SIZE: Large - 15 dealers. *STOCK: General antiques including furniture, porcelain, 19th C watercolours, country and sporting items, luggage and woodworking tools.* LOC: Exeter end of High St. PARK: Nearby. TEL: 0404 42108; home - 0404 850464.

J Barrymore and Co

73-75 High St. (J. and M Ogden) Est: 1979. Open 10-5, Thurs. by appointment only. SIZE: Medium. *STOCK: Silver, 17th-20th C, £100-£15,000; Old Sheffield plate, Victorian electroplate, £100-£4,000; jewellery, £150-£5,000; all 19th C to early 20th C.* LOC: Main st. PARK: Easy. TEL: 0404 42244. VAT: Stan/Spec.

Roderick P Butler BADA

Marwood House. Est: 1948. Open 9.30-5.30. SIZE: Large. *STOCK: Furniture, metalwork, works of art (unusual and interesting items) 17th to early 19th C.* LOC: Adjacent to roundabout at eastern end of High St. PARK: In courtyard. TEL: 0404 42169. VAT: Spec.

Christopher J Button-Stephens Stable Antiques

Plympton House, 59 High St. Open 9.30-1 and 2-5. CL: Sat. p.m. and Thurs. SIZE: Medium. *STOCK: General antiques including copper and brass, from 1800.* LOC: Main St. PARK: Easy. TEL: 0404 42640. VAT: Stan/Spec.

Drury House

50 High St. (J.A.C. and S.J Barnes) Est: 1979. Open 10-4. SIZE: Medium. *STOCK: Country pine, 18th-19th C, £200-£400; Victorian and Edwardian general antiques, decorative items.* PARK: Easy. TEL: 0404 46079; home - 040486 300. VAT: Stan/Spec.

Honiton continued

Fountain Antiques

132 High St. (J Palmer and G York) Open 9.30-5.30. *STOCK: General antiques and pine furniture.* TEL: 0404 42074.

Elizabeth Gilmore Antiques LAPADA

126 High St. Open 10-5, or by appointment. SIZE: Large. *STOCK: Period oak, country furniture and paintings.* TEL: 0404 43565; home - 08847 233. SER: Restoration. VAT: Stan/Spec.

Honiton Antique Toys

38 High St. (L. and S Saunders) Est: 1986. Open 10.30-5. CL: Mon and Thurs. SIZE: Medium. *STOCK: Toys, dolls and teddies.* PARK: Easy. TEL: 0404 41194

.Honiton Fine Art

189 High St. (C.B. and P.R Greenberg) Est: 1974. Open 11-5. SIZE: Medium. *STOCK: English watercolours and oil paintings, 18th-19th C, £300-£5,000; Old Master drawings, Dutch, Italian and French, 16th-18th C, £300-£1,500.* LOC: Town centre. PARK: Easy. TEL: 0404 45942. SER: Valuations; restorations (oil paintings); buys at auction (as stock). VAT: Spec.

Honiton Junction

159 High St. (J Crackston) Est: 1986. Open 10-5.30. SIZE: Medium. *STOCK: Furniture, smalls.* PARK: Nearby. TEL: 0404 43436.

The Honiton Lace Shop

44 High St. Open 9.30-1 and 2-5. *STOCK: Lace including specialist and collectors'; quilts, shawls and other textiles, bobbins and lace making equipment.* TEL: 0404 42416.

L.J Huggett and Son

"Bramble Cross", Exeter Rd. SIZE: Large. *STOCK: Furniture.* TEL: 0404 42043.

Lombard Antiques

14 High St. (L Lombard) Est: 1984. Open 10-5.30. SIZE: Small. *STOCK: 18th-19th C English furniture, porcelain and decorative items.* PARK: Easy. TEL: 0404 42140.

Otter Antiques

69 High St. (G.F Wilkin) Open 9-5.30, Thurs. by appointment only. *STOCK: Silver and plate including cutlery and flatware.* TEL: 0404 42627.

Pilgrim Antiques

145 High St. (G. and J Mills) Est: 1970. Open 9-5.30. SIZE: Large. *STOCK: Period furniture and longcase clocks.* PARK: Easy. TEL: 0404 41219 or 45316/7. SER: Shipping. VAT: Stan/Spec.

Kenneth Sexton Antiques

140 High St. Open 10-5. *STOCK: Country furniture, collectables and pictures.* TEL: 0404 44224.

Honiton continued

Upstairs, Downstairs
12 High St. Open 10-5.30. SIZE: Large. *STOCK: 18th-19th C furniture, porcelain, metalware, pictures and clocks.* PARK: Easy. TEL: 0404 44481.

Mark Westgarth Antiques
167A High St. (M. and M Westgarth) Est: 1982. Open 10-5. SIZE: Small. *STOCK: Furniture, 17th-19th C, from £500.* PARK: Easy. TEL: 0404 46577; home - 0598 52536. SER: Valuations; restorations (furniture); buys at auction (furniture). VAT: Stan/Spec.

Wickham Antiques
191 High St. (J. and E Waymouth) Est: 1986. Open 9.30-5.30. SIZE: Medium. *STOCK: Mahogany and oak country furniture, decorative items.* PARK: Easy. TEL: 0404 44654.

Geoffrey M Woodhead
53 High St. Est: 1950. Open 9.30-5.30. SIZE: Medium. *STOCK: Books and unusual items.* Not Stocked: Coins, stamps, silver, plate. LOC: A30 opposite largest tree in street. PARK: Easy. TEL: 0404 42969. VAT: Stan/Spec.

HORRABRIDGE

Ye Olde Saddlers Shoppe
(R Howes) Est: 1970. SIZE: Small. *STOCK: General antiques, furniture, clocks and watches, collectors' items.* LOC: 4 miles from Tavistock on A386. PARK: Easy. TEL: 0822 852109.

HUXHAM, Nr. Exeter

Austin/Desmond Fine Art
The Old Rectory. (J Austin and W Desmond) Usually open 11-3.30, Sat. 12-6 but prior telephone call advisable. CL: Mon. *STOCK: British paintings, 20th C.* TEL: 0392 841157; 071 242 4443.

INSTOW

Porcupines Bookroom
(S Lowe) Est: 1963. Open by appointment only. *STOCK: Books, 16th-20th C.* TEL: 0271 861158.

JACOBSTOWE, Nr. Okehampton

Taylor-Halsey Antiques
Lower Cadham Farm. (M. and R Halsey) Open by appointment only. SIZE: Medium. *STOCK: Early oak and country furniture, 17th to early 19th C, £50-£3,000; walnut and other 18th C*

Taylor-Halsey Antiques continued

furniture, £100-£4,000; secondhand and out-of-print books on collecting and vernacular architecture, £1-£200. TEL: 0837 85 288; home - same. SER: Valuations; buys at auction. VAT: Stan/Spec.

KENTISBEARE, Nr. Cullompton

Sextons
Dulford Cottage. (B.A. and F.B Ward-Smith) Est: 1979. Open 9-6, Sat. and Sun. by appointment. SIZE: Medium. *STOCK: Country pine and oak, some mahogany, 1720-1900, £50-£2,000; reproduction dressers, £350-£1,200.* LOC: Telephone for directions. PARK: Easy. TEL: 088 46 429; home - same. VAT: Stan. *Trade Only.*

KINGSBRIDGE

Avon House Antiques/Hayward's Antiques
13 Church St. (D.H. and M.S Hayward) Open 10-1 and 2-5. *STOCK: General antiques.* TEL: 0548 853718.

Kingswood Antiques
85 Fore St. (J. and C Hawkins) Open 9.30-4.30. CL: Thurs. p.m. SIZE: Small. *STOCK: Furniture, art nouveau, general small items, £5-£500.* LOC: On A379 Plymouth-Dartmouth road, in one-way section, main street. PARK: Easy, nearby. TEL: 0548 856829.

KINGSWEAR, Nr. Dartmouth

David L.H Southwick Rare Art BADA
Beacon Lodge, Beacon Lane. Open by appointment. *STOCK: Chinese and Japanese works of art.* TEL: 0804 25533; fax - 0804 25535.

LITTLEHEMPSTON, Nr. Totnes

Anthea Knowles (Toys/Dolls)
Jack's Wall. Open by appointment. *STOCK: Toys, locomotives, dolls, mechanical money boxes, late 19th to early 20th C.* TEL: 0803 867319.

LYDFORD, Nr. Okehampton

Skeaping Gallery
Townend House. Est: 1972. Open by appointment. *STOCK: Oils and watercolours.* TEL: 082 282 383. VAT: Spec.

LYNTON

Berry's
42 Lee Rd. (A. and Mrs A. Berry) Est: 1974. Open 10.30-1 and 2-5 (winter - Mon., Wed. and Sat. only), prior telephone call advisable. SIZE: Small. *STOCK: 18th to early 20th C furniture, ceramics, glass and metalware, watercolours, oil paintings and prints, books and bindings, all £20-£1,000.* LOC: Main street. PARK: Easy. TEL: 0598 52633. SER: Valuations.

Bygone Times
1 Castle Hill. (B.P Young) Est: 1976. Open 10.30-1 and 2-5. CL: Sat. p.m. SIZE: Small. *STOCK: General antiques and small items, 17th to early 20th C, £20-£1,500.* LOC: Next to Imperial Hotel. PARK: Easy. TEL: 0598 53232; home - 0598 53280.

Cantabrian Antiques and Architectural Furnishing
Park St. (I.A Williamson) Open 10-5. CL: Mon. *STOCK: Architectural antiques.* TEL: 0598 53282.

Mark Westgarth Antiques
(M and M Westgarth) Est: 1982. Open by appointment. *STOCK: Furniture, 17th-19th C, from £500.* TEL: 0598 52536. SER: Valuations; restorations (furniture); buys at auction (furniture). VAT: Stan/Spec.

MAIDENCOMBE, Nr. Torquay

G.A.Whiteway-Wilkinson
Sunsea, Teignmouth Rd. Est: 1943. Open by appointment only. *STOCK: General antiques, fine art and jewellery.* LOC: Approximately half-way on main Torquay/Teignmouth road. TEL: 0803 329692. VAT: Spec.

MERTON, Nr. Okehampton

Merton Antiques (Barometers)
Quicksilver Barn. (P.R Collins) Est: 1979. Open 8-5, Sat. by appointment. SIZE: Small. *STOCK: Mercurial wheel and stick barometers, 1780-1880, £300-£3,000; aneroid barometers, 1850-1930, £150-£400.* LOC: Between Hatherleigh and Torrington on A386. PARK: Easy. TEL: 08053 443. SER: Valuations; restorations (barometers). VAT: Stan/Spec.

MODBURY Nr. Ivybridge

Bell Inn Antiques
3 Broad St. (Mr and Mrs E Christopher-Walsh) Open 10-5 and by appointment. *STOCK: General antiques, pictures, porcelain, chandeliers, silver, jewellery.* TEL: 0548 830715; home - 0548 830238. VAT: Stan.

Modbury continued

Country Cottage
The Old Smithy, Back St. (T Starkey and P Baker) Est: 1963. Open 9-5. SIZE: Large. *STOCK: Country furniture, 18th-19th C and reproduction.* TEL: 0548 830888/830715. VAT: Stan/Spec.

Fourteen A
14A Broad St. (B Kirke, M Ridsdill and Mr and Mrs H Helmer) Est: 1986. Open 10-5, Wed. in winter 10-1. SIZE: Small. *STOCK: Victorian linen, £1-£150; writing and jewellery boxes, 19th C, £20-£150; china, jewellery, small furniture, tools, luggage, kitchenalia, books and postcards, 19th-20th C.* LOC: Next to Post Office. PARK: Nearby. TEL: Home - 0548 560055/ 830082 or 0752 880489. SER: Restorations (boxes and furniture). FAIRS: Ardingly; Shepton Mallet; Compton (Surrey) (2nd Sun. monthly).

Wild Goose Antiques
34 Church St, Modbury. (Mr and Mrs E Christopher-Walsh) Open 10-5 and by appointment. *STOCK: General antiques, pictures, porcelain, chandeliers, silver, jewellery.* TEL: 0548 830715; home - 0548 830238. VAT: Stan.

MONKTON, Nr. Honiton

Pugh's Farm Antiques
Pugh's Farm. (G Garner and C Cherry) Est: 1974. Open 9.30-5.30, Sun. a.m. by appointment. SIZE: Large. *STOCK: General antiques including country furniture, brass and iron beds and farm bygones.* LOC: A30 2 miles from Honiton. PARK: Easy. TEL: 0404 42860; home - same. VAT: Stan.

MORCHARD BISHOP, Nr. Crediton

Morchard Bishop Antiques
Meadowbank. (J.C. and E.A Child) Resident. Open by appointment. *STOCK: General antiques, metalwork and treen.* LOC: 8 miles west of Crediton, off A377 at Morchard Rd. PARK: Easy. TEL: 036 37 456.

MORETONHAMPSTEAD

The Old Brass Kettle
2-4 Ford St. (H Clark) Est: 1950. Open 9.30-1 and 2.15-5.30. CL: Sun. except by appointment, and Thurs. SIZE: Medium. *STOCK: Pottery, porcelain and furniture, 19th C.* LOC: A382 from Newton Abbot, B3212 from Exeter. TEL: 0647 40334. SER: Buys at auction. VAT: Spec.

NEWTON ABBOT

Newton Abbot Antiques Centre
55 East St. (P. and D Stockman) Est: 1973. Open every Tues. 9-3. SIZE: 50 dealers

Newton Abbot Antiques Centre continued

STOCK: General antiques. LOC: 200yds. from clock tower. PARK: Through arch. TEL: 0626 54074. Below are listed some of the dealers at this market.

Blockley
Decorative objects and furniture.
Bootell Antiques
Smalls.
Robin Brice
General antiques, art nouveau, art deco, pictures.
Camel Antiques
(B and S Murphy) *China, glass, brass and copper, small furniture.* TEL: 0840 212476.
Castle Antiques
Antiquities and objects.
Caunter
Victoriana.
Graham Courtier
Furniture.
Dillon Antiques
Period silver, clocks, china, silver plate.
June Elvin
Plate, china, glass, jewellery.
Forster
Linen, lace, fabrics.
Vyvyan Goode
Furniture and silver, pictures, objets d'art, glass, plate.
R Green
West Country pottery, Doulton, Staffordshire.
Harbourne Antiques
Clocks and small furniture.
Hendrika
General antiques.
Jo Hicks - Bolton Galleries
Furniture, curios, pictures, silver, jewellery.
H Hill
Costume, china, fabrics, lace.
Mr and Mrs Humber
China and pottery.
B Hunt
Silver and china, furniture, period tools.
S Johnson
Small items, china, pottery, silver.
John Lawrence
Furniture and china, metal toys.
Mrs Lock
General antiques, china and pottery.
Mrs Lovell
Linen and lace, small china.
Mr Lovell
Period silver.
McMarells
Small china.
P Mayer
General antiques, china.
G Mosdell
Antiquarian books and prints.
Mr Opie
Cast toys and china.
P & D Antiques
Victorian and shipping furniture.

Newton Abbot Antiques Centre continued

Mrs Payne
Furniture, china.
Mrs Peddie
Silver, jewellery, furniture, china and pottery.
B Pridham
Furniture, china, collectors' items.
Miss Revell
China, dolls, toys, ephemera, dolls' houses.
Mrs Richards
Furniture, bric-a-brac, Victorian and Edwardian.
Roberts
General antiques.
J Ruff
Crown Derby, Doulton, Royal Worcester.
Andrew Shannon
18th and 19th C oak furniture, pewter, brass, treen.
Sherlock
Jewellery.
P Sherman
Furniture, china, brass and copper.
Joy Sleigh
Pottery, china.
Smith
Collectables.
Paul Stockman
Pottery and period porcelain, furniture, flat back, Staffs.
Sheila B Strange
Porcelain, silver plate, brass and copper, small furniture, glass, objets d'art. TEL: Home - 0626 890304.
Village Antiques
Silver, china and furniture.
V Ware
Coloured glass, jewellery.
Liz Wheelekea
General antiques and decor.
Derick Wilson
Jewellery, shipping goods and furniture.
K Wilton
Furniture, china, smalls, shipping goods.
P Winchester
Postcards, china.
Winckworth
Clocks, small furniture, jewellery and chin bottles, Goss.
Wolsey
Furniture, clocks.
P Wright
General antiques, small items.
Mavis Young
Small general antiques.

Old Treasures

126a Queen St. (Mr and Mrs J.F Gordon) Est: 1971. Open 9.30-4.30, Sat. 9.30-3. CL: Thurs. p.m. SIZE: Small. *STOCK: Jewellery, £3-£800; glass, porcelain, portrait miniatures.* Not Stocked: Large furniture, weapons. LOC: On A380, 100yds. from Queen's Hotel. PARK: Easy. TEL: 0626 67181. FAIRS: Wilton House, British International, Birmingham. VAT: Stan/Spec.

NEWTON ST. CYRES, Nr. Exeter

Gordon Hepworth Gallery

Hayne Farm, Sand Down Lane. (C G and M Hepworth) Est: 1990. Open by appointment including Sun. *STOCK: Modern British paintings especially West Country - West Cornwall and St. Ives School, £150-£1,500.* LOC: A377 from Exeter to Barnstaple. After three miles turn left by village sign, into Sand Down Lane, farm entrance on left, after last white house. PARK: Easy. TEL: 0392 851351; home - same. VAT: Spec.

OKEHAMPTON

Alan Jones Antiques

Fatherford Farm. Est: 1971. Open anytime by appointment. SIZE: Large warehouse and showroom. *STOCK: Furniture - all types, paintings, general antiques.* LOC: On A30, one mile from Okehampton. PARK: Easy. TEL: 0837 52970; home - 040 923 428. SER: Valuations. VAT: Stan/Spec.

OTTERY ST. MARY

Georgian House Antiques

13 Silver St. (P. and Mrs S Hampshire) Open 9.30-5.30. SIZE: Large. *STOCK: 17th-20th C furniture, porcelain and collectables.* TEL: 0404 814540; home - same. VAT: Stan/Spec.

William IV rosewood work table with sliding well. 17in. wide. £650. Ibbett Mosely, Sevenoaks. From a Saleroom Report in the May 1991 issue of ***Antique Collecting.***

PAIGNTON

Portobello Department Store
373-377 Torquay Rd. (T.V Martin) Open 9-5.30. *STOCK: General antiques.* TEL: 0803 524955. SER: Shipping.

PLYMOUTH

Alvin Antiques
148 Union St. (A.F.H Gamble) Est: 1936. Open 9.30-1 and 2-5.30. SIZE: Medium. *STOCK: Furniture, George I to Edwardian, £100-£25,000; silver from 1700, £20-£10,000; porcelain, 1650-1930, £2-£5,000.* LOC: From Exeter follow Royal Parade through city centre to join Union St. on way to Davenport. Shop situated half way along Union St. on right. PARK: Easy. TEL: 0752 665628. SER: Valuations. FAIRS: Plymouth. VAT: Stan/Spec.

Annterior Antiques
22 Molesworth Rd, Millbridge. (A Tregenza and R Mascaro) Est: 1982. Open 9.30-5.30, Sat. 9.30-5, or by appointment. SIZE: Small. *STOCK: Stripped pine, 18th-19th C, £50-£3,000; some painted, mahogany and decorative furniture; brass and iron beds, 19th C, £250-£1,500; decorative, small items.* LOC: Follow signs to Torpoint Ferry from North Cross roundabout, turn left at junction of Wilton St. and Molesworth Rd. PARK: Easy. TEL: 0752 558277; home - 0752 562774. SER: Buys at auction; finder. VAT: Stan/Spec.

Antique Fireplace Centre
30 Molesworth Rd, Stoke. (B.F Taylor) Est: 1988. Open 9.30-5.30 or by appointmentment. *STOCK: Fire surrounds - timber, marble, slate, cast iron, £100-£2,000; Georgian and Victorian fire grates, £100-£1,500; accessories including scuttles, coal boxes, fire irons and overmantels.* LOC: 50yds. from Victoria Park, map sent on request. PARK: Easy. TEL: 0752 559441/569061. SER: Valuations. VAT: Stan/Spec.

Barbican Antiques Centre
82-84 Vauxhall St, Barbican. (T Cremer-Price) Open 9.30-5 every day. SIZE: 60+ dealers. *STOCK: Silver and plate, art pottery, porcelain, glass, jewellery, coins, medals, stamps, clocks, collectables.* PARK: Own. TEL: 0752 266927.

A.E Barham
13 The Parade. Open 10-5.30. *STOCK: Furniture, glass, china, pictures; general antiques.* LOC: Opposite Customs House. PARK: Easy. TEL: 0752 663886.

The Bookworm
22b Weston Park Rd, Peverell. (Mrs M.R Kirke) Est: 1978. Open 10-4, Sat. only. SIZE: Small. *STOCK: Books; Victorian and Edwardian furniture; pictures, ceramics, decorative items, from Victorian.* LOC: Main road into city centre. PARK: Easy. TEL: 0752 221715. SER: Valuations.

Plymouth continued

Alan Jones Antiques
Applethorn Slade Farm, Sparkwell. Resident. Est: 1965. Open by appointment. SIZE: Small. *STOCK: Clocks, scientific and marine items, country furniture, primitive and unusual items, 18th-19th C, £5-£500.* LOC: Off A38, phone for directions. PARK: Easy. TEL: 0752 338188. FAIRS: Newton Abbot, Shepton Mallet, Devon County.

M. & A. Antique Exporters
42/44 Breton Side. (M Antonucci) Open 9.30-6; by appointment for export. *STOCK: Pine furniture, general antiques and shipping goods.* TEL: 0752 665419; fax - 0752 228058.

New Street Antique Centre
27 New St, The Barbican. (Richard Hills and Partners Ltd) Est: 1980. Open 10-5, Sun. 2-5 summer months only. SIZE: Medium. *STOCK: Clocks, silver, jewellery, weapons, general antiques.* PARK: Nearby. TEL: 0752 661165; home - 0752 661522. VAT: Stan/Spec.

Colin Rhodes Antiques LAPADA
53 Southside St. Est: 1972. *STOCK: Paintings, period furniture, silver, clocks, general antiques.* TEL: 0752 669079; home - 0752 862232. SER: Valuations. VAT: Spec.

Anne-Marie Scott-Masson
Mount Stone House, Devil's Point. Open by appointment only. *STOCK: Small period pieces, furnishing fabrics and wallpaper.* TEL: 0752 664413. SER: Interior design.

Brian Taylor Antiques
24 Molesworth Rd, Stoke. Est: 1975. Open 9-5.30, Sun. by appointment. SIZE: Medium. *STOCK: Fireplaces and accessories, country furniture, £50-£2,000; clocks, £50-£2,500, all 18th-19th C; gramophones and phonographs, 1885-1930, £100-£1,000.* LOC: 50yds. from Victoria Park, map sent on request. PARK: Easy. TEL: 0752 569061; home - same. SER: Valuations; restorations (clocks and gramophones). VAT: Stan/Spec.

Upstairs Downstairs
Camden St, Greenbank. Open 9.30-5.30. *STOCK: General antiques especially costume, linen and lace.* TEL: 0752 261015.

Victorian Arts
The House that Jack Built, 11 Southside. (A Burrage) Open seven days. *STOCK: Jewellery, glass and silver.* TEL: 0752 603968.

RIDDLECOMBE, Nr. Exeter

Thomas and Dymond LAPADA
Hope Cottage, Cottwood. Open by appointment. *STOCK: English furniture, early 19th C, blue and white transferware and decorative items.* TEL: 076 93 434. FAIRS: West London Jan. and Aug.

SALCOMBE

A-B Gallery

67 Fore St. (A.S. and J.L Arnold-Brown) Est: 1966. Usually open, prior 'phone call advisable. SIZE: Medium. *STOCK: Pictures, oils, mid 19th to 20th C, £500-£8,000; watercolours, late 19th to 20th C, £50-£1,500; etchings and prints, 19th-20th C, £20-£500.* LOC: Central, near Whitestrand car park. TEL: 0548 842764/2728. SER: Valuations. VAT: Spec.

Arabellas Attic

23 Fore St. (J. and M Searle) Open 10.30-1 and 2-5.30, Sun. by appointment. *STOCK: Victorian and Georgian furniture, pine, silver, porcelain and 19th C paintings.* TEL: 0548 2888; home - 0548 550188.

Halsey International Enterprises

BADA

Est: 1950. Consultancy strictly by appointment. *STOCK: 17th-18th C interiors and gardens created in English and Mediterranean manner internationally.* LOC: 1 1/2 miles on A379 Kingsbridge-Dartmouth road. PARK: Easy. TEL: 0548 852440 (24hr. answering service); fax - 0548 857246. SER: Commissions undertaken internationally for interiors (individual rooms or entire houses); customised seminars (April-Sept.).

SEATON

Etceteras Antiques
Beer Rd. (B Warren) Est: 1969. Open 10-4 or by appointment. *STOCK: General antiques.* TEL: 0297 21965.

SHALDON, Nr. Teignmouth

Tempus Fugit
16c Fore St. (R.C Walkley) Est: 1982. Open 10-5, Sat. 10-1, Sun. a.m. by appointment. CL: Thurs. p.m. SIZE: Small. *STOCK: Clocks, 18th-19th C, £25-£6,000; watches, furniture, paintings, jewellery and porcelain.* LOC: From A379 take left turn over bridge to Shaldon. On bend turn left into Fore St., shop on right. PARK: Easy. TEL: 0626 872752. SER: Valuations; restorations (clocks); buys at auction; export facilities. VAT: Stan/Spec.

SIDMOUTH

Copperfields
Pepys House, 1 Church St. (H Halkes) NAG. Est: 1962. Open 10-1 and 2.15-5. CL: Thurs. SIZE: Small. *STOCK: Silver, jewellery, from 17th C, £5-£4,000; Old Sheffield and later silver plate, £5-£750; porcelain and smalls works of art.* Not Stocked: Furniture. LOC: In town centre near church. PARK: Easy. TEL: 0395 512145. SER: Valuations (silver and jewellery). VAT: Stan/Spec.

Gainsborough House Antiques
12 Fore St. (K.S Scratchley) Est: 1937. Open 9-1 and 2-5. CL: Thurs. p.m. (except by appointment) and Sat. p.m. SIZE: Medium. *STOCK: Pottery, porcelain, silver and plate, copper, brass, furniture, Georgian and Victorian, from £10; militaria and medals, 1650 to date, 50p-£500.* LOC: From High St., 100yds. down Fore St. on left. PARK: 75yds. TEL: 0395 514394; home - 0395 515112/513337. SER: Valuations. VAT: Stan/Spec.

Dorothy Hartnell Antiques and Victoriana
38 Mill St. Est: 1974. Open 10-1 and 2-5; Sun. by appointment. CL: Thurs. in winter. SIZE: Medium. *STOCK: Porcelain and pottery, small furniture, brass, pictures, interesting items, £5-£2,500.* LOC: 70yds. off High St., rear Nat. West. Bank. PARK: Nearby. TEL: 0395 512300.

The Lantern Shop
4 New St. (Miss J.M Creeke) Est: 1974. Open 9.45-12.45 and 2.15-4.45. CL: Mon. p.m. and Sat. p.m. SIZE: Medium. *STOCK: Period table lighting, 1750-1950, £45-£1,000; English porcelain, 1800-1915, £5-£1,000; watercolours and oils, 1800-1950, £15-£1,000; small furniture, 1750-1920, £25-£850.* LOC: Town centre, between Market Sq. and Fore St., behind sea front. PARK: Nearby. TEL: 0395 516320. SER:

The Lantern Shop continued

Valuations; restorations (lamps, oil paintings); framing; lamp shade re-covering. VAT: Stan/Spec.

The Lantern Shop Gallery
5 New St. (Miss J.M Creeke) Est: 1974. Open 10-12.45 and 2.15-4.45. CL: Mon. p.m. and Sat. p.m. SIZE: Medium. *STOCK: Topographical prints, especially East Devon and adjacent counties, 1750-1900, £5-£450; decorative prints and engravings, 1750-1960, £5-£300; maps, especially south-west England, West Midlands and Home Counties, 1600-1850, £10-£400.* LOC: Town centre between Market Sq. and Fore St., behind the sea front. PARK: Nearby. TEL: 0395 578462. SER: Valuations; restorations (cleaning and re-framing prints). VAT: Stan.

Sidmouth Antique Market
132 High St. (Mr and Mrs K Downer) Est: 1983. Open 10-4.30. CL: Mon. and Thurs. SIZE: Small. *STOCK: China, linen, 19th-20th C; Torquay ware, pre-1960; toys; all £5-£250.* LOC: Next to Fords. PARK: Nearby. TEL: 0395 577981. SER: Restoration (glass, china).

The Vintage Toy and Train Museum
First Floor, Field's Department Store, Market Pl. (R.D.N., M.E. and J.W Salisbury) Open Easter-October inclusive 10-5. *STOCK: Hornby Gauge O trains, Horby-Dublo, Dinky toys, Meccano and other die-cast and tinplate toys of yesteryear, wooden jig-saw puzzles.* TEL: 0395 515124, ext. 34; home - 0395 513399.

SOUTH BRENT

Philip Andrade Ltd BADA LAPADA
White Oxen Manor, Rattery. Open 9-6; Sat. 9-1 or by appointment. *STOCK: Furniture, 17th to early 19th C, £50-£5,000; English pottery, porcelain, metalware, works of art, 17th to early 19th C.* TEL: 0364 72454. SER: Valuations. VAT: Stan/Spec.

P.M Pollak
Moorview, Plymouth Rd. (Dr R.M Pollak) ABA. Est: 1973. Open by appointment. SIZE: Small. *STOCK: Antiquarian books especially medicine and science; prints, some instruments, £50-£5,000.* LOC: On edge of village, near London Inn. PARK: Own. TEL: 0364 73457; fax - 0364 72918. SER: Valuations; buys at auction; catalogues issued, computer searches.

L.G Wootton Clocks and Watches
2 Church St. Est: 1948. Open by appointment only. *STOCK: Clocks and watches, all periods; small antiques, unusual curios.* LOC: Just off A38. PARK: Easy. TEL: 0364 72553. SER: Valuations; repairs and restorations (clocks).

PHILIP ANDRADE

WHITE OXEN MANOR
RATTERY SOUTH BRENT TQ10 9JX
TELEPHONE: SOUTH BRENT (0364) 72454

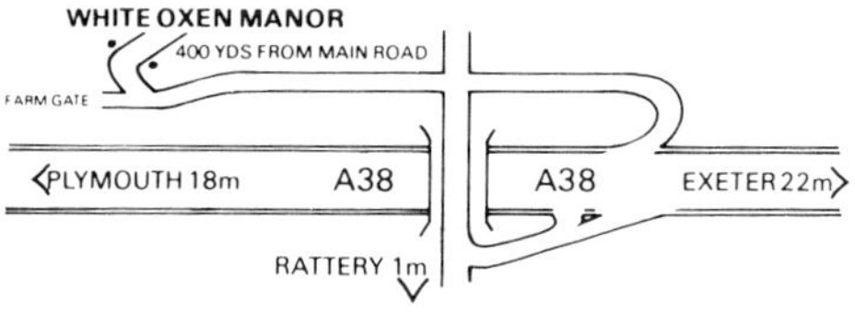
WHITE OXEN MANOR
400 YDS FROM MAIN ROAD
FARM GATE
PLYMOUTH 18m
A38
A38
EXETER 22m
RATTERY 1m

EXTENSIVE STOCK

OF QUALITY ANTIQUE FURNITURE,
ENGLISH AND ORIENTAL PORCELAIN
AND WORKS OF ART

SOUTH MOLTON

The Antiques Parlour
112 East St. *STOCK: Porcelain, ceramics, small furniture, collectable items.* TEL: 076 95 4144.

Architectural Antiques
West Ley, Alswear Old Rd. (A Busek) Est: 1978. Open 9-5. SIZE: Large. *STOCK: Architectural fittings, especially panelled rooms, fire surrounds, marble and stonework, stained glass, pub and shop interiors, decorative items.* LOC: 1 1/2 miles from town centre. PARK: Easy. TEL: 076 95 3342; fax - 076 95 4363. VAT: Stan.

Bellvue House Interiors
Fort House, 36 East St. (A.J Hutter) Est: 1987. Open 9-5. CL: Wed. p.m. in winter. *STOCK: Architectural furnishing, fireplaces, marble and pine surrounds, bathroom fittings, decorators' pieces, 1700-1920, £5-£2,000.* LOC: A361 Taunton side of town. TEL: 076 95 3761. VAT: Stan.

Great Western Pine
99 East St. (B Atwell) Resident. Est: 1987. Open 9-6. SIZE: Medium. *STOCK: Stripped pine, 19th C, £75-£300.* PARK: Easy. TEL: 076 95 2689; home - same. SER: Restorations (pine). VAT: Stan.

Memory Lane Antiques
100 East St. (D Mason) Open 9.30-6, including Sun. in summer. *STOCK: General antiques, china, glass, jewellery.* TEL: 076 95 4288.

South Molton Antiques
103 East St. (D. and W Nicholl) Est: 1976. Open 9-5. *STOCK: Shipping goods, oak, mahogany, Victorian furniture, and pine, £10-£5,000; general antiques.* LOC: B3227, east side of town. TEL: 076 95 3478. VAT: Stan/Spec.

J.R Tredant
50/50a South St. Usually open. *STOCK: General antiques, art deco.* TEL: 076 95 3006; home - 076 95 2416. SER: Valuations; restorations (furniture). VAT: Stan/Spec.

Tredantiques
19 Broad St. (J.C Tredant) Est: 1982. Open 9.30-5, or by appointment. *STOCK: Victorian and Georgian furniture, decorative items, £50-£5,000.* LOC: A361. TEL: 076 95 3841; home - same. VAT: Stan/Spec.

STOCKLAND, Nr. Honiton

Colystock Antiques
Rising Sun Farm. (D.C McCollum) Est: 1975. Open seven days. SIZE: Large. *STOCK: Pine and oak including English, Irish and Continental, 18th-19th C.* TEL: 040 486 271. SER: Container packing and documentation; courier.

TAVISTOCK

King Street Curios
5 King St. (T. and P Bates) Est: 1979. Open 9-5. SIZE: Medium. *STOCK: Pottery, porcelain, collectors' items; art deco, art nouveau, jewellery, up to £100.* LOC: Town centre.

Pendar Antiques
8 Drake Rd. (A.R Martin) Est: 1987. Open 9-5.15, Fri. 9-1 and 1.30-5.15. SIZE: Large. *STOCK: Mahogany, oak and walnut furniture, Victorian, Edwardian and 1920's, £10-£3,000; some Georgian furniture, £300-£1,000; general antiques including fireplaces, 50p-£300.* LOC: Road between Lloyds and Midland Banks. PARK: Nearby. TEL: 0822 617641; home - 0822 617931. SER: Valuations.

Tavistock Fine Art Gallery
77 West St. (D Bruce and T Tucker) Open 10-5, Wed. 10-1, or by appointment. *STOCK: 19-20th C fine paintings and watercolours.* PARK: Easy. TEL: 0822 617952.

TEIGNMOUTH

Charterhouse Antiques
1 Northumberland Pl. (A. and S Webster) Est: 1974. Open 11-1 and 2.15-5, Sat. 10-1 and 2-5. CL: Mon. and Thurs. SIZE: Small. *STOCK: Pottery and porcelain, especially commemoratives, 18th C to 1930s, £1-£200; Victorian jewellery and small silver, 1800-1930, £5-£400; weapons, small furniture, paintings, 1780-1900, £10-£500.* LOC: If facing sea, turn right at Post Office, third left, shop round corner on left. PARK: Easy and nearby. TEL: 0626 54592.

Teignmouth continued

Extence Antiques
2 Wellington St. (T.E. and L.E Extence) Est: 1928. Open 9.30-1 and 2-5.30. SIZE: Medium. *STOCK: Furniture, 18th and early 19th C; jewellery, silver, objets d'art, clocks.* PARK: Limited. TEL: 0626 773353. VAT: Stan/Spec.

Leigh C Extence
2 Wellington St. Est: 1976. Open 9.30-1 and 2-5.30. SIZE: Medium. *STOCK: Clocks, 1690-1880, £500-£20,000.* LOC: Left at lights, left into town centre, right at taxi rank. PARK: Limited. TEL: 0626 773353. SER: Valuations; buys at auction (clocks). VAT: Spec.

Mr. and Mrs. A.M.F. Ritchie
Est: 1954. Open by appointment only. *STOCK: Jewellery, Georgian to 1930.* TEL: 0626 772902

TIVERTON

Bygone Days Antiques
40 Gold St. (N Park) Open 10-1 and 2-5. CL: Thurs. *STOCK: Furniture, Victorian and Georgian; watercolours and oils.* TEL: 0884 252832; home - 0884 255091.

Early Georgian walnut veneered "Tall Boy", circa 1725

Tiverton continued

Chancery Antiques

8-10 Barrington St. Est: 1967. Open 9-5. CL: Sun. and Thurs. except by appointment. SIZE: Large. *STOCK: Furniture, stripped pine, early oak, period mahogany.* PARK: Easy. TEL: 0884 252416; home - 0884 253190. SER: Export facilities. VAT: Stan/Spec.

TOPSHAM, Nr. Exeter

Allnutt Antiques

13 Fore St. (J. and E Gage) Est: 1950. Open 10-5 or by appointment. CL: Wed. *STOCK: Porcelain, 1800-1890; glass, 1780-1890; silver, furniture, 1800-1900.* Not Stocked: Pictures. LOC: 1 mile from Countess Weir roundabout (A377) towards Exmouth. PARK: Own. TEL: 0392 874224; home - 0395 32603. SER: Valuations.

TORQUAY

Birbeck Gallery

45 Abbey Rd. Est: 1922. Open 10-5. CL: Sun. except by appointment. SIZE: Medium. *STOCK: General antiques, Oriental and European; paintings, drawings and prints, 19th to early 20th C, to £10,000.* LOC: 200yds. up Abbey Rd. from main street roundabout at Torquay G.P.O. PARK: Easy or 200yds. TEL: 0803 297144/214836. SER: Valuations; restorations; buys at auction.

Chamberlin Galleries Ltd

1 Victoria Parade. Est: 1947. TEL: 0803 297626. VAT: Stan.

Fortunate Finds

32 Tor Church Rd. (N.E Lythgoe) Est: 1971. CL: Wed. *STOCK: General antiques, Victoriana, coins.* TEL: 0803 297495; home - 0803 292076.

The Gold Shop

24 Torwood St. (D Michele Ltd) Open 10-5.30. *STOCK: Silver and plate, jewellery.* VAT: Stan.

Rocking Horse Pine

3 Laburnum Row. (W Bone) Open 10-5. CL: Mon. *STOCK: Pine, some reproduction; decorative items.* LOC: Off Union St. TEL: 0803 296983.

Sheraton House

1 Laburnum Row, Torre. (K Goodman) *STOCK: Period furniture and decorations.* TEL: 0803 293334.

Spencers Antiques

187 Union St, Torre. *STOCK: General antiques.* TEL: 0803 296598.

Colin Stodgell Fine Art LAPADA

45 Abbey Rd. Open 10-5. CL: Sat. *STOCK: Oil paintings, British and continental, 19th C.* TEL: 0803 292726. SER: Valuations.

Torquay continued

Torre Antique Traders

266 Higher Union St. (P. and Mrs R Curtis and N Boulton) Open 10-5. SIZE: Medium. *STOCK: General antiques.* LOC: Continuation of main shopping area (Union St.). PARK: Easy. TEL: 0803 292184.

TOTNES

Bogan House Antiques

43 High St. (A.T.H Bennett and C Mitchell) Est: 1980. Open 10-5, Fri. 9.15-5. CL: Thurs. and Sat. SIZE: Small. *STOCK: Small silver, especially flatware, 18th-19th C; drinking glasses, 18th to early 19th C, both £10-£200; small decorative items, 17th-19th C, £10-£100; Japanese prints.* LOC: Opposite Civic Hall. PARK: Nearby. TEL: 0803 862075. SER: Valuations (silver and drinking glasses, Japanese woodblock prints).

Collards Books

4 Castle St. (B Collard) Est: 1970. Open 10-5. CL: Thurs. p.m. and lunch hr. in summer, restricted opening in winter. *STOCK: Antiquarian and secondhand books.* LOC: Opposite castle. PARK: Nearby. TEL: Home - 0548 550246.

New Walk House Antiques

1 New Walk, The Plains. (T. and S Hodges) Est: 1972. Open 9.30-5.30. CL: Mon. and Thurs. p.m. SIZE: Medium. *STOCK: Furniture, 18th-19th C; bric-a-brac, china, glass; reproductions.* Not Stocked: Coins, stamps, guns. LOC: Bottom of town, near river. PARK: Easy. TEL: 0803 865096. VAT: Stan/Spec.

Beverley J Pyke - Fine British Watercolours

The Gothic House, Bank Lane. Usually open 10-1 and 2.30-6 Wed. to Sat., and by appointment. SIZE: Small. *STOCK: Watercolours, 20th C, £100-£2,000.* LOC: Opposite P.O. in Fore St. PARK: Nearby. TEL: 0803 864219; home - same.

Rowan Antiques

7 High St. (F Lamont) Open 10-5. *STOCK: English furniture, fine Oriental and European textiles.* TEL: 0803 864897.

WHIMPLE

Anthony James Antiques

The Square. (A.J. and F Mulligan) Open daily or by appointment. SIZE: Medium. *STOCK: Furniture, 17th-18th C; small items, metalware.* PARK: Easy. TEL: 0404 822146. VAT: Spec.

Six various silver and base metal vesta cases including an unusual Aesthetic example decorated in the Japanese style with an applied gilt owl and a bat, the other side depicts an octopus and a fish; unmarked, this was probably made in America, c.1875. The silver examples would sell for £200-£300 each at auction, although the brass novelty vesta case modelled as a swan would only reach £50-£70. They are illustrated with a Victorian 'castle-top' vinaigrette depicting Westminster Abbey, and a plated double sovereign case enamelled with a liner. From an article entitled 'Vesta Cases' by Stephen Helliwell which appeared in the May 1991 issue of ***Antique Collecting.***

WIDECOMBE-IN-THE-MOOR

Barbara Ledger

Cator Court. By appointment only. *STOCK: Watercolours, 19th to early 20th C, £50-£2,500.* TEL: 036 42 324.

WINKLEIGH

L.R Ryce

Cottage Antiques, Chapel Lane. *STOCK: Brass, copper, porcelain, silver, plate and small furniture.* PARK: Easy. TEL: 0837 83231.

WITHERIDGE, Nr. Tiverton

Highcross Antiques

1 North St. (G. and J Pearce) Open by appointment only. *STOCK: General antiques.* TEL: 0884 860898.

WOODBURY, Nr. Exeter

Woodbury Antiques

Church St. (H Jarman) Est: 1966. Open 10-5. CL: Wed. in winter. SIZE: Large. *STOCK: Victorian to Edwardian furniture and items.* PARK: Easy. TEL: 0395 32727. VAT: Stan/Spec.

WOOLACOMBE

Woolacombe Bay Antiques

1 Bay Mews, South St. (B.A. and G Banks) Est: 1963. Open 10.30-1 and 2-5, Tues., Wed. and Thurs. by appointment. SIZE: Medium. *STOCK: Furniture, 18th C to Edwardian, £50-£3,000; clocks, 17th-19th C, £150-£6,000; decorative items, 18th C to Edwardian, £25-£500.* LOC: Town centre. PARK: Easy. TEL: 0271 870167; home - 0271 890639. SER: Valuations; buys at auction (clocks and furniture). VAT: Stan/Spec.

Dorset

Please note this is only a rough map designed to show dealers the number of shops in the various towns, and is not necessarily totally accurate.

Key to number of shops in this area.

- ○ 1–2
- ⊖ 3–5
- ◓ 6–12
- ● 13+

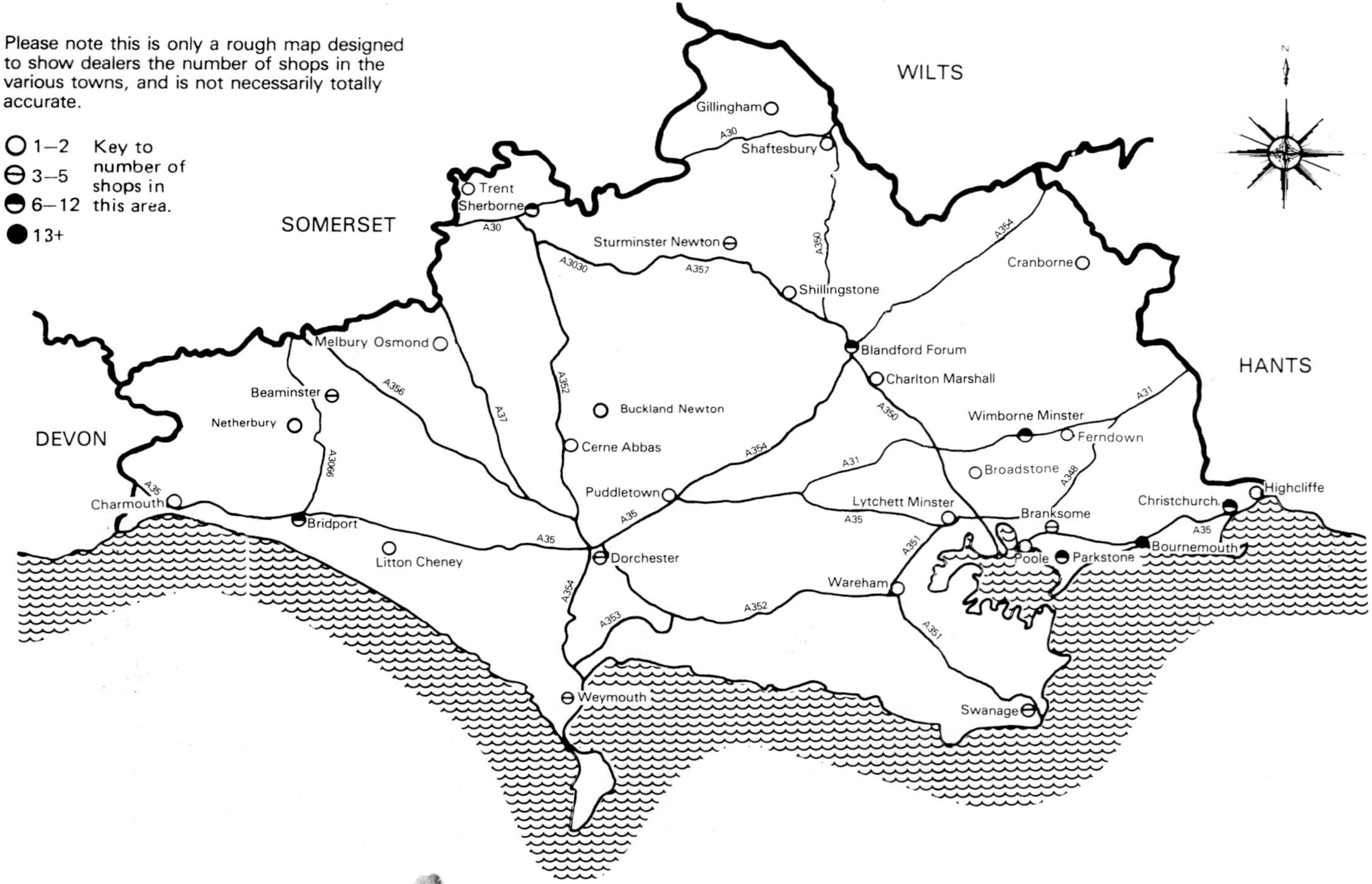
N
WILTS
SOMERSET
HANTS
DEVON
Gillingham
A30
Shaftesbury
Trent
Sherborne
A30
Sturminster Newton
A350
A354
Cranborne
A3030
A357
Shillingstone
Melbury Osmond
Blandford Forum
Charlton Marshall
Beaminster
A356
A350
A31
Wimborne Minster
Ferndown
Netherbury
A37
A352
Buckland Newton
A3066
Cerne Abbas
A354
A31
Broadstone
A348
A35
Charmouth
Puddletown
Lytchett Minster
Highcliffe
Christchurch
Bridport
A35
A35
Branksome
A35
A35
A351
Bournemouth
Litton Cheney
Dorchester
Poole
Parkstone
Wareham
A354
A353
A352
A351
Weymouth
Swanage

BEAMINSTER

Beaminster Antiques
4 Church St. (Mrs T.P.F Frampton)
Est: 1982. Open 9.30-5.30. CL: Wed. SIZE: Small. *STOCK: Small furniture, £20-£1,400; silver, £10-£800; jewellery, £5-£1,400, all Georgian to art deco; objets d'art, porcelain, boxes 18th C to art deco, £5-£1,400; brass and pictures, 18th C to 1920s, £1-£1,000.* Not Stocked: Coins and medals. LOC: Just off square. PARK: Easy. TEL: 0308 862591; home - 093 589 395.

Cottage Antiques
17 The Square. Open 10.30-5.30 or by appointment. CL: Wed. *STOCK: Furniture, paintings, clocks, prints, decorative items.* LOC: A3066. TEL: 0308 862136.

Good Hope Antiques
2 Hogshill St. (D Beney) Est: 1980. Open 9.30-1 and 2-5. CL: Wed. SIZE: Medium. *STOCK: Clocks, especially longcase and bracket, £500-£5,000; furniture, £200-£2,500; all 18th-19th C.* LOC: Town square. PARK: Easy. TEL: 0308 862119; home - same. SER: Valuations; restorations (clocks, including dials). VAT: Spec.

Hennessy LAPADA
Daniels House, Hogshill St. (C. and G.C Hennessy) Resident. Est: 1977. Open 9.30-6, Sun. and evenings by appointment. SIZE: Medium. *STOCK: Pine, oak country, French provincial, decorative and painted furniture, English and continental, 18th-19th C.* LOC: On A3066, 200yds. north of the Square. PARK: Easy. TEL: 0308 862635. VAT: Stan/Spec.

Pines Gallery
Fleet St. (T Frampton) Open 10-4.30. *STOCK: General antiques, oak, mahogany and pine furniture, interior design items, brass and iron beds, glass and smalls.* TEL: 0308 863389; evenings - 0935 89395.

BLANDFORD FORUM

A & D Antiques
21 East St. (A. and D Edgington) Est: 1981. Open 10-5, Sun. by appointment. CL: Mon. and Wed. p.m. SIZE: Small. *STOCK: Drinking glasses, 18th C, £50-£1,000; decanters, 19th C, £15-£100; Lalique, £100-£5,000.* LOC: Town centre on main east-west route (one-way system). PARK: Easy. TEL: 0258 455643; home - same. SER: Valuations (glass); buys at auction (18th C drinking glasses and decanters). VAT: Spec.

Ancient and Modern Bookshop
84 Salisbury St. (Mrs P Davey) Open 9.30-12.30 and 1.30-5.30. CL: Tues., Wed. and Fri. *STOCK: Books and small items.* TEL: 0258 455276.

Blandford Forum continued

Garrets Antiques
18 East St. (M. and P Davey) Open 9.30-12.30 and 1.30-5.30. *STOCK: Small items, collectables, furniture and pictures.* TEL: 0258 455253.

Havelin Antiques
42 Salisbury St. (A Elliot and C Hesketh) Est: 1977. Open 9-5.30, warehouse by appointment. SIZE: Small + warehouse. *STOCK: Furniture, 18th-19th C, £200-£2,000; carpets and textiles, 19th C, £30-£1,000; china, 18th-19th C, £25-£1,000.* LOC: Into Blandford on one-way system, up hill, shop on left. PARK: Nearby. TEL: 0258 452431 and 452880. VAT: Stan/Spec.

Heathcote Antiques
Milborne St. Andrew. (R.J Davis) Open by appointment. *STOCK: Mahogany furniture, 18th-19th C.* TEL: 025 887 695.

Stour Gallery
East St. Gallery, 28 East St. (R Butler) Est: 1966. Open 10-1, and 2-4, Sun. by appointment. CL: Mon. and Wed. p.m. SIZE: Medium. *STOCK: Watercolours, oils and pastels, early 19th to 20th C, £50-£3,000.* LOC: On right-hand side of High St., on one way system. PARK: Opposite. TEL: 0258 456293; home - 0258 860691. SER: Restorations (oil, watercolours, wash line mounts); framing.

Peter Strowger of Blandford LAPADA
13 East St. Est: 1962. Open 10.30-1 and 2-6. SIZE: Medium. *STOCK: Period furniture.* LOC: On A354. PARK: Easy. TEL: 0258 454374.

BOURNEMOUTH

Michael Andrews Antiques
916 Christchurch Rd. Est: 1967. Open 10-5.30. CL: Wed. p.m. SIZE: Medium. *STOCK: Furniture, art nouveau, copper, brass, shipping goods.* PARK: Opposite. TEL: 0202 427615. VAT: Stan.

The Antique Centre
837/839 Christchurch Rd, East Boscombe. (C Williams) Est: 1961. Open 9.30-5.30. SIZE: Large. *STOCK: Silver plate, old Sheffield to art deco; porcelain and pottery, 18th-20th C; art deco pottery especially Clarice Cliff; bric-a-brac, clothes, Victorian to 1960s, £1-£50; furniture, Georgian to art deco, stripped pine, £10-£500; dolls, Victorian and Edwardian, £10-£1,000.* PARK: Easy and at rear. TEL: 0202 421052. SER: Restorations (silver and jewellery repairs, replating); buys at auction.

The Antique Shop
646 Wimborne Rd, Winton. Est: 1946. *STOCK: 0202 527205.*

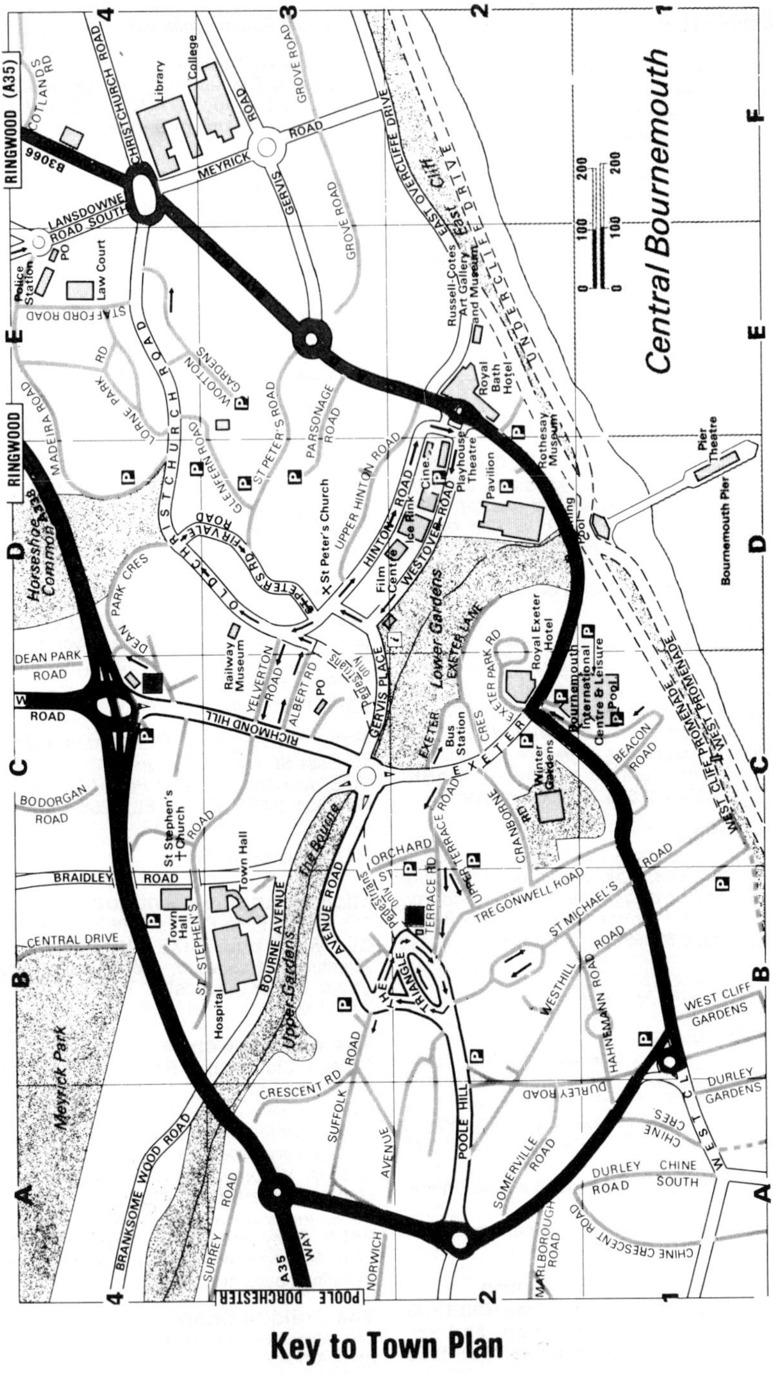
Central Bournemouth
RINGWOOD (A35)
RINGWOOD
B3066
CHRISTCHURCH ROAD
MEYRICK ROAD
LANSDOWNE ROAD SOUTH
Library
College
GROVE ROAD
GERVIS ROAD
EAST OVERCLIFFE DRIVE
East Cliff
UNDERCLIFF DRIVE
Russell-Cotes Art Gallery and Museum
Royal Bath Hotel
Rothesay Museum
Pier Theatre
Bournemouth Pier
Pavilion
Playhouse Theatre
Police Station
PO
Law Court
STAFFORD ROAD
WOOTTON GARDENS
LORNE PARK RD
MADEIRA ROAD
ST PETER'S ROAD
PARSONAGE ROAD
UPPER HINTON ROAD
HINTON ROAD
WESTOVER ROAD
Ice Rink
Cine.
Film Centre
St Peter's Church
OLD CHRISTCHURCH ROAD
FIRVALE ROAD
GLENFERN ROAD
Horseshoe Common
A338
DEAN PARK CRES
DEAN PARK ROAD
Railway Museum
YELVERTON ROAD
ALBERT RD
RICHMOND HILL
GERVIS PLACE
Lower Gardens
EXETER LANE
EXETER PARK RD
Royal Exeter Hotel
Bournemouth International Centre & Leisure Pool
Bus Station
EXETER CRES
EXETER ROAD
Winter Gardens
BEACON ROAD
WEST CLIFF PROMENADE
WEST PROMENADE
BODORGAN ROAD
St Stephen's Church
BRAIDLEY ROAD
Town Hall
ST STEPHEN'S ROAD
CENTRAL DRIVE
Hospital
BOURNE AVENUE
The Bourne
Upper Gardens
AVENUE ROAD
ORCHARD ST
TERRACE RD
UPPER TERRACE ROAD
CRANBORNE RD
TREGONWELL ROAD
ST MICHAEL'S ROAD
WESTHILL ROAD
HAHNEMANN ROAD
THE TRIANGLE
WEST CLIFF GARDENS
DURLEY GARDENS
DURLEY ROAD
CHINE CRES
WEST CL
Meyrick Park
BRANKSOME WOOD ROAD
CRESCENT RD
SUFFOLK ROAD
AVENUE
POOLE HILL
SOMERVILLE ROAD
DURLEY ROAD
CHINE SOUTH
CHINE CRESCENT ROAD
MARLBOROUGH ROAD
NORWICH
SURREY ROAD
A35 WAY
POOLE DORCHESTER

Key to Town Plan

AA Recommended roads		Car Parks	P
Other roads		Parks and open spaces	
Restricted roads		AA Service Centre	AA
Buildings of interest			

Bournemouth continued

Antiques and Furnishings
339 Charminster Rd. (P Neath) Open 10-5.30. *STOCK: Furniture including Victorian stripped pine; brass, copper, china, textiles and decorative objects.* TEL: 0202 527976.

The Artist Gallery
1125 Christchurch Rd, Boscombe. Open 9.30-5. CL: Wed. *STOCK: Limited edition prints - David Shepherd, Sir William Russell Flint, E.R. Sturgeon, Lowry, Gordon King and others.* PARK: Forecourt. TEL: 0202 417066.

Richard Batsford Antiques
121 Gladstone Rd. East, Boscombe. Open 9.30-5.30. *STOCK: General antiques and shipping furniture.* TEL: 0202 397227/303706. *Trade Only.*

Blade and Bayonet
884 Christchurch Rd, Boscombe. (L.M Martin) Resident. Est: 1982. Open 10-12 and 1-5, Fri. 10-12. SIZE: Medium. *STOCK: Militaria, mid 17th to 20th C, £50-£100.* LOC: Near Pokesdown station. PARK: Easy. TEL: 0202 429891. SER: Valuations; restorations (mainly cleaning weapons). FAIRS: Bournemouth, Southsea, Bovington Tank Museum.

Boscombe Antiques
731 Christchurch Rd, East Boscombe. (V Strange and S Morton) Est: 1989. Open 9.30-5.30. SIZE: Large. *STOCK: Decorative porcelain, 1860-1900, £30-£1,000; figures, 1860-1900, £100-£1,500; dinner and tea sets, 1850-1920, £50-£2,000.* LOC: 200yds. east of shopping precinct, on old A35. PARK: Easy. TEL: 0202 398202; home - 0202 887837/421402. VAT: Spec.

Boscombe Militaria
86 Palmerston Rd, Boscombe. (E.A Browne) Est: 1981. Open 10-1 and 1.30-5, Mon. 10-1 and 1.30-4, Wed. 10-1.30. SIZE: Small. *STOCK: German militaria, £10-£500; British and American militaria, £5-£300, all 1914-1918 and 1939-1945.* LOC: Just off Christchurch Rd. PARK: Easy. TEL: 0202 304250; home - same. FAIRS: Winchester, Dorking and major South of England arms.

Collectors Corner
63 Seabourne Rd, Southbourne. (K Goodacre) Est: 1988. Open 10-4.30. CL: Wed. SIZE: Medium. *STOCK: Small items, collectables, bottles, furniture, advertiques and Doulton.* LOC: 100yds. from Pokesdown station. PARK: Easy. TEL: 0202 420945; home - 0425 620794.

Peter Denver Antiques
36 Calvin Rd, Winton. (P Denver-White) Est: 1961. Open 10-5. CL: Mon. SIZE: Small. *STOCK: Furniture, porcelain, pictures, glass, Georgian-Edwardian, £5-£800.* LOC: Off main Wimborne Rd. PARK: Easy. TEL: 0202 532536; home - 0202 513911.

Bournemouth continued

Richard Dunton Antiques
920 Christchurch Rd, Boscombe. (R.D Dunton) Resident. Est: 1980. Open 9-5.30, Sat. and Sun. by appointment. SIZE: Medium. *STOCK: English furniture - oak, mahogany and pine, mainly 19th C; Staffordshire blue and white china, glass, brass and copper, £5-£5,000.* PARK: Easy. TEL: 0202 425963; fax - 0202 418456. SER: Valuations. FAIRS: Birmingham; Olympia. VAT: Stan/Spec. *Trade Only.*

Lionel Geneen Ltd LAPADA
781 Christchurch Rd, Boscombe. Est: 1902. Open 9.15-5, Sat. 9.15-12, other times by appointment. CL: Lunchtimes. SIZE: Large. *STOCK: English, continental and Oriental furniture, china and works of art including bronzes, enamels, ivories, jades, art nouveau and art deco, all 17th C to early 20th C.* LOC: Main road through Boscombe. PARK: Easy. TEL: 0202 422961; home - 0202 520417. SER: Valuations. VAT: Stan/Spec.

Georgian House Antiques
110-112 Commercial Rd. Est: 1967. Open 9-5.30. CL: Wed. p.m. *STOCK: General antiques, silver, coins, jewellery.* TEL: 0202 554175. VAT: Stan.

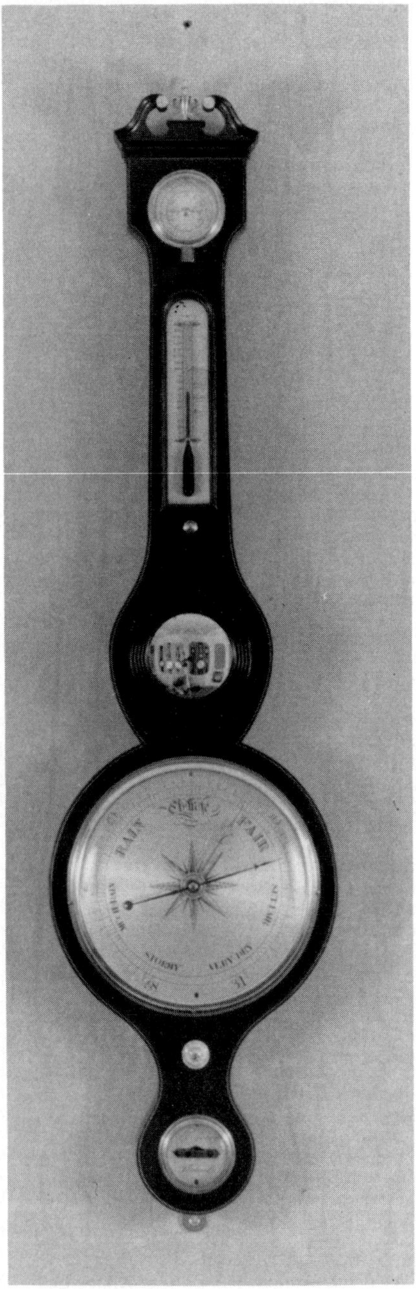
RAIN
FAIR

A high quality wheel or banjo barometer c.1835-45, scroll head, pine carcase with mahogany veneer, strung with black and white lines, five-dial. Correctly and fully restored £850 to £1,000; clean but with evidence of past repairs £450 to £650; distressed, saleroom condition £300 to £500. From an article on banjo (or wheel) barometers by Anita McConnell in the December 1990/January 1991 issue of ***Antique Collecting.*** Photography courtesy of Patrick Marney Barometers.

Bournemouth continued

The Green Room
796 Christchurch Rd, Boscombe. (P.H Richards and E Wright) Est: 1974. Open 10-5.30. SIZE: Medium. *STOCK: Table lamps, old electric lighting, 1880-1950, £25-£2,500; decorative items and furnishings, 1780-1930, £30-£3,000.* PARK: Opposite. TEL: 0202 392634. SER: Valuations; restorations (silver and metalware). VAT: Stan/Spec.

H.L.B. Antiques
139 Barrack Rd. (H.L Blechman) Est: 1969. SIZE: Large. *STOCK: All collectable items.* PARK: Easy. TEL: 0202 429252/482388. VAT: Stan/Spec.

Hampshire Gallery
18 Lansdowne Rd. Est: 1971. *STOCK: Paintings and watercolours, 17th to early 20th C.* TEL: 0202 551211. SER: Valuations; restorations. VAT: Spec.

Hardy's
862 Christchurch Rd, Boscombe. (J Hardy) Open 10-5.30. *STOCK: Period clocks and Clarice Cliff.* TEL: 0202 422407/303030.

Marney's
813 Christchurch Rd, Boscombe. (M Lumb) *STOCK: General antiques, furniture, pottery and porcelain.* TEL: 0202 423907.

Moordown Antiques
885 Wimborne Rd. (T.A Bond) Open Tues. and Thurs. 10-1 and 2.15-5, Sat. 10-1 and 2.15-4. *STOCK: General antiques.* TEL: 0202 513732.

Kenneth Mummery Ltd
9 St. Winifreds Rd. Est: 1917. Open by appointment only. *STOCK: Antiquarian books on music in all languages.* TEL: 0202 555170.

G.B Mussenden and Son, Antiques, Jewellery and Silver
24 Seamoor Rd, Westbourne. Est: 1948. Open 9-5. CL: Wed. SIZE: Medium. *STOCK: Antiques, jewellery, silver.* LOC: Central Westbourne, corner of R.L. Stevenson Ave. PARK: Easy. TEL: 0202 764462. SER: Valuations. VAT: Stan/Spec.

Geo. A Payne and Son Ltd
742 Christchurch Rd, Boscombe. (H.G. and N.G Payne) FGA. Est: 1946. Open 9-5.30. SIZE: Small. *STOCK: Jewellery, 19th-20th C, £10-£3,000; silver, 18th-20th C, £30-£1,000; plate, £10-£200.* LOC: Opposite Browning Ave. and Chessel Ave. PARK: Browning Ave. TEL: 0202 394954. SER: Valuations (gemstone testing); restorations (silver, jewellery, clocks, watches). VAT: Stan/Spec.

R.E Porter
2-6 Post Office Rd. Est: 1934. Open 9.30-5. SIZE: Medium. *STOCK: Silver (including early antique spoons up to modern), Georgian, £20-*

R. E Porter continued

£5,000. Not Stocked: Furniture, paintings, arms, armour, carpets, etc. LOC: Coming from the square, take the Old Christchurch Rd. exit from the roundabout, then first turning on left. PARK: 300yds. at top of Richmond Hill. TEL: 0202 554289. SER: Valuations. VAT: Stan/Spec.

Portique
15/16/17 Criterion Arcade. Est: 1971. *STOCK: Silver, jewellery, china, jade, glass including paperweights, cloisonné.* LOC: Coming from the square take the Old Christchurch Rd. from roundabout, arcade entrance is between first and second turnings on left. TEL: 0202 552979. VAT: Stan/Spec.

Sainsburys of Bournemouth Ltd
23-25 Abbott Rd. Est: 1918. Open 8-1 and 2-6. CL: Sat. p.m. *STOCK: Furniture, especially bookcases and dining tables, 18th C, to £15,000.* PARK: Own. TEL: 0202 529271; home - 0202 763616. VAT: Stan/Spec.

St. Andrew's Market
4a Wolverton Rd, Boscombe. Open 9-5.30. SIZE: 14 units. *STOCK: 18th-19th C furniture and decorative items.* LOC: Next to R.A. Swift and Sons. TEL: 0202 394470.

Sandy's Antiques
790 Christchurch Rd, Boscombe. *STOCK: Oriental items; general antiques; shipping goods, pre-1930.* TEL: 0202 301190; evenings - 0202 470787. VAT: Stan/Spec.

Seabourne Antiques
151 Seabourne Rd. (Mrs A.E Hall) Open 9.30-4.30. CL: Wed. *STOCK: General small antiques and jewellery.* Not Stocked: Furniture. TEL: 0202 422646.

Shickell Antiques
869 Christchurch Rd, Boscombe. (W.J Shickell) Always open. *STOCK: Period jewellery, furniture and general antiques.* TEL: 0202 432331/418497 (24hr. answerphone).

Shickell Antiques Centre
886 Christchurch Rd, Boscombe. (W.J Shickell) Open 10-5.30. CL: Wed. SIZE: 12 dealers. *STOCK: General antiques.* TEL: 0202 418497 (answerphone)/432331.

Shippey's of Boscombe
15-16 Royal Arcade, Boscombe. Est: 1927. Open 9-5. CL: Wed. SIZE: Small. *STOCK: Victorian and later jewellery, objets d'art, silver, china, glass, ivories, £1-£300.* Not Stocked: Pictures. LOC: Centre of Boscombe, at Palmerston Rd. end of Arcade. PARK: Within 200yds. TEL: 0202 396548. SER: Restorations (jewellery). VAT: Spec.

Bournemouth continued

Peter Stebbing
7 Post Office Rd. (P.M Stebbing) Est: 1960. Open 9.30-5. SIZE: Medium. *STOCK: Furniture, £25-£1,000; glass, silver, £1-£100; metalware, jewellery, all 18th-19th C.* LOC: Next to Head Post Office. PARK: 200yds. TEL: 0202 552587. SER: Valuations.

Sterling Coins amd Medals
2 Somerset Rd, Boscombe. (W.V Henstridge) Est: 1969. Open 9.30-4. CL: Wed. p.m. SIZE: Small. *STOCK: Coins, medals, militaria, World War II German items.* LOC: Next to 806 Christchurch Rd. TEL: 0202 423881. SER: Valuations. VAT: Stan.

D.C Stuart Antiques
34-40 Poole Hill. Open 9-5.30. *STOCK: General antiques, hand-carved reproduction furniture.* TEL: 0202 555544.

R.A Swift and Sons **LAPADA**
St. Andrews Hall, 4c Wolverton Rd, Boscombe. Est: 1904. Open 9-5.30, Sat. 9-4. SIZE: Large. *STOCK: English and continental furniture, 18th-19th C; porcelain, pottery, paintings, silver, Sheffield plate, glass, clocks.* TEL: 0202 394470; home - 0202 708321. VAT: Stan/Spec.

Trade Antiques Ltd
957 Christchurch Rd. (K.C Lloyd) Open 9-5.30. *STOCK: Victoriana, shipping and period items, bric-a-brac.* TEL: 0202 292944.

Victorian Chairman
883 Christchurch Rd, Boscombe. (R Leo) Open 9.30-5.30. *STOCK: Furniture, especially chairs and tables.* TEL: 0202 420996. SER: Upholstery.

Victorian Parlour
874 Christchurch Rd, Boscombe. (D.S Lloyd) Est: 1984. Open 9.30-5. SIZE: Large. *STOCK: Furniture, Victorian mahogany and pine, to £500; unusual country bygones, Victorian.* PARK: Easy. TEL: 0202 433928. SER: Restorations (cane and rush seating); buys at auction.

Sydney Wright (Booksellers)
12-13 Royal Arcade, Boscombe. Est: 1905. Open 9-5.30. *STOCK: Antiquarian and secondhand books.* TEL: 0202 397153.

Yesterday Tackle
42 Clingan Rd, Southbourne. (D Dobbyn) Open by appointment. *STOCK: Fishing tackle and associated items including taxidermy; books.* TEL: 0202 476586.

York House Gallery
32 Somerset Rd, Boscombe. (Mrs J Hilliard) Est: 1969. Open 9.30-4.30. SIZE: Small. *STOCK: Oils and watercolours, Victorian to 20th C, £25-£7,000.* LOC: Off Christchurch Rd. PARK: Easy. TEL: 0202 391035; home - 0202 394275. SER: Valuations; buys at auction (pictures).

BRANKSOME

Allen's (Branksome) Ltd
447/449 Poole Rd. (D.L and P.J D'Ardenne) Est: 1948. Open 9-1 and 2.15-6. SIZE: Large. *STOCK: Furniture.* TEL: 0202 763724. VAT: Stan.

Branksome Antiques
370 Poole Rd. (R.E and L.J Maskell and B.A Neal) Est: 1973. Open 10-5. CL: Wed. and Sat. SIZE: Medium. *STOCK: Furniture, 19th-20th C, £50-£200; scientific instruments, 19th C, £100-£300; general antiques and bric-a-brac, £5-£50.* PARK: Easy. TEL: 0202 763324; home - 0258 72296. SER: Buys at auction (as stock). VAT: Stan/Spec.

David Mack Antiques
434-437 Poole Rd, and 43a Langley Rd. Est: 1963. Open 9-5.30 or by appointment. SIZE: Large. *STOCK: 18th-19th C tables, chairs, display cabinets, desks, bureaux, bookcases; later furniture and shipping goods.* LOC: 200yds. from Sainburys Homebase. PARK: Own. TEL: 0202 760005. SER: Restorations. VAT: Stan/Spec.

BRIDPORT

Batten's Jewellers
26 South St. (R Batten) Open 9.30-5. *STOCK: Jewellery and silver.* TEL: 0308 56910. SER: Valuations; repairs.

Bridport Antique Centre
5 West Allington. Open 9-5. SIZE: 12 dealers. *STOCK: Pine and country furniture, lace, linen, books, prints and pictures, postcards, jewellery, etc.* TEL: 0308 25885.

Cox's Corner
40 St. Michael's Lane. (C Cox) SIZE: Large. *STOCK: Furniture, pictures.* TEL: 0308 23451.

Hobby Horse Antiques
29 West Allington. (J Rodber) Resident. Est: 1948. Open mornings and all day Fri. and Sat. SIZE: Large. *STOCK: Mechanical antiques, toys, trains, porcelain, brass, copper, bygones, silver, jewellery.* LOC: West Bridport on south side of A35 between Dorchester and Exeter. PARK: Nearby. TEL: 0308 22801.

PIC's Bookshop
11 South St. CL: Thurs. p.m. *STOCK: Books, engravings and prints.*

Tudor House Antiques **LAPADA**
88 East St. (P Knight and D Burton) Est: 1940. Open 9-1 and 2-5.30, Sun. by appointment. SIZE: Small. *STOCK: General antiques.* LOC: Left hand side of main A35 from Dorchester. PARK: Easy. TEL: 0308 27200; home - same. VAT: Stan/Spec.

Bridport continued

Westdale Antiques

4a St. Michael's Trading Estate. (D Westover and D Dale) Est: 1981. Open 10-4. CL: Thurs. SIZE: Medium. *STOCK: Restored pine furniture, linen and lace, 19th C, £1-£500.* PARK: Nearby. TEL: 0308 27271 (24 hours). SER: Restorations (ceramics).

BROADSTONE

Galerie Antiques

4/4a Station Approach. (R.M. and G.G Black) Est: 1905. Open 10-5, Sat. 10-1. CL: Wed. SIZE: Medium. *STOCK: Royal Doulton, stoneware, figurines, character jugs, seriesware, pottery, porcelain, glass, gold, silver and jewellery, 1880 to date, £5-£500; art deco, Clarice Cliff, Shelley, Wade, Carltonware, Poole pottery, 1920 to date, £5-£350.* Not Stocked: Coins and taxidermy. PARK: Easy. TEL: 0202 695428; home - 0202 886735. SER: Valuations; restorations (clocks, watches and jewellery). FAIRS: Ardingly (Sussex); Alexandra Palace; Doulton; Park Lane Hotel, London.

BUCKLAND NEWTON, Nr. Dorchester

Anthony Harden LAPADA

Castle Hill. (Mr and Mrs A Harden) Open by appointment. *STOCK: Oils and watercolours, 19th to early 20th C.* TEL: 030 05 370. SER: Valuations; restorations (paintings); framing.

CERNE ABBAS

Cerne Antiques

(I Pulliblank) Est: 1972. Open 10-1 and 2-5, Sun. 2-5. CL: Fri. SIZE: Medium. *STOCK: Silver, porcelain, furniture including unusual items, mainly 19th C, £1-£400.* LOC: A352. PARK: Easy. TEL: 0300 341490; home - same.

CHARLTON MARSHALL, Nr. Blandford

Zona Dawson Antiques

The Old Clubhouse. Est: 1958. Open 10-6. CL: Mon. *STOCK: Mainly furniture, clocks, 18th-19th C.* TEL: 0258 453146.

CHARMOUTH, Nr. Bridport

Charmouth Antique Centre

The Street. (R.G Dodd) Open 10-5.30. CL: Sun. and Mon. (Oct.-Mar.). SIZE: Medium. 16 dealers. *STOCK: General antiques.* TEL: 0297 60122.

CHRISTCHURCH

J.L Arditti

88 Bargates. (A. and J.L Arditti) Est: 1964. Open 9-5.30. CL: Sun., except by appointment. SIZE: Medium. *STOCK: Oriental carpets and rugs, 18th to early 20th C, £500-£8,000.* LOC: From town centre take road towards Hurn airport, left side on corner of Bargates and Twynham Avenue. PARK: Twynham Avenue. TEL: 0202 485414. SER: Valuations; restorations; cleaning (Persian rugs). VAT: Stan/Spec.

Christchurch Carpets

55/57 Bargates. (J Sheppard) Est: 1963. Open 9-5.30. SIZE: Large. *STOCK: Persian carpets and rugs, 19th-20th C, £100-£500.* LOC: Main road. PARK: Adjacent. TEL: 0202 482712. SER: Valuations. VAT: Stan/Spec.

Country Flowers - Country Furniture

Purewell House, 113 Purewell. (S Steller) Open 10-6. *STOCK: Stripped pine, country furniture, satinwood, prints, china, cushions.* TEL: 0202 473775.

Hamptons

12 Purewell. (G Hampton) Open 10-6. CL: Sat. a.m. SIZE: Large. *STOCK: Furniture, 18th-19th C; general antiques, clocks, china, silver instruments, metalware, oil paintings, Chinese and Persian carpets and rugs.* PARK: Easy. TEL: 0202 484000.

M. & R. Lankshear Antiques

149 Barrack Rd. (M.I Lankshear) Open 9.30-6. *STOCK: General antiques, especially militaria and swords; collectables, postcards, cigarette cards, medals and paintings.* PARK: Forecourt. TEL: 0202 473091. SER: Valuations.

The Old Stores

West Rd, Bransgore. (Mrs J Collier) Open Thurs.-Sat., 11-5. *STOCK: General antiques.* TEL: 0425 72616.

CRANBORNE, Nr.Wimborne

Tower Antiques

The Square. (P.W Kear and P White) Est: 1975. Open 8.30-5.30. CL: Sat. *STOCK: Georgian and Victorian furniture.* TEL: 072 54 552.

DORCHESTER

Antique Market

Town Hall/Corn Exchange. Est: 1979. Open one Wed. each month (dates in local press). SIZE: 35 stands. *STOCK: General antiques.* TEL: 0963 62478.

Dorchester continued

Books
8 Church St. (D.G.L Johnston) PBFA. Est: 1984. Open 10-5, Thurs. 10-1, Sun. by appointment. SIZE: Medium. *STOCK: Secondhand and antiquarian books, especially on art, literature and Dorset.* LOC: Church St. runs parallel to South St. TEL: 0305 262516. SER: Valuations; restorations (book binding); buys at auction. VAT: Stan.

Colliton Antique and Craft Centre
Colliton St, North Sq. Open daily, Sun. by appointment. SIZE: 8 dealers. *STOCK: 18th-19th C furniture, £25-£3,000; ornaments, brass, copper, bric-a-brac, to £300; jewellery, £20-£1,000.* LOC: By town clock. PARK: Easy. TEL: 0305 269398/266922. SER: Valuations; restorations (cabinet work, upholstery and metalware). VAT: Stan/Spec.

Michael Legg Antiques
15 High East St (Showrooms)and Old Malt House, Bottom-o-Town. (E.M.J Legg) Open 9-5.30 or any time by appointment. SIZE: Medium. *STOCK: 17th-19th C furniture, porcelain, pictures, silver, glass.* TEL: 0305 264596. VAT: Stan/Spec.

Legg of Dorchester
Regency House, 51 High East St. (W. and H Legg) Est: 1930. *STOCK: General antiques, Regency and decorative furniture, stripped pine.* TEL: 0305 264964. VAT: Stan/Spec.

FERNDOWN, Nr. Wimborne

Old Chapel Antiques
552 Wimborne Road East. (A. and K Lloyd) Open 9-5. SIZE: Medium + warehouses. *STOCK: Furniture, china, pictures, jewellery, clocks, 18th-20th C, £50-£25,000.* LOC: A31 north of Bournemouth at junction with Victoria Park Rd. PARK: Forecourt. TEL: 0202 891199; fax - 0425 480123. SER: Containers.

GILLINGHAM

Peter Stride Antiques and Gardens
Wyke. Open 9-5.30. *STOCK: General antiques.* TEL: 0747 824154.

Talisman **LAPADA**
The Old Brewery, Wyke. Open 9-6, Sat. 10-4. SIZE: Large. *STOCK: Unusual and decorative items, garden furniture, architectural fittings, 18th-19th C; English and continental furniture.* TEL: 0747 824423 and 824222; fax - 0747 823544. VAT: Stan/Spec.

HIGHCLIFFE, Nr. Christchurch

M.R Simpson Antiques
Chewton House, Chewton Farm Rd. Est: 1964. Open by telephone appointment only. *STOCK: English furniture, barometers, tea caddies.* TEL: 0425 277105.

Verre Antique
414 Lymington Rd. Est: 1971. Open 10-1 and 2.15-4. *STOCK: Glass, wine decanters, drinking glasses, cruets, clocks, jewellery, watches, silver.* LOC: A337. PARK: Easy. TEL: 0425 272808. SER: Valuations; restorations; polishing and grinding; buys at auction (as stock). FAIRS: Lyndhurst, Bournemouth.

LITTON CHENEY, Nr. Dorchester

Coombe Farm Antiques
(Mrs E.M Percival) Est: 1960. Open 9-5. CL: Sat. *STOCK: 18th-20th C furniture, especially Victorian and Edwardian beds.* Not Stocked: Silver, glass, pictures, jewellery. LOC: Entrance on A35, between Winterbourne Abbas/Bridport. PARK: Own. TEL: 0308 482248.

F Whillock
Court Farm. Open by appointment. *STOCK: Maps and prints.* TEL: 0308 482457. SER: Framing.

LYTCHETT MINSTER

The Old Button Shop
(T Johns) Est: 1970. Open 2-5, Sat. 11-1. CL: Mon. *STOCK: Small antiques, brass, copper, curios, unusual items, and antique Dorset buttons.* TEL: 0202 622169.

MELBURY OSMOND, Nr. Dorchester

Hardy Country
Holt Mill Farm. Est: 1980. SIZE: Large. *STOCK: Stripped pine and country oak, Edwardian and Victorian, £50-£500.* LOC: Off A37. PARK: Easy. TEL: 0935 873361; home - 0935 83440. SER: Valuations; restorations (pine); buys at auction. FAIRS: Bath. VAT: Stan/Spec.

NETHERBURY, Nr. Bridport

Richard and Melissa Bolton Antiques
Ashbee Cottage Workshop, Whitecross. BAFRA. Open by appointment. SIZE: Small. *STOCK: Furniture including country, £100-£2,000; small general antiques, £10-£500; all 18th-19th C.* LOC: 250yds. on right past church. PARK: Easy. TEL: 030 888 474; home - same. SER: Valuations; restorations (furniture); buys at auction. *Trade Only.*

PARKSTONE

Ashley Antiques
176 Ashley Rd. (M Hodson) Open 10-3.30, Sat. 10-4. *STOCK: General antiques.* TEL: 0202 744347.

D.J Burgess
116-116a Ashley Rd. Open 9.30-5.30. CL: Wed. *STOCK: Clocks, watches, jewellery, some furniture.* TEL: 0202 730542. SER: Restorations (clocks and watches); repairs (clocks and watches).

Capricorn Antiques
15 Parr StAshley Cross, Lower Parkstone. (E.B Pugh) Est: 1973. CL: Wed. and Sat. except by appointment. SIZE: Small. *STOCK: Porcelain, glass, small furniture, watercolours, to 1930, £5-£1,000.* LOC: Just off main road. PARK: Easy.

D.J Jewellery
166-168 Ashley Rd. (D.J. and P.M O'Sullivan) NAG. Est: 1978. Open 9-5.30. SIZE: Large. *STOCK: Jewellery, £5-£1,000; silver and plate, £5-£600; clocks, watches, objets d'art.* Not Stocked: Furniture. PARK: Easy. TEL: 0202 745148. SER: Valuations (jewellery); restorations (jewellery, clocks, watches); gem testing. VAT: Stan.

Parkstone continued

Wiffen's Antiques
99/101 Bournemouth Rd. (C A Wiffen) Est: 1960. Open 9-5.30. SIZE: Large. *STOCK: Furniture including shipping; porcelain, pictures, silver and plate, clocks, brass and copper, jewellery, statuary and garden items.* TEL: 0202 736567. SER: Valuations; restorations.

Christopher Williams Antiquarian Bookseller
19 Morrison Ave. *STOCK: Books especially antiques, art, bibliography, cookery, wine, topography.* TEL: 0202 743157. *Postal Only.*

POOLE

Dolphin Antiques
14 High St, Old Poole. (Mrs M Granger and R Samuel) Est: 1978. Open 10-4.30. CL: Wed. Oct.-Mar. SIZE: Large. *STOCK: General antiques, collectors' and decorative items especially Poole pottery.* LOC: Near the quay. PARK: Easy. TEL: 0202 680495.

G.D. and S.T. Antiques
(G.D. and S.T Brown) Open by appointment. *STOCK: General antiques.* TEL: 0202 676340.

PUDDLETOWN

Antique Map and Bookshop
32 High St. (C.D. and H.M Proctor) Open 9-5. *STOCK: Antiquarian and secondhand books, maps, prints and engravings.* TEL: 0305 848633. SER: Postal.

SHAFTESBURY

The Book in Hand (Christopher Driver)
17 Bell St. CL: Wed. *STOCK: Books including antiquarian.* LOC: Opposite car park. SER: Book searches.

Gold Hill Antiques and Collectibles
Gold Hill Parade, Gold Hill. *STOCK: Collectibles.* TEL: 0747 54050.

G.E Johnson and Son (Shaftesbury) Ltd
41-45 High St. Est: 1855. Open 9-5, Wed. 9-1. *STOCK: Furniture.* TEL: 0747 52113.

SHERBORNE

Antique Market
Digby Hall. Open one Thurs. each month (dates in local press). SIZE: 40+ dealers. *STOCK: General antiques, bygones and collectables.* TEL: 0258 840224.

Antiques of Sherborne
1 The Green. (C. and L Greenslade) Open 9.30-5. *STOCK: General antiques, fine furniture, paintings, rugs and collectables.* TEL: 0935 816549; home - 096 321 737. SER: Restorations (furniture, paintings); buys at auction.

Jasper Burton Antiques
23 Cheap St. Est: 1964. Open 9-1 and 2-5. CL: Wed. SIZE: Medium. *STOCK: General antiques, especially furniture.* PARK: Easy. TEL: 0935 814434; home - 0935 812322. VAT: Stan/Spec.

Castleton Country Furniture
Long St. (D Hamilton) Open 9-5.30, Sun. by appointment. *STOCK: Pine.* TEL: 0935 812195.

Country Pine and Antiques
3 The Green. (S Dodge) Open 9-5.30. SIZE: Medium. *STOCK: Finished pine.* LOC: Off A30, 1st shop on left hand side. PARK: Easy. TEL: 0935 815216.

Dodge and Son
28-33 Cheap St. (S Dodge) Open 9-5.30. SIZE: Large. *STOCK: Period furniture, clocks, oils, maps, watercolours, ironwork, statuary, fire accessories including pine mantels.* PARK: At rear. TEL: 0935 815151. VAT: Stan/Spec.

Sherborne continued

Greystoke Antiques
Swan Yard, Off Cheap St. (F.L. and N.E Butcher) Est: 1970. Open 10-4.30. *STOCK: Silver, mainly Georgian, Victorian and later; some 19th C pottery and porcelain, furniture and general antiques.* LOC: Off main street. PARK: Car park adjacent to Swan Yard, or outside shop. TEL: 0935 812833. VAT: Stan/Spec.

Johnsons of Sherborne Ltd
South St. (N.R. and J.J Johnson) Est: 1920. Open 8-5, Sun. by appointment. SIZE: Large. *STOCK: Furniture, 18th to mid-19th C; mahogany and satinwood furniture, late 19th C; art nouveau, export and small items.* LOC: From the west on A30 turn right at centre of Sherborne. PARK: Easy. TEL: 0935 812585. SER: Valuations; restorations (furniture, also upholstery). VAT: Stan/Spec.

The Nook
South St. (B.C Bruton) *STOCK: General antiques - furniture, china, glass, brass and copper.* TEL: 0935 813987.

Old Mermaid Antiques
South St. (R. and D White) Open 8.30-5. SIZE: Medium. *STOCK: Furniture, 18th-19th C; small decorative items.* LOC: Off Cheap St. towards station. PARK: Easy. TEL: 0935 815487. SER: Valuations; restorations. VAT: Stan/Spec.

Sherborne Antique Centre
Mattar Arcade, 17 Newlands. Est: 1965. Open 9-5. SIZE: 12 shops. *STOCK: Fine arts, painting, furniture, rugs, objets d'art, jewellery, gold, silver.* LOC: From A30 via Greenhill. PARK: Easy. TEL: 0935 813464.

The Swan Gallery
51 Cheap St. (S. and Mrs K Lamb) Est: 1977. Open 9.30-5, Wed. 10-1. SIZE: Large. *STOCK: Watercolours, 18th to early 20th C; prints, maps, antiquarian and secondhand books.* PARK: Easy, at rear. TEL: 0935 814465. SER: Valuations; restorations (paintings, watercolours and prints); framing. VAT: Stan/Spec.

SHILLINGSTONE

Ivy House Antiques
The Cross. (A.H.C. and D.C Juett) Est: 1972. Open 9.30-5.30, or by appointment. SIZE: Medium. *STOCK: Furniture, from 17th C, £10-£1,000; porcelain, from George III, £10-£200; silver, from George I, £10-£500; china, glass, jewellery, copper, brass, pictures.* Not Stocked: Weapons, medals, coins. LOC: A357. PARK: Easy. TEL: 0258 860278. VAT: Stan/Spec.

STURMINSTER NEWTON

Quarter Jack Antiques
Bridge St. (A.J Neilson) Est: 1969. SIZE: Small. *STOCK: 18th and 19th C glassware, country oak and mahogany furniture, pictures, walking sticks and horsebrasses.* TEL: 0258 72558; home - same. SER: Restorations.

Toll House
Bagber Lane. (R.E. and L.J Maskell) Est: 1973. Open 9-6 or by appointment. SIZE: Warehouse. *STOCK: Furniture, 19th-20th C, £50-£200; scientific instruments, 19th C, £100-£300; general antiques and bric-a-brac, £5-£50.* PARK: Easy. TEL: 0258 72296/0202 763324. SER: Buys at auction (as stock). VAT: Stan/Spec. *Trade Only.*

Tribe and Son
Bridge St. CMBHI. Resident. Usually open 9-5, Sat. 9-1, but appointment advisable. *STOCK: Longcase clocks.* PARK: At side of shop. TEL: 0258 72311. VAT: Stan/Spec.

SWANAGE

Bishop's of Swanage
31 Station Rd, and 2 Springfield Rd. (G.W. and N.S Bishop) Est: 1950. CL: Thurs. p.m. *STOCK: General antiques, mainly furniture.* TEL: 0929 423245. SER: Buys at auction. VAT: Stan/Spec.

Georgian Gems Antique Jewellers
28 High St. (B Barker) NAG. Est: 1971. Open 9.30-1 and 2.30-5 or by appointment. SIZE: Small. *STOCK: Jewellery, £5-£2,000; silver, £5-£500; both from 1700.* LOC: Town centre. PARK: Nearby. TEL: 0929 424697. SER: Valuations; repairs; gem testing.

The Olde Forge Antiques
273a High St. (D. and J Ferraris) Est: 1967. Open 10-5. CL: Thurs. SIZE: Small. *STOCK: General antiques, pine and bric-a-brac.* LOC: From town centre just over 1/2 mile up the High St. PARK: Easy. TEL: 0929 423319.

Reference Works
12 Commercial Rd. (B Lamb) Open by appointment. SIZE: Small. *STOCK: Reference books on ceramics, new, rare and out-of-print, £5-£700.* TEL: 0929 424423; fax - 0929 422597. SER: Mail order; catalogue available. FAIRS: Wakefield Ceramic.

TRENT, Nr. Sherborne

Old Barn Antiques Co
Flamberts. (G.W Mott and T.E Haines) Resident. Est: 1959. Open by appointment. SIZE: Medium. *STOCK: Furniture, 18th-19th C, £300-£3,000.* PARK: Easy. TEL: 0935 850648. SER: Valuations; restorations; upholstery; polishing; cabinet making. VAT: Spec.

WAREHAM

Heirlooms (Antique Jewellers)
21 South St. (M. and Mrs G Young) F.G.A., R.J. Dip., N.A.G. Est: 1986. Open 9.30-1 and 2.15-5. CL: Wed. SIZE: Medium. *STOCK: Jewellery, Georgian to Edwardian, £10-£1,000; silver, Georgian to Victorian, £20-£500.* LOC: On main thoroughfare. PARK: At rear. TEL: 0929 554207. SER: Valuations; restorations; gem testing.

Judy Wallington-Antiques
28 South St. Est: 1979. Open 10-1 and 2.30-5. CL: Mon. and Wed. except by appointment. SIZE: Medium. *STOCK: Porcelain and pottery, 18th C to art deco, £25-£500; silver and glass, mainly 19th C, £5-£300; jewellery, 19th-20th C, £10-£300; small furniture, Georgian, Victorian and Edwardian.* PARK: Easy and nearby. TEL: 0929 552662; home - 0929 552537. SER: Valuations.

WEYMOUTH

Books Afloat
66 Park St. (J Ritchie) Open 9.30-5.30. CL: Mon. *STOCK: Rare and secondhand books especially nautical; maritime ephemera, ship models, paintings, prints.* LOC: Near railway station. PARK: Nearby. TEL: 0305 779774.

Finesse Fine Art
9 Coniston Cres. (T Wraight and W Flint) Open by appointment only. *STOCK: Pre-war motoring accessories - lamps, badges, metal and Lalique mascots, picnic baskets and other items, from £350-£10,000; Lalique glassware from £1,000-£100,000.* TEL: 0305 770463; fax - 0305 761459.

Lunn's Way Antiques Centre
38 Abbotsbury Rd. (R.J. and Mrs. S.Y Lunn) Est: 1984. Open 9-9. SIZE: Medium. *STOCK: Regency furniture, £200-£500; pairs of vases, 19th C, Samson porcelain figures, both £100-£200.* LOC: Town side of main road towards Abbotsbury. PARK: At rear. TEL: 0305 789193; home - same. SER: Valuations.

North Quay Antique Centre
North Quay. (R.A Shorey) Open 10-5. CL: Mon. SIZE: 8 dealers. *STOCK: General antiques.* TEL: 0305 779313.

Old Harbour Antiques and Nautical Gallery
3 Hope Sq. (D.C Warwick) Est: 1989. Open 10-1 and 2-5.30, Sat. 10-1, Sun. and Mon. and Sat. p.m. by appointment. SIZE: Medium. *STOCK: Nautical items and militaria, 1914 to date, £5-£150.* LOC: Opposite Brewers Quay, adjacent harbour. PARK: Nearby. TEL: 0305 777838; home - 0305 783180. SER: Buys at auction (nautical items).

Weymouth continued

Park Antiquities
Park St. (F. and Mrs. J.R Ballard) *STOCK: General antiques, porcelain, small furniture, treen, advertising items.* LOC: Near railway station. PARK: Nearby. TEL: 0305 787666.

The Treasure Chest
29 East St. (P. Barrett) Open 10-5. CL: Wed. p.m. *STOCK: Maps, prints, general antiques, coins, medals, silver, china.* PARK: Next door. TEL: 0305 772757.

WIMBORNE MINSTER

Antiquatat Antiques LAPADA
The Old Civic Centre, Hanham Rd. (D.W Schwier) Est: 1973. Open 9-4.30. SIZE: Large. *STOCK: Period furniture, silver, porcelain, clocks, containers.* PARK: Own. TEL: 0202 887496.

Barnes House Antiques
West Row. Est: 1980. Open 10-5. SIZE: 4 dealers. *STOCK: Mainly furniture, £5-£5,000.* TEL: 0202 886275.

J Beard
Small Edwardian inlaid furniture and jewellery.
Bryan Chew
Early oak and country furniture and artefacts.
P Emptage
Edwardian furniture and porcelain.
E Simpkiss
Georgian mahogany furniture and silver.

The Bournemouth Gallery Ltd
6 Church St. *STOCK: Limited edition prints.* TEL: 0202 841474. SER: Mail order.

Brights of Nettlebed
(formerly Biggs of Maidenhead)York House, 61-63 Leigh Rd. (R.H Stamp) Open 9-5.30. CL: Mon. SIZE: Large. *STOCK: English furniture, 18th C, from £500; clocks, paintings and objets d'art, pre-1830.* LOC: A31 from Ringwood becomes Leigh Rd. PARK: Easy and at rear via Legg Lane. TEL: 0202 884613. SER: Valuations; restorations. VAT: Stan/Spec.

J.B. Antiques
11 West Row. (J. and Mrs. G Beckett) Est: 1978. Open 10-4, Fri. and Sat. 9.30-4. CL: Wed. SIZE: Small. *STOCK: Copper, £5-£360; brass, £1-£350; furniture, £30-£1,200; all 18th-20th C.* LOC: 2 mins. from Sq. PARK: Nearby. TEL: Home - 0202 882522. SER: Valuations; restorations (metalware); buys at auction (copper).

Minster Antiques
12 Corn Market. (A.A Mason) Est: 1974. Open 10-5. SIZE: Large. *STOCK: Porcelain, china, glass, 19th C, £1-£200; furniture, 18th-19th C, £100-£1,000; brass, copper, collectors' items,*

Minster Antiques continued

18th-20th C. LOC: 100yds. from High St., at back of Minster church. PARK: Easy. TEL: 0202 883355.

T.W. Antiques
12 West Row. (T.E White) Est: 1988. Open 10-4, Fri. and Sat. 9.30-4. CL: Wed. SIZE: Small. *STOCK: Commemoratives, collectables, Doulton and furniture, £5-£500.* LOC: 2 mins. from Sq. PARK: Nearby. TEL: Home - 0202 888958. SER: Valuations; buys at auction (as stock). FAIRS: Sandown; Alexandra Palace, Wimborne Market.

Victoriana Antiques
3 Leigh Rd. (Mrs P Hammer) Open Tues., Thurs. and Fri. 10-1 and 2.30-4. *STOCK: General small antiques, glass, jewellery, silver, brass, objets d'art.* PARK: Easy. TEL: 0202 886739.

West Borough Antiques, Fine Art
36 West Borough. (Mrs K Gale-Yearsley) Open 10-4.30, 10-4 in winter. CL: Wed. *STOCK: General antiques especially porcelain.* TEL: 0202 841167.

Rockingham white cat seated on an oval scroll base flecked with gold, 2½in. (6.4cm) high. Unnumbered. Red griffin mark. 1826-27. From ***English Porcelain Animals of the 19th Century*** by D.G. Rice, published by the **Antique Collectors' Club** in 1989. £25.00.

Durham

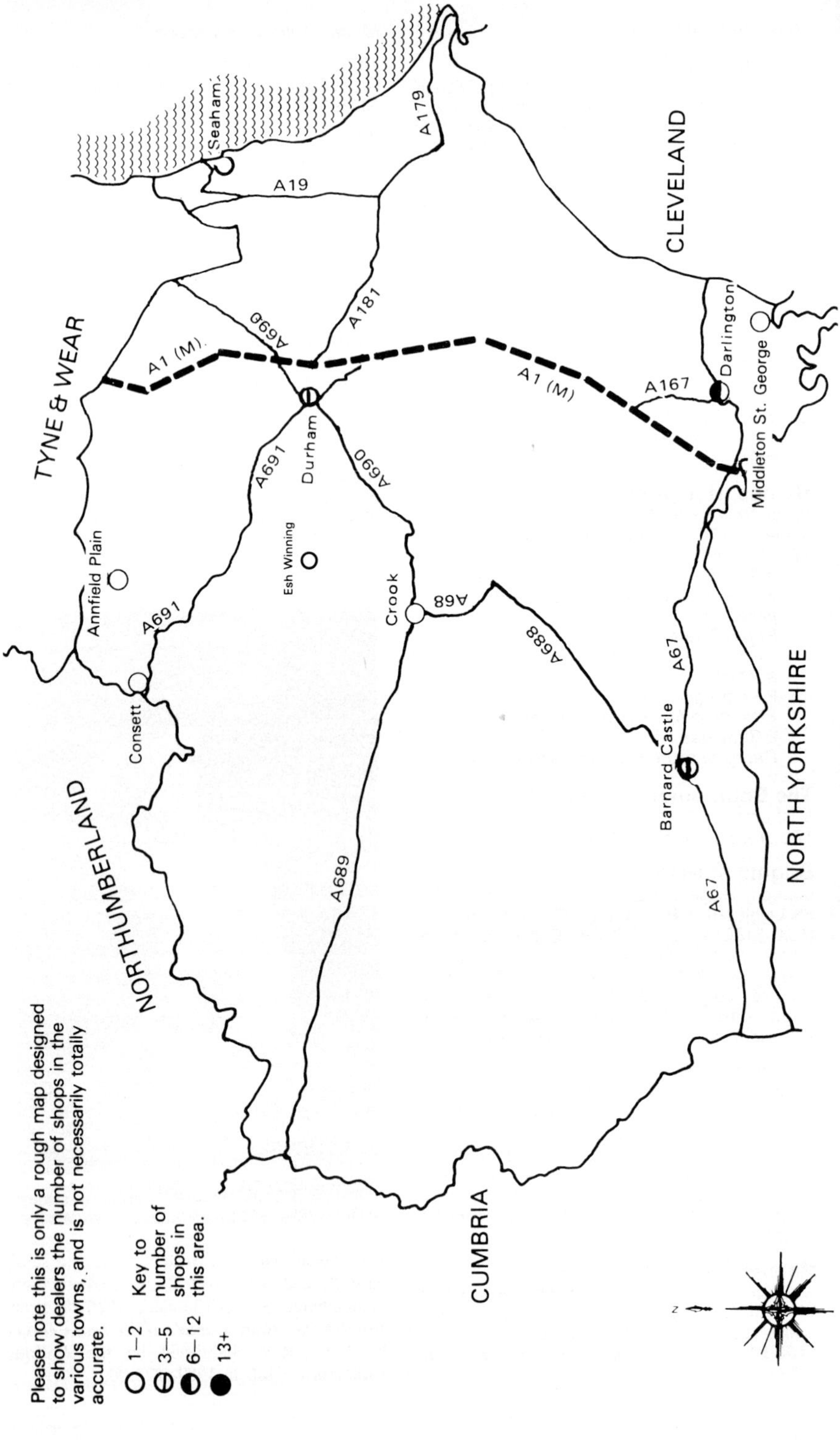

Seaham
A179
A19
CLEVELAND
A181
A690
A1 (M)
TYNE & WEAR
Darlington
Middleton St. George
A167
Durham
A691
Esh Winning
Annfield Plain
Crook
A68
A688
A67
Consett
Barnard Castle
NORTH YORKSHIRE
NORTHUMBERLAND
A689
CUMBRIA

Please note this is only a rough map designed to show dealers the number of shops in the various towns, and is not necessarily totally accurate.

Key to number of shops in this area.

- ○ 1—2
- ⊖ 3—5
- ◐ 6—12
- ● 13+

ANNFIELD PLAIN, Nr. Stanley

Emporium of Art and Age

10 West Rd. (Mrs P.W Halloway) Est: 1978. Open by appointment only. SIZE: Small. *STOCK: Small unusual items, china, glass, silver, books and pictures.* PARK: Easy, opposite. TEL: 0207 239808; home - 091 3863150. SER: Buys at auction.

BARNARD CASTLE

The Collector

Douglas House, The Bank. (R.A Jordan and P.R Hunter) Est: !970. Open 10-5. SIZE: Large. *STOCK: Fine oak country furniture, 17th-18th C; period mahogany furniture, 18th-19th C; watercolours, oils, Georgian silver, Persian rugs, pewter, unusual and collectable items.* TEL: 0833 37783. SER: Restorations. VAT: Spec.

Stephanie Grant Antiques

38-40 The Bank. (S.A Grant) Est: 1977. Open every day 10-5. SIZE: Large. *STOCK: Furniture, paintings, prints (including modern) and decorative items, 16th-18th C.* LOC: A67. PARK: Easy. TEL: 0833 37437. SER: Restorations.

Jackson's Antiques Ltd

Neville House, 10 The Bank. (A. and B Jackson) Est: 1968. Open 10.30-5.30. Sun. by appointment. SIZE: Medium. *STOCK: General antiques - 18th C and Victorian furniture, Victorian coloured glass, porcelain and ceramics.* PARK: Easy. TEL: 0833 37412; home - same. VAT: Stan/Spec.

Town House Antiques

7 Newgate. Est: 1975. Open Wed., Fri. and Sat. *STOCK: Georgian, Victorian and export furniture.* LOC: 100yds. from Market Cross on Bowes Museum Rd. TEL: 0833 37021; 0325 374303. VAT: Stan/Spec.

CONSETT

Harry Raine Antiques

Kelvinside House, Villa Real Rd. Appointment advisable. SIZE: Large. *STOCK: General antiques.* TEL: 0207 503935.

CROOK

Jo Patterson Antiques

(J.W.B Patterson) Est: 1968. Open by appointment. SIZE: Large. *STOCK: Shipping goods, 19th-20th C.* LOC: 4 miles from A68. PARK: Easy. TEL: 0388 746586. *Trade Only.*

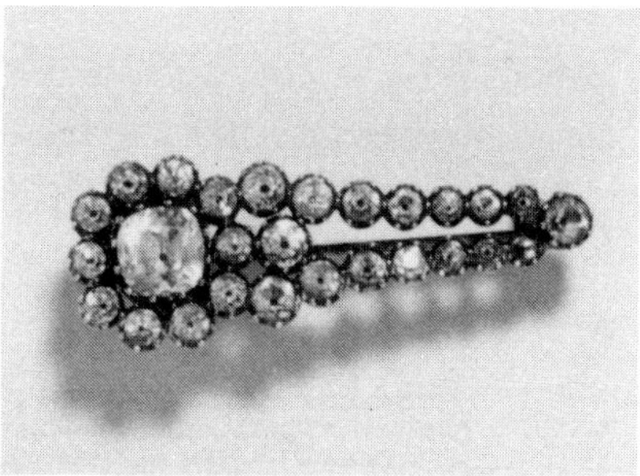

Plate 104. A paste comet brooch, mounted in silver, lined with gold. Like the designs in Knight's *Fancy Ornaments,* it may have been inspired by the sightings of a comet by Sir James South at Kensington and John Herapath at Cranford, Middlesex from 7/26 January 1881 which were reported in *The Times* on 15, 19, 20, 25 and 26 January or by the appearance of Halley's comet in the mid-1830s.

PRIVATE COLLECTION

From ***Jewellery 1789-1910 — The International Era*** by Shirley Bury, published by the **Antique Collectors' Club** in 1991. £47.50 each volume.

DARLINGTON

S Brown and Sons 'The Popular Mart'

26 Hollyhurst Rd. Est: 1976. Open 9.30-5. CL: Wed. p.m. and Sat. p.m., except by appointment. SIZE: Large. *STOCK: General antiques, from late 19th C, £5-£500.* LOC: From town centre, along Woodlands Rd. to Hollyhurst Rd., shop adjacent to Memorial Hospital. PARK: Easy. TEL: 0325 354769; home - 0325 355490. SER: Valuations; buys at auction.

Bygones

3/5 McMullen Rd. (M Pitman and A Walton) Open 10-6, Sun. by appointment. SIZE: Medium. *STOCK: Furniture and fireplaces, Edwardian and Victorian, £100-£2,000; bric-a-brac, curios, country bygones, 1800-1930, £5-£500.* LOC: Off Yarm Road. PARK: Easy. TEL: 0325 461399; home - 0325 380884.

Robin Finnegan (Jeweller)

83 Skinnergate. Est: 1974. Open 10-5.30. SIZE: Medium. *STOCK: Jewellery, general antiques, coins and medals, £1-£2,000.* TEL: 0325 489820. SER: Valuations. VAT: Stan.

Nichol and Hill

20 Grange Rd. Open 10-5. *STOCK: Victorian and Edwardian furniture.* TEL: 0325 357431. SER: Restorations, upholstery, interior decoration.

A Gothick Garden Seat

Robert Manwaring
'The Cabinet and Chair-Maker's Real Friend and Companion', 1765
Plates 31 and 32. 'are two very good Designs for Garden Seats in the Gothic Taste. They will look very genteel painted white intermixed with green. . .' From ***Pictorial Dictionary of British 18th Century Furniture Design — The Printed Sources*** compiled by Elizabeth White and published by the **Antique Collectors' Club** in 1990. £65.00.

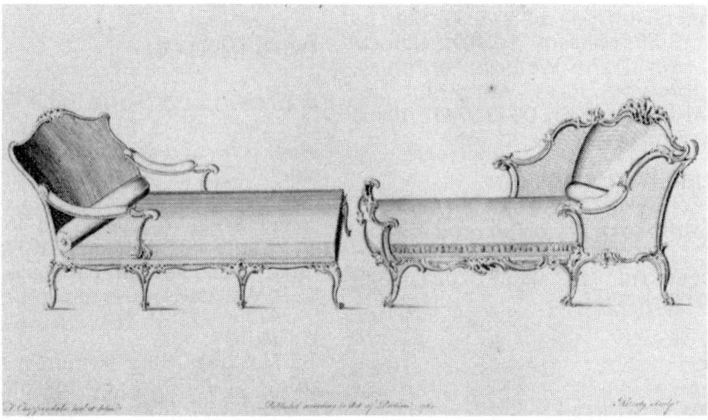

Thomas Chippendale
'The Gentleman and Cabinet-Maker's Director', 3rd Edition, 1763.
Plate XXXII (above) 'What the French call *Pêché-Mortel.* They are sometimes made to take asunder in the middle; one part makes a large Easy-Chair, and the other a Stool, and the feet join in the middle, which looks badly. Therefore I would recommend their being made as in these designs, with a pretty thick mattrass.' Engraving dated 1761. From ***Pictorial Dictionary of British 18th Century Furniture Design — The Printed Sources*** compiled by Elizabeth White and published by the **Antique Collectors' Club** in 1990. £65.00.

Darlington continued

Ronald Richardson
28 Post House Wynd. Est: 1852. Open 9-5. CL: Wed. SIZE: Medium. *STOCK: Jewellery, 19th C; silver, Sheffield plate, clocks and barometers, 18th-19th C.* Not Stocked: Furniture. LOC: One-way street leading into middle of High Row, opposite town clock. PARK: 200yds. in side streets. TEL: 0325 464860. SER: Valuations; restorations (silver, plate, clocks, jewellery). VAT: Stan.

Stella Rutherford Ltd
14 Coniscliffe Rd. (Mrs J Davidson) Est: 1959. Open 10-5, Wed. and Sat. 10-1. SIZE: Medium. *STOCK: Furniture, £50-£500; silver, jewellery, china, glass, £5-£200.* LOC: A167. From south leave motorway at first Darlington exit. Follow one-way system into Coniscliffe Rd. PARK: 30yds. opposite. TEL: 0325 468934. SER: Valuations. VAT: Spec.

DURHAM

J Shotton Antiquarian Books and Prints
89 Elvet Bridge. Est: 1967. Open 9.30-5. CL: Mon. *STOCK: Antiquarian books, prints, maps and paintings.* TEL: 091 3864597.

ESH WINNING, Nr. Durham

Dunelme Coins and Medals
7 Durham Rd. (P.G. and A.E Smith) Est: 1982. Open 9-12 and 1-5. CL: Wed. SIZE: Small. *STOCK: Coins, medals and tokens, from ancient Greek to date, £1-£1,000; regimental badges, stamps, gold and silver, banknotes, pre-1920 postcards, autograph letters, curios and small items.* LOC: Main street. PARK: Easy. TEL: 091 373 4446. SER: Valuations; coin identification; medal ribbons supplied. VAT: Stan/Spec.

MIDDLETON ST. GEORGE, Nr. Darlington

Carousel Antiques
The Red House, Church Lane. (J. and R Winram) Est: 1968. SIZE: Medium. *STOCK: Furniture and general antiques, 18th-19th C, £5-£1,000; porcelain, 19th C, £5-£200.* TEL: 0325 332093. SER: Valuations; buys at auction. FAIRS: Most 3 day fairs in major cities.

SEAHAM

Lynden Antiques
East Farm, Dalton-le-Dale. (D Liddell) Resident, usually available. SIZE: Warehouse. *STOCK: General antiques - shipping goods, furniture including pine and desks, some architectural items.* TEL: 091 5816321.

William Wrighte
'Grotesque Architecture, or Rural Amusement', 1767.
Plate 3. 'Hermit's Cell, with Rustic Seats attached' to be built partly of large stones and Trunks of Trees, set round with ivy and lined with Rushes &c. The Roof should be covered with Thatch, and the Floor paved with small Pebble Stones or Cockle Shells. The Seats attached are intended to be composed of large irregular Stones, Roots of Trees &c.'. From ***Pictorial Dictionary of British 18th Century Furniture Design — The Printed Sources*** compiled by Elizabeth White and published by the **Antique Collectors' Club** in 1990. £65.00.

Essex

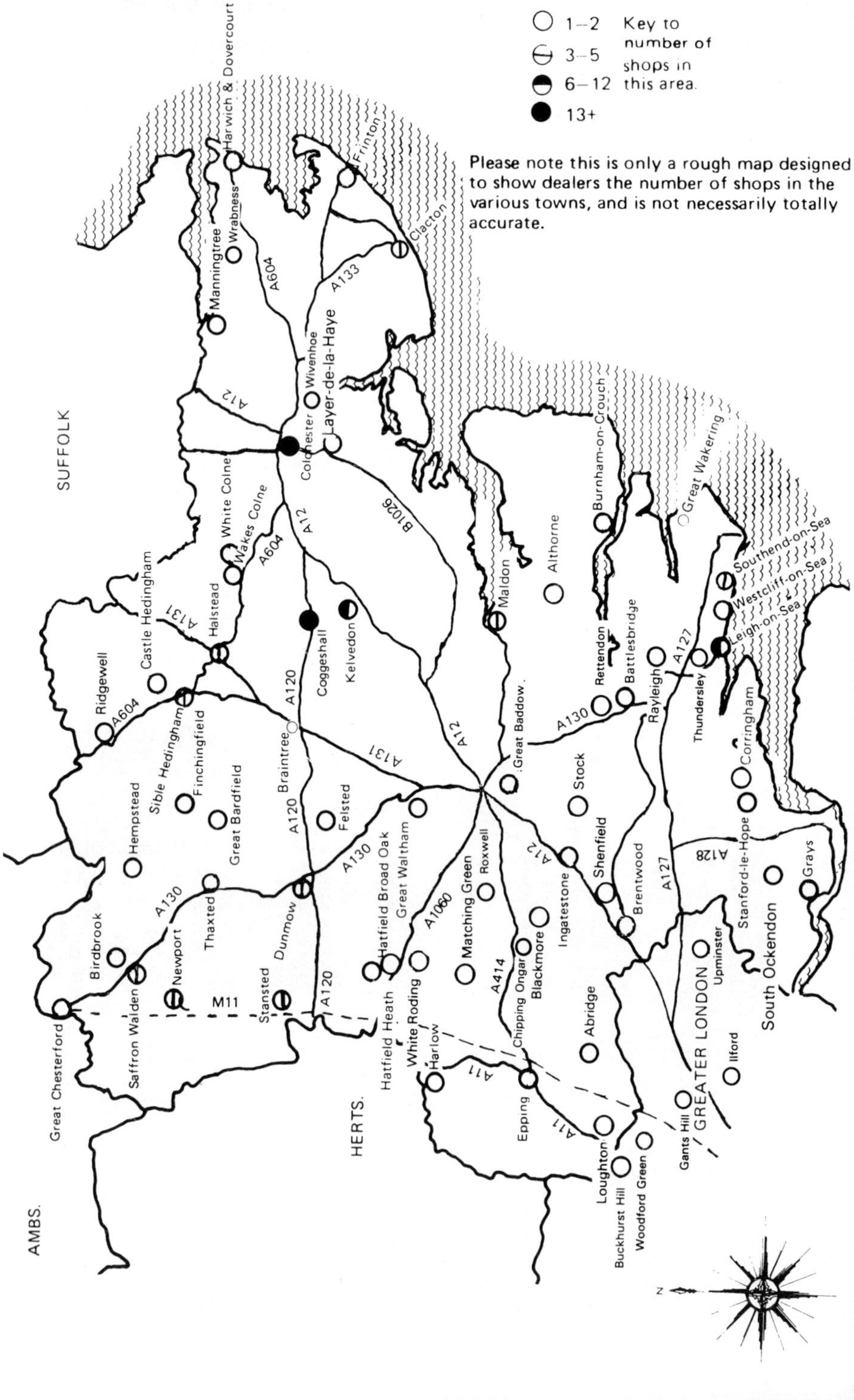
1–2
3–5
6–12
13+
Key to number of shops in this area.
SUFFOLK
HERTS.
AMBS.
GREATER LONDON
Harwich & Dovercourt
Frinton
Wrabness
Clacton
Manningtree
Wivenhoe
Layer-de-la-Haye
Colchester
White Colne
Wakes Colne
Halstead
Castle Hedingham
Ridgewell
Sible Hedingham
Finchingfield
Great Bardfield
Hempstead
Coggeshall
Kelvedon
Braintree
Felsted
Maldon
Althorne
Burnham-on-Crouch
Great Wakering
Southend-on-Sea
Westcliff-on-Sea
Leigh-on-Sea
Thundersley
Rayleigh
Battlesbridge
Rettendon
Great Baddow
Stock
Shenfield
Brentwood
Corringham
Stanford-le-Hope
Grays
South Ockendon
Upminster
Ilford
Gants Hill
Woodford Green
Buckhurst Hill
Loughton
Abridge
Epping
Chipping Ongar
Blackmore
Ingatestone
Roxwell
Matching Green
Great Waltham
Hatfield Broad Oak
White Roding
Hatfield Heath
Harlow
Dunmow
Thaxted
Stansted
Newport
Saffron Walden
Birdbrook
Great Chesterford
A604
A12
A133
A131
A120
B1026
A130
A127
A128
A1060
A414
A11
M11

Please note this is only a rough map designed to show dealers the number of shops in the various towns, and is not necessarily totally accurate.

ABRIDGE

Abridge Antique Centre
Market Pl. (J.S. and F.M Yewman) Est: 1960. Open 10-5, Thurs. 10-1. SIZE: Large, eleven small shops. *STOCK: Clocks, £50-£3,500; furniture, £50-£1,000; both 18th-19th C; small items, china, and porcelain including Doulton, silver, 19th-20th C, £5-£500.* LOC: Chigwell-Ongar road opposite The Rodings Restaurant. PARK: Market Sq. TEL: 0992 813113/812107. FAIRS: Local. VAT: Stan/Spec.

ALTHORNE

John Bailey Antique Clocks
5 Austral Way. Open by appointment. *STOCK: Longcase clocks, £1,000-£3,500; clocks, £100-£1,250; books on horology, art and antiques.* TEL: 0621 740 279. SER: Restorations and repairs.

BATTLESBRIDGE

Battlesbridge Antique Centre
Over 60 dealers with units located in the adjacent premises of Haybarn, Cromwell House, Bridgebarn, the Old Granary and trade warehouse. There are large car parks, furniture restoration workshops and facilities for containers. *STOCK: Wide range, from large furniture to jewellery with specialist dealers for most items, all periods.* LOC: A130, mid-way between Chelmsford and Southend. Junction 29, M25, east on A127 to A130, then north for 3 miles.

Cromwell House Antique Centre
(F Gallie) TEL: 0268 734005. (Office). Ground Floor Dealers - TEL: 0268 762612. First Floor Dealers - TEL: 0268 734030.

Haybarn and Bridgebarn Antique Centres **LAPADA**
(J P Pettitt) TEL: 0268 763500/735884.

Muggeridge Farm Warehouse
(J F Gallie) TEL: 0268 769392.

The Old Granary Antique and Craft Centre
(J F Gallie) Office. TEL: 0268 769392; workshops - 0268 732166; showrooms - 0268 764197.

BIRDBROOK

I Westrope
The Elms. Est: 1958. Open 9-6, Sat. 9-12 or by appointment. *STOCK: Furniture, bric-a-brac, china, dolls, pine, garden ornaments.* LOC: On A604. TEL: 044 085 365; evenings - 044 085 426.

BLACKMORE, Nr. Ingatestone

Haygreen Antiques
Haygreen Farmhouse. (T Harding) Open 9.30-5.30. CL: Mon. *STOCK: Pine, some mahogany and Victorian furniture.* TEL: 0277 821275.

BRAINTREE

Eric Hudes
Paigles, Perry Green, Bradwell. Est: 1946. SIZE: Oriental ceramics and works of art, 10th-19th C; early English and European pottery, 17th-19th C, all £100-£1,000. TEL: 0376 83767. SER: Worldwide postal transactions. FAIRS: Buxton, Harrogate. VAT: Spec. *Postal Only.*

BRENTWOOD

Brandler Galleries
1 Coptfold Rd. (J Brandler) Est: 1973. Open 10-5.30, Sun. by appointment. CL: Mon. SIZE: Medium. *STOCK: British pictures, 20th C, £100-£10,000.* LOC: Near Post Office. PARK: Own at rear. TEL: 0277 222269 (24 hrs.); fax - 222786. SER: Valuations (photographs); restorations (pictures - cleaning, relining, framing); buys at auction (pictures); 2-3 free catalogues annually.

BUCKHURST HILL

Domino Antiques
Challenge House, 57 Queens Rd. (S Parish) Open by appointment. SIZE: Small. *STOCK: Royal Worcester porcelain, 19th to early 20th C, £150-£4,000; watercolours, 19th-20th C, £250-£3,500; English porcelain, £70-£1,000.* PARK: Easy. TEL: 081 505 5071; home - 0702 463892. SER: Buys at auction (as stock). FAIRS: Wakefield Ceramic. VAT: Stan.

BURNHAM ON CROUCH

Quay Antiques
28 High St. (C McMullan) Est: 1961. Open 10-5. CL: Wed. *STOCK: Paintings, prints, china, glass, Victoriana, jewellery, small furniture.* TEL: Home - 0621 782468.

CASTLE HEDINGHAM

Orbell House Gallery
Orbell House. (E. and I Greene) Resident. Est: 1968. Open by appointment. SIZE: Medium plus gallery. *STOCK: Oriental, Persian, Anatolian, Afghan and Caucasian rugs and carpets, £200-£4,000.* PARK: Easy. TEL: 0787 60298. SER: Valuations; repairing and cleaning (Oriental rugs). FAIRS: Castle Hedingham, Bury St. Edmunds and Snape.

CLACTON-ON-SEA

Patina Antiques
32a Frinton Rd, Holland-on-Sea. Open 10-3. CL: Wed. and Thurs. *STOCK: General antiques and bric-a-brac.*

Shaftesbury Antiques
78-80 High St. (R.W. and J.C Dewar) Est: 1977. Open 9.30-1 and 2-5.30, Sun. by appointment. CL: Wed. p.m. SIZE: Small. *STOCK: Small furniture and interesting items, from Victorian, £5-£350; china, pottery and glass, £2-£240.* LOC: From A133 left toward town centre, left at Carnarvon Rd. roundabout, left at second lights into High St., premises 300yds. on right. PARK: Nearby. TEL: 0255 428602; home - same.

L.R Sharman
80B Rosemary Rd. Est: 1973. Open 9.30-5.15. CL: Wed. SIZE: Small. *STOCK: Furniture, 19th C decorative arts, £100-£5,000; jewellery, bronzes, clocks, music boxes, militaria.* LOC: End of Pier Ave., in opposite direction to sea front. PARK: Own. TEL: 0255 424620. SER: Valuations; restorations (furniture and jewellery). VAT: Stan.

COGGESHALL

Antique Metals
12 East St. (R.M. and S.V Chaplin) Est: 1959. Open every day 9-6. *STOCK: Brass, copper, polished steel, especially fenders; brass beds, Georgian and Victorian furniture.* TEL: 0376 562252.

Antique Pine
63/65 West St. (W.T Newton) Resident. Open 7 days 10-6. *STOCK: Victorian stripped pine.* TEL: 0376 561972.

Coggeshall Antiques
Doubleday Corner. Open 10-5, Sun. 2-5. SIZE: Large. *STOCK: Furniture, paintings and decorative items, 18th-19th C.* LOC: A120 opposite White Hart Hotel. PARK: At rear. TEL: 0376 562646; home - 0245 256027.

Elkin Mathews
16 Stoneham St. (D.C Muir) Est: 1887. Open 9.30-1 and 2-4.30, Sat. 10-1 and 2-5. CL: Wed. SIZE: Medium. *STOCK: Antiquarian and secondhand books, 50p-£1,000.* LOC: Just off A120 between Colchester and Braintree. PARK: Own, at rear. TEL: 0376 561730. SER: Valuations; restorations; buys at auction. FAIRS: Major London. VAT: Stan.

Findings
12 Stoneham St. (Mrs R Aylwin) Est: 1973. Open 10-1 and 2-5, Sun. by appointment. CL: Wed. SIZE: Small. *STOCK: Small furniture, all periods, £25-£250; jewellery and silver, £5-£250; linen and lace, £5-£50; bric-a-brac.* LOC: Centre of village. PARK: Easy. TEL: 0376 562351; home - 0376 561537.

Coggeshall continued

Joan Jobson's
5A Church St. (J Corder) Est: 1974. Open 9.30-5; Sun. 2-5 in Summer. SIZE: Medium. *STOCK: Bric-a-brac, Victoriana, general antiques and shipping furniture.* TEL: Home - 0376 561717.

Lindsell Chairs
11 Market Hill. (T.J.L. and A.M Martin) Est: 1982. Open 10.30-6. CL: Sat. SIZE: Large. *STOCK: Chairs and other seating, some tables, mid-18th C to 1914, £75-£4,000+.* Not Stocked: Windsor, caned, rush seated or commode chairs. LOC: Town centre. PARK: Nearby. TEL: 0376 562766; home - 037 184 222. VAT: Stan/Spec.

Mark Marchant Antiques
3 Market Sq. Resident. Est: 1960. Open 11-5, Sun. 2.30-5.30. SIZE: Large. *STOCK: Clocks and decorative works, decor furnishings, all periods.* LOC: A120. PARK: Easy. TEL: 0376 561188. SER: Valuations; restorations; buys at auction. VAT: Spec.

Priors Hall Furniture Ltd
Market Hill, and Priors Way. Open 9.30-5.30 and by appointment. *STOCK: Period furniture.* TEL: 0376 562000.

John Smith Antiques
1 Church St. (J.P Smith) Est: 1973. Open 10-5. SIZE: Medium. *STOCK: Paintings, prints and miniatures, 19th-20th C, £50-£800; furniture, 18th-19th C, £30-£2,000; shipping items, £10-£200.* Not Stocked: Coins, stamps. LOC: Town centre. PARK: Nearby. TEL: 0376 561365; home - 0376 561476. SER: Valuations; restorations (pictures); framing. VAT: Stan/Spec.

COLCHESTER

Anglia Fine Arts
Open by appointment only. *STOCK: Oils and watercolours, 19th-20th C.* TEL: 0206 571995.

Badger Antiques
The Old House, The Street, Elmstead Market. (A Johnson) Resident. Est: 1977. Open 9.30-5.30, Sun. by appointment. SIZE: Medium. *STOCK: Furniture, pine, lace, linen, Victorian underwear, clocks, china, glass.* LOC: 4 miles from Colchester on old A133 Clacton road. PARK: Easy. TEL: 0206 822044. SER: Valuations; restorations (furniture and clocks).

Barntiques
Lampitts Farm, Turkeycock Lane, Stanway. (A Jones and S Doubleday) Resident. Est: 1978. Open weekends. SIZE: Medium. *STOCK: General antiques and pine.* LOC: Turn left at Eight Ash Green from A604. PARK: Easy. TEL: 0206 210486; home - 0206 577031.

Colchester continued

S Bond and Son

14 North Hill. (M. and R Bond) Open 9-5.30. CL: Thurs. p.m.. SIZE: Large. *STOCK: Furniture, oil paintings, watercolours.* TEL: 0206 572925. SER: Restorations. VAT: Stan/Spec.

Elizabeth Cannon

85 Crouch St. Open 9.30-5.30. *STOCK: Jewellery, silver, glass, porcelain, collectors' items, period engravings and furniture.* PARK: Easy. TEL: 0206 575817.

Castle Bookshop

37 North hill. (R.J Green) *STOCK: Antiquarian and secondhand books, maps & prints.* TEL: 0206 577520. VAT: Stan.

The Coin and Stamp Centre

1st Floor13 Centurion House, St. John's St. (R.B Field) Est: 1968. Open 9-5. SIZE: Medium. *STOCK: Coins and stamps; medals, postcards, cigarette cards and accessories.* TEL: 0206 41232. SER: Valuations.

Countrystyle (Coach House Pine)

79 Magdalen Stand 47 London Rd, Lexden. (A Pearce) Est: 1979. Open 10-5, Sat. 9.30-5. *STOCK: Pine.* TEL: 0206 766876.

Davana Original Interiors

88 and 97 Hythe Hill. (D.E Donnelly) Est: 1963. Open 9.30-5. SIZE: Small. *STOCK: Continental decorative items, French furniture, lighting, textiles and curtain accessories, 1800-1930.* PARK: Easy. TEL: 0206 577853. SER: Restorations (metalware); buys at auction (furniture).

Margery Dean Antiques LAPADA

The GalleriesAlma St, Wivenhoe. Est: 1947. Open 9-12.30 and 1.30-5; Sat. 10-12.30 and 2-5. SIZE: Large. *STOCK: Mahogany, country and pine furniture, 18th-19th C.* Not Stocked: Reproductions. LOC: 3 miles from Colchester. Take 1st right by Essex University, old A133 Clacton road, to Wivenhoe. Shop situated before church in side road on left. PARK: Easy. TEL: 0206 822523; home - 0206 250485. SER: Valuations. VAT: Spec.

East Gates Antiques

91A East Hill. (J Latford) Est: 1980. Open 10-6. CL: Sun. and Mon. except by appointment. SIZE: Small. *STOCK: China and glass, 19th to early 20th C, £5-£350; cameras and photographica, pre-1930, £10-£300; general antiques, mainly 19th C.* Not Stocked: Jewellery. LOC: 200 yards from Castle, opposite St. James' church. PARK: 100 yards down hill or multi-storey 100 yards up hill. TEL: 0206 564474; home - 020622 2712.

Essex Antiques Centre

Priory St. (Scalpay Securities Ltd.)Est: 1969. Open 10-5.30. SIZE: Large - 52 dealers. *STOCK: General antiques and collectables.* LOC: Near town centre, off Queen St. Next to

Essex Antiques Centre continued

St. Botolph's Priory. PARK: Easy. TEL: 0206 871150. SER: Restorations (jewellery, furniture, paintings).

Richard Iles Gallery

10a, 10 and 12 Northgate St. (R. and C Iles) Est: 1970. Open 10-1 and 2-4. Thurs. 10-1. SIZE: Small. *STOCK: Watercolours, 19th to early 20th C, £75-£700.* LOC: Off North Hill. PARK: N.C.P. nearby. TEL: 0206 577877. SER: Valuations; restorations (oils, engravings and watercolours); framing; buys at auction. VAT: Stan/Spec.

Cliff Latford Photography

91A East Hill. Est: 1978. Open 10-6. CL: Mon. SIZE: Small. *STOCK: Cameras and photographica, images, photographic books, stereoscopes.* LOC: Opposite St. James' church. TEL: 0206 564474. SER: Valuations; restorations; buys at auction.

Partner and Puxon

7 and 16 North Hill. (S.H. and M Partner) Est: 1937. Open 9-1 and 2.15-5.30. CL: Thurs. p.m. SIZE: Large. *STOCK: English furniture, 16th to early 19th C, £100-£30,000; porcelain and pottery, 18th-19th C, £10-£2,000; period metalware, £50-£1,500; also continental and country furniture, shipping goods, general furnishing items.* LOC: In town centre; North Hill leads from High St. to Railway Station. TEL: 0206 573317. SER: Valuations. VAT: Stan/Spec.

Stock Exchange Antiques

40 Osborne St. (J Mellish and G Dean) Open 10-5. *STOCK: General antiques.* TEL: 0206 561997.

Trinity Antiques Centre

7 Trinity St. Est: 1976. Open 9.30-5. SIZE: 8 dealers. *STOCK: Antiques including small furniture, copper, clocks, brass, porcelain, silver, jewellery, collectors' items, Victoriana, maps and prints, linen, pine furniture.* TEL: 0206 577775.

Trinity Clocks

29 East Hill. (D.R Harker) Open 9.30-5. CL: Thurs. *STOCK: Clocks, watches, furniture, silver, jewellery, china and collectors' items.* TEL: 0206 868623. SER: Repairs (clocks and watches).

CORRINGHAM, Nr. Stanford-le-Hope

Bush House

Church Rd. (F Stephens) Est: 1976. Open by appointment. SIZE: Small. *STOCK: Staffordshire portrait figures, 1837-1901; Staffordshire animals, 1775-1890; pottery animals and other ceramics, 1775-1901; general antiques; all £5-£1,000.* LOC: Opposite the church. PARK: Easy. TEL: 0375 673463; home - same. SER: Valuations; restorations (pottery and porcelain). FAIRS: Park Lane Hotel; Birmingham N.E.C; Monway Ceramic; K.M. Ceramic. VAT: Spec.

DUNMOW

Julia Bennet (Antiques)

Flemings Hill Farm, Gt. Easton. Open by appointment. *STOCK: 18th C mahogany; 17th-19th C oak and country furniture, decorative and garden pieces.* TEL: 0279 850279.

Simon Hilton

Flemings Hill Farm, Gt. Easton. Resident. Est: 1937. Open by appointment. *STOCK: Oil paintings, watercolours and drawings, £100-£10,000; fine prints and sculpture, £50-£5,000; all 17th-20th C.* TEL: 0279 850107/850279. SER: Valuations; restorations (oil paintings, watercolours and drawings); buys at auction. VAT: Spec.

EPPING

Epping Galleries

64 - 66 High St. (P Hellmers) Est: 1972. Open 10-5. CL: Wed. SIZE: Large. *STOCK: Furniture, pine, gramophones, clocks, collectables, linen, 19th-20th C, £5-£300.* LOC: B1393, (A11). PARK: Easy. TEL: 0378 73023/4. SER: Restorations; framing. VAT: Stan/Spec.

Epping Saturday Market

Rear of 64 - 66 High St. (P Hellmers) Est: 1977. Open every Sat. a.m. SIZE: 60 stalls. *STOCK: General antiques and bric-a-brac.* TEL: 0378 73023/4.

FELSTED, Nr. Great Dunmow

Argyll House Antiques

Argyll House, Station Rd. (J Howard and C Lingham) Est: 1978. CL: Wed. SIZE: Medium. *STOCK: Furniture, Victorian and Edwardian, £25-£1,000; porcelain, 19th C to mid-20th C, £5-£500; collectors' items and ephemera, £1-£250.* LOC: Village centre. PARK: Easy. TEL: 0371 820682; home - same.

FINCHINGFIELD, Nr. Braintree

Artisans Gallery

(P. and C.A Shore) Open 10-5.30, Sun. 2-5.30 or by appointment. CL: Mon. *STOCK: Watercolours, oils and prints, 19th-20th C.* TEL: 0371 810709.

Andrew Tate

Great Wincey Farm. Est: 1972. Open 9-5, Sat. 9-1 or by appointment. *STOCK: Stripped pine.* TEL: 0371 810004.

FRINTON-ON-SEA

Dickens Curios

151 Connaught Ave. (Miss M Wilsher) Est: 1970. Open 9.30-1 and 2.15-5.30; Mon. open from 11, Fri. from 10.30; Sat. closed at 5. CL: Wed. p.m. SIZE: Small. *STOCK: Victoriana and earlier items, £5-£200; furniture, 18th-20th C, £5-£300; jewellery, £5-£25; coins and cigarette cards.* Not Stocked: Firearms. LOC: From Frinton Station 1/4 mile down Connaught Ave., opp. Hammond's Garage. PARK: Easy. TEL: 0255 674134.

Frinton Antiques

(K.J. and Mrs. G.M Pethick) Est: 1952. Open by appointment. *STOCK: Small decorative furniture; fine porcelain, silver, glass and pottery.* TEL: 0255 671894. VAT: Stan/Spec.

GANTS HILL

Antique Clock Repair Shoppe

26 Woodford Ave. (K Ashton) Est: 1971. Open 10-5. *STOCK: Clocks, pictures, bric-a-brac.* TEL: 081 550 9540.

GRAYS

Grays Galleries Antiques and Collectors Centre

23 Lodge Lane. Open 10-5.30, incl. some Sundays (telephone for dates). SIZE: 40+ dealers. *STOCK: General antiques, small furniture, jewellery and collectables.* LOC: On A1306 (old A13). TEL: 0375 374883.

GREAT BADDOW

Baddow Antique and Craft Centre

The Bringy, Church St. Est: 1969. Open 9-5, Sun. 11-5. SIZE: 22 dealers. *STOCK: Furniture, general antiques, Victorian brass bedsteads, bric-a-brac and shipping goods.* PARK: Easy. TEL: 0245 76159. SER: Restorations; upholstery.

Micallef Antiques

Warehouse No.1The Bringy, Church St. Open 8.30-5.30. *STOCK: 19th C mahogany and walnut, shipping goods.* TEL: 0245 75050; evenings - 0268 732105.

GREAT BARDFIELD

Golden Sovereign
The Old Police House, High St. (C. and W Leitch) Est: 1969. Open 10-6. CL: Wed. a.m. and Sat. a.m. SIZE: Small. *STOCK: Glass, silver, small furniture, small items, 18th-19th C, from £5.* LOC: B1057. From Dunmow, 100yds. beyond Thaxted turning, 2nd shop on left. PARK: Easy. TEL: 0371 810507; home - same.

Markswood Gallery LAPADA
(E Goodwin) Est: 1978. Open 11-1 and 2.30-5, Sun. 2.30-5, or by appointment. CL: Mon., Wed. and Fri. *STOCK: Watercolours and oil paintings, all periods; small furniture.* TEL: 0371 810106; home - 0371 810329. SER: Restorations; framing; buys at auction.

GREAT CHESTERFORD, Nr. Saffron Walden

C. and J Mortimer and Son
School St. Est: 1962. Open Thurs., Sat. and Sun. 2.30-5, or by appointment. SIZE: Medium. *STOCK: Oak furniture, 16th-18th C, from £400; portrait paintings, 16th-17th C, from £1,500.* LOC: From London on B1383. PARK: Easy. TEL: 0799 30261.

GREAT WAKERING

Times Past
195 High St. (M Sherman and R Gibson) Est: 1976. Open Tues., Thurs. and Sun. 1.30-5.30. *STOCK: Small furniture and decorative items.* TEL: 0702 219752.

GREAT WALTHAM, Nr. Chelmsford

The Stores
(M Webster) Est: 1974. Open 10-5. CL: Sun. and Tues. SIZE: Large. *STOCK: Pine furniture.* LOC: On A130. PARK: At rear. TEL: 0245 360277; home - 0376 26997. VAT: Stan.

HALSTEAD

Helen Blomfield
Hampers, Little Maplestead. Est: 1958. Open by appointment. SIZE: Small. *STOCK: Silver and Sheffield plate, 18th-20th C, £10-£1,000.* LOC: A131 from Halstead towards Sudbury, after one mile turn first left to The Maplesteads, 1/2 mile further, white-gabled farmhouse on right. TEL: 0787 472159. SER: Valuations (silver).

Halstead Antiques
71 Head St. (P Earl) Est: 1973. *STOCK: Small general antiques, glass, bric-a-brac.* TEL: 0787 473265.

Halstead continued

Napier House Antiques
Head St. (V McGregor) Open Wed., Fri., Sat., 9-6, or by appointment. SIZE: Large. *STOCK: Antique beds only.* LOC: Leaving town on A131, shop on right. PARK: Own. TEL: 0787 477346/75280.

Townsford Mill Antiques Centre
The Causeway. (M.T Stuckey) Open 10-5 including Sun. SIZE: 60 dealers. *STOCK: General antiques and collectables.* LOC: On A131 Braintree/Sudbury road. TEL: 0787 474451.

HARLOW

Rundells Antiques
Rundells, London Rd. Est: 1951. Open 10-5. SIZE: Large. *STOCK: 17th-19th C furniture, porcelain, paintings, brass, copper.* LOC: B1393, half-way between Epping and Harlow. PARK: Own. TEL: 0279 422906. VAT: Stan/Spec.

HARWICH

Mayflower Antiques
2 Una Road, Parkeston, and 105 High St., Dovercourt. (J.W Odgers) Est: 1970. Open 10-6. CL: Sat. SIZE: Medium. *STOCK: Clocks, mechanical music, scientific and marine instruments, collectors' items.* LOC: Main road to Parkeston Quay. PARK: Easy. TEL: 0255 504079; mobile - 0860 315101. VAT: Stan/Spec.

HATFIELD BROAD OAK

Tudor Antiques
(R.M. and P.A Wood) Est: 1977. Open 9.30-6.30. *STOCK: Furniture, porcelain, glass, unusual items.* LOC: B183, close to M11 and A120. TEL: 0279 70557.

HATFIELD HEATH, Nr. Bishop's Stortford

Barn Gallery
Parvilles Farm. (H. and M Scantlebury) Est: 1989. Open Wed. and Sat. 10.30-4, other times by appointment. SIZE: Medium. *STOCK: Oil paintings and watercolours, 19th-20th C, £250-£5,000; prints, works by living artists.* LOC: Turning off A1060 at Hatfield Heath, down Matching Green Rd., opposite Down Hall. PARK: Easy. TEL: 0279 730114; home - 0279 731228. SER: Valuations; restorations. VAT: Stan/Spec.

HEMPSTEAD, Nr. Saffron Walden

Michael Beaumont Antiques
Hempstead Hall. Open 10.30-5. CL: Thurs. and Fri. SIZE: Large. *STOCK: Furniture - oak, mahogany, walnut, rosewood, 17th-19th C, £50-£2,500; Oriental rugs.* LOC: On B1054 between Hempstead and Steeple Bumpstead. PARK: Easy. TEL: 0440 730239. SER: Restorations (furniture). VAT: Stan/Spec.

ILFORD

Belgrave Antiques and Bric-a-Brac
77 Belgrave Rd. (Mrs M.M Germain) Est: 1969. Open 10-2 and 3.30-6.30. *STOCK: Furniture, paintings, bric-a-brac, books.* TEL: 081 554 8032.

Flowers Antiques
733 High Rd, Seven Kings. (J.C. and A.D Meeson) Est: 1988. Open 9.30-5.30. CL: Wed. *STOCK: Furniture, Edwardian, Victorian; glass, china.* PARK: Easy. TEL: 081 599 9959. VAT: Stan/Spec.

INGATESTONE

Meyers Gallery LAPADA
66 High St. (Mrs J Meyers) Est: 1972. Open 10-5. CL: Wed. SIZE: Large. *STOCK: Oil paintings and watercolours, 18th-20th C and living artists, £25-£10,000; small Victorian furniture and decorative items.* PARK: Nearby. TEL: 0277 355335. SER: Restorations; framing. VAT: Stan/Spec.

KELVEDON, Nr. Colchester

Kelvedon Antiques BADA
90 High St. (J. and S.E Billings) Est: 1965. Open 9.30-5.30. CL: Sun. except by appointment. SIZE: Medium. *STOCK: Furniture, 18th to early 19th C.* LOC: From London on right hand side of main street. PARK: Easy. TEL: 0376 570557. VAT: Stan/Spec.

Kelvedon continued

Kelvedon Antiques Centre
139 High St. (M Chave) Open 10-5 or by appointment. SIZE: Medium - 6 dealers. *STOCK: Furniture, porcelain, pottery, glass, silver, jewellery, brass, copper, collectors' items, 18th-20th C.* LOC: Off A12 between Chelmsford and Colchester. PARK: Easy. TEL: 0376 570896. FAIRS: Furze Hill, Margaretting.

Millers Antiques Kelvedon LAPADA
46 High St. Est: 1920. Open 9-5.30, Sat. 10-4 or by appointment. SIZE: Large. *STOCK: 17th-19th C mahogany, walnut, fruitwood, oak, English and French furniture.* PARK: Own. TEL: 0376 570098. VAT: Stan/Spec.

The Old Antique Shop
Menai House, 41 High St. (G. and W Boyd-Ratcliff and F Campbell) Est: 1987. Open 10-5.30, Sun. by appointment. SIZE: Medium. *STOCK: Furniture, smalls and decorative items.* TEL: 0376 570223. VAT: Stan/Spec.

G.T Ratcliff Ltd
Whitebarn, Coggeshall Rd. (W.D Boyd-Ratcliff and F.D Campbell) Est: 1935. Open 9-5. CL: Sat. p.m. SIZE: Large. *STOCK: Furniture, mainly 18th and 19th C.* LOC: A12. PARK: Easy. TEL: 0376 570234. VAT: Stan. *Trade Only.*

Thomas Sykes Antiques LAPADA
16 High St. (T.W Sykes and O.P Folkard) Est: 1983. Open 10-5, Sun. by appointment. SIZE: Large. *STOCK: Furniture, 18th-19th C; porcelain, lamps and decorative items; all £300-£25,000.* LOC: Off A12. PARK: Own. TEL: 0376 571969. SER: Valuations; buys at auction. VAT: Spec.

Templar Antiques
6 Peter's House, High St. (P Wilson) Est: 1974. Open 10-5. SIZE: Medium. *STOCK: 18th to early 19th C furniture, prints, pictures and glass, including airtwist wineglasses.* LOC: Village centre, off A12. PARK: Own at rear. TEL: 0376 572101.

LAYER DE LA HAYE

Pugh's Porcelains LAPADA
Layer Fields House, Field Farm Rd. (J. and J Pugh) Resident. Open by appointment. SIZE: Medium. *STOCK: English porcelain, late 18th and early 19th C, £20-£2,500.* LOC: Layer Rd. from Colchester, turn left at The Folly. PARK: Easy. TEL: 0206 348170. SER: Buys at auction. FAIRS: Cheltenham, Wakefield Ceramic, Olympia.

LEIGH-ON-SEA

K.S Buchan
114 The Broadway. Open 10-5. *STOCK: Furniture and general antiques.* TEL: 0702 79440.

Castle Antiques
72 The Broadway. (B.L Zabell and J.A Gair) Open 10-5. CL: Mon. *STOCK: 18th-19th C decorative furniture, pottery and porcelain (especially Staffordshire figures and Masons Ironstone); silver; firearms, edged and ethnic weapons, tribal artifacts, antiquities, cased birds and fish.* TEL: 0702 75732; mobile - 0860 795354.

Collectors' Paradise
993 London Rd. (H.W. and P.E Smith) Est: 1967. Open 10-5.30. CL: Fri. SIZE: Small. *STOCK: Clocks, 1870-1930's, from £45; bric-a-brac; postcards, 1900-1930s; cigarette cards, 1889-1939.* LOC: On A13. PARK: Easy. TEL: 0702 73077.

Pall Mall Antiques
104c/104d Elm Rd. (M Sherman) Open 10-5. *STOCK: Porcelain, copper, brass, glass, general antiques.* TEL: 0702 77235.

Past and Present
81 and 83 Broadway West. (R Banks) Open 9.30-4.30. CL: Tues. and Wed. *STOCK: General antiques.* TEL: 0702 79101.

John Stacey and Sons
86-90 Pall Mall. Est: 1946. Open 9-5.30. CL: Sat. p.m. *STOCK: General antiques.* TEL: 0702 77051. SER: Valuations; exporters; auctioneers. VAT: Stan.

J Streamer Antiques
86 Broadway, and 212 Leigh Rd. Est: 1965. Open 9.30-5.30. CL: Wed. *STOCK: Jewellery, silver, bric-a-brac, small furniture.* TEL: 0702 72895/711633.

Tilly's Antiques
1801 London Rd. (S.T. and R.J Austen) Est: 1972. Open 10-5. CL: Wed. SIZE: Medium. *STOCK: Furniture, 19th C, £100-£500+; Victorian and Edwardian dolls, £100-£500; general antiques, 19th-20th C, £5-£200.* LOC: A13. PARK: Easy. TEL: 0702 557170 (answer-phone). SER: Valuations; restorations (furniture and dolls).

Leigh-on-Sea continued

Richard Wrenn Antiques
113/115 Broadway West. Est: 1950. Open 10.30-5.30. CL: Mon., Wed. and Fri. p.m. SIZE: Large. *STOCK: Furniture, £250-£5,000; porcelain, glass, £30-£1,000; jewellery, silver, objets d'art, £40-£2,000; metalware, brass, copper, £20-£500.* LOC: 250yds. west of Leigh church. TEL: 0702 710745. VAT: Stan/Spec.

LOUGHTON

Pearl Morris
Open by appointment. *STOCK: Doulton, Lambeth and Burslem.* TEL: 081 508 7177.

MALDON

Abacus Antiques
105 High St. (Mrs J Davidson) Open 10-4.30. CL: Wed. SIZE: Large. *STOCK: Jewellery, 19th to early 20th C, £10-£500; porcelain, pottery, glass, small silver and collectors' items, 1800-1930, £5-£250; furniture, 19th C and Edwardian, £20-£2,000.* Not Stocked: Firearms, coins, stamps, books. LOC: Town centre. PARK: Easy. TEL: 0621 850528; home - same. SER: Valuations.

The Antique Rooms
63D High St. (Mrs E Hedley) Est: 1966. Open 10-5, Wed. 10-1. SIZE: Medium. *STOCK: Furniture, pottery, porcelain, glass and silver, costume, linen and lace, jewellery, lace-making equipment, cast-iron fireplaces, fenders, collectors' items.* LOC: Just off High St., in courtyard at rear of Maldon bookshop. PARK: Nearby. TEL: 0621 856985.

Beeleigh Abbey Books (W. and G. Foyle Ltd.)
Beeleigh Abbey. *STOCK: Rare and antiquarian books, all subjects.*

Maldon Antiques and Collectors Market
United Reformed Church Hall, Market Hill. Est: 1975. Open first Sat. every month, 10-5. SIZE: 20 dealers. PARK: Easy. TEL: 07872 22826.

Mayfair Fine Art
Oakwood House, 2 High St. (T.E May) Est: 1985. Open 10.30-3.30, Sat. 10-5, Sun. 2-5. CL: Mon. and Wed. SIZE: Small. *STOCK: Watercolours, oils, sculpture, objets d'art, 19th-20th C, £300-£500.* LOC: Opposite police station. PARK: At rear. TEL: 0621 859074. SER: Valuations; buys at auction (watercolours, oils and sculpture). VAT: Stan/Spec.

MANNINGTREE

"Forty Nine"
High Street. (A Patterson) Open 10-1 and 2-5. *STOCK: General and country antiques.* PARK: Easy. TEL: 0206 396170.

Manningtre continued

F Freestone
"Kiln Tops", 29 Colchester Rd. Open 9-6, appointment advisable. *STOCK: General antiques, furniture, clocks.* TEL: 0206 392998.

MATCHING GREEN, Nr. Harlow

Stone Hall Antiques
Down Hall Rd. Est: 1971. Open 9-5.30, Sat. and Sun. by appointment. SIZE: Warehouse. *STOCK: Furniture, 17th-19th C, £50-£10,000.* LOC: Turning off A1060 at Hatfield Heath. PARK: Own. TEL: 0279 731440; home - same. VAT: Stan. *Trade & Export Only.*

NEWPORT, Nr. Saffron Walden

Brown House Antiques
High St. (B.E. and J Hodgkinson) Est: 1978. Open 10-5. SIZE: Medium. *STOCK: Furniture, from 18th C, £50-£2,500.* LOC: B1383, off M11 at Stansted interchange. PARK: Easy. TEL: 0799 40238; home - same. SER: Valuations; restorations; buys at auction (furniture). VAT: Stan/Spec.

Little Shop Antiques
High St. Est: 1979. Open Tues., Thurs. and Sat. 10-5. *STOCK: General antiques including porcelain, glass, silver, pictures, prints, jewellery, country furniture.* LOC: B1383. TEL: 0799 40633 (after 6 p.m.).

Newport continued

Newport Gallery
High St. (W Kemp and E C Hitchcock) Open 9.30-5. CL: Mon. *STOCK: Watercolours, prints and oils.* LOC: On B1383, two miles from Saffron Walden. PARK: At rear. TEL: 0799 40623.

ONGAR

Robert Bailey Oriental Rugs LAPADA
(R.M Bailey) Est: 1975. Open by appointment. *STOCK: Persian rugs, 19th-20th C, £500-£3,500; Turkoman and Turkish rugs.* Not Stocked: Chinese, Pakistani and Indian rugs. TEL: 0277 362662. SER: Valuations; restorations; cleaning and identification; fairs organiser. VAT: Stan/Spec. *Trade Only.*

RAYLEIGH

F.G Bruschweiler (Antiques) Ltd LAPADA
41-67 Lower Lambricks. Est: 1954. Open 9-5, Sat. by appointment. SIZE: Warehouses. *STOCK: Furniture, 18th-19th C.* LOC: A127 to Weir roundabout through Rayleigh High St. and Hockley Rd., first left past cemetery, then second left, warehouse round corner on left. PARK: Easy. TEL: 0268 773761/773932; home - 062 182 8152; fax - 0268 773318. VAT: Stan. *Trade Only.*

RETTENDON

Antiques Trade Warehouse

Rawlings Farm Buildings, Main Rd. Open 8.30-5.30, or by appointment. CL: Sat. *STOCK: Furniture.* TEL: 0245 400046. The following dealers trade at this warehouse.

F G Bruschweiler (Antiques) Ltd LAPADA
Vic Hall - Junior Antiques
John Sturton - Mr Pickwick
Ian F Vince

RIDGEWELL, Nr. Halstead

Ridgewell Crafts and Antiques

, Ridgewell. (A.A. and C.M.J Godsell and P Crouch) Est: 1952. Open 10-6.30 including Sun. CL: Wed. SIZE: Medium. *STOCK: Clocks and watches, 19th C, £5-£500; china, brass, copper, some furniture.* LOC: On A604, 6 miles from Haverhill towards Colchester. PARK: Easy. TEL: 044 085 272. SER: Clock and watch repairs.

ROXWELL, Nr. Chelmsford

Freeman Antiques

By appointment only. *STOCK: Period oak, especially coffers.* TEL: 024 531 286.

SAFFRON WALDEN

Lankester Antiques and Books

Old Sun InnChurch St, and Market Hill. (J. and P Lankester) Est: 1965. Open 9.30-5.30. SIZE: Large. *STOCK: Furniture, porcelain, pottery, metalwork, general antiques, books, prints and maps.* TEL: 0799 22685. VAT: Stan.

Saffron Walden continued

Littlebury Antiques - Littlebury Restorations Ltd

58/60 Fairycroft Rd. (N.H D'Oyly and M.A Hudson) Est: 1962. Open 9-5. CL: Sat. and Sun. except by appointment. SIZE: Medium. *STOCK: Marine antiques and paintings, clocks, chronometers, chess sets, walking sticks, barometers and curios.* PARK: Easy. TEL: 0799 27961; weekends and evenings 0799 22931; 0279 771530. SER: Valuations; restorations; buys at auction. VAT: Stan/Spec.

Maureen Morris

Open by appointment. *STOCK: Samplers, needleworks, textiles and small country furniture.* TEL: 0799 21338; fax - 0799 22802.

Jane Sumner

9 Market Sq. (Mrs J Sumner) SIZE: Medium. *STOCK: Early oak, Georgian mahogany, metalware, jewellery.* TEL: 0799 23611. FAIRS: Organiser.

SHENFIELD

The Chart House

33 Spurgate, Hutton Mount. (C.C Crouchman) Est: 1974. Open by appointment only. SIZE: Small. *STOCK: Nautical items.* PARK: Easy. TEL: 0277 225012; home - same. SER: Hire of nautical items and equipment; buys at auction. VAT: Stan.

SIBLE HEDINGHAM, Nr. Halstead

Churchgate Antiques

150 Swan St. (B Wilkinson) Est: 1979. Open 10-5, Sun. by appointment. CL: Mon. SIZE: Large. *STOCK: English and Irish period pine, £75-£1,800.* LOC: A604. PARK: Easy. TEL: 0787 62269; home - 0787 61311. SER: Valuations; restorations (stripping). VAT: Stan.

Sible Hedingham continued

Hedingham Antiques
100 Swan St. (P Patterson) Open 10-12.30 and 1.30-5 or by appointment. CL: Wed. p.m. SIZE: Medium. *STOCK: Furniture, 1790-1910; china, glass, silver plate, Victorian to art deco.* LOC: A604, village centre. PARK: Easy. TEL: 0787 60360; home - same.

W.A Pinn and Sons BADA LAPADA
124 Swan St. (K.H. and W.J Pinn) Est: 1943. CL: Sun. except by appointment. SIZE: Medium. *STOCK: Furniture, 17th to early 19th C, £100-£5,000; clocks, 18th to early 19th C, £250-£3,500; interesting items, prior to 1830, £10-£1,500.* LOC: On A604 opposite Shell Garage. PARK: On premises. TEL: 0787 61127. FAIRS: Chelsea Spring and Autumn Antiques; Harrogate. VAT: Stan/Spec.

SOUTH OCKENDEN

Alfred S Allen and Co
P.O. Box No.4. Est: 1964. *STOCK: Coins and accessories, coin jewellery.* SER: Buys at auction. *Mail Order Only.*

SOUTHEND-ON-SEA

Atticus Books
Kickshaws, 20 Alexandra St. (Mrs A.M Eddelin) Est: 1974. Open 11-1 and 2.30-6. CL: Wed. *STOCK: Secondhand and antiquarian books; paintings, maps and prints.* LOC: Town centre, 50yds. from High St. PARK: Meters and opposite. TEL: 0702 353630.

Kickshaws
20 Alexandra St. (Mrs A.M Eddelin) Est: 1974. Open 11-1 and 2.30-6. CL: Wed. SIZE: Small. *STOCK: General antiques, £5-£500.* LOC: Town centre, 50yds. from High St. PARK: Meters and opposite. TEL: 0702 353630.

Lonsdale Antiques
86 Lonsdale Rd, Southchurch. (H.M Clark) Open 9-5.30. CL: Wed. *STOCK: Jewellery, pictures, porcelain, general small antiques.* TEL: 0702 462643.

Reddings Art and Antiques
98 London Rd. (F.H Redding) Resident. Open by appointment only. *STOCK: Oils and watercolours, general antiques.* TEL: 0702 354647.

STANFORD-LE-HOPE

Barton House Antiques
Wharf Rd. (L. and J Pigney) Est: 1973. Open all times but appointment advisable. SIZE: Medium. *STOCK: 17th-19th C furniture; 18th-19th C English porcelain, including English 18th C blue and white, copper, brass and glass.* LOC: Turn

Barton House Antiques continued

off A13 to centre of town, 200yds. on right hand side. PARK: Easy. TEL: 0375 672494. SER: Valuations; buys at auction. VAT: Spec. *Mainly Trade.*

STANSTED

Linden House Antiques
3 and 23 Silver St. (A.W. and K.M Sargeant) Est: 1961. Open 9-5.30. CL: Sun. except by appointment. SIZE: Large. *STOCK: English furniture, 18th-19th C, £100-£10,000; small decorative items, including library and dining room furniture.* LOC: On A11. TEL: 0279 812372. VAT: Spec.

Valmar Antiques
Croft House, High Lane. (J., M. and N Orpin) Resident. Est: 1960. Open 8-5 or by appointment. SIZE: Large. *STOCK: Furniture and decorative items, £50-£10,000.* TEL: 0279 813201; fax - 0279 816962.

Wiskin Antiques LAPADA
18 Silver St. (K. and M Wiskin) Est: 1973. Open 10-5.30, Sun. by appointment. SIZE: Medium. *STOCK: Mahogany, walnut, oak, 18-19th C; pine, £50-£5,000; clocks, silver, small items, £5-£800.* Not Stocked: Reproduction. LOC: B1383 (Old A11), one mile from M11, junction 8. PARK: At rear. TEL: 0279 812376; home - same. SER: Restorations (polishing, pine stripping, re-upholstering). VAT: Spec.

STOCK

Sabine Antiques
38 High St. (C.E Sabine) Est: 1974. Open 10-5 or by appointment. CL: Mon. *STOCK: Furniture, from £50; china and glass, from £5.* LOC: Village centre on B1007. PARK: Easy. TEL: 0277 840553. SER: Valuations; restorations (furniture); silver plating; framing.

THAXTED

Thaxted Galleries
1 Newbiggin St. (J.E Sheppard) Est: 1958. Open 9-5.30. CL: Sun., except by appointment. SIZE: Large. *STOCK: Furniture, £200-£1,000; oak furniture, £250-£1,500; all 17th-18th C; antique lamp bases.* LOC: On B184. PARK: At rear. TEL: 0371 830350.

Turpin's Antiques BADA
4 Stoney Lane. (J.F Braund) SIZE: Large. *STOCK: 17th and 18th C walnut, oak and mahogany, metalware.* TEL: 0371 830495. SER: Restorations; buys at auction. VAT: Spec.

The Princess Royal as an infant, clasping her mother's pearl-set bracelet with a miniature of Prince Albert, in a stipple engraving by James Thomson after a painting by John Lucas, c.1844.
NATIONAL PORTRAIT GALLERY ARCHIVES
From ***Jewellery 1789-1910 — The International Era,*** Volume I, by Shirley Bury, published by the **Antique Collectors' Club** in 1991. £47.50 each volume.

THUNDERSLEY

Bramley Antiques LAPADA

180 Kiln Rd. (S Grater) Est: 1978. Open 11.30-4.30, Sat. 11.30-6. CL: Mon. and Fri. SIZE: Medium. *STOCK: Porcelain and glass, £5-£250; furniture, £30-£2,500; linen, silver, jewellery, brass, £2.50-£500, all 18th to early 20th C.* LOC: A13. PARK: Easy. TEL: 0702 551800. SER: Valuations; restorations. VAT: Stan/Spec.

UPMINSTER

The Old Cottage Antiques

The Old Cottage, Corbets Tey. (R Edwards) Est: 1970. Open 10-5. SIZE: Medium. *STOCK: Furniture, shipping goods, porcelain, silver, general antiques.* Not Stocked: Firearms. PARK: Easy. TEL: 040 22 22867.

WAKES COLNE, Nr. Colchester

Janet Gordon

Wakes Colne House. Resident. Usually open. *STOCK: Furniture, pre-1900, and decorative items.* LOC: A604. PARK: Easy. TEL: 0787 222402. SER: Curtains, covers and fabrics.

WESTCLIFF-ON-SEA

David, Jean and John Antiques

Lincoln House Gallery, 587 London Rd. Est: 1963. Open 10-5. CL: Wed. SIZE: Large. *STOCK: Clocks, furniture, £25-£3,000; porcelain, bronzes, weapons, objets d'art, some shipping goods.* LOC: Opposite Cannon Cinema. TEL: 0702 339106; fax - 0268 560536; home - 0268 733330; evenings - 0268 785815. SER: Valuations; restorations (clocks, barometers and small furniture). VAT: Stan/Spec.

It's About Time

863 London Rd. (R. and V Alps) Est: 1980. Open 9-5.30. CL: Wed. SIZE: Medium. *STOCK: Clocks, 18th-19th C, £200-£4,000; barometers, Victorian and Edwardian furniture.* LOC: A13. PARK: Easy. TEL: 0702 72574; home - 0702 205204.

WHITE COLNE, Nr. Colchester

Compton-Dando (Fine Arts) Limited

Berewyk Hall. (A.C Compton-Dando) Resident. Open by appointment only. *STOCK: Period English and Continental furniture.* LOC: B1024. At 'King's Head' take left turn marked 'Bures' and make for White Colne parish church. Berewyk Hall lies just beyond, on left. PARK: Easy. TEL: 0787 222200. SER: Valuations; buys at auction (furniture). VAT: Stan/Spec.

White Colne continued

Fox and Pheasant Antique Pine
(J. and J Kearin) Est: 1978. Open 10-5, Sun. 12-4. SIZE: Large. *STOCK: Stripped pine.* LOC: A604. PARK: Easy. TEL: 0787 223297. SER: Pine stripping and restorations.

WHITE RODING

White Roding Antiques
'Ivydene', Chelmsford Rd. (F. and J Neill) Est: 1971. Open by appointment. SIZE: Medium. *STOCK: Furniture and shipping goods, 18th-19th C, £10-£1,500.* LOC: A1060 between Bishops Stortford and Chelmsford. PARK: Easy. TEL: 027 976 376; home - same. VAT: Stan/Spec.

WIVENHOE

Antique Furniture Workshop
STOCK: Restored furniture, 18th to early 20th C, £110-£1,000. LOC: 3 miles from Colchester. TEL: 0206 823890. *Trade only.*

WOODFORD GREEN

P. and K.N Blake - Lanehurst Antiques
403 High Rd. Est: 1952. Open Thurs. and Fri., 10-6, Sat. 10-1. SIZE: Medium. *STOCK: Furniture, general antiques.* LOC: A11, close to Castle public house. TEL: 081 504 9264. SER: Valuations; buys at auction. VAT: Stan/Spec.

Galerie Lev
1 The Broadway. Open 10-5. *STOCK: Oils, watercolours, collectors' items, silver plate, porcelain.* LOC: Near Woodford underground station. TEL: 081 505 2226. SER: Framing (trade only).

WRABNESS, Nr. Manningtree

John Drury
Strandlands. Open by appointment. *STOCK: Antiquarian books.* TEL: 0255 886260.

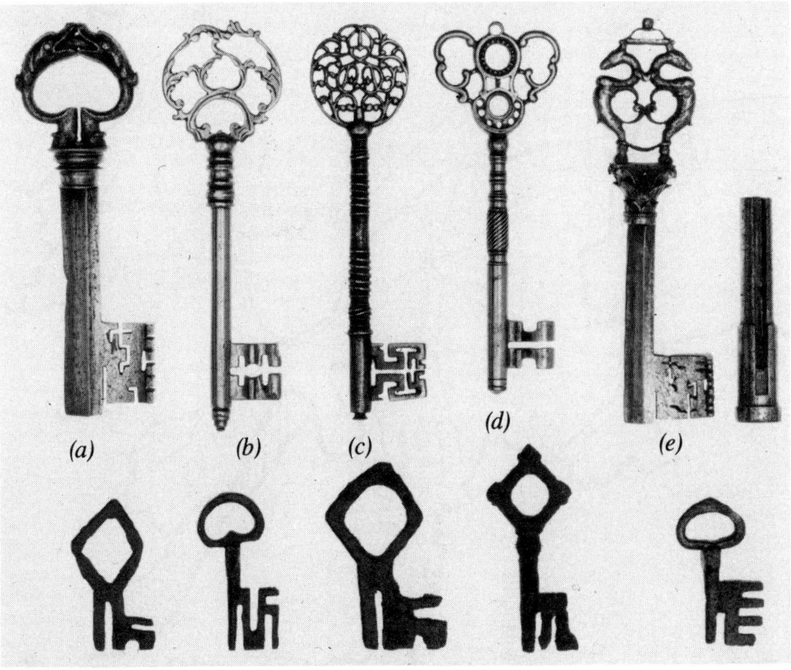
(a)
(b)
(c)
(d)
(e)

(a) 18th century English steel key with triangular shank. (b) 18th century French steel key, 5in., sold for £385 with (d). (c) Early 18th century English steel key, £418. (d) 18th century French steel key. (e) 17th century French steel key and sleeve, £440. (Bottom row) Five 14th/15th century keys. £165. (All Sotheby's, April 1988). From an article entitled 'Prosperity and Security — Decorative Locks and Keys in the 17th and 18th Centuries' by Paul Davidson which appeared in the May 1991 issue of ***Antique Collecting.***

Gloucestershire

Please note this is only a rough map designed to show dealers the number of shops in the various towns, and is not necessarily totally accurate.

Key to number of shops in this area.

- ○ 1–2
- 3–5
- 6–12
- ● 13+

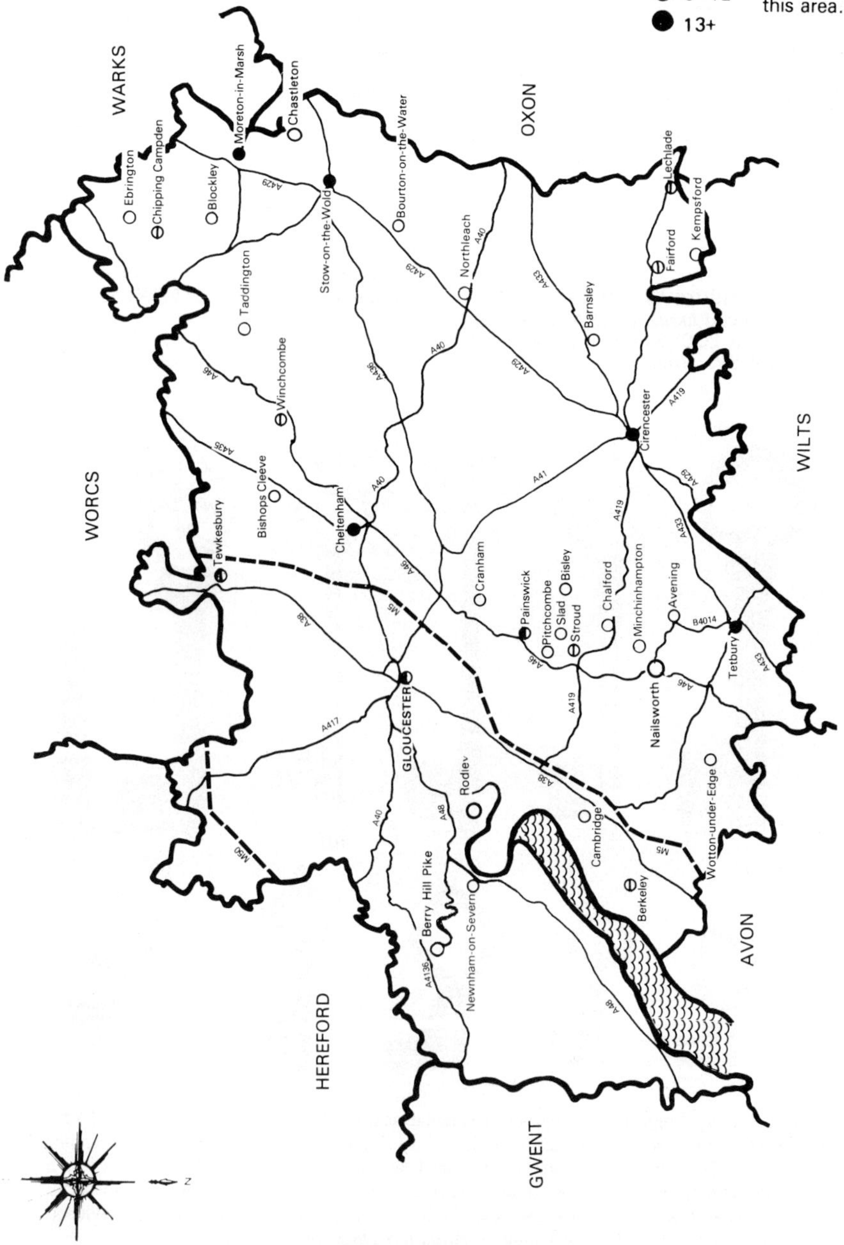

WARKS
OXON
WORCS
WILTS
HEREFORD
GWENT
AVON
Moreton-in-Marsh
Chastleton
Chipping Campden
Ebrington
Blockley
Stow-on-the-Wold
Bourton-on-the-Water
Northleach
Lechlade
Kempsford
Fairford
Taddington
Barnsley
Winchcombe
Cirencester
Bishops Cleeve
Cheltenham
Tewkesbury
Cranham
Painswick
Pitchcombe
Slad
Bisley
Stroud
Chalford
Minchinhampton
Avening
Tetbury
Nailsworth
GLOUCESTER
Rodley
Cambridge
Wotton-under-Edge
Berkeley
Berry Hill Pike
Newnham-on-Severn
A429
A40
A433
A436
A46
A435
A41
A419
A38
M5
A417
A48
A4136
M50
B4014
N

AVENING

Upton Lodge Galleries
Avening House. (J Grant) Est: 1979. Open by appointment. SIZE: Medium. *STOCK: Oils and watercolours, 1880-1950, £100-£5,000.* PARK: Easy. TEL: 045 383 4048.

BARNSLEY, Nr. Cirencester

Denzil Verey
Barnsley House. CADA. Resident. Est: 1980. Open 9.30-5.30, Sat. 10.30-1, other times by appointment. SIZE: Large. *STOCK: Country furniture, including pine, 18th-19th C; treen, country and kitchen bygones, unusual and decorative items.* LOC: 4 miles from Cirencester on A433 to Burford, 1st large house in village, set back off road on the right. PARK: Easy. TEL: 0285 74 402. VAT: Stan/Spec.

BERKELEY

The Antique Shop
11 High St. (H Trueman) Resident. Est: 1976. Open 9.30-5.30. CL: Sat. p.m. Mon. and Wed. SIZE: Small. *STOCK: Small furniture and decorative items, porcelain, glass, needlework and pictures.* LOC: From A38 turn left into High St. past Berkeley Arms Hotel, shop 100yds. on left. PARK: Easy. TEL: 0453 811085.

Berkeley continued

Berkeley Market
(G Hawkins and K Gardiner) Open 9.30-1 and 2-5. CL: Mon. SIZE: Large. *STOCK: General antiques, £1-£1,000.* LOC: Centre of Berkeley, just off A38. PARK: Easy. TEL: 0453 511032. VAT: Stan/Spec.

Newcomb Antiques
17 - 19 High St. (J. and W Newcomb Cryer) Resident. Est: 1978. Open 9.30-5.45. CL: Wed. and Sat. p.m. SIZE: Medium. *STOCK: 18th and 19th C furniture, general antiques, small silver, porcelain.* LOC: From A38 on B4066 past Berkeley Arms Hotel, turn left into High St., last shop 200yds. on left. PARK: Easy. TEL: 0453 810338. VAT: Stan/Spec.

BERRY HILL PIKE, Nr. Coleford

Dean Forest Antiques
The Corner House. (J.R Turner) Est: 1969. Open 8-8 including Sun. SIZE: Medium. *STOCK: Furniture, 18th-20th C, £500-£1,000; porcelain, 18th-20th C, £50-£100; paintings, 19th-20th C, £100-£500.* LOC: A4136, Gloucester/Monmouth road. PARK: Easy. TEL: 0594 33211; home- same. SER: Valuations; restorations (caning and French polishing).

BISHOPS CLEEVE, Nr. Cheltenham

Cleeve Picture Framing
Church Rd. (J Gardner) Open 9-1 and 2-6, Sat. 9-12. *STOCK: Prints and pictures.* TEL: 0242 672785. SER: Framing, cleaning, restoring (oils, watercolours and prints).

The Priory Gallery
The Priory, Station Rd. (R.M. and E James) Est: 1977. Open by appointment only. SIZE: Medium. *STOCK: Watercolours and oils, British and European, late 19th to early 20th C, £1,000-£50,000.* LOC: A435. PARK: Easy. TEL: 0242 673226. SER: Valuations; restorations (watercolours, prints and oils); framing; buys at auction (watercolours, oils). VAT: Stan/Spec.

BISLEY, Nr. Stroud

High Street Antiques
(H Ross) Open 12-6. CL: Wed. and Thurs. SIZE: Small. *STOCK: General antiques, furniture, china, glass, silver, Oriental and Eastern rugs.* TEL: Home - 0452 740275.

CAMBRIDGE, Nr. Gloucester

Bell House Antiques
Bell House. (G. and J Hawkins) Resident. Open 10-1 and 2-5. SIZE: Medium. *STOCK: General antiques including 19th C pine, £5-£500.* LOC: Near Slimbridge, on main A38. PARK: Easy. TEL: 0453 890463. SER: Valuations. VAT: Stan/Spec.

CHALFORD

J. and R Bateman Antiques
Green Court, High St. Est: !975. Open 9-6, other times by appointment. *STOCK: Furniture, oak and country, 17th-19th C; decorative items.* PARK: Easy. TEL: 0453 883234. SER: Restorations; cabinet making, rushing, caning. VAT: Stan/Spec.

Alan du Monceau
Millswood. (A.G.J. and V.G du Monceau) Open by appointment. SIZE: Medium. *STOCK: Oriental rugs, carpets, kelims and textiles, mainly 19th C.* LOC: Off A419. PARK: Easy. TEL: 0453 886979; home - 0453 883787. SER: Valuations; restorations. VAT: Stan/Spec.

CHASTLETON, Nr. Moreton-in-Marsh

Geoffrey Stead
The Dower House. Est: 1963. Open by appointment only. *STOCK: English and continental furniture, decorative objects, paintings.* LOC: 4 miles from Moreton-in-Marsh. TEL: 0608 74364; fax - 0608 74533.

CHELTENHAM

Antiques (Cheltenham) LAPADA
(J Turner) Est: 1950. Open by appointment only. *STOCK: Furniture, porcelain, silver, fine arts.* TEL: 0242 522939. VAT: Stan/Spec.

M.A Bailey Architectural Antiques
16 Suffolk Rd. Open Sat. 10.15-6, weekdays by appointment. *STOCK: Antique and pre-war fixtures, fittings, lighting, advertising items.* LOC: Near Bath Rd. shopping area and colleges. PARK: Nearby. TEL: 0836 278162. SER: Lighting spares.

David Bannister, F.R.G.S
26 Kings Rd. Est: 1962. Open by appointment only. SIZE: Medium. *STOCK: Early maps and prints, 1480-1850, £5-£5,000; decorative and topographical prints; atlases and colour plate books.* TEL: 0242 514287; fax - 0242 513890. SER: Valuations; restorations; lectures; buys at auction. FAIRS: Organiser - Antiquarian Map and Print (Bonnington Hotel). VAT: Stan.

Bed of Roses
12 Prestbury Rd. (M Losh) Est: 1978. Open 9.30-1 and 2-5.30. SIZE: Large. *STOCK: Fine stripped pine.* LOC: 200 metres on town side of roundabout, B4632, close to Pittville Circus. PARK: Easy. TEL: 0242 231918. VAT: Stan/Spec.

John Beer
23 Priory St. Open by appointment only. SIZE: Large. *STOCK: Furniture and objects, 1830-1960's, especially English arts and crafts, Gothic and art deco.* LOC: 200yds. from start of High St. PARK: Easy. TEL: 0242 576080 and 0860 767194. SER: Valuations; buys at auction. VAT: Stan/Spec.

Benson Antiques
Wellesley House, Wellington Sq. Pittville. (H.F. and F Benson) Resident. Est: 1961. Open by appointment only. SIZE: Medium. *STOCK: English and continental furniture, decorative items, 1780-1900.* PARK: Easy. TEL: 0242 517739. VAT: Stan/Spec.

Bottles and Bygones
96 Horsefair St, Charlton Kings. (J. and M Brown) Est: 1974. Open 10-5.30. CL: Mon. and Tues. *STOCK: Bottles, stoneware, pot-lids, commemorative items, jewellery, enamel signs, crested china, postcards, general antiques, furniture, collectors' items, chimney pots and architectural items.* LOC: 1 mile from Cheltenham off Cirencester road. PARK: Easy. TEL: 0242 236393; home - same.

Edward Bradbury and Son
32 High St. (O Bradbury) Resident. Est: 1986. Open by appointment. SIZE: Small. *STOCK: Works of art, tribal art, furniture, 18th-19th C; books on art reference, monographs on artists and photographers, manuscripts.* PARK: Nearby. TEL: 0242 221486. SER: Valuations. VAT: Spec.

Cheltenham continued

Brocante Antiques
197 London Rd, Charlton Kings. *STOCK: Linen, lace, clothes, Edwardian to 1960s.* TEL: 0242 243120.

Butler and Co
111 Promenade. (D.J Butler) Est: 1968. Open Sat. only. SIZE: Small. *STOCK: English coins, 1st to 20th C and world coins, 19th C, both £5-£25; British campaign medals, 19th-20th C, £50-£100.* PARK: Easy. TEL: 0242 522272; home - 0242 234439. SER: Valuations. FAIRS: Bristol and West of England Coin, July and Oct.

Cameo Antiques
31 Suffolk Parade. (R.L Chitty) Est: 1970. Open 10-1 and 2-5. CL: Wed. p.m. SIZE: Small. *STOCK: General antiques, 19th-20th C, £5-£5,000; Victoriana, from £1; collectors' items, art deco, art pottery, Doulton, Moorcroft; furniture, 18th C and decorative.* Not Stocked: Militaria. PARK: Easy. TEL: 0242 233164. VAT: Stan/Spec.

Charlton King Antiques Centre
199 London Rd, Charlton Kings. Est: 1984. Open 9.30-5.30. SIZE: Large - 11 dealers. *STOCK: General antiques, including furniture, china, glass and pictures, £5-£1,000.* LOC: On A40. PARK: Easy. TEL: 0242 510672.

Cheltenham Antique Market
54 Suffolk Rd. (K.J Shave) Est: 1970. Open 9.30-5.30. SIZE: 30 dealers. *STOCK: General antiques.* TEL: 0242 529812.

Cocoa
7 Queens Circus. (O.J Dell) Est: 1973. Open 10-5. SIZE: Small. *STOCK: Lace clothes, fans, interesting small items and jewellery, 19th-20th C, £5-£500.* LOC: Rear of Montpellier, near Queens Hotel. PARK: Easy. TEL: 0242 233588; home - same. SER: Valuations; restorations (period textiles). VAT: Stan.

Country Life Antiques
8 Rotunda Terr, Montpellier St. Open 10-5. *STOCK: Furniture, scientific instruments, decorative accessories, pewter, brass and copper.* PARK: Easy. TEL: 0242 226919.

Greens of Montpellier
15 Montpellier Walk. Est: 1946. Open 9-5. CL: Wed. p.m. SIZE: Medium. *STOCK: Victorian and diamond set jewellery, porcelain, silver, glass, fine books and some furniture.* LOC: Conjunction of Promenade and main shopping centre. PARK: Easy. TEL: 0242 512088. SER: Buys at auction. VAT: Stan/Spec.

Heydens Antiques and Militaria
420 High St. (R.E.J Heyden) Open 10-5.30. *STOCK: General antiques and militaria.* TEL: 0242 582466.

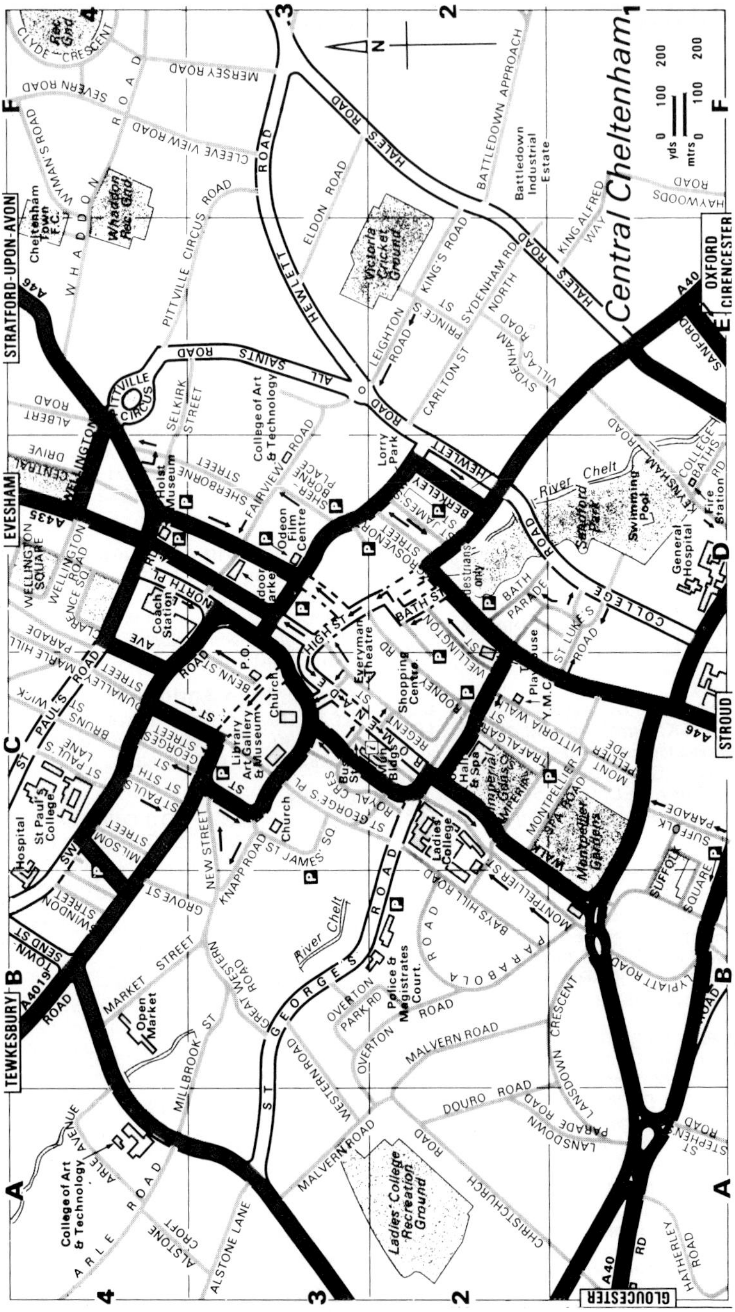
Central Cheltenham
N
STRATFORD-UPON-AVON
EVESHAM
TEWKESBURY
OXFORD CIRENCESTER
STROUD
GLOUCESTER
A46
A435
A4019
A40
HALES ROAD
HEWLETT ROAD
ALL SAINTS ROAD
PITTVILLE CIRCUS
PITTVILLE CIRCUS ROAD
WHADDON ROAD
Whaddon Rec. Gnd.
Cheltenham Town F.C.
Victoria Cricket Ground
Battledown Industrial Estate
BATTLEDOWN APPROACH
College of Art & Technology
Holst Museum
Odeon Film Centre
Coach Station
Everyman Theatre
Shopping Centre
Library Art Gallery & Museum
Church
Bus Stn
Municipal Bldgs
Ladies' College
Imperial Gdns
Montpellier Gardens
Sandford Park
Swimming Pool
General Hospital
Fire Station
St Paul's College
Hospital
Open Market
Police & Magistrates Court
Ladies' College Recreation Ground
River Chelt
HIGH ST
ST GEORGES ROAD
MONTPELLIER WALK
BATH ROAD
COLLEGE ROAD
MALVERN ROAD
CHRISTCHURCH ROAD
ALSTONE LANE
MILLBROOK ST
MARKET STREET
ARLE ROAD
ARLE AVENUE
LANSDOWN CRESCENT
PARABOLA ROAD
DOURO ROAD
OVERTON ROAD
HATHERLEY ROAD
SUFFOLK SQUARE
SUFFOLK PARADE
GREAT WESTERN ROAD
KNAPP ROAD
NEW STREET
GROVE ST
MILSOM STREET
WELLINGTON SQUARE
SELKIRK STREET
CLEEVE VIEW ROAD
MERSEY ROAD
SEVERN ROAD
CLYDE CRESCENT
ELDON ROAD
KING'S ROAD
SYDENHAM RD NORTH
KING ALFRED WAY
HAYWOODS ROAD
yds 0 100 200
mtrs 0 100 200

Key to Town Plan

- AA Recommended roads
- Other roads
- Restricted roads
- Buildings of interest
- Car Parks
- Parks and open spaces
- AA Service Centre

Cheltenham continued

David Howard
42 Moorend Cres. Est: 1983. Open by appointment. *STOCK: Fine oil paintings, watercolours and drawings, 19th-20th C, £500-£5,000.* PARK: Easy. TEL: 0242 243379; home - same. SER: Valuations; buys at auction; research (pictures). VAT: Spec.

H.W Keil (Cheltenham) Ltd BADA
129-131 Promenade. Est: 1953. SIZE: Large. *STOCK: Furniture, paintings, 17th-18th C, metalwork, chandeliers.* LOC: Opp. Queens Hotel, at top of Promenade. PARK: Easy. TEL: 0242 522509. SER: Upholstery. VAT: Spec.

Kyoto House Antiques
14 Suffolk Rd. (Mr and Mrs M Smith-Wood) Open 10.30-5.30, Sun. by appointment. SIZE: Medium. *STOCK: Japanese furniture, £100-£3,000; Japanese collectables, £20-£500; all 18th-19th C, Edo and Meiji period.* TEL: 0242 262549; home - same. SER: Valuations; restorations (furniture).

Latchford Antiques
215 London Rd, Charlton Kings. (K. and R Latchford) Est: 1985. Open 10-5. CL: Wed. SIZE: Small. *STOCK: Stripped pine furniture, mostly Victorian, general furniture, Victorian and Edwardian, £25-£500; china, glass, watercolours, £5-£500.* LOC: 2 miles from Cheltenham, on A40 towards London at Sixways Shopping Centre, on right. PARK: Easy. TEL: 0242 226263. VAT: Stan/Spec.

Leckhampton Antiques
215 Bath Rd. (V Finn) Open 10-4. *STOCK: General antiques.* TEL: 0242 570230.

Manor House Antiques
42 Suffolk Rd. (J.G Benton) Est: 1972. Open 9.30-5. SIZE: Large. *STOCK: Furniture, general antiques, 19th C and Victorian, £50-£1,500; shipping goods.* Not Stocked: Small items, china and jewellery. LOC: A40. PARK: Nearby. TEL: 0242 232780; home - 0684 293222. VAT: Stan/Spec.

Martin and Co. Ltd BADA
19 The Promenade. (I.M. and N.C.S Dimmer) Est: 1890. CL: Sat. p.m. *STOCK: Silver, Sheffield plate, jewellery, objets d'art.* TEL: 0242 522821/239115. VAT: Stan/Spec.

Montpellier Clocks BADA
13 Rotunda Terr, Montpellier. (B Bass) Open 8.30-5.30. *STOCK: Clocks, 17th-19th C; small furniture.* LOC: Close to Queens Hotel. PARK: Easy. TEL: 0242 242178.

Elizabeth Niner Antiques
53 Gt. Norwood St. Est: 1972. Open 9.30-5. SIZE: Medium. *STOCK: Mahogany furniture, 18th-19th C; objets d'art, 1700-1900, £10-£2,000.* LOC: Off Suffolk Rd. PARK: Easy. TEL: 0242 516497. VAT: Stan/Spec.

Cheltenham continued

Patrick Oliver LAPADA
4 Tivòli St. Est: 1896. SIZE: Large. *STOCK: Furniture and shipping goods.* PARK: Easy. TEL: 0242 513392; home - 0242 519538. VAT: Stan/Spec.

Eric Pride Oriental Rugs
44 Suffolk Rd, GMC. Est: 1980. Open 10-6, Mon. and Sat. by appointment. SIZE: Medium. *STOCK: Rugs and carpets, £100-£4,000; kilims, £300-£2,000; saddle-bags and horse covers, £150-£800; all 19th to early 20th C.* LOC: A40 near Cheltenham College. PARK: Easy. TEL: 0242 580822; home - 0242 521057. SER: Valuations; restorations (cleaning and repairs); buys at auction (rugs from Persia, Caucasus and Central Asia; carpets from Turkey and Persia; kelims and bags). VAT: Stan.

Michael Rayner
11 St. Luke's Rd. Open 10-6, other times by appointment. CL: Mon. and Tues. *STOCK: Books, antiquarian and secondhand.* TEL: 0242 512806.

Scott-Cooper Ltd BADA
52 The Promenade. Est: 1912. *STOCK: Silver, plate, jewellery, clocks, ivory, enamel, objets de vertu.* TEL: 0242 522580. SER: Repair and restoration of silver and jewellery. VAT: Stan/Spec.

Sinclair Harding and Co
5 Montpellier Walk. Open 9-5.30. *STOCK: Jewellery, £5-£3,000; silver and especially clocks.* TEL: 0242 524738.

Tapestry
33 Suffolk Parade. (Mrs G Hall) Est: 1980. Open 9.30-5.30. SIZE: Medium. *STOCK: Soft furnishings, furniture, stripped pine, late 18th to early 19th C, £50-£1,000.* LOC: 10 mins. walk from The Promenade. PARK: Easy. TEL: 0242 512191; home - 0242 672274. SER: Valuations; restorations (as stock). FAIRS: Shepton Mallet; British International, Birmingham; Ardingly.

John Townsend
2 Oxford Cottages, Ullenwood. Est: 1969. Open by appointment only. SIZE: Large. *STOCK: Furniture, to 30's, stripped pine, shipping goods, country furniture.* TEL: 024 287 223. SER: Containers. VAT: Stan/Spec.

Triton Gallery
27 Suffolk Parade. (L Bianco) Resident. Open 10-5.30, other times by appointment. *STOCK: Furniture, including decorative.* TEL: 0242 510477.

Joy Turner Antiques
100 Leckhampton Rd. Open by appointment. *STOCK: General antiques.* TEL: 0242 522939.

Cheltenham continued

Turtle Fine Art
29 and 30 Suffolk Parade. (P Field and and W Forsyth) Est: 1983. Open 10-6.30. SIZE: Medium. *STOCK: Watercolours, oils and prints, 19th-20th C, £30-£3,000.* LOC: Off Suffolk Rd. (A40). PARK: Easy. TEL: 0242 241646; home - same. VAT: Stan/Spec.

CHIPPING CAMDEN

Antique Heritage
High St. (D B Smith) Est: 1981. Open 10.30-5, Sat. 10-5, Sun. 11-5. SIZE: Small. *STOCK: Small items, china, porcelain, tables, boxes, Georgian and Victorian, £15-£400.* LOC: Village centre. PARK: Easy. TEL: 0386 840727. VAT: Stan/Spec.

Pedlars
Lower High St. (A Yates) Open 10-5. *STOCK: General antiques.* TEL: 0386 840680.

Saxton House Gallery LAPADA
High St. (S.D. and J Coy) Open 9-5.30. CL: Thurs. SIZE: Medium. *STOCK: Fine English clocks and barometers, unusual carriage clocks, jewellery, Georgian furniture, paintings and watercolours.* LOC: Centre of village. PARK: Easy. TEL: 0386 840278. VAT: Stan/Spec.

School House Antiques LAPADA
School House, High St. (G Hammond) Open 7 days 9.30-5 (June-Spet.). CL: Thurs. (Oct.-May). *STOCK: Clocks, 18th-19th C; furniture including oak and shipping, 17th-19th C.* TEL: 0386 841474; fax - 0386 841367. SER: Restorations.

Stuart House Antiques
High St. (J Collett) Est: 1985. Open 10-1 and 2-5.30 including Sun. SIZE: Medium. *STOCK: China, 19th C; general antiques, from 18th C, all £1-£1,000.* LOC: Opposite market hall. PARK: Easy. TEL: 0386 840995. SER: Valuations.

Swan Antiques
High St. (J Stocker) Est: 1960. Open 9-1 and 2-5.30, Thurs. and Sun. by appointment. SIZE: Medium. *STOCK: Jewellery, including Victorian; silver, George II to 1920; porcelain including Royal Worcester; decorative items, furniture, 17th C oak to 1860 mahogany.* LOC: Village centre. PARK: Easy. TEL: 0386 840759. SER: Gemmologist. Valuations. VAT: Stan/Spec.

CIRENCESTER

Jonathan Beech
Nurses Cottage, Ampney Crucis. Est: 1987. Open 9.30-5.30. SIZE: Small. *STOCK: Clocks, especially wall and country longcase, 1700-1850, £200-£4,500.* LOC: 2 miles from Cirencester, left at The Crown of Crucis, then 200yds. on left. PARK: Easy. TEL: 0285 851495. SER: Restorations (clocks). VAT: Stan/Spec.

Cirencester continued

The Book Room
21-23 Gloucester St. (A.D.J Nielson) Open 9.30-5.30. *STOCK: Furniture, 18th-19th C, and reproduction.* PARK: Easy. TEL: 0285 885227. VAT: Spec.

Walter Bull and Son (Cirencester) Ltd
10 Dyer St. Est: 1815. Open 9-5. SIZE: Small. *STOCK: Silver, from 1700, £50-£3,000; objets d'art.* LOC: Lower end of Market Place. PARK: At rear. TEL: 0285 653875. VAT: Stan/Spec.

Cirencester Antique Market
Market Pl, (Antique Forum Ltd.). Open Fri. SIZE: 60 dealers. *STOCK: General antiques.* TEL: 071 262 5003.

Corner Cupboard Curios
2 Church St. (P Larner) *STOCK: General antiques and gramophonalia.* TEL: 0285 655476.

Forum Antiques
20 West Way, The Forum. (W Mitchell) Est: 1986. Open 9-5.30, Sat. 9.30-5. SIZE: Medium. *STOCK: Furniture - country oak, fruitwood and yew, 16th-19th C; walnut and mahogany, 17th-18th C, £100-£10,000.* LOC: Left at Police Station in Forum car park, near Market Place. PARK: Easy. TEL: 0285 658406; home - 0453 886783. SER: Valuations; restorations (furniture). VAT: Spec.

Jay Gray Antiques
Syrena House, 1 Cheltenham Rd. (Mrs J Gray) Est: 1961. Open 9-6, or by appointment. *STOCK: English and French furniture, English, continental and Oriental porcelain, 18th-19th C; pictures, silver, glass, collectors' items, objets d'art.* Not Stocked: Uniforms, shawls, Goss china. LOC: Junction of A435 and A417. PARK: Easy. TEL: 0285 652755. SER: Buys at auction. VAT: Spec.

Hares LAPADA
17-19 Gosditch St. (J Colborne and and A Hare) Est: 1972. Open 9.30-5.30, Sun. by appointment. SIZE: Large. *STOCK: Furniture, especially dining tables, 18th to early 19th C, £100-£20,000; upholstery and decorative objects.* LOC: Near Market Sq. PARK: Easy. TEL: 0285 640077; home - 0285 653212; 0453 882249. SER: Valuations; restorations; traditional upholstery; buys at auction. VAT: Spec.

W.W Holzgräwe Antiques
Unit 3, Beeches Workshops, Beeches Rd. (W. and A.M Holzgräwe) Est: 1952. Open 8.30-5.30 and by appointment. *STOCK: Furniture and metalwork, 17th to early 19th C.* PARK: Easy. TEL: 0285 659351/658625. SER: Restorations. VAT: Spec.

Cirencester continued

Thomas and Pamela Hudson
At the Sign of the Herald Angel, 19 Park St. CADA. Est: 1959. Open 9-1 and 2-5.30. *STOCK: Old Sheffield, small objets de vertu, netsuke, glass, needlework tools and workboxes, needlework.* LOC: From Market Pl., 100yds. beyond Corinium Museum. TEL: 0285 652972. SER: Valuations; buys at auction. VAT: Spec.

E.C Legg and Son
Unit 3, College Farm, Tetbury Rd. Est: 1902. Open 9-5. CL: Sat. *STOCK: Furniture, 18th-19th C.* TEL: 0285 650695. SER: Restorations (furniture); caning; re-leathering (desks tops, library steps). VAT: Spec.

The William Marler Gallery
36 Dyer St. Est: 1975. Open 9.30-5.30. SIZE: Medium. *STOCK: Wildlife and sporting paintings and watercolours, £100-£20,000; signed proofs and prints, £20-£1,500; all 20th C.* PARK: Easy. TEL: 0285 641641.

A.J Ponsford Antiques
51-53 Dollar St. (A.J. and R.L Ponsford) Est: 1962. Open 8-5.30. CL: Sat. SIZE: Large. *STOCK: Furniture, 1800-1830, £25-£4,000; furniture, 1700-1800, £50-£8,000; copper, brass.* Not Stocked: Silver. LOC: 200yds. from church on left towards Gloucester at junction of

A.J Ponsford Antiques continued

Thomas St. and Spitalgate Lane. PARK: 50yds. opp. TEL: 0285 652355. SER: Valuations; restorations (furniture and oil paintings); rushing, caning, upholstery, picture framing; buys at auction. VAT: Stan/Spec.

John D Rivers
1 Ashcroft Rd. Est: 1973. Open 10-5, Sat. 10-4. CL: Mon. SIZE: Small. *STOCK: Jewellery, 18th-20th C, £25-£1,000.* LOC: Off Cricklade St. PARK: Nearby. TEL: 0285 657616. SER: Valuations; restorations. VAT: Stan/Spec.

Robin Shield Antiques
Carpenters Buildings, The Avenue. (W.R. and P.E Shield) Est: 1974. Open 9.30-5 or by appointment. SIZE: Warehouse. *STOCK: Furniture, £200-£10,000; works of art, £50-£2,000; paintings, £200-£3,000, all 17th-19th C.* LOC: Off Victoria Rd. PARK: Easy. TEL: 0285 885715; home - 0793 750205. SER: Valuations; buys at auction. VAT: Stan/Spec.

William H Stokes BADA
The Cloisters, 6/8 Dollar St. (W.H Stokes and and P.W Bontoft) CADA. Est: 1968. Open 9.30-5.30, Sat. 10-4. *STOCK: Early oak furniture, £1,000-£30,000; brassware, £150-£5,000; all 16th-17th C.* TEL: 0285 653907. FAIRS: Grosvenor House. VAT: Spec.

Cirencester continued

Rankine Taylor Antiques LAPADA
34 Dollar St. (Mrs L Taylor) CADA. Est: 1969. Open 9-5.30, Sun. by appointment. SIZE: Large. *STOCK: Furniture, 17th-19th C, £100-£20,000; glass, 18th-20th C, £10-£250; silver and decorative items, 17th-20th C, £20-£8,000.* Not Stocked: Victoriana, militaria. LOC: From Church, turn right up West Market Place, via Gosditch St. into Dollar St. PARK: Abbey grounds via Spittalgate. TEL: 0285 652529. SER: Valuations; buys at auction (furnishing items). VAT: Spec.

Cirencester continued

P.J Ward Fine Paintings
11 Gosditch St. CADA. Open 9-5. *STOCK: 17th-19th C paintings.* TEL: 0285 658499. SER: Valuations; restorations; framing. VAT: Spec.

Bernard Weaver Antiques
28 Gloucester St. CADA. Open 9.30-6, Sat. 9.30-1. SIZE: Medium. *STOCK: Furniture, 18th-19th C, mahogany and oak; art nouveau and arts and crafts.* LOC: Continuation of Dollar St. PARK: Easy. TEL: 0285 652055; home - same. SER: Valuations.

CRANHAM

Heather Newman Gallery

Milidduwa, Mill Lane. Est: 1969. Open every day by appointment. *STOCK: British watercolours and drawings, 18th-20th C, £50-£5,000.* LOC: Near Prinknash Abbey, just off A46 at Cranham Corner. PARK: Easy. TEL: 0452 812230. SER: Major exhibitions with illustrated catalogues, May and Nov; valuations; buys at auction. FAIRS: "World of Watercolours"; 20th C British Art. VAT: Spec.

EBRINGTON, Nr. Chipping Campden

John Burton Natural Craft Taxidermy

21 Main St. Est: 1973. Open by appointment. SIZE: Small. *STOCK: Taxidermy - cased and uncased fish, birds and mammals, from Victorian, £40-£2,500; glass domes, sporting trophies.* LOC: Village centre. PARK: Easy. TEL: 038678 231; home - same. SER: Valuations; restorations (taxidermy items); buys at auction (taxidermy items). VAT: Stan.

FAIRFORD

Blenheim Antiques

Market Pl. (N Hurdle) CADA. Resident. Est: 1972. Open 9.30-6.30. *STOCK: 18th-19th C furniture, clocks.* TEL: 0285 712094. VAT: Stan/Spec.

Fairford continued

Cirencester Antiques Ltd
High St. (Mr and Mrs R.T.G Chester-Master) CADA. Est: 1959. Open 9-5.30. SIZE: Large. *STOCK: Furniture and works of art, 17th to early 19th C, £50-£50,000.* TEL: 0285 713774.

Gloucester House Antiques Ltd
Market Pl. (Mr and Mrs R Chester-Master) CADA. Est: 1972. Open 9-5.30. SIZE: Large. *STOCK: English and French country furniture in oak, elm, fruitwood, pine; pottery, faiënce and decorative items.* PARK: Easy. TEL: 0285 712790; home - 0285 653066. VAT: Stan/Spec.

GLOUCESTER

Amber Antiques
Unit 16, Antique Centre, Severn Rd. (Mrs E Horton and Mrs S Farrington) Est: 1990. Open 9.30-5, Sat. 9.30-4.30, Sun. 1-4.30. SIZE: Small. *STOCK: Interior gas lights converted to electricity, period telephones, furniture.* TEL: Home - 021 454 3952.

Steven D Bartrick
The Antique Centre, Severn Rd. Est: 1985. Open 9-5, Sat. 9-4.30, Sun. 1-4.30. *STOCK: Topographical prints and some maps.* LOC: Gloucester dock area. PARK: At side of building. TEL: 0452 29716; home - 0242 231691.

E.J Cook and Son Antiques
At the Antique Centre, Severn Rd. (E.J. and C.A Cook) Est: 1949. Open 9.30-5, Sat. 9.30-4.30, Sun. 1-4.30. SIZE: Large. *STOCK: Furniture, clocks, oils and watercolours, small items, 17th-19th C, £50-£6,000.* LOC: On ring road close to dock area. PARK: Easy. TEL: 0452 29716. SER: Restorations (furniture, upholstery and clocks); buys at auction (furniture). VAT: Stan/Spec.

Farr
At the Antique Centre, Severn Rd. (A. and J Farr) Open 9-5, Sun. 1-4.30. *STOCK: Silver, watches, clocks, furniture, brass and glass.* LOC: Gloucester dock area.

Gloucester Antique Centre
Severn Rd. Open 9.30-5, Sat. 9.30-4.30, Sun. 1-4.30. SIZE: 67 dealers. *STOCK: General antiques.* TEL: 0452 29716.

Paul Hayes Architectural Antiques, Antique Warehouse
The Pit, Hare Lane. (P. and A Hayes) Est: 1976. Open 10-6. SIZE: Large. *STOCK: Architectural items especially ecclesiastical, pillars, balcony frontages.* LOC: Off Worcester St. and Northgate St. PARK: Nearby. TEL: 0452 301145; fax - 0452 24722; home - 0594 61267. VAT: Stan.

Gloucester continued

David Kent Antiques
300 Barton St. Est: 1967. Open 10-4.30, Sat. 10-12.30. *STOCK: Victorian shipping items and books.* LOC: Through town, near ring road, east side. PARK: Easy. TEL: 0452 304396; home - 0452 610976. VAT: Stan/Spec.

Lenda Antiques
83 Southgate St. Open 9.30-5.30. *STOCK: General antiques, especially porcelain and pottery.* TEL: 0452 410443.

Paul Medcalf
Shop 29, Gloucester Antique Centre, Severn Rd. Open 9.30-5. Sat. 9.30-4.30, Sun. 1-4.30. *STOCK: English oils especially landscapes and portraits, £50-£1,500; watercolours, £50-£500; etchings, £20-£200.* TEL: 0452 415186.

Military Curios, The Curiosity Shop, HQ84
Southgate Street. (J. and B Williams) Est: 1964. Open 10-5.30. *STOCK: Medals, worldwide militaria, badges, government surplus, gold, silver, miniatures, posters, weapons, blazer badges.* LOC: A38, 350yds. from city centre. PARK: Easy. TEL: 0452 27716. SER: Valuations; medal mounting; finder; costume hire.

Tinkers Antiques
Unit 64, 4th Floor, Gloucester Antique Centre, Severn Rd. (S. and T Hall) Open 9.30-5, Sun. 1-4.30. SIZE: Small. *STOCK: Furniture, 19th C, £150-£350; china and bric-a-brac, £40-£120.* PARK: Easy. TEL: 0452 506758; home - 0993 774383. SER: Valuations. VAT: Stan.

KEMPSFORD, Nr. Fairford

Corinium Antiques
The Old Vicarage. (Mrs H Mahoney) Est: 1980. Open 10-5 or by appointment. SIZE: Large. *STOCK: Country furniture and pine, 17th-19th C; copper, brass, treen, unusual decorative accessories and agricultural items.* PARK: Easy. TEL: 0285 810370.

LECHLADE

Antiques Etcetera
High St. (Mrs C.L Haillay) Est: 1969. Open 10-5, Sun. and evenings by appointment. SIZE: Medium. *STOCK: General antiques, country furniture and artifacts, decorators' items.* PARK: Easy. TEL: 0367 52567; home - 0793 850464.

Bell Fine Arts
Cottar's Barn, Downington. (Mrs R.A Bell) Open by appointment only. *STOCK: Oils, watercolours, Old Master etchings and contemporary items.* TEL: 0367 52255.

Lechlade continued

Gerard Campbell **BADA**
Maple House, Market Pl. (J. and G Campbell) Est: 1980. Open by appointment. SIZE: Large. *STOCK: Clocks especially Biedermeier Vienna regulators, 18th-19th C, £1,500-£15,000; oils, 20th C, £200-£5,000.* PARK: Easy. TEL: 0367 52267; home - same. SER: Valuations; buys at auction. VAT: Spec.

D'Arcy Antiques
High St. (J.W. and Mrs. M.A Corbey) Est: 1986. Open 10-5. SIZE: Medium. *STOCK: Furniture, 1800-1940, £50-£1,000; china, 1800-1960, £2-£100; brass, 1780-1960, £2-£100.* LOC: A361, village centre. PARK: Easy. TEL: 0367 52471; home - 0793 852792.

Lechlade Antiques
5-7 High St. (C Littleton) Open 10-6, including Sun. SIZE: Medium. *STOCK: Furniture, ceramics, brass, copper, pictures and collectables, £10-£500.* TEL: 0367 52832.

Lechlade Antiques Arcade
5, 6 and 7 High St. Open 10-6 including Sun. SIZE: 20 dealers. *STOCK: General antiques.* TEL: 0367 52832. SER: Public commission room.

Peter Whitby Antiques
Ashleigh House, High St. Open 9-5.30. *STOCK: Furniture, metalware, porcelain, items of interest.* PARK: Easy. TEL: 0367 52347. VAT: Spec.

MINCHINHAMPTON, Nr. Stroud

J.V Vosper
20 High St. Est: 1952. *STOCK: Furniture, glass, china, silver, brass, plate, bric-a-brac, 18th-20th C.* TEL: 0453 882480. VAT: Stan.

Mick and Fanny Wright
'The Trumpet', West End. Open 10.30-5.30. CL: Mon. and Tues. SIZE: Medium. *STOCK: Clocks, watches, jewellery, furniture, china and collectables.* LOC: Town centre road to the common. PARK: Nearby. TEL: 0453 883027. VAT: Spec.

MORETON-IN-MARSH

Adams **BADA**
The Old Parsonage, Church St. (Mr and Mrs L Adams) CADA. Open by appointment. *STOCK: 18th C Meissen.* TEL: 0608 51881.

Antique Centre
London House, High St. Est: 1979. Open 10-5, Sun. 12-5. CL: Tues. SIZE: Large. *STOCK: Furniture, paintings, watercolours, prints, domestic artifacts, clocks, silver, jewellery and plate, mainly 17th-19th C, £5-£3,000.* LOC: Centre of High St. (A429). PARK: Easy. TEL: 0608 51084. VAT: Stan/Spec.

Astley House - Fine Art
Astley House, High St. (D. and N Glaisyer) CADA. Est: 1974. Open 9-5.30. SIZE: Medium. *STOCK: Oil paintings and watercolours, 19th-20th C, £200-£10,000.* LOC: Main street. PARK: Easy. TEL: 0608 50601; fax - 0608 51777. SER: Restorations (oils and watercolours); framing; video valuations. VAT: Spec.

Astley House - Fine Art
Astley House, London Rd. (D. and N Glaisyer) CADA. Est: 1974. Open 10-1 and 2-5.30. SIZE: Large. *STOCK: Oil paintings, 19th-20th C; large decorative paintings and portraits.* LOC: Town centre. PARK: Easy. TEL: 0608 50601; fax - 0608 51777. SER: Restorations (oils and watercolours); porcelain framing. VAT: Spec.

The Avon Gallery
High St. (S Creaton) Est: 1978. Open 9.30-5. CL: Wed. *STOCK: Prints, especially sporting; maps.* TEL: 0608 50614. SER: Picture framing.

Simon Brett **BADA**
Creswyke House, High St. Est: 1972. Open 9.30-5.30. *STOCK: English and continental furniture, 17th to early 19th C; works of art, portrait miniatures, old fishing tackle, carved wood fish models.* TEL: 0608 50751; fax - 51791. VAT: Spec.

Paul Cater Antiques **LAPADA**
High St. (P.J.C Cater) Est: 1978. Open 9.30-1 and 2-5, Sun. by appointment. SIZE: Medium. *STOCK: Oak, walnut and mahogany furniture, £50-£7,000; carvings, treen and boxes, £10-*

Paul Cater Antiques continued

£1,000; metalware, £10-£700; all 17th-19th C; silver, 18th-19th C, £5-£1,500; woodworking tools and horse brasses, 19th C. LOC: Northern end of High St. on left of A429. PARK: Easy. TEL: 0608 51888; home - same. VAT: Spec.

Chandlers Antiques
High St. (I Kellam and and P Grout) Open 9.30-1 and 2-5.30. *STOCK: Pottery, porcelain, glass, silver, jewellery, small furniture and general antiques.* TEL: 0608 51347.

Grimes House Antiques
High St. (S. and V Farnsworth) Est: 1978. Open 9.30-1 and 2-5, other times by appointment. CL: Wed. *STOCK: General antiques, Victorian glass especially cranberry.* TEL: 0608 51029.

Lemington House Antiques
Oxford St. (K.W. and Y.F Heath) Open 10-6. *STOCK: Furniture, 17th-19th C; porcelain, glass and decorative smalls.* LOC: Close to junction with High St. PARK: Own. TEL: 0608 51443.

Mrs M.K Nielsen LAPADA
Seaford House, High St. Est: 1965. Open Thur., Fri. and Sat. 9.30-1 and 2-5; other times by appointment. SIZE: Medium. *STOCK: Derby porcelain, £45-£5,000; Worcester, £65-£5,000; furniture, £150-£4,500.* LOC: A429 Fosseway. PARK: Easy. TEL: 0608 50448. VAT: Stan/Spec.

Elizabeth Parker
High St. (P.J King-Smith) CADA. Est: 1975. Open 9-6. SIZE: Large. *STOCK: Furniture, £50-£10,000; English and continental mahogany, satinwood and marquetry, some porcelain, copper and brass, all 18th and 19th C.* LOC: Opposite Manor House Hotel, on Fosseway junction of A44 from Broadway. TEL: 0608 50917. SER: Buys at auction. VAT: Stan/Spec.

Peter Roberts Antiques
High St. Open 10-5.30 or by appointment. SIZE: Large. *STOCK: Decorative furniture, objets d'art, garden furniture, mirrors, beds, 17th-19th C, £50-£10,000.* LOC: Fosseway. PARK: Easy. TEL: 0608 50698. SER: Valuations. VAT: Stan/Spec.

Anthony Sampson BADA
Dale House. Est: 1967. Open 9-1 and 2-5.30, Sun. by appointment. SIZE: Medium. *STOCK: Town and country furniture, to 1830; decorative items.* Not Stocked: Reproductions. LOC: Main street. PARK: Easy. TEL: 0608 50763. VAT: Spec.

Southgate Gallery
Fosse Manor Farm. (J Constable and N Collins) Est: 1968. Open by appointment only. *STOCK: Modern British paintings.* TEL: 0608 50051. SER: Restorations (oils).

NAILSWORTH

Hand Prints and Watercolours Gallery
3 Bridge St. (J Hand) Est: 1988. Open 10-1 and 2-5.30. SIZE: Medium. *STOCK: Victorian watercolours and prints, £5-£1,000; decorative prints, £15-£300.* LOC: A46, 4 miles south of Stroud. PARK: Easy. TEL: 045383 4967. SER: Restorations (as stock); buys at auction (as stock). VAT: Stan.

NEWNHAM-ON-SEVERN

Cottonwood
High Stand The Old House, Lower High St. Open 9.30-1 and 2-5.30. *STOCK: 19th C and Edwardian furniture especially upholstered items, and hand-built reproduction.* PARK: Easy. TEL: 0594 516633; home - 0594 516558. SER: Restorations; re-upholstery.

NORTHLEACH, Nr. Cheltenham

Keith Harding's World of Mechanical Music
The Oak House, High St. (K Harding, FBHI, C.A Burnett, CMBHI and and E Harding) Est: 1961. Articles on clocks, musical boxes. Open 10-6 including Sun. *STOCK: Clocks, musical boxes and automata.* TEL: 0451 60181. SER: Valuations; restorations (musical boxes, clocks); buys at auction. VAT: Stan/Spec.

The Northleach Gallery LAPADA
The Green. (Mr and Mrs P.J Loveday) Open 9.30-4.30. CL: Sat. *STOCK: Prints and etchings including animal, sporting and topographical, pre 18th to early 20th C; some books.* TEL: 0451 60519.

PAINSWICK

Craig Carrington Antiques
Brook House. Est: 1970. Open by appointment. *STOCK: English and continental furniture and works of art.* TEL: 0452 813248. SER: Buys at auction. VAT: Spec.

Greenhouse Antiques
Greenhouse Court Lodge, Bulls Cross. (T.G Stait) Est: 1986. Open 9.30-5.30, Sat. and Sun. by appointment. SIZE: Small. *STOCK: English furniture, garden statuary and ornaments, 18th and 19th C.* LOC: 1/2 mile outside village. PARK: Easy. TEL: 0452 812487; home - same. SER: Buys at auction (furniture). VAT: Spec.

Painswick Antique Centre
New St. (R.J.B Short) Open 10-5, Sat. 9.30-5.30, Sun. 11-5.30. *STOCK: General antiques from jewellery to period furniture.* LOC: A46, near Painswick church. PARK: Easy. TEL: 0452 812431.

Painswick continued

Regent Antiques
Dynevor House, New St. (Mr and Mrs G Coggins) Est: 1960. Open 10-5.30. SIZE: Medium. *STOCK: 17th-18th C, oak, walnut and mahogany, £100-£3,000.* LOC: Main road opp. church. PARK: Easy. TEL: 0452 812543. VAT: Spec. *Trade Only.*

Tibbiwell Antiques
Tibbiwell. (A. and L Major) Est: 1983. Open 10.30-1 and 2.15-5. SIZE: Small. *STOCK: Decorative china, £5-£50; pine furniture, £50-£400, both 19th-20th C.* LOC: Off A46 at church. PARK: Easy. TEL: 0452 813045; home - same.

Weavers Cottage Antiques
Open by appointment. *STOCK: Furniture, copper, decorative items.* TEL: 0452 863291.

PITCHCOMBE, Nr. Stroud

Clifford and Joan Silcocks
Pitchcombe View. (Dr and Mrs C.G Silcocks) Est: 1979. Open by appointment. SIZE: Small. *STOCK: Watercolours, 18th-20th C, £200-£2,000.* LOC: Just off A46, on A4173. PARK: Easy. TEL: 0452 812225.

REDMARLEY D'ABITOT

Forge Antiques
The Granary, Ledbury Rd. (R Pattison) Est: 1981. Open every day 1-8, mornings by appointment. SIZE: Small. *STOCK: 18th-19th C furniture, £500-£5,000.* LOC: On A417 1/2 mile from junction 2, M50. PARK: Easy. TEL: 0531 650520; home - same. SER: Valuations; restorations; buys at auction (furniture). VAT: Stan/Spec.

RODLEY, Nr. Westbury on Severn

Kelly Antiques
Landeck, Goose Lane. (G Kelly) Resident. Always open. *STOCK: Antique pine.* TEL: 045 276 315.

SLAD, Nr. Stroud

Ian Hodgkins and Co. Ltd
Upper Vatch Mill, The Vatch. Open by appointment only. *STOCK: Antiquarian books including pre-Raphaelites and associates, the Brontës; 19th C illustrated, children's art and literature books.* TEL: 0453 764270.

The Kinora viewer is one of the more commonly found optical toys. It appears in a variety of forms with different viewing hoods and wood body. Prices have increased from around £250 to £400 for a basic, working example with one or two picture reels. From an article entitled 'Optical Toys and Persistence of Vision Devices' by Michael Pritchard which appeared in the June 1991 issue of ***Antique Collecting.***

STOW-ON-THE-WOLD

Acorn Antiques
Sheep St. (M Masters) Est: 1987. Open 9.30-1 and 2.15-5. Sat. 9.30-1 and 2.30-5. CL: Wed. p.m. SIZE: Medium. *STOCK: Ceramics and glass, Victorian, £15-£300; furniture, Georgian, Victorian and Edwardian, £50-£2,000; collectables, 19th-20th C, £1-£50.* PARK: Easy. TEL: 0451 31519. SER: Restorations (ceramics).

Ashton Gower Antiques
7a Talbot Court. (R Ashton and C. Gower) Est: 1966. Open 10-1 and 2-5.30 including Sun. SIZE: Large. *STOCK: English furniture, 18th-19th C; French and continental furniture, mirrors, decorative items, copper and brass, china, and smalls.* PARK: Easy. TEL: 0451 870067; home - 0564 777037. SER: Valuations; restorations (furniture). VAT: Stan/Spec.

Baggott Church Street Ltd BADA
Church St. (D.J. and C.M Baggott) CADA. Est: 1978. Open 10-6, Sat. 9.30-5.30 or by appointment. SIZE: Large. *STOCK: English furniture, 17th-19th C; portrait paintings, some metalwork, pottery, treen and decorative items.* LOC: South-west corner of market square. PARK: In market square. TEL: 0451 30370.

Duncan J Baggott
Woolcomber House, Sheep St. CADA. Est: 1967. Open 9.30-5.30 or by appointment. SIZE: Large. *STOCK: 17th-19th C. English oak, mahogany, walnut and fruitwood furniture, paintings, prints and needlework, metalware and domestic items, garden statuary.* PARK: Own. TEL: 0451 30662.

Duncan J Baggott
Huntsmans Yard, Sheep St. CADA. Est: 1967. Open 9-5 or by appointment. CL: Sat. SIZE: Large. *STOCK: 17th-19th C. English and European furniture, portrait and primitive paintings, architectural items and statuary.* LOC: 200yds. from Fosseway entrance on right hand side through coaching gates. PARK: Own. TEL: 0451 30662. *Trade Only.*

Stow-on-the-Wold continued

Colin Brand Antiques
Tudor House, Sheep St. Est: 1985. Open 10-1 and 2-5, Sun. by appointment. CL: Wed. SIZE: Medium. *STOCK: Clocks, small furniture, £200-£4,000; porcelain, £30-£600, all pre-1900.* LOC: Opposite Post Office. PARK: Main square. TEL: 0451 31760; home - same. VAT: Spec.

D Bryden
Sheep St. Est: 1979. Open 10-12.30 and 2-5. CL: Wed. SIZE: Small. *STOCK: English silver, 18th-19th C, £50-£7,000; satinwood, rosewood and mahogany furniture, Georgian, Victorian and Edwardian, £200-£2,000.* LOC: Off A429. PARK: Stow Sq. TEL: 0451 30840. VAT: Stan/Spec.

Burditch Antiques at Park House Antiques
Park St. (J. and C Whelan) Est: 1978. SIZE: Large. *STOCK: English Delftware, 17th-18th C; furniture, 18th C.* LOC: South of market square. PARK: Easy. TEL: 0451 30159; home - 0993 811878. SER: Valuations; buys at auction (English Delftware). FAIRS: Oxford.

J. and J Caspall Antiques
Sheep St. Author of "Making Fire and Light in the Home pre-1820". Est: 1971. Open 9.30-5.30 or by appointment. *STOCK: Period oak, 16th C to 1760; early metalwork, especially lighting and hearth, early woodcarvings, period domestic and decorative items.* PARK: Nearby. TEL: 0451 31160. SER: Valuations. VAT: Spec.

Annarella Clark Antiques
11 Park St. Est: 1968. Open 10-5.30, or by appointment. SIZE: Medium. *STOCK: Wicker and garden, English and French country and painted furniture, needlework, pottery, quilts and decorative objects.* LOC: Park St. leads from Sheep St., 1st right at lights leading into town. PARK: Easy. TEL: 0451 30535; home - same. FAIRS: Olympia, West London, Brighton and Little Chelsea. VAT: Stan/Spec.

Stow-on-the-Wold continued

Christopher Clarke Antiques Ltd
BADA

The Fosse Way. (C.J Clarke) CADA. Est: 1961. Open 9.30-6. SIZE: Medium. *STOCK: Furniture, 17th-19th C, £300-£15,000; walnut, mahogany, metalware, 16th-18th C, £200-£5,000.* Not Stocked: Silver, glass, medals, coins, prints. LOC: Corner of the Fosse Way and Sheep St. PARK: Easy. TEL: 0451 30476.

Cotswold Antiques Centre
The Square. Open 10-5.30. PARK: Easy. TEL: 0451 31585. Below are listed some of the dealers at this centre.

Lesley Bellingham
Art nouveau, jewellery, Victoriana, decorative items.
Country Antiques
Country furniture, baskets, metalware.
Roger Dallimore
Early porcelain, decorative objects, metalware.
A Dodkin
Brass and copper.
Jane Fairfield
Silver and plate, ceramics, metalware.
James Hall
Clocks, especially wall, bracket, mantel and longcase.
J and D Hall
17th-19th C furniture, porcelain, Staffordshire figures.
Pat Johnson
Porcelain, pottery, jewellery.
Adrienne Lambert
18th and 19th C ceramics, country furniture, textiles, decorative items.
Sue London
Ceramics, glass, small furniture, silver and plate, linen and lace.
M J Antiques
Bronze, ormolu, unusual items.
R McQuilkin
18th and 19th C furniture, mainly mahogany, pottery, porcelain, clocks.
T Newman
Pine and country furniture and artefacts.

Cotswold Antiques Centre continued

Olive Green Ltd
General antiques.
Christopher Rose
Period furniture; watercolours, paintings; 18th-19th C glass and ceramics.
J Stanley
Engravings, 19th C porcelain, pottery, glass, furniture, metalware.

The Cotswold Galleries
The Square. (R. and C Glaisyer) CADA. Est: 1961. Open 9-5.30, or by appointment. SIZE: Large. *STOCK: Oil paintings, 19th-20th C landscape.* TEL: 0451 30586. SER: Restoration; framing.

Country Life Antiques
Grey House, The Square. Open 10-5.30. *STOCK: Furniture, oil paintings, scientific instruments, decorative accessories, pewter, brass, copper.* PARK: Easy. TEL: 0451 31564.

The Curiosity Shop
The Square, (Antony Preston Antiques Ltd.). CADA. Est: 1965. Open 9.30-5.30. SIZE: Large. *STOCK: Furniture, clocks, mirrors, 18th to early 19th C, £500-£10,000.* LOC: Off Fosse Way. PARK: Easy. TEL: 0451 31586. VAT: Stan/Spec.

John Davies
(The Church Street Gallery), Church St. Est: 1977. Open 9.30-1 and 2-6. SIZE: Large. *STOCK: British paintings, 1890-1950, including modern, Newlyn school; European paintings and contemporary; all £500-£50,000+.* PARK: In square. TEL: 0451 31698; fax - 0451 32477. SER: Restorations; framing.

Fosse Gallery
The Square. (G O'Farrell and John Lindsey Fine Art Ltd) Est: 1979. Open 10-5.30. SIZE: Large. *STOCK: British post impressionist paintings and watercolours, £100-£10,000.* LOC: Off Fosseway, A429. PARK: Easy. TEL: 0451 31319. SER: Valuations; buys at auction. VAT: Spec.

Stow-on-the-Wold continued

Fosse Way Antiques
Sheep St. (M Beeston) Est: 1969. Open 10-1 and 2-5, Sat. 10-5. SIZE: Small. *STOCK: Furniture, £150-£5,000; bronzes, Sheffield plate, pictures, glass, porcelain and decorative objects, £50-£1,000; all 18th-19th C.* LOC: Opposite Unicorn Hotel. PARK: Easy. TEL: 0451 30776. SER: Valuations; buys at auction. VAT: Stan/Spec.

L Greenwold
"Digbeth", Digbeth St. CADA. Est: 1973. Open 10-5. SIZE: Medium. *STOCK: Jewellery, Oriental porcelain, glass.* LOC: Just off the south east corner of market sq. PARK: Easy. TEL: 0451 30398. SER: Valuations. VAT: Spec.

Keith Hockin (Antiques) Ltd BADA
The Square. CADA. Est: 1968. Open 9-6. CL: Sun. except by appointment. SIZE: Medium. *STOCK: Oak furniture, 1600-1750; country furniture in oak, fruitwoods, yew, 1700-1850; pewter, copper, brass, ironwork, all periods.* Not Stocked: Mahogany. PARK: Easy. TEL: 0451 31058. SER: Buys at auction (oak, pewter, metalwork). VAT: Stan/Spec.

Huntington Antiques Ltd
The Old Forge, Church St. (M.F., S.P. and N.M.J Golding) CADA. Resident. Est: 1974. Open 9-6 or by appointment. *STOCK: Early period and fine country furniture, metalware, treen and textiles, tapestries and works of art.* TEL: 0451 30842. SER: Valuations; buys at auction. FAIRS: Maastricht; Madrid. VAT: Spec.

Martin House Antiques
Sheep St. (G Finney) Resident. Open 10.30-6. CL: Fri. *STOCK: 18th-19th C porcelain; pottery, glass.* TEL: 0451 31217.

Lilian Middleton's Antique Dolls' Shop
Days Stable, Sheep St. Est: 1977. Open 9-5.30, Sun. 11.30-5. *STOCK: Dolls and accessories, including dolls' house furniture.* TEL: 0451 30381. SER: Dolls' hospital and museum.

No. 2 Park Street Antiques
2/3 Park St. (P.R Johnson) Open 9.30-5.30, Sun. 11-5. SIZE: Large - 15 dealers. *STOCK: General antiques including pre-1930 furniture, pictures, brass and copper, china and collectables.* LOC: On main road from town centre towards Chipping Norton. PARK: Easy. TEL: 0451 32311. VAT: Stan/Spec.

Simon W Nutter
Wraggs Row, Fosse Way. Open 9.30-5.30 or by appointment. *STOCK: Furniture, 17th to early 19th C.* TEL: 0451 30658.

Oriental Gallery
1 Digbeth St. (P Catter) Open 10-5, Wed. 10-1. *STOCK: Chinese and Japanese furniture; 19th C Japanese Hina dolls and collectables.* TEL: 0451 30944; fax - 0451 31559.

Stow-on-the-Wold continued

Rudolph Otto
The Little House, Sheep St. (R.O. and E.M Schwager) Est: 1950. Open 9.30-5.30. SIZE: Medium. *STOCK: Early Georgian mahogany furniture, £50-£4,500; Queen Anne, walnut furniture, mirrors, £250-£6,000; oak furniture, 1600-1750, £80-£4,500.* Not Stocked: Victorian bric-a-brac, art nouveau. LOC: Off the Fosseway, opp. the Post Office. PARK: Easy. TEL: 0451 30455. SER: Valuations; restorations. VAT: Stan/Spec.

Park House Antiques
Park St. (G. and B Sutton) Est: 1986. Open 10-5.30, Sun. by appointment only. SIZE: Large. *STOCK: Furniture, watercolours and oils, 18th C onwards; toys and teddy bears; Victorian linens and lace; porcelain, pottery, glass and collectables.* PARK: Easy. TEL: 0451 30159; home - same. VAT: Stan/Spec.

Antony Preston Antiques Ltd BADA LAPADA
The Square. CADA. Est: 1968. Open 9.30-6, or by appointment. *STOCK: English and continental furniture and objects, longcase and bracket clocks, barometers, leather upholstery, all 18th and 19th C.* TEL: 0451 31586/31406. VAT: Stan/Spec.

George III mahogany bow-fronted hanging corner cupboard. £540. Hobbs & Chambers, Cirencester. From a Saleroom Report in the December 1990/January 1991 issue of ***Antique Collecting.***

Stow-on-the-Wold continued

Priests Antiques
The Malt House, Digbeth St. (A.C Priest) Est: 1979. Open 10-5, Sat. 10.30-5. SIZE: Large. *STOCK: Mahogany, 18th and early 19th C; oak, walnut, and fruitwood, 17th-18th C; sporting prints and chromolithographs.* PARK: Easy. TEL: 0451 30592. SER: Valuations. VAT: Spec.

St. Breock Gallery
Digbeth St. (R.G.G Haslam-Hopwood) Est: 1979. Open 10-5. SIZE: Medium. *STOCK: Watercolours, 19th and 20th C, £50-£3,000; furniture, general antiques and objets d'art.* LOC: Just off Market Sq. PARK: Easy. TEL: 0451 30424; home - 071 229 4918. SER: Restorations; buys at auction. VAT: Spec.

Samarkand Galleries
2 Brewery Yard, Sheep St. (B. and L MacDonald) Est: 1980. Open 9.30-6, Sun. and Mon. by appointment. SIZE: Medium. *STOCK: Tribal rugs and artifacts, 19th C, £500-£1,500; fine decorative carpets, 19th-20th C, £1,000-£5,000; kelims, 19th to early 20th C, £200-£700.* LOC: Street adjacent to Market Sq. PARK: Easy. TEL: 0451 32322; home - 0451 31173. SER: Valuations; restorations; cleaning; buys at auction (carpets and rugs). FAIRS: City of London (Nov.); Kenilworth (Mar. and Oct.); Birmingham NEC (Mar.). VAT: Stan/Spec.

Stow-on-the-Wold continued

South Bar Antiques
Digbeth St. (R Deeley) CADA. Est: 1974. Open 9-5.30, Sun. by appointment. SIZE: Large. *STOCK: Clocks, jewellery, furniture, Moorcroft, Wemyss, porcelain, silver, paintings, 1640-1920, £50-£40,000.* PARK: Market Sq. TEL: 0451 30236. FAIRS: Café Royal; Barbican; Olympia; British International, Birmingham; Kenilworth. VAT: Spec.

Stow Antiques
The Square. (Mr and Mrs J Hutton-Clarke) CADA. Resident. Est: 1970. Open 9.30-5.30. SIZE: Large. *STOCK: Furniture, mainly period, £200-£20,000; china, silver and plate, glass, copper, 18th C to 1930, £5-£1,500; highly decorative items, 19th-20th C, £5-£5,000.* PARK: Easy. TEL: 0451 30377. SER: Shipping.

Talbot Court Galleries
Talbot Court. (J.P Trevers) Est: 1988. Open 9.30-1 and 2-5.30; Sun. in summer 11-5. SIZE: Medium. *STOCK: Prints and maps, 1600-1900, £5-£500; restrike engravings, £25-£150.* LOC: Behind Talbot Hotel in precinct between the Square and Sheep St. PARK: Nearby. TEL: 0451 32169. SER: Valuations; restorations (cleaning, colouring); buys at auction (engravings). VAT: Stan.

Stow-on-the-Wold continued

Touchwood International Ltd LAPADA

9 Park St. (K.M., L.A. and P Dixon) Resident. Est: 1830. Open 10-5.30, or by appointment. Sun. by appointment only. SIZE: Medium. *STOCK: Oak, walnut, fruitwood, early period furniture, medieval to early 18th C, £100-£25,000; treen, metalware and pottery, to 1830; works of art, sculptures, carvings.* Not Stocked: Late pine, mahogany. LOC: On A436 just past junction of Digbeth St. and Park St. PARK: Easy. TEL: 0451 30221; 0836 217111. SER: Valuations; restorations (wax polishing, esp. large collections and rare items); upholstery; research medieval to late 17th C furniture; commissions undertaken; finder. VAT: Stan/Spec.

Vanbrugh House Antiques

Park St. (J. and M.M Sands) Resident. Est: 1972. Open 10-6, or by appointment. *STOCK: Furniture and decorative items, 17th to early 19th C; early maps, music boxes, square pianos, clocks and barometers.* LOC: Opposite the Bell Inn. PARK: Easy. TEL: 0451 30797. SER: Valuations. FAIRS: Café Royal; Kenilworth; British International, Birmingham. VAT: Stan/Spec.

STROUD

Gnome Cottage Antiques

55-57 Middle St. (I.A McGrane) Est: 1961. Open 9.30-5.30. *STOCK: General antiques, furniture, prints, glass, china.* TEL: 0453 763669.

R.J.D. Fine Arts

12 Wallbridge. (R.J Dunk) Open 9.30-5. *STOCK: Pictures.* TEL: 0453 764878. SER: Framing.

Shabby Tiger Antiques

18 Nelson St. (S Krucker) Est: 1975. Open 11-6. *STOCK: 19th C furniture, pictures, jewellery, china, glass, metalware, decorative items.* LOC: Nelson St. is adjacent to Parliament St. car park. PARK: Opp. TEL: 0453 759175.

Stroud continued

Ron and Pam Sparrow

Cornermead, Gannicox Rd. Open by appointment. *STOCK: Watercolours, 19th and early 20th C.* TEL: 0453 764379.

Side chair. Painted in yellow ochre with nodes painted in black. Attributed to West Country, c.1800. Seat chamfered below. Seven spindles turned to simulate bamboo. Legs turned with prominent bamboo simulation, joined by H-form stretchers, also simulated. Gouge marks made above each nodal turning to accentuate imitation bamboo.

COLLECTION JAMES AYRES

From ***The English Regional Chair*** by Bernard D. Cotton, published by the **Antique Collectors' Club** in 1990. £49.50.

ARCHITECTURAL HERITAGE

Original and Antique Garden Statuary · Chimney Pieces · Complete Panelled Rooms for Home and Boardroom
Oak and Mahogany Doors · Important Stained Glass · Hotel Restaurant and Bar fitments

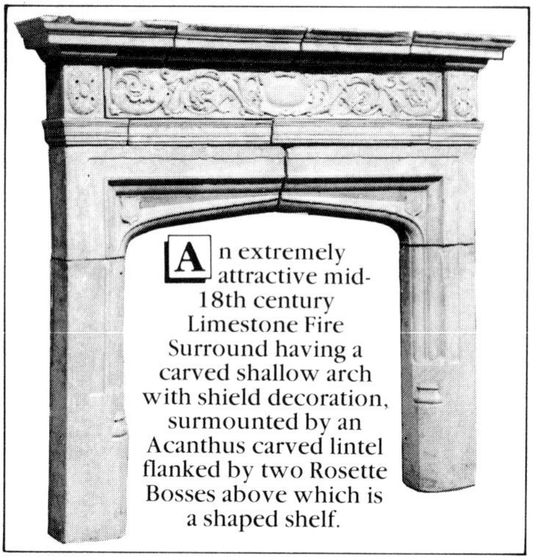

An extremely attractive mid-18th century Limestone Fire Surround having a carved shallow arch with shield decoration, surmounted by an Acanthus carved lintel flanked by two Rosette Bosses above which is a shaped shelf.

A 19th century fired & leaded glass window illustrating a scene from Aesops Fables.

A pair of 19th century Italian White Marble Urns, carved with Greek Warriors above a band of Acanthus foliage.

A 19th century Panelled Room having Dental Cornice and carved top panels; including one door and Oak Fire Surround.

Please be specific with your written enquiries as our stock is constantly changing

Architectural Heritage, Taddington Manor, Taddington,
Nr. Cutsdean, Cheltenham, Gloucestershire, England GL54 5RY
Tel: Stanton (038 673) 414 Telex 43432 DSA-G Ref. AHC Fax (038 673) 236

Open 9.30 – 5.30 Monday to Friday. Closed Saturdays, Sundays & Bank Holidays.

TADDINGTON, Nr. Cutsdean

Architectural Heritage
Taddington Manor. CADA. Est: 1978. Open 9.30-5.30, Sat. 10.30-4.30. SIZE: Large. *STOCK: Period panelling, oak, mahogany and pine; chimney pieces in marble, stone, oak and mahogany; garden statuary, fountains, seats and urns; complete shop and pub interiors, ornamental gates, stained, leaded and etched glass; doors, decorative and unusual items.* PARK: Easy. TEL: 038 673 414; fax - 038 673 236. VAT: Stan.

TETBURY

Antique Interiors
35 Long St. (C.R. and C.J Gee) Est: 1971. Open 9-6, Sun. by appointment. SIZE: Medium. *STOCK: Papier mâché trays on stands, decorative items, period walnut, mahogany, lacquer, Biedermeier and French Empire furniture, mainly 18th-19th C, £30-£3,000.* PARK: Easy. TEL: 0666 504043; home - same. SER: Valuations; courier. VAT: Stan/Spec.

Balmuir House Antiques
14 Long St. (P Whittam) Est: 1969. Open 9.30-5.30, Thurs. and Sun. by appointment. SIZE: Large. *STOCK: Victorian and Edwardian furniture, paintings, mirrors, 19th C, £500-£5,000.* LOC: Town centre. PARK: Easy. TEL: 0666 503822; home - same. SER: Valuations; restorations (furniture, upholstery, paintings). VAT: Stan/Spec.

Breakspeare Antiques LAPADA
36 Long St. (M. and S Breakspeare) CADA. Resident. Est: 1962. Open 9.30-5.30, if closed ring bell. CL: Some Thurs. p.m. SIZE: Medium. *STOCK: English period furniture, mainly mahogany, 18th to early 19th C, some early walnut, longcase clocks, barometers.* PARK: Easy. TEL: 0666 503122. VAT: Stan/Spec. *Mainly Trade.*

J. and M Bristow Antiques
28 Long St. (M.J. and J.A Bristow) Est: 1964. Open 9.30-1 and 2-5.30, but any time by appointment. CL: Thurs. SIZE: Small. *STOCK: Longcase, bracket and lantern clocks; barometers, 17th-18th C; furniture.* Not Stocked: Victoriana, bric-a-brac. LOC: In main street. PARK: Easy. TEL: 0666 502222. VAT: Spec.

The Chest of Drawers
24 Long St. (A. and P Bristow) Resident. Est: 1969. Open 9-5.30. Cl: Thurs. a.m.. SIZE: Medium. *STOCK: Late Georgian, Regency and Victorian furniture; country pieces, 17th-18th C; china and brass.* LOC: On A433. PARK: Easy. TEL: 0666 502105; home - same. VAT: Spec.

Tetbury continued

Colleton House Gallery
16 Long St. Est: 1980. Open 10-1 and 2-5.30. SIZE: Medium. *STOCK: Oils, £300-£5,000; watercolours, £100-£2,000; both 19th to mid-20th C.* PARK: Opposite. TEL: 0666 502048. SER: Valuations; restorations (oils, watercolours, prints); buys at auction.

Country Homes
61 Long St. (C. and D Sayers) Est: 1984. Open 9-5.30, Sun. by appointment. SIZE: Medium. *STOCK: Pine furniture, 19th C, £100-£1,500; treen, 19th C, £10-£150; pictures and metalware, £5-£60.* PARK: Nearby. TEL: 0666 502342. VAT: Stan.

Dolphin Antiques
48 Long St. (P. and L Davis) Est: 1986. Open 10-5.30. SIZE: Small. *STOCK: Mainly 19th C decorative porcelain, general antiques, 1750-1930, £20-£2,000.* Not Stocked: Large furniture. PARK: Nearby. TEL: 0666 504242; home-same.

Jonathan Eaton Antiques
Long St. Est: 1976. Open by appointment. *STOCK: Period and decorative furniture and objects; garden furniture.* TEL: 0666 503685. VAT: Spec.

Elgin House Antiques
1 New Church St. (B Symes) Open everyday 10-5.30. *STOCK: 18th-19th C oak, mahogany and pine furniture; restored brass and iron beds and accessories; upholstered furniture and decorative items.* TEL: 0666 504068.

Hampton Gallery
10 New Church St. (P Downey) Resident. Est: 1969. Open by appointment. SIZE: Large. *STOCK: Weapons, arms and armour, 1700-1880, £50-£5,000.* LOC: Off junction 17, M4. PARK: Easy. TEL: 0666 502971. SER: Valuations; buys at auction (arms). FAIRS: All major. VAT: Spec.

Sylvia Harris Fine Antique Porcelain
Wisteria Cottage, 90 Hampton St. (S.J Harris and M.R Mathews) Resident. Est: 1980. Open by appointment. SIZE: Small. *STOCK: English porcelain, early 19th C; continental porcelain, 18th C, all £250-£10,000.* PARK: Easy. TEL: 0666 503947. FAIRS: Olympia; Café Royal. VAT: Spec.

Paul Nash Antiques BADA
Cherington House, Cherington. (P. and A Gifford Nash) Resident. Est: 1961. Open by appointment only. *STOCK: Fine English furniture, 1680-1840.* LOC: 4 miles from Tetbury. PARK: Own. TEL: 028584 215. VAT: Spec.

Tetbury continued

Old George Antiques and Interiors
3 The Chipping. (Mrs W.M Wild and J Tyndall) CADA. Est: 1974. Open 10-5.30, Sun. by appointment. SIZE: Medium. *STOCK: Mahogany, decorated and walnut furniture, 17th C to Regency, to £5,000+; decorative items, porcelain, lighting, £500-£1,000+; paintings and rugs, to 20th C, £500-£2,000.* LOC: 100yds. from town centre, turn off main street at Snooty Fox Hotel into The Chipping car park. PARK: Easy. TEL: 0666 503405. SER: Valuations; restorations; interior decor and design; buys at auction. VAT: Stan/Spec.

Old Mill Market Shop
12 Church St. (Mr and Mrs M Green) Open 10-5.30, Thurs. 10-1. *STOCK: General antiques and bric-a-brac.* TEL: 0666 503127.

Porch House Antiques
42 Long St. Open 10-1 and 2-5. CL: Thurs. *STOCK: Furniture, 17th-19th C, some paintings and decorative items.* TEL: 0666 502687.

Primrose Antiques
45 Long St. (W.T. and B Stickland) CADA. Est: 1972. Open 9.30-5.30. SIZE: Medium. *STOCK: Oak, mahogany and walnut, brass, copper and pewter, 17th-19th C.* PARK: Easy. TEL: 0666 502440; home - same. VAT: Stan/Spec.

Rudge Antics
46 Long St. (T. and P Rudge) Open 10-5 or by appointment. *STOCK: Pine furniture.* TEL: 0666 503546.

Upton Lodge Galleries
20a Long St. (J Grant) Est: 1979. Open 10-6. SIZE: Medium. *STOCK: Oils and watercolours, from 1900, £100-£5,000.* PARK: Easy. TEL: 0666 503416.

Yeo Antiques **LAPADA**
6 Westonbirt. (B.D. and B.G Ackrill) Open by appointment. *STOCK: Furniture, metalware, clocks, porcelain and pottery.* TEL: 0666 88388. SER: Valuations; restorations. VAT: Stan/Spec.

TEWKESBURY

Abbey Antiques
62 Church St. Est: 1945. CL: Thurs. p.m.. *STOCK: General antiques; Victoriana; trade and shipping goods.* TEL: 0684 292378.

Berkeley Antiques and Replay **LAPADA**
The Wheatsheaf, 132 High St. (P Dennis and R Lane) Open 9.30-5.30. CL: Mon. and Thurs. SIZE: Large. *STOCK: Mahogany, oak, walnut and pine, 17th-19th C, £50-£2,000; brass, copper, silver, china and glass; period clothing, costumes and accessories, fabrics and hangings.* TEL: 0684 292034. SER: Restorations. VAT: Stan/Spec.

Tewkesbury continued

Gainsborough House Antiques
81 Church St. (A. and B Hilson) Open 9.30-5. *STOCK: Furniture, 18th to early 19th C; glass, porcelain.* TEL: 0684 293072. SER: Restoration and conservation.

F.W Taylor
71 Church St. Est: 1972. Open 9-5. SIZE: Medium. *STOCK: Furniture, £150-£4,000; Georgian and Victorian glass and silver, porcelain, pottery, watercolours, prints.* LOC: Close to Abbey. PARK: 100yds. TEL: 0684 295990. SER: Valuations; buys at auction. VAT: Stan/Spec.

Tewkesbury Antique Centre
Tewkesbury Cross Emporium, The Cross, 1 and 2 Church St. (J Preece) Est: 1978. Open 9-5. SIZE: Medium - 10+ units. *STOCK: General antiques.* LOC: Town centre. PARK: At rear. TEL: 0684 850057. SER: Valuations; restorations. VAT: Stan/Spec.

WINCHCOMBE

Kenulf Fine Art
High St. (E. and J Ford) CADA. Est: 1978. Open 9.30-1 and 2-5.30. *STOCK: 19th to early 20th C oil and watercolour paintings and prints.* TEL: 0242 603204/602776. SER: Valuations; restorations (oils and watercolours); period framing.

Muriel Lindsay
Queen Anne House. Resident. Est: 1965. Open 9.30-1 and 2-5.30. *STOCK: Staffordshire, metalwork, glass, small items.* TEL: 0242 602319. VAT: Spec.

Prichard Antiques
16 High St. (K.H. and D.Y Prichard) Est: 1979. Open 9-6, Sun. by appointment. SIZE: Large. *STOCK: Period furniture, £10-£5,000; treen, £1-£500; metalwork, £5-£500, all 17th-19th C.* LOC: On main Broadway to Cheltenham road. PARK: Easy. TEL: 0242 603566. SER: Valuations. VAT: Spec.

WOTTON-UNDER-EDGE

Bell Passage Antiques **LAPADA**
36-38 High St, Wickwar. (Mrs D.V Brand) Est: 1966. Open 8-5, Sun., Mon. and Thurs. by appointment. SIZE: Large. *STOCK: Furniture, £40-£5,000; glass, £1-£100; porcelain, £1-£800; prints, oils and watercolours, £20-£2,000.* LOC: On B4060. PARK: Easy. TEL: 0454 294251. SER: Valuations; restorations. VAT: Stan/Spec.

A pair of gold top and drop earrings finely fretted with foliated scrolls and with crescents attached to the drops. Set with chrysoprase, they perhaps date to about 1845-46, when 'Turkish earrings' were reported fashionable in Paris, or to 1850-60.
VICTORIA AND ALBERT MUSEUM
From ***Jewellery 1789-1910 — The International Era,*** Volume I, by Shirley Bury, published by the **Antique Collectors' Club** in 1991. £47.50 each volume.

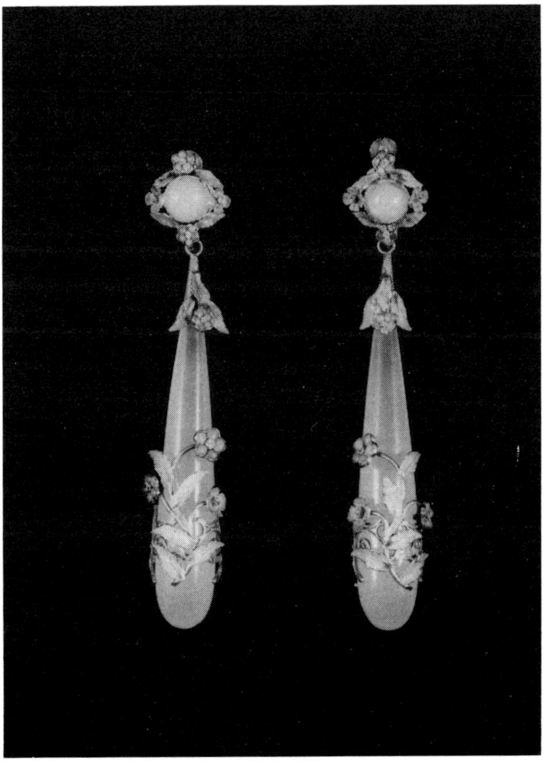

A pair of white chalcedony top and drop earrings with sprays of forget-me-nots in gold and turquoises. They might have been made any time between about 1828-37.
SOTHEBY'S
From ***Jewellery 1789-1910 — The International Era,*** Volume I, by Shirley Bury, published by the **Antique Collectors' Club** in 1991. £47.50 each volume.

Hampshire

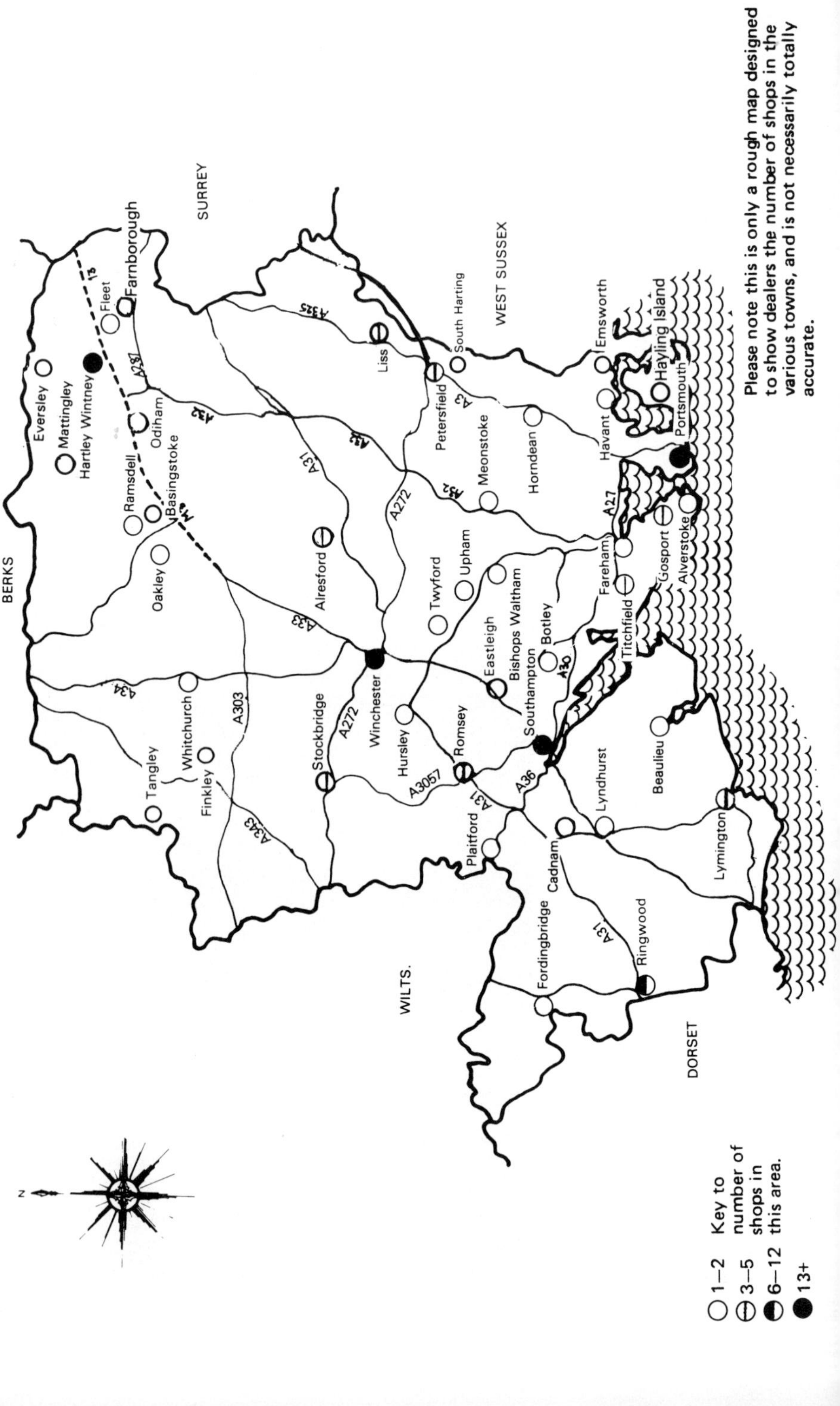
BERKS
SURREY
WEST SUSSEX
WILTS.
DORSET
Eversley
Mattingley
Hartley Wintney
Fleet
Farnborough
Odiham
Ramsdell
Basingstoke
Oakley
Alresford
Liss
South Harting
Petersfield
Meonstoke
Horndean
Emsworth
Havant
Hayling Island
Portsmouth
Gosport
Alverstoke
Fareham
Titchfield
Upham
Twyford
Bishops Waltham
Eastleigh
Botley
Southampton
Winchester
Stockbridge
Whitchurch
Tangley
Finkley
Hursley
Romsey
Plaitford
Cadnam
Lyndhurst
Beaulieu
Lymington
Fordingbridge
Ringwood
M3
A31
A32
A33
A34
A36
A3
A27
A30
A272
A303
A343
A325
A287
A3057
13
N
1–2
3–5
6–12
13+
Key to number of shops in this area.
Please note this is only a rough map designed to show dealers the number of shops in the various towns, and is not necessarily totally accurate.

ALRESFORD

Artemesia LAPADA
16 West St. (D.T.L Wright) Est: 1972. Open 9.30-5. SIZE: Medium. *STOCK: Oriental porcelain, works of art, 10th-19th C, £20-£5,000.* LOC: A31. PARK: Nearby. TEL: 0962 732277. SER: Valuations. VAT: Spec.

Close Antiques BADA
32 East St. (C Baron) Open Wed.-Sat. 9-5 (appointment advisable) and other times by arrangement. SIZE: Medium. *STOCK: 17th-18th C oak, fruitwood, and walnut country furniture; early pottery, Delftware, Staffordshire figures, samplers, early brass, copper, iron and treen.* LOC: A31 on left entering town from east. PARK: At rear. TEL: 0962 733131. VAT: Spec.

Evans and Evans LAPADA
40 West St, (Alresford Clocks Ltd. - D. and N. Evans). Est: 1953. Open Fri. and Sat., other times by appointment. SIZE: Medium. *STOCK: Clocks, watches, 1680-1900, £250-£50,000; musical boxes, 19th C, £500-£12,000; Regency and Victorian barometers, £200-£2,000. Stock only as listed.* LOC: A31. Shop on left going north. PARK: Easy. TEL: 0962 732170. SER: Valuations; buys at auction. VAT: Stan/Spec.

Studio Bookshop and Gallery
17 Broad St. (L Oxley) ABA. Est: 1951. Open 9-1 and 2-5, Wed. 9-1 and 2-4. SIZE: Large. *STOCK: Antiquarian books, £5-£1,500; topographical prints, £2-£250; maps, £5-£400.* LOC: B3046. PARK: Easy. TEL: 0962 732188. SER: Valuations; restorations (oil paintings, prints); framing. FAIRS: Boston, London ABA. VAT: Stan.

Winchester House Antiques
39 Broad St. (D. and P Thompson) Open 9-5 or by appointment. *STOCK: General antiques.* TEL: 0962 733110.

ALVERSTOKE, Nr. Gosport

Alverstoke Antiques
47 Village Rd. Dyer and Follett LtdEst: 1960. Open 9-12.45 and 2.15-5.30. SIZE: Small. *STOCK: Furniture.* PARK: Easy. TEL: 0705 582204. SER: Restorations. VAT: Stan/Spec.

Olive Antiques
2A Church Rd. Est: 1976. Open 8.15-5. SIZE: Medium. *STOCK: Gold, silver, diamonds, jewellery, clocks, barometers, mirrors and porcelain, £10-£1,000.* LOC: Main road from Fareham to Gosport and then to Alverstoke. PARK: Easy. TEL: 0705 522812. SER: Valuations; gem stone testing.

BASINGSTOKE

Squirrell Collectors Centre
9 New St. (A.H. and D.P Stone and Mrs R.A Austen) Est: 1981. Open 10-5.30. SIZE: Small. *STOCK: Small items, wristwatches, jewellery and silver, Victorian and Edwardian, £5-£1,500; collectors items, books.* LOC: Near traffic lights at junction with Winchester St. PARK: Nearby. TEL: 0256 464885. SER: Valuations. FAIRS: Farnham Maltings monthly. VAT: Stan.

BEAULIEU

Beaulieu Fine Arts
The Malt House, High St. (Mr and Mrs S.A Roberts) Est: 1975. Open 9.30-12.30 and 1.30-5.30, Sun. by appointment. SIZE: Medium. *STOCK: Watercolours, mainly 19th and early 20th C, from £200; drawings, prints and etchings, from £16.* LOC: Centre of High St. PARK: High St. TEL: 0590 612089. VAT: Stan/Spec.

BISHOPS WALTHAM

Julia's Antiques
11 Winchester Rd. CL: Mon. and Tues. SIZE: Large. *STOCK: Furniture, including stripped oak to 1940s; bric-a-brac, some silver and jewellery.* PARK: Easy at rear. TEL: 0489 892474.

Bishops Waltham continued

Pinecrafts
4 Brook St. (A Robinson) Open 10-5. SIZE: Large. *STOCK: Pine furniture.* TEL: 0489 892878. SER: Restorations; stripping. VAT: Stan.

BOTLEY, Nr. Southampton

Jane Burnham-Slipper Antiques LAPADA
The Tudor House, 8 Winchester St. Est: 1986. Open 10-12, Sat. 10-4, or by appointment. CL: Wed. SIZE: Small. *STOCK: General antiques, including 18th-19th C furniture, from £300; ceramics and glass, from £35; Georgian silver, from £75.* LOC: 5 minutes from junction 7, M27. PARK: Nearby. TEL: 0489 782354; home - same. FAIRS: Goodwood, Petersfield, Canford Magna, Parham, Warsash and some Wakefield. VAT: Stan/Spec.

CADNAM

C.W Buckingham
Twin Firs, Southampton Rd. Resident. Open 9-6 or by appointment. CL: Thurs. *STOCK: Mainly pine, some period and Victorian furniture.* TEL: 0703 812122.

Hingstons
Minstead Cottage, Romsey Rd. Open 9-5. CL: Sat. SIZE: Warehouse. *STOCK: General antiques, to 1930.* TEL: 0703 812301/812637.

CRAWLEY, Nr. Winchester

Prospect Antiques
Folly Farm. (T.R Baker and G.M Marsh) Open 9-5. *STOCK: General antiques especially pine.* TEL: 0962 72687.

CURDRIDGE, Nr. Botley

Adrienne de Marino-Montero Fine Art and Antiques Ltd
Warwick House. Est: 1989. Open by appointment. SIZE: Large. *STOCK: French furniture, £500-£45,000; French wall lights, ormolu, pictures, portraits, £900-£25,000, all 17th-19th C.* PARK: Easy. TEL: 0489 784326; fax - 0489 782088. SER: Valuations; restorations; French polishing; gilding; buys at auction (Spanish pictures, art deco furniture, 19th-20th C pictures).

EASTLEIGH

Tappers Antiques
186-188 Southampton Rd. (P.A Passell) Open 10-5. *STOCK: General collectables and curios.* LOC: 1 mile off M27. TEL: 0703 643105.

EMSWORTH

Tiffins Antiques
12 Queen St. (Mrs P Hudson) Est: 1987. Open 10-5. SIZE: Small. *STOCK: General antiques, bric-a-brac, clocks.* TEL: 0243 372497; home - same. SER: Restorations (clocks).

EVERSLEY, Nr. Wokingham

Kingsley Barn Antique Centre
Church Lane. (G Bozely) Est: 1988. Open 10.30-5 including Sun. CL: Mon. SIZE: Large. *STOCK: Furniture and crafts.* LOC: 1 mile from A30. PARK: Easy. TEL: 0734 328518. SER: Restorations.

FAREHAM

Elizabethans
58 High St. (Mrs E Keeble) Est: 1961. Open 10-4. *STOCK: Small general antiques, furniture, jewellery.* TEL: 0329 234964 (ansaphone).

FARNBOROUGH

Martin and Parke LAPADA
97 Lynchford Rd. (J Martin and J Warde) Est: 1971. Open 9-5. SIZE: Large. *STOCK: Furniture and shipping goods.* TEL: 0252 515311. VAT: Stan.

FINKLEY, Nr. Andover

Parker Fine Art Ltd
Finkley House. (P.A.R Parker) Open by appointment. *STOCK: Oil paintings, 17th-20th C; frames.* TEL: 0264 352412; fax - 0264 358241; mobile - 0860 323791. SER: Restorations.

FLEET

Fleet Fine Art
1/2 Kings Parade, King's Rd. (A. and M Lewis) Open 9.30-5. CL: Mon. SIZE: Medium. *STOCK: British watercolours, £500-£1,000; oils, £1,500-£2,500; both 1800-1920.* LOC: Between town centre and station. PARK: Easy. TEL: 0252 617500. SER: Valuations; restorations (oils and watercolours); framing; buys at auction (oils and watercolours). FAIRS: Birmingham; Barbican; East Midlands; Arley Hall; some Robert Bailey. VAT: Spec.

FORDINGBRIDGE

Mark Collier BADA
24 High St. Open 10-5.30 or by appointment. *STOCK: General decorative antiques.* Not Stocked: Coins, medals and stamps. TEL: 0425 652555; fax - 0425 656886.

Fordingbridge continued

Quatrefoil
Burgate. (C.D. and Mrs I Aston) Resident. Est: 1972. Always open. SIZE: Large. *STOCK: Early oak furniture, 16th-18th C, £50-£15,000; carvings and sculpture, 13th-17th C, £20-£10,000.* LOC: On A338, adjacent Tudor Rose Inn. PARK: Easy. TEL: 0425 653309. VAT: Stan/Spec.

GOSPORT

E.T Cooper
20 Stoke Rd. Est: 1972. Open 9.30-12.30 and 1.30-5. CL: Wed. p.m. SIZE: Medium. *STOCK: Silver, china, glass, furniture, mechanical music, fairground equipment.* LOC: Main road from Lee-on-Solent through Gosport. PARK: In side road. TEL: 0705 585032. SER: Valuations; buys at auction.

Peter Pan's Bazaar
105 Forton Rd. (S.V Panormo) Est: 1960. CL: Mon., Tues. and Wed. *STOCK: Vintage cameras, early photographica, images, 1850-1950, £5-£500.* LOC: Main road into town. PARK: Easy. TEL: 0705 524254. FAIRS: Main south of England.

Gosport continued

Peter Pan's of Gosport
105c Forton Rd. (J McClaren) Est: 1965. CL: Mon., Tues. and Wed. *STOCK: Jewellery, dolls, toys and miniatures.* LOC: Main road into town. PARK: Easy. TEL: 0705 524254. FAIRS: Main south of England.

HARTLEY WINTNEY

Nicholas Abbott
High St. (C. and A Abbott) Est: 1962. Open 9.30-5.30. SIZE: Large. *STOCK: English furniture, 18th to early 19th C.* LOC: A30. PARK: Easy. TEL: 025 126 2365; home - 0734 326269. VAT: Stan/Spec.

Hartley Wintney continued

Airdale Antiques
at Deva, High St. (E.J Andreae) Est: 1972. *STOCK: Country furniture, 17th-19th C; polished pine.* TEL: 025 126 3538 or 0734 733132.

Andwells LAPADA
High St. (P Heraty) Est: 1967. Open 9-1 and 2-5.30. SIZE: Large. *STOCK: Georgian and Regency furniture, mainly mahogany.* LOC: Main street. PARK: Easy. TEL: 025 126 2305. VAT: Stan/Spec.

Antique House
22 High St. (R.H Campbell and P Weaver) Open 9.30-5.30, Sun. by appointment. *STOCK: Georgian and Victorian furniture, watercolours and prints.* TEL: 025 126 4499; home - 0276 26412. SER: Restorations (furniture).

Cedar Antiques BADA
High St. (D.S Green) Est: 1964. Open 9-6, trade any time. SIZE: Large and warehouse. *STOCK: Fine English oak, walnut and country furniture, 17th-18th C, £50-£10,000; French Provincial furniture; longcase clocks, 1680-1780, £800-£5,000; steel and brass-work, £30-£1,000.* Not Stocked: China, glass, silver. LOC: A30. PARK: Opposite. TEL: 025 126 3252. SER: Valuations; restorations (clocks, period furniture). FAIRS: West of England, Park Lane, Barbican. VAT: Stan/Spec.

Barbara Chitty Antiques at Deva
High St. Open 9.30-5. *STOCK: Pottery, porcelain and small furniture.* TEL: 025 126 3538.

Bryan Clisby at Andwells Antiques
High St. Est: 1976. Open 9.30-1 and 2-5.30. SIZE: Large. *STOCK: Longcase clocks, 1700-1830, £1,500-£10,000; barometers, 1770-1850, £250-£1,500; bracket, wall and mantel clocks.* LOC: A30 village centre. PARK: Easy. TEL: 025 126 2305; home - 0252 716436. SER: Valuations; restorations (clocks and barometers). VAT: Spec.

Hartley Wintney continued

Deva Antiques
High St. (A Gratwick) Open 9.30-5. *STOCK: Walnut and mahogany furniture, 18th C.* TEL: 025 126 3538.

Colin Harris Antiques LAPADA
at Deva, High St. Est: 1966. Open 9-5.30. *STOCK: General antiques, mainly furniture and small decorative items, 18th-19th C, £20-£3,000.* LOC: A30. PARK: Easy. TEL: 025 126 3538; home - 0734 732580. FAIRS: British International, Birmingham; Wilton House, Petersfield. VAT: Spec.

Just the Thing LAPADA
High St. (S Carpenter) Est: 1975. Open 9-5 or by appointment. SIZE: Large. *STOCK: Period mahogany and country furniture; paintings, china, brass, copper, silver and Victorian jewellery.* TEL: 025 126 3393; home - 025 126 2916. VAT: Stan/Spec.

David Lazarus Antiques
High St. Resident. Est: 1973. Open 9.30-5.30; some Sundays, other times by appointment. SIZE: Medium. *STOCK: 17th to early 19th C English and continental furniture; objets d'art.* LOC: Main street. PARK: Nearby. TEL: 025 126 2272. VAT: Stan/Spec.

Millon Antiques LAPADA
High St. (P. and J Millon-Milovanovich) Open 9.30-5. SIZE: Large. *STOCK: English furniture, 1700-1850; including some walnut.* LOC: A30, end of village green. TEL: 025 126 5442. VAT: Spec.

Old Forge Antiques
Old Forge Cottage, The Green. (Mrs M.A.B Gates) Open 10.30-5, but appointment advisable. CL: Wed. and Sat. except by appointment. SIZE: Medium. *STOCK: General antiques, watercolours, oils, prints.* LOC: A30. PARK: Easy. TEL: 025 126 2287.

Hartley Wintney continued

Phoenix Green Antiques
London Rd. (J Biles and P.H.M Hunt) Open 9.30-5.30, Sat. 10-5 or by appointment. SIZE: Large. *STOCK: English and continental country furniture, Georgian mahogany, 18th-19th C.* TEL: 025 126 4430.

Phoenix Green Gallery
London Rd, Phoenix Green. (K Gregory-Smith) Est: 1982. Open 9.30-6, Sat. 10-6. SIZE: Large. *STOCK: Oil paintings and watercolours, 18th-20th C, £500-£1,000+.* LOC: A30 1/2 mile from Hartley Wintney towards Basingstoke. PARK: Easy. TEL: 025 126 2111. SER: Valuations; restorations. FAIRS: Olympia; N.E.C. VAT: Spec.

A.W Porter and Son
High St. (M.A Porter) Est: 1844. Open 9-5.30, Sat. 9-5. *STOCK: Clocks, furniture, silver, jewellery, glass.* LOC: Opposite Lloyds Bank. TEL: 025 126 2676. SER: Restorations (clocks). VAT: Stan/Spec.

Sheila Revell Antiques
at Deva, High St. Open 9-5.30. *STOCK: 18th-19th C decorative objects, small furniture and collectors' items.* TEL: 025 126 3538.

HAVANT

Antiques and Nice Things
40 North St. (M.T Davis-Shaw) Est: 1965. Open 10-5. *STOCK: Paintings, prints, porcelain, copper, brass, silver, Sheffield plate, small furniture, maps, clocks, jewellery, glass.* LOC: Near station. PARK: Own. TEL: 0705 484935; home - 0243 372551. SER: Restorations.

HAYLING ISLAND

Jay Antiques
Open by appointment. *STOCK: Small furniture and small general antiques.* TEL: 0705 465917.

J Morton Lee LAPADA
Cedar House, Bacon Lane. Est: 1984. Open by appointment. *STOCK: Watercolours, 19th-20th C, £50-£10,000.* PARK: Easy. TEL: 0705 464444. SER: Valuations; buys at auction. FAIRS: West London, Jan./Aug., Westminster, Harrogate, Buxton, Surrey, Northern, NEC August, Kensington, City of London, Newcastle, and Goodwood. VAT: Stan/Spec.

HORNDEAN

Goss and Crested China Centre
62 Murray Rd. (N.J Pine) Est: 1968. SIZE: Medium. *STOCK: Goss, 1860-1930, £2-£1,000; other heraldic china, art pottery including Carlton war, Charlotte Rhead, Chamelion, 1890-1930, £1-£1,000.* PARK: Easy. TEL: 0705 597440. SER: Valuations; buys at auction (Goss). VAT: Stan.

HURSLEY, Nr. Winchester

Hursley Antiques
(S Thorne) Est: 1980. Open 10-6. *STOCK: Country furniture, brass, copper, metal.* LOC: 2 1/2 miles from Winchester on Romsey Rd. PARK: Easy. TEL: 0962 75488. SER: Restorations (metalware); repairs (metalware).

LISS

J Du Cros Antiques
Farnham Rd, West Liss. (J. and P Du Cros) Est: 1982. Open 9.30-5.30, Sun. by appointment. SIZE: Medium. *STOCK: English furniture, 1660-1900, £100-£5,000; treen, metalware.* Not Stocked: Glass and porcelain. LOC: Adjacent Spread Eagle public house on village green, A325. PARK: Easy. TEL: 0730 895299. VAT: Stan/Spec.

Pine Collection
71 Station Rd. ((Floydmist Ltd - P Head) Est: 1983. Open 9-1 and 2-5. SIZE: Large. *STOCK: Pine furniture, 18th-20th C, £60-£1,500.* LOC: Next to station. PARK: Easy. TEL: 0730 893743. SER: Restorations; stripping, polishing. VAT: Stan.

Plestor Barn Antiques
Farnham Rd. Open 9-5. SIZE: Large. *STOCK: English furniture, 19th-20th C; silver, plate, china, glass.* LOC: A325. TEL: 0730 893922. VAT: Stan.

LYMINGTON

C.W Buckingham
10 The Square, South St, Pennington. Open 9-6. CL: Thurs. *STOCK: Pine including reproduction.* TEL: 0590 672916.

Captain's Cabin Antiques
1 Quay St. (Mrs D.J Woon) Est: 1989. Open 9.30-5.30. SIZE: Medium. *STOCK: Furniture and pictures, 18th-19th C, £50-£5,000; ceramics, £25-£500; marine items, £80-£1,000; both 18th-19th C; silver, objets d'art, £10-£2,000.* PARK: Nearby. TEL: 0590 672912; home - 0590 677130. SER: Valuations; restorations. VAT: Spec.

Corfield of Lymington Ltd BADA
120 High St. Open 9.15-5.30. SIZE: Large. *STOCK: English furniture, porcelain, English School watercolours and oil paintings, 18th to early 19th C; militaria.* TEL: 0590 673532, 675359 and 677872. SER: Valuations; restorations (furniture, pictures); packing and shipping. VAT: Stan/Spec.

Lymington continued

Hughes and Smeeth Ltd
1 Gosport St. (P Hughes and S Smeeth) ABA. Est: 1976. Open 9.30-5. SIZE: Small. *STOCK: Antiquarian and secondhand books, maps and prints.* LOC: At bottom of High St. PARK: Nearby. TEL: 0590 676324. SER: Valuations; restorations (oil paintings), binding, framing. VAT: Stan.

Lymington Antiques Centre
76 High St. Open 10-5, Sat. 9-5. SIZE: 26 dealers. *STOCK: General antiques and books.* TEL: 0590 670934.

LYNDHURST

The Antiques Gallery
76 High St. (Mr and Mrs K.D.W O'Halloran-Fairgaill) Est: 1988. Open 10-5.30, Sun. 11-6. CL: Mon. *STOCK: Furniture, mainly small, 18th to early 19th C, £50-£2,000; pictures and prints, from 18th C, £30-£1,500; collectables - silver and plate, porcelain and Moorcroft; books, £10-£500.* PARK: Hotel next door. TEL: 0703 282693; home - same. SER: Valuations. VAT: Stan/Spec.

Lita Kaye of Lyndhurst BADA
13 High St. (S. and S Ferder) Est: 1947. Open 9.30-1 and 2.15-5. SIZE: Large. *STOCK: Furniture, clocks, 1690-1820; decorative porcelain, 19th C.* LOC: A35. PARK: 100yds. in High St. TEL: 0703 282337. VAT: Stan/Spec.

MATTINGLEY, Nr. Basingstoke

Anna Hoysted
Goodchilds Farm, Chandlers Green. Open by appointment. *STOCK: English watercolours and drawings, 19th-20th C, £50-£1,500.* LOC: Near Stratfield Saye Estate between A32 and A33. PARK: Easy. TEL: 0256 882355.

MEONSTOKE

W.D Trivess
Heathfield House. Est: 1936. Open by appointment only. *STOCK: Maps and illustrated topography, 16th-19th C.* TEL: 0489 877326. SER: List available. *Postal Only.*

MORESTEAD, Nr. Winchester

Burgess Farm Antiques
(N Spencer-Brayn) Est: 1970. Open 9-5. SIZE: Large. *STOCK: Furniture, especially pine and country, 18th-19th C, £25-£5,000; architectural items - doors, panelling, fire-places.* LOC: 2 miles south of Winchester, off Corehampton road. PARK: Easy. TEL: 0962 777546. SER: Stripping; export. VAT: Stan/Spec.

OAKLEY, Nr. Basingstoke

E.H Hutchins
48 Pardown, East Oakley. Est: 1933. *STOCK: General antiques, Edwardian and later furniture.* Not Stocked: China, jewellery, ornaments. LOC: B3400. PARK: Easy. TEL: 0256 780494. VAT: Stan.

ODIHAM

Monaltrie Antiques
76 High St. (Mrs W Helmore) Est: 1972. Open 10-1 and 2.30-5, Sun. by appointment. CL: Mon. a.m. and Wed. p.m. SIZE: Medium. *STOCK: Furniture, £250-£1,500; copper and brass, £50-£250; silver and collectables, £50-£300, all 18th-19th C.* LOC: 1 1/2 miles junction 5, M3. PARK: Easy. TEL: 0256 702660; home - same. SER: Valuations; buys at auction. VAT: Spec.

The Odiham Gallery
78 High St. (I Walker) Open 10-5, Sat. 10-1. *STOCK: Decorative and Oriental rugs and carpets.* TEL: 0256 703415.

PETERSFIELD

The Barn
Station Rd. (P Gadsden) Est: 1956. Open 9-5. *STOCK: Victoriana, bric-a-brac; also large store of trade and shipping goods.* TEL: 0730 62958. VAT: Stan.

Cull Antiques
62 Station Rd. (J Cull) Est: 1978. Open 10-5.30 or by appointment. *STOCK: 18th C English furniture and metalwork.* TEL: 0730 63670; home - 0730 63471.

Elmore
5 Charles St. (Mr and Mrs L.G Mortimer) Est: 1969. Open 9.30-5. CL: Mon., Wed. and Thurs. *STOCK: Small furniture, porcelain, glass, bric-a-brac, pictures and prints.* TEL: 0730 62383.

Folly Antiques Centre
College St. Est: 1977. Open 9.30-5, Thurs. 9.30-1. SIZE: Several spcialist shops. *STOCK: Antique silver, watercolours, porcelain, glass, furniture, jewellery, brass, copper, period clothes, lace, collectors' items and objets d'art.* LOC: On A3. TEL: 0730 64816.

The Petersfield Bookshop BADA
16a Chapel St. (F Westwood) ABA. Est: 1918. Open 9-5.30. SIZE: Large. *STOCK: Books, old and modern, £1-£500; maps and prints, 1600-1850, £1-£200; oils and watercolours, 19th C, £20-£1,000.* LOC: Chapel St. runs from the Square to Station Rd. PARK: Opposite. TEL: 0730 63438. SER: Restorations and rebinding of old leather books; picture-framing and mount-cutting. FAIRS: Northern and Buxton, Boston and London. VAT: Stan.

PLAITFORD, Nr. Romsey

Plaitford House Gallery
(W.B Yeo) Est: 1960. Open most days and any time by appointment. SIZE: Large. *STOCK: Oil paintings, watercolours, bronzes, 1800-1950, £100-£5,000.* LOC: 1 mile north of A36 midway between Salisbury and Southampton on the road adjoining Landford and Sherfield English. PARK: Easy. TEL: 0794 22221. SER: Valuations; restorations and cleaning of oils and watercolours. VAT: Spec.

PORTSMOUTH

Affordable Antiques
130 Highland Rd, Southsea. (M Gosling) Est: 1987. Open 10.30-5.30. CL: Wed. SIZE: Small. *STOCK: Furniture, Victorian, Edwardian and 1930's; small items, all £2-£850.* LOC: On corner of Highland and Adair Rd., opposite bus depot. PARK: Easy. TEL: 0705 293344; home - 0705 230019. SER: Valuations.

Tony Amos Antiques
239 Albert Rd, Southsea. Open 9-5, Sat. 9-12. *STOCK: General antiques and shipping goods.* TEL: 0705 736818.

R.C Dodson (Exports) Ltd LAPADA
85/87 Fawcett Rd, Southsea. Open 8.30-5.30, Sat. 9.30-5, or by appointment. *STOCK: General antiques.* TEL: 0705 829481.

A Fleming (Southsea) Ltd BADA
The Clock Tower, Castle Rd. Est: 1905. Open 8.30-5. CL: Sat. p.m. SIZE: Large. *STOCK: Furniture, silver, china, porcelain, general antiques, jewellery.* TEL: 0705 822934. SER: Restorations. VAT: Stan/Spec.

The Gallery
11 and 19 Marmion Rd, Southsea. (I Murphy) Open 10-5. *STOCK: At No.19 - Victorian chairs and chesterfields, at No.11 - furniture, mainly Victorian and Edwardian.* PARK: Nearby. TEL: 0705 822016. VAT: Stan.

Leslie's
107 Fratton Rd. (E Lord) Est: 1946. Open 9.30-1 and 2-5.30, Sat. until 6. CL: Wed. p.m. SIZE: Small. *STOCK: Victorian and antique rings, brooches, 1850-1920, £10-£350.* Not Stocked: Furniture, pictures. LOC: Fratton railway station, or 4 shops from main Co-op store in Fratton Rd. PARK: Easy. TEL: 0705 825952. SER: Valuations; restorations (antique jewellery). VAT: Stan.

Colin Macleod Antiques
105 Albert Rd, Southsea. Open 10-5.30. *STOCK: Oriental, continental and English Victorian furniture.* TEL: 0705 864211; fax - 0705 817040.

Portsmouth continued

Oldfield Gallery
76 Elm Grove, Southsea. Est: 1970. Open 10-5. SIZE: Small. *STOCK: Maps and engravings, 16th-19th C, £20-£1,000; decorative prints, 19th-20th C, £5-£50; prints and some paintings, 20th C, £10-£400.* PARK: Easy. TEL: 0705 838042. SER: Valuations; restorations (maps and prints). FAIRS: Bonnington Hotel Map (monthly). VAT: Stan.

Portsmouth Stamp Shop
184 Chichester Rd, North End. (G Coast) Est: 1967. Open 9.15-5.30. *STOCK: Stamps, coins, cigarette cards, postcards, banknotes.* TEL: 0705 663450. VAT: Stan.

Pretty Chairs
189/191 Highland Rd, Southsea. (J Ruffell) Est: !963. Open 10-5. CL: Wed. p.m. SIZE: Large. *STOCK: Victorian chairs, tables, wood boxes, desks, bureaux, sofas, French style furniture and cabriole-legged chairs.* LOC: Off Eastney Rd. PARK: Easy. TEL: 0705 731411. VAT: Stan/Spec.

W.R Priddy
63 Fawcett Rd, Southsea. Open 10-5.30. CL: Sat. *STOCK: General antiques.* TEL: 0705 826135/738906.

Portsmouth continued

W.R Priddy
144 Albert Rd, Southsea. Open 10-4. CL: Wed. and Sat. *STOCK: Bric-a-brac and smalls.* TEL: 0705 738187.

Times Past
141 Highland Rd, Southsea. (S New and S Hemsworth) Open 10-4, Mon. by appointment. *STOCK: General antiques and shipping goods.* TEL: 0705 822701/0831 418488.

Wessex Medical Antiques LAPADA
77 Carmarthen Ave. (Dr D.J Warren) Est: 1984. Open by appointment. SIZE: Small. *STOCK: Medical items, 18th-19th C, £50-£4,000.* LOC: Off Havant Rd., Drayton. PARK: Easy. TEL: 0705 376518; home - same; fax - 0705 201479. SER: Free catalogue; valuations; buys at auction (as stock). FAIRS: Scientific and Medical, Portman Hotel, London. VAT: Stan.

RAMSDELL, Nr. Basingstoke

Ewhurst Gallery LAPADA
(R Mayfield) Est: 1976. Open any time by appointment. *STOCK: Watercolours and drawings, 18th to early 20th C, £100-£5,000.* LOC: 1/4 mile off A339, 5 miles from Basingstoke. PARK: Easy. TEL: 0256 850051. SER: Valuations; buys at auction; finder. VAT: Spec.

RINGWOOD

Barbara Davies Antiques
30A Christchurch Rd. Est: 1985. Open Tues. 10.15-1, Wed. and Fri. 10.15-4. SIZE: Small. *STOCK: Porcelain, 1760-1930, £5-£100; small furniture, 1850-1935, £20-£150; collectors' items.* LOC: Off A31 into Ringwood, turn off roundabout to Moortown, next roundabout, turn right, shop on left 250yds. PARK: Behind Greyfriars Community Centre. TEL: Home - 0202 872268. SER: Valuations (pottery and porcelain).

Ringwood continued

Millers of Chelsea Antiques Ltd LAPADA
Netherbrook House, 86 Christchurch Rd. Est: 1897. Open 9-5.30, Sat. 9-4, other times by appointment. SIZE: Large. *STOCK: Furniture - English and continental country, mahogany and gilt, military, decorative items, 18th-19th C, £25-£3,000.* LOC: On B3347 towards Christchurch. PARK: Own. TEL: 0425 472062; fax - 0425 470892. FAIRS: Decorative Antiques, Olympia. VAT: Stan/Spec.

P.E Palmer Antiques
The Matchbox, 132 Christchurch Rd. Est: 1961. Open 10-4. SIZE: Large. *STOCK: Furniture, collectors' items, 17th-19th C; jewellery, bric-a-brac, guns.* LOC: By the old railway crossing. PARK: Easy. TEL: 0425 472640. SER: Valuations.

Pine Company
104 Christchurch Rd. (D.R. and G.B Smith) Est: 1978. Open 9.30-5.30. SIZE: Large and warehouse. *STOCK: Pine and other wood, 18th-19th C, £30-£1,000; model railways, 19th-20th C, from £5; Chinese furniture.* Not Stocked: Silver, fine china, bric-a-brac. LOC: Almost opposite fire station. PARK: Own. TEL: 0425 476705; home - same; fax - 0425 480467. SER: Restorations. VAT: Stan.

Glen Robinson Interiors and Antiques
62 Christchurch Rd. (Mrs G Robinson) Est: 1980. Open 10-1 and 2-5. SIZE: Medium. *STOCK: Furniture, £500-£1,000; porcelain, £50-£100; both 19th C; decorative objects.* LOC: Opposite council offices. PARK: Easy. TEL: 0425 480450. SER: Valuations; restorations. VAT: Stan/Spec.

The Tennis Bookshop
West Gate, Moyles Court. (A.P.H Chalmers) Resident. Est: 1985. Open by appointment. SIZE: Small. *STOCK: Antiques, books and collectable items relating to racquet sports.* LOC: Ring for details. PARK: Easy. TEL: 0425 480518. SER: Valuations; buys at auction (as stock); catalogue twice a year.

ROMSEY

Bell Antiques

8 Bell St. (M. and B.M Gay) FGA. Est: 1979. Open 9.30-5.30. CL: Wed. p.m. (winter). SIZE: Large. *STOCK: Jewellery and small silver, glass, pottery, porcelain, furniture, prints, mainly 19th and 20th C.* LOC: Near market place. PARK: Adjacent. TEL: 0794 514719. VAT: Stan/Spec.

Cambridge Antiques

5 Bell St. Open 9-4.30. SIZE: Large. *STOCK: Furniture, china, jewellery, watercolours, oils and prints.* LOC: From the West, Romsey by-pass, left into Palmerston St., first left then first right, 100yds. on left. TEL: 0794 523089. VAT: Stan/Spec.

Charles Antiques LAPADA

101 The Hundred. (T.R Cambridge) Est: 1972. Open 9-5.30. SIZE: Large. *STOCK: Furniture, clocks, small china, shipping goods.* LOC: From the west, Romsey by-pass, left into Palmerston St., 1st right into The Hundred. PARK: Easy. TEL: 0794 512885. VAT: Stan/Spec.

Creightons Antique Centre

23-25 Bell St. (K Creighton) Open 9-6. SIZE: 18 stands. *STOCK: General antiques.* TEL: 0794 522758.

"Old Cottage Things"

Broxmore Park, Sherfield English. (M Hyde) Est: 1970. *STOCK: Original building, architectural and garden materials.* LOC: A27. TEL: 0794 884538.

Romsey Medal and Collectors Centre

5 Bell St. (T Cambridge, OMRS) Est: 1980. Open 9-5.30. *STOCK: Medals, militaria, crested and commemorative china, postcards and cigarette cards.* LOC: From the west, Romsey by-pass, left into Palmerston St., first left then first right, 100yds. on left. PARK: Easy. TEL: 0794 512069/512885.

SOUTH HARTING, Nr. Petersfield

Julia Holmes Antique Maps and Prints

South Gardens Cottage. By appointment only. SIZE: Medium. *STOCK: Maps, 1600-1850, £10-£1,000; prints, especially sporting, all periods, to £500.* LOC: End of main street, on the Chichester road. PARK: Opposite. TEL: 0730 825040. SER: Valuations; restorations (cleaning and colouring maps and prints); framing; buys at auction; catalogues. FAIRS: Local and major sporting events. VAT: Stan.

SOUTHAMPTON

Mr Alfred's "Old Curiosity Shop" incorporating James Morris, Fine Art Dealer/Valuer

280 Shirley Rd, Shirley. Est: 1952. Open 9-6. *STOCK: Furniture, 18th-20th C; paintings, porcelain, bronzes, brass, glass, books, silver, jewellery and general antiques.* LOC: On left of main Shirley road, 3/4 mile from Southampton central station. PARK: Outside. TEL: 0703 774772.

Meg Campbell

10 Church Lane, Highfield. Est: 1967. Open by appointment only. *STOCK: English, Scottish and Irish silver, collectors' pieces, old Sheffield plate.* TEL: 0703 557636. SER: Mail order; catalogues available. VAT: Spec.

Cottage Antiques

9 Northam Rd. (K.J Leslie) Open 9.30-4.30. *STOCK: General antiques, furniture, Victorian, trade goods.* TEL: 0703 221546; home - 452246. VAT: Stan.

R.J Elliot

45 Northam Rd. Open 10-5. *STOCK: Silver, plate, small antiques.* TEL: 0703 226642.

Gazelles Art Deco, Interiors

31 Northam Rd, Off St. Mary's St. (A Bellamy) Est: 1986. Open Tues. and Thurs. 9-4.30, Wed., Fri. and Sat. 10-4.30. SIZE: Medium. *STOCK: Art deco ceramics including Clarice Cliff, Susie Cooper, Shelly, Burleigh Ware, Poole, Carlton Ware, Royal Winton, chrome, glass, textiles, furniture, lighting fixtures and fittings.* PARK: Easy. TEL: 0703 780798. FAIRS: Kensington; Greenwich. VAT: Stan.

H.M Gilbert and Son

2 1/2 Portland St. (B.L. and R.C Gilbert) ABA. Est: 1859. Open 8.30-5. *STOCK: Antiquarian and secondhand books, £1-£1,000.* PARK: Easy. TEL: 0703 226420. SER: Valuations; bookbinding; repairs.

Hingstons

11-15 Northam Rd. Open 10-4. CL: Wed. SIZE: Large. *STOCK: General antiques.* TEL: 0703 812301/812637.

R.K Leslie Antiques

23 Northam Rd. Est: 1961. Open 10-4. CL: Wed. p.m. and Sat. *STOCK: Silver, jewellery, curios, china, clocks, furniture.* TEL: 0703 224784. VAT: Stan.

Lodge Road Antiques

71 Lodge Rd. Open 10-5. CL: Wed. SIZE: Large. *STOCK: Antique and fine old furniture for the home.* LOC: Main road between The Avenue and Portswood Rd. PARK: Easy. TEL: 0703 638086. VAT: Stan/Spec.

Southampton continued

L Moody
70 Bedford Pl. (J. and A.H Gubb) Est: 1905. Open 8-5.30. CL: Wed. p.m. SIZE: Large. *STOCK: Furniture, 1650-1910; silver, porcelain, to 1900.* LOC: 1/2 mile north of Civic Centre. PARK: 50yds. in next block. TEL: 0703 333720. SER: Valuations. VAT: Stan/Spec.

Oldfield
34 Northam Rd. (A Downes) Est: 1970. Open 10-5. SIZE: Large. *STOCK: Maps, prints, some books, 16th-20th C, £1-£1,500.* LOC: Near Six Dials. PARK: Easy. TEL: 0703 638916. SER: Valuations; colouring, mounting and framing of maps and prints. FAIRS: Monthly map and print, Bonnington Hotel, London.

Parkhouse and Wyatt Ltd
96 Above Bar. Est: 1794. SIZE: Small. *STOCK: Silver, jewellery.* LOC: City centre. PARK: Meters. TEL: 0703 226653 ext. 25. SER: Valuations; repairs.

Relics Antiques
54 Northam Rd. (R.M Simmonds) Open 9-5. *STOCK: General antiques.* TEL: 0703 221635.

Swaythling Woodcrafts
340 Burgess Rd, Swaythling. (R Brown) Open 9.30-6, Sun. 10-5. SIZE: Medium. *STOCK: Furniture including stripped pine and satinwood, 19th C, £3-£500; clocks, 18th-20th C, £5-£1,000; bric-a-brac.* LOC: Just off M27. PARK: Easy. TEL: 0703 551515; home - same. SER: Valuations; restorations (hand-stripping); pine reproductions to order.

Wellington Antiques
109 St Denys Rd. (G.V Helmer) Open 9-5, Wed. 9-1. *STOCK: Clocks, porcelain, small decorative furniture.* TEL: 0703 553022.

STOCKBRIDGE

Cameron Bucke Antiques
Brookside, High St. (J Corbett) Open 9-5 or by appointment. CL: Mon. *STOCK: Furniture, decorative and unusual objects, 17th C to 1930's.* TEL: 0264 810570.

Lane Antiques
High St. (E.K Lane) Est: 1981. Open 10-5. CL: Wed. SIZE: Small. *STOCK: English and continental porcelain, 18th-19th C, £50-£100; silver and plate, decorative items, glass, small furniture.* PARK: Easy. TEL: 0264 810435; home - same.

Mulberry House Antiques
High St. (R and J Beattie) Est: 1990. Open 9-5. CL: Mon. SIZE: Large. *STOCK: Furniture, clocks and boxes, decorative items including soft furnishings, 18th-19th C, £100-£20,000.* LOC: A272. PARK: Own. TEL: 0264 810357. SER: Valuations; restorations; buys at auction. VAT: Spec.

Stockbridge continued

Stockbridge Antiques
High St. (Mrs P Bradley) Est: 1960. SIZE: Medium. *STOCK: Glass, from 18th C; furniture, 18th-19th C, to £9,000; porcelain, small silver, pictures, rugs.* Not Stocked: Coins, stamps, weapons. LOC: A30. PARK: Easy. TEL: 0264 810829; home - same. VAT: Spec.

Elizabeth Viney BADA
Jacob's House, High St. (Miss E.A Viney, MBE) Est: 1967. Open 9-5. CL: Sun. and some Mon. and Wed., appointment advisable. SIZE: Small. *STOCK: Period furniture - mahogany, walnut, oak and country; treen, brass and copper, especially candlesticks.* Not Stocked: Victoriana. LOC: A30. Opposite old Post Office. PARK: Easy. TEL: 0264 810761. VAT: Stan/Spec.

TITCHFIELD, Nr. Fareham

Gaylords
75 West St. (D.L Hebbard) Est: 1970. Open 9.30-5.30. SIZE: Large. *STOCK: Furniture from 18th C; clocks, shipping goods, £50-£6,000.* LOC: Just off M27. PARK: Easy. TEL: 0329 43402; home - 0329 47134. SER: Valuations; buys at auction (furniture). VAT: Stan/Spec.

Pamela Manley Antique Jewellery
6 and 8 South St. Est: 1965. Open Thurs.-Sat. SIZE: Small. *STOCK: Jewellery, 19th to early 20th C, £5-£500; silver and plate, glass, £10-£500; porcelain, bronzes, boxes.* LOC: 1/4 mile from A27. PARK: Easy. TEL: 0329 42794. SER: Valuations; buys at auction.

Titchfield Antiques Ltd
15 South St. Open 10-7, Sun. 2-6. CL: Mon. *STOCK: Art nouveau, art deco; silver, glass.* PARK: Easy. TEL: 0329 45968. SER: Restorations (as stock).

TWYFORD

Twyford Antiques LAPADA
High St. Open 9.30-5.30. SIZE: Large. *STOCK: Clocks, furniture.* TEL: 0962 713484. SER: Valuations; restorations (clocks).

UPHAM, Nr. Southampton

Susanna Fisher
Spencer. Est: 1971. Open by appointment only. *STOCK: Navigational charts and sailing directions, 16th-19th C.* TEL: 048 96 291. SER: Buys at auction; catalogues available. *Mainly Postal.*

Sharbooks
Farthing Cottages. (Mrs H.D Sharman) Est: 1986. Open by appointment. SIZE: Small. *STOCK: Leather bound books, 18th-20th C, £5-£75.* LOC: 1 mile off B2177. PARK: Easy. TEL: 04896 267; home - same. *Trade Only.*

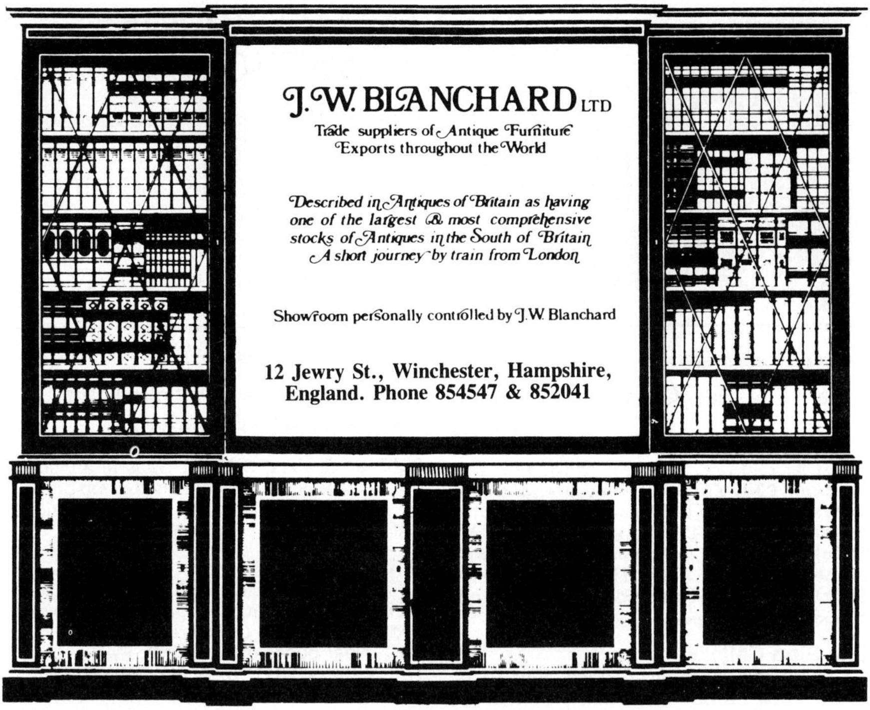
J.W. BLANCHARD LTD
Trade suppliers of Antique Furniture
Exports throughout the World
Described in Antiques of Britain as having one of the largest & most comprehensive stocks of Antiques in the South of Britain
A short journey by train from London
Showroom personally controlled by J.W. Blanchard
12 Jewry St., Winchester, Hampshire, England. Phone 854547 & 852041

WHITCHURCH

Regency House Antiques

Regency House, 14 Church St. (J.W.L Mouat) Resident. Est: 1968. Open 9.30-7. CL: Wed. SIZE: Medium. *STOCK: 17th-19th C, oak, mahogany and pine furniture, longcase clocks; metalwork and bric-a-brac.* LOC: B3400. On Newbury road, coming from Winchester, take first turning on left at crossroads in Whitchurch. PARK: Opposite. TEL: 0256 892149. SER: Valuations; buys at auction. VAT: Spec.

WINCHESTER

Bell Fine Art

67b Parchment St. (K.E. and B Bell) Open 9.30-5.30. *STOCK: Victorian watercolours and oils; prints; all £5-£5,000.* TEL: 0962 860439; home - 0962 733556. SER: Valuations; restorations (oils and watercolours); buys at auction. VAT: Spec.

J.W Blanchard Ltd LAPADA

12 Jewry St. Est: 1940. Open 9-5. SIZE: Large. *STOCK: General antiques, especially breakfront bookcases.* PARK: Own. TEL: 0962 854547/852041; fax - 0962 842572. VAT: Stan/Spec.

Winchester continued

Burns and Graham

4 St. Thomas St. Est: 1971. *STOCK: Furniture, mainly mahogany, 18th to early 19th C, and decorative items.* TEL: 0962 853779. VAT: Stan/Spec.

Peter Daly

at the rear of Thompson Antiques, 20a Jewry St. Open Wed., Fri. and Sat. 10-5. *STOCK: Rare and secondhand books.* TEL: Home - 0962 867732.

Polly de Courcy-Ireland BADA

By appointment only. *STOCK: Early treen, pre-1830 and unusual objects.* TEL: 0962 865716.

Gallery Antiques Ltd

Gallery Corner, St. Thomas St. Open 9-6 or by appointment. SIZE: Large. *STOCK: Furniture especially Regency, 17th to early 19th C, £50-£20,000; paintings, engravings, £50-£10,000; decorative items, £20-£12,000; both 18th-19th C.* LOC: Near public library. TEL: 0962 865039; fax - 0962 867019. VAT: Stan/Spec.

H.M Gilbert

19 The Square. (B.L. and R.C Gilbert) ABA. Open 9-5.30. *STOCK: Antiquarian and secondhand books, £1-£1,000.* TEL: 0962 852832. SER: Valuations; repairs; rebinding.

Winchester continued

Gerald E Marsh (Antique Clocks) BADA

32a The Square. Est: 1947. Open 9.30-5. *STOCK: Clocks, English longcase and bracket, £300-£50,000; French and continental, £200-£10,000; early watches and barometers, £150-£7,000; all 1680-1800.* Not Stocked: Other antiques. LOC: Near Cathedral. PARK: Easy. TEL: 0962 844443. SER: Valuations; restorations (clocks); buys at auction. VAT: Spec.

The Pine Cellars

39 Jewry St. (N Spencer-Brayn) Est: 1970. Open 9-5.30. SIZE: Large and warehouses. *STOCK: Pine and country furniture, 18th-19th C, £10-£2,000; painted furniture, architectural items, panelled rooms.* LOC: One way street, a right turn from top of High St. or St. Georges St., shop 100yds. on right. PARK: Nearby. TEL: 0962 867014/777546. SER: Stripping and export. VAT: Stan/Spec.

Printed Page

2/3 Bridge St. (J. and C Wright) Est: 1977. CL: Mon. SIZE: Small. *STOCK: Antique maps and prints, 17th-19th C, £1-£1,000.* LOC: Bottom of High St., cross over river and shop is on left. PARK: In Water Lane, adjacent to shop. TEL: 0962 854072; fax - 0962 862995. SER: Valuations; picture framing; restorations (prints, oils and watercolours); mount cutting; buys at auction; postal service. VAT: Stan.

Mary Roofe Antiques LAPADA

1 Stonemason's Court, 67 Parchment St. (R. and M Roofe) Est: 1983. Open 10-5, Mon. by appointment. SIZE: Small. *STOCK: 18th and 19th C furniture, boxes, Tunbridgeware, treen, small collectors' items, £5-£2,500.* LOC: 200yds. from High St. and Buttercross. TEL: 0962 840613; home - 0962 862619.

SPCK Bookshops

24 The Square. Open 9-5.30. *STOCK: Books including antiquarian.* TEL: 0962 866617.

Winchester continued

Samuels Spencers Antiques and Decorative Arts Emporium

39 Jewry St. (N Spencer-Brayn) Open 9-5.30. SIZE: 31 dealers. *STOCK: General antiques.* LOC: One way street, right turn from top of High St. or St. George St., shop 100yds. on right. PARK: Nearby. TEL: 0962 867014/777546.

W.G Skipwith

5 Parchment St. Est: 1966. CL: Thurs. p.m. SIZE: Small. *STOCK: Prints, some watercolours and oils, 19th-20th C, from £5; some furniture.* LOC: Near pedestrian precinct. PARK: Easy. TEL: 0962 852911. SER: Valuations; restorations (oils, watercolours, prints). VAT: Stan/Spec.

Thompson Antiques formerly Ships and Sealing Wax

20a Jewry St. Open 9.30-5. SIZE: Large. *STOCK: Victoriana and later furniture, pine, pictures, decorative items, shipping goods.* TEL: 0962 866633; home - 0962 884504.

Todd and Austin Antiques of Winchester

2 Andover Rd. (W Todd and G Austin) Est: 1964. Open 9.30-5. SIZE: Medium. *STOCK: Oriental porcelain, to late 19th C; English and continental glass, 19th to early 20th C; classic French, English and Bohemian paperweights, mid 19th C; boxes including writing cases, tea caddies, knee desks, 18th and 19th C; objets d'art; visiting card cases, snuff boxes, perfume bottles, miniatures painted on ivory, furniture, cabinets, small decorative items, 19th to early 20th C; decorative silver, clocks, Regency to late 19th C.* LOC: 1 minute from Winchester Station. PARK: Easy. TEL: 0962 869824. SER: Valuations.

Webb Fine Arts

6 and 8 Romsey Rd. (D.H Webb) Est: 1955. Open 9-5, Sat. 9-1. SIZE: Large. *STOCK: Oil paintings, Victorian furniture.* LOC: 'The Great Hall' West Gate. PARK: Multi-storey, nearby. TEL: 0962 842273. SER: Valuations; restorations (oil paintings); lining and framing; buys at auction (paintings). VAT: Stan/Spec.

Lanthorns for Wood or Brass.

Thomas Sheraton
'The Cabinet-Maker and Upholsterer's Drawing Book', 1793.
Plate XVII from the Appendix. Horse Dressing Glasses. From ***Pictorial Dictionary of British 18th Century Furniture Design — The Printed Sources*** compiled by Elizabeth White and published by the **Antique Collectors' Club** in 1990. £65.00.

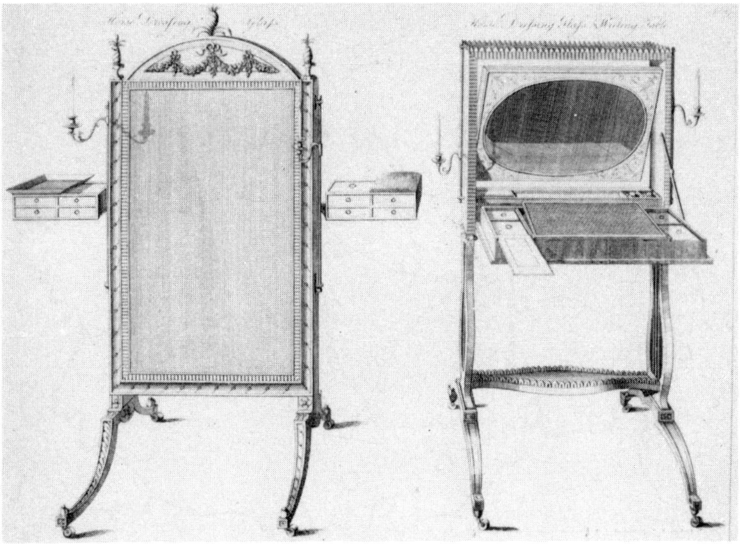

William Ince and John Mayhew
'The Universal System of Household Furniture', 1762.
Lanthorns for Wood or Brass. From ***Pictorial Dictionary of British 18th Century Furniture Design — The Printed Sources*** compiled by Elizabeth White and published by the **Antique Collectors' Club** in 1990. £65.00.

Hereford & Worcester

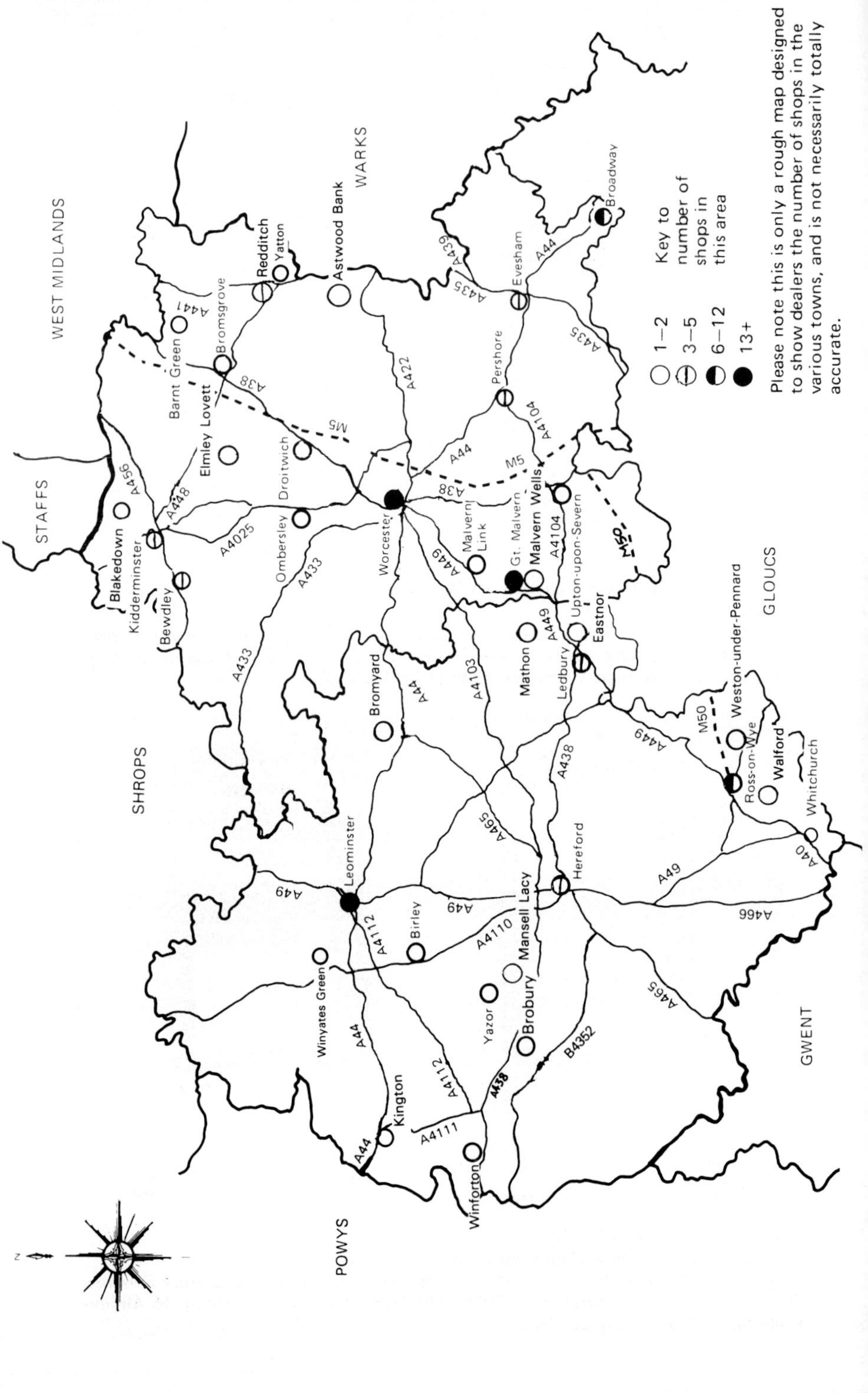

WEST MIDLANDS
STAFFS
WARKS
SHROPS
GLOUCS
GWENT
POWYS
Redditch
Yatton
Astwood Bank
Bromsgrove
Barnt Green
Elmley Lovett
Droitwich
Blakedown
Kidderminster
Bewdley
Ombersley
Worcester
Malvern Link
Gt. Malvern
Malvern Wells
Upton-upon-Severn
Eastnor
Mathon
Ledbury
Pershore
Evesham
Broadway
Bromyard
Leominster
Birley
Mansell Lacy
Hereford
Winyates Green
Yazor
Brobury
Kington
Winforton
Weston-under-Pennard
Ross-on-Wye
Walford
Whitchurch
A441
A38
M5
A456
A448
A4025
A433
A422
A44
A435
A439
A4104
A449
M50
A4103
A438
A465
A49
A40
A466
A4112
A4110
A4111
B4352
Key to number of shops in this area
1–2
3–5
6–12
13+
Please note this is only a rough map designed to show dealers the number of shops in the various towns, and is not necessarily totally accurate.

H.W. KEIL LTD

Telephone
BROADWAY
0386 852408

TUDOR HOUSE
BROADWAY
WORCESTERSHIRE

Member of the British Antique Dealers' Association

17th & 18th Century Furniture · Works of Art

An attractive late 18th century mahogany, 2 drawer writing table with tapered legs and brass castors. Having an excellent depth for practical use. Height 2ft. 4½in. Width 3ft. 6in. Depth 3ft.

Together with a well shaped late 18th century mahogany armchair of the Chippendale period. Having fine proportions.

An excellent mid 18th century oak enclosed dresser with shelves, having interesting cupboards at each side and good detail and warm colour, c.1760. Height 6ft. 5in. Width 8ft. 2in. Depth 1ft. 10in.

Together with a fine range of early pewter and two 17th century single slat back chairs from a set of 6 attractive chairs, of good proportions, c.1690.

Shown from our very varied selection; chosen for their character and colour.

Originators of the well known Keil's dark and light wax polish, available in ½lb and 2lb sizes

In association with H.W. Keil (Cheltenham) Ltd., 129-131 The Promenade, Cheltenham.

ASTWOOD BANK, Nr. Redditch

Bracebridge Gallery
The Old Bakehouse, Langtree Sq.,, 1242 Evesham Rd. CL: Sat. *STOCK: Sporting oil paintings, 20th C, £500-£5,000.* LOC: A441. PARK: Easy. TEL: 0527 893557.

Bracebridge Gallery
'Robindale', 49 The Ridgeway. Est: 1987. Open by appointment only. *STOCK: 18th-20th C oil paintings, and rare signed limited edition prints.* TEL: 0527 893557.

BARNT GREEN, Nr. Birmingham

Barnt Green Antiques
93 Hewell Rd. (N Slater) Est: 1965. Open 9-5.30. SIZE: Medium. *STOCK: Furniture, 17th-19th C, £100-£5,000.* PARK: Easy. TEL: 021 445 4942. SER: Restorations (furniture, clocks, oils); framing; buys at auction. VAT: Stan/Spec.

BEWDLEY

Bewdley Antiques
28 Load St. (P.S Baker) Est: 1984. Open Thurs.-Sat. 10-5, Tues. 10-4. *STOCK: Victorian and Edwardian furniture and effects.* LOC: Opposite St. Ann's Church. PARK: Nearby. TEL: 0299 403731. SER: Valuations; restorations. VAT: Spec.

Clent Books
Rose Cottage, Habberley Rd. (I Simpson) Open by appointment. *STOCK: Antiquarian books, local history, history, topography, £1-£200.* TEL: 0299 401090. SER: Valuations. FAIRS: Waverley Antique and book (Organiser).

Ma's Antiques
89 Welch Gate. (Mrs M Archer) Est: 1987. Open Thurs.-Sat. 10-1 and 2-5. SIZE: Small. *STOCK: Souvenir ware, Victorian; clocks and pocket watches, 1720-1920, £25-£400; brass and copper, £15-£200.* Not Stocked: Jewellery. LOC: Leave A456 (Bewdley by-pass), enter by town centre sign. PARK: Nearby. TEL: 0299 403845. FAIRS: Cirencester.

BIRLEY, Nr. Dilwyn

Gay Walker
Birley Court. Est: 1970. Usually open. Sun., Mon. and Wed. prior telephone call advisable. SIZE: Medium. *STOCK: Mahogany, oak, unstripped pine, treen and unusual items, 17th C to Victorian.* LOC: Large house opposite church, 1/2 mile from the A4110. PARK: Easy. TEL: 056 888 238. SER: Stan/Spec.

BLAKEDOWN, Nr. Kidderminster

Hay Antiques
The Coach House, 20 Birmingham Rd. (J.S Perks) Est: 1984. Open by appointment. SIZE: Small. *STOCK: Furniture, £100-£5,000; watercolours, £200-£300; decorative items, £20-£300; all mainly 19th C.* LOC: A456, village centre. PARK: Easy. TEL: 0562 700791/0831 517178. SER: Restorations (furniture); valuations; buys at auction (19th to early 20th C furniture). FAIRS: British International Birmingham. VAT: Spec.

BROADWAY

Court Antiques
Unit 5, Cotswold Court, The Green. (E Taylor) Open 10-5. *STOCK: General Victorian antiques, especially Staffordshire figures and jugs.* TEL: 0386 853472.

Gavina Ewart BADA
60 High St. (A.J Ewart) Est: 1964. Open 9.30-1 and 2-5.30. SIZE: Medium. *STOCK: Silver cutlery and dining table silver, Sheffield plate; 18th-19th C furniture and porcelain.* PARK: Easy. TEL: 0386 853371; fax - 0386 858948. SER: Valuations; restorations (clocks, furniture and barometers). FAIRS: British International Birmingham; West of England, Bath. VAT: Stan/Spec.

Fenwick and Fisher Antiques
88-90 High St. Est: 1980. Open seven days 10-6. SIZE: Large. *STOCK: Furniture, oak, mahogany and walnut, 17th to early 19th C; samplers, boxes, treen, Tunbridgeware, delft, decorative items.* TEL: 0386 853227; after hours - 0386 853228.

J. and S Gormley Antiques
13A Leamington Rd. Open 10-5, including Sun. CL: Mon. SIZE: Medium. *STOCK: Furniture and related items.* LOC: 400yds. from High St. PARK: Easy. TEL: 0386 853035.

Richard Hagen BADA
Yew Tree House. Open 9.30-5.30, Sun. by appointment. *STOCK: 20th C oils and watercolours.* TEL: 0386 853624/858561; fax - 0386 852172. SER: Valuations; restorations; framing. VAT: Spec.

Hay Loft Gallery
Berry Wormington. (Mrs J.R Pitt and Miss S.A Pitt) Resident. Est: 1984. Open 10.30-5.30 or by appointment. SIZE: Medium. *STOCK: Victorian paintings, £250-£15,000; Victorian watercolours, £250-£3,000.* LOC: From Broadway, 4 miles on B4632 towards Cheltenham, farm on right hand side. PARK: Easy. TEL: 0242 621202. SER: Restorations. VAT: Spec.

Haynes Fine Art BADA
The Bindery Galleries, 69 High St. CADA. Est: 1968. Open 9.30-5.30. SIZE: Large.

Haynes Fine Art continued

STOCK: 16th-20th C British and European paintings, £900-£120,000. **LOC: From Moreton, 50yds. past the Stratford turn off on the left. PARK: Easy. TEL: 0386 852649; home - same. SER: Valuations; restorations; framing. VAT: Spec.**

High Park Antiques
62 High St. Est: 1973. Open Tues.-Sat. 10-5. SIZE: Large. *STOCK: Furniture, early 19th C; silver, china, porcelain, paintings.* LOC: Town centre. PARK: Easy. TEL: 0386 85130; home - 0905 772163. SER: Valuations. VAT: Spec.

Howards of Broadway
27a High St. Open 9.30-5.30 including Sun. SIZE: Small. *STOCK: Jewellery, 1800-1886, £200-£15,000; silver, 1780-1886, £200-£10,000; objects, 1800-1886, £100-£5,000.* PARK: Easy and nearby. TEL: 0386 858924. SER: Valuations; restorations; buys at auction (jewellery and silver). FAIRS: Kenilworth; British International, Birmingham; Barbican; Harrogate. VAT: Stan/Spec.

H.W Keil Ltd BADA
Tudor House, Broad Close, Eadburgha Hall. (V.M Keil) Est: 1925. Open 9-5.30. CL: Thurs. p.m. SIZE: Large. ***STOCK: Walnut, oak and mahogany furniture and works of art, all 17th-18th C.*** **TEL: 0386 852408. VAT: Spec.**

John Noott Fine Paintings LAPADA
14 Cotswold Court, The Green, and 31 High St. CADA. Est: 1972. Open 9-1 and 2-5.30, or by appointment. SIZE: Large. *STOCK: Paintings and watercolours, 19th-20th C, £50-£50,000.* LOC: Centre of village. PARK: Easy. TEL: 0386 852787/858969 (ansaphone 24 hrs.). SER: Valuations; restorations; framing. VAT: Stan/Spec.

Olive Branch Antiques
80 High St. (P. and S Riley) Resident. Est: 1977. Open every day 9.30-6. SIZE: Small. *STOCK: Furniture, to 1900, from £100; clocks, £90-£800; pottery, £5-£150.* LOC: Top end of High St. on A46. PARK: Easy and at rear. TEL: 0386 853440. SER: Restorations (furniture). VAT: Stan/Spec.

Stratford Trevers
The Long Room, 45 High St. Open 9.30-1 and 2.15-5.30, Sun. 2.30-5.30. SIZE: Large. *STOCK: Antiquarian books, maps and prints.* TEL: 0386 853668. SER: Valuations; restorations; framing. VAT: Stan.

BROBURY, Nr. Hay-on-Wye

Brobury House Gallery
(E Okarma) Resident. Est: 1972. Open 9-4.30, 9-4 in winter. *STOCK: Old prints, 17th-20th C; watercolours, 19th-20th C.* PARK: Easy. TEL: 09817 229. SER: Restorations (framing). VAT: Stan.

BROMSGROVE

Strand Antiques
22 The Strand. (D.G Croucher) Est: 1977. Open 9-6. *STOCK: General antiques.* TEL: 0527 72686.

BROMYARD

Arrowsmiths of Bromyard
42-46 Broad St. (P.D Arrowsmith) Open 9.30-1 and 2-5.30, Tues. 9.30-1. *STOCK: Art jewellery and small silver.* TEL: 0885 482478.

Lennox Antiques
3 Broad St. (W.A. and E.S Jones) Est: 1981. Open 10.30-5. CL: Mon., Tues. and Wed. SIZE: Small. *STOCK: Pottery and porcelain, 19th-20th C, £5-£25; glass, £1-£25; small furniture, £10-£200.* LOC: Town centre. PARK: Easy. TEL: 0885 483432; home - 0684 575684. SER: Restorations (pottery, porcelain and cloisonné).

DROITWICH

Grant Fine Art
9A Victoria Sq. Est: 1976. Open by appointment only. SIZE: Small. *STOCK: Golfiana, books, prints, pictures, clubs, £5-£1,000.* TEL: 0905 778155.

Richmond, George (1809-1896)
Toads. Pen and brown ink and watercolour, 10⅜in. x 6¾in. SPINK & SON
From ***The Dictionary of British Watercolour Artists up to 1920,*** Volume III, by H.L. Mallalieu, published by the **Antique Collectors' Club** in 1990. £35.00.

Droitwich continued

H. and B Wolf Antiques Ltd
128 Worcester Rd. (H.G. and B.J Wolf) Est: 1948. Open Fri. and Sat. 9.30-5.30, other days by appointment. SIZE: Medium. *STOCK: Porcelain, pottery, from 1750, £15-£1,500; glass from 1725; general antiques.* Not Stocked: Coins, stamps, medals. LOC: A38. PARK: Easy. TEL: 0905 772320; home - same. VAT: Stan/Spec.

EASTNOR, Nr. Ledbury

Lloyds of Eastnor
Somer Arms. (Mrs P.K Lloyd) Open 9-7 including Sun. SIZE: Large. *STOCK: General antiques.* LOC: A438. TEL: 0531 4878. SER: Shipping.

ELMLEY LOVETT, Nr. Droitwich

Elmley Heritage
Stone House. (J Kramer) Est: 1988. Open by appointment. SIZE: Medium. *STOCK: Fireplaces, 18th-19th C, £300-£800; bathroom fittings, Victorian and Edwardian, £100-£300; architectural items.* LOC: Telephone for directions. PARK: Easy. TEL: 029 923 284; home - same. VAT: Stan.

EVESHAM

Magpie Jewellers and Antiques **LAPADA**
2 Port St, and 61 High St. (R.J. and E.R Bunn) Est: 1975. Open 9.30-5.30. SIZE: Large. *STOCK: Silver, jewellery, furniture and general antiques.* TEL: 0386 41631 any time.

Port Street Antiques
18 Port St. (J and P Nock) Est: 1977. Open 10-5, Wed. 10-1, Fri. 10-3, Sun. by appointment. SIZE: Medium. *STOCK: Pine including reproduction, £75-£500; mahogany, late 19th C, £100-£800; Victorian oak and satinwood, £50-£500.* PARK: Nearby. TEL: 0386 442023; home - 0386 840281. SER: Pine finishing; buys at auction.

Yesterday
79 Port St. (B Jewell) Est: 1981. Open 10.30-5.30, Sat. 9.30-5.30. SIZE: Medium. *STOCK: Pre-1960 clothes and costume jewellery, £5-£50; pottery, 19th-20th C, £10-£50.* LOC: Opposite Swan Inn. PARK: At rear. TEL: 0386 48068; home - same. SER: Valuations.

GREAT MALVERN

Aladdin's Cave
(Mrs A McConnell) Open by appointment. *STOCK: Porcelain, jewellery, silver, small furniture.* TEL: 0684 561746.

Arcadia Antiques
83a and 83c Church St. Est: 1988. Open 10-1 and 2-5. SIZE: Medium. *STOCK: General antiques including furniture, china and glass, pictures, unusual decorative items, 18th to early 20th C, £5-£500.* LOC: Down passageway, off Church St., opposite priory gates. PARK: Nearby. TEL: 0684 572897; home - 0684 560170.

Britannia Restorations
(S.L Malson) Open by appointment. SIZE: Warehouse. *STOCK: Pine, oak and mahogany furniture especially farmhouse and Windsor chairs; metalwork and architectural items.* TEL: 0684 63427 or 0271 882887. SER: Restorations.

Carlton Antiques
43 Worcester Rd. (T Guiver) Open 10-5. *STOCK: Edwardian and Victorian furniture.* TEL: 0684 573092. SER: Valuations.

Church Walk Antiques
5 Church Walk. (C Carmichael) Open 10.30-5. *STOCK: Jewellery, small silver, furniture, decorative items, porcelain and lighting.* TEL: 0684 565192.

Great Malvern continued

Joan Coates of Malvern
26 St. Ann's Rd. Resident. Est: 1969. Open Thurs. and Fri. 10-1 and 2.30-5.30, Sat. 10-1. SIZE: Small. *STOCK: Silver, £5-£250; small furniture, £20-£800; both 18th-20th C; small items.* LOC: From Worcester take A449, in town Foley Arms Hotel on left-hand side, take first right. PARK: Easy. TEL: 0684 575509.

Gray's Antiques of Worcester
Units 24-27, Blackmoore Industrial Estate, Hanley Swan. (D. and M Gray) Open 9-5, weekends and other times by appointment. *STOCK: General antiques and shipping goods.* TEL: 0684 560038; home - 0905 425684; fax - 0684 560038. SER: Containers; storage; export.

Great Malvern Antiques
6 Abbey Rd. (R.J Rice and and L Sutton) Est: 1966. Open 9.30-5.30 or by appointment. CL: Sat. *STOCK: Decorative antiques, furniture, paintings.* LOC: 150yds. from Winter Gardens. PARK: Easy. TEL: 0684 575490; home - same. FAIRS: Olympia; Little Chelsea. VAT: Stan/Spec.

Lismore Gallery
3 Edith Walk. (J. and H Simmonds) Open 10-6. CL: Wed. *STOCK: Watercolours, 19th to early 20th C; decorative Victorian items.* TEL: 0684 568610.

Malvern Arts
43 Worcester Rd. (S.A Conein-Veber) Est: 1988. Open 10-5. SIZE: Small. *STOCK: Watercolours, Victorian and Edwardian, £50-£500; oil paintings, 19th-20th C; £80-£1,000+.* LOC: Town centre. PARK: Easy. TEL: 0684 575889. VAT: Stan/Spec.

Malvern Bookshop
7 Abbey Rd. (J.P. and A.M Gibbs) Est: 1955. Open 9.15-5. CL: Wed. p.m. SIZE: Medium. *STOCK: Antiquarian, secondhand books and remainders.* LOC: Next to Malvern G.P.O. PARK: Easy. TEL: 0684 575915. SER: Valuations; binding; search; buys at auction.

Great Malvern continued

Malvern Studios
56 Cowleigh Rd. (L.M Hall) BAFRA. Open 9-5.15, Fri. and Sat. 9-4.45. *STOCK: Period furniture and general furnishings, Edwardian painted and inlaid furniture.* TEL: 0684 574913. SER: Restorations; woodcarving; polishing; interior design. VAT: Stan/Spec.

Miscellany Antiques
18 and 20 Cowleigh Rd. (R.S. and E.A Hunaban) Resident. Est: 1974. Open 9.30-1 and 2-5.30, trade any time. CL: Sat. and Wed. p.m. SIZE: Medium. *STOCK: Walnut, mahogany, 19th C, £50-£5,000; Victorian, Edwardian and some period furniture; porcelain, silver and plate, jewellery, shipping goods.* LOC: B4219 to Bromyard. PARK: Easy. TEL: 0684 566671. SER: Valuations. VAT: Stan/Spec.

St. James Antiques
193 West Malvern Rd. (H Van Wyngaarden) Open 10-5. *STOCK: Continental and English furniture, lighting and clocks.* PARK: Easy. TEL: 0684 563404; home - 0684 568674. VAT: Stan/Spec.

Treasures of Childhood Past
43 Wyche Rd. (C Tarplett) Est: 1988. Open 10-5, Sat. 11-4. CL: Mon. and Wed. *STOCK: Dolls, doll's house miniatures, teddy bears, children's books, puzzles and related items.* LOC: Opposite car park, 1 mile from town centre. PARK: Easy. TEL: 0684 560010. SER: Doll and teddy bear hospital.

Whitmore
Teynham Lodge, Chase Rd, Upper Colwall. *STOCK: British and foreign coins, 1700-1950, £1-£500; trade tokens, 1650-1900, £1-£200; commemorative medallions, 1600-1950, £1-£200.* TEL: 0684 40651. *Postal Only.*

HEREFORD

I. and J.L Brown Ltd
58-59 Commercial Rd. Open 8-5.30 but appointment advisable. SIZE: Large. *STOCK: Matched sets of period country chairs, £500-£4,000; country and general furniture, including farmhouse tables, decorative items and brass.* LOC: A465, 300 metres from railway station, 100 metres from city ring road. PARK: On premises. TEL: 0432 58895; fax - 0432 275338; home - 0432 70 674. SER: Restorations; re-rushing chairs; container packing. VAT: Stan/Spec.

Great Brampton House Antiques Ltd LAPADA
Great Brampton House, Madley. (P.B Howell) Est: 1969. Open 9-5 or by appointment. SIZE: Large. *STOCK: English and French furniture and fine art.* TEL: 0981 250244; fax - 0981 251333.

Hereford Antique Centre
128 Widemarsh St. (Mrs L F Mitchell) Est: 1991. Open 9-5, Sun. 1-5. SIZE: 40 dealers. *STOCK: General antiques and collectables, £5-£1,000.* PARK: Easy. TEL: 0432 266242. SER: Restorations. VAT: Stan.

Pierpoint Gallery
10 Church St. (A.G. and H.L Beaver) Est: 1969. Open 9.30-5. CL: Thurs. SIZE: Medium. *STOCK: Antiquarian books, maps, prints, 1550-1850, £5-£200.* Not Stocked: Modern reprints and reproductions. LOC: Off Cathedral Precinct. PARK: Nearby. TEL: 0432 267002. VAT: Stan.

G.E Richards and Son Antiques
57 Blueschool St. Est: 1969. Open 9-5. SIZE: Medium. *STOCK: General antiques, £2-£2,000.* LOC: On ring road by traffic signals. PARK: Nearby, but private loading bay at rear. TEL: 0432 267840; home - 0432 355278 /268827. VAT: Stan/Spec.

Warings of Hereford Antiques
43 St. Owen St. (R Waring) Open 9-6 including Sun. *STOCK: Fine 19th C furniture; gold and silver.* TEL: 0432 276241.

KIDDERMINSTER

Antique Centre
11 Towers Buildings, Blackwell St. Est: 1989. Open 10-5. CL: Wed. SIZE: Large - up to 60 dealers. *STOCK: Mainly smalls, jewellery, collectables and toys.* LOC: Town centre, almost opposite multi-storey car park. PARK: Easy. TEL: 0562 829000.

B.B.M. Jewellery and Antiques
8 and 9 Lion St. (W.V. and A Crook) Est: 1977. Open 10-5. CL: Tues. SIZE: Medium. *STOCK: Jewellery, 19th C, £50-£3,000; coins, £5-£1,000; general antiques, £5-£500.* LOC: Adjacent Youth

B.B.M. Jewellery and Antiques continued

Centre, off ring road. PARK: Easy. TEL: 0562 744118. SER: Valuations; restorations (jewellery, porcelain, silver). VAT: Stan/Spec.

Gorst Hall Restoration
Gorst Hall, Barnetts Lane. (J R Callwood) Est: 1984. Open by appointment. SIZE: Medium. *STOCK: English furniture, 18th-19th C, £500-£1,000.* LOC: Off Kidderminster/Bromsgrove road, just off Comberton rd. PARK: Own. TEL: 0562 515880; home -same; mobile - 0831 634602. SER: Valuations; restorations (French polishing, veneering, carving, wood turning, repairs); buys at auction (furniture). VAT: Stan/Spec.

Hi-Felicity
1 Comberton Rd. (J Workman) Open 9-5.30. *STOCK: Antique pine.* TEL: 0562 742549.

Old Curiosity Antiques
11 Towers Buildings, Blackwell St. Est: 1983. Open 10-5. CL: Wed. SIZE: Medium. *STOCK: Smalls, 18th C to 1930's, £5-£500; jewellery, £20-£1,500.* LOC: Town centre, opposite multi-storey car park. PARK: Easy. TEL: 0562 742859.

The Rea Gallery
Lower St, Cleobury Mortimer. (A James-Priday) Open 10-4.30. CL: Thurs. *STOCK: General antiques, jewellery and shipping goods.* TEL: 0299 271099. SER: Restorations; upholstery; shipping; picture framing.

KINGTON

Page Galleries
29 High St. (H Anderson) Open 9.30-5.30. *STOCK: Porcelain, silver, furniture, pictures.* LOC: A44 town centre. PARK: Nearby. TEL: 0544 230551.

LEDBURY

John Nash Antiques and Interiors
1st Floor, Tudor House, 17c High St. (J Nash and L Calleja) Est: 1972. Open 10-5.30, Sun. by appointment. CL: Wed. SIZE: Medium. *STOCK: Mahogany, oak and walnut furniture, 18th-19th C, £300-£5,000; decorative items, fabrics and wallpapers.* TEL: 0531 5714; home - 0684 40432. SER: Valuations; restorations; buys at auction (furniture, silver). VAT: Stan/Spec.

Old George Antiques
Tudor House, 17c High St. (Mrs W Wild and J.G.R Tyndall) CADA. Open 10-5.30, Sat. 10-5, Wed., Sun. and other times by appointment. SIZE: Medium. *STOCK: Furniture, pre-1830, to £2,000; decorative items.* LOC: Tilley's Alley, off High St., opposite Lloyds Bank. PARK: Easy. TEL: 0531 5299 or 0666 503405. SER: Valuations; restorations; buys at auction. FAIRS: Snape; Olympia. VAT: Stan/Spec.

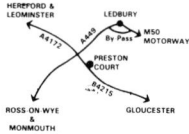

Ledbury continued

Serendipity
The Tythings, Preston Court. (Mrs R Ford) Open 9.30-5 or by appointment. *STOCK: General antiques, 17th-19th C.* LOC: Take A449 from Ledbury, turn left on B4215, premises 500yds. on left behind half-timbered house. TEL: 053184 380/245. SER: Restorations (furniture); buys at auction. FAIRS: Kensington; British International, Birmingham; Olympia. VAT: Stan/Spec.

York House of Ledbury
155 The Homend. Open 9.30-1 and 2-5.30. CL: Wed. *STOCK: Georgian, Victorian and Edwardian furniture, silver plate, copper, brass and decorative items.* LOC: Outskirts of town on Bromyard Rd. PARK: Opposite. TEL: 0531 4687.

LEOMINSTER

Barometer Shop
New St. (R Cookson) Est: 1965. Open 9-5 or by appointment. *STOCK: Barometers, barographs, clocks, scientific instruments.* LOC: Corner of A49 and Broad St. PARK: Easy. TEL: 0568 3652 and 0272 272565. SER: Valuations; restorations; barometers and clock spares.

Leominster continued

Chapman Antiques LAPADA
2 Bridge St. (R Chapman) Est: 1983. Open 9.30-5.30, or by appointment. SIZE: Medium. *STOCK: Furniture including mahogany and dining; clocks including longcase, £100-£15,000.* PARK: Easy. TEL: 0568 5803; mobile - 0836 566146. SER: Valuations; restorations; buys at auction. VAT: Stan/Spec.

Coltsfoot Gallery
Hatfield. (E Collins) Est: 1971. SIZE: Medium. *STOCK: Sporting and wildlife watercolours and prints, £20-£2,000.* PARK: Easy. TEL: 056 882 277; home - same. SER: Restorations (works of art on paper).

Geoffrey Crofts Ltd
10 South St. Est: 1973. Open 9-5.30, Sat. 10-4. SIZE: Medium. *STOCK: Country furniture including pine, 18th-19th C, £100-£3,000; mahogany, Georgian and Victorian, £100-£2,000; decorative items, porcelain and pottery, £5-£500.* LOC: 200yds. from town centre. PARK: Easy. TEL: 0568 611580; home - 0568 5706. SER: Valuations; restorations; buys at auction. VAT: Stan/Spec.

P. and S.N Eddy
22 Etnam St. Resident. Est: 1951. Open 9-6. CL: Sun. except by appointment. SIZE: Small. *STOCK: General antiques, including oak and mahogany furniture, saltglaze stoneware and blue and white pottery, 18th and 19th C; early metalware, treen and bygones.* Not Stocked: Arms, armour, coins, medals, jewellery. LOC: A44. PARK: Easy. TEL: 0568 2813; home - same.

Farmers Gallery
28 Broad St. *STOCK: 18th-19th C paintings, prints, maps, needlework and decorative items.* LOC: Town centre. PARK: Easy. TEL: 0568 611413.

Jeffery Hammond Antiques LAPADA
'Shaftesbury House', 38 Broad St. (J. and E Hammond) Resident. Est: 1970. Open 9-6, Sun. by appointment. SIZE: Medium. *STOCK: Furniture, 1640-1840.* LOC: Town centre. PARK: Easy. TEL: 0568 614876. SER: Valuations; buys at auction (furniture). VAT: Stan/Spec.

Hubbard Antiques BADA
The Golden Lion, Bridge St. (D., T. and P Saunders) Resident. Open 9-5, otherwise ring door bell. *STOCK: 16th-18th C oak furniture; early metalware, period walnut, country furniture, treen, jewellery, patchwork quilts.* LOC: North side of town, junction of A49 and B4361. PARK: Own. TEL: 0568 4362.

Jennings of Leominster
30 Bridge St. (J.R Jennings) Est: 1970. Open 9.30-6. SIZE: Medium. *STOCK: Furniture, 17th-18th C, £500-£3,000; clocks, £200-£2,000;*

Jennings of Leominster continued

paintings, £50-£1,000; both 18th-19th C. PARK: Easy. TEL: 0568 2946; home - same. SER: Valuations; restorations (furniture restoration and gilding, clocks). VAT: Spec.

La Barre Ltd
The Place, 116 South St. Est: 1964. Open 8.30-5.30, Sat. 10-4, other times by appointment. SIZE: Large. *STOCK: Pine, French fruitwood, mahogany, oak and painted furniture, decorative items, 18th-20th C, £50-£5,000.* LOC: On A49 towards Hereford, opp. Cottage Hospital. PARK: Easy. TEL: 0568 4315; home - 0568 2434 or 0432 58432. VAT: Stan/Spec.

Leominster Antiques LAPADA
87 Etnam St. (K. and J Watherington) Resident. Open 9-6, other times by appointment or ring bell. SIZE: Large. *STOCK: Furniture, mainly mahogany, 18th-19th C; decorative items, paintings.* LOC: A44 Worcester Rd. PARK: Easy. TEL: 0568 3217. VAT: Stan/Spec.

Leominster Antiques Market
14 Broad St. Open 10-5. SIZE: 3 floors of showrooms. *STOCK: Antiques including country and painted furniture, mahogany, oak, treen, Staffordshire figures, pottery, porcelain, textiles, metalware, pictures, jewellery and clocks.* TEL: 0568 2189. SER: Restorations (furniture). Below are listed the dealers.

Bradshaw and Smith
Ken Bruce
Mrs P Cox
Cupboard Love
(J Bloomfield)
Mrs O Dyke
Eardisley Antiques
(W E Kinch)
G Hamilton
Barbara Ind
M and J Phillipson
Property Welfare
(D Buchanan)
Don Watson
Jeff Wilson and J Grange

Mayfield Antiques
13 South St. (C.J Scott-Mayfield) Open 9.30-1.30 and 2.30-5.30, Mon. by appointment. *STOCK: Furniture, paintings and decorative items.* TEL: 0568 2127. SER: Interior design; restoration; upholstery; valuations.

Michael Stewart Antiques
Lion Yard, 15 Broad St. Est: 1972. Open daily, Sun. by appointment. *STOCK: Period and Victorian pine for export, country furniture, some oak and mahogany.* TEL: 0568 4946; evenings - 0568 2197.

MALVERN LINK

Kimber and Son
6 Lower Howsell Rd. Est: 1956. Open 9-1 and 2-5, Sat. 9-12.30. *STOCK: Furniture, 18th-19th C; general antiques. Warehouse for trade.* TEL: 0684 574339; home - 0684 572000. SER: Restorations. VAT: Stan/Spec.

MALVERN WELLS

Gandolfi House Interiors
211-213 Wells Rd. (P. and R Weller) Open 10-5.30 or by appointment. CL: Mon. *STOCK: Paintings, mainly watercolours, 19th-20th C; country furniture and general small items.* TEL: 0684 569747.

MANSELL LACY

Bernard Gay
The School House. Open 9-6 including Sun., prior telephone call advisable. *STOCK: Pictures and drawings; small fine objects de vertu.* TEL: 098122 269.

MATHON, Nr. Malvern

Mathon Gallery
Mathon Court, (Phipps and Co. Ltd.). Est: 1980. Open 9.30-5.30 by appointment including Sun. SIZE: Medium. *STOCK: British oils, watercolours and sculpture, 19th-20th C, £100-£30,000.* LOC: Approx. 1 mile west of Malvern, off B4232. TEL: 0684 892242 and 071 352 5381. SER: Valuations; buys at auction (British paintings and sculpture). VAT: Spec.

OMBERSLEY, Nr. Droitwich

Stables Antiques
Coach Yard, Crown and Sandys Hotel. (B. and A Pearce) Est: 1974. Open Tues., Wed. and Sat. 10-5, any time by appointment. SIZE: Medium. *STOCK: Furniture, 17th-19th C, £100-£7,000; china and pottery, 18th-19th C, £10-£1,000; bygones and early metalwares.* LOC: 6 miles north of Worcester on A449. PARK: Easy. TEL: 0905 620353. SER: Valuations; restorations (china, paintings); buys at auction. VAT: Stan/Spec.

PERSHORE

Hansen Chard Antiques
126 High St. (P.W Ridler, MBHI) Est: 1983. Open 10-5, Thurs, 10-1, but appointment advisable. CL: Mon. SIZE: Large. *STOCK: Clocks, pre-1940; longcase clocks, pre-1850, £10-£2,000; barometers £50-£1,000.* LOC: On A44. PARK: Easy. TEL: 0386 553423; home - same. SER: Valuations; restorations (as stock); buys at auction (as stock). VAT: Spec.

Pershore continued

"The Look In" Antiques

134b High St. Est: 1970. Open 10-5 Mon. and Thurs. 12-5, other times by appointment. *STOCK: Furniture, bric-a-brac, china, clocks, prints, watercolours, oils, silver, plate, jewellery, glass, metalware, £3-£800.* TEL: 0386 556776; home - 038 674 588.

Penoyre Antiques

9 and 11 Bridge St. Est: 1969. Open 9.30-1 and 2-5.30, Sat. 9.30-5.30, other times by appointment. CL: Thurs. SIZE: Medium. *STOCK: 18th-19th C mahogany furniture especially dining; chandeliers, mirrors, paintings, framed prints and engravings, £12-£20,000.* PARK: Easy (in main square or opposite). TEL: 0386 553522. VAT: Stan/Spec.

S.W. Antiques

Abbey Showrooms, Newlands. (R.J Whiteside) Est: 1978. Open 9-5, Sun. 2-4.30. SIZE: Large. *STOCK: 19th-20th C furniture including stripped pine, to £3,000.* Not Stocked: Jewellery, small items. LOC: 2 mins. from Abbey. PARK: Own. TEL: 0386 555580; fax - 0386 556205. VAT: Stan/Spec.

Pershore continued

Times Past

84 High St. (J Pollitt) Est: 1977. Open 10-1 and 2-5 (prior telephone call advisable) and by appointment. CL: Wed. and Thur. SIZE: Small. *STOCK: Blue and white transferware pottery, pre-1840; needlework tools and accessories; glass, treen, small silver, jewellery and collectors' items, 1680-1930.* LOC: A44, opposite Pershore Garage. PARK: Easy, 100yds. TEL: 0386 554258; home - same. SER: Valuations. VAT: Stan/Spec.

REDDITCH

The Galleries Antiques Centre

Pickwicks, 503 Evesham Rd, Crabbs Cross. Open 9.30-5, incl. Sun. SIZE: 14 units. *STOCK: A wide range of antiques.* TEL: 0527 550568.

Anne Lemon

Open by appointment. *STOCK: Decorative antiques especially ceramics and glass, 19th-20th C.* TEL: 0527 401777. FAIRS: Sandown, Newark, Ardingly and Alexander Palace.

Aldridge, Frederick James (1850-1933). Making Port. Signed with initials and dated 83, watercolour, 14in. x 10in. Although repetitive and limited, Aldridge's formuli can be well done. SIMON CARTER
From ***The Dictionary of British Watercolour Artists up to 1920,*** Volume III, by H.L. Mallalieu, published by the **Antique Collectors' Club** in 1990. £35.00.

Redditch continued

Pickwicks
503 Evesham Rd, Crabbs Cross. Open 9.30-5, incl. Sun. *STOCK: General antiques.* TEL: 0527 550568.

ROSS-ON-WYE

Baileys Architectural Antiques
The Engine Shed, Ashburton Industrial Estate. (M. and S Bailey) Est: 1978. Open 9-5. SIZE: Large. *STOCK: Architectural antiques including stained and etched glass, cast grates, fireplaces, bathroom fittings, street and garden furniture, doors, pews, panelling, bars, overmantels, counters, beds, tiles, brackets, columns, 18th-19th C.* LOC: Gloucester side of town, just off A40. TEL: 0989 63015; fax - 0989 768172.

Fritz Fryer Antique Lighting LAPADA
12 Brookend St. (F Fryer and J Graham) Est: 1981. Open 9.30-5.30, Sun. by appointment. SIZE: Large. *STOCK: Decorative lighting, original shades, glass chandeliers, Georgian to art deco.* TEL: 0989 67416. SER: Restorations (metalware and glass chandeliers); lighting scheme design. FAIRS: Olympia; N.E.C., Birmingham.

Robert Green Antiques LAPADA
12 Brookend St. Open 10-5. *STOCK: Mainly 18th-19th C mahogany and decorative furniture, especially dining tables and chairs.* TEL: 0989 67504. SER: Valuations.

Robin Lloyd Antiques
23/24 Brookend St. Est: 1970. Open 10-5.30 or any time by appointment. SIZE: Large. *STOCK: 17th-19th C oak and country furniture including dressers and Windsor chairs, French armoires, farmhouse tables, candlesticks, metalware, sporting memorabilia, unusual items, golf clubs, Delft, £5-£5,000.* LOC: 100yds. downhill from Market Hall. PARK: Nearby. TEL: 0989 62123. VAT: Stan/Spec.

Old Pine Shop
Gloucester Rd. (B Miller) Est: 1976. Open 10-5.30 or by appointment. SIZE: Large. *STOCK: Pine furniture, especially dressers, chests, tables, desks, blanket boxes, wardrobes, linen presses, 1830-1930; Victorian brass, iron and wooden bedsteads.* LOC: Last shop on main Gloucester road. PARK: Easy and Cantilupe Rd. TEL: 0989 64738; home - 0989 65131. SER: Restorations (pine stripping).

Palma Court Antique Arcade
27 Brookend St. (R.G Di Palma) Open 10-5. SIZE: 9 shops. *STOCK: General antiques.* TEL: 0989 62752/65949.

Ross-on-Wye continued

Relics
19 High St. (Mr and Mrs I Power) Open 10-5. *STOCK: Jewellery, linen, silver, clocks, smalls and furniture.* TEL: 0989 64539. SER: Restorations and repairs (clocks and jewellery).

Ross Old Book and Print Shop
51 and 52 High St. Open 10-1 and 2-5. *STOCK: Antiquarian and secondhand books, prints and maps.* TEL: 0989 67458.

Trecilla Antiques
36 High St. (Lt. Col. and Mrs I.G Mathews) Est: 1969. Open 9.30-5. CL: Sun. (except by appointment) and Wed. p.m. SIZE: Large. *STOCK: Furniture, longcase clocks, all periods; arms and armour, £50-£7,500; silver, china, glass, metalware, £10-£3,000; prints, maps, militaria and bygones, £1-£500.* LOC: A40. PARK: Private. TEL: 0989 63010; home - 0981 540274. SER: Valuations; restorations; buys at auction. VAT: Stan/Spec.

UPTON-UPON-SEVERN

The Highway Gallery
40 Old St. (J Daniell) Est: 1969. Open 10.30-5, but appointment advisable. CL: Thurs. and Mon. SIZE: Small. *STOCK: Oils, watercolours, 19th-20th C, £100-£10,000.* Not Stocked: Prints. LOC: 100yds. from crossroads towards Malvern. PARK: Easy. TEL: 068 46 2645; home - 068 46 2909. SER: Valuations; restorations (reline and clean); buys at auction (pictures). VAT: Spec.

WALFORD, Nr. Ross-on-Wye

Robson Antiques
Little Howle Farm, Howle Hill. (J Robson) Est: 1982. Open daily including Sun. SIZE: Large. *STOCK: Furniture, from 19th C, £100-£500+.* PARK: Easy. TEL: 0989 768128; home - same. SER: Valuations; buys at auction.

WESTON-UNDER-PENYARD, Nr. Ross-on-Wye

Dolls of Yesterday
Hown Hall. Open by appointment. *STOCK: Dolls, 18th-19th C, from £250.* PARK: Own. TEL: 0989 81271. SER: Valuations. FAIRS: London.

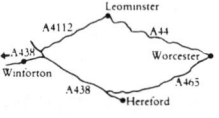

WHITCHURCH, Nr. Ross-on-Wye

Olivers of Whitchurch
Farthing Corner, The Square. (A. and M Oliver) Est: 1983. Open 10-5.30 including Sun. SIZE: Large. *STOCK: Victorian brass and cast-iron beds, fireplaces and architectural; brass and copper, advertising, sporting, musical and unusual collectors items; furniture.* LOC: Village centre, near clock tower. PARK: Easy. TEL: 0600 890662; home - same. SER: Buys at auction.

WINFORTON, Nr. Hereford

Gerald and Vera Taylor
Winforton Court. Est: 1965. Open by appointment. SIZE: Medium. *STOCK: Fully restored longcase clocks, 18th-early 19th C, furniture, mainly mahogany, pre-1840.* LOC: Between Hereford and Brecon on A438. PARK: Easy. TEL: 054 46 226. SER: Valuations; buys at auction. VAT: Stan/Spec.

WINYATES GREEN, Nr. Redditch

Lower House Fine Antiques
Lower House, Far Moor Lane. (Mrs J.B Hudson) Est: 1987. Usually open but prior appointment advisable. SIZE: Small. *STOCK: Furniture, 17th to early 20th C, £100-£4,000; silver and plate,*

Lower House Fine Antiques continued

18th to early 20th C, £10-£1,000; oil lamps, 19th C, £50-£500. Not Stocked: Pine furniture. LOC: 3 miles due east Redditch town centre and 1/2 mile from Coventry Highway island, close to A435. PARK: Own. TEL: 0527 25117; home - same. SER: Valuations; restorations.

WORCESTER

Alma Street Warehouse
Alma St. (D. and G Venn) Open 9.30-1 and 2-4, Sat. 10-3 or by appointment. CL: Mon. p.m. and Thurs. *STOCK: General antiques, stripped pine, satin walnut.* LOC: Off Droitwich Rd. PARK: Easy. TEL: 0905 27493; home - 0905 24943.

Antique Map and Print Gallery
61 Sidbury. (M Nichols) Open 9-5.30. *STOCK: Antiquarian maps, prints and books.* TEL: 0905 612926.

Antique Warehouse
Rear of 74 Droitwich Rd, Barbourne. (D Venn) Open 9-5, Sat. 10-3. *STOCK: General antiques including stripped pine.* TEL: 0905 27493. SER: Stripping pine and walnut.

Antiques and Curios
50 Upper Tything. Open 9.30-5. SIZE: 6 dealers. *STOCK: General antiques.* TEL: 0905 25412.

Barn Antiques
Paynes Heath Farm, Martley Rd, Lower Broadheath. (C.R Fitz-Hugh) Est: 1986. Open 11-5.30, including Sun. CL: Mon., Wed. and Thur. SIZE: Medium. *STOCK: Furniture and clocks, £10-£1,000; collectors' items, £1-£200; all 18th-20th C.* LOC: B4204, 1/2 mile from A443. PARK: Easy. TEL: 0905 355997; home - same. SER: Restorations (clocks and furniture).

Andrew Boyle (Booksellers) Ltd
21 Friar St. Est: 1928. Cl: Thurs. and Sat. Appointment advisable. *STOCK: Antiquarian and secondhand books.* TEL: 0905 611700. SER: Buys at auction.

Bygones by the Cathedral LAPADA
Cathedral Sq. (G Bullock) FGA. Est: 1946. Open 9.30-1 and 2-5.30. *STOCK: Furniture, 17th-19th C; silver, Sheffield plate, jewellery, paintings, glass, English and continental pottery and porcelain, especially Royal Worcester.* LOC: Adjacent main entrance to Cathedral. TEL: 0905 25388.

Bygones (Worcester) LAPADA
55 Sidbury. (G.D Bullock) FGA. Est: 1946. Open 9.30-1 and 2-5.30. *STOCK: Furniture, 17th-19th C; silver, Sheffield plate, jewellery, paintings, glass, English and continental porcelain; pottery, especially Royal Worcester.* LOC: Opposite the public car park in Sidbury and adjacent to the City Walls road junction. TEL: 0905 23132. VAT: Stan/Spec.

Worcester continued

Clive's Curios
48 The Tything. (C Laurence) Open 9-5.30. *STOCK: Furniture especially pine.* TEL: 0905 611323.

Cottage Antiques
17 Friar St. (S.M Wall) Open 9.30-5.30. CL: Thurs. *STOCK: Arms, militaria, country furniture, early lighting, decorative items.* TEL: 0905 24574.

Friars Gate Antiques
19 Friar St. (S.M Cronin) Open 10.30-5. *STOCK: Paintings, small antiques, objets d'art and collectors' items.* TEL: 0905 24192.

Heirlooms
46 Upper Tything. (W MacMillan, G Tarran and A Rumford) Open 9.30-4.30. *STOCK: General antiques, objets d'art, porcelain and prints.* TEL: 0905 23332.

Jean Hodge LAPADA
Peachley Manor, Hallow Lane, Lower Broadheath. Resident. Est: 1969. Open daily including Sun. SIZE: Large. *STOCK: Furniture, 18th-19th C; general antiques, £30-£4,000.* LOC: Off B4204, 3 miles N.W. Worcester. PARK: Easy. TEL: 0905 640255.

Sarah Hodge
Peachley Manor, Hallow Lane, Lower Broadheath. Resident. Est: 1985. Open daily including Sun. SIZE: Large. *STOCK: General antiques, country bygones, pine and kitchenalia.* LOC: Off B4204, 3 miles N.W. Worcester. PARK: Easy. TEL: 0905 640255.

M Lees and Sons LAPADA
Tower House, Severn St. Resident. Est: 1955. Open 9.15-5.15, Sat. by appointment. CL: Thurs. p.m. SIZE: Medium. *STOCK: Furniture, 1780-1880; porcelain, 1750-1920.* LOC: At southern end of Worcester Cathedral adjacent to Edgar Tower; near Royal Worcester Porcelain Museum and factory. PARK: Easy. TEL: 0905 26620; home - 0905 427142. VAT: Stan/Spec.

Meriden House Antiques
41 Upper Tything. Est: 1970. Open 10-5.30. *STOCK: Furniture, £50-£2,000; paintings, silver, metalware, objets d'art.* LOC: A38, extension of Foregate St. TEL: 0905 29014. SER: Restorations (furniture).

The Original Choice Ltd
56 The Tything. (J Ellis) Open 10-6, Thurs. and Fri. 10-7.30, Sun. 11-5.30. *STOCK: Fireplaces, fenders, tiles, stained glass, mirrors and interior fittings.* TEL: 0905 613330.

Worcester continued

St. Georges Antiques
31B Barbourne Rd. Open 10-5.30. TEL: 0905 25915. The following dealers trade from this address.

Collectors World
Coins, medals, badges and other collectables.
Gemma Antiques
Small Victorian furniture and porcelain.
Yestertime
Clocks and time pieces.

Tolley's Galleries
26 College St. (T.M Tolley) *STOCK: Oriental and general antiques, Eastern bronzes, Oriental rugs, 17th-19th C.* PARK: Easy. TEL: 0905 26632. VAT: Stan.

Long Tran Antiques LAPADA
(L Tran) Open by appointment only. *STOCK: British and continental fine porcelain.* TEL: 0905 353840; fax - 0905 776685; mobile - 0831 400685.

W.H.E.A.P. Antiques
17 Bromyard Rd. (P Hooper) Open 9-6 or by appointment. *STOCK: General antiques and shipping goods.* TEL: 0905 427796. SER: Restorations; waxing and French polishing.

YATTON, Nr. Leominster

Moreden Prints
(B Croxton) Open by appointment. *STOCK: Antiquarian and collectable prints and maps.* TEL: 056886 549. SER: Book and print search; mountcutting.

YAZOR

M. and J Russell
The Old Vicarage. Est: 1969. Usually open Fri. to Mon. and evenings, other times appointment advisable. *STOCK: English period oak and country furniture, some garden antiques.* LOC: 7 miles west of Hereford on A480. TEL: 098 122 674. *Mainly Trade.*

Hertfordshire

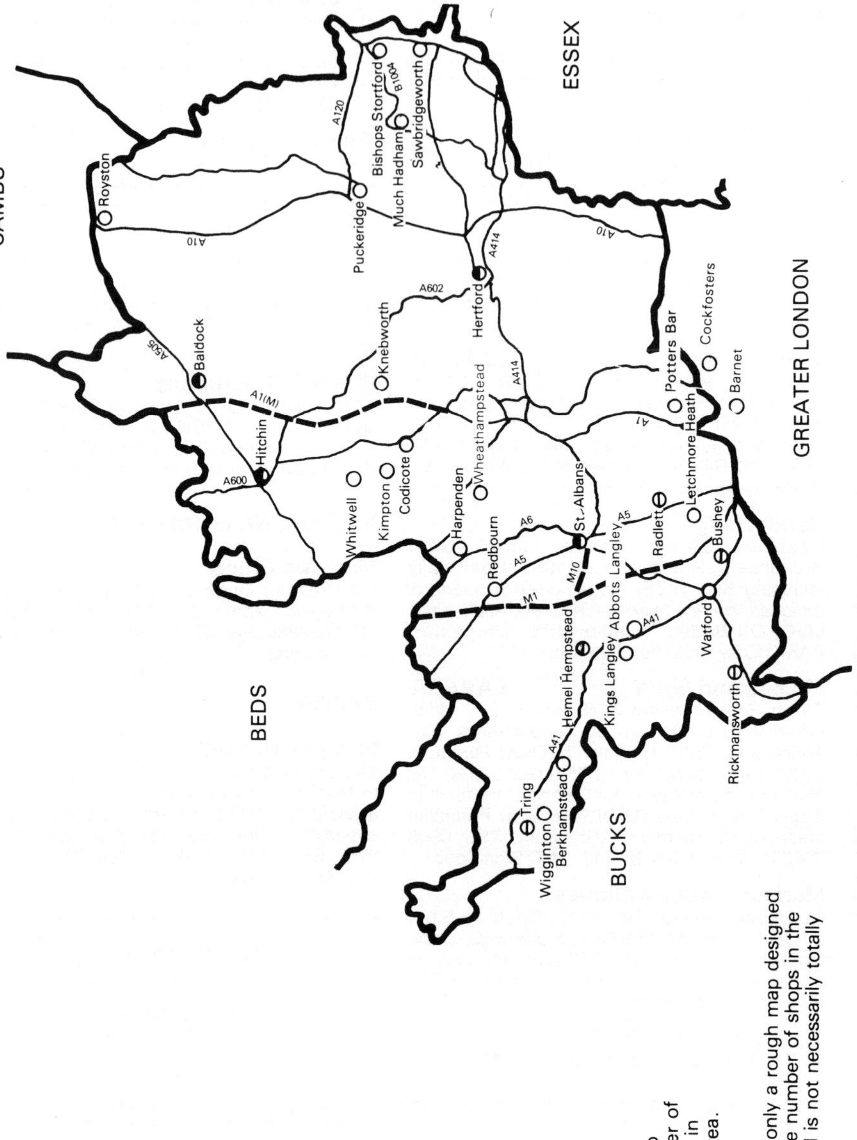
CAMBS
ESSEX
BEDS
BUCKS
GREATER LONDON
Royston
Puckeridge
Bishops Stortford
Much Hadham
Sawbridgeworth
B1004
A120
A10
A10
A414
A414
Hertford
A602
Knebworth
Baldock
A505
A1(M)
Hitchin
A600
Whitwell
Kimpton
Codicote
Wheathampstead
Harpenden
Redbourn
St. Albans
A6
A5
A5
M10
M1
A1
Potters Bar
Cockfosters
Barnet
Letchmore Heath
Radlett
Bushey
Abbots Langley
Watford
Kings Langley
A41
A41
Hemel Hempstead
Berkhamstead
Tring
Wigginton
Rickmansworth

1—2 / 3—5 / 6—12 / 13+ — Key to number of shops in this area.

Please note this is only a rough map designed to show dealers the number of shops in the various towns, and is not necessarily totally accurate.

ABBOTS LANGLEY, Nr. Watford

Dobson's Antiques
53 High St. Est: 1926. Open 8.30-5.30. CL: Tues. p.m. *STOCK: Carved oak, stripped pine, shipping goods, bric-a-brac, £5-£2,000.* LOC: 4 miles north of Watford. TEL: 0923 263186. VAT: Stan/Spec.

BALDOCK

The Attic
20 Whitehorse St. (P Sheppard) Est: 1977. CL: Mon. and Thurs. SIZE: Small. *STOCK: Small furniture, china, brass and copper, dolls and teddy bears, £5-£100.* LOC: 3 minutes from A1(M). PARK: Easy. TEL: 0462 893880.

Anthony Butt Antiques
7/9 Church St. Resident. Est: 1950. Usually open. *STOCK: English furniture, 17th-19th C, £500-£5,000; works of art and objects of interest.* Not Stocked: Bric-a-brac, shipping goods. PARK: Easy. TEL: 0462 895272. SER: Valuations. VAT: Spec.

Howards
33 Whitehorse St. (D.N Howard) Est: 1970. Open 9.30-12.30 and 1-5, Sat. 10-12.30 and 1-5. CL: Mon. *STOCK: Clocks, 18th-19th C, £200-£5,000.* PARK: Easy. TEL: 0462 892385. SER: Valuations. VAT: Spec.

Baldock continued

Ralph and Bruce Moss
26 Whitehorse St. (R.A. and B.A Moss) Est: 1973. Open 9-6. SIZE: Large. *STOCK: Furniture, £50-£5,000; general antiques, £5-£5,000.* LOC: A505, in town centre. PARK: Own. TEL: 0462 892751. VAT: Stan/Spec.

Arthur Porter
31 Whitehorse St. (A.G.R Porter) Est: 1969. Open 9-6 seven days. SIZE: Large. *STOCK: Pine furniture, 18th-20th C; English, continental and decorative items.* LOC: Main street. PARK: Easy. TEL: 0462 895351. SER: Valuations; restorations; stripping; finder. VAT: Stan/Spec.

The Wheelwright
1 Mansfield Rd. (E. and L Hurst) Resident. Est: 1976. Open 9.30-5.30. CL: Thurs. SIZE: Medium. *STOCK: Small porcelain and china, jewellery, small furniture, bric-a-brac, 19th C, £5-£500.* LOC: Off A1. PARK: Easy. TEL: 0462 893876.

BARNET

C Bellinger Antiques
91 Wood St. Est: 1974. Open Thurs., Fri. and Sat., 10-4, or by appointment. SIZE: Medium. *STOCK: Furniture, silver and plate, smalls.* LOC: Opposite Ravenscroft Park. PARK: Within 100yds. TEL: 081 449 3467; home - same. VAT: Stan/Spec.

BERKHAMSTED

Park Street Antiques BADA
350 High St. (M Shanks) Est: 1960. Open 9.30-5.30 or by appointment. CL: Mon. SIZE: Large. *STOCK: Furniture, £100-£30,000; barometers, £100-£10,000; both 17th-19th C; works of art, £30-£3,000; longcase clocks, rugs and carpets.* Not Stocked: Silver, jewellery, coins. LOC: A41. PARK: At west end of town. TEL: 0442 864790; home - 024 029 255. VAT: Stan/Spec.

Yesterday's Pine
61 High St. (N.E Chesters) Est: 1975. Open 10-6, Sun. 2-6. *STOCK: Waxed pine furniture, decorative ceramics, pictures, miscellanea.* TEL: 0442 862042. SER: Furniture made to specification; fitted interiors, bedrooms, and kitchens.

BISHOP'S STORTFORD

Northgate Antiques
21 Northgate End. (Mrs L.B Rawsthorne) Est: 1986. Open 9-5, most Sats. 10-12.30. SIZE: Medium. *STOCK: General antiques and collectables.* LOC: 20yds. north of Sworders auction rooms, 2 miles from Junction 8, M11. PARK: Easy. TEL: 0279 656957; home - 0279 722757.

Bishop's Stortford continued

The Windhill Antiquary
4 High St. (F.W. and G.R Crozier) Est: 1951. Open 10-1 and 2-4, appointment advisable. CL: Wed. p.m. SIZE: Medium. *STOCK: English furniture, 18th C; carved and gilded wall mirrors, 17th-19th C.* Not Stocked: Shipping goods. LOC: Next to George Hotel. PARK: Up hill - first right. TEL: 0279 651587; home - 0920 821316. VAT: Stan/Spec.

BUSHEY, Nr. Watford

Circa Antiques
43 High St, Bushey Village. (K Wildman) Est: 1978. Open 9.30-5.30 or by appointment. SIZE: Medium. *STOCK: General antiques, furniture, porcelain, silver and clocks.* TEL: 081 950 9233.

Country Life Antiques
33a High St. (P Myers) Est: 1981. Open 9.30-5. CL: Wed. p.m. SIZE: Large. *STOCK: Victorian stripped pine and country furniture, general antiques, china, smalls, Victorian and Edwardian watercolours.* PARK: Easy. TEL: 081 950 8575. VAT: Stan.

Thwaites and Co
33 Chalk Hill, Oxhey. Est: 1971. Open 9-5, Sat. 9.30-12.30. *STOCK: Stringed instruments, from violins to double basses.* TEL: 0923 32412. SER: Restorations.

COCKFOSTERS

H Pordes Ltd
383 Cockfosters Rd. *STOCK: Antiquarian books including scientific and learned; remainders.* TEL: 081 449 2524; fax - same, but telephone before transmission. *Postal Only.*

CODICOTE, Nr. Hitchin

Antiques Fair
Peace Memorial Hall. Est: 1975. Open first Sat. monthly 9-4. SIZE: 25 dealers. *STOCK: General antiques.* TEL: 043 871 6892.

Wheldon and Wesley Ltd
Lytton Lodge. Est: 1921. Open by appointment only. *STOCK: Antiquarian books on Natural History.* TEL: 0438 820370; fax - 0438 821478. SER: Buys at auction. *Mail Order Only.*

HARPENDEN

Meg Andrews
20 Holly Bush Lane. Est: 1982. Open by appointment. *STOCK: Worldwide collectable, hangable and wearable antique costume and textiles including Chinese embroideries and woven fabrics, robes, shoes, hats, large hangings, Morris and Arts and Crafts embroideries and woven cloths, Paisley shawls, samplers, silkwork pictures; European costumes and textiles.* LOC: Off Junction 10, M1, south on A1081. PARK: Easy. TEL: 0582 460107; home - same. SER: Valuations; advice; buys at auction. FAIRS: Olympia. VAT: Stan/Spec.

Knights Gallery
38 Station Rd. (J.C Knights) Open 10-4, Sat. 10-1. CL: Wed. *STOCK: Watercolours, oils and prints.* TEL: 0582 460564. SER: Valuations; restorations; framing; buys at auction.

HEMEL HEMPSTEAD

Abbey Antiques and Fine Art LAPADA
97 High St, Old Town. (L., E., S. and C Eames) Est: 1962. Open 9.30-5.30. CL: Wed. p.m. SIZE: Medium. *STOCK: Silver, plate, jewellery, £5-£2,000; early English watercolours, £100-£5,000; furniture, 17th-19th C.* LOC: From London on M1 through main shopping centre to old town. PARK: Easy. TEL: 0442 64667. SER: Valuations; jewellery design and repair; restorations (as stock); buys at auction. VAT: Stan/Spec.

Antique and Collectors Market
Market Pl, (Antique Forum (Birmingham) Ltd.). Open Wed. 9-2. SIZE: 100 dealers. *STOCK: General antiques.* TEL: 071 624 3214.

Hemel Hempstead continued

Carousel
59 High St. (Mr and Mrs J Warrington) Est: 1981. Open 10-12.30 and 1.30-4. CL: Mon. and Wed. p.m. except by appointment. SIZE: Medium. *STOCK: Toys, especially Teddy bears, small items including jewellery, silver, glass, china, some furniture.* LOC: Opposite St. Mary's Church. PARK: Easy. TEL: 0442 219772; home - 0442 242518. SER: Valuations; restorations (Dolls Hospital). FAIRS: Antique Toy and Doll, Kensington Town Hall and Ardingly. VAT: Stan/Spec.

Cherry Antiques
101 - 103 High St. (A. and R.S Cullen and J. and M Payne) Open 9.30-4.30. CL: Wed. p.m. SIZE: Medium. *STOCK: Victorian, Edwardian, and some period furniture, pine, general antiques, collectors' and decorative items, bric-a-brac, needlework tools, dolls, linens, some silver, plate, jewellery, glass, pottery, porcelain, brass, copper, some shipping items.* PARK: Easy. TEL: 0442 64358. VAT: Stan/Spec.

HERTFORD

Beckwith and Son
St. Nicholas Hall, St. Andrew St. (A.K Loveday, FSVA, G.C.M Gray, N.P.J Bunce and P Chappell) Est: 1904. Open 9-1 and 2-5.30. SIZE: Large. *STOCK: General antiques, furniture, silver, pottery, porcelain, prints, weapons, clocks, watches, glass.* Not Stocked: Fabrics. LOC: A602/B158. PARK: Adjacent. TEL: 0992 582079. SER: Valuations; restorations (fine porcelain, furniture, upholstery, silver, clocks). VAT: Stan/Spec.

Georgian House Antiques
42 St. Andrew St. (I.P Defty) Est: 1970. Open 9-5. CL: Thurs. SIZE: Medium. *STOCK: General antiques, 18th C to Edwardian, £100-£1,800.* LOC: Opposite St. Andrew's Church. PARK: Easy. TEL: 0992 583508; home - 0438 86 742. SER: Restorations.

Robert Horton Antiques
13 Castle St. Est: 1972. Open 9-5. *STOCK: Clocks, barometers, furniture, general antiques.* TEL: 0992 587546. VAT: Stan/Spec.

L Partridge Antiques
25 St. Andrew St. (P.L Hodgkinson) Est: 1934. Open 10-1 and 2-6. CL: Thurs. SIZE: Large. *STOCK: Oil paintings, prints, furnishings, silver, jewellery.* PARK: Easy. TEL: 0992 584385; home - 027 974 257. SER: Valuations; restorations (oil paintings, prints, silver, jewellery); upholstery; buys at auction.

Michael Rochford
25 St. Andrew St. Open 10-6. *STOCK: Trade goods including general antiques, furniture.* TEL: 0992 581291.

Hertford continued

Village Green Antiques LAPADA
21 and 23 St. Andrew St, and 6 and 8 Old Cross. (N. and P Petre) Est: 1970. Open 10-5.30. CL: Thurs. p.m. SIZE: Large. *STOCK: Furniture, £50-£10,000; porcelain, metalware, works of art, decorative items.* LOC: 200yds. from A414. PARK: At rear. TEL: 0992 587698; home - 0992 586994. VAT: Stan/Spec.

HITCHIN

The Aspidistra
29 Sun St. (M Plant) Est: 1971. Open 9.30-5.30. *STOCK: Victoriana, pine, jewellery, furniture, bric-a-brac.* TEL: 0462 453817. VAT: Stan.

Bexfield Antiques
13 and 14 Sun St. (A.B Bexfield) Est: 1962. Open 9.30-5. CL: Wed. *STOCK: Jewellery, silver, porcelain, copper, pewter and furniture.* PARK: Nearby. TEL: 0462 432641.

Countrylife Gallery
30 Sun St. (M Morgan and D.B Moore) Open by appointment only. SIZE: Small. *STOCK: Watercolours - botanical, flower and natural history, 1780-1930, £50-£500; oils - flowers and natural history, 1850-1930, £500-£5,000.* LOC: Town square. PARK: 50yds. TEL: 0462 433267; home - same. SER: Valuations; restorations; buys at auction (English watercolours and pictures). FAIRS: Royal Horticultural Soc. VAT: Spec.

Michael Gander
10 Bridge St. Est: 1973. Open 9-6. *STOCK: Period furniture, metalware.* TEL: 0462 432678.

Hitchin Antiques Gallery
37 Bridge St. (R.J Perry) Open 10-5.30. CL: Sun. except by appointment. SIZE: 10 dealers. *STOCK: General antiques including furniture, watercolours, jewellery, Victorian chimney pots and garden items, to £5,000.* PARK: Nearby. TEL: 0462 434525; home - 0582 25546. SER: Valuations; restorations (furniture, re-upholstery, clocks and glass). FAIRS: Luton.

Eric T Moore
24 Bridge St. Open 9.30-1 and 2.15-5.30, Wed. 9-12.30, Sat. all day. *STOCK: Antiquarian books, maps and prints.* TEL: 0462 450497. SER: Picture framing, mount cutting.

R.J Perry Antiques LAPADA
38 Bridge St. Open 10-5.30. SIZE: 3 floors. *STOCK: Metalware, interior decorators' pieces, small furniture, general antiques.* TEL: 0462 434525. SER: Valuations; restorations (furniture, upholstery, metalware). FAIRS: Luton.

Phillips of Hitchin (Antiques) Ltd BADA
The Manor House. (M. and J Phillips) Est: 1884. Open 9-1 and 2-5.30. SIZE: Large.

Phillips of Hitchin (Antiques) Ltd continued

STOCK: Furniture, walnut, oak and mahogany, 17th to early 19th C, £500-£20,000. **LOC: In Bancroft, main street of Hitchin. PARK: Easy. TEL: 0462 432067. SER: Restorations (furniture); books on collecting. FAIRS: Specialist antique exhibitions at the Manor House. VAT: Spec.**

Carole Thomas Fine Arts
First Floor, 32a Sun St. Est: 1977. Open 10.30-5.30. CL: Wed. SIZE: Large. *STOCK: English watercolours, £85-£2,000; Victorian and Edwardian oils, etchings, prints.* LOC: Market Sq. PARK: Market Sq. TEL: 0462 436077. SER: Valuations; restorations (watercolours, oils).

KIMPTON

Annick Antiques
28 High St. (R.V. and A.M Turl) Open seven days 11-5. *STOCK: Victorian, Edwardian and 1930s furniture, country oak, oil paintings, watercolours and general antiques, bric-a-brac.* LOC: Between Wheathampstead and Hitchin. PARK: Easy. TEL: 0438 832491. VAT: Stan.

KING'S LANGLEY

Frenches Farm Antiques
Tower Hill, Chipperfield. (I Cross) Est: 1972. Open 2-6 or by appointment. SIZE: Large. *STOCK: Furniture, including pine, £15-£500; porcelain, Victoriana, copper, brass, £1-£50; mainly 18th-19th C.* Not Stocked: Silver, jewellery, firearms, paintings. LOC: From Chipperfield take Bovingdon Rd. On right 500yds. from Royal Oak public house. PARK: Easy. TEL: 0923 265843.

KNEBWORTH

Hamilton and Tucker Billiard Co. Ltd
Park Lane. (H Hamilton and P Tucker) Est: 1980. Open 9-5, Sat. 10-4, Sun. by appointment. SIZE: Large. *STOCK: Victorian and Edwardian billiard tables, £3,000-£18,000; 19th C convertible billiard/dining tables and accessories, £30-£5,000.* LOC: Near railway station. PARK: Easy. TEL: 0438 811995. SER: Valuations; restorations (billiard tables and assorted furniture); buys at auction (as stock). FAIRS: Distinctive Homes at Alexandra Palace; Cologne International Furniture. VAT: Stan.

LETCHMORE HEATH, Nr. Watford

Anne Barlow Antiques
1 Letchmore Cottages. (Mrs Barlow) Est: 1952. Open 2.30-6.30. CL: Mon. SIZE: Small. *STOCK: Continental and unusual items especially Quimper pottery, country furniture, faience porcelain, toys, clocks, collectors' items, £1-£500.* PARK: Easy. TEL: 0923 855270. SER: Valuations.

MUCH HADHAM

Careless Cottage Antiques
High St. (M Furze) Est: 1979. Open 9.30-5.30, Sun. by appointment. SIZE: Medium. *STOCK: General antiques, oak and country furniture, 17th-19th C, £100-£2,500; china, glass, small and decorative items.* LOC: On B1004, at North end of village. PARK: Easy. TEL: 027 984 2007.

POTTERS BAR

Rodwell Antiques and Reproductions
94 High St. (M.S Rodwell) MGMC. Est: 1985. Open 9-5, Thurs. 9-3, Sat. 9-6, Sun. 11-4. SIZE: Medium. *STOCK: General antiques.* TEL: 0707 55402. SER: Restorations; French polishing.

PUCKERIDGE

St. Ouen Antiques LAPADA
Vintage Corner, Old Cambridge Rd. (V.C.J., J., J. and S.T Blake and Mrs P.B Francis) Est: 1918. Open 10.30-5. SIZE: Large. *STOCK: English and continental furniture, decorative items, silver, porcelain, pottery, glass, clocks, barometers, paintings.* TEL: 0920 821336. SER: Valuations; restorations.

RADLETT

Hasel-Britt Ltd
157 Watling St. (Mrs Britton) Est: 1962. Open 10-5.30. CL: Wed. p.m. *STOCK: General antiques, 19th C; pottery and porcelain.* TEL: 0923 854477.

Old Hat
64 Watling St. (N.G Rogers) Est: 1972. Open 9.30-5.30. CL: Wed. p.m. SIZE: Medium. *STOCK: General antiques, furniture, Victoriana, £50-£5,000; oils, watercolours, porcelain, 18th-19th C, £25-£1,000.* LOC: A5. PARK: Easy. TEL: 0923 855753. VAT: Stan/Spec.

REDBOURN, Nr. St. Albans

J.N Antiques
86 High St. (M. and J Brunning) Est: 1975. Open 9-6. SIZE: Medium. *STOCK: Furniture, 18th-20th C, £5-£3,000; brass and copper, porcelain, 19th C, £5-£100; pictures, 19th and 20th C.* PARK: 50yds. TEL: 0582 793603 (24hrs.). SER: Valuations. VAT: Spec.

Tim Wharton Antiques
24 High St. Est: 1970. Open 10-5.30, Sat. 10-4. CL: Mon. and usually Thurs. *STOCK: Oak and country furniture, 17th-19th C; some mahogany, 18th-early 19th C; copper, brass, ironware and general small antiques.* LOC: On left entering village from St. Albans on A5183. PARK: Easy. TEL: 0582 794371. VAT: Stan/Spec.

RICKMANSWORTH

Clive A Burden
46 Talbot Rd. Est: 1966. Open 9-5, appointment preferred. SIZE: Medium. *STOCK: Maps, 1500-1860, £5-£1,500; natural history, botanical and Vanity Fair, prints, 1720-1870, £1-£1,000; antiquarian books, pre-1870, £10-£5,000.* LOC: In main shopping area. PARK: Nearby. TEL: 0923 778097; home - 0923 772387. SER: Valuations; buys at auction (as stock). VAT: Stan.

David Harriman
Open every day by appointment. *STOCK: Clocks, especially electric, Bulle, Ato, Eureka, Tiffany and Holden. Unrestored cases and movements of brackets and longcases.* TEL: 0923 776919; fax - 0923 773995.

McCrudden Gallery
23 Station Rd. Open 10-5.30. CL: Wed. SIZE: Medium. *STOCK: Fine paintings, watercolours, limited editions prints, etching and engravings.* LOC: Town centre. PARK: Easy. TEL: 0923 772613. SER: Restorations (pictures and frames); buys at auction.

ROYSTON

Royston Antiques
29 Kneesworth St. (J. and M Newnham) Est: 1965. Open 9.30-5. CL: Thurs. SIZE: Medium. *STOCK: Furniture, 1750-1930, £50-£2,500; porcelain, books, £5-£500; collectors' items, pine, metalware, bygones.* TEL: 0763 243876.

ST. ALBANS

By George! Antiques Centre
23 George St. (D.J Pyne) Open 10-5. SIZE: Medium. 15 dealers. *STOCK: A wide range of general antiques, silver, jewellery and fine arts.* LOC: 100yds. from Clock Tower. PARK: Internal courtyard (loading) and nearby. TEL: 0727 53032. SER: Restorations.

The Clock Shop - Philip Setterfield of St. Albans
161 Victoria St. Est: 1974. Open 10.30-6.30, Sat. 10.30-4. CL: Thurs. *STOCK: Clocks and watches.* LOC: City station bridge. TEL: 0727 56633. SER: Restoration; repairs (clocks, watches, barometers). VAT: Stan/Spec.

Dolphin Antiques LAPADA
Garden Cottage, Dolphin Lodge,, Dolphin Yard, off Holywell Hill. (C Constable) Est: 1967. Open by appointment. SIZE: Small. *STOCK: Furniture, 18th-19th C, £100-£4,000; porcelain, £20-£1,000; glass, brass and copper, £10-£300; pictures, prints, £10-£500.* Not Stocked: Coins, medals, weapons. PARK: Nearby. TEL: 0727 863080; home - 0727 861941. VAT: Stan/Spec.

St. Albans continued

James of St Albans
11 George St. (S.N. and W James) Est: 1957. Open 10-5, Thurs. 10-1. *STOCK: Furniture including reproduction; smalls, brass and copper; topographical maps and prints of Hertfordshire.* TEL: 0727 56996. VAT: Stan/Spec.

Leaside Antiques
Shop 5, By George Antique Centre, George St. (T.G Pepper) CL: Thurs. *STOCK: Victorian and Edwardian furniture, ceramics, silver and collectors' items.* TEL: 0727 40653; home - 0582 27957 (answerphone). SER: Repairs (jewellery).

Oriental Rug Gallery Ltd
42 Verulam Rd. (R Mathias and J Blair) Open 9-6, Fri. 9-7, Sun. 10.30-4. *STOCK: Russian, Afghan, Turkish and Persian carpets, rugs and kelims; Oriental objets d'art.* TEL: 0727 41046.

Christopher Perry Antiques
27 College St. Est: 1975. Open Wed. and Sat. 9.30-3.30, other times by appointment. SIZE: Small. *STOCK: Furniture - walnut, mahogany and oak, £50-£2,000; metalware and interesting items, £20-£400; all 1600-1850; prints.* Not Stocked: Bric-a-brac, late Victorian and Edwardian furniture. LOC: From Peahen Hotel A5183/A1081 crossroad into Verulam Rd. Turn left just before pedestrian crossing into Lower Dagnell St., shop 50yds. down on right. PARK: Easy. TEL: 0727 832772; home - same. VAT: Stan/Spec.

Wilkie, Sir David (1785-1841)
A Spaniel. Signed and dated 1835, blue chalk, pen and brown ink, and brown wash heightened with white and red. 9⅝in. x 7⅞in. From the point of view of medium, this drawing has almost everything, and, surprisingly, it works. ANTHONY REED
From ***The Dictionary of British Watercolour Artists up to 1920,*** Volume III, by H.L. Mallalieu, published by the **Antique Collectors' Club** in 1990. £35.00.

St. Albans continued

St. Albans Antique Market
Town Hall, Chequer St. Est: 1978. Open Mon. 9.30-4, including some Bank Holidays. SIZE: 30 stands. *STOCK: A wide variety of antiques.* TEL: 0727 44957.

Stevens Antiques
41 London Rd. (J.E Stevens) Est: 1971. Open 10-5.30, Sat. 9.30-5, Sun. by appointment. CL: Thurs. SIZE: Medium. *STOCK: Stripped pine, £25-£500; small antiques - brass, boxes, china, porcelain, £10-£300, all 19th C; Victorian and Edwardian furniture, 19th to early 20th C, £30-£1,000.* LOC: Off Holywell Hill or Chequer St. PARK: Own, at rear. TEL: 0727 57266; home - 0727 50427. VAT: Stan.

Thomas Thorp
9 George St. Est: 1883. CL: Mon. *STOCK: Antiquarian books, prints.* TEL: 0727 865576.

Stuart Wharton
1 George St. FGA. Est: 1967. Open 9.30-5.30. SIZE: Small. *STOCK: Silver, 18th-20th C, £20-£500; jewellery, mainly modern, £20-£5,000.* LOC: Near clock tower. PARK: Multi-storeys, city centre. TEL: 0727 59489. SER: Valuations (jewellery); goldsmithing, gem testing; buys at auction (silver). VAT: Stan.

SAWBRIDGEWORTH

The Herts and Essex Antique Centre
The Maltings, Station Rd. Est: 1982. Open 10-5, Sat. and Sun. 10.30-6. CL: Mon. SIZE: Large - over 100 dealers. *STOCK: Antiques, from 1780 to date, £1-£1,000.* LOC: Town centre opposite B.R. station. PARK: Easy. TEL: 0279 722044. SER: Restorations.

Papillon Antiques
33A Knight St. (G. and M Jacobs) Open 10-4, Sat. 10-5. CL: Mon. *STOCK: Porcelain, glass, Oriental works of art, paintings, prints, mahogany, oak and pine furniture, 1750-1930.* LOC: Between Harlow and Bishops Stortford. PARK: Easy. TEL: 0279 724633.

TRING

Richard Barrow Antiques
83 High St. Open 9.30-5.30. CL: Wed. *STOCK: General antiques.* TEL: 044 282 6223; home - 044 285 339.

John Bly BADA
50 High St. (F., N., J. and V Bly) Books on furniture and silver. Est: 1891. Open 9-5.30. SIZE: Large. *STOCK: English furniture and silver, 18th C.* TEL: 044 282 3030. VAT: Stan/Spec.

Tring continued

Country Clocks
3 Pendley Bridge Cottages, Tring Station. (T. and J Cartmell) Resident. Est: 1976. Open daily, prior 'phone call advisable. SIZE: Small. *STOCK: Clocks, 18th-19th C.* LOC: One mile from A41, in village, cottage nearest canal bridge. PARK: Easy. TEL: 044 282 5090. SER: Restorations (clocks).

Farrelly Antiques
The Long Barn, 50 High St. (P Farrelly) Open 9-4. *STOCK: Furniture.* TEL: 044 289 1905. SER: Restorations. VAT: Spec.

WATFORD

Copper Kettle Antiques
172 Bushey Mill Lane. (R. and C Barton) Est: 1970. Open 9.30-4.30. CL: Wed. SIZE: Large. *STOCK: General antiques, Victoriana, paintings, watercolours, books, prints, clocks, furniture.* TEL: 0923 248877. VAT: Stan/Spec.

WHEATHAMPSTEAD

Collins Antiques (F.G. and C. Collins Ltd.)
Corner House. (S.J. and M.C Collins) Est: 1907. Open 9-1 and 2-5. SIZE: Large. *STOCK: Furniture, mahogany, 1730-1920, £100-£8,000; oak, 1600-1800, £50-£5,000; walnut, 1700-1740, £75-£3,000.* Not Stocked: Silver. LOC: London, A1(M) junction 4 to B653. PARK: Easy. TEL: 058 283 3111; home - 058 283 3483. VAT: Stan/Spec.

WHITWELL, Nr. Hitchin

Simon Boosey - Persian and Oriental Rugs
The Tun House. Est: 1973. Open by appointment. *STOCK: Persian and Oriental carpets and runners, £500-£5,000; fine village and nomad rugs, £250-£2,000; both 1850-1950; small tribal pieces, pre-1950, £75-£500.* LOC: High St. PARK: Easy. TEL: 0438 871563; home - same. SER: Valuations; restorations; supplier of specialist underlays. VAT: Stan.

WIGGINTON, Nr. Tring

Michael Armson (Antiques) Ltd
Park Farm, The Twist. Open Tues. and Thurs. mornings or by appointment. SIZE: Large. *STOCK: Furniture, 17th-19th C.* TEL: 0442 890990; mobile - 0860 729863; home - 0296 661141.

A rare claret jug, tapering amphora body with stick down handle and trefoil lip, decorated with two acid etched scenes. 'Mercury delivering a message to Calipso' and 'Circe and a handmaiden' from *The Odyssey* of Homer. £500-£800. From an article entitled 'Design Influences on Victorian Glass' by Jeanette Hayhurst published in April 1991 issue of ***Antique Collecting.***

'Limoges Enamel' work by Thomas Bott, the deep blue glazed ground with a portrait head of Agrippina in raised white enamel, c.1858. Bott excelled at this technique and examples are well worth seeking out. From an article entitled 'The Awakening of Worcester Porcelain' by John Sandon published in the February 1991 issue of ***Antique Collecting.***

Humberside

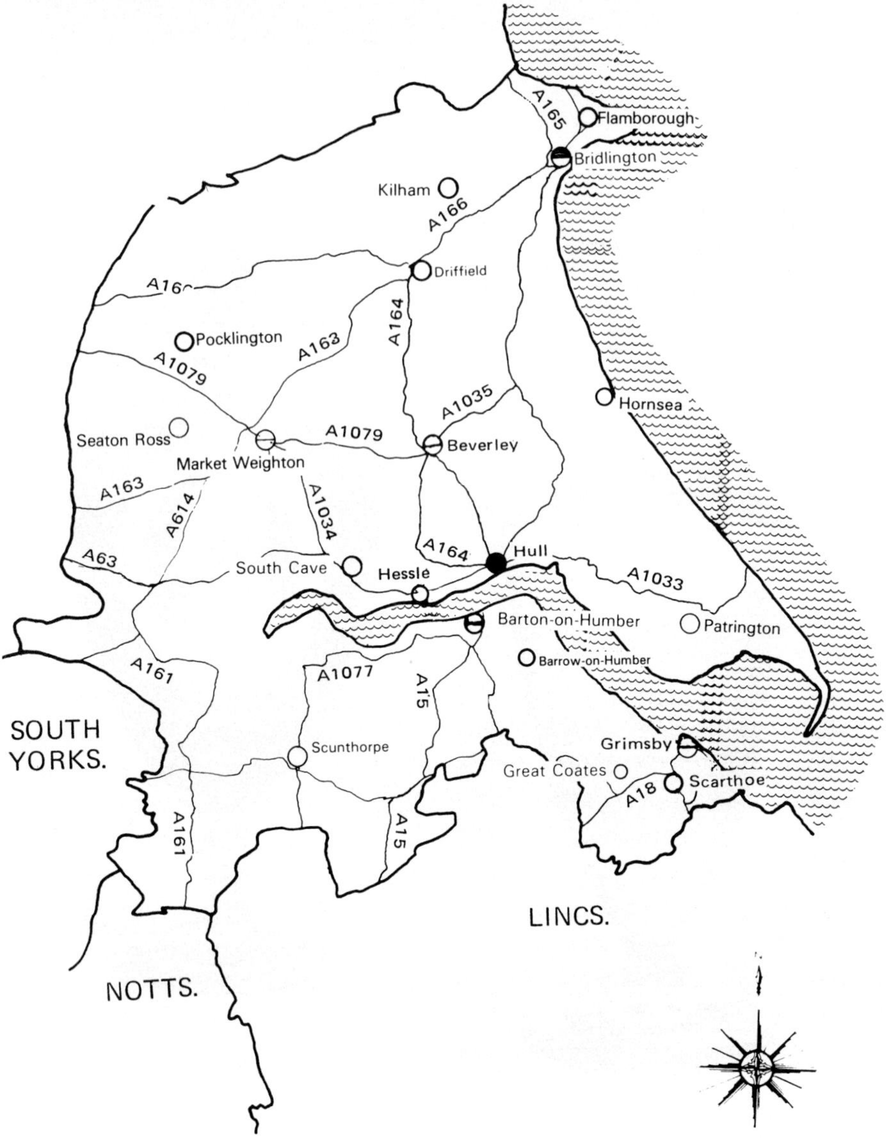

Flamborough
A165
Bridlington
Kilham
A166
Driffield
A16
A164
Pocklington
A163
A1079
A1035
Hornsea
Seaton Ross
A1079
Beverley
Market Weighton
A163
A1034
A614
A164
Hull
A63
South Cave
Hessle
A1033
Barton-on-Humber
Patrington
A161
Barrow-on-Humber
A1077
A15
SOUTH YORKS.
Scunthorpe
Grimsby
Great Coates
A18
Scarthoe
A161
A15
LINCS.
NOTTS.

Please note this is only a rough map designed to show dealers the number of shops in the various towns, and is not necessarily totally accurate.

Key to number of shops in this area.

- ○ 1–2
- ⊖ 3–5
- ◓ 6–12
- ● 13+

BEVERLEY

Hawley Antiques LAPADA
5 North Bar Within. Open 9.30-5. *STOCK: General antiques, furniture, pottery, porcelain, glass, oil paintings, watercolours, silver.* TEL: 0482 868193. VAT: Stan/Spec.

Ladygate Antiques
8 Ladygate. (P. and L Goodman) Est: 1963. Open 9.30-1 and 2-5.30. SIZE: Medium. *STOCK: Furniture, longcase clocks, pottery and porcelain, glass, brass, copperware, pewter, jewellery, maritime relics, silver and plate.* Not Stocked: Militaria, coins. PARK: Easy. TEL: 0482 881494; home - 0482 882299/868857.

Natural Choice Antiques
22 North Bar Without. (J.D. and B Bridges) Est: 1987. Open 9.30-5.30. SIZE: Medium. *STOCK: General antiques - furniture, pottery and porcelain, paintings, silver and plate, clocks, linen, Georgian to Edwardian.* LOC: Outside North Bar, Malton/Driffield road. PARK: Easy. TEL: 0482 862215; home - same. VAT: Stan/Spec.

James H Starkey Galleries
49 Highgate. Est: 1968. Open 10-5, Sat. 10-1 or by appointment. SIZE: Medium. *STOCK: Oil paintings, 16th-19th C; drawings and watercolours, 17th-19th C.* LOC: Opposite Beverley Minster. PARK: Easy. TEL: 0482 881179. SER: Valuations; restorations (paintings); buys at auction. VAT: Stan/Spec.

Well Lane Antiques
10 Well Lane. (S Endley and C Lough) Est: 1969. Open 11-4, Wed. and Thurs. 12.30-3.30, Sat. 10-4. SIZE: Small. *STOCK: General antiques, Victorian, Edwardian and art deco, £5-£250; Victorian linen, £5-£150.* LOC: Off Butcher Row. TEL: 0482 882868; home - 0482 861599 and 0964 550862. FAIRS: Local.

BRIDLINGTON

Antique Militaria
2 Princess Terrace. (B. and I Barker) Open 10-5 in winter, 9-5.30 including Sun. in summer. CL: Thurs. *STOCK: Militaria.* TEL: 0262 676846; home - 0262 601216.

Clockcraft Antiques
13 High St. (P.G Harker) Open 10-5. TEL: 0262 602802.

C.J. and A.J Dixon Ltd
1st Floor, 23 Prospect St. Est: 1969. Open 9-5.30. SIZE: Large. *STOCK: War medals, decorations and coins.* LOC: Town centre. PARK: Easy. TEL: 0262 676877/603348; fax - 0262 606600. SER: Valuations. VAT: Stan/Spec.

Bridlington continued

Priory Antiques
47-49 High St. (P.R Rogerson) Est: 1979. Open 10-5. CL: Thurs. *STOCK: Georgian and Victorian furniture.* TEL: 0262 601365.

Sedman Antiques
Carnaby Court, Off Moor Lane,, Carnaby. (R.H.S. and M.A Sedman) Est: 1971. Open 10-5.30, Sun. by appointment. *STOCK: General antiques, period and shipping furniture, Oriental porcelain, Victorian collectors' items.* LOC: Off A165. TEL: 0262 674039. VAT: Stan/Spec.

Sweet's Antiques
24 West St. (Mrs S.M Sweet) Est: 1950. Open 10-6. *STOCK: General antiques, porcelain, glass.* TEL: 0262 677396.

DRIFFIELD

Breeze Farm Antiques
37 Middle St. South. (M. and S Bishop) Open 9-5.30. CL: Wed. *STOCK: Pine and general antiques.* TEL: 0377 45174.

The Crested China Co
The Station House. (D Taylor) Est: 1978. Open 9-5, Sat. and other times by appointment. *STOCK: Goss and crested china.* TEL: 0377 47042 (24 hr.).

Smith and Smith Designs
58A Middle St. North. (D A and C R Smith and M T Addinall) Est: 1977. Open 9.30-5.30, Sat. 9.30-5, Sun. by appointment. SIZE: Medium + warehouse. *STOCK: Furniture including pine and country, 18th to early 20th C, £50-£2,000; furniture designed and made to order, from £50+.* LOC: Main street. PARK: Easy. TEL: 0377 46321; home - same. SER: Restorations. VAT: Stan/Spec.

FLAMBOROUGH, Nr. Bridlington

Lesley Berry Antiques
The Manor House. (Mrs L Berry) Resident. Est: 1972. Open 9.30-5.30, other times by appointment. SIZE: Small. *STOCK: Furniture, silver, jewellery, amber, Whitby jet, oils, watercolours, prints, copper, brass, textiles, fountain pens.* Not Stocked: Shipping goods. LOC: Shop on corner of Tower St. and Lighthouse Rd. PARK: Easy. TEL: 0262 850943. SER: Buys at auction.

HESSLE

The Antique Parlour
21 The Weir. (S Beercock) Est: 1967. CL: Sun. except to trade. *STOCK: General antiques, Victoriana, bric-a-brac, curios.* TEL: 0482 643329.

HORNSEA

Padgetts Antiques, Photographic and Scientific

19 Hull Rd. (G.R. and D.L Padgett) Est: 1965. Open by appointment. SIZE: Small. *STOCK: Cameras and photographic miscellanea, scientific and ships instruments, mechanical and domestic machines, clocks.* LOC: Overlooking Hornsea Mere. PARK: Easy. TEL: 0964 534086. FAIRS: Newark, Leeds, Manchester.

HULL

'55' Antiques

55 Springbank. (G Etherington) Est: 1960. Open 9-5. SIZE: Medium. *STOCK: Furniture, 17th-19th C, £80-£3,000; paintings, 17th to early 20th C, £40-£3,000; Victoriana, from £20; Victorian garden furniture, vases, urns.* LOC: Take Willerby road; crossroads at north end of town is Springbank. Shop 150yds. on left. PARK: First left, first left again. TEL: 0482 224510. SER: Valuations; restorations (furniture, paintings, clocks, china). VAT: Spec.

Boothferry Antiques LAPADA

388 Wincolmlee. (P. and J.A Smith) Est: 1972. Open 8.30-5, Sat. 9-3, other times by appointment. SIZE: Large. *STOCK: Stripped pine, 1800-1930, £20-£2,000; shipping goods, 1870-1940, £10-£1,000; some period furniture.* Not Stocked: Jewellery and medals. LOC: Turn left at North Bridge, 1/4 mile on right. PARK: Own (rear). TEL: 0482 225220; home - 0482 666033; fax - 0482 211170. SER: Courier; packing, shipping.

De Grey Antiques

96 De Grey St, Beverley Rd. (G Dick) Est: 1962. Open 10.30-1 and 2-5.45. SIZE: Medium. *STOCK: Furniture, clocks, paintings and watercolours, Victorian; glass, china, pewter, brass, copper and oil lamps.* LOC: Off main Beverley Rd., near overhead railway bridge. PARK: Easy. TEL: 0482 442184. SER: Valuations; buys at auction.

Hull continued

Steven Dews Fine Art

66-70 Princes Ave. Open 9-6. CL: Sat. SIZE: Medium. *STOCK: Paintings, 19th-20th C.* TEL: 0482 42424. SER: Valuations; restorations; framing. VAT: Spec.

Grannie's Parlour

33 Anlaby Rd. (Mrs N Pye) Open 11-5. *STOCK: General antiques, ephemera, Victoriana, dolls, toys, kitchenalia.* TEL: 0482 228258; home - 0482 41020.

Grannie's Treasures

1st Floor, 33 Anlaby Rd. (Mrs N Pye) Open 11-5. SIZE: 4 dealers. *STOCK: Advertising items, postcards, tins, bottles, small furniture and pre-1940s clothing.* TEL: 0482 228258; home - 0482 41020.

David K Hakeney Antiques LAPADA

64 George St. Est: 1971. Open 10-6. SIZE: Medium plus warehouse. *STOCK: Georgian, Victorian, Edwardian furniture, smalls, shipping goods.* LOC: City centre. TEL: 0482 228190; mobile - 0860 507774. VAT: Stan/Spec.

Imperial Antiques

397 Hessle Rd. (M Langton) Open 9-5.30. *STOCK: Pine furniture, shipping goods and general antiques.* TEL: 0482 27439.

K. Books of Hull

15 and 17 Hepworth's Arcade, Silver St. Open 10-4.30. *STOCK: Antiquarian books, prints and maps.* TEL: 0482 26457.

Lesley's Antiques

329 Hessle Rd. Est: 1967. Open 10-5.30. SIZE: Medium. *STOCK: General antiques, shipping goods; collectors' items, mostly under £25.* LOC: On main Hull to Hessle Rd. PARK: Easy. TEL: 0482 23986; home - 0482 646280. SER: Restorations; hire.

Hull continued

Geoffrey Mole/Antique Exports
LAPADA

Warehouse 400 Wincolmlee. Est: 1974. Open 9-5. CL: Sat. p.m. SIZE: Large. *STOCK: Shipping furniture, 1850-1920, £5-£2,000; general antiques, 19th C.* LOC: 1/2 mile east off main Beverley Rd. PARK: Easy. TEL: 0482 27858; fax - 0482 218173. SER: Packing, shipping. VAT: Stan.

Pearson Antiques
The Warehouse, 4 Dalton St. (W.B.T Grozier) Est: 1972. Open 10-5, Sat. by appointment. SIZE: Large. *STOCK: Furniture, pottery, brass, silver and plate, stuffed birds, stone figures, late 17th C to Edwardian, £50-£1,000.* LOC: Off Cleaveland St. PARK: Easy. TEL: 0482 29647; home - 0482 862927. SER: Valuations. VAT: Spec. *Trade Only.*

Sandringham Antiques
64a Beverley Rd. (P. and P Allison) Est: 1968. *STOCK: General antiques.* TEL: 0482 847653/20874.

Paul Wilson Ltd **LAPADA**
Perth St. West. Open 8-5.30, Sat. 8.30-11.30, other times by appointment. *STOCK: English, Scottish, Irish, Welsh, German, Austrian and Danish pine.* LOC: Near inner ring road, 10

Paul Wilson Ltd continued

mins. from Humber bridge. Telephone for further details. TEL: 0482 447923/448607. SER: Export and U.K. delivery; catalogue available. VAT: Stan.

KILHAM, Nr. Driffield

The Old Ropery Antique Clocks
East St. *STOCK: Clocks, especially longcase.* PARK: Easy. TEL: 026 282 233. SER: Restorations (furniture and clocks).

MARKET WEIGHTON, Nr. York

Dis & Dat
3 Churchside. (J Plantenga) Open 9-5. CL: Thurs. *STOCK: General small antiques and bric-a-brac.* TEL: 0430 873213.

C.G Dyson and Sons
51 Market Pl. Est: 1966. Open 9-5.30, Sat. till 5. SIZE: Small. *STOCK: Paintings, prints, maps, clocks, jewellery, silver, £5-£600.* Not Stocked: Porcelain. LOC: On main road in centre of town. TEL: 0430 872391. SER: Valuations; restorations.

Grannie's Attic
Kiplingcotes Station. Est: 1964. TEL: 0430 810284.

Market Weighton continued

Houghton Hall Antiques
Houghton Hall, Cliffe Rd. (M.E Watson) Est: 1965. Open daily 8-4, Sun. 11-4. SIZE: Large. *STOCK: Furniture, 17th-19th C, £5-£5,000; china, 19th C, £1-£600; paintings and prints, £20-£1,000; objets d'art.* Not Stocked: Coins, guns. LOC: Turn right on new by-pass from York (left coming from Beverley), signposted North Cave - sign on entrance. PARK: Easy. TEL: 0430 873234. SER: Valuations; restorations (furniture); buys at auction. FAIRS: New York (U.S.A.). VAT: Stan/Spec.

Pieter Plantenga
49 Home Rd. Open 9-5. *STOCK: Stripped pine, general furniture.* TEL: 0430 872473.

PATRINGTON

Clyde Antiques
12 Market Pl. (S M Nettleton) Est: 1978. Open 10-5. CL: Sun., Mon. and Wed. except by appointment. SIZE: Medium. *STOCK: General antiques.* PARK: Easy. TEL: 0964 630650; home - 0964 612471. SER: Valuations. VAT: Stan.

POCKLINGTON

In Retrospect
2 Pavement. (I. and R Barker) Est: 1978. CL: Wed. SIZE: Medium. *STOCK: Furniture, 18th and 19th C, £50-£2,000; paintings and watercolours mainly 19th C, £25-£1,000; ceramics, unusual collectables and ethnographica.* LOC: Next to church. PARK: Easy. TEL: 0759 304894; home - 0759 318559. VAT: Stan/Spec.

SEATON ROSS

Lewis Hickson CMBHI
Antiquarian Horologist, 'Rosewell', South End. Est: 1965. Open by appointment. *STOCK: Longcase and bracket clocks and barometers.* TEL: 0759 318850. SER: Valuations; restorations.

Seaton Ross continued

Rytham Antiques
Rytham Gate House. (Mrs M.M Quirke) Est: 1981. Open 10-5. CL: Mon. SIZE: Small. *STOCK: Silver, small furniture, 19th C, £50-£500; jewellery, late Victorian, £20-£180.* LOC: Off A1079. PARK: Easy. TEL: 0759 318200; home - same.

SOUTH CAVE

The Old Copper Shop
75 Market Pl. (Mrs E.A Featherstone) Est: 1986. Open 9.30-4.30. SIZE: Medium. *STOCK: Furniture, including pine, 19th-20th C; linen, toys, general antiques and collectors' items.* Not Stocked: Militaria, coins. LOC: A1034. PARK: Easy. TEL: 0430 423988; home - 0482 631110. SER: Valuations.

Penny Farthing Antiques
60 Market Pl. (C.E Dennett) Est: 1987. Open 9.30-4.30, Sun. 12.30-4.30. SIZE: Medium. *STOCK: Furniture, 19th-20th C, £25-£2,000; linen, textiles and samplers, 18th-20th C, £5-£500; general collectables, china and glass, 19th-20th C, £5-£500.* Not Stocked: Militaria and coins. LOC: Main road (A1034). PARK: Easy. TEL: 0430 422958; home - 0482 668794. SER: Valuations; buys at auction. FAIRS: Newark.

BARROW-ON-HUMBER

Elegance Antique Exports

Foresters Hall, High St. (G. and M Davey) Open any time by appointment. SIZE: Warehouse. *STOCK: Shipping furniture.* TEL: 0652 635012/660050.

BARTON-ON-HUMBER

Elegance Antiques

Brigg Rd. (G. and M Davey) Est: 1978. Open 9-5.30. SIZE: Large. *STOCK: General shipping items for U.S.A., 1900-1940; Edwardian and Victorian furniture and smalls; German and English pine, £5-£3,000.* LOC: Corner of Market Pl., town centre. PARK: Easy. TEL: 0652 635012/660050. SER: Valuations; restorations; containers; packing. FAIRS: Newark. VAT: Stan. *Trade Only.*

Streetwalker Antiques

35 High St. (J.N Chapman) Open 10.30-12.30 and 2-5. CL: Thurs. SIZE: Small. *STOCK: General antiques, 18th-19th C.* LOC: South bank of Humber Bridge, first exit. PARK: Easy. TEL: 0652 33960/660050. SER: Valuations. VAT: Stan.

Streetwalker Antiques Warehouse

Brigg Rd. (J.N Chapman) Open 9-5.30. SIZE: Large. *STOCK: General antiques and shipping furniture, oak and mahogany.* TEL: 0652 660050/33960. *Trade Only.*

GREAT COATES, Nr. Grimsby

Robin Fowler (Period Clocks)

The Manor House. Open by appointment. SIZE: Large. *STOCK: Clocks and barometers, 17th and 18th C.* TEL: 0472 883264. SER: Restorations (clocks, barometers).

GRIMSBY

Bell Antiques

68 Harold St. (V Hawkey) Est: 1964. Open by appointment, telephone previous evening. SIZE: Large. *STOCK: Pine.* PARK: Easy. TEL: 0472 695110; home - same. VAT: Stan. *Trade Only.*

Goodman Gold

43 Pasture St. (S.N Goodman) Est: 1978. Open 10.15-5. SIZE: Small. *STOCK: Jewellery, £25-£50; smalls, £5-£25; furniture and bric-a-brac, £5-£50; all mainly 19th-20th C.* LOC: Town centre just off Victoria St. PARK: Opposite. TEL: 0472 341301; home - 0472 360740. SER: Valuations (jewellery); buys at auction. FAIRS: Memorial Hall, Cleethorpes and local.

Simon Antiques

7 Saunders St. (S.N Goodman) Open by appointment only. *STOCK: Jewellery, smalls, furniture and bric-a-brac, mainly 19th-20th C, £5-£50.* TEL: 0472 360740. SER: Valuations (jewellery); buys at auction. FAIRS: Memorial Hall, Cleethorpes and local. *Trade Only.*

SCARTHOE, Nr. Grimsby

Scarthoe Antiques

38 Louth Rd. (P Bridges) Est: 1975. Open 10-5. CL: Mon. and Thurs. SIZE: Medium. *STOCK: Jewellery, silver, porcelain, collectors' items, maps, prints, linen.* LOC: A16. PARK: Easy. TEL: 0472 77394.

SCUNTHORPE

Guns and Tackle

251A Ashby High St. (J.A Bowden) Open 9-5.30. CL: Wed. *STOCK: Guns and militaria.* TEL: 0724 865445. SER: Restorations (guns); repairs (guns).

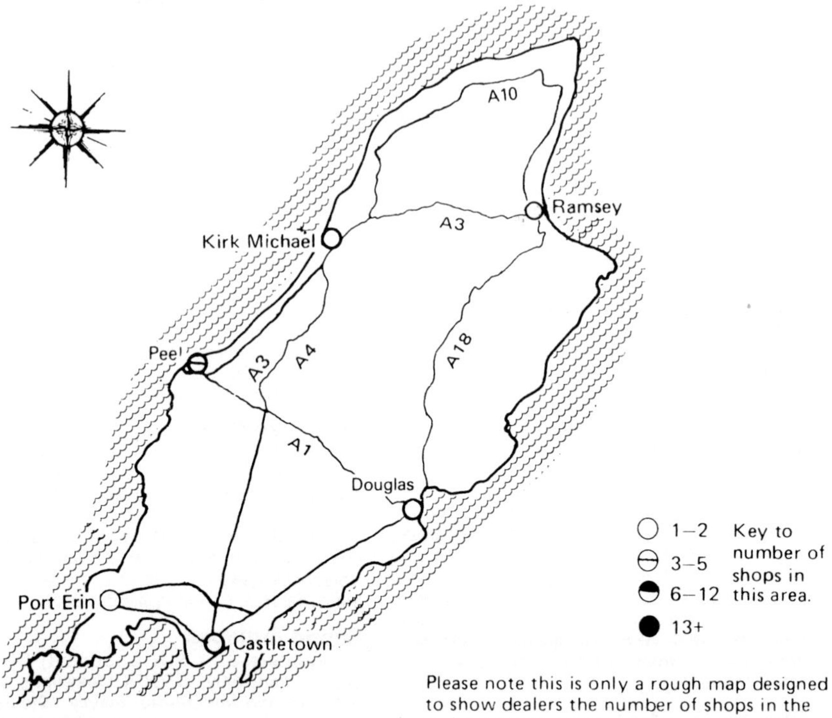
A10
Ramsey
A3
Kirk Michael
A18
Peel
A3
A4
A1
Douglas
Port Erin
Castletown
1–2
3–5
6–12
13+
Key to number of shops in this area.

Please note this is only a rough map designed to show dealers the number of shops in the various towns, and is not necessarily totally accurate.

CASTLETOWN

J. and H Bell Antiques

22 Arbory St. Est: 1965. Open 10-5.30. CL: Tues. and Thurs. SIZE: Medium. *STOCK: Jewellery, silver, china, glass, early metalware, furniture, 18th-20th C, £5-£5,000.* PARK: 50yds. TEL: 0624 823132; home - 822414. SER: Valuations. VAT: Stan/Spec.

DOUGLAS

John Corrin Antiques

73 Circular Rd. Est: 1972. Open Sat. 9-5.30 otherwise by appointment. SIZE: Medium. *STOCK: Furniture, 18th-19th C, £100-£4,500; clocks, barometers, 19th C.* LOC: From the promenade, travel up Victoria St., this becomes Prospect Hill and Circular Rd. is on left. PARK: Easy. TEL: 0624 629655; home - 0624 621382. SER: Valuations; restorations (barometers, clocks, furniture).

KIRK MICHAEL

Church View House Antiques

Main Rd. (P.H Morrison) Est: 1973. Open by appointment. *STOCK: Furniture, porcelain, pictures, glass, silver, 18th-19th C.* LOC: Opposite Parish Church. PARK: Easy. TEL: 0624 878433/663319. SER: Valuations; restorations. VAT: Spec.

PEEL

Bygones Ltd

5 Michael St. (M Boardley) Est: 1975. Open Tues., Wed. and Sat. SIZE: Medium. *STOCK: Small items, silver, plate, porcelain, copper and brass, boxes, art pottery, art nouveau and art deco, small furniture.* PARK: Easy. TEL: 0624 843477.

Circle of Cornelius Johnson, Portrait of Edward Bradhyll of Portfield, Lancashire. Panel, 29in. x 23in. Sold in October 1989 for £2,900. A good example of a provincial repetition of one of Johnson's patterns. The inscription at upper right is a later addition. From an article entitled 'Seventeenth Century Portraits' by Richard Charlton-Jones which appeared in the June 1991 issue of ***Antique Collecting***.

Son of Edward Bradhyll,
of Portfield,
Co Lancast.
BY
C.JANSEN.

Peel continued

Dorothea Horn At The Golden Past
18A Michael St. Est: 1982. Open Summer 10.30-4.30, Winter 11-4.30, Sat. 10.30-4.30. CL: Thurs. Oct.-Mar. SIZE: Medium. *STOCK: Jewellery, porcelain, silver, glass, books, paintings and furniture, 1840-1940, £5-£100.* LOC: Main shopping street. PARK: Easy. TEL: 0624 842170; home - 0624 843839.

Mannin Collections
5 Castle St. (A.E Kelly and K Kemp) Est: 1976. Open 10-5. CL: Thurs. SIZE: Small. *STOCK: Mainly Manx - maps and prints, 18th-19th C, £10-£500; paintings, £50-£2,000; china, 19th-20th C, £5-£200.* LOC: Near Market Pl. PARK: Nearby. TEL: 0624 843897; home - 0624 676116. SER: Valuations; restorations (cleaning and framing); buys at auction. VAT: Stan/Spec.

PORT ERIN

Spinning Wheel
Church Rd. (J.G. and M.B Craig) Est: 1979. Open 10-5. *STOCK: Silver, plate, china, glass, jewellery, pottery, furniture, linen, brass, bric-a-brac, clocks and watches, flatware.* TEL: 0624 833137/835020. SER: Restorations (furniture); French polishing; caning. VAT: Stan.

RAMSEY

P.G Allom and Co. Ltd
3 Parliament St. Est: 1965. *STOCK: Jewellery, silver, some secondhand.* TEL: 0624 812490.

Mrs. P Bourne and Miss V. Corkhill
2 Bourne Pl. Est: 1977. Open 10-5. CL: Wed. *STOCK: General antiques, silver, furniture, copper and brass.* TEL: 0624 812775.

Isle of Wight

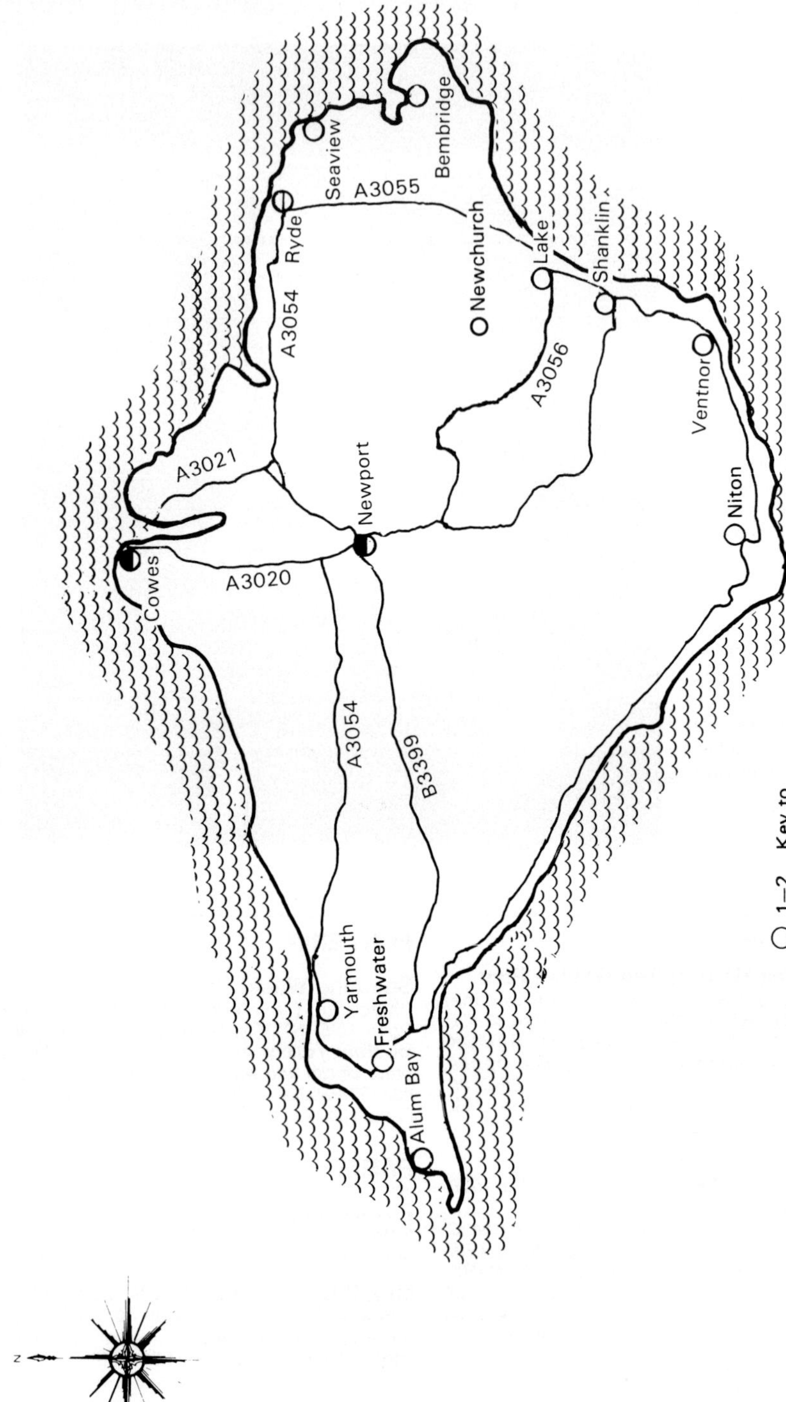
Bembridge
Seaview
A3055
Ryde
Newchurch
Lake
Shanklin
A3054
A3056
Ventnor
A3021
Newport
Niton
Cowes
A3020
A3054
B3399
Yarmouth
Freshwater
Alum Bay
N

○ 1–2 Key to
⊖ 3–5 number of
◐ 6–12 shops in
● 13+ this area.

Please note this is only a rough map designed to show dealers the number of shops in the various towns, and is not necessarily totally accurate.

ALUM BAY

Ron Tayler

'Heatherdown'. Open by appointment. *STOCK: Fine clocks.* PARK: Easy. TEL: 0983 754193.

BEMBRIDGE

Solent Antiques

1 Dennett Rd. (J. and J Van Daal) Est: 1973. Open 10-4, Sat. 10-5. CL: Thurs. p.m. SIZE: Small. *STOCK: Clocks, £200-£3,000; furniture, £200-£1,000; both 19th C.* LOC: Off High St. PARK: Easy. TEL: 0983 872107; home - same. SER: Valuations; restorations.

Windmill Antiques LAPADA

1 Foreland Rd. (E.J de Kort) Est: 1970. CL: Thurs. p.m. SIZE: Medium. *STOCK: Furniture, silver, porcelain, jewellery.* TEL: 0983 873666. SER: Valuations; buys at auction. VAT: Stan/Spec.

COWES

Julia Margaret Cameron Gallery

90B High St. (J Flynn) *STOCK: Antiquarian maps and prints especially local.* TEL: 0983 290404.

Charles Dickens Bookshop

65 High St. *STOCK: Antiquarian and secondhand books, especially 19th C English literature, nautical and children's.* TEL: 0983 293598.

Galerias Segui

75 High St. Est: 1976. Open 9.30-5. SIZE: Medium. *STOCK: Pine furniture, £60-£600; prints and watercolours, £15-£200; bric-a-brac.* LOC: Near Post Office and Red Funnel Pier. PARK: 200yds. TEL: 0983 292148.

The Marine Gallery

1 Bath Rd. Est: 1955. Open 11-1 and 2-5. SIZE: Medium. *STOCK: Marine oils, watercolours, prints, models, £50-£20,000.* LOC: Continuation of High St. leading to esplanade and sea. PARK: Easy. TEL: 0983 200124; fax - 0983 297282. SER: Valuations; restorations; framing. VAT: Stan/Spec.

Chris Watts Antiques

60 High St. Est: 1963. Open by appointment. SIZE: Large. *STOCK: Furniture, paintings, metalwork, £50-£3,000; general small items, £50-£500; all 18th-19th C.* Not Stocked: Jewellery and porcelain. LOC: Adjacent hydrofoil/ferry. PARK: Easy. TEL: 0983 298963; 0860 342558. VAT: Stan/Spec. *Trade Only.*

A.J Whiten

33 Castle St, East Cowes. Open 9-5. *STOCK: General antiques.* TEL: 0983 292098.

FRESHWATER

Aladdin's Cave

147/149 School Green Rd. (Mr and Mrs L.G Dunn) Est: 1984. Open 9.30-4.30. SIZE: Medium. *STOCK: China, collectors' items, glass, linen, clothes, 19th-20th C, £5-£50.* PARK: Easy. TEL: 0983 752934; home - 0983 753846. SER: Restorations (pine stripping). *Trade Only.*

LAKE

Lake Antiques

Sandown Rd. (P Burfield) Est: 1982. Open 10-5, Wed. 10-1. *STOCK: General antiques, Victorian and Edwardian furniture, clocks.* LOC: On the main Sandown-Shanklin Rd. PARK: On forecourt. TEL: 0983 406888/865005.

NEWCHURCH

Vectis Fine Arts

2 Ivy Cottages. (T.R.B Joyner) Est: 1982. Open by appointment only. *STOCK: English watercolours (especially marine) and etchings, 18th-20th C, £150-£5,000.* TEL: 0983 865463. SER: Valuations; restorations; framing; buys at auction (pictures). VAT: Stan/Spec.

NEWPORT

Mike Heath Antiques

3-4 Holyrood St. (M. and B Heath) Est: 1974. Open 9.30-5. CL: Thurs. SIZE: Medium. *STOCK: General antiques and bric-a-brac, 19th-20th C, £5-£500.* LOC: Off High St. PARK: Nearby. TEL: 0983 525748; home - same. SER: Restorations (copper and brass). VAT: Stan/Spec.

Lugley Street Antiques

13 Lugley St. (D.A Newman) Open 9.30-5.30. CL: Thurs. *STOCK: General antiques including clocks.* TEL: 0983 523348.

The Old Firm

68 Pyle St. (M. and T Brett) Est: 1975. Open 9.30-5, Thurs. 9.30-4. SIZE: Medium. *STOCK: Stripped pine, 18th-20th C, £5-£500; Victorian china.* LOC: Opposite Castlehold Lane. PARK: Easy. TEL: 0983 529592; home - 098 370 605. SER: Pine stripping; buys at auction.

Relics

27c Holyrood St. (S Williamson) Est: 1980. Open 10.30-4.30. CL: Thurs. SIZE: Small. *STOCK: Curios, decorative smalls, small furnishing items, 19th-20th C, £5-£100.* LOC: Off High St. PARK: Easy. TEL: 0983 521215. FAIRS: Ardingly.

Newport continued

Marilyn Rose Antiques Centre
87 Pyle St. Est: 1979. Open 10.30-4. *STOCK: Silver, porcelain, jewellery, period clothes and effects, small furniture, copper, brass and bric-a-brac.* LOC: Opposite R.C. Church. PARK: Easy. TEL: 0983 528850; home - 0983 293846.

Watchbell Antiques
Watchbell Lane. (P. and I Matheson and B. and R Julian) Est: 1983. Open 10-3.30, Fri. 10-4.30, Sat. 10-4. CL: Thurs. p.m. SIZE: Small. *STOCK: China and glass, 18th C to 1920, £10-£500; postcards and prints, from 20p; small furniture, copper lustre, commemorative and crested china, to Victorian, £2-£400.* Not Stocked: Large furniture, copper and brass. LOC: Off High St., behind Guildhall. PARK: Nearby. TEL: 0983 852089/526428. SER: Valuations. FAIRS: Shepton Mallet.

Chris Watts Antiques
Heytesbury, Worsley Rd. Open by appointment. *STOCK: Furniture, paintings, clocks and metalwork, £50-£3,000; general small items, £50-£500; all 18th-19th C.* TEL: 0983 822817/298963 or 0860 342558.

NITON

Startime
The Star House, Church St. (R Tapley) Usually open. *STOCK: Clocks, 1750-1930.* TEL: 0983 730823.

RYDE

Decorative Arts
17 Union St. (Mrs D Hoare) Open 10-5.30. *STOCK: Furniture, pictures and works of art, from £20.* TEL: 0983 615463. SER: Valuations. VAT: Spec.

Ryde continued

Hayter's
18, 19 and 20 Cross St. (R.W. and F.L Hayter) Est: 1956. Open 9-1 and 2-5.30. CL: Thurs. SIZE: Large. *STOCK: Furniture including Victorian.* LOC: Through main traffic flow from sea front to town centre. TEL: 0983 63795. VAT: Stan/Spec.

Royal Victoria Arcade
Union St. Open 9-5.30; basement market open Thurs., Fri. and Sat. in summer. TEL: 0983 64661. Below are listed some of the dealers in this Arcade.

Crocus
Collectables, art deco to 1950s.
Echoes
Costume jewellery, militaria and general antiques.
Mary Jane
General antiques.
Moonfleet
General antiques.
Passing Buy
General antiques.
Treasures
General antiques.

Uriah's Heap
9 Royal Victoria Arcade, Union St. (F Cross) Open 10-5. CL: Tues. and Thurs. *STOCK: Small antiques, china, silver, collectables, linen, lace, fountain pens, jewellery.* TEL: 0983 64661.

Vecta Insula
62 High St. (G.L Ruthven) Open 10.30-5. CL: Thurs. *STOCK: Maps, prints, books and watercolours.* TEL: 0983 64362.

SEAVIEW, Nr. Ryde

Seaview Antiques
West St. Open 10.30-1 and 2.30-5, or by appointment. CL: Mon. and Thurs. *STOCK: General antiques, ceramics, furniture, textiles, glass, Victorian jewellery, needlework, tools, violins.* TEL: 0983 612882; home - 0983 613292.

SHANKLIN

Keith Shotter, Collectors Centre
81 Regent St. Est: 1974. Open 9.30-5. *STOCK: Coins, medals, jewellery, bottles, 50 B.C. to 1930.* LOC: 100yds. from railway station. PARK: Easy. TEL: 0983 862334/853620. VAT: Stan.

VENTNOR

Derek R Lord
"St Bedes", 81 Leeson Rd. Open by appointment. *STOCK: Weapons, 16th to mid 19th C, £50-£10,000.* TEL: 0983 854749. SER: Valuations; restorations; buys at auction. FAIRS: All major arms. VAT: Spec.

Ventnor Rare Books
19 Pier St. (N.C.R. and T.A Traylen) ABA. *STOCK: Antiquarian and secondhand books, prints.* TEL: 0983 853706.

YARMOUTH

The Gallery
High St. (G Campbell and S Noakes) Est: 1956. Open 10-1 and 2-5. SIZE: Medium. *STOCK: Watercolours, £75-£1,500; oil paintings, £300-£5,000; both 19th-20th C; maps, engravings and etchings, 18th-20th C, £10-£300.* LOC: Near Common. PARK: Easy. TEL: 0983 760784; home - 0983 78577. SER: Valuations; restorations (oils, watercolours and prints); framing. VAT: Stan/Spec.

Marlborough House Antiques
St. James Sq. (P.A Webb) Est: 1972. *STOCK: Local prints and maps, silver, jewellery, pottery, glass, small furniture.* TEL: 0983 760498.

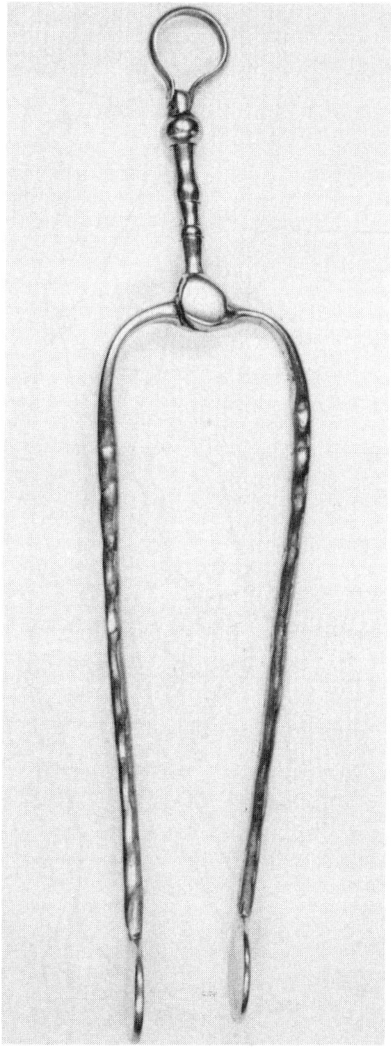

Ember tongs, cast brass, English, second half 18th century. 9in. long. (Jack Casimir Ltd.) From an article on ember tongs by Christopher Bangs in the December 1990/January 1991 issue of ***Antique Collecting.***

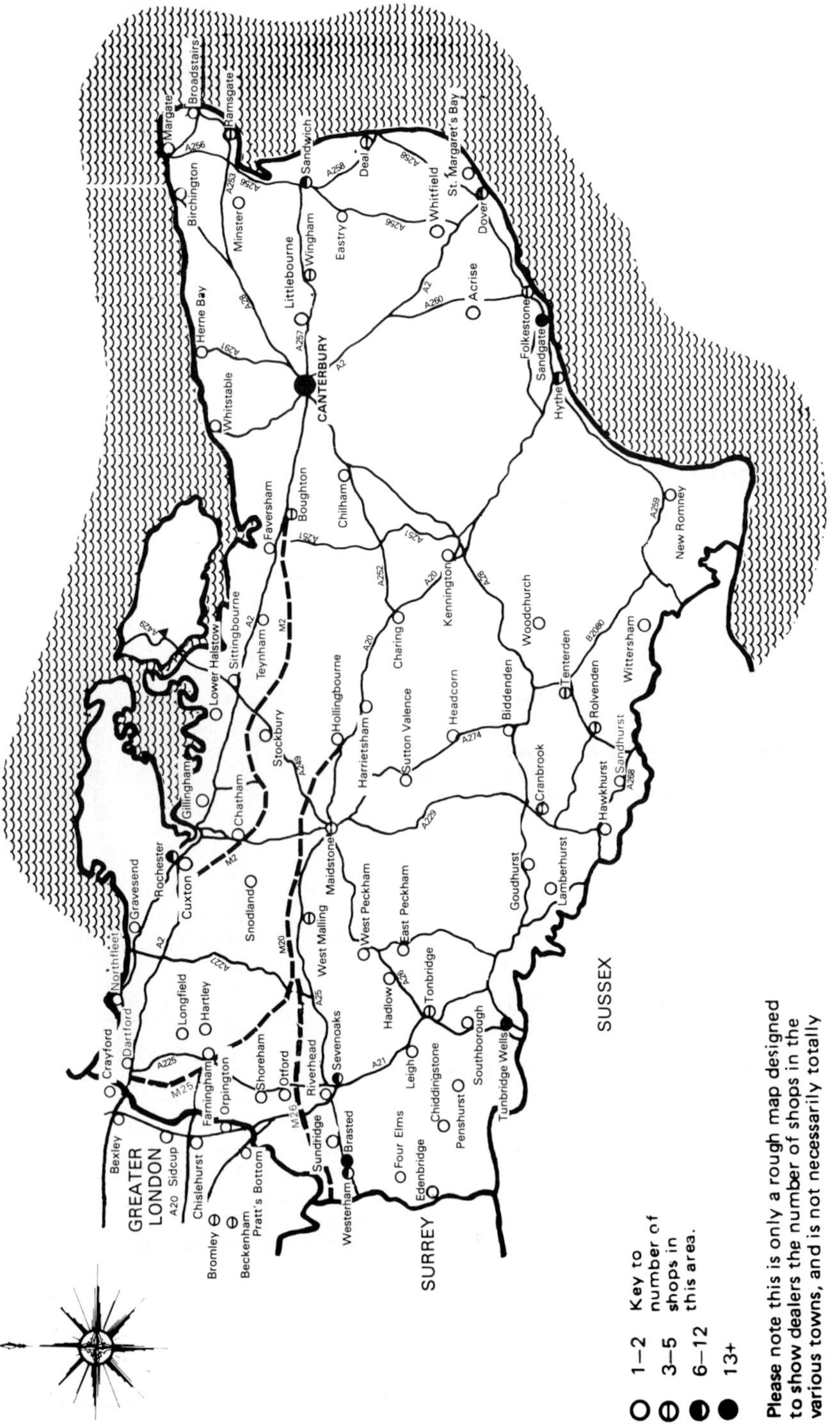

Margate
Broadstairs
Ramsgate
A256
A253
Birchington
Minster
Sandwich
A258
Deal
Eastry
Whitfield
St. Margaret's Bay
Dover
Wingham
Littlebourne
A28
A2
A260
Acrise
Folkestone
Sandgate
Hythe
Herne Bay
A291
Whitstable
A257
CANTERBURY
Boughton
Chilham
Faversham
A251
New Romney
A259
Kennington
A252
A20
Sittingbourne
Lower Halstow
A429
Teynham
M2
Charing
Woodchurch
Tenterden
B2080
Wittersham
Rolvenden
Sandhurst
Hawkhurst
A268
Hollingbourne
Harrietsham
Sutton Valence
Headcorn
A274
Biddenden
Cranbrook
Stockbury
A249
Gillingham
Chatham
Rochester
Maidstone
A229
Gravesend
Cuxton
Snodland
West Malling
West Peckham
East Peckham
Goudhurst
Lamberhurst
Northfleet
Dartford
Crayford
Longfield
Hartley
A227
M20
Hadlow
A26
Tonbridge
Southborough
Tunbridge Wells
SUSSEX
A225
M25
Farningham
Orpington
Shoreham
Otford
Riverhead
Sevenoaks
A21
Leigh
Chiddingstone
Penshurst
M26
Sundridge
Brasted
Four Elms
Edenbridge
Westerham
Bexley
Sidcup
Chislehurst
GREATER LONDON
A20
Pratt's Bottom
Beckenham
Bromley
SURREY

- ○ 1–2
- ⊖ 3–5
- ◐ 6–12
- ● 13+

Key to number of shops in this area.

Please note this is only a rough map designed to show dealers the number of shops in the various towns, and is not necessarily totally accurate.

ACRISE, Nr. Folkestone

R Kirby Antiques
Caroline Cottage, Ridge Row. Open by appointment only. *STOCK: Early period oak.* TEL: 030389 3230.

BECKENHAM

Beckenham Antique Market
Old Council Hall, Bromley Rd. Est: 1979. Open Wed. only 9.30-2. SIZE: 30 stalls. *STOCK: General antiques.* TEL: 081 764 3602.

Horton's LAPADA
428 Croydon Rd. (D. and R Horton) FGA. Est: 1978. CL: Mon. and Wed. SIZE: Medium. *STOCK: Jewellery and silver, 19th-20th C; furniture, late 18th C to Edwardian, all £500-£1,000; British paintings, early to mid 20th C, £250-£750.* LOC: Junction with High St. PARK: Easy. TEL: 081 658 6418. SER: Valuations; restorations (jewellery). VAT: Stan/Spec.

Pepys Antiques
9 Kelsey Park Rd. (H Butler and S.P Elton) Est: 1969. Open 10-5.30. CL: Wed. *STOCK: Furniture, paintings, clocks, silver, porcelain, copper, brass.* LOC: Central Beckenham. TEL: 081 650 0994.

Scallywag
22 High St. (J.A Butterworth) Est: 1970. Open 9.30-5.30. SIZE: Large. *STOCK: Pine, 18th-19th C, £5-£5,000.* LOC: 100yds. from Beckenham Junction station. PARK: Easy. TEL: 081 658 6633. VAT: Stan/Spec.

Norman Witham
2 High St. Est: 1959. Open Fri. and Sat. *STOCK: Porcelain, glass, small furniture, mainly Victorian, £5-£500.* TEL: 081 650 9096; evenings - 081 650 4651. SER: Valuations. VAT: Stan/Spec.

BEXLEY

Argentum Antiques
18-20 High St. (L.T Laklia) Est: 1967. Open 9-5. CL: Thurs. p.m. SIZE: Large. *STOCK: Silver, plate, clocks, porcelain, jewellery, paintings, prints, English and continental furniture.* LOC: A210. From London take the A2 to Bexley. PARK: Easy. TEL: 0322 527915. SER: Valuations; restorations; buys at auction. VAT: Stan.

BIDDENDEN, Nr. Ashford

Two Maids Antiques
6 High St. (J Thornley and R Norris) Est: 1979. Open 10-5 and by appointment. CL: Mon. and Wed. SIZE: Medium. *STOCK: Small furniture, lace bobbins, decorative objects, miniatures, silhouettes, Victorian paintings and frames,*

Two Maids Antiques continued

domestic ironwork, woodcarvings and treen. LOC: A262. PARK: Opposite. TEL: 0580 291807; home - same.

BIRCHINGTON, Nr. Margate

John Chawner
36 Station Approach. Open 10.30-12.30 and 1.30-5. *STOCK: Clocks and smalls.* PARK: Easy. TEL: 0843 43309. SER: Repairs (clocks).

BOUGHTON, Nr. Faversham

The Clock Shop Antiques
187 The Street. (S.G Fowler) MBHI. Resident. Est: 1968. Articles on clocks. Open 10-6. CL: Sun. except by appointment. SIZE: Small. *STOCK: Clocks.* PARK: Easy. TEL: 0227 751258. SER: Repairs (clocks).

Jean Collyer Antiques
194 The Street. (Mrs J.B Collyer) Est: 1977. Open Tues. and Fri. 2-5, Sat. 10-5. SIZE: Small. *STOCK: Porcelain, glass, furniture, general antiques, 18th to mid-19th C.* PARK: Easy. TEL: 0227 751454; home - same. SER: Valuations. VAT: Stan/Spec.

Edward Smith Antiques
202 The Street. Open 10-6 or by appointment. *STOCK: Furniture, curios, clocks, silver, architectural items and models.* TEL: 0227 750395.

BRASTED, Nr. Westerham

The Attic (Sevenoaks) Ltd
The Village House. (R. and J Brydon) ABA. Resident. Est: 1953. Appointment advisable. *STOCK: Antiquarian and out-of-print books.* TEL: 0959 63507.

David Barrington
The Antique Shop. Est: 1947. Open 9-6. SIZE: Medium. *STOCK: Furniture, 18th C.* LOC: A25. PARK: Easy. TEL: 0959 62537. VAT: Stan/Spec.

Brasted Antiques and Interiors
High St. (Mrs R.B Rowlett) Open 10-5.30. *STOCK: Furniture, paintings and bric-a-brac.* TEL: 0959 64863. SER: Interior design.

Elizabeth Brooker Antiques at the Village Gallery
High St. Open 10-6. *STOCK: Fine decorative Georgian furniture, clocks and objets d'art.* TEL: 0959 62503.

Brasted continued

Courtyard Antiques

High St. (H La Trobe) Open 10-5.30. *STOCK: General antiques including silver, jewellery, furniture, especially extending Victorian dining tables, sets of chairs.* PARK: Easy. TEL: 0959 64483. SER: Valuations; restorations (furniture); French polishing and releathering.

Ivy House Antiques

High St. (R Throp and P Welsh) Open 10-6. SIZE: Medium. *STOCK: Furniture, porcelain, paintings, decorative items.* LOC: A25. PARK: Easy. TEL: 0959 64581; home - same. VAT: Stan/Spec.

Keymer Son & Co. Ltd

Swaylands Pl, The Green. Est: 1977. Open 9.30-5.30, Sat. a.m. by appointment. SIZE: Small. *STOCK: Furniture, £100-£500; clocks, £200-£1,000; both 18th-19th C.* LOC: A25. PARK: Easy. TEL: 0959 64203.

Roy Massingham Antiques LAPADA

The Coach House. Open 9-5 or by appointment. *STOCK: 18th-19th C furniture, pictures and decorative items.* TEL: 0959 62408; mobile - 0860 326825.

Old Manor House Antiques

The Green, High St. Open daily. *STOCK: Clocks, barometers, bric-a-brac and general antiques.* TEL: 0959 62536.

Rashleigh LAPADA

High St. (Mrs B.M Jennings) Open 10-5, Sat. 10.30-5.30. *STOCK: General antiques.* TEL: 0959 63938.

Southdown House Antique Galleries

High St. (R. and D Thomas) Est: 1978. Open 9.30-5.30. *STOCK: Furniture, porcelain, glass, metalware, tapestries, 18th-19th C; oils and watercolours, 19th C.* TEL: 0959 63522.

Dinah Stoodley

High St. (Mrs D Stoodley) Est: 1965. Open 9.30-5.30. SIZE: Medium. *STOCK: Oak and country furniture, 17th-19th C, pewter and metalware, pottery.* Not Stocked: Victoriana, jewellery, silver. LOC: A25. PARK: Easy. TEL: 0959 63616. VAT: Stan/Spec.

Tilings Antiques

High St. (H Loveland and P Fawcett) Est: 1974. Open 10-5 .30 or by appointment. SIZE: Medium. *STOCK: Furniture, ceramics, decorative items, 18th-19th C, £20-£2,000.* LOC: Village centre on A25. PARK: Easy. TEL: 0959 64735. VAT: Stan/Spec.

W.W Warner (Antiques) Ltd BADA

The Green. (Mrs C.U Warner) Est: 1957. Open 10-1 and 2-5. SIZE: Medium. *STOCK: English porcelain, 18th-19th C, £5-£1,000; English pottery, 18th to early 19th C, £10-£500; small*

W.W Warner (Antiques) Ltd continued

***mahogany furniture, prior to 1830, £30-£1,000.* Not Stocked: Silver, Victoriana. LOC: A25. PARK: Easy. TEL: 0959 63698. SER: Buys at London auctions. VAT: Spec.**

The Weald Gallery

High St. (S.J. and N.V Turley) Est: 1972. Open 9.30-5.30. SIZE: Small. *STOCK: Watercolours, 1800-1940, £100-£5,000.* LOC: A25. PARK: Easy. TEL: 0959 62672. SER: Valuations; restorations (watercolours, oil paintings and prints). VAT: Stan/Spec.

BROADSTAIRS

Broadstairs Antiques and Collectables

49 Belvedere Rd. (P Edwards) Est: 1980. Open 10.30-4.30 winter, 10-5 summer. CL: Wed. *STOCK: General antiques.* LOC: Opposite Lloyds Bank. TEL: 0843 61965.

BROMLEY

Antica

Rear of 35-41 High St. (L. and P Muccio) Open 10-5.30. *STOCK: General antiques.* LOC: Opposite Debenhams. TEL: 081 464 7661. VAT: Stan.

Bromley Antique Market

Widmore Rd. Est: 1968. Open Thursday 7.30-3. SIZE: 70 stalls. *STOCK: General antiques, jewellery, books, bric-a-brac, copper, brass and clocks, collectors' items, coins, furs, stamps, postcards.* VAT: Stan.

CANTERBURY

Antique and Design

Unit 14, Graham Bell House, Roper Close. (C Whitfield) Est: 1988. Open 9-5.30, Sat. 10-5.30, Sun. by appointment. *STOCK: Pine furniture, decorative items, 1800 to date, £5-£1,500.* LOC: From West Gate along St. Dunstans, over railway crossing, first right then left. PARK: Easy. TEL: 0227 762871. SER: Restorations, buys at auction. VAT: Stan/Spec.

R J Baker

16 Palace St. Est: 1971. Open 9.30-5.30, Wed. 9.30-5. CL: Thurs. SIZE: Small. *STOCK: Silver and jewellery, 18th-19th C, £500-£2,000; handmade modern silverware, modern jewellery.* LOC: 5 minutes from cathedral, opposite The King's School. PARK: Easy. TEL: 0227 463224. SER: Valuations; restorations; gold and silversmiths; manufacturers. VAT: Stan/Spec.

Bell Harry Books

110 Northgate. (J Hubbard) Est: 1977. Open 10-5.30. *STOCK: Secondhand and out of print books.* TEL: 0227 453481; home - 0227 767934.

Canterbury continued

Burgate Antiques
10 Burgate. (Mr and Mrs Winterflood, Mr and Mrs Maddox) Est: 1986. Open 9.30-5.30 including Sun. SIZE: Medium. *STOCK: Furniture, paintings, £5-£2,000; collectors' items including prints, militaria, china, glass and linen; all 19th C.* LOC: City Wall overlooking Cathedral Gardens. TEL: 0227 456500. SER: Valuations; restorations. VAT: Stan/Spec.

Canterbury Rastro
44a High St. (J Coppage) Est: 1981. Open 10-5. SIZE: 6 dealers. *STOCK: General antiques and collectors' items; antiquarian and secondhand books.* LOC: Up narrow lane off High St. PARK: Nearby. TEL: 0227 483537.

Canterbury Weekly Antique Market
Sidney Cooper Centre, St. Peter's St. Open Sat. 8-4.

Chaucer Bookshop
6 Beer Cart Lane. (R Sherston-Baker) ABA, PBFA. Est: 1977. Open 10-5. SIZE: Medium. *STOCK: Books and prints, 18th-20th C, £5-£150; maps, 18th-19th C, £50-£250.* LOC: 5 minutes walk from cathedral, via Mercery Lane and St. Margaret's St. PARK: Castle St. TEL: 0227 453912. SER: Valuations; restorations (book binding); buys at auction (books, maps and prints). VAT: Stan.

Cloisters
26 Palace St. (A De Jaeger) Resident. Est: 1982. Open 10-5.30. SIZE: Small. *STOCK: Prints, especially limited edition topographical, birds, flowers and fashion, 19th C, £5-£25; maps and fine prints, 18th-19th C, £50-£150; modern watercolours and oils.* LOC: Opposite north gate of cathedral. PARK: Multi-storey nearby. TEL: 0227 462729. SER: Restorations; mounting and framing. VAT: Stan.

Coach House Antiques
Duck Lane, St. Radiguns, Northgate. Est: 1975. Open 10-1 and 2-5. SIZE: Large. *STOCK: General antiques, bygones, kitchenalia, juvenilia, small furniture.* PARK: Opposite. TEL: 0227 463117.

Conquest House Antiques LAPADA
17 Palace St. (C.C Hill and D.A Magee) Open 9-6. *STOCK: Furniture and decorative items.* TEL: 0227 464587; fax - 0227 451375.

H.S Greenfield and Son, Gunmakers (Est. 1805)
4/5 Upper Bridge St. (A.G. and T.S Greenfield) Est: 1805. CL: Thurs. p.m. *STOCK: English sporting guns, in pairs and singles; continental sporting guns, firearms, swords, flintlock and percussion pistols.* TEL: 0227 456959. SER: Valuations; restorations (antique firearms). VAT: Stan.

Canterbury continued

The Harvey Centre
22/24 Stour St. (B West and D Gilbert) Est: 1984. Open 9-5.30. SIZE: Medium. *STOCK: Furniture, £50-£1,000; decorative items, £5-£500; both Victorian and Edwardian.* LOC: Off High St. PARK: Nearby. TEL: 0227 452677. VAT: Stan/Spec.

R. and J.L Henley Antiques
37a Broad St. Open 9-6. *STOCK: General antiques, Victorian brass beds.* TEL: 0227 769055. VAT: Stan/Spec.

Leadenhall Gallery
12 Palace St. (D.L Greenaway) Open 9.30-5.30. *STOCK:* Not Stocked: Prints and maps. TEL: 0227 457339.

Nan Leith's Brocanterbury
Errol House, 68 Stour St. *STOCK: Art deco, Victoriana, pressed glass, costume jewellery.* TEL: 0227 454519.

David Miles
37 Northgate. Open 10-5. *STOCK: Antiquarian books, pictures and prints.* TEL: 0227 464773.

Parker-Williams
22 Palace St. (L Parker) CL: Sun. a.m. and Thurs. p.m. SIZE: Medium. *STOCK: Furniture 18th-19th C; porcelain, silver, bronzes, pictures, copper, brass, clocks.* TEL: 0227 768341. VAT: Stan/Spec.

Michael Pearson Antiques
2 The Borough, Northgate. Open 10-6. *STOCK: Early oak, clocks, country furniture, wood carvings.* TEL: 0227 459939. SER: Valuations; restorations (clocks).

The Saracen's Lantern
8-9 The Borough. (W.J Christophers) Est: 1970. *STOCK: General antiques, silver, jewellery, clocks, watches, Victorian bottles and pot-lids, Georgian, Victorian and Edwardian furniture.* LOC: Near Cathedral opp. King's School. PARK: At rear, by way of Northgate and St. Radigun's St. TEL: 0227 451968.

Stablegate Antiques
19 The Borough, Palace St. (Mrs G Giuntini) Est: 1989. Open 10-5.30. SIZE: Small. *STOCK: General antiques, furniture and porcelain, Georgian, Victorian and Edwardian, £5-£1,000; jewellery, glass, objets d'art, collectables.* LOC: Between Mint Yard Gate and King's School. PARK: Nearby. TEL: 0227 764086; home - 0227 831639.

The Victorian Fireplace Ltd
Thanet House, 92 Broad St. (J.J Griffith) Est: 1980. Open 10-5.30, Sun. and Mon. by appointment. SIZE: Medium. *STOCK: Victorian fireplaces and shipping furniture.* LOC: Town centre. PARK: Nearby. TEL: 0227 767723; home - same. SER: Restorations. VAT: Stan/Spec. *Trade Only.*

CHARING

Peckwater Antiques and Interiors
15-17 High St. (F.H. and S.M Tucker) Est: 1983. Open 10-5, other times by appointment. SIZE: Medium. *STOCK: Furniture, decorative items and soft furnishings.* LOC: Off A20. PARK: Easy. TEL: 023 371 2592; home - same. VAT: Stan/Spec.

CHATHAM

John Chawner
44 Chatham Hill. Open 1.30-5. *STOCK: Clocks and general antiques.* PARK: Easy. TEL: 0634 811147/0843 43309. SER: Clock repairs.

CHIDDINGSTONE, Nr. Edenbridge

Barbara Lane Antiques
Tudor Cottage. (Mrs E.B Avery) Est: 1967. Open 10-5. *STOCK: General antiques, furniture, silver and plate, porcelain and 20th C collectables.* LOC: Behind Castle Inn. PARK: Easy. TEL: 0892 870577.

CHILHAM, Nr. Canterbury

Chilham Antiques Ltd
The Square. (Mrs J Green) Est: 1965. Open 9-6, Sun. 12-1 and 3-5. SIZE: Large. *STOCK: Oil paintings, English and continental, 18th-19th C; period furniture, glass, silver, porcelain, objets d'art.* Not Stocked: Firearms. LOC: Follow A20 from London via Maidstone by-pass. PARK: Easy. TEL: 0227 730250/730565. SER: Restorations (cleaning and framing of pictures). VAT: Stan/Spec.

Peacock Antiques
The Square. (S Blacklocks) Open 9.30-6, Sat. 10-6, Sun. 2-6. SIZE: Medium. *STOCK: Furniture, 17th-19th C, £200-£4,000; silver, copper and brass, 18th-19th C, £25-£5,000; china, glass, objets d'art, 19th C, £25-£1,000.* LOC: 1/2 mile off Canterbury to Ashford road and 200yds. off Canterbury to Maidstone road. PARK: Easy. TEL: 0227 730219. VAT: Stan/Spec.

CHISLEHURST

Chislehurst Antiques LAPADA
7 Royal Parade. (Mrs M Crawley) Est: 1976. Open 10-1 and 2-5. SIZE: Medium. *STOCK: Furniture, 1760-1900, some porcelain, glass, brass and copper.* LOC: One mile from A20. PARK: Easy. TEL: 081 467 1530. VAT: Stan/Spec.

Michael Sim LAPADA
1 Royal Parade. Open 9-6 including Sun. SIZE: Medium. *STOCK: English furniture, Georgian and Regency, £500-£50,000; clocks and barometers, £500-£10,000; Oriental works of art, £50-£5,000; pictures, Victorian, £100-£10,000; portrait miniatures, £300-£5,000; animalier bronzes, £1,000-£10,000.* LOC: 50yds. from War Memorial at junction of Bromley Rd. and Centre Common Rd. PARK: Easy. TEL: 081 467 7040; home - same. SER: Valuations; restorations; buys at auction. VAT: Spec.

CRANBROOK

Cranbrook Antique Centre
15 High St. (Mr. and Mrs R Bisram) Open 10-5. SIZE: 7 dealers. *STOCK: General antiques.* TEL: 0580 712173.

Cranbrook Gallery
21B Stone St. (P.A Donovan) Open 9.15-5, Sat. 9.15-4. CL: Mon. *STOCK: Watercolours, prints and maps, 18th-19th C.* TEL: 0580 713021.

The Old Bakery Antiques
BADA LAPADA
The Old Bakery, St. David's Bridge. (D.R. and C Bryan) Est: 1971. Open 9-5.30, Wed. 9-1 and by appointment. SIZE: Medium. *STOCK: Mainly English oak furniture, 17th-18th C; woodcarvings, some metalware.* LOC: Adjacent Tan Yard car park - off road towards Windmill. PARK: Adjacent. TEL: 0580 713103.

Cranbrook continued

Swan Antiques
Stone St. (R.S. and Mrs A White) Resident. Est: 1977. Open 10-1 and 2-5.15, Wed. and Sun. and other times by appointment. SIZE: Medium. *STOCK: English country furniture, mainly small oak, elm and pine, £15-£4,000; English pottery, treen, pictures and collectables; all pre-1890, decorative items, painted furniture.* LOC: Opposite Barclays Bank. PARK: Nearby. TEL: 0580 712720. SER: Valuations; interiors. FAIRS: Brighton; Olympia; Westminster. VAT: Spec.

Wooden Chair Antiques
Waterloo Rd. (Mr and Mrs G Evans) Open 9.30-5.30. *STOCK: General antiques and pine.* LOC: Opposite Cranbrook Public School. PARK: Easy. TEL: 0580 713671. SER: Restorations (furniture); upholstery.

CRAYFORD

Watling Antiques
139 Crayford Rd. Open 10-6.30. *STOCK: General antiques and shipping goods.* TEL: 0322 523620.

CUXTON, Nr. Rochester

Country Pine Antiques
The Barn, Upper Bush Farm, Upper Bush Lane, Upper Bush. (G Bruce) Open by appointment. *STOCK: Antique pine, period sofas and chairs.* TEL: 0634 714198.

DARTFORD

Dartford Antiques
27 East Hill. (M Skudder) Est: 1976. Open 10-4. SIZE: Medium. *STOCK: Furniture, 19th-20th C, £25-£100; collectors' items.* LOC: On hill into town from tunnel. PARK: Easy. TEL: 0322 291350. SER: Valuations.

DEAL

José Morales Antiques
138 High St. Open 9.30-5, Sun. by appointment. CL: Thurs. *STOCK: Furniture, early, Victorian and gilt; prints.* TEL: 0304 361461. SER: Gilding.

The Print Room Gallery
95a Beach St. (M McKenna) Open Mon., Fri. and Sat. 10-1, and 2.30-5.30, other times by appointment. *STOCK: Antiquarian and continental prints and maps.* TEL: 0304 368904.

Quill Antiques
12 Alfred Sq. (A.J. and A.R Young) Open 9-5.30. *STOCK: General antiques, porcelain, postcards.* TEL: 0304 375958.

Deal continued

Serendipity
168/170 High St. (M. and K Short) Est: 1976. Open 10-12 and 2-4, Sat. 9-5 or by appointment. CL: Wed. and Thurs. SIZE: Medium. *STOCK: Oil paintings and watercolours, 1750-1930, £25-£2,000; porcelain, glass and Staffordshire figures, 1780-1930, £30-£300; books, postcards, small furniture, collectables.* PARK: Easy. TEL: 0304 369165; home - 0304 366536. SER: Valuations; restorations.

DOVER

Bonnies
18 Bartholomew St. (P. and R Janes) Est: 1985. Open 9-5. *STOCK: General antiques.* TEL: 0304 204206/830116. SER: Upholstery; restorations.

W.J Morrill Ltd
437 Folkestone Rd. (D Barnes) Est: 1910. Open by appointment. *STOCK: Oil paintings, 18th-20th C, £50-£1,000.* Not Stocked: Watercolours. LOC: 1 1/2 miles from town centre on main Folkestone road. PARK: Easy. TEL: 0304 201989; home - same. SER: Restorations (paintings); relining and framing. VAT: Stan/Spec. *Trade Only.*

J. and L Saunders
196/197 London Rd. Est: 1980. Open 9.30-5.30. *STOCK: General antiques.* TEL: 0304 214003.

Stuff
87 London Rd. (R Bole) Est: 1982. Open 9.30-5.30. CL: Wed. *STOCK: General antiques.* TEL: 0304 215405.

EAST PECKHAM, Nr. Tonbridge

Desmond and Amanda North
The Orchard, Hale St. Est: 1971. Open daily, appointment advisable. SIZE: Medium. *STOCK: Oriental rugs, runners, carpets and cushions, 1800-1939, £60-£3,500.* LOC: On B2015, 150yds. south of junction with B2016. PARK: Easy. TEL: 0622 871353; home - same. SER: Valuations; restorations (reweaving, re-edging, patching, cleaning).

EASTRY

The Plough Pine Shop
High St. (D.A Magee) *STOCK: Stripped pine.* TEL: 0304 617418; fax - 0304 451375.

EDENBRIDGE

Chevertons of Edenbridge Ltd LAPADA

Taylour House, 67 and 69 High St. (D Adam) Open 9-5.30. SIZE: Large. *STOCK: Furniture, 17th-19th C, £100-£15,000.* Not Stocked: Silver, oil paintings, porcelain. LOC: From Westerham, on B2026 to Edenbridge. PARK: Easy. TEL: 0732 863196 and 863358. VAT: Stan/Spec.

FARNBOROUGH, Nr. Orpington

Farnborough (Kent) Antiques BADA

10 Church Rd. (J.M Dewdney) Est: 1970. Open Sat. and by appointment. SIZE: Small. *STOCK: Oak furniture, wood carvings and sculpture, 15th-18th C, £50-£3,000.* Not Stocked: Mahogany and post-1750 furniture. LOC: Off A21 near Bromley, 10 mins. M25. PARK: Easy. TEL: 0689 854286/851834. VAT: Spec.

Pembroke Antiques Ltd LAPADA

3 Church Rd. Open 10-1 and 2.30-5.30. *STOCK: Fine period furniture, 17th to early 19th C; period artifacts.* LOC: Just off A21, 10 mins. from M25. PARK: Easy. TEL: 0689 862846. VAT: Stan/Spec.

FARNINGHAM

P.T Beasley

Forge Yard, High St. (P.T. and R Beasley) Est: 1964. CL: Tues. *STOCK: English furniture, some pewter, brass, Delft, woodcarvings.* LOC: Near the Pied Bull Hotel. TEL: 0322 862453.

FAVERSHAM

Gunpowder House Antiques

78 Lower West St. (E Platt) Est: 1967. Open 9-6, Sun. by appointment. *STOCK: Late 18th-19th C general antiques, £10-£1,000.* LOC: From Ospringe, turn left at Alms Houses, then right into West St. PARK: Opposite. TEL: 0795 534208.

Squires Antiques (Faversham)

3 Jacob Yard, Preston St. (A Squires) Est: 1985. Open 10-5. CL: Wed. and Thurs. *STOCK: General antiques.* TEL: 0795 531503.

FOLKESTONE

Richard Amos

37 Cheriton High St. Open 9.30-12 and 2-5, Wed. 9.30-12. *STOCK: General antiques.* TEL: 0303 275449.

Folkestone continued

Alan Lord Antiques
71 Tontine St. (A.G., J.A. and R.G Lord) Est: 1956. Open 9-1 and 2-4.30. CL: Wed. and Sat. p.m. *STOCK: General antiques, £1-£3,000.* LOC: Road up from harbour. PARK: Easy. TEL: 0303 53674. VAT: Stan/Spec.

G. and D.I Marrin and Sons
149 Sandgate Rd. ABA. Est: 1949. Open 9.30-1 and 2.30-5.30. SIZE: Large. *STOCK: Maps, early engravings, topographical and sporting prints, paintings, drawings, books, engravings.* TEL: 0303 53016; fax - 0303 850956. SER: Restorations; framing. VAT: Stan.

Paul and Karen Rennie
Open by appointment only. *STOCK: Decorative arts, 1880-1960.* TEL: 0303 42090.

Winterdown Books
P.O. Box 106. (G.G Meynell) Est: 1979. *STOCK: Medical and scientific books.* TEL: 0304 853080. SER: Catalogue available.

FOUR ELMS

Treasures
The Cross Roads. (B Ward-Lee) Open 10-5. *STOCK: Copper, brass, glass, porcelain, silver, jewellery, linen, books, toys, pine, small furniture and collectables.* TEL: 073 270 363.

Yew Tree Antiques
The Cross Roads. (P Lewis) Est: 1984. Open 9-5. SIZE: Medium. *STOCK: Porcelain and copper, 19th-20th C, £5-£500; glass, jewellery, linen, small furniture and collectables.* LOC: Off A25 - B269. PARK: Easy. TEL: 0732 70 215.

GILLINGHAM

Dickens Antiques
42 Sturdee Ave. (G Peek) Est: 1979. Open 9-5, Sat. 9-12. CL: Wed. *STOCK: Furniture, jewellery.* TEL: 0634 50950.

T.H. and J Mason
46 Jeffery St. Est: 1948. Open 9-5. CL: Wed. *STOCK: China, glass, jewellery, small furniture, militaria, medals, bric-a-brac.* TEL: 0634 52914.

GOUDHURST

Old Saddlers Antiques
Church Rd. (S Curd) Est: 1969. Open 9.30-12.30 and 2.30-5.30. CL: Tues. SIZE: Small. *STOCK: Small furniture; porcelain, small silver items, 1750-1870; 19th C pictures, prints, copper, horse brasses, jewellery.* Not Stocked: Large furniture. LOC: Opposite Church. PARK: Outside. TEL: 0580 211458. VAT: Spec.

GRAVESEND

Greg Martin Antiques
116 Wrotham Rd. Est: 1982. Open 12-6. CL: Wed. *STOCK: General antiques.* TEL: 0474 566067.

HADLOW, Nr. Tonbridge

The Pedlar's Pack (Hadlow) LAPADA
The Square, Hadlow. (Mrs N Joy) Est: 1976. Open 10-5.30; Mon. and Wed. 10-1. CL: Sun. except by appointment. SIZE: Medium. *STOCK: Country furniture, £50-£400; brass, copper, glass and china, £25-£100; all 18th-19th C; jewellery, objets d'art, small interesting items, 19th-20th C, £25-£300.* LOC: On Tonbridge to Maidstone Rd. PARK: Easy. TEL: 0732 851296; home - same. VAT: Stan/Spec.

HARRIETSHAM, Nr. Maidstone

Judith Peppitt
Chegworth Manor Farm, Chegworth. Open by appointment. *STOCK: English watercolours, 19th-20th C.* TEL: 0622 859313.

HARTLEY, Nr. Dartford

Hartley Antiques
Yew Cottage, Hartley Green. (Mrs E.E Lievesley) Est: 1968. Open 9.30-5. CL: Mon. and Wed. SIZE: Small. *STOCK: Silver, plate, jewellery, copper, brass, china, glass, £1-£100.* Not Stocked: Furniture. LOC: 3/4 mile from Longfield on B260. Between A2 and A20. PARK: Easy. TEL: 04747 2330.

HAWKHURST

Hawkhurst Antiques
Cranbrook Rd. (A Warren) Open 9-5. *STOCK: General antiques, mainly furniture.* PARK: Easy. TEL: 0580 752277. SER: Restorations (furniture).

Septimus Quayles Emporium
Ockley Rd. (Mrs M.R Martin) Est: 1971. Open 9.30-1 and 2.15-5, Wed. 9.30-1, Sat. 10-1 and 2.15-4. *STOCK: General small antiques.* TEL: 0580 752222.

HEADCORN, Nr. Ashford

Penny Lampard
31-33 High St. (Mrs P Lampard) Est: 1981. Open 9.30-5.30. SIZE: Large. *STOCK: Stripped pine furniture, linens, smalls and china.* PARK: Easy. TEL: 0622 890682. FAIRS: Sutton Valence. VAT: Stan.

HERNE BAY

Charlotte Antiques
54 Mortimer St. (P. and I Law) Open 10-3. *STOCK: General antiques and militaria.* TEL: 0227 740964.

Curio Corner Antiques
65 Mortimer St. Est: 1962. Open 9-5. *STOCK: Pine, mahogany and oak furniture; clocks; china; paintings; collectors' items.* PARK: Nearby. TEL: 0227 375892; home - 0227 366653. SER: Valuations. VAT: Stan.

HYTHE

The Den of Antiquity
35 Dymchurch Rd. (R. A Chapman) Est: 1962. Open 9-5 but any time by appointment. CL: Wed. and Thurs. SIZE: Medium. *STOCK: Jewellery, silver, pottery, porcelain, glass, instruments, objets de vertu and d'art, rare and limited pieces of Royal Doulton.* LOC: A259, main coast road from Folkestone to Hastings. PARK: Easy. TEL: 0303 267162.

Homewood Antiques
97 Dymchurch Rd. (D.C. and R.A Homewood) Est: 1984. Open 9-5.30, Sat. 10-4.30. *STOCK: General antiques.* TEL: 0303 265229.

Hythe continued

Hythe Antique Centre
5 High St. Est: 1973. Open 10-4, Sat. 10-5. SIZE: Large. *STOCK: Furniture, china, porcelain, paintings, prints.* LOC: 50yds. from A259 at 1st turning to town centre. PARK: Easy. TEL: 0303 269643.

Kennedy Corporation
148 High St. (M Kennedy) Open by appointment. SIZE: Medium. *STOCK: Oils and watercolours, from 1820, £100-£10,000.* PARK: At rear. TEL: 0303 269323; home - same. SER: Valuations; buys at auction (paintings). VAT: Stan/Spec. *Trade Only.*

Malthouse Arcade
High St. (Mr and Mrs R.M Maxtone Grahame) Est: 1974. Open Fri. and Sat. 10-6. SIZE: Large - 37 stalls. *STOCK: General antiques and collectors' items.* LOC: West end of High St. PARK: 50yds. TEL: 0303 260103; home - 0304 613270.

P.L.B. Enterprises
Open by appointment. *STOCK: Textiles, jewellery, silver and small items.* TEL: 0303 260726.

Radio Vintage
250 Seabrook Rd, Seabrook. (L Riches) *STOCK: Radios, 1920-1950.* TEL: 0303 230693. SER: Repairs.

Hythe continued

Samovar Antiques
158 High St. (Mrs F Clutterbuck) Open 9-5, Wed. 9-1. *STOCK: Clocks, Oriental carpets and rugs, general antiques.* TEL: 0303 264239.

Traditional Furniture
248 Seabrook Rd, Seabrook. (M Hannant) Est: 1977. Open daily. SIZE: Large. *STOCK: Pine, 19th C, £50-£500.* LOC: 1 1/2 miles from end of M20 on A259. PARK: Easy. TEL: 0303 239931; home - 0303 239612. VAT: Stan.

KENNINGTON, Nr. Ashford

Peter Knight
The Mill House. Est: 1968. Open daily but appointment advisable. *STOCK: General antiques.* LOC: On A28, near The Golden Ball public house. TEL: 0233 623009. VAT: Stan/Spec.

LAMBERHURST

The China Locker
(G Wilson) Open by appointment only. SIZE: Small. *STOCK: Prints, 18th-19th C, £5-£40.* TEL: 0892 890555. FAIRS: Hilden Manor, Tonbridge; Spa Hotel, Tunbridge Wells; Penshurst Village Hall.

Lamberhurst Antiques **LAPADA**
Upwey House, School Hill. (M Marks) Resident. Est: 1975. Open 9.30-6, Sun. by appointment. SIZE: Large. *STOCK: Furniture, mirrors and pictures, 18th-19th C, £250-£8,500.* LOC: A21. PARK: Easy. TEL: 0892 890993 or 0836 627282. SER: Valuations; restorations (furniture). VAT: Stan/Spec.

LEIGH, Nr. Tonbridge

Anthony Woodburn **BADA LAPADA**
Orchard House, High St. Est: 1975. Open daily, Sun. by appointment. SIZE: Medium. *STOCK: Clocks and barometers, 17th, 18th and early 19th C.* LOC: Off A21. PARK: Easy. TEL: 0732 832258; fax - 0732 838023. SER: Valuations; buys at auction (clocks). VAT: Spec.

LITTLEBOURNE, Nr. Canterbury

Jimmy Warren Antiques
Cedar Lodge, 28 The Hill. Est: 1969. Open 9-6 including Sun. *STOCK: Mahogany and oak, 1600-1900; decorative garden ornaments.* LOC: A257. PARK: Easy. TEL: 0227 721510. SER: Valuations; restorations. VAT: Stan/Spec.

LONGFIELD, Nr. Dartford

Longfield Antiques
11 Station Rd. (Mrs P Drury) Est: 1977. Open 9.30-5. CL: Thurs. *STOCK: Dolls, jewellery, general antiques.* TEL: 047 47 5076.

LOWER HALSTOW, Nr. Sittingbourne

Halstow Antiques
Green Farm House. (I.P Harvey) Est: 1972. Open 10-8. CL: Tues. SIZE: Small. *STOCK: Oak furniture, 16th-18th C, £100-£1,000; country furniture, £50-£500; copper, silver, brass.* LOC: One mile north of A2 between Rainham and Newington by village green. PARK: Easy. TEL: 0795 842016.

MAIDSTONE

Charles International Antiques **LAPADA**
3 Market St. (Mr and Mrs C Bremner) Est: 1968. Open 10-5. *STOCK: Victorian, Edwardian and shipping goods.* TEL: 0622 682882. SER: Valuations; full container and documentation facilities.

Salmagundi
63 Charlton St. (B.C Shillingford) Est: 1968. Open 11.30-5.30. SIZE: Small. *STOCK: Victoriana, bric-a-brac, collectables, £5-£50.* Not Stocked: Coins, stamps. LOC: From Maidstone, 1 mile up Tonbridge Rd., turn left at Milton St., Charlton St. is second turning on left. PARK: Easy. TEL: 0622 726859; home - same. SER: Valuations.

Maidstone continued

Sutton Valence Antiques **LAPADA**
Unit 4, Haslemere, Parkwood. (T. and N Mullarkey and M Marles) Open 9-5.30. SIZE: Large. *STOCK: Shipping furniture.* PARK: Easy. TEL: 0622 675332/843333/843499. *Trade Only.*

MARGATE

Furniture Mart
Grotto Hill. (R.G Scott) Est: 1971. CL: Wed. SIZE: Large. *STOCK: General antiques £1-£1,500; shipping goods.* LOC: Corner of Bath Place and Grotto Hill. TEL: 0843 220653. SER: Restorations; stripping; restoration materials supplied. VAT: Stan.

Manor House Antiques and Furniture
45/46 Arlington Sq. (D. and G.G Rimington) Open 10-3 during winter, 10-6 including Sun. in summer. *STOCK: China, porcelain, small furniture, copper and brass.* LOC: Near railway station. TEL: 0843 295025.

MINSTER, Nr. Ramsgate

Michael Lamb Antiques
The White Horse, 2 Church St. Est: 1967. Open 9.30-6, or by appointment. CL: Sat. SIZE: Small with store. *STOCK: General antiques, some shipping goods, £20-£1,000.* LOC: 3 miles from Sandwich. PARK: Easy. TEL: 0843 821666. SER: Valuations; restorations (furniture). VAT: Stan.

NEW ROMNEY

Meridian Antiques
22 High St. (N Wilson) Est: 1956. Open 9.30-5.30. CL: Wed. *STOCK: General antiques, small furniture; jewellery, £5-£250; glass, £10-£30; all 1800-1950; porcelain, small Oriental.* Not Stocked: Reproductions. PARK: Easy. TEL: 0679 63675. SER: Valuations.

NORTHFLEET

Northfleet Hill Antiques
36 The Hill. (Mrs M Kilby) Est: 1986. Open Tues., Fri. and Sat. 9.30-5. SIZE: Small. *STOCK: Furniture, 19th C and early 20th C, £30-£800; collectables, £1-£80.* LOC: A226 near junction with B261 and B2175. PARK: Easy (behind Ye Olde Coach and Horses Inn). TEL: 0474 321521.

ORPINGTON

Antica
48 High St, Green Street Green. Open 10-5.30. *STOCK: General antiques.* TEL: 0689 851181.

OTFORD

Darenth Bookshop
8 High St. Est: 1979. Open 9-5. CL: Wed. *STOCK: Secondhand and antiquarian books; prints, maps and watercolours.* TEL: 095 92 2430.

PENSHURST

Bridge House Antiques
Bridge House. (R Binning) Est: 1966. *STOCK: Early country oak and elm furniture.* TEL: 0892 870209. SER: Shipping. VAT: Stan/Spec.

PRATT'S BOTTOM, Nr. Orpington

Celia Jennings **BADA**
3 Mount Pleasant Cottages, Rushmore Hill. Open by appointment. *STOCK: Wood carvings and works of art.* TEL: 0689 853250.

RAMSGATE

Ash House
18 Hereson Rd. (P Wimsett) Est: 1957. Open Fri. and Sat. 11-5, trade by appointment. *STOCK: Stripped pine, general antiques.* TEL: 0843 595480. VAT: Stan.

Patricia Antiques **LAPADA**
2 Grange Rd. (J Pratt) Est: 1960. Open 10-4. CL: Sat. and Thurs. *STOCK: Period furniture and some shipping goods.* TEL: 0843 591222. VAT: Spec. *Mainly Trade.*

Thanet Antiques Trade Centre
45 Albert St. (Mr and Mrs R Fomison) Est: 1971. Open 9-5, Sun. by appointment. SIZE: Large. *STOCK: Furniture and bric-a-brac, 18th-20th C, £1-£5,000.* LOC: From London Rd. right to seafront. With harbour on right turn first left down Addington St., then last right. PARK: Own. TEL: 0843 597336; home - 0843 63394. VAT: Stan.

RIVERHEAD

Amherst Antiques
23 London Rd. (D Brick) Est: 1985. Open 9.30-5. CL: Wed. SIZE: Small. *STOCK: Furniture, £500-£3,000; porcelain, £50-£2,000; silver, £50-£1,000.* LOC: A25. PARK: Nearby. TEL: 0732 455047. FAIRS: Buxton; Guildford; Kensington; Petworth; Charterhouse. VAT: Stan/Spec.

Riverhead continued

Mandarin Gallery
32 London Rd. (J. and Mrs. M.C Liu) Est: 1984. Open 9.30-5. CL: Wed. SIZE: Medium. *STOCK: Chinese rosewood and lacquer furniture, 18th-19th C, £200-£4,000; Oriental porcelain, £35-£3,500; Oriental paintings on silk and paper, £15-£500; both 19th-20th C; jade, stone, ivory and wood carvings.* Not Stocked: Non-Oriental items. LOC: A21. PARK: Easy. TEL: 0732 457399; home - same. SER: Restorations (Chinese furniture); framing.

ROCHESTER

Baggins Book Bazaar
19 High St. Open 10-6 including Sun. *STOCK: Secondhand and antiquarian books.* TEL: 0634 811651.

Cottage Style Antiques
24 Bill Street Rd. (W Miskimmin) Open 9.30-5.30. CL: Wed. *STOCK: General antiques.* TEL: 0634 717623.

Droods
62 High St. (A.J Stewart and C Morgan) Open 10-5.30. *STOCK: General antiques.* TEL: 0634 829000.

Francis Iles
Rutland House, La Providence, High St. (The Family Iles). Est: 1960. Open 9.30-5.30. SIZE: Large. *STOCK: Watercolours and oils, mainly 20th C, £50-£10,000.* LOC: Off central High St. PARK: 40yds. TEL: 0634 843081. SER: Restorations (cleaning and relining); framing. VAT: Stan/Spec.

Langley Galleries
155 High St. (K.J Cook) Est: 1978. Open 9-5.30. *STOCK: Watercolours, oils, 19th-20th C.* TEL: 0634 811802. SER: Restorations and cleaning (watercolours and oils), framing.

Memories
128 High St. (Mrs V.A Lhermette) Est: 1985. Open 9-5.30. SIZE: Medium. *STOCK: Small furniture, £50-£500; china, £5-£75, both 1900-1950; pictures, late Victorian to Edwardian, £20-£70; collectables, bric-a-brac.* PARK: Opposite. TEL: 0634 811044.

Northgate Antiques
48 High St. (P.C Hanks) Est: 1980. Open 10.30-3.30. SIZE: Small. *STOCK: Small items, £1-£100; clocks, £50-£1,000; porcelain and pottery, £1-£250; shipping goods; all 18th C to 1920; postcards, lace, linen, textiles, clothes.* LOC: A2 near Rochester Bridge. PARK: Easy. TEL: 0634 812179/865428. SER: Valuations; buys at auction (porcelain and furniture). VAT: Stan.

Rochester continued

David Rackham (Rochester Fine Arts) LAPADA
88 High St. (D. and J Rackham) Est: 1980. Open daily, Wed. p.m. and Sun. by appointment. SIZE: Medium. *STOCK: Clocks and furniture, 17th-19th C, £20-£150,000.* LOC: A20. Shop centre of High St. PARK: Nearby. TEL: 0634 814129; home - 0622 842981. SER: Valuations; restorations; buys at auction (clocks). FAIRS: Barbican, Olympia, Kenilworth, Goodwood, N.E.C. (August), Café Royal. VAT: Stan/Spec.

Rochester Antiques and Flea Market
Corporation St, (Antique Forum Ltd). Open Sat. 8-1. SIZE: 100 stalls. PARK: Easy. TEL: 071 262 5003.

The Victory
43 High St. (L. and M Petrie) Open 10-5. *STOCK: General antiques.* TEL: 0634 843750.

ROLVENDEN, Nr. Cranbrook

Falstaff Antiques
63-67 High St. (C.M Booth) Est: 1964. Open 9-6. CL: Sun., and Wed. p.m. except by appointment. SIZE: Medium. *STOCK: English furniture, £5-£700; china, metal, glass, silver, £1-£200; all periods.* Not Stocked: Paintings. LOC: On A28, 3 miles from Tenterden, 1st shop on left in village. PARK: Easy. TEL: 0580 241234. SER: Valuations. VAT: Stan/Spec.

Kent Cottage Antiques
39 High St. (Mrs R Amos) Open 9-5.30. *STOCK: Meissen and other continental and English porcelain; silver; jewellery; small furniture.* PARK: Easy. TEL: 0580 241719.

J.D. and R.M Walters
10 Regent St. GMC. Est: 1977. Open 8-6, Sat. p.m. and Sun. by appointment. SIZE: Small. *STOCK: Mahogany furniture, 18th-19th C.* LOC: A28 turn left in village centre onto B2086, shop on left. PARK: Easy. TEL: 0580 241563; home - same. SER: Restorations. VAT: Stan/Spec.

ST. MARGARET'S BAY, Nr. Dover

Impressions and Alexandra's Antiques
1-3 The Droveway. (J Cox-Freeman) Est: 1979. Open 10-1 and 2.15-4.30, Wed. and Sat. p.m. by appointment only. SIZE: Small. *STOCK: Paintings by Victorian and local artists; furniture, porcelain and jewellery.* LOC: Between Dover and Deal at top of hill. PARK: Easy. TEL: 0304 853102; home - 0304 852682.

SANDGATE, Nr. Folkestone

Antiques Etcetera
93 High St. (H. and M.F Brown) Est: 1964. Open 11-1 and 2-5.30, Sun. 11-1. SIZE: Small. *STOCK: Furniture, £5-£100; bric-a-brac and curios, £5-£25; all late 19th C to early 20th C; general antiques, 19th C, £30-£150; secondhand books.* LOC: A259. PARK: Easy. TEL: 0303 49389.

Antiquest
21 High St. (C.M Amos) Est: 1964. Open 10-5.30. SIZE: Medium. *STOCK: Furniture, prints, paintings, general antiques.* LOC: Main road, between Hythe and Folkestone. PARK: Easy. TEL: 0303 49300.

Beaubush House Antiques LAPADA
95 High St. (J Winikus) *STOCK: Small furniture, porcelain and pottery, 18th-19th C.* TEL: 0303 49099/51121.

Mary Brooker 'Marylyn' Antiques and Curios, Gifts
39 High St. (Mrs M Brooker) Est: 1960. Open 10-5.30. CL: Wed. SIZE: Small. *STOCK: Dolls, toys, 18th-19th C, £5-£500; Japanese items, 17th-19th C, £20-£500; jewellery, 18th-20th C, £5-£500; nurses' buckles, silver, 18th-20th C; early brass, china, collectors' items.* Not Stocked: Large furniture. PARK: Easy. TEL: 0303 49207; home - same.

Christopher Buck Antiques
56-60 High St. Est: 1983. Open 10-5. CL: Wed. SIZE: Medium. *STOCK: English furniture, 18th C, £500-£30,000; decorative items, 18th-19th C, £50-£1,000; local interest prints, 17th-19th C, £25-£1,000.* LOC: 5 mins. from M20. PARK: Easy. TEL: 0303 221229. SER: Valuations; restorations (furniture); buys at auction. FAIRS: Olympia, Café Royal. VAT: Stan/Spec.

County Antiques
17 High St. (B Nilson) Open 9.30-5. *STOCK: Furniture.* TEL: 0303 40291; evenings - 0303 813039.

Dench Antiques
Cromwell House, 32 High St. (Mr and Mrs J.W.G Elcombe) Est: 1980. Open 10-6. SIZE: Medium + warehouse. *STOCK: Continental and English furniture, decorator's items.* PARK: Easy. TEL: 0303 40824. SER: Buys at auction. VAT: Stan/Spec.

Michael Fitch Antiques LAPADA
99 High St. Open 10-5.30, Sun. by appointment. *STOCK: Georgian, Victorian and Edwardian furniture and clocks.* TEL: 0303 49600; evenings - 0303 230839.

Freeman and Lloyd Antiques BADA LAPADA
44 High St. (K Freeman and M.R Lloyd) Est: 1968. Open 10-5.30. SIZE: Medium. *STOCK:*

Freeman and Lloyd Antiques continued

***Fine Georgian and Regency English furniture; clocks; paintings and other period items.* LOC: On main coast road between Hythe and Folkestone (A259). PARK: Easy. TEL: 0303 48986 (any time). SER: Valuations. VAT: Stan/Spec.**

Howard Godfrey Antiques Ltd BADA
53 High St. Est: 1965. *STOCK: Paintings, furniture, period silver, clocks, porcelain.* TEL: 0303 49133; fax - same. VAT: Stan/Spec.

Hyron Antiques
86 High St. (R Welsh) Open 9.30-5.30. *STOCK: General antiques.* TEL: 0303 40698. SER: Buys at auction.

Noble Antiques
59A High St. (F.G Noble and 4 other dealers) Est: 1976. Open every day. SIZE: Medium. *STOCK: Clocks, furniture, silver, porcelain, jewellery, bric-a-brac, marine items, telescopes, £5-£1,000.* PARK: Easy. TEL: 0303 49466.

Nordens
43/43a High St. Est: 1946. Open 10-5.30 or by appointment. CL: Wed. p.m. *STOCK: General antiques, Victoriana, bric-a-brac.* LOC: Main Folkestone to Hythe Rd. TEL: 0303 48443.

Old English Pine
100 High St. (A Martin) Open 10-6. *STOCK: Pine furniture and interesting items.* TEL: 0303 48560.

J.T Rutherford and Son
55 High St. Est: 1963. Open 9-6; Sun. 9-2, and by appointment. SIZE: Medium. *STOCK: Furniture, 18th-19th C; longcase clocks; weapons, flintlock, percussion, swords.* LOC: A295. PARK: Easy. TEL: 0303 49515; home - 0303 260822. SER: Restorations (furniture); buys at auction. VAT: Stan/Spec.

Sandgate Antiques Centre
61-63 Sandgate High St. (J Greenwall) Est: 1964. Open 10-6, Sun. 11-6. SIZE: Large. LOC: Folkestone-Brighton road. PARK: Easy. TEL: 0303 48987. SER: Valuations. Below are listed the dealers at this centre.

Jonathan Greenwell Antiques LAPADA
B and T Holmes Antiques
Robin Homewood Antiques
P and D Jennings Antiques
David Lancefield Antiques
Kate Summers Antiques

SANDHURST

Forge Antiques and Restorations
Rye Rd. (J Nesfield) Open 9-6. *STOCK: Victoriana, ceramics, glass, furniture including pine, £1-£5,000.* LOC: A268. PARK: Own. TEL: 0580 850308/850665. SER: Restorations (furniture). VAT: Spec.

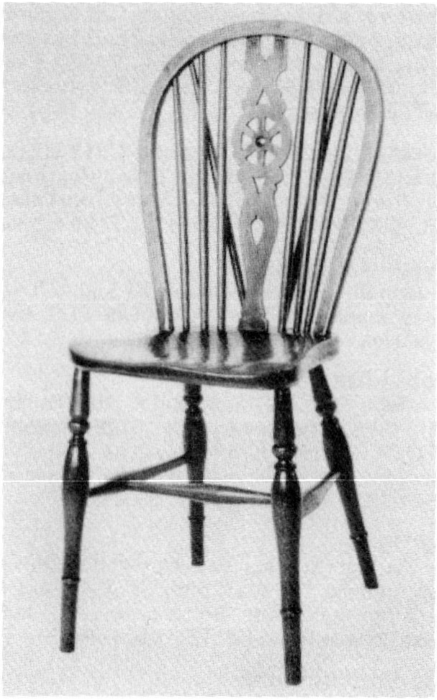

Hoop back Windsor side chair. Beech with ash hoop, fruitwood splat and elm seat with scribed edge line. Stamped 'ST PAUL'S SCHOOL' on edge of seat. Attributed to High Wycombe, c.1820-50. Single ring and concave turned legs with lower ring and straight turned stretchers. Plain hoop supporting three elliptical long spindles either side of central splat with wheel fretted motif and applied roundel. Seat with rear wedge supporting two spindles connected to top of hoop. From ***The English Regional Chair*** by Bernard D. Cotton, published by the **Antique Collectors' Club** in 1990. £49.50.

SANDWICH

James Atkinson Gallery
38 King St. (G.M Carrick) Est: 1977. Open 10-12.30 and 2.15-5 or by appointment. CL: Wed. *STOCK: 19th and early 20th C oils and watercolours.* LOC: Next to Post Office. TEL: 0304 617216. SER: Restorations; framing. VAT: Stan/Spec.

Delf Antiques
36 Harnet St. (Mrs P Wickens) Est: 1972. Open 10-1 and 2-4. CL: Wed. SIZE: Small. *STOCK: Small furniture, decorative items.* LOC: Next to Toy Museum. PARK: Easy. TEL: 0304 612779/615015.

Empire Antiques
Old Council Yard, Gazen Salts, Strand St. (D.A Magee) Open 8-5, Sat. by appointment. *STOCK: Stripped pine and shipping furniture.* TEL: 0304 614474/612395; fax - 0304 451375. SER: Container; import; export; stripping.

Noah's Ark Antique Centre
King St. (Mr and Mrs R.M Maxtone Graham) Est: 1978. Open 10-5. CL: Wed. SIZE: Medium. *STOCK: Staffordshire figures, china, porcelain, antiquarian books, watercolours, oil paintings, prints, small furniture, silver, jewellery, copper and brass.* PARK: Guildhall. TEL: 0304 611144; home - 0304 613270. SER: Valuations.

James Porter Antiques
5 Potter St. Est: 1948. Open 9.30-5.30. CL: Wed. SIZE: Large. *STOCK: Furniture, 18th-19th C.* TEL: 0304 612218.

Nancy Wilson
Monken Quay, Strand St. Open 10-5, other times by appointment. CL: Wed. SIZE: Large. *STOCK: Furniture, 1600-1939, clocks, smalls, £50-£3,000.* LOC: 100yds. from King's Arms public house. PARK: Easy. TEL: 0304 612345; home - same.

SEVENOAKS

The Antiques Centre
120 London Rd. (R Harrison) Est: 1964. Open 9.30-1 and 2-5, Sat. 10-5. SIZE: Several dealers. *STOCK: Mahogany, oak, Oriental and pine furniture, clocks, barometers, paintings, porcelain, dolls, jewellery, glass, silver, copper, brass and decorative items, all 17th-19th C; reference books.* TEL: 0732 452104. VAT: Stan/Spec.

Bradbourne Gallery
4 St. John's Hill (Jane Ross Antiques and Decoration). Open 9.30-5, Sat. 9-1. SIZE: Several dealers. *STOCK: Silver, furniture, ceramics, jewellery, glass, prints and paintings, treen, 18th C to Edwardian.* LOC: 1 mile from town centre, continuation of High St./Dartford Rd. PARK: Easy. TEL: 0732 460756; fax - same.

Sevenoaks continued

A.A Harrison and Son

79 London Rd. (J.E Harrison) Est: 1919. Open 9.30-5, Sat. 10-4. CL: Wed. p.m. *STOCK: General antiques, furniture, paintings.* TEL: 0732 453276. VAT: Stan/Spec.

Sevenoaks Furniture Gallery

53 High St. Est: 1976. Open 9.30-5. *STOCK: Antique pine and country furniture.* TEL: 0732 453030.

Sheldon Ward Antiques

57 St. Johns Hill. (S.A Ward) Est: 1966. Open 10-5.30, Sat. 10-1. CL: Fri. a.m., Mon. and Wed. SIZE: Small. *STOCK: Furniture and bric-a-brac, from 19th C, £5-£500.* LOC: Main road to Dartford Tunnel. PARK: Easy. TEL: 0732 455311; home - same. SER: Valuations; restorations (inlay, marquetry, rushing and caning).

Myola Stead

at The Antiques Centre, 120 London Rd. Open 9-1 and 2-5.30, Sat. 9-5.30. SIZE: Small. *STOCK: Small Edwardian and Victorian furniture, £50-£1,000; small decorative items, including blue and white pottery, silver, boxes, glass and pictures, 19th C, £5-£500; books on antiques and collectables, £5-£100.* PARK: Opposite. TEL: 0732 452104; home - 0732 452040. SER: Book searches undertaken. FAIRS: Newark, Ardingly, Stoneleigh, Sandown Park, Great Danes Hotel, Ashford International Hotel, Tunbridge Wells Spa Hotel.

SHOREHAM, Nr. Sevenoaks

The Porcelain Collector

The Old Pony Stable, High St. (D Porter) Est: 1962. Open by appointment. SIZE: Medium. *STOCK: English and continental porcelain especially Royal Worcester, Royal Doulton, Lambeth, Dresden, S`evres, Royal Vienna, and modern limited editions of military, historial and haute couture subjects; silver, glass, jewellery, metalware, small furniture, toys, clocks, militaria; all from 18th C; art nouveau and art deco.* PARK: Easy. TEL: 095 92 3416. SER: Valuations; restorations (porcelain and furniture); buys at auction.

SITTINGBOURNE

Periwinkle Press

23 East St. (A.L Swain) Est: 1967. SIZE: Medium. *STOCK: Prints, 18th-19th C, £20-£100; maps, watercolours, secondhand books.* TEL: 0795 426242. SER: Restorations (prints and oils); framing. VAT: Stan.

SNODLAND

Aaron Antiques

90 High St. (R.J Goodman) Open 10-5, or by appointment. *STOCK: Clocks and pocket watches, paintings and prints, period and shipping furniture, English, continental and Oriental porcelain; antiquarian books, postcards.* TEL: 0634 241748. VAT: Stan.

SOUTHBOROUGH, Nr. Tunbridge Wells

Henry Baines LAPADA

14 Church Rd. Est: 1968. Open 9.30-5, Sat. 10-4.30. *STOCK: Early oak and country furniture especially sets of chairs; French provincial furniture and decorative items.* PARK: Easy. TEL: 0892 32099. VAT: Stan/Spec.

STOCKBURY

Steppes Hill Farm Antiques BADA

The Hill Farm, South St. (W.F.A Buck) Est: 1965. Always open, appointment advisable. SIZE: Medium. *STOCK: English porcelain, pottery, pot-lids, 18th-20th C, £5-£5,000; small silver; caddy spoons, wine labels, silver boxes, 18th-19th C, to £1,000; furniture, 18th-19th C, £10-£5,000.* LOC: 5 mins. from M2 on A249. Enquire in village for Steppes Hill Antiques. PARK: Easy. TEL: 0795 842205. SER: Valuations; buys at auction. FAIRS: Chelsea; Dorchester; Burlington House; Grosvenor House. VAT: Spec.

SUNDRIDGE, Nr. Sevenoaks

Sundridge Gallery

9 Church Rd. (T. and M Tyrer) Open 10-5.30. *STOCK: Watercolours and oils, 19th and 20th C; some Oriental rugs.* TEL: 0959 64104.

Colin Wilson Antiques

99-103 Main Rd. Open 10-6. *STOCK: Victorian mahogany and inlaid Edwardian furniture.* TEL: 0959 62043. VAT: Stan/Spec.

SUTTON VALENCE, Nr. Maidstone

Sutton Valence Antiques LAPADA

(T. and N Mullarkey and M Marles) Est: 1971. Open 10-5.30. SIZE: Large. *STOCK: Furniture, porcelain, clocks, silver, metalware, shipping items, 18th-19th C.* LOC: On A274 Maidstone/ Tenterden Rd. PARK: Side of shop. TEL: 0622 843333/843499. SER: Valuations. VAT: Stan/Spec.

TENTERDEN

Garden House Antiques
118 High St. (H Kirkham) Resident. Always open. *STOCK: Mainly 18th-19th C furniture, paintings and porcelain; old fishing reels and rods.* PARK: Easy. TEL: 058 06 3664. SER: Valuations; interior design.

The Lace Basket
1a East Cross. (C Walls) Open 10-5. CL: Mon. and Wed. *STOCK: Textiles, Victorian linen and lace.* PARK: Opposite. TEL: 058 06 3923. SER: Valuations.

John McMaster BADA
5 Sayers Sq, Sayers Lane. Est: 1847. CL: Sun. except by appointment. *STOCK: Furniture, engravings, silver, small decorative items.* TEL: 058 06 2941. SER: Valuations.

TEYNAM, Nr. Sittingbourne

Jackson-Grant Antiques
The Old Chapel, 133 London Rd. (D.M Jackson-Grant) Est: 1966. Open 10-9, Tues. 10-7, Sat. 10-6, Sun. 1-5, prior telephone call advisable after 4.30 weekdays. SIZE: Large. *STOCK: Country furniture, oak, 17th-19th C, £50-£1,000; mahogany, £100-£1,000; some*

Jackson-Grant Antiques continued

pine; smalls, 18th C to art deco, £5-£500. LOC: A2 between Faversham and Sittingbourne. PARK: Easy. TEL: 0795 522027; home - same. FAIRS: Newark; Ardingly. VAT: Stan/Spec.

TONBRIDGE

Barden House Antiques
1-3 Priory St. (Mrs B.D Parsons) Open 10-5. SIZE: 6 dealers. *STOCK: General antiques.* TEL: 0732 350142; evenings - 0732 355718.

Derek Roberts Fine Antique Clocks BADA
25 Shipbourne Rd. Author of books on clocks. Est: 1968. Open 9.30-5.30 or by appointment. SIZE: Medium. *STOCK: Fine restored clocks, all types; Tunbridge Ware.* LOC: A227. From London to Tonbridge turn left 20yds. before first set of traffic lights at Tonbridge. Turn left at T junction; showrooms 50yds. on right. PARK: Easy. TEL: 0732 358986. SER: Precision regulators made to order; catalogues available. VAT: Spec.

TUNBRIDGE WELLS

Aaron Antiques
77 St. Johns Rd. (R.J Goodman) Open 9-5. *STOCK: Clocks and pocket watches, paintings and prints; period and shipping furniture; English, continental and Oriental porcelain; antiquarian books, postcards, coins and medals.* TEL: 0634 241748. VAT: Stan/Spec.

D.C Adams LAPADA
at Cowden Antiques, 24 Mount Ephraim Rd. Open 10-5. SIZE: Small. *STOCK: English and Welsh porcelain, 18th to early 19th C, £50-£500.* LOC: Off London road. PARK: Nearby. TEL: 0892 520752. SER: Valuations; buys at auction (as stock). FAIRS: Wakefield Ceramics. VAT: Stan/Spec.

Amadeus Antiques
32 Mount Ephraim. (P.A Davies) Open 10-5, Sun. by appointment. SIZE: Medium. *STOCK: Unusual furniture, to art deco, £50-£1,500; china and bric-a-brac, £25-£100.* LOC: Near hospital. PARK: Easy. TEL: 0892 544406; home - 0892 864884. SER: Valuations.

Annexe Antiques
33 The Pantiles. (M Broad) Est: 1981. Open 9.30-5. CL: Wed. SIZE: Medium. *STOCK: 1820-1920 porcelain, Staffordshire, treen, Tunbridge Ware, pictures, books, toys, silver, glass.* PARK: Nearby. TEL: 0892 547213.

The Antique Pine Shop
2 Mount Sion. (M. and Mrs M Erskine-Hill) Open 9.30-5.30. *STOCK: General antiques, especially pine and porcelain.* TEL: 0892 511591.

Tunbridge Wells continued

Chapel Place Antiques
9 Chapel Pl. (J. and A Clare) Open 9.30-6. *STOCK: Silver, plate, jewellery, dolls, furniture, some porcelain.* TEL: 0892 546561.

Clare Gallery
21 High St. *STOCK: Paintings, 19th-20th C.* LOC: 200yds. from Central Station. TEL: 0892 538717. SER: Valuations; restorations; framing. VAT: Spec.

Collectables
53 Colebrook Rd. (J.R Hickmott) Open 9.30-6. *STOCK: General antiques and bric-a-brac.* TEL: 0892 539085; evenings - 0892 530217.

Corn Exchange Antiques
64 The Pantiles. (B Henderson) Open 9-5.30. *STOCK: Mainly Georgian furniture.* TEL: 0892 539652.

County Antiques
94 High St. (Mr and Mrs P Hale) Open 10-5.30. *STOCK: Small antiques and decorative items.* TEL: 0892 530767.

Cowden Antiques **LAPADA**
24 Mount Ephraim Rd. (A Linstead) Est: 1970. Open 10-5. SIZE: Medium. *STOCK: Furniture, period oak, mahogany, to late 19th C; decorative items.* PARK: Easy. TEL: 0892 520752. SER: Interiors. VAT: Stan/Spec.

Franca Antiques
2 Castle St. Est: 1981. Open 9.30-5.30 or by appointment. CL: Mon. and Wed. *STOCK: Furniture and general antiques, classic maps, prints, postal history and stamps.* TEL: 0892 525779.

Frankham Gallery
4 Nevill St. (M.B Wells) Open 10-5. SIZE: Large. *STOCK: Paintings, 17th-20th C, £25-£5,000; furniture, 18th-19th C, £25-£2,000; bronze and marble sculpture.* LOC: Last shop on right leaving town (A267), gallery backs on to The Pantiles. PARK: Behind gallery. TEL: 0892 529244. VAT: Spec.

Glassdrumman Antiques
Tunbridge Wells Antique Centre, Union Sq, The Pantiles. (G. and A Dyson Rooke) Open 9.30-5, Sat. 9.30-5.30. SIZE: Small. *STOCK: Jewellery, silver, glass, furniture, smalls, 18th and 19th C.* PARK: Nearby. TEL: 0892 533708.

Graham Gallery
4 Castle St. (J Graham) Est: 1987. Open 10.30-5, Sat. 9.30-5.30. CL: Mon. and Wed. SIZE: Small. *STOCK: Watercolours, 19th-20th C, £200-£4,000.* LOC: Off High St., 2nd floor, above Franca Antiques. PARK: Nearby. TEL: 0892 526695; home - 0892 52880

Tunbridge Wells continued

Hadlow Antiques
No. 1 The Pantiles. (M. and L Adler) Est: 1966. Open 10-1 and 2-5. CL: Wed. p.m. and Sat. p.m. SIZE: Small. *STOCK: Clocks, watches, 17th-20th C; dolls and accessories, automata, 18th-20th C; scientific and medical instruments, music boxes, singing birds, gramophones and collectors' items.* LOC: Corner of Nevill St. PARK: Nearby. TEL: 0892 529858. SER: Valuations; restorations; buys at auction. VAT: Stan/Spec.

Hall's Bookshop
20 Chapel Pl. Est: 1898. Open 9.30-5. *STOCK: Antiquarian and secondhand books.* TEL: 0892 527842.

La Trobe and Bigwood Antiques
Motts Farm, Forge Rd, Eridge Green. (H La Trobe and C Bigwood) Open 8.30-5.00. CL: Sat. *STOCK: Dining tables and chairs.* TEL: 0892 863840. SER: Restorations.

Pantiles Antiques
31 The Pantiles. (E.M Blackburn) Est: 1979. Open 10-5.30. CL: Wed. SIZE: Medium. *STOCK: Decorative items, lamps including standard; bronze, copper, brass, furniture, porcelain, pictures.* Not Stocked: Carpets. PARK: Easy. TEL: 0892 531291.

Tunbridge Wells continued

Pantiles Spa Antiques

4-6 Union House, The Pantiles. (J.A Cowpland) Est: 1985. Open 9.30-5, Sat. 9.30-5.30. SIZE: Large. *STOCK: Furniture, £200-£10,000; pictures, £50-£3,000; clocks, £100-£5,000; pianos, £500-£10,000; porcelain, £50-£2,000; jewellery, £50-£200; silver, £50-£1,000; all 17th-19th C.* PARK: Nearby. TEL: 0892 541377. SER: Restorations (furniture). VAT: Spec.

Rare Chairs

37 Quarry Rd. (R G Andrews) Open 10-5.30. *STOCK: General antiques, especially chairs.* TEL: 0892 21783. SER: Restorations; upholstery.

Ian Relf Antiques

132/134 Camden Rd. Open 9.30-1.30 and 2.30-5.30. *STOCK: Mainly furniture.* TEL: 0892 38362.

Patricia Russell Antiques

43 Mount Ephraim. Est: 1969. Open 10-5.30, Sat. 10-5. CL: Mon. *STOCK: Jewellery, silver, glass, porcelain, small furniture.* LOC: Junction of London Rd., and Mount Ephraim, overlooking the common. TEL: 0892 523719; home - 0892 524855.

Graham Stead Antiques Reference Books

Tunbridge Wells Antiques Centre, Union Sq, The Pantiles. Open 9.30-5, Sun. in summer 2-5. SIZE: Small. *STOCK: Reference books on antiques and collectables, £5-£50; small furniture, mainly mahogany, Edwardian and Victorian, £50-£500.* PARK: Nearby. TEL: 0892 533708; home - 0732 452040. SER: Book search. FAIRS: Newark, Ardingly, Stoneleigh, Sandown Park, Great Danes Hotel.

Strawsons Antiques LAPADA

33, 39 and 41 The Pantiles. Est: 1913. Open 9.30-5.30, Wed. 9.30-1. SIZE: Large. *STOCK: Furniture, mahogany, walnut, rosewood, 18th-19th C; silver and plate, Tunbridgeware, boxes, glass.* LOC: Follow directions to Pantiles. PARK: Easy, nearby. TEL: 0892 530607. VAT: Spec.

John Thompson

27 The Pantiles. (J Macdonald and N Thompson) Est: 1982. Open 9.30-1 and 2-5.30. SIZE: Medium. *STOCK: Furniture, 17th to early 19th C; porcelain, pottery, glass, decorative items, 18th to early 19th C; paintings and prints, 17th-19th C.* Not Stocked: Jewellery, silver and militaria. PARK: Warwick Park/Lower Walk Pantiles. TEL: 0892 547215. SER: Restorations (furniture). VAT: Spec.

Tunbridge Wells Antique Centre

Union Sq, The Pantiles. (S.M Maddox) Est: 1977. Open 9.30-5. SIZE: Large. *STOCK: General antiques, £2-£3,000.* PARK: Nearby. TEL: 0892 533708. SER: Valuations. VAT: Stan/Spec.

Tunbridge Wells continued

Up Country

The Corn Stores, 68 St. Johns Rd. (G.J Price and C.M Springett) Est: 1988. Open 9-5.30. SIZE: Large. *STOCK: British and European country furniture, £50-£5,000; associated decorative and interesting items, £5-£500; all 18th-19th C.* LOC: On main London Rd. to Southborough and A21 trunk road which joins M25 and M26 at Sevenoaks intersection. PARK: Own at rear. TEL: 0892 523341. VAT: Stan.

Alan Wood

at Annexe Antiques, 33 The Pantiles. Open 9.30-5. CL: Wed. *STOCK: Ceramics especially Staffordshire and Royal Doulton figures.* TEL: 0892 547213 (Mon. and Sat.) or 0474 533722.

WEST MALLING

The Old Clock Shop

63 High St. (S.L Luck) Est: 1970. Open 9-5. SIZE: Large. *STOCK: Grandfather clocks, 17th-19th C; carriage, bracket and wall clocks.* LOC: 1/4 mile from A20. PARK: Easy. TEL: 0732 843246/840345. VAT: Spec.

Victoria Pataky Antiques and Reproductions

3 The Colonnade, West St. CL: Wed. *STOCK: General antiques, Victoriana.* TEL: 0732 843646.

Scott House Antiques

High St. (M Smith) Est: 1973. CL: Wed. p.m. *STOCK: General antiques, Victoriana, curios, silver, china, furniture, clocks, prints, £5-£1,000.* LOC: Opposite county library. TEL: 0732 841380.

Andrew Smith Antiques

89 High St. Est: 1978. Open 9.30-5.30, Sun. by appointment. SIZE: Medium. *STOCK: Jewellery, English furniture, Victorian-Edwardian, £50-£2,000.* LOC: Off M20, junction 4, A228. PARK: Easy. TEL: 0732 843087; home - same. VAT: Stan/Spec.

WEST PECKHAM, Nr. Maidstone

Langold Antiques

Oxon Hoath. (H.M Bayne-Powell) Est: 1967. Open 9-1 and 2.15-5.30. CL: Sat. SIZE: Medium. *STOCK: English furniture, 18th-19th C.* LOC: Coming from A26, turn left at Carpenters Lane on entering Hadlow. Left at T junction, right at crossroads, 400yds. to lodge gates on right. Showrooms at rear of mansion. PARK: Easy. TEL: 0732 810577. SER: Restorations (furniture). VAT: Spec.

West Peckham continued

"Persian Rugs"
Vines Farm, Matthews Lane. (R. and G King) Resident. Est: 1969. Open 9-7, Sun. by appointment. SIZE: Large. *STOCK: Persian rugs and carpets, to 1900, £100-£750.* LOC: A26 from Tonbridge to Maidstone. Just off Hadlow village turn left then right, premises are first on right. PARK: Easy. TEL: 0732 850228. SER: Valuations; restorations (Oriental carpets); buys at auction (Persian carpets). VAT: Stan.

WESTERHAM

Apollo Galleries **LAPADA**
19 Market Sq. Open 10-5.30. SIZE: Large. *STOCK: Oil and watercolour paintings, bronzes, 19th to early 20th C; English and continental furniture, clocks, 18th-19th C; porcelain, glass, silver.* TEL: 0959 62200. VAT: Spec.

Brazil Antiques Ltd **LAPADA**
2 The Green. *STOCK: Furniture, 18th-20th C.* TEL: 0959 63048. VAT: Stan/Spec.

Castle Antiques Centre
1 London Rd. (Stewart Ward Properties)Est: 1974. Open 10-5. SIZE: Small - 8 dealers. *STOCK: General antiques, £5-£500.* LOC: Just off town centre. PARK: Easy nearby. TEL: 0959 62492. SER: Valuations.

Dunsdale Lodge Antiques
Dunsdale Lodge, Brasted Rd. (Mrs D.M Scott) Est: 1967. Open daily 9-7. SIZE: Small. *STOCK: English porcelain figures, 18th C, £300-£1,500; English pottery figures, 18th-19th C, £50-£2,000; Staffordshire portrait figures, 19th C, £90-£1,000; continental figures, 19th C, £50-£300; lustre; cottages and Toby jugs.* LOC: Shop 500yds. from town on A25. PARK: Easy. TEL: 0959 62160. VAT: Spec.

Westerham continued

Peter Dyke Antiques **LAPADA**
23 High St. Open 10-5.30. CL: Mon. SIZE: Large. *STOCK: Furniture and decorative items, 18th-19th C, £500-£10,000; some paintings, £100-£2,000.* TEL: 0959 62949.

Anthony J Hook
3 The Green. Est: 1948. Open 9-5.30, Sat. 10-4. SIZE: Medium. *STOCK: English furniture, 18th-19th C.* LOC: A25. TEL: 0959 62161. VAT: Stan/Spec.

London House Antiques
4 Market Sq, (Amersham Investment Trust Ltd.). Est: 1977. Open 10-1 and 2.15-5.30, Sun. by appointment. SIZE: Medium. *STOCK: Furniture, 18th-19th C; oil paintings, 18th-20th C; both £500-£4,000. Fine and rare books, fine bindings, 17th-20th C; prints and engravings, 17th-19th C; all £75-£1,000. Rare original copper plates, 17th-19th C, £50-£1,500.* LOC: Off M25, junction 6 on A25 to Westerham. PARK: Easy. TEL: 0959 64479; home - same. SER: Restorations (furniture). VAT: Spec.

Manor Antiques
2a High St. (S Morris) Open 10-5.30 and Sun. 2-5.30. SIZE: Medium. *STOCK: Furniture, paintings, china, brass and copper, 19th C; books.* LOC: A25. PARK: Croydon Rd. TEL: 0959 64810.

Mistral Galleries
12 Market Sq. (J.N Hutchinson) Open 9.30-5.30. SIZE: Large. *STOCK: Pictures, 1750-1920, £2,000-£20,000+; furniture, 1700-1910, £2,000-£7,500+; bronze and porcelain, 1800-1900, £1,000-£5,000+.* LOC: A25. PARK: Easy. TEL: 0959 64477. SER: Valuations; restorations (pictures and furniture). FAIRS: Barbican. VAT: Spec.

Westerham continued

Old Hall (Sphinx Gallery) **LAPADA**
24 Market Sq. (L Van Den Bussche) 10-5.30, other times by appointment. SIZE: Large. *STOCK: Early and Continental oak furniture, metalware, statues, Delft pottery.* PARK: Easy. TEL: 0959 63114.

Denys Sargeant
21 The Green. Est: 1949. Open 9.30-5.30. *STOCK: Glass, especially chandeliers and candelabras, decanters and lustres.* TEL: 0959 62130. SER: Restorations (chandeliers); cleaning (chandeliers). VAT: Stan/Spec.

Taylor-Smith
4 The Grange, High St. Open 10-5. *STOCK: General antiques, books, furniture, paintings, porcelain, glass and decorative items.* TEL: 0959 63100.

Twenty-One Antiques
21 High St. (M Richardson) Open 10-5. SIZE: Small. *STOCK: General antiques, porcelain, £5-£500; small furniture, £25-£1,500; silver, pewter, £10-£1,000; paintings, £50-£1,000.* LOC: A25. PARK: In side road opposite. TEL: 0959 63055.

WHITFIELD, Nr. Dover

Chapman's
St. Margaret's Farm, Napchester Rd. (A.J Chapman) Est: 1989. Open 10-6, Fri. 10-5, Sat. 9.30-5, Sun. and Mon. by appointment. SIZE: Medium. *STOCK: Walnut and mahogany furniture including chests of drawers, tables and chairs, 18th-19th C, to £1,500.* LOC: 5 mins. drive from Whitfield roundabout along A256 Sandwich Rd., right into Napchester Rd. PARK: Easy. TEL: 0304 820170; home - same. SER: Restorations. VAT: Stan/Spec.

WHITSTABLE

Laurens Antiques
17 Harbour St. (G.A Laurens) Est: 1965. Open 9.30-5.30. SIZE: Medium. *STOCK: Furniture, 18th-19th C, £300-£500+.* LOC: Turn off Thanet Way at Longreach roundabout, straight down to one-way system in High St. PARK: Easy. TEL: 0227 261940; home - same. SER: Valuations; restorations (cabinet work); buys at auction.

Magpie
8 Harbour St. (C Davies) Est: 1976. Open 9-1 and 2.30-5.30. CL: Sun. and Wed. except by appointment. PARK: In Sydenham St. opposite. TEL: 0227 273929. SER: Restorations; buys at auction. VAT: Stan/Spec.

WINGHAM, Nr. Canterbury

Bridge Antiques
97 High St. (A. and C Cripps) Resident. Est: 1968. Open 9-5 or by appointment. CL: Wed. SIZE: Large. *STOCK: English and continental furniture, clocks, dolls and toys, books, shipping goods, bric-a-brac.* TEL: 0227 720445.

Lloyd's Bookshop
27 High St. (Mrs J Morrison) ABA. Est: 1958. Open daily. SIZE: Large. *STOCK: Antiquarian and secondhand books, prints, watercolours, ephemera, maps, music.* PARK: Easy. TEL: 0227 720774. SER: Valuations. VAT: Stan.

Silvesters **LAPADA**
33 High St. (S.N Hartley and Mr and Mrs G.M.A Wallis) Est: 1953. Open 9.30-5 by appointment. *STOCK: Furniture, Georgian and Victorian; decorative items, silver, porcelain, glass.* LOC: At main junction in town. TEL: 0227 720278. VAT: Stan/Spec.

WITTERSHAM

Old Corner House Antiques
6 Poplar Rd. (J. and F Shepherd) Open 10-5. CL: Fri. *STOCK: General antiques, country furniture, samplers, 18th and 19th C English pottery, including blue and white and creamware; watercolours, 19th to early 20th C.* PARK: Easy. TEL: 0797 270236.

WOODCHURCH, Nr. Ashford

Woodchurch Antiques
3 The Green. (Mrs K Hewson) Est: 1982. Open 10-5.30, Sun. by appointment. CL: Wed. and Thurs. SIZE: Medium. *STOCK: Continental and English pine, country items, domestic collectables, china, £5-£500.* LOC: At top of green close to church. TEL: 0233 860249; home - same.

Footed tumbler, decorated by John Davenport's patent process with a huntsman loading his rifle, with his dogs, in a wooded landscape, c.1806-10. Height 4½in. (11.4cm). The original use for this shape of glass is not clear. The shape is similar to the caddy bowls in the Richardson pattern book (Plate 38) but that use of the glass seems unlikely as the decoration would rarely be seen once the glass was replaced into the tea caddy box. A more likely use would be to hold the spoons or glass sugar crushers used by the members of gentlemen's drinking clubs or political groups (Plate 50). The shape reappears in pressed glass, later in the century, for that purpose (Colour Plate 44). From ***British Glass 1800-1914*** by Charles R. Hajdamach published by the **Antique Collectors' Club** in 1991. £45.00.

Lancashire

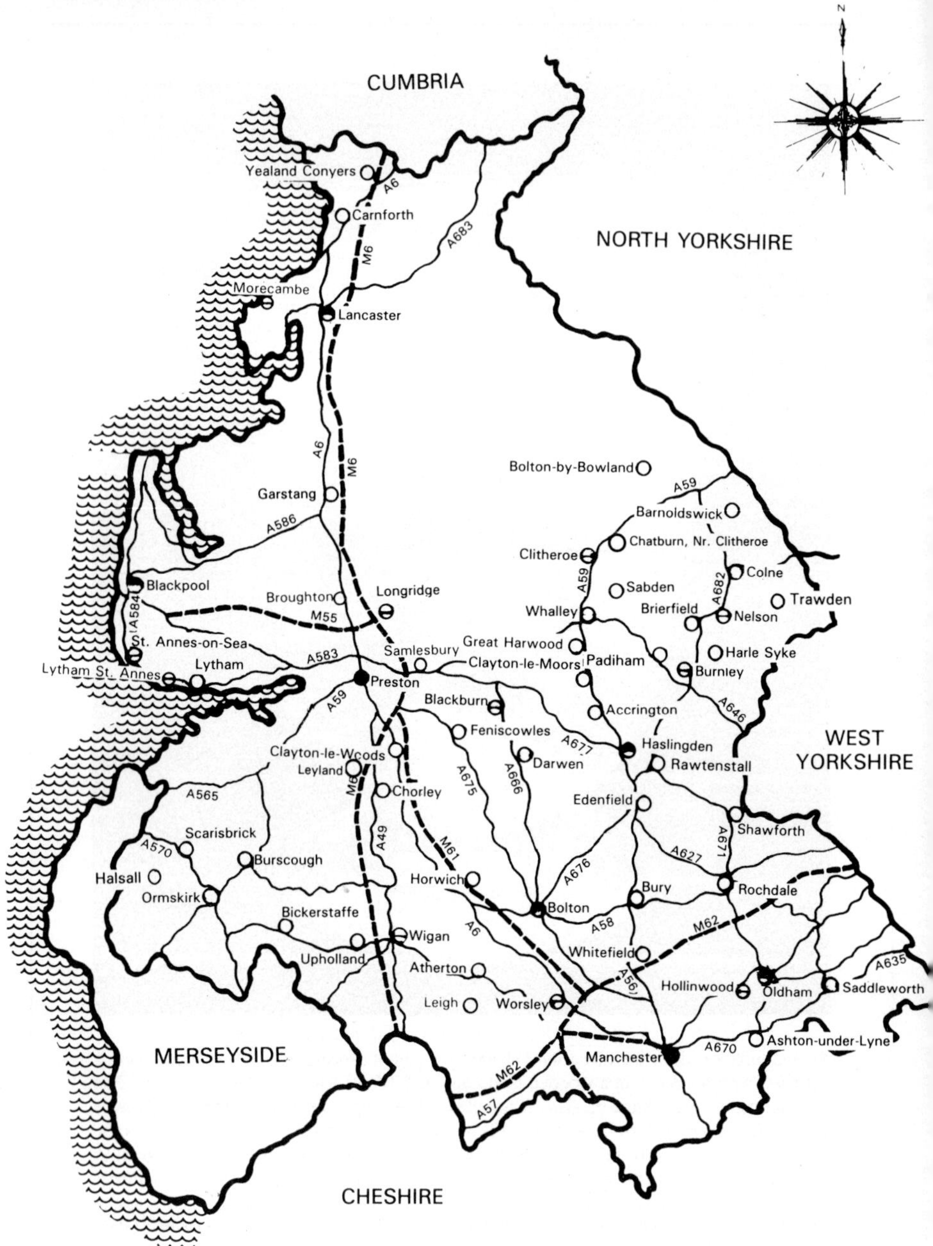
N
CUMBRIA
NORTH YORKSHIRE
WEST YORKSHIRE
MERSEYSIDE
CHESHIRE
Yealand Conyers
Carnforth
Morecambe
Lancaster
Garstang
Blackpool
Broughton
Longridge
St. Annes-on-Sea
Lytham
Lytham St. Annes
Samlesbury
Preston
Clayton-le-Woods
Leyland
Chorley
Scarisbrick
Burscough
Halsall
Ormskirk
Bickerstaffe
Upholland
Wigan
Horwich
Atherton
Leigh
Worsley
Blackburn
Feniscowles
Darwen
Bolton
Bolton-by-Bowland
Barnoldswick
Chatburn, Nr. Clitheroe
Clitheroe
Colne
Sabden
Trawden
Whalley
Brierfield
Nelson
Great Harwood
Harle Syke
Padiham
Clayton-le-Moors
Burnley
Accrington
Haslingden
Rawtenstall
Edenfield
Shawforth
Rochdale
Bury
Whitefield
Hollinwood
Oldham
Saddleworth
Ashton-under-Lyne
Manchester
A6
M6
A683
A586
A584
M55
A583
A59
A565
A570
A49
M61
A675
A666
A677
A676
A58
A627
A671
M62
A56
A635
A670
A57
A646
A682

Please note this is only a rough map designed to show dealers the number of shops in the various towns, and is not necessarily totally accurate.

Key to number of shops in this area.

- 1–2
- 3–5
- 6–12
- 13+

ACCRINGTON

Abbey Antiques
60 and 75 Abbey St. (M.A Capstick) Est: 1976. Open daily. SIZE: Medium. *STOCK: General antiques, Georgian, Victorian and Edwardian mahogany, £200-£10,000.* LOC: Main road. PARK: Easy. TEL: 0254 233280; evenings - 0254 301858. SER: Valuations; buys at auction.

The Coin and Jewellery Shop
129a Blackburn Rd. Est: 1977. Open 10-5.30. CL: Wed. *STOCK: Coins, medals and jewellery.* TEL: 0254 384757.

ASHTON-UNDER-LYNE

Kenworthys Ltd BADA
226 Stamford St. (C.J. and M Collings) Est: 1880. Open 9.30-5. CL: Tues. *STOCK: Silver and jewellery, all periods, £1-£5,000.* PARK: 50yds. away behind shop. TEL: 061 330 3043 (2 lines). SER: Valuations; restorations; buys at auction. FAIRS: Harrogate (E.E.B. and A.D.); Buxton; British International. VAT: Stan/Spec.

Tameside Antiques
Cavendish Mill, 85 Cavendish St. (B Boyle and D Downworth) Est: 1973. Open every day. SIZE: Large and warehouse. *STOCK: Period and Victorian furniture, clocks, works of art, garden statuary.* LOC: On roundabout at Ashton. TEL: 061 344 5477; home - 061 320 9298; 061 308 4445. SER: Valuations; re-upholstery, packing and shipping. VAT: Stan.

ATHERTON

Victoria's
144/146 Bolton Rd. (J Stredder) Open 10-5.30. CL: Mon. *STOCK: General antiques including pine.* TEL: 0942 882311.

BARNOLDSWICK, Nr. Colne

Roy W Bunn LAPADA
34/36 Church St. Est: 1986. *STOCK: Staffordshire figures, 18th-19th C, £45-£2,000.* LOC: Main road. PARK: Easy. TEL: 0282 813703; home - same. SER: Valuations; restorations (ceramics); buys at auction. VAT: Spec.

BICKERSTAFFE, Nr. Ormskirk

E.W Webster BADA
Wash Farm, Rainford Rd. Est: 1975. Open anytime by appointment. SIZE: Large. *STOCK: Furniture, early metal, needlework, treen, decorative items, 1650-1850.* Not Stocked: Bric-a-brac. LOC: Exit 3, M58 on to A570, turn left 100yds. PARK: Easy. TEL: 0695 24326. VAT: Spec.

BLACKBURN

Alpha Supplies Co
108 Whinney Lane. (M Satterthwaite) Est: 1985. Open Mon., Fri. and Sat. afternoon by appointment. SIZE: Small. *STOCK: Ceramics, watches and furniture, £5-£5,000.* LOC: Off duel carriageway (Yewtree Dr.). PARK: Easy. TEL: 0254 249704; home - same. SER: Valuations; restorations (ceramics); buys at auction. FAIRS: Stafford, Newark. VAT: Spec.

Ancient and Modern
56 Bank Top. (D.G Bennett) Est: 1952. Open 9-6. *STOCK: Jewellery, Victorian to date, £20-£500.* LOC: One mile from town centre. PARK: Easy. TEL: 0254 63256. SER: Valuations; restorations; buys at auction (gold, silver, stamps, coins); repairs (jewellery, watches and longcase clocks).

Mitchell's (Lock Antiques)
76 Bolton Rd. (S Mitchell) Open 9-5. *STOCK: General antiques, gold and silver jewellery.* TEL: 0254 664663.

Blackburn continued

Anthony Walmsley Ltd
93 Montague St. (A. and F.A Walmsley) Est: 1968. Open 10-6. CL: Sun., except by appointment. SIZE: Medium. *STOCK: General furniture, clocks.* Not Stocked: Guns or weapons. LOC: 2 minutes from town centre. Montague St. links Preston New Rd. and Preston Old Rd. PARK: Easy. TEL: 0254 698755 any time. SER: Valuations; restorations; buys at auction; shipping and packing; courier service.

BLACKPOOL

Antique Dolls
29a Caunce St. (D Kavanagh) Open 10-5, appointment advisable. *STOCK: Dolls.* TEL: 0253 20701.

Blackpool Antiques Centre
105-107 Hornby Rd. Open 9-5. CL: Sat. SIZE: Large. *STOCK: Irish pine, English hardwood and shipping furniture.* TEL: 0253 752514.

C.B.I. Ltd
521 Lytham Rd. Est: 1965. Open 9-5. CL: Sat. SIZE: Large. *STOCK: Paintings and furniture, English and ancient coins, gold bullion coins, jewellery and silver, £50-£20,000+.* LOC: Lytham Rd. runs from Central Promenade south to Blackpool Airport main gates. Shop is 1/4 mile from airport. PARK: Easy. TEL: 0253 43081. SER: Valuations. VAT: Stan/Spec.

Peter and Ann Christian
400 and 402 Waterloo Rd, South Shore. Open 10-5.30. *STOCK: Decorative art and pine furniture.* TEL: 0253 63268.

Peter Ireland Ltd
31 Clifton St. Open 9-5. *STOCK: Coins, banknotes, war medals and militaria; general antiques, jewellery, pottery, porcelain, commemorative ware, silver.* TEL: 0253 21588.

Lambert's Antiques
378 Talbot Rd. Open 10-5. *STOCK: Furniture mainly Victorian and Edwardian; brass and ceramics.* TEL: 0253 397196. VAT: Stan.

R.H Latham Antiques
45 Whitegate Drive. Resident. Est: 1958. Open 10-5.30. SIZE: Large. *STOCK: Stripped pine, brass, copper and porcelain.* TEL: 0253 33950; home - same. SER: Shipping and courier.

Militaryman Antiques
228 Church St. (M Greenall) Open 9-5, Wed. and Sat. 9-2. *STOCK: Militaria.* TEL: 0253 20077.

Nostalgia
95 Coronation St. (P Jackson) Est: 1978. Open 10-4 including Sun. in summer. SIZE: Small. *STOCK: Commemoratives, 18th-20th C, £2-*

Nostalgia continued

£1,000; crested china, 19th-20th C, £2-£500. LOC: Town centre, near Winter Gardens. PARK: Easy. TEL: 0253 293251. SER: Valuations.

Tom Owen Aquarius Antiques
18 Rawcliffe St, South Shore. Est: 1965. Open 10.30-5.00. *STOCK: Trade items in wood, brass and copper, bric-a-brac, collectors' items.* LOC: Just off south promenade. PARK: Easy. TEL: 0772 716617. VAT: Stan.

Past and Present
126 Harrowside. (A Boyle) Open 10-5.30. *STOCK: General antiques and bric-a-brac.* TEL: 0253 42729.

The Pine Dresser
1 Ball St, South Shore. (D Addison) Est: 1978. Open Sat. 10-5, other times by appointment. SIZE: Small. *STOCK: Pine.* LOC: Off Lytham Rd. PARK: Waterloo Rd. TEL: 0253 403862. SER: Restorations; stripping.

BOLTON

Corner Cupboard
2 Hawarden St. (Mrs E Pratt) Open Tues., Thurs. and Fri. 10-5.30, Sat. 10-2. *STOCK: Bric-a-brac.* TEL: 0204 58948.

Curiosity Shop
832 Bury Rd, Breightmet. (N Riley) Est: 1983. Open Mon. and Tues. 10-4, Wed., Thurs. and Fri. 10-1. SIZE: Small. *STOCK: Shipping goods, £50-£500; bric-a-brac, £1-£100, both 19th C.* LOC: A58, facing Safeways. PARK: Easy. TEL: 0204 21290; home - 0204 592196; mobile - 0860 574808. SER: Valuations. *Trade Only.*

Drop Dial Antiques
Last Drop Village, Hospital Rd, Bromley Cross. (I.W. and I.E Roberts) Est: 1975. Open every afternoon including Sun. SIZE: Small. *STOCK: Clocks, mainly English and French, 18th-20th C, £100-£4,000; mercury barometers, 19th-20th C, £100-£500; paintings, silver and general antiques, £20-£500.* Not Stocked: Stamps and armour. LOC: Beneath Last Drop Collectors Market. PARK: Easy. TEL: 0204 57186; home - 0257 480995. SER: Valuations; restorations (clocks and barometers). VAT: Stan/Spec.

Last Drop Antique and Collectors Club
Last Drop Hotel, Bromley Cross. Open Sun. 11-4. SIZE: 40 dealers. *STOCK: General antiques and collectables.*

Memory Lane Antique Centre
Gilnow Lane, Off Deane Rd. (Mrs M Davies) Open 9-5 including Sun. SIZE: 60 dealers. *STOCK: Wide variety of general antiques.* LOC: Off M61, exit 5. TEL: 0204 380383.

Bolton continued

G Oakes and Son Bolton Ltd
160 Blackburn Rd. Est: 1958. Open 9.30-5.30. CL: Wed. *STOCK: Furniture.* TEL: 0204 26587. SER: Shipping and packing; buys at auction. VAT: Stan.

Park Galleries Antiques, Fine Art and Decor
167 Mayor St. (Mrs S Hunt) Est: 1964. Open Thurs., Fri. and Sat. 10.30-5, or by appointment. SIZE: Medium. *STOCK: English and continental furniture, 17th to early 20th C; English and continental pottery and porcelain, miniatures, glass, brass, silver, copper; paintings, 19th C; decorative and collectable items.* Not Stocked: Weapons, coins, medals, stamps. LOC: On B6202. PARK: Side and rear. TEL: 0204 29827; home - 061 764 5853. SER: Valuations; restorations (furniture; metalwork replating, pottery and porcelain, paintings; frames regilded; clock movements).

BOLTON-BY-BOWLAND, Nr. Clitheroe

Farmhouse Antiques
23 Main St. (M Howard) Est: 1980. Open Sat. and Sun. 12-4.30 or by appointment. SIZE: Small. *STOCK: Textiles, linen and quilts, from 1830; beads and jewellery, small Victorian pottery, china, kitchenalia and brasses.* LOC: Off A59, past Clitheroe, through Sawley to village. PARK: Easy. TEL: 020 07 294; home - 02006 244. FAIRS: Castle and Bailey in Lancs., Yorks. and Cheshire.

Harrop Fold Clocks (F. Robinson)
Harrop Fold, Lane Ends. Est: 1974. Open by appointment. SIZE: Medium. *STOCK: British clocks, barometers, 18th-19th C, £500-£4,000.* LOC: Through Clitheroe to Chatburn and Grindleton. Take Slaidburn road, turn left after 3 miles. PARK: Own. TEL: 020 07 665; home - same. SER: Valuations; restorations (clocks).

BRIERFIELD, Nr. Nelson

Berry's Antiques
17 Colne Rd. (T Berry) Open 10-4.30. CL: Sat. *STOCK: Shipping goods.* TEL: 0282 37086.

J.H Blakey and Sons Ltd (Est. 1905)
Church St. and showrooms at Burnley Rd, Brierfield Centre. Est: 1905. *STOCK: Furniture, brass, copper, pewter, clocks, curios.* TEL: 0282 63593/602493. SER: Restorations. VAT: Stan.

BROUGHTON, Nr. Preston

W.J Cowell and Sons Architectural Antiques
Church Hill House, D'Urton Lane. Open by appointment only. *STOCK: Coloured leaded windows and telephone kiosks.* TEL: 0772 862034. SER: Export.

Broughton continued

Village Antiques
488 Garstang Rd. (W. and L Nelson) Open 9.30-5.30 or by appointment. CL: Sat. *STOCK: General antiques, dolls, jewellery and collectors' items, £5-£1,000.* LOC: 1/2 mile from junction 32, M6 on A6. PARK: Easy. TEL: 0772 862648/862066. SER: Valuations.

BURNLEY

Brun Lea Antiques
3/5 Standish St. (J Waite) Open 9.30-5. CL: Tues. *STOCK: General antiques.* TEL: 0282 32396.

Brun Lea Antiques
Dane House Mill, Dane House Rd. Open 8-6. SIZE: Warehouse. *STOCK: Georgian, Victorian, Edwardian and 1930's furniture.* TEL: 0282 413513.

Mrs S Falik BADA
Est: 1970. Open by appointment only. SIZE: Medium. *STOCK: Fine 18th to early 19th C porcelain.* PARK: Easy. TEL: 0282 65172. SER: Valuations.

BURSCOUGH, Nr. Ormskirk

West Lancs. Antiques LAPADA
Victoria Mill, Victoria St. (W. and B Griffiths) Est: 1959. Open 9-5. SIZE: Large. *STOCK: Shipping furniture.* TEL: 0704 894634/893245; home - 0704 35720. SER: Courier; packing and shipping. VAT: Stan/Spec.

BURY

Newtons
151 The Rock. (C.W Newton) Est: 1931. Open 9-5.30. SIZE: Small. *STOCK: General antiques, 18th-19th C, £5-£500.* Not Stocked: Continental furniture. LOC: From Manchester through Bury town centre, shop is on left 200yds. before Fire Station. PARK: 50yds. behind shop. TEL: 061 764 1863. SER: Valuations; restorations (antique furniture). VAT: Stan.

CARNFORTH

Wm Goodfellow (Antiques) LAPADA
The Green, Over Kellet. Est: 1975. Open 10-6, or by appointment. CL: Wed. SIZE: Small. *STOCK: Small period furniture, £50-£2,000; pottery and porcelain, 1750-1870; silver, glass and metalware, pre-1900, £10-£1,000; decorative and furnishing items.* Not Stocked: Large furniture. LOC: B6254, 1 mile from exit 35, M6. PARK: Easy. TEL: 0524 733030. SER: Valuations; restorations (cabinet work and silver repair); buys at auction. VAT: Stan/Spec.

Carnforth continued

Peter Haworth
Howe Hill, Cow Brow. Open by appointment. *STOCK: English and Scottish paintings and watercolours, 1850-1950; Moorcroft pottery, all £100-£25,000.* LOC: 1/2 mile from junction 36, M6, on Kirkby Lonsdale road. PARK: Easy. TEL: 04487 656.

CHATBURN, Nr. Clitheroe

T Brindle **LAPADA**
6 and 8 Sawley Rd. Open 9.30-5.00, Sat. and other times by appointment. *STOCK: Decorative items.* TEL: 0200 40025; fax - 0200 40090.

CHORLEY

Charisma Curios and Antiques
Tall Trees Cottage, 91 Wigan Rd, Euxton. (N. and V.M Langton) Est: 1977. Open by appointment. *STOCK: General antiques, period furniture.* LOC: A49. PARK: Outside. TEL: 025 72 76845. SER: Restorations (furniture); cane and rush seating.

CLAYTON-LE-MOORS, Nr. Accrington

Edward V Phillips (Antiques)
238 Whalley Rd. Est: 1980. Open 10-12 and 1-5, Tues. and Fri. 1.30-5, Sat. 10-3, Sun. 12-2. SIZE: Medium. *STOCK: Stripped satin walnut, late 19th C, £100-£500; stripped pine, mid to late 19th C, £100-£500; shipping goods, early 20th C, £50-£1,000.* LOC: 1/2 mile from M65 on A680. PARK: Easy. TEL: 0254 396739; home - 0254 384979. SER: Valuations; restorations (hand stripping, finishing and repairs). VAT: Stan/Spec.

Sparth House Antiques
Sparth House, Whalley Rd. (W. and B Coleman) Est: 1967. TEL: 0254 872263.

CLAYTON-LE-WOODS, Nr. Chorley

Carlton Antiques (Exports) **LAPADA**
2 Gough Lane, Clayton Brook Rd. (R.J. and F.J Coventry) Est: 1977. Open daily. CL: Sat. SIZE: Warehouse. *STOCK: Furniture, mainly mahogany, 1750-1900, £100-£4,000.* LOC: Off M6/A6, junction 29, near Esso garage. PARK: Easy. TEL: 0772 34004. SER: Valuations; restorations (cabinet work); buys at auction (Georgian and Victorian furniture); shippers and packers. VAT: Stan.

CLITHEROE

Castle Antiques
15 Moor Lane. (J. and B Tomkinson) Est: 1967. Open 10.30-4.45. CL: Mon. and Wed. SIZE: Large. *STOCK: Shipping goods, stained glass windows, painted pine, Lloyd loom items, clocks, furniture including gateleg tables, large wardrobes and satinwood bedroom suites.* Not Stocked: Arms. TEL: 0200 26568; home - 0254 235820.

Ethos Gallery
4 York St. (F. and P Barnes) Est: 1978. Open 9-5, Wed. and Sun. by appointment. SIZE: Medium. *STOCK: Oil paintings and watercolours, 19th C, £100-£5,000; paintings, £100-£2,000; English crystal £5-£100, both 20th C.* LOC: A59 in town centre. PARK: Own. TEL: 0200 27878; home - 0200 22597. SER: Valuations; restorations (oils and watercolours). VAT: Stan.

M. and N Haworth Ltd
P.O. Box 20. *STOCK: Stamps, coins, post and cigarette cards, medals and memorabilia.* TEL: 0200 23576.

Lee's Antiques
59 Whalley Rd. (A Lee) *STOCK: General antiques.* TEL: 0200 24921; home - 0200 25441.

Rebecca Antiques
22 Moor Lane. (B. and A Donovan) Est: 1967. Open 9-5. CL: Wed. and Sun. except by appointment. SIZE: Medium. *STOCK: Decorative and upholstered items, furniture, £100-£2,000; pictures, brass and objects, £5-£2,000, all 19th-20th C; garden furniture, small architectural items, 18th-20th C, £20-£2,000.* LOC: 15 miles from junction 31, M6, via A59. PARK: Opposite. TEL: 0200 29461; home - 0200 28863. VAT: Stan/Spec.

COLNE

Enloc Antiques
Birchenlee Mill, Lenches Rd. Est: 1978. Open 10-5, Sat. 10-12 or anytime by appointment. SIZE: Warehouse. *STOCK: Pine, 18th-19th C, £5-£1,000; kitchen chairs, 19th C, £20-£40.* TEL: 0282 867101. SER: Restorations (stripping, polishing and joinery). VAT: Stan.

DARWEN

Cranberry Antiques
23 Duckworth St. (J. and M Cunliffe) Est: 1976. Open 10-12 and 1-4. SIZE: Small. *STOCK: Royal Doulton and collectors' items, reference books, glass, general antiques.* LOC: A666. PARK: Easy. TEL: 0254 772678. FAIRS: Stafford, Newark, Charnock Richard, Doncaster Race Course. VAT: Stan/Spec.

Darwen continued

K.C Antiques LAPADA
538 Bolton Rd. (K. and J Anderton) Resident. Open 9-6, Sun. 12-5. *STOCK: Georgian, Victorian and Edwardian furniture and decorative items.* LOC: A666. PARK: Easy. TEL: 0254 772252; home - same. SER: Buys at auction. VAT: Stan/Spec.

ECCLESTON

3 L's Antiques
Unit 4, The Arches, Grove Development Centre. (L Frost) Est: 1989. Open 12-4, Thurs. 12-3, Sun. 10-5. SIZE: Small. *STOCK: Furniture, 1850-1920, £50-£1,000; porcelain, 1850-1950, £5-£200; gramophones, 1900-1930, £50-£250; linen and jewellery.* LOC: Junction 27, M6, village is 2 miles north via Mossy Lea Rd. Shop situated at Bygone Times Centre. PARK: Easy. TEL: Home - 0942 861105. SER: Buys at auction.

Bygone Times
Times House, Grove Mill, The Green. (G Wilson) Open 8-6 including Sun. SIZE: 150 dealers. *STOCK: General antiques including architectural and North American artifacts.* TEL: 0257 453780.

EDENFIELD, Nr. Bury

The Antique Shop
17 Market St. (J. and J.C Salisbury) Est: 1964. Open 10-4. SIZE: Large. *STOCK: General antiques, shipping goods, £1-£10,000.* LOC: On A56. PARK: Easy. TEL: 070 682 3107/2351. SER: Valuations. VAT: Stan/Spec.

FENISCOWLES, Nr. Blackburn

Old Smithy
726 Preston Old Rd. (R.C Lynch) Est: 1967. Open 9-5. SIZE: Large. *STOCK: Period and Victorian fireplaces, pub and architectural items, violins and musical instruments, brass beds, lamps, furniture, shipping items, clothes, Victorian-1950; jewellery, brass, copper, Victorian lace and linen.* LOC: Opposite Fieldens Arms. PARK: Own or nearby. TEL: 0254 209943; home - 0254 580874. SER: Valuations; restorations (wooden items); buys at auction. FAIRS: Park Hall, Charnock Richard.

GARSTANG

Clare's Antiques and Auction Galleries
Wheatsheaf Buildings, Park Hill. (Mrs C.A.L Campbell-Cameron and Mrs C.L Allen) Est: 1960. Open 10-4. CL: Mon. and Wed. SIZE: Large. *STOCK: Royal Worcester porcelain, early 20th C, £150-£4,000; Rudelstadt, Meissen,*

Clare's Antiques and Auction Galleries continued

Dresden figures, 19th C, £500-£2,000; silver, jewellery, small furniture. LOC: Off A6. PARK: Easy. TEL: 0995 605702; home - same. SER: Valuations; restorations (porcelain, jewellery); buys at auction.

GREAT HARWOOD, Nr. Blackburn

Benny Charlesworth's Snuff Box
51 Blackburn Rd. (Mrs A.M and Miss N.M Bartholomew) Est: 1984. Open 10-1 and 2-5, Sat. 10-12.30. CL: Tues. SIZE: Small. *STOCK: Furniture, £25-£900; pottery, £5-£50; both Edwardian and Victorian; metalware, £5-£40; pictures, £5-£200; glass and general antiques.* LOC: 200yds. from town hall clock, off A680. PARK: Easy. TEL: 0254 888550; home - 0254 888743. FAIRS: Charnock Richard, Park Hall.

HALSALL, Nr. Ormskirk

Halsall Hall Ltd
Halsall Hall. (J Nolan) Est: 1970. Open by appointment 7 days and evenings. SIZE: Large. *STOCK: Export items, from £500; interior design, 17th-19th C.* LOC: On A5147 (old A567). TEL: 0704 841065; home - same. SER: Valuations; restorations; buys at auction. VAT: Stan/Spec. *Trade Only.*

HARLE SYKE, Nr. Burnley

The Burnley Antiques Centre
Harle Syke Mill. Est: 1962. Open 8-5, Sat. 10-4, Sun. 1-4. SIZE: Large. *STOCK: Furniture and architectural items.* LOC: Main road from Burnley. PARK: Easy. TEL: 0282 31412; fax - 0282 50605. VAT: Stan.

HASLINGDEN

The Antique Shop
38 Bury Rd. (P Norgrove) Open 9.30-5.30 by prior appointment. *STOCK: Longcase and wall clocks.* TEL: 0706 211995.

Aries Antiques
192 Blackburn Rd. (T Porter) Open 10.30-5. *STOCK: Furniture including shipping; pianos.* TEL: 0706 831651. VAT: Stan/Spec.

P.J Brown Antiques
190 Blackburn Rd. Open 10-5, Sat. and Sun. by appointment. SIZE: Large and warehouse. *STOCK: General antiques and shipping goods.* LOC: A680, parallel to M66 by-pass. PARK: Easy. TEL: 0706 224888. VAT: Stan.

Haslingden continued

Clifton House Antiques
Clifton House, 198 Blackburn Rd. (D Clink) Est: 1958. Open 9-6. CL: Sat. and Sun. SIZE: Medium. *STOCK: General antiques, £5-£500.* PARK: Easy. TEL: 0706 214895. VAT: Stan.

Fieldings Antiques
176, 178 and 180 Blackburn Rd. Est: 1956. Open 9-4.30, Fri. 9-4. CL: Thurs. SIZE: Large. *STOCK: Longcase clocks, £30-£2,000; wall clocks, sets of chairs, pine, period oak, French furniture, glass, shipping goods, toys, steam engines, veteran cars, vintage and veteran motor cycles.* PARK: Easy. TEL: 0254 63358 or 0706 214254.

Speakmans
186 Blackburn Rd. (P Speakman) Est: 1956. Open 9.30-5.30. CL: Sat. SIZE: Small. *STOCK: Furniture, pottery, porcelain, glass, clocks, pictures and unusual items.* PARK: Easy. TEL: 0706 224282; home - 0254 885848.

HOLLINWOOD, Nr. Oldham

Abbey Antiques
299/301 Manchester Rd. (D Mullin) Est: 1969. Open 10-6, Sun. 11-3. SIZE: Large. *STOCK: Stripped pine and general antiques.* LOC: A62. PARK: At side. TEL: 061 681 6538. SER: Restorations; repairs (clocks).

Hollinwood continued

Ace Antiques
293 Manchester Rd. (R. and J O'Brien) Est: 1970. Open 9-5, Sat. 9-12, or by appointment. *STOCK: Furniture, Edwardian and Victorian, shipping goods; general antiques and pianos.* LOC: On main Manchester to Oldham rd. PARK: Opposite. TEL: 061 683 4717; home - 061 626 2062.

Fernlea Antiques
305 Manchester Rd. (A.J. and Mrs B McLaughlin) Open 10-5. *STOCK: General antiques and shipping goods.* TEL: 061 682 0589.

HORWICH, Nr. Bolton

Alan Butterworth (Antiques) Ltd
7 Ardley Rd. Open by appointment. *STOCK: Furniture, 17th-19th C; continental furniture, art nouveau, pottery, porcelain, brass, copper, shipping goods.* TEL: 0204 68094. SER: Export; packing and shipping; courier.

LANCASTER

Article Antiques
134/136 Greaves Rd. (J.W. and L.J Forsyth) Est: 1982. Open 10-5, Sun. 11-4 or by appointment. CL: Mon. and Tues. SIZE: Medium. *STOCK: Furniture, including shipping, £50-£2,000; porcelain, china and glass, £55-£2,000; all 18th-20th C.* LOC: A6 through town from M6, junction 34. PARK: Easy. TEL: 0524 39312; home - 05242 62294. SER: Valuations. VAT: Stan/Spec.

The Assembly Rooms Market
King St. Open Thurs., Fri. and Sat. 10-4.30. SIZE: Several dealers. *STOCK: General antiques, jewellery, collectables, period clothing, books and tools, records and stamps.* TEL: Market Superintendent 0524 66627.

G.W Antiques
47 North Rd., and 4 St. Georges Quay Works, St. Georges Quay. (G Woods) Est: 1978. Open 9-5.30. SIZE: Large and warehouse. *STOCK: Stripped pine, 18th to early 20th C, £30-£1,500; furniture, all periods.* LOC: A6. PARK: 60yds. TEL: 0524 32050/841148. SER: Valuations; restorations (furniture); stripping. VAT: Stan/Spec.

G.B Antiques Ltd
Lancaster Leisure Park, Wyresdale Rd. (Mrs G Blackburn) Open 10-5 including Sun. SIZE: Large - 100+ dealers. *STOCK: Porcelain, glass and silver, late 19th to early 20th C; small furniture, Victorian to early 20th C.* LOC: Off M6, junction 33 or 34. PARK: Easy. TEL: 0524 844734; home - 0772 861593. SER: Valuations; buys at auction. VAT: Stan/Spec.

Lancaster continued

Lancaster Leisure Park Antiques Centre
Wyresdale Rd, (on site of former Hornsea Pottery Plant). Open every day 10-5. SIZE: 20 dealers. *STOCK: A wide range of antiques.* LOC: Off M6, junction 33. TEL: 0524 844734.

Lancastrian Antiques
66 Penny St. (S.P. and H.S Wilkinson) Open 10-5. *STOCK: General antiques.* TEL: 0524 843764.

W.B McCormack
6 and 6a Rosemary Lane. Open 10-5. CL: Wed. *STOCK: Rare and secondhand books.* TEL: 0524 36405.

Studio Arts Gallery
6 Lower Church St. (T. and I Dodgson) Open 9-5.30. *STOCK: Oils and watercolours, 19th-20th C, £50-£25,000; prints, 20th C, £20-£1,000.* TEL: 0524 68014; fax - 0524 844422. SER: Valuations; restorations and cleaning (as stock); framing; buys at auction.

Sun St. Antique Centre
26 Sun St. (Mrs P Bowskill) Est: 1978. Open 9.30-4.30, Sat. 9.30-5. SIZE: Medium. *STOCK: Stripped pine, 19th C, £50-£400; related small items, kitchenalia.* LOC: Off Church St. PARK: Easy. TEL: 0524 37844; home - 0524 733667. VAT: Stan/Spec.

Vicary Antiques
18a Brock St. Est: 1974. Open 10-5. CL: Wed. SIZE: Small. *STOCK: Paintings, prints, art pottery, works of art, 1850-1950; arts and crafts, furniture, quilts.* TEL: 0524 843322. VAT: Stan/Spec.

LEIGH

Leigh Coins, Antiques and Jewellery
4 Queens St. (R Bibby) Open 9.30-5.30, Wed. 9.30-12.30. *STOCK: General antiques and jewellery.* TEL: 0942 607947.

LEYLAND

Hipping Stone Antiques Warehouse
Knowles Mill, Leyland Lane. (N. and V.M Langton) Open 10-5 including Sun. CL: Sat. SIZE: Several dealers. *STOCK: Period furniture, clocks, shipping goods, pine, general antiques, and some smalls.* LOC: 3 mins. M6, junction 28; 10 mins. from Preston. PARK: Easy. TEL: 0772 623110; home - 02572 76845.

LONGRIDGE, Nr. Preston

Charnley Fine Arts
Charnley House, Preston Rd, Alston. (R. and J Crosbie) Est: 1989. Open by appointment. SIZE: Small. *STOCK: 19th and 20th C paintings, £100-*

Charnley Fine Arts continued

£10,000. LOC: Off M55/M6, north of Preston on B6243. PARK: Easy. TEL: 0772 782800; home - same. SER: Restorations.

James Cook Antiques
Office only - The Old Bakery, 36 Inglewhite Rd. Est: 1970. Open by appointment. *STOCK: Complete church interiors, pine and oak pews and furnishings.* TEL: 0772 784290. VAT: Stan/Spec.

The Folly
21 Inglewhite Rd. (E Hamlet) Est: 1982. Open 11-4.30. CL: Wed. SIZE: Medium. *STOCK: Furniture, Georgian, Victorian, Edwardian, £20-£600; mirrors, copper and brass.* LOC: 6 miles from exit 31, M6. PARK: Easy. TEL: 0772 784786; home - 0995 61605. VAT: Stan.

Joy's Shop
83 Berry Lane. (Miss J Hamlet) Resident. Est: 1986. Open 9-5. CL: Wed. SIZE: Small. *STOCK: Art deco china, jewellery, mirrors, lamps; pine furniture, bedding, chests, dressers, tables.* LOC: 6 miles from exit 31, M6. PARK: Nearby. TEL: 0772 782083.

Kitchenalia
'The Old Bakery', Inglewhite Rd. (S Cook) *STOCK: Kitchenalia, brass, copper ware, pottery, pine and oak country furniture, butchers' blocks, Victorian church pews.* TEL: 0772 785411. VAT: Stan/Spec.

LYTHAM

Clifton Antiques
8 Market Sq. (Mrs M.K Howarth and A.P. and D.A Allen) Est: 1975. Open 10.30-5. SIZE: Medium. *STOCK: Small pine furniture, silver, jewellery, £5-£500; brass, copper, crochet work.* Not Stocked: Weapons, coins. PARK: Easy. TEL: 0253 736356.

LYTHAM ST. ANNES

All Our Yesterdays of Lytham
3 Station Rd. (S Brickwood and P Harrison) Open 11-5. CL: Mon. and Wed. *STOCK: General antiques.* TEL: 0253 734748.

Pine Mine Antiques
14 Park Rd. (N. and T Shaw) Open 9-5.30. *STOCK: Pine furniture, 19th C, £150-£700; cast-iron fireplaces, 1890-1930, £200-£500; bric-a-brac, 19th-20th C, £2-£150.* LOC: Between St. Annes Sq. and Wood St. PARK: Nearby. TEL: 0253 720492; home - 0253 693439. SER: Restorations (pine stripping). VAT: Stan.

Snuff Box
5 Market Buildings, Hastings Pl. (Mrs S.C Tayler) Open 10-5. CL: Wed. *STOCK: Silver, jewellery, watches and linen.* TEL: 0253 738656.

Lytham St. Annes continued

Stamford Antiques
29 The Crescent. (Mrs D Travis) Est: 1910. Open Mon., Fri. and Sat. 10-6, other times by appointment. SIZE: Medium. *STOCK: Furniture and clocks.* PARK: Easy. TEL: 0253 728385; home - same. SER: Valuations; restorations (clocks). VAT: Stan/Spec.

MANCHESTER

A.S Antiques
26 Broad St, Salford. (A Sternshine) Est: 1975. Open 10-5.30. CL: Tues. SIZE: Large. *STOCK: Art nouveau and art deco; silver, bronzes, lighting, furniture and general antiques.* Not Stocked: Weapons. LOC: On A6 next to Salford College of Technology, one mile from Manchester city centre. PARK: Easy. TEL: 061 737 5938 or 0836 368230. SER: Valuations; restorations.

Abacus Antiques
259 Monton Rd, Monton. (C.A Mardy) Open 11-5.30, Tues. 2-5. *STOCK: Pottery, glass, furniture, silver plate.* TEL: 061 789 0465.

Acorn Antiques
Coach House, Blackburn St, Prestwich. (R Parish) Open by appointment. *STOCK: Clocks, scientific instruments and general antiques.* TEL: 061 798 7117.

Albion Antiques
643 Stockport Rd, Longsight. (A Collins) Est: 1971. Open 9-6, Sat. by appointment. SIZE: Medium. *STOCK: Furniture, £40-£5,000.* LOC: A6. PARK: Easy. TEL: 061 225 4957. SER: Valuations (furniture, architectural, nautical items, woodworking tools); restorations (furniture and wooden items).

Alpha Antiques
Ginnel Gallery, 16 Lloyd St. (M Satterthwaite) Open 9.30-5.30, Sat. 11-4. SIZE: Large. *STOCK: Furniture, Gothic, Aesthetic, Arts and Crafts, deco, 1950's, art and studio pottery and glass.* SER: Shippers (silver plate).

Antique Fireplaces
1090 Stockport Rd, Levenshulme. (D McMullan) Open 9-6, Sun. 11-5. *STOCK: Fireplaces and architectural items.* TEL: 061 431 8075.

Authentiques
(S.G Rubenstein) Est: 1978. Open by appointment only. SIZE: Small. *STOCK: Decorative items - silver, plate, porcelain, glass, boxes, Staffordshire, watercolours and prints, small furniture, miniatures, brass, curios, early 19th C to 1920s, £50-£500.* LOC: 1/2 mile from junction 17, M62 on A56. PARK: Easy. TEL: 061 773 9601 (ansaphone); fax - 061 725 9579. SER: Valuations; restorations (silver); buys at auction (pictures, silver, furniture). FAIRS: British International, Birmingham.

Manchester continued

The Baron Antiques
373 Bury New Rd, Prestwich. (M Brunsveld) Open 9.30-6. SIZE: Large. *STOCK: 18th C mahogany and early oak furniture, Victorian walnut, clocks, porcelain, objets d'art, shipping goods.* TEL: 061 773 9929. SER: Valuations; restorations.

The Belmont General Stores
20 Ladybarn Rd, Fallowfield. (G Barlow) Open 9.30-5.30. CL: Wed. *STOCK: General antiques.* TEL: 061 224 1117.

Boodle and Dunthorne Ltd
1 King St. Est: 1798. Open 9-5.30. SIZE: Large. *STOCK: Silver, 18th-19th C and Victorian jewellery, £100-£30,000; clocks and clock sets, mid-19th C, £100-£1,000.* Not Stocked: Furniture. TEL: 061 833 9000. VAT: Stan/Spec.

Boothtown Antiques
29 Chaddock Lane, Boothtown. (Mrs J Budgen) Open 10-6. *STOCK: General antiques.* TEL: 061 790 0203; home - 061 799 4814.

Britannia Antiques
754 Stockport Rd, Longsight. (G Zammit and Sons) Open 9-6. *STOCK: Furniture, clocks, architectural and decorative items.* TEL: 061 224 8350/6425. VAT: Stan.

Browzers
14 Warwick St, Prestwich. (A.E. and M Seddon) Open 10-5. CL: Wed. *STOCK: Secondhand books; prints, maps.* TEL: 061 798 0626/773 2327.

Bulldog Antiques
393 Bury New Rd, Prestwich. (P Wordsworth) Est: 1971. Open 10.30-6. CL: Sun. except by appointment. SIZE: Large. *STOCK: Georgian, Victorian and Edwardian furniture, clocks especially longcase and wall clock sets, 18th-19th C, militaria, swords, guns, pistols, shotguns, war medals, pottery, prints, pictures, general antiques and shipping goods.* LOC: Exit 17, M62. PARK: At rear. TEL: 061 798 9277; home - 061 790 7153. SER: Restorations (furniture); French polishing, watch and clock repairs. VAT: Stan.

Cathedral Jewellers
26 Cathedral St. (Mrs R.M Taylor) Open 10-5, Sat. 10-2. *STOCK: Jewellery.* TEL: 061 832 3042.

Chestergate Antiques
1034 Stockport Rd, Levenshulme. (J.G Woods) Open 10-5. *STOCK: Clocks, period and Victorian furniture.* TEL: 061 224 7795; home - 061 442 6795.

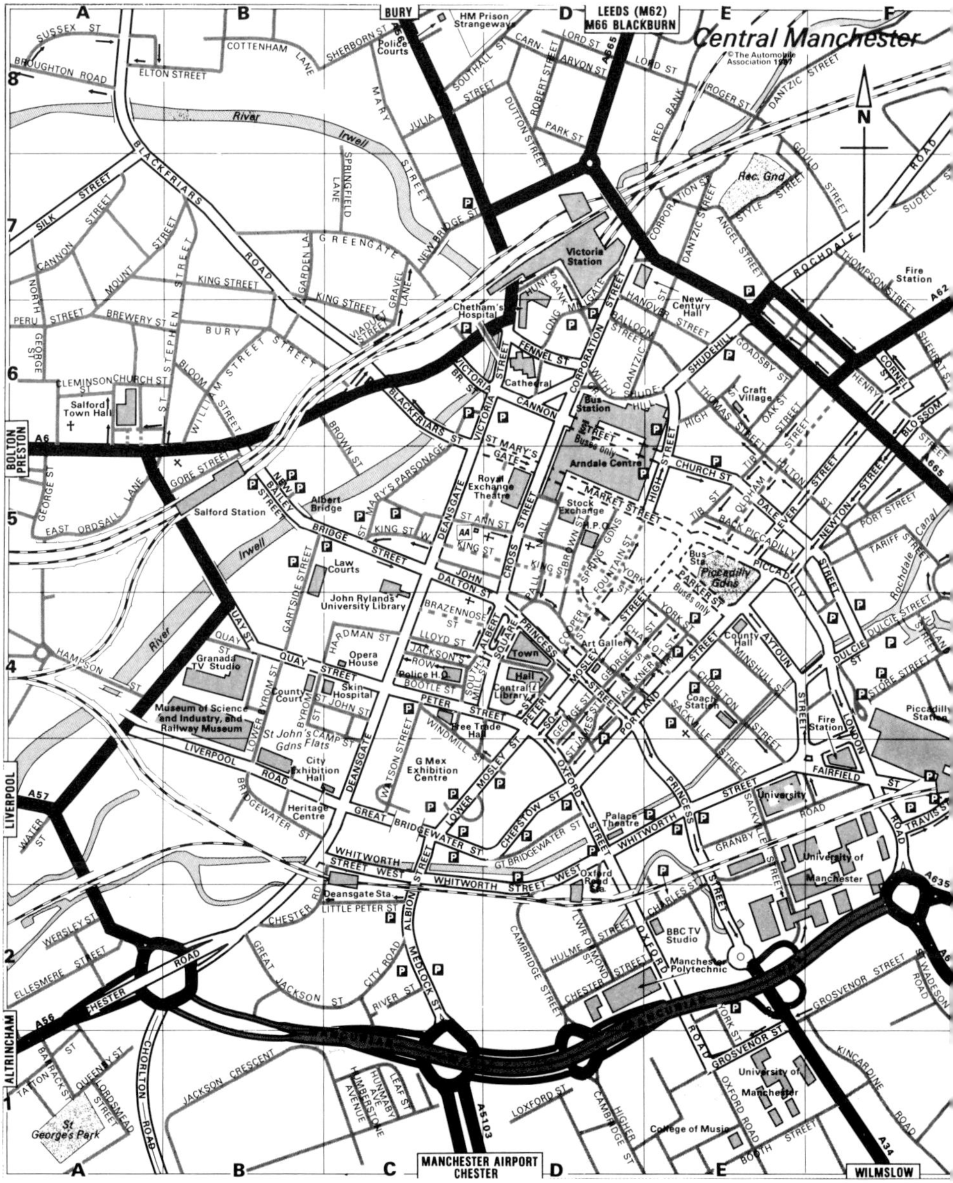
Central Manchester
© The Automobile Association 1987
BURY
LEEDS (M62)
M66 BLACKBURN
BOLTON PRESTON
LIVERPOOL
ALTRINCHAM
MANCHESTER AIRPORT CHESTER
WILMSLOW
A B C D E F
1 2 4 5 6 7 8
N
HM Prison Strangeways
Police Courts
River Irwell
Victoria Station
Chetham's Hospital
Cathedral
Bus Station
Arndale Centre
New Century Hall
Craft Village
Fire Station
Rec. Gnd
Salford Town Hall
Salford Station
Albert Bridge
Royal Exchange Theatre
Stock Exchange
G.P.O.
Law Courts
John Rylands University Library
Piccadilly Gdns
Bus Sta
Buses only
Opera House
Town Hall
Central Library
Art Gallery
Police H.Q.
Granada TV Studio
Museum of Science and Industry, and Railway Museum
County Court
Skin Hospital
St John's Gdns
Flats
City Exhibition Hall
Heritage Centre
Free Trade Hall
G Mex Exhibition Centre
County Hall
Coach Station
Fire Station
Piccadilly Station
University
University of Manchester
Palace Theatre
Oxford Road Sta.
Deansgate Sta.
BBC TV Studio
Manchester Polytechnic
College of Music
St George's Park
DEANSGATE
BLACKFRIARS ROAD
CHESTER ROAD
LIVERPOOL ROAD
QUAY ST
PETER STREET
OXFORD STREET
PORTLAND STREET
PRINCESS STREET
MOSLEY STREET
CORPORATION STREET
ROCHDALE ROAD
WHITWORTH STREET WEST
GREAT BRIDGEWATER ST
LONDON ROAD
OXFORD ROAD
CHORLTON ROAD
MEDLOCK ST
A6 A56 A57 A34 A5103 A635 A665 A62

Key to Town Plan

AA Recommended roads

Other roads

Restricted roads

Buildings of interest

Car Parks

Parks and open spaces

AA Service Centre

Manchester continued

The Connoisseur **LAPADA**
528 Wilmslow Rd. (S Cohen) Est: 1950. Open 10-1 and 2.30-6.30. CL: Wed., and Mon. a.m. *STOCK: English and French furniture and paintings, 18th-19th C; Sèvres and Meissen porcelain, from 19th C.* Not Stocked: Brass, copper, pewter. LOC: From Manchester 4 miles due south down Oxford Rd. - shop situated at corner opp. Withington Fire Station. From south towards city, 150yds. after Christie's Hospital. PARK: Easy. TEL: 061 445 2504. VAT: Stan/Spec.

Crown Antiques
123 Burton Rd, West Didsbury. (C. and D Humphrey) Open 9-5. CL: Wed. *STOCK: Jewellery, pottery and porcelain.* TEL: 061 445 7374.

David H Dickinson Ltd **LAPADA**
17/19 John Dalton St. Est: 1976. Open 9.30-5.30 or by appointment. *STOCK: English and continental furniture, interior decorator items and objets d'art, 18th-19th C.* LOC: Between Albert Sq. and Deansgate. PARK: Easy and multi-storey nearby. TEL: 061 834 1042. SER: Valuations.

Didsbury Antiques (Chorlton)
21 Range Rd, Whalley Range. (J Karczewski-Slowikowski) Est: 1973. Open by appointment. *STOCK: Furniture, pictures, ceramics, 18th-19th C, from £250.* PARK: Easy. TEL: 061 227 9979; home - same. SER: Valuations; buys at auction (furniture, paintings). VAT: Stan.

Family Antiques
405/407 Bury New Rd, Prestwich. (J. and J Ditondo) Open daily. *STOCK: General antiques.* TEL: 061 798 0036.

Forest Books of Cheshire
at The Ginnel Gallery, 16 Lloyd St. (Mrs E Mann) Open 9.30-5.30, Sat. 11-4. CL: Mon. *STOCK: Antiquarian and art books; prints.* TEL: 061 833 9037.

David Friend Antiques
23 Guest Rd, Prestwich. Open by appointment only. *STOCK: Porcelain and works of art.* TEL: 061 773 1382. VAT: Stan/Spec.

The Fulda Gallery
19 Vine St, Salford. (M.J Fulda) Est: 1969. Open by appointment only. *STOCK: Oil paintings, 1500-1950, £500-£30,000; watercolours, 1800-1930, £350-£10,000.* LOC: Near Salford Police Station off Bury New Rd. TEL: 061 792 1962; mobile - 0836 518313. SER: Valuations; restorations; buys at auction.

Garson and Co. Ltd
47 Houldsworth St, Piccadilly. *STOCK: Old and modern masters, watercolours, gold carved mirrors, blackamoors, church altars, telescopes.* TEL: 061 236 9393. SER: Framing (up to 10in. width).

Manchester continued

Gibb's Bookshop Ltd
10 Charlotte St. Est: 1926. *STOCK: Books.* TEL: 061 236 7179.

The Ginnell Gallery
16 Lloyd St. (Mr and Mrs J.K Mottershead) Est: 1973. Open 9.30-5.30, Sat. 11-4. *STOCK: French furniture, art deco, art nouveau, arts and crafts furniture, 1950s pottery and signed glass; antiquarian books.* TEL: 061 833 9037.

Johnsons Antiques
2 Warburton St, Didsbury. (Mrs J Johnson) Open 10-5. *STOCK: General antiques, pine and shipping furniture.* TEL: 061 434 6278.

E. and C.T Koopman and Son Ltd **BADA**
4 John Dalton St. Open 10-5. CL: Sat. *STOCK: Silver, objects d'art, jewellery, porcelain.* TEL: 061 832 9036/834 2420.

Manchester Antique Company
915 Stockport Rd, Levenshulme. (J Long) Est: 1964. Open 10-6. SIZE: Large. *STOCK: Mainly Victorian walnut and mahogany, some period furniture, silver.* LOC: 2 miles from Mersey Square, Stockport, on A6 towards Manchester. PARK: Easy. TEL: 061 224 7923/8018. SER: Valuations; buys at auction (clocks). VAT: Stan. *Trade Only.*

Manchester Antique Hypermarket
Levenhulme Town Hall, 965 Stockport Rd, Levenshulme. Open 10-5. SIZE: 50 dealers. *STOCK: General antiques.* PARK: Easy. TEL: 061 224 2410.

Eric J Morten
Warburton St, Didsbury. Est: 1959. Open 10-6. SIZE: Large. *STOCK: Antiquarian books, 16th-20th C, £5-£5,000.* LOC: Warburton St. is off Wilmslow Rd., near traffic lights in Didsbury village. A34. PARK: Easy. TEL: 061 445 7629 and 0265 277959. SER: Valuations; buys at auction (antiquarian books).

Paul Quentin
626 Manchester Rd, Bury. (D. and P Eccleston) Est: 1965. Open 9-6.30. SIZE: Large. *STOCK: General antiques, weapons, copper, brass, pewter, 1650-1920.* Not Stocked: Fine porcelain. LOC: On A56, 2 miles north of junction 17, M62; 1 mile west of junction 3, M66. PARK: Easy. TEL: 061 766 6673.

Mrs S.J Rigg
Gazebo,106 Burton Rd, Withington. Open 9-6. *STOCK: Jewellery, bric-a-brac, linen and lace.* TEL: 061 445 3802.

Ross Antiques
973 Stockport Rd. (B.J Ross) Open 10-5. *STOCK: General antiques.* TEL: 061 225 4666.

Manchester continued

Royal Exchange Shopping Centre

Antiques Gallery, St. Anne's Sq, Exchange St. Open 9.30-5.30. TEL: 061 834 3731; stallholders - 061 834 1427. Below are listed the dealers at this centre.

Adamas Antiques
Jewellery.
Alexander Antiques
Jewellery, glass and silver.
Antique and Collectables
General antiques.
The Antique Fireplace
Arsenic and Old Lace
Silk and lace wedding dresses.
M Bailey
Stamps.
Callbox
Telephones, pocket watches.
Gary Carey
Jewellery, pottery.
City Jewellers
Jewellery and silver.
Coach Gallery (Scorpio)
Ethnic art, natural history, unusual items.
M Davies
Jewellery, silver, pottery.
Renee Franks
General antiques.
Franks Bookshop
Books and ephemera.
Grenville Art Gallery
Fine paintings.
Joan Grupman
Stripped pine and jewellery.
M and N Haworth Ltd
Stamps, coins, post and cigarette cards, medals and memorabilia. TEL: 061 834 2929; fax - 061 839 4714.
Irving Antiques
Toys and dolls.
Jenny Jones
Jewellery.
Jupiter Antiques
General antiques, bric-a-brac, jewellery.
Linen and Lace
Table linens and lace.
Manchester Coin and Medal Centre
Coins, medals and banknotes.

Royal Exchange Shopping Centre continued

Yvonne Pavion
Jewellery.
Phoenix Antiques
Jewellery and silverware.
David and Karin Ramsden
Furniture, general antiques.
Swan Antiques
Jewellery.

St. James Antiques

41 South King St. *STOCK: Antique jewellery and paintings.* LOC: Off Deansgate, in town centre. TEL: 061 834 9632.

Secondhand and Rare Books

Corner Church St/High St. Open 12-4. *STOCK: Books.* TEL: 061 834 5964 or 0625 861608.

Shaw's Gallery

11 Police St. Est: 1947. Open 9-5.30. SIZE: Large. *STOCK: Pictures, maps and prints.* LOC: Police St. is off King St., between King St. and St. Anne's Sq. PARK: 200yds. away - Kendal Milne car park. TEL: 061 834 7587. SER: Valuations; restorations (pictures); buys at auction; framing.

Village Antiques

416 Bury New Rd, Prestwich. (R Weidenbaum) Est: 1981. Open 10-5, Wed. 10-1. SIZE: Medium. *STOCK: Ornaments and pottery, 19th C, £5-£100; glass, 18th C, porcelain, 18th-19th C, both £50-£100; furniture 18th to early 20th C, £100-£500.* LOC: Village centre, 2 mins. from M62. PARK: Easy and opposite. TEL: 061 773 3612.

Village Furniture Co

58 School Lane, Didsbury. Est: 1978. Open 9-5.30, Sat. 10-4. *STOCK: Pine, 18th-19th C.* PARK: Easy. TEL: 061 445 4747.

MORECAMBE

G.G Exports
25 Middleton Rd, Middleton Village. (G Goulding) Est: 1970. Always available but prior telephone call advisable. SIZE: Large. *STOCK: Shipping goods, £30-£500; Victoriana, £50-£3,000; general antiques and pine.* LOC: On main road between Morecambe promenade and Middleton village. PARK: Easy. TEL: 0524 851565. VAT: Stan. *Trade Only.*

Magpies Nest
Unit 4, Plaza Shopping Arcade, Queen St (B Byrne) Open 9.30-5. CL: Wed. *STOCK: Bric-a-brac, cutlery, china, glass, militaria.* TEL: 0524 423328.

Gino Vescovi
1 Back Abondale Rd. (G. and P Vescovi) Est: 1970. Open by appointment every day. SIZE: Warehouse. *STOCK: Georgian and Victorian items, £50-£5,000.* PARK: Easy. TEL: 0524 416732. SER: Buys at auction. VAT: Stan/Spec.

NELSON

Colin Blakey Galleries
115 Manchester Rd. Est: 1926. Open 9.15-5.30, Sat. 9.30-5. *STOCK: Fireplaces and hearth furniture, French clock sets, 19th C; porcelain figures, prints.* LOC: Exit 12 off M65. PARK: Opposite. TEL: 0282 64941. SER: Restorations (fire furniture). VAT: Stan.

Britton Jewellers, Pawnbrokers and Antiques
34 Scotland Rd. Est: 1970. CL: Tues. *STOCK: Jewellery and general small antiques.* PARK: Opposite. TEL: 0282 697659.

Brooks Antiques
7 Russell St. (D. and S.A Brooks) Est: 1979. Open 9-5.30, Sun. and Tues. by appointment. SIZE: Medium. *STOCK: Furniture, £50-£2,000; smalls, £5-£500; both 1750-1930; postcards, ephemera, early 20th C, to £20.* LOC: 2 mins. from junction 13, M65. Town centre. PARK: Easy. TEL: 0282 698148; home - 0282 866234. SER: Valuations. VAT: Stan.

Margaret's Antique Shop
79a Scotland Rd. (M Owen) Est: 1948. Open 10-6. CL: Tues. SIZE: Small. LOC: Town centre. PARK: Easy.

OLDHAM

Echoes of the Past
1 Plate St. (R Wood) Est: 1981. Open daily. SIZE: Small and warehouse. *STOCK: General antiques, 18th to early 20th C, £5-£5,000.* PARK: Easy. TEL: 061 624 2243. SER: Restorations; buys at auction. VAT: Stan.

Heritage Antiques
123 Milnrow Rd, Shaw. (G James) Open 12-5.30. *STOCK: General antiques.* TEL: 0706 842385.

Oldham continued

Charles Howell Jeweller
2 Lord St. (N.G Howell, NAG) Est: 1870. Open 9.15-5.15. CL: Tues. SIZE: Small. *STOCK: Edwardian and Victorian jewellery, £25-£2,000; silver, early to mid 20th C, £40-£1,500; watches, Victorian to mid 20th C, £50-£800.* LOC: Town centre, off High St. PARK: Limited or by arrangement. TEL: 061 624 1479. SER: Valuations; restorations (jewellery and watches); buys at auction (jewellery and watches). VAT: Stan/Spec.

H.C Simpson and Sons Jewellers (Oldham)Ltd
37 High St. Open 9-5.30. *STOCK: Clocks, jewellery, watches.* TEL: 061 624 7187. SER: Restorations (clocks).

Valley Antiques
Soho St. (R Byron) Est: 1973. Open 10-6. SIZE: Warehouse. *STOCK: General antiques including stripped pine, porcelain, pottery, oak furniture, 19th C, £25-£300.* PARK: Easy. TEL: 061 624 5030. SER: Valuations; restorations (pine stripping, upholstery, clocks).

Waterloo Antiques
16 Waterloo St. (B.J. and S Marks) Est: 1969. Open 10-5. SIZE: Medium. *STOCK: General antiques, jewellery.* LOC: Town centre. TEL: 061 624 5975. SER: Valuations.

ORMSKIRK

Alan Grice Antiques
106 Aughton St. Open 10-6. *STOCK: Period furniture.* PARK: Easy. TEL: 0695 572007.

Revival Pine Stripping
Beacon View, 181 Southport Rd. (N.F. and M.A Sumner) Open by appointment. SIZE: Small. *STOCK: Pine furniture.* TEL: 0695 578308. SER: Stripping.

PADIHAM

C Crowther
47 Higham Hall Rd, Higham. Open by appointment. *STOCK: General antiques.* TEL: 0282 74418.

PRESTON

Donald Allison Antiques LAPADA
115-119 New Hall Lane. Open 9-5.30, Sun. and evenings by appointment. SIZE: Large. *STOCK: English, European and Oriental furniture, paintings, pottery, porcelain and objets d'art.* PARK: Easy. TEL: 0772 701916; fax - 0772 709320. SER: Valuations. VAT: Stan/Spec.

The Antique Centre
56 Garstang Rd. (P Allison) Open 8-7, Sat. and Sun. 9.30-5.30, other times by appointment. SIZE: 24 dealers. *STOCK: Mainly fine art and*

The Antique Centre continued

furniture. TEL: 0772 882078; fax - 0772 709320. SER: Free delivery (UK); worldwide shipping; containers.

Antique and Reproduction Clocks

73 Friargate. (N.E Oldfield, FBHI) TEL: 0772 58465. VAT: Stan.

Barronfield Gallery

47 Friargate. Open 10-5, Thurs. and Sun. by appointment. SIZE: Medium. *STOCK: Victorian and Edwardian watercolours, £100-£10,000.* LOC: Near Ringway on Friargate. PARK: Nearby. TEL: 0772 563465; home - 0772 690512.

Jack Blackburn

41 New Hall Lane. Est: 1968. *STOCK: General antiques.* TEL: 0772 791117. VAT: Stan.

Decoroy

105 New Hall Lane. (R Cummings) Open 9.30-6. *STOCK: Art deco furniture, figures, light fittings, marble clock sets, statues.* TEL: 0772 705371.

Duckworth's Antiques

45 New Hall Lane. (V.K. and M Duckworth) Est: 1960. Open 9.30-6. CL: Sun. except by appointment. SIZE: Medium. *STOCK: General antiques.* Not Stocked: Arms, armour, coins, medals. LOC: Main road leading from M6 motorway. PARK: Easy. TEL: 0772 794336; home - 0772 742720. *Trade Only.*

Betty and Dean Easterby LAPADA

Longton Hall, Longton. Est: 1960. Open 9-5.30, weekends by appointment. *STOCK: Georgian, Victorian and Edwardian furniture; longcase clocks, barometers, mirrors, tea caddies and decorative items.* TEL: 0772 613324. VAT: Stan. *Trade Only.*

Peter Guy 's Antiques and Fine Furniture

26-30 New Hall Lane. Open 9.30-5.30, Sun. 10-4. *STOCK: General antiques, watercolours.* TEL: 0772 703771.

Halewood and Sons

37 Friargate. Est: 1867. CL: Thurs. p.m. *STOCK: Antiquarian books and maps.* TEL: 0772 52603.

North Western Antique Centre

New Preston Mill, (Horrockses Yard), New Hall Lane. (P Allison) Open 8.30-5.30, Sun. 10-4. CL: Sat. SIZE: Over 20 dealers. *STOCK: General antiques, especially Victorian and shipping furniture.* TEL: 0772 794498. Below are listed the dealers.

Aba
Ages Ago Antiques
P Allison
K Almond
Aries

North Western Antique Centre continued

Baron Antiques
J Bowler
G Busato
C J and K Antiques
R Cooke
Paul Doran
R Dunn
Family Antiques
H Fijolek
Fylde Antiques
G W Antiques
Syd and Dave Greenhalgh
Harrington Antiques
C Harrison
N Hickson
A Hobrey
B Hodson
J Lambert
Larkhall Antiques
L Liberati
Lional of France
M McDowell
Jack Moore
The Old Rock
P Oracz
Oxford Antiques
Oxhay
J Patterson
G Pimblett
J Ralstan
Rocking Chair Antiques
M Shalloe
M Stubbings
T Sutcliffe
The Trader Antiques
Frederick Treasure Ltd
Ray Wade
Yates Antiques

Preston Book Co

68 Friargate. Est: 1950. Open 9.30-5.30. *STOCK: Antiquarian books.* TEL: 0772 52603. SER: Buys at auction.

Strange Antiques

100 Church St. (M Strange) Open 9.30-4, Thurs. 9.30-2. *STOCK: General antiques.* TEL: 0772 561121.

Swag

24 Leyland Rd, Penwortham. (M Fletcher) Est: 1967. Open 9-6. CL: Thurs. p.m. SIZE: Small. *STOCK: Dolls, especially 1830-1920, £5-£250; pottery, porcelain, furniture.* LOC: 3 miles from exit 29, M6, following St. Anne's signs. PARK: Easy. TEL: 0772 744970. SER: Restorations (dolls).

Frederick Treasure Ltd LAPADA

The Antique Centre, 56 Garstang Rd. (J.F Treasure) Est: 1908. Open 8-7, Sun. 10-4. SIZE: Large. *STOCK: Furniture, 1650-1900, £20-£10,000.* PARK: Easy. TEL: 0772 882078; office - 0253 736801; mobile - 0860 497850. SER: Valuations. VAT: Stan/Spec.

Preston continued

Ray Wade Antiques LAPADA
111-113 New Hall Lane. Est: 1978. Open 10-5.30, Sat. 10.30-4. SIZE: Medium. *STOCK: Decorative items, objets d'art, furniture, paintings, pottery, porcelain, £5-£5,000.* PARK: Easy. TEL: 0772 792950; fax - 0772 651415; mobile - 0836 291336; home - 0253 700715. SER: Valuations; restorations (as stock); buys at auction. VAT: Stan/Spec.

RAWTENSTALL

Gregory's Antique Pine
Albert Mill, (off Holcombe Rd.). (D Kennedy) Open 9-5, Sat. 12-5. *STOCK: Pine.* TEL: 0706 220049.

ROCHDALE

S.C Falk LAPADA
Open by appointment only. *STOCK: Fine English period furniture.* TEL: 0706 44946. VAT: Stan/Spec.

Owen Antiques
189-193 Oldham Rd. (J.G.T Owen) Est: 1891. Open 11.30-7, Sun. 2-6. *STOCK: Clocks and paintings, 17th-19th C, £100-£5,000; early oak and walnut, spinning wheels, silver, pewter, pistols, phonographs, wireless sets, coins, model ships, orreries and gothic clocks, nautical items, violins, antiquarian books, early ciné equipment.* LOC: A627 from town centre up hill (Oldham road) for 1/2 mile. Next block to high level pavement on left hand side past railway bridge. PARK: 30 mins., otherwise in adjoining side streets. TEL: 0706 48138; home - 0706 353270. SER: Valuations; restorations (clocks and furniture).

SABDEN, Nr. Blackburn

Walter Aspinall Antiques
Pendle Antique Centre, Union Mill, Watt St. Est: 1964. Open 9-5, Sat. and Sun. 11-4, or by appointment. SIZE: Large. *STOCK: Furniture and bric-a-brac.* LOC: On Pendle Hill between Clitheroe and Padiham. TEL: 0282 76311. SER: Export; packing; courier; containers.

SADDLEWORTH, Nr. Oldham

Heyday
Huddersfield Rd, Delph. (H.J Bell) Est: 1972. Open most days including Sun., or by appointment. SIZE: Medium. *STOCK: Furniture and smalls, 19th-20th C including architectural items, fixtures and fittings, £5-£500; art nouveau and art deco items.* LOC: On A62 at road junction to Rochdale. PARK: Easy. TEL: 0457 875849; home - same.

Saddleworth continued

Oldfield Cottage Antiques
Queen Anne Gallery, High St, Uppermill and The Barn, Denshaw Rd., Delph. (Mrs R Potts) Est: 1982. Open every day except Tues., seven days at The Barn. SIZE: Large. *STOCK: Pine furniture and kitchens; blue and white.* PARK: Easy. TEL: 0457 874537/874728.

ST. ANNES-ON-SEA

Cobwebs Antiques
6 St. Andrews Rd. South. (O Furness) Open 10-4.30. CL: Mon. and Wed. *STOCK: Porcelain, small furniture, lace and linen.* LOC: 1st right off The Crescent. TEL: 0253 714255.

J.A Duggan and Co
17a Wood St. Est: 1959. Open 10-5. CL: Sat. *STOCK: Coins - English, European, American and colonial.* TEL: 0253 721233. VAT: Stan/Spec.

Spinning Wheel Antiques
16 St. Davids Rd. (Major C.M Yates) Est: 1945. Open 10-5 or by appointment. CL: Wed. SIZE: Medium. *STOCK: General antiques, porcelain, mid-18th C to 1930, £5-£500; small furniture, silver, early 18th C to 1970s, £5-£2,500.* LOC: From St. Annes Sq. over railway bridge. Turn right at traffic lights into St. Davids Rd., shop 200yds. on right. PARK: Easy. TEL: 0253 724187. SER: Valuations.

The Victorian Shop
19 Alexandria Drive. (G.O Freeman) Open 10-5. *STOCK: General antiques.* TEL: 0253 725700.

SAMLESBURY, Nr. Preston

Samlesbury Hall
Preston New Rd. (Samlesbury Hall Trust)Est: 1969. Open 11.30-5 in summer, 11.30-4 in winter. CL: Mon. SIZE: Large. *STOCK: General collectable antiques.* LOC: Exit 31, M6 on A677 between Preston and Blackburn. PARK: Easy. TEL: 0254 81 2010/2229.

SCARISBRICK

Carrcross Gallery
325 Southport Rd. (G.D Fairclough) Est: 1985. Open daily, by appointment Mon.-Wed. SIZE: Small. *STOCK: Victorian fireplaces, £50-£1,000; Victorian brass/steel beds, £150-£500; furniture, 18th-19th C, £100-£2,000.* PARK: Easy. TEL: 0704 880638; home - 0860 621711. SER: Valuations; restorations (cast-iron, brass). VAT: Stan.

SHAWFORTH, Nr. Rochdale

Shawforth Antiques

193 Market St. (J. and E Bracewell) Est: 1967. Open 9.30-8, Sun. 9.30-5. SIZE: Small. *STOCK: Victoriana, clocks, bric-a-brac.* LOC: On Rochdale to Bacup Rd. PARK: Easy. TEL: 070 685 3402.

TRAWDEN, Nr. Colne

The Old Rock

Keighley Rd. Open 8.30-5.30, Sat. and Sun. by appointment. SIZE: Large. *STOCK: English stained glass, 1800-1930; unusual objects, architectural items.* PARK: Easy. TEL: 0282 869478; home - same. SER: Restorations (stained glass). FAIRS: Main trade and some London decorator. VAT: Stan. *Trade only.*

UPHOLLAND, Nr. Wigan

Lancashire Bygones

12 Parliament St. (Mrs M Rathbone) Est: 1975. Open 10-5. CL: Mon., Tues. and Thurs. SIZE: Medium. *STOCK: General antiques, £5-£1,500; collectors' items, £2-£500.* LOC: On main road near church. PARK: Easy. TEL: 0695 625624/622458.

WHALLEY, Nr. Blackburn

The Abbey Antique Shop

43 and 45 King St. (A.D. and E Austin) Est: 1950. Open 9.30-6. SIZE: Large. *STOCK: Furniture, £10-£450; ceramics, £5-£150; both 18th-19th C; pewter, copper and brass, 17th-18th C.* Not Stocked: Coins and stamps. LOC: A59. PARK: Easy. TEL: 0254 823139. VAT: Stan/Spec.

Davies Antiques

32 King St. (G., E. and P Davies) Est: 1971. Open 10-5. SIZE: Small. *STOCK: British country furniture, and longcase clocks, to £3,000; jewellery, to £500.* Not Stocked: Coins, weapons, continental furniture. LOC: A59. PARK: Easy. TEL: 0254 823764. VAT: Stan/Spec.

WHITEFIELD, Nr. Manchester

Henry Donn Gallery

138/142 Bury New Rd. Est: 1954. Open 9.30-5.30. *STOCK: Paintings, 19th-20th C, £20-£20,000.* LOC: Off motorway M62; junction 17 - towards Bury. TEL: 061 766 8819. SER: Valuations; framing; restorations (pictures). VAT: Stan/Spec.

WIGAN

C de Rouffignac

57 Wigan Lane. Open 10-5. CL: Wed. *STOCK: Furniture, jewellery, oils and watercolours.* TEL: 0942 37927.

Polished with Pride

Unit 3, Peppermill, Darlington St. Open by appointment. *STOCK: Re-polished Victorian and Edwardian furniture.* TEL: 0942 820795. SER: Restorations (as stock).

John Robinson Antiques

172-176 Manchester Rd, Higher Ince. Est: 1965. Open any time. SIZE: Large. *STOCK: General antiques.* LOC: A577 nr. Ince Bar. PARK: Easy. TEL: 0942 47773/41671. SER: Packing for export, etc. VAT: Stan. *Export and Trade Only.*

John Roby Antiques

12 Lord St. Open 10-5. CL: Sat. and Wed. *STOCK: Furniture, to 1940; bric-a-brac.* TEL: 0942 30887.

Whatnot Antiques

90 Wigan Lane. (J., A.L. and R Hargraves) Open 9-5. CL: Wed. *STOCK: General antiques.* TEL: 0942 491880.

WORSLEY

Ambassador House

273 Chorley Rd. (G White) Open 2-6, prior telephone call advisable. *STOCK: Furniture, pottery and porcelain, 17th-18th C.* TEL: 061 794 3806.

H. and M.J Burke

ADA. Est: 1959. Open 10-5, appointment advisable. CL: Sat. *STOCK: Period English furniture.* TEL: 061 794 2093. VAT: Spec.

Wayside Antiques

32 Seddon St, Off Cleggs Lane, Little Hulton. (V Partington) Est: 1983. CL: Tues. and Wed. SIZE: Large. *STOCK: Furniture, £100-£4,000; porcelain, £25-£500; both 19th C. Pictures, 19th-20th C, £100-£400.* LOC: Midway between Salford and Chorley on A6, 300yds. left, off Cleggs Lane. PARK: Easy. TEL: 061 790 3211; home - 061 799 4182. SER: Valuations; buys at auction. FAIRS: Charnock Richard; Newark; Ardingly; Stonleigh; Buxton; Builth Wells; Edinburgh.

YEALAND CONYERS, Nr. Carnforth

M. and I Finch

15/17 Yealand Rd. Est: 1970. SIZE: Medium. *STOCK: Antique and decorative lighting, mirrors, prints, books and furniture.* Not Stocked: Jewellery, silver. LOC: 2 miles from M6, exit 35, just off A6. PARK: Easy. TEL: 0524 73 2212. VAT: Stan/Spec.

Leicestershire

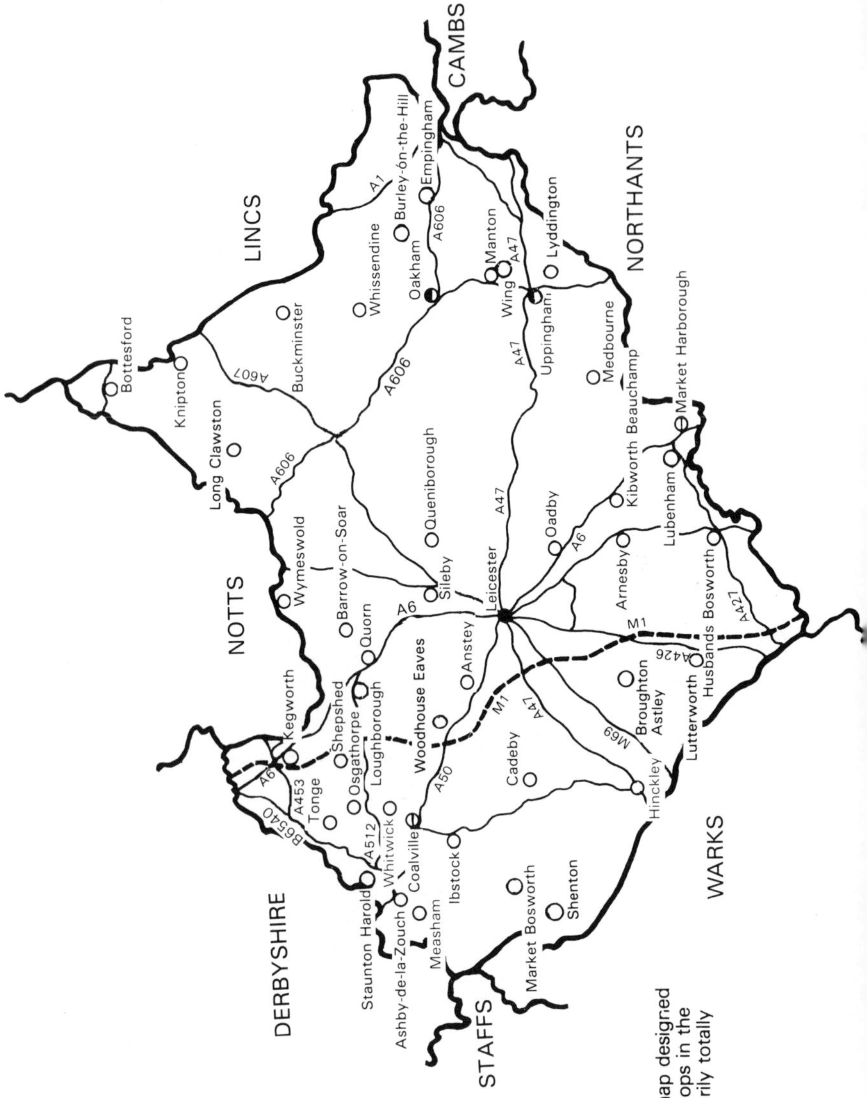
LINCS
CAMBS
NORTHANTS
NOTTS
DERBYSHIRE
STAFFS
WARKS
Bottesford
Knipton
Long Clawston
Buckminster
Whissendine
Oakham
Burley-on-the-Hill
Empingham
Manton
Wing
Lyddington
Uppingham
Medbourne
Market Harborough
Kibworth Beauchamp
Lubenham
Husbands Bosworth
Arnesby
Oadby
Queniborough
Leicester
Sileby
Barrow-on-Soar
Wymeswold
Quorn
Anstey
Woodhouse Eaves
Loughborough
Shepshed
Osgathorpe
Kegworth
Tonge
Whitwick
Coalville
Staunton Harold
Ashby-de-la-Zouch
Measham
Ibstock
Cadeby
Market Bosworth
Shenton
Hinckley
Broughton Astley
Lutterworth
A1
A606
A607
A47
A6
M1
A426
A427
M69
A50
A512
A453
B5540

Please note this is only a rough map designed to show dealers the number of shops in the various towns, and is not necessarily totally accurate.

○	1–2	Key to
⊖	3–5	number of
◐	6–12	shops in
●	12+	this area.

Richard Kimbell

PINE DEALERS FOR OVER 25 YEARS

RIVERSIDE, MARKET HARBOROUGH, LEICESTERSHIRE, LE16 7PT
TEL. (0858) 433444. FAX. (0858) 467627
MON.-FRI. 9am to 6pm, SAT. 9am to 5pm, SUN. 1pm to 4pm

TRADE 9am to 6pm MON.-FRI.

ANSTEY, Nr. Leicester

Antiques in Charnwood LAPADA
68 Bradgate Rd. (B Whadcock and V Bonfield) Est: 1982. Open 10-5. CL: Mon. and Fri. *STOCK: General antiques including fine period furniture, Georgian-Edwardian.* TEL: 0533 350708. VAT: Stan/Spec.

ARNESBY

Leycester Map Galleries Ltd
Well House. (R.A.S Forster) FRGS. Resident. Est: 1978. Open by appointment only. SIZE: Small. *STOCK: World-wide maps and sea charts, 1496-1870, £5-£3,000; atlases, £100-£3,000.* PARK: Easy. TEL: 0533 478462 (24 hour answering service). SER: Valuations; restorations (colouring and cleaning maps); buys at auction. FAIRS: Bonnington Hotel, London (monthly); Imcos. VAT: Stan. *Postal Business.*

ASHBY-DE-LA-ZOUCH

Ivanhoe Antiques LAPADA
53 Market St. (J. and A Mansfield) Est: 1976. Open 10-5, Sun. by appointment. CL: Wed. SIZE: Medium. *STOCK: Furniture, £25-£3,500, porcelain, Derby, Worcester and Coalport, £10-£1,000, all 18th-20th C; silver and oil paintings, 19th C.* LOC: On A50 in centre of town. PARK: Easy. TEL: 0530 415424; home - 0530 412524. VAT: Stan/Spec.

BARROW-ON-SOAR

Bishop Beveridge House
Beveridge St. (T.L Middleton) Open 9-6. *STOCK: Furniture and general antiques.* TEL: 0509 412270. *Trade Only.*

BOTTESFORD

Thomas Keen
51 High St. (T.E Keen, FRSA) Est: 1970. Appointment advisable. *STOCK: Furniture, 17th-19th C; metalwork, oil paintings, decorative items.* TEL: 0949 42177. SER: Restorations, lectures (furniture).

BROUGHTON ASTLEY, Nr. Leicester

Old Bakehouse Antiques and Gallery
10 Green Rd. (S.R Needham) Open Thurs.-Sat. 10-6, Sun. 2-5. *STOCK: Period furniture.* PARK: Easy. TEL: 0455 282276.

BUCKMINSTER, Nr. Grantham

Buckminster Antiques
36 The Row. (Mrs M Wain) Est: 1975. Open Wed., Sat., Sun. and Bank Holidays 2-5. SIZE: Small. *STOCK: General antiques including pottery, porcelain, copper, brass, small furniture, bygones, all £2-£400.* Not Stocked: Coins, medals, firearms. LOC: On B676. PARK: Easy. TEL: Home - 0664 62099.

BURLEY-ON-THE-HILL, Nr. Oakham

Burley Workshop
Home Farm. Est: 1967. Open by appointment. SIZE: Medium. *STOCK: Pine and decorative items, 17th-19th C, £50-£1,000; ironwork, architectural and unusual items.* LOC: On B668, 1/4 mile before village green, on left behind trees, stones mark drive entrance. PARK: Easy. TEL: 0572 757333; home - same. SER: Valuations; restorations (furniture); buys at auction. VAT: Stan/Spec.

CADEBY, Nr. Nuneaton

P Stanworth (Fine Arts)
The Grange. (Mr and Mrs G Stanworth) Resident. Est: 1965. Open by appointment. SIZE: Medium. *STOCK: Oil paintings, 18th to early 20th C, £100-£8,000.* LOC: Just off A447. PARK: Easy. TEL: 0455 291023. VAT: Spec.

COALVILLE

Galleon Antiques
195 Belvoir Rd. (R.J Smith) Open 9-5.30. *STOCK: General antiques.* TEL: 0530 37431. SER: French polishing; upholstery.

Keystone Antiques LAPADA
9 Ashby Rd. (I. and H McPherson, FGA) Est: 1979. Open 10-5, Sat. 10-4. CL: Wed. SIZE: Medium. *STOCK: Jewellery, Victorian and Georgian, £25-£1,500; silver, 1700-1920, £20-£500; small collectable items, 18th-19th C, £15-£300; oil paintings, furniture, cranberry, needlework tools, Victorian and Georgian table glass.* LOC: A50, town centre. PARK: At rear. TEL: 0530 35966. SER: Valuations (jewellery); gem testing. FAIRS: Gamlin Exhibition Services. VAT: Stan/Spec.

Massey's Antiques
26 Hotel St. (Mr and Mrs C.A Irons) Est: 1969. Open 9-5. CL: Wed. SIZE: Small. *STOCK: Bric-a-brac and bygones, small furniture, militaria, 1850-1945.* PARK: Rear. TEL: 0530 32374; home - 0530 32448.

EMPINGHAM, Nr. Oakham

Churchgate Antiques
13 Church St. (R Wheatley) Open Wed., Fri., Sat. and Sun. 10-5. SIZE: Medium. *STOCK: Furniture, mainly 18th-19th C, £50-£5,000; paintings and prints, £10-£2,000; silver and plate, 19th-20th C, £10-£1,000.* LOC: Opposite church, off A606. PARK: Easy. TEL: 078 086 300.

Old Bakery Antiques
Church St. (Mr and Mrs P.B Margerison) Open 9.30-5.30, Sun. 10-4.30. CL: Thurs. SIZE: Medium. *STOCK: Furniture, 17th C to 1920, £50-£6,000; china, 1830-1920, £5-£500; copper and brass, 19th C.* Not Stocked: Jewellery. LOC: 4 miles off A1 on A606 towards Oakham. PARK: Easy. TEL: 078 086 243; home - same. SER: Restorations (furniture); buys at auction. VAT: Stan/Spec.

HINCKLEY

House Things Antiques
Trinity Lane, 44 Mansion St. (P.W Robertson) Est: 1976. Open 10-6. SIZE: Small. *STOCK: Stripped pine, satinwood, oak and walnut, mainly Victorian and Edwardian, £50-£300; small collectors' items, 1860-1930s, £5-£100; cast iron, fireplaces, brass and iron beds, 1890-1920's, £50-£250.* LOC: On inner ring road 200yds. from Leisure Centre. PARK: Easy. TEL: 0455 618518; home - 0455 212797.

Hughes Antiques
(N.K Hughes) Est: 1978. Open by appointment. SIZE: Medium. *STOCK: Period furniture, copper, brass and unusual decorators items.* TEL: 0455 631182. VAT: Stan/Spec. *Trade Only.*

HUSBANDS BOSWORTH, Nr. Market Harborough

Past and Present
High St. (Mrs M Dalloe) Est: 1965. Open 10-5, Sat. 10-1. CL: Tues. and Thurs. SIZE: Small. *STOCK: General antiques, £5-£500.* LOC: A427. PARK: Nearby. TEL: 0858 880506; home - 0858 434428. SER: Restorations (cane seating, porcelain).

IBSTOCK, Nr. Leicester

Mandrake Stephenson Antiques
101 High St. Est: 1979. Open 10-5, Sat. 10-2.30. SIZE: Small. *STOCK: Furniture, Georgian-Edwardian, £50-£500; pottery, pictures.* PARK: Easy. TEL: 0530 60898. SER: Valuations; restorations (furniture).

KEGWORTH

Bonington Clocks
12 Market Pl. (Mrs J McVay) Open Sat. 10-1 or by appointment. *STOCK: Clocks - longcase, dial, wall and mantel; clock movements.* TEL: 0509 672900.

KIBWORTH BEAUCHAMP

Vendy Antiques (Kibworth)
17 Fleckney Rd. (D.R Vendy) Open 10-1 and 2-5, Sat. 11-5. CL: Mon. and Tues. *STOCK: General antiques including furniture and smalls, mainly Victorian, £10-£2,000.* TEL: 0533 796133; home - 0533 713025.

KNIPTON, Nr. Grantham

Anthony W Laywood
ABA. Est: 1967. Open by appointment. SIZE: Medium. *STOCK: Antiquarian books, pre-1850, £20-£2,000.* LOC: 1 1/2 miles off the Grantham-Melton Mowbray road. PARK: Easy. TEL: 0476 870224. SER: Valuations; buys at auction.

LEICESTER

The Antiques Complex
St. Nicholas Pl. (K.W Sansom) Open 9.30-5.30. SIZE: Large. 40 dealers. *STOCK: General antiques including furniture, collectables, clocks, porcelain, glass, jewellery, paintings and decorative items.* LOC: Adjacent to High St., near Holiday Inn. PARK: Own. TEL: 0533 533343; fax - 0533 533347. SER: Container packing.

Leicester continued

Betty's
9 Knighton Fields Rd. West. (A Smith) Est: 1968. Open 9.30-5. SIZE: Small. *STOCK: Satinwood and pine items, brass and copper, pictures.* LOC: Off Saffron Lane. PARK: Easy. TEL: 0533 839048. SER: Valuations; buys at auction.

Birches Art Deco Shop
18 Francis St, Stoneygate. (C. and H Birch) Est: 1978. Open 11-5.30, Sun. by appointment. SIZE: Medium. *STOCK: Art deco, Victoriana and kitchenalia.* LOC: 1 mile south of city centre, off A6. PARK: Easy. TEL: 0533 703235.

Boulevard Antique and Shipping Centre
The Old Diary, Western Boulevard. Open 10-6, Sun. 2-5 or by appointment. SIZE: 10 dealers. *STOCK: Furniture including oak, mahogany, pine and shipping; general antiques and collectables, jewellery, silver and smalls.* LOC: 15 minutes junction 21, M1 on to A46. PARK: Own. TEL: 0533 541201/470396. VAT: Stan/Spec.

Corner Cottage Antiques
At the Antiques Complex, 9 St. Nicholas Pl. (J. and B Roberts) Est: 1969. Open 9-5.30. SIZE: Large. *STOCK: 18th-20th C furniture, oak, walnut and Victorian mahogany furniture for*

Corner Cottage Antiques continued

Australian, American, German, and Japanese markets. LOC: Adjacent to High St., near Holiday Inn. PARK: Easy. TEL: 0455 290344; home - 0455 282583. VAT: Stan/Spec.

Fine Pine
232 Narborough Rd. (Mr and Mrs R.D Branson) Open 9-5. *STOCK: Pine furniture.* TEL: 0533 823970.

Foulds-Field Fine Art
2 Bidford Court, Bidford Close. (P Harris) Est: 1985. Open anytime by appointment. SIZE: Medium. *STOCK: Oils and watercolours, 18th C to 1930, £50-£5,000.* LOC: Off Braunstone Lane (Bidford Rd.) 1/2 mile from Post House Hotel. PARK: Easy. TEL: 0533 824364; home - same. SER: Valuations; buys at auction (paintings). FAIRS: Robert Bailey; Antiques in Britain; Reg Cooper; Bridge. VAT: Stan/Spec.

Letty's Antiques
6 Rutland St. Est: 1952. *STOCK: Silver, jewellery, china and brass.* TEL: 0533 626435.

Montague Antiques
60 Montague Rd, Clarendon Park. (A.R Schlesinger and D.K Moore) Est: 1987. Open 10-7, Sun. 12-5. CL: Wed. SIZE: Small. *STOCK: Furniture, 17th C to 1910, £25-£1,000; ceramics, 18th-20th C; glass, 19th to early 20th C; both £5-£100; silver, plate and general antiques,*

Montague Antiques continued

19th C. Not Stocked: Weapons and jewellery. LOC: From Welford Rd. (A50) to Victoria Pk. to Queens Rd. then Montague Rd. PARK: Easy. TEL: 0533 706485; home - same. SER: Valuations.

Walter Moores and Son
89 Wellington St. (P Moores) Est: 1925. Open 8.30-5.30, Sat. 8.30-12.30. CL: Mon. and Tues. except by appointment. *STOCK: Mainly furniture, 1680-1880, £5-£5,000.* LOC: From London Rd. railway station go up Waterloo Way, first right, then first left and left again. PARK: Easy. TEL: 0533 551402; home - 0533 707552. VAT: Stan/Spec.

Oxford Street Antique Centre Ltd
16-26 Oxford St. Open 10-5.30, Sun. 2-5, or by appointment. SIZE: Large. 50 dealers. *STOCK: Period furniture, shipping goods, silver, bric-a-brac and general antiques, 18th to mid-20th C, 50p-£5,000.* LOC: Main ring road. PARK: Own. TEL: 0533 553006. SER: Container loading facilities; courier. VAT: Stan/Spec.

E Smith (Leicester) Ltd LAPADA
The Antiques Complex, St. Nicholas Pl. (K.W Sansom) Est: 1888. Open 9.30-5.30. SIZE: Large. *STOCK: Furniture, 18th-19th C and Edwardian, £100-£5,000; clocks, smalls and paintings.* LOC: Adjacent High St., near Holiday Inn. PARK: Own. TEL: 0533 533343; fax - 0533 533347. SER: Valuations; buys at auction (18th-19th C furniture and paintings); container packing; courier. VAT: Stan/Spec.

Hammond Smith
32 West Ave, Clarendon Park. Est: 1981. Open by appointment. SIZE: Small. *STOCK: British watercolours, 1750-1950, £300-£10,000; British etchings, 19th-20th C, £100-£500.* TEL: 0533 709020; home - same. SER: Valuations; restorations (watercolours and prints cleaned, mounted and framed); buys at auction (watercolours). VAT: Spec.

Withers of Leicester
142a London Rd. (S Frings) Est: 1860. Open 9-5.30. CL: Thurs. p.m. and Sat. SIZE: Medium. *STOCK: Furniture, 17th-19th C, £50-£3,000; china, 18th-19th C, £10-£300; oil paintings, 19th C, £5-£500.* Not Stocked: Jewellery and coins. LOC: Entering town on main London Rd. PARK: Easy. TEL: 0533 544836. SER: Valuations; restorations (furniture). VAT: Stan/Spec.

LONG CLAWSTON, Nr. Melton Mowbray

Victoriana Architectural
Old Hall Farm, Hose Lane. Open 8.30-5.30. *STOCK: Pine, architectural items.* TEL: 0949 60274. SER: Restorations (oak, mahogany, architectural items, pine stripping).

LOUGHBOROUGH

Copperfield Antiques
221a Derby Rd. (Mrs B Gardner) Est: 1970. Open 10-5. CL: Mon. and Wed. SIZE: Small. *STOCK: Furniture, £50-£1,500; porcelain; £5-£500; both 18th-19th C; brass, copper, china, glass, paintings and boxes, early 19th to early 20th C, £5-£250.* LOC: A6. PARK: Easy. TEL: 0509 232026; home - 0509 239281.

Lowe of Loughborough
37-40 Church Gate. Est: 1846. CL: Sat. SIZE: Large and warehouse. *STOCK: Furniture and period upholstery from early oak c.1600 to Edwardian; mahogany, walnut, oak, £20-£8,000; clocks, bracket and longcase, £95-£2,500; porcelain, pewter, maps, copper and brass.* Not Stocked: Jewellery. LOC: Opposite parish church. PARK: Own. TEL: 0509 212554/217876. SER: Upholstery; restorations; interior design. VAT: Stan/Spec.

LUBENHAM, Nr. Market Harborough

Leicestershire Sporting Gallery and Brown Jack Bookshop
The Old Granary, 62 Main St. (R.L Leete) Est: 1958. When closed apply 87 Lubenham Hill. SIZE: Large. *STOCK: Oil paintings, prints including Vanity Fair and sporting; engravings, maps, furniture, including pine, mahogany and oak; antiquarian books, horse brasses, martingales, swingers.* LOC: Centre of village. PARK: Rear of village green opposite. TEL: 0858 465787. VAT: Stan.

Stevens and Son
Old Post Office, 61 Main St. Resident. Open 9-6. *STOCK: General antiques, mainly furniture.* LOC: A427. TEL: 0858 463521. SER: Restorations (furniture).

LUTTERWORTH

Churchgate Antiques LAPADA
42 Church St. (Mr and Mrs A.P Coupland) Est: 1986. Open by appointment. SIZE: Small. *STOCK: Furniture, 18th-19th C; paintings, pre-1930; both £500-£1,000.* LOC: 1/2 mile junction 20, M1. PARK: Easy. TEL: 0455 553360 (ansaphone); mobile - 0860 543629. FAIRS: NEC; Tatton Park; Stowe; Castle Ashby; Castle Howard. VAT: Stan/Spec.

LYDDINGTON

Timothy Kendrew Antiques LAPADA
Thimble Hall, 3 Thorpe Rd. Open by appointment. *STOCK: Mainly porcelain, £50-£1,000+; small furniture, £50-£2,000+; both 18th to early 19th C; oils and watercolours, £50-£1,000; 18th-19th C.* Not Stocked: Coins, medals, shipping items, silver, jewellery. LOC: 12 miles from A1. TEL: 0572 822558.

MANTON

David Smith Antiques
Old Cottage, 20 St.Mary's Rd. Est: 1953. Open 9-5. CL: Sun., except by appointment. *STOCK: Furniture, glass, silver.* PARK: Easy. TEL: 057 285 244. VAT: Stan/Spec.

MARKET BOSWORTH

Corner Cottage Antiques
5 Market Pl, The Square. (J. and B Roberts) Est: 1969. Open 10-5 or by appointment. *STOCK: 18th-20th C furniture, silver, paintings; clocks, porcelain, glass, brass and copper, general antiques.* PARK: Easy. TEL: 0455 290344; home - 0455 282583. VAT: Stan/Spec.

Country Antiques
4 Main St. (M. and A Boylan) Est: 1980. Open 10-5.30. CL: Tues. SIZE: Medium. *STOCK: Stripped pine.* LOC: Off A447 in market place. PARK: Easy. TEL: 0455 291303; home - same.

MARKET HARBOROUGH

Abbey Antiques
17 Abbey St. (M.A Muckle) Est: 1977. Open 10.30-5. SIZE: Medium. *STOCK: Furniture, 19th C, £50-£1,000; decorative items, bric-a-brac, £1-£150.* LOC: 100yds. off town centre. PARK: Easy. TEL: 0858 462282; home - 0858 464085. SER: Valuations. VAT: Stan/Spec.

Richard Kimbell Ltd
Riverside. Open 8-5.30, Sat. 8-12. SIZE: Large warehouse. *STOCK: Pine and decorative furniture.* TEL: 0858 433444; fax - 0858 467627. SER: Shipping and packing; manufacturer.

J Stamp and Sons
The Chestnuts, 15 Kettering Rd. (M Stamp) Resident. Est: 1948. Open 8-5.30, Sat. 9-12.30 or by appointment. SIZE: Medium. *STOCK: Mahogany and oak furniture, 18th-19th C, £500-£5,000; Victorian furniture, £250-£2,500; Edwardian furniture, £100-£1,000.* LOC: On A6. PARK: Easy. TEL: 0858 462524. SER: Valuations (furniture); restorations (furniture). VAT: Stan/Spec.

Market Harborough continued

Duncan Watts Oriental Rugs
64 St. Mary's Rd. Est: 1984. Open 10-5.30. CL: Wed. SIZE: Medium. *STOCK: Oriental rugs, all periods, £250-£2,000; furniture, 19th C, £250-£1,000; smalls, 19th C, £10-£250.* LOC: Road from town centre to railway station. PARK: Easy. TEL: 0858 432314; home - 0858 462620. SER: Valuations; restorations (furniture and Oriental rugs). VAT: Stan.

MEASHAM, Nr. Burton-upon-Trent

Ashley House Antiques
61 High St. (Mrs P.A Benton) Est: 1976. Open Thurs., Fri. and Sat. 10.30-5. SIZE: Small. *STOCK: Wall clocks - Vienna, English and American, £100-£600; Victorian and Edwardian furniture, 19th C, £100-£375; horse brasses, 19th-20th C, £8-£100; Mason's ironstone, £50-£200; Staffordshire figures, £50-£175; brass and copper, £20-£200.* LOC: A453 between Ashby-de-la-Zouch and Tamworth. PARK: Nearby. TEL: 0530 73568; home - 0543 373655.

MEDBOURNE

E. and C Royall Antiques
10 Waterfall Way. Open 9-6 including Sun. *STOCK: Furniture, pictures, silver, porcelain, glassware, ivories and Oriental bronzes.* TEL: 085 883 744; home - same. SER: Restorations (bronzes, ivories, brassware, metalware, including brass inlay work, woodcarving, upholstery, French polishing).

OADBY

John Hardy Antiques
91 London Rd. Open every day. *STOCK: General antiques.* TEL: 0533 712862. VAT: Stan/Spec.

OAKHAM

Fine Art of Oakham LAPADA
4 and 5 Crown Walk. (A.J Smith) Open 9.30-5 or by appointment. CL: Mon. *STOCK: Continental oils and watercolours, Victorian and 19th C.* TEL: 0572 755221.

Gallery Antiques
17 Mill St. (P.W Jones and G.R Pickett) Open 9.30-5, Sun. 2-5. *STOCK: Furniture, £300-£6,000; porcelain, £25-£750; silver, £20-£10,000; all English 18th-19th C.* TEL: 0572 755094; home - 0572 757252. SER: Valuations; restorations (furniture and porcelain). VAT: Stan/Spec.

Oakham continued

Grafton Country Pictures
153 Brooke Rd. (F Gray) Est: 1967. Open by appointment. *STOCK: Sporting, farming, natural history, decorative prints, 18th and 19th C.* TEL: 0572 757266.

Oakham Antiques
16 Melton Rd. Open 10-3 or by appointment. CL: Tues. and Thurs. *STOCK: Brass, glass, small furniture, postcards, lamps, pictures, prints, silver.* TEL: 066 479 571.

The Old House Gallery
13-15 Market Pl. (R.A Clarke) Est: 1979. Open 9.30-5, Sat. 9.30-4. CL: Thurs. SIZE: Medium. *STOCK: Oil paintings, £50-£3,500; art studio pottery, 1850-1990, £5-£500; watercolours, £25-£2,000; prints and objets d'art, £5-£500; antiquarian county maps, £15-£250.* LOC: In Market Square. PARK: Easy. TEL: 0572 755538. SER: Valuations; restorations (oils, watercolours, prints, frames); framing.

Swans Antique Centre
27 Mill St. (P.W Jones) Est: 1988. Open 9.30-5.30, Sun. 2-5.30. SIZE: Large. 15 dealers. *STOCK: General antiques especially furniture, 1600-1900; pine, silver and plate, oils, watercolours, art deco, linen and rugs, prints, jewellery, porcelain, £5-£5,000.* LOC: 150yds.

Swans Antique Centre continued

from High St. PARK: Easy. TEL: 0572 724364; home - 0572 757252. SER: Valuations; restorations. VAT: Stan/Spec.

Paul Warrington
46 High St. 9-1 and 2-5. *STOCK: Period and decorative furniture, architectural items and garden statuary.* TEL: 0572 722414; mobile - 0860 562879.

OSGATHORPE, Nr. Loughborough

David E Burrows **LAPADA**
Manor House Farm. Est: 1973. *STOCK: Pine, oak, mahogany and walnut furniture, clocks, smalls, £50-£20,000.* LOC: Exit 23, M1, turn right off Ashby road, farm next to church. TEL: 0530 222218; mobile - 0863 598664. VAT: Stan/Spec.

QUENIBOROUGH, Nr. Leicester

J Green and Son

1 Coppice Lane. (R Green) Resident. Est: 1932. Appointment advisable. SIZE: Medium. *STOCK: 18th-19th C English and continental furniture.* LOC: Off A607 Leicester-Melton Mowbray Rd. PARK: Easy. TEL: 0533 606682. SER: Valuations; buys at auction. VAT: Stan/Spec.

QUORN

Mill on the Soar Antiques Ltd

1/3 High St. (T.O. and J York) Open daily, Wed. by appointment. *STOCK: Furniture, 17th-19th C, and associated articles.* LOC: In centre of village, on A6. PARK: Easy. TEL: 0509 414218.

Quorn Pine

16a High St, and 75 Barrow Rd. (S Yates and S Parker) Open 9.30-6. *STOCK: Pine.* TEL: 0509 416031. SER: Stripping and restorations (pine). VAT: Stan/Spec.

SHENTON, Nr. Market Bosworth

Whitemoors Antiques and Fine Art

(C Bethell) Est: 1987. Open 10-5 including Sun. CL: Mon. SIZE: Large. *STOCK: Furniture, £20-£500; smalls, £5-£50; both Victorian and Edwardian; prints, 19th-20th C, £40-£400.* LOC: A5 onto A444 towards Burton-on-Trent, first right then second left. PARK: Easy. TEL: 0455 212250; home - same.

SHEPSHED, Nr. Loughborough

G.K Hadfield

Blackbrook Hill House, Tickow Lane. Resident. Est: 1972. Open daily (books and parts); by appointment (clocks). *STOCK: Clocks, longcase, Act of Parliament, skeleton, Black Forest, American and carriage; in print secondhand and rare horological books.* LOC: 1 3/4 miles along the A512 west of M1, exit 23. PARK: Easy. TEL: 0509 503014; fax - 0509 600136. SER: Restoration materials (antique clocks). VAT: Stan/Spec.

SILEBY, Nr. Loughborough

R.A James Antiques

Ammonite Gallery, 25a High St. *STOCK: Mainly stripped pine, general antiques.* TEL: 050 981 2169.

STAUNTON HAROLD

Ropers Hill Antiques

Ropers Hill Farm. (S. and R Southworth) Est: 1974. Open 9-5.30 every day or by appointment. SIZE: Small. *STOCK: General antiques, shipping goods, silver and metalware.* LOC: On A453. PARK: Easy. TEL: 0530 413919. SER: Valuations.

TONGE, Nr. Melbourne

The Spindles

(Mrs C Reynolds) Est: 1972. Resident. Usually available but telephone call advisable. SIZE: Large. *STOCK: Clocks, watches, 17th-19th C.* LOC: 3 miles from exit 24 M1. PARK: Easy. TEL: 0332 862609. VAT: Stan.

UPPINGHAM

Bay House Antiques

33 High St. East. Est: 1986. Open 10-5. SIZE: Medium. *STOCK: Victorian and Edwardian furniture, porcelain, pottery, glass, metalware and pictures.* LOC: Near Falcon Hotel. PARK: Nearby. TEL: 0572 821045.

Clutter

14 Orange St. (M.C Sumner) Est: 1982. Open 10-5. CL: Thurs. *STOCK: Victorian linen and lace; jewellery; interesting silver, porcelain, glass, small furniture, kitchenalia, 10p-£1,000.* LOC: Take old A47 from by-pass, shop 25yds. from traffic lights. PARK: Opposite. TEL: 0572 823745; home - 057 286 243. SER: Valuations; restorations (furniture, brass, copper, silver).

John Garner

51-53 High St. East. Est: 1967. Open 9-5.30, Sun. by appointment. SIZE: Large, plus warehouse. *STOCK: Oil paintings, furniture,*

John Garner continued

18th-19th C; clocks, bronzes, handcoloured sporting, coaching, marine and genre engravings and etchings. LOC: Just off A47, close to market place. PARK: Easy. TEL: 0572 823607; fax - 0572 821654. SER: Valuations; restorations (pictures, furniture); framing; courier; export, illustrated catalogue available on request. VAT: Stan/Spec.

Gilberts of Uppingham
Ayston Rd. (M Gilbert) Open 9.30-5; Mon., Tues. and Thurs. 9.30-1 and 2-5. *STOCK: General antiques.* TEL: 0572 823486.

Goldmark Books
14 Orange St. (M.M Goldmark) Open 9.30-5.30. *STOCK: Antiquarian and secondhand books.* LOC: Between Market Sq. and traffic lights. PARK: Nearby. TEL: 0572 822694.

Robson Hill
3 Bear Yard. (C.M Hill) Open Fri. and Sat. 10-5. *STOCK: Furniture, china, glass and decorative items, 18th-19th C.* TEL: 0572 821381; home - 0536 511842.

Lapwing Antiques
10 Orange St. (D.L Jones Ltd) Est: 1962. SIZE: Medium + warehouse. *STOCK: Porcelain, 18th-19th C, £20-£1,000; furniture, 17th to early 19th C, £300-£5,000; watercolours and oils, 19th C, £100-£500.* PARK: Nearby. TEL: 0572 821408/822852. SER: Valuations (as stock); restorations; buys at auction (pottery and porcelain). VAT: Spec.

Marie-Ange Martin Antiques
43 High St. East. Est: 1985. Open 10-5, other times by appointment. CL: Thurs. SIZE: Small. *STOCK: Furniture, 17th to early 19th C; some oil paintings, silver, 18th-19th C; all £500-£5,000.* PARK: Easy. TEL: 0572 821359; home - same.

Not Just Books
Market Pl. (R.M. and Mrs F Waknell) Est: 1988. Open 10-5, Sat. 9.30-5.30. SIZE: Large. *STOCK: Books, especially fiction and theology.* TEL: 0572 821306.

T.J Roberts
39/41 High St. East. Resident. Open 9.30-5.30. *STOCK: Furniture, porcelain and pottery, 18th to 19th C; paintings and prints, 19th to early 20th C.* PARK: Easy. TEL: 0572 821493. VAT: Stan/Spec.

E. and C Royall Antiques
Printers Yard, High St. East. Open 10-4.30. CL: Thurs. *STOCK: Furniture, pictures, silver, porcelain, glassware, ivories and Oriental bronzes.* TEL: 085 883 744.

Uppingham continued

Tattersall's
14b Orange St. (J Tattersall) Est: 1985. Open 9-5. CL: Thurs. SIZE: Small. *STOCK: Persian rugs, mirrors, sofas, 19th-20th C.* PARK: Easy, 200yds. TEL: 0572 821171. SER: Restorations (rush and cane work, rugs); upholstery.

Vendy Antiques (Uppingham)
7 Orange St. (T.W Vendy and S.P Phillips) Est: 1964. Open 10-1 and 2-5, Sun. p.m. by appointment. CL: Mon. SIZE: Medium. *STOCK: General antiques including furniture and smalls, mainly Victorian, £10-£2,000.* PARK: Nearby. TEL: 0572 821646; home - 0858 89469. VAT: Stan/Spec.

WHISSENDINE, Nr. Oakham

Old Bakehouse Pine
11 Main St. (E. and W Stevenson) Open seven days, prior phone call advisable. *STOCK: Stripped pine furniture.* LOC: Off A606, opposite village school. TEL: 066 479 691.

WHITWICK

Charles Antiques
3 Market Pl. (N Haydon) Resident. Est: 1971. Open 10-12.30 and 2-5, Mon. 2-5, Sun. by appointment. CL: Wed. SIZE: Medium. *STOCK: Clocks, 18th C, £60-£2,000; general antiques.* LOC: Exit 23, M1. PARK: Easy. TEL: 0530 36932. SER: Valuations; restorations; repairs; buys at auction (clocks). VAT: Stan/Spec.

WING, Nr. Oakham

Robert Bingley Antiques
Home Farm, Church St. Open 9-5, Sun. 11-4. SIZE: Large. *STOCK: Furniture, 17th-19th C, £50-£5,000; glass, clocks, silver and plate, pictures and porcelain.* LOC: Next to church. PARK: Own. TEL: 057 285 725; home - 057 285 314. SER: Valuations; restorations. VAT: Spec.

WOODHOUSE EAVES, Nr. Leicester

Paddock Antiques
The Old Smithy, Brand Hill. (M., C.A. and T.M Bray) Open 10-5.30. CL: Mon. *STOCK: Porcelain, £5-£2,000; prints, small furniture.*

WYMESWOLD, Nr. Loughborough

N Bryan-Peach Antiques
28 Far St. Resident. Open 10-6, Sun. by appointment. SIZE: Medium. *STOCK: Clocks, barometers, watches; 18th-19th C furniture, £50-£5,000.* PARK: Easy. TEL: 0509 880425. SER: Valuations; restorations; buys at auction. VAT: Spec.

Lincolnshire

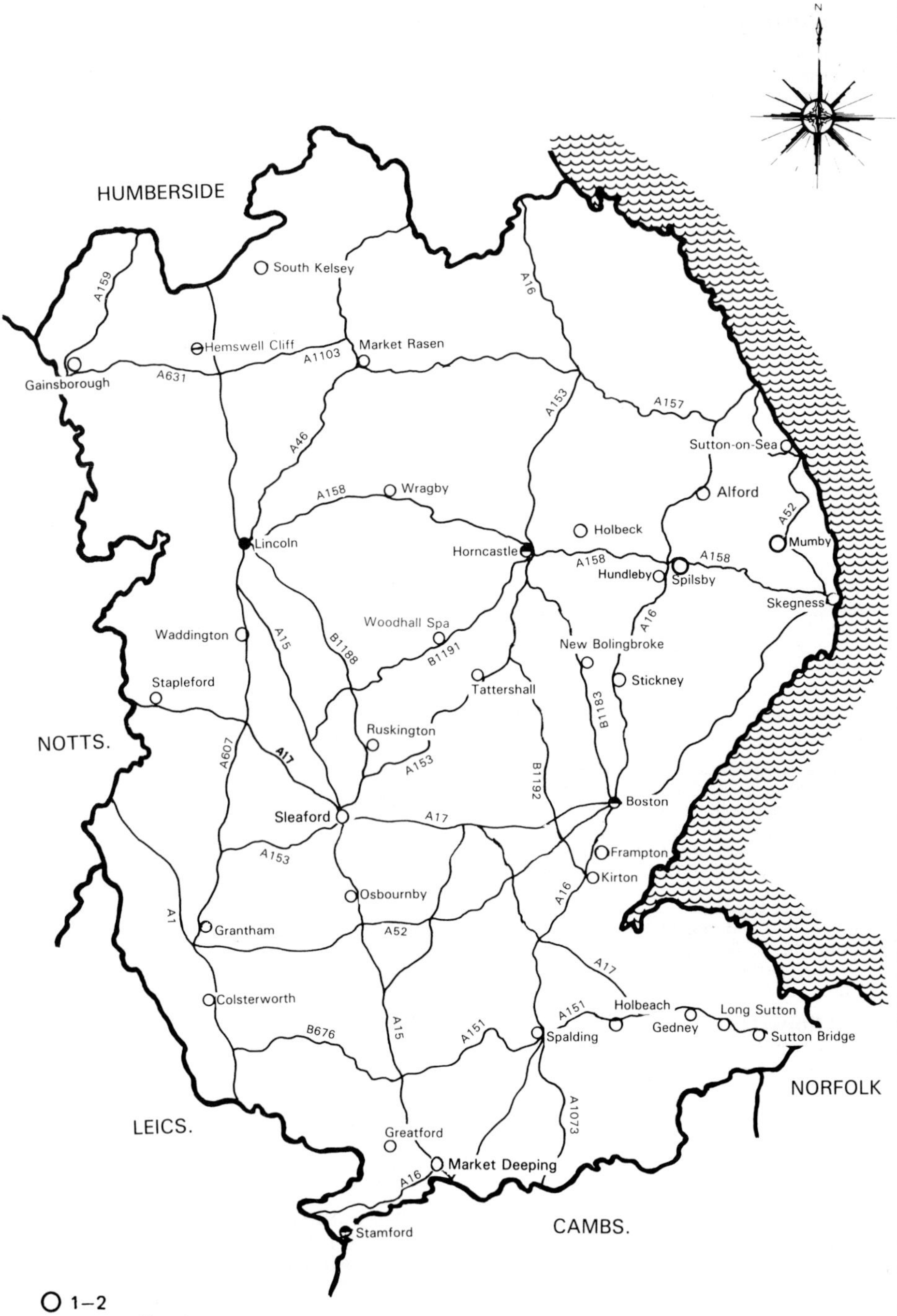

N
HUMBERSIDE
South Kelsey
A159
A16
Hemswell Cliff
Market Rasen
A1103
Gainsborough
A631
A153
A157
A46
Sutton-on-Sea
A158
Wragby
Alford
Holbeck
A52
Lincoln
Horncastle
A158
Mumby
A158
Hundleby
Spilsby
Skegness
Woodhall Spa
A15
B1188
B1191
A16
New Bolingbroke
Waddington
Stapleford
Tattershall
Stickney
B1183
NOTTS.
Ruskington
A607
A17
A153
B1192
Boston
Sleaford
A17
A153
Frampton
Kirton
Osbournby
A16
A1
Grantham
A52
A17
Colsterworth
Holbeach
Long Sutton
A151
Gedney
B676
A15
A151
Spalding
Sutton Bridge
NORFOLK
A1073
LEICS.
Greatford
Market Deeping
A16
Stamford
CAMBS.

O 1–2
⊖ 3–5
◓ 6–12
● 13+

Key to number of shops in this area.

Please note this is only a rough map designed to show dealers the number of shops in the various towns, and is not necessarily totally accurate.

ALFORD

Nainbys Antiques
19 West St. (G.C. and S.E Woodhall) Open Tues. and Fri. 10-4, Sat. 10-1. *STOCK: General antiques, mainly pine.* TEL: 0507 463266.

Talisman Antiques
Regent House, 12 South Market Pl. (M.V Prime) Open 10.30-4.30. CL: Thurs. *STOCK: Silver, jewellery, pine, furniture.* TEL: 0507 463441.

BOSTON

Boston Antiques Centre
12 West St. (R Grant) Est: 1978. Open 9-5. CL: Thurs. SIZE: Medium. *STOCK: Jewellery, silver and plate.* LOC: 2 minutes walk from town centre on Spalding side. PARK: 1 mins. walk. TEL: 0205 361510. SER: Valuations; restorations; export. VAT: Stan.

Mary Holland Antiques
7A Red Lion St. (Mrs M Holland) Est: 1980. Open 10-5, Sun., Mon. and Thurs. by appointment. SIZE: Small. *STOCK: General antiques.* TEL: 0205 363791; home - 0205 353840.

Pen Street Antiques
9A Pen St. (Mrs S.M Taylor) Est: 1976. Open Wed., Fri. and Sat. 10-1 and 2-4. SIZE: Small. *STOCK: China, glass, silver and plate, jewellery, 1830-1930, £2-£200.* LOC: 40 metres from 'New England' Hotel. PARK: Easy. TEL: 0205 364118; home - same. SER: Buys at auction (bric-a-brac).

Portobellow Row Antiques Centre
93-95 High St. Open 10-4. SIZE: 9 dealers. *STOCK: Furniture, pine, shipping goods, '40's-'60's clothing, kitchenalia, postcards, oil lamps and gramophones.* TEL: 0205 369456. SER: Repairs (oil lamps and gramophones).

Quinn Galleries
13 Pen St. (T.P Quinn) Open 9.30-5.30. *STOCK: Oriental carpets, rugs and furniture.* PARK: Nearby. TEL: 0205 352990.

That Little Shop
7 Red Lion St. (L.B Brand) Open Wed. and Fri. 10.30-3.30, Sat. 10.30-4.30. *STOCK: Jewellery and general antiques.* LOC: Behind Woolworths. TEL: Home - 0790 353060.

COLSTERWORTH

Clive Underwood Antiques
46 High St. Est: 1970. Open 9.30-5.30. *STOCK: Furniture, oak, mahogany, 17th-19th C, £45-£10,000; some pictures, glass, porcelain.* LOC: 1/2 mile off A1 between Stamford and Grantham. TEL: 0476 860689. SER: Valuations; restorations; rushing; caning. VAT: Stan/Spec.

FRAMPTON, Nr. Boston

Robert J Kent Antiques
Pinewood, Ralphs Lane. *STOCK: Pine furniture.* LOC: B1391. TEL: 0205 723739. VAT: Stan.

GAINSBOROUGH

G.T.G Ellory Antiques and Shipping
The Old Nick, Cross St. Open 8.30-5. *STOCK: General antiques and shipping furniture.* TEL: 0427 615897.

Mr Van Hefflin
12 High St, Kirton Lindsey. Est: 1820. Open 11-5.30. *STOCK: Pocket and wrist watches; secondhand jewellery.* PARK: Easy. TEL: 0652 648044.

GEDNEY

Paul Johnston BADA
Old Red Lion. Resident. Est: 1975. Open 10-6 or by appointment. SIZE: Small. *STOCK: Early English oak and country furniture.* Not Stocked: Mahogany. LOC: Just off A17 on B1359 at Gedney roundabout. PARK: Easy. TEL: 0406 362414.

GRANTHAM

Grantham Clocks
30 Lodge Way. (R Conder) Resident. Open by appointment. *STOCK: Clocks.* PARK: Easy. TEL: 0476 61784. SER: Restorations.

Grantham Furniture Emporium
4-6 Wharf Rd. (K. and J.E Hamilton) Est: 1970. Open 10-5 including Sun. CL: Mon. SIZE: Large. *STOCK: Victorian and Edwardian furniture, £5-£3,000.* LOC: Town centre, near Post Office. PARK: Own at rear. TEL: 0476 62967.

Harold Nadin
109 London Rd. Open 9.30-5. CL: Sat. p.m. *STOCK: Furniture, 17th to early 19th C; general antiques.* TEL: 0476 63562.

William Redmile Antiques
15 Elmer St. North. (J.W Redmile) Est: 1936. Open 9-6. *STOCK: General antiques.* LOC: From London turn right at Angel Hotel. TEL: 0476 64074. VAT: Stan/Spec.

GREATFORD, Nr. Stamford

The Complete Automobilist
Dept. 1, The Old Rectory. Est: 1967. Open 8.30-5. CL: Sat. *STOCK: Hard-to-get parts for older vehicles.* LOC: East of Stamford. PARK: Easy. TEL: 0778 560312; fax - 0778 560738. SER: Catalogue available.

HEMSWELL CLIFF, Nr. Gainsborough

Hemswell Antiques Centres
Caenby Corner Estate. (P.J. and A.R Miller) Est: 1986. Open 10-5, 7 days a week. SIZE: 270 dealers. *STOCK: Furniture, 17th-19th C; watercolours and oils, 19th C; silver and plate, clocks, porcelain, china, jewellery, dolls, toys, books, prints, clothes.* LOC: A15 from Lincoln then A631 towards Gainsborough, 1 mile from roundabout, follow signs. PARK: Easy. TEL: 042 773 389. SER: Valuations; restorations (oak, mahogany and pine; upholstery); container packing.

Kate
Kate House, Caenby Corner Estate. (Mr Shamsa) Open 10-5 including Sun. *STOCK: Pine including reproduction, general antiques.* TEL: 042 773 724.

Second Time Around
Hemswell Antique Centre, Caenby Corner Estate. (G.L Powis and R Kenyon) Est: 1986. Open 10-5 including Sun. *STOCK: Longcase and bracket clocks, pre 1830, £1,100-£12,000.* LOC: A15 from Lincoln to Caenby Corner roundabout, left towards Gainsborough for 1 mile. (A631). PARK: Easy. TEL: 042 773 389; home - 0522 543167 or 0904 705000. SER: Restorations (clocks). VAT: Spec.

HOLBEACH, Nr. Spalding

All Our Yesterdays Country Antiques and Bygones
North View, Penny Hill. (M.E. and D.C Pearsey) Resident. Open by appointment. *STOCK: Country tools, ironwork.* LOC: Old A17 next to Bulls Neck public house. TEL: 0406 24636.

HOLBECK, Nr. Horncastle

Ann and Michael Heawood
The Quarries. Est: 1982. Open by appointment. *STOCK: Furniture, 17th-19th C; decorative arts, BC to 20th C.* TEL: 065 883 230.

HORNCASTLE

Horncastle Antiques
23 North St. (R Ingram Hill) Est: 1971. Open by appointment only. SIZE: Small. *STOCK: Furniture, 18th-19th C, £50-£500; metalware, 19th C, £50-£200.* LOC: 200yds. from town centre on Louth road. PARK: Easy. TEL: 0507 524415; home - same. VAT: Stan/Spec.

King Antiques
25 Bridge St. (R King) Est: 1986. Open 9.30-5, evenings by appointment. *STOCK: Furniture and decorative items, 18th-19th C.* TEL: 0507 527976.

Horncastle continued

Robert Kitching
9-11 West St. Open 9.30-5. *STOCK: Clocks and general antiques.* TEL: 0507 522120.

The Lincolnshire Antiques Centre
Bridge St. (K Shaw) Open 9-5. SIZE: 30+ dealers. *STOCK: General antiques, £5-£5,000.* LOC: To rear of "The Kitchen Range". PARK: Own. TEL: 0507 527794. VAT: Stan/Spec.

Seaview Antiques
47a East St. (M Chalk) Open 9-5. SIZE: Large. *STOCK: Furniture and smalls, period to shipping, £5-£5,000.* LOC: A158. PARK: Easy. TEL: 0507 523287.

Laurence Shaw Antiques
Spilsby Rd. Open 8.30-5. SIZE: Large. *STOCK: Furniture and general antiques, 17th-20th C, £5-£5,000.* TEL: 0507 527638. SER: Transport, delivery and collections. VAT: Stan/Spec.

Talisman Antiques
51/53 North St. (M.V Prime) Open 10-5. CL: Mon. SIZE: Large. *STOCK: Pine furniture, collectables, satin walnut, model trains.* TEL: 0507 526893.

The Warehouse
Bank St. (Mrs M Brooke and W Cruickshank) Open 10-5. *STOCK: Furniture, pine, oak and mahogany.* TEL: 0507 524569; evenings - 0507 527311.

HUNDLEBY, Nr. Spilsby

Alan Lewis Fine Art
The Old Mill House, 35 Main Rd. (A. and M Lewis) Est: 1987. Open by appointment only. SIZE: Medium. *STOCK: Watercolours, £500-£1,000; oils, £1,500-£2,500; both 1800-1920.* LOC: Just off A16. PARK: Easy. TEL: 0790 52817. SER: Valuations; restorations (oils and watercolours); framing; buys at auction (oils and watercolours). FAIRS: Birmingham; Barbican; East Midlands; Arley Hall; some Robert Bailey. VAT: Spec.

KIRTON

Kirton Antiques LAPADA
3 High St. (A.R Marshall) Est: 1973. Open 8.30-5 or by appointment. CL: Sat. SIZE: Warehouse. *STOCK: Furniture, shipping goods, bric-a-brac, Georgian, Victorian, Edwardian.* TEL: 0205 722595; Cellnet - 0860 531600; evenings - 0205 722134; fax - 0205 722895. VAT: Stan.

LINCOLN

Aladdin Antiques
5 Monks Rd. (M Frith) Open 9-5.30. *STOCK: Victorian and Edwardian pine and continental furniture.* TEL: 0522 533998.

John R Bracey
2 St. Martins St. Open 10-4. *STOCK: Jewellery and silver, decorative art 1880-1930.* PARK: Easy. TEL: 0522 530715.

Michael Brewer
5 Drury Lane. (M.N Brewer) Est: 1954. Open by appointment. SIZE: Medium. *STOCK: Furniture, oil paintings, silver, porcelain, bronzes, works of art.* Not Stocked: Coins. LOC: Close to Cathedral. PARK: 20yds. TEL: 0522 545854. SER: Valuations; buys at auction. VAT: Stan/Spec. *Trade Only.*

Castle Gallery
61 Steep Hill. (A.R Buchanan) Est: 1983. Open 10-5.30, Sun. by appointment. SIZE: Large. *STOCK: Oil paintings, 18th-19th C and modern British, £150-£8,000; watercolours, 18th-20th C, £50-£3,000; antiquarian maps, mirrors.* LOC: 100yds. from Lincoln cathedral. PARK: Easy. TEL: 0522 535078; home - same. SER: Valuations; restorations (oils and watercolours); framing. VAT: Stan/Spec.

Designs on Pine
27 The Strait. (L Copley) Est: 1965. Open 10-5. *STOCK: Pine.* TEL: 0522 529252.

Doyle Antiques
24 Steep Hill. Open 10-5. SIZE: Medium. *STOCK: Period oak and country furniture, paintings, clocks, mainly 17th-18th C.* LOC: Near Cathedral and Castle. TEL: 0522 542226. VAT: Spec.

C Dring
5a Eastgate. Open 10-5.30. CL: Wed. *STOCK: Victorian and Edwardian inlaid furniture; shipping goods, porcelain, clocks.* TEL: 0522 540733/792794.

C. and K.E Dring
111 High St. Open 10-5.30. CL: Wed. *STOCK: Victorian and Edwardian inlaid furniture; shipping goods, porcelain, clocks.* TEL: 0522 540733/792794.

Lincoln continued

Eastgate Antique Centre
6 Eastgate. (N Marris, LAPADA) Est: 1970. Open 9.30-5. SIZE: 12 dealers. *STOCK: Town and country furniture, paintings, jewellery, silver, brass, copper, treen, pottery, porcelain, books and decorative items, 17th-19th C.* Not Stocked: Bric-a-brac, coins and militaria. LOC: Near Cathedral. PARK: Easy. TEL: 0522 544404.

Golden Goose Books
20 and 21 Steep Hill. (W West-Skinn and A Cockram) Est: 1983. Open 10-5.30. *STOCK: Antiquarian books, bookcases, carpets, decorative items, £1-£5,000.* TEL: 0522 522589.

David J Hansord BADA
32 Steep Hill. Est: 1972. Open 9.30-1 and 2-5.30. SIZE: Medium. *STOCK: English and continental furniture, 17th to early 19th C, £100-£10,000; clocks, barometers and scientific instruments, mainly 18th C, from £50.* Not Stocked: Later items. LOC: Few yards from Cathedral. PARK: Easy. TEL: 0522 530044; home - 0522 526983. SER: Valuations; buys at auction. VAT: Stan/Spec.

Harlequin Gallery
22 Steep Hill. (R West-Skinn) Est: 1962. Open 10-5.30. *STOCK: Antiquarian books, prints, maps, 50p-£5,000.* TEL: 0522 522589; home - 0673 858294.

Lincoln continued

Dorrian Lambert Antiques
64/65 Steep Hill. (R Lambert) Est: 1981. Open 10-5, Sat. 10-12.30 and 2-5. CL: Wed. SIZE: Medium. *STOCK: Furniture, clocks, chairs, porcelain, 18th to early 20th C.* PARK: Loading only or nearby. TEL: 0522 545916; home - 042784 686. SER: Valuations; restorations (clocks). FAIRS: Newark Showground.

Lincoln Fine Art
Dernstall House, 33 The Strait. (Mrs D Glen-Doepel) Est: 1973. Open 10-1 and 2-5.30. *STOCK: Oil paintings including decorative portraits, landscapes, marine, watercolours, miniatues, Old Master paintings, drawings, porcelain and objets d'art, 17th-20th C, £80-£10,000.* LOC: Top of High St., opposite Stadz Café. PARK: Nearby. TEL: 0522 533029. SER: Valuations.

Richard Pullen Jeweller
28 The Strait. Est: 1979. Open 10-4.30. CL: Wed. SIZE: Small. *STOCK: Jewellery, silver and plate.* LOC: Top of High St., near Cathedral. PARK: Easy. TEL: 0522 537170. SER: Valuations; repairs (jewellery, including re-threading).

Rowletts of Lincoln
338 High St. (A.H Rowlett) Open 9-5, Wed. 9-1. *STOCK: Coins and jewellery.* TEL: 0522 524139.

The Strait Antiques
5 The Strait. (F.M Davies) Est: 1970. Open 10-4, Sat. 10-5. CL: Mon. and Wed. SIZE: Medium. *STOCK: English pottery and porcelain, 18th-19th C, £25-£200; blue and white transfer ware, early 19th C, £5-£50; general antiques and furniture, 19th to early 20th C; dolls.* LOC: At the start of the ascent to the Cathedral from the top of the High St. PARK: Easy, behind shop. TEL: 0522 523130. VAT: Stan/Spec.

James Usher and Son Ltd
6 Silver St. Open 9-5.30. CL: Wed. *STOCK: Silver, jewellery.* TEL: 0522 527547.

LONG SUTTON

E. and J Northam
15 High St. (Mrs Northam) *STOCK: General antiques, glass, oil lamps, silver.* TEL: 0406 363191.

Trade Antiques
7 Market St. (P.E Poole) Est: 1961. CL: Sat. SIZE: Medium. *STOCK: General shipping goods, clocks and watches.* LOC: A17. PARK: Easy. TEL: 0406 363758. VAT: Stan. *Trade Only.*

MARKET DEEPING

Portland House Antiques
23 Church St. (G.W Cree and V.E Bass) Est: 1987. Open daily, Wed. and Thurs. by appointment. SIZE: Medium. *STOCK: Porcelain, glass, furniture, 18th-19th C, £100-£3,000.* PARK: Easy. TEL: 0778 347129; home - same. SER: Buys at auction. FAIRS: Olympia, Barbican Antiques for Business. VAT: Stan/Spec.

MARKET RASEN

Bothy Antiques
Oxford St. (Mrs M Foster) Est: 1976. Open Fri., Sat. and Sun. 2-4.30. SIZE: Small. *STOCK: Smalls, 19th to early 20th C, £2-£50; prints, watercolours, engravings and oils, 19th C, £10-£100; small Victorian furniture especially oak, some pine, £25-£250.* PARK: Easy. TEL: 067 35 464. SER: Valuations; restorations (pictures and porcelain).

Harwood Tate
Church Mill, Caistor Rd. (J Harwood Tate) Open 9.30-5.30, Sat. 10-1 or by appointment. SIZE: Large. *STOCK: Furniture, mahogany, rosewood, oak; clocks, 18th to early 19th C; ornamental items including pictures and prints, 18th-19th C.* Not Stocked: Shipping goods. LOC: Take A46 from Lincoln, Church Mill is off town centre, north of church. PARK: Easy. TEL: 0673 843579. VAT: Stan/Spec.

MUMBY, Nr. Alford

Barn Antiques
Springfield, Long Lane. (J Miller) Est: 1989. Open 10-5, 10-7 in summer. CL: Wed. in winter. SIZE: Large. *STOCK: Pine and country furniture, 19th-20th C, £50-£300; postcards, linen and haberdashery, 10p to £50; tools, cast iron, collectables.* LOC: B1149, 1/2 mile from A52, 3 1/2 miles from Alford. PARK: Easy. TEL: 0507 490237; home - same. SER: Restorations (pine including stripping). FAIRS: Horncastle.

NEW BOLINGBROKE, Nr. Boston

Junktion
The Old Railway Station. (J Rundle) Est: 1981. Open Tues.-Sat. and by appointment. SIZE: Large. *STOCK: Early advertising, decorative and architectural items; toys, automobilia, mechanical antiques and bygones; early slot machines, wireless telephones, 20th C collectables.* Not Stocked: Porcelain and jewellery. LOC: B1183 Horncastle to Boston road. PARK: Easy. TEL: 0205 480068; home - 0205 480087.

OSBOURNBY

Audley House Antiques
North St. (S Wood) Est: 1948. Open 10-6, Sun. 2-6, or by appointment. *STOCK: Furniture, Georgian, Victorian and some Edwardian; decorative items and treen.* LOC: On A15, 10 miles north of Bourne, turn left into village market place, then right into North St. to far end. PARK: Easy. TEL: 052 95 473/0860 758764. SER: Valuations.

RUSKINGTON

Pinfold Antiques LAPADA
3 Pinfold Lane. (J. and G.D Ballinger) Est: 1981. Open 10-5. SIZE: Medium. *STOCK: Longcase clocks, 17th-19th C, £500-£5,000; period English furniture, weapons, £50-£3,000.* PARK: Easy. TEL: 0526 832200; home - 0526 832057. SER: Valuations; restorations (longcase and bracket clocks, period furniture); buys at auction. FAIRS: Olympia, Merchant Taylors.

SKEGNESS

G.H Crowson
50 High St. Open daily 10-6. *STOCK: General antiques, jewellery.* TEL: 0754 4360. *Mostly Trade.*

Romantiques
87 Roman Bank. (P Davis) Open 9.30-5.30. *STOCK: Clocks and furniture.* PARK: Easy. TEL: 0754 67879. SER: Restoration (as stock).

SLEAFORD

Sleaford Antiques Centre
21 Northgate. Open 10-5. SIZE: 15 dealers. *STOCK: General antiques.* TEL: 0529 414333.

SOUTH KELSEY, Nr. Lincoln

Sykes Antiques
The Old School. (B.G Sykes) Est: 1964. Always open. SIZE: Large. *STOCK: English and continental pine, shipping goods, 19th-20th C, from £10.* LOC: 6 miles off A15. PARK: Easy. TEL: 06527 693; home - same. SER: Export. VAT: Stan. *Trade Only.*

SPALDING

Broad Street Fine Antiques

6 Broad St. (R and Mrs E Cooling) Est: 1991. Open 10-4, Sun. and Thurs. p.m. by appointment. SIZE: Medium. *STOCK: Small decorative Georgian to Victorian furniture, £150-£4,500; fine china including Worcester and Derby, 17th C to Edwardian, £85-£2,000; some oil paintings and watercolours, Victorian to Edwardian, £100-£1,500.* Not Stocked: Oak furniture and bric-a-brac. LOC: From market place to town centre, past NatWest Bank. PARK: 100 yards on left. TEL: 0775 712100; home - 0775 840074.

Dean's Antiques

"The Walnuts", Weston St. Mary's. (Mrs B Dean) Est: 1969. Open daily. SIZE: Medium. *STOCK: General antiques, farm and country bygones, £2-£200.* LOC: On Spalding to Holbeach main road A151. PARK: Easy. TEL: 0406 370429.

SPILSBY

Shaw Antiques

High St. (Mrs J.M Shaw) CL: Tues. *STOCK: Victoriana, silver, glass, general small antiques.* TEL: 0790 52317/52297.

Spilsby Antiques

29 Halton Rd. (D. and C Goodland) Est: 1980. Open by appointment. SIZE: Medium. *STOCK: Jewellery, silver.* PARK: Easy. TEL: 0790 52148. VAT: Stan. *Trade Only.*

STAMFORD

Jane Cox and David Dean

8 The George Mews. Est: 1966. Open 9-1.30 and 2-5.30. SIZE: Medium. *STOCK: Oak, mahogany, carvings, to 18th C, £500-£1,000; textiles, cushions, paintings.* LOC: A1. PARK: Easy. TEL: 0780 63303. SER: Restorations (gilding). FAIRS: Olympia.

Robin Cox Antiques

35-36 St. Peter's St. Est: 1965. Open 9-5, weekends by appointment. *STOCK: English and continental furniture, and works of art, including early oak, mahogany and decorated, wood carvings and sculpture, architectural fittings, garden items, £50-£10,000.* TEL: 0780 64592. VAT: Stan/Spec.

Dawson of Stamford

6 Red Lion Sq. (J Dawson) Open 9-5.30. SIZE: Medium. *STOCK: Jewellery, silver and Georgian furniture.* LOC: Town centre between St. John's church and All Saint's church. TEL: 0780 54166. VAT: Stan/Spec.

George Clocks

9 The George Mews. (J Ballinger and G.K Hadfield) Open 10-5, Sun. by appointment. SIZE: Small. *STOCK: Clocks and barometers,*

George Clocks continued

1650-1820, £200-£15,000; furniture, 1620-1840, £200-£3,500; smalls, 1720-1820, £40-£1,000. Not Stocked: Silver and china. LOC: Behind George Hotel, near station. PARK: Easy. TEL: 0780 66068; home - 0526 832057. SER: Valuations; restorations (clocks); buys at auction (clocks and barometers). VAT: Stan/Spec.

Ivor and Patricia Lewis Antiques and Fine Art Dealers LAPADA

3 St. Mary's St. Open 6 days. *STOCK: English and French furniture - some signed, porcelain, bronzes.* TEL: Evenings - 0733 344567.

Pavilion BADA LAPADA

The George Mews. (Mrs M Brown) Est: 1969. Open 10.30-5. SIZE: Small. *STOCK: English furniture, 18th-19th C, £100-£10,000; decorative items, £100-£500.* LOC: Behind George Hotel. PARK: Easy. TEL: 0780 55405; home - 0664 424209. FAIRS: Olympia; N.E.C.; Harrogate. VAT: Spec.

St. George's Antiques

1 St. George's Sq. (G.H Burns) Est: 1974. Open 9-1 and 2-4.30. CL: Sat. SIZE: Small and trade only warehouse. *STOCK: Period and Victorian furniture, some small items.* TEL: 0780 54117; home - 0476 67492. VAT: Stan/Spec.

St. Mary's Galleries

5 St. Mary's Hill. (Mrs O.M. and R.D Cox) Est: 1961. Open 9.30-5. CL: Thurs. SIZE: Medium. *STOCK: Furniture, 1600-1860, £5-£500; carvings, treen, wooden and metal implements and tools; jewellery, Victorian and Georgian, £2-£130; unusual items, 1600-1900, £1-£30; some textiles, oil paintings and watercolours.* LOC: On old A1 south out of Stamford. PARK: Easy, at rear. TEL: 0780 64159. VAT: Spec.

John Sinclair

11/12 St. Mary's St. (F.J Sinclair) Est: 1970. Open 9-5.30. SIZE: Large. *STOCK: Oak country furniture, 18th C, £200-£3,000; Victorian mahogany furniture, £100-£1,000; Edwardian furniture.* LOC: Near A1. PARK: George Hotel car park. TEL: 0780 65421. VAT: Stan/Spec.

Stamford Antiques Centre

Exchange Hall, Broad St. Open 10-5, Sun. 12-5. SIZE: 30 dealers. *STOCK: General antiques.* LOC: 1 mile from A1. TEL: 0780 62605.

Staniland (Booksellers)

4/5 St. George's St. (M.F. and M.G Staniland) Est: 1973. Open 10-5. SIZE: Large. *STOCK: Books, mainly 19th-20th C, 50p-£500; postcards, 1890-1930, 10p-£30.* LOC: High St. PARK: St. Leonard's St. TEL: 0780 55800; home - 0780 57615.

Stamford continued

Andrew Thomas
Old Granary, 10 North St. Est: 1970. Open 9-6. SIZE: Large. *STOCK: Stripped pine, architectural pine fitments, ironware, oak, mahogany and decorated furniture in original paint.* LOC: From south take old A1 through Stamford. Turn right at second set of traffic lights, warehouse on right. PARK: Opposite. TEL: 0780 62236; home - 0780 410627. VAT: Stan.

STAPLEFORD

Allens Antiques
Moor Farm. Open 9-5, Sat. 9-1. *STOCK: Pine.* LOC: Off A17 Sleaford Rd. TEL: 0522 788392.

STICKNEY

B. and B Antiques
Main Rd. (B.J Whittaker and J Shooter) Open by appointment. *STOCK: General antiques.* PARK: Easy. TEL: 0205 480 204.

SUTTON BRIDGE

Bridge Antiques
30 and 32 Bridge Rd. (A Gittins) Est: 1965. Open 8.30-5.30 or by appointment. CL: Sat. SIZE: Large. *STOCK: Victorian and Edwardian furniture.* LOC: A17. PARK: Easy. TEL: 0406 350704.

Old Barn Antiques Warehouse
New Rd. (S. and Mrs T.J Jackson) Est: 1982. Open 9-5.30, including Sun. SIZE: Large. *STOCK: Furniture and shipping goods including mahogany, walnut, inlaid, oak and pine, £25-£500.* LOC: 1 mile out of village, off old A17 by Barclays Bank. PARK: Own. TEL: 0406 350435; home - same. SER: Restorations (stripping and polishing). *Mainly Trade.*

SUTTON-ON-SEA

Knicks Knacks
41 High St. (Mr and Mrs R.A Nicholson) Est: 1983. Open 10-1 and 2-5, including Sun. CL: Mon. SIZE: Medium + warehouse. *STOCK: Victorian gas lights, brass and iron beds, cast-iron fireplaces, bygones, curios, tools, collectables, pottery, porcelain, art deco, art nouveau, advertising items, furniture and shipping goods, £1-£1,000.* LOC: A52. PARK: Easy. TEL: 0507 441916; home - 0507 441657. VAT: Stan.

TATTERSHALL

Lindum Antiques **LAPADA**
Walnut Farm, Tattershall Thorpe. (D.G. and M Wilby) Est: 1972. Open by appointment only. SIZE: Medium. *STOCK: Pottery and porcelain, 18th-19th C, £30-£2,000.* TEL: 0526 42454. FAIRS: Most major. VAT: Spec.

Wayside Antiques
Market Place. (G Ball) Est: 1969. Open 10-5.30. SIZE: Small. *STOCK: General antiques.* LOC: On A158. PARK: Easy. TEL: 0526 42436. VAT: Stan/Spec.

WADDINGTON, Nr. Lincoln

Kevin McSwiggan **LAPADA**
Garden House, Timms Lane. Est: 1985. Open by appointment. SIZE: Small. *STOCK: Portrait miniatures, 1760-1840; British watercolours, 1850-1920; small furniture, 1790-1840.* LOC: Village centre, first lane on right past 'Horse and Jockey' heading south. PARK: Easy. TEL: 0522 720231; home - same. SER: Valuations; buys at auction (miniatures and watercolours). FAIRS: N.E.C. (Aug.); most Robert Bailey. VAT: Spec.

J. and R Ratcliffe
The Manor, Manor Lane. Est: 1954. *STOCK: Furniture, decorative items, 1600-1830.* PARK: Opposite Horse and Jockey public house. TEL: 0522 720996. VAT: Stan/Spec.

WOODHALL SPA

Best Antiques
The Broadway Centre, The Broadway. (I. and Mrs J.M Pygott) Open 10-5. CL: Wed. SIZE: Medium. *STOCK: Furniture, £100-£3,000; porcelain and china, £5-£1,000; general antiques, £1-£500; pictures, £5-£3,000, all 1750 to date.* LOC: B1191. PARK: Easy. TEL: 0526 53815. VAT: Stan/Spec.

V.O.C. Antiques
27 Witham Rd. (D.J. and C.J Leyland) Resident. Est: 1970. Open 9.30-6, Sun. by appointment. SIZE: Medium. *STOCK: 17th-19th C furniture, to £5,000; period brass and copper, pottery, porcelain and pictures.* LOC: B1191. PARK: Easy. TEL: 0526 52753; home - same. SER: Valuations. VAT: Stan/Spec.

WRAGBY, Nr. Lincoln

Tealby Pine
Goltho Hall, Goltho. (R.G Chesterton-North) Est: 1965. Open every day but appointment preferred. SIZE: Large. *STOCK: Pine, 18th-19th C, £5-£500.* LOC: From Lincoln on A158. 1 mile before Wragby, take right turn signposted Goltho. PARK: Easy. TEL: 0673 858789; fax - 0673 857023. SER: Restorations (furniture stripping). VAT: Stan/Spec. *Trade Only.*

Merseyside

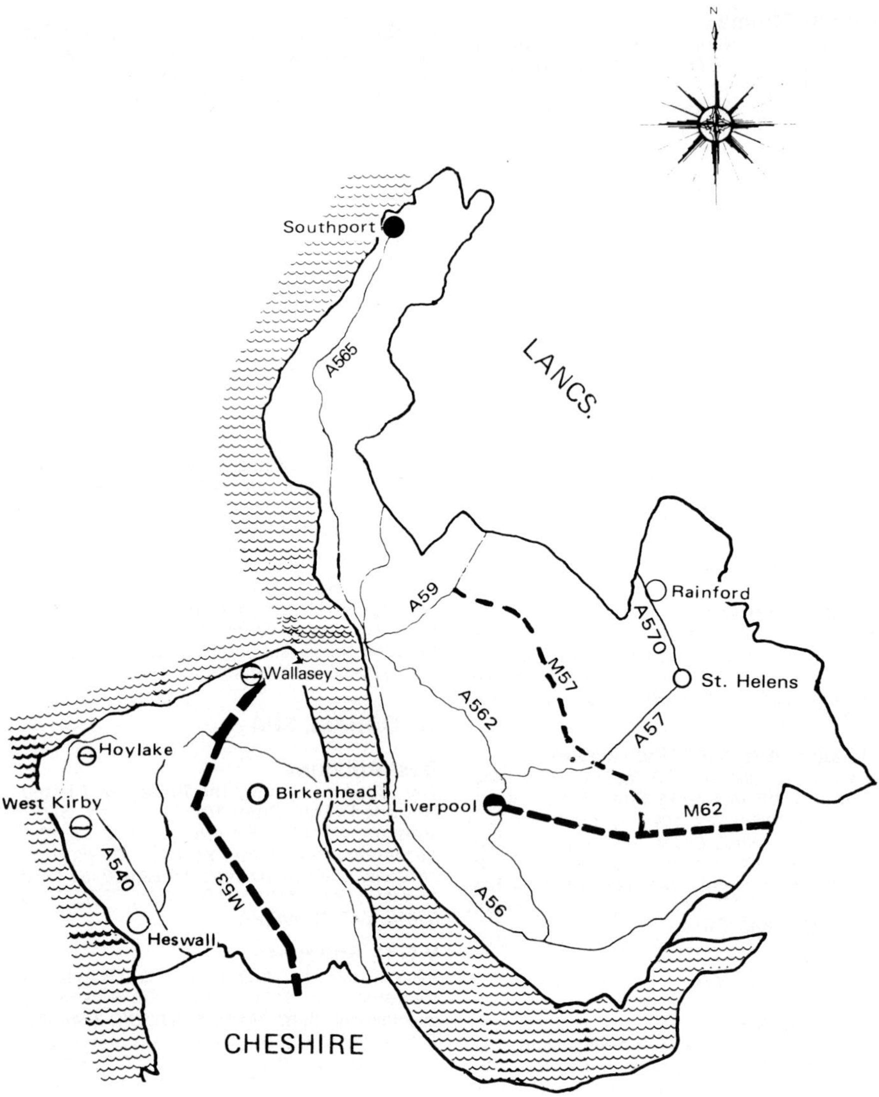

N
Southport
A565
LANCS.
Rainford
A570
A59
M57
St. Helens
Wallasey
A562
A57
Hoylake
Birkenhead
Liverpool
M62
West Kirby
A540
M53
A56
Heswall
CHESHIRE

1–2
3–5
6–12
13+
Key to number of shops in this area.

Please note this is only a rough map designed to show dealers the number of shops in the various towns, and is not necessarily totally accurate.

BIRKENHEAD

Bodhouse Antiques
379 New Chester Rd, Rock Ferry. (G and F M Antonini). Open 9-5, Sat. and Sun. by appointment. SIZE: Large. *STOCK: Furniture, 19th C, ceramics, 19th C and later, silver plated goods, 18th-20th C; all £5-£1,000+; prints and pictures, 19th C, £25-£1,000+.* LOC: 1/2 mile from Birkenhead Tunnel, A41 towards Chester. PARK: Easy. TEL: 051 644 9494; home - 051 327 6233. VAT: Stan/Spec.

William Courtney and Sons LAPADA
Cross/Chester St, Tunnel Entrance, Corner premises including 11-19 Cross St. Est: 1893. Open daily, Sun. and Thurs. p.m. by appointment. SIZE: Large. *STOCK: General antiques, shipping goods, art glass, Staffordshire figures.* PARK: Easy. TEL: 051 647 8693. VAT: Stan.

Rose Mount
2 Rose Mount. (A.J. and L Bampton) Open 10-5. *STOCK: General antiques.* TEL: 051 653 9060.

HESWALL

C Rosenberg
The Antique Shop, 120-122 Telegraph Rd. Est: 1960. Open 10-5.30. CL: Wed. p.m. *STOCK: Jewellery, silver, porcelain, objets d'art.* TEL: 051 342 1053. VAT: Stan.

HOYLAKE

The Clock Shop
7 The Quadrant. (K. and D Whay) Est: 1969. Open 10-5. *STOCK: Clocks and jewellery.* PARK: Easy. TEL: 051 632 1888. SER: Restorations (clock and jewellery repairs). VAT: Stan/Spec.

Hoylake Antique Centre
128-130 Market St. Open 9.15-5.30. *STOCK: Furniture, silver, pictures, porcelain, glass and decorative arts.* LOC: A540, in town centre. PARK: At rear. TEL: 051 632 4231.

Market Antiques
80 Market St. (W Bateman) Est: 1969. Open Thurs. and Fri. 10-1 and 2.15-5, Sat. 10-5, other times by appointment. SIZE: Medium. *STOCK: Furniture, £10-£1,000; trade and shipping goods, silver, glass, china, £2-£250; paintings, prints, £5-£500.* Not Stocked: Weapons, medals, coins. LOC: On main street in town centre A563 or A540. PARK: From Ship Inn forecourt, cars drive in, larger vehicles at rear. TEL: 051 632 4059. VAT: Stan/Spec.

Olde Englande
1 Cable Rd. South. Open 10-5. CL: Wed. p.m. *STOCK: Furniture, curios and general antiques, Victorian and Edwardian.* PARK: Easy. TEL: 051 632 4740. VAT: Stan.

LIVERPOOL

Boodle and Dunthorne Ltd
Boodles House, Lord St. Est: 1798. Open 9-5.30. SIZE: Large. *STOCK: Silver, 18th-19th C, £100-£5,000; clocks and clock-sets, mid-19th C, £200-£4,000; jewellery, Victorian and Georgian, £100-£30,000.* Not Stocked: Furniture. PARK: In Paradise St. TEL: 051 227 2525. VAT: Stan/Spec.

Philip Cowan Antiques
33 Parliament St. Open by appointment only. *STOCK: Fine English furniture, 17th-19th C; mahogany sideboards, long sets of chairs, bureaux, secretaire and breakfront bookcases, partners desks, tea, card and dining tables, linen presses, longcase clocks, settees, armchairs; oak dressers, gateleg and refectory tables, ladder and spindle back rush-seated chairs; decorative and small items.* TEL: Mobile - 0860 741043.

Delta Antiques
175/177 Smithdown Rd. (E.P Jones) Est: 1979. Open 10-12 and 1-5. CL: Sat. a.m and Wed. SIZE: Medium. *STOCK: Stripped pine, 19th C, £50+.* LOC: Ring road, city centre. PARK: Nearby. TEL: 051 734 4277; home - same. SER: Restorations; French polishing.

Edward's Jewellers
45a Whitechapel. (R.A. and E.M Lewis) FGA. Est: 1967. Open by appointment. CL: Sat. SIZE: Small. *STOCK: Jewellery, silver and plate, 19th-20th C, £50-£400.* LOC: City centre. TEL: 051 236 2909. SER: Valuations. VAT: Stan/Spec.

Kensington Tower Antiques Ltd
Christ Church, 170 Kensington. (R Swainbank) Est: 1960. Open 9-5, Sat. and Sun. by appointment. CL: Mon. SIZE: Large. *STOCK: Shipping goods, general antiques.* LOC: A57. PARK: Easy. TEL: 051 260 9466; home - 051 924 6538. VAT: Stan. *Trade Only.*

Liverpool Coin and Medal Co
68 Lime St. (L.J Ross) Est: 1977. Open 10-5. *STOCK: Coins and medals.* TEL: 051 708 8441. SER: Medal sales lists issued (S.A.E.).

Lyver & Boydell Galleries LAPADA
15 Castle St. Est: 1861. Open 10.30-5.30. CL: Sat. SIZE: Medium. *STOCK: Paintings and watercolours, 18th-20th C, £50-£10,000; maps and prints, 16th-19th C, £1-£1,500.* LOC: City centre, opposite Town Hall. PARK: Multi-storey. TEL: 051 236 3256. SER: Valuations; cleaning; framing; restorations; buys at auction. FAIRS: National. VAT: Stan/Spec.

Maggs Antiques Ltd LAPADA
26-28 Fleet St. (G Webster) Est: 1965. Open daily. *STOCK: General antiques, period and shipping smalls, £1-£1,000.* LOC: In town centre by Central station. PARK: Meters. TEL: 051 708 0221; evenings - 09285 64958. SER: Restorations; container packing, courier.

Liverpool continued

E Pryor and Son
110 London Rd. (Mr Wilding) Est: 1876. CL: Wed. *STOCK: General antiques, jewellery, Georgian and Victorian silver, pottery, porcelain, coins, clocks, paintings, ivory and carvings.* TEL: 051 709 1361. VAT: Stan.

Ryan-Wood Antiques
102 Seel St. Est: 1972. Open 9.30-5, Sat. 9.30-3 or by appointment. *STOCK: Furniture, paintings, china, silver, curios, bric-a-brac, Victoriana, Edwardiana, art deco, clothing and furs.* TEL: 051 709 7776; home - 051 709 3203. SER: Restorations. VAT: Stan.

Stefani Antiques
497 Smithdown Rd. (T Stefani) Est: 1969. Open 10-1 and 2-5. CL: Wed. SIZE: Medium. *STOCK: Furniture to 1910, £300-£1,000; jewellery, £25-£500; pottery, silver, old Sheffield plate, porcelain, bronzes.* LOC: On main road. PARK: Easy. TEL: 051 734 1933; home - 051 737 1360. SER: Valuations; restorations.

Swainbanks Ltd
Christchurch, 170 Kensington. Open 9-5 or by appointment. CL: Sat. SIZE: Large. *STOCK: Shipping goods and general antiques.* TEL: 051 260 9466/924 6538. SER: Containers. VAT: Stan.

Theta Gallery
29 and 31 Parliament St. (J Matson) Open by appointment. SIZE: Warehouse. *STOCK: General antiques, especially furniture and clocks.* TEL: 051 708 6375. *Trade Only.*

RAINFORD

Colin Stock BADA
8 Mossborough Rd. Est: 1895. Open by appointment. *STOCK: Furniture, 18th-19th C.* TEL: 074 488 2246.

ST. HELENS

Wedgwoods of St. Helens Ltd
35 Westfield St. Open 10-5. CL: Thurs. *STOCK: Fine jewellery, silver ware, antiques, old toys, coins, stamps, medals, collectables, paintings.* PARK: Nearby. TEL: 0744 55900.

SOUTHPORT

Andersons
14 Wesley St. Open 9-5. SIZE: Small. *STOCK: Watches and clocks.* LOC: Opposite Morrison's. PARK: Nearby. TEL: 0704 540024. SER: Restorations (as stock); repairs.

C.K Broadhurst and Co Ltd
5-7 Market St. Est: 1926. Open 9-5.30. *STOCK: Rare books, first editions, coloured plate books, topography.* TEL: 0704 532064/534110.

Southport continued

Churchtown Antiques
Bow Place, 1 Churchgate,, Churchtown. (R.W. and M.V Burlington) Est: 1977. Open Sat. 10.30-12.30, other times by appointment. *STOCK: General antiques, jewellery, silver and some shipping.* LOC: Close to Botanic Gardens, side of Old Smithy. PARK: Easy. TEL: 0704 536068. SER: Valuations; buys at auction.

Decor Galleries
52 Lord St. (F.D Glover) CL: Tues. *STOCK: Decorative items, furniture, 18th-19th C.* TEL: 0704 535134. VAT: Stan/Spec.

Fine Pine
19 Market St. (R. and W Griffiths) Open 10-4.30. CL: Tues. *STOCK: Pine.* TEL: 0704 538056; evenings - 0704 535720. SER: Shipping, packing and courier.

Molloy's Furnishers Ltd
6-8 St. James St. (P Molloy) Est: 1955. Open daily. SIZE: Large. *STOCK: Mahogany and oak, shipping and Edwardian furniture.* LOC: On A570, Scarisbrick new road. PARK: Easy. TEL: 0704 535204/548101; home - 0704 532857. VAT: Stan.

Osiris Antiques
104 Shakespeare St. (C. and P Wood) Est: 1983. Open 10.45-4.45, Sat. 11-5.15, Sun. by appointment. CL: Tues. SIZE: Small. *STOCK: Art nouveau and art deco, £10-£1,000; period clothing and accessories, 1850-1950, £5-£200; jewellery, 1880-1960, to £150.* LOC: Just out of town, off main road, towards motorway. PARK: Easy. TEL: 0704 500991; home - 0704 60418. SER: Valuations; buys at auction (art nouveau, art deco).

Pinocchio
Prince of Wales Buildings, 2/2a Portland St. Open 9.30-5.30, Sat. 9.15-5.45. SIZE: Medium. *STOCK: Country furniture and pine, £100-£1,000; clocks, 18th-19th C, £250-£3,000; kitchenalia and collectables, 19th-20th C, £5-£500.* LOC: By side entrance of Prince of Wales Hotel, Lord St. PARK: Nearby. TEL: 0704 535028. VAT: Stan/Spec.

The Spinning Wheel
1 Liverpool Rd, Birkdale. (R Bell) Est: 1966. Open 10-5. CL: Tues. SIZE: Small. *STOCK: General antiques, £5-£1,000+.* TEL: 0704 68245; home - 0704 67613. VAT: Stan.

Studio 41
340 Liverpool Rd, Birkdale. (B Sullivan) Open by appointment only. *STOCK: 19th and 20th C oils and watercolours.* TEL: 0704 79132. SER: Valuations; buys at auction.

Southport continued

Tony and Anne Sutcliffe Antiques
130 Cemetery Rd. and Warehouse -, 37A Linaker St. Est: 1969. Open 8.30-5, weekends by appointment. SIZE: Large. *STOCK: Shipping goods, Victorian and period furniture.* LOC: Town centre. TEL: 0704 537068; home - 0704 533465. SER: Containers; courier. VAT: Stan/Spec.

H.S Waine
183 Lord St. Open 10-5. *STOCK: Diamonds, gold, silver, jewellery.* TEL: 0704 532469.

Weldon Antiques and Jewellery
567 Lord St. (H.W. and N.C Weldon) Est: 1914. Open 9.30-5.30. SIZE: Medium. *STOCK: Furniture, clocks, watches, jewellery, silver, coins.* Not Stocked: Militaria. PARK: Easy. TEL: 0704 532191. SER: Valuations; restorations. VAT: Stan.

The White Elephant
22 Kew Rd, Birkdale. (J Wajzner) Est: 1967. *STOCK: General antiques, fine art, ethnographica, collectors' items, weapons, medals, coins, books, postcards.* TEL: 0704 60525.

WALLASEY

Arbiter
10 Atherton St, New Brighton. (W.D.L Scobie and P.D Ferrett) Resident. Est: 1983. Open 11-5, Sat. 2-5, or by appointment. CL: Mon. *STOCK: Arts and crafts movement and decorative arts, £20-£2,000; Oriental, ethnographic and antiquities, £40-£1,500; original prints and drawings, £80-£500.* LOC: Opposite New Brighton station. PARK: Easy. TEL: 051 639 1159. SER: Valuations; buys at auction; consultant.

Decade Antiques
62 Grove Rd. (A.M Duffy) Open 10.30-4.30. SIZE: Large. *STOCK: General antiques, textiles, decorative items, continental furniture.* LOC: Take A554 via promenade, turn along Harrison Drive, right to Grove Rd. TEL: 051 639 6905/8728 or 638 0433.

Harris and Holt Antiques
(S Harris) Open by appointment. *STOCK: Portraits and decorative paintings.* TEL: 051 630 4923.

Roderick Jellicoe Fine Porcelain
Open by appointment. *STOCK: Interesting 18th and early 19th C English porcelain.* TEL: 051 639 2725.

Robbies Antiques
70 Grove Rd. (R Dalby) Open 10.30-1 and 2.15-5. CL: Wed. and Sat. *STOCK: Furniture and ceramics, glass, metalware and general antiques.* TEL: 051 691 1670; home - 051 638 3848. SER: Restorations (furniture); re-upholstery.

WEST KIRBY

Helen Horswill Antiques and Decorative Arts
62 Grange Rd. Open 10-5 or by appointment. SIZE: Medium. *STOCK: Furniture, 17th-19th C; decorative items.* LOC: A540. PARK: Easy. TEL: 051 625 8660/625 2803.

Oliver Antiques
62 Grange Rd. (J.O Horswill) Open 10-5, or by appointment. SIZE: Medium. *STOCK: Furniture, 17th to early 19th C; decorative items.* LOC: A540. PARK: Easy. TEL: 051 625 7111/625 8660.

Trentini Antiques LAPADA
79 Banks Rd. (J Trentini) Open 10.30-4.30 and by appointment. CL: Wed. *STOCK: Decorative items and general antiques.* TEL: 051 625 2122.

Victoria Cottage Antiques
6 Village Rd. (Mrs C Dilger) Est: 1984. Open 10-5, Sun. and Wed. by appointment. SIZE: Medium. *STOCK: Staffordshire figures, 1790-1914, £25-£500; pottery and porcelain, 1780-1920, £10-£150; prints, from 1780, £10-£100; glass, furniture, 1800-1920, £5-£2,000.* LOC: A540 from Chester, turn left into Village Rd. at sandstone monument. PARK: Easy. TEL: 051 625 7517; home - same. SER: Valuations.

An elm stool or a child's table. Elm. Attributed to East Anglia, c.1790-1840. The base stool was made for 2/-, with the embellishment of a drawer which may be 'scratch-beaded, for a further 1/3d' This design of stool would perhaps have been used by a child for eating from, as well as writing or drawing on. The drawer would probably have been used to keep writing materials or playthings in. Flat top. Straight tapered legs and H-frame stretchers. From ***The English Regional Chair*** by Bernard D. Cotton, published by the **Antique Collectors' Club** in 1990. £49.50.

Middlesex

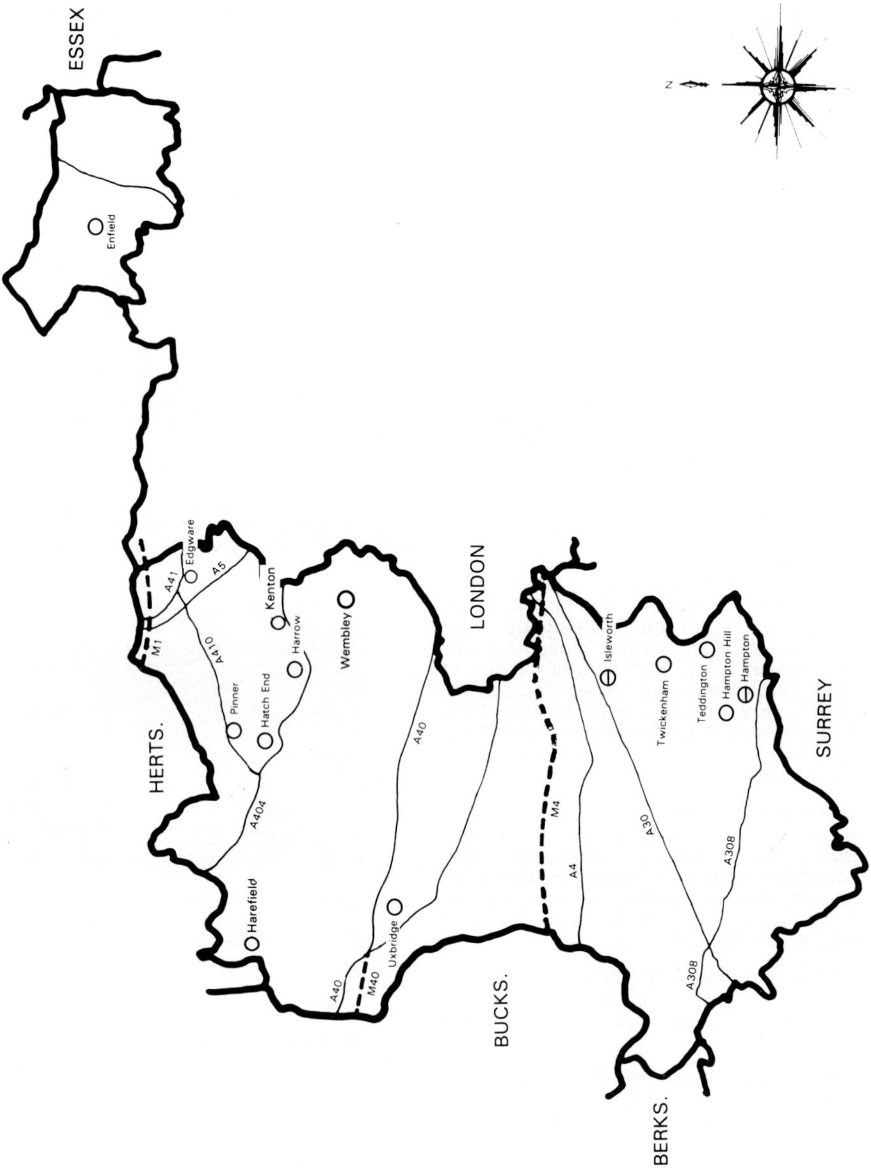
ESSEX
N
Enfield
Edgware
A41
A5
M1
A410
Kenton
Harrow
Wembley
LONDON
Pinner
Hatch End
HERTS.
A404
A40
Harefield
Uxbridge
M40
A40
BUCKS.
M4
A4
A30
Isleworth
Twickenham
Teddington
Hampton Hill
Hampton
SURREY
A308
A308
BERKS.

○ 1–2
⊖ 3–5
◒ 6–12
● 13+

Key to number of shops in this area.

Please note this is only a rough map designed to show dealers the number of shops in the various towns, and is not necessarily totally accurate.

EDGWARE

Edgware Antiques
19 Whitchurch Lane. (E Schloss) Est: 1972. Open 10-5.30. CL: Mon. and Thurs. SIZE: Medium. *STOCK: Furniture, pictures, silver and plate, brass and copper, clocks, bric-a-brac, porcelain and shipping goods.* PARK: Easy. TEL: 081 952 1606; home - 081 952 5924.

Mint & Boxed
110 High St. Open 10.30-5.30. CL: Wed. *STOCK: Antique and collectable toys, mainly automotive.* TEL: 081 952 2002; fax - 081 951 1918.

ENFIELD

Enfield Corner Cupboard
61 Chase Side. Est: 1952. Open 9-5.30, Wed. 9-1. *STOCK: Furniture, silver, china.* TEL: 081 363 6493.

La Trouvaille
1A Windmill Hill. (Mrs C.M Waring) Est: 1982. Open 9.30-5.30. CL: Wed. SIZE: Medium. *STOCK: Small general antiques, collectors' items, furniture and prints, 1800-1930.* Not Stocked: Weapons. LOC: West of town. PARK: Easy. TEL: 081 367 1080.

HAMPTON

Hampton Village Antiques Centre
76 Station Rd. (E Hatvany) Est: 1982. Open 10-5.30. SIZE: Medium - 6 dealers. *STOCK: 19th C furniture, clocks and barometers; 19th-20th C pottery and porcelain, £5-£500.* LOC: Approx. 1 mile west of Hampton Court Palace. PARK: Easy. TEL: 081 979 5871; home - 081 890 7405. SER: Restorations (metal, porcelain, pottery and clocks). FAIRS: Local.

Peco
72 Station Rd. (C.D. and E.S Taylor) Est: 1969. Open 9-1 and 2-5.15, Sat. 9-5.15. SIZE: Large. *STOCK: Doors, 18th-20th C, £50-£100; fireplaces, 18th-19th C, £100-£500.* LOC: 1 1/2 miles from Hampton Court. Turning off Hampton Court/Sunbury Rd. PARK: Own. TEL: 081 979 8310. SER: Restorations (stained glass, cast iron fireplaces, doors); stained glass made to order. VAT: Stan.

Ian Sheridan's Bookshop Hampton
Thames Villa, 34 Thames St. Est: 1960. Open 10.30-7 including Sun. SIZE: Large. *STOCK: Antiquarian and secondhand books.* LOC: 1 mile from Hampton Court Palace. TEL: 081 979 1704.

Valtone Pine
74 Station Rd. (A.P Frost) Open 10-5.30. CL: Mon. *STOCK: Pine.* TEL: 081 979 4060.

HAMPTON HILL

Hampton Hill Gallery Ltd
203 and 205 High St. *STOCK: Watercolours, drawings, prints, 18th-20th C.* TEL: 081 977 1379/5273. SER: Restorations and cleaning (watercolours, prints and paintings); mounting; framing. VAT: Stan/Spec.

HAREFIELD

The Jay's Antique Centre
25/29 High St. Open 10-6, Wed. 10-1. SIZE: 15 dealers. *STOCK: General antiques, bric-a-brac, gold and silver.* TEL: 0895 824738.

HARROW

Kathleen Mann Antiques LAPADA
49 High St. Est: 1973. Open 9-5 or by appointment. CL: Wed. SIZE: Medium. *STOCK: Furniture, 18th-19th C, £25-£3,000; decorative items, £5-£1,000.* LOC: Follow Harrow road, or take A40 turning at Greenford roundabout. PARK: Easy. TEL: 081 422 1892. SER: Buys at auction. VAT: Stan/Spec.

Winston Galleries
68 High St, Harrow Hill. (R. and P Weston) Est: 1970. Open 9.30-5.30, or by appointment. CL: Wed. *STOCK: Furniture, porcelain, 18th-19th C; general antiques, silver, plate, clocks.* TEL: 081 422 4470. VAT: Stan/Spec.

HATCH END

Yesterday's Antiques
357-359 Uxbridge Rd. (M Isenberg) Est: 1973. Open 9-3.30, Tues. and Fri. 10-3.30. CL: Wed. *STOCK: Furniture, 18th-19th C; smalls, decorators' items, painted furniture, bronzes, pictures. Mainly Trade.*

ISLEWORTH

Crowther of Syon Lodge Ltd
Busch Corner, London Rd. Open 9-5, Sat. and Sun. 11-4. SIZE: Large. *STOCK: Period panelled rooms, in pine and oak; chimneypieces in marble, stone and wood; life-sized classical bronze and marble statues; wrought iron entrance gates, garden temples, vases, seats, fountains and other statues.* LOC: Just off the A4, half-way between the West End and London Airport. TEL: 081 560 7978. VAT: Stan/Spec.

Yistelworth Antiques
1 Thornbury Rd. (C.A Gibbs) CL: Mon. *STOCK: General furniture, clocks, pictures, collectables.* LOC: Near Osterley Park, off A4. PARK: Easy. TEL: 081 847 5429.

Mainie Jellett. *Horses Grazing.* National Gallery of Ireland. From ***A Free Spirit — Irish Art 1860-1960*** by Kenneth McConkey, published by the **Antique Collectors' Club** in 1990. £29.50.

Isleworth continued

Yistelworth Antiques

13 Shrewsbury Walk, South St, Old Isleworth. (C.A Gibbs) Est: 1978. Open 10-5.30, Sun. 11.30-3.30. CL: Wed. SIZE: Medium. *STOCK: Furniture, 19th-20th C, £50-£1,000; china, £5-£200; pictures, £25-£500; both 18th-20th C.* LOC: Off Twickenham Rd. at clock tower, shop in square off rear of Castle public house. PARK: Easy. TEL: 081 847 5429; home - 081 560 7793. SER: Valuations.

KENTON, Nr. Harrow

Keith Finch

61 Alicia Ave. Open by appointment only. *STOCK: English furniture and works of art, 18th-19th C.* TEL: 081 907 7655.

PINNER

Artbry's Antiques

44 High St. (A.H Davies and B.E Hill) Est: 1969. Open 9-5.30. CL: Wed. p.m. SIZE: Medium. *STOCK: Furniture, £100-£5,000; crystal, £50-£250; both 18th-19th C; clocks, all types, £50-£3,000; paintings, 17th-19th C, £20-£2,000.* LOC: From Harrow School through Harrow. PARK: Easy. TEL: 081 868 0834. SER: Valuations; restorations (clocks). VAT: Stan/Spec.

Pinner continued

Pinner Antiques

2 East Towers. Open by appointment. *STOCK: General furniture, porcelain, silver, prints.* TEL: 081 866 5546; workshop - 0895 422467.

TEDDINGTON

J.W Crisp Antiques

166 High St. (E Gould and and M Murren) Open 11-4, Sat. 11-3. CL: Wed. *STOCK: Furniture, porcelain and objets d'art, watercolours and oil paintings.* TEL: 081 977 4309. SER: Restorations; French polishing.

TWICKENHAM

Ailsa Gallery

32 Crown Rd. (C.A Wiltshire) Open Thurs., Fri. and Sat. 10-5, other times by appointment. SIZE: Small. *STOCK: Paintings, 19th-20th C, £200-£3,000; bronze, decorative arts, small furniture, silver and glass.* LOC: Off St. Margarets Rd., near station. PARK: Easy. TEL: 081 891 2345; home - 081 892 0188. SER: Buys at auction.

Alberts Cigarette Card Specialists

113 London Rd. (J.A Wooster) Open 10-6, Sat. 10-4. CL: Mon. *STOCK: Original cigarette cards; accessories, film mobilia, Victorian prints, magazines, hand-painted model soldiers, working steam models..* TEL: 081 891 3067. SER: Mail order; shipping; framing; catalogue.

Twickenham continued

Rodney Cook Antiques

58 Richmond Rd. Est: 1969. Open 9.30-6. SIZE: Large. *STOCK: Furniture, pre-1900, £5-£500.* Not Stocked: Silver, jewellery. LOC: 1 mile from Richmond Bridge on main Richmond-Twickenham Rd. TEL: 081 892 6884. VAT: Stan.

Anthony C Hall

30 Staines Rd. Est: 1966. Open 9-5.30. CL: Wed. p.m. and Sat. SIZE: Medium. *STOCK: Antiquarian books.* PARK: Easy. TEL: 081 898 2638.

John Ives Bookseller

5 Normanhurst Drive, St. Margarets. Resident. Est: 1977. Open by appointment at any time. SIZE: Medium. *STOCK: Scarce and out of print books on antiques and collecting, £1-£500.* LOC: Normanhurst Drive is off St. Margarets Rd. near its junction with Chertsey Rd. PARK: Easy. TEL: 081 892 6265. SER: Valuations (as stock).

Marble Hill Gallery

70/72 Richmond Rd. (D. and L Newson) Est: 1974. Open 10-5.30. *STOCK: Victorian watercolours and fireside furniture, French marble mantels, and pine and white Adam style mantels.* LOC: Richmond-Twickenham rd. PARK: Easy. TEL: 081 892 1488. VAT: Stan/Spec.

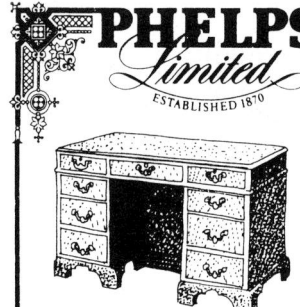

Twickenham continued

David Morley Antiques
371 Richmond Rd. Est: 1968. Open 10-5. CL: Wed. SIZE: Medium. *STOCK:* Not Stocked: Large furniture. LOC: Approx. 200yds. from Richmond Bridge. PARK: In side road (adjacent to shop). TEL: 081 892 2986.

Phelps Ltd LAPADA
133-135 St. Margarets Rd. (R.C Phelps) Est: 1870. Open 9-1 and 2-5.30, Sat. 9-5. SIZE: Large. *STOCK: Victorian and Edwardian furniture and shipping goods.* LOC: Adjacent St. Margaret's station. PARK: Easy. TEL: 081 892 1778/7129. SER: Restorations. VAT: Stan/Spec.

Rita Shenton
148 Percy Rd. Est: 1973. Open by appointment only. SIZE: Medium. *STOCK: Clocks, watches, barometers, automata and ornamental turning books, £1-£1,000.* LOC: Continuation of Whitton High St. PARK: Easy. TEL: 081 894 6888. SER: Valuations; buys at auction (horological books, clocks); catalogues available. *Mainly postal.*

Neil Willcox
113 Strawberry Vale. Open by appointment. *STOCK: Wine, apothecary, medical and other bottles, British and continental, 17th to mid 19th C.* TEL: 081 892 5858 (24 hrs.). SER: Mail order, photos supplied; prop hire; valuations.

Twickenham continued

Zafer
36 Church St. (R.D Zafer) Est: 1971. Open 10-5.30. CL: Wed. SIZE: Small. *STOCK: Jewellery and furniture, £10-£2,000; clocks, £50-£2,000; silver, £10-£300; chairs/sofa frames, £50-£400; all from 17th C.* Not Stocked: Porcelain and early glass. LOC: Off Twickenham High St., parallel to river. TEL: 081 891 3183. SER: Valuations; restorations (upholstery). VAT: Stan.

UXBRIDGE

Antiques Warehouse (Uxbridge)
34-36 Rockingham Rd. Est: 1966. Open 10-6. SIZE: Large. *STOCK: General antiques, shipping items, £1-£4,000.* PARK: Easy. TEL: 0895 56963/71012. VAT: Stan.

Thomas Barnard (A.B.A.)
11 Windsor St. Est: 1944. Open 9.30-5. CL: Wed. *STOCK: General antiquarian books; prints, maps, pictures.* TEL: 0895 58054. SER: Bookbinding, framing.

WEMBLEY

L Kelaty Ltd
Kelaty House, First Way. Est: 1954. Open 8-6, Fri. 8-5. CL: Sat. *STOCK: Rugs and carpets.* TEL: 081 903 9998.

Norfolk

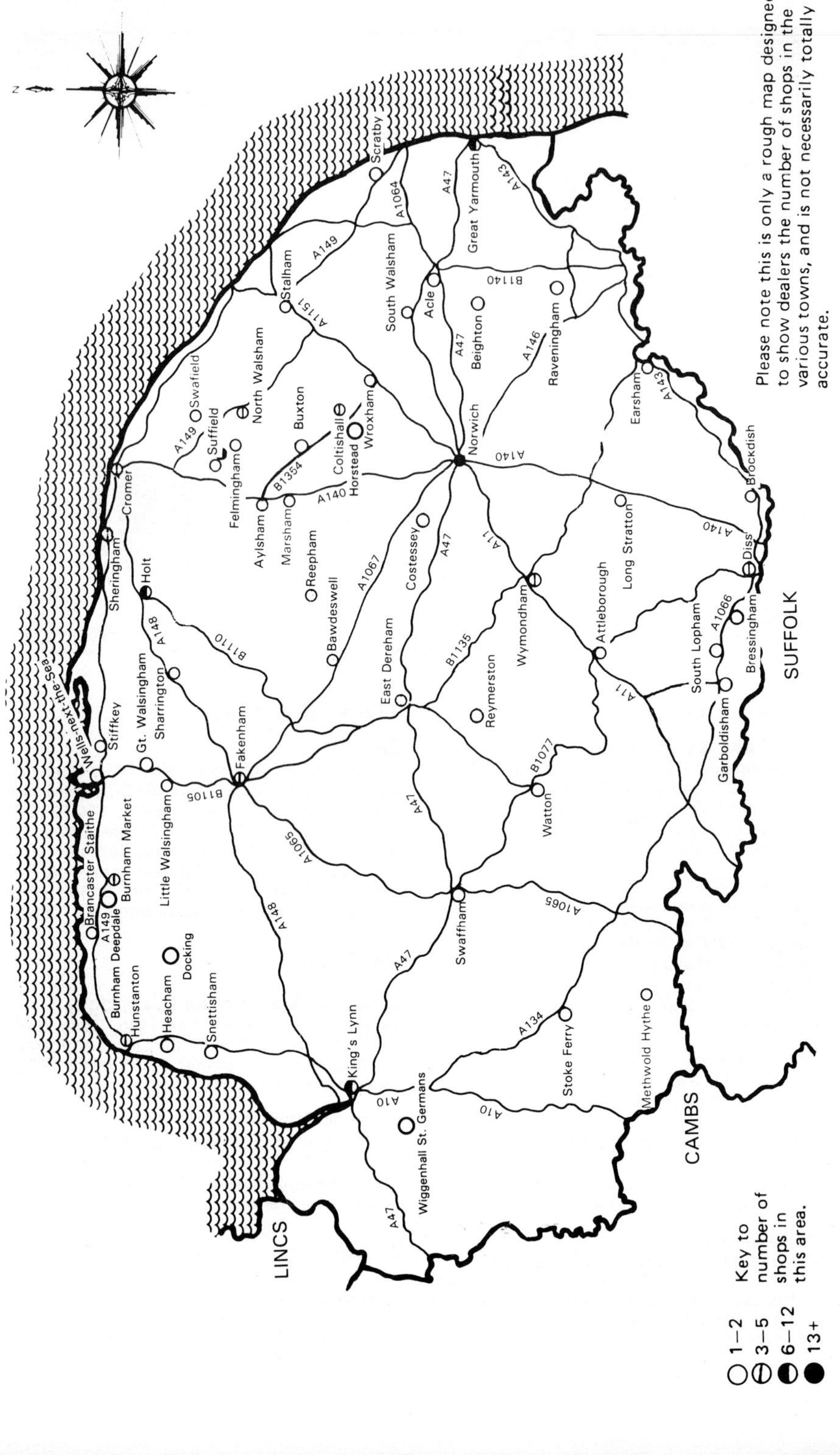

N
Scratby
Great Yarmouth
A47
A143
A1064
A149
Stalham
South Walsham
Acle
B1140
A1151
Beighton
Raveningham
A47
A146
Swafield
North Walsham
Buxton
Wroxham
Coltishall
Horstead
Suffield
A149
Cromer
Felmingham
B1354
Aylsham
Marsham
A140
Norwich
A140
Earsham
A143
Brockdish
Sheringham
Holt
Reepham
Costessey
A47
A11
Long Stratton
A140
Diss
A1067
Bawdeswell
Wymondham
Attleborough
A148
B1110
B1135
Reymerston
A1066
Bressingham
South Lopham
SUFFOLK
Wells-next-the-Sea
Stiffkey
Gt. Walsingham
Sharrington
Fakenham
East Dereham
A11
Garboldisham
B1077
Watton
Brancaster Staithe
Burnham Market
Little Walsingham
B1105
A47
A1065
A149
Burnham Deepdale
Docking
Swaffham
A1065
A148
Hunstanton
Heacham
Snettisham
King's Lynn
A47
A134
Stoke Ferry
Methwold Hythe
A10
A10
Wiggenhall St. Germans
A47
CAMBS
LINCS
Please note this is only a rough map designed to show dealers the number of shops in the various towns, and is not necessarily totally accurate.
Key to number of shops in this area.
1–2
3–5
6–12
13+

ACLE, Nr. Norwich

Ivy House Antiques
Ivy House, The Street. (N Pratt) Est: 1970. Open 9-5. SIZE: Small. *STOCK: Furniture, porcelain, pottery, glass, metalware, 18th-20th C, £25-£2,000; pictures, 19th C; garden furniture, 19th-20th C, both £50-£500.* LOC: Village centre. PARK: Easy. TEL: 0493 750682; home - same. SER: Valuations. FAIRS: Norwich. VAT: Stan/Spec.

Lion Antiques
The Old Sale Ring, Cattle Market. (F Wright) Est: 1947. Open 8.30-5.30, Sat. by appointment only. *STOCK: Furniture, £25-£250; bric-a-brac, from £5, all Victorian to 1930.* LOC: On A47, opposite church. PARK: Easy. TEL: 0493 751836. SER: Restorations (furniture).

ATTLEBOROUGH

A.E Bush and Partners
Vineyards, Leys Lane. (A.G., M.S. and J.A Becker) Est: 1940. Open 9-1 and 2-5.30. *STOCK: Pine and mahogany, 18th-19th C.* LOC: Town outskirts. PARK: Easy. TEL: 0953 454239/452175. SER: Restorations; export and storage; buys at auction. VAT: Stan/Spec.

AYLSHAM

Sheila Hart and John Giles
Open by appointment. *STOCK: Furniture, £200-£5,000; objects, £50-£1,000; all mainly 19th C.* TEL: 0263 768216. FAIRS: Olympia. VAT: Stan/Spec. *Trade Only.*

Pearse Lukies
Bayfield House, White Hart St. Open preferably by appointment. *STOCK: Period oak, sculpture, objects, 18th C furniture.* TEL: 0263 734137. *Trade Only.*

BAWDESWELL, Nr. East Dereham

Norfolk Polyphon Centre
Wood Farm. (N.B Vince) Open weekends, week days preferably by appointment. *STOCK: Mechanical music - polyphons, cylinder musical boxes, organs, orchestrions, automata.* LOC: On B1145, 1 mile east of Bawdeswell village and junction with A1067. TEL: 036 288 230. VAT: Stan/Spec.

BEIGHTON, Nr. Norwich

Old White House Antiques
Denco, Lingwood Rd. (D Hatch) Open by appointment. *STOCK: Furniture.* TEL: 0493 751726. *Trade Only.*

BRANCASTER STAITHE, Nr. King's Lynn

Brancaster Staithe Antiques
Coast Rd. (M.J Wilson) Open every day including Sun. *STOCK: Victorian tables, chairs; oak, unusual pine, bookpresses, art deco.* TEL: 0485 210600.

BRESSINGHAM, Nr. Diss

David Bateson Antiques
Lodge Farm. (D. and P Bateson) Est: 1966. Open by appointment. SIZE: Medium. *STOCK: Country furniture.* LOC: 1 1/2 miles north of Bressingham off A1066 from Diss. PARK: Easy. TEL: 037 988 629. SER: Valuations.

BROCKDISH, Nr. Diss

Brockdish Antiques
Commerce House. (M. and L.E Palfrey) Est: 1975. Open 9-5.30. CL: Wed. *STOCK: Furniture.* LOC: A143. TEL: 037 975 498. SER: Restorations; re-upholstery.

Eekhout Gallery
Rosebrook, Grove Rd. Est: 1964. Open daily by prior appointment. SIZE: Small. *STOCK: Paintings and prints.* LOC: Off A143 Scole to Bungay road, opposite the Green. PARK: Easy. TEL: 037 975 575. SER: Restorations.

BURNHAM DEEPDALE

Steed-Croft Antiques
West End. (J.M Tate) Open Mon., Wed., Fri. and Sat.. *STOCK: Period furniture, decorative items.* TEL: 0485 210812. SER: Interior design.

BURNHAM MARKET

M. and A Cringle
The Old Black Horse. Est: 1965. Open 10-1 and 2-5. CL: Wed. SIZE: Medium. *STOCK: 18th and early 19th C furniture, £50-£2,000; china, glass, pottery, prints, maps, £10-£500.* Not Stocked: Large furniture, Oriental and continental antiques, reproductions. LOC: In village centre. PARK: Easy. TEL: 0328 738456. VAT: Spec.

Anne Hamilton Antiques
North St. (A Hudson) Open 10-1 and 2-5. CL: Wed. SIZE: Medium. *STOCK: Georgian furniture; porcelain, decorative items.* LOC: 20yds. from village green towards coast. PARK: Easy. TEL: 0328 738187. VAT: Stan/Spec.

Burnham Market continued

Market House **BADA**
(J Maufe) Resident. Open 10-6 or by appointment. SIZE: Medium. *STOCK: English furniture - walnut, mahogany, rosewood and some oak, late 17th to mid-19th C, £25-£20,000; works of art, mirrors, small decorative items, some porcelain.* Not Stocked: Silver, jewellery. LOC: B1355, large Queen Anne house on green in village centre. PARK: Easy. TEL: 0328 738475. SER: Valuations; buys at auction. VAT: Spec.

BUXTON, Nr. Norwich

Bygones of Buxton
The Wheatcroft, Mill St. (D Virgo) Resident. Usually open. *STOCK: Porcelain, brass, copper, glass.* PARK: Easy. TEL: 060 546 212.

COLTISHALL

Eric Bates and Sons
High St. Est: 1973. Open 9-5.30. SIZE: Large. *STOCK: General antiques, Georgian, Victorian, Edwardian and shipping furniture.* TEL: 0603 738716. SER: Restorations (furniture); upholstery; container packing. VAT: Stan/Spec.

Roger Bradbury Antiques
Church St. Est: 1967. Open by appointment. *STOCK: Fine period furniture, Nanking cargo, objets d'art.* PARK: Easy. TEL: 0603 737444. VAT: Stan.

Coltishall Antiques Centre
High St. (I Ford) Est: 1980. Open 10-5. SIZE: Large - several specialists. *STOCK: A wide variety of items including porcelain and pottery, silver, jewellery, collectors' items, militaria, glass, Oriental porcelain, plated cutlery, clocks and Georgian, Victorian and Edwardian furniture.* LOC: B1150 on corner of main street. PARK: Easy. TEL: 0603 738306. SER: Valuations; restorations (pottery and porcelain, furniture, objets de vertu, clocks and watches, barometers and upholstery).

Gwendoline Golder
Point House, High St. Est: 1974. Open 11-5. CL: Wed. and Sun., except by appointment. *STOCK: General antiques and collectors' items.* PARK: Easy. TEL: 0603 738099.

Isabel Neal Cabinet Antiques
Bank House, High St. Est: 1968. Open 9.30-5.30. SIZE: Small. *STOCK: Porcelain, pottery, especially blue and white, 17th-20th C; small furniture, watercolours, copper, brass, pewter, collectors' items.* LOC: B1150 towards North Walsham, shop on right. PARK: Easy. TEL: 0603 737379.

COSTESSEY, Nr. Norwich

The Coach House
Townhouse Rd, Old Costessey. (J Hines) Resident. Open by appointment. *STOCK: Modern British paintings; drawings, Victorian watercolours and post-war artists; original prints, etchings, engravings; Baxter and Le Blond.* TEL: 0603 742977. SER: Cleaning prints and watercolours; framing.

CROMER

Bond Street Antiques (Inc. Jas. J. Briggs Est. 1820)
6 Bond St, and 38 Church St. (M.R.T. and J.A Jones) NAG, FGA. Est: 1958. Open 9-1 and 2.15-5.30, Sat. 9-6, Sun. by appointment. SIZE: Medium. *STOCK: Jewellery, silver, porcelain, china, glass, small furniture, 18th-20th C, £50-£5,000.* LOC: From Church St. bear right to Post Office, shop on opposite side on street further along. PARK: Easy. TEL: 0263 513134; home - same. SER: Valuations; restorations (watches and jewellery); gem testing and analysis. VAT: Stan.

Benjamin Rust Antiques
3 St. Margaret's Rd. *STOCK: Furniture, 18th and 19th C, glass, clocks and decorative items.* LOC: Near Norwich Rd. traffic lights. PARK: Own. TEL: 0263 511452. SER: Restorations. VAT: Spec.

A.E Seago
15 Church St. (D.C Seago) Est: 1937. Open 9-1 and 2-5.15. CL: Sun. and Wed. October to April. SIZE: Small. *STOCK: Furniture, 1790-1910, £25-£2,500.* Not Stocked: Silver, garden furniture, oil paintings. LOC: From Sheringham take main coast road, then New St. into High St. PARK: Easy. 50 yds away around church. TEL: 0263 512733. SER: Valuations. VAT: Stan/Spec.

DISS

Diss Antiques **LAPADA**
2 Market Pl. Open 9-1 and 2-5, or by appointment. SIZE: Large. *STOCK: Furniture, barometers, clocks, porcelain, copper, brass.* PARK: Nearby. TEL: 0379 642213; home - 0379 651369. SER: Restorations; restoration materials; export facilities. VAT: Stan/Spec.

Gostling's Antique Centre
13 Market Hill. Open 10-5, Thurs. 10-7, Sun. by appointment. LOC: Town centre, next to Barclays Bank. PARK: Easy. TEL: 0379 650360; after hours - 870367. SER: Valuations; restorations (furniture, clocks and musical boxes). VAT: Stan/Spec. The following are some of the dealers at this centre.

Dennis Chatton
General antiques and small furniture.

Gostling's Antique Centre continued

Corinthian Antiques
Furniture, pictures.
John Crawford
Books, especially relating to both World Wars.
Angela and Brian Grove
General arts, china, porcelain, furniture.
Michael Howe
Books.
Jackie Lane
Country furniture, china, porcelain.
Norah Mayor
Jewellery.
Mrs Netschor
Country oak, early mahogany, prints and paintings.
George Norman
Small and interesting items.
Raymond Norman
Longcase clocks, Victorian and Georgian furniture, music boxes and polyphons.
Vera Sutton
General antiques, porcelain, glass and furniture, 18th-19th C; textiles and decorative objects.

Heywood Antiques and Shipping Co
Unit 3-4, Station Buildings, Burston. (T Hayes and D Rand) Open 9-6. *STOCK: Pine, mahogany, general antiques, bric-a-brac, shipping.* TEL: 0379 740363; fax - 0379 740917. SER: Packing, courier and container facilities.

DOCKING

Dingle Hall Antiques
Brancaster Rd. (A.M Murray) Open 10-5. SIZE: Medium. *STOCK: Jewellery, including costume; plate, porcelain, some furniture.* PARK: Easy. TEL: 04858 675. FAIRS: Alexandra Palace, Newark Showground.

EARSHAM, Nr. Bungay

Earsham Hall Pine
Earsham Hall. (J Derham) Est: 1966. Open 8-5, Sat. and Sun. 10-5. SIZE: Large. *STOCK: Pine furniture.* LOC: On Earsham to Hedenham Rd. PARK: Easy. TEL: 0986 893423; fax - 0986 895656. SER: Container service.

EAST DEREHAM

Dereham Antiques
9 Norwich St. (M. and T Fanthorpe) Est: 1969. Open 10-5. CL: Mon. and Wed. *STOCK: Jewellery, china, glass, small silver items, paintings, furniture.* PARK: Nearby. TEL: 0362 693200.

FAKENHAM

Bygones
6 Norwich Rd. (Mrs S Rivett) Est: 1969. Open 10-1. *STOCK: General antiques and bygones.* LOC: On Norwich Rd. into Fakenham. TEL: 0328 862924; home - 0263 860462.

Fakenham Antique Centre
Old Congregational Chapel, 14 Norwich Rd. (B.D Brewster) Est: 1972. Open 10-5, Thurs. 9-5. SIZE: Large. LOC: Turn off A148 at roundabout to town, turn right at traffic lights, to town centre past Post Office, turn left, centre 50yds. on right. PARK: Easy. TEL: 0328 862941; home - 0263 860543. SER: Restoration (furniture and clocks); polishing. Below are listed the dealers at this centre.

Lesley Adams
Pine and satin walnut. TEL: 0263 713089.
Grace Aldiss
Small furniture, plate and porcelain. TEL: 036 281 239.
William Bennett
Art nouveau glass, china, collectables, small furniture.
Janet Boon
Linen, china, glass and small furniture. TEL: 055 386 229.
Avril Brewster
China, glass, plate, small furniture. TEL: 0263 860543.
Brian Brewster
Furniture, Georgian, Victorian and Edwardian. TEL: 0263 860543.
Gilbert and Edna Briere
Decorative and unusual items, period furniture and pictures. TEL: 0263 732651.
Tony Grover
Clocks, Victorian and Edwardian furniture. TEL: 095 383 654.
Joan Ashton Hall
Victorian and Georgian furniture; decorative items. TEL: 048 58 389.
Rachel Hay
General antiques. TEL: 0553 765432.
Winifred Hunka
Oriental and English porcelain and glass. TEL: 026 371 2667.
Geoff and Lada Kirk
Country furniture, watercolours, Eastern rugs. TEL: 0603 871450.
John Othen
Books mostly Norfolk fieldsports and countryside; ephemera. TEL: 036284 865.
Alfred Vincent
Furniture, Victorian and Edwardian. TEL: 0760 755583.
Joyce Waymouth
General antiques. TEL: 0553 768829.

Market Place Antiques
28 Upper Market Pl. (J Hannent and L.I Wells) Open 10-5, Wed. 10-1. *STOCK: Furniture, porcelain including Doulton, Victorian jewellery, pictures, curios.*

FELMINGHAM, Nr. North Walsham

Solus Marketing (Norfolk)
Cromer Rd. (J.A Ayers) Est: 1973. *STOCK: Silver.* TEL: 0692 402042. *Export Only.*

GARBOLDISHAM, Nr.Diss

Swan House Country Antiques
Hopton Rd. (B Greenway) Open Thurs., Fri. and Sat. 10-5, other times by appointment. *STOCK: Pine, elm, oak and country furniture, copper, brass items and lamps; fireplace accessories and decorators' items; country bygones.* PARK: Own. TEL: 095 381 8188.

GT. WALSINGHAM

Mrs Joan Morton
Open by appointment. *STOCK: Watercolours, 1880-1960.* TEL: 0328 820855.

GT. YARMOUTH

Barry's Antiques
35 King St. Open 9-5.30. SIZE: Large. *STOCK: Jewellery, porcelain, clocks, glass, pictures.* LOC: In main shopping street. PARK: Opposite. TEL: 0493 842713. VAT: Stan/Spec.

David Ferrow
77 Howard St. South. ABA. Est: 1940. Open 9.30-1 and 2.30-5.30, Sat. 9.30-5.30. Telephone call advisable. CL: Thurs. SIZE: Large. *STOCK: Books, some antiquarian maps, local prints, manuscripts.* LOC: From London over river bridge, keep to nearside, turn left and then right to car park. PARK: Easy. TEL: 0493 843800; home - 0493 662247. SER: Valuations; restorations (books and prints). VAT: Stan.

The Ferrow Family Antiques LAPADA
6 and 7 Hall Quay, also 1 George St. Est: 1957. Open 9.15-5.30. *STOCK: General antiques, £50-£5,000.* Not Stocked: Guns, medals, coins, jewellery. LOC: Near Haven Bridge, off A12. TEL: 0493 855391; home - 0493 442093. SER: Valuations; restorations; buys at auction; hire. VAT: Stan/Spec.

Folkes Antiques and Jewellers
74 Victoria Arcade. (Mrs J Baldry) Est: 1946. Open 10-1 and 2-4.30. CL: Thurs. in winter. *STOCK: General antiques especially jewellery and collectables.* LOC: From A47 into town centre, shop on right. PARK: Easy. TEL: 0493 851354. SER: Valuations. FAIRS: Local collectors.

Gold and Silver Exchange
Theatre Plain. (C Birch) Open 9.30-5.15. *STOCK: Coins, medals and secondhand jewellery.* TEL: 0493 859430.

Gt. Yarmouth continued

The Haven Gallery LAPADA
6/7 Hall Quay. (M., J. and P Ferrow) Open 9.15-5.30. *STOCK: Watercolours, drawings, prints, oil paintings, 19th C, £10-£6,000.* LOC: Near Haven Bridge, off A12. TEL: 0493 855391; home - 0493 442093. SER: Valuations, restorations (framing, collections). VAT: Stan/Spec.

John Howkins Antiques
137 and 138 King St. (J.G Howkins) Est: 1973. Open by appointment only. SIZE: Large. *STOCK: Furniture and smalls, 18th to early 20th C, £5-£5,000.* LOC: Main shopping street. PARK: Easy. TEL: 0493 855330; home - 0493 853620/857065. SER: Valuations; restorations (furniture, clocks, upholstery); buys at auction. VAT: Stan/Spec.

Peter Howkins
39, 40, 41 and 135 King St. Est: 1946. Open 9-5.30. SIZE: Large. *STOCK: At 135 King St. - jewellery, Victorian to present day, £5-£5,000; silver, George III to present day, £1-£2,000; at 39 and 40 King St. - furniture, upholstery, Georgian to Victorian, £5-£5,000; at 41 King St. - investment antiques.* LOC: From Norwich through town one-way system to road signposted Lowestoft which intersects King St. PARK: Easy. TEL: 0493 844639. SER: Valuations; restorations (jewellery, special upholstery, silver, gold, furniture). FAIRS: Norwich, Snape and Gt. Yarmouth.

Wheatleys
16 Northgate St, White Horse Plain, and Fullers Hill. Est: 1971. Open 9.30-5, Thurs. 9.30-1. SIZE: Large. *STOCK: Jewellery and general antiques.* LOC: 2 minutes walk from Market Place. PARK: Easy. TEL: 0493 857219. VAT: Stan.

HEACHAM, Nr. King's Lynn

Peter Robinson
Pear Tree House, 7 Lynn Rd. Est: 1880. Open 9-5. Appointment advisable Mon. and Sat. SIZE: Medium. *STOCK: Furniture, 1600-1900, £10-£5,000; china, 1750-1900, metalwork, 1700-1870, both £2-£1,000.* Not Stocked: Late shipping goods. LOC: Shop on left on entry to village. PARK: Easy. TEL: 0485 70228. SER: Valuations; buys at auction. VAT: Stan/Spec.

HOLT

Collectors Cabin
7 Cromer Rd. (J.M.E Codling) Est: 1983. Open 10-1 and 2-4.30. CL: Thurs. p.m. SIZE: Small. *STOCK: Bric-a-brac, bygones, toys, 19th C, £5-£25.* LOC: Near Post Office. PARK: Bull St. TEL: 0263 712241.

Holt continued

R.L Cook
10 Heathfield Rd, High Kelling. Est: 1950. Open by appointment. *STOCK: Antiquarian books.* TEL: 0263 711163.

Dingle Hall Antiques
12 Chapel Yard, Albert St. (A.M Murray) Est: 1966. Open 10-5. SIZE: Medium. *STOCK: Jewellery, including costume; plate, porcelain, some furniture.* LOC: Next to central car park. PARK: Easy. TEL: 0263 712975; home - 0553 810193. SER: Valuations; restorations (furniture, jewellery); re-caning. FAIRS: Alexandra Palace and Newark Showground.

Golden Oldies
29 Norwich Rd. (C.A Wilkins) Open 10-5. CL: Thurs. *STOCK: Victorian and Edwardian furniture, bric-a-brac, china, glass, silver, brass, copper and stripped pine.* TEL: 0263 713614. SER: Buys at auction.

Simon Gough Books
5 Fish Hill. Est: 1976. Open 9.30-5. *STOCK: Antiquarian and secondhand books; bindings.* TEL: 0263 712650.

Humbleyard Fine Art
3 Fish Hill. (J.D Layte) Est: 1971. Open 10-5. CL: Fri. SIZE: Medium. *STOCK: Scientific and medical instruments, 1700-1900, £5-£2,000; paintings, 1850-1950, £30-£500; samplers, corkscrews, small furniture, pottery, nautical and unusual items, non painted pictures.* PARK: Easy. TEL: 0263 713362. SER: Valuations; restorations (watercolours, prints); buys at auction (paintings and instruments). FAIRS: Olympia. VAT: Spec.

In the Picture (The Golf Collection)
16 Chapel Yard. (T. and D Groves) Open 9.30-5. SIZE: Medium. *STOCK: Decorative prints, limited editions, maps, sporting (especially golf), £5-£500.* PARK: Easy. TEL: 0263 713720/822265; home - 0263 82478; fax - 0263 822097. SER: Golf collection by appointment (catalogue). VAT: Stan.

Richard Scott Antiques
30 High St. Est: 1967. Open 10-1 and 2-5. CL: Thurs. SIZE: Medium. *STOCK: Pottery and porcelain, rare and unusual objects, furniture.* LOC: On A148. PARK: Easy. TEL: 0263 712479. SER: Valuations; conservation advice. VAT: Stan.

HORSTEAD, Nr. Coltishall

Liz Allport-Lomax
Open by appointment only. *STOCK: Objets de vertu, collectors' items, porcelain, pottery and silver, 18th-19th C; glass, watercolours and oils, all £5-£1,000; copper, brass and furniture, 19th C, £5-£2,000.* TEL: 0603 737631.

HUNSTANTON

Delawood Antiques
10 Westgate. (Mrs J.E Woodhouse) Est: 1975. Open 10-5 or by appointment. CL: Mon., Tues. and Thurs. SIZE: Small. *STOCK: General antiques, furniture, jewellery, collectors' items, £1-£1,000.* LOC: Near town centre and bus station. PARK: Easy. TEL: 0485 532903; home - same. SER: Valuations.

Old Bakery Antiques
1 Church St. Est: 1968. Open 11-1 and 2-4. CL: Thurs. and Fri. SIZE: Small. *STOCK: Small items, Victorian and Edwardian; embroideries, Staffordshire figures.* PARK: Easy. TEL: Home - 0485 210396. FAIRS: Snape and Bury St. Edmunds.

R.C Woodhouse (Antiquarian Horologist)
10 Westgate. MBHI and BWCG. Est: 1975. CL: Mon., Tues. and Thurs. except by appointmnt. SIZE: Small. *STOCK: Georgian, Victorian and Edwardian longcase, dial, wall and mantle clocks; some watches.* LOC: Near town centre and bus station. PARK: Easy. TEL: 0485 532903; home - same. SER: Valuations; restorations (longcase, bracket, chimney, carriage, French); church and stable clocks locally.

KING'S LYNN

Tim Clayton Jewellery
23 Chapel St. Open 9-5. *STOCK: Jewellery, clocks, watches, furniture and pictures, pre 1900.* TEL: 0553 772329. SER: Restorations (silver); bespoke jewellery made to order.

Norfolk Galleries
Railway Rd. (B Houchen and G.R Cumbley) Open 8.30-5.30, Sat. by appointment. *STOCK: Victorian and Edwardian furniture.* PARK: Nearby. TEL: 0553 765060.

Old Curiosity Shop
25 St. James St. (Mrs R.S Wright) Est: 1980. Open 10.30-5, Sat. 9.30-6. SIZE: Small. *STOCK: General collectable smalls, glass, clothing, linen, jewellery, lighting, art deco and nouveau, furniture, prints, stripped pine and paintings, pre 1930, £1-£500.* LOC: Off Saturday market place towards London Rd. PARK: At rear or nearby. TEL: 0553 766591. FAIRS: Alexandra Palace, Newark and local.

The Old Granary Antique and Collectors Centre
King Staithe Lane, off Queens St. Open 10-5. *STOCK: China, glass, books, silver, jewellery, brass, copper, postcards, linen, some furniture, and general antiques.* PARK: Easy. TEL: 0553 775509.

King's Lynn continued

Silverton Antiques
23 Chapel St. (Mrs S Clayton) Open 9-5. *STOCK: Glass, porcelain, clocks, furniture and paintings.* TEL: 0553 772329. SER: Restorations (clocks).

Tower Gallery
Middleton Tower. (T.H. and J Barclay) Est: 1963. SIZE: Large. *STOCK: General antiques including furniture, china, glass, silver, prints, pictures.* LOC: One mile off A47. PARK: Easy. TEL: 0553 840203/840581.

LITTLE WALSINGHAM

Howard Fears t/a Pilgrim's Progress
51 High St. Always available. *STOCK: Antiquarian and secondhand books, ephemera, stamps, prints.* SER: Buys at auction.

LONG STRATTON

Old Coach House
Ipswich Rd. Est: 1976. Open 10-1 and 2-5. CL: Mon. *STOCK: General antiques, pine, Victorian and Edwardian export furniture, paintings, copper, brass, china.* TEL: 0508 30942.

MARSHAM

L.W Pead
The Highlands, High St. Est: 1969. Open by appointment. *STOCK: General antiques.* TEL: 0263 732841; home - 0263 732292.

METHWOLD HYTHE

The Hythe Antiques
6 Old Severalls Rd. (J Livingstone) Open 10-5. CL: Tues. *STOCK: Victorian and Edwardian furniture, bric-a-brac, clocks.* TEL: 0366 728644.

NORTH WALSHAM

Anglia Antique Exporters
Trade Warehouse, Station Yard, Norwich Rd. (J Connaughton and P Keegan) SIZE: Large. *STOCK: Victorian, Edwardian, pine and general shipping goods, £10-£1,500.* TEL: 0692 406266; home - 026378 568.

Eric Bates and Sons
Melbourne House, Bacton Rd. Est: 1973. Open 8-5.30. SIZE: Large. *STOCK: General antiques, Victorian, Edwardian, shipping furniture.* TEL: 0692 403221. SER: Restorations (furniture); upholstery; shipping and container packing. VAT: Stan/Spec.

Cromwellian lobster tailed helmet 'pot', very good condition. £850. Wallis & Wallis, Lewes. From a Saleroom Report in the December 1990/January 1991 issue of ***Antique Collecting.***

North Walsham continued

North Walsham Antique Gallery
29 Grammar School Rd. (M.B. and I.F Hicks) Est: 1970. Open 9-1 and 2-5. CL: Wed. p.m. SIZE: Medium. *STOCK: China, glass, silver, collectors' items, small furniture.* TEL: 0692 405059. SER: Valuations; restorations. VAT: Stan/Spec.

NORWICH

William Allchin Antiques
22-24 St. Benedict St. Est: 1978. Open 10-5. *STOCK: Victorian and early 20th C lighting, brass and iron beds, bathroom furniture, fireplaces, soft furnishings.* Not Stocked: Silver. LOC: Close to St. Andrew's Hall. PARK: Easy. TEL: 0603 660046; fax - same. SER: Restorations (metal polishing, repairs and re-upholstery). VAT: Stan.

Another One incorporating Fagins Alley
140 Magdalen St. (J.S Lee) Open 10.30-5.30. *STOCK: General antiques and bric-a-brac.* TEL: 0603 615302.

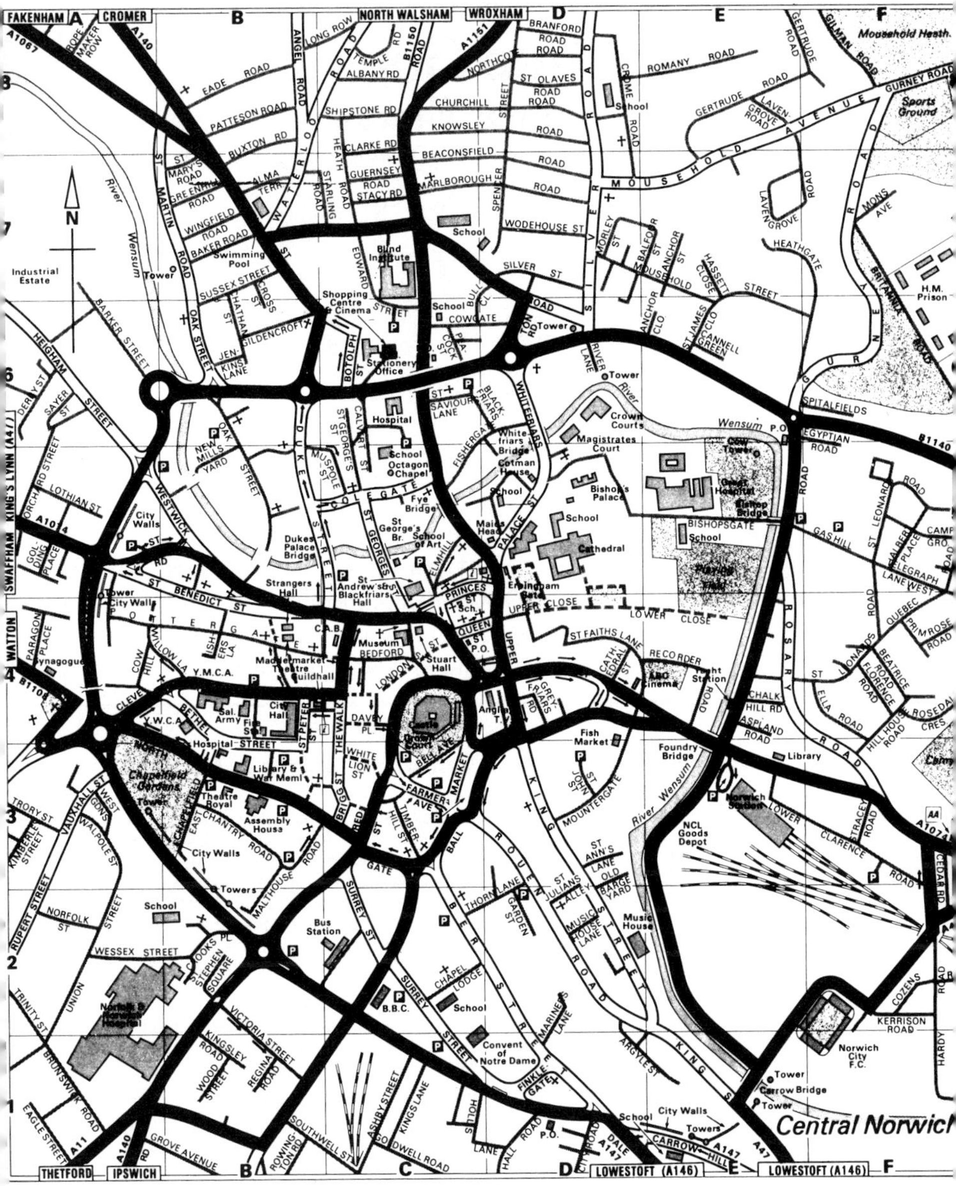
FAKENHAM
CROMER
NORTH WALSHAM
WROXHAM
A1067
A140
A1151
B1150
Mousehold Heath
Sports Ground
ROPE MAKER ROW
LONG ROW
TEMPLE RD
ALBANY RD
BRANFORD ROAD
NORTHCOTE ROAD
ST OLAVES ROAD
ROMANY ROAD
GERTRUDE ROAD
GURNEY ROAD
EADE ROAD
PATTESON ROAD
SHIPSTONE RD
CHURCHILL ROAD
KNOWSLEY ROAD
BEACONSFIELD ROAD
MARLBOROUGH ROAD
CLARKE RD
GUERNSEY ROAD
STACY RD
BUXTON RD
ST MARY'S ROAD
GREEN HILL ROAD
ALMA TERR
WINGFIELD ROAD
BAKER ROAD
Swimming Pool
WATERLOO ROAD
STARLING ROAD
HEATH ROAD
SPENCER STREET
CROME ROAD
School
MOUSEHOLD AVENUE
LAVENGROVE ROAD
WODEHOUSE ST
SILVER ST
SILVER ROAD
MONS AVE
BRITANNIA ROAD
H.M. Prison
HEATHGATE
STREET
HASSETT CLOSE
MORLEY ST
BALFOUR ST
ANCHOR ST
MOUSEHOLD
ANCHOR CLO
ST JAMES CLO
CANNELL GREEN
River Wensum
Industrial Estate
Tower
Blind Institute
EDWARD STREET
Shopping Centre Cinema
BARKER STREET
SUSSEX STREET
CROSS ST
CHATHAM ST
GILDENCROFT
JENKINS LANE
OAK STREET
School
COWGATE
BULL CL
PEACOCK ST
BOTOLPH ST
Stationery Office
Tower
RIVER LANE
HEIGHAM STREET
SAYER ST
DERBY ST
ST SAVIOURS LANE
BLACKFRIARS ST
WHITEFRIARS
Crown Courts
Magistrates Court
Wensum
Hospital
School
Octagon Chapel
NEW MILLS YARD
DUKE STREET
MUSPOLE ST
ST GEORGE'S ST
CALVERT ST
FISHERGATE
Whitefriars Bridge
Cotman House
School
Bishop's Palace
Cow Tower
Great Hospital
Bishop Bridge
EGYPTIAN ROAD
SPITALFIELDS
B1140
GAS HILL
ST LEONARDS ROAD
ORCHARD STREET
LOTHIAN ST
A1074
KING'S LYNN (A47)
SWAFFHAM
GOLDING PLACE
City Walls
WESTWICK
COLEGATE
Fye Bridge
St George's Br.
School of Art
ELM HILL
Maids Head
PALACE ST
School
Cathedral
BISHOPSGATE
School
Dukes Palace Bridge
Strangers Hall
St Andrew's & Blackfriars Hall
Erpingham Gate
UPPER CLOSE
LOWER CLOSE
ROSARY ROAD
ALBERT PLACE
TELEGRAPH LANE WEST
QUEBEC ROAD
PRIMROSE ROAD
Tower
City Walls
ST BENEDICT ST
POTTERGATE
PRINCES ST
QUEEN ST
C.A.B.
Museum
BEDFORD
ST FAITHS LANE
RECORDER ROAD
CATHEDRAL ST
WATTON
PARAGON PLACE
Synagogue
B1108
COW HILL
WILLOW LA
Y.M.C.A.
Maddermarket Theatre
Guildhall
Stuart Hall
LONDON ST
UPPER KING ST
Freight Station
ABC Cinema
CHALK HILL RD
ASPLAND ROAD
BEATRICE ROAD
FLORENCE ROAD
HILL HOUSE ROAD
ROSEDALE CRES
ELLA ROAD
CLEVELAND
BETHEL ST
Y.W.C.A.
Sal. Army
Fire Stn
City Hall
ST PETER ST
THE WALK
DAVEY PL.
Castle
Crown Court
Anglia T.V.
GREYFRIARS RD
Fish Market
Foundry Bridge
Library
NORTH
Hospital
STREET
Chapelfield Gardens
Library & War Meml
WHITE LION ST
BELL AVE
MARKET AVE
FARMERS AVE
TIMBERHILL
ST JOHN ST
MOUNTERGATE
River Wensum
Norwich Station
NCL Goods Depot
LOWER CLARENCE ROAD
STRACEY ROAD
A1074
CEDAR RD
TRORY ST
KIMBERLEY STREET
VAUXHALL ST
WEST GDNS
WALPOLE ST
Theatre Royal
Tower
CHAPELFIELD ROAD
EAST CHANTRY ROAD
Assembly House
BRIGG ST
RED LION ST
GATE
ROUEN ROAD
ST ANN'S LANE
OLD BARGE YARD
ST JULIANS ALLEY
Music House Lane
Music House
KING STREET
City Walls
Towers
MALTHOUSE ROAD
RUPERT STREET
NORFOLK ST
School
Bus Station
SURREY ST
THORN LANE
GARDEN ST
BER STREET
WESSEX STREET
COOKS PL
STEPHEN SQUARE
Norfolk & Norwich Hospital
UNION STREET
TRINITY ST
CHAPEL LODGE
School
B.B.C.
SURREY STREET
Convent of Notre Dame
MARINE LANE
ARGYLE ST
KING ST
COZENS ROAD
KERRISON ROAD
Norwich City F.C.
HARDY
VICTORIA STREET
KINGSLEY ROAD
REGINA ROAD
WOOD STREET
FINKLE GATE
Tower
Carrow Bridge
Tower
BRUNSWICK ROAD
EAGLE STREET
A11
A140
GROVE AVENUE
SOUTHWELL ST
ROWINGTON RD
ASHBY STREET
KINGS LANE
GOLDWELL ROAD
HOLLS LANE
HALL ROAD
P.O.
CITY ROAD
DALE
A147
School
City Walls
Towers
CARROW HILL
A147
A47
Central Norwich
THETFORD
IPSWICH
LOWESTOFT (A146)
LOWESTOFT (A146)
A
B
C
D
E
F

Key to Town Plan

AA Recommended roads		Car Parks	P
Other roads		Parks and open spaces	
Restricted roads		AA Service Centre	AA
Buildings of interest			

Norwich continued

As Time Goes By Antique and Tower Clocks

5 Wrights Court, Elm Hill. (S Phillips, MBHI) Est: 1981. Open 9.30-5, Sat. 10-4. SIZE: Medium. *STOCK: Clocks, £150-£8,000.* LOC: Small courtyard on right at bottom of Elm Hill. TEL: 0603 666508. SER: Valuations (clocks); restorations (clocks).

The Bank House Gallery LAPADA

71 Newmarket Rd. (R.S Mitchell) Resident. Est: 1979. Open by appointment. *STOCK: English and continental oil paintings especially Norwich and Suffolk schools, 19th C, £1,000-£50,000.* LOC: On A11 between city centre and ring road. PARK: Own. TEL: 0603 633380. SER: Valuations; restorations; buys at auction (paintings). VAT: Stan/Spec.

Arthur Brett and Sons Ltd BADA

40/44 St. Giles St. Est: 1870. Open 9.30-5, Sat. by appointment. SIZE: Large. *STOCK: Antique furniture, mahogany, walnut and oak, sculpture, metalwork.* LOC: Near City Hall. PARK: Easy. TEL: 0603 628171; fax - 0603 630245. FAIRS: Grosvenor House and Harrogate. VAT: Stan/Spec.

Norwich continued

Carrow Hill Antique and Bygone Centre

Carrow Hill. (The Edwards Family) Est: 1968. CL: Mon. and Thurs. SIZE: Large. *STOCK: Furniture including hand stripped, dining tables, chairs, dressers, bedroom; brass and iron beds, sofas, bygones, bric-a-brac, Victorian to 1930.* LOC: Off King St. PARK: Easy. TEL: 0603 628628. SER: Restorations (Victorian tables and chests); French polishing; upholstery.

Cathedral Gallery

93 Upper St. Giles St. (P Crowe) Open 10-5.15. *STOCK: Antique maps and prints.* TEL: 0603 624800.

Cloisters Antiques Fair

St. Andrew's and Blackfriars Hall, St. Andrew's Plain. (Norwich City Council) Est: 1976. Open Wed. only 9.30-3.30. SIZE: 23 dealers. *STOCK: General antiques.* PARK: Easy. TEL: 0603 628477; fax - 0603 762182.

Country and Eastern

8 Redwell St. (J Millward) Est: 1978. Open daily. *STOCK: Oriental rugs, kelims and textiles, late 19th C to early 20th C, £50-£500; primitive and country furniture, 18th-19th C, £25-£500; woolwork pictures, 17th-19th C, £10-£200; bygones, 18th-19th C, £2-£75.* LOC: Top of Elm Hill. PARK: Nearby. TEL: 0603 623107. VAT: Stan/Spec.

Norwich continued

Crome Gallery and Frame Shop
34 Elm Hill. (J Willis) Est: 1971. Open 9.30-5. SIZE: Medium. *STOCK: Watercolours, £50-£350; oils, £150-£500; prints, £10-£150; all 18th-20th C.* LOC: Near cathedral. PARK: Easy. TEL: 0603 622827/614781. SER: Valuations; restorations (oils, watercolours, prints). VAT: Stan/Spec.

Peter Crowe, Antiquarian Book Seller
75-77 Upper St. Giles St. Open 9-6. *STOCK: Antiquarian books, 17th-18th C, calf, 19th C, cloth and fine bindings, travel, topography and Norfolk.* TEL: 0603 624800.

Charles Cubitt
10 All Saints Green. (Mrs A.E.C Hunter) Est: 1868. Open 9.30-5. SIZE: Medium. *STOCK: Jewellery, silver, plate, china, glass, antiquarian books.* LOC: Opposite Bond's store. PARK: Behind Bond's store. TEL: 0603 622569.

D'Amico Antiques Ltd
20 Highland Rd, off Colman Rd. (J.E Wrightson and Mrs P Mawtus) NAWCC. Resident. Est: 1947. SIZE: Small. *STOCK: Clocks, 17th-20th C.* LOC: Off Colman Rd. (part of Norwich ring road) near Unthank Rd. traffic lights. PARK: Easy. TEL: 0603 52320. SER: Restorations (clocks). VAT: Stan/Spec.

Clive Dennett Coins
66 St. Benedicts St. BNTA. Est: 1970. CL: Thurs. a.m. and lunchtime. SIZE: Small. *STOCK: Coins and medals, ancient Greek to date, £5-£5,000; jewellery, 19th-20th C; banknotes, 20th C; both £5-£1,000.* PARK: Easy. TEL: 0603 624315. SER: Valuations; buys at auction (as stock). FAIRS: All Simmons; Cumberland Hotel, London; Coinex; Marriott Hotel, London; Tienan, Belgium.

Elm Hill Antiques
20 Elm Hill. (A.E Gray) Est: 1976. Open 10-5.30, Sat. 10-4. SIZE: Medium. *STOCK: Furniture and decorative items, 18th and 19th C.* LOC: Near cathedral. PARK: Easy. TEL: 0603 664339. VAT: Spec.

Englishman's Antiques
86 St. Benedicts St. (R. and M.K Kimp) Est: 1979. Open 10-5. CL: Mon. SIZE: Medium. *STOCK: Furniture, mainly Victorian and Edwardian, £50-£5,000; small items, £3-£1,000; English watercolours, 19th-20th C, £50-£700.* LOC: Near city centre, bottom of Grapes Hill. PARK: Easy. TEL: 0603 633411; home - 0263 78464. SER: Valuations. VAT: Stan/Spec.

The Fairhurst Gallery
13 Bedford St. Est: 1951. Open 10-6. SIZE: Large. *STOCK: Oil paintings, £5-£5,000; watercolours, £5-£2,000, both 19th-20th C; frames, 18th-20th C.* LOC: Behind Travel Centre and Travel Australia. TEL: 0603 614214. SER: Valuations; restorations; cleaning; framemakers. VAT: Spec.

Norwich continued

Gallery 45
45 St. Benedicts St. (J Hines) Open 11-3, Sat. 11-4 or by appointment. CL: Mon. *STOCK: Modern British and continental art.* TEL: 0603 763771.

Michael Hallam Antiques
17 Magdalen St. (M.J Hallam) Est: 1969. Open 10.30-5. SIZE: Small. *STOCK: Furniture, porcelain, pictures and small items, mainly 19th C, £10-£2,000.* LOC: Near cathedral. TEL: 0603 413692. SER: Valuations. VAT: Stan/Spec.

Nigel Handley
32 Elm Hill. (N.S Handley) Est: 1986. Open 10-5. CL: Mon. SIZE: Medium. *STOCK: Furniture, 18th-19th C, £10-£3,000; china, pictures and decorative items.* LOC: Near cathedral. PARK: Easy. TEL: 0603 628100. VAT: Stan/Spec.

Donna Hannent
86 St. Benedicts St. Est: 1980. Open 10-5. CL: Mon. SIZE: Small. *STOCK: Jewellery, 1800-1940, £25-£1,000; collectors' items and small silver.* LOC: City centre. PARK: Easy. TEL: 0603 633411. SER: Valuations.

G Jarrett
12-14 Old Palace Rd. Est: 1961. TEL: 0603 625847; home - 0603 618244.

Henry Levine and Co BADA
55 London St. (D. and L Levine) Est: 1865. Open 9.30-5. CL: Thurs. *STOCK: Silver, jewellery, Sheffield plate.* TEL: 0603 628709. SER: Valuations (especially Norwich silver). VAT: Stan/Spec.

The Little Gallery
38 Elm Hill. (I Hook) Est: 1968. *STOCK: Watercolours, drawings, etchings.* TEL: 0603 625809. SER: Buys at auction. VAT: Spec.

Robert Lowe Antiques
54 St. Benedicts St. Open 9.30-5. *STOCK: Victorian and Edwardian lighting, brass and iron beds, bathroom fittings, furniture and fireplaces.* TEL: 0603 624806.

Maddermarket Antiques
18c Lower Goat Lane. Est: 1955. Open 9.30-4.30. *STOCK: Jewellery, silverware.* TEL: 0603 620610.

Mandell's Gallery BADA
Elm Hill. Est: 1964. Open 9-5.30. SIZE: Large. *STOCK: Oils, watercolours, specialising in Norwich and Suffolk schools.* LOC: Near shopping centre, close to cathedral. PARK: Easy. TEL: 0603 626892/629180. SER: Valuations; restorations; framing. VAT: Spec.

Norwich continued

The Movie Shop
Antiquarian and Nostalgia Centre, 11 St. Gregory's Alley. Open 10-5. SIZE: Large. *STOCK: Books, magazines and movie ephemera; furniture, porcelain, pre-1940 clothes and textiles, general antiques.* TEL: 0603 615239.

Ninety-One
91 Upper St. Giles St. Open 9.30-5.30. *STOCK: Furniture including pine and oak.* SER: French spoken.

Norwich Antique and Collectors Centre
Quayside, Fye Bridge. (R.A Dazeley and I.J Ford) Est: 1982. Open 10-5 including Bank Holidays. SIZE: Large - 25 dealers. *STOCK: General antiques and collectors items, 2p-£5,000+.* LOC: Near the cathedral. PARK: Nearby. TEL: 0603 612582. SER: Valuations; restorations; framing.

Queen of Hungary Antiques
49 St. Benedicts St. (V O'Grady) Resident. Est: 1981. Open 10-5.30. *STOCK: Pine, oak, mahogany and walnut furniture.* TEL: 0603 625082.

Stephen Reiss Fine Art
14 Bridewell Alley. (Stephen Reiss Fine Art Ltd) Est: 1985. Open daily, Sun. and Mon. by appointment. SIZE: Medium. *STOCK: Paintings and drawings - 19th C British, £1,000-£10,000; selected 20th C, £500-£5,000; Dutch, 17th C, from £4,000.* LOC: Pedestrian alley between London St. and St. Andrew's St. PARK: Duke St. multi-storey. TEL: 0603 615357; home - 0728 452499. SER: Valuations; restorations (oils and watercolours); buys at auction. VAT: Stan/Spec.

St. Michael at Plea Antiques Centre
Bank Plain. (B Godsafe) Est: 1974. Open 9.30-5. SIZE: Medium - 30 dealers. *STOCK: General antiques, pre 1940, £5-£1,000.* LOC: Bank Plain, top of London St. PARK: Multi-storey nearby. TEL: 0603 619129. SER: Restorations (furniture, re-upholstery and recaning).

The Scientific Anglian (Bookshop)
30-30a St. Benedict St. (N.B Peake) Est: 1965. Open 10-5.30. CL: Mon. a.m. and Thurs. a.m. SIZE: Large. *STOCK: Secondhand books, old and modern, 30p-£200; antiquarian items, 1500-1900, from £1.* Not Stocked: Maps or prints. LOC: 3 minutes walk from City Hall straight down Upper Goat Lane, turn left into St. Benedict's. PARK: Limited nearby or multi-storey St. Andrew's St. TEL: 0603 624079. SER: Valuations; buys at auction. VAT: Stan.

Oswald Sebley
20 Lower Goat Lane. (P.H Knights) Est: 1895. Open 9-5.15. CL: Thurs. SIZE: Small. *STOCK: Silver, 18th-20th C, £15-£2,000; jewellery, Victorian, £10-£4,000.* LOC: 150yds. to right of City Hall, down paved street. PARK: Nearby. TEL: 0603 626504. SER: Valuations; restorations (silver and gold jewellery). VAT: Stan/Spec.

This and That
56 Bethel St. (G Francis) Open 10.30-5.30. *STOCK: General antique and pine furniture.* TEL: 0603 632201.

James and Ann Tillett **LAPADA**
12 and 13 Tombland. Est: 1972. Open 9-6, Sat. 9-1.30. *STOCK: English domestic silver and flatware, from 17th C; mustard pots, collectors' items, barometers, barographs, longcase clocks, jewellery, from 18th C.* LOC: Opposite Erpingham Gate, Norwich Cathedral and Maid's Head Hotel. TEL: 0603 624914. SER: Valuations; restorations (silver); export facilities. VAT: Stan/Spec.

Thomas Tillett & Co
17 St. Giles St. (A Grigg) Est: 1971. Open daily. SIZE: Medium. *STOCK: Diamond jewellery, 19th-20th C, £50-£2,000; silver, 18th-19th C, £20-£1,000.* PARK: Easy. TEL: 0603 625922. SER: Valuations; restorations (jewellery, silver). VAT: Stan/Spec.

The Tombland Bookshop
8 Tombland. (J.G. and A Freeman) Open 9.30-5. *STOCK: Antiquarian and secondhand books, maps and prints.* TEL: 0603 760610.

Tooltique
54 Waterloo Rd. (M Jacobs) Open 9-5.30. CL: Thurs. *STOCK: Tools including secondhand.* TEL: 0603 414289.

Tudor Galleries
14 Bank St. (Mrs P Dickerson) Est: 1987. Open 10-5, Sat. 10-4. SIZE: Medium. *STOCK: Paintings, late 19th C to contemporary, £200-£5,000.* LOC: Between Upper King St. and Bank Plain. PARK: Multi-storey nearby. TEL: 0603 760041. SER: Buys at auction (oils and watercolours).

Malcolm Turner
15 St. Giles St. Open 9.30-5. SIZE: Small. *STOCK: Staffordshire, Imari, English and Oriental ceramics, silver, mostly 19th C, £50-£300.* PARK: Nearby. TEL: 0603 627007. SER: Valuations. VAT: Stan/Spec.

Yesteryear
24D Magdalen St. (Mrs E Watson) Est: 1980. Open 10-5. *STOCK: General antiques, pictures, oils, watercolours, prints, collectors' items, bygones, bric-a-brac, Doulton figures and character jugs, art deco, art nouveau, small furniture.* PARK: Nearby. TEL: 0603 622908 or 0263 721169.

Norwich continued

Robert Young Antiques LAPADA
4A Exchange St. (K. and R Young) Est: 1970. Open 10-4. CL: Mon. *STOCK: Jewellery 18th-20th C, £5-£5,000.* LOC: Off Market Sq. opposite Jarrolds. PARK: Nearby. TEL: 0603 618605. VAT: Stan.

RAVENINGHAM

M.D Cannell Antiques
Castell Farm. Resident. Open 9-9 including Sun. SIZE: Large. *STOCK: Georgian and Victorian furniture, metalwork, 17th-19th C; garden and decorative items.* LOC: On B1140. PARK: Easy. TEL: 050 846 441. VAT: Stan/Spec.

Roderic Haugh Antiques LAPADA
1 Castell Farm. Open by appointment. *STOCK: Furniture, painted and 18th-19th C; architectural items.* TEL: Home - 0603 35347.

REEPHAM

The Chimes
Market Pl. (D. and H McDonell) Open 9.30-5. CL: Thurs. p.m. SIZE: Medium. *STOCK: General antiques and Victoriana, scientific and optical instruments, paintings.* PARK: Easy. TEL: 0603 870480; home - same.

REYMERSTON, Nr. Norwich

Xanthus Gallery
(P Goodman) Est: 1982. Open by appointment. SIZE: Medium. *STOCK: English pictures and drawings, 1750-1950, £100-£6,000.* LOC: 10 minutes from A47. PARK: Easy. TEL: 0362 850862; home - same. SER: Valuations; restorations (paintings); buys at auction (paintings). VAT: Stan.

SCRATBY, Nr. Gt. Yarmouth

Keith Lawson Antiques
Scratby Garden Centre, Beach Rd. Est: 1988. Open seven days, 9-6. SIZE: Large barn. *STOCK: General antiques.* LOC: B1159. PARK: Easy. TEL: 0493 730950. SER: Valuations; restorations. VAT: Stan/Spec.

SHARRINGTON, Nr. Holt

Sharrington Antiques
(P Coke) Est: 1944. Open by chance 9.30-5.00, or by appointment. CL: Jan.-Mar. SIZE: Medium. *STOCK: Small and interesting items, £5-£1,500; china, pictures, embroideries, treen, papier mâché.* LOC: 3 miles west of Holt. PARK: Easy. TEL: 0263 861411; home - 0263 860719.

SHERINGHAM

Rose Denis
20 High St. *STOCK: Jewellery and silver.* TEL: 0263 823699.

Dorothy's Antiques
23 Waterbank Road. (Mrs D.E Collier) Est: 1975. *STOCK: Glass, especially cranberry; Royal Worcester, Meissen, Sitzendorf porcelain, commemoratives, Goss china, brass, copper, small furniture, clocks, cased birds, ribbon plates, porcelain shoes, collectors' items.* TEL: 0263 822319; home - 0263 823018.

Parriss
20 Station Rd. (J.H Parriss) Est: 1947. Open 9-5.30. CL: Wed. SIZE: Medium. *STOCK: Jewellery, £30-£2,500; silver, £40-£2,000; clocks, £100-£3,000.* LOC: A1082, in main street. PARK: Within 150yds. TEL: 0263 822661. SER: Valuations; restorations (jewellery, silver, clocks). VAT: Stan.

The Westcliffe Gallery
2-8 Augusta St. (Parks, Bollon & Vinsen) Resident. Est: 1979. Open 9.30-1 and 2-5.30, Sat. 9.30-5.30. CL: Wed. SIZE: Medium. *STOCK: Oils, watercolours and drawings, 19th-20th C, £100-£15,000.* LOC: Town centre. PARK: Easy. TEL: 0263 824320. SER: Valuations; restorations (oils, watercolours, prints); gilding. VAT: Stan/Spec.

SNETTISHAM, Nr. King's Lynn

Jasper Antiques
11A Hall Rd. (M Norris) Est: 1975. Open 10.30-1, afternoons by appointment, Sat. 10.30-1 and 2-4. CL: Tues. and Thurs. SIZE: Medium. *STOCK: Decorative items including ceramics, £5-£2,000; furniture, £50-£3,000; mirrors, £20-£1,500; all 18th-19th C; jewellery, 19th C, £5-£250.* LOC: Narrow passageway from Market Sq. to Hall Rd. PARK: Easy and Market Sq. TEL: 0485 41485. SER: Valuations; restorations (ceramics, jewellery, clocks and watches, silver-plating and furniture); buys at auction.

SOUTH LOPHAM, Nr. Diss

Angel Antique Centre
Pansthorn Farmhouse, Redgrave Rd. (J.R. and A Saxon) Open 9.30-6 including Sun. SIZE: Large - 12 dealers. *STOCK: Victorian, Edwardian and pine furniture, linen, porcelain, clocks, glassware and collectables.* PARK: Own. TEL: 037 988 317. SER: Restorations (furniture).

The Gallery and Things
The Street. (H. and E Chalk) Open 9.30-5.30 including Sun. and Bank Holidays. CL: Mon. *STOCK: 19th C watercolours, some oils and prints, antiquarian books.* LOC: A1066 Diss/Thetford Rd. TEL: 037 988 761. SER: Framing.

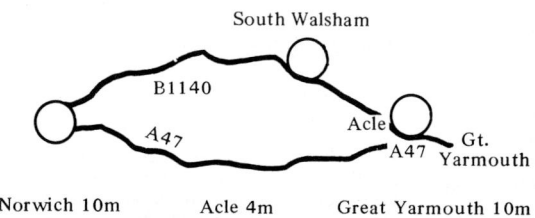

SOUTH WALSHAM

Leo Pratt and Son
Old Curiosity Shop. (R. and E.D Pratt) Est: 1890. Open 9-1 and 2-5.30. SIZE: Large. *STOCK: Furniture, from 1700; porcelain, glass, pottery, 1830; shipping furniture, metalware.* PARK: Easy. TEL: 060 549 204. SER: Restorations (furniture); buys at auction. FAIRS: Norwich. VAT: Stan/Spec.

STALHAM

Stalham Antique Gallery
High St. (M.B. and I.F Hicks) Est: 1970. Open 9-1 and 2-5. SIZE: Medium. *STOCK: Furniture, Regency to 19th C; some early oak; pictures, china, glass.* Not Stocked: Reproductions. PARK: Easy. TEL: 0692 80636. SER: Valuations; restorations. VAT: Spec.

STIFFKEY

Stiffkey Antiques
The Old Methodist Chapel. Open by arrangement with Stiffkey Lamp Shop. *STOCK: Victorian and Edwardian bathroom fittings; fireplaces, fenders and fire irons, door furniture, books, bric-a-brac, Japanese and other tinplate toys, many boxed and mint.* PARK: Easy. TEL: 0328 830460; fax - 0328 830005.

Stiffkey continued

The Stiffkey Lamp Shop
Townshend Arms. (R Belsten and D Mann) Est: 1976. Open 10.30-6 (winter 10-5), Sun. 11-6. SIZE: Medium. *STOCK: Lamps, gas, electric and oil, 1800-1920, £25-£2,000; rare lamp fittings.* LOC: Coast road near Wells-on-Sea. PARK: Easy. TEL: 0328 830460; fax - 0328 830005. SER: Restorations (lamp fittings). VAT: Stan.

STOKE FERRY, Nr. King's Lynn

Farmhouse Antiques
White's Farmhouse, Barker's Drove, off Oxborough Rd. (P Philpot) Resident. Est: 1969. Usually open, prior telephone call advisable. *STOCK: General antiques, especially desks and writing tables.* TEL: 0366 500588. SER: Restorations.

SUFFIELD, Nr. Aylsham

G. and E Briere
Keepers Cottage. Resident. Est: 1966. Open by appointment. SIZE: Medium. *STOCK: Period furniture, paintings, unusual decorative items.* LOC: First fork left past the garage on Aylsham-North Walsham Rd. TEL: 0263 732651.

SWAFFHAM

Cranglegate Antiques
Market Pl. (K.W Buckie) Resident. Est: 1960. Open Tues. and Sat. 10-1 and 2-5.30. SIZE: Small. *STOCK: General antiques and collectors' items, 17th-20th C, £5-£1,000.* LOC: A47. PARK: In square opposite or in passage at rear. TEL: Home - 0760 721052. FAIRS: Local.

Swaffham Antiques Supplies
66-68 London St. (M. and R Cross) Est: 1959. Open 10-5. CL: Mon. SIZE: Large. *STOCK: General antiques, 18th-19th C, shipping furniture, £100-£5,000.* LOC: Off A47. PARK: Easy. TEL: 0760 721697; home - same.

SWAFIELD, Nr. North Walsham

Staithe Lodge Gallery
Staithe Lodge. (M.C.A Foster) Resident. Est: 1976. Open 9-5, Sun. by appointment. CL: Wed. p.m. SIZE: Medium. *STOCK: Watercolours, paintings and prints, 1800-1950, £30-£250; furniture, 1750-1900, £75-£300; plateware, glass and small items, 1800-1900, £10-£75.* LOC: On B1145 at the Mundesley end of the North Walsham by-pass. PARK: Easy. TEL: 0692 402669. SER: Restorations; framing; buys at auction (mainly watercolours). VAT: Stan/Spec.

WATTON

Clermont Antiques
Clermont Hall. (P Jones) Resident. Est: 1983. Open daily. SIZE: Large. *STOCK: Furniture, decorative items, 18th to early 19th C.* LOC: Down farm track, off B1108. PARK: Easy. TEL: 0953 882189. VAT: Spec.

WELLS-NEXT-THE-SEA

Church Street Antiques
2 Church St. (P. and G Crowe, P. and B Ford and L.A Irons) Est: 1974. Open 10-5 including Sun., Mon. by appointment. SIZE: Small. *STOCK: General antiques, £5-£1,000.* LOC: A149 main coast road. PARK: Easy. TEL: 0328 711698; home - 04858 606. FAIRS: Blakeney Hotel, Blakeney and Petwood Hotel, Woodhall Spa.

Wells Antique Centre
The Old Mill, Maryland. Open 10-5 including Sun. SIZE: 13 dealers. *STOCK: General antiques.* PARK: Easy. TEL: 0328 711433.

WIGGENHALL ST. GERMANS, Nr. King's Lynn

Wiggenhall Antiques
The Old Clubroom, Surrey St. (P.A. and L.S Oliver) Est: 1985. Open 10-9, May-Sept; otherwise 10-5. CL: Mon. and Tues. SIZE: Medium. *STOCK: Furniture, 19th C, £50-£2,500; china, 19th to early 20th C, £5-£500; general antiques, 19th C, £5-£500.* LOC: Approx. 4 miles south of King's Lynn. PARK: Easy. TEL: 0553 85308; home - same. SER: Valuations; restorations (furniture); French polishing; upholstery; buys at auction. VAT: Spec.

WROXHAM

T.C.S Brooke BADA
The Grange. (M.A., S.T. and L.A.P Brooke) Est: 1932. Open 9.30-1 and 2.15-5.30. CL: Wed. *STOCK: English porcelain, 18th C, furniture (mainly Georgian), silver, glass, works of art, Oriental rugs.* PARK: Easy. TEL: 0603 782644. SER: Valuations. VAT: Spec.

WYMONDHAM

King
Market Pl. (M King) Est: 1969. Open 9-5. CL: Mon. and Wed., except by appointment. *STOCK: General antiques, furniture, copper, brass, silver, jewellery, porcelain.* PARK: Easy. TEL: 0953 604758; evenings - 0953 602427. VAT: Stan/Spec.

M.E. and J.E Standley
"Acorns"23 Norwich Rd, and warehouses at Chandlers Hill. Open Sat., otherwise by appointment. *STOCK: Furniture, 17th-19th C and Victorian.* TEL: 0953 602566.

Turret House
27 Middleton St. (Dr and Mrs D.H Morgan) PBFA. Resident. Est: 1972. SIZE: Small. *STOCK: Antiquarian books, especially science and medical; scientific instruments.* LOC: Corner of Vicar St., adjacent to War Memorial. TEL: 0953 603462. SER: Buys at auction. FAIRS: London (monthly) and major provincial PBFA. VAT: Stan/Spec.

Wymondham Antique Centre
No. 1 Town Green. Open 10-5. SIZE: 17 dealers. *STOCK: General antiques and collectables.* TEL: 0953 604817.

Northamptonshire

Please note this is only a rough map designed to show dealers the number of shops in the various towns, and is not necessarily totally accurate.

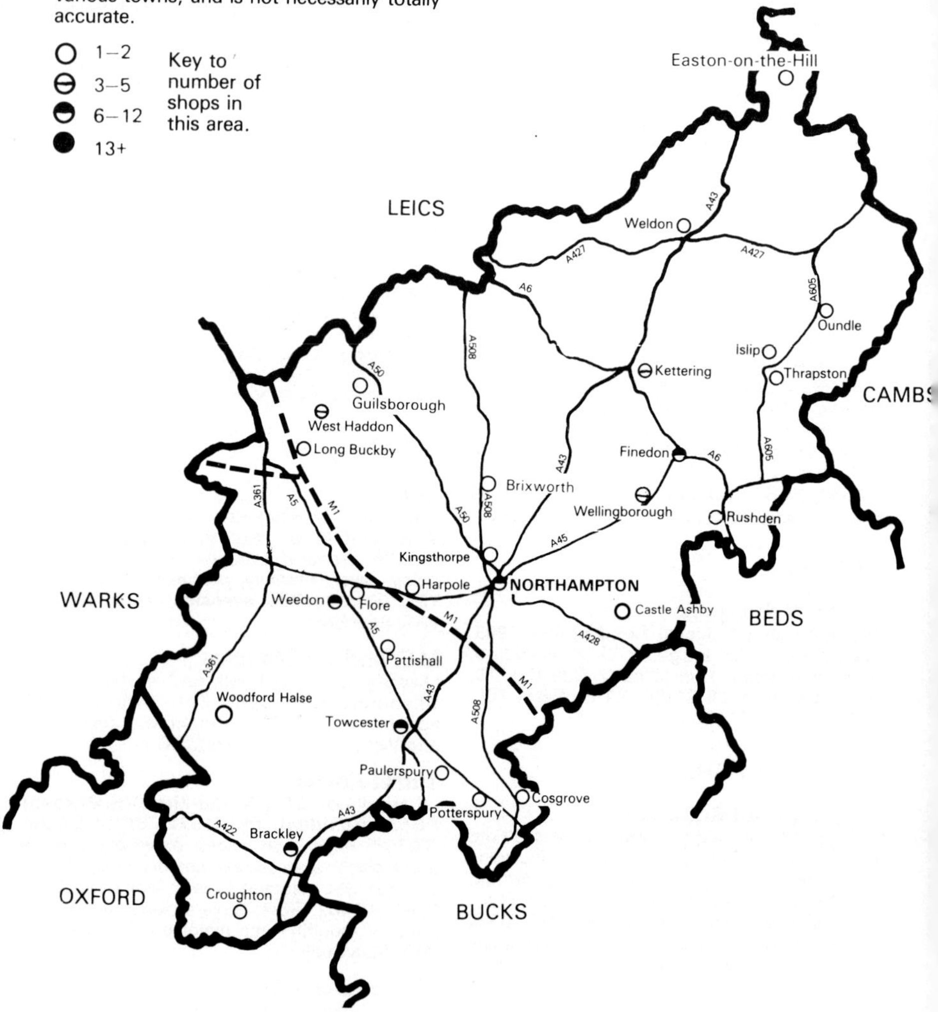
1–2
3–5
6–12
13+
Key to number of shops in this area.
LEICS
Easton-on-the-Hill
Weldon
A43
A427
A427
A6
A605
Oundle
Islip
Thrapston
Kettering
CAMBS
A508
A50
Guilsborough
West Haddon
Long Buckby
A43
Finedon
A6
A605
Brixworth
Wellingborough
Rushden
A361
A5
M1
A50
A508
A45
Kingsthorpe
Harpole
NORTHAMPTON
WARKS
Weedon
Flore
M1
Castle Ashby
BEDS
A5
A428
Pattishall
A361
A43
A508
M1
Woodford Halse
Towcester
Paulerspury
Cosgrove
Potterspury
A43
A422
Brackley
OXFORD
Croughton
BUCKS

N

BRACKLEY

Brackley Antiques
69 High St. (Mrs B.H Nutting) Est: 1977. Open 10-6, Wed. 10-12, Sun. by appointment. SIZE: Medium. *STOCK: Furniture, especially traditionally upholstered, 19th C, £50-£2,000; ceramics, 18th-20th C, £2-£400; interesting and unusual items.* LOC: A43. PARK: Easy. TEL: 0280 703362; home - same. SER: Restorations (furniture and upholstery).

Peter Jackson Antiques
3 Market Pl. Open 10.30-1 and 2-5. *STOCK: English and continental porcelain and pottery, 18th-19th C; furniture, paintings, silver, jewellery, glass, watercolours and prints.* TEL: 0280 703259/0993 882415. SER: Valuations; restorations.

Juno's Antiques
4 Bridge St. Open 10-1 and 2-5. CL: Wed. *STOCK: General antiques.* LOC: Northampton/Oxford road. TEL: 0280 700639.

Patrick Nutting Books
69 High St. Est: 1990. Open 10-6, Wed. 10-12, Sun. by appointment. *STOCK: Antiquarian and secondhand books.* LOC: A43. PARK: Easy. TEL: 0280 703362.

The Old Hall Bookshop
32 Market Pl. (J and Lady Juliet Townsend) Est: 1977. Open 9.30-1 and 2-5.30. SIZE: Large. *STOCK: Antiquarian, secondhand and new books.* LOC: Town centre on east side of Market Place. PARK: Easy. TEL: 0280 704146. VAT: Stan.

Right Angle
24 Manor Rd. Open 9.30-5.30, Wed. 9.30-1. *STOCK: Watercolours, oils, prints and maps.* TEL: 0280 702462. SER: Framing.

BRIXWORTH, Nr. Northampton

B.R Gunnett
128 Northampton Rd. Open by appointment. *STOCK: Furniture, bric-a-brac.* TEL: 0604 880057.

CASTLE ASHBY

Castle Ashby Gallery
The Old Farmyard. (G S Wright - Fine Paintings) Open 10-6. CL: Mon. *STOCK: Oil paintings - British, 1850-1950, £200-£20,000; continental, £1,500-£10,000.* LOC: Adjacent to Castle Ashby House. PARK: Easy. TEL: 060129 787; fax - same. SER: Valuations; restorations (oils). VAT: Spec.

COSGROVE, Nr. Milton Keynes

Restall Brown and Clennell Ltd
LAPADA

(S Brown) Est: 1905. Open Mon.-Fri. 8.30-5.30, appointment advisable; other times by appointment. *STOCK: English furniture, 17th-19th C.* LOC: Off A5, trains can be met at Central Milton Keynes Station. TEL: 0908 565888. VAT: Stan/Spec.

CROUGHTON, Nr. Brackley

Croughton Antiques
29 High St. (L.T. and N Cross) Est: 1971. Open Wed.-Sun. 10-6 or by appointment. SIZE: Medium. *STOCK: General antiques, decorators' items and shipping goods.* LOC: B4031. PARK: Easy. TEL: 0869 810203. VAT: Stan/Spec.

FINEDON

Baroq at Jean Burnett Antiques
37 High St. (B Dawson) Open 10.30-5, appointment advisable. *STOCK: Pottery and porcelain, £10-£500; paintings and watercolours, £100-£1,000; furniture, £100-£2,000.* TEL: 0933 680430/0234 240448.

Jean Burnett Antiques
37 High St. Est: 1967. Usually open, appointment advisable. *STOCK: Samplers and other embroideries, needlework tools and accessories, decorative items.* TEL: 0933 680430/681882.

M.C Chapman
3 and 3a Church St and Old Cinema, 12-20 Regent St. Est: 1967. Open 9-5.30. CL: Sat. p.m. SIZE: Large. *STOCK: Furniture, 18th-19th C; clocks, 18th-20th C, both £100-£3,000; decorative items, 19th-20th C, £100-£1,000.* LOC: On A6. PARK: Easy. TEL: 0933 681260. SER: Valuations; buys at auction. FAIRS: Newark. VAT: Stan/Spec.

Finedon Antiques (Antiques Centre)
3 Church St. (M.C Chapman) Est: 1973. Open 9.30-5.30, Sun. 2-5. SIZE: Large - 20 dealers. *STOCK: Ceramics, glass, paintings, prints and clocks, furniture, silver and plate, mainly 18th to early 20th C.* LOC: From roundabout at junction of A6 and A510 take A6 towards Kettering, turn left after 30yds., follow to bottom hill, premises on left. PARK: Easy. TEL: 0933 681260. SER: Export facilities. VAT: Stan/Spec.

Noton Antiques
1 High St. Est: 1978. Open Mon., Wed. and Sat. 10-5.30 or by appointment. *STOCK: General antiques.* TEL: 0933 680973. SER: Storage.

Finedon continued

Quaker Lodge Antiques
28 Church St. (S Banks) Resident. *STOCK: Period, Victorian and Edwardian furniture and general antiques.* TEL: 0933 680371. VAT: Stan/Spec.

Thorpe Antiques
Old Cinema Site, 12-20 Regent St. (M.R Clow) Open daily and Sat. a.m., other times by appointment. SIZE: Large. *STOCK: Georgian, Victorian and Edwardian mahogany furniture.* TEL: 0933 681688. SER: Restorations; cabinet making; French polishing; buys at auction. VAT: Stan/Spec.

FLORE

Flore House Antiques Ltd LAPADA
Flore House. (P.G Norman) Est: 1968. Open 9.30-6. SIZE: Large. *STOCK: Decorative furniture and accessories.* Not Stocked: Jewellery, gold, silver. LOC: Turn left at bollards into The Avenue for Flore House. PARK: Easy. TEL: 0327 40585; fax - 0327 349909. VAT: Stan. *Trade Only.*

V. and C Madeira
The Huntershields. Est: 1968. Open 9-7, Sun. by appointment. SIZE: Large. *STOCK: Furniture, 17th-19th C, £50-£5,000; decorative items, 19th C, £50-£2,000; metalware, 18th-19th C, £10-£1,000.* LOC: Off M1, junction 16, into Flore, last turning on left, premises on right next to Flore House Antiques. PARK: Easy. TEL: 0327 40718; home - same; fax: 0327 349263. VAT: Stan/Spec. *Trade Only.*

GUILSBOROUGH

Nick Goodwin Exports
The Firs, Nortoft Rd. Open every day by appointment. SIZE: Warehouse. *STOCK: Oak, mahogany, walnut, stripped and painted pine, smalls.* TEL: 0280 813115/0604 740234 (telephone/fax). SER: Restorations and pine stripping; export; shipping; packing; courier.

HARPOLE

Inglenook Antiques
23 High St. (T and P Havard) Est: 1971. Open 10-7. CL: Wed. SIZE: Small. *STOCK: Jewellery, £1-£75; stripped pine furniture, £15-£175; general antiques, £1-£200.* LOC: In main street. PARK: Easy. TEL: 0604 830007.

ISLIP

J Roe Antiques
The Old Furnace Site, Kettering Rd. (Mr and Mrs J Roe) Est: 1968. Open 6 days a week. *STOCK: General antiques; continental and American shipping goods.* TEL: 080 12 2937. VAT: Stan.

KETTERING

Albion Antiques
36 Duke St. (Mr and Mrs N Walmsley) Est: 1980. Open Mon., Fri. and Sat. 10-6. SIZE: Small. *STOCK: General bric-a-brac and furniture, Georgian-1930s, £5-£100.* LOC: Off Rockingham Rd. PARK: Easy. TEL: 0536 516220; home - same. SER: Valuations; restorations; caning; rushing; upholstery.

Antiques Warehouse
53-56 Havelock St. (M Coles) Open 8.30-6. *STOCK: Pine, porcelain, china, shipping goods.* TEL: 0536 411394/510522. SER: Stripping; furniture and kitchens made to order.

Alexis Brook
74 Lower St. (Mrs A Brook) Est: 1959. Open from 10 onwards, appointment advisable. CL: Sun. a.m. SIZE: Medium. *STOCK: General antiques, £1-£3,000.* LOC: On A6 from Market Harborough. House halfway up hill on left before main shopping centre. PARK: At Collingwood Motors, adjacent. TEL: 0536 513854.

Dragon Antiques
85 Rockingham Rd. (A.P Jones) Open 10-5. CL: Thurs. *STOCK: General antiques especially watercolours, oils and Oriental items.* TEL: 0536 517017.

Rockingham Road Antiques
103 Rockingham Rd. (C.M Hill) Resident. Est: 1985. Open 10.30-6, Mon.-Thurs. by appointment. SIZE: Medium. *STOCK: Furniture, 18th-19th C, £25-£5,000; decorative items, 18th-20th C, £25-£2,500; stone and marble.* LOC: From town centre towards Corby, shop on left, corner of Duke St. PARK: Easy. TEL: 0536 511842. SER: Valuations; restorations (marble and stone); buys at auction (furniture and stone items).

C.W Ward Antiques
Deene House, 40 Lower St. (Mrs J Wilson) Est: 1912. Open 9-5. SIZE: Small. *STOCK: General antiques, furniture; pottery, porcelain, pewter, glass, bygones and pictures.* LOC: 25yds. from GPO on A6. PARK: Opposite. TEL: 0536 513537. SER: Valuations; restorations (furniture, silver, porcelain); upholstery and curtain making. VAT: Stan/Spec.

KINGSTHORPE, Nr. Northampton

Laila
25 Welford Rd. (L Gray) Open 9-5.30. *STOCK: Pine.* TEL: 0604 715277. SER: Waxing; stripping.

The Old Brigade
10a Harborough Rd. (S.C Wilson) Est: 1978. Open by appointment. SIZE: Small. *STOCK: Military items, 1890's to 1945, £10-£10,000.* LOC: Junction 15, M1. PARK: Easy. TEL: 0604 719389; home- same. SER: Valuations. VAT: Stan/Spec.

LONG BUCKBY

R.E Thompson
17 Church St. Est: 1968. Open 8-5. SIZE: Large. *STOCK: Shipping goods, furniture, 19th-20th C; stripped pine, clocks, £1-£1,000.* PARK: Easy. TEL: 0327 842242/843487. VAT: Stan.

NETHER HEYFORD

Heyford Antiques
7 Church St. (J and J Bland) Est: 1987. Open 10-5 including Sun., evenings and Thurs. by appointment. SIZE: Small. *STOCK: Early English pottery, toby jugs, 1770-1840, £100-£3,000; Staffordshire portrait figures and pot-lids, 1840-1870, £60-£1,000; bargeware, brass and copper, small furniture, 19th C, £100-£500.* LOC: 1 mile junction 16, M1, 1 mile from A5. PARK: Easy. TEL: 0327 40749; home - same. SER: Buys at auction. FAIRS: NEC; Radley College, Oxford.

NORTHAMPTON

Adne and Naxos
71-73 Kingsthorpe Rd, Kingsthorpe Hollow. (P Scott) Open 9-5.30, Sat. 10-4.30. *STOCK: Fine art and furniture.* TEL: 0604 710740.

Buley Antiques
164 Kettering Rd. Est: 1966. Open 10.30-4.45, Thurs. by appointment. SIZE: Medium. *STOCK: Victoriana, £5-£200.* PARK: Nearby. TEL: 0604 31588; home - 0604 491577. SER: Valuations. VAT: Stan.

F. and C.H Cave
111 Kettering Rd. Est: 1879. Open 9-5.30. CL: Thurs. SIZE: Large. *STOCK: Furniture - Georgian, Victorian and decorative; general antiques and paintings.* LOC: Near town centre, 1/4 mile beyond pedestrianised area. PARK: Adjoining side streets. TEL: 0604 38278. VAT: Stan/Spec.

Northampton continued

Michael Jones Jeweller
1 Gold St. Est: 1919. *STOCK: Silver, gold and gem jewellery, French and carriage clocks.* TEL: 0604 32548. VAT: Stan/Spec.

Nostalgia Antiques
190 Kettering Rd. (T.W Harris) Open 9-5. CL: Thurs. *STOCK: General antiques, clocks.* PARK: Easy. TEL: 0604 33823.

Occultique
73 Kettering Rd. (M.J Lovett) Est: 1973. Open 10-5. SIZE: Small. *STOCK: Books, 50p-£500.* PARK: Nearby. TEL: 0604 27727. VAT: Stan.

Penny's Antiques
83 Kettering Rd. (Mrs P Mawby) Est: 1976. Open 11-4, Sat. 10-5. CL: Thurs. SIZE: Small. *STOCK: Shipping goods, kitchen chairs, pictures, army badges, furniture, china, smalls, glass, brass; Victorian to 1940, £5-£100.* LOC: On A43 near town centre. PARK: Easy. TEL: 0604 32429.

Regent House
Royal Terrace. (G Cave) Est: 1951. Open 9-1 and 2-5.30. CL: Sat. SIZE: Medium. *STOCK: Mainly furniture, 1660-1890, especially Georgian, £100-£18,000.* LOC: Near town centre, just north of Regent Square (road to Leicester); white detached house 100yds. on left hand side (west). PARK: Half-circle drive. TEL: 0604 37992. VAT: Spec.

R.S.J Savage and Son LAPADA
Alfred St. (M.J Savage) Est: 1905. Open 9-5.15, Sat. 9-12.30. *STOCK: Oils and watercolours, 18th C to date; antiquarian maps and prints, mirrors, framed pot lids, work by local artists.* LOC: Turn at mini roundabout on Billing Rd., into Alfred St. near hospital. Victorian building on left. PARK: Adjoining streets. TEL: 0604 20327. SER: Restorations (paintings); framing; brochure available.

Wootton Billingham
79 St. Giles St. (D.J Veryard) Est: 1897. Open 10-5. *STOCK: Antiquarian and secondhand books.* TEL: 0604 34531.

OUNDLE, Nr. Peterborough

Chancery Antiques
50 Glapthorne Rd. (R Andrews) Est: 1973. Open by appointment. *STOCK: Furniture, £50-£500; clocks, £10-£500, both 1780-1900; decorative items, 1850-1930, £10-£100.* TEL: 0832 273734.

Howard Antiques
46/46A West St. Est: 1964. Open 10-4.30. CL: Mon. SIZE: Medium. *STOCK: Clocks, furniture, £25-£1,000; collectors' items, china, glass, metalwork, £5-£200, all 17th-19th C.* PARK: Easy. TEL: 0832 274239; home - 0234 711106.

Quinn Galleries
36 Market Place. (T.P Quinn) Open 9.30-5.30. *STOCK: Oriental carpets, rugs and furniture.* TEL: 0832 273744.

PATTISHALL, Nr. Towcester

F King
Fosters Booth Road. Open by appointment only. *STOCK: Furniture, English and continental pictures, 18th-19th C.* LOC: Between Towcester and Weedon on A5. TEL: 0327 830326. VAT: Spec.

PAULERSPURY, Nr. Towcester

The Antique Galleries BADA
Watling St. (M Cameron) Est: 1948. Open 9-5.30. SIZE: Large. *STOCK: English furniture, 1650-1830; barometers, 1780-1830.* LOC: 3 miles south of Towcester on A5. PARK: Own. TEL: 032 733 238. VAT: Spec.

POTTERSPURY, Nr. Towcester

Reindeer Antiques Ltd BADA LAPADA
43 Watling St. (J.W Butterworth) Est: 1959. Open 9-6. SIZE: Large. *STOCK: Period English furniture, paintings, metal, clocks, garden furniture and statuary.* LOC: A5. TEL: 0908 542407. VAT: Stan/Spec.

RUSHDEN

D.W Sherwood Antiques Ltd
59 Little St. Est: 1960. *STOCK: General antiques.* TEL: 0933 53265.

Shire Antiques
111 High St. South. (J.V Preston) Open Fri., Sat. and Sun. 10-5. *STOCK: General antiques.* TEL: 0933 315567.

THRAPSTON, Nr. Kettering

J Roe Antiques
Unit 1, Cottingham Way. (Mr and Mrs J Roe) Open 9-6, Sat. 10-4. *STOCK: General antiques; continental and American shipping goods.* TEL: 080 12 2937. VAT: Stan.

TOWCESTER

Acorn Antiques
The Old Mill, Moat Lane. (I.B Porter) Open 10-5. SIZE: Large. *STOCK: Pine and hardwood country furniture, architectural items.* PARK: Easy. TEL: 0327 52788; fax - 0327 359543. SER: Valuations; restorations (pine stripping and repairs, French polishing). VAT: Stan.

Clark Galleries
215 Watling St. (A Clark) Est: 1964. Open 8.30-5.30, Sat. 9.30-4. SIZE: Medium. *STOCK: Landscape paintings, 18th C, £500-£15,000; portraits, 17th-18th C, £500-£5,000.* LOC: M1, junction 15, on A5. PARK: Easy and at rear. TEL: 0327 52957. SER: Valuations (oil paintings); restorations and re-lining (oil paintings). VAT: Stan/Spec.

Ron Green
209, 227-239 Watling St. West. Est: 1952. Open 9-6 or by appointment. SIZE: Large. *STOCK: English and continental furniture, £30-£30,000; oil paintings, £100-£10,000; decorative items.* TEL: 0327 50387.

John and Jennifer Jones
2 Watling St. Est: 1961. Open 9-6, Sat. 9-5, Sun. by appointment. SIZE: Medium. *STOCK: Furniture, 18th-19th C, £200-£750; shipping goods, 19th C, £25-£200; pictures and china.* LOC: A5. PARK: Easy. TEL: 0327 51898; home - 0327 51675. VAT: Spec.

R. and M Nicholas
161 Watling St. Open 9.30-6. SIZE: Small. *STOCK: 18th-19th C porcelain, silver and glass.* TEL: 0327 50639. VAT: Stan/Spec.

Shelron Collectors Shop
9 1/2 Brackley Rd. (R Grosvenor and N Saunders) PTA. Resident. Est: 1973. Open 10-5. CL: Mon. SIZE: Small. *STOCK: Postcards, from 1890; cigarette and trade cards, from 1880; ephemera, bric-a-brac, books, prints, models, £1-£100.* LOC: Leave M1, junction 15 or 16, 100yds. from A5 traffic lights going west. PARK: Easy. TEL: 0327 50242. SER: Valuations (postcards and cigarette cards). FAIRS: Covent Garden Jubilee Market, BIPEX and other specialist.

WEEDON

Robert Gray (Antique Dealer)
High St. Open most days and by appointment. *STOCK: General antiques.* TEL: Home - 0327 77802.

Weedon continued

Helios & Co (Antiques)
25/27 High St. (J Skiba and B Walters) Open 9-6 including Sun. SIZE: Large. *STOCK: English and continental furniture, especially dining tables; decorative accessories.* PARK: Easy. TEL: 0327 40264; evenings - 0525 270247. VAT: Spec.

Christopher Jones Antiques
The Lawn Works, High St. Open 10-5. *STOCK: Decorative and general antiques.* TEL: 0327 42165.

Sergio Lovato Antiques
23 High St. Open 10-7 including Sun, and by appointment. *STOCK: Furniture, decorative objects, paintings, mirrors.* TEL: 0327 40570. SER: Restorations.

Private Room
25 High St. (P Norman) Open 10.30-5, Thurs. 10.30-2.30, Sat. 10.30-4.30. *STOCK: Collectable and decorative antiques.* TEL: 0327 349277.

Rococo Antiques and Interiors
5 New St, Lower Weedon. (N.K Griffiths) Resident, usually available. *STOCK: Ironwork, including brass and iron beds, and architectural items.* LOC: 3 miles junction 16, M1, 1/4 mile off A5. PARK: Easy. TEL: 0327 41288. VAT: Stan/Spec.

Thirty-Eight Antiques Ltd
Building 14, Royal Ordnance Dept. (E.S. and N Saunders) Open 8-5.30, Sat. 8-12, other times by appointment, telephone call advisable. SIZE: Large. *STOCK: French decorative and English furniture, mostly light woods, some mahogany; pine and mahogany reproductions; panelled rooms, architectural items, stained glass, painted furniture.* TEL: 0327 40766; fax - 0327 40808. SER: Furniture made to order.

The Village Antique Market
62 High St. (E.A. and J.M Saunders) Est: 1967. Open 9.30-5.30, Sun. 10.30-5.30. SIZE: Large - 40 dealers. *STOCK: General antiques and interesting items.* LOC: On A45, just off A5. PARK: At side of market. TEL: 0327 42015. VAT: Stan.

WELDON

Loft Emporium
15-17 High St. (C.H Oliver) Open 10-5, Sun. by appointment. SIZE: 7 units. *STOCK: Mechanical objects, clocks, furniture, curios, books, pictures, radios, fire accessories, lighting, fixtures and antique related items.* TEL: 0536 65855. SER: Valuations; restorations.

WELLINGBOROUGH

Antiques and Bric-a-Brac Market
Market Sq, Town Centre. Open Tues. 9-4. SIZE: 135 stalls. *STOCK: General antiques and collectables.* TEL: 0905 611321.

Wellingborough continued

Park Book Shop
12 Park Rd. (J.A Foster) Est: 1979. Open 10-5, Thurs. 10-2. SIZE: Medium. *STOCK: Books, 19th C maps and prints, £5-£25; postcards, 20th C, 10p-£5.* PARK: Easy. TEL: 0933 222592. SER: Valuations.

Park Gallery
16 Cannon St. (Mrs J Foster) Est: 1988. Open 10-5. CL: Thurs. SIZE: Medium. *STOCK: Prints, maps, 18th-19th C, £5-£50.* LOC: Continuation of A510 into town. PARK: Easy. TEL: 0933 222592. VAT: Stan.

Bryan Perkins Antiques
Finedon Rd. (B.H. and J Perkins) Est: 1971. Open 9-5. CL: Sat. p.m. SIZE: Large. *STOCK: Furniture and paintings, 19th C, £200-£2,000; small items.* PARK: Easy. TEL: 0933 228812; home - 0536 790259. SER: Valuations; restorations (furniture). VAT: Spec. *Trade Only.*

WEST HADDON

Antiques
9 West End. Est: 1978. Open 10-5.30. CL: Sun., except by appointment. SIZE: Medium. *STOCK: Country furniture, period metalwork, brass and copper, treen and other domestic items.* LOC: A428. PARK: Easy. TEL: 0788 510772; home - 0788 822330. VAT: Spec.

The Country Pine Shop
The Romney Building, Northampton Rd. (H.J. and S.M Walters) Est: 1985. Open 8.30-5.30. SIZE: Large. *STOCK: English and continental stripped pine, £50-£800.* LOC: A428. TEL: 0788 510430.

Paul Hopwell Antiques BADA
30 High St. Est: 1974. Open 9-6. CL: Sun. except by appointment. SIZE: Large. *STOCK: 17th and 18th C oak and walnut country furniture, longcase clocks, metalware, oil paintings and prints mainly sporting and country pursuits.* LOC: A428. PARK: Easy. TEL: 0788 510636. SER: Valuations; restorations (furniture and metalware); buys at auction. VAT: Spec.

WOODFORD HALSE, Nr. Daventry

The Corner Cupboard
18 Station Rd. (T.R. and Mrs H.M Stuart) Est: 1980. Open 9-6.30, Sun. 9.30-6.30, Mon., Tues. and Wed. by appointment. SIZE: Medium. *STOCK: English and continental stripped pine, Victorian and Edwardian, £50-£1,000; iron and brass beds, Victorian, £175-£650; sofas, chairs, chesterfields, Victorian, £50-£450.* LOC: Off A361 towards village. After 1 mile turn right up Phipps Rd. to village centre, shop in parade at top of hill. PARK: Easy. TEL: 0327 60725; home - same. SER: Restorations (cabinet, upholstery, contract joinery).

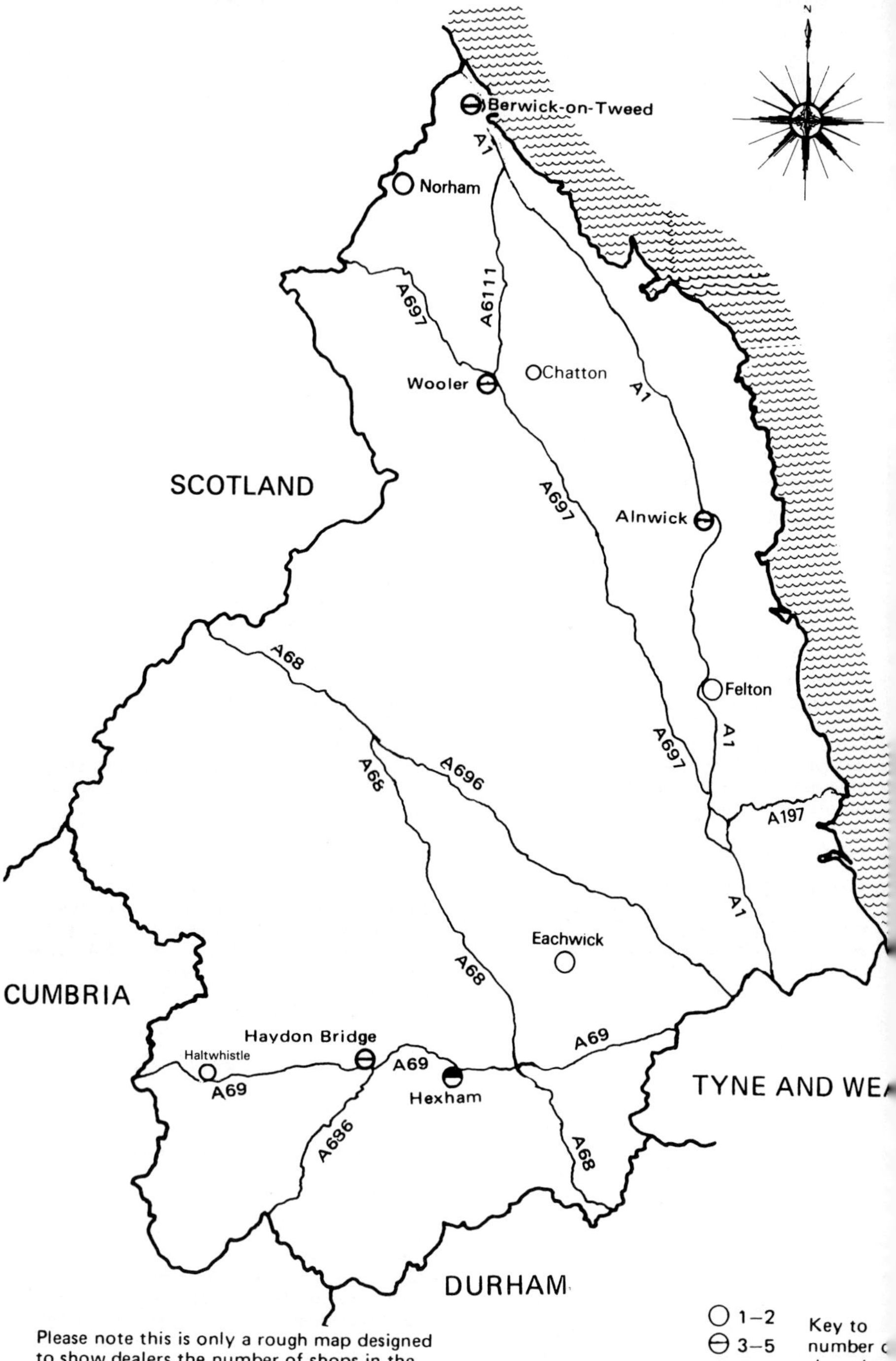
N
Berwick-on-Tweed
A1
Norham
A697
A6111
Wooler
Chatton
A1
SCOTLAND
A697
Alnwick
A68
Felton
A1
A697
A68
A696
A197
A1
Eachwick
A68
CUMBRIA
Haydon Bridge
Haltwhistle
A69
A69
A69
Hexham
TYNE AND WE
A686
A68
DURHAM
1–2
3–5
6–12
13+
Key to
number
shops in
this area.

Please note this is only a rough map designed to show dealers the number of shops in the various towns, and is not necessarily totally accurate.

ALNWICK

Country Pine Antiques
22 Bailiffgate. (J. and T Higson and J Storey) Est: 1980. Open 10-5. CL: Wed. SIZE: Large. *STOCK: Country pine furniture.* LOC: Opposite the castle. PARK: Easy. TEL: 0665 603616. SER: Valuations; restorations; buys at auction. VAT: Stan.

Pottergate Antiques
24 Narrowgate. (Mrs L Shell) Open 10-5 or by appointment. CL: Wed. SIZE: Medium. *STOCK: General antiques and Oriental rugs, £1-£2,500.* LOC: Near castle. TEL: 0665 510034; home - 0665 604212. VAT: Stan/Spec.

Ian A Robertson
Castle Corner, Narrowgate. *STOCK: English oak, mahogany furniture, glass, china and brass, 18th-19th C.* TEL: 0665 602725.

Tamblyn
12 Bondgate Without. (Mrs S.M Hirst) Est: 1981. Open 10-4.30. SIZE: Medium. *STOCK: General antiques including country furniture, pottery, pictures; antiquities, glass, to 20th C, £5-£450.* LOC: Diagonally opposite war memorial at southern entrance to town. PARK: Easy. TEL: 0665 603024; home - same. SER: Valuations.

BERWICK-ON-TWEED

The Antique Shop
31 Bridge St. (J Roberts and T Charlesworth) Est: 1983. Open 10.30-4.30, other times by appointment. CL: Mon. and Thurs. SIZE: Medium. *STOCK: Oak and mahogany furniture, porcelain and glass, 18th-19th C; silver, watercolours and prints, mirrors and light fittings, brass and copper including fenders and fire-irons; screens, needlework pictures and samplers.* TEL: 0289 302648; home - 0668 213610.

Castlegate Antiques
83 Castlegate. (R. and A Fairbairn) Est: 1973. Open 9-1 and 2-5 or by appointment. CL: Sat. p.m. SIZE: Medium. *STOCK: Clocks, furniture, shipping items, general antiques, Victorian, £1-£1,000.* Not Stocked: Militaria. LOC: Old A1, at junction to Berwick railway station. PARK: Easy. TEL: 0289 306009.

Treasure Chest
44 Castlegate. (Y Scott) Est: 1988. Open 10-3, Thurs. 10-1 and Sat. 11.30-3. SIZE: Small. *STOCK: China, jewellery, glass, silver plate and small furniture, from 1860, £5-£150.* LOC: Approximately 1 mile from A1. PARK: Easy. TEL: Home - 0289 307736. SER: Restorations (china). FAIRS: Local.

CHATTON, Nr. Alnwick

Country Pine Antiques
Church House. (J Railton) Est: 1980. Open 10-5 or anytime by appointment. SIZE: Warehouse. *STOCK: Pine, oak and country furniture, 18th-19th C, £50-£5,000; architectural items.* PARK: Easy. TEL: 066 85 323. SER: Valuations; restorations; buys at auction. VAT: Stan/Spec.

EACHWICK

Hazel Cottage Clocks
Hazel Cottage. (E. and M Charlton) Open every day 9.30-6. SIZE: Medium. *STOCK: Clocks, £150-£8,000.* LOC: Just off Darras Hall to Stamfordham road, opp. Wylam turn-off. PARK: Easy. TEL: 0661 852415. SER: Restorations (longcase clocks). VAT: Spec.

FELTON, Nr. Morpeth

Felton Park Antiques
Felton Park. (D. and A Burton) Resident. Est: 1973. *STOCK: Small Georgian furniture, pottery and porcelain - mainly Sunderland lustre, Newhall, blue and white transfer ware.* PARK: Easy. TEL: 0670 787319. SER: Valuations; restorations; polishing. VAT: Spec.

HALTWHISTLE

Armstrong Antiques of Haltwhistle
Sycamore House, Station Rd. (R Armstrong) Est: 1986. Open 10-5, Sun. 1.30-4.30. CL: Mon. and Wed. SIZE: Small. *STOCK: Furniture, Georgian, Victorian and Edwardian, £50-£1,000; china and decorative items, pictures and clocks, 19th-20th C, £5-£500.* LOC: Just off A69. PARK: Easy. TEL: 0434 321787. SER: Valuations; buys at auction. FAIRS: Newark; Charnock Richards.

HAYDON BRIDGE, Nr. Hexham

Haydon Bridge Antiques
3 Shaftoe St. (J. and J Smith) Est: 1974. Open 10.30-5 and by appointment. CL: Mon. and Thurs. SIZE: Large. *STOCK: Stripped pine, £5-£500; Victorian and Edwardian oak and mahogany, shipping goods, Victorian oils and watercolours.* PARK: Easy. TEL: 0434 684200; home - 0434 684461. VAT: Stan.

Haydon Gallery
3 Shaftoe St. (J Smith) Est: 1975. Open 10.30-5.30; Sun., Mon. and Thurs. by appointment. SIZE: Small. *STOCK: Oils and watercolours by North Eastern artists and others, mainly 19th C; some bronzes.* TEL: 0434 684200; home - 0434 684461. SER: Valuations; restorations (oil paintings).

Haydon Bridge continued

Revival Beds
Oddfellows Workshop, Shaftoe St. (I Coulson) *STOCK: Fourposters, half testers, traditional wood beds.* PARK: Easy. TEL: 0434 684755.

HEXHAM

Arthur Boaden Antiques LAPADA
29 and 30 Market Pl. (R.J Boaden) Est: 1948. Open 9-12.30 and 1.30-5. SIZE: Large. *STOCK: Small furniture, Georgian, Regency, Victorian, £50-£3,000; Victorian bric-a-brac, £1-£100; paintings, 19th-20th C, £50-£1,000; Victorian jewellery, from £10.* LOC: Opposite Hexham Abbey, off A69. PARK: Nearby. TEL: 0434 603187. SER: Valuations; jewellery repairs. VAT: Stan/Spec.

Gordon Caris
16 Market Pl. Est: 1972. Open 9-5. CL: Thurs. *STOCK: Clocks and watches.* TEL: 0434 602106. SER: Restorations (clocks and watches).

Hallstile Antiques
17 Hallstile Bank. (Mrs P Neuman) Est: 1982. Open 10-5. CL: Thurs. SIZE: Large. *STOCK: Furniture, 17th to early 19th C, £50-£7,000; paintings and prints, £15-£600; clocks, silver plate, china, porcelain and glass.* LOC: Town centre, just off Market Place. PARK: Nearby. TEL: 0434 602239. SER: Buys at auction.

Hexham continued

J.A. and T Hedley

3 St. Mary's Chare. (D Hall and W.H Jewitt) Est: 1819. Open 9-5. CL: Thurs. p.m. SIZE: Medium. *STOCK: 17th C to Victorian furniture; 18th C to Edwardian porcelain, silver, glass, china.* LOC: Off Battle Hill (A69). PARK: 400yds. TEL: 0434 602317. SER: Valuations; restorations (furniture); buys at auction (furniture). VAT: Stan/Spec.

Hexham Antiques (Inc. Hotspur Antiques)

6 Rear Battle Hill. (J. and D Latham) Est: 1977. Open 10.30-4.30, Sat. 9.30-4.30. CL: Sun. and Thurs., except by appointment. SIZE: Large. *STOCK: Furniture, clocks, pictures, glass, china, boxes and collectors' items, to art deco.* LOC: Main shopping street, opposite National Westminster Bank. PARK: 400 metres. TEL: 0434 603851; home - 0434 604813. SER: Valuations; buys at auction. VAT: Spec.

Top Drawer

19 Hallstile Bank. (E Elliott) Open 11-4.30. CL: Wed. and Thurs. *STOCK: General antiques especially hand-stitched quilts; linen and some stripped pine.* TEL: 0434 605669.

Turn of the Century Antiques

8 Market St. (E Alston and P Pearce) Est: 1975. Open Tues., Fri. and Sat. 11-5. *STOCK: Books, country bygones, china, glass, shipping items, furniture; all £1-£200.* PARK: Market Sq. TEL: 0434 607621/603988.

The Violin Shop

31a Hencotes. (N Cain) Est: 1970. Open 10-5 or by appointment. *STOCK: Violins, violas, cellos and bows.* TEL: 0434 607897.

John Walker Antiques

Stable Buildings, Station Rd. Open 9.30-4.30. CL: Thurs. *STOCK: General antiques, shipping goods and architectural items.* TEL: 0434 608520; home - 0661 842945. VAT: Stan/Spec.

NORHAM, Nr. Berwick-on-Tweed

J. and D Stewart

6 and 8 West St. Resident. Est: 1969. SIZE: Medium. *STOCK: China, glass, collectors items, mainly Victorian.* LOC: 7 miles north of Berwick-on-Tweed. PARK: Easy. TEL: 0289 382376.

WOOLER

Border Sporting Gallery

25 High St. (D. and T Ross) Open 9-5. CL: Sat. SIZE: Medium. *STOCK: Sporting oils and prints, Snaffles, L. Edwards, Tom Carr, Thorburn, 1925 and earlier, £10-£20,000.* LOC: Main St. PARK: Easy. TEL: 0668 81872. SER: Valuations; restorations. VAT: Stan/Spec.

Wooler continued

W.J Miller and Son

1-5 Church St. (J Miller) Est: 1947. Open any time by appointment. SIZE: Large, and warehouses. *STOCK: Georgian and Victorian furniture, clocks, paintings.* LOC: A697. PARK: Nearby. TEL: 0668 81500; home - 066 87 281. VAT: Stan/Spec. *Trade Only.*

E.D. and M.A Redpath

Dovecot House, The Peth. Open 10-5. Available any time to trade. *STOCK: Furniture, clocks, porcelain, silver, trade and shipping goods.* TEL: 0668 81396. SER: Buys at auction. VAT: Stan.

Geo. III mahogany balloon bracket timepiece by Robert Gibson, London, c.1800, 16¼in. high. From an article on balloon clocks by Richard Garnier in the December 1990/January 1991 issue of ***Antique Collecting.***

Nottinghamshire

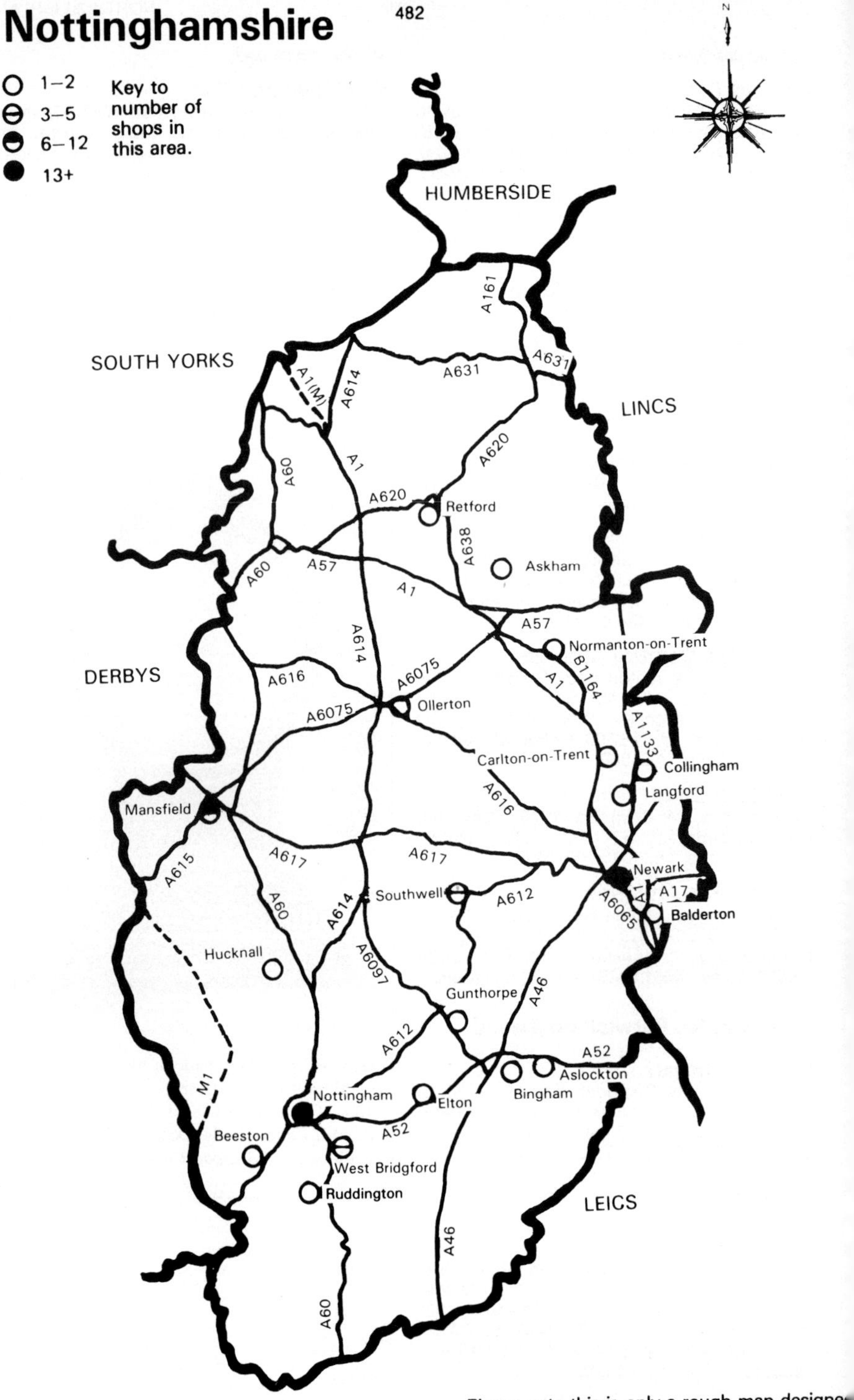
N
1–2
3–5
6–12
13+
Key to number of shops in this area.
HUMBERSIDE
SOUTH YORKS
LINCS
DERBYS
LEICS
A161
A631
A631
A1(M)
A614
A1
A60
A620
A620
Retford
A638
Askham
A60
A57
A1
A57
Normanton-on-Trent
B1164
A1
A614
A616
A6075
Ollerton
A6075
A1133
Carlton-on-Trent
Collingham
Langford
A616
Mansfield
A615
A617
A617
Newark
A17
A1
A6065
Balderton
A60
A614
Southwell
A612
Hucknall
A6097
Gunthorpe
A46
A612
M1
A52
Aslockton
Bingham
Nottingham
Elton
A52
Beeston
West Bridgford
Ruddington
A46
A60

Please note this is only a rough map designed to show dealers the number of shops in the various towns, and is not necessarily totally accurate.

ASKHAM, Nr. Newark

Sally Mitchell Fine Arts
Thornlea. Est: 1967. Author of the Dictionary of British Equestrian Artists. Appointment advisable. SIZE: Medium. *STOCK: Mainly 20th C sporting paintings and prints, some 17th-19th C sporting paintings.* LOC: 5 miles from Retford; 5 mins. from Markham Moor roundabout on A1. PARK: Easy. TEL: 077 783 234. SER: Valuations; restorations; framing; lectures; buys at auction.

ASLOCKTON, Nr. Nottingham

Jane Neville Gallery
Elm House, Abbey Lane. (R Repetto-Wright and J Neville) Resident. Est: 1979. Open 10-4, Sat., Sun. and Mon. by appointment. SIZE: Medium. *STOCK: Paintings and prints including sporting, 19th-20th C, £50-£5,000.* LOC: A52. PARK: Easy. TEL: 0949 50220. SER: Valuations; restorations; framing; research; print publishers; buys at auction (sporting paintings). VAT: Stan/Spec.

BALDERTON

Blacksmiths Forge
74 Main St. (Mrs J Sheppard) Est: 1982. Open 12-5, Sat. 9.30-6, Wed. and Sun. by appointment. SIZE: Medium. *STOCK: Pine, beech, satin walnut bedroom furniture, Victorian-Edwardian, £50-£100; smalls, Victorian-1920, £5-£100; fireplaces, cast-iron and pine surrounds, Georgian-1920, £20-£300.* LOC: Off A1, follow signs to village, turn right at traffic lights, shop on right next to church. PARK: Easy. TEL: 0636 700008; home - same. SER: Valuations; restorations; stripping; polishing; buys at auction (furniture). FAIRS: Newark.

BEESTON

Elizabeth Bailey
33 Chilwell Rd. Est: 1966. Open 10-5.30, Mon. 2-5.30. CL: Thurs. SIZE: Small. *STOCK: Furniture, 18th C to 1930's shipping; general smalls and decorative items, hand-stripped pine.* TEL: 0602 255685; home - 0602 259259. SER: Restorations (furniture and longcase clocks). VAT: Stan/Spec.

BINGHAM

E.M Cheshire BADA LAPADA
The Manor House, Market Pl. Open 9.30-5.30. CL: Wed. p.m. *STOCK: Furniture, 17th C oak; 18th-19th C mahogany, early metalware.* TEL: 0949 838861. VAT: Stan/Spec.

CARLTON-ON-TRENT, Nr. Newark

Tudor Rose Antiques
(D.H and Mrs C Rose) Resident. Est: 1984. Open by appointment only. SIZE: Medium.

Tudor Rose Antiques continued

STOCK: Furniture, 18th-19th C, £50-£2,500; interesting items, 18th-20th C, £1-£500. LOC: 1/4 mile from Sutton-on-Trent turning off A1. PARK: Easy. TEL: 0636 821841. SER: Restorations (furniture). FAIRS: Local.

COLLINGHAM, Nr. Newark

The Barn
(J Richardson) Open by appointment. *STOCK: 18th-19th C furniture and furnishings, treen, textiles, linen and lace, Baxter prints and licencees, Stevengraphs.* TEL: 0636 892884.

Paul Merrill Antiques
The Laurels, High St. Open 9-5, Sun. 10-2. *STOCK: Period and garden furniture.* TEL: 0636 893013.

ELTON, Nr. Nottingham

Rectory Bungalow Workshop
Main Rd. (E.M and Mrs M.G Mackie) Est: 1981. Open Sat. 10-5 in summer, 10-12 and 2-3 in winter, other times by appointment. SIZE: Small. *STOCK: Furniture, 17th-19th C; hand-painted, decorative items.* LOC: A52 between Nottingham and Grantham, near Granby/Orston crossroads. PARK: Easy. TEL: 0949 50330/50878; home - same. SER: Restorations (cane and rush seating). VAT: Spec.

HUCKNALL

Curiosity Corner
53a Watnall Rd. (C Channer) Open 9.15-5, Wed. 9.15-12, Sat. 10.15-2. *STOCK: General antiques.* TEL: 0602 630789.

LANGFORD, Nr. Newark

T Baker
Langford House Farm. Est: 1966. CL: Sun. except by appointment and Sat. SIZE: Medium. *STOCK: Victoriana, period furniture and oak.* LOC: A1133. PARK: Own. TEL: 0636 704026. *Trade Only.*

MANSFIELD

Antiques Warehouse
375 Chesterfield Rd. North, Pleasley. (B Lowe and M Walsh) Est: 1976. Open 8-6, weekends by appointment. SIZE: Large. *STOCK: Victorian shipping furniture, £30-£1,000.* LOC: Off M1, junction 29. PARK: Easy. TEL: 0623 810480; home - 0773 874525/875273. SER: Valuations; restorations. VAT: Stan.

The Book Shelf
16 Albert St. (F.B and S Payton) Open 9.30-5. CL: Wed. SIZE: Medium. *STOCK: Antiquarian and secondhand books.* LOC: Town centre. TEL: 0623 648231; home - 0623 640601. SER: Buys at auction (books).

Mansfield continued

Fair Deal Antiques

138 Chesterfield Rd. North. (D Lowe) Est: 1972. Open 9.30-5.30. CL: Sat. p.m. and Sun. except by appointment. SIZE: Large. *STOCK: Shipping goods, £50-£100; furniture, mainly mahogany, Victorian, £100-£1,000; period furniture, metalware and small items.* PARK: Easy. TEL: 0623 653768/512419. VAT: Stan. *Trade Only.*

Mansfield Antiques

49-51 Ratcliffe Gate. Est: 1964. Open 9-5.30 and by appointment. SIZE: Large. *STOCK: Furniture.* LOC: On A617 Newark Rd. PARK: Easy and adjacent. TEL: 0623 27475; home - 0623 632108. SER: Valuations; buys at auction. VAT: Stan/Spec.

Omega Antiques of Mansfield

8 Lansdowne Ave. (J. and J McCarron) Est: 1986. Open 9-5, Sat. 9-1. SIZE: Small. *STOCK: English furniture, 18th-19th C, £50-£500; English and European porcelain and ceramics, 17th-19th C, £25-£500; paintings and prints, 19th-20th C, £25-£1,000.* LOC: Just off A60. PARK: Easy. TEL: 0623 650989; home - same. SER: Valuations; restorations (furniture). FAIRS: Newark, Stafford, N.E.C., Swallow Hotel. VAT: Stan.

Sheppards Antiques

122-124 Chesterfield Rd. North. (J. and B Sheppard) Est: 1970. Open 9.30-5.30, Sat. 9.30-1. CL: Wed. *STOCK: Furniture, period to shipping, mainly Victorian for Australian and continental markets, £10-£2,500; general small items.* LOC: 4 miles from M1, exit 29. PARK: Forecourt. TEL: 0623 31691. VAT: Stan/Spec.

NEWARK

Castle Gate Antiques Centre

55 Castle Gate. Est: 1985. Open 9-5.30. SIZE: Large. LOC: A46 through town, 250yds. from castle. PARK: Easy. TEL: 0636 700076. Below are listed the dealers at this centre.

Colin C Bowdell LAPADA
17th-19th C arms, armour, militaria, truncheons and tipstaves. TEL: Home - 0476 63206. SER: Valuations. VAT: Stan/Spec.

N Bryan-Peach Antiques
18th-19th C furniture, clocks and barometers, metalware, £50-£3,000. TEL: Home - 0509 880425. VAT: Stan/Spec.

Evelyn Buckle Antiques
Oak and mahogany furniture, 18th-19th C; decorative items. TEL: Home - 0949 42057. VAT: Stan/Spec.

James Dobie Antiques
18th-19th C town and country furniture; 19th-20th C oils and watercolours, pottery and porcelain, to 1930; decorative items. TEL: Home - 0476 76143. SER: Valuations. VAT: Stan/Spec.

Fearn Antiques LAPADA
18th-19th C town and country furniture; 19th to early 20th C watercolours; decorative items. TEL: 0606 775090. VAT: Stan/Spec.

Castle Gate Antiques Centre continued

Parkside Antiques
18th-19th C mahogany and walnut furniture; 19th to early 20th C paintings. VAT: Stan/Spec.

Michael Thompson Antiques
18th-19th C oak and mahogany furniture, decorative items, £50-£2,000. TEL: Home - 0949 50204. VAT: Stan/Spec.

Margaret M Thompson Antiques
19th C oak and mahogany furniture, pictures and decorative items. TEL: Home - 0949 50204. SER: Valuations. VAT: Stan/Spec.

D. and G Antiques

11 Kings Rd. (Mr and Mrs D Stutchbury) Est: 1982. Open 9.30-5. CL: Mon. SIZE: Large. *STOCK: Furniture, mainly 19th C, £50-£500; porcelain and glass, 19th C, £5-£100; pictures, Victorian, £20-£150.* LOC: From Market Sq. 500yds., opposite school playing fields. PARK: Easy. TEL: 0636 702782. SER: Restorations; buys at auction.

D. and V Antiques

4A Northgate. (D. and V Whitehead) Est: 1982. Open 9.30-5. CL: Fri. SIZE: Small. *STOCK: Furniture, Victorian and Edwardian, £50+; small items, clocks, oil lamps.* LOC: A46 before town centre (Lincoln side). TEL: 0636 71888; home - 0636 76880.

R.R Limb Antiques

31-35 Northgate. Open 9-6. *STOCK: General antiques and pianos.* TEL: 0636 74546.

Newark Antique Warehouse

Kelham Rd. Open 8.30-5.30, Sat. 10-4. LOC: Just off A1. PARK: Easy. TEL: 0636 74869. Below are listed the dealers at this warehouse. *Trade Only.*

A & J Antiques
17th-19th C country furniture. VAT: Stan/Spec.

A M Antiques
Period furniture. VAT: Stan/Spec.

T and L Baker
Victorian mahogany and walnut furniture and longcase clocks. VAT: Stan/Spec.

B Benson
Furniture and decorative items.

David E Burrows
Georgian mahogany and country furniture. VAT: Stan/Spec.

John Dench Antiques
17th-19th C furniture, English pottery, decorative items, longcase clocks, £50-£10,000. VAT: Stan/Spec.

Dukeries Antiques
(J and J Coupe) *17th-19th C furniture; vintage and classic cars.* VAT: Stan/Spec.

Genesis
Continental items, wicker, cane and decorative furniture.

J Sheppard
Georgian, Victorian and Edwardian furniture. VAT: Stan/Spec.

P R Straw
Georgian, Victorian and shipping furniture. VAT: Stan/Spec.

Wickersley Antiques
Mainly Victorian furniture. VAT: Stan/Spec.

Newark continued

Newark Antiques Centre
Regent House, Lombard St. Open 9.30-5. SIZE; 52 dealers. *STOCK: Georgian and Victorian furniture, art deco, pottery, porcelain, glass, swords, militaria, coins, stamps, clocks, pictures, books; Victoriana, silver, jewellery and general antiques.* TEL: 0636 605504.

Portland Antiques
20 Portland St. (C Duckworth) Est: 1968. Open 9.30-5, Fri. and Sat. 9.30-5.30, Mon. and Thurs. by appointment. SIZE: Medium. *STOCK: General antiques and smalls, shipping items, pine, collectors' items, £5-£1,000.* LOC: A46,2 mins. from town centre. PARK: At rear. TEL: 0636 701478; home - 0636 72972. SER: Valuations.

Roger Sarsby and Michael Pickering Fine Art
Mill Farm, Kirklington. Open by appointment. *STOCK: British and continental watercolours, 18th and 19th C.* TEL: 0636 813394.

Second Time Around
Newark Antiques Centre, Regent House, Lombard St. (G.L Powis and R Kenyon) Est: 1985. Open 9.30-5. SIZE: Medium. *STOCK: Clocks, mainly longcase and bracket, to 1830, £1,100-£12,000.* LOC: A46 town centre, opposite bus station entrance. PARK: Easy. TEL: 0636 605504; home - 0522 543167 or 0904 705000. SER: Restorations (as stock). VAT: Spec.

Newark continued

Jack Spratt Antiques
Unit 5, George St. Open 8-5.30, Sat. 8-12. SIZE: Warehouse. *STOCK: Pine and oak.* PARK: Easy. TEL: 0636 707714/74853. VAT: Stan.

TGM Antiques Warehouse
5 Victoria St. (T.G Marsh) Est: 1980. Open 9-5 or by appointment. SIZE: Large. *STOCK: Furniture including pine.* LOC: A46. PARK: Easy. TEL: 0636 701686; home - same. SER: Valuations; restorations; export packing. VAT: Stan/Spec.

T.T. Antiques
Warehouse, Hatchett Lane off Lincoln Rd. (T Tunstall) Open 9-5 or by appointment. *STOCK: Pine and period furniture, clocks.* TEL: 0636 77291; evenings - 0636 704030.

Wade-Smith and Read
1-3 Castlegate. (A Wade-Smith and A Read) Open 9-5. *STOCK: 17th-18th C furniture; decorative items; Eastern rugs.* TEL: 0636 73792.

NORMANTON-ON-TRENT, Nr. Newark

F.J McCarthy Ltd
The Grange. Est: 1946. CL: Sat. *STOCK: Furniture, English and continental 18th C; works of art.* TEL: 0636 821382. VAT: Stan/Spec.

NOTTINGHAM

Antiques and General Trading Co
145 Lower Parliament St. (C. and M Drummond-Hoy) Est: 1965. Open 10-5. CL: Thurs. SIZE: Large. *STOCK: Furniture, from 17th C oak to decorative furniture and objects, £50-£5,000.* LOC A52. PARK: At side. TEL: 0602 585971; home - 0664 62184. SER: Valuations; restorations (furniture). VAT: Stan/Spec.

B Armstrong
19 Bentinck Rd, Hyson Green. Open 10-5.30. CL: Thurs. *STOCK: Collectors' items, militaria, badges, medals, coins, cigarette cards, toys.* TEL: 0602 789062.

Breck Antiques
726 Mansfield Rd, Woodthorpe. (P.H.K Astill) Est: 1969. Open Tues., Fri. and Sat., other times by appointment. SIZE: Small. *STOCK: Furniture and porcelain, 18th-19th C.* LOC: Main Mansfield road. PARK: Forecourt. TEL: 0602 605263; home - 0602 621197. SER: Valuations.

N.J Doris
170 Derby Rd. Open 10-4.30. CL: Thurs. *STOCK: Books, antiquarian and secondhand; county maps, postcards and music.* TEL: 0602 781194.

The Golden Cage
99 Derby Rd. (J Pearson and J Paradise) Open 10-5. *STOCK: Beaded dresses, Victorian clothes, tweeds, coats, dinner jackets.* TEL: 0602 411600/289521.

Granny's Attic
308 Carlton Hill, Carlton. (Mrs A Pembleton) Open Tues., Thurs. and Fri. 9-3.30; Sat. 9.30-4. *STOCK: Dolls, miniatures, general antiques and furniture.* TEL: 0602 265204.

Sheila Harris Antiques
3 Canning Circus, Derby Rd. Est: 1975. Open 10.30-5. CL: Thurs. SIZE: Medium. *STOCK: Furniture, porcelain, metalware, all 19th C.* PARK: Nearby. TEL: 0602 412094; home - 0602 473099. FAIRS: Thoresby Hall; Harlaxton Manor; N.E.C. and Wellbeck Abbey.

Nottingham continued

Hockley Coins
170 Derby Rd. (D.T Peake) Open 10-4. CL: Thurs. *STOCK: Coins, medals, badges, postcards, cigarette cards, toys, silver, collectables.* TEL: 0602 790667.

Melville Kemp Ltd LAPADA
79-81 Derby Rd. Est: 1900. Open 9.30-1 and 2-5.30. CL: Sat. p.m. and Thurs. SIZE: Small. *STOCK: Jewellery, Victorian; silver, Georgian and Victorian, both £5-£5,000; ornate English and continental porcelain, Sheffield plate.* Not Stocked: Furniture. LOC: From Nottingham on main Derby Rd. PARK: Easy. TEL: 0602 417055; fax - 0602 417055. SER: Valuations; restorations (silver, china, jewellery); buys at auction. VAT: Stan/Spec.

Lustre Metal Antiques Nottingham Donsign Ltd
Canning Circus, Derby Rd. Est: 1957. Open 9-4.30. *STOCK: Copper, brass, silver, plated and cast iron items, especially fireplaces and beds.* TEL: 0602 704385/500316; evenings - 0602 211046. SER: Restorations; repairs and polishing.

Anthony Mitchell Fine Paintings BADA LAPADA
Sunnymede House, 11 Albemarle Rd, Woodthorpe. (A. and M Mitchell) Est: 1965. Open by appointment. *STOCK: Oil paintings, £2,000-£100,000; watercolours, £500-£30,000.* LOC: North on Nottingham ring road to junction with Mansfield road, turn right, then 3rd left. PARK: Easy. TEL: 0602 623865; home - same. SER: Valuations; restorations. FAIRS: Olympia, N.E.C., Harrogate, Cafe Royal, Barbican and Bath. VAT: Spec.

Nottingham Antique Centre
British Rail Goods Yard, London Rd. (P.G Murdoch) Est: 1969. Open 9-5, Sat. a.m. by appointment. CL: Sat. p.m. SIZE: Large. *STOCK: Shipping furniture, Georgian and Victorian, £50-£200; clocks and pottery, Edwardian, £50-£500; bric-a-brac, Victorian, £5-£25.* LOC: From city centre, head south via Lower Parliament St. to Canal St. island. Carry on to London Rd., turn left at 2nd set of traffic lights. PARK: Easy. TEL: 0602 504504/505548. VAT: Stan.

Nottingham continued

Parkside Antiques

140 Derby Rd, (Canning Circus). (M. and C Hufton) Est: 1983. Open 10-5, Tues. and Wed. 2-5. CL: Thurs. SIZE: Medium. *STOCK: Furniture, especially tables, chairs and other seating, £50-£3,500.* PARK: At rear. TEL: 0602 609685 (evenings). FAIRS: British International, Birmingham; Robert Bailey; Barnsdale Country Club, Rutland Water.

Pegasus Antiques

62 Derby Rd. (P. and J Clewer) Open 9.30-5. *STOCK: Fine 18th-19th C furniture, paintings, general antiques.* TEL: 0602 474220.

S Pembleton

306 Carlton Hill, Carlton. Open Tues., Thurs. and Fri. 9-5, Sat. 10-5. *STOCK: General antiques.* TEL: 0602 265204.

Mike Pollock

110 Derby Rd. Open 10.30-3.30. *STOCK: General antiques, Victoriana, clocks, mechanical and steam models, toys, bygones.* TEL: 0602 474266.

David and Carole Potter Antiques

76 Derby Rd. Est: 1966. Open 10-4. CL: Thurs. SIZE: Medium. *STOCK: Clocks, 18th-19th C, £50-£5,000; period furniture, 17th-19th C; pottery, porcelain and glass, 18th-19th C, £20-£7,000; trade and shipping goods.* LOC: From Nottingham centre, take main Derby Rd., shop on right. PARK: Easy. TEL: 0602 417911; home - 0602 211084. VAT: Stan/Spec.

Val Smith Coins and Antiques

170 Derby Rd. Open 10-4.30. CL: Thurs. *STOCK: Coins, medals, badges, postcards, cigarette cards, toys, collectables, books and general antiques.* TEL: 0602 781194.

Station Pine Antiques

103 Carrington St. Open 9.30-5.30. SIZE: Large. *STOCK: Stripped pine and satin walnut furniture.* LOC: Near Midland Station. TEL: 0602 582710.

Top Hat Antiques Centre

66-72 Derby Rd. (Top Hat Exhibitions Ltd) Est: 1978. Open 9.30-5. SIZE: Large. *STOCK: Furniture, Georgian to Edwardian; small porcelain and metal items, to art deco; oils, watercolours and prints, 19th-20th C, £30-£1,000.* LOC: A52 town centre. PARK: Easy. TEL: 0602 419143; home - 0602 258769/259841. VAT: Stan/Spec.

Trade Wind Antiques

1A Arkwright St. (Mr and Mrs M Storer) Est: 1965. Open 10-4. SIZE: Large. *STOCK: Clocks and general antiques.* TEL: 0602 862850.

Trident Arms

74 Derby Rd. Est: 1970. Open 9.30-5, Sat. 10-4. SIZE: Large. *STOCK: Arms and armour of all ages and nations.* LOC: From city centre take main Derby Rd., shop on right. PARK: Easy. TEL: 0602 474137; fax - 0602 414199. SER: Valuations. VAT: Stan/Spec.

OLLERTON

Hamlyn Lodge

Station Rd. (N., J.S. and M.J Barrows) Open 10-5, Sun. 12-5. CL: Mon. SIZE: Small. *STOCK: General antiques, 18th-19th C, £100-£3,000.* LOC: Off A614. PARK: Easy. TEL: 0623 823600. SER: Restorations (furniture).

RETFORD

Franco Antiques

Riverside Lodge, London Rd. (F Franco) Open daily. *STOCK: English and continental porcelain, music boxes, furniture, 1700-1930.* PARK: Own. TEL: 0777 705688. SER: Restorations (porcelain).

RUDDINGTON, Nr. Nottingham

Arthur and Ann Rodgers

7 Church St. Est: 1958. SIZE: Small. *STOCK: Maps and prints, pottery and china, books.* LOC: Village centre. PARK: Easy. TEL: Home - 0602 216214. SER: Valuations; restorations; buys at auction. VAT: Stan.

SOUTHWELL

Strouds (of Southwell Antiques)

3-7 Church St. (V.N. and J Stroud) Est: 1972. Open 10-5, Sun. by appointment. SIZE: Large and warehouse. *STOCK: Furniture, clocks, metalware, paintings, 17th-19th C, £10-£10,000.* LOC: Town centre. PARK: Easy. TEL: 0636 815001; home - 0636 814194. VAT: Stan/Spec.

WEST BRIDGFORD

Bridgford Antiques

2A Rushworth Ave. Open 10-5, Sat. 10-1. SIZE: Medium. *STOCK: Furniture and general antiques, pictures, books and postcards.* LOC: Opposite County Hall. TEL: 0602 821835; home - 0602 817161.

Joan Cotton (Antiques)

5 Davies Rd. Est: 1969. Open 9-5. CL: Wed. *STOCK: General antiques, Victoriana, jewellery, silver, china, glass and bygones.* LOC: 1/2 mile along Bridgford Rd. from Trent Bridge, in town centre. PARK: On forecourt. TEL: 0602 813043.

Moulton's Antiques

5 Portland Rd. (J Moulton) Open 10-5.30. CL: Mon. *STOCK: General antiques.* TEL: 0602 814354; home - 0602 815973. SER: Restorations (furniture); stripping (pine); pine furniture made to order.

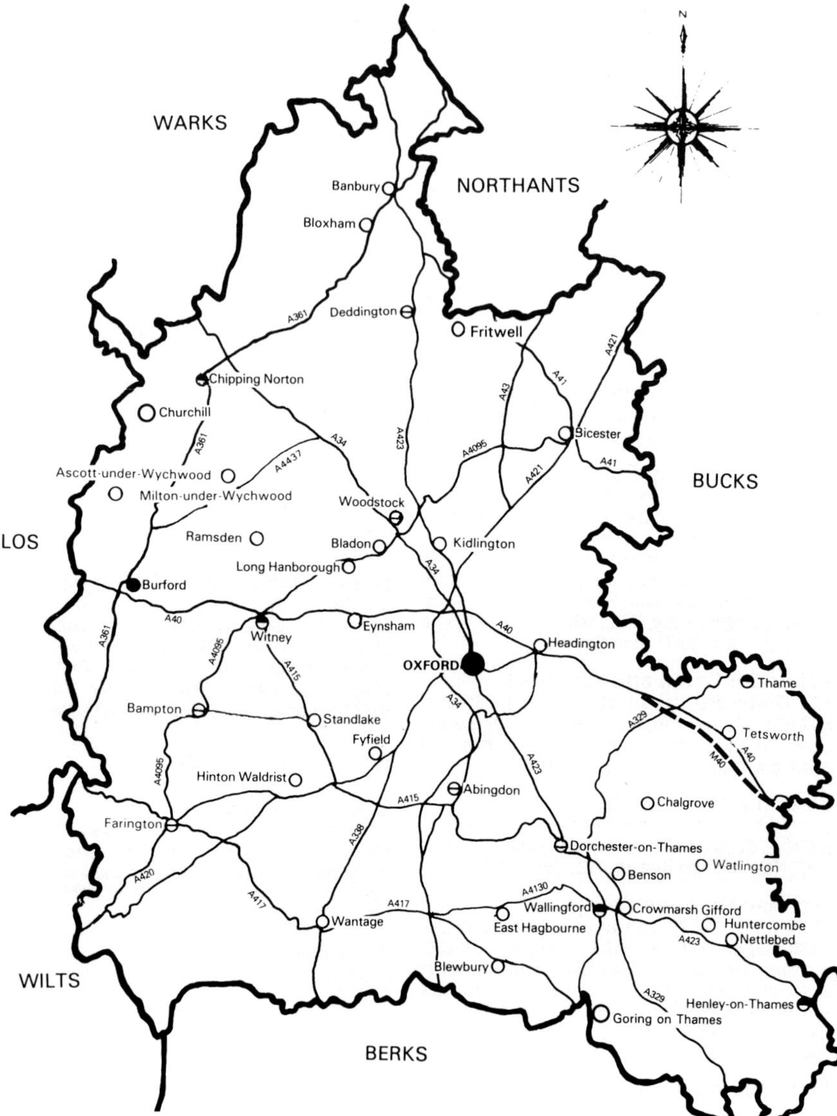
WARKS
NORTHANTS
BUCKS
GLOS
WILTS
BERKS
N
Banbury
Bloxham
Deddington
Fritwell
Chipping Norton
Churchill
Ascott-under-Wychwood
Milton-under-Wychwood
Ramsden
Woodstock
Bladon
Kidlington
Long Hanborough
Burford
Witney
Eynsham
Bicester
Headington
OXFORD
Thame
Tetsworth
Bampton
Standlake
Fyfield
Hinton Waldrist
Abingdon
Chalgrove
Faringdon
Dorchester-on-Thames
Benson
Watlington
Wallingford
Crowmarsh Gifford
Huntercombe
Nettlebed
Wantage
East Hagbourne
Blewbury
Henley-on-Thames
Goring on Thames
A361
A34
A423
A43
A41
A421
A4095
A4437
A40
A415
A329
M40
A420
A417
A338
A4130

○ 1–2
⊖ 3–5
◓ 6–12
● 13+

Key to number of shops in this area.

Please note this is only a rough map designed to show dealers the number of shops in the various towns, and is not necessarily totally accurate.

ABINGDON

Checker Books
2 Checker Walk. (Weir) Est: 1955. Open by appointment. *STOCK: Antiquarian books.* TEL: 0235 528172.

Melrose Antiques
45 Stert St. (Mrs P Schneider) Resident. Est: 1969. CL: Wed. and Thurs. *STOCK: Furniture, porcelain, pictures, jewellery and unusual items.* LOC: A415. TEL: 0235 520146.

R.R Morris Antiques
29 Broad St. Est: 1934. Open 9-5.30. CL: Thurs. *STOCK: Furniture, 17th to early 19th C, general antiques.* TEL: 0235 520766; evenings - 0235 848386. VAT: Spec.

ASCOTT-UNDER-WYCHWOOD

Wychwood Antiques
Four Centuries, London Lane. Open by appointment only. *STOCK: English country furniture and decorative items.* TEL: 0993 831571.

BAMPTON

Angela John Antiques
Market Sq. Est: 1975. Open Tues., Thurs. and Sat. 10-4. SIZE: Medium. *STOCK: Mahogany and oak, 19th C; brass, copper, glass, porcelain and collectables, £5-£500.* LOC: A4095. PARK: Easy. TEL: 0993 850436; home - 0993 772448.

Jean Lathbury Antiques
South Elms, Broad St. Resident. Open by appointment only. *STOCK: English pottery, Staffordshire lustre, creamware; English Delft tiles; watercolours and drawings, glass, collectors' items.* TEL: 0993 850406.

Wheelgate House Antiques
Market Sq. (M House) Open 8.30-6. *STOCK: General antiques.* PARK: Opposite. TEL: 0993 850243.

BANBURY

Sunloch Gallery
6 West Bar. (C Lester) Open 10-12.30 and 1.30-5. *STOCK: Victorian and Edwardian china; some silver, 19th C.* TEL: 0295 255746.

Judy Vedmore Furniture and Antiques
42 Parson's St. (J Vedmore, E.J.A. Patterson Co. Ltd) Est: 1978. Open 10-5. SIZE: Medium. *STOCK: Furniture, Georgian-1930's, £15-£600; collectable and unusual items, books, from 1800, £2-£600.* LOC: Parallel to High St. TEL: 0295 890342.

Late 19th century Meissen porcelain clock case, white enamel dial and French 8-day striking movement signed 'S. Marti & Cie, number 103112'. £4,400. From an Auction Feature on the sale of the remaining contents of Donnington Grove, Newbury, Berkshire, by Dreweatt Neate on 1st May 1991, published in the June 1991 issue of ***Antique Collecting.***

BENSON

Bygones
Paddock House, Brook St. (M.A. and J.O Cleland) Est: 1968. Open 10-6+, including Sun. CL: Wed. SIZE: Medium. *STOCK: General antiques.* LOC: On B4009 opp. Farmer's Man. PARK: Easy. TEL: 0491 38307.

BICESTER

The Barn
Crumps Butts, off Bell Lane. (E Latimer) Est: 1975. CL: Sat. and lunchtimes. SIZE: Medium. *STOCK: Furniture, including shipping items, 18th-20th C, £50-£500.* LOC: Town centre. PARK: Easy. TEL: 0869 252958. SER: Restorations; veneering and polishing; buys at auction.

Lisseter of Bicester
3 Kings End. (D Lisseter) Est: 1945. Open 9-5.30. *STOCK: Furniture, all periods; Victoriana.* PARK: Easy, opposite. TEL: 0869 252402. VAT: Stan/Spec.

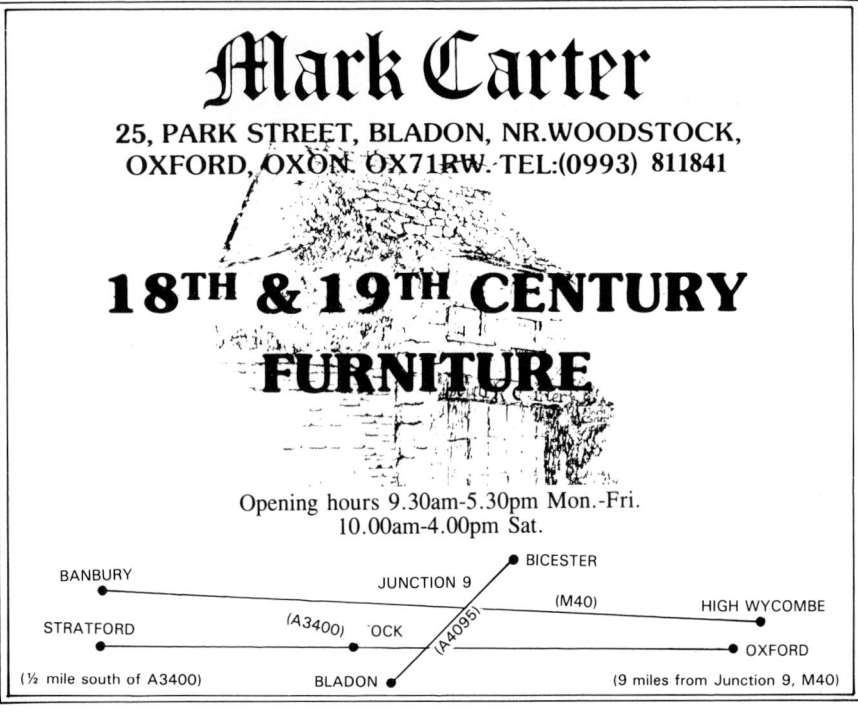

BLADON, Nr. Woodstock

Mark Carter Antiques
25 Park St. Est: 1979. Open 9.30-5.30, Sat. 10-4, other times by appointment. SIZE: Medium. *STOCK: English mahogany, oak and fruitwood furniture, 17th-19th C, £300-£5,000.* LOC: From Woodstock on A3400, through the village, shop on left. PARK: Opposite. TEL: 0993 811841; home - same. SER: Valuations. VAT: Spec.

Park House Antiques
26 Park St. (H., M. and J Roseby) Resident. Est: 1978. Open 9-7.30, trade any time. *STOCK: Walnut, mahogany, satinwood and rosewood furniture, early 18th to early 19th C, £200-£7,000; decorative objects, £50-£500.* PARK: Easy. TEL: 0993 812817. VAT: Spec.

BLEWBURY

Blewbury Antiques
London Rd. (S. and E Richardson) Est: 1973. Open 10-6, including weekends. CL: Tues. *STOCK: General antiques, books, Victoriana, bric-a-brac.* TEL: 0235 850366.

BLOXHAM, Nr. Banbury

H.C Dickins
High St. (P. and H.R Dickins) Open 10-5.30, Sat. 10-1. *STOCK: 19th-20th C British sporting and landscape paintings, watercolours, drawings and prints.* TEL: 0295 721949.

BURFORD

The Ark Angel
48 High St. (D Leroy) Open 10-6. *STOCK: Naïve paintings and artefacts; country furniture, unusual and decorating items.* TEL: 099 382 2342.

Burford Antiques
134 High St. Open 9.30-5.30. SIZE: Large. *STOCK: Furniture, 18th-19th C; metalwork, ceramics, clocks, mirrors.* TEL: 099 382 2552/2135. SER: Valuations; restorations. VAT: Stan/Spec.

The Burford Gallery
Classica House, High St. (B Etheridge) Est: 1976. Open 10-6. SIZE: Medium. *STOCK: British and continental watercolours, 18th-20th C, £40-£6,000.* LOC: 400yds. from A40 roundabout. PARK: Easy. TEL: 099 382 2305; home - same. SER: Valuations; framing and mounting; buys at auction (watercolours). VAT: Spec.

Burford continued

Cotswold Gateway Antique Centre ·

Cheltenham Rd. Open 10-5.30, Sun. p.m. to 5.30. LOC: On roundabout (A40) Oxford/ Cheltenham road. PARK: Easy. TEL: 099 382 3678. Below are listed the dealers at this centre.

Ashton Gower Antiques
Units 1 and 2. (C Gower) Est: 1987. Open 10-5.30. *English and continental furniture, mirrors and decorative accessories, 18th-20th C, £25-£5,000.* TEL: 099 382 2450; home - 0993 883279. SER: Valuations; restorations; buys at auction. VAT: Stan/Spec.

Gateway Antiques
(M C Ford, P Brown) Est: 1986. *English and continental furniture, 18th and 19th C, and decorative accessories.* TEL: 099 382 3678. SER: Valuations. VAT: Stan/Spec.

West Street Antiques
(Mr and Mrs R C Wakefield) Est: 1987. Open 10-5.30, Sun. 12-5. *Fine period furniture, 17th-19th C, £100-£5,000; decorative objects, 19th-20th C, £5-£500; metalware and paintings, 18th-20th C, £50-£500.* TEL: 099 382 2721. VAT: Stan/Spec.

Burford continued

The Crypt Antiques

109 High St. (P Matthey and M Schotten) CADA. Est: 1957. Open 9.30-1 and 2-5.30 or by appointment. *STOCK: 18th-19th C furniture, antique fishing tackle, golfing collectables.* TEL: 099 382 2302; home - 0993 830254. SER: Restorations.

Denver House Antiques and Collectables

Denver House, Witney St. (T. and B Radman) Resident. Est: 1976. Open 10-5.30, Sun. by appointment. SIZE: Medium. *STOCK: Coins and medals, B.C. to date; orders, medals, badges, decorations, military books, police and fire brigade memorabilia, stamps and paper money, 1560 to date; maps, books.* PARK: Easy and nearby. TEL: 099 382 2040 (24 hours); fax - 099 382 2769. SER: Valuations; restorations (maps and bank notes); buys at auction (coins, stamps, medals, sovereign and stamp cases, maps, covers and tokens). VAT: Stan.

Burford continued

Jonathan Fyson Antiques
44 and 50 High St. (J.R Fyson) CADA. Est: 1972. Open 9.30-1 and 2-5.30. SIZE: Small. *STOCK: English and continental furniture, decorative brass and steel including lighting and fireplace accessories; papier mâché, tôle, treen, porcelain, glass, jewellery.* LOC: A361. Coming from London on A40 between Oxford and Cheltenham at junction with A361. PARK: Easy. TEL: 099 382 3606/3204; home - 036786 223. SER: Valuations. VAT: Spec.

Horseshoe Antiques and Gallery
97 High St. (B. and Mrs P Evans) Open 9-5.30. CL: Wed. and Sun. except by appointment. SIZE: Medium. *STOCK: Early oak and country furniture, metalware; 19th-20th C watercolours, oil paintings, longcase clocks.* LOC: East side of High St. PARK: Easy. TEL: 099 382 3244; home - 099 382 2429. VAT: Spec.

Howards of Burford
51 High St. Open 9-5.30 including Sun. SIZE: Large. *STOCK: Jewellery, 1800-1886, £200-£15,000; silver, 1780-1886, £200-£10,000; objects, 1800-1886, £100-£5,000; furniture and other general antiques.* PARK: Easy. TEL: 099 382 3172.

Anthony Nielsen Antiques
80 High St. Est: 1977. Open 9.30-1 and 2-5.30. SIZE: Large. *STOCK: Furniture, mahogany,*

Anthony Nielsen Antiques continued

walnut, rosewood, oak, William and Mary-Edwardian, £200-£20,000; copper, brass, £20-£500. PARK: Easy. TEL: 099 382 2014; after hours (0451) 21710.

Peter Norden Antiques
High St. Est: 1960. Open 9.30-5.30. SIZE: Medium. *STOCK: Early oak and country furniture, period walnut, metalware, treen, pottery, period firearms, especially blunderbusses, and armour, 16th to mid-19th C.* Not Stocked: Silver, bronze, shipping goods. PARK: Easy. TEL: 099 382 2121. VAT: Spec.

David Pickup **BADA**
115 High St. CADA. Est: 1977. Open 9.30-1 and 2-5.30, Sat. 10-1 and 2-4. SIZE: Medium. *STOCK: Fine furniture, from £1,000+; works of art, £500-£10,000; decorative objects, from £100+; all late 17th-19th C.* PARK: Easy. TEL: 099 382 2555. FAIRS: New York International. VAT: Spec.

Brian Sinfield Gallery
128 High St. Open 10-5.30. *STOCK: Early watercolours and paintings, Victorian to contemporary.* TEL: 099 382 2603. SER: Valuations; buys at auction.

Burford continued

Geoffrey Stead
158 High St. Est: 1963. Open 9.30-5.30 or by appointment. SIZE: Medium. *STOCK: English and continental furniture; decorative objects and paintings.* PARK: Easy. TEL: 0993 822352; home - 0608 74364; fax - 0608 74533. SER: Valuations; buys at auction. VAT: Spec.

Swan Gallery
High St. (J. and D Pratt) CADA. Est: 1966. Open 9.30-5.30. SIZE: Large. *STOCK: Furniture - oak, yew, fruitwood and walnut, 17th-19th C, £500-£8,000; oil paintings, sculpture and watercolours, 19th-20th C, £100-£8,000; metalwork, blue and white pottery and porcelain, small decorative items, 18th-20th C, £50-£800.* PARK: Easy. TEL: 099 382 2244. SER: Valuations; restorations (furniture). VAT: Mainly Spec.

Zene Walker, Burford BADA
The Bull House, High St. (P Walker) Est: 1954. Open 9-5.30. SIZE: Large. *STOCK: 18th C furniture, English, Welsh, continental and Oriental ceramics and works of art.* TEL: 099 382 3284. VAT: Stan/Spec.

Frank Williams
The Old Post Office, High St. Est: 1933. Open 9.30-5.30. SIZE: Large. *STOCK: General antiques, furniture, decorative items.* TEL: 099 382 2128. VAT: Spec.

Wren Gallery
4 Bear Court, High St. (S Hall and G Mitchell) Est: 1986. Open 10-5.30. SIZE: Medium. *STOCK: 19th-20th C watercolours and drawings.* TEL: 099 382 3495. SER: Valuations; restorations (watercolours); buys at auction (watercolours). VAT: Spec.

CHALGROVE, Nr. Oxford

Antiques Warehouse
Warpsgrove. (P. and R Hitchcox) Est: 1957. Open 9-5, Sun. 2-5 or by appointment. SIZE: Large. *STOCK: Furniture, 1700-1930.* LOC: Halfway between Oxford and Henley, just off the B480, 4 miles M40. TEL: 0865 890241. VAT: Stan/Spec.

CHIPPING NORTON

Broughton House Antiques
Hill Lawn House, Off New St. (J Duff) Open 9-6, Sun. by appointment. *STOCK: Furniture, 18th-19th C; some paintings and porcelain.* TEL: 0608 643219.

Bugle Antiques LAPADA
9 Horsefair. (M. and D Harding-Hill) Est: 1971. Open 9.30-6. *STOCK: English and French country furniture in oak, elm and fruitwood; Windsor chairs, dressers, bureaux and large tables.* TEL: 0608 643322. VAT: Stan/Spec.

Chipping Norton continued

Chipping Norton Antique Centre
Ivy House, 1 Middle Row. (G Wissinger) Open 10-5 including Sun. SIZE: 28 dealers. *STOCK: A wide variety of smalls and furniture.* PARK: Own. TEL: 0608 644212.

Chipping Norton Books and Prints
21 High St. (T Perkins, M.G Manwaring and E Kirby) Open 10-5.30. *STOCK: Antiquarian and secondhand books; antiquarian prints, maps, engravings, 1600-1900.* TEL: 0608 644325 (prints); 0608 641724 (books).

The Emporium
26 High St. Open 9.30-5. *STOCK: Bric-a-brac, postcards and prints, memorabilia.* TEL: 0608 643103.

Georgian House Antiques
21 West St. Open 9-6. *STOCK: 17th-19th C furniture and paintings.* TEL: 0608 641369.

Jonathan Howard
21 Market Pl. (J.G Howard) Est: 1979. Open by appointment or ring bell. SIZE: Small. *STOCK: Clocks - longcase, wall and carriage, 18th-19th C.* PARK: Easy. TEL: 0608 643065. SER: Valuations; restorations (movement, dials and cases). VAT: Stan/Spec.

Key Antiques BADA
11 Horse Fair. (D. and M Robinson) CADA. Resident. Open 9.30-6 or by appointment. SIZE: Medium. *STOCK: Period oak and country furniture, domestic metalware including kitchenware and lighting, early pottery, paintings, needlework, carvings.* LOC: On main road. PARK: Easy. TEL: 0608 643777. VAT: Spec.

Packer House Antiques
28 High St. (T. and S Jones) Est: 1979. Open 9.30-6. SIZE: Medium. *STOCK: Oak country furniture, 17th-19th C; copper and brass, 18th-19th C.* PARK: Opposite. TEL: 0608 643255; home - same.

Peter Stroud Antiques
35 New St. CADA. Open 9-5.30. SIZE: Medium. *STOCK: 17th-19th C period furniture, oak, walnut, fruitwood and mahogany including tables, chairs, dressers and bureaux.* LOC: 150yds. from Town Hall down hill on the right. PARK: Own. TEL: 0608 642571. SER: Valuations. VAT: Stan/Spec.

Peter Wiggins
Raffles, Southcombe. Est: 1969. Usually available. *STOCK: Barometers.* LOC: 1 mile from Chipping Norton on A34. TEL: 0608 642652; home - same. SER: Valuations; restorations (barometers, clocks, automata); buys at auction.

CHURCHILL

John Parker

2 Old Cottages, Merriscourt. Est: 1968. Open by appointment only. *STOCK: Furniture, objets d'art, metalwork.* TEL: 0831 492946. SER: Courier service.

CROWMARSH GIFFORD, Nr. Wallingford

The Pennyfarthing

49 The Street. (N. and S Lewis) Open 9.30-6. CL: Wed. *STOCK: Furniture including pine; copper, brass, porcelain, glass, scientific and general antiques.* PARK: Easy. TEL: 0491 37470.

DEDDINGTON

Castle Antiques Ltd LAPADA

Manor Farm, Clifton. (J. and J Vaughan) Est: 1968. Open 10-5. SIZE: Large. *STOCK: Furniture, £25-£3,000; silver, metalware, £10-£1,000; pottery, porcelain, £10-£200; kitchenalia.* LOC: B4031 (Aynho Road), 6 miles from junction 10, M40. PARK: Easy. TEL: 0869 38688; evenings - 0869 38294. VAT: Stan/Spec.

The Deddington Antique Centre

Laurel House, Bull Ring, Market Sq. (G Newark) Est: 1972. Open 10-5. SIZE: Medium -16 dealers. *STOCK: 18th-19th C furniture, oils, watercolours, porcelain, silver and plate, country furniture and related items, linen, lace and collectors' items.* LOC: Off A423 Oxford to Banbury road at Deddington traffic lights. PARK: Easy. TEL: 0869 38968. SER: Valuations. FAIRS: Henley and Oxford.

J and B Antiques LAPADA

Clydesdale Market Pl. (J.E Green) Est: 1978. Open 10-1 and 2-6. CL: Mon. SIZE: Small. *STOCK: Porcelain and pottery, 18th to early 19th C, £25-£1,500; objets d'art and virtue, 18th-19th , £25-£2,000; furniture, 17th to early 19th C, £500-£10,000.* PARK: Easy. TEL: 0869 38382; mobile - 0836 684133. SER: Valuations; buys at auction. FAIRS: Olympia; Oxford. VAT: Stan/Spec.

Tuckers Country Store (Grove Galleries)

Market Pl. (R Gregory) Open daily, Sun. mornings only. SIZE: Medium. *STOCK: Furniture including country pine, collectors' items, 18th-19th C, £25-£500; oils and watercolours, mainly 19th C, £50-£1,000; clocks, wall and mantel; Victorian linen.* PARK: Outside. TEL: 0869 38215; home - 38397. SER: Valuations; restorations; cleaning (oil paintings); buys at auction (paintings and furniture). FAIRS: Oxford, Newark, Abingdon and London. VAT: Spec.

DORCHESTER-ON-THAMES

Dorchester Galleries

Rotten Row. (D Knipe) Est: 1978. Open 10-6, Sun. and Wed. by appointment only. *STOCK: Paintings, £35-£900; prints, £10-£350, both 18th-20th C; glass and china, 19th-20th C, £1-£50; maps, 16th-19th C, £30-£350.* LOC: Off Henley-Oxford road, opposite Dorchester Abbey. PARK: Easy. TEL: 0865 341116. SER: Valuations; restorations; buys at auction (pictures, prints).

Giffengate Antiques

16 High St. (E.M. and S.A Reily-Collins) Est: 1978. Open 9-5. SIZE: Large. *STOCK: English and continental porcelain, silver, glass, pictures and furniture, 17th-19th C, £50-£20,000.* PARK: Own. TEL: 0865 340028. SER: Valuations; restorations. FAIRS: Olympia and Park Lane. VAT: Stan/Spec.

Hallidays Antiques Ltd LAPADA

The Old College, High St. Est: 1950. SIZE: Large. *STOCK: Furniture, 17th-19th C, £100-£20,000; paintings, 18th-19th C, £100-£4,000; decorative and small items, pine and marble mantelpieces, firegrates, fenders, 18th-20th C; room panelling.* PARK: At rear. TEL: 0865 340028. FAIRS: Olympia and Park Lane. VAT: Stan/Spec.

Shambles Antiques and Interiors

3 High St. (Z Lebentz) Est: 1982. Open daily, including Sun. CL: Mon. SIZE: Medium. *STOCK: English and European pine and decorative items, 18th-19th C, £5-£3,000.* LOC: Opposite abbey, just off main Oxford/Wallingford by-pass. PARK: Easy. TEL: 0865 341373; home - 0491 680233.

EAST HAGBOURNE, Nr. Didcot

E.M Lawson and Co

Kingsholm. (W.J. and K.M Lawson) Est: 1921. Usually open 10-5 but appointment preferred. CL: Sat. *STOCK: Antiquarian and rare books, 1500-1900.* PARK: Easy. TEL: 0235 812033. VAT: Stan.

EYNSHAM, Nr. Oxford

David John Ceramics

11 Acre End St. (J Twitchett and D Holborough) CADA. Est: 1959. CL: Mon. SIZE: Medium. *STOCK: English ceramics, 18th-20th C, £15-£5,000; small furniture, decorative items.* TEL: 0865 880786. VAT: Stan/Spec.

John Wilson (Autographs) Ltd

50 Acre End St. ABA. Est: 1967. Open 9-6, Sat. by appointment. SIZE: Large. *STOCK: Autograph letters, historical documents, manuscripts, £10-£50,000.* LOC: From Oxford, off the A40 towards Cheltenham. PARK: Easy. TEL: 0865 880883. SER: Valuations; commissions. FAIRS: ABA London. VAT: Stan/Spec.

THE PERFECT FIND

A magnificent George I period walnut Tallboy with well veneered moulded cornice and below three short and three long figured crossbanded drawers between canted corners and standing on a chest of three long drawers with similar decorations and all retaining its original brasswork. 40in.W x 21in.D x 72½in.H., c.1725

Find a wide selection of 'Perfect Finds' in more than 20 beautiful showroom settings at Dorchester-on-Thames. Or, write or phone for our colour brochure to:

HALLIDAYS

Hallidays Antiques Ltd.,
The Old College,
Dorchester-on-Thames,
Oxfordshire OX10 7HL.
Tel: (0865) 340028/68
Telex: 83147
Fax: (0865) 341149

FARINGDON

A. and F Partners BADA

20 London St. Open 9.30-6. SIZE: Medium. *STOCK: English furniture, 17th-19th C, works of art, £100-£20,000.* Not Stocked: Victoriana. LOC: A420. PARK: Easy, within 20yds. TEL: 0367 240078. SER: Valuations. VAT: Spec.

Faringdon Gallery

21 London St. (G.E Lott) Usually open, appointment preferred. CL: Thurs. *STOCK: Watercolours, oils, etchings and books, 19th-20th C, £50-£6,000.* LOC: A420. PARK: Market Sq. TEL: 0367 242030; home - same. SER: Valuations; restorations (framing and mounting); buys at auction (paintings and prints). VAT: Spec.

La Chaise Antique

30 London St. (Roger Clark) Est: 1968. Open 10-6. CL: Sun., except by appointment. SIZE: Large. *STOCK: Chairs, pre-1860; furniture, 18th and 19th C; general antiques, decorators' items.* Not Stocked: Silver, porcelain and glass. LOC: A420. PARK: At rear. TEL: 0367 240427; mobile - 0831 205002. SER: Valuations; restorations; upholstery (leather and fabrics); table top liners. FAIRS: Oxford, Brighton, High Wycombe, N.E.C., Decorative and Antiques Fair and Henley (organiser). VAT: Spec.

FRITWELL, Nr. Bicester

Tollgate Antiques

61 North St. (M.K Palmer) Open by appointment. *STOCK: Furniture, pictures, copper, brass, collectables.* TEL: 0869 346955.

FYFIELD, Nr. Abingdon

Blackwell's Rare Books

Fyfield Manor. Est: 1879. Open 9-5.15. *STOCK: Antiquarian and rare books.* LOC: A420 adjacent to village green. PARK: Easy. TEL: 0865 390692. SER: Valuations; binding; buys at auction. VAT: Stan/Spec.

GORING-ON-THAMES

Goring Antique Centre

16 High St. (Mrs A.E Newton) Est: 1981. Open 10-5, Thurs. 10-1 and 2-5, Sat. 11-5. CL: Wed. p.m. SIZE: Small. *STOCK: General antiques and collectables, £1-£500.* LOC: Next to Midland Bank. PARK: Nearby. TEL: 0491 873300; home - 0734 698084. SER: Valuations; buys at auction. VAT: Stan.

HEADINGTON, Nr. Oxford

Ancient & Modern

6 Cherwell Dr. (M.H Harwood) Est: 1976. Open 9.30-6. SIZE: Medium. *STOCK: Furniture and china, £50-£100; collectables, £25-£50, all 19th C.* LOC: Near John Radcliffe Hospital. PARK: Easy. TEL: 0865 66408; home - 0865 56643. VAT: Stan.

Barclay Antiques

107 Windmill Rd. (C Barclay) Est: 1979. Open 10-5.30. CL: Wed. SIZE: Small. *STOCK: Porcelain, silver and jewellery, 18th-19th C, £50-£100; period lamps, 20th C, £50-£500.* PARK: Easy. TEL: 0865 69551. SER: Valuations. FAIRS: Oxford.

HENLEY-ON-THAMES

The Barry M. Keene Gallery

12 Thameside. Est: 1971. Open 9.30-5.30 and by appointment. *STOCK: Watercolours, paintings, etchings, prints, 18th to early 20th C, contemporary works and sculpture, £15-£15,000.* LOC: Junction 8/9 M4, over bridge, immediate left, 5th building on right. TEL: 0491 577119. SER: Restorations; framing, cleaning, relining, gilding, export. VAT: Stan/Spec.

Richard J Kingston BADA LAPADA

95 Bell St. Open 9-5.30, Sat. 9.30-5 or by appointment. SIZE: Medium. *STOCK: Furniture, 17th to early 19th C; silver, porcelain, paintings, antiquarian and secondhand books.* LOC: A423 some 1/2 mile from town centre traffic lights. PARK:Easy. TEL: 0491 574535; home - 0491 573133. SER: Restorations. FAIRS: Surrey, Buxton. VAT: Stan/Spec.

Henley-on-Thames continued

B.R Ryland
75 Reading Rd. Est: 1945. Open 9-5.30. CL: Wed. SIZE: Large. *STOCK: Furniture, Victorian and later, £20-£500; copper, brass, clocks, £10-£200; china and glass, all periods, £5-£50.* LOC: A4155. From Reading first shop on right on entering Henley. From London M4 turn left after Henley bridge, follow the river past station, then turn left, last shop on the parade. PARK: Opposite. TEL: 0491 573663. VAT: Stan/Spec.

Saturdays Antiques
2 Friday St. (D.C McGregor) Open 10-5.30. SIZE: Medium. *STOCK: Country furniture, 17th-19th C; associated decorative items, cast-iron and architectural items.* LOC: Opposite main post office. PARK: Easy. TEL: 0491 574104. SER: Valuations; buys at auction. VAT: Stan/Spec.

Selkirk
7 Friday St. (C Selkirk) Est: 1976. CL: Mon. SIZE: Small. *STOCK: Decorative paintings, £250-£2,500; works of art, £10-£500; all 18th-19th C.* LOC: From junction 8/9 M4, over Henley Bridge, sharp left, then first right. PARK: Easy. TEL: 0491 574077. SER: Valuations; restorations; buys at auction; design. VAT: Spec.

Thames Gallery
Thameside. (S Came) Open 10-5. *STOCK: Georgian and Victorian silver; paintings, 19th C.* TEL: 0491 572449.

Thames Oriental Rug Co
Thames Carpet Cleaners Ltd, 48/56 Reading Rd. (J. and D Benardout and C Aigin) Resident. Est: 1955. Open 9-12.30 and 1.30-5, Sat. 9-12.30. SIZE: Medium. *STOCK: Oriental rugs, mid-19th C to modern.* PARK: Easy. TEL: 0491 574676. SER: Valuations; restorations (carpets); cleaning (carpets). VAT: Stan.

HINTON WALDRIST

Antony Davenport
The Grange. Open by appointment only. *STOCK: English furniture, 17th-19th C.* TEL: 0865 820227.

HUNTERCOMBE

The Country Seat LAPADA
Huntercombe Manor Barn. (W Clegg and H Ferry) TVADA. Est: 1969. Open 9-5.30, Sun. by appointment. *STOCK: Garden statuary, fountains, garden furniture and architectural fittings; panelled rooms and associated furniture, decorative items, all 1700-1900; 19th C English furniture.* LOC: A423 1 1/2 miles from Nettlebed towards Wallingford. PARK: Easy. TEL: 0491 641349. SER: Valuations; restorations; buys at auction. VAT: Spec.

KIDLINGTON

Handtiques
120 Mill St. (K Hand) Open 9-5.30. *STOCK: Mainly ceramics, general antiques.* PARK: Easy. TEL: 086 75 6942.

LONG HANBOROUGH

David A Hallett Antiques (Hanborough Antiques)
125 and 127 Main Rd. Open 10-5, Sun. 2-5. CL: Mon. SIZE: Medium. *STOCK: Furniture, country and period; pottery, porcelain, Victoriana, rural and domestic bygones, brass and copper, collectors' items.* LOC: Going north from Oxford on A34 turn left before Woodstock on to A4095 near Witney. PARK: Easy. TEL: 0993 882767.

MILTON-UNDER-WYCHWOOD

John Jackson LAPADA
3 The Old School, Church Rd. (J.H Jackson) Open by appointment. *STOCK: Furniture, 18th-19th C and Oriental; Oriental works of art; watercolours, 19th to early 20th C.* TEL: 0993 831678.

NETTLEBED

Harvey Ferry and William Clegg Antiques BADA LAPADA
The Barns, 1 High St. (H Ferry and W Clegg) Est: 1965. Open 9-5.30, Sat. 10-4. SIZE: Large and warehouse. *STOCK: English furniture, 1630-1830, £100-£10,000; associated items, 1680-1850, £10-£1,000; trade goods, 1630-1850, £100-£10,000, garden and architectural items.* LOC: A423, Henley to Oxford, Barns at rear of first house on left in Nettlebed. PARK: Easy. TEL: 0491 641533. SER: Valuations; restorations (furniture); buys at auction. VAT: Spec.

Selkirk
22A High St. SIZE: Medium. *STOCK: Decorative and interior design items, £200-£5,000.* PARK: Easy. TEL: 0491 641780.

OXFORD

Reginald Davis Ltd BADA
34 High St. Est: 1941. Open 9-5. CL: Thurs. *STOCK: Silver, English and continental, 17th to early 19th C; jewellery, Sheffield plate, Georgian and Victorian.* Not Stocked: Glass, china, pewter. LOC: On A40. PARK: Easy. TEL: 0865 248347. SER: Valuations; restorations (silver, jewellery). VAT: Stan/Spec.

Oxford continued

Jeremy's (Oxford Stamp Centre)
98 Cowley Rd. Open 10-12.30 and 2-5. *STOCK: Stamps and postcards.* TEL: 0865 241011.

Christopher Legge Oriental Carpets
25 Oakthorpe Rd, Summertown. (C.T Legge) Est: 1970. SIZE: Medium. *STOCK: Rugs, various sizes, mainly 19th C, £100-£6,000.* LOC: Near shopping parade. PARK: Easy. TEL: 0865 57572; fax - 0865 54877. SER: Valuations; restorations (re-weaving). VAT: Stan.

Laurie Leigh Antiques
36 High St. (L., D. and W Leigh) Est: 1963. Open 11-6. CL: Thurs. *STOCK: English clocks, keyboard musical instruments.* TEL: 0865 244197. VAT: Stan/Spec.

Roger Little
White Lodge, Osler Rd. (Dr R Little) Est: 1988. Open by appointment except Sun. SIZE: Small. *STOCK: English and continental pottery and tiles, £50-£5,000; medieval English pottery, £100-£500; studio pottery, 1850-1960, £50-£500; Islamic pottery and glass, 1500-1850, £50-£1,000.* Not Stocked: Anything other than above. LOC: Near town centre. PARK: Easy. TEL: 0865 62317; home - same. SER: Valuations; restorations (pottery); buys at auction (English pottery and tiles).

Magna Gallery
41 High St. (B Kentish) Est: 1965. Open 10-5.30. SIZE: Medium. *STOCK: Maps, prints, 1570-1870, 50p-£1,500.* TEL: 0865 245805. SER: Valuations. VAT: Stan.

P. Audley Miller
46 High St. Open 9.30-5. *STOCK: General antiques, glass, china; longcase, mantel and bracket clocks.* TEL: 0865 247952. FAIRS: Oxford (organiser). VAT: Stan/Spec.

Niner and Hill Rare Books
43 High St. (P Hill and M Niner) Open 10-5.30. *STOCK: Antiquarian and rare books especially on travel and the arts.* TEL: 0865 726105.

Number Ten/Oxford Antiques
10 North Parade. (Mrs P Clewett) Est: 1979. Open 10-1.30 and some afternoons, prior telephone call advisable. CL: Sun. except by appointment. SIZE: Small. *STOCK: English porcelain and pottery, 1780-1920, £1-£400; small general antiques, including furniture, 1600-1920, £1-£1,000.* LOC: North Parade is second left turning from central Oxford on Banbury road. PARK: 50yds. TEL: 0865 512816; home - same. VAT: Stan/Spec.

The Oxford Antique Trading Co
40/41 Park End St. (D.A Jones and R.S.J Howse) Open 9-5.30. SIZE: Large - 60 dealers. *STOCK: General antiques, from 18th C to 1930s, £50-£5,000.* LOC: 150yds. from railway station. PARK: Easy. TEL: 0865 793927; home - 0865 717576. SER: Valuations; restorations (furniture, upholstery). VAT: Stan/Spec.

Oxford continued

Oxford Antiques Centre
The Jam Factory, 27 Park End St. Open 10-5 and 1st Sun. monthly. CL: Mon. SIZE: 35 dealers. *STOCK: General antiques 18th-19th C including furniture, silver, brass and copper, watercolours and oils, prints, kelims and other Oriental rugs, period clothes, luggage, pens, jewellery, porcelain, ceramics, toys, antiquities, books.* LOC: Opposite railway station. TEL: 0865 251075. SER: Restorations; repairs (jewellery, clocks and watches); valuations; shipping.

Oxford Architectural Antiques
The Old Depot, Nelson St, Jericho. (K.D Edmonds) Est: 1972. CL: Wed. SIZE: Large. *STOCK: Architectural items, especially Victorian fireplaces, bathrooms, ironwork, stained glass, garden ornaments and terraced house items.* LOC: 1/2 mile from city centre. PARK: Easy. TEL: 0865 53310. SER: Restorations; fitting undertaken. VAT: Stan.

Payne and Son (Goldsmiths) Ltd
BADA
131 High St. (G.N., E.P. and J.D Payne) Est: 1790. Open weekdays 9-5. SIZE: Medium. *STOCK: British silver, antique, Victorian, modern and secondhand; jewellery, all £50-£10,000+.* LOC: Town centre near Carfax traffic lights. PARK: 800yds. TEL: 0865 243787. SER: Restorations (English silver). VAT: Stan/Spec.

A Rosenthal Ltd
9-10 Broad St. Est: 1936. Open 9-5.15, Sat. by appointment. *STOCK: Continental literature; Judaica; autograph letters.* TEL: 0865 243093; fax - 0865 794197. SER: Buys at auction.

Rowell of Oxford Ltd
12 Turl St. Open 9-5. SIZE: Medium. *STOCK: Silver; Sheffield plate, late 18th and 19th C, to £150.* PARK: 200yds. TEL: 0865 242187. SER: Valuations; restorations (silver, jewellery, clocks and watches); buys at auction. VAT: Stan/Spec.

Sanders of Oxford Ltd
104 High St. CL: Sat. p.m. SIZE: Large. *STOCK: Prints, maps, antiquarian books and manuscripts.* TEL: 0865 242590. VAT: Stan/Spec.

A.J Saywell Ltd. (The Oxford Stamp Shop)
15 Hollybush Row. (I.H. and H.J Saywell) Est: 1943. Open 10-5.30, Thurs. 10-1. SIZE: Small. *STOCK: Stamps, accessories, coins and some medals.* LOC: Off Park End St. near railway station. PARK: Easy. TEL: 0865 248889. SER: Valuations. VAT: Stan.

Thorntons of Oxford Ltd
11 Broad St. Open 9-6. *STOCK: Antiquarian books.* TEL: 0865 242939.

Oxford continued

Titles Old and Rare Books
15/1 Turl St. Est: 1972. Open 9.30-5.30. *STOCK: Antiquarian and secondhand books, general subjects, especially literature, agriculture, travel and natural history.* TEL: 0865 727928.

Robin Waterfield Ltd
36 Park End St. Open 9.30-5.30. *STOCK: Antiquarian and secondhand books, especially academic in the humanities; 17th-18th C English books; philosophy.* TEL: 0865 721809.

RAMSDEN, Nr. Oxford

Janus Antiques
Open by appointment only. *STOCK: 17th-19th C English and continental decorative antiques.* TEL: 099 386 230 or 0836 509930.

Richard Purdon BADA
The Gallery, Wilcote Lane. Open by appointment. SIZE: Large. *STOCK: Antique Eastern and European carpets, village and tribal rugs, flatweaves, runners and needlework.* LOC: Off Witney to Charlbury road. TEL: 099 386 777. SER: Valuations; restorations. VAT: Stan/Spec.

STANDLAKE, Nr. Witney

Manor Farm Antiques
Manor Farm. (C.W Leveson-Gower) Est: 1964. Open daily, Sun. by appointment. SIZE: Large. *STOCK: Victorian brass and iron beds.* PARK: Easy, in Farmyard. TEL: 0865 300303.

TETSWORTH, Nr. Oxford

Tetsworth Antiques
High St. (M. and D Vine) Open 11-5, including Sun., Sat. 10-5. CL: Mon. and Wed. SIZE: Medium. *STOCK: Furniture, china, glass, pine, clocks, £1-£4,000.* LOC: A40. PARK: Easy. TEL: 084 428 636. SER: Valuations; restorations. VAT: Stan/Spec.

THAME

Michael Priest Antiques and Fine Arts
60 North St. (M.G Priest) Est: 1979. Open 10-1 and 2.15-5, Sat. 10-5. SIZE: Large. *STOCK: Mahogany, 18th C; early walnut and oak, 17th-18th C; oil paintings and primitives, Victorian.* PARK: Easy. TEL: 084 421 4461. SER: Valuations. VAT: Spec.

Thame continued

Rosemary and Time
42 Park St. Open 9-6. *STOCK: Clocks, watches, barometers.* TEL: 084 421 6923. SER: Valuations; restorations; old spare parts. VAT: Stan/Spec.

H. and D Smith Sons and Daughters
1 Upper High St. Est: 1960. Open 9.30-5.30. CL: Wed. SIZE: Large. *STOCK: Pine, mirrors, rugs, china.* TEL: 084 421 2035. VAT: Stan/Spec.

Telling Time Antiques
57 North St. (S Telling) Est: 1978. *STOCK: Longcase clocks, 17th-20th C, £850-£4,000; watches, £10-£2,000; wall, mantel, carriage and French clocks, £50-£3,500; furniture, jewellery, general antiques.* LOC: Off M40, junction 6. PARK: Easy. TEL: 084 421 3007. SER: Valuations. VAT: Stan/Spec.

Thame Antique and Art Galleries
11-12 High St. Open 9-5.30. SIZE: Large. *STOCK: Furniture, 18th and 19th C; Victorian oil paintings and watercolours.* TEL: 084 421 2725.

Thame Pine
1 Upper High St. (D Smith) Open 9.30-5.30. CL: Mon. and Wed. *STOCK: Pine and garden stoneware.* TEL: 084 421 5914.

WALLINGFORD

The Antique Shop
20 High St. (L O'Donnell) Open 10-1 and 2-5. SIZE: Medium. *STOCK: Furniture, 18th-19th C, to £1,000; small items, 18th C to art deco, £1-£500; books, £1-£100.* LOC: Into town over Wallingford Bridge, 150yds. along High St. on left-hand side. PARK: Thames St. TEL: 0491 39332. FAIRS: Organiser of Portcullis Fairs (Oxfordshire).

County Antiques
101 High St. (Mrs A Reed) Est: 1984. Open 10-5.30. CL: Wed. SIZE: Medium. *STOCK: Furniture, late 18th to 19th C, £100-£1,000; porcelain and pottery, 18th-19th C, £50-£500; jewellery and silver, 19th to early 20th C, £25-£500.* LOC: Next to Wallingford bridge. PARK:

County Antiques continued

Opposite. TEL: 0491 32450; home - 0491 36426. SER: Commission sales. FAIRS: Castle; Caroline Penman; Robert Bailey. VAT: Stan/Spec.

Michael and Jane de Albuquerque
12 High St. Open 10-5. *STOCK: Furniture and decorative items, 18th-19th C.* PARK: At rear. TEL: 0491 32322.

The Lamb Arcade
High St. Open 10-5, Sat. 10-5.30, Wed. 10-4. TEL: 0491 35048/35166. SER: Restoration (furniture). Below are listed some of the dealers at this centre.

Alicia Antiques
(A Collins) *China, silver and collectors' items.* TEL: 0491 33737; home - 0865 340382.

Antiqus
18th-19th C upholstered furniture, pictures, silver and porcelain figures.

Anne Brewer Antiques
Furniture, china, silver, jewellery and objets d'art. TEL: 0491 38486.

Toby English
Antiquarian and secondhand books. TEL: 0491 36389.

Great Expectations
(N McKie) *Victorian brass bedsteads, linens and bedroom furnishings.* TEL: 0491 39909.

Kay Harcus
General antiques, copper and brass.

Hill Top Farm Antiques
(M Biesley) *Victorian furniture, pine.* TEL: 0491 33555.

Nicola Antiques
Period and Victorian furniture, ornamental items.

Hilda Perry/Gretel Stone
Small furniture, porcelain, silver, pictures and objets d'art.

Margaret Richmond
Small 17th-19th C oak country furniture, accessories and decorative items. TEL: 0491 35166.

Julie Strachey
Pine. TEL: 0491 35166.

The Lamb Arcade continued

Tags
(T and A Green) *Collectors' items, curios, jewellery, militaria, scientific instruments and furniture*. TEL: 0491 35048; home - 0491 872962.

Rosemary Toop
Boxes, Victorian furniture, collectors' items and lighting. TEL: 0491 35166.

MGJ Antiques LAPADA
1A St. Martins St. (Mrs M Jane) Est: 1971. Open 10-4.30, Sat. 10-5. SIZE: Small. *STOCK: Jewellery, Victorian and secondhand, £100-£1,000.* LOC: Town centre. PARK: Nearby. TEL: 0491 34336; home - 0235 848444. SER: Valuations. VAT: Stan/Spec.

Mike Ottrey Antiques
16 High St. (M.J Ottrey) Est: 1955. Open 9-5.30. SIZE: Large. *STOCK: Furniture, 17th-19th C; oil paintings, copper and brass, decorative and unusual items.* LOC: A429. PARK: At rear. TEL: 0491 36429. VAT: Stan/Spec.

Wallingford continued

Second Time Around Antiques
6 St. Peters St. (C O'Donnell) Est: 1974. Open 9.30-1 and 2-5. CL: Mon. and Wed. SIZE: Medium. *STOCK: Furniture, 18th to early 20th C, to £2,000; clocks, £50-£1,000; small collectors' items - porcelain, silver and brass, £1-£200; linen, some stripped pine.* LOC: Into town centre over Wallingford Bridge, turn left into Thames St., then first right. PARK: Easy. TEL: 0491 39345.

Wallingford continued

Summers, Davis and Son Ltd BADA LAPADA

Calleva House, 6 High St. (M.S Baylis and G Wells) CINOA, TVADA. Est: 1917. Open 8-5.30. SIZE: Large. *STOCK: English and continental decorative furniture, 17th-19th C.* Not Stocked: Silver, shipping goods. LOC: From London, shop is on left, 50yds. from Thames Bridge. PARK: Opposite, behind castellated gates. TEL: 0491 36284; fax - 0491 33443. VAT: Spec.

WANTAGE

Arts and Antiques (Oxford) Ltd

33 Wallingford St. (J.F.W King) Est: 1947. Open 9.30-6 or by appointment. CL: Thurs. p.m. SIZE: Medium. *STOCK: Furniture, oil paintings, watercolours, sculpture, bronzes, general antiques including unusual items, £5-£9,000.* PARK: Easy. TEL: 023 57 2676. SER: Valuations; restorations (oil paintings). VAT: Spec.

WATLINGTON, Nr. Oxford

Cross Antiques

37 High St. (R.A. and Mrs I.D Crawley) Est: 1986. Open 10-6, Sun. and Wed. by appointment. SIZE: Small. *STOCK: Furniture,*

Cross Antiques continued

1700-1900, £100-£2,000; garden urns, seats and figures, 19th C, £200-£2,000; decorative items, pictures, 18th-19th C, £10-£1,000. LOC: Off B4009. PARK: Easy and at rear. TEL: 049 161 2324; home - same. SER: Valuations; restorations (furniture and porcelain); buys at auction. FAIRS: High Wycombe, Reading.

Stephen Orton Antiques LAPADA

The Antiques Warehouse, Shirburn Rd. Open 9-5, or by appointment. SIZE: Large. *STOCK: 18th and 19th C furniture and some decorative items.* LOC: 2 mins. from exit 6, M40. TEL: 049161 3752. SER: Valuations; restorations; buying agent. VAT: Stan/Spec.

WITNEY

Country Pine Antiques

14A West End. (M.L Parker and P Littlewood) Est: 1986. Open 9.30-5.30, Sun. 2-5 or by appointment. SIZE: Medium. *STOCK: Pine, 19th C, £100-£2,000.* LOC: Just off A40 straight over mini roundabout (Oxford Hill), shop on right. PARK: Easy. TEL: 0993 778584. SER: Valuations; restorations (pine). VAT: Stan/Spec.

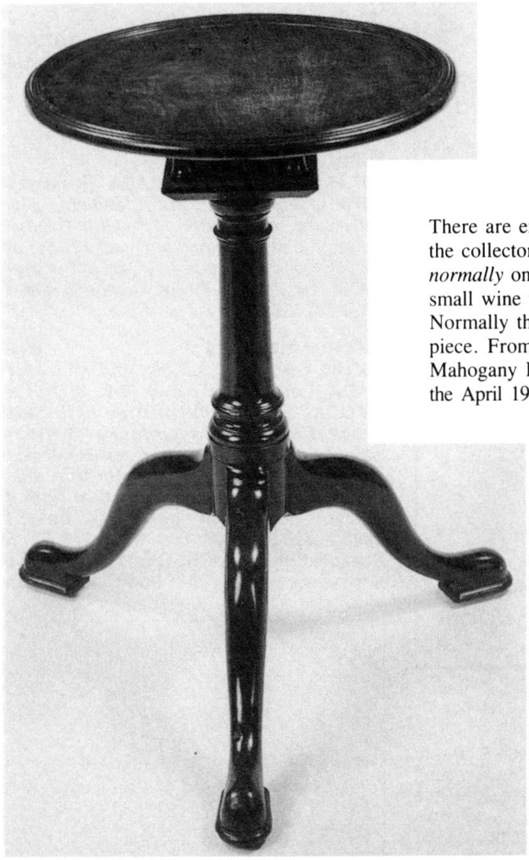

There are endless variations in design, but the collector should be aware that *normally* one does not expect to see a small wine table with a birdcage under. Normally the top is fixed through a turned piece. From an article entitled 'Early Mahogany Furniture' by James Storm in the April 1991 issue of ***Antique Collecting.***

17th century oak hanging livery or glass cupboard. £2,640. Phillips, Chester. From a Saleroom Report in the May 1991 issue of ***Antique Collecting.***

Witney continued

Colin Greenway Antiques

90 Corn St. Resident. Est: 1975. Open 9.30-6 or by appointment. SIZE: Large. *STOCK: Furniture, 17th-20th C; clocks, metalware, decorative and unusual items.* LOC: Along High St. to town centre, turn right, shop 400yds. on right. PARK: Easy. TEL: 0993 705026. VAT: Stan/Spec.

Ian Pout Antiques

99 High St. (I. and J Pout) CADA. Open 10-5.30. *STOCK: 18th and 19th C furniture, decorative objects, vintage teddy bears.* TEL: 0993 702616; home - 0869 40205. VAT: Spec.

Relics

35 Bridge St. (B Wiles and R Russell) Est: 1978. Open 9-5.30, Sun. by appointment. SIZE: Large. *STOCK: General antiques and shipping items, 50p-£500.* LOC: Main road. PARK: Easy. TEL: 0993 704611; home - 0993 841477/779557.

Anthony Scaramanga Antiques BADA

108 Newland. CADA. Est: 1969. Open 10-5. CL: Fri. a.m. and Sun. except by appointment. *STOCK: Samplers, 17th-19th C; needlework pictures, lace, small furniture, Staffordshire figures, blue and white pottery.* LOC: From Oxford on A40, turn off bypass onto A4022, shop on left before coming to A147 and Witney. PARK: Easy. TEL: 0993 703472. VAT: Spec.

Witney continued

Joan Wilkins Antiques

158 Corn St. (Mrs J Wilkins) Est: 1973. Open 10-5. CL: Tues. *STOCK: Furniture, 18th-19th C, £150-£2,500; 19th C glass, metalware, £10-£500.* LOC: Town centre. PARK: Easy. TEL: 0993 704749. VAT: Spec.

Windrush Antiques

107 High St. (B Tollett) CADA. Resident. Est: 1978. Open 10-5.30. SIZE: Medium. *STOCK: Furniture, especially 17th-18th C oak and country chairs; Georgian mahogany, some metalware and porcelain.* LOC: A40, corner of Mill St. and High St. PARK: Private at rear. TEL: 0993 772536.

Witney Antiques BADA

96/100 Corn St. (L.S.A. and C.J Jarrett) CADA. Est: 1962. Open 9.30-5. SIZE: Large. *STOCK: English furniture, 17th-18th C; bracket and longcase clocks, mahogany, oak and walnut, metalware, needleworks and works of art.* LOC: From Oxford on old A40 through Witney via High St., turn right at T-junction, 400yds. on right. PARK: Easy. TEL: 0993 703902/703887; fax - 0993 779852. SER: Restorations. FAIRS: Chelsea; Park Lane; Grosvenor House. VAT: Spec.

The hongs at Canton, attributed to Lam Qua. Oil on canvas. Circa 1830-35. Many of the painters working in a western style for a western market are mysterious figures, about whom little is known. Lam Qua emerges as a real personality in Carl Crossman's ***The Decorative Arts of the China Trade***, published in 1991 by the **Antique Collectors' Club.** £45.00. Lam Qua's self-portrait in the book depicts a handsome though hefty man with an expansive face and pleasant smile. He became the most celebrated Chinese painter in the English style in Canton, and the painting illustrated is one of the finest and most imaginative 19th century views of Canton.

ANTHONY SCARAMANGA ANTIQUES

108 Newland · Witney · Oxon OX8 6JN · (0993) 703472

One of our showrooms in which we have between 70 to 80 samplers and needlework pictures in stock at any time. We also have a wide selection of marked blue and white transfer ware, early 19th century Victorian Staffordshire figures, and a representative collection of small, good quality 18th and 19th century furniture.

SAMPLERS

We specialise in 17th to 19th century samplers, fine early needlework, stumpwork, lace, etc.

Colour prints of samplers and needlework pictures from our extensive stock available on request. Samplers crated and sent airmail to all parts of the world at reasonable rates.

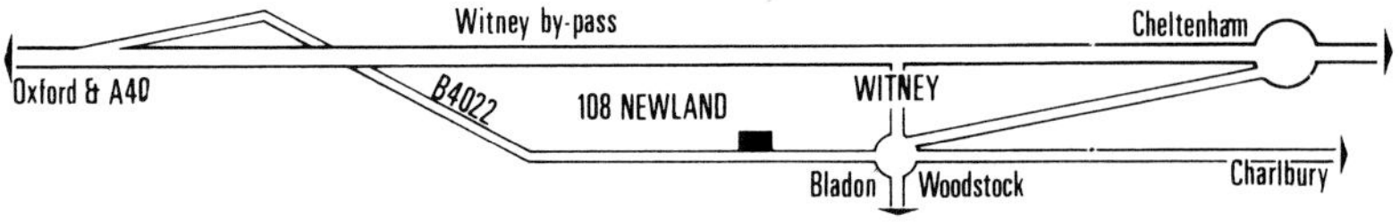
Witney by-pass
Cheltenham
Oxford & A40
B4022
108 NEWLAND
WITNEY
Bladon
Woodstock
Charlbury

WOODSTOCK

Fox House

30/32 Oxford St. (J Coles) Resident. Est: 1977. Open 9.30-5.30. CL: Wed. SIZE: Large. *STOCK: General antiques, interesting items, silver and plate, Victoriana, furniture, objets d'art.* LOC: A34, next to Marlborough Hotel. PARK: Easy. TEL: 0993 811377. SER: Valuations; restorations; buys at auction. VAT: Stan/Spec.

Museum Bookshop

County Museum, Fletcher's House, (Oxfordshire County Council). Est: 1966. Oct.-April. Open 10-4, Sat. 10-5, Sun. 2-5. CL: Mon.; May-Sept. Open 10-5, Sat. 10-6, Sun. 2-6. SIZE: Small. *STOCK: Books on antiquities, crafts, archaeology, local history, original fine art, mainly pictures.* LOC: In town centre, between P.O. and Barclays Bank. PARK: Easy. TEL: 0993 811456. VAT: Stan.

Span Antiques

6 Market Pl. Est: 1978. Open 10-1 and 2-5 including Sun. CL: Wed. SIZE: Medium. LOC: Near Town Hall. PARK: Easy. TEL: 0993 811332. SER: Valuations. Below are listed some of the dealers selling from these premises.

Derek Bramwell
Silver and Chinese porcelain.
Doreen Caudwell
Table linen and textiles.

Span Antiques continued

Andrew Crawforth
Kitchen antiques, iron, copper, brass and farming bygones.
R and M Eden
Georgian furniture.
Four Seasons Antiques
English porcelain.
Maureen Gough
Decorative desk items.
Lis Hall-Bakker
Art nouveau and deco.
Jasper Antiques
Small silver and objets d'art.
Alan Stuart-Mobey
Furniture and bric-a-brac.

Thistle House Antiques

14 Market Pl. Open 10-6. *STOCK: 18th and 19th C furniture, porcelain, pictures.* TEL: 0993 811736. SER: Restorations.

Woodstock Antiques LAPADA

11 Market St. (C Mason-Pope) Est: 1979. Open 9.30-5.30, Sun. 1-5.30, other times by appointment. CL: Mon. SIZE: Medium. *STOCK: Staffordshire figures and animals, £150-£6,000; small furniture, £200-£2,000; decorative objects, pictures and prints, £100-£500, all 18th and early 19th C.* LOC: Town centre. PARK: Easy. TEL: 0993 811494; home - same. VAT: Stan/Spec.

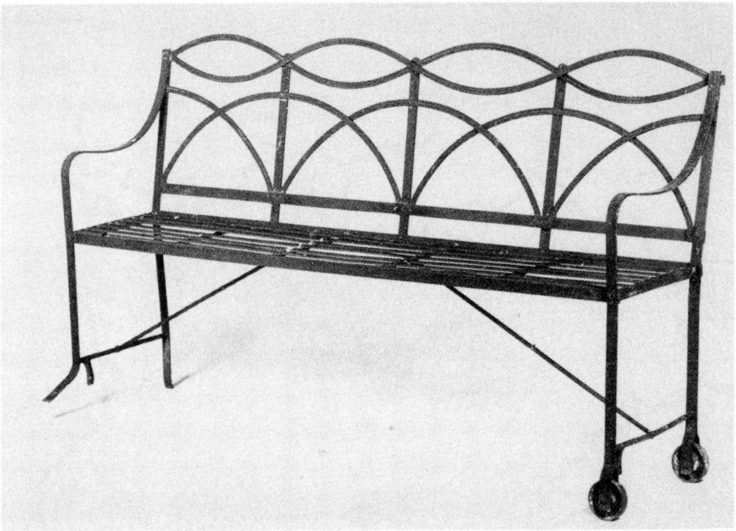

Early 19th century wrought-iron garden bench, 80in. £2,035. From an Auction Feature on the sale of the remaining contents of Donnington Grove, Newbury, Berkshire, by Dreweatt Neate on 1st May 1991, published in the June 1991 issue of ***Antique Collecting.***

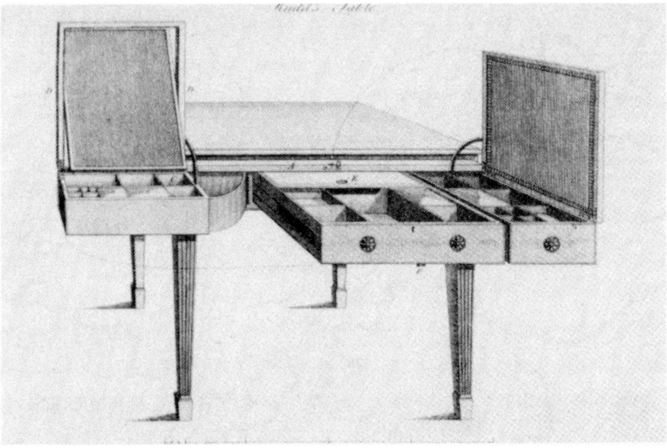

A. Hepplewhite & Co.
'The Cabinet-Maker and Upholsterer's Guide', 1st Edition, 1788. 2nd Edition, 1789. 3rd Edition, 1794.
Plate 79. Rudd's Table 'or reflecting dressing table'. This is the most complete dressing table made, possessing every convenience which can be wanted, or mechanism and ingenuity supply. It derives its name from a once popular character, for whom it is reported it was first invented.' From ***Pictorial Dictionary of British 18th Century Furniture Design — The Printed Sources*** compiled by Elizabeth White and published by the **Antique Collectors' Club** in 1990. £65.00.

Shropshire

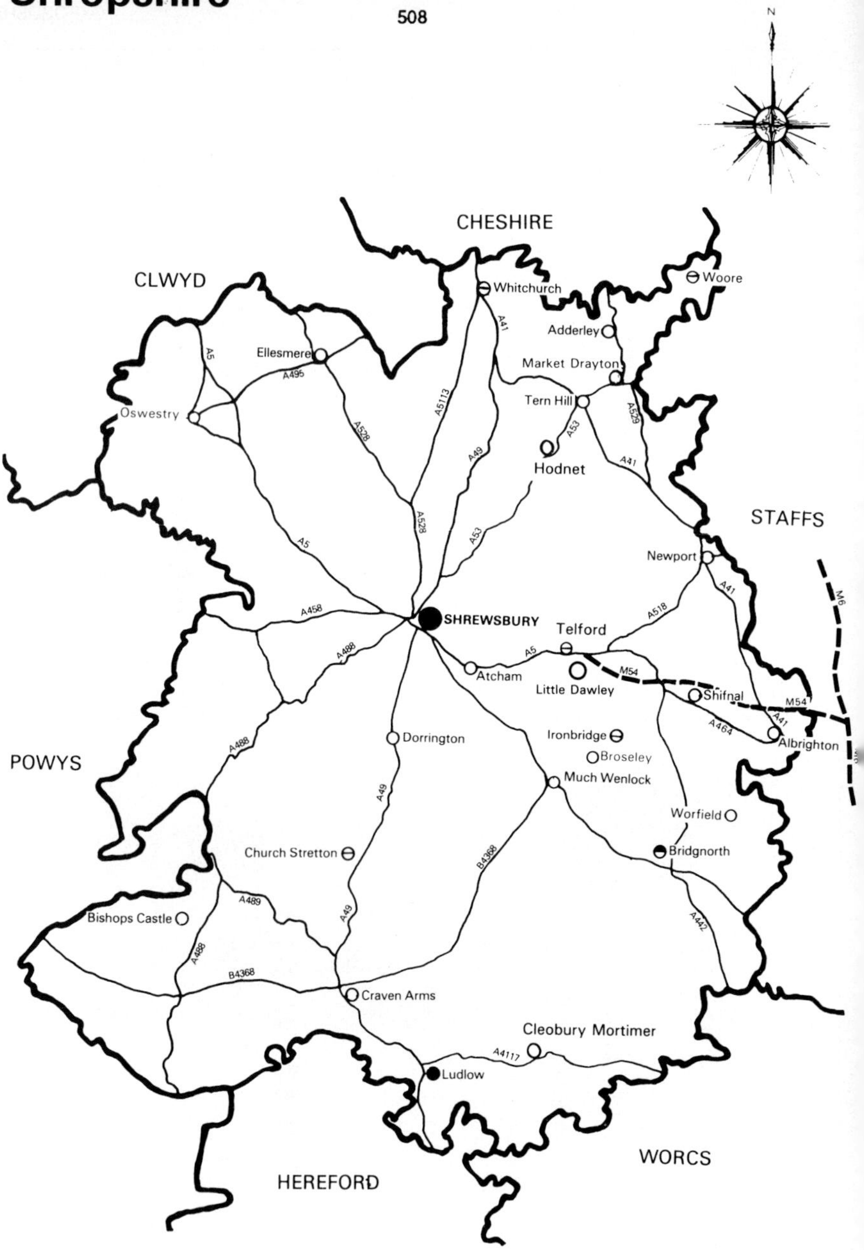
N
CHESHIRE
CLWYD
STAFFS
POWYS
HEREFORD
WORCS
Whitchurch
Woore
Adderley
Market Drayton
Tern Hill
Hodnet
Ellesmere
Oswestry
Newport
SHREWSBURY
Telford
Atcham
Little Dawley
Shifnal
Albrighton
Dorrington
Ironbridge
Broseley
Much Wenlock
Worfield
Bridgnorth
Church Stretton
Bishops Castle
Craven Arms
Cleobury Mortimer
Ludlow
A5
A495
A528
A5113
A41
A53
A529
A49
A458
A488
A518
M54
M6
A464
A489
B4368
A442
A4117

Please note this is only a rough map designed to show dealers the number of shops in the various towns, and is not necessarily totally accurate.

Key to number of shops in this area.

- ○ 1–2
- ⊖ 3–5
- ◓ 6–12
- ● 13+

ADDERLEY, Nr. Market Drayton

Doreen Elkington Antiques

(Mrs D.E Elkington) Est: 1979. Open 10-5, or by appointment. CL: Mon. and Thurs. SIZE: Small. *STOCK: Furniture, £120-£700; silver, plate and collectors' items, 18th-20th C; porcelain, glass, brass, copper, 19th C; all £20-£300.* LOC: A529 from Market Drayton to Audlem. TEL: 0630 5433; home - same. SER: Valuations.

ALBRIGHTON (Neachley)

Doveridge House of Neachley BADA

Long Lane, (alongside RAF Cosford). (Cdr and Mrs H.E.R Bain) CINOA. Est: 1967. Open 9-6 seven days a week and/or by appointment. SIZE: Large. *STOCK: 17th-19th C English and continental furniture, fine art, clocks, decorative artifacts.* LOC: From London M1 to M6. Junction 10A via M54 for North and Mid Wales. Leave at Junction 3 (A41) in Wolverhampton/Cosford direction. 1/2 a mile see Neachley signpost, turn immediately right into Long Lane, 4th entrance. From the North, M6 Junction 11, A460 towards Wolverhampton. Join M54 at Junction 1 then as Junction 3 above. PARK: Easy. TEL: 0902 373131/2. SER: Valuations; restorations (furniture and oils); interior design; export.

ATCHAM, Nr. Shrewsbury

Mytton Antiques

Norton Cross Roads. (M.A., E.A. and J.M Nares) Est: 1972. Open 10.30-5 or by appointment. SIZE: Medium. *STOCK: General antiques, especially longcase clocks and reference books.* LOC: On A5 between Shrewsbury and Wellington. PARK: Own. TEL: 0952 86229 (24hrs.). SER: Buys at auction. VAT: Stan/Spec.

BRIDGNORTH

Bakehouse Antiques

6 St. John St, Low Town. (C.P Dixon) Est: 1971. Open 10-5.30. SIZE: Medium. *STOCK: Country furniture, brass, copper, pine, toys, dolls, general antiques including jewellery.* LOC: In one-way street, 1/4 mile from by-pass, close to river. PARK: Easy. TEL: 0746 763227.

English Heritage

2 Whitburn St, High Town. (P.J Wainwright) Open 9.30-5. SIZE: Medium. *STOCK: Jewellery and general antiques, militaria.* LOC: Just off High St. PARK: High St. TEL: 0746 762097. SER: Framing. VAT: Stan/Spec.

Bridgnorth continued

Micawber Antiques
64 St. Mary's St. (M. and N Berthoud) Open 10-5, other days by appointment. CL: Mon. and Thurs. SIZE: Medium. *STOCK: English porcelain and pottery, £5-£500; small furniture, £100-£1,000; decorative items, £5-£500.* LOC: 100yds. west of town hall in High St. PARK: Easy. TEL: 0746 763254; home - same. SER: Valuations; buys at auction (English porcelain).

Pauline Norton Galleries
Bank St. Est: 1963. Open 10.30-1 and 2-5.30 or by appointment. CL: Thurs. SIZE: Medium. *STOCK: Oil and watercolour paintings, 19th C, £5-£3,000.* LOC: Bank St. is opposite G.P.O. in High St. PARK: Listley St. TEL: 0746 764889. SER: Restorations (paintings); framing. FAIRS: Local. VAT: Spec. *Trade Only.*

Parmenter Antiques
5 Central Court, High St. (J Parmenter) Open 10-1 and 2-5, Sat. 10-5. CL: Thurs. SIZE: Medium. *STOCK: Furniture, 17th C to Edwardian, £50-£4,000; pictures and objects, £5-£350.* LOC: Off M6, junction 10 on A454. PARK: Nearby. TEL: 0746 765599; home - 0746 764208. SER: Buys at auction (furniture). FAIRS: N.E.C., Birmingham.

Tatters Decorative Antiques
2 West Castle St. (M. and M Logan) Est: 1986. Open 10-5, Sat. 10-4. CL: Thurs. SIZE: Small. *STOCK: Staffordshire pottery, textiles, fringing, mirrors and giltware, small furniture.* PARK: Easy. TEL: 0746 761918. SER: Restorations (painted furniture). FAIRS: N.E.C.; Stafford County Showground.

BROSELEY

Gallery 6
6 Church St. (J.A Boulton) Resident. Est: 1983. Open 9-5, Sun. 2-5. SIZE: Medium. *STOCK: Oils, watercolours and prints, late 19th C to contemporary, £100-£2,500.* LOC: Junction 4, M54, take A442. PARK: Easy. TEL: 0952 882860. FAIRS: Buxton; British International, Birmingham; Shrewsbury; Edinburgh.

CHURCH STRETTON

Antiques on the Square
2 Sandford Court, Sandford Ave. (C.J Radford) Est: 1985. Open 9-5.30, Sun. 10-4.30. SIZE: Medium. *STOCK: Period furniture, art deco, applied arts furniture, glass, ceramics, 1680-1930, £5-£3,000; collectors items, £5-£500; decorative items, £5-£1,000; both pre-1900.* Not Stocked: Armour, stamps. LOC: Off A49. PARK: Easy. TEL: 0694 724111; home - 0694 723072. SER: Valuations; restorations (furniture and ceramics); buys at auction (English furniture pre-1830). FAIRS: Nottingham and Greenwich (London) Deco. VAT: Stan/Spec.

Church Stretton continued

George Hofman Antiques
at the Sign of the Black Cat, 17 High St. Open Thurs., Fri. and Sat. 9.30-5.30, other times by appointment. *STOCK: General antiques and decorative items.* PARK: Easy. TEL: 0694 722604. VAT: Stan/Spec.

Old Barn Antiques LAPADA
High St. (Lt. Col. and Mrs D.W Witting) Est: 1980. Open every day by appointment. SIZE: Medium. *STOCK: Furniture, 18th and early 19th C; general antiques, porcelain.* Not Stocked: Coins, jewellery, silver, clocks, books and militaria. LOC: Off A49. PARK: Bucks Head car park at rear. TEL: 0694 723742; home - 0694 72229 (ansaphone). VAT: Stan/Spec.

Stretton Antiques and Militaria
7 High St. (H.A. and J Davies) Open 10.30-5. SIZE: Large. *STOCK: General antiques, militaria.* PARK: Easy. TEL: 0694 723526.

Stretton Antiques Market
36 Sandford Ave. (P. and L Forbes) Est: 1986. Open 9.30-5.30, Sun. and Bank Holidays 10.30-4.30. SIZE: Large - 55 dealers. *STOCK: General antiques, shipping items and collectables.* LOC: Town centre. PARK: Easy. TEL: 0694 723718. SER: Valuations; buys at auction.

CLEOBURY MORTIMER, Nr. Kidderminster

Cleobury Mortimer Antique Centre
Childe Rd. Open 10-5 including Sun. SIZE: Several dealers. *STOCK: General antiques including Georgian, Victorian and Edwardian pine furniture and smalls.* PARK: Own. TEL: 0299 270513; evenings - 0299 266350.

CRAVEN ARMS

I. and S Antiques
Stokesay, Shrewsbury Rd. (J Briscoe) Open 9-5; Sun. 10.30-4.30 in summer. *STOCK: Unstripped pine, shipping goods, treen, country items, bric-a-brac, 19th to early 20th C.* TEL: 0588 672263; home - 05884 374.

Pym Antiques
6 Market St. (J. and S Pym) Resident. Est: 1980. Open 10-1 and 2-5. CL: Wed. SIZE: Medium. *STOCK: China, glass, jewellery, silver, 19th-20th C, £10-£500.* LOC: Off A49. PARK: Nearby. TEL: 0588 672497.

DORRINGTON, Nr. Shrewsbury

D.J Wakeman and Co. Ltd LAPADA
Grove Farmhouse. Est: 1977. CL: Sat. and Sun., except by appointment. SIZE: Medium. *STOCK: Furniture, to 19th C.* LOC: On A49. TEL: 074 373 388. VAT: Stan/Spec.

ELLESMERE

Wharf Road Antiques

Wharf Rd. (A Fraser-Welch) Est: 1984. Open 10-1 and 2-5.30 including Sun. CL: Wed. SIZE: Medium. *STOCK: Furniture, £50-£1,000; Goss, crested and Wedgwood pottery, £5-£100; books, £1-£50; all 19th to early 20th C.* PARK: Easy. TEL: 0691 623227 (ansaphone); home - 0691 657667. SER: Valuations; restorations (polishing and upholstery); buys at auction (furniture). VAT: Stan.

White Lion Antiques

Market St. (Mrs D Wheeldon) Est: 1966. *STOCK: Furniture, clocks, pottery, porcelain, glass.* TEL: 0691 622335.

HODNET, Nr. Market Drayton

Hodnet Antiques

13a and 19a Shrewsbury St. (Mrs J Scott) Est: 1976. Open Tues. and Fri. 10.30-2.30, other days and school holidays by appointment. SIZE: Small. *STOCK: General antiques - china, glass, silver, jewellery, pictures, brass and copper, £3-£500; Victorian and Edwardian furniture, £25-£1,000.* LOC: A53. PARK: Easy. TEL: Home - 063 083 591. SER: Valuations; buys at auction.

IRONBRIDGE

Bill Dickenson

Tudor House Antiques, 11 Tontine Hill. Open 10-5.30, Sun. 2.30-5.30. *STOCK: General antiques especially porcelain, including Caughley and Coalport.* LOC: Opposite bridge. TEL: 0952 433783.

Ironbridge Antique Centre

Dale End. (F.G Cooke) Est: 1968. Open 10-5, Sun. 2-5. SIZE: Large. *STOCK: Porcelain, 1800-1950, £1-£3,000; furniture, £20-£1,000; pictures, jewellery, general antiques and bric-a-brac, 50p-£1,000; all 1700-1930.* PARK: Easy. TEL: 0952 433784. SER: Valuations; restorations (cabinet making); buys at auction.

Peter Whitelaw

Tudor House Antiques, 11 Tontine Hill. Open 10-5.30, Sun. 2.30-5.30. *STOCK: General antiques especially porcelain including Caughley and Coalport.* LOC: Opposite bridge. TEL: 0952 433783.

LITTLE DAWLEY

C.J Antiques LAPADA

(Mr and Mrs S Williamson) Open by appointment only. *STOCK: British porcelain, 19th to early 20th C.* TEL: 0952 595403. SER: Valuations; restorations (porcelain).

A hot water jug, Charles Wright, London, 1778 with an applied medallion on either side illustrative of land and sea. This jug, which was bought for £4,180 at Sotheby's London, 23rd May, 1991, was not expensive when condition and design combined with usability are considered. This type of distinctive Adam design should be a prime candidate for a handsome return in the long term. From an article on Georgian Silver by Peter Waldron, author of ***The Price Guide to Antique Silver,*** published in the July/August 1991 issue of ***Antique Collecting.***

LUDLOW

Antique Corner
12 Old St. (J. and A Clegg) Resident. Est: 1960. Open 9-5.30. *STOCK: Country and other period furniture, metalware and decorative items.* TEL: 0584 873176.

Architectural Antiques and Interiors
140 Corve St. (R.G. and J Dickinson) Open 9.30-1 and 2-5. *STOCK: Bathrooms, fireplaces, lighting, doors and other architectural antiques.* TEL: 0584 876207.

D.W. and A.B Bayliss
22 Old St. Resident. *STOCK: Furniture, 18th-19th C; silver, decorative items.* TEL: 0584 873634. SER: Valuations.

R.G Cave and Sons Ltd BADA LAPADA
17 Broad St. Resident. Est: 1962. Open 9.30-5.30. *STOCK: Furniture, 1630-1830; clocks, barometers, metalwork, fine art and collectors' items.* PARK: Easy. TEL: 0584 873568. SER: Valuations. VAT: Spec.

The Corve Galleries
12 Corve St. (R Painter) Open 9-5.30. SIZE: 4 dealers. *STOCK: 19th C paintings, furniture and decorative items and general antiques.* TEL: 0584 873420; home - 0584 79301 or 0299 400947; fax - 0562 825249. SER: Valuations; restorations (furniture and pictures).

Ludlow continued

The Curiosity Shop
127 Old St. (J Luffman) Resident. Open 9.30-5 or by appointment. *STOCK: Country furniture, clocks, paintings and militaria, £5-£7,000.* TEL: 0584 875927. SER: Valuations; buys at auction (militaria, paintings). VAT: Spec.

G. & D Ginger
5 Corve St. Open 9-5. SIZE: Large. *STOCK: Country and mahogany furniture; decorative and associated items.* TEL: 0584 876939.

The Jane Marler Gallery
Dawes Mansion, Church St. Est: 1975. Open 10-5. CL: Thurs. SIZE: Medium. *STOCK: Wildlife, sporting and contemporary paintings and watercolours, £100-£15,000; signed proofs and prints, £5-£1,000; all 19th-20th C.* LOC: Town centre near church. PARK: Nearby. TEL: 0584 874160. SER: Valuations; restorations (oil paintings, watercolours and prints); framing. VAT: Stan/Spec.

Mitre House Antiques
Corve Bridge. (L Jones) Open 9-5.30. *STOCK: Clocks, pine and general antiques.* TEL: 0584 872138.

Ludlow continued

Pepper Lane Antique Centre
Pepper Lane. (Mr and Mrs K.L Morris) Est: 1985. Open 9-5.30, Sun. by appointment. SIZE: Large. *STOCK: Furniture, £50-£3,000; porcelain, silver, plate, clocks, paintings, jewellery, collectors' items, £5-£1,000; all 18th to early 20th C.* Not Stocked: Linen. LOC: Rear of Boots in King St. PARK: Easy. TEL: 0584 876494; home - 074 632 292. SER: Restorations (furniture, upholstery, clocks).

Olivia Rumens **BADA**
30 Corve St. Resident. Open 10-5. CL: Thurs. *STOCK: English and continental oil paintings, 17th-19th C.* TEL: 0584 873952. SER: Restorations. VAT: Spec.

St. Leonards Antiques
Corve St. (A Smith) Open 9-5. SIZE: 8 dealers. *STOCK: Furniture, silver, jewellery, porcelain, clocks, pictures, Oriental carpets, brass, copper and interesting bygones.* TEL: 0584 875573. SER: Restorations (clocks and furniture).

Paul Smith
The Old Chapel, Old St. (P. and B Smith) Est: 1944. Appointment advisable. LOC: Town centre. PARK: Easy, in archway. TEL: 0584 872666.

Ludlow continued

M. and R Taylor (Antiques)
53 Broad St. (M Taylor) Est: 1977. Open from 9 a.m. including evenings. SIZE: Medium. *STOCK: Furniture, mahogany, oak and walnut, Persian rugs, brass and copper, 17th-19th C.* PARK: Nearby. TEL: 0584 874169; home - same. VAT: Stan/Spec.

Teme Valley Antiques
1 The Bull Ring. (C.S Harvey) Est: 1979. Usually open 10-5.30, Sun. by appointment. SIZE: Medium. *STOCK: English and continental porcelain, 18th to early 20th C, £25-£2,500; furniture, oil and watercolour paintings, 17th to early 20th C, £50-£2,500; silver, plate, metalware and glass, 17th to early 20th C, £10-£3,500.* Not Stocked: Militaria, coins and carpets. LOC: Town centre opposite Boots. PARK: Easy. TEL: 0584 874686. SER: Valuations; buys at auction (porcelain). VAT: Stan/Spec.

MARKET DRAYTON

Adams Antiques **LAPADA**
77 Cheshire St. (S. and N Summers) Est: 1975. Open 10-5, Thurs. 10-1. SIZE: Medium. *STOCK: Oak, mahogany and walnut, mainly 17th-19th C; longcase clocks, desks, chairs, porcelain, silver, lamps, watercolours and paintings, jewellery and decorative items, £10-*

Adams Antiques continued

£15,000. LOC: Town centre. PARK: Easy. TEL: 0630 653893; home - 0270 812093. SER: Valuations. VAT: Stan/Spec.

MUCH WENLOCK

Cruck House Antiques

23 Barrow St. (Mrs B Roderick Smith) Est: 1985. Open 9.30-5.30. CL: Wed. SIZE: Small. *STOCK: Silver and watercolours, 19th-20th C, £25-£300; furniture, 19th C, £50-£500; general antiques.* Not Stocked: Weapons and gold. LOC: Near Sq. PARK: Easy. TEL: 0952 727165.

Wenlock Fine Art

2 The Square. (J Redman and P Cotterill) Est: 1990. Open 10-5 (including Sun. in summer). CL: Mon., Tues. and Wed. SIZE: Small. *STOCK: Modern British paintings, mainly 20th C, some late 19th C, £100-£6,000.* PARK: Nearby. TEL: 0952 728232; home - 0782 281598 or 0584 73270. SER: Valuations; restorations (cleaning); mounting; framing; buys at auction (as stock). VAT: Spec.

NEWPORT

Worth's

34 St. Mary's St. (G.F.E Worth) Resident. Est: 1932. CL: Thurs. and lunch hours. SIZE: Medium. *STOCK: General antiques, 19th C; shipping goods, antiquarian books.* LOC: Opposite church on main A41. PARK: Easy. TEL: 0952 810122. VAT: Stan/Spec.

OSWESTRY

The Antique Shop

King St. Est: 1963. Open 9-5, Sun. by appointment. *STOCK: General antiques and secondhand goods; Victoriana, bric-a-brac.* TEL: 0691 653011.

The Oswald Road Antique and Reproduction Centre

Oswald Rd. (M. and J Clifford) Open 9.30-5.30. SIZE: Large. *STOCK: Wide range of general antiques.* TEL: 0691 670690.

SHIFNAL

Broadway Antiques

25 Broadway. (Mrs E Onions) Resident. Est: 1968. SIZE: Medium. *STOCK: Oak and country furniture, 17th-19th C; brass, copper, metalware.* LOC: Town centre on Newport Rd. PARK: Easy. TEL: 0952 460997. VAT: Stan/Spec.

SHREWSBURY

Candle Lane Books

28-29 Princess St. (J Thornhill) Open 9.30-5. *STOCK: Antiquarian and secondhand books.* TEL: 0743 65301.

Castle Antiques (Militaria)

20B Castle Gates. Open 10-5. CL: Thurs. *STOCK: Medals, militaria and military books.* TEL: 0743 66570/61180.

Expressions

17 Princess St. (O.J Foster) Open 10.30-4.30. CL: Thurs. *STOCK: Art deco originals, ceramics, furniture, jewellery, lighting, mirrors, prints.* TEL: 0743 351731.

Hutton Antiques

18 Princess St. (Mrs P.I Hutton) Est: 1978. Open 9.30-1 and 2-5. CL: Thurs. SIZE: Medium. *STOCK: Silver, porcelain and glass, 18th-19th C, £50-£500; small furniture, £50-£1,300; Victorian jewellery.* LOC: Off square, near Music Hall. PARK: Easy. TEL: 0743 245810. SER: Valuations.

The Little Gem

18 St. Mary's St. (M.A Bowdler) Est: 1969. Open 9-5.30. CL: Thurs. (except Dec.). SIZE: Medium. *STOCK: Georgian and Victorian jewellery.* Not Stocked: Weapons, coins, medals, furniture. LOC: Opposite St. Mary's Church along from G.P.O. PARK: In side road (St. Mary's Place) opposite shop. TEL: 0743 52085.

F.C Manser and Son Ltd LAPADA

53/54 Wyle Cop. (G Manser and family) Est: 1944. Open 9-1 and 2-5.30. CL: Thurs. p.m. SIZE: Large. *STOCK: Furniture, 17th-20th C, £150-£12,000; Oriental items, 15th-20th C, £5-£3,000; silver, plate, copper, 18th-20th C, £5-£6,000; jewellery, 19th-20th C, £50-£4,000.* Not Stocked: Coins, books. LOC: 150yds. town side of English bridge. PARK: Own. TEL: 0743 51120/245730; fax - 0743 271047. SER: Valuations; restorations. VAT: Stan/Spec.

Raleigh House

23 Belle Vue Rd. (R. and E Handbury-Madin) GADAR. Est: 1968. Open 10-5. *STOCK: Furniture, pottery, porcelain, glass, jewellery, silver.* PARK: Easy. TEL: 0743 59552. SER: Valuations; restorations (furniture, clocks).

Severn Fine Art

67 Abbey Foregate. (G Hancock) Open by appointment. SIZE: Small. *STOCK: Oil paintings and watercolours, 19th to early 20th C, £500-£10,000.* LOC: Town centre. PARK: Easy. TEL: 0743 247514. SER: Valuations; restorations; buys at auction (19th-20th C pictures).

Shrewsbury continued

Shrewsbury Antique Centre
15 Princess House, The Sq. (J Langford) Est: 1978. Open 9.30-5.30. SIZE: Large - 37 dealers. *STOCK: General antiques and collectables.* LOC: Town centre just off the Sq. PARK: Nearby. TEL: 0743 247704. SER: Valuations; restorations (furniture, pictures and silver).

Shrewsbury Antique Market
Frankwell Quay Warehouse. (J Langford) Open 9.30-5. SIZE: Large. 45 lock-up and open units. *STOCK: Wide range of general antiques and collectors' items, £1-£2,000.* LOC: Alongside Frankwell Quay car park. PARK: Easy. TEL: 0743 350916.

Tiffany Antiques
Unit 3, Shrewsbury Antique Centre, 15 Princess House, The Sq. (A Wilcox) Est: 1988. Open 9.30-5.30. SIZE: Small. *STOCK: Glass and china, silver plate, curios, £10-£200.* LOC: Town centre. PARK: Nearby. TEL: Home - 0270 257425. FAIRS: Newark, Peterborough and Ardingly.

Vintage Fishing Tackle Shop and Angling Art Gallery incorporating Coleham Marine
103 Longden Coleham. (C Partington) Resident. Est: 1977. Open Sat. 10-5, other days by appointment. SIZE: Small. *STOCK: Angling items, from 1496 to date, mainly under £100; ancient craft, coracles.* LOC: Near Greyfriars footbridge. PARK: Nearby. TEL: 0743 69373. SER: Valuations; restorations (rods, reel); buys at auction. VAT: Stan/Spec.

Wyle Cop Antiques and Reproductions
The Old School, off Wyle Cop. (J Clifford) Open 10-5.30. *STOCK: Stripped pine, oak, mahogany and satin walnut furniture, late Georgian to Edwardian; wall and grandfather clocks.* TEL: 0743 231180.

TELFORD

Haygate Gallery
40 Haygate Rd, Wellington. (Mrs M Kuznierz) Open 9-5, Sat. 9-1. CL: Wed. *STOCK: Watercolours, oils and general antiques.* TEL: 0952 48553.

Bernie Pugh Antiques
120 High St, Wellington. Resident. Open 9.30-1.30 and 2.30-5.30. *STOCK: General antiques.* TEL: 0952 56184.

Telford Antiques Centre
High St, Wellington. (J Langford) Open 10-5, Sun. 2-5. SIZE: 60+ dealers. *STOCK: General antiques.* LOC: 2 mins. from M54. PARK: Easy. TEL: 0952 56450.

TERN HILL, Nr. Market Drayton

L Onions - White Cottage Antiques
White Cottage, 8 Tern Hill. Est: 1965. Open 9.30-5.30. SIZE: Medium. *STOCK: Furniture, oak and some walnut, brass, 16th-18th C.* LOC: On A41, 200yds. from roundabout at Tern Hill cross roads. PARK: Easy. TEL: 063 083 222. VAT: Stan/Spec.

WHITCHURCH

Audrey and Brian Bingham Antiques
Ellesmere House, 28 Dodington. Resident, usually open daily. *STOCK: Oak, 17th-18th C, £50-£3,000.* TEL: 0948 6068. SER: Valuations. VAT: Stan/Spec.

Civic Antiques
The Dairy Farm, Heath Rd, Prees Heath. (J Simcox) Resident. Est: 1970. Open 9-5, Sun. and evenings by appointment. SIZE: Large. *STOCK: Pine furniture, from 19th C, £100-£500; continental furniture, £800-£1,000.* LOC: South of Whitchurch A41/A49, southbound lane of dual carriageway. PARK: Easy. TEL: 0948 3668; home - 0948 2626; fax - 0948 3604. SER: Valuations; restorations (pine); buys at auction. VAT: Stan.

Whitchurch continued

Dodington Antiques

15 Dodington, and The Old Music Hall. (G MacGillivray) Resident. Est: 1978. Always open. SIZE: Large. *STOCK: Oak, fruitwood, walnut country, and 18th to early 19th C mahogany furniture, longcase clocks, barometers, £10-£6,000.* LOC: On fringe of town centre. PARK: Easy. TEL: 0948 3399. SER: Buys at auction. VAT: Stan/Spec.

Robert Whitney Antiques

Withinlee, Alport Rd. Open by appointment. SIZE: Medium. *STOCK: Early oak and country furniture, related items.* TEL: 0948 4084.

WOORE, Nr. Crewe

The Mount

12 Nantwich Rd. Est: 1978. CL: Wed. SIZE: Small. *STOCK: County maps, prints and engravings including national history, fashion and hunting, from 17th C, £2-£500; Victorian artwork.* LOC: Junction of A51 and A525. PARK: Easy. TEL: 063 081 274; home - same. SER: Framing; finder (maps and topography).

Woore continued

Scot Hay House Antiques

7 Nantwich Rd. (D. and J Belcher) Est: 1983. Open daily, Sun. by appointment. CL: Mon. and 12.30-1.30. SIZE: Medium. *STOCK: Kitchenalia and fine country furniture, £25-£1,000; blue and white pottery, £5-£50; garden furniture, £50-£500; all 18th to early 20th C.* LOC: Junction A51 and A525. PARK: Easy. TEL: Home - 0782 629708. FAIRS: N.E.C. (Aug.); Bath (April); Shrewsbury; Hereford; Bingley Hall. VAT: Spec.

Peter Wain BADA

7 Nantwich Rd. Open 10-1 and 2-5. CL: Mon. and Tues. SIZE: Medium. *STOCK: European and Oriental ceramics and works of art, 16th-20th C, £50-£5,000.* LOC: A51, opposite church. PARK: Easy. TEL: 0630 817118. SER: Restorations (ceramics); valuations (as stock). VAT: Spec.

Somerset

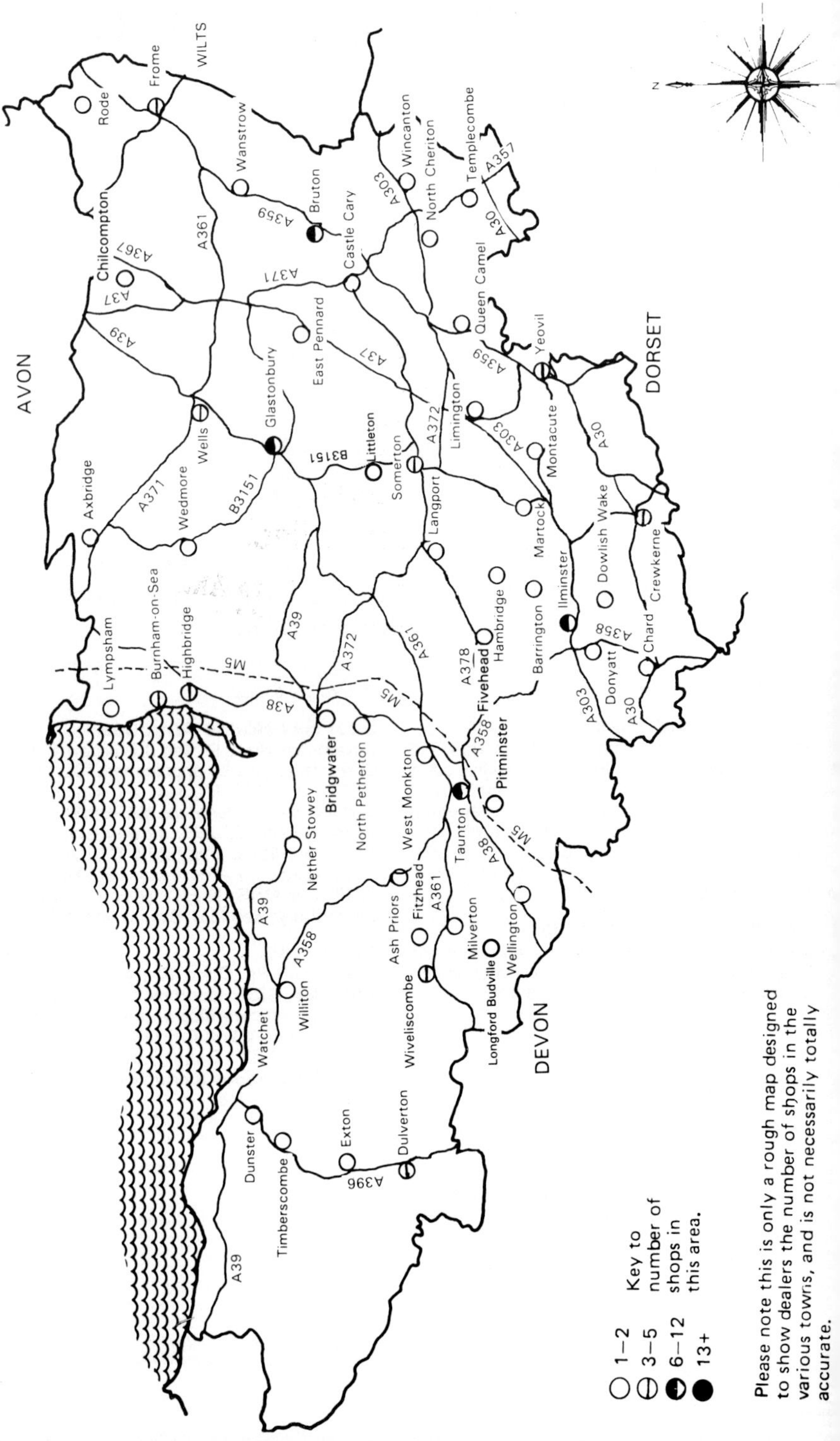
AVON
WILTS
DORSET
DEVON
N
Rode
Frome
Wanstrow
Wincanton
Templecombe
North Cheriton
Bruton
Castle Cary
Chilcompton
Queen Camel
East Pennard
Yeovil
Glastonbury
Wells
Limington
Montacute
Littleton
Somerton
Axbridge
Wedmore
Langport
Martock
Dowlish Wake
Crewkerne
Ilminster
Hambridge
Barrington
Chard
Donyatt
Lympsham
Burnham-on-Sea
Highbridge
Fivehead
Pitminster
Bridgwater
North Petherton
West Monkton
Nether Stowey
Taunton
Wellington
Fitzhead
Ash Priors
Milverton
Longford Budville
Wiveliscombe
Williton
Watchet
Dulverton
Exton
Dunster
Timberscombe
A361
A359
A367
A37
A39
A371
A303
A357
A30
A372
B3151
A378
A358
A38
A396
M5
○ 1–2
⊖ 3–5
◐ 6–12
● 13+
Key to number of shops in this area.

Please note this is only a rough map designed to show dealers the number of shops in the various towns, and is not necessarily totally accurate.

ASH PRIORS, Nr. Taunton

The Granary Galleries

Court House. (R Hall) Est: 1969. Open 8.30-5.30. SIZE: Large. *STOCK: Period items, general antiques, 18th-19th C furniture, some shipping goods.* PARK: Easy. TEL: 0823 432402; home after 6.30 (0823) 432816. VAT: Stan/Spec.

Hall's Antiques

Court House. (A.R. and J.M Hall) Est: 1945. Open 8.30-5.30. CL: Sun. except by appointment. SIZE: Large. *STOCK: English and continental furniture, 18th-19th C; oil paintings, watercolours, 17th-19th C; all £25-£10,000; shipping goods.* LOC: On A358. PARK: Easy. TEL: 0823 432402; home - same. SER: Valuations; buys at auction. VAT: Stan/Spec.

AXBRIDGE

The Old Post House

Weare, Bridgewater Rd. (R. and M Seaman) *STOCK: General antiques and country furniture.* TEL: 0934 732372.

BARRINGTON, Nr. Ilminster

Stuart Interiors (Antiques) Ltd

Barrington Court. Open 9-5, Sat. 10-5. SIZE: Large. *STOCK: Oak furniture, £100-£10,000; accessories, £50-£2,500; both pre-1720.* Not

Stuart Interiors (Antiques) Ltd continued

Stocked: 18th C mahogany. LOC: Between A303 and M5, 5 miles north-east of Ilminster. House is National Trust property, signposted in area. PARK: Easy. TEL: 0460 40349. SER: Valuations; buys at auction (early oak furniture and accessories, interior design and architectural items including oak panelling). VAT: Spec.

BRIDGWATER

Bridgwater Antiques Market

Marycourt Shopping Mall. (C.P Munro) Est: 1988. Open Fri. 9-5 and Sat. 10-5. SIZE: 20 stalls. *STOCK: Secondhand and antiquarian books and a wide range of small antiques and bygones.* LOC: Town centre, opposite St. Mary's church. PARK: Nearby. TEL: 0823 451433.

BRUTON

Bruton Gallery

(M. and S le Marchant) SIZE: Large. *STOCK: 19th-20th C European sculpture and contemporary European paintings.* TEL: 0749 812205. VAT: Stan/Spec.

Bruton continued

Gallery 16
16 High St. (Mrs P.S Wilson) Open 9-5. *STOCK: Oils and watercolours, 19th-20th C.* TEL: 0749 812269.

Harlequin Antiques
Harlequin Arcade, High St. Open 9-5.30. *STOCK: Decorative and small items.* TEL: 0749 813653.

Michael Lewis Gallery
17 High St. Est: 1953. Open 9-6, Sun. by appointment. SIZE: Large. *STOCK: Maps, 1575-1850, £20-£500; prints, 1700-1900, £10-£250.* LOC: A359. PARK: Easy. TEL: 0749 813557; home - same. SER: Picture framing. VAT: Stan.

M.G.R. Exports
Station Rd. Open 8.30-6, weekends by appointment. SIZE: Large. *STOCK: Georgian, Victorian, Edwardian and shipping items, barley twist oak, Lloyd loom and smalls.* PARK: Easy. TEL: 0749 812460/813728.

James Ribbons
Unit 1, Station Yard. SIZE: Large. *STOCK: Furniture, mainly 17th-19th C; small items, glass and porcelain, all £50-£5,000.* PARK: Easy. TEL: 0749 73964. SER: Valuations; restorations; buys at auction. VAT: Stan/Spec.

W.P.S. (Bruton) Ltd
The Old Mill, Station Rd. Open 8.30-6, weekends by appointment. SIZE: Large. *STOCK: Victorian, Edwardian, shipping goods.* PARK: Easy. TEL: 0749 812785.

BURNHAM-ON-SEA

Adam Antiques
30 Adam St. (R Coombes) Open 9-5. SIZE: Large. *STOCK: Furniture, clocks, brass, porcelain and shipping goods.* PARK: Easy. TEL: 0278 783193.

Castle Antiques LAPADA
(T.C Germain) Open by appointment. *STOCK: Jewellery, silver.* TEL: 0278 785031.

C.T Culverwell
Victoria St. (B.G. and C.P Blake) Est: 1920. Open 9-1 and 2-5.30. SIZE: Large. *STOCK: Furniture, £5-£1,000; silver, £1-£1,000; jewellery, £1-£800.* LOC: Next to church and GPO. PARK: Easy. TEL: 0278 782307; home - 0278 784662. VAT: Stan/Spec.

Heape's Antiques
39 Victoria St. (Mrs M.M Heap) Open 10-1 and 2.30-4.30. *STOCK: Small furniture, fine arts, porcelain, glass, memorabilia.* TEL: 0278 782131.

CASTLE CARY

Cary Antiques Ltd
2 High St. (Mrs J.A Oldham) Est: 1977. Open 10-5.30. CL: Wed. SIZE: Small. *STOCK: Furniture, Victorian and Edwardian, £30-£500; china, brass and copper, glass, bric-a-brac, pictures, 18th-19th C, £5-£150.* LOC: Town centre, B3152. PARK: Easy. TEL: 0963 50437. SER: Valuations; picture framing; caning and rushing; repairs (china).

John Martin Antiques
High St. Est: 1975. Open 9.30-5. CL: Mon. and Thurs. *STOCK: Clocks, watches, copper and brass, oil lamps, decorative items, jewellery, furniture.* TEL: 0963 50733.

CHARD

Guildhall Antique Market
The Guildhall. Open Thurs. 8-4. SIZE: 6 dealers. *STOCK: General antiques.*

Holyrood Antiques
54 Holyrood St. (S. and E Milner) Open 10-4.30. CL: Mon. and Wed. *STOCK: Victorian silver, jewellery, small furniture, glass and china.* TEL: 0460 67004.

CHILCOMPTON, Nr. Bath

Mendip Pine and Antiques
Knitts Farm, Stock Hill Rd. (N. and S Day) CL: Mon. and Wed. *STOCK: Pine.* TEL: 0761 233282. SER: Restorations; stripping; kitchens made from reclaimed pine.

COXLEY, Nr. Wells

Wells Reclamation
The Old Cider Farm. (H Davies) Est: 1984. Open 9-5.30. SIZE: Large. *STOCK: Architectural items, 18th-19th C.* LOC: A39 towards Glastonbury from Wells. PARK: Easy. TEL: 0749 77087; home - 0749 77484. SER: Valuations. VAT: Stan.

CREWKERNE

Antique and Country Pine
14 East St. (R.W.H. and M.J Wheeler) Open 10-5, Thurs. 10-1. *STOCK: Country pine.* TEL: 0460 75623.

Julian Armytage
Open by appointment only. *STOCK: Fine sporting, marine and decorative prints.* TEL: 0460 73449.

Crewkerne Furniture Emporium
Viney Bridge, South St. (A.P Bucke) Est: 1974. Open 9-5.30. *STOCK: Furniture, shipping goods, collectors' items, agricultural bygones.* TEL: 0460 75319.

Crewkerne continued

Oscars
13-15 Market Sq, and North St. (B.J. and H.M Hall) Est: 1966. Open 10-5.30. SIZE: Large. *STOCK: Victoriana, Georgiana furniture; shipping goods.* LOC: Centre of the square on A30. PARK: Easy. TEL: 0460 72718. VAT: Stan/Spec.

DONYATT, Nr. Ilminster

Something Old
Church Cottage. (Mrs M.A Wood) Resident. Est: 1980. Open by appointment. SIZE: Medium. *STOCK: Pottery and porcelain, small furniture, 18th-19th C.* LOC: 1/2 mile off A303, on A358. PARK: Easy. TEL: 0460 54283.

DOWLISH WAKE, Nr. Ilminster

Dowlish Wake Antiques
(Mrs G Estling) Est: 1973. Open 10-1 and 2.30-5.30, Sun. by appointment. SIZE: Medium. *STOCK: Ceramics only - English porcelain and pottery, late 18th C to early 20th C.* LOC: Take Ilminster/Crewkerne road and turn off at Kingstone corner, downhill to village. PARK: Easy. TEL: 0460 52784; home - same. VAT: Stan/Spec.

DULVERTON

Acorn Antiques
39 High St. (P Hounslow) Est: 1984. Open 9.30-6. SIZE: Medium. *STOCK: Furniture, textiles and china, 18th-20th C, £5-£100.* LOC: Town centre. PARK: Nearby. TEL: 0398 23286; home - same. SER: Valuations; buys at auction (decorative items). FAIRS: Brocante, Newark, Ardingly, Shepton Mallet.

Guy Dennler Antiques
Hele House. Open by appointment. *STOCK: Fine decorative objects, 18th and 19th C English furniture, papier mâché, tôle, pictures, porcelain and lamps.* TEL: 0398 23736.

Dulverton Antique Centre
Lower Town Hall. Open 10-5. SIZE: Small. *STOCK: Furniture, 18th-19th C, £100-£2,700; silver, 18th-20th C, £5-£500; oil paintings, £50-£2,500; watercolours, £20-£250.* LOC: Town centre. PARK: Easy, nearby. TEL: 0398 23522. SER: Valuations; restorations; buys at auction. VAT: Spec.

Faded Elegance
39 High St. (M Delbridge) Open 9.30-6. *STOCK: Textiles and decorative interior design items.* TEL: 0398 23286.

Dulverton continued

Rothwell and Dunworth
2 Bridge St. (Mrs C Rothwell and M Dunworth) ABA. Est: 1975. Open 10.30-1 and 2.30-5, Thurs. 10.30-1. SIZE: Medium. *STOCK: Antiquarian and secondhand books especially on hunting and horses.* LOC: 1st shop in village over River Barle. PARK: 100yds. SER: Valuations.

DUNSTER, Nr. Minehead

Antiques
21 High St. Est: 1968.

EAST PENNARD, Nr. Shepton Mallet

Pennard House
(M. and S Dearden) Resident. Est: 1979. Open by appointment. SIZE: Large. *STOCK: Pine furniture, 18th-19th C, £100-£2,000; French provincial tables, armoires, buffets, £300-£3,000.* LOC: From Shepton Mallet, 4 miles south off A37. PARK: Easy. TEL: 074 986 266; home - same. SER: Valuations; restorations (pine and country furniture). VAT: Stan/Spec. *Trade Only.*

EXTON, Nr. Dulverton

A Lodge-Mortimer
The Old School House. Open by appointment only. *STOCK: Porcelain and pottery, especially English Delftware and Oriental porcelain, £5-£2,000; objets d'art, £5-£1,000; watercolours.* LOC: Just off A396 from Bridgetown on Dunster/Tiverton road. TEL: 064 385 358. SER: Valuations; buys at auction; commissions undertaken; author and lecturer.

FITZHEAD, Nr. Taunton

J.C White
Est: 1960. *STOCK: Country furniture and clocks.* TEL: 0823 400427.

FIVEHEAD, Nr. Taunton

Peter Kennedy
1 Langford Close. ABA. Est: 1975. Open by appointment. SIZE: Small. *STOCK: Illustrated antiquarian books on natural history, botany, travel, topography, atlases, especially colour plate books; decorative prints.* LOC: Midway between Taunton and Langport, 10 mins. from M5, exit 25. PARK: Easy. TEL: 04608 479; home - same; fax - 04608 829. SER: Valuations; restorations (cleaning and colouring of prints); buys at auction (as stock); lists and catalogues issued. VAT: Stan.

FROME

Old Curiosity Shop
15 Catherine Hill. (R. and B Hackett) Open 10-1 and 2-5. CL: Thurs. *STOCK: Antiquarian books.* TEL: 0373 64482.

Sutton and Sons
15 and 33 Vicarage St. *STOCK: Furniture, 18th-19th C; clocks, pictures, decorative pieces.* TEL: 0373 62062. SER: Restorations and upholstery. VAT: Stan/Spec.

Jill and David Swale
37 Butts Hill. Open Wed. 10-4, or by appointment. *STOCK: Watercolours, 19th-20th C.* TEL: 0373 65067.

GLASTONBURY

Abbey Antiques
52-54 High St. (G.E Browning and Son) Est: 1952. Open 9-5.30. SIZE: Medium. *STOCK: Glass and furniture.* TEL: 0458 31694. VAT: Stan.

Abbots House
Benedict St. (Mrs P Elliott) Est: 1973. *STOCK: Jewellery, silver; china, glass.* TEL: 0458 32123.

Antiques Fair
Glastonbury Abbey Car Park, Market Pl. Est: 1960. Open 9.30-6 (7 days in summer). *STOCK: Unusual and decorative items; furniture, Georgian and Victorian; jewellery.* TEL: 0458 32939.

Antiques Market
Town Hall. Open one Sat. each month (dates in local press). SIZE: Several stands. *STOCK: Antiques, collectables and general antiques.* TEL: 0963 62478.

Kings Farm Antiques
1 The Monarch, 15 High St. (D. and G Rogers) Open daily or by appointment. CL: Mon. SIZE: Large. *STOCK: Textiles, quilts, linen and lace, period clothing, £5-£300; watercolours and samplers, £20-£300; country furniture, £50-£1,000.* LOC: Off High St., next to Midland Bank. TEL: 0458 210021/34522. SER: Buys at auction. FAIRS: Wells, Glastonbury, Shepton Mallet.

Monarch Antiques
15 High St. (J.A Badman) Est: 1970. Open 9.45-5.45. SIZE: Medium. *STOCK: General antiques and collectors' items, religious items including icons, coins, military items, antiquities and weapons, £5-£1,000.* LOC: On A39. PARK: At rear. TEL: 0458 32498. SER: Valuations. VAT: Stan/Spec.

Matthew Willis Antique Clocks
88 Bove Town. Open by appointment. *STOCK: English, French and American clocks.* TEL: 0458 32103.

HAMBRIDGE, Nr. Langport

Chalon U.K. Ltd **LAPADA**
Old Hambridge Mill. (M. and T Chalon) Est: 1974. Appointment preferred. SIZE: Large. *STOCK: 18th-19th C pine - painted British and European.* TEL: 0458 252374; fax - 0458 251192.

HIGHBRIDGE

Colin Dyte Exports Ltd **LAPADA**
Huntspill Rd. Open 7-6.30 or by appointment. *STOCK: Mahogany, 18th-20th C.* PARK: Easy. TEL: 0278 788590/788605; home - 0278 683761. SER: Packing; transport; documentation.

T.M Dyte Antiques
2B Isleport Business Park. Open 8.30-5.30. CL: Sat. *STOCK: Shipping goods.* TEL: 0278 786495.

Terence Kelly Antiques
Huntspill Court, West Huntspill. Open by appointment. *STOCK: Furniture, decorative and collectors' items.* TEL: 0278 785052.

The Treasure Chest Ltd
The Jays, 19 Alstone Lane. (R.J. and V Rumble) Est: 1964. CL: Sun., except by appointment. SIZE: Medium. *STOCK: General antiques including furniture, 17th-20th C; smalls especially musical boxes.* LOC: Off A38 down lane by Royal Artillery public house, 200yds. on left. PARK: Easy. TEL: 0278 787267. SER: Valuations; restorations (pictures); buys at auction. VAT: Stan/Spec. *Trade Only.*

ILMINSTER

Ray Best Antiques **LAPADA**
North St. House. (R. and W Best) Est: 1964. Open 9.30-6, Sat. 11-3. Trade any time by appointment. SIZE: Medium. *STOCK: Furniture, £50-£6,000; clocks, £50-£2,000; metalware, £30-£2,000, all 17th-19th C; porcelain, glass, 18th-19th C, £20-£2,000; silver, country items.* Not Stocked: Coins, stamps, medals. LOC:

Ray Best Antiques continued

Town centre, 2nd turning on left down one way street, off Market Sq. next to George Hotel. PARK: Easy. TEL: 0460 52194. SER: Valuations; buys at auction. VAT: Spec.

County Antiques Centre
21-23 West St. (Mrs J.P Barnard) Resident. Est: 1981. Open 10-5, or by appointment. SIZE: Medium - 8 dealers. *STOCK: 18th-19th C pottery, porcelain, metalwork, furniture and decorative antiques.* LOC: West of town at traffic lights crossing. PARK: At rear. TEL: 0460 54151; home - 0460 52269. SER: Upholstery.

Ilminster continued

Clare Hutchinson

1A West St. (C.C Hutchinson) Est: 1978. Open 10-5.30, Sat. 10-2. CL: Thurs. SIZE: Small. *STOCK: Oil paintings, 18th-20th C, £100-£5,000; gilt frames, 18th-19th C, £40-£500; watercolours, 19th-20th C, £50-£1,000.* LOC: From Market sq., down Silver St., shop on left. PARK: Easy. TEL: 0460 53369; home - 0460 21368. SER: Restorations (pictures and frames). VAT: Spec.

James Hutchison

5 West St. *STOCK: Pictures, frames, china and glass, collectables, furniture.*

Moolham Mill Antiques BADA

Moolham Mill, Moolham Lane. (R Cropper) Est: 1966. Open by appointment. SIZE: Medium. *STOCK: Oak furniture, 17th-18th C; mahogany furniture, 18th to early 19th C; Delft, pewter, 18th-19th C; metalwork, treen, decorative items, needleworks, samplers.* Not Stocked: Silver, Victorian furniture. LOC: From Ilminster on A303 take A3037 for Chard. One mile from centre of Ilminster take road signposted to Dowlish Wake/Kingstone. Premises 300yds. on right. PARK: Easy. TEL: 0460 52834. SER: Valuations; buys at auction. VAT: Spec. *Mainly Trade.*

Plympton Gallery

31 West St. (J. and E Van Den Bergh) Est: 1987. Open 10-1 and 2-5, Sat. 10-1. CL: Mon. and Thurs. SIZE: Small. *STOCK: Fine watercolours, some 19th C and early 20th C, £150-£3,500; prints, £35-£350; sculptures, £100-£5,000; all mainly contemporary.* LOC: 1 mile east from Southfields roundabout on A303, corner of Brewery Lane. PARK: Easy. TEL: 0460 54437. SER: Picture framing and restoration; valuations; buys at auction (mainly pictures). VAT: Stan/Spec.

J.A Stancomb

Bullen Court, Broadway. Est: 1965. Appointment advisable. *STOCK: Silver.* LOC: From London A303, 2 miles beyond Ilminster. The Five Dials Inn on right, turn right around inn and 400yds. to river bridge. Gate at left on bridge. TEL: 0460 52640.

West End House Antiques

34-36 West St. (T.H Sabine) Est: 1964. Open 9.30-5. SIZE: Large. *STOCK: Furniture, 18th to early 20th C, £50-£700; art deco china including Clarice Cliff, £5-£1,000; pictures, 19th-20th C, £10-£500.* LOC: Old A303. PARK: Easy. TEL: 0460 52793; home - 0404 42140. SER: Valuations; buys at auction.

LANGFORD BUDVILLE, Nr. Wellington

Trevor Micklem Antiques Ltd BADA

Harpford Mill. (C.T., S.E.M. and T.J.M Micklem) Est: 1962. Open by appointment. *STOCK: Early furniture, delft ware, pottery, pewter, needlework and metalware.* TEL: 0823 660236; home - 0823 672710.

LANGPORT

King's House Antiques

The King's House, Bow St. (Mrs D Desmond) Est: 1976. Open 9-5, Sat. 9-2, Sun. by appointment. CL: Wed. SIZE: Small. *STOCK: Small collectables, £5-£25.* LOC: Taunton to Yeovil road. PARK: Easy and nearby. TEL: 0458 250350; home - same. SER: Buys at auction (smalls, pictures). FAIRS: Yeovil.

LIMINGTON, Nr. Yeovil

Genges Farm Antiques

Genges Farm. (R Gilbert) Resident. Est: 1965. Always available. SIZE: Medium. *STOCK: Pine and country furniture especially Irish and period; French provincial furniture and decorative items; period oak and elm.* LOC: Off A37. PARK: Easy. TEL: 0935 840464 or 0458 250193.

LITTLETON, Nr. Somerton

Cains Antiques LAPADA

Littleton House. (T. and M.C Finlay) Est: 1956. Open 10-5, Sun. by appointment. SIZE: Medium. *STOCK: Furniture, 18th-19th C, £25-£10,000; Oriental porcelain, ironstone china, designer lamps.* LOC: B3151, approx. 1 1/2 miles north of Somerton. PARK: Easy. TEL: 0458 72341; home - same. SER: Valuations; restorations (furniture and antique lighting fixtures). VAT: Stan/Spec.

Westville House Antiques

Westville House. (D. and M Stacey) Est: 1986. Open daily, Sun. by appointment. SIZE: Small. *STOCK: Furniture - pine, £300-£700; satinwood and ash, £200-£500; all 19th C.* LOC: B3151, approx. 1 1/2 miles north of Somerton. PARK: Easy. TEL: 0458 73376; home - same. SER: Valuations; buys at auction. FAIRS: Bath and West; North Somerset. VAT: Stan/Spec.

LYMPSHAM, Nr. Weston-Super-Mare

Baytree House Antiques

Stevens Lane. (N. and S Adams) Est: 1982. Open 9-6. SIZE: Large. *STOCK: Stripped pine furniture, some smalls.* LOC: Off A370 - turn left immediately after first Jeff Brown garage, premises about 3/4 mile on right. PARK: Easy. TEL: 0934 750367. VAT: Stan/Spec.

Cains Antiques
Antique furniture, Decorative Accessories, Designer Lamps
Appointment advisable
Littleton House, Littleton, Somerset, TA11 6NP
Telephone: 0458 72341

One of a pair of Staffordshire hedgehogs, with applied sherds to simulate spines, on rocky bases flecked with gold, 3in. (7.6cm) long, c.1830-40. SOTHEBY'S
From ***English Porcelain Animals of the 19th Century*** by D.G. Rice published by the **Antique Collectors' Club** in 1989. £25.00.

MARTOCK

Martock Gallery
Treasurer's House. (G.I Palmer) Est: 1971. *STOCK: Watercolours, 18th-19th C, some oil paintings, prints, £20-£200.* LOC: Opposite church. TEL: 0935 823288. SER: Buys at auction.

MILVERTON, Nr. Taunton

Milverton Antiques
Fore St. (A Waymouth) Est: 1972. Resident, open any time. SIZE: Medium. *STOCK: Pine and oak country furniture, longcase clocks, interesting china, copper, brass and treen.* LOC: 8 miles from Taunton on B3227 Barnstaple road. PARK: 50yds. TEL: 0823 400597. VAT: Stan/Spec.

MONTACUTE, Nr. Yeovil

Gerald Lewis BADA
The Old Brewery, The Old Estate Yard. (G. and B Lewis) Open by appointment. *STOCK: 18th and early 19th C furniture and clocks.* TEL: 0935 825435.

Montacute continued

Montacute Antiques
April Cottage, 12 South St. (E.M. and J.K Warrick) Open 9-6 including Sun. *STOCK: Small furniture, porcelain, glass, pictures, metalware, decorative and interesting items.* PARK: Easy. TEL: 0935 824786.

NETHER STOWEY, Nr. Bridgwater

House of Antiquity
St. Mary St. (M.S Todd) Est: 1967. Open 10-5 or by appointment. SIZE: Medium. *STOCK: Philatelic literature, world topographical, maps, handbooks, postcards, ephemera, postal history.* LOC: A39. PARK: Easy. TEL: 0278 732426. SER: Valuations; buys at auction. VAT: Stan.

NORTH CHERITON, Nr. Templecombe

Joy Lee Antiques LAPADA
The Stables. (Mr and Mrs U Worle) Est: 1979. Open by appointment. SIZE: Medium. *STOCK: 18th-19th C English furniture and decorative accessories including paintings, boxes, caddies, English and Oriental pottery and porcelain, brass, decorators' items.* LOC: From A303, 2 miles along A357. PARK: Easy. TEL: 0963 33779; home - same. SER: Valuations; buys at auction (as stock). VAT: Spec.

NORTH PETHERTON, Nr. Bridgwater

Kathleen's Antiques
60 Fore St. (K Pocock) Resident. Est: 1971. Open 9-6.30. SIZE: Medium. *STOCK: Furniture, clocks, 18th-19th C, £50-£650; oil paintings, watercolours, sporting prints, £10-£250; silver, £10-£250; china, glass, copper, brass, Victorian, £10-£125.* LOC: A38. PARK: Easy. TEL: 0278 662535.

PITMINSTER, Nr. Taunton

Pitminster Studio
(Mr and Mrs T Everett) Est: 1946. Open 10-4 or by appointment. *STOCK: Modern and contemporary British paintings and sculpture, £200-£10,000.* LOC: 3 miles south of Taunton, between pub and church. PARK: Easy. TEL: 0823 42710. VAT: Stan/Spec.

QUEEN CAMEL, Nr. Yeovil

R Bonnett Antiques
The Thatch, High St. Open 9-5.30, Sun. and other times by appointment. *STOCK: Furniture and smalls pre-1900.* LOC: A359. TEL: 0935 850724. SER: Courier.

Queen Camel continued

Steven Ferdinando
The Old Vicarage. Open by appointment. *STOCK: Antiquarian and secondhand books.* TEL: 0935 850210.

RODE, Nr. Bath

Keyford Antiques
Southfield House, 16 High St. (F O'Dwyer) Open by appointment. *STOCK: Georgian and Victorian mahogany and pine furniture, oak and decorative items.* TEL: 0373 830531. *Trade Only.*

SOMERTON

John Gardiner Antiques
Monteclefe House. Appointment advisable. *STOCK: General antiques; Edwardian and quality old reproduction furnishings.* LOC: A303. TEL: 0458 72238 or 0836 592108.

The London Cigarette Card Co. Ltd
Sutton Rd. (I.A. and E.K Laker, F.C Doggett and Y Berktay) Est: 1927. CL: Sat. SIZE: Medium. *STOCK: Cigarette cards, 1885 to date; sets from £2; other cards, from 15p.* PARK: Easy. TEL: 0458 73452. SER: Mail order.

Valetta House Antiques
West St. (Mrs J Gardiner) Open 10-5. CL: Wed. *STOCK: Small general antiques and furniture.* TEL: 0458 74015.

TAUNTON

Philip Barrett Antiques and Prints
Rowford Cottage, Cheddon Fitzpaine. (P. and P Barrett) Open by appointment. *STOCK: Maps; topographic and sporting prints; Vanity Fair cartoons, country and stripped pine furniture, pottery, porcelain and watercolours.* TEL: 0823 451248.

Caroline's Antiques
17 East Reach. (Mrs C Hunt) Open 9.30-5. CL: Tues. *STOCK: General antiques and collectables.* TEL: 0823 321255.

Jeremiah Antiques
19A Staplegrove Rd. (D.W Jeremiah) Open 11-4. *STOCK: Small items, silver and jewellery.* TEL: 0823 336903; home - 0823 282924.

Joshua Antiques
Paul St. *STOCK: Decorative furnishings.* TEL: 0823 332874.

Rothwell and Dunworth
14 Paul St. (Mrs C Rothwell and M Dunworth) ABA. Est: 1975. Open 11-5.30. SIZE: Medium. *STOCK: Antiquarian and secondhand books.* LOC: Off A38, opposite multi-storey car park, behind County Hotel. TEL: 0823 282476. SER: Valuations; book-binding.

Taunton continued

Selwoods
Queen Anne Cottage, Mary St. Est: 1927. Open 9-5. SIZE: Large. *STOCK: Furniture, including Victorian and Edwardian.* TEL: 0823 272780.

Staplegrove Lodge Antiques
Staplegrove Lodge. (T Atkins) Est: 1958. Open by appointment only. SIZE: Medium. *STOCK: General antiques, furniture, silver, porcelain, pot-lids.* LOC: Pink house just off A361 Taunton/Barnstaple road up No Through Road just before the Cross Keys inn. PARK: Own. TEL: 0823 331153; home - same.

L.M. and D.G Stroud
(Stroud's of Taunton). NAG. Open by appointment. *STOCK: Jewellery.* TEL: 0823 284452. FAIRS: Chelsea, Olympia, British International, Birmingham, West London, Harrogate, Barbican.

Taunton Silver Street Antiques Centre
27/29 Silver St, (Atlantic Antiques Centres Ltd.). Est: 1978. Open Mon. 9-4. SIZE: 130 dealers. *STOCK: General antiques and collectables, including specialists in most fields.* LOC: 1 1/2 miles from junction 25, M5, toward town centre, 100yds. from Sainsbury Superstore. PARK: Easy. TEL: 0823 289327; enquiries (071) 351 5353.

TEMPLECOMBE

Yewtree Antiques
Park House, High St. (B Hayden) Open 9.30-6. *STOCK: General antiques.* TEL: 0963 70505.

TIMBERSCOMBE, Nr. Minehead

Zwan Antiques
(M. van Zwanenberg) Open Tues., Thurs. and Sun. p.m. or by appointment. *STOCK: Jewellery, 18th-20th C, £1-£2,000; porcelain, 18th-19th C, £5-£1,000; hunting prints and riding items, 19th-20th C, £1-£500; some original sporting pictures, £50-£1,000; small items.* LOC: 2 miles out of Dunster on A396. PARK: Outside. TEL: 064 384 608. SER: Valuations; buys at auction.

WANSTROW, Nr. Shepton Mallet

Fred Milton Antiques
Open Sat. and Sun., other times by appointment. SIZE: Large. *STOCK: Furniture, Victorian and later.* TEL: 074 985 433. VAT: Stan.

WATCHET

Clarence House Antiques
41 Swain St. Est: 1970. Open 10-6.30. CL: Sun. in winter. SIZE: Medium. *STOCK: General*

Clarence House Antiques continued

antiques, pine, brass, copper, bric-a-brac, upholstered furniture. TEL: 0984 31389. VAT: Stan.

Nick Cotton Antiques and Fine Art
Beechstone House, 47 Swain St. Est: 1970. Open 10-5.30, Sun. by appointment. SIZE: Medium. *STOCK: Paintings, 1750-1950; period furniture.* TEL: 0984 31814 (any time). SER: Restorations; framing; research. VAT: Spec.

WEDMORE

Coach House Gallery
Church St. (Mrs V Davies) Est: 1976. Open 9-6 or by appointment. SIZE: Small. *STOCK: English watercolours, 19th and early 20th C; small furniture, English porcelain; glass and silver, 18th C.* LOC: Opposite St. Mary's Church. TEL: 0934 712718; home - same.

WELLINGTON

Michael and Amanda Lewis Oriental Carpets and Rugs LAPADA
8 North St. Est: 1982. Open 10-1 and 2-5.30, Mon. and weekends by appointment. SIZE: Medium. *STOCK: Oriental carpets and rugs, mainly 19th-20th C, £25-£25,000.* PARK: 100yds. TEL: 0823 667430. SER: Valuations; restorations (as stock); repairs and cleaning.

Oxenhams
74 Mantle St. Open 9-9, Sun. by appointment. CL: Thurs. p.m. *STOCK: General antiques.* LOC: On A38. PARK: Easy. TEL: 0823 662592.

WELLS

Shelagh Berryman Music Boxes
15 Market Pl. Open 10-5.30 or by appointment. *STOCK: Music boxes, clocks and general antiques, mainly 19th C.* TEL: 0749 76203.

Bernard G House (Mitre Antiques)
Market Pl. Est: 1963. Open 9.30-5.30. SIZE: Medium. *STOCK: Barometers and scientific instruments, furniture including miniatures and apprentice pieces, 18th-19th C; longcase and bracket clocks, metalware, decorative and architectural items.* PARK: In Market Place. TEL: 0749 72607. SER: Restorations. VAT: Stan/Spec.

Lovejoys
Queen St. (T and J Oliver) Est: 1991. Open 9-4, Sun. by appointment. SIZE: Small. *STOCK: Paintings, Edwardian and Victorian furniture, Victorian china.* PARK: Nearby. TEL: 0749 670706. SER: Restorations. VAT: Stan/Spec.

Edward A Nowell BADA
12 Market Pl. Est: 1952. Open 9-1 and 2-5.30. SIZE: Large. *STOCK: Furniture, clocks, barometers, 17th to early 19th C; jewellery, silver, porcelain, English and continental, all*

Edward A. Nowell continued

***prices.* Not Stocked: Victoriana, bric-a-brac, curios, weapons, books. LOC: From any direction, turn left into Market Place (one-way system). PARK: 20yds. facing shop. TEL: 0749 72415. SER: Valuations; restorations (furniture, silver, clocks and jewellery); re-upholstery. VAT: Stan/Spec.**

Marcus Nowell **LAPADA**
21 Market Pl. Est: 1973. Open 9.30-5.30. SIZE: Medium. *STOCK: Furniture and decorative items, 18th-19th C, £50-£10,000.* PARK: Easy. TEL: 0749 78051. SER: Valuations; restorations (furniture); buys at auction (furniture). VAT: Stan/Spec.

WEST MONKTON, Nr. Taunton

William Morley Antiques
Musgrave's Old Farm. (W.H Morley) Est: 1970. Open daily, appointment advisable. SIZE: Medium. *STOCK: Oak and country furniture, 17th to early 19th C; early brass and metalware.* LOC: From A38 or A361, second house on right on road to village before Monkton Inn. PARK: Easy. TEL: 0823 412751. SER: Valuations; buys at auction; specialist finder.

WILLITON

Edward Venn
52 Long St. Est: 1979. Open 10-5. *STOCK: Furniture, 18th C; clocks.* TEL: 0984 32631 (ansaphone). SER: Restorations (furniture, barometers and clocks).

WINCANTON

Barry M Sainsbury
17 High St. Est: 1958. CL: Thurs. p.m. *STOCK: Oak and mahogany furniture, china, glass, pictures, decorative items.* TEL: 0963 32289. SER: Restorations; cabinet makers. VAT: Stan/Spec.

WIVELISCOMBE

The Carousel Pig
9 High St. (A McKinley) CL: Mon. and Wed. *STOCK: General antiques, unusual and decorative items, textiles, taxidermy, £5-£2,000.* PARK: Easy. TEL: 0984 24556. SER: Restorations (china and taxidermy); taxidermy commission.

J.C Giddings
Open by appointment only. SIZE: Large warehouses. *STOCK: Furniture, mostly 18th-19th C.* TEL: 0984 23703. VAT: Stan. *Mainly Trade.*

Heads 'n' Tails
'Bournes House', 41 Church St. (D. and A McKinley) Resident. Open by appointment.

Heads 'n' Tails continued

STOCK: Taxidermy including Victorian cased and uncased birds, mammals and fish, £5-£2,000; decorative items, glass domes. LOC: Opposite church. PARK: Easy. TEL: 0984 23097 or 0860 741185. SER: Taxidermy; restorations; commissions. VAT: Spec.

Peter Lee Antiques
1 Silver St. (P. and A Lee) Open 9-5. CL: Sat. p.m. *STOCK: Furniture, china, general antiques, fine arts and unsual items.* LOC: B3227, town centre. PARK: Nearby. TEL: 0984 24055.

YEOVIL

Fox and Co
30 Princes St. Est: 1970. *STOCK: Antiquities, coins, medals and militaria, reference books.* PARK: Easy. TEL: 0935 72323. VAT: Stan/Spec.

John Hamblin
Unit 315 Oxford Rd, Penn Mill Trading Estate. (J. and M.A Hamblin) Est: 1980. Open 8.30-5. CL: Sat. SIZE: Small. *STOCK: Furniture, 1750-1900, £300-£3,000.* PARK: Easy. TEL: 0935 71154; home - 76673. SER: Restorations (furniture); cabinet work. VAT: Stan.

Mactaggart Books
Little Brympton, Brympton d'Evercy. Est: 1971. Usually open but telephone call advisable. *STOCK: Secondhand and antiquarian books.* TEL: 0935 86 2609.

Watercolour World
4 Parcroft Gdns. (D Fowles) Open 10-5. *STOCK: Victorian oils and watercolours.* TEL: 0935 72384.

Staffordshire

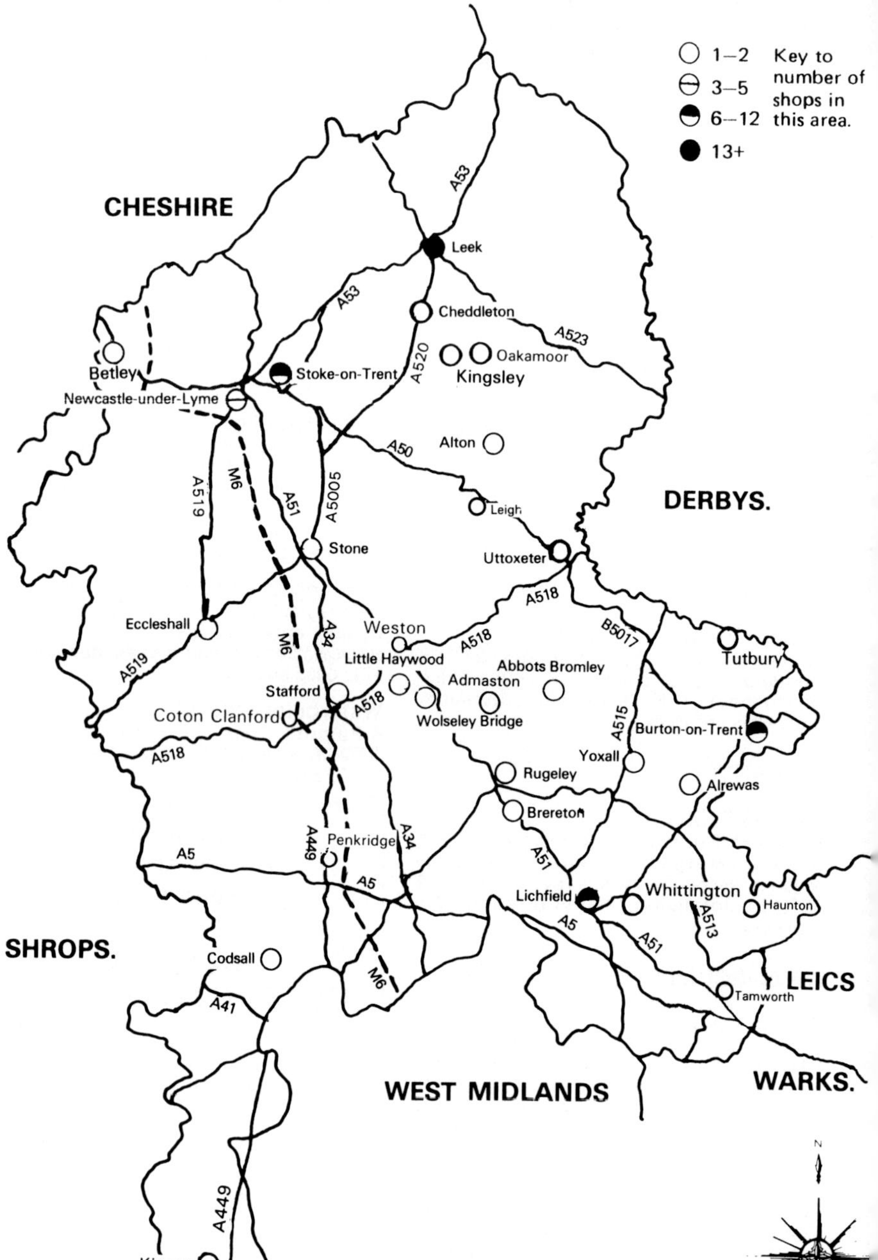

1–2
3–5
6–12
13+
Key to number of shops in this area.
CHESHIRE
DERBYS.
SHROPS.
LEICS
WARKS.
WEST MIDLANDS
Leek
Cheddleton
Oakamoor
Kingsley
Stoke-on-Trent
Betley
Newcastle-under-Lyme
Alton
Leigh
Stone
Uttoxeter
Eccleshall
Weston
Little Haywood
Abbots Bromley
Admaston
Tutbury
Stafford
Coton Clanford
Wolseley Bridge
Burton-on-Trent
Yoxall
Rugeley
Alrewas
Brereton
Penkridge
Lichfield
Whittington
Haunton
Codsall
Tamworth
Kinver
A53
A520
A523
A50
A5005
A51
A519
M6
A34
A518
B5017
A515
A449
A5
A513
A41
N

Please note this is only a rough map designed to show dealers the number of shops in the various towns, and is not necessarily totally accurate.

ABBOTS BROMLEY, Nr. Rugeley

Birchwood Antiques

Bromleys, Bagot St. (V Edwards) Open daily. *STOCK: General antiques, especially blue and white and lace.* TEL: 0283 840288.

Ivy House Antiques

Ivy House, High St. (Mrs B.A Hammersley) Est: 1959. Open 10-6, Sat. and Sun. 2-6. SIZE: Small. *STOCK: General antiques, porcelain, glass, china, small furniture and bygones.* PARK: Easy. TEL: 0283 840259.

ADMASTON, Nr. Rugeley

G Julian Allen

Admaston Farm. Open by appointment only. SIZE: Large. *STOCK: Georgian, Victorian and Edwardian furniture.* PARK: Own. TEL: 0889 500232.

ALREWAS, Nr. Burton-on-Trent

Poley Antiques

5 Main St. (D.T. and A.G Poley) Est: 1977. Open 10-5, and by appointment. CL: Wed. SIZE: Small. *STOCK: General antiques, furniture, silver, jewellery, china, glass, copper, brass.* Not Stocked: Stamps, coins and militaria. LOC: 20yds. from A38, between Lichfield and Burton, on A513. PARK: Own. TEL: 0283 791151; home - same. VAT: Stan/Spec.

ALTON

M.J. and I Cope

Open daily 9-6. *STOCK: Victorian and Edwardian furniture, pottery, brass and copper; pine and shipping items.* LOC: Centre of village, 1/2 mile from Alton Towers. PARK: Easy. TEL: 0538 702524.

BETLEY, Nr. Crewe

Betley Court Gallery

Main Rd. (Prof G.N Brown and Dr F Brown) Resident. Est: 1980. Open afternoons or by appointment anytime. CL: Mon. SIZE: Large. *STOCK: Oils, watercolours, prints, £20-£5,000; ceramics, especially Doulton Lambeth and Wedgwood, £20-£2,500; both 18th-20th C; furniture, Georgian, Regency, Victorian, £20-£2,500.* Not Stocked: Militaria, clocks. LOC: Village centre. PARK: Easy. TEL: 0270 820652. SER: Buys at auction.

B. and A.E Lightfoot

Bank House Antiques, Main Rd. Open by appointment. *STOCK: General antiques.* TEL: 0270 820397.

BRERETON, Nr. Rugeley

Rugeley Antique Centre

161/3 Main Rd. Open 9-5. SIZE: Large - 28 units. *STOCK: China, glass, pottery, pictures, furniture, pine, treen, linen and shipping goods.* LOC: A51, one mile south of Rugeley town, opposite Cedar Tree Hotel. PARK: Own. TEL: 0889 577166. VAT: Stan/Spec.

BURTON-ON-TRENT

Broadway Studios

127 New St. (F.H Dyson) Est: 1969. CL: Wed. SIZE: Medium. *STOCK: Prints, watercolours, oil paintings, £1-£500.* TEL: 0283 41802. SER: Picture framing and mount cutting. VAT: Stan.

Burton Antiques

1 and 2 Horninglow Rd. (C.H Armett) Est: 1977. Open 10-5 every day. SIZE: Large. *STOCK: Shipping and pine furniture.* LOC: A50. PARK: Nearby. TEL: 0283 42331. SER: Valuations; pine stripping; buys at auction.

Holloways Antiques and Interior Design

138 Derby St. Open 10-5. CL: Wed. *STOCK: Mainly 18th-19th C furniture, clocks, pictures, silver plate, porcelain.* PARK: Easy. TEL: 0283 36648. SER: Soft furnishings supplied; interior design. VAT: Stan/Spec.

Justin Pinewood

The Maltings, Wharf Rd. (S Silvester) Open 9-5.30. *STOCK: Stripped pine furniture.* TEL: 0283 510860.

H.J Richards and Son

Abbey Arcade, High St. Est: 1896. Open 9-5.30, Sat. 9-4.30. SIZE: Small. *STOCK: Jewellery, mainly Victorian and Edwardian, £50-£2,500; silver.* LOC: Market Place end of main shopping thoroughfare. PARK: Limited and nearby. TEL: 0283 65921. SER: Valuations; restorations (silver, jewellery and clocks). VAT: Stan.

C. and R Scattergood

132 Branston Rd. Open 9-6. *STOCK: Decorative antiques.* TEL: 0283 46695.

CHEDDLETON, Nr. Leek

Jewel Antiques

'Whitegates', Basford Bridge Lane. (B. and D.J Smith) Est: 1967. Open by appointment. *STOCK: Paintings, prints, jewellery, oil lamps, small furniture and clocks, 18th-19th C, £25-£2,000.* PARK: Easy. TEL: 0538 360744/361247. SER: Buys at auction.

R.G Wragg

319 Cheadle Rd. Est: 1970. Resident, usually available. *STOCK: Books, 19th C, £5-£200.* TEL: 0538 360044.

CODSALL

Dam Mill Antiques

Birches Rd. (G. and H Bassett) Est: 1977. Open 10-1 and 2.30-5.30. CL: Tues. and Thurs. SIZE: Small. *STOCK: General antiques, small furniture, china, glass, copper, brass, silver and jewellery.* PARK: Easy. TEL: 090 74 3780.

COTON CLANFORD, Nr. Stafford

C. and J Mowe

Stokingate Farm. Est: 1970. Open by appointment. *STOCK: Shipping goods, pine and general antiques.* TEL: 0785 282799. VAT: Stan/Spec. *Trade Only.*

ECCLESHALL

B Timmis and Son

1 The Beehive, High St. Open 10-5. CL: Wed. *STOCK: Small antiques, shipping goods, longcase clocks, pine, metals.* LOC: In main street. PARK: Easy. TEL: 0785 850883. VAT: Stan/Spec.

HAUNTON, Nr. Tamworth

Heart of England Antiques

The Manor Barn. (R Gilbert and Miss P Crockett) Est: 1985. Open 10-5.30, Sun. by appointment. SIZE: Large. *STOCK: Furniture, 18th-19th C, £500-£3,000; paintings, £50-£1,000; silver, plate, £5-£200; both 19th C.* LOC: Next to the Manor. PARK: Easy. TEL: Home - 0860 434003. SER: Valuations; restorations (furniture, including re-upholstery); buys at auction (furniture and paintings). FAIRS: Chestford Grange (May); St. Johns Hotel, Solihull; N.E.C. (Aug.); Stafford 3 day. VAT: Stan/Spec.

KINGSLEY, Nr. Leek

Country Cottage Interiors

Newhall Farmhouse, Hazels Crossroads. (L Salmon) Resident. Est: 1972. Open 10-5. SIZE: Medium. *STOCK: Pine, £5-£500; kitchenalia, 25p-£100.* LOC: Off A52. PARK: Own. TEL: 0538 754762.

KINVER

The Antique Centre

128 High St. (R Harris) Open 10-5.30. SIZE: 10 dealers. *STOCK: Stripped pine, clocks, china, glass, bric-a-brac, furniture, pianos.* TEL: 0384 877441. SER: Stripping.

LEEK

Antiques and Objets d'Art of Leek

70 St. Edwards St. Est: 1955. Open 10-6. CL: Thurs. *STOCK: English and continental furniture; porcelain, silver, glass, oil paintings.* TEL: 0538 382587. FAIRS: Buxton. VAT: Spec.

Anvil Antiques

Cross St. Mill, Cross St. (K.L. and J.S Spooner) Est: 1975. Open 9-6. SIZE: Large. *STOCK: Stripped pine, architectural and oak, mahogany, bric-a-brac, decorative items and painted furniture, prints and art gallery.* LOC: Ashbourne Rd., from town centre roundabout, turn first left, Victorian mill on right. PARK: Easy. TEL: 0538 371657. VAT: Stan.

Aspleys Antique Market

Compton Mill, Compton. (J Aspley) Est: 1976. Open 9.6. CL: Sun. except by appointment. SIZE: Large. *STOCK: General antiques, especially pine, shipping items, bric-a-brac, mainly Victorian and Edwardian.* PARK: Own. TEL: 0538 373396. SER: Restorations (mainly pine); shipping and packing; courier service. VAT: Stan.

Sylvia Chapman Antiques

4 St. Edward St. Open 12-5.30. CL: Thurs. *STOCK: General small and collectors' items, especially 19th to early 20th C pottery and porcelain, Staffordshire figures and jugs, glass, treen, copper and brass.* PARK: Opposite. TEL: 0538 399116.

Cyril Cox Antiques

76/78 St. Edward St. Est: 1971. Open 10-6. CL: Thurs. SIZE: Medium. *STOCK: General antiques including furniture, porcelain, glass, china, gold and silver, pictures, jewellery and linen.* LOC: At junction with Brook St. PARK: Nearby. TEL: 0538 399924; home - 0782 511169. SER: Valuations; restorations (furniture).

Directmoor Ltd

Albany House, Abbey Green Rd. Open 9-6. SIZE: Large and warehouse. *STOCK: English, Irish and continental pine, objets d'art, small and decorative items, oils and watercolours.* LOC: A523 Macclesfield Rd. PARK: Easy. TEL: 0538 387474/399876; fax - 0538 371307.

England's Gallery

Ball Haye House, 1 Ball Haye Terr. (F.J. and S England) Est: 1968. Open 10-5.30. CL: Mon. SIZE: Large. *STOCK: Oils and watercolours, 18th-19th C, £500-£10,000; etchings, engravings, lithographs, mezzotints, £50-£4,000.* LOC: Towards Ball Haye Green from A523 turn at lights. PARK: Nearby. TEL: 0538 373451; home - 0538 386352. SER: Valuations; restorations (cleaning, relining, regilding); framing, mount cutting; buys at auction (paintings). VAT: Stan.

Leek continued

Gemini Trading
Limes Mill, Abbotts Rd. (T.J Lancaster and Mrs Y.A Goldstraw) Est: 1981. Open daily, Sun. by appointment only. SIZE: Large. *STOCK: Pine, £25-£600; kitchenalia, £5-£35; both 19th C.* LOC: Turn off A53 along Abbotts Rd. before town centre. PARK: Easy. TEL: 0538 387834. VAT: Stan.

Gilligans Antiques
59 St. Edward St. (M.T Gilligan) Est: 1977. *STOCK: Victorian and Edwardian furniture.* TEL: 0538 384174.

Grosvenor Antiques
Overton Bank House. Open 9-4.30. *STOCK: Clocks, watches and barometers; some furniture.* TEL: 0538 385669.

Roger Haynes - Antiques Finder
31 Compton. Open 9.30-6; Sat. 9.30-5 or by appointment. *STOCK: Pine, small general and decorative items.* TEL: 0538 385161.

Johnson's
Park Works, Park Rd. (P. and Mrs J Johnson) Est: 1976. Open 9-6. SIZE: Medium. *STOCK: Pine and country furniture, £50-£1,000; decorative accessories, quilts, needlework and samplers, £50-£500; all 18th-19th C; domestic items, 19th C, £5-£50.* LOC: Off M6, exit 14 on

Johnson's continued

to A520, just off A523 Macclesfield road. PARK: Easy. TEL: 0538 386745. SER: Restorations (pine). VAT: Stan.

The Leek Bookshop
4 Brook St. (R.G Wragg) SIZE: Large. *STOCK: Books, 19th C, £5-£200.* TEL: 0538 373391.

Willott Antiques
1 Clerk Bank. (J Willott) Est: 1977. Open 10-4.30. SIZE: Medium. *STOCK: General antiques, including oak and mahogany furniture and pottery.* LOC: Main Macclesfield road into Leek. PARK: Easy. TEL: 0538 371519; home - 0782 504609. VAT: Stan.

Pat Wood
Stanley St. CL: Thurs. *STOCK: Paintings and prints.* TEL: 0538 385696. SER: Restorations (pictures); framing.

LEIGH, Nr. Stoke-on-Trent

John Nicholls
Open by appointment only. *STOCK: Oak furniture and related items, 17th-18th C.* LOC: 2 miles from Uttoxeter, just off A50 towards Stoke-on-Trent. SER: 0889 502351; mobile - 0836 244024.

LICHFIELD

Mike Abrahams Books
Cranmere Court, Walsall Rd. PBFA. Est: 1975. Open by appointment. SIZE: Large. *STOCK: Books, especially Midlands topography, 17th C to date, £2-£1,000; documents, ephemera, 17th-20th C, £2-£50.* LOC: On left hand bend of A51 from Rugeley. PARK: Easy. TEL: 0543 256200; home - same. SER: Valuations. FAIRS: Bingley Hall, Stafford and PBFA. Book. Organiser - Midland Antiquarian Book.

The Antique Shop LAPADA
31 Tamworth St. (Mrs P.M Rackham) Open 9.30-1.30 and 2.30-5.30. SIZE: Medium. *STOCK: Furniture, pottery, porcelain, silver, prints, paintings, copper and brass, jewellery, glass, £5-£700.* PARK: Easy. TEL: 0543 268324.

Cordelia and Perdy's Antique Junk Shop
53 Tamworth St. (C.R.J. and P.J Mellor) *STOCK: General antiques and trade shipping goods.* TEL: 0543 263223.

Images - Peter Stockham
at The Staffs Bookshop, 4 & 6 Dam St. Open 9.30-5.30. *STOCK: Early children's books, art and illustrated books, printed ephemera; antique toys, mainly wooden; games and associated items; fine printing; prints and wood engravings.* TEL: 0543 264093.

Lichfield continued

James A Jordan
7 The Corn Exchange. CMBHI. Open 9-5.30. *STOCK: Clocks especially longcase; watches and barometers.* TEL: 0543 416221; fax - 021 522 2004. SER: Valuations; restorations (clocks and chronometers).

L Royden Smith
Church View, Farewell Lane, Burntwood. Est: 1972. Open Wed. and Sat. 10.30-5 or by appointment. *STOCK: Antiquarian books, general antiques, bric-a-brac, shipping goods.* TEL: 0543 682217.

The Staffs Bookshop
4 & 6 Dam St. Open 9.30-5.30. *STOCK: Rare, secondhand and antiquarian books, especially 18th-19th C.* TEL: 0543 264093.

LITTLE HAYWOOD, Nr. Stafford

Jalna Antiques
Coley Lane. Resident. Est: 1974. Open most times. *STOCK: Furniture, pre-1900.* Not Stocked: Shipping goods. LOC: 1/2 mile off A51, 12 miles north of Lichfield. TEL: 0889 881381. SER: Restorations; re-upholstery. VAT: Spec.

NEWCASTLE-UNDER-LYME

Antique Market
The Stones, (Antique Forum (Birmingham) Ltd.). Open Tues. 9-4. SIZE: 50 dealers. *STOCK: General antiques.* TEL: 088 97 527.

Errington Antiques
63 George St, (corner of George and Albert St.). (G.K Errington) Open 10-12.30 and 2-5. CL: Thurs. *STOCK: Arms, Oriental furniture and general antiques.* TEL: 0782 632822.

Hood and Broomfield
Lyme Galleries, 29 Albert St. (J Hood and G.H Broomfield) Open 10-5.30, Sat. 10-4, Thurs. by appointment. *STOCK: Oils and watercolours, 19th and early 20th C.* TEL: 0782 626859. SER: Restorations; framing. VAT: Spec.

Richard Midwinter Antiques
13 Brunswick St. (Mr and Mrs R Midwinter) Est: 1987. Open 10-5.30, Thurs. by appointment. SIZE: Medium. *STOCK: Furniture - oak, walnut, mahogany and garden, 17th-19th C, £50-£10,000; longcase, mantel and wall clocks, £150-£4,000; paintings, £35-£3,000, both 18th-19th C; ceramics and watercolours, 19th C, £15-£1,500.* Not Stocked: Pine and ephemera. LOC: Almost opposite swimming baths. TEL: 0782 712483; home - 0630 872289. SER: Valuations; restorations (framing, clock repair); buys at auction (furniture). VAT: Spec.

OAKAMOOR, Nr. Stoke-on-Trent

Directmoor Ltd
The Coppice Farm, Nr. Moorcourt Farley Rd. (D Johnson) Est: 1977. Open by appointment. SIZE: Warehouse. *STOCK: Stripped and restored pine furniture - English, Irish, continental and reproduction; country furnishing items.* LOC: Follow Alton Towers signs from motorways. PARK: Easy. TEL: 0538 702419; home - same. SER: Valuations; restorations; container packing and shipping. VAT: Stan. *Trade Only.*

PENKRIDGE, Nr. Stafford

Golden Oldies
1 and 5 Crown Bridge. (W.A. and M.A Knowles) Open 10-5.30, Sun. and Mon. 10-2. PARK: Easy. TEL: 0785 714722. VAT: Stan/Spec.

RUGELEY

Evelyn Winter
1 Wolseley Rd. (Mrs E Winter) Est: 1962. Open 10.30-5.30. SIZE: Small. *STOCK: Staffordshire figures, pre-Victorian, from £90; Victorian, £30-£500; copper, brass, glass and general antiques.* Not Stocked: Coins and weapons. LOC: Coming from Lichfield or Stafford stay on A51 and avoid town by-pass. PARK: Easy and at side of shop. TEL: 0889 583259.

STAFFORD

Browse
127 Lichfield Rd. (H Barnes) Est: 1981. Open 9.30-5. SIZE: Large. *STOCK: Furniture, 1860-1940 and reproduction.* LOC: Outskirts of town. PARK: Easy. TEL: 0785 41097; home - 0785 660336. SER: Valuations; restorations (caning and rushing).

STOKE-ON-TRENT

Ann's Antiques
24 Leek Rd, Stockton Brook. Open 10-5. CL: Thurs. *STOCK: Victorian furniture, brass, copper, jewellery, paintings, pottery and unusual items.* TEL: 0782 503991. VAT: Stan.

Antiques Workshop and Boulton's Antiques
43-45 Hope St, Hanley. (H. and S Oakes and J Rowley) Est: 1974. Open 9.30-5.30, Sun. by appointment. SIZE: Medium. *STOCK: Furniture including pine, mahogany and oak; pottery, 18th-20th C; general antiques and bric-a-brac.* PARK: Own at rear. TEL: 0782 273645. SER: Valuations; restorations (pine stripping, upholstery, polishing).

Barclay House Antiques
14-16 Howard Pl, Shelton. (P Lumley and D Latham) Open 9.30-6. SIZE: Large. *STOCK: Furniture and collectables.* LOC: City centre 1 mile; 1/2 mile from railway station towards Hanley city centre. TEL: 0782 274747.

Castle Antiques
113 Victoria St, Hartshill. (J Taylor) Est: 1965. Open 10-5.30. CL: Thurs. SIZE: Medium. *STOCK: Edwardian and Victorian furniture and clocks, £100-£1,000.* LOC: 300yds. from main road. PARK: 100yds. TEL: 0782 625168. VAT: Stan/Spec.

Five Towns Antiques
17 Broad St, Hanley. (B. and B Arkinstall) Open 10-5.30. CL: Thurs. SIZE: Small. *STOCK: 1930's pottery and porcelain, general antiques.* PARK: Nearby. TEL: 0782 272930.

Old Flames Architectural Antiques
133/139 Church St. (W Buckley Jnr, R.J Stevenson, S.F Molloy and P Machin, (Art and Art)) Est: 1989. Open 10-6. SIZE: Large. *STOCK: Fireplaces - marble, slate, cast-iron; fire surrounds, 1800-1930, £50-£10,000; art nouveau and art deco pottery including Carlton ware, Charlotte Rhead, Doulton.* LOC: Off M6, junction 15 on A500, opposite Spode factory. PARK: Own. TEL: 0782 744985; fax - 0782 747165. SER: Restorations (marble decoration, graining and rag rolling). VAT: Stan.

W.G Steele
20 Piccadilly, Hanley. Est: 1770. Open 9-6. *STOCK: Victorian and Edwardian jewellery.* Not Stocked: Furniture. TEL: 0782 213216.

Stoke-on-Trent continued

The Tinder Box

61 Lichfield St, Hanley. (Mr and Mrs G.E Yarwood) Est: 1969. Open 10-5. CL: Sat. SIZE: Large. *STOCK: Victorian oil lamps and spare parts; early brass and copper, jewellery, furniture and unusual items.* PARK: Easy. TEL: 0782 261368/550508. SER: Cleaning (brass and copper).

STONE

Stone-Wares Antiques

24 Radford St. (G Wheeler) Est: 1978. Open 9-6, Sun. by appointment. CL: Sat. p.m. SIZE: Medium. *STOCK: Period and reproduction country and pine furniture; longcase clocks, £100-£10,000.* LOC: A520 north of Stone. PARK: Easy. TEL: 0785 815000. VAT: Stan/Spec.

TAMWORTH

Bridle Antiques

Bro-Dawel House, Kettlebrook Rd. (W.G.V Turner) Est: 1988. Open by appointment seven days. SIZE: Small. *STOCK: Furniture, £500-£2,000; porcelain and ceramics, £100-£1,000; engravings and prints, £50-£500; all 18th-19th C; watercolours and oils, 19th C, £50-£500.* LOC: 2 1/2 miles junction 10, M42, via A5 to A51. PARK: Nearby. TEL: 0827 53031; home - same. SER: Valuations; restorations (furniture and paintings); buys at auction (furniture). FAIRS: West Midlands; Stafford County Showground.

TUTBURY, Nr. Burton-on-Trent

Town and Country Antiques

40 Monk St. (A.J Pym) Est: 1985. Open 9.30-5.30, including Sun. *STOCK: Stripped pine, £50-£500; Victorian/Edwardian linen and lace, £5-£150; reproduction pine, £15-£800.* TEL: 0283 520556. SER: Valuations. VAT: Stan.

Tutbury Mill Antiques

6 Lower High St. (F.J. and G.J Allen) Open seven days 9-6. SIZE: Warehouse. *STOCK: Georgian, Victorian and Edwardian furniture.* LOC: A50. Part of Georgian cobbled mews. PARK: Own. TEL: 0283 815999; home - 0889 270891.

UTTOXETER

Pine Antiques

52 Bridge St. (M.A. and A Groves) Open 9.30-5. *STOCK: English country pine and satinwood, pottery, linen and kitchenalia.* TEL: 0889 565374; home - 0889 564898.

WESTON, Nr. Stafford

Weston Antique Gallery

Boat Lane. (Mr and Mrs F Rabone) Est: 1976. Open 10-5.30 and by appointment. SIZE: Small. *STOCK: Maps and prints, 17th-19th C, £5-£500; Staffordshire pottery and porcelain, small silver and glass, 19th-20th C, £5-£100; small furniture and items, 19th C, £50-£500.* LOC: On A518. PARK: Easy. TEL: 0889 270450; home - same. SER: Restorations, framing.

WHITTINGTON, Nr. Lichfield

Milestone Antiques

5 Main St. (H. and E Crawshaw) Resident. Est: 1988. Open Thurs.-Sat. 10-6, Sun. 11-3, other times by appointment. *STOCK: Furniture, porcelain, pottery, pictures, brass and copper, 18th-19th C.* LOC: A51 Lichfield/Tamworth road, turn north at Whittington Barracks, shop 50yds. past crossroads in village. PARK: Outside. TEL: 0543 432248. VAT: Stan/Spec.

WOLSELEY BRIDGE, Nr. Rugeley

Jalna Antiques

The Old Barn. (G. and D Hancox) Open 10-5. *STOCK: Furniture and smalls.* LOC: Junction A51/A513. TEL: 0889 881381.

YOXALL

Armson's of Yoxall Antiques

LAPADA

The Hollies. (F.R.B. and P.K Armson) Est: 1955. Open 9-5, Sat. and other times by appointment. SIZE: Large. *STOCK: Period furniture and shipping goods.* LOC: On A515. TEL: 0543 472352. VAT: Stan/Spec.

H.W Heron and Son Ltd

The Antique Shop, 1 King St. (H.N.M. and J Heron) Est: 1949. Open 9-6, Sat. 10.30-5.30, Sun. 2-6. SIZE: Large. *STOCK: Furniture, porcelain, glass, pictures, all prices.* LOC: On A515 in centre of village, opp. church. PARK: Easy. TEL: 0543 472266; home - same. SER: Valuations. VAT: Stan/Spec.

IS YOUR ENTRY CORRECT?
If there is even the slightest inaccuracy in your entry, *please* let us know before 1st January 1992.
GUIDE TO THE
ANTIQUE SHOPS OF BRITAIN
5 Church Street, Woodbridge, Suffolk.
Tel: (0394) 385501

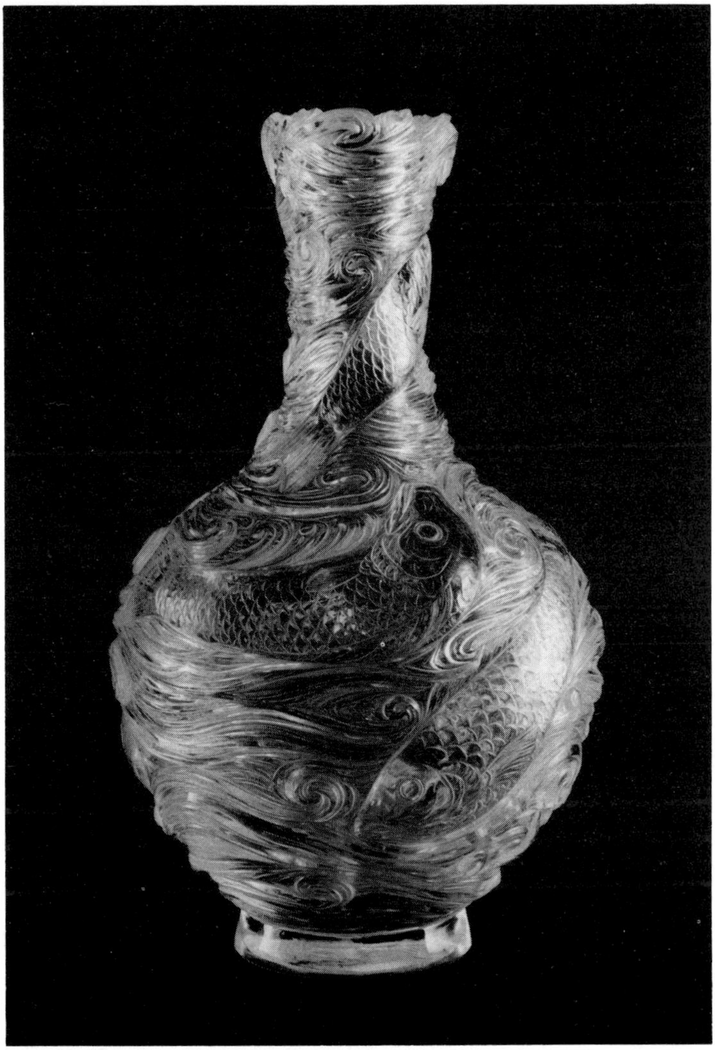

Vase, cut and engraved rock crystal with fish amid waves. Recorded in the Webb pattern books, no. 17415 'Flint vase engd. RC' and in the price book '25.3.89. 12″ vase flint carved £34.00'. Thomas Webb and Sons, possibly engraved by George Woodall, 1889. Height 12in. (30.6cm). From ***British Glass 1800-1914*** by Charles R. Hajdamach published by the **Antique Collectors' Club** in 1991. £45.00.

Suffolk

Please note this is only a rough map designed to show dealers the number of shops in the various towns, and is not necessarily totally accurate.

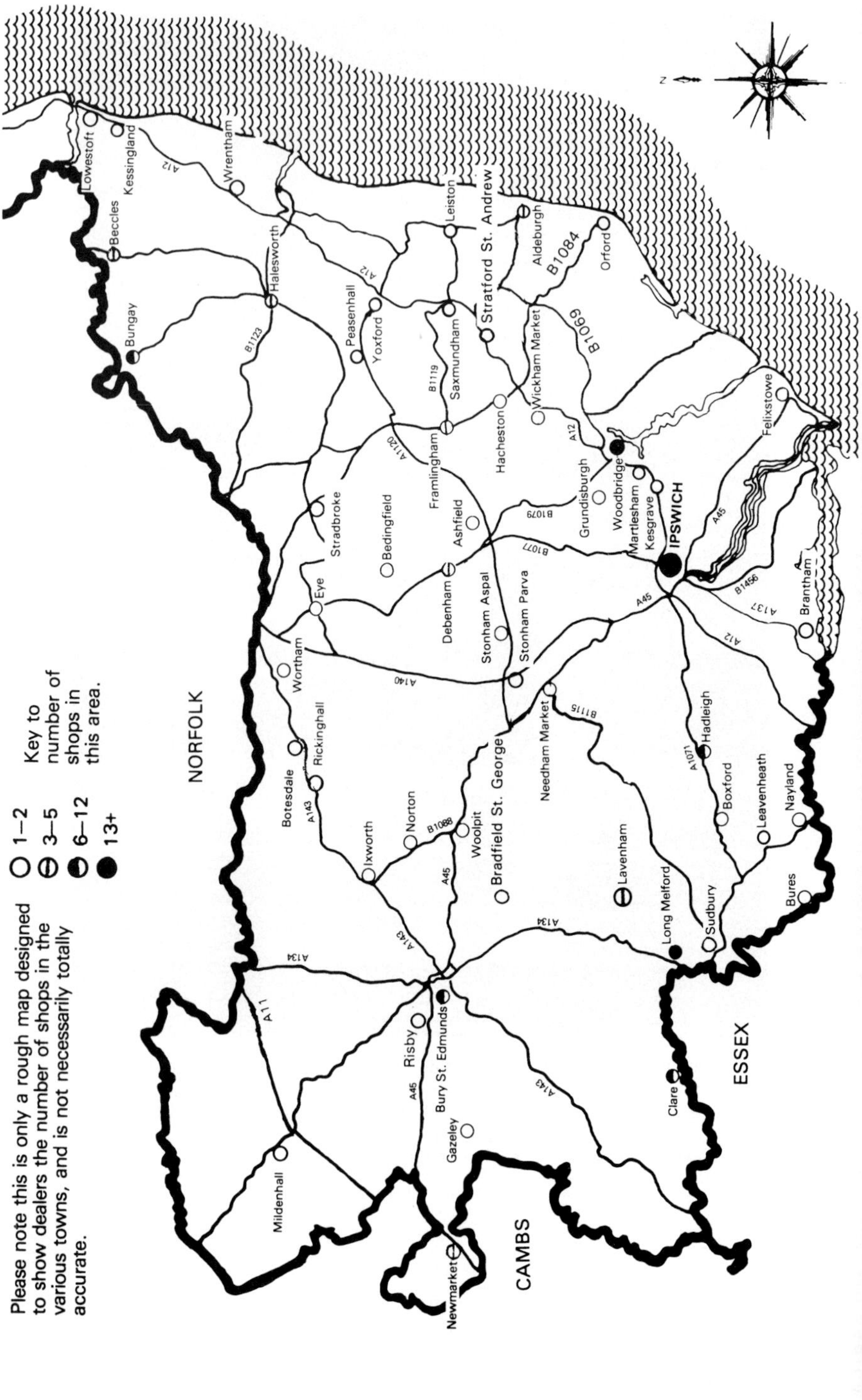

Key to number of shops in this area.
1–2
3–5
6–12
13+
NORFOLK
ESSEX
CAMBS
Lowestoft
Kessingland
Wrentham
Beccles
Halesworth
Bungay
Leiston
Aldeburgh
Orford
Stratford St. Andrew
Peasenhall
Yoxford
Saxmundham
Wickham Market
Hacheston
Framlingham
Felixstowe
Woodbridge
Grundisburgh
Martlesham
Kesgrave
IPSWICH
Brantham
Stradbroke
Bedingfield
Ashfield
Debenham
Eye
Stonham Aspal
Stonham Parva
Wortham
Rickinghall
Botesdale
Needham Market
Hadleigh
Boxford
Leavenheath
Nayland
Bures
Sudbury
Long Melford
Lavenham
Bradfield St. George
Woolpit
Norton
Ixworth
Bury St. Edmunds
Risby
Gazeley
Mildenhall
Newmarket
Clare
A12
A45
A140
A134
A143
A11
A1071
A1120
A137
B1123
B1119
B1084
B1069
B1079
B1077
B1115
B1088
B1456
N

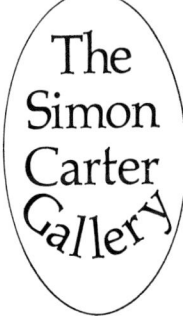

The Simon Carter Gallery

23 MARKET HILL
WOODBRIDGE SUFFOLK
IP12 4LX

Telephone Woodbridge 382242

LARGE STOCK OF OIL PAINTINGS, WATERCOLOURS & DRAWINGS OF ALL PERIODS; SPECIALISING IN PORTRAITS.

ANTIQUE FURNITURE & DECORATIVE ITEMS WITH A PENCHANT FOR THE UNUSUAL

OPEN MONDAY—SATURDAY
9.15 a.m.—5.30 p.m.

FRENCH, GERMAN AND ITALIAN SPOKEN

THE GALLERY IS 1¼ HOURS BY TRAIN FROM LIVERPOOL STREET STATION, LONDON.

ALDEBURGH

Aldeburgh Galleries
132 High St. (Mr and Mrs W Dandy and Mr and Mrs S Haslam) Open 10-5. *STOCK: Jewellery, silver, collectables, Steiff bears, general antiques.* TEL: 0728 453963.

Guillemot
134/136 High St. (L Weaver) Est: 1973. Open 10-1 and 2-5, Sat. 10-1 and 2-6, Wed. p.m. and Sun. by appointment. SIZE: Medium. *STOCK: Pine, elm, oak and fruitwood country furniture, dressers, tables and treen.* LOC: Town centre. PARK: Easy. TEL: 0728 453933. VAT: Stan/Spec.

Mole Hall Antiques
102/104 High St. (P Weaver) Est: 1976. Open 10-5.30, Wed. 10-1, Sun. and other times by appointment. SIZE: Small. *STOCK: Early country furniture and unusual decorative items.* PARK: Easy. TEL: 0728 452361; home - same. VAT: Stan/Spec.

Thompson's Gallery
175 High St. (J. and S Thompson) Open 10-5, or by appointment. SIZE: Medium. *STOCK: Oils and watercolours, 18th-19th C; furniture, 18th to early 20th C; both £300-£10,000.* PARK: Easy. TEL: 0728 453743. SER: Valuations; restorations; framing; buys at auction. VAT: Spec.

ASHFIELD, Nr. Stowmarket

Mrs. A.M Ponsonby
Upham House. Est: 1963. Open by appointment. SIZE: Medium. *STOCK: Furniture, 18th to early 19th C, to £10,000; furnishing pieces, fine handworked bed and table linen.* Not Stocked: Clocks, firearms. LOC: Off main Ipswich to Framlingham road, 2 1/2 miles short of Earl Soham, on by-road to Cretingham. PARK: Easy. TEL: 072 882 200. SER: Restorations (cabinet making).

BECCLES

Art and Antiques
6 The Walk. Open 10-5. SIZE: Medium. *STOCK: General antiques, silver, bric-a-brac.* LOC: Town centre opp. church. PARK: 2 hours outside shop. TEL: 0502 713300.

Beccles Gallery
Saltgate House. (S. and F.T Abrehart) Open 10-1 and 2-5. CL: Mon. *STOCK: Prints, oils and watercolours, 19th-20th C.* TEL: 0502 714017. SER: Restorations and cleaning (oils, watercolours); framing.

Besleys Books
Saxon Bookshop, 4 Blyburgate. (P.A. and P.F Besley) Est: 1978. Open 9.30-1 and 2-5. CL: Wed. SIZE: Medium. *STOCK: Books, 50p-£1,000; prints, £7-£50; maps, £3-£100; all 17th-20th C.* LOC: Town centre. PARK: Nearby. TEL:

Besleys Books continued

0502 715762; home - 0502 75649. SER: Valuations; restorations (book binding); buys at auction (books). FAIRS: Various PBFA.

Saltgate Antiques
11 Saltgate. (A.M Ratcliffe) Resident. Est: 1971. Open 10-5. CL: Wed. p.m. SIZE: Medium. *STOCK: Furniture, 17th-19th C, £100-£3,000; clocks, collectors' items, brass, copper, Staffordshire figures, paintings and prints, 19th C bric-a-brac, £5-£300.* LOC: Town centre opp. bus station. PARK: Easy. TEL: 0502 712776.

Waveney Antiques Centre
Peddars Lane. Open 10-5.30. SIZE: 26 dealers. *STOCK: General antiques, books, furniture, jewellery, silver, clocks and collectors' items.* PARK: Easy. TEL: 0502 716147.

BEDINGFIELD, Nr. Eye

The Olde Red Lion
The Street. Est: 1973. Open by appointment. *STOCK: Furniture and general antiques.* LOC: 3 miles from Eye, 2 miles from Debenham. TEL: 072 876 491. SER: Restorations (furniture, oil paintings, ceramics, snuff boxes, wood carvings).

BOTESDALE

Botesdale Antiques
Crown Hill. (J Ransome and S Davis) SIZE: Small. *STOCK: Furniture, ceramics, paintings and collectables, from £5.* LOC: A143 opposite church. PARK: Easy. TEL: 0379 898894; home - same.

BOXFORD

The Corner Cupboard
The Old Bakery. Open by appointment only. *STOCK: Victoriana, papier mâché, samplers, beadwork and small furniture.* PARK: Easy. TEL: 0787 210123.

BRADFIELD ST. GEORGE, Nr. Bury St. Edmunds

Denzil Grant Antiques
Hubbards Corner. Est: 1979. Open anytime. *STOCK: Furniture, 16th to early 19th C; tapestry, metalware.* LOC: Off A45 between Bury St. Edmunds and Ipswich. PARK: Easy. TEL: 0449 736576.

BRANTHAM, Nr. Manningtree

Brantham Mill Antiques
(C Webber) Open Wed.-Sun. *STOCK: Pine, mahogany and country furniture, 18th-19th C, £50-£1,000.* LOC: B1070. VAT: Stan/Spec.

BUNGAY

Black Dog Antiques
51 Earsham St. (K Button) Est: 1986. Open daily. *STOCK: General antiques including period oak, mahogany and pine, china, linen and collectables, £1-£100+.* LOC: Opposite Post Office. PARK: Easy. TEL: 0986 895554; home - 0986 894489. SER: Valuations.

Bridge Street Antiques
24 Bridge St. (P.L. and W.B Foulger) Est: 1967. Open Tues. and Sat. 9.30-12.30 and 2-5. SIZE: Small. *STOCK: Satin walnut, stripped and pine furniture, 19th-20th C, £75-£500.* LOC: A144. PARK: Easy. TEL: Home - 0986 894449.

Broad Street Antiques
Broad St. (J Stamp) Est: 1971. Open 10-1 and 2-5, Sat. 10-1. *STOCK: General antiques, bric-a-brac.* TEL: 0986 892960 evenings. VAT: Stan.

Cork Brick Antiques
6 Earsham St. (G. and K Skipper) Open 10-5.30. *STOCK: Country and decorative antiques; architectural decoration.* PARK: Easy. TEL: 0986 894873; home 0502 712646.

Country House Antiques
30 Earsham St. Est: 1979. CL: Mon. and Wed. and Sat. p.m. except by appointment. SIZE: Medium and trade warehouse. *STOCK: Mahogany, inlaid, oak and walnut furniture,*

Country House Antiques continued

18th-19th C; 19th C porcelain and collectables. LOC: Near Post Office. PARK: Easy. TEL: 0986 892875; home and warehouse - 0508 58144.

Cransford Gallery
20 Broad St. (H.M. and V.J Vincent) Est: 1978. Open Thurs.-Sat. 10-5 or by appointment. SIZE: Small. *STOCK: Fine 19th-20th C watercolours, £50-£3,000.* LOC: Near town centre. PARK: Easy. TEL: 0986 892043. VAT: Spec.

Pine Apples
4b Earsham St. (B Feraille) Open 10-5.30. *STOCK: General antiques, reproduction pine and beech furniture.* TEL: 0986 893312.

BURES

Bures Antiques
1 Bridge St. Est: 1973. Open 9.30-5.30, Sun. by appointment. SIZE: Large. *STOCK: General antiques, from 17th C to art deco, furniture, porcelain, glass, metalware, £5-£5,000.* PARK: Own. TEL: 0787 227858; home - 0206 210215. SER: Restorations (furniture and metalwork). VAT: Stan/Spec.

BURY ST. EDMUNDS

Corner Shop Antiques
1 Guildhall St. Open 10-5. *STOCK: Victoriana, porcelain, jewellery, silver, clocks and collectors' items.* LOC: Corner of Abbeygate and Guildhall St., opposite Corn Exchange. TEL: 0284 701007.

Guildhall Gallery — LAPADA
1 and 1a Churchgate St. (P.N Hewes) Est: 1965. Open 10-1 and 2-5.30. CL: Thurs. SIZE: Large. *STOCK: Oil paintings, £100-£5,000; watercolours, £50-£400; sporting prints and others, £10-£250; all 19th C.* PARK: Easy. TEL: 0284 762366. SER: Valuations; restorations; framing. VAT: Stan/Spec.

Guildhall Street Antiques
27 Guildhall St. (Mrs T Cutting) Est: 1965. Open 9.30-5.30. CL: Mon. a.m., Tues. and Thurs. SIZE: Medium. *STOCK: General antiques, bric-a-brac, £25-£2,500.* LOC: From town centre down Guildhall St. to below Churchgate St. junction. PARK: Easy. TEL: 0284 703060/ 735278.

Peppers Period Pieces
23 Churchgate St. (M.E Pepper) Est: 1975. Open 10-5. STOCK: Furniture, oak, elm, yew, fruitwood, mahogany, 16th-19th C; English domestic implements in brass, copper, lead, tin, iron, pewter and treen, 16th to early 20th C;

Peppers Period Pieces continued

some pottery and porcelain, bygones and collectables, late 19th to early 20th C. Not Stocked: Reproductions. PARK: Easy. TEL: 0284 768786; home - 0359 50606. SER: Valuations; repairs and polishing of all types. VAT: Spec.

R.N Usher
42 Southgate St. Est: 1938. Open 9-5.30. Ring bell any time. CL: Sun., except by appointment. SIZE: Small. *STOCK: Furniture, mahogany (mainly) and painted, 1720-1840, £20-£10,000; china, glass, 18th-19th C, £25-£1,500; architectural items, mainly mantelpieces, £50-£5,000.* Not Stocked: Brass, copper, reproductions. LOC: South side of town on A45 to Ipswich. PARK: Opposite. TEL: 0284 754838. SER: Caning and gilding; buys at auction. VAT: Spec.

Winston Mac (Silversmith)
65 St. John's St. (E.W McKnight) Est: 1978. Open 9-5. CL: Sun. except by appointment and Sat. SIZE: Small. *STOCK: Silver tea services, creamers, salts.* PARK: Easy. TEL: 0284 767910. SER: Restorations (silver and plating). VAT: Stan/Spec.

CLARE, Nr. Sudbury

Agnus
41A Nethergate St. (R. and Mrs S Lamb) Est: 1988. Open 10-1 and 2-5. CL: Wed. SIZE: Small. *STOCK: Early oak furniture, 17th to early 18th C; treen and candlesticks, 17th to early 19th C; Victorian and Georgian jewellery.* Not Stocked: Pine and 20th C furniture, silver and ceramics. LOC: Village centre, next to post office. PARK: Easy. TEL: 0787 278547. VAT: Spec.

Clare Antique Warehouse
The Mill, Malting Lane. (D Edwards and J Tanner) Est: 1974. Open 9.30-5.30. SIZE: Large - over 40 dealers. *STOCK: 17th-19th C furniture, textiles, paintings, porcelain, glass, silver, clocks, decorative items, £5-£20,000.* LOC: 100yds. from High St. Follow signs for Clare Castle, Country Park. PARK: Easy. TEL: 0787 278449. SER: Valuations; restorations. VAT: Stan/Spec.

The Clare Collector — LAPADA
1 Nethergate St. (J Verney) Est: 1979. Open 10-1 and 2-5.30. SIZE: Medium. *STOCK: English and continental oak, walnut, mahogany and fruitwood furniture, 17th-19th C; pottery and porcelain, prints and watercolours, Oriental and tribal rugs, unusual and decorative items.* PARK: Easy. TEL: 0787 277909; home - 0787 277494. VAT: Spec.

Clare continued

The Clare Hall Company
The Barns, Clare Hall, Cavendish Rd. Open 9-5 or by appointment. CL: Sat. SIZE: Medium. *STOCK: Interesting and unusual antique pine; Victorian sofas and easy chairs.* LOC: A1092. PARK: Easy. TEL: 0787 277510; home - 0787 278445. VAT: Stan/Spec.

Granny's Attic
22 High St. (M Sadler-Chapman) Est: 1972. Open Sat. 10.30-5 and April-Dec., Tues., Thurs. and Fri. 2-5. *STOCK: Victorian to 1940's cottage bygones, linens, collectors' items, fashions and accessories.* LOC: Off main road, opposite church tower doorway. PARK: Easy. TEL: 0787 277740.

Michael Moore Workshops
The Barns, Clare Hall, Cavendish Rd. Est: 1970. Open 9-5 or by appointment. CL: Sat. *STOCK: Hand-made copies of floor standing and table globes.* LOC: A1092. PARK: Easy. TEL: Office - 0787 277510; home/workshops - 0787 278445. SER: Full cabinet making; restorations. VAT: Stan/Spec.

F.D Salter Antiques
1-2 Church St. Est: 1959. Open 9-5. CL: Wed. p.m. SIZE: Medium. *STOCK: Oak and mahogany furniture, English porcelain, 18th to early 19th C, £50-£2,000.* LOC: A1092. PARK:

F.D Salter Antiques continued

Easy. TEL: 0787 277693. SER: Valuations; restorations (furniture). FAIRS: Snape, Bury St. Edmunds and Barbican. VAT: Stan/Spec.

Trinder's Booksellers
Malting Lane. (P Trinder) Est: 1975. Open Tues., Thurs. and Sat. 10-1 and 2-5, other times by appointment. SIZE: Medium. *STOCK: Books including British Isles topography, architecture, art reference, Folio Society, true crime, 19th-20th C.* PARK: Nearby. TEL: 0787 277130; home - same.

DEBENHAM

Debenham Antique Centre
Foresters Hall, High St. (G Adams and P Massey) Open 10-5.30, Sun. 2-5. SIZE: Large - several dealers. *STOCK: Furniture - oak and country, Georgian, Victorian, and Edwardian and 19th C pine; silver, china, glass, brass, pictures and decorators' items; all £10-£10,000.* PARK: Car park nearby. TEL: 0728 860777. SER: Restorations (furniture). VAT: Stan/Spec.

Debenham Gallery
1 High St. (Mrs P Staines) Est: 1987. Open 9.30-5.30, Sun. by appointment. *STOCK: Fine art oil paintings and watercolours, 17th-20th C, £50-£20,000; furniture, 17th-19th C, £100-£5,000; Persian and Oriental rugs, 19th-20th C, £200-£2,000; clocks and pianos.* TEL: 0728 860707. SER: Valuations; restorations; buys at auction (oil paintings). VAT: Stan/Spec.

Fleming's Antiques
High St. *STOCK: Furniture, including garden.* PARK: Easy. TEL: 0728 860422. VAT: Spec.

N Lanchester
21 High St. Open every day. *STOCK: General antiques, 18th-19th C shipping goods and smalls.* TEL: 0728 860756.

EXNING, Nr. Newmarket

Derby Cottage Collectables
Fordham Rd. (V Cole) Open 9-7 including Sun. SIZE: Medium. *STOCK: Furniture and ceramics, 19th to early 20th C, £5-£1,000; bygones and collectors' items, £1-£100.* LOC: Just off A45 Newmarket by-pass on A142 to Ely. PARK: Easy. TEL: 0638 578422; home - same. VAT: Stan/Spec.

EYE

The Corner Shop
Castle St. (Mrs O.M Whalley) Est: 1969. CL: Tues. TEL: 0379 870614/870261.

FELIXSTOWE

John McCulloch Antiques
1a Hamilton Rd. Open 9.30-5, Wed. 9.30-1. *STOCK: Furniture, copper, brass, pictures, clocks and bric-a-brac.* LOC: Main street, sea front end at top of Bent Hill. PARK: Around corner. TEL: 0394 283126; home - 0394 272179.

FRAMLINGHAM

Bed Bazaar
29 Double St. (B Goodbrey) Open 9-5.30, appointment advisable. Sun. by appointment only. *STOCK: Victorian brass and iron beds.* LOC: Up Church St. towards Framlingham

Bed Bazaar continued

Castle. Opposite church gates turn right into Double St. PARK: Easy. TEL: 0728 723756. SER: Restorations (beds); polishing (brass, copper).

Muriel Clover Antiques
14 Bridge St. Resident. CL: Wed. *STOCK: Oak and mahogany furniture, small items, glass and porcelain.* TEL: 0728 723159.

Goodbreys
29 Double St. (R. and M Goodbrey) Est: 1965. Open Sat. 9-5.30, other times by appointment. SIZE: Large. *STOCK: Decorative items including sleighbeds, upholstery, Biedermeier, simulated bamboo, painted cupboards, lighting, garden furniture, country pieces; pottery, glass, textiles, mirrors, bric-a-brac.* LOC: Up Church St. towards Framlingham Castle. Opposite church gates turn right into Double St. PARK: Easy. TEL: 0728 723756. VAT: Mainly Spec. *Mainly Trade.*

Regency House
(T Fleming) Est: 1962. Open by appointment. *STOCK: Furniture and oil paintings.* LOC: Opposite Church. PARK: Easy. TEL: 0728 723553.

GRUNDISBURGH, Nr. Woodbridge

Bond's Manor Antiques
Bond's Manor. (T.K. and W.E Hickford) Est: 1983. Open by appointment. SIZE: Small. *STOCK: Furniture and accessories, 17th to early 19th C.* LOC: 1 mile west of village green. PARK: Easy. TEL: 047 335 357; home - same.

The Coach House
(R. and S Foster-Pegg) Open Thurs.-Sun. 10-5. *STOCK: Fine furniture, porcelain, glass, bric-a-brac and silverware.* TEL: 047 335 569.

HACHESTON, Nr. Wickham Market

Joyce Hardy Pine and Country Furniture
Resident. Open 9.30-5.30. CL: Sun. except by appointment. *STOCK: Pine, especially period dressers and corner cupboards.* LOC: B1116, Framlingham Rd. PARK: Easy. TEL: 0728 746485. SER: Hand-made furniture from old pine.

HADLEIGH, Nr. Ipswich

Barn End Antiques
(P.M Skoulding) Est: 1958. *STOCK: Small furniture, silver, glass, china, treen, metal, bygones, firearms and allied items.* PARK: Easy. TEL: 0473 823164. SER: Valuations.

Hadleigh continued

Playthings of the Past

102a High St. (T.M Marcangelo and Mrs P.A Orchard) Resident. Est: 1986. Open 9.30-1 and 2-5.30, Wed. p.m. and Sun. by appointment. *STOCK: Collectable toys including trains, dolls, teddy bears.* PARK: Nearby. TEL: 0473 824435. SER: Valuations.

Randolph BADA

97 and 99 High St. (B.F. and H.M Marston) Est: 1921. Open 9-5.30, but appointment advisable. Sun. only by appointment. SIZE: Medium. *STOCK: Furniture, 1600-1830, £50-£25,000; brass, copper, porcelain, delftware, treen.* Not Stocked: Silver. PARK: Easy. TEL: 0473 823789. SER: Valuations; restorations (furniture). FAIRS: Grosvenor House; Harrogate. VAT: Spec.

Isobel Rhodes

69-73 Angel St. *STOCK: Furniture, oak, country, mahogany; brassware.* TEL: 0473 823754; home - 0473 310409. VAT: Spec.

Gordon Sutcliffe BADA

11 High St. Est: 1952. Open 9.30-5.30. *STOCK: Furniture, 1620-1820, £100-£10,000; porcelain.* Not Stocked: Victorian furniture, bric-a-brac, reproductions. TEL: 0473 823464. SER: Valuations. FAIRS: Chelsea. VAT: Spec.

Tara's Hall

Victoria House, Market Place. (B O'Keefe) Est: 1977. Open 10-5. CL: Wed. SIZE: Medium. *STOCK: Textiles and linen, jewellery, art nouveau and art deco, small items.* PARK: Easy. TEL: 0473 824031. SER: Valuations; buys at auction (jewellery, art nouveau objects).

HALESWORTH

Ash Tree Antiques

Ash Tree Farm, Wissett. (P.M. and A.M.F.T Lambert) Est: 1980. Open Sat. and Sun. 10-5, other times by appointment. SIZE: Medium. *STOCK: Small pine and country furniture, 18th C to date, £5-£100; pottery and porcelain, £5-*

Ash Tree Antiques continued

£50. LOC: 1 mile from Halesworth P.O. on Wissett Rd. PARK: Easy. TEL: 0986 872867; home - same. SER: Buys at auction.

Blyth Bygones

8 Station Rd. Est: 1966. Open 10-5. CL: Thurs. *STOCK: General antiques especially pine.* TEL: 0986 873397. SER: Pine stripping.

Number Six Antiques

Chediston St. (S Simpkin) Open 10.30-5, Mon. 10.30-3. CL: Thurs. *STOCK: Furniture including pine, small and decorative items, bric-a-brac, china and glass, £5-£500.* PARK: Easy. TEL: 0986 875492.

IPSWICH

A Abbott Antiques

757 Woodbridge Rd. (C Lillistone) Est: 1965. Open 10.30-5. CL: Wed. SIZE: Medium. *STOCK: Small items, especially clocks and jewellery; Victorian, Edwardian and shipping furniture, £5-£1,000.* PARK: Easy. TEL: 0473 728900; home - same.

Tony Adams Bygones Shop

175 Spring Rd. Open 10-5. CL: Wed. *STOCK: Bygones, especially wireless sets; toy trains, cameras.*

Ashley Antiques

20A Fore St. (A.M Warren) Open 9-1 and 2-5, Sat. 10-1. SIZE: Small. *STOCK: Furniture, 18th-19th C, £200-£4,000; clocks, 18th-20th C, £200-£3,000; porcelain and glass, 19th C, £20-£200.* Not Stocked: Silver and jewellery. LOC: Off Star Lane. PARK: Easy. TEL: 0473 251696; home - 0473 253041. SER: Buys at auction (furniture, clocks and china). FAIRS: Local.

Atfield and Daughter

17 St. Stephen's Lane. (D.A. and Miss S.F Atfield) Est: 1920. Open 9.30-5.30. SIZE: Large. *STOCK: Furniture, clocks, metal, pottery, £5-£500; pistols, swords, guns, militaria, scientific instruments, £10-£800; books on collecting, £5-£15.* LOC: Opposite bus station, Old Cattle Market. PARK: Nearby. TEL: 0473 251158. SER: Valuations; restorations (general cabinet work); buys at auction. VAT: Stan.

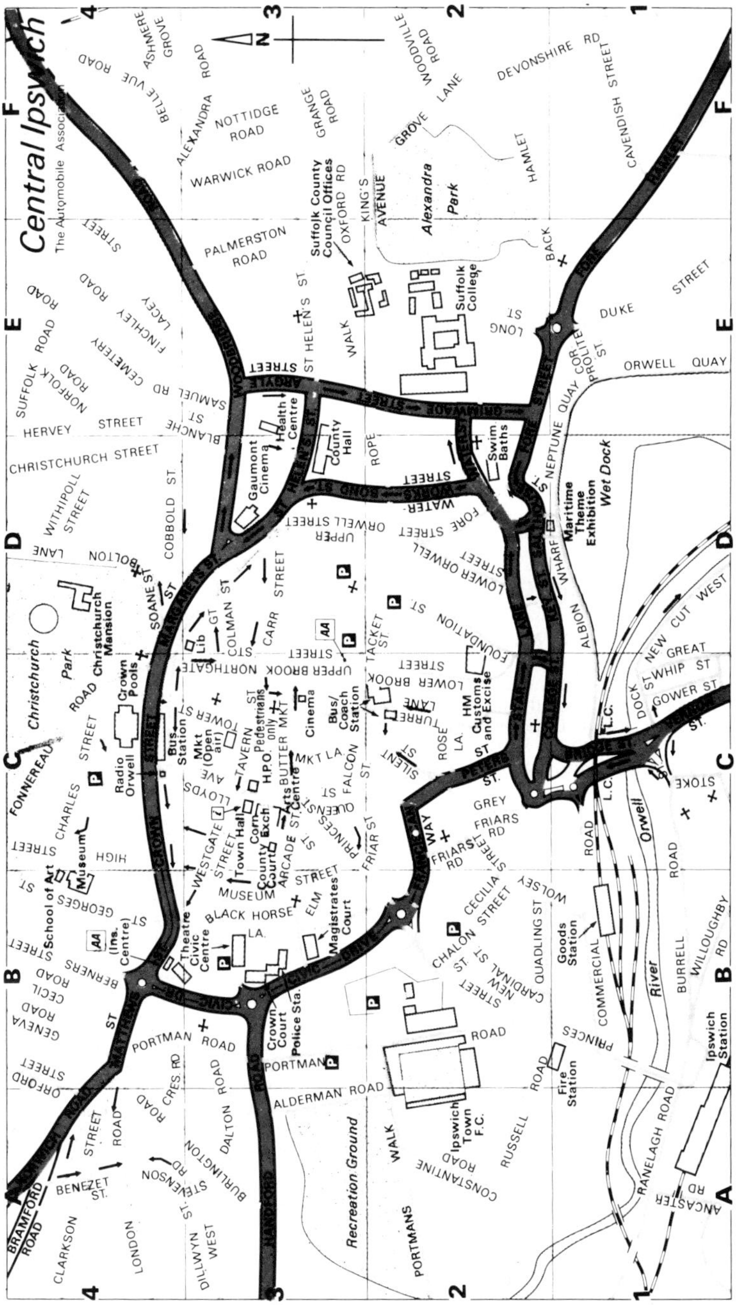
Central Ipswich
The Automobile Association
Alexandra Park
Christchurch Park
Christchurch Mansion
Recreation Ground
Ipswich Town F.C.
Wet Dock
Maritime Theme Exhibition
River Orwell
Ipswich Station
Suffolk County Council Offices
Suffolk College
County Hall
Health Centre
Gaumont Cinema
Bus/Coach Station
HM Customs and Excise
Town Hall
Corn Exch
County Court
Museum
Magistrates Court
Crown Court
Police Sta.
Theatre Civic Centre
Goods Station
Fire Station
Swim Baths
Crown Pools
Radio Orwell
School of Art
Museum

Key to Town Plan

AA Recommended roads

Other roads

Restricted roads

Buildings of interest

Car Parks

Parks and open spaces

AA Service Centre

Ipswich continued

Paul Bruce Antiques

Frobisher Rd. Est: 1972. Open by appointment. SIZE: Warehouse. *STOCK: Oak, walnut and mahogany, paintings, general antiques, £20-£6,500.* TEL: 0473 255400/233671; fax - 0473 233656. VAT: Stan/Spec.

Sonia Cordell Antiques

13 St. Peters St. Est: 1961. Open 10-4.30 or by appointment. CL: Most Sats. *STOCK: Small decorative bygones, treen, jewellery, English and foreign silver, needlework tools, ephemera and toys, prints and paintings, especially 20th C British.* PARK: Nearby. TEL: 0473 219508; home - 0394 282254.

Country Bygones and Antiques

13c St. Peters St. (P Adams) Open 10-5, including most Sats. *STOCK: Domestic, country and decorative items, silver, plate, some jewellery, prints and pictures; porcelain, 18th-19th C; some Studio pottery.* PARK: In street and nearby. TEL: 0473 253683; home - 03948 392.

Claude Cox at College Gateway Bookshop

3 Silent St. Open 10-5. CL: Wed. SIZE: Medium. *STOCK: Books, from 1470; some local maps and prints.* LOC: Leave Inner Ring Road at Bridge St. double roundabout; 2nd right is Silent St., shop on left. PARK: Opposite and just past shop. TEL: 0473 254776. SER: Valuations; restorations (rebinding); buys at auction, catalogue available.

Croydon and Sons Ltd

50-56 Tavern St. Est: 1865. Open 9-5.30. SIZE: Large. *STOCK: Jewellery, £10-£25,000; silver, 18th and 19th C, £5-£5,000.* LOC: Opposite Great White Horse Hotel. TEL: 0473 256514; fax - 0473 231565. SER: Valuations; restorations (silver, plate, clocks, watches and jewellery). VAT: Stan/Spec.

The Edwardian Shop

556 Spring Rd. *STOCK: 1930s oak furniture.* TEL: 0473 7216576; evenings - 0473 7212890.

The Fortescue Gallery

27 St. Peter's St. (L Fortescue) Open 10-4. CL: Mon. except by appointment. *STOCK: 19th C pictures.* PARK: Easy. TEL: 0473 251342.

John Gazeley Associates Fine Art

17 Fonnereau Rd. Est: 1966. Usually open but appointment advisable. SIZE: Small. *STOCK: Decorative oil paintings, watercolours and prints, 18th to early 20th C, £5-£500; topographical engravings of local interest.* LOC: Central Ipswich off Crown St., east side of Christchurch Park. PARK: Easy. TEL: 0473 252420; home - same. SER: Restorations (cleaning, re-lining paintings); framing.

Ipswich continued

Hubbard Antiques

16 St. Margarets Green. Est: 1964. Open 9-6. SIZE: Large. *STOCK: General antiques, period furniture, mahogany, oak, paintings.* PARK: Easy. TEL: 0473 226033. SER: Valuations; restorations. VAT: Stan/Spec.

Hyland House Antiques

45 Felixstowe Rd. (J Burton) Open 10.30-5.30, Sat. 9.30-5.30. CL: Wed. and Thurs. SIZE: Large. *STOCK: Pre-war furniture and bric-a-brac.* TEL: 0473 210055/251723/712536.

Majors Galleries

6 St. Helens St. (M Weiner) Est: 1982. Open 9.30-5.30. SIZE: Medium. *STOCK: Furniture, 19th C; art deco and art nouveau, £1-£1,000; decorative small items including clocks, ornaments, plates and pictures, 19th C.* LOC: Opposite Odeon theatre. PARK: Nearby. TEL: 0473 221190.

Orwell Galleries

1 Upper Orwell St. (M Weiner) Open 9.30-5.30. CL: Wed. SIZE: Medium. *STOCK: Furniture and pine.* TEL: 0473 221190.

Orwell Paint Strippers

Halifax Mill, 427 Wherstead Rd. (M Weiner) Open 8.30-5.30, Sat. 8.30-5. *STOCK: Pine.* TEL: 0473 680091. SER: Restorations; stripping; pine furniture made to order from old wood.

Pine Interiors incorporating Countrystyle

18 St. Margaret's Green. (R.J Hubbard) Open 9-6. *STOCK: Pine.* TEL: 0473 226033.

Tom Smith Antiques

33A St. Peter's St. Est: 1959. *STOCK: Period furniture, accessories, shipping goods, £5-£2,000.* TEL: 0473 210172.

Spring Antiques

436 Spring Rd. (S Bullard) Est: 1970. Open 9.30-1. CL: Thurs. SIZE: Small. *STOCK: Clocks, brass, silver and plate, china, jewellery.* Not Stocked: Coins, stamps. LOC: From Woodbridge on A1214, bear left at 2nd roundabout for town centre then take left fork at Lattice Barn Inn. Shop opp. Inskil school. PARK: 50yds. in adjacent streets. TEL: 0473 725606.

Thompson's

418 Norwich Rd. (D. and Mrs S Thompson) Est: 1978. Open 10-5.30. CL: Sun. except by appointment. SIZE: Medium. *STOCK: Furniture, mainly late Victorian and shipping, 1870 to date, £10-£400.* LOC: 1 mile from town centre, on corner at traffic lights next to railway bridge. PARK: Own, at side of premises. TEL: 0473 747793; home - 0473 259199. SER: Valuations; buys at auction (shipping items). VAT: Stan/Spec.

Ipswich continued

Thompson's Antiques

386 Spring Rd. (D. and Mrs S Thompson) Open 10-1 or by appointment. CL: Sun. except by appointment. *STOCK: General antiques mainly bric-a-brac and china, some furniture.* LOC: 1 mile from town centre towards Woodbridge. TEL: 0473 725742; home - 0473 259199. SER: Valuations; buys at auction (shipping items).

C.A Wall

11 St. Peter's St. Est: 1972. Open 9.30-5.30. *STOCK: Furniture, £50-£1,000.* LOC: Past Town Hall, down Queen St., St. Nicholas St. to St. Peter's St. PARK: Silent St. TEL: 0473 214366. VAT: Stan/Spec.

Gerald Weir Antiques LAPADA

7-11 Vermont Rd. Open by appointment only. SIZE: Large. *STOCK: Georgian and Victorian furniture.* TEL: 0473 252606/255572.

IXWORTH, Nr. Bury St. Edmunds

E.W Cousins and Son LAPADA

27 High St, and The Old School. CL: Sat. p.m. SIZE: Large and warehouse. *STOCK: General antiques, 18th-19th C, £50-£6,000; shipping items.* LOC: A143. Opposite Methodist Chapel. PARK: Easy. TEL: 0359 30254. SER: Valuations; restorations. VAT: Stan/Spec.

Ixworth Antiques

17 High St. (M Ginders) Open 10-5. *STOCK: Victorian and Edwardian furniture, brass and silver plate.* PARK: Easy. TEL: 0359 31691. SER: Polishing (brass); plating (silver).

KESGRAVE

Mainline Furniture

83 Main Rd. (Mr and Mrs R.S Rust) Est: 1977. Open 9-6. CL: Wed. p.m. *STOCK: Furniture, Victorian to 1950's; china and collectables, clocks.* TEL: 0473 623092.

KESSINGLAND

Kessingland Antiques

36A High St. Est: 1976. Open 10-5.30. SIZE: Large. *STOCK: Edwardian, Victorian furniture, general antiques and collectables, watches, clocks, jewellery, shipping goods.* LOC: On A12, 3 miles south of Lowestoft. PARK: On forecourt and own. TEL: 0502 740562. VAT: Stan/Spec.

LAVENHAM

R.G Archer

7 Water St. Est: 1970. Open 9-5, Sun. 10-5. *STOCK: Antiquarian and secondhand books.* TEL: 0787 247229.

J. and J Baker

12-14 Water St, and 3a High St. (C.J. and Mrs B.A.J Baker) Est: 1960. Open 9-1 and 2-5.30. SIZE: Medium. *STOCK: Oak and mahogany furniture, 1600-1870, £100-£10,000; oils and watercolours, 19th C, £150-£5,000; English porcelain and metalware, 18th-19th C, £20-£1,000; collectors' items, £20-£1,000.* LOC: Below Swan Hotel at T junction of A1141 and B1071. PARK: Easy. TEL: 0787 247610. VAT: Stan/Spec.

Motts of Lavenham

8 Water St. (J.G. and D.M Mott) Est: 1980. Open 10-4.30, Sun. by appointment. SIZE: Small. *STOCK: Furniture, £20-£1,000; pottery and porcelain, £5-£350, all 19th C; metal toys and diecasts, 20th C, 20p-£100.* LOC: Off High St. by Swan Hotel, shop 200yds. on left. PARK: Easy. TEL: 044 93 637; home - same. SER: Buys at auction (tinplate and diecasts). VAT: Stan.

Tom Smith Antiques

36 Market Pl. Est: 1959. SIZE: Large and warehouse. *STOCK: Furniture, early Staffordshire figures, rugs.* TEL: 0787 247463. SER: Valuations; restorations. VAT: Stan/Spec.

LEAVENHEATH

Clock House

Locks Lane. (A.G Smeeth) Est: 1983. Open by appointment. SIZE: Small. *STOCK: English clocks, 17th to early 19th C, £1,000-£5,000; French and English clocks, Victorian and Edwardian, £200-£1,000.* PARK: Easy. TEL: 0206 262187; home - same. SER: Valuations; restorations (clocks and furniture); buys at auction (clocks and furniture).

LEISTON

Leiston Furniture Warehouses

High St. (J.R Warren) Est: 1980. CL: Wed. and Sat. p.m. except by appointment. SIZE: Medium. *STOCK: Furniture, Georgian, Victorian, Edwardian and shipping oak, £20-£2,000.* Not Stocked: Clocks, china, brass and bric-a-brac. LOC: Off High St., driveway beside Geaters Florists. PARK: Easy. TEL: 0728 831414; home - same. SER: Valuations; restorations (furniture). VAT: Stan/Spec.

Leiston Trading Post

21a Cross St. (A.E Moore) Est: 1967. Open 10-1 and 2-5, other times by appointment. CL: Wed. SIZE: Small. *STOCK: Bric-a-brac, Victoriana, Victorian and Edwardian furniture.* PARK: Easy. TEL: 0728 830081; home - 0728 830281. VAT: Stan.

LONG MELFORD

Antique Clocks by Simon Charles

Little St. Mary's Court, Hall St. Est: 1970. Open 9.30-1 and 2-5.30, Sat. 9.30-5, Wed. by appointment. SIZE: Medium. *STOCK: Clocks, especially longcase, 17th-19th C, £150-£10,000; barometers, 18th-19th C, £150-£1,000.* LOC: Opposite fire station on main road. PARK: Easy. TEL: 0787 880040; home - 0787 75931. SER: Valuations; restorations (clock movements and cases); buys at auction (clocks). FAIRS: Snape and Bury St. Edmunds. VAT: Stan/Spec.

Ashley Gallery

Belmont House, Hall St. Est: 1965. Open 9.30-5.30, or by appointment. SIZE: Medium. *STOCK: Paintings, watercolour drawings, furniture, porcelain, Oriental rugs.* LOC: A134, opposite Crown Hotel. PARK: Easy. TEL: 0787 75434. VAT: Spec.

Raine Bell

Little St. Marys. Est: 1978. Open 10-1 and 2-5. SIZE: Small. *STOCK: Mahogany furniture, paintings, early 19th C, £500-£1,000.* LOC: Main road opposite fire station. PARK: Easy. TEL: 0787 880040; home - 0787 248298. SER: Restorations. VAT: Spec.

Long Melford continued

Roger Carling and Tess Sinclair
Coconut House, Hall St. Resident. Usually open 10-1 and 2-5, other times by appointment. *STOCK: Furniture, mahogany and oak, 18th-19th C; general antiques, metalware, clocks, barometers, textiles, mirrors, decorative items.* TEL: 0787 312012.

Chater-House Gallery
Foundry House, Hall St. (A.D Chater-House) Open 10-5. SIZE: 14 showrooms. *STOCK: Furniture, Georgian, Victorian and Edwardian; pianos.* TEL: 0787 79831. SER: Valuations; restorations (furniture); upholstery.

Compton-Dando (Fine Arts) Ltd
Hall St. (A.C Compton-Dando) Open 9.30-12.45 and 2-5.30. *STOCK: Period English and continental furniture.* PARK: Easy. TEL: 0787 312610/222200. SER: Valuations; buys at auction (furniture); packing, insurance and transport. VAT: Stan/Spec.

Bruno Cooper Antiques
Little St. Marys Court. Est: 1984. Open 10-5.30. SIZE: Medium. *STOCK: Period furniture and works of art, late 17th to early 19th C, £500-£15,000; paintings and bronzes, £500-£15,000.* Not Stocked: Silver, Victoriana and bric-a-brac. LOC: Near Fire Station on main road. PARK: Easy. TEL: 0787 312613; home - 0603 54038. VAT: Spec.

Long Melford continued

Country Antiques
10 Westgate St. (R Ford, I Bury and B Raymond) Est: 1967. SIZE: Small. *STOCK: 18th-19th C decorative items.* LOC: On outskirts of Long Melford, on road to Clare, nr. church. PARK: Easy. TEL: 0787 71358.

Country Collectables
Hall St. (K Steers) Open 11-5. *STOCK: General antiques and collectables, Georgian to art deco.* LOC: Next to Old Maltings Antiques Co. TEL: 0787 310140; evenings - 0206 250442.

The Enchanted Aviary
63 Hall St. (C.C Frost) Est: 1970. Open most days, but appointment advisable. SIZE: Medium. *STOCK: Cased and uncased mounted birds, animals, fish, mostly late Victorian, £15-£800.* PARK: Easy. TEL: 0787 78814. VAT: Spec.

The Goff Galleries
Hall St. (B Goff Gillings) Est: 1958. SIZE: Medium. *STOCK: Furniture, 18th C, £500-£25,000; oil paintings, 1580-1830, £400-£8,000.* Not Stocked: Victorian items. LOC: On main A134, opp. Bull Hotel. PARK: Easy. TEL: 0787 78228. SER: Valuations. VAT: Spec.

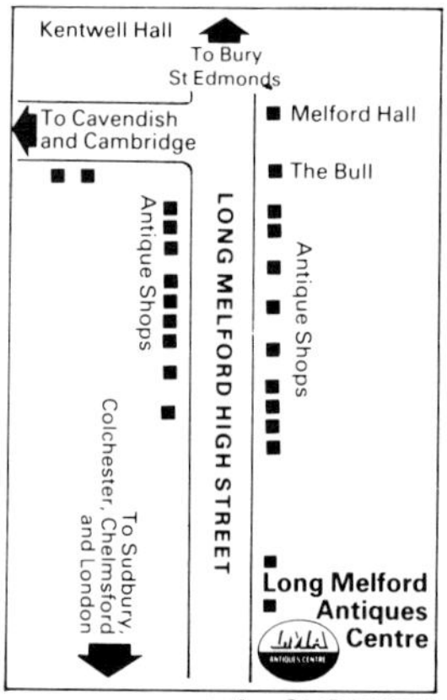
Kentwell Hall
To Bury St Edmonds
To Cavendish and Cambridge
Melford Hall
The Bull
Antique Shops
LONG MELFORD HIGH STREET
Antique Shops
To Sudbury, Colchester, Chelmsford and London
Long Melford Antiques Centre

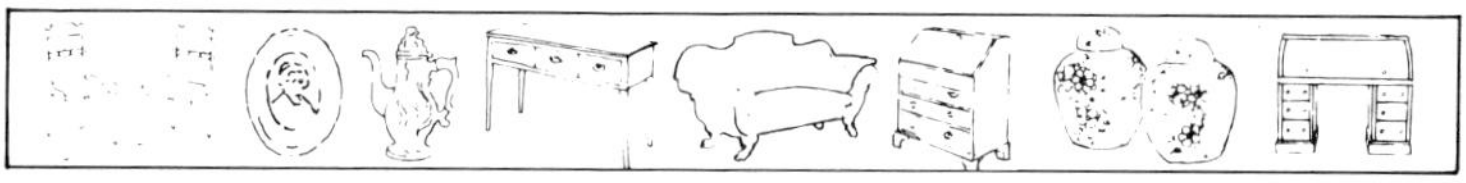

Long Melford continued

Long Melford Antiques Centre

The Chapel Maltings, and the adjacent White Hart Annexe. (Baroness V von Dahlen) Est: 1984. Open 10-5.30 or by appointment. SIZE: Large - 55 dealers. *STOCK: Furniture - early oak, Queen Anne, Georgian, Edwardian and Victorian; silver, china, glass, clocks, dolls, toys and decorators' items, £5-£10,000.* LOC: A134, Sudbury end of village. PARK: Ample, behind White Hart. TEL: 0787 79287/310316. SER: Valuations; restorations (furniture); packing and shipping; buys at auction. VAT: Stan/Spec.

Alexander Lyall Antiques

Belmont House, Hall St. (A.J Lyall) Est: 1977. Open 9.30-5.30. SIZE: Medium. *STOCK: Furniture, 18th-19th C.* LOC: A134 opposite Crown Hotel. PARK: Easy. TEL: 0787 75434; home - same. SER: Restorations (furniture); buys at auction (English furniture). VAT: Stan/Spec.

Magpie Antiques

Hall St. (Mrs P Coll) Est: 1985. Open 10.30-1 and 2.30-5, Sat. 10-5.30. CL: Mon. and Wed. SIZE: Small. *STOCK: Smalls including hand-painted china; furniture, Victorian and stripped pine.* LOC: Main street. PARK: Easy. TEL: 0787 310581; home - same.

Long Melford continued

Patrick Marney

The Gate House, Melford Hall. Est: 1964. Open by appointment. SIZE: Small. *STOCK: Fine barometers, 18th-19th C, £1,000-£5,000; pocket aneroids, 19th C, £150-£1,000; scientific instruments, 18th-19th C, £250-£2,000; all fully restored.* LOC: A134. PARK: Easy. TEL: 0787 880533; home - 0787 79193. SER: Valuations; restorations (mercury barometers). VAT: Stan.

Melford Fine Arts

Little St. Mary's. (L Chambers∑ D Keens) Open 10-1 and 2-5.30, Sun. 2-5. CL: Mon. *STOCK: General antiques.* TEL: 0787 312174.

Neptune Antiques

Hall St. (P. and M Horsman) Est: 1969. Open 10-5.30, Sun. by appointment. SIZE: Large. *STOCK: Furniture, £500-£15,000; objects, £100-£2,000; both 17th-18th C.* LOC: A134 near Bull Hotel. TEL: 0787 75787; home - 0473 251110. SER: Valuations; restorations (17th-18th C furniture); buys at auction (17th-18th C furniture). FAIRS: Olympia, Barbican, British International, Birmingham. VAT: Spec.

Obelisk Antiques

Little St. Marys, Hall St. (A Collins) Open 9.30-1 and 2-5.30 or by appointment. *STOCK: Furniture and works of art, 17th-19th C.* LOC: Next to fire station. TEL: 0787 72864. SER: Transport provided from Colchester railway station.

Long Melford continued

The Old Forge
Bridge St. (C. and I Chilton) Open 9.30-5. SIZE: Medium. *STOCK: Mahogany and oak, 17th-20th C, £5-£1,500.* LOC: On A134, 2 1/2 miles from Long Melford. TEL: 0787 247083. VAT: Stan/Spec.

Old Maltings Antique Company
Old Maltings, Hall St. (D Edwards and J Tanner) SIZE: Large. *STOCK: Antique and decorative items.* TEL: 0787 79636.

St. Mary's Antiques LAPADA
St. Mary's Court, Little St. Mary's. (F. and A Collins, N Bush) Est: 1963. Open 10-1 and 2-5.30. SIZE: Medium. *STOCK: Furniture and works of art, 17th-19th C, £100-£20,000.* LOC: A134. PARK: Easy. TEL: 0787 881810. SER: Valuations; buys at auction. VAT: Stan/Spec.

Seabrook Antiques Ltd
Old Maltings, Hall St. (D Edwards and J Tanner) Open 9.30-5.30. *STOCK: Oak country furniture, continental and English mahogany, decorative items, 17th-20th C.* TEL: 0787 76876.

Oswald Simpson LAPADA
Hall St. Est: 1971. Open 9.30-5.30, other times by appointment. *STOCK: Early oak and country furniture, £25-£10,000; brass, copper, pewter and country items, £10-£500; all 17th-19th C; samplers and needlework, 17th-20th C, £25-£1,000.* PARK: Easy. TEL: 0787 77523; home - 0449 740030. SER: Valuations; restorations. VAT: Spec.

Suthburgh Antiques
Red House, Hall St. (R.P Alston) Est: 1977. Open 10-5. CL: Sun. except by appointment. SIZE: Medium. *STOCK: Furniture, £300-£6,000; Georgian barometers and clocks, £400-£5,000; antiquarian maps and prints, 1600-1850, £25-£450; small collectors' items, boxes, glass, brass, copper, £50-£400.* Not Stocked: Victorian furniture and later items. LOC: Opposite Bull Hotel, A134. PARK: Easy. TEL: 0787 74818; home - same. SER: Valuations; restorations (furniture, barometers); buys at auction. VAT: Stan/Spec.

Times Past
Hall St. (V.C Waine) Open Tues., Thurs. and Sat. 11-5. *STOCK: Art nouveau, art deco and unusual items.* LOC: Next to The Old Maltings Antique Co. PARK: Easy. TEL: 0787 310140; home and fax: - 0376 71078.

Tudor Antiques
Little St. Marys. (A.H Denton-Ford) Est: 1974. Open 9.30-5.30. SIZE: Large. *STOCK: General antiques, £5-£2,000; curios, silver, objets d'art, small furniture, bygones.* LOC: Sudbury end of Long Melford, shop with yellow blind. PARK: Easy. TEL: 0787 75950. SER: Valuations; metal polishing; repairs (metal, clocks, barometers). VAT: Stan/Spec.

Village Clocks
Little St. Mary's. (J.C Massey) Est: 1975. Open 10-5, Sat. 9.30-5. CL: Wed. SIZE: Small.

Village Clocks continued

STOCK: Clocks - longcase, bracket, wall and mantle, 18th-19th C, £500-£2,500; carriage, 19th C, £500-£1,000. PARK: Easy. TEL: 0787 75896. SER: Valuations; restorations (as stock); buys at auction (clocks). FAIRS: Uxbridge Horological, Brunel University.

Ward Antiques plc
Hall St. Est: 1982. Open 10-1 and 2-5.30, Sun. by appointment. SIZE: Large. *STOCK: Furniture, 17th to early 19th C, £100-£40,000.* Not Stocked: Silver and glass. LOC: A134. PARK: Easy. TEL: 0787 78265; home - 0787 312549. SER: Valuations; restorations; buys at auction (furniture). VAT: Stan/Spec.

LOWESTOFT

W Taylor Antiques
13 St. Peter's St. (W.D.J Taylor) Est: 1965. Open Tues., Fri. and Sat. 10-4. SIZE: Small. *STOCK: Furniture, 1840-1910, £5-£250; pictures, 1830-1920, £3-£100; bygones and bric-a-brac, £1-£100.* LOC: Opposite Market Place, High St., A12. PARK: 100yds. opp. TEL: 0502 3374; home - 0502 730421.

Windsor Gallery
167 London Rd. South. (R.W Glanfield) Open 9-5. *STOCK: Paintings.* TEL: 0502 512278.

MARTLESHAM, Nr. Woodbridge

Martlesham Antiques
The Thatched Roadhouse. (R.F Frost) Est: 1973. Open daily, Sun. by appointment. SIZE: Large. *STOCK: Furniture and decorative items, 17th-20th C, £25-£3,000.* LOC: A1214 opposite Red Lion public house. PARK: Own. TEL: 03943 386732; fax - 03943 382959.

MILDENHALL

Hunt and Clement
10 North Terrace. Open 10-5.30, Sun. 2-5. *STOCK: Pine, Victorian, Edwardian and 1920s shipping goods.* TEL: 0638 718025.

NEEDHAM MARKET

Roy Arnold
77 High St. Est: 1974. Open 9.30-5.30, appointment advisable, Sun. by appointment. SIZE: Medium. *STOCK: Woodworkers' and craftsmen's tools, scientific instruments and books, including antiquarian, £10-£5,000.* LOC: A45, centre of High St. PARK: Easy. TEL: 0449 720110. VAT: Stan/Spec.

The Old Town Hall Antique Centre
High St. (S. and R Abbott) Open 10-5. SIZE: Several dealers. *STOCK: General antiques.* TEL: 0449 720773. SER: Repairs (jewellery).

NEWMARKET

Equus Art Gallery
Sun Lane. (L EveleighΣ T Minahan) Est: 1989. Open 9.30-5.30. CL: Wed. p.m. SIZE: Medium. *STOCK: Equine oils, watercolours and sculpture, 19th-20th C, £300-£1,000; equine prints, 18th-20th C, £50-£2,000.* LOC: Off High St. PARK: Nearby. TEL: 0638 560445; home - 0638 666637. VAT: Stan.

Jemima Godfrey
5 Rous Rd. (Miss A Lanham) Est: 1968. Open Thurs. and Fri. 10-1 and 2-4.30. SIZE: Small. *STOCK: Small antiques and jewellery, 19th C.* LOC: Just off High St., nr. clock tower. PARK: Easy. TEL: 0638 663584.

Newmarket Gallery
156 High St. (N.R Herbert) Resident. Open 9.30-1 and 2-5, Sun. and Wed. by appointment. SIZE: Small. *STOCK: Sporting prints, drawings, pictures.* LOC: A11 at south end of High St. PARK: Easy. TEL: 0638 661183. SER: Valuations; restorations; buys at auction.

Northwold Gallery
Rear of 30 High St. (C.G. and J.A Troman) Est: 1973. Open 10-1 and 2-5. CL: Sat. p.m. and Wed. SIZE: Medium. *STOCK: Paintings and prints, 19th C to contemporary, to £900.* LOC: Behind Waggon and Horses public house. PARK: Easy. TEL: 0638 668758; home - 0638 663471. SER: Framing; restorations (oils, watercolours and prints).

R.E. and G.B Way
Brettons, Burrough Green. Open 8.30-5.30, but appointment advisable. *STOCK: Antiquarian and secondhand books on shooting, fishing, horses, racing and hunting and small general section.* TEL: 0638 507217.

NORTON, Nr. Bury St. Edmunds

E.J Everitt
Long Reach, Ashfield Rd. Open 9-5. SIZE: Large. *STOCK: Georgian, Victorian and shipping furniture.* LOC: Just off A45 between Ipswich and Bury St. Edmunds. TEL: 0359 41581.

ORFORD

Castle Antiques
Market Sq. (S Simpkin) Est: 1969. Open daily including Sun. 11-4.30. SIZE: Medium. *STOCK: Furniture, general small antiques, bric-a-brac, glass, china, clocks.* TEL: 0394 450100.

PEASENHALL, Nr. Saxmundham

Peasenhall Art and Antiques Gallery
The Street. (A. and M Wickins) Resident. Est: 1972. Open every day. *STOCK: 19th C watercolours and oils; country furniture, all*

Peasenhall Art and Antiques Gallery continued

woods; walking sticks. TEL: 072 879 224; home - same. SER: Restorations (oils, watercolours, furniture). VAT: Spec.

RICKINGHALL, Nr. Diss

Joan Adams Antiques
Rossendale Cottage, The Street. Est: 1975. Open 10-6 including Sun. CL: Mon. except by appointment. SIZE: Small. *STOCK: Furniture, 17th to early 19th C, £100-£1,500; early woodcarvings, £100-£500; pictures, embroideries and metalware; early children's furniture.* LOC: A143, between Diss and Bury St. Edmunds. PARK: Easy. TEL: 0379 898485; home - same.

The Pump House Antiques
(V Sutton) Open Sat. 10-5, or by appointment. *STOCK: General antiques; porcelain, glass and furniture, 18th-19th C; textiles and decorative objects.* PARK: Easy. TEL: 0379 898964.

RISBY, Nr. Bury St. Edmunds

The Risby Barn
(R. and S Martin) Open seven days 10-5. SIZE: 24 dealers. *STOCK: Furniture, porcelain, metalware, tools, pine, art deco.* LOC: Just off A45 west of Bury St. Edmunds. TEL: 0284 811126.

SAXMUNDHAM

Antiques and Country Things
The Old Shop, 49 North Entrance, (High St.). (K Veness) Est: 1982. Open 10-5.30. CL: Thurs. p.m. SIZE: Large. *STOCK: General antiques including small furniture, collectables, bric-a-brac, jewellery, 18th-19th C, £1-£1,000.* LOC: Opposite bus station, near bridge. TEL: 0728 604171. SER: Restorations.

STONHAM ASPAL, Nr. Stowmarket

The Caldecott Gallery
Stonham Barns, Pettaugh Rd. (M.J Banks) Est: 1985. SIZE: Small. *STOCK: 19th and 20th C art, £50-£100; general antiques, £5-£100.* LOC: 3 miles off A140 on A1120 going east. PARK: Easy. TEL: 0449 711005. SER: Framing; buys at auction.

STONHAM PARVA, Nr. Stowmarket

E.T Webster
Mill Barn, Church Lane. Open by appointment. *STOCK: Antiquarian books relating to English literature, 16th-20th C; oak for restoration.* TEL: 0449 711397.

STRADBROKE, Nr. Eye

Mary Palmer Antiques
The Cottage Farm, New St. (Mrs M Palmer Stones) Resident. Est: 1980. Open 9-9, Sun. by appointment. SIZE: Small. *STOCK: English glass, 1750-1850; furniture, 1700-1900.* LOC: B1117. PARK: Easy. TEL: 037 984 8100. SER: Valuations; restorations (furniture).

SUDBURY

Antique Clocks by Simon Charles
The Limes, 72 Melford Rd. Open by appointment only. *STOCK: Clocks, especially quality English longcase, 16th-19th C, £500-£5,000.* TEL: 0787 75931. SER: Valuations; restorations; repairs.

Napier House Antiques
Church St. Resident. Open 9-5 or by appointment. SIZE: Large. *STOCK: Georgian and Victorian furniture, £100-£3,000.* Not Stocked: Smalls. TEL: 0787 75280/477346.

WICKHAM MARKET

Crafers Antiques
The Hill. (Mrs E Davies) Est: 1970. Open Mon., Wed., Fri. and Sat. 9.30-6, Tues. and Thurs. 9.30-1 and 2-6. *STOCK: 18th-20th C porcelain and pottery, glass, silver, jewellery, furniture and collectors' items.* LOC: Opposite church. TEL: 0728 747347 (anytime).

Roy Webb
179 High St. Open Mon., Thurs. and Sat. 10-6 or by appointment. *STOCK: Furniture, 18th-19th C; clocks.* TEL: 0728 746077; home - 039 43 2697. VAT: Stan.

WOODBRIDGE

Antique Furniture Warehouse
Old Maltings, Crown Pl. (H.T. and R.E Ferguson) Est: 1976. Usually open 9-5. CL: Sat., Sun. except by appointment. SIZE: Large. *STOCK: Furniture, 17th to early 20th C, £200-£10,000; small items.* LOC: In centre of town, off Quay St. First warehouse in Crown Place. TEL: 0394 387222; home - 0394 460237. VAT: Stan/Spec. *Trade and Export Only.*

Richard Arden Antiques
19 Market Hill. Est: 1966. Open 9-1 and 2-4.30. CL: Wed. SIZE: Small. *STOCK: Furniture, pictures, interesting and decorative objects, 18th-19th C; garden furniture.* PARK: Easy. TEL: 0394 382068. VAT: Spec.

Bagatelle
40 Market Hill. (N Lambert) Est: 1990. Open 10.30-5.30, Wed. 10.30-1. CL: Thurs. SIZE: Small. *STOCK: Orientalia, watercolours and engravings, 19th-20th C; small furniture and collectables, 18th-20th C; all £10-£5,000.* PARK: Nearby. TEL: 0394 380204.

Woodbridge continued

Simon Carter Gallery
23 Market Hill. Est: 1960. Open 9.15-5.30. SIZE: Large. *STOCK: English and continental oil paintings, 17th-20th C; English watercolours and drawings, 18th-20th C; furniture, oak and mahogany, 17th-19th C; decorative objects, studio pottery, some porcelain and prints.* Not Stocked: Clocks, silver. PARK: 60yds. behind gallery in Theatre St. TEL: 0394 382242; home - 0394 411894. SER: Three exhibitions held annually. VAT: Spec.

David Gibbins Antiques BADA
21 Market HIlll. Est: 1964. Open 9.30-5.30, Wed. 9.30-1. *STOCK: English furniture, late 16th to early 19th C, £300-£15,000; English pottery and porcelain, metalwork.* PARK: Own in Theatre St. TEL: 0394 383531; home - 0394 382685. SER: Valuations; buys at auction. VAT: Spec.

Hamilton Antiques
5 Church St. (H.T. and R.E Ferguson) Est: 1976. Open 9.30-1 and 2-5, Sat. 9.30-1 and 2-4.30. CL: Wed. p.m. except by appointment. *STOCK: Furniture - mahogany, walnut, oak, fruitwood, 17th-20th C, £200-£10,000.* TEL: 0394 387222; home - 0394 460237. VAT: Stan/Spec.

Housewives' Choice
26 The Street, Melton. Open Thurs., Fri., Sat. 10-5.30, Sun. 2-5.30. *STOCK: Pine, bygones, kitchenalia, beds, bric-a-brac.* LOC: Next door to Melton P.O. TEL: 0394 385158.

Anthony Hurst Antiques LAPADA
13 Church St. (A.H.B Hurst) Est: 1957. Open 9.30-1 and 2-5.30. CL: Wed. p.m. SIZE: Large. *STOCK: English furniture, oak, walnut and mahogany, 1600-1900, £100-£5,000.* PARK: Easy. TEL: 0394 382500. SER: Valuations; restorations (furniture); buys at auction. VAT: Stan/Spec.

Jenny Jackson Antiques
30 Market Hill. Est: 1960. Open 10.30-1 and 2-5, Sun. by appointment. CL: Mon. SIZE: Medium. *STOCK: Furniture and rugs, 18th-19th C, £100-£2,000; oil paintings, 17th-18th C, £1,000-£10,000; decorative objects, £25-£500.* LOC: Town centre. PARK: Easy. TEL: 0394 380667. VAT: Spec.

Lambert's Barn
24A Church St. Open 9.30-1 and 2-5. CL: Wed. p.m. SIZE: Large. *STOCK: Mainly Victorian and 20th C furniture, miscellaneous items.* PARK: Easy. TEL: 0394 382380.

Edward Manson
8 Market Hill. Open 10-5.30, Wed. 10-1. *STOCK: Clocks.* TEL: 0394 380235. SER: Restorations (clocks).

HAMILTON ANTIQUES

5 Church Street
Woodbridge
Suffolk
telephone
(0394) 387222

Always a good selection of
18th, 19th and 20th century good
quality furniture at reasonable prices

¾ hour from Harwich
½ hour from Felixstowe

Woodbridge continued

Melton Antiques
Kingdom HallMelton Rd, Melton. (A Harvey-Jones) Est: 1975. Open 9.30-5.30. SIZE: Small. *STOCK: Silver, collector's items, £5-£500; decorative items and furniture, £15-£500; both 18th-19th C; Victoriana and general antiques, 19th C, £5-£500.* LOC: On right hand-side coming from Woodbridge. PARK: Easy. TEL: 0394 386232.

Sarah Meysey-Thompson Antiques
10 Church St. Est: 1962. Open 10-5, Wed. 10-4, Sun. by appointment. SIZE: Medium. *STOCK: Small furniture, late 18th to early 19th C; china, glass, decorative items, 19th C; textiles and curtains.* PARK: Easy. TEL: 0394 382144; home -0394 386410. VAT: Spec.

A.G Voss
24 Market Hill. Est: 1965. Open 10-1 and 2-5. CL: Wed. *STOCK: Furniture, 17th to early 19th C, from £65; longcase clocks, 18th C, from £400.* PARK: Nearby and at rear. TEL: 0394 385830. SER: Valuations; restorations. VAT: Spec.

The Woodbridge Trading Co
7 Bakers Lane. Open 10-5, Sat. 10-4, Wed. and other times by appointment. SIZE: Medium. *STOCK: Furniture, period mirrors, decorative lighting and general antiques.* LOC: Off Church St., lane opposite Barclays Bank. PARK: Limited at rear. TEL: 0394 382426; fax - 0728 747426.

WOOLPIT, Nr. Bury St. Edmunds

J.C Heather
The Old Crown. Est: 1946. Open every day 9-8. SIZE: Large. *STOCK: Furniture, 18th-19th C, £20-£1,000.* Not Stocked: China. LOC: Near centre of village on right. PARK: Easy. TEL: 0359 40297. VAT: Stan/Spec.

Woolpit Antiques
The Street. Open Thurs.-Sat., or by appointment. *STOCK: Furniture, including painted, decorative items, Victoriana, £5-£500.* TEL: 0359 40895.

WORTHAM, Nr. Diss

The Falcon Gallery
Honeypot Farm. (N Smith) Resident. Est: 1974. Open by appointment seven days. SIZE: Medium. *STOCK: Watercolours and oils, 19th C.* LOC: South side of A143 in village centre, 4 miles west of Diss. PARK: Easy. TEL: 037 983 312. SER: Valuations; restorations (oils, watercolours); framing. VAT: Stan/Spec.

WRENTHAM, Nr. Beccles

Wren House Antiques
1 High St. (J. and W Pipe) Open Tues., Thurs. and Sat. 10-5. *STOCK: Clocks, china, glass, maps, prints, jewellery.* TEL: 050 275 276. SER: Repairs (clocks).

Wrentham Antiques
40-44 High St. (B Spearing) Always open. SIZE: Large. *STOCK: Victorian, Georgian, Edwardian and decorative furniture.* LOC: A12. PARK: Easy. TEL: 0502 75583; home - 0502 513633; fax - 0502 75707. SER: Buys at auction. VAT: Stan/Spec.

YOXFORD

Red House Antiques
The Red House, Old High Rd. (J and Mrs M Trotter) Est: 1987. Open 10-1 and 2-6, Mon. and Wed. by appointment. SIZE: Small. *STOCK: Ceramics, 18th-19th C, £5-£1,000; watercolours, 19th-20th C, £100-£800; small furniture, late 18th to early 19th C; objets d'art.* Not Stocked: Stamps, arms, silver and clocks. LOC: Off either A1120 or A12, opposite churchyard. PARK: Easy. TEL: 072 877 615; home - same.

Joan Stevens, Bookseller
Rosslyn House, High St. By appointment only. *STOCK: Books on literature, art and humanities.* SER: Catalogues on request.

Suffolk House Antiques
2 High St. (A Singleton) Open 10-1 and 2.15-5.15. CL: Wed. *STOCK: Early European furniture and works of art, country furniture.* TEL: 072 877 8122; home - 072 879 467.

WRENTHAM ANTIQUES

Wholesale & Export

Barry C. Spearing

40-44 High Street, Wrentham, nr. Beccles, Suffolk
Telephone: (0502) 75583 or (0502) 513633 evenings
Fax: 0502 75707

Large stock of period Victorian, Edwardian and shipping furniture.

Container packing service

Suffolk House Antiques

Early European Furniture and Works of Art

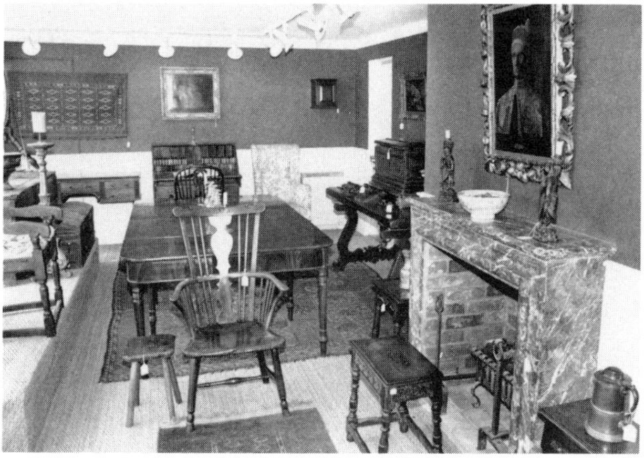

Suffolk House Antiques

High Street, Yoxford, Suffolk.
IP17 3EP. Tel: (072877) 8122

Surrey

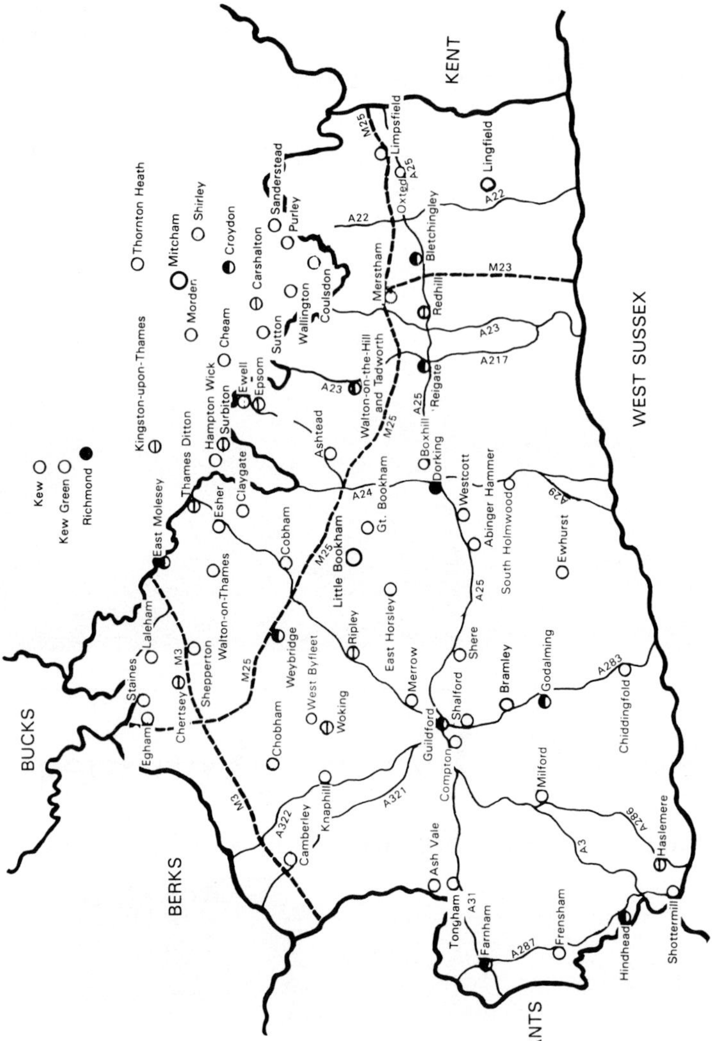
BUCKS
BERKS
HANTS
KENT
WEST SUSSEX
Kew
Kew Green
Richmond
Kingston-upon-Thames
Thornton Heath
Mitcham
Shirley
Morden
Croydon
Carshalton
Sanderstead
Purley
Cheam
Sutton
Wallington
Coulsdon
Hampton Wick
Surbiton
Ewell
Epsom
Thames Ditton
Claygate
Esher
East Molesey
Ashtead
Walton-on-the-Hill and Tadworth
Merstham
Bletchingley
Oxted
Limpsfield
Lingfield
Redhill
Reigate
Boxhill
Dorking
Westcott
Abinger Hammer
South Holmwood
Ewhurst
Gt. Bookham
Little Bookham
Cobham
Walton-on-Thames
Laleham
Staines
Egham
Chertsey
Shepperton
Weybridge
West Byfleet
Woking
Chobham
Ripley
East Horsley
Merrow
Guildford
Shalford
Shere
Bramley
Godalming
Chiddingfold
Compton
Milford
Haslemere
Shottermill
Hindhead
Frensham
Farnham
Tongham
Ash Vale
Camberley
Knaphill
M3
M25
M23
A22
A23
A24
A25
A29
A217
A283
A286
A3
A31
A287
A321
A322

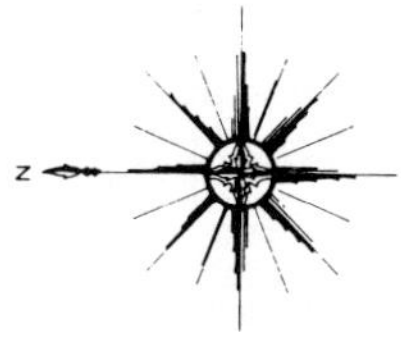

1–2	Key to
3–5	number of
6–12	shops in
13+	this area.

Please note this is only a rough map designed to show dealers the number of shops in the various towns, and is not necessarily totally accurate.

ABINGER HAMMER

Abinger Bazaar
Guildford Rd. (C. and G Field) Est: 1978. Open 11.30-5, Thurs., Sat. and Sun. SIZE: Medium. *STOCK: Porcelain, glass, metal, Victorian, Edwardian, 30's and 50's, £1-£300; books to £50.* LOC: A25 next to trout farm. PARK: Nearby. TEL: 0306 730756.

Stirling Antiques
Aberdeen House. (V.S Burrell) Est: 1968. Open 9.30-6.30. CL: Thurs. *STOCK: Stained glass, furniture, copper, brass, jewellery, silver, curios, dolls.* PARK: Easy. TEL: 0306 730706. VAT: Stan.

ASH VALE

House of Christian Antiques
5-7 Vale Rd. (A Bail) Est: 1970. Open 10-5.30. SIZE: Medium. *STOCK: Pine, 19th-20th C, from £30; mahogany and oak furniture, 19th C, £30-£800.* LOC: Take Tongham turning from A31 (Hogs Back), right after bridge, over roundabout, left at next roundabout, 1st on left after canal bridge. PARK: Easy. TEL: 0252 314478; home - same. SER: Valuations; restorations; stripping.

ASHTEAD

Memory Lane Antiques
102 The Street. (J Lock) Est: 1984. Open 10-5. CL: Wed. *STOCK: General antiques, pre-1920, £5-£1,000.* PARK: Easy. TEL: 0372 273436.

BLETCHINGLEY

Cider House Galleries Ltd
Norfolk House, 80 High St. (T Roberts) Est: 1967. Open 9.30-5.30. CL: Sat. p.m. and Sun. except by appointment. SIZE: Large. *STOCK: Paintings, 17th-20th C, from £200.* LOC: A25, behind F.G. Lawrence Auctioneers. PARK: Own. TEL: 0883 742198; home - 0737 768187; fax - 0883 744014. SER: Valuations. VAT: Stan/Spec.

Elias Clark Antiques Ltd BADA
1 The Cobbles, High St. (L.D. and J.M Clark) Est: 1978. Open 10-1 and 2.30-5, other times by appointment. CL: Mon. *STOCK: Oak and country furniture, 17th, 18th and early 19th C, £100-£5,000; English pottery, especially figures, jugs, prattware, 18th and early 19th C, £50-£3,000; sporting prints, 18th and 19th C.* LOC: Village centre. PARK: Easy. TEL: 0883 743714. VAT: Spec.

John Anthony Antiques
71 High St. (J.A. and N Hart) Resident. Open 10-6, prior telephone call advisable. *STOCK: 18th to early 19th C furniture.* TEL: 0883 743197.

Bletchingley continued

Simon Marsh
The Old Butchers Shop, High St. Est: 1970. Open 10-6. *STOCK: Grandfather clocks; 18th and 19th C, furniture.* PARK: Easy. TEL: 0883 743350. SER: Restorations (furniture and clocks); upholstery.

Post House Antiques LAPADA
32 High St. (P. and V Bradley) Open daily, Sun. by appointment. *STOCK: General antiques, mirrors, fenders, decorative items, shipping goods.* LOC: A25. PARK: Easy. TEL: 0883 743317. VAT: Stan/Spec.

Quill Antiques
86 High St. (Mrs J Davies) Est: 1971. Open 10-1 and 2-5.30, other times by appointment. CL: Wed. p.m. *STOCK: General antiques including copper, brass, china, farming bygones, kitchenalia, linen and lace, 50p-£500.* LOC: A25. PARK: Easy. TEL: 0883 743755; home - same.

BRAMLEY, Nr. Guildford

Drummonds of Bramley Architectural Antiques Ltd
Birtley Farm, Horsham Rd. (D.J.H Shaw) Est: 1988. Open 9-6, Sun. 10-6. *STOCK: Architectural items, mainly 19th C, £50-£30,000; original bathroom equipment, 1830-1930, £30-£8,000; period building materials, pre-1930.* LOC: 1 mile south of Bramley on A281, on left. PARK: Easy. TEL: 0483 898766. SER: Restorations (blacksmithing and stone work). VAT: Stan/Spec.

Memories
High St. (P Kelsey) Est: 1984. Open 10-5. SIZE: Small - 7 dealers. *STOCK: Victorian and Edwardian furniture, china and glass, silver, linen and lace, collectables and bygones, kitchenalia, stripped pine furniture, art deco.* LOC: South of Guildford on A281. PARK: Easy. TEL: 0483 892205.

CAMBERLEY

235 Antiques
235 London Rd. (R.G. and P.T Ellis) Est: 1977. Open 10-1 and 2-4. CL: Mon. and Wed. SIZE: Small. *STOCK: Furniture, clocks and silver, 19th-20th C, £20 upwards.* LOC: A30. PARK: Easy. TEL: 0276 24071/32123. SER: Restorations (furniture and clocks).

The Pedlar
231 London Rd. (Z da Costa) Open 10-5. *STOCK: Georgian and Victorian furniture; general antiques, Chinese porcelain.* TEL: 0276 64750.

CARSHALTON

Antiques
314 Carshalton Rd. (E.M Marshall) CL: Wed. p.m. *STOCK: General antiques, especially Victorian and Edwardian oil lamps.* TEL: 081 642 2108.

Carshalton Antique Galleries
5 High St. (B.A Gough) Est: 1968. Open 9-5. CL: Wed. SIZE: Large. *STOCK: General antiques, furniture, clocks, glass, china, pictures.* Not Stocked: Silver, jewellery, bronze, firearms. PARK: 50yds. opposite, or 60yds. down High St. TEL: 081 647 5664; home - 0306 887187. VAT: Stan/Spec.

Cherub Antiques
312 Carshalton Rd. (M Wisdom) Open 10.30-5.30. CL: Wed. *STOCK: Pine.* TEL: 081 643 0028.

D.H McDonald
376 Carshalton Rd. (D.H. and Mrs. S McDonald) Est: 1984. Open 10.30-6. SIZE: Medium. *STOCK: Furniture, shipping goods, collectables, gold and silver, pictures.* LOC: Adjacent Windsor Castle public house. PARK: Easy. TEL: 081 669 7402; home - 081 788 4981.

CHEAM

Rogers Antiques and Rogers Antique Interiors
22 Ewell Rd, Cheam Village. (M. and C Rogers) Est: 1971. Open 10-5.30. SIZE: Medium. *STOCK: Furniture, 18th-19th C, £100-£2,000; upholstered and boardroom furniture, Tillman dining tables.* LOC: Village centre, just off Sutton by-pass, A217. PARK: 50yds. TEL: 081 643 8466. SER: Valuations; interior design. VAT: Stan/Spec.

CHERTSEY

Chertsey Antiques
8 Windsor St. (Mrs S Langmead and Mrs S Ryan) Open 10-5.30, Wed. 12-5.30. *STOCK: General antiques.* TEL: 0932 563565. SER: Picture framing.

Mister Sun Antiques
96 Guildford St. (R Lee) Open 10-5.30. CL: Mon. *STOCK: General antiques.* TEL: 0932 566323.

Surrey Antiques Centre
10 Windsor St. (P.L Allen) Open 10-5. SIZE: 7 dealers. *STOCK: Furniture, jewellery, glass, pottery and porcelain, silver, pictures, kitchenalia, books.* TEL: 0932 563313; home - 841097.

CHIDDINGFOLD, Nr. Godalming

Manor House Interiors
1 Petworth Rd. (T Art and M Pendleton) *STOCK: Small English and continental antiques, collectables, paintings, mirrors, lighting, silver, interior design accessories and decorative items. Some furniture.* LOC: On A283, near village green. PARK: Easy. TEL: 0428 682727.

CHOBHAM

Greengrass Antiques LAPADA
Hookstone Farm, Hookstone Lane, West End. (D Greengrass) Open by appointment only. *STOCK: Decorative items; furniture, 19th C; works of art; shipping goods.* TEL: 0276 857582.

Penny Farthing Antiques and Pretty Things
The Doll's House, 71 High St. (S Blackburn) Est: 1978. SIZE: Small. *STOCK: Victorian and early oak and pine, £50-£500; porcelain, china, glass, brass and copper and early country pieces, £5-£50; silver, £7-£50; lace, lace pillows, silk flowers.* PARK: Easy, behind shop or opposite. TEL: 0276 857718.

The Tarrystone
40-42 High St. (Mrs D Hanbury) Est: 1960. Open 9-1 and 2-5, Sat. 9-2. *STOCK: Furniture, brass, porcelain.* PARK: Easy. TEL: 0276 857494.

CLAYGATE

Keeble Ltd
22 The Parade. (F.J Keeble) Open 9.30-5. CL: Sat. *STOCK: Furniture, late 18th C; light fittings.* TEL: 0372 68966. VAT: Stan.

COBHAM

Antics
44 Portsmouth Rd. (K Needham) Est: 1967. Open 9.30-1 and 2-5.30. SIZE: Large. *STOCK: Pine furniture, rustic and farmhouse antiques; shipping goods.* LOC: A3. PARK: Easy. TEL: 0932 865505. VAT: Stan.

Cobham Galleries
65 Portsmouth Rd. (Mrs T.B Boyle and Mrs M.F Pound) Open 10-5, Sun. 11-5. CL: Mon. *STOCK: Period and country furniture, longcase clocks, watercolours, oils.* TEL: 0932 867909. SER: Buys at auction.

COMPTON, Nr. Guildford

The Old Post Office Antiques LAPADA
The Street, Compton. (D Ford) Open Thurs., Fri. and Sat. 10-5.30. *STOCK: Furniture, English, continental and decorative, £100-£3,000; bronzes and porcelain, pictures and*

The Old Post Office Antiques continued

decorative items. LOC: A3 beyond Guildford from London, left on to B3000, shop 300yds. on left. PARK: Easy. TEL: 0483 810303; home - same. SER: Valuations. VAT: Stan/Spec.

COULSDON

Decodream
Open by appointment only. *STOCK: Pottery - Clarice Cliff, Shelley, Foley, F. and C. Rhead and Carlton ware.* TEL: 0737 556079.

David Potashnick Antiques LAPADA
7 The Parade, Stoats Nest Rd. Open 9-5.30, Sat. 9-12 or by appointment. *STOCK: General antiques.* TEL: 081 660 8403. SER: Restorations (furniture).

CRANLEIGH

Barbara Rubenstein Fine Art
Smithwood House, Smithwood Common. Open by appointment. *STOCK: Watercolours and some oils, 19th-20th C, £250-£7,500.* TEL: 0483 267969; fax - 0483 267535.

CROYDON

Apollo Galleries LAPADA
65/67 South End. (G.W Barr) Open 9.30-5. CL: Sun. except by appointment. SIZE: Large. *STOCK: 19th-20th C oil and watercolour paintings; 19th C bronzes; 18th-19th C English and continental furniture and clocks, porcelain, glass and silver.* LOC: Through Croydon on left on A23. PARK: Own. TEL: 081 681 3727. SER: Restorations (pictures). VAT: Spec.

Collectors Corner Antiques
43 Brighton Rd, South Croydon. (R. and A Pope) Est: 1980. CL: Mon. and Wed. *STOCK: Dolls, tin toys, dinkies, lead soldiers and animals, furniture, bric-a-brac.* TEL: 081 680 7511.

G.E Griffin
43a Brighton Rd, South Croydon. (E.J.H Robinson) Est: 1896. Open 8-5.30, Sat. 9-5. SIZE: Large. *STOCK: General antiques.* TEL: 081 688 3130. SER: Restorations, upholstery.

Paul Keen Antiques LAPADA
195-197 Brighton Rd. (P.A. and G Keen) Est: 1965. Open 10-5. SIZE: Large. *STOCK: Furniture, furnishings, William IV, Victorian, Edwardian, £5-£2,000; Georgian furniture 1700-1830, £25-£4,000; bric-a-brac, paintings, all periods, £1-£500.* Not Stocked: Coins, medals, stamps. LOC: From London take main Brighton Road through Croydon (not by-pass). Shop on left on leaving Croydon. PARK: Easy. TEL: 081 688 1316. SER: Valuations. VAT: Stan/Spec.

Croydon continued

Trengrove
46 South End. Est: 1890. Open 9-6. SIZE: Large. *STOCK: General antiques, Victoriana; oils, watercolours, 18th-19th C.* LOC: On main road through Croydon. TEL: 081 688 2155. SER: Valuations. VAT: Stan/Spec.

The Whitgift Galleries LAPADA
77 South End. Est: 1945. *STOCK: Paintings, 19th-20th C.* TEL: 081 688 0990. SER: Conservation, restoration, framing. VAT: Spec.

DORKING

Roy Breeden Antiques LAPADA
7 West St. Open 9-5.30. CL: Wed. *STOCK: Furniture and decorative items.* TEL: 0306 882552.

Noel Collins
15 West St. Est: 1975. Open 10-5. CL: Wed. *STOCK: Jewellery.*

T.M Collins
70 High St. Est: 1963. SIZE: Medium. *STOCK: Jewellery, 1800-1900, £25-£3,000.* LOC: Opposite Boots chemist. PARK: Behind shop. TEL: 0306 880790. SER: Valuations; restorations (jewellery). VAT: Stan.

J. and M Coombes
44 West St. Est: 1965. Open 9.30-5.30. *STOCK: General antiques.* TEL: 0306 885479. VAT: Stan.

Dorking Antique Centre
17/18 West St. (Mrs G.D Emburey) Est: 1989. Open 10-5.30. SIZE: 30 dealers. *STOCK: Period and pine furniture, silver, porcelain, jewellery, copper and brass, pictures and prints, decorative and collectors' items.* LOC: Continuation of High St. into one-way system. PARK: Opposite. TEL: 0306 740915. SER: Restorations.

Dorking Antiques
58 West St. (E Hutton and P Norman) Est: 1947. Open 9.30-1 and 2-6, or by appointment. CL: Wed. *STOCK: 18th-19th C English furniture, clocks, glass, pewter, maps.* LOC: From London on A24, then follow one-way system into West St. PARK: 100yds. in Church St. off West St. TEL: 0306 883777. VAT: Stan/Spec.

Dorking Desk Shop LAPADA
41 West St. (J.G Elias) Est: 1969. Open 8-1 and 2-5.30, Sat. 10.30-1 and 2-5. SIZE: Large. *STOCK: Desks, especially partners, cylinder bureaux, davenports, kneehole and pedestal, 18th to mid-20th C, £100-£10,000.* PARK: Nearby. TEL: 0306 883327 or evenings 0306 880535; fax - 0306 75363. VAT: Stan/Spec.

Dorking continued

Dorking Emporium Antiques Centre
1A West St. (Mrs S.M Kenny) Est: 1982. Open 10-5. SIZE: Medium. *STOCK: Furniture, mainly mahogany, 18th-19th C, £100-£5,000; art deco items, including furniture, £15-£700; country bygones, books, collectables.* LOC: A25. PARK: Nearby. TEL: 0306 76646; home - 0883 627270.

Douglas Antiques
62a West St. (R.M Douglas) Est: 1959. Open 10-1 and 2-5. SIZE: Medium. *STOCK: English furniture, 17th to early 19th C; decorative objects.* LOC: A25. From London A24 to Dorking High St., follow one-way system to West St. PARK: 100yds. TEL: 0306 881217; home - 081 394 2361. VAT: Stan/Spec.

Hampshires of Dorking
51/52 West St. (Thorpe and Foster plc) Open 9.30-6. SIZE: Large. *STOCK: English walnut, mahogany and satinwood furniture, 18th C, £500-£25,000.* PARK: At rear. TEL: 0306 887076. VAT: Spec.

E Hollander Ltd **BADA**
The Dutch House, Horsham Rd, South Holmwood. (D.J. and B Pay) CINOA, BHI. Open by appointment. *STOCK: Longcase and bracket clocks, 1750-1825; silver, Sheffield plate, English barometers, 18th-*

E Hollander Ltd continued

***19th C.* TEL: 0306 888921. SER: Restorations (clock mechanisms and cases, barometers). VAT: Stan/Spec.**

Eleanor Hutton (Jewellers and Silversmiths)
59 West St. Open 9-1 and 2-5.30. CL: Wed. SIZE: Medium. *STOCK: Jewellery, silver, glass and collectors' items, from 18th C.* LOC: From London on A24, then follow one-way system into West St. TEL: 0306 883777. SER: Valuations; restorations; re-plating. VAT: Stan/Spec.

King's Court Galleries
54 West St. (Mrs J Joel) Open 9.30-5.30. *STOCK: Antique maps, engravings, decorative and sporting prints.* TEL: 0306 881757. SER: Framing.

King's Court Galleries **LAPADA**
19 West St. (C Joel) Open 10-5.30, Sat. 10-6. *STOCK: Fine 18th to early 19th C furniture.* TEL: 0306 886466.

John Lang Antiques
Old King's Head Court, High St. Est: 1985. *STOCK: 17th and 18th C country oak, brass, copper and decorators' items.* TEL: 0306 882203.

Norfolk House Antiques
5 West St. (M Share) Open 10-5, Wed. 10-1. *STOCK: Furniture, especially Georgian and Victorian dining tables and chairs.* TEL: 0306 881028; home - 0273 681841.

Nostalgia
1 West St. (Y Hungerford-Boyle) Open 9.30-5.30, Wed. 9.30-1.30. *STOCK: Vintage clothing, textiles, lace, linen, theatrical costume.* TEL: 0306 880022; home - 0273 681841. SER: Hire.

Ockley Antiques
43 West St. (P. and A Atkinson) Est: 1970. Open 9.30-1 and 2-5. SIZE: Large. *STOCK: Pine, 17th-20th C, £50-£1,000.* LOC: Half way down West St. PARK: Nearby. TEL: 0306 712266/885007; home - 0306 7111271. VAT: Stan.

Oriental Carpets and Decorative Arts
37 West St. (A. and C Gilchrist and Associates) Open 10.30-6, Wed. by appointment. *STOCK: Fine and tribal Oriental carpets and rugs.* TEL: 0306 76370. SER: Valuations (rugs, carpets); repairs and cleaning (rugs and carpets).

The Owl House
4 Lyons Court. (M Hicks and A Burrill) Est: 1978. Open 10-1 and 2-5, Wed. and Fri. 10-1, evenings by appointment. SIZE: Small. *STOCK: Country furniture mainly pine, 19th C, £15-£1,300; oak and mahogany, 18th-19th C, £200-£500; decorative items, £25-£200; longcase*

The Owl House continued

clocks, from £800. LOC: Off High St. by Lloyds Bank. PARK: Nearby. TEL: 0306 740239; home - 040372 2267 and 0372 375864. SER: Buys at auction (longcase clocks). FAIRS: Ardingly and Brocante Decorative, Kensington. VAT: Stan/Spec.

The Quilt Room
20 West St. (P Lintott and R Miller) Open 9.30-5. *STOCK: Quilts.* TEL: 0306 740739.

Elaine Saunderson Antiques
18/18a Church St. (Mrs E.C Saunderson) Est: 1988. Open 9.30-1 and 2-5.30, Sun. and Wed. by appointment. SIZE: Medium. *STOCK: Furniture, late 18th to early 19th C, £50-£10,000; decorative items.* Not Stocked: Silver and jewellery. LOC: Turn left into North St. at end of West St. one-way. 100yds. up North St., opposite junction with Church St. PARK: Easy. TEL: 0306 881231/886082; home - same. SER: Valuations; restorations (furniture). VAT: Spec.

Philip Spooner Antiques
55 West St. (P.J Spooner) Est: 1984. Open 9.30-1 and 2.15-5.30. SIZE: Medium. *STOCK: Furniture, 17th-19th C, £50-£5,000; collectors' fishing tackle, garden furniture.* PARK: Easy. TEL: 0306 881773. SER: Valuations. VAT: Stan/Spec.

Thorpe and Foster plc
49 West St. Open 9.30-6. SIZE: Large. *STOCK: English walnut, mahogany and satinwood furniture, 18th C, £500-£25,000.* LOC: On A24. PARK: At rear. TEL: 0306 881029. VAT: Spec.

Upstairs, Downstairs Antiques
Old King's Head Court, High St. (Mrs J Sayer and Mrs T Harrison) Open 9.30-5. SIZE: Medium. *STOCK: Furniture, to £5,000, porcelain and Staffordshire, to £1,000, both 18th-19th C; decorative items, jewellery and silver, to £1,500.* LOC: Opposite NatWest Bank, through archway. PARK: At rear in North St. TEL: 0306 888849. SER: Valuations; restorations (furniture and porcelain).

Dorking continued

Victoria and Edward Antiques Centre
61 West St. Est: 1972. Open 9.30-5.30. SIZE: Medium - 28 dealers. *STOCK: General antiques.* PARK: Nearby. TEL: 0306 889645.

Pauline Watson Antique Jewellery and Silver
Old King's Head Court. FGA, NAG. Est: 1960. Open 9.30-5.30. SIZE: Small. *STOCK: Jewellery and silver especially Victorian; reproduction silver frames and earrings.* LOC: Off west end of High St. PARK: Behind shop in North St. TEL: 0306 885452. SER: Valuations; restorations (jewellery); buys at auction (jewellery and silver). VAT: Stan/Spec.

West Street Antiques
63 West St. (J.G Spooner and R Ratner) Est: 1980. Open 9.30-1 and 2.15-5.30. SIZE: Medium. *STOCK: Furniture, 17th to early 20th C, £100-£5,000; arms, 17th-19th C, £100-£5,000; brass, copper, ceramics, collectors' items.* Not Stocked: Jewellery and carpets. LOC: West St. (A25) one-way system. PARK: Nearby. TEL: 0306 883487; home - 0306 730182 and 0372 52877. VAT: Stan/Spec.

Patrick Worth Antiques BADA
11 West St. (B.P Meyer) Est: 1967. Open 9.30-5.30. CL: Wed. SIZE: Large. *STOCK: Period furniture, decorative items, mainly 18th to early 19th C.* Not Stocked: Silver, glass and jewellery. LOC: A25. TEL: 0306 884484. VAT: Spec.

EAST HORSLEY

A.E Gould and Sons (Antiques) Ltd LAPADA
Old Rectory Cottage, Ockham Rd. South. (D. and P Gould) Est: 1949. Open 9.30-5, Sun. by appointment. SIZE: Large. *STOCK: Furniture, 18th C, £200-£5,000; 19th C, £100-£3,000; barometers, garometers.* PARK: Easy. TEL: 048 65 3747; home - 081 949 4251. VAT: Stan.

EAST MOLESEY

Abbott Antiques
75 Bridge St. Est: 1970. *STOCK: Clocks.* TEL: 081 941 6398.

The Antiques Arcade
77 Bridge Rd. (J.L Abbott) Open 10-5. SIZE: 14 dealers. *STOCK: General antiques.* TEL: 081 979 7954.

B.S. Antiques
39 Bridge Rd. (S Anderman) Est: 1983. Open 10-5. CL: Wed. SIZE: Medium. *STOCK: Clocks, barometers, prints, some furniture.* LOC: Near Hampton Court. PARK: Easy. TEL: 081 941 1812. SER: Valuations; restorations (clocks and barometers). VAT: Spec.

The Court Gallery
16 Bridge Rd. (J Clark) Est: 1980. Open 9-5. CL: Mon. SIZE: Small. *STOCK: Oils, watercolours and drawings, 19th-20th C, £50-£1,000; Staffordshire pottery, 19th C, £35-£200.* LOC: From Scilly Isles roundabout turn into Hampton Court Way, Bridge Rd. is on left by Hampton Court Bridge. PARK: Easy. TEL: 081 941 2212. SER: Valuations; restorations (oils and watercolours); framing.

The Gooday Shop and Studio
48-50 Bridge Rd. (R Gooday) CL: Wed. and mornings. *STOCK: Collectors' items, 1900-1930.* TEL: 081 979 9971.

Hampton Court Antiques
75 Bridge Rd, Hampton Court. (H Abbott) Open 10-5. *STOCK: General antiques including clocks, furniture, lamps and decorative objects.* TEL: 081 941 6398.

Howard Hope Phonographs and Gramophones
21 Bridge Rd. Open Fri. and Sat. 10-5 and by appointment. *STOCK: Mechanical and musical items.* LOC: Close by Hampton Court Palace. TEL: 081 941 2472; 081 398 7130. SER: Spare parts.

Nicholas Antiques
31 Bridge Rd. Open 9.30-5. CL: Wed. p.m. *STOCK: Furniture, general antiques and decorative items.* TEL: 081 979 0354. VAT: Stan/Spec.

The Sovereign Antique Centre
53 Bridge Rd. CL: Wed. p.m. SIZE: 10 dealers. *STOCK: Furniture, pictures and objets d'art.* LOC: Near Hamilton Court. TEL: 081 783 0595.

Martin Speed
5 Bridge Rd. Open 10-5, prior telephone call advisable. CL: Sat. *STOCK: General antiques and fine furniture.* LOC: Near Hampton Court Bridge. TEL: 081 979 6690/1087. VAT: Stan/Spec.

EGHAM

Fishers of Surrey
94 High St. (R. and E.S Fisher) Est: 1972. Open 9-5. CL: Wed. SIZE: Medium. *STOCK: General antiques, Victorian and Edwardian.* LOC: Next to Police Station. PARK: Easy. TEL: 0784 432981. SER: Valuations.

Pastimes (Egham) Ltd
86 Hgh St. (A.S Carlyon-Gibbs) Est: 1976. Open 10-6. SIZE: Large. *STOCK: Postage stamps - Aden, Bahamas, Barbados, Egypt, Ghana, Hungary, India, Jamaica, Monserrat, Newfoundland, Great Britain, Australia, Papua New Guinea, Mauritius, USA, Eire, Israel, Germany, France, Hong Kong, Gibraltar, Ceylon, Gold Coast, Canada, Austria, Belgium; watercolours, oils and prints, mainly Victorian, £10-£3,000; longcase, bracket, wall, and carriage clocks, watches; furniture, especially chairs, 17th-20th C; porcelain, copper and brass, cloisonné, silver and gold, £5-£500.* PARK: Easy. TEL: 0784 436290; home - 0628 39353. SER: Valuations; restorations (pictures and furniture); framing; clock and watch repairs, French polishing, upholstery; buys at auction.

EPSOM

Fogg Antiques
75 South St. (R Fogg and M Hughes) Est: 1982. Open 9-6, Sat. 10-6. SIZE: Medium. *STOCK: English and continental pine, Victorian to 1900s, £50-£1,000.* LOC: A24. TEL: 0372 726931. SER: Pine stripping (furniture). VAT: Stan.

Link Gold Ltd
95 High St. (A.C Thiele and G.M Reed) Open 9.30-4, Sat. 9.30-3.30. *STOCK: Gold including jewellery, from 1900, £50-£500; silver, from 1800, £15-£200; silver plate, from 1900, £5-£100; general antiques, £5-£100.* TEL: 0372 729970.

Vandeleur Antiquarian Books
6 Seaforth Gdns. (E.H Bryant) Open by appointment only. *STOCK: Antiquarian and secondhand books on all subjects, prints and maps.* TEL: 081 393 7752. SER: Valuations; catalogues issuee; searches undertaken. VAT: Stan.

ESHER

Kensington Galleries LAPADA
Badgers Wood, West End Lane. (J.S Bates) Open by appointment only. *STOCK: Oil paintings especially sporting; animalier bronzes, 19th C.* TEL: 0372 64407. SER: Valuations; restorations.

EWELL

J.W McKenzie
12 Stoneleigh Park Rd. Est: 1971. Appointment advisable. *STOCK: Antiquarian books on theatre and cricket.* TEL: 081 393 7700.

Token House Antiques LAPADA
7 Market Parade, High St. (Mrs D Walker) Est: 1966. Open 11-5. CL: Wed. *STOCK: Furniture, 18th-19th C; porcelain, decorative items, metalware and general antiques.* LOC: Opp. post office. PARK: At rear. TEL: 081 393 9654. VAT: Stan/Spec.

EWHURST, Nr. Cranleigh

Cranleigh Antiques
Milkhill, The Street. (R Hoskin) Est: 1976. Open 10-5, Sat. 10-1 and Sun. by appointment. SIZE: Medium. *STOCK: Oak and mahogany furniture, 18th-19th C, £5-£1,000; general antiques and bygones.* PARK: Easy. TEL: 0483 277318. SER: Valuations. VAT: Stan.

FARNHAM

Bits and Pieces
82 West St. (Mrs C.J Wickins) CL: Wed. p.m. *STOCK: Victoriana, furniture, art nouveau, art deco.* TEL: 0252 722355/715043. SER: Costume hire.

Bourne Mill Antiques
Guildford Rd, (Premises shared by 75 dealers). Est: 1971. Open 10-5.30 every day. *STOCK: Stripped pine, general antiques, bric-a-brac, linen, watercolours, oil paintings, architectural and collectors' items.* TEL: 0252 716663.

Casque and Gauntlet Antiques Ltd
55/59 Badshot Lea Rd, Badshot Lea. (R Colt) Est: 1957. SIZE: Large. *STOCK: Militaria, arms, armour.* LOC: On Aldershot to Farnham road. PARK: Easy. TEL: 0252 20745, ext. 2. SER: Restorations (metals); re-gilding. VAT: Stan/Spec.

Farnham continued

Christopher's Antiques
Sandford Lodge, 39a West St. (Mr and Mrs C.M Booth) Resident. Est: 1972. Open 8-1 and 2-5.30, weekends by appointment. SIZE: Large. *STOCK: Fruitwood country and mahogany furniture, 18th-19th C; walnut furniture, 17th-18th C.* LOC: From Guildford on the A31, turn right at second roundabout. PARK: Easy. TEL: 0252 713794. SER: Valuations; restorations (furniture). VAT: Stan/Spec.

Farnham Antique Centre
27 South St. (Miss M.A Stanford) Est: 1976. Open 9.30-5. SIZE: Large. 12 dealers. *STOCK: General antiques, including silver, jewellery, porcelain, brass and copper, clocks, dolls, toys, textiles, pine, Oriental items, small period furniture and collectors' items.* LOC: On the one-way system into Farnham, large corner site. PARK: At rear. TEL: 0252 724475.

Heytesbury Antiques LAPADA
P.O. Box 222. (I. and S Ingall) Est: 1974. Open by appointment only. SIZE: Medium. *STOCK: Pre-1830 mahogany, walnut and rosewood furniture, and 19th C decorative furniture, textiles and associated items, £200-£12,000; paintings and bronzes, 19th C, £100-£2,000.* TEL: 0252 850893. FAIRS: West London, Olympia, Kensington, Decorators and others. VAT: Mainly Spec.

P. and B Jordan
90 West St. (P.A. and W.E Jordan) Est: 1962. Open 9.30-1, Sat. 9.30-1 and 2-5.30 or by appointment. SIZE: Medium. *STOCK: Furniture and ceramics, from 1750, £50-£500; oil paintings, prints, from 1700, £5-£500; glass, brass fenders, from 1700, £5-£50.* Not Stocked: Carpets, tapestries. LOC: On main road through town centre. PARK: Round corner, 'The Hart' Rd. TEL: 0252 716272. VAT: Stan/Spec.

Lion and Lamb Gallery at Biggs of Farnham
West St. (C. and S Neville) Est: 1975. *STOCK: Landscape, marine, sporting and wildlife pictures, 20th C.* TEL: 0252 714154; home - 0420 477894. SER: Restorations (oils and watercolours); framing; mounting.

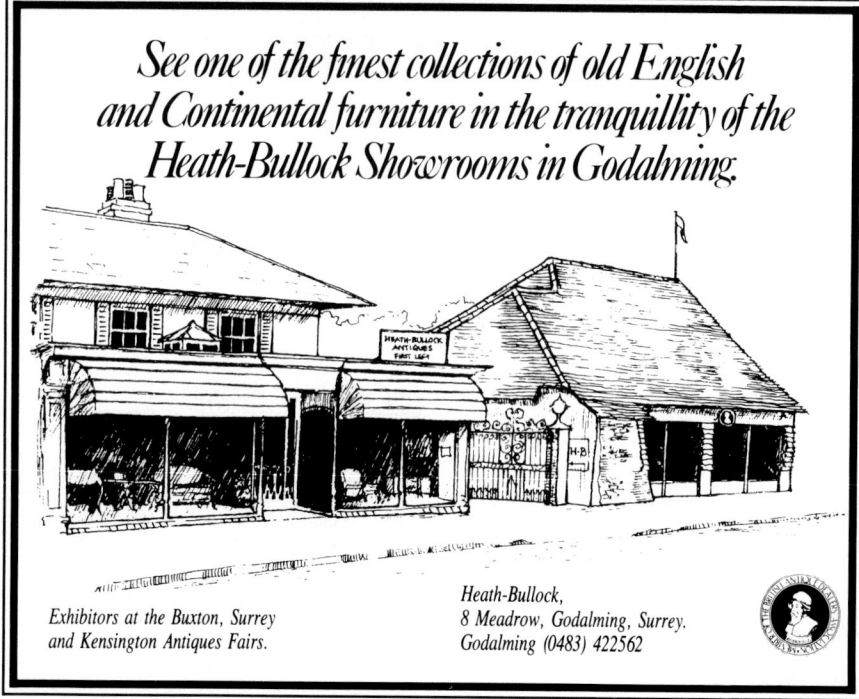

Farnham continued

Maltings Monthly Market

Bridge Sq. Est: 1969. First Sat. monthly. SIZE: 150 stalls. *STOCK: 60% of the dealers sell a wide variety of antiques, bric-a-brac, postcards and collectables.* LOC: Follow signs to Wagon Yard car park, Maltings over footbridge. TEL: 0252 726234.

R. and M Putnam

60 Downing St. Est: 1957. Open 10-1 and 2-5.30; 5 on Sat. CL: Sun. except by appointment. SIZE: Medium. *STOCK: Period pine furniture, 18th-19th C; Staffordshire pottery, 19th C; brass, copper, oil and watercolour paintings, oak and mahogany furniture, country items.* LOC: Town centre. PARK: Easy. TEL: 0252 715769; home - 0252 715485. SER: Restorations (furniture); buys at auction. VAT: Stan/Spec.

Village Pine

32 West S. (S McGrath) Est: 1981. Open 10-5. SIZE: Large. *STOCK: Pine furniture including dressers, chests of drawers and boxes, unusual and small items, Victorian, £35-£650.* LOC: On left past Bishops Table Hotel. PARK: Easy. TEL: 0252 726660.

Karel Weijand Fine Oriental Carpets LAPADA

Lion and Lamb Courtyard. Est: 1963. Open 9.30-5.30. SIZE: Medium. *STOCK: Fine antique*

Karel Weijand Fine Oriental Carpets continued

and modern Oriental and Persian rugs and carpets, from £100. LOC: Off West St. PARK: Easy. TEL: 0252 726215. SER: Valuations; restorations. VAT: Stan/Spec.

Wrecclesham Antiques

47 Wrecclesham Rd. (A Vallis and J Hudson) Est: 1979. Open daily, Sun. by appointment. SIZE: Medium. *STOCK: Pine, 19th C, £50-£450; clocks, 17th-19th C, £150-£800; Victorian furniture, 19th C, £60-£300.* LOC: A325. PARK: Easy. TEL: 0252 716468; home - same.

FRENSHAM

Douglas Franks

St. Anthony's. Est: 1949. Open by appointment. *STOCK: Furniture and accessories.* TEL: 025 125 2467. VAT: Stan/Spec.

GODALMING

Cry for the Moon

31 High St. (J.L Ackroyd) Est: 1977. Open 9.30-5.30. SIZE: Medium. *STOCK: Mainly jewellery, £50-£10,000; silver and objets d'art.* TEL: 0483 426201; fax - 0483 860117. SER: Valuations (jewellery, silver); repairs (jewellery); jewellery commissions undertaken. VAT: Stan/Spec.

Godalming continued

P. and J Goldthorpe
Bicton Croft, Deanery Rd. Open by appointment only. *STOCK: Paintings, mainly English and Dutch, 17th-18th C.* TEL: 0483 414356.

Heath-Bullock BADA
8 Meadrow. (R.J. and M.E Heath-Bullock) Est: 1926. Open 10-1 and 2-4, Sun. by appointment. SIZE: Large. *STOCK: English and continental furniture, garden ornaments, works of art.* LOC: A3100. From Guildford on the left side approaching Godalming. PARK: Own. TEL: 0483 422562; fax - 0483 426077. SER: Valuations (furniture); restoration; upholstery. FAIRS: Exhibitors at and organisers of Buxton, Surrey and Kensington.

The Olde Curiosity Shoppe
99 High St. *STOCK: Silver, brass, copper, china, collectables and jewellery.* TEL: 0483 415889.

Priory Antiques
29 Church St. (P Rotchell) Open 10-4. CL: Wed. *STOCK: General antiques.* TEL: 0483 421804.

David White Antiques
34 Meadrow. (D. and Y White) Resident. Est: 1981. Open 9.30-5 and by appointment. CL: Wed. p.m. SIZE: Medium. *STOCK: English country furniture, especially fruitwood and yew and unusual chairs, 17th to early 19th C, £50-£5,000; copper, brass and treen, from £20.* LOC: A3100, opposite Pickfords Depository. PARK: Easy. TEL: 0483 420957. VAT: Stan/Spec.

GREAT BOOKHAM, Nr. Leatherhead

Bookham Galleries
Leatherhead Rd. (J Rowe) Est: 1969. Open by appointment only. SIZE: Large. *STOCK: Furniture, 18th-19th C.* LOC: A246. PARK: Easy. TEL: 0372 52668. VAT: Stan/Spec.

Roger A Davis Antiquarian Horologist
19 Dorking Rd. Est: 1971. Open 9.30-12.30 and 2-5.30. CL: Mon. and Wed., Fri. p.m. and Sun. a.m. except by appointment. SIZE: Small. *STOCK: Clocks, 18th-19th C, £100-£4,000.* LOC: From Leatherhead A246 to centre of village, turn left at sign for Polesden Lacey, shop 1/4 mile along Dorking Rd. PARK: Easy. TEL: 0372 57655; home - 0372 53167. SER: Valuations; restorations (mechanical and case work); buys at auction (antique clocks).

GUILDFORD

The Antiques Centre
22 Haydon Pl, Corner of Martyr Rd. (Mrs S.D.J Pullen) Est: 1969. Open 10-4. CL: Mon. and Wed. LOC: Close to Surrey Advertiser. PARK: 100yds. on left from North St. TEL: 0483 67817. The wide variety of goods offered is shown by

The Antiques Centre continued

the principal items of stock which follow the names of some of the dealers listed below.

Peter Bradley
Pine, kitchenalia and clocks.
Jennifer Carter
China, collectables, bygones.
Elaine Chandler
Tom Thumb miniatures, doll's houses and dolls' house miniatures.
Joan Goggin
China, collectables, bygones.
Beryl Joyce
Oriental and European ceramics, glass, antiquities, pictures and decorative items.
Helen McHugh
Lace, baby gowns, general antiques, lace cushions.
Sylvia Pullen
Silver, jewellery, Devon ware.

Bijoux Jewellers
12 Epsom Rd. (Mrs N.C Harper) Est: 1968. Open daily 10-5.30. *STOCK: Jewellery, including secondhand and modern; silver.* LOC: Near Odeon cinema. TEL: 0483 32992. VAT: Stan.

Denning Antiques
1 Chapel St. Open 10-5. *STOCK: Silver, lace, linen, pre-1930 clothes, textiles, collectors' items.* LOC: Off High St. PARK: Nearby. TEL: 0483 39595.

Gillingham Antiques
'Lyndhurst', 148 London Rd. Est: 1920. Open 9-1 and 2-5.30. CL: Sat. SIZE: Medium. *STOCK: Mahogany, oak and walnut furniture, 17th-19th C.* Not Stocked: Reproductions or Victoriana. LOC: 3 doors from A.A. Office. PARK: Easy. TEL: 0483 61952. FAIRS: Guildford. VAT: Stan/Spec.

Horological Workshops BADA
204 Worplesdon Rd. (M.D Tooke) Est: 1968. Open 8.30-5.30, Sat. 9-12.30 or by appointment. *STOCK: Clocks, watches, barometers.* TEL: 0483 576496. SER: Buys at auction.

Thomas Thorp Bookseller
170 High St. Est: 1883. Open 9-5, 5.30 on Sat. SIZE: Large. *STOCK: Books including antiquarian and out-of-print.* LOC: At traffic lights at top of High St. PARK: Road running parallel High St. 200yds. away. TEL: 0483 62770. SER: Valuations; buys at auction (antiquarian books). Private collections bought.

Charles W Traylen
Castle House, 49/50 Quarry St. Est: 1945. Open 9-1 and 2-5. CL: Mon. SIZE: Large. *STOCK: Fine books and manuscripts, 13th C to date.* PARK: 200yds. TEL: 0483 572424. SER: Valuations; restorations (bindings); buys at auction. VAT: Stan.

HAMPTON WICK

Hampton Wick Antiques
48 High St. Est: 1957. Open 10-5. *STOCK: Clocks and barometers, general antiques.* TEL: 081 977 3178.

HASLEMERE

Allen Avery Interiors
1 High St. Est: 1971. Open 9-1 and 2.15-5. CL: Sat. p.m. and Wed. *STOCK: English furniture.* TEL: 0428 643883.

J.K Glover (Antiques)
Grayswood. LOC: Village Green. TEL: 0428 642184.

Surrey Clock Centre
3 Lower St. (C Ingrams and S Haw) Est: 1962. Open 9-1 and 2-5. SIZE: Large. *STOCK: Grandfather clocks, 1680-1850, £900-£3,500; carriage clocks, 1790-1900, £150-£2,000; bracket clocks, 1680 and after, from £150; barometers, £400-£1,200.* PARK: Easy. TEL: 0428 651313. SER: Valuations; restorations (clocks, brass and painted dials to the trade); buys at auction. VAT: Stan/Spec.

Wood's Wharf Antiques Bazaar
56 High St. SIZE: 12 dealers. *STOCK: A wide selection of antiques.* LOC: Opposite The Georgian Hotel. TEL: 0428 2125.

HINDHEAD

Albany Antiques Ltd
8-10 London Rd. (T Winstanley) Est: 1965. Open 9-6. CL: Sun. except by appointment. *STOCK: Furniture, 17th-18th C, £20-£400; china (also Chinese), £5-£400; metalware, £7-£50, both 18th-19th C.* Not Stocked: Silver. LOC: On A3. PARK: Easy. TEL: 0428 605528. VAT: Stan/Spec.

Peter Borton Fine Arts
Moorlands, Linkside West. Est: 1969. Open by appointment. *STOCK: Collector paintings and watercolours.* TEL: 0428 605033.

M.J Bowdery BADA
12 London Rd. Est: 1970. Always available, prior telephone call advisable. *STOCK: Furniture, 18th-19th C.* TEL: 0428 606376; home - 0428 605244. VAT: Stan/Spec.

Oriel Antiques
3 Royal Parade, Tilford Rd. (J Gear) Est: 1974. Open 9-5.30. CL: Wed. p.m.. *STOCK: Furniture and pictures, 18th-19th C.* TEL: 0428 606281.

"Second Hand Rose"
Portsmouth Rd, Bramshott Chase. (S.J. and S.Y Ridout) Est: 1980. Open 9.30-5.30 and by appointment. SIZE: Large. *STOCK: Furniture, paintings, bric-a-brac, 18th-20th C.* LOC: On A3, 1 mile S.W. of Hindhead. PARK: Easy. TEL: 0428 604880; home - same. VAT: Stan/Spec.

Hindhead continued

What Not Antiques
Crossways Rd, Grayshot. (Mrs M Wylie) Open 9-5.30. *STOCK: General antiques and pine.* TEL: 0428 604871.

HORLEY

Horley Antiques and Collectables Centre
12 Station Rd. (Mrs R Smith) Open 9.30-5. SIZE: 4 dealers. *STOCK: General antiques.* TEL: 0293 774182.

KEW

Lloyds of Kew
9 Mortlake Terrace. (D Lloyd) Open 10-5.30. CL: Wed. *STOCK: Out-of-print books on gardening, botany and some general.* PARK: Easy. TEL: 081 940 2512. SER: Annual catalogues (Oct.).

KEW GREEN

Andrew Davis
6 Mortlake Terrace. Est: 1969. *STOCK: Decorative and functional items, especially clocks, furniture, ceramics.* TEL: 081 948 4911. SER: Framing.

KINGSTON-UPON-THAMES

Glencorse Antiques LAPADA
321 Richmond Rd, Ham Parade, Ham Common. (M Igel and B.S Prydall) Open 10-5.30. *STOCK: Watercolours, oils and furniture, 18th-19th C.* PARK: Easy. TEL: 081 541 0871.

Glydon and Guess Ltd
14 Apple Market. Est: 1940. Open 9.30-5. CL: Wed. *STOCK: Jewellery, small silver, £100-£5,000.* LOC: Town centre. TEL: 081 546 3758. SER: Restorations; valuations. VAT: Stan.

Kingston Antiques
170 London Rd. (T. and H Deveson and G.M Reed) Est: 1977. Open 10-7. SIZE: Small. *STOCK: Mahogany, walnut and rosewood furniture, 18th-19th C, £200-£1,500; clocks and objets d'art, 19th C, £300-£1,000; porcelain and bric-a-brac, 19th-20th C, £10-£200.* LOC: At foot of Kingston Hill. PARK: Easy. TEL: 081 549 5876; home - same. SER: Valuations; restorations (cabinet work and polishing).

Link Gold Ltd
13 Apple Market. (A.C Thiele and G.M Reed) Est: 1981. Open 9.30-5. SIZE: Small. *STOCK: Gold including jewellery, from 1900, £50-£500; silver, from 1800, £15-£200; silver, plate, from 1900, £5-£100; general antiques, £5-£100.* Not Stocked: Large furniture. LOC: Above Holland & Barrett.

Link Gold Ltd continued

PARK: Union St. car park. TEL: 081 549 5551 or 081 398 1237. SER: Valuations (jewellery); buys at auction (as stock). FAIRS: Kempton Park, Sunbury. VAT: Stan/Spec.

KNAPHILL, Nr. Woking

Knaphill Antiques

38 High St. (P.W. and J.A Bethney) Open 8.30-6. CL: Mon. SIZE: Small and warehouse. *STOCK: Barometers, clocks, Georgian, Victorian and Edwardian furniture.* LOC: Off A322 turn right after the Fox Public House at Bisley towards Knaphill, shop oppposite Crown public house. TEL: 048 67 3179; home - 0483 811616.

LALEHAM, Nr. Staines

Laleham Antiques

23 Shepperton Rd. (H. and E Potter) Est: 1970. Open 10-5. SIZE: Medium. *STOCK: Period furniture, pine, porcelain, general and trade antiques.* LOC: B376. PARK: Easy. TEL: 0784 450353. VAT: Stan.

LIMPSFIELD

Limpsfield Watercolours

High St. (Mrs C Reason) FATG. Est: 1985. Open Thurs., Fri. and Sat. 9.30-2. SIZE: Small. *STOCK: Watercolours, £15-£5,000; prints and etchings, £5-£200; all 1850-1940 and contemporary.* Not Stocked: Oils. LOC: From junction 6, M25 on B269. PARK: Easy. TEL: 0883 717010. SER: Valuations; restorations (prints, watercolours, oils); framing; mounting. VAT: Spec.

LINGFIELD

Lingfield Antiques

4 East Grinstead Rd. (A.F Robertson) Open 9-5. CL: Wed. p.m. *STOCK: General antiques, furniture, porcelain and silver.* TEL: 0342 834501.

LITTLE BOOKHAM

Alanna Staton Antiques LAPADA

The Old Barn, 120 Little Bookham St. (P.T Station) Est: 1967. Open by appointment only. *STOCK: 18th and 19th C furniture, objets d'art, copper, brass, plate, silver, jewellery, glass.* LOC: A246 from Leatherhead to Guildford, across National Trust common. PARK: Easy. TEL: 0372 58567. VAT: Stan/Spec.

MERROW, Nr. Guildford

The Pine Shop

174 Epsom Rd. (S Hamilton) Open 10-1 and 2-5. CL: Wed. *STOCK: Pine furniture.* TEL: 0483 572533.

MERSTHAM

The Old Smithy Antique Centre

7 High St. (S.M Davidson) 10-5. SIZE: 12 dealers. *STOCK: General antiques and collectables.* PARK: Easy. TEL: 0737 642306.

MILFORD, Nr. Godalming

Michael Andrews Antiques

Portsmouth Rd. Est: 1974. Open daily, Sun. by appointment. SIZE: Small. *STOCK: Furniture, 18th to early 19th C.* LOC: Corner of Cherry Tree Rd. PARK: Easy. TEL: 0483 420765; home - same. VAT: Stan/Spec.

MITCHAM

Cherub Antiques

177 Streatham Rd. (M Wisdom) Open 10.30-5.30. *STOCK: Pine.* TEL: 081 640 7179.

MORDEN

A Burton-Garbett

35 The Green. Est: 1959. By appointment only. Prospective clients met (at either Morden or Wimbledon tube station) by car. *STOCK: Books on travel, the arts, antiquities of South and Central America, Mexico and the Caribbean, 16th-20th C, £5-£5,000.* TEL: 081 540 2367. SER: Buys at auction (books, pictures, fine arts, ethnographica). VAT: Stan.

OXTED

Antiques and Interiors

64 Station Rd. East. (G.P. and S.M Maddox) Est: 1977. Open 9-5. SIZE: Large. *STOCK: Mahogany, walnut, rosewood and oak furniture, 19th C; porcelain, prints, watercolours, silver and collectable items.* LOC: Off A25. PARK: Easy. TEL: 0883 712806. SER: Valuations; restorations. VAT: Stan/Spec.

Treasures

151 Station Rd. East. Open 10-5. *STOCK: Copper, brass, glass, porcelain, silver, jewellery, linen, books, pine, toys, small furniture and collectables.* TEL: 0883 713301.

PURLEY

Michael Addison Antiques

28-30 Godstone Rd. (M. and N Addison) Est: 1981. Open 10-5. CL: Wed. p.m. SIZE: Medium. *STOCK: Furniture, 1780-1930, £200-£2,000.* Not Stocked: Bric-a-brac. LOC: A22, 1 mile east of Purley. PARK: Easy. TEL: 081 668 6714. SER: Valuations; restorations; upholstery. VAT: Stan/Spec.

REDHILL

Ivelet Books Ltd
18 Fairlawn Dr. *STOCK: Old, rare and out-of-print architecture, applied arts, illustrated, gardening; landscape and garden history; prints.* TEL: 0737 768282; fax - 0737 764520. SER: Catalogues available. *Postal Only.*

F.G Lawrence and Sons
89 Brighton Rd. Est: 1871. Open 9-1 and 2-5, Sat. 10-1. CL: Wed. p.m. SIZE: Large. *STOCK: Edwardian, Victorian and Georgian furniture.* LOC: On A23. PARK: Own. TEL: 0737 764196. SER: Valuations; buys at auction. VAT: Stan.

Redhill Antiques Warehouse
89 Brighton Rd. (E.L Pritchard) Open 9-5.30 or by appointment. *STOCK: Period, Victorian and shipping furniture.* TEL: 0737 762053.

REIGATE

Antique Dresser
57 High St. (T Wilcox) Open 10-5.30. *STOCK: General antiques.* TEL: 0737 222654.

Bourne Gallery Ltd LAPADA
31/33 Lesbourne Rd. (J Robertson) Est: 1970. Open 10-1 and 2-5.30. SIZE: Large. *STOCK: 19th and 20th C oils and watercolours, £250-£25,000.* PARK: Easy. TEL: 0737 241614. SER: Restorations (oil paintings). VAT: Spec.

Heath Antiques
15 Flanchford Rd. (J. and P Gibson) Resident, but prior telephone call advisable. SIZE: Small. *STOCK: Porcelain including Mason's Ironstone and blue and white, 18th-20th C, £5-£250; silver, general antiques, small furniture.* LOC: Reigate Heath, just off A25 main Reigate-Dorking road. PARK: Easy. TEL: 0737 244230; home - same. SER: Valuations.

Bertram Noller (Reigate)
14a London Rd. (A.M Noller) Est: 1970. Open 9.30-1 and 2-5.30. CL: Tues. and Wed. SIZE: Small. *STOCK: Collectors' items, furniture, grates, fenders, mantels, copper, brass, glass, pewter, £1-£500.* LOC: West side of one-way traffic system. Opposite Upper West St. car park. PARK: Opposite. TEL: 0737 242548. SER: Valuations; restorations (furniture, clocks, marble).

Reigate Galleries Ltd
45a Bell St. (J.S Morrish) Est: 1958. Open 9-5.30, Wed. 9-1. SIZE: Large. *STOCK: Old prints, engravings, antiquarian books.* PARK: Opposite. TEL: 0737 246055. SER: Picture framing. VAT: Stan.

Showcase
27 Croydon Rd. (L Blackford and J Butler) Open 10-4. *STOCK: General antiques.* TEL: 0737 222305.

Reigate continued

Victoriana Dolls LAPADA
(Mr and Mrs C Bond) Open by appointment. *STOCK: Dolls and accessories.* TEL: 0737 249525.

RICHMOND

Antique Mart
72-74 Hill Rise. (G. and Y Katz) Open 10-5, Sun. 2-6. CL: Wed. SIZE: Large. *STOCK: Furniture, 18th-19th C.* TEL: 081 940 6942. SER: Buys at auction. VAT: Stan/Spec.

Antiques Arcade
22 Richmond Hill. Est: 1984. Open 10.30-5.30, Sun. 2-5.30. CL: Wed. SIZE: Medium. *STOCK: Mahogany, rosewood and walnut furniture, some country, 18th, 19th C and Edwardian; fine porcelain and pottery, children's furniture, from 17th C; Staffordshire figures, porcelain, pictures, prints, general antiques, collectors' items, jewellery.* PARK: Easy. TEL: 081 940 2035.

Bridge Antiques
24 Hill Rise. (C.A Bodmer and D.M Andrews) Est: 1985. Open 10.30-5.30, Sun. 2.30-5.30. CL: Wed. SIZE: Small. *STOCK: Furniture, £200-£6,000; clocks, £400-£3,000, both 18th-19th C; glass, £20-£500; early Masons ironstone, £50-£500; pictures, lamps and chandeliers, 19th-20th C, £50-£3,000.* LOC: Bottom of Richmond Hill. PARK: Nearby. TEL: 081 948 6802. VAT: Stan/Spec.

Brookville Antiques
222 Sandycombe Rd. (Z Malcolm and A.K Khan) Open 10-6. *STOCK: Decorative items, clocks, furniture and stained glass.* LOC: Near Kew Gardens. TEL: 081 940 6230; home - same.

Court Antiques (Richmond)
12/14 Brewers Lane, and 13 The Green. (A. and L Coombs) Est: 1958. Open 9.30-5.30. SIZE: Small. *STOCK: General antiques, jewellery, furniture, silver.* Not Stocked: Coins and stamps. LOC: From Richmond station turn left along the Quadrant into George St., Brewers Lane is on the right. PARK: 30yds. turn left. TEL: 081 940 0515. VAT: Stan.

Dukes Yard Antique Market
1A Duke St. (C Hendley) Open 10-6. CL: Mon. SIZE: 74 stands. *STOCK: General antiques.* TEL: 081 332 1051.

Mollie Evans
82 Hill Rise. Est: 1965. Open Thurs.-Sat. 10.30-5.30, Sun. 2.30-5.30 and by appointment. SIZE: Medium. *STOCK: Early country and painted furniture, pottery, some textiles, interesting bygones, unusual bold decorative items including sculpture, to 1930, £50-£4,000.* LOC: From centre of Richmond, take A307 towards Kingston (Petersham Rd.). Fork left up hill

Mollie Evans continued

immediately after passing Richmond Bridge on right. PARK: Meters. TEL: 081 948 0182 (ansaphone). SER: Buys at auction. VAT: Spec.

Peter and Debbie Gooday
20 Richmond Hill. Est: 1971. Open 11-5.30, Sun. (trade only) 2-5.30. CL: Mon., Wed. and Fri., except by appointment. SIZE: Medium. *STOCK: Decorative items and jewellery, art nouveau and art deco; art nouveau metalwork especially Liberty pewter, 1880-1950, £5-£2,000.* LOC: 100yds. from Richmond Bridge. PARK: Easy. TEL: 081 940 8652. SER: Buys at auction.

Roland Goslett Gallery
139 Kew Rd. Est: 1974. Open Thurs. and Fri. 10-6, Sat. 10-2, otherwise by appointment. SIZE: Small. *STOCK: English watercolours and oil paintings, 19th to early 20th C, £100-£5,000.* PARK: Easy. TEL: 081 940 4009. SER: Valuations; restorations (oils, watercolours and frames); framing. VAT: Spec.

Hill Rise Antiques LAPADA
26 Hill Rise. (P Hinde and D Milewski) Est: 1978. Open 10.30-5.30, Sun. (trade only) 2.30-5.30. CL: Wed. SIZE: Large. *STOCK: 18th and 19th C walnut and mahogany furniture and longcase clocks, £100-£10,000; silver and plate, bronzes, mirrors, boxes and glassware.* LOC: 1 mile from A316 (M3). PARK: At rear by arrangement. TEL: 081 332 2941; home - same. FAIRS: Olympia (June and Oct.), City Fair, Barbican. VAT: Stan/Spec.

Horton's
2 Paved Court, The Green. (D. and R Horton) FGA. CL: Wed. *STOCK: Jewellery and silver, 18th-20th C; all £500-£1,000; British paintings, early to mid-20th C, £250-£750.* TEL: 081 332 1775. SER: Valuations.

Hugh Evelyn Ltd
36a Friar's Stile Rd. Open by appointment. *STOCK: Prints, 17th-19th C, £20-£1,000; watercolours, 19th C, £50-£850.* PARK: Easy. TEL: 081 948 4031 (24 hours). SER: Restorations (prints, watercolours and pastels). VAT: Stan.

Kingabys
15 Paved Court. (A Glazebrook) Est: 1960. Open 10-5.30. SIZE: Small. *STOCK: Jewellery, £20-£4,000; silver, £10-£2,000; pictures, £20-£600.* LOC: Pedestrian alley leading off Richmond Green. PARK: 150yds. in Friars Lane off Richmond Green. TEL: 081 940 6533. VAT: Stan.

F. and T Lawson Antiques
13 Hill Rise. Resident. Est: 1965. Open 10-5.30, Sat. 10-5. CL: Wed. and Sun. a.m. SIZE: Medium. *STOCK: Furniture, 1680-1870; paintings and watercolours, both £30-£1,500; clocks, 1650-1930, £50-£2,000; bric-a-brac, £5-*

F. and T Lawson Antiques continued

£300. LOC: Near Richmond Bridge at bottom of Hill Rise on the river side, overlooking river. PARK: Further up Hill Rise, and limited for loading and unloading. TEL: 081 940 0461. SER: Valuations; buys at auction.

Layton Antiques
1 Paved Court, The Green. (Lady Layton) Est: 1967. Open 10-5. CL: Wed. and Sun. except by appointment. SIZE: Medium. *STOCK: 18th and 19th C furniture, silver and decorative items.* LOC: Off The Green at Prince's Head public house. PARK: Easy. TEL: 081 940 2617. VAT: Stan/Spec.

Lion Antiques
16 Brewers Lane. Open 9-5. *STOCK: Silver and jewellery.* TEL: 081 940 8069.

Marryat
88 Sheen Rd, (Marryat (Richmond) Ltd.). Est: 1990. Open 10-5.30. SIZE: Large. *STOCK: English and continental furniture, watercolours and oils, 19th C, £100-£1,000; ceramics and glass, 18th-19th C, £10-£100.* LOC: Follow M3/A316 towards Richmond, first left into Church Rd. then left again. PARK: Easy. TEL: 081 332 0262. SER: Valuations; restorations. VAT: Stan/Spec.

Palmer Galleries
10 Paved Court. (C.D. and V.J Palmer) Est: 1984. Open 10-5. SIZE: Medium. *STOCK: Prints, watercolours and engravings, 19th-20th C, £50-£1,000.* PARK: Richmond Green. TEL: 081 948 2668; home - 081 998 0901. VAT: Stan/Spec.

Piano Nobile Fine Paintings
26 Richmond Hill, (Travers Partnership). Est: 1986. Open Thurs.-Sun. 10-6.. SIZE: Medium. *STOCK: Fine 19th C Impressionist and early 20th C Post-Impressionist and Modernist British and continental oil paintings, specialising in Les Petits Maitres of the Paris Schools, £500-£50,000.* PARK: Easy. TEL: 081 940 2435. SER: Valuations; restorations (oil paintings and watercolours); framing; buys at auction (19th-20th C oil paintings). FAIRS: Grosvenor. VAT: Stan/Spec.

Richmond Traders
28, 30/32 Hill Rise. Open 10.30-5.30, Sun. 2-5. CL: Wed. SIZE: 16 dealers. *STOCK: General antiques.* TEL: 081 948 4638.

Rowan Antiques
4 Worple Way. Open 10-6. CL: Mon. and Tues. *STOCK: Furniture, Georgian to Victorian; clocks, watercolours.* TEL: 081 332 1167.

RIPLEY

Cedar House Gallery
Est: 1987. *STOCK: Watercolours and oils, 19th to early 20th C, £500-£10,000; clocks, £500-£1,500; objets d'art, £100-£500; both 19th C.* LOC: 1/2 mile M25/A3 junction. PARK: Easy. TEL: 0483 211221. SER: Restorations.

J Hartley Antiques Ltd
186 High St. Est: 1949. Open 8.45-5, Sat. 9.45-2.45. *STOCK: Queen Anne and Georgian furniture.* TEL: 0483 224318. VAT: Stan.

Manor House
High St. Est: 1952. SIZE: Medium. *STOCK: Furniture, 18th C; copper and brass, 18th-19th C; clocks, prints mostly sporting and military; china, glass.* LOC: A3. PARK: Easy. TEL: 0483 225350. VAT: Stan/Spec.

Ripley Antiques LAPADA
67 High St. (H Denham) Est: 1960. Open 9.30-1 and 2-5.15, Sun. by appointment. SIZE: Large. *STOCK: Furniture, decorative items, American shipping goods mainly early 18th-19th C.* LOC: 2 mins. from junction 10 at M25/A3 interchange. PARK: Easy. TEL: 0483 224981/224333. SER: Valuations; restorations. VAT: Stan/Spec.

Ripley continued

Sage Antiques and Interiors LAPADA
The Green Cottage, High St. (H. and C Sage) GMC. Est: 1971. Open 9.30-1 and 2-5.30, Sat. all day. SIZE: Large. *STOCK: Furniture, mahogany, oak, walnut, 1600-1900, £150-£8,000; oil paintings, £100-£5,000; watercolours, £50-£1,000, china, £2-£500, all 18th-19th C; silver, Sheffield plate, brass, pewter, decorative items, 18th-19th C, £50-£1,000.* LOC: Village centre, on main road. PARK: Easy. TEL: 0483 224396; fax - 0483 211978. SER: Restorations (furniture, pictures); interior furnishing. VAT: Stan.

Anthony Welling Antiques BADA
Broadway Barn, High St. Est: 1970. Open 9-1 and 2-5.30 and evenings by appointment. CL: Sun. except by appointment. SIZE: Large. *STOCK: English oak, 17th-18th C, £250-£8,000; country furniture, 18th C, £200-£6,000; brass, copper, pewter, 18th C, £100-£750.* Not Stocked: Glass, china, silver. LOC: Turn off A3 at Ripley, shop in centre of village on service road. PARK: Easy. TEL: 0483 225384. VAT: Spec.

SANDERSTEAD

Shirley Warren BADA LAPADA
The Antique Glass Shop, 333b Limpsfield Rd. (Mrs S Warren) ADA. Open 10-5 or by appointment. CL: Mon. *STOCK: English and*

Shirley Warren continued

***continental glass, antiquity to 19th C, £100-£10,000; reference books.* LOC: B269, 10 mins. from M25, junction 6. PARK: Easy. TEL: 081 651 5180; home - 081 657 1751. SER: Valuations. FAIRS: British International, Birmingham NEC (April); Olympia (June); International Ceramic (June); London Antique Dealers', Cafe Royal (Feb. and Sept.); Park Lane Hotel (Oct.). VAT: Spec.**

SHALFORD, Nr. Guildford

M Granshaw
Ye Olde Malt House, The Street. Est: 1895. Open every day 9.30-5.30. *STOCK: English furniture, 17th-19th C; stripped pine, metalware and garden ornaments, statuary, glass, silver, jewellery, general antiques.* LOC: A281. 1 mile from Guildford, opposite Seahorse Inn. TEL: 0483 61462.

SHEPPERTON

Rickett & Co. Antiques
Church Sq. (A.L Spencer) Est: 1968. Open 10-5, Wed. 10-1, prior telephone call advisable. *STOCK: Brass and copper, 18th-19th C, £100-£300; fenders and fire tools, oil lamps, inkwells, chandeliers, grandfather clocks.* LOC: 10 mins. from London airport. PARK: Easy. TEL: 0932 243571; home - 0932 222508. SER: Restorations (metal repairs and polishing). VAT: Spec.

SHERE, Nr. Guildford

Asters Antique Centre
Middle St. (J Watson) Est: 1983. Open 10-5, Sat. 10-5.30, Sun. 11-5.30. SIZE: Large. *STOCK: Victorian and Edwardian items, £5-£500.* LOC: A25. PARK: Easy. TEL: 048 641 2846. VAT: Stan/Spec.

Yesterdays Pine
Gomshall Lane. (J. and V Stuart) Open 10-5.30. *STOCK: Victorian pine.* TEL: 048 641 3198.

SHIRLEY

Shirley Antiques
574 Wickham Rd. (R. and I Manzi) Est: 1976. Open 9.30-5.30. *STOCK: General antiques and shipping goods.* TEL: 081 777 8335; home - 081 462 4107.

Spring Park Jewellers
284 Wickham Rd. (M McCamley MGA) Est: 1965. Open 10-5.30. CL: Wed. SIZE: Small. *STOCK: Jewellery, paintings, prints, silver, furniture.* LOC: 2 miles from central Croydon on road to West Wickham. PARK: Easy. TEL: 081 656 2800. SER: Valuations; clock, watch and jewellery repairs; buys at auction.

SHOTTERMILL, Nr. Haslemere

Grannie's Attic
Checkerboards, Hindhead Rd. (A.G.J Buckland) Open 9.30-6. *STOCK: Small general antiques, bric-a-brac.* TEL: 0428 4572.

SOUTH HOLMWOOD, Nr. Dorking

Holmwood Antiques
Norfolk Rd. (R Dewdney) Open 9-6.30, evenings and weekends by appointment. *STOCK: Georgian and Victorian furniture.* TEL: 0306 888174/888468.

STAINES

K.W Dunster Antiques LAPADA
23 Church St. Open 9.30-5.30. CL: Thurs. SIZE: Medium. *STOCK: Clocks, furniture, general antiques, interior decor, jewellery, nautical items.* TEL: 0784 453279; home - 0784 483146. VAT: Stan/Spec.

Margaret Melville Watercolours
11 Colnebridge Close, Market Sq. Est: 1980. By appointment only. *STOCK: English watercolours, 1850-1950, £75-£10,000.* TEL: 0784 455395. SER: Valuations; commissions. FAIRS: Bellhouse, Beaconsfield, High Wycombe, Mentmore Towers. VAT: Spec.

SURBITON

House of Mallett
77 Brighton Rd. (K Mallett) Est: 1974. Open Mon., Fri. and Sat. 10-5, Sun. (trade only) 10-1. SIZE: Large. *STOCK: Mahogany furniture, general antiques and art pottery, arts and crafts.* PARK: Easy. TEL: 081 390 3796.

B.M Newlove
139-141 Ewell Rd. Est: 1958. Open 9.30-5.30. CL: Wed. SIZE: Medium and store. *STOCK: Furniture, 17th-19th C, especially early oak and Georgian mahogany, £200-£5,000; china, 18th-19th C, £75-£200; paintings, all periods, £50-£2,000; longcase clocks, Georgian barometers.* Not Stocked: Pot-lids, fairings. LOC: Down Kingston by-pass at Tolworth underpass, turn right into Tolworth Broadway, then into Ewell Rd. Shop one mile on. PARK: Easy. TEL: 081 399 8857. VAT: Stan/Spec.

Laurence Tauber Antiques
131 Ewell Rd. Open 9.30-5. CL: Wed. p.m. *STOCK: General antiques, especially for Trade.* PARK: Easy. TEL: 081 390 0020. VAT: Stan.

SUTTON

S Warrender and Co
4 and 6 Cheam Rd. (F.R Warrender) Est: 1953. Open 9-5.30. CL: Wed. SIZE: Medium. *STOCK:*

S Warrender and Co continued

Jewellery, 1790 to date, £10-£1,500; silver, 1762 to date, £10-£1,000; carriage clocks, 1860-1900, £115-£800. TEL: 081 643 4381. SER: Valuations; restorations (jewellery, silver, quality clocks). VAT: Stan.

Whittington Galleries **LAPADA**
22 Woodend. (M Wakely) Open by appointment. *STOCK: 18th-19th C English pottery and porcelain, blue and white transferware.* TEL: 081 644 9327.

THAMES DITTON

The David Curzon Gallery
1 High St. Open 10-6 (Sun. 12-4, May-Aug.). CL: Mon. SIZE: Medium. *STOCK: 18th, 19th C and modern British oil paintings and watercolours, landscape, marine, figurative, £750-£20,000; traditional contemporary works, £50-£1,500.* LOC: 5 mins. walk from station. PARK: Easy. TEL: 081 398 7860. VAT: Spec.

Fern Cottage Antique Centre
28/30 High St. Est: 1960. Open 10-5.30. SIZE: Large. 20 dealers. *STOCK: General antiques, 18th-19th C furniture, maps, prints, porcelain, silver, jewellery.* TEL: 081 398 2281.

Elizabeth Gant
52 High St. ABA. PBFA. Est: 1981. CL: Wed. SIZE: Small. *STOCK: Antiquarian, secondhand and illustrated books, especially childrens; ephemera, toys, 10p-£1,000.* PARK: Nearby. TEL: 081 398 0962; 081 398 5107. SER: Valuations; buys at auction (books). FAIRS: PBFA (London).

THORNTON HEATH

Corner Cabinet
446 Whitehorse Rd. (R Thomas) Est: 1977. Open 10-5. CL: Mon. *STOCK: General antiques and furniture.* LOC: End of Thornton Heath High St., at junction Whitehorse Rd. and Whitehorse Lane, opposite parish church. TEL: 081 684 3156.

TONGHAM, Nr. Farnham

Glover and Stacey Ltd
Grange Farm, Grange Rd. (G.A Hooke) Est: 1979. Open 9-5, Sun. 10-1. SIZE: Large. *STOCK: Architectural salvage including statues, ironwork, doors, fireplaces, panelling, staircases.* LOC: Off A31. TEL: 02518 2993/2804. SER: Restorations (architectural salvage); buys at auction. VAT: Stan/Spec.

WALLINGTON

The Attic
7 Parkgate Rd. Open 9.30-5, Sat. 9.30-1. CL: Mon. and Wed. *STOCK: General antiques, shipping goods, dolls and toys.* TEL: 081 669 9656.

Wallington continued

Manor Antiques
75A Manor Rd. (M Webb) Open 10-5. CL: Wed. *STOCK: General antiques.* TEL: 081 669 5970.

WALTON-ON-THAMES

Susan Becker **LAPADA**
P O Box 160, (S. Becker Fleming). Est: 1959. Open by appointment only. SIZE: Small. *STOCK: Porcelain, English and continental, 18th-20th C, £200-£25,000; glass and fine objects.* LOC: 10 minutes A3, M25, M4. PARK: Easy. TEL: 0932 227820; mobile - 0860 279380. SER: Valuations; buys at auction. FAIRS: Cumberland Ceramics. VAT: Stan/Spec.

Boathouse Gallery
The Towpath, Manor Rd. (B.E Clark) CL: Mon. *STOCK: Oil paintings, watercolours, engravings.* TEL: 0932 242718. SER: Picture framing, mounting and restoration. VAT: Stan.

WALTON-ON-THE-HILL AND TADWORTH

Ian Caldwell **LAPADA**
9a Tadworth Green, Dorking Rd. Resident. Est: 1978. Open 10-5.30. CL: Wed. SIZE: Medium. *STOCK: Oak, walnut and mahogany furniture especially Georgian.* LOC: 2 miles from M25, 1/4 mile from A217 on B2032 in Dorking direction. PARK: Easy. TEL: 0737 813969. SER: Valuations; restorations. VAT: Stan/Spec.

William Cooper and Son
Avondale, Dorking Rd, Tadworth. Est: 1945. Open 9-5. CL: Wed. SIZE: Small. *STOCK: Furniture, general antiques.* PARK: Easy. TEL: 073 781 3861. VAT: Stan/Spec.

Country Shop Antiques
20 Walton St. (Mrs J Allam) Est: 1972. Open 10.30-4. CL: Wed. and Sat. SIZE: Small. *STOCK: General antiques, small furniture.* PARK: Easy. TEL: 073 781 3393.

WEST BYFLEET

Academy Antiques
5 Camphill Ind. Estate. (R Donnachie) Open anytime by appointment. *STOCK: Billiard/snooker tables and accessories.* TEL: 0932 352067; fax - 0932 353904.

WESTCOTT, Nr. Dorking

Westcott Antiques
The Studio, Parsonage Lane. Est: 1968. Open 9.30-5. CL: Sun. p.m. SIZE: Large. *STOCK: Oak and walnut furniture, 1600-1800; mahogany furniture, 1700-1820.* LOC: A25. Two miles west of Dorking on road to Guildford. PARK: Easy. TEL: 0306 881900. SER: Valuations; restorations (furniture); buys at auction. VAT: Stan/Spec.

The Westcott Gallery
4 Guildford Rd. (Mr and Mrs A Wakefield) Est: 1989. Open 9-5, Sat. 10-5. SIZE: Medium. *STOCK: Oils and watercolours, 19th-20th C, from £250; contemporary paintings, from £50.* LOC: On A25, between Dorking and Guildford. PARK: Opposite. TEL: 0306 76261. SER: Valuations; restorations (oils, watercolours and frames). VAT: Stan.

WEYBRIDGE

Church House Antiques LAPADA
42 Church St. (M.I Foster) Est: 1886. Open Thurs., Fri., Sat. 10-5.30. SIZE: Medium. *STOCK: Furniture, 18th-19th C, £95-£7,000; jewellery, 18th-19th C, some modern, £30-£5,000; pictures, silver, plate, decorative items.* Not Stocked: Coins and stamps. PARK: Behind library. TEL: 0932 842190. VAT: Stan/Spec.

The Clock Shop Weybridge
64 Church St. Est: 1970. Open 9.30-6. SIZE: Medium. *STOCK: Clocks, 1685-1900, from £500; French carriage clocks, from £300.* LOC: Opposite Midland Bank on corner. PARK: Easy. TEL: 0932 840407/855503. SER: Valuations; restorations (clocks). VAT: Stan/Spec.

Weybridge continued

Edward Cross - Fine Paintings
128 Oatlands Drive. Est: 1973. Open Fri. 10-12.30 and 2-4, Sat. 10-12.30. SIZE: Medium. *STOCK: Oil paintings and watercolours, 19th-20th C, £500-£30,000.* LOC: A3050. PARK: Opposite. TEL: 0932 851093. SER: Valuations; restorations (watercolours and oil paintings); buys at auction (pictures). VAT: Spec.

Hatch Antiques LAPADA
49 Church St. (B.D Hatch) Est: 1968. Open 10-1 and 2-5.30, Sat. to 5, Wed. p.m. by appointment. CL: Mon. SIZE: Large. *STOCK: Furniture, clocks, general antiques, 17th C to Edwardian.* PARK: Easy. TEL: 0932 846782; home - 0932 849623. SER: Valuations; restorations (furniture and clocks). VAT: Stan/Spec.

Jandora
112 Oatlands Drive, Oatlands Village. (J Silverstone) Est: 1985. Open 10-1 and 2.15-5. CL: Wed. SIZE: Medium. *STOCK: China, silver, dolls, prints, collectables, furniture, curios.* PARK: Easy. TEL: 0932 851858; home - 0932 842175. FAIRS: Local and Ardingly.

Not Just Silver
16 York Rd. (Mrs S Hughes) Est: 1969. Open 9.30-5.30, Sun. by appointment. *STOCK: Silver, from Georgian, £50-£2,000; Old Sheffield plate, £60-£800; English and continental porcelain, 18th-19th C, £30-£800; objets d'art including bronze, to £1,000; furniture, paintings.* LOC: Opposite car park, just off Queens Rd. TEL: 0932 842468; home - 0932 228011. SER: Valuations; restorations (re-plating, metalwork, glass and porcelain); buys at auction (English and European silver and porcelain).

R Saunders BADA
71 Queen's Rd. (J.B Tonkinson) Est: 1878. Open 9.30-1 and 2.30-5. CL: Wed. SIZE: Medium. *STOCK: English mahogany, oak and walnut furniture, wheel and stick barometers, 1650-1830, £50-£5,000; glass, porcelain, silver, watercolours, pewter and brass.* Not Stocked: Reproductions. PARK: 150yds. in York Rd. TEL: 0932 842601. SER: Valuations; restorations (furniture). VAT: Spec.

Weybridge continued

Weybridge Antiques
43 Church St, The Quadrant. (P Pocock) Est: 1974. Open 9.30-5.30. SIZE: Large. *STOCK: Furniture, oils and watercolours.* LOC: From M25 into town, Church St. is first right. PARK: At rear. TEL: 0932 852503. SER: Valuations; restorations (oil paintings, furniture); gilding. VAT: Stan/Spec.

WINDLESHAM

Country Antiques
Country Gardens Garden Centre, London Rd. (Mrs M Usher, S Sommers, S Webber and C Martin) Est: 1990. Open 10-5, including Sun. SIZE: Large. *STOCK: Victorian and Edwardian, some Georgian, furniture, £50-£2,000; china and glass, collectables including lace and prints, pine, Victorian to 1930's, £2-£100.* LOC: A30, between Sunningdale and Bagshot; off M3, junction 3. PARK: Easy. TEL: 0344 874143. SER: Restorations.

WOKING

Bakers of Maybury Ltd
42 Arnold Rd. (K.R Baker) *STOCK: General antiques.* TEL: 0483 767425/761168.

Woking continued

Chattels
156 High St, Old Woking. (J Kendall) Open by appointment only. SIZE: Small. *STOCK: Clocks, barometers, some small furniture.* LOC: Two miles off A3 at Ripley. PARK: Own. TEL: 0483 771310. SER: Restorations (English clocks, furniture).

Manor Antiques and Restorations
2 New Shops, High St, Old Woking. (A.V Wellstead and P Thomson) Open 10-5, Sat. 10-4.30. *STOCK: General antiques, pine, china and glass.* TEL: 0483 724666. SER: Valuations; restorations (furniture); picture framing; caning and re-rushing.

The Venture
High St, Old Woking. (D Wilkins and D Law) Resident. Est: 1946. Always open. *STOCK: General antiques, pre-1920, especially pine.* TEL: 0483 772103.

Wych House Antiques LAPADA
Aberdeen House, Wych Hill. (A. and C Perry) Est: 1965. Open 9-6, Sat. 9-1. SIZE: Large and warehouses. *STOCK: Continental and English furniture, pine, decorative items, paintings, kitchenalia.* TEL: 0483 764636. VAT: Stan.

Sussex East

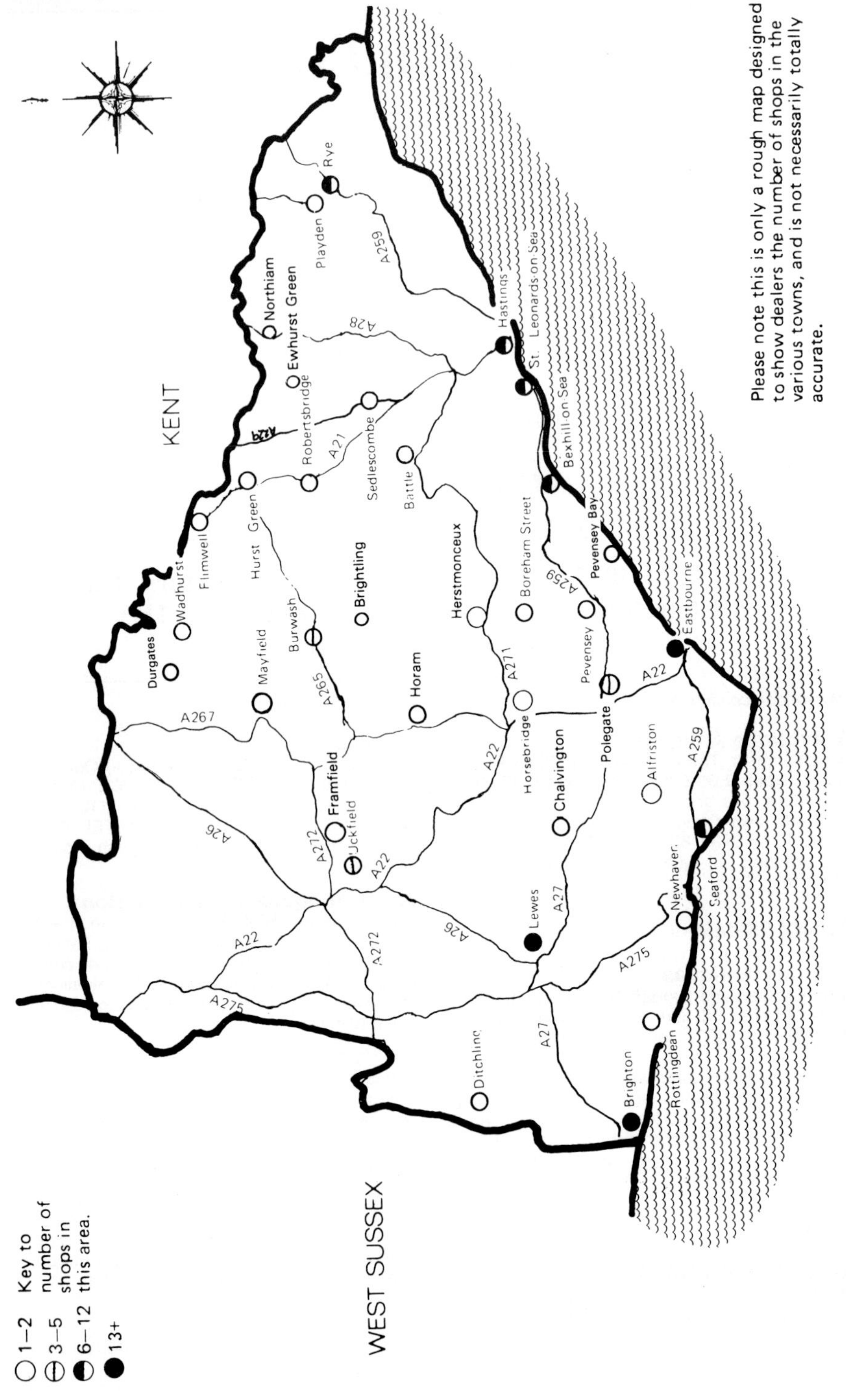

KENT
WEST SUSSEX
Rye
Playden
A259
Northiam
Ewhurst Green
A28
Hastings
St. Leonards-on-Sea
Robertsbridge
A229
A21
Sedlescombe
Battle
Bexhill-on-Sea
Flimwell
Hurst Green
Brightling
Herstmonceux
Boreham Street
Pevensey Bay
Wadhurst
Burwash
Pevensey
Eastbourne
Durgates
Mayfield
A265
Horam
A271
A22
A267
Horsebridge
Polegate
Framfield
Chalvington
Alfriston
A259
A26
A272
Uckfield
A22
Lewes
A27
Newhaven
Seaford
A22
A272
A26
A275
A275
Ditchling
A27
Rottingdean
Brighton
Key to number of shops in this area.
1–2
3–5
6–12
13+
Please note this is only a rough map designed to show dealers the number of shops in the various towns, and is not necessarily totally accurate.

ALFRISTON, Nr. Polegate

Alfriston Antiques
The Square. (J Tourell) Est: 1967. Open 10.30-1 and 2-5.30, appointment advisable during winter months. CL: Mon. and Tues. SIZE: Small. *STOCK: Collectors' items, vinaigrettes, snuff boxes, caddy spoons, silver, plate, carriage and other clocks, jewellery, paintings, pot-lids, copper, brass.* PARK: Easy. TEL: 0323 870498. VAT: Stan/Spec.

Radford Antiques
Twytton House, High St. (Mrs P.J Radford) Open 10.30-5. SIZE: Medium. *STOCK: Metalware, weapons, glass, china, jewellery, prints and maps.* PARK: Nearby. TEL: 0323 870440.

BATTLE

Magpie Antiques
38 Mount St. (C. and G Huckvale) *STOCK: General antiques, Victoriana, bric-a-brac.* TEL: 042 46 2194; home - 042 46 2341.

BEXHILL-ON-SEA

Barclay Antiques LAPADA
7 Village Mews, Little Common. (R. and M Barclay) Est: 1971. Open 10-4.30. CL: Wed.

Barclay Antiques continued

SIZE: Medium. *STOCK: Pottery and porcelain especially Worcester, Derby and Coalport, £75-£400; small furniture including desks and secretaires; watercolours and oils, £500-£2,500; all 18th-19th C; treen including Tunbridgeware, 19th C, £50-£1,800; slag glass, £10-£200.* LOC: Coast road. PARK: Easy. TEL: Home - 0797 222734. SER: Valuations; restorations (furniture and porcelain, exceptional pieces only); buys at auction (porcelain). FAIRS: Kensington; British International, Birmingham; Buxton; Snape; Brighton; Bath; Bury St. Edmunds; Olympia. VAT: Spec.

Bexhill Antique Exporters
56 Turkey Rd. (H and K Abbott) Open 8-5.30. CL: Sat. SIZE: Warehouse. *STOCK: Antique and shipping furniture.* TEL: 0424 225103/ 210182; fax - 0424 731430. SER: Container packing

IS YOUR ENTRY CORRECT?
If there is even the slightest inaccuracy in your entry, *please* let us know before 1st January 1992.
GUIDE TO THE ANTIQUE SHOPS OF BRITAIN
5 Church Street, Woodbridge, Suffolk.
Tel: (0394) 385501

Bexhill-on-Sea continued

Bexhill Antiques Centre
Quaker's Mill, Old Town. (H. and K Abbott) Est: 1972. Open 10-5.30, Sun. by appointment. LOC: A259 coast road. PARK: Opposite. TEL: 0424 210182/225103; fax - 0424 731430. Below are listed some of the dealers at this centre.

H and K Abbott
General and shipping furniture.
K Abbott
Silver and plate.
E Broad
Kitchenalia, brass.
M J Buckton
Upholstery.
P and J Gardner
Porcelain, china and smalls.
A Harmer
Kitchenalia, sporting memorabilia.
N Little
Dolls' furniture and smalls.
N Slater
General furniture.

Coppers
No. 4 Village Mews, Little Common. (Mrs E Pinner) Open 10-5. *STOCK: Maps, porcelain, glass, boxes, slopes, small furniture.*

The Gallery
18 Endwell Rd. (Mrs D Kelly) Est: 1980. Open 9-5. SIZE: Warehouse *STOCK: Furniture, porcelain, glass, from 18th C.* TEL: 0424 212127.

The Old Mint House LAPADA
45 Turkey Rd. (J.C Nicholson) Est: 1960. Open 8.30-5.30, Sat. and Sun. by appointment. SIZE: Large. *STOCK: Carved oak and mahogany, American and Australian shipping goods, 18th-19th C, £10-£1,500.* PARK: Easy. TEL: 0424 216056; 0323 762337. SER: Buys at auction; container packing. VAT: Stan.

Stewart Gallery
48 Devonshire Rd. Open 9-5.30. *STOCK: Paintings and ceramics, 19th-20th C, £5-£25,000; onyx and glassware.* TEL: 0424 223410. SER: Valuations; restorations (paintings and frames). VAT: Stan/Spec.

Village Antiques
2 and 4 Cooden Sea Rd, Little Common. (Mr and Mrs D Cowpland) Est: 1975. Open 10-5. CL: Wed. SIZE: Large. *STOCK: Furniture.* LOC: A259. TEL: 042 43 5214/042 46 2035. SER: Restorations. VAT: Stan.

BOREHAM STREET, Nr. Hailsham

Camelot Antiques
(Mrs B.C Chambers) Est: 1968. Open 10-1 and 2.15-5.30. CL: Wed. SIZE: Small. *STOCK: Porcelain and pottery, 1800-1930, £5-£300; small furniture, 19th-20th C, £25-£600; silver,*

Camelot Antiques continued

copper, brass, glass, Victorian, £5-£300. Not Stocked: Firearms, stamps, medals. PARK: Easy. TEL: 0323 833460. FAIRS: Various county.

BRIGHTLING

John Hunt Galleries
Perch Hill Farm, Willingford Lane. (J.A.E Hunt) Est: 1989. Open by appointment only. SIZE: Medium. *STOCK: Oil paintings and watercolours, 19th-20th C, £100-£5,000.* LOC: South of A265 at Burwash Weald between Burwash and Heathfield. Premises one mile along Willingford Lane. PARK: Easy. TEL: 042 482 239; home - same. VAT: Spec.

BRIGHTON

Adrian Alan Ltd LAPADA
Unit 3, The Grange Industrial Estate, Southwick. Est: 1963. Open 8.30-5.30, Sat. 9-1. SIZE: Large. *STOCK: English and continental furniture, clocks, barometers, bronzes and metalware.* TEL: 0273 870250; fax - 0273 870533. VAT: Stan/Spec.

Alexandria Antiques
3 Hanover Pl, Lewes Rd. (A.H Ahmed) Open 9.30-6, Sat. 9-12. *STOCK: Georgian and Victorian furniture; Oriental and European porcelain; oil and watercolour paintings; Oriental carpets, objets d'art.* TEL: 0273 688793.

Ashton's Antiques
1-3 Clyde Rd, Preston Circus. (R Ashton) Open 9.30-5, Wed. 9.30-1, Sat. 10-2. *STOCK: Victorian, Edwardian upholstery and pine; general trade and shipping goods.* TEL: 0273 605253. VAT: Stan/Spec.

Attic Antiques
23 Ship St. (F.B. and M.J Moorhead) Est: 1965. Open 11-1 and 2.15-5, Sat. 12-1, prior telephone call advisable. *STOCK: General antiques, 1720-1920, £15-£1,500; paintings, clocks, barometers, Oriental antiques, bronzes, English and continental china, tantalus, Victorian oil lamps, copper, brass, pewter; Imari, Canton, Satsuma and Worcester china; Georgian, Victorian, Edwardian and continental furniture.* TEL: 0273 26378. VAT: Stan. *Mainly Trade.*

H Balchin and Son
18-19 Castle St. (C.B Balchin) Resident. Est: 1930. Open 9.30-1 and 2.30-5.30. CL: Thurs. and Sat. p.m. SIZE: Large. *STOCK: General antiques, 18th-19th C.* LOC: From Western Rd., down Preston St., Castle St. is second turning on left. PARK: Loading only. SER: Valuations. VAT: Stan/Spec.

Bell-Air Antiques
18 St. Georges Rd, Kemp Town. (Mrs C Nolan) Open 9-5.30. CL: Wed. and Sat. p.m. *STOCK: General antiques.* TEL: 0273 687238.

Bexhill Antique Exporters

Offering one of the largest stocks of antique and shipping furniture in the South East. Comprehensive container service available

Bexhill Antique Centre
Quakers Mill, Old Town
Bexhill on Sea, East Sussex
Telephone: 0424 210182/225103
Fax: 0424 731430

Bexhill Antique Exporters
56 Turkey Road
Bexhill on Sea, East Sussex
Telephone: 0424 225103/210182
Fax: 0424 731430

**Open at Warehouse:
8.00 to 5.30 Mon.-Fri.
At Antique Centre:
10.00-5.00 Mon.-Sat.
By appointment on Sun.**

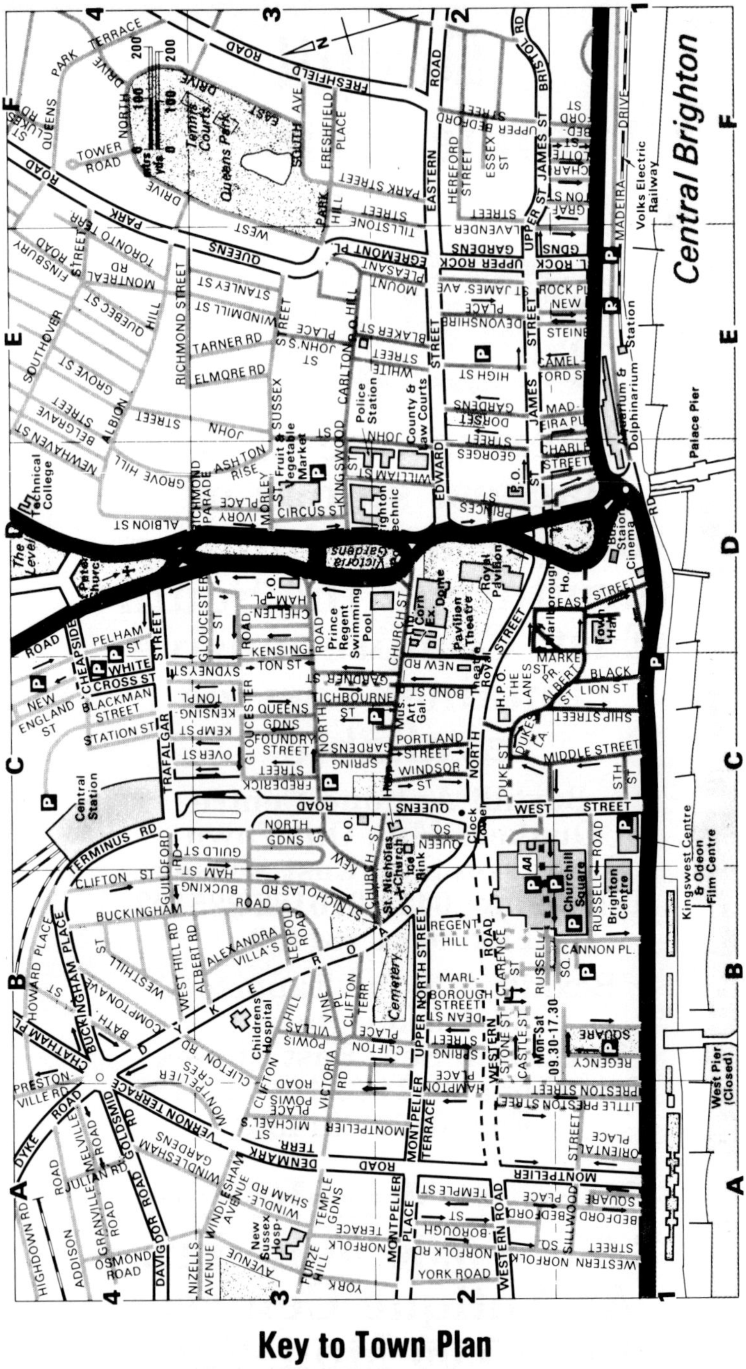
Central Brighton
Volks Electric Railway
Palace Pier
West Pier (Closed)
Kingswest Centre & Odeon Film Centre
Brighton Centre
Churchill Square
Central Station
Queens Park
Tennis Courts
Victoria Gardens
Royal Pavilion
Pavilion Theatre
Dome
Corn Ex.
Town Hall
Theatre Royal
Prince Regent Swimming Pool
Police Station
County & Law Courts
Fruit & Vegetable Market
Technical College
The Level
St Peter's Church
St. Nicholas Church
Ice Rink
Clock Tower
Cemetery
Childrens Hospital
New Sussex Hosp.
Aquarium & Dolphinarium
Mon-Sat 09.30-17.30
MADEIRA DRIVE
WESTERN ROAD
NORTH STREET
QUEENS ROAD
WEST STREET
DYKE ROAD
EDWARD STREET
EASTERN ROAD
MONTPELIER ROAD
TRAFALGAR STREET
RICHMOND STREET
TERMINUS RD
KINGSWAY

Key to Town Plan

AA Recommended roads
Other roads
Restricted roads
Buildings of interest
Car Parks
Parks and open spaces
AA Service Centre

Brighton continued

Brighton Antique Wholesalers
39 Upper Gardner St. SIZE: Several dealers. *STOCK: 18th-19th C furniture, £50-£5,000.* LOC: Off North Rd. PARK: Easy. TEL: 0273 695457.

Brighton Antiques Gallery
41 Meeting House Lane. Est: 1975. Open 10-5.30. SIZE: 22 stalls. *STOCK: Antiques including Georgian and Victorian silver, porcelain, paintings, glass, jewellery, copper and brass, small furniture, unusual collectors' items, coins, ephemera.* TEL: 0273 26693/21059. VAT: Stan/Spec.

Brighton Architectural Salvage
33-34 Gloucester Rd. (L F Moore) Open 9.30-5, Sat. 10-4.30. *STOCK: Restored architectural items including pine furniture; fireplaces and surrounds - marble, pine, mahogany, cast-iron Victorian tiled and cast inserts and over-mantels; doors, stained glass, panelling; cast-iron balcony and street railings, spiral staircases; stonework, lamp posts and light fittings; garden seats and ornaments.* TEL: 0273 681656.

Bryde & Co
53 Meeting House Lane. Est: 1934. *STOCK: Gold, diamonds, Victorian jewellery, silver, watches, objets de vertu, general antiques.* TEL: 0273 27973. VAT: Stan.

P Carmichael **LAPADA**
33 Upper North St. (H Mileham) Est: 1946. Open 9.30-5.30. CL: Sat. p.m. *STOCK: Furniture, 18th-19th C.* TEL: 0273 28072. VAT: Stan/Spec.

Sheila Cashin Gallery
40 Upper North St. Est: 1982. Open 10-5, Sat. 10-1. SIZE: Small. *STOCK: Restored bamboo furniture, especially lacquer tables, £50-£1,000; painted and decorative furniture; tapestry pictures, decorative items, especially mirrors, £10-£500.* PARK: Meters nearby. TEL: 0273 26619; home - same.

Circus Antiques
2B Clyde Rd, Preston Circus. (Mrs A Jones) Est: 1990. Open 9.30-5, Sat. 10-4. CL: Wed. SIZE: Small. *STOCK: Porcelain and glass, English and continental, mainly 18th-19th C, some 20th C Doulton, £100-£1,000; decorative furniture, sofas and chairs, mainly 19th C to early 20th C, £300-£1,500; lamps and pictures, 19th C, £50-£500.* LOC: A23 just past Preston Park on one-way system. PARK: London Rd. TEL: 0273 696553; home - 0403 211121. SER: Valuations; buys at auction (porcelain and furniture). FAIRS: Wakefield Ceramic; Weybridge, Cheltenham, Felbridge, Wilton, Wakefield, Cranleigh and various Sun. VAT: Stan/Spec.

Connoisseur Antique Gallery
113 Church Rd, Hove. *STOCK: General antiques.* TEL: 0273 777398.

Brighton continued

Christopher G Cowen Antiques **LAPADA**
60 Middle St. (C. and S Cowen) Open 9.30-5.30, Sat. 10-4. SIZE: Medium. *STOCK: Edwardian, Victorian and Georgian furniture, decorative and Oriental items.* LOC: 2 mins. walk from seafront. PARK: Nearby. TEL: 0273 205757; home - same. SER: Valuations; restorations (furniture); buys at auction. FAIRS: Brighton; Ardingly; Bath. VAT: Stan/Spec.

Graham Deane Antiques **LAPADA**
39 Upper North St. Open by appointment. *STOCK: Furniture, china, brass, general antiques.* TEL: 0273 207207.

Graham Deane Antiques **LAPADA**
18/19 Marlborough St. Open 9.30-5.30, Sat. 10-1. *STOCK: Furniture, china, brass, general antiques.* TEL: 0273 207207.

Harry Diamond and Son
9 Union St, The Lanes. (R. and H Diamond) Est: 1937. Open 9-5. *STOCK: Diamond jewellery, antique silver and 19th C French clocks, £50-£20,000.* Not Stocked: Coins, furniture. TEL: 0273 29696. VAT: Stan.

James Doyle Antiques
10 Union St, The Lanes. (J.R Doyle) Est: 1975. Open 9.30-6. *STOCK: Jewellery, silver.* TEL: 0273 23694; fax - 0273 24330.

D.H Edmonds Ltd
27 and 28 Meeting House Lane, The Lanes. Est: 1965. Open 10-5.30. SIZE: Large. *STOCK: Jewellery, silver, objets d'art, watches, £50-£20,000.* TEL: 0273 27713/28871. VAT: Stan.

Alan Fitchett Antiques
5-5A Upper Gardner St. Est: 1969. Open 9-5.30. CL: Sat. SIZE: Large. *STOCK: Furniture, 18th-20th C, £50-£10,000; silver plate and works of art.* LOC: Near station. PARK: Easy. TEL: 0273 600894. SER: Valuations; restorations. VAT: Stan.

Paul Goble
44 Meeting House Lane, The Lanes. Est: 1965. Open 9-5.30, Sun. 10-5.30 or by appointment. *STOCK: Jewellery, watches, silver, pictures and prints, teddy bears and dolls.* TEL: 0273 202801; fax - 0273 202736. SER: Export. VAT: Stan.

The Gold and Silversmiths of Hove
3 Planet House1 The Drive, Hove. Est: 1910. Open 9-5.30. CL: Mon. *STOCK: Jewellery and silver.* TEL: 0273 738489.

Brighton continued

Robert Hale Antiques
217 Preston Rd. (R.N Hale) Est: 1976. Open 10-1 and 2-5.30, Sat. 10-1. SIZE: Large. *STOCK: Furniture and objects, town and country, period and decorative, English and continental in chestnut, walnut, fruitwood, rosewood and mahogany, 17th-19th C, £100-£5,000.* LOC: Main London Rd., opposite Preston Manor. PARK: Nearby. TEL: 0273 559221; workshop - 0273 566479; home - 0273 478423. SER: Valuations; restorations (furniture); buys at auction. VAT: Stan/Spec.

Douglas Hall Ltd
23 Meeting House Lane. (A.M Longthorne) Est: 1968. Open 9.30-5. *STOCK: Silver, jewellery.* TEL: 0273 25323. VAT: Stan.

Hallmarks
4 Union St, The Lanes. (J Hersheson) Est: 1966. Open 9-5. SIZE: Small. *STOCK: Silver and plate, jewellery and clocks.* PARK: Meters. TEL: 0273 725477. VAT: Stan/Spec.

Simon Hatchwell Antiques LAPADA
94 Gloucester Rd. Est: 1961. CL: Sat. SIZE: Large. *STOCK: English and European antiques, paintings, chandeliers, bronzes, carpets, clocks, barometers, grandfather clocks, all 17th-20th C.* Not Stocked: Jewellery. PARK: Own. TEL: 0273 691164. SER: Restorations (barometers and furniture); re-gilding. VAT: Stan/Spec.

David Hawkins (Brighton) Ltd LAPADA
15B Prince Albert St, The Lanes. Est: 1958. Open 9-5. SIZE: Large. *STOCK: General antiques, fine art, silver and Sheffield plate, decorative and collectors' items, arms and armour, £10-£7,500.* LOC: Large detached building at south entrance of The Lanes. TEL: 0273 21357. VAT: Stan/Spec.

Holleyman and Treacher Ltd
21a and 22 Duke St. Est: 1937. Open 9-5. *STOCK: Books including antiquarian, music.* TEL: 0273 28007.

The House of Antiques LAPADA
17 Prince Albert St. (A Margiotta) Open 10-5.30. *STOCK: Jewellery and silver.* TEL: 0273 27680/24961. VAT: Stan.

Dudley Hume
46 Upper North St. Est: 1973. CL: Sat. and Sun. except by appointment. SIZE: Medium. *STOCK: Period and Victorian furniture, metal, light fittings.* LOC: Parallel to the Western Rd., one block to the north. TEL: 0273 23461. VAT: Stan/Spec.

Hyndford Antiques
143 Edward St. (Mrs M.C Skelson) Est: 1968. Open 10.30-4.30 or by appointment. CL: Mon. and Tues. SIZE: Small. *STOCK: Small collectables especially Oriental carvings,*

Hyndford Antiques continued

bygones and china, £1-£150; prints, ephemera, postcards, 50p-£60; all 19th-20th C. LOC: Edward St. east at right angles to Brighton Pavilion. PARK: Meters, near shop. TEL: 0273 679936/602220. FAIRS: Ardingly and Brighton Centre.

Jubilee Antique Cellars and Collectors Market
Gardner St, (Sherman and Waterman Assoc. Ltd.). Open 9-5. SIZE: 25 units. *STOCK: General antiques.* TEL: 0273 600574/071 836 3186/2136.

Kingsbury Antiques
Hallmarks, 4 Union St. (J.J Hersheson) Est: 1966. Open 9-5. *STOCK: Old Sheffield plate, silver, jewellery, glass; clocks.* TEL: 0273 725477. VAT: Stan/Spec.

Kollect-o-Mania
25 Trafalgar St. Open 10-5. SIZE: 10 dealers. *STOCK: A wide range of general antiques, records, books, dolls' houses, miniature furniture, toys, collectables.* LOC: Near station. TEL: 0273 694229.

Le Jazz Hot
14 Prince Albert St. (A Davis and D Herbert) Est: 1988. Open 10.30-5.30, Sun. by appointment. SIZE: Large. *STOCK: Art deco and art nouveau including mirrors, lamps, figures, china, glass, bakelite, costume jewellery, furniture and fittings, £50-£1,000.* LOC: Adjacent to Lanes. PARK: Easy. TEL: 0273 206091; home - 0273 676709. SER: Valuations. VAT: Stan/Spec.

Leoframes
70 North Rd. (H. and Mrs A Schofield and S Round) Open 9-5.30. *STOCK: Prints.* TEL: 0273 695862. SER: Restorations; framing.

The Leopard
35 Kensington Gdns. (A. and A Leppard) Est: 1973. Open 9-4, Wed. 9-1, Sat. 9-5. SIZE: Medium. *STOCK: Costume, 19th C, £50-£200; lace, table and bed linen, 19th-20th C, £5-£50; period clothing, early 20th C, £5-£100.* LOC: Pedestrian street at bottom of Gloucester Rd. PARK: Easy. TEL: 0273 695427; home - 0273 507619.

Harry Mason LAPADA
21A Prince Albert St. Est: 1954. Open 9.30-5.15, Sat. 10-2, Sun. by appointment. SIZE: Large. *STOCK: Silver and plate, 18th-20th C; jewellery, 19th-20th C.* LOC: Adjacent to The Lanes. PARK: Nearby. TEL: 0273 29540/735750. SER: Valuations; restorations (silver and jewellery); buys at auction (as stock); buyers of scrap silver and gold. FAIRS: Sunday London Hotel. VAT: Stan/Spec.

H Miller (Antiques) Ltd
22a Ship St. Est: 1947. Open 10-5, Sat. 9-1. *STOCK: Silver, jewellery, Sheffield silver, plate.* TEL: 0273 26255. VAT: Stan/Spec.

Brighton continued

Patrick Moorhead Antiques
22 and 59A Ship St. Open 10-5, Sat. 11-4.30 or by appointment. *STOCK: General antiques, paintings, furniture, marbles, bronzes; porcelain, English, Continental and especially Oriental, 18th-19th C.* TEL: 0273 26062.

Michael Norman Antiques
17/18 Bond St. (M.P Keehan) Open 9-5.30. CL: Sat. SIZE: Large. *STOCK: Furniture, 19th C.* TEL: 0273 697716; fax - 0273 206556.

Michael Norman Antiques Ltd BADA

15 Ship St. Est: 1965. Open 9-5.30. *STOCK: English furniture.* TEL: 0273 29253/4 or 26712; fax - 0273 206556. VAT: Stan/Spec.

Oasis Antiques
39 Kensington Gdns. (I. and A Stevenson) Est: 1970. Open 10-5, Mon. 11-5, Sat. 8-5. SIZE: Medium. *STOCK: Lighting and furniture, to 1930, £1-£5,000; European and Oriental items including bronzes, art glass, period clothes, linen and lace, gramophones, art nouveau, art deco.* LOC: Off North Road from railway station, centre of north Lanes. PARK: Nearby. TEL: 0273 683885. SER: Restorations (furniture, metals and ceramics); polishing.

Brian Page Antiques
8 Foundry St. Open by appointment only. *STOCK: English and continental decorative arts; art nouveau, arts and crafts furniture, 1870-1940; Japanese items including screens, antiques, prints, books and furniture.* TEL: 0273 609310; fax - 0273 620055.

Colin Page Antiquarian Books
36 Duke St. (C.G Page) Est: 1971. Open 10-5.30. *STOCK: Antiquarian and secondhand books, especially British topography, travel, natural history, illustrated and bindings, 16th-20th C, £1-£5,000.* LOC: Town centre. PARK: Meters or nearby. TEL: 0273 25954; fax - 0273 746246.

Dermot and Jill Palmer Antiques
7 and 8 Union St, The Lanes. Resident. Est: 1963. Open 9-6, Sun. by appointment. *STOCK: French and English furniture, textiles, architectural and garden objects, screens, mirrors, pictures, £50-£5,000.* TEL: 0273 28669. FAIRS: Olympia. VAT: Stan/Spec.

Parsons & Edwards
34A Providence Place. (P Parsons and K Edwards) Est: 1973. Open 7.30-6. CL: Sat. p.m. SIZE: Medium. *STOCK: Victorian and Edwardian furniture especially chests of drawers, £100-£1,000; reproductions.* LOC: 1/4 mile south of Preston Circus. Turn right up York Hill. PARK: Easy. TEL: 0273 621001. SER: Restorations (furniture). VAT: Stan.

Brighton continued

Sue Pearson
13 1/2 Prince Albert St. Open 10-4. SIZE: Small. *STOCK: Antique dolls, teddy bears, dolls' house miniatures.* LOC: Lanes area. PARK: Meters or N.C.P. TEL: 0273 29247. SER: Valuations; restorations; buys at auction (dolls and bears). FAIRS: Major London Doll. VAT: Stan/Spec.

Ben Ponting Antiques
53 Upper North St. Open 9.30-5.30, Sat. 10-1. *STOCK: Furniture, 18th-19th C.* TEL: 0273 29409.

Prinny's Antique Gallery
3 Meeting House Lane, The Lanes. Open 9.30-5. SIZE: 26 stands. *STOCK: General antiques, porcelain, jewellery, books, toy soldiers.* TEL: 0273 204554. SER: Restorations (watches and clocks).

Pyramid
9a Kensington Gdns. (C Slater) Est: 1984. Open 10-5, Sat. 9-5.30. SIZE: Medium. *STOCK: Art deco and 20th C collectors items; china and glass, £10-£600; furniture and furnishings, £50-£1,500; lighting and pictures, £15-£200.* LOC: Between Gloucester and North roads. PARK: Gloucester Rd., Sydney or Tidy St. TEL: 0273 607791. SER: Valuations; restoration (china).

Recollections
1a Sydney St. (B Bagley and P Tooley) Est: 1973. Open 10.30-4.30, Sat. 10.30-5.30. SIZE: Small. *STOCK: Small collectable items, 19th-20th C, £5-£250; brass and copper especially fireplace furniture; Victorian oil lamps.* LOC: From railway station down Trafalgar St. last turning on right. PARK: Opposite in Belmont St. TEL: 0273 681517. SER: Valuations; restorations (metal, china, oil lamps).

Resners' BADA LAPADA
1 Meeting House Lane. (S. and G.R Resner) Est: 1918. Open 9.50-5.30. SIZE: Small. *STOCK: Jewellery, £250-£5,000; objets d'art, £250-£1,000; silver, £150-£2,500; all 18th-19th C.* LOC: The Lanes. PARK: Nearby. TEL: 0273 29127. SER: Valuations; restorations (jewellery). FAIRS: Jewellery, Dorchester; Kensington, Chelsea, British International, Birmingham; Buxton, Kenilworth, Barbican, Harrogate, Inhorgenta, Munich. VAT: Stan/Spec.

Retro
52 George St. (F Vincent) Est: 1982. Open 10.30-5.30. SIZE: Small. *STOCK: Small Victorian tea sets, £5-£100; Victorian writing slopes, £50-£100; clocks, art deco items, to 1930's, £500-£1,000; some furniture.* LOC: Near American Express headquarters. PARK: Easy. TEL: 0273 603809. SER: Restorations (woodwork and ceramics). FAIRS: Ardingly. VAT: Stan.

Brighton continued

Robinson's Bookshop Ltd

11 Bond St. (Mrs S Robinson, T.P. and P.M Brown) Est: 1958. Open 9-5.30. *STOCK: Books on antiques and art; general and technical books.* LOC: North Lanes area. TEL: 0273 29012.

Rodney Arthur Classics

Rear of 64-78 Davigdor Rd, Hove. (R.A Oliver) Est: 1979. Open 8.15-12.15 or by appointment. SIZE: Medium. *STOCK: Furniture, mainly Victorian and Edwardian shipping, £35-£850.* LOC: From Seven Dials, Davigdor Rd. is the exit to the west. PARK: Easy. TEL: 0273 26550. VAT: Stan. *Trade Only.*

Clive Rogers Oriental Rugs

22 Brunswick Rd, Hove. Est: 1974. Open by appointment. SIZE: Medium. *STOCK: Oriental rugs, carpets, textiles; Oriental and Islamic works of art.* LOC: Off Western Rd. PARK: Easy. TEL: 0273 738257; home - same; fax - 0273 738687. SER: Valuations; restorations (as stock); historical analysis commission agents; buys at auction. VAT: Stan/Spec.

Rutland Antiques

48 Upper North St. Open 10.30-5.30, Sun. by appointment. SIZE: Small. *STOCK: Furniture, porcelain, textiles and general antiques.* LOC: North of and parallel to Western Rd. PARK: Reasonable. TEL: 0273 29991.

'The Sentry Box'

Prinny's Antiques Gallery, 3 Meeting House Lane, The Lanes. (G Weiner) Est: 1962. Open 10-4.30, Sun. by appointment. SIZE: Small. *STOCK: Orders, decorations, badges and insignia of Imperial Germany and Austrian states; pikelhaubes and head-dress; Third Reich orders, decorations, badges and weapons; firearms and edged weapons; Imperial and Nazi German head-dress and accoutrements; British Victorian and French Napoleonic militaria including medals and badges; classic automobilia, all £5-£2,000.* TEL: 0273 204554/601960. SER: Valuations; restorations (edged weapons); buys at auction (militaria); mail order catalogues available 50p (U.K.), £1 (overseas) subscription on request. FAIRS: London Arms, London West Hotel; Bedford Arms; Nottingham Arms.

Shelton Arts

4 Islingword Rd. (G.S Hodgkison) Est: 1952. Open 9-6. *STOCK: Antiquarian prints, pictures.* PARK: Easy. TEL: 0273 698345. SER: Framing; mount cutting; dry mounting, head laminations; restorations (fine art).

Shop of the Yellow Frog

10/11 The Lanes. (J.N Chalcraft) Est: 1946. Open 9-6, and Sun. during season. SIZE: Small. *STOCK: 19th C jewellery, from £10; 18th-19th C silver, 18th C porcelain, both £5-£500.* Not Stocked: Large furniture. LOC: Near Brighton

Shop of the Yellow Frog continued

Pavilion. TEL: 0273 25497. SER: Valuations; restorations (watches, jewellery, furniture); buys at auction.

S. and L Simmons LAPADA

9 Meeting House Lane, The Lanes. (L.M. and S.L Simmons) NAG. Est: 1948. Open 9.30-5.30. *STOCK: Jewellery and silver, 19th C.* TEL: 0273 27949. VAT: Stan.

Raymond J Smith (Antiques)

50 Upper North St. Open 10-5.30, Sat. 10-2. *STOCK: Furniture and decorative items, 18th-19th C.* TEL: 0273 204958/721936.

The Sussex Commemorative Ware Centre

88 Western Rd, Hove. (R Prior) Est: 1974. Open 9-12, Sat. 9-12 and 2-3.30, other times by appointment. *STOCK: Antique and modern Royal commemoratives including Doulton and limited editions; Parian.* TEL: 0273 773911. SER: Catalogues.

Tapsell Antiques LAPADA

10 Ship St. Gdns, Coachhouse, 59 and 59a Middle St. Est: 1948. Open 9-5.30, other times by appointment. SIZE: Large. *STOCK: Oriental and continental porcelain, English and continental furniture, clocks, bronzes, general antiques.* TEL: 0273 28341. VAT: Stan/Spec.

Michael Tidey Antiques

87 St. Georges Rd, Kemptown. Resident. *STOCK: English furniture.* TEL: 0273 602389.

Graham Webb

59 Ship St. Est: 1961. Open 10-5. CL: Mon. SIZE: Small. *STOCK: Cylinder and disc musical boxes, all mechanical musical instruments, £150-£8,000.* LOC: Close to the Lanes. PARK: Middle St. TEL: 0273 21803; home - 0273 772154. VAT: Stan/Spec.

Stephen and Sonia Welbourne

43 Denmark Villas, Hove. Open by appointment *STOCK: Watercolours and oil paintings, mainly English, some continental, 19th and early 20th C* LOC: Near Hove station. TEL: 0273 722518. VAT Spec.

E. and B White

43-47 Upper North St, and warehouse at 3[illegible] Robertson Rd. Est: 1962. Open 9.30-5. CL: Sat p.m. SIZE: Medium. *STOCK: Oak furniture, £50 £2,000.* LOC: Upper North St. runs parallel to and north of Western Rd. (the main shopping street). TEL: 0273 28706. VAT: Spec.

David Wigdor

30 Trafalgar St. Est: 1968. Open 10-1 and 2-5 Sat. and Sun. by appointment. *STOCK: General antiques.* TEL: 0273 677272. VAT: Stan/Spec.

Brighton continued

The Witch Ball

48 Meeting House Lane. (Mrs G Daniels and Miss G Glassman) Est: 1966. Open 10.30-6. *STOCK: 18th-19th C cartoons and prints; 16th-19th C maps.* TEL: 0273 26618. VAT: Stan.

L Woolman Antiques

29 Gloucester Rd, North Lanes. Est: 1973. Open 9-5, Sat. 8 a.m.-10 a.m.. SIZE: Medium. *STOCK: Continental, Oriental and English porcelain, bronzes, clocks, paintings and decorative furniture, 18th-19th C, £25-£5,000.* LOC: Near station. PARK: Easy. TEL: 0273 609645; home - 0273 779866. SER: Valuations; buys at auction (clocks and watches). VAT: Stan. *Trade Only.*

Yellow Lantern Antiques Ltd LAPADA

34 Holland Rd, Hove. (B.R. and E.A Higgins) Est: 1950. Open 9-1 and 2.15-5.30, Sat. 9-4. SIZE: Medium. *STOCK: Mainly English furniture, £50-£3,000; French and English clocks; both to 1850; bronzes, 19th C, £100-£1,500; continental porcelain, 1820-60, £50-£1,000.* Not Stocked: Pottery, oak, 18th C porcelain. LOC: From Brighton seafront to Hove, turn right at Hotel Alexander, shop 100yds. on left past traffic lights (opposite Maples furnishing store.). PARK: Easy. TEL: 0273 771572; home - 0273 455476. SER: Valuations; restorations; buys at auction. FAIRS: Buxton; Harrogate; Guildford; Kensington; City of London. VAT: Spec.

Zebrak at Barnes Jewellers

24 Meeting House Lane, The Lanes. (T. and A Zebrak) Est: 1978. Open daily, Sat. and Sun. by appointment. SIZE: Small. *STOCK: Jewellery, £5-£50,000; watches, silver and objets d'art, 1800-1950, £5-£50,000.* PARK: Nearby. TEL: 0273 202929; fax - 0273 21021; home - 0273 722140. SER: Valuations; restorations; buys at auction. FAIRS: Olympia. VAT: Stan/Spec.

BURWASH, Nr. Etchingham

Chateaubriand Antiques Centre

High St. Open 10-5, Sun. 2-5. SIZE: 15 dealers. *STOCK: Lace, linen, furniture, country oak, glass, bronzes, paintings, smalls.* LOC: A265. TEL: 0435 882535. SER: Shipping.

Chaunt House

High St. (M Walsh) Est: 1976. CL: Mon. SIZE: Small. *STOCK: Clocks, 19th C, £50-£1,000; watches and barometers.* LOC: A265. PARK: Easy. TEL: 0435 882221; home - same. SER: Valuations; restorations; buys at auction (as stock). VAT: Stan/Spec.

Lime Tree Antiques

High St. (S. and A Vickery) Est: 1967. Open 9-6, usually open Sun. but appointment advisable. SIZE: Medium. *STOCK: Old oak, silver, clocks, glass, porcelain, firearms, rugs, antiquarian books, prints, oils and watercolours, £5-£5,000.*

Lime Tree Antiques continued

PARK: Easy. TEL: 0435 882385. SER: Restorations (paintings, prints and furniture). VAT: Stan/Spec.

Popes Cottage Antiques

High St. (Mr and Mrs T.B Thornhill) Open 10-5 including Sun. SIZE: Small. *STOCK: Furniture, Victorian and Edwardian, £50-£500; porcelain, plates and coffee cans, Victorian and Edwardian, £25-£400; small silver and jewellery, £25-£400.* Not Stocked: Postcards, stamps and large furniture. LOC: A265 Hurst Green, Heathfield Rd., near Batemans N.T. PARK: Easy. TEL: 0435 882906; home - same.

CHALVINGTON

Steve Powell Antiques

Chalvington House. Open by appointment. *STOCK: English and continental furniture, metalware and decorative items.* TEL: 032 183 334.

DITCHLING

Dycheling Antiques

34 High St. (E.A Hudson) Est: 1977. Open 10.30-6. SIZE: Large. *STOCK: Georgian, Victorian, Edwardian and country furniture, especially dining chairs, £25-£4,000.* LOC: Off A23, at Kings Head on B2116. PARK: Easy. TEL: 07918 2929; home - same. VAT: Stan/Spec.

Nona Shaw Antiques

4 and 8 West St. Est: 1954. SIZE: Medium. *STOCK: Porcelain, furniture, silver, copper and brass.* TEL: 07918 3290. VAT: Stan/Spec.

DURGATES, Nr. Wadhurst

Park View Antiques

High St. (B Ross) Est: 1985. Open 10-5, Sat. 10-5.30, Wed. and Sun. by appointment. SIZE: Small. *STOCK: Pine, oak and country furniture, 18th-19th C, £100-£500; decorative items, 1930's, £25-£150; iron and metalware, 17th-19th C, £25-£250.* LOC: On B2099 Frant-Hurst Green road. PARK: Easy. TEL: 089 288 3630; home - 0892 740264. SER: Valuations; restorations (furniture).

EASTBOURNE

Anglo Am Warehouse

2a Beach Rd. (L Williams and H Hoevelmann) Est: 1976. Open 9.30-5, Sat. and Sun. by appointment. SIZE: Large. *STOCK: Shipping furniture, 1850-1920, £50-£2,000; period furniture, pre 1850, £500+; general antiques.* LOC: Off Seaside Rd. PARK: Easy. TEL: 0323 648661; 0892 36627; 043 53 2126; fax - 0323 648658. SER: Restorations. VAT: Stan. *Trade Only.*

Eastbourne continued

Antique Market

Leaf Hall, Seaside. (R Evenden) Open Tues. and Sat. 9-5. SIZE: 16 stallholders. *STOCK: General antiques.* TEL: 0323 27530.

Douglas Barsley Antiques LAPADA

44 Cornfield Rd. Est: 1966. Open 10-1 and 2-5, Sat. 10-12.30. *STOCK: Small collectors' items, silver, porcelain, small fine furniture.* TEL: 0323 33666.

Douglas Barsley Antiques LAPADA

214-216 Seaside. Est: 1966. Open 9-5, Sat. 9-1. *STOCK: General antiques and shipping furniture.* TEL: 0323 26834.

Bell Antiques

47 South St. (Mrs M.J Everett) Open 10-1 and 2-4, Wed. and Sat. 10-12. SIZE: Small. *STOCK: Porcelain and small bijou items, 18th-19th C, £5-£150; furniture, Victorian and Edwardian, £40-£200; paintings and prints, to 1930, £8-£100.* LOC: Road opposite Town Hall. PARK: Easy. TEL: 0323 641339. SER: Valuations.

Wm Bruford and Son Ltd BADA

11/13 Cornfield Rd. Est: 1883. Open 9-1 and 2-5.30. SIZE: Medium. *STOCK: Jewellery, Victorian, late Georgian; some silver, clocks (bracket, carriage), watches, from 1750, £50-£1,000.* Not Stocked: China, glass, brass, pewter, furniture. TEL: 0323 25452. SER: Valuations; restorations (clocks and silver). VAT: Stan/Spec.

Bygones

24 Willingdon Rd, Old Town. (J.A Gearing) Est: 1986. Open 10.30-5. CL: Fri. and Wed. SIZE: Medium. *STOCK: Costume and accessories, 1900-early 1950's, £5-£150.* LOC: At the end of A22. PARK: Nearby. TEL: 0323 37537; home - 0323 39199. SER: Valuations.

Camilla's Bookshop

57 Grove Rd. (C Francombe and S Broad) Est: 1976. Open 10-6. *STOCK: Books, including antiquarian and on art, antiques and collectables, and especially naval, military, aviation, technical, needlework, broadcasting.* LOC: Next to police station. TEL: 0323 36001. SER: Valuations.

John Cowderoy Antiques LAPADA

42 South St. (J.H., R., D.J. and R.A Cowderoy) GMC. Est: 1972. Open 9.30-1 and 2.30-5. CL: Wed. p.m. and Sat. p.m. SIZE: Large. *STOCK: Clocks, musical boxes, furniture, porcelain, silver and plate, jewellery, copper, brass, paintings.* LOC: 150yds. from Town Hall. PARK: Easy. TEL: 0323 20058. SER: Restorations (clocks, music boxes and furniture). VAT: Stan/Spec.

Crest Antiques

52 Grove Rd. (C Powell) Open 10-6. *STOCK: General antiques and collectables.* TEL: 0323 21185.

Eastbourne continued

John Day of Eastbourne Fine Art

9 Meads St. Est: 1964. Open 9.30-1 and 2-5. CL: Wed. and Sat. p.m. SIZE: Medium. *STOCK: East Anglian paintings, watercolours, English and continental paintings, all 19th C.* LOC: Meads village, west end of Eastbourne. PARK: Easy. TEL: 0323 25634. SER: Restorations; framing (oils and watercolours).

Roderick Dew

10 Furness Rd. Est: 1971. *STOCK: Antiquarian books, especially on art and antiques.* TEL: 0323 20239. *Postal Only.*

Eastbourne Antiques Market

80 Seaside. (C French) Est: 1969. Open 10-5.30. SIZE: Large. 42 stalls. *STOCK: A wide selection of general antiques.* PARK: Easy. TEL: 0323 20128. FAIRS: Eastbourne and others. VAT: Stan.

Elliott and Scholz Antiques

12 Willingdon Rd. (C.R Elliott and K.V Scholz) Est: 1981. Open 9.30-5, Wed. and Sat. 9.30-2. SIZE: Small. *STOCK: Small furniture, £500-£1,000; clocks, £100-£300; bric-a-brac, £50-£100, all 19th-20 C.* LOC: A22. PARK: Easy. TEL: 0323 32200; home - 0323 639063. SER: Valuations.

Fountain Antiques

124 Pevensey Rd. (C.F Wilson and A.M Parks) Est: 1990. Open 10-1 and 2-5, Sat. 10-1, Sun. and other times by appointment. SIZE: Large. *STOCK: Formal, decorative, country and oak furniture, 17th-20th C, £50-£10,000; jewellery, £20-£1,000; garden furniture and stoneware, period and reproduction, £50-£2,000; period accessories, £20-£1,000.* LOC: Behind seafront, just east of pier. PARK: Easy. TEL: 0323 35010. SER: Valuations; restoration; shipping.

London and Sussex Antiquarian Book and Print Services

Open by appointment. *STOCK: Books, including colour plate, prints and literature, 19th-20th C.* TEL: 0323 30857.

James Ludby Antiques

25 Ocklynge Rd. (G Ludby) Est: 1967. Open daily, Wed. p.m., Sat. p.m., lunchtimes and Sun. by appointment. SIZE: Small. *STOCK: Furniture, small items, china, glass and brass, unusual interesting items, 18th C to 1930, £5-£500.* LOC: In 'Old Town'. PARK: Easy. TEL: 0323 32073. SER: Valuations. FAIRS: Brighton.

Jonathan Owen

42 Cornfield Rd. Open 10-5. *STOCK: Jewellery.* TEL: 0323 649170.

Timothy Partridge Antiques

46 Ocklynge Rd. Open 10-5, Sat. 10-1. *STOCK: General antiques.* LOC: In old town, near St. Mary's Church. PARK: Easy. TEL: 0323 638731.

Eastbourne continued

Pharoahs Antiques Centre
28 South St. (W. and J Pharoah) Est: 1973. Open 10-5. SIZE: Medium. 14 stallholders. *STOCK: A wide range of antiques including jewellery, pine, kitchenalia, china, curios, lace, linen, books, ephemera, Victorian furniture, original light fittings and lamps.* LOC: Near Town Hall. PARK: Easy. TEL: 0323 38655. FAIRS: Ardingly.

Ernest Pickering
44 South St. Est: 1946. Open 9-5. CL: Wed. p.m. and Sat. p.m. *STOCK: Furniture, porcelain, grandfather clocks.* TEL: 0323 30483. VAT: Stan/Spec.

Premier Gallery
26 South St. (D Mazzoli) Est: 1983. Open 10-5.30, Sun. by appointment. SIZE: Large. *STOCK: Oil paintings, £200-£2,000; watercolours, £150-£1,500; both 19th-20th C.* LOC: Near station. PARK: Easy. TEL: 0323 36023. SER: Valuations; restorations (oil paintings and watercolours); buys at auction (modern British paintings). VAT: Stan.

Raymond Smith
30 South St. (J.R. and T Smith) Resident. Est: 1963. Open 9-5.30. CL: Wed. SIZE: Large. *STOCK: Secondhand and antiquarian books, 16th-20th C, 5p-£1,000; publishers' remainders, 75p-£30; maps and prints, 17th-20th C, 50p-£350.* LOC: 200yds. east of Town Hall. PARK: Easy. TEL: 0323 34128. SER: Valuations. VAT: Stan.

E Stacy-Marks Ltd **BADA**
24 Cornfield Rd. Est: 1889. SIZE: Large. *STOCK: Paintings, English, Dutch and continental schools, 18th-20th C.* TEL: 0323 20429/32653. VAT: Stan.

Stewart Gallery
25 Grove Rd, (Gallery Laraine Ltd.). Est: 1970. Open 9-5.30, Sun. 11-5. SIZE: Large. *STOCK: Paintings and ceramics, 19th-20th C, £5-£25,000; onyx and glassware.* LOC: Next to library, 150yds. from station. PARK: Easy. TEL: 0323 29588; home - same. SER: Valuations; restorations (paintings and frames); buys at auction (paintings). VAT: Stan/Spec.

Time for Everyone
44 Ocklynge Rd, Old Town. (D Lincoln) Est: 1969. Open Fri. 1-5, Sat. 9-1, other times by appointment. SIZE: Small. *STOCK: English, French, German and American wall and mantel clocks, mostly late 19th C, £25-£750.* LOC: A259. PARK: Easy. TEL: 0323 35714 (ansaphone); home - same. SER: Valuations; restorations (clocks).

W.H Weller - Restoration Centre
12 North St. (D Rothwell) Est: 1892. Open 9.15-5. *STOCK: Metalware, brass, silver, trophies.* TEL: 0323 410972. SER: Restorations; polishing; silver plating; engraving.

EWHURST GREEN, Nr. Bodiam

Ewhurst Gallery
Court Lodge. (C Churton) Resident. Open 10-6 including Sun., prior telephone call advisable. *STOCK: 19th-20th C oils, watercolours and drawings.* LOC: 1 mile from Bodiam Castle (N.T.). TEL: 0580 830213.

FLIMWELL

Graham Lower
Stonecrouch Farmhouse. Open 9-6 or by appointment. *STOCK: English and continental 17th-18th C oak furniture.* LOC: A21. TEL: 058 087 535. SER: Valuations. VAT: Spec.

FRAMFIELD, Nr. Uckfield

Andrea de Montal
Open by appointment. *STOCK: Country house furniture and objects, specialising in 19th C re-upholstered furniture covered in antique textiles.* TEL: 0825 890797; fax - 0825 890697.

HASTINGS

Abbey Antiques
364 Old London Rd. (A.T. and Y.M Dennis) Est: 1960. Open 10.30-4.30. CL: Wed. *STOCK: Victorian, Edwardian and shipping furniture, porcelain, brass and copper, glass, linen, lace, curios, clocks, barometers, pictures.* LOC: A21 from Dover, 1 mile before Hastings. PARK: Easy. TEL: 0424 429178. VAT: Stan/Spec.

George Street Antiques Centre
47 George St. (F Stanley and P Heuduk) Est: 1969. Open 9-5, Sun. 11-4. SIZE: Medium - 20 dealers. *STOCK: Small items, 19th-20th C, £5-£100.* LOC: In old town, parallel to seafront. PARK: Seafront. TEL: 0424 429339; home - 0424 813526/713300.

Hallstand
23 Courthouse St. Open 10-5.30. *STOCK: Crested china, jewellery, collectables, small furniture.* LOC: Old Town.

Howes Bookshop
Trinity Hall, Braybrooke Terrace. ABA. Est: 1920. Open 9.30-1 and 2.15-5. CL: Sat. p.m. *STOCK: Antiquarian and academic books in literature, history, arts, bibliography.* TEL: 0424 423437. FAIRS: ABA.

Nakota Curios
12 Courthouse St. (D.E Taylor) Est: 1964. Open 10.30-1 and 2.30-5. CL: Wed. SIZE: Medium. *STOCK: General trade items, decorative china, furniture, Victoriana, jewellery.* Not Stocked: Coins, medals. PARK: Easy. TEL: 0424 438900.

Hastings continued

J Radcliffe
40 Cambridge Rd. Open 10-1 and 2-5. CL: Wed. p.m. *STOCK: General antiques, trade goods.* TEL: 0424 426361.

HERSTMONCEUX

W.F Bruce Antiques
Gardner St. Est: 1977. Open 9-6 by appointment including Sun. SIZE: Medium. *STOCK: Clocks, early 18th to late 19th C, £100-£5,000; clock movements, early 18th to late 19th C, £100-£2,000; decorative items, mainly 19th C, £100-£1,000.* LOC: A271 towards Batttle. PARK: Easy. TEL: 0323 833718; home - same. SER: Buys at auction (clocks, decorative items). VAT: Stan/Spec.

Touchwood
1 The Square. (M.E Long and S Miles) Est: 1975. Open 10-4.30, Sun. 10-1. CL: All day Wed, Mon. p.m. SIZE: Medium. *STOCK: Victorian pine furniture, £5-£1,000, kitchenalia and bric-a-brac.* LOC: A271 off A23. PARK: Easy. TEL: 0323 832020; home - same. SER: Stripping. FAIRS: Ardingly. VAT: Stan/Spec.

HORAM, Nr. Heathfield

John Botting Antiques
Winstan House, High St. SIZE: Medium. *STOCK: Victorian, Edwardian and some Georgian furniture, mahogany, oak and pine; bric-a-brac.* TEL: 04353 3553.

HORSEBRIDGE, Nr. Hailsham

Horsebridge Antiques Centre
1 North St. (R Lane) Resident. Est: 1978. Open 10-1 and 1.30-5. SIZE: Large. *STOCK: General antiques including furniture, silver, glass, pottery, brass and copper.* LOC: A271. PARK: Easy. TEL: 0323 844414. SER: Valuations.

HURST GREEN

Delmas
Little Bernhurst. (P.D Stimpson) Est: 1973. Open 10-6.30. CL: Wed. *STOCK: English and continental furniture and paintings.* TEL: 058 086 345. VAT: Stan/Spec.

Pigeon House Antiques **LAPADA**
52 London Rd. (D.K. and R.M Wiltshire) Resident. Est: 1974. *STOCK: English and continental furniture, rosewood, satinwood, maple, mahogany, 18th-19th C; decorative items.* LOC: On A21, next to the Royal George. PARK: Easy. TEL: 058 086 474. VAT: Stan/Spec.

LEWES

John Bird Antiques
Norton House, Iford. Est: 1970. Open anytime by appointment. *STOCK: Furniture, country pine, oak, fruitwood, painted architectural and garden paintings, needlework, fabric.* TEL: 0273 483366.

Bow Windows Book Shop
128 High St. (A. and J Shelley) Open 9-5. SIZE: Large. *STOCK: Books including natural history, English literature, travel, topography.* LOC: Off A27. TEL: 0273 480780. FAIRS: Antiquarian Book.

Charleston Antiques
4 Lansdown Pl. (M. and S Ball) Est: 1980. Open Mon.-Sat. 10-5, Sun. by appointment. SIZE: Medium. *STOCK: Georgian, Victorian and Edwardian furniture, art nouveau, arts and crafts, garden furniture and ornaments, £50-£1,500.* LOC: On one-way system towards railway station. PARK: Friars Walk or station. TEL: 0273 477916; home - 0273 483670. VAT: Stan/Spec.

Celia Charlotte's
7 Malling St. (C.C Russell) Est: 1976. SIZE: Medium. *STOCK: Antique lace, needlework, embroideries, textiles, wall hangings, christening gowns, lace veils, bedspreads, lace tablecloths, period costume, fans, shawls, dolls, pictures, small miscellaneous items.* LOC: A27, bottom of Cliffe High St. PARK: Easy. TEL: 0273 473303/474311.

Lewes continued

Cliffe Antiques Centre
47 Cliffe High St. (Miss P Harrison) Est: 1984. Open 9.30-5. SIZE: Medium - 16 dealers. *STOCK: General antiques, £5-£1,000.* LOC: Follow town centre signs, turning left at traffic lights. PARK: Easy. TEL: 0273 473266.

Coombe House Antiques **BADA LAPADA**
Coombe House, 121 Malling St. (L.P. and S.Y Cato) Resident. Est: 1975. Open daily, Sun. by appointment. SIZE: Medium. *STOCK: English and continental furniture, mirrors, period decorative works of art, garden furniture.* LOC: Opposite Esso petrol station on A26. PARK: Private forecourt. TEL: 0273 473862. SER: Valuations; restorations. VAT: Stan/Spec.

A.J Cumming
84 High St. Est: 1976. Open 10-1 and 2-5. *STOCK: Antiquarian and out of print books.* TEL: 0273 472319. SER: Buys at auction.

H.P Dennison and Son
22 High St. (D.H Dennison) Est: 1933. Open 8.30-5. CL: Wed. p.m. SIZE: Medium. *STOCK: Mahogany furniture, early 19th C.* PARK: Easy. TEL: 0273 480655. SER: Valuations; restorations (furniture). VAT: Stan/Spec.

The Drawing Room
53 High St. Open 9.30-5.30. SIZE: Large. *STOCK: Furniture, pictures, objets d'art.* TEL: 0273 478560.

Felix Gallery
Corner of Sun St. and Lancaster St. (W.S.H. and Mrs M.M Whitehead) Est: 1981. Open 10-6, Sun. 12-6. SIZE: Small. *STOCK: Cats only - pottery, porcelain, bronze and silver, pictures, general objets d'art. English and continental.* LOC: 2 mins. from town centre. PARK: Easy. TEL: 0273 472668; home - same.

Fifteenth Century Bookshop
99 High St. (S Mirabaud) Est: 1938. *STOCK: Antiquarian and general secondhand books and prints, teddy bears and soft toys.* TEL: 0273 474160.

Foundry Lane Antiques Centre
15 Cliffe High St. (D Wall) Open 10-5. CL: Mon. *STOCK: 19th and 20th C decorative arts, furniture, metal, pottery, china, glass, fabric, jewellery.* TEL: 0273 475361.

Renée and Roy Green **BADA**
Ashcombe House, Lewes Rd. *STOCK: Furniture and objects, 17th to early 19th C.* LOC: From Brighton A27, entrance on left-hand side 500yds. before Lewes (A275) turn-off. TEL: 0273 474794.

Lewes continued

Lewes Antique Centre
20 Cliffe High St. (C Keen) Est: 1968. Open 9.30-5. SIZE: Large - 42 stallholders. *STOCK: Furniture, china, copper and metalware, glass, clocks.* LOC: A27, from London to Brighton, follow one-way system in town to end of Little East St. Turn left over traffic lights. PARK: Easy. TEL: 0273 476148. SER: Shipping facilities.

Pastorale Antiques
15 Malling St. (O Soucek) Open 10-6 or by appointment. SIZE: Large. *STOCK: Pine and European country furniture, mahogany and decorative items.* TEL: 0273 473259; home - 04352 3044; fax - 0273 473259.

Mary Sautter Pine Furniture
6 Station St. (M. and M Sautter) Est: 1970. Open 9.30-1 and 2-5. CL: Sat. and Wed. afternoons. SIZE: Large. *STOCK: Pine furniture, 18th-19th C, £150-£1,500; longcase clocks.* LOC: From railway station, in town centre. PARK: Easy, own. TEL: 0273 474842. VAT: Stan.

Southdown Antiques
48 Cliffe High St. (Miss P.I. and K.A Foster) Est: 1969. Open by appointment. SIZE: Medium. *STOCK: Small antiques, especially 18th-19th C English, continental and Oriental porcelain, objets d'art, works of art, glass, papier mâché trays, silver plate, £50-£350,000.* LOC: A27. One-way street north. PARK: Easy. TEL: 0273 472439. VAT: Stan/Spec.

Trevor **BADA**
Trevor House, 110 High St. Est: 1946. Open by appointment. *STOCK: Furniture, 17th to early 19th C; works of art.* VAT: Spec.

Lionel Young Antiques
1 South St, Cliffe Corner. Est: 1920. CL: Wed. *STOCK: General antiques, furniture, china, glass, pictures, prints and plate.* TEL: 0273 472455.

MAYFIELD

Wm. J Gravener Antiques
High St. (Mr and Mrs Gravener) Resident. Est: 1965. *STOCK: Furniture, longcase clocks.* TEL: 0435 873389. VAT: Spec.

NEWHAVEN

Newhaven Flea Market
28 South Way. (R Mayne and A Wilkinson) Est: 1971. Open every day except 25th Dec. 10-5.30. *STOCK: Victoriana, Edwardian, bric-a-brac.* TEL: 0273 517207/516065.

Newhaven continued

Leonard Russell **BADA**
21 Kings Ave, Mount Pleasant. Resident. Est: 1981. Open by appointment. SIZE: Small. *STOCK: English pottery figures, groups, animals, busts, lustre, 1720-1840, £80-£1,000; English Toby jugs, 1765-1840, £400-£3,000; Prattware including plaques, Toby and serving jugs, money boxes, animals, cow creamers, £100-£1,000; English commem-orative pottery, 1770-1840.* LOC: 500 yards from A259 South Coast Rd., 3/4 mile from town centre. PARK: Easy. TEL: 0273 515153. SER: Valuations; restorations (pottery); buys at auction (pottery). FAIRS: Olympia; Kensington; West London; Wilton House; Tatton Park; Radley College (ceramic fair); Stowe School.

NORTHIAM

Sheena Canham Fine Art
Spanyard's Farm, Adams Lane. (Mrs S Canham) Open by appointment only. SIZE: Medium. *STOCK: Watercolours, 18th-20th C.* LOC: Between A28 and B2165. PARK: Own. TEL: 0580 830265.

PEVENSEY

The Old Mint House **LAPADA**
(J.C Nicholson) Est: 1901. Open 9-5.30, Sun. by appointment. SIZE: Large and warehouse. *STOCK: Furniture, porcelain, clocks, 18th-19th C, £20-£10,000.* LOC: A259 coast road. PARK: Own. TEL: 0323 762337. SER: Buys at auction. VAT: Stan/Spec.

PEVENSEY BAY

Murray-Brown
Silverbeach, Norman Rd. (G. and J Murray-Brown) Open by appointment only. *STOCK: Paintings and prints.* TEL: 0323 764298; mobile - 0836 775128. SER: Valuations; restorations; cleaning.

PLAYDEN, Nr. Rye

Old Post House Antiques
Old Post House. (D Cooke) Est: 1957. Open any time by appointment. SIZE: Medium. *STOCK: Oil paintings.* LOC: A268, opp. Peace and Plenty public house. PARK: Easy. TEL: 079 78 303. SER: Valuations; restorations; packing and shipping. VAT: Spec.

POLEGATE

Monarch Antiques
A27 Antiques Complex, Chaucer Industrial Estate, Dittons Rd. (J.H King) Open 9-6, Sat. 10-4. *STOCK: Furniture, from Georgian, £5-£2,000.* TEL: 03212 7167. VAT: Stan.

Polegate Antiques Centre
97 Station Rd. (R Tolhurst) Open 9-5. CL: Sat. SIZE: 8 dealers. *STOCK: General antiques.* TEL: 03212 5277.

Graham Price Antiques Ltd
4 Chaucer Industrial Estate, Dittons Rd. Open 9-6. SIZE: Large. *STOCK: Mainly furniture - pine, country, decorative, French, Irish, European, period and Victorian oak, mahogany and walnut; bric-a-brac and kitchenalia.* LOC: Between Hastings and Brighton on A27. TEL: 03212 7167/7681; fax - 03212 3904. SER: Export, packing, shipping and courier; restoration.

ROBERTSBRIDGE

De Montfort
49 High St. (E.D. and A.A Sloane) Est: 1961. Open 10.30-5.30. SIZE: Large. *STOCK: English and continental furniture, 1500-1800; Islamic and ancient art; Oriental carpets, kelims, and textiles.* Not Stocked: Any items not included above. LOC: A21. PARK: Easy. TEL: 0580 880698. VAT: Spec.

ROTTINGDEAN

Trade Wind
Little Crescent. (R Morley Smith) Est: 1974. Open by appointment only. *STOCK: Small furniture mainly mahogany, 1760-1850; period silver caddy spoons, wine labels, sifter spoons, sauce and spice ladles.* TEL: 0273 31177.

RYE

Bragge and Sons
Landgate House. (N.H. and J.R Bragge) Est: 1840. Open 9-5. CL: Tues. p.m. *STOCK: 18th C*

Bragge and Sons continued

furniture and works of art. LOC: Entrance to town - Landgate. TEL: 0797 223358. SER: Valuations; restorations. VAT: Spec.

Ron and Mel Dellar
Western House, Winchelsea Rd. Resident. Est: 1969. Open by appointment only. *STOCK: Paintings, prints, furniture, decorative items, lace and linen.* TEL: 0797 223419.

Herbert Gordon Gasson
The Lion Galleries, Lion St. (T.J Booth) Est: 1909. Open 9-1 and 2-5.30. CL: Tues. p.m. SIZE: Large. *STOCK: 17th-18th C oak and walnut; Staffordshire and Chinese porcelain.* Not Stocked: Silver and glass. PARK: Easy. TEL: 0797 222208. SER: Restorations. VAT: Stan/Spec.

Grist Mill Interiors
The Grist Mill, Strand Quay. (P Kemp) Open 10-6.30 including Sun. *STOCK: Oriental antiques, fine wood carvings, porcelain.* PARK: Easy. TEL: 0797 225784; fax - 0797 225793. SER: Shipping; courier.

Landgate Antiques LAPADA
22 Landgate. (R. and J Jones) Est: 1987. Open 9-5.30. *STOCK: Desk and writing accessories; furniture, clocks, decorative items.* TEL: 0797 224746.

Ann Lingard - Rope Walk Antiques LAPADA
18-22 Rope Walk, and 17 Tower St. Est: 1972. Open 9-5.30. CL: Sun. except by appointment. SIZE: Large. *STOCK: English pine furniture and accessories, to 1870; kitchenalia.* Not Stocked: Jewellery, silver and plate. PARK: Own, and public next door. TEL: 0797 223486. VAT: Stan/Spec.

Mint Dolls and Toys
71 The Mint. Est: 1970. Open 10-5 every day. *STOCK: Dolls, toys, Steiff, miniatures.* TEL: 0797 222237/225952.

Rye continued

Rye Antiques
93 High St. (Mrs D Turner) Est: 1966. Open 9-6. CL: Sun. except by appointment. SIZE: Small. *STOCK: Small oak, walnut and mahogany furniture, 17th-19th C, £50-£1,000; clocks, longcase, bracket, wall, £30-£1,500; metalware, jewellery, silver and plate, 17th-19th C, £5-£1,000.* Not Stocked: Glass, coins, bric-a-brac. PARK: Easy. TEL: 0797 222259. VAT: Stan/Spec.

ST. LEONARDS-ON-SEA

Aarquebus Antiques
46 Norman Rd. (Mr and Mrs G Jukes) Resident. Est: 1957. Open 9-6 every dy. SIZE: Medium. *STOCK: Furniture, 18th C, £500-£1,000; shipping goods, Victorian to 1930, £5-£500; glass, gold and silver, 18th-19th C, £5-£1,000.* LOC: Take A2100 to St. Leonards-on-Sea, turn right after main post office. PARK: Easy. TEL: 0424 433267. SER: Valuations; restorations (furniture); pine stripping; buys at auction.

Banner Antiques
56 Norman Rd. (G.M Schofield) Est: 1972. Open 10-1 and 2.15-5.30. CL: Wed. SIZE: Large. *STOCK: Furniture, porcelain, pottery, copper, brass, watercolours.* Not Stocked: Jewellery, silver, weapons. PARK: Easy. TEL: 0424 420050.

Chapel Antiques
Chapel House, 1 London Rd. (E.R Alff) Est: 1946. Open 9-5. SIZE: Large. *STOCK: Furniture, china, glass and paintings, 17th-19th C, £100-£5,000.* PARK: Easy. TEL: 0424 440025. SER: Valuations; restorations (furniture). VAT: Stan/Spec.

Cirdeco
24 North St. (M Gowen) Est: 1988. Open 10-5. CL: Wed. SIZE: Medium. *STOCK: Books, mainly secondhand.* LOC: Just off seafront. PARK: Nearby. TEL: 0424 421187. SER: Searches undertaken.

Filsham Farmhouse Antiques
111 Harley Shute Rd. (J.H Yorke) Open 9-5.30. *STOCK: Furniture especially oak; brass, copper, clocks and shipping goods.* TEL: 0424 433109. VAT: Stan.

Galleon Antiques
19 Marina. *STOCK: Furniture, some Chinese.* LOC: A259 - seafront. TEL: 0424 440974/424145/714981. SER: Restorations.

Galleon Antiques
70 Sedlescombe Rd. North. *STOCK: Early Chinese and Japanese furniture, carvings, silks, bronzes.* LOC: On A21. TEL: 0424 424145/ 714981.

Galleria Fine Arts Ltd
77 Norman Rd. Open 10-6. *STOCK: Decorative art and furniture, 18th-19th C.* TEL: 0424 722317.

St. Leonards-on-Sea continued

The Hastings Antique Centre
59-61 Norman Rd. (R.J Amstad) Open 10-5.30, Sun. by appointment. TEL: 0424 428561; home - 0424 752922. Below are listed some of the dealers at this centre.

R J Amstad
Furniture.
R Armstrong
1930-1950 collectables.
V Bevan-Jones
Decorative items.
C Booth
Furniture.
E Broad
Brass and copper.
C Clements
Paintings and prints.
P Clements/K Harding
Decorative items and textiles.
I Copeland/S Longmead
Furniture.
C Cunliffe
Furniture.
S Dahms
Clocks.
W Dazeley
Pine furniture and kitchenalia.
F Fowler/S Slater
Decorative items.
K Gumbrell
Decorative items.
Horsebridge Antiques
China, furniture, decorative items.
G Howlett/J Kinsella
Furniture, decorative items.
T Lee
Porcelain, china.
C Lonsdale
Art deco, art nouveau.
G Mennis
Sporting, leather goods.
M Neech
Decorative items, china, jewellery.
P Tassell
1930-1950 clothing.
Tiffany Antiques
Furniture.
S Todd
Decorative items.
J Ziebell
Tools, kitchenalia, pine.

John Lang and Tiffany Antiques
65 Norman Rd. (J. and C Lang) Open 10-5, Sat. 10-1. *STOCK: General antiques.* TEL: 0424 714848.

Monarch Antiques
6 Grand Parade. (J.H King) Est: 1983. Open 9-5, Sat. 9-1. SIZE: Medium. *STOCK: Furniture, from Victorian, £5-£2,000.* LOC: A259. PARK: Easy. TEL: 0424 445841; home - 0424 214158. SER: Valuations.

St. Leonards-on-Sea continued

K Nunn
106 Bohemia Rd. Open Mon., Tues. and Thurs. 9-5. *STOCK: General antiques, weapons and unusual items.* TEL: 0424 431093. SER: Buys at auction. VAT: Stan/Spec.

SEAFORD

Molly Alexander
Crouch House, Crouch Lane. Est: 1967. *STOCK: Paintings, watercolours and antiquities.* LOC: Opposite new Constitutional Club. PARK: Opposite. TEL: 0323 896577.

Richard Alexander
Crouch House, Crouch Lane. Est: 1948. Open by appointment. *STOCK: Oriental items, oils and watercolours, £25-£500.* PARK: Easy. TEL: 0323 896577.

The Courtyard Antiques Market
13, 15, 17 High St. (Mrs S.E Barrett) Open 8.30-5.30. SIZE: Medium - 8 dealers. *STOCK: General antiques.* TEL: 0323 892091.

The Old House
13, 15, 17 High St. (P.R. and S.M Barrett) Est: 1928. Open 8.30-5.30. SIZE: Large. *STOCK: 18th-19th C furniture, china and glass, £5-£5,000.* LOC: Near Railway Station. PARK: In own yard in South St. TEL: 0323 892091; home - 0323 898364. SER: Valuations; restorations (furniture); shippers. VAT: Stan/Spec.

Seaford's "Barn Collectors' Market" and Studio Bookshop
The Barn, Church Lane. Est: 1967. Open Tues., Thurs. and Sat. 10-4.30. SIZE: Several dealers. *STOCK: Collectables including buttons, ephemera, books, post and cigarette cards.* LOC: Off High St. TEL: 0323 890010.

Steyne House Antiques
35 Steyne Rd. (J.R Deakin) Est: 1969. Open 10.30-5, Sat. 10.30-4. CL: Sun. and Mon. except by appointment. SIZE: Small. *STOCK: Staffordshire figures, pottery and porcelain, copper and brass, £20-£250+; country furniture, £50-£750+; decorative agricultural and domestic items, £20-£80+; all 18th-19th C.* LOC: Off A259 into Broad St., take 2nd right into High St., then 3rd left. PARK: Easy and opposite. TEL: 0323 895088; home -same. SER: Restorations (china).

SEDLESCOMBE

Holmes House Antiques
The Green. (F.J Fleischer) Est: 1973. Open 10-12 and 3-6 including Sun. CL: Mon. SIZE: Small. *STOCK: Watercolours and oil paintings, £100-£1,000; small silver, £10-£100; both 19th C; furniture, 19th-20th C, £300-£500.* PARK: Easy. TEL: 0424 870450.

Sedlescombe continued

Mrs C Kinloch
Bulmer House, The Green. *STOCK: Dolls, teddies and associated items.* TEL: 0424 870364.

UCKFIELD

Barnes Gallery
8 Church St. (S.J. and A.R Barnes) Est: 1984. Open 10-5.30. CL: Mon. SIZE: Medium. *STOCK: 19th to early 20th C watercolours and oils, £200-£20,000.* PARK: Nearby. TEL: 0825 762066. SER: Restorations; cleaning. VAT: Spec.

Nicholas Bowlby
Owl House, Poundgate. Est: 1981. Open every day by appointment. SIZE: Medium. *STOCK: English watercolours and drawings, 18th-20th C, £50-£4,000.* LOC: Just off A26, 1 1/2 miles south of Crowborough. PARK: Easy. TEL: 0892 653722. SER: Valuations; restorations; buys at auction (watercolours and drawings). VAT: Spec.

Ivan R Deverall
Duval HouseThe Glen, Cambridge Way. *STOCK: Maps.* TEL: 0825 762474. SER: Catalogue available; colouring. VAT: Stan.

Georgian House Antiques
222 High St. (Mr and Mrs P Hale) Resident. Est: 1976. Open 10-6, Sun. and evenings by appointment. CL: Some Weds. SIZE: Large. *STOCK: English domestic oak and country furniture and related decorative items, 1600-1860.* Not Stocked: Bric-a-brac. LOC: A22. PARK: Nearby. TEL: 0825 765074. SER: Furniture made from 17th C timber. VAT: Spec.

Ringles Cross Antiques
Ringles Cross. (C. and J Dunford) Est: 1965. Open 9.30-6 or by appointment. *STOCK: Oriental items and English furniture, 17th-18th C.* LOC: 1 mile north of Uckfield. PARK: Easy. TEL: 0825 762909. VAT: Spec.

WADHURST

Art and Antiques (Wadhurst)
High St. (D Maskell) Open Tues., Thurs. and Sat. 10.30-5. *STOCK: Lace, period clothes, brass, pewter, copper, porcelain, old English pottery, dolls, furniture, prints, documents and textiles.* TEL: 089 288 2091.

Sussex West

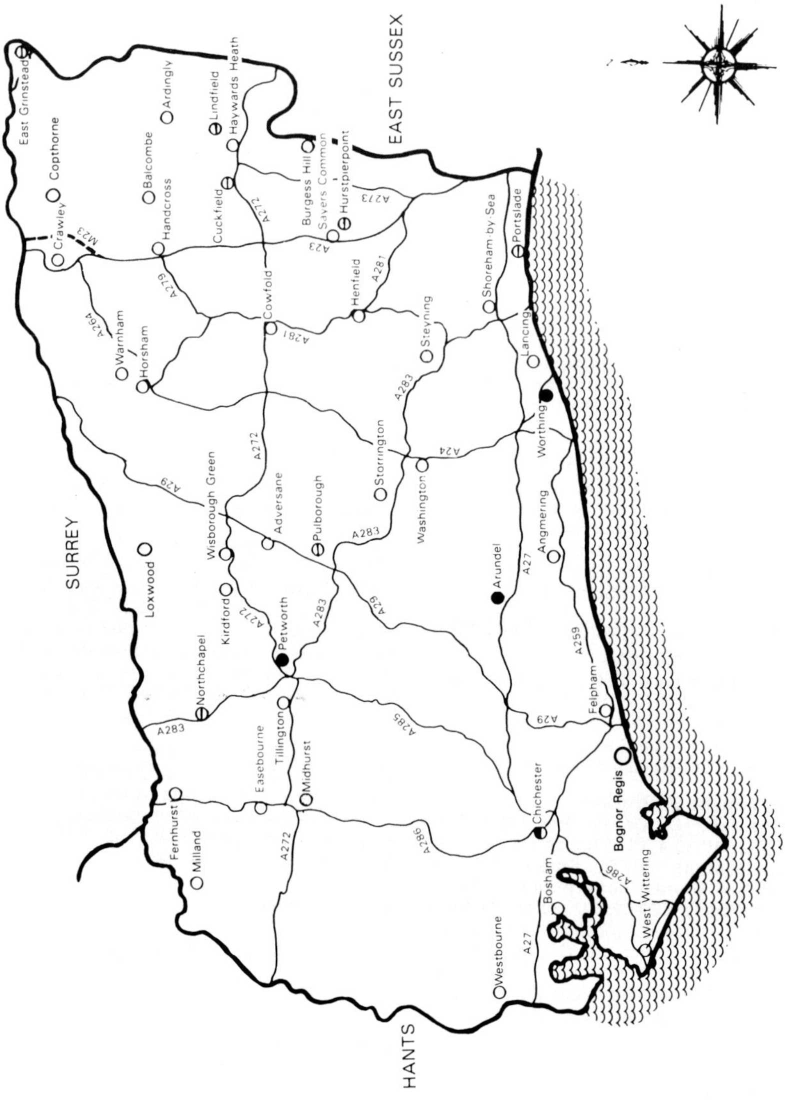
EAST SUSSEX
SURREY
HANTS
East Grinstead
Copthorne
Crawley
M23
Balcombe
Ardingly
Lindfield
Haywards Heath
Handcross
Cuckfield
Burgess Hill
Sayers Common
Hurstpierpoint
A272
A273
A23
Henfield
A281
Shoreham-by-Sea
Portslade
A264
Warnham
Horsham
A219
Cowfold
Steyning
Lancing
A283
Worthing
Storrington
A24
Washington
A29
Wisborough Green
Adversane
Pulborough
Loxwood
Arundel
A27
Angmering
Kirdford
Petworth
A259
Northchapel
Felpham
A283
Tillington
A285
Easebourne
Midhurst
Chichester
Bognor Regis
Fernhurst
Milland
A286
West Wittering
Bosham
Westbourne

Please note this is only a rough map designed to show dealers the number of shops in the various towns, and is not necessarily totally accurate.

Key to number of shops in this area.

- ○ 1–2
- ⊖ 3–5
- ◒ 6–12
- ● 13+

AVERSANE, Nr. Billingshurst

Antique Centre and Collectors Market
Old House. Open daily including Sun. SIZE: 22 stallholders. *STOCK: General antiques and collectors' items.* PARK: Easy. TEL: 0403 783594/782186.

ANGMERING

Bygones
The Square. (R.A. and Mrs L.R Whittaker) Est: 1965. Open 10-1 and 2.15-5, Sat. 10-12. CL: Wed. SIZE: Medium. *STOCK: Furniture, £50-£1,000; china, £5-£150; silver, £10-£250; linen, £5-£75; all 1800-1920.* LOC: A280. PARK: Easy. TEL: 0903 786152; home - same. SER: Valuations; buys at auction (furniture).

ARDINGLY, Nr. Haywards Heath

Ardingly Antiques
64 High St. (Mrs P Gordon) Est: 1972. Open 10.30-1 and 2.30-5.30, Sun. 2.30-5.30 or by appointment. CL: Mon. and Wed. SIZE: Medium. *STOCK: Georgian and Victorian furniture; button back chairs, porcelain, silver and glass, clocks.* LOC: On B2028. PARK: Large forecourt. TEL: 0444 892680/892089.

ARUNDEL

Armstrong-Davis Gallery
The Square. *STOCK: Fine sculptures of all periods; original bronze sculptures by 19th-20th C masters.* TEL: 0903 882752. SER: Commissions accepted for sculpture in relation to architectural, industrial and private projects. Represented in Italy and Switzerland.

Baynton-Williams
69 Ford Rd. (R.H. and S.C Baynton-Williams) *STOCK: Maps, views, sporting, marine and decorative prints.* TEL: 0903 882898. SER: Valuations; cataloguing. *Postal Only.*

Country Life by Bursig
1 Tarrant Sq, Tarrant St. (R.H Bursig) Est: 1978. Open 9.30-5, Sun. 2-5. SIZE: Large. *STOCK: Furniture, oak, mahogany and walnut, 17th-19th C, £50-£2,000; oil paintings and watercolours, £50-£500; porcelain, pewter and brass, £5-£200, all 19th C.* PARK: Easy. TEL: 0903 883456; home - 0243 822045. VAT: Spec.

Richard Davidson Antiques BADA
Romsey House, 51 Maltravers St. Open by appointment only. *STOCK: Fine furniture, decorative accessories, oil paintings.* TEL: 0428 78566; fax - 0428 788121. SER: Restoration. VAT: Spec.

Gallery 88
15 Tarrant St. (Mrs B Driver) *STOCK: Paintings, silver, plate, porcelain, glass.* TEL: 0903 882921.

Arundel continued

Pat Golding
6 Castle Mews, Tarrant St. Open 10-1 and 2-5. *STOCK: Ceramics and glass, 18th-20th C.*

Lasseters
8a High St. Est: 1780. *STOCK: Jewellery, silver.* TEL: 0903 882651. VAT: Stan/Spec.

Mamie's Antiques Centre
5 River Rd. (Mrs M Eyers) Open Sat. 9-5. SIZE: 30+ dealers. *STOCK: General antiques.* PARK: Easy. TEL: 0903 882012. The following businesses operate from this address.

The Courtyard
Open Sat. 9-5. *Garden statuary.*

The Gallery
Open Sat. 9-5. *Period items including fine furniture and porcelain.*

The Studio
Open by appointment. *Furniture and general antiques.*

Serendipity Antiques
27 Tarrant St. (A.G Brown) Est: 1972. Open 9.30-1 and 2-6. CL: Sun. a.m. SIZE: Medium. *STOCK: Victorian prints, watercolours, oils and maps.* Not Stocked: China, glass, brass. LOC: Opposite Norfolk Hotel, turn left for Chichester. PARK: Easy. TEL: 0903 882047. SER: Restorations (oil paintings); colouring (maps and prints). VAT: Stan/Spec.

Spencer Swaffer LAPADA
30 High St. Est: 1974. Open 9-6. SIZE: Large. *STOCK: Unusual decorative items, traditional items, brass, blue and white, Staffordshire, dinner services, pine, oak dressers, marble tables, bamboo, shop fittings, candlesticks, majolica, French, English, painted and garden furniture.* PARK: Easy. TEL: 0903 882132. VAT: Stan/Spec.

Sussex Fine Art
7 Castle Mews, Tarrant St. (G.C. and P.A Miller) Est: 1987. Open Fri. and Sat. 10.30-5.30, Sun. 12-5, other days by appointment. SIZE: Small. *STOCK: English watercolours, 1760-1930, from £100.* LOC: Off High St. PARK: 50yds. TEL: 0903 884055. SER: Framing; buys at auction. VAT: Spec.

Tarrant Gallery
10 Tarrant St. (Mrs M Selbach and Mrs C Ellis) Est: 1981. Open 10.30-1 and 2-5, Sat. 10-5.30. *STOCK: Furniture, 1700-1900, £500-£1,000; decorative items including lamps and pictures, £100-£500; china and metalware, £50-£100; both 1820-1920.* LOC: Town centre. PARK: Nearby. TEL: 0903 884236; home - 0243 514508 and 0273 673921. FAIRS: Goodwood House; Parham House.

Arundel continued

Tarrant Street Antique Centre

Nineveh House, Tarrant St. (Miss J Millar and A Pugh) Open 9.30-5, Sun. 11-5. SIZE: Large. 14 dealers. *STOCK: A wide range of general antiques including Edwardian and Victorian, country and pine furniture, jewellery and silver, paintings and prints, china and glass, luggage and Oriental rugs.* LOC: Off A27 and A29 into town then second left off High St. PARK: Own forecourt. TEL: 0903 884307. SER: Valuations; restorations. VAT: Stan/Spec.

Treasure House Antiques

31 High St, and 5/7 Tarrant St. (Mrs Henderson) Est: 1969. CL: Wed. *STOCK: General antiques and collectors' items including Victoriana, pocillovy, commemoratives, Goss and crested china.* PARK: Crown Yard behind High St. TEL: 0903 883101.

Treasure House Antiques and Collectors Market

31b High St, and Crown Yard car park. Est: 1972. Open 9-5; Crown Yard Sat. 9-5 only. CL: Wed. *STOCK: Victoriana, domestic bygones, porcelain, lace, cameras, lamps, curios, silver, jewellery, clocks, metalware, small furniture.* PARK: Easy. TEL: 0903 883101.

Upstairs Downstairs Antique Market

29 Tarrant St. Open 10-5 including Sun. SIZE: 7 dealers. *STOCK: General antiques.* TEL: 0903 883749.

Whitehouse Antique Interiors

4 Tarrant Square, Tarrant St. (G.G Cross) Open 10-5. *STOCK: Furniture, porcelain, decorative items.* TEL: 0903 882443.

BALCOMBE

Pine and Design

Haywards Heath Rd. (J.M Nelson and G Lindsay-Stewart) Est: 1974. CL: Sun. a.m. SIZE: Medium. *STOCK: Stripped pine furniture, mirrors, sofas, pictures, lace, 18th-19th C, £25-£500.* LOC: B2036. PARK: Easy. TEL: 0444 811700. SER: Restorations and interior design, handmade kitchens and furniture from old pine. VAT: Stan.

Woodall and Emery Ltd

Haywards Heath Rd. Est: 1884. TEL: 0444 811608. VAT: Stan.

BOGNOR REGIS

Gough Bros. Art Shop and Gallery

71 High St. (S Neal) Est: 1975. CL: Wed. p.m. SIZE: Medium. *STOCK: Watercolours, £50-£1,000; oils, £100-£1,500; miniatures, £150-£400; all 19th to early 20th C.* LOC: Off High St., behind Unicorn public house. PARK: Nearby. TEL: 0243 823773. SER: Valuations; restor-

Gough Bros. Art Shop and Gallery continued

ations (oils and watercolours, frames and gilding); buys at auction (oils, watercolours and drawings). VAT: Stan/Spec.

BOSHAM

Bosham Antiques

(L.M. and M.D Lain) Open 9.30-5.30, other times by appointment. *STOCK: General antiques, upholstered and shipping goods.* LOC: A259 at Bosham roundabout. PARK: Own. TEL: 0243 572005. VAT: Stan/Spec.

BURGESS HILL

British Antique Exporters Ltd

LAPADA

School Close, Queen Elizabeth Ave. Est: 1963. Open 9-5.30. SIZE: Large. *STOCK: General antiques.* LOC: Off Queen Elizabeth Ave. TEL: 0444 245577. VAT: Stan.

British Antique Replicas

School Close, Queen Elizabeth Ave. Est: 1962. Open 8-5.30, Sat. 9-5.30. SIZE: Large. *STOCK: Furniture, £100-£20,000.* LOC: 3 miles west A23. PARK: Easy. TEL: 0444 245577. SER: Valuations; restorations; bespoke furniture. VAT: Stan.

CHICHESTER

Almshouses Arcade

19 The Hornet. Est: 1983. Open 9.30-4.30. LOC: 200yds. from Cattle Market at eastern end of city. On one-way system (A286) just before traffic lights at Market Ave. PARK: Easy. Below are listed the dealers at these premises.

R K Barnett
Antiques and collectables including small furniture. TEL: 0243 528089.

Beachcroft Models
(B Rolfe) *Model railways, Dinky toys, collectors' items.* TEL: 0243 776409.

Madeline Cocks
General antiques and collectables, especially ceramics and glass; small furniture.

Overlord
(D Rowe) *Militaria, some general antiques, £5-£100.*

Antique Shop

Frensham House, Hunston. (J.M Riley) Est: 1956. Open 9-6. *STOCK: English furniture, 1700-1830, £200-£3,000; bureaux, chests of drawers, tables, chairs.* LOC: One mile south of Chichester by-pass on B2145. PARK: Easy. TEL: 0243 782660.

The Canon Gallery

4 Newtown. (J Green) Open 9-5.15. *STOCK: 19th and 20th C watercolours and oils.* TEL: 0243 786063. SER: Valuations; restorations; framing.

Chichester continued

Gallery Six Antiques at Nigel Purchase Gallery

The Hornet. (R.G Chambers) Open 9.30-5.30. *STOCK: Fine art, porcelain, furniture, local artists.* TEL: 0243 782018.

Gems Antiques

39 West St. (M.L Hancock) Open 10-1 and 2-5. *STOCK: Period furniture, Staffordshire and porcelain figures, books and pictures.* TEL: 0243 786173.

Green and Stone of Chichester

1 North House, North St. (R.J.S Baldwin) Open 9-5.30. *STOCK: Artists' and writing materials, 19th C engravings, watercolours.* TEL: 0243 533953.

Peter Hancock Antiques

40-41 West St. Articles on coins. Est: 1950. Open 9.30-5.30. SIZE: Medium. *STOCK: Silver, jewellery, porcelain, furniture, £20-£2,000; pictures, glass, clocks, books, £5-£500; all 18th-19th C; enthnographica, art nouveau, art deco, 19th-20th C, £5-£500.* LOC: From Chichester Cross, 17 doors past Cathedral. PARK: Easy. TEL: 0243 786173. SER: Valuations. VAT: Stan/Spec.

Heritage Antiques

77D St. Pancras. (D.R. and D.A Grover) Open 9.30-5.30. *STOCK: Furniture and smaller items.* TEL: 0903 783470.

St. Pancras Antiques

150 St. Pancras. (R.F. and M Willatt) Est: 1980. Open 9.30-1 and 2-5. CL: Thurs. p.m. SIZE: Small. *STOCK: Militaria, arms and armour, medals, documents, uniforms and maps, 1600-1914, £5-£1,000; china, pottery and ceramics, 1800-1930, £2-£100; small furniture, 18th-19th C, £20-£800; coins, ancient to date.* Not Stocked: Silver and carpets. TEL: 0243 787645. SER: Valuations; restorations (arms and armour); buys at auction (militaria).

COPTHORNE, Nr. Crawley

Copthorne Group Antiques

Copthorne Bank. (Mrs M Denman) Open 10-5.30. *STOCK: General antiques including furniture, dolls, china, jewellery, collectables, Victorian watercolours, oils.* LOC: 10 minutes from Gatwick. Off M23, junction 10. TEL: 0342 712802.

COWFOLD

Cowfold Clocks

The Olde House, The Street. (F.M Henderson) Open 9.30-5.30. CL: Mon. *STOCK: Clocks - English dial, lacquer tavern, bracket, mantel and longcase, 18th-20th C.* TEL: 0403 864505 (24hr.). SER: Repairs (clocks); dial painting and restoration.

Cowfold continued

Squires Pantry Antiques

Station Rd. (L.M Lasham) Open 10-1 and 2-5. *STOCK: Pine.* TEL: 0403 864869. VAT: Stan/Spec.

CRAWLEY

Alan and Jennie Hardman Antiques

Spikemead Farm, Poles Lane, Lowfield Heath. Est: 1971. Open by appointment, including Sun. SIZE: Large. *STOCK: French furniture, country and formal, mainly 19th C, £100-£1,500.* LOC: Off A23 Gatwick. PARK: Easy. TEL: 0293 560294. SER: Containers. VAT: Stan/Spec. *Trade Only.*

Splinters

1 London Rd, Northgate. (Mr and Mrs D Ringrose) Est: 1987. Open 9-6. SIZE: Small. *STOCK: Pine, 19th C, £100-£1,000.* LOC: A23 in town centre. PARK: Easy. TEL: 0293 565555. SER: Valuations. VAT: Stan.

CUCKFIELD

David Foord-Brown AntiquesLAPADA

High St. Est: 1988. Open 10-5.30. SIZE: Medium. *STOCK: Furniture, 1780-1880, £300-£5,000; porcelain, 1800-1850, £20-£1,500.* Not Stocked: Country furniture. LOC: A272. PARK: Easy. TEL: 0444 414418. SER: Valuations. VAT: Stan/Spec.

John Hopkins (Antiques) Ltd BADA

1 The Courtyard, Ockenden Manor. (J., M. and A Hopkins) Est: 1956. Open by appointment only. *STOCK: English and continental furniture, 17th-19th C, £600-£5,000; watercolours, 19th C, £250-£2,500; glass candelabra, 18th-19th C, £1,800-£5,000.* LOC: Turn off London-Brighton road at Bolney crossroads, towards Cuckfield. PARK: Easy. TEL: 0444 454323/456140. SER: Valuations; buys at auction (English and continental furniture). FAIRS: Most major. VAT: Stan/Spec.

Richard Usher Antiques

23 South St. Est: 1978. Open 10-5.30. CL: Wed. p.m. and Sat. p.m. SIZE: Medium. *STOCK: Furniture, 17th-19th C, £50-£2,000; decorative items.* LOC: A272. PARK: Easy. TEL: 0444 451699. SER: Valuations; restorations.

EASEBOURNE, Nr. Midhurst

Easebourne Antiques

Easebourne Lane. (J Fynes) Est: 1971. Open daily, Sun. by appointment. SIZE: Medium. *STOCK: General antiques, 19th-20th C, to £500.* LOC: A286. PARK: Easy. TEL: 0730 816240; home - 0798 42353. SER: Valuations.

EAST GRINSTEAD

The Antique Atlas
31A High St. Open 10-5. *STOCK: Maps, charts, plans and views worldwide.* LOC: Entrance Cantelupe Rd. TEL: 0342 315813.

The Antique Print Shop
11 Middle Row. (A.A.W Daszewski and Mrs A.C Keddie) Est: 1988. Open 9.30-6. SIZE: Small. *STOCK: Prints, pre-1880, £5-£100; maps especially British county, 1500-1870, £10-£1,000; English watercolours and drawings, 1700-1880, £100-£700.* LOC: On island in middle High St., opposite St. Swithins church. PARK: Lewes Rd. TEL: 0342 410501; fax - 0342 322149. SER: Restorations; buys at auction (as stock); framing. FAIRS: Monway Fairs, London, City of London Antiques (Barbican).

Keith Atkinson Antiques
Moorhawes Farm. Open by appointment. SIZE: Large. *STOCK: Furniture, 19th to early 20th C.* TEL: 0342 87765; fax - 0342 87767. SER: Restorations (furniture); packing and shipping. *Trade Only.*

FELPHAM, Nr. Bognor Regis

Susan and Robert Botting
'Rosedene', 38 Firs Ave. (S.M. and R.M.D Botting) Est: 1979. Open by appointment. SIZE: Small. *STOCK: Watercolours and oil paintings,*

Susan and Robert Botting continued

19th C, £500-£15,000. LOC: Off A259. PARK: Easy. TEL: 0243 584515; home - same. SER: Valuations; restorations. FAIRS: Kensington; Petworth; Westminster; Harrogate; Petersfield. VAT: Spec.

FERNHURST, Nr. Haslemere

Sheelagh Hamilton
9b Midhurst Rd. Open 10-5. *STOCK: Period pine furniture, pictures.* TEL: 0428 653253.

HANDCROSS

Handcross Antiques
High St. Est: 1978. Open 9-4.30. CL: Mon. all day, Wed. p.m. *STOCK: General antiques.* TEL: 0444 400784.

HAYWARDS HEATH

David Burkinshaw
Sugworth Farmhouse, Borde Hill Lane. Open by appointment. *STOCK: Pedestal and partner desks, 1820-1880.* TEL: 0444 459747.

Ramm Antiques
43 Sussex Rd. (R.E Ramm) *STOCK: Collectables and general antiques.* TEL: 0444 451393.

HENFIELD

Alexander Antiques
Post House, Small Dole. (Mrs J.A Goodinge) Est: 1971. CL: Sun. except by appointment. SIZE: Medium. *STOCK: Country furniture, brass, copper, pewter, samplers, small collectors' and decorative items, treen.* LOC: A2037. PARK: Easy. TEL: 0273 493121; home - same. VAT: Stan/Spec.

HORSHAM

L.E Lampard and Sons
23-31 Springfield Rd. Est: 1920. Open 8-1 and 2-5. SIZE: Medium. *STOCK: Mahogany and oak furniture, firebacks, grates.* TEL: 0403 54012/64332. VAT: Stan/Spec.

Saranno
20 Queen St. (Mr and Mrs R.A Smith) Est: 1989. Open 9.30-5, Sun. by appointment. SIZE: Medium. *STOCK: General antiques and collectables.* TEL: 0403 41298; home - 0342 716361. SER: Valuations.

HURSTPIERPOINT

Chimera Books
17 High St. (R. and J Lyon) Open by appointment only. SIZE: Large. *STOCK: Antiquarian books especially Oriental art, reference and travel.* TEL: 0273 832255.

Hurstpierpoint continued

The Clock Shop
36 High St. Est: 1974. CL: Wed. p.m. and Mon. *STOCK: Clocks.* TEL: 0273 832081. SER: Restorations (clocks and furniture).

Julian Antiques
124 High St. Est: 1964. Open 9-5. CL: Sat. *STOCK: French clocks, bronzes, art deco, fireplaces, mirrors, furniture.* TEL: 0273 832145.

Michael Miller
The Lamb, 8 Cuckfield Rd. (M. and V Miller) Est: 1880. Open Sat. 9.30-5, other times appointment advisable. *STOCK: Arms and armour, post-1460, from £5; general antiques.* TEL: 0273 834567. SER: Buys at auction; exporters.

KIRDFORD, Nr. Billingshurst

Sheila Hinde Fine Art LAPADA
Idolsfold House. *STOCK: Fine paintings and watercolours, animalier bronzes.* TEL: 0403 77576. VAT: Spec.

LANCING

Crabtree Antiques
67 Crabtree Lane. (R East) Open 9.30-4, Sat. 9.30-1. CL: Tues. *STOCK: General antiques and bric-a-brac.* TEL: 0903 754648.

LINDFIELD

Alma Antiques
79 High St. Est: 1976. Open 10.30-5. CL: Wed. *STOCK: Small collectable items, porcelain, glass, silver, copper, brass, furniture, watercolours and prints.*

The Corner Gallery
99 High St. (R Mulcare) Est: 1974. Open 9.30-5.30. CL: Sun. a.m. SIZE: Medium. *STOCK: Furniture, £25-£200; glass, £2-£50; china, porcelain, £5-£100, all 19th-20th C.* Not Stocked: Books. LOC: A272 Haywards Heath, turn off to B2028. PARK: Nearby. TEL: 0444 482483.

Lindfield Galleries BADA
59 High St. (D Adam) Est: 1972. Open 9-5.30. *STOCK: Oriental carpets.* TEL: 0444 483817. VAT: Stan/Spec.

LOXWOOD, Nr. Billingshurst

Loxwood Antiques
High St. (D Haines) Open 9.30-5.30. CL: Wed. *STOCK: Victorian, Edwardian and decorative antiques.* TEL: 0403 753370.

MIDHURST

Church Hill Clocks
Church Hill. (W.P. and Dr. E Tyrrell) Open 9-4.30, Wed. 9-1. *STOCK: Clocks.* TEL: 0730 813891 (ansaphone). SER: Restorations; repairs.

Eagle House Antiques Market
Market Sq. (J.H Brown) Open daily. SIZE: Medium - 15 dealers. *STOCK: General antiques, furniture, silver, porcelain, pictures and glass, £5-£1,000.* PARK: Easy. TEL: 0730 812718.

Foord Antiques LAPADA
P.O. Box 14. (C.G. and E.S Foord) Open by appointment. *STOCK: Furniture, boxes, treen, metalware, decorative items, 18th to early 19th C.* TEL: 079 86 351 or 0836 533655.

Midhurst Antiques Market
Knockhundred Row. (D.M Brindle-Wood-Williams) Est: 1974. Open 9.30-5. TEL: 0730 814231.

West Street Antiques
West St. (A Goodman) Est: 1984. Open 10-1 and 2-5. CL: Wed. SIZE: Medium. *STOCK: Decorative and country furniture, brass, pottery and porcelain; some oil paintings and early prints, quilts, rugs and jewellery, £5-£4,000.* PARK: Easy. TEL: 0730 815232. SER: Buys at auction.

MILLAND, Nr. Liphook

The Plough
Maysleith. (Mrs I Morton-Smith) Est: 1980. Open by appointment only. SIZE: Medium. *STOCK: Decorative and collectable agricultural implements, including horsedrawn ploughs, wooden harrows, haysweeps, £50-£150; hand tools - saws, hay-knives, wheelwrights, blacksmiths, £3-£20; barn and domestic appliances - mangles, cheese presses, butter workers, pulpers, cake crackers, £50-£150; all mainly Victorian and Edwardian.* LOC: 1/2 mile off A3 just north of Petersfield, Hants., telephone for directions. PARK: Easy. TEL: 042 876 323; home - same. SER: Buys at auction (agricultural implements). VAT: Stan.

NORTHCHAPEL, Nr. Petworth

D. and A Callingham Antiques
Est: 1966. CL: Wed. *STOCK: English furniture.* LOC: On A283. TEL: 042 878 379. VAT: Stan/Spec.

N. and S Callingham Antiques
Est: 1979. Open 9-5.30. CL: Wed. SIZE: Medium. *STOCK: Furniture, 1700-1900, £10-£10,000.* LOC: London Road 5 miles north of Petworth. PARK: Easy. TEL: 042 878 379; home - 0903 724233. SER: Valuations; restorations. VAT: Stan/Spec.

Northchapel continued

Krüger Smith Fine Art
(M.C Krüger and H.E Smith) Est: 1983. Open by appointment. *STOCK: Watercolours, 19th C; oils, 19th-20th C; both £100-£4,000; contemporary paintings.* LOC: Just north of Petworth. TEL: 042 878 265 or 0962 771019. SER: Valuations; restorations (watercolours, oils and frames); buys at auction (pictures).

PETWORTH

Majid Amini - Persian Carpet Gallery
Church St. Open 9.30-5. *STOCK: Oriental rugs.* LOC: A272. PARK: Nearby. TEL: 0798 43344. SER: Valuations; restorations; cleaning.

The Bacchus Gallery
Lombard St. (R. and A Gillett) Est: 1988. Open 10-1 and 2.15-5.30. CL: Mon. and Wed. except by appointment. SIZE: Small. *STOCK: Wine related items.* LOC: Cobbled street leading off town square. PARK: Town square. TEL: 0798 42844; fax - 0798 42634. SER: Buys at auction (as stock). VAT: Stan/Spec.

Baskerville Antiques
Saddlers House, Saddlers Row. (A. and E Baskerville) Est: 1968. Open 9.30-6, Sun. by appointment. SIZE: Medium. *STOCK: English clocks, barometers and furniture, £1,000-£15,000; decorative items and instruments,*

Baskerville Antiques continued

£500-£5,000; all 18th-19th C. LOC: Town centre. PARK: Public, adjoining shop. TEL: 0798 42067; home - same. SER: Restorations (English clocks and furniture). VAT: Spec.

Nigel Bassett
Swan House, Market Sq. (N.J Bassett) Est: 1990. Open 10-1 and 2-5.30. SIZE: Small. *STOCK: Dining room antiques, 18th-19th C.* PARK: Easy. TEL: 0798 44121. VAT: Stan/Spec.

Lesley Bragge Antiques
Fairfield House, High St. Est: 1974. Open 10-1 and 2-5.30. SIZE: Medium. *STOCK: Decorative furniture, 18th-19th C; silver and plate, porcelain, textiles, ormolu, brass, copper, objets d'art, garden furniture.* LOC: Off Golden Square. PARK: Nearby. TEL: 0798 42324. SER: Valuations; restorations; upholstery. VAT: Stan/Spec.

Mark Chapman Antiques LAPADA
New St. Open 10-5.30 or by appointment. *STOCK: Oak and country furniture, 17th-18th C; brass including 18th C base metal candlesticks, pictures, 19th C; decorative items.* TEL: 0798 42283; fax - 0798 43878; home - 0243 572862. SER: Restorations (furniture, metal, paintings).

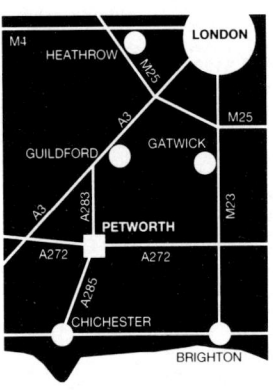

Petworth continued

Philip Cooper Antiques
The Nook, Golden Sq. (P Cooper and S Harrison) Est: 1971. Open by appointment. SIZE: Medium. *STOCK: Oak, walnut, fruitwood and mahogany furniture, 17th-18th C, from £500.* LOC: Lower end of High St. PARK: Nearby. TEL: 0798 42033. VAT: Spec.

Nigel Cracknell (Antiques) Ltd **BADA**
Lombard St. (N.O Cracknell) Est: 1965. Open 9.30-5, Sat. 10-5. SIZE: Large. *STOCK: 18th C mahogany and 19th C rosewood, £1,000-£40,000; 18th C walnut, £1,000-£40,000+; 17th-18th C oak, £1,000-£25,000.* PARK: Easy. TEL: 0798 44188; home - 0672 512912. SER: Valuations; restorations; buys at auction. VAT: Stan/Spec.

Flora Dora Antiques
Lombard St. (J. and P Waldy) Est: 1978. Open 10-5.30. *STOCK: Small furniture, collectors' items including pot lids, stevengraphs, Baxter prints and Le Blond prints, Staffordshire figures, horse brasses.* PARK: Easy. TEL: 0798 43109; home - same. VAT: Stan/Spec.

Frith Antiques
New St. (H.A. and Mrs M.A Frith) Est: 1974. Open 10-5. SIZE: Small. *STOCK: Oak and mahogany country furniture, £50-£3,000;*

Frith Antiques continued

copper, brass, steel and pewter, £10-£500; all 17th-19th C; fishing tackle, 18th-19th C. Not Stocked: Silver. LOC: 50yds. Town Square. PARK: Nearby. TEL: 0798 43155; home - 0798 831606. FAIRS: West London - Jan. and Aug., Olympia. VAT: Stan/Spec.

Granville Antiques **BADA**
High St. (I.E.G Miller) Est: 1979. Open 10-5.30, Wed. 10-2.30 or by appointment. SIZE: Medium. *STOCK: Period furniture, pre-1840, £50-£15,000; accessories and pictures.* Not Stocked: Militaria and jewellery. LOC: 100yds. from market square. PARK: Nearby. TEL: 0798 43250; home - 0243 542293. SER: Valuations (furniture); restorations (furniture); buys at auction. FAIRS: Olympia and Surrey. VAT: Spec.

Griffin Antiques
Squires Holt, Church St. (R. and C Wilson) Est: 1981. Open 10-1 and 2-5.30. SIZE: Medium. *STOCK: English oak, 17th-19th C, £400-£5,000; English pine, £50-£500, domestic metalware, £20-£500, both 18th-19th C.* LOC: Town centre. PARK: Easy. TEL: 0798 43306; home - same. VAT: Stan/Spec.

Grove House Antiques
Middle St. (D Houghton-Connell) Est: 1977. Open 10-1 and 2-5.30, Sun. by appointment. SIZE: Medium. *STOCK: Oak and pine country*

Grove House Antiques continued

furniture, unusual decorative items, treen, lace and quilts. LOC: Between High St. and New St. PARK: Easy. TEL: 0798 43151; home - 0798 42563. SER: Restorations (furniture, paintings). VAT: Stan/Spec.

William Hockley Antiques LAPADA
East St. (D. and V Thrower) Est: 1974. *STOCK: Fine 18th to early 19th C furniture and decorative items; early English pottery.* TEL: 0798 43172.

Howes Gallery
The Square. (B.K Wigg) Est: 1968. Open 10-1 and 2-5.15. SIZE: Medium. *STOCK: Oil paintings, 19th -20th C, £200-£8,000; watercolours, 19th C to early 20th C, £100-£4,000.* LOC: Town centre. PARK: Easy and 200yds. TEL: 0798 43523. VAT: Spec.

Humphry Antiques
North St. (J. and M Humphry) Open 10-1 and 2-5.30, Sun. by appointment. SIZE: Medium. *STOCK: Early English oak and country furniture, 16th-18th C; wood carvings and sculpture, tapestry, metalwork, unusual and decorative items.* LOC: Opposite St. Mary's Church. PARK: Own. TEL: 0798 43053; home - 0798 42944.

Lewis and Lloyd BADA
Swan House, Market Sq. (J.D. and P.C Lewis) Est: 1968. Open 10-5.30. CL: Wed.

Lewis and Lloyd continued

SIZE: Medium. *STOCK: Furniture, 18th-19th C, £1,500-£25,000.* LOC: Town centre. PARK: Easy. TEL: 0798 42896. VAT: Spec.

The Madison Gallery
Swan House, Market Sq. (J. and S Drayson) Open 10-5.30, Sun. by appointment. SIZE: Large. *STOCK: Furniture, including decorative; pictures, accessories.* PARK: Easy. TEL: 0798 43638. SER: Restorations; upholstery. VAT: Stan/Spec.

Millhouse
The Square. (E.G. and C.F Rawnsley) Open 10-5 or by appointment. SIZE: Medium. *STOCK: Fine period furniture and works of art.* PARK: Own - in front of shop. TEL: 0798 43080. SER: Commission search and vetting. VAT: Spec.

John G Morris Ltd BADA
Market Sq. Est: 1962. Open 10-5.30 or by appointment. CL: Wed. p.m. SIZE: Medium. *STOCK: Furniture, English and continental, 1660-1850, from £250; English clocks, 18th-19th C, £2,000-£10,000; English barometers, £800-£4,000; French animalier bronzes, 19th C, £500-£5,000; some porcelain.* Not Stocked: Bric-a-brac, jewellery, Edwardian articles. LOC: On A272. PARK: Easy. TEL: 0798 42305. SER: Valuations; buys at auction. VAT: Stan/Spec.

Petworth continued

Petworth Antique Market
East St. (D.M. and P.J Rayment) Est: 1968. Open 10-5.30. SIZE: Large - 36 dealers. *STOCK: General antiques, books, furniture, brass, copper, pictures, textiles.* LOC: Near church. PARK: Adjoining. TEL: 0798 42073. VAT: Stan/Spec.

Ernest Streeter and Daughter
The Clock House, Lombard St. Est: 1888. CL: Wed. *STOCK: Silver, jewellery.* TEL: 0798 42239. VAT: Stan.

J.C Tutt Antiques
Angel St. Est: 1968. Open 10-5.30. SIZE: Large. *STOCK: Mahogany and country furniture, and accessories.* PARK: Nearby. TEL: 0798 43221. VAT: Stan/Spec.

Michael Wakelin and Helen Linfield **BADA LAPADA**
10 New St. Est: 1968. Open 10-5.30. *STOCK: Fine English country furniture - oak, ash, elm, yew and fruitwood; metalwork, wood carvings, treen, needlework, primitive pictures, lighting; formal mahogany and walnut.* TEL: 0798 42417. VAT: Spec.

T.G Wilkinson Antiques Ltd
1 Pound St. (T. and S Wilkinson) Est: 1979. Open 10-5.30. SIZE: Medium. *STOCK: English and continental furniture, paintings and works of*

T.G Wilkinson Antiques Ltd continued

art, 17th-19th C, £500-£15,000. LOC: On Chichester Rd. from town centre. PARK: Town centre. TEL: 0798 42967. VAT: Stan/Spec.

Jeremy Wood Fine Art
East St. Est: 1974. Open 10-1 and 2-5. *STOCK: Oils and watercolours, etchings, 1880-1950, £5-£500; art reference books, illustrated art and travel books, motoring/motor racing art and books, £1-£50.* TEL: 0798 43408. VAT: Spec.

PORTSLADE

Peter Marks Antique Warehouse
1/11 Church Rd. Est: 1965. Open 9.30-6, Sat. 9.30-1. SIZE: Large. *STOCK: General antiques, shipping goods.* TEL: 0273 415471. VAT: Stan.

J Powell (Hove) Ltd **LAPADA**
20 Wellington Rd. Est: 1949. Open 9-6. CL: Sun. and Sat. p.m. except by appointment. SIZE: Large. *STOCK: Bookcases, display cabinets, £110-£1,500; writing tables and desks, £120-£1,200; longcase and bracket clocks, £50-£2,000; general furniture, shipping goods, 18th-20th C, £5-£1,500.* Not Stocked: Porcelain, jewellery, silver. LOC: 150yds. west of Boundary Rd., on seafront. PARK: Easy. TEL: 0273 411599; home - 0273 593274. SER: Restorations (furniture). VAT: Stan.

Portslade continued

Peter Semus Crafting Antiques
The Warehouse, Gladstone Rd. Open 8-6, Sat. 8-12. *STOCK: General antiques, furniture including reproduction.* PARK: Easy. TEL: 0273 420154; fax - 0273 430355.

PULBOROUGH

Mare Hill Galleries
Mare Hill. (C. and V Trewin) Est: 1970. Open 10-5. *STOCK: Furniture, paintings, porcelain, Oriental works of art.* Not Stocked: Silver, jewellery. TEL: 079 82 2006. VAT: Stan/Spec.

Mulberry House Galleries
Mulberry House, Codmore Hill. Est: 1974. Open 9-6; Wed. p.m., Sat. p.m. and Sun. by appointment. *STOCK: Fine art, prints, oil paintings and watercolours.* LOC: A29, 1 mile north of Pulborough. PARK: Own. TEL: 079 82 2463.

RUDGWICK, Nr. Horsham

Brocante
Clare Cottage Barn, Somersbury Lane, Ellens Green. (J. and M Hicks) Est: 1984. Open Thurs., Fri. and Sat., other days by appointment. SIZE: Medium. *STOCK: Pine, 19th-20th C, £15-£1,500; country and decorative smalls, £5-£100.* LOC: Between Horsham and Guildford - telephone for exact details. PARK: Easy. TEL: 040 372 2267; home - same. SER: Valuations; buys at auction (clocks). VAT: Stan/Spec.

SAYERS COMMON

Recollect Studios
The Old School, London Rd. (Mr & Mrs J Jackman) Est: 1970. Open 10-5. CL: Mon. *STOCK: Dolls, dolls house miniatures, books, doll restoration materials.* LOC: A23. PARK: Own. TEL: 0273 833314. SER: Restorations (dolls); catalogues available.

SHOREHAM-BY-SEA

Tudor Cottage Antiques
Upper Shoreham Rd. (Mrs J Perrett) Resident. Est: 1967. Open daily (also evenings). *STOCK: General antiques, curios.* LOC: Near Amsterdam Restaurant. TEL: 0273 453554.

STEYNING

David R Fileman
Squirrels, Bayards. Open daily. *STOCK: Table glass, £20-£1,000; chandeliers, candelabra, £500-£20,000; all 18th-19th C. Collectors' items, 17th-19th C, £25-£2,000; paperweights, 19th C, £50-£5,000.* LOC: A283 to north of Steyning village. TEL: 0903 813229. SER: Valuations; restorations (chandeliers and candelabra). VAT: Stan/Spec.

Steyning continued

Penfold Gallery and Antiques
30 High St. (Mrs J Exley-Turner) Open 9.30-4.30. *STOCK: Watercolours, oils, prints, etchings, etc; general antiques.* TEL: 0903 815595.

STORRINGTON

Storrington Antiques
46 West St. (D.J Bond) Est: 1967. Open 9.30-5 daily. *STOCK: Furniture and general antiques.* TEL: 0903 742193.

Thakeham Furniture
Orchardway Stables, Rock Rd. (T.J.G Chavasse) Est: 1988. Open 8.30-5, Sat. and Sun. by appointment. SIZE: Small. *STOCK: Furniture, 1750-1880, £20-£3,000.* LOC: Off B2193, one mile north of Storrington. PARK: Easy. TEL: 0903 745474. SER: Restorations (furniture); buys at auction (furniture). VAT: Stan/Spec.

TILLINGTON, Nr. Petworth

Loewenthal Antiques
Tillington Cottage. CL: Wed. *STOCK: 18th C furniture and objets d'art.* LOC: A272, 1 mile west of Petworth. TEL: 0798 42969.

WARNHAM

Warnham Antiques
24 Church St. (J.A Kay) Est: 1977. Open 10-1 and 2-5. CL: Mon. and Fri. SIZE: Medium. *STOCK: Chests, tables, chairs, bureaux, clocks and pictures, 18th-19th C, to £700.* LOC: Off A24. PARK: Easy. TEL: 0403 52802; home - 0403 60767.

WASHINGTON, Nr. Pulborough

Chanctonbury Antiques
Clematis Cottage. (G Troche) Est: 1961. Open 10-5.30. CL: Sun. and Tues. except by appointment. SIZE: Medium. *STOCK: Porcelain, needlework, glass, furniture, objets de vertu.* LOC: Just off A24. PARK: Easy. TEL: 0903 892233.

Sandhill Barn Antiques (Pine and Country)
Est: 1969. Open from 9.30-5.30. SIZE: Large. *STOCK: Pine and old painted country furniture, bygones, early iron, brass, copper, treen, kitchen items.* Not Stocked: Silver, jewellery, mahogany. LOC: At the Washington roundabout (crossroads of A24 and A283), take the Steyning road and turn left immediately into cul-de-sac. PARK: Easy. TEL: 0903 892888. SER: Stripping (pine). VAT: Stan.

WEST WITTERING

Buck's Barn Antiques
(M Wallace and M Sheldrick) Resident. CL: Mon. *STOCK: General small antiques.* TEL: 0243 513729.

WESTBOURNE, Nr. Emsworth

Westbourne Antiques
3 Lamb Buildings, The Square. (H.J. and V.J Lain) Est: 1951. Open Thurs., Fri. and Sat. 9-5. SIZE: Large. *STOCK: Silver, jewellery, collectors' items.* PARK: Nearby. TEL: 0243 373711. SER: Valuations; repairs (jewellery and watches).

WISBOROUGH GREEN, Nr. Billingshurst

Wisborough Green Antiques
Billingshurst Rd. (A Hughes) Est: 1975. Open 10.30-1 and 2.15-4.30. CL: Mon. SIZE: Medium. *STOCK: Georgian and Victorian furniture, pine, porcelain, sewing items, lace, jewellery, paintings, rugs.* LOC: A272. Next to Three Crowns public house. PARK: Easy. TEL: 0403 700650.

WORTHING

7-9 The Arcade
(R Law) Open 10-5. CL: Some Wed. *STOCK: Victorian and Edwardian fine jewellery, silver, porcelain dolls, furniture, collectables.* TEL: 0903 200274.

A Biscoe
122 Montague St. (R Byskou) Open 10-6. *STOCK: Furniture, silver, porcelain, 18th-19th C; jewellery, clocks and objets d'art.* TEL: 0903 202489; home - 0903 782723.

Cheriton Antiques LAPADA
21 New Broadway, Tarring Rd. (A.C Biggs and Mrs M.D Edwardes) Open 9.30-5.30. CL: Wed. *STOCK: Mahogany, walnut and rosewood furniture, 18th-19th C; porcelain, glass, upholstered chairs, couches, lighting.* Not Stocked: Jewellery, silver. LOC: 200yds. east of West Worthing railway station. TEL: 0903 35463 (ansaphone). VAT: Stan/Spec.

Chloe Antiques
61 Brighton Rd. (Mrs D Peters) Est: 1960. Open 9.30-12.30 and 2-5. SIZE: Small. *STOCK: General antiques, furniture, jewellery, china, glass, bric-a-brac.* LOC: From Brighton, on main rd. just past Beach House Park on corner. PARK: Opposite. TEL: 0903 202697.

Crosshall Gallery
47 Arlington Ave, Goring-by-Sea. (S Briggs) Est: 1979. Open by appointment. *STOCK: Watercolours, mainly 19th C.* TEL: 0903 44291. VAT: Spec.

Worthing continued

Geoffrey Godden Chinaman BADA
19a Crescent Rd. (G.A Godden) Est: 1900. Open by appointment. *STOCK: Ceramics, 18th-19th C.* LOC: Town centre. PARK: Easy. TEL: 0903 35958/31901. VAT: Spec.

Godden of Worthing Ltd BADA
19a Crescent Rd. (G. and J Godden) Est: 1900. Open by appointment. *STOCK: Ceramics, 18th-19th C.* PARK: Easy. TEL: 0903 35958/31901. VAT: Spec.

A. de Saye Hutton Antiques
Est: 1963. By appointment only. *STOCK: English porcelain especially New Hall, 18th-19th C.* PARK: Easy. TEL: 0903 502651.

Rococo Antiques
21 Warwick Rd. (K.P Jakes) Open 11-5. CL: Fri. *STOCK: General antiques.* TEL: 0903 35896.

Steyne Antique Gallery
29 Brighton Rd. (H.W. and V.I Melling) Open 9.30-5.30. CL: Mon. *STOCK: Furniture, porcelain, clocks and general antiques.* TEL: 0903 200079.

Robert Warner and Son Ltd
1-13 South Farm Rd. Est: 1940. CL: Wed. p.m. SIZE: Large. *STOCK: Furniture, bric-a-brac.* TEL: 0903 32710. VAT: Stan.

Whitehouse Antiques Ltd
87 Rowlands Rd. (G.G Cross) Est: 1959. Open 9.30-1 and 2-5 or by appointment. CL: Wed. and Sat. p.m. SIZE: Large. *STOCK: Furniture, shipping goods, china, silver, pewter, brass.* LOC: Near seafront. PARK: Easy. TEL: 0903 30844. VAT: Stan/Spec.

Wilsons Antiques LAPADA
57/59 Broadwater Rd. (F Wilson) Est: 1936. Open 9-5. SIZE: Large. *STOCK: Period furniture, 18th-19th C, £100-£10,000; Edwardian furniture, £50-£4,000; decorative items, 19th C, £10-£750.* Not Stocked: Pine. PARK: At rear. TEL: 0903 202059. SER: Valuations; restorations (furniture). FAIRS: N.E.C. (April); Olympia (June and Oct.); Barbican. VAT: Stan/Spec.

Tumbler engraved with a portrait of Buffalo Bill, c.1903. The engraving is attributed to W.O. Bowen who worked at J. & J. Northwood's decorating shop in Wordley and later became its manager. Height 5¼in. (13.6cm). HULBERT OF DUDLEY COLLECTION

Tyne and Wear

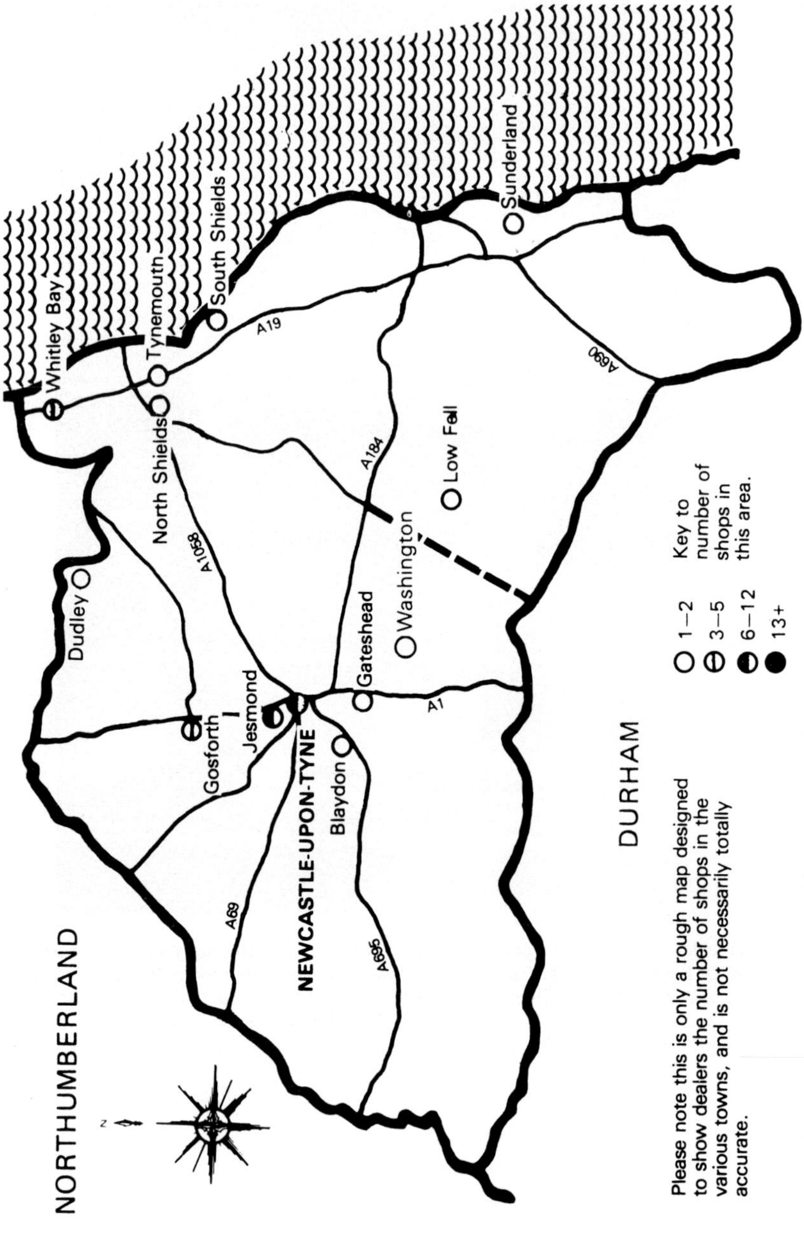
Whitley Bay
Tynemouth
South Shields
Sunderland
A19
North Shields
A184
Low Fell
A690
Dudley
A1058
Gateshead
Washington
Gosforth
Jesmond
NEWCASTLE-UPON-TYNE
Blaydon
A1
A69
A695
NORTHUMBERLAND
DURHAM
N
1–2
3–5
6–12
13+
Key to number of shops in this area.

Please note this is only a rough map designed to show dealers the number of shops in the various towns, and is not necessarily totally accurate.

BLAYDON, Nr. Newcastle-upon-Tyne

Blaydon Antique Centre
Bridge House, Bridge St. (Mrs E Bradshaw) Est: 1978. Open 10-5. SIZE: Large. *STOCK: Furniture, 18th-20th C, £5-£3,000, including pianos; china, brass, pictures.* PARK: Easy. TEL: 091 4143535 (24 hrs.). SER: Valuations. FAIRS: Local.

DUDLEY

Weetslade Fine Art
High Weetslade. Open by appointment. *STOCK: Oils and watercolours, 19th-20th C.* TEL: 091 2500174. SER: Restorations; framing.

GATESHEAD

Boadens of Hexham
28 The Boulevard, Antique Village, Metrocentre. (R.J Boaden) Open 10-8, Thurs, 10-9, Sat. 9-6. *STOCK: Small general antiques, china, glass, silver, paintings, jewellery and reproductions.* TEL: 091 460 0358.

Metro Antiques
31 The Boulevard, Antiques Court, Antique Village, Metrocentre. (R Welch) Open 10-8, Thurs. 10-9, Sat. 9-6. *STOCK: Furniture, china, jewellery, prints and bric-a-brac, including reproduction.* TEL: 091 460 0340.

Sovereign Antiques
35 The Boulevard, Antiques Court, The Antique Village, Metrocentre. Open 10-8, Thurs. 10-9, Sat. 9-6. *STOCK: Fine jewellery, silver, prints and maps.* TEL: 091 460 9604.

The Windmill
223 Coatsworth Rd. (G Taylor) Est: 1978. Open 10-5.30, Sat. 10-3. SIZE: Medium. *STOCK: General antiques - furniture, pictures, clocks, bric-a-brac, £5-£500.* Not Stocked: Jewellery. LOC: Corner of Whitehall Rd. PARK: Easy. TEL: 091 4772300; home - 091 4774161. SER: Valuations; restorations (oil paintings and watercolours); framing.

GOSFORTH, Nr. Newcastle-upon-Tyne

Causey Antique Shop
Causey St. *STOCK: Furniture, 19th C; Victoriana and collectors' items.*

H. and S. Collectables
149 Salters Rd. (H. and Mrs S Shorrick) Est: 1989. Open 10-5, Sun. by appointment. SIZE: Small. *STOCK: Collectables, 1800-1930, £5-£900.* LOC: Off High St. PARK: Easy. TEL: 091 2846626; home - 091 2863498. SER: Valuations.

Gosforth continued

Anna Harrison Fine Antiques LAPADA
Grange Park, Great North Rd. Est: 1976. Open 10-4.30. SIZE: Large. *STOCK: English furniture, porcelain, silver, oils and watercolours.* LOC: A6125, 3 miles north of city centre, near Regent Centre. PARK: Forecourt. TEL: 091 2843202; home - 091 2367652. SER: Valuations; restorations. VAT: Stan/Spec.

H Krolick
Est: 1947. Open by appointment. TEL: 091 2856741.

MacDonald Fine Art
2 Ashburton Rd. (T. and C MacDonald) Est: 1976. Open 10-1 and 2.30-5.30. CL: Wed. SIZE: Medium. *STOCK: Watercolours and oils, mainly north-eastern artists, English and Scottish, 18th-20th C.* LOC: 1 mile west of A1. PARK: Easy. TEL: 091 2844214; home - 091 2856188. SER: Valuations; restorations (watercolours and oils); framing; buys at auction (watercolours and oils). VAT: Spec.

JESMOND, Nr. Newcastle-upon-Tyne

Bewick Antiques
14 Clayton Rd. (C Seaton) Est: 1974. Open 10.30-4.30. SIZE: Large. *STOCK: Furniture, £50-£1,000; decorative items and textiles, £20-£500, all 19th C; antiquarian books, £5-£1,000.* LOC: 200yds. from A1. PARK: Easy. TEL: 091 2812711; home - 067072 276. VAT: Stan/Spec.

Clayton Antiques
15a Clayton Rd. (D. and J Westle) Est: 1979. Open 11-5 or by appointment. CL: Wed. SIZE: Small. *STOCK: Small furniture, 18th and 19th C, glass, decorative items and collectables.* LOC: Off Osborne Rd. PARK: Easy. TEL: 091 2817416. VAT: Stan/Spec.

Geoffrey Hugall
19 Clayton Rd. Est: 1970. Open 10-5 or by appointment. SIZE: Medium. *STOCK: General antiques, furniture, china, period and decorative items.* Not Stocked: Weapons, musical instruments. PARK: Easy. TEL: 091 2818408. VAT: Stan/Spec.

Owen Humble LAPADA
11-12 Clayton Rd. Est: 1958. Open 6 days. SIZE: Large and warehouse. *STOCK: Furniture, general antiques.* PARK: Easy. TEL: 091 2814602. SER: Restorations. VAT: Stan/Spec.

Osborne Art and Antiques
18c Osborne Rd. (F.T. and S Jackman) Est: 1974. Open 10-5.15. *STOCK: Victorian oil paintings, watercolours, drawings, engravings and maps.* TEL: 091 2816380. SER: Restorations; picture framing. VAT: Stan/Spec.

Jesmond continued

W. and J Walker
231 Jesmond Rd. Est: 1976. Open 10-5. CL: Mon. SIZE: Medium. *STOCK: Furniture, clocks, bric-a-brac, all 19th C.* LOC: Main road to east coast. PARK: Osborne Ave. - around corner. TEL: 091 2817286. VAT: Stan.

LOW FELL, Nr. Gateshead

N Jewett
639/643 Durham Rd. Est: 1948. Large. SIZE: Antique and reproduction furniture, glass, china, £5-£5,000. LOC: On A6127, 3 miles south of Newcastle-upon-Tyne. PARK: On hill opp. TEL: 091 4877636. SER: Valuations. VAT: Stan/Spec.

NEWCASTLE-UPON-TYNE

Antiques Centre
8-10 St. Mary's Place East. (B. and G Punton) Est: 1985. Open 10-5. CL: Mon. SIZE: 18 dealers. *STOCK: General antiques and collectables.* LOC: Opp. Civic Centre. PARK: Nearby. TEL: 091 2323821/2329832. SER: Valuations; restorations; metal polishing. FAIRS: York, Leeds, Glasgow. VAT: Stan.

Davidson's The Jewellers Ltd
94 and 96 Grey St. Open 9-5. *STOCK: Jewellery, silver.* TEL: 091 2322551/2322895.

Newcastle-upon-Tyne continued

The Dean Gallery
42 Dean St. (A.P Graham) Est: 1970. Open 10-5. CL: Sat. p.m. SIZE: Large. *STOCK: Oils, watercolours, local and national, 18th to early 20th C, £100-£10,000.* LOC: Going north over Tyne Bridge, turn left, and left again. PARK: Easy. TEL: 091 2321208. SER: Valuations; restorations; framing. VAT: Stan/Spec.

Intercoin
99 Clayton St. Open 9-4.30. CL: Wed. *STOCK: Coins and items of numismatic interest; jewellery, silver.* LOC: City centre. TEL: 091 2322064.

Owen's Jewellers
14 Shields Rd, Byker. (D.W Robertson) Est: 1968. Open 9-5. *STOCK: Jewellery.* TEL: 091 2654332.

W Robinson (Newcastle) Ltd
49-53 Grainger Market. Est: 1881. Open 9-5, Wed. 9-3. *STOCK: Antiquarian books.* TEL: 091 2322978.

Shiners Architectural Reclamation
123 Jesmond Rd. (B. and A Lawson) Open 9-5. SIZE: Large. *STOCK: Architectural items including Victorian and Edwardian fireplaces.* LOC: On main road. PARK: Easy. TEL: 091 2816474. SER: Valuations; metal polishing.

Newcastle-upon-Tyne continued

Spicker Jewellers
75 Grainger Market, Alley No.2. *STOCK: Pottery, china, silver, objets d'art, textiles, quilts.* TEL: 091 2325057.

R.D Steedman
9 Grey St. Est: 1907. CL: Sat. p.m. *STOCK: Rare books.* TEL: 091 2326561.

Warner Fine Art
208 Wingrove Rd, Fenham. (S. and M Warner) Est: 1989. Open by appointment only. SIZE: Medium. *STOCK: Watercolours, 19th and 20th C, £300-£10,000; oils, 18th-20th C, to £4,000; prints and etchings, decorative objects, 18th-20th C, £50-£500.* LOC: Off A69, Westgate Rd. PARK: Easy. TEL: 091 273 8030 (24 hrs.). SER: Valuations; restorations (watercolours, oils, frames); buys at auction (watercolours, oils, prints, ship models, maritime objects mainly northern).

NORTH SHIELDS

Peter Coulson Antiques
8-10 Queen Alexandra Rd. Est: 1977. Open 10-5. CL: Wed. *STOCK: General antiques; clocks and watches.* TEL: 091 2579761. SER: Repairs.

Maggie May's
Incorporating Tynemouth Fine Art, 49 Kirton Park Terrace. (Miss M.L Hayes) Est: 1960. Open 10.30-5.30. CL: Wed. SIZE: Medium. *STOCK: General antiques and collectors' items, art deco, Victorian and Edwardian furniture, china, glass; 19th C paintings and watercolours, especially Northumbrian artists, 1800-1950; continental furniture, glassware, porcelain, decorative items, gramophones.* LOC: Opposite The Gunner Inn, near Preston Hospital. TEL: 091 2570076. SER: Valuations; restorations; framing; French polishing.

SOUTH SHIELDS

The Curiosity Shop
16 Frederick St. Est: 1969. CL: Wed. *STOCK: General antiques, paintings, jewellery, furniture, Royal Doulton.* TEL: 091 4565560.

William White
20A Frederick St. Open 9.30-4. TEL: 091 2568461.

SUNDERLAND

Peter Smith Antiques **LAPADA**
12-14 Borough Rd. Est: 1968. Open 9.30-4.30, Sat. 9.30-12, other times by appointment. SIZE: Warehouse. *STOCK: Georgian, Victorian, Edwardian longcase clocks, shipping goods, £5-£15,000.* LOC: Towards docks/Hendon from

Peter Smith Antiques continued

town centre. PARK: Easy. TEL: 091 5673537/5677842; fax - 091 5142286; home - 091 5140008. SER: Valuations; restorations; some shipping; buys at auction. VAT: Stan/Spec.

TYNEMOUTH

Renaissance Antiques
11 Front St. (E. and N Moore) Est: 1977. Open 10.30-1 and 2-4. CL: Wed.-Fri. SIZE: Medium and trade goods store. *STOCK: Furniture, Victorian to art deco, £50-£1,000; china and porcelain, silver, brass and copper, £5-£100; shipping goods.* LOC: Main coast road from Newcastle. PARK: Easy. TEL: 091 2595555; home - 091 2574073. SER: Valuations.

Ian Sharp Antiques **LAPADA**
23 Front St. Open 9.30-5.30, or by appointment. *STOCK: Furniture, 18th to early 20th C; British oil paintings, pottery and watercolours; Northern ceramics, 18th to early 20th C.* TEL: 091 296 0656.

David R Strain Antiques **LAPADA**
66 Front St. Est: 1983. Open 9.30-5. CL: Sat. p.m. SIZE: Medium. *STOCK: Furniture and general antiques, Edwardian, Victorian, Georgian, £5-£2,000.* Not Stocked: Weapons, books, silver and jewellery. LOC: Main coast road from Newcastle, 10 mins. from Tyne tunnel. PARK: Easy. TEL: 091 2592459; home - 091 2590300. SER: Valuations; buys at auction (furniture). VAT: Stan/Spec.

WASHINGTON

Harold J Carr Antiques **LAPADA**
Field House, Rickleton. Open by appointment. *STOCK: General antiques and furniture.* TEL: 091 3886442.

WHITLEY BAY

The Bric-a-Brac
195 Park View. (C Rawes) Est: 1953. Open 10-5. SIZE: Medium. *STOCK: General antiques.* TEL: 091 2526141.

Northumbria Pine
54 Whitley Rd. (C. and V Dowland) Est: 1979. Open 9.30-5. CL: Wed. SIZE: Medium. *STOCK: Stripped pine, 19th C, £100-£700.* LOC: Cullercoats end of Whitley Rd., behind sea front. PARK: Easy. TEL: 091 2524550. VAT: Stan.

Treasure Chest
2 and 4 Norham Rd. Est: 1974. Open 10.30-1 and 2-4. CL: Wed. and Thurs. SIZE: Small. *STOCK: General antiques.* LOC: Just off main shopping area of Park View, leading to Monkseaton Railway Station. PARK: Easy. TEL: 091 2512052.

Warwickshire

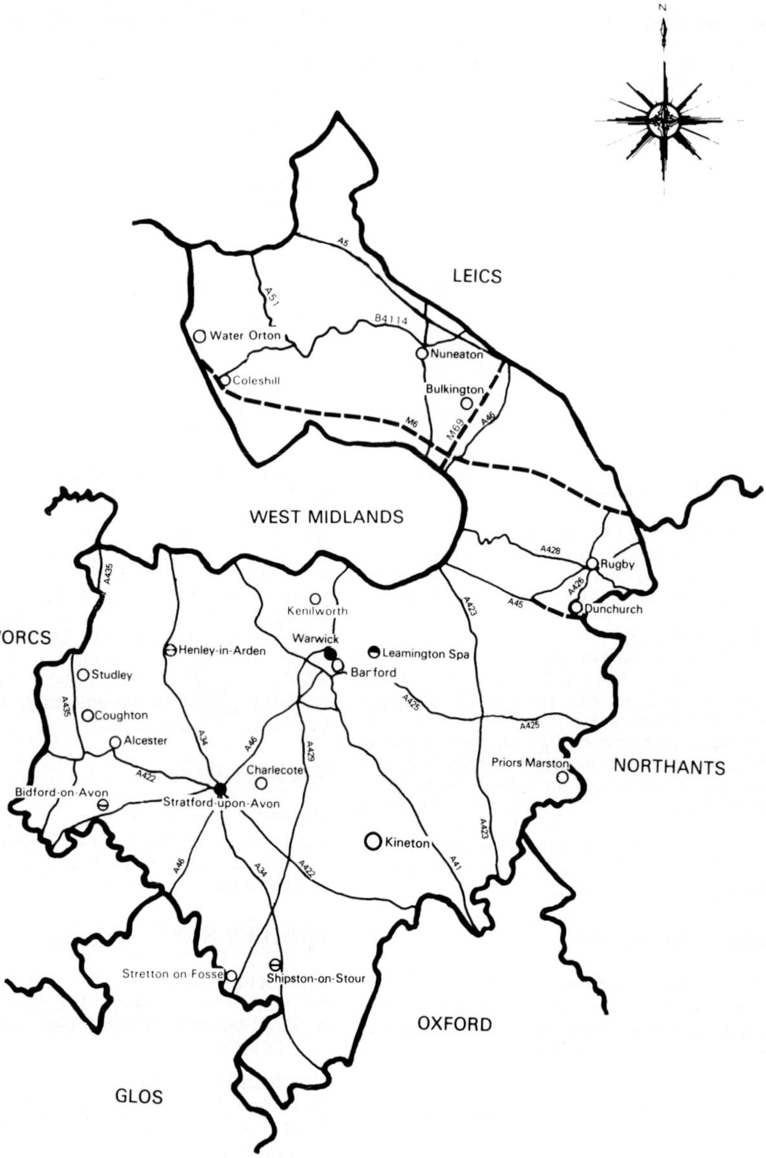
N
LEICS
A5
A51
B4114
Water Orton
Nuneaton
Coleshill
Bulkington
M6
M69
A46
WEST MIDLANDS
A428
Rugby
A426
A45
Dunchurch
A435
A423
WORCS
Kenilworth
Warwick
Henley-in-Arden
Leamington Spa
Studley
Barford
A425
Coughton
A425
A34
A46
A429
Alcester
Priors Marston
NORTHANTS
Charlecote
A422
Bidford-on-Avon
Stratford-upon-Avon
Kineton
A423
A41
A46
A34
A422
Stretton on Fosse
Shipston-on-Stour
OXFORD
GLOS

Please note this is only a rough map designed to show dealers the number of shops in the various towns, and is not necessarily totally accurate.

Key to number of shops in this area.

- ○ 1–2
- ⊖ 3–5
- ◓ 6–12
- ● 13+

ALCESTER

High St. Antiques
11A High St. (P Payne) Est: 1979. Open Sat. 11-1 and 2.30-5, weekdays by appointment. SIZE: Small. *STOCK: Glass and china, 18th-20th C, but mainly 19th C, £5-£200; brass, copper and silver, 19th-20th C, £5-£100+; postcards and art deco china.* LOC: On left-hand side near church coming from Stratford-on-Avon road. PARK: Rear of High St. TEL: 0789 764009; home - same. SER: Valuations.

Malthouse Antiques Centre
Market Pl. (R.T. and P Adkins) Est: 1982. Open 10-5, Sun. 2-5. SIZE: Large. *STOCK: Victorian pine furniture, £25-£300; furniture, from Georgian, £100-£1,000; paintings and prints, £25-£1,000.* LOC: Off High St. PARK: Easy. TEL: 0789 764032. SER: Restorations; buys at auction.

BARFORD, Nr. Warwick

Goodsons Antiques
Ingsley Bank, Wellesbourne Rd. (C.A Goodson) Open by appointment. *STOCK: Furniture, silver and jewellery.* TEL: 0926 624044. SER: Restorations.

BIDFORD-ON-AVON

The Antiques Centre
High St. (M Davison) Est: 1983. Open 10-5, Sun. 2-5.30. SIZE: 11 dealers. *STOCK: Furniture, china, glass, jewellery, paintings, bygones, clocks.* PARK: Easy. TEL: 0789 773680.

Crown Antiques
14 High St. (J. and C Ford) Resident. Est: 1980. Open 10-5.30, Sat. 10-4.30, Sun. by appointment. CL: Thurs. SIZE: Medium. *STOCK: Furniture, 18th-19th C, up to £6,000; Edwardian inlaid, £50-£3,000; general antiques.* LOC: 100yds. off A439. PARK: Easy. TEL: 0789 772939. SER: Valuations; buys at auction (furniture); courier. VAT: Stan/Spec.

BULKINGTON, Nr. Nuneaton

Sport and Country Gallery LAPADA
Northwood House. (R. and S Hill) Open any time by appointment. *STOCK: 19th-20th C oils and watercolours.* TEL: 0203 314335. VAT: Spec.

CHARLECOTE

Country Furniture
Kingsmead Farm. (Mrs J Seccombe) Resident. Est: 1970. Open Sat. and Sun., other times by appointment. SIZE: Medium. *STOCK: Pine, bric-a-brac, country furniture.* TEL: 0789 840254. SER: Valuations. VAT: Stan.

Jack Goodchild using a razor sharp adze to create the saddle shaped seats for which Windosrs are noted. The seat maker or 'bottomer' held the seat in position on the floor with his feet, and needed great skill not only to produce the required shaping, but also to avoid injuring himself.

MUSEUM OF ENGLISH RURAL LIFE, UNIVERSITY OF READING

From ***The English Regional Chair,*** by Bernard D. Cotton, published by the **Antique Collectors' Club** in 1990. £49.50.

COLESHILL

Coleshill Antiques & Interiors Ltd LAPADA
14 High St. (A.J Webster) Open 9.30-5. *STOCK: Porcelain, furniture, jewellery and silver.* PARK: Easy. TEL: 0675 462931; 0675 467416. VAT: Stan/Spec.

Geostran Antiques
Middle Lane, Whitacre Heath. (A. and A.M Potter) Est: 1983. Open 10-5, Sat., Sun. and other times by appointment. SIZE: Small. *STOCK: Small furniture, pre Edwardian, £100+; clocks and collectors' items, 19th C, £20+.* LOC: Junction 4, M6, to Coleshill, then B4114, follow signs to Whiteacre Heath. PARK: Easy. TEL: 0675 81483; home - same. SER: Restorations (clocks and small furniture). FAIRS: British International, Birmingham; Belfry Hotel, Warks.

COUGHTON, Nr. Alcester

Coughton Galleries Ltd
Coughton Court. (Lady Isabel Throckmorton) Est: 1968. Open 10-5.30, Wed., Thurs., Sat. and Sun., or by appointment. SIZE: Medium. *STOCK: Modern British and Irish oil paintings and watercolours.* TEL: 0789 762642. VAT: Spec.

DUNCHURCH, Nr. Rugby

Dunchurch Antique Centre
16/16a Daventry Rd. (M. and Mrs G Vandervelden) Est: 1981. Open 7 days, 10-5. SIZE: Medium - 18 dealers. *STOCK: Mainly pre-1930 house furnishings and fitments, collectors items, silver, plate and jewellery.* LOC: Opposite Guy Fawkes cottage. PARK: Easy. TEL: 0788 817147. SER: Valuations; buys at auction (clocks, barometers and watches). VAT: Stan/Spec.

HENLEY-IN-ARDEN

Arden Gallery
(G.B Horton) Est: 1963. Open 1-6. CL: Sat. SIZE: Medium. *STOCK: Oil paintings, Victorian, £20-£1,000; watercolours, all periods, to £1,500; portrait miniatures.* LOC: A34. PARK: Easy. TEL: 0564 792520. VAT: Spec.

The Chadwick Gallery
Doctors Lane. (R Barnes) Open 10-5. CL: Mon. and Thurs. p.m. *STOCK: 19th to early 20th C watercolours, etchings and engravings; some contemporary works.* TEL: 0564 794820.

Colmore Galleries Ltd LAPADA
52 High St. Open 11-5.30. *STOCK: Pictures, 19th-20th C.* TEL: 0564 792938. SER: Valuations; restorations; framing.

Lacy Gallery
56 High St. Open 10-1 and 2-5.30. CL: Fri. and Sat. *STOCK: Period frames; sporting and decorative paintings, watercolours and prints, 18th-20th C; art reference books.* TEL: 0564 793073.

Henley-in-Arden continued

Jasper Marsh BADA
3 High St. (P.R.J Marsh) Est: 1967. Open 10-5.30, Sun. p.m. by appointment. *STOCK: English furniture, Georgian, oak and mahogany, 17th to early 19th C, English and Oriental porcelain, Chinoiserie and Oriental art.* TEL: 0564 792088. VAT: Spec.

KENILWORTH

The Allen Gallery
38 Castle Hill. (N.P Allen) Est: 1975. Open 11.30-5.30, including Sun., Tues. and Wed. by appointment. CL: Mon. and Thurs. SIZE: Medium. *STOCK: Paintings, watercolours and etchings, 19th-20th C; period frames, Oriental carpets, furniture, objets d'art.* PARK: Easy. TEL: 0926 851435; home - same. SER: Valuations; restorations; buys at auction (paintings). FAIRS: Local; some Robert Bailey.

Castle Gallery
32 Castle Hill. (M. and M Lloyd-Smith) Open 11-5 including Sun., other times by appointment. CL: Mon. and Thurs. *STOCK: Watercolours, drawings.* TEL: 0926 58727. SER: Conservation framing.

Janice Paull Antiques LAPADA
125 Warwick Rd. Est: 1965. Open by appointment. SIZE: Medium. *STOCK: Mason's Ironstone, 1813-1880; pottery and porcelain, 1780-1890; Baxter and Le Blond prints; all from £100.* LOC: Main st. PARK: Easy. TEL: 0926 55253. SER: Valuations. FAIRS: Cafe Royal, N.E.C., Kenilworth. VAT: Spec.

KINETON

Jeremy Venables
The Old Mill, Mill Lane. Est: 1977. Open 9.15-5.30 and by appointment. CL: Sat. SIZE: Large. *STOCK: Victorian, Georgian, Edwardian and shipping furniture.* LOC: Junction 12, M40, 2 miles Kineton, past Carpenter's Arms, 1st left. PARK: Easy. TEL: 0926 640971. SER: Export. VAT: Stan.

LEAMINGTON SPA

John Goodwin and Sons
Blackdown Mill, Blackdown. Open 9.30-5.30. *STOCK: Victorian and Edwardian furniture.* TEL: 0926 450687.

Hague Antiques
2 Regent St. (J Hague) Est: 1967. Open 9.30-1 and 2-5. SIZE: Medium. *STOCK: Furniture, copper and brass, dolls, unstripped pine.* LOC: One of the main roads which cross the Parade. PARK: Easy. TEL: 0926 37236. VAT: Stan/Spec.

David Hooper Antiques
20 Regent St. Open 9-6. *STOCK: General antiques.* TEL: 0926 429679.

COLESHILL ANTIQUES & INTERIORS LTD

EST 1958

VENDORS & PURCHASERS OF FINE ANTIQUES

LAPADA
MEMBER

Part of our extensive collection from one of our showrooms

2 MINUTES FROM NATIONAL EXHIBITION CENTRE

Trade welcome to sell

14 HIGH ST.,
COLESHILL, WARWICKSHIRE

ANTIQUES 0675 462931 INTERIORS 0675 467416

Leamington Spa continued

Leamington Pine and Antique Centre
20 Regent St. Open 9-6. SIZE: 12 dealers. *STOCK: General antiques.* TEL: 0926 429679.

Lions Den
Open by appointment. *STOCK: Moorcroft pottery, porcelain, oil paintings and water-colours.* TEL: 0926 339498.

Spa Antiques
4 Windsor St. (A Jackson) Open 9.30-6. *STOCK: Oak furniture.* TEL: 0926 422927.

Trading Post
39 Chandos St. (B Morris) Est: 1949. Open 10-12 and 2-4. CL: Thurs. p.m. *STOCK: Small general antiques, Victorian jewellery.* TEL: 0926 421857.

Percy F Wale Ltd
32 and 34 Regent St. (B.A., P.G. and G.S Barton) Est: 1918. Open 9-1 and 2-6, Sat. 9-6. SIZE: Large. *STOCK: Late Georgian, Victorian and Edwardian furniture, £500-£6,000; quality reproduction furniture, silver and plate.* LOC: Regent St. crosses main Parade in centre of town, shop situated at Western end. PARK: Easy. TEL: 0926 421288. SER: Restorations (upholstery, furniture). VAT: Stan/Spec.

Yesterdays
21 Portland St. (D. and Mrs K Norbury) Est: 1986. Open 10-5. CL: Mon. and Tues. SIZE: Small.

Yesterdays continued

STOCK: Furniture, George III to Edwardian, £75-£1,000; china, prints, 1850-1910, £10-£100. Not Stocked: Pine. LOC: Parallel to The Parade. PARK: Easy. TEL: 0926 450238; home - 0926 316565.

NUNEATON

Vivian Antiques
32 Coton Rd. (C Vivian) Est: 1973. Open 10-4.30, Sat. 10-1 or by appointment. CL: Thurs. SIZE: Medium. *STOCK: Furniture, 18th-19th C; shipping goods.* LOC: A444. PARK: Easy. TEL: 0203 381945; home - 0203 346795. SER: Restorations (furniture).

PRIORS MARSTON, Nr. Rugby

Daneby House Antiques
Daneby House, (Daneby Antiques Ltd.). Est: 1965. Open 9-6, or by appointment. CL: Tues. and Thurs. SIZE: Small. *STOCK: Furniture, Queen Anne to Victorian, £100-£1,500; china, glass, £20-£100; metalware, silver, £20-£200; all Georgian to Victorian.* LOC: 6 miles from Daventry. PARK: Easy. TEL: 0327 60347.

RUGBY

Rugby Antiques Centre
22 Railway Terrace. (R. and M Dennis) Open 10-5.30. CL: Wed. SIZE: 20 stalls. *STOCK: General antiques, especially books, juvenalia, pictures, prints, art deco, furniture, 1790-1940, £2-£2,000.* PARK: Easy, multi-storey opp. SER: Restorations.

SHIPSTON-ON-STOUR

Fine-Lines (Fine Art) LAPADA
The Old Rectory, 31 Sheep St. (L.W. and R.M Guthrie) Est: 1975. Open seven days appointment only. SIZE: Medium. *STOCK: British and European watercolours, pastels, drawings and selected oils, from 1850, £300-£10,000.* LOC: On main one-way street. PARK: Easy. TEL: 0608 62323; home - same. SER: Restorations; cleaning; framing; buys at auction (paintings, watercolours and drawings). VAT: Spec.

The Grandfather Clock Shop
2 Bondgate House, West St, Granville Court. (M.S Chambers) Est: 1978. Open 9.30-5. CL: Mon. and Thurs. p.m. SIZE: Medium. *STOCK: Clocks - longcase, pre-1800, £1,000-£4,000; wall, £250-£1,000; mantle and bracket, 1790-1890, £200-£2,000; barometers, 1790-1860, £350-£1,000; furniture including oak, 17th-18th C.* PARK: Easy. TEL: 0608 62144; home - 0926 57487.

'Time in Hand'
11 Church St. (F.R Bennett) Open 9.30-1 and 2-5.30 or by appointment. SIZE: Medium. *STOCK: Longcase, carriage and wall clocks, barometers.* PARK: Town centre. TEL: 0608 62578. SER: Restorations (clocks, watches, barometers and mechanical instruments).

STRATFORD-UPON-AVON

Abode
Shrieve's House, 40 Sheep St. (Mrs A. and J Bannister) Est: 1975. Open 9-5.30. SIZE: Large. *STOCK: Furniture, pine, interior design items.* LOC: Town centre. TEL: 0789 268755. SER: Buys at auction (furniture). FAIRS: Decorex International (Interior Design). VAT: Stan/Spec.

The Antique Arcade
4 Sheep St. (R Chambers) Est: 1979. Open 10-5.30. SIZE: 14 dealers. *STOCK: Jewellery, silver, furniture, books, toy soldiers, lace.* TEL: 0789 297249.

Arbour Antiques Ltd BADA
Poet's Arbour, Sheep St. (R.J Wigington) Est: 1952. Open 9-5.30, Sat. by appointment. *STOCK: Arms, armour.* LOC: From town centre towards Theatre and River, behind Bobby Brown's Restaurant through archway at right. PARK: Easy. TEL: 0789 293453. VAT: Spec.

Art Deco Ceramics Ltd
Upstairs at The Antique Arcade, 4 Sheep St. (H. and P Watson). Open 10-5.15 including Sun., Sat. 10-5.45. SIZE: Medium. *STOCK: Art deco pottery, figurines, face masks, lamps.* Not Stocked: Militaria, coins, stamps. PARK: Nearby. TEL: 0789 297249. SER: Finder. FAIRS: Loughborough Art Deco; Alexandra Palace; London Decorative Arts; Kensington; Greenwich World of Art Deco; Greenwich Antiques and Decorative Arts Fair.

Stratford-upon-Avon continued

Jean A Bateman LAPADA
41 Sheep St. Open 9.30-5. *STOCK: Victorian and Georgian jewellery, objets d'art and vertu, including scent bottles.* TEL: 0789 298494. SER: Valuations. VAT: Stan/Spec.

Bow Cottage Antiques
Antique Arcade, 4 Sheep St. (R Harvey-Morgan) Open 10.30-5.30. *STOCK: English porcelain, 18th-19th C, £5-£200; glass and English silver, 18th-20th C, £5-£150+; oil paintings, watercolours; engravings, maps; general antiques, small furniture.* TEL: 0789 297249. Messages can be left at 0789 205883. VAT: Stan.

Burman Antiques LAPADA
5 Trinity St. (J. and J Burman Holtom) Est: 1973. Open by appointment only. SIZE: Small. *STOCK: Clocks, pot lids, Staffordshire paintings, prints, horse brass, copper and fishing tackle.* LOC: Near Shakespeare Memorial Theatre. PARK: Easy. TEL: 0789 295164. SER: Restorations (clocks). VAT: Spec.

Miles Ferneyhough BADA LAPADA
11 Chapel St. (M.H Ferneyhough) Est: 1959. Open 9-5. SIZE: Medium. *STOCK: Mahogany furniture, pictures, works of art, 18th to early 19th C, £500-£20,000.* LOC: Town centre. PARK: Easy. TEL: 0789 293928. SER: Valuations. FAIRS: Kenilworth, N.E.C., Olympia, Café Royal and Harrogate. VAT: Spec.

Stratford-upon-Avon continued

Tim Harrison Wholesale Exports
Hatton Rock. Est: 1971. CL: Sat. SIZE: Warehouse. *STOCK: Shipping goods and large Victorian and Edwardian furniture.* PARK: Easy. TEL: 0789 292921. *Trade Only.*

Howards Jewellers
44a Wood St, (A. Howard Antiques Ltd.). Est: 1985. Open 9.30-5.30. *STOCK: Jewellery, silver, objets d'art, 19th C.* LOC: Town centre. PARK: Nearby. TEL: 0789 205404. SER: Valuations; restorations (as stock); buys at auction (as stock). FAIRS: British International, Birmingham; Barbican; Harrogate; Kenilworth. VAT: Stan/Spec.

Jazz
Shop 2, Civic Hall,, Rother St. (Mrs S Hill) Est: 1988. Open 10-6. CL: Mon. SIZE: Small. *STOCK: Art deco ceramics, lighting, jewellery and furniture, £10-£1,500.* LOC: From island in town centre follow Wood St. PARK: Easy. TEL: 0789 298362; home - 021 705 9858. SER: Valuations. FAIRS: Decorative Arts, Kensington Town Hall; Art Deco, Loughborough; N.E.C. (August).

La-di-da
6c Union St. (P.M Barber) Open 9-5. *STOCK: Period interior decorators and architectural items.* TEL: 0789 267521/092 684 3127. SER: Restorations (pine); interior design; finder. VAT: Stan/Spec.

Lions Den
31 Henley St. (T. and E Hitchcox and S Gould) Open 9.30-6 including Sun. *STOCK: Moorcroft pottery, porcelain, oil paintings and water-colours.* TEL: 0789 415802; fax - 0789 415853.

The Loquens Gallery
The Minories, Rother St. (S. and J Loquens) Est: 1975. Open 9.15-5, Sun. by appointment. SIZE: Medium. *STOCK: English watercolours, some oil paintings, late 18th to early 20th C, to £3,000.* LOC: From island in town centre, follow Wood St. to Rother St. junction, entrance to Minories is on right. PARK: Easy. TEL: 0789 297706; home - 0789 750469. SER: Valuations; restorations (cleaning watercolours, relining oils); framing. VAT: Stan/Spec.

Rich Designs
The Antique Arcade, Sheep St. (R Green and D Jones) Est: 1988. Open 10-5.30 or by appointment, Sat. 10-5.30. SIZE: Small. *STOCK: Clarice Cliff pottery, £25-£2,500.* PARK: Easy. TEL: 0789 772111; home - 0789 720950. SER: Valuations; restorations; buys at auction (as stock). FAIRS: Greenwich Deco; Kensington Deco; Loughborough Deco.

Rosemary Antiques and Paper Moon Books
Antique Arcade, 4 Sheep St. (Mrs R.E Fletcher) Est: 1977. Open 10-5.30 and occasional Sun. SIZE: Small. *STOCK: Pottery and porcelain, £5-*

Rosemary Antiques and Paper Moon Books continued

£200; small furniture, £40-£300; both late 19th C to 1940; books - children's illustrated and poetry, from Victorian, £5-£100. Not Stocked: Silver, brass and copper, glass and jewellery. TEL: 0789 297249; home - 0386 438827.

Stratford Antique Centre
Ely St. (N Sims) Open 10-5.30 every day. SIZE: 60 dealers. *STOCK: General antiques.* TEL: 0789 204180.

Robert Vaughan
20 Chapel St. (R. and C.M Vaughan) ABA. Est: 1953. Open 9.30-6. SIZE: Medium. *STOCK: Antiquarian and out-of-print books, maps and prints.* LOC: Town centre. PARK: Easy. TEL: 0789 205312. SER: Valuations; buys at auction (books). VAT: Stan.

James Wigington
'Winchester 73', 276 Alcester Rd. Open by appointment. *STOCK: General antiques, arms and armour, cannons, early fishing tackle.* TEL: 0789 293881.

STRETTON-ON-FOSSE, Nr. Moreton-in-Marsh

Astley House - Fine Art
The Old School. (D. and N Glaisyer) CADA. Est: 1974. Open by appointment. SIZE: Large. *STOCK: Large decorative oil paintings, 19th-20th C.* LOC: Village centre. PARK: Easy. TEL: 0608 50601; fax - 0608 51777. SER: Valuations; restorations; framing; exhibitions; mailing list. VAT: Spec.

STUDLEY

Prospect Antiques
Chester House, Alcester Rd. (R.T Felix) Open 10-5. CL: Sat. p.m. SIZE: Large. *STOCK: General furniture, porcelain, glass, bronzes, Oriental items.* LOC: A435. PARK: Easy. TEL: 052 785 2494. VAT: Stan/Spec.

WARWICK

Duncan M Allsop
26 Smith St. ABA. Est: 1965. Open 9.30-5.30. SIZE: Medium. *STOCK: Antiquarian and modern books.* LOC: 50yds. east of Eastgate. PARK: Nearby. TEL: 0926 493266.

Apollo Antiques Ltd LAPADA
The Saltisford, Birmingham Rd. (R.H Mynott) Est: 1968. Open 9-6, Sat. 9.30-12.30. SIZE: Large and warehouse. *STOCK: Period, decorative English and continental furniture, sculpture, paintings, decorative objects, works of art; Victorian furniture.* PARK: Easy. TEL: 0926 494746; fax - 0926 401477. VAT: Stan/Spec.

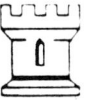

Warwick continued

John Bolton

Est: 1972. Open by appointment only. *STOCK: Furniture; longcase clocks.* TEL: 029588 439.

H.H Bray Ltd

9 Jury St. (B. and I Harper) Est: 1929. Open 9.30-5.30. *STOCK: Silver, jewellery, Sheffield plate.* LOC: On main Stratford to Warwick road. PARK: Easy. TEL: 0926 492791. SER: Valuations. VAT: Stan/Spec.

Eastgate Fine Arts

6 Smith St. (K Pittaway) Open 10-5.30. *STOCK: Original maps, prints, paintings.* TEL: 0926 499777.

John Goodwin and Sons

Unit F, Budbrooke Road Industrial Estate. Open 8.30-5.30, Sat. by appointment. *STOCK: Victorian and Edwardian furniture.* TEL: 0926 491191.

Russell Lane Antiques

2-4 High St. (R.G.H Lane) Open 11-5. *STOCK: Jewellery, silver, porcelain, furniture.* TEL: 0926 494494.

Mason-Watts Fine Art

60 Smith St. (C.N.S Mason-Watts and R Dover) Est: 1980. Open 10-5. SIZE: Small. *STOCK: British art including English and Scottish Royal Academicians, 1900 to contemporary, £300-*

Mason-Watts Fine Art continued

£50,000. LOC: 200yds. from Warwick Castle. PARK: Easy. TEL: 0926 403160; home - 0926 316192. SER: Valuations; restorations; buys at auction (paintings and sculpture). VAT: Stan/Spec.

Patrick and Gillian Morley Antiques LAPADA

62 West St. Est: 1968. Open 9-5.30. CL: Sat. SIZE: Large. *STOCK: Furniture, 17th to late 19th C; unusual and decorative items, sculpture, carvings and textiles; all £50-£20,000.* LOC: Almost opposite Warwick Castle 2nd car park. PARK: Easy. TEL: 0926 494464; home - 0926 54191; fax - 0926 400531. SER: Valuations; buys at auction. VAT: Mainly Spec.

Peggy Nesbitt

Open by appointment. *STOCK: Dolls.* TEL: 0926 491600. SER: Restorations and repairs.

Warwick continued

Martin Payne Antiques LAPADA
30 Brook St. Est: 1971. Open 10-5.30. CL: Wed. SIZE: Small. *STOCK: Silver and canteens, 18th-19th C, £50-£10,000.* LOC: Between High St. and Market Pl. PARK: Easy. TEL: 0926 494948; home - 0608 61282. SER: Valuations; restorations (silver repairs and re-plating). VAT: Stan/Spec.

Pine Design
33 The Saltisford. (C Mynott) Open 9.30-5.30. *STOCK: Pine; decorative items.* TEL: 0926 494666.

Warwick continued

James Reeve
at Quinneys of Warwick, 9 Church St. Est: 1865. Open 9.30-5.30. CL: Sat. p.m. *STOCK: Furniture, mahogany, oak, and rosewood, 17th-18th C, £80-£8,000; furniture, 19th C, £50-£3,500; glass, copper, brass, pewter, china.* TEL: 0926 498113. VAT: Stan/Spec.

Chris Rhodes Antiques
19 West Rock, Saltisford. SIZE: Medium. *STOCK: Fine furniture, 18th and 19th C, £50-£5,000; paintings, clocks; quality smalls, decorative and unusual items.* LOC: A425 Birmingham to Warwick road. PARK: Easy. TEL: 0926 492079; home - 0926 511836. SER: Valuations. VAT: Stan/Spec.

Smith St. Antiques Centre
7 Smith St. (E Brook and W Mechilli) Est: 1971. Open 10-5.30. SIZE: Large. LOC: Corner position, Smith St. is an extension of High St. PARK: Easy and at rear. TEL: 0926 497864; home - 0926 882060. VAT: Stan/Spec. Below are listed the dealers at this centre.

Simon Bowler
Oriental porcelain, silver and furniture.

Erol Brook
Silver and plate, decanters, curios, barometers.

Eleanor Antiques
(Mrs E W E Creed) *Porcelain, 18th to early 20th C, £5-£500; glass, 18th to early 20th C, £2-£75; needlework tools, 19th-20th C, £2-£25.* TEL: 0926 400554.

Mick Howe
Cigarette cards. SER: Framing.

Chris James
Military medals, swords, guns.

Walter Mechilli
Silver, plate, porcelain and golf collectables.

Joyce Smith
Porcelain, silver, jewellery, small furniture.

Don Spencer
Furniture, clocks, barometers and jewellery.

Jean Stapley
Silver, porcelain, Doulton figures, jewellery.

Turtons Antiques
Jewellery, silver, gold.

Warwick continued

Don Spencer Antiques
Unit 2, 20 Cherry St. Est: 1963. Open by appointment only. SIZE: Large. *STOCK: Desks, 1850-1920, £500-£5,000; dining furniture and bookcases, 1800-1920, £500-£3,000.* PARK: Easy. TEL: 0926 499857; home - 0564 775470. VAT: Stan/Spec.

The Tao Antiques
66a Smith St. (Mrs J Black) Open 11-6. *STOCK: General antiques.* TEL: 0926 495029.

Vintage Antique Market
36 Market Pl. (R Thompson) Est: 1977. Open 10-5. SIZE: Gallery. *STOCK: Watercolours 1800-1920 and 14 stands selling a wide range of goods including furniture, pine, clocks, porcelain, bric-a-brac, jewellery.* TEL: 0926 491527.

The Warwick Antique Centre
20-22 High St. Open 6 days a week. SIZE: Approx. 30 dealers. *STOCK: General antiques.* TEL: 0926 495704.

Warwick Antiques
16-18 High St. (M Morrison) Est: 1969. Open 9-5, Sat. 10-5. SIZE: Large and warehouses. *STOCK: Furniture, mahogany, oak, Chinese; metalware, copper, brass, pewter, glass, china, bygones, curios, statuary, garden furniture, shipping goods.* LOC: Midway between E. and W. Gate clock towers. PARK: At rear. TEL: 0926 492482; fax - 0926 493867. SER: Restorations (furniture). VAT: Stan/Spec.

Warwick Desks
20 West Rock. (Mrs C Mynott) Est: 1977. Open 9.30-1 and 2-6, Sat. 9.30-1. SIZE: Large and warehouse. *STOCK: Desks, bookcases, chairs and library furniture.* LOC: Off Birmingham Rd. PARK: Easy. TEL: 0926 494666. VAT: Stan/Spec.

Westgate Antiques LAPADA
28 West St. (D.M Cunningham) Open 10-5.30, Sat. 10-1. *STOCK: Silver - Sheffield and plate; canteens, mahogany furniture, glass, decorative items and boxes, all 18th-19th C.* LOC: Near town centre, beyond the West Gate. PARK: Easy. TEL: 0926 494106. SER: Valuations; restorations (silver, including re-plating, and furniture). VAT: Stan/Spec.

WATER ORTON

J Mason Antique Clocks
Glympton House, 3 New Rd. Est: 1986. Open 9-2.30 including Sun., or by appointment. CL: Thurs. SIZE: Small. *STOCK: Longcase and bracket clocks, 18th-19th C, £600-£5,000.* LOC: Junction 4, M6, north on A446, left on to A4117. Shop in village centre. PARK: Easy. TEL: 021 747 5751; home - same. SER: Valuations; restorations. VAT: Spec.

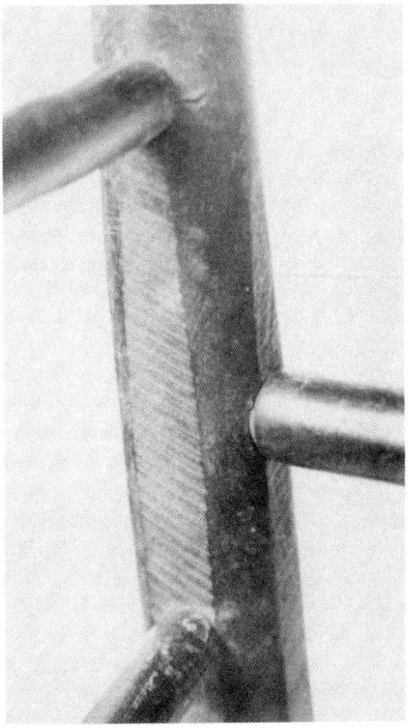

The inside facet of a front leg from a Lancashire spindle back chair, c.1800, showing circular saw teeth marks which indicate that, in common with the usual practice in this region's chair making, the chair leg was turned from sawn seasoned timber, rather than from cleft 'green' wood. From ***The English Regional Chair*** by Bernard D. Cotton, published by the **Antique Collectors' Club** in 1990. £49.50.

West Midlands

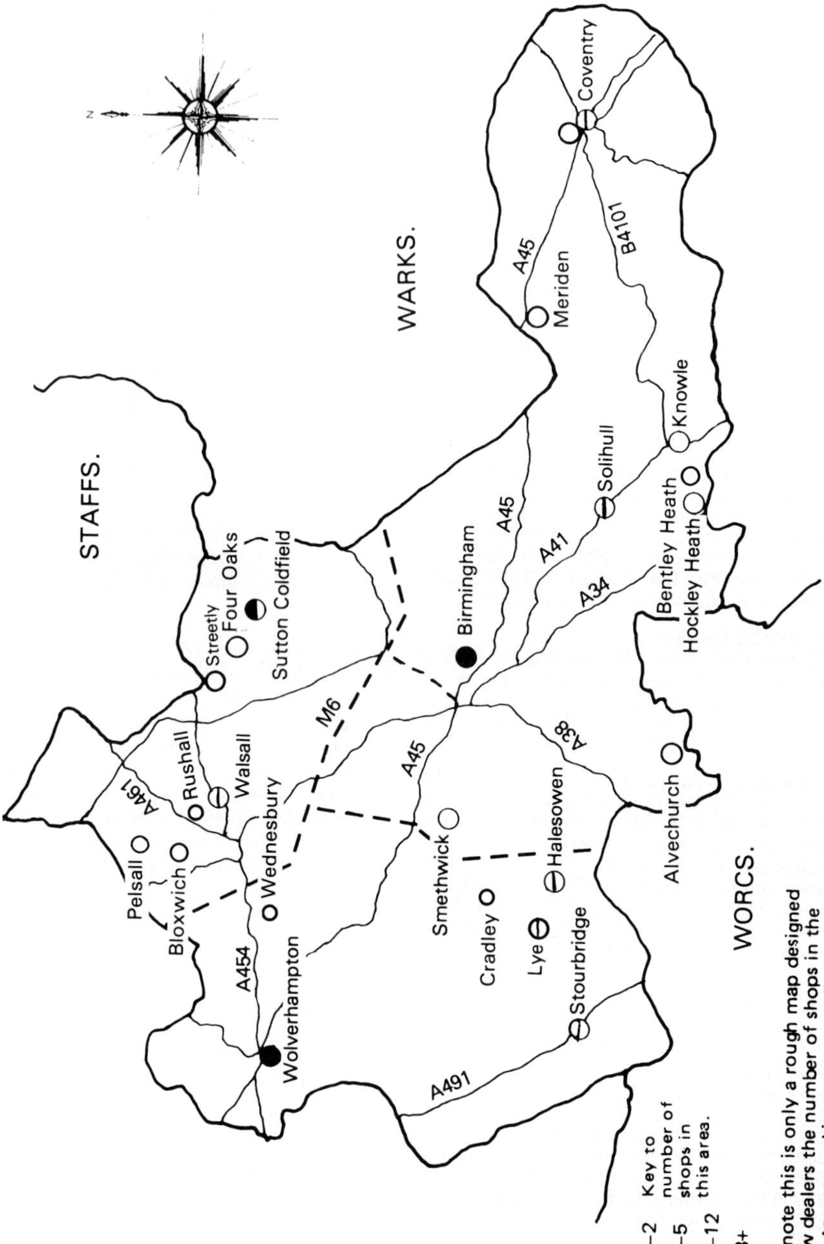

STAFFS.
WARKS.
WORCS.
Coventry
Meriden
A45
B4101
Knowle
Solihull
Bentley Heath
Hockley Heath
A41
A34
A45
Birmingham
Four Oaks
Streetly
Sutton Coldfield
M6
Rushall
Walsall
A461
Pelsall
Bloxwich
Wednesbury
A454
Wolverhampton
A45
A38
Smethwick
Halesowen
Alvechurch
Cradley
Lye
Stourbridge
A491

○ 1–2
⊖ 3–5
◐ 6–12
● 13+

Key to number of shops in this area.

Please note this is only a rough map designed to show dealers the number of shops in the various towns, and is not necessarily totally accurate.

ALVECHURCH

Woodland Fine Art LAPADA
16 The Square. (C Haynes and A Smith) Est: 1971. Open 10-6, Sun. by appointment. SIZE: Medium. *STOCK: Oil paintings, fine watercolours, and decorative prints, 19th to early 20th C, £20-£2,000; decorative lamps and mirrors, 19th C, £50-£500; collectables, trunks, brass and porcelain, 19th-20th C, £5-£200.* LOC: Exit 4, M42, then A34, 4 miles on right. PARK: Easy. TEL: 021 445 5886. SER: Valuations; restorations; framing; buys at auction. FAIRS: British International, Birmingham; Bailey, Shepton, Bob Harris. VAT: Stan/Spec.

BENTLEY HEATH, Nr. Solihull

Roger Widdas Fine Paintings LAPADA
7 Bullivents Close. Open by appointment. *STOCK: Drawings, oil paintings and watercolours including British, all 19th to early 20th C.* TEL: 0564 773217.

BIRMINGHAM

Always Antiques
285 Vicarage Rd, Kings Heath. (R. and D Messenger) Open Mon. 2-6, Thurs.-Sat. 9-6, other times by appointment. *STOCK: Victorian and Edwardian furniture, dolls, linen, lace and curios.* TEL: 021 444 8701.

Amber Antiques
Leeming House, 27 Frederick Rd, Edgbaston. (Mrs E Horton and Mrs S Farrington) Est: 1990. Open 9.30-5, Sat. 9.30-4.30, Sun. 1-4.30. SIZE: Small. *STOCK: Interior gas lights converted to electricity, period telephones, furniture.* LOC: Off M5. PARK: Own. TEL: 021 454 3952; home - same.

Archives
496 Bristol Rd, Selly Oak. (S.D. and I.J Healy and D Heywood) Open 9.30-5.30 including Sun. *STOCK: Victorian and Edwardian furniture; clocks and upholstery, to 1930.* TEL: 021 472 4026.

Peter Asbury Antiques
162 Vicarage Rd, Langley. Open 9-5. CL: Wed. p.m. *STOCK: General antiques.* TEL: 021 552 1702.

Ashleigh House Antiques
Ashleigh House, 5 Westbourne Rd. (P. and R Hodgson) Est: 1974. Open by appointment. SIZE: Large. *STOCK: Furniture, oils and watercolours, £200-£5,000; clocks, £300-£2,000; objets d'art, £75-£2,000, all 1700-1880.* LOC: From Five Ways Edgbaston take Calthorpe Rd. and bear right into Westbourne Rd., premises 150 yards on left. PARK: Easy. TEL: 021 454 6283; home - same. SER: Valuations; restorations (furniture and paintings); buys at auction. FAIRS: Most dateline, Midlands area. VAT: Stan/Spec.

Birmingham continued

Austy House Antiques
Princes Corner, Harborne Park Rd, Harborne. (R.P Cooke) Open 10-6, Sun. by appointment. *STOCK: French furniture, oil paintings, porcelain, chandeliers, general antiques.* PARK: Albert Rd. TEL: 021 427 5325. VAT: Spec.

Paul Baxter
Open by appointment only. *STOCK: Oriental ceramics and general antiques.* TEL: 0564 824920.

Birmingham Bookshop
567 Bristol Rd, Selly Oak. *STOCK: Out-of-print books, all periods.* TEL: 021 472 8556. VAT: Stan.

Cameo
4 Lonsdale Rd, Harborne. Open Thurs. and Fri. 9.15-5.30, Sat. 9.15-4. *STOCK: General antiques especially ceramics.* TEL: 021 426 6900.

Carleton Gallery
91 Vivian Rd, Harborne. (D Dunnett) Open 9-5.30, Wed. 9-1. *STOCK: Maps and prints.* TEL: 021 427 2487.

Chesterfield Antiques
181 Gravelly Lane. (A.I Beddard) Est: 1977. Open 10-5.30. CL: Wed. *STOCK: General antiques.* TEL: 021 373 3876.

The City of Birmingham Antique Market
St. Martins Market, Edgbaston St, (Antique Forum (Birmingham) Ltd.). Est: 1976. Open Mon. 6.30-2. SIZE: Large. Several dealers. *STOCK: General antiques, art deco, 5p-£5,000.* LOC: Adjacent to Bull Ring. PARK: Multi-storey nearby. TEL: 071 624 3214. SER: Valuations.

Peter Clark Antiques LAPADA
36 St. Mary's Row, Moseley. Open 9-5.30. SIZE: Medium. *STOCK: Furniture, mid-17th C to early 20th C, £175-£2,500; silver, early 19th C to early 20th C, £100-£500.* LOC: Centre of Moseley. PARK: At rear. TEL: 021 449 8245. SER: Valuations; restorations (furniture). VAT: Stan/Spec.

The Collectors Shop
63 Station St. (J Cash) Est: 1967. Open 10-4. CL: Wed. p.m. SIZE: Small. *STOCK: Coins, militaria, secondhand jewellery, silver, small items.* LOC: One minute from New St. Station. PARK: Nearby. TEL: 021 631 2072. SER: Valuations; buys at auction (coins). FAIRS: Most major coin. VAT: Stan/Spec.

R Collyer
185 New Rd, Rubery. Open 9-5.30. *STOCK: Clocks, including longcase, watches, barometers, secondhand jewellery.* LOC: 1 mile from Lydiate Ash roundabout. TEL: 021 453 2332. SER: Valuations; restorations.

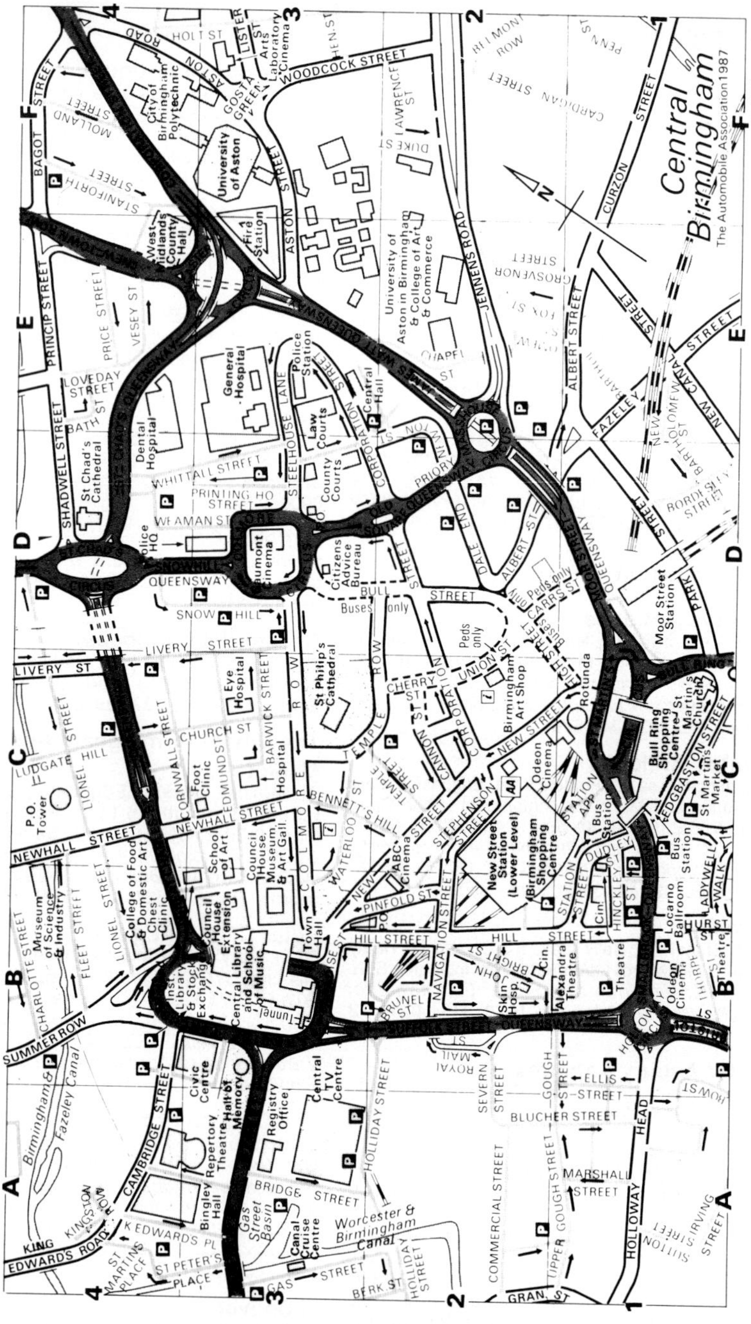
Central Birmingham
The Automobile Association 1987
A
B
C
D
E
F
1
2
3
4
HOLT ST
ASTON ROAD
LISTER ST
Arts Laboratory Cinema
WOODCOCK STREET
GOSTA GREEN
City of Birmingham Polytechnic
University of Aston
BAGOT STREET
MOLLAND STREET
STANIFORTH STREET
West Midlands County Hall
Fire Station
ASTON STREET
LAWRENCE ST
DUKE ST
University of Aston in Birmingham & College of Art & Commerce
JENNENS ROAD
BELMONT ROW
PENN ST
CARDIGAN STREET
CURZON STREET
GROSVENOR STREET
FOX ST
ALBERT STREET
FAZELEY STREET
NEW CANAL STREET
BARTHOLOMEW ST
PRINCIP STREET
PRICE STREET
VESEY ST
LOVEDAY STREET
BATH ST
ST CHAD'S QUEENSWAY
General Hospital
Police Station
STEELHOUSE LANE
Law Courts
Central Hall
CORPORATION STREET
CHAPEL ST
SHADWELL STREET
St Chad's Cathedral
Dental Hospital
WHITTALL STREET
PRINTING HO STREET
WEAMAN ST
County Courts
PRIORY QUEENSWAY
DALE END
ALBERT ST
MOOR STREET QUEENSWAY
BORDESLEY STREET
Police HQ
SNOW HILL QUEENSWAY
Beaumont Cinema
Citizens Advice Bureau
BULL STREET
Buses only
Peds only
CARRS ST
Moor Street Station
PARK STREET
SNOW HILL
LIVERY STREET
LIVERY ST
Eye Hospital
BARWICK STREET
St Philip's Cathedral
TEMPLE ROW
CHERRY ST
UNION ST
Birmingham Art Shop
HIGH STREET
Rotunda
ST MARTIN'S QUEENSWAY
BULL RING
Bull Ring Shopping Centre
St Martin's Church
CHURCH ST
CORNWALL STREET
LUDGATE HILL
LIONEL STREET
EDMUND ST
Foot Clinic
Hospital
TEMPLE STREET
CANNON ST
NEW STREET
Odeon Cinema
STATION APP
Bus Station
EDGBASTON STREET
St Martin's Market
P.O. Tower
NEWHALL STREET
BENNETT'S HILL
WATERLOO ST
COLMORE ROW
STEPHENSON STREET
New Street Station (Lower Level)
Birmingham Shopping Centre
DUDLEY ST
Bus Station
LADYWELL WALK
Museum of Science & Industry
College of Food & Domestic Art
Chest Clinic
School of Art
Council House, Museum, & Art Gall.
ABC Cinema
NEW ST
PINFOLD ST
NAVIGATION STREET
STATION STREET
HINCKLEY ST
Locarno Ballroom
HURST ST
CHARLOTTE STREET
FLEET STREET
Council House Extension
Town Hall
HILL STREET
JOHN BRIGHT ST
Alexandra Theatre
Theatre
Odeon Cinema
Theatre
THORP ST
Inst. Library & Stock Exchange
Central Library and School of Music
Tunnel
BRUNEL ST
Skin Hosp.
SUFFOLK STREET QUEENSWAY
SMALLBROOK QUEENSWAY
HOLLOWAY CIRCUS
SUMMER ROW
Birmingham & Fazeley Canal
CAMBRIDGE STREET
Civic Centre
Hall of Memory
Central TV Centre
Registry Office
HOLLIDAY STREET
ROYAL MAIL ST
SEVERN STREET
GOUGH STREET
ELLIS STREET
BLUCHER STREET
HOWE ST
Repertory Theatre
Bingley Hall
BRIDGE STREET
MARSHALL STREET
HOLLOWAY HEAD
KINGSTON ROW
KING EDWARDS ROAD
K EDWARDS PL
Gas Street Basin
Canal Cruise Centre
Worcester & Birmingham Canal
COMMERCIAL STREET
UPPER GOUGH STREET
SUTTON STREET
IRVING STREET
ST MARTINS PLACE
ST PETER'S PLACE
GAS STREET
BERK ST
GRAN. ST

Key to Town Plan

AA Recommended roads

Other roads

Restricted roads

Buildings of interest

Car Parks

Parks and open spaces

AA Service Centre

© Automobile Association 1988.

Birmingham continued

Dalton Street Antiques
66 Dalton St. (M.L Chandler) Open 10-6 or by appointment. *STOCK: General antiques, stripped pine, satinwood, fireplaces, beds, architectural items.* LOC: City centre. PARK: Easy. TEL: 021 236 2479/745 6562. SER: Restorations; valuations.

Dolly Mixtures
Open by appointment. SIZE: Dolls and teddies. TEL: 021 422 6959.

Eden Coins
P.O. Box 73, Oldbury. (R Pratt) Est: 1979. Open by appointment. *STOCK: Coins, medals and tokens, 18th-20th C, £1-£100.* LOC: 1 mile M5, junction 3. TEL: 021 422 5357; home - same. FAIRS: Cumberland Coin.

Edgbaston Gallery
42 Islington Row, Five Ways, Edgbaston. (I Bethell) Est: 1976. Open 12.30-5.30. CL: Sat. and Sun. except by appointment. SIZE: Medium. *STOCK: Oil paintings and watercolours, £50-£1,000; small furniture, clocks, collectors' items, all 19th C.* LOC: Junction of Islington Row and Frederick Rd. PARK: In Frederick Rd. TEL: 021 454 4244; home - 021 459 3568. SER: Valuations; restorations; framing; buys at auction (paintings).

Maurice Fellows
21 Vyse St, Hockley. *STOCK: Objets d'art, jewellery.* TEL: 021 554 0211; fax - 021 507 0807. SER: Valuations; restorations.

Fine Pine
75 Mason Rd, Erdington. (H Duignan) Open 8.30-5.30. *STOCK: Pine and satin walnut furniture, iron tiled fireplaces and surrounds, general antiques.* TEL: 021 373 6321.

Format of Birmingham Ltd
18 Bennetts Hill. (G Charman and D Vice) Open 9.30-5. CL: Sat. *STOCK: Coins, medals.* PARK: New St. station. VAT: Stan/Spec.

G.V.R. Antiques Ltd
Unit L68 Wyrley Rd, Witton. Open 9-5 or by appointment. CL: Sat. SIZE: Warehouse. *STOCK: Victorian and shipping furniture, pianos.* LOC: 3 minutes from Spaghetti junction (M6, junction 6). PARK: Easy. TEL: 021 327 2701/449 6869.

Garratt Antiques
35 Stephenson St. Est: 1958. *STOCK: Jewellery, brass, silver, copper, pewter, silver plate, china, crystal, dolls and bric-a-brac.* TEL: 021 643 9507.

Genesis Antiques
(M.K Davis and C.A Booth) Est: 1977. Open by appointment. SIZE: Medium. *STOCK: European furniture - shipping goods, art nouveau, art deco, wicker, bentwood, beech, oak and mahogany, £5-£1,000; crystal and brass, lighting and*

Genesis Antiques continued

mirrors, £50-£500; textiles and clothing, decorative arts, objects and jewellery, 1850-1950. TEL: 021 454 1968.

Christopher Gordon Antiques
133 School Rd, Moseley. Est: 1974. Open Sat. only 10-5. *STOCK: Architectural and decorative items, £5-£500; early shop and pub fixtures and fittings; early advertising items, signs and mirrors, all 19th-20th C; pine, stained glass, fireplaces.* LOC: 5 mins. from Moseley Village. PARK: Easy. TEL: 021 444 4644. SER: Courier.

The Graves Gallery
3 The Spencers, Augusta St, Hockley. (P Cassidy) Open 10.30-5.30 or by appointment. CL: Mon. *STOCK: 18th-20th C oil paintings and watercolours.* TEL: 021 212 1635.

The Halcyon Gallery
59 The Pallasades. (L., P. and R Green) Open 9-5.30. *STOCK: Modern British oils, watercolours and limited editions - Sir William Russell Flint, David Shepherd, Lowry.* TEL: 021 643 4474.

Harborne Place Antiques
22-24 Northfield Rd, Harborne. Open 9.30-5.30. CL: Sun. except by appointment. *STOCK: Period and Victorian furniture, shipping goods and general antiques.* TEL: 021 427 5788. SER: Restorations; re-upholstery; buys at auction. VAT: Stan/Spec.

Bob Harris and Sons, Antiques LAPADA
2071 Coventry Rd, Sheldon. (R.E Harris) Resident. Est: 1953. Open 9-6. CL: Sun. except by appointment. *STOCK: 18th-19th C furniture and general antiques.* TEL: 021 743 2259. VAT: Stan/Spec.

Houghtons of Moseley
115 Alcester Rd, Moseley. (A Prior and G Waldron) Open 10-5.30. *STOCK: Period clothes, Victorian to 1970.* TEL: 021 449 9953.

John Hubbard Antiques LAPADA
224-226 Court Oak Rd, Harborne. Est: 1968. Open 9-6. SIZE: Large. *STOCK: Furniture, 17th-19th C, £50-£5,000; paintings, £50-£2,000.* LOC: 3 miles from city centre. PARK: Easy. TEL: 021 426 1694. SER: Valuations; restorations; leather linings. VAT: Stan/Spec.

James Antiques - Canalside
Gas St. Basin. (P. and D James) Est: 1969. Open 12-6 Wed. to Sat. or by appointment. SIZE: Small. *STOCK: Decorative antiques, small furniture, stained glass, tiles, painted goods, folk art, general, some 18th, mainly 19th C, to £500.* LOC: Central, near International Convention Centre. TEL: 021 643 3131; home - 021 444 4628. SER: Valuations; restorations; stained glass repairs; buys at auction.

Birmingham continued

Rex Johnson and Sons
28 Lower Temple St. (D Johnson) Open 9.30-5.30, Sat. 9.30-5. *STOCK: Silver, jewellery, porcelain and glass.* TEL: 021 643 9674.

Rex Johnson and Sons
23 Union Street. (R Johnson) Open 9.30-5.15. *STOCK: Silver, jewellery, porcelain and glass.* TEL: 021 643 7503.

Jomarc Pianos Ltd. and Pianorama
Unit 123, Newtown Shopping Centre, Newtown Row, Aston. (P Hoskinson) Open 9.30-5.30, Sat. 9.30-4. *STOCK: Pianos.* TEL: 021 359 2895; home - 0922 743292.

Kestrel House Antiques
72 Gravelly Hill North, Erdington. (E.C Jones) Est: 1895. Open 9-6. SIZE: Large. *STOCK: Oil paintings of all schools, 19th C; shipping furniture.* TEL: 021 373 2375. SER: Picture cleaning, relining and restoration; restoration of frames and framing. VAT: Stan.

March Medals
113 Gravelly Hill North, Erdington. (M.A March) Est: 1975. Open 10-5, Sat. 10-2. *STOCK: Orders, decorations, campaign medals, militaria and military books.* TEL: 021 384 4901. SER: Catalogues issued. VAT: Stan/Spec.

Maxwells Book Shop
22 Shaftmoor Lane, Acocks Green. (C.M Prickett) Open 10.30-4.45. CL: Mon. *STOCK: Antiquarian and secondhand books.* TEL: 021 706 8379.

Moseley Antiques
Unit 5 Woodbridge Rd, Moseley. (Mrs H Benstead) Est: 1972. Open 10-6. CL: Wed. *STOCK: Furniture and clocks.* TEL: 021 449 6186.

The Moseley Gallery
6 Ernest St, Holloway Head. (M. and C Ashton) Est: 1985. Open 9-5.30, Sat. and Sun. by appointment. SIZE: Medium. *STOCK: Watercolours and drawings, 18th-20th C, £100-£3,000+.* LOC: City centre. PARK: Easy. TEL: 021 622 3986; fax - 021 666 6630. SER: Valuations; restorations; mounting, framing. VAT: Spec.

Birmingham continued

Nathan and Co. (Birmingham) Ltd
31 Corporation St. Est: 1857. Open 9-5. SIZE: Medium. *STOCK: Silver and jewellery, £35-£25,000.* LOC: A31. PARK: New St. Station. TEL: 021 643 5225. SER: Valuations; restorations (silver and jewellery); buys at auction. FAIRS: British International (Birmingham). VAT: Stan/Spec.

The Old Clock Shop
32 Stephenson St. (M.L. and S.R. Durham) Open 10.30-5. *STOCK: Clocks especially longcase, mantle and wall; scientific instruments, microscopes and sextants, all 18th-19th C; optical instruments, vintage wrist watches and antique pocket watches; £100-£10,000.* TEL: 021 632 4864. SER: Valuations; restorations (clocks). VAT: Stan/Spec.

The Original Choice Ltd
1340 Stratford Rd, Hall Green. (J Ellis) Est: 1978. Open Mon., Thurs. and Fri. 11-6, Sat. 10-6 or by appointment. *STOCK: Fireplaces, fenders, tiles, stained glass, mirrors and interior fittings.* TEL: 021 778 3821. SER: Installations.

Piccadilly Jewellers
Piccadilly Arcade, New St. (R. and R Johnson) Open 10-5. *STOCK: Jewellery, silver and objects.* TEL: 021 643 5791.

S.R. Furnishing and Antiques
18 Stanley Rd, Oldbury. (S Willder) Est: 1975. *STOCK: General antiques and shipping furniture.* TEL: 021 422 9788.

Smithsonia
14-16 Piccadilly Arcade, Off New St. (V Smith and M Ferguson) Open 10-5.15. *STOCK: Jewellery, collectables, prints.* TEL: 021 643 8405.

Station Road Emporium
47 Station Rd, Erdington. (H Moore) Open 9-7. *STOCK: Furniture and bric-a-brac, 1780-1900.* TEL: 021 373 2725.

Stuart House Fine Art
123 Queens Park Rd, Harborne. Open 9-6. SIZE: Small. *STOCK: Furniture, 17th to early 19th C, £100-£5,000; paintings, £200-£2,000.*

Stuart House Fine Art continued

LOC: 3 miles from city centre. PARK: Easy. TEL: 021 426 3300. SER: Valuations; restorations. VAT: Spec.

Tatters of Tyseley
590 Warwick Rd, Tyseley. (N Smith and G Jinks) Open 10-5, Fri. 10-7. CL: Mon. *STOCK: Fire surrounds, grates and fireplaces.* TEL: 021 707 4351.

Treasure Chest
1407 Pershore Rd, Stirchley, and 636 Bristol Rd., Selly Oak. Est: 1960. Open 8.30-6. *STOCK: General antiques, shipping furniture.* TEL: 021 458 3705/414 1544.

Victoria's Curios
287 Bearwood Rd, Bearwood, Warley. Open 10-6. *STOCK: Furniture, mahogany, satin and pine; Victorian tiled cast-iron fireplaces and surrounds; costume jewellery, silver, bric-a-brac, textiles.* TEL: 021 429 8661.

Yesterdays Antiques
125 Potbury Rd, Oldbury. (D.P Hipkins) Open 9-6. *STOCK: General antiques.* TEL: 021 420 3980.

BLOXWICH

Cobwebs
639d Bloxwich Rd, Leamore. (Mrs M Hannaway) Open 10.30-4.30. CL: Thurs. *STOCK: Bric-a-brac.* PARK: Easy. TEL: 0922 493670.

COVENTRY

The Antique Shop
107 Spon End. (J Branagh) Open 9-5.30. *STOCK: General antiques.* TEL: 0203 525915.

Memories Antiques
400A Stoney Stanton Rd. (R.D Seymour) Est: 1964. Open 9.30-5, Sun. 10-2. CL: Wed. *STOCK: General antiques, Victorian and Edwardian furniture, shipping goods, stripped pine, china, gold, silver, paintings and collectors' items.* TEL: 0203 687994/440215.

Milton Antiques
93 Dane Rd. (A.P Ross) Est: 1971. Open by appointment. SIZE: Large. *STOCK: Furniture, shipping goods.* Not Stocked: Glass, china, silver, pictures. LOC: Off A46. PARK: Easy. TEL: 0203 456285. *Trade Only.*

Spon End Antiques
115-116 Spon End. (N. and J Green) Open 10.30-4.30. *STOCK: Furniture, jewellery, pianos, china, dolls, teddy bears, pre-50's clothes.* TEL: 0203 228379/447628.

Sports Programmes
P.O. Box 74, Chapel St. (A Stanford) *STOCK: Football programmes.* TEL: 0203 228672. *Postal Only.*

CRADLEY HEATH

J.B. Antiques
205 Halesowen Rd, Old Hill. (J Turner) Open 8.30-5.30 including Sun. *STOCK: Furniture, china, glass, jewellery, 18th to early 20th C.* TEL: 0384 411121.

FOUR OAKS, Nr. Sutton Coldfield

M Allen Watch and Clock Maker
76A Walsall Rd. (M.A Allen) Est: 1969. Open 9-5.30, Sun. by appointment. SIZE: Small. *STOCK: Clocks - longcase, 1780-1840; French decorative mantle, 1820-1880; Vienna regulators, 1840-1880; pocket watches, 1700 onwards.* LOC: By Sutton Park, close to television mast. PARK: Easy. TEL: 021 308 6117; home - 021 308 8134. SER: Valuations; restorations (clocks and watches). FAIRS: Solihull, Penns Hall Hotel, Sutton Coldfield, Puckrup Hall, Tewkesbury, Park House Hotel, Shifnal. VAT: Stan/Spec.

Robert Taylor
Windy Ridge, Worcester Lane. Est: 1983. Open 9-6 by appointment only. *STOCK: Old toys including clockwork, tinplate, diecast and Dinky, £5-£1,000.* PARK: Easy. TEL: 021 308 4209; home - same. SER: Valuations; restorations; buys at auction. FAIRS: Donnington, Buxton, Gloucester.

HALESOWEN

Martyn Brown Antiques
130 Hagley Rd, Hayley Green. Open 9.30-5. CL: Wed. *STOCK: Furniture, clocks, paintings and collectables.* TEL: 021 585 5758.

Clent Books
52 Summer Hill. (I Simpson) Est: 1978. Open 10-4. CL: Wed. SIZE: Small. *STOCK: Antiquarian books, local history, topography, £1-£200.* LOC: Town centre. PARK: Opposite. TEL: 021 550 0309; home - 0299 401090. SER: Valuations. FAIRS: Waverley Antique and Book (Organiser).

Robert Withers Antiques
248 Hagley Rd, Hasbury. Open 9-5.30. CL: Wed. and Thurs. *STOCK: Furniture, works of art, clocks; oil paintings and watercolours, 19th C.* PARK: Easy. TEL: 021 550 4588; evenings - 021 550 9033.

HOCKLEY HEATH, Nr. Solihull

Magpie House
2212 Stratford Rd. (D.P Fair) Est: 1958. CL: Sat. except by appointment. SIZE: Medium. *STOCK: Oak and mahogany.* LOC: A34 to Stratford-on-Avon, 1 mile from M42 junction. PARK: Easy. TEL: 0564 782005. VAT: Stan/Spec. *Trade Only.*

KNOWLE

Chadwick Antiques
Chadwick End. (Mrs P Tibenham) Resident. Est: 1973. Open 10-5, also some Sun. SIZE: Medium. *STOCK: Furniture, 18th-19th C; collectors' items, general antiques.* Not Stocked: Oil paintings. LOC: A41. PARK: Easy. TEL: 0564 782096. SER: Valuations.

Richard Lukeman Fine Art
1673-1675 High St. Est: 1980. Open 9.30-5.30. SIZE: Medium. *STOCK: Watercolours and oil paintings, 19th C; furniture, porcelain, collectors' items, silver, £10-£2,000.* LOC: Main Warwick/Birmingham road. PARK: Own and rear of premises. TEL: 0564 774302. SER: Restorations (paintings); framing. VAT: Stan/Spec.

LYE, Nr. Stourbridge

The Lye Curios, Inc. Lye Antique Furnishings
181 High St. (Mr and Mrs P Smith) Est: 1979. Open 9-5. SIZE: Medium. *STOCK: Furniture, china, glass, metalware.* PARK: Easy. TEL: 0384 897513; home - 0384 62788. SER: Valuations.

Lye continued

Retro Products
Antique Warehouse, The Yard, Star St. (M McHugo) Est: 1980. Open 10-5. CL: Sat. SIZE: Large. *STOCK: Furniture - Victorian, Edwardian, garden and shipping, £5-£1,000; cast iron metalwork; architectural items.* LOC: Off Stourbridge to Birmingham Rd. PARK: Easy. TEL: 0384 894042; home - 0384 373332. FAIRS: Ardingly and Newark. VAT: Stan.

Smithfield Antiques
20 Stourbridge Rd. (R Harling) Open 9-5.30, other times by appointment. *STOCK: General antiques and shipping goods.* TEL: 0384 897821.

MERIDEN, Nr. Coventry

Meriden Antiques and Curios
The Old Library, The Green. (W.J. and B.V Doherty) Open 10-5. CL: Wed. *STOCK: General antiques especially pine.* TEL: 0676 23482.

PELSALL, Nr. Walsall

L.P. Furniture (Mids) Ltd
152 Lime Lane. (P Farouz) Est: 1982. Open daily including Sun., Tues. by appointment. SIZE: Warehouse. *STOCK: Mahogany, Victorian and Edwardian, £50-£750; shipping, to*

L.P. Furniture (Mids) Ltd continued

1950, £25-£750; pine, Victorian and reproduction, £60-£500. Not Stocked: Smalls, clocks, paintings and carpets. LOC: Junction 12, M6, take A5 towards Cannock, right at second roundabout on B4154, shop 150yds. on left. PARK: Easy. TEL: 0543 370256; home - 0922 495155. SER: Courier, packing, shipping. VAT: Stan.

RUSHALL, Nr. Walsall

P. and K Turner Antiques
107 Lichfield Rd. (P.M. and K.L Turner) Est: 1981. CL: Tues. SIZE: Medium. *STOCK: Furniture including oak and shipping, 18th C to 1930's, £20-£2,000; china, £5-£500; brass and copper, £5-£300.* LOC: A461 2 1/2 miles north of Walsall, 4 1/2 miles, junction 10, M6. PARK: Easy. TEL: 0922 720871; home - 0543 274176. SER: Valuations; restorations (furniture including French polishing, repair and inlay); buys at auction. FAIRS: Newark. VAT: Stan/Spec.

SMETHWICK, Nr. Warley

Grannies Attic Antiques
437 Bearwood Rd. (B.A Seymour) Est: 1965. Open 10-6 or by appointment to trade. CL: Wed. SIZE: Medium. *STOCK: Dolls, oak, mahogany and walnut furniture, curios, art deco, Victorian and Edwardian clothes, porcelain, books, pictures, fans, toys, records, stuffed animals, brass, copper, jewellery, tools, mirrors, smalls and shipping items, pre-1930, £5-£1,000.* LOC: Off Hagley Rd. PARK: Easy. TEL: 021 429 4180; home - 021 454 7507. SER: Valuations; buys at auction. *Mainly Trade.*

SOLIHULL

Geoffrey Hassall Antiques
20 New Rd. Est: 1972. Open 9.30-1 and 2-5.30. CL: Mon. SIZE: Small. *STOCK: Furniture, 18th-19th C.* Not Stocked: Books, jewellery. PARK: Easy. TEL: 021 705 0068. SER: Restorations (furniture).

Renaissance
18 Marshall Lake Rd, Shirley. (S.K Macrow) MGMC. Est: 1981. Open 9.30-5.30. SIZE: Small. *STOCK: General antiques.* LOC: Near Stratford Rd. TEL: 021 745 5140. SER: Restorations (repairs, re-upholstery and polishing).

Tilleys Antiques LAPADA
(S.A Alpren) Open by appointment. *STOCK: British glass, Oriental pottery, porcelain, shipping goods; silver, 19th C; Worcester.* TEL: 021 704 1813. SER: Restorations (jewellery, silver); repairs (clock, watch).

STOURBRIDGE

Bridge Antiques
32A Market St. (D.P. and B Deeley) Est: 1976. Open Tues., Fri. and Sat. 10-5. SIZE: Small. *STOCK: General antiques, especially china - Prattware, Worcester, Doulton; small furniture, jewellery, glass and silver, £3-£1,000.* LOC: 1st right off ring road, 1st right into Market St. PARK: Nearby. TEL: 0384 379495.

Colin J Clarke LAPADA
8 Exford Close, Amblecote. Open by appointment. *STOCK: Furniture, paintings, silver.* TEL: 0384 894546. VAT: Stan/Spec.

Kennerley Antiques Ltd
81 Worcester St. (G.T Callwood) Open 10-5, Mon. 12-5. CL: Thurs. *STOCK: General antiques.* TEL: 0384 371444/375338 (workshop). SER: Restoration and stripping.

Oldswinford Gallery
106 Hagley Rd, Oldswinford. (A.R Harris) Open 9.30-5. *STOCK: 18th-20th C oil paintings, watercolours and prints.* TEL: 0384 395577. SER: Restorations and framing.

S.O.S. Militaria
Curio Corner, 32 Park St. (B.J Smale) Open 9.30-5. *STOCK: Medals, badges, militaria.* TEL: 0384 379652; evenings - 029 93 5795.

STREETLY, Nr. Sutton Coldfield

Hardwick Antiques
Chester Rd. (R.J Cassidy) Open afternoons. CL: Wed. *STOCK: General antiques.* LOC: Opposite Ruby Rest. TEL: 021 353 1489.

SUTTON COLDFIELD

Thomas Coulborn and Sons BADA
Vesey Manor, 64 Birmingham Rd. (P Coulborn) Est: 1939. Open 9-5.30. SIZE: Medium. *STOCK: General antiques, 1600-1830; English furniture, 17th-18th C; paintings and clocks.* Not Stocked: 19th C bric-a-brac. LOC: 3 miles from Spaghetti Junction. From Birmingham A5127 through Erdington, premises on main road opposite cinema. PARK: Easy. TEL: 021 354 3974/021 354 3139. SER: Valuations; restorations (furniture and paintings); buys at auction. FAIRS: British International, Birmingham (Spring). VAT: Spec.

Stancie Cutler Antique and Collectors Fair
Town Hall. Est: 1981. Open one Wed. monthly 11-8, trade 10-8, prior telephone call advisable. SIZE: 70 stands. *STOCK: Antiques from large furniture to thimbles, mostly pre-1940.* TEL: Home - 0270 624288.

Sutton Coldfield continued

Driffold Gallery
78 Birmingham Rd. (D Gilbert) Open 10-5.30. CL: Thurs. *STOCK: Oil paintings and watercolours, 19th-20th C.* TEL: 021 355 5433.

Kelford Antiques
14a Birmingham Rd. (E.S Kelsall) Est: 1968. Open 9-5. CL: Thurs p.m. *STOCK: General antiques, Georgian and Victorian furniture, silver, porcelain, Staffordshire figures, pot-lids, jewellery.* TEL: 021 354 6607. VAT: Stan/Spec.

Osborne Antiques
91 Chester Rd, New Oscott. (C Osborne) Est: 1976. Open 9-5, Sat. 9-1. CL: Mon. *STOCK: Barometers, clocks and furniture.* TEL: 021 355 6667. SER: Restorations; spares (clocks, barometers).

H. and R.L Parry Ltd
23 Maney Corner. (H Parry) Est: 1925. Open 9.30-5.30. SIZE: Medium. *STOCK: Porcelain, silver and jewellery, all periods; metalware, paintings.* LOC: A38 from Birmingham road into Sutton. Cinema on right, on corner of service road in which premises are situated. TEL: 021 354 1178. SER: Valuations. VAT: Stan/Spec.

WALSALL

Nicholls Jewellers and Antiques
57 George St. (R Nicholls) Open 9-5. *STOCK: Antique and secondhand jewellery, curios.* TEL: 0922 641081.

Past and Present
66 George St. (G. and Mrs A.J Ellis) Open 9.30-5. *STOCK: Satin, walnut, mahogany and oak furniture, curios, collectables, linen, ceramics, pottery, porcelain.* LOC: Opposite Sainsbury's car park. TEL: 0922 611151.

Jon and Kate Rutter
The Doghouse, 309 Bloxwich Rd. Open 9-5.30, Sun. by appointment. SIZE: Large. *STOCK: General antiques.* TEL: 0922 30829/24263. VAT: Stan.

Toad Hall
70 Queen St. (S. and S Rutter) Est: 1967. Open 9.30-5.30. SIZE: Large. *STOCK: General antiques and shipping goods.* LOC: 5 minutes from junction 10, M6. PARK: Easy. TEL: 0922 724100. VAT: Stan/Spec.

Walsall Antiques Centre
7A The Digbeth Arcade. (J.M Shaw and S.P Swaine) Est: 1989. Open 10-6. SIZE: Large - 45 dealers. *STOCK: Porcelain, 1850-1940, £25-£250; furniture, 1800-1930, £50-£2,000; Royal commemoratives, 1820-1937, £10-£500.* LOC: In Victorian arcade by the Digbeth St. outdoor market. PARK: Nearby. TEL: 0922 725163/725165. SER: Valuations; buys at auction (Royal commemoratives). FAIRS: Alexandra Palace, N.E.C., Bingley Hall (Stafford), Wembley Easter. VAT: Stan/Spec.

WEDNESBURY

Brett Wilkins Antiques
81 Holyhead Rd. Est: 1983. Open Fri. and Sat., other days (including Sun.) by appointment. SIZE: Medium. *STOCK: Shipping items, 1900-1940, £5-£250; Victorian mahogany, 19th C, £100-£500; some pine, 19th-20th C, £100-£500.* LOC: 2 miles off M6, junction 9 on A41. PARK: Easy. TEL: 021 502 0720; home - 0860 541260. FAIRS: All major. VAT: Stan.

WOLVERHAMPTON

Baron Antiques
26 Queen Sq. (P., A. and M Hackner) Open 9-5.30. *STOCK: Victorian jewellery, silver, glass, china, watches.* TEL: 0902 21818/28603.

Broad Street Gallery
16 Broad St. (J.E. and J.T Hill) FATG. Est: 1975. Open 9-5.30. CL: Thurs. p.m. *STOCK: Prints, watercolours, oils, £50-£1,000.* LOC: 3 minutes from St. Peter's Church. PARK: Easy. TEL: 0902 24977. SER: Restorations; framing. VAT: Stan.

Collectors' Paradise Ltd
56a Worcester St. (D Hoppett and R Butlin) Est: 1963. Open 10-5. CL: Thurs. p.m. *STOCK: Arms, armour, militaria, uniforms, bric-a-brac.* TEL: 0902 20315.

Alan M France
Open by appointment only. *STOCK: Clocks and pocket watches.* TEL: 0902 731167.

Galata Coins Ltd
Park House, 77 Albert Rd. (P. and B Withers) BNTA. Est: 1967. Open 9-5. CL: Sat. SIZE: Small. *STOCK: Greek and Roman coins, 450 B.C. to 500 A.D., £10-£500; British coins, 800 A.D. to 1953, £5-£500; world coins, especially Scandinavian, 850 A.D. to 1960, £1-£1,000.* LOC: Near 'Halfway House' on Tettenhall Rd. (A41) towards Newport. PARK: Easy. TEL: 0902 771118. SER: Valuations; buys at auction (coins). FAIRS: BNTA Coin, Europa Hotel. VAT: Stan/Spec.

Gemini Antiques
18a Upper Green, Tettenhall. (J Pettitt) Open 11-4. *STOCK: General antiques.* TEL: 0902 742523; home - 09073 73334.

Golden Oldies
5 St. Georges Parade. (W.A. and M.A Knowles) Open 10-5.30. CL: Mon. *STOCK: Victorian, Edwardian and later furniture, £25-£2,000; paintings, decorative items.* PARK: Easy. TEL: 0902 22397. VAT: Stan/Spec.

Martin-Quick Antiques Ltd LAPADA
323 Tettenhall Rd. Est: 1965. Open 9-6, Sat. 9.30-4. SIZE: Large. *STOCK: 18th-19th C furniture, shipping goods, architectural items, stripped pine, silver plate.* Not Stocked: Militaria,

Martin-Quick Antiques Ltd continued

coins. LOC: One mile from town centre on A41. PARK: Easy. TEL: 0902 754703/090 74 3015; home - 0902 752908; fax - 0902 756889. VAT: Stan/Spec.

Brian Oates Fine Paintings
Open by appointment only. *STOCK: 19th-20th C oil paintings and etchings; Oriental ceramics.* TEL: 0902 743499.

Pendeford House Antiques
1 Pendeford Ave, Claregate, Tettenhall. (Mrs B Tonks) Est: 1980. Open 10.30-5, Wed. 10.30-6.30. CL: Thurs. SIZE: Medium. *STOCK: China and porcelain, £5-£500; furniture and clocks, £50-£1,500; oil paintings and watercolours, £50-£500; all 19th-20th C; glass, linen, brass and copper, jewellery and silver.* LOC: From main Tettenhall Rd., turn at traffic lights towards Codsall. At first small traffic island, take 3rd exit, shop next to Jet Garage. PARK: Easy. TEL: 0902 756175; home - same.

Rainbow Antiques
75-76 Dudley Rd. Est: 1968. Open 10-6. *STOCK: General antiques.* TEL: 0902 59800.

The Red Shop
7 Hollybush Lane, Penn. (B Savage) Open 9.30-5.30. *STOCK: Furniture including pine.* TEL: 0902 342915.

Ring Road Antiques
116 School St. (R G Hill) Open 9.30-3. CL: Mon. and Thurs. *STOCK: General antiques and shipping goods.* TEL: 0902 313684.

Second Thoughts
1-3 Coalway Rd, Penn. (Mr and Mrs C.R Turley) Est: 1977. Open 9.30-1 and 2-4.30, or by appointment. CL: Wed. SIZE: Small. *STOCK: Furniture, 18th-19th C; porcelain, glass, watercolours and prints.* LOC: A449, 3/4 mile from town centre. PARK: Easy. TEL: 0902 337748/337366. SER: Valuations. VAT: Stan/Spec.

Treasure Chest
21 High St, Bilston. (M Saunders) Open 10-4, Sat. 10-5. CL: Thurs. p.m. *STOCK: General antiques and bric-a-brac.* TEL: 0902 409782.

Wakeman and Taylor Antiques
LAPADA
140b Tettenhall Rd. Est: 1967. Open 8.30-5.30, or by appointment. CL: Sat. SIZE: Large. *STOCK: Furniture, 1700-1900, £100-£10,000.* LOC: One mile from town centre on A41. PARK: Easy. TEL: 0902 751166; home - 0902 372991/0785 284539. VAT: Stan/Spec. *Trade Only.*

A George III mahogany tallboy chest, 3ft.8in. wide. These pieces have not recently been in strong demand and now carry very attractive auction estimates. Although they normally require quite a large room, they are handsome and functional and should see a strengthening of value over the next year. From an article on 18th century mahogany furniture by Philip Duckworth published in the July/August issue of ***Antique Collecting.***

Wiltshire

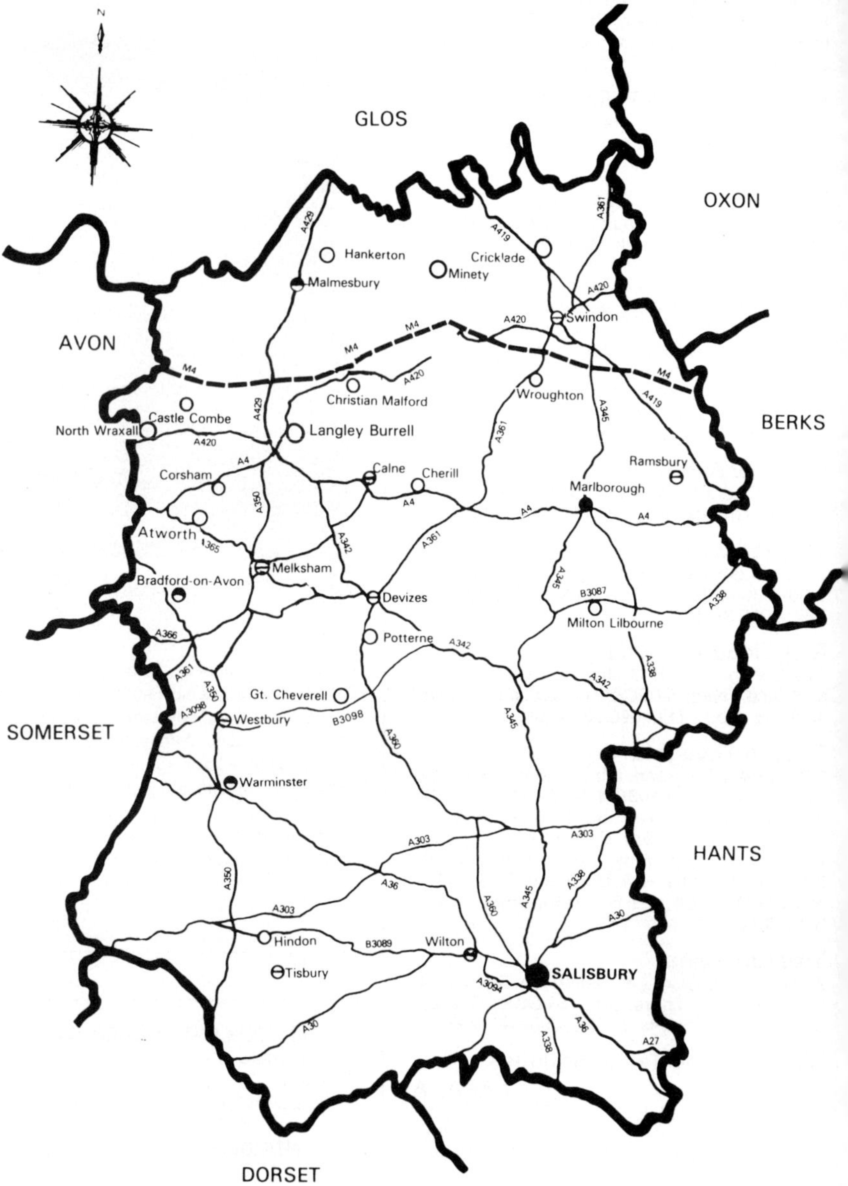
N
GLOS
OXON
AVON
BERKS
SOMERSET
HANTS
DORSET
Hankerton
Malmesbury
Minety
Cricklade
Swindon
Wroughton
Christian Malford
Castle Combe
North Wraxall
Langley Burrell
Corsham
Calne
Cherill
Ramsbury
Marlborough
Atworth
Melksham
Bradford-on-Avon
Devizes
Milton Lilbourne
Potterne
Gt. Cheverell
Westbury
Warminster
Hindon
Tisbury
Wilton
SALISBURY
M4
A4
A420
A429
A419
A361
A345
A350
A342
A365
A366
A3098
B3098
B3087
A338
A360
A303
A36
A30
B3089
A3094
A27

Please note this is only a rough map designed to show dealers the number of shops in the various towns, and is not necessarily totally accurate.

Key to number of shops in this area.

- ○ 1–2
- ⊖ 3–5
- ◒ 6–12
- ● 13+

ATWORTH, Nr. Melksham

Peter Campbell Antiques
59 Bath Rd. (P.R Campbell) Est: 1976. Open 10-5, Sun. and Thurs. by appointment. SIZE: Medium. *STOCK: General antiques and decorative items, 18th-19th C.* Not Stocked: Silver and jewellery. LOC: Between Bath and Melksham on A350. PARK: Easy. TEL: 0225 709742; home - same. VAT: Stan/Spec.

BRADFORD-ON-AVON

Avon Antiques BADA
25-27 Market St. (V. and A Jenkins, BA) Est: 1960. Open 9.45-5.30, Sun. by appointment. SIZE: Large. *STOCK: English and some continental furniture, 1600-1880; metalwork, treen, clocks, barometers, some textiles, painted and lacquer furniture.* LOC: A363, main street of town. PARK: Opposite. TEL: 022 16 2052. FAIRS: Grosvenor House. VAT: Spec.

Harp Antiques LAPADA
17 Woolley St. (H.A. and J Roland-Price) Resident. Est: 1973. Open daily 9-6. SIZE: Medium. *STOCK: Georgian and Regency furniture, £100-£8,000; English pottery and porcelain, £30-£3,000; silver, £5-£300.* LOC: B3107, 300yds. from town centre. PARK: Easy. TEL: 022 16 5770; home - same. SER: Valuations (silver, furniture). VAT: Spec.

Mac Humble Antiques BADA LAPADA
7-9 Woolley St. (W. Mc. A. and B.J Humble) Open 9-6, Sat. 9-5. SIZE: Large. *STOCK: 17th-19th C oak, mahogany, fruitwoods, metalware, treen, samplers, silkwork pictures, decorative objects.* TEL: 022 16 6329. SER: Valuations; restorations. VAT: Stan/Spec.

Moxhams Antiques LAPADA
17, 23 and 24 Silver St. (R. and J Bichard) Est: 1966. Open 9-5.30 or by appointment. SIZE: Large. *STOCK: English and continental furniture, clocks, 1650-1830, £50-£15,000; European and Oriental pottery and porcelain, 1700-1830, £10-£3,000; metals, treen, decorative items, 1600-1900, £5-£5,000.* Not Stocked: Silver, jewellery. PARK: Own, at rear. TEL: 022 16 2789; home - 0380 828677. SER: Valuations. VAT: Stan/Spec.

Richard and Pamela Nadin
'Audleys', 5 Woolley St. Est: 1970. Open 9.30-5.30 or by appointment. SIZE: Medium. *STOCK: Unusual furniture and decorations, carpets, fittings, upholstery, 18th and 19th C.* PARK: Easy. TEL: 022 16 2476. SER: West Kensington, Chelsea, Marlborough, Olympia. VAT: Stan/Spec.

Rodney and Susan Otway
Dutch Barton Cottage, Church St. ABA. Open 10-1 and 2-5.30. CL: Wed. *STOCK: English literature, 17th-19th C.* TEL: 022 16 3885.

Cedric says yew wood like these chairs

CALNE

Calne Antiques
2a London Rd. (M Blackford) Open 9-5 including Sun. *STOCK: Furniture and shipping goods, collectors' items.* LOC: Next to White Hart Hotel. TEL: 0249 816311.

Cottage Comforts
37 Quemerford. (D Swan) Est: 1977. Open 10-5, Sat. 2-5. CL: Tues. and Wed. SIZE: Small. *STOCK: Jewellery, 1800-1930, £10-£100; small furniture, £10-£50; small decorative items, £5-£40.* LOC: A4. PARK: Easy. TEL: 0249 816371; home - same.

Clive Farahar and Sophie Dupré - Rare Books, Autographs and Manuscripts
14 The Green. Open by appointment. SIZE: Medium. *STOCK: Rare books on voyages and travels, autograph letters and manuscripts, 15th-20th C, £5-£5,000.* LOC: Off A4 in town centre. PARK: Easy. TEL: 0249 821121; fax - 0249 821202. SER: Valuations; buys at auction (as stock). FAIRS: ABA; Universal Autograph Collectors' Club. VAT: Stan.

Hilmarton Manor Press
Hilmarton Manor. (H Baile de Laperriere) Est: 1967. Book on Silver Auction Records. Open 9-6. SIZE: Medium. *STOCK: New and out of print art and photography reference books, some*

Hilmarton Manor Press continued

antiquarian. LOC: 3 miles from Calne on A3102 towards Swindon. PARK: Easy. TEL: 024 976 208. SER: Buys at auction.

CASTLE COMBE, Nr. Chippenham

Combe Cottage Antiques BADA
(B. and A Bishop) Est: 1960. Open 10-1 and 2-6. SIZE: Medium. *STOCK: Country furniture, £20-£5,000; metalware, £10-£2,000; both 17th to early 19th C; treen, pottery, 18th-19th C, £5-£500; early lighting devices.* Not Stocked: Mahogany furniture, glass, silver, Victoriana. LOC: A420 from Chippenham towards Bristol. After 3 miles bear right on B4039. PARK: 20yds. TEL: 0249 782250. SER: Valuations. Specialists in cottage furnishings. VAT: Spec.

IS YOUR ENTRY CORRECT?
If there is even the slightest inaccuracy in your entry, *please* let us know before 1st January 1992.
GUIDE TO THE
ANTIQUE SHOPS OF BRITAIN
5 Church Street, Woodbridge, Suffolk.
Tel: (0394) 385501

CHERHILL, Nr. Calne

P.A. Oxley Antique Clocks and Barometers LAPADA
The Old Rectory, Main Rd. Est: 1971. Open 9.30-5, other times by appointment. CL: Wed. SIZE: Large. *STOCK: Longcase, bracket, carriage clocks and barometers, 17th-19th C, £250-£30,000.* LOC: A4, not in village. PARK: Easy. TEL: 0249 816227; fax - 0249 821285. VAT: Spec.

CHRISTIAN MALFORD, Nr. Chippenham

Harley Antiques LAPADA
The Comedy. (G.J Harley) Est: 1959. Open 9-6 or by appointment. SIZE: Large. *STOCK: Furniture, 18th-19th C, £150-£3,000; decorative objects, £30-£1,000.* LOC: B4069, 4 miles off M4, junction 17. PARK: Own. TEL: 0249 720112; home - same. SER: Colour brochure available (export only). VAT: Stan. *Trade Only.*

CODFORD, Nr. Warminster

Tina's Antiques
75 High St. (T.A Alder) Open 9-6, Sat. 9-1. *STOCK: General antiques.* TEL: 0985 50828. VAT: Spec.

CORSHAM

Robin and Matthew Eden
Pickwick Village. Resident. Est: 1947. SIZE: Large. *STOCK: 17-19th C country house furniture and garden items.* TEL: 0249 713335. VAT: Spec.

CRICKLADE, Nr. Swindon

Edred A.F Gwilliam
Candletree House, Bath Rd. Est: 1976. Open by appointment. SIZE: Medium. *STOCK: Arms and armour, swords, pistols, long guns, £30-£10,000+.* PARK: Easy. TEL: 0793 750241. SER: Valuations; buys at auction. FAIRS: Major arms. VAT: Stan/Spec.

Robin Shield Antiques
23 High St. (W.R. and P.E Shield) Est: 1974. Usually open, appointment advisable. SIZE: Large. *STOCK: Furniture, £200-£10,000; works of art, £100-£5,000; paintings, £500-£10,000; all 17th-19th C.* LOC: Adjacent to church. PARK: Easy. TEL: 0793 750205; home - same. SER: Valuations; buys at auction. VAT: Stan/Spec.

DEVIZES

Cross Keys Jewellers
The Ginnel, Market Pl. (D. and D Pullen) NAG. Est: 1967. Open 9.30-5.30. *STOCK: Jewellery, silver.* LOC: Alley adjacent Nationwide Building Socy. PARK: Easy. TEL: 0380 726293. VAT: Stan.

Devizes continued

Saville Antiques
37 Long St. (P.M Bruce) Est: 1962. Open 9.30-1 and 2-6, Sat. 9.30-12.30, Sun., Mon. and other times by appointment. SIZE: Small. *STOCK: Furniture, 17th to early 19th C, £50-£5,000; clocks, pictures, decorative items, 18th to early 19th C.* LOC: Near museum. PARK: Easy. TEL: 0380 723559. SER: Valuations. VAT: Spec.

Elizabeth Newby Vincent
Nursteed Pl. Open by appointment. *STOCK: Furniture, 18th to early 19th C; garden and decorative pieces.* TEL: 0380 723844.

GT. CHEVERELL, Nr. Devizes

Mary Manners Antiques
The Barn, Laurel House, 48 High St. Est: 1976. Open by appointment or by chance. SIZE: Small. *STOCK: Small decorative items, Staffordshire figures, pewter, blue and white transferware, textiles, £20-£300; furniture, £100-£800, all 18th-19th C.* LOC: Opposite Bell Inn. PARK: Easy. TEL: 0380 812301; home - same. FAIRS: Chelsea, Shepton Mallet. VAT: Spec.

HANKERTON, Nr. Malmesbury

North Wilts Exporters
Cloatley Manor, Cloatley Rd. (M Thornbury) Est: 1972. Open Mon.-Sat. or by appointment. *STOCK: American and continental shipping goods, pine, 18th-19th C.* LOC: Via A429. TEL: 0666 77870. SER: Valuations; shipping. VAT: Stan.

HINDON, Nr. Salisbury

Monkton Galleries
High St. (J. and B Dempsey) Resident. Est: 1967. CL: Sat. p.m. SIZE: Medium. *STOCK: Early oak and country furniture; metalware, longcase clocks.* PARK: Easy. TEL: 074 789 235. SER: Valuations; restorations (metalware, prints and pictures). FAIRS: Buxton; Surrey; British International, Birmingham. VAT: Spec.

LANGLEY BURRELL, Nr. Chippenham

Harriet Fairfax Fireplaces and General Antiques
Langley Green. Open by appointment only. *STOCK: China, glass, dolls, furniture, fabrics and needlework; architectural items and fittings, brass and iron knobs, knockers; fireplaces, pine and iron, 1780-1950.* TEL: 0249 652030. SER: Polishing; welding; design consultancy.

Robertson – Dundee
Fine mahogany longcase clock. 8-day with painted dial, c.1810.

P. A. Oxley

Antique Clocks & Barometers

The Old Rectory · Cherhill · Near Calne
Wiltshire SN11 8UX
Telephone (0249) 816227 Fax (0249) 821285

P.A. Oxley is one of the longest established and largest antique clock and barometer dealers in the U.K. with over 100 quality antique clocks and barometers including over 50 longcase clocks.

It is not our policy to exhibit at Antique Fairs and therefore our extensive stock can only be viewed at our large showrooms on the main A4 London to Bath road at Cherhill.

Full shipping facilities are available to any country in the world. U.K. customers are provided with a free delivery and setting up service combined with a twelve month guarantee.

If your desire is for a genuine antique clock or barometer then we will be pleased to see you at Cherhill where you can examine our large stock and discuss your exact requirement. If time is short and you cannot visit us we will send you a selection of photographs from which you can buy with confidence.

Hours of opening are 9.30-5.00 every day except Wednesday. Sunday and evening appointments can easily be arranged. We look forward to welcoming you to our establishment.

Michael & Patricia Oxley
Member of the London & Provincial Antique Dealers' Association

James Pike – Newton Abbot
Fine mahogany 8-day longcase clock with rocking ship automata, c.1770.

MALMESBURY

Antiques - Rene Nicholls

56 High St. (Mrs R Nicholls) Est: 1980. Open 10-5.30, Sun. by appointment. SIZE: Small. *STOCK: English pottery and porcelain, 18th to early 19th C, £50-£900; small furniture.* PARK: Opposite. TEL: 0666 823089; home - same.

Belinda Ballantine (Painted Furniture)

The Abbey Brewery, Market Cross. Est: 1987. Open 10-5. SIZE: Medium. *STOCK: Painted furniture, lamps, clock faces and accessories, £10-£1,000.* PARK: Nearby. TEL: 0666 822047. SER: Hand painted furniture. VAT: Stan.

Batstone Books

12 Gloucester St. (D. and M.E Batstone) Est: 1982. Open every day 10-1 and 2-5. SIZE: Small. *STOCK: Books, some antiquarian, to £400.* LOC: Turn left top of High St., shop by traffic mirror. PARK: Outside Bell Hotel. TEL: 0666 823072. FAIRS: P.B.F.A.

Andrew Britten Antiques

48 High St. (T.M Tyler and T.A Freeman) Est: 1975. Open 9.30-6, Sun. by appointment. SIZE: Medium. *STOCK: Furniture, 1700-1900, £100-£1,500; decorative brass, wood, glass and porcelain items, £15-£500.* Not Stocked: Jewellery, militaria. PARK: Opposite. TEL: 0666 823376. VAT: Spec.

Malmesbury continued

Cross Hayes Antiques LAPADA

The Antique and Furniture Warehouse, 19 Bristol St. (D Brooks) Est: 1975. Open 8.30-5. SIZE: Warehouse. *STOCK: Georgian to 1920s furniture - oak, mahogany, walnut and pine; books including antiquarian, bric-a-brac.* TEL: 0666 824260; home - 0666 822062; fax - 0666 823020. SER: Valuations. VAT: Stan/Spec.

Dovetail Antiques

67/69 High St. (C.R Perrin) Resident. Est: 1987. Open 10-5.30. SIZE: Small. *STOCK: Early oak and country furniture; metalware and treen; mahogany and walnut town furniture, 18th-19th C; Oriental and unusual items, 19th C.* Not Stocked: Jewellery and bric-a-brac. PARK: Nearby. TEL: 0666 822191. VAT: Spec.

J.P Kadwell

Silver St. Est: 1981. Open 8.15-5.30, Sun. by appointment. CL: Thurs. except by appointment. SIZE: Medium. *STOCK: General antiques, £5-£500.* PARK: Easy. TEL: 0666 823589; home - same. SER: Restorations (wood); buys at auction. VAT: Stan/Spec.

Malmesbury Antiques

Westport House, Gloucester Rd. (P. von Fullman) Est: 1974. Open 9.30-5.30 or by appointment. SIZE: Medium. *STOCK: Furniture, 18th-19th C, £100-£5,000; lamps, paintings, fabrics and decorative objects, £15-£2,000.* PARK: Nearby. TEL: 0666 824656. VAT: Stan/Spec.

Malmesbury continued

Relic Antiques at Brillscote Farm

Brillscote Farm, Lea. (M Gliksten and G Gower) Est: 1975. Open 9-5, Sat. and Sun. by appointment. SIZE: Large. *STOCK: Old shop and pub fronts and interiors, doors, screens and bars, stained and engraved glass windows and architectural fittings, provincial and country furniture, fairground animals and scenery, 19th C; garden ornaments, nautical and aeronautical models, etc.* LOC: Take left turn to Lea off Wootton Bassett Rd., 2nd house on right. PARK: On premises. TEL: 0666 822332. SER: Valuations; buys at auction. VAT: Stan.

MARLBOROUGH

The Antique and Book Collector

Katharine House, The Parade. (C.C Gange) Est: 1983. Open 9.45-8.30, Sun. by appointment. SIZE: Medium. *STOCK: Furniture, 17th-19th C, £200-£2,000; decorative items, £100-£1,000; glass, silver, brass, china, 18th-19th C, £20-£500; paintings and prints, £10-£1,000; books, £5-£500.* PARK: Easy. TEL: 0672 514040; home - same. FAIRS: PBFA monthly; Oxfam annually. VAT: Stan/Spec.

Carousel Antiques

72 High St. Est: 1964. Open daily. *STOCK: Porcelain, glass, bric-a-brac, pictures, prints, some small furniture.* TEL: 0672 513496.

Cellaigh Antiques

4 Silverless St. (J. and L Legge) Resident. Est: 1983. Open 10-5.30, Sun. by appointment. SIZE: Small. *STOCK: Pine and country furniture, garden stoneware.* LOC: 50yds. from High St. via Kingsbury Rd. PARK: Easy. TEL: 0672 514860. SER: Buys at auction.

Cook of Marlborough Fine Art Ltd LAPADA

High Trees House, Savernake Forest. (W.J Cook) Est: 1963. Open 10-5, Sat. and Sun. by appointment. SIZE: Medium. *STOCK: Furniture, 18th to early 19th C; objets d'art, 18th-19th C; pictures, 19th-20th C.* LOC: 1 1/2 miles from Marlborough on A346 towards Burbage. PARK: Easy. TEL: 0672 513017; fax - 0672 514455. SER: Valuations; restorations (furniture including polishing and gilding); buys at auction (furniture). FAIRS: Cafe Royal; Olympia; Barbican; Harrogate. VAT: Stan/Spec.

Nigel Cracknell (Antiques) Ltd

Cavendish House, 138 High St. Resident. Est: 1965. Trade anytime, appointment advisable. SIZE: Large. *STOCK: 18th and early 19th C English furniture, some oak; brass and decorative items, £500-£30,000.* PARK: Easy. TEL: 0672 512912. VAT: Stan/Spec.

Marlborough continued

Clifford and Roger Dade

4 Kingsbury St. Est: 1987. Open 9.30-5.30, Sun. by appointment. SIZE: Medium. *STOCK: English mahogany furniture and accessories, pre-1830.* LOC: On A4, near Town Hall. PARK: Nearby. TEL: 0672 515727; home - 0672 513198. VAT: Stan/Spec.

Robert Kime Antiques

Upper Farm, Fosbury. Est: 1968. Open 10-6, Sat. by appointment. *STOCK: Decorative, period furniture.* TEL: 026489 268. VAT: Spec.

Lacewing Fine Art Gallery

124 High St. (N James) Open 10-5.30. CL: Wed. *STOCK: Paintings and watercolours, 16th-19th C, £200-£10,000.* TEL: 0672 514580.

The Marlborough Parade Antique Centre

The Parade. (T Page and N Cannon) Est: 1985. Open every day 10-5. SIZE: 57 dealers. *STOCK: Good quality furniture, paintings, silver, porcelain, glass, clocks, jewellery, copper, brass and pewter, £5-£5,000.* LOC: Adjacent A4 in town centre. PARK: Easy. TEL: 0672 515331. SER: Valuations; restorations (furniture, porcelain, copper, brass); buys at auction. VAT: Stan/Spec.

Marlborough Sporting Gallery and Bookshop

6 Kingsbury St. Est: 1977. Open 10-5, Sun. by appointment. SIZE: Medium. *STOCK: Sporting oils, watercolours, £50-£5,000; sporting prints, £10-£500, all 1800-1975; books, 1750 to date, £3-£500.* LOC: Up hill above Town Hall. PARK: Easy. TEL: 0672 514074; fax - 0672 516435. SER: Valuations; restorations (oils, watercolours, prints); buys at auction. FAIRS: Major equestrian events. VAT: Spec.

The Military Parade Bookshop

The Parade. (G. and P Kent) *STOCK: Military history books especially regimental histories and World Wars 1 and 2.* LOC: Next to The Lamb. TEL: 0672 515470.

Principia Arts and Sciences

5 London Rd. (M Forrer) Open 9.30-5.30 and by appointment. *STOCK: Collectors' items, scientific instruments, treen, small country furniture, pictures and clocks.* TEL: 0672 512072; fax - 0672 512153.

Stuart Gallery

4 London Rd. (A.B Loncraine) Est: 1968. Open 9-6.30, Thurs., Fri. and Sat. *STOCK: General antiques especially small collectables, watercolours, oils and prints, china, glass, interior design pieces, books, garden items.* PARK: Easy. TEL: 0672 513593.

RELIC ANTIQUES
AT
BRILLSCOTE FARM
LEA VILLAGE, NR MALMESBURY, WILTSHIRE

Tel: 0666-822332 Fax: 0666-825598

ARCHITECTURAL ANTIQUES
COUNTRY FURNITURE
GARDEN ORNAMENTS
PERIOD SHOP & BAR INTERIORS
FAIRGROUND ART
VINTAGE ADVERTISING & TRADE SIGNS
NAÏVE & FOLK ART
DECORATORS' PIECES

(8 miles from M4 Motorway at Exits 16 & 17)

OPEN DAILY 9am – 5.30pm
Weekends by appointment

ANNUAL BRILLSCOTE FARM AUCTION
14th & 15th OCTOBER 1991

Further information & catalogues from Brillscote Farm Auction,
127 Pancras Road, London N.W.1
Telephone: 071-387-6039 Fax: 071-388-2691

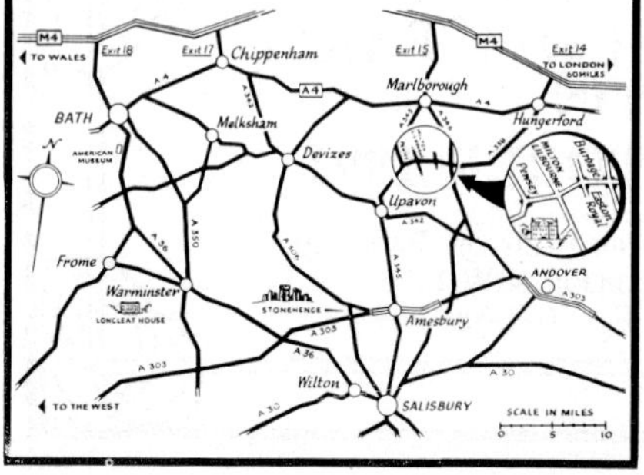
M4
TO WALES
Exit 18
Exit 17
Chippenham
Exit 15
M4
Exit 14
TO LONDON
Marlborough
Hungerford
BATH
Melksham
Devizes
Upavon
Frome
Warminster
ANDOVER
STONEHENGE
Amesbury
Wilton
SALISBURY
TO THE WEST
SCALE IN MILES
0
5
10

Marlborough continued

Annmarie Turner Antiques

22 Salisbury Rd. Est: 1960. Open 9-6, Sat. 9-5, Sun. by appointment. SIZE: Large. *STOCK: Country and Welsh primitive furniture, £50-£1,000; English treen, kitchen, trade and architectural items, £10-£200; paintings and decorative items, £20-£400; all 17th-19th C.* Not Stocked: Jewellery, silver and weapons. LOC: Left side of first roundabout approaching town centre from Hungerford on A4. PARK: Easy and George Lane. TEL: 0672 515396; home - same. SER: Valuations. VAT: Spec.

MELKSHAM

Sue and Roy Dann Antiques Ltd

Avonside Enterprise Park, New Broughton Rd. Open 8.30-5.30. SIZE: Large. *STOCK: 18th-19th C furniture and accessories for the American market.* TEL: 0225 707329; home - 0380 2695.

Alan Jaffray

16 Market Pl. Est: 1956. Open 10-1 and 2-5, Sat. by appointment. SIZE: Large. *STOCK: Furniture and smalls, 18th-19th C, £50-£2,000.* LOC: Main Bath to Devizes Rd. PARK: Easy. TEL: 0225 702269; fax - 0225 790413. VAT: Stan/Spec.

Tamaree Antiques

'Tamaree', 59 King St. (B Gillet) Resident. Est: 1965. Open by appointment. CL: Wed. SIZE: Small. *STOCK: Silver and jewellery, 19th-20th C; porcelain, pottery, glass, early Victorian to art deco.* LOC: 100yds. from Market Place. PARK: Easy. TEL: 0225 703746. FAIRS: Local.

MILTON LILBOURNE, Nr. Pewsey

Rupert Gentle Antiques BADA

The Manor House. Est: 1954. Open 9.15-6. SIZE: Medium. *STOCK: 18th C furniture, needlework, domestic accessories, especially English and continental brass, 1600-1800.* LOC: From Hungerford on A4 take A338 for Pewsey. PARK: Easy. TEL: 0672 63344. SER: Valuations; buys at auction. VAT: Stan/Spec.

MINETY, Nr. Malmesbury

Sambourne House Antiques

Sambourne House. (T Cove) Est: 1984. Open daily, Sun. by appointment. SIZE: Large. *STOCK: Pine, 1800-1910, £75-£400; furniture, 20th C, £50-£200; reproduction decorative items, £10-£300.* LOC: 10 mins. from M4, junction 16. PARK: Easy. TEL: 0666 860288; home - 0666 822271. SER: Valuations; restorations (pine, renovating, stripping and finishing); buys at auction; export arranged (especially Chicago, U.S.A.). FAIRS: Period Homes and Interiors. VAT: Stan. *Trade Only.*

NORTH WRAXHALL, Nr. Chippenham

Delomosne and Son Ltd BADA

Court Close. (M.C.F Mortimer and T.N Osborne) Est: 1905. Articles on chandeliers, glass and porcelain. Open 9.30-5.30. SIZE: Large. *STOCK: English and Irish glass, pre-1830, £20-£20,000; glass, chandeliers, English and European porcelain, needle-work, papier mâché and treen.* LOC: Off A420 between Bath and Chippenham. PARK: Easy. TEL: 0225 891505; fax - 0225 891907. SER: Valuations; buys at auction. FAIRS: International Ceramic. VAT: Spec.

POTTERNE, Nr. Devizes

Antiques and Interiors

Open Wed.-Sat. 10.30-5.30, other times by appointment. *STOCK: Furniture and decorative accessories.* LOC: On A360, centre of village. TEL: 0380 722880. VAT: Spec.

RAMSBURY, Nr. Marlborough

Heraldry Today

Parliament Piece. Est: 1954. Open 9.30-4.30; weekends by appointment. *STOCK: Heraldic and genealogical books and manuscripts, 50p-£2,000.* TEL: 0672 20617; fax - 0672 20163.

Inglenook Antiques

59 High St. (D White) Est: 1969. Open 10-5.30, Sun. by appointment. CL: Mon. p.m. *STOCK: Clocks, barometers, fire irons, brass, copper, oil lamps, some furniture.* LOC: 7 miles east of Marlborough off the A4. TEL: 0672 20261. SER: Restorations (longcase clock movements).

Bryan Mann Antiques

The Square. (B.K Mann) Est: 1973. SIZE: Medium. *STOCK: Period and country, English and continental furniture; decorative objects and unusual items.* Not Stocked: Coins, arms, glass. LOC: Approx. 4 1/2 miles from Hungerford. PARK: Easy. TEL: 0672 20552. VAT: Stan/Spec.

SALISBURY

Joan Amos Antiques

7a St. John St. Est: 1983. Open 9.30-12.30 and 1.30-5, Sat. 9.30-1. CL: Wed. SIZE: Small. *STOCK: Porcelain, £20-£200; small furniture, £100-£1,000; both late 19th C.* LOC: On right hand side when entering city from south (A354). PARK: Limited. TEL: 0722 330888.

Antique and Collectors Market

37 Catherine St. Open 9-5. SIZE: Large. *STOCK: Silver, plate, china, glass, toys, books, taxidermy, postcards, etc.* TEL: 0722 326033.

The Avonbridge Antiques and Collectors Market

United Reformed Church Hall, Fisherton St. Open Tues. 9-4. SIZE: 15 dealers. *STOCK: General antiques.* LOC: Opposite hospital.

The Barn Book Supply

88 Crane St. (J. and J Head) Est: 1958. Open every day 9-4. *STOCK: Antiquarian books on angling, shooting, horses, deerstalking.* TEL: 0722 327767.

D.M Beach

52 High St. (A Beach) Est: 1930. Open 9-5.30. SIZE: Large. *STOCK: Antiquarian books, 1500 to date, 5p-£1,000; maps, prints, oils and watercolours, to £1,500.* LOC: From Bournemouth into city, take first possible turn left. Shop is on next corner. PARK: 120yds. down Crane St. TEL: 0722 333801. SER: Valuations; restorations (leather bindings); buys at auction. FAIRS: U.S.A. and London.

Derek Boston Antiques LAPADA

223 Wilton Rd, also warehouse at Wilton. Est: 1964. Open 9.30-5. SIZE: Large. *STOCK: Furniture.* TEL: 0722 322682; home - 0722 324426. VAT: Stan/Spec.

Robert Bradley

71 Brown St. Est: 1970. Open 9.30-5.30. CL: Sat. p.m. *STOCK: Furniture, 17th and 18th C; decorative items.* TEL: 0722 333677. VAT: Spec.

Salisbury continued

Ronald Carr

6 St. Francis Rd. (R.G Carr) Est: 1983. Open by appointment. SIZE: Small. *STOCK: Modern British etchings, £5-£1,000.* LOC: 1 mile north of city on A345. PARK: Easy. TEL: 0722 328892; home - same. SER: Buys at auction.

Castle Galleries

81 Castle St. (J.C Lodge) Est: 1971. Open 9.30-5, Sat. 9.30-1. CL: Wed. *STOCK: General antiques, coins and medals.* PARK: Easy. TEL: 0722 333734. VAT: Stan/Spec.

Ian G Hastie BADA

46 St. Ann St. Est: 1952. *STOCK: English and continental furniture, 17th to early 19th C; works of art, 18th and 19th C.* TEL: 0722 322957.

Edward Hurst Antiques

Stirling House, Paynes Hill. Est: 1983. Open 9.30-5.30, Sat. 9.30-1.30. SIZE: Medium. *STOCK: Country house furniture and decorative items, 1650-1820.* LOC: Just off St. Anne's St. PARK: Easy. TEL: 0722 320595. VAT: Spec.

Mr. Micawber's Attic

73 Fisherton St. (Mr and Mrs E.M Johnson and others) Est: 1981. Open 9.30-5. CL: Wed. SIZE: Large - approx. 20 stalls. *STOCK: General antiques including jewellery, silver, furniture, clocks, coins and medals, books, porcelain,*

Mr. Micawber's Attic continued

pine, bottles, glass, lace, linen and clothes, minerals, ironwork, stained glass. LOC: 300yds. from railway station towards town centre. PARK: Opposite, behind shops. TEL: 0722 337822. SER: Valuations; restorations (furniture); repairs (watches and jewellery). FAIRS: Local.

T.J Newsam

St. Martin's House, 49 St. Ann St. Est: 1979. Open by appointment. SIZE: Medium. *STOCK: Longcase and bracket clocks, £500-£15,000.* LOC: Near cathedral. PARK: Easy. TEL: 0722 411059; home - same. SER: Valuations (clocks); buys at auction (English clocks). VAT: Spec.

St. John Street Gallery

7 St. John St. (Viscount Folkestone) Est: 1987. SIZE: Medium. *STOCK: Furniture, £50-£2,000, objects, £10-£1,000; both 1700-1850; pictures, Victorian watercolours, modern British, £10-£1,000.* LOC: Opposite Queen Anne's Gate. PARK: Nearby. TEL: 0722 412310; home - 0722 411616. SER: Valuations; buys at auction (furniture).

Salisbury Clock Shop

107 Exeter St. (A Dolby and M.S Thompson) Open 10-1 and 2-4.30, Sat. 10-12.30. CL: Mon. SIZE: Medium. *STOCK: Clocks and period furniture.* TEL: 0722 337076. SER: Restorations.

Salisbury continued

Maria Villacampa-Ascaso
Manor House, Winterbourne Dauntsey. Open 10-6, Sun. by appointment. *STOCK: Furniture, 18th-19th C, £40-£1,400; ceramics, from 18th C, £20-£450; paintings.* LOC: A338. PARK: Own. TEL: 0980 611334; home - same. SER: Courier. VAT: Spec.

Chris Wadge Clocks
142 Fisherton St. Open 9-5. CL: Mon. *STOCK: Clocks, movements and spare parts.* TEL: 0722 334467. SER: 400 day specialist.

SWINDON

Antiques and All Pine
11 Newport St, Old Town. (J. and M Brown) Open 10-5.30. CL: Mon. and Wed. SIZE: Medium. *STOCK: Pine, china, lace, linen and costume jewellery, general antiques.* LOC: From M4, junction 15 or 16 follow signs to Old Town. PARK: 100yds. TEL: 0793 520259. VAT: Stan/Spec.

Allan Smith Antique Clocks
162 Beechcroft Rd, Upper Stratton. Est: 1988. Open by appointment. SIZE: Medium. *STOCK: Longcase, £695-£6,950, wall, bracket and lantern clocks, weight driven Vienna's; some furniture and smalls; occasionally specialist clocks to £25,000.* LOC: Near Baker Arms Inn. PARK: Easy. TEL: 0793 822977. SER: Restorations (clocks). VAT: Spec.

Victoria Bookshop
30 Wood St. (S Austin) Est: 1965. Open 9-5.30. SIZE: Large. *STOCK: Books, most subjects, old postcards.* LOC: From Marlborough, Chippenham or M4, follow signs to Old Town. PARK: 200yds. reached by pedestrian way. TEL: 0793 527364.

TISBURY

Jennifer Browne
Staple House, High St. *STOCK: English watercolours, decorative pictures, country furniture.*

Edward Marnier Antiques
17 High St. (E.F Marnier) Est: 1989. Open 10-6, Sun. 10-12, Sun. and Mon. p.m. by appointment. CL: Wed. *STOCK: English and continental furniture, £20-£2,000; pictures, carpets and mirrors, £25-£3,000; decorative items, all 18th-19th C.* PARK: Easy. TEL: 0747 871074; home - 072 276 716810. SER: Valuations; buys at auction. VAT: Spec.

May and May Ltd
Arundell House, High St. Est: 1963. Open by appointment. *STOCK: Antiquarian music and music literature.* TEL: 0747 870353; fax - 0747 871425. SER: Buys at auction.

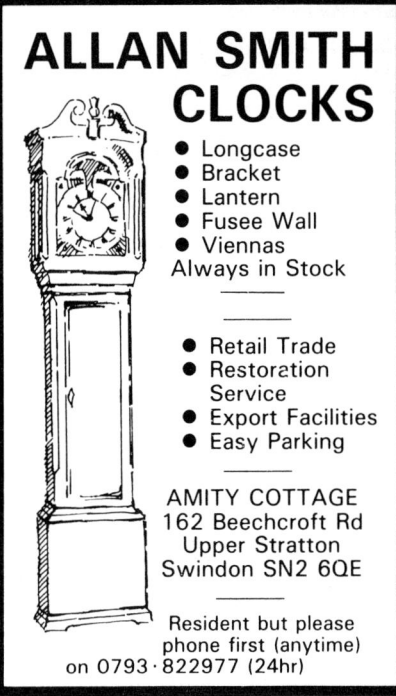

Tisbury continued

Carol Pearson Antiques
4 High St. Est: 1984. Open 10-1 and 2-5, Wed. by appointment. SIZE: Large. *STOCK: Georgian, Victorian and Edwardian furniture, £25-£3,000; paintings, £10-£2,000; porcelain, 18th-19th C.* PARK: Easy. TEL: 0747 870710. SER: Restorations (ceramics and furniture).

WARMINSTER

The Antique Warehouse
61 East St. (P.A. and D Gale) Open 8.30-5.30, other times by appointment. CL: Sat. SIZE: Large. *STOCK: General antiques and shipping goods.* PARK: Easy. TEL: 0985 219460. SER: Restorations; shipping and packing.

Bishopstrow Antiques
55 East St. (A., M. and J.M Stewart-Cox) Est: 1974. Open 10-1 and 2-5.30. SIZE: Medium. *STOCK: Furniture including pine and country; porcelain, boxes, small silver, decorative items, all 18th-19th C.* LOC: On left of old A36 leaving Warminster on Salisbury road, opposite Esso garage. PARK: Easy. TEL: 0985 212683; home - 0985 40877. VAT: Spec.

Warminster continued

Britannia Antiques Exports

Furlong House, 61 East St. (T.A Goodsman and P.A Gale) Open 8.30-5.30, other times by appointment. CL: Sat. SIZE: Large. *STOCK: General antiques.* TEL: 0985 219360. SER: Restorations; packing; shipping.

Century Antiques

10 Silver St. (N Giltsoff) Open 10-5.30. *STOCK: General antiques.* TEL: 0985 217031.

Choice Antiques

4 Silver St. (Mrs A.M Bailey) Open 10-1 and 2-5.30, Sat. 10-1 and 2-5. SIZE: Medium. *STOCK: General antiques and decorative items, 18th-19th C, £25-£6,000.* PARK: Easy. TEL: 0985 218924; home - 0225 782209. VAT: Stan/Spec.

Peter Houghton Antiques LAPADA

33 Silver St. (P.J Houghton) Est: 1985. Open 10-12.30 and 2-5.30, Sun. by appointment. SIZE: Medium. *STOCK: Fine English furniture, 18th C, £500-£1,500; clocks and watercolours, 19th C.* LOC: West end of town centre at Frome/Bath fork. PARK: Easy. TEL: 0985 213451; home - 0985 216288. SER: Valuations; buys at auction. FAIRS: Olympia, N.E.C., Westminster, City of London Fine Arts. VAT: Spec.

Obelisk Antiques

2 Silver St and The Old Bakery, Silver St. (P Tanswell) Open 10-1 and 2-5.30. SIZE: Large and warehouse. *STOCK: English and continental furniture, 18th-19th C; decorative items, objets d'art.* TEL: 0985 846646.

J.R Vernon Antiques

16a Silver St. Est: 1974. Open 10-5.30. SIZE: Medium. *STOCK: Furniture, 19th C, £50-£2,000.* LOC: A36. PARK: Easy. TEL: 0985 218933. VAT: Stan/Spec.

K. and A Welch

1A Church St. Est: 1967. Open 8-6, Sat. 9-1. SIZE: Large. *STOCK: Shipping furniture, 18th-19th C, £10-£2,000.* LOC: A36 west end of town. PARK: Own. TEL: 0985 214687; home - 0985 213433. VAT: Stan. *Trade Only.*

WESTBURY

Booth Gallery and Titanic Signals Archive

30 Edenvale Rd. Est: 1970. Open by appointment only. *STOCK: Maps and prints.* TEL: 0373 823271; home - same. SER: Valuations; restorations; mounting and framing; print colouring; 350 archive signals on exhibition. VAT: Stan.

Bratton Antiques LAPADA

Market Pl. (J.A.W. and F.A Hyde) Est: 1976. Open 10-1 and 2.15-5, Sat. 10-1. CL: Wed. SIZE: Small. *STOCK: Staffordshire figures and*

Bratton Antiques continued

animals, furniture, both 18th-19th C; country and domestic bygones. Not Stocked: Jewellery, silver and weapons. LOC: Close to A350. PARK: Easy. TEL: 0373 823021. VAT: Stan/Spec.

Ray Coggins Antiques

1 Fore St. Open 9-5.30. *STOCK: Period, pine country furniture and decorative, architectural items.* TEL: 0373 826574.

WILTON, Nr. Salisbury

Ian J Brook, Antiques and Picture Gallery

26 North St. Resident. Est: 1962. Open after hours to trade by appointment. CL: Wed. p.m. *STOCK: Furniture, oil paintings and watercolours, £5-£5,000.* TEL: 0722 743392. VAT: Stan/Spec.

Earle

47 North St. (B Earle) Est: 1960. Open 9.30-5.30. CL: Wed. SIZE: Small. *STOCK: General antiques.* Not Stocked: Large furniture. LOC: From market place turn directly into North St. PARK: Easy. TEL: 0722 743284.

Pamela Lynch

18 West St. Resident. Open 10-5, Sat. 10-1. CL: Wed. *STOCK: Small furniture, needlework pictures, decorative items, objets de vertu.* TEL: 0722 744113.

Carol Pearson Antiques

14 West St. Est: 1984. Open 10-1 and 2-5. SIZE: Small. *STOCK: Furniture - Georgian, Victorian and Edwardian, £25-£3,000; paintings, £10-£2,000; porcelain, 18th-19th C.* LOC: 100yds. from traffic lights. PARK: Easy. TEL: 0722 742451. SER: Restorations (ceramics and furniture).

A.J Romain and Sons

The Old House, 11 and 13 North St. *STOCK: Furniture, mainly 17th-18th C; early oak, walnut and marquetry; clocks, copper, brass and miscellanea.* TEL: 0722 743350. VAT: Stan/Spec.

WROUGHTON, Nr. Swindon

Wroughton Antique Centre

23 High St. (H Sutton) Open 10-5 or by appointment. CL: Wed. SIZE: Medium. *STOCK: Chests, general antiques, bric-a-brac.* LOC: A361. PARK: Easy. TEL: 0793 813232; home - 0793 721235.

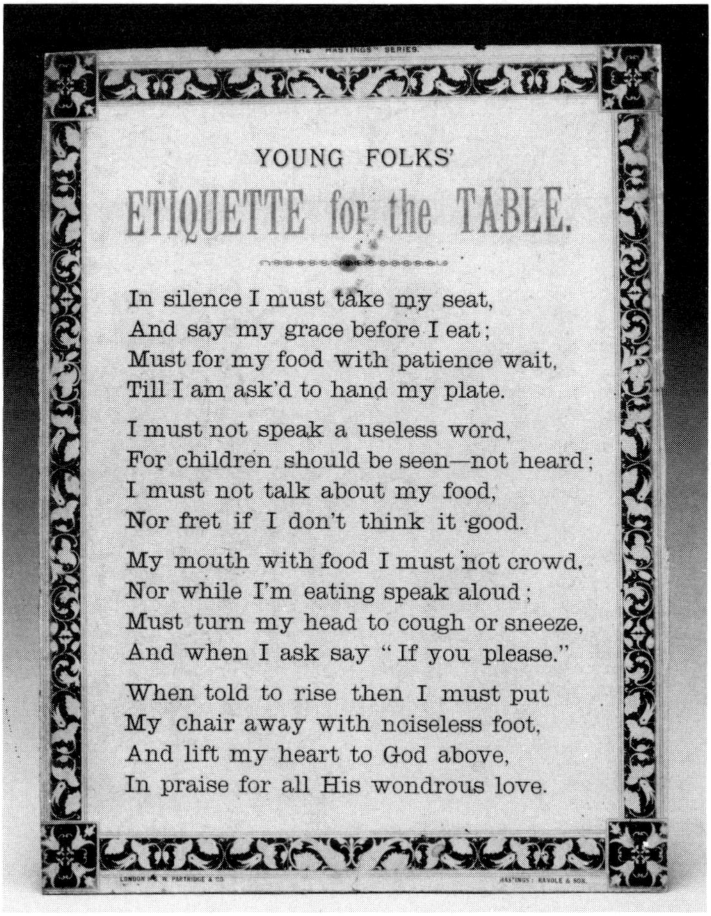
YOUNG FOLKS'
ETIQUETTE for the TABLE.
In silence I must take my seat,
And say my grace before I eat;
Must for my food with patience wait,
Till I am ask'd to hand my plate.
I must not speak a useless word,
For children should be seen—not heard;
I must not talk about my food,
Nor fret if I don't think it good.
My mouth with food I must not crowd,
Nor while I'm eating speak aloud;
Must turn my head to cough or sneeze,
And when I ask say "If you please."
When told to rise then I must put
My chair away with noiseless foot,
And lift my heart to God above,
In praise for all His wondrous love.

A late Victorian card printed with verses instructive of good table manners, which no doubt hung in a nursery. It endorses the Victorian philosophy that children should be seen and not heard. c.1880. CAMBRIDGE AND COUNTY FOLK MUSEUM
From ***Yesterday's Children*** by Sally Kevill-Davies published by the **Antique Collectors' Club** in 1991. £25.00.

Yorkshire North

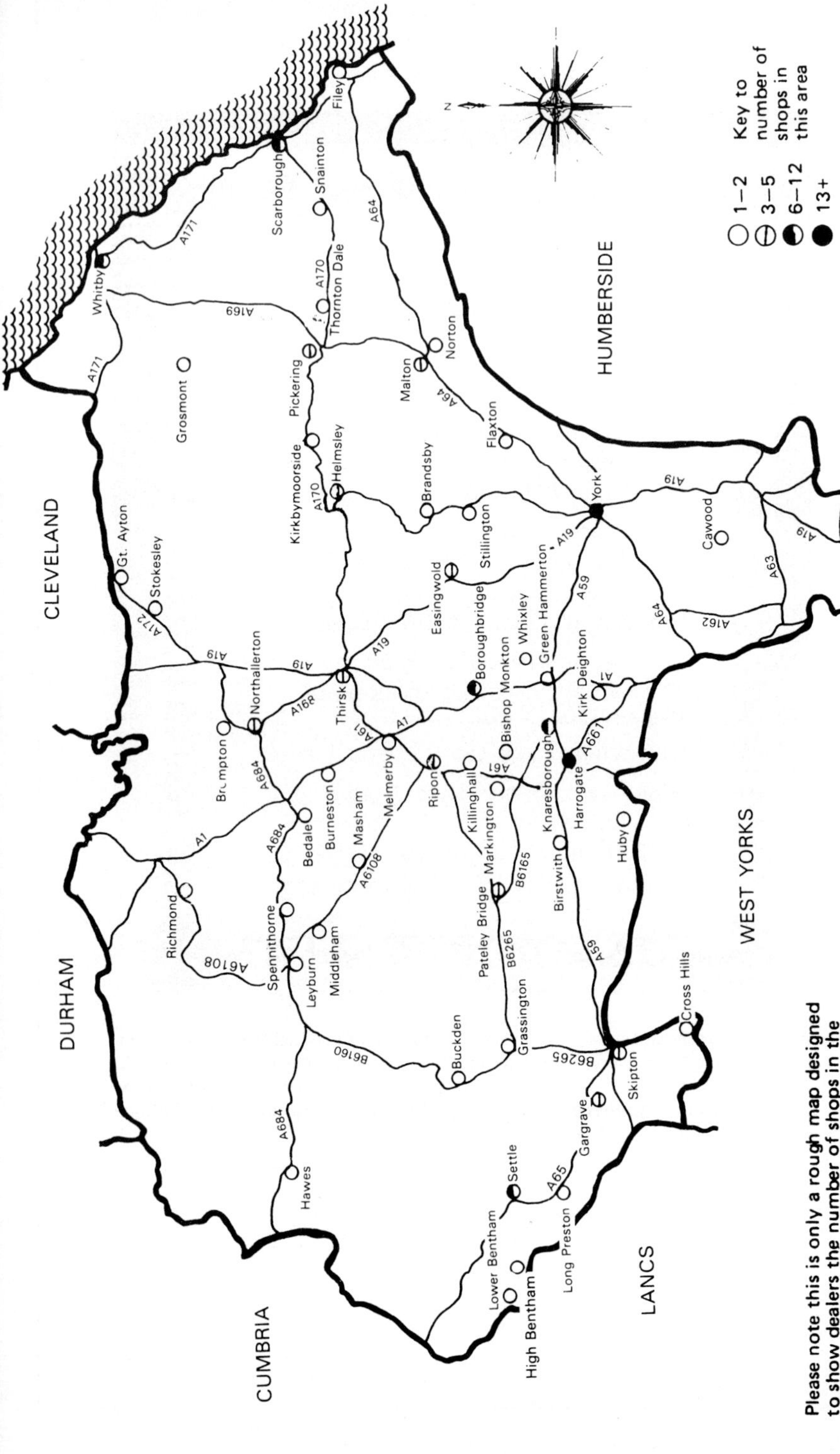

CLEVELAND
DURHAM
CUMBRIA
LANCS
WEST YORKS
HUMBERSIDE
N
Whitby
Scarborough
Filey
Snainton
Thornton Dale
Pickering
Grosmont
Malton
Norton
Flaxton
Kirkbymoorside
Helmsley
Brandsby
Stillington
York
Cawood
Gt. Ayton
Stokesley
Easingwold
Boroughbridge
Green Hammerton
Whixley
Northallerton
Thirsk
Bishop Monkton
Kirk Deighton
Brompton
Melmerby
Ripon
Killinghall
Knaresborough
Harrogate
Bedale
Burneston
Masham
Markington
Birstwith
Huby
Richmond
Spennithorne
Leyburn
Middleham
Pateley Bridge
Grassington
Buckden
Skipton
Cross Hills
Gargrave
Hawes
Settle
Long Preston
Lower Bentham
High Bentham
A171
A169
A170
A64
A19
A172
A168
A61
A1
A684
A6108
B6160
B6265
B6165
A59
A661
A162
A63
A65
1–2
3–5
6–12
13+
Key to number of shops in this area

Please note this is only a rough map designed to show dealers the number of shops in the various towns, and is not necessarily totally accurate.

BEDALE

Bedale Antiques

12 Market Pl. (G.G Hopgood) Est: 1989. Open 9.30-5. CL: Wed. SIZE: Small. *STOCK: Furniture, 19th C, £200-£4,000; ceramics, jewellery and books, 19th-20th C, £5-£700.* LOC: Bedale centre. PARK: Easy. TEL: 0677 23150.

Thornton Gallery

Snape. (Mr and Mrs W.H Turnbull) Est: 1970. Open by appointment. SIZE: Small. *STOCK: Oil paintings, £200-£3,000; watercolours, £50-£1,500; all 19th-20th C.* Not Stocked: Furniture, silver, pewter. LOC: 5 miles from A1 at Leeming Motel. PARK: Easy. TEL: 0677 70318. SER: Valuations; restorations (oil paintings); buys at auction. VAT: Spec.

BIRSTWITH, Nr. Harrogate

John Pearson Antique Clock Restoration

Church Cottage. Est: 1978. Open by appointment. *STOCK: Longcase, bracket and wall clocks, 18th C.* LOC: Off A59. PARK: Easy. TEL: 0423 770828; home - same. SER: Restorations (clocks, cases, movements and especially dials).

BISHOP MONKTON, Nr. Harrogate

Pine Finds

The Old Cornmill. (G. and J Pitt) Est: 1979. Open 9-5, Sun. 10-5. SIZE: Large. *STOCK: Pine and country smalls, 18th-19th C, £10-£1,000.* LOC: 5 miles west of A1. TEL: 0765 87159; fax - 0765 87056. SER: Restorations (pine). VAT: Stan.

BOROUGHBRIDGE

Jeffery Bates Antiques

The Stone Yard, Fishergate. Est: 1966. Open 10.30-5. CL: Thurs. SIZE: Small. *STOCK: Small items and silver including snuff boxes and objets de vertu, £10-£350; pictures, £40-£500; furniture, £150-£1,000; walking sticks, £15-£250, all 18th-19th C.* LOC: 1 mile from A1. PARK: Own. TEL: 0423 324258. SER: Valuations; buys at auction (silver and general antiques). FAIRS: Olympia; Harrogate; Heritage in the West End. VAT: Stan/Spec.

Country Antiques

High St. (J.P. and P.W Raine) Est: 1969. CL: Thurs. and lunch times. SIZE: Medium. *STOCK: Silver, 18th-20th C; furniture and metalware, 17th to early 19th C.* PARK: Easy. TEL: 0423 324017. VAT: Stan/Spec.

Joan Eyles Antiques BADA

The Stone Yard, Fishergate. (J.M. and J.C.H Eyles) Est: 1962. Open 11-5.30. CL: Thurs.

Joan Eyles Antiques continued

***STOCK: Pottery, furniture, general antiques, especially fenders, treen, sewing equipment, textiles.* Not Stocked: Weapons. PARK: Own. TEL: 0423 323357; home - 0423 322487. VAT: Spec.**

Galloway Antiques LAPADA

High St. (Mr and Mrs J.E Gay) Est: 1977. Open 9.30-5.30, Sun. p.m. by appointment. SIZE: Large. *STOCK: Furniture, 18th-20th C, £50-£3,000; paintings, 19th-20th C, £75-£2,000; decorative items including Wemyss, 18th-20th C, £5-£500.* Not Stocked: Arms and medals. LOC: 1 mile off A1. PARK: Easy. TEL: 0423 324602; home - 0423 506719. SER: Valuations; restorations (furniture and upholstery). FAIRS: Castle, N.E.C. (Aug.); Wembley.

St. James House Antiques

St. James Sq. (J.D Wilson) Est: 1989. Open 9-5.30, Thurs. 9-12.30, Sun. by appointment. SIZE: Medium. *STOCK: Furniture, £50-£10,000; brass and copper, £5-£750, all 1750-1920; china, 1740-1900, £5-£1,500.* Not Stocked: Guns. LOC: Town centre. PARK: Easy. TEL: 0423 322508; home - same. SER: Valuations; restorations (furniture); upholstery. VAT: Stan/Spec.

R.S Wilson and Sons BADA

High St. Est: 1917. Open 9-5.30. CL: Thurs. p.m. *STOCK: Furniture, 17th-19th C; porcelain and pottery.* TEL: 0423 322417; home - 0423 322654. VAT: Stan/Spec.

BRANDSBY

L.L Ward and Son

Bar House. (R Ward) Est: 1970. Open 8.30-5. *STOCK: Pine.* TEL: 034 75 651.

BROMPTON, Nr. Northallerton

Country Pine Antiques

Unit 45, The Old Mill. (C Tindler) Open Wed. and Sat. 9-6, other times by appointment. *STOCK: Victorian pine.* TEL: 0609 774322.

BUCKDEN, Nr. Skipton

Greystones Antiques

(W. and S Griffiths) Open Thurs., Fri., Sat. and some Sun., other times by appointment. *STOCK: Lace-collars, stoles, veils, christening gowns; table and bed linen; prints, Yorkshire watercolours, collectors' items, model railways.* LOC: Centre of Yorkshire Dales National Park. TEL: 075 676 847. SER: Commissions and export.

BURNESTON, Nr. Bedale

Simon Greenwood Antiques

(S. and C Greenwood) Est: 1976. Open by appointment. *STOCK: Furniture, including upholstered items, 17th-20th C, £5-£1,000; decorative items and textiles.* LOC: 1/4 mile from A1. PARK: Easy. TEL: Home - 0677 22554; 076 584 571. SER: Valuations; buys at auction. VAT: Stan/Spec.

W Greenwood (Fine Art)

Oak Dene, Church Wynd. Est: 1978. Open by appointment. *STOCK: Paintings and watercolours, 19th and 20th C, £100-£5,000; frames, £20-£500; mirrors.* LOC: Take B6285 left off A1 northbound, house 1/4 mile on right. PARK: Easy. TEL: 0677 23217. SER: Valuations; restorations (paintings), framing.

CAWOOD, Nr. Selby

Cawood Antiques

Sherburn St. (J.E Gilham) Open 9-6 including Sun. *STOCK: General antiques, shipping, furniture, copper, brass, porcelain, pictures, collectors' items.* PARK: Easy. TEL: 0757 268533.

CROSS HILLS, Nr. Keighley

Heathcote Antiques

1 Aire St. (M Webster) Resident. Est: 1979. Open 10-5.30, Sun. 12.30-4. CL: Mon. and Tues. SIZE: Medium. *STOCK: Pine, Victorian furniture and small items, £5-£500.* PARK: Easy. TEL: 0535 635250. SER: Valuations.

EASINGWOLD

Bow Antiques

94 Long St. (J.W. and R.E Ager-Harris) Est: 1987. Open 9.30-5. CL: Wed. SIZE: Medium. *STOCK: Furniture, £50-£3,000; glass, £10-£150; both 18th-19th C; porcelain and pottery, 18th-20th C, £15-£300.* Not Stocked: Pictures, jewellery, militaria and gold. LOC: A19. PARK: Easy. TEL: 0347 22596; home - 0347 22478 or 03473 8178.

Easingwold continued

Chapman Medd and Sons

Market Pl. Est: 1865. Open 8-12 and 1-5. Open at any time in summer. *STOCK: Country furniture, oak and mahogany.* TEL: 0347 21370.

Mrs B.A.S Reynolds

42 Long St. *STOCK: General antiques, Victorian.* TEL: 0347 21078.

White House Farm Antiques

Thirsk Rd. (G Hood) Resident. Est: 1960. Usually open but prior 'phone call advisable. *STOCK: Rural and domestic bygones, stone troughs, architectural reclamation and garden ornaments.* LOC: Two miles north of Easingwold, on A19. PARK: Easy. TEL: 0347 21479.

FILEY

Cairncross and Sons

31 Bellevue St. (G Cairncross) Open 9.30-12.45 and 2-4.30. CL: Wed. p.m. *STOCK: Medals, uniforms, insignia, cap badges.* Not Stocked: Weapons. TEL: 0723 513287.

Filey Antiques

1 Belle Vue St. Est: 1970. Open daily 10.30-4.30 in summer, 11-4 in winter, Thurs. to Sat. only. SIZE: Small. *STOCK: Small furniture, prints, china, bric-a-brac, jewellery.* Not Stocked: Coins, militaria. LOC: Town centre, at corner of Belle Vue St. and West Ave. PARK: Easy. TEL: 0723 513440.

FLAXTON, Nr. York

Elm Tree Antiques

(R. and J Jackson) Est: 1975. Open 9-5, Sun. 10-5. SIZE: Large. *STOCK: Furniture, 17th C to Edwardian; small items, £5-£5,000.* LOC: 1 mile off A64. PARK: Easy. TEL: 090486 462; home - same. SER: Valuations; restorations (cabinet making, polishing and upholstery).

GARGRAVE, Nr. Skipton

Antiques at Forge Cottage
22A High St. Est: 1989. Open most days 11-4.30 or by appointment. *STOCK: Porcelain, glass, metalware and lighting; collectors' items.* LOC: A65. PARK: Easy.

H Blackburn
9 East St. Open anytime by appointment. *STOCK: Furniture, pottery, metalware, pictures.* LOC: First left turn off A65 from Skipton after petrol station. TEL: 0756 749796. SER: Valuations; container packing; courier; finder.

Bernard Dickinson
Estate Yard, West St. Resident. Est: 1958. Open 9-6 or by appointment. *STOCK: Early English oak and walnut furniture.* PARK: Easy. TEL: 0756 748257/749285. VAT: Spec.

Gargrave Gallery
48 High St. (B Herrington) Appointment advisable. *STOCK: General antiques.* PARK: Easy. TEL: 0756 749641.

Myers Galleries BADA
Endsleigh House, High St. (R.N Myers and Son) Est: 1890. Open 9-5.30 or by appointment. SIZE: Medium. *STOCK: Furniture, oak, mahogany, 17th to early 19th C; pottery, porcelain and metalware.* Not Stocked: Victoriana, weapons, coins, jewellery. LOC: A65. Skipton-Settle road. PARK: Behind shop and opposite. TEL: 0756 749587. SER: Valuations. VAT: Spec.

GRASSINGTON, Nr. Skipton

Fairings
Lucy Fold. (D. and M.A Byrne) Est: 1979. CL: Thurs. SIZE: Small. *STOCK: Georgian and Victorian country antiques, including brass, copper, blue and white china, small oak, mahogany and pine furniture, £5-£750.* LOC: Opposite Black Horse Hotel. PARK: Easy. TEL: 0756 752755.

GREAT AYTON

The Great Ayton Bookshop
47 High St. (M.S Jones) Est: 1978. Open 10-5.30, Wed. 10-2, Sun. 2-5.30. CL: Mon. SIZE. Small. *STOCK: Books, antiquarian and secondhand, 50p-£100; postcards, pre-1930, 10p-£20; prints and local maps, 10p-£50.* LOC: 7 miles south of Middlesbrough off Stokesley road. PARK: Easy. TEL: 0642 723358. SER: Valuations. FAIRS: P.B.F.A. VAT: Stan.

GREEN HAMMERTON, Nr. York

The Main Pine Co
Grangewood. (C. and K.M Main) Est: 1976. Open 9-5. SIZE: Large. *STOCK: Pine furniture,*

The Main Pine Co continued

18th-19th C, £100-£1,500; architectural pine, 19th-20th C, £50-£1,000; china, linen and bric-a-brac, 18th-20th C, £5-£100. LOC: Just off A59. PARK: Easy. TEL: 0423 330451; home - 0423 331078; fax: - 0423 331278. SER: Restorations (pine). VAT: Stan.

GROSMONT, Nr. Whitby

Country Connections (Esk House Arts)
Esk House. (D.R. and J.M Stonehouse) Open 10-5 including Sun. *STOCK: Fine art prints and oil paintings.* TEL: 0947 85319.

HARROGATE

Ann-tiquities
12 Cheltenham Parade. (Mrs A Wilkinson) Open 10-4. CL: Wed. *STOCK: Bric-a-brac, linen, silver, brass, copper, small items.* TEL: 0423 503567.

Antique and Furniture Centre
46 Back Cheltenham Mount. (R Maynard) Open 10.30-5, Sun. and Mon. by appointment. *STOCK: 19th C mahogany, pine and oak furniture, collectables, linen, shipping items, £5-£2,000.* LOC: Opposite conference centre. TEL: 0423 509708. VAT: Stan.

Antiques and Collectables
37/39 Cheltenham Crescent. (G Nimmo) Open 9.30-5.30. *STOCK: Jewellery, silver, furniture, watches, collectors' items.* TEL: 0423 521897.

Armstrong BADA LAPADA
10-11 Montpellier Parade. (M.A. and C.J Armstrong) Est: 1976. Open 10-5.30. SIZE: Medium. *STOCK: Fine English furniture, 18th to early 19th C; glasses and works of art, 18th C.* PARK: Easy. TEL: 0423 506843. FAIRS: Olympia (June); Café Royal. VAT: Spec.

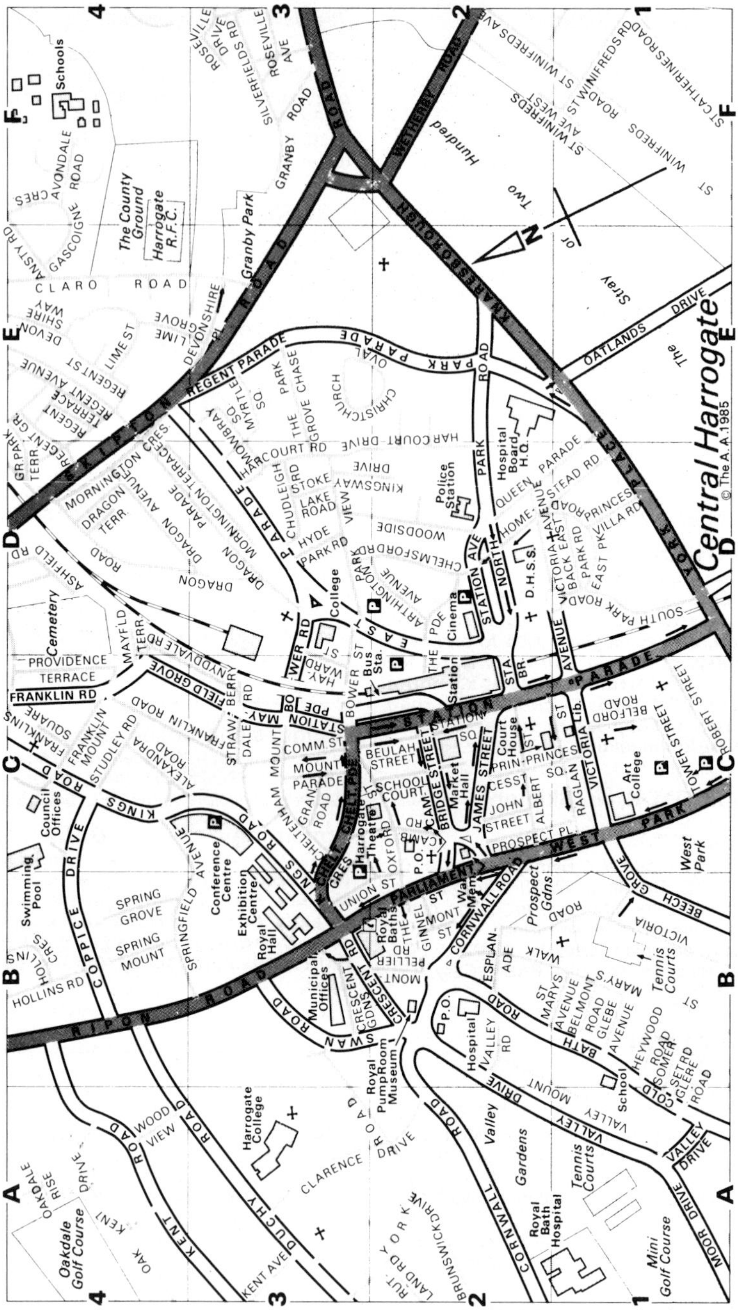
Central Harrogate
© The A.A. 1985
A
B
C
D
E
F
1
2
3
4
RIPON ROAD
SKIPTON ROAD
KNARESBOROUGH ROAD
WETHERBY ROAD
YORK PLACE
STATION PARADE
WEST PARK
PARLIAMENT ST
KINGS ROAD
EAST PARADE
PARK PARADE
REGENT PARADE
CLARO ROAD
FRANKLIN RD
PROVIDENCE TERRACE
CONFERENCE CENTRE
Exhibition Centre
Royal Hall
Municipal Offices
Royal PumpRoom Museum
Harrogate College
Valley Gardens
Royal Bath Hospital
Mini Golf Course
Oakdale Golf Course
Tennis Courts
West Park
Prospect Gdns
The Stray
The County Ground Harrogate R.F.C.
Granby Park
Cemetery
Council Offices
Swimming Pool
Police Station
Hospital Board H.Q.
Art College
Court House
Market Hall
Harrogate Theatre
Royal Baths
Station
Bus Sta.
Cinema
College
Schools
Hospital
School
DUCHY ROAD
CORNWALL ROAD
VALLEY DRIVE
VICTORIA AVENUE
OATLANDS DRIVE
CHRISTCHURCH OVAL
HARCOURT DRIVE
Two Hundred

Key to Town Plan

- AA Recommended roads
- Other roads
- Restricted roads
- Buildings of interest
- Car Parks
- Parks and open spaces
- AA Service Centre

Harrogate continued

Bill Bentley
16 Montpellier Parade. Open 9.30-5.30 or by appointment. SIZE: Large. *STOCK: Oak furniture, 1600-1800; country furniture, 1700-1800; period metalwork and treen.* PARK: Easy. TEL: 0423 564084; home - 0423 564564. SER: Restorations. VAT: Spec.

Bloomers
41 Cheltenham Crescent. (G.R. and M Cooper) Est: 1973. Open 11-5. CL: Wed. SIZE: Small. *STOCK: Textiles including quilts, samplers, linen, fans, period clothing and accessories, lace.* LOC: Corner of King's Rd., almost opposite new conference centre. PARK: Nearby. TEL: 0423 569389.

Harrogate continued

Cottage Antiques
3 Devonshire Pl, Skipton Rd. (Mrs S Evans) Open 10-5, other times by appointment. CL: Fri. SIZE: Large. *STOCK: Period oak, pine, country furniture, 17th-19th C; country and dairy items, treen, brass, copper, pottery, 18th-19th C; domestic cast iron, 19th C.* LOC: A59, 100yds. from Westmoreland St. traffic lights. PARK: Easy. TEL: 0423 568195; home - 0937 72694. VAT: Stan/Spec.

John Daffern Antiques
38 Forest Lane Head, Starbeck. Open 10-5. CL: Tues. and Thurs. SIZE: Small. *STOCK:*

John Daffern Antiques continued

Mahogany furniture, £250-£5,000; longcase clocks, tea caddies, bronzes, £100-£1,000; pottery and porcelain, £25-£1,000, all 18th-19th C. LOC: Adjacent to Harrogate Golf Club. PARK: Easy. TEL: 0423 889832; home - 076 586 329. VAT: Stan/Spec.

Derbyshire Antiques Ltd
27 Montpellier Parade. (R.C. and M.T Derbyshire) Est: 1960. Open 10-5.30. SIZE: Medium. *STOCK: Early oak and walnut, 16th-18th C; Georgian furniture to 1820; decorative items.* TEL: 0423 503115/564242; mobile - 0860 580836. VAT: Spec.

Dragon Antiques
10 Dragon Rd. (P.F Broadbelt) Resident. Est: 1954. Open 11-6. Always available. SIZE: Small. *STOCK: Victorian art glass, £30-£300; art pottery, postcards, G.B. and foreign.* LOC: 5 mins. from town centre, opp. Dragon Road car park. PARK: Easy. TEL: 0423 562037.

Fox's Antique Pine and Country Furniture
83 Knaresborough Rd. (M. and P Fox) Est: 1958. Open 9-1 and 2.15-6. SIZE: Large. *STOCK: Pine furniture.* LOC: A59. PARK: Easy. TEL: 0423 888116. SER: Stripping (pine).

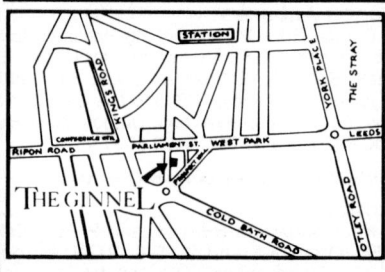

Harrogate continued

Garth Antiques LAPADA
2 Montpellier Mews. (I Chapman) Open 10-5.30. SIZE: Medium. *STOCK: Furniture, 18th-19th C, £50-£3,000; brass and copper, 19th C, £1-£500; oils and watercolours, £5-£3,000.* LOC: Turn left from Montpellier Parade at Montpellier public house. TEL: 0423 530573. VAT: Stan/Spec.

The Ginnel
Harrogate Antique Centre, The Ginnel. (P Stephenson) Open 9.30-5.30. SIZE: 40 dealers. *STOCK: Furniture, pottery, porcelain, jewellery, clocks, oils, watercolours, prints, silver, glass, arms, armour, lace and antiquities.* LOC: Off Parliament St. opp. Debenhams. TEL: 0423 508857. SER: Courier.

W.F Greenwood and Sons Ltd BADA
2 and 3 Crown Pl. Est: 1829. Open 9-1 and 2.15-5.30. CL: Wed. p.m. SIZE: Large. *STOCK: Furniture, 1660-1850, £25-£15,000; pottery and porcelain, 1740-1830, £15-£800; silver and jewellery, £10-£3,500.* TEL: 0423 504467. SER: Valuations. VAT: Stan/Spec.

Grove Collectors Centre
Grove Rd. Open 10-4.30. CL: Tues. SIZE: 8 dealers. *STOCK: General antiques including silver, porcelain, cigarette cards, collectables and furniture.* TEL: 0423 561680.

Harrogate Fine Arts
77 Station Parade. (M Reid and C Long) CL: Mon. Otherwise open but Sun. by appointment. *STOCK: Fine art, 19th-20th C.* TEL: 0423 530355.

Haworth Antiques
26 Cold Bath Rd. (G. and J White) Open 10-5 or by appointment. CL: Mon. SIZE: Medium. *STOCK: Clocks, 18th-19th C, £100-£2,000; small furniture, Georgian and Victorian, £50-£1,000.* LOC: 300yds. from Crown Hotel. PARK: Easy. TEL: 0423 521401; home - 0423 734293. SER: Restorations (clocks, dials, re-painted and re-silvered). VAT: Stan/Spec.

R.B Kendal-Greene
2A Chudleigh Rd. Est: 1964. *STOCK: General antiques.* TEL: 0423 562497; home - 0423 883504. VAT: Stan/Spec. *Trade and Export Only.*

Rodney Kent LAPADA
20 West Park. Open 10-1 and 2-5. CL: Mon. *STOCK: Paintings, drawings and watercolours, 16th-20th C; continental and English furniture, 18th-19th C.* TEL: 0423 560352.

David Lawes
125 Cold Bath Rd. Est: 1962. Open 9-1 and 2.30-5.30. CL: Wed. p.m. and Sat. p.m. SIZE: Small. *STOCK: Philatelic items.* PARK: Easy. TEL: 0423 568428. SER: Valuations.

London House Oriental Rugs and Carpets
9 Montpellier Parade. (N.C Ries) Est: 1981. Open 10-5.30. CL: Mon. SIZE: Medium. *STOCK: Persian, Turkish, Indian, Afghan and Chinese rugs*

London House Oriental Rugs and Carpets continued

and carpets, 19th-20th C, £25-£5,000; kelims and camel bags, 19th-20th C, £25-£2,000. LOC: Town centre on The Stray. PARK: Easy. TEL: 0423 567167; home - 0937 845123. SER: Valuations; restorations (handmade rugs). VAT: Stan.

David Love BADA LAPADA

10 Royal Parade. (Mr and Mrs D.A Love) Est: 1969. Open 9-1 and 2-6. SIZE: Large. *STOCK: Furniture, English, 17th-19th C; pottery and porcelain, English and continental; decorative items, all periods.* LOC: Opposite Pump Room Museum. PARK: Easy. TEL: 0423 565797. SER: Valuations; buys at auction. VAT: Stan/Spec.

Harrogate continued

Charles Lumb and Sons Ltd BADA

2 Montpellier Gardens. (F. and A.R Lumb) Est: 1920. Open 9-1 and 2-6. SIZE: Medium. *STOCK: Furniture, 17th to early 19th C; metalware, period accessories.* PARK: 20yds. immediately opposite. TEL: 0423 503776; home - 0423 863281; fax - 0423 530074. FAIRS: Harrogate. VAT: Spec.

McTague of Harrogate

17/19 Cheltenham Mount. (P McTague) Open 9.30-1 and 2-5.30. CL: Mon. SIZE: Medium. *STOCK: Prints, some oil paintings, drawings and watercolours, 17th-19th C.* LOC: From Conference Centre on Kings Rd., go up Cheltenham Parade and turn first left. PARK: Easy. TEL: 0423 567086. VAT: Stan/Spec.

Harrogate continued

D Mason & Son
7/8 Westmoreland St. FGA, NAG. Open 9-5. *STOCK: Victorian, Edwardian and secondhand jewellery; clocks.* TEL: 0423 567305. SER: Repairs (clocks and jewellery).

Montpellier Mews Antique Market
Montpellier St. Open 9.30-5.30. SIZE: Various dealers. *STOCK: A wide variety of antiques - porcelain, jewellery, furniture, paintings, Oriental carpets and cushions.* LOC: Behind Weatherells. TEL: 0423 530484.

Ogden of Harrogate Ltd BADA
38 James St. Est: 1893. Open 9-5. SIZE: Large. *STOCK: English silver, Sheffield plate and jewellery, oil paintings, English and continental, 19th C.* TEL: 0423 504123. VAT: Stan/Spec.

Omar (Harrogate) Ltd
8 Crescent Rd. (P McCormick) Est: 1946. Open 9-5.30. SIZE: Medium. *STOCK: Persian, Turkish, Caucasian rugs and carpets, £50-£5,000.* PARK: Easy. TEL: 0423 503675. SER: Valuations; restorations (Oriental carpets); buys at auction. VAT: Stan.

Paraphernalia
38a Cold Bath Rd. (P.F Hacker and J.P Boyes-Watson) Open 10-5. SIZE: Postcards; small furniture, collectors' items, crested china, bric-a-brac. TEL: 0423 567968 (evenings only).

Paul M Peters Antiques
15a Bower Rd. Est: 1967. Open 10-5. CL: Sat. SIZE: Medium. *STOCK: Chinese and Japanese ceramics and works of art, 17th-19th C; European ceramics and glass, 18th-19th C; European metalware, scientific instruments and unusual objects.* LOC: Town centre, at bottom of Station Parade. PARK: Easy. TEL: 0423 560118. SER: Valuations. VAT: Stan/Spec.

Elaine Phillips Antiques Ltd BADA
1 and 2 Royal Parade. Open 9.30-5.30. SIZE: Large. *STOCK: Oak furniture, 1600-1800; country furniture, 1700-1800; some mahogany, 18th and early 19th C; period metal work and decoration.* LOC: Opposite Crown Hotel. PARK: Easy. TEL: 0423 569745. VAT: Spec.

Pianorama (Harrogate) Ltd
1-3-5 Omega St, Ripon Rd. (M Sellers) Open 9-5. *STOCK: Period pianos.* TEL: 0423 567573.

John H Preston and Sons
39 James St. Open 9-5.30 but appointment advisable. *STOCK: Precision instruments, barographs, barometers, compasses, microscopes, cameras.* TEL: 0423 503187.

Regency Fine Art
123 Wetherby Rd. (G.B Wright) Resident. Est: 1966. Open by appointment. SIZE: Medium. *STOCK: English and continental oil paintings, 18th-20th C, £100-£400.* PARK: Easy at rear. TEL: 0423 883178. SER: Valuations; restorations.

Harrogate continued

Rippon Bookshop
1st Floor, 6 Station Bridge. (Mrs A Rawson) Est: 1980. Open 10-5. SIZE: Medium. *STOCK: Antiquarian books - local history, £25-£150; local topography and general £5-£25.* LOC: Near Railway station and opposite Odeon Cinema. PARK: Nearby. TEL: 0423 501835; home - 0765 4848. SER: Valuations; restorations (book binding); finder.

F.B Shaftoe
17-18 Regent Parade. Est: 1945. Open 9-5.30. CL: Sat. SIZE: Small. *STOCK: Brown 19th C furniture.* TEL: 0423 502151. VAT: Stan/Spec. *Trade and Export Only.*

Shaw Bros
21 Montpellier Parade. (J. and C Shaw) CL: Wed. p.m. *STOCK: English and continental porcelain, 18th-19th C; silver, jewellery, Meissen, Dresden vases and figures.* TEL: 0423 567466.

Singing Bird Antiques
19 Knaresborough Rd. (A.M Sagar) Est: 1964. Open 10-4.30. CL: Sat. SIZE: Medium. *STOCK: Furniture, silver, pewter, 18th C; pottery, porcelain.* LOC: On A59, 1 mile out of Harrogate on left, just before pedestrian crossing. PARK: Easy. TEL: 0423 888292; home - 0423 885715.

Smith's ("The Rink") Ltd
Dragon Rd. Est: 1906. Open 9-5.30. SIZE: Large. *STOCK: General antiques, 1750-1820, £150; Victoriana 1830-1900, £50.* LOC: From Leeds, right at Prince of Wales crossing, left at Skipton Rd. and left before railway bridge. PARK: Easy. TEL: 0423 503217. VAT: Stan/Spec.

Sutcliffe Galleries BADA
5 Royal Parade. Est: 1947. Open 10-5. *STOCK: Paintings, 19th C.* LOC: Opposite Crown Hotel. TEL: 0423 562976; home - 075 672 663. SER: Valuations; restorations; framing.

Thorntons of Harrogate LAPADA
1 Montpellier Gdns. Open 9.30-5.30. *STOCK: 17th-18th C furniture, metalware, clocks, paintings, porcelain, arms and armour, scientific instruments.* TEL: 0423 504118. VAT: Spec.

Traditional Interiors
Library House, Regent Parade. (M Green) Est: 1976. Open 8.30-5.30, Sat. 8.45-4, Sun. by appointment. SIZE: Medium. *STOCK: Pine furniture, Georgian, Victorian, Edwardian, £5-£2,000; treen, kitchenalia and collectors' items.* LOC: Overlooking the Stray. PARK: Easy. TEL: 0423 560452. SER: Valuations; restorations; stripping. VAT: Stan/Spec.

Walker Galleries Ltd BADA
6 Montpellier Gdns. Est: 1972. Open 9.30-1 and 2-5.30. SIZE: Medium. *STOCK: Oil paintings and watercolours, 18th C furniture.*

Walker Galleries Ltd continued

TEL: 0423 567933. SER: Valuations; restorations; framing. FAIRS: Chelsea, Harrogate, British International, Birmingham, Northern (Harrogate), Barbican, Olympia. VAT: Spec.

Christopher Warner BADA
15 Princes St. (C.C. Warner, I.P Legard and G.S.M Brown) Est: 1770. Open 9.30-5. SIZE: Small. *STOCK: Jewellery, 1740-1890; silver, 1720-1840, both £50-£12,000.* PARK: Easy. TEL: 0423 503617. SER: Valuations; restorations (silver and jewellery); buys at auction. FAIRS: Harrogate and British International (Birmingham). VAT: Stan/Spec.

Weatherell's of Harrogate Antiques and Fine Arts LAPADA
29 Montpellier Parade. Open 9-5.30. SIZE: Large. *STOCK: Period and fine decorative furniture.* TEL: 0423 507810/525004; fax - 0423 520005.

Windmill Antiques LAPADA
4 Montpellier Mews, Montpellier St. (B. and J Tildesley) Est: 1980. Open 10-5.30. SIZE: Small. *STOCK: Furniture, £250-£5,000; copper and brass, £20-£500; boxes, inkstands, rocking horses and children's chairs, £50-£2,000; all 18th-19th C.* LOC: Behind Montpellier Parade. PARK: Nearby. TEL: 0423 530502; home - 0845 401330. VAT: Spec.

HAWES

Sturman's Antiques
Main St. (A., M.M. and P.J Sturman) Open 10-5 including Sun. *STOCK: Victorian and Edwardian furniture, porcelain, pictures and paintings.* TEL: 0969 667742.

HELMSLEY

Rievaulx Books
18 High St. (C Howard) Est: 1986. Open 10.30-5. CL: Mon. SIZE: Medium. *STOCK: Antiquarian books, especially on natural history, field sports, Yorkshire, art and antiques.* LOC: From Market Sq., past church, shop 100 yards past Feversham Arms inn. PARK: Easy. TEL: 0439 70912; home - same.

Pauline Stephenson
Bondgate. Est: 1974. Open Fri., Sat. or by appointment. *STOCK: Furniture, Georgian-Edwardian, £50-£1,000; copper, brass, porcelain and glass, £20-£2,000.* LOC: 150yds. from Market Place on A170 towards Scarborough. TEL: 0439 70351; home - same. VAT: Spec.

Westway Cottage Restored Pine
Ashdale Rd. (J. and J Dzierzek) Est: 1986. Open Fri., Sat. and Mon. 9-5.30, Sun. 1-5.30, other times by appointment. SIZE: Small.

Westway Cottage Restored Pine continued

STOCK: Pine furniture, 19th C, £50-£700. LOC: From A170 from Scarborough, first left into town, then left again at bottom of Ashdale Rd. PARK: Easy. TEL: 0439 70172; home - same. SER: Valuations; restorations (pine).

York Cottage Antiques LAPADA
7 Church St. (G. and E.M Thornley and G.E Cooper) Est: 1976. Open daily April-Dec. 10-4. CL: Wed. Open Fri. and Sat. only Jan.-March, other times by appointment. *STOCK: Early oak furniture and country items; metalware 18th-19th C; pottery and porcelain, especially Ironstone, blue and white and lustre, cranberry glass; collectors' and commemorative items.* LOC: Opposite church. PARK: Adjacent. TEL: 0439 70833; home - same.

HIGH BENTHAM

Articles Antiques
Pyes Mill. (J.W. and L.J Forsyth) Open by appointment. SIZE: Warehouse. *STOCK: Furniture including shipping.* LOC: Near railway station. PARK: Easy. TEL: 0524 39312; home - 05243 62294.

HUBY, Nr. Leeds

Haworth Antiques
Harrogate Rd. (G. and J White) BWCMG. Est: 1969. Open 9-6 or by appointment. CL: Mon. *STOCK: Clocks - wall, longcase and bracket, 18th-20th C, £15-£2,000; small furniture.* Not Stocked: Porcelain, pottery and paintings. LOC: A658. PARK: Own. TEL: 0423 734293. SER: Restorations (clocks and clock dials). VAT: Stan/Spec.

KILLINGHALL, Nr. Harrogate

Norwood House Antiques
88 Ripon Rd. (R.M Mallaby) Resident. Est: 1981. Open 10-5, other times by appointment. CL: Wed. *STOCK: English and continental furniture, 19th C; porcelain, clocks, silver, decorative items.* PARK: Easy. TEL: 0423 506468.

KIRK DEIGHTON, Nr. Wetherby

Elden Antiques
23 Ashdale View. (E. and D Broadley) Est: 1970. Open 9-11.30 and 12.30-5.30, Sat. 12-5.30. SIZE: Medium. *STOCK: General antiques including small furniture.* LOC: Main road between Wetherby and Knaresborough. PARK: Easy. TEL: 0937 584770; home - same.

KIRKBYMOORSIDE, Nr. Helmsley

Crown Square Antiques
3 Crown Sq. (T Cooper) Resident. Est: 1988. CL: Thurs., otherwise open, appointment advisable. SIZE: Medium. *STOCK: Oak and country furniture (mostly tables and chairs), 18th-19th C, £50-£3,500; associated decorative items, 18th-19th C, £20-£800.* Not Stocked: Pine. LOC: Off Market Pl., behind memorial hall. PARK: Easy. TEL: 0751 33295.

KNARESBOROUGH

Robert Aagaard Ltd
Frogmire House, Stockwell Rd. Est: 1961. Open 9-5, Sat. 10-4. SIZE: Medium. *STOCK: Chimney pieces, marble fire surrounds and interiors.* LOC: Town centre. PARK: Own. TEL: 0423 864805. VAT: Stan.

Bowkett
9 Abbey Rd. (E.S Starkie) Resident. Est: 1919. Open 9-6. SIZE: Medium. *STOCK: Chairs, small furniture, brass, copper, pot-lids, Goss, books.* LOC: By the river at the lower road bridge. PARK: Easy. TEL: 0423 866112. SER: Restorations (upholstery and small furniture). VAT: Stan/Spec.

Cheapside Antiques
4 Cheapside. (Mrs M.E Hanson) Open 10-5. CL: Thurs. *STOCK: Furniture, porcelain, metalware and small collectors' items, 1750-1900.* TEL: 0423 867779. VAT: Spec.

The Emporium
Market Flat Lane, Lingerfield. (N Wadley) Open by appointment. SIZE: Medium and warehouse. *STOCK: Pine and general antiques.* PARK: Easy. TEL: 0423 868539. SER: Packing; shipping; courier. VAT: Stan.

Milton J Holgate
36 Gracious St. Est: 1972. Open 9-5.30, or by appointment. CL: Thurs. *STOCK: Georgian furniture, longcase clocks.* PARK: Easy. TEL: 0423 865219. VAT: Mainly Spec. *Mainly Trade.*

Kellys of Knaresborough
Rear of 96 High St. (D.C Kelly) Est: 1969. Open Mon., Fri. and Sat. 10-5 or by appointment. SIZE: Large. *STOCK: Chandeliers, wall lights, general lighting, candle sticks, lustres, 19th and early 20th C.* LOC: A59. PARK: Own. TEL: 0423 862041. 24hr. (ansaphone). SER: Buys at auction. VAT: Stan/Spec.

The Northern Kilim Centre
24 Finkle St. Open 10.30-5, Sun. 2-5. CL: Thurs. *STOCK: Persian, Turkish, Afghan and Central Asian flat woven rugs and nomadic carpets.* TEL: 0423 866219/866502. SER: Valuations; restorations.

Knaresborough continued

Pictoriana
88 High St. (Mrs A Wadley) Est: 1982. Open 9.30-5.30, Sun. 10.30-4.30. SIZE: Large. *STOCK: Pine including reproduction, £20-£1,000; wood carvings and kitchenalia, £5-£100.* LOC: A59. PARK: Nearby. TEL: 0423 866116; home - 0423 884175. SER: Restorations (pine). VAT: Stan.

The Gordon Reece Gallery
Finkle St. Est: 1981. Open 10.30-5, Sun. 2-5 or by appointment. CL: Thurs. SIZE: Large. *STOCK: Architectural items, furniture, metalware, carvings and rare textiles, £5-£4,000.* LOC: Town centre. PARK: Own. TEL: 0423 866219/866502; home - same. SER: Exhibitions organised and mounted; touring exhibitions. VAT: Stan.

Reflections
23 Waterside. (J. and M.V McNamara) Resident. Est: 1977. Open Tues.-Sun. 9.30-6, other times by appointment. SIZE: Small. *STOCK: Furniture, 19th C; paintings, 19th to early 20th C, both £50-£1,000; bric-a-brac and brassware; books, 19th to early 20th C, £1-£100.* LOC: Turn off A59 at World's End Inn. PARK: Easy. TEL: 0423 862005.

Charles Shaw
The Old Vicarage, 2 Station Rd. Est: 1981. Open daily including Sun. p.m. SIZE: Medium. *STOCK: Taxidermy, £25-£5,000; country and sporting pictures, £20-£5,000; both 19th-20th C; out-of-print, country and sporting books, £5-£500; small antiques and furniture, 18th-20th C.* LOC: Off High St. A59. PARK: Own. TEL: 0423 867715. SER: Valuations; buys at auction. VAT: Stan/Spec.

Swadforth House LAPADA
Gracious St. (J Thompson) Est: 1968. *STOCK: General antiques.* TEL: 0423 864698. VAT: Spec.

LEYBURN

Cottage Antiques
High St. (M. and S Hardcastle) Est: 1972. CL: Tues. and Wed. SIZE: Medium. *STOCK: Furniture, £45-£1,000; small items.* LOC: A684. PARK: Easy. TEL: 0969 23555.

LONG PRESTON

Gavèls
Summerfield, Station Rd. (G.K Blissett) Open by appointment. *STOCK: Paintings, water-colours, etchings, 19th and 20th C.* TEL: 072 94 384.

LOWER BENTHAM

Low Mill Antiques
Mill Lane. (G Garman) Est: 1987. Open 9.30-5.30 prior telephone call advisable; Sun. by appointment. SIZE: Medium. *STOCK: English, Irish and continental pine, 18th-20th C, £10-£1,000.* LOC: Off M6, junction 34 onto B6480, 15 miles to village, turn right after 2nd bridge. PARK: Own. TEL: 05242 61152; home - 05242 61286. SER: Valuations; restorations; pine stripping. VAT: Stan/Spec.

W.T. and J Spencer
Arundel House. *STOCK: Stripped pine, oak, mahogany, pottery, porcelain.* LOC: B6480. TEL: 0468 61058.

MALTON

Malton Antique Market
2 Old Maltongate. (Mrs M.A Cleverly) Est: 1970. Open 9.30-12.30 and 2-5. CL: Thurs. SIZE: Medium. *STOCK: Furniture, Georgian to Victorian, to £1,500; glass, bric-a-brac, porcelain, pottery, copper and brass.* LOC: From York take A64, shop is at main traffic light junction in Malton. PARK: 20yds. further. TEL: 0653 692732. SER: Commission sales.

Malton continued

Matthew Maw Antiques
18 Castlegate. Open 9-5. CL: Thurs. p.m. *STOCK: Furniture including shipping.* LOC: A64. TEL: 0653 694638. VAT: Stan/Spec.

Talents Fine Arts Ltd
7 Market Pl. (J Burrows) Est: 1986. Open daily. SIZE: Medium. *STOCK: Oils, watercolours and prints, 19th C, £20-£500; contemporary local artists.* LOC: A64 near church. PARK: Easy. TEL: 0653 600020. SER: Restorations; framing. VAT: Stan/Spec.

MANFIELD

Trade Antiques. D.D. White
Lucy Cross Cottage. Est. 1975. *STOCK: Georgian, Victorian and export furniture.* LOC: B6275, Scotch Corner to Piercebridge road, on left 3 1/2 miles after leaving A1. PARK: Easy. TEL: (0325) 374303 or (0833) 37021. VAT: Stan/Spec.

MARKINGTON, Nr. Harrogate

Daleside Antiques
Hinks Hall Lane. Est: 1978. Open 8-5, Sat. and Sun. by appointment. *STOCK: Pine furniture, decorative items, architectural features and fittings, 18th-19th C, £50-£3,500; Georgian, mahogany furniture; Victorian shop fittings.* TEL: 0765 87888; fax - 0765 87886. SER: Containers; courier; restorations. VAT: Stan.

MASHAM, Nr. Ripon

Aura Antiques

1-3 Silver St. (R. and R Sutcliffe) Est: 1985. Open 9.15-5.15, Sun. by appointment. SIZE: Medium. *STOCK: Furniture especially mahogany, 18th to mid-19th C, £50-£5,000; metalware - brass and copper, fenders, £5-£250; china, glass, silver and decorative objects, £5-£1,000; all 18th-19th C.* LOC: Corner of Market Sq. PARK: Easy. TEL: 0765 89315; home - 0765 838192. SER: Valuations; buys at auction (mahogany period furniture). VAT: Spec.

MELMERBY, Nr. Ripon

Terry Kindon Antiques Ltd LAPADA

Unit 23, Melmerby Industrial Estate, Green Lane. Open 9.30-5, other times by appointment. CL: Sat. *STOCK: Mainly furniture and pine.* TEL: 076 584 522. SER: Containers.

MIDDLEHAM, Nr. Leyburn

White Boar Antiques and Books

Kirkgate. (J. and G Armstrong) Est: 1983. Open 10-6. Winter - open 10-4.30 or by appointment. CL: Mon. SIZE: Small. *STOCK: Furniture, clocks and porcelain, 18th-19th C, £500-£1,000; silver, copper, brass, pewter and glass, 19th C,*

White Boar Antiques and Books continued

£50-£150; books including antiquarian, 17th-20th C, £1-£450+. LOC: A6108 towards Leyburn. PARK: Opposite. TEL: 0969 23901; home - same. SER: Book search.

NORTHALLERTON

Alverton Antiques

7 South Parade. (Mrs M.C Matson) Est: 1981. Open Wed., Fri. and Sat. 10-5.30, other times by appointment. SIZE: Small. *STOCK: Clocks, 17th-19th C, £100-£3,000; period English furniture, £200-£2,000.* LOC: Town centre. PARK: Easy. TEL: 0609 780402; home - same. SER: Valuations; restorations (clocks); buys at auction (clocks and furniture).

The Antique and Art

7 Central Arcade. (Mrs J Willoughby) Open 10-5. CL: Thurs. *STOCK: Porcelain, pottery, silver, jewellery, glass, prints and paintings.* TEL: 0609 772051; home - 0609 774157.

Collectors Corner

145/6 High St. (J Wetherill) Est: 1972. Open Tues., Wed. and Fri. 10-4; Sat. 10-5, or by appointment. *STOCK: General antiques, collectors' items.* LOC: Opposite GPO. TEL: 0609 777623; home - 0609 775199.

Yorkshire Pine

220A High St. (J.M Haw) Open 9-5. *STOCK: Pine.* TEL: 0609 772374.

NORTON

D. and M.H Lindley

69 Commercial St. Est: 1958. Open 9-5. CL: Thurs. p.m. *STOCK: Furniture, china.* TEL: 0653 693220.

PATELEY BRIDGE

Cat in the Window Antiques

22 High St. (Mrs S Morgan) Est: 1976. Open 12.30-5. CL: Mon. and Wed. *STOCK: Small furniture, metalware, glass, ceramics, art nouveau, art deco, amber, coral, jet etc., pictures, sewing items, linen, lace and collectors' items.* PARK: Easy. TEL: 0423 711343.

Brian Loomes

Calf Haugh Farm. Est: 1966. Open 9-5 by appointment. SIZE: Medium. *STOCK: British clocks, especially longcase, wall, bracket and lantern, pre-1840, £500-£10,000.* Not Stocked: Foreign clocks. LOC: From Pateley Bridge, first private lane on left on Grassington Rd. (B6265). PARK: Own. TEL: 0423 711163; home - same. VAT: Spec.

Pateley Bridge continued

Squirrels and Early Days
4 King's Court. (Mrs S.A Warner) Est: 1981. Open 12.30-5.30 incl. Sun., and other times by appointment. CL: Mon. and Thurs. SIZE: Medium. *STOCK: Pine and country furniture, 1860-1920, £40-£600; treen, collectables, £5-£65.* LOC: Off main street, at bottom of hill. PARK: Easy. TEL: 0423 711661; home - 0423 780387. SER: Valuations; restorations (furniture).

PICKERING

Antiques & Things
South Gate. (J Whitaker) Open 10-5. CL: Wed. *STOCK: General antiques, dolls, linen.* PARK: At rear. TEL: 0751 76142.

John Hague
18 Hallgarth. Est: 1959. Open by appointment. *STOCK: Furniture, porcelain and general antiques, prints and pictures.* TEL: 0751 72829.

C.H Reynolds
122 Eastgate. Open 9.30-5.30, Sun. by appointment. *STOCK: General antiques.* TEL: 0751 72785.

RICHMOND

Brown's Antiques LAPADA
2 New Rd. (G.P. and Mrs J.A Brown) Open 10-4, Sun. and Wed. by appointment. SIZE: Medium. *STOCK: Furniture, Georgian and Victorian; paintings, porcelain, some silver.* LOC: Top of Market Place, opposite Castle Walk. PARK: Opposite. TEL: 0748 4095; home - 0748 3577. SER: Restorations (furniture). VAT: Stan/Spec.

RIPON

Balmain Antiques
13 High Skellgate. Open 10-4. *STOCK: Bronzes, furniture, paintings, silver and porcelain.* TEL: 0765 701294.

Pinetree Antiques
44 North St. (M.P Dunn) Open 9.30-5. *STOCK: Pine furniture.* TEL: 0765 2905.

Rose Fine Art and Antiques
13 Kirkgate. (Mr and Mrs S Rose) Est: 1984. Open daily, Sun. by appointment. CL: Wed. SIZE: Medium. *STOCK: Pictures, 18th to early 20th C, £5-£2,000; furniture, £50-£1,000; porcelain and glass, £5-£500; both 19th to early 20th C.* LOC: Between Market Place and cathedral. PARK: Nearby. TEL: 0765 690118; home - same. SER: Valuations; restorations (pictures); buys at auction (pictures and prints); framing. VAT: Stan.

Ripon continued

Sigma Antiques and Fine Art
Water Skellgate. (D Thomson) Est: 1963. Open 9-5.30. *STOCK: Furniture, 17th-19th C; glass, paintings, 18th-19th C; jewellery, silver, European and Eastern pottery and porcelain; jades, ivories, fine objets d'art, bronzes; continental furniture, ornaments, 18th-19th C; decorators' items.* PARK: Nearby. TEL: 0765 3163; fax - 0765 690933.

Skellgate Curios
2 Low Skellgate. (J.I Wain and P.S Gyte) Est: 1974. Open 11-5. CL: Wed. *STOCK: General antiques, silver, jewellery and curios.* TEL: 0765 701290; home - 0765 85336/5345. VAT: Stan/Spec.

Yesteryear
6 and 7 High Skellgate. (J Rowlay) Open 10-4.30. CL: Wed. *STOCK: Small furniture, copper, brass, china, jewellery, silver, linen.* TEL: 0765 707801.

SCARBOROUGH

Bar Antiques
14 Bar St. (C Armstrong) Open 10-5. *STOCK: Silver, porcelain and glass.* TEL: 0723 351487.

Browns Antiques
6 Seamer Road Corner. (P. and Mrs L Brown) Est: 1973. Open 10-5. SIZE: Medium. *STOCK: Furniture, pictures, porcelain, pottery, objets d'art, Victorian to Georgian, £5-£4,500; art deco, art nouveau.* LOC: At junction of Seamer Rd. and Falsgrave Rd. PARK: Nearby. TEL: 0723 377112. VAT: Stan.

Gerards
14 Bar St. (H Armstrong) Open 10-5. *STOCK: Jewellery and bullion.* TEL: 0723 351487.

Hanover Antiques
10 Hanover Rd. Est: 1976. Open 10-4. CL: Wed. *STOCK: Militaria, medals, badges and general small items, Dinky toys, 50p-£500.* PARK: Easy. TEL: 0723 374175.

Shuttleworths
7 Victoria Rd. (L.R Shuttleworth) Open 10-4. CL: Wed. *STOCK: General antiques.* TEL: 0723 366278.

SETTLE

H.I Milnthorpe
Kirkgate. Est: 1974. Open 9-12.30 and 1.30-5. CL: Wed. SIZE: Medium. *STOCK: English furniture, 17th to early 19th C, £100-£10,000; pottery and porcelain, pre-1850, £20-£1,500.* Not Stocked: Victorian furniture, guns, coins and jewellery. LOC: A65. PARK: Easy. TEL: 0729 823046. SER: Valuations. VAT: Spec.

Settle continued

Mary Milnthorpe and Daughters Antique Shop

Market Pl. Est: 1958. Open 9.30-5. CL: Wed. SIZE: Small. *STOCK: Jewellery and silver, 18th-19th C and secondhand.* LOC: Opp. Town Hall. PARK: Easy. TEL: 0729 822331. VAT: Stan/Spec.

Nanbooks

Roundabout, Duke St. (N.M Midgley) Resident. Est: 1955. Open Tues., Fri. and Sat. 11-12.30 and 2-5.30. SIZE: Small. *STOCK: English pottery, porcelain, glass, some Oriental porcelains, general small antiques, 17th-19th C, to £150; bric-a-brac, 19th-20th C; some antiquarian books.* Not Stocked: Jewellery. LOC: A65. PARK: Easy. TEL: 0729 823324.

Roy Precious

King William House, High St. Resident. Est: 1972. Open 10-5.30 or by appointment. CL: Wed. SIZE: Medium. *STOCK: Oak and country furniture, some walnut and mahogany, 17th-19th C, £30-£6,000; oil paintings, specialising in portraits, 17th-19th C, £300-£5,000; some pottery and prints.* LOC: Opposite Post Office, on the old High St. PARK: Easy. TEL: 0729 823946. SER: Valuations. VAT: Stan/Spec.

E Thistlethwaite

The Antique Shop, Market Sq. Est: 1972. Open 9-5. CL: Wed. SIZE: Medium. *STOCK: Country furniture and metalware, 18th-19th C.* LOC:

E Thistlethwaite continued

Town centre, A65. PARK: Forecourt. TEL: 0729 822460. VAT: Stan/Spec.

Well Cottage Antiques

Well Cottage, High St. (Mrs J Lassey) Est: 1987. CL: Mon. and Wed. *STOCK: Porcelain and pottery, pine, 19th-20th C, £5-£100; framed cigarette cards, 20th C, £40-£70.* LOC: Town centre. PARK: Easy. TEL: 0729 823593; home - same. SER: Framing.

SKIPTON

Adamson Armoury

Newmarket St. (J.K Adamson) Est: 1975. Open 10-6 including Sun. SIZE: Medium. *STOCK: Weapons, 18th-19th C, £10-£300; militaria, 19th-20th C, 50p-£50.* LOC: A65, 200yds. from town centre. PARK: Rear. TEL: 0756 791355; home - 0756 798859. SER: Valuations. FAIRS: Leeds, Liverpool, Nottingham, Birmingham.

Corn Mill Antiques

High Corn Mill, Chapel Hill. (Mrs M Hawkridge) Est: 1984. Open 10-4. CL: Tues. and Wed. SIZE: Medium. *STOCK: Oak, mahogany and walnut furniture, £100-£2,000; porcelain, silver plate, prints, pictures, brass and copper, £5-£500; Victorian to 1930s.* Not Stocked: Jewellery, gold and silver. LOC: From town centre, take

Corn Mill Antiques continued

Grassington road, shop on right, just across bridge. PARK: Easy. TEL: 0756 792440; home - 072 93 489. SER: Valuations. VAT: Spec.

Craven Books
23 Newmarket St. (Miss K Farey and Miss M.G Fluck) Open 9.30-12.30 and 1.30-5, Sat. 9-12.30 and 1.30-4.30. CL: Tues., and first and last Mon., every month. *STOCK: Northern topography, maps and prints.* TEL: 0756 792677. SER: Finder.

Pine Mine Antiques
3 Albert St. (K Manger) Open 10-5. CL: Tues. *STOCK: Pine furniture, 19th C, £150-£700; cast-iron fireplaces, 1890-1930, £200-£500; bric-a-brac, 19th-20th C, £2-£150.* TEL: 0756 799754.

SNAINTON, Nr. Scarborough

Cottage Antiques
19 High St. (Mrs M.J Whittaker and Mrs E.A Shackleton) Resident. Est: 1984. CL: Sat. p.m. SIZE: Small. *STOCK: Georgian furniture, pine, clocks, china, glass, jewellery, pictures and unusual cottage items, £1-£1,600.* Not Stocked: Weapons and stamps. LOC: A170, equidistant Scarborough and Pickering. PARK: Easy. TEL: 0723 859724; home - 0723 859577. SER: Valuations; restorations (cabinet work).

SPENNITHORNE, Nr. Leyburn

N.J. and C.S Dodsworth
Thorney Hall. Est: 1973. Open by appointment. SIZE: Medium. *STOCK: English furniture and longcase clocks, 18th to early 19th C.* LOC: Off A684. TEL: 0969 22277. VAT: Stan/Spec.

STILLINGTON

Pond Cottage Antiques
Brandsby Rd. (C.M. and D Thurstans) Resident. Est: 1972. *STOCK: Pine, kitchenalia, country furniture, treen, metalware, brass, copper.* TEL: 0347 810796. SER: Pine stripping.

STOKESLEY

Three Tuns Antiques
2 Three Tuns Wynd. (E. and L.C Payman) Est: 1972. Open 10.30-5. *STOCK: Small furniture, jewellery, silver, general small antiques, ceramics, glass.* TEL: 0642 711377; home - 0642 724284.

THIRSK

Cottage Antiques and Curios
1 Market Pl. (Mrs E.H. and S.R Ballard) Est: 1970. Open 9-5. CL: Wed. *STOCK: Victorian porcelain and glass, £5-£250; furniture, from*

Cottage Antiques and Curios continued

1750, £5-£1,000; brass, copper, silver and plated ware, £3-£300. PARK: Easy. TEL: 0845 522536/523212; home - 0845 577461.

Kirkgate Picture Gallery
18 Kirkgate. (R Bennett) Est: 1979. Open Mon., Thurs. and Sat. 10-1 and 2-5 and by appointment. SIZE: Small. *STOCK: Oil paintings, £50-£3,000; watercolours, £50-£1,000; both 19th to early 20th C.* LOC: Joins Market Place. PARK: Nearby. TEL: 0845 524085; home - same. SER: Restorations (oil paintings); buys at auction; framing.

B Ogleby
35, 36 and 37 The Green. Open by appointment only. SIZE: Large. *STOCK: Furniture, 17th-20th C.* TEL: 0845 522676/524120. SER: Shipping and packing. VAT: Stan/Spec. *Trade and Export Only.*

Potterton Books
The Old Rectory, Sessay. (C Jameson) Open 9-5. SIZE: Large. *STOCK: Classic reference works on art, architecture, interior design, antiques and collecting.* TEL: 0845 401218; fax - 0845 401439. SER: Library accessories; book search; decorative bindings; catalogues issued. FAIRS: Major London.

THORNTON LE DALE, Nr. Pickering

Stable Antiques
4 Pickering Rd. (Mrs S Kitching Walker) Open 2.15-5, mornings by appointment. CL: Mon. SIZE: Small. *STOCK: Porcelain, £5-£150; furniture, £20-£300; silver, glass, brass, plate, copper, collectors' items, £5-£150, all 19th C to 1930's.* LOC: A170. PARK: Easy. TEL: 0751 74435. SER: Valuations. FAIRS: Downe Arms, Wykeham; Clifton Hotel, Scarborough.

WHITBY

Aird-Gordon Antiques
15 Baxtergate. Open daily. *STOCK: Glass, jewellery, jet, china, small furniture.* TEL: 0947 601515.

The Bazaar
7 Skinner St. (F.A Doyle) Est: 1970. Open 9.30-5.30. *STOCK: Jewellery, furniture, general antiques, 19th C.* TEL: 0947 602281. VAT: Stan/Spec.

'Bobbins' Wool Craft Antiques
Wesley Hall, Church St. (D. and P Hoyle) Open 10.30-5 every day February to Christmas. SIZE: Small. *STOCK: General antiques, especially oil lamps, 19th-20th C.* LOC: Between Market Place and steps to Abbey. PARK: Nearby. TEL: 0947 600585. SER: Repairs and spares (oil lamps). VAT: Stan.

Lady Nicotine

Advertising tobacco-jar, c.1897-1900. Height 5½in. From an article entitled 'British Pottery Tobacco-Jars' by Roger Fresco-Corbu published in the April 1991 issue of ***Antique Collecting.***

Whitby continued

Caedmon House
14 Station Sq. (E.M Stanforth) Est: 1977. Open 10-5, until 7 in summer and Sun. until Nov. 2-6. SIZE: Medium. *STOCK: General, mainly small, antiques including jewellery, dolls and china, to £1,200.* PARK: Easy. TEL: 0947 602120; home - 0947 603930. SER: Valuations; restorations (upholstery and china). VAT: Stan/Spec.

Castle Antiques
157 Church St. (P.A Clayton) Open 9.30-5, seven days. *STOCK: Stripped pine and general antiques.* TEL: 0947 603020.

Coach House Antiques
Coach Rd, Sleights. (C.J Rea) Resident. Est: 1973. Open 10-5 (winter months 10.30-4.30). CL: Sun. and Thurs. except by appointment. SIZE: Small. *STOCK: Furniture, especially oak and country; glass, jewellery, linen, metalware, paintings, porcelain, silver, unusual and decorative items.* LOC: On A169, 3 miles south west of Whitby. TEL: 0947 810313.

Jowsey and Roe
7 Sandgate. (T Roe) Open 9-5 including Sun. in summer. *STOCK: Jewellery especially Victorian Whitby jet.* TEL: 0947 602252.

The Mount Antiques
Khyber Pass. (M. and B Bottomley) Est: 1973. Open 9.30-5. SIZE: Large. *STOCK: Period*

The Mount Antiques continued

mahogany and country oak furniture, pine and kitchenalia, dining tables and chairs, fireplaces and architectural items, clocks, pictures, lighting and smalls. PARK: Own. TEL: 0947 604516. VAT: Stan/Spec.

WHIXLEY

Garth Antiques
The Old School, Franks Lane. (I Chapman) Est: 1978. Open by appointment. SIZE: Medium. *STOCK: Furniture, 18th-19th C, £50-£3,000; brass and copper, 19th C, £1-£500; oils and watercolours, £5-£3,000.* LOC: A59, turn left at Whixley Hospital, then left opposite The Anchor public house, into old village. PARK: Easy. TEL: 0423 331055. VAT: Stan/Spec.

YORK

Acomb Antiques
3 Westview Close, Boroughbridge Rd and warehouse - 12a Limegarth, Upper Poppleton. (J.F. and A James) Est: 1969. SIZE: Large. *STOCK: Furniture, clocks, barometers and dolls, 17th-19th C, £50-£2,000; shipping goods.* LOC: Off Harrogate road, just outside York boundary, near ring road. PARK: Easy. TEL: 0904 791999/781510.

Barbican Bookshop
24 Fossgate. Est: 1961. Open 9.15-5.30. *STOCK: Antiquarian books.* TEL: 0904 653643/644878. VAT: Stan.

Barker Court Antiques and Bygones
44 Gillygate. (Mrs D Yates) Est: 1970. Open 10.30-4.30. CL: Sun. and Wed. except by appointment. SIZE: Small. *STOCK: Pottery and porcelain, glass, plated items, Victorian to 1930, £3-£100.* LOC: 3 mins. walk from York Minster. PARK: Gillygate. TEL: 0904 622611.

Bishopsgate Antiques
23/24 Bishopsgate St. (R Wetherill) Open 9.15-6. *STOCK: General antiques.* TEL: 0904 623893.

'Bobbins'
31-33 Goodramgate. (D Hoyle) Open 10-5.30. SIZE: Small. *STOCK: Rush seated country chairs, tools and bygones, small furniture, general antiques, art deco, clocks, oil lamps, 18th-20th C.* LOC: Opposite York Minster at junction with Deansgate. PARK: Outside city walls. TEL: 0904 653597. SER: Spares (oil lamps). VAT: Stan.

Barbara Cattle BADA
45 Stonegate. Open 9-5.30. CL: Wed. (Sept. to May). *STOCK: Jewellery and silver, Georgian to date.* TEL: 0904 623862.

The Chaucer Head
41 Low Petergate. (D McDowell) Est: 1972. Open 9-12.30 and 1.30-5. *STOCK: Books especially economics, science and medicine.* TEL: 0904 622000.

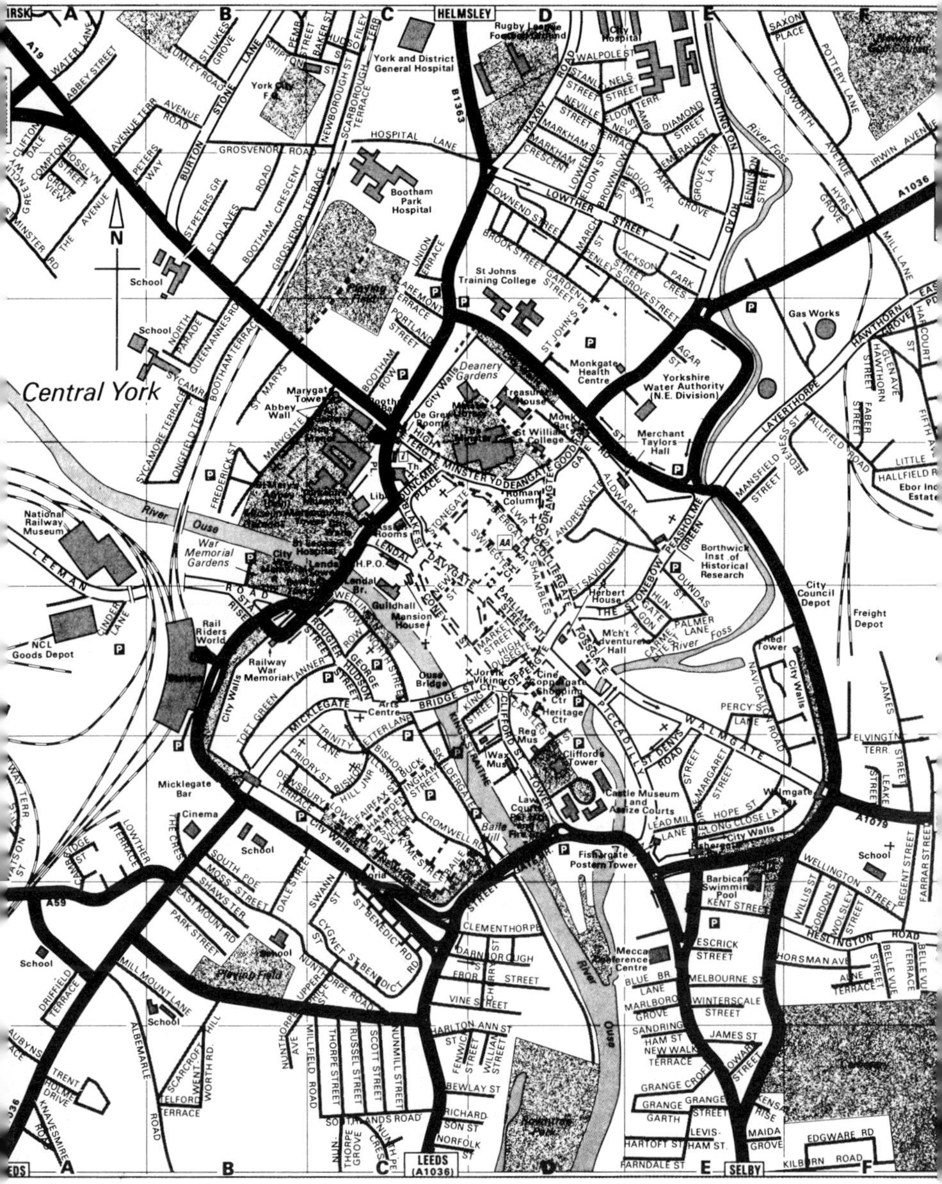
Central York
HELMSLEY
LEEDS (A1036)
SELBY
A19
A1036
A1079
A59
B1363
York and District General Hospital
Bootham Park Hospital
York City F.C.
Rugby League Football Ground
City Hospital
St Johns Training College
Gas Works
Yorkshire Water Authority (N.E. Division)
Monkgate Health Centre
Merchant Taylors Hall
Deanery Gardens
Treasurers House
The Minster
St Williams College
De Grey Rooms
Roman Column
Marygate Tower
Abbey Wall
National Railway Museum
War Memorial Gardens
River Ouse
River Foss
Borthwick Inst of Historical Research
City Council Depot
Freight Depot
Herbert House
M'ch't Adventurers Hall
Guildhall
Mansion House
Ouse Bridge
Arts Centre
Rail Riders World
Railway War Memorial
NCL Goods Depot
City Walls
Micklegate Bar
Cinema
School
Jorvik Viking Ctr
Coppergate Shopping Ctr
Heritage Ctr
Reg Mus
Wax Mus
Clifford's Tower
Castle Museum and Assize Courts
Law Courts
Baile Hill
Fishergate Postern Tower
Barbican Swimming Pool
Mecca Conference Centre
Walmgate Bar
Playing Field
Ebor Ind Estate
Red Tower
MICKLEGATE
PICCADILLY
WALMGATE
LOWTHER STREET
BOOTHAM
GILLYGATE
THE STONEBOW
PARLIAMENT STREET
CONEY ST
LENDAL
BLOSSOM STREET
HESLINGTON ROAD
LAYERTHORPE
LEEMAN ROAD
FISHERGATE
A B C D E F

Key to Town Plan

AA Recommended roads		Car Parks	P
Other roads		Parks and open spaces	
Restricted roads		AA Service Centre	AA
Buildings of interest			

York continued

Clocks and Gramophones

11 Walmgate. (P McAulay) Est: 1987. Open 10.30-4.30. CL: Mon. SIZE: Small. *STOCK: Wind-up gramophones, 1905-1940's, £50-£600; clocks, 1800-1940, £40-£2,000; 78 records, 1905-1950's, £1-£10.* PARK: Nearby. TEL: 0904 611924. SER: Restorations (clocks and gramophones).

Coulter Galleries

Open by appointment only. *STOCK: Watercolours and oils, pre-1900; frames.* TEL: 0904 702101.

Danby Antiques

61 Heworth Rd. (N. and Mrs J Banks) Resident. Est: 1985. Open seven days (telephone first). SIZE: Small. *STOCK: Boxes, 18th-19th C; writing accessories including fountain pens and pencils; unusual collectables, all 19th-20th C.* LOC: 1 mile from city centre on A1036 (Scarborough), turn right signed Heslington (university), shop 100 yards on left just before traffic lights/church. PARK: Easy. TEL: 0904 415280. SER: Buys at auction. FAIRS: London, Newark, Stafford, Harrogate, Birmingham (N.E.C.). VAT: Spec.

Fettes Fine Art

(T. and G Thornton) Open by appointment. SIZE: Small. *STOCK: Pictures - early Victorian, £3,000-£10,000; European schools, 18th C, £3,000-£5,000; 20th C, to £5,000.* TEL: 0904 641344. VAT: Stan/Spec.

French Fine Arts

1 Goodramgate. (C.W Sykes) Open 9-5, other times by appointment. *STOCK: Oil paintings.* TEL: 0904 654266.

Robert M Himsworth

28 The Shambles. Est: 1949. Open 9-5. SIZE: Small. *STOCK: Antique jewellery.* TEL: 0904 625089. VAT: Stan/Spec.

Holgate Antiques

Holgate Rd. (T Betts) Est: 1980. Open 10-5, Sat. 10-4. *STOCK: General antiques, furniture, bric-a-brac.* TEL: 0904 30005.

Minster Gate Bookshop

8 Minster Gates. (N Wallace) Est: 1970. Open 9.30-5.30. SIZE: Large. *STOCK: Antiquarian and secondhand books.* LOC: Opposite south door of York Minster. PARK: Nearby. TEL: 0904 621812. SER: Valuations; restorations; book finding.

Robert Morrison and Son BADA

Trentholme House, 131 The Mount. (C Morrison) Est: 1890. Open 9-5, Sat. 9-12. SIZE: Large. *STOCK: English furniture, 1700-1900, porcelain and clocks.* LOC: Near racecourse, one mile from city centre on Leeds Rd. From A1, take A64 to outskirts of York, then take A1036 York west road. PARK: Easy. TEL: 0904 655394. VAT: Stan/Spec.

York continued

O'Flynn Antiquarian Booksellers

35 Micklegate. Open 9-6. *STOCK: Prints and maps, many hand coloured; antiquarian and secondhand books on history, travel, natural history, sciences, poetry, biographies, literary criticism, general fiction and Scotland.* TEL: 0904 641404.

St. John Antiques

26 Lord Mayor's Walk. (R. and J Bell) Open 10-5. CL: Mon. *STOCK: Victorian stripped pine and satinwood furniture.* PARK: At rear. TEL: 0904 644263.

Ken Spelman

70 Micklegate. (P Miller and A Fothergill) ABA. Est: 1948. SIZE: Large. *STOCK: Secondhand and antiquarian books especially fine arts and literature, 50p-£5,000.* PARK: Easy. TEL: 0904 624414. SER: Valuations; buys at auction (books). FAIRS: Bath, Oxford, York, Harrogate and London PBFA and ABA. VAT: Spec.

Stonegate Fine Arts

47 Stonegate. (Mr and Mrs A.B Short) Est: 1970. Open 9.30-5.30; April-Oct. Sun. 11-3. SIZE: Medium. *STOCK: Pictures, from £500+.* LOC: City centre. PARK: Nearby. TEL: 0904 643771. SER: Valuations; restorations. VAT: Stan.

Taikoo Books Ltd

29 High Petergate. (D Chilton) Open 10-5.30 but appointment advisable. *STOCK: Antiquarian and secondhand books especially on mountaineering, polar, Africiana, Oriental and big game hunting.* TEL: 0904 641213.

Thacker's Antiques

42 Fossgate. Open 10-5. SIZE: Large. *STOCK: Furniture and bric-a-brac, £5-£5,000.* LOC: In city centre, next to Merchant Adventurer's Hall. PARK: Loading only. TEL: 0904 633077.

Inez M.P Yates

5 The Shambles. Est: 1948. Open 10.30-5. CL: Wed. *STOCK: Small furniture, porcelain, paintings, jewellery, unusual small collectors' items.* LOC: City centre, by Kings Sq. TEL: 0904 654821.

Yon Antiques

Whip-ma-Whop-ma-Gate, (Next to The Shambles). (A.G Macdonald) Est: 1968. Open 9.30-6. SIZE: Small. *STOCK: General antiques, Georgian to art nouveau, £5-£25+.* Not Stocked: Extra large furniture. LOC: Off Stonebow. PARK: Easy. TEL: 0904 627928; home - 0423 30240. SER: Buys at auction.

York Antiques Centre

2 Lendal. Open summer 9.30-5.30, winter 10-5. SIZE: 20 dealers. *STOCK: Antiques and collectable items, 18th-20th C.* LOC: Opposite the museum gardens. PARK: Easy. TEL: 0904 641582/641445.

Tennis art, especially prior to 1900, is likely to rise in value in the coming year. This bronze statue by Rudolf Marcuse sold for £1,980 in September 1989 at Phillips West Two. From an article on sporting memorabilia by Angus Gull published in the July/August 1991 issue of ***Antique Collecting.***

Yorkshire South

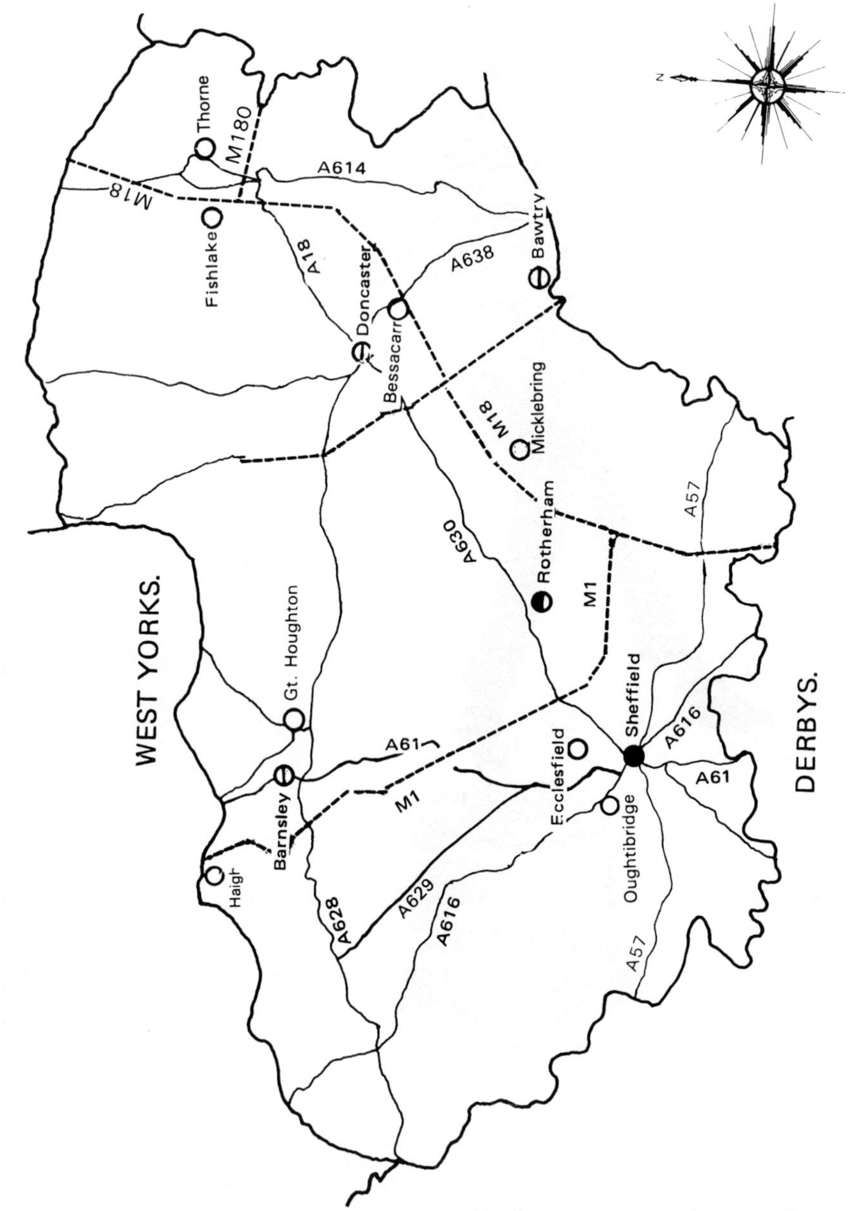
Thorne
M180
M18
A614
Fishlake
A18
Doncaster
A638
Bawtry
Bessacarr
Micklebring
M18
Rotherham
A630
A57
M1
WEST YORKS.
Gt. Houghton
Sheffield
A616
DERBYS.
A61
Ecclesfield
Barnsley
M1
Oughtibridge
Haigh
A628
A629
A616
A57

1–2
3–5
6–12
13+

Key to number of shops in this area.

Please note this is only a rough map designed to show dealers the number of shops in the various towns, and is not necessarily totally accurate.

BARNSLEY

Armchair Antiques
152 Sheffield Rd. (S Law) Open 9-5. *STOCK: Stripped furniture.* TEL: 0226 296777.

Charisma Antiques Trade Warehouse
St. Paul's former Methodist ChapelMarket St, Hoyland. (J.C Simmons) Est: 1980. Open 10-5. SIZE: Large. *STOCK: Furniture, shipping goods, pictures.* LOC: 1 1/2 miles off M1 exit 36. PARK: Easy. TEL: 0226 747599; home - 0226 790482. VAT: Stan/Spec.

Angela Charlesworth Antiques LAPADA
99 Dodworth Rd. (B Charlesworth) Est: 1971. Open Tues., Wed. and Sat. p.m., or by appointment. SIZE: Medium. *STOCK: English pottery and porcelain especially Yorkshire factories, 18th-19th C, £25-£400; furniture, 18th-19th C, £100-£2,000; collectors' items, 18th C to 1900s, £5-£100.* LOC: Exit 37, M1, follow Barnsley signs for approximately 1 mile on main road. PARK: Easy. TEL: 0226 282097; home - 0226 203688.

Christine Simmons Antiques
St. Paul's Former Methodist Chapel, Market St, Hoyland. Est: 1976. Open 10-4. SIZE: Medium. *STOCK: Smalls and pictures.* LOC: 1 1/2 miles from exit 36, M1. PARK: Easy. TEL: 0226 747599/790482.

Summer Lane Antiques
87a Summer Lane. (G Warttig) Open 10-6. *STOCK: Edwardian and Victorian furniture, art deco items.* TEL: 0226 293013. SER: Restorations.

BAWTRY, Nr. Doncaster

Doyle Antiques
9a Swan St. (A.G Doyle) Est: 1974. Open Fri., Sat. and Sun., other times by appointment. SIZE: Medium. *STOCK: Period oak and country furniture, paintings, clocks, mainly 17th-18th C.* LOC: Just off A1. PARK: Easy. TEL: Evenings - 0302 710524. VAT: Spec.

Swan Antiques
2 Swan St. Open 10-5, other times by appointment. SIZE: Large. *STOCK: Furniture, silver, porcelain, scientific instruments, collectables, taxidermy.* PARK: Easy. TEL: 0302 710301; evenings - 0302 710400.

Treasure House Antiques Centre
4-10 Swan St. Est: 1982. Open 10-5 including Sun. and Bank Holidays. SIZE: Large - various dealers. *STOCK: Silver, porcelain, furniture, carnival glass, postcards and general antiques.* PARK: Easy. TEL: 0302 710621.

Timothy D Wilson BADA
Grove House, Wharf St. Est: 1926. Open 9-5, Sun. by appointment. SIZE: Large. *STOCK: English oak and country furniture, 17th-18th*

Timothy D Wilson continued

***C; Windsor chairs, metalware, Mason's ironstone, decorative items and textiles.* PARK: Easy. TEL: 0302 710040. VAT: Spec.**

BESSACARR, Nr. Doncaster

Keith Stones Grandfather Clocks
5 Ellers Drive. Est: 1988. Open by appointment. SIZE: Small. *STOCK: Grandfather clocks especially painted dial with 30 hour and 8 day movements, Georgian to early 19th C, £500-£1,500.* LOC: Take A638 Bawtry road off racecourse roundabout, through traffic lights after 3/4 mile, take second right into Ellers Rd. then second left. PARK: Easy. TEL: 0302 535258; home - same. SER: Valuations.

DONCASTER

Antiques and Bargain Stores
6 Sunny Bar, Market Pl. Open 9.45-5. CL: Thurs. *STOCK: Dolls, toys, china, pistols, swords, small antiques.* TEL: 0302 344857.

Castaways
137 Balby Rd. (Mrs S.E Hill) Est: 1979. Open 10-3. *STOCK: General antiques, curios, collectables.* TEL: 0302 841086.

Danum Antique Centre
199 Carr House Rd. Open 10-5.30. SIZE: 8 dealers. *STOCK: General antiques including clocks, paintings, furniture, pottery and porcelain.* TEL: 0302 341670.

Doncaster Sales and Exchange
20 Copley Rd. Open 9.30-5. CL: Thurs. *STOCK: General small antiques.* TEL: 0302 344857. VAT: Stan.

Francis Sinclair Ltd
39 Hallgate. Open 9.30-5.30, Thurs. 9.30-1. *STOCK: Clocks.* TEL: 0302 367260.

ECCLESFIELD, Nr. Sheffield

John R Wrigley
185 The Wheel. Est: 1961. Postal only, catalogue issued monthly. *STOCK: Antiquarian books; gramophone records.* TEL: 0742 460275.

FISHLAKE

Fishlake Antiques
Pinfold Lane. Resident. Est: 1972. Open by appointment. SIZE: Medium. *STOCK: Rural furniture especially stripped pine; clocks including longcase and wall clocks, Victorian to mid-19th C, £30-£1,000; small Victoriana - writing boxes, lamps, £3-£70; rural collectors' items - cartwheels, ploughs, wheelwright and carpenters' tools, 19th and 20th C, £1-£50.* LOC: Off A63. PARK: Own. TEL: 0302 841411.

GREAT HOUGHTON, Nr. Barnsley

Capricorn
7 High St. (Mr and Mrs G Craven) Open 10-5. *STOCK: General antiques, stripped pine, satin walnut.* TEL: 0226 754057.

HAIGH

Mallglade Antiques LAPADA
Haigh Hall. Open by appointment. CL: Sat. SIZE: Medium. *STOCK: Georgian, Victorian, Edwardian furniture, £30-£3,000.* LOC: 1/4 mile from exit 38, M1. PARK: Own. TEL: 0924 830516. VAT: Stan/Spec. *Trade Only.*

MICKLEBRING, Nr. Rotherham

Robert Clark LAPADA
Sunnyside House. (R.R Clark) Est: 1955. Open by appointment. *STOCK: English pottery and porcelain, silver spoons, furniture, metalware, prints and watercolours, 17th-19th C.* LOC: From M18 junction 1 turn towards Maltby and Bawtry, take 1st left then over crossroads into village, 2nd building on left. PARK: Own. TEL: 0709 812540; home - same. FAIRS: Snape, Cheltenham, Thoresby and Castle. VAT: Spec.

OUGHTIBRIDGE, Nr. Sheffield

Julie Goddard Antiques
7-9 Langsett Rd. South. (Miss J.P Goddard) Est: 1982. Open 10-4.30. CL: Wed. SIZE: Large. *STOCK: Furniture - Victorian, Edwardian, £50-£5,000; Georgian, William IV, £100-£3,000.* Not Stocked: Jewellery and silver. LOC: 12 minutes from M1, exit 36 towards Sheffield, shop situated in one-way system (A616). PARK: Easy. TEL: 0742 862261. SER: Restorations (furniture - polishing, veneering, caning and re-rushing); buys at auction (furniture); framing.

ROTHERHAM

Roger Appleyard Ltd LAPADA
Fitzwilliam Rd, Eastwood Trading Estate. Open 8-6, Sat. 8-1. SIZE: Large. *STOCK: General antiques, £5-£1,500.* LOC: A630. PARK: Easy. TEL: 0709 367670/377770; fax - 0709 829395. SER: Packing and shipping. VAT: Stan/Spec. *Trade Only.*

John Mason Jewellers Ltd
36 High St. Open 9-5.30. *STOCK: Silver, jewellery.* TEL: 0709 382311. SER: Valuations; repairs. VAT: Spec.

John Shaw Antiques Ltd
The Old Methodist Chapel, Parkgate. Open 9.30-4.30. CL: Sat. SIZE: Large. *STOCK: General antiques, £5-£9,000.* TEL: 0709 522340. VAT: Stan.

Rotherham continued

South Yorkshire Antiques
88-94 Broad St. (A Swindells) Est: 1955. Open 9.30-4.30. *STOCK: General antiques and shipping furniture.* PARK: Easy. TEL: 0709 585854/526514; 24 hr. ansaphone 0709 582688. SER: Valuations; restorations. VAT: Stan.

Philip Turnor Antiques
94a Broad St, Parkgate. Open 9-5; Sat. 9-3. *STOCK: Shipping furniture, 1830-1930.* TEL: 0709 524640.

Wickersley Antiques
Unit 4, Foundry St, Parkgate. (N. and S Butler) Est: 1970. Open by appointment. SIZE: Large and warehouse. *STOCK: Furniture, 17th-20th C, £25-£3,000; general antiques, clocks, export furniture including mahogany, walnut and oak, pianos.* LOC: 1 mile from Rotherham on A633 towards Barnsley. PARK: Easy. TEL: 0742 851486 or 0836 320549. SER: Valuations. VAT: Stan/Spec.

SHEFFIELD

A. and C. Antiques
239 Abbeydale Rd. (C.E Maltby) Est: 1984. Open 10.30-5.30. SIZE: Medium. *STOCK: General antiques, smalls, jewellery, £30-£500.* LOC: Main rd. south of city centre, towards Chesterfield. PARK: Easy. TEL: 0742 589161.

Anita's Holme Antiques
144 Holme Lane, Hillsborough. (A.L Spalton) Est: 1986. Open 10.30-5.30. SIZE: Medium. *STOCK: General antiques, 19th C, £50-£100.* LOC: A61, turn left at traffic lights opposite Owlerton Sports Stadium, shop 1 1/2 miles on right. PARK: Easy. TEL: 0742 336698.

Arcade Antiques Ltd
14 The Sheaf Market. (Mr and Mrs J.W.H Lee) Est: 1963. Open 9-5, Fri. 9-5.45, Sat. 9-5.30. CL: Thurs. SIZE: Small. *STOCK: Jewellery, 1900 to date, £5-£100; pottery, including Victorian and reproduction Staffordshire; clocks, 18th C, and watches.* LOC: From M1 take Catcliffe turning, down dual carriageway to roundabout. PARK: Adjacent to market. TEL: 0742 737651. SER: Valuations; restorations (especially jewellery). VAT: Stan.

Canterbury Place Antiques and Sheffield Pine Centre
356/358 South Rd and Unit E, Lowfield Cutlery Forge, Guernsey Rd. (P Coldwell) Open 9-6. SIZE: Large. *STOCK: Stripped pine and general antiques.* TEL: 0742 336103/587458.

Chimney Piece Antique Fires
262 South Rd, Walkley. (J Young) Open 9.30-5. CL: Wed. *STOCK: Fireplaces.* TEL: 0742 346085.

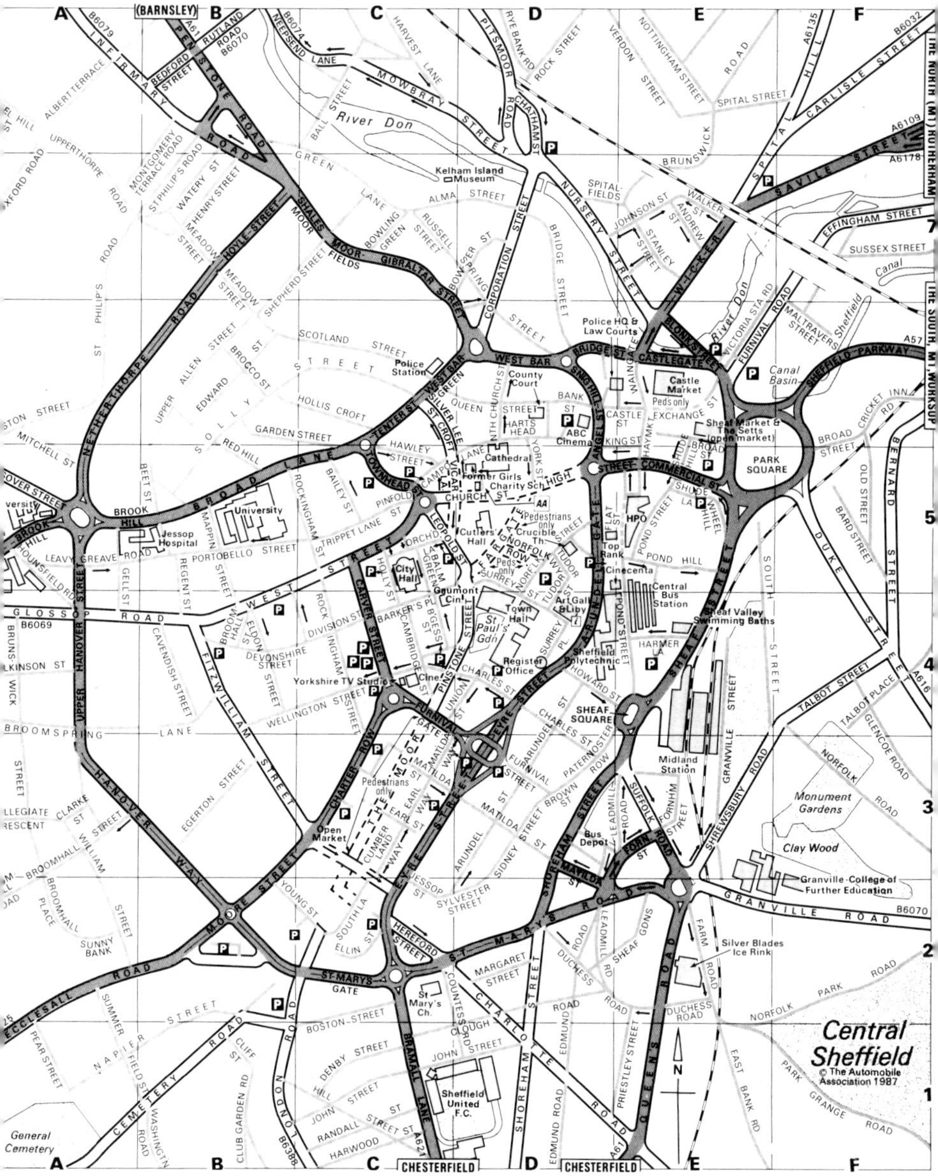

(BARNSLEY)
A
B
C
D
E
F
THE NORTH (M1) ROTHERHAM
THE SOUTH, M1, WORKSOP
1
2
3
4
5
7
INFIRMARY ROAD
B6079
PENISTONE ROAD
A61
RUTLAND ROAD
B6070
BEDFORD STREET
NEEPSEND LANE
B6074
HARVEST LANE
MOWBRAY STREET
River Don
BALL STREET
GREEN LANE
Kelham Island Museum
ALMA STREET
RUSSELL STREET
BOWLING GREEN
PITSMOOR ROAD
RYE BANK RD
ROCK STREET
CHATHAM ST
NURSERY STREET
VERDON STREET
NOTTINGHAM STREET
SPITAL STREET
SPITAL HILL
A6135
CARLISLE STREET
B6032
SAVILE STREET
A6109
A6178
BRUNSWICK ROAD
SPITAL FIELDS
JOHNSON ST
ANDREW ST
STANLEY STREET
WALKER ST
WICKER
EFFINGHAM STREET
SUSSEX STREET
Canal
ALBERT TERRACE
UPPERTHORPE ROAD
MONTGOMERY TERRACE ROAD
ST PHILIP'S ROAD
WATERY ST
HENRY STREET
MEADOW STREET
SHALESMOOR
MOOR FIELDS
GIBRALTAR STREET
HOYLE STREET
SHEPHERD STREET
BOWER SPRING
CORPORATION STREET
BRIDGE STREET
Police HQ & Law Courts
NETHERTHORPE ROAD
SCOTLAND STREET
Police Station
WEST BAR
BRIDGE ST
CASTLEGATE
BLONK STREET
VICTORIA STA RD
FURNIVAL ROAD
MALTRAVERS STREET
Sheffield
A57
SHEFFIELD PARKWAY
Canal Basin
UPPER ALLEN STREET
EDWARD ST
BROCCO ST
SOLLY STREET
HOLLIS CROFT
GARDEN STREET
RED HILL
TENTER ST
WEST BAR GREEN
SILVER ST
QUEEN STREET
County Court
CHURCH ST
BANK ST
HARTS HEAD
SNIG HILL
WAINGATE
Castle Market
Peds only
EXCHANGE
CASTLE ST
KING ST
Sheaf Market & The Setts (open market)
PARK SQUARE
BROAD STREET
CRICKET INN RD
BERNARD STREET
OLD STREET
MITCHELL ST
BROAD LANE
HAWLEY STREET
Cathedral
Former Girls Charity Sch
HIGH ST
ANGEL ST
COMMERCIAL ST
HAYMKT
SHUDE HILL
SHUDE LA
WHEEL HILL
University
BROOK HILL
Jessop Hospital
BEET ST
MAPPIN ST
ROCKINGHAM ST
BAILEY ST
TOWNHEAD ST
PINFOLD ST
TRIPPET LANE
CAMPO LANE
VICAR LA
CHURCH ST
Pedestrians only
Cutlers' Hall
Crucible Th.
NORFOLK ROW
HPO
FLAT ST
POND STREET
POND HILL
BARD STREET
DUKE STREET
LEAVY GREAVE ROAD
PORTOBELLO STREET
GELL ST
REGENT ST
ORCHARD LA
LEOPOLD ST
City Hall
BALM GREEN
Gaumont Cin
SURREY ST
Peds only
TUDOR ST
Top Rank
Cinecenta
Central Bus Station
SOUTH STREET
GLOSSOP ROAD
B6069
UPPER HANOVER STREET
WEST STREET
CARVER STREET
HOLLY ST
BARKER'S POOL
Town Hall
St Paul's Gdn
Art Gall & Liby
ARUNDEL GATE
POND ST
Sheaf Valley Swimming Baths
BROOMHALL ST
ELDON ST
DEVONSHIRE STREET
DIVISION ST
CAMBRIDGE ST
BURGESS ST
Register Office
Sheffield Polytechnic
HARMER LA
CAVENDISH STREET
FITZWILLIAM STREET
Yorkshire TV Studio
Cine
PINSTONE STREET
CHARLES ST
UNION ST
HOWARD ST
SHEAF SQUARE
SHEAF STREET
WELLINGTON STREET
FURNIVAL GATE
NORFOLK ST
CHARLES ST
TALBOT STREET
TALBOT PLACE
A616
BROOMSPRING LANE
EGERTON STREET
CHARTER ROW
THE MOOR
MATILDA WAY
ECCLESALL ROAD
EYRE STREET
FURNIVAL STREET
ARUNDEL ST
PATERNOSTER ROW
Midland Station
GRANVILLE STREET
SHREWSBURY ROAD
GLENCOE ROAD
NORFOLK ROAD
Monument Gardens
CLARKE ST
WILLIAM STREET
BROOMHALL ST
HANOVER WAY
Open Market
Pedestrians only
EARL WAY
EARL ST
CUMBERLAND WAY
MATILDA ST
BROWN ST
SIDNEY ST
SHOREHAM STREET
Bus Depot
LEADMILL ROAD
SUFFOLK ROAD
FORNHAM STREET
FORN ST
Clay Wood
Granville College of Further Education
GRANVILLE ROAD
B6070
BROOMHALL PLACE
SUNNY BANK
MOORE STREET
YOUNG ST
SOUTH LA
ELLIN ST
JESSOP ST
SYLVESTER STREET
MAVILDA ST
HEREFORD STREET
ST MARY'S ROAD
DUCHESS ROAD
LEADMILL RD
SHEAF GDNS
FARM ROAD
Silver Blades Ice Rink
ST MARYS GATE
MARGARET STREET
St Mary's Ch.
COUNTESS RD
CHARLOTTE ROAD
EDMUND ROAD
DUCHESS ROAD
NORFOLK PARK ROAD
SUMMER STREET
NAPIER STREET
CLIFF ST
BOSTON STREET
CLOUGH RD
JOHN STREET
DENBY STREET
HILL STREET
JOHN ST
RANDALL ST
HARWOOD ST
BRAMALL LANE
A621
Sheffield United F.C.
SHOREHAM STREET
PRIESTLEY STREET
QUEENS ROAD
A61
EAST BANK RD
N
Central Sheffield
© The Automobile Association 1987
PARK GRANGE ROAD
PEAR STREET
CEMETERY ROAD
WASHINGTON ROAD
FIELD ST
CLUB GARDEN RD
LONDON ROAD
B6388
General Cemetery
CHESTERFIELD
CHESTERFIELD

Key to Town Plan

AA Recommended roads		Car Parks	P
Other roads		Parks and open spaces	
Restricted roads		AA Service Centre	AA
Buildings of interest			

Sheffield continued

Cobwebs
208 Whitham Rd, Broomhill. (S.L Sleath) Est: 1978. Open 10-5. CL: Thurs. and Tues. SIZE: Small. *STOCK: Ceramics, small furniture, jewellery, pictures, 19th C, £5-£300.* LOC: Main road near university. PARK: Nearby. TEL: 0742 681923. SER: Valuations; upholstery.

The Doll's House Antiques
(Mrs S Gray) Est: 1960. Open by appointment. SIZE: Small. *STOCK: Furniture, small general antiques, 18th to early 20th C, £5-£2,000; dolls, 19th to early 20th C; jewellery, Victorian and Edwardian clothes and accessories, collectors' items; oil paintings and watercolours.* Not Stocked: Stamps, books, coins. TEL: 0742 360061. SER: Restorations (dolls, antique fabrics and garments, porcelain, silver, plate, jewellery, furniture, pictures); buys at auction.

Dronfield Antiques
375-377 Abbeydale Rd. (H.J Greaves) Est: 1968. Open 10.30-5.30. CL: Thurs. and Sat. except by appointment. SIZE: Large + warehouses. *STOCK: Trade and shipping goods, Victoriana, glass, china.* LOC: A621, 1 mile south of city centre. PARK: Easy. TEL: 0742 550172/581821; home - 0742 556024. VAT: Stan.

Ellis's
144 Whitham Rd. Est: 1943. Open 9-6. *STOCK: Oriental carpets and rugs.* TEL: 0742 662920. VAT: Stan.

Fillibuster and Booth Ltd
749 Ecclesall Rd. Open 10.30-5.30. CL: Thurs. *STOCK: General antiques and collectors' items, oils and watercolours, 1880-1920.* TEL: 0742 682653.

Findley Antiques
314 Langsett Rd. (B Findley) Est: 1973. Open 9.30-5.30, Sun. by appointment. SIZE: Medium. *STOCK: Shipping items, 1900-1940, £25-£35; bric-a-brac, 1850-1950, £2-£10; general antiques, Victoriana, £100-£150.* LOC: 1 mile from city centre on A616. PARK: Easy. TEL: 0742 346088; home - same. VAT: Stan.

Fulwood Antiques and The Basement Gallery
7 Brooklands Ave. (Mrs H.J Wills) Est: 1977. Open Wed. and Fri. 10-5, Sat. 10-1. SIZE: Medium. *STOCK: General small items, fine furniture; oil paintings and watercolours, 19th-20th C, £50-£5,000.* LOC: From city centre towards Broomhill, Fulwood Rd., Nethergreen and straight on for Fulwood. PARK: Easy. TEL: 0742 307387; home - 0742 301346. SER: Valuations; restorations (ceramics, metal and pictures).

Fun Antiques
72 Abbeydale Rd. (B Harrap) Est: 1978. Open by appointment. SIZE: Medium. *STOCK:*

Fun Antiques continued

Unusual and collectable items including sporting items, toys, advertising, Christmas, arcade and fairground items, 20th C, £5-£1,000. PARK: Easy. TEL: 0742 553424. SER: Valuations; buys at auction (as stock). FAIRS: Harrow, Ardingly, Newark, Stoneleigh, Alexandra Palace. VAT: Stan. *Trade Only.*

Gilbert and Sons
16 Abbeydale Rd. (B. and C Gilbert) Open 9.30-5. *STOCK: Shipping items.* TEL: 0742 552043.

G.H Green LAPADA
334-6 Abbeydale Rdand warehouse, The Chapel, Broadfield Rd. Est: 1962. Open 9-5.30. *STOCK: Period and shipping goods.* TEL: 0742 550881; home - 0742 660494. VAT: Stan/Spec. *Trade Only Warehouse.*

Hibbert Bros. Ltd
117 Norfolk St. (P.A Greaves) Open 9-5.30. *STOCK: Oils and watercolours.* TEL: 0742 722038.

Alan Hill Books, Sheffield
261 Glossop Rd. Est: 1980. Open 10.30-5.30. *STOCK: Antiquarian books, maps and prints.* TEL: 0742 780594.

Hinson Fine Paintings BADA
290 Glossop Rd. Open 9-5, Sat. 9-12. *STOCK: Oil paintings, watercolours, fine antiques, 19th C.* TEL: 0742 722082. VAT: Spec.

A.E Jameson and Co LAPADA
257 Glossop Rd. (P Jameson) Est: 1883. Open 9-5.45. SIZE: Large. *STOCK: Furniture, pre-1820, £20-£15,000; glass, china, weapons.* LOC: A57. TEL: 0742 723846; home - 0742 726189. SER: Valuations; restorations (furniture); buys at auction. VAT: Stan/Spec.

Peter Kelsey
629/631 Abbeydale Rd. Est: 1920. Open 10-5. CL: Thurs. *STOCK: Furniture, 18th-19th C, silver, shipping goods.* TEL: 0742 587288. SER: Valuations. VAT: Stan/Spec.

Oriel Antiques
185 Abbeydale Rd. (A Black) Est: 1970. Open 10-4.30. CL: Thurs. SIZE: Small. *STOCK: Pottery and porcelain, early 19th C; copper and brass, 18th-19th C; all £5-£25. Furniture, 17th-19th C, £5-£100.* LOC: A621. PARK: Easy. SER: Buys at auction.

The Oriental Rug Shop
763 Abbeydale Rd. (A Hazaveh) Open 10-5. *STOCK: Rugs and carpets.* TEL: 0742 552240/589821.

Paraphernalia
66/68 Abbeydale Rd. Est: 1972. *STOCK: General antiques, stripped pine, lighting, brass and iron beds.* TEL: 0742 550203. VAT: Stan.

Sheffield continued

Peter James Antiques
112 and 114 London Rd. (P.J Conboy) Est: 1980. Open 9.30-5. SIZE: Large. *STOCK: Furniture - mahogany, walnut, pine, oak and satin walnut, 1800-1920.* PARK: Easy. TEL: 0742 700273. SER: Restorations. VAT: Stan.

Porter Prints (Broomhill)
205 Whitham Rd. *STOCK: Maps and prints.* TEL: 0742 685751.

Pot-Pourri
647 Ecclesall Rd, Hunters Bar. (Mrs M Needham) Est: 1972. Open 10-5.30. *STOCK: Old and antique jewellery, silver, plate including Sheffield.* TEL: 0742 669790. VAT: Stan.

Richards Furniture Sales
94 Abbeydale Rd. (B Wardley) Est: 1963. Open 9-5.30. CL: Thurs. SIZE: Large. *STOCK: General antiques and reproduction furniture.* LOC: On road south out of Sheffield. PARK: Easy. TEL: 0742 550720. SER: Valuations; restorations; re-leathering; buys at auction. VAT: Stan.

N.P. and A Salt Antiques LAPADA
Unit 1 and 2, Barmouth Rd. Open 9.30-4.30. CL: Sat. SIZE: Large. *STOCK: Victorian furniture, shipping goods, smalls and toys.* TEL: 0742 582672. SER: Valuations; packing; shipping; courier. *Trade Only.*

Tilley's Vintage Magazine Shop
281 Shoreham St. (A.G.J. and A.A.J.C Tilley) Est: 1979. Open Tues., Fri. and Sat. 9-5, other times by appointment. SIZE: Large. *STOCK: Magazines, comics, newspapers, books, postcards, cigarette cards, prints, ephemera.* LOC: Opposite Sheffield United F.C. PARK: Easy. TEL: 0742 752442. SER: Mail order.

Turn of the Century
48-50 Barber Rd, Crookesmoor. Open 10-6, Sun. and other times by appointment (prior telephone call advisable). SIZE: Medium. *STOCK: English furniture, 18th-19th C, £100-£4,000; longcase clocks, 18th to early 19th C, £1,500-£3,500; wall clocks, 19th C, from £500; oil paintings and watercolours, 19th C, from £150; general antiques and collectors items, 18th-19th C, £20-£500.* Not Stocked: Books, coins, militaria. LOC: Follow A57 or inner ring road (Upper Hanover St.-Netherthorpe Rd.) to University roundabout, exit into Bolsover St., continue for 1/2 mile, over traffic lights, shop 150 yards on right. PARK: Easy. TEL: 0742 670947. VAT: Mainly Spec.

Paul Ward Antiques
Owl House, 8 Burnell Rd, Owlerton. Resident. Est: 1976. Open by appointment. SIZE: Large. *STOCK: Matched sets of Victorian dining and kitchen chairs, country chairs, general antiques.* LOC: 2 miles north of city on A61. TEL: 0742 335980. VAT: Stan.

THORNE, Nr. Doncaster

Canterbury House
24 Finkle St. (J.R Holgate) Est: 1977. Open 8.45-5. *STOCK: General antiques, watches and clocks.* TEL: 0405 812102.

Bone china vase in imitation of Japanese lacquer, with stork in pâte-sur-pâte after Christopher Dresser, 1880.
THOMAS GOODE & CO. LTD.
From ***The Dictionary of Minton*** by Paul Atterbury and Maureen Batkin, published by the **Antique Collectors' Club** in 1990. £35.00.

Yorkshire West

Please note this is only a rough map designed to show dealers the number of shops in the various towns, and is not necessarily totally accurate.

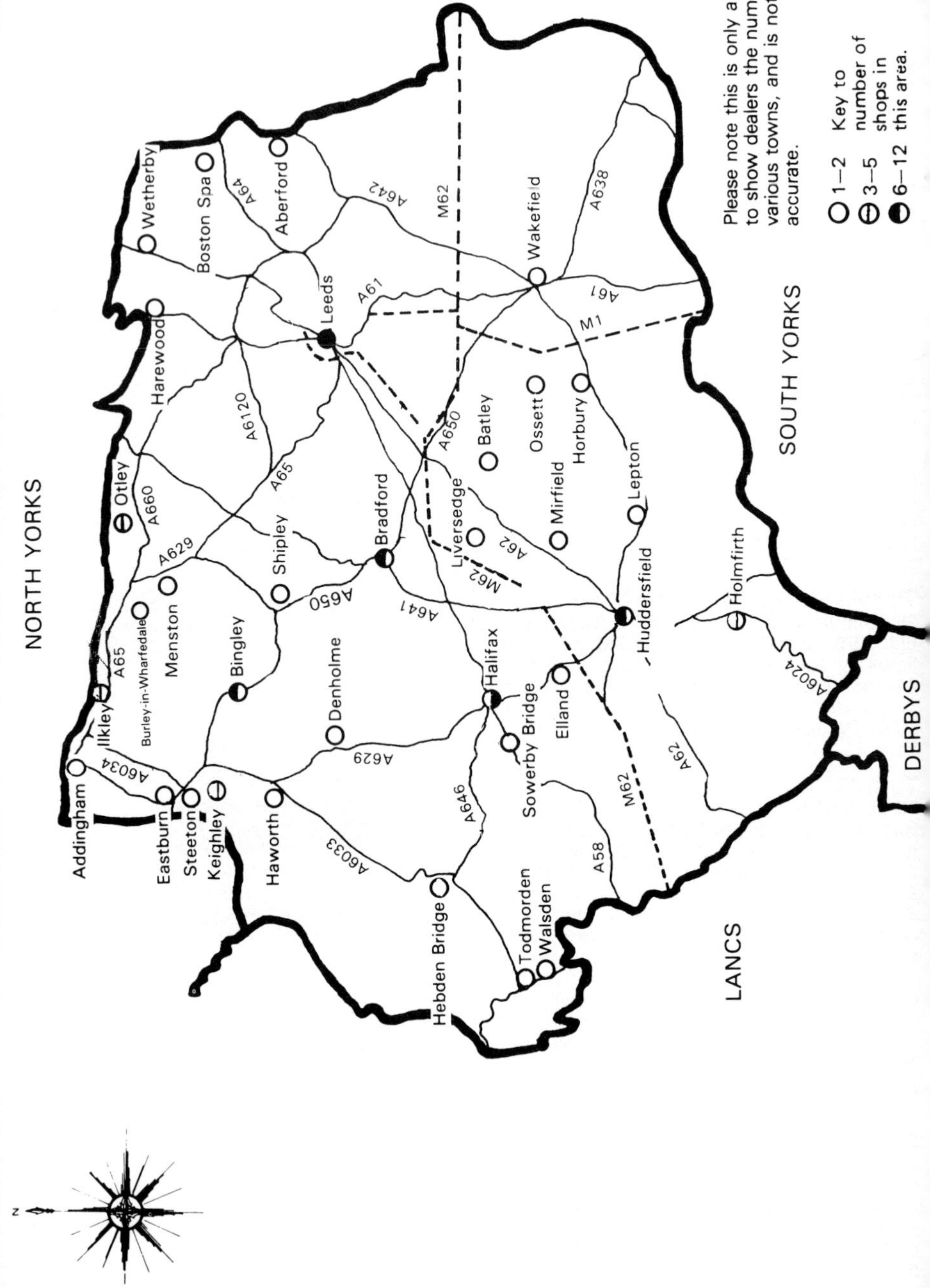
NORTH YORKS
SOUTH YORKS
LANCS
DERBYS
Wetherby
Boston Spa
Aberford
Leeds
Harewood
Otley
Wakefield
Batley
Ossett
Horbury
Mirfield
Lepton
Liversedge
Bradford
Shipley
Menston
Burley-in-Wharfedale
Ilkley
Addingham
Eastburn
Steeton
Keighley
Haworth
Bingley
Denholme
Halifax
Sowerby Bridge
Elland
Huddersfield
Holmfirth
Hebden Bridge
Todmorden
Walsden
A64
A642
M62
A638
A61
M1
A6120
A650
A65
A660
A629
A62
A641
A6024
A6034
A646
A6033
A58
N

○ 1–2 Key to
⊖ 3–5 number of
◐ 6–12 shops in this area.

ABERFORD

Aberford Antiques Ltd
Hicklam House. (J.W.H Long and C.A Hebb) Est: 1973. Open 9-5.30, Sundays 10-5.30. SIZE: Large. *STOCK: Stripped pine, Victorian and period, £10-£1,500; Victoriana, £5-£1,000; local prints and maps; Victorian oil paintings.* LOC: Opposite Almshouses at entrance of village. PARK: Easy. TEL: 0532 813209. SER: Fitted pine kitchens. VAT: Stan/Spec.

ADDINGHAM, Nr. Ilkley

Addingham Antiques
70-72 Main St. (G.J Estevez) Open by appointment. SIZE: Large. *STOCK: Furniture, 17th-19th C; clocks, 18th-19th C; musical boxes; oil paintings, 19th-20th C; scientific instruments, Doulton studio pottery.* LOC: A65. PARK: Opposite. TEL: 0943 830788 (24 hrs.). SER: Restorations (clocks, musical boxes, furniture, paintings).

Manor Barn Pine
Burnside Mill, Main St, (Rose Farm Furniture Ltd.). Est: 1972. Open 8-5.30. SIZE: Warehouse. *STOCK: Pine, 17th-19th C and reproduction; oak and shipping goods.* PARK: Easy. TEL: 0943 830176. VAT: Stan/Spec.

BATLEY

Leon Cooper LAPADA
21 Commercial St. Est: 1952. Open 9-5 or by appointment. CL: Sat. *STOCK: Jewellery, watches, miniatures, clocks, weapons.* LOC: Off B6124, near Hick Lane traffic lights. TEL: 0924 442291; fax: - 0924 472093. SER: Valuations. VAT: Stan.

BINGLEY

Bingley Antiques Centre
Keighley Rd. (J.B. and J Poole) Est: 1965. Open 9.30-5, Tues. 10-4, Sun. 2-5. SIZE: Large. *STOCK: Furniture, 18th-19th C; pottery, porcelain, shipping goods, garden furniture.*

Bingley Antiques Centre continued

LOC: On A650, opposite parish church. PARK: Easy. TEL: 0274 567316. SER: Valuations. VAT: Stan/Spec.

E Carrol
5 Ryshworth Hall, Keighley Rd, Crossflatts. Est: 1970. Open by appointment. SIZE: Small. *STOCK: Oil paintings, watercolours.* LOC: A650. PARK: Easy. TEL: 0274 568800. VAT: Stan.

Cottingley Antiques
Unit C, Ebor Mills, Dubb Lane. (P Nobbs) Open 9-5. *STOCK: General antiques and pine.* TEL: 0274 561406.

Curio Cottage
3 Millgate. (Mrs W.J Windle) Open 2.30-5.30. CL: Tues. and Fri. SIZE: Small. *STOCK: Victoriana, curios and stripped pine.* TEL: Home - 0274 612975.

J. & H. Antiques
82/84 Main St. Open 10-5, Sun. 1-5. *STOCK: Pine, general antiques, bric-a-brac.* TEL: 0274 563134.

Juliana
92 Main St. (J. and T Capstick) *STOCK: Silver, jewellery, small collectors' items.* TEL: 0535 272193. *Postal Only.*

Victorian House Shop
88 Main St. (J Foster) Open 11-5, Sun. 2-5. CL: Mon. and Tues. *STOCK: Victorian and reproduction fireplaces, general antiques, bric-a-brac.* TEL: 0274 569278.

BOSTON SPA, by Wetherby

London House Oriental Rugs and Carpets
London House, High St. (M.A. and Mrs I.T.H Ries) Open 10-5.30 including Sun. CL: Mon. SIZE: Medium. *STOCK: Caucasian, Turkish, Afghan and Persian rugs, runners and carpets, £50-£3,750; kelims, tapestries and textiles.* LOC: Off A1, south of Wetherby. PARK: Easy. TEL: 0937 845123; home - same. SER: Valuations; restorations (Oriental carpets and rugs); buys at auction (Oriental carpets and rugs). VAT: Stan/Spec.

BRADFORD

Bradford Antiques and Curio Centre
132 Sunbridge Rd. Open 10-5. SIZE: 12 dealers on two floors. *STOCK: Pine, period sofas, general antiques, linen and period clothes.* TEL: 0274 391249; home - 0274 670611. SER: Re-upholstery.

Carlton Antiques and Fine Art
1 Hammond Sq, Emm Lane, Heaton. (M Gray) Open Tues. and Thurs. 2-4.30, Sat. and Sun. 2-5. SIZE: Small. *STOCK: Oils and watercolours, 19th to early 20th C, £500-£2,000; mahogany and walnut furniture, 19th C, £400-£800; English and continental porcelain, 19th-20th C, £50-£500.* LOC: A650 Keighley road, turn left at Norman Arch. PARK: Easy. TEL: 0274 496853; home - 0274 545745. SER: Restorations (porcelain). VAT: Stan/Spec.

Carlton Antiques and Fine Art
280 Keighley Rd, Frizinghall. (M Gray) Open 10.30-12.30 and 2-5.30, Sun. 2-6. CL: Wed. and Fri. *STOCK: Oils and watercolours, 19th to early 20th C, £500-£2,000; mahogany and walnut furniture, 19th C, £400-£800; English and continental porcelain, 19th-20th C, £50-£500.* LOC: A650, 400 yards on right beyond Norman arch travelling out of the city. TEL: 0274 482953; home - 0274 545745.

Collectors' Corner
5-7 Frizinghall Rd. (C. and G Douthwaite) Est: 1970. Open 2-7., or by appointment. CL: Mon. and Thurs. *STOCK: Victoriana, bric-a-brac, postcards.* PARK: Easy. TEL: 0274 487098.

The Corner Shop
89 Oak Lane. (Miss Badland) Est: 1961. Open Tues. 2-5.30, Thurs. and Sat. 11-5.30. *STOCK: Pottery, small furniture, clocks and general items.*

Langley's (Jewellers) Ltd
59 Godwin St. TEL: 0274 722280. VAT: Stan.

Low Moor Antiques
233 and 234 Huddersfield Rd, Low Moor. (J.A Bowler) Est: 1972. Open 9-12 and 2-5. CL: Wed. and Sat. p.m. *STOCK: Shipping furniture, pine, silver plate and general antiques.* TEL: 0274 671047/604835.

BURLEY-IN-WHARFEDALE

Burtique
72 Main St. (J.B. and L.L Burrows) Est: 1990. Open 9.30-5.30. CL: Mon. SIZE: Medium. *STOCK: Furniture, 18th C, £200-£7,000; copper and brass, 19th C, £50-£200; ceramics, 18th C, £10-£500.* LOC: A65 between Otley and Ilkley. PARK: Nearby. TEL: 0943 863639. SER: Restorations; buys at auction (furniture and decorative items). VAT: Spec.

DENHOLME, Nr. Bradford

Ye Olde Curiosity Shop
23 New Rd. (F Weatherill) Est: 1964. Open 11-5. SIZE: Medium. *STOCK: Curios, general antiques, shipping goods.* LOC: 7 miles from Bradford, via Thornton Rd. PARK: 20yds. on side of main road. TEL: Home - 0274 542756.

EASTBURN, Nr. Keighley

M Kelly Antiques
41 Main Rd. Est: 1968. Open 9.30-5. SIZE: Medium. *STOCK: English and continental pine, darkwoods and small items, 19th C, to £1,000.* PARK: Easy. TEL: 0535 653002. SER: Restorations (pine stripping). VAT: Stan.

ELLAND

Oldfield Cottage Antiques
Southgate, St. Pauls Buildings. (Mrs R Potts) Est: 1987. Open Wed.-Sat. 10.30-5. *STOCK: Pine furniture and kitchens; blue and white.* TEL: 0422 370320.

Andy Thornton Architectural Antiques Ltd
Marshfield Mill, Dewsbury Rd. Est: 1973. Open 8-5; Sat. 9-3. SIZE: Large. *STOCK: Architectural antiques - doors, stained glass, fireplaces, panelling, garden furniture, light fittings, pews.* PARK: Easy. TEL: 0422 377314/375595. VAT: Stan.

HALIFAX

Ken Balme Antiques
12 Keighley Rd, Ovenden. Est: 1986. Open 9-5, Wed. 1-5. *STOCK: General antiques especially Victorian glass and commemorative ware.* TEL: 0422 344193/244830.

Boulevard Reproductions
369 Skircoat Green Rd. (T Bright) Open 9.30-7pm, Sun. for viewing. *STOCK: Furniture.* TEL: 0422 368628.

Jean Brear
19 Causeway Head, Burnley Rd. Est: 1955. *STOCK: Antiquarian books; maps, atlases, prints, oils, manuscripts, small antiques.* TEL: 0422 366144.

Halifax continued

Collectors Old Toys and Antiques
89 Northgate. (J Haley) Open 10-5. *STOCK: Collectors toys, general and shipping antiques, small items, china, glass, clocks.* TEL: 0422 822148/360434.

Halifax Antiques Centre
Queens Rd. Est: 1981. Open 10-5 Tues.-Sat. SIZE: Large and two warehouses. 30 dealers. *STOCK: Furniture, porcelain, pottery, jewellery, art deco, linen, mechanical music, collectables, decorative items, general antiques.* LOC: 1 mile from town centre, corner Queens Rd. and Gibbet St. (not the Piece Hall) near Kings Cross. PARK: Own. TEL: 0422 366657. SER: Export.

Muir Hewitt Art Deco Originals
Halifax Antiques Centre, Queens Rd. Open 10-5. CL: Mon. *STOCK: Pottery including Susie Cooper, Charlotte Rhead and Clarice Cliff; Shelley ceramics; furniture, lighting and mirrors.* LOC: 1 mile west of town centre on the A58 (A646), turn right into Queens Rd. at Trafalgar Inn traffic lights, centre is at next traffic lights (opp. Lloyds Bank).. PARK: Easy. TEL: 0422 366657; home - 0274 882051.

Hillside Antiques
Denholme Gate Rd, Hipperholme. (M. and J Preston) Est: 1981. Open 10-12.15 and 2-5.15. CL: Wed. SIZE: Small. *STOCK: Pottery,*

Hillside Antiques continued

porcelain, small furniture, copper, brass, brass, glass, 1870-1940. Not Stocked: Linen, clothing and gold. LOC: A644, 150yds. north of Hipperholme crossroads. PARK: Easy. TEL: Home - 0422 202744. FAIRS: Local.

North Bridge Antiques
5 North Bridge. (S Lester) Open 9-5, Thurs. 9-1. *STOCK: Shipping goods.* TEL: 0422 358474.

Scott and Varey
10 Prescott St. (W.B Scott) Est: 1963. Open 9-5.30, Sun. 10-4. SIZE: Large. *STOCK: Furniture, 1740-1940.* LOC: Town centre near Halifax Building Society. PARK: Easy. TEL: 0422 366928 (24hrs.); fax - 0422 340 277.

HAREWOOD, Nr. Leeds

Harewood Cottage Antiques
26/27 Harrogate Rd. (D Wilson) Open 10-6. CL: Sun., Mon. and Thurs. except by appointment. *STOCK: Furniture, porcelain, collectors' items, 18th to early 20th C, £5-£2,000.* LOC: Opposite Harewood House Gates. PARK: At rear. TEL: 0532 886327.

HAWORTH

Haworth Antiques

Lees Mill, Lees Lane. (R. Smith.) Open 8.30-4.30, weekends by appointment. SIZE: Large. *STOCK: General antiques and shipping goods, 1850-1930.* LOC: Main road into Haworth. PARK: Easy. TEL: 643535; home - 644144. SER: Valuations, restorations (furniture). VAT: Stan. *Trade Only.*

HEBDEN BRIDGE, Nr. Halifax

Cornucopia Antiques

9 West End. (C Nassor) Open Thurs., Fri. and Sun. 1-5, Sat. 11-5. *STOCK: Pine, oak and mahogany furniture, art deco, lamps, lighting, pottery, bric-a-brac, kitchenware.* LOC: Town centre behind Pennine Information Centre. PARK: Easy. TEL: 0422 844497.

Larkhall Antiques

39 Market St. (J Blom) Open 10-5, Sat. 11-5, Sun. 1-5. CL: Tues. *STOCK: General antiques especially furniture.*

G.J Saville

Foster Clough. Open by appointment only. *STOCK: Maps and prints, 1500-1850.* TEL: 0422 882808. SER: Valuations; buys at auction. FAIRS: British International, Birmingham; Barbican; Tatton Park; West London; Olympia.

HOLMFIRTH, Nr. Huddersfield

Andrew Spencer Bottomley

The Coach House, Huddersfield Rd. Open by appointment. *STOCK: Arms and armour including pistols, swords, daggers, helmets and suits of armour.* TEL: 0484 685234. SER: Valuations and television and film hire.

Chapel House Fireplaces

Netherfield House, St. Georges Rd, Scholes. Open strictly by appointment within the following times - Tues. 9-7, Wed.-Sat. 9-5. *STOCK: Georgian, Victorian and Edwardian grates and mantels; French chimneypieces.* TEL: 0484 682275.

The Toll House Bookshop

32/34 Huddersfield Rd. (E.V Beardsell) Est: 1978. Open 10-5. *STOCK: Books including antiquarian.* TEL: 0484 686541.

Upperbridge Antiques

9 Huddersfield Rd. (Mrs M Coop and I Ridings) Open 1-5, Sun. 2-5. CL: Tues. SIZE: Small. *STOCK: Pottery, linen, metalware, interesting items, Victorian to art deco, £5-£150.* Not Stocked: Jewellery. LOC: A635. PARK: Nearby. TEL: 0484 687200.

HORBURY, Nr. Wakefield

The Old Tithe Barn

16 Tithe Barn St. (J S Ingham) Est: 1945. Open daily. CL: Wed. *STOCK: General antiques, especially furniture.* LOC: Between Ossett and Wakefield. PARK: Easy. TEL: 0924 274362; home - same. SER: Restorations (upholstery, French polishing, furniture repairs). VAT: Stan.

HUDDERSFIELD

20th Century Antiques

462 Wakefield Rd, Waterloo. (S.J Marten) Est: 1970. SIZE: Large and warehouse. *STOCK: Furniture, export and shipping items, pianos and clocks, Georgian to 1920s, £5-£1,000.* PARK: Easy. TEL: 0484 515166. VAT: Stan/Spec.

Beau Monde Antiques

343a Bradford Rd, Fartown. (R.M Schofield) Est: 1963. Open 9.30-6, Sat. 9.30-5. CL: Wed. pm. SIZE: Medium. *STOCK: Furniture, general antiques, bric-a-brac, £5-£500.* LOC: On A641, 1 mile from town centre. PARK: Easy. TEL: 0484 427565.

Berry Brow Antiques

90/92 Dodds Royd, Woodhead Rd, Berry Brow. (M Griffiths) Est: 1972. Open 10-2. SIZE: Medium. *STOCK: Victorian and Edwardian furniture, china, bric-a-brac.* LOC: 2 miles from town centre on Holmfirth Rd. PARK: Easy. TEL: 0484 663320.

Collectors Corner (Yorkshire Jewellery Ltd.)

13 Market Ave. Est: 1977. Open 9-5. *STOCK: Jewellery, coins, small items.* LOC: Opposite Boots, chemist. TEL: 0484 428359.

D.W Dyson (Antique Weapons)

Wood Lea, Shepley. Est: 1974. Open by appointment only. *STOCK: Antique weapons including cased duelling pistols, armour, miniature arms, rare and unusual items.* LOC: Off A616. PARK: Easy. TEL: 0484 607331; home - same. SER: Valuations; buys at auction (antique weapons); special presentation items made to order in precious metals; advice on restoration. FAIRS: Dorchester Hotel, London; Dortmund, Stuttgart and other major foreign. VAT: Spec.

Fillans (Antiques)

2 Market Walk. (G Neary) NAG. Est: 1852. Open 8.45-5.30. SIZE: Small. *STOCK: English silver, 1700-1980; Sheffield plate, 1760-1840, £10-£500; jewellery, £50-£10,000.* Not Stocked: Other than above. PARK: Town centre multi-storey. TEL: 0484 531609. SER: Valuations; restorations; buys at auction (English silver and jewellery). VAT: Stan/Spec.

Heritage Antiques

10 Byram Arcade, Westgate. (Mrs H Beaumont and Mrs B Noble) Open 10-5. CL: Wed. *STOCK: General antiques.* TEL: 0484 514667.

Huddersfield continued

Huddersfield Antiques
170 Wakefield Rd, Moldgreen. Est: 1971. Open 10.30-4.30, or by appointment. SIZE: Medium. *STOCK: Victoriana, bric-a-brac, collectors' items, postcards; warehouse of trade and shipping goods.* PARK: Easy. TEL: 0484 539747. SER: Valuations; buys at auction.

Paragon Antiques
Open by appointment only. *STOCK: Georgian and Victorian furniture; early blue and white porcelain and china.* LOC: 1/2 mile from junction 24, M62. TEL: 0484 606014. SER: Restorations (furniture).

Second Childhood
20 Byram Arcade, Westgate. (E Hoy) Est: 1984. Open 10.30-3.30 or by appointment. CL: Mon. and Wed. SIZE: Small. *STOCK: Victorian and Edwardian dolls, dolls' houses, toys, teddy bears, Victorian to 1950s; associated items.* LOC: 100 yards from railway and bus stations. PARK: Easy. TEL: 0484 530117; home - 0484 603854. SER: Valuations; restorations (dolls' hospital and teddy repairs). FAIRS: Major U.K. dolls.

ILKLEY

Antiques Centre
34 Leeds Rd. (D Carmichael, G Higgins and A Speak) Est: 1986. Open 10-5, Sun. 2-5. CL:

Antiques Centre continued

Mon. SIZE: Large. *STOCK: General antiques including furniture, brass and iron bedsteads, paintings, prints, books, fireplaces.* LOC: On A65. PARK: Easy. TEL: 0943 601394.

J.H Cooper and Son (Ilkley) Ltd
LAPADA

33-35 Church St, and 50 Leeds Rd. Est: 1910. Open 9-1 and 2-5.30. SIZE: Large. *STOCK: English furniture, pre-1830, £100-£10,000; porcelain and silver, pictures.* Not Stocked: Post-1880 items. LOC: A65. PARK: Easy. TEL: 0943 608020. SER: Valuations; restorations (furniture); buys at auction. VAT: Stan/Spec.

Keith Richardson Antiques
26 Leeds Rd. Est: 1974. Open 9-5. CL: Wed. SIZE: Medium. *STOCK: Jewellery, dolls, glass, furniture, Victoriana, commemorative ware.* PARK: Adjacent street. TEL: 0943 600045.

Jack Shaw and Co
The Old Grammar School, Skipton Rd. Est: 1945. Open 9.30-12.45 and 2-5.30. *STOCK: Silver, furniture.* TEL: 0943 609467. VAT: Spec.

Simon
25 Church St. (S.G.H Pratt) SIZE: Medium. *STOCK: Furniture and clocks, 17th-19th C, £50-£5,000.* Not Stocked: Coins, weapons, jewellery. PARK: Adjacent street. TEL: 0943 602788. SER: Valuations; buys at auction. VAT: Stan/Spec.

KEIGHLEY

Barleycote Hall Antiques LAPADA
2 Janet St, Crossroads. (R Hoskins) Resident. Est: 1968. Open 11-5, trade may call evenings. CL: Mon. *STOCK: Georgian and Victorian furniture, porcelain, metalwork, paintings, jewellery, Victorian and Edwardian clothing, clocks of all types.* LOC: A629, turn right towards Haworth, 600yds. on right. TEL: 0535 644776. VAT: Stan/Spec.

Keighleys of Keighley
153 East Parade. (B Keighley and Son) Est: 1939. Open 9-5. CL: Tues. *STOCK: Furniture, jewellery, gold and silver, china.* LOC: Next to the Victoria Hotel. PARK: Easy. TEL: 0535 663439; home - 0535 607180. VAT: Stan.

Real Macoy
2 Janet St. (D Seal) Open 11-5 including Sun. CL: Mon. and Sat. *STOCK: Quilts, textiles, period clothing.* TEL: 0535 644776.

D Richardson Antiques
72 Haworth Rd, Crossroads. Open 9-5. CL: Sat. *STOCK: General antiques and shipping goods.* PARK: Easy at rear. TEL: 0535 644982.

Scar Top Antiques incorporating T.J. Timber Ltd
Moor Lodge, Stanbury. (T. and S Johnston) Est: 1971. Open 9-5 seven days. SIZE: Large. *STOCK: Pine, 18th-20th C.* LOC: Haworth/Colne road. PARK: Easy. TEL: 0535 646427/642585. SER: Stripping; timber reclamation; reproductions from old timber. VAT: Stan.

LEEDS

19 Nort Blob inc. Serendipity
28 Gledhow Wood Ave. (G Mackintosh) *STOCK: General antiques and shipping goods.* TEL: 0532 683355 or 0831 351921 (mobile).

Aladdin's Cave
19 Queens Arcade. (P. and S Isaacs) Est: 1954. CL: Mon. SIZE: Small. *STOCK: Jewellery, £15-£250; collectors' items; all 19th-20th C.* LOC: Town centre. PARK: 100 yards. TEL: 0532 457903; home - 0532 842425. SER: Valuations. VAT: Stan.

Andrew's Antique Shop inc. Exchange Jewellers
56 North St. (A.W.D Rogers and K.A Humphrey) Est: 1969. Open 9.30-4.30. CL: Sat. SIZE: Large and warehouse. *STOCK: General antiques, jewellery, shipping goods.* TEL: 0532 430870. VAT: Stan.

The Antique Exchange
400 Kirkstall Rd. (S Wood) Est: 1976. Open 10.30-3. CL: Tues. and Wed. SIZE: Medium. *STOCK: Furniture including satin walnut and ash, 19th-20th C, £150-£1,500.* LOC: Kirkstall Rd. is 1/2 mile west of Yorkshire Television Studios. PARK: Easy. TEL: 0532 743513. VAT: Stan/Spec.

Leeds continued

Batty's Antiques
3 Stanningley Rd. (R.J. and S.M Batty) Open 10-5, Thurs. 10-8. *STOCK: Period and reproduction furniture.* TEL: 0532 639011.

Bishop House Antiques
169 Town St, Rodley. (Mrs J.M Bishop) Est: 1977. Open Sat. 2-5.30, or by appointment. *STOCK: General antiques, porcelain and glass.* TEL: 0532 563071.

Boston Pine Co.
Unit 9, Globe Mills, Back Row and Unit 10, Granary Wharf, The Dark Arches. (Mrs K Harper and K Burns) Open 10-6, Sat. 11-4.30. *STOCK: Pine.* TEL: 0532 441650/428007. SER: Furniture made from old timber; restorations; stripping.

Calverley Antiques
34 Salisbury St, Calverley. (S Lawton) Open 10-5. CL: Wed. *STOCK: General antiques, pine.* TEL: 0532 562779. SER: Pine stripping.

Clifton Antiques
854 Leeds Rd, Bramhope. (A.S Ambler) Est: 1972. Open 9.45-6. SIZE: Medium. *STOCK: Furniture, china, pictures.* Not Stocked: Stamps, medals and coins. LOC: A660. PARK: Easy. TEL: 0532 673765; home - 0943 464801. VAT: Stan/Spec.

Coins International and Antiques International
1 and 2 Melbourne St. (J.M Harrison) Open 9-5. CL: Sat. *STOCK: Coins, medals, silver, gold, general antiques, jewellery.* PARK: Easy. TEL: 0532 434230; fax - 0532 345544.

Geary Antiques
114 Richardshaw Lane, Stanningley, Pudsey. (J.A Geary) Est: 1933. Open 10-5.30. CL: Wed. SIZE: Warehouse. *STOCK: Furniture, Georgian, Victorian and Edwardian; copper and brass.* LOC: 300yds. from South Leeds Ring Rd. PARK: Easy. TEL: 0532 564122. SER: Restorations (furniture). VAT: Stan/Spec.

William Goldsmith
23 County Arcade. (R.F Chesterman) Est: 1961. Open 9-5.30. SIZE: Medium. *STOCK: Jewellery, 19th-20th C, £50-£500; clocks, 19th C, £100-£1,000; samplers and prints, 18th-19th C, £25-£100.* LOC: Town centre. PARK: Nearby. TEL: 0532 451345; home - 0532 680275. SER: Valuations; restorations. VAT: Stan.

Kingsway Antiques
223 New Rd. Side, Horsforth. (T Waddington) Est: 1929. Open by appointment. *STOCK: General antiques, clocks, jewellery.* TEL: 0532 587674. SER: Buys at auction.

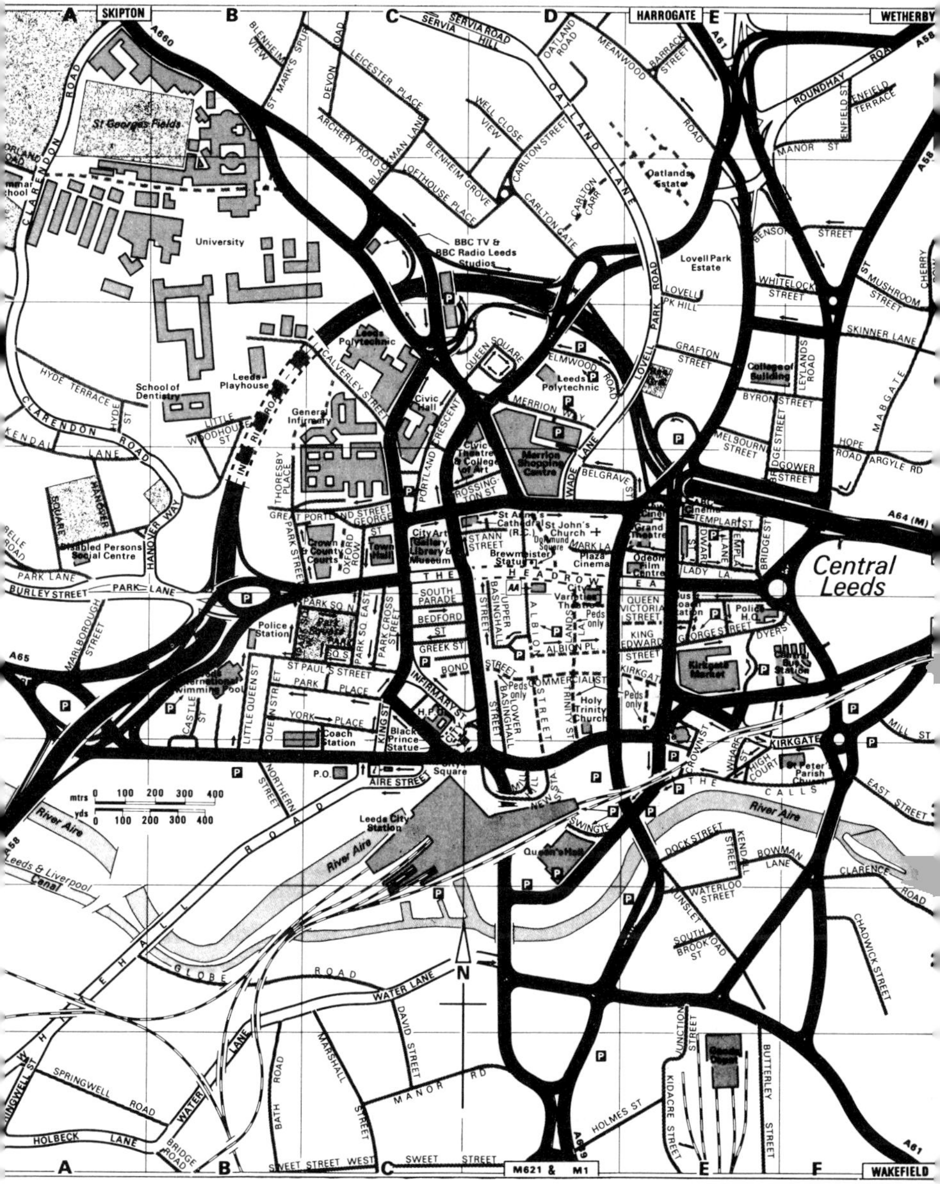

SKIPTON
HARROGATE
WETHERBY
A660
A61
A58
St Georges Fields
University
School of Dentistry
Leeds Playhouse
General Infirmary
Leeds Polytechnic
Civic Hall
BBC TV & BBC Radio Leeds Studios
Lovell Park Estate
Oatlands Estate
College of Building
Merrion Shopping Centre
Civic Theatre & College of Art
St Anne's Cathedral (R.C.)
St John's Church
City Art Gallery Library & Museum
Town Hall
Crown & County Courts
Disabled Persons Social Centre
Brewmeister Statue
Plaza Cinema
Grand Theatre
Odeon Film Centre
City Varieties Theatre
Peds only
Police Station
Police H.Q.
Bus Station
Central Bus Station
Kirkgate Market
Holy Trinity Church
St Peter's Parish Church
International Swimming Pool
Coach Station
Black Prince Statue
H.P.O.
P.O.
City Square
Leeds City Station
Queen's Hall
River Aire
Leeds & Liverpool Canal
Central Leeds
A64 (M)
A65
A58
A61
M621 & M1
WAKEFIELD
CLARENDON ROAD
HYDE TERRACE
KENDAL LANE
PARK LANE
BURLEY STREET
MARLBOROUGH STREET
HANOVER WAY
PARK SQUARE
GREAT GEORGE STREET
PORTLAND CRESCENT
CALVERLEY STREET
BLENHEIM VIEW
ST MARK'S SPUR
SERVIA ROAD
SERVIA HILL
DEVON ROAD
LEICESTER PLACE
ARCHERY ROAD
BLACKMAN LANE
BLENHEIM GROVE
LOFTHOUSE PLACE
WELL CLOSE VIEW
CARLTON STREET
CARLTON GATE
CARLTON CARR
OATLAND ROAD
OATLAND LANE
MEANWOOD ROAD
BARRACK STREET
ROUNDHAY ROAD
ENFIELD STREET
ENFIELD TERRACE
MANOR ST
BENSON STREET
WHITELOCK STREET
MUSHROOM STREET
SKINNER LANE
GRAFTON STREET
LEYLANDS ROAD
BYRON STREET
MELBOURNE STREET
BRIDGE STREET
GOWER STREET
HOPE ROAD
ARGYLE RD
MARGATE
LOVELL PARK ROAD
LOVELL PK HILL
QUEEN SQUARE
ELMWOOD ROAD
MERRION WAY
WADE LANE
BELGRAVE ST
TEMPLAR ST
THE HEADROW
LADY LA
VICAR LANE
BRIGGATE
ALBION STREET
ALBION PL.
COMMERCIAL ST
KIRKGATE
BOAR LANE
TRINITY ST
NEW STATION ST
SWINEGATE
THE CALLS
EAST STREET
MILL ST
CROWN ST
HIGH COURT
DOCK STREET
KENDALL STREET
BOWMAN LANE
WATERLOO STREET
CLARENCE ROAD
CHADWICK STREET
HUNSLET ROAD
SOUTH BROOK ST
JUNCTION STREET
KIDACRE STREET
BUTTERLEY STREET
HOLMES ST
A639
WHITEHALL ROAD
GLOBE ROAD
WATER LANE
DAVID STREET
MANOR RD
MARSHALL STREET
BATH ROAD
SWEET STREET WEST
SWEET STREET
SPRINGWELL ROAD
HOLBECK LANE
BRIDGE ROAD
NORTHERN STREET
AIRE STREET
INFIRMARY ST
KING ST
QUEEN ST
YORK PLACE
PARK PLACE
ST PAUL'S STREET
BOND ST
GREEK ST
BEDFORD ST
SOUTH PARADE
EAST PARADE
PARK CROSS STREET
PARK SQ. EAST
PARK ST
OXFORD ROW
THORESBY PLACE
LITTLE QUEEN ST
CASTLE ST
LITTLE WOODHOUSE ST
INNER RING ROAD
UPPER BASINGHALL STREET
LOWER BASINGHALL STREET
QUEEN VICTORIA STREET
KING EDWARD STREET
GEORGE STREET
DYERS
mtrs 0 100 200 300 400
yds 0 100 200 300 400
N

Key to Town Plan

AA Recommended roads	▬▬	Car Parks	P
Other roads	═	Parks and open spaces	▱
Restricted roads	─ ─ ─	AA Service Centre	AA
Buildings of interest	☐		

Leeds continued

Kirkstall Antiques
366 Kirkstall Rd. (S.R. and A Gibson) Est: 1973. Open 10.30-3. CL: Tues. and Wed. SIZE: Medium. *STOCK: Stripped and painted pine, shipping goods, £5-£500; general small items, £1-£100.* LOC: A65. PARK: Easy. TEL: 0532 757367. VAT: Stan/Spec.

M.D. Antiques
68a Lowtown, Pudsey. (M Drayton) *STOCK: Furniture, 18th-19th C.* TEL: 0532 557544.

Memorabilia
Booths Yard, Pudsey. (G Tomlinson) Est: 1986. Open 9.30-5, Mon., Wed. and Sun. by appointment. SIZE: Medium. *STOCK: General antiques, ephemera, bric-a-brac, historical artefacts, £5-£500; Victorian prints, engravings and old photographs, £10-£200.* LOC: Between Leeds and Bradford. PARK: Easy. TEL: 0532 563653. SER: Valuations; restorations; buys at auction.

Oakwood Gallery
613 Roundhay Rd, Oakwood. Open 9-6. *STOCK: Fine paintings and prints.* PARK: Easy. TEL: 0532 401348. SER: Framing; restorations; conservation.

Leeds continued

Originals
193 Meanwood Rd. Open Thurs.-Sat. 10-3, other times by appointment. *STOCK: Fireplaces; spare parts for Victorian fireplaces.* TEL: 0532 431613.

Parker Gallery
450 Roundhay Rd, Oakwood. Open Fri. and Sat., or by appointment. *STOCK: Oils, 19th to early 20th C, £200-£10,000.* TEL: 0532 350384; home - 0532 657123.

The Piano Shop
39 Holbeck Lane. (M Besbrode and B Seals) Open 9-5. *STOCK: Pianos.* TEL: 0532 443685. SER: Restorations; French polishing; hire.

Roses the Jewellers
107-108 Briggate. (J Crowther) Open 9-5.30. *STOCK: Victorian, antique and secondhand gold, silver, jewellery and diamonds.* TEL: 0532 439767.

Bryan Smith
26-28 Chapeltown, Pudsey. Open 10-5.30. CL: Sat. *STOCK: Furniture, porcelain, pottery, oils and watercolours, glass and collectable items.* PARK: Easy. TEL: 0532 555815; mobile - 0860 393260.

Leeds continued

Thirkill Antiques
Springfield CottageWest End Lane, Horsforth. Est: 1963. *STOCK: Paintings, smalls, musical.* LOC: 10 mins. south of Leeds and Bradford Airport. TEL: 0532 589160.

Waterloo Antiques Centre
Waterloo House, Crown St. Open 10-5. CL: Mon. SIZE: 45 dealers. *STOCK: General antiques.* LOC: Back of Corn Exchange. TEL: 0532 444187.

Windsor House Antiques (Leeds) Ltd. LAPADA
18-20 Benson St. (D.K Smith) Est: 1959. Open 9-5. CL: Sat. SIZE: Large. *STOCK: English furniture, 18th-19th C; paintings, objects.* PARK: Easy. TEL: 0532 444666; fax - 0532 426394. VAT: Stan/Spec.

Year Dot
15 Market St. Arcade. (P Davis) Open 9.30-5. *STOCK: Oriental pottery and porcelain, paintings, clocks, barometers, glass, copper, brass, bric-a-brac, jewellery, watches.* TEL: 0532 460860.

LEPTON, Nr. Huddersfield

K.L.M. & Co. Antiques
The Antique Shop, Wakefield Rd. (K.L. & J Millington) Est: 1980. Open 10.30-5, other times by appointment. SIZE: Large and warehouse. *STOCK: Furniture, including stripped pine, to 1930s, £25-£1,000; pianos.* LOC: A642 Wakefield road from Huddersfield, shop opposite village church. PARK: Easy and at rear. TEL: 0484 607763; home - 0484 607548. SER: Valuations. VAT: Stan.

MENSTON

Antiques
101 Bradford Rd. (W. and J Hanlon) Est: 1974. *STOCK: Handworked linen, textiles, pottery, porcelain, art nouveau, art deco, silver, plate, jewellery, small furniture, collectors items, barometers.* PARK: Forecourt. TEL: 0943 677634; home - 0943 463693.

Park Antiques
2 North View, Main St. (P. and J Roe) Resident. Est: 1975. Open 10-6.30, Sat. 10-6. CL: Mon. SIZE: Medium. *STOCK: Furniture, Georgian to Edwardian, £75-£2,500; glass and porcelain, 1850-1900; metal ware and decorative items, 1800-1900; all £50-£500; clocks, 1800-1900, £200-£1,500.* Not Stocked: Pine, silver. LOC: Opposite the park. PARK: Easy. TEL: 0943 872392. VAT: Stan/Spec.

MIRFIELD

David Brooke Antiques
9A Pratt Lane. Est: 1980. Open by appointment. SIZE: Small. *STOCK: Royal commemoratives,*

David Brooke Antiques continued

silver plate, 18th-19th C, furniture, general antiques, £5-£1,000. LOC: Off Lee Green. PARK: Easy. TEL: 0924 492483; home - same. SER: Valuations. FAIRS: Alexandra Palace; Shepton Mallet; Stafford.

OSSETT, Nr. Wakefield

Keith R Oldroyd Antiques
Est: 1979. Open by appointment. SIZE: Warehouse. *STOCK: Furniture, £5-£500; pottery and porcelain, clocks and mechanical music, 18th-20th C, £25-£500.* PARK: Easy. TEL: 0924 272163.

OTLEY, Nr. Leeds

Butterchurn Antiques
32-36 Bondgate. (G.M Dolan) Est: 1980. Open 9.30-3.30. SIZE: Small. *STOCK: Stripped pine furniture, general antiques.* TEL: 0943 462579. SER: Restorations (furniture); paint stripping.

H. and M Suttle
16 Market Pl. (D.M Allott and S.M Tankard) Est: 1887. Open 10-5. CL: Wed. *STOCK: China, silver, jewellery, coloured glass, furniture.* Not Stocked: Stamps, coins and postcards. TEL: 0943 462313. VAT: Stan/Spec.

Yap, Yap and Yap
7 Kirkgate Arcade. (C Wolfenden) Open 10-3, Fri. and Sat. 10-5. CL: Wed. *STOCK: General antiques especially linen.* TEL: 0943 467495.

SALTAIRE, Nr. Shipley

The Titus Gallery
1 Daisy Pl, Saltaire Rd. (C A Grice) Est: 1975. Open 10-5.30, Sun. 11-5.30 or by appointment. SIZE: Medium. *STOCK: Oil paintings and watercolours, 18th-20th C, £100-£35,000; occasional furniture, 18th-19th C, £400-£5,000; objets d'art, 18th-20th C, £50-£2,000.* LOC: Near roundabout, at junction of A650 and A657. PARK: Own. TEL: 0274 581894; home - same. SER: Valuations; restorations (oil paintings, watercolours and frames); buys at auction (as stock). VAT: Stan/Spec.

SHIPLEY

R Bell and Son
37 Briggate. TEL: 0274 582602.

Price Less Antiques
2 Gaisby Lane. (Mrs P Lee) Open 10-6. *STOCK: General antiques and jardinières.* TEL: 0274 581760.

SOWERBY BRIDGE, Nr. Halifax

Memory Lane
69 Wakefield Rd. (L Robinson) Open 9-5. SIZE: Warehouse and showroom. *STOCK: Pine and dolls.* TEL: 0422 833223.

Talking Point Antiques
66 West St. (P. and L Austwick) Open Mon., Thur., Fri., Sat. 10-5.30, other days by appointment. *STOCK: Restored gramophones and phonographs, 78rpm records and sheet music, related items; small furniture; pottery, porcelain and curios.* TEL: 0422 834126.

STEETON

Owls Antiques
1-3 Station Rd. (G.C Bradley) Open 10-7.30. CL: Tues. *STOCK: Furniture, general antiques, paintings and taxidermy.* TEL: 0535 652614.

TODMORDEN

Echoes
650a Halifax Rd, Eastwood. (P. and R Oldman) Est: 1980. CL: Tues. SIZE: Medium. *STOCK: Costume, textiles, linen and lace, £5-£500; jewellery, £5-£150; all 19th-20th C.* LOC: A646. PARK: Easy. TEL: 0706 817505; home - same. SER: Valuations; restorations (costume); buys at auction (as stock). VAT: Stan.

From an article on miniatures by Daphne Foskett published in the December 1990/ January 1991 issue of ***Antique Collecting.*** Daphne Foskett is the author of ***Miniatures: Dictionary and Guide*** published by the **Antique Collectors' Club** in 1987. £45.00.

Todmorden continued

Pennine Antiques
58 Burnley Rd. (K. and L Chapman and K Man) Open Sat. 10.30-6. *STOCK: Metalware, paintings, prints, porcelain and pottery, glass, treen, interesting and unusual items.* TEL: 0706 813773.

Todmorden Fine Art
27 Water St. (Mr Middleton and Mr Gunning) Est: 1981. Usually open but prior telephone call advisable. SIZE: Small. *STOCK: Oil paintings and watercolours, mainly 19th C, £50-£5,000.* LOC: Off M62, junction 20. PARK: Hall St. opposite. TEL: 0706 814723; home - same. SER: Valuations; restorations; framing. VAT: Spec.

WAKEFIELD

Robin Taylor Fine Arts
36 Carter St. Open 9.30-5.30. *STOCK: Oils and watercolours.* TEL: 0924 381809.

D.K Tuckwell
45 Regent St. Open 10-6 including Sun. *STOCK: General antiques.* PARK: Easy. TEL: 0924 377467.

WALSDEN, Nr. Todmorden

Cottage Antiques (1984) Ltd
788 Rochdale Rd. (G Slater) Resident. Est: 1978. Open daily, Tues. and Wed. by appointment. CL: Mon. SIZE: Medium. *STOCK: Pine furniture, kitchenalia, 19th C, £5-£1,000; general antiques.* PARK: Easy. TEL: 070 681 3612. SER: Restorations; pine stripping; import and export of continental pine.

WETHERBY

Mitchell-Hill Gallery
2 Church St. (D.G Mitchell-Hill) Open 9-1 and 2-5, Wed. 9-1. *STOCK: Oils, watercolours and pastels from early 1800.* TEL: 0937 585929.

Raymond Tomlinson (Antiques) Ltd. and Period Furniture Ltd. (Wetherby Antiques) LAPADA
Northfield Buildings, Northfield Pl. Est: 1971. Open 8-4.30, Sat. 9-12.30 or by appointment. SIZE: Large. *STOCK: Furniture, £5-£5,000; clocks, £10-£3,000.* LOC: A1 Wetherby roundabout, Wetherby exit, take 8th turning left, warehouse on left behind "Fields" joiners. PARK: Easy. TEL: 0937 584866/584870; fax - 0937 580204. SER: Export; restoration; container packing. VAT: Stan/Spec. *Trade Only.*

CHANNEL ISLANDS

Channel Islands are exempt from V.A.T.

Guernsey

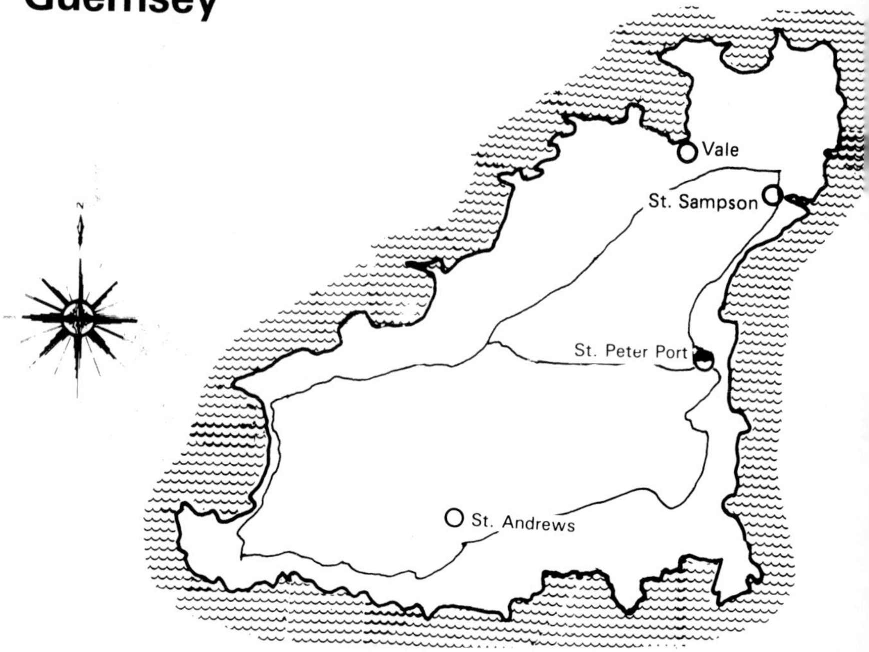
N
Vale
St. Sampson
St. Peter Port
St. Andrews

Jersey

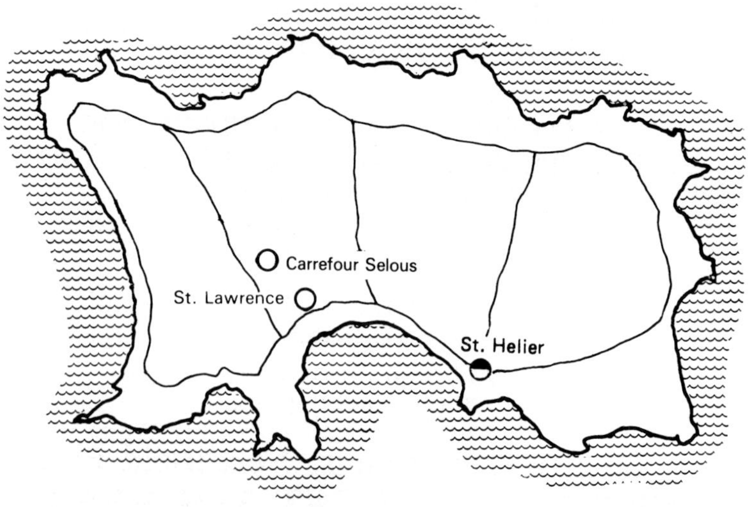
Carrefour Selous
St. Lawrence
St. Helier

Please note this is only a rough map designed to show dealers the number of shops in the various towns, and is not necessarily totally accurate.

○ 1–2
⊖ 3–5
◓ 6–12
● 13+

Key to number shops in this area

ALDERNEY

Victoria Antiques
"St. Catherine's", Victoria St. (P.A Nightingale) Open 10-12.30 and 2.30-4.30. *STOCK: Period and Victorian furniture, glass, silver, china, jewellery, small objets d'art.* TEL: 048 182 3260. SER: Valuations (furniture and silver).

GUERNSEY

ST. ANDREWS

Alexander Antiques
Open by appointment. *STOCK: Fine English furniture, 17th-19th C; mahogany sideboards, long sets of chairs, bureaux, secretaire and breakfront bookcases, partners desks, tea, card and dining tables, linen presses, longcase clocks, settees, armchairs; oak dressers, gateleg and refectory tables, ladder and spindle back rush-seated chairs; decorative and small items.* TEL: Mobile - 0860 741043.

ST. PETER PORT

Mark Blower Antiques
3 Tower Hill. Est: 1978. Appointment advisable. SIZE: Small. *STOCK: English furniture, 18th C, £1,000-£10,000; decorative furnishings, 19th C, to £1,000.* LOC: Off Bordage St. PARK: Nearby. TEL: 0481 25638 and 0860 741472. SER: Valuations; restorations (furniture); buys at auction (furniture).

Channel Islands Galleries Ltd
Trinity Sq. Centre, Trinity Sq. (G.P. and Mrs C Gavey) Est: 1967. Open 10-12.30 and 2-5, or by appointment. CL: Thurs. p.m.. *STOCK: Antique maps, sea charts and prints of the Channel Islands; oil paintings, watercolours, Channel Islands' books, illustrated, historical, social, geographical and natural history.* Not Stocked: General antiques. TEL: 0481 23247; home - 0481 47337.

Grange Antiques
7/8 The Grange. (Mrs K.M Carré) Est: 1968. Open 9.30-5. CL: Sat. p.m., Thurs. and Sun., except by appointment. SIZE: Medium. *STOCK: Objets d'art, and small furniture, 18th-19th C, £25-£1,000; pottery and porcelain, 18th C to art deco, £5-£500; jewellery, antique and secondhand, £1-£500; linens, silver and plate.* LOC: One of main roads from harbour going inland, shop opposite the Elizabeth College. PARK: 50yds. on right. TEL: 0481 721480. SER: Valuations; buys at auction.

The Pine Collection
17 Mansell St. (P Head) Est: 1986. Open 9.30-5.30. *STOCK: Pine.* TEL: 0481 26891.

David Proctor Antiques
12 Mansell St. Est: 1973. Open 10-1 and 2-5. CL: Thurs. p.m. SIZE: Small. *STOCK: Period,*

David Proctor Antiques continued

Victorian and Edwardian furniture, clocks, nautical items, oils, watercolours, silver and plate, items of local interest. PARK: Nearby. TEL: 0481 726808; home - 0481 46025.

St. James's Gallery Ltd
18-20 The Bordage. (AP.H. and C.O Whittam) Est: 1945. CL: Thurs. p.m. and lunch times. SIZE: Large. *STOCK: Furniture, £100-£20,000; porcelain, both 18th-19th C; paintings, 18th-20th C.* TEL: 0481 720070; home - 0481 723999. SER: Valuations; restorations (furniture, upholstery, pictures, framing); buys at auction.

Thesaurus
15 Tudor House, Mill St./Bordage. *STOCK: Antiquarian and out of print books, maps and prints.* LOC: Town centre. TEL: 0481 720217.

ST. SAMPSON

The Old Curiosity Shop
Commercial Rd. Est: 1978. CL: Mon. and Thurs. *STOCK: Old books, prints, postcards, ephemera, paintings, small furniture, china, glass, silver, brass, £1-£5,000.* TEL: 0481 45324.

VALE

Anne Drury Antiques
Rue de Passeur, L'Ancresse. Est: 1960. Open 10-12 and 2-4, Mon., Tues., Thurs. by appointment. SIZE: Medium. *STOCK: Furniture, 18th C to 1920, £50-£6,000; porcelain, 17th C to 1920, £10-£2,000; silver and jewellery, 18th C to 1920, £10-£4,000.* LOC: Off main L'Ancresse Rd. by Copperfields Restaurant. PARK: Easy. TEL: 0481 48386; home - 0481 47814. SER: Valuations; buys at auction. FAIRS: Local and London.

Geoffrey P Gavey
Les Clospains, Rue de L'Ecole. Est: 1967. Open by appointment. *STOCK: Maps, sea charts and prints of the Channel Islands; oil and watercolour paintings; Channel Islands books, illustrated, historical, social, geographic and natural history.* Not Stocked: General antiques. TEL: 0481 47337.

A Steiff felt covered golly, German, c.1913. 23in. high, which sold for £2,090 on 9th May 1991 at Sotheby's. From an article on dolls by Bunny Campione published in the July/August 1991 issue of **Antique Collecting.**

JERSEY

CARREFOUR SELOUS, ST. LAWRENCE

David Hick Antiques
Alexandra House. Est: 1977. Open 9.30-5. CL: Mon. SIZE: Large and warehouse. *STOCK: Furniture and small items.* TEL: 0534 65965; fax - 0534 65448.

ST. HELIER

John Blench & Son
50 Don St. *STOCK: Fine bindings, local maps and prints.* TEL: 0534 25281.

John Cooper Antiques
16 The Market. *STOCK: General antiques.* TEL: 0534 23600.

Grange Gallery and Fine Arts Ltd
39 New St. (G.J Morris) Est: 1974. Open 9-5.30. CL: Sun., Tues. and Thurs. except by appointment. SIZE: Medium. *STOCK: Oil paintings, 18th and 19th C, local prints, 19th C, £100-£9,000.* LOC: Antique area of St. Helier. PARK: Multi-storey 100yds. TEL: 0534 20077. SER: Valuations; restorations (pictures); buys at auction; framing.

John Rae Antiques
Savile St. Est: 1947. Open daily. *STOCK: General antiques, furniture, pictures, pine, clocks.* TEL: 0534 32171/58071.

Lance and Marcus Rae Antiques
Savile St. Open daily. SIZE: Large. *STOCK: General antiques, furniture, pictures, clocks, silver.* TEL: 0534 32171.

Sheila Rae Antiques
Clare St. Open mornings only. *STOCK: China, glass, pictures, silver, fabrics, small furniture.* TEL: 0534 58071/32171.

St. Helier Galleries Ltd BADA
9 James St (J.H Appleby) Est: 1953. Open 8.30-5.30. CL: Sat. *STOCK: Paintings, 17th-20th C, all schools; early English watercolours, continental and colonial drawings,*

St. Helier Galleries Ltd continued

***from £400+; Channel Island and modern limited edition prints.* LOC: By Minden Place car park. TEL: 0534 67048. SER: Valuations; restorations.**

The Selective Eye Gallery
50 Don St. (J. and P Blench) Est: 1958. Open 9-5. CL: Thurs. and Sat. p.m. SIZE: Medium. *STOCK: Oil paintings, 19th-20th C; maps, prints and antiquarian books, 16th-18th C.* Not Stocked: General antiques. LOC: Town centre. PARK: Multi-storey 100yds. TEL: 0534 25281. SER: Valuations; restorations (pictures). FAIRS: Jersey.

Shepherds Antiques
76 Val Plaisant. (J Shepherd) Est: 1967. Open 11-5, Sat. 9-5. *STOCK: General antiques.* TEL: 0534 22713.

Thesaurus (Jersey) Ltd
3 Burrard St. (I Creaton) Est: 1973. Open 8.30-6. SIZE: Large. *STOCK: Antiquarian and out of print books, £1-£2,000; maps and prints.* Not Stocked: General antiques. LOC: Town centre. PARK: 100yds. TEL: 0534 37045. SER: Buys at auction. VAT: Spec.

Joan Thomson Antiques
39 Don St. Est: 1967. Open 10-5. SIZE: Medium. *STOCK: Furniture, £200-£3,000; smalls, £10-£500; linen and lace, from £10.* PARK: Nearby. TEL: 0534 80603. SER: Valuations; buys at auction.

Union Street Antique Market
8 Union St. (A.L Thomson) Est: 1965. Open 10-5. SIZE: Large - several dealers. *STOCK: General antiques.* PARK: 150yds. TEL: 0534 73805; home - 0534 22475. SER: Buys at auction.

ST. LAWRENCE

I.G.A. Old Masters Ltd
5 Kimberley Grove, Rue de Haut. (I.G. and Mrs C.B.V Appleby) Est: 1953. Open by appointment. *STOCK: Old Master and 19th C paintings.* LOC: Near glass church. PARK: Easy. TEL: 0534 24226; home - same.

NORTHERN IRELAND

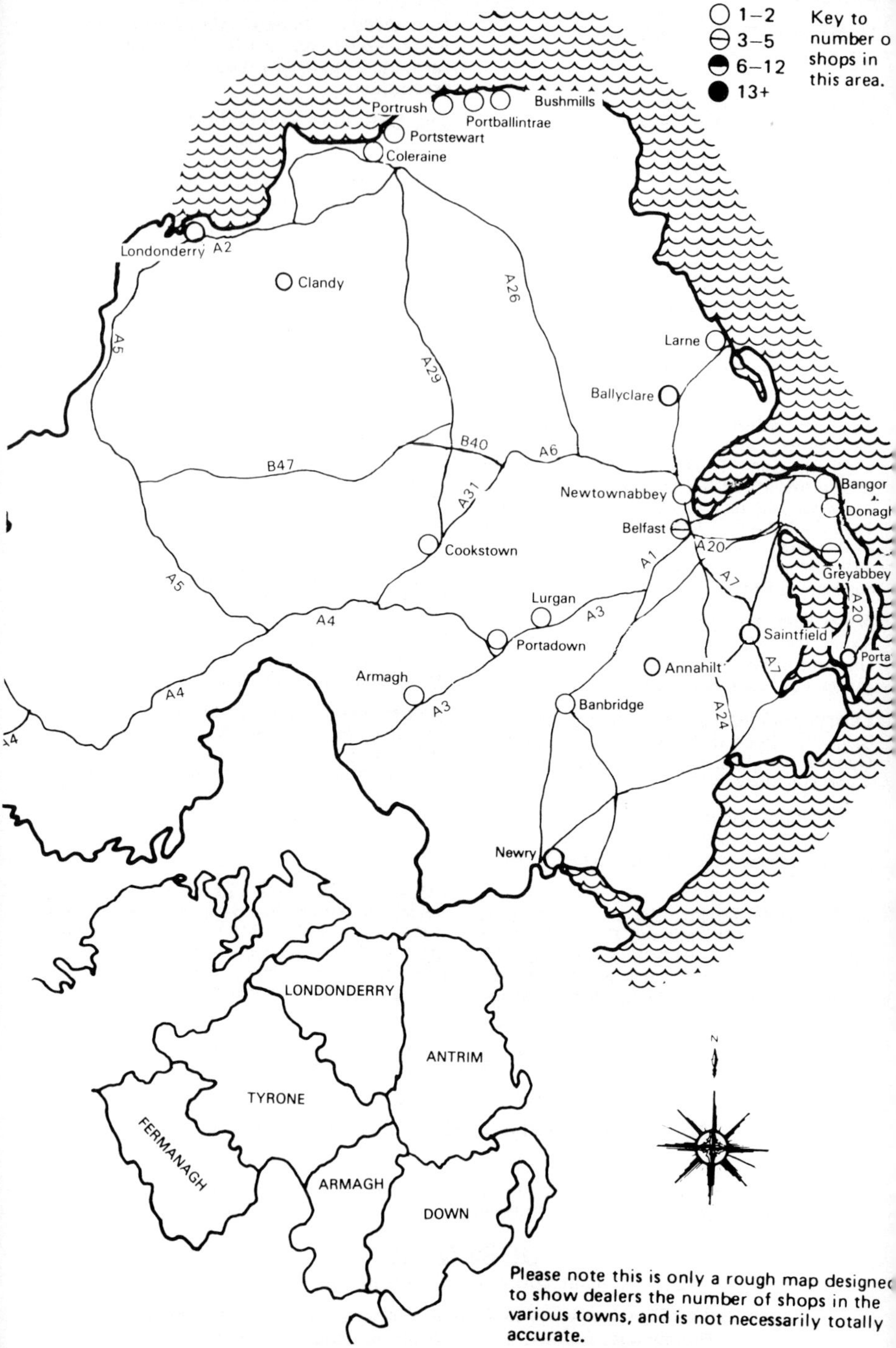
1–2
3–5
6–12
13+
Key to number o
shops in
this area.
Portrush
Portballintrae
Bushmills
Portstewart
Coleraine
Londonderry
A2
Clandy
A26
A5
A29
Larne
Ballyclare
B40
A6
B47
A31
Newtownabbey
Bangor
Donagh
Belfast
A20
Cookstown
A1
A7
Greyabbey
A5
Lurgan
A3
A20
A4
Saintfield
Portadown
Porta
Annahilt
A7
Armagh
Banbridge
A4
A3
A24
Newry
LONDONDERRY
ANTRIM
TYRONE
FERMANAGH
ARMAGH
DOWN
N

Please note this is only a rough map designed to show dealers the number of shops in the various towns, and is not necessarily totally accurate.

BELFAST

The Bell Gallery
13 Adelaide Park. (J.N Bell) Est: 1964. Open 10-6. SIZE: Medium. *STOCK: British and Irish art, 19th-20th C.* LOC: Off Malone Rd. TEL: 0232 662998. SER: Valuations; restorations (paintings); buys at auction. VAT: Stan/Spec.

Emerald Isle Books
539 Antrim Rd. Est: 1966. Open by appointment. *STOCK: Travel, Ireland, theology.* TEL: 0232 370798. SER: Catalogues available.

T.H Kearney & Sons
123 University St. Resident. *STOCK: Small antiques.* TEL: 0232 231055. SER: Restorations and upholstery. VAT: Stan.

Charlotte and John Lambe
41 Shore Rd. Open 10-5. CL: Sat. *STOCK: English and French furniture, 19th C; pictures and works of art.* TEL: 0232 370761.

Sinclair's Antique Gallery
19 Arthur St. Est: 1900. Open 9-5.30. CL: Sat. SIZE: Small. *STOCK: Victorian jewellery, china, glass, £10-£1,000; silver, coins.* LOC: 100yds. from city centre. TEL: 0232 322335. VAT: Stan.

County Antrim

BALLYCLARE

Antique Shop
64a Main St. (T Heaney) Est: 1971. Open 10-5. *STOCK: 18th-19th C, furniture and clocks, £20-£1,000; pottery, glass.* TEL: 096 03 52550. SER: Restorations (clocks and furniture). VAT: Spec.

BUSHMILLS

Dunluce Antiques
33 Ballytober Rd. (Mrs C Ross) Est: 1978. Open 2-8, or by appointment. SIZE: Small. *STOCK: Furniture, £50-£1,000; porcelain and glass, £1-£1,000; silver, £5-£500; all Georgian to Edwardian; paintings, mainly Irish, £50-£10,000.* LOC: 1 1/2 miles off Antrim coast rd. at Dunluce Castle. PARK: Easy. TEL: 026 57 31140. SER: Restorations (porcelain).

LARNE

Albert Graham Ltd
89/91 Main St. (A. and A Graham) Est: 1960. Open 9.30-5.30 or by appointment. CL: Tues. SIZE: Large + large warehouse. *STOCK: Furniture, clocks, 18th-20th C, £25-£3,000.* LOC: Beside Agnew St. car park. TEL: 0574 76655/73134. VAT: Stan/Spec.

NEWTOWNABBEY

New Abbey Antiques
Caragh Lodge, Glen Rd., Jordanstown. (A MacHenry) IADA. Est: 1964. Open 9.30-5.30 or by appointment. SIZE: Medium. *STOCK: General antiques, mostly furniture.* LOC: 6 miles from Belfast to Whiteabbey village, fork left at traffic lights on dual carriageway; turn left into Old Manse Rd. and continue into Glen Rd. PARK: Easy. TEL: 0232 862036. SER: Valuations. FAIRS: Dublin, Belfast and Irish. VAT: Stan/Spec.

PORTBALLINTRAE, Nr. Bushmills

Brian R Bolt, Collectors Antiques
88 Ballaghmore. Business by post or appointment only. *STOCK: Small and unusual silver, objects of vertu, snuff boxes, table silver, vesta cases, Scottish and Irish provincial silver, treen, tortoiseshell, bon-bon dishes, cruets.* TEL: 026 57 31129. SER: Search; catalogue and glass list available.

PORTRUSH

Alexander Antiques
108 Dunluce Rd. (R. and Mrs M., and D Alexander) Est: 1974. Open 10-6. CL: Sun. except by appointment. SIZE: Large. *STOCK: Furniture including pine, silver, porcelain, fine art, 18th-20th C; oils and watercolours, 19th-20th C.* Not Stocked: Militaria, jewellery, coins. LOC: 1 mile from Portrush on A2 to Bushmills. PARK: Easy. TEL: 0265 822783. SER: Valuations; buys at auction. VAT: Stan/Spec.

Seaview Antiques
16 Ballyreagh Rd. (Mrs W Macafee) Est: 1981. Open 2-5.30, Sat. 11-6; July and Aug. 11-6. CL: Sun. except by appointment. *STOCK: Furniture, jewellery, silver, linen and porcelain, 19th-20th C.* Not Stocked: Militaria and coins. LOC: 1 mile from Portrush on coast road to Portstewart. PARK: Easy. TEL: 0265 824944; home - 0265 52153.

County Armagh

ARMAGH

The Hole-in-the-Wall
Market St. (I Emerson) Est: 1953. *STOCK: General antiques.* LOC: City centre. VAT: Stan/Spec.

LURGAN

Charles Gardiner Antiques
48 High St. Est: 1968. Open 9-1 and 2-6. CL: Wed. *STOCK: Clocks, furniture and general antiques.* PARK: Own. TEL: 0762 323934.

PORTADOWN

Moyallon Antiques
54 Moyallon Rd. Est: 1975. Usually open. SIZE: Medium. *STOCK: Furniture, 19th C, £50-£500; pine and country furniture, 18th-19th C, £50-£250; ceramics and bric-a-brac, £5-£100.* LOC: Portadown - Gilford Rd., 1 mile from Gilford on right-hand side. PARK: Easy. TEL: 0762 831615.

County Down

ANNAHILT

Period Architectural Features and Antiques
263 Ballynahich Rd. (J Cousans) Open 9.30-5.30. SIZE: Large. *STOCK: Marble chimney pieces, early 18th to late 19th C, £5-£1,000; period panelling and pine pews, stained glass, Victorian bathrooms, decorative architectural items.* TEL: 0846 638091. SER: Valuations; restorations (marble); pine stripping; French polishing; buys at auction. VAT: Stan.

BANBRIDGE

Cameo Antiques
41 Bridge St. (D. and J Bell) Est: 1966. TEL: 082 06 23241.

BANGOR

Phyllis Arnold Studio Gallery
24 Dufferin Ave. Est: 1968. Open Wed. and Fri. 10-1.30, Sat. 11-5 and by appointment. *STOCK: Decorative antiques especially maps and prints of Ireland; 19th and 20th C watercolours.* TEL: 0247 469899; home - 0247 853322. SER: Restorations (maps, prints, watercolours); hand colouring; framing. FAIRS: Culloden. VAT: Stan/Spec.

DONAGHADEE

Furney Antiques
4 Shore St. (B. and I Furney) Est: 1976. Open Wed., and Thurs. 2-5.30, Fri. and Sat. 11-5.30 or by appointment. *STOCK: Georgian, Regency and early Victorian furniture; Victorian china, silver.* TEL: 0247 883517.

GREYABBEY, Nr. Newtownards

The Antique Shop
9 Main St. (M McAuley) Est: 1968. *STOCK: General antiques.* TEL: Home - 02477 38333.

B B Antiques
Hoops Courtyard, 5-7 Main St. (B Beasant) Est: 1989. Open Wed., Fri. and Sat. 11-5. SIZE: Small. *STOCK: Furniture, mahogany, 19th C, £300-£500; linen and lace, 19th C to early 20th C, £30-£80.* PARK: Easy. TEL: Home - 0232 654145. FAIRS: Templeton Hotel (Spring) and Culloden Hotel (Autumn). VAT: Stan.

B B Antiques continued

Greyabbey Timecraft Ltd
18 Main St. Est: 1976. Open 11-5.30. CL: Sun. and Thurs., except by appointment. SIZE: Small. *STOCK: Clocks and watches, 19th C, £100-£2,000; jewellery, 19th-20th C, £10-£500.* LOC: Opposite G.P.O. PARK: Easy. TEL: 024 774 416; home - 024 774 252. SER: Valuations; restorations; buys at auction (clocks and watches).

Old Cross Antiques
3-5 Main St. (C.J Auld) Est: 1966. Open 11.30-5.30, other times by appointment. CL: Mon. and Thurs. SIZE: Medium. *STOCK: Silver, 1750-1920, £25-£800; porcelain and Staffordshire, 1800-1920, £5-£500; small furniture, 1800-1920, £10-£1,500; unusual and interesting bric-a-brac.* Not Stocked: Books, stamps, coins, medals. LOC: Village centre. PARK: Easy. TEL: 024 774 346; home -same.

NEWRY

Downshire House Antiques
62 Downshire Rd. (H. and R McCabe) Open 9-6. *STOCK: General antiques including furniture and porcelain, 18th-19th C, £50-£1,000.* TEL: 0693 66689; home - 0693 5178. SER: Valuations; restorations (furniture). FAIRS: Conway Hotel, Lisburn; Drumkeen Hotel, Belfast. VAT: Stan.

McCabes Antique Galleries
11-12 St. Mary's St. (H. and R McCabe) Est: 1910. Open 9.30-1 and 2-5.30, Wed., Sun. and evenings by appointment. SIZE: Large and warehouse. *STOCK: General antiques including furniture and porcelain, 18th-19th C, £50-£10,000.* PARK: Own. TEL: 0693 62695/66689/69199; home - 0693 5178. SER: Valuations; restorations (furniture). FAIRS: Conway Hotel, Lisburn; Drumkeen Hotel, Belfast. VAT: Stan.

PORTAFERRY

Rock Angus Antiques
2 Ferry St. (D Dunlop) Open Wed., Fri., Sat. (and Sun. Easter-Sept.) 12-5.30 or by appointment. SIZE: Small. *STOCK: Clocks, £50-£2,000; furniture, 18th-19th C, £50-£2,500; Irish paintings, 19th-20th C, £50-£2,000; nautical memorabilia, £50-£500.* LOC: A20 from Newtownards through Greyabbey. PARK: Easy. TEL: 02477 28935; home - same. SER: Valuations; restorations (clocks); buys at auction (clocks).

SAINTFIELD

Albert Forsythe
66 Carstown Rd. Resident. Usually open. *STOCK: Irish, French provincial and country pine furniture, 18th-19th C.* TEL: 0238 510398. SER: Container; courier.

County Londonderry

CLAUDY

K.O Hagan
'Bensara'162 Foreglen Rd. *STOCK: Georgian, Victorian and Edwardian furniture, especially pine.* TEL: 0504 338506.

COLERAINE

The Forge Antiques
24 Long Commons. (M.W Walker) Est: 1977. Open 10-5.30. CL: Thurs. *STOCK: General antiques, silver, clocks, jewellery, porcelain, paintings.* TEL: 0265 51339. VAT: Stan.

LONDONDERRY

Richmond Antiques
Richmond Centre and Lisnagelvin Shopping Centre. (A Fullam) Open 9-5.30, Thurs. and Fri. 9-9, Lisnagelvin - Wed. 9-9, Sat. 9-6. *STOCK: Georgian and Victorian jewellery, furniture, linen, books, silver, china.* TEL: 0504 260562/48206; home - 0504 52140.

PORTSTEWART

The Forge Antiques
Cappagh, 182 Coleraine Rd. (Mrs M.W Walker) Est: 1967. Open 2-6. SIZE: Large. *STOCK: Jewellery, 19th-20th C, £5-£4,000; furniture, silver, porcelain, Belleek, bric-a-brac.* LOC: Main road between Coleraine and Portstewart. PARK: Easy. TEL: 026 583 2209; home - 0265 42438. VAT: Stan.

County Tyrone

COOKSTOWN

Cookstown Antiques
46 James St. (T.H Jebb) Est: 1976. Open 9-5.30. SIZE: Small. *STOCK: Jewellery, silver, £10-£1,000; coins, £5-£100; pictures, ceramics and militaria, £5-£500; general antiques, all 19th and 20th C.* Not Stocked: Large furniture. LOC: Opposite Post Office, in town centre. PARK: Easy. TEL: 064 87 65279; home - 064 87 62926. SER: Valuations; buys at auction. FAIRS: All Northern Ireland.

The Saddle Room Antiques
4 Coagh St. (C.J Leitch) Est: 1968. Open 10-6. CL: Mon. and Wed. *STOCK: China, silver, furniture, glass, jewellery.* TEL: 064 87 62033.

SCOTLAND NORTH

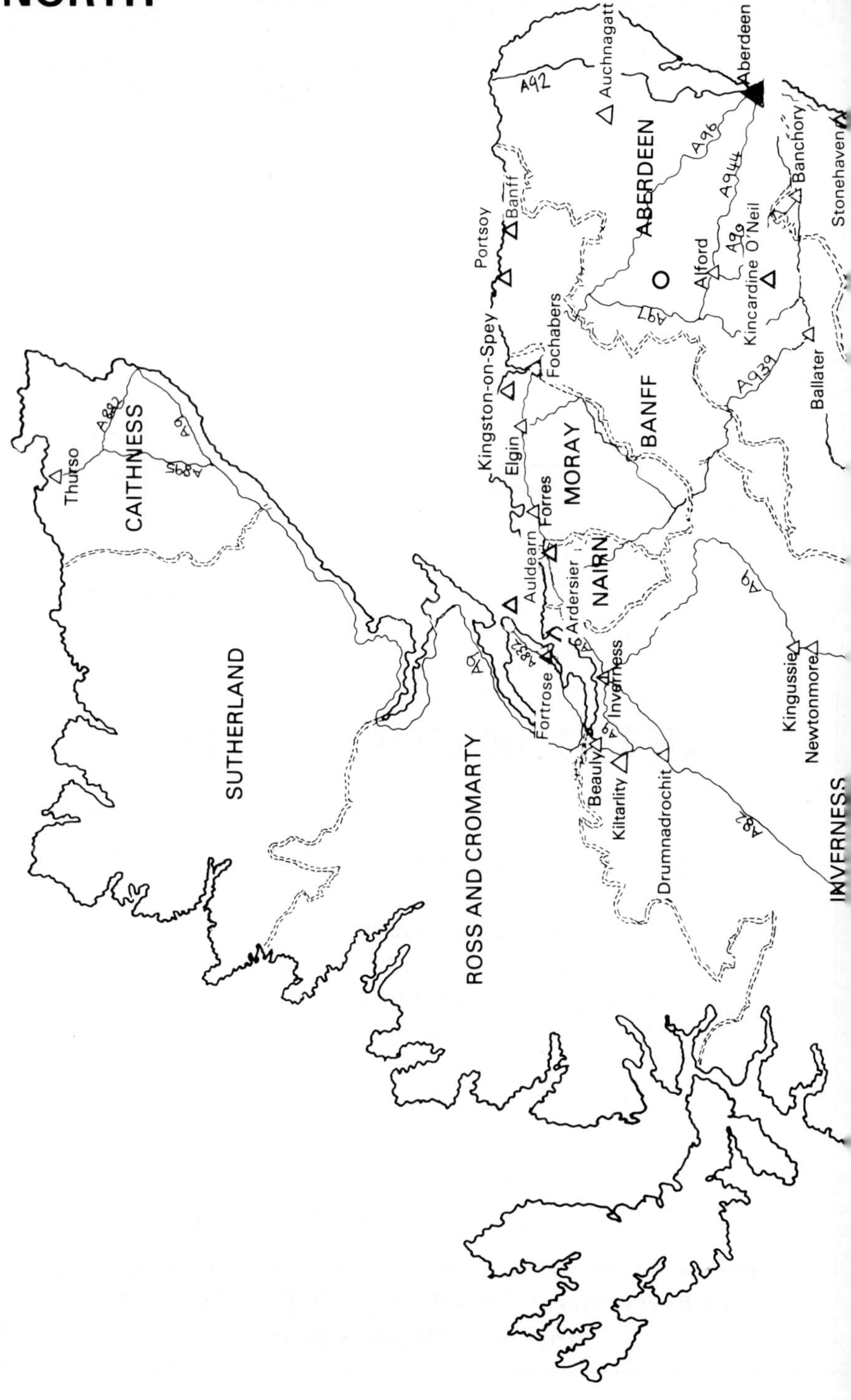
CAITHNESS
Thurso
A882
A9
A895
SUTHERLAND
ROSS AND CROMARTY
A9
A832
Fortrose
Inverness
Beauly
Kiltarlity
Drumnadrochit
A82
INVERNESS
Ardersier
Auldearn
NAIRN
Forres
MORAY
Elgin
Kingston-on-Spey
Fochabers
Portsoy
Banff
BANFF
A9
Kingussie
Newtonmore
ABERDEEN
Auchnagatt
A92
Aberdeen
A96
A944
A97
Alford
A99
Kincardine O'Neil
A939
Ballater
Banchory
Stonehaven

SCOTLAND

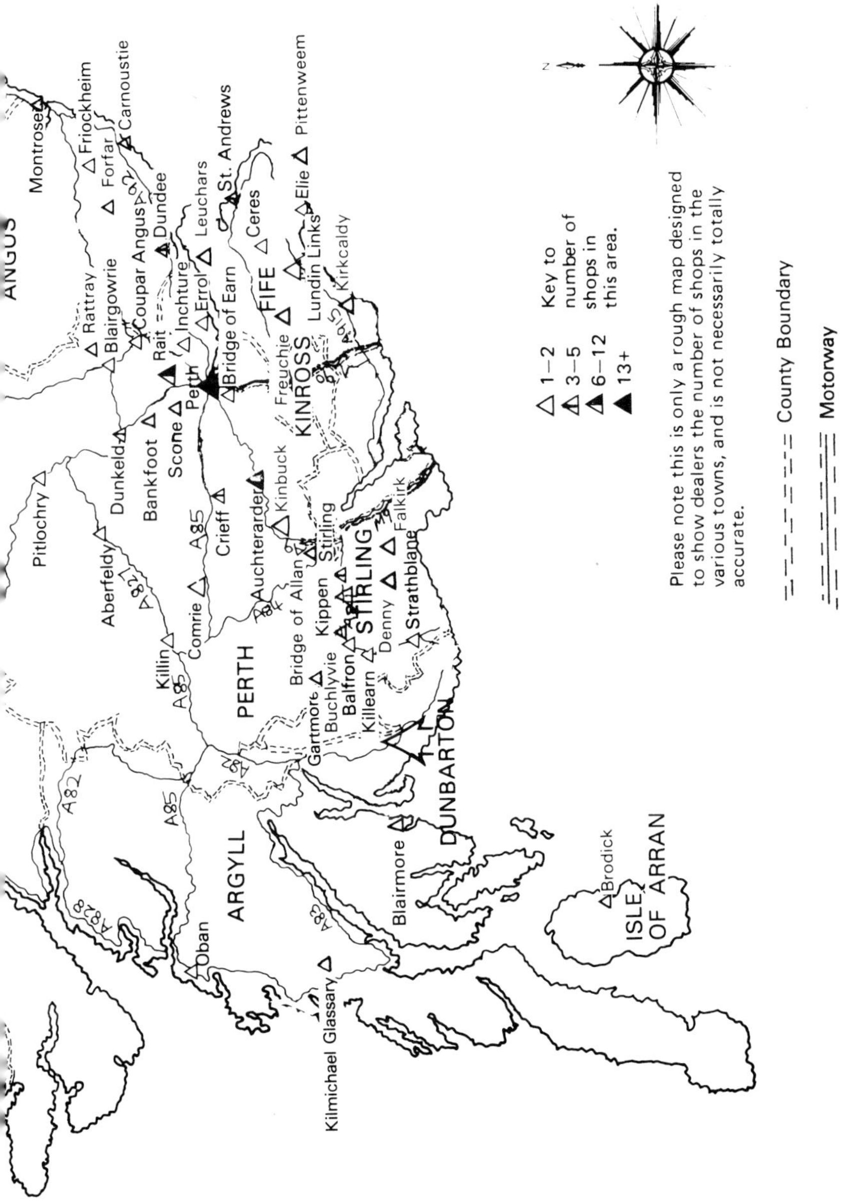
ANGUS
Montrose
Friockheim
Carnoustie
Forfar
Dundee
Rattray
Blairgowrie
Coupar Angus
Leuchars
St. Andrews
Pittenweem
Elie
Ceres
Inchture
Errol
Rait
Perth
Bridge of Earn
FIFE
Lundin Links
Kirkcaldy
Freuchie
KINROSS
Pitlochry
Dunkeld
Bankfoot
Scone
Aberfeldy
Crieff
Auchterarder
Kinbuck
Stirling
Falkirk
Comrie
Killin
Bridge of Allan
Kippen
STIRLING
Denny
Strathblane
PERTH
Buchlyvie
Balfron
Killearn
Gartmore
DUNBARTON
ARGYLL
Oban
Blairmore
Kilmichael Glassary
Brodick
ISLE OF ARRAN
A85
A82
A828
A83
A822
A9
A92
A91
M9
A84
A915
Key to number of shops in this area.
1–2
3–5
6–12
13+
Please note this is only a rough map designed to show dealers the number of shops in the various towns, and is not necessarily totally accurate.
County Boundary
Motorway

SCOTLAND SOUTH

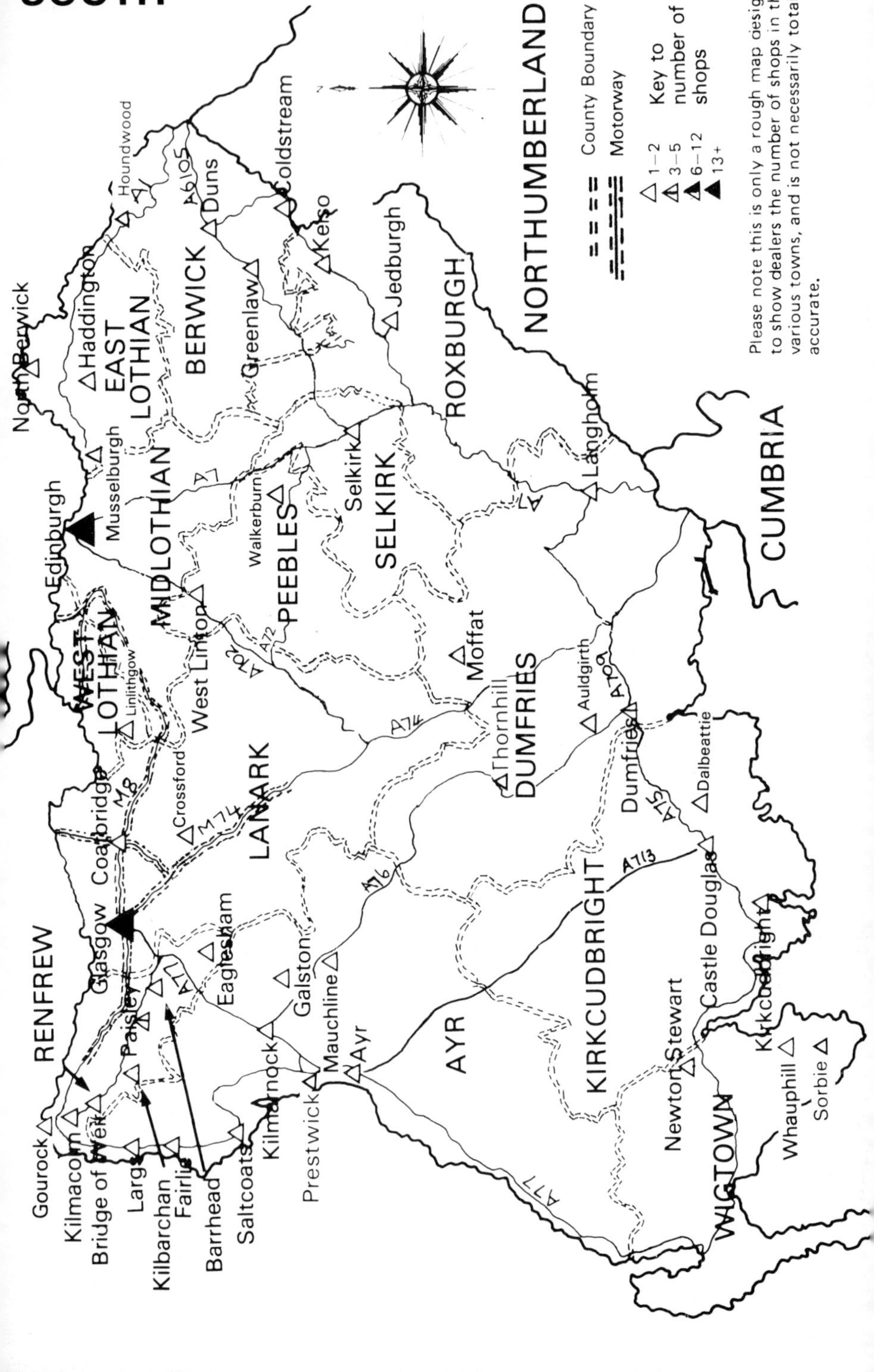
RENFREW
WEST LOTHIAN
MIDLOTHIAN
EAST LOTHIAN
BERWICK
PEEBLES
SELKIRK
ROXBURGH
NORTHUMBERLAND
CUMBRIA
LANARK
DUMFRIES
AYR
KIRKCUDBRIGHT
WIGTOWN
North Berwick
Haddington
Houndwood
Duns
Coldstream
Kelso
Greenlaw
Jedburgh
Musselburgh
Edinburgh
Walkerburn
Selkirk
Langholm
Linlithgow
West Linton
Moffat
Auldgirth
Thornhill
Dumfries
Dalbeattie
Crossford
Coatbridge
Glasgow
Eaglesham
Galston
Mauchline
Castle Douglas
Kirkcudbright
Newton Stewart
Whauphill
Sorbie
Paisley
Kilmarnock
Ayr
Prestwick
Saltcoats
Barrhead
Fairlie
Kilbarchan
Largs
Bridge of Weir
Kilmacolm
Gourock
A1
A6105
A7
A72
A702
A74
A76
A77
A709
A75
A713
M8
M74
County Boundary
Motorway
1–2
3–5
6–12
13+
Key to number of shops
Please note this is only a rough map designed to show dealers the number of shops in the various towns, and is not necessarily totally accurate.

SCOTTISH COUNTY BOUNDARIES

CAITHNESS
SUTHERLAND
ROSS AND CROMARTY
SKYE
NAIRN
MORAY
BANFF
ABERDEEN
INVERNESS
KINCARDINE
ANGUS
ARGYLL
PERTH
DUNBARTON
KINROSS
FIFE
STIRLING
RENFREW
W. LOTHIAN
MIDLOTHIAN
EAST LOTHIAN
ARRAN
LANARK
BERWICK
PEEBLES
AYR
SELKIRK
ROXBURGH
DUMFRIES
WIGTOWN
KIRKCUDBRIGHT

ABERDEEN
(Aberdeenshire)

Atholl Antiques
322 Great Western Rd. Open 10.30-1 and 2.30-6, or by appointment. *STOCK: Scottish paintings and furniture.* TEL: 0224 593547. VAT: Stan/Spec.

John Bell of Aberdeen Ltd
Balbrogie by Blackburn, Kinellar. Est: 1899. Open 9-5. CL: Sat. SIZE: Large. *STOCK: Furniture, 18th C.* LOC: On A96, 8 miles from city centre. TEL: 0224 790209. VAT: Stan/Spec.

James Benzie
651 George St. Est: 1953. Open 1-4. *STOCK: Small items, glass, china, pottery, copper, brass, silver, pictures.*

Gallery
41 Justice St. (J.H Wells) Est: 1981. Open 10.30-5.30, Sat. 10.30-4.30. SIZE: Large. *STOCK: Pre-1920 furniture; jewellery, post-1850; curios and Victoriana; paintings and prints, post-1800, from £25.* LOC: Between Castlegate and Beach Boulevard. PARK: Easy. TEL: 0224 625909. SER: Valuations; restorations and repairs (jewellery). VAT: Stan.

McCalls (Aberdeen)
11 Castle St. (B McCall) Est: 1948. PARK: Nearby. TEL: 0224 641916.

Aberdeen continued

McCalls Limited
11 Bridge St. Open 9.30-5.30, Thurs. 9.30-8. *STOCK: Jewellery.* TEL: 0224 584577.

The Rendezvous Gallery
100 Forest Ave. Est: 1973. Open 10-1.30 and 2.30-6. CL: Fri. SIZE: Medium. *STOCK: Art nouveau, art deco, glass, jewellery, bronzes, furniture, £100-£5,000; paintings, watercolours, Scottish School, £200-£5,000.* LOC: Just off Great Western Rd. to Braemar. PARK: Easy. TEL: 0224 323247. VAT: Stan/Spec.

Mr. Reynolds
162/164 Skene St. Resident. *STOCK: General antiques.*

Thistle Antiques **LAPADA**
28 Esslemont Ave. Est: 1967. TEL: 0224 634692. VAT: Spec.

Elizabeth Watt
69 Thistle St. Est: 1976. Open 10-1 and 2.30-5, Sat. 10-1. SIZE: Small. *STOCK: General antiques.* LOC: Off the west end of Union St. PARK: Nearby. TEL: 0224 647232. SER: Restorations (china, glass).

The Waverley Gallery
18 Victoria St. (G Wood) Open 9.30-6. *STOCK: Oil paintings and watercolours, £50-£6,000; prints, £20-£2,000; etchings, £40-£400; all 18th-20th C.* LOC: Corner of Waverley Pl. TEL: 0224 640633. SER: Valuations; restorations; framing.

Colin Wood (Antiques) Ltd
25 Rose St. Est: 1968. Open 10-12.30 and 2.15-5, Sat. 10-12 and 2.15-4. SIZE: Medium. *STOCK: Furniture, 17th-19th C; works of art, Scottish paintings and silver.* PARK: Multi-storey in Chapel St. TEL: 0224 643019; home - 0224 640640. VAT: Stan/Spec.

Wm Young (Antiques) Ltd **BADA**
1 Gaelic Lane, Belmont St. Est: 1887. Open 9.30-5.30, Sat. 10-4. *STOCK: Fine furniture, 17th-19th C; paintings and objets d'art.* TEL: 0224 644757.

ABERFELDY
(Perthshire)

Denis Young Antiques
Glenlyon. (D.E. and Mrs J.M Young) Est: 1979. Open by appointment only. *STOCK: Oriental porcelain, 1200-1800; English porcelain and pottery, 1750-1840; English glass, pre-1840; small items.* Not Stocked: Silver, jewellery. TEL: 08877 232. SER: Valuations.

ABERNYTE
(Perthshire)

Fine Antique Glass
Smithy Cottage. (S.D Hole) Open by appointment. SIZE: Small. *STOCK: Decanters and bowls, £40-£1,500; drinking glasses, £20-£1,000; candelabra and chandeliers, £200+; all 1750-1900.* LOC: A85 from Perth, then north on B953. Cottage has stone pillars and is opposite duck pond. TEL: 082886 350.

ALFORD
(Aberdeenshire)

R.S Gordon (Antiques)
Main St. (R. and J Gordon) Est: 1959. Open 9-5.30. *STOCK: General antiques; clocks, musical boxes, Victoriana, bric-a-brac.* LOC: Between Aberdeen and Huntly on the A944. TEL: 09755 62404. VAT: Stan/Spec.

ARDERSIER
(Inverness-shire)

Ardersier Antiques
Ardersier Cottage. (M. and H Galleitch) Est: 1979. Open 9-6, evenings by appointment. SIZE: Small. *STOCK: Paintings, £25-£1,000; toys and dolls, curios, £5-£100; all 19th C.* LOC: A96, near Fort George. PARK: Easy. TEL: 0667 62237; home - same. SER: Valuations; restorations (paintings and furniture stripping); buys at auction.

AUCHTERARDER
(Perthshire)

Antiques and Fine Art
14 Townhead. (Mrs S Drysdale) Open 10-1 and 2-5. CL: Wed. p.m. *STOCK: Furniture, paintings, silver, general antiques, French paperweights.* PARK: Easy. TEL: 0764 63035; home - 0764 2653. SER: Valuations. VAT: Spec.

Paul Hayes Gallery
71 High St. PADA. Est: 1962. Open 10-1 and 2-5 or by appointment. CL: Wed. *STOCK: Fine paintings, 18th-20th C, especially sporting, marine and Scottish post-impressionist.* TEL: 0764 62320/63442. VAT: Spec.

Susan Procter
47/51 The Feus. PADA. *STOCK: Interesting and unusual items for interior decoration; garden statuary, Staffordshire figures.* TEL: 0764 62532. VAT: Spec.

K Stanley and Son
Regal Buildings, Townhead. (Mr and Mrs Kasiewicz) Est: 1957. Open 10-1 and 2-5. SIZE: Large. *STOCK: Furniture, porcelain, bric-a-brac, shipping goods.* VAT: Stan.

Auchterarder continued

Times Past Antiques
Broadfold Farm. (J.M Brown) Est: 1970. Open 8-5, weekends by appointment. SIZE: Large. *STOCK: Stripped pine, 19th-20th C, from £50; shipping goods, £5-£500.* LOC: From town centre take Abbey Rd. to flyover A9 at T junction. Turn left, 1st farm on left. PARK: Easy. TEL: 0764 63166; home - same. SER: Restorations (pine); courier; container-packing. VAT: Stan.

John Whitelaw and Sons Antiques
120 High St. Open 9-5.30. *STOCK: General antiques; furniture, 17th-19th C.* PARK: Easy. TEL: 0764 62482. VAT: Stan/Spec.

AULDEARN, Nr. Nairn
(Nairnshire)

Auldearn Antiques
Dalmore Manse, Lethen Rd. Est: 1980. Open 10-6 including Sun. SIZE: Medium. *STOCK: Victorian linen and lace, kitchenalia, china, furniture, architectural items.* LOC: 1 mile from village. TEL: 0667 53087; home - same.

AULDGIRTH, Nr. Dumfries (Dumfriesshire)

Allanton Antiques

Allanton House. (Mr and Mrs T.L Burford) Est: 1987. Open 9.30-5.30 including Sun., or by appointment. SIZE: Medium. *STOCK: General antiques and collectors items, linen and lace, kitchenalia, furniture and bric-a-brac, 18th-20th C, 50p-£1,500.* LOC: A76, approximately 7 miles north of Dumfries, 1/4 mile drive to house. PARK: Own. TEL: 038 774 509; home - same. SER: Buys at auction. FAIRS: Edinburgh, Carlisle, Durham, Gateshead, Sunderland, Blackpool.

AYR (Ayrshire)

Antiques

39 New Rd. (T Rafferty) Est: 1970. Open 10-5. *STOCK: General antiques.* TEL: 0292 265346.

The Old Curiosity Shop

27 Crown St. (B.D Kelly and D.S Davie) Est: 1970. Open 9-5, Sat. 10-4. SIZE: Medium. *STOCK: Furniture and paintings, 19th C, £50-£5,000.* LOC: Cross 'Auld Brig' leaving Ayr for Prestwick, 1st left after traffic lights. PARK: Easy. TEL: 0292 280222. SER: Valuations; restorations (French polishing, re-upholstery). VAT: Stan/Spec.

BALFRON (Stirlingshire)

Amphora Galleries

16-20 Buchanan St. (L Ruglen) Resident. Est: 1961. Open 10-5.30 and by appointment. SIZE: Large. *STOCK: General antiques, furniture, decorative items.* LOC: On A81. TEL: 0360 40329.

BALLATER (Aberdeenshire)

The McEwan Gallery LAPADA

Bridge of Gairn. (D. and P McEwan) Est: 1968. Usually open. SIZE: Medium. *STOCK: Oil paintings, watercolours, £50-£50,000; prints, £5-£300; all 18th-20th C; etchings, 17th-19th C, £5-£300; Scottish and natural history books.* LOC: First house on the east side of A939 after its junction with A93 outside Ballater. PARK: Easy. TEL: 03397 55429; fax - 03397 55995. SER: Valuations; restorations (framing); buys at auction (paintings, watercolours, books). FAIRS: Buxton, Harrogate, Game, and exhibitions in Canada. VAT: Spec.

BANCHORY (Kincardineshire)

Bygones

6 Dee St. (V Watt and P Reid) Est: 1983. Open 10-1 and 2-5, Sat. 10-5.30. SIZE: Medium. *STOCK: Victoriana, bric-a-brac, small furniture, to £500.* LOC: Town centre. PARK: Easy. TEL: 033 02 3095. SER: Valuations. VAT: Stan/Spec.

BANKFOOT (Perthshire)

Antiques and Bygones

Tighvallich, Dunkeld Rd. (W Wright) Est: 1989. Open 9.15-6, Sun. 10.15-6. SIZE: Small. *STOCK: Oil lamps, 19th C, £30-£300; scales and balances, 19th to early 20th C, £40-£300; tools and instruments, 19th C, £10-£400.* LOC: Off A9. PARK: Easy. TEL: 0738 87452; home - same. SER: Restorations (oil lamps, instruments); buys at auction (as stock).

Athollbank Antiques

Main St. (J. and P Morrison) Est: 1970. Open 10-7 every day, 10-5 in winter. SIZE: Medium. *STOCK: Furniture, 18th-20th C, £150-£1,000; pottery and porcelain, 18th-19th C, £10-£400; paintings and prints, 19th-20th C, £50-£500.* LOC: 1 mile from A9. PARK: Easy. TEL: 0738 87253; home - same. SER: Valuations; restorations (furniture); buys at auction (furniture and porcelain).

BARRHEAD, Nr. Glasgow (Renfrewshire)

C.P.R. Antiques and Services

96 Main St. (Mr and Mrs Porterfield) Est: 1965. Open 10-1 and 1.30-5. CL: Tues. SIZE: Medium. *STOCK: Brass, furniture and curios, 19th-20th C, to £5,000.* PARK: Easy. TEL: 041 881 5379. SER: Restorations (brass, copper, pewter); spare parts for oil lamps.

BEAULY (Inverness-shire)

Iain Marr Antiques

3 Mid St. (I. and A Marr) HADA. Est: 1975. Open 10.30-1 and 2-5.30. CL: Thurs. *STOCK: Silver, jewellery, clocks, porcelain, scientific instruments, arms, oils, watercolours, small furniture.* LOC: Off Square, on left going north, next to Priory stores. TEL: 0463 782372. VAT: Stan/Spec.

BLAIRGOWRIE (Perthshire)

Roy Sim, Antiques

21 Allan St. PADA. Est: 1977. Open 9.30-1 and 2-5.30. SIZE: Large and warehouse. *STOCK:*

Roy Sim, Antiques continued

Furniture, jewellery, silver and plate, clocks, scientific and nautical instruments, weapons, brass and copper, oriental items, shipping furniture, £1-£2,000. TEL: 0250 3860; home - 0250 3700. VAT: Stan/Spec.

BLAIRMORE, Nr. Dunoon (Argyllshire)

Fyne Antiques

2 Pierhead. (M.P Glenn) Est: 1984. Open 1.30-5.30. CL: Tues., Wed., Thurs. and Dec. and Jan. SIZE: Small. *STOCK: Pine and country items, £5-£200; mahogany and oak furniture, Staffordshire and Scottish pottery.* LOC: From Dunoon, take A880 Ardentinny road, shop opposite pier. PARK: Easy. TEL: 036 984 563; home - 0369 3510. SER: Valuations; restorations (pine).

BRIDGE OF ALLAN, Nr. Stirling (Stirlingshire)

Athole House Antiques

64 Henderson St. (F. and N Wernham) Est: 1988. Open 10-1 and 2-5, Sun. 11-1 and 3-5. CL: Mon. SIZE: Medium. *STOCK: Furniture, late 18th to Edwardian, £50-£2,000; general antiques, mainly 19th C, £10-£500.* LOC: Just off end of M8, town centre, opposite Royal Hotel. PARK: Easy. TEL: 0786 833959. SER: Valuations; restorations (furniture); upholstery. VAT: Stan/Spec.

BRIDGE OF EARN (Perthshire)

Imrie Antiques LAPADA

Back St. (Mr and Mrs I Imrie) Est: 1969. Open 10-1 and 2-5.30. SIZE: Large. *STOCK: Victorian and 18th C shipping goods.* PARK: Easy. TEL: 0738 812784. VAT: Stan.

BRIDGE OF WEIR (Renfrewshire)

Castle Fine Art

4/5 Castle Terr. (Mrs L Higgins) Est: 1978. Open 10.30-1 and 2.30-5.30, Sat. 10-1, Sun. 2.30-5.30, Mon., Tues. and Wed. by appointment. SIZE: Medium. *STOCK: Oil paintings, £50-£20,000; watercolours, £20-£2,000; both 19th-20th C.* LOC: Leave M8 at Linwood, follow signs to village. Turn sharp left on entering village. PARK: Easy. TEL: 0505 690951; home - 050 587 3450. SER: Valuations; restorations; framing; buys at auction. VAT: Stan/Spec.

BRODICK (Isle of Arran)

Village Studio

Kames Cottage, Shore Rd. (C Mason) Open 10-12.30 and 2-4.30. *STOCK: Bric-a-brac, collectables, objets d'art, gold and silver jewellery.* TEL: 0770 2213.

BUCHLYVIE (Stirlingshire)

Amphora Galleries

Main St. (L Ruglen) Est: 1961. Open 10-5.30 or by appointment. SIZE: Large. *STOCK: Furniture and decorative items.* TEL: 0360 85203; home - 0360 40329.

CARNOUSTIE (Angus)

Decorative Antiques/The Corner Shop

95 Dundee St. Open 11-5. CL: Wed. *STOCK: Furniture, fireplaces, clocks, bric-a-brac, general antiques, shipping goods.* TEL: 0241 55750; home - 0382 79968.

CASTLE DOUGLAS (Kirkcudbrightshire)

Bendalls Antiques

221-223 King St. (R.A Mitchell) Est: 1949. Open 9.30-12.30 and 1.30-5. CL: Thurs. p.m. and Sat. p.m. TEL: 0556 2113. VAT: Stan/Spec.

Chapel Fine Art and Antiques at McGill Duncan Gallery

231 King St. (A Bradley) Open 9-5. *STOCK: Small fine antiques and paintings.* TEL: 0556 2468.

CERES (Fife)

Ceres Antiques

19 Main St. (Mrs E Norrie) SIZE: Medium. *STOCK: General antiques, china.* PARK: Easy. TEL: 033 482 384.

COATBRIDGE (Lanarkshire)

Michael Stewart Antiques

Hornock Cottages, Gartsherry Rd. Est: 1968. Open by appointment. *STOCK: Georgian, Victorian and shipping furniture and smalls.* TEL: 0236 22532.

COLDSTREAM
(Berwickshire)

Coldstream Antiques LAPADA
44 High St. (Mr and Mrs J Trinder) Resident. Open daily. SIZE: Large. *STOCK: Furniture, 17th-20th C; general antiques, clocks, silver and shipping goods, 17th-19th C.* LOC: A697. TEL: 0890 2552. VAT: Stan/Spec.

COMRIE
(Perthshire)

The Coach House
Dundas St. (Mrs M Chilcott) Resident. Est: 1972. Open 10.30-12.30 and 2.30-5. CL: Wed. Outside hours and winter months by appointment only. SIZE: Small. *STOCK: Pottery and porcelain, £5-£100, from early 19th C; decorative items.* LOC: On main road, Crieff to Loch Earn (and Oban). PARK: Easy. TEL: 0764 70765.

COUPAR ANGUS
(Perthshire)

Henderson Antiques
35 Lintrose. Est: 1984. *STOCK: Furniture.* TEL: 0828 27450. VAT: Stan.

CRIEFF
(Perthshire)

Antiques and Fine Art
11 Comrie St. (Mrs S Drysdale) Open 10-1 and 2-5. CL: Wed. p.m. SIZE: Medium. *STOCK: Furniture, paintings, silver, general antiques, French paperweights.* LOC: A85. PARK: Easy. TEL: 0764 4496; home - 0764 2653. VAT: Spec.

Crieff Antiques
Comrie Rd. (Mrs J Cormack) Est: 1968. Open 10-12.30 and 2-4.30 and some Sat. CL: Wed. p.m. SIZE: Medium. *STOCK: Victorian porcelain, paraffin lamps, £5-£150; music boxes, clocks and small furniture, £10-£500; motor mascots, lamps, badges, collectors advertising items, enamel signs, 20th C, £5-£300.* Not Stocked: Large furniture. LOC: On A85 next to Gordon Motors. PARK: Nearby. TEL: 0764 3322/3271.

Strathearn Antiques
2 Comrie St. (R Torrens) Est: 1977. Open 10-5. SIZE: Medium. *STOCK: General antiques, curios, jewellery, coins, medals, books, Royal Doulton items.* PARK: Easy. TEL: 0764 4344; home - 0764 3592. SER: Valuations (jewellery). VAT: Stan.

CROSSFORD
(Lanarkshire)

The Antiquarian
Clyde Valley Country Estate. (H Mulholland) Est: 1988. Open 1-5 including Sun. and by

The Antiquarian continued

appointment. CL: Mon. SIZE: Small. *STOCK: Furniture, 19th C, £500-£1,000; silver, plate and brass, china and glass, £50-£100.* LOC: A72. PARK: Easy. TEL: 055586 833; 0698 64077. SER: Valuations; buys at auction (furniture).

The Antique Shop
Silver Birch Garden Centre. (J. and J Laughlan) Est: 1986. Open Sat. and Sun. 1-5, other days by appointment. SIZE: Small. *STOCK: Small unusual items, jewellery, £5-£100; furniture, £50-£200; all 19th-20th C.* LOC: Near main Clyde Valley Rd. PARK: Easy. TEL: 0698 885360; home - same. SER: Valuations; restorations; buys at auction.

DALBEATTIE
(Kirkcudbrightshire)

Wildman's Antiques
3 Maxwell St. (P. and M Wildman) Est: 1960. Open 10-12.30 and 1.30-5. SIZE: Medium. *STOCK: Jewellery, £50-£500; furniture, £100-£1,500; silver and plate, £50-£1,500, all 19th-20th C.* LOC: A711. PARK: Easy. TEL: 0556 610260. SER: Valuations. VAT: Stan/Spec.

DENNY
(Stirlingshire)

Century Antiques
Viewfield, 74 Glasgow Rd. (I Burton) Open by appointment only anytime including Sat., Sun. and evenings. SIZE: Large. *STOCK: Furniture, clocks and general smalls.* LOC: From M80, junction 4 or junction 9, M9, on main road through village, corner house opposite fire station. PARK: Easy. TEL: 0324 823333. VAT: Stan/Spec.

DINGWALL
(Ross-shire)

Dingwall Antiques
6 Church St. (I Leslie) Est: 1988. Open 10-5. SIZE: Medium. *STOCK: Books, secondhand; china and glass, maps and prints, £1-£200.* PARK: Easy. TEL: 0463 782220. VAT: Stan.

DOLLARBEG, Nr. Dollar
(Stirlingshire)

Dollarbeg Decorative Arts
(R. and C Conn) Open 10-5. *STOCK: Pottery and porcelain especially Wedgwood and Fairyland lustre.* PARK: Easy. TEL: 025594 3441.

DRUMNADROCHIT
(Inverness-shire)

Joan Frere Antiques
Drumbuie House. (Mrs J Frere) Open daily 9-8 May-October, other times by appointment. SIZE: Medium. *STOCK: Furniture, especially English oak, pre-1800.* Not Stocked: Victoriana, reproductions. LOC: On Loch Ness just before Drumnadrochit village, on A82. PARK: Easy. TEL: 045 62 210; home - same.

DUMFRIES
(Dumfriesshire)

I.G Anderson
Gribton. Open by appointment only. *STOCK: Antiquarian and secondhand books.* LOC: From Dumfries, take B729 Moniaive road, after 1/4 miles take Newtonairds road. First entry on left. TEL: 0387 721071.

Cairnyard Antiques
Cairnyard, Beeswing. (B Farnell) Est: 1971. Open daily or by appointment. SIZE: Medium. *STOCK: General antiques, furniture and clocks.* LOC: A711, 5 miles S.W. of Dumfries (follow Dalbeattie signs). PARK: Easy. TEL: 038773 218; home - same.

Dix Antiques
100 English St. (B. and M Hughes) Est: 1965. Open 10-4.30. CL: Thurs. SIZE: Small and store. *STOCK: General antiques, £5-£1,000.* LOC: Near cinema. TEL: 0387 64234; home - 0387 65259.

DUNDEE
(Angus)

Angus Antiques
4 St. Andrews St. Est: 1964. Open 10-4. CL: Sat. *STOCK: Militaria, badges, medals, swords, jewellery, silver, gold, collectors items, art nouveau, art deco, advertising and decorative items, tins, toys, teddy bears.* TEL: 0382 22128.

Neil P Livingstone
Unit 9, South Grove Works, Brewery Lane. Open 9-5. CL: Sat. *STOCK: Furniture, 19th-20th C, £100-£5,000.* TEL: 0382 29295. *Trade Only.*

Mac's Antiques
218 Hilltown. (J McDonell) Open 9.30-5. SIZE: Large. *STOCK: Victorian and Edwardian furniture, silver, plate, shipping goods.* TEL: 0382 26332. SER: Container packing.

Westport Gallery
3 Old Hawkhill, and 48 Westport. (N Livingstone) Est: 1976. Open 9-5. SIZE: Medium. *STOCK: Decorative items including paintings.* LOC: At city centre end of Perth Road, turn into Tay St. and bear left, shop on the right. PARK: Easy. TEL: 0382 22033. SER:

Westport Gallery continued

Valuations; restorations (furniture, ceramics, paintings); buys at auction (paintings). VAT: Stan/Spec.

DUNKELD
(Perthshire)

Dunkeld Antiques
Tay Terr. (D Dytch) Est: 1986. Open 10-5.30, Sun. 12-5.30. SIZE: Large. *STOCK: General antiques especially boxes, office and library furniture, books, 19th-20th C, £1-£1,500.* LOC: Overlooking River Tay, premises are a converted church. PARK: Easy. TEL: 035 02 8832; home - same. SER: Valuations; buys at auction (clocks and furniture). VAT: Stan/Spec.

Dunkeld Interiors
14 Bridge St. (Mrs B Cowe) Est: 1984. Open daily, Sat. and Sun. by appointment. CL: Mon. *STOCK: Furniture, 18th-19th C, £500-£2,500; prints, 18th-20th C, £30-£300; decorative items, 19th-20th C.* LOC: 2 mins. off A9, Perth to Inverness road. PARK: Easy. TEL: 035 02 582; home - same. SER: Finder. VAT: Stan/Spec.

K Stanley and Son
High St. Est: 1962. *STOCK: General antiques and curios.* VAT: Stan.

DUNS
(Berwickshire)

Bygones
5 Market Sq. (S.J. and V.E Schooling) Est: 1989. Open 10-1 and 2-5, Sun. by appointment. CL: Wed. p.m. SIZE: Medium. *STOCK: Smalls including china, pictures and books, £5-£50; small furniture, £20-£500; both 19th-20th C.* LOC: Off A1 on B6051. PARK: Nearby. TEL: 0361 83229; home - 0361 83679. SER: Stripping (small furniture); buys at auction. FAIRS: Ednam House Hotel, Kelso; Ingliston, Edinburgh. VAT: Stan.

Country Shop Antiques
The Coach House, Murray Cres. (T.P. and K Burns) Est: 1965. *STOCK: Period furniture, dolls, paintings; longcase clocks, jewellery, silver.* TEL: 0361 82240.

Wedderburn Castle Antiques
Wedderburn Castle. (G. and L Whitla) Est: 1980. Open 10-5, Sun. 1-5, Sat. by appointment. SIZE: Large. *STOCK: Furniture, 18th-19th C, £300-£5,000; lights and fittings, £100-£500; collectors' items, £50-£1,000; both 19th-20th C.* LOC: Off A1 at Berwick and A68 at Coldstream. PARK: Easy. TEL: 0361 82981; home - same. SER: Valuations; restorations (furniture, clocks, musical boxes); buys at auction (furniture and clocks). VAT: Stan.

EAGLESHAM (Renfrewshire)

Eaglesham Antiques Ltd
73 Montgomery St. (M.F Finlay) Est: 1966. Open 12-5. CL: Mon. *STOCK: Porcelain, silver, glass, objets d'art, paintings, small furniture.* LOC: Original village past Eglington Arms Hotel. PARK: Easy. TEL: 035 53 2814.

EDINBURGH (Midlothian)

Another World
25 Candlemaker Row. (D Harrison) Est: 1974. Open Wed., Fri. and Sat. 12-4.30 or by appointment. *STOCK: Netsuke and Oriental art.* TEL: 031 225 1988. VAT: Spec.

Antiques
38 Victoria St. (E Humphrey) Est: 1946. Open 10-4, Sat. 10-12.30 or by appointment. *STOCK: Paintings, glass, china, curios, postcards.* TEL: 031 226 3625.

'Artisan'
65A Dundas St. (R Forrest) Open 12-6. *STOCK: Stripped pine furniture, antiques, curios and prints.* TEL: 031 556 4253. SER: Restorations.

Edinburgh continued

Behar Carpets
12a Howe St. (M. and Mrs P Slater) Est: 1920. Open 9-5.30. *STOCK: Oriental carpets and rugs, 19th C, from £200.* TEL: 031 225 1069. SER: Valuations; restorations (cleaning and repairs). VAT: Stan.

Laurance Black Ltd
45 Cumberland St. Est: 1967. Open 10-5, Sat. 10-1. SIZE: Small. *STOCK: Scottish furniture and decorative items, £50-£5,000; pottery and porcelain, £5-£1,000; paintings and prints, £50-£20,000; all 18th-19th C.* PARK: Easy. TEL: 031 557 4545. VAT: Spec.

Joseph Bonnar, Jewellers
72 Thistle St. Open 10.30-5 or by appointment. SIZE: Medium. *STOCK: Antique and period jewellery.* LOC: Parallel with Princes St. PARK: Own. TEL: 031 226 2811. VAT: Stan/Spec.

Bourne Fine Art Ltd
4 Dundas St. (P Bourne) Est: 1978. Open 10-6, Sat. 10-1. SIZE: Medium. *STOCK: British paintings, 1800-1950; decorative arts, 1860-1930.* PARK: Easy. TEL: 031 557 4050. SER: Valuations; restorations; buys at auction; framing. VAT: Stan/Spec.

Margaret Brown
14-16 St. Stephen St. Est: 1971. TEL: 031 225 9357.

Calton Gallery
10 Royal Terr. (A. and S Whitfield) Est: 1979. Open 10-6, Sat. 10-1. SIZE: Large. *STOCK: Paintings, especially marine, and watercolours, £50-£30,000; prints, £10-£1,000, all 19th C to early 20th C; sculpture, 19th and early 20th C, to £5,000.* PARK: Easy. TEL: 031 556 1010; home - same; fax - 031 558 1150. SER: Valuations; restorations (oils, watercolours, prints); buys at auction (paintings). VAT: Stan/Spec.

Cinders
51 St. Stephen St. (A Mutch) Open 1.30-5, Sat. 10-4. CL: Mon. *STOCK: Period fireplaces.* TEL: 031 225 3793 or 031 558 3141 (evenings).

The Carson Clark Gallery Scotia Maps - Mapsellers
173 Canongate, The Royal Mile. (A Carson Clark) FRGS. Est: 1971. Open 10.30-5.30. *STOCK: Maps and sea charts.* TEL: 031 556 4710. SER: Valuations.

Classic Telephones
7 West Crosscauseway. (S Maitland) Open 11-1 and 2-6. SIZE: Small. *STOCK: Bakelite reconditioned telephones, 1930's to 1950's, £50-£500; candlestick telephones, 1920's; telephone signs, gadgets and other telephonology; some 19th C telephones.* PARK: Nearby. TEL: 0592 890235; 031 668 2927. SER: Valuations; restorations (as stock); mail order; illustrated catalogue.

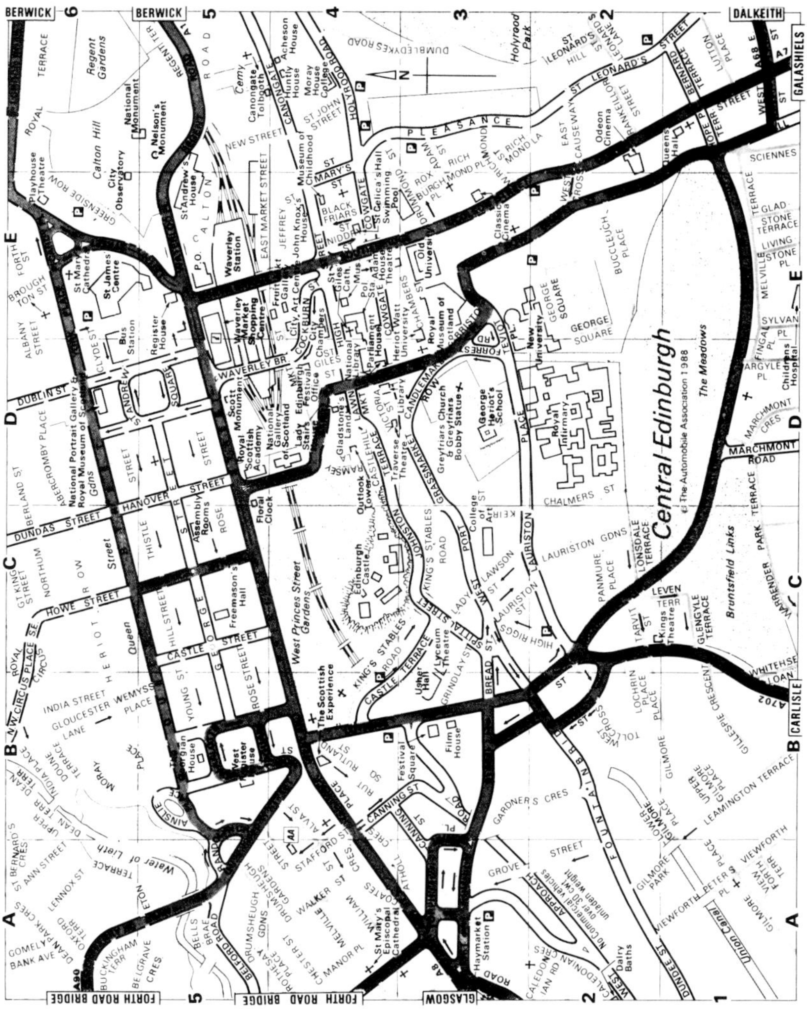
Central Edinburgh
© The Automobile Association 1988
BERWICK
DALKEITH
GALASHIELS
CARLISLE
GLASGOW
FORTH ROAD BRIDGE
Calton Hill
Regent Gardens
Holyrood Park
Waverley Station
West Princes Street Gardens
Edinburgh Castle
The Meadows
Bruntsfield Links
George Square
Royal Infirmary
Haymarket Station
Union Canal
Queen Street
George Street
Princes Street
Lauriston Place
Grassmarket
Canongate
Holyrood Road
Pleasance
Cowgate
St Mary's Cathedral
St James Centre
Register House
Scott Monument
National Gallery of Scotland
Assembly Rooms
Usher Hall
Lyceum Theatre
Film House
Kings Theatre
Water of Leith
Dundee St
Lothian Road

Key to Town Plan

- AA Recommended roads
- Other roads
- Restricted roads
- Buildings of interest
- Car Parks
- Parks and open spaces
- AA Service Centre

Edinburgh continued

The Collectors Shop

49 Cockburn St. (D Cavanagh) Est: 1960. Open 11-5. *STOCK: Coins, medals, militaria, cigarette and postcards, small collectors' items, jewellery, silver and plate.* Not Stocked: Postage stamps. TEL: 031 226 3391. SER: Buys at auction.

Court Curio Shop

519 Lawnmarket. TEL: 031 225 3972.

Curio Corner

30 West Preston St. (J Casey) Est: 1979. Open 10-6. SIZE: Medium. *STOCK: Furniture, 18th-19th C; brass, copper and pewter, 17th-19th C; cameras, 1880's to 1970's; all £5-£500.* LOC: Into town up Dalkeith road, past Commonwealth Pool, 1st left over traffic lights into West Preston St. PARK: Easy. TEL: 031 667 1210; home - 031 667 8515. SER: Valuations; restorations (metal polishing and repairs).

Eric Davidson (Antiques) Ltd

4 Grassmarket. (E.C Davidson) Est: 1967. Open 9-5.30. SIZE: Large. *STOCK: Furniture, mostly period but also Edwardian and Victorian; porcelain and silver, oil paintings, 18th-19th C.* LOC: From West End of Edinburgh, straight along Kings Stable Rd. behind the castle. PARK: Easy. TEL: 031 225 5815. VAT: Stan/Spec.

Alan Day Antiques LAPADA

13c Dundas St. Open 1-6, Fri. 12-5. CL: Sat. *STOCK: Furniture, 19th C; general antiques.* TEL: 031 557 5220.

A.F Drysdale Ltd

20 and 35 North West Circus Pl. Est: 1974. Open 10-1 and 2-5, Sat. 10-1. *STOCK: Small antiques, lamps, decorative furniture.* TEL: 031 225 4686. VAT: Stan.

George Duff Antiques

254 Leith Walk. Open by appointment. *STOCK: Shipping goods, pre-1940.* TEL: 031 554 8164; home - 031 337 1422. VAT: Stan. *Export Only.*

Dunedin Antiques Ltd

4 North West Circus Pl. (D Ingram and G Niven) Est: 1973. Open 9.30-1 and 2.30-5.30. SIZE: Large. *STOCK: Furniture, period items, chimney pieces, architectural fittings, 18th-19th C, £100-£15,000.* Not Stocked: Porcelain. LOC: From Princes St. down Frederick St. PARK: Easy. TEL: 031 220 1574; home - 031 556 8140. SER: Valuations; buys at auction (furniture, weapons). VAT: Stan/Spec.

Edinburgh Coin Shop

2 Polwarth Cres. (T.D Brown) Open 10-5. CL: Sun. *STOCK: Coins, medals, badges, militaria, postcards, cigarette cards, stamps, jewellery, clocks and watches, general antiques, bullion dealers.* TEL: 031 229 3007/229 2915. VAT: Stan.

Edinburgh continued

Donald Ellis Antiques

9 Bruntsfield Pl. (D.G. and C.M Ellis) Est: 1970. *STOCK: Furniture, 18th to early 19th C, £20-£1,000; silver, porcelain, £5-£500; brass, copper, £1-£100.* LOC: Opp. Links Garage at Bruntsfield Links. PARK: Nearby. TEL: 031 229 1819.

Tom Fidelo

49 Cumberland St. Open 2-6, Sat. 12-6. *STOCK: Paintings, works of art, 18th-20th C.* LOC: Left at corner of Dundas St. and Cumberland St. PARK: Easy. TEL: 031 557 2444.

Fine Art Gallery

41 Dundas St. (P.G Ross) Est: 1968. Open 10-5, Sat. 10-1. SIZE: Medium. *STOCK: Pictures - Scottish, British and continental, 18th-20th C, £100-£100,000.* LOC: Dundas St. is continuation of Hanover St., coming off Princes St. PARK: Easy. TEL: 031 557 4569. SER: Valuations; restorations.

The Fine Art Society plc BADA

137 George St. Est: 1876. Open 9.30-5.30, Sat. 10-1. SIZE: Large. *STOCK: Paintings, watercolours, drawings, sculpture, and Scottish furniture, from 1770.* TEL: 031 220 6370. VAT: Spec.

E.B Forrest and Co. "Antiques"

3 Barclay Terr. *STOCK: Jewellery, plate, cutlery, brass, copper, silver, china, art pottery, glass, linen and lace.* TEL: 031 229 3156.

Fyfe's Antiques

41 Thistle St. *STOCK: 18th and 19th C furniture, oil paintings, silver, porcelain.* TEL: 031 225 4287. VAT: Stan/Spec.

Galloways (Edinburgh) Ltd

Galloway House, Corner of St. Stephens St, Stockbridge. Est: 1949. Open 9.30-5.30. CL: Sat. p.m. SIZE: Large. *STOCK: Furniture, Victorian, Georgian and Regency, £100-£3,000; sundries, £10-£100.* LOC: From Forth Bridge, fork left at Blackhall for London Rd. Turn right in Princes St. for Frederick St. PARK: Easy. TEL: 031 225 3221. VAT: Stan.

R.B Garriock

At the Edinburgh Antique Market, 58 St. Stephen St. Open daily 10-5.30. *STOCK: Furniture, porcelain, Victoriana, curios.* TEL: 031 669 4836.

Georgian Antiques LAPADA

10 Pattison St, Leith Links. Est: 1976. Open 8.30-5.30, Sat. and other times by appointment. SIZE: Large. *STOCK: Furniture, Georgian, Victorian, inlaid, Edwardian; shipping goods, smalls, £10-£10,000.* LOC: Off Leith Links. PARK: Easy. TEL: 031 553 7286 (24 hrs.); fax - 031 553 6299. SER: Valuations; restorations; buys at auction; packing; shipping; courier. VAT: Stan/Spec.

Edinburgh continued

Gladrags
17 Henderson Row. (K Cameron) Est: 1977. Open Thurs., Fri. and Sat. 12-6. *STOCK: Period clothes, linen, lace, beadwork, shawls, costume jewellery, silks and satins, cashmeres and accessories.* TEL: 031 557 1916.

Goodwin's Antiques Ltd
15 and 16 Queensferry St. Est: 1952. Open 9.30-5.30, Sat. 9.30-1. *STOCK: Jewellery, silver.* LOC: Off Princes St., West end. TEL: 031 225 4717. VAT: Stan/Spec.

Hand in Hand
3 North West Circus Pl, Edinburgh. (Mr and Mrs O Hand) Est: 1969. Open 10-5.30. CL: Mon. *STOCK: Victorian linen, embroidery, furnishings, lace, shawls (including Paisley), and period costume, 1800-1955.* TEL: 031 226 3598. VAT: Stan/Spec.

Michael Hart
30 St. Stephen St. Est: 1940. TEL: 031 220 1036.

Herrald Antiques
38 Queen St. Est: 1882. Open 9-5. CL: Sat. p.m. SIZE: Medium. *STOCK: Furniture, Persian rugs.* TEL: 031 225 5939. SER: Restorations. VAT: Stan.

Malcolm Innes Gallery
67 George St. Est: 1981. CL: Sat. *STOCK: Scottish landscape, sporting and natural history pictures.* TEL: 031 226 4151. SER: Valuations; restorations; buys at auction; framing. VAT: Spec.

Kenneth Jackson
66 Thistle St. Est: 1969. *STOCK: English and continental furniture, 17th to early 19th C.* TEL: 031 225 9634. VAT: Stan/Spec.

Jacksonville Warehouse
83 Causewayside. (N.T.C Clarke) Est: 1974. Open 10-6. SIZE: Large. *STOCK: Furniture, bric-a-brac, shipping goods, 1850-1950, £5-£500.* PARK: Easy. TEL: 031 667 0616; home - 031 667 3632. SER: Valuations. VAT: Stan.

Letham Antiques
20 Dundas St. (Mrs J Letham) Est: 1966. Open 10-5.30. CL: Mon. SIZE: Medium. *STOCK: Furniture, late 18th C to Art Deco, £50-£4,000; glass, pottery, porcelain, silver, 18th-20th C, £20-£4,000.* LOC: From Princes St., north along Hanover St. to Dundas St. PARK: Easy. TEL: 031 556 6565. SER: Buys at auction. VAT: Stan/Spec.

David Letham BADA
65 Queen Charlotte St. Est: 1960. Open by appointment. *STOCK: Furniture, decorative objects, collectors' items.* TEL: 031 554 6933. VAT: Spec.

Edinburgh continued

William MacAdam BADA
86 Pilrig St. Est: 1976. Open by appointment only. SIZE: Small. *STOCK: Collectors drinking glasses, 17th-19th C, £50-£6,000; coloured glass, 18th-19th C, £15-£250; usable and pressed glass, £5-£200; interesting and unusual items.* LOC: Off Leith Walk, halfway down. PARK: Easy. TEL: 031 553 1364. SER: Valuations. FAIRS: Most major. VAT: Spec.

William Macintosh & Co
5-5a Johnston Terr. (P. and Mrs J London) Est: 1964. Open 10-6, Sun. 2-5 in summer. SIZE: Large. *STOCK: Brass architectural and light fittings, fenders, pine, panelling, mantelpieces, furniture, Victorian, £5-£100.* LOC: Left at the top of Royal Mile. PARK: Easy. TEL: 031 225 6113. VAT: Stan.

McNaughtan's Bookshop
3a and 4a Haddington Pl. Est: 1957. Open 9.30-5.30. CL: Mon. *STOCK: Antiquarian books.* TEL: 031 556 5897.

John Mathieson and Co
48 Frederick St. Open 9-5.30, Sat. 9-4.30. *STOCK: Paintings, watercolours, prints.* TEL: 031 225 6798. SER: Restorations (framing, gilding). VAT: Stan/Spec.

Mulherron Antiques
83 Grassmarket. (F., A. and J Mulherron) Est: 1970. Open 10-6. SIZE: Large. *STOCK: Furniture, 18th C to Regency, £250-£10,000; Oriental carpets and rugs, £250-£7,500; decorative objects to art deco, £50-£350.* PARK: Easy. TEL: 031 226 5907; home - 031 667 4119. SER: Valuations; restorations (furniture); buys at auction (furniture and Oriental rugs). VAT: Stan/Spec.

John O Nelson
22-24 Victoria St. Est: 1957. Open 10-12 and 1.30-5, Sat. 10-1 and 2-4. *STOCK: Antiquarian maps, prints, watercolours.* LOC: First turning off George IV Bridge on right, past Royal Mile. Victoria St. leads down to Grassmarket. PARK: Castle Terrace, west end. TEL: 031 225 4413; evenings - 031 667 5275. VAT: Stan.

Now and Then (Toy Centre)
7 and 9 West Crosscauseway. Open 11-6, Sat. 10-6. *STOCK: Telephones, tin and diecast toys, clockwork and electric model trains, collectable mechanical ephemera, automobilia, juvenalia, clocks, gold and silver watches, small furniture, old advertisements, bric-a-brac.* LOC: City centre off A68. PARK: Nearby. TEL: 031 668 2927 (answer machine); 031 226 2867. SER: Valuations; buys at auction.

Old Golf Shop Inc
13 Albany St. (M.W Olman) Open by appointment only. *STOCK: Pre-1910 woodshaft clubs, golf related items including oil paintings, art work, books, bronzes, pottery, silver, medals; tennis items.* TEL: 031 663 7647.

Edinburgh continued

Open Eye Gallery Ltd
75/79 Cumberland St. (T. and P Wilson) Est: 1976. Open 10-6, Sat. 10-4. SIZE: Medium. *STOCK: Early 20th C etchings, contemporary paintings, ceramics and jewellery.* LOC: From Princes St. go east, left into Frederick St. right at bottom of hill. PARK: Easy. TEL: 031 557 1020. SER: Valuations; restorations (paintings and ceramics); buys at auction. VAT: Mainly Spec.

H Parry
Castle Antiques, 330 Lawnmarket. *STOCK: Silver, porcelain, English and continental furniture, clocks.* TEL: 031 225 7615.

Quadrant Antiques
5 North West Circus Pl, Stockbridge. (M Leask) Est: 1965. Open 10-5, Mon. 12-5. SIZE: Medium. *STOCK: Nautical items, general antiques including trade and shipping goods, furniture, clocks, brass beds, 18th-19th C.* PARK: Easy. TEL: 031 226 7282. VAT: Spec.

Alan Rankin
72 Dundas St. Est: 1964. Open by appointment. SIZE: Small. *STOCK: Antiquarian books, £5-£500; out-of-print scholarly books from 1850, £1-£40; prints, maps from earliest times to 1860, £1-£200.* LOC: From Princes St., down Hanover St. to first block on left past Gt. King St. PARK: Easy. TEL: 031 556 3705; home - same. SER: Valuations; buys at auction.

Chris Ratter Antiques
10 Bonnington Rd. Lane, Leith. Open 9-5. CL: Sat. *STOCK: General antiques.* TEL: 031 553 2564.

Royal Mile Curios
363 High St. (L Bosi and R Eprile) Open 10.30-5. *STOCK: Jewellery and silver.* TEL: 031 226 4050.

James Scott
43 Dundas St. Est: 1964. Open 12-1 and 2.30-5.30. CL: Thurs. p.m. *STOCK: Curiosities, unusual items, silver, jewellery, small furniture.* TEL: 031 556 8260. VAT: Stan.

The Scottish Gallery
Aitken Dott plc, 94 George St. Est: 1842. Open 10-6, Sat. 10-1 (10-5 during Festival and December). *STOCK: 20th C and contemporary Scottish art, crafts, studio ceramics and jewellery.* LOC: Off Princes St. TEL: 031 225 5955. VAT: Stan/Spec.

Serendipity
118 West Bow. *STOCK: Small silver, plate, bijouterie, china, glass, prints.*

Daniel Shackleton
17 Dundas St. *STOCK: Paintings, watercolours, prints.* TEL: 031 557 1115. VAT: Spec.

Edinburgh continued

Stockbridge Antiques and Fine Art
8 Deanhaugh St, Stockbridge. (D Urquhart and J.D Ross) Est: 1988. Open 2-5.30. CL: Mon. SIZE: Small. *STOCK: Furniture and paintings, 17th to 20th C, £50-£30,000; fine French and German dolls, mid 19th C to 20th C, £100-£6,000; teddy bears, 1905-1940's; tin plate toys, clockwork trains, juvenalia, miniature items, 19th C to mid 20th C, £20-£1,000; ceramics, glass, small collectables, Oriental items and textiles, Victorian whitework, christening robes, beadwork items etc., £10-£1,000.* Not Stocked: Silver, jewellery and militaria. LOC: 1/2 mile north of Princes St. PARK: Easy. TEL: 031 332 1366. SER: Valuations; buys at auction.

James Thin (Booksellers)
53-59 South Bridge. Est: 1848. Open Mon.-Sat. *STOCK: Antiquarian and secondhand books.* TEL: 031 556 6743. FAIRS: Buys at auction.

This and That Antiques and Bric-a-Brac
22 Argyle Pl. Open 2.30-5.30. CL: Mon.-Wed. *STOCK: Porcelain, silver, small furniture, Scottish pottery, bric-a-brac.* TEL: 031 229 6069; home - 031 447 1309.

The Thrie Estaits
49 Dundas St. Est: 1970. CL: Sat. *STOCK: Pottery, porcelain, glass, unusual and decorative items, some furniture.* TEL: 031 556 7084.

Unicorn Antiques
65 Dundas St. (N Duncan) Est: 1967. Usually open 11-6. SIZE: Medium. *STOCK: Glass, china, curios, household items, prints, paintings, metalware, bric-a-brac, pre-1950, 10p-£500.* Not Stocked: Weapons, coins, jewellery. LOC: From Princes St. turn into Hanover St. Dundas St. is a continuation of Hanover St. PARK: Easy. TEL: 031 556 7176; home - 031 332 9135.

West Bow Antiques
102 West Bow. Open 10-5.30. *STOCK: Furniture, pottery, porcelain, glass, brass, decorative items.* TEL: 031 226 2852 (24 hrs.). VAT: Stan/Spec.

John Whyte
116b Rose St. Est: 1928. Open 9.30-5.15, Sat. 9.30-12.30. *STOCK: Jewellery, watches, silver.* TEL: 031 225 2140. VAT: Stan.

Whytock and Reid
Sunbury House, Belford Mews. (J.C. and D.C Reid) Est: 1807. Open 9-5.30. CL: Sat. p.m. SIZE: Large. *STOCK: Furniture, English and continental, 18th to early 19th C, £50-£20,000; Eastern rugs, carpets, £50-£10,000.* Not Stocked: Victorian furniture. LOC: 1/2 mile from West End, off Belford Rd. PARK: Own. TEL: 031 226 4911. SER: Valuations; restorations (furniture, rugs); buys at auction; interiors. VAT: Stan/Spec.

Edinburgh continued

Aldric Young
49 Thistle St. *STOCK: General antiques; English and continental furniture, paintings, 18th-19th C.* TEL: 031 226 4101. VAT: Spec.

Young Antiques
36 Bruntsfield Pl. (T.C Young) Est: 1979. Open 10.30-1.30 and from 2.30. CL: Wed. p.m. SIZE: Medium. *STOCK: Victorian and Edwardian furniture, £50-£1,000; ceramics, £20-£2,000; Persian rugs, oils and watercolours, £50-£1,500.* LOC: Near Lothian Rd. PARK: Easy. TEL: 031 229 1361. SER: Valuations; buys at auction (Persian rugs, art pottery).

ELGIN
(Morayshire)

West End Antiques
35 High St. (F Stewart) HADA. Est: 1969. Open daily 9-5.30, Wed. 9-1. *STOCK: Silver, clocks and watches, Victorian jewellery, bric-a-brac.* TEL: 0343 547531; home - 0343 543216. VAT: Stan/Spec.

ELIE
(Fife)

Malcolm Antiques
5 Bank St. Est: 1965. *STOCK: Victoriana, collectors' items, curios, clocks.* TEL: 0333 330116.

ERROL
(Perthshire)

Errol Antiques
The Cross. (A Knox) PADA. Est: 1949. Open 8.30-12 and 1-4.30. CL: Sat. and Sun. except by appointment. SIZE: Small. *STOCK: Furniture, 18th-19th C, £50-£5,000; paintings, 17th-20th C, £25-£3,000.* Not Stocked: Porcelain. LOC: 2 miles off A85. PARK: Easy. TEL: 082 12 391. SER: Valuations; restorations (cabinet making); buys at auction (furniture, paintings). VAT: Stan/Spec.

Greycroft Antiques
Greycroft, Station Rd. (D. and Mrs. J Pickett) Est: 1981. Open 10-5.30, Sun. and other times by appointment. SIZE: Medium. *STOCK: Furniture including desks, bureaux and sofas, to mid-19th C, £500-£8,000; tables, chairs, Oriental porcelain, £50-£1,000; porcelain, brass, copper and bronze, £15-£150.* LOC: A85 between Perth and Dundee. PARK: Easy. TEL: 082 12 221; home - same. SER: Restorations (furniture); buys at auction (furniture). VAT: Stan/Spec.

FAIRLIE
(Ayrshire)

Antiques
86 Main Rd. (E.A Alvarino) Est: 1976. Open 11-5. CL: Mon. SIZE: Small. *STOCK: Bric-a-brac, £5-£300; small furniture, clocks and silver, £10-£500; jewellery; all Victorian or Edwardian.* LOC: A78. PARK: 25yds. TEL: 0475 568613. SER: Valuations; buys at auction. VAT: Stan.

FALKIRK
(Stirlingshire)

James Finlay
178 Grahams Rd. Est: 1966. Open 9.30-4, Wed. and Sat. 9.30-12. SIZE: Small. *STOCK: Bric-a-brac, 1880-1950; shipping furniture.* LOC: 1/4 mile from town centre. PARK: Easy. TEL: 0324 31505; home - 0324 20264 or 0324 37868.

FOCHABERS
(Morayshire)

The Antique Market
George St. Open 10-5. CL: Wed. and Sun. except July and Aug. SIZE: 4 dealers. *STOCK: General antiques.*

Antiques Etcetera
18 The Sq. (D. and E Gordon) Est: 1977. Open 10-1 and 2-5. CL: Wed. p.m. SIZE: Small. *STOCK: Furniture and paintings, 19th C, £50-£700; smalls, 19th-20th C, from £3.* LOC: Village centre. PARK: Easy. TEL: 0343 821269; home - same.

Granny's Kist
Hadlow House, 22 The Sq. (M Hill) Est: 1985. Open 9-5. CL: Wed. SIZE: Medium. *STOCK: Kitchenalia and tools, £5-£25; furniture, £50-£100; all 19th-20th C.* LOC: A96 village centre. PARK: Easy. TEL: 0343 820838; home - 0542 34218. FAIRS: Inverness, Elgin, Aberdeen.

Inverspey Arts
22 The Sq. (J. and M Holstead) Est: 1983. Open 10-1 and 2-5, Mon. 10-1 and 2-4. CL: Wed. SIZE: Medium. *STOCK: General collectables - Oriental, clocks including longcase, glass, European, art nouveau; furniture, from 18th C oak to 1930's.* PARK: Easy. TEL: 0343 820; home - 0343 820572. FAIRS: Drummossie, Inverness, Haddo House, Banchory, Edinburgh, Tree Tops.

Michael Low Antiques
89 High St. Est: 1967. TEL: 0343 820238.

Murray-Tait Antiques
64 High St. (B. and E Forsyth) Open 10-5. *STOCK: General antiques, paintings and soft furnishings.* TEL: 0343 821387.

Fochabers continued

Pringle Antiques
High St. (G.A Christie) Est: 1983. Open 9.30-1 and 2-6 every day, closing at 5p.m in winter. SIZE: Medium. *STOCK: Furniture, Victorian, £20-£1,000; general antiques, pictures, brass, pottery, silver and jewellery.* Not Stocked: Books and clothing. LOC: A96, premises are a converted church. PARK: Easy. TEL: 0343 820362; home - 0343 820599. VAT: Stan/Spec.

Marianne Simpson
61/63 High St. (M.R Simpson) Est: 1990. Open 9-1 and 2-5, Sun. by appointment. Winter - open Tues., Thurs. and Sat. 10-1 and 2-4. SIZE: Small. *STOCK: Books, 19th-20th C, prints, 19th C; ephemera, 19th-20th C, all £1-£50.* LOC: A95. PARK: Easy. TEL: 0343 821192; home - same.

Victoriana
The Red House, High St. (L Barnard) Open 10-1 and 2-5.30 or by appointment. CL: Mon. *STOCK: Lace and linen; clothes, to 1940, christening robes, Victorian nightgowns, petticoats, etc., accessories.* TEL: 0343 821133.

FORRES
(Morayshire)

Michael Low Antiques
45 High St. Est: 1967. TEL: 0309 73696. VAT: Stan.

FORTROSE
(Ross and Cromarty)

Black Isle Antiques
(Mrs N.J Stokes and Mrs V Hourston) HADA. Open Fri. and Sat. or by appointment. SIZE: Small. *STOCK: China, glass, general small items.* PARK: Easy. TEL: 0381 20407. SER: Valuations.

FREUCHIE
(Fife)

Freuchie Antiques
Oxley House, Main St. (C.P Wakefield) Est: 1980. CL: Wed. SIZE: Medium. *STOCK: Mainly small collectables, linen, lace and postcards, £5-£100.* PARK: Easy. TEL: 0337 57348.

FRIOCKHEIM, Nr. Arbroath
(Angus)

M.J. and D Barclay
29 Gardyne St. Est: 1965. Open 10.30-1 and 2-5.30. CL: Thurs. *STOCK: General antiques including furniture, jewellery, silver, porcelain and clocks.* Not Stocked: Stamps, books, coins. PARK: Easy. TEL: 024 12 365. VAT: Stan.

GALSTON
(Ayrshire)

Galleries de Fresnes
Cessnock Castle. (The Baron de Fresnes) D.A. (Glas.). Articles on drawings and paintings. Est: 1934. Open 10-6. SIZE: General antiques, to 1850; silver, glass, oil paintings, 20th C; reproduction pine. LOC: Approximately 600yds. on Sorn road out of Galston, 6 miles from Kilmarnock. PARK: Easy. TEL: 0563 820314. SER: Valuations; restorations (paintings); buys at auction; courier for overseas traders. *Mainly Trade.*

GARTMORE, Nr. Aberfoyle
(Stirlingshire)

Robert and Vashti Lewis Antiques
Blarnaboard Farm. Est: 1975. Resident - always open but prior telephone call advisable. SIZE: Medium. *STOCK: Pine, £25-£1,000; farm and kitchen items, £5-£100; all 18th-20th C; general antiques, £5-£1,000.* LOC: First farm outside village on Drymen road, off A81. PARK: Easy. TEL: 087 72 374. SER: Valuations; restorations; pine stripping.

GLASGOW
(Lanarkshire)

Albany Antiques **LAPADA**
1347 Argyle St. (P.J O'Loughlin) Est: 1969. Open Mon.-Fri. 9.30-5.30 or by appointment. *STOCK: Chinese and Japanese porcelain, Georgian, Victorian and Edwardian furniture, shipping goods.* TEL: 041 339 4267. VAT: Stan/Spec.

Bath Street Antiques Galleries

E A Alvarino Antiques
Edwardian, Victorian and Georgian furniture and accessories; general antiques, silver, clocks, instruments and paintings. TEL: 041 221 1888.

Brown's Clocks Ltd
(Wilson J) FBHI *Longcase, wall and mantel clocks, £30-£5,000.* TEL: 041 248 6760. SER: Valuations; restorations; buys at auction. VAT: Stan/Spec.

Glenburn Antiques
Jewellery, silver, porcelain.

David Gray
Architectural Antiques. TEL: 0360 22244.

John Green Fine Art
19th and 20th C British and Continental oils, watercolours and etchings. TEL: 041 221 6025. SER: Restorations; framing.

Cooper Hay Rare Books
Antiquarian books and prints. TEL: 041 226 3074.

Pauline Jamieson
Staffordshire figures, Scottish pottery, general antiques.

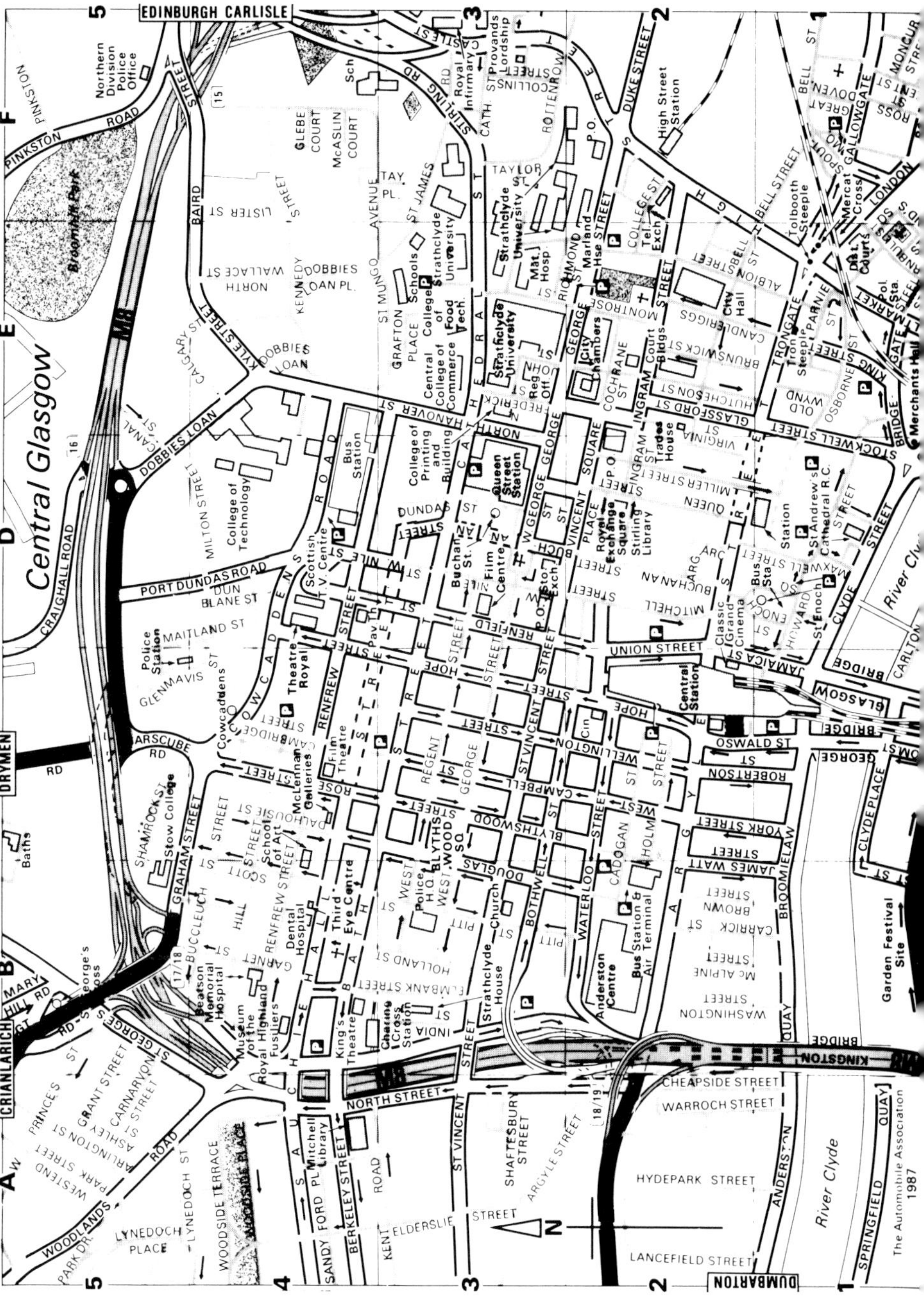

Central Glasgow
EDINBURGH CARLISLE
DRYMEN
CRIANLARICH
DUMBARTON
Broomhill Park
PINKSTON ROAD
Northern Division Police Office
BAIRD STREET
GLEBE COURT
McASLIN COURT
LISTER ST
NORTH WALLACE ST
KENNEDY STREET
DOBBIES LOAN
DOBBIES LOAN PL.
KYLE STREET
CALGARY ST
CANAL ST
CRAIGHALL ROAD
PORT DUNDAS ROAD
DUN BLANE ST
MAITLAND ST
Police Station
GLENMAVIS ST
College of Technology
MILTON STREET
Cowcaddens
COWCADDENS
GARSCUBE RD
Theatre Royal
Scottish T.V. Centre
Bus Station
ST MUNGO AVENUE
TAY PL.
ST JAMES
Strathclyde University
GRAFTON PLACE
Central College of Commerce
College of Food Tech.
College of Printing and Building
STIRLING RD
Royal Infirmary
CATH. ST
Provands Lordship
COLLINS STREET
ROTTENROW
TAYLOR ST
Mat. Hosp.
RICHMOND ST
Marland Hse
GEORGE STREET
City Chambers
COCHRANE ST
INGRAM ST
Court Bldgs
HIGH STREET
DUKE STREET
High Street Station
COLLEGE ST
Tel. Exch.
ALBION STREET
BELL STREET
City Hall
CANDLERIGGS
BRUNSWICK ST
HUTCHESON ST
GLASSFORD ST
Trades House
VIRGINIA ST
Tolbooth Steeple
Mercat Cross
TRONGATE
Tron Steeple
OLD WYND
OSBORNE ST
KING STREET
Merchants Hall
STOCKWELL STREET
GALLOWGATE
LONDON
Dist. Courts
Pol. Sta.
HANOVER ST
NORTH FREDERICK ST
Reg. Off.
Queen Street Station
DUNDAS STREET
W. NILE ST
Buchanan St.
Film Centre
W. GEORGE
VINCENT PLACE
Royal Exchange Square
Stirling Library
QUEEN STREET
MILLER STREET
Sto. Exch.
P.O.
BUCHANAN
ARGYLE
St Andrew's Cathedral R.C.
MAXWELL STREET
Bus Sta.
St Enoch
HOWARD ST
MITCHELL STREET
Classic Grand Cinema
UNION STREET
RENFIELD STREET
JAMAICA ST
Central Station
GLASGOW BRIDGE
CLYDE STREET
River Clyde
CARLTON
OSWALD ST
ROBERTSON ST
YORK STREET
JAMES WATT STREET
BROOMIELAW
CLYDE PLACE
Garden Festival Site
HOPE STREET
WELLINGTON
WEST CAMPBELL ST
BLYTHSWOOD SQ.
WEST GEORGE
REGENT ST
DOUGLAS ST
CADOGAN ST
HOLM ST
WATERLOO STREET
BOTHWELL ST
Church
PITT ST
Strathclyde House
Anderston Centre
Bus Station & Air Terminal
CARRICK ST
BROWN STREET
McALPINE STREET
WASHINGTON STREET
KINGSTON BRIDGE
CHEAPSIDE STREET
WARROCH STREET
HYDEPARK STREET
LANCEFIELD STREET
ANDERSTON QUAY
SPRINGFIELD QUAY
Pav. Th.
SAUCHIEHALL STREET
RENFREW STREET
CAMBRIDGE STREET
Film Theatre
ROSE STREET
McLennan Galleries
DALHOUSIE ST
School of Art
SCOTT STREET
Stow College
SHAMROCK ST
Baths
GRAHAM STREET
BUCCLEUCH ST
HILL ST
GARNET ST
Dental Hospital
Beatson Memorial Hospital
Museum of the Royal Highland Fusiliers
WEST Police H.Q.
Third Eye Centre
HOLLAND ST
ELMBANK STREET
King's Theatre
Charing Cross Station
INDIA ST
NORTH STREET
Mitchell Library
ST VINCENT ST
SHAFTESBURY STREET
ARGYLE STREET
ELDERSLIE STREET
KENT RD
BERKELEY STREET
SANDYFORD PL
WOODSIDE PLACE
WOODSIDE TERRACE
LYNEDOCH ST
LYNEDOCH PLACE
PARK DR.
WOODLANDS ROAD
WESTEND PARK STREET
ARLINGTON ST
ASHLEY ST
CARNARVON ST
GRANT STREET
PRINCE'S ST
ST GEORGE'S RD
St George's Cross
MARY HILL RD
The Automobile Association 1987

Key to Town Plan

AA Recommended roads		Car Parks	P
Other roads		Parks and open spaces	
Restricted roads		AA Service Centre	AA
Buildings of interest			

Bath Street Antiques Galleries continued

Kilgour Antiques
(Mrs C G Kilgour) *18th-19th C European and oriental ceramics, jewellery and silver including Scottish; glass, miniatures, samplers and other objects d'art.* TEL: 041 249 4396.
Barclay Lennie Fine Art Ltd LAPADA
Oil paintings, watercolours and sculpture, mainly Scottish, 19th-20th C. TEL: 041 226 5413.
Murray McIlroy
Pottery, porcelain, Scottish paintings, furniture and decorative objects 1650-1950. TEL: 041 221 4004.
Sundance Antiques
Dolls, jewellery, silver, pottery, furniture including pine.
Karen Thom
Jewellery, silver, ornaments.

Behar Carpets
15 Bath St. (M. and Mrs. P Slater) Est: 1920. Open 9-5.30. SIZE: Large. *STOCK: Oriental carpets and rugs, 19th C.* PARK: Multi-storey. TEL: 041 332 2858. SER: Valuations; restorations (cleaning and repairs). VAT: Stan.

Butler's Furniture Galleries Ltd
24-26 Millbrae Rd, Langside. (L Butler) Open 9.30-5.30 or by appointment. CL: Sat. *STOCK: Furniture, Georgian, Victorian, Edwardian; small decorative items.* TEL: 041 632 9853. SER: Valuations.

The Den of Antiquity
61 Dixon Ave, Crosshill. Est: 1960. Open 10-5. CL: Sat. and Sun., except by appointment. *STOCK: General antiques.* TEL: 041 423 0375; evenings - 041 637 4434. VAT: Stan/Spec.

Duophone Antiques
Virginia Galleries, 31 Virginia St. (J.E Cavanagh) Open 10-5. SIZE: Small. *STOCK: General furniture and shipping goods, mechanical music and clocks, paintings, silver, 18th-20th C.* LOC: Near Argyle St. railway station. PARK: Fair. TEL: 041 552 7757.

The Fine Art Society plc BADA
134 Blythswood St. Est: 1876. Open 9.30-5.30, Sat. 10-1. SIZE: Large. *STOCK: British paintings, watercolours, drawings, sculpture, especially Scottish, from 1800.* TEL: 041 332 4027. VAT: Spec.

James Forrest and Co (Jewellers) Ltd
53 West Nile St. Est: 1957. CL: Sat. p.m. *STOCK: Silver, jewellery, clocks.* LOC: City centre. TEL: 041 221 0494. VAT: Stan.

Heritage House Antiques
Unit 6a, Yorkhill Quay. Open 9-5. SIZE: 10 dealers. *STOCK: General antiques, furnishings, smalls and fine arts.* TEL: 041 334 4924.

Hour Hand Furniture and Antiques
287 High St. Est: 1971. Open 9-5. SIZE: Medium. *STOCK: General antiques.* PARK:

Hour Hand Furniture and Antiques continued

Easy. TEL: 041 552 2332; evenings - 041 946 1866. SER: Restorations (period house and architectural).

Keep Sakes
27 Gibson St. (Mrs R Currie) Est: 1971. Open 10-5, Mon. 10-2. *STOCK: General antiques, jewellery.* TEL: 041 334 2264. SER: Upholstery; French polishing; repairs (jewellery). VAT: Stan.

Caroline Kerr Antiques
103 Niddrie Rd, Queens Park. Open 9.30-5. CL: Sat. *STOCK: General antiques.* TEL: 041 424 0444; home - 041 946 3787. SER: Buys at auction.

Gordon J Kerr Antiques
103 Niddrie Rd, Queens Park. Open 9.30-5. CL: Sat. *STOCK: General antiques.* TEL: 041 424 0444; home - 03552 21101. SER: Buys at auction.

I.E Lovatt Antiques
100 Torrisdale St. Est: 1963. CL: Sat. SIZE: Large. *STOCK: General antiques, Victoriana, shipping goods.* LOC: Adjacent Queen's Park railway station. TEL: 041 423 6497; home - 041 638 0302. SER: Valuations; buys at auction. VAT: Stan/Spec.

Jean Megahy
481 Great Western Rd. (F.G Halliday) Open 10-5. CL: Sat. p.m. *STOCK: Furniture, brass, silver, Oriental items.* TEL: 041 334 1315. VAT: Stan/Spec.

Mercat-Hughes Antiques
85 Queen St, 1 Royal Exchange Court. (P Hughes and C Forrester) Open 10-5.30, or by appointment. CL: Sat. *STOCK: Small furniture, brass, ceramics, clocks, watches, E.P. and silver, jewellery and trade items.* TEL: 041 204 0851; home - 041 770 4572.

Muirhead Moffat and Co
182 West Regent St. (D.J Brewster and J.D Hay) Est: 1896. Open 10-12.30 and 1.30-5. CL: Sat. and Sun. except by appointment. SIZE: Medium. *STOCK: Period furniture, barometers and jewellery; clocks, silver, weapons, porcelain, tapestries and pictures.* LOC: Off Blythswood Sq. PARK: Easy. TEL: 041 226 4683/226 3406. SER: Valuations; restorations (furniture, clocks, barometers and jewellery); buys at auction. VAT: Stan/Spec.

Nice Things Old and New
1010 Pollokshaws Rd. (J. and E Lake) Est: 1961. Open 12-6. *STOCK: Interesting and unusual pieces.* LOC: Facing Langside Halls and Marlborough House (Shawlands). TEL: 041 649 3826. FAIRS: Organiser.

Nithsdale Antiques
103 Niddrie Rd, Queens Park and 79 St. George's Rd. (W McDonald) Open 9.30-5.30. *STOCK: General antiques.* TEL: 041 424 0444/333 9272; home - 041 637 9366. SER: Buys at auction.

Glasgow continued

Pettigrew and Mail **LAPADA**
7 The Loaning, Whitecraigs, Giffnock. (S Mail and C Pettigrew) Est: 1966. Open by appointment only. *STOCK: Scottish impressionist, Victorian, English and continental paintings, 19th-20th C, from £500.* LOC: Just off A77. PARK: Easy. TEL: 041 639 2989/4592. SER: Valuations; restorations; commissions undertaken. VAT: Spec.

R.L Rose and Co
19 Waterloo St. Open 9-4. *STOCK: Oriental carpets and rugs.* TEL: 041 248 3313. SER: Restorations (as stock).

Frank Russell and Son Antiques
1 Rutherglen Rd. Est: 1972. Open by appointment. SIZE: Large. *STOCK: Georgian, Victorian, Edwardian, art deco and bric-a-brac, £5-£5,000.* LOC: Near sign for Atlas Express. Close to Shawfield Greyhound Stadium. TEL: 041 647 9608; home - 0236 736385. VAT: Stan.

Saratoga Trunk
1st Floor, 136 Renfield St. (C McLay) Est: 1977. Open 10.30-5, Sat. 10.30-4. SIZE: Large. *STOCK: Linen and textiles, Victorian to 1940s, £2-£500; costume, £5-£500; jewellery, £10-£200; both Victorian to 1950s.* LOC: Opposite S.T.V. Studios. PARK: Easy. TEL: 041 331 2707. SER: Valuations. VAT: Stan.

John Smith and Son (Glasgow) Ltd
57-61 St. Vincent St. Est: 1751. Open 9-5.30. SIZE: Medium. *STOCK: Antiquarian books and prints.* LOC: City centre. TEL: 041 221 7472. SER: Buys at auction (antiquarian books); out of print book search.

Stenlake and McCourt
1 Overdale St, Langside. Est: 1984. Open 11-6. SIZE: Small. *STOCK: Edwardian postcards; cigarette cards, to 1950; ephemera, 1700-1930.* LOC: 50yds. from Battlefield monument. PARK: Easy. TEL: 041 632 2304. SER: Valuations (as stock). FAIRS: Bipex; Scottish Philatelic Congress and others. VAT: Stan.

Temptations Unlimited
127 Douglas St. (S.O Lind) Est: 1981. Open 10-5.30, Sat. 10-5. SIZE: Medium. *STOCK: Jewellery, glass and pictures, 19th C, £50-£100.* LOC: Second right after Christie's (Glasgow), Bath St., 20yds. on left. PARK: Meters. TEL: 041 332 4403; home - 041 332 4400. SER: Valuations; buys at auction. FAIRS: Antiques in Britain. VAT: Stan/Spec.

The Victorian Village
53 and 57 West Regent St. (J.D McArdle) Open 10-5, Sat. 10-1. SIZE: 30 dealers. LOC: Near Renfield St. PARK: Meters. TEL: 041 332 0808. VAT: Stan/Spec.

Ann's Antiques
Bric-a-brac and jewellery.
Terry Black
Silver, plate.

The Victorian Village continued

Ian Frame
Militaria.
House of Tarot
Postcards.
Jade Antiques
Ornaments.
Marjory Kerr
Jewellery, china.
Putting on the Ritz
20s clothing, jewellery.
Rosamund Rotherford
Jewellery, Victorian lace.
Tony Wallis
Clothes.

Virginia Antique Galleries
31/33 Virginia St, (Off Argyle St.). (M Robinson) Open 10-5, Sun. 12-5. SIZE: 20 dealers. *STOCK: Furniture, glass, jewellery, silver, porcelain and brass.* TEL: 041 552 2573/8640; office - 041 552 5840.

West of Scotland Antique Centre Ltd
Langside Lane, 539 Victoria Rd, Queens Park (Wosac Ltd.). Est: 1969. Open 9.30-5.30, Sun. 12-5. SIZE: Large - 8 dealers. *STOCK: Pine, Georgian to Edwardian, £50-£3,000.* PARK: Easy. TEL: 041 422 1717. VAT: Stan/Spec.

Tim Wright Antiques
147 Bath St. (T. and J Wright) Est: 1971. Open 9.30-5, Sat. 10.30-1.30. *STOCK: Porcelain, pottery and glass, continental, British and Oriental, some 18th but mainly 19th C, £25-£1,500; brass and metalware, £20-£500; small furniture and collectors items, £50-£2,000; silver and plate, £20-£1,500.* LOC: On opposite corner to Christie's, Glasgow. PARK: Multi-storey opposite. TEL: 041 221 0364. SER: Valuations; buys at auction (as stock). VAT: Mainly Spec.

Yesteryear
158 Albert Drive. (I.C Taylor) Open 11-6. *STOCK: General antiques.* TEL: 041 429 3966.

GOUROCK
(Lanarkshire)

Bygones
59 Shore St. (R PcPhail) Open 9.30-5.30. *STOCK: General antiques.* TEL: 0475 31114.

GREENLAW
(Berwickshire)

Greenlaw Antiques
(Mr and Mrs A Brotherston) Est: 1970. Open Mon. to Fri. and by appointment. SIZE: Large. *STOCK: General antiques, £5-£500.* PARK: Easy. TEL: 036 16 220. VAT: Stan/Spec.

Greenlaw continued

Greenlaw Antiques

The Town Hall. (Mr and Mrs A Brotherston) Open Sun. and Wed. 2-5. *STOCK: General antiques, £5-£500.*

HADDINGTON (East Lothian)

Elm House Antiques

The Sands, Church St. (Mrs I MacDonald) Est: 1972. Open daily, appointment advisable, and Sat. 10-1 and 2-5. SIZE: Small. *STOCK: English porcelain and pottery, 18th and 19th C, £20-£600; blue and white earthenware, Scottish pottery, £20-£900; boxes, furniture, £25-£800.* LOC: Off A1, end of High St. PARK: Easy. TEL: 062 082 3413; home - same.

Leslie and Leslie

Open 9-1 and 2-5. CL: Sat. *STOCK: General antiques*. TEL: 062 082 2241; fax - same. VAT: Stan.

HOUNDWOOD (Berwickshire)

Houndwood House AntiquesLAPADA

Houndwood House. (R. and I Gourlay) Resident. Est: 1982. Open daily including evenings. SIZE: Large. *STOCK: Furniture, late 18th C to Edwardian, £100-£5,500; paintings, 18th C to 1920, £150-£3,500; smalls, Georgian-Edwardian, £10-£500; decorative items.* LOC: On A1, 13 miles north of Berwick-on-Tweed. PARK: Easy. TEL: 08907 61232. SER: Valuations; restorations (furniture and porcelain especially Wemyss ware); buys at auction. FAIRS: Castle (Scotland, Yorkshire and The South); Antiques in Britain (Scotland). VAT: Spec.

INCHTURE (Perthshire)

C.S Moreton (Antiques)

Inchmartine House. (P.M. and Mrs M Stephens) Est: 1922. Open 9-5.30. CL: Sat. *STOCK: Furniture, £50-£10,000; carpets and rugs, £50-£3,000; ceramics, metalware; all 16th C to 1860; silver and plate, paintings, weapons.* LOC: Take A85 Perth/Dundee road, entrance on left at Lodge. PARK: Easy. TEL: 0828 86412; home - same. SER: Valuations. VAT: Stan/Spec.

INVERNESS (Inverness-shire)

The Attic

Riverside, 17 Huntly St. (P Gratton) HADA. Est: 1976. Open 10.30-1 and 2-5. CL: Wed., Jan.-Mar. Mon. and Wed. SIZE: Small. *STOCK: Art deco china, jewellery, linen, textiles, period*

The Attic continued

clothes, Victorian to 1940's, from £5. PARK: The Riverside. TEL: 0463 243117/240224. SER: Valuations. FAIRS: Aberdeen.

Frasers Antiques and Reproductions

28/30 Church St. Est: 1900. Open 9-1 and 2-5. SIZE: Small. STOCK: Furniture, from 1800; oil paintings, prints, £50-£2,000; china, brass, copper, £2-£750. LOC: Town centre. PARK: Restricted (delivery and collection). TEL: 0463 233634. SER: Valuations; buys at auction. VAT: Stan.

Highland Antiques

15 Tomnahurich St. (J. and H Hesling) HADA, PBFA. Est: 1962. Open 10.30-5. CL: Wed. *STOCK: Furniture, £100-£1,000; paintings, £50-£1,000; both 19th C; general antiques, 18th-19th C, £20-£1,000; antiquarian books especially of Scottish interest.* LOC: Town centre. TEL: 0463 231316; home - 046385 250. SER: Valuations; buys at auction. VAT: Stan/Spec.

Past and Present

19 Market Brae. (Mr and Mrs J.A Kemlo) Open 10-5. *STOCK: Porcelain, brass, prints, jewellery, silver and lace.* TEL: 0463 226185; home - 0463 233148.

JEDBURGH (Roxburghshire)

Mainhill Gallery

Carnessie, Ancrum. (B. and D Bruce) Est: 1981. Open 10.30-5.30, prior telephone call advisable, or by appointment. SIZE: Medium. *STOCK: Oil paintings, watercolours and etchings, 19th-20th C, some prints, £35-£7,000.* LOC: Just off A68, 3 miles north of Jedburgh, centre of Ancrum. PARK: Easy. TEL: 083 53 518. SER: Valuations; buys at auction. VAT: Spec.

R. and M Turner (Antiques and Fine Art) Ltd LAPADA

34/36 High St. Est: 1965. Open 10-5.30. CL: Sun. except by appointment. SIZE: Large. *STOCK: Furniture, clocks, porcelain, paintings, silver, jewellery, 17th-20th C.* LOC: On A68 to Edinburgh. PARK: Own. TEL: 0835 63445. SER: Valuations; restorations (furniture, pottery, porcelain); packing; shipping; interior design. VAT: Stan/Spec.

KILBARCHAN (Renfrewshire)

Gardner's The Antique Shop LAPADA

Wardend House, Kibbleston Rd. (G.D. and R.K.F Gardner) Est: 1950. Open to the trade 7 days a week. Retail 10-1 and 2-6, Sat. 10-1. SIZE: Large. *STOCK: General antiques.* LOC: 12 miles from Glasgow, at far end of Tandlehill Rd. 10 mins. from Glasgow Airport. TEL: 050 57 2292.

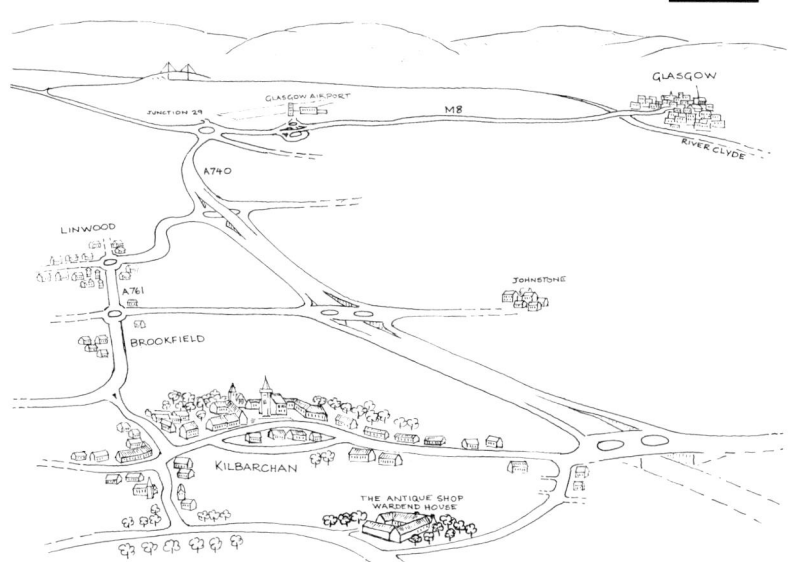

Kilbarchan continued

Marjorie McDougall
10 The Cross. Est: 1968. Open Thurs. to Sun. 1-5, other days by appointment. *STOCK: Textiles, 19th C, £50-£500; furniture, 18th-19th C, £50-£2,000; beds, 19th C, £200-£700+.* LOC: 1st turning off M8 after airport towards Linwood. PARK: Easy. TEL: 050 57 2229; home - same. VAT: Stan/Spec.

KILLEARN, Nr. Glasgow (Stirlingshire)

Country Antiques
(Lady J Edmonstone) Est: 1975. SIZE: Small. *STOCK: Small antiques and decorative items, Victoriana and textiles.* LOC: A81. In main st. PARK: Easy. TEL: Home - 0360 70215.

KILLIN (Perthshire)

Maureen H Gauld
Cameron Buildings, Main St. Est: 1975. Open Mar.-Oct. 10-5.30. SIZE: Small. *STOCK: General antiques, silver and paintings, £5-£2,000.* PARK: Easy. TEL: 056 72 475; home - 056 72 605.

KILMACOLM (Renfrewshire)

Kilmacolm Antiques Ltd
Stewart Pl. (H Maclean) Est: 1973. Open 10-1 and 2.30-5. CL: Sun. and Wed. except by appointment. SIZE: Medium. *STOCK: Furniture, 18th-19th C, £100-£8,000; objets d'art, 19th C; jewellery, £5-£5,000; paintings, £100-£5,000.* LOC: First shop on right when travelling from Bridge of Weir. PARK: Easy. TEL: 050 587 3149. SER: Restorations (furniture, silver, jewellery, porcelain). FAIRS: Hopetown House, Perth, Roxburghe, Edinburgh. VAT: Stan/Spec.

KILMARNOCK (Ayrshire)

MacInnes Antiques
1 Gibson St. (Mrs M MacInnes) Est: 1973. Open by appointment. *STOCK: General antiques.* TEL: 0563 26739.

KILMICHAEL GLASSARY, By Lochgilphead (Argyllshire)

Rhudle Mill
(D Murray) Est: 1979. Open daily, weekends by appointment. SIZE: Medium. *STOCK: Furniture, 18th C to art deco, £30-£3,000; small items and bric-a-brac, £5-£500.* LOC: Signposted 3 miles south of Kilmartin on A816 Oban to

Rhudle Mill continued

Lochgilphead road. PARK: Easy. TEL: 054 684 284; home - same. SER: Restorations (furniture); French polishing; buys at auction.

KILTARLITY, By Beauly (Inverness-shire)

Old Pine Furniture and Jouet
Fuaranbuie, 8 Kinerras. (J. and A Jeorrett) Open by appointment. *STOCK: Restored pine including Victorian, £25-£600+.* TEL: 046 374 261.

KINBUCK (Perthshire)

Kings of Kinbuck
The Old Mill, Main St. (H King) Est: 1983. Open 9-6, Sat. 10-2. SIZE: Medium. *STOCK: Victorian chaise longues, sofas, chairs, rugs, general antiques and secondhand books.* LOC: Off A9. PARK: Easy. TEL: 0786 822915. SER: Restorations; stripping (pine and hardwoods); upholstery and canework.

Old Mill Antiques Ltd
The Old Mill. (G Dobbie and S Hughes) Open 9-5, Sat. 9-1. SIZE: Large. *STOCK: Architectural antiques, specialising in fireplaces, and reproduction furniture.* LOC: North of Dunblane, 2 miles off A9. PARK: Easy. TEL: 0786 823 811. SER: Fire installations.

KINCARDINE O'NEIL, Nr. Aboyne (Aberdeenshire)

Amber Antiques
1 Southside, Old Turnpike. (V Watson) Est: 1982. Open 10.30-6, Sun. 1.30-5. SIZE: Small. *STOCK: Jewellery especially amber, Victorian and Edwardian, £25-£500; silver, Georgian-Edwardian, £10-£500; Oriental objets d'art, £5-£1,000; pictures, 16th-20th C, £25-£500; antiquarian books.* LOC: On North Deeside Rd. PARK: Easy. TEL: 033 984 277; home - 03398 84338. SER: Valuations; buys at auction. FAIRS: Aberdeen, Inverness, Banchory, Newark.

KINGHORN (Fife)

The Pend Antiques
53 High St. Est: 1990. Open 10-1 and 2-5.30, Wed. 1-5.30, Sun. 2-5. SIZE: Large. *STOCK: Pre 1940's furniture, prints, china, glass, textiles and general collectables, £1-£400.* PARK: Easy. TEL: 0592 890207; home - 0592 890140. SER: Valuations; restorations; stripping, waxing, small repairs; buys at auction (furniture).

KINGSTON-ON-SPEY
(Morayshire)

Collectables
Lein Rd. (J Penman and B Taylor) Est: 1987. Open daily and last Sun. of month, prior telephone call required. SIZE: Small. *STOCK: Militaria and jewellery, lap desks, china, collectables, small furniture, all from Victorian, £5-£200.* LOC: On B9105. PARK: Easy. TEL: 034 387 462; home - same. SER: Valuations. FAIRS: Inverness and Aberdeen.

KINGUSSIE
(Inverness-shire)

Mostly Pine
Gynack Cottage, High St. Est: 1980. Open 10-5 including Sun. in summer. *STOCK: Stripped pine and country furniture, decorative items, small collectables.* LOC: A9. TEL: 0540 661838. SER: Restorations (pine). VAT: Stan/Spec.

Colin Murdoch
56 High St. Est: 1968. Open 9.30-1 and 2.30-5.30. In winter by appointment. CL: Wed. p.m. SIZE: Small. *STOCK: Oil and watercolour paintings, 18th-20th C; prints and maps, books, some furniture.* LOC: Main St., signposted from new A9. PARK: Easy. TEL: 0540 661552; home - 0540 661300. SER: Valuations; buys at auction. VAT: Stan.

KINROSS
(Kinross)

Miles Antiques **LAPADA**
16 Mill St. (K. and S Miles) Est: 1979. Open 9-5, weekends by appointment. SIZE: Large. *STOCK: Furniture, including decorative, 19th C, Victorian and Edwardian, £500-£5,000; china and pottery, £50-£500.* LOC: Off M90, junction 6. Take right at High St. then second left. PARK: Easy. TEL: 0577 64858; home - 0577 63881. SER: Restorations (upholstery, polishing, small repairs). VAT: Stan/Spec.

KIPPEN
(Stirlingshire)

Robert Ainslie
"Glenora", Main St. Resident. Est: 1949. SIZE: Large. *STOCK: Furniture, brass, copper, shipping goods.* LOC: 9 miles from Stirling. PARK: Easy. TEL: 078 687 368. VAT: Stan.

KIRKCALDY
(Fife)

Langtown Antiques
Millie St. (G Hutchinson) Open 10-5. CL: Mon. *STOCK: General antiques.* PARK: Easy. TEL: 0592 204733.

Kirkcaldy continued

Graham Proudlock
49 Loughborough Rd. Est: 1986. Open by appointment. *STOCK: Kitchen, laundry and collectors' items, country and craftsmen's tools and garden items.* PARK: Easy. TEL: 0592 51546. SER: Valuations; buys at auction. VAT: Stan/Spec.

KIRKCUDBRIGHT
(Kirkcudbrightshire)

Chapel Antiques
Chapel Farm. (A Bradley) Est: 1981. Open 9-5 and by appointment. SIZE: Small. *STOCK: China, small and shipping furniture, silver, brass and copper, 18th-20th C, £5-£1,000.* LOC: 200yds. off A75 between Ringford and Twynholm on A762, 2 1/2 miles from Kirkcudbright. PARK: Easy. TEL: 055722 281.

Osborne **LAPADA**
41 Castle St. (R.A Mitchell) Est: 1948. Open 9-12.30 and 1.30-5. CL: Thurs. p.m and Sat. p.m. TEL: 0557 30441. VAT: Stan/Spec.

LANGHOLM
(Dumfriesshire)

The Antique Shop
High St. (R. and V Baird) Est: 1970. Open 10.30-5.30. CL: Wed. p.m. SIZE: Small. *STOCK: China, glass, pictures, 18th-20th C; jewellery, rugs, 19th-20th C; also Trade Warehouse of furniture, shipping goods, nearby.* LOC: 20 miles north of Carlisle on A7. PARK: 100yds. TEL: 038 73 80238.

The Steeple Bookshop
High St. (R. and V Baird) Est: 1984. Open Sat., May-Oct. 10-4, other times by appointment. TEL: 038 73 80238.

LARGS
(Ayrshire)

Narducci Antiques
11 Waterside St. (G Narducci) Open 2.30-5.30 or by appointment. SIZE: Warehouse. *STOCK: General antiques and shipping goods.* TEL: 0475 672612/0294 61687. SER: Packing; export. *Mainly Trade and Export.*

LESLIE BY INSCH
(Aberdeenshire)

C.S. Antiques
New Leslie. Open by appointment. SIZE: Medium. *STOCK: Pine, oak and mahogany furniture, 19th C, £50-£500.* LOC: Telephone for directions. PARK: Easy. TEL: 0464 20567; home - same. FAIRS: Tree Tops Hotel, Aberdeen.

LEUCHARS, Nr. St. Andrews
(Fife)

Earlshall Castle
(The Baron of Earlshall) Est: 1963. Open by appointment only. SIZE: Small. *STOCK: Arms and armour especially Scottish basket hilted swords and dirks, 16th-19th C, £200-£20,000.* LOC: Signposted on A91 at Guardbridge and in village. PARK: Easy. TEL: 0334 839205; home - same. SER: Valuations; restorations (wood, metal, engraving, chiselling and casting); buys at auction (weapons). VAT: Stan/Spec.

LINLITHGOW
(West Lothian)

Heritage Antiques
222 High St. (Mrs A.G Dunbar) Open 10-5. CL: Wed. *STOCK: China, glass, small furniture, jewellery, medals, silver, collectors' items.* TEL: 0506 847460.

LUNDIN LINKS
(Fife)

Bits 'n' Bobs Antiques
19 Leven Rd. Est: 1968. SIZE: Small. *STOCK: General antiques.* PARK: Easy. TEL: 0333 320266.

MOFFAT
(Dumfriesshire)

T.W Beaty LAPADA
22 Well St. Open 9.30-5; trade any time by appointment. SIZE: Large and warehouse. *STOCK: Furniture, china, glass, brass, pictures, 18th-20th C.* TEL: 0683 20380. VAT: Stan/Spec.

Harthope House Antiques
Church Gate. (Mrs M Owens) Est: 1979. Open 10-5. CL: Wed. *STOCK: Furniture, general antiques especially Victorian jewellery.* TEL: 0683 20710.

MONTROSE
(Angus)

Red Rose Antiques
47 Ferry St. (R Noller) Est: 1969. Open 10-5. CL: Sun. except by appointment. *STOCK: General antiques, smalls and furniture.* Not Stocked: Coins, stamps. LOC: 1 block south, 3 1/2 blocks east of Montrose Steeple. PARK: Easy. TEL: 0674 73076; home - same.

MUSSELBURGH
(East Lothian)

Paul Couts Ltd BADA
Linkfield House, 8-10 High St. Open 9-1 and 2.30-5, Sat. by appointment. *STOCK: Furniture, 18th C, £200-£20,000.* LOC: 15 mins. from Edinburgh. PARK: Easy. TEL: 031 665 7759; fax - 031 665 0836.

NEWTON STEWART
(Wigtownshire)

Brown's Antique Shop
44 and 53 Queen St. (M.B Brown) Est: 1946. *STOCK: General antiques.* TEL: 0671 2052. SER: Valuations; restorations; re-upholstery, repairs, auctioneers (furniture). VAT: Stan.

Pathbrae Antiques
20 Albert St. (R. and D Williamson, W. and M Plunkett) Est: 1985. Open 10.30-12.45 and 1.45-5. CL: Wed. p.m. SIZE: Small. *STOCK: Porcelain, 19th-20th C, from £5; jewellery, silver and plate.* LOC: Main street (A75). PARK: Easy. TEL: 0671 3429. SER: Valuations. VAT: Stan/Spec.

NEWTONMORE (Inverness-shire)

The Antique Shop
Main St. (F Dodd) HADA. Est: 1964. Open 9.30-5.30. SIZE: Medium. *STOCK: Small furniture, £20-£500; glass, china, silver, plate, copper, brass, secondhand books.* LOC: On A86 opposite Mains Hotel. PARK: Easy. TEL: 054 03 272; home - 054 04 256.

Highland House Antiques
Main St. (J L Ashford) Est: 1985. Open 9-1 and 2-5.30. SIZE: Small. *STOCK: Paintings, £500-£1,000; vintage fishing tackle, £100-£200; silver, £50-£100; all 19th-20th C.* LOC: 1 1/2 miles off A9. PARK: Easy. TEL: 05403 375.

NORTH BERWICK (East Lothian)

Fraser Antiques
129 High St. Est: 1968. Open 10-5. CL: Mon. SIZE: Medium. *STOCK: Porcelain, glass, pictures, silver, small furniture, general antiques.* LOC: From Berwick-on-Tweed via A1 follow A198 4 miles north of Dunbar. PARK: Easy. TEL: 0620 2722. SER: Restorations (paintings, clocks, furniture).

OBAN (Argyllshire)

The McIan Gallery (Campbell-Gibson Fine Arts)
10 Argyll Sq. Est: 1973. Open 9-5.30. *STOCK: Victorian and early 20th C watercolours and oil paintings, Scottish and continental, from £200.* TEL: 0631 66755/62303. SER: Restorations; framing; valuations; buys at auction.

Oban Antiques
35 Stevenson St. (P. and P Baker) Est: 1970. Open 9.30-5.30. SIZE: Medium. *STOCK: Mainly 19th C furniture, smalls, collectables, art deco items, £5-£1,500; some secondhand books.* LOC: Off George (main) St. PARK: Easy. TEL: 0631 66203; home - 0631 77215. SER: Valuations.

PAISLEY (Renfrewshire)

Corrigan Antiques
Woodlands, High Calside. Open by appointment. SIZE: Medium. *STOCK: General antiques and decorative items.* LOC: Near town centre. TEL: 041 887 7542. SER: Valuations. VAT: Stan/Spec.

Heritage Antiques
Walker St. (C.W Anderson) Est: 1963. Open Mon., Tues., Wed. 10-3; trade anytime by

Heritage Antiques continued

appointment. SIZE: Large. *STOCK: Furniture, late 18th-19th C; shipping goods and small items.* LOC: Off High St. PARK: Own. TEL: 041 889 3661 (24hrs.) and 041 880 8309. SER: Valuations. VAT: Stan/Spec.

Paisley Fine Books
17 Corsebar Cres. (Mr and Mrs B Merrifield) Est: 1985. Open by appointment. SIZE: Small. *STOCK: Books on architecture, art, antiques and collecting.* TEL: 041 884 2661; home - same. SER: Free book search; catalogues issued.

PERTH (Perthshire)

Ainslie's Antique Warehouse
Unit 3, Gray St. (T.S. and A Ainslie) Open 9-5, by appointment at weekends. SIZE: Large. *STOCK: General antiques.* TEL: 0738 36825.

Atholl Antiques
80 Princess St. (M. and L Gallagher) Open 9.30-1 and 2-5, Sat. 9.30-1. *STOCK: General antiques.* TEL: 0738 20054.

Coach House Antiques Ltd
77 Kinnoull St. (J Walker) PADA. Est: 1971. Open 9.30-5.30. SIZE: Large. *STOCK: Furniture, furnishings and decorative items, 18th-19th C; sporting prints; £20-£5,000.* PARK: Nearby. TEL: 0738 29835; home - 0738 828627. VAT: Spec.

A.S Deuchar and Son
10-12 South St. (A.S. and A.W.N Deuchar) Open 10-1 and 2-5. CL: Sat. p.m. SIZE: Large. *STOCK: Victorian shipping goods, furniture; 19th C paintings; china, brass, silver and plate.* LOC: Glasgow to Aberdeen Rd., near Queen's Bridge. PARK: Easy. TEL: 0738 26297; home - 0738 51452. VAT: Stan/Spec.

Forsyth Antiques
8 St. Paul's Sq. (A McDonald Forsyth) Est: 1961. Open 10-5. SIZE: Medium. *STOCK: Silver, 18th-19th C, £5-£1,000; jewellery, 19th-20th C, £5-£750; Monart glass, 20th C, £5-£500.* LOC: Behind St. Paul's Church, junction of High St. and Methven St. PARK: Easy. TEL: 0738 22173; home - 08214 570. SER: Valuations; buys at auction (silver). VAT: Stan/Spec.

Gallery One
1/2 St. Paul's Sq. (A McDonald Forsyth) Est: 1990. Open 10-5. *STOCK: Scottish pictures, Monart glass, jewellery, furniture.* LOC: Junction of High St. and Methven St. PARK: Easy. TEL: 0738 24877. SER: Valuations.

The George Street Gallery
38 George St. (M Hardie) PADA. Open 10-1 and 2-5. CL: Wed. and Sat. p.m. *STOCK: Oil paintings, watercolours, prints and etchings by Scottish artists, late 19th to early 20th C.* TEL: 0738 38953.

Perth continued

Hardie Antiques
25 St. John St. (T.G Hardie) PADA. Est: 1980. Open 9.30-5.15, Sat. 10-1. SIZE: Medium. *STOCK: Jewellery and silver, 18th-20th C, £5-£5,000.* PARK: Nearby. TEL: 0738 33127; home - 0738 51764. SER: Valuations. VAT: Stan/Spec.

Henderson
5 North Methven St. (J.G Henderson) Est: 1935. Open 9-5.30. CL: Wed. p.m. SIZE: Small. *STOCK: Porcelain, glass, 1720-1900, £5-£50; silver, jewellery, 1800-1900, £2-£200; coins, medals and stamps, £1-£100.* Not Stocked: Furniture. LOC: On A9. PARK: Easy. TEL: 0738 24836; home - 0738 21923. SER: Valuations. VAT: Stan.

Ian Murray Antiques Warehouse
21 Glasgow Rd. Open 9-5. CL: Sat. SIZE: Large - 8 dealers. *STOCK: General antiques, Victorian, Edwardian and shipping items.* PARK: Easy. TEL: 0738 37222. VAT: Stan/Spec.

Robertson and Cox Antiques
60 George St. PADA. Open 9.30-1 and 2-5. CL: Wed. p.m. and Sat. p.m. SIZE: Medium. *STOCK: Furniture, 18th and 19th C; paintings, porcelain, Oriental rugs, smalls.* TEL: 0738 26300. VAT: Spec.

Tay Street Gallery
70 Tay St. (I.C Ingram) Est: 1972. Open 9.30-1 and 2-5, Sat. 10-1, other times by appointment. CL: Wed. p.m. SIZE: Small. *STOCK: Furniture, mostly Georgian, £100-£3,000; pictures and prints, £100-£2,000; china, glass, metalware, decorative items, £10-£2,000.* LOC: Overlooking River Tay. PARK: Easy. TEL: 0738 20604. VAT: Stan/Spec.

PITLOCHRY
(Perthshire)

Blair Antiques
14 Bonnethill Rd. (A.C Huie) PADA. Est: 1976. Open 9-5. CL: Thurs. p.m. *STOCK: Period furniture, Scottish oil paintings, silver - some provincial, curios, clocks, pottery and porcelain.* LOC: Beside Scotlands Hotel, off A9 to Inverness. TEL: 0796 2624. SER: Valuations; buys at auction. VAT: Stan/Spec.

PITTENWEEM
(Fife)

Pittenweem Antiques and Fine Art
15 East Shore, The Harbour. (K.M McKillop and D.O MacNeal) Est: 1974. Open 10-5, Sun. 2-6. SIZE: Medium. *STOCK: Fine art and paintings of Scottish school, late 19th C to early 20th C, £500-£1,000; furniture, £500-£1,000, and Scottish pottery, both mid-19th C; small items.* PARK: Easy. TEL: 0333 312054. SER: Valuations.

PORTSOY
(Aberdeenshire)

Other Times
17 Seafield St. (D McLean and T Mathieson) Est: 1986. Open 10-5, including Sun. *STOCK: General antiques, 1700-1950.* TEL: 0261 42866. VAT: Stan.

PRESTWICK
(Ayrshire)

The Pine Village
By Quickstrip, 399-413 Spey Rd, Prestwick Airport. (J.R Cunningham and D.A Johnson) Est: 1980. Open 9-5.30, Sat. 9-5. SIZE: Medium. *STOCK: Furniture including stripped pine, 18th-19th C; shipping goods, 1930-1950.* LOC: Off main Prestwick Rd. PARK: Easy. TEL: 0292 74377. SER: Restorations (French polishing, upholstery, stripping); buys at auction (furniture). VAT: Stan.

Yer Granny's Attic
176 Main St. (Mr and Mrs B Dickson) Est: 1986. Open 10-6, Sun. by appointment. SIZE: Small. *STOCK: General antiques, collectables, bric-a-brac and linen, from Victorian, £5-£25.* LOC: Opposite large sandstone church. PARK: Nearby. TEL: 0292 76312. SER: Restorations (stained glass).

RAIT
(Perthshire)

The Bothy
Rait Antiques Centre. (C McCallum) Est: 1986. SIZE: Small. *STOCK: Georgian, Victorian, Edwardian pine furniture, small and decorative items, textiles.* LOC: Off A85. PARK: Easy. TEL: 082 17 205. SER: Buys at auction.

Carse Antiques
Rait Antiques Centre. (Mr and Mrs M Murray Threipland) PADA. Est: 1983. Open 10-1 and 2-5. CL: Sun., except by appointment. SIZE: Large. *STOCK: Furniture, especially early oak and country, £25-£25,000; decorative items especially Wemyss ware, 17th-20th C, £5-£500.* Not Stocked: Silver and jewellery. LOC: 1 mile north of A85 between Perth and Dundee. PARK: Easy. TEL: 082 17 205; home - 082 17 227; fax - 082 17 201. VAT: Stan/Spec.

Fair Finds
Rait Antiques Centre. (J Mitchell and L Templeman) SIZE: Large. *STOCK: Furniture, smalls, textiles, upholstered furniture and pine.* TEL: 082 17 379.

Keith Antiques
Rait Antiques Centre. (D. and S Keith) Est: 1979. Open 9-5, Sun. by appointment. SIZE: Small. *STOCK: 18th-19th C furniture, clocks, porcelain, £500-£5,000.* PARK: Easy. TEL: 082 17 386. SER: Valuations; buys at auction. VAT: Stan/Spec.

Rait continued

Murray-Tait Antiques
Rait Antiques Centre. Open 9.30-5, Sat. 10-5. *STOCK: General antiques, soft furnishings, decorative items.* TEL: 082 17 344; mobile - 0860 605392.

Templemans
The Mill Room, Rait Antiques Centre. Est: 1967. Open 9.30-5. *STOCK: Period and decorative furniture, £200-£20,000.* TEL: 082 17 344; home - 0828 86268. SER: Valuations; museum acquisitions. VAT: Spec.

RATTRAY, Nr. Blairgowrie (Perthshire)

Architectural Recycling Co
Craighall. (A.I Rattray) Open by appointment. *STOCK: Architectural items and salvage.* PARK: Easy. TEL: 0250 4749.

ST. ANDREWS (Fife)

Bygones
68 South St. (Mrs J Guest) Open 10-4.30, Sun. 2-4.30. CL: Thurs. *STOCK: Furniture, smalls, silver, bric-a-brac.* LOC: Near town hall. PARK: Easy. TEL: 0334 75849.

Circa Antiques
211 South St. (C McDonald Craig) Est: 1978. Open 10-1 and 2-5. SIZE: Medium. *STOCK: General antiques, mainly British, 1800-1900, £5-£1,000.* Not Stocked: Postcards, crested china, militaria and weapons. PARK: Nearby. TEL: 0334 76798.

Old St. Andrews Gallery
9 Albany Pl. (Mr and Mrs D.R Brown) Est: 1973. CL: 1-2 daily. SIZE: Medium. *STOCK: Golf memorabilia, 19th C, £100-£5,000; silver, jewellery especially Scottish 19th-20th C, £100-£3,000; general antiques, from 18th C, £50-£5,000.* LOC: Main street. PARK: Easy. TEL: 0334 77840. SER: Valuations; restorations (jewellery, silver); buys at auction (golf memorabilia). VAT: Stan.

Old St. Andrews Gallery
10 Golf Place. Open 9-1 and 2-5. *STOCK: Golf memorabilia, art and books, from 18th C, to £10,000.* TEL: 0334 77840.

St. Andrews Fine Art
84a Market St. (J Carruthers) Open 10-1 and 2-5. *STOCK: Scottish 19th and 20th C paintings, drawings and watercolours.* TEL: 0334 74080.

SALTCOATS (Ayrshire)

Narducci Antiques
57 Raise St. (G Narducci) Est: 1972. Open 10-1

Narducci Antiques continued

and 2.30-5.30, or by appointment. *STOCK: General antiques and shipping goods.* TEL: 0294 61687/67137. SER: Packing, export. *Mainly Trade and Export.*

SCONE, Nr. Perth (Perthshire)

Robert Ainslie Antiques
80 Perth Rd. Open 9-5, Sat., Sun. and other times by appointment. SIZE: Medium. *STOCK: Georgian, Victorian and Edwardian furnishings and smalls, especially longcase clocks.* TEL: 0738 52438.

SELKIRK (Selkirkshire)

Heatherlie Antiques
6/8 Heatherlie Terr. (A.F.D Scott) Est: 1979. Open 9-12.30 and 1.30-5. CL: Sat. p.m. SIZE: Medium. *STOCK: Furniture, £50-£1,000; pottery and porcelain, general antiques, brass, bric-a-brac and copper, £5-£250; all 19th-20th C.* LOC: Leave A7 at Selkirk market place and take Moffat/Peebles road for 1/2 mile. PARK: Easy. TEL: 0750 20114. VAT: Stan/Spec.

SORBIE, Nr. Newton Stewart (Wigtownshire)

R.G Williamson & Co LAPADA
Old Church. Est: 1965. Open 2-4, April-Sept., other times by appointment. SIZE: Large. *STOCK: Furniture, from 1700, from £20; small items, from 18th C, from £5.* LOC: Off A75. PARK: Easy. TEL: 098 885 275; home - same. SER: Valuations; buys at auction. VAT: Stan/Spec.

STIRLING (Stirlingshire)

Campbell Antiques
35 Friars St. (S Campbell) Resident. Est: 1980. Open 10-5. SIZE: Small. *STOCK: Jewellery, £10-£2,000; furniture including pine, £20-£1,000; paintings, £50-£1,000; bric-a-brac, £1-£100; coins and medals, £1-£1,000; all 18th-20th C.* LOC: Off Murray Pl., part of main thoroughfare. PARK: Nearby. TEL: 0786 71832; home - 0786 70595. SER: Valuations; restorations (china, furniture, jewellery); buys at auction (paintings, furniture, jewellery).

Monument Antiques
75 Wallace St. (Mr and Mrs G Oddy) Open 11.30-5. CL: Wed. *STOCK: General antiques especially clocks.* TEL: 0786 70317.

Elizabeth Paterson Antiques LAPADA
52 1/2 Spittal St. (E. and J Paterson) Est: 1976.

Elizabeth Paterson Antiques continued

Open 11-5. CL: Sat. and Sun. except by appointment. SIZE: Large. *STOCK: Furniture including pine; Oriental porcelain.* LOC: On road to Stirling Castle. TEL: 0786 50648. SER: Valuations; export and packing worldwide.

STONEHAVEN (Kincardineshire)

Kotobuki Antiques

66 Allardice St. (L Cameron) Open 9.30-5.30. *STOCK: Oriental items.* PARK: Easy. TEL: 0569 66589.

STRATHBLANE (Stirlingshire)

Whatnots

16 Milngavie Rd. (F Bruce) Est: 1965. *STOCK: Furniture, paintings, jewellery, silver and plate, clocks, small items, shipping goods, horse drawn and old vehicles.* LOC: 25 miles from Stirling and 10 miles from Glasgow. PARK: Easy. TEL: 0360 70310/50218. VAT: Stan/Spec.

THORNHILL, Nr. Dumfries (Dumfries-shire)

Thornhill Gallery Antique Centre

47-48 Drumlanrig St. (A.S.B Crawford) Est: 1984. Open 9-5.30 or by appointment. SIZE: Medium - 6 dealers. *STOCK: Furniture, 18th-20th C; watercolours and oil paintings; glass; porcelain; silver and plate; bronzes; pine country furniture and related items; linen; Oriental carpets and rugs.* LOC: A76 in village centre. PARK: Easy. TEL: 0848 30566; home - same. VAT: Stan/Spec.

THURSO (Caithness)

Thurso Antiques

Drill Hall, Sinclair St. (G. and J Atkinson) HADA. Est: 1971. Open 10-1 and 2-5, Thurs. 10-1. SIZE: Small. *STOCK: Porcelain, 1700-1920, £5-£1,500; jewellery, 1700-1930, £25-£1,000; silver, 1750-1900, £25-£1,000; coins, 1500-1900, £2-£500; paintings, 1750-1920, £25-£1,500; fiddles, 1740-1930, £50-£1,000; medals.* LOC: Near Post Office. PARK: Easy. TEL: 0847 63291. SER: Valuations; restorations; cleaning (paintings); silver, jewellery and fiddle repairs.

WALKERBURN (Peebleshire)

Townhouse Antiques

(B Brett and J Juett) Open 10.30-4.30. CL: Wed. *STOCK: Textiles, collectables, china, furniture.* LOC: On A72, 7 miles east of Peebles. TEL: 089 687 694/371.

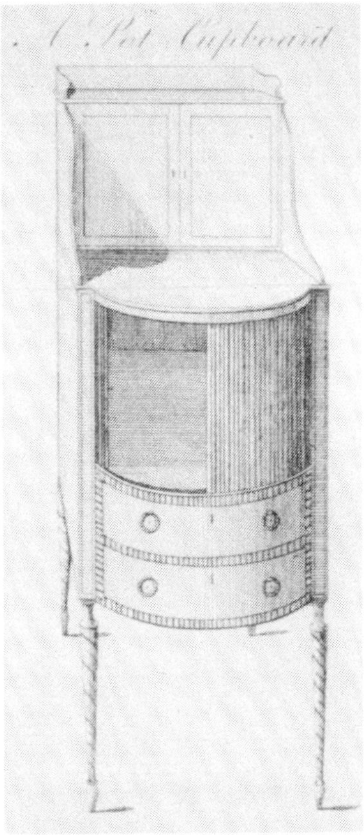

Thomas Sheraton
'The Cabinet-Maker and Upholsterer's Drawing Book', 1793.
Plate XLIII from Part III. Pot Cupboard. 'These are used in genteel bedrooms, and are sometimes finished in satinwood, and in a style a little elevated above their use . . . Sometimes there are folding doors to the cupboard part, and sometimes a curtain of green silk, fixed on a brass wire at top and bottom; but in this design a tambour door is used, as preferable. The upper cupboard contains shelves, and is intended to keep medicines to be taken in the night, or to hold other little articles which servants are not permitted to overlook.'
From ***Pictorial Dictionary of British 18th Century Furniture Design — The Printed Sources*** compiled by Elizabeth White and published by the **Antique Collectors' Club** in 1990. £65.00.

WALES

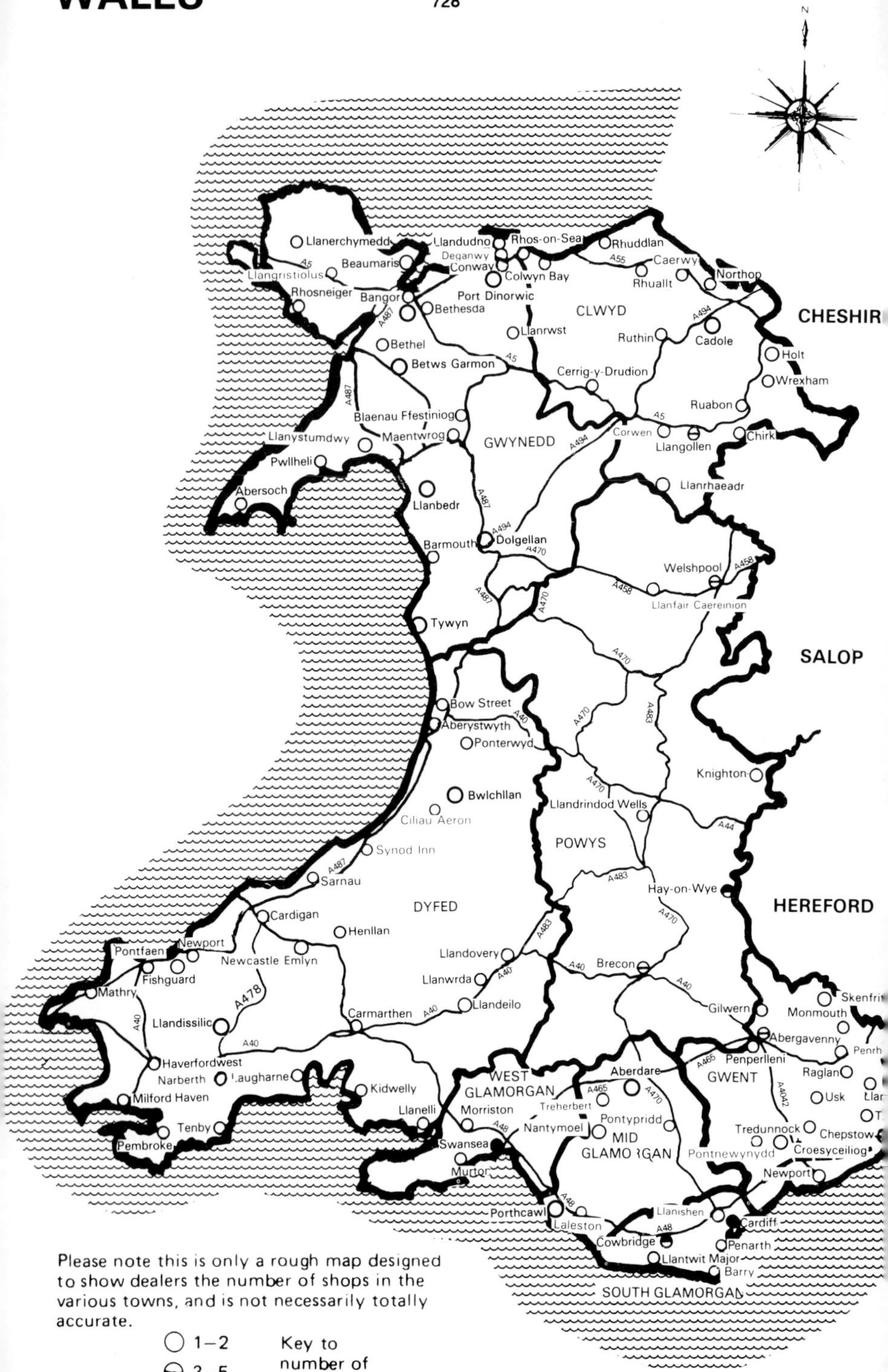

N
Llanerchymedd
Llandudno
Rhos-on-Sea
Rhuddlan
Deganwy
Conway
Colwyn Bay
Caerwys
Northop
Beaumaris
Llangristiolus
A5
A55
Rhuallt
Rhosneiger
Bangor
Port Dinorwic
Bethesda
CLWYD
CHESHIRE
A487
A494
Llanrwst
Ruthin
Cadole
Bethel
Holt
Betws Garmon
A5
Cerrig-y-Drudion
Wrexham
Ruabon
Blaenau Ffestiniog
Corwen
Llangollen
Chirk
Llanystumdwy
Maentwrog
GWYNEDD
Pwllheli
Abersoch
Llanbedr
Llanrhaeadr
Barmouth
Dolgellau
A470
Welshpool
A458
Llanfair Caereinion
Tywyn
SALOP
Bow Street
Aberystwyth
Ponterwyd
A483
Knighton
Bwlchllan
Llandrindod Wells
Ciliau Aeron
A44
POWYS
Synod Inn
Sarnau
Hay-on-Wye
DYFED
Cardigan
HEREFORD
Henllan
Newport
Pontfaen
Newcastle Emlyn
Llandovery
Fishguard
A40
Brecon
Llanwrda
A478
Mathry
Llandissilic
Llandeilo
Gilwern
Carmarthen
Monmouth
Abergavenny
Haverfordwest
Penperlleni
Narberth
Laugharne
Aberdare
WEST GLAMORGAN
GWENT
A465
Raglan
Milford Haven
Kidwelly
Usk
Llanelli
Morriston
Treherbert
A4042
Pontypridd
Tenby
A48
Nantymoel
MID GLAMORGAN
Tredunnock
Chepstow
Pembroke
Swansea
Pontnewynydd
Croesyceiliog
Murton
Newport
Porthcawl
Llanishen
Cardiff
Laleston
Cowbridge
Penarth
Llantwit Major
Barry
SOUTH GLAMORGAN

Please note this is only a rough map designed to show dealers the number of shops in the various towns, and is not necessarily totally accurate.

Key to number of shops in this area.

- ○ 1–2
- ⊖ 3–5
- ◓ 6–12
- ● 13+

Clwyd

BAGILLT

Mayfair Antiques
Green Park House, Green Park, High St. (H Edwards) Open by appointment. *STOCK: General antiques.* TEL: 0352 711891.

CADOLE, Nr. Mold

Rocking Chair Antiques
Cwr-y-Coed, Ruthin Rd. (G Baines) Open by appointment. *STOCK: Stripped pine furniture.* TEL: 035285 568. SER: Export.

CAERWYS, Nr. Mold

Tom Lloyd-Roberts
Old Court House. Est: 1967. *STOCK: Antiquarian books, £2-£2,000.* TEL: 0352 720276.

CERRIG-Y-DRUDION, Nr. Corwen

Michael Main Ltd. Architectural Antiques
The Old Rectory. Resident. Open 8-4.30, Sat. 8-1 or by appointment. SIZE: Large. *STOCK: Period doors, fire surrounds, ballustrades, panelling, stained glass and other architectural items.* LOC: On A5. PARK: Easy. TEL: 049 082 491. VAT: Stan/Spec.

CHIRK

Seventh Heaven
Chirk Mill. (Mr and Mrs J.J Butler) Est: 1971. Open every day. SIZE: Large. *STOCK: Brass, iron and wooden beds including half-tester, four-poster and canopied, mainly 19th C.* LOC: On A5 as it crosses Welsh border. PARK: Easy. TEL: 0691 777622/773563; fax - 0691 777313. VAT: Stan.

COLWYN BAY

North Wales Antiques - Colwyn Bay
56-58 Abergele Rd. (F Robinson) Est: 1971. Open 9-5. SIZE: Large warehouse. *STOCK: Shipping items, Victorian, early oak, mahogany and pine.* LOC: On A55. PARK: Easy. TEL: 0492 530521, evenings - 0492 516141. VAT: Stan.

CORWEN

Caxton House Antiques
Bridge St. (M Holmes Field) Open 10-4.30. CL: Sat. *STOCK: Small furniture, china, pottery, Staffordshire figures, prints, oil lamps, Victorian clothing.* LOC: On A5. TEL: 0490 3276.

HOLT, Nr. Wrexham

Norman Davies
Rock Cottage, Bridge St. Open Sat. and Sun. 10-5, other times by appointment. *STOCK: Furniture, 18th-19th C.* TEL: 0829 270210.

LLANGOLLEN

M Gallagher (Antiques)
Hall St. Open by appointment. *STOCK: General antiques.* TEL: 0978 860655.

J. and R Langford
12 Bridge St. (P. and M Silverston) Est: 1960. CL: Thurs. p.m. and 1-2 daily. SIZE: Medium. *STOCK: Furniture, £100-£3,000; pottery and porcelain, £50-£700; silver, general antiques, clocks, brass and paintings, £20-£2,000; all 18th-19th C.* LOC: Turn right at Royal Hotel, shop on right. PARK: Easy. TEL: 0978 860182; home - 0978 860493. SER: Valuations. VAT: Stan/Spec.

Oak Chest
1 Oak St. Est: 1950. *STOCK: Victorian jewellery and silver.* TEL: 0978 860095. VAT: Stan.

Passers Buy (Marie Evans)
Oak St/Chapel St. (Mrs M Evans) Est: 1970. Open 10-5, Sun. by appointment. SIZE: Medium. *STOCK: Pottery, porcelain, furniture, copper, brass and prints.* LOC: Just off A5. Junction of Chapel St. and Oak St. PARK: Easy. TEL: 0978 860861. FAIRS: Portmeirion Spring and Autumn.

Victoria House Antiques
Oak St. (E.M. and R Evans) Open 10-5 (if closed contact shop next door), Sun. by appointment. *STOCK: Mainly furniture.* TEL: 0978 860861.

LLANRHAEADR

Minstrel Gallery
Church St. (R.D. and B.S Hilton) Est: 1987. Open 10.30-1 and 2.30-5.30, Sun. 2.30-5. In winter Fri. and Sat. only or by appointment. SIZE: Small. *STOCK: Porcelain and glass, country furniture, 18th-19th C, £5-£500; brass, copper and jewellery, unusual items.* LOC: A5 from Shrewsbury, left at Knockin turn-off. Cross A483 at Llynclys by White Lion. Village straight ahead, gallery is at far corner at back of church. PARK: Nearby. TEL: 069 189 455; home - same. SER: Buys at auction (furniture and smalls). FAIRS: Silhouette.

MOLD

Mold Antiques and Interiors
The Old Chapel, 91 Wrexham St. (A Terry) Est: 1984. CL: Thurs. SIZE: Large. *STOCK: Furniture, early Victorian and Edwardian, some*

Mold Antiques and Interiors continued

Georgian and Regency, £50-£2,500. LOC: From Mold Cross into Wrexham St., premises 1/4 mile on right. PARK: Easy. TEL: 0352 2979; home - 0244 380512. FAIRS: Wilmslow Moat House Sunday monthly. VAT: Stan/Spec.

NORTHOP, Nr. Mold

James H Morris and Co

Old Village School, The Green. Appointment advisable. *STOCK: Furniture, clocks.* LOC: A55. TEL: 035 286 508; home - 035 286 768. SER: Valuations.

RHOS-ON-SEA

Clwyd Coins and Stamps

12 Colwyn Cres. (J.H Jones) Open by appointment. *STOCK: Coins, stamps and postcards.* TEL: 0492 40610.

Shelagh Hyde

11 Rhos Rd. Est: 1960. Open 10-1 and 2.30-5. CL: Wed. p.m. *STOCK: Trade selection of general antiques; furniture, porcelain, glass.* TEL: 0492 48879.

RHUALLT, Nr. St. Asaph

John Trefor Antiques

Rhuallt Hall Farm. Est: 1967. Open by appointment any time. SIZE: Medium. *STOCK: Oak, walnut and mahogany furniture especially Welsh dressers, longcase clocks, some shipping goods, £5-£6,500.* Not Stocked: Jewellery, cards and medals. LOC: On A55, 3 miles from St. Asaph towards Chester, next to village shop. PARK: Easy. TEL: 0745 583604. VAT: Stan/Spec.

RUTHIN

Castell Delmar Antiques

Wrexham Rd. (W.T Jones) Open by appointment. SIZE: Warehouse. *STOCK: Pre-1930 furniture and shipping goods.* TEL: 082 42 4484.

Ruthin continued

Old Tyme Antiques

21 Clwyd St. (G. and J Vaughan) Open 10.30-5. CL: Thurs. p.m. in winter. *STOCK: Wall and mantel clocks; British, European and Oriental porcelain, Imari ware, cranberry, gaudy Welsh china, brass, silver, jewellery, postcards and bric-a-brac.* LOC: 100yds. from town square. PARK: Nearby. TEL: Home - 082 42 2902. VAT: Stan.

R. and S.M Percival Antiques

Porth-y-Dwr, 65 Clwyd St. Est: 1979. Open daily, Sun. and Mon. by appointment. SIZE: Medium. *STOCK: Pine, mahogany and oak furniture and decorative smalls, 18th-19th C, £100-£1,000+.* PARK: Behind shop. TEL: 082 42 4454; home - 097 888 370. SER: Valuations; buys at auction (furniture). FAIRS: Newark. VAT: Stan/Spec.

WREXHAM

Smith Antiques

2 New Rd, Rhosddu. (Mrs J Price) *STOCK: Collectors and shipping items, needlework, 19th C furniture.* SER: Clock repairs; buys at auction. VAT: Stan.

Dyfed

ABERAERON

Colectomania

Corner Shop, Albert St. (K. and J Whiteland) Est: 1957. Open 10.30-5.30. CL: Thurs. SIZE: Medium. *STOCK: Furniture and small items including brass, copper, china, 19th C, £5-£1,000.* LOC: Off A487. PARK: Easy. TEL: Home - 0570 470 597. SER: Valuations.

ABERYSTWYTH

The Furniture Cave
33 Cambrian St. (P David) Est: 1975. Open 9-5, Wed. 9-3, Sat. 10-4. *STOCK: Pine, 1700-1930, from £100; general antiques, Victorian and Edwardian, £30-£300; small items, 19th C, £10-£50.* LOC: First right off Terrace Rd., at railway station end. PARK: Nearby. TEL: 0970 611234. SER: Restorations.

Howards of Aberystwyth LAPADA
10 Alexandra Rd. Open 10-5.30. *STOCK: Furniture, jewellery, Welsh pottery and copper lustre, gaudy Welsh and early pottery, Staffordshire groups, blue and white, cranberry, glass, silver, prints and maps of Cardiganshire, collectables and decorative items, especially country.* TEL: 0970 624973.

Chris Mann Antiques
Westminster Yard, High St. *STOCK: Furniture and decorative items, especially longcase clocks.*

AMMANFORD

Amman Antiques
29 Station Rd. (B Haines) Open by appointment only. *STOCK: General antiques.* TEL: 0269 592730.

BOW STREET

Garn House Antiques
Garn House. (Mrs M Hagarty) Est: 1969. Open Mon.-Sat. but to the Trade any time. *STOCK: General antiques, furniture, Victoriana, copper, brass, porcelain, glass, collectors' items and Victorian jewellery.* TEL: 0970 828562/828885.

BWLCHLLAN, Nr. Lampeter

Jansons Antiques
Aelybryn. (J.C Jansons) Usually open but prior telephone call advisable. *STOCK: Furniture - Welsh oak, original painted pine, primitive Welsh country; brass and iron beds.* TEL: 0570 470549.

CARDIGAN

Bayvil House Antiques
39 High St. (R.L.V. and G.V Smith) Est: 1940. Open 9-5.30. CL: Wed. p.m. *STOCK: Furniture, especially oak and mahogany, 18th-19th C; pottery, porcelain, copper and brass.* LOC: First shop on right when entering town from river bridge. TEL: 0239 612654. VAT: Stan/Spec.

Cardigan Antiques
(P Griffiths) By appointment only. *STOCK: Oak and country furniture, 18th C.* TEL: 0239 820680/86202.

Cardigan continued

Chapel House Antiques

11 Pendre. (M Kitson) Resident. Est: 1963. Open 10-5, Wed. 10-1, Sun. by appointment. SIZE: Medium. *STOCK: Pine and country furniture, kitchenalia, decoys, rugs, late 18th C to 1920, £5-£2,500.* LOC: Continuation of High St. PARK: Nearby. TEL: 0239 613268/614868. SER: Valuations; restorations; buys at auction (pre-1850 and unusual furniture). FAIRS: Newark, Builth Wells. VAT: Stan/Spec.

Chapel House Antiques

32 Pentood Estate. (M Kitson) Open by appointment from 8-6, Sat. 10-5. SIZE: Warehouse. *STOCK: Pine and country furniture.* PARK: Own. TEL: 0239 614868. SER: Restoration (including stripping and polishing); packing; shipping and courier. VAT: Stan/Spec.

CARMARTHEN

John Carpenter

Resident. Est: 1973. Open by appointment. *STOCK: Musical instruments, furniture, general antiques.* TEL: 0267 234895. SER: Buys at auction.

Cwmgwili Mill

Bronwydd Arms. (M.J Sandell) Est: 1950. Open 9-1 and 2-6, Sat. 9-1 and 2-6, Sun. by appointment. SIZE: Large. *STOCK: Furniture, oak, mahogany and country including dressers, coffers, long tables, and court cupboards, 17th-19th C, £50-£1,000.* PARK: Easy. TEL: 0267 231500; home - 0267 237215. VAT: Spec.

Merlins Antiques

Albion Arcade, Blue St. (Mrs J.R Perry) Open 10.15-4.30. CL: Thurs. *STOCK: Small items - porcelain, pottery and postcards.* TEL: 0267 237728.

CILIAU AERON, Nr. Lampeter

K.W Finlay Antiques

The Forge, Neuaddlwyd. Est: 1969. Usually open but prior telephone call advisable. SIZE: Large. *STOCK: Furniture, 18th-20th C, £50-£3,000; smalls.* Not Stocked: Militaria, jewellery. LOC: A482. PARK: Easy. TEL: 0545 570536; home - same. VAT: Stan/Spec. *Trade Only.*

FISHGUARD

Hermitage Antiquities

10 West St. (J.B Thomas) Est: 1976. Open 9.30-1 and 2-5.30. CL: Wed. and Sat. p.m. SIZE: Small. *STOCK: Arms, armour and militaria - full suits of armour, 16th-17th C; military long-guns, pistols, swords; cased pistol sets, military headgear, ethnographica, 16th-19th C, £50-£5,000; antiquities, jewellery, objets d'art.* LOC: 50yds. on right after leaving Square on Harbour road (West St.). PARK: 300yds.

Buckle, enamelled and gilt, designed by Josef Hoffmann and executed by the Wiener Werkstätte; 1909.

LANDESGEWERBEAMT, BADEN-WURTEMBERG, STUTTGART

From ***Jewellery 1789-1910 - The International Era,*** Volume II, by Shirley Bury published by the **Antique Collectors' Club** in 1991. £47.50 each volume.

Hermitage Antiques continued

TEL: 0348 873037; home - 0348 872322. SER: Valuations; restorations (arms and armour, inlay work on wheel locks, flintlock parts re-built, woodwork repairs); buys at auction (arms and armour). VAT: Spec.

Manor House Antiques

Main St. (R.E Davies) Open 9.15-5.30. *STOCK: General antiques especially porcelain and pottery.* TEL: 0348 873260.

HAVERFORDWEST

Gerald Oliver Antiques

14 Albany Terr, St. Thomas Green. Est: 1957. Open 9.30-1 and 2-5. CL: Thurs. p.m. SIZE: Small. *STOCK: Furniture, pre-1890, £5-£3,000; ceramics, metalwork, small silver, from 35; unusual, decorative and local interest items.* LOC: Via by-pass and up Merlins Hill to St. Thomas Green. PARK: Easy. TEL: 0437 762794. SER: Valuations. VAT: Spec.

Pine Design Workshop

19 Bridgend Sq. (B. and J Palmer and K.L Thomas) Open 9.30-5.30. *STOCK: Pine.* TEL: 0437 765676.

HENLLAN, Nr. Newcastle Emlyn

Richard Lloyd **LAPADA**
Dolhaidd Mansion. Est: 1969. Open 9-5, prior telephone call advisable. SIZE: Large. *STOCK: Country furniture, shipping goods, general antiques, bygones.* LOC: On A484, 2 miles Newcastle Emlyn. TEL: 0559 370791/370582. VAT: Stan/Spec. *Trade Only.*

Tortoiseshell Antiques
Trebedw Guest House. (Mrs P Taylor) Est: 1972. Open by appointment only. SIZE: Small. *STOCK: Carved European ivories, £45-£1,500; jewellery and objects, £35-£500; textiles, samplers, needlework tools, £40-£1,000; all 18th to early 19th C.* LOC: Off Carmarthen/Cardigan Rd. PARK: Easy. TEL: 0559 370943; home - same. SER: Valuations; restorations (jewellery). FAIRS: Olympia, NEC, West London, Buxton, Kensington, Snape, Tatten Park, Bath, City of London (Barbican), Wilton House, High Wycombe, and major provincial. VAT: Spec.

KIDWELLY

Country Antiques **LAPADA**
Old Castle Mill. (R. and L Bebb) Open 10-5. CL: Mon. SIZE: Large. *STOCK: Welsh country furniture and artefacts; longcase clocks, brass and copper.* LOC: Just off A484. PARK: Easy. TEL: 0554 890534. SER: Valuations. VAT: Stan/Spec.

Kidwelly continued

Country Antiques **LAPADA**
31 Bridge St. (R. and L Bebb) Open 10-5. CL: Mon. SIZE: Large. *STOCK: Georgian and Victorian furniture and accessories; Persian carpets; collectables.* LOC: On A484. PARK: Easy. TEL: 0554 890328. VAT: Stan/Spec.

LAMPETER

Barn Antiques
2 Market St. (N Megicks) Est: 1980. Open 9-5.30, Wed. 9-1. SIZE: Medium. *STOCK: Pine, oak, mahogany, mainly 19th C, £50-£1,000; reproduction pine and oak.* LOC: Pedestrianised street just off town centre. PARK: Easy. TEL: 0570 423526. SER: Valuations; restorations (re-veneering, inlay work, French polishing, pine stripping and finishing). VAT: Stan/Spec.

LAUGHARNE

Neil Speed Antiques
The Strand. Est: 1975. Open Fri. and Sat. 11-5, and some other days in summer, or by appointment. *STOCK: General antiques, country furniture and associated items.* TEL: 0994 427412.

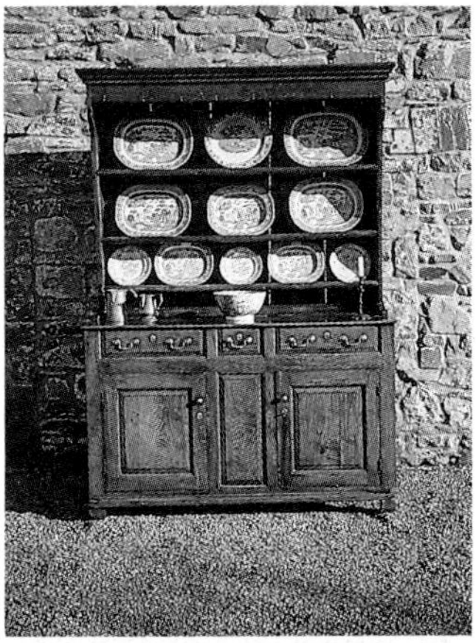

LLANDEILO

Jim and Pat Ash

The Warehouse, 5 Station Rd. Est: 1977. Open 9.30-5. SIZE: Large. *STOCK: Furniture, oak, Welsh country, walnut, cherrywood and European pine.* LOC: 50yds. off A40. PARK: Easy. TEL: 0558 823726; home - 0269 850119. SER: Valuations; shipping; courier; buys at auction. VAT: Stan/Spec.

LLANDISSILIO, Nr. Clynderwen

Jeremiah Antiques

The Old Saddlery. (S. and S Jeremiah) Est: 1980. Open by appointment only. SIZE: Small. *STOCK: Mahogany furniture, 19th C, £50-£2,500.* LOC: Halfway through village on A478. PARK: Easy. TEL: 09916 848; home - same. SER: Restorations (furniture, excluding pine); buys at auction.

LLANDOVERY

Dyfri Antiques

11 High St. (B Leach) Est: 1968. SIZE: Small. *STOCK: Small general antiques, china, pottery, collectors' items, old dolls.* TEL: 0550 20602.

Ovell Antiques

1 Kings Rd. Open 9.30-5. *STOCK: Antiquarian maps, prints, smalls and Victorian jewellery.* TEL: 0550 20928/21013.

LLANELLI

Alice's Antiques

24 Upper Park St. (Mrs A Davies) Est: 1940. Open 10-1 and 2-6. CL: Tues. p.m. SIZE: Small. *STOCK: General antiques, 1850-1950, £5-£50; paintings, silver, Georgian and Victorian, china, metalware.* LOC: On main road in town centre. PARK: At rear. TEL: 0554 773045. SER: Valuations; buys at auction. VAT: Stan.

LLANWRDA

Maclean Antiques

Tiradda, Llansadwrn. (D.J Thorpe) Resident. Est: 1972. Open 9.30-6. SIZE: Large. *STOCK: Period pine, country furniture, treen, brass, period metal.* PARK: Easy. TEL: 0550 777509. VAT: Spec.

MATHRY

Cartrefle Antiques

(M Hughes and Y Chesters) Open in summer 10-5.30; in winter Tues.-Sat. 10.30-4, evenings by appointment. *STOCK: General antiques especially jewellery.* PARK: Easy. TEL: 0348 831591.

MILFORD HAVEN

Milford Haven Antiques
Robert St. Est: 1968. Open 10-5. *STOCK: General antiques.* TEL: 0646 692152.

NARBERTH

Barn Court Antiques
12 High St. (A. and M Evans) Est: 1989. Open 10-5. CL: Mon. SIZE: Medium. *STOCK: Oak, mahogany, walnut and rosewood furniture, Georgian to late Victorian, £100-£3,000; oils and watercolours, £100-£3,000; china, glass and silver, mainly Victorian, £10-£300.* Not Stocked: Pine furniture. LOC: Off A40 on A478. PARK: Easy. TEL: 0834 861421.

Cheriton Antiques LAPADA
32 High St. (Mr and Mrs P.R Thomas) Est: 1985. Open 9-5.30. SIZE: Large. *STOCK: Early oak and walnut furniture, £100-£25,000; metalwork, British pottery, needlework, country and decorative furnishings; early paintings.* Not Stocked: Jewellery, medals and militaria. PARK: Easy. TEL: 0834 860660; home - 0646 651728. SER: Valuations; restorations (furniture and pictures); buys at auction (as stock). VAT: Stan/Spec.

NEWCASTLE EMLYN

Castle Antiques
Market Sq. (Mr and Mrs B.G Houser) Est: 1986. Open 9.30-5.30. SIZE: Small. *STOCK: Furniture, 1700 to 1920s, £500-£2,000; china and glass, Victorian to 1920s; kitchenalia, 18th-19th C; both £5-£200.* LOC: Main road, under clock tower. PARK: Castle St. TEL: 0239 710420; home - same. VAT: Stan/Spec.

NEWPORT

Newport Antiques
Market St. (R Atkinson) Est: 1970. *STOCK: Small furniture, pine, silver, plate, brass, copper, porcelain and jewellery.* LOC: A487. TEL: 0239 820351.

PEMBROKE

Northgate Antiques
10 Northgate St. (J.P. and J Howells) Est: 1956. Open 10-5. CL: Wed. p.m. *STOCK: Furniture, oak, mahogany, 18th-20th C; general antiques, copper, brass, china and jewellery.* TEL: 0646 684416; home - 0646 672388/681502. VAT: Stan.

Pembroke Antique Centre
The Hall, Hamilton Terr. (M Davis) Open 10-5. SIZE: 30 dealers. *STOCK: Oak, pine and mahogany furniture, china, porcelain, clocks, prints, collectors' items.* LOC: Old chapel on main st. PARK: Easy. TEL: 0646 687017.

PEMBROKE DOCK

Glyn Jones Antiques
25 Pembroke St. Resident. Open daily. SIZE: Large. *STOCK: Pine, shipping furniture and smalls.* LOC: 1/4 mile from Irish ferry terminal. TEL: 0646 621732; home - 0646 621934. SER: Restorations; pine stripping; container packing.

PONTERWYD, Nr. Aberystwyth

Doggie Hubbard's Bookshop
Ffynnon Cadno. (C.L.B Hubbard) ABA. Est: 1946. Open 10-5, Sun. by appointment. SIZE: Medium. *STOCK: Rare books on dogs, 16th-19th C, £50-£500; scarce books on dogs, 19th-20th C, £25-£100; other books on dogs, 20th C, £5-£25.* LOC: 1/2 mile form Ponterwyd westwards on A44. PARK: Easy. TEL: 097 085 224; home - same. SER: Valuations; buys at auction (rare dog books). FAIRS: New York and Boston.

PONTFAEN, Nr. Fishguard

The Old Vicarage
(T.C. and C.M Dunn) Est: 1985. Open 9-6, Mar.-Oct. only, other times by appointment. CL: Mon. *STOCK: Garden furniture, £100-£5,000; statuary, £50-£5,000; both 19th-20th C.* LOC: Just off B4313. PARK: Easy. TEL: 0348 881363; home - same. SER: Restorations (metalwork and stone); buys at auction (as stock). VAT: Spec.

SARNAU

Ffynnon Las
(P. and G Palmer) Est: 1971. Open at any time. SIZE: Small. *STOCK: Decorated furniture in American and European styles, 19th to early 20th C.* LOC: Off A487 9 miles north of Cardigan, down track. PARK: Easy. TEL: 0239 654648; home - same.

SYNOD INN

Forge Antiques
The Old Forge. (P Williams) Est: 1982. Open 10-5 or by appointment. SIZE: Medium. *STOCK: General antiques, furniture and decorative items, Welsh quilts, 19th-20th C, £5-£1,500.* LOC: 1 mile south of Synod Inn on A487. PARK: Easy. TEL: 0545 580707/580604. VAT: Stan/Spec.

TENBY

Audrey Bull
15 Upper Frog St. Open 10-5. CL: Wed. *STOCK: Period and Welsh country furniture, general antiques, especially jewellery and silver.* TEL: 0834 3114; home - 0834 813425. VAT: Spec.

Tenby continued

Clareston Antiques
Warren St. (K. and Mrs M.J.A Hunt) Est: 1964. Open 10-5, or by appointment. CL: Wed. SIZE: Small. *STOCK: Georgian and Victorian furniture; English and Welsh porcelain and pottery; silver and models.* LOC: Town centre, near police station. PARK: Easy. TEL: 0834 3350; home - same. SER: Valuations.

Mid Glamorgan

ABERDARE

Aberdare Park Antiques
Cemetery Rd (J.A Toms) Open Tues. and Wed. 10.30-4. *STOCK: General antiques.* LOC: Opposite top gates of park. TEL: 0685 878197.

BRIDGEND

Meeks Antiques Ltd
Market St. Open 9-5. *STOCK: General antiques.* TEL: 0656 654469.

Meeks Antiques Ltd
Tresaison House, St Mary Hill. (N T Meek) Open 10-5. *STOCK: General antiques.* TEL: 0656 860273; fax - same; mobile - 0850 701418.

CAERPHILLY

G.J Gittins and Son
10 Clive St. Open 9-5, Sat. 10-5. CL: Wed. *STOCK: General antiques and shipping goods.* TEL: 0222 868835.

NANTYMOEL, Nr. Bridgend

Quest Antiques
1 Ogwy St. (K. and Mrs L Bellamy) Est: 1988. Open 9.30-5 including Sun. SIZE: Small. *STOCK: General antiques, Victoriana, bric-a-brac, £5-£100.* Not Stocked: Large furniture. LOC: M4, junction 36 onto A4061. PARK: Easy. TEL: 0656 840403; home - same. FAIRS: Local.

PONTYPRIDD

Pontypridd Antiques
Old Bakery, Shepherd St, Pwllgwuan. (P Cooke) Open 9-5, Sat. 9-12. *STOCK: Stripped pine, china, brass and copper, Victorian and Edwardian, £5-£500.* TEL: 0443 407616. *Mainly Trade.*

PORTHCAWL

Harlequin Antiques
Dock St. (J Ball) Open 9-5. *STOCK: General antiques.* TEL: 065 671 5910.

TONYPANDY

Token Antiques
11 Llunpia Rd. (K.D Rose) Open 10-4. CL: Sat. *STOCK: General antiques.* TEL: 0443 441299.

TREHERBERT

Steven Evans Antiques
The Warehouse, Abertonllwyd St. Est: 1981. Open by appointment. SIZE: Warehouse. *STOCK: Large furniture - Victorian mahogany, Edwardian inlaid, American shipping, £5-£5,000.* LOC: Junction 34, M4, then A4110. PARK: Own. TEL: 0443 776410/777045; evenings - 0831 341634. SER: Valuations; restorations; North American specialists; container packing and shipping. VAT: Stan.

TREORCHY

Steven Evans Antiques
Regent St. Open 9-5, Sun. by appointment. SIZE: Warehouse. *STOCK: Victorian mahogany, Edwardian inlaid, American shipping, £5-£5,000.* LOC: Junction 34, M4, then A4110. PARK: Own. TEL: 0443 776410/777045/431756; evenings - 0831 341634. SER: Valuations; restorations; North American specialists; container packing and shipping. VAT: Stan.

South Glamorgan

BARRY

Hawkins Bros. Antiques
5, 21 and 22, Romily Buildings, Barry Docks and Gwalia Buildings. Open 8-5.30, weekends and other times by appointment. *STOCK: General antiques.* TEL: 0446 746561/721444/749880; evenings - 0446 721393/730878/745205 or 0222 513717.

Irena Art and Antiques
111 Broad St. (Mrs I Halabuda) Est: 1977. Open daily. SIZE: Small. *STOCK: Furniture, 18th-19th C, £50-£1,000; porcelain and glass, general antiques and art deco, £50-£100.* PARK: Easy. TEL: 0446 747626; home - 0446 732517. SER: Valuations; restorations (cane and rush seating, painted furniture, lacquerware, gold-leafing and gilding); buys at auction (18th C cottage oak furniture, Bergere settees, chairs).

CARDIFF

Alexander Antiques
312 Whitchurch Rd. (J.R Bradley) Open 10-5.30. *STOCK: Jewellery, clocks and furniture.* TEL: 0222 621824.

Back to the Wood
Old Post Office Sorting Office, West Canal Wharf. (I Cooling) Open 9-5. *STOCK: Pine and fireplaces.* LOC: Next door to Jacobs Antique Centre. TEL: 0222 390939. SER: Restorations (fireplaces); pine stripping.

A Burge Antiques
54 Crwys Rd. Open 9-5.30. CL: Wed. *STOCK: General antiques including clocks.* TEL: 0222 383268.

Charlotte's Wholesale Antiques
129 Woodville Rd, Cathays. (P.G Cason) Open 9.30-4. SIZE: Large and warehouse. *STOCK: Shipping goods, general antiques, period furniture.* TEL: 0222 759809/ 224632.

Cronin Antiques
12 Mackintosh Pl, Roath. (J Cronin) Open 9.30-4.30. *STOCK: General antiques, silver and jewellery.* TEL: 0222 498929.

Rhys Davies Antiques
2a Pontcanna St. (Mr and Mrs R Davies) Est: 1970. Open 9-6, or by appointment. SIZE: Medium. *STOCK: Furniture, 17th-19th C, £50-£3,000; silver and plate, 18th-19th C, £20-£2,000; copper, brass, clocks, 18th-19th C.* LOC: From Castle towards Cowbridge through traffic lights and first right after St. Davids Hospital. PARK: Easy. TEL: 0222 340022; home - 0633 681096. VAT: Stan/Spec.

W.H Douglas
161 Cowbridge Rd. East. *STOCK: General antiques, Victoriana, trade and shipping goods.* TEL: 0222 224861. *Trade Only.*

Dovetail Antiques
182 King's Rd and 1 Pontcanna St, Canton. (P Cooke) Est: 1978. Open 10-4, Sat. 10-5.30. CL: Wed. SIZE: Medium. *STOCK: Stripped pine, china, brass and copper, Victorian and Edwardian, £5-£500.* LOC: Off Cathedral Rd. at end of Pontcanna St. PARK: Easy. TEL: 0222 225165. VAT: Stan/Spec.

Grandma's Goodies
31 Mortimer Rd, Pontcanna. (R Gronow) Est: 1981. Open Thurs., Fri. and Sat. 10-1 and 2-5, or by appointment. SIZE: Medium. *STOCK: Linen, china and bric-a-brac, £5-£200.* LOC: 5 minutes by car from town centre to Cathedral Rd. PARK: Easy. TEL: 0222 383142; home - 0222 340901. SER: Prop hire.

Heritage Antiques and Stripped Pine
83 Pontcanna St. (D Gluck) Est: 1974. Open 9-6. SIZE: Medium. *STOCK: Pine and general antiques, 19th C, £50-£500.* LOC: 1st turning by

Heritage Antiques and Stripped Pine continued

shops at top end of Cathedral Rd. PARK: Easy. TEL: 0222 390097. SER: Restorations (mainly pine). FAIRS: Sophia Gardens, Cardiff. VAT: Stan.

Jacobs Antique Centre
West Canal Wharf. Open Wed.-Sat. 9.30-5. SIZE: Large - 80 dealers. *STOCK: General antiques, stripped pine and furniture.* LOC: 2 mins. from main railway and bus stations. PARK: 100yds. TEL: Thurs. and Sat. only 0222 390939. SER: Valuations; restorations; buys at auction.

Kings Antiques
163 Cowbridge Rd. East, Canton. (A Munro and B Quinn) Est: 1984. SIZE: Medium. *STOCK: Fireplaces, including 19th C French marble, £50-£1,000; furniture including reproduction; Victorian and Edwardian bathroom suites.* LOC: Main road in Canton on west side of city. PARK: Opposite. TEL: 02222 225014. SER: Valuations; restorations (furniture and fireplaces); fireplace installations. VAT: Stan.

Kings Fireplaces & Architectural Antiques
All Saints Church, Adamsdown Sq., Splott. (A Munro and B Quinn) *STOCK: Fireplaces, including 19th C French marble, £50-£1,000; furniture, including reproduction; Victorian and Edwardian bathroom suites.* TEL: 0222 492439. SER: Restoration (19th C cast iron).

The Light Brigade and Penylan Antiques
3 Wellfield Rd. (J Stockton) Open 9.30-5.30. *STOCK: General antiques, lighting, furnishings and jewellery.* TEL: 0222 499156. VAT: Stan.

Llanishen Antiques
26 Crwys Rd, Cathays. (Mrs J Boalch) Open 10.30-4.30. CL: Wed. except by appointment. *STOCK: Furniture, silver, china, glass, bric-a-brac.* TEL: 0222 397244.

Manor House Fine Arts
73 Pontcanna St, Pontcanna. (S.K Denley-Hill) Est: 1976. Open 10.30-5.30. CL: Mon., Wed. and Sun. except by appointment. SIZE: Medium. *STOCK: Watercolours, oil paintings and prints, £50-£2,000; general antiques and smalls, £10-£1,000, all 1800-1960.* LOC: Pontcanna St. is at north end of Cathedral Rd. PARK: Easy. TEL: 0222 227787. SER: Valuations; restorations; framing and mounting; buys at auction. VAT: Stan/Spec.

Past and Present
242 Whitchurch Rd, Heath. (C. and J Rowles) Est: 1970. Open 10.30-5, Sat. till 5.30. CL: Mon. (except to trade) and Wed. SIZE: Medium. *STOCK: Clocks, 19th C, £50-£1,000+; furniture, 18th-19th C, £5-£1,000+; china and bric-a-brac, £5-£500.* LOC: From M4 along eastern avenue by-pass, city turn-off by University Hospital, 1st left into Whitchurch Rd. PARK: Nearby. TEL: 0222 621443; home - 0222 759529. SER: Valuations; restorations (French polishing, clock and small furniture); buys at auction. FAIRS: Some local. VAT: Stan.

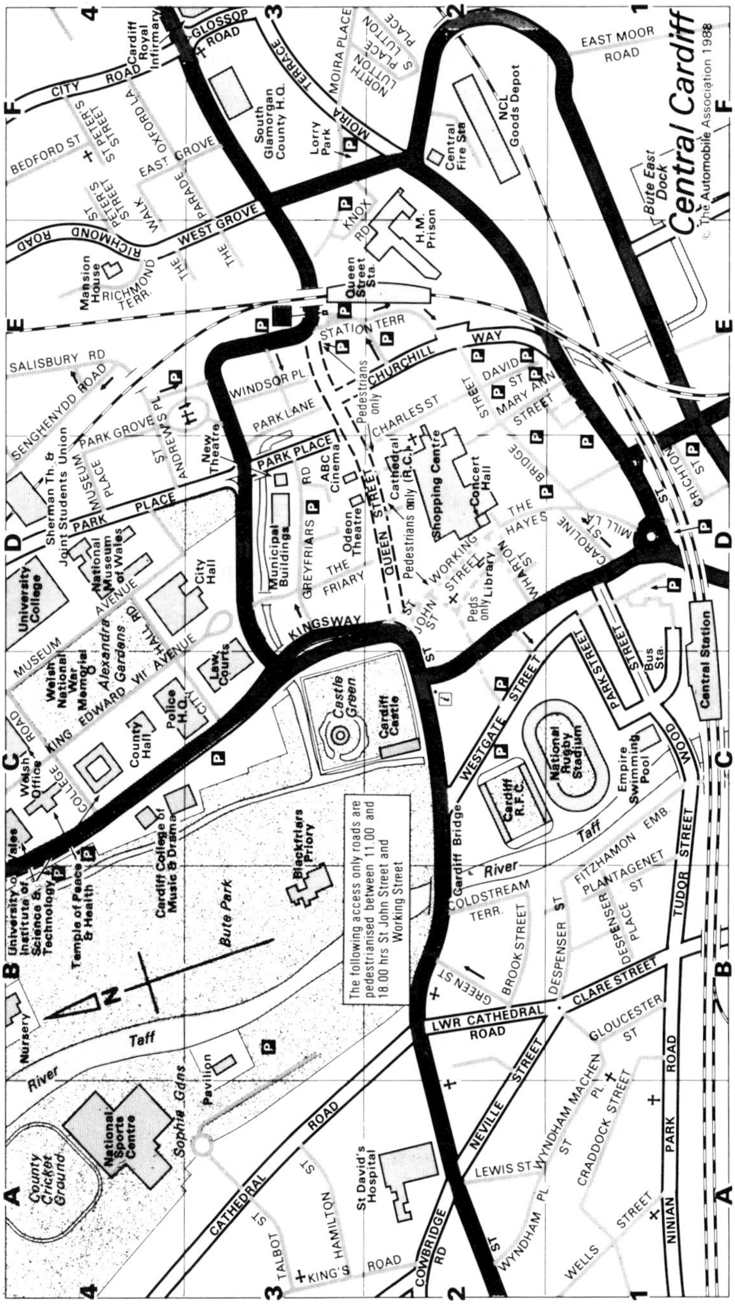

Central Cardiff
© The Automobile Association 1988
EAST MOOR ROAD
NCL Goods Depot
Central Fire Sta
Bute East Dock
NORTH LUTTON PLACE
S LUTTON PLACE
MOIRA PLACE
MOIRA TERRACE
Lorry Park
South Glamorgan County H.Q.
GLOSSOP ROAD
CITY ROAD
Cardiff Royal Infirmary
BEDFORD ST
ST PETER'S STREET
OXFORD LA.
EAST GROVE
WEST GROVE
RICHMOND ROAD
RICHMOND TERR.
Mansion House
THE PARADE
THE WALK
KNOX RD
H.M. Prison
Queen Street Sta.
STATION TERR
CHURCHILL WAY
SALISBURY RD
SENGHENYDD ROAD
WINDSOR PL.
PARK LANE
PARK GROVE
ST ANDREWS PL
New Theatre
PARK PLACE
MUSEUM PLACE
Sherman Th. & Joint Students Union
ABC Cinema
CHARLES ST
Pedestrians only
Cathedral (R.C.)
Shopping Centre
Concert Hall
DAVID ST
MARY ANN STREET
BRIDGE STREET
THE HAYES
CAROLINE ST
MILL LA
CRICHTON ST
Municipal Buildings
GREYFRIARS RD
Odeon Theatre
THE FRIARY
QUEEN STREET
WORKING STREET
Library
WHARTON ST
ST JOHN ST
Peds only
KINGSWAY
University College
National Museum of Wales
City Hall
MUSEUM AVENUE
Alexandra Gardens
Welsh National War Memorial
KING EDWARD VII AVENUE
Law Courts
Police H.Q.
County Hall
Castle Green
Cardiff Castle
WESTGATE STREET
PARK STREET
Bus Sta.
Central Station
National Rugby Stadium
Cardiff R.F.C.
Empire Swimming Pool
WOOD ST
COLLEGE ROAD
Welsh Office
Cardiff College of Music & Drama
Blackfriars Priory
The following access only roads are pedestrianised between 11.00 and 18.00 hrs St John Street and Working Street
Bute Park
University of Wales Institute of Science & Technology
Temple of Peace & Health
Cardiff Bridge
River Taff
COLDSTREAM TERR.
FITZHAMON EMB.
PLANTAGENET ST
DESPENSER PLACE
DESPENSER ST
TUDOR STREET
BROOK STREET
GREEN ST
CLARE STREET
LWR CATHEDRAL ROAD
GLOUCESTER ST
Nursery
Pavilion
Sophia Gdns
National Sports Centre
County Cricket Ground
CATHEDRAL ROAD
NEVILLE STREET
LEWIS ST
WYNDHAM ST
MACHEN PL.
CRADDOCK STREET
NINIAN PARK ROAD
St David's Hospital
HAMILTON ST
TALBOT ST
KING'S ROAD
COWBRIDGE RD
WYNDHAM PL.
WELLS STREET
A B C D E F
1 2 3 4

Key to Town Plan

AA Recommended roads	Car Parks
Other roads	Parks and open spaces
Restricted roads	AA Service Centre
Buildings of interest	© Automobile Association 1988.

Cardiff continued

San Domenico Stringed Instruments
175 Kings Rd, Canton. (H Morgan) Open 10-1 and 2-5. CL: Sat. p.m. SIZE: Small. *STOCK: Fine violins, violas, cellos and bows, mainly 18th-19th C, £300-£20,000.* LOC: Off Cathedral Rd. or Cowbridge Rd. PARK: Easy. TEL: 0222 235881; home - 0222 777156; fax - 0222 344510. SER: Valuations; restorations; buys at auction. VAT: Stan/Spec.

COWBRIDGE

Cowbridge Antiques
55 Eastgate. (J. and S Owen) Open 10-5.30, Sat. 10-5. CL: Wed. p.m. *STOCK: Furniture.* TEL: 0446 774774.

Eastgate Antiques
87 Eastgate. (L Herbert) Est: 1984. Open 10-1 and 2-5.30. CL: Wed. SIZE: Medium. *STOCK: Furniture, silver, jewellery, oils and watercolours, 18th C to Edwardian.* LOC: Off A48. PARK: Nearby. TEL: 0446 775111; home - 0446 773505. SER: Buys at auction (furniture). VAT: Stan/Spec.

Jenny Wren Antiques
23 High St. (Mrs A Roberts) Est: 1976. Open 10-1 and 2-5.30. CL: Wed. SIZE: Medium. *STOCK: Furniture, copper, brass, silver.* LOC: Off A48. PARK: 50yds. TEL: 0446 774165; home - 0446 772118. VAT: Stan/Spec.

John Owen Gallery
55 Eastgate. (J. and P Owen) Open 10-5. CL: Wed. p.m. *STOCK: Oils and watercolours.* TEL: 0446 774774. SER: Framing and restoration.

Renaissance Antiques
The Arcade, 49 High St. (R. and J Barnicott) Est: 1984. Open 10-1 and 2.15-5.30, other times by appointment. CL: Wed. SIZE: Small. *STOCK: Small furniture, Georgian, Victorian and Edwardian, £100-£3,000; brass, copper, plate, decorative ceramics, objets d'art, 18th to 20th C, £5-£500.* Not Stocked: Coins, militaria, reproductions. LOC: Main street, in new arcade opp. Electricity Showroom. PARK: 200 yards. TEL: 0446 773893; home - 0446 774656. SER: Caning. VAT: Stan/Spec.

The Watercolour Gallery
Old Wool Barn, Verity's Court. (P Allin) Est: 1987. Open from 11. CL: Mon., and Wed. p.m. SIZE: Small. *STOCK: Watercolours, £30-£1,000; occasional oil paintings, all 19th-20th C.* LOC: Off High St. PARK: Nearby. TEL: 0446 775683.

LLANISHEN, Nr. Cardiff

Arch Antiques
1 Fidlas Rd. (D Arch) Open 11-5.30. CL: Wed. *STOCK: General antiques including gramophones.* LOC: 1 1/4 miles off M4 Pentwyn turn-off, shop at Rhyd-y-Penau roundabout. TEL: 0222 765122/756311.

LLANTWIT MAJOR

Argosy Antiques
9 Church St. (R.S Cottle) Est: 1968. Open 10-4.30. CL: Mon. and Wed. p.m. *STOCK: Furniture, 18th-19th C; general antiques, jewellery, including secondhand.* PARK: Next to church. TEL: 0446 796667; home - 0656 767103.

PENARTH

Corner Cupboard Antiques
4a Station Approach. (Mrs M Green) Open 10-5. CL: Wed. *STOCK: General antiques.* TEL: 0222 705392.

Stanwells Antiques and Jewellery
36 Windsor Terr. (J. and M Waters) Open 9.30-1 and 2-5.30. CL: Wed. p.m. *STOCK: China, porcelain, pictures, silver and jewellery.* TEL: 0222 706906.

West Glamorgan

GORSEINON, Nr. Swansea

Gold and Silver Shop
Cross St. (E Paine) Open 10-1 and 2-4. *STOCK: Gold and silver, general antiques.* TEL: 0792 891874.

MORRISTON, Nr. Swansea

Aaron Antiques
62-66 Martin St. (A Davies) Est: 1971. Open 10-5. *STOCK: Furniture, longcase clocks, shipping goods.* TEL: 0792 773271. VAT: Stan.

MURTON, Nr. Swansea

West Wales Antiques LAPADA
18 Manselfield Rd. (W.H. and J.I Davies) Est: 1956. Open 10-1 and 2-5. CL: Mon. *STOCK: Porcelain, 18th C, £20-£800; Welsh porcelain, 1814-1820, £20-£1,000; dolls, 1880-1920; 18th-19th C furniture, silver, pottery, glass, jewellery and collectors' items.* LOC: M4-A4067-B4436, entrance to Gower Peninsula. TEL: 044 128 4318; home - 0639 644379. VAT: Stan/Spec.

SOUTHGATE

Southgate Antiques
65a Southgate Rd. (J. and P Sharples) Est: 1989. Open 10-1 and 2.15-5. CL: Mon. SIZE: Small. *STOCK: Pottery including Staffordshire figures, £50-£800; furniture, £60-£1,000; tea caddies, brassware, copper, silver, glass, paintings, prints, £60-£200; all Victorian.* LOC: Main road through village, on Gower Peninsula. PARK: Easy. TEL: 044 128 3212; home - 044 128 3513. SER: Valuations; restorations (clocks).

SWANSEA

James Allan
22 Park St. (S.J Allan) Est: 1929. Open 9.30-4.45. SIZE: Small. *STOCK: Jewellery, 1850 to date, £50-£5,000.* LOC: Off Kingsway, round corner from Mothercare. PARK: Nearby. TEL: 0792 652176. SER: Valuations. VAT: Stan.

Antique Centre
21 Oxford St. Open 10-5 although dealers' times vary. TEL: 0792 466854. Below are listed some of the 18 dealers at this centre.

Artefacts
Pictures, paintings.
Bijou Antiques
General antiques.
Blue Lady
General antiques.
City Antiques
Jewellery. SER: Repairs.
Forget-me-Not
China and bric-a-brac.
Geoff Militaria
Mair's Antiques
Jewellery, glass, china, brass, gold and silver.
Nadia's Antiques
General antiques.
Number Ten
Toys.
Past Times
(G. Richards) *Porcelain, Doulton, militaria and postcards.*
Purdy and Lloyd Antiques
Silver, porcelain, pottery, glass, furniture and collectables. TEL: 0792 648883; home - 0792 799906.
Bobby Roberts
Furniture and general antiques
Allan Treharne
Jewellery. SER: Repairs.
Winkies
Pre-1950s clothes.

Bygone Antiques
Basement of Homeflair, 37-39 St. Helens Rd. (C.A Oliver) Open 9.30-5. *STOCK: China, furniture, linen and collectors' items.* TEL: 0792 468248.

Keith Chugg Antiques
Gwydr Lane, Uplands. Open 9-5.30, Sat. 9-1. *STOCK: Pianos and general antiques including furniture.* TEL: 0792 472477.

Clydach Antiques
83 High St, Clydach. (R.T Pulman) Open 10-5, Sat. 10-1. *STOCK: General antiques.* TEL: 0792 843209.

Philip Davies
130 Overland Rd, Mumbles. Open by appointment. *STOCK: British watercolours and oil paintings, 1850-1950, maps and prints, all £25-£10,000.* TEL: Home - 0792 361766 (24hrs). SER: Valuations; restorations (paintings and frames).

Swansea continued

Dylan's Bookshop
Salubrious Passage. (J.M Towns) Open 10-5. *STOCK: Antiquarian books on Welsh history and topography, Anglo/Welsh literature and general books.* TEL: 0792 655255.

Elizabeth Antiques
504 Mumbles Rd. (W Wickstead) Open 11-5.30. *STOCK: Jewellery and general antiques.* TEL: 0792 361909; home - 0792 798978.

Grand View Antiques
220A Oxford St. SIZE: Several dealers. *STOCK: General antiques and small furniture, pre-1940, £5-£500.* Not Stocked: Knives, swords and guns. TEL: 0792 648883.

Elizabeth Hughes Antiques
76 St. Helens Rd. Est: 1977. Open 10-1 and 2.30-5. CL: Sat. p.m. *STOCK: Pine, mahogany and oak furniture, cast-iron grates, general antiques.* TEL: 0792 654697, home - 0792 361687.

Eynon Hughes Antiques
Henrietta St. (E. and M Hughes) Est: 1984. Open 10-5. *STOCK: Longcase clocks, £500-£2,500; brass and cast iron beds, £100-£500; furniture, 18th-19th C, £200-£1,000.* PARK: Easy. TEL: 0792 651446; home - 099 427 253. SER: Buys at auction (furniture).

Anne and Colin Hulbert (Antiques and Firearms)
17 Approach Rd, Manselton. Est: 1962. CL: Sun. p.m. SIZE: Small. *STOCK: Shipping goods and general antiques.* PARK: Easy. TEL: 0792 653818; home - same. SER: Valuations; buys at auction (furniture). *Trade Only.*

Mackays Antiques
1388b Neath Rd, Hafod. (S Mackay) Open 10-4, Sat. 9-12. *STOCK: Pine.* TEL: 0792 655413. SER: Restorations.

Magpie Antiques
57 St. Helens Rd. (H Hallesy) Est: 1984. Usually open 10-5. *STOCK: Ceramics including Swansea, Llanelly and other Welsh potteries; oak and country furniture.* PARK: Easy. TEL: 0792 648722. SER: Valuations; restorations (furniture).

Kim Scurlock
25 Russell St. (A.K Scurlock) Est: 1982. Open 9.30-5, Mon. 9.30-4.30, Sat. 9.30-1. SIZE: Medium. *STOCK: Victorian pine and country furniture, £25-£1,000; some reproduction pine and mainly Edwardian and Victorian oak and mahogany furniture, £50-£1,000.* LOC: Between Walters Rd. and St. Helens Rd. PARK: Easy. TEL: 0792 643085. SER: Restorations. VAT: Stan.

Swansea continued

Thicke Galleries **LAPADA**
(T.G Thicke) Est: 1981. By appointment only. SIZE: Medium. *STOCK: Oils and watercolours, 19th C and early 20th C, to £8,000.* LOC: Coast road to West Swansea. PARK: Easy. TEL: 0792 207515. SER: Valuations; restorations (oils and watercolours). FAIRS: British International, Birmingham; West London; Castle. VAT: Spec.

Gwent

ABERGAVENNY

Henry H Close
36 Cross St. (Mr and Mrs H Close) Est: 1968. Open 9-5, and by appointment. *STOCK: 18th-19th C furniture, porcelain, pottery, glass, brass, copper, jewellery, silver, prints.* TEL: 0873 3583. VAT: Stan.

H.K Lockyer
22 Monk St. Open 9.30-5.30. *STOCK: Pottery, porcelain, silver, antiquarian books.* PARK: Opposite. TEL: 0873 5825. VAT: Stan/Spec.

ABERTILLERY

David's Antiques
64-66 Somerset St. (D Webb) Est: 1975. Open 9.30-4, Sun. by appointment. CL: Wed. and Thurs. SIZE: Medium. *STOCK: General antiques.* LOC: Take Risca road off M4. PARK: Nearby. TEL: 0495 215888; home - 0495 212393. SER: Valuations; restorations (furniture). FAIRS: Tredegar House.

CHEPSTOW

Davies Antiques Centre **LAPADA**
12 St. Mary's St. (-J.F Davies) Est: 1963. Open 10-5. SIZE: Large - 10+ dealers. *STOCK: Furniture and shipping goods, glass, china, clocks, metalware and collectors items.* PARK: Easy. TEL: 0291 625957; home - 060 083 343. SER: Valuations; buys at auction. VAT: Stan/Spec.

Glance Back Bookshop
17 Upper Church St. Open 10-5.30, plus Bank Holidays and Sun. (Easter to Oct.). SIZE: Large. *STOCK: Books including antiquarian; stamps, coins, tokens, medals, postcards, banknotes, pens.* LOC: Town centre. PARK: Easy.

Glance Gallery
17a Upper Church St. Open 10-5.30, Sun. in summer 1-5.30. SIZE: Large. *STOCK: Antiquarian prints and maps.* LOC: Town centre. PARK: Easy. SER: Valuations; restorations (canvas, board or paper); framing; hand-colouring.

Chepstow continued

Nash Antiques
(C. and D Huish) Est: 1966. Open by appointment. SIZE: Large. *STOCK: General antiques, 17th-20th C, £1-£5,000.* TEL: 0594 52426. SER: Valuations; restorations; furniture made. VAT: Stan/Spec.

Plough House Interiors
11 Upper Church St. (Mr and Mrs P Jones) Est: 1972. Open 10-5, Sat. 10-4.30, Sun. by appointment. CL: Wed. SIZE: Large. *STOCK: Victorian and Edwardian furniture and shipping goods.* LOC: 2 miles from Severn Bridge and M4. PARK: Easy. TEL: 0291 625200; home - same. SER: Valuations; restorations; buys at auction. VAT: Stan/Spec.

GILWERN, Nr. Abergavenny

Gilwern Antiques
Powell Bros, Main Rd. Est: 1968. CL: Mon. *STOCK: General antiques including furniture, clocks, porcelain, pottery, glass, some silver and jewellery.* LOC: Leave A465 at Aberbaiden Caravan Park roundabout, 1/2 mile along A4077 to top end of Gilwern. PARK: Nearby. TEL: 0873 830276/830384.

LLANDOGO

Llandogo Antiques
(R. and J Hall) Resident. Est: 1965. Open 10-1 and 2-5. CL: Tues. SIZE: Small. *STOCK: Ceramics, glass, general antiques and small furniture.* Not Stocked: Large furniture. LOC: Last shop in village going south A466. PARK: 50yds. TEL: 0594 530213.

MONMOUTH

Carol Freeman Antiques
The Gallery, Nailers Lane. Open 10-5. CL: Mon. *STOCK: General antiques.* TEL: 0600 72252.

Monmouth Antiques **LAPADA**
The Old Gaol, Hereford Rd. Est: 1971. Open 9-12.30 and 4-7, Sun. and other times by appointment. SIZE: Small. *STOCK: Furniture, £50-£1,000; clocks; all 18th-19th C.* LOC: Near town centre. PARK: Own. TEL: 0600 6568. SER: Valuations; restorations (furniture and clocks). VAT: Spec.

NEWPORT

Antiques of Newport
82 Chepstow Rd. (Mr and Mrs J.M Duggan) Est: 1953. Open 9.30-5.30. CL: Thurs. *STOCK: Furniture, pottery, porcelain, silver, jewellery, maps, prints, fine art.* TEL: 0633 259935.

Newport continued

Beechwood Antiques
418 Chepstow Rd. (W.J Samuel) Open 10-12.30 and 2-5.30. *STOCK: General antiques.* TEL: 0633 279192.

Rex Moreton Studio
Mountjoy Rd. Open by appointment only. SIZE: Medium. *STOCK: Furniture, 18th-19th C, £20-£1,000; Doulton stoneware, 19th-20th C, £15-£500; pictures.* Not Stocked: Collectors' items. LOC: Near town centre in cul-de-sac, behind junction Cardiff Rd. and Commercial Rd. PARK: Easy. TEL: 0633 255078; home - 0633 267887. SER: Valuations; restorations (furniture); buys at auction. VAT: Stan/Spec.

Treasure Trove Antiques
23/25 Commercial Rd. (B.A Baggott) Open 10-6. *STOCK: General antiques especially furniture.* TEL: 0633 255353.

PENRHOS, Nr. Raglan

Lott and Gerrish
The Firs. Open by appointment. *STOCK: 19th-20th C British etchings and engravings.* TEL: 0600 85239.

PONTNEWYNYDD, Nr. Pontypool

The Pine Barn
Gillingham House, Freeholdland. Open 10-5. *STOCK: General antiques and stripped pine furniture.* TEL: 0495 752256; home - same. SER: Restorations; stripping.

PONTYPOOL

Pine Barn
Freehold Land. (L.M. and R.C Brean) Open 9.30-5.30. *STOCK: Pine.* TEL: 0495 752256.

RAGLAN

Raglan Antiques
High St. (W. and M Phillips) Est: 1954. Open 10-5 or by appointment. CL: Thurs. SIZE: Small. *STOCK: Furniture and clocks, 17th-18th C; early glass, porcelain, blue and white china including Delft, silver, jewellery, pewter, metalware, smokers' pipes, paintings, prints.* LOC: A40. PARK: Easy. TEL: 0291 690327. SER: Valuations; buys at auction. VAT: Stan/Spec.

TINTERN

Abbey Antiques
(D. and H Ford) FGA. Open daily including Sun. CL: Mon. SIZE: Large and warehouse. *STOCK: Country oak, pine and mahogany, shipping furniture, clocks, jewellery, silver, plate, bric-a-brac, china.* LOC: A466, opposite Tintern Abbey. TEL: 0291 689233.

TREDUNNOCK

Betty Williams
Tyr Eglwys. Est: 1975. Open by appointment only. *STOCK: 19th and 20th C watercolours.* TEL: 063 349 301.

USK

Castle Antiques
41 Old Market St. (S Lockyer) Open 12-5 or by appointment. *STOCK: General antiques, especially English and Welsh pottery, porcelain, blue and white transfer ware.* TEL: 029 13 2424;

Gwynedd

ABERSOCH

Annteaks
Main St. (H Duke) Est: 1946. Open 9-8. Always open to the Trade. *STOCK: General antiques from collectors' items to shipping goods.* LOC: Opposite Midland Bank. TEL: 075 881 2353. SER: Buys at auction.

ARTHOG

Gothick Dream Fine Art
Arthog Hall. (L.W Harcourt) Est: 1983. Open by appointment. SIZE: Medium. *STOCK: Paintings, furniture, 1760-1960, £200-£15,000.* PARK: Easy. TEL: 0341 250168. SER: Valuations; restorations (paintings and frames). VAT: Spec.

BANGOR

Wellfield Antique Centre
Wellfield Court. (T Andrew) Open Thurs.-Sat. 10-5. SIZE: 20 stands. TEL: 0248 361360.
Bangor continued

David Windsor Gallery
201 High St. Est: 1970. Open 10-5. CL: Wed. *STOCK: Oils and watercolours, 18th-20th C; maps, engravings, lithographs.* TEL: 0248 364639. SER: Restorations; framing; mounting. VAT: Stan/Spec.

BEAUMARIS

Castle Antiques
13 Church St. (J. and S Jones) Open 9-5.30, Sun. in summer. *STOCK: Country furniture, metalware, prints, brass and collectables.* LOC: Opposite P.O. TEL: 0248 810474.

Museum of Childhood
1 Castle St. *STOCK: Children's toys and memorabilia collectables.* TEL: 0248 712498.

BETHEL, Nr. Caernarfon

W.W Griffiths
Ivy Cottage. Resident, prior telephone call advisable. Est: 1978. *STOCK: Clocks, £300-£1,500; furniture, metalware, porcelain, some shipping goods.* LOC: After entering village from Caernarfon, turn left 200yds., then 1st right. TEL: 0248 670556. SER: Valuations. VAT: Stan/Spec.

BETHESDA

Ogwen Antiques
10 High St. (R. and J Ostle) Est: 1970. Open 10-6. CL: Sun. except by appointment. SIZE: Small. *STOCK: Victoriana, prints (topographical including North Wales), clocks, glass, china, art deco and art nouveau, paintings, 1800-1930; stripped pine, bottles, militaria, railwayana, postcards, advertising, old tools, photographs, brass, copper, toys.* PARK: Easy. TEL: 0248 600460/600549. SER: Valuations; restorations (oil paintings, watercolours); clock repairs.

BETWS GARMON

Revival
Salem Chapel. (G Yorath) Est: 1982. Usually open, prior telephone call advisable. SIZE: Small. *STOCK: Furniture, to 1925; china, bric-a-brac.* LOC: A4085 near village Post Office. PARK: Easy. TEL: 028 685 397; home - same. SER: Restorations and re-gilding.

BLAENAU FFESTINIOG

The Antique Shop
74A Manod Rd. (Mrs R Roberts) Est: 1971. *STOCK: Victoriana, furniture, brass and copper, oil lamps, clocks.* TEL: 0766 830629.

BODORGAN (Anglesey)

Michael Webb Fine Art **LAPADA**
Open by appointment only. *STOCK: Victorian and 20th C oil paintings and watercolours.* TEL: 0407 840336. SER: Valuations; restorations; framing. VAT: Spec.

CONWAY

Black Lion Antiques
11 Castle St. (M.A Wilks-Jones) Est: 1957. Open 10-5 and by appointment. SIZE: Small. *STOCK: Small furniture, including stripped pine, china, coloured glass, Victoriana, books, brass, shipping goods, metalware.* LOC: A55. PARK: Easy. TEL: 0492 592470. FAIRS: 3-day dateline.

Conway Antiques
17 Bangor Rd. (D.E Calligan) Open 10.30-5. *STOCK: General antiques.* TEL: 0492 592461.

Paul Gibbs Antiques and Decorative Arts
25 Castle St. Open 10-5. *STOCK: Art deco and art nouveau pottery, 1880-1940; Doulton, Moorcroft, unusual teapots.* TEL: 0492 593429.

DEGANWY

Acorn Antiques LAPADA
Castle Buildings. (K.S Bowers-Jones) Open 10-5. *STOCK: Ceramics, glass, furniture, pictures, brass and copper, 19th C.* TEL: 0492 584083.

DOLGELLAU

The Antique Shop
Plas yn Dre. (R Barman) Open 10-4. CL: Wed. *STOCK: Furniture, including pine and country; kitchenalia.* TEL: 0341 422753.

LLANBEDR, Nr. Harlech

Artro Antiques
Maes Artro (R.W Jones) *STOCK: General antiques.* TEL: 0341 280691.

LLANDUDNO

The Antique Shop
24 Vaughan St. (C.G Lee) Est: 1938. Open 9-5.30. SIZE: Medium. *STOCK: Jewellery, silver, porcelain, glass, ivories, metal goods, from 1700; period furniture, shipping goods.* LOC: Near promenade. PARK: Easy. TEL: 0492 75575.

Madoc Antiques and Art Gallery
48 Madoc St. (H. and L Aldridge) Est: 1975. SIZE: Medium. *STOCK: English watercolours, 18th-20th C, £200-£3,000; furniture, Edwardian, Victorian and Georgian, £100-£4,000; porcelain, silver, pre-1930, £2-£600; longcase clocks, £450-£3,000.* PARK: Opposite. TEL: 0492 79754; home - 0492 79760. SER: Valuations; restorations (clocks). VAT: Stan/Spec.

A silver and 'Scottish pride' brooch by James Fenton of Birmingham which is stamped with a lozenge shaped Registry. Mark on the reverse showing that the design was registered on 14 October 1865. The 'pebbles' are agates, cut into slivers, fitted into recesses cut into the metal and then polished flat. The silver mounts are variously engraved and decorated with the aid of the knurling machine.

VICTORIA AND ALBERT MUSEUM

From ***Jewellery 1789-1910 — The International Era,*** Volume II, by Shirley Bury published by the **Antique Collectors' Club** in 1991. £47.50 each volume.

LLANERCHYMEDD

Tony Andrew

8 High St. Est: 1976. Open by appointment only. SIZE: Small + warehouse. *STOCK: Signed limited edition prints by Charles Tunnicliffe; furniture, horse-drawn vehicles.* LOC: Centre of Isle of Anglesey. PARK: Easy. TEL: 0248 470204; home - same; warehouse - 0248 470666. SER: Framing; buys at auction.

LLANRWST

Snowdonia Antiques LAPADA

(J Collins) Est: 1961. Open 10-5. CL: Thurs. p.m. SIZE: Medium. *STOCK: Period furniture especially longcase clocks.* LOC: Turn off A5 just before Betws-y-Coed on to A496 for 4 miles. PARK: Easy. TEL: 0492 640789. SER: Restorations (furniture); repairs (grandfather clocks).

LLANYSTUMDWY, Nr. Criccieth

Roger Day Antiques

Y-Glyn (R. and Mrs A Day) Est: 1975. Open by appointment. SIZE: Medium. *STOCK: Oak and country furniture, early pottery, metalware, treen, some period mahogany.* LOC: A497. PARK: Easy. TEL: 0766 522988; home - same. VAT: Stan/Spec. *Trade Only.*

MAENTWROG

Harvey-Owen Antiques

The Old School (Mr and Mrs J.L. and L Harvey) Est: 1972. Open 10-5. *STOCK: General antiques.* TEL: 076 685 310.

PORT DINORWIC (Y Felinheli)

Burling Antiques

(C. and S Burling) Est: 1987. Open strictly by appointment only. SIZE: Medium. *STOCK: Oak and country furniture, 17th-19th C, £100-£5,000; some mahogany furniture, 18th-19th C; unusual and decorative items.* Not Stocked: Silver and jewellery. LOC: Edge of village, mid way

Burling Antiques continued

between Bangor and Caenarfon (A487). PARK: Easy. TEL: 0248 671313; home - same. VAT: Stan/Spec.

PWLLHELI

Rodney Adams Antiques

Hall Pl, 10 Penlan St. Resident. Est: 1965. CL: Sun. except by appointment. *STOCK: Period furniture; longcase clocks.* TEL: 0758 613173; evenings - 0758 614337. VAT: Stan/Spec.

RHOSNEIGR

Fan-Fayre Antiques

High St (S Richards) Resident. Est: 1976. Open 10-5.30, prior telephone call advisable during winter months. SIZE: Small. *STOCK: Jewellery, porcelain, silver, collectable items, 19th C, £25-£500.* LOC: 5 miles off A5 from the Holyhead Rd., on Anglesey Island. PARK: Easy. TEL: 0407 810580 (24hr. anwer phone). SER: Valuations. FAIRS: St. Martins, Birmingham; Portmeirion, Wales; Newark and Nottinghamshire Showground; Ardingley, Sussex.

TYWYN

Wynn Cato

(M.K.W Cato) Open by appointment only. *STOCK: Welsh paintings, 1550-1950; general antiques and curiosities relating to Wales.* TEL: 0799 550236; home - 071 736 5002.

Powys

BRECON

Hazel of Brecon

2 Dukes Arcade. (H Hillman) Est: 1969. Open 10-5. CL: Wed. SIZE: Small. *STOCK: Jewellery, 19th-20th C, £50-£1,000.* LOC: Town centre, just off main sq. PARK: Easy. TEL: 0874 5274 (24 hour answering service). SER: Valuations.

Brecon continued

Lace Lady
3 Market Arcade, High St. (P Palmer) Est: 1960. Open 9-4.30, Thurs. and Sat. 10.30-3. CL: Mon. and Wed. SIZE: Small. *STOCK: Lace and linen, to £200; jewellery, porcelain, silver and furniture.* PARK: Nearby. TEL: Home - 0874 638162. SER: Valuations.

Maps, Prints and Books
7 The Struet. (Mr and Mrs D.G Evans) Est: 1961. Open 9-1 and 2-5. CL: Wed. SIZE: Large. *STOCK: Books, maps, prints, 17th C, £5-£500.* LOC: A438, near Boots the Chemist. PARK: Opposite. TEL: 0874 2714. VAT: Stan.

Ship Street Galleries
14 Ship St. (T.R. and C Constantinescu) Est: 1974. Open by appointment only. *STOCK: Period furniture, pine, shipping goods, 18th-19th C; glass and general antiques.* TEL: 0874 3926.

Silver Time
2 Dukes Arcade. (L Hillman) Open 10-5. CL: Wed. SIZE: Small. *STOCK: Silver and gold watches and 19th-20th C silver and plate.* LOC: Town centre, just off main square. PARK: Easy. TEL: 0874 5274 (24 hour answering service). SER: Valuations.

CRICKHOWELL

Gallop and Rivers Architectural Antiques
Ty'r Ash, Brecon Rl. (G P Gallop and R A Rivers) Open 9.30-5.30. *STOCK: Architectural items, pine and country furniture.* TEL: 0873 811084. VAT: Stan.

HAY-ON-WYE

Antiques Market
6 Market St. Open 10-5. SIZE: 18 dealers. *STOCK: General antiques and collectables.* LOC: By the Butter Market. TEL: 0497 820175.

Richard Booth's Bookshop
The Limited Bookshop. Five Star Bookshop (Military), Hay Castle Bookshop (American Indians, art, photography, transport) Est: 1974. Open 7 days 9.30-5.30, later at weekends and during summer. SIZE: Large. *STOCK: Books.* LOC: Town centre. TEL: 0497 820322.

The Corner Shop
5 St. John's Pl. (E Okarma) Open 10-5. *STOCK: Prints, oils and watercolours, 19th-20th C.* TEL: 0497 820045. SER: Framing. VAT: Stan.

Hay-on-Wye continued

Hebbards of Hay
7 Market St. (G.B Hebbard) Est: 1958. Open Wed.-Sat. 10-5, other times by appointment. SIZE: Small. *STOCK: Pottery and porcelain.* LOC: A438, opp. the Post Office. PARK: Own. TEL: 0497 820413.

Tamara Le Bailly Antiques
5 Market St. Open 10.30-5.30. *STOCK: General antiques and country furniture.* PARK: Nearby. TEL: 0497 820656.

Mark Westwood Antiquarian Books
High Town. (M. and C Westwood) ABA; PBFA. Est: 1976. Open 12.30-5.30, prior telephone call advisable in winter. *STOCK: Antiquarian books especially on science and medicine, 16th-20th C, £50-£500.* TEL: 0497 820068. SER: Valuations; buys at auction (antiquarian books). VAT: Stan.

Wigington Antiques
Powys House, 15 Broad St. (B Wigington) BAFRA. Est: 1961. Open 10-5. SIZE: Small. *STOCK: General antiques, mainly furniture, 17th-19th C, to £5,000.* LOC: Next to clocktower. PARK: Nearby. TEL: 0497 820545 (24hr. ansaphone). SER: Valuations; restorations (furniture).

KNIGHTON

Offa's Dyke Antique Centre
4 High St. (M McAvoy, M Samuel, I Watkins and Mrs S.D Yeomans) Est: 1985. Open 9.30-1 and 2-5. SIZE: Medium - 16 dealers. *STOCK: Pottery, bijouterie and 18th and 19th C furniture, £5-£500.* LOC: Near town clocks. PARK: Easy. TEL: 0547 528635; evenings 0547 528940 or (05477) 240. VAT: Stan.

Islwyn Watkins
1 High St. Est: 1978. Open 10-1 and 2.30-5, prior telephone call advisable, Tues. and Wed. by appointment. SIZE: Small. *STOCK: Pottery including studio, 18th-20th C, £25-£350; country and domestic bygones, treen, 18th-20th C, £5-£100; small country furniture, 18th-19th C, £20-£400.* Not Stocked: Jewellery, silver, militaria. LOC: By town clock. PARK: Easy. TEL: 0547 520145; home - 0547 528940. SER: Valuations. VAT: Stan/Spec.

LLANDRINDOD WELLS

Euston House Galleries and Roma Antiques
1, 2 and 3 High St. (A.H Helliwell) Est: 1969. Open 9-9. CL: Wed. p.m. SIZE: Medium. *STOCK: Cottage antiques, country furniture, metal implements, arms and silver.* LOC: Near County Hall, off A483. PARK: Easy. TEL: 0597 2046.

LLANFAIR CAEREINION, Nr. Welshpool

Heritage Restorations
Maes y Glydfa. (J. and Mrs F Gluck) Est: 1970. Open 9-5.30. SIZE: Large. *STOCK: Pine and country furniture, £50-£2,000; some oak and architectural items, all 18th-19th C.* LOC: A458 from Shrewsbury through village. After 2 miles take first left after river bridge, follow signs. PARK: Easy. TEL: 0938 810384; home - same. SER: Restorations (furniture including pine stripping). VAT: Stan/Spec.

MONTGOMERY

Mike Butcher Antiques
Gaol Rd. Always open. *STOCK: Mahogany, oak, brass and copper.* TEL: 0686 668064; home - same.

WELSHPOOL

F.E Anderson and Son LAPADA
5-6 High St. (D. and I Anderson) Open daily. *STOCK: Furniture, 17th-18th C; English and Chinese ceramics, glass, silver, paintings, early metalware.* TEL: 0938 553340; home - 0938 553324/75509.

Horley Antiques
19 High St. (C Darnell) Est: 1970. Open 9.30-1 and 2.15-4.30, Sat. 9.30-1. SIZE: Small. *STOCK: Paintings, 19th C, £5-£500; general, mainly small, items.* PARK: Easy. TEL: 0938 552421.

School House Antiques
21 High St. (M.L.G Robinson) Est: 1977. Open 10.30-1.30 and 2.30-4.30, Thurs. and Sat. 10.30-1.30. SIZE: Medium. *STOCK: Furniture, 18th-19th C, £250-£5,000; oils and watercolours, 19th C, £100-£1,000; silver and plate, 18th-19th C, £100-£500.* LOC: Town at junction of A458, A483 and A490. PARK: Easy. TEL: 0938 554858; home - 093 874 267. SER: Valuations; restorations (rush and cane seating). VAT: Spec.

Waterloo Antiques LAPADA
Salop Rd. (R. and N Robinson) Est: 1979. SIZE: Medium. *STOCK: Porcelain, furniture, paintings, metalware.* LOC: On A483 on entering town from the east. PARK: Easy. TEL: 0938 553999 (24hr.); home - 0938 555468. VAT: Spec.

YSTRADGYNLAIS, Nr. Swansea

Margaret's Astoria Antiques
38a Brecon Rd. (M Williams) Est: 1979. Open 10-5, Sat. 10-1. CL: Mon. SIZE: Small. *STOCK: Jewellery, £75-£500; china, £5-£100; small furniture, £50-£100; all Victorian to 1930s.* LOC: A4067 Swansea/Brecon road. PARK: Easy. TEL: 0639 849946. SER: Buys at auction (jewellery). FAIRS: David Robinson, local.

Mrs Norton, one of the beautiful Sheridan sisters, was a wit as well as a beauty. She became a writer, marrying Sir William Stirling-Maxwell as a widow in old age. Etty's portrait of her must have been painted in the 1840s (she had her fortieth birthday in 1848). Her gold bar archaeological brooch was then unusual in England. It is inscribed SALVE (Hail!). STIRLING-MAXWELL COLLECTION POLLOK HOUSE GLASGOW

Index of Packers and Shippers: Exporters of Antiques (Containers)

LONDON

Anglo Pacific (Fine Art) Ltd. LAPADA
Units 1 and 2, Bush Industrial Estate, Standard Rd., NW10 6DF. Tel. (081) 965 0667. Fax. (081) 965 4954. *(Packers and shippers of antiques, fine art, household effects and cars. All destinations).*

Baker Britt and Co. Ltd.
Unit 2, Marshgate Trading Estate, Marshgate Lane, E15 2NG. Tel. (081) 534 2266. Telex. 21940. *(Freight forwarders, overseas removals.)* VAT: Stan.

James Bourlet & Sons Ltd.
(See entry under Middlesex.)

Bullens Ltd.
Unit 9 Cranford Way, Tottenham Lane, Hornsey, N8. Tel. (071 272 6671. *(Specialist comprehensive removal service.)*

London continued

Davies Turner Worldwide Movers Ltd.
Overseas House, Stewarts Rd., SW8 4UG. Tel. (071) 622 4393. Telex. 28471. Fax. (071) 720 3897. *(Fine art and antiques packers and shippers. Courier and finder service. Full container L.C.L. and groupage service worldwide. In house travel and insurance depts.)*

IS YOUR ENTRY CORRECT?
If there is even the slightest inaccuracy in your entry, *please* let us know before 1st January 1992.
GUIDE TO THE
ANTIQUE SHOPS OF BRITAIN
5 Church Street, Woodbridge, Suffolk.
Tel: (0394) 385501

London continued

Featherston Shipping Ltd. LAPADA
24 Hampton House, 15-17 Ingate Pl., SW8 3NS. Tel. (071) 720 0422. Fax. (071) 720 6330. *(Antiques and fine art packed and shipped or airfreighted worldwide; security storage.)*

C.R. Fenton and Co. Ltd.
Beachy Rd., Old Ford., E3 2NX. Tel. (081) 533 2711. Telex. Fenton G. 8812859. Fax. (081) 985 6032. *(Packers and shippers.)*

IS YOUR ENTRY CORRECT?
If there is even the slightest inaccuracy in your entry, *please* let us know before 1st January 1992.
GUIDE TO THE
ANTIQUE SHOPS OF BRITAIN
5 Church Street, Woodbridge, Suffolk.
Tel: (0394) 385501

Three SylvaC dogs, £165.
Sworder's, Bishop's Stortford.
From a Saleroom Report published in the February 1991 issue of **Antique Collecting.**

Fentons please!
AUCTION CATALOGUE
A RARE COLLECTION OF ANTIQUES AND FINE ART
Tuesday 21st
19
LONDON • NEW YORK • PARIS
MEMO
Who do you want to pack and ship?
Fentons please
FENTONS
FINE ART PACKING & SHIPPING
ESTD. 1938
C.R. FENTON & CO. LTD., BEACHY ROAD,
LONDON E3 2NX. Tel: 081-533 2711. Telex: 8812859 FENTON G.
Fax: 081-985 6032

Our only rival.

*Gander & White have only one rival. The walnut.
Nature has created in the walnut, the perfect model for individual high-quality packaging. Each walnut shell provides tailor-made protection for its contents; in the same way we create unique individual packing for every work of art entrusted to our care.*

Specialised packing and shipping of antiques and works of art

Groupage container services by air and sea to North America

Weekly door-to-door road groupage services to major European cities

Household removals

High security storage

Gander & White. In a nutshell, specialist packing, total protection.

Gander & White

PACKERS & SHIPPERS

*Gander & White Shipping Ltd., 21 Lillie Road, London SW6 1UE.
Tel: 071 381 0571 Fax: 071 381 5428
New Pound, Wisborough Green, Billingshurst, West Sussex RH14 0AY
Tel: 0403 784911 Fax: 0403 784873
Gander & White Inc., 33-31 Greenpoint Avenue, Long Island City, N.Y. 11101
Tel: 718 784 8444 Fax: 718 784 9337*

One of a pair of 19th century cut glass two branch table lustres, 13in. high (one damaged). £825. From an Auction Feature on the sale of the remaining contents of Donnington Grove, Newbury, Berkshire, by Dreweatt Neate on 1st May 1991, published in the June 1991 issue of **Antique Collecting.**

London continued

Gander and White Shipping Ltd.
Head Office, 21 Lillie Rd., SW6 1UE. Tel. (071) 381 0571. Fax. (071) 381 5428. *(Specialist packers and shipper of antiques and works of art.)*

Gander and White Shipping Ltd.
14 Mason's Yard, Duke St., St. James's, SW1Y 6BU. Tel. (071) 930 5383. Fax. (071) 920 4145. Cables: Gandite.

Hedleys Humpers Ltd. **LAPADA**
Units 3 and 4, 97 Victoria Rd., North Acton NW10 6ND. Tel. (081) 965 8733 (10 lines). Telex. 25229. Fax. (081) 965 0249. *(Weekly deliveries, door-to-door service to Europe, and part load shipments by air and sea to U.S.A.)*

Interdean Ltd.
3/5 Cumberland Ave., NW10 7RU. Tel. (081) 961 4141; Telex: 922119. *(Antiques and fine art packed, shipped and airfreighted worldwide. Storage and international removals. Full container L.C.L. and groupage service worldwide.)*

London continued

Lockson Services Ltd. **LAPADA**
29 Broomfield St., Limehouse, E14 6BX. Tel. (071) 515 8600 (6 lines). Telex. 884222. Fax. (071) 515 4043. *(Full service to the antique trade including dealers, decorators, collectors: couriers, collection, packing; shipping and insurance.)*

Masterpack Ltd.
16 Paddington Green, W2 1LG. Tel. (071) 724 5822. Telex. 8813271 GECOMS G. *(Fine art packers and shippers. Personal service guaranteed.)*

Mat Transport Ltd.
Arnold House, 36-41 Holywell Lane, EC2P 2EQ. Tel. (071) 247 6500. Telex. 886051. *(International freight forwarders and transport operators.)*

Stephen Morris Shipping Ltd.
318 Green Lanes, N4 1BX. Tel. (071) 354 1212. Telex. 261707. Fax. (081) 802 4110. *(Worldwide shippers and packers. Groupage services to U.S.A. and Australasia.)*

Nelson Shipping
7 Glasshouse Walk, Vauxhall, SE11 5ES. Tel. (071) 587 0265. *(Expert export and packing service.)*

The Packing Shop
Plaza G13, 535 Kings Rd., SW10. Tel: (071) 352 2021. *Fine art and general antiques shipped worldwide, especially United States and Europe.*

The Packing Shop
Unit L, London Stone Business Estate, Broughton St., SW8. Tel: (071) 498 3255.

Pitt and Scott Ltd. **LAPADA**
20/24 Eden Grove, N7 8ED. Tel. (071) 607 7321. Telex. 21857. Fax. (071) 607 0566. *(Packers and shippers of antiques and fine art. Shipping, forwarding and airfreight agents. Comprehensive service provided for visiting antique dealers. Insurance arranged.)*

L.J. Roberton Ltd. **LAPADA**
Marlborough House, Cooks Rd., Stratford, E15 2PW. Tel. (081) 519 2020. Telex. 8953984. Fax. (081) 519 8571.

Robinsons International **LAPADA**
24 Somerton Rd., London, NW2 1SA. Tel. (081) 452 5441. Telex. 8814998. Fax. (081) 452 6664. *(Specialist packers and shippers of antiques and fine art worldwide. Established over 90 years.)*

T. Rogers and Co. (Packers) Ltd.
1A Broughton St., London, SW8 3QJ. Tel. (071) 622 9151. Fax (071) 627 3318. Telex 915243. *(Specialists in storage, packing, removal, shipping and forwarding antiques and works of art. Insurance.)*

Trans-Euro Fine Art Division **LAPADA**
Drury Way, Brent Park, London, NW10 0JN. Tel. (081) 784 0100. Telex. 923368. Fax. (081) 451 0061. *(Specialist packing and worldwide shipping services by air, sea or road. Single items, part loads or full containers. Courier and buyer services.)*

London continued

Wingate and Johnston Ltd. **LAPADA**
78 Broadway, Stratford, E15 1NG. Tel. (081) 555 8123 and (081) 519 3211. Telex 897545. Fax. (081) 519 8115. *(Specialists in the international movement of antiques and fine arts for over a hundred and fifty years — services incorporate all requirements from case making to documentation and insurance. Freight groupage specialists.)*

AVON

M. & M. Services
Vale Lane, Hartcliffe Way, Bristol, BS3 5RU. Tel. (0272) 666991. *(Worldwide shippers and packers.)*

Robinsons International
Silverthorne Wharf, Silverthorne Lane, Bristol. BS2 0QD. Tel. (0272) 723020. *(Specialist packers and shippers of antiques and fine art worldwide. Established over 90 years.)*

A.J. Williams (Shipping) **LAPADA**
607 Sixth Ave., Central Business Park, Hengrove, Bristol BS14 9BZ. TEL: (0272) 892166. Fax. (0272) 891333.

BUCKINGHAMSHIRE

Goyabam Translocations
214 Desborough Ave., High Wycombe. Tel. (0494) 446383. *(Worldwide container shipping & packing.)*

Paget Freight Ltd.
Spaceregal Centre, Coln Industrial Estate, Old Bath Rd., Colnbrook, SL3 0NJ. Tel. (0753) 682426. Telex. 847514. Fax. (0753) 686367. *(Packing and shipping of antiques and works of art worldwide especially Bermuda and North and South America.)*

CHESHIRE

The Rocking Chair
Unit 3/6, St. Peters Way, Warrington. Tel. (0925) 52409.

DEVON

Blatchpack Ltd.
Lodge Trading Estate, Broadclyst, Exeter, EX5 3EA. Tel. (0392) 61721. Fax. (0392) 61724. *(International fine art packers and shippers.)*

DORSET

Alan Franklin Transport **LAPADA**
Unit 8, 27 Blackmoor Rd., Ebblake Industrial Estate, Verwood, BH21 6AX. Tel. (0202) 826539. Fax. (0202) 827337. *(Container packing and shipping. Weekly door to door European service.)*

ESSEX

Geo. Copsey and Co.Ltd. **LAPADA**
Danes Rd., Romford. Tel: (0708) 740714 or (081) 592 1003. *(Worldwide packers and shippers.)*

Scott Packing and Warehousing Co. Ltd.
Security House, Abbey Wharf Industrial Estate, Kingsbridge Rd., Barking, IG11 0BT. Tel. (081) 591 3388. Telex. 897325. Fax. (081) 594 4571. *(Packers and shippers — 12 offices throughout U.K.)*

Stekelman Art Services (Shipping) Ltd.
Unit 3, Pacific Wharf, Hertford Rd., Barking. Tel. (081) 594 4474. Fax. (081) 594 9229. *(Fine art consultants, packers, shippers worldwide. Overseas removals. Import/export documentation. Specialised Spanish service.)*

GLOUCESTERSHIRE

The Removal Company — Barndy & Bendell
Unit D, Ashville Trading Estate, The Runnings, Cheltenham, GL51 9PT. Tel. (0242) 523362.

J.N. Oakey
Unit 6, Barret Industrial Park, St. Oswalds Rd., Gloucester, GL1 2SR. Tel. (0452) 507427/ 507414. *(Nationwide haulage, removals and storage — household goods, antiques and fine arts.)*

HAMPSHIRE

Cantay Group Ltd.
Head Office — Unit D, Telford Rd., Houndmills Industrial Estate, Basingstoke, RG21 2YU. Tel. (0256) 465533. Also at 95 Fleet Rd., Fleet, GU13 8PJ. Tel. (0252) 811884. *(Specialist packers and shippings.)*

Colin Macleod's
105 Albert Rd., Southsea, Portsmouth. Tel. (0705) 864211. Fax. (0705) 817040. *(Worldwide shippers.)*

Robinsons International
Guildford St., Southampton, SO9 4UW. Tel. (0703) 220069. *(Specialist packers and shippers of antiques and fine art worldwide. Established over 90 years.)*

HUMBERSIDE

Peter Smith t/a Boothferry Antiques
388 Wincolmlee, Hull, HU2 0QL. Tel. (0482) 225220/666033. *(Antiques, shipping goods and stripped pine, single items or container loads. Couriers covering North of England. Full documentation.)*

LANCASHIRE

Alan Butterworth (Antiques) Ltd.
7 Ardley Rd., Horwich, Bolton, BL6 6QF. Tel. (0204) 68094.

Robinsons International Removers Ltd.
Unit (one) Egremont Cl., Moss Lane Industrial Estate, Whitefield, Manchester, M25 6FH. Tel. (061) 766 8414. *(Specialist packers and shippers of antiques and fine art worldwide. Established over 90 years.)*

Lancashire continued

Anthony Walmsley Antiques
93 Montagu St., Blackburn. Tel. (0254) 698755.

LEICESTERSHIRE

Richard Kimbell Ltd.
Riverside, Market Harborough, LE16 7PT. Tel: (0858) 433444. Telex. 32376. Fax. (0858) 467627. *(Container packers and shippers. Speedy despatch — competitive rates.)*

MERSEYSIDE

John Mason International Ltd. LAPADA
35 Wilson Rd., Huyton, Liverpool, L36 6AE. Tel. (051) 449 3938. *(Specialist packer, full and part container loads, groupage services worldwide, courier and finder service.)*

MIDDLESEX

Air Service Packing and Forwarding
Unit 29, Central Trading Estate, Bedfont, TW18 4XG. Tel. (0784) 457764. Fax. (0784) 243575. *(Specialist packers of art and antiques; worldwide shipping.)*
James Bourlet and Sons Ltd. LAPADA
3 Space Waye, Pier Rd., Feltham. TW14 0TY. Tel. (081) 751 1155. Telex. 935242. Fax. (081) 890 1735. *(Fine art packing, freight*

James Bourlet and Sons Ltd. continued

forwarding and transport. Full responsibility undertaken for the complexities of shipments at all stages.)
Cantay (London) Ltd.
Cantay House, Third Cross Rd., Twickenham, TW2 5EB. Tel. (081) 893 3303. Fax. (081) 893 3068. Telex. 933662. *(Specialist packers and shippers.)*
Phelps Ltd. LAPADA
133-135 St. Margarets Rd., Twickenham. TW1 1RF. Tel. (01) 892 1778/7129.
Vulcan International Services Ltd. LAPADA
Unit 8, Ascot Rd., Clockhouse Lane, Feltham. TW14 8QF. Tel. (0784) 244152. Telex 295888. Fax. (0784) 248183. *(Fine art packers and shippers worldwide.)*
W.B. Airfreight Ltd. LAPADA
Unit 3, Blackburn Trading Estate, Nathin Close, Stanwell, Staines. Tel. (0784) 240666. Fax. (0784) 248457. Telex. 934876. *(Worldwide by sea and air.)*

OXFORDSHIRE

Cantay Group Ltd.
Unit 1, Oakfield Industrial Estate, Stanton Harcourt Rd., Eynsham, Oxford OX8 1TN. Tel. (0865) 882989. Fax. (0865) 883310. Telex. 837614.

Oxfordshire continued

Cotswold Carriers
Unit 9, Worcester Rd. Industrial Estate, Chipping Norton, OX7 5YF. Tel. and Fax. (0608) 642856. *(Removals, storage, shipping, door-to-door Continental deliveries.)*

J.N. Oakey
See details under Gloucestershire.

Robinson International Removers Ltd.
Nuffield Way, Abingdon, OX14 1TN. Tel. (0235) 524992. *(Specialist packers and shippers of antiques and fine art worldwide. Established over 90 years.)*

SOMERSET

Colin Dyte Exports Ltd.
Huntspill Rd., Highbridge, TA9 3DE. Tel. (0278) 788590.

W.P.S. (Bruton) Ltd.
The Old Mill, Station Rd., Bruton, BA10 0EH. Tel. (0749) 812785. Open 8.30–6, Sat. 8.30–12.30. *(Specialised collection, valuation, packing, shipping and export service worldwide especially U.S.A., Canada, Australia, South Africa.)*

SURREY

W. Ede & Co.
9 Bath House Rd., Beddington Lane, Croydon, CR0 4TT. Tel. (081) 684 7555. Telex. 946667. *(Worldwide packing and shipping, complete documentation and removals service, container packing.)*

SUSSEX

Bexhill Antique Exporters
56 Turkey Rd., Bexhill-on-Sea, East Sussex. TN39 5HB. Tel. (0424) 225103/210182. Fax. (0424) 731430. Approx. 8,000 sq. ft. General and shipping furniture. *(Packing facilities for 20ft. and 40ft. containers, all documentation. Worldwide shipping.)*

British Antique Exporters Ltd.
School Close, Queen Elizabeth Ave., Burgess Hill, West Sussex, RH15 9RX. Tel. (0444) 245577. *(Packers and shippers.)*

Gander and White Shipping Ltd.
Newpound, Wisborough Green, Billinghurst, West Sussex. Tel. (0403) 784911. Telex. 878310. Fax. (0403) 784873. *(Specialist packers and shippers of fine art and antiques.)*

Global Services
West St., Lewes, East Sussex. BN7 2NJ. Tel. (0273) 475903. *(Packers and shippers of antiques, arms, armour and fine works of art.)*

Martells International
32 London Rd., East Grinstead, RH19 4DW. Tel. (0342) 321303. Fax. (0342) 317522. Telex. 946305. *(International removers, export packers and shippers.)* VAT: Stan.

Sussex continued

Peter Semus Antiques
The Warehouse, Gladstone Rd. Portslade, East Sussex, BN4 1LJ. Tel. (0273) 420154. Fax. (0273) 430355. Open Mon.–Fri. 8–6. *(Packers and shippers of antiques and household effects worldwide. Containers only. No small shipments.)*

TYNE AND WEAR

Owen Humble (Packing and Shipping) Ltd.
Clayton House, Walbottle Rd., Lemington, Newcastle-upon-Tyne, NE15 9RU. Tel. (091) 2677220. *(Worldwide service.)*

WARWICKSHIRE

Scott Packing and Warehousing Co. Ltd.
Unit 9, Ratcliffe Road Industrial Estate, Ratcliffe Rd., Atherstone, CV9 1JA. Tel. (0827) 714631.

WEST MIDLANDS

Robinsons International
585 Moseley Rd., Birmingham, B12 9BJ. Tel. (021) 449 4731. Telex. 338804. Fax. (021) 449 9942. *(Specialist packers and shippers of antiques and fine art worldwide. Established over 90 years.)*

YORKSHIRE

H. Blackburn
9 East St., Gargrave, BD23 3RS. Tel. (0756) 749796. *(Export, packers, shippers, courier service.)*

Turnbulls (Removals) Ltd.
287 Roundhay Rd., Leeds. Tel. (0532) 495828. *(Worldwide service.)*

SCOTLAND

Elizabeth Paterson Antiques, Shipping and Packing
52½ Spittal St., Stirling, FK8 1DU. Tel. (0786) 50648/823779. *(Packing, shipping and export service worldwide.)*

Scott Packing and Warehousing Co. Ltd.
Beaverbank Pl., Edinburgh, EH7 4ET. Tel. (031) 557 2000. *(Packers and shippers.)*

Scott Packing and Warehousing Co. Ltd.
Kilsyth Rd., Kirkintilloch, Glasgow, G66 1TJ. Tel. (041) 776 5194. Telex. 778940. *(Packers and shippers.)*

WALES

James and Patricia Ash
The Warehouse, Station Rd., Llandeilo, Dyfed, SA19 7AM. Tel. (0558) 823726. *(Shipping and container service. Supply and packing for overseas clients.)*

Index of Auctioneers

LONDON

Academy Auctioneers and Valuers
Northcote House, Northcote Ave., Ealing, London, W5 3UR. Tel. (081) 579 7466/9997. *Monthly sales of antiques, collectables, works of art, furniture, jewellery and silver.* Open 9–5. Valuations.

Bloomsbury Book Auctions
3 and 4 Hardwick St., EC1R 4RY. Tel. (071) 833 2636/7 and (071) 636 1945. *Twenty sales per year of books, manuscripts and maps, and especially disposal of academic libraries. Occasional sales of prints and drawings. Sellers commission 12½% (trade 10%); buyers premium 10%.*

Bonhams Knightsbridge
Montpelier St., Knightsbridge, SW7 1HH. Tel. (071) 584 9161. Fax. (071) 589 4072. *Regular sales of watercolours, Old Masters, European and modern pictures, prints, carved frames, furniture, clocks, Oriental, European and contemporary ceramics, art deco, art nouveau, objects of art, tribal art and antiquitities, silver, jewellery, objects of vertu, furs. Annual theme sales to coincide with Cowes Week, The Boat Show, Crufts, Chelsea Flower Show and National Cat Show. Pictures, sculptures and related works of art. Viewing Mon. 8.45–7, Tues.–Fri. 8.45–6, Sun. 12–5.*

Bonhams Chelsea
65–69 Lots Rd., Chelsea, SW10 0RN. Tel. (071) 584 9161. Fax. (071) 589 4072. *Regular sales of pictures, prints, furniture, carpets, books, maps, ceramics, silver, jewellery, erotic arts, militaria, sporting, fishing, cameras, toys, vintage pens, writing equipment, textiles and dolls. Viewing Mon. 8.45–7, Tues.–Fri. 8.45–5, Sat. and Sun. 10–1.*

Christie's
8 King St., St. James's, SW1Y 6QT. Tel. (071) 839 9060. *Porcelain, pottery, objets d'art and miniatures, pictures including Old Masters, English, Victorian, continental, impressionist, contemporary, prints, drawings, watercolours, art deco, art nouveau; Japanese and Chinese, Islamic and Persian works of art; glass, silver, jewellery, books, modern guns, arms and armour. Furniture, carpets, tapestries and wine. Other specialist sales periodically.* Christie's are the oldest fine art saleroom in the world.

Christie's South Kensington Ltd.,
85 Old Brompton Rd., SW7 3LD. Tel. (071) 581 7611. Telex. 922061. Fax. (071) 584 0431. *Sales of jewellery; silver; pictures; watercolours, drawings and prints; furniture and carpets; ceramics and works of art;*

Christie's South Kensington Ltd. continued

printed books; costume, textiles and embroidery. Toys and games; dolls; wines; art nouveau and art deco; cameras. Periodic sales of automata, mechanical music and vintage machines; motoring and aeronautical items including car mascots; Staffordshire portrait figures, pot-lids and Goss; miniatures; antiquities and cigarette cards and postcards.

Dowell Lloyd and Co. Ltd.
118 Putney Bridge Rd., Putney, SW15 2NQ. Tel. (081) 788 7777. *Two sales a week of general antique and modern items.* VAT: Stan.

Forrest and Co.
79–85 Cobbold Rd., Leytonstone, E11 3NS. Tel. (081) 534 2931. *Sales of antique and quality furniture, china, glassware, clocks, clock sets and works of art at fortnightly intervals.*

Stanley Gibbons Auctions Ltd.
399 Strand, WC2R 0LX. Tel. (071) 836 8444. *About 15 sales each year in London and overseas venues including popular general collections especially Gt. Britain, British Empire and Postal History. Catalogue subscription £25 p.a. (£30 Europe, £45 overseas) including prices realised lists. Postal bidding service available through catalogues, which also provide current market prices.*

Glendining and Co.
101 New Bond St., W1Y 9LG. Tel. (071) 493 2445. *Specialist auctioneers of coins and medals. About sixteen sales each year of coins; minimum four sales each year of military medals.*

Harmers of London Stamp Auctioneers Ltd.,
91 New Bond St., W1A 4EH. Tel. (071) 629 0218. Fax. (071) 495 0260. *The London division of the Harmer organisation who hold auctions in London, Zurich and New York. Sales of postage stamps, postal history and associated material held normally monthly from September to July. Fully illustrated catalogue produced for each sale. Philatelic insurance. "Guarantee" scheme for vendors.*

Lots Road Galleries
71 Lots Rd., Chelsea, SW10 0RN. Tel. (071) 351 7771. *Auction sales every Monday at 6p.m., approx. 350 lots of antique, traditional and decorative furniture, Oriental carpets, curtains, paintings, prints, ceramics, clocks, glass, silver, objets d'art. On view Fridays 10–4p.m., Saturdays and Sundays 10–1 and Mondays 10–6. Items accepted Wednesday–Friday. (Settlement within one week of sale.)* LOC: Off King's Rd, Worlds End. PARK: Easy. SER: Valuers and consultants: carrier service. VAT registered. S.A.E. for catalogue.

London continued

Phillips
101 New Bond St. and Blenstock House, 7 Blenheim St., W1Y OAS. Tel. (071) 629 6602. Telex. 298855. Fax. (071) 629 8876. *Furniture, carpets, works of art: two sales a week. Pictures, ceramics and glass, silver, weekly. Many specialist sales covering all aspects of art, antiques and collectors' items at frequent intervals, mostly monthly.*

Phillips West Two
10 Salem Rd., W2 4DL. Tel. (071) 229 9090. *Sales of furniture, porcelain and works of art each Thursday with the exception of four pre-arranged dates reserved for pianos. Sales of pictures alternate with those of collector's items on a Wednesday. Viewing a minimum of one day prior. Buyers premium 10% plus VAT.*

Rippon Boswell and Co.
The Arcade, South Kensington Station, SW7 2NA. Tel. (071) 589 4242. *International specialist auctioneers of old and antique Oriental carpets. Approx. two auctions a year in London. Also in Germany, Switzerland, U.S.A. and Far East.*

Rosebery Fine Art Ltd.
The Old Railway Booking Hall, Crystal Palace, Station Rd., SE19 2AZ. Tel. (081) 778 4024. *Sales of antique and modern furniture, ceramics, glass and works of art held twice a month.*

Sotheby's
34—35 New Bond St., W1A 2AA. Tel. (071) 493 8080. *Open for free valuations Mon.-Fri. 9-4.30. Sales daily of paintings, drawings, watercolours, prints, books and manuscripts, European sculpture and works of art, antiquities, silver, ceramics and glass, jewellery, Oriental works of art, furniture, musical instruments, clocks and watches, vintage cars, wine, postage stamps, coins, medals, toys and dolls and other collectors' items.*

Southgate Auction Rooms
Munro House, Munro Drive, Cline Rd., N11 2LZ. Tel. (081) 886 7888. *Weekly sales on Thursdays at 6.30 p.m. of jewellery, silver, china/porcelain, paintings, furniture.* (Viewing from 9a.m. on the day.)

AVON

Alder King — Black Horse Agencies
The Old Malthouse, Comfortable Pl., Upper Bristol Rd., Bath, BA1 3AJ. Tel. (0225) 447933. *Regular sales of antique furniture and works of art. Frequent auctions of Victorian and later furnishings. Monthly jewellery sales; quarterly musical instrument sales. Valuations.*

Aldridges, Bath
The Auction Galleries, 130—132 Walcot St., Bath, BA1 5BG. Tel. (0225) 462830. *Sales are held on Tuesdays and are broken down*

Aldridges, Bath continued

into specialist categories: Antique furniture to include clocks and Oriental carpets; silver and porcelain including glass and metalware; paintings and prints; Victorian and general furniture. Viewing Saturday mornings and Mondays. Catalogues available upon annual subscription. Large clients' car park.

Allen & Harris with Osmond Tricks
Bristol Auction Rooms, St. John's Place, Apsley Rd., Clifton, Bristol, BS8 2ST. Tel. (0272) 737201. *Six-weekly auctions of antique furniture, clocks, rugs, textiles, paintings, prints, musical instruments, glass, pottery, porcelain, silver, objects of vertu, toys and collectables. View day prior to sale from 10a.m. till 7p.m. and day of auction from 9a.m. until sale commences at 10.30a.m. Fortnightly auctions of Victorian and modern household furniture and effects. View day prior to sale from noon to 5p.m. and day of auction from 9a.m. until sale commences at 10.30a.m. Specialist auctions and house sales held throughout the year. Catalogue subscription service. Buyer's premium.*

Hoddell Pritchard (Est. 1785) G.A. Property Services
Clevedon Salerooms, Tickton Lodge, 8 Belle Vue Rd., Clevedon. BS21 7NT. Tel. (0272) 876699. *Bi-monthly auctions of antique furniture, fine art and collectors items. Fortnightly sales of Victorian, Edwardian and general furniture and effects. Occasional specialist sales and sales held on vendors property. Valuations given.*

Phillips Auctioneers — Bath
1 Old King St., Bath, BA1 2JT. Tel. (0225) 310609 and 310709. *Members of the Phillips Auction Group. Regular specialised sales of antique furniture, clocks, Oriental rugs, porcelain, silver, paintings, and collectors' sales. Programme of future sales sent on request.*

Phillips Auctioneers
71 Oakfield Rd., Clifton, Bristol, BS8 2BE. Tel. (0272) 734052. *Quarterly specialist antiques sales. Victorian sales monthly.*

Taviner's Auction Rooms
Prewett St., Redcliffe, Bristol, BS1 6PB. Tel. (0272) 265996. *Specialist sales of antiques, collectables, books, postcards and cigarette cards monthly. General furniture and effects every Friday.*

Woodspring Auctions
Churchill Rd. Weston-super-Mare. Tel. (0934) 628419. *Fortnightly sales of Edwardian and general household furniture, brass, copper, glass, china, coins, medals and bric-a-brac.*

BEDFORDSHIRE

Wilson Peacock
The Auction Centre, 26 Newnham St., Bedford, MK40 3JR. Tel. (0234) 266366. *Antique sale first Friday of every month. Viewing Thursday prior 9a.m.—6p.m. General sales every Saturday at 1.30a.m.* SER: Buys at auction.

BERKSHIRE

Robin Elliott, FRICS, IRRV incorporating Chancellors Fine Art
32 High St., Ascot, SL5 7HG. Tel. (0344) 872588. *Regular sales of antique furniture, porcelain, clocks, glass, silver, plate, oil paintings, watercolours, prints and jewellery.*
Dreweatt — Neate
Donnington Priory, Donnington, Newbury. RG13 2JE. Tel. (0635) 31234. Fax. (0635) 528195. *Sales at Donnington Priory mostly on a weekly basis. General furnishing — fortnightly on Tuesday. Antique furniture — eight per annum. Paintings, books, prints, silver and jewellery — three of each per annum. Members of the Society of Fine Art Auctioneers. Buyer's premium, 10%.*
Holloways
12 High St., Streatley, Reading. RG8 9HY. Tel. (0491) 872318. *Sales of antique furniture, ceramics, paintings etc., at Goring Village Hall. Approx. every five weeks.*
Martin and Pole
12 Milton Rd., Wokingham. Tel. (0734) 790460. *Auctions of antiques and collectables held on third Wednesday every month at Wokingham Auction Galleries, Milton Rd.*
Thimbleby and Shorland
31 Great Knollys St., Reading, RG1 7HU. Tel. (0734) 508611. *Collective sales of antique and modern furniture and effects held monthly on Saturdays at Reading Cattle Market. Also four specialist sales of horse-drawn vehicles, harness, horse brasses, driving sundries, whips and lamps etc.*
Duncan Vincent
105 London St., Reading, RG1 4LF. Tel. (0734) 589502. *About six collective sales of antique, Victorian and all good quality modern furniture and effects, about 700 lots, during the year at Memorial Hall, Shiplake.*

BUCKINGHAMSHIRE

Barnard and Learmount
18 Bathhurst Walk, Iver, SL0 9AZ. Tel. (0753) 652024. *Book and furniture auctions.*
Downer Ross (Auctioneers)
Charter House, 426 Avebury Boulevard, Milton Keynes, MK9 2HS. Tel. (0908) 679900. *Sales every four to six weeks.*
D.S. Johnson & Co. Auctions
31 West St., Buckingham, MK18 1HE. Tel. (0280) 822535.

Buckinghamshire continued

Nationwide Anglia — Amersham
The Amersham Auction Rooms, 125 Station Rd., Amersham, HP6 5BD. Tel. (0494) 729292. *Weekly general sales. Monthly selected antique sales. Sale day Thursday at 10.30p.m.*

CAMBRIDGESHIRE

Cheffins, Grain and Comins
The Cambridge Saleroom, 2 Clifton Rd., Cambridge, CB1 4BW. Tel. (0223) 213343 (10 lines). *Regular weekly and other specialist sales of furniture, clocks, porcelain, silver, pictures, sporting items, wine, rural and domestic bygones.*
Cheffins, Grain and Comins
Clifton Rd., Cambridge, CB1 4BW. Tel. (0223) 358721. *Sales of antique furniture, silver, china, glass, bric-a-brac etc., at Ely Maltings every two to three months (approx. four sales per annum). Also weekly (Thurs.) sales of household furniture.*
Grounds and Co.
2 Nene Quay, Wisbech, PE13 1AG. Tel. (0945) 585041/2. *Two specialist sales a year. Each sale comprises approx. 1,800 lots.*
Hammond and Co.
Cambridge Pl., Cambridge. Tel. (0223) 356067. *Weekly sales of furniture, smalls and antiques on Fridays from 10 a.m.*
Phillips (St. Ives)
The Saleroom, Station Rd., St. Ives, PE17 4JF. Tel. (0480) 68144. *Regular sales of good furniture, pictures, silver, jewellery, ceramics and Victoriana. Sales on Tuesdays at 11a.m., enquiries to Richard Haywood.* Also at The Golden Rose, 17 Emmanuel Rd., Cambridge, CB1 1JW. Tel. (0223) 66523 enquiries to Charles Simpson.

CHESHIRE

Andrew, Hilditch and Son Ltd.
Hanover House, 1A The Square, Sandbach, CW11 0AP. Tel. (0270) 767246 and 762048. *Quarterly sales of fine pictures and period furnishings. General and Edwardian furniture. Sales held weekly.*
Robert I. Heyes and Associates
Hatton Buildings, Lightfoot St., Hoole, Chester. Tel. (0244) 328 941. *Auctions first Tuesday each month.*
Brian Lightfoot & Co.
Betley Auctions, Betley Village Hall. Tel. (0270) 820397. *Monthly sales of general antiques, 3rd Saturday at 10a.m. Viewing from 8.15a.m.*
Frank R. Marshall and Co.
Marshall House, Church Hill, Knutsford, WA16 6DH. Tel. (0565) 653284. *Regular sales of antique furniture, objets d'art, silver, pewter, glassware, porcelain, pictures, brass and copper. Monthly household collective sales including bric-a-brac. Specialised sales at The Knutsford Auction Salerooms.*

Cheshire continued

Phillips in Chester
New House, 150 Christleton Rd., Chester, CH3 5TD. Tel. (0244) 313936 (4 lines). Fax. (0244) 340028. 35 branches countrywide including Chester.
Sotheby's
Booth Mansion, 28-30 Watergate St., Chester, CH1 2NA and Saltney, Chester. Tel. (0244) 315531. *Specialist sales of silver, jewellery, ceramics, furniture, clocks, collectors' items, miniatures, objects of vertu, glass, rugs and carpets. Insurance valuations.*
Wright Manley
Beeston Sales Centre, Beeston Castle Smithfield, Tarporley, CW6 0DR. Tel. (0829) 260318. *Fortnightly general sales and bi-monthly fine art and furniture sales.*

CORNWALL

Collins & Harris
The Auction Rooms, The Parade, Trengrove Way, Helston. TR13 8ER. Tel. (0872) 76611. *Auctions held on first Tuesday monthly.* Office — 29 Coinagehall St., Helston.
Jefferys
5 Fore St., Lostwithiel, PL22 0BP. Tel. (0208) 872245. *Sales alternate Wednesdays. Viewing on Tuesday and morning of sale. All sales commence at 10a.m*
Jefferys
Belmont Auction Rooms, Wadebridge. PL27 7NY. Tel. (020 881) 2131. *Sales of general antiques, collectors items, books and stamps every 12 weeks at 10a.m.*
Lambrys
incorporating R.J. Hamm A.S.V.A., Polmorla Walk, Wadebridge, PL27 7AE. Tel. (020 881) 3593. *Fortnightly sales of antiques and objets d'art.* Illustrated catalogues issued.
W.H. Lane and Son
Fine Art Auctioneers and Valuers. 65 Morrab Rd., Penzance, TR18 2QT. Tel. (0736) 61447. *Twelve sales each year of antiques and objets d'art. Two specialist book sales per year. Six picture sales per year (specialists in the Newlyn and St. Ives Schools of Art). Two specialist toy sales per year. Frequent house sales.*
David Lay A.S.V.A.
The Penzance Auction House, Alverton, Penzance, TR18 4RE. Tel. (0736) 61414. Fax. (0736) 60035. *Sales of fine art, antiques and collectors' items every two weeks.*
M.G.A. Auctions
The Camborne Auction House, West Charles St., Camborne, TR14 8JG. Tel. (0209) 711065. *Sales every Thursday at 6p.m.*
Phillips Cornwall
Cornubia Hall, Par, PL24 2AQ. Tel. (072 681) 4047. *Selected monthly Tuesday sales of antiques. Fortnightly Thursday sales of Victorian, pine and general household furnishings. Collectors sales, Feb., April, Aug., Dec.*
Pooley and Rogers
Regent Auction Rooms, Abbey St. Penzance. Tel. Office — (0736) 63816/7 or 795451. Saleroom — (0736) 68814. *Bi-monthly sales of antique furniture, objets d'art, silver and jewellery.*

CUMBRIA

Cumbria Auction Rooms
12 Lowther St., Carlisle. CA3 8DA. Tel. (0228) 25259. *Weekly sales of Victorian and later furniture and effects. Catalogue sales of antiques and works of art every ten weeks.*
Mossops
Loughrigg Villa, Kelsick Rd., Ambleside. LA22 0BZ. Tel. (0966) 33015. *Collective sales of antiques, works of art and older style country furnishings at intervals throughout the year. Also catalogue sales on premises. Full valuation service.*
James Thompson
64 Main St., Kirkby Lonsdale, LA6 2AJ. Tel. (05242) 71555. *Monthly two day sales of silver, ceramics, general antiques. Special picture sales six times a year.*
Thomson, Roddick and Laurie Ltd.
24 Lowther St., Carlisle. CA3 8DA. Tel. (0228) 28939 and 39636. *Bi-monthly catalogue sales of antiques and collectors' items at Dumfries and Carlisle, Cumbria. Occasional specialist sales at Carlisle and Dumfries, particularly antiquarian books, sporting guns, silver and pictures. Monthly general furniture sales at Wigton, Brampton (Cumbria) and Annan, Dumfriesshire.*

DERBYSHIRE

Neales
The Derby Salerooms, Becket St., Derby, DE1 1HW. Tel. (0332) 43286. *Regular sales of antique, Victorian, Edwardian and reproduction furniture and furnishings, pictures, silver, jewellery, ceramics (especially Derbyshire factories), glass, decorative arts and collectors' items.*
Wheatcrofts
Matlock Auction Gallery, Old English Rd., off Dale Rd., Matlock, DE4 3LX. Tel. (0629) 584591. *Monthly sales antiques and general.*

DEVON

Bearne's
Rainbow, Avenue Rd., Torquay TQ2 5TG. Tel. (0803) 296277. *Regular sales of antique furniture, works of art, silver, jewellery, collectors' items, clocks and watches, paintings, ceramics and glass, carpets and rugs. Illustrated catalogues published three weeks prior to sale.*

Devon continued

Bonhams — West Country
Dowell St., Honiton, EX14 8LX. Tel. (0404) 41872.

Peter J. Eley, F.S.V.A.
Western House, 98-100 High St., Sidmouth, EX10 8EF. Tel. (0395) 512552. *Sales of antiques, silver, pictures and china every four to five weeks.*

Kingsbridge Auction Sales (J.A.S. Hawkins) inc. Charles Head & Son
Auctioneers office: 85 Fore St., Kingsbridge, TQ7 1AB. Tel. (0548) 856829. *Regular sales of antique and general household furniture and effects.*

Lyme-Bay Auction Galleries
28 Harbour Rd., Seaton. Tel. (0297) 22453. *General household and antique auctions held every 4–6 weeks.*

Michael Newman Central Auction Rooms
Kinterbury House, St. Andrews Cross, Plymouth. PL1 2DG. Tel. (0752) 669298. *Collective antique sales second Tues. of each month. Six picture sales, three coin sales and three book sales per year.*

Phillips
Alphin Brook Rd., Alphington, Exeter. EX2 8TH. Tel. (0392) 439025. Fax. (0392) 410361. *Thursday sales of antique and reproduction furniture and furnishings; oil paintings, watercolours and good quality prints; silver, silver plate and jewellery; porcelain and glass, Victoriana and objets d'art. Book sales held four times a year; sporting sale held once a year.*

Phillips Fine Art Auctioneers
Armada St., North Hill, Plymouth, PL4 8LS. Tel. (0752) 673504.

Potburys of Sidmouth
The Auction Rooms, Temple St., Sidmouth. EX10 8LH. Tel. (0395) 515555. *Twice monthly plus private house sales.*

Rendells
Stone Park, Ashburton, TQ13 7RH. Tel. (0364) 53017. *Regular sales of antique furniture, silver, jewellery, porcelain, glass, clocks, pictures, plate, copper, brass, miscellanea.*

John Smale and Co. Ltd.
11 High St., Barnstaple. EX31 1BG. Tel. (0271) 42000. *Intermittently throughout the year. Private house sales only.*

Taylor's
Honiton Galleries, 205 High St., Honiton, EX14 8LF. Tel. (0404) 42404. *Sales of paintings and prints, antiques, silver, books, porcelain every seven weeks.*

Ward and Chowen
1 Church Lane, Tavistock, PL19 8AB. Tel. (0822) 612458.

Whitton and Laing
32 Okehampton St., Exeter, EX4 1DY. Tel. (0392) 52621. *Antique auctions monthly. Book auctions quarterly. Coins, silver, jewellery, every six weeks. General weekly.*

DORSET

Cottees, Bullock and Lees
The Market, East St., Wareham. Tel. (0929) 552826. *Furniture and effects every two weeks.*

Hy. Duke and Son (Fox Holdings Group)
Fine Art Salerooms, Weymouth Ave., Dorchester. DT1 1DG. Tel. (0305) 265080. *Regular sales every six weeks including specialist sections of silver and jewellery, Oriental and English porcelain, English and Continental furniture, pictures, books, or Oriental rugs.* Also at Weymouth Furniture Saleroom, St. Nicholas St., Weymouth. Tel. (0305) 783488. *Regular sales of Victorian and later shipping furniture and effects.*

House and Son
Lansdowne House, Christchurch Rd., Bournemouth, BH1 3JW. Tel. (0202) 556232. *Sales fortnightly of selected furniture, pictures, books, silver, porcelain and glass. Catalogues £1.50 inc. postage.*

Wm. Morey & Sons
Salerooms, St. Michaels Lane, Bridport, DT6 3RB. Tel. (0308) 22078. *Antique and general sales held every three to four weeks.*

Riddetts of Bournemouth
Richmond Hill, Bournemouth Sq., Bournemouth, BH2 6EJ. Tel. (0202) 555686. *Sales fortnightly including fine antiques, jewellery, silver, plate, pictures. Illustrated sale programme free. Catalogue subscription £25p.a.*

Southern Counties Auctioneers
The Livestock Market, Christys Lane, Shaftesbury, SP7 8JL. Tel. Shaftesbury (0747) 52720. *Regular sales of antique furniture and effects.*

DURHAM

Denis Edkins
Auckland Auction Rooms, 58 Kingsway, Bishop Auckland, DL14 7JF. Tel. (0388) 603095. *General sales in Auckland Auction Rooms. Antique sales from time to time.*

G. Tarn Bainbridge and Son
Northern Rock House, High Row, Darlington, DL3 7QN. Tel. (0325) 462633 and 462553. *Three to four collective sales per year and regular country house sales.*

Thomas Watson and Son
Northumberland St., Darlington, DL3 7HJ. Tel. (0325) 462559/5 (two lines). *Regular sales of antiques and good quality house contents.*

ESSEX

Abridge Auction Rooms
Market Pl., Abridge, Romford, RM4 1UA. *3 weekly sales a month at 7p.m. and bi-monthly sales of jewellery, Victorian and Edwardian furniture and Doulton. (No sale on last Wed. of month).* Tel. (0992) 813113/812107.

Essex continued

Black Horse Agencies — Ambrose
149 High Rd., Loughton. IG10 4LZ. Tel. (081) 508 2121 or 502 3951. *Sales held on last Thursday of month.*
William H. Brown
11-14 East Hill, Colchester, CO1 2QX. Tel. (0206) 868070. *Weekly sales of antique and modern furniture, china, glass, silver and decorative items.*
G.A. Fine Arts and Chattels
1 Market St., Saffron Walden. CB10 1JB. Tel. (0799) 513281. *Sales of antique and fine furniture, antique effects and objets d'art, held every month.*
Hamptons Fine Art — J.M. Welch and Sons
Old Town Hall, Great Dunmow. CM6 1AU. Tel. (0371) 872117. Fax. (0371) 875936. Salerooms at Chequers Lane, Gt. Dunmow. *Selected antique furniture and effects, sales every two months and monthly sales of collectables and household furniture. Catalogue subscription service available.*
Cooper Hirst Auctions
The Granary Salerooms, Victoria Rd., Chelmsford. Tel. (0245) 260535. *Regular sales every six weeks of antiques and weekly Friday sales of Victoriana, bric-a-brac etc. Catalogue subscription scheme.*
Reemans
Head Gate Auction Rooms, 12 Head Gate, Colchester, CO3 3BT. Tel. (0206) 574271/2. *Sales held every Wednesday. Viewing 9—7 Tuesday prior. Evening sale last Tuesday of month.*
Simon H. Rowland
Chelmsford Auction Rooms, 42 Mildmay Rd., Chelmsford. CM2 ODZ. Tel. (0245) 354251. *Regular sales by order of the Sheriff of Essex and private vendors.*
John Stacey and Sons
Leigh Auction Rooms, 86-90 Pall Mall, Leigh-on-Sea, SS9 1RG. Tel. (0702) 77051. *Monthly auctions of furniture, works of art and collectors items. Catalogue subscription scheme £21p.a.*

GLOUCESTERSHIRE

Bruton, Knowles
Albion Chambers, 111 Eastgate St., Gloucester, GL1 1PZ. Tel. (0452) 21267. *Fine art auctioneers and valuers. House and collective sales held throughout the year. Valuations and inventories prepared.*
Corinium Galleries
25 Gloucester St., Cirencester, GL7 2DJ. Tel. (0285) 659057. *Monday auctions of postcards and small collectables every five weeks.*
Fraser, Glennie and Partners
The Old Rectory, Siddington, Cirencester, GL7 6HL. Tel. (0285) 659677. *Monthly sales of*

Fraser, Glennie and Partners continued

antiques, other furniture, collectors' items and musical instruments, at the Bingham Hall, Cirencester.
Mallams Fine Art Auctioneers and Valuers
26 Grosvenor St., Cheltenham, GL52 2SG. Est. 1788. Tel. (0242) 235712. *Regular sales of furniture, ceramics, paintings, textiles, rugs and works of art.*
Moore, Allen and Innocent
33 Castle St., Cirencester. GL7 1QD. Tel. (0285) 651831. *Monthly: collective sales of over 1,000 lots of antique and other furniture. Bi-annual specialist picture sales, and specialist sporting sales, Fridays at 10a.m. Viewing: day prior 10.30a.m.-8.00p.m. No buyers premium.*
Short Graham & Co.
City Chambers, 4/6 Clarence St., Gloucester, GL1 1EA. Tel. (0452) 21177. *Sales of general antiques, household and outdoor effects, books, objets d'art and collectables every four to six weeks.*
Wotton Auction Rooms (Sandoes)
Tabernacle Rd., Wotton-under-Edge, GL12 7EB. Tel. (0453) 844733. *Ten collective sales of antiques. Picture sales and house contents sales as instructed. Catalogues by subscription.*

HAMPSHIRE

Austin and Wyatt Nationwide Anglia
The Square, Bishop's Waltham, Southampton, SO3 1GG. Tel. (0489) 896333. *Occasional private house sales.*
Basingstoke Auction Rooms
82-84 Sarum Hill, Basingstoke, RG21 1ST. Tel. (0256) 840707. *Regular sales of antiques and fine art and fortnightly general sales. Occasional specialist sales. Catalogues available. Buyer's premium 10%.*
Fox & Sons
5 and 7 Salisbury St., Fordingbridge, SP6 1AD. Tel. (0425) 652121. Fax. (0425) 656690. *Monthly sales of antique and later furniture, silver, plate, metalware, ceramics, pictures, etc.*
G.A. Property Services
Furniture and Fine Art Dept., 86 The Hundred, Romsey, SO51 8BX. (Manager — Michael G. Baker, F.S.V.A.) Tel. (0794) 513331. The Romsey Auction Rooms, 86 The Hundred, Romsey. *Monthly sales of antique and period furniture and effects, silver, jewellery and plate.*
Hants and Berks Auctions
82-84 Sarum Hill, Basingstoke. Tel. (0256) 840707. *Monthly sales at Heckfield Village Hall, on Saturday at 10.30a.m. Viewing on previous day 11a.m. — 9p.m. Sales include antiques, reproduction and household furniture, clocks, porcelain, glass, silver, pictures, etc. Occasional specialist sales. Catalogues available.*

Hampshire continued

Jacobs and Hunt
Lavant St., Petersfield. GU32 3EF. Tel. (0730) 62744/5. *General antique sales every six to eight weeks on Fridays.*

May and Son
18 Bridge St., Andover, SP10 1BH. Tel. (0264) 323417 and 363331. *Monthly sales of antique furniture and effects at Penton Mewsey Village Hall. (Lots from private sources only.) Private house contents sales.*

Nationwide Fine Art and Furniture
New Forest Auction Rooms, Emsworth Rd., Lymington, SO4 9ZE. Tel. (0590) 677225. *Fortnightly sales of antique and modern furniture and effects. Special quarterly sales of antique and reproduction furniture, pottery and porcelain, silver and plated items, paintings, etc. Occasional house contents sales.*

D.M. Nesbit and Co.
7 Clarendon Rd., Southsea, PO5 2ED. Tel. (0705) 864321. *Monthly sales of antique furniture, silver, porcelain, and pictures.*

Phillips
54 Southampton Rd., Ringwood, BH24 1JD. Tel. (0425) 473333. *Regular sales, usually monthly.*

Phillips Fine Art Auctioneers
The Red House, Hyde St., Winchester, SO23 7DX. Tel. (0962) 862515. Fax. (0962) 865166. *Bi-monthly sales of fine furniture, pictures, silver, jewellery, ceramics, metalware, clocks, rugs and works of art. Fortnightly sales of antique, Victorian and Edwardian furniture, ceramics, pictures and objects.*

HEREFORD AND WORCESTER

Griffiths and Co.
57 Foregate St., Worcester, WR1 1DZ. Tel. (0905) 26464.

Hamptons Fine Art — Pocock and Lear
The Malvern Sale Room, Barnards Green Rd., Malvern. Tel. (0684) 892314/5. *Bi-monthly catalogued antique and fine art auctions. Fortnightly general sales. Specialist sales of Worcester porcelain (single items or collections.) Valuations.*

Hereford and Worcester continued

Phipps and Pritchard
Bank Buildings, Kidderminster, DY10 1BU. Tel. (0562) 822244/5/6 and 822187. *Regular monthly sales of antique furniture; water-colours and oil paintings; copper, brass and glassware, china and porcelain; stamps; coins and weapons etc. Private house sales also conducted.*

Russell, Baldwin and Bright
The Fine Art Saleroom, Ryelands Rd., Leominster. HR6 8NZ. Tel. (0568) 611166. *Monthly sales mostly two-day of fine antiques and collector's items.*

Sandoe-Nationwide Anglia
41-43 High St., Broadway, WR12 7DP. Tel. (0386) 852456. *Collective antique and modern furniture sales bi-monthly. Specialist sales of silver and porcelain twice yearly.*

HERTFORDSHIRE

Brown & Merry
41 High St., Tring, HP23 5AB. Tel. (044282) 6446. *Fortnightly Saturday sales of antiques and collectables held at The Cattle Market, Brook St., Tring. Monthly fine art sales held on Fridays.*

Norris and Duvall — Furniture and Fine Art Auctioneers and Valuers
106 Fore St., Hertford, SG14 1AH. Tel. (0992) 582249. *Monthly sales of antique furniture, china, glass, silver, jewellery, pictures, clocks, linen, lace, collectors items, oriental rugs at Castle Hall, Hertford. Selected entries invited from private customers, details to be received at least ten days before each sale. Annual catalogue subscription £17. No buyer's premium.*

Pamela and Barry Auctions
Antiques and collectors auctions held on the first and third Tuesdays of each month at Village Hall, Sandridge, St. Albans, AL4 9ST. Viewing 3p.m. until the start at 7p.m. Tel. (0727) 861180 for details.

Hertfordshire continued

G.E. Sworder and Sons
15 Northgate End, Bishops Stortford, CM23 2ET. Tel. (0279) 651388. *Monthly auctions of antique furniture, ceramics, silver, pictures, decorative items. Viewing Saturday prior to sale 9a.m.—12 noon, Monday prior to sale 9a.m.—4p.m.*

HUMBERSIDE NORTH

Gilbert Baitson
"The Edwardian Auction Galleries", 194 Anlaby Rd, Hull, HU3 2RJ. Tel. (0482) 223355/6, after hours (0482) 645241. *Sales of antique and modern furnishings every Wednesday at 10.30a.m. Viewing, day prior until 8p.m.*

Black Horse Agencies — Storey, Sons & Parker
18 Quay Rd., Bridlington. YO15 2AP. Tel. (0262) 676724 (24hrs.). *General auctions every Thursday. Regular sales of antiques and fine arts.*

Dee and Atkinson — Agricultural and Fine Arts
The Exchange Saleroom, Driffield, YO25 7LJ. Tel. (0377) 43151. *Regular sales of general antiques. Victorian furniture, silver, jewellery, etc. Viewing 2 days prior. Bi-monthly antique sales, silver, jewellery etc. at 10.30a.m.*

H. Evans and Sons
1 St. James's St., Hessle Rd., Hull, HU3 2DH. Tel. (0482) 23033. *Five antiques sales per annum, fortnightly general furniture and effects.*

HUMBERSIDE SOUTH

Dickinson, Davy and Markham
New Saleroom, Elwes St., Brigg, DN20 8JH. Tel. (0652) 53666. *Fine art and antique auctions held every six to eight weeks, also Victorian and household effects sold every two weeks. Catalogue subscription service available.*

A.E. Dowse and Son
Foresters' Galleries, Falkland Way, Barton upon Humber, DN18 5RL. Tel. (0652) 32335. *Monthly sales of general antiques and collectors' items.*

ISLE OF WIGHT

Watson, Bull and Porter
Auction Rooms, 79 Regent St., Shanklin, PO37 7AP. Tel. (0983) 863441. *Monthly auctions of antiques and fine arts.*

Ways
The Auction House, Garfield Rd., Ryde, PO33 2NQ. Tel. (0983) 62255. *Bi-monthly sales of general antiques, furniture, paintings, silver, porcelain, etc. Monthly sales of antique and modern furnishings.*

KENT

Albert Andrews Auctions and Sales
Maiden Lane, Crayford, Dartford. DA1 4LX. Tel. (0322) 528868. *Weekly auctions on Wednesdays at 10.00a.m. — viewing Tuesdays 4.30p.m.—8.30p.m. — including antiques, Victorian and Edwardian furniture, bric-a-brac, paintings, clocks etc.*

Black Horse Agencies
Geering and Colyer, Highgate, Hawkhurst, TN18 4AD. Tel. (0580) 753463/753181. *Regular sales by auction; sales also held on owner's premises. Valuations prepared. Catalogues (£1.80 by post) and further details from the auctioneers.*

Bracketts
27-29 High St., Tunbridge Wells, TN1 1UU. Tel. (0892) 33733. *Weekly sale of antiques and general household furniture on Fridays. Special sales of antiques and sales on the premises.*

G.A. Property Services
The Canterbury Auction Galleries, 40 Station Rd. West, Canterbury, CT2 8AN. Tel. (0227) 763337. *Specialist fine art and antiques auctions held bi-monthly and monthly auctions of Victorian, Edwardian and quality modern furniture and effects. Professional valuations for insurance, probate and family division.*

Halifax Property Services
53 High St., Tenterden, TN30 6BG. Tel. (058 06) 3200. *Antique and modern furniture and effects in the first Wednesday of each month.*

Halifax Property Services continued

Evening sales of antiques, pictures, porcelain, silver, objets d'art, etc., on the second Wednesday bi-monthly. Also fine art sales at Cranbrook announced in the press.

Hobbs Parker
Romney House, Ashford Market, Ashford, TN23 1PG. Tel. (0233) 622222. Fax. (0233) 46642. *Monthly sales of antiques and household furniture.*

Ibbett, Mosely
125 High St., Sevenoaks, TN13 1UT. Tel. (0732) 456731. *Antiques and objets d'art.*

Kennedy Auctioneers
St. Johns St. Auction Rooms, Folkestone. Tel. (0303) 269323, home and office.

Lambert & Foster
102 High St., Tenterden, TN30 6AU. Tel. (058 06) 3233. Also 21 offices throughout Kent and Sussex. *Monthly general sales of good quality antique furniture and effects. Special contents sales at private residences in the county. Fine art evening sales.*

Phillips
11 Bayle Parade, Folkestone, CT20 1SQ. Tel. (0303) 45555. *Fortnightly fine art and Victoriana sales.*

Phillips Son & Neale
49 London Rd., Sevenoaks, TN13 1AR. Tel. (0732) 740310. *Monthly sales of antiques and collectors' items.*

Messrs. Stewart, Gore
100/102 Northdown Rd., Margate, 137 Canterbury Rd., Westbrook, 161 Northdown Rd., Cliftonville and 95 High St., Broadstairs. Auction Rooms: Clifton Place, Margate. Tel. (0843) 221528/9. *Monthly collective sales of antiques. Specialist sales according to demand. Private house sales.*

LANCASHIRE

Capes Dunn and Co.
The Auction Galleries, 38 Charles St., Manchester, M1 7DB. Tel. (061) 273 1911. Fine Art Auctioneers founded 1826. *Catalogues of weekly specialist sales available on request.*

Entwistle Green (Black Horse Agencies)
The Galleries, Kingsway, Ansdell, Lytham St. Annes, FY8 1AB. Tel. (0253) 735442. *Sales of antique, reproduction and modern furnishings and appointments held fortnightly on Tuesday and Wednesday. Average 400—600 lots commencing 10a.m. each day. View Saturday morning before noon and Monday to 3.45p.m. Buyers premium 10%.*

McKennas, Auctioneers and Valuers
Bank Salerooms, Harris Court, Clitheroe, BB7 1BJ. Tel. (0200) 22695. *Antique and later furniture, pictures, silver, pottery, bric-a-brac and related items. Monthly sales at Pendleton Village Hall nr. Clitheroe on Thursdays at 10a.m. Viewing Wed. 10-8p.m. Valuations for probate, insurance, etc.*

Lancashire continued

J.R. Parkinson Son and Hamer Auctions
The Auction Room, Rochdale Rd., Bury. Tel. (061) 761 1612/7372. *Specialised auctions of antiques, Victoriana and Edwardiana on a six to eight week basis throughout the year.*

Phillips — Manchester
Trinity House, 114 Northenden Rd., Manchester M33 3HD. Tel. (061) 962 9237. *Regular sales of antique jewellery, clocks, watches, scientific instruments, paintings and watercolours, Period, Victorian and modern furnishings; Chinese and Japanese furnishings, porcelain, collectors' items. Auctions held Wednesdays commencing 10a.m. Viewing previous and same day.*

John E. Pinder and Son
48 Berry Lane, Longridge, Preston, PR3 3JP. Tel. (0772) 782282/783993. *Mixed antique, period and general furnishings monthly.*

LEICESTERSHIRE

William H. Brown
The Warner Auction Rooms, 16/18 Halford St., Leicester, LE1 1JB. Tel. (0533) 519777. *Regular sales of antiques, pictures, porcelain, silver, etc., in our rooms; outside sales by arrangement.*

Freckeltons
1 Leicester Rd., Loughborough. LE11 2AE. Tel. (0509) 214564. *Monthly sales of general antiques.*

Gilding's Auctioneers and Valuers
Roman Way, Market Harborough, LE16 7PQ. Tel. (0858) 410414. *Monthly sales of antiques, fortnightly sales of Victoriana and collectables.*

N.H. Noton & Associates
4 Market Pl., Oakham, LE15 6DT. Tel. (Office) (0572) 723377. 96 South St., Oakham (Saleroom) Tel. (0572) 722222. *General sales fortnightly (alternate Thursdays). Special sales of antique furniture, silver, china, jewellery etc. every six weeks.*

LINCOLNSHIRE

William H. Brown
Westgate Hall, Grantham, NG31 6LT. Tel. (0476) 68861. *Bi-monthly antique and fine art sales. Occasional specialist and house contents sales. Fortnightly sales of general household furniture and effects.*

C.J. Daykin, F.R.I.C.S.
69 Northgate, Sleaford, NG34 7BB. Tel. (0529) 413954. *General sale Mondays (exc. B.H.) and monthly Thursday sales.*

James Eley and Son
1 Main Ridge West, Boston, PE21 6QQ. Tel. (0205) 361687. *Regular sales at Boston and Skegness.*

Escritt and Barrell
The Saleroom, Dysant Rd., Grantham, NG31 7DD. Tel. (0476) 66991. *Three-weekly general shipping and antique sales. Frequent antique sales.*

Lincolnshire continued

Thomas Mawer and Son
63 Monks Rd., Lincoln, LN2 5HP. Tel. (0522) 524984. *General sales every fortnight. Catalogued antique sales monthly.*

Nationwide Anglia Fine Art & Furniture
Auction Rooms, Spalding Rd., Bourne, PE10 9LE. Tel. (0778) 422686. *Antiques sales every month. Antique and modern sales every Saturday.*

MERSEYSIDE

A.J. Cobern
The Grosvenor Salerooms, 93B Eastbank St., Southport, PR8 1DG. Tel. (0704) 500515. *Sales of antique, reproduction and modern furnishings held every three-four weeks. Average 600/700 lots commencing 10a.m. Viewing weekend and two days prior to sale.*

Kingsley and Co. Auctioneers
3/4 The Quadrant, Hoylake, Wirral, L47 2EE. Tel. (051) 632 5821. *Sales every Tuesday of antiques, fine art and general chattels.*

Outhwaite and Litherland
"Kingsway Galleries", Fontenoy St., Liverpool, L3 2BE. Tel. (051) 236 6561/3. *Victorian, Edwardian and modern furnishings — weekly Tuesday. General antiques and fine quality reproductions — fortnightly Wednesday. Fine art sales including all works illustrative of the fine arts — monthly Wednesday. Specialist sales of books, wines, stamps etc. — periodically. Members of The Society of Fine Art Auctioneers.*

NORFOLK

Hugh Best Auctions
The Cornhall, Cattle Market St., Fakenham. Tel. (0328) 851557. *Weekly sales of antique and other furniture every Thursday at 11a.m. Annual evening picture sale around the end of March. Country house sales as instructed.*

Clowes, Nash and Thurgar
6 Tombland, Norwich, NR3 1HE. Tel. (0603) 627261. *Antiques and general furniture weekly sales.*

Ewings
Market Pl., Reepham, Norwich, NR10 4JJ. Tel. (0603) 870473. *Periodic sales of antique and modern furniture and effects.*

Thos. Wm. Gaze and Son
Diss Auction Rooms, Roydon Rd., Diss, IP22 3LN. Tel. (0379) 650306. *Weekly catalogue sales of antique and cottage furniture on Fridays at 10.30a.m. and bi-monthly special catalogue sales.*

Glennie's
Merchants Court, St. George's St., Norwich, NR3 1AB. Tel. (0603) 633558. Fax. (0603) 760080. *Regular catalogue sales of fine art, antiques and collectors' items.*

Norfolk continued

Nigel F. Hedge
28B Market Pl., North Walsham, NR28 9BS. Tel. (0692) 402881. *Fortnightly general and antique sales.*

Hilham's
43 Baker St., Gorleston-on-Sea, NR31 6QT. Tel. (0493) 662152/600700/604104. *Art auctions held regularly. Antiques and Victoriana sales every month.*

James — Norwich Auctions Ltd.
(Member of the James Group)
Head Office — 33 Timberhill, Norwich NR1 3LA. Tel. (0603) 624817. *Regular sales of antiques and collectors' items. Catalogues available.*

G.A. Key
Incorporated Auctioneers, 8 Market Pl., Aylsham, NR11 6EH. Tel. (0263) 733195. *Sales operating from Aylsham salerooms. Three weekly sales of period antique, Victorian furniture, silver, porcelain, etc. Bi-monthly pictures sales for all classes of oils, watercolours, prints, etc. Six book and collectors sales annually. Weekly sales of shipping and secondhand furniture. Further details of all sales from auctioneers' offices as above.*

NORTHAMPTONSHIRE

Goldsmiths
15 Market Pl., Oundle, PE8 4BA. Tel. (0832) 272349. *Approximately bi-monthly.*

Heathcote Ball & Co
Albion Auction Rooms, Commercial St., Northampton, NN1 1PJ. Tel. (0604) 37263/4. *Regular fine art and antiques sales, fortnightly general sales, specialist sales. Mailing subscription £8 per annum.*

R.L. Lowery and Partners
24 Bridge St., Northampton. NN1 1NT. Tel. (0604) 21561. *Country and town house sales. Collective sales mainly to wind up estates. Approx. eight sales p.a. Fine art valuations for probate and family division.*

Southams Established 1900
Corn Exchange, Thrapston, Nr. Kettering, NN14 4JJ. Tel. (08012) 4486. *Sales of antiques and superior furniture, silver, silver plate, copper, brass, fine china, glass, Oriental rugs, oil paintings, watercolours and prints. Catalogues £1 incl. p. & p. Yearly subscription £12 incl. p. & p. First Thursday each month. Viewing Wednesday 9.30a.m. to 8p.m. No buyer's premium.*

H. Wilford Ltd.
Midland Rd., Wellingborough, NN8 1NB. Tel. (0933) 222760/222762. *Weekly sales of antique and modern furniture, shipping goods, jewellery, etc. every Thursday.*

NOTTINGHAMSHIRE

Arthur Johnson and Sons (Auctioneers)
The Nottingham Auction Centre, Meadow Lane, Nottingham, NG2 3GY. Tel. (0602) 869128. *About 1,000 lots weekly on Saturday at 10a.m. of antique and shipping furniture, silver, gold, porcelain, metalwares and collectables.*
Neales
192-194 Mansfield Rd., Nottingham, NG1 3HU. Tel. (0602) 624141. *Specialist sales of paintings, drawings, prints and books; silver, jewellery, bijouterie and watches; European and Oriental ceramics and works of art, glass; furniture and decoration; metalwork, fabrics, needlework, carpets and rugs; collectors' toys and dolls; stamps, coins and medals, postcards and cigarette cards, autographs and collectors' items. Weekly collective sales (Monday) of general antique and later furnishings, shipping goods, reproduction furnishings. Period and later ceramics, glass and decorative effects. Sales on the premises of the contents of town and country properties.*
John Pye and Sons
Furniture and General Auctions, Corn Exchange, Cattle Market, London Rd., Nottingham. Tel. (0602) 866261/865238.
C.B. Sheppard and Son
The Auction Gallery, Chatsworth St., Sutton-in-Ashfield. Tel. (0773) 872419. Saledays (0623) 556310. *Monthly sales of antiques, collectors' items, jewellery and works of art. No buyers premium.*
Henry Spencer and Sons — Fine Art Auctioneers
20 The Square, Retford, DN22 6BX. Tel. (0777) 708633. *Specialist sales of furniture, carpets, ornamental items, works of art; paintings, drawings and prints; porcelain and glass. Silver, jewellery and bijouterie. Non-specialist sales of furniture and effects held three times a month. Sales on the premises at town and country houses.*
Richard Watkinson and Partners
17 Northgate, Newark, NG24 1EX. Tel. (0636) 77154. *Monthly sales of antique and Victorian furniture, oil paintings, silver, etc. Weekly sales of early 20th C and general household furniture.*

OXFORDSHIRE

Green and Co.
33 Market Pl., Wantage, OX12 8AL. Tel. (023 57) 3561/2. *Regular sales of antiques and other furniture, copper, brass, china, glass, silver and plate, clocks and objets d'art, both in private houses and at salerooms.*
Holloways
49 Parsons St., Banbury, OX16 8PF. Tel. (0295) 253197. *Sales at least three times monthly.*

Oxfordshire continued

Mallams
Fine Art Auctioneers, Bocardo House, 24A St. Michael's St., Oxford, OX1 2EB. Tel. (0865) 241358. *Frequent sales of furniture, silver, paintings and works of art. House sales arranged on the premises.*
Messenger's
Messenger's Salerooms, 27 Sheep St., Bicester, OX6 7JF. Tel. (0869) 252901. *Antique furniture and effects each month. Specialist sales of carpentry tools, collectors items and domestic bygones.*
Phillips Fine Art Auctioneers
39 Park End St., Oxford, OX1 1JD. Tel. (0865) 723524. Fax. 791064. *Fortnightly sales of Victoriana and general effects. Specialist sales of fine furniture, rugs, works of art, silver, jewellery, ceramics and fine wines throughout the year.*

SHROPSHIRE

Cooper and Green
3 Barker St., Shrewsbury, SY1 1QF. Tel. (0743) 232244 and at The Square, Church Stretton, SY6 6DA. Tel. (0694) 722458.
Hall, Wateridge and Owen
Welsh Bridge Salerooms, Shrewsbury. Tel. (0743) 231212. *Regular Victoriana and household (Fridays). Bi-monthly selected antiques and collectables.*
Ludlow Antique Auctions Ltd.
29 Corve St., Ludlow, SY8 1DA. Tel. (0584) 875157; (0584) 873496. *Specialist fine art and antique auctions every six weeks (Tuesdays) on the premises.*
Perry and Phillips
Newmarket Salerooms, Newmarket Buildings, Listley St., Bridgnorth, WV16 4AW. Tel. (0746) 762248. *Weekly (Tuesday) sales of good quality household furniture and effects. Monthly sales of antique furniture, Victoriana, china, porcelain, pictures etc. Regular specialist sales and house contents sales.*

SOMERSET

W.R.J. Greenslade & Co.
Priory Saleroom, Winchester St., Taunton, TA1 1RN. Tel. (0823) 277121. *Monthly sales of antique and good quality furniture, silver, plate, copper, brass, china, glassware, pictures, prints etc. Catalogues subscription £10 p.a.*
Gribble Booth and Taylor
32 The Avenue, Minehead, TA24 5AZ. Tel. (0643) 702281. *Regular sales every three weeks of antique and other furniture and effects at Mart Rd. Salerooms, Minehead. Tel. (0643) 703646. Occasional house clearance sales.*
Lawrence Fine Art of Crewkerne
South St., Crewkerne TA18 8AB. Tel. (0460) 73041. *Specialist auctioneers and valuers. Regular sales of antiques and fine art. Weekly general sales.*

Somerset continued

The London Cigarette Card Co. Ltd.
Sutton Rd., Somerton, TA11 6QP. Tel. (0458) 73452. *Suppliers of thousands of different series of cigarette and trade cards, and special albums. Publishers of catalogues, reference books, and monthly magazine. Regular auctions in London. S.A.E. for details. Mail order, open by appointment.*

Nationwide Anglia Fine Art & Furniture
Frome Market Auction Rooms, Standerwick, Frome, BA11 2PY. Tel. (0373) 831010. *Collective sales of antiques and fine art on the second Friday monthly at 11a.m. Weekly general household sales. Haulage service.*

Nuttall Richards and Co.
The Town Hall, Axbridge, BS26 2AR. Tel. (0934) 732969. *Bi-monthly sales of privately entered fine art and selected antiques of all categories. Extra sales conducted on owners premises when instructed.* SER: Valuations; inventories prepared.

Tamlyn and Son
56 High St., Bridgwater, TA6 3BN. Tel. (0278) 458241/2.

Wellington Salerooms
Mantle St., Wellington, TA21 8AR. Tel. (0823) 664815. *Bi-monthly sales of general antiques. Fortnightly sales of Victorian, Edwardian and shipping goods.*

STAFFORDSHIRE

Bagshaws Agriculture
17 High St., Uttoxeter. Tel. (0889) 562811. *Monthly collective sales of antique and household furniture. Special house sales and farmhouse sales on the premises as required.*

John German
The Rotunda, Burton-on-Trent, DE14 1LN. Tel. (0283) 42051. *Occasional sales of major house contents; specialist fine art valuation department.*

Hall and Lloyd, Auctioneers. Est. 1882
South St., Stafford. ST16 2DZ. Tel. (0785) 58176. *Regular fortnightly sales at South St. auction rooms of antique and general household furniture and effects. 1,000 or more lots every other Thursday. Special catalogued sales of antiques held quarterly.*

Louis Taylor Britannia
Britannia House, 10 Town Rd., Hanley, Stoke-on-Trent. Tel. (0782) 260222. *Quarterly fine art sales which include furniture, pictures, pottery, porcelain, silver and objets d'art. Specialist Royal Doulton auctions. General Victoriana auctions held every two weeks.*

Wintertons
Lichfield Auction Centre, Woodend Lane, Fradley. Lichfield, WS13 8NF. Tel. (0543) 263256. *Monthly sales of antiques and fine art of various specialised categories and twice monthly sales of Victorian and general furniture and effects.*

SUFFOLK

Abbotts Auction Rooms
Campsea Ashe, nr. Woodbridge, IP13 0PS. Tel. (0728) 746323. *Sales every Monday, except some Bank Holidays, at 11a.m. comprising 600 lots; antique and cottage furniture, Victoriana and bric-a-brac. Monthly sales in new saleroom comprising 600 lots; Georgian and other antique furniture, porcelain, pictures, silver and objets d'art. Viewing Saturdays 9a.m. — 11a.m. for Monday sales. Monthly sales normally Wednesday, viewing previous Monday 2p.m. — 8p.m.* SER: Buys at auction.

H.A. Adnams
The Auction Room, 98 High St., Southwold. Tel. (0502) 723292.

Boardman — Fine Art Auctioneers
Station Road Corner, Haverhill, CB9 0EY. Tel. (0440) 730414. Fax. (0440) 730505. *Large sales held bi-monthly specialising in selected fine furniture, clocks and paintings.*

William H. Brown
Olivers Rooms, Burkitts Lane, Sudbury. CO10 6HB. Tel. (0787) 880305. *Weekly sales of antique and household furniture and shipping goods. Regular sales of good quality antiques. Illustrated fine arts review published annually. Enquiries to: James Fletcher, F.R.I.C.S. Furniture and Fine Art Dept.*

Diamond Mills and Co. Fine Art Auctioneers
117 Hamilton Rd., Felixstowe, IP11 7BL. Tel. (0394) 282281 (3 lines). *Quarterly fine art sales. Monthly general sales. Auctions at The Orwell Hall, Orwell Rd., Felixstowe.*

Durrant's
10 New Market, Beccles, NR34 9HA. Tel. (0502) 712122. *Antique and general furniture auctions every Friday at own showroom Gresham Rd., Beccles.*

Lacy Scott (Fine Art Dept.)
10 Risbygate St., Bury St. Edmunds, IP33 3AA. Tel. (0284) 763531. Fax. (0284) 704713. *Quarterly sales of fine art including antique and decorative furniture, silver, pictures, ceramics, etc. on behalf of executors and private vendors. Regular (every two/three weeks). Sales of Victoriana and general household contents. Also quarterly sales of diecast and tinplate toys (2 of which include working steam scale models) and annual sales of fine wines.*

Neal Sons and Fletcher
26 Church St., Woodbridge, IP12 1DP. Tel. (0394) 382263. *Two special mixed antiques sales per year. Individual specialised sales and complete house contents sales as required. Household furniture sales monthly.*

Phillips inc. Garrod Turner
Dover House, Wolsey St., Ipswich, IP1 1TP. Tel. (0473) 55137, and 21 St. Peter's St., Ipswich, IP1 1XF. Tel. (0473) 254664/255137. *Three specialist sales per month.*

Suffolk continued

Tuohy and Son
Denmark House, 18 High St., Aldeburgh. Tel. (0728) 452066. *Collective sales six times a year or by arrangement. Jan., Mar., May, July, Sept., Nov. Antique sales by arrangement.*
H.C. Wolton and Son
6 Whiting St., Bury St. Edmunds. IP33 1PB. Tel. (0284) 762099. *High class sales of selected antiques. Sixty years experience of Fine Art sales.* SER: Valuations.

SURREY

Chancellors Auctions (formerly Bonsor Penningtons)
74 London Rd., Kingston, KT2 6PX. Tel. (081) 541 4139. *Weekly sales on Thursdays. One fine art and antiques each month. Viewing previous Tuesday 2p.m.—8p.m. and Wednesday 9a.m.—5p.m. Sales start at 10. Three general sales each month, viewing Wednesday 2p.m.—8p.m. and Thursday 9a.m.—12 noon. Sales start at 12 noon.*
Clarke Gammon Fine Art Auctioneers
The Guildford Auction Rooms, Bedford Rd., Guildford. GU1 4SJ. Tel. (0483) 572266/66458.
Croydon Auction Rooms (Rosan and Co.) (incorporating E. Reeves Auctions)
144/150 London Rd., Croydon, CR0 2TD. Tel. (081) 688 1123/4/5. *Collective sales every Saturday 10a.m.*
Hamptons Fine Art
93 High St., Godalming, GU7 1AL. Tel. (0483) 423567. *Fine art at 93 High St. Antique and household goods at Queen St. and Bridge St., Godalming.* SER: Valuations.
Lawrences' — Auctioneers
Norfolk House, 80 High St., Bletchingley, RH1 4PA. Tel. (0883) 743323. Fax. (0883) 744578. *Six-weekly antique and reproduction furniture and effects.*
Parkins
18 Malden Rd., Cheam, SM3 8SD. Tel. (081) 644 6633 and (081) 644 6127 (Auction Room). *Weekly sales of general household furniture and effects on Mondays at 10a.m. Viewing Friday 2—4 and Saturday 10—4p.m. Special antique and collectors sales first Monday in month. Small antiques and collectors' sales on third Friday evening in month at 7p.m.*
Wentworth Auction Galleries
21 Station Approach, Virginia Water. GU25 4DW. Tel. (0344) 843711. *Antique and general sales every four to six weeks.*
P.F. Windibank
18—20 Reigate Rd., Dorking. RH4 1SG. Tel. (0306) 884556. *Fine art auctions held every four to six weeks throughout the year.*

SUSSEX EAST

Burstow and Hewett
Abbey Auction Galleries and Granary Sale Rooms, Battle TN33 0AT. Tel. (04246) 2302/2374. *Monthly sales of antique furniture, silver, jewellery, porcelain, brass, rugs, etc., at the Abbey Auction Galleries. Also monthly evening sales of fine oil paintings, watercolours, prints and engravings. At the Granary Sale Rooms — monthly sales of furniture, china, silver, brass, etc.*
Clifford Dann Auction Galleries
Fine Art Auction Galleries, 20-21 High St., Lewes. BN7 2LN. Tel. (0273) 480111. *General sales of period furniture, oil paintings, watercolour drawings, porcelain, carpets, silver, jewellery, books, etc. every six weeks on Tuesdays.*
Fryer's Auction Galleries
Terminus Rd., Bexhill-on-Sea, TN39 3CR. Tel. (0424) 212994. *Fortnightly sales of collective household goods including shipping goods. Antiques and collectors' items sold every six weeks.*
Gorringe's Auction Galleries
15 North St., Lewes, BN7 2PD. Tel. (0273) 472503. *Sales approx. every six weeks of period furniture, Oriental carpets and rugs, oil paintings, watercolour drawings and prints, decorative china, glass, silver plate, jewellery etc.*
Graves, Son and Pilcher Fine Arts
71 Church Rd., Hove, BN3 2GL. Tel. (0273) 735266. *Monthly sales of fine art including antique furniture, pictures, silver, Oriental carpets and rugs and ornamental items. Specialised sales of primitive art, coins, books and jewellery.*
Edgar Horn
Auction Galleries, 46/50 South St., Eastbourne, BN21 4QJ. Tel. (0323) 410419. *Approx. ten sales per year, each including antique furniture, porcelain, glass and collectors' items, Oriental rugs and carpets. Specialist sales of silver and jewellery, oil paintings and watercolours, prints, etc.*
Raymond P. Inman
The Auction Galleries, 35 and 40 Temple St., Brighton. BN1 3BH. Tel. (0273) 774777. *Monthly collective sales, including silver and jewellery.*
Lewes Auction Rooms (Julian Dawson)
56 High St., Lewes, BN7 1XE. Tel. (0273) 478221. *Antique furniture and effects every six weeks. General furniture and effects every Monday.*
South Eastern Auctions Ltd.
The Auction Galleries, 39 High St., Hastings, TN34 3ER. Tel. (0424) 434220. *Monthly antiques, collectors and paintings sales.*

Sussex East continued

Wallis and Wallis
West Street Auction Galleries, West St., Lewes, BN7 2NJ. Tel. (0273) 473137. *Nine annual sales of arms and armour, militaria, coins and medals. Specimen catalogue £4.25. Current combined catalogues £7. Die cast and tin plate toys — catalogues £2.50.*

SUSSEX WEST

R.H. Ellis and Sons
44/46 High St., Worthing, BN11 1LL. Tel. (0903) 38999. *Monthly specialist auctions of antique, Victorian and Edwardian furniture, porcelain. Quarterly auctions of silver, water-colours, paintings, Oriental rugs and carpets.*

Garth Denham and Associates
Horsham Auction Galleries, Warnham, RH12 3RZ. Tel. (0403) 53837. *Two day antique sales. Monthly on Tues. and Wed. sales of good furniture of all periods, silver, jewellery, European and Oriental ceramics and collectors' items, paintings, drawings, prints and bronzes, metalware, and Oriental carpets and rugs. Also monthly sales of general antiques, modern and shipping furniture. Periodic sales of books, stamps, coins and medals, arms and armour and specialist collections as advertised.*

G.A. Property Services — Worthing Auction Galleries
31 Chatsworth Rd., Worthing, BN11 1LY. Tel. (0903) 205565. *Fortnightly general antique furniture sales and specialist sales every six to eight weeks. Viewing Saturdays 9—12a.m. and Mondays 9—1 and 2—4, prior to sale Tuesdays/Wednesdays commencing 9.30a.m.*

Nationwide Anglia — King and Chasemore
West St., Midhurst, GU29 9NG. Tel. (073081) 2456/7/8. *General sales of antique and modern furniture and effects every six weeks.*

Phillips Fine Art Salerooms
Baffins Hall, Baffins Lane, Chichester, PO19 1UA. Tel. (0243) 787548. *Sales monthly on Thursday sales of antique and reproduction furniture, clocks, paintings, Persian and other carpets. Sales commence at 10a.m. View day prior to sale. Occasional sales of silver and porcelain.*

Sotheby's Sussex
Summers Pl., Billingshurst, RH14 9AD. Tel. (0403) 783933. Fax. (0403) 785153. Telex. Gavel 87210. *Weekly sales of paintings, furniture, carpets, clocks, ceramics, glass, silver, jewellery, vertu, sporting guns, weapons, coins, toys, dolls, books, maps, Oriental items and garden statuary.*

Stride and Son
Southdown House, St. John's St., Chichester, PO19 1XQ. Tel. (0243) 780207. *Last Friday of each month — antiques and general sales.*

Sussex West continued

Sussex Auction Galleries
59 Perrymount Rd., Haywards Heath, RH16 3DR. Tel. (0444) 414935. *Auctions of antiques and reproduction furniture and effects, including ceramics, silver, jewellery, clocks, Persian rugs, Victoriana. Annual subscription £6.50 for catalcgues. No buyers premium.*

TYNE AND WEAR

Anderson and Garland
Fine Art Salerooms, Marlborough House, Marlborough Crescent, Newcastle-upon-Tyne, NE1 4EE. Tel. (091) 232 6278. Fax. (091) 261 8665. *Regular sales of antique furniture and effects. Fortnightly sales of Victorian and later furniture.*

Boldon Auction Galleries
24a Front St., East Boldon. NE36 OSJ. Tel. (091) 537 2630. *Quarterly antique auctions.*

Thomas N. Miller
18—22 Gallowgate, Newcastle-upon-Tyne, NE1 4SN. Tel. (091) 232 5617. *Auctions of antiques every Wednesday and every fourth Thursday.*

WARWICKSHIRE

Bigwood Auctioneers Ltd.
The Old School, Tiddington, Stratford-upon-Avon, CV37 7AW. Tel. (0789) 69415. *Auction sales held every Friday at 11a.m. Monthly sales of paintings, furniture. Quarterly sales of wine. Catalogue subscription rates available on request. Valuations undertaken.*

Black Horse Agencies — Locke and England
1 and 2 Euston Pl., Leamington Spa, CV32 4RT. Tel. (0926) 427988. Salerooms: Walton House, 11 The Parade, Leamington Spa. *Antique furniture, porcelain, pictures, silver, etc., each month. Shipping goods, Victorian and Edwardian furniture, household and effects. Weekly Thursdays at 11a.m. house contents sales. Phone for full details.*

John Briggs and Calder
133 Long St., Atherstone. CV9 1AD. Tel. (0827) 718911. Also at Clinton House, Coleshill, Birmingham, B46 3BP. Tel. (0675) 462355, and 1 Victoria Rd., Tamworth (Staffordshire), B79 7HN. Tel. (0827) 61144. *Auctions on clients' instructions.*

Henley in Arden Auction Sales Ltd.
The Estate Office, Warwick Rd., Henley-in-Arden. B95 5BH. Tel. (0564) 793211. *Regular Saturday sales of antique and modern furniture and effects.*

Warwick and Warwick Ltd.
Chalon House, 2 New St., Warwick, CV34 4RX. Tel. (0926) 499031. *Philatelic auctioneers and private treaty specialists. Auctions normally held on the first Wednesday of every month with philatelic material covering the whole world, also picture postcards, ephemera and cigarette cards.*

WEST MIDLANDS

Biddle and Webb
Ladywood Middleway, Birmingham, B16 OPP. Tel. (021) 455 8042. *Fine art sales first Friday of every month at 11a.m., antique sales on second Friday of every month at 11a.m., silver, jewellery, medals, coins and watches sales on fourth Friday of every month at 11a.m., quarterly sales of antique photographica and scientific instruments. Quarterly (on Saturdays 11a.m.) sales of toys and juvenilia. Weekly sales of Victoriana and collectables. Tuesdays at 10.30a.m.*

Cariss Residential
20/22 High St., Kings Heath, Birmingham B14 7JU. Tel. (021) 444 0088. *General sales of antique furniture, chattles, etc., and periodical specialist sales.*

Codsall Antique Auctions
Codsall Village Hall, Nr. Wolverhampton. Tel. (0902) 606728. *Alternate Wednesday evening sales of Victorian antiques and shipping goods.*

Fellows and Sons
Augusta House, 19 Augusta St., Hockley, Birmingham, B18 6JA. Tel. (021) 212 2131. Fax. (021) 212 1249. *Auctioneers and valuers of jewels, silver, fine art, fine wines and spirits.*

James and Lister Lea, Est'd. 1846
42 Bull St., Birmingham, B4 6AF. Tel. (021) 200 1100. *Approx. four sales a year of contents of country and town houses as required. All sale items are from private sources with an emphasis on the more unusual collectors' items. Buyer's premium 8% plus VAT.*

Phillips Midlands
The Old House, Station Rd., Knowle, Solihull, B93 OHT. Tel. (0564) 776151. *Specialised weekly sales of (a) fine furniture and works of art, (b) silver and jewellery, (c) Victoriana, (d) paintings, (e) collectors' items, (f) ceramics and 19th and 20th C decorative arts, (g) books. Free sales programme and subscription on request.*

Weller and Dufty Ltd.
141 Bromsgrove St., Birmingham, B5 6RQ. Tel. (021) 692 1414. Fax. (021) 622 5605. *Ten sales per annum, approximately every five weeks, of antique and modern firearms, edged weapons, militaria, etc. Periodic sales of specialist items, books, wine and fine art. Postal bids accepted. Illustrated catalogue available.*

WILTSHIRE

Allen and Harris
The Planks Salerooms, Old Town, Swindon, SN3 1QP. Tel. (0793) 615915. *Bi-monthly auctions of antique furniture, shipping goods, china, glass and collectors' items on Saturdays.*

Wiltshire continued

Hampton Fine Art
Incorporating Pocock & Lear
20 High St., Marlborough, SN8 1AA. Tel. (0672) 513471. *Antique and quality furniture and effects sales on first Wednesday in each month, general household furniture and effects on second Wednesday each month.*

Woolley and Wallis
Salisbury Salerooms, Castle St., Salisbury, SP1 3SU. Tel. (0722) 411422. *Monthly sales of antique furniture, porcelain, and pottery, glass and metalwork. Special sales of Eastern carpets and rugs, books and maps, also paintings, watercolours and prints, textiles, fans, dolls and toys, Oriental furniture, Oriental ceramics and works of art. Quarterly sales of silver and plated items, jewellery, objects of art, etc.*

YORKSHIRE NORTH

Boulton and Cooper Ltd.
St. Michaels House, Market Pl., Malton, YO17 OLR. Tel. (0653) 692151. Members of S.O.F.A.A. *Monthly antiques sales at Malton and Seamer. Fortnightly general sales at Pickering and Seamer.*

H.C. Chapman and Son
The Auction Mart, North St., Scarborough, YO11 1DL. Tel. (0723) 372424. Fax. (0723) 500697. *Members of S.O.F.A.A. Monthly special sales of antiques and fine art held on Tuesdays, viewing Friday 4-7p.m., Saturday 10a.m.-4p.m., Monday 9a.m.-12 noon. Annual catalogue subscription £30. Weekly sales of Edwardian and later shipping furniture and bric-a-brac, and modern furnishings held on Mondays. Viewing Saturday 10a.m.-4p.m. and Monday from 9a.m.*

G.A. Fine Arts & Chattels Ward Price
The Royal Auction Rooms, 14-15 Queen St., Scarborough, YO11 1HA. Tel. (0723) 353581. *Regular sales of antiques, Victoriana and later furniture, silver, jewellery and household effects. Sales commence at 10a.m. Viewing 2 days prior to sale.*

Paul Hirst Auctions
Scarthingwell Centre, Scarthingwell, Nr. Tadcaster, LS24 9PT. Tel./Fax. (0937) 817742. *Evening antique sales held 1st and 3rd Monday of each month (approximately 500 lots). Catalogues and viewing over weekend. Sales held on vendor's premises and household sales, both at regular intervals. Specialist sales of jewellery (Nov.).*

Hutchinson-Scott
The Grange, Marton-le-Moor, Ripon. HG4 5AT. Tel. (0423) 324264. *Periodic general sales plus two or three catalogue sales per year. Specialist in fine antiques and works of art.*

Yorkshire North continued

James Johnston
The Square, Boroughbridge, YO5 9AS. Tel. (0423) 322382. *Occasional private dispersal sales. Also twice monthly collective auction sales at the old saleroom Coltsgate Hill, Ripon T/A Joplings & Johnston.*

Morphets
(William H. Brown) 4-6 Albert St., Harrogate, HG1 1JL. Tel. (0423) 530030. *Sales of antiques and works of art bi-monthly, interspersed with regular sales of general furniture and effects. Catalogue subscription scheme.*

Nationwide Anglia — Wells Cundall
27 Flowergate, Whitby. YO21 3AX. Tel. (0947) 603433. *Monthly antiques sales. VAT: Stan. No buyers premium.*

Stephenson and Son
20 Castlegate, York, YO1 1RT. Tel. (0904) 625533. *Six sales annually of antique and Victorian furniture, silver and paintings.*

Geoffrey Summersgill, A.S.V.A.
8 Front St., Acomb, York, YO2 3BZ and at Market Pl., Easingwold. Tel. (0904) 791131 and (0347) 21366. *Auctions of antiques and household effects. Collectors' items.*

Tennants
27 Market Pl., Leyburn, DL8 5AS. Tel. (0969) 23780. *Sales held every other Saturday at Middleham Salerooms (antiques and later residual house contents — approx. 600 lots.) No catalogues. View Fridays. Catalogue sales held at Richmond Salerooms. Sales frequently held on vendors' premises during summer months.*

YORKSHIRE SOUTH

A.E. Dowse and Son Sheffield
Cornwall Galleries, Scotland St., Sheffield, S3 7DE. Tel. (0742) 725858. *Monthly Saturday and quarterly Monday sales of antiques. Quarterly sales of diecast, tin plate and collectors' toys. Fortnightly sales of modern furniture and shipping goods.*

Eadon Lockwood and Riddle
Western Saleroom, Crookes, Sheffield S10 1UA. Tel. (0742) 686294. *General sales each month. Occasional collective antique sales.*

YORKSHIRE WEST

Armitage, Hewitt and Hellowell
32 Queen St., Huddersfield. Tel. (0484) 426118. *Occasional antique sales.*

Ernest R. de Rome
12 New John St., Westgate, Bradford, BD1 2QY. Tel. (0274) 734116/9. *Weekly sales.*

Garside, Waring and Robinson
17 Alexandra St., Halifax. HX1 1BS. Tel. (0422) 353527/362138.

Andrew Hartley Fine Arts
Victoria Hall Salerooms, Little Lane, Ilkley, LS29 8EA. Tel. (0943) 816363. *Fifty sales per year including six good antique and fine art and other specialist sales.*

Yorkshire West continued

Phillips at Hepper House
17A East Parade, Leeds, LS1 2BU. Tel. (0532) 448011. *Monthly sales of antique furniture and objects of art and regular speciality sales of pictures, ceramics, silver/jewellery, books, etc.*

John H. Raby and Son
Salem Auction Rooms, 21 St. Mary's Rd., Bradford, BD8 7QL. Tel. (0274) 491121. *Sales of antique furniture and pictures every four to six weeks.*

CHANNEL ISLANDS

David Procter Auctions
12 Mansell St., The Old Quarter, St. Peter Port, Guernsey. Tel. (0481) 726808; home — (0481) 46025. *Occasional auctions of property and/or their contents, plus bi-annual catalogue auctions of items of Channel Island interest.*

Langlois
Westaway Chambers, Don St., St. Helier, Jersey. Tel. (0534) 22441. Fax. (0534) 39354. *Periodic antique sales. Weekly household sales.*

SCOTLAND

John Anderson Auctioneers
33 Cross St., Fraserburgh, Aberdeens., AB43 5EQ. Tel. (0346) 28878. *Weekly furniture sales held Tuesday evenings at Strichen.*

Brown's
Carsluith Hall, Carsluith by Newton Stewart, Wigtownshire. Tel. (0671) 2052. *Sales held on the last Wed. and Thurs. each month except Dec. and Jan.*

Christie's Scotland
164-166 Bath St., Glasgow, G2 4TG. Tel. (041) 332 8134. Fax. (041) 332 5759. Telex 779901. *Regular specialist sales of jewellery, silver, porcelain, furniture, paintings, prints, books, collectors' items and stamps, together with sales of particular Scottish interest.*

Frasers (Auctioneers)
28-30 Church St., Inverness. IV1 1EH. Tel. (0463) 232395. *Sales every two weeks on Thursday and Friday.*

Leslie and Leslie
Haddington, East Lothian, EH41 3JJ. Tel./Fax. (062 082) 2241. *General auctions every three months.*

Loves Auction Rooms
52-54 Canal St., Perth, Perthshire PH2 8LF. Tel. (0738) 33337. *Regular sales of antique and decorative furniture, jewellery, silver, plate, ceramics, works of art, metalware, glass, pictures, clocks, mirrors, pianos, Eastern carpets and rugs, garden furniture, architectural items. Weekly sales of Victorian and household effects (Friday at 10.30a.m.) Specialist sales of books, collectors' items. Valuations.*

Scotland continued

Lyon and Turnball Ltd.
51 George St., Edinburgh, Midlothian, EH2 2HT. Tel. (031) 225 4627.

John Milne
9 North Silver St., Aberdeen, AB1 1RJ. Tel. (0224) 639336. *Weekly general sales, regular catalogue sales of antiques, silver, paintings, books, jewellery and collectors' items.*

Robert Paterson and Son
8 Orchard St., Paisley, PA1 1UZ, Renfrewshire. Tel. (041) 889 2435. *Every second Tuesday.*

Phillips Scotland
207 Bath St., Glasgow, G2 4HD. Tel. (041) 221 8377. *Antique and reproduction furniture, pictures, Oriental and Continental ceramics, silver, jewellery, works of art and carpets — fortnightly.* And at 65 George St., Edinburgh, EH2 2JL. Tel. (031) 225 2266. *Oil paintings, furniture, Oriental rugs, works of art, silver — all monthly. Continental ceramics, glass, Oriental ceramics and works of art, books, watercolours and prints, jewellery, postcards and maps — bi-monthly. Dolls and textiles — three a year.*

L.S. Smellie and Sons Ltd.
The Furniture Market, Lower Auchingramont Rd., Hamilton, Lanarks., ML10 6BE. Tel. (0698) 282007. *Fine antiques auctions (3rd Thursday in Feb., May, Aug. and Nov.).*

Taylor's Auction Rooms
11 Panmure Row, Montrose, Angus, DD10 8HH. Tel. (0674) 72775. *Antique sales held every second Saturday.*

Thomson, Roddick and Laurie Ltd.
60 Whitesands, Dumfries, DG1 2RS. Tel. (0387) 55366. *Catalogued antique and sporting sales.* Also at 20 Murray St., Annan, DG12 6EG. Tel. (0461) 202575.

WALES

Dodds Property World
Victoria Auction Galleries, Mold, Clwyd, CH7 1EB. Tel. (0352) 2552. *Weekly auctions of general furniture, shipping goods on Wednesdays at 10.30a.m. Bi-monthly auctions of antique furniture, silver, porcelain and pictures etc. on Wednesday evenings at 5.45p.m. Catalogues available.*

Spencer John Francis
Curiosity Sale Rooms, King St., Carmarthen, Dyfed, SA31 1BH. Tel. (0267) 233456/7. *Antique sales every six weeks. Household sales at regular intervals.*

Grimwades Auctions
4 and 5 Stadium Close, Penarth Rd., Cardiff, S. Glam., CF1 7TS. Tel. (0222) 220914. *General sales fortnightly. Catalogue sales every six weeks, and property auctions every eight weeks.*

Wales continued

King Thomas, Lloyd Jones and Co.
Bangor House, High St., Lampeter, Dyfed, SA48 7BB. Tel. (0570) 422550/422855. *Monthly sales of general antiques. No buyer's premium.*

Harry Ray and Co.
Lloyds Bank Chambers, Welshpool, Powys, SY21 7RR. Tel. (0938) 552555. *Fortnightly country sales.*

Rennies
1 Agincourt St., Monmouth, Gwent, NP5 3DZ. Tel. (0600) 2916. *Periodic sales of antique furniture and effects, usually on Thursday.*

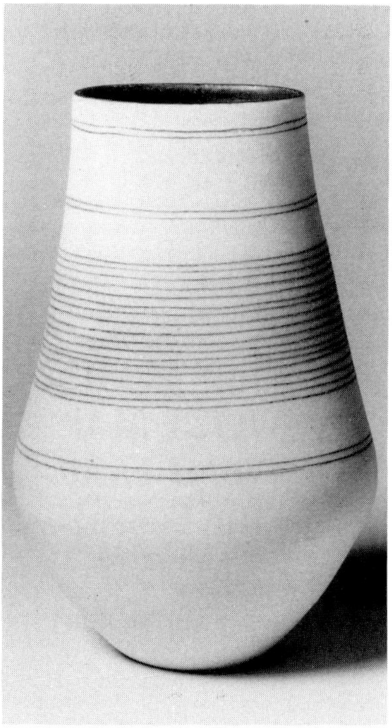

This porcelain vase by Dame Lucie Rie sold in March for £3,960. Her work is increasingly in demand internationally, a reflection of her great contribution to 20th century ceramics. From an article on contemporary ceramics by Alastair Nicolson published in the July/August issue of **Antique Collecting.**

Because this list has been compiled well in advance, alterations or cancellations to the Fairs listed can occur. We strongly advise anyone wishing to attend a Fair, especially if they have to travel any distance, to telephone the organiser to confirm the details given. Details have been listed alphabetically and under county order. Unless stated, all dates refer to 1991.

LONDON

Adams Antique Fairs - 071 254 4054
Antiques Fair, The New Royal Horticultural Hall, Vincent Square, Victoria, S.W.1 - **September 1**
Antiques Fair, The Old Royal Horticultural Hall, Vincent Square, Victoria, S.W.1 - **September 29; October 27; November 17; December 1**

Bagatelle Fairs - 081 391 2339/042 868 5452
The London Decorative Arts Fair, The Kensington Town Hall, Off Kensington High Street, W.8 - **September 7; December 7**
The Kensington Brocante Antiques Fair, The Kensington Town Hall, Off Kensington High Street, W.8 - **September 21; November 23**
The Kensington Vanity Antiques Fair, The Kensington Town Hall, Off Kensington High Street, W.8 - **October 19; December 21**

David Bannister - 0242 514287
The Antiquarian Map and Print Fair, The Bonnington Hotel, Southampton Row, W.C.1 - **2nd Mon. monthly**

London continued

Cultural Exhibitions Ltd - 0483 422562
The 40th Kensington Antiques Fair, The New Town Hall, Hornton Street, Kensington, W.8 - **November 5/10**

Peter Delahar - 081 866 8659
The Eleventh International Scientific and Medical Instrument Fair, The Portman Hotel, Portman Square, W.1 - **October 27**

Raymond Gubbay Exhibitions Ltd - 081 441 8940
The City of London Antiques and Fine Art Fair, The Barbican Exhibition Halls, Barbican Centre, E.C.2 - **November 20/25**

Heritage Antiques Fairs - 071 624 5173
Antiques Fair, The Kensington Hilton, 179 - 199 Holland Park Avenue, W.11 - **1st Sun. monthly**
Antiques Fair, The Kensington Palace Hotel, De Vere Gardens, Kensington High Street, W.8. - **September 8; October 27; December 8**
Antiques Fair, The London Marriott Hotel, Grosvenor Square, W.1 - **3rd Sun. monthly**
Decorative Antiques and Textiles Fair, Chelsea Harbour, Lots Road, S.W.6 - **September 18/22**
Antiques Fair, The Cafe Royal, 68 Regent Street, W.1. - **September 22; November 24**
Antiques Fair, The Hilton on Park Lane, 22 Park Lane, W.1 - **September 29; October 13; November 10**

Historic & Heritage Antiques Fayres - 081 398 5324
The Bi-Annual Antique Doll and Toy Fair, The Cumberland Hotel, Marble Arch, W.1 - **October 27**

P & J Hobbs - 081 542 4675
Antiques and Collectors' Fair, St Mark's Church Hall, Compton Road, Wimbledon, S.W.19 - **September 28; October 26; November 30; December 14**

The Italian Connection Antiques - 081 543 5075/8970
Antiques and Collectors' Fair, The British Red Cross Centre, 28 Worple Road, Wimbledon, S.W.19 - **3rd Sun. monthly**

Joshua Hodgetts at work on the intaglio lathe carving a vase very similar to the vase in Colour Plate 31, early 20th century. From ***British Glass 1800-1914*** by Charles R. Hajdemach published by the **Antique Collectors' Club** in 1991. £45.00.

London continued

Jax Fairs - 0444 400570
Antiques and Collectors' Fair, Picketts-Lock Leisure Centre, Picketts-Lock Lane, (off Montague Road), Edmonton, N.9. - **1st Sun. monthly**

Heather McConnell - 071 493 6420
The 20th Century British Art Fair, The Royal College of Art, Kensington Gore, S.W.7 - **September 25/29; September 23/27, 1992**
The Park Lane Antiques Fair, The Park Lane Hotel, Piccadilly, W.1 - **October 2/7; September 30/October 5, 1992**

M & S Enterprises - 081 440 2330
Antiques and Collectors' Fairs, Chase Side, Southgate, N.14 - **3rd Thurs. monthly**
Collectors' Fair, The Muswell Hill Centre, Off Summerland Gardens, Muswell Hill, N.10 - **September 28; October 26; November 23; December 8**

Monway Limited - 071 603 0380
Antiques Fair, The Park Lane Hotel, Piccadilly, W.1 - **September 1, 15, 29; October 20; November 3, 17; December 1, 15**
Antiques Fair, The Sheraton Park Tower, 101 Knightsbridge, S.W.1. - **September 8; October 6; November 10; December 8**
Antiques Fair, The Rembrandt Hotel, Thurloe Place, S.W.7 - **4th Sun. monthly**
The National Porcelain, Pottery and Glass Fair, The Rembrandt Hotel, Thurloe Place, S.W.7 - **October 13**

London continued

Penman Antiques Fairs - 0444 482514
The Chelsea Antiques Fair, Chelsea Old Town Hall, King's Road, Chelsea, S.W.3 - **September 10/21; March 20/21, September 15/26, 1992**
The L.A.P.A.D.A. Antiques Show, The Royal College of Art, Kensington Gore, S.W.7 - **October 16/20; October 14/18, 1992**
The West London Antiques Fair, Kensington Town Hall, Hornton Street,W.8 - **January 16/19, August 13/16, September 15/26, 1992**
The Annual Westminster Antiques Fair, The Royal Horticultural Old Hall, Vincent Square, S.W.1 - **April 30/May 3, 1992**

Penman & Partners Ltd - 071 724 2818
The 33rd London Antiquarian Book Fair, The Park Lane Hotel, Piccadilly, W.1 - **June 1992**

Philbeach Events Limited - 071 370 8211/8234
The Fine Art and Antiques Fair, The Grand Hall, Olympia Exhibition Centre, Hammersmith Road, W.14 - **October 8/13**

Pig & Whistle Promotions - 081 883 7061
Antiques and Collectors' Fair, The Great Hall, Alexandra Palace, Wood Green, N.22 - **September 15; November 10**

Ravenscott Fairs - 071 727 5045
The Little Chelsea Antiques Fair, Chelsea Town Hall, Kings Road, S.W.3 - **September 30/October 1; December 2/3**

London continued

1st Royal Eltham Scout Group - 081 850 4384
Antiques and Collectables' Fair, Thames Polytechnic, Avery Hill Road, Eltham, S.E.9 - **October 19**

Evan Steadman Communications Group Ltd - 0799 26699
The Grosvenor House Antiques Fair (Under the patronage of Her Majesty Queen Elizabeth The Queen Mother), Grosvenor House, Park Lane, W.1 - **June 1992**

Jane Sumner and John Braund - 0799 23611
The London Antique Dealers Fair, The Cafe Royal, 68 Regent Street, W.1 - **September 3/8; February 11/16, 1992**

Wakefield Antiques Fairs - 0634 723461
Antiques Fair, The Cumberland Hotel, Marble Arch, W.1 - **1st Sun. monthly**

West Promotions - 081 641 3224
The London Paper Money Fair and Bond & Share Fair, The Mount Royal Hotel, Bryanston Street, W.1 - **November 17**

Angela Wynn - 071 491 8806
The World of Drawings and Watercolours, The Park Lane, Piccadilly, W.1 - **January 22/26 1992; January 20/24 1993**

AVON

Robert Bailey Antiques Fairs - 0277 362662
The City of Bath Antiques Fair, The Pavilion, Bath - **September 25/28**

Evergreen Promotions - 0934 636648
Antiques and Collectors' Fair, The Webbington Hotel and Country Club, Near Weston-super-Mare - **3rd Sun. monthly**

Melba Fairs - 0934 624854
The Giant Antiques and Collectors' Flea Markets, The Winter Gardens Pavillion, Sea Front, Weston-super-Mare - **September 21**
The First West of England Antiques and Decorative Arts Fair, The Bristol Exhibition Centre, Canons Marsh, Central Bristol - **October 5/6**

Talisman Fairs - 0225 872522
Antiques and Collectors' Fair, The Pavilion, North Parade, Bath -**September 7; October 26; November 23; December 7**
Antiques and Collectables Fair, The Brunel Great Train Shed, Temple Meads, Bristol - **September 8; October 13; November 10; December 8, 29**

Louise Stroud Walker - 0423 567933
The Bath Antique and Fine Art Fair, The Assembly Rooms, Bath - **October 23/26**

BEDFORDSHIRE

Bartholomew Fairs - 0279 600005
Antiques and Collectors' Fair, The Putteridge Recreation Centre, Putteridge Lane, Stopsley, Luton - **September 8; December 8**

Bedfordshire continued

Biggleswade Antiques Fairs - 0234 857317
Antiques Fairs, The Weatherley Centre, Eagle Farm Road, Biggleswade (A1) - **3rd Sun. monthly**

Reg Cooper Antiques Fairs - 0672 515558
The Bedford County Antiques Fair, Woburn Abbey - **October 28/29**

Herridges Antiques and Collectors' Fairs Limited - 0234 45725
Antiques Fair, The Corn Exchange, Bedford - **September 15; October 27**

Sovereign Fairs - 0234 350600
Antiques Fair, The Mander College, Bedford - **September 15; October 6; November 3; December 1**

BERKSHIRE

Chiltern Fairs - 0753 890301
Antiques Fair, The Racecourse, Maidenhead Road, Windsor - **2nd and 4th Sun. monthly**

Lindifayre - 0734 694679
Antiques, Collectors' and Furniture Fair, The Loddon Hall, Twyford - **Last Sun. monthly**

Gill McDonald - 0734 345495
Flea Market/Collectors' Fair, Loddon Hall, Loddon Hall Road, Twyford - **September 15; October 20; November 10; December 15**

Magnum Antiques Fairs - 0491 681009
Antiques Fair, The Wellington College Sports Centre, Crowthorne - **October 20; November 17; December 29**

Silhouette Fairs - 0635 44338
Antiques and Collectors' Fair, Royal Enclosure Rooms, Racecourse, Ascot - **September 1; October 6; November 3; December 1**
Antiques and Collectors' Fair, The Town Hall, Hungerford - **4th Sun. monthly**

Mrs Wyatt - 0734 833020
Antiques and Collectors' Fair, St Crispins Sports Centre, J10, M4, A329, Wokingham - **1st Sun. monthly**

BUCKINGHAMSHIRE

Chiltern Fairs - 0753 890301
Antiques and Collectors' Fair, The Centre for Epilepsy, Chalfont St. Peter - **1st Sun. monthly**

Harries & May - 0296 624633
Antiques Fair, The Memorial Hall, Great Missenden - **2nd Sat. monthly**
Antiques Fair, The Memorial Hall, Shiplake, Near Henley - **3rd Sun. monthly**

King Collectables - 0933 311313
Antiques Fair and Flea Market, The Bull Hotel, Olney - **September 14/15; October 12/13; November 17; December 1, 29**

Buckinghamshire continued

M J Fairs - 0494 726879/0923 242907
Antiques and Collectors' Fair, The Masonic Centre, Beaconsfield - **1st Sun. monthly**
Antiques and Collectors' Fair, The Village Hall, Little Chalfont -**September 21; October 19; November 16; December 14**

Norton Antiques - 0494 673674
The High Wycombe Autumn Antiques Fair, The Royal Grammer School, Hamilton Road, High Wycombe - **October 31/November 2**

CAMBRIDGESHIRE

Biggleswade Antique Fairs - 0234 857317
Antiques Fair, The Priory Centre, St Neots - **September 1; November 3**

County Fairs - 0533 879688
Antiques Fair, The Haycock Hotel, Wansford - **November 10**

Herridges Antiques and Collectors' Fairs Limited - 0234 45725
Antiques Fair, The St Ivo Recreation Centre, St Ives - **October 6; November 16/17**

CHESHIRE

Robert Bailey Antiques Fairs - 0277 362662
The Tatton Park Antiques Fair, Tatton Park (The Tenants Hall and Victorian Rooms), Knutsford - **September 11/15**
Antiques Fair, Peckforton Castle, Chester - **November 8/10**

Bygones Of The Cloud - 0565 632323/651784
Antiques and Collectors' Fair, The Leisure Centre, Priory Lane, Macclesfield - **September 28; November 2; December 7**

Reg Cooper Antiques Fairs - 0672 515558
The Cheshire County Antiques Fair, Arley Hall, Knutsford - **October 12/13**

Penman Antiques Fairs - 0444 482514
The Chester Antiques Show, The Grandstand, Chester Racecourse, Chester - **February 20/23, 1992**

Pine Promotions - 0565 873769/632323
Antiques and Collectors' Fair, The Community Centre, Woodford, Near Wilmslow - **September 1; October 12; December 1**
Antiques and Collectors' Fair, The Village Hall, Marthall, Near Knutsford - **2nd Sun. monthly**
Antiques and Collectors' Fair, The Masonic Hall, Wellington Road South, Stockport - **September 14**
Antiques and Collectors' Fair, The Bowdon Rooms, The Firs, Bowdon - **September 15; November 17**
Antiques and Collectors' Fair, The Civic Centre, Knutsford - **October 20; December 15**

Pamela Robertson - 0244 678106
Antique and Collectors' Fair, The Northgate Arena, Victoria Road, Chester - **September 28; October 26; November 16; December 7, 28**

CORNWALL

Vanity Fairs - 0208 872 909
Antiques and Collectors' Fair, The Leisure World, Carlyon Bay, St. Austell - **1st Sun. monthly**

West Country Antiques and Collectors Fairs - 0364 52182
The Truro Antiques and Collectors' Fair, The City Hall, Truro - **October 4/5; December 5/6**

CUMBRIA

Albany Fairs - 091 584 2934/0836 531108
Antiques and Collectables Fair, The Village Hall, Pooley Bridge, Ullswater - **September 13/15; October 25/27; December 31/January 1**

Robert Bailey Antiques Fairs - 0277 362662
Antiques Fair, The Holker Hall, Near Grange-over-Sands - **November 15/17**

Lakeland Quality Fairs - 07684 86676/0287 622385
Antiques Fair, The Prince of Wales Hotel, Grasmere - **September 8, 15**
The Autumn Fair, The Prince of Wales Hotel, Grasmere - **October 20/23**

DERBYSHIRE

Cultural Exhibitions Ltd - 0483 422562
Buxton Antiques Fair, Pavilion Gardens - **May 9/16, 1992**

Peak Fairs - 062981 2449
Antiques and Collectors' Fair, The Town Hall, Bakewell - **September 2, 7/8, 9, 26, 21/22, 23, 30; October 6, 7, 14, 19/20, 21, 28; November 4, 9/10, 11, 18, 24, 25; December 2, 8/9, 16, 28/January 2**

Unicorn Fairs - 061 773 7001
Antiques and Collectors' Fair, The Pavilion Gardens, Buxton - **September 28/29; November 9/10; December 28/29**

Wakefield Ceramics Fairs - 0634 723461
Ceramics Fair, The Royal Crown Derby Museum, Osmaston Road, Derby - **September 7/8**

DEVON

Anchor Fairs - 0297 445540
Antiques and Collectors' Fair, The Mariners Hall, Beer - **September 22; October 20**

Devon County Antiques Fairs - 0363 82571
Antiques and Collectors' Fair, The New Exeter Livestock Centre, Matford Park, Marsh Barton, Exeter - **September 7; November 9, 30**
The Southwest of England Antiques Fair, The Westpoint Exhibition Centre, Clyst St Mary, Exeter - **October 12/13**

Sheila Hyson - 064 723 459
Antiques and Collectors' Fair, The Jubilee Hall, Chagford (in aid of Leukaemia) - **September 28; November 23**

Devon continued

Kernow Fairs - 0726 842957
Antiques Fair, The Elfordleigh Hotel and Country Club, Colebrook, Near Plymouth - **1st Sun. monthly**

West Country Antiques and Collectors Fairs - 0364 52182
The Exmouth Antiques and Collectors' Fair, The Pavilion, The Sea Front, Exmouth - **2nd Sun. monthly; every Sun. July, August, September**
The Barnstaple Antiques and Collectors' Fair, The Queens Hall, Barnstaple - **Every Fri.**
The Newton Abbot Giant Antiques, Collectors' and Book Fair, The Racecourse, Newton Abbot - **September 11/12; November 30/December 1**
The Budleigh Salterton Antiques, Collectors' and Book Markets, The Masonic Hall, Budleigh Salterton - **September 14**
The Exeter Annual Antiques Fair, The Imperial Hotel, St Davids Hill, Exeter - **September 26/27**
The West of England Dolls House, Dolls, Toys, and Miniatures Fair, The Pavilion, The Sea Front, Exmouth - **October 6**
The Devon and Somerset Antiques, Collectors' and Book Fair, Toad Hall, Cullompton - **October 20; November 17; December 15, 29**
The Powderham Castle Antiques Fair, Powderham Castle, Near Exeter - **October 26/27**
The South Devon and Dartmoor Autumn Antiques and Collectors' Fair, The Moorland Hotel, Haytor, Bovey Tracey - **November 16/17**

DORSET

Anchor Fairs - 0297 445540
Antiques and Collectors' Fair, The Corfe Castle, Village Hall, Corfe - **2nd Sun. monthly**

Antiques In Britain Fairs - 0273 423355
The 4th Annual Autumn Antiques Fair, The Coach House Inn, Tricketts Cross, Ferndown, - **October 5/6**

Reg Cooper Antiques Fairs - 0672 515558
The Dorset County Antiques Fair, Bryanston School, Blandford - **November 1/2**
Devon County Antiques Fairs - 0363 82571
Antiques Fair, Sherborne School, Sherborne - **October 26/27**

Forest Fairs - 0202 875167
Collectors' Market, The Druitt Hall, Christchurch - **weekly on Mon.**
Antiques and Collectors' Fair, The Allendale Centre, Wimborne - **September 15; November 10**
Antiques and Collectors' Fair, The Coach House Inn, Ferndown - **September 29; December 8**
Antiques and Collectors' Fair, The Kings Arms Hotel, Christchurch - **October 6; November 17**
Antiques and Collectors' Fair, The Littledown Centre, Castle Lane, Bournemouth - **December 28/29**

Dorset continued

Grandma's Attic Fairs - 0590 677687
Antique and Collectors' Fair, The Dorset College of Agriculture and Horticulture, Kingston Maurward, Dorchester - **October 13**
Antique and Collectors' Fair, The Allendale Centre, Wimborne - **December 29**

DURHAM

Albany Fairs - 091 584 2934/0836 531108
Antiques and Collectables Fair, Community Centre, Lanchester - **October 6, December 26**

ESSEX

Bartholomew Fairs - 0279 600005
Antiques and Collectors' Fair, The Moat House Hotel, Southern Way, Harlow - **1st Sun. monthly**
Antiques and Collectors' Fair, Sir James Hawkey Hall, Broadmead Road, Woodford Green - **September 21; November 23**
Antiques and Collectors' Fair, The Sport Centre, Near The Town Centre, Harlow - **September 22; December 29**
Antiques and Collectors' Fair, The Assembly Hall, The Green, Chingford - **October 5; November 10**
Antiques and Collectors' Fair, The Town Hall, Highbridge Street, Waltham Abbey - **October 13**
Antiques and Collectors' Fair, The Sportcentre, Harrow Lodge Park, Hornchurch - **October 27**

Emporium Fairs - 0440 704632
Antiques Fair, Furze Hill Banqueting Centre, Margaretting, Near Chelmsford - **September 8; October 13; November 10; December 1**

Hallmark Fairs - 0702 586262
Antiques and Collectors' Fair, The Hollywood Restaurant, Shipwrights Drive, Benfleet - **September 22**
Antiques and Collectors' Fair, The Arlington Rooms, London Road, Westcliff - **September 29**
Antiques and Colectors' Fair, The Courage Hall (Brentwood Public School), Middleton Hall Lane Entrance, Brentwood - **October 6**
Antiques and Collectors' Fair, The Dolphin Centre, Main Road, Romford - **November 24**
Antiques and Collectors' Fair, The Runnymede Hall, Kiln Road, Benfleet - **December 1**
Antiques and Collectors' Fair, The Freight House, Bradley Way, Rochford - **December 15**

D J Major - 0782 222826
Antiques and Collectors' Market, United Reformed Church Hall, Market Hill, Maldon - **1st Sat. monthly**

M & S Enterprises - 081 440 2330
Fleamarket and Collectors' Fair, The Town Hall, High Road, Ilford -**September 12, 26; October 3, 10, 24, 25; November 28; December 5, 28**

Sandway Fairs - 0206 579658
Antiques and Collectors' Fair, The Sports Centre, Langham - **October 13**
Antiques and Collectors' Fair, Orpen Hall, West Bergholt, Colchester - **November 17**

GLOUCESTERSHIRE

Robert Bailey Antiques Fairs - 0277 362662
The Cotswolds Antiques Fair, The Pittville Pump Rooms, Cheltenham - **October 30/November 2**

Dragon Fairs - 0666 503043
Antiques Fair, The Hare and Hounds, Westonbirt - **September 29; October 13**

Keith Smith Fairs - 0684 575126
Antiques and Collectors' Fair, The Bingham Hall, Cirencester -**2nd Sun. monthly**

Talisman Fairs - 0225 872522
Antiques and Collectors' Fair The Leisure Centre, Gloucester - **September 29**

HAMPSHIRE

Antiques In Britain Fairs - 0273 423355
The Andover Antiques Fair, John Hanson School, Andover - **30/September 1**

Athena Fayres - 0489 584633
Antique and Collectors' Fair, The Community Centre, Sarisbury Green - **1st Sun. monthly**
Antique and Collectors' Fair, The Village Hall, Minstead, Near Cadnam - **Sun. monthly**
Collectors' Fair, The Lockswood Centre, Locks Heath - **usually 3rd Sat. monthly**
Antique and Collectors' Fair, The Community Centre, Mill Lane, Wickham - **Last Sun. monthly**

Forest Fairs - 0202 875167
Antique and Collectors' Fair, The Balmer Lawn Hotel, Brockenhurst - **September 8; November 3**
Antique and Collectors' Fair, The Romsey Show, Broadlands, Romsey - **September 14**
Antique and Collectors' Fair, The Ringwood Recreation Centre, Ringwood - **October 13**

Gamlin Exhibition Services - 0452 862557
Antiques Fair, The Town Hall, Petersfield - **September 5/7**

Grandma's Attic Fairs - 0590 677687
Antiques and Collectors' Fair, The Potters Heron Hotel, Ampfield - **1st Sun. monthly**
Antiques and Collectors' Fair, The Masonic Hall, Lymington - **September 14; October 12, 19; November 2, 9; December 14**
Antiques and Collectors' Fair, The Lanz at Riverside, Ringwood - **September 15; December 1**
Antique and Collectors' Fair, The Brockenhurst Village Hall, Brockenhurst - **September 22; October 20; November 10; December 8**
Antiques and Collectors' Fair, The St Thomas Church Hall, Lymington - **September 28; October 26; November 23; December 14**
Antiques and Collectors' Fair, The Lyndhurst Park Hotel, Lyndhurst - **September 29; October 27; November 24; December 15**

Magnum Antiques Fairs - 0491 681009
Antiques Fair, The Village Hall, Old Basing, Near Basingstoke - **September 8; October 13; November 17; December 8**
Antiques Fair, The River Park Leisure Centre, Winchester - **September 29**

Hampshire continued

Shandos O'Flynn Promotions - 0329 661780
Antiques and Collectors' Fair, The Pyramids on Clarence Esplanade, Southsea - **2nd Sun. monthly**
Antiques and Collectors' Fair, The Botley Park and Country Club, Botley - **September 15; November 3**

Southsea Antiques Fairs - 0705 825807/0243 376196
Antiques & Collectors Fairs, The Portsmouth Guildhall, Southsea - **September 22; October 20; November 17; December 29**

Mrs Wyatt - 0734 833020
Antiques and Collectors' Fair, The Victoria Hall, A30, Hartley Wintney - **October 13; November 10; December 8**

HEREFORD AND WORCESTER

Antiques In Britain Fairs - 0273 423355
The 21st Annual Hereford & Worcestershire Antiques Fair, Bank House Hotel, Bransford - **October 8/10**

C J Antiques Fairs - 0952 595403
Antiques Fair, The Gainsborough House Hotel, Bewdley Hill, Kidderminster - **November 3**

Classic Antique Fairs - 021 476 5798
Antiques Fair, The Stone Manor Hotel, A448, Near Kidderminster -**September 15; November 10; December 29**

Wakefield Ceramics Fair - 0634 723461
Ceramics Fair, The Dyson Perrins Museum, Severn Street, Worcester - **October 19/20**

Waverley Fairs - 0905 620697
Antiques and Collectors' Fair, The Bromsgrove Market Hall, Bromsgrove - **Every Wed.**

Worcestershire Book Fairs - 0905 620697
Book Fair, The Three Counties Showground Complex, Malvern - **September 8; December 8**

HERTFORDSHIRE

Robert Bailey Antiques Fairs - 0277 362662
The Hatfield House Antiques Fair, Hatfield - **September 6/8**

Bartholomew Fairs - 0279 600005
Antiques and Collectors' Fair, The Red Lion, Great North Road, Hatfield - **3rd Sun. monthly**
Antiques and Collectors' Fair, The Grundy Park Leisure Centre, Windmill Lane, Cheshunt - **September 29; November 24**

Biggleswade Antique Fairs - 0234 857317
Antiques Fair, Blakemore Hotel, Little Wymondley, Hitchin/Stevenage - **October 6; December 1**

Camfair - 0440 704632
Antiques and Collectors' Fair, The Castle Hall, The Wash, Hertford -**September 28; October 26; November 23; December 14**

Hertfordshire continued

Chiltern Fairs - 0753 890301
Antiques Fair, The Memorial Hall, Common Road, Chorleywood - **1st Sat. monthly**
Antiques Fair, The Polytechnic, College Lane, Hatfield - **3rd Sun. monthly**
Antiques Fair, The Public Hall, Harpenden - **usually last Tues. monthly**
Antiques Fair, The Town Hall, Watford - **usually last Sat. monthly**
Antiques Fair, The St Clement Danes School, Chorleywood - **October 19**

G & Y Services - 0438 355049
Antiques and Collectors' Fair, The Village Hall, Knebworth, Near Stevenage - **usually 2nd Sun. monthly**

Harlequin Fairs - 0462 671688
Antiques Fair, Haberdashers' Aske's School for Girls, Aldenham Road, Elstree - **3rd Sun. monthly**

Herridges Antiques and Collectors' Fairs Limited - 0234 45725
Antiques Fair, The Plinston Hall, Letchworth - **October 13**

International Antique and Collectors' Fair Co Ltd - 0636 702326
The Antique and Collectors' Fair, The Hertfordshire County Showground, Redbourn - **November 19**

M J Fairs - 0494 726879/0923 242907
Antiques and Collectors' Fair, The Village Hall, Chipperfield - **September 14; October 12; November 9; December 7**
Antiques and Collectors' Fair, The Village Hall, Sarratt - **September 22; October 20; November 24; December 29**
Antiques and Collector' Fair, The Sports Centre, Berkhamsted -**September 29**

M & S Enterprises - 081 440 2330
Antiques and Collectors' Fair, The Wesley Hall, Stapylton Road, Barnet - **Wed. monthly**
Fleamarket and Collectors' Fair, The Corn Exchange, Fore Street, Hertford - **2nd Sat. monthly**
Fleamarket and Collectors' Fair, The Times Club Roaring Meg Retail Park, London Road, Stevenage - **September 21; November 30**
Fleamarket and Collectors' Fair, The Town Hall, Chequers Street, St Albans - **September 25; October 16, 19, 30; November 13, 16, 27; December 11, 18, 21**
Fleamarket and Collectors' Fair, The Drill Hall, Amwell End, Ware - **October 5; November 2; December 7**

NORTH HUMBERSIDE

Abbey Antiques Fairs - 0482 445785/0831 449731
Antiques and Collectors' Fair, The Willerby Manor, Hull - **September 22; October 27; November 24; December 22**

KENT

Antiques and Collectors' Club - 0293 782020
Antique and Collectors' Fair, The Hilden Manor, London Road, Tonbridge - **1st Sun. monthly**

Cross Country Fairs Ltd - 0474 834120
Antiques Fair, The Metropole, The Leas, Folkestone - **1st Sun. monthly**
Antiques Fair, The Spa Hotel, Mount Ephraim, Tunbridge Wells - **3rd Sun. monthly**
Antiques Fair, The Ashford International Hotel, Simone Weil Avenue, Ashford - **September 22; October 27; November 24; December 29**

Mr B Holmes - 0843 595484
Antiques and Collectors' Fair, Northdown House, Northdown Park, Cliftonville, Margate - **Last Sun. monthly**
Antiques and Collectors' Fair, The Kent County Cricket Club, Old Dover Road, Canterbury - **October 13; November 10; December 8**

Wakefield Antiques Fairs - 0634 723461
Antiques and Collectors' Fair, The Great Danes Hotel, Hollingbourne, Near Maidstone - **September 8; October 13; November 10; December 7**

LANCASHIRE

Robert Bailey Antiques Fairs - 0277 362662
Antiques Fair, Hoghton Tower, Preston - **November 22/24**

Castle Fairs Ltd - 0937 845829
The Lancashire Antique Dealer's Fair, Stoneyhurst, Near Whalley - **October 25/27**

Unicorn Fairs - 061 773 7001
Antiques and Collectors' Fair, The Exhibition Halls, Park Hall, Charnock Richard, Near Chorley - **Every Sun.**

LEICESTERSHIRE

County Fairs - 0533 879688
Antiques Fair, The Village Hall, Broughton Astley - **September 1; November 17**
Antiques Fair, The High School, Market Bosworth - **September 8**
Antiques Fair, The Community College, Kibworth - **September 15; November 24**
Antiques Fair, The Stage Hotel, Wigston Fields - **September 29; December 8**
Antiques Fair, The Bardon Hall Hotel, Bardon - **October 27; December 29**
Antiques Fair, The Willoughby Hotel, Upper Broughton - **October 13; December 1; January 1**
Antiques Fair, The Town Hall, Loughborough - **October 20**
Antiques Fair, The Crest Hotel, Corby - **November 3**
Antiques Fair, The Bosworth College, Desford - **December 15**

LINCOLNSHIRE

Robert Bailey Antiques Fairs - 0277 362662
Antiques Fair, The Harlaxton Manor, Grantham - **October 4/6**

MIDDLESEX

Chiltern Fairs - 0753 890301
Antiques and Collectors' Fair, The Mount Vernon Hospital, Northwood - **September 29; November 10**

NORFOLK

King Collectables - 0933 311313
Antiques Fair and Flea Market, The Poachers Pocket, Walcott - **October 20**
Antiques Fair and Flea Market, The Town Hall, Aylsham - **October 26**

Tradex Fairs - 0728 79531
Antiques and Collectors' Fair, The Corn Hall, Diss - **November 2**

Vivid Fairs - 0379 852777
Crafts and Antiques Fair, The Swan Hotel, The Thoroughfare, Harleston - **October 12; December 14**

NORTHAMPTONSHIRE

King Collectables - 0933 311313
Antiques Fair and Flea Market, The Alfred Street School, Rushden - **November 30**

Magpie Fairs - 0604 890107
Antiques and Collectors' Fair, The Cogenhoe Village Hall, Near Northampton - **September 22; October 20; November 17; December 15**

Sovereign Fairs - 0234 350600
Antiques Fair, The Moathouse Hotel, Northampton - **September 28; October 26; November 30**

NOTTINGHAMSHIRE

International Antique and Collectors' Fair Company Ltd - 0636 702326
The Famous International Fair, The Newark and Nottinghamshire Showground, Newark - **October 22**
The Christmas International Fair, The Newark and Nottinghamshire Showground, Newark - **December 10**

Wakefield Ceramics Fairs - 0634 723461
Ceramics Fair, The Worksop College, Worksop, Nottingham - **October 26/27**

Whittington Exhibitions - 081 644 9327
The Thoresby Antiques Fair, Thoresby Exhibition Centre, Thoresby Park, Ollerton - **September 20/22**

OXFORDSHIRE

Harries & May - 0296 625335
Antiques Fair, The Cokethorpe School, Whitney - **September 29**

Jay Fairs - 0235 815633
The Flea Market, The Regal Centre, Wallingford - **September 21; November 23**
The Drayton Antiques and Collectors' Fair, Drayton Hall, Drayton, Abingdon - **September 29; November 17**
Antiques and Collectors' Fair, The Fawley Court, Henley-on-Thames - **November 10**

Oxfordshire continued

Mayfairs - 0865 511579
Antique and Collectors' Fair, The Langdale Hall, Witney - **1st Sun. monthly**
Antique and Collectors' Fair, The Marlborough School, Woodstock - **2nd Sun. monthly**
Antique and Collectors' Fair, The Wheatley Park School, Wheatley - **4th Sun. monthly**

Silhouette Fairs - 0635 44338
Antiques and Collectors' Fair, The Abbey Hall, Abingdon - **September 15, 29; October 20; November 17; December 8**

Wakefield Ceramics Fairs - 0634 723461
Ceramics Fair, Henley Town Hall, Henley on Thames - **October 10/12**

SOMERSET

Reg Cooper Antiques Fairs - 0672 515558
The Somerset County Antiques Fair, Dillington House, Ilminster - **September 14/15**

Devon County Antiques Fairs - 0363 82571
Antiques Fair, The Millfield School, Street - **December 14/15**

Merlin Fairs - 0278 691616
Antiques and Collectors' Fair, The Royal Bath & West Showground, Shepton Mallet - **September 3; November 16/17**

West Country Antiques and Collectors Fairs - 0364 52182
The Wells Antiques and Collectors' Fair, The Star Hotel, Wells - **September 2/3; November 22/23**
The Annual Antiques and Collectors' Fair, The Indoor School, The County Cricket Ground, Taunton - **October 11/12**
The Wells Antiques Fair, The Bishops Palace, Wells - **November 1/2**
Taunton Annual Antiques and Collectors Fair, County Cricket Ground, Taunton - **October 11/12**

STAFFORDSHIRE

Bowmans Antique Fairs - 0532 843333/0943 465782
The Stafford Ceramics and Glass Fair, The Bingley Hall County Showground, Stafford - **August 31/September 1**
The Stafford Giant Three Day Antiques Fair, The Bingley Hall, County Showground, Stafford - **October 4/6; December 13/15**

Bygones Of The Cloud - 0565 632323/651784
Antiques and Collectors' Fair, Olivers Southbank Street, Leek - **October 6; November 17**

Waverley Fairs - 0905 620697
Antiques Fair, The Kinver Community Centre, Stourbridge - **1st Sun. monthly**
Book Fair, The Kinver Community Centre, Stourbridge - **3rd Sun. monthly**

SUFFOLK

Anglian Arts and Antiques - 0986 872368
The St Edmunds Antiques Fair, Bury St Edmunds - **October 24/26**

Antiques In Britain Fairs - 0273 423355
The 25th Annual East Anglia Antiques Fair, The Athenaeum, Angel Hill, Bury St. Edmunds - **September 5/7**

Dedham Fairs - Waldringfield 674
Antiques and Collectors' Fair, The Hewitt Hall, Dedham - **September 28; November 9; December 14**

International Antique & Collectors Fair Co Ltd - 0636 702326
The Ipswich International Fair, The Suffolk Showground, Bucklesham Road, Ipswich - **September 10**

Kyson Fairs - 047 335 528
Antiques and Collectors' Fair, The Woodbridge Community Hall, Station Road, Woodbridge - **October 13; November 17; December 15**

Lorna Quick Four Season Fairs - 0787 281855
Antique and Collectors' Fair, The Officers' Club, Tactical Operational Base, R.A.F. Bentwaters, Woodbridge - **September 8**
Antique and Collectors' Fair, The American Elementary School, R.A.F. Lakenheath, Near Brandon - **September 22; November 3; December 29**
Antique and Collectors' Fair, The Bob Hope Recreation Centre, R.A.F. Mildenhall - **October 27**

Sandway Fairs - 0206 579658
Antiques and Collectors' Fair, The Constable Hall, East Bergholt - **September 29; December 8**
Antiques and Collectors Fair, The Village Hall, Bures - **October 27**

SURREY

Reg Cooper Antiques Fairs - 0672 515558
The Surrey County Antiques Fair, Gordon's School, Near Lightwater - **October 19/20**

Cultural Exhibitions Ltd - 0483 422562
The Surrey Antiques Fair, The Civic Hall, Guildford - **October 4/8; October 2/6, 1992**

Leatherheads Antiques and Collectors' Fairs - 0372 379795
Antique and Collectors' Fair, St Mary's Parish Hall, Church Road, Leatherhead - **September 21; October 19; November 16**

Wonder Whistle Enterprises - 071 249 4050
Antique and Collectors' Fair, The Exhibition Centre, Sandown Park Racecourse, Esher - **October 15; December 3**

SUSSEX

Antiques and Collectors' Club - 0293 782020
Antique and Collectors' Fair, The Gatwick Manor Hotel, London Road, Crawley - **3rd Sun. monthly**
Antique and Collectors' Fair, The Corn Exchange, Pavillion Gardens, Brighton - **September 17; November 19**

Sussex continued

Antiques In Britain Fairs - 0273 423355
The 3rd Annual Autumn Antiques Fair, The Wivelsfield Green Village Hall, Near Haywards Heath - **October 26/27**

Robert Bailey Antiques Fairs - 0277 362662
Antiques Fair, Seaford College, Petworth - **August 30/September 1; December 28/31**
The Lancing College Antiques Fair, Near Worthing - **October 25/27**

Castle Fairs - 0937 845829
The Antiques and Decorative Arts Fair at Parham, Parham Park - **November 1/3**
The South East Counties Antique Dealers Fair, Goodwood House, Chichester - **November 22/24**

Clinton Hall Antiques & Collectors' Fairs - 0273 514454
Antiques and Collectors' Fair, The Clinton Hall, Broad Street, Seaford - **4th Sun. monthly**

International Antiques and Collectors' Fair Company Ltd - 0636 702326
The Ardingly Fair, The South of England Showground, Ardingly - **September 25; November 6**

King Collectables - 0933 311313
Antiques Fair and Flea Market, The Memorial Hall, Yardley, Hastings - **September 29; November 3**

Brenda Ley - 0798 813822
Antiques Fair, The Brighton Centre, Seafront Entrance, Kings Road, Brighton - **September 15; December 4**

Magnum Antiques Fairs - 0491 681009
Antiques Fair, The Grange Centre, Midhurst - **October 6; December 1**

Wakefields Antiques Fair - 0634 723461
Antiques and Collectors' Fair, The Felbridge Hotel, East Grinstead -**September 30; October 27; November 24; December 21**

Wakefield Ceramics Fairs - 0634 723461
Ceramics Fair, The Felbridge Hotel, East Grinstead - **September 21/22**

TYNE & WEAR

Albany Fairs - 091 584 2934/0836 531108
Antiques and Collectables Fair, The Community Centre, Lanchester, Co Durham - **October 6; December 26**

Great Northern Antiques and Collectors' Fairs Ltd - 0642 550268
Antiques and Collectors' Fair, The Scotch Corner Hotel, A1 A66 Junction, Darlington - **September 29; November 10**
Antiques and Collectors' Fair, The Hogarth Manor Hotel, Durham City, Durham - **October 6; December 29**
Antiques and Collectors' Fair, The Lancastrian Suite, Federation, Gateshead - **November 17**

WARWICKSHIRE

Classic Antiques Fairs - 021 476 5798
Antiques Fair, The Charlecote Pheasant Hotel, A429 Midway Warwick/Stratford - **September 1; October 13; December 1**

International Antique and Collectors' Fair Company Ltd - 0636 702326
The Royal Showground Winter International Fair, The Royal Showground, Stoneleigh, Near Kenilworth - **October 8**

Jane Sumner and John Braund - 0799 23611
The Kenilworth Antiques Fair, Chesford Grange, Kenilworth - **October 22/26; March 3/7, 1992**

Wakefield Antiques Fair - 0634 723461
Antiques and Fine Art Fair, The Ragley Hall, Alcester - **November 29/December 1**

WEST MIDLANDS

A K Fairs - 021 744 4385
Antiques Fair, The Greswolde Hotel, High Street, Knowle, Near Solihull - **2nd Sun. monthly**

C J Antique Fairs - 0952 595403
The Midlands Autumn Antique and Fine Art Fair The National Motorcycle Museum, Coventry Road, (M42, Junction with A45), Bickenhill - **September 6/8**

Linda Colban - 021 780 4141 ext 2760
The British International Antiques Fair, The National Exhibition Centre, Birmingham - **April 9/15; August 6/9, 1992**

Bob Harris & Sons - 021 743 2259
Antiques Fair, The Warwickshire County Cricket Ground, Edgbaston, Birmingham - **September 26/28; November 7/9**
Collectors Market, The Warwickshire County Cricket Ground, Edgbaston, Birmingham - **December 28**

Willow Fairs - 0905 620697
Book Fair, The Leisure Centre, Wombourne, Wolverhampton - **Last Sun. monthly**

WILTSHIRE

Wakefield Ceramics Fair - 0634 723461
Ceramics Fair, The Michael Herbert Hall, Wilton - **November 22/24**

NORTH YORKSHIRE

Abbey Antiques Fairs - 0482 445785/0831 449731
Antiques and Collectors' Fair, The Old Swan Hotel, Harrogate - **September 1, 29; October 20; November 10; December 1, 29**

Aston Antique Fairs - 0532 666498/692213
Antiques Fair, The Granby Hotel, Harrogate - **Usually 4th Sun. monthly**

Robert Bailey Antiques Fairs - 0277 362662
The Castle Howard Antiques Fair, York - **November 27/December 1**

North Yorkshire continued

Castle Fairs - 0937 845829
Antiques Eurofair, Hazelwood Castle, Near Tadcaster - **September 13/15**
Antiques and Decorative Arts at Settrington, The Orangery, Near Malton - **September 27/29**
Antiques and Decorative Arts at Rudding, Rudding House, Harrogate - **November 8/10**

Great Northern Antiques and Collectors Fairs Ltd - 0642 550268
Antiques and Collectors' Fair, The Great Yorkshire Showground, Harrogate - **September 6/8; November 1/3**

Orion Antique Fairs - 0274 566196
Antiques Fair, The Lounge Hall, Harrogate - **September 7**
Antiques Fair, The Granby Hotel, Harrogate - **September 15; October 13; November 10; December 29**
Antiques Fair, The Cairn Hotel, Harrogate - **September 22; October 27; November 24; December 15**

Evan Steadman Communications Group Ltd - 0799 26699
The Northern Antiques Fair, The Royal Baths Assembly Rooms, Harrogate - **September 26/October 2**

Wakefield Ceramics Fairs - 0634 723461
Ceramics Fair, The Crown Hotel, Crown Place, Harrogate - **November 8/10**

WEST YORKSHIRE

Abbey Antiques Fairs - 0482 445785/0831 449731
Antiques and Collectors' Fair, The Bankfield Hotel, Bingley - **September 15; October 6; November 17; December 8**
Antiques and Collectors' Fair, The Hilton National Hotel, Garforth, Leeds - **November 3; December 8**

Robert Bailey Antiques Fairs - 0277 362662
The Ilkley Antiques Fair, Kings Hall and Wintergardens, Ilkley -**December 6/8**

Great Northern Antiques and Collectors' Fairs Ltd - 0642 550268
Antiques and Collectors' Fair, The Sports Centre, Leeds University, Leeds - **November 23**

SOUTH YORKSHIRE

Abbey Antiques Fairs - 0483 445785/0831 449731
Antiques and Collectors' Fair, The Keresforth Hall, Barnsley - **September 8; October 13; November 17; December 15**

SCOTLAND

Albany Fairs - 091 584 2934/0836 531108
Antiques and Collectables Fair, The Town Hall, Moffat, Annandale - **September 20/22; October 12/13**

Scotland continued

Antiques In Britain Fairs - 0273 423355
The 14th Annual Edinburgh Winter Antiques Fair, The Roxburghe Hotel Charlotte Square, Edinburgh - **November 15/17**

Castle Fairs - 0937 845829
The Antique Dealers Fair of Scotland, Hopetoun House, South Queensferry - **October 11/13**

Scotfairs - Crieff 3592
Antiques and Collectors' Fair, The Skean Dhu Hotel, Farburn Terrace, Dyce - **1st Sun. monthly**
Antiques and Collectors' Fair, The Mitchell Theatre, Granville Street, Glasgow - **September 1, 22; October 6, 27; November 24; December 1, 22**
Antiques and Collectors' Fair, The Dam Park Hall, Ayr - **Usually 2nd Sat. monthly**
Antiques and Collectors' Fair, The Marryat Hall, Dundee - **September 8; October 27; November 17; December 22**
Antiques and Collectors' Fair The City Hall, Candleriggs, Glasgow - **September 8; October 20; November 3; December 15**
Antiques and Collectors' Fair, The Albert Halls, Stirling - **September 14, 28; October 19; November 16; December 7, 21**
Antiques and Collectors' Fair, The Assembly Rooms, George Street, Edinburgh - **September 14; October 5**

Val Watson - 03398 84277
Antiques and Collectors' Fair, The Victoria Hall, Station Square, Ballater, Aberdeenshire - **September 7**
Antiques and Collectors' Fair, The Burnett Arms Hotel, High Street, Banchory, Aberdeenshire - **2nd Sun. monthly**

WALES

Antiques In Britain Fairs - 0273 423355
The 22nd Annual Welsh Antiques Fair, The Castle of Brecon Hotel, Castle Square, Brecon, Powys - **September 12/14**

Melba Fairs - 0934 624854
The Second South Wales Premier Antiques and Collectors' Drive-in Fair, The Racecourse, Chepstow - **September 10**

Puzzle House Fairs - 0594 60653
The Chepstow Antiques Fair, The Leisure Centre, Crossway Green, Chepstow, Gwent - **Usually 4th Sun. monthly**

David Robinson Fairs - 0222 620520
Antiques Fair, Seabank Hotel, Promenade, Porthcawl - **September 8**
Antiques Fair, The Glyn Clydach Hotel, Longford Road, Neath Abbey, Neath - **3rd Sun. monthly**
Antiques Fair, The Exchange Hall, Mount Stuart Square, Cardiff - **September 22**
Antiques Fair, The New House Country Hotel, Thornhill, Cardiff - **October 6; November 3**
Antiques Fair, The Rest, Rest Bay, Porthcawl - **December 1**

IRELAND

L & M Fairs Ltd - 0238 528428
Antiques Fair, The Methodist Church Hall, 262 Lisburn Road, Belfast - **Usually 1st Sat. monthly**
Antiques, Collectables and Jewellery, Gallery 88, 88 Main Street, Portrush - **September 8**
Antiques Fair, The USPCA, Larne - **September 21**
Antiques Fair, The USPCA, Hillsborough Court House - **October 12**
Antiques Fair, Silverbirch Hotel, Omagh - **October 17**
Antiques Fair, The Town Hall, Coleraine - **October 19**
Antiques Fair, The Town Hall, Ballymena - **November 9**
Antiques Fair, The Community Centre USPCA, Armagh - **November 23**

OVERSEAS

Brian & Anna Haughton - 071 734 5491
The International Antique Dealers Show, The Seventh Regiment Armory, Park Avenue at 67th Street, New York City - **October 18/24**

ALPHABETICAL LIST OF TOWNS AND VILLAGES WITH THE COUNTIES UNDER WHICH THEY APPEAR IN THIS GUIDE

A

Abbots Bromley, Staffs.
Abbots Langley, Herts.
Abbots Leigh, Avon.
Aberaeron, Dyfed, Wales.
Aberdare, Mid-Glamorgan, Wales.
Aberdeen, Aberd., Scot.
Aberfeldy, Perths., Scot.
Aberford, W. Yorks.
Abergavenny, Gwent, Wales.
Abernyte, Perths., Scot.
Abersoch, Gwynedd, Wales.
Abertillery, Gwent, Wales.
Aberystwyth, Dyed, Wales.
Abingdon, Oxon.
Abinger Hammer, Surrey.
Abridge, Essex.
Accrington, Lancs.
Acle, Norfolk.
Acrise, Kent.
Adderley, Shrops.
Addingham, W. Yorks.
Admaston, Staffs.
Adversane, W. Sussex.
Albrighton, Shrops.
Alcester, Warks.
Alderney, C.I.
Aldeburgh, Suffolk.
Alderley Edge, Cheshire.
Alford, Aberd., Scot.
Alford, Lincs.
Alfriston, E. Sussex.
Allonby, Cumbria.
Alnwick, Northumb.
Alresford, Hants.
Alrewas, Staffs.
Althorne, Essex.
Alton, Staffs.
Altrincham, Cheshire.
Alum Bay, Isle of Wight.
Alvechurch, W. Midlands.
Alverstoke, Hants.
Amersham, Bucks.
Ammanford, Dyfed, Wales.
Ampthill, Beds.
Angarrack, Cornwall.
Angmering, W. Sussex.
Annfield Plain, Durham.
Anstey, Leics.
Ardersier, Inver., Scot.
Ardingly, W. Sussex.
Armagh, Co. Armagh, N. Ireland.
Arnesby, Leics.
Arreton, Isle of Wight.
Arthog, Gwynedd, Wales.
Arundel, W. Sussex.
Ash Priors, Somerset.
Ascott-under-Wychwood, Oxon.
Ash Vale, Surrey.
Ashbourne, Derbys.
Ashburton, Devon.
Ashby de la Zouch, Leics.
Ashfield, Suffolk.
Ashtead, Surrey.
Ashton-under-Lyne, Lancs.
Askham, Notts.
Aslockton, Notts.
Astwood Bank, Hereford and Worcs.
Atcham, Shrops.
Atherton, Lancs.
Attleborough, Norfolk.
Atworth, Wilts.
Auchterarder, Perths., Scot.
Audlem, Cheshire.
Auldearn, Nairn., Scot.
Auldgirth, Dumfriess., Scot.
Avening, Glos.
Aveton Gifford, Devon.
Axbridge, Devon.
Aylesbury, Bucks.
Aylsham, Norfolk.
Ayr, Ayr., Scot.

B

Bagilt, Clwyd, Wales.
Bakewell, Derbys.
Balcombe, W. Sussex.
Balderton, Notts.
Baldock, Herts.
Balfron, Stirlings., Scot.
Ballater, Aberd., Scot.
Ballyclare, Co. Antrim, N. Ireland.
Bampton, Devon.
Bampton, Oxon.
Banbridge, Co. Down, N. Ireland.
Banbury, Oxon.
Banchory, Kincard., Scot.
Banff, Banff., Scot.
Bangor, Co. Down, N. Ireland.
Bangor, Gwynedd, Wales.
Bankfoot, Perths., Scot.
Barford, Warks.
Barkham, Berks.
Barnard Castle, Durham.
Barnet, Herts.
Barnoldswick, Lancs.
Barnsley, Glos.
Barnsley, S. Yorks.
Barnstaple, Devon.
Barnt Green, Hereford and Worcs.
Barrhead, Renfrews., Scot.
Barrington, Somerset.
Barrow-in-Furness, Cumbria.
Barrow-on-Humber, S. Humberside.
Barrow-on-Soar, Leics.
Barry, S. Glamorgan, Wales.
Barton, Cheshire.
Barton-on-Humber, S. Humberside.
Basingstoke, Hants.
Baslow, Derbys.
Bassingbourn, Cambs.
Bath, Avon.
Batley, W. Yorks.
Battle, E. Sussex.
Battlesbridge, Essex.
Bawdeswell, Norfolk.
Bawtry, S. Yorks.
Beaconsfield, Bucks.
Beaminster, Dorset.
Beaulieu, Hants.
Beauly, Inver., Scot.
Beaumaris, Gwynedd, Wales.
Beccles, Suffolk.
Beckenham, Kent.
Bedale, N. Yorks.
Bedford, Beds.
Bedingfield, Suffolk.
Beeston, Notts.
Beetham, Cumbria.
Beighton, Norfolk.
Belfast, N. Ireland.
Belper, Derbys.
Bembridge, Isle of Wight.
Benson, Oxon.
Bentley Heath, W. Mids.
Berkeley, Glos.
Berkhamsted, Herts.
Berry Hill Pike, Glos.
Berwick-on-Tweed, Northumb.
Bessacar, S. Yorks.
Bethel, Gwynedd, Wales.
Bethesda, Gwynedd, Wales.
Betley, Staffs.
Betwys Garmon, Gwynedd, Wales.
Bevereley, N. Humberside.
Bewdley, Hereford and Worcs.
Bexhill-on-Sea, E. Sussex.
Bexley, Kent.
Bicester, Oxon.
Bickerstaffe, Lancs.
Biddenden, Kent.
Bideford, Devon.
Bidford-on-Avon, Warks.
Biggleswade, Beds.
Billingham, Cleveland.
Bingham, Notts.

Bingley, W. Yorks.
Birchington, Kent.
Birdbrook, Essex.
Birkenhead, Merseyside.
Birley, Hereford and Worcs.
Birmingham, W. Mids.
Birstwith, N. Yorks.
Bishop Monkton, N. Yorks.
Bishops Castle, Shrops.
Bishops Cleeve, Glos.
Bishop's Stortford, Herts.
Bishops Waltham, Hants.
Bisley, Glos.
Blackburn, Lancs.
Blackmore, Essex.
Blackpool, Lancs.
Bladon, Oxon.
Blaenau Ffestiniog, Gwynedd, Wales.
Blairgowrie, Perths., Scot.
Blairmore-by-Dunoon, Argyll, Scot.
Blakedown, Hereford and Worcs.
Blandford Forum, Dorset.
Blaydon, Tyne and Wear.
Bletchingley, Surrey.
Blewbury, Oxon.
Blockley, Glos.
Bloxham, Oxon.
Bloxwich, W. Mids.
Bognor Regis, W. Sussex.
Bolton, Lancs.
Bolton-by-Bowland, Lancs.
Boreham Street, E. Sussex.
Boroughbridge, N. Yorks.
Bosham, W. Sussex.
Boston, Lincs.
Boston Spa, W. Yorks.
Botesdale, Suffolk.
Botley, Hants.
Bottesford, Leics.
Bottisham, Cambs.
Boughton, Kent.
Bournemouth, Dorset.
Bourton-on-the-Water, Glos.
Bow Street, Dyfed, Wales.
Bowdon, Cheshire.
Bowness-on-Windermere, Cumbria.
Boxford, Suffolk.
Boxhill, Surrey.
Brackley, Northants.
Bradfield St. George, Suffolk.
Bradford, W. Yorks.
Bradford-on-Avon, Wilts.
Bradstone, Devon.
Braintree, Essex.
Bramley, Surrey.
Brampton, Cambs.
Brampton, Cumbria.
Brancaster Staithe, Norfolk.
Brandsby, N. Yorks.
Branksome, Dorset.
Brantham, Suffolk.
Brassington, Derbys.
Brasted, Kent.
Braunton, Devon.
Brecon, Powys, Wales.
Brentwood, Essex.
Brereton, Staffs.
Bressingham, Norfolk.
Bridge of Allan, Stirlings., Scot.
Bridge of Earn, Perths., Scot.
Bridge of Weir, Renfrews., Scot.
Bridgend, Mid. Glam., Wales.
Bridgnorth, Shrops.
Bridgwater, Somerset.
Bridlington, N. Humberside.
Bridport, Dorset.
Brierfield, Lancs.
Brightling, E. Sussex.
Brighton, E. Sussex.
Bristol, Avon.
Brixham, Devon.
Brixworth, Northants.
Broadstairs, Kent.
Broadstone, Dorset.
Broadway, Hereford and Worcs.
Brobury, Hereford and Worcs.
Brockdish, Norfolk.
Brodick, Isle of Arran, Scot.
Bromley, Kent.
Brompton, N. Yorks.
Bromsgrove, Hereford and Worcs.
Bromyard, Hereford and Worcs.
Broseley, Shrops.
Broughton, Lancs.
Broughton Astley, Leics.
Broughton in Furness, Cumbria.
Bruton, Somerset.
Buckden, N. Yorks.
Buckfastleigh, Devon.
Buckhurst Hill, Essex.
Buckingham, Bucks.
Buckland Newton, Dorset.
Buchlyvie, Stirlings., Scot.
Buckminster, Leics.
Budleigh Salteron, Devon.
Bulkington, Warks.
Bungay, Suffolk.
Bures, Suffolk.
Burford, Oxon.
Burgess Hill, W. Sussex.
Burghfield Common, Berks.
Burley-in-Wharfdale, W. Yorks.
Burley-on-the-Hill, Leics.
Burneston, N. Yorks.
Burnham Deepdale, Norfolk.
Burnham Market, Norfolk.
Burnham-on-Crouch, Essex.
Burnham-on-Sea, Somerset.
Burnley, Lancs.
Burscough, Lancs.
Burton-on-Trent, Staffs.
Burwash, E. Sussex.
Burwell, Cambs.
Bury, Lancs.
Bury St. Edmunds, Suffolk.
Bushey, Herts.
Bushmills, Co. Antrim, N. Ireland.
Buxton, Derbys.
Buxton, Norfolk.
Bwlchllan, Dyfed, Wales.

C

Cadeby, Leics.
Cadnam, Hants.
Cadole, Clwyd, Wales.
Caernarvon, Gwynedd, Wales.
Caerphilly, Mid. Glamorgan, Wales.
Caerwys, Clwyd, Wales.
Callington, Cornwall.
Calne, Wilts.
Camberley, Surrey.
Camborne, Cornwall.
Cambridge, Cambs.
Cambridge, Glos.
Canterbury, Kent.
Cardiff, S. Glamorgan, Wales.
Cardigan, Dyfed, Wales.
Carlisle, Cumbria.
Carlton-on-Trent, Notts.
Carmarthen, Dyfed, Wales.
Carnforth, Lancs.
Carnon Downs, Cornwall.
Carrefour Selous, Jersey, C.I.
Carnoustie, Angus, Scot.
Carshalton, Surrey.
Cartmel, Cumbria.
Castle Cary, Somerset.
Castle Combe, Wilts.
Castle Douglas, Kirkcud., Scot.
Castle Hedingham, Essex.
Castleton, Derbys.
Castletown, Isle of Man.
Castor, Cambs.
Caversham, Berks.
Cawood, N. Yorks.
Ceres, Fife, Scot.
Cerne Abbas, Dorset.
Cerrig-y-Drudion, Clwyd, Wales.
Chagford, Devon.
Chalfont St. Giles, Bucks.
Chalford, Glos.
Chalgrove, Oxon.
Chalvington, E. Sussex.
Chapel-en-le-Frith, Derbys.
Chard, Somerset.
Charing, Kent.
Charlecote, Warks.
Charlton Marshall, Dorset.
Charmouth, Dorset.
Chastleton, Glos.
Chatburn, Lancs.

Chatham, Kent.
Chatton, Northumb.
Cheadle, Cheshire.
Cheadle, Staffs.
Cheadle Hulme, Cheshire.
Cheam, Surrey.
Cheddleton, Staffs.
Cheltenham, Glos.
Chepstow, Gwent, Wales.
Cherhill, Wilts.
Chertsey, Surrey.
Chesham, Bucks.
Chester, Cheshire.
Chesterfield, Derbys.
Chichester, W. Sussex.
Chiddingfold, Surrey.
Chiddingstone, Kent.
Chilcompton, Somerset.
Chilham, Kent.
Chipping Campden, Glos.
Chipping Norton, Oxon.
Chirk, Clwyd, Wales.
Chislehurst, Kent.
Chittering, Cambs.
Chobham, Lancs.
Christchurch, Dorset.
Christian Malford, Wilts.
Chulmleigh, Devon.
Church Stretton, Shrops.
Ciliau Aeron, Dyfed, Wales.
Cirencester, Glos.
Clacton on Sea, Essex.
Clare, Suffolk.
Claygate, Surrey.
Clayton-le-Moors, Lancs.
Clayton-le-Woods, Lancs.
Cleobury Mortimer, Shrops.
Clevedon, Avon.
Clitheroe, Lancs.
Clutton, Avon.
Coalville, Leics.
Coatbridge, Lanarks., Scot.
Cobham, Surrey.
Cockermouth, Cumbria.
Cockfosters, Herts.
Codford, Wilts.
Codicote, Herts.
Codsall, Staffs.
Coggeshall, Essex.
Colchester, Essex.
Coldingham, Berwicks., Scot.
Coldstream, Berwicks., Scot.
Coleraine, Co. Londonderry, N. Ireland.
Colne, Lancs.
Coleshill, Warks.
Collingham, Notts.
Colsterworth, Lincs.
Coltishall, Norfolk.
Colwyn Bay, Clwyd, Wales.
Colyton, Devon.
Combe Martim, Devon.
Comberton, Cambs.
Compton, Surrey.
Comrie, Perths., Scot.
Congleton, Cheshire.
Congresbury, Avon.
Coniston, Cumbria.
Consett, Durham.
Conway, Gwynedd, Wales.
Cookham, Berks.
Cookstown, Co. Tyrone, N. Ireland.
Copthorne, W. Sussex.
Corby Hill, Cumbria.
Corringham, Essex.
Corsham, Wilts.
Corwen, Clwyd, Wales.
Cosgrove, Northants.
Costessey, Norfolk.
Coton Clanford, Staffs.
Coughton, Warks.
Coulsdon, Surrey.
Coupar Angus, Perths., Scot.
Coventry, W. Mids.
Cowbridge, S. Glamorgan, Wales.
Cowes, Isle of Wight.
Cowfold, W. Sussex.
Cowley, Oxon.
Cradley, W. Mids.
Cranborne, Dorset.
Cranbrook, Kent.
Cranham, Glos.
Craven Arms, Shrops.
Crawley, W. Sussex.
Crayford, Kent.
Cremyll, Cornwall.
Crewkerne, Somerset.
Cricklade, Wilts.
Crieff, Perths., Scot.
Cromer, Norfolk.
Crook, Durham.
Crosby Ravensworth, Cumbria.
Crossford, Lanarks., Scot.
Cross Hills, N. Yorks.
Croughton, Northants.
Crowmarsh Gifford, Oxon.
Croydon, Surrey.
Cuckfield, W. Sussex.
Cullompton, Devon.
Cuxton, Kent.

D

Dalbeattie, Kircudbrightshire, Scot.
Darlington, Durham.
Dartford, Kent.
Dartmouth, Devon.
Darwen, Lancs.
Datchet, Berks.
Deal, Kent.
Debenham, Suffolk.
Deddington, Oxon.
Deganwy, Gwynedd, Wales.
Denham Village, Bucks.
Denholme, W. Yorks.
Denny, Stirlings., Scot.
Derby, Derbys.
Dingwall, Ross-shire, Scot.
Disley, Cheshire.
Diss, Norfolk.
Ditchling, E. Sussex.
Docking, Norfolk.
Doddington, Cambs.
Dolgellau, Gwynedd, Wales.
Dollarbeg, Stirlingshire, Scot.
Donaghadee, Co. Down, N. Ireland.
Doncaster, S. Yorks.
Donyatt, Somerset.
Dorchester, Dorset.
Dorchester-on-Thames, Oxon.
Dorking, Surrey.
Dorney, Berks.
Dorrington, Shrops.
Douglas, Isle of Man.
Dover, Kent.
Dowlish Wake, Somerset.
Draperstown, Co. Londonderry, N. Ireland.
Driffield, N. Humberside.
Droitwich, Hereford and Worcs.
Dronfield, Derbys.
Drumnadrochit, Inver., Scot.
Dudley, Tyne and Wear.
Duffield, Derbys.
Dulford, Devon.
Dulverton, Somerset.
Dumfries, Dumfries., Scot.
Dunchurch, Warks.
Dundee, Angus, Scot.
Dunkeld, Perths., Scot.
Dunmow, Essex.
Duns, Berwicks., Scot.
Dunstable, Beds.
Dunster, Somerset.
Durgates, E. Sussex.
Durham, Durham.
Duxford, Cambs.

E

Eachwick, Northumb.
Eaglescliffe, Cleveland.
Eaglesham, Renfrews., Scot.
Earsham, Norfolk.
Easebourne, W. Sussex.
Easingwold, N. Yorks.
East Budleigh, Devon.
East Dereham, Norfolk.
East Grinstead, W. Sussex.
East Hagbourne, Oxon.
East Horsley, Surrey.
East Molesey, Surrey.
East Peckham, Kent.
East Pennard, Somerset.
Eastbourne, E. Sussex.
Eastburne, W. Yorks.
Eastleigh, Hants.
Eastnor, Hereford and Worcs.
Easton-on-the-Hill, Northants.
Eastry, Kent.
Ebrington, Glos.
Ecclesfield, S. Yorks.

Eccleshall, Staffs.
Eccleston, Lancs.
Edenbridge, Kent.
Edenfield, Lancs.
Edgware, Middx.
Edinburgh, Midloth., Scot.
Egham, Surrey.
Elgin, Moray., Scot.
Elie, Fife, Scot.
Elland, W. Yorks.
Ellesmere, Shrops.
Elmley Lovett, Hereford and Worcs.
Elton, Notts.
Ely, Cambs.
Empingham, Leics.
Emsworth, Hants.
Endmoor, Cumbria.
Enfield, Middx.
Epping, Essex.
Epsom, Surrey.
Errol, Perths., Scot.
Esh Winning, Durham.
Esher, Surrey.
Eton, see Windsor and Eton, Berks.
Eversley, Hants.
Evesham, Hereford and Worcs.
Ewell, Surrey.
Ewhurst, Surrey.
Ewhurst Green, E. Sussex.
Exeter, Devon.
Exmouth, Devon.
Exning, Suffolk.
Exton, Somerset.
Eye, Suffolk.
Eynsham, Oxon.

F

Fairford, Glos.
Fairlie, Ayr., Scot.
Fakenham, Norfolk.
Falkirk, Stirlings., Scot.
Falmouth, Cornwall.
Fareham, Hants.
Faringdon, Oxon.
Farnborough, Kent.
Farnborough, Hants.
Farndon, Cheshire.
Farnham, Surrey.
Farnham Common, Bucks.
Farningham, Kent.
Faversham, Kent.
Felixstowe, Suffolk.
Felmingham, Norfolk.
Felpham, W. Sussex.
Felsted, Essex.
Felton, Northumb.
Feniscowles, Lancs.
Ferndown, Dorset.
Fernhurst, W. Sussex.
Filey, N. Yorks.
Finchingfield, Essex.
Finedon, Northants.
Finkley, Hants.
Fishguard, Dyfed, Wales.
Fishlake, S. Yorks.
Fitzhead, Somerset.
Fivehead, Somerset.
Flamborough, N. Humberside.
Flaxton, N. Yorks.
Fleet, Hants.
Flimwell, E. Sussex.
Flore, Northants.
Fochabers, Moray., Scot.
Folkestone, Kent.
Fordham, Cambs.
Fordingbridge, Hants.
Forfar, Angus, Scot.
Forres, Moray., Scot.
Fortrose, Ross and Crom., Scot.
Four Elms, Kent.
Four Oaks, W. Midlands.
Fowlmere, Cambs.
Framfield, E. Sussex.
Framlingham, Suffolk.
Frampton, Lincs.
Frensham, Surrey.
Freshford, Avon.
Freuchie, Fife, Scot.
Frinton-on-Sea, Essex.
Friockheim, Angus, Scot.
Fritwell, Oxon.
Frodsham, Cheshire.
Frome, Somerset.
Fyfield, Oxon.

G

Gainsborough, Lincs.
Galston, Ayr., Scot.
Gants Hill, Essex.
Garboldisham, Norfolk.
Gargrave, N. Yorks.
Garstang, Lincs.
Gartmore, Stirlings., Scot.
Gateshead, Tyne and Wear.
Gazeley, Suffolk.
Gedney, Lincs.
Gerrards Cross, Bucks.
Gillingham, Dorset.
Gillingham, Kent.
Gilwern, Gwent, Wales.
Glasgow, Lanarks., Scot.
Glastonbury, Somerset.
Glossop, Derbys.
Gloucester, Glos.
Godalming, Surrey.
Gorseinon, W. Glamorgan, Wales.
Gosforth, Cumbria.
Gosforth, Tyne and Wear.
Gosport, Hants.
Goudhurst, Kent.
Gourock, Lanarks., Scot.
Grampound, Cornwall.
Grantham, Lincs.
Grasmere, Cumbria.
Grassington, N. Yorks.
Gravesend, Kent.
Grays, Essex.
Great Ayton, N. Yorks.
Great Baddow, Essex.
Great Bardfield, Essex.
Great Bookham, Surrey.
Great Chesterford, Essex.
Great Cheverell, Wilts.
Great Coates, S. Humberside.
Great Harwood, Lancs.
Great Houghton, S. Yorks.
Great Malvern, Hereford and Worcs.
Great Missenden, Bucks.
Great Shefford, Berks.
Great Urswick, Cumbria.
Great Wakering, Essex.
Great Walsingham, Norfolk.
Great Waltham, Essex.
Great Yarmouth, Norfolk.
Greatford, Lincs.
Green Hammerton, N. Yorks.
Greenlaw, Berwicks., Scot.
Greyabbey, Co. Down, N. Ireland.
Greystoke, Cumbria.
Grimsby, S. Humberside.
Grosmont, N. Yorks.
Grundisburgh, Suffolk.
Guildford, Surrey.
Guilsborough, Northants.
Guisborough, Cleveland.
Gullane, E. Loth., Scot.
Gunnislake, Cornwall.
Gunthorpe, Notts.

H

Hacheston, Suffolk.
Haddenham, Bucks.
Haddington, E. Loth., Scot.
Hadleigh, Suffolk.
Hadlow, Kent.
Haigh, S. Yorks.
Halesowen, W. Mids.
Halesworth, Suffolk.
Halifax, W. Yorks.
Halsall, Lancs.
Halstead, Essex.
Haltwhistle, Northumb.
Hambridge, Somerset.
Hampton, Middx.
Hampton Hill, Middx.
Hampton Wick, Surrey.
Handcross, W. Sussex.
Hankerton, Wilts.
Harbertonford, Devon.
Hare Hatch, Berks.
Harefield, Middx.
Harewood, W. Yorks.
Harle Syke, Lancs.
Harlington, Beds.
Harlow, Essex.
Harpenden, Herts.
Harpole, Northants.
Harrietsham, Kent.
Harrogate, N. Yorks.
Harrow, Middx.
Harston, Cambs.
Hartley, Kent.
Hartley Wintney, Hants.

Harwich and Dovercourt, Essex.
Haslemere, Surrey.
Haslingden, Lancs.
Hastings, E. Sussex.
Hatch End, Middx.
Hatfield Broad Oak, Essex.
Hatfield Heath, Essex.
Hatherleigh, Devon.
Havant, Hants.
Haverfordwest, Dyfed, Wales.
Hawes, N. Yorks.
Harkhurst, Kent.
Haworth, W. Yorks.
Hay on Wye, Powys, Wales.
Haydon Bridge, Northumb.
Hayfield, Derbys.
Hayle, Cornwall.
Hayling Island, Hants.
Haywards Heath, W. Sussex.
Hazel Grove, Cheshire.
Hazlemere, Bucks.
Heacham, Norfolk.
Headcorn, Kent.
Headington, Oxon.
Heanor, Derbys.
Heath and Reach, Beds.
Hebden Bridge, W. Yorks.
Helmsley, N. Yorks.
Hemel Hempstead, Herts.
Hempstead, Essex.
Hemswell Cliff, Lincs.
Henfield, W. Sussex.
Henley-in-Arden, Warks.
Henley-on-Thames, Oxon.
Henllan, Dyfed, Wales.
Hereford, Hereford and Worcs.
Hermitage, Berks.
Herne Bay, Kent.
Herstmonceux, E. Sussex.
Hertford, Herts.
Hessle, N. Humberside.
Heswall, Merseyside.
Hexham, Northumb.
High Bentham, N. Yorks.
High Wycombe, Bucks.
Highbridge, Somerset.
Highcliffe, Dorset.
Hinckley, Leics.
Hindhead, Surrey.
Hindon, Wilts.
Hinton Waldrist, Oxon.
Hitchin, Herts.
Hockley Heath, W. Mids.
Hodnet, Shrops.
Holbeach, Lincs.
Holbeck, Lincs.
Hollingbourne, Kent.
Hollinwood, Lancs.
Holme, Cumbria.
Holmfirth, W. Yorks.
Holsworthy, Devon.
Holt, Clwyd, Wales.
Holt, Norfolk.
Honiton, Devon.
Horam, E. Sussex.
Horbury, W. Yorks.
Horley, Surrey.
Horncastle, Lincs.
Horndean, Hants.
Hornsea, N. Humberside.
Horrabridge, Devon.
Horsebridge, E. Sussex.
Horstead, Norfolk.
Horwich, Lancs.
Houndwood, Berwicks., Scot.
Hoylake, Merseyside.
Huby, N. Yorks.
Hucknall, Notts.
Huddersfield, W. Yorks.
Hughendon Valley, Bucks.
Hull, N. Humberside.
Hundleby, Lincs.
Hungerford, Berks.
Hunstanton, Norfolk.
Huntercombe, Oxon.
Hursley, Hants.
Hurst, Berks.
Hurst Green, E. Sussex.
Hurstpierpoint, W. Sussex.
Husbands Bosworth, Leics.
Huxham, Devon.
Hyde, Cheshire.
Hythe, Kent.

I

Ibstock, Leics.
Ickleton, Cambs.
Ilford, Essex.
Ilkeston, Derbys.
Ilkley, W. Yorks.
Ilminster, Somerset.
Inchture, Perths., Scot.
Ingatestone, Essex.
Instow, Devon.
Inverness, Inver., Scot.
Ipswich, Suffolk.
Ironbridge, Shrops.
Isleworth, Middx.
Islip, Northants.
Iver, Bucks.
Ixworth, Suffolk.

J

Jacobstowe, Devon.
Jedburgh, Roxbs., Scot.
Jesmond, Tyne and Wear.

K

Kegworth, Leics.
Keighley, W. Yorks.
Kelvedon, Essex.
Kempsford, Glos.
Kempston, Beds.
Kendal, Cumbria.
Kenilworth, Warks.
Kennington, Kent.
Kentisbeare, Devon.
Kenton, Middx.
Kesgrave, Suffolk.
Kessingland, Suffolk.
Keswick, Cumbria.
Kettering, Northants.
Kew, Surrey.
Kew Green, Surrey.
Kibworth Beauchamp, Leics.
Kidderminster, Hereford and Worcs.
Kidlington, Oxon.
Kidwelly, Dyfed, Wales.
Kilbarchan, Renfrews., Scot.
Kilham, N. Humberside.
Killamarsh, Derbys.
Killearn, Stirls., Scot.
Killin, Perths., Scot.
Killinghall, N. Yorks.
Kilmalcolm, Renfrews., Scot.
Kilmarnock, Ayr, Scot.
Kilmichael Glassary, Argyll, Scot.
Kiltarlity, Inver., Scot.
Kimpton, Herts.
Kinbuck, Perths., Scot.
Kincardine O'Neil, Aberdeens., Scot.
Kineton, Warks.
Kinghorn, Fife, Scot.
Kings Langley, Herts.
Kings Lynn, Norfolk.
Kingsand, Cornwall.
Kingsbridge, Devon.
Kingsley, Staffs.
Kingsthorpe, Northants.
Kingston-on-Spey, Moray, Scot.
Kingston-upon-Thames, Surrey.
Kingswear, Devon.
Kington, Hereford and Worcs.
Kingussie, Inver., Scot.
Kinver, Staffs.
Kippen, Stirls., Scot.
Kirdford, W. Sussex.
Kirk Deighton, N. Yorks.
Kirk Michael, Isle of Man.
Kirkby Lonsdale, Cumbria.
Kirkby Stephen, Cumbria.
Kirkbymoorside, N. Yorks.
Kirkcaldy, Fife, Scot.
Kirkcudbright, Kirkcud., Scot.
Kirton, Lincs.
Knaphill, Surrey.
Knaresborough, N. Yorks.
Knebworth, Herts.
Knighton, Powys, Wales.
Knowle, W. Mids.
Knutsford, Cheshire.

L

Lake, Isle of Wight.
Laleham, Surrey.
Laleston, Mid Glamorgan, Wales.

Lamberhurst, Kent.
Lampeter, Dyfed, Wales.
Lampeter Velfry, Dyfed, Wales.
Lancaster, Lancs.
Lancing, W. Sussex.
Landbeach, Cambs.
Lane End, Bucks.
Langford, Avon.
Langford, Notts.
Langholm, Dumfries., Scot.
Langley Burrell, Wilts.
Langport, Somerset.
Langford Budville, Somerset.
Largs, Ayr., Scot.
Larne, Co. Antrim, N. Ireland.
Laugharne, Dyfed, Wales.
Launceston, Cornwall.
Lavenham, Suffolk.
Layer-de-la-Haye, Essex.
Leafield, Oxon.
Leamington Spa, Warks.
Leavenheath, Suffolk.
Lechlade, Glos.
Ledbury, Hereford and Worcs.
Leeds, W. Yorks.
Leedstown, Cornwall.
Leek, Staffs.
Leicester, Leics.
Leigh, Kent.
Leigh, Lancs.
Leigh-on-Sea, Essex.
Leighton Buzzard, Beds.
Leiston, Suffolk.
Leominster, Hereford and Worcs.
Lepton, W. Yorks.
Leslie, Aberdeens., Scot.
Letchmore Heath, Herts.
Leuchars, Fife, Scot.
Lewes, E. Sussex.
Leyburn, N. Yorks.
Leyland, Lancs.
Lichfield, Staffs.
Limington, Somerset.
Limpsfield, Surrey.
Lincoln, Lincs.
Lindfield, W. Sussex.
Lingfield, Surrey.
Linlithgow, West Lothian, Scot.
Linslade, Beds.
Liss, Hants.
Little Abington, Cambs.
Little Bookham, Surrey.
Little Budworth, Cheshire.
Little Dawley, Shrops.
Little Haywood, Staffs.
Little Walsingham, Norfolk.
Littlebourne, Kent.
Littlehempston, Devon.
Litton Cheney, Dorset.
Liverpool, Merseyside.
Liversedge, W. Yorks.
Llanbedr, Gwynedd, Wales.
Llandeilo, Dyfed, Wales.
Llandissilio, Dyfed, Wales.
Llandogo, Gwent, Wales.
Llandovery, Dyfed, Wales.
Llandrindod Wells, Powys, Wales.
Llandudno, Gwynedd, Wales.
Llanelli, Dyfed, Wales.
Llanerchymedd, Gwynedd, Wales.
Llanfair Caereinion, Powys, Wales.
Llangollen, Clwyd, Wales.
Llanishen, S. Glamorgan, Wales.
Llanrhaeadr, Clwyd, Wales.
Llanrwst, Gwynedd, Wales.
Llantwit Major, S. Glamorgan, Wales.
Llanwrda, Dyfed, Wales.
Llanystumdwy, Gwynedd, Wales.
Londonderry, Co. Londonderry, N. Ireland.
Long Buckby, Northants.
Long Clawston, Leics.
Long Crendon, Bucks.
Long Eaton, Derbys.
Long Hanborough, Oxon.
Long Melford, Suffolk.
Long Preston, N. Yorks.
Long Stratton, Norfolk.
Longfield, Kent.
Longridge, Lancs.
Looe, Cornwall.
Lostwithiel, Cornwall.
Loughborough, Leics.
Loughton, Essex.
Low Fell, Tyne and Wear.
Lower Bentham, N. Yorks.
Lower Halstow, Kent.
Lower Kinnerton, Cheshire.
Lowestoft, Suffolk.
Loxwood, W. Sussex.
Lubenham, Leics.
Ludlow, Shrops.
Lundin Links, Fife, Scot.
Lurgan, Co. Armagh, N. Ireland.
Luton, Beds.
Lutterworth, Leics.
Lyddington, Leics.
Lydford, Devon.
Lye, W. Mids.
Lymington, Hants.
Lympsham, Somerset.
Lyndhurst, Hants.
Lynton, Devon.
Lychett Minster, Dorset.
Lytham, Lancs.
Lytham St. Annes, Lancs.

M

Macclesfield, Cheshire.
Maentwrog, Gwynedd, Wales.
Magherafelt, Co. Londonderry, N. Ireland.
Maidencombe, Devon.
Maidenhead, Berks.
Maidstone, Kent.
Maldon, Essex.
Malmesbury, Wilts.
Malpas, Cheshire.
Malton, N. Yorks.
Malvern Link, Hereford and Worcs.
Manchester, Lancs.
Manningtree, Essex.
Mansell Lacy, Hereford and Worcs.
Mansfield, Notts.
Manton, Leics.
March, Cambs.
Margate, Kent.
Market Bosworth, Leics.
Market Deeping, Lincs.
Market Drayton, Shrops.
Market Rasen, Lincs.
Market Harborough, Leics.
Market Weighton, N. Humberside.
Markington, N. Yorks.
Marlborough, Wilts.
Marlow, Bucks.
Marple, Cheshire.
Marsham, Norfolk.
Marshfield, Avon.
Martlesham, Suffolk.
Martock, Somerset.
Marton, Cleveland.
Masham, N. Yorks.
Matching Green, Essex.
Mathan, Hereford and Worcs.
Mathry, Dyfed, Wales.
Mattingley, Hants.
Mayfield, E. Sussex.
Measham, Leics.
Medbourne, Leics.
Melbourn, Cambs.
Melbourne, Derbys.
Melbury Osmond, Dorset.
Melksham, Wilts.
Melmerby, N. Yorks.
Menston, W. Yorks.
Meonstoke, Hants.
Meriden, W. Midlands.
Merrow, Surrey.
Merstham, Surrey.
Merton, Devon.
Methwold Hythe, Norfolk.
Mevagissey, Cornwall.
Micklebring, S. Yorks.
Middleham, N. Yorks.
Middlesbrough, Cleveland.
Middleton St. George, Durham.
Midhurst, W. Sussex.
Midsomer Norton, Avon.
Milburn, Cumbria.
Mildenhall, Suffolk.
Milford, Surrey.
Milford Haven, Dyfed, Wales.
Milland, W. Sussex.

Milnthorpe, Cumbria.
Milton Keynes, Bucks.
Milton Lilbourne, Wilts.
Milton-under-Wychwood, Oxon.
Milverton, Somerset.
Minchinhampton, Glos.
Minster, Kent.
Minety, Wilts.
Mirfield, W. Yorks.
Mitcham, Surrey.
Mobberley, Cheshire.
Modbury, Devon.
Moffat, Dumfries, Scot.
Monkton, Devon.
Monmouth, Gwent, Wales.
Montacute, Somerset.
Montgomery, Powys, Wales.
Montrose, Angus, Scot.
Monyash, Derbys.
Morden, Surrey.
Morchard Bishop, Devon.
Morecambe, Lancs.
Morestead, Hants.
Moreton-in-the-Marsh, Glos.
Moretonhampstead, Devon.
Morriston, W. Glamorgan, Wales.
Mousehole, Cornwall.
Much Hadham, Herts.
Much Wenlock, Shrops.
Mumby, Lincs.
Murton, W. Glamorgan, Wales.
Musselburgh, E. Loth., Scot.

N

Nailsworth, Glos.
Nantwich, Cheshire.
Nantymoel, Mid Glamorgan, Wales.
Naphill, Bucks.
Narbeth, Dyfed, Wales.
Neath, W. Glamorgan, Wales.
Needham Market, Suffolk.
Nelson, Lancs.
Neston, Cheshire.
Nether Heyford, Northants.
Nether Stowey, Somerset.
Netherbury, Dorset.
Nettlebed, Oxon.
New Bolingbroke, Lincs.
New Mills, Derbys.
New Romney, Kent.
Newark, Notts.
Newbury, Berks.
Newby Bridge, Cumbria.
Newcastle Emlyn, Dyfed, Wales.
Newcastle-under-Lyme, Staffs.
Newcastle-upon-Tyne, Tyne and Wear.
Newchurch, Isle of Wight.
Newhaven, E. Sussex.
Newmarket, Suffolk.
Newnham-on-Severn, Glos.
Newport, Dyfed, Wales.
Newport, Essex.
Newport, Gwent, Wales.
Newport, Isle of Wight.
Newport, Shrops.
Newry, Co. Down, N. Ireland.
Newton Abbot, Devon.
Newton St. Cyres, Devon.
Newton Stewart, Wigtowns., Scot.
Newtonmore, Inver., Scot.
Newtown, Cheshire.
Newtownabbey, Co. Antrim, N. Ireland.
No Man's Heath, Cheshire.
Norham, Northumb.
Normanton on Trent, Notts.
North Berwick, E. Loth., Scot.
North Cheriton, Somerset.
North Petherton, Somerset.
North Petherwin, Cornwall.
North Shields, Tyne & Wear.
North Walsham, Norfolk.
North Wraxall, Wilts.
Northallerton, N. Yorks.
Northam, E. Sussex.
Northampton, Northants.
Northchapel, W. Sussex.
Northfleet, Kent.
Northleach, Glos.
Northop, Clwyd, Wales.
Norton, Suffolk.
Norton, N. Yorks.
Norwich, Norfolk.
Nottingham, Notts.
Nuneaton, Warks.

O

Oadby, Leics.
Oakamoor, Staffs.
Oakham, Leics.
Oakley, Hants.
Oban, Argyll, Scot.
Odiham, Hants.
Okehampton, Devon.
Oldham, Lancs.
Ollerton, Notts.
Olney, Bucks.
Olveston, Avon.
Ombersley, Hereford and Worcs.
Ongar, Essex.
Orford, Suffolk.
Orkskirk, Lancs.
Orpington, Kent.
Orwell, Cambs.
Osbournby, Lincs.
Osgathorpe, Leics.
Ossett, W. Yorks.
Oswestry, Shrops.
Otford, Kent.
Otley, W. Yorks.
Ottery St. Mary, Devon.
Oughtibridge, S. Yorks.
Oundle, Northants.
Outwell, Cambs.
Oxford, Oxon.
Oxted, Surrey.

P

Padiham, Lancs.
Padstow, Cornwall.
Paignton, Devon.
Painswick, Glos.
Pailton, Warks.
Paisley, Renfrews., Scot.
Parkstone, Dorset.
Pateley Bridge, N. Yorks.
Patrington, N. Humberside.
Pattishall, Northants.
Paulerspury, Northants.
Peasenhall, Suffolk.
Peel, Isle of Man.
Pelsall, W. Midlands.
Pembroke, Dyfed, Wales.
Pembroke Docks, Dyfed, Wales.
Penarth, S. Glamorgan, Wales.
Penkridge, Staffs.
Penn, Bucks.
Penrhos, Gwent, Wales.
Penrith, Cumbria.
Penryn, Cornwall.
Penshurst, Kent.
Penzance, Cornwall.
Perranarworthal, Cornwall.
Perranporth, Cornwall.
Pershore, Hereford and Worcs.
Perth, Perths., Scot.
Peterborough, Cambs.
Petersfield, Hants.
Petworth, W. Sussex.
Pevensey, E. Sussex.
Pevensey Bay, E. Sussex.
Pickering, N. Yorks.
Pill, Avon.
Pinner, Middx.
Pitchcombe, Glos.
Pitlochry, Perths., Scot.
Pitminster, Somerset.
Pittenween, Fife, Scot.
Plaitford, Hants.
Playden, E. Sussex.
Plumley, Cheshire.
Plymouth, Devon.
Pocklington, N. Humberside.
Polegate, E. Sussex.
Ponterwyd, Dyfed, Wales.
Pontfaen, Dyfed, Wales.
Pontnewynydd, Gwent, Wales.
Pontypool, Gwent, Wales.
Pontypridd, Mid Glam., Wales.
Poole, Dorset.
Port Dinorwic, Gwynedd, Wales.

Port Erin, Isle of Man.
Port Isaac, Cornwall.
Portadown, Co. Armagh, N. Ireland.
Portaferry, County Down, N. Ireland.
Portballintree, C. Antrim, N. Ireland.
Porthcawl, Mid. Glamorgan, Wales.
Portrush, Co. Antrim, N. Ireland.
Portscatho, Cornwall.
Portslade, W. Sussex.
Portsmouth, Hants.
Portsoy, Aberdeens., Scot.
Portstewart, Co. Londonderry, N. Ireland.
Potterne, Wilts.
Potterspury, Northants.
Poynton, Cheshire.
Pratt's Bottom, Kent.
Prestbury, Cheshire.
Preston, Lancs.
Prestwick, Ayr, Scot.
Princes Risborough, Bucks.
Priors Marston, Warks.
Puckeridge, Herts.
Puddletown, Dorset.
Pulborough, W. Sussex.
Pulford, Cheshire.
Pulloxhill, Beds.
Purley, Surrey.
Pwllheli, Gwynedd, Wales.

Q

Queen Camel, Somerset.
Queniborough, Leics.
Quorn, Leics.

R

Radlett, Herts.
Raglan, Gwent, Wales.
Rainford, Merseyside.
Rait, Perths., Scot.
Ramsbury, Wilts.
Ramsdell, Hants.
Ramsden, Oxon.
Ramsey, Cambs.
Ramsey, Isle of Man.
Ramsgate, Kent.
Rattray, Perths., Scot.
Raveningham, Norfolk.
Ravenstonedale, Cumbria.
Rawtenstall, Lancs.
Rayleigh, Essex.
Reach, Cambs.
Reading, Berks.
Redbourn, Herts.
Redcar, Cleveland.
Reddish, Cheshire.
Redditch, Hereford and Worcs.
Redhill, Surrey.
Redland, Avon.
Redruth, Cornwall.
Reepham, Norfolk.
Reigate, Surrey.
Retford, Notts.
Rettendon, Essex.
Reymerston, Norfolk.
Rhosneigr, Gwynedd, Wales.
Rhos-on-Sea, Clwyd, Wales.
Rhuallt, Clwyd, Wales.
Richmond, Surrey.
Richmond, N. Yorks.
Rickinghall, Suffolk.
Rickmansworth, Herts.
Riddlescombe, Devon.
Ridgewell, Essex.
Ringway, Cheshire.
Ringwood, Hants.
Ripley, Surrey.
Ripon, N. Yorks.
Risby, Suffolk.
Riverhead, Kent.
Robertsbridge, E. Sussex.
Rochdale, Lancs.
Rochester, Kent.
Rode, Somerset.
Rodley, Glos.
Rolvenden, Kent.
Ramsey, Hants.
Ross-on-Wye, Hereford and Worcs.
Rotherham, S. Yorks.
Rottingdean, E. Sussex.
Roxwell, Essex.
Royston, Herts.
Rudgwick, W. Sussex.
Rugby, Warks.
Rugeley, Staffs.
Ruskington, Lincs.
Rumford, Cornwall.
Runcorn, Cheshire.
Rushall, W. Mids.
Rushden, Northants.
Ruthin, Clwyd, Wales.
Ryde, Isle of Wight.
Rye, E. Sussex.

S

Sabden, Lancs.
Saddleworth, Lancs.
Saffron Walden, Essex.
St. Agnes, Cornwall.
St. Albans, Herts.
St. Andrews, Guernsey, C.I.
St. Anne's-on-Sea, Lancs.
St. Austell, Cornwall.
St. Gerrans, Cornwall.
St. Helens, Merseyside.
St. Helier, Jersey, C.I.
St. Ives, Cambs.
St. Ives, Cornwall.
St. Lawrence, Jersey, C.I.
St. Leonards-on-Sea, E. Sussex.
St. Margaret's Bay, Kent.
St. Neots, Cambs.
St. Peter Port, Guernsey, C.I.
St. Sampson, Guernsey, C.I.
Saintfield, Co. Down, N. Ireland.
Salcombe, Devon.
Salisbury, Wilts.
Saltburn, Cleveland.
Saltcoats, Ayr., Scot.
Samlesbury, Lancs.
Sanderstead, Surrey.
Sandford, Devon.
Sandgate, Kent.
Sandhurst, Kent.
Sandwich, Kent.
Sarnau, Dyfed, Wales.
Sawbridgeworth, Herts.
Saxmundham, Suffolk.
Sayers Common, W. Sussex.
Scarborough, N. Yorks.
Scarisbeck, Lancs.
Scarthoe, S. Humberside.
Scone, Norfolk.
Scratby, Norfolk.
Scunthorpe, S. Humberside.
Seaford, E. Sussex.
Seaham, Durham.
Seaton, Devon.
Seaton Ross, N. Humberside.
Seaview, Isle of Wight.
Sedburgh, Cumbria.
Sedlescombe, E. Sussex.
Selkirk, Selks., Scot.
Settle, N. Yorks.
Sevenoaks, Kent.
Shaftesbury, Dorset.
Shaldon, Devon.
Shalford, Surrey.
Shanklin, Isle of Wight.
Shardlow, Derbys.
Sharrington, Norfolk.
Shawforth, Lancs.
Sheffield, S. Yorks.
Shefford, Beds.
Shenfield, Essex.
Shenton, Leics.
Shepperton, Surrey.
Shepshed, Leics.
Sherborne, Dorset.
Shere, Surrey.
Sheringham, Norfolk.
Shifnal, Shrops.
Shillingstone, Dorset.
Shipley, W. Yorks.
Shipston-on-Stour, Warks.
Shirley, Derbys.
Shirley, Surrey.
Shoreham, Kent.
Shoreham-by-Sea, W. Sussex.
Shottermill, Surrey.
Shrewsbury, Shrops.
Sible Hedingham, Essex.
Sidmouth, Devon.
Sileby, Leics.
Sittingbourne, Kent.
Skegness, Lincs.
Skewen, W. Glamorgan, Wales.

Skipton, N. Yorks.
Slad, Glos.
Sleaford, Lincs.
Smethwick, W. Mids.
Snainton, N. Yorks.
Snettisham, Norfolk.
Snodland, Kent.
Soham, Cambs.
Solihull, W. Mids.
Somerton, Somerset.
Sonning-on-Thames, Berks.
Sorbie, Wigtown, Scot.
South Brent, Devon.
South Cave, N. Humberside.
South Harting, Hants.
South Holmwood, Surrey.
South Kelsey, Lincs.
South Lopham, Norfolk.
South Molton, Devon.
South Ockendon, Essex.
South Shields, Tyne & Wear.
South Walsham, Norfolk.
Southampton, Hants.
Southborough, Kent.
Southend-on-Sea, Essex.
Southgate, W. Glamorgan, Wales.
Southport, Merseyside.
Southwell, Notts.
Sowerby Bridge, W. Yorks.
Spalding, Lincs.
Spennithorne, N. Yorks.
Spilsby, Lincs.
Stafford, Staffs.
Staines, Surrey.
Staithes, Cleveland.
Stalham, Norfolk.
Stamford, Lincs.
Standlake, Oxon.
Stanford Dingley, Berks.
Stanford-le-Hope, Essex.
Stansted, Essex.
Stapleford, Lincs.
Staunton Harold, Leics.
Steeple Clayton, Bucks.
Steeton, W. Yorks.
Steyning, W. Sussex.
Stickney, Lincs.
Stiffkey, Norfolk.
Stillington, N. Yorks.
Stirling, Stirlings., Scot.
Stock, Essex.
Stockbridge, Hants.
Stockbury, Kent.
Stockland, Devon.
Stockport, Cheshire.
Stoke Ferry, Norfolk.
Stoke-on-Trent, Bucks.
Stokesley, N. Yorks.
Stone, Staffs.
Stonham Aspal, Suffolk.
Stonham Parva, Suffolk.
Stony Stratford, Bucks.
Storrington, W. Sussex.
Stourbridge, W. Mids.
Stow-on-the-Wold, Glos.
Stradbroke, Suffolk.
Stratford-upon-Avon, Warks.
Strathblane, Stirlings., Scot.
Streatley, Berks.
Streetly, W. Mids.
Stretton, Cheshire.
Stretton-on-Fosse, Warks.
Stroud, Glos.
Sturminster Newton, Dorset.
Sudbury, Suffolk.
Suffield, Norfolk.
Sunderland, Tyne and Wear.
Sundridge, Kent.
Sunninghill, Berks.
Surbiton, Surrey.
Sutton, Surrey.
Sutton Bridge, Lincs.
Sutton Coldfield, W. Mids.
Sutton-on-Sea, Lincs.
Sutton Valence, Kent.
Swaffham, Norfolk.
Swaffham Prior, Cambs.
Swafield, Norfolk.
Swanage, Dorset.
Swanbourne, Bucks.
Swansea, W. Glamorgan, Wales.
Swindon, Wilts.
Synod Inn, Dyfed, Wales.

T

Taddington, Glos.
Tangley, Herts.
Tarporley, Cheshire.
Tattershall, Lincs.
Taunton, Somerset.
Tavistock, Devon.
Teddington, Middx.
Teignmouth, Devon.
Tenby, Dyfed, Wales.
Tenterden, Kent.
Tern Hill, Shrops.
Tetbury, Glos.
Tetsworth, Oxon.
Tewkesbury, Glos.
Teynham, Kent.
Thame, Oxon.
Thames Ditton, Surrey.
Thatcham, Berks.
Thaxted, Essex.
Thirsk, N. Yorks.
Thornaby, Cleveland.
Thorne, S. Yorks.
Thornhill, Dumfries., Scot.
Thornton Heath, Surrey.
Thornton-le-Dale, N. Yorks.
Thrapston, Northants.
Thundersley, Essex.
Thurso, Caithness, Scot.
Ticknall, Derbys.
Tideswell, Derbys.
Tillington, W. Sussex.
Tilston, Cheshire.
Timberscombe, Somerset.
Tingewick, Bucks.
Tintern, Gwent, Wales.
Tisbury, Wilts.
Titchfield, Hants.
Tiverton, Devon,
Toddington, Beds.
Todmorden, W. Yorks.
Tonbridge, Kent.
Tonge, Leics.
Tongham, Surrey.
Tonypandy, Mid. Glamorgan, Wales.
Topsham, Devon.
Torquay, Devon.
Towcester, Northants.
Trawden, Lancs.
Tredunnock, Gwent, Wales.
Tregony, Cornwall.
Treherbert, Mid. Glam., Wales.
Trent, Dorset.
Treorchy, Mid. Glamorgan, Wales.
Tring, Herts.
Truro, Cornwall.
Tunbridge Wells, Kent.
Turvey, Beds.
Tutbury, Staffs.
Twickenham, Middx.
Twyford, Berks.
Twyford, Bucks.
Twyford, Hants.
Tynemouth, Tyne and Wear.
Tywyn, Gwynedd, Wales.

U

Uckfield, E. Sussex.
Ulverston, Cumbria.
Unstone, Derbys.
Upham, Hants.
Upholland, Lancs.
Upminster, Essex.
Uppingham, Leics.
Upton-upon-Severn, Hereford and Worcs.
Usk, Gwent, Wales.
Uttoxeter, Staffs.
Uxbridge, Middx.

V

Vale, Guernsey, C.I,
Ventnor, Isle of Wight.

W

Waddesdon, Bucks.
Waddington, Lincs.
Wadebridge, Cornwall.
Wadhurst, E. Sussex.
Wakefield, W. Yorks.
Wakes Colne, Essex.
Walford, Hereford and Worcs.
Walkerburn, Peebles., Scot.
Wallasey, Merseyside.
Wallingford, Oxon.
Wallington, Surrey.
Walsall, W. Mids.

Walsden, W. Yorks.
Walton on Thames, Surrey.
Walton-on-the-Hill and Tadworth, Surrey.
Wansford, Cambs.
Wanstrow, Somerset.
Wantage, Oxon.
Warboys, Cambs.
Wareham, Dorset.
Wargrave, Berks.
Warminster, Wilts.
Warnham, W. Sussex.
Warrington, Cheshire.
Warwick, Warks.
Washington, W. Sussex.
Washington, Tyne and Wear.
Watchet, Somerset.
Water Orton, Warks.
Watford, Herts.
Watlington, Oxon.
Watton, Norfolk.
Wavendon, Bucks.
Wedmore, Somerset.
Wednesbury, W. Mids.
Weedon, Bucks.
Weedon, Northants.
Weldon, Northants.
Wellingborough, Northants.
Wellington, Somerset.
Wells, Somerset.
Wells-next-the-Sea, Norfolk.
Welshpool, Powys, Wales.
Wembley, Middx.
Wendover, Bucks.
West Bridgford, Notts.
West Byfleet, Surrey.
West Haddon, Northants.
West Harptree, Avon.
West Kirby, Merseyside.
West Knoyle, Wilts.
West Malling, Kent.
West Monkton, Somerset.
West Peckham, Kent.
West Wittering, W. Sussex.
Westbourne, W. Sussex.
Westbury, Wilts.
Westcliff-on-Sea, Essex.
Westcott, Surrey.
Westerham, Kent.
Weston, Staffs.
Weston-super-Mare, Avon.
Weston-under-Pennard, Hereford and Worcs.
Wetherby, W. Yorks.
Weybridge, Surrey.
Weymouth, Dorset.
Whaley Bridge, Derbys.
Whalley, Lancs.
Wheathampstead, Herts.
Whimple, Devon.
Whissendine, Leics.
Whitby, N. Yorks.
Whitchurch, Bucks.
Whitchurch, Hants.
Whitchurch, Hereford and Worcs.
Whitchurch, Shrops.
White Colne, Essex.
White Roding, Essex.
White Waltham, Berks.
Whitefield, Lancs.
Whitegate, Cheshire.
Whitehaven, Cumbria.
Whitfield, Kent.
Whitley Bay, Tyne and Wear.
Whitstable, Kent.
Whittington, Staffs.
Whitwell, Herts.
Whitwick, Leics.
Whixley, N. Yorks.
Wickham Market, Suffolk.
Widecombe-in-the-Moor, Devon.
Widegates, Cornwall.
Wigan, Lancs.
Wiggenhall St. Germans, Norfolk.
Wigton, Cumbria
Willingham, Cambs.
Williton, Somerset.
Wilmslow, Cheshire.
Wilshamstead, Beds.
Wilton, Wilts.
Wimborne Minster, Dorset.
Wincanton, Somerset.
Winchcombe, Glos.
Winchester, Hants.
Windermere, Cumbria.
Windlesham, Surrey.
Windsor and Eton, Berks.
Winforton, Hereford and Worcs.
Wing, Leics.
Wingham, Kent.
Winkleigh, Devon.
Winslow, Bucks.
Winyates Green, Hereford and Worcs.
Wisbech, Cambs.
Wisborough Green, W. Sussex.
Witheridge, Devon.
Witney, Oxon.
Wittersham, Kent.
Wiveliscombe, Somerset.
Wivenhoe, Essex.
Woburn, Beds.
Woburn Sands, Bucks.
Woking, Surrey.
Wolseley Bridge, Staffs.
Wolverhampton, W. Mids.
Woodbridge, Suffolk.
Woodbury, Devon.
Woodchurch, Kent.
Woodford Green, Essex.
Woodford Halse, Northants.
Woodhall Spa, Lincs.
Woodhouse Eaves, Leics.
Woodstock, Oxon.
Woodville, Derbys.
Woolacombe, Devon.
Wooler, Northumb.
Woolhampton, Berks.
Woolpit, Suffolk.
Woore, Shrops.
Worcester, Hereford and Worcs.
Worsley, Lancs.
Wortham, Suffolk.
Worthing, W. Sussex.
Wotton-under-Edge, Glos.
Wrabness, Essex.
Wragby, Lincs.
Wraysbury, Berks.
Wrentham, Suffolk.
Wrexham, Clwyd, Wales.
Wrington, Avon.
Wroughton, Wilts.
Wroxham, Norfolk.
Wymeswold, Leics.
Wymondham, Norfolk.

Y

Yarm, Cleveland.
Yarmouth, Isle of Wight.
Yatton, Avon.
Yatton, Hereford and Worcs.
Yazor, Hereford and Worcs.
Yealand Conyers, Lancs.
Yeaveley, Derbys.
Yeovil, Somerset.
York, N. Yorks.
Yoxall, Staffs.
Yoxford, Suffolk.
Ystradgynlais, Powys, Wales.

DEALERS' INDEX

ALPHABETICAL LIST OF SHOPS AND DEALERS AND THE NAME OF THE TOWN AND COUNTY UNDER WHICH THEY APPEAR IN THIS GUIDE

In order to facilitate reference to dealers, this index lists separately both the names of dealers and their trade names, i.e. the name of their shop or business, as well as the towns and counties under which they are to be found in this Guide. Thus A.E. Jones and C. Smith of High St. Antiques will be indexed under

Jones, A.E., Town, County
Smith, C., Town, County
and High St. Antiques, Town, County

Where there are a large number of dealers in one town, the shop name has been added in brackets after the dealer, i.e.

A.E. Jones, Town, County (High Street Antiques).

Stallholders at markets are indicated by abbreviations after their listing.

i.e. Smith, J., London, W.8. Ant. Hyp.
= J. Smith is to be found as a stallholder under entry for Antique Hypermarket, London, W.8.

Market Abbreviations

Alf. Ant. Mkt.	=	Alfies's Antique Market.
Ant. Ant. Mkt.	=	Antiquarius Antique Market.
Ant. C.	=	Antique Centre.
Ant. Mkt.	=	Antique Market.
B. Ant. Mkt.	=	Bath Antique Market.
B. St. Ant. G.	=	Bath Street Antiques Galleries.
B. St. Ant. C.	=	Bond Street Antique Centre.
B. St. Silv. Galls.	=	Bond Street Silver Galleries.
Ber. Ant. Whse.	=	Bermondsey Antique Warehouse.
Bex. Ant. C.	=	Bexhill Antique Centre.
C. Ant. and Craft C.	=	Carlisle Antique and Craft Centre.
Chen. Gall.	=	Chenil Galleries.
Clift. Ant. Mkt.	=	Clifton Antique Market.
C. Ant. C.	=	Cotswold Antiques Centre.
G. Ant. Mkt.	=	Grays Antique Market.
G. Mews	=	Grays Mews Antique Market.
G. Port	=	Grays Portobello.
Gt. West. Ant. C.	=	Great Western Antique Centre.
Gt. West. Ant. C. Wed. Mkt.	=	Great Western Antique Centre Wednesday Market.
Ham. Ant. Emp.	=	Hampstead Antique Emporium.
Hastings A.C.	=	Hastings Antique Centre
L. Arc.	=	The Lamb Arcade.
L. Ant. Mkt.	=	Leominster Antique Market.
Lon. Silv. Vts.	=	London Silver Vaults.
Mid. Ant. Mkt.	=	Midhurst Antique Market.
N. Ant. Wrhse.	=	Newark Antique Warehouse.
N. A. Ant. C.	=	Newton Abbot Antique Centre.
N.W. Ant. C.	=	North Western Antique Centre.
Royal Ex. S.C.	=	Royal Exchange Shopping Centre.
S. Ant. C.	=	Sandgate Antiques Centre.
Smith St. A.C.	=	Smith Street Antique Centre.
Tor. Ant. C.	=	Torquay Antique Centre.
Vict. Vill.	=	The Victorian Village.
W. Pk. Ant. Pav.	=	West Park Antiques Pavilion.
Wob. Ab. Ant. C.	=	Woburn Abbey Antiques Centre.

A

3 L's Antiques, Eccleston, Lancs.
7-9 The Arcade, Worthing, W. Sussex.
19 Nort Blob incorporating Serendipity, Leeds, W. Yorks.
20th Century, Cambridge, Cambs.
20th Century Antiques, Huddersfield, W. Yorks.
20th Century Gallery, London, S.W.6.
"27a", Bath, Avon.
(55) for Decorative Living, London, S.W.6.
"55" Antiques, Hull, N. Humberside.
139 Antiques, London, N.16.
235 Antiques, Camberley, Surrey.
634 Kings Road, London, S.W.6.
A1A Antiques, Ulverston, Cumbria.
A. and C. Antiques, Sheffield, S. Yorks.
A. & D. Antiques, Blandford Forum, Dorset.
A.D.C. Heritage Ltd., London, W.1.
A.E. Gallery, London, W.8. Kensington Church St. Ant. C.
A. & F. Partners, Faringdon, Oxon.
A. & G. Antiques, London, W.1. G. Ant. Mkt.
A. and J. Antiques, Newark, Notts. N. Ant. Wrhse.
A.M. Antiques, Newark, Notts. N. Ant. Wrhse.
A.S. Antiques, Manchester, Lancs.
A Thing of Beauty, Farnham Common, Bucks.
Aagaard Ltd., Robert, Knaresborough, N. Yorks.
Aalders, M. and E., London, W.5.
Aaron Antiques, Morriston, W. Glam., Wales.
Aaron Antiques, Snodland, Kent.
Aaron Antiques, Tunbridge Wells, Kent.
Aaron (London) Ltd., Didier, London, S.W.1.
Aaron Gallery, London, W.1.
Aaron, M. & D., London, W.1.
Aarquebus Antiques, St. Leonards-on-Sea, E. Sussex.
A-B Gallery, Salcombe, Devon.
Aba, Preston, Lancs. N.W. Ant. C.
Abacus Antiques, London, W.1. G. Ant. Mkt.
Abacus Antiques, Maldon, Essex.
Abacus Antiques, Manchester, Lancs.
Abbey Antique Shop, Whalley, Lancs.
Abbey Antiques, Accrington, Lancs.
Abbey Antiques, Glastonbury, Somerset.
Abbey Antiques, Hastings, E. Sussex.
Abbey Antiques, Hollinwood, Lancs.
Abbey Antiques, Ickleton, Cambs.
Abbey Antiques, Market Harborough, Leics.
Abbey Antiques, Ramsey, Cambs.
Abbey Antiques, Tewkesbury, Glos.
Abbey Antiques, Tintern, Gwent, Wales.
Abbey Antiques and Fine Art, Hemel Hempstead, Herts.
Abbey Galleries, Bath, Avon.
Abbey House, Derby, Derbys.
Abbots House, Glastonbury, Somerset.
Abbott Antiques, A., Ipswich, Suffolk.
Abbott Antiques and Country Pine (formerly Olwen Carthew), London, S.E.26.
Abbott, C. and A., Hartley Wintney, Hants.
Abbott, H., East Molesey, Surrey.
Abbott and Holder, London, W.C.1.
Abbott, H. and K., Bexhill-on-Sea, E. Sussex. Bex. Ant. C.
Abbott, J.L., East Molesey, Surrey.
Abbott, K., Bexhill-on-Sea, E. Sussex. Bex. Ant. C.
Abbott, Nicholas, Hartley Wintney, Hants.
Abbott, S. & R., Needham Market, Suffolk.
Abe, Emmy, London, W.1. B. St. Ant. C.
Aderdare Park Antiques, Aberdare, Mid-Glam., Wales.
Aberdeen House Antiques, London, W.5.
Aberford Antiques Ltd., Aberford, W. Yorks.
Abinger Bazaar, Abinger Hammer, Surrey.
Abington Books, Little Abington, Cambs.
Abode, Stratford-upon-Avon, Warks.
Abrahams Books, Mike, Lichfield, Staffs.
Abramov, Eli, London, W.1. B. St. Ant.C.
Abrehart, S. and F.T., Beccles, Suffolk.
Abridge Antique Centre, Abridge, Essex.
Abstract, London, W.8. Kensington Church St. Ant. C.
Aby, R., Penzance, Cornwall.
Acanthus Antiques, London, S.W.19.
Academy Antiques, West Byfleet, Surrey.
Accossato, G., London, S.W.3., Chen. Gall.
Accurate Trading Co., London, W.1. B. St. Ant. C.
Ace Antiques, Hollinwood, Lancs.
Ackerman and Son Ltd., Arthur, London, W.1.
Ackrill, B.D. and B.G., Tetbury, Glos.
Ackroyd, J.L., Godalming, Surrey.
Acomb Antiques, York, N. Yorks.
Acorn Antiques, Deganwy, Gwynedd, Wales.
Acorn Antiques, Bideford, Devon.
Acorn Antiques, Dulverton, Somerset.
Acorn Antiques, London, S.E.21.
Acorn Antiques, Manchester, Lancs.
Acorn Antiques, Stow-on-the-Wold, Glos.
Acorn Antiques, Towcester, Northants.
Acquisitions (Fireplaces) Ltd., London, N.W.1.
Adam Antiques, Burnham-on-Sea, Somerset.
Adam, D., Edenbridge, Kent.
Adam, D., Lindfield, W. Sussex.
Adam Gallery, Bath, Avon.
Adamas Antiques, Manchester, Lancs. Royal Ex. S.C.
Adams, Moreton-in-Marsh, Glos.
Adams Antiques, Chester, Cheshire
Adams Antiques, London, N.W.1.
Adams Antiques, Market Drayton, Shrops.
Adams Antiques, St. Ives, Cambs.
Adams, Beth, London, N.W.8. Alf. Ant. Mkt.
Adams, B. and T., Chester, Cheshire.
Adams, D., London, W.C.2. (Tooley, Adams & Co. Ltd.)
Adams Antiques, D.C., Tunbridge Wells, Kent.
Adams, G., Debenham, Suffolk.
Adams, J., London, S.W.14.
Adams Antiques, Joan, Rickinghall, Suffolk.

Adams, Lesley, Fakenham, Norfolk. Ant. C.
Adams, Mr. and Mrs. L., Moreton-in-Marsh, Glos.
Adams Ltd., Norman, London, S.W.3.
Adams, N. and S., Lympsham, Somerset.
Adams, N.W. and S.M., Weston-super-Mare, Avon.
Adams, P., Ipswich, Suffolk. (Country Bygones and Antiques)
Adams Antiques, Rodney, Pwllheli, Gwynedd, Wales.
Adams Room Antiques Ltd., London, S.W.19.
Adams Bygones Shop, Tony, Ipswich, Suffolk.
Adams Antiques, Yvonne, Ashbourne, Derbys.
Adams, Mrs. Y.S., Ashbourne, Derbys.
Adamson, Alexander, Kirkby Lonsdale, Cumbria.
Adamson Armoury, J.K., Skipton, N. Yorks.
Addinall, M.T., Driffield, N. Humb.
Addingham Antiques, Addingham, W. Yorks.
Addison, D., Blackpool, Lancs.
Addison Fine Art, London, W.1.
Addison Antiques, Michael, Purley, Surrey.
Addison, M. and N. Purley, Surrey.
Addison-Ross Gallery, London, S.W.1.
Addrison, Mr. and Mrs., Windsor and Eton, Berks.
Addrison Bros., Windsor and Eton, Berks.
Adkins, R.T. and P., Alcester, Warks.
Adler, L. and M., Tunbridge Wells, Kent (Hadlow Antiques).
Adne and Naxos, Northampton, Northants.
Afford, S. and J., London, N.1. The Mall.
Affordable Antiques, Portsmouth, Hants.
Afshar, Sormeh, London, N.W.8. Alf Ant. Mkt.
Age of Elegance, London, S.W.14.
Ager, A., Ashburton, Devon.
Ager-Harris, J.W. and R.E. Easingwold, N. Yorks.
Ages Ago Antiques, Preston, Lancs. N.W Ant. C.
Ages Ago Antiques, St. Agnes, Cornwall.
Agnew, A., London, W.8. (Stocksprings Antiques).
Agnew and Son Ltd., Thomas, London, W.1.
Agnus, Clare, Suffolk.
Ahmed, A.H., Brighton, E. Sussex. (Alexandria Antiques)
Ahuan (U.K.) Ltd., London, S.W.1.
Aigin, C., Henley-on-Thames, Oxon.
Ailsa Gallery, Twickenham, Middx.
Aindow, R. and A.O., Kendal, Cumbria.
Ainslie, Robert, Kippen, Stirls., Scot.
Ainstie Antiques, Robert, Perth, Perths., Scot.
Ainslie, T.S. and A., Perth, Perths., Scot.
Ainslie's Antique Warehouse, Perth, Perths., Scot.
Aird-Gordon Antiques, Whitby, N. Yorks.
Airdale Antiques, Hartley Wintney, Hants.
Al Mashreq Galleries, London, W.8.
Ala Ryba, London, N.W.3. Ham. Ant. Emp.
Aladdin Antiques, Lincoln, Lincs.
Aladdin's Cave, Freshwater, I. of Wight.
Aladdin's Cave, Grasmere, Cumbria.
Aladdin's Cave, Great Malvern, Hereford and Worcs.
Aladdin's Cave, Leeds, W. Yorks.
Alan Ltd., Adrian, Brighton, E. Sussex.
Alan, Manfred, London, N.W.8. Alf. Ant. Mkt.
Albany Antiques, Glasgow, Lanarks., Scot.
Albany Antiques Ltd., Hindhead, Surrey.
Albemarle Gallery, London, W.1.
Albert and Victoria, London, E.4.
Albert's Cigarette Card Specialists, Twickenham, Middx.
Albion Antiques, Kettering, Northants.
Albion Antiques, Manchester, Lancs.
Aldbrook, M., London, W.8. (Paravent).
Aldeburgh Galleries, Aldeburgh, Suffolk.
Alder, T.A. Codford, Wilts.
Alderley Antiques, Alderley Edge, Cheshire.
Alderson, Bath, Avon.
Alderson, C.J.R., Bath, Avon.
Aldiss, Grace, Fakenham, Norfolk. Ant. C.
Aldred, L.J., Cambridge, Cambs. (Dolphin Antiques).
Aldridge, H. and L., Llandudno, Gwynedd, Wales.
Alexander Antiques, Cardiff, Glam., Wales.
Alexander Antiques, Henfield, W. Sussex.
Alexander Antiques, Manchester, Lancs. Royal Ex. S.C.
Alexander Antiques, Portrush, Co. Antrim, N. Ireland.
Alexander Antiques, St. Andrews, Guernsey, C.I.
Alexander and Berendt Ltd., London, W.1.
Alexander Gallery, Bristol, Avon.
Alexander, G., London, S.W.3. Ant. Ant. Mkt.
Alexander, Molly, Seaford, E. Sussex.
Alexander, Richard, Seaford, E. Sussex.
Alexander, R. and Mrs., M. and D., Portrush, Co. Antrim, N. Ireland.
Alexandria Antiques, Brighton, E. Sussex.
Alff, E.R., St. Leonards-on-Sea, E. Sussex.
Alfies Antique Market, London, N.W.8.
Alfred's Old Curiosity Shop, Mr., incorporating James Morris, Fine Art Dealer, Southampton, Hants.
Alfriston Antiques, Alfriston, E. Sussex.
Ali Baba, Bristol, Avon. Clift. Ant. Mkt.
Alice's, London, W.11.
Alice's Antiques, Llanelli, Dyfed, Wales.
Alicia Antiques, Wallingford, Oxon. L. Arc.
All Our Yesterdays Country Antiques and Bygones, Holbeach, Lincs.
All Our Yesterdays of Lytham, Lytham St. Annes, Lancs.
Allam, Mrs. J., Walton-on-the-Hill and Tadworth, Surrey.
Allan, C., Cheadle Hume, Cheshire.
Allan, James, Swansea, W. Glam., Wales.
Allan, S.J., Swansea,W. Glam., Wales.
Allan's Antiques and Reproductions, Cheadle Hume, Cheshire.
Allanton Antiques, Auldgirth, Scot.
Allchin Antiques, William, Norwich, Norfolk.
Allcroft, Antiques, Michael, Hayfield, Derbys.

Allen, Armin B., London, S.W.1.
Allen, A.P. and D.A., Lytham, Lancs.
Allen and Co., Alfred S., South Ockendon, Essex.
Allen Avery Interiors, Haslemere, Surrey.
Allen, Mrs. C.L., Garstang, Lancs.
Allen, F.J. and G. J., Tutbury, Staffs.
Allen Gallery, The, Kenilworth, Warks.
Allen, G. Julian, Admaston, Staffs.
Allen and Co. (The Horseman's Bookshop) Ltd., J.A., London, S.W.1.
Allen Watch and Clock Maker, M., Four Oaks, W. Mids.
Allen, M.A., Four Oaks, W. Mids.
Allen, N.P., Kenilworth, Warks.
Allen Antiques Ltd., Peter, London, S.E.15.
Allen, P.L., Chertsey, Surrey.
Allen, Mrs. S., Monyash, Derbys.
Allen, Trevor, London, S.W.3. Ant. Ant. Mkt.
Allen, Trevor, London, S.W.3. Chen. Gall.
Allen's Antiques, Stapleford, Lincs.
Allen's (Branksome) Ltd., Branksome, Dorset.
Allin, P., Cowbridge, S. Glam, Wales.
Allison Antiques, Donald, Preston, Lancs.
Allison, P. and P., Hull, N. Humberside.
Allison, P. and P., Preston, Lancs. N.W. Ant. C.
Allison Antiques, Paul, Preston, Lancs. N.W. Ant. C.
Allison, Philip and R., London, S.W.10 (Furniture Cave).
Allison's, London, W.1. G. Mews.
Allnutt Antiques, Topsham, Devon.
Allom and Co. Ltd., P.G., Ramsey, I. of Man.
Allott, D.M., Otley, W. Yorks.
Allport-Lomax, Liz, Horstead, Norfolk.
Allsebrook, R., Shirley, Derbys.
Allsop, Duncan M., Warwick, Warks.
Allsopp Antiques, John, London, S.W.1.
Alma Antiques, Lindfield, W. Sussex.
Alma Antiques, London, N.1. The Mall.
Alma Street Warehouse, Worcester, Hereford and Worcs.
Almond, K., Preston, Lancs. N.W. Ant. C.
Almshouses Arcade, Chichester, W. Sussex.
Alpha Antiques, Manchester, Lancs.
Alpha Supplies Co., Blackburn, Lancs.
Alpren, S.A., Solihull, W. Mids.
Alps, R. & V., Westcliff-on-Sea, Essex.
Alresford Clocks Ltd., Alresford, Hants.
Alston, E., Hexham, Northumb.
Alston, R.P., Long Melford, Suffolk.
Alton Gallery, London, S.W.13.
Alvarino, E.A., Fairlie, Ayr., Scot.
Alvarino Antiques, E.A. Glasgow, Lanarks., Scot. B. St. Ant. G.
Alverstoke Antiques, Alverstoke, Hants.
Alverton Antiques, Northallerton, N. Yorks.
Alves, Mrs. M., London, S.W.3. Chen. Gall.
Alvin Antiques, Plymouth, Devon.
Alway, Marian and John, Datchet, Berks.
Always Antiques, Birmingham, W. Mids.
Amadeus Antiques, Tunbridge Wells, Kent.
Amadeus Gallery, London, N.W.8.
Amati, E., London, S.W.1 (Antiquus).
Amato, L., London, N.W.1.
Amazing Grates, London, N.2.
Ambassador House, Worsley, Lancs.
Amber Antiques, Birmingham, W. Mid.
Amber Antiques, Gloucester, Glos.
Amber Antiques, Kincardine O'Neil, Aberd., Scot.
Ambler, A.S., Leeds, W. Yorks.
Amell Ltd., Verner, London, S.W.1.
Amend Antiques, Stokenchurch, Bucks.
Amend, B., Stokenchurch, Bucks.
Amersham Antiques and Collectors Centre, Amersham, Bucks.
Amersham Investment Trust Ltd., Westerham, Kent.
Amherst Antiques, Riverhead, Kent.
Amini-Persian Carpet Gallery, Majid, Petworth, W. Sussex.
Amman Antiques, Ammanford, Dyfed, Wales.
Amor Ltd., Albert, London, S.W.1.
Amor, M., Princes Risborough, Bucks.
Amos, C.M., Sandgate, Kent.
Amos Antiques, Joan, Salisbury, Wilts.
Amos, Mrs. R., Rolvenden, Kent.
Amos, Richard, Folkestone, Kent.
Amos Antiques, Tony, Portsmouth, Hants.
Amphora Galleries, Balfron, Stirls., Scot.
Amphora Galleries, Buchlyvie, Stirls., Scot.
Ampthill Antiques, Ampthill, Beds.
Ampthill Emporium, Ampthill, Beds.
Amstad, R.J., St. Leonards-on-Sea, E. Sussex.
An Eye for Art, London, N.W.8. Alf. Ant. Mkt.
Ancestors, Bath, Avon. Gt. West. Ant. C.
Anchor Antiques Ltd., London, W.C.2.
Anchor, S., London, N.W.1. (Spatz).
Anchor, S., London, W.C.2.
Ancient and Modern, Blackburn, Lancs.
Ancient and Modern, Headington, Oxon.
Ancient and Modern, St. Austell, Cornwall.
Ancient and Modern Bookshop, Blandford Forum, Dorset.
And So To Bed, Keswick, Cumbria.
And So To Bed Ltd., London, S.W.6.
Anderman, S., East Molesey, Surrey.
Andersen, G. and V., London, W.8 (The Lacquer Chest).
Anderson, Mr. and Mrs. A., Bath, Avon (Trimbridge Galleries).
Anderson, C.W., Paisley, Renfrews., Scot.
Anderson, D. and I., Welshpool, Powys, Wales.
Anderson and Son, F.E., Welshpool, Powys, Wales.
Anderson, H., Kington, Hereford and Worcs.
Anderson, I.G., Dumfries, Dumfries., Scot.
Andersons, Southport, Merseyside.
Anderson's Antiques Ltd., St. Helier, Jersey, C.I.
Anderton, K. and J., Darwen, Lancs.
Andipa Icon Gallery, Maria, London, S.W.3.
Andrade Ltd., Philip, South Brent, Devon.
Andrea, K., London, S.W.3., Chen. Gall.
Andreae, E.J., Hartley Wintney, Hants.
Andrew, T., Bangor, Gwynedd, Wales.

Andrew, Tony, Llanerchymedd, Gwynedd, Wales.
Andrews, A., London, S.E.1. Ber. Ant. Wrhse.
Andrew's Antique Shop incorporating Exchange Jewellers, Leeds, W. Yorks.
Andrews, D.M., Richmond, Surrey.
Andrews, Meg, Harpenden, Herts.
Andrews Antiques, Michael, Bournemouth, Dorset.
Andrews Antiques, Michael, Milford, Surrey.
Andrews, R., Oundle, Northants.
Andrews, R.G., Tunbridge Wells, Kent.
Andwells, Hartley Wintney, Hants.
Andy's All Pine, London, W.14.
Angel Antique Centre, South Lopham, Norfolk.
Angel Arcade, London, N.1
Angela John Antiques, Bampton, Oxon.
Angeli, Patricia, London, W.1., G. Mews.
Anglia Antique Exporters, North Walsham, Norfolk.
Anglia Fine Arts, Colchester, Essex.
Anglo Am Warehouse, Eastbourne, E. Sussex.
Anglo-Persian Carpet Co., London, S.W.7.
Angus Antiques, Dundee, Ang., Scot.
Anita's Holme Antiques, Sheffield, S. Yorks.
Annal, E. and M., Glossop, Derbys.
Annesley, F., London, N.1. (Commemoratives.)
Anness, A. and A., Cambridge, Cambs. (Rose Cottage Antiques).
Annexe Antiques, Tunbridge Wells, Kent.
Annick Antiques, Kimpton, Herts.
Annie's Antique Clothes, London, N.1.
Anno Domini Antiques, London, S.W.1.
Ann's Antiques, Glasgow, Scot. Vict. Vill.
Ann's Antiques, Stoke-on-Trent, Staffs.
Annteaks, Abersoch, Gwynedd, Wales.
Annterior Antiques, Plymouth, Devon.
Ann-tiquities, Harrogate, N. Yorks.
Another One incorporating Fagins Alley, Norwich, Norfolk.
Another World, Edinburgh, Midloth., Scot.
Anson, Stephen, London, S.W.5.
Anthemion — The Antique Shop, Cartmel, Cumbria.
Anthony James Antiques, Whimple, Devon.
Antica, Bromley, Kent
Antica, Orpington, Kent.
Antichi, G., London, W.11.
Antics, Cobham, Surrey.
Antiquarian, The, Crossford, Scot.
Antiquarius, London, S.W.3.
Antiquatat Antiques, Wimborne Minster, Dorset.
Antiquated, London, S.W.20.
Antique Arcade, The, Stratford-upon-Avon, Warks.
Antique and Art, Northallerton, N. Yorks.
Antique Atlas, The, East Grinstead, W. Sussex.
Antique Beds, Bristol, Avon.
Antique and Book Collector, The, Marlborough, Wilts.
Antique Carpets Gallery, London, S.W.6.
Antique Centre, The, Bournemouth, Dorset.
Antique Centre, Kidderminster, Hereford and Worcs.
Antique Centre, The, Kinver, Staffs.
Antique Centre, Moreton-in-Marsh, Glos.
Antique Centre, The, Preston, Lancs.
Antique Centre, The, Sevenoaks, Kent.
Antique Centre, Swansea, W. Glam. Wales
Antique Centre, Abingdon House, The, Honiton, Devon.
Antique Centre and Collectors Market, Adversane, W. Sussex.
Antique Centre on the Quay, The, Exeter, Devon.
Antique City, London, E.17.
Antique Clock Repair Shoppe, Gants Hill, Essex.
Antique Clocks, Harston, Cambs.
Antique Clocks by Simon Charles, Long Melford, Suffolk.
Antique Clocks by Simon Charles, Sudbury, Suffolk.
Antique Clocks — Terence Plank, London, N.1. The Mall.
Antique and Collectables, Manchester, Lancs. Royal Ex. S. C.
Antiques and Collectors Market, Salisbury, Wilts.
Antique and Collectors Market, Hemel Hempstead, Herts.
Antique and Collectors Pieces, Barnstaple, Devon.
Antique Connoisseur p.l.c., The, London, W.11. G. Mews.
Antique Corner, Ludlow, Shrops.
Antique and Design, Canterbury, Kent.
Antique Dolls, Blackpool, Lancs.
Antique Dresser, Reigate, Surrey.
Antique Exchange, The, Leeds, W. Yorks.
Antique Exporters U.K., Shirley, Derbys.
Antique Exporters of Chester, Chester, Cheshire.
Antique Fireplace, The, Manchester, Lancs. Royal Ex. S.C.
Antique Fireplace Centre, Plymouth, Devon.
Antique Fireplaces, Manchester, Lancs.
Antique Forum (Birmingham) Ltd., Birmingham, W. Mids.
Antique Forum (Birmingham) Ltd., Hemel Hempstead, Herts.
Antique Forum (Birmingham) Ltd., Newcastle-under-Lyme, Staffs.
Antique Forum Ltd., Rochester, Kent.
Antique and Furniture Centre, Harrogate, N. Yorks.
Antique Furniture Warehouse, Stockport, Cheshire.
Antique Furniture Warehouse, Woodbridge, Suffolk.
Antique Furniture Workshop, Wivenhoe, Essex.
Antique Galleries, The, Paulerspury, Northants.
Antique Heritage, Chipping Campden, Glos.
Antique Home, London, W.8.
Antique House, Hartley Wintney, Hants.
Antique Interiors, Tetbury, Glos.
Antique Linen and Lace, Bath, Avon. Gt. West. Ant. C.
Antique Map and Bookshop, Puddletown, Dorset.
Antique Map and Print Gallery, Worcester, Hereford and Worcs.

Antique Market, Dorchester, Dorset.
Antique Market, Eastbourne, E. Sussex.
Antique Market, The, Fochabers, Morays., Scot.
Antique Market, Newcastle-under-Lyme, Staffs.
Antique Market, Sherborne, Dorset.
Antique Mart, Richmond, Surrey.
Antique Metals, Coggeshall, Essex.
Antique Mini-Market, London, S.E.10.
Antique Militaria, Bridlington, N. Humberside.
Antique and Modern Furniture Ltd., London, S.W.5.
Antique Parlour, Hessle, N. Humberside.
Antique Patchwork Quilts, London, S.W.10.
Antique Pine, Coggeshall, Essex.
Antique Pine Shop, The, Tunbridge Wells, Kent.
Antique Porcelain Co. Ltd., London, W.1.
Antique Print Shop, The, East Grinstead, W. Sussex.
Antique and Reproduction Clocks, Preston, Lancs.
Antique Rooms, The, Maldon, Essex.
Antique Shop, Ballyclare, Co. Antrim, N. Ireland.
Antique Shop, The, Berkeley, Glos.
Antique Shop, The, Berwick-on-Tweed, Northumbs.
Antique Shop, The, Blaenau Ffestiniog, Gwynedd, Wales.
Antique Shop, The, Bournemouth, Dorset.
Antique Shop, Chichester, W. Sussex.
Antique Shop, The, Coltishall, Norfolk.
Antique Shop, The, Coventry, W. Mids.
Antique Shop, The, Crossford, Scot.
Antique Shop, The, Dolgellau, Gwynedd, Wales.
Antique Shop, Edenfield, Lancs.
Antique Shop, The, Greyabbey, Co. Down, N. Ireland.
Antique Shop, The, Haslingden, Lancs.
Antique Shop, The, Langholm, Dumfries, Scot.
Antique Shop, The, Lichfield, Staffs.
Antique Shop, The, Llandudno, Gwynedd, Wales.
Antique Shop, Milnthorpe, Cumbria.
Antique Shop, The, Newtonmore, Inver., Scot.
Antique Shop, The, Oswestry, Shrops.
Antique Shop, The, Wallingford, Oxon.
Antique Shop (Valantique), The, London, N.2.
Antique Textile Company, The, London, W.11.
Antique Trader, The, London, N.1.
Antique Warehouse, London, S.E.1.
Antique Warehouse, London, S.E.8.
Antique Warehouse, The, Warminster, Wilts.
Antique Warehouse, Worcester, Hereford and Worcs.
Antiques, Ayr, Ayr., Scot.
Antiques, Barrow-in-Furness, Cumbria.
Antiques, Carshalton, Surrey.
Antiques, Dunster, Somerset.
Antiques, Edinburgh, Midloth., Scot.
Antiques, Fairlie, Ayr., Scot.
Antiques, Menston, W. Yorks.
Antiques, West Haddon, Northants.
Antiques 132, London, W.4.
Antiques and All Pine, Swindon, Wilts.
Antiques Arcade, The, East Molesey, Surrey,
Antiques Arcade, Richmond, Surrey.
Antiques at Budleigh House, East Budleigh, Devon.
Antiques at Forge Cottage, Gargrave, N. Yorks.
Antiques at Wendover, Wendover, Bucks.
Antiques and Bargain Stores, Doncaster, S. Yorks.
Antiques and Bric-a-Brac, Wellingborough, Northants.
Antiques and Bygones, Bankfoot, Perths., Scot.
Antiques Centre, The, Bidford-on-Avon, Warks.
Antiques Centre, The, Guildford, Surrey.
Antiques Centre, Ilkley, W. Yorks.
Antiques Centre, Newcastle-upon-Tyne, Tyne and Wear.
Antiques Centre, The, Sevenoaks, Kent.
Antiques (Cheltenham), Cheltenham, Glos.
Antiques and Collectables, Harrogate, N. Yorks.
Antiques Complex, The, Leicester, Leics.
Antiques and Country Pine, Crewkerne, Somerset.
Antiques and Country Things, Saxmundham, Suffolk.
Antiques and Curios, Worcester, Hereford and Worcs.
Antiques Etc., Cambridge, Cambs.
Antiques Etc., Stretton, Cheshire.
Antiques Etcetera, Lechlade, Glos.
Antiques Etcetera, Fochabers, Scot.
Antiques Etcetera, Sandgate, Kent.
Antiques Fair, Glastonbury, Somerset.
Antiques and Fine Art, Auchterarder, Perths., Scot.
Antiques and Fine Art, Crieff, Perths., Scot.
Antiques for All, Glossop, Derbys.
Antiques and Furnishings, Bournemouth, Dorset.
Antiques Gallery, The, Lyndhurst, Hants.
Antiques and General Trading Co., Nottingham, Notts.
Antiques (Hendon) Ltd., London, N.W.4.
Antiques in Charnwood, Anstey, Leics.
Antiques and Interiors, Oxted, Surrey.
Antiques and Interiors, Potterne, Wilts.
Antiques Market, Glastonbury, Somerset.
Antiques Market, Hay-on-Wye, Powys, Wales.
Antiques — Rene Nicholls, Malmesbury, Wilts.
Antiques and Nice Things, Havant, Hants.
Antiques and Objets d'Art of Leek, Leek, Staffs.
Antiques of Ascot, Sunninghill, Berks.
Antiques of Newport, Newport, Gwent, Wales.
Antiques of Penrith, Penrith, Cumbria.
Antiques of Sherborne, Sherborne, Dorset.

Antiques on the Square, Church Stretton, Shrops.
Antiques Parlour, The, South Molton, Devon.
Antiques and Pine, Horncastle, Lincs.
Antiques — Sheila White, Sandhurst, Berks.
Antiques Shop, The, Whitegate, Cheshire.
Antiques and Things, London, S.W.11.
Antiques and Things, Pickering, N. Yorks.
Antiques Trade Warehouse, Rettendon, Essex.
Antiques Warehouse, Chalgrove, Oxon.
Antiques Warehouse, Kettering, Northants.
Antiques Warehouse, Mansfield, Notts.
Antiques Warehouse (Uxbridge), Uxbridge, Middx.
Antiques Workshop and Boulton's Antiques, Stoke-on-Trent, Staffs.
Antiquest, Sandgate, Kent.
Antiquités, London, S.W.1.
Antiques, Wallingford, Oxon. L. Arc.
Antiquum, London, N.W.5.
Antiquus, London, S.W.1.
Antiquus, Windsor and Eton, Berks.
Antonini, G., Birkenhead, Merseyside.
Antonucci, M., Plymouth, Devon.
Antrobus Ltd., Philip, London, W.1.
Anvil Antiques, Leek, Staffs.
Apollo Antiques Ltd., Warwick, Warks.
Apollo Galleries, Croydon, Surrey.
Apollo Galleries, Westerham, Kent.
Apple Market, London, W.C.2.
Appleby, I.G. and Mrs. C.B.V., St. Lawrence, Jersey, C.I.
Appleby (A. Lee and Co.), London, W.1. B. St. Ant. C.
Appleby, J.H., St. Helier, Jersey, C.I.
Appleby, K., Chester, Cheshire (Farmhouse Antiques).
Appleby, Michael, London, S.W.1.
Appleby, M.A., London, S.W.1.
Appleby, Nigel, London, S.W.3. Ant. Ant. Mkt.
Applecross Antiques, Woburn, Beds. Wob. Ab. Ant. C.
Appleton, E., London, S.W.13.
Appleyard Ltd., Roger, Rotherham, S. Yorks.
Applin Antiques, Jess, Cambridge, Cambs.
Apter, B. and Mrs. C., London, S.W.3.
Apter Fredericks Ltd., London, S.W.3.
Aqua Libra, London, W.1.
Arabella's Attic, Salcombe, Devon.
Arbiter, Wallasey, Merseyside.
Arbour Antiques Ltd., Stratford-upon-Avon, Warks.
Arca, London, W.1. G. Ant. Mkt.
Arcade Antiques Ltd., Sheffield, S. Yorks.
Arcadia Antiques, Gt. Malvern, Hereford and Worcs.
Arch Antiques, Llanishen, S. Glam., Wales.
Arch, D., Llanishen, S. Glam. Wales.
Archer, Mrs. M., Bewdley, Hereford and Worcs.
Archer, R.G., Lavenham, Suffolk.
Architectural Antiques, London, W.6.
Architectural Antiques, South Molton, Devon.
Architectural Antiques and Interiors, Ludlow, Shrops.
Architectural Heritage, Taddington, Glos.
Architectural Recycling Co., Rattray, Perths., Scot.
Archives, Birmingham, W. Mids.
Arden Antiques, Brenda, Tarporley, Cheshire.
Arden Gallery, Henley-in-Arden, Warks.
Arden Antiques, Richard, Woodbridge, Suffolk.
Ardersier Antiques, Ardersier, Invern., Scot.
Ardingly Antiques, Ardingly, W. Sussex.
Arditti, A. and J.L., Christchurch, Dorset.
Arditti, J.L., Christchurch, Dorset.
Arena, S., London, S.W.3. Ant. Ant. Mkt.
Argentum Antiques, Bexley, Kent.
Argosy Antiques, Llantwit Major, S. Glam., Wales.
Argyll Etkin Gallery, London, W.1.
Argyll Etkin Ltd., London, W.1.
Argyll House Antiques, Felsted, Essex.
Aries Antiques, Haslingden, Lancs.
Aries, Preston, Lancs. N.W. Ant. C.
Arieta, Valerie, London, W.8.
Aristo-Cat, Gerrards Cross, Bucks.
Aritake, S., London, S.W.3. Ant. Ant. Mkt.
"Ark Angel", The, Burford, Oxon.
Arkea Antiques, Bath, Avon.
Arkinstall, B. and B., Stoke-on-Trent, Staffs.
Armada Antiques, London, W.1. G. Ant. Mkt.
Armand Antiques, London, W.1. G. Mews.
Armchair Antiques, Barnsley, S. Yorks.
Armelin Interiors, Christopher, London, S.W.10.
Armelin Antiques, Karin, London, S.W.6.
Armett, C.H. Burton-on-Trent, Staffs.
Armigers, Woburn, Beds. Wob. Ab. Ant. C.
Armitage, London, W.1.
Armitage, Clayre, London, W.1. B. St. Ant. C.
Armitage, Mrs. M., Chester, Cheshire (Richmond Galleries).
Armitage, Tim, Nantwich, Cheshire.
Armitage, T.J., Nantwich, Cheshire.
Armour-Winston Ltd., London, W.1.
Armoury Antiques, London, W.1. G. Ant. Mkt.
Armoury of St. James, Military Antiquarians, The, London, S.W.1.
Arms and Armour/Chris Seidler, London, W.1. G. Mews.
Armson, F.R.B. and P.K., Yoxall, Staffs.
Armson Antiques, Mike, Woburn, Beds. Wob. Ab. Ant. C.
Armson (Antiques) Ltd., Michael, Wigginton, Herts.
Armsons of Yoxall Antiques, Yoxall, Staffs.
Armstrong, Harrogate, N. Yorks.
Armstrong, B., Nottingham, Notts.
Armstrong, C., Scarborough, N. Yorks.
Armstrong, H., Scarborough, N. Yorks.
Armstrong, J. and G., Middleham, N. Yorks.
Armstrong, M.A. and C.J., Harrogate, N. Yorks. (Armstrong Antiques).
Armstrong, R., St. Leonards-on-Sea, E. Sussex. Hastings Ant. C.
Armstrong-Davis Gallery, Arundel, W. Sussex.

Armytage, Julian, Crewkerne, Somerset.
Arnold Gallery, Peter, Wingrave, Bucks.
Arnold Studio Gallery, Phyllis, Bangor, Co. Down, N. Ireland.
Arnold, Roy, Needham Market, Suffolk.
Arnold, Sean, London, W.1. G. Ant. Mkt.
Arnold-Brown, A.S. &. J.L., Salcombe, Devon.
Arrowsmith, P.D., Bromyard, Hereford and Worcs.
Arrowsmiths of Bromyard, Bromyard, Hereford and Worcs.
Arsenic & Old Lace, Manchester, Lancs. Royal Ex. S.C.
Art and Antiques, Beccles, Suffolk.
Art and Antiques (Wadhurst), Wadhurst, E. Sussex.
Art and Art, Stoke-on-Trent, Staffs.
Art Deco, Carlisle, Cumbria. C. Ant. and Craft C.
Art Deco Ceramics Ltd., Stratford-upon-Avon, Warks.
Art Furniture (London) Ltd., London, N.W.1.
Art, T., Chiddingfold, Surrey.
Art-Antica, London, W.1. B.St. Ant. C.
Artavia Gallery, Barnstaple, Devon.
Artbry's Antiques, Pinner, Middx.
Artemesia, Alresford, Hants.
Artemis Fine Arts Limited, London, S.W.1.
Articles Antiques, High Bentham, N. Yorks.
Articles Antiques, Lancaster, Lancs.
Artifacts, Swansea, W. Glam., Wales. Ant. C.
Artisan, Edinburgh, Midloth., Scot.
Artisans Gallery, Finchingfield, Essex.
Artist Gallery, The, Bournemouth, Dorset.
Artro Antiques, Llanbedr, Gwynedd, Wales.
Arts and Antiques (Oxford) Ltd., Wantage, Oxon.
Arwas, V., London, W.1 (Editions Graphiques Gallery).
As Time Goes By, London, N.1.
As Time Goes By Antique and Tower Clocks, Norwich, Norfolk.
Asbury Antiques, Peter, Birmingham, W. Mids.
Ash Brothers Antiques, Exeter, Devon (Exeter Antique Wholesalers).
Ash House, Ramsgate, Kent.
Ash, Jim and Pat, Llandeilo, Dyfed, Wales.
Ash Rare Books, London, E.C.3.
Ash Tree Antiques, Halesworth, Suffolk.
Ashbourne Fine Art, Ashbourne, Derbys.
Ashbrook Antiques, Ken, Penzance, Cornwall.
Ashburton Marbles, Ashburton, Devon.
Ashburton Rare Books, Ashburton, Devon.
Ashcroft, Nan S., London, N.W.3.
Ashford, J.L., Newtonmore, Invern., Scot.
Ashleigh House Antiques, Birmingham, W. Mids.
Ashley Antiques, Hungerford, Berks.
Ashley Antiques, Ipswich, Suffolk.
Ashley Antiques, Parkstone, Dorset.
Ashley Gallery, Long Melford, Suffolk.
Ashley House Antiques, Measham, Leics.
Ashton, Christopher, London, N.1. The Mall.
Ashton Gower Antiques, Stow-on-the-Wold, Glos.
Ashton Gower Antiques, Burford, Oxon. Cots. Gateway A.C.
Ashton, K., Gants Hill, Essex.
Ashton, M. and C., Birmingham, W. Mids. (The Moseley Gallery).
Ashton, R., Brighton, E. Sussex.
Ashton, R., Stow-on-the-Wold, Glos.
Ashton's Antiques, Brighton, E. Sussex.
Aspidistra, Bath, Avon.
Aspidistra, The, Hitchin, Herts.
Aspinall Antiques, Walter, Sabden, Lancs.
Aspley, J., Leek, Staffs.
Aspleys Antique Market, Leek, Staffs.
Asprey (City Branch) Ltd., London E.C.3.
Asprey Ltd., Maurice, London, S.W.1.
Asprey p.l.c., London, W.1.
Assad, Elias, London, W.1. G. Mews.
Assembly Rooms Market, The, Lancaster, Lancs.
Asta, J. and V., Long Crendon, Bucks.
Astarte Gallery, London, W.1.
Asters Antique Centre, Shere, Surrey.
Astill, P.H.K., Nottingham, Notts.
Astley, David, London, S.E.1. Ant. Whse.
Astley House — Fine Art, Moreton-in-Marsh, Glos.
Astley House — Fine Art, Stretton-on-Fosse, Warks.
Astley's, London, S.W.1.
Aston, C.D. and Mrs. I., Fordingbridge, Hants.
At the Sign of the Chest of Drawers, London, N.1.
Atfield and Daughter, Ipswich, Suffolk.
Atfield, D.A. and Miss S.F., Ipswich, Suffolk.
Athole House Antiques, Bridge of Allan, Stirls., Scot.
Atholl Antiques, Aberdeen, Aberd., Scot.
Atholl Antiques, Perth, Perths., Scot.
Athollbank Antiques, Bankfoot, Perths., Scot.
Atkin, Miss D.J., Nantwich, Cheshire.
Atkins, T., Taunton, Somerset.
Atkinson, G. and J., Thurso, Caith., Scot.
Atkinson Gallery, James, Sandwich, Kent.
Atkinson Antiques, Keith, East Grinstead, W. Sussex.
Atkinson, P. and A., Dorking, Surrey.
Atkinson, R., Newport, Dyfed, Wales.
Atlantic Antiques Centres Ltd., London, W.1. (Bond Street Antiques Centre).
Atlantic Antiques Centres Ltd., London, W.11. (Rogers Antiques Gallery).
Atlantic Antiques Centres Ltd., London, S.E.1.
Atlantic Antiques Centres Ltd., London, N.1.
Atlantic Antiques Centres Ltd., London, S.W.3. (Antiquarius).
Atlantic Antiques Centres Ltd., London, S.W.3. (Chenil Galleries).
Atlantic Antiques Centres Ltd., London, E.1.
Atlantic Antiques Centres Ltd., Bath, Avon.
Atlantic Antiques Centres Ltd., Taunton, Somerset.
Atlantic Bay Carpets, London, W.1.
Atlantis Bookshop, London, W.C.1.
Atrium Antiques, Guisborough, Cleveland.

Atrium Antiques and Interiors Ltd., Woburn, Beds.
Attic, The, Baldock, Herts.
Attic, The, Inverness, Inver., Scot.
Attic, The, Wallington, Surrey.
Attic Antiques, Brighton, E. Sussex.
Attic Antiques, Penzance, Cornwall.
Attic Antiques, Wisbech, Cambs.
Attic Cellar, St. Ives, Cornwall.
Attic Gallery, Wisbech, Cambs.
Attic (Sevenoaks) Ltd., A.B.A., The, Brasted, Kent.
Atticus Books, Southend-on-Sea, Essex.
Atwell, B., South Molton, Devon.
Audley Art, London, N.1. The Mall.
Audley House Antiques, Osbournby, Lincs.
Audraw Ltd., Soham, Cambs.
Audus L., Soham, Cambs.
Auld, C.J., Greyabbey, Co. Down, N. Ireland.
Auld, Ian, London, N.1.
Auldearn Antiques, Auldearn, Nairns., Scot.
Aune Valley Antiques, Aveton Gifford, Devon.
Aura Antiques, Masham, N. Yorks.
Aust, B., London, S.E.20.
Austen, Mrs. R.A., Basingstoke, Hants.
Austen, S.T. and R.J.., Leigh-on-Sea, Essex.
Austin, A.D. and E., Whalley, Lancs.
Austin/Desmond Fine Art, Huxham, Devon.
Austin/Desmond Fine Art, London, W.C.1.
Austin/Desmond Fine Art, Sunninghill, Berks.
Austin, G., Winchester, Hants.
Austin and Sons Ltd., G., London, S.E.15.
Austin, H., A., D. and V., London, S.E.15.
Austin, J., Huxham, Devon.
Austin, J., London, W.C.1.
Austin, J., Sunninghill, Berks.
Austin, S., Swindon, Wilts.
Austin-Kaye, A.M., Chester, Cheshire.
Austwick, P. and L., Sowerby Bridge, W. Yorks.
Austy House Antiques, Birmingham, W. Mids.
Authentiques, Manchester, Lancs.
Avalon Postcard and Stamp Shop, Chester, Cheshire.
Avery, Mrs. E.B., Chiddingstone, Kent.
Avon Antiques, Bradford-on-Avon, Wilts.
Avon Gallery, The, Moreton-in-Marsh, Glos.
Avon House Antiques/Hayward's Antiques, Kingsbridge, Devon.
Avonbridge Antiques and Collectors Market, The, Salisbury, Wilts.
Avril Antiques, Bath, Avon. Gt. West. Ant. C.
Axia Art Consultants Ltd., London, W.11.
Ayers, J.A., Felmingham, Norfolk.
Ayers, L., Wansford, Cambs.
Aylwin, Mrs. R., Coggeshall, Essex.
Aytac, Osman, London, W.1. G. Ant. Mkt.
Aytag, G., London, S.W.3. Ant. Ant. Mkt.

B

B.B. Antiques, Greyabbey, Co. Down, N. Ireland.
B. and B. Antiques, Stickney, Lincs.
B.B.M. Jewellery and Antiques, Kidderminster, Hereford and Worcs.
B.C. Metalcrafts Ltd., London, N.W.9.
B.D.I., London, S.W.10 (Furniture Cave).
B.S. Antiques, East Molesey, Surrey.
B. and T. Antiques, London, W.11.
Babic, Natasha, London, S.W.1. Ant. Ant. Mkt.
Bacchus Antiques — In the Service of Wine, Cartmel, Cumbria.
Bacchus Gallery, The, Petworth, W. Sussex.
Bach, Mr. and Mrs., London, S.W.3., Ant. Ant. Mkt.
Bach Antiques, Lane End, Bucks.
Back to the Wood, Cardiff, S. Glam., Wales.
Bacon, D., London, W.1 (G. Heywood Hill Ltd.).
Baddiel, Colin, London, W.1., G. Mews.
Baddiel Golfiana, London, W.1., G. Mews.
Baddow Antique and Craft Centre, Gt. Baddow, Essex.
Badger, The, London, W.5.
Badger Antiques, Colchester, Essex.
Badgers Antiques, London, S.E.10.
Badir, R. and R., London, W.1. G. Ant. Mkt.
Badland, Miss, Bradford, W. Yorks.
Badman, J.A., Glastonbury, Somerset.
Badraie, E., London, N.W.8.
Bagatelle, Woodbridge, Suffolk.
Baggins Book Bazaar, Rochester, Kent.
Baggott, B.A., Newport, Gwent, Wales.
Baggott Church Street Ltd., Stow-on-the-Wold, Glos.
Baggott Duncan J., Stow-on-the-Wold, Glos.
Baggott, D.J. and C.M., Stow-on-the-Wold, Glos.
Bagley, B., Brighton, E. Sussex (Recollections).
Bagnall, W., Chulmleigh, Devon.
Bagshaw Antiques, G., Macclesfield, Cheshire.
Bagshawe, N., London, S.W.3. (Walker-Bagshawe.)
Bail, A., Ash Vale, Surrey.
Baile de Laperriere, H., Calne, Wilts.
Bailey, Mrs. A.M., Warminster, Wilts.
Bailey, C., London, W.11. G. Port.
Bailey, Elizabeth, Beeston, Notts.
Bailey Antique Clocks, John, Althorne, Essex.
Bailey, M., Manchester, Lancs. Royal Ex.S.C.
Bailey Architectural Antiques, M.A., Cheltenham, Glos.
Bailey, M. and S., Ross-on-Wye, Hereford & Worcs.
Bailey, R.M., Ongar, Essex.
Bailey Oriental Rugs, Robert, Ongar, Essex.
Baileys Architectural Antiques, Ross-on-Wye, Hereford & Worcs.
Bailie Antiques, Alexander, London, N.1. The Mall.
Baillache, Serge, London, W.11.
Bain, Cdr. and Mrs. H.E.R., Albrighton, Shrops.
Baines, G., Cadole, Clwyd, Wales.
Baines of Bath, G.A., Bath, Avon.

Baines, G. and J., Bath, Avon.
Baines, Henry, Southborough, Kent.
Baird, R. and V., Langholm, Dumfries, Scot.
Bakehouse Antiques, Bridgnorth, Shrops.
Baker Antiques, Anthony, Alderley Edge, Cheshire.
Baker, C.J. and B.A.J., Lavenham, Suffolk.
Baker, David, London, W.1. G. Mews.
Baker, David, London, W.11. G. Port.
Baker Oriental Works of Art, Gregg, London, W.1.
Baker Antiques, John, Newbury, Berks.
Baker, J. and J., Lavenham, Suffolk.
Baker, K.R., Woking, Surrey.
Baker, P., Modbury, Devon.
Baker, P. and P., Oban, Scot.
Baker, P.S., Bewdley, Hereford and Worcs.
Baker, R.J., Canterbury, Kent.
Baker, T., Langford, Notts.
Baker, T.R., Crawley, Hants.
Baker, T. and L., Newark, Notts. N. Ant. Wrhse.
Bakers of Maybury Ltd., Woking, Surrey.
Balchin, C.B., Brighton, E. Sussex.
Balchin and Son, H., Brighton, E. Sussex.
Baldry, Mrs. J., Gt. Yarmouth, Norfolk.
Baldwin and Sons Ltd., A.H., London, W.C.2.
Baldwin, G.E. and J.E., London, W.11.
Baldwin, R.J.S., Chichester, W. Sussex.
Baldwin, R.J.S., London, S.W.3. (Green and Stone).
Balfour-Lynn, A., London, W.C.1.
Ball Antique & Fine Art, David, Leighton Buzzard, Beds.
Ball, D. & J., Leighton Buzzard, Beds.
Ball, G., Tattershall, Lincs.
Ball, J., Porthcawl, Mid. Glam., Wales.
Ball, M. and S., Lewes, E. Sussex.
Ballantine (Painted Furniture), Belinda, Malmesbury, Wilts.
Ballard, Mrs. E.H. and S.R., Thirsk, N. Yorks.
Ballard, F. & Mrs. J.R., Weymouth, Dorset.
Ballinger, J., Stamford, Lincs.
Ballinger, J. and G.D., Ruskington, Lincs.
Balmain Antiques, Ripon, N. Yorks.
Balme Antiques, Ken, Halifax, W. Yorks.
Balmuir House Antiques, Tetbury, Glos.
Balster, Shaun, London, S.W.3. Ant. Ant. Mkt.
Bamad, Rahmet, London, W.11. G. Port.
Bampton Antiques, Bampton, Devon.
Bampton, A.J. and L., Birkenhead, Merseyside.
Banbury Fayre, London, N.1.
Bandini, L., London, W.1 (Eskenazi Ltd.).
Bangs, Christopher, London, S.W.11.
Bank House Gallery, The, Norwich, Norfolk.
Banks, B.A. and G., Woolacombe, Devon.
Banks, M.J., Stonham Aspal, Suffolk.
Banks, N. and Mrs. J., York, N. Yorks. (Danby Antiques).
Banks, P.M.L., London, S.W.15.
Banks, R., Leigh-on-Sea, Essex.
Banks, S., Finedon, Northants.
Banner Antiques, St. Leonards-on-Sea, E. Sussex.
Bannister, Mrs. A. and J., Stratford-upon-Avon, Warks.
Bannister, David, Cheltenham, Glos.
Bannister, Louise, London, N.1. The Mall.
Bar Antiques, Scarborough, N. Yorks.
Barbagallo, Sebastiano, London, S.E.1.
Barbara, London, N.W.3. Ham. Ant. Emp.
Barber, P.M., Stratford-upon-Avon, Warks.
Barbican Antiques Centre, Plymouth, Devon.
Barbican Bookshop, York, N. Yorks.
Barclay Antiques, Bexhill-on-Sea, E. Sussex.
Barclay Antiques, Headington, Oxon.
Barclay, C., Headington, Oxon.
Barclay House Antiques, Stoke-on-Trent, Staffs.
Barclay, Mr. & Mrs. K., London, N.W.8.
Barclay, M.J. and D., Friockheim, Ang., Scot.
Barclay, R. and M., Bexhill-on-Sea, E. Sussex.
Barclay Samson Ltd., London, S.W.6.
Barclay, T.H. and J., King's Lynn, Norfolk.
Bardawil, Eddy, London, W.8.
Bardawil, E.S., London, W.8.
Barden House Antiques, Tonbridge, Kent.
Barder Antiques, Richard, Hermitage, Berks.
Barder, R.C.R., and P.A., Hermitage, Berks.
Bardwell Antiques, Dronfield, Derbys.
Bardwell, S., Dronfield, Derbys.
Bargain Box, Luton, Beds.
Barham Antiques, London, W.11.
Barham, A.E., Plymouth, Devon.
Barham, P.R., London, W.11.
Barker, B., Swanage, Dorset.
Barker, B., London, S.W.3. Ant. Ant. Mkt.
Barker, B. and I., Bridlington, N. Humberside.
Barker Court Antique and Bygones, York, N. Yorks.
Barker, D., Beaconsfield, Bucks.
Barker, I. & R., Pocklington, N. Humberside.
Barker, L., Ampthill, Beds.
Barker-Mill Design Associates, London, W.8.
Barkes and Barkes, London, N.W.1.
Barkes, J.N. and P.R., London, N.W.1.
Barkham Antique and Craft Centre, Barkham, Berks.
Barkoff, B., London, S.W.3. Ant. Ant. Mkt.
Barley Antiques, Robert, London, S.W.6.
Barley, R.A., London, S.W.6.
Barleycote Hall Antiques, Keighley, W. Yorks.
Barling of Mount Street Ltd., London, W.1.
Barlow, Anne, London, W.11. G. Port.
Barlow Antiques, Anne, Letchmore Heath, Herts.
Barlow, E., London, S.W.1. (General Trading Co. Ltd.)
Barlow, G., Manchester, Lancs. (The Belmont General Stores).
Barlow, J., Alderley Edge, Cheshire.
Barlow, Peter, London, W.11. G. Port.
Barman, R., Dolgellau, Gwynedd, Wales.
Barn, The, Bicester, Oxon.
Barn, The, Collingham, Notts.
Barn, The, Petersfield, Hants.
Barn Antiques, Lampeter, Dyfed, Wales.
Barn Antiques, Mumby, Lincs.

Barn Antiques, Worcester, Hereford and Worcs.
Barn Book Supply, The, Salisbury, Wilts.
Barn Court Antiques, Narberth, Dyfed, Wales.
Barn End Antiques, Hadleigh, Suffolk.
Barn Gallery, Hatfield Heath, Essex.
Barnard, Mrs. J.P., Ilminster, Somerset.
Barnard, L., Fochabers, Morays., Scot.
Barnard, Thomas, Uxbridge, Middx.
Barnes, D., Dover, Kent.
Barnes, F. & P., Clitheroe, Lancs.
Barnes Gallery, Uckfield, E. Sussex.
Barnes, H., Stafford, Staffs.
Barnes House Antiques, Wimborne Minster, Dorset.
Barnes, J.A.C. and S.J., Honiton, Devon.
Barnes, R., Henley-in-Arden, Warks.
Barnes Antiques, R.A., London, S.W.15.
Barnes, S.J. and A.R., Uckfield, E. Sussex.
Barnet Antiques, London, W.8.
Barnett, J.P., London, W.11 (S. Lampard & Son Ltd.).
Barnett, Roger, Windsor and Eton, Berks.
Barnett, R.K., Chichester, W. Sussex.
Barnicott, R. and J., Cowbridge, S. Glam., Wales.
Barnt Green Antiques, Barnt Green, Hereford and Worcs.
Barntiques, Colchester, Essex.
Barometer Fair, London, W.C.1.
Barometer Shop, The, Bristol, Avon.
Barometer Shop, Leominster, Hereford and Worcs.
Baron Antiques, Altrincham, Cheshire.
Baron Antiques, The, Manchester, Lancs.
Baron Antiques, Preston, Lancs. N.W. Ant. C.
Baron Antiques, Wolverhampton, West Mids.
Baron, C., Alresford, Hants.
Baron Fine Art, Chester, Cheshire.
Baron, H., London, N.W.6.
Baron of Earlshall, The, Leuchars, Scot.
Baron, S. and R., Chester, Cheshire.
Baron, V., London, N.W.8.
Baroq Antiques, Little Brickhill, Bucks.
Baroq at Jean Burnett Antiques, Finedon, Northants.
Barr, R. W., Croydon, Surrey.
Barrett, I. and B., Widegates, Cornwall.
Barrett and James, London, W.1.
Barrett, P., Weymouth, Dorset.
Barrett Antiques and Prints, Philip, Taunton, Somerset.
Barrett, P. and P., Taunton, Somerset.
Barrett, P.R. and S.M., Seaford, E. Sussex.
Barrett, Mrs. S.E., Seaford, E. Sussex.
Barrie, K., London, N.W.6.
Barrington, David, Brasted, Kent.
Barrington, D., London, N.1 (Yesterday Child).
Barrington, N., M. and J., Warrington, Cheshire.
Barron and Sons, J., Mevagissey, Cornwall.
Barronfield Gallery, Preston, Lancs.
Barrow Antiques, Richard, Tring, Herts.
Barrows, N., J.S. and M.J., Ollerton, Notts.
Barrymore & Co., J., Honiton, Devon.
Barry's Antiques, Gt. Yarmouth, Norfolk.
Barsley Antiques, Douglas, Eastbourne, E. Sussex.
Bartholomew, Mrs. A.M. and Miss N.M., Great Harwood, Lancs.
Bartlett, Nigel A., London, S.E.1.
Barlett Street Antique Centre, Bath, Avon.
Bartman, F., London, S.W.1 (Anno Domini Antiques).
Barton, B.A., P.G. and G.S., Leamington Spa, Warks.
Barton House Antiques, Stanford-le-Hope, Essex.
Barton, R. and C., Watford, Herts.
Bartram, Albert, Chesham, Bucks.
Bartrick, Steven D., Gloucester, Glos.
Barwick, T., London, N.1 (Old Woodworking Tools).
Basey, S., Bristol, Avon. (Relics.)
Bashir, M., London, S.W.3. Ant. Ant. Mkt.
Baskerville Antiques, Petworth, W. Sussex.
Baskerville, A. and B., Petworth, W. Sussex.
Bass, B., Cheltenham, Glos. (Montpellier Clocks).
Bass, V.E., Market Deeping, Lincs.
Bassett, G. and H., Codsall, Staffs.
Bassett, Nigel, Petworth, W. Sussex.
Bassett, N.J., Petworth, W. Sussex.
Bastillo, J., London, S.W.11. (Just a second Antiques Ltd.)
Bate, A.C., London, W.1 (Scarisbrick & Bate Ltd.).
Bate, C.J. and J.A., Kirkby Stephen, Cumbria.
Bateman, Jean A., Stratford-upon-Avon, Warks.
Bateman Antiques, J. and R., Chalford, Glos.
Bateman, W., Hoylake, Merseyside.
Bates & Sons, Eric, Coltishall, Norfolk.
Bates & Sons, Eric, North Walsham, Norfolk.
Bates Antiques, Jeffrey, Boroughbridge, N. Yorks.
Bates, J.S., Esher, Surrey.
Bates, M. and W., Carnon Downs, Cornwall.
Bates, T. and P., Tavistock, Devon.
Bates, V., London, W.11. (Virginia).
Bateson Antiques, David, Bressingham, Norfolk.
Bateson, D. and P., Bressingham, Norfolk.
Bath Antiques Market, Bath, Avon.
Bath Chair, The, Woolhampton, Berks.
Bath Galleries, Bath, Avon.
Bath Saturday Antiques Market, Bath, Avon.
Bath Stamp and Coin Shop, Bath, Avon.
Bath Street Antiques Galleries, Glasgow, Lanarks., Scot.
Bathurst, D., London, S.W.1. (The St. James Art Group).
Batley, T.C., Knutsford, Cheshire.
Batsford Antiques, Richard, Bournemouth, Dorset.
Batstone Books, Malmesbury, Wilts.
Batstone, D. and M.E., Malmesbury, Wilts.
Batten, R., Bridport, Dorset.

Bell Antiques, Eastbourne, E. Sussex.
Bell Antiques, Grimsby, S. Humberside.
Bell Antiques, Romsey, Hants.
Bell Book and Radmall, London, W.C.2.
Bell, D. and J., Banbridge, Co. Down, N. Ireland.
Bell, E., Cockermouth, Cumbria.
Bell Fine Art, Winchester, Hants.
Bell Fine Arts, Lechlade, Glos.
Bell Gallery, Belfast, N. Ireland.
Bell House Antiques, Cambridge, Glos.
Bell Harry Books, Canterbury, Kent.
Bell, H.J., Saddleworth, Lancs.
Bell, I., London, E.2.
Bell Inn Antiques, Modbury, Devon.
Bell Antiques, J. and H., Castletown, I. of Man.
Bell, J.N., Belfast, N. Ireland.
Bell of Aberdeen Ltd., John, Aberdeen, Aberd., Scot.
Bell, K.E. and B., Winchester, Hants.
Bell, N.J., Redcar, Cleveland.
Bell Passage Antiques, Wotton-under-Edge, Glos.
Bell, Raine, Long Melford, Suffolk.
Bell, R., Southport, Merseyside.
Bell, Mrs. R.A., Lechlade, Glos.
Bell, R. and J., York, N. Yorks. (St. John's Antiques).
Bell and Son, R., Shipley, W. Yorks.
Bell Street Antiques Centre, Princes Risborough, Bucks.
Bell-Air Antiques, Brighton, E. Sussex.
Bellamy, A., Romsey, Hants.
Bellamy, K. and Mrs. L., Nantymoel, Mid-Glam., Wales.
Bellevue House Interiors, South Molton, Devon.
Bellinger Antiques, C., Barnet, Herts.
Bellingham, Lesley, Stow-on-the-Wold, Glos. C. Ant. C.
Bellis Antiques, Mary, Hungerford, Berks.
Bellord, E., London, W.1. (A.D.C. Heritage Ltd.)
Belmont General Stores, The, Manchester, Lancs.
Belmont-Maitland, R., London, W.1 (Tradition Military Antiques).
Below Stairs, Hungerford, Berks.
Below Stairs, Kendal, Cumbria.
Belsten, Roger, Stiffkey, Norfolk.
Belton, Anthony, London, W.8.
Benardout, J. and D., Henley-on-Thames, Oxon.
Benardout, Raymond, London, S.W.1.
Bendall's Antiques, Castle Douglas, Kirkcud., Scot.
Bendon, H.V., Buckfastleigh, Devon.
Benet Gallery, Cambridge, Cambs.
Beney, D., Beaminster, Dorset.
Benjamin/Cook, London, W.1. G. Ant. Mkt.
Benjamin, Ronald, London, W.1. B. St. Ant. C.
Benjamin, R.S., London, N.W.8. Alf. Ant. Mkt.
Benjamin, S., London, W.1 (Halcyon Days).
Benjamin, S., London, E.C.3.
Bennett, Bath, Avon. B. Ant. Mkt.
Bennett, A., Truro, Cornwall.
Bennett, A.T.H., Totnes, Devon.
Bennett, David, London, N.W.8. Alf. Ant. Mkt.
Bennett, D.G., Blackburn, Lancs.
Bennett, F.R., Shipston-on-Stour, Warks.
Bennett G., Alderley Edge, Cheshire.
Bennett (Antiques), Julia, Dunmow, Essex.
Bennett, Paul, London, W.1.
Bennett, R., Thirsk, N. Yorks.
Bennett, William, Fakenham, Norfolk. Ant. C.
Bennison, London, S.W.1.
Benosiglio, Mr. and Mrs. S., London, W.5.
Benosiglio Ltd., S., London, W.5.
Bensley, John, Hungerford, Berks.
Benson Antiques, Cheltenham, Glos.
Benson, B., Newark, Notts. N. Ant. Wrhse.
Benson, H.F. & F., Cheltenham, Glos.
Benstead, Mrs. H., Birmingham, W. Mids. (Moseley Antiques).
Bentel, Miss B., London, S.W.3. Ant. Ant. Mkt.
Bentley, Bill, Harrogate, N. Yorks.
Bentley and Co. Ltd., London, W.1.
Bentley, M.R., Knutsford, Cheshire.
Bently Antiques, Pat, Ampthill, Beds.
Benton, J.G., Cheltenham, Glos. (Manor House Antiques)
Benton, Mrs. P.A., Measham, Leics.
Benzie, James, Aberdeen, Aberd., Scot.
Beresford-Clark, London, S.W.6.
Beresiner, Y., London, N.1. (Intercol London).
Berge, I., London, W.8. (Little Winchester Gallery)
Berger, Clark, London, S.W.3. Ant. Ant. Mkt.
Berger, Ursula and Jurgen, London, N.W.8. Alf. Ant. Mkt.
Berkeley Antiques and Replay, Tewkesbury, Glos.
Berkeley Market, Berkeley, Glos.
Berkshire Metal Finishers Ltd., Sandhurst, Berks.
Berktay, Y., Somerton, Somerset.
Bermondsey Antique Market, London, S.E.1.
Bermondsey Antique Warehouse, London, S.E.1.
Bernard, L.S., London, S.W.3 (Chelsea Rare Books).
Bernheimer Fine Arts Ltd., London, W.1.
Bernheimer, K.O., London, W.1.
Bertelsen, P., London, S.W.3. (Gallery Arcticus).
Berry, A. and Mrs. A., Lynton, Devon.
Berry Brow Antiques, Huddersfield, W. Yorks.
Berry, F.E., Disley, Cheshire.
Berry, Mrs. L., Flamborough, N. Humberside.
Berry Antiques, Lesley, Flamborough, N. Humberside.
Berry, T., Brierfield, Lancs.
Berryman Music Boxes, Shelagh, Wells, Somerset.
Berry's, Lynton, Devon.
Berry's Antiques, Brierfield, Lancs.
Berthoud, M. and N., Bridgnorth, Shrops.
Besbrode, M., Leeds, W. Yorks. (The Piano Shop)

Beslali, London, W.1. G. Mews.
Besley, P.A. and P.F., Beccles, Suffolk.
Besleys Books, Beccles, Suffolk.
Best Antiques, Woodhall Spa, Lincs.
Best Antiques, Ray, Ilminster, Somerset.
Best, R. and W., Ilminster, Somerset.
Bethell, C., Shenton, Leics.
Bethell, I., Birmingham, W. Mids. (Edgbaston Gallery).
Bethney, P.W. and J.A., Knaphill, Surrey.
Betley Court Gallery, Betley, Staffs.
Bett, H., London, W.1 (Maggs Bros. Ltd.)
Betts, T., York, N. Yorks. (Holgate Antiques).
Betty's, Leicester, Leics.
Bevan-Jones, V., St. Leonards-on-Sea, E. Sussex. Hastings Ant. C.
Beverley, London, N.W.8.
Beverley Brook Antiques, London, S.W.13.
Bevins, J.R., Ulverston, Cumbria.
Bewdley Antiques, Bewdley, Hereford and Worcs.
Bewick Antiques, Jesmond, Tyne and Wear.
Bexfield Antiques, A.B., Hitchin, Herts.
Bexhill Antique Exporters, Bexhill-on-Sea, E. Sussex.
Bexhill Antiques Centre, Bexhill-on-Sea, E. Sussex.
Bianco, L., Cheltenham, Glos. (Triton Gallery).
Bibby, R., Leigh, Lancs.
Bichard, R. and J., Bradford-on-Avon, Wilts.
Bickersteth, David, Bassingbourn, Cambs.
Biddulph, Peter, London, W.1.
Bieganski, Z., Woburn, Beds.
Biesley, M., Wallingford, Oxon. L. Arc.
Big Ben Antique Clocks, London, S.W.6.
Biggs, A.C., Worthing, W. Sussex.
Biggs, J. J. and P., Bideford, Devon.
Biggs, P.S., Bristow, Bristol, Avon. Clift. Ant. Mkt.
Bigozzi, A., London, S.W.6. (D.M.T. Antiques)
Bigwood, C., Tunbridge Wells, Kent.
Bijou Antiques, Swansea, W. Glam., Wales. Ant. C.
Bijoux Jewellers, Guildford, Surrey.
Bilby, D., London, W.1.
Bilby and Holloway, London, W.1.
Biles, J., Hartley Wintney, Hants.
Billing, D., London, S.W.3. Ant. Ant. Mkt.
Billings, J. and S.E., Kelvedon, Essex.
Binder, D. and A., London, N.W.8.
Bingham Antiques, Audrey and Brian, Whitchurch, Shrops.
Bingham, Tony, London, N.W.3.
Bingley Antiques Centre, Bingley, W. Yorks.
Bingley Antiques, Robert, Wing, Leics.
Bingley, S., Aberystwyth, Dyfed, Wales.
Binning, R., Penshurst, Kent.
Birbeck Gallery, Torquay, Devon.
Birch, C., Gt. Yarmouth, Norfolk.
Birch, C. & H., Leicester, Leics.
Birches Art Deco Shop, Leicester, Leics.
Birchwood Antiques, Abbots Bromley, Staffs.
Bird, John, Lewes, E. Sussex.
Birdcage Antiques, The, Windermere, Cumbria.
Birmingham Bookshop, Birmingham, W. Mids.
Biscoe, A., Worthing, W. Sussex.
Bishop, B. and A., Castle Combe, Wilts.
Bishop Beveridge House, Barrow on Soar, Leics.
Bishop, G.W. and N.S., Swanage, Dorset.
Bishop, J., London, W.4.
Bishop, Mrs. J.M., Leeds, W. Yorks.
Bishop, M. & S., Driffield, N. Humberside.
Bishop House Antiques, Leeds, W. Yorks.
Bishop's Antiques, London, W.4.
Bishop's of Swanage, Dorset.
Bishops Park Antiques, London, S.W.6.
Bishopsgate Antiques, York, N. Yorks.
Bishopstrow Antiques, Warminster, Wilts.
Bisram, Mr. and Mrs. R., Cranbrook, Kent.
Bits 'n' Bobs Antiques, Lundin Links, Scot.
Bits and Pieces, Farnham, Surrey.
Bizarre, London, N.W.8.
Bizarre Antiques, Bristol, Avon.
Black, A., Sheffield, S. Yorks. (Oriel Antiques).
Black Ltd., Arthur, London, W.1. B. St. Silv. Galls.
Black Cat, London, S.E.20.
Black Dog Antiques, Bungay, Suffolk.
Black Oriental Carpets, David, London, W.11.
Black Isle Antiques, Fortrose, Ross and Cromarty, Scot.
Black, Mrs. J., Warwick, Warks.
Black Lion Antiques, Conway, Gwynedd, Wales.
Black Ltd., Laurance, Edinburgh, Midloth., Scot.
Black, Manley Joseph, London, N.W.8. Alf. Ant. Mkt.
Black, Oonagh, London, N.W.8. Alf. Ant. Mkt.
Black, R.M. and G.G., Broadstone, Dorset.
Black Terry, Glasgow, Lanarks., Scot. Vict. Vill.
Blackburn, E.M., Tunbridge Wells, Kent. (Pantiles Antiques).
Blackburn, Mrs. G., Lancaster, Lancs.
Blackburn, H., Gargrave, N. Yorks.
Blackburn, Jack, Preston, Lancs.
Blackburn, Norman, London, W.11.
Blackburne, L., Neston, Cheshire.
Blackford, L., Reigate, Surrey.
Blackford, M., Calne, Wiltshire.
Blacklocks, S., Chilham, Kent.
Blackpool Antiques Centre, Blackpool, Lancs.
Blacksmith's Forge, Balderton, Notts.
Blackwell's Rare Books, Fyfield, Oxon.
Blade and Bayonet, Bournemouth, Dorset.
Bladud House Antiques, Bath, Avon.
Blaik, J., Princes Risborough, Bucks.
Blair Antiques, Pitlochry, Perths., Scot.
Blair, J., St. Albans, Herts.
Blairman and Sons Ltd., H., London, W.1.
Blake, B.G. and C.P., Burnham-on-Sea, Somerset.
Blake, K.N. and P. — Old Cottage Antiques, London, E.11.
Blake, P. and K.N. — Lanehurst Antiques, Woodford Green, Essex.
Blake, V.C.J., J.J. and S.T., Puckeridge, Herts.

Booth Gallery and Titanic Signals Archive, Westbury, Wilts.
Booth, Joanna, London, S.W.3.
Booth, J., Princes Risborough, Bucks.
Booth Antiques and Restorations, L., Stockport, Cheshire.
Booth, T.J., Rye, E. Sussex.
Boothferry Antiques, Hull, N. Humberside.
Booth's Bookshop, Richard, Hay-on-Wye, Powys. Wales.
Boothtown Antiques, Manchester, Lancs.
Bord (Gold Coin Exchange) M., London, W.C.2.
Border Sporting Gallery, Wooler, Northumb.
Bornoff, Claude, London, W.2.
Borton Fine Arts, Peter, Hindhead, Surrey.
Bosch, Milena, London, S.W.3. (Natasha Barbic) Ant. Ant. Mkt.
Boscombe Militaria, Bournemouth, Dorset.
Bosham Antiques, Bosham, W. Sussex.
Bosi, L., Edinburgh, Midloth., Scot. (Royal Mile Curios.)
Bosley, S., London, N.1.
Bosson Antiques, Peter, Wilmslow, Cheshire.
Boston Antiques Centre, Boston, Lincs.
Boston Antiques, Derek, Salisbury, Wilts.
Boston and Martine, Nicholas, London, S.W.3. Chen. Gall.
Boston Pine Co., Leeds, W. Yorks.
Botesdale Antiques, Botesdale, Suffolk.
Bothy, The, Rait, Perths., Scot.
Bothy Antiques, Market Rasen, Lincs.
Botting Antiques, John, Horam, E. Sussex.
Botting, S.M. and R.M.D., Felpham, W. Sussex.
Botting, Susan and Robert, Felpham, W. Sussex.
Bottles and Bygones, Cheltenham, Glos.
Bottomley, Andrew Spencer, Holmfirth, W. Yorks.
Bottomley, M. and B., Whitby, N. Yorks.
Bottrill, Sonia, London, N.1. The Mall.
Boulevard Antique and Shipping Centre, Leicester, Leics.
Boulevard Reproductions, Halifax, W. Yorks.
Boulton, J.A., Broseley, Shrops.
Boulton, N., Torquay, Devon.
Bourdon-Smith Ltd., J.H., London, S.W.1.
Bourne Fine Art, London, S.W.1.
Bourne Fine Art Ltd., Edinburgh, Midloth., Scot.
Bourne Gallery Ltd., Reigate, Surrey.
Bourne Mill Antiques, Farnham, Surrey.
Bourne, P., Edinburgh, Midloth., Scot. (Bourne Fine Art Ltd.).
Bourne, Mrs. P., Ramsey, Isle of Man.
Bournemouth Gallery Ltd., The, Wimborne Minster, Dorset.
Bousfield, Guy, Windsor and Eton, Berks.
Boustead Antiques, Olwyn, Chester, Cheshire.
Boustead, Mrs. O.L., Chester, Cheshire.
Boutique Fantasque, London, N.1.
Bouyamourn, Z., Redland, Avon.
Bow Antiques, Easingwold, N. Yorks.
Bow Cottage Antiques, Stratford-upon-Avon, Warks.
Bow House Antiques, Hungerford, Berks.
Bow Windows Book Shop, Lewes, E. Sussex.
Bowdell, Colin, London, W.1. G. Ant. Mkt.
Bowdell, Colin C., Newark, Notts. Castle G.A.C.
Bowden, David, London, W.1. G. Ant. Mkt.
Bowden, David, London, N.1. The Mall.
Bowden, J.A., Scunthorpe, S. Humberside.
Bowdery, M.J., Hindhead, Surrey.
Bowdler, M.A., Shrewsbury, Shrops.
Bowen, Mrs. S., Wilshamstead, Beds.
Bowerman, Mrs. E., Davenham, Cheshire.
Bowers-Jones, K.S., Deganwy, Gwynedd, Wales.
Bowie, Mrs. A., Bath, Avon. Bath Ant. Mkt.
Bowkett, Knaresborough, N. Yorks.
Bowlby, Nicholas, Uckfield, E. Sussex.
Bowler, J., Preston, Lancs. N.W. Ant. C.
Bowler, J.A., Bradford, W. Yorks.
Bowler, Mrs. R., Woodville, Derbys.
Bowler, Simon, Warwick, Warks. Smith St. A. C.
Bowles, A., London, S.W.6.
Bowman, B. and A., London, N.W.8.
Bowman, H., London, W.5.
Bowood Antiques, Wendover, Bucks.
Bowmoore Gallery, London, S.W.1.
Bowry, Stanhope, London, W.1. G. Ant. Mkt.
Bowskill, Mrs. P., Lancaster, Lancs.
Box House Antiques, London, S.W.1.
Boxer, Henry, London, W.8. Kensington Church St. Ant.
Boycott-Enigma, B., London, S.W.3. Chen. Gall.
Boyd-Carpenter, Patrick, London, W.1. G. Ant. Mkt.
Boyd-Ratcliff, G. and W., Kelvedon, Essex.
Boyer, R., Nantwich, Cheshire.
Boyes-Watson, J.P., Harrogate, N. Yorks. (Paraphenalia)
Boylan, M. and A., Market Bosworth, Leics.
Boyle, A., Blackpool, Lancs.
Boyle (Booksellers) Ltd., Andrew, Worcester, Hereford and Worcs.
Boyle, B., Ashton-under-Lyne, Lancs.
Boyle & Co., John, London, S.W.10.
Boyle, Mrs. T.B., Cobham, Surrey.
Boys, Rob, London, W.11. G. Port.
Boys Shipping, Robin, London, S.E.1. Ant. Wrhse.
Bozely, G., Eversley, Hants.
Bracebridge Gallery, Astwood Bank, Hereford and Worcs.
Bracewell, J. and E., Shawforth, Lancs.
Bracey, John R., Lincoln, Lincs.
Brackley Antiques, Brackley, Northants.
Bradbourne Gallery, Sevenoaks, Kent.
Bradbury and Son, Edward, Cheltenham Glos.
Bradbury, O., Cheltenham, Glos.
Bradbury Antiques, Roger, Coltishall, Norfolk.
Bradford Antiques and Curio Centre, Bradford, W. Yorks.
Bradley, A., Castle Douglas, Kirkcud., Scot.
Bradley, A., Kirkcudbright, Kirkcud., Scot.

Bradley, G.C., Steeton, W. Yorks.
Bradley, J.R., Cardiff, S. Glam., Wales. (Alexander Antiques)
Bradley, Peter, Guildford, Surrey. Ant. C.
Bradley, P., Middlesbrough, Cleveland.
Bradley, Mrs. P., Stockbridge, Hants.
Bradley, P. and V., Bletchingley, Surrey.
Bradley, Robert, Salisbury, Wilts.
Bradley, R.J., Ampthill, Beds.
Bradley's Antiques and Jewellery, Middlesbrough, Cleveland.
Bradshaw, Mrs. E., Blaydon, Tyne & Wear.
Bradshaw and Smith, Leominster, Hereford & Worcs. L. Ant. Mkt.
Braemar Antiques Ltd., White Waltham, Berks.
Bragg Antiques, John, Lostwithiel, Cornwall.
Bragge Antiques, Lesley, Petworth, W. Sussex.
Bragge, N.H. and J.R., Rye, E. Sussex.
Bragge and Sons, Rye, E. Sussex.
Braithwaite, Catherine, London, N.W.8. Alf. Ant. Mkt.
Bramley Antiques, Thundersley, Essex.
Brampton Mill Antiques, Brampton, Cambs.
Bramwell, Derek, Woodstock, Oxon.
Bramwell, R.H., Cambridge, Cambs. (Dolphin Antiques).
Branagh, J., Coventry, W. Mids.
Brancaster Staithe Antiques, Brancaster Staithe, Norfolk
Brand Antiques, Colin, Stow-on-the-Wold, Glos.
Brand, Mrs. D.V., Wotton-under-Edge, Glos.
Brand, L.B., Boston, Lincs.
Brandl, E., London, S.W.6.
Brandler Galleries, Brentwood, Essex.
Brandler, J., Brentwood, Essex.
Brandt Oriental Antiques, London, S.W.6.
Brandt, R., London, S.W.6. (Brandt Oriental Antiques).
Branksome Antiques, Branksome, Dorset.
Branson, Mr. and Mrs. R.D., Leicester, Leics.
Brantham Mill Antiques, Brantham, Suffolk.
Brass & Son, Lawrence, Bath, Avon.
Brassington, Mr. and Mrs., Yeaveley, Derbys.
Brasted Antiques and Interiors, Brasted, Kent.
Bratton Antiques, Westbury, Wilts.
Braund, J.F., Thaxted, Essex.
Braverman, B., Runcorn, Cheshire.
Bray, Ltd., H.H., Warwick, Warks.
Bray, M., C.A. and T.M., Woodhouse Eaves, Leics.
Brazier, T.R.G., London, N.W.3.
Brazil Antiques Ltd., Westerham, Kent.
Breakspeare Antiques, M. and S., Tetbury, Glos.
Brean, L.M. and R.C., Pontypool, Gwent, Wales.
Brear, Jean, Halifax, W. Yorks.
Breck Antiques, Nottingham, Notts.
Breeden Antiques, Roy, Dorking, Surrey.
Breese, Ursula, Woburn, Beds. Wob. Ab. Ant. C.
Breeze Farm Antiques, Driffield, N. Humberside.
Breeze, G.E., London, S.W.10. (Furniture Cave)
Bremner, Mr. and Mrs. C., Maidstone, Kent.
Bret-Day, Philip, London, W.1. (Patrick Boyd-Carpenter). G. Ant. Mkt.
Brett and Sons Ltd., Arthur, Norwich, Norfolk.
Brett, B., Walkerburn, Peebles., Scot.
Brett, M. & T., Newport, I. of Wight.
Brett, Simon, Moreton-in-Marsh, Glos.
Brewer Antiques, Ann, Wallingford, Oxon. L. Arc.
Brewer, Michael, Lincoln, Lincs.
Brewer, M.N., Lincoln, Lincs.
Brewster, Avril, Fakenham, Norfolk. Ant. C.
Brewster, Brian, Fakenham, Norfolk. Ant. C.
Brewster, B.D., Fakenham, Norfolk. Ant. C.
Brewster, D.J., Glasgow, Lanarks., Scot. (Muirhead Moffat and Co.).
Brian Antiques, Luigi, London, W.C.2. Lon. Silv. Vaults.
Bric-a-Brac, The, Whitley Bay, Tyne and Wear.
Brice, Robin, Newton Abbot, Devon. N.A. Ant. C.
Brick, D., Riverhead, Kent.
Brickman, L., Brighton, E. Sussex (Prinny's Antique Gallery).
Brickwood, S., Lytham St. Annes, Lancs.
Bridge Antiques, Richmond, Surrey.
Bridge Antiques, Stourbridge, W. Mids.
Bridge Antiques, Sutton Bridge, Lincs.
Bridge Antiques, Wingham, Kent.
Bridge Antiques, Christine, London, S.W.13.
Bridge House Antiques, Nantwich, Cheshire.
Bridge House Antiques, Penshurst, Kent.
Bridge Street Antiques, Bungay, Suffolk.
Bridges, J.D. and B., Beverley, N. Humberside.
Bridges, P., Scarthoe, S. Humberside.
Bridgford Antiques, West Bridgwood, Notts.
Bridgwater Antiques Market, Bridgwater, Somerset.
Bridgwater, David, Marshfield, Avon.
Bridle Antiques, Tamworth, Staffs.
Bridport Antique Centre, Bridport, Dorset.
Briere, Gilbert and Edna, Fakenham, Norfolk. Ant. C.
Briere, G. and E., Suffield, Norfolk.
Brigg, Miss M., Sedbergh, Cumbria.
Briggs Ltd., F.E.A., London, W.11.
Briggs Ltd., F.E.A., London, W.11. (Wellington Antiques).
Briggs, S., Worthing, W. Sussex.
Brigham, R. Loftus, London, W.13.
Bright Antiques, Carl, Stockport, Cheshire.
Bright, T., Halifax, W. Yorks.
Brighton Antique Wholesalers, Brighton, E. Sussex.
Brighton Antiques Gallery, Brighton, E. Sussex.
Brighton Architectural Salvage, Brighton, E. Sussex.
Brights of Nettlebed (formerly Biggs of Maidenhead), Wimborne Minster, Dorset.
Brindle, J., Bristol, Avon. Clift. Ant. Mkt.
Brindle, T, Chatburn, Lancs.
Brindle-Wood-Williams, D.M., Midhurst, W. Sussex. Mid. Ant. Mkt.

Brine, L., Bath, Avon. (L.B. Antiques). Gt. West. Ant. C.
Briscoe, J., Craven Arms, Shrops.
Briscoe-Knight, M.E., London, S.W.3. (O.F. Wilson Ltd.).
Brise, J., London, S.W.6. (Pryce & Brise Antiques).
Brisigotti Antiques Ltd., London, S.W.1.
Bristol Antique Market, Bristol, Avon.
Bristol Guild of Applied Art Ltd., Bristol, Avon.
Bristol Trade Antiques, Bristol, Avon.
Bristow, A. and P., Tetbury, Glos.
Bristow Antiques, J. and M., Tetbury, Glos.
Bristow and Jane, M., London, S.W.3. Chen. Gall.
Bristow, M.J. and J.A., Tetbury, Glos.
Bristow, S., Bristol, Avon. (P. Briggs). Clift. Ant. Mkt.
Britannia, London, W.1. G. Ant. Mkt.
Britannia Antique Exports, Warminster, Wilts.
Britannia Antiques, Manchester, Lancs.
Britannia Restorations, Combe Martin, Devon.
Britannia Restorations, Gt. Malvern, Hereford and Worcs.
Britcastle Antiques and Interiors, Bedford, Beds.
British Antique Exporters Ltd., Burgess Hill, W. Sussex.
British Antique Replicas, Burgess Hill, W. Sussex.
Britten Antiques, Andrew, Malmesbury, Wilts.
Brittle, M., London, W.8. (Paravent)
Britton, Mrs., Radlett, Herts.
Britton's Jewellers, Pawnbrokers and Antiques, Nelson, Lancs.
Broad, E., St. Leonards-on-Sea, E. Sussex. Hastings A.C.
Broad, E., Bexhill-on-Sea, E. Sussex. Bex. Ant. C.
Broad, M., Tunbridge Wells, Kent. (Annexe Antiques).
Broad, S., Eastbourne, E. Sussex.
Broad Street Antiques, Bungay, Suffolk.
Broad Street Fine Antiques, Spalding, Lincs.
Broad Street Gallery, Penryn, Cornwall.
Broad Street Gallery, Wolverhampton, W. Mids.
Broadbelt, P.F., Harrogate, N. Yorks. (Dragon Antiques).
Broadhurst and Co. Ltd., C.K., Southport, Merseyside.
Broadley, E. and D., Kirk Deighton, N. Yorks.
Broadstairs Antiques and Collectables, Broadstairs, Kent.
Broadway Antiques, St. Ives, Cambs.
Broadway Antiques, Shifnal, Shrops.
Broadway Studios, Burton-on-Trent, Staffs.
Brobbin, L.M. and H.C., Whaley Bridge, Derbys.
Brobury House Gallery, Brobury, Hereford and Worcs.
Brocante, Rudgwick, W. Sussex.
Brocante Antiques, Cheltenham, Glos.
Brockdish Antiques, Brockdish, Norfolk.
Brocklehurst, Aubrey, London, S.W.7.
Brod Gallery, London, S.W.1.
Bromage, Mrs. P., London, S.W.1. (Oakstar Ltd.)
Bromley Antique Market, Bromley, Kent.
Brook, Alexis, Kettering, Northants.
Brook, Mrs. A., Kettering, Northants.
Brook, Erol, Warwick, Warks. Smith St. A.C.
Brook Antiques and Picture Gallery, Ian J., Wilton, Wilts.
Brook Lane Antiques, Alderley Edge, Cheshire.
Brooke Antiques, David, Mirfield, W. Yorks.
Brooke Antiques, Rodney, London, S.W.18.
Brooke, M.A., S.T. and L.A.P., Wroxham, Norfolk.
Brooker Antiques at the Village Gallery, Elizabeth, Brasted, Kent.
Brooker "Marylyn" Antiques and Curios, Gifts, Mary, Sandgate, Kent.
Brookfield Gallery, Colyton, Devon.
Brooks, A., London, W.C.1.
Brooks Antiques, Nelson, Lancs.
Brooks, David, Malmesbury, Wilts.
Brooks, D. and S.A., Nelson, Lancs.
Brooks, Philip, Macclesfield, Cheshire.
Brooks, Mr. Temple, London, N.W.6.
Brookstone, M. and J., London, S.W.1. (Julian Simon Fine Art Ltd.).
Brookville Antiques, Richmond, Surrey.
Broomfield, G.H., Newcastle-under-Lyme, Staffs.
Brotherston, Mr. and Mrs. A., Greenlaw, Berwicks., Scot.
Broughton House Antiques, Chipping Norton, Oxon.
Brower Antiques, David, London, W.8.
Brown, Avril, Bath, Avon. Gt. West. Ant. C.
Brown, A., London, W.1. (Connaught Brown plc.).
Brown, A., London, S.W.3. Chen. Gall.
Brown Antiques, Alasdair, London, S.W.6.
Brown Antiques, Alasdair, Datchet, Berks.
Brown, A.G., Arundel, W. Sussex.
Brown, A.J.C., London, S.W.6.
Brown, D. and C., Penzance, Cornwall.
Brown, Mr. and Mrs. D.R., St. Andrews, Fife, Scot.
Brown, G.D. and S.T., Poole, Dorset.
Brown, Prof. G.N. and Dr. F., Betley, Staffs.
Brown, G.P. and Mrs. J.A., Richmond, N. Yorks.
Brown, G.M.S., Harrogate, N. Yorks. (Christopher Warner.)
Brown House Antiques, Newport, Essex.
Brown, H. and M.F., Sandgate, Kent.
Brown, I. and J.L., London, S.W.6.
Brown Ltd., I. and J.L., Hereford, Hereford and Worcs.
Brown, Jean, London, S.W.10 (Furniture Cave).
Brown, J.H., Midhurst, W. Sussex.
Brown, J.M., Auchterarder, Perths., Scot.
Brown, J. & M., Cheltenham, Glos. (Bottles and Bygones).
Brown, J. and M., Swindon, Wilts.

Brown, Mrs. M., Chipping Sodbury, Avon.
Brown, Margaret, Edinburgh, Midloth., Scot.
Brown, Mrs. M., Stamford, Lincs.
Brown Antiques, Martyn, Halesowen, W. Mids.
Brown, M.B., Newton Stewart, Wigtowns., Scot.
Brown, P., Burford, Oxon. Cotswold Gateway A.C.
Brown Antiques, P.J., Haslingden, Lancs.
Brown, P. and Mrs. L., Scarborough, N. Yorks.
Brown, R., Southampton, Hants.
Brown, Sue, London, W.1. G. Mews.
Brown, S., Cosgrove, Northants.
Brown and Sons, S., The Popular Mart, Darlington, Durham.
Brown, T.D., Edinburgh, Midloth., Scot. (Edinburgh Coin Shop).
Brown, T.P. and P.M., Brighton, E. Sussex (Robinson's Bookshop Ltd.)
Brown, Mrs. V.M., Pershore, Hereford and Worcs.
Brown, William McLeod, London, S.W.3. Ant. Ant. Mkt.
Browne, E.A., Bournemouth, Dorset. (Boscombe Militaria)
Browne, Jennifer, Tisbury, Wilts.
Browning and Son, G.E., Glastonbury, Somerset.
Brown's, London, S.W.10 (Furniture Cave).
Brown's Antiques, Richmond, N. Yorks.
Brown's Antiques, Scarborough, N. Yorks.
Brown's Antique Shop, Newton Stewart, Wigtowns., Scot.
Brown's Number Three Ltd., Arthur, London, S.W.6.
Brown's Clocks Ltd., Glasgow, Lanarks., Scot. B. St. Ant. G.
Brown's Galleries, Penzance, Cornwall.
Browns of West Wycombe, High Wycombe, Bucks.
Browse, Stafford, Staffs.
Browse & Darby Ltd., London, W.1.
Browzers, Manchester, Lancs.
Bruce, B. & D., Jedburgh, Roxburghs., Scot,
Bruce, D., Bradstone, Devon.
Bruce, D., Tavistock, Devon.
Bruce, F., Strathblane, Stirls., Scot.
Bruce, G., Cuxton, Kent.
Bruce, Ken, Leominster, Hereford and Worcs. L. Ant. Mkt.
Bruce Antiques, Paul, Ipswich, Suffolk.
Bruce, P.M., Devizes, Wilts.
Bruce Antiques, W.F., Herstmonceux, E. Sussex.
Bruendel, K.N., Windsor and Eton, Berks. (Compton Gallery).
Bruford and Heming Ltd., London, W.1.
Bruford and Son Ltd., Wm., Eastbourne, E. Sussex.
Bruford and Son Ltd., Wm., Exeter, Devon.
Brun Lea Antiques, Burley, Lancs.
Brunel Antiques, Bath, Avon. Gt. West. Ant. C.
Brunning, M. and J., Redbourn, Herts.
Bruno, B., London, N.W.8. Alf. Ant. Mkt.
Brunsveld, Mr., Manchester, Lancs. (The Baron Antiques).
Brunswick, S., London, N.W.8. Alf. Ant. Mkt.
Bruschweiler (Antiques) Ltd., F.G., Rayleigh, Essex.
Bruschweiler (Antiques) Ltd., F.G., Rettendon, Essex.
Bruton, B.C., Sherborne, Dorset.
Bruton Gallery, Bruton, Somerset.
Bryan, D.R. and C., Cranbrook, Kent.
Bryan, Mr. and Mrs. V.C., Endmoor, Cumbria.
Bryan-Peach Antiques, N., Newark, Notts. Castle G.A.C.
Bryan-Peach Antiques, N., Wymeswold, Leics.
Bryant, D., Lostwithiel, Cornwall.
Bryant, E.H., Epsom, Surrey.
Bryde and Co., Brighton, E. Sussex.
Bryden, D., Stow-on-the-Wold, Glos.
Brydon, R.and J., Brasted, Kent.
Bryers Antiques, Bath, Avon.
Bryers, S., Bath, Avon.
Buchan, K.S., Leigh-on-Sea, Essex.
Buchanan, A.R., Lincoln, Lincs.
Buchanan, D., Leominster, Hereford and Worcs. L. Ant. Mkt.
Buchanan, J., Penzance, Cornwall.
Buchingen, Miss T., London, S.W.3. Ant. Ant. Mkt.
Buck, Mrs. B., Chalfont St. Giles, Bucks.
Buck Antiques, Christopher, Sandgate, Kent.
Buck and Payne Ltd., London, N.1.
Buck, R., London, W.11. (Rod's Antiques).
Buck, W.F.A., Stockbury, Kent.
Buck, W.M., London, N.1.
Bucke, A.P., Crewkerne, Somerset.
Buckie, G.McC., and P.R., Cambridge, Cambs.
Buckie, K.W., Swaffham, Norfolk.
Buckie's, Cambridge, Cambs.
Buckingham Books, Buckingham, Bucks.
Buckingham, C.W., Cadnam, Hants.
Buckingham, C.W., Lymington, Hants.
Buckland, A.G.J., Shottermill, Surrey.
Buckle Antiques, Evelyn, Newark, Notts. Castle G.A.C.
Buckle Ltd., T.F. London, S.W.10.
Buckley Jnr., W., Stoke-on-Trent, Staffs.
Buckley Antiques Exports, W., Congleton, Cheshire.
Buckminster Antiques, Buckminster, Leics.
Buck's Barn Antiques, West Wittering, W. Sussex.
Bucks House, Chalfont St. Giles, Bucks.
Buckton, M.J., Bexhill-on-Sea, E. Sussex. Bex. Ant. C.
Budgen, Mrs. J., Manchester, Lancs. (Boothtown Antiques).
Budhu, H.P., London, S.W.3. Ant. Ant. Mkt.
Bugle Antiques, Chipping Norton, Oxon.
Buhler Galleries, London, S.W.6.
Buhler, M., London, S.W.6.
Buley Antiques, Northampton, Northants.
Bulka, S., London, W.C.2. Lon. Silv. Vts. (David S. Shure and Co.).
Bull, Audrey, Tenby, Dyfed, Wales.

Bull (Antiques) Ltd., John, London, W.11.
Bull (Antiques) Ltd., John, London, W.1. B. St. Silv. Galls.
Bull and Son (Cirencester) Ltd., Walter, Cirencester, Glos.
Bullard, S., Ipswich, Suffolk (Spring Antiques).
Bulldog Antiques, Manchester, Lancs.
Bullock, G., Worcester, Hereford and Worcs.
Bullock, G.D., Worcester, Hereford and Worcs.
Bunce, N.P.J., Hertford, Herts.
Bunce, S. and S., Barkham, Berks.
Bunn, R.J. and E.R., Evesham, Hereford and Worcs.
Bunn, Roy W., Barnoldswick, Lancs.
Bunting, Miss J.L., Belper, Derbys.
Bunting Antiques, Peter, Hyde, Cheshire.
Bunzl, Tony, London, S.W.3.
Burden Antiques, Anthony, Dartmouth, Devon.
Burden, Clive A., Rickmansworth, Herts.
Burden Ltd., Clive A., London, S.W.1.
Burditch Antiques at Park House Antiques, Stow-on-the-Wold, Glos.
Burdon, Alyson, London, W.14.
Bures Antiques, Bures, Suffolk.
Burfield P., Lake, I. of Wight.
Burford Antiques, Burford, Oxon.
Burford Gallery, The, Burford, Oxon.
Burford, Mr. and Mrs. T.L., Auldgirth, Scot.
Burgan, Mrs. S.E.M., Yatton, Avon.
Burgate Antiques, Canterbury, Kent.
Burge Antiques, A., Cardiff, S. Glam., Wales.
Burgess, D.J., Parkstone, Dorset.
Burgess Farm Antiques, Morestead, Hants.
Burke, H. and M.J., Worsley, Lancs.
Burkinshaw, David, Haywards Heath, W. Sussex.
Burley Workshops, Burley-on-the-Hill, Leics.
Burling Antiques, Port Dinorwic, Gwynedd, Wales.
Burling, Clive and Sue, Port Dinorwic, Gwynedd, Wales.
Burlington Gallery Ltd., London, W.1.
Burlington Paintings Ltd., London, W.1.
Burlington, R.W. and M.V., Southport, Merseyside. (Churchtown Antiques).
Burman Antiques, Stratford-upon-Avon, Warks.
Burn, J., March, Cambs.
Burne, Mrs. G., R.V. and A.T.G., London, S.W.3.
Burne (Antique Glass) Ltd., W.G.T., London, S.W.3.
Burness Antiques, Marie Louise, London, S.W.1.
Burness Antiques and Scientific Instruments, Victor, London, S.E.1.
Burness, V.G., London, S.E.1.
Burnett, C.A., Northleach, Glos.
Burnett Antiques, Jean, Finedon, Northants.
Burnham-Slipper Antiques, Jane, Botley, Hants.
Burnley Antiques Centre, The, Harle Syke, Lancs.
Burns, Alisdair, London, S.W.3. Ant. Ant. Mkt.
Burns and Graham, Winchester, Hants.
Burns, G.H., Stamford, Lincs.
Burns, K., Leeds, W. Yorks.
Burns, T.P. and K., Duns, Berwicks., Scot.
Burnstock, Ursula, London, N.W.8. Alf. Ant. Mkt.
Burrage, A., Plymouth, Devon.
Burrell Antiques, High Wycombe, Bucks.
Burrell, G. and P., High Wycombe, Bucks.
Burrell, V.S., Abinger Hammer, Surrey.
Burrill, A., Dorking, Surrey.
Burrows, David, E., Newark, Notts. N. Ant. Wrhse.
Burrows, David E., Osgathorpe, Leics.
Burrows, J., Malton, N. Yorks.
Burrows, J.B. and L.L., Burley-in-Wharfedale, W. Yorks.
Bursig, R.H., Arundel, W. Sussex.
Burtique, Burley-in-Wharfedale, W. Yorks.
Burton Antiques, Burton-on-Trent, Staffs.
Burton, D., Bridport, Dorset.
Burton, D. and A., Felton, Northumb.
Burton, I., Denny, Stirls., Scot.
Burton, J., Ipswich, Suffolk. (Hyland House Antiques).
Burton Antiques, Jasper, Sherborne, Dorset.
Burton Natural Craft Taxidermy, John, Ebrington, Glos.
Burton, Mr. and Mrs. S., London, W.1. (Young and Stephens Ltd.)
Burton-Garbett, A., Morden, Surrey.
Bury, I., Long Melford, Suffolk.
Bury Street Gallery, London, S.W.1.
Busato, G., Preston, Lancs. N.W. Ant. C.
Busek, A., South Molton, Devon.
Bush, A., London, N.1 (Bushwood Antiques).
Bush and Partners, A.E., Attleborough, Norfolk.
Bush House, Corringham, Essex.
Bush, N., Long Melford, Suffolk.
Bushe Antiques, London, N.1.
Bushwood Antiques, London, N.1.
Butcher, F.L. and N.E., Sherborne, Dorset.
Butcher Antiques, Mike, Montgomery, Powys, Wales.
Butchoff Antiques, London, W.11.
Butler and Co., Cheltenham, Glos.
Butler, D.J., Cheltenham, Glos.
Butler, H., Beckenham, Kent.
Butler, J., Reigate, Surrey.
Butler, Mr. and Mrs. J.J., Chirk, Clwyd, Wales.
Butler, J.J., Honiton, Devon.
Butler, L., Glasgow, Lanarks., Scot. (Butler's Furniture Galls. Ltd.)
Butler, N. and S., Rotherham, S. Yorks.
Butler, R., Blandford Forum, Dorset.
Butler, Robin, Bristol, Avon.
Butler, Roderick P., Honiton, Devon.
Butler, Mrs. S.A., London, S.E.23.
Butler and Wilson, London, S.W.3.
Butler's Furniture Galleries Ltd., Glasgow, Lanarks., Scot.
Butlin, R., Wolverhampton, W. Mids.
Butt Antiques, Anthony, Baldock, Herts.
Butterchurn Gallery, Otley, W. Yorks.

Butterworth (Antiques) Ltd., Alan, Horwich, Lancs.
Butterworth, C., London, S.W.3. Ant. Ant. Mkt.
Butterworth, J.A., Beckenham, Kent.
Butterworth, J.A., London, S.W.9.
Butterworth, J.W., London, W.8. (Reindeer Antiques)
Butterworth, J.W., Potterspury, Northants.
Butterworth, M. and J., Woburn, Beds.
Butterworths, Woburn, Beds.
Buttifant, Mrs. P., Heanor, Derbys.
Buttons and Beads, Carlisle, Cumbria. C. Ant. and Craft C.
Button, K., Bungay, Suffolk.
Button Queen, The, London, W.1.
Button-Stephens, Christopher J., Honiton, Devon.
Buxton Ltd., Helen, London, W.1.
By George! Antiques Centre, St. Albans, Herts.
Bye Antiques, Ann, Reading, Berks.
Byers, Mrs. M., Carlisle, Cumbria.
Bygone Antiques, Swansea, W. Glam., Wales.
Bygone Bathrooms, London, S.E.23.
Bygone Days Antiques, Tiverton, Devon.
Bygone Times, Eccleston, Lancs.
Bygone Times, Lynton, Devon.
Bygones, Angmering, W. Sussex.
Bygones, Banchory, Kincard., Scot.
Bygones, Benson, Oxon.
Bygones, Darlington, Durham.
Bygones, Duns, Scot.
Bygones, Eastbourne, E. Sussex.
Bygones, Fakenham, Norfolk.
Bygones, Gourock, Lanarks, Scot.
Bygones, Heanor, Derbys.
Bygones, St. Andrews, Fife, Scot.
Bygones by the Cathedral, Worcester, Hereford, and Worcs.
Bygones Ltd., Peel, Isle of Man.
Bygones of Buxton, Buxton, Norfolk.
Bygones (Worcester), Worcester, Hereford and Worcs.
Byles, Robert, Bampton, Devon.
Byrne, B., Morecambe, Lancs.
Byrne, D. and M.A., Grassington, N. Yorks.
Byrne, Patricia, London, W.1. G. Ant. Mkt.
Byron, R., Oldham, Lancs.
Byskou, R., Worthing, W. Sussex.

C

C.B.I. Ltd., Blackpool, Lancs.
C.J. Antiques, Little Dawley, Shrops.
C.J. and K. Antiques, Preston, Lancs. N.W. Ant. C.
C.K. Antiques, Woburn, Beds. Wob. Ab. Ant. C.
C.P.R. Antiques and Services, Barrhead, Renfrews., Scot.
C.S. Antiques, Leslie, Scot.
Caedmon House, Whitby, N. Yorks.
Caelt Gallery, London, W.11.
Cain, N., Hexham, Northumbs.
Cains Antiques, Littleton, Somerset.
Cairncross, G., Filey, N. Yorks.
Cairncross and Sons, Filey, N. Yorks.
Cairnyard Antiques, Dumfries, Dumfriess., Scot.
Caldecott Gallery, The, Stonham Aspal, Suffolk.
Caldwell, Ian, Walton on the Hill and Tadworth, Surrey.
Callbox, Manchester, Lancs. Royal Ex. S.C.
Calleja, L., Ledbury, Hereford and Worcs.
Callingham Antiques, D. and A., North Chapel, W. Sussex.
Calligan, D.E., Conway, Gwynedd, Wales.
Callingham, N. and S., North Chapel, W. Sussex.
Callwood, G.T., Stourbridge, W. Mids.
Callwood, J.R., Kidderminster, Herefords. and Worcs.
Calne Antiques, Calne, Wilts.
Calton Gallery, Edinburgh, Midloth., Scot.
Calverley Antiques, Leeds, W. Yorks.
Calvert Antiques, Endmoor, Cumbria.
Camberwell Antiques Market, London, S.E.5.
Cambridge Antiques, Romsey, Hants.
Cambridge Fine Art Ltd., Cambridge, Cambs.
Cambridge Pine, Bottisham, Cambs.
Cambridge, T., Romsey, Hants.
Cambridge, T.R., Romsey, Hants.
Camden Art Gallery, London, N.W.8.
Camden Lock Antiques Centre, The, London, N.W.1. (Relic Antiques.)
Camden Passage Antiques Centre, London, N.I.
Came, S., Henley-on-Thames, Oxon.
Camel Antiques, Newton Abbot, Devon. N. A. Ant. C.
Camelot Antiques, Boreham Street, E. Sussex.
Cameo, Birmingham, W. Mids.
Cameo Antiques, Banbridge, Co. Down, N. Ireland.
Cameo Antiques, Cheltenham, Glos.
Cameo Antiques, London, W.8.
Camerer Cuss and Co., London, S.W.1.
Cameron Bucke Antiques, Stockbridge, Hants.
Cameron, Jasmin, London, S.W.3. Ant. Ant. Mkt.
Cameron Gallery, Julia Margaret, Cowes, Isle of Wight.
Cameron, K., Edinburgh, Midloth., Scot. (Gladrags)
Cameron, L., Stonehaven, Scot.
Cameron, M., Paulerspury, Northants.
Cameron, Peter, London, W.1. B. St. Silv. Galls.
Camilla's Bookshop, Eastbourne, E. Sussex.
Campbell Antiques, Stirling, Stirls., Scot.
Campbell, F., Kelvedon, Essex.
Campbell, F.D., Kelvedon, Essex.
Campbell, Gerard, Lechlade, Glos.
Campbell, G., Yarmouth, I. of Wight.
Campbell, J. and G., Lechlade, Glos.
Campbell, Picture Frames Ltd., John, London, S.W.3.
Campbell Gallery, The Lucy B., London, W.8.

Campbell, Meg, Southampton, Hants.
Campbell Antiques, Peter, Atworth, Wilts.
Campbell, P.R., Atworth, Wilts.
Campbell, R.H., Hartley Wintney, Hants.
Campbell, S., Stirling, Stirls., Scot.
Campbell-Cameron, Mrs. C.A.L., Garstang, Lancs.
Campion, London, S.W.13.
Campion, R.J., London, S.W.6. (Old World Trading Co.).
Candle Lane Books, Shrewsbury, Shrops.
Canham, Mrs. S., Northiam, E. Sussex.
Canham Fine Art, Sheena, Northiam, E. Sussex.
Cannell Antiques, M.D., Raveningham, Norfolk.
Cannell, R.H., Ampthill, Beds.
Cannon, Elizabeth, Colchester, Essex.
Cannon, N., Marlborough, Wilts.
Canon Gallery, The, Chichester, W. Sussex.
Canonbury Antiques, London, N.1.
Canonbury Antiques Ltd., London, W.11.
Cantabrian Antiques & Architectural Furnishing, Lynton, Devon.
Canterbury House, Thorne, S. Yorks.
Canterbury Place Antiques and Sheffield Pine Centre, Sheffield, S. Yorks.
Canterbury Rastro, Canterbury, Kent.
Canterbury Weekly Antique Market, Canterbury, Kent.
Capital Clocks, London S.W.8.
Capon, Patric, London, N.1.
Capricorn, Great Houghton, S. Yorks.
Capricorn Antiques, Parkstone, Dorset.
Capstick, J. and T., Bingley, W. Yorks.
Capstick, M.A., Accrington, Lancs.
Capstick-Dale, R., London, W.1. (Albemarle Gallery).
Captain's Cabin Antiques, Lymington, Hants.
Caray Antiques, London, N.W.3. Ham. Ant. Emp.
Cardiff Antiques Centre, Cardiff, S. Glam., Wales.
Cardigan Antiques, Cardigan, Dyfed, Wales.
Careless Cottage Antiques, Much Hadham, Herts.
Carey, A. and L., Cambridge, Cambs. (Collectors' Centre).
Carey, Charles, London, W.11. G. Port.
Carey, Gary, Manchester, Lancs. Royal Ex. S.C.
Caris, Gordon, Hexham, Northumb.
Carless, R. and J., London, S.W.6.
Carleton Gallery, Birmingham, W. Mids.
Carling, Roger and Tess Sinclair, Long Melford, Suffolk.
Carlisle Antique & Craft Centre, Carlisle, Cumbria.
Carlton Antiques, Great Malvern, Hereford and Worcs.
Carlton Antiques (Exports), Clayton-le-Woods,Lancs.
Carlton Antiques and Fine Arts, Bradford, W. Yorks.
Carlyon-Gibbs, A.S., Egham, Surrey.
Carmichael, D., Ilkley, W. Yorks.
Carmichael, P., Brighton, E. Sussex.
Carnell, Paul, London, W.11. G. Port.
Carnival Antiques, Bristol, Avon.
Carol and Jeffrey and Groomsbridge, London, W.1. G. Ant. Mkt.
Caroline's Antiques, Taunton, Somerset.
Carousel, Hemel Hempstead, Herts.
Carousel Antiques, Marlborough, Wilts.
Carousel Antiques, Middleton St. George, Durham.
Carousel Pig, The, Wiveliscombe, Somerset.
Carpenter, John, Carmarthen, Dyfed, Wales.
Carpenter, S., Hartley Wintney, Hants.
Carr Antiques, Harold J., Washington, Tyne and Wear.
Carr, Ronald, Salisbury, Wilts.
Carr, R.G., Salisbury, Wilts.
Carrcross Gallery, Scarisbrick, Lancs.
Carré, Mrs. K.M., St. Peter Port, Guernsey, C.I.
Carrick, G.M., Sandwich, Kent.
Carrington Antiques, Craig, Painswick, Glos.
Carrington and Co. Ltd., London, W.1.
Carritt Limited, David, London, S.W.1.
Carrol, E., Bingley, W. Yorks.
Carroll, Mrs. V., London, S.W.3. Ant. Ant. Mkt.
Carrow Hill Antique and Bygone Centre, Norwich, Norfolk.
Carruthers, C.J., Carlisle, Cumbria.
Carruthers, J., St. Andrews, Scot.
Carruthers, J., C. and F.E., Carlisle, Cumbria.
Carruthers, Lindsay, Buxton, Derbys.
Carse Antiques, Rait, Perths., Scot.
Carshalton Antique Galleries, Carshalton, Surrey.
Carter, A.W., London, W.1. (Bluett and Sons Ltd.)
Carter, D., London, W.11. (Alice's)
Carter, D.R., Woolhampton, Berks.
Carter Antiques, George, Wells, Somerset.
Carter, Jennifer, Guildford, Surrey. Ant. C.
Carter Antiques, Mark, Bladon, Oxon.
Carter Gallery, Simon, Woodbridge, Suffolk.
Cartmell, T. and J., Tring, Herts.
Cartner, J., Carlisle, Cumbria.
Cartographia Ltd., London, W.C.1.
Cartrefle Antiques, Mathry, Dyfed, Wales.
Cary Antiques Ltd., Castle Cary, Somerset.
Casemate, Bath, Avon.
Casey, F.G. and A.P., Wilmslow, Cheshire.
Casey, J., Edinburgh, Scot. (Curio Corner).
Cash, J., Birmingham, W. Mids. (The Collectors Shop).
Cashin Gallery, Sheila, Brighton, E. Sussex.
Casimir Ltd., Jack, London, W.11.
Casolani, David, London, N.W.8. Alf. Ant. Mkt.
Cason, P.G., Cardiff, S. Glam., Wales. (Charlotte's Wholesale Antiques).
Caspall Antiques, J. and J., Stow-on-the-Wold, Glos.
Casque and Gauntlet Antiques Ltd., Farnham, Surrey.
Cassidy, P., Birmingham, W. Mids. (The Graves Gallery).
Cassidy, R.J., Streetly, W. Mids.
Cassio Antiques, London, W.11.
Castaways, Doncaster, S. Yorks.

Castell Delmar Antiques, Ruthin, Clwyd, Wales.
Castle Antiques, Beaumaris, Gwynedd, Wales.
Castle Antiques, Burnham-on-Sea, Somerset.
Castle Antiques, Clitheroe, Lancs.
Castle Antiques, Newcastle Emlyn, Dyfed, Wales.
Castle Antiques, Newton Abbot, Devon. N. A. Ant. C.
Castle Antiques, Orford, Suffolk.
Castle Antiques, Stoke-on-Trent, Staffs.
Castle Antiques, Usk, Gwent, Wales.
Castle Antiques, Whitby, N. Yorks.
Castle Antiques Centre, Westerham, Kent.
Castle Antiques Ltd., Deddington, Oxon.
Castle Antiques (Militaria), Shrewsbury, Shrops.
Castle Ashby Gallery, Castle Ashby, Northants.
Castle Bookshop, Colchester, Essex.
Castle Coins and Chiltern International Antiques, Dunstable, Beds.
Castle Fine Art, Bridge of Weir, Renfrews, Scot.
Castle Galleries, Salisbury, Wilts.
Castle Gallery, Kenilworth, Warks.
Castle Gallery, Lincoln, Lincs.
Castle Gate Antiques Centre, Newark, Notts.
Castle, Simon, London W.8.
Castlegate Antiques, Berwick-on-Tweed, Northumb.
Castleton Country Furniture, Sherborne, Dorset.
Cat in the Window Antiques, Pateley Bridge, N. Yorks.
Cater Antiques, Paul, Moreton-in-Marsh, Glos.
Cater, P.J.C., Moreton-in-Marsh, Glos.
Cathedral Gallery, Norwich, Norfolk.
Cathedral Jewellers, Manchester, Lancs.
Catherine and Mary Antiques, Penzance, Cornwall.
Catherine and Michael, London, S.W.3.
Catley, B.R., London, S.W.3. (W.J. Sparrow.) Chen. Gall.
Cato, L.P. and S.Y., Lewes, E. Sussex.
Cato, M.K.W., Tywyn, Gwynedd, Wales.
Cato, Wynn, Tywyn, Gwynedd, Wales.
Catter, P., Stow-on-the-Wold, Glos.
Cattle, Barbara, York, N. Yorks.
Catto Gallery, The, London, N.W.3.
Catto, Mrs. G., London, N.W.3.
Caudwell, Doreen, Woodstock, Oxon.
Caunter, Newton Abbot, Devon. N.A. Ant. C.
Causey Antique Shop, Gosforth, Tyne & Wear.
Cavanagh, D., Edinburgh, Midloth., Scot.
Cavanagh, J.E., Glasgow, Lanarks., Scot. (Duophone Antiques).
Cave, F. and C.H., Northampton, Northants.
Cave, G., Northampton, Northants.
Cave and Sons Ltd., R.G., Ludlow, Shrops.
Cavendish Fine Arts, Twyford, Berks.
Cavendish, Odile, London, S.W.1.
Cavendish Antiques, Rupert, London, S.W.6.
Cavet, C., London, S.W.6. (D.M.T. Antiques)
Cavey, C., London, W.1. B. St. Ant. C.
Cawood Antiques, Cawood, N. Yorks.
Caxton House Antiques, Corwen, Clwyd, Wales.
Cazalet Ltd., Lumley, London, W.1.
Cecil, Mrs. C., Four Elms, Kent.
Cedar Antiques, Hartley Wintney, Hants.
Cedar House Gallery, Ripley, Surrey.
Cekay Antiques, London, W.1. G. Ant. Mkt.
Celia Charlottes, Lewes, E. Sussex.
Cellaigh Antiques, Marlborough, Wilts.
Centaur Gallery, London, N.6.
Century Antiques, Denny, Stirls., Scot.
Century Antiques, Warminster, Wilts.
Century Antiques and Victoria Galleries, Windermere, Cumbria.
Century Galleries, Bideford, Devon.
Century Gallery, London, S.W.3.
Cerberus, London, W.1. G. Ant. Mkt.
Ceres Antiques, Ceres, Fife, Scot.
Cerne Antiques, Cerne Abbas, Dorset.
Chadwick Antiques, Knowle, W. Mids.
Chadwick Gallery, The, Henley-in-Arden, Warks.
Chagnon, Mrs. L., London, W.1. (Lydia and Anita's Antiques). B. St. Ant. C.
Chair Co., The, London, S.W.6.
Chalcraft, J.N., Brighton, E. Sussex (The Shop of the Yellow Frog).
Chalk, H. and E., South Lopham, Norfolk.
Chalk, M., Horncastle, Lincs.
Challis, R., London, S.E.10.
Chambers, M.B., Bideford, Devon.
Chalmers, A.P.H., Ringwood, Hants.
Chalon, M. and T., Hambridge, Somerset.
Chalon UK Ltd., Hambridge, Somerset.
Chamberlin Galleries Ltd., Torquay, Devon.
Chambers, Mrs. B.C., Boreham Street, E. Sussex.
Chambers, L., Long Melford, Suffolk.
Chambers, M.S., Shipston-on-Stour, Warks.
Chambers, R., Stratford-upon-Avon, Warks.
Chambers, R.G., Chichester, W. Sussex.
Chan, K.L., London, S.W.3. Ant. Ant. Mkt.
Chancery Antiques, Oundle, Northants.
Chancery Antiques, Tiverton, Devon.
Chancery Antiques Ltd., London, N.1.
Chanctonbury Antiques, Washington, W. Sussex.
Chandler, Elaine, Guildford, Surrey. Ant. C.
Chandler, M.L., Birmingham, W. Mids. (Dalton Street Antiques.)
Chandlers Antiques, Moreton-in-Marsh, Glos.
Channel Islands Galleries Ltd., St. Peter Port, Guernsey, C.I.
Channer, C., Hucknall, Notts.
Chanticleer Antiques, London, W.11.
Chantry Bookshop and Gallery, Dartmouth, Devon.
Chapel Antiques, Kirkcudbright, Kirkcud., Scot.
Chapel Antiques, Nantwich, Cheshire.
Chapel Antiques, Penzance, Cornwall.
Chapel Antiques, St. Leonards-on-Sea, E. Sussex.

Chesters, N.E., Ampthill, Beds.
Chesters, N.E., Berkhamsted, Herts.
Chesters, N.E., Buckingham, Bucks.
Chesters, N.E., Stony Stratford, Bucks.
Chesters, N.E., Woburn, Beds.
Chesters, Y., Mathry, Dyfed, Wales.
Chesterton, Mrs. Margaret, St. Austell, Cornwall.
Chesterton-North, R.G., Wragby, Lincs.
Chevenix-Trench Antiques, London, N.1.
Chevenix-Trent, S., London, N.1.
Chevertons of Edenbridge Ltd., Edenbridge, Kent.
Chew, Bryan, Wimborne Minster, Dorset.
Chighine, G. and B., London, W.11. (L'Acquaforte).
Chilcott, Mrs. M., Comrie, Perths., Scot.
Child, P., London, N.1. (Swan Fine Art).
Child, Rachel, London, W.1. B. St. Ant. C.
Chilham Antiques Ltd., Chilham, Kent.
Chilton, C. and I., Long Melford, Suffolk.
Chilton, D., York, N. Yorks. (Taikoo Books Ltd.)
Chilvers, Sylvia, London, N.W.8. Alf. Ant. Mkt.
Chimera Books, Hurstpierpoint, W. Sussex.
Chimes, The, Reepham, Norfolk.
Chimney Piece Antique Fires, Sheffield, S. Yorks.
Chimney Pieces, London, W.11.
Chin, P.Y. , London, N.W.8. Alf. Ant. Mkt.
China Locker, The, Lamberhurst, Kent.
China Repairers, incorporating Mair and Drayson Antiques, London, N.W.8.
Chipping Norton Antique Centre, Chipping Norton, Oxon.
Chipping Norton Books and Prints, Chipping Norton, Oxon.
Chislehurst Antiques, Chislehurst, Kent.
Chiswick Antiques, London, W.13.
Chitty Antiques at Deva, Barbara, Hartley Witney, Hants.
Chitty, R.L., Cheltenham, Glos. (Cameo Antiques).
Chloe Antiques, Worthing, W. Sussex.
Choice Antiques, Warminster, Wilts.
Christchurch Carpets, Christchurch, Dorset.
Christensen, H.O., London, S.W.1. (Watts and Christensen).
Christian, Peter and Ann, Blackpool, Lancs.
Christian, S., London, N.21.
Christie, G.A., Focabers, Morays., Scot.
Christie, J., London, W.1.
Christie, P.S., London, W.1.
Christophe, J., London, W.1 (Harcourt Antiques.)
Christopher Alan, London, S.E.10.
Christopher Antiques, London, S.W.11.
Christopher's Antiques, Farnham, Surrey.
Christophers, W.J., Canterbury, Kent.
Christopher-Walsh, Mr. and Mrs. E., Modbury, Devon.
Chugg Antiques, Keith, Swansea, W. Glam., Wales.
Chugg, Mrs. M., Braunton, Devon.
Church Hill Clocks, Midhurst, W. Sussex.
Church House Antiques, Weybridge, Surrey.
Church Street Antiques, Broughton-in-Furness, Cumbria.
Church Street Antiques, London, N.W.8.
Church Street Antiques, Wells-next-the-Sea, Norfolk.
Church Street Galleries Ltd., London W.8.
Church View House Antiques, Kirk Michael, I. of Man.
Church Walk Antiques, Great Malvern, Hereford and Worcs.
Churchgate Antiques, Empingham, Leics.
Churchgate Antiques, Lutterworth, Leics.
Churchgate Antiques, Sible Hedingham, Essex.
Churchstoke Booksellers, Bath, Avon. Gt. West. Ant. C.
Churchtown Antiques, Southport, Merseyside.
Churton, C., Ewhurst Green, E. Sussex.
Ciancimino Ltd., London, S.W.1.
Cider House Galleries Ltd., The, Bletchingley, Surrey.
Cinders, Edinburgh, Midloth., Scot.
Cinema Bookshop, London W.C.1.
Circa Antiques, Bushey, Herts.
Circa Antiques, St. Andrews, Fife, Scot.
Circus Antiques, Brighton, E. Sussex.
Cirdeco, St. Leonards-on-Sea, E. Sussex.
Cirencester Antique Market, Cirencester, Glos.
Cirencester Antiques Ltd., Fairford, Glos.
City Antiques, Swansea, W. Glam., Wales. Ant. C.
City Clocks, London, E.C.1.
City Jewellers, Manchester, Lancs. Royal Ex. S.C.
City of Birmingham Antique Market, Birmingham, W. Mids.
Civic Antiques, Whitchurch, Shrops.
Claessens, G. and J., Buxton, Derbys.
Clare Antique Warehouse, Clare, Suffolk.
Clare Collector, The, Clare, Suffolk.
Clare Gallery, Tunbridge Wells, Kent.
Clare Hall Company Ltd., The, Clare, Suffolk.
Clare, J. and A., Tunbridge Wells, Kent.
Clare, Mr. and Mrs. M.E., Stretton, Cheshire.
Clarence House Antiques, Watchet, Somerset.
Clare's Antiques and Auction Galleries, Garstang, Lancs.
Clareston Antiques, Tenby, Dyfed, Wales.
Clark, A., Towcester, Northants.
Clark Antiques, Annarella, Stow-on-the-Wold, Glos.
Clark, A. Carson, Edinburgh, Midloth., Scot. (The Carson Clark Gallery — Scotia Maps).
Clark, B.E., Walton-on-Thames, Surrey.
Clark, Brenda Klare Gerwat, London, N.W.8. Alf. Ant. Mkt.
Clark Gallery, Scotia Maps — Mapsellers, Carson, Edinburgh, Midloth., Scot.
Clark, D., London S.E.6.
Clark, D.E., Brampton, Cambs.
Clark Antiques Ltd., Elias, Bletchingley, Surrey.
Clark Galleries, Towcester, Northants.
Clark Antiques, Gerald, London N.W.7.

Clark, G.J., London N.W.7.
Clark, H., Moretonhampstead, Devon.
Clark, H.M., Southend-on-Sea, Essex.
Clark, J., East Molesey, Surrey.
Clark, Jonathan, London, S.W.10.
Clark, L.D. and J.M., Bletchingley, Surrey.
Clark, Malcolm G., Cambridge, Cambs.
Clark Antiques, Peter, Birmingham, W. Mids.
Clark, P.B. & A.L., Penrith, Cumbria.
Clark, R., Faringdon, Oxon.
Clark, Ruth, London, W.1. G. Mews.
Clark, Robert, Micklebring, S. Yorks.
Clark, R.R. Micklebring, S. Yorks.
Clark, Steve, London, S.W.3. Chen. Gall.
Clarke Antiques Ltd., Christopher, Stow-on-the- Wold, Glos.
Clarke, Colin J., Stourbridge, W. Mids.
Clarke, C.J., Stow-on-the-Wold, Glos.
Clarke, Janet, Freshford, Avon.
Clarke, M., Warboys, Cambs.
Clarke, N.T.C., Edinburgh, Scot. (Jacksonville Warehouse).
Clarke, R.A., Oakham, Leics.
Clarke-Hall Ltd., J., London, E.C.4.
Classic Telephones, Edinburgh, Scot.
Clay, John, London, S.W.6.
Clay, P., Peterborough, Cambs.
Clayton Antiques, Jesmond, Tyne and Wear.
Clayton, P.A., Whitby, N. Yorks.
Clayton, Mrs. S., Kings Lynn, Norfolk.
Clayton, Teresa, London, W.1. G. Mews.
Clayton Jewellery, Tim, Kings Lynn, Norfolk.
Cleeve Antiques, Bristol, Avon.
Cleeve Picture Framing, Bishops Cleeve, Glos.
Clegg, J. and A., Ludlow, Shrops.
Clegg, W., Huntercombe, Oxon.
Clegg, W., Nettlebed, Oxon.
Cleland, M.A. and J.O., Benson, Oxon.
Cleland, R., London, W.11. (Court Galleries). Stouts Ant. Arc.
Clements, C., St. Leonards-on-Sea, E. Sussex. Hastings Ant. C.
Clements, James W., Carlisle, Cumbria.
Clements, P., St. Leonards-on-Sea, E. Sussex. Hastings Ant. C.
Clements, V. and R., Plumley, Cheshire.
Clent Books, Bewdley, Hereford and Worcs.
Clent Books, Halesowen, W. Mids.
Cleobury Mortimer Antique Centre, Cleobury Mortimer, Shrops.
Clermont Antiques, Watton, Norfolk.
Clevedon Fine Arts (with Clevedon Books.), Clevedon, Avon.
Cleveland, S.F., Preston, Lancs. N.W. Ant. C.
Cleverly, M.A., Malton, N. Yorks.
Clewer, P. and J., Nottingham, Notts.
Clewett, Mrs. P., Oxford, Oxon.
Clewlow, Miss J., Nantwich, Cheshire.
Cliffe Antiques Centre, Lewes, E. Sussex.
Clifford, M. and J., Oswestry, Shrops.
Clifford, J., Shrewsbury, Shrops.
Clifford and Son Ltd., T.J., Bath, Avon (Paragon Antiques and Collectors Market).
Clifton Antiques, Leeds. W. Yorks.
Clifton Antiques, Lytham, Lancs.
Clifton Antiques Market, Bristol, Avon.
Clifton, F., London, N.16.
Clifton House Antiques, Haslingden, Lancs.
Clink, D., Haslingden, Lancs.
Clisby at Andwells Antiques, Bryan, Hartley Wintney, Hants.
Clive's Curios, Worcester, Hereford and Worcs.
Clock Clinic Ltd., The, London, S.W.15.
Clock House, The, Chapel-en-le-Frith, Derbys.
Clock House, Leavenheath, Suffolk.
Clock Shop, The, Hoylake, Merseyside.
Clock Shop, The, Hurstpierpoint, W. Sussex.
Clock Shop, The, Weybridge, Surrey.
Clock Shop Antiques, The, Boughton, Kent.
Clock Shop — Phillip Setterfield of St. Albans, The, St. Albans, Herts.
Clock Tower Antiques, Tregony, Cornwall.
Clockcraft Antiques, Bridlington, N. Humberside.
Clocks and Gramophones, York, N. Yorks.
Cloisters, Canterbury, Kent.
Cloisters Antiques Fair, Norwich, Norfolk.
Close Antiques, Alresford, Hants.
Close, Henry H., Abergavenny, Gwent, Wales.
Clover Antiques, Fordham, Cambs.
Clover Antiques, Muriel, Framlingham, Suffolk.
Clow, M.R., Finedon, Northants.
Clunes Antiques, London, S.W.19.
Clutter, Uppingham, Leics.
Clutterbuck, Mrs. F., Hythe, Kent.
Clwyd Coins and Stamps, Rhos-on-Sea, Clwyd, Wales.
Clydach Antiques, Swansea, W. Glam., Wales.
Clyde Antiques, Patrington, Hull, N. Humberside.
Coach Gallery (Scorpio), Manchester, Lancs. Royal Ex. S.C.
Coach House, The, Comrie, Perths., Scot.
Coach House, The, Costessey, Norfolk.
Coach House, The, Grundisburgh, Suffolk.
Coach House Antiques, Canterbury, Kent.
Coach House Antiques, Whitby, N. Yorks.
Coach House Antiques, Wisbech, Cambs.
Coach House Antiques Ltd., Perth, Perths., Scot.
Coach House Gallery, Wedmore, Somerset.
Coach House (Scorpio), Manchester, Lancs. Royal Ex. S.C.
Coakley, P., London, N.1. (Style).
Coakley, Tony, London, S.W.3. Chen. Gall.
Coakley, T., London, N.W.8. Alf. Ant. Mkt.
Coast, G., Portsmouth, Hants.
Coates of Malvern, Joan, Great Malvern, Hereford and Worcs.
Coats, A., London, W.8. (Coats Oriental Carpets and Co. Ltd.)
Coats, Dick, London, W.4.
Coats Oriental Carpets, London, W.8.
Cobblers, London, E.15.
Cobblers Hall Antiques, Toddington, Beds.
Cobham Galleries, Cobham, Surrey.
Cobra and Bellamy, London, S.W.1.
Cobweb Antiques, Cullompton, Devon.
Cobwebs, Bloxwich, W. Mids.
Cobwebs, Sheffield, S. Yorks.

Cobwebs Antiques, St. Annes-on-Sea, Lancs.
Cochrane Antiques, Fergus, London, S.W.6.
Cochrane, F.V., London, S.W.6.
Cockermouth Antiques, Cockermouth, Cumbria.
Cockermouth Antiques Market, Cockermouth, Cumbria.
Cockram, A., Lincoln, Lincs.
Cocks, Madeline, Chichester, W. Sussex.
Cocoa, Cheltenham, Glos.
Cocozza, G., London, W.11 (Westbourne Gallery)
Codling, Mrs. J.M.E., Holt, Norfolk.
Coggeshall Antiques, Coggeshall, Essex.
Coggins, Mr. and Mrs. G., Painswick, Glos.
Coggins Antiques, Ray, Westbury, Wilts.
Cohen and Sons, B., London, S.W.1. (Trafalgar Galleries)
Cohen, Edward, London, S.W.1.
Cohen, Eli, London, S.W.3. Ant. Ant. Mkt.
Cohen, Joanne, London, N.W.8. Alf. Ant. Mkt.
Cohen, M., London, W.11.
Cohen and Pearce (Oriental Porcelain), London, W.11.
Cohen, S., Manchester, Lancs. (The Connoisseur).
Cohen, Yonna, London, W.1. G. Mews.
Cohn, George and Peter, London, W.C.1.
Coin and Jewellery Shop, The, Accrington, Lancs.
Coin and Stamp Centre, The, Colchester, Essex.
Coins International and Antiques International, Leeds, W. Yorks.
Coke, P., Sharrington, Norfolk.
Colborne, J., Cirencester, Glos.
Colborne, J., London, S.W.10. (Hares Antiques).
Coldstream Antiques, Coldstream, Berwicks., Scot.
Coldwell, P., Sheffield, S. Yorks. (Canterbury Place Antiques).
Cole (Fine Paintings) Ltd., Christopher, Beaconsfield, Bucks.
Cole, J., London, N.1. (House of Steel Antiques).
Cole at Twenty-Eight Camden Passage, Judy, London, N.1.
Cole, V., Exning, Suffolk.
Colefax and Fowler, London, W.1.
Coleman, Garrick D., London, W.2.
Coleman, G.D. & G.E., London, W.2.
Coleman, P., Chesterfield, Derbys.
Coleman Antiques, Robin and Jan, Bath, Avon.
Coleman Antiques, Simon, London, S.W.13.
Colemans W. and B., Clayton-le-Moors, Lancs.
Coles, D.A., Clevedon, Avon. (Beech Antiques.)
Coles, J., Woodstock, Oxon.
Coles, M., Kettering, Northants.
Coles, Mrs. P., Bristol, Avon. Clift. Ant. Mkt.
Coles, S., Bristol, Avon. Clift. Ant. Mkt.
Coleshill Antiques and Interiors Ltd., Coleshill, Warks.
Coll, Mrs. P., Long Melford, Suffolk.
Collard, B., Totnes, Devon.
Collard's Books, Totnes, Devon.
Collectables, Kingston-on-Spey, Morays., Scot.
Collectables, London, N.1. The Mall.
Collectables, Tunbridge Wells, Kent.
Collection, London, W.1. B. St. Ant. C.
Collections, Bath, Avon. B. Ant. Mkt.
Collectomania, Aberaeron, Dyfed, Wales.
Collector, The, Barnard Castle, Durham.
Collectors Cabin, Holt, Norfolk.
Collectors Centre, Cambridge, Cambs.
Collectors Centre, Gunnislake, Cornwall.
Collectors' Corner, Bournemouth, Dorset.
Collectors' Corner, Bradford, W. Yorks.
Collectors' Corner, Northallerton, N. Yorks.
Collectors' Corner, Waddesdon, Bucks.
Collectors' Corner Antiques, Croydon, Surrey.
Collectors' Corner — Militaria, London, S.E.22.
Collectors Corner (Yorkshire Jewellery Ltd.), Huddersfield, W. Yorks.
Collectors Gallery, The, Caversham, Berks.
Collectors' Market, Cambridge, Cambs.
Collectors Market, London, N.W.8. Alf. Ant. Mkt.
Collectors Old Toys and Antiques, Halifax, W. Yorks.
Collectors' Paradise, London, N.W.8. Alf. Ant. Mkt.
Collectors' Paradise Ltd., Leigh-on-Sea, Essex.
Collectors' Paradise Ltd., Wolverhampton, W. Mids.
Collectors' Shop, The, Birmingham, W. Mids.
Collectors' Shop, The, Edinburgh, Midloth., Scot.
Collectors' Treasures Ltd., Marlow, Bucks.
Collectors World, Worcester, Hereford and Worcester.
Colleton House Gallery, Tetbury, Glos.
Collett, J., Chipping Campden, Glos.
Collicott, R., Ashburton, Devon.
Collier, Mrs. D.E., Sheringham, Norfolk.
Collier, Mrs. J., Christchurch, Dorset.
Collier, Mark, Fordingbridge, Hants.
Collings and Ashford, London, N.1. B. St. Ant. C.
Collings, C.J. and M., Ashton-under-Lyne, Lancs.
Collingwood of Bond Street Ltd., London, W.1.
Collino, Julie, London, S.W.7.
Collins, A., Long Melford, Suffolk.
Collins, A., Manchester, Lancs. (Albion Antiques).
Collins, A., Wallingford, Oxon. L. Arc.
Collins Antiques (F.G. and C. Collins Ltd.), Wheathampstead, Herts.
Collins, B.L., London, W.C.2. Lon. Silv. Vts.
Collins and Clark, Cambridge, Cambs.
Collins, E., Leominster, Hereford and Worcs.
Collins, F. and A., Long Melford, Suffolk.
Collins, John, Hare Hatch, Berks.
Collins, J., Llanrwst, Gwynedd, Wales.
Collins, J., London, W.1. (Maggs Bros. Ltd.)

Collins, J.G., Cambridge, Cambs.
Collins and Son, J., Bideford, Devon.
Collins, Kate, Hare Hatch, Berks.
Collins, Noel, Dorking, Surrey.
Collins, N., Moreton-in-Marsh, Glos.
Collins, Peter, London, S.W.6.
Collins, P.R., Merton, Devon.
Collins, S., London, S.W.3. Ant. Ant. Mkt.
Collins, S.J. and M.C., Wheathampstead, Herts.
Collins, T.M., Dorking, Surrey.
Colliton Antique and Craft Centre, Dorchester, Dorset.
Collyer Antiques, Jean, Boughton, Kent.
Collyer, Mrs. J.B., Boughton, Kent.
Collyer, R., Birmingham, W. Mids.
Colmore Galleries Ltd., Henley-in-Arden, Warks.
Colnaghi and Co. Ltd., P. and D., London, W.1.
Colt, R., Farnham, Surrey.
Coltishall Antiques Centre, Coltishall, Norfolk.
Coltsfoot Gallery, Leominster, Hereford and Worcs.
Colystock Antiques, Stockland, Devon.
Combe Cottage Antiques, Castle Combe, Wilts.
Comberton Antiques, Comberton, Cambs.
"Commemoratives", London, N.1.
Compactum, The, London, S.E.1.
Complete Automobilist, The, Greatford, Lincs.
Compton Gallery, The, Windsor and Eton, Berks.
Compton-Dando, A.C., Long Melford, Suffolk.
Compton-Dando, A.C., White Colne, Essex.
Compton-Dando (Fine Arts) Ltd., Long Melford, Suffolk.
Compton-Dando (Fine Arts) Ltd., White Colne, Essex.
Conboy, P.J., Sheffield, S. Yorks. (Peter James Antiques).
Conder, R., Grantham, Lincs.
Conein-Veber, S.A., Great Malvern, Hereford and Worcs.
Congleton Antiques, Congleton, Cheshire.
Conn, R. and C., Dollarbeg, Scot.
Connaught Brown plc., London, W.1.
Connaught Galleries, London, W.2.
Connaughton, J., North Walsham, Norfolk.
Connell, J., Wargrave, Berks.
Connie and Steven, London, N.W.8. Alf. Ant. Mkt.
Connoisseur, The, Manchester, Lancs.
Connoisseur Antique Gallery, Brighton, E. Sussex.
Connoisseur Gallery, The, London, S.W.1.
Conquest House Antiques, Canterbury, Kent.
Conquy, Hilary, London, S.W.3. (W. Harvey). Ant. Ant. Mkt.
Constable, C., St. Albans, Herts.
Constable, J., Moreton-in-Marsh, Glos.
Constant Reader Bookshop, The, London, S.W.6.
Constantinescu, T.R. and C., Brecon, Powys, Wales.
Constantinidi, P., London, W.1. (Eskenazi Ltd.)
Continuum, Joy, London, W.1. G. Ant. Mkt.
Conway Antiques, Conway, Gwynedd, Wales.
Cook, E.J. and C.A., Gloucester, Glos.
Cook and Son Antiques, E.J., Gloucester, Glos.
Cook Antiques, James, Longridge, Lancs.
Cook, K.J., Rochester, Kent.
Cook of Marlborough Fine Art Ltd., Marlborough, Wilts.
Cook Antiques, Rodney, Twickenham, Middx.
Cook, R.L., Holt, Norfolk.
Cook, S., Longridge, Lancs.
Cook, Sheila, London, W.14.
Cook, W., East Budleigh, Devon.
Cook, W.J., Marlborough, Wilts.
Cooke, D., Playden, E. Sussex.
Cooke, F.G., Ironbridge, Shrops.
Cooke Antiques Ltd., Mary, London, W.8.
Cooke, P., Cardiff, Glam., Wales. (Dovetail Antiques).
Cooke, P., Pontypridd, M. Glam., Wales.
Cooke, Roger, Preston, Lancs. N.W. Ant. C.
Cooke, R.P., Birmingham, W. Mids. (Austy House Antiques).
Cookson, R., Bristol, Avon. (The Barometer Shop).
Cookson, R., Leominster, Hereford and Worcs.
Cookstown Antiques, Cookstown, Co. Tyrone, N. Ireland.
Cooling, I., Cardiff, S. Glam., Wales. (Back to the Wood)
Cooling, R. and Mrs. E., Spalding, Lincs.
Coombe Farm Antiques, Litton Cheney, Dorset.
Coombe House Antiques, Lewes, E. Sussex.
Coombes, J. and M., Dorking, Surrey.
Coombes, R., Burnham-on-Sea, Somerset.
Coombs, A. and L., Richmond, Surrey.
Coop, Mrs. M., Holmfirth, W. Yorks.
Cooper Antiques, Bruno, Long Melford, Suffolk.
Cooper Antiques, Eileen, Braunton, Devon.
Cooper, E.T., Gosport, Hants.
Cooper Fine Arts Ltd., London, S.W.6.
Cooper, G.E., Helmsley, N. Yorks.
Cooper, G.R. and M., Harrogate, N. Yorks. (Bloomers).
Cooper, J., London, S.W.10.
Cooper Antiques, John, St. Helier, Jersey, C.I.
Cooper and Son (Ilkley) Ltd., J.H., Ilkley, W. Yorks.
Cooper, J.P., Disley, Cheshire.
Cooper, Leon, Batley, W. Yorks.
Cooper Antiques, Philip, Petworth, W. Sussex.
Cooper, t/a Sheila Smith Antiques, Sheila, Bath, Avon.
Cooper, T., Kirkbymoorside, N. Yorks.
Cooper and Son, William, Walton-on-the-Hill and Tadworth, Surrey.
Coote Tapestries, Belinda, London, W.8.
Cope, M.J. and I., Alton, Staffs.

Cope-Brown, S.J., Cambridge, Cambs. (Hyde Park Corner Antiques)
Copeland/S. Longmead, I., St. Leonards-on-Sea, E. Sussex. Hastings Ant. C.
Copley, L., Lincoln, Lincs.
Coppage, J, Canterbury, Kent.
Coppelia Antiques, Plumley, Cheshire.
Copper Kettle Antiques, Watford, Herts.
Copperfield Antiques, Loughborough, Leics.
Copperfield, Robert, Macclesfield, Cheshire.
Copperfields, Sidmouth, Devon.
Copperhouse Gallery, W. Dyer and Sons, Hayle, Cornwall.
Coppers, Bexhill-on-Sea, E. Sussex.
Copthorne Group Antiques, Copthorne, W. Sussex.
Corbett, J., Stockbridge, Hants.
Corbey, J.W. and Mrs. M.A., Lechlade, Glos.
Cordas, S., London, S.W.3. (Mrs. E. Mitchell). Ant. Ant. Mkt.
Cordelia and Perdy's Antique Junk Shop, Lichfield, Staffs.
Cordell Antiques, Sonia, Ipswich, Suffolk.
Corder, J., Coggeshall, Essex.
Corfield of Lymington Ltd., Lymington, Hants.
Corinium Antiques, Kempsford, Glos.
Corinthian Antiques, Diss, Norfolk.
Cork Brick Antiques, Bungay, Suffolk.
Corkhill, V., Ramsey, Isle of Man.
Cormack, Mrs. J., Crieff, Perths., Scot.
Corn Exchange Antiques, Tunbridge Wells, Kent.
Corn Mill Antiques, Skipton, N. Yorks.
Corner Cabinet, Thornton Heath, Surrey.
Corner Cottage Antiques, Leicester, Leics.
Corner Cottage Antiques, Market Bosworth, Leics.
Corner Cupboard, Bolton, Lancs.
Corner Cupboard, The, Boxford, Suffolk.
Corner Cupboard, The, London, N.W.2.
Corner Cupboard, The, Woodford Halse, Northants.
Corner Cupboard Antiques, Penarth, S. Glam., Wales.
Corner Cupboard Curios, Cirencester, Glos.
Corner Gallery, The, Lindfield, W. Sussex.
Corner Portobello Antiques Supermarket, London, W.11.
Corner Shop, Bradford, W. Yorks.
Corner Shop, Eye, Suffolk.
Corner Shop, The, Hay-on-Wye, Powys, Wales.
Corner Shop Antiques, Bury St. Edmunds, Suffolk.
Cornerways, Penrith, Cumbria.
Corney House Antiques, Penrith, Cumbria.
Cornish, James R., Langford, Avon.
Cornucopia, London, S.W.1.
Cornucopia Antiques, Hebden Bridge, W. Yorks.
Coronel, H.S., London, W.11. (Fleur de Lys Gallery).
Corridor Stamp Shop, Bath, Avon.
Corrigan Antiques, London, N.1.
Corrigan Antiques, Paisley, Renfrews., Scot.
Corrin Antiques, John, Douglas, I. of Man.
Corry, E.I., Derby, Derbys.
Corve Galleries, The, Ludlow, Shrops.
Cossa Antiques, Gabor, Cambridge, Cambs.
Cotham Galleries, Bristol, Avon.
Cotham Hill Bookshop, Bristol, Avon.
Cotswold Antiques Centre, Stow-on-the-Wold, Glos.
Cotswold Galleries, The, Stow-in-the-Wold, Glos.
Cottage Antiques, Beaminster, Devon.
Cottage Antiques, Cambridge, Cambs.
Cottage Antiques, Harrogate, N. Yorks.
Cottage Antiques, Kendal, Cumbria.
Cottage Antiques, Leyburn, N. Yorks.
Cottage Antiques, Ringway, Cheshire.
Cottage Antiques, Snainton, N. Yorks.
Cottage Antiques, Southampton, Hants.
Cottage Antiques, Woburn, Beds. Wob. Ab. Ant. C.
Cottage Antiques, Worcester, Hereford and Worcs.
Cottage Antiques (1984) Ltd., Walsden, W. Yorks.
Cottage Antiques and Curios, Thirsk, N. Yorks.
Cottage Comforts, Calne, Wilts.
Cottage Curios, Allonby, Cumbria.
Cottage Curios, Chesterfield, Derbys.
Cottage Style Antiques, Rochester, Kent.
Cottage Things, Kingsand, Cornwall.
Cotterill, P., Much Wenlock, Shrops.
Cottingley Antiques, Bingley, W. Yorks.
Cottle, R.S., Llanwit Major, S. Glam., Wales.
Cotton, Barry, London, N.1. The Mall.
Cotton (Antiques), Joan, West Bridgford, Notts.
Cotton Antiques and Fine Art, Nick, Watchet, Somerset.
Cottonwood, Newnham-on-Severn, Glos.
Coughton Galleries Ltd., Coughton, Warks.
Coulborn, P., Sutton Coldfield, W. Mids.
Coulborn and Sons, Thomas, Sutton Coldfield, W. Mids.
Coulson, I., Haydon Bridge, Northumbs.
Coulson Antiques, Peter, North Shields, Tyne and Wear.
Coulter Galleries, York, N. Yorks.
Country Antiques, Boroughbridge, N. Yorks.
Country Antiques, Kidwelly, Dyfed, Wales.
Country Antiques, Killearn, Stirling, Scot.
Country Antiques, Long Melford, Suffolk.
Country Antiques, Market Bosworth, Leics.
Country Antiques, Stow-on-the-Wold, Glos. C. Ant. C.
Country Antiques, Tunbridge Wells, Kent.
Country Antiques, Windlesham, Surrey.
Country Bygones and Antiques, Ipswich, Suffolk.
Country Clocks, Tring, Herts.
Country Collectables, Long Melford, Suffolk.
Country Connections (Esk House Arts), Grosmont, N. Yorks.
Country Cottage, Modbury, Devon.
Country Cottage Interiors, Kingsley, Staffs.
Country and Eastern, Norwich, Norfolk.
Country Flowers — Country Furniture, Christchurch, Dorset.
Country Furniture, Charlecote, Warks.

Craven, Mr. and Mrs. G., Gt. Houghton, S. Yorks.
Craven Gallery, London, W.2.
Craven, K. and B., Farnham Common, Bucks.
Crawford, Alistair, London, W.1. B. St. Silv. Galls.
Crawford, A.S.B., Thornhill, Dumfriess., Scot.
Crawford, John, Diss, Norfolk.
Crawforth, Andrew, Woodstock, Oxon.
Crawley and Asquith, London, W.1.
Crawley, Mrs. M., Chislehurst, Kent.
Crawley, R.A. and Mrs. I.D., Watlington, Oxon.
Crawshaw, E.T., London, W.11 (Caelt Gallery).
Crawshaw, H. and E., Whittington, Staffs.
Creaton, I., St. Helier, Jersey, C.I.
Creaton, S., Moreton-in-Marsh, Glos.
Cree, G.W., Market Deeping, Lincs.
Creed Books Ltd., Ann, London, W.C.2.
Creed, Mrs. E.W.E., Warwick, Warks. (Eleanor Antiques) Smith St. A.C.
Creeke, Miss J.M., Sidmouth, Devon.
Creese-Parsons, S.H., Bath, Avon. (Jadis Ltd.).
Creighton, K., Romsey, Hants.
Creighton's Antique Centre, Romsey, Hants.
Cremer-Price, Mrs., London, S.W.3. Ant. Ant. Mkt.
Cremer-Price, T., Plymouth, Devon.
Cremyll Antiques, Cremyll, Cornwall.
Crescent Antiques, Disley, Cheshire.
Crest Antiques, Eastbourne, E. Sussex.
Crested China Co., The, Driffield, N. Humberside.
Crewe-Read, D., London, S.W.6. (The Pine Mine (Crewe-Read Antiques)).
Crewkerne Furniture Emporium, Crewkerne, Somerset.
Crick, Mrs. M.E., London, W.8.
Criddle, G.H. and J., Cambridge, Cambs. (Benet Gallery).
Crieff Antiques, Crieff, Perths., Scot.
Cringle, M. and A., Burnham Market, Norfolk.
Cripps, A. & C., Wingham, Kent.
Crisford, A., London, W.1 (Bobinet Ltd.).
Crisp Antiques, J.W., Teddington, Middx.
Crisp, R.B., Bath, Avon. Gt. West. A.C. Wed. Mkt.
Crispin Antiques, Ian, London, N.W.1.
Crockett, Miss P., Haunton, Staffs.
Crocodile Shop, London, S.W.3. Ant. Ant. Mkt.
Crocus, Ryde, I. of Wight.
Croesus/Westleigh Antiques, London, W.1. G. Ant. Mkt.
Croft Antiques, John, Bath, Avon.
Crofter's Lane Ltd., London, W.2.
Crofton Antiques, Bath, Avon. Gt. West. Ant. C.
Crofts Ltd., Geoffrey, Leominster, Hereford and Worcs.
Crofts, Peter A., Wisbech, Cambs.
Crome Gallery and Frame Shop, Norwich, Norfolk.
Cromwell House Antique Centre, Battlesbridge, Essex.
Cronan Ltd., Sandra, London, W.1.
Cronin Antiques, Cardiff, S. Glam., Wales.
Cronin, J., Cardiff, S. Glam., Wales. (Cronin Antiques)
Cronin, S.M., Worcester, Hereford and Worcs.
Crook, W.V. and A., Kidderminster, Hereford and Worcs.
Cropper, R., Ilminster, Somerset.
Cropper, Stuart, London, W.1. G. Mews.
Crosbie, R. and J., Longridge, Lancs.
Crosbie-Smith, Mrs. P., Exeter, Devon.
Cross Antiques, Watlington, Oxon.
Cross (Fine Art), David, Bristol, Avon.
Cross — Fine Paintings, Edward, Weybridge, Surrey.
Cross, F., Ryde, I. of Wight.
Cross, G.G., Arundel, W. Sussex.
Cross, G.G., Worthing, W. Sussex.
Cross Hayes Antiques, Malmesbury, Wilts.
Cross, I., Kings Langley, Herts.
Cross Keys Jewellers, Devizes, Wilts.
Cross, L.T. and N., Croughton, Northants.
Cross, M. and R., Swaffham, Norfolk.
Crosse, Jeanne, Bristol, Avon. Clift. Ant. Mkt.
Crosshall Gallery, Worthing, W. Sussex.
Crossley, M., Great Missenden, Bucks.
Crotty and Son Ltd., J., London, S.W.6.
Crouch End Antiques, London, N.8.
Crouch, P., Ridgewell, Essex.
Croucher, D.G., Bromsgrove, Hereford and Worcs.
Crouchman, C.C., Shenfield, Essex.
Croughton Antiques, Croughton, Northants.
Crowe, P., Norwich, Norfolk. (Cathedral Gallery).
Crowe Antiquarian Book Seller, Peter, Norwich, Norfolk.
Crowe, P. and G., Wells-next-the-Sea, Norfolk.
Crowley, Mrs. D., and Mrs. A. Fothergill, London, S.W.3. Chen. Gall.
Crown Antiques, Bidford-on-Avon, Warks.
Crown Antiques, Manchester, Lancs.
Crown Square Antiques, Kirkbymoorside, N. Yorks.
Crowson, G.H., Skegness, Lincs.
Crowther, C., Padiham, Lancs.
Crowther, J., Leeds, W. Yorks. (Roses the Jewellers).
Crowther of Syon Lodge Ltd., Isleworth, Middx.
Crowther and Son Ltd., T., London, S.W.6.
Crowther, Mrs. V., London, S.W.11.
Croxton, B., Yatton, Hereford and Worcs.
Croydon and Sons Ltd., Ipswich, Suffolk.
Crozier, F.W. and G.R., Bishops Stortford, Herts.
Cruck House Antiques, Much Wenlock, Shrops.
Cruickshank, W., Horncastle, Lincs.
Crump, G., Bideford, Devon.
Cry for the Moon, Godalming, Surrey.
Cryer, J. and W. Newcomb, Berkeley, Glos.
Crypt Antiques, The, Burford, Oxon.

Crystal Palace Collectors Market, London, S.E.19.
Csakys Antiques, London, S.W.1.
Csaky's Antiques, Sonning-on-Thames, Berks.
Cubitt, Charles, Norwich, Norfolk.
Cull Antiques, Petersfield, Hants.
Cull, J., Petersfield, Hants.
Cull, Phillip, London, W.1. B. St. Silv. Galls.
Cullen, A. and R.S., Hemel Hempstead, Herts.
Cullimore, Jill, Bath, Avon. Gt. West. Ant. C. Wed. Mkt.
Cullompton Antiques Ltd., Cullompton, Devon.
Cullompton Old Tannery Antiques Ltd., Cullompton, Devon.
Culverwell, C.T., Burnham-on-Sea, Somerset.
Cumbley, G.R., King's Lynn, Norfolk
Cumming, A.J., Lewes, E. Sussex.
Cummings, R., Preston, Lancs.
Cunliffe, C., St. Leonards-on-Sea, E. Sussex. Hastings Ant. C.
Cunliffe, J. and M., Darwen, Lancs.
Cunningham, D.M., Warwick, Warks.
Cunningham Antiques, E., Falmouth, Cornwall.
Cunningham, J.R., Prestwick, Ayr, Scot.
Cupboard Antiques, The, Amersham, Bucks.
Cupboard Love, Leominster, Hereford and Worcs. L. Ant. Mkt.
Cura Antiques, London W.11.
Cura, D., London W.11.
Curbishley, John and Nick, Stockport, Cheshire.
Curd, S., Goudhurst, Kent.
Curio Corner Antiques, Herne Bay, Kent.
Curio Corner, Edinburgh, Scot.
Curio Cottage, Bingley, W. Yorks.
Curiosity, Stockport, Cheshire.
Curiosity Antiques, Portscatho, Cornwall.
Curiosity Corner, Hacknall, Notts.
Curiosity Shop, Bolton, Lancs.
Curiosity Shop, The, South Shields, Tyne & Wear.
Curiosity Shop, The, Stow-on-the-Wold, Glos.
Curious Grannies, London, E.8.
Currie, Mrs. R., Glasgow, Lanarks., Scot. (Keep Sakes).
Curtis, P. and Mrs. R., Torquay, Devon.
Curzon Gallery, The David, Thames Ditton, Surrey.
Cuss Clock Co. Ltd., The, London, S.W.1.
Cutler Antique and Collectors Fairs, Stancie, Nantwich, Cheshire.
Cutler Antique and Collectors Fairs, Stancie, Sutton Coldfield, W. Mids.
Cutler Street Antique Market, London, E.1.
Cutting, Mrs. T., Bury St. Edmunds, Suffolk.
Cwmgwili Mill, Carmarthen, Dyfed, Wales.

D

D. & G. Antiques, Newark, Notts.
D.J. Jewellery, Parkstone, Dorset.
D.M.E. Antiques, Congresbury, Avon.
D.M. Restorations, Weston-super-Mare, Avon.
D. and V. Antiques, Newark, Notts.
Da Costa, Z., Camberley, Surrey.
Dade, Clifford and Roger, London, S.W.17.
Dade, Clifford and Roger, Marlborough, Wilts.
Daffern Antiques, John, Harrogate, N. Yorks.
D'Agar Antiques, Miles, London, S.W.10 (Furniture Cave).
Dahms, S., St. Leonards-on-Sea, E. Sussex. Hastings Ant. C.
Daisie's Antiques, Carlisle, Cumbria.
Dalby, R., Wallasey, Merseyside.
Dale, D., Bridport, Dorset.
Dale, John, London, W.11.
Dale Ltd., Peter, London, S.W.1.
Daleside Antiques, Markington, N. Yorks.
D'Alessandro and Bessant, London, W.8. Ant. Hyp.
Dallimore, Roger, Stow-on-the-Wold, Glos. C. Ant. C.
Dalloe, Mrs. M., Husbands Bosworth, Leics.
Dalton Street Antiques, Birmingham, W. Midlands.
Daly, M. and S., Wadebridge, Cornwall.
Daly, Peter, Winchester, Hants.
Dam Mill Antiques, Codsall, Staffs.
D'Amico Antiques Ltd., Norwich, Norfolk.
Danby Antiques, York, N. Yorks.
Dando, Andrew, Bath, Avon.
Dando, G. and V., Bath, Avon.
Dandy, Mr. and Mrs. W., Aldeburgh, Suffolk.
Daneby Antiques Ltd., Priors Marston, Warks.
Daneby House Antiques, Priors Marston, Warks.
Daniel, A., London, N.1. (Heritage Antiques).
Daniel, P., London, W.C.2. Lon. Silv. Vts.
Daniell, J., Upton-on-Severn, Hereford and Worcs.
Daniels, Mr., London, W.1. (Resners) B. St. Ant. C.
Daniels, Mrs. G., Brighton, E. Sussex (The Witch Ball).
Daniels, M., Brighton, E. Sussex. (Resners).
Dann, S. & M. Hatherleigh, Devon.
Dann Antiques Ltd., Sue and Roy, Melksham, Wilts.
Danum Antique Centre, Doncaster, S. Yorks.
Daphne's Antiques, Penzance, Cornwall.
D'Arcy Antiques, Lechlade, Glos.
D'Ardenne, D.L. and P.J., Branksome, Dorset.
Dare, George, London, W.8.
Darenth Bookshop, Otford, Kent.
Darer, Alan, London, W.1. G. Mews.
Darnell, C., Welshpool, Powys, Wales.
Dartford Antiques, Dartford, Kent.
Dartmoor Antiques Centre, Ashburton, Devon.
Daszewski, A.A.W., East Grinstead, W. Sussex.
Davana Original Interiors, Colchester, Essex.

Davar, Zal, London, S.W.3.
Davenham Antique Centre, Davenham, Cheshire.
Davenport, Antony, Hinton Waldrist, Oxon.
Davey, G. and M., Barrow-on-Humber, S. Humberside.
Davey, G. and M., Barton-on-Humber, S. Humberside.
Davey, M. and P., Blandford Forum, Dorset.
Davey, Mrs. P., Blandford Forum, Dorset.
David Alexander Antiques, London, S.W.6.
David, G., Cambridge, Cambs.
David John Ceramics, Eynsham, Oxon.
David, Jean & John Antiques, Westcliff-on-Sea, Essex.
David, P., Aberystwyth, Dyfed, Wales.
David's Antiques, Abertilley, Gwent, Wales.
Davidson Ltd., Arthur, London, S.W.1.
Davidson, A. and L., London, S.W.1.
Davidson Brothers, London, N.1.
Davidson (Antiques) Ltd., Eric, Edinburgh Midloth., Scot.
Davidson, E.C., Edinburgh, Midloth., Scot.
Davidson, Mrs. J., Darlington, Durham.
Davidson, J., Maidenhead, Berks.
Davidson, Mrs. J., Maldon, Essex.
Davidson, Michael, London, W.11.
Davidson, Morelle, London, W.1. (Eli Abramov). B. St. Ant. C.
Davidson Antiques, Richard, Arundel, W. Sussex.
Davidson, S. and C., London, N.1.
Davidson, S.M., Merstham, Surrey.
Davidson's The Jewellers, Ltd., Newcastle-upon-Tyne, Tyne and Wear.
Davie, D.S., Ayr., Ayr., Scot.
Davies, Mrs., London, W.11. G. Port.
Davies Antiques, London W.8.
Davies Antiques, Whalley, Lancs.
Davies Antiques Centre, Chepstow, Gwent, Wales.
Davies, A., Morriston, W. Glam., Wales.
Davies, Mrs. A., Llanelli, Dyfed, Wales.
Davies, A.G., London, W.1 (Astarte Gallery).
Davies, A.H., Pinner, Middx.
Davies, Barry, London, W.1.
Davies Antiques, Barbara, Ringwood, Hants.
Davies, C., London, S.W.3. (Christine Schell).
Davies, C., Whitstable, Kent.
Davies, C. and W., Swansea, W. Glam., Wales. Ant. Centre. (Goldcraft).
Davies, Mrs. E., Wickham Market, Suffolk.
Davies, F.M., Lincoln, Lincs.
Davies, G., Cockermouth, Cumbria.
Davies, G., E. and P., Whalley, Lancs.
Davies, H., Coxley, Somerset.
Davies, H.A. and J., Church Stretton, Shrops.
Davies, H.Q.V., London W.8.
Davies, John, Stow-on-the-Wold, Glos.
Davies, John F., Chepstow, Gwent, Wales.
Davies (Jewellers) Ltd., J.M., London, W.1. G. Ant. Mkt.
Davies, Mrs. M., Bolton, Lancs.
Davies, M., Manchester, Lancs. Royal Ex. S.C.
Davies, Norman, Holt, Clwyd, Wales.
Davies, Philip, Swansea, W. Glam. Wales.
Davies, P.A., Tunbridge Wells, Kent. (Amadeus Antiques).
Davies, Mr. and Mrs. R., Cardiff, S. Glam., Wales. (Rhys Davies Antiques).
Davies Antiques, Rhys, Cardiff, S. Glam., Wales.
Davies, R. and D., Wendover, Bucks.
Davies, R.E., Fishguard, Dyfed, Wales.
Davies, Mrs. V., Wedmore, Somerset.
Davies, W.H. and J.I., Murton, W. Glam., Wales.
Davighi, N., London, W.6.
Davis, A., Brighton, E. Sussex. (Le Jazz Hot).
Davis, Andrew, Kew Green, Surrey.
Davis Ltd., A.B., London, W.1.
Davis and Davis Architectural Antiques, London, S.E.5.
Davis, Mrs. J., Bletchingley, Surrey.
Davis, Jesse, London, S.W.3. Chen. Gall.
Davis Antiques, John E., Barkham, Berks.
Davis, Kenneth, London, S.W.1.
Davis, K. and D., London, S.E.5.
Davis, M., Pembroke, Dyfed, Wales.
Davis, M.K., Birmingham, W. Mids. (Genesis Antiques.)
Davis, P., Leeds., W. Yorks.
Davis, P., Skegness, Lincs.
Davis, P. and L., Tetbury, Glos.
Davis, Ruth, London, N.W.8. Alf. Ant. Mkt.
Davis Ltd., Reginald, Oxford, Oxon.
Davis Antiquarian Horologist, Roger A., Gt. Bookham, Surrey.
Davis, R.J., Blandford Forum, Dorset.
Davis, S., Botesdale, Suffolk.
Davis, Mrs. S., London, W.1 (Venners Antiques).
Davis p.l.c., Tony, London, S.W.11.
Davis-Shaw, M.T., Havant, Hants.
Davison, J., London, S.E.10.
Davison, M., Bidford-on-Avon, Warks.
Davison, R. and M.D., Chester, Cheshire (Chester Antiques).
Davson, Mrs. K. and C.M.E., London, S.W.1. (Kate Foster Ltd.)
Dawson, B., Finedon, Northants.
Dawson, B., Little Brickhill, Bucks.
Dawson, J., Stamford, Lincs.
Dawson of Stamford, Stamford, Lincs.
Dawson Antiques, Zona, Charlton Marshall, Dorset.
Day Antiques, Alan, Edinburgh, Midloth., Scot.
Day of Eastbourne Fine Art, John, Eastbourne, E. Sussex.
Day, M., London, W.1. (Burlington Paintings Ltd.)
Day, N. and S., Chilcompton, Somerset.
Day Antiques, Roger, Llanystumdwy, Gwynedd, Wales.
Day, R. and Mrs. A., Llanystumdwy, Gwynedd, Wales.
Day Ltd., Richard, London, W.1.
Day Ltd., Shirley, London, S.W.1.
Dazeley, R.A., Norwich, Norfolk. (Norwich Antique and Collectors Centre).

Dazeley, W., St. Leonards-on-Sea, E. Sussex. Hastings Ant. C.
De Albuquerque, Michael and Jane, Wallingford, Oxon.
de Boilley Oriental Art, Jehanne, London, W.1.
De Cacqueray, A., London, S.W.1. (Antiquités).
De Courcy-Ireland, Polly, Winchester, Hants.
De Fresnes, The Baron, Galston, Ayr., Scot.
De Grey Antiques, Hull, N. Humberside.
De Havilland, Adele, London, W.1. B. St. Ant. C.
De Havilland (Antiques) Ltd., London, S.W.1.
De Jaeger, A., Canterbury, Kent.
De Kort, E.J., Bembridge, Isle of Wight.
De Lotz, P.G., London, N.W.3.
De Montal, Andrea, Framfield, E. Sussex.
De Montfort, Robertsbridge, E. Sussex.
De Perez, J., London, W.11. Stouts Ant. Arc.
De Rin, V., London, S.W.3 (Rogers de Rin).
De Rouffignac, C., Wigan, Lancs.
De Saye Hutton Antiques, A., Worthing, W. Sussex.
De Sousa, Jo, London, W.11. G. Port.
Deacon, S., London, W.1. B. St. Ant. C.
Deakin, J.R., Seaford, E. Sussex.
Dean, Mrs. B., Spalding, Lincs.
Dean, David, Stamford, Lincs.
Dean Gallery, The, Newcastle-upon-Tyne, Tyne and Wear.
Dean, G., Colchester, Essex. (Stock Exchange Antiques)
Dean, M. and H., London, W.C.1.
Dean Antiques, Margery, Colchester, Essex.
Dean Forest Antiques, Berry Hill Pike, Glos.
Deane Antiques, Whaley Bridge, Derbys.
Deane Antiques, Graham, Brighton, E. Sussex.
Dean's Antiques, Spalding, Lincs.
Dearden, M. and S., Bath, Avon. (Pennard House Antiques).
Dearden, M. and S., East Pennard, Somerset.
Debenham Antique Centre, Debenham, Suffolk.
Debenham Gallery, Debenham, Suffolk.
Deblinger and Co., Robert, London, W.1. B. St. Ant. C.
Deborah, London, N.W.3. Hm. Ant. Emp.
Decade Antiques, Wallasey, Merseyside.
Decodence, London, N.1. The Mall.
Decodream, Coulsdon, Surrey.
Decor Galleries, Southport, Merseyside.
Decorative Antiques/The Corner Shop, Carnoustie, Angus, Scot.
Decorative Arts, Ryde, I. of Wight.
Decoroy, Preston, Lancs.
Deddington Antique Centre, Deddington, Oxon.
Deeley, D.P. and B., Stourbridge, W. Mids.
Deeley, R., Stow-on-the-Wold, Glos.
Deerstalker Antiques, Whitchurch, Bucks.
Dee's Antiques, Windsor and Eton, Berks.
Defresne, P., London, S.W.3. Ant. Ant. Mkt.
Defty, I.P., Hertford, Herts.
Deighton, Bell and Co., Cambridge, Cambs.
Deighton, James, London, N.W.8. Alf. Ant. Mkt.
Deja Vu, Bath, Avon.
Del Grosso, Jo, London, N.W.8. Alf. Ant. Mkt.
Dela-Ware, Bath, Avon.
Delawood Antiques, Hunstanton, Norfolk.
Delbridge, M., Dulverton, Somerset.
Delehar, London, W.11.
Delehar, Peter, London, W.11.
Delf Antiques, Sandwich, Kent.
Delieb Antiques Ltd., London, N.W.11.
Delieb, E., London, N.W.11.
Delightful Muddle, The, London, S.W.1.
Dell, O.J., Cheltenham, Glos. (Cocoa).
Dellar, Ron and Mel, Rye, E. Sussex.
Dellow, H., Bath, Avon. (Dela-Ware.)
Delmas, Hurst Green, E. Sussex.
Delomosne and Son Ltd., North Wraxhall, Wilts.
Delta Antiques, Liverpool, Merseyside.
Demas, London, W.1.
Demetzy Books, London, W.11.
Dempsey, J. and B., Hindon, Wilts.
Dempsey, P.D. and J.M., London, S.E.10.
Den of Antiquity, Glasgow, Lanarks., Scot.
Den of Antiquity, The, Hythe, Kent.
Dench Antiques, Sandgate, Kent.
Dench Antiques, John, Newark, Notts. N. Ant. Wrhse.
Denham Gallery, John, London, N.W.6.
Denham, Mrs. M., Copthorne, W. Sussex.
Denis, Rose, Sheringham, Norfolk.
Denley-Hill, S.K., Cardiff, S. Glam. Wales. (Manor House Fine Arts).
Dennett Coins, Clive, Norwich, Norfolk.
Dennett, C.E., South Cave, N. Humb.
Denney, L., London, W.11. G. Port. (J. Hill).
Denning Antiques, Guildford, Surrey.
Dennis, A.T. and Y.M., Hastings, E. Sussex.
Dennis, B.W., Bath, Avon. (Haliden Oriental Rug Shop)
Dennis, P., Tewkesbury, Glos.
Dennis, Richard, London, W.8.
Dennis, R. and M., Rugby, Warks.
Dennison Antiques, Bev, Grasmere, Cumbria.
Dennison, D.H., Lewes, E. Sussex.
Dennison and Son, H.P., Lewes, E. Sussex.
Dennler Antiques, Guy, Dulverton, Somerset.
Denny Ltd., Colin, London, S.W.3.
Denton Antiques, London, W.8.
Denton (Antiques) J., Luton, Beds.
Denton, M.T. and M.E., London, W.8.
Denton-Ford, A.H., Long Melford, Suffolk.
Denver House Antiques & Collectables, Burford, Oxon.
Denver Antiques, Peter, Bournemouth, Dorset.
Denvir, J., London, W.11. (Old Father Time Clock Centre).
Derby Antique Centre, Derby, Derbys.
Derby Antiques Market, Derby, Derbys.
Derby Cottage Collectables, Exning, Suffolk.
Derbyshire Antiques Ltd., Harrogate, N. Yorks.

Derbyshire Clocks, Glossop, Derbys.
Derbyshire, R.C. and M.T., Harrogate, N. Yorks.
Dereham Antiques, East Dereham, Norfolk.
Derham, J., Earsham, Norfolk.
Designs on Pine, Lincoln, Lincs.
Desmond, Mrs. D., Langport, Somerset.
Desmond, W., Huxham, Devon.
Desmond, W., London, W.C.1.
Desmond, W., Sunninghill, Berks.
Desmonde, Kay, London, W.8.
Deuchar, A.S. and A.W.N., Perth, Perths., Scot.
Deuchar and Son, A.S., Perth, Perths., Scot.
Deutsch Antiques, H. and W., London, W.8.
Deva Antiques, Hartley Wintney, Hants.
Deverall, Ivan, R., Uckfield, E. Sussex.
Deveson, T. and H., Kingston-upon-Thames, Surrey.
Dew, Roderick, Eastbourne, E. Sussex.
Dewar, R.W. and J.C., Clacton-on-Sea, Essex.
Dewart, Glen, London, S.W.3. Chen. Gall.
Dewdney, J.M., Farnborough, Kent.
Dewdney, R., South Holmwood, Surrey.
Dewdney, Mrs. V., Bristol, Avon. (Antique Beds).
Dews Fine Art, Steven, Hull, N. Humberside.
Di Michele Antiques, E. and A., London, W.11.
Di Palma, R.G., Ross-on-Wye, Hereford and Worcs.
Dial Marylebone, The, London, W.1.
Diamond and Son., Harry, Brighton, E. Sussex.
Diamond, R. and H., Brighton, E. Sussex.
Diana, London, N.W.3. Ham. Ant. Emp.
Dick, G., Hull, N. Humberside.
Dickens Antiques, Gillingham, Kent.
Dickens Curios, Frinton, Essex.
Dicken's Old Curiosity Shop, London, W.C.2.
Dickenson, Bill, Ironbridge, Shrops.
Dickerson, Mrs. P., Norwich, Norfolk. (Tudor Galleries)
Dickins, H.C., Bloxham, Oxon.
Dickins, P. and H.R., Bloxham, Oxon.
Dickinson, Bernard, Gargrave, N. Yorks.
Dickinson Ltd., David H., Manchester, Lancs.
Dickinson, D. and B., Bath, Avon.
Dickinson, R.G. and J., Ludlow, Shrops.
Dickinson, Sandy, London, W.1. G. Mews.
Dickinson, S.G., D., N.W. and Mrs. E.M., Bath, Avon.
Dickson, Mr. and Mrs. B., Prestwick, Ayr., Scot.
Dickson, R., Bath, Avon. (Abbey Galleries).
Dickson Antiques Ltd., Robert, London, S.W.3.
Didier Antiques, London, W.8. Kensington Church St. A.C.
Didsbury Antiques (Chorlton), Manchester, Lancs.
Dike, L., Bristol, Avon. (Bristol Trade Antiques).
Dilger, Mrs. C., West Kirby, Merseyside.
Dillon Antiques, Newton Abbot, Devon. N.A. Ant. C.
Dimmer, I.M. and N.C.S., Cheltenham, Glos. (Martin and Co. Ltd.)
Dingle Hall Antiques, Docking, Norfolk.
Dingle Hall Antiques, Holt, Norfolk.
Dingwall Antiques, Dingwall, Scot.
Dining Room Shop, The, London, S.W.13.
Directmoor Ltd., Leek, Staffs.
Directmoor Ltd., Oakamoor, Staffs.
Dis and Dat, Market Weighton, N. Humberside.
Diss Antiques, Diss, Norfolk.
Ditondo, J. and J., Manchester, Lancs. (Family Antiques).
Dix Antiques, Dumfries, Dumfries., Scot.
Dix, S., London, S.W.6. (Spice.)
Dixon Ltd., C.J. and A.J., Bridlington, N. Humberside.
Dixon, C.P., Bridgnorth, Shrops.
Dixon, K.M., L.A. and P., Stow-on-the-Wold, Glos.
Dixon, Mr. and Mrs. N., London, S.W.1.
Dixon, P., London, S.W.6. (Chelsea Clocks and Antiques).
Dixon's Antique Centre, London, S.W.14.
Dobbie, G., Kinbuck, Perths., Scot.
Dobbyn, D., Bournemouth, Dorset.
Dobie Antiques, James, Newark, Notts. Castle G.A.C.
Doble, I., Exeter, Devon.
Dobson, Mrs. C.M., London, N.W.8.
Dobson's Antiques, Abbots Langley, Herts.
Dockerill Ltd., A. and R., London, S.W.15.
Dodd, F., Newtonmore, Inverns., Scot.
Dodd, J., London, W.1. (Waterhouse and Dodd).
Dodd, Maurice, Carlisle, Cumbria.
Dodd, R.G., Charmouth, Dorset.
Doddington Antiques, Bub, Wadebridge, Cornwall.
Doddington House Antiques, Doddington, Cambs.
Dodge Interiors Ltd., Martin, Bath, Avon.
Dodge, M.J., Bath, Avon.
Dodge, S., Sherborne, Dorset.
Dodge and Son, Sherborne, Dorset.
Dodgson, T. and I., Lancaster, Lancs.
Dodington Antiques, Whitchurch, Shrops.
Dodkin, A., Stow-on-the-Wold, Glos. C. Ant. C.
Dodo Old Advertising, London, W.11.
Dodson (Exports) Ltd., R.C., Portsmouth, Hants.
Dodsworth, N.J. and C.S., Spennithorne, N. Yorks.
D'Offay Gallery, Anthony, London, W.1.
Doggett, F.C., Somerton, Somerset.
Doherty, W.J. and B.V., Meriden, W. Mids.
Dolan, G.M., Otley, W. Yorks.
Dolby, A., Salisbury, Wilts.
Dollarbeg Decorative Arts, Dollarbeg, Scot.
Dolleris, A.J., London, S.W.15.
Dollin and Daines, Bath, Avon.
Doll's House Antiques, The, Sheffield, S. Yorks.
Dolls House Toys Ltd., The, London, W.C.2.
Dolls of Yesteryear, Weston-under-Pennard,Hereford and Worcs.
Dolls and Toys of Yesteryear, Hungerford, Berks.

Dolly Mixtures, Birmingham, W. Mids.
Dolphin Antiques, Cambridge, Cambs.
Dolphin Antiques, Poole, Dorset.
Dolphin Antiques, St. Albans, Herts.
Dolphin Antiques, Tetbury, Glos.
Dolphin Antiques, Woburn, Beds. Wob. Ab. Ant. C.
Dolphin Arcade, London, W.11.
Dolphin Coins, London, N.W.3.
Dombey, Philip, London, W.8.
Dome Antiques (Exports) Ltd., London, N.1.
Domino Antiques, Buckhurst Hill, Essex.
Domus, London, W.1. G. Mews.
Donay Antiques, London, N.1.
Donay, N., London, N.1.
Doncaster Sales and Exchange, Doncaster, S. Yorks.
Donelly, Mrs. J., Whaley Bridge, Derbys.
Donn Gallery, Henry, Whitefield, Lancs.
Donnachie, R., West Byfleet, Surrey.
Donnelly, D.E., Colchester, Essex.
Donohoe, London, W.1. G. Mews.
Donovan, B. and A., Clitheroe, Lancs.
Donovan, J., London, W.11 (A.M. Web).
Donovan, J., London, N.1. (Rumours Decorative Arts)
Donovan, P.A., Cranbrook, Kent.
Doran, Paul, Preston, Lancs. N.W. Ant. C.
Dorchester Galleries, Dorchester-on-Thames, Oxon.
Doris, N.J., Nottingham, Notts.
Dorking Antique Centre, Dorking, Surrey.
Dorking Antiques, Dorking, Surrey.
Dorking Desk Shop, The, Dorking, Surrey.
Dorking Emporium Antiques Centre, Dorking, Surrey.
Dorling, T., Truro, Cornwall.
Dorothy's Antiques, Sheringham, Norfolk.
Dorrian Lambert Antiques, Lincoln, Lincs.
D'Orsai Ltd., Sebastian, London, W.C.1.
Doubleday, S., Colchester, Essex.
Douch, A., London, W.1.
Douglas Antiques, Dorking, Surrey.
Douglas, R.M., Dorking, Surrey.
Douglas, W.H., Cardiff, S. Glam., Wales.
Douthwaite, C. and G., Bradford, W. Yorks.
Douwes Fine Art Ltd., London, S.W.1.
Dover, R., Warwick, Warks.
Doveridge House of Neachley, Albrighton, Shrops.
Dovetail Antiques, Cardiff, S. Glam., Wales.
Dovetail Antiques, Malmesbury, Wilts.
Dower House Antiques, Kendal, Cumbria.
Dowland, C. and V., Whitley Bay, Tyne and Wear.
Dowling, G., Bristol, Avon. Clift. Ant. Mkt.
Dowling, J. and P., London, W.1. G. Ant. Mkt.
Dowling and Bray, Looe, Cornwall.
Dowling, Paul, London, S.W.3. Chen. Gall.
Dowlish Wake Antiques, Dowlish Wake, Somerset.
Downer, Mr. and Mrs. K., Sidmouth, Devon.
Downes, A., Southampton, Hants.
Downes Antiques, Brian and Angela, Bath, Avon.
Downey, P., Tetbury, Glos.
Downie, U.,London, W.11. (Graham and Green).
Downshire House Antiques, Newry, Co. Down, N.Ireland.
Downworth, D., Ashton-under-Lyne, Lancs.
Downworth, M., Bath, Avon. Gt. West. A. C. Wed. Mkt.
Doyle Antiques, Bawtry, S. Yorks.
Doyle Antiques, Lincoln, Lincs.
Doyle, A.G., Bawtry, S. Yorks.
Doyle, F.A., Whitby, N. Yorks.
Doyle Antiques, James R., Brighton, E. Sussex.
D'Oyly, N.H., Saffron Walden, Essex.
Dragon Antiques, Harrogate, N. Yorks.
Dragon Antiques, Kettering, Northants.
Dragons of Walton St. Ltd., London, S.W.3.
Drake, London, N.W.8. Alf. Ant. Mkt.
Drake, B., Harrogate, N. Yorks. W. Pk. Ant. Pav.
Drawing Room, The, Lewes, E. Sussex.
Drayson, J. and S., Petworth, W. Sussex. (The Madison Gallery)
Drayton, M., Leeds, W. Yorks. (M.D. Antiques).
Dreams, London, N.W.1.
Drecker, L.C.M., London, N.W.9.
Drewett, R., Bath, Avon. (Town and Country Antiques).
Drey, G., London, S.W.3. Chen. Gall.
Driffold Gallery, Sutton Coldfield, W. Mids.
Dring, C., Lincoln, Lincs.
Dring, C. and K.E., Lincoln, Lincs.
Driver, Mrs. B., Arundel, W. Sussex.
Dronfield Antiques, Sheffield, S. Yorks.
Droods, Rochester, Kent.
Drop Dial Antiques, Bolton, Lancs.
Drown, William R., London, S.W.1.
Druks, M., London, N.W.8. Alf. Ant. Mkt.
Drummond, D.B., London, W.C.2 (Pleasures of Past Times).
Drummond, J.N., London, N.W.8.
Drummond/Wrawby Moor Art Gallery Ltd., Nicholas, London, N.W.8.
Drummond-Hoy, C. & M., Nottingham, Notts.
Drummonds of Bramley Architectural Antiques Ltd., Bramley, Surrey.
Drury Antiques, Anne, Vale, Guernsey, C.I.
Drury, Mrs. C., Kingsand, Cornwall.
Drury House, Honiton, Devon.
Drury, John, Wrabness, Essex.
Drury, P., Conway, Gwynedd, Wales.
Drury, Mrs. P., Longfield, Kent.
Dryden Ltd., Peter, Bath, Avon.
Drysdale Ltd., A.F., Edinburgh, Midloth., Scot.
Drysdale, Mrs. S., Auchterarder, Perths., Scot.
Drysdale, Mrs. S., Crieff, Perths., Scot.
Du Cros Antiques, J., Liss, Hants.
Du Cros, J. and P., Liss, Hants.
du Monceau, Alan, Chalford, Glos.
du Monceau, A.G.T. and V.G., Chalford, Glos.
Dubiner, M., London, W.1 (Paul Bennett).
Duc, G.P.A., London, W.6.
Duck, S., Bristol, Avon. (Oldwoods).

Duckworth, C., Newark, Notts.
Duckworth, V.K. and M., Preston, Lancs.
Duckworths Antiques, Preston, Lancs.
Duda, M., Hughenden Valley, Bucks.
Dudley, A.F. and J.A., Reach, Cambs.
Dudley's Antiques and Home Interiors, Reach, Cambs.
Duff Antiques, George, Edinburgh, Midloth., Scot.
Duff, J., Chipping Norton, Oxon.
Duffy, A.M., Wallasey, Merseyside.
Duggan, David, London, W.1. B. St. Ant. C.
Duggan and Co., J.A., St. Annes-on-Sea, Lancs.
Duggan, Mr. and Mrs. J.M., Newport, Gwent, Wales.
Duggan, Stuart, London, S.W.10 (Furniture Cave).
Duigian, H., Birmingham, W. Mids. (Fine Pine.)
Duke, H., Abersoch, Gwynedd, Wales.
Dukeries Antiques, Newark, Notts. N. Ant. Wrhse.
Dukes Yard Antique Market, Richmond, Surrey.
Dulverton Antique Centre, Dulverton, Somerset.
Dunbar, Mrs. A.G., Linlithgow, West. Loth., Scot.
Duncan House Antiques, Woburn, Beds. Wob. Ab. Ant. C.
Duncan, N., Edinburgh, Midloth., Scot. (Unicorn Antiques).
Duncan, S., Bideford, Devon.
Dunchurch Antique Centre, Dunchurch, Warks.
Dunedin Antiques Ltd., Edinburgh, Midloth., Scot.
Dunelme Coins and Medals, Esh Winning, Durham.
Dunford, C., and J., Uckfield, E. Sussex.
Dunk, R.J., Stroud, Glos.
Dunkeld Antiques, Dunkeld, Perths., Scot.
Dunkeld Interiors, Dunkeld, Perths., Scot.
Dunlop, D., Portaferry, Co. Down, N. Ireland.
Dunluce Antiques, Bushmills, Co. Antrim, N. Ireland.
Dunn, Mr. and Mrs. L.G., Freshwater, I. of Wight.
Dunn, M.P., Ripon, N. Yorks.
Dunn, R., Preston, Lancs. N.W. Ant. C.
Dunn, T.C. and C.M., Pontfaen, Dyfed, Wales.
Dunnett, D., Birmingham, W. Mids. (Carleton Gallery).
Dunsdale Lodge Antiques, Westerham, Kent.
Dunster Antiques, K.W., Staines, Surrey.
Dunton Antiques, Richard, Bournemouth, Dorset.
Dunton, R.D., Bournemouth, Dorset.
Dunworth, M., Dulverton, Somerset.
Dunworth, M., Taunton, Somerset.
Duophone Antiques, Glasgow, Lanarks., Scot.
Dupré, Sophie, Calne, Wilts.
Durante, Tony, and Claude Colot, London, S.W.3. Chen. Gall.
Durham, M.L. and S.R., Birmingham, W. Mids. (The Old Clock Shop.)
Duriez, L., Exeter, Devon.
Durrant, D. and E., Stockport, Cheshire.
Dux Antiques, Frank, Bath, Avon.
Dwyer, S., London, S.W.3. (T. Giorgi) Ant. Ant. Mkt.
Dycheling Antiques, Ditchling, E. Sussex.
Dye, P. and P., Bath, Avon. (Adam Gallery)
Dyer, A.P., Hayle, Cornwall.
Dyer and Follett Ltd., Alverstoke, Hants.
Dyer and Sons, W., Hayle, Cornwall.
Dyer and Son, W., Redruth, Cornwall.
Dyfri Antiques, Llandovery, Dyfed, Wales.
Dyke, Mrs. O., Leominster, Hereford and Worcs. L. Ant. Mkt.
Dyke Antiques, Peter, Westerham, Kent.
Dylan's Bookshop, Swansea, W. Glam., Wales.
Dymond, J., Meshaw, Devon.
Dyson and Sons, C.G., Market Weighton, N. Humberside.
Dyson (Antique Weapons), D.W., Huddersfield, W. Yorks.
Dyson, F.H., Burton-on-Trent, Staffs.
Dyson, K., London, S.W.13.
Dystelegh Antiques, Disley, Cheshire.
Dytch, D., Dunkeld, Perths., Scot.
Dyte Exports Ltd., Colin, Highbridge, Somerset.
Dyte Antiques, T.M., Highbridge, Somerset.
Dzierzek, J. and J., Helmsley, N. Yorks.

E

E. and A. Antiques, Woburn, Beds. Wob. Ab. Ant. C.
E.R. Antiques Centre, Stockport, Cheshire.
Eagle House Antiques Market, Midhurst, W. Sussex.
Eaglesham Antiques Ltd., Eaglesham, Renfrews., Scot.
Ealing Gallery, London, W.5.
Eames, L., E., S. and C., Hemel Hempstead, Herts.
Eardisley Antiques, Leominster, Hereford and Worcs. L. Ant. C.
Earl, Mrs. E., London, S.W.3. Ant. Ant. Mkt.
Earl, P., Halstead, Essex.
Earle, B., Wilton, Wilts.
Earlshall Castle, Leuchars, Fife, Scot.
Earsham Hall Pine, Earsham, Norfolk.
Easebourne Antiques, Easebourne, W. Sussex.
East Gates Antiques, Colchester, Essex.
East Gates Antiques, London, N.W.8. Alf. Ant. Mkt.
East, R., Lancing, W. Sussex.
East-Asia Co, London, N.W.1.
Eastbourne Antiques Market, Eastbourne, E. Sussex.
Easterby, Betty and Dean, Preston, Lancs.
Eastgate Antique Centre, Lincoln, Lincs.
Eastgate Antiques, Cowbridge, S. Glam., Wales.
Eastgate Fine Arts, Warwick, Warks.
Easton, F.M. and A., Reading, Berks.
Eaton Gallery, London, S.W.1.

Eaton Antiques, Jonathan, Tetbury, Glos.
Eaton Booksellers Ltd., Peter, Weedon, Bucks.
Eaton, P. and P., Windsor and Eton, Berks.
Eatons of Eton Ltd., Windsor and Eton, Berks.
Ebbinkhuyson, P., London, N.W.1. (Spatz).
Ebbinkhuyson, P., London, W.C.2.
Ebrich, Rosemary, London, W.1. G. Mews.
Eccles, J., London, N.W.1 (Jazzy Art Deco).
Eccles Road Antiques, London, S.W.11.
Eccleston, D. and P., Manchester, Lancs.
Echoes, Ryde, I. of Wight.
Echoes, Todmorden, W. Yorks.
Echoes of the Past, Oldham, Lancs.
Eddelin, Mrs. A.M., Southend-on-Sea, Essex.
Eddy, P. and S.N., Leominster, Hereford and Worcs.
Ede Ltd., Charles, London, W.1.
Edelstein at Robin Symes, Annamaria, London, S.W.1.
Eden Coins, Birmingham, W. Mids.
Eden, Robin and Matthew, Corsham, Wilts.
Eden, R. and M., Woodstock, Oxon.
Edgar Gallery, Owen, London, S.W.1.
Edgbaston Gallery, Birmingham, W. Mids.
Edgington, A. and D., Blandford Forum, Dorset.
Edgware Antiques, Edgware, Middx.
Edinburgh Coin Shop, Edinburgh, Midloth., Scot.
Editions Graphiques Gallery, London, W.1.
Edmonds Ltd, D.H., Brighton, E. Sussex.
Edmonds Ltd., D.H., London, W.1.
Edmonds, K.D., Oxford, Oxon.
Edmonstone, Lady J., Killearn, Stirling, Scot.
Edmunds, Andrew, London, W.1.
Edwardes, Mrs. M.D., Worthing, W. Sussex.
Edwardian Shop, The, Ipswich, Suffolk.
Edwards Antique Exports, Brian, Lower Kinnerton, Cheshire.
Edwards, B.H. Lower Kinnerton, Cheshire.
Edwards, Charles, London, S.W.6.
Edwards Ltd., Christopher, London, S.W.1.
Edwards, D., Clare, Suffolk.
Edwards, D., Long Melford, Suffolk.
Edwards Family, The, Norwich, Norfolk. (Carrow Hill Antique and Bygone Centre).
Edwards, H., Bagillt, Clwyd, Wales.
Edwards, Josephine, London, N.1. The Mall.
Edward's Jewellers, Liverpool, Merseyside.
Edwards, K., Brighton, E. Sussex. (Parsons and Edwards).
Edwards and Gloria, K., London, W.1. B. St. Ant. C.
Edwards Antiques, Keith D., Kendal, Cumbria.
Edwards, P., Broadstairs, Kent.
Edwards, R., Upminster, Essex.
Edwards, V., Abbots Bromley, Staffs.
Eekhout Gallery, Brockdish, Norfolk.
Eichler, R.J. and L.L., Whitchurch, Bucks.
Eimer, Christopher, London, N.W.11.
Eisler, R.J. and D.M., Marlow, Bucks.
Ekstein, L., London, S.W.1.
Ekstein Ltd., M., London, S.W.1.
Elcombe, Mr. and Mrs. J.W.G., Sandgate, Kent.
Elden Antiques, Kirk Deighton, N. Yorks.
Eldridge, B., London, E.C.1.
Eldridge London, London, E.C.1.
Eleanor Antiques, Warwick, Warks. Smith St. A.C.
Elegance Antique Exports, Barrow-on-Humber, S. Humberside.
Elegance Antiques, Barton-on-Humber, S. Humberside.
Elgin House Antiques, Tetbury, Glos.
Elias, J.G., Dorking, Surrey.
Eliot Antiques, Stanford Dingley, Berks.
Elisabeth's Antiques, London, W.1. B. St. Ant. C.
Elithorn, S., London, N.W.5.
Elizabeth Antiques, Swansea, W. Glam., Wales.
Elizabeth & Son, Ulverston, Cumbria.
Elizabethans, Fareham, Hants.
Elkin Mathews, Coggeshall, Essex.
Elkington Antiques, Doreen, Adderley, Shrops.
Elkington, Mrs. D.E., Adderley, Shrops.
Elliott, A., Blandford Forum, Dorset.
Elliot, R.J., Southampton, Hants.
Elliott, A. and C., London, W.11 (E.R. O'Connor).
Elliott, C.R., Eastbourne, E. Sussex.
Elliott, E., Hexham, Northumbs.
Elliott, Mrs. P., Glastonbury, Somerset.
Elliott, S., London, S.W.14.
Elliott and Scholz Antiques, Eastbourne, E. Sussex.
Elliott and Snowdon Ltd., London, W.11.
Ellis, Mrs. C., Arundel, W. Sussex.
Ellis Antiques, Donald, Edinburgh, Midloth., Scot.
Ellis Antiques, D.G. and C.M., Edinburgh, Midloth., Scot.
Ellis, G. and Mrs. A.J., Walsall, W. Mids.
Ellis, G.E., Chester, Cheshire. (Avalon Postcard and Stamp Shop).
Ellis, J., Birmingham, W. Mids. (The Original Choice.)
Ellis, J., Worcester, Hereford and Worcs.
Ellis, R.G. and P.T., Camberley, Surrey.
Ellis's, Sheffield, S. Yorks.
Ellory Antiques and Shipping, G.T.G., Gainsborough, Lincs.
Elm Hill Antiques, Norwich, Norfolk.
Elm House Antiques, Haddington, E. Loth., Scot.
Elm Tree Antiques, Flaxton, N. Yorks.
Elmes Antiques, Margaret, Denham Village, Bucks.
Elmey Heritage, Elmey Lovett, Hereford and Worcs.
Elmore, Petersfield, Hants.
Elsom Antiques, Pamela, Ashbourne, Derbys.
Elsworth, Mrs. J., Beaconsfield, Bucks.
Elsworth Beaconsfield Ltd., June, Beaconsfield, Bucks.
Elton, S.P., Beckenham, Kent.
Elvin, June, Newton Abbot, Devon. N.A. Ant. C.
Emanouel Antiques Ltd., London, W.1.
Embden, K.B., London, W.C.2 (Anchor Antiques Ltd.).

Emburey, Mrs. G.D., Dorking, Surrey.
Emerald Isle Books, Belfast, N. Ireland.
Emerson, I., Armagh, Co. Armagh, N. Ireland.
Emerson, S., London, S.W.3. Ant. Ant. Mkt.
Emery, Valérie, London, W.C.2 (Travis and Emery).
Emm, Anthony, Bath, Avon.
Emmerson, Mrs. J., Colyton, Devon.
Empire Antiques, Sandwich, Kent.
Emporium, The, Chipping Norton, Oxon.
Emporium, The, Knaresborough, N. Yorks.
Emporium of Age and Art, Annfield Plain, Durham.
Emptage, P., Wimborne Minster, Dorset.
Enchanted Aviary, The, Long Melford, Suffolk.
Endeavour Antiques, Saltburn, Cleveland.
Endley, S., Beverley, Beverley, N. Humberside.
Enfield Antiques, London, S.E.1.
Enfield Corner Cupboard, Enfield, Middx.
England, F.J. and S., Leek, Staffs.
England's Gallery, Leek, Staffs.
English Country Furnishings, Mobberley, Cheshire.
English Heritage, Bridgnorth, Shrops.
English Period Interiors, London, S.W.6.
English, Toby, Wallingford, Oxon. L. Arc.
Englishman's Antiques, Norwich, Norfolk.
Enloc Antiques, Colne, Lancs.
Entwistle, London, W.1.
Epping Galleries, Epping, Essex.
Epping Saturday Market, Epping, Essex.
Eprile, R., Edinburgh, Midloth., Scot. (Royal Mile Curios.)
Equus Art Gallery, Newmarket, Suffolk.
Ermitage Ltd., London, W.1.
Errington Antiques, Newcastle-under-Lyme, Staffs.
Errington, G.K., Newcastle-under-Lyme, Staffs.
Errol Antiques, Errol, Perths., Scot.
Erskine-Hill, M. and Mrs. M., Tunbridge Wells, Kent. (The Antique Pine Shop)
Eskenazi, J.E., London, W.1.
Eskenazi Ltd., London, W.1.
Essex Antiques Centre, Colchester, Essex.
Essex Antiques, Richard, Bristol, Avon.
Essie Carpets, London, W.1.
Ester and Leslie, London, W.1. G. Mews.
Estevez, G.J., Addingham, W. Yorks.
Estling, Mrs. G., Dowlish Wake, Somerset.
Etceteras Antiques, Seaton, Devon.
Etheridge, B., Burford, Oxon.
Etherington, G., Hull, N. Humberside.
Ethos Gallery, Clitheroe, Lancs.
Eton Antique Bookshop, Windsor and Eton, Berks.
Eton Cottage Antiques, Windsor and Eton, Berks.
Eton Gallery Antiques, Windsor and Eton, Berks.
Eureka Antiques and Interiors, Bowdon, Cheshire.
Euston House Galleries and Roma Antiques, Llandrindod Wells, Powys, Wales.
Evans, A. and M., Narberth, Dyfed, Wales.
Evans, B. and Mrs. P., Burford, Oxon.
Evans, D., London, W.4. (Antiques 132).
Evans, Mr. and Mrs. D.G., Brecon, Powys, Wales
Evans, D. and N. Alresford, Hants.
Evans and Evans, Alresford, Hants.
Evans, E.M. and R. Llangollen, Clwyd, Wales.
Evans, Mr. and Mrs. G., Cranbrook, Kent.
Evans, Mrs. M., Llangollen, Clwyd, Wales.
Evans, Mollie, Richmond, Surrey.
Evans, Patricia, London, S.W.3. Ant. Ant. Mkt.
Evans, Peter, Hare Hatch, Berks.
Evans, Mrs. S., Harrogate, N. Yorks. (Cottage Antiques.)
Evans, Stewart, Malpas, Cheshire.
Evans Antiques, Steven, Treherbert, Mid-Glam., Wales.
Evans Antiques, Steven, Treorchy, Mid-Glam., Wales.
Evanson, P., London, S.W.6. (R. and H. Short).
Eve, J., Cambridge, Cambs. (Gabor Cossa Antiques.)
Eveleigh, L., Newmarket, Suffolk.
Evenden, R., Eastbourne, E. Sussex.
Everett, Mrs. M.J., Eastbourne, E. Sussex.
Everett, Mr. and Mrs. T., Pitminster, Somerset.
Everitt, E.J., Norton, Suffolk.
Eves, I.A., Broadway, Hereford and Worcs.
Evonne, London, W.1. G. Ant. Mkt.
Ewart, A.J., Broadway, Hereford and Worcs.
Ewart, Gavina, Broadway, Hereford and Worcs.
Ewen, D., London, W.11. (Pembridge Art Gallery).
Ewer, William, London, W.1. G. Ant. Mkt.
Ewhurst Gallery, Ewhurst Green, E. Sussex.
Ewhurst Gallery, Ramsdell, Hants.
Ewing, J.F., London, W.11. (Portobello Antique Store).
Exeter Antique Wholesalers, Exeter, Devon.
Exeter Rare Books, Exeter, Devon.
Exley-Turner, Mrs. J., Steyning, W. Sussex.
Expressions, Shrewsbury, Shrops.
Extence Antiques, Teignmouth, Devon.
Extence, Leigh C., Teignmouth, Devon.
Extence, T.E. and L.E., Teignmouth, Devon.
Eyers, Mrs. M., Arundel, W. Sussex.
Eyles Antiques, Joan, Boroughbridge, N. Yorks.
Eyles, J.M. and J.C.H., Boroughbridge, N. Yorks.

F

Facade, The, London, W.11.
Faded Elegance, Dulverton, Somerset.
Fagiani, A., London, S.E.15.
Fagin's Antiques, Exeter, Devon.
Fahimian, E., London, W.1. (Accurate Trading Co.). B. St. Ant. C.
Fair Deal Antiques, Mansfield, Notts.
Fair, D.P., Hockley Heath, W. Mids.

Fair Finds, Rait, Perths., Scot.
Fairbairn, R. and A., Berwick-on-Tweed, Northumb.
Fairclough, G.D., Scarisbrick, Lancs.
Fairfax Fireplaces and Antiques, London, S.W.6.
Fairfax, H., London, S.W.6, (Fairfax Fireplaces and Antiques.)
Fairfax Fireplaces and General Antiques, Harriett, Langley Burrell, Wilts.
Fairfield, Jane, Stow-on-the-Wold, Glos. C. Ant. C.
Fairhurst Gallery, The, Norwich, Norfolk.
Fairings, The, Harrogate, N. Yorks.
Fairman (Carpets) Ltd., Jack, London, W.11.
Fakenham Antique Centre, Fakenham, Norfolk.
Falcon Gallery, The, Wortham, Suffolk.
Falconer, P., St. Austell, Cornwall.
Falik, Mrs. S., Burnley, Lancs.
Falk, S.C., Rochdale, Lancs.
Falloon, Ronald, London, W.1. G. Ant. Mkt.
Falstaff Antiques, Rolvendon, Kent.
Family Antiques, Manchester, Lancs.
Family Antiques, Preston, Lancs. N.W. Ant. C.
Fan-Fayre Antiques, Rhosneigr, Gwynedd, Wales.
Fanthorpe, M. and T., East Dereham, Norfolk.
Fantiques, Amersham, Bucks.
Farahar and Sophie Dupré, Clive, Calne, Wilts.
Fardon, J.A., Bristol, Avon. (Alexander Gallery).
Farey, Miss K., Skipton, N. Yorks.
Faringdon Gallery, Faringdon, Oxon.
Farmers Gallery, Leominster, Hereford and Worcs.
Farmhouse Antiques, Bolton-by-Bowland, Lancs.
Farmhouse Antiques, Chester, Cheshire.
Farmhouse Antiques, Stoke Ferry, Norfolk.
Farnborough (Kent) Antiques, Farnborough, Kent.
Farnell, B., Dumfries, Dumfriess., Scot.
Farnes, C., Penzance, Cornwall.
Farnham Antique Centre, Farnham, Surrey.
Farnham, P.M., Bath, Avon. ("27a").
Farnsworth, S. and V., Moreton-in-Marsh, Glos.
Farouz, P., Pelsall, W. Mids.
Farr, A. and J., Gloucester, Glos.
Farrelly Antiques, Tring, Herts.
Farrelly, P., Tring, Herts.
Farrelly, S., London, S.W.16.
Farrelly, Stephen, London, N.W.3.
Farington, Mrs. S., Birmingham, W. Mids. (Amber Antiques).
Farrington, Mrs. S., Gloucester, Glos.
Farrow, D.H., Hungerford, Berks. (Medalcrest Ltd.)
Farrow, E., London, W.11. (Dodo Old Advertising).
Farrow, Peter, Great Missenden, Bucks.
Farrow and Werth, London, N.W.8. Alf. Ant. Mkt.
Farthings Antiques, Nantwich, Cheshire.
Faustus Fine Art Ltd., London, S.W.1.
Fawcett, L., London, W.11. (Themes and Variations).
Fawcett, P., Brasted, Kent.
Fawkes, K., London, N.W.3.
Fearfield, Miss A., Budleigh Salterton, Devon.
Fearn Antiques, Newark, Notts. Castle G.A.C.
Fears t/a Pilgrims' Progress, Howard, Little Walsingham, Norfolk.
Featherstone, Mrs. E.A., South Cave, N. Humberside.
Feldman Ltd., R., London, W.C.2. Lon. Silv. Vts.
Felix Gallery, Lewes, E. Sussex.
Felix, R.T., Studley, Warks.
Fell Antiques, Mary, Brampton, Cumbria.
Fellows, Maurice, Birmingham, W. Mids.
Felton Park Antiques, Felton, Northumb.
Fenlan Antiques, Turvey, Beds.
Fenn Ltd., London, W.8. (Abstract). Kensington Ch. St. A.C.
Fenwick and Fisher Antiques, Broadway, Hereford and Worcs.
Fenwick, M., London, S.W.6 (Sensation Ltd.).
Feraille, B., Bungay, Suffolk.
Ferder, S. and S., Lyndhurst, Hants.
Ferdinando, Steven, Queen Camel, Somerset.
Fereday, N., Ashburton, Devon;
Ferguson, Brian, Carlisle, Cumbria.
Ferguson, H.T. and R.E., Woodbridge, Suffolk.
Ferguson, M., Birmingham, W. Mids. (Smithsonia)
Fern Cottage Antique Centre, Thames Ditton, Surrey.
Fernandes and Marche, London, S.W.1.
Ferneyhough, Miles, Stratford-upon-Avon, Warks.
Ferneyhough, M.H., Stratford-upon-Avon, Warks.
Fernlea Antiques, Hollinwood, Lancs.
Ferrant Antiques, D.J., London, N.1.
Ferrant, J., London, N.1.
Ferrara, G., Newton Abbot, Devon. N.A. Ant. C.
Ferrett, P.D., Wallasey, Merseyside.
Ferrow, David, Great Yarmouth, Norfolk.
Ferrow Family Antiques, The, Great Yarmouth, Norfolk.
Ferrow, M., J. and P., Great Yarmouth, Norfolk.
Ferry, H., Huntercombe, Oxon.
Ferry and William Clegg Antiques, Harvey, Nettlebed, Oxon.
Ferry, H., Nettlebed, Oxon.
Fettes Fine Art, York, N. Yorks.
Few, Ted, London, S.W.17.
Ffynnon Las, Sarnau, Dyfed, Wales.
Fidelo, Tom, Edinburgh, Midloth., Scot.
Field, C. and G., Abinger Hammer, Surrey.
Field, M. Holmes, Corwen, Clwyd, Wales.
Field, P., Cheltenham, Glos. (Turtle Fine Art).
Field, R.B., Colchester, Essex.

Fielden, Brian, London, W.1.
Fielden, David, London, S.W.3. Ant. Ant. Mkt.
Fiell, Peter, London, S.W.3. Chen. Gall.
Fieldings Antiques, Haslingden, Lancs.
Fifteenth Century Bookshop, Lewes, E. Sussex.
Fijolek, H., Preston, Lancs. N.W. Ant. C.
Fileman, David R., Steyning, W. Sussex.
Filey Antiques, Filey, N. Yorks.
Filkins Antiques, Chester, Cheshire.
Fillans (Antiques), Huddersfield, W. Yorks.
Fillibuster and Booth Ltd., Sheffield, S. Yorks.
Filsham Farmhouse Antiques, St. Leonards-on-Sea, E. Sussex.
Final Whistle, London, N.W.8. Alf. Ant. Mkt.
Finch, Keith, Kenton, Middx.
Finch, M. and I., Yealand Conyers, Lancs.
Finch, N., London, N.W.3.
Finch, N., London, N.W.8.
Finchley Fine Art Galleries, London, N.12.
Findings, Coggeshall, Essex.
Findley Antiques, Sheffield, S. Yorks.
Findley, B., Sheffield, S. Yorks. (Findley Antiques.)
Fine Art Gallery, Edinburgh, Midlothian, Scot.
Fine Antique Glass, Abernyte, Scot.
Fine Art Investments, London, W.8.
Fine Art of Oakham, Oakham, Leics.
Fine Art Society p.l.c., The, Edinburgh, Midloth., Scot.
Fine Art Society p.l.c., The, Glasgow, Lanarks., Scot.
Fine Art Society p.l.c., The, London, W.1.
Fine China (London) Ltd., London, W.C.2.. Lon. Silv. Vts.
Fine Jewellery at Liberty's, London, W.1.
Fine Pine, Birmingham, W. Mids.
Fine Pine, Carlisle, Cumbria. C. Ant. and Craft. C.
Fine Pine, Leicester, Leics.
Fine Pine, Southport, Merseyside.
Fine Pine Antiques, Harbertonford, Devon.
Finedon Antiques (Antiques Centre), Finedon, Northants.
Fine-Lines (Fine Art), Shipston-on-Stour, Warks.
Finer, E., London, W.C.2 (Frognal Rare Books).
Finesse Fine Art, Weymouth, Dorset.
Finlay, James, Falkirk, Stirls., Scot.
Finlay Antiques, K.W., Cilau Aeron, Dyfed, Wales.
Finlay, M.F., Eaglesham, Renfrews., Scot.
Finlay, T. and M.C., Littleton, Somerset.
Finn, V., Cheltenham, Glos. (Leckhampton Antiques)
Finnegan (Jeweller), Robin, Darlington, Durham.
Finney, G., Stow-on-the-Wold, Glos.
Finney Antique Prints and Books, Michael, London, N.1.
Fire Place (Hungerford) Ltd., The, Hungerford, Berks.
Firmin, Rodney, Swaffham Prior, Cambs.
First Floor, London, S.W.10 (Furniture Cave).
First, Jack, London, W.1. G. Ant. Mkt.
Fischelis, R., London, N.W.2.
Fisher, R., London, S.W.3 (Dragons of Walton St. Ltd.).
Fisher, R. and E.S., Egham, Surrey.
Fisher and Sperr, London, N.6.
Fisher, Susanna, Upham, Hants.
Fisher Street Antiques, Carlisle, Cumbria.
Fisher, W.I.J., Penzance, Cornwall.
Fishers of Surrey, Egham, Surrey.
Fishlake Antiques, Fishlake, S. Yorks.
Fitch Antiques, Michael, Sandgate, Kent.
Fitchett Antiques, Alan, Brighton, E. Sussex.
Fitter, M.C., Bath, Avon. Gt. West. Ant. C. Wed. Mkt.
Fitzgerald-Moore, T.E., Beetham, Cumbria.
Fitz-Hugh, C.R., Worcester, Hereford and Worcs.
Five Five Six Antiques, London, S.W.6.
Five Towns Antiques, Stoke-on-Trent, Staffs.
Flappers, Buckingham, Bucks.
Flappers, Cambridge, Cambs.
Fleamarket, The, London, N.1.
Fleet Fine Art, Fleet, Hants.
Flegg Antiques, Sue, London, W.1. G. Mews.
Fleischer, F.J., Sedlescombe, E. Sussex.
Fleming (Southsea) Ltd., A., Portsmouth, Hants.
Fleming and Bea. Korniczky, Jean, London, N.W.8. Alf. Ant. Mkt.
Fleming, S. Becker, Walton-on-Thames, Surrey.
Fleming, T., Framlingham, Suffolk.
Fleming's Antiques, Debenham, Suffolk.
Fletcher, H.M., London, W.C.2.
Fletcher, M., Preston, Lancs.
Fletcher, Mrs. R.E., Stratford-upon-Avon, Warks.
Fleur de Lys Gallery, London, W.11.
Flight of Fancy, London, S.W.3. Chen. Gall.
Flint, W., Weymouth, Dorset.
Flint Galleries Ltd., Sir William Russell, Wrington. Avon.
Flintlock Antiques, Stockport, Cheshire.
Flora Dora Antiques, Petworth, W. Sussex.
Flore House Antiques Ltd., Flore, Northants.
Flowerdew at Trianon, Liliane, London, W.1.
Flowers Antiques, Ilford, Essex.
Floyd Ltd., George, London, S.W.6.
Floydmist Ltd., Liss, Hants.
Fluck, Miss M.G., Skipton, N. Yorks.
Fluitman, Mrs. A., Woburn, Beds.
Fluss and Charlesworth Ltd., London, W.9.
Fluss, E., London, W.9.
Flyn, J.C., Cowes, I. of Wight.
Foddy, D., Derby, Derbys.
Fogg Antiques, Epsom, Surrey.
Fogg, Mrs. P.M., London, N.W.8. Alf. Ant. Mkt.
Fogg, R., Epsom, Surrey.
Fogg, Sam, London, W.1.
Foley, C., London, W.1. (Lane Fine Art Ltd.).
Folkard, O.P., Kelvedon, Essex.
Folkes Antiques and Jewellers, Gt. Yarmouth, Norfolk.

Folkestone, Viscount, Salisbury, Wilts.
Folly, The, Longridge, Lancs.
Folly Antiques Centre, Petersfield, Hants.
Fomison, Mr. and Mrs. R., Ramsgate, Kent.
Foord Antiques, Midhurst, W. Sussex.
Foord, C.G., Petersfield, Hants.
Foord, C.G. and E.S., Midhurst, W. Sussex.
Foord-Brown Antiques, David, Cuckfield, W. Sussex.
For Pine, Chesham, Bucks.
Forbes, P. and L., Church Stretton, Shrops.
Ford, D., Compton, Surrey.
Ford, D. and H., Tintern, Gwent, Wales.
Ford, E. and J., Winchcombe, Glos.
Ford and Son Ltd., G.W., Unstone, Derby.
Ford and Son Ltd., G.W., Woburn, Beds. Wob. Ab. Ant. C.
Ford, I., Coltishall, Norfolk.
Ford, I.J., Norwich, Norfolk. (Norfolk Antique and Collectors' Centre.)
Ford, J. and C., Bidford-on-Avon, Warks.
Ford, M.C., Burford, Oxon. Cots. Gateway A.C.
Ford, P. and B., Wells-next-the-Sea, Norfolk.
Ford, Mrs. R., Ledbury, Hereford and Worcs.
Ford, R., Long Melford, Suffolk.
Foreman, Mr. and Mrs. A.M., Carlisle, Cumbria.
Forest Books of Cheshire, Manchester, Lancs.
Forge Antiques, The, Coleraine, Co. Londonderry, N. Ireland.
Forge Antiques, Portstewart, Co. Londonderry, N. Ireland.
Forge Antiques, Redmarley D'Abitot, Glos.
Forge Antiques, Synod Inn, Dyfed, Wales.
Forge Antiques and Restorations, Sandhurst, Kent.
Forget-me-Not, Swansea, W. Glam., Wales. Ant. C.
Forman, Adrian, London, W.1. G. Ant. Mkt.
Forman of Piccadilly Ltd., London, W.1.
Format of Birmingham Ltd., Birmingham, W. Mids.
Forrer, M., Marlborough, Wilts.
Forrest and Co:, E.B., Edinburgh, Midloth., Scot.
Forrest and Co. (Jewellers) Ltd., James, Glasgow, Lanarks., Scot.
Forrest, R., Edinburgh, Midloth., Scot. (Artisan)
Forrester, C., Glasgow, Scot. (Mercat-Hughes Antiques)
Forster, Newton Abbot, Devon. N.A. Ant. C.
Forster, B., London, S.W.1. (M. Ekstein Ltd.)
Forster, J.M.W., London, W.C.1.
Forster, R.A.S., Arnesby, Leics.
Forster, W., London, N.16.
Forsyth Antiques, Perth., Perths., Scot.
Forsyth, A. McDonald, Perth, Perths., Scot.
Forsyth, B. and E., Fochabers, Morays., Scot.
Forsyth, J.W. and L.J., High Bentham, N. Yorks.
Forsyth, J.W. and L.J., Lancaster, Lancs.
Forsyth, W., Cheltenham, Glos. (Turtle Fine Art).
Forsythe, Albert, Saintfield, Co. Down, N. Ireland.
Fortescue Gallery, The, Ipswich, Suffolk.
Fortescue, L. (The Fortescue Gallery), Ipswich, Suffolk.
Fortnum and Mason p.l.c., London, W.1.
Fortunate Finds, Torquay, Devon.
Fortunoff Silver Sales Incorporated, London, W.1. B. St. Silv. Galls.
Forty Eight Walton St., London, S.W.3.
Forty Nine, Manningtree, Essex.
Forum Antiques, Cirencester, Glos.
Fosse Gallery, Stow-on-the-Wold, Glos.
Fosse Way Antiques, Stow-on-the-Wold, Glos.
Foster, A. and E., Naphill, Bucks.
Foster Antiques, Gene and Sally, Bath, Avon.
Foster, Mrs. J., Wellingborough, Northants.
Foster, J.A., Wellingborough, Northants.
Foster Ltd., Kate, London, S.W.1.
Foster, Michael, London, S.W.3.
Foster, Mrs. M., Market Rasen, Lincs.
Foster, M.C.A., Swafield, Norfolk.
Foster, M.I., Weybridge, Surrey.
Foster, O.J., Shrewsbury, Shrops.
Foster, P., Dorking, Surrey.
Foster, Miss P.I. and Keith A., Lewes, E. Sussex.
Foster, Miss S., Bristol, Avon. Clift. Ant. Mkt.
Foster-Pegg, R. and S., Grundisburgh, Suffolk.
Fothergill, A., York, N. Yorks. (Ken Spelman)
Foulds-Field Fine Art, Leicester, Leics.
Foulger, P.L. and W.B., Bungay, Suffolk.
Foundry Lane Antiques Centre, Lewes, E. Sussex.
Fountain Antiques, Eastbourne, E. Sussex.
Fountain Antiques, Honiton, Devon.
Four Seasons Antiques, Woodstock, Oxon.
Fourteen A., Modbury, Devon.
Fowle, A.C., London, S.W.16.
Fowle, A. and J., London, S.W.16.
Fowler, F., St. Leonards-on-Sea, E. Sussex. Hastings Ant. C.
Fowler (Period Clocks), Robin, Great Coates, S. Humberside.
Fowler, S.G., Boughton, Kent.
Fowles, D., Yeovil, Somerset.
Fox and Co., Yeovil, Somerset.
Fox House, Woodstock, Oxon.
Fox, Judy, London, W.11.
Fox, M. and P., Harrogate, N. Yorks. (Fox's Antique Pine and Country Furniture).
Fox and Pheasant Antique Pine, White Colne, Essex.
Fox, Sally, London, N.W.8. Alf. Ant. Mkt.
Fox's Antique Pine and Country Furniture, Harrogate, N. Yorks.
Foye Gallery, Luton, Beds.
Foyle Ltd., W. and G., London, W.C.2.
Frame, Ian, Glasgow, Lanarks., Scot. Vict. Vill.
Frampton, T., Beaminster, Dorset.
Frampton, Mrs. T.P.F., Beaminster, Dorset.
Franca Antiques, Tunbridge Wells, Kent.

France, Alan M., Wolverhampton, W. Mids.
Francis, G., Norwich, Norfolk. (This and That).
Francis, Peter, London, W.1.
Francis, Mrs. P.B., Puckeridge, Herts.
Franco Antiques, Retford, Notts.
Franco, F., Retford, Notts.
Francombe, C., Eastbourne, E. Sussex.
Frankham Gallery, Tunbridge Wells, Kent.
Frankl, G., London, N.W.4.
Frankland, B.A., Doddington, Cambs.
Franklin (Antiques), N. and I., London, W.1. B. St. Silv. Galls.
Franklin, R., London, S.E.5.
Franklins, Camberwell Antique Market, London, S.E.5.
Franklyn, S., London, W.11. (The Antique Textile Company).
Franks Book Shop, Manchester, Lancs. R. Ex. S.C.
Franks, Douglas, Frensham, Surrey.
Franks, I., London, W.C.2. Lon. Silv. Vts.
Franks Ltd., J.A.L., London, S.W.1.
Franks Ltd., J.A.L., London, W.C.1.
Franks, Renee, Manchester, Lancs. Royal Ex. S.C.
Franses and Sons, Robert, London, N.W.8.
Franses Ltd., S., London, S.W.1.
Franses Conservation, S., London, W.2.
Franses Gallery, Victor, London, S.W.1.
Frasco International Ltd., London, S.W.1. (Moreton St. Gallery)
Fraser Antiques, North Berwick, E. Loth., Scot.
Fraser Antiques, Douglas B., Glasgow, Lanarks., Scot. B. St. Ant. G.
Frasers Antiques and Reproductions, Inverness, Inver., Scot.
Fraser-Welch, A., Ellesmere, Shrops.
Frayling, G., Bath, Avon. Gt. West. Ant. C.
Frazer Antiques, Malcolm, Cheadle, Cheshire.
Fredericks and Son, C., London, S.W.3.
Fredericks and Son, J.A., London, W.1.
Fredericks, J.A. and C.J., London, W.1.
Fredericks, R.F., London, S.W.3.
Freedman, Gerald, London, S.W.6.
Freedman, Mrs. H., London, N.21.
Freeman Antiques, Roxwell, Essex.
Freeman Antiques, Carol, Monmouth, Gwent, Wales.
Freeman, G.O., St. Annes-on-Sea, Lancs.
Freeman, J., London, W.11.
Freeman, J.G. and A., Norwich, Norfolk.
Freeman, K., Sandgate, Kent.
Freeman and Lloyd Antiques, Sandgate, Kent.
Freeman Antiques, Simon, Bath, Avon.
Freeman, T.A., Malmesbury, Wilts.
Freeman, Vincent, London, N.1.
Freestone, E., London, N.W.8. Alf. Ant. Mkt.
Freestone, F., Manningtree, Essex.
French, C., Eastbourne, E. Sussex.
French Fine Arts, York, N. York.
French Glasshouse, The, London, W.8.
French-Greenslade, S., Tilston, Cheshire.
Frenches Farm Antiques, Kings Langley, Herts.
Frere Antiques, Joan, Drumnadrochit, Inver., Scot.
Freuchie Antiques, Freuchie, Fife, Scot.
Friargate Pine and Antiques Centre, Derby, Derbys.
Friars Gate Antiques, Worcester, Hereford and Worcs.
Friedner, M., London, W.C.2. (Linden and Co. (Antiques) Ltd.). Lon. Silv. Vts.
Friend Antiques, David, Manchester, Lancs.
Frings, S., Leicester, Leics.
Frinton Antiques, Frinton-on-Sea, Essex.
Frith, M., Lincoln, Lincs.
Frith Antiques, H.A. and Mrs. M.A., Petworth, W. Sussex.
Frith, T. and M., London, W.1 (The Button Queen).
Fritz-Denneville Fine Arts Ltd., H., London, W.1.
Frocks and Tails, Bristol, Avon.
Frognal Rare Books, London, W.C.2.
Frontiers, London, S.W.3. Ant. Ant. Mkt.
Frost, A.P., Hampton, Middx.
Frost, C.C., Long Melford, Suffolk.
Frost, L., Eccleston, Lancs.
Frost, Paddy, London, S.W.3. Ant. Ant. Mkt.
Frost, P.J., Iver, Bucks.
Frost, R.F., Martlesham, Suffolk.
Frost and Reed Ltd., London, W.1.
Fry, M., London, N.W.2.
Frydman, O., London, W.1. B. St. Silv. Galls.
Fryer, F., Ross-on-Wye, Hereford and Worcs.
Fryer Antique Lighting, Fritz, Ross-on-Wye, Hereford and Worcs.
Fulda Gallery Ltd., Manchester, Lancs.
Fulda, M.J., Manchester, Lancs.
Fullam, A., Londonderry, Co. Londonderry, N. Ireland.
Fulwood Antiques and The Basement Gallery, Sheffield, S. Yorks.
Fun Antiques, Sheffield, S. Yorks.
Furness, O., St. Annes-on-Sea, Lancs.
Furney Antiques, Donaghadee, Co. Down, N. Ireland.
Furney, B. and I., Donaghadee, Co. Down, N. Ireland.
Furniture Cave, The, Aberystwyth, Dyfed, Wales.
Furniture Cave, London, S.W.10.
Furniture Mart, Margate, Kent.
Furniture Store Ltd., The, London, N.W.8.
Furniture Store/St. Austell Antiques Centre, The, St. Austell, Cornwall.
Furniture Vault, London, N.1.
Furze, M., Much Hadham, Herts.
Fyfe's Antiques, Edinburgh, Midloth., Scot.
Fylde Antiques, Preston, Lancs. N.W. Ant. C.
Fyne Antiques, Blairmore, Argyll, Scot.
Fynes, J., Easebourne, W. Sussex.
Fyson Antiques, Jonathan, Burford, Oxon.
Fyson, J.R., Burford, Oxon.

G

G.B. Antiques Ltd., Lancaster, Lancs.
G.D. and S.T. Antiques, Poole, Dorset.
G.G. Exports, Morecambe, Lancs.
G. and J. Antiques, Buxton, Derbys.
G.V.R. Antiques Ltd., Birmingham, W. Mids.
G.W. Antiques, Lancaster, Lancs.
G.W. Antiques, Preston, Lancs. N.W. Ant. C.
Gadsden, P., Petersfield, Hants.
Gage (Works of Art) Ltd., Deborah, London, W.1.
Gage, J. and E., Topsham, Devon.
Gainsborough House Antiques, Sidmouth, Devon.
Gainsborough House Antiques, Tewkesbury, Glos.
Galata Coins Ltd., Wolverhampton, W. Mids.
Gale, E. and S., Portscatho, Cornwall.
Gale, P.A., Warminster, Wilts.
Gale, P.A. and D., Warminster, Wilts.
Galerias Segui, Cowes, I. of Wight.
Galerie 1900, London, N.W.1.
Galerie Antiques, Broadstone, Dorset.
Galerie Harounoff, London, W.1. G. Mews.
Galerie Lev, Woodford Green, Essex.
Galerie Moderne Ltd., London, S.W.1.
Gale-Yearsley, Mrs. K., Wimborne Minster, Dorset.
Gallagher (Antiques), M., Llangollen, Clwyd, Wales.
Gallagher, M. and L., Perth, Perths., Scot.
Galleitch, M. and H., Ardersier, Inverns., Scot.
Galleon, The, Bath, Avon.
Galleon Antiques, Coalville, Leics.
Galleon Antiques, Hastings, E. Sussex.
Galleon Antiques, St. Leonards-on-Sea, E. Sussex.
Galleria Fine Arts Ltd., St. Leonards-on-Sea, E. Sussex.
Galleries Antiques Centre, The, Redditch, Hereford and Worcs.
Galleries de Fresnes, Galston, Ayrs., Scot.
Gallery, Aberdeen, Aberd., Scot.
Gallery, The, Arundel, W. Sussex.
Gallery, The, Bexhill-on-Sea, E. Sussex.
Gallery, The, Penrith, Cumbria.
Gallery, The, Portsmouth, Hants.
Gallery, The, Yarmouth, Isle of Wight.
Gallery 6, Broseley, Shrops.
Gallery 16, Bruton, Somerset.
Gallery 25, London, S.W.1.
Gallery 45, Norwich, Norfolk.
Gallery 88, Arundel, W. Sussex.
Gallery 287 and Gallery 289, London, W.11.
Gallery Antiques, Oakham, Leics.
Gallery Antiques Ltd., Winchester, Hants.
Gallery Arcticus, London, S.W.3.
Gallery Kaleidoscope, London, N.W.6.
Gallery Laraine Ltd., Eastbourne, E. Sussex.
Gallery Lingard, London, S.W.1.
Gallery of Antique Costume and Textiles, The, London, N.W.8.
Gallery on Church Street, The, London, N.W.8.
Gallery One, Perth, Scot.
Gallery Six Antiques at Nigel Purchase Gallery, Chichester, W. Sussex.
Gallery and Things, The, South Lopham, Norfolk.
Gallery Three, March, Cambs.
Gallery Tonkin and Gallery Lyonesse, Penzance, Cornwall.
Gallie, F., Battlesbridge, Essex.
Gallie, J.F., Battlesbridge, Essex.
Gallop, G.P., Crickhowell, Powys, Wales.
Gallop and Rivers, Architectural Antiques, Crickhowell, Powys, Wales.
Galloway Antiques, Boroughbridge, N. Yorks.
Galloway and Porter Ltd., Cambridge, Cambs.
Galloways (Edinburgh) Ltd., Edinburgh, Midloth., Scot.
Gamble, A.F.H., Plymouth, Devon.
Game Advice, London, N.W.5.
Gander, Michael, Hitchin, Herts.
Gandolfi House Interiors, Malvern Wells, Hereford and Worcs.
Gange, C.C., Marlborough, Wilts.
Gant, Elizabeth, Thames Ditton, Surrey.
Gaphar, S.A., London, S.W.18.
Garbett, M., Bristol, Avon. (Cotham Hill Bookshop).
Garden House Antiques, Tenterden, Kent.
Gardiner Antiques, London, E.4.
Gardiner Antiques, Charles, Lurgan, Co. Armagh, N. Ireland.
Gardiner Antiques, Helen, London, N.W.8. Alf. Ant. Mkt.
Gardiner, Mrs. J., Somerton, Somerset.
Gardiner Antiques, John, Somerton, Somerset.
Gardiner, K., Berkeley, Glos.
Gardiner, Robin, London, N.W.8. Alf. Ant. Mkt.
Gardner, A.J., London, S.W.3 (The Purple Shop).
Gardner, Mrs. B., Loughborough, Leics.
Gardner, E., London, N.W.3. Hamp. Ant. Emp.
Gardner, G.D. and R.K.F., Kilbarchan, Renfrews., Scot.
Gardner, J., Bishops Cleeve, Glos.
Gardner, J., London, N.1. The Mall.
Gardner, P. and J., Bexhill-on-Sea, E. Sussex. Bex. Ant. C.
Gardner's The Antique Shop, Kilbarchan, Renfrews., Scot.
Gargrave Gallery, Gargrave, N. Yorks.
Garman, G., Lower Bentham, N. Yorks.
Garn House Antiques, Bow Street, Dyfed, Wales.
Garner, G., Monkton, Devon.
Garner, John, Uppingham, Leics.
Garner Antiques, P.R., Landbeach, Cambs.
Garrard and Co. Ltd., (The Crown Jewellers), London, W.1.
Garratt Antiques, Birmingham, W. Mids.
Garratt (Fine Paintings), Stephen, London, W.14
Garraway, William, London, N.W.8. Alf. Ant. Mkt.

Garrets Antiques, Blandford Forum, Dorset.
Garrick Antiques, Philip, London, W.11.
Garriock, R.B., Edinburgh, Midloth., Scot.
Garrow, Marilyn, London, S.W.13.
Garrow Antique Textiles, Marilyn, London, W.1.
Garson and Co. Ltd., Manchester, Lancs.
Garth Antiques, Harrogate, N. Yorks.
Garth Antiques, Whixley, N. Yorks.
Garvin Antiques, London, N.W.3. Ham. Ant. Emp.
Gasson, Herbert Gordon, Rye, E. Sussex.
Gatehouse Antiques, Macclesfield, Cheshire.
Gates, Mrs. M.A.B., Hartley Wintney, Hants.
Gates, Mrs. M.A.B., London, N.1. (Boutique Fantasque).
Gateway Antiques, Burford, Oxon.
Gateway Antiques II, Burford, Oxon.
Gauld, Maureen H., Killin, Perths., Scot.
Gaunt, Peter, London, W.1. B. St. Silv. Galls.
Gavèls, Long Preston, N. Yorks.
Gavey, Geoffrey P., Vale, Guernsey, C.I.
Gavey, G.P. and Mrs. C., St. Peter Port, Guernsey, C.I.
Gavin, J.M., Penryn, Cornwall.
Gay, Bernard, Mansell Lacy, Hereford and Worcs.
Gay, Mr. and Mrs. J.E., Boroughbridge, N. Yorks.
Gay, M. and B.M., Romsey, Hants.
Gaylords, Titchfield, Hants.
Gay's (Hazel Grove) Antiques Ltd., Hazel Grove, Cheshire.
Gazeley Associates Fine Art, John, Ipswich, Suffolk.
Gazelle's Art Deco Interiors, Southampton, Hants.
Gealer, Mrs. R., Falmouth, Cornwall.
Gealer, Cdr. R., Falmouth, Cornwall.
Gear, J., Hindhead, Surrey.
Gearing, J.A., Eastbourne, E. Sussex.
Geary Antiques, Leeds, W. Yorks.
Geary, J.A., Leeds, W. Yorks.
Geddes, Mrs D., London, W1. (Addison Fine Art).
Gee, C.R. and C.J., Tetbury, Glos.
Gee, Mrs. W., Melbourne, Derbys.
Gemini Antiques, Great Missenden, Bucks.
Gemini Antiques, Wolverhampton, W. Mids.
Gemini Trading, Leek, Staffs.
Gemma Antiques, Worcester, Hereford and Worcs.
Gems Antiques, Chichester, W. Sussex.
Geneen Ltd., Lionel, Bournemouth, Dorset.
General Trading Co. Ltd., London, S.W.1.
Genesis, Newark, Notts. N. Ant. Wrhse.
Genesis Antiques, Birmingham, W. Mids.
Genges Farm Antiques, Limington, Somerset.
Genie, London, N.W.8. Alf. Ant. Mkt.
Gentle Antiques, Rupert, Milton Lilbourne, Wilts.
Geoff Militaria, Swansea, W. Glam, Wales. Ant. C.
George, A., London, S.W.6.
George, C., London, S.W.8.
George Clocks, Stamford, Lincs.
George, D., London, S.W.1. (Eaton Gallery)
George Leuchars, London, S.W.6.
George Street Antiques Centre, Hastings, E. Sussex.
George Street Gallery, The, Perth, Perths., Scot.
George's Antiquarian and Secondhand Bookshop, Bristol, Avon.
Georgian Antiques, Edinburgh, Midloth., Scot.
Georgian Gems Antique Jewellers, Swanage, Dorset.
Georgian House, Kendal, Cumbria.
Georgian House Antiques, Bournemouth, Dorset.
Georgian House Antiques, Chipping Norton, Oxon.
Georgian House Antiques, Hertford, Herts.
Georgian House Antiques, Ottery St. Mary, Devon.
Georgian House Antiques, Uckfield, E. Sussex.
Georgian Village, London, N.1.
Georgian Village Antiques Market, London, E.17.
Georgina's Antiques, London, E.17.
Geostran Antiques, Coleshill, Warks.
Gerards, Scarborough, N. Yorks.
Geris, S.A., London, S.W.3. Ant. Ant. Mkt.
Germain, Mrs. M.M., Ilford, Essex.
Germain, T.C., Burnham-on-Sea, Somerset.
German, Michael G., London, W.8.
Gerry, R., London, W.8. (Barnet Antiques).
Get Stuffed, London, N.1.
Gewirtz, J., London, N.1. (John Laurie)
Ghassemi, F. and V., London, W.1. (South Audley Antiques).
Ghiggini, Nina, London, W.6.
Gholam, J. and J.M., Ringway, Cheshire.
Gibb, A., London, W.14.
Gibbins Antiques, David, Woodbridge, Suffolk.
Gibbon, Richard, London, N.W.8. Alf. Ant. Mkt.
Gibbons, Derek, Cambridge, Cambs.
Gibbons, Stanley, London, W.C.2.
Gibb's Bookshop Ltd., Manchester, Lancs.
Gibbs, C.A., Isleworth, Middx.
Gibbs Ltd., Christopher, London, W.1.
Gibbs, J.P. and A.M., Great Malvern, Hereford and Worcs.
Gibbs, Norman, London, N.1. The Mall.
Gibbs Antiques and Decorative Arts, Paul, Conway, Gwynedd, Wales.
Gibbs, W.T., Kempston, Beds.
Gibson, C., London, S.W.3. Ant. Ant. Mkt.
Gibson, David, Bath, Avon.
Gibson, J. and P., Reigate, Surrey.
Gibson, N., Bowden, Cheshire.
Gibson, R., Great Wakering, Essex.
Gibson, Roderick, Nantwich, Cheshire.
Gibson, S.R. & A., Leeds, W. Yorks.
Gibson Fine Art Ltd., Thomas, London, W.1.
Giddings, J.C., Wiveliscombe, Somerset.
Giffengate Antiques, Dorchester-on-Thames, Oxon.
Gifford-Mead, N.J.A., London, S.W.10 (Furniture Cave).

Gilbert, B. and C., Sheffield, S. Yorks. (Gilbert and Sons).
Gilbert, B.L. and R.C., Southampton, Hants.
Gilbert, B.L. and R.C., Winchester, Hants.
Gilbert, D., Canterbury, Kent.
Gilbert, D., Sutton Coldfield, W. Mids.
Gilbert, H.M., Winchester, Hants.
Gilbert and Son, H.M., Southampton, Hants.
Gilbert, M., Uppingham, Leics.
Gilbert, R., Limington, Somerset.
Gilbert, R., Haunton, Staffs.
Gilbert and Sons, Sheffield, S. Yorks.
Gilbert, Trevor, London, W.1. G. Mews.
Gilberti, Attilio, London, W.1.
Gilberts of Uppingham, Uppingham, Leics.
Gilchrist and Associates, A. and C., Dorking, Surrey.
Gilded Lily, The, London, W.1. G. Ant. Mkt.
Giles, John, London, W.9. (Sheila Hart)
Gilham, J.E., Cawood, N. Yorks.
Gill, Mr., London, S.W.3. Ant. Ant. Mkt.
Gill, D., London, S.W.3.
Gill, D., Hungerford, Berks. (Mary Bellis Antiques).
Gillespie, V., Olveston, Avon. (Green Farm Antiques).
Gillet, B., Melksham, Wilts.
Gillett, R. and A., Petworth, W. Sussex. (The Bacchus Gallery).
Gilligan, M.T., Leek, Staffs.
Gilligans Antiques, Leek, Staffs.
Gillingham Antiques, Guildford, Surrey.
Gillingham Ltd., G. and F., London, N.W.2.
Gillingham, J.L., Mousehole, Cornwall.
Gillingham, R. Harrogate, N. Yorks. W. Pk. Ant. Pav.
Gillings, B. Goff, Long Melford, Suffolk.
Gilmore Antiques, Elizabeth, Honiton, Devon.
Giltsoff, N., Warminster, Wilts.
Gilwern Antiques, Gilwern, Gwent.
Ginders, M., Ixworth, Suffolk.
Ginger, G. and D., Ludlow, Shrops.
Ginnel, The, Harrogate, N. Yorks.
Ginnel Gallery, The, Manchester, Lancs.
Ginsberg, P., Prestbury, Cheshire.
Ginty, John, Woburn, Beds. Wob. Ab. Ant. C.
Giordani, Maurizzio and Loretta, London, S.W.3. Ant. Ant. Mkt.
Giorgi, T., London, S.W.3. Ant. Ant. Mkt.
Gittings, A., Sutton Bridge, Lincs.
Gittins and Son, G.J., Caerphilly, Mid-Glam., Wales.
Giuntini, Mrs. G., Canterbury, Kent.
Glade Antiques, London, N.W.8. Alf. Ant. Mkt.
Gladrags, Edinburgh, Midloth., Scot.
Glaisyer, D. and N., Moreton-in-Marsh, Glos.
Glaisyer, D. and N., Stretton-on-Fosse, Warks.
Glaisyer, R. and C., Stow-on-the-Wold, Glos.
Glance Back Bookshop, Chepstow, Gwent, Wales.
Glance Gallery, Chepstow, Gwent, Wales.
Glanfield, R.W., Lowestoft, Suffolk.
Glasby and Son Antiques, A.W., Leedstown, Cornwall.
Glasby, D.E., Leedstown, Cornwall.
Glassdrumman Antiques, Tunbridge Wells, Kent.
Glassman, Miss R., Brighton, E. Sussex (The Witch Ball).
Glassman, R., London, W.C.2.
Glazebrook, A., Richmond, Surrey.
Glazebrook, M., London, W.1. (Albemarle Gallery).
Glenburn Antiques, Glasgow, Lanarks., Scot. B. St. Ant. G.
Glencorse Antiques, Kingston-upon-Thames, Surrey.
Glendale, M. and R., London, W.1.
Glen-Doepel, Mrs. D., Lincoln, Lincs.
Glenn, M.P., Blairmore, Argyll, Scot.
Glenville Antiques, Yatton, Avon.
Gliksten, M., Malmesbury, Wilts.
Gliksten, M., London, N.W.1. (Relic Antiques Trade Warehouse).
Glossop Antique Centre, Glossop, Derbys.
Glossop, F., St. Ives, Cornwall.
Gloucester Antique Centre, Gloucester, Glos.
Gloucester House Antiques Ltd., Fairford, Glos.
Glover, F.D., Southport, Merseyside. (Decor Galleries).
Glover (Antiques), J.K., Haslemere, Surrey.
Glover and Stacey Ltd., Tongham, Surrey.
Gluck, D., Cardiff, S. Glam., Wales (Heritage Antiques and Stripped Pine).
Gluck, J. and Mrs. F., Llanfair Caereinion, Powys, Wales.
Glydon and Guess Ltd., Kingston-upon-Thames, Surrey.
Glynn Interiors, Knutsford, Cheshire.
Gmur, Helen, London, N.W.8. Alf. Ant. Mkt.
Gnome Cottage Antiques, Stroud, Glos.
Goble, Paul, Brighton, E. Sussex.
Goddard, Miss J.P., Oughtibridge, S. Yorks.
Goddard Antiques, Julie, Oughtibridge, S. Yorks.
Godden at Klaber and Klaber, Geoffrey, London, W.8.
Godden Chinaman, Geoffrey, Worthing, W. Sussex.
Godden, G.A., Worthing, W. Sussex.
Godden, G. and J., Worthing, W. Sussex.
Godden of Worthing Ltd., Worthing, W. Sussex.
Godfrey Antiques Ltd., Howard, Sandgate, Kent.
Godfrey, Jemima, Newmarket, Suffolk.
Godsafe, B., Norwich, Norfolk. (St. Michael at Plea Antiques Market)
Godsell, A.A. and C.M.J., Ridgewell, Essex.
Godson and Coles Ltd., London, S.W.3.
Goff Galleries, The, Long Melford, Suffolk.
Goggin, Joan, Guildford, Surrey.
Gold Hill Antiques and Collectibles, Shaftesbury, Dorset.
Gold Shop, The, Torquay, Devon.
Gold and Silver Exchange, Exeter, Devon.
Gold and Silver Exchange, Gt. Yarmouth, Norfolk.
Gold and Silver Shop, Gorseinon, W. Glam., Wales.

Gold and Silversmiths of Hove, The, Brighton, E. Sussex.
Goldband, D. and T., London, W.C.2 (Old Curiosity Shop).
Golden Cage, The, Nottingham, Notts.
Golden Drop Antiques, The, Warboys, Cambs.
Golden Goose Books, Lincoln, Lincs.
Golden Oldies, Holt, Norfolk.
Golden Oldies, Penkridge, Staffs.
Golden Oldies, Wolverhampton, W. Mids.
Golden Sovereign, Great Bardfield, Essex.
Golder, Gwendoline, Coltishall, Norfolk.
Golding, D., London, W.C.2. Lon. Silv. Vts.
Golding, Eric, Wisbech, Cambs.
Golding and Co., Jules, London, W.C.2. Lon. Silv. Vts.
Golding, M., Stockport, Cheshire.
Golding, M., Manchester, Lancs. (Zippy Antiques)
Golding, M.F., S.P. and N.M.J., Stow-on-the-Wold, Glos.
Golding, Pat, Arundel, W. Sussex.
Goldmark Books, Uppingham, Leics.
Goldmark, M.M., Uppingham, Leics.
Goldsmith, A., London, W.11.
Goldsmith & Perris, London, N.W.8. Alf. Ant. Mkt.
Goldsmith, William, Leeds, W. Yorks.
Goldstone, Michael, Bakewell, Derbys.
Goldstraw, Mrs. Y.A., Leek, Staffs.
Goldstrom, T. and A., London, N.1. The Mall.
Goldthorpe, P. and J., Godalming, Surrey.
Golebiowski, Z., London, W.1. (Atlantic Bay Carpets).
Good Fairy Open Air Market, The, London, W.11.
Good Hope Antiques, Beaminster, Dorset.
Good, Mrs. K., Waddesdon, Bucks.
Goodacre Engraving Ltd., Long Eaton, Derbys.
Goodacre, K., Bournemouth, Dorset. (Collectors Corner)
Gooday, Peter and Debbie, Richmond, Surrey.
Gooday, R., East Molesey, Surrey.
Gooday Shop and Studio, The, East Molesey, Surrey.
Goodbrey, B., Framlingham, Suffolk.
Goodbrey, R. and M., Framlingham, Suffolk.
Goodbreys, Framlingham, Suffolk.
Goode and Co. Ltd., Thomas, London, W.1.
Goode, Vyvyan, Newton Abbot, Devon. N.A. Ant. C.
Goodfellow (Antiques), William, Carnforth, Lancs.
Gooding-Lapworth Clocks, G. Buxton, Lapworth, Warks.
Goodinge, Mrs. J.A., Henfield, W. Sussex.
Goodlad, Anthony D., Chesterfield, Derbys.
Goodland, D. and C., Spilsby, Lincs.
Goodman, A., Midhurst, W. Sussex.
Goodman Gold, Grimsby, S. Humberside.
Goodman, K.E., Torquay, Devon.
Goodman, P., Reymerston, Norfolk.
Goodman, P. and L., Beverley, N. Humberside.
Goodman, R.J., Snodland, Kent.
Goodman, R.J., Tunbridge Wells, Kent.
Goodman, S.N., Grimsby, S. Humberside.
Goodsman, T.A., Warminster, Wilts.
Goodson, C.A., Barford, Warks.
Goodson's Antiques, Barford, Warks.
Goodwin, E., Great Bardfield, Essex.
Goodwin, G.A. and A.M., London, N.W.2.
Goodwin and Sons, John, Leamington Spa, Warks.
Goodwin and Sons, John, Warwick, Warks.
Goodwin, M., Alderley Edge, Cheshire.
Goodwin, M., Buckingham, Bucks.
Goodwin Exports, Nick, Guilsborough, Northants.
Goodwin, P., London, S.W.6.
Goodwin & Wadhwa, London, S.W.6.
Goodwins Antiques Ltd., Edinburgh, Midloth., Scot.
Gooley, P., London, W.9.
Gordon, A. and F., London, W.1.
Gordon, Brian, London, S.W.3. Chen. Gall.
Gordon Antiques, Christopher, Birmingham, W. Mids.
Gordon, D. and E., Fochabers, Scotland.
Gordon, G., London, N.W.3.
Gordon, G., London, N.W.8.
Gordon, Janet, Wakes Colne, Essex.
Gordon, Mr. and Mrs. J.F., Newton Abbot, Devon.
Gordon, Ora, London, W.1. G. Mews.
Gordon, Mrs. P., Ardingley, W. Sussex.
Gordon, R. and J., Alford, Aberd. Scot.
Gordon (Antiques), R.S., Alford, Aberd., Scot.
Gore, Teresa, London, N.W.8. Alf. Ant. Mkt.
Goring Antique Centre, Goring-on-Thames, Oxon.
Gorman, Mrs. J.M., Chesterfield, Derbys.
Gormley Antiques, J. and S., Broadway, Hereford and Worcs.
Gorst Hall Restoration, Kidderminster, Hereford and Worcs.
Goslett Gallery, Roland, Richmond, Surrey.
Gosling, C. and A., Budleigh Salterton, Devon.
Gosling, M., Portsmouth, Hants.
Goss and Crested China Centre., Horndean, Hants.
Gostling's Antique Centre, Diss, Norfolk.
Gothick Dream Fine Art, Arthog, Gwynedd, Wales.
Gottlieb, Marie, London, N.W.8.Alf. Ant. Mkt.
Gouby, M., London, W.8 (Michael Coins).
Gough, B.A., Carshalton, Surrey.
Gough Bros. Art Shop and Gallery, Bognor Regis, W. Sussex.
Gough, Maureen, Woodstock, Oxon.
Gough Books, Simon, Holt, Norfolk.
Gould and Sons (Antiques) Ltd., A.E., East Horsley, Surrey.
Gould Antiques and Julian Gonnevmann, Betty, London, N.6.
Gould, D. and P., East Horsley, Surrey.
Gould, E., Teddington, Middx.
Gould, Gillian, London, W.1.

Gould, Patrick and Susan, London, W.1. G. Mews.
Gould, S., Stratford-upon-Avon, Warks.
Goulding, G., Morecambe, Lancs.
Goullet, J., London, S.W.3. Ant. Ant. Mkt.
Gourlay, R. and I., Houndwood, Berwicks., Scot.
Gowen, M., St. Leonards-on-Sea, E. Sussex.
Gower, C., Burford, Oxon.
Gower, Christopher, London, S.W.3. Ant. Ant. Mkt.
Gower, C., Stow-on-the-Wold, Glos.
Gower, G., Malmesbury, Wilts.
Gower, G., London, N.W.1. (Relic Antiques Trade Warehouse).
Grace, Mr. and Mrs. S. Staley, Ramsey, Cambs.
Grafton Country Pictures, Oakham, Leics.
Graham, A., London, W.11. (Graham and Green).
Graham, A. and A., Larne, Co. Antrim, N. Ireland.
Graham Ltd., Albert, Larne, Co. Antrim, N. Ireland.
Graham, A.P., Newcastle-upon-Tyne, Tyne and Wear. (The Dean Gallery).
Graham, Daphne, London, S.W.3.
Graham Gallery, David, London, N.1.
Graham Gallery, Burghfield Common, Berks.
Graham Gallery, Tunbridge Wells, Kent.
Graham Gallery Ltd., Gavin, London, W.11.
Graham and Green, London, W.11.
Graham, Imogen, London, S.W.6.
Graham, Joss, London, S.W.1.
Graham, J., Ross-on-Wye, Hereford and Worcs.
Graham, J., Tunbridge Wells, Kent.
Graham and Oxley (Antiques) Ltd., London, W.8.
Graham, Mr. and Mrs. R.M. Maxtone, Hythe, Kent.
Graham, Mr. and Mrs. R.M. Maxtone, Sandwich, Kent.
Graham-Stewart, M., London, W.11.
Grahame, Eila, London, W.8.
Gramophone Workshop, London, N.W.8. Alf. Ant. Mkt.
Granary Galleries, The, Ash Priors, Somerset.
Grand View Antiques, Swansea, W. Glam., Wales.
Grandfather Clock Shop, The, Shipston-on-Stour, Warks.
Grandma's Goodies, Cardiff, S. Glam., Wales.
Grange Antiques, St. Peter Port, Guernsey, C.I.
Grange Gallery and Fine Arts Ltd., St. Helier, Jersey, C.I.
Grange, J., Leominster, Hereford and Worcs. L. Ant. Mkt.
Granger, Mrs. M., Poole, Dorset.
Grannies Attic, Market Weighton, N. Humberside.
Grannie's Attic, Shottermill, Surrey.
Grannie's Attic Antiques, Smethwick, W. Mids.
Grannie's Parlour, Hull, N. Humberside.
Grannie's Treasures, Hull, N. Humberside.
Granny's Attic, Clare, Suffolk.
Granny's Attic, Nottingham, Notts.
Granny's Kist, Fochabers, Scotland.
Granshaw, M., Shalford, Surrey.
Grant Antiques, Denzil, Bradfield St. George, Suffolk.
Grant Fine Art, Droitwich, Hereford and Worcs.
Grant, J., Avening, Glos.
Grant, J., Tetbury, Glos.
Grant, K.N., London, W.1. G. Ant. Mkt.
Grant, Mrs. P., London, S.W.1 (Ning Ltd.).
Grant, R., Boston, Lincs.
Grant Antiques, Stephanie, Barnard Castle, Durham.
Grant, Sylvia, Woburn, Beds. Wob. Ab. Ant. C.
Grant, S.A., Barnard Castle, Durham.
Grant, Mrs. V., Waddesdon, Bucks.
Grantham Clocks, Grantham, Lincs.
Grantham Furniture Emporium, Grantham, Lincs.
Grant-Peterkin, K., London, W.1. (A.D.C. Heritage Ltd.)
Granville Antiques, Petworth, W. Sussex.
Grasvenor Antiques, London, S.E.1. Ber. Ant. Wrhse.
Grate Expectations, Camborne, Cornwall.
Grater, S., Thundersley, Essex.
Gratton, P., Inverness, Inver., Scot.
Gratwick, A., Hartley Wintney, Hants.
Graus Antiques, London, W.1.
Graus, E. and H., London, W.1.
Gravelly Bank Pine Antiques, Yeaveley, Derbys.
Gravener Antiques, Wm. J., Mayfield, E. Sussex.
Graves Gallery, The, Birmingham, W. Mids.
Gray, Anthony, London, W.1. G. Mews.
Gray, Mr. and Mrs. A., Penrith, Cumbria.
Gray Antique Centre, Weedon, Northants.
Gray, A.E., Norwich, Norfolk. (Elm Hill Antiques).
Gray, B., London, N.W.8. Alf. Ant. Mkt.
Gray, David, Glasgow, Scotland. B. St. Ant. G.
Gray, D. and M., Great Malvern, Hereford and Worcs.
Gray, F., Oakham, Leics.
Gray, G.C.M., Hertford, Herts.
Gray, Mrs. J., Cirencester, Glos.
Gray Antiques, Jay, Cirencester, Glos.
Gray, L., Kingsthorpe, Northants.
Gray, M., Bradford, W. Yorks.
Gray, Marion, London, N.4.
Gray Antiques, Robert, London, S.W.6.
Gray (Antique Dealer), Robert, Weedon, Northants.
Gray, Mrs. S., Sheffield, S. Yorks. (The Dolls House Antiques).
Gray, Solveig and Anita, London, W.1. G. Ant. Mkt.
Grayling, David, A.H., Crosby Ravensworth, Cumbria.
Graylow and Co., Bath, Avon.
Grays Antique Market, London, W.1.
Gray's Antiques of Worcester, Great Malvern, Hereford and Worcs.

Grays Galleries Antiques and Collectors' Centre, Grays, Essex.
Grays Mews, London, W.1.
Grays Portobello, London, W.11.
Great Ayton Bookshop, The, Great Ayton, N. Yorks.
Great Brampton House Antiques Ltd., Hereford, Hereford and Worcs.
Great Expectations, Wallingford, Oxon. L. Arc.
Great Malvern Antiques, Great Malvern, Hereford and Worcs.
Great Western Antique Centre Ltd., Bath, Avon.
Great Western Antique Centre Ltd. - The Wednesday Market, Bath, Avon.
Great Western Pine, South Molton, Devon.
Greaves, H.J., Sheffield, S. Yorks. (Dronfield Antiques).
Greaves, P.A., Sheffield, S. Yorks. (Hibbert Bros. Ltd.)
Greco, Linette, London, N.W.8. Alf. Ant. Mkt.
Green Antiques, Anthony, London, W.1. B. St. Ant. C.
Green Gallery, David, E., London, S.E.26.
Green, D.S., Hartley Wintney, Hants.
Green Antiques, Ena, London, N.W.8. Alf. Ant. Mkt.
Green, E.M., London, W.1. (Garrard and Co. Ltd.)
Green Farm Antiques, Olveston, Avon.
Green, G.H., Sheffield, S. Yorks.
Green, J., Chichester, W. Sussex.
Green, Mrs. J., Chilham, Kent.
Green, J.E., Deddington, Oxon.
Green Fine Art, John, Glasgow, Lanarks., Scot. B. St. Ant. G.
Green and Son, J., Queniborough, Leics.
Green, L., P. and R., Birmingham, W. Mids. (The Halcyon Gallery).
Green, M., Harrogate, N. Yorks. (Traditional Interiors).
Green, Mrs. M., Penarth, S. Glam., Wales.
Green, Mr. and Mrs. M., Tetbury, Glos.
Green, N. and J., Coventry, W. Mids.
Green Parrot, The, London, S.E.10.
Green, Richard, London, W.1.
Green, R., Newton Abbot, Devon. N.A. Ant. C.
Green, R., Queniborough, Leics.
Green, R., Stratford-upon-Avon, Warks.
Green, Ron, Towcester, Northants.
Green Room, The, Bournemouth, Dorset.
Green Antiques, Robert, Ross-on-Wye, Hereford and Worcs.
Green, R.J., Colchester, Essex. (Castle Bookshop).
Green, Renée and Roy, Lewes, E. Sussex.
Green, S., London, W.8.
Green and Stone, London, S.W.3.
Green and Stone of Chichester, Chichester, W. Sussex.
Green, T. and A., Wallingford, Oxon. L. Arc.
Green, T. and S., St. Gerrans, Cornwall.
Greenall, M., Blackpool, Lancs.
Greenaway, D.L., Canterbury, Kent.
Greenaway, T., London, W.1 (Blunderbuss Antiques).
Greenberg, C.B. and P.R., Honiton, Devon.
Greene, E. and I., Castle Hedingham, Essex.
Greenfield, A.G. and T.S., Canterbury, Kent.
Greenfield and Son, H.S., Canterbury, Kent.
Greenfield, K., London, W.1. B. St. Ant. C.
Greengrass Antiques, Chobham, Surrey.
Greengrass, D., Chobham, Surrey.
Greengrass, D., London, N.W.8.
Greenhalgh, P., London, W.1. B. St. Silv. Galls.
Greenhalgh, Syd and Dave, Preston, Lancs. N.W. Ant. C.
Greenhouse Antiques, Painswick, Glos.
Greenlaw Antiques, Greenlaw, Berwicks., Scot.
Greenman, S., London, N.12.
Green's Antique Galleries, London, W.8.
Green's of Montpellier, Cheltenham, Glos.
Greenwall Antiques, Jonathan, Sandgate, Kent. S. Ant. C.
Greenway, B., Garboldisham, Norfolk.
Greenway Antiques, Colin, Witney, Oxon.
Greenwich Antiques and Ironware Co., London, S.E.10.
Greenwich Antiques Market, London, S.E.10.
Greenwich Gallery, The, London, S.E.10.
Greenwold, L., Stow-on-the-Wold, Glos.
Greenwood, Judy, London, S.W.6.
Greenwood Antiques, Simon, Burneston, N. Yorks.
Greenwood, S. and C., Burneston, N. Yorks.
Greenwood (Fine Art), W., Burneston, N. Yorks.
Greenwood and Sons Ltd., W.F., Harrogate, N. Yorks.
Greer, Robin, London, S.W.3.
Greg, Meriel de M., Bath, Avon. B. Ant. Mkt.
Gregory, Bottley and Lloyd, London, S.W.6.
Gregory, George, Bath, Avon.
Gregory, H., London, W.11. (Portobello Antique Store).
Gregory, J., London, W.6.
Gregory, M., London, S.W.1. (Arnold Wiggins and Sons Ltd.).
Gregory Gallery, Martyn, London, S.W.1.
Gregory, N., Wendover, Bucks.
Gregory Gallery, Noel, Farnham Common, Bucks.
Gregory, R., Deddington, Oxon.
Gregory's Antique Pine, Rawtenstall, Lancs.
Gregory-Smith, K., Hartley Wintney, Hants.
Gregson, D. and M., St. Agnes, Cornwall.
Grenville Art Gallery, Manchester, Lancs. Royal Ex. S.C.
Grenville Street Bookshop, Stockport, Cheshire.
Gresham, R.A., Bath, Avon. Gt. West. Ant. C.
Gretton, K., London, S.W.11.
Greyabbey Timecraft Ltd., Greyabbey, Co. Down, N. Ireland.
Greycroft Antiques, Errol, Scotland.
Grey-Harris and Co., Bristol, Avon.
Greystoke Antiques, Sherborne, Dorset.
Greystones Antiques, Buckden, N. Yorks.

Grice Antiques, Alan, Ormskirk, Lancs.
Grice, C.A., Saltaire, W.Yorks.
Gridley, Gordon, London, N.1.
Griffen Antiques, London, N.1. The Mall.
Griffin Antiques, Petworth, W. Sussex.
Griffin, G.E., Croydon, Surrey.
Griffin, R., Bath, Avon. Gt. West. Ant. C. (Roy's Watches).
Griffin Antiques Ltd., Simon, London, W.1.
Griffin, S.J., London, W.1.
Griffith, J.J., Canterbury, Kent.
Griffiths, D., London, N.1 (Number Nineteen).
Griffiths, J., Bath, Avon (Bath Galleries).
Griffiths, M., Huddersfield, W. Yorks.
Griffiths, Mary, London, N.W.8. Alf. Ant. Mkt.
Griffiths, N.K., Weedon, Northants.
Griffiths, P., Cardigan, Dyfed, Wales.
Griffiths, R. and W., Southport, Merseyside.
Griffiths, Mrs. T.A., Windermere, Cumbria.
Griffiths, W. and B., Burscough, Lancs.
Griffiths, W. and S., Buckden, N. Yorks.
Griffiths, W.W., Bethel, Gwynedd, Wales.
Griffons Court, Newbury, Berks.
Grigg, A., Norwich, Norfolk. (Thomas Tillett and Co.).
Grimes Militaria, Chris, Bristol, Avon.
Grimes House Antiques, Moreton-in-Marsh, Glos.
Grist Mill Interiors, Rye, E. Sussex.
Grodzinski, W., London, W1. (Atlantic Bay Carpets).
Gronow, R., Cardiff, S. Glam., Wales. (Grandma's Goodies)
Gross, Colin, London, W.1. G. Mews.
Grosvenor Antiques, Leek, Staffs.
Grosvenor Antiques Ltd., London, W.8.
Grosvenor Antiques of Chester, Chester, Cheshire.
Grosvenor House Interiors, Beaconsfield, Bucks.
Grosvenor Jewellery, London, W.1. B. St. Ant. C.
Grosvenor Prints, London, W.C.2.
Grosvenor, R., Towcester, Northants.
Grothier, Robert, London, S.W.10 (Furniture Cave).
Groucott, M., Peterborough, Cambs.
Grout, P., Moreton-in-Marsh, Glos.
Grove Antiques, London, N.1.
Grove Antiques, London, S.W.1.
Grove, Angela and Brian, Diss, Norfolk.
Grove Collectors Centre, Harrogate, N. Yorks.
Grove Gallery, Windsor and Eton, Berks.
Grove House Antiques, Petworth, W. Sussex.
Grove Side Antiques, Bristol, Avon. Clift. Ant. Mkt.
Grover, D.R. and D.A., Chichester, W. Sussex.
Grover, Tony, Fakenham, Norfolk. Ant. C.
Groves, M.A. and A. Uttoxeter, Staffs.
Groves, T. and D., Holt, Norfolk.
Grozier, W.B.T., Hull, N. Humbs.
Grupman, Joan, Manchester, Lancs. Royal Ex. S.C.
Gubb, J. and A.H., Southampton, Hants.
Guest, Mrs. J., St. Andrews, Fife, Scot.
Guildhall Antique Market, Chard, Somerset.
Guildhall Fair, Chester, Cheshire.
Guildhall Gallery, Bury St. Edmunds, Suffolk.
Guildhall Street Antiques, Bury St. Edmunds, Suffolk.
Guillemot, Aldeburgh, Suffolk.
Guinevere Antiques, London, S.W.6.
Guittot, B., London, S.W.3. Ant. Ant. Mkt.
Guiver, T., Great Malvern, Hereford and Worcs.
Gulessarian, Alice, London, W.1. G. Mews.
Gumb, Linda, London, N.1.
Gumbrell, K., St. Leonards-on-Sea, E. Sussex. Hastings A.C.
Gun Powder House Antiques, Faversham, Kent.
Gunn, Mrs. B., London, S.W.3. Ant. Ant. Mkt.
Gunnett, B.R., Brixworth, Northants.
Gunning, Mr., Todmorden, W. Yorks.
Guns and Tackle, Scunthorpe, S. Humberside.
Gunson, P., Kendal, Cumbria.
Gunter Fine Art, London, N.W.2.
Gurl, Bath, Avon. Gt. West. Ant. C.
Guthrie, L.W. and R.M., Shipston-on-Stour, Warks.
Guy, A.R. and D.E., Amersham, Bucks.
Guy's Antiques and Fine Furniture, Peter, Preston, Lancs.
Gwilliam, D.L., Bath, Avon (The Galleon).
Gwilliam, Edred A.F., Cricklade, Wilts.
Gwydir St. Antiques, Cambridge, Cambs.
Gwyneth Lloyd, London, S.W.3.
Gyles, D.E., Bath, Avon. Gt. West. A. C. Wed. Mkt.
Gyte, P.S., Ripon, N. Yorks.

H

H.L.B. Antiques, Bournemouth, Dorset.
HRW Antiques, London, S.W.4.
H. and S. Collectables, Gosforth, Tyne and Wear.
Haas, Otto, (A. and M. Rosenthal), London, N.W.3.
Habberley, Vera, London, N.W.8. Alf. Ant. Mkt.
Hacker, P.F., Harrogate, N. Yorks. (Paraphenalia)
Hackett, R. and B., Frome, Somerset.
Hackner, P.A. and M., Wolverhampton, W. Mids.
Hackney House Antiques, Chesterfield, Derbys.
Hadfield, G.K., Shepshed, Leics.
Hadfield, G.K., Stamford, Lincs.
Hadji Baba Ancient Art, London, W.1.
Hadleigh Jewellers, London, W.1.
Hadlow Antiques, Tunbridge Wells, Kent.
Hagan, K.O., Claudy, Co. Londonderry, N. Ireland.
Hagarty, Mrs. M., Bow Street, Dyfed, Wales.
Hage, Mrs E., London, W.1. (Elisabeth's Antiques) B. St Ant. C.
Hagen., Richard, Broadway, Hereford and Worcs.

Hague Antiques, Leamington Spa, Warks.
Hague, J., Leamington Spa, Warks.
Hague, John, Pickering, N. Yorks.
Hahn, P., London, W.1
Hahn and Son Fine Art Dealers, London, W.1.
Haig-Harrison, A.G., Bristol, Avon. (Frocks and Tails).
Haillay, Mrs. C.L., Lechlade, Glos.
Haines, B., Ammanford, Dyfed, Wales.
Haines, D., Loxwood, W. Sussex.
Haines Antiques Ltd., John, London, S.W.13.
Haines, J. and S.D., London, S.W.13.
Haines, Susan, London, W.1. G. Ant. Mkt.
Haines, T.E., Trent, Dorset.
Hakeney Antiques, David K., Hull, N. Humberside.
Halabuda, Mrs. I., Barry, S. Glam., Wales.
Halcyon Days, London, W.1.
Halcyon Days, London, E.C.3.
Halcyon Gallery, The, Birmingham, W. Mids.
Haldane, J., Little Abington, Cambs.
Hale, Mr and Mrs. P., Tunbridge Wells, Kent.
Hale, Mr. and Mrs. P., Uckfield, E. Sussex.
Hale Antiques, R., Brighton, E. Sussex.
Hale, R.N., Brighton, E. Sussex.
Hales Antiques, Mark, London, W.11.
Hales Antiques Ltd., Robert, London, W.8.
Halewood and Sons, Preston, Lancs.
Haley, J., Halifax, W. Yorks.
Haliden Oriental Rug Shop, Bath, Avon.
Halifax Antiques Centre, Halifax, W. Yorks.
Halkes, H. Sidmouth, Devon.
Hall, Anthony C., Twickenham, Middx.
Hall, Mrs. A.E., Bournemouth, Dorset. (Seabourne Antiques).
Hall, A.R. and J.M., Ash Priors, Somerset.
Hall, B.J. and H.M., Crewkerne, Somerset.
Hall, D., Hexham, Northumb.
Hall Ltd., Douglas, Brighton, E. Sussex.
Hall, Ewa, London, W.1. G. Port.
Hall, Mrs. G., Cheltenham, Glos. (Tapestry).
Hall, J., London, N.W.8. Alf. Ant. Mkt.
Hall, Joan Ashton, Fakenham, Norfolk. Ant. C.
Hall, James, Stow-on-the-Wold, Glos. C. Ant. C.
Hall, J. and D., Stow-on-the-Wold, Glos. C. Ant. C.
Hall, L.M., Great Malvern, Hereford and Worcs.
Hall, R., Ash Priors, Somerset.
Hall, Robert, London, W.9.
Hall, R. and J., Llandogo, Gwent, Wales.
Hall, S., Burford, Oxon.
Hall, S. and T., Gloucester, Glos.
Hall-Bakker, Lis, Woodstock, Oxon.
Hall-Junior Antiques, Vic, Rettendon, Essex.
Hallam Antiques, Michael, Norwich, Norfolk.
Hallam Gallery, London, S.W.14.
Hallam, M.J., Norwich, Norfolk.
Hallam, P., London, S.W.14.
Hallesy, H., Swansea, W. Glam., Wales. (Magpie Antiques).
Hallett Antiques, David, A., Long Hanborough, Oxon.
Hallett, Laurence, London, S.W.1.
Halliday, F.G., Glasgow, Lanarks., Scot. (Jean Megahy).
Halliday's, London, S.W.3.
Halliday's Antiques Ltd., Dorchester-on-Thames, Oxon.
Hallmark, London, W.1. G. Ant. Mkt.
Hallmarks, Brighton, E. Sussex.
Halloway, Mrs. P.W., Annfield Plain, Durham.
Hall's Antiques, Ash Priors, Somerset.
Hall's Bookshop, Tunbridge Wells, Kent.
Hallstand, Hastings, E. Sussex.
Hallstile Antiques, Hexham, Northumb.
Halo Antiques, Altrincham, Cheshire.
Halsall Hall Ltd., Halsall, Lancs.
Halsey International Enterprises, Salcombe, Devon.
Halsey International Enterprises, London, S.W.1.
Halsey, M. and R., Jacobstowe, Devon.
Halstead Antiques, Halstead, Essex.
Halstow Antiques, Lower Halstow, Kent.
Hamandani, Mrs. B., London, S.W.3. Ant. Ant. Mkt.
Hamblin, John, Yeovil, Somerset.
Hamblin, J. and M.A., Yeovil, Somerset.
Hamilton Antiques, London, W.C.2. Lon. Silv. Vts.
Hamilton Antiques, Woodbridge, Suffolk.
Hamilton Antiques, Anne, Burnham Market, Norfolk.
Hamilton, D., Sherborne, Dorset.
Hamilton Fine Arts, London, W.11.
Hamilton, G., Leominster, Hereford and Worcs. L. Ant. Mkt.
Hamilton, H., Knebworth, Herts.
Hamilton, John, London, N.W.8. Alf. Ant. Mkt.
Hamilton, K. and J.E., Grantham, Lincs.
Hamilton, P. and W., London, S.W.20.
Hamilton, Rosemary, London, S.W.1.
Hamilton Ltd. Antiques, Ross, London, S.W.1.
Hamilton, Sheelagh, Fernhurst, W. Sussex.
Hamilton, S., Merrow, Surrey.
Hamilton and Tucker Billiard Co. Ltd., Knebworth, Herts.
Hamilton, V., London, W.11.
Hamilton's Corner, London, S.W.20.
Hamlet, E., Longridge, Lancs.
Hamlet, Miss J., Longridge, Lancs.
Hamlyn Lodge, Ollerton, Notts.
Hammer, Mrs. P., Wimborne Minster, Dorset.
Hammersley, Mrs. B.A., Abbots Bromley, Staffs.
Hammond, Carol, and David Somerville, London, W.8. Ken. Church St. Ant. C.
Hammond, D. and R., Buxton, Derbys.
Hammond, G., Chipping Campden, Glos.
Hammond Antiques, Jeffery, Leominster, Hereford and Worcs.
Hammond, J. and E., Leominster, Hereford and Worcs.
Hampshire Gallery, Bournemouth, Dorset.

Hampshire, P. and Mrs. S., Ottery St. Mary, Devon.
Hampshires of Dorking, Dorking, Surrey.
Hampstead Antique Emporium, London, N.W.3.
Hampton Court Antiques, East Molesey, Surrey.
Hampton, G., Christchurch, Dorset.
Hampton Gallery, Tetbury, Glos.
Hampton Hill Gallery Ltd., Hampton Hill, Middx.
Hampton Village Antiques Centre, Hampton, Middx.
Hampton Wick Antiques, Hampton Wick, Surrey.
Hamptons, Christchurch, Dorset.
Hanbury, Mrs. D., Chobham, Surrey.
Hancock, G., Shrewsbury, Shrops.
Hancock Gallery, London, W.11.
Hancock, M.L., Chichester, W. Sussex.
Hancock Antiques, Peter, Chichester, W. Sussex.
Hancocks and Co. (Jewellers) Ltd., London, W.1.
Hancox, G. and D., Wolseley Bridge, Staffs.
Hancox, G. and R., Wansford, Cambs.
Hancox, P.E., Wansford, Cambs.
Hand in Hand, Edinburgh, Midloth., Scot.
Hand, J., Nailsworth, Glos.
Hand, K., Kidlington, Oxon.
Hand, Mr. and Mrs. O., Edinburgh, Midloth., Scot. (Hand in Hand).
Hand Prints and Watercolours Gallery, Nailsworth, Glos.
Handbury-Madin, R. and E., Shrewsbury, Shrops.
Handcross Antiques, Handcross, W. Sussex.
Handford Antiques, William, London, S.W.3.
Handford Antiques, William, London, S.W.10.
Handley, Nigel, Norwich, Norfolk.
Handley, N.S., Norwich, Norfolk.
Handtiques, Kidlington, Oxon.
Hanks, P.C., Rochester, Kent.
Hanlin, London, N.W.3. Ham. Ant. Emp.
Hanlon, W. and J., Menston, W. Yorks.
Hannant, M., Hythe, Kent.
Hannaway, Mrs. M., Bloxwich, W. Mids.
Hannen, L.G., London, W.1. (H. Blairman and Son Ltd.).
Hannent, Donna, Norwich, Norfolk.
Hannent, J., Fakenham, Norfolk.
Hanover Antiques, Scarborough, N. Yorks.
Hansen Chard Antiques, Pershore, Hereford and Worcs.
Han-Shan Tang Ltd., London, S.W.6.
Hanson, Mrs. M.E., Knaresborough, N. Yorks.
Hansord, David J., Lincoln, Lincs.
Harari and Johns Ltd., London, S.W.1.
Harborne Place Antiques, Birmingham, W. Midlands.
Harbottle, Patricia, London, W.11.
Harbottle, Mrs. P., London, W.11.
Harbourne Antiques, Newton Abbot, Devon. N.A. Ant. C.
Harby, Diane, London, W.1. G. Ant. Mkt.
Harcourt Antiques, London, W.1.
Harcourt, L.W., Arthog, Gwynedd, Wales.
Harcourt, P., London, W.1. (Maggs Bros. Ltd.)
Harcus, Kay, Wallingford, Oxon. L. Arc.
Hardcastle, M. and S., Leyburn, N. Yorks.
Harden, Anthony, Buckland Newton, Dorset.
Harden, Mr. and Mrs. A., Buckland Newton, Dorset.
Hardie Antiques, Perth, Perths., Scot.
Hardie, M., Perth, Perths., Scot.
Hardie, T.G., Perth, Perths., Scot.
Hardiman, M. and G.A., Melbourn, Cambs.
Hardiman, P.N., Melbourn, Cambs.
Harding, E., Northleach, Glos.
Harding, Mrs. J., Duffield, Derbys.
Harding, J., London, W.11. (Gallery 287 and Gallery 289).
Harding, K., Northleach, Glos.
Harding, K., St. Leonards-on-Sea, E. Sussex. Hastings Ant. C.
Harding, R., London, W.1. (Maggs Bros. Ltd.)
Harding, T., Blackmore, Essex.
Harding-Hill, M. and D., Chipping Norton, Oxon.
Harding's World of Mechanical Music, Keith, Northleach, Glos.
Hardman Antiques, Alan and Jennie, Crawley, W. Sussex.
Hardwick Antiques, Streetly, W. Mids.
Hardwick, Mrs. P., Audlem, Cheshire.
Hardy Antiques, John, Oadby, Leics.
Hardy and Co., James, London, S.W.3.
Hardy Country, Melbury Osmond, Dorset.
Hardy, J., Bournemouth, Dorset.
Hardy Pine and Country Furniture, Joyce, Hacheston, Suffolk.
Hardy, P., London, N.1. (William Bedford plc).
Hardy's, Bournemouth, Dorset.
Hare, A., Cirencester, Glos.
Hare, A., London, S.W.10. (Hares Antiques).
Hares, Cirencester, Glos.
Hares Antiques, London, S.W.10.
Harewood Cottage Antiques, Harewood, W. Yorks.
Hargraves, J., A., L. and R., Wigan, Lancs.
Harker, D.R., Colchester, Essex.
Harker, P.G., Bridlington, N. Humberside.
Harkins, Brian, London, W.1. G. Ant. Mkt.
Harlequin Antiques, Bruton, Somerset.
Harlequin Antiques, Porthcawl, Mid-Glam., Wales.
Harlequin Gallery, Lincoln, Lincs.
Harley Antiques, Christian Malford, Wilts.
Harley, G.J., Christian Malford, Wilts.
Harling, R., Lye, W. Mids.
Harman Antiques, Robert, Ampthill, Beds.
Harmandian, G., Bath, Avon (Arkea Antiques).
Harmer, A. Bexhill-on-Sea, E. Sussex. Bex. Ant. C.
Harms, A., London, N.1. (At the Sign of the Chest of Drawers)
Harold's Place, London, W.5.
Harp Antiques, Bradford-on-Avon, Wilts.
Harper, B. and I., Warwick, Warks.
Harper, Erica and Hugo, Chester, Cheshire.

Harper Fine Paintings, Poynton, Cheshire.
Harper, Mrs. K., Leeds, W. Yorks.
Harper Antiques, Martin and Dorothy, Bakewell, Derbys.
Harper, M.R., Bristol, Avon. (Bristol Ant. Mkt.)
Harper, Mrs. N.C., Guildford, Surrey.
Harper, P.R., Poynton, Cheshire.
Harrap, B., Sheffield, S. Yorks. (Fun Antiques).
Harriman, David, Rickmansworth, Herts.
Harrington Antiques, Preston, Lancs. N.W. Ant. C.
Harrington Gallery, David, London, W.1.
Harrington, Mrs. M., London, S.W.3. (Old Church Galleries)
Harris, A.R., Stourbridge, W. Mids.
Harris, Mrs. B., Hungerford, Berks.
Harris Antiques, Bibi, Hungerford, Berks.
Harris, B.C. and R.H., London, W.1. (S.H. Harris and Son (London) Ltd.).
Harris and Sons Antiques, Bob, Birmingham, W. Mids.
Harris Antiques, Colin, Hartley Wintney, Hants.
Harris, Essie C., London, E.C.1.
Harris, E.C. and D., London, E.C.1.
Harris and Holt, Wallasey, Merseyside.
Harris, I., London, W.1 (N. Bloom and Son Ltd.).
Harris, I., London, S.W.1. (N. Bloom and Son (Antiques) Ltd.)
Harris, Jonathan, London, W.8.
Harris, M.G., London, W.11 (K. and M. Antiques). Stouts Arc.
Harris and Sons, M., London, S.W.1.
Harris, Nicholas, London, S.W.6.
Harris, P., Leicester, Leics.
Harris, R., Bath, Avon. Gt. West. Ant. C.
Harris, R., Kinver, Staffs.
Harris, R.E., Birmingham, W. Mids.
Harris, R.M., London, S.W.1.
Harris, S., Wallasey, Merseyside.
Harris Antiques, Sheila, Nottingham, Notts.
Harris Fine Antique Porcelain, Sylvia, Tetbury, Glos.
Harris and Son (London) Ltd., S.H., London, W.1.
Harris, S.J., Tetbury, Glos.
Harris, T.W., Northampton, Northants.
Harris, V. and H., Penryn, Cornwall.
Harrison Fine Antiques, Anna, Gosforth, Tyne and Wear.
Harrison and Son, A.A., Sevenoaks, Kent.
Harrison, B. and S.L., Turvey, Beds.
Harrison, C., Preston, Lancs. N.W. Ant. C.
Harrison, D., Edinburgh, Midloth., Scot. (Another World).
Harrison, J.E., Sevenoaks, Kent.
Harrison, J.M., Leeds, W. Yorks. (Coins International).
Harrison, Marguerite, London, W.11. G. Port. (Anne Barlow)
Harrison, Miss P., Lewes, E. Sussex.
Harrison, P., Lytham St. Annes, Lancs.
Harrison, R., London, W.11. (Graham and Green).
Harrison, Richard, London, N.W.8. Alf. Ant. Mkt.
Harrison, R., Sevenoaks, Kent.
Harrison, S., Petworth, W. Sussex. (Philip Cooper Antiques).
Harrison, Mrs. T., Dorking, Surrey.
Harrison Wholesale Exports, Tim, Stratford-upon-Avon, Warks.
Harrods Ltd., London, S.W.1.
Harrogate Fine Arts, Harrogate, N. Yorks.
Harrop Fold Clocks, Bolton-by-Bowland, Lancs.
Hart, E., London, N.1.
Hart, J.A. and N., Bletchingley, Surrey.
Hart, Michael, Edinburgh, Midloth., Scot.
Hart, Rosemary, London, N.1.
Hart and Rosenberg, London, N.1.
Hart and John Giles, Sheila, Aylsham, Norfolk.
Harthope House Antiques, Moffat, Dumfries., Scot.
Hartley Antiques, Hartley, Kent.
Hartley Antiques Ltd., J., Ripley, Surrey.
Hartley, S.N., Wingham, Kent.
Hartnell Antiques and Victoriana, Dorothy, Sidmouth, Devon.
Hartnoll, Julian, London, S.W.1.
Harvesters Barn Antiques, Four Elms, Kent.
Harvey, C.S., Ludlow, Shrops.
Harvey Centre, The, Canterbury, Kent.
Harvey, E., London, W.11. (The Old Haberdasher).
Harvey and Gore, London, W.1.
Harvey, I.P., Lower Halstow, Kent.
Harvey, Mr. and Mrs. J. and L., Maentwrog, Gwynedd, Wales.
Harvey, J.M., Aylesbury, Bucks.
Harvey Antiques, Morton, Aylesbury, Bucks.
Harvey, W., London, S.W.3. Ant. Ant. Mkt.
Harvey and Co. (Antiques) Ltd., W.R., London, W.1.
Harvey, W.R., G.M. and A.D., London, W.1.
Harvey-Jones, A., Woodbridge, Suffolk.
Harvey-Lee, Elizabeth, London, N.W.2.
Harvey-Morgan, R., Stratford-upon-Avon, Warks.
Harvey-Owen Antiques, Maentwrog, Gwynedd, Wales.
Harvie-Watt, R., London, S.W.13.
Harwood Antiques, London, S.W.15.
Harwood, A. and D.B.M., Weston-super-Mare, Avon.
Harwood, G.M., London, S.W.15.
Harwood, J., Grasmere, Cumbria.
Harwood, M.H., Headington, Oxon.
Harwood West End Antiques, Weston-super-Mare, Avon.
Hasel-Britt Ltd., Radlett, Herts.
Haslam, Mr. and Mrs. S., Aldeburgh, Suffolk.
Haslam and Whiteway, London, W.8.
Haslam-Hopgood, R.G.G., Stow-on-the-Wold, Glos.
Haslam-Hopwood, R.G.G., Wadebridge, Cornwall.
Hassall Antiques, Geoffrey, Solihull, W. Mids.
Hastie, Ian G., Salisbury, Wilts.
Hastie, Robert and Georgina, Hungerford, Berks.

Hastings Antique Centre, The, St. Leonards-on-Sea, E. Sussex.
Hastings-Spital, K., Bath, Avon. (Quiet St. Antiques)
Hatch Antiques, Weybridge, Surrey.
Hatch, B.D., Weybridge, Surrey.
Hatch, D., Beighton, Norfolk.
Hatcher, Sherry, London, N.1.
Hatchwell Antiques, Simon, Brighton, E. Sussex.
Hatherleigh Antiques, Hatherleigh, Devon.
Hatvany, E., Hampton, Middx.
Haugh Antiques, Roderic, Raveningham, Norfolk.
Haughey Antiques, D.M., Kirkby Stephen, Cumbria.
Haughton Antiques, Brian, London, W.1.
Havard, T. and P., Harpole, Northants.
Havelin Antiques, Blandford Forum, Dorset.
Haven Gallery, The, Great Yarmouth, Norfolk.
Havenplan's Architectural Emporium, Killamarsh, Derbys.
Haverstock Antiques, London, N.W.1.
Haw, J.M., Northallerton, N. Yorks.
Haw, S., Haslemere, Surrey.
Hawkey, V., Grimsby, S. Humberside.
Hawkhurst Antiques, Hawkhurst, Kent.
Hawkin, London, W.1. G. Mews.
Hawkins Bros. Antiques, Barry, S. GLam., Wales.
Hawkins Antiques, Brian, London, N.1.
Hawkins (Brighton) Ltd., David, Brighton, E. Sussex.
Hawkins, G., Berkeley, Glos.
Hawkins, G. and J., Cambridge, Glos.
Hawkins, J. and C., Kingsbridge, Devon.
Hawkridge, Mrs. M., Skipton, N. Yorks.
Hawley Antiques, Beverley, N. Humberside.
Hawley Antique Clocks, John and Carol, Clevedon, Avon.
Haworth Antiques, Harrogate, N. Yorks.
Haworth Antiques, Huby, N. Yorks.
Haworth Antiques, Haworth, W. Yorks.
Haworth Ltd., M. and N., Clitheroe, Lancs.
Haworth, M. and N., Manchester, Lancs. R. Ex. S.C.
Haworth, Peter, Carnforth, Lancs.
Hay Antiques, Blakedown, Hereford and Worcs.
Hay Rare Books, Cooper, Glasgow, Lanarks., Scot. B. St. Ant. G.
Hay, J.D., Glasgow, Lanarks, Scot. (Muirhead Moffat and Co.).
Hay Loft Gallery, Broadway, Hereford and Worcs.
Hay, Rachael, Fakenham, Norfolk. Ant. C.
Haybarn and Bridgebarn Antiques Centre, Battlesbridge, Essex.
Hayden, B., Templecombe, Somerset.
Haydon Bridge Antiques, Haydon Bridge, Northumb.
Haydon Gallery, Haydon Bridge, Northumberland.
Haydon House Antiques, Woburn Sands, Bucks.
Haydon, N., Whitwick, Leics.
Hayes, Miss M.L., North Shields, Tyne and Wear.
Hayes, Architectural Antiques, Paul, Gloucester, Glos.
Hayes, P. and A., Gloucester, Glos.
Hayes Gallery, Paul, Auchterarder, Perths., Scot.
Hayes, T., Diss, Norfolk.
Haygate Gallery, Telford, Shrops.
Haygreen Antiques, Blackmore, Essex.
Hayhurst Fine Glass, Jeanette, London, W.8.
Haylett, A.P. and M.A., Outwell, Cambs.
Hayman and Hayman, London, S.W.3. Ant. Ant. Mkt.
Haynes, C., Alvechurch, W. Mids. (Woodland Fine Art).
Haynes Fine Art, Broadway, Hereford and Worcs.
Haynes, Antique Finder, Roger, Leek, Staffs.
Hayter, R.W. and F.L., Ryde, I. of Wight.
Hayters, Ryde, I. of Wight.
Hayward, D.H. and M.S., Kingsbridge, Devon.
Haywood, Pamela, London, S.W.3. Chen. Gall.
Hazandras, J.A., London, W.1. (The Sladmore Gallery).
Hazareh, A., Sheffield, S. Yorks. (The Oriental Rug Shop)
Hazel Cottage Clocks, Eachwick, Northumb.
Hazel of Brecon, Brecon, Powys, Wales.
Hazlitt, Gooden & Fox Ltd., London, S.W.1.
Heacock, J.A., Stockport, Cheshire.
Head, J. and J., Salisbury, Wilts.
Head, P., Liss, Hants.
Head, P., St. Peter Port, Guernsey, C.I.
Heads 'n' Tails, Wiveliscombe, Somerset.
Healey, Mrs. I., Bristol, Avon. (Silver Stall.) Clift. Ant. Mkt.
Healey, M., London, S.W.3. Ant. Ant. Mkt.
Healy, S.D. and I., Birmingham, W. Mids. (Archives).
Heaney, T., Ballyclare, Co. Antrim, N. Ireland.
Heap, Mrs. M.M., Burnham-on-Sea, Somerset.
Heap's Antiques, Burnham-on-Sea, Somerset.
Hearne, E.W.A. and R.E.W., Beaconsfield, Bucks.
Heart of England Antiques, Haunton, Staffs.
Hearth and Home, London, N.W.1.
Heath Antiques, Reigate, Surrey.
Heath Antique Centre, Heath and Reach, Beds.
Heath, A.R., Bristol, Avon.
Heath, B., London, E.C.1.
Heath, C., London, N.W.1. (Hearth and Home).
Heath, K.W. and Y.F., Moreton-in-Marsh, Glos.
Heath Antiques, Mike, Newport, I. of Wight.
Heath, M. and B., Newport, I. of Wight.
Heath-Bullock, Godalming, Surrey.
Heath-Bullock, R.J. and M.E., Godalming, Surrey.
Heathcote Antiques, Blandford Forum, Dorset.
Heathcote Antiques, Crosshills, N. Yorks.

Heather Antiques, London, N.1.
Heather, J.C., Woolpit, Suffolk.
Heatherlie Antiques, Selkirk, Selkirks., Scot.
Heawood, Ann and Michael, Holbeck, Lincs.
Hebb, C.A., Aberford, West. Yorks.
Hebbard, D.L., Titchfield, Hants.
Hebbard, G.B., Hay-on-Wye, Powys, Wales.
Hebbards of Hay, Hay-on-Wye, Powys, Wales.
Hedingham Antiques, Sible Hedingham, Essex.
Hedley, Mrs. E., Maldon, Essex.
Hedley, J.A. and T., Hexham, Northumb.
Heelis, J., Milburn, Cumbria.
Heffer, W., Cambridge, Cambs. (Antiques Etc.).
Heffers Booksellers, Cambridge, Cambs. (Deighton Bell and Co.).
Heian Gallery, London, W.1. G. Mews.
Heidareh/A. Bagdhi, M., London, N.W.8. Alf. Ant. Mkt.
Heim Gallery, London, S.W.1.
Heirloom and Howard Ltd., Bath, Avon.
Heirlooms, Worcester, Hereford and Worcs.
Heirlooms (Antique Jewellers), Wareham, Dorset.
Helios and Co. (Antiques), Weedon, Northants.
Helius Antiques, London, S.W.14.
Helliwell, A.H., Llandrindod Wells, Powys, Wales.
Hellmers, P., Epping, Essex.
Hellon, D., Chester, Cheshire. (St. Peter's Fine Art Gallery Ltd.).
Helm Antiques, Linda, London, N.1.
Helmer, G.V., Southampton, Hants.
Helmer, Mr. and Mrs. H., Modbury, Devon.
Helmore, Mrs. W., Odiham, Hants.
Helton Antiques, Heath and Reach, Beds.
Hemswell Antiques Centres, Hemswell Cliff, Lincs.
Hemsworth, S., Portsmouth, Hants.
Henderson, Perth, Perths., Scot.
Henderson, Mrs., Arundel, W. Sussex.
Henderson Antiques, Coupar Angus, Perths., Scot.
Henderson, B., Tunbridge Wells, Kent (Corn Exchange Antiques).
Henderson, F.M., Cowfold, W. Sussex.
Henderson, G., London, S.W.1. (Clarendon Gallery)
Henderson, J.G., Perth, Perths., Scot.
Henderson, Milne, London, N.W.8.
Henderson, S. Milne, London, N.W.8.
Henderson Gallery, Marina, London, S.W.10.
Hendy, Alastair, London, N.W.8. Alf. Ant. Mkt.
Heneage and Co. Ltd., Thomas, London, S.W.1.
Hendley, C., Richmond, Surrey.
Hendrika, Newton Abbot, Devon. N.A. Ant. C.
Henham (Antiques), Martin, London, N.2.
Henley House Antiques, Rumford, Cornwall.
Henley Antiques, R. and J.L., Canterbury, Kent.
Hennell Ltd., (incorporating Frazer and Haws (1868) and E. Lloyd Lawrence (1830)), London, W.1.
Hennessy, C. and G.C., Beaminster, Dorset.
Henning, Tina, London, N.W.8. Alf. Ant. Mkt.
Henson, R., London, S.W.3. Ant. Ant. Mkt.
Henstridge, W.V., Bournemouth, Dorset. (Sterling Coins and Medals).
Hepburn, T. and N., Beaconsfield, Bucks.
Hepner, R.P., Knutsford, Cheshire.
Hepworth, C.G. and I.M., Newton St. Cyres, Devon.
Hepworth Gallery, Gordon, Newton St. Cyres, Devon.
Heraldry Today, Ramsbury, Wilts.
Heraty, P., Hartley Wintney, Hants.
Heraz, London, S.W.1.
Herbert, D., Brighton, E. Sussex. (Le Jazz Hot).
Herbert, Mrs. E., Saltburn, Cleveland.
Herbert, L., Cowbridge, S. Glam., Wales.
Herbert, Peter, London, N.W.8. Alf. Ant. Mkt.
Herbert, N.R., Newmarket, Suffolk.
Hereford Antique Centre, Hereford, Hereford & Worcs.
Heritage Antiques, Chichester, W. Sussex.
Heritage Antiques, Huddersfield, W. Yorks.
Heritage Antiques, Linlithgow, West Loth., Scot.
Heritage Antiques, London, N.1.
Heritage Antiques, Oldham, Lancs.
Heritage Antiques, Paisley, Renfrews., Scot.
Heritage Antiques and Restorations, Great Missenden, Bucks.
Heritage Antiques and Stripped Pine, Cardiff, S. Glam., Wales.
Heritage House Antiques, Glasgow, Scotland.
Heritage Restorations, Llanfair Caereinion, Powys, Wales.
Hermitage Antiques, London, S.W.1.
Hermitage Antiquities, Fishguard, Dyfed, Wales.
Heron, C., Thatcham, Berks.
Heron, H.N.M. and J., Yoxall, Staffs.
Heron and Son Ltd., H.W., Yoxall, Staffs.
Herrald Antiques, Edinburgh, Midloth., Scot.
Herring, W., North Petherwin, Cornwall.
Herrington, B., Gargrave, N. Yorks.
Herrington, D.M., Hungerford, Berks. (Dolls and Toys of Yesteryear).
Herrington, L.R., Hungerford, Berks. (Bow House Antiques).
Hersheson, J., Brighton, E. Sussex. (Hallmarks).
Hersheson, J.J., Brighton, E. Sussex (Kingsbury Antiques).
Hershkowitz Ltd., Robert, London, S.W.7.
Herts. and Essex Antique Centre, The, Sawbridgeworth, Herts.
Hesketh, C., Blandford Forum, Dorset.
Heskia, London, W.1.
Hesling, J. and H., Inverness, Inverns., Scot.
Heuduk, P., Hastings, E. Sussex.
Hewes, P.N., Bury St. Edmunds, Suffolk.
Hewitt Art Deco Originals, Muir, Halifax, W. Yorks.
Hewlett, T.A, London, W.11.
Hewson, Mrs. K., Woodchurch, Kent.
Hexham Antiques (inc. Hotspur Antiques), Hexham, Northumb.

Heyday, Saddleworth, Lancs.
Heyden, R.E.J., Cheltenham, Glos.
Heyden's Antiques and Militaria, Cheltenham, Glos.
Heyford Antiques, Nether Heyford, Northants.
Heytesbury Antiques, Farnham, Surrey.
Heywood Antiques and Shipping Co., Diss, Norfolk.
Heywood, D., Birmingham, W. Mids. (Archives).
Heywood, E., London, S.W.3. (Monro Heywood Ltd.)
Hibbert Bros Ltd., Sheffield, S. Yorks.
Hick Antiques, David, Carrefour Selous, Jersey, C.I.
Hickey Maurice, London, S.W.3. Ant. Ant. Mkt.
Hickford, T.K. and W.E., Grundisburgh, Suffolk.
Hickmott, Mrs. F., Glossop, Derbys.
Hickmott, J.R., Tunbridge Wells, Kent.
Hicks, D., London, N.21.
Hicks Gallery, London, S.W.19.
Hicks, J. and A., London, S.W.19.
Hicks, J. and M., Rudgwick, W. Sussex.
Hicks, M., Dorking, Surrey.
Hicks-Bolton Galleries, Jo, Newton Abbot, Devon. N.A. Ant. C.
Hicks, M.B. and I.F., North Walsham, Norfolk.
Hicks, M.B. and I.F., Stalham, Norfolk.
Hickson, Lewis, CMBHI, Antiquarian Horologist, Seaton Ross, N. Humberside.
Hickson, N., Preston, Lancs. N.W. Ant. C.
Hidden Gem, Macclesfield, Cheshire.
Hi-Felicity, Kidderminster, Hereford and Worcs.
Higgins, B.R. and E.A., Brighton, E. Sussex (Yellow Lantern Antiques Ltd.).
Higgins, G., Ilkley, W. Yorks.
Higgins, Mrs. L., Bridge of Weir, Renfrews., Scot.
Higgins, R., Bridport, Dorset.
High Park Antiques, Broadway, Hereford and Worcs.
High Street Antiques, Alcester, Warks.
High Street Antiques, Bisley, Glos.
High Street Antiques and Decor, Falmouth, Cornwall.
Higham, J., Carlisle, Cumbria.
Highcross Antiques, Witheridge, Devon.
Highland Antiques, Hazel Grove, Cheshire.
Highland Antiques, Inverness, Inverns., Scot.
Highland House Antiques, Newtonmore, Invern., Scot.
Highmoor, Mrs. E.M., Cambridge, Cambs. (Collectors Market).
Highway Gallery, The, Upton-on-Severn, Hereford and Worcs.
Higson, J. and T., Alnwick, Northumbs.
Hildreth, Ltd., W., London, W.11.
Hiley, W., London, S.W.6. (William Sheppee).
Hill Books, Alan, Bakewell, Derbys.
Hill Books, Alan, Sheffield, S. Yorks.
Hill, A.R., Bristol, Avon. (The Oriental Carpet Centre)
Hill, B.E., Pinner, Middx.
Hill, C.C., Canterbury, Kent.
Hill, C.C., London, N.1.
Hill, C.M., Kettering, Northants.
Hill, C.M., Uppingham, Leics.
Hill, David, Kirkby Stephen, Cumbria.
Hill, D., Macclesfield, Cheshire.
Hill Ltd., G. Heywood, London, W.1.
Hill, G. M., and J., London, S.W.1. (Jeremy Ltd..).
Hill, H., Newton Abbot, Devon. N.A. Ant. C.
Hill, J. and Denney, L., London, W.11. G. Port.
Hill, J.E. and J.T., Wolverhampton, W. Mids.
Hill, M., Fochabers, Scotland.
Hill, P., Oxford, Oxon.
Hill, Robson, Uppingham, Leics.
Hill Rise Antiques, Richmond, Surrey.
Hill, R.G., Wolverhampton, W. Mids.
Hill, R. Ingram, Horncastle, Lincs.
Hill, R. and S., Bulkington, Warks.
Hill, Mrs. S., Stratford-upon-Avon, Warks.
Hill, Mrs. S.E., Doncaster, S. Yorks.
Hill Top Farm Antiques, Wallingford, Oxon. L. Arc.
Hill and Sons, W.E., Great Missenden, Bucks.
Hilliard, Mrs. J., Bournemouth, Dorset. (York House Gallery)
Hillman, H., Brecon, Powys, Wales.
Hillman, L., Brecon, Powys, Wales.
Hill-Reid, J., London, S.W.6.
Hills Antiques, Macclesfield, Cheshire.
Hills and Partners Ltd., Richard, Plymouth, Devon.
Hillside Antiques, Halifax, W. Yorks.
Hillyers, London, S.E.26.
Hilmarton Manor Press, Calne, Wilts.
Hilson, A. and B., Tewkesbury, Glos.
Hilton, R.D. and B.S. LLanrhaeadr, Clywd, Wales.
Hilton, Simon, Dunmow, Essex.
Himsworth, Robert M., York, N. Yorks.
Hinde, P., Richmond, Surrey.
Hinde Fine Art, Sheila, Kirdford, W. Sussex.
Hines, J., Costessey, Norfolk.
Hines, J., Norwich, Norfolk. (Gallery 45)
Hines, Mrs. W.C.M., London, N.1. (Grove Antiques).
Hines, Mrs. W.C.M., London, S.W.1. (Grove Antiques)
Hingston's, Cadman, Hants.
Hingston's, Southampton, Hants.
Hinson Fine Paintings, Sheffield, S. Yorks.
Hipkins, D.P., Birmingham, W. Mids. (Yesterdays Antiques).
Hipping Stone Antiques Warehouse, Leyland, Lancs.
Hirschhorn, Robert, London, N.1.
Hirsh, A., London, E.C.1.
Hirsh Fine Jewels, London, E.C.1.
Hirst Antiques, London, W.11.
Hirst, Mrs. S.M., Alnwick, Northumb.
Hitchcock, E.C., Newport, Essex.
Hitchcox, P. and R., Chalgrove, Oxon.
Hitchcox, T. and E., Stratford-upon-Avon, Warks.

Hitchin Antiques Gallery, Hitchin, Herts.
Hoare, Mrs. D., Ryde, Isle of Wight.
Hoare, Oliver, London, S.W.1 (Ahuan U.K. Ltd.).
Hobart, A. and M., London, S.W.1 (Pyms Gallery).
Hobbs, Carlton, London, S.W.1.
Hobby Horse Antiques, Bridport, Dorset.
Hobrey, A., Preston, Lancs. N.W. Ant. C.
Hobson, Platon, London, N.W.3.
Hockin (Antiques) Ltd., Keith, Stow-on-the-Wold, Glos.
Hockley Coins, Nottingham, Notts.
Hockley Antiques, William, Petworth, W. Sussex.
Hodge, Jean, Worcester, Hereford and Worcs.
Hodge, Sarah, Worcester, Hereford and Worcs.
Hodges, T. and S., Totnes, Devon.
Hodgkins and Co. Ltd., Ian, Slad, Glos.
Hodgkinson, B.E. and J., Newport, Essex.
Hodgkinson, P.L., Hertford, Herts.
Hodgkison, G.S., Brighton, E. Sussex. (Shelton Arts)
Hodgson, J., Great Shefford, Berks.
Hodgson, P. and R., Birmingham, W. Mids. (Ashley House Antiques).
Hodnet Antiques, Hodnet, Shrops.
Hodsoll McKenzie, London, S.W.1.
Hodson, B., Preston, Lancs. N.W. Ant. C.
Hodson, M., Parkstone, Dorset.
Hoevelmann, H., Eastbourne, E. Sussex.
Hoffman, London, W.1. B St. Ant. C.
Hoffman Antiques, London, W.1. G. Ant. Mkt.
Hoffman, J.E., London, E.5.
Hofgartner, S., Hungerford, Berks. (Below Stairs).
Hofman Antiques, George, Church Stretton, Shrops.
Hogg, David, London, W.1. G. Ant. Mkt.
Holborough, D., Eynsham, Oxon.
Holder, D., London, W.C.1.
Hole-in-the-Wall, The, Armagh, Co. Armagh, N. Ireland.
Hole-in-the-Wall Antiques, Stockport, Cheshire.
Hole, S.D., Abernyte, Scotland.
Holgate Antiques, York, N. Yorks.
Holgate, J.R., Thorne, S. Yorks.
Holgate, Milton J., Knaresborough, N. Yorks.
Hollamby, M., London, W.2. (Connaught Galleries).
Holland Antiques, London, W.1. G. Ant. Mkt.
Holland and Holland Ltd., London, W.1.
Holland Antiques, Mary, Boston, Lincs.
Hollander Ltd., E., South Holmwood, Surrey.
Hollender, K., London, W.1. (The Scripophily Shop).
Hollett, R.F.G. and C.G., Sedbergh, Cumbria.
Holett and Son, R.F.G., Sedbergh, Cumbria.
Holleyman and Treacher Ltd., Brighton, E. Sussex.
Hollings Antiques, Irene, Woburn, Beds. Wob. Ab. Ant. C.
Hollingshead and Co., London, S.W.6.
Hollingshead, D., London, S.W.6.
Hollington Antiques, Long Crendon, Bucks.
Holloway, B., London, W.1. (Bilby and Holloway).
Holloways Antiques and Interior Design, Burton-on-Trent, Staffs.
Hollywood Road Gallery, London, S.W.10.
Holme Fire Co., The, Holme, Cumbria.
Holmes Antiques, Cockermouth, Cumbria.
Holmes, Brian and Lynn, London, W.1. G. Ant. Mkt.
Holmes Antiques, B. and T., Sandgate, Kent. S. Ant. C.
Holmes, C. and S., Cockermouth, Cumbria.
Holmes, D., London, W.8.
Holmes, D., Port Isaac, Cornwall.
Holmes House Antiques, Sedlescombe, E. Sussex.
Holmes, J., Perranporth, Cornwall.
Holmes Antique Maps and Prints, Julia, South Harting, Hants.
Holmes, Ltd., London, W.1.
Holmes, Mrs. M., Bristol, Avon. (Silver Stall). Clift. Ant. Mkt.
Holmes, R., Cullompton, Devon.
Holmwood Antiques, South Holmwood, Surrey.
Holstead, J. and M., Fochabers, Scotland.
Holt, R., London, W.1. B. St. Silv. Galls.
Holt and Co. Ltd., R., London, E.C.1.
Holtom, J. and J. Burman, Stratford-upon-Avon, Warks.
Holyome, A.C., London, N.1 (Canonbury Antiques).
Holyrood Antiques, Chard, Somerset.
Holzgrawe, W. and A.M., Cirencester, Glos.
Holzgrawe Antiques, W.W., Cirencester, Glos.
Home to Home, London, N.6.
Homewood Antiques, Hythe, Kent.
Homewood, D.C. and R.A., Hythe, Kent.
Homewood Antiques, Robin, Sandgate, Kent. S. Ant. C.
Hone Watercolours, Angela, Marlow, Bucks.
Honiton Antique Toys, Honiton, Devon.
Honiton Fine Art, Honiton, Devon.
Honiton Junction, Honiton, Devon.
Honiton Lace Shop, The, Honiton, Devon.
Hood and Broomfield, Newcastle-under-Lyme, Staffs.
Hood, G., Easingwold, N. Yorks.
Hood and Co., Helena, Bath, Avon.
Hood, J., Newcastle-under-Lyme, Staffs.
Hood, Mrs. L.M., Bath, Avon.
Hook, Anthony J., Westerham, Kent.
Hook, I., Norwich, Norfolk (The Little Gallery).
Hook, P., London, S.W.1. (The St. James Art Group).
Hooke, G.A., Tongham, Surrey.
Hooper Antiques, David, Leamington Spa, Warks.
Hooper and Purchase, London, S.W.3.
Hooper, P., Worcester, Hereford and Worcs.
Hope and Glory, London, W.8.

Hope Phonographs and Gramophones, Howard, East Molesey, Surrey.
Hopkins (Antiques) Ltd., John, Cuckfield, W. Sussex.
Hopkins, J., M. and A., Cuckfield, W. Sussex.
Hopkins, M., Bath, Avon. (Frank Dux Antiques).
Hoppen Ltd., Stephanie, London, S.W.3.
Hoppett, D., Wolverhampton, W. Mids.
Hopwell Antiques, Paul, West Haddon, Northants.
Hopwood, D. and R., Windermere, Cumbria.
Hopwood, G.G., Bedale, N. Yorks.
Horley Antiques, Welshpool, Powys, Wales.
Horley Antiques and Collectables Centre, Horley, Surrey.
Horn Antiques, Audlem, Cheshire.
Horn at the Golden Past, Dorothea, Peel, Isle of Man.
Horncastle Antiques, Horncastle, Lincs.
Horne, Jonathan, London, W.8.
Hornsey Ltd., Adrian, Twyford, Bucks.
Hornsey Ltd., Adrian, London, W.4.
Horological Workshops, Guildford, Surrey.
Horsebridge Antiques, St. Leonards-on-Sea, E. Sussex. Hastings Ant. C.
Horsebridge Antiques Centre, Horsebridge, E. Sussex.
Horseshoe Antiques and Gallery, Burford, Oxon.
Horsman, P. and M., Long Melford, Suffolk.
Horswell, E.F. and J., London, W.1 (The Sladmore Gallery).
Horswill Antiques and Decorative Arts, Helen, West Kirby, Merseyside.
Horswill, J.O., West Kirby, Merseyside.
Horton, D. and R., Beckenham, Kent.
Horton, D. and R., Richmond, Surrey.
Horton, Mrs. E., Birmingham, West Mids. (Amber Antiques).
Horton, Mrs. E., Gloucester, Glos.
Horton, G.B., Henley-in-Arden, Warks.
Horton Antiques, Robert, Hertford, Herts.
Horton's, Beckenham, Kent.
Horton's, Richmond, Surrey.
Horwood, R., Bristol, Avon (Sedan Chair Antiques).
Hosains Books and Antiques, London, W.2.
Hoskin, C., Padstow, Cornwall.
Hoskin, R., Ewhurst, Surrey.
Hoskins, R., Keighley, W. Yorks.
Hoskinson, P., Birmingham, W. Mids. (Jomarc Pianos Ltd. and Pianorama)
Hotspur Ltd., London, S.W.1.
Hotz Fine Art, Dennis, London, W.1.
Houchen, B., King's Lynn, Norfolk.
Houghton Hall Antiques, Market Weighton, N. Humberside.
Houghton Antiques, Peter, Warminster, Wilts.
Houghton, P.J., Warminster, Wilts.
Houghton-Connell, D., Petworth, W. Sussex. (Grove House Antiques)
Houghtons of Moseley, Birmingham, W. Mids.
Houlding, Frances, London, N.W.8. Alf. Ant. Mkt.
Houndwood House Antiques, Houndwood, Berwicks., Scot.
Hounslow, P., Dulverton, Somerset.
Hour Hand Furniture and Antiques, Glasgow, Lanarks., Scot.
Hourston, Mrs. V., Fortrose, Scotland.
House (Mitre Antiques), Bernard G., Wells, Somerset.
House, Kate, London, S.W.15.
House, M., Bampton, Oxon.
House of Antiques, Brighton, E. Sussex.
House of Antiquity, Nether Stowey, Somerset.
House of Buckingham (Antiques), London, E.C.1.
House of Christian Antiques, Ash Vale, Surrey.
House of Frames, London, S.W.3. Ant. Ant. Mkt.
House of Mallett, Surbiton, Surrey.
House of Mirrors, London, S.W.6.
House of Steel Antiques, London, N.1.
House of Tarot, Glasgow, Scotland. Vict. Vill.
House Thing Antiques, Hinckley, Leics.
Houser, Mr. and Mrs. B.G., Newcastle Emlyn, Dyfed, Wales.
Housewive's Choice, Woodbridge, Suffolk.
How, Mrs. G.E.P., London, W.1.
How of Edinburgh, London, W.1.
Howard Antiques, London, W.1.
Howard Antiques, Oundle, Northants.
Howard Antiques Ltd., A., Stratford-upon-Avon, Warks.
Howard B., Bath, Avon (Churchstoke Booksellers). Gt. West. Ant. C.
Howard Antiques, Barbara, Penzance, Cornwall.
Howard, C., Helmsley, N. Yorks.
Howard, David, Cheltenham, Glos.
Howard, D.N., Baldock, Herts.
Howard, D.S., Bath, Avon. (Heirloom and Howard Ltd.).
Howard, H., London, N.W.8.
Howard, Jonathan, Chipping Norton, Oxon.
Howard, J., Felsted, Essex.
Howard, J., London, N.W.8. Alf. Ant. Mkt.
Howard, J.G., Chipping Norton, Oxon.
Howard, M., Bolton-by-Bowland, Lancs.
Howard, Valerie, London, W.8.
Howard-Jones, H., London, W.8.
Howards, Baldock, Herts.
Howards Jewellers, Stratford-upon-Avon, Warks.
Howards of Aberystwyth, Aberystwyth, Dyfed, Wales.
Howards of Broadway, Broadway, Hereford and Worcs.
Howards of Burford, Burford, Oxon.
Howarth, Mrs. M.K., Lytham, Lancs.
Howe, C., London, S.W.1.
Howe, Dudley, London, N.W.8. Alf. Ant. Mkt.
Howe, Mick, Warwick, Warks. Smith St. A.C.
Howe, Michael, Diss, Norfolk.
Howell Jeweller, Charles, Oldham, Lancs.
Howell, N.G., Oldham, Lancs.

Howell, P.B., Hereford, Hereford and Worcs.
Howells, J.P. and J., Pembroke, Dyfed, Wales.
Howes Bookshop, Hastings, E. Sussex.
Howes Gallery, Petworth, W. Sussex.
Howes, R., Horrabridge, Devon.
Howkins Antiques, John, Gt. Yarmouth, Norfolk.
Howkins, J.G., Gt. Yarmouth, Norfolk.
Howkins, Peter, Gt. Yarmouth, Norfolk.
Howlett, G./J. Kinsella, St. Leonards-on-Sea, E. Sussex. Hastings. Ant. C.
Howse, R.S.J., Oxford, Oxon.
Hoy, E., Huddersfield, W. Yorks.
Hoyer-Millar, Virginia, London, N.W.8. Alf. Ant. Mkt.
Hoylake Antique Centre, Hoylake, Merseyside.
Hoyle, D. and P., Whitby, N. Yorks.
Hoyle, D., York, N. Yorks. (Bobbins).
Hoysted, Anna, Mattingley, Hants.
Hubbard Antiques, Leominster, Hereford and Worcs.
Hubbard Antiques, Ipswich, Suffolk.
Hubbard, C.L.B., Ponterwyd, Dyfed, Wales.
Hubbard, J., Canterbury, Kent.
Hubbard Antiques, John, Birmingham, W. Mids.
Hubbard's Bookshop, Doggie, Ponterwydd, Dyfed, Wales.
Hubbard, R.J., Ipswich, Suffolk. (Pine Interiors incorporating Countrystyle).
Huberts, Burford, Oxon.
Huckett, A.G. and N.E., Toddington, Beds.
Huckvale, C. and G., Battle, E. Sussex.
Huddersfield Antiques, Huddersfield, W. Yorks.
Hudes, Eric, Braintree, Essex.
Hudes, Eric, London, W.11.
Hudson, Lady Cathleen, Stanford Dingley, Berks.
Hudson, E.A., Ditchling, E. Sussex.
Hudson, F.R., London, W.8. (Roundfield House Antiques Ltd.)
Hudson, J., Farnham, Surrey.
Hudson, Mrs. J.B., Winyates Green, Hereford and Worcs.
Hudson, M.A., Saffron Walden, Essex.
Hudson, Mrs. P., Emsworth, Hants.
Hudson, Thomas and Pamela, Cirencester, Glos.
Hufton, M. and C., Nottingham, Notts.
Hugall, G., Jesmond, Tyne and Wear.
Huggett and Son, L.J., Honiton, Devon.
Hugh Evelyn Ltd., Richmond, Surrey.
Hughes Antiques, Hinckley, Leics.
Hughes, A., London, S.W.13.
Hughes, A., Wisborough Green, W. Sussex.
Hughes, B. and M., Dumfries, Dumfries., Scot.
Hughes Antiques, Elizabeth, Swansea, W. Glam. Wales.
Hughes Antiques, Eynon, Swansea, W. Glam., Wales.
Hughes, E. and M., Swansea, W. Glam., Wales.
Hughes, M., Epsom, Surrey.
Hughes, M., Mathry, Dyfed, Wales.
Hughes, M.A. and D.A., Bath, Avon.
Hughes, N.K., Hinckley, Leics.
Hughes, P., Glasgow, Lanarks., Scot. (Mercat Antiques).
Hughes, P., Lymington, Hants.
Hughes, Textiles, Paul, London, W.2.
Hughes, S., Kinbuck, Scotland.
Hughes, Mrs. S., Weybridge, Surrey.
Hughes and Smeeth Ltd., Lymington, Hants.
Huie, A.C., Pitlochry, Perths., Scot.
Huish, C. and D., Chepstow, Gwent, Wales.
Hulbert, (Antiques and Firearms), Anne and Colin, Swansea, W. Glam., Wales.
Hull Gallery, Christopher, London, S.W.1.
Hull, Mrs. P., Budleigh Salterton, Devon.
Hulme, J. Alan, Chester, Cheshire.
Humber, Mr. and Mrs., Newton Abbot, Devon. N. A. Ant. C.
Humble Antiques, Mac, Bradford-on-Avon, Wilts.
Humble, Owen, Jesmond, Tyne and Wear.
Humble, W. McA. and B.J., Bradford-on-Avon, Wilts.
Humbleyard Fine Art, Holt, Norfolk.
Hume, Dudley, Brighton, E. Sussex.
Humphrey, C. and D., Manchester, Lancs. (Crown Antiques)
Humphrey, E., Edinburgh, Midloth., Scot. (Antiques).
Humphrey, K.A., Leeds, W. Yorks. (Andrew's Antique Shop).
Humphry Antiques, J. and M., Petworth, W. Sussex.
Humphrys, Brian, Penzance, Cornwall.
Hunaban, R.S. and E.A., Great Malvern, Hereford and Worcs.
Hünersdorff Rare Books and Manuscripts, London, S.W.10.
Hungerford Arcade, Hungerford, Berks.
Hungerford-Boyle, Y., Dorking, Surrey.
Hunka, Winifred, Fakenham, Norfolk. Ant. C.
Hunnings, P.J.M., Penn, Bucks.
Hunt, B., Newton Abbot, Devon, N.A. Ant. C.
Hunt and Clement, Mildenhall, Suffolk.
Hunt, Mrs. C., Taunton, Somerset.
Hunt, J.A.E., Brightling, E. Sussex.
Hunt Galleries, John, Brightling, E. Sussex.
Hunt, K. and Mrs. M.J.A., Tenby, Dyfed, Wales.
Hunt, P.H.M., Hartley Wintney, Hants.
Hunt, Mrs. S., Bolton, Lancs.
Hunter, Mrs. A.E.C., Norwich, Norfolk (Charles Cubitt).
Hunter, P.R., Barnard Castle, Co. Durham.
Hunter Fine Art, Sally, London, S.W.1.
Hunter, T., London, S.W.1. (Cobra and Bellamy).
Huntington Antiques Ltd., Stow-on-the-Wold, Glos.
Huntley, Diana, London, N.1.
Hunwick, P.F., Hungerford, Berks. (The Old Malthouse).
Hurdle, N., Fairford, Glos.
Hurford, Peter, London, S.W.6.

Hursley Antiques, Hursley, Hants.
Hurst, A.H.B., Woodbridge, Suffolk.
Hurst Antiques, Anthony, Woodbridge, Suffolk.
Hurst Antiques, Edward, Salisbury, Wilts.
Hurst, E. and L., Baldock, Herts.
Hutchin, D., Chesham, Bucks.
Hutchings, D.W. and E.J., Reading, Berks.
Hutchins, E.H., Oakley, Hants.
Hutchinson, Clare, Ilminster, Somerset.
Hutchinson, C.C., Ilminster, Somerset.
Hutchinson, J.N., Westerham, Kent.
Hutchinson, P. and M., London, W.11.
Hutchinson-Shire, Mr. and Mrs. N.A., Endmoor, Cumbria.
Hutchinson, G., Kirkcaldy, Fife, Scot.
Hutchison, J., Ilminster, Somerset.
Hutter, Adrienne, London, W.1. G. Ant. Mkt.
Hutter, A.J., South Molton, Devon.
Hutton Antiques, Shrewsbury, Shrops.
Hutton (Jewellers and Silversmiths), Eleanor, Dorking, Surrey.
Hutton, Mrs. P.I., Shrewsbury, Shrops.
Hutton-Clarke, Mr. and Mrs. J., Stow-on-the-Wold, Glos.
Hyams, M., London, W.11. (Nanking Porcelain Co.)
Hyde, J.A.W. and F.A., Westbury, Wilts.
Hyde, M., Romsey, Hants.
Hyde Park Antiques, London, W.11.
Hyde Park Corner Antiques (Antiques Centre), Cambridge, Cambs.
Hyde, Shelagh, Rhos-on-Sea, Clwyd, Wales.
Hyde, W., London, N.W.8.
Hyder, Steven, London, W.11. G. Port.
Hyland House Antiques, Ipswich, Suffolk.
Hyndford Antiques, Brighton, E. Sussex.
Hyron Antiques, Sandgate, Kent.
Hythe Antique Centre, Hythe, Kent.
Hythe Antiques, The, Methwold Hythe, Norfolk.

I

1A Gallery, London, S.W.10.
I.G.A. Old Masters Ltd., St. Lawrence, Jersey, C.I.
I. and S., Antiques, Craven Arms, Shrops.
Iconastas, London, S.W.1.
Idenden, R.S., London, W.1 (South Audley Antiques).
Igel, M., Kingston-upon-Thames, Surrey.
Igel Fine Arts Ltd., Manya, London, W.2.
Iglesis, D., London, S.W.1 (Gallery '25.)
Il Libro, London, S.W.3. Chen. Gall.
Iles Family, The, Rochester, Kent.
Iles, Francis, Rochester, Kent.
Iles Gallery, Richard, Colchester, Essex.
Iles, R. and C., Colchester, Essex.
Illingworth, V.E., London, N.5.
Illuminated Objects, Bath, Avon.
Ilsley, R., London, N.W.3.
Images in Watercolours, Chalfont St. Giles, Bucks.
Images — Peter Stockham, Lichfield, Staffs.
Imperial Antiques, Hull, N. Humberside.
Imperial Antiques, Stockport, Cheshire.
Impressions and Alexandra's Antiques, St. Margaret's Bay, Kent.
Imrie Antiques, Bridge of Earn, Perths., Scot.
Imrie, Mr. and Mrs. I., Bridge of Earn, Perths., Scot.
In Retrospect, Pocklington, N. Humberside.
In the Picture (The Golf Collection), Holt, Norfolk.
Incisioni, London, N.W.8. Alf. Ant. Mkt.
Ind, Barbara, Leominster, Hereford and Worcs. L. Ant. Mkt.
Ing, J., Wisbech, Cambs.
Ingall, I. and S., Farnham, Surrey.
Ingham, J.S., Horbury, W. Yorks.
Inglenook Antiques, Harpole, Northants.
Inglenook Antiques, Ramsbury, Wilts.
Inglis, Brand, London, S.W.1.
Ingram, D., Edinburgh, Midloth., Scot. (Dunedin Antiques Ltd.).
Ingram, I.C., Perth, Perths., Scot.
Ingrams, C., Haslemere, Surrey.
Inheritance, London, N.1.
Innes Gallery, Malcolm, London, S.W.3.
Innes Gallery, Malcolm, Edinburgh, Midloth., Scot.
Intercoin, Newcastle-upon-Tyne, Tyne and Wear.
Intercol London, London, N.1.
Inverspey Antiques, Fochabers, Scotland.
Iona Antiques, London, W.8.
Irani, M.Z., London, S.W.1. (The Connoisseur Gallery.)
Ireland Ltd., Peter, Blackpool, Lancs.
Irena Art and Antiques, Barry, S. Glam., Wales.
Iris Antiques, London, N.W.8. Alf. Ant. Mkt.
Ironbridge Antique Centre, Ironbridge, Shrops.
Irons, Mr. and Mrs. C.A., Coalville, Leics.
Irons, L.A., Wells-next-the-Sea, Norfolk.
Irving Antiques, Manchester, Lancs. Royal Ex. S.C.
Irving, Giulia, London, W.1. Grays A.M.
Irwin, C. and M., Ravenstonedale, Cumbria.
Isaacs, P. and S., Leeds, W. Yorks.
Isbell, S., Bath, Avon. (Queen's Parade Antiques Ltd.)
Isenberg, M., Hatch End, Middx.
Islington Artefacts, London, N.1.
It's About Time, Carlisle, Cumbria. C. Ant. and Craft C.
It's About Time, Westcliff-on-Sea, Essex.
Ivanhoe Antiques, Ashby de la Zouch, Leics.
Ivelet Books Ltd., Redhill, Surrey.
Ives Bookseller, John, Twickenham, Middx.
Ivy House Antiques, Abbots Bromley, Staffs.
Ivy House Antiques, Acle, Norfolk.
Ivy House Antiques, Brasted, Kent.
Ivy House Antiques, Gt. Shefford, Berks.
Ivy House Antiques, Shillingstone, Dorset.
Ixworth Antiques, Ixworth, Suffolk.

J

J.A.G., London, W.8. Ken. Church St. Ant. C.
J. and B. Antiques, Deddington, Oxon.
J.B. Antiques, Cradley Heath, W. Mids.
J.B. Antiques, Wimborne Minster, Dorset.
J.C. Antiques, London, E.10.
J. and G. Antiques, London, N.W.8. Alf. Ant. Mkt.
J. and H. Antiques, Bingley, W. Yorks.
J.N. Antiques, Redbourn, Herts.
Jack, J., Glasgow, Lanarks., Scot. (Mercat Antiques).
Jackdaw Antiques, Thatcham, Berks.
Jackman, F.T. and S., Jesmond, Tyne and Wear.
Jackman, Mr. and Mrs. J., Sayers Common, W. Sussex.
Jackson, A., Leamington Spa, Warks.
Jackson Antiques, London, N.W.3. Ham. Ant. Emp.
Jackson, A. and B., Barnard Castle, Durham.
Jackson, Miss A.E., Chesham, Bucks.
Jackson, F., London, W.10.
Jackson, John, Milton-under-Wychwood, Oxon.
Jackson Antiques, Jenny, Woodbridge, Suffolk.
Jackson, J.H., Milton-under-Wychwood, Oxon.
Jackson, Kenneth, Edinburgh, Midloth., Scot.
Jackson, P., Blackpool, Lancs.
Jackson, P., Windsor and Eton, Berks. (Times Past Antiques Ltd.).
Jackson Antiques, Peter, Brackley, Northants.
Jackson, P. and V.F., London, S.W.3. (O.F. Wilson Ltd.).
Jackson, R. and J., Flaxton, N. Yorks.
Jackson Antiques, S.I., Wigton, Cumbria.
Jackson, S. and Mrs. T.J., Sutton Bridge, Lincs.
Jackson, T.C. and Mrs., Newbury, Berks.
Jackson-Grant Antiques, Teynham, Kent.
Jackson-Grant, D.M., Teynham, Kent.
Jackson's Antiques Ltd., Barnard Castle, Co. Durham.
Jacksonsville Warehouse, Edinburgh, Midloth., Scot.
Jacobi, Mrs. P.M., Chester, Cheshire. (Grosvenor Antiques of Chester)
Jacobs Antique Centre, Cardiff, S. Glam., Wales.
Jacobs, G., Newark, Notts.
Jacobs, G. and M., Sawbridgeworth, Herts.
Jacobs, M., Norwich, Norfolk (Tooltique).
Jacques, Peter, London, N.W.8. Alf. Ant. Mkt.
Jade Antiques, Glasgow, Scotland. Vict. Vill.
Jadis Ltd., Bath, Avon.
Jaffa, John, London, W.1. G. Ant. Mkt.
Jaffray, Alan, Melksham, Wilts.
Jakes, K.P., Worthing, W. Sussex.
Jalna Antiques, Little Haywood, Staffs.
Jalna Antiques, Wolseley Bridge, Staffs.
Jamandic Ltd., Chester, Cheshire.
James Antiques — Canalside, Birmingham, W. Mids.
James and Son Ltd., Anthony, London, S.W.3.
James, Chris, Warwick, Warks. Smith St. A.C.
James, D. and E., London, S.W.1.
James (Fine Victorian Watercolours), David, London, S.W.1.
James, G., Oldham, Lancs.
James Antiques, Joseph, Penrith, Cumbria.
James, J.F., and A., York, N. Yorks. (Acomb Antiques).
James, N., Marlborough, Wilts.
James of St. Albans, St. Albans, Herts.
James, P. and D., Birmingham, W. Mids. (James Antiques — Canalside)
James, P.L., London, S.W.6.
James Antiques, R.A., Sileby, Leics.
James, R.M. and E., Bishops Cleeve, Glos.
James, S.N. and W., St. Albans, Herts.
James-Priday, A., Kidderminster, Hereford and Worcs.
Jameson and Co., A.E. Sheffield, S. Yorks.
Jameson, C., Thirsk, N. Yorks.
Jameson, P., Sheffield, S. Yorks.
Jamieson, Pauline, Glasgow, Lanarks., Scot. B. St. Ant. G.
Jandora, Weybridge, Surrey.
Jane, Mrs. M., Wallingford, Oxon.
Janes, P. and R., Dover, Kent.
Jansons Antiques, Bwlchllan, Dyfed, Wales.
Jansons, J.C., Bwlchllan, Dyfed, Wales.
Janus Antiques, London, S.W.3. Chen. Gall.
Janus Antiques, Ramsden, Oxon.
Japanese Gallery, London, N.1.
Japanese Gallery, London, W.8.
Jarman, H., Woodbury, Devon.
Jarona Antiques, London, S.W.3 (Nigel Appleby). Ant. Ant. Mkt.
Jarrett, G., Norwich, Norfolk.
Jarrett, L.S.A. and C.J., Witney, Oxon.
Jartelius, M., London, N.1. The Mall.
Jarvis, Timothy, Woburn, Beds. Wob. Ab. Ant. C.
Jasper Antiques, Snettisham, Norfolk.
Jasper Antiques, Woodstock, Oxon.
Jasper's Fine Arts Ltd., Maidenhead, Berks.
Jasper's Fine Arts, Windsor and Eton, Berks.
Jay Antiques, Hayling Island, Hants.
Jay, C.G., Looe, Cornwall.
Jay Antiques and Objets d'Art, Melvyn, London, W.8.
Jay's Antique Centre, The, Harefield, Middx.
Jazy Antiques, London, N.1. The Mall.
Jazz, Stratford-upon-Avon, Warks.
Jazzy Art Deco, London, N.W.1.
Jebb, T.H., Cookstown, Co. Tyrone, N. Ireland.
Jefferson, Patrick, London, S.W.6.
Jeffs at Nicholas Harris, Peter, London, S.W.6.
Jellicoe Fine Porcelain, Roderick, Wallasey, Merseyside.
Jellinek, T., London, W.8. (Lindsay Antiques.)
Jemms, Colyton, Devon.

Jenkins, J., London, S.E.26.
Jenkins, V. and A., Bradford-on-Avon, Wilts.
Jenner, J., London, S.W.3. Ant. Ant. Mkt.
Jennings, Mrs. B.M., Brasted, Kent.
Jennings, Celia, Pratt's Corner, Kent.
Jennings, J.R., Leominster, Hereford and Worcs.
Jennings Antiques, Paul, Angarrack, Cornwall.
Jennings Antiques, P. and D., Sandgate, Kent. S. Ant. C.
Jennings of Leominster, Leominster, Hereford and Worcs.
Jennings, R., Bideford, Devon.
Jennings, R.J., Pulloxhill, Beds.
Jenny Wren Antiques, Cowbridge, S. Glam. Wales.
Jennywell Hall Antiques, Crosby Ravensworth, Cumbria.
Jeorrett, J. and A., Kiltarlity, Inver., Scot.
Jeremiah Antiques, Llandissilio, Dyfed, Wales.
Jeremiah Antiques, Taunton, Somerset.
Jeremiah, D.W., Taunton, Somerset.
Jeremiah, S. and S., Llandissilio, Dyfed, Wales.
Jeremy Ltd., London, S.W.1.
Jeremy's (Oxford Stamp Centre), Oxford, Oxon.
Jesse., John, London, W.8.
Jessie's Button Box, Bath, Avon. Gt. West. Ant. C.
Jessop Classic Photographica, London, W.C.1.
Jewel Antiques, Cheddleton, Staffs.
Jewell, B., Evesham, Hereford and Worcs.
Jewell Ltd., S. and H., London, W.C.2.
Jewett, N. Low Fell, Tyne and Wear.
Jewitt, W.H., Hexham, Northumb.
Jinks, G., Birmingham, W. Mids. (Tatters of Tyseley).
Joan of Art Ltd., London, S.W.3. (Forty-Eight Walton St.).
Jobson's, Joan, Coggeshall, Essex.
Joel, C., Dorking, Surrey.
Joel, Mrs. J., Dorking, Surrey.
John Antiques, Angela, Bampton, Oxon.
John Anthony Antiques, Bletchingley, Surrey.
John (Rare Rugs) Ltd., C., London, W.1.
John, P.R., London, N.W.8.
Johns, T., Lytchett Minster, Dorset.
Johnson, A., Colchester, Essex.
Johnson, Mrs. A., Much Wenlock, Shrops.
Johnson, A., Windsor and Eton, Berks.
Johnson, D., Birmingham, W. Mids. (Rex Johnson and Sons).
Johnson, D., Oakamoor, Staffs.
Johnson, D.A., Prestwick, Ayr, Scot.
Johnson, D. and S., Bath, Avon. (Beau Nash House Antiques).
Johnson, Mr. and Mrs. E.M., Salisbury, Wilts.
Johnson Antiques Ltd., George, London, W.11.
Johnson and Son (Shaftesbury) Ltd., G.E., Shaftesbury, Dorset.
Johnson, Mrs. J., Manchester, Lancs.
Johnson, Mrs. J.A., Cartmel, Cumbria.
Johnson Ltd., Oscar and Peter, London, S.W.1.
Johnson, P. and J., Leek, Staffs.
Johnson, P.R., Stow-on-the-Wold, Glos.
Johnson, R., Birmingham, W. Mids.
Johnson, Robert, London, W.1. G. Ant. Mkt.
Johnson, R. and R., Birmingham, W. Mids. (Piccadilly Jewellers).
Johnson and Sons, Rex, Birmingham, W. Mids.
Johnson, S., Newton Abbot, Devon. N.A. Ant. C.
Johnson, T.L., Maidenhead, Berks.
Johnson, T.L., Windsor and Eton, Berks.
Johnson, Walker and Tolhurst Ltd., London, W.1.
Johnson's, Leek, Staffs.
Johnson's Antiques, Manchester, Lancs.
Johnsons of Sherborne Ltd., Sherborne, Dorset.
Johnston, Mrs. B., London, S.W.3. Ant. Ant. Mkt.
Johnston, D., Windsor and Eton, Berks. (Dee's Antiques)
Johnston, D.G.L., Dorchester, Dorset.
Johnston, Paul, Gedney, Lincs.
Johnston, T. and S., Keighley, W. Yorks.
Johnstone, W., Barrhead, Renfrews., Scot.
Jolliffe, Patricia, Hare Hatch, Berks.
Jomarc Pianos Ltd. and Pianorama, Birmingham, W. Mids.
Jones, London, W.11.
Jones, Mrs. A., Brighton, E. Sussex. (Circus Antiques).
Jones, A., Colchester, Essex.
Jones, Annabel, London, S.W.3.
Jones Antiques, Alan, Okehampton, Devon.
Jones Antiques, Alan, Plymouth, Devon.
Jones, A.P., Kettering, Northants.
Jones Antiques, Christopher, Weedon, Northants.
Jones, D., Kendal, Cumbria.
Jones, D., Stratford-upon-Avon, Warks.
Jones, D.A., Oxford, Oxon.
Jones Ltd., D.L., Uppingham, Leics.
Jones, E., Chester, Cheshire.
Jones, E.C., Birmingham, W. Mids. (Kestrel House Antiques).
Jones, E.P., Liverpool, Merseyside.
Jones, G., London, S.W.6.
Jones, Mrs. Gwyneth, London, S.W.3. Chen. Gall.
Jones, Miss G., Looe, Cornwall.
Jones Antiques, Glyn, Pembroke Dock, Dyfed, Wales.
Jones, Howard, London, W.8.
Jones, J., London, W.11.
Jones, Jenny, Manchester, Lancs. Royal Ex. S.C.
Jones, J.H., Rhos-on-Sea, Clwyd, Wales.
Jones, John and Jennifer, Towcester, Northants.
Jones, J. and S., Beaumaris, Gwynedd, Wales.
Jones, L., Ludlow, Shrops.
Jones, M., Hazlemere, Bucks.

Jones, Jeweller, Michael, Northampton, Northants.
Jones, M.R.T. and Mrs. J.A., Cromer, Norfolk.
Jones, M.S., Great Ayton, N. Yorks.
Jones, Orlando, Bath, Avon.
Jones, P., Bristol, Avon. Clift. Ant. Mkt.
Jones, Mr. and Mrs. P., Chepstow, Gwent, Wales.
Jones, P., London, S.W.3. Chen. Gall.
Jones, Paul, London, S.W.3.
Jones, P., Watton, Norfolk.
Jones, P. and A., Nantwich, Cheshire.
Jones, P.W., Oakham, Leics.
Jones, R., Bristol, Avon. Clift. Ant. Mkt.
Jones, Roderick, London, N.W.8. Alf. Ant. Mkt.
Jones, R. and J., London, S.W.1.
Jones, R. and J., Rye, E. Sussex.
Jones and Son, Roy, Exeter, Devon (Exeter Antique Wholesalers).
Jones, R.W., Llanbedr, Gwynedd, Wales.
Jones, T. and S., Chipping Norton, Oxon.
Jones, W., London, W.11.
Jones, W.A. and E.S., Bromyard, Hereford and Worcs.
Jones and Son (Antiques) Ltd., W., London, W.11.
Jones, W.T., Ruthin, Clwyd, Wales.
Jordan, James, A., Lichfield, Staffs.
Jordan, P.A. and W.E., Farnham, Surrey.
Jordan, P. and B., Farnham, Surrey.
Jordan, R.A., Barnard Castle, Durham.
Jordan (Fine Paintings), T.B. and R., Eaglescliffe, Cleveland.
Jorgen Antiques, London, S.W.15.
Joseph Antiquarian Bookseller, E., London W.1.
Joseph, John, London, W.1. G. Ant. Mkt.
Joseph and Pearce Ltd., London, E.C.1.
Josephine, Bath, Avon.
Joshua Antiques, Taunton, Somerset.
Joslin, Richard, London, W.14.
Joslyn, J.H., London, S.E.22.
Jouques, P., Bath, Avon. Gt. West. Ant. C.
Jowsey and Roe, Whitby, N. Yorks.
Joy, Mrs. N., Hadlow, Kent.
Joyce, Beryl, Guildford, Surrey. Ant. C.
Joyner, T.R.B., Newchurch, Isle of Wight.
Joy's Shop, Longridge, Lancs.
Jubb, Mrs. M., Bristol, Avon, Clift. Ant. Mkt.
Jubilee, London, N.1.
Jubilee Antique Cellars and Collectors Market, Brighton, E. Sussex.
Juett, A.H.C. and D.C., Shillingstone, Dorset.
Juett, J., Walkerburn, Peebles., Scot.
Jukes, Mr. and Mrs. G., St. Leonards-on-Sea, E. Sussex.
Julian Antiques, Hurstpierpoint, W. Sussex.
Julian Antiques, London, N.1.
Julian, B. and R., Newport, I. of Wight.
Juliana, Bingley, W. Yorks.
Julia's Antiques, Bishops Waltham, Hants.
Junk Shop, The, London, E.17.
Junktion, New Bolingbroke, Lincs.
Juno's Antiques, Brackley, Northants.
Jupiter Antiques, Manchester, Lancs. Royal Ex. S.C.
Juran and Co., Alexander, London, W.1.
Jury, D., Bristol, Avon. (Cotham Galleries).
Just a Second Antiques Ltd., London, S.W.11.
Just Desks, London, N.W.3.
Just Desks, London, N.W.8.
Just the Thing, Hartley Wintney, Hants.
Justin Pinewood, Burton-on-Trent, Staffs.

K

K. Books of Hull, Hull, N. Humberside.
K.C. Antiques, Darwen, Lancs.
K.L.M. and Co. Antiques, Lepton, W. Yorks.
K. and M. Antiques, London, W.11. Stouts Arc.
K. and M. Antiques, London, S.W.3. Ant. Ant. Mkt.
Kaczer, T., London, W.1. B. St. Ant. C.
Kadwell, J.P., Malmesbury, Wilts.
Kailas, M., London, S.W.6. (Richardson and Kailas)
Kairis, M.V., London, N.8.
Kaplan Associates Ltd., Lewis M., London, S.W.3.
Kara Antiques, M., Newark, Notts. N. Ant. Wrhse.
Karczewski-Slowikowski, J., Manchester, Lancs. (Didsbury Antiques (Chorlton)).
Kasiewicz, Mr. and Mrs., Auchterarder, Perths., Scot.
Kaskimo, Mrs. P.A., London, S.W.3. Ant. Ant. Mkt.
Kasmin, J., London, S.W.10.
Kate, Hemswell Cliff, Lincs.
Kathleen's Antiques, North Petherton, Somerset.
Katz, G. and Y., Richmond, Surrey.
Kausmally, A., London, N.1.
Kausmally Antiques, London, N.1.
Kavanagh, D., Blackpool, Lancs.
Kay, J.A., Warnham, W. Sussex.
Kaye, A.M., Chester, Cheshire.
Kaye of Lyndhurst, Lita, Lyndhurst, Hants.
Kaye Ltd., Simon, London, W.1 (I. Freeman and Son.)
Kayes of Chester, Chester, Cheshire.
Kear, P.W., Cranborne, Dorset.
Kearin, J. and J., White Colne, Essex.
Kearney, Felicity, London, W.1. G. Ant. Mkt.
Kearney and Sons, T.H., Belfast, N. Ireland.
Keates, G.W. and V.A., Carlisle, Cumbria.
Keats, London, W.1. G. Mews.
Keays, Mary, London, N.W.8. Alf. Ant. Mkt.
Keddie, Mrs. A.C., East Grinstead, W. Sussex.
Keeble, Mrs. E., Fareham, Hants.
Keeble, F.J., Claygate, Surrey.
Keeble Ltd., Claygate, Surrey.
Keegan, P., North Walsham, Norfolk.
Keehan, M.P., Brighton, E. Sussex (Michael Norman Antiques).
Keen, C., Lewes, E. Sussex.
Keen Antiques, Cassandra, London, N.1.

Kilbane, E., Bath, Avon. Gt. West. A. C. Wed. Mkt.
Kilby, Mrs. M., Northfleet, Kent.
Kilgour Antiques, Glasgow, Lanarks., Scot. B. St. Ant. G.
Kilgour, Mrs. C.G., Glasgow, Lanarks., Scot. B. St. Ant. G.
Kilim House, The, London, S.W.6.
Kilim Warehouse Ltd., The, London, S.W.12.
Killinger Antiques, Sue, Woburn, Beds. Wob. Ab. Ant. C.
Kilmacolm Antiques Ltd., Kilmacolm, Renfrews., Scot.
Kimbell Ltd., Richard, Market Harborough, Leics.
Kimber and Son, Malvern Link, Hereford and Worcs.
Kime Antiques, Robert, Marlborough, Wilts.
Kimp, R. and M.K., Norwich, Norfolk. (Englishman's Antiques).
Kinch, W.E., Leominster, Hereford and Worcs. L. Ant. Mkt.
Kindon Antiques Ltd., Terry, Melmerby, N. Yorks.
King, Wymondham, Norfolk.
King, Ann, Bath, Avon.
King Antiques, Horncastle, Lincs.
King, B., London, S.W.3. (Christine Schell.)
King, D. and A., London, S.W.1.
King Antique Glass, Dominic, London, S.W.1.
King Antiques, Eric, London, S.W.6.
King, F., London, W.14.
King, F., Pattishall, Northants.
King, H., Kinbuck, Perths., Scot.
King, J., London, W.C.2. (Thomas Kettle Ltd.).
King, J.F.W., Wantage, Oxon.
King, J.H., Polegate, E. Sussex.
King, J.H., St. Leonards-on-Sea, E. Sussex.
King, M., Wymondham, Norfolk.
King, R., Horncastle, Lincs.
King Antiques, Roger, Hungerford, Berks.
King, Mr. and Mrs. R.F., Hungerford, Berks.
King, R. and G., West Peckham, Kent.
King Street Curios, Tavistock, Devon.
King Street Galleries, London, S.W.1.
Kingaby's, Richmond, Surrey.
Kingham, Mrs. G., London, S.E.21.
Kings Antiques, Cardiff, S. Glam., Wales.
Kings Court Galleries, Dorking, Surrey.
Kings Farm Antiques, Glastonbury, Somerset.
Kings Fireplaces and Architectural Antiques, Cardiff, S. Glam., Wales.
Kings House Antiques, Langport, Somerset.
Kings of Kinbuck, Kinbuck, Perths., Scot.
Kings Road Gallery, London, S.W.10. Furn. Cave.
Kingsbury Antiques, Brighton, E. Sussex.
Kingsley Barn Antique Centre, Eversley, Hants.
Kingsley Galleries, Bath, Avon.
King-Smith, P.J., Moreton-in-Marsh, Glos.
King-Smith, Thomas, Burford, Oxon.
Kingston Antiques, Kingston-upon-Thames, Surrey.
Kingston, D., London, S.W.3. Chen. Gall.
Kingston, Mrs. E., London, S.W.19.
Kingston, Richard J., Henley-on-Thames, Oxon.
Kingsway Antiques, Leeds, W. Yorks.
Kingswood Antiques, Kingsbridge, Devon.
Kingswood, T., London, W.C.2.
Kinloch, Mrs. C., Sedlescombe, E. Sussex.
Kirby Antiques, R., Acrise, Kent.
Kirk, B. and D., Penzance, Cornwall.
Kirk, Geoff and Lada, Fakenham, Norfolk. Ant. C.
Kirkby, J., Greystoke, Cumbria.
Kirkdale Pianos, London, S.E.26.
Kirke, B., Modbury, Devon.
Kirke, Mrs. M.R., Plymouth, Devon.
Kirkgate Picture Gallery, Thirsk, N. Yorks.
Kirkham, H., Tenterden, Kent.
Kirkland, G., London, S.W.6. (Whiteway & Waldron Ltd.).
Kirkstall Antiques, Leeds, W. Yorks.
Kirsch, Marcus, London, W.2.
Kirsh Ltd., Marcus, London, W.2.
Kirton Antiques, Kirton, Lincs.
Kitchenalia, Longridge, Lancs.
Kitching, Robert, Horncastle, Lincs.
Kitson, M., Cardigan, Dyfed, Wales.
Kitts Corner Antiques, Penzance, Cornwall.
Klaber, Mrs. B. and Miss P., London, W.8.
Klaber and Klaber, London, W.8.
Kleanthous Antiques, London, W.11. Stouts Arc.
Kleanthous, C. and C., London, W.11. Stouts Arc.
Klein, M., London, S.W.3. Ant. Ant. Mkt.
Kleinman, Patricia, London, N.1. The Mall.
Kluth, Simon, London, N.W.8. Alf. Ant. Mkt.
Knaphill Antiques, Knaphill, Surrey.
Knick Knacks, Sutton-on-Sea, Lincs.
Knight and Son, B.R., St. Ives, Cambs.
Knight, D., Macclesfield, Cheshire.
Knight, F. and Mrs. B., Swanbourne, Bucks.
Knight, J.C., Harpenden, Herts.
Knight, John C., Luton, Beds.
Knight, M., St. Ives, Cornwall.
Knight, P., Bridport, Dorset.
Knight, Peter, Kennington, Kent.
Knights Antiques, Brassington, Derbys.
Knight's Gallery, Harpenden, Herts.
Knights' Gallery, Luton, Beds.
Knights, P.H., Norwich, Norfolk (Oswald Sebley).
Knightsbridge Coins, London, S.W.1.
Knipe, D., Dorchester-on-Thames, Oxon.
Knowl Hill Galleries, Hare Hatch, Berks.
Knowles (Toys/Dolls), Anthea, Littlehampton, Devon.
Knowles, W.A. and M.A., Penkridge, Staffs.
Knowles, W.A. and M.A., Wolverhampton, W. Mids.
Knox, A., Errol, Perths., Scot.
Knutsford Gallery Antiques, Knutsford, Cheshire.
Knutsford Road Antiques, Wilmslow, Cheshire.
Kollect-o-Mania, Brighton, E. Sussex.
Koopman and Son Ltd., E. and C.T., London, W.C.2. Lond. Silv. Vts.

Koopman and Son Ltd., E. and C.T., Manchester, Lancs.
Kopriva, A., London, S.W.6. (Pageant Antiques).
Korn, E., London, N.10.
Korn, M.E., London, N.10.
Korniczky, Bea, London, N.W.8. Alf. Ant. Mkt. (J. Fleming).
Kotobuki, London, N.W.8. Alf. Ant. Mkt.
Kotobuki Antiques, Stonehaven, Scotland.
Kramer, J., Elmey Lovett, Hereford and Worcs.
Kreckovic, L. and E., London, S.W.6.
Krell, Mrs. V., London, S.W.3. Chen. Gall. Wear.
Krolick, H., Gosport, Tyne and Wear.
Krolle, Mrs. D., Amersham, Bucks.
Krucker, S., Stroud, Glos.
Kruml, Richard, London, W.1.
Kusnierz, Mrs. M., Telford, Shrops.
Kyle Antiques, S., London, W.C.2. Lon. Silv. Vts.
Kyoto House Antiques, Cheltenham, Glos.
Kyriacou, K. and T., London, N.W.5.

L

L.B. Antiques, Bath, Avon. Gt. West. Ant. C.
L.P. Furniture (Mids) Ltd., Pelsall, W. Mids.
La Barre Ltd., Leominster, Hereford and Worcs.
La Chaise Antiques, Faringdon, Oxon.
La Trobe, H., Brasted, Kent.
La Trobe and Bigwood Restorers, Tunbridge Wells, Kent.
La Trouvaille, Enfield, Middx.
La Verite Ltd., London, S.W.3. Ant. An. Mkt.
Lace Basket, The, Tenterden, Kent.
Lace Lady, Brecon, Powys, Wales.
Lacewing Fine Art Gallery, Marlborough, Wilts.
Lacey Gallery, Stephen, London, S.W.10.
Lacey, S.W.H., London, S.W.10.
Lacis, Budleigh Salterton, Devon.
L'Acquaforte, London, W.11.
Lacquer Chest, The, London, W.8.
Lacy Gallery, Henley-in-Arden, Warks.
Lacy Gallery, London, W.11.
Ladd's Gallery, Hare Hatch, Berks.
La-di-da, Stratford-upon-Avon, Warks.
Lady Newborough, London, W.1.
Ladygate Antiques, Beverley, N. Humberside.
Lagden, J., Penzance, Cornwall.
L'Aiglon Antique Centre, London, W.11.
Laila, Kingsthorpe, Northants.
Lain, H.J. and V.J., Westbourne, W. Sussex.
Lain, L.M. and M.D., Bosham, W. Sussex.
Lak Ltd., Mahine, London, W.14.
Lake Antiques, Lake, I. of Wight.
Lake, J. and E., Glasgow, Lanarks., Scot. (Nice Things Old and New).
Lake, P., Bristol, Avon. (The Tudor Gallery of Bristol).
Laker, I.A. and E.K., Somerton, Somerset.
Laklia, L.T., Bexley, Kent.
Laleham Antiques, Laleham, Surrey.
Lamari, R., London, S.W.3. Ant. Ant. Mkt.
Lamb Arcade, The, Wallingford, Oxon.
Lamb, B., Swanage, Dorset.
Lamb Antiques, Michael, Minster, Kent.
Lamb, R. and Mrs. S., Clare, Suffolk.
Lamb, S. and Mrs. K., Sherborne, Dorset.
Lambden, J., Warboys, Cambs.
Lambe, Charlotte and John, Belfast, N. Ireland.
Lamberhurst Antiques, Lamberhurst, Kent.
Lambert, Adrienne, Stow-on-the-Wold, Glos. C. Ant. C.
Lambert, John, Preston, Lancs. N.W. Ant. C.
Lambert, N., Woodbridge, Suffolk.
Lambert, P.M. and A.M.F.T., Halesworth, Suffolk.
Lambert, R., Lincoln, Lincs.
Lambert's Antiques, Blackpool, Lancs.
Lambert's Barn, Woodbridge, Suffolk.
Lamont Antiques Ltd., London, S.E.10.
Lamont, F., Totnes, Devon.
Lamont, N., London, S.E.10.
Lamp Gallery, The, London, S.W.6.
Lampard and Sons, L.E., Horsham, W. Sussex.
Lampard, Penny, Headcorn, Kent.
Lampard, Mrs. P., Headcorn, Kent.
Lampard and Son Ltd., S., London, W.11.
Lampert, B., London, W.C.2. Lon. Silv. Vts.
Lancashire Bygones, Upholland, Lancs.
Lancaster, Barbara, London, W.1. G. Ant. Mkt.
Lancaster Leisure Park Antiques Centre, Lancaster, Lancs.
Lancaster, T.J., Leek, Staffs.
Lancastrian Antiques, Lancaster, Lancs.
Lancefield Antiques, David, Sandgate, Kent. S. Ant. C.
Lancer, Marilyn, London, N.W.8. Alf. Ant. Mkt.
Lanchester, N., Debenham, Suffolk.
Landgate Antiques, Rye, E. Sussex.
Lane Antiques, Stockbridge, Hants.
Lane Antiques, Barbara, Chiddingstone, Kent.
Lane, E.K., Stockbridge, Hants.
Lane Fine Art Ltd., London, W.1.
Lane, Jackie, Diss, Norfolk.
Lane, Mrs. N., London, W.5. (Ealing Gallery).
Lane, R., Horsebridge, E. Sussex.
Lane, R., Tewkesbury, Glos.
Lane Antiques, Russell, Warwick, Warks.
Lane, R.H.G., Warwick, Warks.
Lang Antiques, John, Dorking, Surrey.
Lang, J. and C., St. Leonards-on-Sea, E. Sussex.
Lang and Tiffany Antiques, John, St. Leonards-on-Sea, E. Sussex.
Langford, London, S.W.10.
Langford, J., Shrewsbury, Shrops.
Langford, J., Telford, Shrops.
Langford, J. and R., Llangollen, Clwyd, Wales.

Langford, L.L., London, S.W.10.
Langfords, London, W.C.2. Lon. Silv. Vts.
Langham Ltd., Marion, Woburn, Beds. Wob. Ab. Ant. C.
Langley Antiques, Corby Hill, Cumbria.
Langley Galleries, Rochester, Kent.
Langley's (Jewellers) Ltd., Bradford, W. Yorks.
Langmead, Mrs. S., Chertsey, Surrey.
Langold Antiques, West Peckham, Kent.
Langton, M., Hull, N. Humberside.
Langton, N. and V.M., Chorley, Lancs.
Langton, N. and V.M., Leyland, Lancs.
Langtown Antiques, Kirkcaldy, Fife, Scot.
Lanham, Miss A., Newmarket, Suffolk.
Lankester Antiques and Books, Saffron Walden, Essex.
Lankester, J. and P., Saffron Walden, Essex.
Lankshear, M.I., Christchurch, Dorset.
Lankshear Antiques, M. and R., Christchurch, Dorset.
Lansdown Antiques, Bath, Avon.
Lantern Gallery, Bath, Avon.
Lantern Shop, The, Sidmouth, Devon.
Lantern Shop Gallery, The, Sidmouth, Devon.
Lapwing Antiques, Uppingham, Leics.
Large Gallery, George, Woburn, Beds.
Larkhall Antiques, Hebden Bridge, W. Yorks.
Larkhall Antiques, Preston, Lancs. N.W. Ant. C.
Larner, P., Cirencester, Glos.
Lascelles, R., London, S.W.6. (Big Ben Antique Clocks).
Lasham, L.M., Cowfold, W. Sussex.
Lasher, C., London, W.1. (M. and L. Silver Co. Ltd.)
Lask, Anthony, London, N.W.8. Alf. Ant. Mkt.
Lassalle, Judith, London, N.1.
Lasseters, Arundel, W. Sussex.
Lassey, Mrs. J., Settle, N. Yorks.
Lassota, M., London, S.W.6.
Last Drop Antique and Collectors Club, Bolton, Lancs.
Lastlodge Ltd., London, W.11 (Wynyards Antiques.)
Latchford Antiques, Cheltenham, Glos.
Latchford, K. and R., Cheltenham, Glos. (Latchford Antiques).
Latford Photography, Cliff, Colchester, Essex.
Latford, J., Colchester, Essex. (Eastgates Antiques).
Latham, D., Stoke-on-Trent, Staffs.
Latham, J. and D., Hexham, Northumb.
Latham Antiques, R.H., Blackpool, Lancs.
Lathbury Antiques, Jean, Bampton, Oxon.
Latimer, E., Bicester, Oxon.
Latreville, Claude and Martine, London, S.W.3. Chen. Gall.
Laughlan, J. and J., Crossford, Scot.
Laura's Bookshop, Derby, Derbys.
Laurence, C., Worcester, Hereford and Worcs.
Laurence Corner Militaria, London, N.W.1.
Laurence Ltd., Victor, London, N.W.1 (Laurence Corner Militaria.)
Laurens Antiques, G.A., Whitstable, Kent.
Laurie, John, London, N.1.
Laurie Antiques, Peter, London, S.E.10.
Lavender Antiques Ltd., D.S., London, W.1.
Lavian, Joseph, London, N.W.5.
Law, D., Woking, Surrey.
Law, P. and I., Herne Bay, Kent.
Law, R., Worthing, W. Sussex.
Law, S., Barnsley, S. Yorks.
Lawes, David, Harrogate, N. Yorks.
Lawrence and Sons, F.G., Redhill, Surrey.
Lawrence, John, Newton Abbot, Devon. N.A. Ant. C.
Lawrence, L.D., London, N.6.
Lawrence, Madeline, London, N.W.8. Alf. Ant. Mkt.
Lawrence R., London, S.W.1. (Gallery 25).
Lawson, Mrs. A., Glossop, Derbys.
Lawson and Co., E.M., East Hagbourne, Oxon.
Lawson Antiques, F. and T., Richmond, Surrey.
Lawson Antiques, Keith, Scratby, Norfolk.
Lawson, W.J. and K.M., East Hagbourne, Oxon.
Lawton, S., Leeds, W. Yorks. (Calverley Antiques).
Layne, A.C., Carlisle, Cumbria.
Layte, J.D., Holt, Norfolk.
Layton, Lady, Richmond, Surrey.
Layton Antiques, Richmond, Surrey.
Laywood, Anthony W., Knipton, Leics.
Lazarus Antiques, D., Hartley Wintney, Hants.
Le Bailly Antiques, Tamara, Hay-on-Wye, Powys, Wales.
Le Jazz Hot, Brighton, E. Sussex.
Le Marchant, M. and S., Bruton, Somerset.
Le Rougetel, B. and P., Chester, Cheshire. (Filkins Antiques).
Leach, B., Llandovery, Dyfed, Wales.
Leadenhall Gallery, Canterbury, Kent.
Leadlay Gallery, Warwick, London, S.E.10.
Leamington Pine and Antique Centre, Leamington Spa, Warks.
Leaside Antiques, Luton, Beds.
Leaside Antiques, St. Albans, Herts.
Leask, M., Edinburgh, Midloth., Scot. (Quadrant Antiques).
Leatherland Antiques, P.D., Reading, Berks.
Lebentz, Z., Dorchester-on-Thames, Oxon.
Lechlade Antiques, Lechlade, Glos.
Lechlade Antiques Arcade, Lechlade, Glos.
Leckhampton Antiques, Cheltenham, Glos.
Ledger, Barbara, Widecombe-in-the-Moor, Devon.
Ledger, M. and A., Stockport, Cheshire.
Lee, A., Clitheroe, Lancs.
Lee, C.G., Llandudno, Gwynedd, Wales.
Lee, G., London, W.11. (Noble Antiques).
Lee Antiques, Joy, North Cheriton, Somerset.
Lee, J. Morton, Hayling Island, Hants.
Lee, J.S., Norwich, Norfolk. (Another One)
Lee, Mr. and Mrs. J.W.H., Sheffield, S. Yorks. (Arcade Antiques Ltd.).
Lee, Mrs. P., Shipley, W. Yorks.
Lee Antiques, Peter, Wiveliscombe, Somerset.
Lee, P. and A., Wiveliscombe, Somerset.

Lee, R., Chertsey, Surrey.
Lee (Fine Arts) Ltd., Ronald A., London, W.1.
Lee, R.A. and C.B., London, W.1.
Lee and Stacey, London, N.W.3. Ham. Ant. Emp.
Lee, T. St. Leonards-on-Sea, E. Sussex. Hastings Ant. C.
Leek Bookshop, The, Leek, Staffs.
Lee's Antiques, Clitheroe, Lancs.
Lees, J.A. and T.P., Glossop, Derbys.
Lees and Sons, M., Worcester, Hereford and Worcs.
Leete R.L., Lubenham, Leics.
Lefevre Gallery, London, W.1.
Lefevre Ltd., London, W.1.
Legard, I.P., Harrogate, N. Yorks. (Christopher Warner).
Leger Galleries Ltd., The, London, W.1.
Legg and Son, E.C., Cirencester, Glos.
Legg, E.M.J., Dorchester, Dorset.
Legg Antiques, Michael, Dorchester, Dorset.
Legg of Dorchester, Dorchester, Dorset.
Legg, W. and H., Dorchester, Dorset.
Leggatt Brothers, London, S.W.1.
Leggatt, Sir Hugh, London, S.W.1.
Legge, C.T., Oxford, Oxon.
Legge Oriental Carpets, Christopher, Oxford, Oxon.
Legge, J. and L., Marlborough, Wilts.
Lehan, Mr. and Mrs., London, S.W.3. Ant. Ant Mkt.
Lehmann, Peter, London, N.1. The Mall.
Leicestershire Sporting Gallery and Brown Jack Bookshop, Lubenham, Leics.
Leigh Coins, Antiques and Jewellery, Leigh, Lancs.
Leigh and Son, G.E. and J.E., Reddish, Cheshire.
Leigh and Son, G.E., Reddish, Cheshire.
Leigh, Joan, London, W.11.
Leigh Antiques, Laurie, Oxford, Oxon.
Leigh, L., D., and W., Oxford, Oxon.
Leiston Furniture Warehouse, Leiston, Suffolk.
Leiston Trading Post, Leiston, Suffolk.
Leitch, C.J., Cookstown, Co. Tyrone, N. Ireland.
Leitch, C. and W., Great Bardfield, Essex.
Leith's Brocanterbury, Nan, Canterbury, Kent.
Leloup, Diane, London, W.11. G. Port.
Lemington House Antiques, Moreton-in-Marsh, Glos.
Lemkow, Sara, London, N.1.
Lemon, Ann, Redditch, Hereford and Worcs.
Lenda Antiques, Gloucester, Glos.
Lennard Antiques, Tingewick, Bucks.
Lennard, Pat, London, W.1. G. Ant. Mkt.
Lennie Fine Art Ltd., Barclay, Glasgow, Lanarks., Scot. B. St. Ant. G.
Lennox Antiques, Bromyard, Hereford & Worcs.
Lenson, Nellie and Smith, Roy, London, N.1.
Leo, R., Bournemouth, Dorset. (Victorian Chairman)
Leoframes, Brighton, E. Sussex.
Leominster Antiques, Leominster, Hereford and Worcs.
Leominster Antiques Market, Leominster, Hereford and Worcs.
Leon Antiques Ltd., London, W.C.2. Lon. Silv. Vts.
Leon, Mrs. N., London, S.W.3. (Miss E. Pollock) Ant. Ant. Mkt.
Leong, Ken, London, W.11. G. Port.
Leopard, The, Brighton, E. Sussex.
Leppard, A. and A., Brighton, E. Sussex (The Leopard.)
Leroy, D., Burford, Oxon.
Lesley's Antiques, Hull, N. Humberside.
Leslie, I., Dingwall, Scotland.
Leslie, K. J., Southampton, Hants.
Leslie and Leslie, Haddington, E. Loth., Scot.
Leslie Antiques, R.K., Southampton, Hants.
Leslie, Stanley, London, S.W.3.
Leslie's, Portsmouth, Hants.
Lester, C., Banbury, Oxon.
Lester, S., Halifax, W. Yorks.
Letham Antiques, Edinburgh, Midloth., Scot.
Letham, David, Edinburgh, Midloth., Scot.
Letham, Mrs. J., Edinburgh, Midloth., Scot.
Letty's Antiques Ltd., Leicester, Leics.
Leuchars, H., London, S.W.6.
Lev, Mrs., London, W.8.
Lev (Antiques) Ltd., London, W.8.
Levene Ltd., M.P., London, S.W.7.
Leveridge-Koh, Mrs. T., London, W.1. (Meileng Collection). B. St. Ant. C.
Leveson-Gower, C.W., Standlake, Oxon.
Levine, D. and L., Norwich, Norfolk.
Levine and Co., Henry, Norwich, Norfolk.
Levine, Jenny, London, W.11. G. Port.
Levinsky, J., London, E.15.
Levy, A., London, S.W.6.
Levy, Mrs. C., London, N.1. (Collectables). The Mall.
Levy, Celia,/Sheila Hart, London, N.W.8. Alf. Ant. Mkt.
Levy, G.J., M.P. and W.Y., London, W.1 (H. Blairman and Sons Ltd.)
Levy, M., London, W.8. (Cameo Gallery)
Lewes Antique Centre, Lewes, E. Sussex.
Lewis, A., Fleet, Hants.
Lewis Antiques, Buxton, Derbys.
Lewis Fine Art, Alan, Hundleby, Lincs.
Lewis, A. and M., Hundleby, Lincs.
Lewis, Arthur, S., London, S.W.1.
Lewis, Mrs. B., London, W.11. (B. and T. Antiques).
Lewis, Gerald, Montacute, Somerset.
Lewis Antiques, Gerald, Woburn, Beds. Wob. Ab. Ant. C.
Lewis, G. and B., Montacute, Somerset.
Lewis Antique and Fine Art Dealers, Ivor and Patricia, Peterborough, Cambs.
Lewis Antique and Fine Art Dealers, Ivor and Patricia, Stamford, Lincs.
Lewis, J.D. and P.C., Petworth, W. Sussex.
Lewis, J. and S., Buxton, Derbys.
Lewis and Lloyd, Petworth, W. Sussex.
Lewis Antiques, Michael, London, N.1.
Lewis – Oriental Carpets and Rugs, Michael and Amanda, Wellington, Somerset.
Lewis, M. and D., London, W.11.
Lewis, M. and D., London, S.W.1.
Lewis Gallery, Michael, Bruton, Somerset.

Lewis, N. and S., Crowmarsh Gifford, Oxon.
Lewis, P., Four Elms, Kent.
Lewis, R.A. and E.M., Liverpool, Lancs. (Edward's Jewellers).
Lewis Antiques, Robert and Vashti, Gartmore, Stirlings., Scot.
Lewis, Sara, London, N.W.8. Alf Ant. Mkt.
Lewis, Miss S., London, W.1. (Grosvenor Jewellery) B. St. Ant. C.
Lewzey, J.A., Woolhampton, Berks.
Lexton, M., London, S.W.3. Ant. Ant. Mkt.
Leycester Map Galleries Ltd., Arnesby, Leics.
Leyland, D.J. and C.J., Woodhall Spa, Lincs.
Lhermette, Mrs. V.A., Rochester, Kent.
Li, Wan, London, N.1.
Liberati, L., Preston, Lancs. N.W. Ant. C.
Liberty, London, W.1.
Libra Antiques, London, W.8.
Libson, L.J., London, W.1 (Leger Galleries Ltd.)
Licht and Morrison, London, W.1. G. Ant. Mkt.
Liddell, D., Seaham, Durham.
Liddiard Antiques, Susan, Pill, Avon.
Liddiard, V.A., Woolhampton, Berks.
Lieber, Ian, London, W.2.
Lievesley, Mrs. E.E., Hartley, Kent.
Light Brigade and Penylan Antiques, The, Cardiff, S. Glam., Wales.
Lightbody, P., Callington, Cornwall.
Lightfood, B. and A.E., Betley, Staffs.
Lighthouse Ltd., The, London, S.W.19.
Lillistone, C., Ipswich, Suffolk (A. Abbott Antiques.)
Lim, T., Weston-super-Mare, Avon.
Limb Antiques, R.R., Newark, Notts.
Lime Tree Antiques, Burwash, E. Sussex.
Limner Antiques, London, W.1. B. St. Ant. C.
Limpsfield Watercolours, Limpsfield, Surrey.
Lincoln, Christopher, Bath, Avon. Gt. West Ant. C.
Lincoln, D., Eastbourne, E. Sussex.
Lincoln Fine Art, Lincoln, Lincs.
Lincolnshire Antique Centre, The, Horncastle, Lincs.
Lind, S.O., Glasgow, Lanarks., Scot. (Temptations Unlimited).
Linden and Co. (Antiques) Ltd., London, W.C.2. Lon. Silv. Vts.
Linden, H., F., H.M. and S.C., London, W.C.2. Lon. Silv. Vts.
Linden House Antiques, Stansted, Essex.
Lindfield Galleries, Lindfield, W. Sussex.
Lindley, D. and M.H., Norton, N. Yorks.
Lindsay Antiques, London, W.8.
Lindsay, Muriel, Winchcombe, Glos.
Lindsay-Stewart, G., Balcombe, W. Sussex.
Lindsell Chairs, Coggeshall, Essex.
Lindsey Fine Arts Ltd., John, Stow-on-the-Wold, Glos.
Lindum Antiques, Tattershall, Lincs.
Lineham, Andrew, London, N.1. The Mall.
Lineham and Sons, Eric, London, W.8.
Linen and Lace, Manchester, Lancs. Royal Ex. S.C.
Linfield, Helen, Petworth, W. Sussex.
Linford, Carr, Bath, Avon.
Linford, N.J. and A. Carr, Bath, Avon.
Ling, Susan, Hare Hatch, Berks.
Lingard — Rope Walk Antiques, Ann, Rye, E. Sussex.
Lingard, T.P., London, S.W.1. (Gallery Lingard.)
Lingfield Antiques, Lingfield, Surrey.
Lingham, C., Felsted, Essex.
Link Gold Ltd., Epsom, Surrey.
Link Gold Ltd., Kingston-upon-Thames, Surrey.
Linslade Antiques and Curios, Linslade, Beds.
Linsley, Mrs. C.M., Gosforth, Cumbria.
Linstead, A., Tunbridge Wells, Kent (Cowden Antiques).
Lintott, P., Dorking, Surrey.
Lion Antiques, Acle, Norfolk.
Lion Antiques, Richmond, Surrey.
Lion Gallery and Bookshop, Knutsford, Cheshire.
Lion and Lamb Gallery, Farnham, Surrey.
Lion, Witch and Lampshade, London, S.W.1.
Lional of France, Preston, Lancs. N.W. Ant. C.
Lions Den, Leamington Spa, Warks.
Lions Den, Stratford-upon-Avon, Warks.
Lions and Unicorns, Nantwich, Cheshire.
Lipitch Ltd., J., London, W.11.
Lipitch Ltd., Michael, London, S.W.3.
Lipitch Ltd., Peter, London, S.W.3.
Lipka Ltd., W., London, W.11. Corn. Port. Ant. Sup.
Lis, J., London, S.W.5.
Lismore Gallery, Great Malvern, Hereford and Worcs.
Lisseter, D., Bicester, Oxon.
Lisseter of Bicester, Bicester, Oxon.
Little Curiosity Shop, The, London, N.21.
Little Gallery, The, Norwich, Norfolk.
Little Gem, The, Shrewsbury, Shrops.
Little Jem's, Penzance, Cornwall.
Little, N., Bexhill-on-Sea, E. Sussex. Bex. Ant. C.
Little Roger, Oxford, Oxon.
Little, Dr. R., Oxford, Oxon.
Little Shop Antiques, Newport, Essex.
Little Winchester Gallery, London, W.8.
Littlebury Antiques — Littlebury Restorations Ltd., Saffron Walden, Essex.
Littlejohn, Mrs. R., Bristol, Avon. Clift. Ant. Mkt.
Littleton, C., Lechlade, Glos.
Littlewood, P., Witney, Oxon.
Liu, Mrs., London, W.11. G. Port.
Liu, J. and Mrs. M-C., Riverhead, Kent.
Livani, P., Bath, Avon. Gt. West Ant. C.
Liverpool Coin and Medal Co., Liverpool, Merseyside.
Livesley, W.H., Macclesfield, Cheshire.
Livingstone, J., Methwold Hythe, Norfolk.
Livingstone, N., Dundee, Angus, Scot.
Livingstone, Neil P., Dundee, Angus, Scotland.
Liza Doolittle's, London, E.12.
Llandogo Antiques, Llandogo, Gwent, Wales.

Lowe Antiques, Robert, Norwich, Norfolk.
Lowe, S., Instow, Devon.
Lowe, Mrs. S., London, W.8. (Kensington Fine Arts)
Lowe and Sons, Chester, Cheshire.
Lowe, W.F., London, W.8. (Fine Art Investments)
Lower, Graham, Flimwell, E. Sussex.
Lower House Fine Antiques, Winyates Green, Herford and Worcs.
Lowes, E. and K., Barkham, Berks.
Loxwood Antiques, Loxwood, W. Sussex.
Lucas, Fay, London, S.W.3. Ant. Ant. Mkt.
Lucas, N., Amersham, Bucks.
Lucbernet, C., London, W.1. G. Ant. Mkt.
Lucerne Gallery, London, W.8.
Luck, S., London, W.C.2. (Tooley, Adams and Co. Ltd.)
Luck, S.L., West Malling, Kent.
Luczyc-Wyhowska, J., London, S.W.12.
Ludby, G., Eastbourne, E. Sussex.
Ludby Antiques, James, Eastbourne, E. Sussex.
Luffman, J., Ludlow, Shrops.
Lugley Street Antiques, Newport, I. of Wight.
Lukeman Fine Art, Richard, Knowle, W. Mids.
Lukies, Pearse, Aylsham, Norfolk.
Lumb and Sons Ltd., Charles, Harrogate, N. Yorks.
Lumb, F. and A.R., Harrogate, N. Yorks.
Lumb, M., Bournemouth, Dorset. (Marney's).
Lumley, P., Stoke-on-Trent, Staffs.
Lummis Fine Art, Sandra, London, N.8.
Lummis, Mrs S. and Dr. T., London, N.8.
Lundie, L., London, W.11. (The Old Haberdasher).
Lunn Antiques, London, S.W.6.
Lunn, R.J. and Mrs. S.Y., Weymouth, Dorset.
Lunn, S., London, S.W.6.
Lunn's Way Antiques Centre, Weymouth, Dorset.
Lury, R. and J., Cambridge, Cambs. (Cambridge Fine Art Ltd.).
Lustigman, Myra, London, S.W.3. Chen. Gall.
Lustre Metal Antiques Nottingham Donsign Ltd., Nottingham, Notts.
Lyall Antiques, Alexander J., Long Melford, Suffolk.
Lye Curios Inc. Lye Antique Furnishings, The, Lye, W. Mids.
Lymington Antiques Centre, Lymington, Hants.
Lynch, Pamela, Wilton, Wilts.
Lynch, R.C., Feniscowles, Lancs.
Lynden Antiques, Seaham, Durham.
Lyon, R. and J., Hurstpierpoint, W. Sussex.
Lyons, Elizabeth, Bath, Avon. Gt. West. Ant. C.
Lyons, H., London, W.8. (Bloomsbury Antiques). Kensington Ch. St. A.C.
Lyons, John, London, N.W.8. Alf. Ant. Mkt.
Lyons Gallery, John, London, N.W.3.
Lythgoe, N.E., Torquay, Devon.
Lyver and Boydell Galleries, The, Liverpool, Merseyside.

M

M. and A. Antique Exporters, Plymouth, Devon.
M.C.N. Antiques, London, W.11.
M.D. Antiques, Leeds, W. Yorks.
M.G.J. Antiques, Wallingford, Oxon.
M.G.R. Exports, Bruton, Somerset.
M.J. Antiques, Stow-on-the-Wold, Glos. C. Ant. C.
M. and L. Silver Co. Ltd., London, W.1.
M.S.M. Antiques, London, S.W.10 (Furniture Cave).
Maas Gallery, London, W.1.
Maas, J., London, S.W.1. (Box House Antiques)
Maas, J.S., London, W.1.
MacAdam, William, Edinburgh, Midloth., Scot.
McAdam-Thomson, Mr. and Mrs., Broughton-in-Furness, Cumbria.
Macadie, Mrs. M., Crosby Ravensworth, Cumbria.
Macafee, Mrs. W., Portrush, Co. Antrim, N. Ireland.
McAleer, M., London, W.2.
McAleer, M.J. & Mrs M., London, W.2.
McArdle, J.D., Glasgow, Lanarks., Scot. Vict. Vill.
McAskie, P.H., London, W.1. G. Mews.
McAuley, P., York, N. Yorks. (Clocks and Gramophones).
McAuley, M., Greyabbey, Co. Down, N. Ireland.
MacAuliffe, J., Saltburn, Cleveland.
McAvoy, M., Knighton, Powys, Wales.
McBain and Sons, I.G.S., Exeter, Devon. (Exeter Antique Wholesalers.)
McBains of Exeter (Antique Wholesalers), Exeter, Devon. (Exeter Antique Wholesalers.)
Macbeth, Bath, Avon. Gt. West. Ant. C.
McCabe, H. and R., Newry, Co. Down, N. Ireland.
McCabe's Antique Galleries, Newry, Co. Down, N. Ireland.
McCall, B., Aberdeen, Aberd., Scot.
McCall's (Aberdeen), Aberdeen, Aberd., Scot.
McCall's Limited, Aberdeen, Aberd., Scot.
McCallum, C., Rait, Perths., Scot.
McCamley, M., Shirley, Surrey.
McCarron, J. and J., Mansfield, Notts.
McCarthy Ltd., F.J., Normanton-on-Trent, Notts.
McCarthy, Ian and Diane, Clutton, Avon.
McClaren, J., Gosport, Hants.
McClean, Marie and Gerry, London, S.W.3. Chen. Gall.
Macclesfield Antiques, Macclesfield, Cheshire.
McCollum, D.C., Stockland, Devon.
MacConnal-Mason Gallery, London, S.W.1.

MacConnal-Mason Gallery, London, W.1.
McConnell, Mrs. A., Great Malvern, Hereford and Worcs.
McCormack, W.B., Lancaster, Lancs.
McCormick, N., London, S.W.13.
McCormick, P., Harrogate, N. Yorks. (Omar (Harrogate) Ltd.)
MrCrone, Miss J.M., Keswick, Cumbria.
McCrudden Gallery, D., Rickmansworth, Herts.
McCulloch Antiques, John, Felixstowe, Suffolk.
McDermott, Mr. and Mrs. J., London, E.14.
McDonald, Carshalton, Surrey.
MacDonald, A.G., York, N. Yorks. (Yon Antiques).
MacDonald, A. and Mrs. M., Amersham, Bucks.
MacDonald, B. and L., Stow-on-the-Wold, Glos.
MacDonald, D.H. and Mrs. S., Carshalton, Surrey.
MacDonald Fine Art, Gosforth, Tyne and Wear.
MacDonald, Mrs. I., Haddington, E. Loth., Scot.
MacDonald, Joy, London, S.W.13.
McDonald, June, London, S.E.1. Ant. Whse.
MacDonald, J., Tunbridge Wells, Kent. (John Thompson)
MacDonald, J., London, N.W.8. Alf. Ant. Mkt.
MacDonald, Nigel, London, N.W.8. Alf. Ant. Mkt.
MacDonald, T. and C., Gosforth, Tyne and Wear.
McDonald, W., Glasgow, Lanarks., Scot. (Nithsdale Antiques)
McDonald-Hobley, Mrs. N., London, S.W.3. Ant. Ant. Mkt.
McDonell, D. and H., Reepham, Norfolk.
McDonell, J., Dundee, Angus, Scot.
MacDonnell, Finbar, London, N.1.
McDougall, Marjorie, Kilbarchan, Renfrews., Scot.
McDowell, D., York, N. Yorks. (The Chaucer Head).
Mace, R., Gunnislake, Cornwall.
McEvoy, Mrs. M., Comberton, Cambs.
McEvoy, Maureen, London, N.1. The Mall.
McEwan Gallery, The, Ballater, Aberd., Scot.
McEwan, P. and D., Ballater, Aberd., Scot.
MacGillivray, G., Whitchurch, Shrops.
McGrane, I.A., Stroud, Glos.
McGrath, S., Farnham, Surrey.
McGregor, D.C., Henley-on-Thames, Oxon.
McGregor, V., Halstead, Essex.
MacHenry, A., Newtownabbey, Co. Antrim, N. Ireland.
Machin, P., Stoke-on-Trent, Staffs.
McHugh, Helen, Guildford, Surrey. Ant. C.
McHugo, M., Lye, W. Mids.
McIan Gallery (Campbell-Gibson Fine Arts), The, Oban, Renfrews., Scot.
Macinnes, A., Campbell, Bath, Avon. (Lantern Gallery).
MacInnes Antiques, Kilmarnock, Ayr., Scot.
MacInnes, Mrs. M., Kilmarnock, Ayr, Scot.
Macintosh & Co., William, Edinburgh, Midloth., Scot.
Mack Antiques, David, Branksome, Dorset.
MacKay, N.A., Bath, Avon. (Jadis Ltd.).
McKay, R.I., London, E.C.1.
Mackay, S., Swansea, W. Glam., Wales.
Mackays Antiques, Swansea, W. Glam., Wales.
McKenna and Co., London, S.W.3.
McKenna, M., Deal, Kent.
McKenna, M., London, S.W.3.
McKenzie, J.W., Ewell, Surrey.
Mackenzie-Smith, P., Bristol, Avon. Clift. Ant. Mkt.
Mackie, E.M. & Mrs. M.G., Elton, Notts.
McKie, N., Wallingford, Oxon. L. Arc.
McKillop, K.M., Pittenweem, Fife, Scot.
McKinley, A., Wiveliscombe, Somerset.
McKinley, D. and A., Wiveliscombe, Somerset.
McKintosh, G., Leeds, W. Yorks. (19 Nort Blob).
McKnight, E.W., Bury St. Edmunds, Suffolk.
McKoy, Robert, London, N.W.8. Alf. Ant. Mkt.
McLaughlin, A.J. and Mrs. B., Hollingwood, Lancs.
McLay, C., Glasgow, Lanarks., Scot. (Saratoga Trunk).
Maclean Antiques, Llanwrda, Dyfed, Wales.
Mclean/Black/Somerville, London, N.W.8. Alf. Ant. Mkt.
Maclean, D., Portsoy, Aberd., Scot.
Maclean, H., Kilmacolm, Renfrews., Scot.
McLean, Mrs. M., London, S.W.3. Ant. Ant. Mkt.
McLennan, Rodd, London, S.W.1.
Macleod Antiques, Colin, Portsmouth, Hants.
Macleod, M., London, N.W.8. Alf. Ant. Mkt.
McMarells, Newton Abbot, Devon. N.A. Ant. C.
McMaster, John, Tenterden, Kent.
Macmillan, C., London, S.W.3. (McKenna and Co.).
MacMillan, W., Worcester, Hereford and Worcs.
McMullan, C., Burnham-on-Crouch, Essex.
McMullan, D., Manchester, Lancs. (Antique Fireplaces).
McNamara, J. and M.V., Knaresborough, N. Yorks.
McNaughtan's Bookshop, Edinburgh, Midloth., Scot.
MacNeal, D.O., Pittenweem, Fife, Scot.
McNeill Fine Art, Agnes, London, S.W.3. Chen. Gall.
McPhail, R., Gourock, Lanarks., Scot.
McPherson, I. and H., Coalville, Leics.
McPherson, Mrs. J., Woburn, Beds. Wob. Ab. Ant. C.
McPherson, Robert, London, W.1. G. Mews.
McQuilkin, R., Stow-on-the-Wold, Glos. C. Ant. C.
Macrae-Stewart, L., Bath, Avon. (Country Interiors). Gt. West. Ant. C.
Macrow, S.K., Solihull, W. Mids.
Mac's Antiques, Dundee, Angus, Scot.

Mac-Smith, Bristol, Avon. Clift. Ant. Mkt.
McSwiggan, Kevin, Waddington, Lincs.
Mactaggart Books, Yeovil, Somerset.
McTaque of Harrogate, Harrogate, N. Yorks.
McTague, P., Harrogate, N. Yorks.
McVay, Mrs. J., Kegworth, Leics.
McVeigh and Charpentier, London, S.W.10.
McWhirter, A.J.K., London, S.W.10.
MacWhirter, Rob, Petworth, W. Sussex.
Maddermarket Antiques, Norwich, Norfolk.
Maddon, Sue, London, W.1. G. Ant. Mkt.
Maddox, Mr. and Mrs., Canterbury, Kent.
Maddox, G.P. and S.M., Oxted, Surrey.
Maddox, S.M., Tunbridge Wells, Kent.
Made of Honour, Chester, Cheshire.
Madeira Antiques, V. and C., Flore, Northants.
Madison Gallery, The, Petworth, W. Sussex.
Madoc Antiques and Art Gallery, Llandudno, Gwynedd, Wales.
Magee, D.A., Canterbury, Kent.
Magee, D.A., Eastry, Kent.
Magee, D.A., London, N.1.
Magee, D.A., Sandwich, Kent.
Maggie May's, North Shields, Tyne and Wear.
Maggs Antiques Ltd., Liverpool, Merseyside.
Maggs Bros. Ltd., London, W.1.
Maggs, John, Falmouth, Cornwall.
Maggs, J.F., B.D. and E.F., London, W.1.
Magna Carta Antiques, London, S.W.3. Ant. Ant. Mkt.
Magna Gallery, Oxford, Oxon.
Magpie, Whitstable, Kent.
Magpie Antiques, Battle, E. Sussex.
Magpie Antiques, Davenham, Cheshire.
Magpie Antiques, Long Melford, Suffolk.
Magpie Antiques, Swansea, W. Glam., Wales.
Magpie House, Hockley Heath, W. Mids.
Magpie Jewellers and Antiques, Evesham, Hereford and Worcs.
Magpies, London, S.W.6.
Magpies Nest, Morecambe, Lancs.
Magus Antiques, London, W.11.
Magus Antiques, London, N.W.8.
Mahboubian Gallery, London, W.1.
Mahboubian, H., London, W.1.
Mahgerefteh, J., London, N.W.8. Alf. Ant. Mkt.
Mahoney, Mrs. H., Kempsford, Glos.
Mail, S., Glasgow, Lanarks., Scot. (Pettigrew and Mail).
Main, C. & K.M., Green Hammerton, N. Yorks.
Main Ltd. Architectural Antiques, Michael, Cerrig-y-Drudion, Clwyd, Wales.
Main Pine Co., The, Green Hammerton, N. Yorks.
Main Street Antiques, London, S.E.10.
Mainhill Gallery, Jedburgh, Roxburghs., Scot.
Mainline Furniture, Kesgrave, Suffolk.
Mair, P., London, N.W.8.
Mair's Antiques, Swansea, W. Glam., Wales. Ant. C.
Maitland, S., Edinburgh, Scotland.
Major, A.H., London, W.8.
Major, A. and L., Painswick, Glos.
Major (Antiques) Ltd., C.H., London, W.8.
Majors Galleries, Ipswich, Suffolk.
Maker, B.J., Redruth, Cornwall.
Maker, J.P., Camborne, Cornwall.
Malcolm Antiques, Elie, Fife, Scot.
Malcolm, Z., Richmond, Surrey.
Maldon Antiques and Collectors Market, Maldon, Essex.
Malik and Son Ltd., David, London, N.W.10.
Malkin, Mary, Woburn, Beds. Wob. Ab. Ant. C.
Mall Antiques Arcade, The, London, N.1.
Mall Galleries, The, London, S.W.1.
Mall Gallery, The, Bristol, Avon.
Mall Jewellers, The, Bristol, Avon.
Mallaby, R.M., Killinghall, N. Yorks.
Mallett at Bourdon House Ltd., London, W.1.
Mallett, K., Surbiton, Surrey.
Mallett and Son (Antiques) Ltd., London, W.1.
Mallglade Antiques, Haigh, W. Yorks.
Mallory and Son Ltd., E.P., Bath, Avon.
Malmed, Mrs. V., London, S.W.1 (Old London Galleries).
Malmesbury Antiques, Malmesbury, Wilts.
Malone, Peggy, London, W.1. G. Ant. Mkt.
Malsom, S.L., Combe Martin, Devon.
Malsom, S.L., Gt. Malvern, Hereford and Worcs.
Maltby, C.E., Sheffield, S. Yorks. (A. and C. Antiques).
Malthouse Antiques Centre, Alcester, Warks.
Malthouse Arcade, Hythe, Kent.
Maltings Monthly Market, Farnham, Surrey.
Malton Antique Market, Malton, N. Yorks.
Malvasi, T., London, W.11.
Malvern Arts, Great Malvern, Hereford and Worcs.
Malvern Bookshop, Great Malvern, Hereford and Worcs.
Malvern Studios, Great Malvern, Hereford and Worcs.
Maman, Daniel, London, N.W.8. Alf. Ant. Mkt.
Mamie's Antique Centre, Arundel, W. Sussex.
Mammon, C. and T., London, W.C.2. Lon. Silv. Vts.
Mammon Antiques, J., London, W.C.2. Lon. Silv. Vts.
Man, H., London, S.W.3. Chen. Gall.
Man, K., Todmorden, W. Yorks.
Manchester Antique Company, Manchester, Lancs.
Manchester Antique Hypermarket, Manchester, Lancs.
Manchester Coin & Medal Centre, Manchester, Lancs. Royal Ex. S.C.
Mandarin Gallery, Riverhead, Kent.
Mandell's Gallery, Norwich, Norfolk.
Mander, J.P., London, E.2.
Mandrake Stephenson Antiques, Ibstock, Leics.
Mangate Gallery, London, W.4.
Manger, K., Skipton, N. Yorks.
Manheim (Peter Manheim) Ltd., D.M. and P., London, N.6.

Manheim, P., London, N.6.
Manion Antiques, Ashbourne, Derbys.
Manion, Mrs. V.J., Ashbourne, Derbys.
Mankowitz, Daniel, London, W.2.
Mankowitz, London, W.1. G. Mews.
Manley, J., Windsor and Eton, Berks.
Manley Antique Jewellery, Pamela, Titchfield, Hants.
Mann Antiques, Bryan, Ramsbury, Wilts.
Mann, B.K., Ramsbury, Wilts.
Mann Antiques, Chris, Aberystwyth, Dyfed, Wales.
Mann, David, Stiffkey, Norfolk.
Mann, Mrs. E., Manchester, Lancs. (Forest Books of Cheshire).
Mann Antiques, Kathleen, Harrow, Middx.
Manners, E. and H., London, W.8.
Manners Antiques, Mary, Gt. Cheverell, Wilts.
Mannin Collections, Peel, I. of Man.
Manor Antiques, Wallington, Surrey.
Manor Antiques, Westerham, Kent.
Manor Antiques, Wilshamstead, Beds.
Manor Antiques and Restorations, Woking, Surrey.
Manor Barn Pine, Addingham, W. Yorks.
Manor Farm Antiques, Standlake, Oxon.
Manor House, Ripley, Surrey.
Manor House Antiques, Cheltenham, Glos.
Manor House Antiques, Fishguard, Dyfed, Wales.
Manor House Antiques and Furniture, Margate, Kent.
Manor House Fine Arts, Cardiff, S. Glam., Wales.
Manor House Interiors, Chiddingfold, Surrey.
Mansell, William C., London, W.2.
Manser and Son Ltd., F.C., Shrewsbury, Shrops.
Manser and Family, G., Shrewsbury, Shrops.
Mansfield Antiques, Mansfield, Notts.
Mansfield, J. and A., Ashby-de-la-Zouch, Leics.
Manson, Edward, Woodbridge, Suffolk.
Mansour Gallery, London, W.1.
Mantoura, J.H., London, W.8 (Al Mashreq Galleries.)
Manussis, V., London, S.W.1. (Cobra and Bellamy).
Manwaring, M.G., Chipping Norton, Oxon.
Manzi, R. and I., Shirley, Surrey.
Map House, The, London, S.W.3.
Maps, Prints and Books, Brecon, Powys, Wales.
Mara, M., London, S.W.3. Ant. Ant. Mkt.
Marble Hill Gallery, Twickenham, Middx.
Marcangelo, T.M., Hadleigh, Suffolk.
March Medals, Birmingham, W. Mids.
March, M.A., Birmingham, W. Mids.
Marchant Antiques, Mark, Coggeshall, Essex.
Marchant, R.P., London, W.8.
Marchant and Son, S., London, W.8.
Marchmont Bookshop, London, W.C.1.
Mardy, C.A., Manchester, Lancs. (Abacus Antiques).
Mare Hill Galleries, Pulborough, W. Sussex.
Margaret's Astoria Antiques, Ystradgynlais, Powys, Wales.
Margaret's Antique Shop, Nelson, Lancs.
Margerison, Mr. and Mrs. P.B., Empingham, Leics.
Margiotta, A., Brighton, E. Sussex (The House of Antiques).
Margolis, Iris, London, N.W.8. Alf. Ant. Mkt.
Marianski, N.J., Derby, Derbys.
Marine Gallery, The, Cowes, I. of Wight.
Mariners Antiques, The, Staithes, Cleveland.
Marino-Montero Fine Art and Antiques Ltd., Adrienne, Curdridge, Hants.
Mark Gallery, London, W.2.
Mark, H., London, W.2.
Market Antiques, Hoylake, Merseyside.
Market House, Burnham Market, Norfolk.
Market Place Antiques, Fakenham, Norfolk.
Market Square Antiques, Olney, Bucks.
Markov, M., London, S.W.3. Ant. Ant. Mkt.
Marks, A., London, W.1.
Marks Antiques Ltd., London, W.1.
Marks, B.J. and S., Oldham, Lancs.
Marks Ltd., Barrie, London, N.W.5.
Marks, M., Lamberhurst, Kent.
Marks Antique Warehouse, Peter, Portslade, W. Sussex.
Markswood Gallery, Great Bardfield, Essex.
Marlborough Fine Art (London) Ltd., London, W.1.
Marlborough House Antiques, Yarmouth, I. of Wight.
Marlborough Parade Antique Centre, The, Marlborough, Wilts.
Marlborough Rare Books Ltd., London, W.1.
Marlborough Sporting Gallery and Bookshop, Marlborough, Wilts.
Marler Gallery, The, Jane, Ludlow, Shrops.
Marler Gallery, The, William, Cirencester, Glos.
Marles, M., Maidstone, Kent.
Marles, M., Sutton Valence, Kent.
Marlow Antiques Centre, Marlow, Bucks.
Marney, Patrick, Long Melford, Suffolk.
Marney's, Bournemouth, Dorset.
Marnier Antiques, Edward, Tisbury, Wilts.
Marnier, E.F., Tisbury, Wilts.
Marno, F., London, W.8. (Stocksprings Antiques).
Marpole, A., Burwell, Cambs.
Marr Antiques, Iain, Beauly, Inver., Scot.
Marr, I. and A., Beauly, Inver., Scot.
Marrin and Sons, G. and D.I., Folkestone, Kent.
Marriott Ltd., Michael, London, S.W.6.
Marriott, T.I., Beaconsfield, Bucks.
Marris, N., Lincoln, Lincs.
Marryat, Richmond, Surrey.
Marryat (Richmond) Ltd., Richmond, Surrey.
Marsden, K., London, W.C.1.
Marsh and Son, A.V., London, S.W.15.
Marsh (Antique Clocks), Gerald E., Winchester, Hants.
Marsh, G.M., Crawley, W. Sussex.
Marsh, Jasper, Henley-in-Arden, Warks.
Marsh, P.R.J., Henley-in-Arden, Warks.
Marsh, Simon, Bletchingley, Surrey.

Marsh, T.G., Newark, Notts.
Marshall, A.R., Kirton, Lincs.
Marshall, E.M., Carshalton, Surrey.
Marshall Antiques, Tim, Tingewick, Bucks.
Marston, B.F. and H.M., Hadleigh, Suffolk.
Marten, S.J., Huddersfield, W. Yorks.
Martin, A., Sandygate, Kent.
Martin Antiques, Alan, Olney, Bucks.
Martin, A.D., Olney, Bucks.
Martin, A.R., Tavistock, Devon.
Martin, C., Windlesham, Surrey.
Martin (Coins) Ltd., C.J., London, N.14.
Martin and Co. Ltd., Cheltenham, Glos.
Martin, D., London, S.W.3. Chen. Gall.
Martin, E., London, N.2.
Martin Antiques, Greg, Gravesend, Kent.
Martin House Antiques, Stow-on-the-Wold, Glos.
Martin, J., Farnborough, Hants.
Martin Antiques, John, Castle Cary, Somerset.
Martin, L.M., Bournemouth, Dorset. (Blade and Bayonet)
Martin Antiques, Marie-Ange, Uppingham, Leics.
Martin, Mrs. M.R., Hawkhurst, Kent.
Martin, Nigel, London, N.W.8. Alf. Ant. Mkt.
Martin and Parke, Farnborough, Hants.
Martin, P.E., Bath, Avon. Gt. West. Ant. C. Wed. Mkt.
Martin, Peter J., Windsor and Eton, Berks.
Martin, Robin, London, W.11.
Martin, R. and S., Risby, Suffolk.
Martin, Tony, Looe, Cornwall.
Martin, T.J.L. and A.M., Coggeshall, Essex.
Martin, T.V., Paignton, Devon.
Martin-Quick Antiques Ltd., Wolverhampton, W. Mids.
Martin's Gallery, Hazlemere, Bucks.
Martin-Taylor Antiques, David, London, S.W.6.
Martire, Francesca, London, N.W.8. Alf. Ant. Mkt.
Martlesham Antiques, Martlesham, Suffolk.
Martock Gallery, The, Martock, Somerset.
Mary Jane, Ryde, I. of Wight.
Maryan and Daughters, Richard, London, S.W.19.
Ma's Antiques, Bewdley, Hereford and Worcs.
Mascaro, R., Plymouth, Devon.
Maskell, D., Wadhurst, E. Sussex.
Maskell, R.E. and L.J., Branksome, Dorset.
Maskell, R.E. and L.J., Sturminster Newton, Dorset.
Mason, A.A., Wimborne Minster, Dorset.
Mason, C., Brodick, I. of Arran, Scot.
Mason, D., South Molton, Devon.
Mason & Son, D., Harrogate, N. Yorks.
Mason, Harry, Brighton, E. Sussex.
Mason Antique Clocks, J., Water Orton, Warks,
Mason Jewellers Ltd., John, Rotherham, S. Yorks.
Mason, Oriental Art, Jeremy J., London, W.1.
Mason, P., London, S.W.1.
Mason Gallery, Paul, London, S.W.1.
Mason, T.H. and J., Gillingham, Kent.
Mason-Pope, C., Woodstock, Oxon.
Mason-Watts, C.N.S., Warwick, Warks.
Mason-Watts Fine Art, Warwick, Warks.
Massada Antiques, London, W.1.
Massey and Son, D.J., Alderley Edge, Cheshire.
Massey & Son, D.J., Cheadle, Cheshire.
Massey & Son, D.J. Macclesfield, Cheshire.
Massey, J.C., Long Melford, Suffolk.
Massey, P., Debenham, Suffolk.
Massey's Antiques, Coalville, Leics.
Massingham Antiques, R., Brasted, Kent.
Masters, M., Stow-on-the-Wold, Glos.
Mathaf Gallery Ltd., London, S.W.1.
Mather, Mrs. P., Corby Hill, Cumbria.
Matheson, P. and I., Newport, I. of Wight.
Mathews, Lt. Col. I.G. and Mrs., Ross-on-Wye, Hereford and Worcs.
Mathews, M.R., Tetbury, Glos.
Mathias, G.S., London, S.W.3. Ant. Ant. Mkt.
Mathias, R., St. Albans, Herts.
Mathieson and Co., John, Edinburgh, Midloth., Scot.
Mathieson, T., Portsoy, Aberd., Scot.
Mathon Gallery, London, S.W.3.
Mathon Gallery, Mathon, Hereford and Worcs.
Matsell Antiques Ltd., Ilkeston, Derbys.
Matsell Antiques Ltd., Woburn, Beds. Wob. Ab. Ant. C.
Matsell, B. and P., Ilkeston, Derbys.
Matson, J., Liverpool, Merseyside (Theta Gallery).
Matson, Mrs. M.C., Northallerton, N. Yorks.
Matthey, P., Burford, Oxon.
Matthiesen Fine Art Ltd. and Matthiesen Works of Art Ltd., London, S.W.1.
Maude, R.M.C., London, S.W.15.
Maude Tools, Richard, London, S.W.15.
Maufe, J., Burnham Market, Norfolk.
Maw Antiques, Matthew, Malton, N. Yorks.
Mawby, Mrs. P., Northampton, Northants.
Mawer, Mr. and Mrs., Penrith, Cumbria.
Mawtus, Mrs. P., Norwich, Norfolk. (D'Amico Antiques Ltd.).
Maxim Antiques, Woburn, Beds. Wob. Ab. Ant. C.
Maxwells Book Shop, Birmingham, W. Mids.
May, J. and J., London, W.8.
May and May Ltd., Tisbury, Wilts.
May, T.E., Maldon, Essex.
Mayer, P., Newton Abbot, Devon. N.A. Ant. C.
Mayfair Antiques, Bagillt, Clwyd, Wales.
Mayfair Carpet Gallery Ltd., London, W.1.
Mayfair Fine Art, Maldon, Essex.
Mayfair Gallery, London, W.1.
Mayfield Antiques, Leominster, Hereford and Worcs.
Mayfield, R., Ramsdell, Hants.
Mayflower Antiques, Harwich and Dovercourt, Essex.
Mayflower Antiques, London, W.11.
Mayflower Antiques, Padstow, Cornwall.
Maynard, Adrian, London, S.W.1.
Maynard Antiques, Mark, London, S.W.6.

Maynard, R., Harrogate, N. Yorks.
Mayne, R., Newhaven, E. Sussex.
Mayor, Norah, Diss, Norfolk.
Mayorcas, J.D. and L.G., London, S.W.1.
Mayorcas Ltd., London, S.W.1.
Mazure and Co. Ltd., I.J., London, S.W.1.
Mazzoli, D., Eastbourne, E. Sussex.
Meadowcroft Antiques, Stephen, Farndon, Cheshire.
Meadway Books, London, N.W.3. Ham. Ant. Emp.
Mears and Boyer, Woburn, Beds. Wob. Ab. Ant. C.
Mechilli, Walter, Warwick, Warks. Smith St. A.C.
Medalcrest Ltd., Hungerford, Berks.
Medcalf, N.K.T., Woburn Sands, Bucks.
Medcalf, Paul, Gloucester, Glos.
Medda, G., London, W.11. (Themes and Variations).
Medina Antiquarian Maps and Prints, Winslow, Bucks.
Mee, R., London, W.8. (Roderick Antique Clocks).
Mee, R., London, S.W.3. Ant. Ant. Mkt.
Meeson, J.C. and A.D., Ilford, Essex.
Meeks Antiques Ltd., Bridgend, Mid-Glam., Wales.
Megahy, Jean, Glasgow, Lanarks., Scot.
Megicks, N., Lampeter, Dyfed, Wales.
Mehta, A., London, S.W.3. Ant. Ant. Mkt.
Meileng Collection, London, W.1. B. St. Ant. C.
Melbourne Gallery, Melbourne, Derbys.
Melbourne Treasure Chest, Melbourne, Derbys.
Meldrum, D., Chagford, Devon.
Melford Fine Arts, Long Melford, Suffolk.
Melliar-Smith, M.V., Honiton, Devon.
Melling, H.W. and V.I., Worthing, W. Sussex.
Mellish, J., Colchester, Essex. (Stock Exchange Antiques)
Mellor and A.L. Baxter, D., London, W.8.
Mellor, C.R.J. and P.J., Lichfield, Staffs.
Mellor, R., Bath, Avon. (Antique Linen and Lace). Gt. West. Ant. C.
Melody, M., Chester, Cheshire.
Melody's Antique Galleries, Chester, Cheshire.
Melrose Antiques, Abingdon, Oxon.
Melton Antiques, Woodbridge, Suffolk.
Melton's, London, W.1.
Melville Watercolours, Margaret, Staines, Surrey.
Meltzer, L., London, W.11.
Memorabilia, Leeds, W. Yorks.
Memories, Bramley, Surrey.
Memories, Rochester, Kent.
Memories Antiques, Coventry, W. Mids.
Memory Lane, Sowerby Bridge, W. Yorks.
Memory Lane Antiques, Ashtead, Surrey.
Memory Lane Antiques, South Molton, Devon.
Memory Lane Antique Centre, Bolton, Lancs.
Mendez incorporating Craddock and Barnard, Christopher, London, S.W.1.
Medina Gallery, Bideford, Devon.
Mendip Pine and Antiques, Chilcompton, Somerset.
Mendoza, Antonio, London, S.E.1.
Mendoza, S., London, N.W.3. Ham. Ant. Emp.
Mendoza, Sybil, Woburn, Beds. Wob. Ab. Ant. C.
Mennis, G., St. Leonards-on-Sea, E. Sussex. Hastings A.C.
Mercat-Hughes Antiques, Glasgow, Lanarks., Scot.
Mercury Antiques, London, W.11.
Mere Antiques, Fowlmere, Cambs.
Meredith, John and A., Chagford, Devon.
Meriden Antiques and Curios, Meriden, W. Mids.
Meriden House Antiques, Worcester, Hereford and Worcs.
Meridian Antiques, New Romney, Kent.
Merkel, M.P., Dartmouth, Devon.
Merlin Antiques, Kirkby Lonsdale, Cumbria.
Merlins Antiques, Carmarthen, Dyfed, Wales.
Merola, M., London, S.W.3.
Merrifield, Mr. and Mrs. B., Paisley, Renfrew, Scot.
Merrill Antiques, Paul, Collingham, Notts.
Merton Antiques (Barometers), Merton, Devon.
Messenger, R. and D., Birmingham, W. Mids. (Always Antiques).
Messum, David, London, W.1.
Metcalfe, A., Bristol, Avon. (Grove Side Antiques) Clift. Ant. Mkt.
Metcalf, June, London, S.W.10 (Furniture Cave).
Metro Antiques, Gateshead, Tyne and Wear.
Mexborough, Lord and Countess of, London, S.W.3. (The Map House).
Meyer, B.P., Dorking, Surrey.
Meyer, G.A., London, W.8 (Church Street Galleries Ltd.)
Meyer, T., London, W.8. (Pamela Teignmouth and Son)
Meyer, Vicky, London, W.11. Corn. Port. Ant. Sup.
Meyers Gallery, Ingatestone, Essex.
Meyers, Mrs. J., Ingatestone, Essex.
Meynell, G.G., Folkestone, Kent.
Meysey-Thompson Antiques, Sarah, Woodbridge, Suffolk.
Miall, Margaret, London, N.W.8. Alf. Ant. Mkt.
Micallef Antiques, Gt. Baddow, Essex.
Micawber, London, N.W.3. Ham. Ant. Emp.
Micawber Antiques, Bridgnorth, Shrops.
Micawber's Attic, Mr., Salisbury, Wilts.
Michael Coins, London, W.8.
Michael's Antiques, Bristol, Avon.
Michell, T.J.B., Penzance, Cornwall.
Michele Ltd., D., Torquay, Devon.
Michelson, Mrs. E., London, W.1. (Nonesuch Antiques).
Micklem, C.T., S.E.M. and T.J.M., Langford Budville, Somerset.

Micklem Antiques Ltd., Trevor, Langford Budville, Somerset.
Middlebridge Antiques Ltd., Romsey, Hants.
Middleton, Mr., Todmorden, W. Yorks.
Middleton Ltd., Arthur, London, W.C.2.
Middleton, T.L., Barrow-on-Soar, Leics.
Middleton's Antique Doll Shop, Lilian, Stow-on-the-Wold, Glos.
Midgley, N.M., Settle, N. Yorks.
Midhurst Antiques Market, Midhurst, W. Sussex.
Midwinter, Mr. and Mrs. R., Newcastle-under-Lyme, Staffs.
Midwinter Antiques, Richard, Newcastle-under-Lyme, Staffs.
Mighell, J., London, N.1 (Strike One Ltd).
Mildred, J. and S., Bath, Avon. Gt. West. Ant. C.
Mildwurf and Partners, L., Penrith, Cumbria.
Mileham, H., Brighton, E. Sussex (P. Carmichael).
Miles Antiques, Kinross, Kinross., Scot.
Miles Bookshop, Archie, Gosforth, Cumbria.
Miles, David, Canterbury, Kent.
Miles, David, London, N.W.1.
Miles, J., London, N.W.8. Alf. Ant. Mkt.
Miles, K. and S., Kinross, Kinross., Scot.
Miles Antiques, Richard, London, W.1.
Miles Gallery, Roy, London, W.1.
Miles, S., Herstmonceux, E. Sussex.
Milestone Antiques, Whittington, Staffs.
Milewski, D., Richmond, Surrey.
Milford Haven Antiques, Milford Haven, Dyfed, Wales.
Military Curios, The Curiosity Shop, HQ84, Gloucester, Glos.
Military Parade Bookshop, The, Marlborough, Wilts.
Militaryman Antiques, Blackpool, Lancs.
Mill Farm Antiques, Disley, Cheshire.
Mill House Antiques, Beetham, Cumbria.
Mill House Antiques, London, S.W.6.
Mill on the Soar Antiques Ltd., Quorn, Leics.
Millar, Miss J., Arundel, W. Sussex.
Miller, A., Woburn, Beds. Wob. Ab. Ant. C.
Miller, A.M., Woburn, Beds. Wob. Ab. Ant. C.
Miller, Bill, London, N.W.8. Alf. Ant. Mkt.
Miller, B., Ross-on-Wye, Hereford & Worcs.
Miller Fine Arts, Duncan R., London, N.W.3.
Miller, G.C. and P.A., Arundel, W. Sussex.
Miller (Antiques) Ltd., H., Brighton, E. Sussex.
Miller (Ants.) Ltd., H., London, W.C.2. Lond. Silv. Vts.
Miller, I.E.G., Petworth, W. Sussex. (Granville Antiques).
Miller, J., Mumby, Lincs.
Miller, J., Wooler, Northumb.
Miller, M., London, N.W.8. Alf. Ant. Mkt.
Miller, Michael, Hurstpierpoint, W. Sussex.
Miller, M. and V., Hurstpierpoint. W. Sussex.
Miller, N., Cullompton, Devon.
Miller, P., London, S.W.3. Ant. Ant. Mkt.
Miller, P. Audley, Oxford, Oxon.
Miller, P.B., York, N. Yorks. (Ken Spelman).
Miller, P.J. and A.R., Hemswell Cliff, Lincs.
Miller, R., Dorking, Surrey.
Miller and Son, W.J., Wooler, Northumb.
Millers Antiques, Kelvedon, Essex.
Millers of Chelsea (Antiques) Ltd., Ringwood, Hants.
Millgreen Antiques, Wargrave, Bucks.
Millhouse, Petworth, W. Sussex.
Millington, K.L. and J., Lepton, W. Yorks.
Millon Antiques, Hartley Wintney, Hants.
Millon-Milovanovich, P. and J., Hartley Wintney, Hants.
Mills Antiques, Cullompton, Devon.
Mills Antiques, Mrs., Ely, Cambs.
Mills, E.T., Ely, Cambs.
Mills, G. and J., Honiton, Devon.
Mills Architectural Antiques Ltd., Robert, Bristol, Avon.
Millward, J., Norwich, Norfolk. (Country and Eastern).
Milne and Moller, London, W.11.
Milne Ltd., Nigel, London, W.1.
Milner Antiques, J., Marple, Cheshire.
Milner, S. and E., Chard, Somerset.
Milnthorpe, H.I., Settle, N. Yorks.
Milnthorpe and Daughters Antique Shop, Mary, Settle, N. Yorks.
Milton Antiques, Coventry, W. Mids.
Milton Antiques, Fred, Wanstrow, Somerset.
Milverton Antiques, Milverton, Somerset.
Minahan, T., Newmarket, Suffolk.
Minoo and Andre, London, W.1. (G. Mews).
Minoo Mog, London, N.W.8. Alf. Ant. Mkt.
Minster Antiques, Wimborne Minster, Dorset.
Minster Gate Bookshop, York, N. Yorks.
Minstrel Gallery, Llanhaeadr, Clwyd, Wales.
Mint and Boxed, Edgware, Middx.
Mint Dolls and Toys, Rye, E. Sussex.
Mirabaud, S., Lewes, E. Sussex.
Miscellanea, Maidenhead, Berks.
Miscellany Antiques, Great Malvern, Hereford and Worcs.
Miskimmin, W., Rochester, Kent.
Miss Elany, Long Eaton, Derbys.
Missenden, D., Woburn Sands, Bucks.
Mister Sun Antiques, Chertsey, Surrey.
Mistral Galleries, Westerham, Kent.
Mitchell Fine Paintings, Anthony, Nottingham, Notts.
Mitchell, A. and M., Nottingham, Notts.
Mitchell, C., Totnes, Devon.
Mitchell, Mrs. E., London, S.W.3. Ant. Ant. Mkt.
Mitchell, G., Burford, Oxon.
Mitchell, J., Rait, Perths., Scot.
Mitchell and Son, John, London, W.1.
Mitchell Antiques, Laurence, London, N.1.
Mitchell, Mrs. L.F., Hereford, Herefs. and Worcs.
Mitchell, L.P.J., London, N.1.
Mitchell Ltd., Paul, London, W.1.
Mitchell, R.A., Castle Douglas, Kirkcud., Scot.
Mitchell, R.A., Kirkcudbright, Kirkcud., Scot.

Mitchell, R.S., Norwich, Norfolk (The Bank House Gallery).
Mitchell, S., Blackburn, Lancs.
Mitchell Fine Arts, Sally, Askham, Notts.
Mitchell, W., Cirencester, Glos.
Mitchell-Hill, D.G., Wetherby, W. Yorks.
Mitchell-Hill Gallery, Wetherby, W. Yorks.
Mitchell's (Lock Antiques), Blackburn, Lancs.
Mitre House Antiques, Ludlow, Shrops.
Mitton, B. and W., Carlisle, Cumbria. C. Ant. and Craft C.
Mizza, P., London, S.W.3. Chen. Gall.
Moggach Antiques, Ian, London, S.W.6.
Mohamed Ltd., Bashir, London, W.1.
Mohamed, M.O., London, N.W.8. Alf. Ant. Mkt.
Mohammed, A., London, W.11. G. Port.
Mohammed, Ali, London, W.1. G. Mews.
Moira, London, W.1.
Mokhtarzadeh, M., London, W.1 (Mansour Gallery).
Mold Antiques and Interiors, Mold, Clwyd, Wales.
Mole Antique Exports, Geoffrey, Hull, N. Humberside.
Mole Hall Antiques, Aldeburgh, Suffolk.
Moller, Mr. and Mrs. C., London, W.11. (Milne and Moller).
Molloy, P., Southport, Merseyside.
Molloy, S.F., Stoke-on-Trent, Staffs.
Molloy, T.M., London, S.W.3. Ant. Ant. Mkt.
Molloy's Furnishers Ltd., Southport, Merseyside.
Molony, J., London, W.1. (The Richmond Gallery)
"Mon Galerie", Amersham, Bucks.
Mona Antiqua, Beaumaris, Gwynedd, Wales (Tudor Rose).
Monaltrie Antiques, Odiham, Hants.
Monarch Antiques, Glastonbury, Somerset.
Monarch Antiques, Polegate, E. Sussex.
Monarch Antiques, St. Leonards-on-Sea, E. Sussex.
Money (Antiques) Ltd., Lennox, London, S.W.1.
Money, L.B., London, S.W.1.
Monika, London, N.1. The Mall.
Monk and Son, D.C., London, W.8.
Monkton Galleries, Hindon, Wilts.
Monmouth Antiques, Monmouth, Gwent, Wales.
Monro Heywood Ltd., London, S.W.3.
Monro, J., London, S.W.3. (Monro Heywood Ltd.)
Monro Ltd., Mrs., London, S.W.1.
Montacute Antiques, Montacute, Somerset.
Montague Antiques, Leicester, Leics.
Montilla and Acevedoa, A., London, S.W.3. Chen. Gall.
Montpellier Clocks, Cheltenham, Glos.
Montpellier Mews Antiques Market, Harrogate, N. Yorks.
Monument Antiques, Stirling, Stirlings., Scot.
Moody, L., Southampton, Hants.
Moolham Mill Antiques, Ilminster, Somerset.
Moon, Michael, Whitehaven, Cumbria.
Moon, M. and S., Whitehaven, Cumbria.
Mooney, Riro, D., Duxford, Cambs.
Moonfleet, Ryde, I. of Wight.
Moor, M. and A., Middlesbrough, Cleveland.
Moordown Antiques, Bournemouth, Dorset.
Moore, A.E., Leiston, Suffolk.
Moore, D., Congresbury, Avon.
Moore, D.B., Hitchin, Herts.
Moore, D.K., Leicester, Leics.
Moore, Eric, T., Hitchin, Herts.
Moore, H., Birmingham, W. Mids. (Station Rd. Emporium).
Moore, Jack, Preston, Lancs. N.W. Ant. C.
Moore, J.C., Bowness-on-Windermere, Cumbria.
Moore, L.F., Brighton, E. Sussex. (Brighton Architectural Salvage).
Moore, Mrs. M., Horncastle, Lincs.
Moore Workshop, Michael, Clare, Suffolk.
Moore Antiques, Marcus, No Man's Heath, Cheshire.
Moore, M.G.J. and M.P., No Man's Heath, Cheshire.
Moore, N. and E., Tynemouth, Tyne and Wear.
Moores, P., Leicester, Leics.
Moores and Son, Walter, Leicester, Leics.
Moorhead, F.B. and M.J., Brighton, E. Sussex (Attic Antiques).
Moorhead Antiques, Patrick, Brighton, E. Sussex.
Moorland Antiques, Weston-super-Mare, Avon.
Morales Antiques, José, Deal, Kent.
Morchard Bishop Antiques, Morchard Bishop, Devon.
Moreden Prints, Yatton, Hereford and Worcs.
Moreton (Antiques), C.S., Inchture, Perths., Scot.
Moreton Studio, Rex, Newport, Gwent, Wales.
Moreton Street Gallery, London, S.W.1.
Morgan, C., Rochester, Kent.
Morgan, Dr. and Mrs. D.H., Wymondham, Norfolk.
Morgan, Gavin, London, N.W.8. Alf. Ant. Mkt.
Morgan, H., Cardiff, S. Glam., Wales. (San Domenico Stringed Instruments).
Morgan, J., Chesham, Bucks.
Morgan Antiques, Linda, London, N.1. The Mall.
Morgan, M., Hitchin, Herts.
Morgan, Mrs. S., Pateley Bridge, N. Yorks.
Morley Antiques, David, Twickenham, Middx.
Morley Antiques, Patrick and Gillian, Warwick, Warks.
Morley and Co. Ltd., Robert, London, S.E.13.
Morley Antiques, William, West Monkton, Somerset.
Morley, W.H., West Monkton, Somerset.
Morrill Ltd., W.J., Dover, Kent.
Morris, B., Leamington Spa, Warks.
Morris, G.J., St. Helier, Jersey, C.I.
Morris, Ian, Chesterfield, Derbys.
Morris Ltd., John G., Petworth, W. Sussex.

Morris and Co., James H., Northop, Clwyd, Wales.
Morris, Mr. and Mrs. K.L., Ludlow, Shrops.
Morris, Maureen, Saffron Walden, Essex.
Morris, Pearl, Loughton, Essex.
Morris Antiques, R.R., Abingdon, Oxon.
Morris, S., Westerham, Kent.
Morrish, J.S., Reigate, Surrey.
Morrison, Mrs., London, S.W.3. Ant. Ant. Mkt.
Morrison, C., York, N. Yorks.
Morrison, Guy, London, S.W.1.
Morrison, Jan, Bristol, Avon. Clift. Ant. Mkt.
Morrison, Mrs. J., Wingham, Kent.
Morrison, J. and P., Bankfoot, Perths., Scot.
Morrison, M., Warwick, Warks.
Morrison, P.H., Kirk Michael, Isle of Man.
Morrison and Son, Robert, York, N. Yorks.
Morse and Son Ltd., Terence, London, W.11.
Morten, Eric J., Manchester, Lancs.
Mortimer, Brian, Exeter, Devon.
Mortimer and Sons, C. & J., Great Chesterford, Essex.
Mortimer, Mr. and Mrs. L.G., Petersfield, Hants.
Mortimer, M.C.F., North Wraxhall, Wilts.
Mortimore-Hooper, A.J., London, S.W.3 (Hooper and Purchase).
Mortlake Antiques, Kirkby Stephen, Cumbria.
Morton, Mrs. Joan, Great Walsingham, Norfolk.
Morton, S., Bournemouth, Dorset. (Boscombe Antiques).
Morton-Smith, Mrs. I., Milland, W. Sussex.
Mosdell, Newton Abbot, Devon. N. A. Ant. C.
Mosdell, G., Ashburton, Devon.
Moseley Antiques, Birmingham, W. Mids.
Moseley Gallery, The, Birmingham, W. Mids.
Moss, A., London, N.1 (Annie's Antiques and Clothes).
Moss End Antique Centre, Warfield, Berks.
Moss Galleries — Rachel Moss, London, S.W.3.
Moss, P.G. and E.M., London, W.1.
Moss, R.A. and B.A., Baldock, Herts.
Moss, Ralph and Bruce, Baldock, Herts.
Moss, S., Bath, Avon. (Casemate).
Moss Ltd., Sydney L., London, W.1.
Mostly Boxes, Windsor & Eton, Berks.
Mostly Pine, Kingussie, Inverns., Scot.
Mote, H.C., London, S.W.3. (H.W. Newby)
Mott, G.W., Trent, Dorset.
Mott, J.G. and D.M., Lavenham, Suffolk.
Mottershead, Mr. and Mrs. J.K., Manchester, Lancs. (The Ginnel Gallery).
Mottershead, D., and Mrs., Long Eaton, Derby.
Motts of Lavenham, Lavenham, Suffolk.
Mouat, J.W.L., Whitchurch, Hants.
Mould Ltd., Anthony, London, W.1.
Moulton, J., West Bridgford, Notts.
Moulton's Antiques, West Bridgford, Notts.
Mount, The, Woore, Shrops.
Mount Antiques, The, Whitby, N. Yorks.
Mount Gallery, London, N.W.3. Ham. Ant. Emp.
Mounter, G., Dulford, Devon.
Movie Shop, The, Norwich, Norfolk.
Mowe, C. and J., Coton Clanford, Staffs.
Moxhams Antiques, Bradford-on-Avon, Wilts.
Moy, R.F., London, S.E.10.
Moyallon Antiques, Portadown, Co. Armagh, N. Ireland.
Muccio, L. and P., Bromley, Kent.
Muckle, M.A., Market Harborough, Leics.
Muddiman, A.R.T., Chesham, Bucks.
Muggeridge Farm Warehouse, Battlesbridge, Essex.
Muggleton, Mrs. R., London, S.W.3. Chen. Gall.
Muir, D.C., Coggeshall, Essex.
Muirhead Moffat and Co., Glasgow, Lanarks., Scot.
Mulberry House Antiques, Stockbridge, Hants.
Mulberry House Galleries, Pulborough, W. Sussex.
Mulcare, R., Lindfield, W. Sussex.
Mulder, Frederick, London, N.W.3.
Mulherron Antiques, Edinburgh, Midloth., Scot.
Mulherron, F., A. and J., Edinburgh, Midloth., Scot.
Mulholland, H., Crossford, Scotland.
Mullarkey, T. and N., Maidstone, Kent.
Mullarkey, T. and N., Sutton Valence, Kent.
Mullett, G. and A., London, S.W.6. (The Constant Reader Bookshop).
Mulligan, A.J., and F., Whimple, Devon.
Mullin, D., Hollinwood, Lancs.
Mummery Ltd., Kenneth, Bournemouth, Dorset.
Munro, A., Cardiff, S. Glam., Wales. (Kings Lynn)
Munro, C.P., Bridgwater, Somerset.
Murdoch, Colin, Kingussie, Inver., Scot.
Murdoch, P.G., Nottingham, Notts. (Nottingham Antique Centre).
Murphy, B. and S., Newton Abbot, Devon, N. A. Ant. C.
Murphy, I., Portsmouth, Hants.
Murphy, T.H., London, W.4.
Murray, A.M., Docking, Norfolk.
Murray, A.M., Holt, Norfolk.
Murray, D., Kilmichael Glassary, Argyll, Scot.
Murray Antiques Warehouse, Ian, Perth, Perths., Scot.
Murray McIlroy, Glasgow, Scotland. B. St. Ant. G.
Murray-Brown, Pevensey Bay, E. Sussex.
Murray-Brown, G. and J., Pevensey Bay, E. Sussex.
Murray-Tait Antiques, Fochabers, Morays., Scot.
Murray-Tait Antiques, Rait, Perths., Scot.
Murren, M., Teddington, Middx.
Museum Bookshop, Woodstock, Oxon.
Museum of Childhood, Beaumaris, Gwynedd, Wales.
Mussenden and Son Antiques, Jewellery and Silver, G.B., Bournemouth, Dorset.
Mutch, A., Edinburgh, Midloth., Scot. (Cinders).

Myers, Fiandaca, London, W.1. G. Ant. Mkt.
Myers Galleries, Gargrave, N. Yorks.
Myers, P., Bushey, Herts.
Myers and Son, R.N., Gargrave, N. Yorks.
Mynott, C., Warwick, Warks.
Mynott, Mrs. C., Warwick, Warks.
Mynott, R.H., Warwick, Warks.
Myra Antiques and JLA Ltd., London, W.1. B. St. Ant. C.
Myriad Antiques, London, W.11.
Mytton Antiques, Atcham, Shrops.

N

Nadia's Antiques, Swansea, W. Glam., Wales. Ant. C.
Nadin, Harold, Grantham, Lincs.
Nadin, Richard and Pamela, Bradford-on-Avon, Wilts.
Naghi, E., London, W.1 (Emanouel Antiques Ltd.).
Nagioff (Jewellery), I. and R., London, W.C.2. Lond. Silv. Vts.
Nagle and Mottesham, Newark, Notts. (Retford Pine). Newark Ant Wrhse.
Nahum, Peter, London, S.W.1.
Nainbys Antiques, Alford, Lincs.
Nakota Curios, Hastings, E. Sussex.
Namdar, V., London, W.1. G. Mews.
Nanbooks, Settle, N. Yorks.
Nanking Porcelain Co., London, W.11.
Nantwich Antique Centre, Nantwich, Cheshire.
Nantwich Art Deco and Decorative Arts, Nantwich, Cheshire.
Nanwani and Co., London, E.C.3.
Napier House Antiques, Halstead, Essex.
Napier House Antiques, Sudbury, Suffolk.
Napier Ltd., Sylvia, London, S.W.6.
Narducci Antiques, Largs, Ayr., Scot.
Narducci Antiques, Saltcoats, Ayr., Scot.
Narducci, G., Largs, Ayr., Scot.
Narducci, G., Saltcoats, Ayr., Scot.
Nares, M.A., E.A. and J.M., Atcham, Shrops.
Nash Antiques, Chepstow, Gwent, Wales.
Nash Antiques and Interiors, John, Ledbury, Hereford and Worcs.
Nash Antiques, Paul, Tetbury, Glos.
Nash, P. and A. Gifford, Tetbury, Glos.
Nassor, C., Hebden Bridge, W. Yorks.
Nat Leslie Ltd., London, W.C.2. Lon. Silv. Vts.
Nathan and Co. (Birmingham) Ltd., Birmingham, W. Mids.
Nathan Antiques, John, Exeter, Devon.
Natural Choice Antiques, Beverley, N. Humberside.
Neal, B.A., Branksome, Dorset.
Neal, C., London, W.1. (Meltons).
Neal Cabinet Antiques, Isabel, Coltishall, Norfolk.
Neal, Stephen, Bognor Regis, W. Sussex.
Neale, A.N., B.J. and I.J., London, W.1 (Holmes Ltd.)
Neale, P., Rumford, Cornwall.
Neary, G., Huddersfield, W. Yorks.
Neath, P., Bournemouth, Dorset. (Antiques and Furnishings)
Necus, R.S. and S., London, S.W.3. Ant. Ant. Mkt.
Neech, M., St. Leonards-on-Sea, E. Sussex. Hastings Ant. C.
Needham, A. and A., Buxton, Derbys.
Needham, K., Cobham, Surrey.
Needham, Mrs. M., Sheffield, S. Yorks. (Pot Pourri).
Needham, S.R., Broughton Astley, Leics.
Neill, F. and J., White Roding, Essex.
Neilson, A.J., Sturminster Newton, Dorset.
Nels, P.J., London, W.1.
Nels Ltd., Paul, London, W.1.
Nelson, A., London, W.1. (Lane Fine Art Ltd.).
Nelson, G., London, S.W.3. Chen. Gall.
Nelson, J.M., Balcombe, W. Sussex.
Nelson, John O., Edinburgh, Midloth., Scot.
Nelson, W. and L., Broughton, Lancs.
Neptune Antiques, Long Melford, Suffolk.
Nesbitt, Peggy, Warwick, Warks.
Nesfield, J., Sandhurst, Kent.
Nethercott, A., Bath, Avon. Gt. West. A. C. Wed. Mkt.
Netherley Cottage Antiques, Milburn, Cumbria.
Netscher, Mrs., Diss, Norfolk.
Nettleton, S.M., Patrington, N. Humberside.
Neumann, Mrs. P., Hexham, Northumbs.
Nevill Fine Paintings Ltd., Guy, London, S.W.3.
Nevill, Miss S.M., Budleigh Salterton, Devon.
Neville, C. and S., Farnham, Surrey.
Neville Antiques, Howard, London, W.1. G. Ant. Mkt.
Neville Gallery, Jane, Aslockton, Notts.
Neville's Antiques, Woburn Sands, Bucks.
New Abbey Antiques, Newtownabbey, Co. Antrim, N. Ireland.
New Gallery, Budleigh Salterton, Devon.
New Generation Antiques Market, Penzance, Cornwall.
New Grafton Gallery, London, S.W.13.
New King's Road and Hurlingham Gallery, London, S.W.6.
New, S., Portsmouth, Hants.
New Street Antique Centre, Plymouth, Devon.
New Street Antiques, Penzance, Cornwall.
New Street Antiques Ltd., Altrincham, Cheshire.
New Walk House Antiques, Totnes, Devon.
Newark Antique Warehouse, Newark, Notts.
Newark Antiques Centre, Newark, Notts.
Newark, G., Deddington, Oxon.
Newborough, Lady, London, W.1.
Newby, H.W., (A.J. Waller) and H.C. Mote, London, S.W.3.
Newcomb Antiques, Berkeley, Glos.
Newcomb, Pat, London, N.W.8. Alf. Ant. Mkt.
Newcombe, P.J., Barnstaple, Devon.
Newell-Smith, S. and D., London, N.1. (Tadema).
Newhaven Flea Market, Newhaven, E. Sussex.

Newland and Son, L., London, W.1.
Newlove, B.M., Surbiton, Surrey.
Newman and Cooling Ltd., London, N.W.3.
Newman, D.A., Newport, I. of Wight.
Newman Gallery, Heather, Cranham, Glos.
Newman, T., Stow-on-the-Wold, Glos. Cots. Ant. C.
Newmarket Gallery, Newmarket, Suffolk.
Newnham, J. and M., Royston, Herts.
Newport Antiques, Newport, Dyfed, Wales.
Newport Gallery, Newport, Essex.
Newsam, T.J., Salisbury, Wilts.
Newson, D. and L., Twickenham, Middx.
Newton Abbot Antiques Centre, Newton Abbot, Devon.
Newton, Mrs. A.E., Goring-on-Thames, Oxon.
Newton, C.W., Bury, Lancs.
Newton, J., London, N.W.1. (Haverstock Antiques)
Newton, W.T., Coggeshall, Essex.
Newtons, Bury, Lancs.
Nice Things Old and New, Glasgow, Lanarks., Scot.
Nichol and Hill, Darlington, Durham.
Nicholas Antiques, East Molesey, Surrey.
Nicholas, R. and M., Towcester, Northants.
Nicholl, D. and W., South Molton, Devon.
Nicholls, John, Leigh, Staffs.
Nicholls Jewellers and Antiques, Walsall, W. Mids.
Nicholls, Mrs. R., Malmesbury, Wilts.
Nicholls, R., Walsall, W. Mids.
Nichols, M., Worcester, Hereford and Worcs.
Nicholson, J.C., Bexhill-on-Sea, E. Sussex.
Nicholson, J.C., Pevensey, E. Sussex.
Nicholson, Richard A., Chester, Cheshire.
Nicholson, Mr. and Mrs. R.A., Sutton-on-Sea, Lincs.
Nick Nack Antiques, Bideford, Devon.
Nickerson, S., London, W.11. (Myriad Antiques).
Nicola Antiques, Wallingford, Oxon. L. Arc.
Nielsen Antiques, Anthony, Burford, Oxon.
Nielsen, A.D.J., Cirencester, Glos.
Nielsen, Mrs. M.K., Moreton-in-Marsh, Glos.
Nieradzik Antiques, Eva, London, W.11.
Nightingale, P.A., Alderney, C.1.
Nihon Token, London, W.C.1.
Nilson, B., Sandgate, Kent.
Nimbus Antiques, Whaley Bridge, Derbys.
Nimmo, G., Harrogate, N. Yorks.
Niner Antiques, Elizabeth, Cheltenham, Glos.
Niner and Hill Rare Books, Oxford, Oxon.
Niner, M., Oxford, Oxon.
Ninety-One, Norwich, Norfolk.
Ning Ltd., London, S.W.1.
Nithsdale Antiques, Glasgow, Lanarks., Scot.
Niven, G., Edinburgh, Midloth., Scot. (Dunedin Antiques Ltd.).
No. 2 Park Street Antiques, Stow-on-the-Wold, Glos.
No. 12, Queen St., Bath, Avon.
Noah's Ark Antique Centre, Sandwich, Kent.
Noakes, S., Yarmouth, I. of Wight.
Nobbs, P., Bingley, W. Yorks.
Noble, Avril, London, W.C.2.
Noble Antiques, London, W.11.
Noble Antiques, Sandgate, Kent.
Noble, Mrs. B., Huddersfield, W. Yorks.
Noble, F.G., Sandgate, Kent.
Nock, J. and P., Evesham, Hereford and Worcs.
Nolan, Mrs. C., Brighton, E. Sussex (Bell-Air Antiques).
Nolan, J., Halsall, Lancs.
Noller, A.M., Reigate, Surrey.
Noller (Reigate), Bertram, Reigate, Surrey.
Noller, R., Montrose, Ang., Scot.
Nonesuch Antiques, London W.1. B. St. Ant. C.
Nook, The, Sherborne, Dorset.
Noonstar Ltd., London, W.8. (Abstract). Kensington Ch. St. A.C.
Noortman, London, W.1.
Noott Fine Paintings, John, Broadway, Hereford and Worcs.
Norbury, D. and Mrs. K., Leamington Spa, Warks.
Norcliffe Fine Art, London, N.W.8. Alf. Ant. Mkt.
Norden Antiques, Peter, Burford, Oxon.
Nordens, Sandgate, Kent.
Nordmark and King, London, N.W.8. Alf. Ant. Mkt.
Norfolk Galleries, King's Lynn, Norfolk.
Norfolk House Antiques, Dorking, Surrey.
Norfolk Polyphon Centre, Bawdeswell, Norfolk.
Norgrove, P., Haslingden, Lancs.
Norman, B.E., London, W.1 (Harvey and Gore).
Norman, George, Diss, Norfolk.
Norman Antiques, Ltd., Michael, Brighton, E. Sussex.
Norman, P., Dorking, Surrey.
Norman, P., Weedon, Northants.
Norman Antiques and Restorations, Peter, Burwell, Cambs.
Norman, P.G., Flore, Northants.
Norman, Raymond, Diss, Norfolk.
Norman, Sue, London, S.W.3. Ant. Ant. Mkt.
Norrie, Mrs. E., Ceres, Fife, Scot.
Norris, M., Snettisham, Norfolk.
Norris, R., Biddenden, Kent.
North, Amanda and Desmond, East Peckham, Kent.
North Bridge Antiques, Halifax, W. Yorks.
North London Clock Shop Ltd., London, N.5.
North Quay Antique Centre, Weymouth, Dorset.
North Wales Antiques, Colwyn Bay, Clwyd, Wales.
North Walsham Antique Gallery, North Walsham, Norfolk.
North Western Antique Centre, Preston, Lancs.
North Wilts Exporters, Hankerton, Wilts.
Northam, E. and J., Long Sutton, Lincs.
Northcote Road Antiques Market, London, S.W.11.
Northern Kilim Centre, The, Knaresborough, N. Yorks.

Northfleet Hill Antiques, Northfleet, Kent.
Northgate Antiques, Bishops Stortford, Herts.
Northgate Antiques, Pembroke, Dyfed, Wales.
Northgate Antiques, Rochester, Kent.
Northleach Gallery, The, Northleach, Glos.
Northumbria Pine, Whitley Bay, Tyne and Wear.
Northwold Gallery, Newmarket, Suffolk.
Norton Antiques, Beaconsfield, Bucks.
Norton, B.R., St. Ives, Cambs.
Norton, M.S., N.E.L., J.P. and F.E., London, W.1. (S.J. Phillips Ltd.)
Norton Galleries, Pauline, Bridgnorth, Shrops.
Nortonbury Antiques, London, W.C.1.
Norwich Antique and Collectors Centre, Norwich, Norfolk.
Norwood House Antiques, Killinghall, N. Yorks.
Nostalgia, Blackpool, Lancs.
Nostalgia, Dorking, Surrey.
Nostalgia Antiques, Northampton, Northants.
Nostalgia Architectural Antiques, Stockport, Cheshire.
Nosworthy, P., Grampound, Cornwall.
Nosworthy, P. and R., Holsworthy, Devon.
Nosworthy, R., St. Austell, Cornwall.
Not Cartier, Bath, Avon. Gt. West. Ant. C.
Not Just Books, Uppingham, Leics.
Not Just Silver, Weybridge, Surrey.
Noton Antiques, Finedon, Northants.
Nottingham Antique Centre, Nottingham, Notts.
Notts Pine, Jeff and Lindy, Bath, Avon. Gt. West. Ant. C.
Now and Then (Toy Centre), Edinburgh, Midloth., Scot.
Nowell, Edward A., Wells, Somerset.
Nowell, Marcus, Wells, Somerset.
Number Nineteen, London, N.1.
Number Ten, Swansea, W. Glam., Wales. Ant. C.
Number Ten Oxford Antiques, Oxford, Oxon.
Number Six Antiques, Halesworth Suffolk.
Nunan, M.P., Bath, Avon. (Deja Vu). Gt. West. Ant. C.
Nunn, C.C., Falmouth, Cornwall.
Nunn, K., St. Leonards-on-Sea, E. Sussex.
Nunn/Christine McCabe, Michael, London, N.W.8. Alf. Ant. Mkt.
Nutter, Simon W., Stow-on-the-Wold, Glos.
Nutting, Mrs. B.H., Brackley, Northants.
Nutting Books, Patrick, Brackley, Northants.
Nye, Pat, London, W.11.
Nyman and Co. Ltd., Chas. L., London, N.W.1.

O

Oak Chest, Llangollen, Clwyd, Wales.
Oakes and Son, G., Bolton, Lancs.
Oakes, H. & S., Stoke-on-Trent, Staffs.
Oakes, J., Bristol, Avon. Clift. Ant. Mkt.
Oakley, Ms. N., London, N.W.8. Alfies.
Oakham Antiques, Oakham, Leics.
Oakstar Ltd., London, S.W.1.
Oakwood Gallery, Leeds, W. Yorks.
Oasis Antiques, Brighton, E. Sussex.
Oates Fine Paintings, Brian, Wolverhampton, W. Mids.
Oban Antiques, Oban, Scotland.
Obelisk, London, N.W.8. Alf. Ant. Mkt.
Obelisk Antiques, Long Melford, Suffolk.
Obelisk Antiques, Warminster, Wilts.
O'Brien, R. and J., Hollinwood, Lancs.
O'Callaghan, J., London, W.1. G. Mews.
Occultique, Northampton, Northants.
Ockley Antiques, Ockley, Surrey.
O'Connor Brothers, Windsor and Eton, Berks.
O'Connor, E.R., London, W.11.
Oddiquities, London, S.E.23.
Oddy, Mr. and Mrs. G., Stirling, Stirlings., Scot.
Odgers, J.W., Harwich and Dovercourt, Essex.
Odger, J.W., London, W.11 (Mayflower Antiques).
Odiham Gallery, The, Odiham, Hants.
Odling, David, London, W.1. G. Ant. Mkt.
O'Donnell, A., London, S.E.13.
O'Donnell, A.J., Bowdon, Cheshire.
O'Donnell, C., Wallingford, Oxon.
O'Donnell, L., Wallingford, Oxon.
O'Donnell, Steven, London, W.1. G. Ant. Mkt.
O'Dwyer, F., Rode, Somerset.
O'Dwyer, E., London, N.W.3. Ham. Ant. Emp.
O'Farrell, G., Stow-on-The Wold, Glos.
Off the Rails, Bath, Avon. Gt. West. Ant. C.
Offa's Dyke Antique Centre, Knighton, Powys, Wales.
O'Flynn Antiquarian Booksellers, York, N. Yorks.
Ogden, J. and M., Honiton, Devon.
Ogden of Harrogate Ltd., Harrogate, N. Yorks.
Ogden Ltd., Richard, London, W.1.
Ogleby, B., Thirsk, N. Yorks.
O'Grady, V., Norwich, Norfolk. (Queen of Hungary Antiques).
Ogwen Antiques, Bethesda, Gwynedd, Wales.
O'Halloran-Fairgaill, Mr. and Mrs. K.D.W., Lyndhurst, Hants.
O'Karma, E., Brobury, Hereford and Worcs.
O'Karma, E., Hay-on-Wye, Powys, Wales.
O'Keefe, B., Hadleigh, Suffolk.
O'Keefe, E., London, W.11. (Chimney Pieces).
O'Kelly, A. and J., London, E.8.
Okker, Nadine, London, W.1. G. Ant. Mkt.
Okolski, Z.J., London, W.3.
Old Antique Shop, The, Budleigh Salterton, Devon.
Old Antique Shop, The, Kelvedon, Essex.
Old Bakehouse Pine, Whissendine, Leics.
Old Bakehouse Antiques and Gallery, Broughton Astley, Leics.
Old Bakery, The, Woolhampton, Berks.
Old Bakery Antiques, Cranbrook, Kent.
Old Bakery Antiques, Empingham, Leics.
Old Bakery Antiques, Hunstanton, Norfolk.
Old Barn Antiques, Church Stretton, Shrops.
Old Barn Antiques Co., Trent, Dorset.

Old Barn Antiques Warehouse, Sutton Bridge, Lincs.
Old Brass Kettle, Moretonhampstead, Devon.
Old Brigade, The, Kingsthorpe, Northants.
Old Button Shop, The, Lytchett Minster, Dorset.
Old Chapel Antiques, Ferndown, Dorset.
Old Church Galleries, London, S.W.3.
Old Cinema Antique Store, The, London, W.4.
Old Clock Shop, The, Birmingham, W. Mids.
Old Clock Shop, The, West Malling, Kent.
Old Coach House, Long Stratton, Norfolk.
Old Copper Shop, The, South Cave, N. Humberside.
Old Corner House Antiques, Wittersham, Kent.
Old Cottage Antiques, The, Upminster, Essex.
Old Cottage Things, Romsey, Hants.
Old Cross Antiques, Greyabbey, Co. Down, N. Ireland.
Old Cross Gallery, Glossop, Derbys.
Old Curiosity Antiques, Kidderminster, Hereford and Worcs.
Old Curiosity Shop, The, Ayr, Ayr., Scot.
Old Curiosity Shop, Beaconsfield, Bucks.
Old Curiosity Shop, Frome, Somerset.
Old Curiosity Shop, King's Lynn, Norfolk.
Old Curiosity Shop, The, St. Sampson, Guernsey, C.I.
Old Curiosity Shop (Antiques), The, Axminster, Devon.
Old English Pine, Sandgate, Kent.
Old Ephemera and Newspaper Shop, London, S.W.1.
Old Father Time Clock Centre, London, W.11.
Old Firm, The, Newport, I. of Wight.
Old Flames Architectural Antiques, Stoke-on-Trent, Staffs.
Old Forge, The, Long Melford, Suffolk.
Old Forge Antiques, Hartley Wintney, Hants.
Old George Antiques, Ledbury, Hereford and Worcs.
Old George Antiques and Interiors, Tetbury, Glos.
Old Golf Shop Inc., Edinburgh, Midloth., Scot.
Old Granary Antique and Collectors Centre, Kings Lynn, Norfolk.
Old Granary Antique & Craft Centre, The, Battlesbridge, Essex.
Old Haberdasher, The, London, W.11.
Old Hall Bookshop, The, Brackley, Northants.
Old Hall (Sphinx Gallery), Brasted, Kent.
Old Harbour Antiques and Nautical Gallery, Weymouth, Dorset.
Old Hat, Radlett, Herts.
Old House, The, Seaford, E. Sussex.
Old House Antiques, Wansford, Cambs.
Old House Gallery, The, Oakham, Leics.
Old London Galleries, London, S.W.1.
Old Malthouse, The, Hungerford, Berks.
Old Maltings Antique Company, Long Melford, Suffolk.
Old Man Antiques, The, Coniston, Cumbria.
Old Manor House Antiques, Brasted, Kent.
Old Maps and Prints, London, S.W.1.
Old Mermaid Antiques, Sherborne, Dorset.
Old Mill Antiques Ltd., Kinbuck, Perths., Scot.
Old Mill Gallery, The, Neston, Cheshire.
Old Mill Market Shop, Tetbury, Glos.
Old Mint House, The, Bexhill-on-Sea, E. Sussex.
Old Mint House, The, Pevensey, E. Sussex.
Old Palace Antiques, Lostwithiel, Cornwall.
Old Pine, London, S.W.6.
Old Pine Furniture and Jouet, Kiltarlity, Inver., Scot.
Old Pine Loft, The, Luton, Beds.
Old Pine Shop, Ross-on-Wye, Hereford and Worcs.
Old Post House, The, Axbridge, Somerset.
Old Post House Antiques, Playden, E. Sussex.
Old Post House Antiques, Woolhampton, Berks.
Old Posthouse, The, Penzance, Cornwall.
Old Post Office Antiques, Compton, Surrey.
Old Rock, The, Preston, Lancs. N.W. Ant. C.
Old Rock, The, Trawden, Lancs.
Old Ropery Antique Clocks, The, Kilham, N. Humberside.
Old Saddlers Antiques, Goudhurst, Kent.
Old St. Andrews Gallery, St. Andrews, Fife, Scot.
Old School Antiques, The, Dorney, Berks.
Old Smithy, Feniscowles, Lancs.
Old Smithy Antique Centre, The, Merstham, Surrey.
Old Soke Books, Peterborough, Cambs.
Old Stores, The, Christchurch, Dorset.
Old Tithe Barn, The, Horbury, W. Yorks.
Old Town Hall Antique Centre, The, Needham Market, Suffolk.
Old Treasures, Newton Abbot, Devon.
Old Vicarage, The, Pontfaen, Dyfed, Wales.
Old White House Antiques, Beighton, Norfolk.
Old Woodworking Tools, London, N.1.
Old World Trading Co., London, S.W.6.
Olde Curiosity Shoppe, The, Godalming, Surrey.
Olde Englande, Hoylake, Merseyside.
Olde Forge Antiques, The, Swanage, Dorset.
Olde Red Lion, The, Bedingfield, Suffolk.
Olde Tyme Antiques, Ruthin, Clwyd, Wales.
Oldfield, Southampton, Hants.
Oldfield Cottage Antiques, Elland, W. Yorks.
Oldfield Cottage Antiques, Marple, Cheshire.
Oldfield Cottage Antiques, Saddleworth, Lancs.
Oldfield Gallery, Portsmouth, Hants.
Oldfield, N.E., Preston, Lancs.
Oldham, Mrs. J.A., Castle Cary, Somerset.
Oldman, P. and R., Todmorden, W. Yorks.
Oldroyd Antiques, Keith R., Ossett, W. Yorks.
Oldswinford Gallery, Stourbridge, W. Mids.
Oldwoods, Bristol, Avon.
Olive Antiques, Alverstoke, Hants.

Olive Branch Antiques, Broadway, Hereford and Worcs.
Olive Green Ltd., Stow-on-the-Wold, Glos. C. Ant. C.
Oliver Antiques, West Kirby, Merseyside.
Oliver, A., London, W.8 (Oliver-Sutton Antiques).
Oliver, A. and M., Whitchurch, Hereford and Worcs.
Oliver, C.A., Swansea, W. Glam., Wales.
Oliver, C.H., Weldon, Northants.
Oliver Antiques, Gerald J., Haverfordwest, Dyfed, Wales.
Oliver, Patrick, Cheltenham, Glos.
Oliver, P.A. and L.S., Wiggenhall St. Germans, Norfolk.
Oliver, R.A., Brighton, E. Sussex. (Rodney Arthur Classics).
Oliver, Susan, London, N.W.8. Alf. Ant. Mkt.
Oliver, T. and J., Wells, Somerset.
Oliver, Tony L., Windsor and Eton, Berks.
Olivers of Whitchurch, Whitchurch, Hereford and Worcs.
Oliver-Sutton Antiques, London, W.8.
Olman, M.W., Edinburgh, Midloth., Scot. (Old Golf Shop Inc.)
Olney, A., Ampthill, Beds.
Olney Antique Centre, Olney, Bucks.
O'Loughlin, P.J., Glasgow, Lanarks., Scot. (Albany Antiques).
Omar (Harrogate) Ltd., Harrogate, N. Yorks.
Omega Antiques of Mansfield, Mansfield, Notts.
Omell Galleries, London, S.W.1.
Omell, N.R., London, S.W.1.
Omniphil, London, W.1. G. Ant. Mkt.
Omniphil Ltd., Chesham, Bucks.
Ondaatje, Miss J., London, S.W.3. Chen. Gall.
O'Nians, Hal, London, S.W.1. (King St. Galleries).
Onions, L. — White Cottage Antiques Tern Hill, Shrops.
Onions, Mrs. E., Shifnal, Shrops.
Oola Boola Antiques London, London, S.E.1.
Oosthuizen, Jacqueline, London, S.W.3.
Oosthuizen, Jacqueline, London, N.1.
Open Eye Gallery Ltd., Edinburgh, Midloth., Scot.
Opie, Mr., Newton Abbot, Devon. N.A. Ant. C.
Oracz, P., Preston, Lancs, N.W. Ant. C.
Orbell House Gallery, Castle Hedingham, Essex.
Orchard Antiques, London, W.2.
Orchard, Mrs. P.A., Hadleigh, Suffolk.
Orchard, R., London, W.2.
Organ, G.H. and S.M., Bath, Avon (Corridor Stamp Shop).
Organ, R., Bristol, Avon. (Triangle Antiques).
Oriel Antiques, Hindhead, Surrey.
Oriel Antiques, Sheffield, S. Yorks.
Oriel Gallery, The, Cambridge, Cambs.
Oriental Bronzes Ltd., London, W.1.
Oriental Carpet Centre, The, Bristol, Avon.
Oriental Carpets and Decorative Arts, Dorking, Surrey.
Oriental Gallery, Stow-on-the-Wold, Glos.
Oriental Rug Gallery Ltd., St. Albans, Herts.
Oriental Rug Shop, The, Sheffield, S. Yorks.
Original Choice, The, Birmingham, W. Mids.
Original Choice, Penryn, Cornwall.
Original Choice Ltd., The, Worcester, Hereford and Worcs.
Originals, Leeds, W. York.
Originals, The, London, N.W.8. Alf. Ant. Mkt.
Orion Antiques, London, W.1. G. Mews.
Ormonde, F., London, W.11. (Ormonde Gallery).
Ormonde Gallery, London, W.11.
Orpin, J., M. and N., Stansted, Essex.
Orrsich, Paul, London, S.W.6.
Orton, R.J., London, N.4.
Orton Antiques, Stephen, Watlington, Oxon.
Orwell Galleries, Ipswich, Suffolk.
Orwell Paint Strippers, Ipswich, Suffolk.
Osborne, Kirkcudbright, Kirkcud., Scot.
Osborne Antiques, Sutton Coldfield, W. Mids.
Osborne Art and Antiques, Jesmond, Tyne and Wear.
Osborne, C., Sutton Coldfield, W. Mids.
Osborne, T.N.M., North Wraxhall, Wilts.
Oscar's, Crewkerne, Somerset.
O'Shea Gallery, London, S.W.1
Osiris Antiques, Southport, Merseyside.
Osman, Aytac, London, S.W.3. Ant. Ant. Mkt.
Ossowski, A. and M., London, S.W.1.
Osterly Antiques Ltd., London, S.W.6.
Ostle, R., Bethesda, Gwynedd, Wales.
O'Sullivan, D.J. and P.M., Parkstone, Dorset.
Oswald Road Antique and Reproduction Centre, The, Oswestry, Shrops.
Othen, John, Fakenham, Norfolk. Ant. C.
Other Times, Portsoy, Aberd., Scot.
Otter Antiques, Honiton, Devon.
Otto, Rudolph, Stow-on-the-Wold, Glos.
Ottrey Antiques, Mike, Wallingford, Oxon.
Ottrey, M.J., Wallingford, Oxon.
Otway, Rodney and Susan, Bradford-on-Avon, Wilts.
Oulton, P.M.C. and T., Altrincham, Cheshire.
Out of Time Antiques, Ashbourne, Derbys.
Outred, Anthony, London, S.W.10 (Furniture Cave).
Ovell Antiques, Llandovery, Dyfed, Wales.
Overland Antiques, John, Olney, Bucks.
Overlord, Chichester, W. Sussex.
Owen, Mrs. A., Cambridge, Cambs. (Cottage Antiques).
Owen Antiques, Rochdale, Lancs.
Owen, J., Brighton, E. Sussex (Prinny's Antique Gallery).
Owen, Jonathan, Eastbourne, E. Sussex.
Owen Gallery, John, Cowbridge, S. Glam., Wales.
Owen, J.G.T., Rochdale, Lancs.
Owen, J. and P., Cowbridge, S. Glam., Wales.
Owen, M., Nelson, Lancs.
Owen, Aquarius Antiques, Tom, Blackpool, Lancs.

Owen's Jewellers, Newcastle-upon-Tyne, Tyne and Wear.
Owens, Mrs. M., Moffat, Dumfries, Scot.
Owens, Mrs. M.J., Sedbergh, Cumbria.
Owl House, The, Dorking, Surrey.
Owls Antiques, Steeton, W. Yorks.
Oxenhams, Wellington, Somerset.
Oxford Antique Trading Company, The, Oxford, Oxon.
Oxford Antiques, Preston, Lancs. N.W. Ant. C.
Oxford Antiques Centre, Oxford, Oxon.
Oxford Architectural Antiques, Oxford, Oxon.
Oxford Street Antique Centre Ltd., Leicester, Leics.
Oxfordshire County Council, Woodstock, Oxon.
Oxhay, Preston, Lancs. N.W. Ant. C.
Oxley, L., Alresford, Hants.
Oxley Antique Clocks and Barometers, P.A., Cherhill, Wilts.

P

P. and D. Antiques, Newton Abbot, Devon. N.A. Ant. C.
P.L.B. Enterprises, Hythe, Kent.
Packer House Antiques, Chipping Norton, Oxon.
Paddock Antiques, Woodhouse Eaves, Leics.
Padgett, G.R. and D.L., Hornsea, N. Humberside.
Padgetts Antiques, Photographic and Scientific, Hornsea, N. Humberside.
Paessler, S.D. and R.J., Marlow, Bucks.
Page Antiques, Stockport, Cheshire.
Page, A. and H., London, S.W.7.
Page Antiques, Brian, Brighton, E. Sussex.
Page Antiquarian Books, Colin, Brighton, E. Sussex.
Page, C.G., Brighton, E. Sussex (Colin Page Antiquarian Books).
Page, D.R.J. and S.J., London, W.11 (J. Fairman (Carpets) Ltd.)
Page Galleries, Kington, Hereford and Worcs.
Page Oriental Art, Kevin, London, N.1.
Page, T., Marlborough, Wilts.
Pageant Antiques, London, S.W.6.
Pain, B, Cambridge, Cambs. (Artisan Antiques & Collectables).
Pain Gallery, Jean, Cambridge, Cambs.
Paine, E., Gorseinon, W. Glam., Wales.
Painswick Antique Centre, Painswick, Glos.
Painter, R., Ludlow, Shrops.
Paisley Fine Books, Paisley, Renfrew., Scot.
Palfrey, M. and L.E., Brockdish, Norfolk.
Pall Mall Antiques, Leigh-on-Sea, Essex.
Palma Court Antique Arcade, Ross-on-Wye, Hereford and Worcs.
Palmer, B. and J., Haverfordwest, Dyfed, Wales.
Palmer, C.D. and V.J., Richmond, Surrey.
Palmer Antiques, Dermot and Jill, Brighton, E. Sussex.
Palmer Galleries, Richmond, Surrey.
Palmer, G.I., Martock, Somerset.
Palmer, H.J. and Miss J., London, S.W.3. Ant. Ant. Mkt.
Palmer, J., Honiton, Devon.
Palmer, M., Penzance, Cornwall.
Palmer Antiques, Mary, Stradbroke, Suffolk.
Palmer, M.K., Fritwell, Oxon.
Palmer, P., Brecon, Powys, Wales.
Palmer Antiques, P.E., Ringwood, Hants.
Palmer, P. and G., Sarnau, Dyfed, Wales.
Panormo, S.V., Gosport, Hants.
Pantelli, A., London, N.1 (Inheritance).
Pantiles Antiques, Tunbridge Wells, Kent.
Pantiles Spa Antiques, Tunbridge Wells, Kent.
Papillon Antiques, Sawbridgeworth, Herts.
Paradise, J., Nottingham, Notts.
Paragon Antiques, Huddersfield, W. Yorks.
Paragon Antiques and Collectors Market, Bath, Avon.
Paraphernalia, Harrogate, N. Yorks.
Paraphernalia, Sheffield, S. Yorks.
Paravent, London, W.8.
Paravicini, Hungerford, Berks.
Pardoe, Stuart, London, W.11.
Parikian, D., London, W.14.
Parish, R., Manchester, Lancs. (Acorn Antiques).
Parish, S., Buckhurst Hill, Essex.
Park Antiques, Menston, W. Yorks.
Park Antiquities, Weymouth, Dorset.
Park Book Shop, Wellingborough, Northants.
Park Galleries, London, N.3.
Park Galleries Antiques, Fine Art and Decor, Bolton, Lancs.
Park Gallery, Wellingborough, Northants.
Park House Antiques, Bladon, Oxon.
Park House Antiques, Stow-on-the-Wold, Glos.
Park, N., Tiverton, Devon.
Park Street Antiques, Berkhamsted, Herts.
Park View Antiques, Durgates, E. Sussex.
Park Walk Gallery, London, S.W.10.
Parker, Elizabeth, Moreton-in-Marsh, Glos.
Parker Fine Art Ltd., Finkley, Hants.
Parker Gallery, Leeds. W. Yorks.
Parker Gallery, The, London, S.W.1.
Parker, John, Churchill, Oxon.
Parker, L., Canterbury, Kent.
Parker, M.L., Witney, Oxon.
Parker Antiques, Michael and Margaret, London, S.W.7.
Parker, P.A.R., Finkley, Hants.
Parker, S., Quorn, Leics.
Parker Ltd., Thomas H., London, S.W.1.
Parker-Williams, Canterbury, Kent.
Parkhouse Antiques and Jewellery, Mark, Barnstaple, Devon.
Parkhouse and Wyatt Ltd., Southampton, Hants.
Parkin, J., Derby, Derbys.
Parkin Fine Art Ltd., Michael, London, S.W.1.
Parkin, P.J., Bristol Avon. (Bizarre Antiques).
Parkins, Mrs. G., Budleigh Salterton, Devon.
Parkinson, E. & D., Chalfont St. Giles, Bucks.
Parkinson-Large, P., Woburn, Beds.

Parks, A.M., Eastbourne, E. Sussex.
Parks, Bollon and Vinsen, Sheringham, Norfolk.
Parkside Antiques, Newark, Notts. Castle G.A.C.
Parkside Antiques, Nottingham, Notts.
Parmenter Antiques, Bridgnorth, Shrops.
Parmenter, J., Bridgnorth, Shrops.
Parriss, J.H., Sheringham, Norfolk.
Parry, H., Edinburgh, Midloth., Scot.
Parry Ltd., H. and R.L., Sutton Coldfield, W. Mids.
Parry, R., Exeter, Devon.
Parsons, A.L. and R.F., London, W.1. (Tessiers Ltd.)
Parsons, Mrs. B.D., Tonbridge, Kent.
Parsons and Edwards, Brighton, E. Sussex.
Parsons, P., Brighton, E. Sussex.
Parsonson, R.S., Launceston, Cornwall.
Partington, C., Shrewsbury, Shrops.
Partington, V., Worsley, Lancs.
Partner and Puxton, Colchester, Essex.
Partner, S.H. and M., Colchester, Essex.
Partners, A.F., London, N.W.8. Alf. Ant. Mkt.
Partridge Fine Arts plc, London, W.1.
Partridge Antiques, L., Hertford, Herts.
Partridge Antiques, Timothy, Eastbourne, E. Sussex.
Partridges, Amersham, Bucks.
Partt, J., Bath, Avon. Gt. West. Ant. C.
Pash and Son, A., London, W.1. B. St. Silv. Galls.
Paskin, David, London, W.1. G. Ant. Mkt.
Passell, P.A., Eastleigh, Hants.
Passers Buy (Marie Evans), Llangollen, Clwyd, Wales.
Passing Buy, Ryde, I. of Wight.
Past and Present, Blackpool, Lancs.
Past and Present, Cardiff, S. Glam., Wales.
Past and Present, Husbands Bosworth, Leics.
Past and Present, Inverness, Inverns., Scot.
Past and Present, Leigh-on-Sea, Essex.
Past and Present, Walsall, W. Mids.
Past Times, Swansea, W. Glam., Wales. Ant. Centre.
Pastimes (Egham) Ltd., Egham, Surrey.
Pastorale Antiques, Lewes, E. Sussex.
Pataky Antiques and Reproductions, Victoria, West Malling, Kent.
Patchwork Dog, The and The Calico Cat Ltd., London, N.W.1.
Paterson Antiques, Elizabeth, Stirling, Stirlings., Scot.
Paterson, E. and J., Stirling, Stirlings., Scot.
Pathbrae Antiques, Newton Stewart, Wigtown, Scot.
Patina Antiques, Clacton-on-Sea, Essex.
Patricia Antiques, Ramsgate, Kent.
Patterson, A., Manningtree, Essex.
Patterson, E.J.A., Banbury, Oxon.
Patterson, J., Preston, Lancs. N.W. Ant. C.
Patterson Antiques, Jo., Crook, Durham.
Patterson, J.W.B., Crook, Durham.
Patterson, P., Sible Hedingham, Essex.
Patterson Fine Arts Ltd., W.H., London, W.1.
Patterson, W.H. and Mrs. P.M., London, W.1.
Pattison, R., Redmarley, D'Abitot, Glos.
Paul, Mrs. E., London, W.1 (Demas).
Paull Antiques, Janice, Kenilworth, Warks.
Pauw Antiques, M., London, S.W.6.
Pavilion, Stamford, Lincs.
Pavion, Yvonne, Manchester, Lancs. Royal Ex. S.C.
Pawle Ltd., Julian, London, W.1. B. St. Silv. Galls.
Pawsey and Payne, London, S.W.1.
Pay, D.J. and B., South Holmwood, Surrey.
Payman, E. and L.C., Stokesley, N. Yorks.
Payne, Mrs., Newton Abbot, Devon. N. A. Ant. C.
Payne and Son Ltd., Geo. A., Bournemouth, Dorset.
Payne, G.N., E.P. and J.D., Oxford, Oxon.
Payne, H.G. and N.G., Bournemouth, Dorset. (Geo. A. Payne and Son Ltd.).
Payne, J. and M., Hemel Hempstead, Herts.
Payne Antiques, Martin, Warwick, Warks.
Payne, M.H., London, N.1.
Payne, M.S., London, N.W.8. Alf. Ant. Mkt.
Payne, P., Alcester, Warks.
Payne, P., Peterborough, Cambs.
Payne, S., Grampound, Cornwall.
Payne and Son (Goldsmiths), Ltd., Oxford, Oxon.
Payton, F.B. and S., Mansfield, Notts.
Payton Antiques, Mary, Chagford, Devon.
Peacock Antiques, Chilham, Kent.
Peacock, G.A., Winslow, Bucks.
Pead, L.W., Marsham, Norfolk.
Peake, D.T., Nottingham, Notts.
Peake, Geoffrey, London, N.W.8. Alf. Ant. Mkt.
Peake, N.B., Norwich, Norfolk (The Scientific Anglian Bookshop).
Pearce, A., Colchester, Essex.
Pearce, B. and A., Ombersley, Hereford and Worcs.
Pearce, G. and J., Witheridge, Devon.
Pearce, P., Hexham, Northumb.
Pearce, R., London, W.11 (Cohen and Pearce).
Pearl Cross Ltd., London, W.C.2.
Pearman, John, London, S.W.3. Chen. Gall.
Pearsey, M.E. and D.C., Holbeach, Lincs.
Pearson Antiques, Hull, N. Humbs.
Pearson Antiques, Carol, Tisbury, Wilts.
Pearson Antiques, Carol, Wilton, Wilts.
Pearson Antique Clock Restoration, John, Birstwith, N. Yorks.
Pearson, J., Nantwich, Cheshire.
Pearson, J., Nottingham, Notts.
Pearson Ltd., John A., Windsor and Eton, Berks.
Pearson Antiques, Michael, Canterbury, Kent.
Pearson, Sue, Brighton, E. Sussex.
Pearson Antiques and Paintings, Sebastian, Cambridge, Cambs.
Pearson, Frasco International Ltd., W.M., London, S.W.1. (Moreton Street Gallery).
Peasenhall Art and Antiques Gallery, Peasenhall, Suffolk.

Phelps, R.C., Twickenham, Middx.
Philip and Sons Ltd., Trevor, London, S.W.1.
Phillips, Bob and Angela, London, N.W.8. Alf. Ant. Mkt.
Phillips, E., London, N.W.8.
Phillips Antiques Ltd., Elaine, Harrogate, N. Yorks.
Phillips and Sons, E.S., London, W.11.
Phillips (Antiques), Edward V., Clayton-le-Moors, Lancs.
Phillips, Henry, London, W.8.
Phillips, Howard, Woburn, Beds. Wob. Ab. Ant. C.
Phillips, M. and J., Hitchin, Herts.
Phillips of Hitchin (Antiques) Ltd., Hitchin, Herts.
Phillips Ltd., Ronald, London, W.1.
Phillips, S., Norwich, Norfolk. (As Time Goes By Antiques).
Phillips Ltd., S.J., London, W.1.
Phillips, S.P., Uppingham, Leics.
Phillips, V., Altrincham, Cheshire.
Phillips, W. and M., Raglan, Gwent, Wales.
Phillips and Sons, Cookham, Berks.
Phillipson, M. and J., Leominster, Hereford and Worcs. L. Ant. Mkt.
Philp, R., London, W.11.
Philpot, P., Stoke Ferry, Norfolk.
Phipps and Co. Ltd., London, S.W.3 (Mathon Gallery.)
Phipps and Co. Ltd., Mathon, Hereford and Worcs.
Phoenix, London, N.W.8. Alf. Ant. Mkt.
Phoenix Antiques, Fordham, Cambs.
Phoenix Antiques, London, W.11 (Philip and Paul Allison Antiques Ltd.)
Phoenix Antiques, Manchester, Lancs. Royal Ex. S.C.
Phoenix Green Antiques, Hartley Wintney, Hants.
Phoenix Green Gallery, Hartley Wintney, Hants.
Piano Nobile Fine Paintings, Richmond, Surrey.
Piano Shop, The, Leeds, W. Yorks.
Pianorama (Harrogate) Ltd., Harrogate, N. Yorks.
Picasso, Matteo, London, N.W.8. Alf. Ant. Mkt.
Piccadilly Gallery, London, W.1.
Piccadilly Jewellers, Birmingham, W. Mids.
Pickering, B., Allonby, Cumbria.
Pickering and Chatto Ltd., Incorporating Dawsons of Pall Mall, London, S.W.1.
Pickering, Ernest, Eastbourne, E. Sussex.
Pickering Fine Art, Michael, Newark, Notts.
Pickersgill, A. and C., Barnstaple, Devon.
Pickett, D. and Mrs. J., Errol, Perths., Scot.
Pickett, G.R., Oakham, Leics.
Pickup, David, Burford, Oxon.
Pickwick Antiques, London, N.W.3. Ham. Ant. Emp.
Pickwick Antiques, Mr., London, S.E.1. Ber. Ant. Whse.
Pickwicks, Redditch, Hereford and Worcs.
Pic's Bookshop, Bridport, Dorset.
Pictoriana, Knaresborough, N. Yorks.
Pictures (Chris Crowe Fine Art), Macclesfield, Cheshire.
Pictures and Things, Penzance, Cornwall.
Pieces of Eight, Conway, Gwynedd, Wales.
Piermont Antiques Ltd., London, N.21.
Pierpoint Gallery, Hereford, Hereford and Worcs.
Piersenne,G. and K., London, N.21.
Pigeon House Antiques, Hurst Green, E. Sussex.
Pigney, L. and J., Stanford-Le-Hope, Essex.
Pike, D., Weston-super-Mare, Avon.
Pike, Valerie, Woburn, Beds. Wob. Ab. Ant. C.
Pilgrim Antiques, Honiton, Devon.
Pilkington, P., London, E.C.2.
Pillory House, Nantwich, Cheshire.
Pimblett, G., Preston, Lancs. N.W. Ant. C.
Pine Antiques, Uttoxeter, Staffs.
Pine Apples, Bungay, Suffolk.
Pine Barn, The, Pontnewynydd, Gwent, Wales.
Pine Barn, Pontypool, Gwent, Wales.
Pine Cellars, The, Winchester, Hants.
Pine Collection, Liss, Hants.
Pine Collection, The, St. Peter Port, Guernsey, C.I.
Pine Company, Ringwood, Hants.
Pine and Country Antiques, North Petherwin, Cornwall.
Pine and Design, Balcombe, W. Sussex.
Pine Design, Warwick, Warks.
Pine Design Workshop, Haverfordwest, Dyfed, Wales.
Pine Dresser, The, Blackpool, Lancs.
Pine Finds, Bishop Monkton, N. Yorks.
Pine Interiors incorporating Countrystyle, Ipswich, Suffolk.
Pine Merchants, The, Great Missenden, Bucks.
Pine Mine, The, (Crewe-Read Antiques), London, S.W.6.
Pine Mine Antiques, Lytham St. Annes, Lancs.
Pine Mine Antiques, Skipton, N. Yorks.
Pine, N.J., Horndean, Hants.
Pine Parlour, The, Ampthill, Beds.
Pine Parlour, The, Truro, Cornwall.
Pine and Period Furniture, Grampound, Cornwall.
Pine Reflections, Hughenden Valley, Bucks.
Pine Shop, The, Merrow, Surrey.
Pine Time, Hare Hatch, Berks.
Pine Too, Congleton, Cheshire.
Pinetree Antiques, Ripon, N. Yorks.
Pine Village, The, London, S.W.6.
Pine Village, The, Prestwick, Ayr., Scot.
Pinecrafts, Bishops Waltham, Hants.
Pines Gallery, Beaminster, Dorset.
Pinewood Studio, Penzance, Cornwall.
Pinfold Antiques, Ruskington, Lincs.
Pinhas, Ms., London, S.W.3. Chen. Gall.
Pink Cottage Antiques, Widegates, Cornwall.
Pinn, K.H. and W.J., Sible Hedingham, Essex.
Pinn and Sons, W.A., Sible Hedingham, Essex.
Pinner Antiques, Pinner, Middx.

Potterton Books, Thirsk, N. Yorks.
Potts, Mrs. R., Elland, W. Yorks.
Potts, Mrs. R., Marple, Cheshire.
Potts, Mrs. R., Saddleworth, Lancs.
Poulter and Son, H.W., London, S.W.10.
Pound, Mrs. M.F., Cobham, Surrey.
Pout Antiques, Ian, Witney, Oxon.
Pout, I. and J., Witney, Oxon.
Powell, C., Eastbourne, E. Sussex.
Powell (Hove) Ltd., J., Portslade, W. Sussex.
Powell Antiques, Steve, Chalvington, E. Sussex.
Power, Tom, London, N.W.8. Alf. Ant. Mkt.
Power, Mr. and Mrs. I., Ross-on-Wye, Hereford and Worcs.
Powis, G.L., Hemswell Cliff, Lincs.
Powis, G.L., Newark, Notts.
Pratt, Mrs. E., Bolton, Lancs.
Pratt, J., Ramsgate, Kent.
Pratt, J. and D., Burford, Oxon.
Pratt and Son, Leo, South Walsham, Norfolk.
Pratt, N., Acle, Norfolk.
Pratt, R., Birmingham, W. Midlands. (Eden Coins).
Pratt Antiques, Rosemary, Woburn, Beds. Wob. Ab. Ant. C.
Pratt, R. and Mrs. E.D., South Walsham, Norfolk.
Pratt, S.G.H., Ilkley, W. Yorks.
Precious, Roy, Settle, N. Yorks.
Preece, J., Tewkesbury, Glos.
Preiss, Shoshi, London, N.W.8. Alf. Ant. Mkt.
Premier Gallery, Eastbourne, E. Sussex.
Prestbury Antiques, Prestbury, Cheshire.
Prestige Antiques, John, Brixham, Devon.
Preston Antiques Ltd., Antony, Stow-on-the-Wold, Glos.
Preston Book Co., Preston, Lancs.
Preston and Sons, John H., Harrogate, N. Yorks.
Preston, J.V., Rushden, Northants.
Preston, L., London, N.W.8. Alf. Ant. Mkt.
Preston, M. and J., Halifax, W. Yorks.
Preston, N. and I., Launceston, Cornwall.
Pretty Chairs, Portsmouth, Hants.
Price Antiques Ltd., Graham, Polegate, E. Sussex.
Price, G.D.A., Alderley Edge, Cheshire.
Price, G.J., Tunbridge Wells, Kent.
Price, Mrs. J., Wrexham, Clwyd, Wales.
Price, K., Sunninghill, Berks.
Price Less Antiques, Shipley, W. Yorks.
Price, M. & A. Harlington, Beds.
Price, Richard, London, W.11.
Prichard Antiques, K.H. and D.Y., Winchcombe, Glos.
Prickett, C.M., Birmingham, W. Mids. (Maxwells Book Shop).
Priddy, W.R., Portsmouth, Hants.
Pride Oriental Rugs, Eric, Cheltenham, Glos.
Prides of London, London, S.W.3.
Pridham, B., Newton Abbott, Devon. N. A. Ant. C.
Priest, A.C., Stow-on-the-Wold, Glos.
Priest Antiques, Michael, London, S.W.1.
Priest, Michael, Antiques and Fine Arts, Thame, Oxon.
Priest, M.G. and A.C., Thame, Oxon.
Priestly, M., London, W.8 (The Antique Home).
Priests Antiques, Stow-on-the-Wold, Glos.
Prime, M.V., Alford, Lincs.
Prime, M.V., Horncastle, Lincs.
Primrose Antiques, Tetbury, Glos.
Princedale Antiques, London, N.7.
Principia Arts and Sciences, Marlborough, Wilts.
Pringle Antiques, Fochabers, Morays., Scot.
Pringle, T., London, W.1. (The Richmond Gallery)
Prinny's Antique Gallery, Brighton, E. Sussex.
Print Room, The, Deal, Kent.
Print Room, The, London, W.C.1.
Printed Page, Winchester, Hants.
Prior, A., Birmingham, W. Mids. (Houghtons of Moseley).
Prior, R., Brighton, E. Sussex (The Sussex Commemorative Ware Centre).
Priors Hall Furniture Ltd., Coggeshall, Essex.
Priory Antiques, Bridlington, N. Humberside.
Priory Antiques, Exeter, Devon.
Priory Antiques, Godalming, Surrey.
Priory Antiques, London, E.C.1.
Priory Gallery, The, Bishops Cleeve, Glos.
Pritchard, E.L., Redhill, Surrey.
Pritchard, Mary, London, S.W.3 (Mr. Gill.) Ant. Ant. Mkt.
Private Room, Weedon, Northants.
Probsthain, Arthur, London, W.C.1.
Procter Antiques, David, St. Peter Port, Guernsey, C.I.
Procter, Susan, Auchterarder, Perths., Scot.
Proctor, A. and H., Windsor and Eton, Berks. (Windsor Antiques and Design).
Proctor, C.D. & H.M. Puddletown, Dorset.
Property Welfare, Leominster, Hereford and Worcs. L. Ant. Mkt.
Prospect Antiques, Crawley, Hants.
Prospect Antiques, Studley, Warks.
Prothero, P. and M., Neston, Cheshire.
Proudlock, Graham, Kircaldy, Fife, Scot.
Provincial Antique Silver Co., London, W.C.2. Lon. Silv. Vts. (E. and C.T. Koopman).
Pruskin Gallery, The, London, W.8.
Pryce and Brise Antiques, London, S.W.6.
Pryce, N., London, S.W.6.
Prydal, B.S., Kingston-upon-Thames, Surrey.
Prydal, B.S., London, W.2.
Pryor and Son, E., Liverpool, Merseyside.
Pugh, A., Arundel, W. Sussex.
Pugh Antiques, Bernie, Telford, Shrops.
Pugh Antiques, Christopher, Chester, Cheshire.
Pugh, E.B., Parkstone, Dorset.
Pugh, J. and J., Layer de la Haye, Essex.
Pugh, Robert, Bath, Avon.
Pugh's Farm Antiques, Monkton, Devon.
Pughs' Porcelains, Layer de la Haye, Essex.
Pullen, D. and D., Devizes, Wilts.
Pullen Jeweller, Richard, Lincoln, Lincs.
Pullen, Sylvia, Guildford, Surrey. Ant. C.

Pullen, Mrs. S.D.J., Guildford, Surrey. Ant. C.
Pulliblank, I., Cerne Abbas, Dorset.
Pulman, R.T., Swansea, W. Glam., Wales.
Pulton, J.J.A. and D.A., London, S.W.6 (Through the Looking Glass Ltd.).
Pulton, J.J.A. and D.A., London, W.8.
Pump House Antiques, The, Rickinghall, Suffolk
Purcell, A., London, N.7.
Purchase, S., London, S.W.3 (Hooper and Purchase).
Purdon, Richard, Ramsden, Oxon.
Purdy and Lloyd Antiques, Swansea, W. Glam., Wales. Antique Centre.
Purple Shop, London, S.W.3.
Purple Shop, The, London, S.W.3. Ant. Ant. Mkt.
Putnam, London, N.W.8. Alf. Ant. Mkt.
Putnam, R. and M., Farnham, Surrey.
Putnams, London, N.W.1.
Puttick, M.J., London, S.W.1. (Heraz).
Putting on the Ritz, Glasgow, Lanarks., Scot. Vict. Vill.
Puzzle House Antiques, London, W.1. G. Ant. Mkt.
Pydar Antiques and Gallery, Truro, Cornwall.
Pye, Mrs. N. Hull, N. Humberside.
Pye, Ross, London, N.W.3. Ham. Ant. Emp.
Pygott, I. and Mrs. J.M., Woodhall Spa, Lincs.
Pyke — Fine British Watercolours, Beverley, J., Totnes, Devon.
Pym Antiques, Craven Arms, Shrops.
Pym, A.J., Tutbury, Staffs.
Pym, J. and S., Craven Arms, Shrops.
Pyms Gallery, London, S.W.1.
Pyne, D.J., St. Albans, Herts.
Pyrah, Mr., London, S.W.3. Chen. Gall.
Pyramid, Brighton, E. Sussex.

Q

Quadrant Antiques, Edinburgh, Midloth., Scot.
Quaker Lodge Antiques, Finedon, Northants.
Quaradeghini, C. and A., London, W.2.
Quaradeghini, T., London, N.W.1. (Regent Antiques).
Quaritch Booksellers Ltd., Bernard, London, W.1.
Quarter Jack Antiques, Sturminster Newton, Dorset.
Quastel, D., London, N.W.3. Ham. Ant. Emp.
Quatrefoil, Fordingbridge, Hants.
Quay Antiques, Burnham-on-Sea, Essex.
Quay Gallery, The, Exeter, Devon.
Quayles Emporium, Septimus, Hawkhurst, Kent.
Queen Adelaide Gallery, Kempston, Beds.
Queen Anne House, Chesham, Bucks.
Queen of Hungary Antiques, Norwich, Norfolk.
Queens Parade Antiques Ltd., Bath, Avon.
Queens Road Antiques, Bristol, Avon.
Quentin, Paul, Manchester, Lancs.
Quest Antiques, London, W.13.
Quest Antiques, Nantymoel, Mid-Glam., Wales.
Questor, Woburn, Beds.
Quiet Street Antiques, Bath, Avon.
Quill Antiques, Bletchingley, Surrey.
Quill Antiques, Deal, Kent.
Quilt Room, The, Dorking, Surrey.
Quilter, Michael, Amersham, Bucks.
Quinn, B., Cardiff, S. Glam., Wales. (Kings Antiques)
Quinn Antiques, Barrie, London, S.W.6.
Quinn, B.J., London, S.W.6.
Quinn Galleries, Boston, Lincs.
Quinn Galleries, Oundle, Northants.
Quinn, N.J., London, W.4. (Stratton-Quinn Antiques Etc.).
Quinn, T.P., Boston, Lincs.
Quinn, T.P., Oundle, Northants.
Quinney's, Budleigh Salterton, Devon.
Quinney's Jewellery, Bristol, Avon.
Quinto of Cambridge, Cambridge, Cambs.
Quirke, Mrs. M.M., Seaton Ross, N. Humberside.
Quorn Pine, Quorn, Leics.

R

R.B.R. Group, London, W.1. G. Ant. Mkt.
R.J.D. Fine Arts, Stroud, Glos.
R.M.B. Art, London, N.W.8. Alf. Ant. Mkt.
Rabi Gallery Ltd., London, W.1.
Rabone, Mr. and Mrs. F., Weston, Staffs.
Rachel, Bristol, Avon. Clift. Ant. Mkt.
Rackham, D. and J., Rochester, Kent.
Rackham (Rochester Fine Arts), Rochester, Kent.
Rackham, Mrs. P.M., Lichfield, Staffs.
Radcliffe, J., Hastings, E. Sussex.
Radford Antiques, Alfriston, E. Sussex.
Radford, C.J., Church Stretton, Shrops.
Radford, Mrs. P.J., Alfriston, E. Sussex.
Radio Vintage, Hythe, Kent.
Radman, T. and B., Burford, Oxon.
Radnor House, Grampound, Cornwall.
Radosenska, Mrs. E., Bath, Avon (Bladud House Antiques.)
Rae Antiques, John, St. Helier, Jersey, C.I.
Rae Antiques, Lance and Marcus, St. Helier, Jersey, C.I.
Rae Antiques, Sheila, St. Helier, Jersey, C.I.
Raeymaekers, F. and T., London, W.1. (A.D.C. Heritage).
Raffaelli, G., London, S.W.3. Chen. Gall.
Rafferty, T., Ayr, Ayr., Scot.
Raffety Ltd., London, W.8.
Raffles Antiques, London, N.W.8.
Raglan Antiques, Raglan, Gwent, Wales.
Railton, J., Chatton, Northumbs.
Rainbow Antiques, Wolverhampton, W. Mids.
Raine Antiques, Harry, Consett, Durham.
Raine, J.P. and P.W., Boroughbridge, N. Yorks.
Rainsford, P.R., Bath, Avon.
Raleigh House, Shrewsbury, Shrops.
Ralstan, J., Preston, Lancs. N.W. Ant. C.
Ramm Antiques, Haywards Heath, W. Sussex.
Ramm, R.E., Haywards Heath, W. Sussex.

Ramsden, David and Karin, Manchester, Lancs. Royal Ex. S.C.
Ramsey Antiques, Alan, Thornaby, Cleveland.
Rand, D., Diss, Norfolk.
Randall, Lily, London, W.1. G. Mews.
Randalls Antiques, London, S.W.13.
Randerson, J., London, S.E.10.
Randolph, Hadleigh, Suffolk.
Randolph Antiques Ltd., David, London, S.W.10.
Rankin, Alan, Edinburgh, Midloth., Scot.
Rankin Coin Co. Ltd., George, London, E.2.
Rankin, Piers, London, N.1. The Mall.
Ransome, B.G., Wisbech, Cambs.
Ransome, J., Botesdale, Suffolk.
Rapley Antiques, John, Woburn, Beds. Wob. Ab. Ant. C.
Rapscallion Antiques Ltd., London, S.W.16.
Rare Art, London, W.C.2. Lon. Silv. Vts.
Rare Carpets Gallery, London, S.W.10.
Rare Chairs, Tunbridge Wells, Kent.
Rashleigh, Brasted, Kent.
Ratcliff, D.V. and W.D. Boyd, Kelvedon, Essex.
Ratcliff Ltd., G.T., Kelvedon, Essex.
Ratcliffe, A.M., Beccles, Suffolk.
Ratcliffe, J. and R., Waddington, Lincs.
Rathbone, Mrs. M., Upholland, Lancs.
Ratner, R., Dorking, Surrey.
Ratter Antiques, Chris, Edinburgh, Midloth., Scot.
Rattray, A.L., Rattray, Perths., Scot.
Rau, H., London, S.W.14.
Raven, K., M. and P., Amersham, Bucks.
Raw, W.I., Keswick, Cumbria.
Rawes, C., Whitley Bay, Tyne and Wear.
Rawlings-Gibson, G., Bath, Avon (Automobilia). Gt. West. Ant. C.
Rawnsley, E.G. and C.F., Petworth, W. Sussex. (Millhouse).
Rawson, Mrs. A., Harrogate, N. Yorks. (Rippon Bookshop).
Rawsthorne, Mrs. L.B., Bishops Stortford, Herts.
Rayment Antiques, Derek, Barton, Cheshire.
Rayment, D.J. and K.M., Barton, Cheshire.
Rayment, D.M. and P.J., Petworth, W. Sussex. (Petworth Antique Market).
Raymond, B., Long Melford, Suffolk.
Raynor, D., London, S.W.3. Ant. Ant. Mkt.
Rayner, Michael, Cheltenham, Glos.
Ray's, Bath, Avon. Gt. West. Ant. C.
Rea, C.J., Whitby, N. Yorks.
Rea Gallery, The, Kidderminster, Hereford and Worcs.
Read, A., Newark, Notts.
Read Antique Sciences, Mike, St. Ives, Cornwall.
Reading Emporium, Reading, Berks.
Real Macoy, Keighley, W. Yorks.
Reason, Mrs. C., Limpsfield, Surrey.
Rebecca Antiques, Clitheroe, Lancs.
Recollect Studios, Sayers Common, W. Sussex.
Recollections, Brighton, E. Sussex.
Rectory Bungalow Workshop, Elton, Notts.
Red House Antiques, Bideford, Devon.
Red House Antiques, Yoxford, Suffolk.
Red Lion Market (Portobello Antiques Market), London, W.11.
Red Rose Antiques, Montrose, Ang., Scot.
Red Shop, The, Wolverhampton, W. Mids.
Redcar Antiques, Redcar, Cleveland.
Redding, F.H., Southend-on-Sea, Essex.
Reddings Art and Antiques, Southend-on-Sea, Essex.
Re-Design, London, N.W.8. Alf. Ant. Mkt.
Redford, S. and R., Altrincham, Cheshire.
Redford, William, London, W.1.
Redhill Antiques Warehouse, Redhill, Surrey.
Redman, J., Much Wenlock, Shrops.
Redmile Ltd., Anthony, London, S.W.10. (Furniture Cave)
Redmile, J.W., Grantham, Lincs.
Redmile Antiques, William, Grantham, Lincs.
Redpath, E.D. and M.A., Wooler, Northumb.
Reece Gallery, The Gordon, Knaresborough, N. Yorks.
Reed, Mrs. A., Wallingford, Oxon.
Reed, G.M., Epsom, Surrey.
Reed, G.M., Kingston-upon-Thames, Surrey.
Rees, T.G., Bristol, Avon. (The Vintage Wireless Co.)
Reeve at Quinneys of Warwick, James, Warwick, Warks.
Reeves, Paul, London, W.8.
Reeves, R.J. and S.E., Cullompton, Devon.
Reeves Bookseller Ltd., William, London, S.W.16.
Reference Works, Swanage, Dorset.
Reflections, Knaresborough, N. Yorks.
Regan, Angela, London, N.W.8. Alf. Ant. Mkt.
Regency Fine Art, Harrogate, N. Yorks.
Regency House, Framlingham, Suffolk.
Regency House Antiques, Whitchurch, Hants.
Regent Antiques, London, N.W.1.
Regent Antiques, Painswick, Glos.
Regent House, Northampton, Northants.
Regent House Antiques, New Mills, Derbys.
Regent House Antiques, Newtown, Cheshire.
Reid, A., London, W.1 (Lefevre Gallery).
Reid, J.C. and D.C., Edinburgh, Midloth., Scot. (Whytock and Reid).
Reid, M., Harrogate, N. Yorks. (Harrogate Fine Arts).
Reid, P., Banchory, Kincard, Scot.
Reigate Galleries Ltd., Reigate, Surrey.
Reilly, K., London, S.W.3. Ant. Ant. Mkt.
Reily-Collins, E.M. and S.A., Dorchester-on-Thames, Oxon.
Reindeer Antiques Ltd., Potterspury, Northants.
Reindeer Antiques (Reindeer International Ltd.), London, W.8.
Reiss Fine Art, Stephen, Norwich, Norfolk.
Reiss Fine Art Ltd., Stephen, Norwich, Norfolk.
Relcy Antiques, London, S.E.10.
Relf Antiques, Ian, Tunbridge Wells, Kent.
Relic Antiques at Brillscote Farm, Malmesbury, Wilts.
Relic Antiques Trade Warehouse, London, N.W.1.
Relics-Pine Furniture, Bristol, Avon.

Relics, Newport, I. of. Wight.
Relics, Ross-on-Wye, Hereford and Worcs.
Relics, Witney, Oxon.
Relics Antiques, Southampton, Hants.
Relph, S., Bath, Avon. (Off the Rails). Gt. West. Ant. C.
Remember When, London, W.1. G. Mews.
Remember When Ltd., London, S.W.13.
Remington, Reg and Philip, London, W.C.2.
Renaissance, Solihull, W. Mids.
Renaissance Antiques, Cowbridge, S. Glam., Wales.
Renaissance Antiques, Tynemouth, Tyne and Wear.
Rendall Antiques, Lesley, London, S.W.6.
Rendezvous Gallery, The, Aberdeen, Aberd., Scot.
Rendlesham Antiques Ltd., London, S.W.10.
Rendlesham, Lord, London, S.W.10.
Rennie, Paul and Karen, Folkestone, Kent.
Repetto-Wright, R., Aslockton, Notts.
Resner, S. and G.R., Brighton, E. Sussex.
Resners', Brighton, E. Sussex.
Restall Brown and Clennell Ltd., Cosgrove, Northants.
Retro, Brighton, E. Sussex.
Retro Products, Lye, W. Mids.
Retrospect Antiques, Combe Martin, Devon.
Reubens, London, S.E.23.
Reubens, R.E., London, S.E.23.
Revell Antiques, Sheila, Hartley Wintney, Hants.
Revell, Miss, Newton Abbot, Devon, N. A. Ant. C.
Revival, Betws Garmon, Gwynedd, Wales.
Revival Antiques and Collectables, Carlisle, Cumbria. C Ant. and Craft C.
Revival Beds, Haydon Bridge, Northumbs.
Revival Pine Stripping, Ormskirk, Lancs.
Rex Antiques, London, W.11.
Reynold, A., London, W.C.2.
Reynolds, Mr., Aberdeen, Aberd., Scot.
Reynolds, B.A.S., Easingwold, N. Yorks.
Reynolds, C., London, N.W.8. Alf. Ant. Mkt.
Reynolds, Mrs. C., Tonge, Leics.
Reynolds, C.H., Pickering, N. Yorks.
Reynolds, Peter, London, S.W.6.
Rezai Persian Carpets, A., London, W.11.
Rhodes Antiques, Colin, Plymouth, Devon.
Rhodes Antiques, Chris, Warwick, Warks.
Rhodes, Isobel, Hadleigh, Suffolk.
Rhodes, Mrs. J., London, S.W.6.
Rhodes, Patricia and Simon Thorpe, London, S.W.3. Chen. Gall.
Rhudle Mill, Kilmichael Glassary, Argyll, Scot.
Ribbons, James, Bruton, Somerset.
Rice, R.J., Great Malvern, Hereford and Worcs.
Rich Designs, Stratford-upon-Avon, Warks.
Rich, S., London, S.W.1. (Peter Tillou Works of Art).
Richards, Mrs., Newton Abbot, Devon, N.A. Ant. C.
Richards, D., Penzance, Cornwall.
Richards and Sons, David, London, W.1.
Richards Furniture Sales, Sheffield, S. Yorks.
Richards, G., Swansea, W. Glam., Wales. Ant. C.
Richards and Son Antiques, G.E., Hereford, Hereford and Worcs.
Richards and Son, H.J., Burton-on-Trent, Staffs.
Richards, J., London, S.W.13.
Richards, L., London, W.11 (Mercury Antiques).
Richards, M., H. and E., London, W.1.
Richards, Paul, London, S.W.6.
Richards, P.H., Bournemouth, Dorset. (The Green Room)
Richards, S., Rhosneigr, Gwynedd, Wales.
Richards, S. and S. Willis, London, S.W.3. Chen. Gall.
Richards, W.J., London, W.11. (St. John's Collection Ltd.).
Richardson, B., Bristol, Avon (Quinney's).
Richardson, C., London, S.W.6. (Richardson and Kailas)
Richardson Antiques, D., Keighley, W. Yorks.
Richardson, J., Collingwood, Notts.
Richardson and Kailas, Icons, London, S.W.6.
Richardson Antiques, Keith, Ilkley, W. Yorks.
Richardson, M., Westerham, Kent.
Richardson, Pat, London, W.1. G. Mews.
Richardson, Ronald, Darlington, Durham.
Richardson, S. and E., Blewbury, Oxon.
Richardson, W.L. and M.G., Guisborough, Cleveland.
Riches, Pulloxhill, Beds.
Riches, L., Hythe, Kent.
Richmond Antiques, Londonderry, Co. Londonderry, N. Ireland.
Richmond Galleries, Chester, Cheshire.
Richmond Gallery, The, London, W.1.
Richmond, Margaret, Wallingford, Oxon. L. Arc.
Richmond Traders, Richmond, Surrey.
Rickett and Co. Antiques, Shepperton, Surrey.
Ridgewell Crafts and Antiques, Ridgewell, Essex.
Ridings, I., Holmfirth, W. Yorks.
Ridler, P.W., Pershore, Hereford and Worcs.
Ridout, S.J. and S.Y., Hindhead, Surrey.
Ridsdill, M., Modbury, Devon.
Ries, M.A. and Mrs. I.T.H., Boston Spa, W. Yorks.
Ries, N.C., Harrogate, N.Yorks. (London House Oriental Rugs and Carpets)
Rievaulx Books, Helmsley, N. Yorks.
Rigg, Mrs. S.J., Manchester, Lancs.
Right Angle, Brackley, Northants.
Riley Antiques, London, N.1. The Mall.
Riley, G., London, N.1. The Mall.
Riley, Mrs. G.M., London, S.W.3. Ant. Ant. Mkt.
Riley, J.M. Chichester, W. Sussex.
Riley, N., Bolton, Lancs.
Riley, P. and S., Broadway, Hereford and Worcs.
Rimes, R., Wansford, Cambs.
Rimington, D. and G.G., Margate, Kent.
Ring Road Antiques, Wolverhampton, W. Mids.

Ringles Cross Antiques, Uckfield, E. Sussex.
Ringrose, Mr. and Mrs. D., Crawley, W. Sussex.
Ripley Antiques, Ripley, Surrey.
Rippingale, S. and R., London, S.W.6 (Old Pine).
Rippon Bookshop, Harrogate, N. Yorks.
Risby Barn, The, Risby, Suffolk.
Risdale, Mrs. M., Bristol, Avon. Clift. Ant. Mkt.
Risky Business, London, N.W.8.
Ritchie, A.M.F. and Mrs., Teignmouth, Devon.
Ritchie, J., Weymouth, Dorset.
Ritchie, S., Kendal, Cumbria.
Ritchie, V., Kendal, Cumbria.
Ritzy, London, N.1. The Mall.
Rivers, John D., Cirencester, Glos.
Riverside Antiques, Bideford, Devon.
Riverside Antiques, Hungerford, Berks.
Rivett, Mrs. S., Fakenham, Norfolk.
Rix, H., London, S.W.11.
Robbies Antiques, Wallasey, Merseyside.
Robbins, Guy, London, W.11. G. Port. (Pat Bedford).
Roberts, Newton Abbot, Devon. N.A. Ant. C.
Roberts, Mrs. A., Cowbridge, S. Glam., Wales.
Roberts Antiques, Ann, Ampthill, Beds.
Roberts, Bobby, Swansea, W. Glam., Wales. Ant. C.
Roberts, C., Bath, Avon. (No.12 Queen St.)
Roberts, D., Nantwich, Cheshire.
Roberts Antiques, David, Leominster, Hereford and Worcs.
Roberts Fine Antique Clocks, Derek, Tonbridge, Kent.
Roberts, Gareth, London, N.W.8. Alf. Ant. Mkt.
Roberts, I.W. and I.E., Bolton, Lancs.
Roberts, J., Berwick-on-Tweed, Northumbs.
Roberts Bookshop, John, Bristol, Avon.
Roberts, J. and B., Leicester, Leics.
Roberts, J. and B., Market Bosworth, Leics.
Roberts, J.T., Bristol, Avon (John Roberts).
Roberts Antiques, Peter, Moreton-in-Marsh, Glos.
Roberts, Mrs. R., Blaenau Ffestiniog, Gwynedd, Wales.
Roberts, Mr. and Mrs. S.A., Beaulieu, Hants.
Roberts, T., Bletchingley, Surrey.
Roberts, T.J., Uppingham, Leics.
Robertson, A.F., Lingfield, Surrey.
Robertson and Cox Antiques, Perth, Perths., Scot.
Robertson, D.W., Newcastle-upon-Tyne, Tyne and Wear. (Owen's Jewellers).
Robertson, E., Woburn, Beds. Wob. Ab. Ant. C.
Robertson, Ian A., Alnwick, Northumbs.
Robertson, J., Reigate, Surrey.
Robertson Antiques, Leon, Penryn, Cornwall.
Robertson, P.W., Hinckley, Leics.
Robertson, R.D.A., London, S.W.6 (David Alexander Antiques).
Robinson, London, W.1. G.M. Ant. Mkt.
Robinson, A., Bishops Waltham, Hants.
Robinson, Mrs. A., Monyash, Derbys.
Robinson, C., London, N.W.8. Alf. Ant. Mkt.
Robinson, D.A., London, N.W.8.
Robinson, D. and M., Chipping Norton, Oxon.
Robinson, E.J.H. Croydon, Surrey.
Robinson, F., Bolton-by-Bowland, Lancs.
Robinson, F., Colwyn Bay, Clwyd, Wales.
Robinson, G., London, N.W.8.
Robinson, Mrs. G., Ringwood, Hants.
Robinson Antiques, Gerald, London, W.11. (Colin Smith).
Robinson Interiors and Antiques, Glen, Ringwood, Hants.
Robinson, Jonathan, London, W.1. G. Mews.
Robinson, Jo, London, N.W.8. Alf. Ant. Mkt.
Robinson Antiques, John, Wigan, Lancs.
Robinson, L., Sowerby Bridge, W. Yorks.
Robinson, M., Glasgow, Lanarks., Scot. (Virginia Antique Galleries)
Robinson, M.L.G., Welshpool, Powys, Wales.
Robinson, Peter, Heacham, Norfolk.
Robinson, R. and N., Welshpool, Powys, Wales.
Robinson, Mrs. S., Brighton, E. Sussex.
Robinson, T.E., Bath, Avon.
Robinson (Newcastle) Ltd., W., Newcastle-upon-Tyne, Tyne and Wear.
Robinson's Bookshop Ltd., Brighton, E. Sussex.
Robson Antiques, Walford, Hereford and Worcs.
Robson, J., Walford, Hereford and Worcs.
Roby Antiques, John, Wigan, Lancs.
Rochefort Antiques Gallery, London, N.21.
Rochester Antiques and Flea Market, Rochester, Kent.
Rochford, Michael, Hertford, Herts.
Rock Angus Antiques, Portaferry, Co. Down, Ireland.
Rocking Chair Antiques, Cadole, Clwyd, Wales.
Rocking Chair Antiques, Preston, Lancs. N.W. Ant. C.
Rocking Chair Antiques, The, Warrington, Cheshire.
Rocking Horse Pine, Torquay, Devon.
Rockingham Road Antiques, Kettering, Northants.
Rockman, A.C., London, N.W.8. Alf. Ant. Mkt.
Rockman, B.M., London, N.W.8. Alf. Ant. Mkt.
Rococo Antiques and Interiors, Weedon, Northants.
Rococo Antiques, Worthing, W. Sussex.
Rodber, J., Bridport, Dorset.
Roderick Antique Clocks, London, W.8.
Rodgers, Arthur and Ann, Ruddington, Notts.
Rodney Arthur Classics, Brighton, E. Sussex.
Rod's Antiques, London, W.11.
Rodwell Antiques and Reproductions, Potters Bar, Herts.
Rodwell, M.S., Potters Bar, Herts.
Roe Antiques, Guy, Woburn, Beds. Wob. Ab. Ant. C.

Roe, Mr. and Mrs. J., Islip, Northants.
Roe, Mr. and Mrs. J., Thrapston, Northants.
Roe Antiques, J., Islip, Northants.
Roe Antiques, J., Thrapston, Northants.
Roe, P. and J., Menston, W. Yorks.
Roe, P.S., London, S.W.1 (Trove).
Roe, T., Whitby, N. Yorks.
Roffe, V., London, W.1 (Vigo-Sternberg Galleries).
Roger, J., London, W.8.
Roger (Antiques) Ltd., J., London, W.8.
Rogers Antique Gallery, London, W.11.
Rogers Antiques and Rogers Antique Interiors, Cheam, Surrey.
Rogers, A.W.D., Leeds, W. Yorks. (Andrew's Antique Shop).
Rogers, C. and M., Cheam, Surrey.
Rogers Oriental Rugs, Clive, Brighton, E. Sussex.
Rogers, D. and G., Glastonbury, Somerset.
Rogers de Rin, London, S.W.3.
Rogers, Eva, Kempston, Beds.
Rogers, N.G., Radlett, Herts.
Rogers Turner Books Ltd., London, S.E.10.
Rogerson, P.R., Bridlington, N. Humberside.
Rogerson, T.H. and B.A., Whitegate, Cheshire.
Roland-Price, H.A. and J., Bradford-on-Avon, Wilts.
Rolfe, B., Chichester, W. Sussex.
Rolleston, B.T.W., London, W.8 (The Antique Home).
Romain and Sons, A.J., Wilton, Wilts.
Romantiques, Skegness, Lincs.
Romsey Medal and Collectors Centre, Romsey, Hants.
Ronay, Edina, London, S.W.3. Ant. Ant. Mkt.
Roofe Antiques, Mary, Winchester, Hants.
Roofe, R. and M., Winchester, Hants.
Rooke, G. and A. Dyson, Tunbridge Wells, Kent.
Rookery Farm Antiques, London, N.1.
Ropers Hill Antiques, Staunton Harold, Leics.
Rosa Antiques, London, W.11. Stouts Ants. Arc.
Rose Antiques, Ashbourne, Derbys.
Rose, B., London, N.W.1. (Galerie 1900).
Rose, Christopher, Stow-on-the-Wold, Glos. C. Ant. C.
Rose Cottage Antiques, Cambridge, Cambs.
Rose, Dorothy, London, S.W.15.
Rose, D.H. and Mrs. C., Carlton-on-Trent, Notts.
Rose, Mrs. E., London, E.12.
Rose Farm Furniture Ltd., Addingham, W. Yorks.
Rose Fine Art and Antiques, Ripon, N. Yorks.
Rose Ltd., Geoffrey, London, S.W.1.
Rose, K.D., Tonypandy, Mid-Glam., Wales.
Rose Antiques Centre, Marilyn, Newport, I. of Wight.
Rose Mount Antiques, Birkenhead, Merseyside.
Rose, R.E., London, S.E.9.
Rose and Co., R.L., Glasgow, Lanarks., Scot.
Rose, Mr. and Mrs. S., Ripon, N. Yorks.
Roseby, H., M. and J., Bladon, Oxon.
Rosemary Antiques and Paper Moon Books, Stratford-upon-Avon, Warks.
Rosemary and Time, Thame, Oxon.
Rosenberg, C., Heswall, Merseyside.
Rosenberg, H., London, N.1 (Hart and Rosenberg).
Rosenthal Ltd., A., Oxford, Oxon.
Rose's the Jewellers, Leeds, W. Yorks.
Rosina's, Falmouth, Cornwall.
Ross, Alvin, London, N.W.8. Alf. Ant. Mkt.
Ross Antiques, London, W.1. B. St. Silv. Galls.
Ross Antiques, Manchester, Lancs.
Ross, A.P., Coventry, W. Mids.
Ross, B., Durgates, E. Sussex.
Ross, B.J., Manchester, Lancs.
Ross, Mrs. C., Bushmills, Co. Antrim, N. Ireland.
Ross, D. and T., Wooler, Northumb.
Ross, H., Bisley, Glos.
Ross Antiques and Decoration, Jane, Sevenoaks, Kent.
Ross, J.D., Edinburgh, Midloth., Scot. (Stockbridge Antiques and Fine Art).
Ross, L.J., Liverpool, Merseyside (Liverpool Coin and Medal Co.).
Ross Antiques, Marcus, London, N.1.
Ross Old Book and Print Shop, Ross-on-Wye, Hereford and Worcs.
Ross, P.G., Edinburgh, Midloth., Scot. (Fine Art Gallery).
Ross, T.C.A. and D.A.A., London, S.W.1. (Addison-Ross Gallery).
Rosser-Rees, S., Bath, Avon. (Ancestors). Gt. West. Ant. C.
Rosson, J., London, E.C.1.
Rota Ltd., Bertram, London, W.C.2.
Rotchell, P., Godalming, Surrey.
Rote, R. and D., London, N.1 (Chancery Antiques Ltd.).
Rothera, D., London, N.1 (Antique Trader).
Rotherford, Rosamund, Glasgow, Lanarks. Scot. Vict. Vill.
Rothman, London, S.W.1.
Rothman, Joel, London, S.W.3. Ant. Ant. Mkt.
Rothman, J.A.F. and S.P.J., London, S.W.1.
Rothschild, Miranda, London, W.11. G. Port.
Rothwell, Mrs. C., Dulverton, Somerset.
Rothwell, Mrs. C., Taunton, Somerset.
Rothwell and Dunworth, Dulverton, Somerset.
Rothwell, D., Eastbourne, E. Sussex.
Rothwell and Dunworth, Taunton, Somerset.
Round, S., Brighton, E. Sussex. (Leoframes).
Roundfield House Antiques Ltd., London, W.8.
Rout, Mrs. D., London, W.4.
Rovati, P., London, W.1. (Art-Antica). B. St. Ant. C.
Rowan Antiques, Richmond, Surrey.
Rowan Antiques, Totnes, Devon.
Rowan, Mrs. Michele, London, S.W.3. Ant. Ant. Mkt.

Rowe, D., Chichester, W. Sussex.
Rowe, J., Great Bookham, Surrey.
Rowe, J.H. and J., London, S.W.6 (Bookham Galleries.)
Rowe and Lorenzo, London, N.W.8. Alf. Ant. Mkt.
Rowell of Oxford Ltd., Oxford, Oxon.
Rowlands, Mrs. M., London, S.W.14.
Rowlay, J., Ripon, N. Yorks.
Rowles, C. and J., Cardiff, S. Glam., Wales.
Rowlett, A.H., Lincoln, Lincs.
Rowlett, Mrs. R.B., Brasted, Kent.
Rowlett's of Lincoln, Lincoln, Lincs.
Rowley, J., Stoke-on-Trent, Staffs.
Royal Exchange Art Gallery, London, E.C.3.
Royal Exchange Shopping Centre, Manchester, Lancs.
Royal Mile Curios, Edinburgh, Midloth., Scot.
Royal Victoria Arcade, Ryde, I. of Wight.
Royall Antiques, E. and C., Medbourne, Leics.
Royall Antiques, E. and C., Uppingham, Leics.
Royle, Mrs. M., Beaconsfield, Bucks.
Royston Antiques, Royston, Herts.
Rubin, A. and L., London, S.W.3 (Pelham Galleries).
Rubenstein Fine Art, Barbara, Boxhill, Surrey.
Rubinstein, S.G., Manchester, Lancs. (Authentiques).
Rudge Antics, Tetbury, Glos.
Rudge, T. and P., Tetbury, Glos.
Ruff, J., Newton Abbot, Devon. N. A. Ant. C.
Ruffell, J., Portsmouth, Hants.
Rugby Antiques Centre, Rugby, Warks.
Rugeley Antique Centre, Brereton, Staffs.
Ruglen, L., Balfron, Stirls., Scot.
Ruglen, L., Buchlyvie, Stirls., Scot.
Rumble, R.J. and V., Highbridge, Somerset.
Rumble Antiques, Simon and Penny, Chittering, Cambs.
Rumens, Olivia, Ludlow, Shrops.
Rumford, A., Worcester, Hereford and Worcs.
Rumours Decorative Arts, London, N.1.
Rundells Antiques, Harlow, Essex.
Rundle, A., Bedford, Beds.
Rundle, J., New Bolingbroke, Lincs.
Rupert's, London, W.13.
Rush, R.D., London, W.1. (Aqua Libra).
Rush, R.D., London, W.1. (Lady Newborough).
Rushton, E. and B., Pulford, Cheshire.
Ruskin, L.M.A., Bristol, Avon.
Ruskins, Bristol, Avon.
Russell, C., London, W.1.
Russell, Miss C.C., Lewes, E. Sussex.
Russell and Son Antiques, Frank, Glasgow, Lanarks., Scot.
Russell, Leonard, Newhaven, E. Sussex.
Russell, M. and J., Yazor, Hereford and Worcs.
Russell, P., Tunbridge Wells, Kent.
Russell, R., Witney, Oxon.
Russell Rare Books, London, W.1.
Rust Antiques, Benjamin, Cromer, Norfolk.
Rust, Mr. and Mrs. R.S., Kesgrave, Suffolk.
Rutherford and Son, J.T., Sandgate, Kent.
Rutherford Ltd., Stella, Darlington, Durham.
Ruthven, G.L., Ryde, I. of Wight.
Rutland Antiques, Brighton, E. Sussex.
Rutland Gallery, London, W.1.
Rutter Antiques, Jon and Kate, Walsall, W. Mids.
Rutter, S. and S., Walsall, W. Mids.
Ryan, Mrs. S., Chertsey, Surrey.
Ryan-Wood Antiques, Liverpool, Merseyside.
Ryce, L.R., Winkleigh, Devon.
Rye Antiques, Rye, E. Sussex.
Ryecroft Antiques, Amersham, Bucks.
Ryland, B.R., Henley-on-Thames, Oxon.
Rynsard, R., Woburn, Beds. Wob. Ab. Ant. C.
Rytham Antiques, Seaton Ross, N. Humberside.

S

S.A.G. Art Galleries, London, S.W.18.
S.D.P., London, W.1. G. Ant. Mkt.
S. and G. Antiques, London, W.11.
S. and G. Antiques, London, S.W.3. Ant. Ant. Mkt.
S. and H. Antiques, London, N.W.8.
S.O.S. Militaria, Stourbridge, W. Mids.
SPCK Bookshops, Winchester, Hants.
SPV Antiques, London, N.W.8. Alf. Ant. Mkt.
S.R. Furnishing and Antiques, Birmingham, W. Mids.
S.W. Antiques, Pershore, Hereford and Worcs.
Saadat, R. Tadj, London, W.1 (Armitage).
Saalmans, J.A. and K.M., Grasmere, Cumbria.
Saatcioglu, Yakup, London, N.W.8. Alf. Ant. Mkt.
Sabin Galleries Ltd., London, W.8.
Sabin, S.F., E.P. and P.G., London, W.8.
Sabin and Vanderkar (Fine Paintings) Ltd. and G.B. Vanderkar, London, S.W.1.
Sabine Antiques, C.E., Stock, Essex.
Sabine, T.H., Ilminster, Somerset.
Sackin, L., London, W.1. (Schwartz Sackin and Co. Ltd.).
Saddle Room Antiques, The, Cookstown, Co. Tyrone, N. Ireland.
Sadi and Nasser, London, W.1. B. St. Ant C.
Sadler-Chapman, M., Clare, Suffolk.
Sagar, A.M., Harrogate, N. Yorks. (Singing Bird Antiques).
Sage Antiques and Interiors, Ripley, Surrey.
Sage, H. and C., Ripley, Surrey.
Sainsbury, Barry, London, S.W.1.
Sainsbury, Barry M., Wincanton, Somerset.
Sainsbury, M., Bath, Avon.
Sainsburys of Bournemouth Ltd., Bournemouth, Dorset.
St. Albans Antique Market, St. Albans, Herts.
St. Andrews Fine Art, St. Andrews, Scotland.

St. Andrew's Market, Bournemouth, Dorset.
St. Breock Gallery, Stow-on-the-Wold, Glos.
St. Breock Gallery, Wadebridge, Cornwall.
St. George's Antiques, Perranporth, Cornwall.
St. George's Antiques, Stamford, Lincs.
St. Georges Antiques, Worcester, Hereford and Worcs.
Saint George's Gallery Books Ltd., London, S.W.1.
St. Helier Galleries Ltd., St. Helier, Jersey, C.I.
St. James Antiques, Great Malvern, Hereford and Worcs.
St. James Antiques, Manchester, Lancs.
St. James Art Group, The, London, S.W.1.
St. James's Gallery Ltd., St. Peter Port, Guernsey, C.I.
St. James House Antiques, Boroughbridge, N. Yorks.
St. John Antiques, York, N. Yorks.
St. John Street Gallery, Salisbury, Wilts.
St. John's Collection Ltd., London, W.11.
St. Jude's Antiques, London, W.8.
St. Leonards Antiques, Ludlow, Shrops.
St. Mary's Antiques, Long Melford, Suffolk.
St. Mary's Galleries, Stamford, Lincs.
St. Michael at Plea Antiques Centre, Norwich, Norfolk.
St. Nicholas Galleries Ltd. (Antiques and Jewellery), Carlisle, Cumbria.
St. Nicholas Galleries (Antiques) Ltd., Carlisle, Cumbria.
St. Ouen Antiques, Puckeridge, Herts.
St. Pancras Antiques, Chichester, W. Sussex.
St. Peter's Fine Art Gallery Ltd., Chester, Cheshire.
St. Peters Organ Works, London, E.2.
Sakhai, E., London, W.1 (Essie Carpets).
Salisbury Clock Shop, Salisury, Wilts.
Salisbury, J. and J.C., Edenfield, Lancs.
Salisbury, R.D.N., M.E. and J.W., Sidmouth, Devon.
Salmagundi, Maidstone, Kent.
Salmon, D., London, S.W.5.
Salmon, L., Kingsley, Staffs.
Salt Antiques, N.P. and A., Sheffield, S. Yorks.
Salter Antiques, F.D., Clare, Suffolk.
Salter, S., London, E.4.
Saltgate Antiques, Beccles, Suffolk.
Salveson, Dick, London, N.W.8. Alf. Ant. Mkt.
Samarkand Galleries, Stow-on-the-Wold, Glos.
Sambourne House Antiques, Minety, Wilts.
Samic, London, N.W.8. Alf. Ant. Mkt.
Samiramis Ltd.,London, W.1. G. Mews.
Samlesbury Hall, Samlesbury, Lancs.
Samlesbury Hall Trust, Samlesbury, Lancs.
Samne, H., London, W.C.2 (Anchor Antiques Ltd.)
Samovar Antiques, Hythe, Kent.
Sampson, Anthony, Moreton-in-Marsh, Glos.
Sampson Antiques Ltd. inc. Tobias Jellinek Antiques, Alistair, London, S.W.3.
Sampson, A.H., London, S.W.3.
Samuel, M., Knighton, Powys, Wales.
Samuel, R., Poole, Dorset.
Samuel, W.J., Newport, Gwent, Wales.
Samuels and Sons Ltd., C., Exeter, Devon.
Samuels Spencers Antiques and Decorative Arts Emporium, Winchester, Hants.
San Domenico Stringed Instruments, Cardiff, S. Glam., Wales.
San Fairy Anne, London, E.14.
Sanaiy Carpets, London, S.W.1.
Sanaiy, H., London, S.W.1.
Sanchez-Martin, Mrs. A.M., London, W.1. (Xelana Antiques). B. St. Ant. C.
Sandberg Antiques, Patrick, London, W.8.
Sandberg, P.C.F., London, W.8.
Sandell, M.J., Carmarthen, Dyfed, Wales.
Sanders of Oxford Ltd., Oxford, Oxon.
Sanders and Sons, Robin, London, S.W.6.
Sanders Penzance Gallery and Antiques, Tony, Penzance, Cornwall.
Sandgate Antiques Centre, Sandgate, Kent.
Sandhill Barn Antiques (Pine and Country), Washington, W. Sussex.
Sandringham Antiques, Hull, N. Humberside.
Sands, J. and M.M., Stow-on-the-Wold, Glos.
Sands, R., London, W.1. (M. and R. Glendale)
Sandy's Antiques, Bournemouth, Dorset.
Sansean, C., Warboys, Cambs.
Sansom, K.W., Leicester, Leics.
Santos, A.V., London, W.8.
Saracen's Lantern, The, Canterbury, Kent.
Saranno, Horsham, W. Sussex.
Saratoga Trunk, Glasgow, Lanarks., Scot.
Sargeant, A.W. and K.M., Stansted, Essex.
Sargeant, Denys, Westerham, Kent.
Sarsby and Michael Pickering Fine Art, Roger, Newark, Notts.
Sarti Antiques Ltd., G., London, W.11.
Sassower, G., London, N.1. The Mall.
Satchell, S., Kendal, Cumbria.
Satoe, London, W.1. G. Ant. Mkt.
Satterthwaite, M., Blackburn, Lancs.
Satterthwaite, M., Manchester, Lancs. (Alpha Antiques).
Sattin Ltd., Gerald, London, S.W.1.
Sattin, G. and M., London, S.W.1.
Saturdays Antiques, Henley-on-Thames, Oxon.
Saunders Antiques, Charles, London, S.W.3.
Saunders, D., T. and P., Leominster, Hereford and Worcs.
Saunders, E.A. and J.M., Weedon, Northants.
Saunders, E.S. and N., Weedon, Northants.
Saunders, J. and L., Dover, Kent.
Saunders, L. and S., Honiton, Devon.
Saunders, M., Wolverhampton, W. Mids.
Saunders, N., Towcester, Northants.
Saunders, Ric, London, W.11. Stouts Arc.
Saunders, R., Weybridge, Surrey.
Saunders, R.A., Bristol, Avon.
Saunderson Antiques, Elaine, Dorking, Surrey.
Saunderson, Mrs. E.C., Dorking, Surrey.
Sautter, M. and M., Lewes, E. Sussex.
Sautter Pine Furniture, Mary, Lewes, E. Sussex.

Savage, B., Wolverhampton, W. Mids.
Savage, M.J., Northampton, Northants.
Savage and Son, R.S.J., Northampton, Northants.
Savage Antiques, Sam, Ticknall, Derbys.
Savage, S. and M., Ticknall, Derbys.
Savile, Hon. C.A. and Mrs., London, S.W.3. (The Map House).
Savile, D.M., London, S.W.6.
Savile Pine, London, S.W.6.
Savill, P.M., Nantwich, Cheshire.
Saville Antiques, Devizes, Wilts.
Saville, G.J., Hebden Bridge, W. Yorks.
Saville House plc, Bath, Avon.
Sawers, Robert G., London, W.1.
Sawyer, Chas. J., London, W.1. (E. Joseph).
Saxon, J.R. and A., South Lopham, Norfolk.
Saxton House Gallery, Chipping Campden, Glos.
Sayer, Mrs. J., Dorking, Surrey.
Sayers, C. and D., Tetbury, Glos.
Saywell Ltd. (The Oxford Stamp Shop), A.J., Oxford, Oxon.
Saywell, I.H. and H.J., Oxford, Oxon.
Scales, R. and S., London, S.E.1.
Scallywag, Beckenham, Kent.
Scallywag, London, S.W.9.
Scalpay Securities Ltd., Colchester, Essex.
Scantlebury, H. and M., Hatfield Heath, Essex.
Scar Top Antiques incorporating T.J. Timber Ltd., Keighley, W. Yorks.
Scaramanga Antiques, Anthony, Witney, Oxon.
Scarisbrick and Bate Ltd., London, W.1.
Scarthoe Antiques, Scarthoe, S. Humberside.
Scattergood, C. and R., Burton-on-Trent, Staffs.
Schanzer, R.P., London, N.W.1 (This and That Furniture).
Schell, Christine, London, S.W.3.
Schiff, London, W.1. (P. Hamilton), G. Mews.
Schlesinger, A.R., Leicester, Leics.
Schloss, E., Edgware, Middx.
Schneider, Mrs. P., Abingdon, Oxon.
Schofield, G.M., St. Leonards-on-Sea, E. Sussex.
Schofield, H. and Mrs. A., Brighton, E. Sussex. (Leoframes).
Schofield, R.M., Huddersfield, W. Yorks.
Scholz, K.V., Eastbourne, E. Sussex.
School House Antiques, Chipping Campden, Glos.
School House Antiques, Welshpool, Powys, Wales.
Schooling, S.J. and V.E., Duns, Scot.
Schotten, M., Burford, Oxon.
Schrager, G.R. and H.J., London, W.11. (Schredds of Portobello).
Schredds of Portobello, London, W.11.
Schroder Ltd., Timothy, London, S.W.1.
Schuster Gallery, The, London, W.1.
Schuster, Thomas E., London, W.1.
Schwager, R.O. and E.M., Stow-on-the-Wold, Glos.
Schwartz, N., London, W.5.
Schwartz Sackin and Co. Ltd., London, W.1.
Schwier, D.W., Wimborne Minster, Dorset.
Scientific Anglian (Bookshop), The, Norwich, Norfolk.
Scobie, W.D.L., Wallasey, Merseyside.
Scola, Patrick, London, N.W.8. Alf. Ant. Mkt.
Scope Antiques, London, N.W.6.
Scorpio Antiques, London, N.W.3. Ham. Ant. Emp.
Scot Hay House Antiques, Woore, Shrops.
Scott Antiques, Bath, Avon.
Scott, A.F.D., Selkirk, Selkirks., Scot.
Scott, Mrs. D.M., Westerham, Kent.
Scott House Antiques, West Malling, Kent.
Scott, Miss J., London, S.W.3. Ant. Ant. Mkt.
Scott, James, Edinburgh, Midloth., Scot.
Scott, Mrs. J., Hodnet, Shrops.
Scott, J.D., West Harptree, Avon.
Scott, P., Northampton, Northants.
Scott Antiques, Richard, Holt, Norfolk.
Scott, R.G., Margate, Kent.
Scott and Varey, Halifax, W. Yorks.
Scott, W.B., Halifax, W. Yorks.
Scott, Y., Berwick-on-Tweed, Northumbs.
Scott-Cooper Ltd., Cheltenham, Glos.
Scott-Masson, Anne-Marie, Plymouth, Devon.
Scott-Mayfield, C.J., Leominster, Hereford and Worcs.
Scottish Gallery, The, Edinburgh, Midloth., Scot.
Scottish Gallery, The, London, W.1.
Scratchley, K.S., Sidmouth, Devon.
Scripophily Shop, The, London, W.1.
Scudder Antiques, Terry, Woburn, Beds. Wob. Ab. Ant. C.
Scudders Emporium, Bideford, Devon.
Scull, T. and S.E., Bristol, Avon (Cleeve Antiques).
Scurlock, A.K., Swansea, W. Glam., Wales.
Scurlock, Kim, Swansea, W. Glam., Wales.
Seabourne Antiques, Bournemouth, Dorset.
Seabrook Antiques Ltd., Long Melford, Suffolk.
Seaby Ltd., B.A., London, W.1.
Seafords Barn Collectors Market and Studio Book Shop, Seaford, E. Sussex.
Seager, A.A., London, W.8.
Seager Antiques Ltd., Arthur, London, W.8.
Seago, London, S.W.1.
Seago, A.E., Cromer, Norfolk.
Seago, D.C., Cromer, Norfolk.
Seago, T.P. and L.G., London, S.W.1.
Seal, D., Keighley, W. Yorks.
Seale Antiques, Jeremy, London, S.W.13.
Seales, Anthony, Windsor and Eton, Berks.
Seals, B., Leeds, W. Yorks. (The Piano Shop)
Seaman, R. and M., Axbridge, Somerset.
Searle and Co. Ltd., London, E.C.3.
Searle, E.A., Cambridge, Cambs. (The Bookroom (Cambridge)).
Searle, J. and M., Salcombe, Devon.
Sears, M.D., London, W.1. (M. and R. Glendale)

Seaton, C., Jesmond, Tyne and Wear.
Seaview Antiques, Horncastle, Lincs.
Seaview Antiques, Portrush, Co. Antrim, N. Ireland.
Seaview Antiques, Seaview, I. of Wight.
Sebley, Oswald, Norwich, Norfolk.
Seccombe, Mrs. J., Charlecote, Warks.
Second Childhood, Huddersfield, W. Yorks.
Second Hand Rose, Hindhead, Surrey.
Second Thoughts, Wolverhampton, W. Mids.
Second Time Around, Hemswell Cliff, Lincs.
Second Time Around, Newark, Notts.
Second Time Around Antiques, Wallingford, Oxon.
Secondhand Alley, Shefford, Beds.
Secondhand and Rare Books, Manchester, Lancs. Royal Ex. S.C.
Secondhand Rose, London, S.W.8.
Sedan Chair Antiques, Bristol, Avon.
Sedbergh Antiques and Collectables, Sedbergh, Cumbria.
Seddon, A.E. and M., Manchester, Lancs. (Browzers).
Sedler, H., London, S.W.3. Ant. Ant. Mkt.
Sedman Antiques, Bridlington, N. Humberside.
Sedman, R.H.S. and M.A., Bridlington, N. Humberside.
Sefton Antiques, Woburn, Beds. Wob. Ab Ant. C.
Selbach, Mrs. M., Arundel. W. Sussex.
Select Antiques Gallery Ltd., London, W.8.
Selective Eye Gallery, The, St. Helier, Jersey, C.I.
Seligmann, M. and D., London, W.8.
Selkirk, Henley-on-Thames, Oxon.
Selkirk, C., Henley-on-Thames, Oxon.
Selkirk, Nettlebed, Oxon.
Sellefyan, Mrs. F., London, S.W.3. Ant. Ant. Mkt.
Sellers, M., Harrogate, N. Yorks. (Pianorama (Harrogate) Ltd).
Selwoods, Taunton, Somerset.
Semus Crafting Antiques, Peter, Portslade, W. Sussex.
Senhouse, H.P., Carlisle, Cumbria.
Senior, Mark, London, S.W.3.
Sensation Ltd., London, S.W.6.
Sentry-Box, The, Brighton, E. Sussex.
Serendipity, Deal, Kent.
Serendipity, Edinburgh, Midloth., Scot.
Serendipity, Ledbury, Hereford and Worcs.
Serendipity Antiques, Arundel, W. Sussex.
Serendipity Emporium, London, E.15.
Sessacar, B., London, S.E.10.
Setterfield of St. Albans, Philip, St. Albans, Herts.
Sevenoaks Furniture Gallery, Sevenoaks, Kent.
Seventh Heaven, Chirk, Clwyd, Wales.
Severn, D., Truro, Cornwall.
Severn Fine Art, Shrewsbury, Shrops.
Seville, R., Bristol, Avon. (Relics).
Sewell, Jeremy, London, N.W.8. Alf. Ant. Mkt.
Sewell (Antiques) Ltd., Jean, London, W.8.
Sewell R. and J., London, W.8.
Sexton Antiques, Kenneth, Honiton, Devon.
Sexton's, Kentisbeare, Devon.
Seyfried Antiques, David, London, S.W.6.
Seymour, B.A., Smethwick, W. Mids.
Seymour, R.D., Coventry, W. Mids.
Shabby Tiger Antiques, Stroud, Glos.
Shackleton, Daniel, Edinburgh, Midloth., Scot.
Shackleton, Mrs. E.A., Snainton, N. Yorks.
Shadad Antiques, London, W.1. G. Mews.
Shaftesbury Antiques, Clacton-on-Sea, Essex.
Shaftoe, F.B., Harrogate, N. Yorks.
Shaikh, M., London, W.1.
Shaikh and Son (Oriental Rugs) Ltd., London, W.1.
Shalloe, M., Preston, Lancs. N.W. Ant. C.
Shambles Antiques and Interiors, Dorchester-on-Thames, Oxon.
Shamsa, Mr., Hemswell Cliff, Lincs.
Shamsa, M., London, S.W.15.
Shand, L., London, W.8. (Lindsay Antiques).
Shanks, M., Berkhamsted, Herts.
Shannon, Andrew, Newton Abbot, Devon. N.A. Ant. C.
Shapero Rare Books, Bernard T., London, W.11.
Shapiro and Co., London, W.1. G. Ant. Mkt.
Sharbooks, Upham, Hants.
Shardlow Antiques Warehouse, Shardlow, Derbys.
Share, M., Dorking, Surrey.
Share, Trudi and Bob, London, N.W.8. Alf. Ant. Mkt.
Sharman, Mrs. H.D., Upham, Hants.
Sharman, L.R., Clacton-on-Sea, Essex.
Sharp Antiques, Ian, Tynemouth, Tyne and Wear.
Sharpe, J. and E., Aveton Gifford, Devon.
Sharples, J. and P., Southgate, W. Glam., Wales.
Sharrington Antiques, Sharrington, Norfolk.
Shave, K.J., Cheltenham, Glos. (Chelt. Ant. Mkt.)
Shaw Antiques, Spilsby, Lincs.
Shaw Bros., Harrogate, N. Yorks.
Shaw, Charles, Knaresborough, N. Yorks.
Shaw, D., Congleton, Cheshire.
Shaw, D.J.H., Bramley, Surrey.
Shaw Antiques Ltd., John, Rotherham, S. Yorks.
Shaw and Co., Jack, Ilkley, W. Yorks.
Shaw, J. and C., Harrogate, N. Yorks.
Shaw, Mrs. J.M., Spilsby, Lincs.
Shaw, J.M., Walsall, W. Mids.
Shaw Antiques, Laurence, Horncastle, Lincs.
Shaw, Matthew, London, S.W.3. Chen. Gall.
Shaw, Nona, Ditchling, E. Sussex.
Shaw, N.R., London, W.1. (Julian Pawle Ltd). B. St. Silv. Gall.
Shaw, N. and T., Lytham St. Annes, Lancs.
Shawforth Antiques, Shawforth, Lancs.
Shaw's Gallery, Manchester, Lancs.
Sheen Gallery, London, S.W.14.
Shelagh Antiques, London, N.W.3. Ham. Ant. Emp.
Sheldrick, M., West Wittering, W. Sussex.
Shell, Mrs. L., Alnwick, Northumbs.
Shelley, A. and J., Lewes, E. Sussex.

Shelton Collectors Shop, Towcester, Northants.
Shelton Arts, Brighton, E. Sussex.
Shenny, D., London, W.1. (Place Vendome). B. St. Ant. C.
Shenton, Rita, Twickenham, Middx.
Shepherd, F., Wittersham, Kent.
Shepherd, J., St. Helier, Jersey, C.I.
Shepherd, J., Wittersham, Kent.
Shepherd Antiques, Peter, Hurst, Berks.
Shepherds Antiques, St. Helier, Jersey, C.I.
Sheppard and Cooper Ltd., London, W.1.
Sheppard, Mrs. J., Balderton, Notts.
Sheppard, J., Christchurch, Dorset.
Sheppard, J. and B., Mansfield, Notts.
Sheppard, J.E., Thaxted, Essex.
Sheppard, J., Newark, Notts. N. Ant. Wrhse.
Sheppard, P., Baldock, Herts.
Sheppards Antiques, Mansfield, Notts.
Sheppee, William, London, S.W.6.
Sheraton House, Torquay, Devon.
Sherborne Antique Centre, Sherborne, Dorset.
Sherena Cedar Gallery, London, W.1.
Sheridan's Bookshop Hampton, Ian, Hampton, Middx.
Sherlock, Newton Abbot, Devon. N.A. Ant. C.
Sherlock, George, London, S.W.6.
Sherman, M., Great Wakering, Essex.
Sherman, M., Leigh-on-Sea, Essex.
Sherman, P., Newton Abbot, Devon. N.A. Ant. C.
Sherman and Waterman Associates Ltd., London, W.C.2.
Sherman and Waterman Assoc. Ltd., Brighton, E. Sussex (Jubilee Antique Cellars and Collectors Market.)
Sherston-Baker, R., Canterbury, Kent.
Sherwood (Antiques) Ltd., D.W., Rushden, Northants.
Shickell Antiques, Bournemouth, Dorset.
Shickell Antiques Centre, Bournemouth, Dorset.
Shickell, W.J., Bournemouth, Dorset.
Shield and Allen Ltd., London, S.W.6.
Shield Antiques, Robin, Cirencester, Glos.
Shield Antiques, Robin, Cricklade, Wilts.
Shield, W.R. and P.E., Cirencester, Glos.
Shield, W.R. and P.E., Cricklade, Wilts.
Shillingford, B.C., Maidstone, Kent.
Shindler, A., Chester, Cheshire (Watergate Antiques).
Shine, A. and Z., London, N.W.8. Alf. Ant. Mkt.
Shiners Architectural Reclamation, Newcastle-upon-Tyne, Tyne and Wear.
Ship Street Galleries, Brecon, Powys, Wales.
Shippeys' of Boscombe, Bournemouth, Dorset.
Shire Antiques, Newby Bridge, Cumbria.
Shire Antiques, Rushden, Northants.
Shire, B. and Mrs. J., Newby Bridge, Cumbria.
Shirley Antiques, Shirley, Surrey.
Shockett, J., London, W.1. (Collection). B. St. Ant. C.
Shooter, J., Stickney, Lincs.
Shop of the Yellow Frog, Brighton, E. Sussex.
Shore, P. and C.A., Finchingfield, Essex.
Shorey, R.A., Weymouth, Dorset.
Shorn (Scalpay Ltd.), D., London, S.W.3. Ant. Ant. Mkt.
Shorrick, H. and S., Gosforth, Tyne and Wear.
Short, Mr. and Mrs. A.B., York, N. Yorks.
Short, M. and K., Deal, Kent.
Short, R. and H., London, S.W.6.
Short, R.J.B., Painswick, Glos.
Shortmead Antiques, Biggleswade, Beds.
Shotter Collectors Centre, Keith, Shanklin, I. of Wight
Shotton Antiquarian Books and Prints, J., Durham, Durham.
Showcase, Reigate, Surrey.
Shrewsbury Antique Centre, Shrewsbury, Shrops.
Shrewsbury Antique Market, Shrewsbury, Shrops.
Shrives Gallery, Monyash, Derbys.
Shrubsole, C.J., London, W.C.1.
Shrubsole Ltd., S.J., London, W.C.1.
Shure and Co., David S., London, W.C.2. Lon. Silv. Vts.
Shuster, S., London, N.W.8.
Shuttleworth, J.M., Preston, Lancs. N.W. Ant. C.
Shuttleworth, L.R., Scarborough, N. Yorks.
Shuttleworths, Scarborough, N. Yorks.
Siden, G.T. London, N.W.6.
Sidmouth Antique Market, Sidmouth, Devon.
Sigma Antiques and Fine Art, Ripon, N. Yorks.
Silbert, C., London, S.W.6 (The Gallery).
Silcocks, Clifford and Joan, Pitchcombe, Glos.
Silcocks, Dr. and Mrs. C.G., Pitchcombe, Glos.
Silstar, London, W.C.2. Lond. Silv. Vts.
Silver, A., London, N.W.8.
Silver, B., London, W.1.
Silver Belle, London, N.W.8.
Silver Mouse Trap, The, London, W.C.2.
Silver Sixpence, London, S.E.6.
Silver Stall, The, Bristol, Avon. Clift. Ant. Mkt.
Silver Thimble, The, Kendal, Cumbria.
Silver Time, Brecon, Powys, Wales.
Silverman, B., London, W.C.2. Lon. Silv. Vts.
Silverman, Michael, London, S.E.3.
Silverman, S. and R., London, W.C.2. Lon. Silv. Vts.
Silverston, P. and M., Llangollen, Clwyd, Wales.
Silverstone, J., Weybridge, Surrey.
Silverton Antiques, Kings Lynn, Norfolk.
Silvester, S., Burton-on-Trent, Staffs.
Silvesters, Wingham, Kent.
Singleton, Andrew, Yoxford, Suffolk.
Sim, Michael, Chislehurst, Kent.
Sim Antiques, Roy, Blairgowrie, Perths., Scot.

Simcox, J., Whitchurch, Shrops.
Simmonds, C., Chesham, Bucks.
Simmonds, J. and H., Great Malvern, Hereford and Worcs.
Simmonds, R.M., Southampton, Hants.
Simmons Antiques, Christine, Barnsley, S. Yorks.
Simmons, J.C., Barnsley, S. Yorks.
Simmons, L.M. and S.L., Brighton, E. Sussex.
Simmons Antiques, S. and L., Brighton, E. Sussex.
'Simon', Ilkley, W. Yorks.
Simon Antiques, Grimsby, S. Humberside.
Simon Fine Art Ltd., Julian, London, S.W.1.
Simon, M., Nantwich, Cheshire.
Simons, Jack (Antiques) Ltd., London, W.C.2. London Silv. Vts.
Simpkin, S., Halesworth, Suffolk.
Simpkin, S., Orford, Suffolk.
Simpkiss, E., Wimborne Minster, Dorset.
Simply Capital, London, E.18.
Simpson, D., London, S.W.3 (A. Lianos.) Ant. Ant. Mkt.
Simpson and Sons Jewellers (Oldham) Ltd., H.C., Oldham, Lancs.
Simpson, I., Bewdley, Hereford and Worcs.
Simpson I., Halesowen, W. Mids.
Simpson, M., London, S.W.3. Ant. Ant. Mkt.
Simpson, Marianne, Fochabers, Scotland.
Simpson Ltd., Michael, London, W.1.
Simpson, M.R., Fochabers, Scotland.
Simpson Antiques, M.R., Highcliffe, Dorset.
Simpson, Oswald, Long Melford, Suffolk.
Simpson, R., London, W.11. G. Port.
Simpsons — Pine Mirrors, London, W.14.
Simpsons Textiles, London, W.11. G. Port.
Sims, D., London, S.W.6.
Sims, N., Stratford-upon-Avon, Warks.
Sims, Robin, London, N.1.
Sims, Reed Ltd., London, S.W.1.
Sinai Antiques Ltd., London, W.8.
Sinai, E. and M., London, W.8.
Sinai, M., London, W.1. (Mayfair Gallery).
Sinclair, F.J., Stamford, Lincs.
Sinclair Ltd., Francis, Doncaster, S. Yorks.
Sinclair, G., London, N.W.8.
Sinclair Harding & Co., Cheltenham, Glos.
Sinclair, John, Stamford, Lincs.
Sinclair, Tess, Long Melford, Suffolk.
Sinclair-Hill, Mrs. J.C., Windsor and Eton, Berks. (John A. Pearson Ltd.).
Sinclair's Antique Gallery, Belfast, N. Ireland.
Sinfield Gallery, Brian, Burford, Oxon.
Sinfield, S.E., Biggleswade, Beds.
Singer, A.J., London, N.1. The Mall.
Singing Bird Antiques, Harrogate, N. Yorks.
Singing Tree, The, London, S.W.6.
Siptroth, Roswitha, London, N.W.8. Alf. Ant. Mkt.
Sirett Antiques Ltd., London, W.11. Stouts Arc.
Sirett, Mrs. A.M., London, W.11. Stouts Arc.
Sirett, G., London, W.11. Stouts Arc.
Sitch, H., London, W.1 (W. Sitch and Co. Ltd.)
Sitch and Co. Ltd., W., London, W.1.
Skeaping Gallery, Lydford, Devon.
Skeel Antiques and Eccentricities, Keith, London, N.1.
Skeel Antiques Warehouse, Keith, London, N.1.
Skellgate Curios, Ripon, N. Yorks.
Skelson, Mrs. M.C., Brighton, E. Sussex. (Hyndford Antiques).
Skiba, John, Weedon, Northants.
Skipper, G. and K., Bungay, Suffolk.
Skipwith, W.G., Winchester, Hants.
Skoob Books Ltd., London, W.C.1.
Skoob Two t/a I.K. Ong, London, W.C.1.
Skoulding, P.M., Hadleigh, Suffolk.
Skrebowski, Justin, London, W.11.
Skudder, M., Dartford, Kent.
Slade, Bristol, Avon. Clift. Ant. Mkt.
Slade, Miss N., Bristol, Avon. Clift. Ant. Mkt.
Sladmore Gallery, The, London, W.1.
Slater, C., Brighton, E. Sussex. (Pyramid).
Slater, David, London, W.11.
Slater, G., Walsden, W. Yorks.
Slater, M. and Mrs. P., Edinburgh, Midloth., Scot. (Behar Carpets.)
Slater, M. and Mrs. P., Glasgow, Lanarks., Scot. (Behar Carpets.)
Slater, N., Barnt Green, Hereford and Worcs.
Slater, N., Bexhill-on-Sea, E. Sussex. Bex. Ant. C.
Sleaford Antiques Centre, Sleaford, Lincs.
Sleath, S.L., Sheffield, S. Yorks.
Sleigh, Joy, Newton Abbot, Devon. N.A. Ant. C.
Sloane, E.D. and A.A., Robertsbridge, E. Sussex.
Sloane, Peter, London, W.11. G. Port.
Smale, B.J., Stourbridge, W. Mids.
Smale, Rosemary and Clare, London, N.W.8. Alf. Ant. Mkt.
Small, Murray, London. N.W.8. Alf. Ant. Mkt.
Small, Miss P.M., Exeter, Devon.
Smeeth, A.G., Leavenheath, Suffolk.
Smeeth, S., Lymington, Hants.
Smily, Mr. and Mrs. T., Bath, Avon. (Illuminated Objects)
Smith, Newton Abbot, Devon. N.A. Ant. C.
Smith, A., Alvechurch, W. Mids.
Smith, A., Bristol, Avon (Triangle Antiques).
Smith, A., Leicester, Leics.
Smith, A., Ludlow, Shrops.
Smith Antiques, Wrexham, Clwyd, Wales.
Smith Antique Clocks, Allan, Swindon, Wilts.
Smith Antiques, Andrew, West Malling, Kent.
Smith, A.J., Oakham, Leics.
Smith Antiques, Bryan, Leeds, W. Yorks.
Smith, B. and D.J., Cheddleton, Staffs.
Smith, B.J. and R., Tingewick, Bucks.
Smith, Mrs. B. Roderick, Much Wenlock, Shrops.
Smith, C., Turvey, Beds.
Smith and Gerald Robinson Antiques, Colin, London, W.11.
Smith, D., Thame, Oxon.

Smith Antiques, David, Manton, Leics.
Smith, D.A. and C.R., Driffield, N. Humb.
Smith, D.B., Chipping Campden, Glos.
Smith, D.K., Leeds, W. Yorks. (Windsor House Antiques (Leeds) Ltd.).
Smith, D.R. and G.B., Ringwood, Hants.
Smith Antiques, Edward, Boughton, Kent.
Smith, E.B. and E.M., Hungerford, Berks (The Fire Place (Hungerford) Ltd.)
Smith (Leicester) Ltd., E., Leicester, Leics.
Smith and Sons (Peterborough) Ltd., G., Peterborough, Cambs.
Smith, Hammond, Leicester, Leics.
Smith Sons and Daughters, H. and D., Thame, Oxon.
Smith, H.W. and P.E., Leigh-on-Sea, Essex.
Smith, J., Haydon Bridge, Northumbs.
Smith, Joyce, Warwick, Warks. Smith St. A.C.
Smith, J., Windsor and Eton, Berks. (Eton Gallery Antiques).
Smith Antiques, John, Coggeshall, Essex.
Smith, John Carlton, London, S.W.1.
Smith, J. and J., Haydon Bridge, Northumb.
Smith, J.P., Coggeshall, Essex.
Smith, J.P.D., London, S.W.1 (Trove).
Smith, J.R. and T., Eastbourne, E. Sussex.
Smith and Son (Glasgow Ltd.), John, Glasgow, Lanarks., Scot.
Smith, K., St. Neots, Cambs.
Smith, L. Royden, Lichfield, Staffs.
Smith, Michael, London, W.1. B. St. Silv. Galls.
Smith, M., West Malling, Kent.
Smith, M.A., London, S.W.13.
Smith, M.P.W., London, N.W.1. (Hearth and Home)
Smith, N., Birmingham, W. Mids. (Tatters of Tyseley)
Smith, N., Wortham, Suffolk.
Smith, Paul, Ludlow, Shrops.
Smith, Mr. and Mrs. P., Lye, W. Mids.
Smith Antiques, Peter, Sunderland, Tyne and Wear.
Smith, P. and B., Ludlow, Shrops.
Smith (Bookseller), Peter Bain, Cartmel, Cumbria.
Smith, P.G. and A.E., Esh Winning, Durham.
Smith, P. and J.A., Hull, N. Humberside.
Smith, Raymond, Eastbourne, E. Sussex.
Smith, R., Haworth, W. Yorks.
Smith, Mrs. R., Horley, E. Sussex.
Smith, Roy, London, N.1. (Nellie Lenson and Roy Smith).
Smith, Mr. and Mrs. R.A., Horsham, W. Sussex.
Smith, R.J., Coalville, Leics.
Smith, R. and J., Ramsey, Cambs.
Smith (Antiques), Raymond J., Brighton, E. Sussex.
Smith, R.L.V. and G.V., Cardigan, Dyfed, Wales.
Smith, R. Morley, Rottingdean, E. Sussex.
Smith, R.W., Fowlmere, Cambs.
Smith Antiques, Sheila, Bath, Avon.
Smith Street Antiques Centre, Warwick, Warks.
Smith, S.A. and D.J., Ashbourne, Derbys.
Smith and Smith Designs, Driffield. N. Humb.
Smith, T., Chalfont St. Giles, Bucks.
Smith Antiques, Tom, Ipswich, Suffolk.
Smith Antiques, Tom, Lavenham, Suffolk.
Smith, Val, Nottingham, Notts.
Smith, V., Birmingham, W. Mids. (Smithsonia)
Smithfield Antiques, Lye, W. Mids.
Smith's (The Rink) Ltd., Harrogate, N. Yorks.
Smithsonia, Birmingham, W. Mids.
Smith-Wood, Mr. and Mrs. M., Cheltenham, Glos.
Smurthwaite, T. and S., Holme, Cumbria.
Smyth — Antique Textiles, Peta, London, S.W.1.
Snook, T.B. and H.J., Caversham, Berks.
Snowden Antiques, Ruby, Yarm, Cleveland.
Snowden, R.H., Yarm, Cleveland.
Snowdonia Antiques, Llanrwst, Gwynedd, Wales.
Snuff Box, Lytham St. Annes, Lancs.
Snyder, B., London, W.1. (Spring Antiques).
Snyder, B., London, N.1.
Sodbury Antiques, Chipping Sodbury, Avon.
Soleimani, R.R., London, W.1 (Hadji Baba Ancient Art.)
Solent Antiques, Bembridge, I. of Wight.
Soleymani, R. and V., London, W.1 (Rabi Gallery).
Solus Marketing (Norfolk), Felmingham, Norfolk.
Somerset, B., London, W.1. (The Dial Marylebone).
Somervale Antiques, Midsomer Norton, Avon.
Somerville Ltd., Stephen, London, W.1.
Something Old, Donyatt, Somerset.
Something Old, Something New, Redland, Avon.
Somlo Antiques, London, S.W.1.
Somlo, G. and S., London, S.W.1.
Sommers, S., Windlesham, Surrey.
Sonmez, N., London, S.W.3. Chen. Gall.
Sosna, Boris, London, W.1. G. Mews.
Sotheran Limited, Henry, London, W.1.
Sotherans, London, S.W.1.
Soucek, O., Lewes, E. Sussex.
South Audley Antiques, London, W.1.
South Bar Antiques, Stow-on-the-Wold, Glos.
South London Antique and Book Centre, London, S.E.10.
South Molton Antiques, South Molton, Devon.
South Yorkshire Antiques, Rotherham, S. Yorks.
Southdown Antiques, Lewes, E. Sussex.
Southdown House Antique Galleries, Brasted, Kent.
Southern, J., Bath, Avon. Gt. West. Ant. C.
Southgate Antiques, Southgate, W. Glam., Wales.
Southgate Gallery, Moreton-in-Marsh, Glos.
Southwell, J., London, S.W.6.
Southwick Rare Art, David, L.H., Kingswear, Devon.
Southworth, S. and R., Staunton Harold, Leics.

Souvenir Antiques, Carlisle, Cumbria.
Sovereign Antiques, Gateshead, Tyne and Wear.
Sovereign Antique Centre, The, East Molesey, Surrey.
Sovereign Art, Woburn, Beds. Wob. Ab. Ant. C.,
Spa Antiques Market, Leamington Spa, Warks.
Spalton, A.L., Sheffield, S. Yorks. (Anita's Holme Antiques).
Span Antiques, Woodstock, Oxon.
Sparks Ltd., John, London, W.1.
Sparrow, R. and P., Stroud, Glos.
Sparth House Antiques, Clayton-le-Moors, Lancs.
Spatz, London, N.W.1.
Spatz, London, W.C.2.
Speak, A., Ilkley, W. Yorks.
Speakman, P., Haslingden, Lancs.
Speakmans, Haslingden, Lancs.
Spearing, B., Wrentham, Suffolk.
Speed, J., Ripley, Surrey.
Speed (Maps), John, London, S.E.11.
Speed, Martin, East Molesey, Surrey.
Speed Antiques, Neil, Laugharne, Dyfed, Wales.
Speelman, Alfred, London, W.1.
Speelman Ltd., Edward, London, W.1.
Speight, Connie, London, N.W.8. Alf. Ant. Mkt.
Spellman, D. and S., London, W.1 (The Welbeck Gallery).
Spelman, Ken, York, N. Yorks.
Spencer, Aylesbury, Bucks.
Spencer, A.L., Shepperton, Surrey.
Spencer, Charles, London, W.9.
Spencer Antiques, Don, Warwick, Warks.
Spencer, Don, Warwick, Warks. Smith St. A.C.
Spencer, M., Aylesbury, Bucks.
Spencer, W.T. and J., Lower Bentham, N. Yorks.
Spencer-Bowles Antiques, London, S.W.6.
Spencer-Brayn, N., Morestead, Hants.
Spencer-Brayn, N., Winchester, Hants.
Spencers Antiques, Torquay, Devon.
Spero, Simon, London, W.8.
Sperr, J.R., London, N.6.
Spice, London, S.W.6.
Spicker Jewellers, Newcastle-upon-Tyne, Tyne and Wear.
Spigard, A., London, N.W.1.
Spillers Ltd., H.J., London, W.1.
Spilsby Antiques, Spilsby, Lincs.
Spindles, The, Tonge, Leics.
Spink, John, London, S.W.6.
Spink Ltd., Michael and Henrietta, London, S.W.1.
Spink and Son Ltd., London, S.W.1.
Spinning Wheel, The, Beaconsfield, Bucks.
Spinning Wheel, Port Erin, Isle of Man.
Spinning Wheel, The, Southport, Merseyside.
Spinning Wheel Antiques, St. Annes-on-Sea, Lancs.
Splinters, Crawley, W. Sussex.
Spon End Antiques, Coventry, W. Mids.
Spooner, J.G., Dorking, Surrey.
Spooner, Kelvin, London, N.W.8. Alf. Ant. Mkt.
Spooner, K.L. and J.S., Leek, Staffs.
Spooner Antiques, Philip, Dorking, Surrey.
Spooner, P.J., Dorking, Surrey.
Sport and Country Gallery, Bulkington, Warks.
Sports Programmes, Coventry, W. Mids.
Spratt Antiques, Jack, Newark, Notts.
Spread Eagle Antiques, London, S.E.10.
Spring Antiques, Ipswich, Suffolk.
Spring Antiques, London, W.1.
Spring Park Jewellers, Shirley, Surrey.
Springett, C.M., Tunbridge Wells, Kent.
Spurrier-Smith Antiques, Ashbourne, Derbys.
Spurrier-Smith, I., Ashbourne, Derbys.
Spyer and Son (Antiques) Ltd., Gerald, London, S.W.1.
Squires Antiques, Altrincham, Cheshire.
Squires, A., Faversham, Kent.
Squires Antiques (Faversham), Faversham, Kent.
Squires Pantry Antiques, Cowfold, W. Sussex.
Squirrel Collectors Centre, Basingstoke, Hants.
Squirrels and Early Days, Pateley Bridge, N. Yorks.
Stable Antiques, Sedbergh, Cumbria.
Stable Antiques, Thornton le Dale, N. Yorks.
Stablegate Antiques, Canterbury, Kent.
Stables, The, Grasmere, Cumbria.
Stables Antiques, Ombersley, Hereford and Worcs.
Stables, K., Bath, Avon. (No.12 Queen St.).
Stacey, D. and M., Littleton, Somerset.
Stacey and Sons, John, Leigh-on-Sea, Essex.
Stacy-Marks Ltd., E., Eastbourne, E. Sussex.
Stafford, Ulla, Windsor and Eton, Berks.
Staffs Bookshop, The, Lichfield, Staffs.
Stage Door Prints, London, W.C.2.
Staines, Mrs.P., Debenham, Suffolk.
Stair and Company Ltd., London, W.1.
Stait, T.G., Painswick, Glos.
Staithe Lodge Gallery, Swafield, Norfolk.
Stalham Antique Gallery, Stalham, Norfolk.
Stamford Antiques, Lytham St. Annes, Lancs.
Stamford Antiques Centre, Stamford, Lincs.
Stamp, J., Bungay, Suffolk.
Stamp and Sons, J., Market Harborough, Leics.
Stamp, M., Market Harborough, Leics.
Stamp, R.H., Wimborne Minster, Dorset.
Stancomb, J.A., Ilminster, Somerset.
Standley, M.E. and J.E., Wymondham, Norfolk.
Stanford, A., Coventry, W. Mids.
Stanford, Miss M.A., Farnham, Surrey.
Stanforth, E.M., Whitby, N. Yorks.
Staniland (Booksellers), Stamford, Lincs.
Staniland, M.F. and M.G., Stamford, Lincs.
Stanley, F., Hastings, E. Sussex.
Stanley, J., Stow-on-the-Wold, Glos. C. Ant. C.
Stanley, Ian and Mandy, London, W.1. G. Mews.

Stanley and Son, K., Auchterarder, Perths., Scot.
Stanley and Son, K., Dunkeld, Perths., Scot.
Stanton, Louis, London, W.11.
Stanton, L., London, S.W.3. Chen. Gall.
Stanton, L.R. and S.A., London, W.11.
Stanton Antiques Restoration, Peter, Truro, Cornwall.
Stanton, P. and V., Truro, Cornwall.
Stanwells Antiques and Jewellery, Penarth, S. Glam., Wales.
Stanworth, Mr. and Mrs. G., Cadeby, Leics.
Stanworth (Fine Arts), P., Cadeby, Leics.
Staplegrove Lodge Antiques, Taunton, Somerset.
Stapleton, D.H., Bedford, Beds.
Stapleton Antiques, Serena, London, S.W.15.
Stapleton's Antiques, Bedford, Beds.
Stapley, Jean, Warwick, Warks. Smith St. A. C.
Starkey, James H., Beverley, N. Humberside.
Starkey, T., Modbury, Devon.
Starkie, E.S., Knaresborough, N. Yorks.
Startime, Niton, I. of Wight.
Statham, Jacqueline, Woburn, Beds. Wob. Ab. Ant. C. (Christina Tooley).
Station Pine Antiques, Nottingham, Notts.
Station Road Emporium, Birmingham, W. Mids.
Staton Antiques, Alanna, Little Bookham, Surrey.
Staton, P.T., Cobham, Surrey.
Stead, Geoffrey, Burford, Oxon.
Stead, Geoffrey, Chastleton, Glos.
Stead Antiques Reference Books, Graham, Tunbridge Wells, Kent.
Stead, Myola, Sevenoaks, Kent.
Stebbing, Peter, Bournemouth, Dorset.
Steed-Croft Antiques, Burnham Deepdale, Norfolk.
Steedman, R.D., Newcastle-upon-Tyne, Tyne and Wear.
Steeds, J., Burghfield Common, Berks.
Steel, Jeremy and Guy, London, S.W.1.
Steel, N., London, N.1. (Banbury Fayre)
Steel, Mrs. V., London, N.2.
Steele, W.G., Stoke-on-Trent, Staffs.
Steenson, M., London, W.11. (Books and Things).
Steeper, L., London, W.9.
Steeple Bookshop, The, Langholm, Dumfriess., Scot.
Steer, Colin George, London, N.W.8. Alf. Ant. Mkt.
Steers, K., Long Melford, Suffolk.
Stefani Antiques, London, S.W.19.
Stefani Antiques, Liverpool, Merseyside.
Stefani, K., London, S.W.19.
Stefani, Mrs. T., Liverpool, Merseyside.
Stein, M.W., Bristol, Avon. Clift. Ant. Mkt.
Steller, Mrs. D., Christchurch, Dorset.
Stenlake and McCourt, Glasgow, Lanarks., Scot.
Stent, J., Amersham, Bucks.
Stephens, F. Corringham, Essex.
Stephens, P.M. and Mrs. M., Inchture, Perths., Scot.
Stephenson, P., Harrogate, N. Yorks. (The Ginnel)
Stephenson, Pauline, Helmsley, N. Yorks.
Stephenson Decorative Carpets and Kilims, Robert, London, S.W.3. (Daphne Graham)
Steppes Hill Farm Antiques, Stockbury, Kent.
Sterling Books, Weston-super-Mare, Avon.
Sterling Coins and Medals, Bournemouth, Dorset.
Stern Art Dealers, London, W.11.
Stern, H., London, W.C.2. Lon. Silv. Vts. (Silstar).
Stern and Son, M., London, W.11.
Sternberg, C., London, W.1 (Vigo-Sternberg Galleries).
Sternshine, A., Manchester, Lancs. (A.S. Antiques).
Stevens Antiques, St. Albans, Herts.
Stevens Bookseller, Joan, Yoxford, Suffolk.
Stevens Antiques, J.E., St. Albans, Herts.
Stevens and Son, Lubenham, Leics.
Stevens, Malcolm D., London, N.1. The Mall.
Stevens-Wilson, L.W. and Mrs., London, N.21.
Stevenson, E. and W., Whissendene, Leics.
Stevenson, I. and A., Brighton, E. Sussex. (Oasis Antiques).
Stevenson, R.J., Stoke-on-Trent, Staffs.
Stewart, Mr. and Miss, London, E.15.
Stewart, A.J., Rochester, Kent.
Stewart, F., Elgin, Moray., Scot.
Stewart Gallery, Bexhill-on-Sea, E. Sussex.
Stewart Gallery, Eastbourne, E. Sussex.
Stewart, J. and D., Norham, Northumb.
Stewart – Fine Art, Lauri, London, N.2.
Stewart Antiques, Michael, Coatbridge, Lanarks., Scot.
Stewart Antiques, Michael, Leominster, Hereford and Worcs.
Stewart, W., London, S.W.3. Ant. Ant. Mkt.
Stewart-Cox, A., J.M. and M., Warminster, Wilts.
Steyne Antique Gallery, Worthing, W. Sussex.
Steyne House Antiques, Seaford, E. Sussex.
Stickland, W.T. and B., Tetbury, Glos.
Stiffkey Antiques, Stiffkey, Norfolk.
Stiffkey Lamp Shop, The, Stiffkey, Norfolk.
Stimpson, P.D., Hurst Green, E. Sussex.
Stirling Antiques, Abinger Hammer, Surrey.
Stobo, Constance, London, W.8.
Stock, Colin, Rainford, Merseyside.
Stock Exchange Antiques, Colchester, Essex.
Stockbridge Antiques, Stockbridge, Hants.
Stockbridge Antiques and Fine Art, Edinburgh, Midloth., Scot.
Stocker, C.J., Harston, Cambs.
Stocker, J., Chipping Campden, Glos.
Stockham at Images, Peter, Lichfield, Staffs.
Stockland, M., Hungerford, Berks. (Riverside Antiques).
Stockman, Paul, Newton Abbot, Devon. N.A. Ant. C.
Stockman, P. and D., Newton Abbot, Devon. N. A. Ant. C.
Stockspring Antiques, London, W.8.
Stockton, J., Cardiff, S. Glam., Wales (The Light Brigade and Penylan Antiques.)

Stodel, Jacob, London, W.8.
Stodel, S. and J., London, W.C.2. Lon. Silv. Vts.
Stodgell Fine Art, Colin, Torquay, Devon.
Stokes, Mrs. N.J., Fortrose, Ross and Cromarty, Scot.
Stokes, William H., Cirencester, Glos.
Stone Antiques, Alan, London, S.W.15.
Stone, A.H. and D.P., Basingstoke, Hants.
Stone, Mrs Barbara, London, S.W.3. Ant. Ant. Mkt.
Stone Hall Antiques, Matching Green, Essex.
Stonegate Fine Arts, York, N. Yorks.
Stonehouse, D.R. and J.M., Grosmont, N. Yorks.
Stones, A., London, N.1. (Rumours Decorative Arts)
Stones, Grandfather Clocks, Keith, Bessacarr, S. Yorks.
Stones, Mrs. M. Palmer, Stradbroke, Suffolk.
Stones, Mrs. S., Wisbech, Cambs.
Stone-Wares Antiques, Stone, Staffs.
Stoodley, Mrs. Dinah, Brasted, Kent.
Stoppenbach and Delestre Ltd., London, W.1.
Storer, Mr. and Mrs. M., Nottingham, Notts. (Trade Wind Antiques).
Stores, The, Great Waltham, Essex.
Storey, J., Alnwick, Northumbs.
Storey, Harold T., London, W.C.2.
Storey, M. and J., London, S.W.1. (The Delightful Muddle).
Storrington Antiques, Storrington, W. Sussex.
Stour Gallery, Blandford Forum, Dorset.
Stove Shop, The, London, N.W.2.
Stow Antiques, Stow-on-the-Wold, Glos.
Strachey, Julie, Wallingford, Oxon. L. Arc.
Strain Antiques, David R., Tynemouth, Tyne and Wear.
Strait Antiques, The, Lincoln, Lincs.
Strand Antiques, Bromsgrove, Hereford and Worcs.
Strand Antiques, London, W.4.
Strange, A., London, W.11. G. Port.
Strange Antiques, Preston, Lancs.
Strange, D., London, W.C.2 (Pearl Cross Ltd.).
Strange, M., Preston, Lancs.
Strange, Sheila B., Newton Abbot, Devon. N. A. Ant. C.
Strange, V.H., Bampton, Devon.
Strange, V., Bournemouth, Dorset. (Boscombe Antiques)
Stratford Antique Centre, Stratford-upon-Avon, Warks.
Strathearn Antiques, Crieff, Perths., Scot.
Stratton-Quinn Antiques Etc., London, W.4.
Straw, P.R., Newark, Notts. N. Ant. Wrhse.
Strawson's Antiques, Tunbridge Wells, Kent.
Streamer Antiques, J., Leigh-on-Sea, Essex.
Streatham Traders and Shippers Market, London, S.W.16.
Streather, Pamela, London, S.W.1.
Stredder, J., Atherton, Lancs.
Streeter and Daughter, Ernest, Petworth, W. Sussex.
Streetwalker Antiques, Barton-on-Humber, S. Humberside.
Streetwalker Antiques Warehouse, Barton-on-Humber, S. Humberside.
Stretton Antiques Market, Church Stretton, Shrops.
Stretton Antiques and Militaria, Church Stretton, Shrops.
Strickland and Dorling, Truro, Cornwall.
Strickland, P., Truro, Cornwall.
Stride Antiques and Gardens, Peter, Gillingham, Dorset.
Strike One (Islington) Ltd., London, N.1.
Strong, C.J., Exmouth, Devon.
Stroud, L.M. and D.G., Taunton, Somerset.
Stroud of Southwell (Antiques), Southwell, Notts.
Stroud Antiques, Peter, Chipping Norton, Oxon.
Stroud, V.N. and J., Southwell, Notts.
Stroud's of Taunton, London, S.W.3. (Louise Stroud).
Strover Antiques, Cambridge, Cambs.
Strover, B.J., Cambridge, Cambs.
Strowger of Blandford, Peter, Blandford Forum, Dorset.
Stuart Antiques, London, S.E.10.
Stuart Antiques, D.C., Bournemouth, Dorset.
Stuart House Antiques, Chipping Campden, Glos.
Stuart Gallery, Marlborough, Wilts.
Stuart House Fine Art, Birmingham, W. Mids.
Stuart Interiors (Antiques) Ltd., Barrington, Somerset.
Stuart, J. and V., Shere, Surrey.
Stuart, T.R. and Mrs. H.M., Woodford Halse, Northants.
Stuart-Mobey, Alan, Woodstock, Oxon.
Stubbings, M., Preston, Lancs. N.W. Ant. C.
Stuckey, M.T., Halstead, Essex.
Studio, The, Arundel, W. Sussex.
Studio, The, London, N.1.
Studio 41, Southport, Merseyside.
Studio 101, Windsor and Eton, Berks.
Studio Arts Gallery, Lancaster, Lancs.
Studio Bookshop and Gallery, Alresford, Hants.
Stuff, Dover, Kent.
Sturgeon, J.A. and Mrs. J., Sandhurst, Berks.
Sturman, A., M.M. and P.J., Hawes, N. Yorks.
Sturman's Antiques, Hawes, N. Yorks.
Sturton, J., London, S.E.1. Ber. Ant. Whse.
Sturton — Mr. Pickwick, John, Rettendon, Essex.
Stutchbury, Mr. and Mrs. D., Newark, Notts.
Style, London, N.1.
Styles, P. and D., Hungerford, Berks.
Styles Silver, Hungerford, Berks.
Suddaby Fine Art, Leon, Penzance, Cornall.
Suffolk House Antiques, Yoxford, Suffolk.
Sukmano Antiques, London, W.8.
Sulaiman, Mr., London, S.W.3. Ant. Ant. Mkt. (Mr. Garcia)
Sullivan, B., Southport, Merseyside.

Summer Antiques, Kate, Sandgate, Kent. S. Ant. C.
Summer Lane Antiques, Barnsley, S. Yorks.
Summers, Davis and Son Ltd., Wallingford, Oxon.
Summers, S. and N., Market Drayton, Shrops.
Sumner, Mrs. Jane, Saffron Walden, Essex.
Sumner, M.C., Uppingham, Leics.
Sumner, N.F. and M.A., Ormskirk, Lancs.
Sun Street Antique Centre, Lancaster, Lancs.
Sundance Antiques, Glasgow, Lanarks., Scot. B. St. Ant. G.
Sundial Antiques, Amersham, Bucks.
Sundridge Gallery, Sundridge, Kent.
Sunloch Gallery, Banbury, Oxon.
Sunset Country Antiques, Cullompton, Devon.
Surena Antiques, London, W.1. G. Mews.
Surrey Antiques Centre, Chertsey, Surrey.
Surrey Clock Centre, Haslemere, Surrey.
Surya, K., London, W.C.1.
Sussex Commemorative Ware Centre, The, Brighton, E. Sussex.
Sussex Fine Art, Arundel, W. Sussex.
Sutcliffe Galleries, Harrogate, N. Yorks.
Sutcliffe, Gordon, Hadleigh, Suffolk.
Sutcliffe, R. and R., Masham, N. Yorks.
Sutcliffe, Tony, Preston, Lancs. N.W. Ant. C.
Sutcliffe Antiques, Tony and Anne, Southport, Merseyside.
Suthburgh Antiques, Long Melford, Suffolk.
Suttle, H. and M., Otley, W. Yorks.
Sutton, B.D., Windsor and Eton, Berks. (Compton Gallery).
Sutton, G. and B., Stow-on-the-Wold, Glos.
Sutton, H., Wroughton, Wilts.
Sutton, L., Great Malvern, Hereford and Worcs.
Sutton, L. and M., London, W.11.
Sutton P., London, W.8 (Oliver-Sutton Antiques).
Sutton and Sons, Frome, Somerset.
Sutton, Vera, Diss, Norfolk.
Sutton, V., Rickinghall, Suffolk.
Sutton Valence Antiques, Maidstone, Kent.
Sutton Valence Antiques, Sutton Valence, Kent.
Swadforth House, Knaresborough, N. Yorks.
Swaffer, Spencer, Arundel, W. Sussex.
Swaffham Antiques Supplies, Swaffham, Norfolk.
Swag, Preston, Lancs.
Swain, A.L. Sittingbourne, Kent.
Swainbank, R., Liverpool, Merseyside.
Swainbank's Ltd., Liverpool, Merseyside.
Swaine, S.P., Walsall, W. Mids.
Swale, Jill and David, Frome, Somerset.
Swan Antiques, Bawtry, S. Yorks.
Swan Antiques, Chipping Campden, Glos.
Swan Antiques, Cranbrook, Kent.
Swan Antiques, Manchester, Lancs. Royal Ex. S. C.
Swan, D., Calne, Wilts.
Swan Fine Art, London, N.1.
Swan Gallery, Burford, Oxon.
Swan Gallery, The, Sherborne, Dorset.
Swan House Country Antiques, Garboldisham, Norfolk.
Swanbourne Antiques and Cottage Tearooms, Swanbourne, Bucks.
Swann Galleries, Oliver, London, S.W.3.
Swans Antique Centre, Oakham, Leics.
Swaythling Woodcrafts, Southampton, Hants.
Sweet, E., Penzance, Cornwall.
Sweet, S.M., Bridlington, N. Humberside.
Sweeting, K.J., Belper, Derbys.
Sweeting's (Antiques 'n' Things), Belper, Derbys.
Sweet's Antiques, Bridlington, N. Humberside.
Swift, M., Camborne, Cornwall.
Swift and Sons, R.A., Bournemouth, Dorset.
Swindells, A., Rotherham, S. Yorks.
Swindells, H. and A., Bath, Avon. (Bath Stamp and Coin Shop).
Swonnell (Silverware) Ltd., E., London, W.1. B. St. Silv. Galls.
Swycher, Marion, London, N.W.8. Alf. Ant. Mkt.
Sydney House Antiques, Wansford, Cambs.
Sydney, Norma, Leominster, Hereford and Worcs. L. Ant. Mkt.
Sykes Antiques, South Kelsey, Lincs.
Sykes, B.G., South Kelsey, Lincs.
Sykes Antiques, Christopher, Woburn, Beds.
Sykes, C. and M., Woburn, Beds.
Sykes, C.W., York, N. Yorks. (French Fine Art).
Sykes, G.M., London, N.7.
Sykes, Mrs. I., Bristol, Avon. Clift. Ant. Mkt.
Sykes Antiques, Thomas, Kelvedon, Essex.
Sykes, T.W., Kelvedon, Essex.
Symes, B., Tetbury, Glos.
Symes, John and Sheila, Bristol, Avon.
Symes Ltd., Robin, London, S.W.1.

T

T.F.S. Ltd., Chalfont St. Giles, Bucks.
T.G.M. Antiques Warehouse, Newark, Notts.
TMT Antiques, London, S.E.1.
T.T. Antiques, Newark, Notts.
T.W. Antiques, Wimborne Minster, Dorset.
Tadema Gallery, London, N.1.
Tagg, M. and P., Hare Hatch, Berks.
Tags, Wallingford, Oxon. L. Arc.
Taikoo Books Ltd., York, N. Yorks.
Tait, L. and V., Nantwich, Cheshire.
Talbot Court Galleries, Stow-on-the-Wold, Glos.
Talents Fine Arts Ltd., Malton, N. Yorks.
Talisman, Gillingham, Dorset.
Talisman Antiques, Alford, Lincs.
Talisman Antiques, Horncastle, Lincs.
Talking Machine, London, N.W.4.
Talking Point Antiques, Sowerby Bridge, W. Yorks.
Tamar Gallery (Antiques and Fine Art), Launceston, Cornwall.
Tamaree Antiques, Melksham, Wilts.

Tamblyn, Alnwick, Northumb.
Tameside Antiques, Ashton-under-Lyne, Lancs.
Tanglewood, Ashbourne, Derbys.
Tankard, S.M., Otley, W. Yorks.
Tanner, J., Clare, Suffolk.
Tanner, J., Long Melford, Suffolk.
Tanswell, P., Warminster, Wilts.
Tao Antiques, The, Warwick, Warks.
Tapestry, Cheltenham, Glos.
Tapley, R., Niton, I. of Wight.
Tappers Antiques, Eastleigh, Hants.
Tapsell Antiques, Brighton, E. Sussex.
Tapsell Antiques, London, W.1. G. Mews.
Tara Antiques, London, N.W.8.
Taramasco, A., London, N.W.8.
Tara's Hall, Hadleigh, Suffolk.
Taregwian, M., London, S.W.6. (Antique Carpets Gallery)
Tarplett, Mrs. C., Great Malvern, Hereford and Worcs.
Tarran, G., Worcester, Hereford and Worcs.
Tarrant Gallery, Arundel, W. Sussex.
Tarrant Street Antique Centre, Arundel, W. Sussex.
Tarrystone, The, Chobham, Surrey.
Tassell, P., St. Leonards-on-Sea, E. Sussex. Hastings A.C.
Tassles, Bath, Avon. Gt. West. Ant. C.
Tate, Andrew, Finchingfield, Essex.
Tate, J. Harwood, Market Rasen, Lincs.
Tate, J.M., Burnham Deepdale, Norfolk.
Tatters Decorative Antiques, Bridgnorth, Shrops.
Tatters of Tyseley, Birmingham, W. Mids.
Tattersall, J., Uppingham, Leics.
Tattersall's, Uppingham, Leics.
Tauber Antiques, Laurence, Surbiton, Surrey.
Taunton Silver Street Antiques Centre, Taunton, Somerset.
Tavistock Antiques, St. Neots, Cambs.
Tavistock Fine Art Gallery, Tavistock, Devon.
Tay Street Gallery, Perth, Perths., Scot.
Tayler, Ron, Alum Bay, I. of Wight.
Tayler, Mrs. S.C., Lytham St. Annes, Lancs.
Taylor, B., Kingston-on-Spey, Morays., Scot.
Taylor Antiques, Brian, Plymouth, Devon.
Taylor, B.F., Plymouth, Devon.
Taylor, C., Thatcham, Berks.
Taylor, C.D. and E.S., Hampton, Middx.
Taylor, D., Driffield, N. Humberside.
Taylor, D., London, S.W.18.
Taylor, D.E., Hastings, E. Sussex.
Taylor, E., Broadway, Herefs. and Worcs.
Taylor, Elsie, London, N.W.8. Alf. Ant. Mkt.
Taylor, F.W., Tewkesbury, Glos.
Taylor, G., Gateshead, Tyne and Wear.
Taylor Gallery Ltd., The, London, W.1.
Taylor, Gerald and Vera, Winforton, Hereford and Worcs.
Taylor, I.C., Glasgow, Lanarks., Scot. (Yesteryear).
Taylor, J., London, W.1. (The Taylor Gallery Ltd.).
Taylor, Mrs. J., Stockton Heath, Cheshire.
Taylor, J., Stoke-on-Trent, Staffs.
Taylor, Mr. and Mrs. J.C., Melbourne, Derbys.
Taylor, Mrs. L., Cirencester, Glos.
Taylor, M., London, S.W.12.
Taylor, M., Ludlow, Shrops.
Taylor (Antiques), M. and R., Ludlow, Shrops.
Taylor, Mrs. P., Henllan, Dyfed, Wales.
Taylor, Robert, Four Oaks, W. Mids.
Taylor Antiques, Rankine, Cirencester, Glos.
Taylor Fine Arts, Robin, Wakefield, W. Yorks.
Taylor, R.I.G., London, S.W.10.
Taylor, Mrs. R.M., Manchester, Lancs. (Cathedral Jewellers).
Taylor, Steven J., Bath, Avon. B. Ant. Mkt.
Taylor, Mrs. S.M., Boston, Lincs.
Taylor, V., Bath, Avon. (Victoria) Gt. West Ant. C.
Taylor Antiques, W., Lowestoft, Suffolk.
Taylor, W.D.J., Lowestoft, Suffolk.
Taylor-Halsey Antiques, Jacobstowe, Devon.
Taylor-Smith, Westerham, Kent.
Tealby Pine, Wragby, Lincs.
Teignmouth and Son, Pamela, London, W.8.
Telfer-Smollett, M. and C., London, W.11.
Telford Antiques Centre, Telford, Shrops.
Telling, S., Thame, Oxon.
Telling Time Antiques, Thame, Oxon.
Teltscher Ltd., F., London, W.1.
Teme Valley Antiques, Ludlow, Shrops.
Templar Antiques, Kelvedon, Essex.
Temple Gallery, London, W.11.
Temple Lighting, Milton Keynes, Bucks.
Temple Antiques, Jeanne, Milton Keynes, Bucks.
Temple, R.C.C., London, W.11
Templeman, L., Rait, Perths., Scot.
Templemans, Rait, Perths, Scot.
Temptations Unlimited, Glasgow, Lanarks, Scot.
Tempus Fugit, Shaldon, Devon.
Tennis Bookshop, The, Ringwood, Hants.
Terrace Antiques, London, W.5.
Terrett, S., Truro, Cornwall.
Terry Antiques, London, W.4.
Terry, A., Mold, Clwyd, Wales.
Tessa's Antiques, Saltburn, Cleveland.
Tessiers Ltd., London, W.1.
Tethers End Antiques, Tutbury, Staffs.
Tetsworth Antiques, Tetsworth, Oxon.
Tewkesbury Antique Centre, Tewkesbury, Glos.
Thacker's Antiques, York, N. Yorks.
Thakeham Furniture, Storrington, W. Sussex.
Thame Antique and Art Galleries, Thame, Oxon.
Thame Pine, Thame, Oxon.
Thames Gallery, Henley-on-Thames, Oxon.
Thames Oriental Rug Co., Henley-on-Thames, Oxon.
Thanet Antiques Trade Centre, Ramsgate, Kent.
That Little Shop, Boston, Lincs.
Thaxted Galleries, Thaxted, Essex.
Themes and Variations, London, W.11.
Thesaurus, St. Peter Port, Guernsey, C.I.

Thesaurus (Jersey) Ltd., St. Helier, Jersey, C.I.
Theta Gallery, Liverpool, Merseyside.
Thicke Galleries, Swansea, W. Glam., Wales.
Thicke, T.G., Swansea, W. Glam., Wales.
Thiele, A.C., Epsom, Surrey.
Thiele, A.C., Kingston-upon-Thames, Surrey.
Thimble Society, London, W.1. G. Ant. Mkt.
Thin (Booksellers), James, Edinburgh, Midloth., Scot.
Thirkill Antiques, Leeds, W. Yorks.
Thirty Eight Antiques Ltd., Weedon, Northants.
This and That, Norwich, Norfolk.
This and That Antiques and Bric-a-Brac, Edinburgh, Midloth., Scot.
This and That (Furniture), London, N.W.1.
Thistle Antiques, Aberdeen, Aberd., Scot.
Thistle House Antiques, Woodstock, Oxon.
Thistlethwaite, E., Settle, N. Yorks.
Thom, A.W., Chapel-en-le-Frith, Derbys.
Thom, Karen, Glasgow, Lanarks., Scot. B. St. Ant G.
Thomas, Andrew, Stamford, Lincs.
Thomas, Alan G., London, S.W.3.
Thomas, Mrs. C., Windsor and Eton, Berks.
Thomas (Fine Arts), Carole, Hitchin, Herts.
Thomas and Dymond, Riddlecombe, Devon.
Thomas, Mrs. E., London, W.1.
Thomas, G.M., London, W.11. G. Port.
Thomas, J.B., Fishguard, Dyfed, Wales.
Thomas, K.L., Haverfordwest, Dyfed, Wales.
Thomas, M. and V., Penn, Bucks.
Thomas Antiques, Nicholas, London, W.11.
Thomas Fine Paintings, Paul, Wokingham, Berks.
Thomas, Mr. and Mrs. P.R., Narberth, Dyfed, Wales.
Thomas, R., Thornton Heath, Surrey.
Thomas, R. and D., Brasted, Kent.
Thomas, Wing Cdr. R.G., Midsomer Norton, Avon.
Thomas, R.N., Meshaw, Devon.
Thompson Antiques formerly Ships and Sealing Wax, Winchester, Hants.
Thompson, B., London, N.1 (Antique Trader).
Thompson, D. and P., Alresford, Hants.
Thompson, D. and Mrs. S., Ipswich, Suffolk.
Thompson, J., Knaresborough, N. Yorks.
Thompson, John, Tunbridge Wells, Kent.
Thompson, J. and S., Aldeburgh, Suffolk.
Thompson, L.E., Stockport, Cheshire.
Thompson Antiques, Margaret M., Newark, Notts. Castle G.A.C.
Thompson Antiques, Michael, Newark,Notts. Castle G.A.C.
Thompson, M.S., Salisbury, Wilts.
Thompson, N., Tunbridge Wells, Kent (John Thompson.)
Thompson, N.F., Tideswell, Derbys.
Thompson, R., Warwick, Warks.
Thompson, R.E., Long Buckby, Northants.
Thompson, Sue, London, S.W.3. Ant. Ant. Mkt.
Thompson's, Ipswich, Suffolk.
Thompson's Antiques, Ipswich, Suffolk.
Thompson's Gallery, Aldeburgh, Suffolk.
Thomson Antiques, Perranarworthal, Cornwall.
Thomson, A.L., St. Helier, Jersey, C.I.
Thomson — Albany Gallery, Bill, London, S.W.1.
Thomson, D., Ripon, N. Yorks.
Thomson, I.G.F., Unstone, Derbys.
Thomson Antiques, Joan, St. Helier, Jersey, C.I.
Thomson Ltd., Murray, London, W.8.
Thomson, P., Woking, Surrey.
Thomson, W.B., London, S.W.1. (Bill Thomson — Albany Gallery).
Thorn, David J., Budleigh Salterton, Devon.
Thornberry, R.C., London, W.1 (Wilberry Antiques).
Thornbury, M., Hankerton, Wilts.
Thorne, S., Hursley, Hants.
Thornhill Galleries Ltd., London, S.W.6.
Thornhill Galleries Ltd., London, S.W.15.
Thornhill Gallery Antique Centre, Thornhill, Dumfriess., Scot.
Thornhill, J., Shrewsbury, Shrops.
Thornhill, Mr. and Mrs. T.B., Burwash, E. Sussex.
Thornley, G. and E.M., Helmsley, N. Yorks.
Thornley, J., Biddenham, Kent.
Thornton Architectural Antiques Ltd., Andy, Elland, W. Yorks.
Thornton Gallery, Bedale, N. Yorks.
Thornton, J., London, S.W.6 (634 Kings Road.)
Thornton Antiques, Joseph, Windermere, Cumbria.
Thornton, J.W., Ulverston, Cumbria.
Thornton, J.W., Windermere, Cumbria.
Thornton Antiques Supermarket, J.W., Bowness-on-Windermere, Cumbria.
Thornton, T. and G., York, N. Yorks. (Fettes Fine Art)
Thorntons of Harrogate, Harrogate, N. Yorks.
Thorntons of Oxford Ltd., Oxford, Oxon.
Thorp, Thomas, St. Albans, Herts.
Thorp, Bookseller, Thomas, Guildford, Surrey.
Thorpe, A., Dorking, Surrey.
Thorpe Antiques, Finedon, Northants.
Thorpe, D.J., Llanwrda, Dyfed, Wales.
Thorpe and Foster plc., Dorking, Surrey.
Thorpe, S., London, S.W.3. Ant. Ant. Mkt.
Three Tuns Antiques, Stokesley, N. Yorks.
Threipland, Mr. and Mrs. M. Murray, Rait, Perths., Scot.
Thrie Estaits, The, Edinburgh, Midloth., Scot.
Throckmorton, Lady Isabel, Coughton, Warks.
Throp, R. Brasted, Kent.
Through the Looking Glass Ltd., London, S.W.6.
Through the Looking Glass, London, W.8.
Thrower, D. and V., Petworth, W. Sussex. (William Hockley Antiques).
Thuillier, William, London, S.W.1.
Thurlow, K., London, S.W.6 (David Alexander Antiques).

Thurso Antiques, Thurso, Caith., Scot.
Thurstans, C.M. and D., Stillington, N. Yorks.
Thwaites and Co., Bushey, Herts.
Tibbiwell Antiques, Painswick, Glos.
Tibenham, Mrs. P., Knowle, W. Mids.
Tidey Antiques, Michael, Brighton, E. Sussex.
Tiernan, Eugene, London, N.1.
Tiffany Antiques, St. Leonards-on-Sea, E. Sussex. Hastings Ant. C.
Tiffany Antiques, Shrewsbury, Shrops.
Tiffins Antiques, Emsworth, Hants.
Tildesley, B. and J., Harrogate, N. Yorks. (Windmill Antiques).
Tilings Antiques, Brasted, Kent.
Till, M., London, N.1 (Vane House Antiques).
Tillett, James and Ann, Norwich, Norfolk.
Tillett and Co., Thomas, Norwich, Norfolk.
Tilley, A.G.J. and A.A.J.C., Chesterfield, Derbys.
Tilley, A.G.J. and A.A.J.C., Sheffield, S. Yorks.
Tilley, Mrs. P., Macclesfield, Cheshire.
Tilley's Antiques, Solihull, W. Mids.
Tilley's Vintage Magazine Shop, Chesterfield, Derbys.
Tilley's Vintage Magazine Shop, Sheffield, S. Yorks.
Tillman Ltd., William, London, S.W.1.
Tillou Works of Art, Peter, London, S.W.1.
Tilly Manor Antiques, West Harptree, Avon.
Tilly's Antiques, Leigh-on-Sea, Essex.
Time for Everyone, Eastbourne, E. Sussex.
Time in Hand, Shipston-on-Stour, Warks.
Times Past, Great Wakering, Essex.
Times Past, Long Melford, Suffolk.
Times Past, Pershore, Hereford and Worcs.
Times Past, Portsmouth, Hants.
Times Past Antiques, Auchterarder, Perths., Scot.
Times Past Antiques Ltd., Windsor and Eton, Berks.
Timmis and Son, B., Eccleshall, Staffs.
Timm's Antiques, S. and S., Woburn, Beds. Wob. Ab. Ant. C.
Timms Antiques Ltd., S. and S., Ampthill, Beds.
Timothy, P., London, E.C.1.
Tina Art, London, N.W.8. Alf. Ant. Mkt.
Tina's Antiques, Codford, Wilts.
Tinder Box, The, Stoke-on-Trent, Staffs.
Tindler, C., Brompton, N. Yorks.
Tingewick Antiques Centre, Tingewick, Bucks.
Tinkers Antiques, Gloucester, Glos.
Tinne, G., Bath, Avon. Gt. West. Ant. C. (Not Cartier)
Tipping, Brian, London, S.W.3. Ant. Ant. Mkt.
Titchfield Antiques Ltd., Titchfield, Hants.
Titchner and Sons, John, Littleton, Cheshire.
Titles Old and Rare Books, Oxford, Oxon.
Titmuss, E.L., London, W.8. (Hope and Glory).
Titus Gallery, The, Saltaire, W. Yorks.
Toad Hall, Walsall, W. Mids.
Tobias and the Angel, London, S.W.13.
Toby's Antiques, Weston-super-Mare, Avon.
Tociapski, Igor, London, W.11.
Todd, A., Stockport, Cheshire.
Todd and Austin Antiques of Winchester, Winchester, Hants.
Todd, E., Hazel Grove, Cheshire.
Todd, M.S., Nether Stowey, Somerset.
Todd, S., St. Leonards-on-Sea, E. Sussex. Hastings Ant. C.
Todd, W., Winchester, Hants.
Todmorden Fine Art, Todmorden, W. Yorks.
Token Antiques, Tonypandy, Mid-Glam., Wales.
Token House Antiques, Ewell, Surrey.
Tolhurst, R., Polegate, E. Sussex.
Tolkien, Mr. and Mrs. S., London, S.W.3. Chen. Gall.
Toll House, Sturminster Newton, Dorset.
Toll House Bookshop, The, Holmfirth, W. Yorks.
Tollett, B., Witney, Oxon.
Tolley, T.M., Worcester, Hereford and Worcs.
Tolley's Galleries, Worcester, Hereford and Worcs.
Tollgate Antiques, Fritwell, Oxon.
Tombland Bookshop, The, Norwich, Norfolk.
Tomkinson, J. and B., Clitheroe, Lancs.
Tomkinson, S., London, N.W.1.
Tomkinson's Stained Glass and Architectural Antiques, London, N.W.1.
Tomlin, D.S., London, N.5.
Tomlinson and Son, F., Stockport, Cheshire.
Tomlinson, G., Leeds, W. Yorks.
Tomlinson Antiques Ltd. and Period Furniture Ltd., Raymond, (Wetherby Antiques), Wetherby, W. Yorks.
Toms, J.A., Aberdare, Mid-Glam., Wales.
Tonkinson, J.B., Weybridge, Surrey.
Tonks, Mrs. B., Wolverhampton, W. Mids.
Tooke, M.D., Guildford, Surrey.
Tooley, Adams and Co. Ltd., London, W.C.2.
Tooley, Christina, Woburn, Beds. Wob. Ab. Ant. C.
Tooley, M.V., Chesham, Bucks.
Tooley, P., Brighton, E. Sussex (Recollections).
Tooltique, Norwich, Norfolk.
Toop, Rosemary, Wallingford, Oxon. L. Arc.
Top Drawer, Hexham, Northumb.
Top Hat Antiques Centre, Nottingham, Notts.
Top Hat Exhibitions Ltd., Nottingham, Notts.
Torr, D., London, S.W.6. (Chelsea Clocks and Antiques.)
Torre Antique Traders, Torquay, Devon.
Torrens, R., Crieff, Perths., Scot.
Tortoiseshell Antiques, Henllan, Dyfed, Wales.
Toth, Ferenc, London, S.W.6.
Toth, F. and E., London, S.W.6.
Totteridge Gallery, The, London, N.20.
Toubian Antiques Ltd., London, W.8.
Toubian, N., London, W.8.
Touchwood, Herstmonceux, E. Sussex.
Touchwood International Ltd., Stow-on-the-Wold, Glos.

Tourell, J., Alfriston, E. Sussex.
Tovey, N., London, S.W.3 (L'Odeon.)
Tower Antiques, Cranborne, Dorset.
Tower Antiques, London, W.10.
Tower Bridge Antique Warehouse Ltd., London, S.E.1.
Tower Gallery, King's Lynn, Norfolk.
Town and Country Antiques, Bath, Avon.
Town and Country Antiques, Tutbury, Staffs.
Town and Country Antiques, Woburn, Beds. Wob. Ab. Ant. C.
Town and Country Antiques Ltd., Tingewick, Bucks.
Town House Antiques, Barnard Castle, Durham.
Townhead Antiques, Newby Bridge, Cumbria.
Townhouse Antiques, Walkerburn, Peebles., Scot.
Townley, Mrs. C.H. and C.P., Newby Bridge, Cumbria.
Towns, J.M., Swansea, W. Glam., Wales.
Townsend, John, Cheltenham, Glos.
Townsend, J. and Lady Juliet, Brackley, Northants.
Townsend, M., London, N.W.1.
Townsend, M., London, N.W.8.
Townsend's, London, N.W.1.
Townsend's, London, N.W.8.
Townsford Mill Antiques Centre, Halstead, Essex.
Townwell House Antiques, Nantwich, Cheshire.
Toynbee-Clarke, G. and D., London, W.1.
Toynbee-Clarke Interiors Ltd., London, W.1.
Tracy Gallery, Simon, London, N.W.8.
Trade Antiques, Long Sutton, Lincs.
Trade Antiques — D.D. White, Manfield, N. Yorks.
Trade Antiques Ltd., Bournemouth, Dorset.
Trade Wind, Rottingdean, E. Sussex.
Trade Wind Antiques, Nottingham, Notts.
Trader Antiques, London, N.13.
Trader Antiques, Preston, Lancs. N.W. Ant. C.
Trading Places, London, N.W.8.
Trading Post, Leamington Spa, Warks.
Tradition Military Antiques, London, W.1.
Traditional Furniture, Hythe, Kent.
Traditional Homes, London, N.W.1.
Trafalgar Galleries, London, S.W.1.
Tran Antiques, Long, Worcester, Hereford and Worcs.
Travers Partnership, Richmond, Surrey.
Travis, Mrs. D., Lytham St. Annes, Lancs.
Travis and Emery, London, W.C.2.
Traylen, Charles W., Guildford, Surrey.
Traylen, N.C.R. and T.A., Ventnor, I. of Wight.
Treadaway Antiques, Paul, Woburn, Beds. Wob. Ab. Ant. C.
Treasure Chest, Berwick-on-Tweed, Northumbs.
Treasure Chest, Birmingham, W. Mids.
Treasure Chest, The, Weymouth, Dorset.
Treasure Chest, Whitley Bay, Tyne and Wear.
Treasure Chest, Wolverhampton, W. Mids.
Treasure Chest Ltd., The, Highbridge, Somerset.
Treasure Ltd., Frederick, Preston, Lancs.
Treasure Ltd., Frederick, Preston, Lancs. N.W. Ant. C.
Treasure House Antiques, Arundel, W. Sussex.
Treasure House Antiques Centre, Bawtry, S. Yorks.
Treasure House Antiques and Collectors Market, Arundel, W. Sussex.
Treasure, J.F., Preston, Lancs.
Treasure, L., Exmouth, Devon.
Treasure Trove Antiques, Newport, Gwent, Wales.
Treasures, Exmouth, Devon.
Treasures, Four Elms, Kent.
Treasures, Oxted, Surrey.
Treasures, Ryde, I. of Wight.
Treasures of Childhood Past, Great Malvern, Hereford and Worcs.
Trecilla Antiques, Ross-on-Wye, Hereford and Worcs.
Tredant, J.C., South Molton, Devon.
Tredant, J.R., South Molton, Devon.
Tredantiques, South Molton, Devon.
Trefor Antiques, John, Rhualt, Clwyd, Wales.
Tregenza, A., Plymouth, Devon.
Treharne, Allan, Swansea, W. Glam., Wales. Ant. C.
Tremayne Ltd., David, London, S.W.5.
Trench Enterprises, London, W.11.
Trenchard Ltd. Charterhouse Gallery, Graham, Heath and Reach, Beds.
Trengove, Croydon, Surrey.
Trentini Antiques, West Kirby, Merseyside.
Trentini, J., West Kirby, Merseyside.
Trevers, J.P., Stow-on-the-Wold, Glos.
Trevers, Stratford, Broadway, Hereford and Worcs.
Trevor, Lewes, E. Sussex.
Trevor-Venis, P., Hexham, Northumb.
Trewin, C. and V., Pulborough, W. Sussex.
Triangle Antiques, Bristol, Avon.
Trianon, London, W.1. G. Ant. Mkt.
Tribe and Son, Tom, Sturminster Newton, Dorset.
Trickey, S., Bristol, Avon. Clift. Ant. Mkt.
Trident Arms, Nottingham, Notts.
Trimbridge Galleries, Bath, Avon.
Trinder, Mr. and Mrs. J., Coldstream, Berwicks., Scot.
Trinder, P., Clare, Suffolk.
Trinder's Booksellers, Clare, Suffolk.
Trinity Antiques Centre, Colchester, Essex.
Trinity Clocks, Colchester, Essex.
Trio, The, London, N.W.3. Ham. Ant. Emp.
Triton Gallery, Cheltenham, Glos.
Trivess, W.D., Meonstoke, Hants.
Troche, G., Washington, W. Sussex.
Troman, C.G. and J.A., Newmarket, Suffolk.
Tron (Antiques) Ltd., David, London, S.W.3.
Trotter, J. and Mrs. M., Yoxford, Suffolk.
Trotter/Parsons, London, W.1. G. Mews.
Trove, London, S.W.1.
Trowbridge Gallery, London, S.W.3.
Trowbridge, M., London, S.W.3.
Trueman, H., Berkeley, Glos.
Truscott, Christina, London, W.11.

U

V

Valley Antiques, Oldham, Lancs.
Vallis, A., Farnham, Surrey.
Valls Ltd., Rafael, London, S.W.1.
Valmar Antiques, Stansted, Essex.
Valtone Pine, Hampton, Middx.
Van Daal, J. and J., Bembridge, I. of Wight.
Van Den Bergh, J. and E., Ilminster, Somerset.
Van Den Bussche, L., Brasted, Kent.
Van Der Breggen, F.J., London, N.1. (Grove Antiques).
Van Der Breggen, F.J. London, S.W.1. (Grove Antiques)
Van der Steen, Mrs. C., London, S.W.3. Chen. Gall.
Van Haeften Ltd., Johnny, London, S.W.1.
Van Haeften, J. and S., London, S.W.1.
Van Hefflin, Mr., Gainsborough, Lincs.
Van Kloof Fine Art, Bradstone, Devon.
Van Riemsdijk, B., Wavendon, Bucks.
Van Riemsdijk Fine Art, Wavendon, Bucks.
Van Vredenburgh Ltd., Edric, London, S.W.1.
Van Wyngaarden, H., Great Malvern, Hereford and Worcs.
Van Zwanenberg, M., Timberscombe, Somerset.
Vanbrugh House Antiques, Stow-on-the-Wold, Glos.
Vandekar Antiques, London, W.1. G. Mews.
Vandekar, Betty and Vera, London, W.1. G. Mews.
Vandekar Antiques Ltd., Nicholas, W.1.
Vandeleur Antiquarian Books, Epsom, Surrey.
Vandenberg, Anita, London, W.11. G. Port.
Vander (Antiques) Ltd., C.J., London, E.C.1.
Vandervelden, M. and Mrs. G., Dunchurch, Warks.
Vane House Antiques, London, N.1.
Vanity Fayre, Mousehole, Cornwall.
Varcoe, Myles, St. Austell, Cornwall.
Vargha, M., London, W.8. (Select Antiques Gallery Ltd.)
Varnham, H.J. and R.P., London, S.E.3.
Vaseroy, London, W.1. B. St. Ant. C.
Vaughan, London, S.W.6.
Vaughan, G. and J., Ruthin, Clwyd, Wales.
Vaughan, J. and J., Deddington, Oxon.
Vaughan, M.J. and Mrs. L.M., London, S.W.6.
Vaughan, Robert, Stratford-upon-Avon, Warks.
Vaughan, R. and C.M., Stratford-upon-Avon, Warks.
Vecta Insula, Ryde, I. of Wight.
Vectis Fine Arts, Newchurch, I. of Wight.
Vedmore Furniture and Antiques, Judy, Banbury, Oxon.
Vella, J.D. and H., Olney, Bucks.
Venables, Jeremy, Kineton, Warks.
Vendy Antiques (Kibworth), Kibworth Beauchamp, Leics.
Vendy Antiques (Uppingham), Uppingham, Leics.
Vendy, D.R., Kibworth Beauchamp, Leics.
Vendy, T.W., Uppingham, Leics.
Veness, K., Saxmundham, Suffolk.
Venn, D., Worcester, Hereford and Worcs.
Venn, D. and G., Worcester, Hereford and Worcs.
Venn, Edward, Williton, Somerset.
Venners Antiques, London, W.1.
Ventnor Rare Books, Ventnor, I. of Wight.
Venture, The, Woking, Surrey.
Verey, Denzil, Barnsley, Glos.
Verney, J., Clare, Suffolk.
Vernon Antiques, J.R., Warminster, Wilts.
Verrall and Co., Brian R., London, S.W.17.
Verre Antique, Highcliffe, Dorset.
Verve Gallery, The, Kirkby Lonsdale, Cumbria.
Veryard, D.J., Northampton, Northants.
Vescovi, Gina, Morecambe, Lancs.
Vescovi, G. and P., Morecambe, Lancs.
Vicary Antiques, Lancaster, Lancs.
Vice, D., Birmingham, W. Mids. (Format of Birmingham Ltd.).
Vickers, John, Woburn, Beds. Wob. Ab. Ant. C.
Vickery, S. and A., Burwash, E. Sussex.
Victoria, Bath, Avon. Gt. West. Ant C.
Victoria Antiques, Alderney, C.1.
Victoria Antiques, Holsworthy, Devon.
Victoria Antiques, Wadebridge, Cornwall.
Victoria Books, Reading, Berks.
Victoria Bookshop, Swindon, Wilts.
Victoria Cottage Antiques, West Kirby, Merseyside.
Victoria and Edward Antiques Centre, Dorking, Surrey.
Victoria Gallery, Camborne, Cornwall.
Victoria Gallery/Victoria Books, Redruth, Cornwall.
Victoria House Antiques, Llangollen, Clwyd, Wales.
Victorian Antiques, London, S.E.1. Ant. Wrhse.
Victorian Arts, Plymouth, Devon.
Victorian Chairman, Bournemouth, Dorset.
Victorian Fireplace Ltd., The, Canterbury, Kent.
Victorian House Shop, Bingley, W. Yorks.
Victorian Parlour, Bournemouth, Dorset.
Victorian Pine and Antiques, Peterborough, Cambs.
Victorian Shop, The, St. Annes-on-Sea, Lancs.
Victorian Village, The, Glasgow, Lanarks., Scot.
Victoriana, Fochabers, Morays., Scot.
Victoriana Antiques, Stockton Heath, Cheshire.
Victoriana Antiques, Wimborne Minster, Dorset.
Victoriana Architectural, Long Clawston, Leics.
Victoriana Dolls, Reigate, Surrey.
Victoria's, Atherton, Lancs.
Victoria's Bedroom, Hungerford, Berks.
Victoria's Curios, Birmingham, W. Mids.
Victory, The, Rochester, Kent.
Vieux-Pernon, B., London, S.W.1 (Heritage).
Vigo Carpet Gallery, London, W.1.
Vigo-Sternberg Galleries, London, W.1.
Villacampa-Ascaso, Maria, Salisbury, Wilts.

Village Antique Market, The, Weedon, Northants.
Village Antiques, Bexhill-on-Sea, E. Sussex.
Village Antiques, Broughton, Lancs.
Village Antiques, Manchester, Lancs.
Village Antiques, Newton Abbot, Devon. N.A. Ant. C.
Village Antiques, Stockton Heath, Cheshire.
Village Clocks, Long Melford, Suffolk.
Village Furniture Co., Manchester, Lancs.
Village Gallery, London, W.11.
Village Green Antiques, Hertford, Herts.
Village Pine, Farnham, Surrey.
Village Studio, Brodick, I. of Arran, Scot.
Village Time, London, S.E.7.
Vince, Ian F., Rettendon, Essex.
Vince, N.B., Bawdeswell, Norfolk.
Vincent, Alfred, Fakenham, Norfolk. Ant. C.
Vincent, Elizabeth Newby, Devizes, Wilts.
Vincent, F., Brighton, E. Sussex. (Retro)
Vincent, H., Barrow-in-Furness, Cumbria.
Vincent, H.M. and V.J., Bungay, Suffolk.
Vinci Antiques, London, W.1. B. St. Ant. C.
Vine Cottage Antiques, Streatley, Berks.
Vine House Antiques, Neston, Cheshire.
Vine, M. and D., Tetsworth, Oxon.
Viney, Elizabeth, Stockbridge, Hants.
Vintage, London, W.1. G. Ant. Mkt.
Vintage Antique Market, The, Warwick, Warks.
Vintage Cameras Ltd., London, S.E.26.
Vintage Fishing Tackle Shop and Angling Art Gallery inc. Coleham Marine, Shrewsbury, Shrops.
Vintage Sounds, London, N.W.8. Alf. Ant. Mkt.
Vintage Toy and Train Museum, The, Sidmouth, Devon.
Vintage Wireless Co. Ltd., The, Bristol, Avon.
Violin Shop, The, Hexham, Northumbs.
Vipul, London, W.1. B. St. Ant. C.
Virginia, London, W.11.
Virginia Antique Galleries, Glasgow, Lanarks., Scot.
Virgo, D., Buxton, Norfolk.
Viventi, G., London, S.E.1. Ber. Ant. Wrhse.
Viventi, Sara, London, N.W.8. Alf. Ant. Mkt.
Vivian Antiques, C., Nuneaton, Warks.
Von Dahlen, Baroness, V., Long Melford, Suffolk.
Von der Berg, C., London, S.W.6. (Han-Shan Tang Ltd.).
von Fullman, P., Malmesbury, Wilts.
Von Lobkowitz, I.K., London, S.W.19. (Acanthus Antiques)
Von Pflugl Antiques, Johnny, London, W.11.
Von Wallwitz, Angela Grafin, London, W.1.
Von Westenholz, P., London, S.W.1. (Westenholz Kime Ltd.)
Vosburgh, B., London, N.1 (Jubilee).
Vosper, J.V., Michinhampton, Glos.
Voss, A.G., Woodbridge, Suffolk.

W

W.13 Antiques, London, W.13.
W.H.E.A.P. Antiques, Worcester, Hereford and Worcs.
W.P.S. (Bruton) Ltd., Bruton, Somerset.
Wace Ancient Art Ltd., Rupert, London, S.W.1.
Waddington, T., Leeds, W. Yorks. (Kingsway Antiques).
Wade, Ray, Preston, Lancs. N.W. Ant. C.
Wade Antiques, Ray, Preston, Lancs.
Wade, Valerie, London, S.W.3.
Wade-Smith, A., Newark, Notts.
Wade-Smith and Read, Newark, Notts.
Wadge Clocks, Chris, Salisbury, Wilts.
Wadham, Peter, Exeter, Devon.
Wadhwa, M., London, S.W.6.
Wadley, Mrs. A., Knaresborough, N. Yorks.
Wadley, N., Knaresborough, N. Yorks.
Waggoner, J. and J., Bath, Avon (Aspidistra Antiques).
Wagner Antiques, London, S.W.8.
Wagner, D., London, S.W.8.
Wain, J.I., Ripon, N. Yorks.
Wain, Mrs. M., Buckminster, Leics.
Wain, Peter, Woore, Shrops.
Waine, V.C., Long Melford, Suffolk.
Wainwright, P.J., Bridgnorth, Shrops.
Waite, J., Burnley, Lancs.
Wajzner, John, Southport, Merseyside. (The White Elephant).
Wakefield, Mr. and Mrs. A., Westcott, Surrey.
Wakefield, C.P., Freuchie, Fife, Scot.
Wakefield, Mr. and Mrs. R.C., Burford, Oxon. Cots. Gateway A.C.
Wakelin, Michael and Helen Linfield, Petworth, W. Sussex.
Wakely, M., Sutton, Surrey.
Wakeman and Co. Ltd., D.J., Dorrington, Shrops.
Wakeman and Taylor Antiques, Wolverhampton, W. Mids.
Wakerley, A., Cambridge, Cambs. (The Oriel Gallery).
Waknell, R.M. and Mrs F., Uppingham, Leics.
Walcot Reclamation, Bath, Avon.
Waldron, G., Birmingham, W. Mids. (Houghtons of Moseley)
Waldy, J. and P., Petworth, W. Sussex. (Flora Dora Antiques).
Wale Ltd., Percy F., Leamington Spa, Warks.
Walford, G.W., London, N.5.
Walker, C., London, S.W.3. (Walker-Bagshawe)
Walker, Mrs. D., Ewell, Surrey.
Walker, Gay, Birley, Hereford and Worcs.
Walker Galleries Ltd., Harrogate, N. Yorks.
Walker, G.R., Penrith, Cumbria.
Walker, I., Odiham, Hants.
Walker, J., Perth, Perths., Scot.
Walker Antiques, John, Hexham, Northumbs.
Walker Gallery, Meldrum, London, S.W.6.
Walker, M. and D., Meldrum, London, S.W.6.
Walker, M.W., Coleraine, Co. Londonderry, N. Ireland.
Walker, Mrs. M.W., Portstewart, Co. Londonderry, N. Ireland.

Walker, P., Burford, Oxon.
Walker, Sue, West Knoyle, Wilts.
Walker, Mrs. S., Kitching, Thornton le Dale, N. Yorks.
Walker, W.E., London, N.W.1.
Walker, W. and J., Jesmond, Tyne and Wear.
Walker, Zene, Burford, Oxon.
Walker-Bagshawe, London, S.W.3.
Walkley, R.C., Shaldon, Devon.
Wall, C.A., Ipswich, Suffolk.
Wall, D., Lewes, E. Sussex.
Wall, S.M., Worcester, Hereford and Worcs.
Wallace Antiques Ltd., London, S.E.3.
Wallace, M., West Wittering, W. Sussex.
Wallace, N., York, N. Yorks. (Minster Gate Bookshop).
Wallbank-Fox, J.A. and M.A., Hungerford, Berks. (Victoria's Bedroom).
Waller, A.J., London, S.W.3 (H.W. Newby).
Wallington-Antiques, Judy, Wareham, Dorset.
Wallis, Catherine, London, N.W.8. Alf. Ant. Mkt.
Wallis, D., London, N.W.8. Alf. Ant. Mkt.
Wallis, Derek and Glenda, Bath, Avon.
Wallis, G.M.A. and Mrs., Wingham, Kent.
Wallis, Tony, Glasgow, Scotland. Vict. Vill.
Wallop, L.N.J., London, S.W.1 (Pawsey and Payne Ltd.).
Wallop, Hon. N.V.B., London, S.W.1 (Pawsey and Payne Ltd.).
Walls, C., Tenterden, Kent.
Walmsley Antiques, Anthony, Blackburn, Lancs.
Walmsley, A. and F.A., Blackburn, Lancs.
Walmsley, Mr. and Mrs. N., Kettering, Northants.
Walne, H.S., Southport, Merseyside.
Walpole Gallery, London, W.1.
Walpole, G.R., London, W.11. (Magus Antiques)
Walsall Antiques Centre, Walsall, W. Mids.
Walsh Ltd., Bernard, Chester, Cheshire.
Walsh, M., Burwash, E. Sussex.
Walsh, M., Mansfield, Notts.
Walter, R.W., London, W.C.2. Lon. Silv. Vts.
Walter Antiques Ltd., William, London, W.C.2. Lon. Silv. Vts.
Walters, B., Weedon, Northants.
Walters, H.J. and S.M., West Haddon, Northants.
Walters, J.D. and R.M., Rolvenden, Kent.
Walton, A., Darlington, Durham.
Walwyn Antiques, Howard, London, S.W.11.
Wandle's Workshop, Mr., London, S.W.18.
Wansford Antiques and Oriental Pottery, Wansford, Cambs.
Warboys Antiques, Warboys, Cambs.
Warburton, E., Stockport, Cheshire.
Ward Antiques, London, S.E.7.
Ward Antiques plc, Long Melford, Suffolk.
Ward, Charles H., Derby, Derbys.
Ward Antiques, C.W., Kettering, Northants.
Ward, D.N., London, S.W.6.
Ward and Son, L.L., Brandsby, N. Yorks.
Ward, M.G., Derby, Derbys.
Ward Antiques, Paul, Sheffield, S. Yorks.
Ward Fine Paintings, P.J., Cirencester, Glos.
Ward, R., Brandsby, N. Yorks.
Ward, S.A., Sevenoaks, Kent.
Ward Antiques, Sheldon, Sevenoaks, Kent.
Ward Properties, Stewart, Westerham, Kent.
Ward, T. and M., London, S.E.7.
Wardle, J., Farnborough, Hants.
Wardle, M.S., London, S.W.14.
Wardle, T., Ashbourne, Derbys.
Ward-Lee, B., Four Elms, Kent.
Wardley, B., Sheffield, S. Yorks. (Richards Furniture Sales).
Wardrope, J., Carlisle, Cumbria. C. Ant. and Craft C.
Ward-Smith, B.A. and F.B., Kentisbeare, Devon.
Ware, V., Newton Abbot, Devon. N.A. Ant. C.
Warehouse, The, Horncastle, Lincs.
Wargrave Antiques, Wargrave, Berks.
Waring, Mrs. C.M., Enfield, Middx.
Waring, R., Hereford, Hereford and Worcs.
Warings of Hereford Antiques, Hereford, Hereford and Worcs.
Warne Family, The, Tregony, Cornwall.
Warner, Christopher, Harrogate, N. Yorks.
Warner, C.C., Harrogate, N. Yorks.
Warner, Carol, London, N.W.8. Alf. Ant. Mkt.
Warner, Mrs. C.U., Brasted, Kent.
Warner Fine Art, Newcastle-upon-Tyne, Tyne and Wear.
Warner, Marie, London, N.W.8. Alf. Ant. Mkt.
Warner and Son Ltd., Robert, Worthing, W. Sussex.
Warner, Mrs. S.A., Pateley Bridge, N. Yorks.
Warner, S. and M., Newcastle-upon-Tyne, Tyne and Wear.
Warner (Antiques) Ltd., W.W., Brasted, Kent.
Warnham Antiques, Warnham, W. Sussex.
Waroujian, M.L., London, W.6.
Warren, A., Hawkhurst, Kent.
Warren, Ailie, London, W.1. G. Mews.
Warren, A.M., Ipswich, Suffolk. (Ashley Antiques).
Warren, B., Seaton, Devon.
Warren, C.R.H., Bristol, Avon (The Mall Gallery).
Warren, Dr. D.J., Portsmouth, Hants.
Warren Antiques, Jimmy, Littlebourne, Kent.
Warren, J.R., Leiston, Suffolk.
Warren Antiques, Leigh, London, S.W.6.
Warren, M., London, N.1.
Warren, Shirley, Sanderstead, Surrey.
Warrender, F.R., Sutton, Surrey.
Warrender and Co., S., Sutton, Surrey.
Warrick, E.M. and J.K., Montacute, Somerset.
Warrington, Mr. and Mrs. J., Hemel Hempstead, Herts.
Warrington, Paul, Easton-on-the-Hill, Northants.
Wartski Ltd., London, W.1.
Warttig, G., Barnsley, S. Yorks.

Warwick Antique Centre, The, Warwick, Warks.
Warwick Antiques, Carlisle, Cumbria. C. Ant. and Craft C.
Warwick Antiques, Warwick, Warks.
Warwick Desks, Warwick, Warks.
Warwick, D.C., Weymouth, Dorset.
Watchbell Antiques, Newport, I. of Wight.
Water Lane Antiques, Bakewell, Derbys.
Watercolour Gallery, The, Cowbridge, S. Glam., Wales.
Watercolour World, Yeovil, Somerset.
Waterfield Ltd., Robin, Oxford, Oxon.
Waterfront Antiques Market, Falmouth, Cornwall.
Watergate Antiques, Chester, Cheshire.
Waterhouse and Dodd, London, W.1.
Waterhouse, R., London, W.1. (Waterhouse and Dodd)
Waterloo Antiques, Oldham, Lancs.
Waterloo Antiques, Welshpool, Powys, Wales.
Waterloo Antiques Centre, Leeds, W. Yorks.
Waterman Fine Art Ltd., London, S.W.1.
Waterman, T. and R., London, S.W.1. (Trevor Philip and Sons Ltd.).
Waters, J. and M., Penarth, S. Glam., Wales.
Waterside Antiques, Ely, Cambs.
Waterway Galleries, Leominster, Hereford and Worcs.
Watherington, K. and J., Leominster, Hereford and Worcs.
Watkins Books Ltd., London, W.C.2.
Watkins, I., Knighton, Powys, Wales.
Watkins, Islwyn, Knighton, Powys, Wales.
Watling Antiques, Crayford, Kent.
Watson, Don, Leominster, Hereford and Worcs. L. Ant. Mkt.
Watson, Mrs. E., Norwich, Norfolk. (Yesteryear).
Watson, G.D., London, S.W.3. (Lewis M. Kaplan Associates Ltd.)
Watson, H. and P., Stratford-upon-Avon, Warks.
Watson, J., Shere, Surrey.
Watson, M.E., Market Weighton, N. Humberside.
Watson Antique Jewellery and Silver, Pauline, Dorking, Surrey.
Watson, Steven, London, N.W.8. Alf. Ant. Mkt.
Watson, V., Kincardine O'Neil, Aberd., Scot.
Watt, Mrs. Elizabeth, Aberdeen, Aberd., Scot.
Watt, V., Banchory, Kincard., Scot.
Watts Antiques, Chris, Cowes, I. of Wight.
Watts Antiques, Chris, Newport, I. of Wight.
Watts and Christensen, London, S.W.10.
Watts, C.E.H., London, S.W.1.
Watts Oriental Rugs, Duncan, Market Harborough, Leics.
Watts, P.J., St. Austell, Cornwall.
Waveney Antiques, London, S.W.10. (Furniture Cave)
Waveney Antiques Centre, Beccles, Suffolk.
Waverley Gallery, The, Aberdeen, Aberd., Scot.
Way, R.E. and G.B., Newmarket, Suffolk.
Waymouth, A., Milverton, Somerset.
Waymouth, Joyce, Fakenham, Norfolk. Ant. C.
Waymouth, J. and E., Honiton, Devon.
Wayne, The Razor Man, Neil, Belper, Derbys.
Wayside Antiques, Duffield, Derbys.
Wayside Antiques, Tattershall, Lincs.
Wayside Antiques, Worsley, Lancs.
Waywell, M., Amersham, Bucks.
Weald Gallery, The, Brasted, Kent.
Wearn and Son Ltd., R., London, S.W.3.
Weatherell's of Harrogate Antiques and Fine Arts, Harrogate, N. Yorks.
Weatherill, F., Denholme, W. Yorks.
Weaver Antiques, Bernard, Cirencester, Glos.
Weaver, L., Aldeburgh, Suffolk.
Weaver, P., Aldeburgh, Suffolk.
Weaver, P., Hartley Wintney, Hants.
Weaver, Trude, London, W.11.
Weavers Cottage Antiques, Painswick, Glos.
Web, A.M., London, W.11.
Webb, D., Abertillery, Gwent, Wales.
Webb, D.H., Winchester, Hants.
Webb Fine Arts, Winchester, Hants.
Webb, Graham, Brighton, E. Sussex.
Webb, G.P., London, E.17.
Webb, M., London, N.1. (Style)
Webb, M., London, N.13.
Webb, M., Wallington, Surrey.
Webb Fine Art, Michael, Bodorgan, Gwynedd, Wales.
Webb, P.A., Yarmouth, I. of Wight.
Webb, Roy, Wickham Market, Suffolk.
Webber, C., Brantham, Suffolk.
Webber, S., Windlesham, Surrey.
Webster, A.J., Coleshill, Warks.
Webster, A. and S., Teignmouth, Devon.
Webster, E.T., Stonham Parva, Suffolk.
Webster, E.W., Bickerstaffe, Lancs.
Webster, G., Liverpool, Merseyside (Maggs Antiques).
Webster, M., Crosshills, N. Yorks.
Webster, M., Great Waltham, Essex.
Webster-Speakman, S.J., Cambridge, Cambs.
Wedderburn Castle Antiques, Duns, Berwicks., Scot.
Wedgwoods of St. Helens Ltd., St. Helens, Merseyside.
Weedon, Mike, London, N.1. The Mall.
Weetslade Fine Art, Dudley, Tyne and Wear.
Weidenbaum, R., Manchester, Lancs. (Village Antiques).
Weijand Fine Oriental Carpets, Karel, Farnham, Surrey.
Weiner, G., Brighton, E. Sussex (The Sentry Box).
Weiner, M., Ipswich, Suffolk. (Majors Galleries)
Weiner, M., Ipswich, Suffolk. (Orwell Galleries).
Weiner, M., Ipswich, Suffolk. (Orwell Paint Strippers).
Weir, Abingdon, Oxon.
Weir, Mr. and Mrs. D., Bottisham, Cambs.
Weir Antiques, Gerald, Ipswich, Suffolk.
Weiss, A. and G., London, W.C.2. Lon. Silv. Vts.

Weiss Gallery, The, London, W.1.
Weiss, Peter K., London, W.C.2. Lon. Silv. Vts.
Welbeck Gallery, The, London, W.1.
Welbourne, Stephen and Sonia, Brighton, E. Sussex.
Welch, K. and A., Warminster, Wilts.
Welch, R., Gateshead, Tyne and Wear.
Weldon Antiques and Jewellery, Southport, Merseyside.
Weldon, H.W. and N.C., Southport, Merseyside.
Well Cottage Antiques, Settle, N. Yorks.
Well House Antiques, Tilston, Cheshire.
Well Lane Antiques, Beverley, N. Humberside.
Wellard, Mary, London, W.1. G. Ant. Mkt.
Wellby Ltd., H.S., Haddenham, Bucks.
Wellby, C.S., Haddenham, Bucks.
Weller, P. and R., Malvern Wells, Herefords. and Worcs.
Weller — Restoration Centre, W.H., Eastbourne, E. Sussex.
Wellfield Antique Centre, Bangor, Gwynedd, Wales.
Welling Antiques, Anthony, Ripley, Surrey.
Wellington Antiques, London, W.11.
Wellington Antiques, Southampton, Hants.
Wellington Gallery, London, N.W.8.
Wells Antique Centre, Wells-next-the-Sea, Norfolk.
Wells, G., Wallingford, Oxon.
Wells, J.H., Aberdeen, Aberd., Scot.
Wells, L.I., Fakenham, Norfolk.
Wells, M.B., Tunbridge Wells, Kent (Frankham Gallery).
Wells Reclamation, Coxley, Somerset.
Wellstead, A.V., Woking, Surrey.
Welsh, P., Brasted, Kent.
Welsh, R., Sandgate, Kent.
Wendover Antiques, Wendover, Bucks.
Wenlock Fine Art, Much Wenlock, Shrops.
Wentworth, J., London, W.11. (The Antique Textile Company).
Wernham, F. and N., Bridge of Allan, Stirls., Scot.
Wertheim, C., London, W.11. G. Port.
Wertheim, Mr. and Mrs. C.D., London, W.8 (Japanese Gallery).
Wessex Medical Antiques, Portsmouth, Hants.
West Borough Antiques, Fine Art, Wimborne Minster, Dorset.
West, B., Canterbury, Kent.
West Bow Antiques, Edinburgh, Midloth., Scot.
West Country Antiques and Collectors Fairs, Ashburton, Devon.
West End Antiques, Elgin, Moray, Scot.
West End Antiques Market, Redruth, Cornwall.
West End Galleries, Buxton, Derbys.
West End House Antiques, Ilminster, Somerset.
West Farm Antiques, Orwell, Cambs.
West Quay Curios, Looe, Cornwall.
West Lancs. Antiques, Burscough, Lancs.
West Antiques, Marie, London, N.1.
West-Cobb Antiques Ltd., Mark J., London, S.W.19.
West-Cobb Antiques Ltd., Mark J., London, N.1.
West of Scotland Antique Centre Ltd., Glasgow, Lanarks., Scot.
West Street Antiques, Burford, Oxon.
West Street Antiques, Dorking, Surrey.
West Street Antiques, Midhurst, W. Sussex.
West Wales Antiques, Murton, W. Glam. Wales.
Westbourne Antiques, Westbourne, W. Sussex.
Westbourne Gallery, London, W.11.
Westcliffe Gallery, The, Sheringham, Norfolk.
Westcott Antiques, Westcott, Surrey.
Westcott Gallery, The, Westcott, Surrey.
Westdale Antiques, Bridport, Dorset.
Westenholz Kime Ltd., London, S.W.1.
Westfield Antiques, Baslow, Derbys.
Westgarth Antiques, Mark, Lynton, Devon.
Westgarth, M. and M., Lynton, Devon.
Westgate Antiques, Warwick, Warks.
Westland, G., London, E.C.2.
Westland Pilkington, London, E.C.2.
Westle, D. and J., Jesmond, Tyne and Wear.
Westleigh Antiques, London, W.1. (Croesus). G. Ant. Mkt.
Westley-Richards, W., London. S.W.3. (Century Gallery).
Westminster Group, London, W.1. G. Ant. Mkt.
Weston Antique Gallery, Weston, Staffs.
Weston Ltd., David, London, S.W.1.
Weston, D.A., London, S.W.1.
Weston, R. and P., Harrow, Middx.
Weston Gallery, William, London, W.1.
Westover, D., Bridport, Dorset.
Westport Gallery, Dundee, Angus, Scot.
Westrope, I., Birdbrook, Essex.
West-Skinn, R., Lincoln, Lincs.
West-Skinn, W., Lincoln, Lincs.
Westville House Antiques, Littleton, Somerset.
Westward Country Pine, Launceston, Cornwall.
Westway Cottage Restored Pine, Helmsley, N. Yorks.
Westwood, F., Petersfield, Hants.
Westwood Antiquarian Books, Mark, Hay-on-Wye, Powys, Wales.
Westwood, M. and C., Hay-on-Wye, Powys, Wales.
Wetherill, J., Northallerton, N. Yorks.
Wetherill, R., York, N. Yorks. (Bishopsgate Antiques).
Weybridge Antiques, Weybridge, Surrey.
Weysom, John, London, W.1. (Sue Brown) G. Mews.
Whadcock, B., Anstey, Leics.
Whalley, Mrs. O.M., Eye, Suffolk.
Wharf Road Antiques, Ellesmere, Shrops.
Wharton, Stuart, St. Albans, Herts.
Wharton Antiques, Tim, Redbourn, Herts.
What Not Antiques, Hindhead, Surrey.
What Now Antiques, Buxton, Derbys.
Whatnot Antiques, Wigan, Lancs.

Whatnots, Strathblane, Stirls., Scot.
Whay, K. and D., Hoylake, Merseyside.
Wheatley Antiques, London, W.1. G. Ant. Mkt.
Wheatley, Mr. and Mrs. K., Mobberley, Cheshire.
Wheatley, R., Empingham, Leics.
Wheatley's, Gt. Yarmouth, Norfolk.
Wheeldon, Mrs. D., Ellesmere, Shrops.
Wheelekea, Liz, Newton Abbot, Devon. N.A. Ant. C.
Wheeler, G., Stone, Staffs.
Wheeler, R.W.H. and M.J., Crewkerne, Somerset.
Wheelgate House Antiques, Bampton, Oxon.
Wheelwright, The, Baldock, Herts.
Whelan, J. and C., Stow-on-the-Wold, Glos.
Wheldon and Wesley Ltd., Codicote, Herts.
Whiddons Antiques and Tearooms, Chagford, Devon.
Whillock, F., Litton Cheney, Dorset.
Whitaker, J., Pickering, N. Yorks.
Whitby, C. and Mrs. B., Lane End, Bucks.
Whitby Antiques, Peter, Lechlade, Glos.
White, London, N.W.8. Alf. Ant. Mkt.
White, A. and D., Weston-super-Mare, Avon.
White Furnishings, Andrew, London, W.10.
White Boar Antiques and Books, Middleham, N. Yorks.
White, B.B., London, E.C.1.
White Cottage Antiques, Tern Hill, Shrops.
White, Doreen, London, N.1. The Mall.
White D., Ramsbury, Wilts.
White Antiques, David, Godalming, Surrey.
White, D.D., Manfield, N. Yorks.
White, D. and Y., Godalming, Surrey.
White Elephant, The, Southport, Merseyside.
White Elephant Antiques, Bowness-on-Windermere, Cumbria.
White, E. and B., Brighton, E. Sussex.
White, G., Worsley, Lancs.
White, G. and J., Harrogate, N. Yorks. (Haworth Antiques).
White House Antiques, Princes Risborough, Bucks.
White House Farm Antiques, Easingwold, N. Yorks.
White, Howard, London, W.1. B. St. Silv. Galls.
White, J., London, W.1. (W.H. Patterson Fine Arts Ltd.)
White, John, London, N.W.8. Alf. Ant. Mkt.
White, J.C., Fitzhead, Somerset.
White, J.C., White Waltham, Berks.
White, J. and G., Huby, N. Yorks.
White, J.J., London, N.W.8. Alf. Ant. Mkt.
White Lion Antiques, Ellesmere, Shrops.
White, P., Cranborne, Dorset.
White, P. Denver, Bournemouth, Dorset. (Peter Denver Antiques)
White Roding Antiques, White Roding, Essex.
White, R. and D., Sherborne, Dorset.
White, R.S. and Mrs. A., Cranbrook, Kent.
White, S., Derby, Derbys.
White, T.E., Wimborne Minster, Dorset.
White, W., South Shields, Tyne and Wear.
Whitehead, D. and V., Newark, Notts.
Whitehead, Joyce and Rod, Chester, Cheshire.
Whitehead, W.S.H., and Mrs. M.M., Lewes, E. Sussex.
Whitehouse Antique Interiors, Arundel, W. Sussex.
Whitehouse Antiques Ltd., Worthing, W. Sussex.
Whiteland, K. and J., Aberaeron, Dyfed, Wales.
Whitelaw and Sons Antiques, John, Auchterarder, Perths., Scot.
Whitelaw, Peter, Ironbridge, Shrops.
Whitemoors Antiques and Fine Art, Shenton, Leics.
Whiten, A.J., Cowes, I. of Wight.
Whiteside, R.J., Pershore, Hereford and Worcs.
Whitestone, S., London, W.1 (Bobinet Ltd.).
Whiteway, M., London, S.W.6. (Whiteway and Waldron Ltd.).
Whiteway, T.M., London, W.8 (Haslam and Whiteway).
Whiteway and Waldron Ltd., London, S.W.6.
Whiteway-Wilkinson, G.A., Maidencombe, Devon.
Whitfield, A. and S., Edinburgh, Midloth., Scot. (Calton Gallery).
Whitfield, C., Canterbury, Kent.
Whitfield Antiques, Robert, London, S.E.10.
Whitgift Galleries, Croydon, Surrey.
Whitla, G. and L., Duns, Berwicks., Scot.
Whitmore, Great Malvern, Hereford and Worcs.
Whitney Antiques, Robert, Whitchurch, Shrops.
Whittaker, B.J., Stickney, Lincs.
Whittaker, Mrs. M.J., Snainton, N. Yorks.
Whittaker, R.A. and Mrs. L.R., Angmering, W. Sussex.
Whittal, G., London, N.1. The Mall.
Whittam, A.P.H. and C.O., St. Peter Port, Guernsey, C.I.
Whittam, P., Tetbury, Glos.
Whittingham, A., Bath, Avon. (Bath Saturday Antiques Mkt.).
Whittingham, Bath, Avon. Gt. West. A. C. Wed. Mkt.
Whittington Galleries, Sutton, Surrey.
Whitton, A.T., Exeter, Devon.
Whitworth and O'Donnell Ltd., London, S.E.13.
Whylie, Mrs. M., Hindhead, Surrey.
Whyte, John, Edinburgh, Midloth., Scot.
Whyte, Philip, London, S.W.1.
Whytock and Reid, Edinburgh, Midloth., Scot.
Wibroe Antiques Ltd., Neil, London, W.11.
Wickens, Mrs. P., Sandwich, Kent.
Wickersley Antiques, Newark, Notts. N. Ant. Wrhse.
Wickersley Antiques, Rotherham, S. Yorks.
Wickham Antiques, Honiton, Devon.
Wickins, A. and M., Peasenhall, Suffolk.
Wickins, Mrs. C.J., Farnham, Surrey.
Wickstead, W., Swansea, W. Glam., Wales.

Widcombe, Antiques and Pine, Bath, Avon.
Widdas Fine Paintings, Roger, Bentley Heath, W. Mids.
Widmerpool House Antiques, Maidenhead, Berks.
Wieliczko, J. and D., London, N.6.
Wiffen, C.A., Parkstone, Dorset.
Wiffen's Antiques, Parkstone, Dorset.
Wigdor, David, Brighton, E. Sussex.
Wigek, Z., London, S.W.6. (House of Mirrors).
Wigg, B.K., Petworth, E. Sussex. (Howes Gallery).
Wiggenhall Antiques, Wiggenhall St. Germans, Norfolk.
Wiggins and Sons Ltd., Arnold, London, S.W.1.
Wiggins, Peter, Chipping Norton, Oxon.
Wigington Antiques, Hay-on-Wye, Powys., Wales.
Wigington, B., Hay-on-Wye, Powys., Wales.
Wigington, James, Stratford-upon-Avon, Warks.
Wigington, R.J., Stratford-upon-Avon, Warks.
Wigram, Francis, Penn, Bucks.
Wilbourg, London, W.1. (Mankowitz). G. Mews.
Wilby, D.G. and M., Tattershall, Lincs.
Wilcocks, Norman, London, N.W.8. Alf. Ant. Mkt.
Wilcox, A., Shrewsbury, Shrops.
Wilcox, S., Bristol, Avon. (Oldwoods).
Wilcox, T., Reigate, Surrey.
Wild Goose Antiques, Modbury, Devon.
Wild, Mrs. W., Ledbury, Hereford and Worcs.
Wild, Mrs. W.M., Tetbury, Glos.
Wildenstein and Co. Ltd., London, W.1.
Wilder, M.P., Chesham, Bucks.
Wilding, Mr., Liverpool, Merseyside (E. Pryor and Son).
Wilding, R.D., Wisbech, Cambs.
Wildish, Lt. Col. V. and Mrs. A., Dorney, Berks.
Wildman, K., Bushey, Herts.
Wildman, P. and M., Dalbeattie, Scotland.
Wildman's Antiques, Dalbeattie, Scotland.
Wiles, B., Witney, Oxon.
Wiles, Bret, Woodstock, Oxon.
Wilkins Antiques, Brett, Wednesbury, W. Mids.
Wilkin, G.F., Honiton, Devon.
Wilkins, C.A., Holt, Norfolk.
Wilkins, D., Woking, Surrey.
Wilkins, Mrs. J., Witney, Oxon.
Wilkins Antiques, Joan, Witney, Oxon.
Wilkins, M., London, W.1.
Wilkins and Wilkins, London, W.1.
Wilkinson, Mrs. A., Harrogate, N. Yorks. (Ann-tiquities).
Wilkinson, A., Newhaven, E. Sussex.
Wilkinson, B., Sible Hedingham, Essex.
Wilkinson, P.J. and Mrs J., Bowness-on-Windermere, Cumbria.
Wilkinson, P.J. and Mrs. J., Holme, Cumbria.
Wilkinson and Son, R., London, S.E.6.
Wilkinson, S., London, W.11 (Chanticleer Antiques.)
Wilkinson, S.P. and H.S., Lancaster, Lancs.
Wilkinson Antiques Ltd., T.G., Petworth, W. Sussex.
Wilkinson, T. and S., Petworth, W. Sussex.
Wilks-Jones, M.A., Conway, Gwynedd, Wales.
Willatt, R.F. and M., Chichester, W. Sussex.
Willcocks, C.A., London, S.W.3. Chen. Gall.
Willcocks, Mrs. Y.P., London, S.W.3. Chen. Gall.
Willcox, Neil, Twickenham, Middx.
Willder, S., Birmingham, W. Mids. (S.R. Furnishing and Antiques).
William, G., Winster, Derbys.
Williams, A., London, S.W.3. Ant. Ant. Mkt.
Williams, A.J., Bristol, Avon (Carnival Antiques).
Williams, Betty, Tredunnock, Gwent, Wales.
Williams, C., Bournemouth, Dorset (The Antique Centre.)
Williams Antiques, Catherine, London, S.W.3. Ant. Ant. Mkt.
Williams Antiquarian Bookseller, Christopher, Parkstone, Dorset.
Williams, Frank, Burford, Oxon.
Williams, J. and B., Gloucester, Glos.
Williams, J.R., London, W.1.
Williams, L., Eastbourne, E. Sussex.
Williams, Margaret, Woburn, Beds. Wob. Ab. Ant. C.
Williams, M., Ystradgynlais, Powys, Wales.
Williams, P., Synod Inn, Dyfed, Wales.
Williams, P., Winslow, Bucks.
Williams, R. and Y., Coniston, Cumbria.
Williams and Son, London, W.1.
Williams, Tony, London, S.W.3. (Shaun Balster) Ant. Ant. Mkt.
Williams Antiques Ltd., Thomas, Bideford, Devon.
Williams (Fine Art) Ltd., Thomas, London, S.W.7.
Williamson, Aura, London, W.1. G. Mews.
Williamson, I.A., Lynton, Devon.
Williamson, R. and D., Newton Stewart, Wigtowns., Scot.
Williamson and Co., R.G., Sorbie, Wigtowns., Scot.
Williamson, Mr. and Mrs. S., Little Dawley, Shrops.
Williamson, S., Newport, I. of Wight.
Willingham Antiques and Collectors Market, Willingham, Cambs.
Willis, Henry, London, W.1. B. St. Silv. Galls.
Willis, J., Norwich, Norfolk. (Crome Gallery and Frame Shop).
Willis Antique Clocks, Matthew, Glastonbury, Somerset.
Willott Antiques, J., Leek, Staffs.
Willoughby, Mrs. J., Northallerton, N. Yorks.
Willow Collectables, Woburn, Beds. Wob. Ab. Ant. C.
Willow Farm Pine Centre, Harlington, Beds.
Wills, Mrs. H.J., Sheffield, S. Yorks. (Fulwood Antiques).
Willson, E., Hungerford, Berks. (Mary Bellis Antiques).

Wilsher, Miss M., Frinton, Essex.
Wilshire, J., Great Missenden, Bucks.
Wilson Antiques, Colin, Sundridge, Kent.
Wilson, C.F., Eastbourne, E. Sussex.
Wilson, D., Harewood, W. Yorks.
Wilson, Derick, Newton Abbot, Devon. N.A. Ant. C.
Wilson, F., Worthing, W. Sussex.
Wilson, G., Eccleston, Lancs.
Wilson, G., Lamberhurst, Kent.
Wilson Antiques, Ian, London, S.E.1.
Wilson, J., Glasgow, Lanarks., Scot. (Brown's Clocks Ltd.) B. St. Ant. G.
Wilson, Mrs. J., Kettering, Northants.
Wilson, Jeff, Leominster, Hereford and Worcs. L. Ant. Mkt.
Wilson (Autographs) Ltd., John, Eynsham, Oxon.
Wilson, J. and A.M., Glasgow, Lanarks., Scot. (Browns of Argyle Street Ltd.).
Wilson, J.D., Boroughbridge, N. Yorks.
Wilson, K., Ickleton, Cambs.
Wilson, M.J., Brancaster Staithe, Norfolk.
Wilson, N., New Romney, Kent.
Wilson, Nancy, Sandwich, Kent.
Wilson, O., Bideford, Devon.
Wilson Ltd., O.F., London, S.W.3.
Wilson, P., Kelvedon, Essex.
Wilson Ltd., Paul, Hull, N. Humberside.
Wilson, Mrs. P.S., Bruton, Somerset.
Wilson, R. and C., Petworth, W. Sussex. (Griffin Antiques).
Wilson and Sons, R.S., Boroughbridge, N. Yorks.
Wilson, S.C., Kingsthorpe, Northants.
Wilson, Timothy D., Bawtry, S. Yorks.
Wilson, T. and P., Edinburgh, Midloth., Scot. (Open Eye Gallery Ltd.).
Wilson's Antiques, Worthing, W. Sussex.
Wilton, K., Newton Abbot, Devon. N.A. Ant. C.
Wiltshire, C.A., Twickenham, Middx.
Wiltshire, D.K. and R.M., Hurst Green, E. Sussex.
Wimpole Antiques, London, W.1. G. Ant. Mkt.
Wimsett, P., Ramsgate, Kent.
Winchester House Antiques, Alresford, Hants.
Winchester, P., Newton Abbot, Devon. N.A. Ant. C.
Winchmore Antiques Ltd., London, N.21.
Winckworth, Newton Abbot, Devon. N. A. Ant. C.
Windebank, R., Bath, Avon. (Quiet St. Antiques)
Windhill Antiquary, The, Bishops Stortford, Herts.
Windle, Mrs. W.J., Bingley, W. Yorks.
Windmill, The, Gateshead, Tyne and Wear.
Windmill Antiques, Bembridge, I. of Wight.
Windmill Antiques, Harrogate, N. Yorks.
Windrush Antiques, Witney, Oxon.
Windsor Antiques, Windsor and Eton, Bucks.
Windsor Gallery, Lowestoft, Suffolk.
Windsor Gallery, David, Bangor, Gwynedd, Wales.
Windsor House Antiques (Leeds) Ltd., Leeds, W.Yorks.
Wingfield, Mrs. M., London, S.W.4.
Wingfield Sporting Gallery, London, S.W.4.
Winikus, J., Sandgate, Kent.
Winkie's, Swansea, W. Glam., Wales. Ant. Centre.
Winkworth Antiques, Richard, Redruth, Cornwall.
Winkworth Antiques, Richard, Truro, Cornwall.
Winram, J. and R., Middleton St. George, Durham.
Winstanley, T., Hindhead, Surrey.
Winster Arts, Winster, Derbys.
Winston Galleries, Harrow, Middx.
Winston Mac (Silversmith), Bury St. Edmunds, Suffolk.
Winstone, D., Bath, Avon. Gt. West. Ant. C.
Winstone Stamp Co. and S.D. Postcards, Bath, Avon. Gt. West. Ant. C.
Winter, Eveline, Rugeley, Staffs.
Winter, Mrs. F.J., Bath, Avon (Widcombe Antiques and Pine).
Winterdown Books, Folkestone, Kent.
Winterflood, Mr. and Mrs., Canterbury, Kent.
Winters' Antiques, Weston-super-Mare, Avon.
Winters, R.N., E.P. and L.B., Weston-super-Mare, Avon.
Wirth, P. and C., London, S.W.19.
Wisborough Green Antiques, Wisborough Green, W. Sussex.
Wisdom, M., Carshalton, Surrey.
Wisdom, M., Mitcham, Surrey.
Wise, Mary, London, W.8.
Wise Owl Bookshop, The, Bristol, Avon.
Wisehall, Michael, Knutsford, Cheshire.
Wiskin Antiques, Stansted, Essex.
Wiskin, K. and M, Stansted, Essex.
Wissinger, George and Antonio Mandoza, London, S.E.1.
Wissinger, G., Chipping Norton, Oxon.
Witch Ball, The, Brighton, E. Sussex.
Witch Ball, The, London, N.W.9.
Witchball, The, London, W.C.2.
Witham, Norman, Beckenham, Kent.
Withers of Leicester, Leicester, Leics.
Withers, P. and B., Wolverhampton, W. Mids.
Withers Antiques, Robert, Halesowen, W. Mids.
Witney Antiques, Witney, Oxon.
Witting, Lt. Col. and Mrs. D.W. Church Stretton, Shrops.
Woburn Abbey Antiques Centre, Woburn, Beds.
Woburn Fine Arts, Woburn, Beds.
Woda, A., London, N.W.8.
Wolf Antiques Ltd., H. and B., Droitwich, Hereford and Worcs.
Wolf, H.G. and B.J., Droitwich, Hereford and Worcs.
Wolfe (Jewellery), London, W.C.2. Lond. Silv. Vts.
Wolfenden, C., Otley, W. Yorks.
Wolfers, D., London, S.W.13.
Wolfson, Lady Ruth, London, N.1. (Chapter One).

Wolkowinski, R., London, W.1. G. Mews.
Wolsey, Newton Abbot, Devon. N.A. Ant. C.
Wood, Alan, Tunbridge Wells, Kent.
Wood (Antiques) Ltd., Colin, Aberdeen, Aberd., Scot.
Wood Gallery, Christopher, London, S.W.1.
Wood, G., Aberdeen, Aberd., Scot.
Wood Fine Art, Jeremy, Petworth, W. Sussex.
Wood, J. and S., Cartmel, Cumbria.
Wood Antiques, Lilian, Great Urswick, Cumbria.
Wood, Mrs. M.A., Donyatt, Somerset.
Wood, Pat, Leek, Staffs.
Wood, P. and C., Southport, Merseyside.
Wood, R., Oldham, Lancs.
Wood, R.M. and P.A., Hatfield Broad Oak, Essex.
Wood, S., Leeds, W. Yorks. (The Antique Exchange)
Wood, S., Osbournby, Lincs.
Woodage, Graham, London, N.1. The Mall.
Woodall and Emery Ltd., Balcombe, W. Sussex.
Woodbridge, Nick, Bath, Avon.
Woodbridge Trading Co., The, Woodbridge, Suffolk.
Woodburn, Anthony, Leigh, Kent.
Woodbury Antiques, Woodbury, Devon.
Woodchurch Antiques, Woodchurch, Kent.
Wooden Box Antiques, Woodville, Derbys.
Wooden Chair Antiques, Cranbrook, Kent.
Woodford, Mike, Bath, Avon. Gt. West. Ant. C.
Woodhall, G.C. and S.E., Alford, Lincs.
Woodhead, Geoffrey M., Honiton, Devon.
Woodhouse, A., London, W.C.2 (The Silver Mouse Trap).
Woodhouse, Mrs. J.E., Hunstanton, Norfolk.
Woodhouse (Antiquarian Horologist), R.C., Hunstanton, Norfolk.
Woodland Fine Art, Alvechurch, W. Mids.
Woods, J.G., Manchester, Lancs. (Chestergate Antiques).
Wood's Wharf Antiques Bazaar, Haslemere, Surrey.
Woodstock Antiques, Woburn, Beds. Woburn Ab. Ant. C.
Woodstock Antiques, Woodstock, Oxon.
Woolacombe Bay Antiques, Woolacombe, Devon.
Woolf, P., A. and P., London, N.1 (Dome Antiques).
Woolley, Rod, London, N.W.8. Alf. Ant. Mkt.
Woolman Antiques, L., Brighton, E. Sussex.
Woolpit Antiques, Woolpit, Suffolk.
Woon, Mrs. D.J., Lymington, Hants.
Wooster, B.R. and P.A., Streatley, Berks.
Wooster, J.A., Twickenham, Middx.
Wootton Billingham, Northampton, Northants.
Wootton Clocks and Watches, L.G., South Brent, Devon.
Wordsworth, P., Manchester, Lancs. (Bulldog Antiques).
Workman, J., Kidderminster, Hereford and Worcs.
World Famous Portobello Market, London, W.11.
Worle, Mr. and Mrs. U., North Cheriton, Somerset.
Worms, L., London, E.C.3.
Worth, G.F.E., Newport, Shrops.
Worth Antiques, Patrick, Dorking, Surrey.
Worthington, R., Bristol, Avon. (The Barometer Shop).
Worth's, Newport, Shrops.
Wosac Ltd., Glasgow, Lanarks., Scot. (West of Scotland Ant. Centre Ltd.)
Wragg, R.G., Cheddleton, Staffs.
Wragg, R.G., Leek, Staffs.
Wraight, T., Weymouth, Dorset.
Wray's Lighting Emporium, Christopher, London, S.W.6.
Wrecclesham Antiques, Farnham, Surrey.
Wren Antiques, London, S.W.13.
Wren Gallery, Burford, Oxon.
Wren House Antiques, Wrentham, Suffolk.
Wren, M.J., Bath, Avon (The Galleon).
Wrenn Antiques, Richard, Leigh-on-Sea, Essex.
Wrentham Antiques, Wrentham, Suffolk.
Wrigglesworth, Linda, London, W.1. G. Mews.
Wright Antiques, Alen, Wigton, Cumbria.
Wright Antiques Ltd., Clifford, London, S.W.3.
Wright, D.T.L., Alresford, Hants.
Wright, E., Bournemouth, Dorset. (The Green Room)
Wright, F., Acle, Norfolk.
Wright, G.B., Harrogate, N. Yorks. (Regency Fine Art).
Wright (Fine Paintings), G.S., Castle Ashby, Northants.
Wright, J., London, N.1. (Number Nineteen)
Wright, J. and C., Winchester, Hants.
Wright, Mick and Fanny, Minchinhampton, Glos.
Wright, P., Newton Abbot, Devon. N.A. Ant. C.
Wright, Mrs. R.S., King's Lynn, Norfolk.
Wright (Booksellers), Sidney, Bournemouth, Dorset.
Wright Antiques, Tim, Glasgow, Lanarks., Scot.
Wright, T. and J., Glasgow, Lanarks., Scot.
Wright, W., Bankfoot, Perths., Scot.
Wrightson, J.E., Norwich, Norfolk (D'Amico Antiques Ltd.).
Wrigley, John R., Ecclesfield, S. Yorks.
Wroughton Antique Centre, Wroughton, Wilts.
Wych House Antiques, Woking, Surrey.
Wyche House Antiques, Nantwich, Cheshire.
Wychwood Antiques, Ascott-under-Wychwood, Oxon.
Wykeham Galleries, The, London, S.W.13.
Wyle Cop Antiques and Reproductions, Shrewsbury, Shrops.
Wylie, Mrs. M., Hindhead, Surrey.
Wyllie Gallery, The, London, W.11.
Wyllie, J.G., London, W.11. (The Wyllie Gallery).
Wymondham Antique Centre, Wymondham, Norfolk.
Wyncoll, Craig, London, N.1. The Mall.
Wyncoll, Craig, London, W.1. G. Ant Mkt.
Wyndham, H., London, S.W.1. (The St. James Art Group.)
Wynsave Investments Ltd., Hungerford, Berks. (Hungerford Arcade).
Wynter Ltd. Arts and Sciences, Harriet, London, S.W.10.

Wynter Ltd. Arts and Sciences, Harriet, London, S.W.10.
Wynyards Antiques, London, W.11.
Wyrardisbury Antiques, Wraysbury, Berks.

X

Xanthus Gallery, Reymerston, Norfolk.
Xelana Antiques, London, W.1. B. St. Ant. C.

Y

Yacobi, B. and C., London, W.1 (Massada Antiques.)
Yacob's Gallery, London, W.8.
Yandell, Mrs. A., Cambridge, Cambs. (Cottage Antiques).
Yap, Yap and Yap, Otley, W. Yorks.
Yardley, B., Bristol, Avon. Clift. Ant. Mkt.
Yardley, K.A.C., London, E.17.
Yardy, S., London, W.14.
Yarwood, Mr. and Mrs. G.E., Stoke-on-Trent, Staffs.
Yates, A., Chipping Campden, Glos.
Yates Antiques, Preston, Lancs. N.W. Ant. C.
Yates Antiques, Brian, Chesterfield, Derbys.
Yates, Major, C.M., St. Annes-on-Sea, Lancs.
Yates, Mrs. D., York, N. Yorks. (Barker Court Antiques and Bygones).
Yates, Inez M.P., York, N. Yorks.
Yates, S., Quorn, Leics.
Ye Olde Curiosity Shop, Denholme, W. Yorks.
Ye Olde Saddlers Shoppe, Horrabridge, Devon.
Year Dot, Leeds, W. Yorks.
Yellow Lantern Antiques Ltd., Brighton, E. Sussex.
Yendell, J.M., Bampton, Devon.
Yeo Antiques, Tetbury, Glos.
Yeo, G.A., Hazel Grove, Cheshire.
Yeo, W.B., Plaitford, Hants.
Yeomans, Mrs. S.D., Knighton, Powys, Wales.
Yer Granny's Attic, Prestwick, Ayr, Scot.
Yesterday, Evesham, Hereford and Worcs.
Yesterday Antiques, Tideswell, Derbys.
Yesterday Child, London, N.1.
Yesterday Tackle, Bournemouth, Dorset.
Yesterdays, Leamington Spa, Warks.
Yesterdays Antiques, Birmingham, W. Mids.
Yesterdays Antiques, Hatch End, Middx.
Yesterday's Antiques, London, S.W.14.
Yesterday's Pine, Ampthill, Beds.
Yesterday's Pine, Berkhamsted, Herts.
Yesterday's Pine, Buckingham, Bucks.
Yesterday's Pine, Shere, Surrey.
Yesterday's Pine, Stony Stratford, Bucks.
Yesterday's Pine, Woburn, Beds.
Yestertime, Worcester, Hereford and Worcs.
Yesteryear, Glasgow, Lanarks., Scot.
Yester-year, Iver, Bucks.
Yesteryear, Norwich, Norfolk.
Yesteryear, Ripon, N. Yorks.
Yesteryear, Stoke-on-Trent, Staffs. Barclay House.
Yesteryear Antiques, Ramsey, Cambs.
Yew Tree Antiques, Four Elms, Kent.
Yewman, J.S. and F.M., Abridge, Essex.
Yewtree Antiques, Templecombe, Somerset.
Yistelworth Antiques, Isleworth, Middx.
Yon Antiques, York, N. Yorks.
Yorath, G., Betws Garmon, Gwynedd, Wales.
York Antique Centre, York, N. Yorks.
York Arcade, London, N.1.
York Cottage Antiques, Helmsley, N. Yorks.
York, G., Honiton, Devon.
York House Gallery, Bournemouth, Dorset.
York House of Ledbury, Ledbury, Hereford and Worcs.
York, T.O. and J., Quorn, Leics.
Yorke, J.H., St. Leonards-on-Sea, E. Sussex.
Yorkshire Pine, Northallerton, N. Yorks.
Youll, B., Exeter, Devon.
Youll's Antique Centre, Exeter, Devon.
Youlten, Vivien C., London, W.2.
Young, Aldric, Edinburgh, Midloth., Scot.
Young Antiques, Edinburgh, Midloth., Scot.
Young, A.J. and A.R., Deal, Kent.
Young, B.P., Lynton, Devon.
Young Antiques, Denis, Aberfeldy, Perths., Scot.
Young, D.E., and Mrs. J.M., Aberfeldy, Perths., Scot.
Young, J., Sheffield, S. Yorks. (Chimney Piece Antique Fires).
Young and Son (Antiques), John, Keswick, Cumbria.
Young, K. and Mrs. M., Willingham, Cambs.
Young, K. and R., Norwich, Norfolk.
Young Antiques, Lionel, Lewes, E. Sussex.
Young, Mavis, Newton Abbot, Devon. N.A. Ant. C.
Young, Michael, London, N.1. The Mall.
Young, M. and Mrs. G., Wareham, Dorset.
Young, M.M. and R.S., Wadebridge, Cornwall.
Young Antiques, Robert, London, S.W.11.
Young Antiques, Robert, Norwich, Norfolk.
Young and Stephens Ltd., London, W.1.
Young, T.C., Edinburgh, Midloth., Scot. (Young Antiques).
Young (Antiques) Ltd., Wm., Aberdeen, Aberd., Scot.
Youssefian, A., London, W.8. (Select Antiques Gallery Ltd.)

Z

Zadah Gallery, London, W.1.
Zafer, R.D., Twickenham, Middx.
Zammit and Sons, G., Manchester, Lancs. (Britannia Antiques).
Zarzycka, Basia, London, S.W.3. Chen. Gall.
Zagiemski, Mrs. J., London, N.1. The Mall.
Zebrak at Barnes Jewellers, Brighton, E. Sussex.
Zebrak, T. and A., Brighton, E. Sussex.
Zeno Booksellers & Publishers, London, W.C.2.
Zentner, F., London, W.C.1.
Ziebell, J., St. Leonards-on-Sea, E. Sussex. Hastings. Ant. C.
Zinni-Lask, J., London, N.W.1. (The Patchwork Dog and The Calico Cat Ltd.)
Zippy Antiques, Stockport, Cheshire.
Zoulfaghari, London, N.W.5.
Zwan Antiques, Timberscombe, Somerset.
Zwemmer Ltd., A., London, W.C.2.

SPECIALIST DEALERS

Most antique dealers in Britain sell a wide range of goods from furniture, through porcelain and pottery, to pictures, prints and clocks. Much of the interest in visiting antique shops comes from this diversity. However, there are a smaller number of dealers who obtain their livelihood by specialising, and the following is a list of these dealers. Most of them will always have in stock a representative selection of the items under their classification.

The name of the business together with the area of London or the town and county under which the detailed entry can be found are given in the listing. Again, we would like to repeat the advice given in the introduction that, if readers are looking for a particular object, they would be well advised to telephone around before making long journeys.

CLASSIFICATIONS

Antique Centres
Antiquities
Antiquarian Books (see Books)
Architectural Items
Arms and Militaria
Art Deco and Art Nouveau
Barometers
Books (Antiquarian)
Brass (see Metalwork)
Bronzes
Carriages and Cars
Carpets and Rugs
Chinese Art (see Oriental Art)
Clocks and Watches
Coins and Medals
Dolls and Toys
Frames
Furniture
- Continental (especially French)
- Country
- Georgian
- Oak
- Pine
- Victorian

Garden Furniture, Ornaments and Statuary
Glass
Horn Items
Icons (see Russian Art)
Islamic Art
Japanese Art (see Oriental Art)
Jewellery (see Silver and Jewellery)
Lighting
Maps and Prints
Metalwork
Miniatures
Mirrors
Musical Boxes, Instruments and Literature
Nautical Instruments (see Scientific Instruments)
Needlework (see Tapestries)
Netsuke (see Oriental Art)
Oil Paintings
Oriental Art
Photographs and Equipment
Playing Cards
Porcelain
Pottery (see also Porcelain)
Prints (see Maps)
Rugs (see Carpets)
Russian Art
Scientific Instruments
Sculpture
Shipping Goods and Period Furniture for the Trade
Silver and Jewellery
Sporting Items and Associated Memorabilia
Sporting Paintings and Prints
Stamps
Tapestries, Textiles and Needlework
Tools (including Needlework and Sewing)
Toys (see Dolls and Toys)
Trade Dealers (see Shipping Goods)
Treen
Vintage Cars (see Carriages and Cars)
Watercolours
Wholesale Dealers (see Shipping Goods)
Wine Related Items

Antiques Centres

Bond Street Antique Centre, London, W.1.
Grays Antique Market, London, W.1.
Grays Mews, London, W.1.
The Corner Portobello Antiques Supermarket, London, W.11.
The Good Fairy Open Air Market, London, W.11.
Grays Portobello, London, W.11.
L'Aigton Antique Centre, London, W.11.
The Red Lion Market (Portobello Antiques Market), London, W.11.
Roger's Antiques Gallery, London, W.11.
Stouts Antique Arcade, London, W.11.
World Famous Portobello Market, London, W.11.
Antiquarius, London, S.W.3.
Chelsea Antique Market, London, S.W.3.
Chenil Galleries, London, S.W.3.
Dixon's Antique Centre, London, S.W.14.
Streatham Traders and Shippers Market, London, S.W.16.
Bermondsey Antique Market, London, S.E.1.
Franklins Camberwell Antiques Market, London, S.E.5.
Greenwich Antiques Market, London, S.E.10.
Crystal Palace Collectors Market, London, S.E.19.
Cutler Street Antique Market, London, E.1.
Georgian Village Antiques Market, London, E.17.
Angel Arcade, London, N.1.
Georgian Village, London, N.1.
London Militaria Market, London, N.1.
The Mall Antiques Arcade, London, N.1.
York Arcade, London, N.1.
Hampstead Antique Emporium, London, N.W.3.
Alfies Antiques Market, London, N.W.8.
Apple Market, London, W.C.2.
Covent Garden Flea Market, London, W.C.2.
The London Silver Vaults, London, W.C.2.
Bartlett Street Antique Centre, Bath, Avon.
Bath Antique Market, Bath, Avon.
Bath Saturday Antiques Market, Bath, Avon.
Great Western Antique Centre, Bath, Avon.
Paragon Antiques and Collectors Market, Bath, Avon.
Bristol Antique Market, Bristol, Avon.
Clifton Antiques Market, Bristol, Avon.
Ampthill Antiques Centre, Ampthill, Beds.
Heath Antique Centre, Heath and Reach, Beds.
The Woburn Abbey Antiques Centre, Woburn, Beds.
Ladd's Gallery, Hare Hatch, Berks.
Hungerford Arcade, Hungerford, Berks.
Reading Emporium, Reading, Berks.
Amersham Antiques and Collectors Centre, Amersham, Bucks.
Olney Antique Centre, Olney, Bucks.
Bell Street Antiques Centre, Princes Risborough, Bucks.
Tingewick Antiques Centre, Tingewick, Bucks.
Antiques at Wendover, Wendover, Bucks.
Collectors Market, Cambridge, Cambs.
Willingham Antiques and Collectors Market, Willingham, Cambs.
Guildhall Fair, Chester, Cheshire.
Davenham Antiques Centre, Davenham, Cheshire.
Stancie Cutler Antique and Collectors Fairs, Nantwich, Cheshire.
Nantwich Antique Centre, Nantwich, Cheshire.
E.R. Antiques Centre, Stockport, Cheshire.
Waterfront Antique Complex, Falmouth, Cornwall.
New Generation Antique Market, Penzance, Cornwall.
West End Antiques Market, Redruth, Cornwall.
Attic Cellar, St. Ives, Cornwall.
Carlisle Antique and Craft Centre, Carlisle, Cumbria.
Cockermouth Antiques Market, Cockermouth, Cumbria.
Derby Antiques Centre, Derby, Derbys.
Derby Antiques Market, Derby, Derbys.
Glossop Antique Centre, Glossop, Derbys.
Dartmoor Antiques Centre, Ashburton, Devon.
The Antique Centre on the Quay, Exeter, Devon.
Youll's Antiques Centre, Exeter, Devon.
Antique Centre, Honiton, Devon.
Newton Abbot Antique Centre, Newton Abbot, Devon.
Barbican Antiques Centre, Plymouth, Devon.
New Street Antique Centre, Plymouth, Devon.
Sidmouth Antique Market, Sidmouth, Devon.
Antique Centre, Bournemouth, Dorset.
Bridport Antique Centre, Bridport, Dorset.
Antique Market, Dorchester, Dorset.
Colliton Antique and Craft Centre, Dorchester, Dorset.
Antique Market, Sherborne, Dorset.
Sherborne Antique Centre, Sherborne, Dorset.
Lunn's Way Antiques Centre, Weymouth, Dorset.
North Quay Antiques Centre, Weymouth, Dorset.
Barnes House Antiques, Wimborne Minster, Dorset.
Abridge Antique Centre, Abridge, Essex.
Battlesbridge Antique Centre, Battlesbridge, Essex.
Trinity Antiques Centre, Colchester, Essex.
Epping Saturday Market, Epping, Essex.
Grays Galleries Antiques and Collectors Centre, Grays, Essex.
Baddow Antique and Craft Centre, Gt. Baddow, Essex.
Kelvedon Antiques Centre, Kelvedon, Essex.
Maldon Antiques and Collectors' Market, Maldon, Essex.
Charlton Kings Antique Centre, Cheltenham, Glos.
Cheltenham Antique Market, Cheltenham, Glos.
Cirencester Antique Market, Cirencester, Glos.

Antique Centre, Moreton-in-Marsh, Glos.
Painswick Antique Centre, Painswick, Glos.
Cotswold Antiques Centre, Stow-on-the-Wold, Glos.
Lymington Antiques Centre, Lymington, Hants.
Folly Antiques Centre, Petersfield, Hants.
Antique Centre, Kidderminster, Hereford and Worcs.
Leominster Antiques Market, Leominster, Hereford and Worcs.
Antique and Collectors' Market, Hemel Hempstead, Herts.
Hitchin Antiques Gallery, Hitchin, Herts.
By George! Antiques Centre, St. Albans, Herts.
St. Albans Antique Market, St. Albans, Herts.
The Herts and Essex Antique Centre, Sawbridgeworth, Herts.
Beckenham Antique Market, Beckenham, Kent.
Bromley Antique Market, Bromley, Kent.
Canterbury Rastro, Canterbury, Kent.
Canterbury Weekly Antique Market, Canterbury, Kent.
Hoodeners Antiques and Collectors Market, Canterbury, Kent.
Cranbrook Antique Centre, Cranbrook, Kent.
Hythe Antique Centre, Hythe, Kent.
Malthouse Arcade, Hythe, Kent.
Rochester Antiques and Flea Market, Rochester, Kent.
Sandgate Antiques Centre, Sandgate, Kent.
Noah's Ark Antique Centre, Sandwich, Kent.
The Antiques Centre, Sevenoaks, Kent.
Bradbourne Gallery, Sevenoaks, Kent.
Barden House Antiques, Tonbridge, Kent.
Tudor Cottage Antiques Centre, Tonbridge, Kent.
Tunbridge Wells Antique Centre, Tunbridge Wells, Kent.
Castle Antiques Centre, Westerham, Kent.
Westerham Antique Centre, Westerham, Kent.
Last Drop Antique Club Collectors Market, Bolton, Lancs.
Burnley Antique Centre, Harle Syke, Lancs.
The Assembly Rooms Market, Lancaster, Lancs.
Lancaster Leisure Park Antiques Centre, Lancaster, Lancs.
Sun Street Antique Centre, Lancaster, Lancs.
Manchester Antique Hypermarket, Manchester, Lancs.
Royal Exchange Shopping Centre, Manchester, Lancs.
North Western Antique Centre, Preston, Lancs.
Walter Aspinall Antiques, Sabden, Lancs.
The Antiques Complex, Leicester, Leics.
Oxford Street Antique Centre Ltd., Leicester, Leics.
Swans Antique Centre, Oakham, Leics.
Boston Antiques Centre, Boston, Lincs.
Hemswell Antique Centre, Hemswell Cliff, Lincs.
Lincolnshire Antique Centre, Horncastle, Lincs.
Eastgate Antique Centre, Lincoln, Lincs.
Stamford Antiques Centre, Stamford, Lincs.
Hampton Village Antiques Centre, Hampton, Middx.
The Jay's Antique Centre, Harefield, Middx.
Coltishall Antiques Centre, Coltishall, Norfolk.
Fakenham Antique Centre, Fakenham, Norfolk.
Old Granary Antique and Collectos Centre, Kings Lynn, Norfolk.
Cloisters Antiques Fair, Norwich, Norfolk.
Norwich Antique and Collectors Centre, Norwich, Norfolk.
Angel Antique Centre, South Lopham, Norfolk.
Swaffham Antiques Centre, Swaffham, Norfolk.
Wymondham Antique Centre, Wymondham, Norfolk.
Finedon Antiques (Antiques Centre), Finedon, Northants.
Village Antique Market, Weedon, Northants.
Antiques and Bric-a-Brac, Market Wellingborough, Northants.
Castle Gate Antiques Centre, Newark, Notts.
Newark Antiques Centre, Newark, Notts.
Nottingham Antique Centre, Nottingham, Notts.
Top Hat Antiques Centre, Nottingham, Notts.
Cotswold Gateway Antique Centre, Burford, Oxon.
Cotswold Gateway Antique Cente, Chipping Norton, Oxon.
Deddington Antique Centre, Deddington, Oxon.
Oxford Antiques Centre, Oxford, Oxon.
Oxford Antique Trading Co., Oxford, Oxon.
The Lamb Arcade, Wallingford, Oxon.
Span Antiques, Woodstock, Oxon.
Stretton Antiques Market, Church Stretton, Shrops.
Ironbridge Antique Centre, Ironbridge, Shrops.
Pepper Lane Antique Centre, Ludlow, Shrops.
St. Leonards Antiques, Ludlow, Shrops.
Shrewsbury Antique Centre, Shrewsbury, Shrops.
Shrewsbury Antique Market, Shrewsbury, Shrops.
Bridgwater Antiques Market, Bridgwater, Somerset.
Guildhall Antique Market, Chard, Somerset.
Crewkerne Antique Centre, Crewkerne, Somerset.
Dulverton Antique Centre, Dulverton, Somerset.
Country Antique Centre, Ilminster, Somerset.
Taunton Silver Street Antiques Centre, Taunton, Somerset.
Rugeley Antique Centre, Brereton, Staffs.
The Antique Centre, Kinver, Staffs.
Antique Market, Newcastle-under-Lyme, Staffs.

Waveney Antiques Centre, Beccles, Suffolk.
Clare Antique Warehouse, Clare, Suffolk.
Debenham Antique Centre, Debenham, Suffolk.
Long Melford Antiques Centre, Long Melford, Suffolk.
The Old Town Hall Antique Centre, Needham Market, Suffolk.
Surrey Antiques Centre, Chertsey, Surrey.
Victoria and Edward Antiques Centre, Dorking, Surrey.
The Antiques Arcade, East Molesey, Surrey.
Sovereign Antique Centre, The, East Molesey, Surrey.
Farnham Antique Centre, Farnham, Surrey.
Maltings Monthly Market, Farnham, Surrey.
The Antique Centre, Guildford, Surrey.
Wood's Wharf Antiques Bazaar, Haslemere, Surrey.
Old Smithy Antique Centre, Merstham, Surrey.
Antiques Arcade, Richmond, Surrey.
Fern Cottage Antique Centre, Thames Ditton, Surrey.
Bexhill Antiques Centre, Bexhill-on-Sea, Sussex East.
Brighton Antiques Gallery, Brighton, Sussex East.
Jubilee Antique Cellars and Collectors Market, Brighton, Sussex East.
Kollect-o-Mania, Brighton, Sussex East.
Prinny's Antique Gallery, Brighton, Sussex East.
Chateaubriand Antiques Centre, Burwash, Sussex East.
Antique Market, Eastbourne, Sussex East.
Eastbourne Antiques Market, Eastbourne, Sussex East.
Pharoah's Antiques Centre, Eastbourne, Sussex East.
George Street Antiques Centre, Hastings, Sussex East.
Cliffe Antiques Centre, Lewes, Sussex East.
Lewes Antiques Centre, Lewes, Sussex East.
Polegate Antiques Cente, Polegate, Sussex East.
Hastings Antique Centre, St. Leonards-on-Sea, Sussex East.
Seaford "Barn Collectors Market", Seaford, Sussex East.
Antique Centre and Collectors Market, Adversane, Sussex West.
Mamie's Antiques Centre, Arundel, Sussex West.
Tarrant Street Antique Centre, Arundel, Sussex West.
Treasure House Antiques and Collectors Market, Arundel, Sussex West.
Upstairs Downstairs Antique Market, Arundel, Sussex West.
Almhouses Arcade, Chichester, Sussex West.
Eagle House Antiques Market, Midhurst, Sussex West.
Midhurst Antiques Market, Midhurst, Sussex West.
Petworth Antique Market, Petworth, Sussex West.
The Antiques Centre, Bidford-on-Avon, Warks.
Dunchurch Antique Centre, Dunchurch, Warks.
Spa Antiques Market, Leamington Spa, Warks.
Rugby Antiques Centre, Rugby, Warks.
The Antique Arcade, Stratford-upon-Avon, Warks.
Stratford Antique Centre, Stratford-upon-Avon, Warks.
Smith St. Antique Centre, Warkwick, Warks.
Vintage Antique Market, Warwick, Warks.
The Warwick Antique Centre, Warwick, Warks.
The City of Birmingham Antique Market, Birmingham, West Midlands.
Stancie Cutler Antique and Collectors' Fair, Sutton Coldfield, West Midlands.
Walsall Antiques Centre, Walsall, W. Mids.
Marlborough Parade Antique Centre, Marlborough, Wilts.
Antique and Collectors Market, Salisbury, Wilts.
The Avonbridge Antiques and Collectors Market, Salisbury, Wilts.
Mr. Micawber's Attic, Salisbury, Wilts.
The Ginnel, Harrogate, Yorkshire North.
Grove Collectors Centre, Harrogate, Yorkshire North.
Montpellier Mews Antique Market, Harrogate, Yorkshire North.
York Antiques Centre, York, Yorkshire North.
Treasure House Antiques Centre, Bawtry, Yorkshire South.
Bingley Antiques Centre, Bingley, Yorkshire West.
Bradford Antiques and Curio Centre, Bradford, Yorkshire West.
Halifax Antiques Centre, Halifax, Yorkshire West.
Antiques Centre, Ilkley, Yorkshire West.
Waterloo Antiques Centre, Leeds, Yorkshire West.
Union Street Antique Market, St. Helier, Jersey, Channel Islands.
Bath Street Antiques Galleries, Glasgow, Scotland.
The Victorian Village, Glasgow, Scotland.
Virginia Antique Galleries, Glasgow, Scotland.
West of Scotland Antique Centre Ltd., Glasgow, Scot.
Pembroke Antique Centre, Pembroke, Dyfed, Wales.
Jacob's Antique Market, Cardiff, S. Glam, Wales.
Antique Centre, Swansea, W. Glam., Wales.
Wellfield Antique Centre, Bangor, Gwynedd, Wales.

Antiquities

Astarte Gallery, London, W.1.
Charles Ede Ltd., London, W.1.
Hadji Baba Ancient Art, London, W.1.

Mansour Gallery, London, W.1.
Sheppard and Cooper Ltd., London, W.1.
Ahuan (U.K.) Ltd., London, S.W.1.
Robin Symes Ltd., London, S.W.1.
Rupert Wace Ancient Art Ltd., London, S.W.1.
Ian Auld, London, N.1.
M. Sainsbury, Bath, Avon.
Tamblyn, Alnwick, Northumbs.
A. Burton-Garbett, Morden, Surrey.
Richard Alexander, Seaford, Sussex East.

Antiquarian Books (See Books)

Architectural Items

Architectural Antiques, London, W.6.
E.S. Phillips and Sons, London, W.11.
J. Crotty and Son Ltd., London, S.W.6.
T. Crowther and Son, London, S.W.6.
Fairfax Fireplaces and Antiques, London, S.W.6.
Hollingshead and Co., London, S.W.6.
Old World Trading Co., London, S.W.6.
Pageant Antiques, London, S.W.6.
Thornhill Galleries Ltd., London, S.W.6.
Whiteway and Waldron, London, S.W.6.
Scallywag, London, S.W.9.
T.F. Buckle Ltd., London, S.W.10.
Furniture Cave, London, S.W.10.
H.W. Poulter and Son, London, S.W.10.
A. and R. Dockerill Ltd., London, S.W.15.
Thornhill Galleries Ltd., London, S.W.15.
Davis and Davis Architectural Antiques, London, S.E.5.
Lamont Antiques Ltd., London, S.E.10.
London Architectural Salvage and Supply Co. Ltd., London, E.C.2.
Westland Pilkington, London, E.C.2.
Townsends, London, N.W.1.
Townsends, London, N.W.8.
Walcot Reclamation, Bath, Avon.
Robert Mills, Bristol, Avon.
David Bridgewater, Marshfield, Avon.
Town and Country Antiques Ltd., Tingewick, Bucks.
Nostalgia, Stockport, Cheshire.
Grate Expectations, Callington, Cornwall.
The Holme Fire Co., Holme, Cumbria.
Havenplan's Architectural Emporium, Killamarsh, Derbys.
Ashburton Marbles, Ashburton, Devon.
Catabrian Antiques and Architectural Furnishing, Lynton, Devon.
Antique Fireplace Centre, Plymouth, Devon.
Brian Taylor Antiques, Plymouth, Devon.
Architectural Antiques, South Molton, Devon.
Bellevue House Interiors, South Molton, Devon.
Talisman, Gillingham, Dorset.
Hayes Architectural Antiques, Paul, Gloucester, Glos.
Architectural Heritage, Taddington, Glos.
Old Cottage Things, Romsey, Hants.
The Pine Cellars, Winchester, Hants.
Burgess Farm Antiques, Morestead, Hants.
Elmey Heritage, Elmey Lovett, Hereford and Worcs.
Bailey's Architectural Antiques, Ross-on-Wye, Hereford and Worcs.
Olivers of Whitchurch, Whitchurch, Hereford and Worcs.
The Original Choice, Worcester, Hereford and Worcs.
W.J. Cowell and Sons Architectural Antiques, Broughton, Lancs.
Bygone Times, Eccleston, Lancs.
Old Smithy, Feniscowles, Lancs.
Ralph A. Sutcliffe, Harle Syke, Lancs.
James Cook Antiques, Longridge, Lancs.
Antique Fireplaces, Manchester, Lancs.
Britannia Antiques, Manchester, Lancs.
The Old Rock, Trawden, Lancs.
Victoriana Architectural, Long Clawston, Leics.
Crowther of Syon Lodge Ltd., Isleworth, Middx.
The Country Seat, Huntercombe, Oxon.
Architectural Antiques, Ludlow, Shrops.
Anvil Antiques, Leek, Staffs.
Old Flames Architectural Antiques, Stoke-on-Trent, Staffs.
Drummonds of Bramley Architectural Antiques Ltd., Bramley, Surrey.
Glover and Stacey, Tongham, Surrey.
Brighton Architectural Salvage, Brighton, Sussex East.
Shiners Architectural Reclamation, Newcastle-upon-Tyne, Tyne and Wear.
La-di-da, Stratford-upon-Avon, Warks.
Dalton Street Antiques, Birmingham, West Midlands.
Christopher Gordon Antiques, Birmingham, West Midlands.
James Antiques, Canalside, Birmingham, West Midlands.
Original Choice Ltd., Birmingham, West Midlands.
Tatters of Tyseley, Birmingham, West Midlands.
Martin-Quick Antiques Ltd., Wolverhampton, W. Mids.
Harriett Fairfax Fireplaces, Langley Burrell, Wilts.
Relic Antiques at Brillscote Farm, Malmesbury, Wilts.
Ray Coggins Antiques, Westbury, Wilts.
White House Farm Antiques, Easingwold, Yorkshire North.
Robert Aagaard Ltd., Knaresborough, Yorkshire North.
Daleside Antiques, Markington, Yorkshire North.
Andy Thornton Architectural Antiques Ltd., Elland, Yorkshire West.
Chapel House Fireplaces, Holmfirth, Yorkshire West.
Period Architectural Features and Antiques, Annahilt, Co. Down, N.I.
Dunedin Antiques Ltd., Edinburgh, Scotland.
Old Mill Antiques, Kinbuck, Scotland.
Michael Main Ltd., Architectural Antiques, Cerrig-y-Drudion, Clwyd, Wales.

Arms and Militaria

Blunderbuss Antiques, London, W.1.
Forman Piccadilly Ltd., London, W.1.
Holland and Holland Ltd., London, W.1.

Tradition — Military Antiques, London, W.1.
Under Two Flags, London, W.1.
Michael German, London, W.8.
Robert Hales Antiques Ltd., London, W.8.
The Armoury of St. James, London, S.W.1.
Peter Dale Ltd., London, S.W.1.
Peter Tillou Works of Art, London, S.W.1.
Collectors Corner — Militaria, London, S.E.22.
London Militaria Market, London, N.1.
Nihon Token, London, W.C.1.
Tony L. Oliver, Windsor and Eton, Berks.
Sundial Antiques, Amersham, Bucks.
Hollington Antiques, Long Crendon, Bucks.
Terence H. Porter, Steeple Claydon, Bucks.
Antron House Antiques, Penzance, Cornwall.
Anthony D. Goodlad, Chesterfield, Derbys.
John Meredith, Chagford, Devon.
Gainsborough House Antiques, Sidmouth, Devon.
Charterhouse Antiques, Teignmouth, Devon.
Sterling Coins and Medals, Bournemouth, Dorset.
M. and R. Lankshear Antiques, Christchurch, Dorset.
Epping Galleries, Epping, Essex.
David, Jean and John Antiques, Westcliff-on-Sea, Essex.
Heydens Antiques and Militaria, Cheltenham, Glos.
Military Curios, Gloucester, Glos.
Hampton Galery, Tetbury, Glos.
Romsey Medal and Collectors Centre, Romsey, Hants.
Cottage Antiques, Worcester, Hereford and Worcs.
Guns and Tackle, Scunthorpe, Humberside South.
Hawley Antiques, Beverley, Humberside North.
Antique Militaria, Bridlington, Humberside North.
H.S. Greenfield and Son, Canterbury, Kent.
T.H. and J. Mason, Gillingham, Kent.
Militaryman Antiques, Blackpool, Lancs.
Bulldog Antiques, Manchester, Lancs.
Massey's Antiques, Coalville, Leics.
Pinfold Antiques, Ruskington, Lincs.
Trident Arms, Nottingham, Notts.
Monarch Antiques, Glastonbury, Somerset.
Fox and Co., Yeovil, Somerset.
Errington Antiques, Newcastle-under-Lyme, Staffs.
Barn End Antiques, Hadleigh, Suffolk.
Atfield and Daughter, Ipswich, Suffolk.
West Street Antiques, Dorking, Surrey.
Casque and Gauntlet Antiques Ltd., Farnham, Surrey.
The Sentry Box — Military Antiques, Brighton, Sussex East.
St. Pancras Antiques, Chichester, Sussex West.
Michael Miller, Hurstpierpoint, Sussex West.
Arbour Antiques Ltd., Stratford-upon-Avon, Warks.
March Medals, Birmingham, W. Midlands.
Collectors' Paradise Ltd., Wolverhampton, W. Midlands.
Edred A.F. Gwillian, Cricklade, Wilts.
Military Parade Bookshop, Marlborough, Wilts.
Cairncross and Sons, Filey, Yorkshire North.
Hanover Antiques, Scarborough, Yorkshire North.
Adamson Armoury, Skipton, Yorkshire North.
Andrew Spencer Bottomley, Holmfirth, Yorkshire West.
D.W. Dyson, Huddersfield, Yorkshire West.
Angus Antiques, Dundee, Scotland.
Earlshall Castle, Leuchars, Scotland.
Hermitage Antiquities, Fishguard, Dyfed, Wales.

Art Deco and Art Nouveau

Editions Graphiques Gallery, London, W.1.
Liberty, London, W.1.
Mayfair Gallery, London, W.1.
Young and Stephen Ltd., London, W.1.
Antiques 132, London, W.4.
Cameo Gallery, London, W.8.
John Jesse, London, W.8.
The Pruskin Gallery, London, W.8.
Joan Leigh, London, W.11.
Jones, London, W.11.
Cobra and Bellamy, London, S.W.1.
Galerie Moderne Ltd., London, S.W.1.
Gallery 25, London, S.W.1.
Lewis M. Kaplan Associates Ltd., London, S.W.3.
L'Odeon, London, S.W.3.
Twentieth Century, London, S.W.12.
The Studio, London, N.1.
Tadema Gallery, London, N.1.
John Beer, London, N.6.
Art Furniture (London) Ltd., London, N.W.1.
Jazzy Art Deco, London, N.W.1.
John Lyons Gallery, London, N.W.3.
The Furniture Store Ltd., London, N.W.6.
Alfies Antique Market, London, N.W.8.
Beverley, London, N.W.8.
Bizarre, London, N.W.8.
Simon Tracy Gallery, London, N.W.8.
Fantiques, Amersham, Bucks.
20th Century, Cambridge, Cambs.
B.R. Knight and Sons, St. Ives, Cambs.
Nantwich Art Deco and Decorative Arts, Nantwich, Cheshire.
Honiton Antique Toys, Honiton, Devon.
Beaminster Antiques, Beaminster, Dorset.
The Antique Centre, Bournemouth, Dorset.
Galerie Antiques, Broadstone, Dorset.
Johnsons of Sherborne Ltd., Sherborne, Dorset.
Finesse Fine Art, Weymouth, Dorset.
Davana Original Interiors, Colchester, Essex.
Bell Antiques, Romsey, Hants.
Titchfield Antiques Ltd., Titchfield, Hants.
The Folly, Longridge, Lancs.
Joy's Shop, Longridge, Lancs.
A.S. Antiques, Manchester, Lancs.
Decoroy, Preston, Lancs.
Heyday, Saddleworth, Lancs.
Birches Art Deco Shop, Leicester, Leics.
Arbiter, Wallasey, Merseyside.
Bits and Pieces, Farnham, Surrey.

Peter and Debbie Gooday, Richmond, Surrey.
Decodream, Coulsdon, Surrey.
Le Jazz Hot, Brighton, Sussex East.
Brian Page Antiques, Brighton, Sussex East.
Pyramid, Brighton, Sussex East.
Foundry Lane Antiques Centre, Lewes, Sussex East.
Cirdeco, St. Leonards-on-Sea, Sussex East.
Armstrong-Davis Gallery, Arundel, Sussex West.
Jazz, Stratford-upon-Avon, Warks.
Art Deco Ceramics Ltd., Stratford-upon-Avon, Warks.
Muir Hewitt, Halifax, Yorkshire West.
Rendezvous Gallery, Aberdeen, Scotland.
Gothick Dream Fine Art, Arthog, Gwynedd, Wales.
Paul Gibbs Antiques and Decorative Arts, Conway, Gwynedd, Wales.

Barometers (Most clock dealers also sell barometers)

John Carlton Smith, London, S.W.1.
Aubrey Brocklehurst, London, S.W.7.
Howard Walwyn Antiques, London, S.W.11.
Patric Capon, London, N.1.
Strike One (Islington) Ltd., London, N.1.
Barometer Fair, London, W.C.1.
Barometer Shop, Bristol, Avon.
Medalcrest Ltd., Hungerford, Berks.
The Old Malthouse, Hungerford, Berks.
Eton Gallery Antiques, Windsor and Eton, Berks.
Anthony Seales, Windsor and Eton, Berks.
John Beazor and Sons Ltd., Cambridge, Cambs.
Derek Rayment Antiques, Barton, Cheshire.
Chester Antiques, Chester, Cheshire.
Antiques Etc., Stretton, Cheshire.
Peter Bosson Antiques, Wilmslow, Cheshire
Mike Read Antique Sciences, St. Ives, Cornwall.
The Old Man Antiques, Coniston, Cumbria.
Merton Antiques, Merton, Devon.
M.R. Simpson Antiques, Highcliffe, Dorset.
Ronald Richardson, Darlington, Durham.
Littlebury Antiques, Saffron Walden, Essex.
It's About Time, Westcliff-on-Sea, Essex.
Saxton House Gallery, Chipping Campden, Glos.
Vanbrugh House Antiques, Stow-on-the-Wold, Glos.
Evans and Evans, Alresford, Hants.
Olive Antiques, Alverstoke, Hants.
Bryan Clisby, Hartley Wintney, Hants.
Gerald E. Marsh (Antique Clocks), Winchester, Hants.
Barometer Shop, Leominster, Hereford and Worcs.
Hansen Chard Antiques, Pershore, Hereford and Worcs.
Park Street Antiques, Berkhamstead, Herts.
Robert Horton Antiques, Hertford, Herts.
Robin Fowler, Gt. Coates, S. Humbs.
John Corrin Antiques, Douglas, I. of Man.
Michael Sim, Chislehurst, Kent.
Anthony Woodburn, Leigh, Kent.
Drop Dial Antiques, Bolton, Lancs.
Harrop Fold Clocks, Bolton-by-Bowland, Lancs.
The Antique Galleries, Paulersbury, Northants.
Peter Wiggins, Chipping Norton, Oxon.
R.G. Cave and Sons Ltd., Ludlow, Shrops.
Bernard G. House, Wells, Somerset.
Edward A. Nowell, Wells, Somerset.
Patrick Marney, Long Melford, Suffolk.
Suthburgh Hall, Long Melford, Suffolk.
E. Hollander Ltd., Dorking, Surrey.
A.E. Gould and Sons (Antiques) Ltd., East Horsley, Surrey.
Horological Workshops, Guildford, Surrey.
Knaphill Antiques, Knaphill, Surrey.
Dial Antiques, Shere, Surrey.
R. Saunders, Weybridge, Surrey.
Chattels, Woking, Surrey.
Adrian Alan Ltd., Brighton, Sussex East.
P. Carmichael, Brighton, Sussex East.
Simon Hatchwell Antiques, Brighton, Sussex East.
Chaunt House, Burwash, Sussex East.
Baskerville Antiques, Petworth, Sussex West.
John G. Morris Ltd., Petworth, Sussex West.
The Grandfather Clock Shop, Shipston-on-Stour, Warks.
Osborne Antiques, Sutton Coldfield, West Midlands.
P.A. Oxley Antique Clocks, Cherhill, Wilts.

Books (Antiquarian)

Sam Fogg, London, W.1.
M. & R. Glendale, London, W.1.
G. Heywood Hill Ltd., London, W.1.
E. Joseph, London, W.1.
Maggs Bros. Ltd., London, W.1.
Marlborough Rare Books Ltd., London, W.1.
Jonathan Potter Ltd., London, W.1.
Bernard Quaritch Ltd., London, W.1.
Robert G. Sawers, London, W.1.
Schuster, Thomas E., London, W.1.
Henry Sotheran Ltd., London, W.1.
Bayswater Books, London, W.2.
Hosains Books and Antiques, London, W.2.
D. Mellor and A.L. Baxter, London, W.8.
Books and Things, London, W.11.
Demetzy Books, London, W.11.
Bernard T. Shapero Rare Books, London, W.11.
J. Allen and Co. (The Horseman's Bookshop) Ltd., London, S.W.1.
Clive A. Burden Ltd., London, S.W.1.
The Connoisseur Gallery, London, S.W.1.
Thomas Heneage and Co. Ltd., London, S.W.1.
O'Shea Gallery, London, S.W.1.
Pickering and Chatto Ltd., London, S.W.1.
Saint George's Gallery Books Ltd., London, S.W.1.
Sims, Reed Ltd., London, S.W.1.
Spink and Son Ltd., London, S.W.1.
Chelsea Rare Books, London, S.W.3.
Robin Greer, London, S.W.3.
Stephanie Hoppen Ltd., London, S.W.3.
Alan G. Thomas, London, S.W.3.
634 Kings Road, London, S.W.6.
The Constant Reader Bookshop, London, S.W.6.

Han-Shan Tang Ltd., London, S.W.6.
John Boyle and Co., London, S.W.10.
Hünersdorff Rare Books and Manuscripts, London, S.W.10.
Harriett Wynter Ltd., London, S.W.10.
David Loman Ltd., London, S.W.13.
Michael Phelps, London, S.W.15.
The Warwick Leadley Gallery, London, S.E.10.
Rogers Turner Books Ltd., London, S.E.10.
Ash Rare Books, London, E.C.3.
J. Clarke-Hall Ltd., London, E.C.4.
Chapter One, London, N.1.
Intercol London, London, N.1.
G.W. Walford, London, N.5.
Fisher and Sperr, London, N.6.
M.E. Korn, London, N.10.
W. Forster, London, N.16.
East-Asia Co., London, N.W.1.
P.G. de Lotz, London, N.W.3.
Keith Fawkes, London, N.W.3.
Otto Haas, London, N.W.3.
Frederick Mulder, London, N.W.3.
Barrie Marks Ltd., N.W.5.
Atlantis Bookshop, London, W.C.1.
Louis W. Bondy, London, W.C.1.
Marchmont Bookshop, London, W.C.1.
The Print Room, London, W.C.1.
Arthur Probsthain, London, W.C.1.
Skoob Books Ltd., London, W.C.1.
Bell, Book and Radmell, London, W.C.2.
Ann Creed Books Ltd., London, W.C.2.
H.M. Fletcher, London, W.C.2.
W. and G. Foyle Ltd., London, W.C.2.
Frognal Rare Books, London, W.C.2.
Henry Pordes Books Ltd., London, W.C.2.
Reg and Philip Remington, London, W.C.2.
Bertram Rota Ltd., London, W.C.2.
Harold T. Storey, London, W.C.2.
Watkins Books Ltd., London, W.C.2.
Zeno Booksellers and Publishers, London, W.C.2.
A. Zwemmer Ltd., London, W.C.2.
George Baytun, Bath, Avon.
George Gregory, Bath, Avon.
Derek and Glenda Wallis, Bath, Avon.
Cotham Hill Bookshop, Bristol, Avon.
George's Antiquarian and Secondhand Bookshop, Bristol, Avon.
A.R. Heath, Bristol, Avon.
John Roberts Bookshop, Bristol, Avon.
Wise Owl Bookshop, Bristol, Avon.
Janet Clarke, Freshford, Avon.
Sterling Books, Weston-super-Mare, Avon.
William Smith (Booksellers) Ltd., Reading, Berks.
Buckingham Books, Buckingham, Bucks.
Penn Barn, Penn, Bucks.
Peter Eaton Booksellers Ltd., Weedon, Bucks.
David Bickersteth, Bassingbourn, Cambs.
The Bookroom, Cambridge, Cambs.
G. David, Cambridge, Cambs.
Deighton Bell and Co., Cambridge, Cambs.
Galloway and Porter Ltd., Cambridge, Cambs.
Derek Gibbons, Cambridge, Cambs.
Abington Books, Little Abington, Cambs.
Old Soke Books, Peterborough, Cambs.
Eric Golding, Wisbech, Cambs.
Lion Gallery and Bookshop, Knutsford, Cheshire.
Greville Street Bookshop, Stockport, Cheshire.
Norman Kerr-Gatehouse Bookshop, Cartmel, Cumbria.
Peter Bain Smith, Cartmel, Cumbria.
David A.H. Grayling, Crosby Ravensworth, Cumbria.
Book House, Ravenstonedale, Cumbria.
Michael Moon, Whitehaven, Cumbria.
Laura's Bookshop, Derby, Derbys.
Ashburton Rare Books, Ashburton, Devon.
Exeter Rare Books, Exeter, Devon.
Geoffrey M. Woodhead, Honiton, Devon.
Collards Books, Totnes, Devon.
Kenneth Mummery, Bournemouth, Dorset.
Sydney Wright, Bournemouth, Dorset.
Books, Dorchester, Dorset.
Antique Map and Bookshop, Puddletown, Dorset.
The Book in Hand, Shaftesbury, Dorset.
Reference Works, Swanage, Dorset.
Books Afloat, Weymouth, Dorset.
J. Shotton, Durham, Co. Durham.
Elkin Matthews, Coggeshall, Essex.
Ian Hodgkins and Co. Ltd., Slad, Glos.
Studio Bookshop and Gallery, Alresford, Hants.
Hughes and Smith, Lymington, Hants.
The Petersfield Bookshop, Petersfield, Hants.
H.M. Gilbert and Son, Southampton, Hants.
Peter Daly, Winchester, Hants.
SPCK Bookshops, Winchester, Hants.
Stratford Trevers, Broadway, Hereford and Worcs.
Grant Fine Art, Droitwich, Hereford and Worcs.
Malvern Bookshop, Gt. Malvern, Hereford and Worcs.
Pierpoint Gallery, Hereford, Hereford and Worcs.
Ross Old Book and Print Shop, Ross-on-Wye, Hereford and Worcs.
Andrew Boyle (Booksellers) Ltd., Worcester, Hereford and Worcs.
H. Pordes Ltd., Cockfosters, Herts.
Eric T. Moore, Hitchin, Herts.
Clive A. Burden, Rickmansworth, Herts.
Thomas Thorp, St. Albans, Herts.
K. Books of Hull, Hull, N. Humberside.
The Attic (Sevenoaks) Ltd., Brasted, Kent.
Bell Harry Books, Canterbury, Kent.
Chaucer Bookshop, Canterbury, Kent.
Winterdown Books, Folkestone, Kent.
Darenth Bookshop, Otford, Kent.
Baggins Book Bazaar, Rochester, Kent.
Hall's Bookshop, Tunbridge Wells, Kent.
Lloyds Bookshop, Wingham, Kent.
Browzers, Manchester, Lancs.
Forest Books of Cheshire, Manchester, Lancs.
Gibb's Bookshop Ltd., Manchester, Lancs.
Eric J. Morten, Manchester, Lancs.
Halewood and Sons, Preston, Lancs.
Preston Book Co., Preston, Lancs.
Anthony W. Laywood, Knipton, Leics.
Lubenham Antiques and The Brown Jack Bookshop, Lubenham, Leics.

Goldmark Books, Uppingham, Leics.
Golden Goose Books, Lincoln, Lincs.
Harlequin Gallery, Lincoln, Lincs.
Stanilands, Stamford, Lincs.
C.K. Broadhurst and Co. Ltd., Southport, Merseyside.
Ian Sheridan's Bookshop, Hampton, Middx.
Anthony C. Hall, Twickenham, Middx.
John Ives Bookseller, Twickenham, Middx.
Rita Shenton, Twickenham, Middx.
Thomas Barnard, Uxbridge, Middx.
David Ferrow, Great Yarmouth, Norfolk.
R.L. Cook, Holt, Norfolk.
Simon Gough, Holt, Norfolk.
Howard Fears, Little Walsingham, Norfolk.
Cathedral Gallery, Norwich, Norfolk.
Peter Crowe, Norwich, Norfolk.
The Scientific Anglian (Bookshop), Norwich, Norfolk.
The Tombland Bookshop, Norwich, Norfolk.
Turret House, Wymondham, Norfolk.
Old Hall Bookshop, Brackley, Northants.
Occultique, Northampton, Northants.
Wootton Billingham, Northampton, Northants.
Park Bookshop, Wellingborough, Northants.
The Bookshelf, Mansfield, Notts.
Checker Books, Abingdon, Oxon.
E.M. Lawson and Co., East Hagbourne, Oxon.
Blackwell's Rare Books, Fyfield, Oxon.
Niner and Hill Rare Books, Oxford, Oxon.
A. Rosenthal Ltd., Oxford, Oxon.
Sanders of Oxford Ltd., Oxford, Oxon.
Thorntons of Oxford Ltd., Oxford, Oxon.
Titles Old and Rare Books, Oxford, Oxon.
Robin Waterfield Ltd., Oxford, Oxon.
Museum Bookshop, Woodstock, Oxon.
Candle Lane Books, Shrewsbury, Shrops.
Rothwell and Dunworth, Dulverton, Somerset.
Old Curiosity Shop, Frome, Somerset.
House of Antiquity, Nether Stowey, Somerset.
Old Zion Chapel, Somerton, Somerset.
Rothwell and Dunworth, Taunton, Somerset.
MacTaggart Books, Yeovil, Somerset.
R.G. Wragg, Cheddleton, Staffs.
Leek Bookshop, The, Leek, Staffs.
Mike Abrahams, Lichfield, Staffs.
Images — Peter Stockham, Lichfield, Staffs.
The Staffs Bookshop, Lichfield, Staffs.
Besley Books, Beccles, Suffolk.
Trinder's Booksellers, Clare, Suffolk.
Claude Cox at College Gateway Bookshop, Ipswich, Suffolk.
R.G. Archer, Lavenham, Suffolk.
R.E. and G.B. Way, Newmarket, Suffolk.
E.T. Webster, Stonham Parva, Suffolk.
Vandeleur Antiquarian Books, Epsom, Surrey.
J.W. McKenzie, Ewell, Surrey.
Thomas Thorp Bookseller, Guildford, Surrey.
Charles W. Traylen, Guildford, Surrey.
Ivelet Books Ltd., Redhill, Surrey.
Elizabeth Gant, Thames Ditton, Surrey.
Holleyman and Treacher Ltd., Brighton, Sussex East.
Colin Page Antiquarian Books, Brighton, Sussex East.
Robinson's Bookshop Ltd., Brighton, Sussex East.
Roderick Dew, Eastbourne, Sussex East.
London and Sussex Antiquarian Book and Print Services, Eastbourne, Sussex East.
Raymond Smith, Eastbourne, Sussex East.
Howes Bookshop, Hastings, Sussex East.
Bow Windows Book Shop, Lewes, Sussex East.
A.J. Cumming, Lewes, Sussex East.
Fifteenth Century Bookshop, Lewes, Sussex East.
Chimera Books, Hurstpierpoint, Sussex West.
W. Robinson, Newcastle-upon-Tyne, Tyne and Wear.
R.D. Steedman, Newcastle-upon-Tyne, Tyne and Wear.
Robert Vaughan, Stratford-upon-Avon, Warks.
Duncan M. Allsop, Warwick, Warks.
Birmingham Bookshop, Birmingham, West Midlands.
Maxwells Book Shop, Birmingham, West Midlands.
Clent Books, Halesowen, West Midlands.
Rodney and Susan Otway, Bradford-on-Avon, Wilts.
Clive Farahar and Sophie Dupré, Calne, Wilts.
Hilmarton Manor Press, Calne, Wilts.
Batstone Books, Malmesbury, Wilts.
Marlborough Sporting Gallery and Bookshop, Marlborough, Wilts.
Heraldy Today, Ramsbury, Wilts.
The Barn Book Supply, Salisbury, Wilts.
D.M. Beach, Salisbury, Wilts.
Victoria Bookshop, Swindon, Wilts.
Great Ayton Bookshop, Great Ayton, Yorkshire North.
Rippon Bookshop, Harrogate, Yorkshire North.
Rievaulx Books, Helmsley, N. Yorks.
Charles Shaw, Knaresborough, Yorkshire North.
White Boar Antiques and Books, Middleham, Yorkshire North.
Potterton Books, Thirsk, Yorkshire North.
Barbican Bookshop, York, Yorkshire North.
The Chaucer Head, York, Yorkshire North.
Minster Gate Bookshop, York, Yorkshire North.
O'Flynn Antiquarian Booksellers, York, Yorkshire North.
Ken Spelman, York, Yorkshire North.
Taikoo Books Ltd., York, Yorkshire North.
John R. Wrigley, Ecclesfield, Yorkshire South.
Alan Hill Books, Sheffield, Yorkshire South.
Jean Brear, Halifax, Yorkshire West.
Tollhouse Bookshop, Holmfirth, Yorkshire West.
Channel Islands Galleries Ltd., St. Peter Port, Guernsey, C.I.
Thesaurus, St. Peter Port, Guernsey, C.I.
Geoffrey P. Gavey, Vale, Guernsey, C.I.
John Blench and Son, St. Helier, Jersey, C.I.

Thesaurus (Jersey) Ltd., St. Helier, Jersey, C.I.
Emerald Isle Books, Belfast, N. Ireland.
I.G. Anderson, Dumfries, Scotland.
McNaughton's Bookshop, Edinburgh, Scotland.
Alan Rankin, Edinburgh, Scotland.
James Thin (Booksellers), Edinburgh, Scotland.
John Smith and Son (Glasgow) Ltd., Glasgow, Scotland.
Paisley Fine Books, Paisley, Scotland.
Tom Lloyd-Roberts, Caerwys, Clwyd, Wales.
Doggie Hubbard's Bookshop, Ponterwyd, Dyfed, Wales.
Dylan's Bookshop, Swansea, W. Glam., Wales.
Glance Back, Chepstow, Gwent,Wales.
Maps, Prints and Books, Brecon, Powys, Wales.
Richard Booth's Bookshop, Hay-on-Wye, Powys, Wales.
Mark Westwood, Hay-on-Wye, Powys, Wales.

Brass (See Metalwork)

Bronzes

J. Christie, London, W.1.
Barry Davies, London, W.1.
Editions Graphiques Gallery, London, W.1.
Eskenazi Ltd., London, W.1.
A. and F. Gordon, London, W.1.
William Redford, London, W.1.
The Sladmore Gallery, London, W.1.
South Audley Antiques, London, W.1.
David Brower Antiques, London, W.8.
Cameo Gallery, London, W.8.
H. and W. Deutsch Antiques, London, W.8.
Melvyn Jay Antiques, London, W.8.
Howard Jones, London, W.8.
Pruskin Gallery, London, W.8.
Mary Wise, London, W.8.
J. Lipitch Ltd., London, W.11.
Marie Louise Burness Antiques, London, S.W.1.
Victor Franses Gallery, London, S.W.1.
Rodd McLennan, London, S.W.1.
Peter Nahum, London, S.W.1.
Gerald Spyer and Son (Antiques) Ltd., London, S.W.1.
Trove, London, S.W.1.
Anthony James & Son Ltd., London, S.W.3.
Cooper Fine Arts Ltd., London, S.W.6.
Inheritance, London, N.1.
Nellie Lenson and Roy Smith, London, N.1.
West End Galleries, Buxton, Derbys.
Architectural Heritage, Taddington, Glos.
Michael Sim, Chislehurst, Kent.
Mistral Galleries, Westerham, Kent.
Bruno Cooper Antiques, Long Melford, Suffolk.
Apollo Galleries, Croydon, Surrey.
Armstrong-Davis Gallery, Arundel, Sussex West.
Sheila Hinde Fine Art, Kirdford, Sussex West.
John G. Morris Ltd., Petworth, Sussex West.

Carriages and Cars

Brian R. Verrall and Co., London, S.W.17.
Architectural Heritage, Taddington, Glos.
Nostalgia, Bridlington, N. Humberside.
Fieldings Antiques, Haslingden, Lancs.
Whatnots, Strathblane, Scotland.

Carpets and Rugs

Aaron Gallery, London, W.1.
Atlantic Bay Carpets, London, W.1.
Bernheimer Fine Arts Ltd., London, W.1.
Essie Carpets, London, W.1.
Attilio Gilberti, London, W.1.
Hadji Baba Ancient Art, London, W.1.
Heskia, London, W.1.
C. John (Rare Rugs) Ltd., London, W.1.
Alexander Juran and Co., London, W.1.
Kennedy Carpets and Kelims, London, W.1.
Mayfair Carpet Gallery Ltd., London, W.1.
Paul Nels Ltd., London, W.1.
Rabi Gallery Ltd., London, W.1.
Shaikh and Son (Oriental Rugs) Ltd., London, W.1.
Vigo Carpet Gallery, London, W.1.
Vigo-Sternberg Galleries, London, W.1.
Zadah Gallery, London, W.1.
S. Franses Conservation, London, W.2.
S. Bensiglio Ltd., London, W.5.
M.L. Waroujian, London, W.6.
Barker-Mill Design Associates, London, W.8.
Coats Oriental Carpets, London, W.8.
Clive Loveless, London, W.10.
David Black Oriental Carpets, London, W.11.
J. Fairman (Carpets) Ltd., London, W.11.
A. Rezai Persian Carpets, London, W.11.
Raymond Benardout, London, S.W.1.
S. Franses (Carpets) Ltd., London, S.W.1.
Victor Franses Gallery, London, S.W.1.
Heraz, London, S.W.1.
Mayorcas Ltd., London, S.W.1.
Sanaiy Carpets, London, S.W.1.
Robert Stephenson Decorative Carpets and Kilims, London, S.W.3.
Anglo Persian Carpet Co., London, S.W.7.
Rare Carpets Gallery, London, S.W.10.
Y. and B. Bolour, London, N.W.5.
Joseph Lavian, London, N.W.5.
Zoulfaghari, London, N.W.5.
Robert Franses and Sons, London, N.W.8.
Haliden Oriental Rug Shop, Bath, Avon.
Peter Norman Antiques and Restorations, Burwell, Cambs.
Robert Copperfield, Macclesfield, Cheshire.
Imperial Antiques, Stockport, Cheshire.
J.L. Arditti, Christchurch, Dorset.
Christchurch Carpets, Christchurch, Dorset.
Orbell House Gallery, Castle Hedingham, Essex.
Robert Bailey Oriental Rugs, Ongar, Essex.
Alan du Monceau, Chalford, Glos.
Brookfield Antiques, Cheltenham, Glos.
Eric Pride, Oriental Rugs, Cheltenham, Glos.
Odiham Gallery, Odiham, Hants.
Tolley's Galleries, Worcester, Hereford and Worcs.

Park Street Antiques, Berkhamsted, Herts.
Northgate Antiques, Bishops Stortford, Herts.
Oriental Rug Gallery Ltd., St. Albans, Herts.
Simon Boosey, Whitwell, Herts.
Desmond and Amanda North, East Peckham, Kent.
Samovar Antiques, Hythe, Kent.
Persian Rugs, West Peckham, Kent.
Duncan Watts Oriental Rugs, Market Harborough, Leics.
L. Kelaty Ltd., Wembley, Middx.
Christopher Legge, Oxford, Oxon.
Michael and Amanda Lewis, Wellington, Somerset.
Debenham Gallery, Debenham, Suffolk.
Karel Weijand, Farnham, Surrey.
Bookham Galleries, Great Bookham, Surrey.
Clive Rogers Oriental Rugs, Brighton, Sussex East.
Lindfield Galleries, Lindfield, Sussex West.
Majid Amini, Petworth, Sussex West.
London House Oriental Carpets and Rugs, Harrogate, N. Yorks.
Omar (Harrogate) Ltd., Harrogate, Yorkshire North.
Northern Kilim Centre, Knaresborough, Yorkshire North.
Gordon Reece Gallery, Knaresborough, Yorkshire North.
Ellis's, Sheffield, Yorkshire South.
The Oriental Rug Shop, Sheffield, Yorkshire South.
London House Oriental Rugs and Carpets, Boston Spa, Yorkshire West.
Behar Carpets, Edinburgh, Scotland.
Herrald Antiques, Edinburgh, Scotland.
Whytock and Reid, Edinburgh, Scotland.
Behar Carpets, Glasgow, Scotland.
Country Antiques, Kidwelly, Dyfed, Wales.

Chinese Art (See Oriental Art)

Clocks and Watches

Armour-Winston Ltd., London, W.1.
Asprey p.l.c., London, W.1.
Bobinet Ltd., London, W.1.
Carrington and Co. Ltd., London, W.1.
Collingwood of Bond Street Ltd., London, W.1.
'The Dial', Marylebone, London, W.1.
Garrard and Co. Ltd. (The Crown Jewellers), London, W.1.
Graus Antiques, London, W.1.
Ronald A. Lee (Fine Arts) Ltd., London, W.1.
Mallett at Bourdon House Ltd., London, W.1.
The Badger, London, W.5.
Philip Dombey, London, W.8.
Raffety Ltd., London, W.8.
Roderick Antique Clocks, London, W.8.
Old Father Time Clock Centre, London, W.11.
Richard Price, London, W.11.
Igor Tociapski, London, W.11.
Camerer Cuss and Co., London, S.W.1.
Arthur S. Lewis, London, S.W.1.
John Carlton Smith, London, S.W.1.
Somlo Antiques, London, S.W.1.
Philip Whyte, London, S.W.1.
Big Ben Antique Clocks, London, S.W.6.
Chelsea Clocks and Antiques, London, S.W.6.
Aubrey Brocklehurst, London, S.W.7.
Capital Clocks, London, S.W.8.
Howard Walwyn Antiques, London, S.W.11.
The Clock Clinic Ltd., London, S.W.15.
Village Time, London, S.E.7.
R.E. Rose, London, S.E.9.
Hoffman, London, E.5.
City Clocks, London, E.C.1.
Bushe Antiques, London, N.1.
Patric Capon, London, N.1.
Strike One Ltd., London, N.1.
North London Clock Shop Ltd., London, N.5.
Mr. Temple Brooks, London, N.W.6.
Thomas Kettle Ltd., London, W.C.2.
John Croft Antiques, Bath, Avon.
David Gibson Antiques, Bath, Avon.
Quiet St. Antiques, Bath, Avon.
Barometer Shop, Bristol, Avon.
John and Carole Hawley Antique Clocks, Clevedon,Avon.
James R. Cornish, Langford, Avon.
Richard Barder Antiques, Hermitage, Berks.
John Bensley, Hungerford, Berks.
Robert and Georgina Hastie, Hungerford, Berks.
Medalcrest Ltd., Hungerford, Berks.
Eton Gallery Antiques, Windsor and Eton, Berks.
Anthony Seales, Windsor and Eton, Berks.
Times Past Antiques Ltd., Windsor and Eton, Berks.
Windsor Antiques and Design, Windsor and Eton, Berks.
Wyrardisbury Antiques, Wraysbury, Berks.
Norton Antiques, Beaconsfield, Bucks.
M.V. Tooley, Chesham, Bucks.
Alan Martin Antiques, Olney, Bucks.
Robin Unsworth Antiques, Olney, Bucks.
Courtyard Clocks, Winslow, Bucks.
S.J. Webster-Speakman, Cambridge, Cambs.
Rodney Firmin, Swaffham Prior, Cambs.
Adams Antiques, Chester, Cheshire.
Boodle and Dunthorne Ltd., Chester, Cheshire.
Chester Antiques, Chester, Cheshire.
Mill Farm Antiques, Disley, Cheshire.
Cranford Clocks, Knutsford, Cheshire.
Cheshire Antiques, Macclesfield, Cheshire.
Chapel Antiques, Nantwich, Cheshire.
Coppelia Antiques, Plumley, Cheshire.
G.E. Leigh and Son, Reddish, Cheshire.
Antiques Etc., Stretton, Cheshire.
The Antiques Shop, Whitegate, Cheshire.
Peter Bosson Antiques, Wilmslow, Cheshire.
Paul Jennings Antiques, Angarrack, Cornwall.
Merlin Antiques, Kirkby Lonsdale, Cumbria.
David Hill, Kirkby Stephen, Cumbria.
The Clock House, Chapel-en-le-Frith, Derbys.
Derbyshire Clocks, Glossop, Derbys.
Goodacre Engraving Ltd., Long Eaton, Derbys.

Nimbus Antiques, Whaley Bridge, Derbys.
W.G. Potter and Son, Axminster, Devon.
John Nathan Antiques, Exeter, Devon.
Alan Jones Antiques, Plymouth, Devon.
Brian Taylor, Plymouth, Devon.
Tempus-Fugit, Shaldon, Devon.
Good Hope Antiques, Beaminster, Dorset.
D.J. Burgess, Parkstone, Dorset.
Old Mermaid Antiques, Sherborne, Dorset.
Tom Tribe and Son, Sturminster Newton, Dorset.
John Bailey, Althorne, Essex.
Mark Marchant Antiques, Coggeshall, Essex
Antique Clock Repair Shoppe, Gants Hill, Essex.
Collectors Paradise, Leigh-on-Sea, Essex.
W.A. Pinn and Sons, Sible Hedingham, Essex.
David Jean and John Antiques, Westcliff-on-Sea, Essex.
It's About Time, Westcliff-on-Sea, Essex.
Colin Elliott, Cheltenham, Essex.
Montpellier Clocks, Cheltenham, Glos.
Saxton House Gallery, Chipping Campden, Glos.
Jonathan Beech, Cirencester, Glos.
Gerald Campbell, Lechlade, Glos.
Keith Harding's World of Mechanical Music, Northleach, Glos.
Colin Brand Antiques, Stow-on-the-Wold, Glos.
J. and M. Bristow Antiques, Tetbury, Glos.
Evans and Evans, Alresford, Hants.
Bryan Clisby, Hartley Witney, Hants.
A.W. Porter and Son, Hartley Witney, Hants.
Swaythling Woodcrafts, Southampton, Hants.
Gaylords, Titchfield, Hants.
Twyford Antiques, Twyford, Hants.
Gerald E. Marsh (Antique Clocks), Winchester, Hants.
Todd and Austin Antiques of Winchester, Winchester, Hants.
Ma's Antiques, Bewdley, Hereford and Worcs.
Hansard Chard Antiques, Pershore, Hereford and Worcs.
Trecilla Antiques, Ross-on-Wye, Hereford and Worcs.
Gerald and Vera Taylor, Winforton, Hereford and Worcs.
Howards, Baldock, Herts.
Park Street Antiques, Berkhamstead, Herts.
Robert Horton Antiques, Hertford, Herts.
David Harriman Antiques, Rickmansworth, Herts.
The Clock Shop, St. Albans, Herts.
Country Things, Tring, Herts.
The Old Ropery Antique Clocks, Kilham, N. Humberside.
Robin Fowler, Gt. Coates, S. Humberside.
Lewis Hickson, Seaton Ross, N. Humberside.
John Corrin Antiques, Douglas, I. of Man.
Ron Tayler, Alum Bay, I. of Wight.
John Chawner, Birchington, Kent.
The Clock Shop Antiques, Boughton, Kent.
Old Manor House Antiques, Brasted, Kent.
John Chawner, Chatham, Kent.
Michael Sim, Chislehurst, Kent.
Roy Massingham, Hawkhurst, Kent.
Anthony Woodburn, Leigh, Kent.
Northgate Antiques, Rochester, Kent.
David Rackham (Rochester Fine Arts), Rochester, Kent.
Derek Roberts Fine Antique Clocks, Tonbridge, Kent.
Hadlow Antiques, Tunbridge Wells, Kent.
The Old Clock Shop, West Malling, Kent.
Drop Dial Antiques, Bolton, Lancs.
Harrop Fold Clocks, Bolton-by-Bowland, Lancs.
J.H. Blakey and Sons Ltd., Brierfield, Lancs.
The Antique Shop, Haslingden, Lancs.
Boodle and Dunthorne Ltd., Manchester, Lancs.
Bulldog Antiques, Manchester, Lancs.
Manchester Antique Co., Manchester, Lancs.
Antique and Reproduction Clocks, Preston, Lancs.
Jack Blackburn, Preston, Lancs.
Bonington Clocks, Kegworth, Leics.
Lowe of Loughborough, Loughborough, Leics.
Ashley House Antiques, Measham, Leics.
David E. Burrows, Osgathorpe, Leics.
G.K. Hadfield, Shepshed, Leics.
The Spindles, Tonge, Leics.
Charles Antiques, Whitwick, Leics.
N. Bryan-Peach Antiques, Wymeswold, Leics.
Grantham Clocks, Grantham, Lincs.
Robert Hitching, Horncastle, Lincs.
Pinfold Antiques, Ruskington, Lincs.
George Clocks, Stamford, Lincs.
The Clock Shop, Hoylake, Merseyside.
Boodle and Dunthorne, Liverpool, Merseyside.
Artbry's Antiques, Pinner, Middx.
Zafer, Twickenham, Middx.
Norfolk Polyphon Centre, Bawdeswell, Norfolk.
R.C. Woodhouse, Hunstanton, Norfolk.
As Time Goes By Antique Clocks, Norwich, Norfolk.
D'Amico Antiques Ltd., Norwich, Norfolk.
Parriss, Sheringham, Norfolk.
Michael Jones Jeweller, Northampton, Northants.
Howard Antiques, Oundle, Northants.
Hazel Cottage Clocks, Eachwick, Northumbs.
Gordon Caris, Hexham, Northumbs.
David and Carole Potter Antiques, Nottingham, Notts.
Trade Winds Antiques, Nottingham, Notts.
Horseshore Antiques and Gallery, Burford, Oxon.
Jonathan Howard, Chipping Norton, Oxon.
P. Audley Miller, Oxford, Oxon.
Rosemary and Time, Thame, Oxon.
Telling Time Antiques, Thame, Oxon.
Second Time Around Antiques, Wallingford, Oxon.

Witney Antiques, Witney, Oxon.
Mytton Antiques, Atcham, Shrops.
Mitre House Antiques, Ludlow, Shrops.
Matthew Willis, Antique Clocks, Glastonbury, Somerset.
Ray Best Antiques, Ilminster, Somerset.
Gerald Lewis, Montacute, Somerset.
Edward A. Nowell, Wells, Somerset.
Croydon and Sons Ltd., Ipswich, Suffolk.
Clock House, Leavenheath, Suffolk.
Antique Clocks by Simon Charles, Long Melford, Suffolk.
Suthburgh Antiques, Long Melford, Suffolk.
Village Clocks, Long Melford, Suffolk.
Antique Clocks by Simon Charles, Sudbury, Suffolk.
Edward Manson, Woodbridge, Suffolk.
A.G. Voss, Woodbridge, Suffolk.
Simon Marsh, Bletchingley, Surrey.
E. Hollander Ltd., Dorking, Surrey.
Abbott Antiques, East Molesey, Surrey.
Roger A. Davis, Antiquarian Horologist, Gt. Bookham, Surrey.
Horological Workshops, Guildford, Surrey.
Surrey Clock Centre, Haslemere, Surrey.
Knaphill Antiques, Knaphill, Surrey.
S. Warrender and Co., Sutton, Surrey.
The Clock Shop, Weybridge, Surrey.
Chattels, Woking, Surrey.
Simon Hatchwell Antiques, Brighton, Sussex East.
Chaunt House, Burwash, Sussex East.
Wm. Bruford and Son Ltd., Eastbourne, Sussex East.
John Cowderoy Antiques, Eastbourne, Sussex East.
W.F. Bruce Antiques, Herstmonceux, Sussex East.
Rye Antiques, Rye, Sussex East.
Cowfold Clocks, Cowfold, Sussex East.
The Clock Shop, Hurstpierpoint, Sussex West.
Baskerville Antiques, Petworth, Sussex West.
Lewis and Lloyd, Petworth, Sussex West.
John G. Morris Ltd., Petworth, Sussex West.
J. Powell (Hove) Ltd., Portslade, Sussex West.
The Grandfather Clock Shop, Shipston-on-Stour, Warks.
Time in Hand, Shipston-on-Stour, Warks.
J. Mason, Water Orton, Warks.
Ashley House Antiques, Birmingham, West Midlands.
R. Collyer, Birmingham, West Midlands.
Old Clock Shop, Birmingham, West Midlands.
M. Allen Watch and Clock Maker, Four Oaks, West Midlands.
Osborne Antiques, Sutton Coldfield, West Midlands.
Alan M. France, Wolverhampton, West Midlands.
Moxhams Antiques, Bradford-on-Avon, Wilts.
P.A. Oxley Antique Clocks and Barometers, Cherhill, Wilts.
Monkton Galleries, Hindon, Wilts.
T.J. Newsam, Salisbury, Wilts.
Salisbury Clock Shop, Salisbury, Wilts.
Chris Wadge Clocks, Salisbury, Wilts.
Allan Smith Antique Clocks, Swindon, Wilts.
Peter Houghton Antiques, Warminster, Wilts.
John Pearson, Birstwith, Yorkshire North.
D. Mason and Son, Harrogate, Yorkshire North.
Haworth Antiques, Huby, Yorkshire North.
Alverton Antiques, Northallerton, Yorkshire North.
Brian Loomes, Pateley Bridge, Yorkshire North.
Acomb Antiques, York, Yorkshire North.
Francis Sinclair Ltd., Doncaster, Yorkshire South.
Fishlake Antiques, Fishlake, Yorkshire South.
Leon Cooper, Batley, Yorkshire West.
Simon, Ilkley, Yorkshire West.
William Goldsmith, Leeds, Yorkshire West.
Park Antiques, Menston, Yorkshire West.
Raymond Tomlinson (Antiques) Ltd., Wetherby, Yorkshire West.
Antique Shop, Ballyclare, Co. Antrim, N. Ireland.
Greyabbey Timecraft Ltd., Greyabbey, Co. Down, N. Ireland.
Country Shop Antiques, Duns, Scotland.
Brown's Clocks Ltd., Glasgow, Scotland. Bath St. Antiques Galleries.
Monument Antiques, Stirling, Scotland.
Chris Mann Antiques, Aberystwyth, Dyfed, Wales.
W.W. Griffiths, Bethel, Gwynedd, Wales.
Rodney Adams Antiques, Pwllheli, Gwynedd, Wales.

Coins and Medals

A. Douch, London, W.1.
B.A. Seaby Ltd., London, W.1.
Michael Coins, London, W.8.
The Armoury of St. James's, London, S.W.1.
Knightsbridge Coins, London, S.W.1.
Spink and Son Ltd., London, S.W.1.
Beaver Coin Room, London, S.W.5.
Intercol, London, N.1.
C.J. Martin (Coins) Ltd., London, N.14.
Dolphin Coins, London, N.W.3.
A.H. Baldwin and Sons Ltd., London, W.C.2.
M. Bord (Gold Coin Exchange), London, W.C.2.
Bath Stamp and Coin Shop, Bath, Avon.
Potters Antiques and Coins, Bristol, Avon.
Castle Coins, Dunstable, Beds.
Lowe and Sons Ltd., Chester, Cheshire.
Hills Antiques, Macclesfield, Cheshire.
Vanity Fair, Mousehole, Cornwall.
Souvenir Antiques, Carlisle, Cumbria.
Penrith Coin and Stamp Centre, Penrith, Cumbria.
Gainsborough House Antiques, Sidmouth, Devon.
Sterling Coins and Medals, Bournemouth, Dorset.
Robin Finnegan (Jeweller), Darlington, Durham.

Samuel Roper – Oakhill
Fine mahogany 8-day longcase clock with moonphase, c.1805

P. A. Oxley

Antique Clocks & Barometers

The Old Rectory · Cherhill · Near Calne
Wiltshire SN11 8UX
Telephone (0249) 816227 Fax (0249) 821285

P.A. Oxley is one of the longest established and largest antique clock and barometer dealers in the U.K. with over 100 quality antique clocks and barometers including over 50 longcase clocks.

It is not our policy to exhibit at Antique Fairs and therefore our extensive stock can only be viewed at our large showrooms on the main A4 London to Bath road at Cherhill.

Full shipping facilities are available to any country in the world. U.K. customers are provided with a free delivery and setting up service combined with a twelve month guarantee.

If your desire is for a genuine antique clock or barometer then we will be pleased to see you at Cherhill where you can examine our large stock and discuss your exact requirement. If time is short and you cannot visit us we will send you a selection of photographs from which you can buy with confidence.

Hours of opening are 9.30-5.00 every day except Wednesday. Sunday and evening appointments can easily be arranged. We look forward to welcoming you to our establishment.

Michael & Patricia Oxley
Member of the London & Provincial Antique Dealers' Association

Joseph Miles – Shaston
Fine oak 8-day brass dial longcase clock, c.1770

Dunelme Coins and Medals, Esh Winning, Durham.
Coin and Stamp Centre, Colchester, Essex.
Dickens Curios, Frinton-on-Sea, Essex.
Alfred S. Allen & Co., South Ockendon, Essex.
Butler and Co., Cheltenham, Glos.
Military Curios, Gloucester, Glos.
Portsmouth Stamp Shop, Portsmouth, Hants.
Whitmore, Gt. Malvern, Hereford and Worcs.
B.B.M. Jewellery and Antiques, Kidderminster, Hereford and Worcs.
C.J. and A.J. Dixon Ltd., Bridlington, N. Humberside.
Keith Shotton, Shanklin, I. of Wight.
Coins of Canterbury, Canterbury, Kent.
C.B.I. Ltd., Blackpool, Lancs.
M. and N. Howarth Ltd., Clitheroe, Lancs.
J.A. Duggan and Co., St. Annes-on-Sea, Lancs.
Rowletts of Lincoln, Lincoln, Lincs.
Liverpool Coin and Medal Co., Liverpool, Merseyside.
Gold and Silver Exchange, Gt. Yarmouth, Norfolk.
Clive Dennent Coins, Norwich, Norfolk.
B. Armstrong, Nottingham, Notts.
Hockley Coins, Nottingham, Notts.
Denver House Antiques and Collectables, Burford, Oxon.
Fox and Co., Yeovil, Somerset.
St. Pancras Antiques, Chichester, Sussex West.
The Collectors' Shop, Birmingham, West Midlands.
Eden Coins, Birmingham, W. Midlands.
Format of Birmingham Ltd., Birmingham, West Midlands.
March Medals, Birmingham, West Midlands.
Galata Coins Ltd., Wolverhampton, West Midlands.
Military Parade Bookshop, Marlborough, Wilts.
Castle Galleries, Salisbury, Wilts.
Cairncross and Sons, Filey, Yorkshire North.
Hanover Antiques, Scarborough, Yorkshire North.
Coins International, Leeds, Yorkshire West.
Cookstown Antiques, Cookstown, Co. Tyrone, N. Ireland.
Collectors Shop, Edinburgh, Scotland.
Edinburgh Coin Shop, Edinburgh, Scotland.
Henderson, Perth, Scotland.
Thurso Antiques, Thurso, Scotland.
Glance Back, Chepstow, Gwent, Wales.

Dolls and Toys

Under Two Flags, London, W.1.
Kay Desmonde, London, W.8.
Trench Enterprises, London, W.11.
A.M. Web, London, W.11.
The Singing Tree, London, S.W.6.
Judith Lassalle, London, N.1.
Yesterday Child, London, N.1.
Game Advice, London, N.W.5.
Dolls and Toys of Yesteryear, Hungerford, Berks.
Tim Armitage, Nantwich, Cheshire.
Abbey House, Derby, Derbys.
Honiton Antique Toys, Honiton, Devon.
Anthea Knowles, Littlehempston, Devon.
Vintage Toy and Train Museum, Sidmouth, Devon.
The Antique Centre, Bournemouth, Dorset.
Hobby Horse Antiques, Bridport, Dorset.
Lilian Middleton's Antique Doll Shop, Stow-on-the-Wold, Glos.
Old Dolls House Antiques, Gosport, Hants.
Peter Pan's of Gosport, Gosport, Hants.
Treasures of Childhood Past, Gt. Malvern, Hereford and Worcs.
Dolls of Yesterday, Weston-under-Penyard, Hereford and Worcs.
The Attic, Baldock, Herts.
Cherry Antiques, Hemel Hempstead, Herts.
Grannie's Parlour, Hull, N. Humberside.
Longfield Antiques, Longfield, Kent.
Mary Brooker 'Marylyn' Antiques and Curios, Gifts, Sandgate, Kent.
Hadlow Antiques, Tunbridge Wells, Kent.
Bridge Antiques, Wingham, Kent.
Antique Dolls, Blackpool, Lancs.
Swag, Preston, Lancs.
Mint and Boxed, Edgeware, Middx.
Granny's Attic, Nottingham, Notts.
Mike Pollock, Nottingham, Notts.
Playthings of the Past, Hadleigh, Suffolk.
Motts of Lavenham, Lavenham, Suffolk.
Memory Lane Antiques, Ashtead, Surrey.
Gooday Shop and Studio, East Molesey, Surrey.
Victoria Fine Art, Godalming, Surrey.
Victoriana Dolls, Reigate, Surrey.
Elizabeth Gant, Thames Ditton, Surrey.
Sue Pearson, Brighton, Sussex East.
Mint Dolls and Toys, Rye, Sussex East.
Recollect Studios, Sayers Common, Sussex West.
Dolly Mixtures, Birmingham, West Midlands.
Robert Taylor, Four Oaks, West Midlands.
Collectors Old Toys and Antiques, Halifax, Yorkshire West.
Second Childhood, Huddersfield, Yorkshire West.
Now and Then (Toy Centre), Edinburgh, Scotland.

Frames

Paul Mitchell Ltd., London, W.1.
H.J. Spillers Ltd., London, W.1.
Lacy Gallery, London, W.11.
Paul Mason Gallery, London, S.W.1.
Arnold Wiggins and Sons Ltd., London, S.W.1.
The Fairhurst Gallery, Norwich, Norfolk.

Furniture

Continental (mainly French)

Alexander and Berendt Ltd., London, W.1.
Antique Porcelain Co., London, W.1.
Barling of Mount Street Ltd., London, W.1.
Bernheimer Fine Arts Ltd., London, W.1.

H. Blairman and Sons Ltd., London, W.1.
Antoine Cheneviere Fine Arts, London, W.1.
A. and F. Gordon, London, W.1.
Howard Antiques, London, W.1.
Mallett at Bourdon House Ltd., London, W.1.
Partridge Fine Arts p.l.c., London, W.1.
William Redford, London, W.1.
South Audley Antiques, London, W.1.
Toynbee-Clarke Interiors Ltd., London, W.1.
M. Turpin Ltd., London, W.1.
Claude Bornoff, London, W.2.
Daniel Mankowitz, London, W.2.
Architectural Antiques, London, W.6.
Bonrose Antiques, London, W.6.
David Brower Antiques, London, W.8.
Jonathan Harris, London, W.8.
Melvyn Jay Antiques and Objets d'art, London, W.8.
Reindeer Antiques (Reindeer International Ltd.), London, W.8.
Select Antiques Gallery Ltd., London, W.8.
Jacob Stodel, London, W.8.
Murray Thomsom Ltd., London, W.8.
Serge Baillache, London, W.11.
Barham Antiques, London, W.11.
P.R. Barham, London, W.11.
Cura Antiques, London, W.11.
E. and A. Di Michele Antiques, London, W.11.
The Facade, London, W.11.
M. and D. Lewis, London, W.11.
J. Lipitch Ltd., London, W.11.
Nicholas Thomas Antiques, London, W.11.
Trude Weaver, London, W.11.
Didier Aaron (London) Ltd., London, S.W.1.
Antiquities, London, S.W.1.
Blanchard and Alan Ltd., London, S.W.1.
Marie-Louise Burness Antiques, London, S.W.1.
Csasky's Antiques, London, S.W.1.
Arthur Davidson Ltd., London, S.W.1.
Grove Antiques, London, S.W.1.
Hermitage Antiques, London, S.W.1.
Carlton Hobbs, London, S.W.1.
Jeremy Ltd., London, S.W.1.
M. and D. Lewis, London, S.W.1.
Watts and Christensen, London, S.W.1.
Tony Bunzl, London, S.W.3.
Forty-Eight Walton St., London, S.W.3.
William Handford Antiques, London, S.W.3.
Hooper and Purchase, London, S.W.3.
Anthony James and Son Ltd., London, S.W.3.
Peter Lipitch Ltd., London, S.W.3.
Pelham Galleries, London, S.W.3.
O.F. Wilson Ltd., London, S.W.3.
Karin Armelin Antiques, London, S.W.6.
Bishops Park Antiques, London, S.W.6.
Alasdair Brown Antiques, London, S.W.6.
I. and J.L. Brown, London, S.W.6.
Rupert Cavendish Antiques, London, S.W.6.
David Alexander Antiques, London, S.W.6.
Charles Edwards, London, S.W.6.
Goodwin and Wadhwa, London, S.W.6.
Sylvia Napier Ltd., London, S.W.6.
M. Pauw Antiques, London, S.W.6.
Michael and Margaret Parker Antiques, London, S.W.6.
M. Turpin Ltd., London, S.W.6.
Furniture Cave, London, S.W.10.
Rendlesham Antiques Ltd., London, S.W.10.
Simon Coleman Antiques, London, S.W.13.
Jorgen Antiques, London, S.W.15.
Adams Room Antiques Ltd., London, S.W.19.
Greenwich Antiques and Ironware Co., London, S.E.10.
Stuart Antiques, London, S.E.10.
The Antique Trader, London, N.1.
Chevenix-Trench Antiques, London, N.1.
Grove Antiques, London, N.1.
Robert Hirschhorn, London, N.1.
Cassandra Keen, London, N.1.
Thomas Kerr Antiques Ltd., London, N.1.
Swan Fine Art, London, N.1.
Adams Antiques, London, N.W.1.
Chas L. Nyman and Co. Ltd., London, N.W.1.
G. and F. Gillingham Ltd., London, N.W.2.
Jadis Ltd., Bath, Avon.
Pennard House Antiques, Bath, Avon.
Queens Parade Antiques Ltd., Bath, Avon.
Mary Bellis Antiques, Hungerford, Berks.
Bibi Harris Antiques, Hungerford, Berks.
Ulla Stafford, Windsor and Eton, Berks.
Pine Reflections, Hughenden Valley, Bucks.
Phoenix Antiques, Fordham, Cambs.
Ivor and Patricia Lewis, Peterborough, Cambs.
Adams Antiques, St. Ives, Cambs.
Adams Antiques, Chester, Cheshire.
Imperial Antiques, Stockport, Cheshire.
C. Kerfoot Antiques, Stockport, Cheshire.
Utopia Antiques Ltd., Holme, Cumbria.
G. and J. Antiques, Buxton, Derbys.
West End Galleries, Buxton, Derbys.
Colystock Antiques, Stockland, Devon.
Hennessy, Beaminster, Dorset.
Lionel Geneen Ltd., Bournemouth, Dorset.
R.A. Swift and Sons, Bournemouth, Dorset.
Millers Antiques, Kelvedon, Essex.
Compton-Dando (Fine Arts) Ltd., White Colne, Essex.
Geoffrey Stead, Chastleton, Glos.
Benson Antiques, Cheltenham, Glos.
Jay Gray Antiques, Cirencester, Glos.
Trouthouse Antiques Ltd., Eastleach, Glos.
Gloucester House Antiques Ltd., Fairford, Glos.
Simon Brett, Moreton-in-Marsh, Glos.
Elizabeth Parker, Moreton-in-Marsh, Glos.
Duncan J. Baggott, Stow-in-the-Wold, Glos.
Annarella Clark Antiques, Stow-in-the-Wold, Glos.
Anthony Preston Antiques Ltd., Stow-in-the-Wold, Glos.
Adrienne de Marino-Montero Fine Art and Antiques Ltd., Curdridge, Hants.
Cedar Antiques, Hartley Wintney, Hants.
David Lazarus Antiques, Hartley Wintney, Hants.
Phoenix Green Antiques, Hartley Wintney, Hants.
Colin Macleod Antiques, Portsmouth, Hants.
Pretty Chairs, Portsmouth, Hants.
Miller of Chelsea Antiques Ltd., Ringwood, Hants.
St. James Antiques, Great Malvern, Hereford and Worcs.

Great Brampton House Antiques Ltd., Hereford, Hereford and Worcs.
La Barre Ltd., Leominster, Hereford and Worcs.
Robin Lloyd Antiques, Ross-on-Wye, Hereford and Worcs.
St. Ouen Antiques, Puckeridge, Herts.
Old Hall (Sphinx Gallery), Brasted, Kent.
Roy Massingham Antiques, Brasted, Kent.
Antique and Design, Canterbury, Kent.
Dench Antiques, Sandgate, Kent.
Henry Baines, Southborough, Kent.
Up Country, Tunbridge Wells, Kent.
Bridge Antiques, Wingham, Kent.
David H. Dickinson Ltd., Manchester, Lancs.
The Ginnel Gallery, Manchester, Lancs.
Donal Allison Antiques, Preston, Lancs.
J. Green and Son, Queniborough, Leics.
David J. Hansord, Lincoln, Lincs.
Robin Cox Antiques, Stamford, Lincs.
Ivor and Patricia Lewis Antiques and Fine Art Dealers, Stamford, Lincs.
Ron Green, Towcester, Northants.
Helios and Co. (Antiques), Weedon, Northants.
Thirty-Eight Antiques Ltd., Weedon, Northants.
F.J. McCarthy Ltd., Normanton-on-Trent, Notts.
Ashton Gower Antiques, Burford, Oxon. (Cots. Gateway A.C.).
Jonathan Fyson Antiques, Burford, Oxon.
Bugle Antiques, Chipping Norton, Oxon.
Summers, Davis and Son Ltd., Wallingford, Oxon.
Doveridge House of Neachley, Albrighton, Shrops.
The Granary Galleries, Ash Priors, Somerset.
Hall's Antiques, Ash Priors, Somerset.
Pennard House, East Pennard, Somerset.
Genges Farm Antiques, Limington, Somerset.
George Carter Antiques, Wells, Somerset.
Edward A. Nowell, Wells, Somerset.
The Clare Collector, Clare, Suffolk.
Debenham Antique Centre, Debenham, Suffolk.
Compton-Dando (Fine Arts) Ltd., Long Melford, Suffolk.
Seabrook Antiques Ltd., Long Melford, Suffolk.
Manor House Interiors, Chiddingfold, Surrey.
The Old Post Office Antiques, Compton, Surrey.
Heath-Bullock, Godalming, Surrey.
Whittingdon Galleries, Sutton, Surrey.
Wych House Antiques, Woking, Surrey.
Adrian Alan Ltd., Brighton, Sussex East.
Tapsell Antiques, Brighton, Sussex East.
Steve Powell Antiques, Chalvington, Sussex East.
Graham Lower, Flimwell, Sussex East.
Delmas, Hurst Green, Sussex East.
Coombe House Antiques, Lewes, Sussex East.
Graham Price Antiques Ltd., Polegate, Sussex East.
De Montford, Robertsbridge, Sussex East.
Alan and Jennie Hardman Antiques, Crawley, Sussex West.
John Hopkins (Antiques) Ltd., Cuckfield, Sussex West.
John G. Morris Ltd., Petworth, Sussex West.
Apollo Antiques Ltd., Warwick, Warks.
Patrick and Gillian Morley, Warwick, Warks.
Austy House Antiques, Birmingham, West Midlands.
Moxhams Antiques, Bradford-on-Avon, Wilts.
Bryan Mann Antiques, Ramsbury, Wilts.
Ian G. Hastie, Salisbury, Wilts.
Obelisk Antiques, Warminster, Wilts.
Norwood House Antiques, Killinghall, Yorkshire North
Charlotte and John Lambe, Belfast, N. Ireland.
Kenneth Jackson, Edinburgh, Midloth., Scot.
Whytock and Reid, Edinbugh, Midloth., Scot.
Aldric Young, Edinburgh, Midloth., Scot.

Country (For 16th and 17th century furniture also see Oak)

M. and D. Seligmann, London, W.8.
Alistair Sampson Antiques, London, S.W.3.
Stephen Anson, London, S.W.5.
I. and J.L. Brown, London, S.W.6.
Howard Walwyn Antiques, London, S.W.11.
Robert Young Antiques, London, S.W.11.
Simon Coleman Antiques, London, S.W.13.
Tobias and The Angel, London, S.W.13.
Haverstock Antiques, London, N.W.1.
This and That (Furniture), London, N.W.1.
Lansdown Antiques, Bath, Avon.
No.12 Queen Street, Bath, Avon.
Pennard House Antiques, Bath, Avon.
Green Farm Antiques, Olveston, Avon.
Tilly Manor Antiques, West Harptree, Avon.
Margaret Elmes Antiques, Denham Village, Bucks.
Simon and Penny Rumble Antiques, Chittering, Cambs.
West Farm Antiques, Orwell, Cambs.
Farmhouse Antiques, Chester, Cheshire.
Peter Bunting, Hyde, Cheshire.
English Country Furnishings, Mobberley, Cheshire.
David Hill, Kirkby Stephen, Cumbria.
John Meredith, Chagford, Devon.
Britannia Restorations, Combe Martin, Devon.
Hatherleigh Antiques, Hatherleigh, Devon.
Taylor-Halsey Antiques, Jacobstowe, Devon.
Brian Taylor, Plymouth, Devon.
Hennessy, Beaminster, Dorset.
Margery Dean Antiques, Colchester, Essex.
Denzil Verey, Barnsley, Glos.
Gloucester House Antiques Ltd., Fairford, Glos.
Paul Cater Antiques, Moreton-in-Marsh, Glos.
Anthony Sampson, Moreton-in-Marsh, Glos.
Keith Hockin (Antiques) Ltd., Stow-on-the-Wold, Glos.
Huntingdon Antiques Ltd., Stow-on-the-Wold, Glos.

Touchwood Antiques Ltd., Stow-on-the-Wold, Glos.
Close Antiques, Alresford, Hants.
Airedale Antiques, Hartley Wintney, Hants.
Cedar Antiques, Hartley Wintney, Hants.
Phoenix Green Antiques, Hartley Wintney, Hants.
Hursley Antiques, Hursley, Hants.
Millers of Chelsea Antiques Ltd., Ringwood, Hants.
Elizabeth Viney, Stockbridge, Hants.
Burgess Farm Antiques, Morestead, Hants.
The Pine Cellars, Winchester, Hants.
H.W. Keil Ltd., Broadway, Hereford and Worcs.
I. and J.L. Brown, Hereford, Hereford and Worcs.
Geoffrey Crofts Ltd., Leominster, Hereford and Worcs.
Michael Stewart, Leominster, Hereford and Worcs.
M. and J. Russell, Yazor, Hereford and Worcs.
Country Life Antiques, Bushey, Herts.
Village Green Antiques, Hertford, Herts.
Dinah Stoodley, Brasted, Kent.
Old Bakery Antiques, Cranbrook, Kent.
Pedlar's Pack, Hadlow, Kent.
Halstow Antiques, Lower Halstow, Kent.
Henry Baines, Southborough, Kent.
Jackson-Grant Antiques, Teynham, Kent.
E.W. Webster, Bickerstaffe, Lancs.
Davies Antiques, Whalley, Lancs.
David E. Burrows, Osgathorpe, Leics.
Clive Underwood Ltd., Colsterworth, Lincs.
Paul Johnston, Gedney, Lincs.
Burghley Antiques, Stamford, Lincs.
Robin Cox Antiques, Stamford, Lincs.
John Sinclair, Stamford, Lincs.
David Bateson, Bressingham, Norfolk.
Antiques, West Haddon, Northants.
Paul Hopwell Antiques, West Haddon, Northants.
Clement House Antiques, Burford, Oxon.
Jonathan Fyson Antiques, Burford, Oxon.
Horseshoe Antiques and Gallery, Burford, Oxon.
Peter Norden Antiques, Burford, Oxon.
Swan Gallery, Burford, Oxon.
Bugle Antiques, Chipping Norton, Oxon.
Key Antiques, Chipping Norton, Oxon.
Country Furniture, Dorchester-on-Thames, Oxon.
Genges Farm Antiques, Limington, Somerset.
William Morley Antiques, West Monkton, Somerset.
John Nicholls, Leigh, Staffs.
Edward Venn, Williton, Somerset.
Guillemot, Aldeburgh, Suffolk.
Mole Hall Antiques, Aldeburgh, Suffolk.
Peppers Period Pieces, Bury St. Edmunds, Suffolk.
Michael Moore Antiques, Clare, Suffolk.
Oswald Simpson, Long Melford, Suffolk.
Elias Clark Antiques Ltd., Bletchingley, Surrey.
King's Court Galleries, Dorking, Surrey.
David White Antiques, Godalming, Surrey.
Mollie Evans, Richmond, Surrey.
Anthony Welling Antiques, Ripley, Surrey.
Georgian House Antiques, Uckfield, Sussex East.
Mark Chapman Antiques, Petworth, Sussex West.
Frith Antiques, Petworth, Sussex West.
Humphry Antiques, Petworth, Sussex West.
Michael Wakelin and Helen Linfield, Petworth, Sussex West.
Combe Cottage Antiques, Castle Combe, Wilts.
Monkton Galleries, Hindon, Wilts.
Annmarie Turner, Marlborough, Wilts.
Chapman Medd and Sons, Easingwold, Yorkshire North.
Bill Bentley, Harrogate, Yorkshire North.
Cottage Antiques, Harrogate, Yorkshire North.
Elaine Phillips Antiques Ltd., Harrogate, Yorkshire North.
Roy Precious, Settle, Yorkshire North.
Doyle Antiques, Bawtry, Yorkshire South.
Country House Antiques, Belfast, N. Ireland.
Carse Antiques, Rait, Scotland
Country Antiques, Kidwelly, Dyfed, Wales.
James and Pat Ash, Llandeilo, Dyfed, Wales.
Rodney Adams Antiques, Pwllheli, Gwynedd, Wales.

Georgian (1714–1830)

Asprey p.l.c., London, W.1.
Bernheimer Fine Arts Ltd., London, W.1.
H. Blairman & Son Ltd., London, W.1.
Bobinet Ltd., London, W.1.
Brian Fielden, London, W.1.
Fortnum and Mason plc, London, W.1.
Peter Francis, London, W.1.
W.R. Harvey and Co. (Antiques) Ltd., London, W.1.
Mallett and Son (Antiques) Ltd., London, W.1.
Stair and Co. Ltd., London, W.1.
Toynbee-Clarke Interiors Ltd., London, W.1.
M. Turpin, London, W.1.
Claude Bornoff, London, W.2.
The Antique Home, London, W.8.
Church St. Galleries Ltd., London, W.8.
C.H. Major (Antiques) Ltd., London, W.8.
Henry Phillips, London, W.8.
Patrick Sandberg Antiques, London, W.8.
Murray Thomson Ltd., London, W.8.
Serge Baillache, London, W.11.
Butchoff Antiques, London, W.11.
Graham Charge Antiques, London, W.11.
John Dale, London, W.11.
Michael Davidson, London, W.11.
Keith Finch, London, W.11.
Philip Garrick Antiques, London, W.11.
George Johnson Antiques Ltd., London, W.11.
J. Lipitch Ltd., London, W.11.
Terence Morse and Son Ltd., London, W.11.
Didier Aaron (London) Ltd., London, S.W.1.
Anno Domini Antiques, London, S.W.1.

John Bly, London, S.W.1.
Arthur Davidson Ltd., London, S.W.1.
Fernandes and Marche, London, S.W.1.
General Trading Co. Ltd., London, S.W.1.
M. Harris and Sons, London, S.W.1.
Hotspur Ltd., London, S.W.1.
Howe, London, S.W.1.
Jeremy Ltd., London, S.W.1.
Priest Antiques, Michael, London, S.W.1.
Geoffrey Rose Ltd., London, S.W.1.
Westenholz Kime Ltd., London, S.W.1.
Norman Adams Ltd., London, S.W.3.
Apter Fredericks Ltd., London, S.W.3.
H.C. Baxter and Sons, London, S.W.3.
Richard Courtney Ltd., London, S.W.3.
C. Fredericks and Son, London, S.W.3.
Halliday's, London, S.W.3.
Anthony James and Son Ltd., London, S.W.3.
John Keil Ltd., London, S.W.3.
Michael Lipitch Ltd., London, S.W.3.
Pelham Galleries, London, S.W.3.
David Pettifer Ltd., London, S.W.3.
O.F. Wilson Ltd., London, S.W.3.
David Tron (Antiques) Ltd., London, S.W.5.
Alasdair Brown Antiques, London, S.W.6.
John Clay, London, S.W.6.
Fergus Cochrane Antiques, London, S.W.6.
Charles Edwards, London, S.W.6.
Goodwin and Wadhwa, London, S.W.6.
George Leuchars, London, S.W.6.
Patrick Jefferson, London, S.W.6.
Michael Marriott Ltd., London, S.W.6.
Ian Moggach Antiques, London, S.W.6.
David Seyfried Antiques, London, S.W.6.
Furniture Cave, London, S.W.10.
John Haines Antiques, London, S.W.13.
Wren Antiques, London, S.W.13.
Serena Stapleton Antiques, London, S.W.15.
Clifford and Roger Dade, London, S.W.17.
Relcy Antiques, London, S.E.10.
Westland Pilkington, London, E.C.2.
The Antique Trader, London, N.1.
Alexander Bailie Antiques, London, N.1. (The Mall)
William Bedford p.l.c., London, N.1.
Peter Chapman Antiques, London, N.1.
D.J. Ferrant Antiques, London, N.1.
Haverstock Antiques, London, N.W.1.
Regent Antiques, London, N.W.1.
W.E. Walker, London, N.W.1.
Patricia Beckman, London, N.W.3.
Antiquum, London, N.W.5.
Wellington Gallery, London, N.W.8.
S. and H. Jewell Ltd., London, W.C.2.
Beau Nash House Antiques, Bath, Avon.
Saville House plc, Bath, Avon.
John Croft Antiques, Bath, Avon.
Brian and Angela Downes, Bath, Avon.
Anthony Emm, Bath, Avon.
David Gibson Antiques, Bath, Avon.
Jadis Ltd., Bath, Avon.
Queens Parade Antiques Ltd., Bath, Avon.
Quiet St. Antiques, Bath, Avon.
Robin Butler, Bristol, Avon.
Robert Harman Antiques, Ampthill, Beds.
S. and S. Timms Antiques Ltd., Ampthill, Beds.
F. and M. O'Dell, Shefford, Beds.
Butterworths, Woburn, Beds.
Christopher Sykes Antiques, Woburn, Beds.
Alasdair Brown Antiques, Datchet, Berks.
Old School Antiques, Dorney, Berks.
Roger King Antiques, Hungerford, Berks.
Medalcrest Ltd., Hungerford, Berks.
The Old Malthouse, Hungerford, Berks.
Paravicini, Hungerford, Berks.
Griffons Court, Newbury, Berks.
Cavendish Fine Arts, Twyford, Berks.
Guy Bousfield, Windsor and Eton, Berks.
Eton Gallery Antiques, Windsor and Eton, Berks.
John A. Pearson Ltd., Windsor and Eton, Berks.
Norton Antiques, Beaconsfield, Bucks.
Period Furniture Showrooms, Beaconsfield, Bucks.
Margaret Elmes Antiques, Denham Village, Bucks.
Bowood Antiques, Wendover, Bucks.
Haydon House (Antiques), Woburn Sands, Bucks.
S. Webster Speakman, Cambridge, Cambs.
Simon and Penny Rumble Antiques, Chittering, Cambs.
Eureka Antiques and Interiors, Bowdon, Cheshire.
Adams Antiques, Chester, Cheshire.
Cheshire Antiques, Macclesfield, Cheshire.
Alan Bennett, Truro, Cornwall.
Pydar Antiques and Gallery, Truro, Cornwall.
Peter Stanton Antiques Restorations, Truro, Cornwall.
Brian Ferguson, Carlisle, Cumbria.
Anthemion, Cartmel, Cumbria.
Haughey Antiques, Kirkby Stephen, Cumbria.
Shire Antiques, Newby Bridge, Cumbria.
Townhead Antiques, Newby Bridge, Cumbria.
Matsell Antiques Ltd., Ilkeston, Derbys.
Shardlow Antiques Warehouse, Shardlow, Derbys.
G.W. Ford and Son Ltd., Unstone, Derbys.
Nimbus Antiques, Whaley Bridge, Derbys.
J. Collins and Son, Bideford, Devon.
David J. Thorn, Budleigh Salterton, Devon.
Roderick P. Butler, Honiton, Devon.
Philip Andrade Ltd., South Brent, Devon.
Extence Antiques, Teignmouth, Devon.
Good Hope Antiques, Beaminster, Dorset.
R.A. Swift and Sons, Bournemouth, Dorset.
Johnsons of Sherborne Ltd., Sherborne, Dorset.
Antiquatat Antiques, Wimborne Minster, Dorset.
Jackson's Antiques Ltd., Barnard Castle, Durham.
Margery Dean Antiques, Colchester, Essex.
Partner and Puxon, Colchester, Essex.
Kelvedon Antiques, Kelvedon, Essex.
Millers Antiques, Kelvedon, Essex.
Thomas Sykes Antiques, Kelvedon, Essex.
Stone Hall Antiques, Matching Green, Essex.
W.A. Pinn and Son, Sible Hedingham, Essex.
Compton-Dando, White Colne, Essex.

H.W. Keil (Cheltenham) Ltd., Cheltenham, Glos.
Hares, Cirencester, Glos.
W.W. Holzgrawe Antiques, Cirencester, Glos.
Rankine Taylor Antiques, Cirencester, Glos.
Bernard Weaver, Cirencester, Glos.
Simon Brett, Moreton-in-Marsh, Glos.
Paul Cater Antiques, Moreton-in-Marsh, Glos.
Elizabeth Parker, Moreton-in-Marsh, Glos.
Anthony Sampson, Moreton-in-Marsh, Glos.
Craig Carrington, Painswick, Glos.
Greenhouse Antiques, Painswick, Glos.
Colin Brand Antiques, Stow-on-the-Wold, Glos.
Christopher Clarke Antiques, Stow-on-the-Wold, Glos.
Rudolph Otto, Stow-on-the-Wold, Glos.
Vanbrugh House Antiques, Stow-on-the-Wold, Glos.
Breakspeare Antiques, Tetbury, Glos.
Close Antiques, Alresford, Hants.
Jane Burnham-Slipper Antiques, Botley, Hants.
Adrienne Marino-Montero Fine Art, Curdridge, Hants.
Nicholas Abbott, Hartley Wintney, Hants.
Andwells, Hartley Wintney, Hants.
Deva Antiques, Hartley Wintney, Hants.
Millon Antiques, Hartley Wintney, Hants.
Phoenix Green Antiques, Hartley Wintney, Hants.
J. du Cros Antiques, Liss, Hants.
Corfield of Lymington Ltd., Lymington, Hants.
Lita Kaye of Lyndhurst, Lyndhurst, Hants.
Joseph William Blanchard Ltd., Winchester, Hants.
Elizabeth Viney, Stockbridge, Hants.
Gallery Antiques Ltd., Winchester, Hants.
Barnt Green Antiques, Barnt Green, Hereford and Worcs.
H.W. Keil Ltd., Broadway, Hereford and Worcs.
Great Brampton House Antiques, Hereford, Hereford and Worcs.
John Nash Antiques and Interiors, Ledbury, Hereford and Worcs.
Stables Antiques, Ombersley, Hereford and Worcs.
Bygones (Worcester), Worcester, Hereford and Worcs.
Anthony Butt Antiques, Baldock, Herts.
Ralph and Bruce Moss, Baldock, Herts.
M. and S. Armson, Berkhamsted, Herts.
Park Street Antiques, Berkhamsted, Herts.
Phillips of Hitchin (Antiques) Ltd., Hitchin, Herts.
Dolphin Antiques, St. Albans, Herts.
John Bly, Tring, Herts.
Collins Antiques (F.G. and C. Collins Ltd.), Wheathampstead, Herts.
Boothferry Antiques, Hull, N. Humbs.
In Retrospect, Pocklington, N. Humbs.
Michael Sim, Chislehurst, Kent.
Peacock Antiques, Chilham, Kent.
Chevertons of Edenbridge Ltd., Edenbridge, Kent.
Old Forge, Hollingbourne, Kent.
David Rackham (Rochester Fine Arts), Rochester, Kent.
Sutton Valence Antiques, Sutton Valence, Kent.
Langold Antiques Ltd., West Peckham, Kent.
Anthony J. Hook, Westerham, Kent.
Mistral Galleries, Westerham, Kent.
E.W. Webster, Bickerstaffe, Lancs.
Park Galleries Antiques, Bolton, Lancs.
Wm. Goodfellow (Antiques), Carnforth, Lancs.
Carlton Antiques Exports, Clayton-le-Woods, Lancs.
Alan Butterworth (Antiques) Ltd., Horwich, Lancs.
Bulldog Antiques, Manchester, Lancs.
The Connoisseur, Manchester, Lancs.
Dickinson Ltd., David H., Manchester, Lancs.
Manchester Antique Co., Manchester, Lancs.
Betty and Dean Easterby, Preston, Lancs.
Frederick Treasure Ltd., Preston, Lancs.
Antiques in Charnwood, Anstey, Leics.
Ivanhoe Antiques, Ashby de la Zouch, Leics.
Corner Cottage Antiques, Leicester, Leics.
Walter Moores and Son, Leicester, Leics.
E. Smith (Leicester) Ltd., Leicester, Leics.
Lowe of Loughborough, Loughborough, Leics.
Corner Cottage Antiques, Market Bosworth, Leics.
J. Green and Son, Queniborough, Leics.
Lapwing Antiques, Uppingham, Leics.
T.J. Roberts, Uppingham, Leics.
Robert Bingley Antiques, Wing, Leics.
Anthony Cotton, Lincoln, Lincs.
David J. Hansord, Lincoln, Lincs.
Pinfold Antiques, Ruskington, Lincs.
Colin Stock, Rainford, Merseyside.
Market House, Burnham Market, Norfolk.
Peter Robinson, Heacham, Norfolk.
Arthur Brett and Sons Ltd., Norwich, Norfolk.
Leo Pratt and Son, South Walsham, Norfolk.
T.C.S. Brooke, Wroxham, Norfolk.
Restall Brown and Clennell Ltd., Cosgrove, Northants.
M.C. Chapman, Finedon, Northants.
V. and C. Madeira, Flore, Northants.
F. and C.H. Cave, Northampton, Northants.
Regent House, Northampton, Northants.
The Antique Galleries, Paulerspury, Northants.
Reindeer Antiques Ltd., Pottersbury, Northants.
Archway Antiques, Towcester, Northants.
Arthur Boaden Antiques, Hexham, Northumbs.
E.M. Cheshire, Bingham, Notts.
Zene Walker, Burford, Oxon.
Peter Stroud, Chipping Norton, Oxon.
Hallidays Antiques Ltd., Dorchester-on-Thames, Oxon.
Mark Carter Antiques, Bladon, Oxon.
Park House Antiques, Bladon, Oxon.

Clement House Antiques, Burford, Oxon.
A. and F. Partners, Faringdon, Oxon.
La Chaise Antique, Faringdon, Oxon.
Henley Antiques Gallery, Henley-on-Thames, Oxon.
Richard J. Kingston, Henley-on-Thames, Oxon.
Antony Davenport, Hinton Waldrist, Oxon.
Harvey Ferry and William Clegg, Nettlebed, Oxon.
Michael Priest Antiques and Fine Arts, Thame, Oxon.
Summers, Davis and Son Ltd., Wallingford, Oxon.
Doveridge House of Neachley, Albrighton, Shrops.
R.G. Cave and Sons Ltd., Ludlow, Shrops.
Paul Smith, Ludlow, Shrops.
F.C. Manser and Son Ltd., Shrewsbury, Shrops.
L. Onions, Tern Hill, Shrops.
Granary Galleries, Ash Priors, Somerset.
Halls Antiques, Ash Priors, Somerset.
James Ribbons, Bruton, Somerset.
Ray Best Antiques, Ilminster, Somerset.
Moolham Mill Antiques, Ilminster, Somerset.
Edward A. Nowell, Wells, Somerset.
J.C. Giddings, Wiveliscombe, Somerset.
R.N. Usher, Bury St. Edmunds, Suffolk.
The Clare Collector, Clare, Suffolk.
Randolph, Hadleigh, Suffolk.
Gordon Sutcliffe, Hadleigh, Suffolk.
Hubbards Antiques, Ipswich, Suffolk.
Roger Carling and Tess Sinclair, Long Melford, Suffolk.
Compton-Dando (Fine Arts) Ltd., Long Melford, Suffolk.
Bruno Cooper Antiques, Long Melford, Suffolk.
The Goff Galleries, Long Melford, Suffolk.
Neptune Antiques, Long Melford, Suffolk.
Suthburgh Antiques, Long Melford, Suffolk.
Ward Antiques plc., Long Melford, Suffolk.
Antique Furniture Warehouse, Woodbridge, Suffolk.
David Gibbins Antiques, Woodbridge, Suffolk.
Hamilton Antiques, Woodbridge, Suffolk.
Anthony Hurst Antiques, Woodbridge, Suffolk.
A.G. Voss, Woodbridge, Suffolk.
John Anthony Antiques, Bletchingley, Surrey.
Paul Keen Antiques, Croydon, Surrey.
Dorking Desk Shop, Dorking, Surrey.
Hampshires of Dorking, Dorking, Surrey.
Kennedy and Spooner Antiques, Dorking, Surrey.
Elaine Saunderson Antiques, Dorking, Surrey.
Thorpe and Foster Ltd., Dorking, Surrey.
Upstairs, Downstairs Antiques, Dorking, Surrey.
West Street Antiques, Dorking, Surrey.
Patrick Worth Antiques, Dorking, Surrey.
A.E. Gould and Sons (Antiques) Ltd., East Horsley, Surrey.
Christopher's Antiques, Farnham, Surrey.
P. and B. Jordan, Farnham, Surrey.
Heath-Bullock, Godalming, Surrey.
M.J. Bowdery, Hindhead, Surrey.
Knaphill Antiques, Knaphill, Surrey.
Hill Rise Antiques, Richmond, Surrey.
B.M. Newlove, Surbiton, Surrey.
J. Hartley Antiques Ltd., Ripley, Surrey.
Ripley Antiques, Ripley, Surrey.
Sage Antiques and Interiors, Ripley, Surrey.
Anthony Welling Antiques, Ripley, Surrey.
Ian Caldwell, Walton-on-the-Hill and Tadworth, Surrey.
Hatch Antiques, Weybridge, Surrey.
R. Saunders, Weybridge, Surrey.
Weybridge Antiques, Weybridge, Surrey.
Brighton Antique Wholesalers, Brighton, Sussex East.
Alan Fitchett Antiques, Brighton, Sussex East.
Michael Norman Antiques, Brighton, Sussex East.
Yellow Lantern Antiques Ltd., Brighton, Sussex East.
Pigeon House Antiques, Hurst Green, Sussex East.
Coombe House Antiques, Lewes, Sussex East.
Renée and Ray Green, Lewes, Sussex East.
Trevor, Lewes, Sussex East
Old Mint House, Pevensey, Sussex East.
Trade Wind, Rottingdean, Sussex East.
Bragge and Sons, Rye, Sussex East.
Rye Antiques, Rye, Sussex East.
The Old House, Seaford, Sussex East.
Ardingly Antiques, Ardingly, Sussex West.
Country Life by Bursig, Arundel, Sussex West.
British Antique Replicas, Burgess Hill, Sussex West.
Antique Shop, Chichester, Sussex West.
John Hopkins (Antiques) Ltd., Cuckfield, Sussex West.
Baskerville Antiques, Petworth, Sussex West.
Mark Chapman Antiques, Petworth, Sussex West.
Philip Cooper Antiques, Petworth, Sussex West.
Frith Antiques, Petworth, Sussex West.
Granville Antiques, Petworth, Sussex West.
William Hockley Antiques, Petworth, Sussex West.
Humphry Antiques, Petworth, Sussex West.
Lewis and Lloyd, Petworth, Sussex West.
The Madison Gallery, Petworth, Sussex West.
Millhouse, Petworth, Sussex West.
John G. Morris Ltd., Petworth, Sussex West.
J.C. Tutt Antiques, Petworth, Sussex West.
Warnham Antiques, Warnham, Sussex West.
Wilson's Antiques, Worthing, Sussex West.
Jasper Marsh, Henley-in-Arden, Warks.
Jeremy Venables, Kineton, Warks.
Percy F. Wale Ltd., Leamington Spa, Warks.
Burman Antiques, Stratford-upon-Avon, Warks.
Miles Ferneyhough, Stratford-on-Avon, Warks.

Patrick and Gillian Morley, Warwick, Warks.
James Reeve, Warwick, Warks.
Ashleigh House Antiques, Birmingham, West Midlands.
Bob Harris and Sons Antiques, Birmingham, West Midlands.
John Hubbard Antiques, Birmingham, West Midlands.
Stuart House Fine Art, Birmingham, West Midlands.
Thomas Coulborn and Sons, Sutton Coldfield, West Midlands.
H. and R.L. Parry Ltd., Sutton Coldfield, West Midlands.
Martin-Quick Antiques Ltd., Wolverhampton, West Midlands.
Wakeman and Taylor Antiques, Wolverhampton, West Midlands.
Avon Antiques, Bradford-on-Avon, Wilts.
Harp Antiques, Bradford-on-Avon, Wilts.
Moxhams Antiques, Bradford-on-Avon, Wilts.
Harley Antiques, Christian Malford, Wilts.
Robin and Matthew Eden, Corsham, Wilts.
Robin Shield Antiques, Cricklade, Wilts.
Andrew Britten Antiques, Malmesbury, Wilts.
Cross Hayes Antiques, Malmesbury, Wilts.
Dovetail Antiques, Malmesbury, Wilts.
Malmesbury Antiques, Malmesbury, Wilts.
Nigel Cracknell (Antiques) Ltd., Marlborough, Wilts.
Robert Kime Antiques, Marlborough, Wilts.
Rupert Gentle Antiques, Milton Lilbourne, Wilts.
Bryan Mann Antiques, Ramsbury, Wilts.
Robert Bradley, Salisbury, Wilts.
Ian G. Hastie, Salisbury, Wilts.
Edward Hurst Antiques, Salisbury, Wilts.
St. John Street Gallery, Salisbury, Wilts.
Peter Houghton Antiques, Warminster, Wilts.
A.J. Romain and Sons, Wilton, Wilts.
R.S. Wilson and Sons, Boroughbridge, Yorkshire North.
Bernard Dickinson, Gargrave, Yorkshire North.
Myers Galleries, Gargrave, Yorkshire North.
Armstrong, Harrogate, Yorkshire North.
W.F. Greenwood and Sons Ltd., Harrogate, Yorkshire North.
David Love, Harrogate, Yorkshire North.
Charles Lumb and Sons Ltd., Harrogate, Yorkshire North.
Windmill Antiques, Harrogate, Yorkshire North.
H.I. Milnthorpe, Settle, Yorkshire North.
Robert Morrison and Son, York, Yorkshire North.
Doyle Antiques, Bawtry, Yorkshire South.
Wickersley Antiques, Rotherham, Yorkshire North.
A.E. Jameson and Co., Sheffield, Yorkshire South.
Addingham Antiques, Addingham, Yorkshire West.
J.H. Cooper and Son (Ilkley) Ltd., Ilkley, Yorkshire West.
Simon, Ilkley, Yorkshire West.
Geary Antiques., Leeds, Yorkshire West.
Windsor House Antiques (Leeds) Ltd., Leeds, Yorkshire West.
Raymond Tomlinson (Antiques) Ltd., Wetherby, Yorkshire West.
St. James's Gallery Ltd., St. Peter Port, Guernsey, C.I.
Antique Shop, Ballyclare, Co. Antrim, N. Ireland.
Dunluce Antiques, Bushmills, Co. Antrim, N. Ireland.
Albert Graham Ltd., Larne, Co. Antrim, N. Ireland.
Furney Antiques, Donaghadee, Co. Down, N. Ireland.
John Bell of Aberdeen Ltd., Aberdeen, Scotland.
Coldstream Antiques, Coldstream, Scotland.
Dunkeld Interiors, Dunkeld, Scotland.
Laurance Black Ltd., Edinburgh, Scotland.
Eric Davison (Antiques) Ltd., Edinburgh, Scotland.
Dunedin Antiques Ltd., Edinburgh, Scotland.
Galloways (Edinburgh) Ltd., Edinburgh, Scotland.
Georgian Antiques, Edinburgh, Scotland.
Kenneth Jackson, Edinburgh, Scotland.
Letham Antiques, Edinburgh, Scotland.
Whytock and Reid, Edinburgh, Scotland.
Greycroft Antiques, Errol, Scotland.
Butler's Furniture Galleries Ltd., Glasgow, Scotland.
Muirhead Moffat and Co., Glasgow, Scotland.
C.S. Moreton Antiques, Inchture, Scotland.
Kilmacolm Antiques Ltd., Kilmacolm, Scotland.
Paul Couts Ltd., Musselburgh, Scotland.
Coach House Antiques Ltd., Perth, Scotland.
Tay Street Gallery, Perth, Scotland.
Keith Antiques, Rait, Scotland.
Templemans, Rait, Scotland.
Country Antiques, Kidwelly, Dyfed, Wales.
James and Pat Ash, Llandeilo, Dyfed, Wales.

Oak (i.e. furniture prior to 1700)
Barling of Mount Street, London, W.1.
Ronald A. Lee (Fine Arts) Ltd., London, W.1.
Daniel Mankowitz, London, W.2.
M. and D. Seligmann, London, W.8.
Louis Stanton, London, W.11.
Anno Domini Antiques, London, S.W.1.
Csaky's Antiques, London, S.W.1.
Arthur Davidson Ltd., London, S.W.1.
Pamela Streather, London, S.W.1.
Joanna Booth, London, S.W.3.
Alistair Sampson Antiques, London, S.W.3.
Stephen Anson, London, S.W.5.
David Alexander, London, S.W.6.
Rendlesham Antiques, London, S.W.10.
Howard Walwyn Antiques, London, S.W.11.
Robert Young Antiques, London, S.W.11.
No.12 Queen Street, Bath, Avon.
Green Farm Antiques, Olveston, Avon.
Mary Bellis Antiques, Hungerford, Berks.
Paravicini, Hungerford, Berks.

John Baker Antiques, Newby, Berks.
Albert Bartram, Chesham, Bucks.
Simon and Penny Rumble Antiques, Chittering, Cambs.
Peter Bunting, Hyde, Cheshire.
Kendal Studios Antiques, Kendal, Cumbria.
Shire Antiques, Newby Bridge, Cumbria.
Beedham Antiques Ltd., Bakewell, Derbys.
K. Chappell Antiques and Fine Art, Bakewell, Derbys.
Michael Goldstone, Bakewell, Derbys.
Robert Byles, Bampton, Devon.
J. Collins and Son, Bideford, Devon.
John Meredith, Chagford, Devon.
Priory Antiques, Exeter, Devon.
Hatherleigh Antiques, Hatherleigh, Devon.
Roderick P. Butler, Honiton, Devon.
Taylor-Halsey Antiques, Jacobstowe, Devon.
Philip Andrade Ltd., South Brent, Devon.
South Molton Antiques, South Molton, Devon.
C. and J. Mortimer and Sons, Great Chesterford, Essex.
H.W. Keil (Cheltenham) Ltd., Cheltenham, Glos.
William H. Stokes, Cirencester, Glos.
Rankine Taylor Antiques, Cirencester, Glos.
Gloucester House Antiques Ltd., Fairford, Glos.
Simon Brett, Moreton-in-Marsh, Glos.
Paul Cater Antiques, Moreton-in-Marsh, Glos.
Anthony Sampson, Moreton-in-Marsh, Glos.
Baggott Church St. Ltd., Stow-on-the-Wold, Glos.
Duncan Baggott Antiques, Stow-on-the-Wold, Glos.
J. and J. Caspall Antiques, Stow-on-the-Wold, Glos.
Christopher Clarke Antiques Ltd., Stow-on-the-Wold, Glos.
Keith Hockin, Stow-on-the-Wold, Glos.
Huntingdon Antiques Ltd., Stow-on-the-Wold, Glos.
Touchwood International Ltd., Stow-on-the-Wold, Glos.
Close Antiques, Alresford, Hants.
Quatrefoil, Fordingbridge, Hants.
Cedar Antiques, Hartley Wintney, Hants.
Elizabeth Viney, Stockbridge, Hants.
H.W. Keil Ltd., Broadway, Hereford and Worcs.
Hubbard Antiques, Leominster, Hereford and Worcs.
La Barre Ltd., Leominster, Hereford and Worcs.
M. and J. Russell, Yazor, Hereford and Worcs.
Dobson's Antiques, Abbots Langley, Herts.
Phillips of Hitchin (Antiques) Ltd., Hitchin, Herts.
Christopher Perry Antiques, St. Albans, Herts.
Collins Antiques, Wheathampstead, Herts.
Old Hall (Sphinx Gallery), Brasted, Kent.
Diana Stoodley, Brasted, Kent.
Old Bakery Antiques, Cranbrook, Kent.
Swan Antiques, Cranbrook, Kent.
Farnborough (Kent) Antiques, Farnborough, Kent.
Halstow Antiques, Lower Halstow, Kent.
Bridge House Antiques, Penshurst, Kent.
Henry Baines, Southborough, Kent.
Jackson-Grant Antiques, Teynham, Kent.
H. and M.J. Burke, Worsley, Lancs.
Lowe of Loughborough, Loughborough, Leics.
David E. Burrows, Osgathorpe, Leics.
Paul Johnston, Gedney, Lincs.
Pinfold Antiques, Ruskington, Lincs.
Robin Cox Antiques, Stamford, Lincs.
John Sinclair, Stamford, Lincs.
A.E. Bush and Partners, Attleborough, Norfolk.
Pearse Lukies, Aylsham, Norfolk.
Arthur Brett and Sons Ltd., Norwich, Norfolk.
Regent House, Northampton, Northants.
Paul Hopwell Antiques, West Haddon, Northants.
Country Pine Antiques, Alnwick, Northumbs.
Country Pine Antiques, Chatton, Northumbs.
E.M. Cheshire, Bingham, Notts.
Mark Carter Antiques, Bladon, Oxon.
Jonathan Fyson Antiques, Burford, Oxon.
Horseshoe Antiques and Gallery, Burford, Oxon.
Peter Norden Antiques, Burford, Oxon.
Swan Gallery, Burford, Oxon.
Bugle Antiques, Chipping Norton, Oxon.
Key Antiques, Chipping Norton, Oxon.
Packer House Antiques, Chipping Norton, Oxon.
Peter Stroud Antiques, Chipping Norton, Oxon.
Michael Priest Antiques and Fine Arts, Thame, Oxon.
Witney Antiques, Witney, Oxon.
Audrey and Brian Bingham Antiques, Whitchurch, Shrops.
Stuart Interiors (Antiques) Ltd., Barrington, Somerset.
Ray Best Antiques, Ilminster, Somerset.
Moolham Mill Antiques, Ilminster, Somerset.
Milverton Antiques, Milverton, Somerset.
Barry M. Sainsbury, Wincanton, Somerset.
Oswald Simpson, Long Melford, Suffolk.
Peppers Period Pieces, Bury St. Edmunds, Suffolk.
The Clare Collector, Clare, Suffolk.
Randolph, Hadleigh, Suffolk.
J. and J. Baker, Lavenham, Suffolk.
Neptune Antiques, Long Melford, Suffolk.
Elias Clark Antiques Ltd. Bletchingley, Surrey.
King's Court Galleries, Dorking, Surrey.
Thorpe and Foster Ltd., Dorking, Surrey.
Anthony Welling Antiques, Ripley, Surrey.
B.M. Newlove, Surbiton, Surrey.
Graham Lower, Flimwell, Sussex East.
Georgian House, Uckfield, Sussex East.
Mark Chapman, Petworth, Sussex West.
Frith Antiques, Petworth, Sussex West.
Griffin Antiques, Petworth, Sussex West.
Humphry Antiques, Petworth, Sussex West.
J.C. Tutt, Petworth, Sussex West.

Jasper Marsh, Henley-in-Arden, Warks.
James Reeve, Warwick, Warks.
Avon Antiques, Bradford-on-Avon, Wilts.
Monkton Galleries, Hindon, Wilts.
Edward Hurst Antiques, Salisbury, Wilts.
R.S. Wilson and Sons, Boroughbridge, Yorkshire North.
Chapman Medd and Sons, Easingwold, Yorkshire North.
Bill Bentley, Harrogate, Yorkshire North.
Cottage Antiques, Harrogate, Yorkshire North.
W.F. Greenwood and Sons Ltd., Harrogate, Yorkshire North.
Elaine Phillips Antiques Ltd., Harrogate, Yorkshire North.
Roy Precious, Settle, Yorkshire North.
Doyle Antiques, Bawtry, Yorkshire South.
Timothy D. Wilson, Bawtry, Yorkshire South.
Joan Frere Antiques, Drumnadrochit, Scotland.
Carse Antqiues, Rait, Scotland
Country Antiques, Kidwelly, Dyfed, Wales.
Cheriton Antiques, Narbeth, Dyfed, Wales.

Pine

Stratton-Quinn Antiques Etc., London, W.4.
Andy's All Pine, London, W.14.
(55) For Decorative Living, London, S.W.6.
Bishops Park Antiques, London, S.W.6.
Old Pine, London, S.W.6.
The Pine Mine (Crewe Read Antiques), London, S.W.6.
The Pine Village, London, S.W.6.
Savile Pine, London, S.W.6.
Town and Country Antiques, London, S.W.6.
Nicholas Beech, London, S.W.8.
Scallywag, London, S.W.9.
Remember When, London, S.W.13.
Islington Artefacts, London, N.1.
Michael Lewis Antiques, London, N.1.
Adams Antiques, London, N.W.1.
Lansdown Antiques, Bath, Avon.
Pennard House Antiques, Bath, Avon.
Widcombe Antiques and Pine, Bath, Avon.
Oldwoods, Bristol, Avon.
Relics, Bristol, Avon.
Bay Tree Antiques, Weston-super-Mare, Avon.
The Pine Parlour, Ampthill, Beds.
Yesterday's Pine, Ampthill, Beds.
Willow Farm Pine Centre, Harlington, Beds.
The Old Pine Loft, Luton, Beds.
Yesterday's Pine, Woburn, Beds.
Yesterday's Pine, Buckingham, Bucks.
The Pine Merchants, Gt. Missenden, Bucks.
Pine Reflections, Hughendon Valley, Bucks.
Bach Antiques, Lane End, Bucks.
The Antique Shop, Tingewick, Bucks.
Adams Antiques, St. Ives, Cambs.
The Golden Drop Antiques, Warboys, Cambs.
Brook Lane Antiques, Alderley Edge, Cheshire.
Richmond Galleries, Chester, Cheshire.
Pine Too, Congleton, Cheshire.
Stewart Evans, Malpas, Cheshire.
English Country Furnishings, Mobberley, Cheshire.
Pine and Period Furniture, Grampound, Cornwall.
Westward Country Pine, Launceston, Cornwall.
Pine and Country Antiques, North Petherwin, Cornwall.
Utopia Antiques Ltd., Holme, Cumbria.
Tanglewood, Ashbourne, Derbys.
Gravelly Bank Pine Antiques, Yeaveley, Derbys.
Petticombe Manor Antiques, Bideford, Devon.
Cobweb Antiques, Cullompton, Devon.
Sunset Country Antiques, Cullompton, Devon.
G. Mounter, Dulford, Devon.
Fagins Antiques, Exeter, Devon.
Fine Pine Antiques, Harbertonford, Devon.
Great Western Pine, South Molton, Devon.
South Molton Antiques, South Molton, Devon.
Colystock Antiques, Stockland, Devon.
Rocking Horse Pine, Torquay, Devon.
Hennessy, Beaminster, Dorset.
Castleton Country Furniture, Sherborne, Dorset.
Country Pine and Antiques, Sherborne, Dorset.
Countrystyle, Colchester, Essex.
Margery Dean Antiques, Colchester, Essex.
Andrew Tate, Finchingfield, Essex.
Churchgate Antiques, Halstead, Essex.
Fox and Pheasant Antique Pine, White Colne, Essex.
Denzil Verey, Barnsley, Glos.
Bed of Roses, Cheltenham, Glos.
Pinecrafts, Bishops Waltham, Hants.
Pine Collection, Liss, Hants.
Burgess Farm Antiques, Morestead, Hants.
Millers of Chelsea Antiques Ltd., Ringwood, Hants.
Pine Company, Ringwood, Hants.
Swaythling Woodcrafts, Southampton, Hants.
Pine Cellars, Winchester, Hants.
Paul Somers Interiors, Great Malvern, Hereford and Worcs.
Hi-Felicity, Kidderminster, Hereford and Worcs.
Old Pine Shop, Ross-on-Wye, Hereford and Worcs.
Arthur Porter, Baldock, Herts.
Yesterday's Pine, Berkhamsted, Herts.
Stevens Antiques, St. Albans, Herts.
Boothferry Antiques, Hull, N. Humberside.
Paul Wilson Old and Antique Pine, Hull, N. Humberside.
Pieter Plantenga, Market Weighton, N. Humberside.
Elegance Antiques, Barton-on-Humber, S. Humberside.
Bell Antiques, Grimsby, S. Humberside.
Scallywag, Beckenham, Kent.
Enloc Antiques, Colne, Lancs.
G.W. Antiques, Lancaster, Lancs.
Pine Mine Antiques, Lytham St. Annes, Lancs.

Village Furniture Co., Manchester, Lancs.
Revival Pine Stripping, Ormskirk, Lancs.
Walter Aspinall Antiques, Sabden, Lancs.
Oldfield Cottage Antiques, Saddleworth, Lancs.
Burley Workshops, Burley-on-the-Hill, Leics.
House Things Antiques, Hinckley, Leics.
Vendy Antiques (Kibworth), Kibworth, Leics.
Fine Pine, Leicester, Leics.
Richard Kimbell Ltd., Market Harborough, Leics.
David E. Burrows, Osgathorpe, Leics.
R.A. James Antiques, Sileby, Leics.
Old Bakehouse Pine, Whissendene, Leics.
Fenn End Antiques, Horncastle, Lincs.
Designs on Pine, Lincoln, Lincs.
Sykes Antiques, South Kelsey, Lincs.
Andrew Thomas, Stamford, Lincs.
Tealby Pine, Wragby, Lincs.
Delta Antiques, Liverpool, Merseyside.
Fine Pine, Southport, Merseyside.
Valtone Pine, Hampton, Middx.
Earsham Hall Pine, Earsham, Norfolk.
Country Pine Shop, West Haddon, Northants.
Country Pine Antiques, Alnwick, Northumbs.
Country Pine Antiques, Chatton, Northumbs.
Haydon Bridge Antiques, Haydon Bridge, Northumbs.
Castle Antiques, Newark, Notts.
Retford Pine, Newark, Notts.
Jack Spratt Antiques, Newark, Notts.
T.T. Antiques, Newark, Notts.
Trent Antiques, Newark, Notts.
Gatehouse, Nottingham, Notts.
Station Pine Antiques, Nottingham, Notts.
Thame Pine, Thame, Oxon.
Pennard House, East Pennard, Somerset.
Chalon U.K. Ltd., Hambridge, Somerset.
Genges Farm Antiques, Limington, Somerset.
Bay Tree House Antiques, Lympsham, Somerset.
Milverton Antiques, Milverton, Somerset.
Justin Pinewood, Burton-on-Trent, Staffs.
Country Cottage Interiors, Kingsley, Staffs.
Anvil Antiques, Leek, Staffs.
Aspleys Antique Market, Leek, Staffs.
Directmoor Ltd., Leek, Staffs.
Gemini Trading, Leek, Staffs.
Johnson's, Leek, Staffs.
Directmoor Ltd., Oakamoor, Staffs.
Michael Moore Antiques, Clare, Suffolk.
Joyce Hardy Pine and Country Furniture, Hacheston, Suffolk.
Countrystyle, Ipswich, Suffolk.
Ockley Antiques, Dorking, Surrey.
Fogg Antiques, Epsom, Surrey.
Village Pine, Farnham, Surrey.
The Pine Shop, Merrow, Surrey.
House of Pine, Eastbourne, Sussex East.
Mary Sautter, Lewes, Sussex East.
Mary Sautter Pine Furniture, Lewes, Sussex East.
Grist Mill Interiors, Rye, Sussex East.
Ann Lingard, Rope Walk Antiques, Rye, Sussex East.
Pine and Design, Balcombe, Sussex West.
Sheelagh Hamilton, Fernhurst, Sussex West.
Griffin Antiques, Petworth, Sussex West.
Sandhill Barn Antiques (Pine and Country), Washington, Sussex West.
Northumbria Pine, Whitley Bay, Tyne and Wear
Spa Antiques Market, Leamington Spa, Warks.
Pine Design, Warwick, Warks.
Always Antiques, Birmingham, West Midlands.
Cross Hayes Antiques, Malmesbury, Wilts.
Pine Finds, Bishop Monkton, Yorkshire North.
L.L. Ward and Son, Brandsby, Yorkshire North.
Country Pine Antiques, Brompton, Yorkshire North.
The Main Pine Co., Green Hammerton, Yorkshire North.
Fox's Antique Pine and Country Furniture, Harrogate, Yorkshire North.
Traditional Interiors, Harrogate, Yorkshire North.
Westway Cottage Restored Pine, Helmsley, Yorkshire North.
Low Mill Antiques, Lower Bentham, Yorkshire North.
Daleside Antiques, Markington, Yorkshire North.
Yorkshire Pine, Northallerton, Yorkshire North.
Squirrels and Early Days, Pateley Bridge, Yorkshire North.
Pine Mine Antiques, Skipton, Yorkshire North.
Fishlake Antiques, Fishlake, Yorkshire South.
Canterbury Place Antiques and Sheffield Pine Centre, Sheffield, Yorkshire South.
Aberford Antiques Ltd., Aberford, Yorkshire West.
Manor Barn Pine, Addingham, Yorkshire West.
M. Kelly Antiques, Eastburn, Yorkshire West.
Oldfield Cottage Antiques, Elland, Yorkshire West.
Scar Top Antiques, Keighley, Yorkshire West.
Boston Pine Co., Leeds, Yorkshire West.
Kirkstall Antiques, Leeds, Yorkshire West.
K.L.M. and Co. Antiques, Lepton, Yorkshire West.
Butterchurn Gallery, Otley, Yorkshire West.
Memory Lane Antiques, Sowerby Bridge, Yorkshire West.
Cottage Antiques (1984) Ltd., Walsden, Yorkshire West.
The Pine Collection, St. Peter Port, Guernsey, C.I.
Albert Forsythe, Saintfield, Co. Down, N.I.
K.O. Hagan, Claudy, Co. Londonderry, N.Ireland.
Artisan, Edinburgh, Scotland.
Robert and Vashti Lewis, Gartmore, Scotland.
Old Pine Furniture and Jouet, Kiltarlity, Scotland.

Mostly Pine, Kingussie, Scotland.
The Pine Village, Prestwick, Scotland.
James and Pat Ash, Llandeilo, Dyfed, Wales.

Victorian (1830-1901)

Terrace Antiques, London, W.5.
Cameo Gallery, London, W.8.
Butchoff Antiques, London, W.11.
Rex Antiques, London, W.11.
Zal Davar, London, S.W.3.
Furniture Cave, London, S.W.10.
Just a Second Antiques, London, S.W.11.
Wren Antiques, London, S.W.13.
A. and J. Fowle, London, S.W.16.
Bermondsey Antique Warehouse, London, S.E.1.
Tower Bridge Antique Warehouse, London, S.E.1.
Antique Warehouse, London, S.E.8.
Peter Allen Antiques Ltd., London, S.E.15.
Bushwood Antiques, London, N.1.
Brian Hawkins Antiques, London, N.1.
Kausmally Antiques, London, N.1.
Home to Home, London, N.6.
Finchley Fine Art Galleries, London, N.12.
Haverstock Antiques, London, N.W.1.
Antiquum, London, N.W.5.
The Furniture Store Ltd., London, N.W.6.
Church Street Antiques, London, N.W.8.
The Witch Ball, London, N.W.9.
Mendip Antiques, Bath, Avon (Gt. West Ant. C.).
Manor Antiques, Wilshamstead, Beds.
Paravicini, Hungerford, Berks.
Peter Farrow, Gt. Missenden, Bucks.
Sydney House Antiques, Wansford, Cambs.
Pydar Antiques and Gallery, Truro, Cornwall.
Pink Cottage Antiques, Widegates, Cornwall.
Haughley Antiques, Kirkby Stephen, Cumbria.
Petticombe Manor Antiques, Bideford, Devon
Alan Jones Antiques, Okehampton, Devon.
South Molton Antiques, South Molton, Devon.
Jackson's Antiques Ltd., Barnard Castle, Durham.
Balmuir House Antiques, Tetbury, Glos.
Corfield of Lymington Ltd., Lymington, Hants.
R.C. Dodson (Exports) Ltd., Portsmouth, Hants.
The Gallery, Portsmouth, Hants.
Pretty Chairs, Portsmouth, Hants.
Bewdley Antiques, Bewdley, Hereford and Worcs.
Carlton Antiques, Gt. Malvern, Hereford and Worcs.
Miscellany Antiques, Gt. Malvern, Hereford and Worcs.
Warings of Hereford Antiques, Hereford, Hereford and Worcs.
Country Life Antiques, Bushey, Herts.
Cherry Antiques, Hemel Hempstead, Herts.
Annick Antiques, Kimpton, Herts.
Leaside Antiques, St. Albans, Herts.
David K. Hakeney Antiques, Hull, N. Humberside.
Charles International, Maidstone, Kent.
David Rackham (Rochester Fine Arts), Rochester, Kent.
Brazil Antiques Ltd., Westerham, Kent.
Bulldog Antiques, Manchester, Lancs.
Walter Aspinall, Sabden, Lancs.
Polished with Pride, Wigan, Lancs.
Old Bakery Antiques, Empingham, Leics.
House Things Antiques, Hinckley, Leics.
Corner Cottage Antiques, Leicester, Leics.
Ashley House Antiques, Measham, Leics.
King Antiques, Horncastle, Lincs.
Laurence Shaw Antiques, Horncastle, Lincs.
John Sinclair, Stamford, Lincs.
Tony and Anne Sutcliffe Antiques, Southport, Merseyside.
Phelps Ltd., Twickenham, Middx.
Brancaster Staithe Antiques, Brancaster Staithe, Norfolk.
Eric Bates and Sons, Coltishall, Norfolk.
Eric Bates and Sons, North Walsham, Norfolk.
Thorpe Antiques, Finedon, Northants.
Arthur Boaden Antiques, Hexham, Northumbs.
Fair Deal Antiques, Mansfield, Notts.
John B. Sheppard Antiques, Mansfield, Notts.
The Country Seat, Huntercombe, Oxon.
Cobbles Antiques, Bishops Castle, Shrops.
M.G.R. Exports, Bruton, Somerset.
W.P.S. (Bruton) Ltd., Bruton, Somerset.
Cary Antiques Ltd., Castle Cary, Somerset.
M.J. and I. Cope, Alton, Staffs.
Wrentham Antiques, Wrentham, Suffolk.
Dudley Hume, Brighton, Sussex East.
Don Spencer Antiques, Warwick, Warks.
Archives, Birmingham, W. Mids.
L.P. Furniture (Mids.) Ltd., Pelsall, W. Mids.
Cross Hayes Antiques, Malmesbury, Wilts.
K. and A. Welch, Warminster, Wilts.
Geary Antiques, Leeds, Yorkshire West.
Mac's Antiques, Dundee, Scotland.
Laurance Black Ltd., Edinburgh, Scotland.
Young Antiques, Edinburgh, Scotland.
Errol Antiques, Errol, Scotland.
Pringle Antiques, Fochabers, Scotland.
Butler's Furniture Galleries Ltd., Glasgow, Scotland.
Houndwood House Antiques, Houndwood, Scotland.
Kings of Kinbuck, Kinbuck, Scotland.
Heritage Antiques, Paisley, Scotland.
A.S. Deuchar and Son, Perth, Scotland.
Elizabeth Paterson Antiques, Stirling, Scotland.
Thornhill Gallery Antiques Centre, Thornhill, Scotland.
North Wales Antiques, Colwyn Bay, Clwyd, Wales.
Country Antiques, Kidwelly, Dyfed, Wales.

See also Shipping Goods and Period Furniture for the Trade.

Garden Furniture, Ornaments and Statuary

Christopher Gibbs Ltd., London, W.1.
Mallett of Bourdon House Ltd., London, W.1.
Seago, London, S.W.1.
T. Crowther and Son Ltd., London, S.W.6.
Charles Edwards, London, S.W.6.
N.J.A. Gifford-Mead and Miles d'Agar Antiques, London, S.W.10. Furniture Cave.
London Architectural Salvage and Supply Co. Ltd., London, E.C.2.
Westland Pilkington, London, E.C.2.
Judy Cole, London, N.1.
House of Steel Antiques, London, N.1.
Townsends, London, N.W.8.
Robert Pugh, Bath, Avon.
David Bridgwater, Marshfield, Avon.
Anthemion, Cartmel, Cumbria.
Haughey Antiques, Kirkby Stephen, Cumbria.
Townhead Antiques, Newby Bridge, Cumbria.
Talisman, Gillingham, Dorset.
I. Westrope, Birdbrook, Essex.
Greenhouse Antiques, Painswick, Glos.
Duncan J. Baggott, Stow-on-the-Wold, Glos.
Architectural Heritage, Taddington, Glos.
Crowther of Syon Lodge ltd., Isleworth, Middx.
The Country Seat, Huntercombe, Oxon.
M. Granshaw, Shalford, Surrey.
Robin and Matthew Eden, Corsham, Wilts.
The Old Vicarage, Pontfaen, Dyfed, Wales.

Glass

Thomas Goode and Co. (London) Ltd., London, W.1.
Mayfair Gallery, London, W.1.
Sheppard and Cooper, London, W.1.
Nicholas Vandekar Antiques Ltd., London, W.1.
Cameo Gallery, London, W.8.
Mrs. M.E. Crick, London, W.8.
Denton Antiques, London, W.8.
The French Glasshouse, London, W.8.
Eila Grahame, London, W.8.
Jeanette Hayhurst, London, W.8.
Eric Lineham and Sons, London, W.8.
Patricia Harbottle, London, W.11.
Anno Domini Antiques, London, S.W.1.
Galerie Moderne Ltd., London, S.W.1.
Gallery '25, London, S.W.1.
Dominic King Antique Glass, London, S.W.1.
Gerald Sattin Ltd., London, S.W.1.
W.G.T. Burne (Antique Glass) Ltd., London, London, S.W.3.
Pryce and Brise Antiques, London, S.W.6.
Christine Bridge Antiques, London, S.W.13.
The Dining Room Shop, London, S.W.13.
Mark J. West — Cobb Antiques Ltd., London, S.W.19.
R. Wilkinson & Son, London, S.E.6.
Mark J. West — Cobb Antiques Ltd., London, N.1.
Frank Dux Antiques, Bath, Avon.
Somervale Antiques, Midsomer Norton, Avon.
Old House Antiques, Wansford, Cambs.
A. and D. Antiques, Blandford Forum, Dorset.
Finesse Fine Art, Weymouth, Dorset.
Templar Antiques, Kelvedon, Essex.
Stockbridge Antiques, Stockbridge, Hants.
Todd & Austin Antiques of Winchester, Winchester, Hants.
H. and B. Wolf Antiques Ltd., Droitwich, Hereford and Worcs.
Watchbell Antiques, Newport, I. of Wight.
Denys Sargeant, Westerham, Kent.
Ethos Gallery, Clitheroe, Lancs.
Montague Antiques, Leicester, Leics.
Artbry's Antiques, Pinner, Middx.
Neil Willcox, Twickenham, Middx.
Allport-Lomax, Liz, Horstead, Norfolk.
Dorothy's Antiques, Sheringham, Norfolk.
Hutton Antiques, Shrewsbury, Shrops.
Ray Best Antiques, Ilminster, Somerset.
James Ribbons, Bruton, Somerset.
Shirley Warren, Sanderstead, Surrey.
David R. Fileman, Steyning, Sussex West.
Delomosne and Son Ltd., North Wraxhall, Wilts.
Kellys of Knaresborough, Knaresborough, Yorkshire North.
Ken Balme Antiques, Halifax, Yorkshire West.
The Rendezvous Gallery, Aberdeen, Scotland.
William MacAdam, Edinburgh, Scotland.
Wynn Cato, Tywyn, Gwynedd, Wales.

Horn Items

Horn Antiques, Audlem, Cheshire.

Icons (see Russian Art)

Islamic Art

Aaron Gallery, London, W.1.
Emanouel Antiques Ltd., London, W.1.
Hadji Baba Ancient Art, London, W.1.
Mansour Gallery, London, W.1.
Bashir Mohamed Ltd., London, W.1.
Rabi Gallery Ltd., London, W.1.
Hosains Books and Antiques, London, W.2.
Al Mashreq Galleries, London, W.8.
Robert Hales Antiques Ltd., London, W.8.
Yacob's Gallery, London, W.8.
Ahuan (U.K.) Ltd., London, S.W.1.
Connoisseur Gallery, London, S.W.1.
Michael and Henrietta Spink Ltd., London, S.W.1.

Japanese Art (See Oriental Art)

Jewellery (See Silver and Jewellery)

Lighting

W. Sitch & Co. Ltd., London, W.1.
Stair and Company, London, W.1.
N. Davighi, London, W.6.
Mrs. M. Crick, London, W.8.
Eric Lineham and Sons, London, W.8.
The Facade, London, W.11.
Jones, London, W.11.
Carlton Hobbs, London, S.W.1.

Howe, London, S.W.1.
Jeremy Ltd., London, S.W.1.
Lion, Witch and Lampshade, London, S.W.1.
Lennox Money (Antiques) Ltd., London, S.W.1.
W.G.T. Burne (Antique Glass) Ltd., London, S.W.1.
Hooper and Purchase, London, S.W.3.
The Lamp Gallery, London, S.W.6.
Paul Richards, London, S.W.6.
Vaughan, London, S.W.6.
Christopher Wray, London, S.W.6.
Period Brass Lights, London, S.W.7.
M. Turpin Ltd., London, S.W.7.
H.W. Poulter and Son, London, S.W.10.
Christopher Bangs, London, S.W.11.
The Lighthouse Ltd., London, S.W.19.
R. Wilkinson & Son, London, S.E.6.
Oddiquities, London, S.E.23.
Turn On Lighting Ltd., London, N.1.
The Antique Shop (Valantiques), London, N.2.
B.C. Metalcrafts Ltd., London, N.W.9.
David Malik and Son Ltd., London, N.W.10.
George and Peter Cohn, London, W.C.1.
Queens Parade Antiques Ltd., Bath, Avon.
Ian & Dianne McCarthy, Clutton, Avon.
Manor Antiques, Wilshamstead, Beds.
Antrium Antiques, Woburn, Beds.
Compton Gallery, Windsor and Eton, Berks.
Sundial Antiques, Amersham, Bucks.
Jeanne Temple Antiques, Milton Keynes, Bucks.
White House Antiques, Princes Risborough, Bucks.
Old House Antiques, Wansford, Cambs.
E. and B. Rushton, Pulford, Cheshire.
The Lantern Shop, Sidmouth, Devon.
The Green Room, Bournemouth, Dorset.
Marino-Montero Fine Art, Adrienne, Curdridge, Hants.
Fritz Fryer, Ross-on-Wye, Hereford and Worcs.
Denys Sargeant, Westerham, Kent.
Stiffkey Lamp Shop, Stiffkey, Norfolk.
James Ribbons, Bruton, Somerset.
The Tinder Box, Stoke-on-Trent, Staffs.
Bruno Cooper Antiques, Long Melford, Suffolk.
Oasis Antiques, Brighton, Sussex East.
Delomosne and Son Ltd., North Wraxhall, Wilts.
Kellys of Knaresborough, Knaresborough, N. Yorks.

Maps and Prints

Burlington Gallery Ltd., London, W.1.
Lumley Cazalet Ltd., London, W.1.
Day Ltd., Richard, London, W.1.
Andrew Edmunds, London, W.1.
Omniphil (Grays A. Mkt.), London W.1.
Jonathan Potter Ltd., London, W.1.
The Schuster Gallery, London, W.1.
The Welbeck Gallery, London, W.1.
Bayswater Books, London, W.2.
Connaught Galleries, London, W.2.
Davies Antiques, London, W.8.
Charles Spencer, London, W.9.
Norman Blackburn, London, W.11.
L'Acquaforte, London, W.11.
St. John's Collection Ltd., London, W.11.
Clive A. Burden Ltd., London, S.W.1.
J.A.L. Franks Ltd., London, S.W.1.
Graham and Oxley, London, S.W.1.
David Ker Fine Art, London, S.W.1.
Paul Mason Gallery, London, S.W.1.
Christopher Mendez, London, S.W.1.
Old London Galleries, London, S.W.1.
Old Maps and Prints, London, S.W.1.
O'Shea Gallery, London, S.W.1.
The Parker Gallery, London, S.W.1.
Michael Parkin Fine Art Ltd., London, S.W.1.
Sotheran's, London, S.W.1.
John Campbell Picture Frames Ltd., London, S.W.3.
Stephanie Hoppen Ltd., London, S.W.3.
The Map House, London, S.W.3.
Old Church Galleries, London, S.W.3.
Paul Orssich, London, S.W.6.
Francois Valcke, London, S.W.6.
John F.C. Phillips, London, S.W.12.
The Warwick Leadlay Gallery, London, S.E.10.
John Speed (Maps), London, S.E.11.
Ash Rare Books, London, E.C.3.
Intercol, London, N.1.
Judith Lassalle, London, N.1.
Finbar MacDonnell, London, N.1.
Elizabeth Harvey-Lee, London, N.W.2.
Frederick Mulder, London, N.W.3.
Cartographia Ltd., London, W.C.1.
Sebastian D'Orsai Ltd., London, W.C.1.
The Print Room, London, W.C.1.
Grosvenor Prints, London, W.C.2.
Avril Noble, London, W.C.2.
Stage Door Prints, London, W.C.2.
Tooley, Adams and Co. Ltd., London, W.C.2.
The Witch Ball, London, W.C.2.
Lantern Gallery, Bath, Avon.
Trimbridge Galleries, Bath, Avon.
John Roberts Bookshop, Bath, Avon.
Clevedon Fine Arts, Clevedon, Avon.
Sir William Russell Flint Galleries Ltd., Wrington, Avon.
Graham Gallery, Burghfield Common, Berks.
Paravicini, Hungerford, Berks.
Jaspers Fine Arts Ltd., Maidenhead, Berks.
Jaspers Fine Arts, Windsor and Eton, Berks.
Fantiques, Amersham, Bucks.
Omniphil Ltd., Chesham, Bucks.
Collectors Treasures Ltd., Marlow, Bucks.
Penn Barn, Penn, Bucks.
Benet Gallery, Cambridge, Cambs.
Jean Pain Gallery, Cambridge, Cambs.
Quinto of Cambridge, Cambridge, Cambs.
Coach House Antiques, Wisbech, Cambs.
J. Alan Hulme, Chester, Cheshire.
Richard A. Nicholson, Chester, Cheshire.
Lion Gallery and Bookshop, Knutsford, Cheshire.
Harper Fine Paintings, Poynton, Cheshire.
John Maggs, Falmouth, Cornwall.

Kendal Studios Antiques, Kendal, Cumbria.
Laura's Bookshop, Derby, Derbys.
Ashburton Rare Books, Ashburton, Devon.
Artavia Gallery, Barnstaple, Devon.
Medina Gallery, Bideford, Devon.
New Gallery, Budleigh Salterton, Devon.
C. Samuels & Sons Ltd., Exeter, Devon.
The Little Lantern Shop, Sidmouth, Devon.
The Artist Gallery, Bournemouth, Dorset.
Antique Map and Bookshop, Puddletown, Dorset.
Swan Gallery, Sherborne, Dorset.
J. Shotton, Durham, Co. Durham.
Castle Bookshop, Colchester, Essex.
Simon Hilton, Dunmow, Essex.
Artisans Gallery, Finchingfield, Essex.
Newport Gallery, Newport, Essex.
Atticus Books, Southend-on-Sea, Essex.
Cleeve Picture Framing, Bishops Cleeve, Glos.
David Bannister, Cheltenham, Glos.
William Marler Gallery, Cirencester, Glos.
Avon Gallery, Moreton-in-Marsh, Glos.
The Northleach Gallery, Northleach, Glos.
Talbot Court Galleries, Stow-on-the-Wold, Glos.
Vanbrugh House Antiques, Stow-on-the-Wold, Glos.
Bell Passage Antiques, Wotton-under-Edge, Glos.
Hughes and Smeeth Ltd., Lymington, Hants.
W.D. Trivess, Meonstoke, Hants.
The Petersfield Bookshop, Petersfield, Hants.
Oldfield Gallery, Portsmouth, Hants.
Julia Holmes Antique Maps and Prints, South Harting, Hants.
Oldfield, Southampton, Hants.
Bell Fine Art, Winchester, Hants.
Printed Page, Winchester, Hants.
W.G. Skipworth, Winchester, Hants.
Gavina Ewart, Broadway, Hereford and Worcs.
Stratford Trevers, Broadway, Hereford and Worcs.
Brobury House Gallery, Brobury, Hereford and Worcs.
Pierpoint Gallery, Hereford, Hereford and Worcs.
Coltsfoot Gallery, Leominster, Hereford and Worcs.
Ross Old Book and Print Shop, Ross-on-Wye, Hereford and Worcs.
Antique Map and Print Gallery, Worcester, Hereford and Worcs.
Eric T. Moore, Hitchin, Herts.
Clive A. Burden, Rickmansworth, Herts.
James of St. Albans, St. Albans, Herts.
Thomas Thorp, St. Albans, Herts.
Mannin Collections, Peel, I. of Man.
The Gallery, Yarmouth, I. of Wight.
Chaucer Bookshop, Canterbury, Kent.
Cloisters, Canterbury, Kent.
Leadenhall Gallery, Canterbury, Kent.
G. and D.I. Marrin and Sons, Folkestone, Kent.
Darenth Bookshop, Otford, Kent.
Periwinkle Press, Sittingbourne, Kent.
Lloyds Bookshop, Wingham, Kent.
Shaw's Bookshop Ltd., Manchester, Lancs.
Leycester Map Galleries Ltd., Arnesby, Leics.
Old Bakery Antiques, Empingham, Leics.
Leicestershire Sporting Gallery, Lubenham, Leics.
Grafton Country Pictures, Oakham, Leics.
Old House Gallery, Oakham, Leics.
Harlequin Gallery, Lincoln, Lincs.
Lyver & Boydell Galleries, Liverpool, Merseyside.
Thomas Barnard, Uxbridge, Middx.
M. and A. Cringle, Burnham Market, Norfolk.
The Coach House, Costessey, Norfolk.
David Ferrow, Great Yarmouth, Norfolk.
Cathedral Gallery, Norwich, Norfolk.
Peter Crowe, Norwich, Norfolk.
Tombland Bookshop, Norwich, Norfolk.
R.S.J. Savage and Son, Northampton, Northants.
Park Book Shop, Wellingborough, Northants.
Border Sporting Gallery, Wooler, Northumbs.
Arthur and Ann Rogers, Ruddington, Notts.
Barry M. Keene Gallery, Henley-on-Thames, Oxon.
Magna Gallery, Oxford, Oxon.
Sanders of Oxford Ltd., Oxford, Oxon.
Jane Marler Gallery, Ludlow, Shrops.
The Mount, Woore, Shrops.
Plympton Gallery, Ilminster, Somerset.
Michael Lewis Gallery, Woore, Somerset.
Weston Antique Gallery, Weston, Staffs.
Beccles Gallery, Beccles, Suffolk.
Guildhall Gallery, Bury St. Edmunds, Suffolk.
Newmarket Gallery, Newmarket, Suffolk.
Northwold Gallery, Newmarket, Suffolk.
King's Court Galleries, Dorking, Surrey.
Reigate Galleries Ltd., Reigate, Surrey.
J. and J. Speed, Ripley, Surrey.
Holleyman and Treacher Ltd., Brighton, Sussex East.
Shelton Frames and Pictures, Brighton, Sussex East.
The Witch Ball, Brighton, Sussex East.
Raymond Smith, Brighton, Sussex East.
London and Sussex Antiquarian Book and Print Services, Eastbourne, Sussex East.
Ivan R. Deverall, Uckfield, Sussex East.
Baynton-Williams, Arundel, Sussex West.
Serendipity Antiques, Arundel, Sussex West.
The Antique Atlas, East Grinstead, Sussex West.
The Antique Print Shop, East Grinstead, Sussex West.
Burman Antiques, Stratford-upon-Avon, Warks.
Robert Vaughan, Stratford-upon-Avon, Warks.
Duncan M. Allsop, Warwick, Warks.
Carleton Gallery, Birmingham, West Midlands.
D.M. Beach, Salisbury, Wilts.
Booth Gallery, Westbury, Wilts.
Great Ayton Bookshop, Great Ayton, Yorkshire North.
McTague of Harrogate, Harrogate, Yorkshire North.
Craven Books, Skipton, Yorkshire North.
Alan Hill Books, Sheffield, Yorkshire South.

Porter Prints (Broomhill), Sheffield, Yorkshire South.
Jean Brear, Halifax, Yorkshire West.
Channel Islands Galleries Ltd., St. Peter Port, Guernsey, C.I.
Thesaurus, St. Peter Port, Guernsey, C.I.
Geoffrey P. Gavey, Vale, Guernsey, C.I.
John Blench and Son, St. Helier, Jersey, C.I.
Grange Gallery and Fine Arts Ltd., St. Helier, Jersey, C.I.
St. Helier Galleries Ltd., St Helier, Jersey, C.I.
The Selective Eye Gallery, St. Helier, Jersey, C.I.
Thesaurus (Jersey) Ltd., St. Helier, Jersey, C.I.
Phyllis Arnold Studio Gallery, Bangor, Co. Down, N. Ireland.
The Waverley Gallery, Aberdeen, Scotland.
The McEwan Gallery, Ballater, Scotland.
Calton Gallery, Edinburgh, Scotland.
Carson Clark Gallery, Edinburgh, Scotland.
Tom Fidelo, Edinburgh, Scotland.
John O. Nelson, Edinburgh, Scotland.
Alan Rankin, Edinburgh, Scotland.
Colin Murdoch, Kingussie, Scotland.
Ovell Prints Ltd., Llandovery, Dyfed, Wales.
Cheriton Antiques, Narberth, Dyfed, Wales.
Philip Davies, Swansea, W. Glam., Wales.
Glance Gallery, Chepstow, Gwent, Wales.
Tony Andrew, Llanerchymedd, Gwynedd, Wales.
Maps, Prints and Books, Brecon, Powys, Wales.

Metalwork

Jack Casimir Ltd., London, W.11.
E.R. O'Connor and A. and C. Elliott, London, W.11.
Alistair Sampson Antiques, London, S.W.3.
Christopher Bangs, London, S.W.11.
Judy Cole, London, N.1.
Heritage Antiques, London, N.1.
House of Steel, London, N.1.
Brian and Caroline Craik, Bath, Avon.
Christopher Sykes Antiques, Woburn, Beds.
The Fireplace (Hungerford) Ltd., Hungerford, Berks.
Medalcrest Ltd., Hungerford, Berks.
Berkshire Metal Finishers Ltd., Sandhurst, Berks.
Peter J. Martin, Windsor and Eton, Berks.
Sundial Antiques, Amersham, Bucks.
Albert Bartram, Chesham, Bucks.
A. and E. Foster, Naphill, Bucks.
Dolphin Antiques, Cambridge, Cambs.
Phoenix Antiques, Fordham, Cambs.
David Bedale, Knutsford, Cheshire.
Michael Wisehall, Knutsford, Cheshire.
Victoriana Antiques, Stockton Heath, Cheshire.
Shire Antiques, Newby Bridge, Cumbria.
Stable Antiques, Sedbergh, Cumbria.
Pamela Elsom, Ashbourne, Derbys.
Spurrier-Smith Antiques, Ashbourne, Derbys.
Water Lane Antiques, Bakewell, Derbys.
Ashburton Marbles, Ashburton, Devon.
Roderick P. Butler, Honiton, Devon.
Morchard Bishop Antiques, Morchard Bishop, Devon.
Philip Andrade Ltd., South Brent, Devon.
Antique Metals, Coggeshall, Essex.
Partner and Puxon, Colchester, Essex.
Richard Wrenn Antiques, Leigh-on-Sea, Essex.
Berkeley Antiques, Berkeley, Glos.
Studio Antiques, Bourton-on-the-Water, Glos.
W.W. Holzgrawe, Cirencester, Glos.
William H. Stokes, Cirencester, Glos.
Paul Cater Antiques, Moreton-in-Marsh, Glos.
J. and J. Caspall Antiques, Stow-on-the-Wold, Glos.
Country Life Antiques, Stow-on-the-Wold, Glos.
Fox House Antiques, Stow-on-the-Wold, Glos.
Keith Hockin (Antiques) Ltd., Stow-on-the-Wold, Glos.
Huntington Antiques Ltd., Stow-on-the-Wold, Glos.
Touchwood International Ltd., Stow-on-the-Wold, Glos.
Prichard Antiques, Winchcombe, Glos.
Close Antiques, Alresford, Hants.
Cedar Antiques, Hartley Wintney, Hants.
Hursley Antiques, Hursley, Hants.
Monaltrie Antiques, Odiham, Hants.
Cull Antiques, Petersfield, Hants.
Elizabeth Viney, Stockbridge, Hants.
Regency House Antiques, Whitchurch, Hants.
P. and S.N. Eddy, Leominster, Hereford and Worcs.
Hubbard Antiques, Leominster, Hereford and Worcs.
Stables Antiques, Ombersley, Hereford and Worcs.
Michael Gander, Hitchin, Herts.
R.J. Perry Antiques, Hitchin, Herts.
Christopher Perry Antiques, St. Albans, Herts.
Old Hall (Sphinx Gallery), Brasted, Kent.
Dinah Stoodley, Brasted, Kent.
The Old Forge, Hollingbourne, Kent.
E.W. Webster, Bickerstaffe, Lancs.
Ivanhoe Antiques, Ashby de la Zouch, Leics.
Thomas Keen, Bottesford, Leics.
Burley Workshops, Burley-on-the-Hill, Leics.
House Things Antiques, Hinckley, Leics.
Hughes Antiques, Hinckley, Leics.
Lowe of Loughborough, Loughborough, Leics.
Paul Johnston, Gedney, Lincs.
Peter Robinson, Heacham, Norfolk.
Arthur Brett and Sons Ltd., Norwich, Norfolk.
V. and C. Madeira, Flore, Northants.
Antiques, West Haddon, Northants.
Jonathan Fyson Antiques, Burford, Oxon.
Horseshoe Antiques and Gallery, Burford, Oxon.
Peter Norden Antiques, Burford, Oxon.
Key Antiques, Chipping Norton, Oxon.
Mike Ottrey Antiques, Wallingford, Oxon.

Joan Wilkins Antiques, Witney, Oxon.
Broadway Antiques, Shifnal, Shrops.
Sandhill Barn Antiques (Pine and Country), Washington, Sussex West.
Rupert Gentle Antiques, Milton Lilbourne, Wilts.
Elaine Phillips Antiques Ltd., Harrogate, Yorkshire North.
Tim Wright Antiques, Glasgow, Scotland.

Miniatures

D.S. Lavender (Antiques) Ltd., London, W.1.
Limner Antiques, London, W.1 (B. St. Ant. C.).
S.J. Phillips Ltd., London, W.1.
Maurice Asprey Ltd., London, S.W.1.
Simon Brett, Moreton-in-Marsh, Glos.
Michael Sim, Chislehurst, Kent.
Park Galleries Antiques, Bolton, Lancs.
Arden Gallery, Henley-in-Arden, Warks.

Mirrors (Most furniture dealers also sell Mirrors)

Anne Bloom Jewellers, London, W.1.
Brian Fielden, London, W.1.
W.R. Harvey and Co. (Antiques) Ltd., London, W.1.
Stair and Company Ltd., London, W.1.
Valerie Howard, London, W.8.
J. Roger (Antiques) Ltd., London, W.8.
Through the Looking Glass Ltd., London, W.8.
Chimney Pieces, London, W.11.
Simpsons — Pine Mirrors, London, W.11.
Anno Domini Antiques, London, S.W.1.
Burness Antiques, Marie Louise, London, S.W.1.
Fernandes and Marche, London, S.W.1.
Oakstar Ltd., London, S.W.1.
A. and M. Ossowski, London, S.W.1.
Gerald Spyer, London, S.W.1.
Norman Adams Ltd., London, S.W.3.
Anthony James and Son Ltd., London, S.W.3.
Clifford Wright Antiques Ltd., London, S.W.3.
Chelsea Fine Furniture Ltd., London, S.W.6.
Charles Edwards, London, S.W.6.
House of Mirrors, London, S.W.6.
P.L. James, London, S.W.6.
Old World Trading Co., London, S.W.6.
Paul Richards, London, S.W.6.
Through the Looking Glass Ltd., London, S.W.6.
Ferenc Toth, London, S.W.6.
M. Turpin Ltd., London, S.W.7.
David Randolph Antiques Ltd., London, S.W.10.
Alexander Bailie Antiques, London, N.1. The Mall.
Townsends, London, N.W.1.
Peter Roberts Antiques, Moreton-in-Marsh, Glos.
The Curiosity Shop, Stow-on-the-Wold, Glos.
Rudolph Otto, Stow-on-the-Wold, Glos.
Balmuir House Antiques, Tetbury, Glos.
The Windmill Antiquary, Bishops Stortford, Herts.

Musical Boxes, Instruments and Literature

John and Arthur Beare (J. and A. Beare Ltd.), London, W.1.
Peter Biddulph, London, W.1.
Arthur S. Lewis, London, S.W.1.
Pelham Galleries, London, S.W.3.
William Reeves Bookseller Ltd., London, S.W.16.
Robert Morley and Co. Ltd., London, S.E.13.
Kirkdale Pianos, London, S.E.26.
St. Peters Organ Works, London, E.2.
Curios Grannies, London, E.8.
David Miles, London, N.W.1.
Tony Bingham, London, N.W.3.
Talking Machine, London, N.W.4.
Otto Haas, London, N.W.3.
H. Baron, London, N.W.6.
Travis and Emery, London, W.C.2.
Aspidistra, Bath, Avon.
Dollin and Daines, Bath, Avon.
W.E. Hill and Sons, Great Missenden, Bucks.
Miss Elany, Long Eaton, Derbys.
Kenneth Mummery Ltd., Bournemouth, Dorset.
Mayflower Antiques, Harwich and Dovercourt, Essex.
Colin Elliott, Cheltenham, Glos.
Keith Harding's World of Mechanical Music, Northleach, Glos.
Vanbrugh House Antiques, Stow-on-the-Wold, Glos.
Evans and Evans, Alresford, Hants.
Julian Thwaites and Co., Bushey, Herts.
Hadlow Antiques, Tunbridge Wells, Kent.
Old Smithy, Feniscowles, Lancs.
Norfolk Polyphon Centre, Bawdeswell, Norfolk.
The Violin Shop, Hexham, Northumb.
Franco Antiques, Retford, Notts.
Laurie Leigh Antiques, Oxford, Oxon.
The Treasure Chest Ltd., Highbridge, Somerset.
Shelagh Berryman, Wells, Somerset.
Graham Webb, Brighton, Sussex East.
John Cowderoy Antiques, Eastbourne, Sussex East.
G.V.R. Antiques Ltd., Birmingham, West Midlands.
Jomarc Pianos Ltd. and Pianorama, Birmingham, West Midlands.
May and May Ltd., Tisbury, Wilts.
Pianorama (Harrogate) Ltd., Harrogate, Yorkshire North.
The Piano Shop, Leeds, Yorkshire West.
San Domenico Stringed Instruments, Cardiff, S. Glam., Wales.

Nautical Instruments (See Scientific Instruments)

Needlework (See Tapestries)

Netsuke (See Oriental Art)

Oil Paintings

Arthur Ackermann and Son Ltd., London, W.1.
Addison Fine Art, London, W.1.
Thomas Agnew and Sons Ltd., London, W.1.
Albemarle Gallery, London, W.1.
Browse and Darby Ltd., London, W.1.
Burlington Paintings Ltd., London, W.1.
P. and D. Colnaghi and Co. Ltd., London, W.1.
Connaught Brown p.l.c., London, W.1.
Crawley and Asquith, London, W.1.
Anthony d'Offay, London, W.1.
Editions Graphiques Gallery, London, W.1.
Entwistle, London, W.1.
Fine Art Society p.l.c., London, W.1.
H. Fritz-Denneville Fine Arts Ltd., London, W.1.
Frost and Reed Ltd., London, W.1.
Deborah Gage (Works of Art) Ltd., London, W.1.
Christopher Gibbs Ltd., London, W.1.
Thomas Gibson Fine Art Ltd., London, W.1.
Richard Green, London, W.1.
Hahn and Son Fine Art Dealers, London, W.1.
Lane Fine Art Ltd., London, W.1.
Lefevre Gallery, London, W.1.
The Leger Galleries Ltd., London, W.1.
Maas Gallery, London, W.1.
MacConnal Mason Gallery, London, W.1.
Marlborough Fine Art (London) Ltd., London, W.1.
David Messum, London, W.1.
Roy Miles Gallery, London, W.1.
John Mitchell and Son, London, W.1.
Anthony Mould Ltd., London, W.1.
Noortman, London, W.1.
Partridge (Fine Arts) Ltd., London, W.1.
W.H. Patterson Fine Arts Ltd., London, W.1.
The Richmond Gallery, London, W.1.
Schwartz Sackin and Co. Ltd., London, W.1.
Michael Simpson Ltd., London, W.1.
Stephen Somerville Ltd., London, W.1.
South Audley Antiques, London, W.1.
Edward Speelman Ltd., London, W.1.
Stoppenbach and Delestre Ltd., London, W.1.
The Taylor Gallery Ltd., London, W.1.
Walpole Gallery, London, W.1.
Waterhouse and Dodd, London, W.1.
The Weiss Gallery, London, W.1.
Wildenstein & Co. Ltd., London, W.1.
Wilkins & Wilkins, London, W.1.
Williams and Son, London, W.1.
Manya Igel Fine Arts Ltd., London, W.2.
Z.J. Okolski, London, W.3.
Mangate Gallery, London, W.4.
Ealing Gallery, London, W.5.
Baumkotter Gallery, London, W.8.
George Dare, London, W.8.
Iona Antiques, London. W.8.
Little Winchester Gallery, London, W.8.
Sabin Galleries Ltd., London, W.8.
Caelt Gallery, London, W.11.
Fleur de Lys Gallery, London, W.11.
Gavin Graham Gallery, London, W.11.
Hamilton Fine Arts, London, W.11.
Hancock Gallery, London, W.11.
Philp, London, W.11.
Portland Gallery, London, W.11.
Stern Art Dealers, London, W.11.
The Wyllie Gallery, London, W.11.
Stephen Garratt (Fine Paintings), London, W.14.
Richard Joslin, London, W.14.
Didier Aaron (London) Ltd., London, S.W.1.
Verner Amell Ltd., London, S.W.1.
Artemis Fine Arts Ltd., London, S.W.1.
Beaton-Brown Fine Paintings, London, S.W.1.
Belgrave Gallery, London, S.W.1.
Bourne Fine Art, London, S.W.1.
Bowmoore Gallery, London, S.W.1.
Brisigotti Antiques Ltd., London, S.W.1.
Brod Gallery, London, S.W.1.
David Carritt Ltd., London, S.W.1.
Chaucer Fine Arts Inc., London, S.W.1.
Cox and Company, London, S.W.1.
Douwes Fine Art Ltd., London, S.W.1.
W.R. Drown, London, S.W.1.
Eaton Gallery, London, S.W.1.
Faustus Fine Art Ltd., London, S.W.1.
Martyn Gregory Gallery, London, S.W.1.
Harari and Johns Ltd., London, S.W.1.
Julian Hartnoll, London, S.W.1.
Hazlett, Gooden and Fox Ltd., London, S.W.1.
Heim Gallery, London, S.W.1.
Christopher Hull Gallery, London, S.W.1.
Oscar and Peter Johnson Ltd., London, S.W.1.
R. and J. Jones, London, S.W.1.
David Ker Fine Art, London, S.W.1.
King Street Galleries Ltd., London, S.W.1.
Leggatt Brothers, London, S.W.1.
MacConnal Mason Gallery, London, S.W.1.
The Mall Galleries, London, S.W.1.
Paul Mason Gallery, London, S.W.1.
Mathaf Gallery Ltd., London, S.W.1.
Matthiesen Fine Art Ltd., London, S.W.1.
Moreton Street Gallery, London, S.W.1.
Guy Morrison, London, S.W.1.
Murray-Brown, London, S.W.1.
Peter Nahum, London, S.W.1.
Omell Galleries, London, S.W.1.
N.R. Omell, London, S.W.1.
The Parker Gallery, London, S.W.1.
Michael Parkin Fine Art Ltd., London, S.W.1.
Pawsey and Payne Ltd., London, S.W.1.
Polak Gallery, London, S.W.1.
Michael Priest Antiques, London, S.W.1.
Pyms Gallery, London, S.W.1.
Sabin and Vanderkar (Fine Paintings) Ltd., London, S.W.1.
The St. James Art Group, London, S.W.1.
Julian Simon Fine Art, London, S.W.1.
William Thuillier, London, S.W.1.
Peter Tillou Works of Art, London, S.W.1.
Trafalgar Galleries, London, S.W.1.
Rafael Valls Ltd., London, S.W.1.
Johnny Van Haeften Ltd., London, S.W.1.

Whitford and Hughes, London, S.W.1.
Christopher Wood Gallery, London, S.W.1.
Century Gallery, London, S.W.3.
Colin Denny Ltd., London, S.W.3.
Stephanie Hoppen Ltd., London, S.W.3.
Malcolm Innes Gallery, London, S.W.3.
Mathon Gallery, London, S.W.3.
Guy Neville Fine Art Ltd., London, S.W.3.
Oliver Swann Galleries, London, S.W.3.
Walker-Bagshawe, London, S.W.3.
20th Century Gallery, London, S.W.6.
Barclay Samson Ltd., London, S.W.6.
Cooper Fine Arts Ltd., London, S.W.6.
New King's Road and Hurlingham Gallery, London, S.W.6.
Jonathan Clark, London, S.W.10.
IA Gallery, London, S.W.10.
Lacey Gallery, Stephen, London, S.W.10.
Park Walk Gallery, London, S.W.10.
New Grafton Gallery, London, S.W.13.
Alton Gallery, London, S.W.13.
Sheen Gallery, London, S.W.14.
S.A.G. Art Galleries, London, S.W.18.
Hicks Gallery, London, S.W.19.
The Greenwich Gallery, London, S.E.10.
Royal Exchange Art Gallery, London, E.C.3.
Swan Fine Art, London, N.1.
Centaur Gallery, London, N.6.
Sandra Lummis Fine Art, London, N.8.
Finchley Fine Art Galleries, London, N.12.
The Totteridge Gallery, London, N.20.
Gunter Fine Art, London, N.W.2.
Duncan R. Miller Fine Arts, London, N.W.3.
Newman and Cooling Ltd., London, N.W.3.
John Denham Gallery, London, N.W.6.
Gallery Kaleidoscope, London, N.W.6.
Amadeus Gallery, London, N.W.8.
Camden Art Gallery, London, N.W.8.
Nicholas Drummond, London, N.W.8.
Austin/Desmond Fine Art, London, W.C.1.
Adam Gallery, Bath, Avon.
Beau Nash House Antiques, Bath, Avon.
Martin Dodge Interiors Ltd., Bath, Avon.
William Pelly, Bath, Avon.
Nick Woodbridge, Bath, Avon.
David Cross (Fine Art), Bristol, Avon.
The Mall Gallery, Bristol, Avon.
Pelter/Sands Art Gallery, Bristol, Avon.
Graham Trenchard Ltd., Heath and Reach, Beds.
Queen Adelaide Gallery, Kempston, Beds.
Christopher Sykes Antiques, Woburn, Beds.
Woburn Fine Arts, Woburn, Beds.
Graham Gallery, Burghfield Common, Berks.
The Collectors Gallery, Caversham, Berks.
Phillips and Sons, Cookham, Berks.
Marian and John Alway, Datchet, Berks.
Paravicini, Hungerford, Berks.
Jaspers Fine Arts Ltd., Maidenhead, Berks.
Austin/Diamond fine Art, Sunninghill, Berks.
Paul Thomas Fine Paintings, Wokingham, Berks.
Christopher Cole, Beaconsfield, Bucks.
Baroq Antiques, Little Brickhill, Bucks.
Penn Barn, Penn, Bucks.
Van Riemsdijk Fine Art, Wavendon, Bucks.
Peter Arnold Gallery, Wingrave, Bucks.
Brook Hall Gallery, Winslow, Bucks.
Cambridge Fine Art Ltd., Cambridge, Cambs.
The Oriel Gallery, Cambridge, Cambs.
Baron Fine Art, Chester, Cheshire.
St. Peters Fine Art Gallery Ltd., Chester, Cheshire.
Philip Brooks, Macclesfield, Cheshire.
Harper Fine Paintings, Poynton, Cheshire.
T.B. and R. Jordan (Fine Paintings), Eaglescliffe, Cleveland.
Tamar Gallery, Launceston, Cornwall.
Tony Sanders Penzance Gallery and Antiques, Penzance, Cornwall.
Myles Varcoe, St. Austell, Cornwall.
The Gallery, Penrith, Cumbria.
Ashbourne Fine Art, Ashbourne, Derbys.
Kenneth Upchurch, Ashbourne, Derbys.
K. Chappell, Bakewell, Derbys.
Charles H. Ward, Derby, Derbys.
Melbourne Gallery, Melbourne, Derbys.
Shrives Gallery, Monyash, Derbys.
J. Collins and Son, Bideford, Devon.
Van Kloof Fine Art, Bradstone, Devon.
New Gallery, Budleigh Salterton, Devon.
Honiton Fine Art, Honiton, Devon.
Thomas and Dymond, Riddlecombe, Devon.
A-B Gallery, Salcombe, Devon.
The Lantern Shop, Sidmouth, Devon.
Tavistock Fine Art Gallery, Tavistock, Devon.
Birbeck Gallery, Torquay, Devon.
Colin Stodgell Fine Art, Torquay, Devon.
Stour Gallery, Blandford Forum, Dorset.
Hampshire Gallery, Bournemouth, Dorset.
York House Gallery, Bournemouth, Dorset.
Brandler Galleries, Brentwood, Essex.
John Smith Antiques, Coggeshall, Essex.
Simon Hilton, Dunmow, Essex.
Markswood Gallery, Gt. Bardfield, Essex.
C. and J. Mortimer and Son, Gt. Chesterford, Essex.
Barn Gallery, Hatfield Heath, Essex.
Meyers Gallery, Ingatestone, Essex.
Michael Tubbs, Little Baddow, Essex.
Newport Gallery, Newport, Essex.
Upton Lodge Galleries, Avening, Glos.
The Priory Gallery, Bishops Cleeve, Glos.
David Howard, Cheltenham, Glos.
Turtle Fine Art, Cheltenham, Glos.
The William Marler Gallery, Cirencester, Glos.
Robin Shields Antiques, Cirencester, Glos.
P.J. Ward, Cirencester, Glos.
Bell Fine Arts, Lechlade, Glos.
Gerard Campbell, Lechlade, Glos.
Astley House — Fine Art, Moreton-in-Marsh, Glos.
Southgate Gallery, Moreton-in-Marsh, Glos.
The Cotswold Galleries, Stow-on-the-Wold, Glos.
John Davies, Stow-on-the-Wold, Glos.
Fosse Gallery, Stow-on-the-Wold, Glos.
Park House Antiques, Stow-on-the-Wold, Glos.
Balmuir House Antiques, Tetbury, Glos.
Colleton House Gallery, Tetbury, Glos.
Upton Lodge Galleries, Tetbury, Glos.

Beaulieu Fine Arts, Beaulieu, Hants.
Fleet Fine Art, Fleet, Hants.
Phoenix Green Gallery, Hartley Wintney, Hants.
Corfield of Lymington Ltd., Lymington, Hants.
Marino-Montero Fine Art, Adrienne, Curdridge, Hants.
Petersfield Bookshop, Petersfield, Hants.
Plaitford House Gallery, Plaitford, Hants.
Bell Fine Art, Winchester, Hants.
Gallery Antiques Ltd., Winchester, Hants.
Webb Fine Arts, Winchester, Hants.
Bracebridge Gallery, Astley Bridge, Hereford and Worcs.
Richard Hagen, Broadway, Hereford and Worcs.
Hay Loft Gallery, Broadway, Hereford and Worcs.
Haynes Fine Arts, Broadway, Hereford and Worcs.
John Noott,, Broadway, Hereford and Worcs.
Highbury House Antiques, Leominster, Hereford and Worcs.
Mathon Gallery, Mathon, Hereford and Worcs.
The Barn Gallery, Powick, Hereford and Worcs.
Highway Gallery, Upton-upon-Severn, Hereford and Worcs.
Countrylife Gallery, Hitchin, Herts.
Carole Thomas (Fine Arts), Hitchin, Herts.
McCrudden Gallery, Rickmansworth, Herts.
James H. Starkey Galleries, Beverley, N. Humberside.
Steven Dews Fine Art, Hull, N. Humberside.
Houghton Hall Antiques, Market Weighton, N. Humberside.
In Retrospect, Pocklington, N. Humberside.
Vectis Fine Arts, Newchurch, Isle of Wight.
Marine Gallery, Cowes, Isle of Wight.
The Gallery, Yarmouth, Isle of Wight.
Chilham Antiques Ltd., Chilham, Kent.
W.J. Morrill Ltd., Dover, Kent.
Francis Iles, Rochester, Kent.
Langley Galleries, Rochester, Kent.
James Atkinson Gallery, Sandwich, Kent.
Sundridge Gallery, Sundridge, Kent.
Frankham Gallery, Tunbridge Wells, Kent.
Peter Dyke Antiques, Westerham, Kent.
Mistral Gallery, Westerham, Kent.
Peter Howarth, Carnforth, Lancs.
Ethos Gallery, Clitheroe, Lancs.
Studio Arts Gallery, Lancaster, Lancs.
Fulda Gallery Ltd., Manchester, Lancs.
Garson and Co. Ltd., Manchester, Lancs.
Henry Donn Gallery, Whitefield, Lancs.
P. Stanworth (Fine Arts), Cadeby, Leics.
Foulds-Field Fine Art, Leicester, Leics.
Leicestershire Sporting Gallery, Lubenham, Leics.
Old House Gallery, Oakham, Leics.
Castle Gallery, Lincoln, Lincs.
Alan Lewis Fine Art, Hundleby, Lincs.
Lincoln Fine Art, Lincoln, Lincs.
Lyver and Boydell Galleries, Liverpool, Merseyside.
Jays, Fine Art Dealers, Southport, Merseyside.
Studio 41, Southport, Merseyside.
Eekhout Gallery, Brockdish, Norfolk.
The Coach House, Costessey, Norfolk.
The Haven Gallery, Great Yarmouth, Norfolk.
Bank House Gallery, Norwich, Norfolk.
Crome Gallery and Frame Shop, Norwich, Norfolk.
The Fairhurst Gallery, Norwich, Norfolk.
Mandell's Gallery, Norwich, Norfolk.
Stephen Reiss Fine Art, Norwich, Norfolk.
Xanthus Gallery, Reymerston, Norfolk.
Westcliffe Gallery, Sheringham, Norfolk.
The Gallery and Things, South Lopham, Norfolk.
Staithe Lodge Gallery, Swafield, Norfolk.
Regent House, Northampton, Northants.
Brian Perkins Antiques, Wellingborough, Northants.
Jane Neville Gallery, Aslockton, Notts.
Horseshoe Antiques and Gallery, Burford, Oxon.
Swan Gallery, Burford, Oxon.
Dorchester Galleries, Dorchester-on-Thames, Oxon.
Hallidays Antiques Ltd., Dorchester-on-Thames, Oxon.
Faringdon Gallery, Faringdon, Oxon.
Barry M. Keene Gallery, Henley-on-Thames, Oxon.
Selkirk, Henley-on-Thames, Oxon.
Michael Priest Antiques and Fine Arts, Thame, Oxon.
Thame Antique and Art Galleries, Thame, Oxon.
Arts and Antiques (Oxford) Ltd., Wantage, Oxon.
Pauline Norton Galleries, Bridgnorth, Shrops.
Gallery 6, Broseley, Shrops.
The Jane Marler Gallery, Ludlow, Shrops.
Olivia Rumens, Ludlow, Shrops.
Teme Valley Antiques, Ludlow, Shrops.
Severn Fine Art, Shrewsbury, Shrops.
Haygate Gallery, Wellington, Shrops.
Hall's Antiques, Ash Priors, Somerset.
Clare Hutchinson, Ilminster, Somerset.
Pitminster Studio, Pitminster, Somerset.
Nick Cotton Antiques and Fine Art, Watchet, Somerset.
Betley Court Gallery, Betley, Staffs.
England's Gallery, Leek, Staffs.
Hood and Broomfield, Newcastle-under-Lyme, Staffs.
Thompson's Gallery, Aldeburgh, Suffolk.
Beccles Gallery, Beccles, Suffolk.
Cransford Gallery, Bungay, Suffolk.
Guildhall Gallery, Bury St. Edmunds, Suffolk.
Debenham Gallery, Debenham, Suffolk.
John Gazeley, Ipswich, Suffolk.
J. and J. Baker, Lavenham, Suffolk.
Peasenhall Art and Antiques Gallery, Peasenhall, Suffolk.
Simon Carter Gallery, Woodbridge, Suffolk.
The Falcon Gallery, Wortham, Suffolk.
Cider House Galleries Ltd., Bletchingley, Surrey.

The Court Gallery, East Molesey, Surrey.
Pastimes (Egham) Ltd., Egham, Surrey.
Lion and Lamb Gallery, Farnham, Surrey.
P. and J. Goldthorpe, Godalming, Surrey.
Bourne Gallery, Reigate, Surrey.
Sage Antiques and Interiors, Ripley, Surrey.
Anthony Welling Antiques, Ripley, Surrey.
Boathouse Gallery, Walton-on-Thames, Surrey.
The Westcott Gallery, Westcott, Surrey.
Edward Cross, Weybridge, Surrey.
Barclay Antiques, Bexhill-on-Sea, Sussex East.
John Day of Eastbourne Fine Arts, Eastbourne, Sussex East.
Premier Gallery, Eastbourne, Sussex East.
E. Stacy-Marks Ltd., Eastbourne, Sussex East.
Old Post House Antiques, Playden, Sussex East.
Holmes House Antiques, Sedlescombe, Sussex East.
Barnes Gallery, Uckfield, Sussex East.
Canon Gallery, Chichester, Sussex West.
Susan and Robert Botting, Felpham, Sussex West.
Sheila Hinde Fine Art, Kirdford, Sussex West.
Howes Gallery, Petworth, Sussex West.
Jeremy Wood Fine Art, Petworth, Sussex West.
Mulberry House Galleries, Pulborough, Sussex West.
Weetslade Fine Art, Dudley, Tyne and Wear.
Macdonald Fine Art, Gosforth, Tyne and Wear.
The Dean Gallery, Newcastle-upon-Tyne, Tyne and Wear.
Warner Fine Art, Newcastle-upon-Tyne, Tyne and Wear.
Sport and Country Gallery, Bulkington, Warks.
Coughton Galleries Ltd., Coughton, Warks.
Arden Gallery, Henley-in-Arden, Warks.
Colmore Galleries Ltd., Henley-in-Arden, Warks.
Lacy Gallery, Henley-in-Arden, Warks.
Fine-Lines (Fine Art), Shipston-on-Stour, Warks.
Burman Antiques, Stratford-upon-Avon, Warks.
Astley House — Fine Art, Stretton-on-Fosse, Warks.
Mason-Watts Fine Art, Warwick, Warks.
Woodland Fine Art, Alvechurch, West Midlands.
Roger Widdas Fine Paintings, Bentley Heath, West Midlands.
Ashleigh House Antiques, Birmingham, West Midlands.
Edgbaston Gallery, Birmingham, West Midlands.
The Graves Gallery, Birmingham, West Midlands.
Halcyon Gallery, Birmingham, West Midlands.
John Hubbard Antiques, Birmingham, West Midlands.
Kestrel House Antiques, Birmingham, West Midlands.
Stuart House Fine Art, Birmingham, West Midlands.
Robert Withers Antiques, Halesowen, West Midlands.
Richard Lukeman Fine Art, Knowle, West Midlands.
Oldswinford Gallery, Stourbridge, West Midlands.
Driffold Gallery, Sutton Coldfield, West Midlands.
Brian Oates Fine Paintings, Wolverhampton, West Midlands.
Lacewing Fine Art Gallery, Marlborough, Wilts.
Ian J. Brook, Wilton, Wilts.
Thornton Gallery, Bedale, Yorkshire North.
W. Greenwood (Fine Art), Burneston, Yorkshire North.
Garth Antiques, Harrogate, Yorkshire North.
Rodney Kent, Harrogate, Yorkshire North.
McTague of Harrogate, Harrogate, Yorkshire North.
Regency Fine Art, Harrogate, Yorkshire North.
Sutcliffe Galleries, Harrogate, Yorkshire North.
Walker Galleries Ltd., Harrogate, Yorkshire North.
Reflections, Knaresborough, Yorkshire North.
Charles Shaw, Knaresborough, Yorkshire North.
Rose Fine Art and Antiques, Ripon, Yorkshire North.
Kirkgate Picture Gallery, Thirsk, Yorkshire North.
Coulter Galleries, York, Yorkshire North.
Fettes Fine Art, York, Yorkshire North.
French Fine Arts, York, Yorkshire North.
Stonegate Fine Arts, York, Yorkshire North.
Hibbert Bros. Ltd., Sheffield, Yorkshire South.
Hinson Fine Paintings, Sheffield, Yorkshire South.
E. Carrol, Bingley, Yorkshire West.
Carlton Antiques and Fine Art, Bradford, Yorkshire West.
Parker Gallery, Leeds, Yorkshire West.
The Titus Gallery, Saltaire, Yorkshire West.
Todmorden Fine Art, Todmorden, Yorkshire West.
Mitchell-Hill Gallery, Wetherby, Yorkshire West.
Channel Islands Galleries Ltd., St. Peter Port, Guernsey, C.I.
Geoffrey P. Gavey, Vale, Guernsey, C.I.
Grange Gallery and Fine Arts Ltd., St. Helier, Jersey, C.I.
St. Helier Galleries, St. Helier, Jersey, C.I.
The Selective Eye Gallery, St. Helier, Jersey, C.I.
I.G.A. Old Masters Ltd., St. Lawrence, Jersey, C.I.
The Bell Gallery, Belfast, N. Ireland.
Dunluce Antiques, Bushmills, Co. Antrim, N. Ireland.
Atholl Antiques, Aberdeen, Scotland.
The Waverley Gallery, Aberdeen, Scotland.
Paul Hayes Gallery, Auchterarder, Scotland.

The McEwan Gallery, Ballater, Scotland.
Castle Fine Art, Bridge of Weir, Scotland.
Westport Ltd., Dundee, Scotland.
Bourne Fine Art Ltd., Edinburgh, Scotland.
The Calton Gallery, Edinburgh, Scotland.
Fine Art Gallery, Edinburgh, Scotland.
The Fine Art Society plc., Edinburgh, Scotland.
Malcolm Innes Gallery, Edinburgh, Scotland.
John Mathieson and Co., Edinburgh, Scotland.
Open Eye Gallery Ltd., Edinburgh, Scotland.
Daniel Shackleton, Edinburgh, Scotland.
Errol Antiques, Errol, Scotland.
Fine Art Society p.l.c., Glasgow, Scotland.
Pettigrew and Mail, Glasgow, Scotland.
The Mainhill Gallery, Jedburgh, Scotland.
Colin Murdoch, Kingussie, Scotland.
The Mclan Gallery (Campbell-Gibson Fine Arts), Oban, Scotland.
Pittenweem Antiques and Fine Art, Pittenweem, Scotland.
Manor House Fine Arts, Cardiff, S. Glam., Wales.
Philip Davies, Swansea, W. Glam., Wales.
Gothick Dream Fine Art, Arthog, Gwynedd, Wales.
David Windsor Gallery, Bangor, Gwynedd, Wales.
Michael Webb, Bordorgan, Gwynedd, Wales.

Oriental Art

Gregg Baker Oriental Works of Art, London, W.1.
Barling of Mount Street Ltd., London, W.1.
Bernheimer Fine Arts Ltd., London, W.1.
H. Blairman and Co., London, W.1.
Bluett and Sons Ltd., London, W.1.
Helen Buxton Ltd., London, W.1.
Barry Davies, London, W.1.
de Boilley Oriental Art, Jehanne, London, W.1.
Eskenazi Ltd., London, W.1.
Robin Kennedy, London, W.1.
Richard Kruml, London, W.1.
Jeremy J. Mason Oriental Art, London, W.1.
Sydney L. Moss Ltd., London, W.1.
Oriental Bronzes Ltd., London, W.1.
John Sparks Ltd., London, W.1.
Alfred Speelman, London, W.1.
Toynbee-Clarke Interiors Ltd., London, W.1.
David Brower Antiques, London, W.8.
Robert Hales Antiques Ltd., London, W.8.
Japanese Gallery, London, W.8.
Peter Kemp, London, W.8.
S. Marchant and Son, London, W.8.
D.C. Monk and Son, London, W.8.
A.V. Santos, London, W.8.
Mary Wise, London, W.8.
Robert Hall, London, W.9.
Cohen and Pearce (Oriental Porcelain), London, W.11.
Grays Portobello, London, W.11.
Eric Hudes, London, W.11.
M.C.N. Antiques, London, W.11.
Nanking Porcelain Co., London, W.11.
Ormonde Gallery, London, W.11.
Christina Truscott, London, W.11.
Odile Cavendish Gallery, London, S.W.1.
Ciancimino Ltd., London, S.W.1.
Shirley Day Ltd., London, S.W.1.
Christopher Edwards Ltd., London, S.W.1.
Barry Sainsbury, London, S.W.1.
Spink and Son Ltd., London, S.W.1.
Edric Van Vredenburgh Ltd., London, S.W.1.
David Tremayne Ltd., London, S.W.5.
Brandt Oriental Antiques, London, S.W.6.
Gerald Freeman, London, S.W.6.
Goodwin and Wadha, London, S.W.6.
The Lighthouse Ltd., London, S.W.19.
R. Holt and Co. Ltd., London, E.C.1.
Chancery Antiques, London, N.1.
Hart and Rosenberg, London, N.1.
Japanese Gallery, London, N.1.
Wan Li, London, N.1.
Laurence Mitchell Antiques, London, N.1.
Kevin Page Oriental Art, London, N.1.
East-Asia Co., London, N.W.1.
Milne Henderson, London, N.W.8.
Nihon Token, London, W.C.1.
Gabor Cossa, Cambridge, Cambs.
Highland Antiques, Hazel Grove, Cheshire.
Imperial Antiques, Stockport, Cheshire.
David L.H. Southwick Rare Art, Kingswear, Devon.
Eric Hudes, Braintree, Essex.
Kyoto House Antiques, Cheltenham, Glos.
Artemesia, Alresford, Hants.
Todd and Austin Antiques of Winchester, Winchester, Hants.
Tolley's Galleries, Worcester, Hereford and Worcester.
Northgate Antiques, Bishop's Stortford, Herts.
Michael Sim, Chislehurst, Kent.
Mandarin Gallery, Riverhead, Kent.
John Hardy Antiques, Oadby, Leics.
Country and Eastern, Norwich, Norfolk.
F.C. Manser and Son Ltd., Shrewsbury, Shrops.
Galleon Antiques, Hastings, Sussex East.
De Montfort, Robertsbridge, Sussex East.
Ringles Cross Antiques, Uckfield, Sussex East.
Richard Lukeman Fine Art, Knowle, West Midlands.
Paul M. Peters Antiques, Harrogate, Yorkshire North.
Sigma Antiques and Fine Art, Ripon, Yorkshire North.
Denis Young, Aberfeldy, Scotland.
Another World, Edinburgh, Scotland.
Albany Antiques, Glasgow, Scotland.
Elizabeth Paterson Antiques, Stirling, Scotland.

Photographs and Equipment

Bayswater Books, London, W.2.
Robert Hershkowitz, London, S.W.7.
Vintage Cameras, London, S.E.26.
Jubilee, London, N.1.
Finchley Fine Art Galleries, London, N.12.
Jessop Classic Photographica, London, W.C.1.
Artavia Gallery, Barnstaple, Devon.
Medina Gallery, Bideford, Devon.
East Gates Antiques, Colchester, Essex.
Cliff Latford Photography, Colchester, Essex.
Peter Pan's Bazaar, Gosport, Hants.
Padgett's Antiques, Hull, N. Humberside.

Playing Cards
Intercol, London, N.1.
Game Advice, London, N.W.5.

Porcelain
Antique Porcelain Co. Ltd., London, W.1.
Bernheimer Fine Arts Ltd., London, W.1.
H. Blairman and Sons Ltd., London, W.1.
Thomas Goode and Co. (London) Ltd., London, W.1.
Harcourt Antiques, London, W.1.
Brian Haughton Antiques, London, W.1.
Giulia Irving, London, W.1. (Grays A.M.).
Nicholas Vandekar Antiques Ltd., London, W.1.
Venners Antiques, London, W.1.
Angela Gräfin von Wallwitz, London, W.1.
The Badger, London, W.5.
Harold's Place, London, W.5.
David Brower Antiques, London, W.8.
H. and W. Deutsch Antiques, London, W.8.
Geoffrey Godden, London, W.8.
Grosvenor Antiques Ltd., London, W.8.
Claire Hobson Antiques, London, W.8.
Hope and Glory, London, W.8.
Valerie Howard, London, W.8.
Melvyn Jay Antiques and Objets d'art, London, W.8.
Peter Kemp, London, W.8.
Klaber and Klaber, London, W.8.
Eric Lineham and Sons, London, W.8.
J. and J. May, London, W.8.
St. Jude's Antiques, London, W.8.
Arthur Seager Antiques Ltd., London, W.8.
Jean Sewell (Antiques) Ltd., London, W.8.
Simon Spero, London, W.8.
Stockspring Antiques, London, W.8.
Mary Wise, London, W.8.
Magus Antiques, London, W.11.
Mercury Antiques, London, W.11.
Schredds of Portobello, London, W.11.
Armin B. Allen, London, S.W.1.
Albert Amor Ltd., London, S.W.1.
Burness Antiques, Marie Louise, London, S.W.1.
Kate Foster, London, S.W.1.
Graham and Oxley (Antiques) Ltd., London, S.W.1.
Christopher Hodsoll, London, S.W.1.
Ning Ltd., London, S.W.1.
Gerald Sattin Ltd., London, S.W.1.
H.W. Newby (A.J. Waller) and H.C. Mote, London, S.W.3.
Gerald Freedman, London, S.W.6.
The Dining Room Shop, London, S.W.13.
R.A. Barnes Antiques, London, S.W.15.
Harwood Antiques, London, S.W.15.
Audley Art Ltd., London, N.1. The Mall.
Corrigan Antiques, London, N.1.
Diana Huntley, London, N.1.
Inheritance, London, N.1.
Laurence Mitchell Antiques, London, N.1.
Persian Market, London, N.1.
Martin Henham (Antiques), London, N.2.
D.M. and P. Manheim (Peter Manheim) Ltd., London, N.6.
Finchley Fine Art Galleries, London, N.12.
Rochefort Antiques Gallery, London, N.21.
Gerald Clark Antiques, London, N.W.7.
China Repairers, London, N.W.8.
Magnus Antiques, London, N.W.8.
S. and H. Antiques, London, N.W.8.
Anchor Antiques, London, W.C.2.
Andrew Dando, Bath, Avon.
Brian and Angela Downes, Bath, Avon.
Heirloom and Howard Ltd., Bath, Avon.
Quiet Street Antiques, Bath, Avon.
The Tudor Gallery of Bristol, Bristol, Avon.
Cobblers Hall Antiques, Toddington, Beds.
The Old School Antiques, Dorney, Berks.
Chapel Antiques, Hungerford, Berks.
Old Malthouse, Hungerford, Berks.
The Compton Gallery, Windsor and Eton, Berks.
Fantiques, Amersham, Bucks.
Baroq Antiques, Little Brickhill, Bucks.
Bowood Antiques, Wendover, Bucks.
Collins and Clark, Cambridge, Cambs.
Gabor Cossa Antiques, Cambridge, Cambs.
Gallery Three, March, Cambs.
Abbey Antiques, Ramsey, Cambs.
Sydney House Antiques, Wansford, Cambs.
Peter A. Crofts, Wisbech, Cambs.
Made of Honour, Chester, Cheshire.
Christopher Pugh Antiques, Chester, Cheshire.
Lions and Unicorns, Nantwich, Cheshire.
Zippy Antiques, Stockport, Cheshire.
The Antiques Shop, Whitegate, Cheshire.
Knutsford Road Antiques, Wilmslow, Cheshire.
E. and N.R. Charlton Fine Art and Porcelain Marton, Cleveland.
Redcar Antiques, Redcar, Cleveland.
Endeavour Antiques, Saltburn, Cleveland.
Tamar Gallery (Antiques and Fine Art), Launceston, Cornwall.
Tony Martin, Looe, Cornwall.
Ages Ago Antiques, St. Agnes, Cornwall.
Clock Tower Antiques, Tregony, Cornwall.
Alan Bennett, Truro, Cornwall.
Mary Fell Antiques, Brampton, Cumbria.
Croft Head Antiques, Caldbeck, Cumbria.
Brian Ferguson, Carlisle, Cumbria.
Souvenir Antiques, Carlisle, Cumbria.
Kendal Studios Antiques, Kendal, Cumbria.
Alexandra Adamson, Kirkby Lonsdale, Cumbria.
K. Chappell Antiques and Fine Art, Bakewell, Derbys.
Derby Antique Centre, Derby, Derbys.
Westfield Antiques, Baslow, Derbys.
David J. Thorn, Budleigh Salterton, Devon.
Mary Payton Antiques, Chagford, Devon.
Hatherleigh Antiques, Hatherleigh, Devon.
Kingswood Antiques, Kingsbridge, Devon.
Alvin Antiques, Plymouth, Devon.
The Lantern Shop, Sidmouth, Devon.
Philip Andrade, South Brent, Devon.
Charterhouse Antiques, Teignmouth, Devon.
Allnutt Antiques, Topsham, Devon.
Galerie Antiques, Broadstone, Dorset.
Greystoke Antiques, Sherborne, Dorset.
Ivy House Antiques, Shillingstone, Dorset.

Reference Works, Swanage, Dorset.
Judy Wallington Antiques, Wareham, Dorset.
Partner and Puxon, Colchester, Essex.
Rundells Antiques, Harlow, Essex.
Pugh's Porcelains, Layer de la Haye, Essex.
Peter and Audrey Edwick, Layer Marney, Essex.
Barton House Antiques, Stanford-le-Hope, Essex.
Pamela Rowan, Blockley, Glos.
Studio Antiques Ltd., Bourton-on-the-Water, Glos.
Jay Gray Antiques, Cirencester, Glos.
Adams, Moreton-in-Marsh, Glos.
Mrs. M.K. Nielsen, Moreton-in-Marsh, Glos.
Colin Brand Antiques, Stow-on-the-Wold, Glos.
Freeman, Stow-on-the-Wold, Glos.
L. Greenwold, Stow-on-the-Wold, Glos.
Martin House Antiques, Stow-on-the-Wold, Glos.
South Bar Antiques, Stow-on-the-Wold, Glos.
Sylvia Harris Fine Antique Porcelain, Tetbury, Glos.
Old George Antiques and Interiors, Tetbury, Glos.
F.W. Taylor, Tewkesbury, Glos.
Bell Passage Antiques, Wotton-under-Edge, Glos.
Close Antiques, Alresford, Hants.
Goss and Crested China Centre, Horndean, Hants.
Corfield of Lymington Ltd., Lymington, Hants.
Lita Kaye of Lyndhurst, Lyndhurst, Hants.
Lane Antiques, Stockbridge, Hants.
Todd and Austin Antiques of Winchester, Winchester, Hants.
Gavina Ewart, Broadway, Hereford and Worcs.
H. and B. Wolf Antiques Ltd., Droitwich, Hereford and Worcs.
M. Lees and Sons, Worcester, Hereford and Worcs.
Dolphin Antiques, St. Albans, Herts.
The Crested China Co., Driffield, N. Humberside.
Houghton Hall Antiques, Market Weighton, N. Humberside.
Watchbell Antiques, Newport, I. of Wight.
W.W. Warner (Antiques) Ltd., Brasted, Kent.
Beaubush House Antiques, Sandgate, Kent.
The Porcelain Collector, Shoreham, Kent.
Steppes Hill Farm Antiques, Stockbury, Kent.
D.C. Adams Antiques, Tunbridge Wells, Kent.
Dunsdale Lodge Antiques, Westerham, Kent.
Mistral Galleries, Westerham, Kent.
Park Galleries Antiques, Bolton, Lancs.
Mrs. S. Falik, Burnley, Lancs.
Wm. Goodfellow (Antiques), Carnforth, Lancs.
The Connoisseur, Manchester, Lancs.
David Friend Antiques, Manchester, Lancs.
Wayside Antiques, Worsley, Lancs.
Ivanhoe Antiques, Ashby de la Zouch, Leics.
Timothy Kendrew Antiques, Lyddington, Leics.
Lapwing Antiques, Uppingham, Leics.
Paddock Antiques, Woodhouse Eaves, Leics.
The Strait Antiques, Lincoln, Lincs.
Best Antiques, Woodhall Spa, Lincs.
Roderick Jellicoe Fine Porcelain, Wallasey, Merseyside.
Allport-Lomax, Liz, Horstead, Norfolk.
Isabel Neal Cabinet Antiques, Coltishall, Norfolk.
Market Place Antiques, Fakenham, Norfolk.
Peter Robinson, Heacham, Norfolk.
Richard Scott Antiques, Holt, Norfolk.
Dorothy's Antiques, Sheringham, Norfolk.
T.C.S. Brooke, Wroxham, Norfolk.
Peter and Heather Jackson Antiques, Brackley, Northants.
Felton Park Antiques, Felton, Northumbs.
David and Carole Potter Antiques, Nottingham, Notts.
Franco Antiques, Retford, Notts.
Giffengate Antiques, Dorchester-on-Thames, Oxon.
David John Ceramics, Eynsham, Oxon.
Roger Little, Oxford, Oxon.
Bill Dickenson, Ironbridge, Shrops.
Peter Whitelaw, Ironbridge, Shrops.
Teme Valley Antiques, Ludlow, Shrops.
Dowlish Wake Antiques, Dowlish Wake, Somerset.
A. Lodge-Mortimer, Exton, Somerset.

Ray Best Antiques, Ilminster, Somerset.
Zwan Antiques, Timberscombe, Somerset.
Five Towns Antiques, Stoke-on-Trent, Staffs.
Cransford Gallery, Bungay, Suffolk.
Gordon Sutcliffe, Hadleigh, Suffolk.
Patrick Taylor, Ipswich, Suffolk.
J. and J. Baker, Lavenham, Suffolk.
Motts of Lavenham, Suffolk.
Templar Antiques, Nayland, Suffolk.
Pump House Antiques, Rickinghall, Suffolk.
Red House Antiques, Yoxford, Suffolk.
Upstairs, Downstairs Antiques, Dorking, Surrey.
P. and B. Jordan, Farnham, Surrey.
Heath Antiques, Reigate, Surrey.
Not Just Silver, Weybridge, Surrey.
Barclay Antiques, Bexhill-on-Sea, Sussex East.
Tapsell Antiques, Brighton, Sussex East.
Yellow Lantern Antiques Ltd., Brighton, Sussex East.
Stewart Gallery, Eastbourne, Sussex East.
Southdown Antiques, Lewes, Sussex East.
Geoffrey Godden Chinaman, Worthing, Sussex West.
Eleanor Antiques, Warwick, Warks. Smith St. A.C.
Bridge Antiques, Stourbridge, West Midlands.
Pendeford House Antiques, Wolverhampton, West Midlands.
Harp Antiques, Bradford-on-Avon, Wilts.
Moxhams Antiques, Bradford-on-Avon, Wilts.
Antiques — Rene Nicholls, Malmesbury, Wilts.
Carol Pearson Antiques, Wilton, Wilts.
Myers Galleries, Gargrave, Yorkshire North.
W.F. Greenwood and Sons Ltd., Harrogate, Yorkshire North.
David Love, Harrogate, Yorkshire North.
Shaw Bros., Harrogate, Yorkshire North.
Pauline Stephenson, Helmsley, Yorkshire North.
H.I. Milnthorpe, Settle, Yorkshire North.
Angela Charlesworth, Barnsley, Yorkshire South.
Robert Clark, Micklebring, Yorkshire South.
Hillside Antiques, Halifax, Yorkshire West.
H. and M. Suttle, Otley, Yorkshire West.
Dunluce Antiques, Bushmills, Co. Antrim, N.I.
Old Cross Antiques, Greyabbey, Co. Down, N.I.
Denis Young, Aberfeldy, Scotland.
Tim Wright Antiques, Glasgow, Scotland.
Elm House Antiques, Haddington, Scotland.
Pathbrae Antiques, Newton Stewart, Scotland.
Thurso Antiques, Thurso, Scotland.
Old Tyme Antiques, Ruthin, Clwyd, Wales.
Castle Antiques, Usk, Gwent, Wales.

Pot-Lids

Oliver-Sutton Antiques, London, W.8.
Gavina Ewart, Broadway, Hereford and Worcs.
The Old Forge, Hollingbourne, Kent.
Steppes Hill Farm Antiques, Stockbury, Kent.
Ivanhoe Antiques, Ashby de la Zouch, Leics.

Pottery (See also Porcelain)

Aqua Libra, London, W.1.
Brian Haughton Antiques, London, W.1.
Nicholas Vandekar Antiques Ltd., London, W.1.
Venners Antiques, London, W.1.
Angela Gräfin von Wallwitz, London, W.1.
St. Peters Browsery, London, W.4.
Richard Dennis, London, W.8.
Geoffrey Godden, London W.8.
Claire Hobson Antiques, London, W.8.
Jonathan Horne, London, W.8.
Valerie Howard, London, W.8.
Libra Antiques, London, W.8.
Lindsay Antiques, London, W.8.
J. and J. May, London, W.8.
Oliver-Sutton Antiques, London, W.8.
Arthur Seager Antiques Ltd., London, W.8.
M. and D. Seligmann, London, W.8.
Jean Sewell (Antiques) Ltd., London, W.8.
Stockspring Antiques, London, W.8.
Eric Hudes, London, W.11.
Mercury Antiques, London, W.11.
Graham and Oxley (Antiques) Ltd., London, S.W.1.
Armin B. Allen, London, S.W.1.
Christopher Hodsoll, London, S.W.1.
Christopher Wood Gallery, London, S.W.1.
The Purple Shop, London, S.W.3.
Rogers de Rin, London, S.W.3.
Alistair Sampson Antiques, London, S.W.3.
Gerald Freedman, London S.W.6.
Robert Young Antiques, London, S.W.11.
Tobias and The Angel, London, S.W.13.
R.A. Barnes Antiques, London, S.W.15.
Vale Stamps and Antiques, London, S.E.3.
Commemoratives, London, N.1.
Corrigan Antiques, London, N.1.
Carol Ketley Antiques, London, N.1.
Laurence Mitchell Antiques, London, N.1.
Finchley Fine Art Galleries, London, N.12.
Gerald Clark Antiques, London, N.W.7.
China Repairers, London, N.W.8.
Andrew Dando, Bath, Avon.
Robert Pugh, Bath, Avon.
The Compton Gallery, Windsor and Eton, Berks.
Baroq Antiques, Little Brickhill, Bucks.
Sydney House Antiques, Wansford, Cambs.
Farmhouse Antiques, Chester, Cheshire.
Made of Honour, Chester, Cheshire.
Christopher Pugh Antiques, Chester, Cheshire.
J. Milner Antiques, Marple, Cheshire.
Lions and Unicorns, Nantwich, Cheshire.
The Antiques Shop, Whitegate, Cheshire.
Knutsford Road Antiques, Wimslow, Cheshire.
Endeavour Antiques, Saltburn, Cleveland.
Tamar Gallery (Antiques and Fine Art), Launceston, Cornwall.
Kendal Studios Antiques, Kendal, Cumbria.
K. Chappell Antiques and Fine Art, Bakewell, Derbys.

Mary Payton Antiques, Chagford, Devon.
Kingswood Antiques, Kingsbridge, Devon.
Thomas and Dymond, Riddlescombe, Devon.
Philip Andrade Ltd., South Brent, Devon.
Charterhouse Antiques, Teignmouth, Devon.
Hardy's, Bournemouth, Dorset.
Galerie Antiques, Broadstone, Dorset.
Judy Wallington Antiques, Wareham, Dorset.
Eric Hudes, Braintree, Essex.
Partner and Puxon, Colchester, Essex.
Bush House, Corringham, Essex.
Pamela Rowan, Blockley, Glos.
The Little Window, Nailsworth, Glos.
Burditch Antiques at Park House Antiques, Stow-on-the-Wold, Glos.
L. Greenwood, Stow-on-the-Wold, Glos.
South Bar Antiques, Stow-on-the-Wold, Glos.
F.W. Taylor, Tewkesbury, Glos.
Muriel Lindsay, Winchcombe, Glos.
Close Antiques, Alresford, Hants.
Olive Branch Antiques, Broadway, Hereford and Worcs.
H. and B. Wolf Antiques Ltd., Droitwich, Hereford and Worcs.
Stables Antiques, Ombersley, Hereford and Worcs.
Times Past, Pershore, Hereford and Worcs.
Oakley Antiques, Berkhamsted, Herts.
Ann Barlow Antiques, Letchmore Heath, Herts.
W.W. Warner (Antiques) Ltd., Brasted, Kent.
The Old Forge, Hollingbourne, Kent.
Beaubush House Antiques, Sandgate, Kent.
Steppes Hill Farm Antiques, Stockbury, Kent.
Alan Wood, Tunbridge Wells, Kent.
Dunsdale Lodge Antiques, Westerham, Kent.
Roy W. Bunn Antiques, Barnoldswick, Lancs.
Wm. Goodfellow (Antiques), Carnforth, Lancs.
Manor House Antiques Ltd., Oakham, Leics.
The Strait Antiques, Lincoln, Lincs.
Allport-Lomax, Liz, Horstead, Norfolk.
Isabel Neal Cabinet Antiques, Coltishall, Norfolk.
Richard Scott Antiques, Holt, Norfolk.
Peter Jackson, Brackley, Northants.
Felton Park Antiques, Felton, Northumbs.
David and Carole Potter, Nottingham, Notts.
Giffengate Antiques, Dorchester-on-Thames, Oxon.
Woodstock Antiques, Woodstock, Oxon.
Dowlish Wake Antiques, Dowlish Wake, Somerset.
A. Lodge-Mortimer, Exton, Somerset.
Trevor Micklem Antiques Ltd., Langford Budville, Somerset.
Betley Court Gallery, Betley, Staffs.
Eveline Winter, Rugeley, Staffs.
Five Towns Antiques, Stoke-on-Trent, Staffs.
Weston Antique Gallery, Weston, Staffs.
Templar Antiques, Nayland, Suffolk.
Elias Clark Antiques Ltd., Bletchingley, Surrey.
Barclay Antiques, Bexhill-on-Sea, Sussex East.
Leonard Russell, Newhaven, Sussex East.
Steyne House Antiques, Seaford, Sussex East.
Treasure House Antiques, Arundel, Sussex West.
Geoffrey Godden Chinaman, Worthing, Sussex West.
Eleanor Antiques, Warwick, Warks. Smith St. A.C.
Bridge Antiques, Stourbridge, West Midlands.
Harp Antiques, Bradford-on-Avon, Wilts.
Moxhams Antiques, Bradford-on-Avon, Wilts.
Antiques — Rene Nicholls, Malmesbury, Wilts.
Nigel Cracknell (Antiques) Ltd., Marlborough, Wilts.
Bratton Antiques, Westbury, Wilts.
Myers Galleries, Gargrave, Yorkshire North.
W.F. Greenwood and Sons Ltd., Harrogate, Yorkshire North.
David Love, Harrogate, Yorkshire North.
H.I. Milnthorpe, Settle, Yorkshire North.
Angela Charlesworth Antiques, Barnsley, Yorkshire South.
Robert Clark, Micklebring, Yorkshire South.
Muir Hewitt, Halifax, Yorkshire West.
Hillside Antiques, Halifax, Yorkshire West.
Tim Wright Antiques, Glasgow, Scotland.
Elm House Antiques, Haddington, Scotland.
Howards of Aberystwyth, Dyfed, Wales.
Rex Moreton Studio, Newport, Gwent, Wales.
Castle Antiques, Usk, Gwent, Wales.
Paul Gibbs Antiques and Decorative Arts, Conway, Gwynedd, Wales.
Islwyn Watkins, Knighton, Powys, Wales.

Prints (See Maps)

Rugs (See Carpets)

Russian Art
C. Barrett and Co., London, W.1.
Antoine Cheneviere Fine Arts, London, W.1.
Ermitage Ltd., London, W.1.
David Harrington Gallery, London, W.1.
Roy Miles Gallery, London, W.1.
Wartski Ltd., London, W.1.
The Mark Gallery, London, W.2.
Temple Gallery, London, W.11.
Richard Joslin, London, W.13.
Maurice Asprey Ltd., London, S.W.1.
Carlton Hobbs, London, S.W.1.
Iconastas, London, S.W.1.
I.J. Mazure and Co. Ltd., London, S.W.1.
Omell Galleries, London, S.W.1.
Maria Andipa Icon Gallery, London, S.W.3.

Scientific Instruments
I. Freeman and Son, London, W.1.
Eila Grahame, London, W.8.
Peter Delehar, London, W.11.
Mayflower Antiques, London, W.11.
Rod's Antiques, London, W.11.
Igor Tociapski, London, W.11.

Arthur Davidson Ltd., London, S.W.1.
Trevor Philip and Sons Ltd., London, S.W.1.
David Weston Ltd., London, S.W.1.
Goodwin and Wadha, London, S.W.6.
Langfords, London, S.W.10.
Harriet Wynter Ltd., London, S.W.10.
Victor Burness Antiques and Scientific Instruments, London, S.E.1.
Peter Laurie Antiques, London, S.E.10.
Reubens, London, S.E.23.
Vintage Cameras Ltd., London, S.E.26.
Gordon Gridley, London, N.1.
Finchley Fine Art Galleries, London, N.12.
Barometer Fair, London, W.C.1.
Arthur Middleton, London, W.C.2.
The Barometer Shop, Bristol, Avon.
Christopher Sykes Antiques, Woburn, Beds.
Phoenix Antiques, Fordham, Cambs.
Malcolm Frazer Antiques, Cheadle, Cheshire.
Filkins Antiques, Chester, Cheshire.
Flintlock Antiques, Stockport, Cheshire.
High Street Antiques and Decor, Falmouth, Cornwall.
Mike Read Antique Sciences, St. Ives, Cornwall.
Branksome Antiques, Branksome, Dorset.
Toll House, Sturminster Newton, Dorset.
Mayflower Antiques, Harwich and Dovercourt, Essex.
Country Life Antiques, Stow-on-the-Wold, Glos.
Peter Whitby Antiques, Lechlade, Glos.
Country Life Antiques, Stow-on-the-Wold, Glos.
Wessex Medical Antiques, Portsmouth, Hants.
Padgett's Antiques, Hull, Humberside North.
Hadlow Antiques, Tunbridge Wells, Kent.
David T. Hansord, Lincoln, Lincs.
Pinfold Antiques, Ruskington, Lincs.
Humbleyard Fine Art, Holt, Norfolk.
The Chimes, Reepham, Norfolk.
Turret House, Wymondham, Norfolk.
Bernard G. House, Wells, Somerset.
Patrick Marney, Long Melford, Suffolk.
The Old Clock Shop, Birmingham, West Midlands.
Principia Arts and Sciences, Marlborough, Wilts.
Paul M. Peters Antiques, Harrogate, Yorkshire North.
John H. Preston and Sons, Harrogate, Yorkshire North.
Roy Sim Antiques, Blairgowrie, Scotland.
Quadrant Antiques, Edinburgh, Scotland.

Sculpture

Thomas Agnew & Son Ltd., London, W.1.
Albemarle Gallery, London, W.1.
Barling of Mount Street Ltd., London, W.1.
Browse and Darby Ltd., London, W.1.
J. Christie, London, W.1.
P. and D. Colnaghi and Co. Ltd., London, W.1.
Anthony d'Offay, London, W.1.
Eskenazi Ltd., London, W.1.
The Fine Art Society p.l.c., London, W.1.
Peter Francis, London, W.1.
W.H. Patterson Fine Arts Ltd., London, W.1.
Sladmore Gallery, The, London, W.1.
Stoppenbach and Delestre, London, W.1.
Philp, London, W.11.
Louis Stanton, London, W.11.
Chaucer Fine Arts Inc., London, S.W.1.
Hazlitt, Gooden and Fox Ltd., London, S.W.1.
Heim Gallery, London, S.W.1.
Matthiesen Fine Arts Ltd., London, S.W.1.
Edric Van Vredenburgh Ltd., London, S.W.1.
Joanna Booth, London, S.W.3.
Mathon Gallery, London, S.W.3.
Pageant Antiques, London, S.W.6.
Ted Few, London, S.W.17.
Westland Pilkington, London, E.C.2.
Gordon Gridley, London, N.1.
The Studio, London, N.1.
Tadema Galley, London, N.1.
Centaur Gallery, London, N.6.
Tara Antiques, London, N.W.8.
Nihon Token, London, W.C.1.
Pelter/Sands Art Gallery, Bristol, Avon.
New Gallery, Budleigh Salterton, Devon.
Simon Hilton, Dunmow, Essex.
Touchwood Antiques Ltd., Stow-on-the-Wold, Glos.
Kenulf Fine Art, Winchcombe, Glos.
Mathon Gallery, Mathon, Hereford and Worcs.
Frankham Gallery, Tunbridge Wells, Kent.
Bruton Gallery, Bruton, Somerset.
Armstrong-Davis Gallery, Arundel, Sussex West.

Shipping Goods and Period Furniture for the Trade

Daniel Mankowitz, London, W.2.
Chelsea Bric-a-Brac Shop Ltd., London, S.W.19.
Hamilton's Corner, London, S.W.20.
Oola Boola Antiques, London, S.E.1.
Penny Farthing Antiques, London, S.E.1.
Tower Bridge Antique Warehouse, London, S.E.1.
Lamont Antiques Ltd., London, S.E.10.
Bushwood Antiques, London, N.1.
Keith Skeel Antique Warehouse, London, N.1.
Regent Antiques, London, N.W.1.
Dela-Ware, Bath, Avon.
Helton Antiques, Heath and Reach, Beds.
Eva Rogers, Kempston, Beds.
J. Denton (Antiques), Luton, Beds.
Secondhand Alley, Shefford, Beds.
The Woburn Abbey Antiques Centre, Woburn, Beds.
Adrian Hornsey Ltd., Twyford, Bucks.
Brampton Mill Antiques, Brampton, Cambs.
Halo Antiques, Altrincham, Cheshire.
Grosvenor Antiques, Chester, Cheshire.
Melody's Antique Galleries, Chester, Cheshire.
Brian Edwards Antique Exports, Lower Kinnerton, Cheshire.
Polyera Antiques, Middlesbrough, Cleveland.
Radnor House, Grampound, Cornwall.
Richard Winkworth, Redruth, Cornwall.
Sweeting's, Belper, Derbys.
Shardlow Antiques Warehouse, Shardlow, Derbys.

Antique Exporters (Derby) U.K., Shirley, Derbys.
G. Mounter, Dulford, Devon.
Exeter Antique Wholesalers, Exeter, Devon.
Alan Jones Antiques, Okehampton, Devon.
M. and A. Antique Exporters, Plymouth, Devon.
South Molton Antiques, South Molton, Devon.
Richard Batsford Antiques, Bournemouth, Dorset.
Sandy's Antiques, Bournemouth, Dorset.
David Mack Antiques, Branksome, Dorset.
Tower Antiques, Cranborne, Dorset.
Jo Patterson Antiques, Crook, Durham.
Lynden Antiques, Seaham, Durham.
Partner and Puxon, Colchester, Essex.
Rundells Antiques, Harlow, Essex.
F.G. Bruschweiler (Antiques) Ltd., Rayleigh, Essex.
Antiques Trade Warehouse, Rettendon, Essex.
Valmar Antiques, Stansted, Essex.
David, Jean and John Antiques, Westcliff-on-Sea, Essex.
White Roding Antiques, White Roding, Essex.
Manor House Antiques, Cheltenham, Glos.
Patrick Oliver, Cheltenham, Glos.
John Townsend, Cheltenham, Glos.
David Kent Antiques, Gloucester, Glos.
Regent Antiques, Painswick, Glos.
Duncan J. Baggott, Stow-on-the-Wold, Glos.
Breakspeare Antiques, Tetbury, Glos.
Martin and Parke, Farnborough, Hants.
The Barn, Petersfield, Hants.
R.C. Dodson (Exports) Ltd., Portsmouth, Hants.
Millers of Chelsea Antiques Ltd., Ringwood, Hants.
Hingstons, Southampton, Hants.
Gaylords, Titchfield, Hants.
Thompsons Antiques, Winchester, Hants.
Miscellany Antiques, Gt. Malvern, Hereford and Worcs.
I. and J.L. Brown, Hereford, Hereford and Worcs.
Dobson's Antiques, Abbots Langley, Herts.
Annick Antiques, Kimpton, Herts.
Dolphin Antiques, St. Albans, Herts.
Collins Antiques, Wheathampstead, Herts.
Sedman Antiques, Bridlington, N. Humberside.
Boothferry Antiques, Hull. N. Humberside.
Imperial Antiques, Hull, N. Humberside.
Geoffrey Mole, Hull, N. Humberside.
Elegance Antiques, Barton-on-Humber, S. Humberside.
Silvesters, Birchington, Kent.
Charles International Antiques, Maidstone, Kent.
Sutton Valence Antiques, Maidstone, Kent.
Patricia Antiques, Ramsgate, Kent.
Northgate Antiques, Rochester, Kent.
Empire Antiqies, Sandwich, Kent.
Berry's Antiques, Brierfield, Lancs.
West Lancs. Antiques, Burscough, Lancs.
Castle Antiques, Clitheroe, Lancs.
K.C. Antiques, Darwen, Lancs.
G.W. Antiques, Lancaster, Lancs.
Manchester Antique Co., Manchester, Lancs.
G.G. Exports, Morecambe, Lancs.
Betty and Dean Easterby, Preston, Lancs.
North Western Antique Centre, Preston, Lancs.
John Robinson Antiques, Wigan, Lancs.
Hughes Antiques, Hinckley, Leics.
Corner Cottage Antiques, Leicester, Leics.
Laurence Shaw Antiques, Horncastle, Lincs.
Kirton Antiques, Kirton, Lincs.
C. and K.E. Dring, Lincoln, Lincs.
Trade Antiques, Long Sutton, Lincs.
Sykes Antiques, South Kelsey, Lincs.
Burghley Antiques, Stamford, Lincs.
William Courtney and Sons, Birkenhead, Merseyside.
Kensington Tower Antiques Ltd., Liverpool, Merseyside.
Swainbanks Ltd., Liverpool, Merseyside.
Theta Gallery, Liverpool, Merseyside.
Molloy's Furnishers, Southport, Merseyside.
Tony and Anne Sutcliffe Antiques, Southport, Merseyside.
Phelps Ltd., Twickenham, Middx.
Antiques Warehouse, Uxbridge, Middx.
A.E. Bush and Partners, Attleborough, Norfolk.
Eric Bates and Sons, Coltishall, Norfolk.
John Howkins, Great Yarmouth, Norfolk.
Leo Pratt and Son, South Walsham, Norfolk.
Thorpe Antiques, Finedon, Northants.
V. and C. Madeira Antiques, Flore, Northants.
R.E. Thompson, Long Buckby, Northants.
J. Roe Antiques, Thrapston, Northants.
John Walker Antiques, Hexham, Northumbs.
W.J. Miller and Son, Wooler, Northumberland.
Fair Deal Antiques, Mansfield, Notts.
Sheppards Antiques, Mansfield, Notts.
M.G.R. Exports, Bruton, Somerset.
W.P.S. (Bruton) Ltd., Bruton, Somerset.
Moolham Mill Antiques, Ilminster, Somerset.
Keyford Antiques, Rode, Somerset.
C. and J. Mowe, Coton Clanford, Staffs.
B. Timmis and Son, Eccleshall, Staffs.
Anvil Antiques, Leek, Staffs.
Aspleys Antique Market, Leek, Staffs.
Armsons of Yoxall Antiques, Yoxall, Staffs.
Goodbreys, Framlingham, Suffolk.
E.W. Cousins and Son, Ixworth, Suffolk.
Antique Furniture Warehouse, Woodbridge, Suffolk.
Wrentham Antiques, Wrentham, Suffolk.
Ripley Antiques, Ripley, Surrey.
Weybridge Antiques, Weybridge, Surrey.
Wych House Antiques, Woking, Surrey.
Village Antiques, Bexhill-on-Sea, Sussex East.
Ashton's Antiques, Brighton, Sussex East.
Christopher G. Cowen Antiques, Brighton, Sussex East.
Rodney Arthur Classics, Brighton, Sussex East.
L. Woolman Antiques, Brighton, Sussex East.

Anglo Am Warehouse, Eastbourne, Sussex East.
Abbey Antiques, Hastings, Sussex East.
John Botting, Horam, Sussex East.
British Antique Exporters Ltd., Burgess Hill, Sussex West.
Keith Atkinson Antiques, East Grinstead, Sussex West.
Peter Marks Antique Warehouse, Portslade, Sussex West.
J. Powell (Hove) Ltd., Portslade, Sussex West.
Wilson's Antiques, Worthing, Sussex West.
Peter Smith Antiques, Sunderland, Tyne and Wear.
Crown Antiques, Bidford-on-Avon, Warks.
Tim Harrison, Stratford-upon-Avon, Warks.
GVR Antiques Ltd., Birmingham, West Midlands.
Bob Harris and Sons Antiques, Birmingham, West Midlands.
Milton Antiques, Coventry, West Midlands.
Smithfield Antiques, Lye, West Midlands.
L.P. Furniture (Mids) Ltd., Pelsall, West Midlands.
Brett Wilkins Antiques, Wednesbury, West Midlands.
Martin-Quick Antiques Ltd., Wolverhampton, West Midlands.
Wakeman and Taylor Antiques, Wolverhampton, West Midlands.
North Wilts Exporters, Hankerton, Wilts.
Cross Hayes Antiques, Malmesbury, Wilts.
K. and A. Welch, Warminster, Wilts.
R.B. Kendal-Green, Harrogate, Yorkshire North.
F.B. Shaftoe, Harrogate, Yorkshire North.
Terry Kindon Antiques Ltd., Melmerby, Yorkshire North.
B. Ogleby, Thirsk, Yorkshire North.
Acomb Antiques, York, Yorkshire North.
Mallglade Antiques, Haigh, Yorkshire South.
Roger Appleyard Ltd., Rotherham, Yorkshire South.
South Yorkshire Antiques, Rotherham, Yorkshire South.
Philip Turnor Antiques, Rotherham, Yorkshire South.
Wickersley Antiques, Rotherham, Yorkshire South.
Dronfield Antiques, Sheffield, Yorkshire South.
Gilbert and Sons, Sheffield, Yorkshire South.
G.H. Green, Sheffield, Yorkshire South.
N.P. and A. Salt Antiques, Sheffield, Yorkshire South.
Scott and Varey, Halifax, Yorkshire West.
Barleycote Hall Antiques, Keighley, Yorkshire West.
Geary Antiques, Leeds, Yorkshire West.
Windsor House Antiques (Leeds) Ltd., Leeds, Yorkshire West.
K.L.M. and Co. Antiques, Lepton, Yorkshire West.
Raymond Tomlinson (Antiques) Ltd., Wetherby, Yorkshire West.
Imrie Antiques, Bridge of Earn, Scotland.
Michael Stewart Antiques, Coatbridge, Scotland.
Mac's Antiques, Dundee, Scotland.
George Duff Antiques, Edinburgh, Scotland.
Georgian Antiques, Edinburgh, Scotland.
Jacksonville Warehouse, Edinburgh, Scotland.
Errol Antiques, Errol, Scotland.
James Findlay, Falkirk, Scotland.
Albany Antiques, Glasgow, Scotland.
Gardner's The Antique Shop, Kilbarchan, Scotland.
The Antique Shop, Langholm, Scotland.
Narducci Antiques, Largs, Scotland.
T.W. Beaty, Moffat, Scotland.
Heritage Antiques, Paisley, Scotland.
A.S. Deuchar and Son, Perth, Scotland.
Ian Murray Antiques Warehouse, Perth, Scotland.
Narducci Antiques, Saltcoats, Scotland.
Elizabeth Paterson Antiques, Stirling, Scotland.
North Wales Antiques, Colwyn Bay, Clwyd, Wales.
Shelagh Hyde, Rhos-on-Sea, Clwyd, Wales.
John Trefor Antiques, Rhuallt, Clwyd, Wales.
Richard Lloyd, Henllan, Dyfed, Wales.
Country Antiques, Kidwelly, Dyfed, Wales.
Jim and Pat Ash, Llandeilo, Dyfed, Wales.
Castle Antiques, Newcastle Emlyn, Dyfed, Wales.
Steven Evans Antiques, Treherbert, Mid-Glam., Wales.
Steven Evans Antiques, Treorchy, Mid-Glam., Wales.
Charlotte's Wholesale Antiques, Cardiff, S. Glam., Wales.
W.H. Douglas, Cardiff, S. Glam., Wales.
Ann and Colin Hubert, Swansea, W. Glam., Wales.
John F. Davies, Chepstow, Gwent, Wales.
Abbey Antiques, Tintern, Gwent, Wales.
Annteaks (Antiques), Abersoch, Gwynedd, Wales.
Roger Day Antiques, Llanystumdwy, Gwynedd, Wales.
Rodney Adams Antiques, Pwllheli, Gwynedd, Wales.

Silver and Jewellery

A.D.C. Heritage Ltd., London, W.1.
Philip Antrobus, London, W.1.
Armitage, London, W.1.
Armour-Winston Ltd., London, W.1.
Asprey p.l.c, London, W.1.
Astarte Gallery, London, W.1.
Barrett and James, London, W.1.
Brian Beet, London, W.1.
Paul Bennett, London, W.1.
Bentley and Co. Ltd., London, W.1.
Bilby and Holloway, London, W.1.
Anne Bloom Jewellers, London, W.1.
N. Bloom and Son (Antiques) Ltd., London, W.1.
Bond Street Antique Centre, London, W.1.

Bond Street Silver Galleries, London, W.1.
Bruford and Heming Ltd., London, W.1.
Carrington and Co., London, W.1.
Collingwood of Bond Street Ltd., London, W.1.
Sandra Cronan Ltd., London, W.1.
A.B. Davis Ltd., London, W.1.
Demas, London, W.1.
A. Douch, London, W.1.
D.H. Edmonds Ltd., London, W.1.
Ermitage Ltd., London, W.1.
Fine Jewellery at Liberty's, London, W.1.
Liliane Flowerdew at Trianon, London, W.1.
Garrard and Co. Ltd., (The Crown Jewellers), London, W.1.
Graus Antiques, London, W.1.
Grays Antique Market, London, W.1.
Grays Mews, London, W.1.
Simon Griffin Antiques Ltd., London, W.1.
Hadleigh Jewellers, London, W.1.
Hancocks and Co. (Jewellers) Ltd., London, W.1.
S.H. Harris and Son (London) Ltd., London, W.1.
Harvey and Gore, London, W.1.
Hennell Ltd., Founded 1736 (incorporating Frazer and Hawes (1868) and E. Lloyd Lawrence (1830)), London, W.1.
Holmes Ltd., London, W.1.
How of Edinburgh, London, W.1.
Johnson, Walker and Tolhurst Ltd., London, W.1.
Lady Newborough, London, W.1.
D.S. Lavender (Antiques) Ltd., London, W.1.
Liberty, London, W.1.
M. and L. Silver Co. Ltd., London, W.1.
Marks Antiques Ltd., London, W.1.
Massada Antiques, London, W.1.
Nigel Milne Ltd., London, W.1.
Moira, London, W.1.
L. Newland and Son, London, W.1.
Richard Ogden Ltd., London, W.1.
S.J. Phillips Ltd., London, W.1.
David Richards and Sons, London, W.1.
Silver, London, W.1.
Tessiers Ltd., London, W.1.
Wartski Ltd., London, W.1.
Young and Stephens Ltd., London, W.1.
M. McAleer, London, W.2.
William C. Mansell, London, W.2.
Mary Cooke Antiques Ltd., London, W.8.
H. and W. Deutsch Antiques, London, W.8.
Green's Antique Galleries, London, W.8.
Lev (Antiques) Ltd., London, W.8.
E. and A. Di Michele Antiques, London, W.11.
J. Freeman, London, W.11.
Hyde Park Antiques, London, W.11.
S. Lampard and Son Ltd., London, W.11.
Schredds of Portobello, London, W.11.
Stouts Antique Arcade, London, W.11.
L. and M. Sutton, London, W.11.
Maurice Asprey Ltd., London, S.W.1.
J.H. Bourdon-Smith Ltd., London, S.W.1.
Cornucopia, London, S.W.1.
Kenneth Davis, London, S.W.1.
De Haviland (Antiques) Ltd., London, S.W.1.
M. Ekstein Ltd., London, S.W.1.
Brand Inglis, London, S.W.1.
Paul Longmire Ltd., London, S.W.1.
Gerald Sattin Ltd., London, S.W.1.
Timothy Schroder Ltd., London, S.W.1.
Michael and Henrietta Spink Ltd., London, S.W.1.
Spink and Son Ltd., London, S.W.1.
Antiquarius, London, S.W.3.
Boodle and Dunthorne Ltd., London, S.W.3.
Chenil Galleries, London, S.W.3.
James Hardy and Co., London, S.W.3.
Annabel Jones, London, S.W.3.
Stanley Leslie, London, S.W.3.
McKenna and Co., London, S.W.3.
The Purple Shop, London, S.W.3.
Nicholas Harris, London, S.W.6.
Peter Jeffs, London, S.W.6.
M.P. Levene Ltd., London, S.W.7.
A. and H. Page, London, S.W.7.
Whitworth and O'Donnell Ltd., London, S.E.13.
Cutler Street Antique Market, London, E.1.
Essie C. Harris, London, E.C.1.
Hirsh Fine Jewels, London, E.C.1.
Joseph and Pearce Ltd., London, E.C.1.
R.I. McKay, London, E.C.1.
Priory Antiques, London, E.C.1.
A.R. Ullmann Ltd., London, E.C.1.
C.J. Vander (Antiques) Ltd., London, E.C.1.
Asprey (City Branch) Ltd., London, E.C.3.
Nanwani and Co., London, E.C.3.
Searle and Co. Ltd., London, E.C.3.
David Graham, London, N.1.
Rosemary Hart, London, N.1.
Heather Antiques, London, N.1.
John Laurie, London, N.1.
Linda Morgan Antiques, London, N.1. The Mall.
The Corner Cupboard, London, N.W.2.
Delieb Antiques Ltd., London, N.W.11.
S.J. Shrubsole Ltd., London, W.C.1.
Thomas Kettle Ltd., London, W.C.2.
The London Silver Vaults, London, W.C.2.
Pearl Cross Ltd., London, W.C.2.
H. Perovetz Ltd., London, W.C.2.
The Silver Mouse Trap, London, W.C.2.
Abbey Galleries, Bath, Avon.
Bath Galleries, Bath, Avon.
Bladud House Antiques, Bath, Avon.
D. and B. Dickinson, Bath, Avon.
M.A. and D.A. Hughes, Bath, Avon.
E.P. Mallory and Son Ltd., Bath, Avon.
Grey-Harris and Co., Bristol, Avon.
The Mall Jewellers, Bristol, Avon.
Quinneys Jewellery, Bristol, Avon.
R.A. Saunders, Bristol, Avon.
Victoria's Emporium, Bristol, Avon.
Styles Silver, Hungerford, Berks.
Eatons of Eton, Windsor and Eton, Berks.
Turks Head Antiques, Windsor and Eton, Berks.
Victoria Antiques, Windsor and Eton, Berks.
Benedict Jewellers, Amersham, Bucks.
Spencer, Aylesbury, Bucks.
Aristocat, Gerrards Cross, Bucks.
Collectors Corner, Waddesdon, Bucks.
Buckie's, Cambridge, Cambs.
Attic Gallery, Wisbech, Cambs.

Coach House Antiques, Wisbech, Cambs.
Alderley Edge Antiques, Alderley Edge, Cheshire.
D.J. Massey and Son, Alderley Edge, Cheshire.
D.J. Massey and Son, Cheadle, Cheshire.
Boodle and Dunthorne Ltd., Chester, Cheshire.
Grosvenor Antiques, Chester, Cheshire.
Kayes of Chester, Chester, Cheshire.
Lowe and Sons, Chester, Cheshire.
Bernard Walsh Ltd., Chester, Cheshire.
Watergate Antiques, Chester, Cheshire.
D.J. Massey and Son, Macclesfield, Cheshire.
G.E. Leigh and Son, Reddish, Cheshire.
The Silver Thimble, Kendal, Cumbria.
Jane Pollock Antiques, Penrith, Cumbria.
Timothy Coward, Braunton, Devon.
Wm. Bruford and Son Ltd., Exeter, Devon.
Gold and Silver Exchange, Exeter, Devon.
Brian Mortimer, Exeter, Devon.
John Nathan Antiques, Exeter, Devon.
Boase and Vaughan, Exmouth, Devon.
J. Barrymore and Co., Honiton, Devon.
Otter Antiques, Honiton, Devon.
Alvin Antiques, Plymouth, Devon.
Copperfields, Sidmouth, Devon.
Philip Andrade, South Brent, Devon.
Charterhouse Antiques, Teignmouth, Devon.
Extence Antiques, Teignmouth, Devon.
Bogan House Antiques, Totnes, Devon.
Beaminster Antiques, Beaminster, Dorset.
Georgian House Antiques, Bournemouth, Dorset.
G.B. Mussenden & Son, Bournemouth, Dorset.
Geo. A. Payne and Son, Bournemouth, Dorset.
R.E. Porter, Bournemouth, Dorset.
Portique, Bournemouth, Dorset.
Seabourne Antiques, Bournemouth, Dorset.
Peter Stebbing, Bournemouth, Dorset.
Battens, Bridport, Dorset.
D.J. Jewellery, Parkstone, Dorset.
Arndale Antiques, Poole, Dorset.
Greystoke Antiques, Sherborne, Dorset.
Georgian Gems Antique Jewellers, Swanage, Dorset.
Heirlooms, Wareham, Dorset.
Robert Finnegan, Darlington, Durham.
Ronald Richardson, Darlington, Durham.
Bishops Antiques, Basildon, Essex.
Helen Blomfield, Halstead, Essex.
Richard Wrenn Antiques, Leigh-on-Sea, Essex.
Abacus Antiques, Malden, Essex.
Green's of Montpellier, Cheltenham, Glos.
Martin and Co. Ltd., Cheltenham, Glos.
Scott-Cooper Ltd., Cheltenham, Glos.
Swan Antiques, Chipping Camden, Glos.
Walter Bull and Son (Cirencester) Ltd., Cirencester, Glos.
John D. Rivers, Cirencester, Glos.
Rankine Taylor Antiques, Cirencester, Glos.
Paul Cater Antiques, Moreton-in-Marsh, Glos.
L. Greenwold, Stow-on-the-Wold, Glos.
Olive Antiques, Alverstoke, Hants.
Squirrel Collectors Centre, Basingstoke, Hants.
A. Fleming (Southsea) Ltd., Portsmouth, Hants.
Leslie's, Portsmouth, Hants.
Meg Campbell, Southampton, Hants.
R.J. Elliot, Southampton, Hants.
R.K. Leslie Antiques, Southampton, Hants.
Parkhouse and Wyatt, Southampton, Hants.
Lane Antiques, Stockbridge, Hants.
Pamela Manley, Titchfield, Hants.
Todd and Winchester Antiques, Winchester, Hants.
Gavina Ewart, Broadway, Hereford and Worcs.
Howard of Broadway, Broadway, Hereford and Worcs.
Arrowsmith of Bromyard, Bromyard, Hereford and Worcs.
Magpie Jewellers and Antiques, Evesham, Hereford and Worcs.
B.B.M. Jewellery and Antiques, Kidderminster, Hereford and Worcs.
Bygones (Worcester), Worcester, Hereford and Worcs.
Bygones by the Cathedral, Worcester, Hereford and Worcs.
Howards, Baldock, Herts.
Abbey Antiques and Fine Art, Hemel Hempstead, Herts.
Neale Antiques, Hertford, Herts.
Bexfield Antiques, Hitchin, Herts.
Stuart Wharton, St. Albans, Herts.
John Bly, Tring, Herts.
C.J. and A.J. Dixon Ltd., Bridlington, N. Humberside.
Lesley Berry Antiques, Flamborough, N. Humberside.
Rytham Antiques, Seaton Ross, N. Humberside.
Goodman Gold, Grimsby, S. Humberside.
J. and H. Bell Antiques, Castletown, I. of Man.
P.G. Allom and Co. Ltd., Ramsey, I. of Man.
Marilyn Rose Antiques Centre, Newport, I. of Wight.
Marlborough House Antiques, Yarmouth, I. of Wight.
Peacock Antiques, Chilham, Kent.
Hartley Antiques, Hartley, Kent.
Den of Antiquity, Hythe, Kent.
PLB Enterprises, Hythe, Kent.
Meridian Antiques, New Romney, Kent.
Mary Brooker Antiques, Sandgate, Kent.
Howard Godfrey Antiques, Sandgate, Kent.
Steppes Hill Farm Antiques, Stockbury, Kent.
Kenworthys Ltd., Ashton-under-Lyne, Lancs.
Snuff Box, Lytham St. Annes, Lancs.
Boodle and Dunthorne, Manchester, Lancs.
Cathedral Jewellers, Manchester, Lancs.
E. and C.T. Koopman and Son Ltd., Manchester, Lancs.
St. James Antiques, Manchester, Lancs.
Charles Howell Jeweller, Oldham, Lancs.
H.C. Simpson and Sons, Oldham, Lancs.
Keystone Antiques, Coalville, Leics.

Letty's Antiques, Leicester, Leics.
Richard Pullen Jeweller, Lincoln, Lincs.
Rowletts, Lincoln, Lincs.
James Usher and Son Ltd., Lincoln, Lincs.
C. Rosenberg, Heswall, Merseyside.
The Clock Shop, Hoylake, Merseyside.
Boodle and Dunthorne, Liverpool, Merseyside.
Edward's Jewellers, Liverpool, Merseyside.
H.S. Walne, Southport, Merseyside.
Weldon Antiques and Jewellery, Southport, Merseyside.
Zafer, Twickenham, Middx.
Solus Marketing, Felmingham, Norfolk.
Peter Howkins, Gt. Yarmouth, Norfolk.
Donna Hannent, Norwich, Norfolk.
Henry Levine and Co., Norwich, Norfolk.
Maddermarket Antiques, Norwich, Norfolk.
Thomas Tillett & Co., Norwich, Norfolk.
Oswald Sebley, Norwich, Norfolk.
James and Ann Tillett, Norwich, Norfolk.
Robert Young Antiques, Norwich, Norfolk.
Parriss, Sheringham, Norfolk.
Michael Jones Jeweller, Northampton, Northants.
Melville Kemp Ltd., Nottingham, Notts.
Twemlow and Co. Ltd., Nottingham, Notts.
Reginald Davis Ltd., Oxford, Oxon.
Payne and Son (Goldsmiths) Ltd., Oxford, Oxon.
Rowell and Son Ltd., Oxford, Oxon.
M.G.J. Antiques, Wallingford, Oxon.
The Little Gem, Shrewsbury, Shrops.
C.T. Culverwell, Burnham-on-Sea, Somerset.
J.A. Stancomb, Ilminster, Somerset.
Zwan Antiques, Timberscombe, Somerset.
Edward A. Nowell, Wells, Somerset.
H.J. Richards and Son, Burton-on-Trent, Staffs.
W.G. Steele, Stoke-on-Trent, Staffs.
Winston Mac (Silversmith), Bury St. Edmunds, Suffolk.
Croydon and Sons Ltd., Ipswich, Suffolk.
Old Post Office Antiques, Compton, Surrey.
Noel Collins, Dorking, Surrey.
E. Hollander Ltd., Dorking, Surrey.
Eleanor Hutton, Dorking, Surrey.
Link Gold Ltd., Epsom, Surrey.
Cry for the Moon, Godalming, Surrey.
Glydon and Guess Ltd., Kingston-upon-Thames, Surrey.
Link Gold Ltd., Kingston-upon-Thames, Surrey.
Kingabys, Richmond, Surrey.
Lion Antiques, Richmond, Surrey.
Spring Park Jewellers, Shirley, Surrey.
S. Warrender and Co., Sutton, Surrey.
Not Just Silver, Weybridge, Surrey.
Bryde and Co., Brighton, Sussex East.
Harry Diamond and Son, Brighton, Sussex East.
James Doyle Antiques, Brighton, Sussex East.
D.H. Edmonds Ltd., Brighton, Sussex East.
Paul Goble, Brighton, Sussex East.
Douglas Hall Ltd., Brighton, Sussex East.
Hallmarks, Brighton, Sussex East.
Kingsbury Antiques, Brighton, Sussex East.
Harry Mason, Brighton, Sussex East.
H. Miller (Antiques) Ltd., Brighton, Sussex East.
Resner's, Brighton, Sussex East.
Shop of the Yellow Frog, Brighton, Sussex East.
S. and L. Simmons, Brighton, Sussex East.
Wm. Bruford and Son Ltd., Eastbourne, Sussex East.
Lasseters, Arundel, Sussex West.
Peter Hancock Antiques, Chichester, Sussex West.
Ernest Streeter and Daughter, Petworth, Sussex West.
Westbourne Antiques, Westbourne, Sussex West.
Davidson's The Jewellers Ltd., Newcastle-upon-Tyne, Tyne and Wear.
Owen's Jewellers, Newcastle-upon-Tyne, Tyne and Wear.
Spicker Jewellers, Newcastle-upon-Tyne, Tyne and Wear.
Jean A. Bateman, Stratford-upon-Avon, Warks.
Howards Jewellers, Stratford-upon-Avon, Warks.
H.H. Bray Ltd., Warwick, Warks.
Russell Lane Antiques, Warwick, Warks.
Martin Payne Antiques, Warwick, Warks.
Westgate Antiques, Warwick, Warks.
Garratts Antiques, Birmingham, West Midlands.
Rex Johnson and Sons, Birmingham, West Midlands.
Nathan and Co. (Birmingham) Ltd., Birmingham, West Midlands.
Piccadilly Jewellers, Birmingham, West Midlands.
H. and R.L. Parry Ltd., Sutton Coldfield, West Midlands.
Nicholls Jewellers and Antiques, Walsall, West Midlands.
Baron Antiques, Wolverhampton, West Midlands.
Cross Keys Jewellers, Devizes, Wilts.
Tamaree Antiques, Melksham, Wilts.
Jeffery Bates Antiques, Boroughbridge, Yorkshire North.
Antiques and Collectables, Harrogate, Yorkshire North.
W.F. Greenwood and Sons Ltd., Harrogate, Yorkshire North.
D. Mason and Son, Harrogate, Yorkshire North.
Ogden of Harrogate Ltd., Harrogate, Yorkshire North.
Christopher Warner, Harrogate, Yorkshire North.
Jowsey and Roe, Whitby, Yorkshire North.
Robert M. Himsworth, York, Yorkshire North.
John Mason Jewellers Ltd., Rotherham, Yorkshire South.
Pot-Pourri, Sheffield, Yorkshire South.
Juliana, Bingley, Yorkshire West.
Collectors Corner, Huddersfield, Yorkshire West.
Fillans (Antiques), Huddersfield, Yorkshire West.

Aladdin's Cave, Leeds, Yorkshire West.
Coins International, Leeds, Yorkshire West.
William Goldsmiths, Leeds, Yorkshire West.
Roses the Jewellers, Leeds, Yorkshire West.
H. and M. Suttle, Otley, Yorkshire West.
Sinclair's Antique Gallery, Belfast, N. Ireland.
Brian R. Bolt, Portballintrae, Co. Antrim, N. Ireland.
Greyabbey Timecraft Ltd., Greyabbey, Co. Down, N. Ireland.
Old Cross Antiques, Greyabbey, Co. Down, N. Ireland.
The Forge Antiques, Portstewart, Co. Londonderry, N. Ireland.
Cookstown Antiques, Cookstown, Co. Tyrone, N. Ireland.
Gallery, Aberdeen, Scotland.
Joseph Bonnar, Jewellers, Edinburgh, Scotland.
Goodwins Antiques Ltd., Edinburgh, Scotland.
Letham Antiques, Edinburgh, Scotland.
Royal Mile Curios, Edinburgh, Scotland.
John Whyte, Edinburgh, Scotland.
West End Antiques, Elgin, Scotland.
James Forrest and Co. (Jewellers) Ltd., Glasgow, Scotland.
Tim Wright Antiques, Glasgow, Scotland.
Amber Antiques, Kincardine O'Neil, Scotland.
Forsyth Antiques, Perth, Scotland.
Hardie Antiques, Perth, Scotland.
Old St. Andrews Gallery, St. Andrews, Scotland.
Thurso Antiques, Thurso, Scotland.
Oak Chest, Llangollen, Clwyd, Wales.

Sporting Items and Associated Memorabilia

Risky Business, London, N.W.8.
Warboys Antiques, Warboys, Cambs.
Simon Brett, Moreton-in-Marsh, Glos.
The Tennis Bookshop, Ringwood, Hants.
Grant Fine Art, Droitwich, Hereford and Worcs.
Hamilton and Tucker Billiard Co. Ltd., Knebworth, Herts.
The Crypt, Burford, Oxon.
Vintage Fishing Tackle Shop, Shrewbury, Shrops.
Academy Antiques, West Byfleet, Surrey.
Sports Programmes, Coventry, West Midlands.
Old Golf Shop Inc., Edinburgh, Scotland.
Old St. Andrews Gallery, St. Andrews, Scotland.

Sporting Paintings and Prints

Arthur Ackermann and Son Ltd., London, W.1.
Burlington Gallery Ltd., London, W.1.
Frost and Reed Ltd., London, W.1.
Richard Green, London, W.1.
Lane Fine Art Ltd., London, W.1.
Wilkins and Wilkins, London, W.1.
Iona Antiques, London, W.8.
Lacy Gallery, London, W.11.
Addison-Ross Gallery, London, S.W.1.
Paul Mason Gallery, London, S.W.1.
Old Maps and Prints, London, S.W.1.
O'Shea Gallery, London, S.W.1.
Trove, London, S.W.1.
Malcolm Innes Gallery, London, S.W.3.
Guy Nevill Pictures, London, S.W.3.
Wingfield Sporting Gallery, London, S.W.4.
The William Marler Gallery, Cirencester, Glos.
The Avon Gallery, Moreton-in-Marsh, Glos.
Priests Antiques, Stow-on-the-Wold, Glos.
Julia Holmes Antique Maps and Prints, South Harting, Hants.
Border Sporting Gallery, Wooler, Northumb.
Sally Mitchell Fine Paintings, Askham, Notts.
Jane Neville Gallery, Aslockton, Notts.
The Jane Marler Gallery, Ludlow, Shrops.
Kensington Galleries, Esher, Surrey.
Lion and Lamb Gallery, Farnham, Surrey.
Sheila Hinde Fine Art, Kirdford, Sussex West.
Sport and Country Gallery, Bulkington, Warks.
Lacy Gallery, Henley-in-Arden, Warks.
Marlborough Sporting Gallery and Bookshop, Marlborough, Wilts.
Malcolm Innes Gallery, Edinburgh, Scotland.

Stamps

Argyll Etkin Gallery, London, W.1.
Michael Coins, London, W.8.
J.A.L. Franks, London, S.W.1.
J.A.L. Franks, London, W.C.1.
Stanley Gibbons, London, W.C.2.
Corridor Stamp Shop, Bath, Avon.
Avalon Postcard and Stamp Shop, Chester, Cheshire.
Penrith Coin and Stamp Centre, Penrith, Cumbria.
Coin and Stamp Centre, Colchester, Essex.
Portsmouth Stamp Shop, Portsmouth, Hants.
Pastimes (Egham) Ltd., Egham, Surrey.
Glance Back, Chepstow, Gwent, Wales.

Tapestries, Textiles and Needlework

Bernheimer Fine Arts Ltd., London, W.1.
Marilyn Garrow, London, W.1.
Holland and Holland, London, W.1.
Heskia, London, W.1.
C. John (Rare Rugs) Ltd., London, W.1.
Alexander Juran and Co., London, W.1.
Mallett and Son (Antiques) Ltd., London, W.1.
Paul Nels Ltd., London, W.1.
Stair and Co., London, W.1.
Vigo Carpet Gallery, London, W.1.
Vigo-Sternberg Galleries, London, W.1.
John Fell-Clark, London, W.2.
S. Franses Conservation, London, W.2.
Paul Hughes Textiles, London, W.2.
Daniel Mankowitz, London, W.2.
Vivian C. Youlten, London, W.2.
Aberdeen House Antiques, London, W.5.
Nina Ghiggini, London, W.6.
Barker-Mill Design Associates, London, W.8.
Coats Oriental Carpets, London, W.8.
Belinda Coote Tapestries, London, W.8.
Eila Grahame, London, W.8.

Jonathan Horne, London, W.8.
Clive Loveless, London, W.10.
Antique Textile Co., London, W.11.
David Black, London, W.11.
Jack Fairman (Carpets) Ltd., London, W.11.
Eva Nieradzik Antiques, London, W.11.
Pat Nye, London, W.11.
The Old Haberdasher, London, W.11.
Virginia, London, W.11.
Trude Weaver, London, W.11.
Alyson Burdon, London, W.14.
Charleville Gallery, London, W.14.
Sheila Cook, London, W.14.
Anno Domini Antiques, London, S.W.1.
Raymond Benardout, London, S.W.1.
Box House Antiques, London, S.W.1.
Victor Franses Gallery, London, S.W.1.
S. Franses, London, S.W.1.
Joss Graham, London, S.W.1.
Heraz, London, S.W.1.
Mayorcas Ltd., London, S.W.1.
Peta Smyth-Antique Textiles, London, S.W.1.
Joanna Booth, London, S.W.3.
Graham, Daphne, London, S.W.3.
Paul Jones, London, S.W.3.
Gwyneth Lloyd, London, S.W.3.
Pelham Galleries, London, S.W.3.
Alistair Sampson Antiques, London, S.W.3.
Robert Barley, London, S.W.6.
Beresford-Clark, London, S.W.6.
Alistair Brown, London, S.W.6.
Buhler Galleries, London, S.W.6.
Five Five Six Antiques, London, S.W.6.
Robert Gray Antiques, London, S.W.6.
Judy Greenwood, London, S.W.6.
The Kilim House, London, S.W.6.
Lunn Antiques, London, S.W.6.
Rare Carpets Gallery, London, S.W.10.
Antiques and Things, London, S.W.11.
Campion, London, S.W.13.
Age of Elegance, London, S.W.14.
Harwood Antiques, London, S.W.15.
Linda Gumb, London, N.1.
Putnams, London, N.W.1.
Spatz, London, N.W.1.
Platon Hobson, London, N.W.3.
Joseph Lavian, London, N.W.5.
Robert Franses and Son, London, N.W.8.
Gallery of Antique Costume and Textiles, London, N.W.8.
Spatz, London, W.C.2.
Blyth Antiques, Bath, Avon.
Gene and Sally Foster, Bath, Avon.
Ann King, Bath, Avon.
No.12 Queen Street, Bath, Avon.
Sheila Cooper t/a Sheila Smith Antiques, Bath, Avon.
Robert and Georgina Hastie, Hungerford, Berks.
Bowood Antiques, Wendover, Bucks.
Filkins Antiques, Chester, Cheshire.
Robert Copperfield, Macclesfield, Cheshire.
Daisie's Antiques, Carlisle, Cumbria.
Eileen Cooper Antiques, Braunton, Devon.
Lacis, Budleigh Salterton, Devon.
Pirouette, Exeter, Devon.
Honiton Lace Shop, Honiton, Devon.
Rowan Antiques, Totnes, Devon.
Badger Antiques, Colchester, Essex.
The Antique Rooms, Maldon, Essex.
Brocante Antiques, Cheltenham, Glos.
Annarella Clark Antiques, Stow-on-the-Wold, Glos.
Meg Andrews, Harpenden, Herts.
Anthony Scaramanga Antiques, Witney, Oxon.
Trevor Micklem Antiques Ltd., Langford Budville, Somerset.
Bloomers, Harrogate, Yorkshire North.

Tools (including needlework and sewing)

Richard Maude Tools, London, S.W.15.
Old Woodworking Tools, London, N.12.
Sheila Cooper t/a Sheila Smith, Bath, Avon.
Norton Antiques, Aylesbury, Bucks.
Filkins Antiques, Chester, Cheshire.
Woolmarket Antiques, Chipping Campden, Glos.
Thomas and Pamela Hudson, Cirencester, Glos.
Paul Cater Antiques, Moreton-in-Marsh, Glos.
Tooltique, Norwich, Norfolk.
Jean Burnett Antiques, Finedon, Northants.
Roy Arnold, Needham Market, Suffolk.
The Plough, Milland, Sussex West.

Toys (See Dolls and Toys)

Trade Dealers (See Shipping Goods)

Treen

Halcyon Days, London, W.1.
Simon Castle, London, W.8.
Arthur Seager Antiques Ltd., London, W.8.
M. and D. Seligman, London, W.8.
Wynyards Antiques, London, W.11.
Robert Young Antiques, London, S.W.11.
Halcyon Days, London, E.C.3.
Linda Helm Antiques, London, N.1.
Thomas Franklins Antiques, Hungerford, Berks.
A. and E. Foster, Naphill, Bucks.
Simon and Penny Rumble Antiques, Chittering, Cambs.
Phoenix Antiques, Fordham, Cambs.
A.P. and M.A. Haylett, Outwell, Cambs.
Daphne's Antiques, Penzance, Cornwall.
Shire Antiques, Newby Bridge, Cumbria.
Denzil Verey, Barnsley, Glos.
Paul Cater Antiques, Moreton-in-Marsh, Glos.
Baggott Church Street Ltd., Stow-on-the-Wold, Glos.
Huntington Antiques Ltd., Stow-on-the-Wold, Glos.
Touchwood Antiques Ltd., Stow-on-the-Wold, Glos.
Prichard Antiques, Winchcombe, Glos.
J. Du Cros Antiques, Liss, Hants.
Elizabeth Viney, Stockbridge, Hants.
Polly de Courcy-Ireland, Winchester, Hants.
Mary Roofe Antiques, Winchester, Hants.
Gay Walker, Birley, Hereford and Worcs.
Barclay Antiques, Bexhill-on-Sea, Sussex East.

Vintage Cars (See Carriages and Cars)

Watercolours

Thomas Agnew and Sons Ltd., London, W.1.
Burlington Paintings Ltd, London, W.1.
P. and D. Colnaghi and Co. Ltd., London, W.1.
Connaught-Brown plc., London W.1.
Crawley and Asquith, London, W.1.
Editions Graphiques Gallery, London, W.1.
The Fine Art Society p.l.c., London, W.1.
Frost and Reed Ltd., London, W.1.
Richard Green, London, W.1.
E. Joseph, London, W.1.
The Leger Galleries Ltd., London, W.1.
Maas Gallery, London, W.1.
David Messum, London, W.1.
John Mitchell and Son, London, W.1.
Piccadilly Gallery, London, W.1.
Michael Simpson Ltd., London, W.1.
Waterhouse and Dodd, London, W.1.
Manya Igel Fine Arts Ltd., London, W.2.
Mangate Gallery, London, W.4.
Ealing Gallery, London, W.5.
George Dare, London, W.8.
Sabin Galleries Ltd., London, W.8.
Simon Spero, London, W.8.
Beryl Kendall, London, W.9.
L'Acquaforte, London, W.11.
Stephen Garratt (Fine Paintings), London, W.14.
Chris Beetles Ltd. Watercolours and Paintings, London, S.W.1.
Bowmoore Gallery, London, S.W.1.
Martyn Gregory Gallery, London, S.W.1.
David James (Fine Victorian Watercolours), London, S.W.1.
Oscar and Peter Johnson Ltd., London, S.W.1.
David Ker Fine Art, London, S.W.1.
King Street Galleries, London, S.W.1.
Moreton Street Gallery, London, S.W.1.
Guy Morrison, London, S.W.1.
Peter Nahum, London, S.W.1.
Michael Parkin Fine Art Ltd., London, S.W.1.
Pawsey and Payne, London, S.W.1.
Polak Gallery, London, S.W.1.
Spink and Son Ltd., London, S.W.1.
Christopher Wood Gallery, London, S.W.1.
Colin Denny, London, S.W.3.
Stephanie Hoppen Ltd., London, S.W.3.
Mathon Gallery, London, S.W.3.
Moss Galleries-Rachel Moss, London, S.W.3.
Mark Senior, London, S.W.3.
Oliver Swann Galleries, London, S.W.3.
Walker-Bagshaw, London, S.W.3.
Barclay Samson, London, S.W.6.
Rupert Cavendish Antiques, London, S.W.6.
Cooper Fine Arts Ltd., London, S.W.6.
New King's Road and Hurlingham Gallery, London, S.W.6.
John Spink, London, S.W.6.
Francois Valcke, London, S.W.6.
Meldrum Walker Gallery, London, S.W.6.
IA Gallery, London, S.W.10.
Lacey Gallery, Stephen, London, S.W.10.
Park Walk Gallery, London, S.W.10.
Alton Gallery, London, S.W.13.
Hallam Gallery, London, S.W.14.
Sheen Gallery, London, S.W.14.
S.A.G. Art Galleries, London, S.W.18.
Hicks Gallery, London, S.W.19.
The Greenwich Gallery, London, S.E.10.
David E. Green Gallery, London, S.E.26.
Royal Exchange Art Gallery, London, E.C.3.
Park Galleries, London, N.3.
Centaur Gallery, London, N.6.
Finchley Fine Art Galleries, London, N.12.
The Totteridge Gallery, London, N.20.
Gunter Fine Art, London, N.W.2.
The Catto Gallery, London, N.W.3.
John Denham Gallery, London, N.W.6.
Gallery Kaleidscope, London, N.W.6.
Camden Art Gallery, London, N.W.8.
Abbott and Holder, London, W.C.1.
Austin/Desmond Fine Art, London, W.C.1.
Sebastian D'Orsai Ltd., London, W.C.1.
Beau Nash House Antiques, Bath, Avon.
Martin Dodge Interiors Ltd., Bath, Avon.
Kingsley Gallery, Bath, Avon.
William Pelly, Bath, Avon.
Trimbridge Galleries, Bath, Avon.
The Mall Gallery, Bristol, Avon.
Pelter/Sands Art Gallery, Bristol, Avon.
Sir William Russell Flint Galleries Ltd., Wrington, Avon.
Graham Trenchard Ltd., Heath and Reach, Beds.
Queen Adelaide Gallery, Kempston, Beds.
David Ball Antique and Fine Art, Leighton Buzzard, Beds.
Foye Gallery, Luton, Beds.
Knights Gallery, Luton, Beds.
Woburn Fine Arts, Woburn, Beds.
Graham Gallery, Burghfield Common, Berks.
The Collectors Gallery, Caversham, Berks.
Marian and John Alway, Datchet, Berks.
Paravicini, Hungerford, Berks.
Jaspers Fine Arts Ltd., Maidenhead, Berks.
Paul Thomas Fine Paintings, Wokingham, Berks.
"Mon Galerie", Amersham, Bucks.
Christopher Cole, Beaconsfield, Bucks.
Images in Watercolour, Chalfont St. Giles, Bucks.
Noel Gregory Gallery, Farnham Common, Bucks.
Baroq Antiques, Little Brickhill, Bucks.
Angela Hone Watercolours, Marlow, Bucks.
Penn Barn, Penn, Bucks.
Van Riemsdijk Fine Art, Wavendon, Bucks.
Peter Arnold Gallery, Wingrave, Bucks.
Cambridge Fine Art Ltd., Cambridge, Cambs.
Baron Fine Art, Chester, Cheshire.
St. Peters Fine Art Gallery Ltd., Chester, Cheshire.
Philip Brooks, Macclesfield, Cheshire.
Pictures (Chris Crowe Fine Art), Macclesfield, Cheshire.
Harper Fine Paintings, Poynton, Cheshire.
T.B. and R. Jordan (Fine Paintings), Eaglescliffe, Cleveland.

E. and N.R. Charlton Fine Art and Porcelain, Marton, Cleveland.
Copperhouse Gallery, Hayle, Cornwall.
Tamar Gallery (Antiques and Fine Art), Launceston, Cornwall.
Tony Sanders Penzance Gallery and Antiques, Penzance, Cornwall.
Penandrea Gallery, Redruth, Cornwall.
Myles Varcoe, St. Austell, Cornwall.
St. Breock Gallery, Wadebridge, Cornwall.
The Gallery, Penrith, Cumbria.
Ashbourne Fine Art, Ashbourne, Derbys.
Kenneth Upchurch, Ashbourne, Derbys.
Melbourne Gallery, Melbourne, Derbys.
Shrives Gallery, Monyash, Derbys.
J. Collins and Son, Bideford, Devon.
Van Kloof Fine Art, Bradstone, Devon.
New Gallery, Budleigh Salterton, Devon.
Honiton Fine Art, Honiton, Devon.
A-B Gallery, Salcombe, Devon.
The Lantern Shop, Sidmouth, Devon.
Tavistock Fine Art Gallery, Tavistock, Devon.
Birbeck Gallery, Torquay, Devon.
Beverley J. Pyke, Totnes, Devon.
Barbara Ledger, Widecombe-in-the-Moor, Devon.
Stour Gallery, Blandford Forum, Dorset.
The Artist Gallery, Bournemouth, Dorset.
Hampshire Gallery, Bournemouth, Dorset.
York House Gallery, Bournemouth, Dorset.
Swan Gallery, Sherborne, Dorset.
Richard Iles Gallery, Colchester, Essex.
Simon Hilton, Dunmow, Essex.
Markswood Gallery, Gt. Bardfield, Essex.
Barn Gallery, Hatfield Heath, Essex.
Meyers Gallery, Ingatestone, Essex.
Newport Gallery, Newport, Essex.
Upton Lodge Galleries, Avening, Glos.
The Priory Gallery, Bishops Cleeve, Glos.
David Howard, Cheltenham, Glos.
Turtle Fine Art, Cheltenham, Glos.
Cirencester Antiques Ltd., Cirencester, Glos.
The William Marler Gallery, Cirencester, Glos.
Heather Newman, Cranham, Glos.
Bell Fine Arts, Lechlade, Glos.
Gerard Campbell, Lechlade, Glos.
Astley House Fine Art, Moreton-in-Marsh, Glos.
Clifford and Joan Silcocks, Pitchcombe, Glos.
Fosse Gallery, Stow-on-the-Wold, Glos.
Park House Antiques, Stow-on-the-Wold, Glos.
St. Breock Gallery, Stow-on-the-Wold, Glos.
Ron and Pam Sparrow, Stroud, Glos.
Colleton House Gallery, Tetbury, Glos.
Upton Lodge Galleries, Tetbury, Glos.
Kenulf Fine Art, Winchcombe, Glos.
Fleet Fine Art, Fleet, Hants.
Phoenix Green Gallery, Hartley Wintney, Hants.
J. Morton Lee, Hayling Island, Hants.
Corfield of Lymington Ltd., Lymington, Hants.
Anna Hoysted, Mattingley, Hants.
Petersfield Bookshop, Petersfield, Hants.
Plaitford House Gallery, Plaitford, Hants.
Ewhurst Gallery, Ramsdell, Hants.
Bell Fine Art, Winchester, Hants.
Haynes Fine Art, Broadway, Hereford and Worcs.
Bindery Galleries, Broadway, Hereford and Worcs.
Richard Hagen, Broadway, Hereford and Worcs.
Hay Loft Gallery, Broadway, Hereford and Worcs.
John Noott, Broadway, Hereford and Worcs.
Brobury House Gallery, Brobury, Hereford and Worcs.
Lismore Gallery, Great Malvern, Hereford and Worcs.
Coltsfoot Gallery, Leominster, Hereford and Worcs.
Mathon Gallery, Mathon, Hereford and Worcs.
The Barn Gallery, Powick, Hereford and Worcs.
Highway Gallery, Upton-upon-Severn, Hereford and Worcs.
Knight's Gallery, Harpenden, Herts.
Abbey Antiques and Art, Hemel Hempstead, Herts.
Country Life Gallery, Hitchin, Herts.
Carole Thomas (Fine Arts), Hitchin, Herts.
McCrudden Gallery, Rickmansworth, Herts.
Vectis Fine Arts, Newchurch, I. of Wight.
Galerias Segui, Cowes, I. of Wight.
Marine Gallery, Cowes, I. of Wight.
The Gallery, Yarmouth, I. of Wight.
The Weald Gallery, Brasted, Kent.
Kennedy Corporation, Hythe, Kent.
Francis Iles, Rochester, Kent.
Langley Galleries, Rochester, Kent.
James Atkinson Gallery, Sandwich, Kent.
Sundridge Gallery, Sundridge, Kent.
Graham Gallery, Tunbridge Wells, Kent.
Peter Dyke Antiques, Westerham, Kent.
Peter Howarth, Carnforth, Lancs.
Ethos Gallery, Clitheroe, Lancs.
Studio Arts Gallery, Lancaster, Lancs.
Fulda Gallery Ltd., Manchester, Lancs.
Barronfield Gallery, Preston, Lancs.
Foulds-Field Fine Art, Leicester, Leics.
Hammond Smith, Leicester, Leics.
Old House Gallery, Oakham, Leics.
Alan Lewis Fine Art, Hundleby, Lincs.
Castle Gallery, Lincoln, Lincs.
Lincoln Fine Art, Lincoln, Lincs.
Lyver and Boydell Galleries, Liverpool, Merseyside.
Studio 41, Liverpool, Merseyside.
Jays, Fine Art Dealers, Southport, Merseyside.
The Coach House, Costessey, Norfolk.
Mrs. Joan Morton, Great Walsingham, Norfolk.
The Haven Gallery, Great Yarmouth, Norfolk.
Crome Gallery and Frame Shop, Norwich, Norfolk.
The Fairhurst Gallery, Norwich, Norfolk.
The Little Gallery, Norwich, Norfolk.
Mandell's Gallery, Norwich, Norfolk.

The Westcliffe Gallery, Sheringham, Norfolk.
The Gallery and Things, South Lopham, Norfolk.
Staithe Lodge Gallery, Swafield, Norfolk.
The Burford Gallery, Burford, Oxon.
Horseshoe Antiques and Gallery, Burford, Oxon.
Swan Gallery, Burford, Oxon.
Wren Gallery, Burford, Oxon.
Faringdon Gallery, Faringdon, Oxon.
Barry M. Keene Gallery, Henley-on-Thames, Oxon.
Thame Antique and Art Galleries, Thame, Oxon.
Art and Antiques (Oxford) Ltd., Wantage, Oxon.
Pauline Norton Galleries, Bridgnorth, Shrops.
Gallery 6, Broseley, Shrops.
Jane Marler Gallery, Ludlow, Shrops.
Teme Valley Antiques, Ludlow, Shrops.
Severn Fine Art, Shrewsbury, Shrops.
Haygate Gallery, Telford, Shrops.
Old Vicarage Gallery, Worfield, Shrops.
Hall Antiques, Ash Priors, Somerset.
Claire Hutchinson, Ilminster, Somerset.
Plympton Gallery, Ilminster, Somerset.
Martock Gallery, Martock, Somerset.
Pitminster Studio, Pitminster, Somerset.
Coach House Antiques, Wedmore, Somerset.
Betley Court Gallery, Betley, Staffs.
Broadway Studios, Burton-on-Trent, Staffs.
England's Gallery, Leek, Staffs.
Hood and Broomfield, Newcastle-under-Lyme, Staffs.
Cransford Gallery, Bungay, Suffolk.
Guildhall Gallery, Bury St. Edmunds, Suffolk.
Peasenhall Art and Antiques Gallery, Peasenhall, Suffolk.
Simon Carter Gallery, Woodbridge, Suffolk.
The Falcon Gallery, Wortham, Suffolk.
Red House Antiques, Yoxford, Suffolk.
Barbara Rubenstein Fine Art, Boxhill, Surrey.
The Court Gallery, East Molesey, Surrey.
Past Times, Egham, Surrey.
Limpsfield Watercolours, Limpsfield, Surrey.
Bourne Gallery, Reigate, Surrey.
Margaret Melville Watercolours, Staines, Surrey.
The David Curzon Gallery, Thames Dutton, Surrey.
Boathouse Gallery, Walton-on-Thames, Surrey.
The Westcott Gallery, Westcott, Surrey.
Edward Cross, Weybridge, Surrey.
Barclay Antiques, Bexhill-on-Sea, Sussex East.
Stephen and Sonia Welbourne, Brighton, Sussex East.
John Day of Eastbourne Fine Art, Eastbourne, Sussex East.
Premier Gallery, Eastbourne, Sussex East.
Ewhurst Gallery, Ewhurst Green, Sussex East.
Holmes House Antiques, Sedlescombe, Sussex East.
Barnes Gallery, Uckfield, Sussex East.
Nicholas Bowlby, Uckfield, Sussex East.
Sussex Fine Art, Arundel, Sussex West.
Canon Gallery, Chichester, Sussex West.
John Hopkins (Antiques) Ltd., Cuckfield, Sussex West.
The Antique Print Shop, East Grinstead, Sussex West.
Sheila Hinde Fine Art, Kirdford, Sussex West.
Susan and Robert Botting, Felpham, Sussex West.
Howes Gallery, Petworth, Sussex West.
Jeremy Wood Fine Art, Petworth, Sussex West.
Mulberry House Galleries, Pulborough, Sussex West.
Crosshall Gallery, Worthing, Sussex West.
Weetslade Fine Art, Dudley, Tyne and Wear.
MacDonald Fine Art, Gosforth, Tyne and Wear.
The Dean Gallery, Newcastle-upon-Tyne, Tyne and Wear.
Warner Fine Art, Newcastle-upon-Tyne, Tyne and Wear.
Sport and Country Gallery, Bulkington, Warks.
Coughton Galleries Ltd., Coughton, Warks.
Arden Gallery, Henley-in-Arden, Warks.
The Chadwick Gallery, Henley-in-Arden, Warks.
Lacy Gallery, Henley-in-Arden, Warks.
Fine-Lines (Fine Art), Shipston-on-Stour, Warks.
The Loquens Gallery, Stratford-upon-Avon, Warks.
Mason-Watts Fine Art, Warwick, Warks.
Woodland Fine Art, Alvechurch, West Midlands.
Roger Widdas Fine Paintings, Bentley Heath, West Midlands.
Ashleigh House Antiques, Birmingham, West Midlands.
Edgbaston Gallery, Birmingham, West Midlands.
The Graves Gallery, Birmingham, West Midlands.
Halcyon Gallery, Birmingham, West Midlands.
The Moseley Gallery, Birmingham, West Midlands.
Robert Withers Antiques, Halesowen, West Midlands.
Richard Lukeman Fine Art, Knowle, West Midlands.
Oldswinford Gallery, Stourbridge, West Midlands.
Driffold Gallery, Sutton Coldfield, West Midlands.
Lacewing Fine Art Gallery, Marlborough, Wilts.
St. John Street Gallery, Salisbury, Wilts.
Ian J. Brook, Wilton, Wilts.
Thornton Gallery, Bedale, Yorkshire North.
W. Greenwood (Fine Art), Burneston, Yorkshire North.
Garth Antiques, Harrogate, Yorkshire North.
Rodney Kent, Harrogate, Yorkshire North.
McTague of Harrogate, Harrogate, Yorkshire North.

Walker Galleries Ltd., Harrogate, Yorkshire North.
Gavèls, Long Preston, Yorkshire North.
Kirkgate Picture Gallery, Thirsk, Yorkshire North.
Robert Coulter, York, Yorkshire North.
Hibbert Bros. Ltd., Sheffield, Yorkshire South.
Hinson Fine Paintings, Sheffield, Yorkshire South.
E. Carrol, Bingley, Yorkshire West.
Carlton Antiques and Fine Art, Bradford, Yorkshire West.
Parker Gallery, Leeds, Yorkshire West.
The Titus Gallery, Saltaire, Yorkshire West.
Todmorden Fine Art, Todmorden, Yorkshire West.
Mitchell-Hill Gallery, Wetherby, Yorkshire West.
Channel Islands Galleries Ltd., St. Peter Port, Guernsey, C.I.
Geoffrey P. Gavey, Vale, Guernsey, C.I.
St. Helier Galleries, St. Helier, C.I.
The Bell Gallery, Belfast, N. Ireland.
Dunluce Antiques, Bushmills, Co. Antrim, N. Ireland.
Phyllis Arnold Studio Gallery, Bangor, Co. Down, N. Ireland.
The Rendezvous Gallery, Aberdeen, Scotland.
The Waverley Gallery, Aberdeen, Scotland.
The McEwan Gallery, Ballater, Scotland.
Castle Fine Art, Bridge of Weir, Scotland.
Laurance Black Ltd., Edinburgh, Scotland.
The Calton Gallery, Edinburgh, Scotland.
Fine Art Society plc., Edinburgh, Scotland.
John Mathieson and Co., Edinburgh, Scotland.
John O. Nelson, Edinburgh, Scotland.
Open Eye Gallery Ltd., Edinburgh, Scotland.
Daniel Shackleton, Edinburgh, Scotland.
Fine Art Society plc., Glasgow, Scotland.
Mainhill Gallery, Jedburgh, Scotland.
Colin Murdoch, Kingussie, Scotland.
The McIan Gallery (Campbell-Gibson Fine Art), Oban, Scotland.
Manor House Fine Arts, Cardiff, S. Glam., Wales.
Philip Davies, Swansea, W. Glam., Wales.
Betty Williams, Tredunnock, Gwent, Wales.
David Windsor Gallery, Bangor, Gwynedd, Wales.
Michael Webb Fine Art, Bodorgan, Gwynedd, Wales.

Wholesale Dealers (See Shipping Goods)

Wine Related Items
Brian Beet, London, W.1.
Patricia Harbottle, London, W.11.
Richard Kihl Wine Antiques and Accessories, London, N.W.1.
Nan Ashcroft, London, N.W.3.
Robin Butler, Bristol, Avon.
Christopher Sykes Antiques, Woburn, Beds.
Bacchus Antiques — In the Service of Wine, Cartmel, Cumbria.
Neil Willcox, Twickenham, Middx.
The Bacchus Gallery, Petworth, Sussex West.
Wynn Cato, Tywyn, Gwynedd, Wales.

STOP PRESS AND AMENDMENTS

London W.1

Claire Hobson Antiques
at Thomas Goode & Co. Ltd., 19 South Audley St. Open 9.30–5.30. *STOCK: English porcelain and pottery, some continental, late 18th to early 19th C, £10–£10,000.* TEL: 071 499 2823.

London W.2

Whitford and Hughes
(A. Mibus and D. Hughes.) Open by appointment only. *STOCK: Oil paintings, late 19th to 20th C.* TEL: 071 221 8097.

London S.W.1

Lesley Rendall Antiques BADA
69 Pimlico Rd. Open 10–6. *STOCK: Furniture, 18th to mid 19th C; decorative objects.* TEL: 071 730 7206. FAIRS: Olympia. VAT: Stan/Spec.

London S.W.6

Lesley Rendall Antiques
Moved to S.W.1 – see entry above.

London S.E.1

The Antiques Pavilion
175 Bermondsey St. (Capital City Investments Ltd.) Est: 1966. Open 9.30–6, Fri. 7–6, Sat. 9–2. SIZE: Large. *STOCK: Furniture, Georgian to 1930's, £25–£25,000.* LOC: Near Bermondsey Market, close to Tower Bridge. PARK: Easy. TEL: 071 403 2021. SER: Restorations (leathering, French polishing); buys at auction. VAT: Stan.

Berkshire

THATCHAM

Richard Kimbell
Country Gardens, Turnpike Rd. (R. and F. Kimbell) Open 9–6 including Sun. SIZE: Large. *STOCK: Antique pine, £10–£3,000; reproduction pine and country accessories.* PARK: Easy. TEL: 0635 74822.

Cumbria

HOLME, Via Carnforth

JBW Antiques
Green Farm, Duke St. (J. Benson-Wilson.) Resident. Est: 1991. Open 9–12.30 and 1–5, Sat. 9–12.30 and 1–4. SIZE: Small. *STOCK: Pottery, porcelain and glass, silver and plate, mainly 19th C, from £5; militaria, small (and some selected large) furniture, 18th–19th C.* LOC: A6070 from Carnforth through Burton. Shop opposite public house in village centre. PARK: Easy. TEL: 0524 781377. SER: Valuations; restorations; buys at auction.

Devon

HONITON

L.J. Huggett and Son
Bramble Cross, Exeter Rd. Now trading from Stamps Building, King St. Open 9.30–5, Sat. 9.30–1. *STOCK: 18th–19th C furniture.* TEL: 0404 42043; home – 0404 47117.

SOUTH MOLTON

The Lace Shop
Bay House, 33 East St. (F. Sadler.) Est: 1971. CL: Mon. *STOCK: Lace, 18th–19th C, £5–£500; linens, bridal veils, head-dresses and dresses, 19th–20th C, £5–£1,000.* PARK: Easy. TEL: 07695 3184; home – same. SER: Valuations; restorations (handmade lace and embroidery). VAT: Stan/Spec.

Mole Gallery
32 East St. (A. and G. Fry.) Est: 1977. Open 9.30–5. SIZE: Large. *STOCK: Period and contemporary paintings, 19th–20th C; prints; frames.* PARK: Easy. TEL: 07695 3845; home – same. SER: Valuations; restorations. VAT: Stan/Spec.

Essex

ALRESFORD

Rita M. Wilkinson Antiques
Heath Farm House, Station Rd. Resident. Open by appointment. *STOCK: Mainly 19th and some selected 20th C furniture especially Victorian dining tables.* LOC: Just off B1027. PARK: Own. TEL: 0206 822805; mobile – 0860 775680.

Hampshire

STOCKBRIDGE

George Hofman Antiques at the Sign of the Black Cat
Brookside, High St. Est: 1973. Open Tues., Thurs., Fri. and Sat. 10—5.30 or by appointment. SIZE: Medium. *STOCK: General antiques and decorative items.* LOC: A30. PARK: At rear. TEL: 0264 810570; home — same. VAT: Stan/Spec.

Kent

DEAL

Decors
67 Beach St. (N. Loftus-Potter.) Est: 1973. Open by appointment. CL: Mon. SIZE: Small. *STOCK: Decorative items, general antiques and fabrics, mainly 18th-19th C, £5—£5,000.* PARK: Easy. TEL: 0304 368030; home — same. SER: Valuations; restorations (gilding).

SMEETH, Nr. Ashford

Ashbourn and Hirsch Ltd
Evegate Mill, Station Rd. (F. and L. Ashbourn, C. Hirsch.) Open 9—6, Sun. by appointment. SIZE: Large. *STOCK: Furniture especially continental salon suites, consul and hall tables, £1,000—£4,000; dining tables and chair sets, 19th C, £500—£1,500; chandeliers and gasoliers, £100—£3,000; mirrors including pier, £200—£2,000; both 19th C.* LOC: Off junction 10, M20 onto A20, take third turning right into Station Rd., mill 1 mile. PARK: Easy. TEL: 0233 720055; fax — 0233 720155. VAT: Stan/Spec.

Northamptonshire

NORTHAMPTON

Talent Pastimes Ltd. (Collectors Shop)
85 Kettering Rd. (M.L. Watts PTS.) Est: 1977. Open 9—5, Thurs. 9—2. SIZE: Small. *STOCK: Stamps, from 1840; postal history, from 1600's; covers, from, 1840's; all 5p to £500; post and cigarette cards, 20p to £100; toy soldiers and figurines, mainly modern, from £20 set; accessories.* LOC: A43 near town centre. PARK: Easy. TEL: 0604 36396. VAT: Stan.

Shropshire

CHURCH STRETTON

George Holme Antiques
17 High St. Business closed. See entry under Stockbridge, Hants. in this section.

Somerset

TAUNTON

The Belvedere Gallery
10 Belvedere Rd. (J. and D. Phillips.) Est: 1990. Open 9.30—5.30, Sat. 10—1, Sun. by appointment. SIZE: Small. *STOCK: Watercolours, from 1850; oils, from 1600; both £50—£10,000; small furniture, carvings and etchings, 1600—1900, £50—£5,000.* LOC: Opposite The Council House, 2 minutes from station. PARK: Easy and NCP nearby. TEL: 0823 323563; home — 0823 698113. SER: Valuations; restorations; buys at auction (pictures). FAIRS: Shepton Mallet. VAT: Stan/Spec.

East Sussex

BEXHILL-ON-SEA

Springfield Antiques
127 Ninfiler Rd., Sidley. (C. and C.J. Georgiou.) Open 9—5.30, Sat. 9—1 or by appointment. *STOCK: Silver and plate, smalls, pine, oak and mahogany furniture.* TEL: 0424 211225.

Wiltshire

WARMINSTER

Swans Antiques
8 Silver St. (E. and J. Hurley.) Est: 1970. Open 10—5, Wed. 10—1. SIZE: Medium. *STOCK: Decorative furnishings, 19th C, £25—£1,000; textiles, 18th—19th C, £25—£1,000.* LOC: From Bath or Frome road, 200 yards past obelisk monument on right-hand side. PARK: Nearby. TEL: 0985 219726; home — 0373 51351. SER: Restorations (china, upholstery). FAIRS: Shepton Mallet, Cheltenham, Bristol, Sandown Park.

North Yorkshire

YORK

Newgate Antiques Centre

14 Newgate. (M.S. and D.J. Smith.) Est: 1983. Open 9–5.30. SIZE: Small. LOC: Adjacent to York market, off Parliament St. PARK: Multi-storey. TEL: 0904 679844. VAT: Stan. Below are listed the dealers at this market.

Circle Antiques
Art deco, general antiques.
Golden Memories of York
Antique and secondhand jewellery.
Howard Johnson Antiques
China, clocks, toys.
Rose Richards
Prints, pictures and linen.
Thackers of York
Small furniture, brass and collectables.
Traditions
Period costume jewellery.

Scotland

NEWBURGH (Fife)

Newburgh Antiques

222 High St. (Miss D.L. Fraser.) Est: 1991. Open 10–12 and 1–5.30. SIZE: Small. *STOCK: Wemyss ware, 1860–1920, £100–£1,500; Scottish watercolours and oil paintings, 1800–1950's, £100–£1,500; furniture, 1750–1900, £200–£2,000.* LOC: A913. PARK: Easy. TEL: 0337 41026; home – 0337 40725. SER: Valuations.

Dealers' Index — Stop Press

FOR A NEW OR SUBSTANTIALLY ALTERED ENTRY USE THIS FORM

Please complete and return this form; there is no charge

NAME OF SHOP ....

ADDRESS OF SHOP ....

....
full address including actual county (not postal area)

Name (or names) and initials of proprietor(s) ....
(Mr/Mrs/Miss/or title)

Previous trading address (if applicable) ....

....

State whether 'Trade Only' (Yes or No) ....

BADA (Yes or No) .... LAPADA (Yes or No) ....

Year Established .... Resident on premises (Yes or No) ....

OPENING HOURS: (One entry, e.g. '9.30—5.30' if open all day or part day. Two entries, e.g. '9.30—1.00, 2,00—5.30' if closed for lunch)

Please put 'CLOSED' and 'BY APPT.' where applicable

	Morning	Afternoon
Sunday	....	....
Monday	....	....
Tuesday	....	....
Wednesday	....	....
Thursday	....	....
Friday	....	....
Saturday	....	....

SIZE OF SHOWROOM

Small (up to 600 sq.ft.) ....

Medium (600 to 1,500 sq.ft.) ....

Large (over 1,500 sq.ft.) ....

HOW TO GET TO YOUR SHOP (BUSINESS)

Brief helpful details from the nearest well-known road:

....

....

....

....

OF WHAT DOES YOUR STOCK CHIEFLY CONSIST?

(A) Please list in order of importance	(B) Approximate period or date of stock	(C) Indication of price range of stock eg £50—£100 or £5—£25
1. (Principal stock)		
2.		
3.		

IS PARKING *OUTSIDE* YOUR SHOP (BUSINESS) Easy (Yes or No) ....

TELEPHONE NUMBER: Business ....

Home ....

(only if customers can ring for appointments outside business hours)

V.A.T. scheme operated — Standard/Special/Both ....

SERVICES OFFERED:

Valuations (Yes or No) ....

Restorations (Yes or No) ....

Type of work ....

Buying specific items at auction for a commission (Yes or No) ....

Type of item ....

FAIRS:

At which fairs (if any) do you normally exhibit? ....

....

....

CERTIFICATION:

The information given above is accurate and you may publish it in the Guide. I understand that this entry is entirely free.

Signed ....

Date ....

ENGLISH COUNTY BOUNDARIES

Map showing county boundaries of England. For county boundary details of Northern Ireland, Scotland and Wales see maps at start of relevant sections.

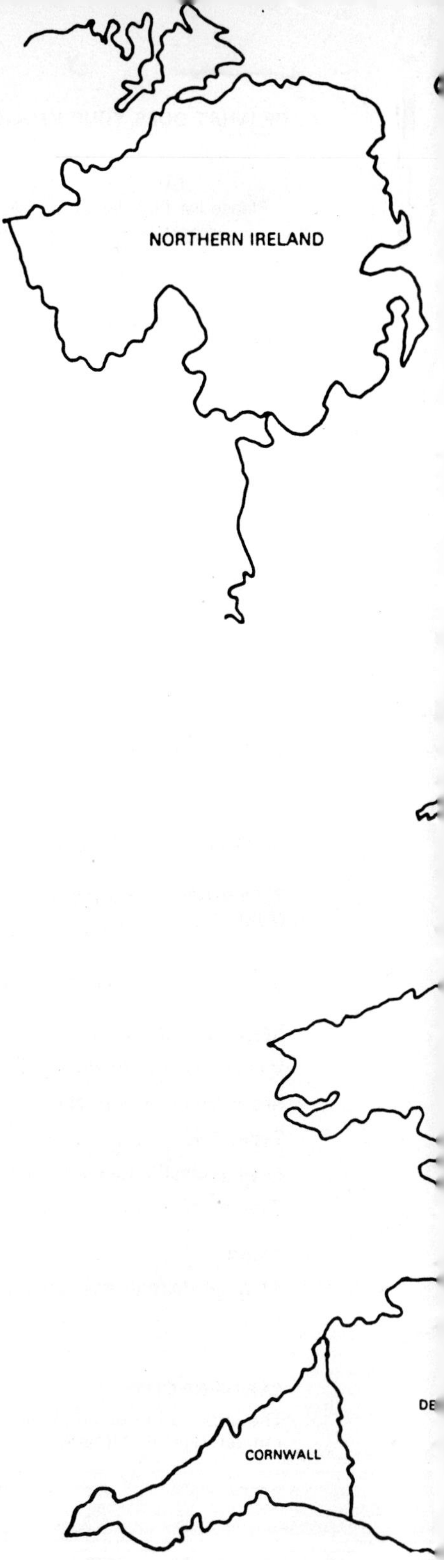
NORTHERN IRELAND
CORNWALL